The Sports Encyclopedia:
Pro Football
The Modern Era, 1960 to the present

Other Books Authored By Sports Products Inc.

THE SPORTS ENCYCLOPEDIA: BASEBALL
THE SPORTS ENCYCLOPEDIA: PRO BASKETBALL
THE ALL-SPORTS WORLD RECORD BOOK
THE WORLD BOOK OF ODDS
THE COMPLETE ALL-TIME BASEBALL REGISTER
THE COMPLETE ALL-TIME PRO BASEBALL REGISTER
MONDAY MORNING QUARTERBACK
PRO FOOTBALL: THE EARLY YEARS

The Sports Encyclopedia:
Pro Football
The Modern Era, 1960 to the present

by David S. Neft, Richard M. Cohen, Jordan A. Deutsch

Editorial and photographic assistance by *Pro Football Weekly*

GROSSET & DUNLAP
A Filmways Company

Publishers • New York

Portions of this book were originally published in
THE SPORTS ENCYCLOPEDIA: PRO FOOTBALL, 1974
THE SPORTS ENCYCLOPEDIA: PRO FOOTBALL, 1976

All photographs used by permission of *Pro Football Weekly*

Contents

LEADERS AND FEATURES 391

Preface

Pro Football, The Modern Game is a complete statistical record of professional football from 1960 to the present. All years prior to 1960 may be found in the companion book, *Pro Football, The Early Years.* The authors have also produced other sports references and encyclopedia historie s.

The authors have taken the liberty to arrange the material into two distict periods (1960-1969, and 1970-present) The split with this period is natural due to the total merger of the AFL and NFL.

Within each period the fan has the opportunity to guage football history in a much better perspective. In each period, the authors have included a statistical matter and text, arranged in an easy to follow year-by-year and division-by-division format. In addition, there are register sections, Championship Games, Super Bowls, single season leaders by category, lifetime leaders by category as well as a host of other featured material, all of which serves to make *Pro Football, The Modern Game,* the most complete book of its kind.

For the authors, who could not have undertaken this project alone, there are many individuals and former professional players to thank whose assistance was necessary in helping to make this book a reality. Their contributions are extensive, and range from supplying demographic information to some of the color as it actually took place on the field. To these individuals, the authors express their deep appreciation that finally there is a book where you can "go and look it up."

Chief consultants in preparation of the written manuscript and for procurement and layout of photos —

Pro Football Weekly—
  Art Arkush,, Publisher
  Dan Arkush
  Neil Warner

Director of Research and coordinator for earlier editions —
  Roland T. Johnson

Special consultant—
  John G. Hogrogian

Pro Football Hall of Fame —
  Jim Campbell, Research Librarian, who made available not only his facility, but also his endless knowledge, time, and co-operation in seeing this book to its fruition.
  Don Smith, Public Relations Director

Stan Grosshandler — An independent contributor who coordinated and served as liaison with the following former professional players:

Chuck Bednarik	Dick Hoerner
Jack Christiansen	Henry Jordan
Dutch Clark	Don Kindt
Chuck Conerly	Joe Kopcha
Jack Cronin	Dante Lavelli
Ed Danowski	Jim Mutscheller
Art DeCarlo	Ernie Nevers
Art Donovan	Curly Oden
Benny Friedman	Johnny Sisk
Buckets Goldenberg	Hank Soar
Otto Graham	Ken Strong
Pat Harder	Y. A. Tittle
Mel Hein	Em Tunnell
Clarke Hinkle	Alex Wojciechowicz
Crazy Legs Hirsch	

Bob Carroll — His years of research have provided the first set of consistent data for the years 1920-1925.

Independent Contributors —
  Bob Allen   Joel Bussert
  Mark Swayne   John Crelli
  Irving d. Shapiro

University of Rhode Island Library — inter-library loan department

The Notre Dame Int'l Sports and Games Reseach Collection
  Herb Juliano, Corator

Cover art by Bill Hoffman

The authors' wives, (a special thanks for once again displaying their faith and cooperation throughout the project); Naomi Neft, and Thea Deutsch.

Since such a book of this magnitude will include errors the authors would appreciate, for the purpose of keeping future editions as accurate and complete as possible, if the readers will send any corrections and additions to:

SPORTS PRODUCTS, INC.
415 Main Street
Ridgefield, CT. 06877

Codes and Explanations

In each section of the book, unfamiliar abbreviations, and bold facing may be shown. The following, by section, is an explanation of this matter:

Yearly Sections

Age — The age shown for each player is as Sept. 1 of that year.

Traded Players — Shown only on the team which the player played for most, along with a "from or to" reference.

Bold Facing — Indicates league leaders.

Team Name Line — Shown alongside the name of each team is the team Won-Lost-Tied record and the head coaches.

Home Team Indication — In a team's game-by-game scores, certain opponents appear in upper case. This means that the opponent played at that team's home park.

Opponent's Score — In a team's game-by-game scores the opponent's score always appears in the right hand column.

Rosters — Attempts to include, in a year, only those who actually played in a league game. The limitations of data, however, may have accidentally included men who did not get into a league game.

Position Abbreviations — (Applies to all sections. If a man played more than one position, the listing is in order of amount played at each position):

BB — Blocking back
C   — Center
DB — Defensive back
DE — Defensive end
DG — Defensive guard
DT — Defensive tackle
NT — Nose tackle
FB — Fullback
FL — Flanker
G   — Offensive and defensive guard
HB — Halfback
K   — Punter or place kicker (and did not play any other position in a particular year)
LB — Linebacker
MG — Middle Guard
NT — Nose Tackle
OG — Offensive guard
OE — Offensive end
OT — Offensive tackle
QB — Quarterback
T   — Offensive and defensive tackle
TB — Tailback
TE — Tight end
WB — Wingback
WR — Wide receiver

Career Interruptions — Fully explained, but only covers a full year or career end interruption.

Team Abbreviations — (Applies to all sections)

Akr — Akron
Atl — Atlanta

Bal — Baltimore
Bkn — Brooklyn
Bos — Boston
Buf — Buffalo
Can — Canton
ChiB — Chicago Bears and Chicago Staleys
ChiC — Chicago Cardinals
ChiT — Chicago Tigers
Cin — Cincinnati
Cle — Cleveland
Col — Columbus
C-T — Chicago Cardinals-Pittsburgh Steelers (merged
C-S — Cincinnati Reds and St. Louis Gunners
Dal — Dallas
Day — Dayton
Dec — Decatur
Den — Denver
Det — Detroit
Dul — Duluth
Eva — Evansville
Fra — Frankford
GB — Green Bay
Ham — Hammond
Har — Hartford
Hou — Houston
KC — Kansas City
Ken — Kenosha
LA — Los Angeles
Lou — Louisville
Mia — Miami
Mil — Milwaukee
Min — Minnesota or Minneapolis
Mun — Muncie
NE — New England
NO — New Orleans
Nwk — Newark
NYB — New York Bulldogs
NYG — New York Giants
NYJ — New York Jets
NYT — New York Titans
NYY — New York Yankees
Oak — Oakland
Oor — Oorang (Marion, Ohio)
Ora — Orange
Phi — Philadelphia
Pit — Pittsburgh
P-P — Philadelphia Eagles-Pittsburgh Steelers (merged)
Port — Portsmouth
Pott — Pottsville
Prov — Providence
Rac — Racine
RI — Rock Island
Roch — Rochester
SD — San Diego
Sea — Seattle
SF — San Francisco
SI — Staten Island
StL — St. Louis
TB — Tampa Bay
Was — Washington

Championship Section

Giveaways — Passes that were intercepted and fumbles lost.

Takeaways — Passes intercepted and opposing fumbles recovered.

Note: These two categories apply to team statistics only.

TAP — Indicates Tackled Attempting to Pass.

Register Sections

Players have been assigned to the various register sections according to what time period they played in most.

Register sections, by period, are divided into an alphabetical register, and then into various statistical registers. In the alphabetical register, alongside each man's name are one or more reference numbers (1, 2, 3, 4, 5). These reference numbers are to serve as guides as where to find the player's statistical record (if there is no reference number it means the player did not have enough minimum statistics to rate a ranking). The following are the reference numbers and their identification:

> 1 Passing
> 2 Rushing and receiving
> 3 Punt returns and kickoff returns
> 4 Punting
> 5 Kicking

The register sections are broken down into two periods, 69, and 1970-77.

Some of the unfamiliar information which appears in each alphabetical register is as follows:

Last name, Use name (name player was known as), nicknames which appear in parenthesis ( ):
> Bailey, Howard (Screeno)

If a player used another name other than that he was "born as," his real name is indicated in parenthesis ( ) after the last name. Such as in the case of Rocky Thompson:
> Thompson (born Symonds), Rocky

Weight — Average weight for career.

HC — Indicates, for year or years, that the player was a head coach.

PC — Indicates, for year or years, that the player was a head coach while actively playing.

League Abbreviations — A (American Football League), AA (All-American Football Conference).

Other Major League Sports — Certain players also played professional basketball or major league baseball. The basketball information is indicated with the league in abbreviations: NBL—National Basketball League, NBA—National Basketball Association, BAA—Basketball Association of American, ABL—American Basketball League.

Career Interruptions — If an abbreviation other than a league follows the year played, it means that only a full year was missed or a career end because of certain prevailing reasons. The codes and explanations follow:

AA	— Injured in automobile accident
AJ	— Broken collarbone
BA	— Broken arm
BC	— Broken collarbone
BG	— Broken finger
BH	— Broken bone in hand
BL	— Broken leg
BN	— Broken ankle
BQ	— Broken neck
BW	— Broken or dislocated wrist
CFL	— Jumped to Canadian Football League
FJ	— Foot or heel injury
HJ	— Hand injury
HO	— Holdout
IL	— Illness
JJ	— Injury — type of injury unknown
KJ	— Knee injury
LJ	— Leg or thigh injury
MS	— Military service
NJ	— Ankle injury
PJ	— Hip injury
RJ	— Finger injury
SJ	— Shoulder injury or shoulder separation
SL	— Suspended by commissioner
VR	— Voluntarily retired
WFL	— Jumped to World Football League
XJ	—Back injury
ZJ	—Neck injury

Use Name (Nicknames) – Positions	Team by Year	See Section	Hgt.	Wgt.	College	Int	Pts
Agajanian, Ben (The Toeless Wonder) K	45Phi 45Pit 47-48LA-AA 49NYG 53LA 54-57NYG 60LA-A 61DalA 61GB 62OakA 64SD-A	5	6'	215	New Mexico		655
Ameche, Alan (The Horse) FB	55-60Bal	2	6'	218	Wisconsin		264
Austin, Bill OG-T	49-50NYG 51-52MS 53-57NYG HC66-68Pit HC70Was		6'1"	223	Oregon State	1	
Barnes, Larry FB-DE	57SF 60OakA	5	6'1"	228	Colorado State		55
Barnett, Tom HB-DB	59-60Pit	2	5'11"	190	Purdue		12
Barry, Al OG	54GB 55-56MS 57GB 58-59NYG 60LA-A		6'2"	230	Southern Calif.		
Baugh, Sammy QB-TB-DB	37-52Was HC60-61NY-A HC64HouA	12 4	6'2"	182	Texas Christian	28	55
Beatty, Ed C	55-56SF 57-61Pit 61Was		6'3"	229	Mississippi		
Beck, Ken DT-DE	59-60GB		6'2"	245	Texas A&M		
Bednarik, Chuck LB-C	49-62Phi		6'3"	233	Pennsylvania	20	6
Bell, Eddie DB	55-58Phi 59CFL 60NY-A		6'1"	212	Pennsylvania	11	6
Bernardi, Frank DB-HB	55-57ChiC 60DenA	3	5'9"	181	Colorado	4	12
Bernet, Ed OE	55Pit 60DalA	2	6'3"	203	S.M.U.		6
Bettis, Tom LB	55-61GB 62Pit 63ChiB HC77KC		6'2"	228	Purdue	1	
Bielski, Dick OE-FB	55-59Phi 60-61Dal 62-63Bal	2 5	6'1"	224	Maryland		208
Biscaha, Joe OE	59NYG 60BosA		6'1"	190	Richmond		
Bishop, Bill DT-OT	52-60ChiB 61Min		6'4"	248	North Texas State	2	6
Boll, Don OT-OG	53-59Was 60NYG		6'2"	270	Nebraska		
Borden, Nate DE	55-59GB 60-61Dal 62BufA		6'	234	Indiana		
Boydston, Max OE	55-58ChiC 60-61DalA 62OakA	2	6'2"	210	Oklahoma		48
Braatz, Tom LB-OE	57Was 58LA 58-59Was 60Dal		6'1"	216	Marquette	2	
Brettschneider, Carl LB	56-59ChiC 60-63Det		6'1"	223	Iowa State	3	
Brewster, Darrell (Pete) OE	52-58Cle 59-60Pit	2	6'3"	210	Purdue		126
Brito, Gene DE-OE	51-53Was 54CFL 55-58Was 59-60LA	2	6'1"	226	Loyola (L.A.)	1	12
Brookshier, Tom DB	53Phi 54-55MS 56-61Phi		6'	196	Colorado	20	
Brown, Ed QB-DB	54-61ChiB 62-65Pit 65Bal	12 4	6'2"	209	San Francisco		94
Brown, Hardy LB-DB-FB	48BknAA 49ChiAA 50Bal 50Was 51-56SF 56ChiC 60DenA	5	6'	193	Tulsa	13	43
Brown, Paul	HC46-49CleAA HC50-62Cle HC68-69CinA HC70-75Cin				Miami (Ohio)		
Brown, Ray DB-QB	58-60Bal	4	6'2"	195	Mississippi	13	
Brown, Rosey OT	53-65NYG		6'3"	249	Morgan State		
Brubaker, Dick OE-DE	55,57ChiC 60BufA	2	6'	202	Ohio State		6
Brueckman, Charlie LA	58Was 60LA-A		6'2"	223	Pittsburgh		
Bruney, Fred DB	53SF 54-55MS 56-57Pit 58LA 60-62BosA	3	5'10"	184	Ohio State	15	6
Campbell, Dick LB	58-60Pit		6'1"	227	Marquette	3	
Campbell, Marion DT-DE-OT	54-55SF 56-61Phi HC74-76Atl		6'3"	250	Georgia	3	
Campbell, Stan OG	52Det 53-54MS 55-58Det 59-61Phi 62OakA		6'	226	Iowa State		
Carmichael, Al HB	53-58GB 60-61DenA	23	6'1"	192	Southern Calif.		84
Carpenter, Ken HB-OE	50-53Cle 60DenA	23	6'	195	Oregon State		108
Carpenter, Lew HB-FB-FL-OE-DB	53-55Det 56MS 57-58Cle 59-63GB	23	6'1"	209	Arkansas	1	126
Carson, Johnny OE	54-59Was 60HouA	2	6'3"	202	Georgia		90
Cassady, Hopalong HB-FL	56-61Det 62Cle 62Phi 63Det	23	5'10"	183	Ohio State		144
Chorovich, Dick OT	55-56Bal 60LA-A		6'4"	260	Miami (Ohio)		
Christiansen, Jack DB-HB	51-58Det HC63-67SF	3	6'1"	190	Colorado State	46	78
Churchwell, Don OT-DT	59Was 60OakA		6'1"	253	Mississippi		
Clarke, Leon OE-FL	56-59LA 60-62Cle 63Min	2	6'4"	232	Southern Calif.		114
Clatterbuck, Bobby QB	54-57NYG 60LA-A	12	6'3"	195	Houston		6
Collins, Ray DT-OT	52-52SF 54NYG 55-59CFL 60-61DalA		5'11"	238	Louisiana State		
Cone, Fred FB-K	51-57GB 60Dal	2 5	5'11"	199	Clemson		494
Consright, Bill (Red) C-LB-OE-DE	37-38ChiB 39-42Cle 43Was 43Bkn 44Cle HC62OakA		6'1"	203	Oklahoma	4	6
Conner, Clyde OE	56-63SF	2	6'2"	193	U. of Pacific		108
Connolly, Ted OG	54SF 55MS 56-62SF 63Cle		6'3"	240	Tulsa, Santa Clara		
Cronin, Gene DE-OG-LB	56-59Det 60Dal 61-62Was		6'2"	229	U. of Pacific	1	
Cross, Bob OT-DT	52ChiB 53MS 54-55LA 56-57SF 58-59ChiC 60BosA		6'4"	248	Kilgore J.C.		
Crow, Lindon DB	55-57ChiC 58-60NYG 61-64LA	3	6'1"	195	Southern Calif.	38	20
D'Agostino, Frank OG-OT	56Phi 60NY-A		6'1"	245	Auburn		
Davis, Milt DB	57-60Bal		6'1"	188	U.C.L.A.	27	18
DeCarlo, Art DB-OE	53Pit 54-55MS 56-57Was 57-60Bal		6'2"	196	Georgia	7	
Derby, Dean DB-HB	57-61Pit 61-62Min		6'	187	Washington	21	21
Dimmick, Tom C-OT-LB	56Phi 60DalA		6'6"	253	Houston		
Dittrich, John OG	56ChiC 57-58MS 59GB 60DalA 61BufA		6'1"	236	Wisconsin		
Dooley, Jim OE-FL-HB-DB	52-54ChiB 55MS 56-57ChiB 58BN 59-62, HC68-71ChiB	2	6'4"	198	Miami (Fla.)	5	96
Doran, Jim OE-DE	51-59Det 60-61Dal	2	6'2"	201	Iowa State	1	150
Dorow, Al QB	54-56Was 57Phi 58-59CFL 60-61NY-A 62BufA	12	6'	193	Michigan State		96
Doyle, Dick DB	55Pit 60DenA		6'	193	Ohio State	2	
Drulis, Chuck LB-OG	42ChiB 43-44MS 45-49ChiB 50GB HC61StL		5'10"	216	Temple	4	
Dublinski, Tom QB	52-54Det 56-57CFL 58NYG 60DenA	12	6'2"	197	Utah		6
Dupre, L.G. (Long Gone) HB	55-59Bal 60-61Dal	2 4	5'11"	190	Baylor		108
Fears, Tom OE-DB	48-56LA HC67-70NO	2 5	6'2"	213	U.C.L.A.	2	249
Felton, Ralph LB-FB	54-60Was 61-62BufA	5	5'11"	210	Maryland	7	19
Ferguson, Howie FB	53-58GB 60LA-A	2	6'2"	214	none		78
Filchock, Frankie TB-QB-DB-HB	38Pit 38-41Was 42-43MS 44-45Was 46NYG 47-49DE 50Bal HC60-61DenA	12	5'11"	193	Indiana	1	18
Fry, Bob OT-OG	53LA 54-55MS 56-59LA 60-64Dal		6'4"	235	Kentucky		
Fuller, Frank DT-OG-C-DE	53,55,57-58LA 59ChiC 60-62StL 63Phi		6'4"	244	Kentucky		2
Gain, Bob DT-DE-OG-OT-LB	52Cle 53MS 54-64Cle		6'3"	256	Kentucky	1	9
George, Bill LB-OG-DT	52-65ChiB 66LA	5	6'2"	237	Wake Forest	18	26
Gibron, Abe OG-DG	49BufAA 50-56Cle 56-57Phi 58-59, HC72-74ChiB		5'11"	243	Purdue		
Gifford, Frank HB-FL-DB	52-60NYG 61VR 62-64NYG	123 5	6'1"	197	Southern Calif.	1	484
Gilmer, Harry QB-HB-DB	48-52Was 53JJ 54Was 55-56, HC65-66Det	12	6'	169	Alabama	5	12
Glick, Gary DB-HB	56-59Pit 59-61Was 61Bal 63SD-A	5	6'2"	195	Colorado State	14	65
Gob, Art DE	59-60Was 60LA-A		6'4"	230	Pittsburgh		2
Gordon, Bobby DB	58ChiC 60HouA	4	6'	193	Tennessee	5	
Graham, Otto QB-DB	46-49CleAA 50-55Cle HC66-68Was 45-46 played in N.B.L.	12	6'1"	196	Northwestern	7	256
Grant, Bud OE-DE	51-52Phi 53CFL HC67-77Min 49-51 played in N.B.A.	2	6'3"	199	Minnesota		42
Griffin, Bob LB-C	53-57LA 61DenA 61StL		6'3"	235	Arkansas	1	2
Groza, Lou (The Toe) OT-DT-K	46-49CleAA 50-59Cle 60VR 61-67Cle	5	6'3"	240	Ohio State		1608
Guy, Buzz OG-DT-OT	58-59NYG 60Dal 61HouA 61DenA		6'3"	248	Duke		
Halas, George OE-DE	PC20Dec PC21-18, HC29, 33-42ChiB 43-45MS HC46-55,58-68ChiB		6'	175	Illinois		68
Hanner, Dave DT	52-64GB		6'2"	257	Arkansas	4	2

Use Name (Nicknames) – Positions	Team by Year	See Section	Hgt.	Wgt.	College	Int	Pts
Hansen, Wayne LB-C-OG-OT-DT	50-58ChiB 60DalA		6'2"	231	Texas-El Paso	6	6
Harris, Jimmie DB	57Phi 58LA 60DalA 61DenA		6'1"	178	Oklahoma	11	6
Hatley, John OG-DT	53ChiB 54-55ChiC 60DenA		6'3"	249	Sul Ross State		
Hauser, Art DT-OG	54-57LA 59ChiC 59NYG 60BosA 61DenA		6'	237	Xavier-Ohio		6
Hecker, Norb DB-OE	51-53LA 54CFL 55-57Was HC66-68Atl		6'2"	193	Baldwin-Wallace	28	20
Heinrich, Don QB	54-59NYG 60Dal 62OakA	12	6'	182	Washington		30
Helluin, Jerry DT	52-53Cle 54-57GB 60HouA		6'2"	272	Tulane	1	6
Henke, Ed DE-LB-OG-DG-OT-DT	49LA-AA 51-52SF 53-54MS 55CFL 56-60SF 61-63StL		6'3"	227	Southern Calif.		
Herchman, Bill DT	56-59SF 60-61Dal 62HouA		6'2"	246	Texas Tech	1	6
Hickey, Red OE-DE	41Cle 42-44MS 45Cle 46-48LA HC59-63SF	2	6'2"	204	Arkansas		96
Hill, Harlon OE-DB	54-61ChiB 62Pit 62Det	2	6'3"	199	Florence State	3	240
Holovak, Mike FB-LB	46LA 47-48ChiB HC61-68BosA	2	6'1"	213	Boston College	1	36
Howell, Jim Lee OE-DE	37-42NYG 43-45MS 46-48,HC54-60NYG	2	6'6"	210	Arkansas		42
Howton, Billy OE	52-58GB 59Cle 60-63Dal	2	6'2"	191	Rice		366
Hudson, Bob LB-DB-OE	51-52NYG 53-55Phi 56VR 57-58Phi 59Was 60DalA 60-61DenA		6'4"	225	Clemson	19	
Hughes, Ed DB	54-55LA 56-58NYG HC71Hou		6'1"	184	Tulsa	3	
Ivy, Pop DE-OE	40Pit 40-42ChiC 43-44MS 45-47ChiC HC58-59ChiC HC60-61StL HC62-63HouA	2	6'3"	208	Oklahoma	3	20
Jackson, Charlie DB	58ChiC 60DalA		5'11"	180	S.M.U.	1	
Jessup, Bill OE-FL	51-52SF 53MS 54SF 55HJ 56-58SF 60DenA	2 4	6'1"	195	Southern Calif.		42
Johnson, Bill C-LB	48-49SF-AA 50-56SF HC76-77Cin		6'3"	228	Tyler J.C.	2	6
Johnson, Harvey LB-BB-FB-G	46-49NY-AA 51NYY HC68BufA HC71Buf	5	5'11"	212	William & Mary	1	262
Johnson, Jack DB	57-59ChiB 60-61BufA 61DalA	4	6'3"	198	Miami (Fla.)	8	
Johnson, Joe HB-DE-FL	54-58GB 60-61BosA	2	6'	185	Boston College		48
Jones, Jim DB-FB	58LA 61OakA		6'1"	204	Washington		
Joyce, Don DE-DT	51-53ChiC 54-60Bal 61Min 62DenA		6'3"	253	Tulane	1	
Karilivacz, Carl DB	53-57Det 58NYG 59-60LA		6'	188	Syracuse	13	12
Kinard, Billy DB-HB	56Cle 57-58GB 60BufA		6'	189	Mississippi	4	6
King, Don OT-DT	54Cle 55CFL 56Phi 56GB 60DenA		6'3"	260	Kentucky	2	
Knafelc, Gary OE	54ChiC 54-62GB 63SF	2	6'4"	217	Colorado		138
Konovsky, Bob OG-DE-OT	56-58ChiC 60ChiB 61DenA		6'2"	246	Wisconsin		
Krouse, Ray DT-DE-OT	51-55NYG 56-57Det 58-59Bal 60Was		6'3"	263	Maryland		
Krutko, Larry FB	58-60Pit	2	6'	220	West Virginia		24
Kuchta, Frank C-LB	58-59Was 60DenA		6'2"	225	Notre Dame		
Kuharich, Joe G-LB	40-41ChiC 42-44MS 45,HC52ChiC HC54-58Was HC64-68Phi	5	5'11"	195	Notre Dame	1	12
Landry, Tom DB-HB-QB	49NY-AA 50-55NYG HC60-77Dal	12 4	6'1"	195	Texas	32	36
Lane, Night Train DB-OE	52-53LA 54-59ChiC 60-65Det		6'1"	194	Scottsbluff J.C.	68	50
Lansford, Buck OG-OT	55-57Phi 58-60LA		6'2"	232	Texas		
Larson, Paul QB	57ChiC 60OakA		5'11"	183	California		
Lary, Yale DB	52-53Det 54-55MS 56-64Det	34	6'	187	Texas A&M	50	36
Layne, Bobby QB	48ChiB 49NYB 50-58Det 58-62Pit	12 5	6'1"	201	Texas		372
LeBaron, Eddie QB	52-53Was 54CFL 55-59Was 60-63Dal	12 4	5'9"	166	U. of Pacific		60
Lewis, Woodley DB-OE-HB	50-55LA 56-59ChiC 60Dal	23	6'	193	Oregon	26	108
Lipscomb, Big Daddy DT-DE	53-55LA 56-60Bal 61-62Pit died May 10, 1963		6'6"	284	none	1	2
Long, Bob LB-DE	55-59Det 60-61LA 62Dal		6'3"	232	U.C.L.A.	7	2
Macon, Eddie HB-DB	52-53ChiB 54-59CFL 60OakA	2	6'	177	U. of Pacific	9	36
Mairs, Gil DT-DE	54-61Det		6'2"	243	Murray State		
Mangum, Pete LB	54NYG 60DenA		6'	219	Mississippi		
Marchetti, Gino DE-DT-OT	52Dal 53-64Bal 65VR 66Bal		6'4"	244	San Francisco	1	20
Marchibroda, Ted QB	54-56Pit 57ChiC HC75-77Bal	12	5'10"	178	St. Bonaventure, Detroit		18
Martin, Jim LB-OG-DE-OT-K	50Cle 51-61Det 62VR 63Bal 64Was	5	6'2"	227	Notre Dame	6	434
Mathews, Ray HB-OE-FL-DB	51-59Pit 60Dal	123	6'	190	Clemson	2	261
Matson, Ollie HB-FB-DB-FL	52ChiC 53MS 54-58ChiC 59-62LA 63Det 64-66Phi	23	6'2"	210	San Francisco	3	438
Matuszak, Marv LB-OG	53Pit 54MS 55-56Pit 57-58SF 58GB 59-61Bal 62-63BufA 64DenA		6'3"	232	Tulsa	14	
McCabe, Richie DB	55Pit 56MS 51-58Pit 59Was 60-61BufA		6'1"	185	Pittsburgh	9	6
McCafferty, Don OE-DE	46NYG HC70-72Bal HC73Det		6'4"	220	Ohio State		6
McClairen, Jack OE	55-60Pit	2	6'4"	213	Bethune-Cookman		18
McClung, Willie OT-DT	55-57Pit 58-59Cle 60-61Det		6'2"	250	Florida A&M		
McCormack, Mike OT-DG-DT	51NYY 52-53MS 54-62Cle HC73-75Phi		6'4"	246	Kansas	1	
McElhenny, Hugh (Hurryin' Hugh, The King) HB	52-60SF 61-62Min 63NYG 64Det	23	6'1"	197	Washington		360
McHan, Lamar QB	54-58ChiC 59-60GB 61-63Bal 63SF 64CFL	12	6'1"	201	Arkansas		72
McIlhenny, Don HB	56Det 57-59GB 60-61Dal 61SF	23	6'	197	S.M.U.		84
McPeak, Bill DE	49-57Pit HC61-65Was		6'1"	206	Pittsburgh		6
Meilinger, Steve OE	56-57Was 58GB 59BA 60GB 61Pit 61StL	2	6'2"	227	Kentucky		48
Michaels, Walt LB	51GB 52-61Cle 63NY-A HC77NYJ		6'	231	Washington & Lee	11	12
Middleton, Dave OE-HB-FL	55-60Det 61Min	2	6'1"	194	Auburn		
Miller, Johnny OT-DT-DE	56Was 57MS 58-59Was 60GB		6'5"	253	Boston College		2
Miller, Paul DE-C	54-57LA 60-61DalA 62SD-A		6'2"	226	Louisiana State	1	
Modzelewski, Dick (Little Mo) DT	53-54Was 55Pit 56-63NYG 64-66,HC77Cle		6'	258	Maryland		4
Moegle, Dick DB-HB	55-59SF 60Pit 61Dal	2	6'	190	Rice	28	42
Morris, Jack DB	58-60LA 60Pit 61Min	5	6'	189	Oregon	8	30
Mutscheller, Jim OE-DE	54-61Bal	2	6'1"	213	Notre Dame		240
Myhra, Steve OG-LB	57-61Bal	5	6'1"	237	North Dakota		312
Nagler, Gern OE	53ChiC 54MS 55-58ChiC 59Pit 60-61Cle	2	6'2"	190	Santa Clara		168
Nix, Doyle DB	55GB 56-57MS 58-59Was 60LA-A 61DalA		6'1"	191	S.M.U.	16	6
Nixon (born Nicksick), Mike DB-HB-WB	35Pit 42Bkn HC59-61Was HC65Pit		5'11"	181	Pittsburgh		
Nolan, Dick DB	54-57NYG 58ChiC 59-61NYG 62Dal HC68-75SF		6'1"	185	Maryland	23	2
Noll, Chuck LB-OG-C	53-59Cle HC69-77Pit		6'1"	218	Dayton	8	14
North, John OE-DB	48-49BalAA 50Bal HC73-75NO	2	6'2"	199	Vanderbilt	1	36
Norton, Jerry DB-HB	54-58Phi 59ChiC 60-61StL 62Dal 63-64GB	234	5'11"	195	S.M.U.	35	42
Nutter, Buzz C-LB	54-60Bal 61-64Pit 65Bal		6'4"	230	Virginia Tech		
O'Connell, Tom QB	53ChiB 54-55MS 56-57Cle 60-61BufA	12	5'11"	187	Illinois		26
Olszewski, Johnny (Johnny O) FB-HB	53-57ChiC 58-60Was 61Det 62DenA	2	5'11"	200	California		114
O'Neil, Bob OG-DE	56-57Pit 61NY-A		6'1"	229	Notre Dame		
Palumbo, Sam LB-C	55-56Cle 57GB 60BufA		6'2"	226	Notre Dame	1	
Panfil, Ken OT-DT	56-58LA 59ChiC 60-62StL		6'6"	242	Purdue		
Parker, Buddy BB-LB-FB-DB	35-36Det 37-43,HC49ChiC HC51-56Det HC57-64Pit	2	6'	193	Centenary	2	28
Patera, Jack LB-OG	55-57Bal 58-59ChiC 60-61Dal HC76-77Sea		6'1"	234	Oregon	6	

Pre-1960 Players & Coaches
(Who overlap into the Modern Era)

Use Name (Nicknames) – Positions	Team by Year	See Section	Hgt	Wgt	College	Int	Pts
Pellington, Bill LB-OG	53-64Bal		6'2"	234	Rutgers	21	6
Perry, Jerry DT-DE-OT-OG	54Det 55MS 56-59Det 60-62StL	5	6'4"	237	California		190
Perry, Joe FB-DB	48-49SF-AA 50-60SF 61-62Bal 63SF	23	6'	203	Compton J.C.	1	513
Peters, Volney DT-OT-DE	62-63ChiC 54-57Was 58Phi 60LA-A 61OakA		6'4"	237	Southern Calif.		6
Pitts, Hugh LB	56LA 60HouA		6'2"	223	Texas Christian	3	
Podoley, Jim HB-OE	57-60Was 61JJ	2	6'2"	200	Central Michigan		78
Powell, Charley DE-LB-OE	52-53SF 54MS 55-57SF 58-59 retired for pro boxing career 60-61OakA		6'2"	226	none		2
Pricer, Billy FB	57-60Bal 61DalA	2	5'10"	208	Oklahoma		18
Putnam, Duane OG-LB	52-59LA 60Dal 61Cle 62LA		6'	228	U. of Pacific		
Ramsey, Buster OG-LB	46-51ChiC HC60-61BufA		6'1"	219	William & Mary	7	2
Rauch, Johnny QB-DB	49NYB 50-51NYY 51Phi HC66-68OakA HC69BufA HC70Buf	1	6'	197	Georgia	2	6
Rechichar, Bert DB-LB-HB-OE	52Cle 53-59Bal 60Pit 61NY-A	345	6'1"	209	Tennessee	31	179
Renfro, Will DT-DE-OT	57-59Was 60Pit 61Phi		6'5"	233	Memphis State		
Reynolds, Billy HB	53-54Cle 55-56MS 57Cle 58Pit 60OakA	23	5'10"	195	Pittsburgh		42
Richardson, Jess DT	53-56Phi 57JJ 58-61Phi 62-64BosA		6'2"	261	Alabama	1	
Richter, Les LB	54-62LA	5	6'3"	238	California	16	193
Riley, Lee DB	55Det 56,58-59Phi 60NYG 61-62NY-A	3	6'1"	192	Detroit	23	
Robustelli, Andy DE	51-55LA 56-64NYG		6'1"	230	Arnold	2	32
Romine, Al DB-HB	55,58GB 60DenA 61BosA		6'2"	191	Florence State	4	
Rote, Kyle OE-HB	51-61NYG	2	6'	199	S.M.U.		312
Rote, Tobin QB	50-56GB 57-59Det 60-62CFL 64SD-A 66DenA	12	6'3"	211	Rice		228
Rush, Clive OE	53GB HC69BosA HC70Bos	2 4	6'2"	197	Miami (Ohio)		
Rymkus, Lou OT-DT	43Was 44-45MS 46-49CleAA 50-51Cle HC60HouA		6'4"	231	Notre Dame	1	12
Saban, Lou LB-FB	46-49CleAA HC60-61BosA HC62-65BufA HC67-69DenA HC70-71Den HC72-76Buf	5	6'	202	Indiana	13	27
St. Claire, Bob OT	53-63SF 64FJ		6'9"	263	Tulsa, San Francisco		
Schmidt, Joe LB	53-65,HC67-72Det		6'1"	220	Pittsburgh	24	18
Schnelker, Bob OE	53Phi 54-60NYG 61Min 61Pit	2	6'3"	214	Bowling Green		204
Schrader, Jim C-OT	54Was 55MS 56-61Was 62-64Phi		6'2"	244	Notre Dame		
Scott, Tom DB-DE	53-58Phi 59-64NYG		6'2"	219	Virginia	8	18
Scudero, Scooter DB-HB	54-58Was 60Pit	23	5'10"	173	San Francisco	10	18
Sears, Jimmy HB-DB	54ChiC 55-56MS 57-58ChiC 60LA-A	23	5'11"	183	Southern Calif.	2	18
Sewell, Harley OG-LB	53-62Det 63LA		6'1"	230	Texas	1	6
Shaw, Buck	HC46-49SF-AA HC50-54SF HC58-60Phi				Notre Dame		
Sherman, Allie QB-DB	43P-P 44-47Phi 61-68NYG	12	5'11"	170	C.U.N.Y.-Bklyn.	2	24
Sherman, Will DB-HB	52Dal 54-60LA 61Min		6'2"	197	St. Mary's	29	24
Shula, Don DB-HB	51-52Cle 53-56Bal 57Was HC63-69Bal HC70-77Mia		5'11"	190	John Carroll	21	
Simerson, John C-OT	57-58Phi 58Pit 60HouA 61BosA		6'3"	257	Purdue		
Skorich, Nick G-LB	46-48Pit HC61-63Phi HC71-74Cle		5'9"	197	Cincinnati		
Spencer, Ollie OT-OG-C	53Det 54-55MS 56Det 57-58GB 59-61Det 63OakA		6'2"	245	Kansas		
Spinney, Art OG-DE-OE	50Bal 51-52MS 53-60Bal		6'	230	Boston College		
Stits, Bill DB-HB	54-56Det 57-58SF 59Was 59-61NYG	23	6'	194	U.C.L.A.	15	6
Striegel, Bill OG-OT-LB	59Phi 60BosA 60OakA		6'2"	235	U. of Pacific		
Stroud, Jack OG-OT	53-64NYG		6'1"	235	Tennessee		
Sugar, Leo DE	54-59ChiC 60StL 61Phi 62Det		6'1"	214	Purdue	1	18
Summerall, Pat DE-OE-K	52Det 53-57ChiC 58-61NYG	5	6'4"	228	Arkansas		563
Sumner, Charlie DB	55ChiB 56-57MS 58-60ChiB 61-62Min		6'1"	194	William & Mary	21	6
Sutherin, Don DB	59NYG 59-60Pit		5'10"	193	Ohio State	1	
Sutton, Ed HB-DB	57-59Was 60NYG	2	6'1"	205	North Carolina	1	60
Svare, Harland (Swede) LB-OT	53-54LA 55-60NYG HC62-65LA HC71-73SD		6'	214	Washington State	9	6
Taseff, Carl DB-HB	51Cle 52MS 53-61Bal 61Phi 62BufA	23	5'11"	192	John Carroll	20	48
Taylor, Hugh (Bones) OE	47-54Was HC65HouA	2	6'4"	194	Oklahoma City		348
Temp, Jim DE	57-60GB		6'4"	245	Wisconsin	1	
Thomas, Jessee DB	55-57Bal 60LA-A		5'10"	180	Michigan State	4	6
Tittle, Y.A. (Ya-Ya, The Bald Eagle) QB	48-49BalAA 50Bal 51-60SF 61-64NYG	12	6'	192	Louisiana State		234
Toneff, Bob DT-DG-DE-OT-OG	52SF 53MS 54-58SF 59-64Was		6'2"	260	Notre Dame	2	
Triplett, Mel FB	55-60NYG 61-62Min	2	6'1"	215	Toledo		108
Tunnell, Em (Emlen the Gremlin) DB-HB	48-58NYG 59-61GB	3	6'1"	193	Iowa	79	60
Turner, Bulldog C-LB-OG-OT-HB	40-52ChiB HC62NY-A		6'1"	237	Hardin-Simmons	16	24
Van Brocklin, Norm (The Dutchman) QB	49-57LA 58-60Phi HC61-66Min HC68-74Atl	12 4	6'1"	199	Oregon		66
Waller, Ron HB	55-58LA 59KJ 60LA-A HC73SD	23	5'11"	180	Maryland		54
Wallner, Fred LB-OG	51-52ChiC 53MS 54-55ChiC 60HouA		6'2"	231	Notre Dame	3	
Walston, Bobby OE-FL-HB	51-62Phi	2 5	6'	190	Georgia		881
Waterfield, Bob QB-DB	45Cle 46-52,HC60-62LA	12 45	6'1"	196	U.C.L.A.	20	573
Weatherall, Jim DT-OT	55-57Phi 58Was 59-60Det		6'4"	245	Oklahama		
Weber, Chuck LB-DE-OG	55-56Cle 56-58ChiC 59-61Phi		6'1"	229	West Chester St.	10	6
Webster, Alex (Big Red) HB-FB	55-64,HC69-73NYG	2	6'3"	218	N. Carolina State		336
Wegert, Ted HB	55-56Phi 60NY-A 60DenA 60BufA	2	5'11"	202	none		30
Wells, Billy HB	54Was 55MS 56-57Was 57Pit 58Phi 60BosA	23	5'9"	176	Michigan State		54
Wietecha, Ray C-LB	53-62NYG		6'1"	225	Northwestern	1	
Wilkins, Roy LB-DE	58-59LA 60-61Was		6'3"	224	Georgia		
Williams, Fred DT-OG	52-63ChiB 64-65Was		6'4"	249	Arkansas	2	
Williams, Jerry HB-DB	49-52LA 53-54,HC69-71Phi	23	5'10"	175	Washington State	15	108
Wilson, Billy OE-FL	61-70SF	2	6'3"	191	San Jose State		294
Wilson, George OE-DE 39-40 played in N.B.L.	37-46ChiB HC57-64Det HC66-69MiaA	2	6'1"	199	Northwestern	3	108
Wilson, Jerry LB-DE	59-60Phi 60SF		6'3"	238	Auburn		
Wilson, Tom (Touchdown Tommy) HB-FB	56-61LA 62Cle 63Min	23	6'	203	none		144
Womble, Roye HB-FL	54-57Bal 60LA-A	2	6'	185	North Texas State		54
Wren, Junior DB	56-59Cle 60Pit 61NY-A	4	6'	192	Missouri	14	8
Youngelman, Sid DT-DE	55SF 56-58Phi 59Cle 60-61NY-A 62-63BufA		6'3"	257	Alabama		
Zucco, Vic DB	57-60ChiB	3	6'	187	Michigan State	8	6

Lifetime Statistics – Players from Pre 1960 Section 1 – **PASSING**
(All men with 25 or more passing attempts)

Name	Years	Att.	Comp.	Comp. Pct.	Yards	Yds/ Att.	TD	Int.	Pct. Int.
Sammy Baugh	37-52	2995	1693	56.5	21886	7.3	188	203	6.8
Ed Brown	54-65	1987	949	47.8	15600	7.9	102	138	6.9
Bobby Clatterbuck	54-57,60	149	77	51.7	1032	6.9	8	9	6.0
Al Dorow	54-57,60-62	1207	572	47.4	7708	6.4	64	93	7.7
Tom Dublinski	52-54,58,60	177	93	52.5	1300	7.3	8	13	7.3
Frankie Filchock	38-41,44-46,50	677	342	50.5	4921	7.3	47	79	11.7
Frank Gifford	52-60,62-64	63	29	46.0	823	13.1	14	6	9.5
Harry Gilmer	48-52,54-56	579	263	45.4	3786	6.5	23	45	7.8
Otto Graham	46-55	2626	1464	55.8	23584	9.0	174	135	5.1
Don Heinrich	54-60,62	406	164	40.4	2287	5.6	17	23	5.7
Tom Landry	49-55	47	11	23.4	172	3.7	1	7	14.9
Bobby Layne	48-62	3700	1814	49.0	26768	7.2	196	243	6.6
Eddie LeBaron	52-53,55-63	1796	897	49.9	13399	7.5	104	141	7.9
Ted Marchibroda	54-57	385	172	44.7	2169	5.6	16	29	7.5
Ray Mathews	51-60	51	19	37.3	350	6.9	2	2	3.9
Lamar McHan	54-64	1351	610	45.2	9449	7.0	72	108	8.0
Tom O'Connell	53,56-57,60-61	423	204	48.2	3261	7.7	21	34	8.0
Johnny Rauch	49-51	170	70	41.2	959	5.6	8	9	5.3
Tobin Rote	50-59,63-64,66	2907	1329	45.7	18850	6.5	148	191	6.6
Allie Sherman	43-47	135	66	48.9	823	6.1	9	9	6.7
Y.A. Tittle	48-64	4395	2427	55.2	33070	7.5	242	248	5.6
Norm Van Brocklin	49-60	2895	1553	53.6	23611	8.2	173	178	6.1
Bob Waterfield	45-52	1617	813	50.3	11849	7.3	98	127	7.9

Lifetime Statistics – Players from Pre 1960 Section 2 – **RUSHING and RECEIVING**
(All men with 25 or more rushing attempts or 10 or more receptions)

		RUSHING				RECEIVING			
Name	Years	Att.	Yards	Avg.	TD	Rec.	Yards	Avg.	TD
Alan Ameche	55-60	964	4045	4.2	40	101	733	7.3	4
Tom Barnett	59-60	81	263	3.2	1	7	52	7.4	1
Sammy Baugh	37-52	318	324	1.0	9	1	0	0.0	0
Ed Bernet	55-60					26	325	12.5	1
Dick Bielski	55-63	80	229	2.9	2	107	1305	12.2	10
Max Boydston	55-58,60-62					97	1328	13.7	8
Darrell Brewster	52-60					210	3758	17.9	21
Gene Brito	51-53,55-60					47	618	13.1	2
Ed Brown	54-65	265	920	3.6	14				
Dick Brubaker	55,57,60					13	200	15.4	1
Al Carmichael	53-58,60-61	222	947	4.3	4	112	1633	14.6	8
Ken Carpenter	50-53,60	242	1199	5.0	11	71	823	11.6	6
Lew Carpenter	53-55,57-63	468	2025	4.3	16	87	782	9.0	4
Johnny Carson	54-60					173	2591	15.0	15
Hopalong Cassady	56-63	316	1229	3.9	6	111	1601	14.4	18
Leon Clarke	56-63	1	–4	–4.0	0	141	2215	15.7	18
Bobby Clatterbuck	54-57,60	29	–27	–0.9	1				
Fred Cone	51-57,60	347	1156	3.3	12	75	852	11.4	4
Clyde Connor	56-63					203	2643	13.0	18
Jim Dooley	52-54,56-57,59-62	1	0	0.0	0	211	3172	15.0	16
Jim Doran	51-61	3	57	19.7	0	212	3667	17.3	24
Al Dorow	54-57,60-62	284	864	3.1	16				
Tom Dublinski	52-54,58,60	28	118	4.2	1				
L.G. Dupre	55-61	476	1761	3.7	11	104	1131	10.9	7
Tom Fears	48-56	5	15	3.0	0	400	5397	13.5	38
Howie Ferguson	53-58,60	670	2558	3.8	10	148	1247	8.4	3
Frankie Filchock	38-41,44-46,50	477	1478	3.1	6	8	88	11.0	0
Frank Gifford	52-60,62-64	840	3609	4.3	34	367	5434	14.8	43
Harry Gilmer	48-52,54-56	201	923	4.6	1	20	220	11.0	1
Otto Graham	46-55	405	882	2.2	44				
Bud Grant	51-52					56	997	17.8	7
Don Heinrich	54-60,62	27	24	0.9	5				
Red Hickey	41,45-48	7	7	1.0	1	75	1288	17.2	16
Harlon Hill	54-62	12	103	8.6	0	233	4717	20.2	40
Mike Holovak	46-48	136	720	5.3	6	13	155	11.9	0
Jim Lee Howell	37-42,46-47					61	921	15.1	7
Billy Howton	52-63	5	29	5.8	0	503	8459	16.8	61
Pop Ivy	40-42,45-47					53	513	9.7	1
Bill Jessup	51-52,54,56-58,60	1	–5	–5.0	0	61	994	16.3	7
Joe Johnson	54-58,60-61	93	376	4.0	0	84	920	11.0	8
Gary Knafelc	54-63					154	2162	14.0	23
Larry Krutko	58-60	96	331	3.4	4	14	108	7.7	0
Tom Landry	49-55	36	131	3.6	1	6	109	18.2	0
Bobby Layne	48-62	611	2451	4.0	25				
Eddie LeBaron	52-53,55-63	202	650	3.2	9				
Woodley Lewis	50-60	47	188	4.0	0	123	1885	15.3	12
Eddie Macon	52-53,60	70	324	4.6	2	14	49	3.5	2
Ted Marchibroda	53,55-57	50	176	3.5	3				

Name	Years	RUSHING Att.	Yards	Avg.	TD	RECEIVING Rec.	Yards	Avg.	TD
Ray Matthews	51-60	300	1057	3.5	5	233	3963	17.0	34
Ollie Matson	52,54-66	1170	5173	4.4	40	222	3285	14.8	23
Jack McClairen	55-60					85	1253	14.7	3
Hugh McElhenny	52-64	1124	5281	4.7	38	264	3247	12.3	20
Lamar McHan	54-63	239	849	3.6	12	0	1	—	0
Don McIlhenny	56-61	414	1581	3.8	7	70	655	9.4	7
Steve Meilinger	56-58,60,61	1	6	6.0	0	60	863	14.4	8
Dave Middleton		67	210	3.1	2	183	2966	16.2	17
Dick Moegle	55-61	60	310	5.2	6	8	185	23.1	0
Jim Mutscheller	54-61					220	3684	16.7	40
Gern Nagler	53,55-61					196	3119	15.9	28
John North	48-50					38	784	20.6	5
Jerry Norton	54-64	47	341	7.3	1	11	125	11.4	1
Tom O'Connell	53,56-57,60-61	67	27	0.4	4				
Johnny Olszewski	53-62	837	3320	4.0	16	104	988	9.5	3
Buddy Parker	35-43	180	489	2.7	4	40	378	9.5	0
Joe Perry	49-63	1929	9723	5.0	71	260	2021	7.8	12
Jim Podoley	57-60	209	746	3.6	2	78	1461	18.7	11
Billy Pricer	57-61	97	316	3.3	2	15	115	7.7	1
Billy Reynolds	53-54,57-58,60	176	585	3.3	7	24	252	10.5	0
Kyle Rote	51-61	231	871	3.8	4	300	4797	16.0	48
Tobin Rote	50-59,63-64,66	635	3128	4.9	37	2	28	14.0	1
Clive Rush	53	1	-6	-6.0	0	14	190	13.6	0
Bob Schnelker	53-61					211	3667	17.4	33
Scooter Scudero	54-58,60	43	139	3.2	0	6	62	10.3	1
Jimmy Sears	54,57-58,60-61	34	119	3.5	1	18	253	14.1	2
Allie Sherman	43-47	92	-44	-0.5	4				
Bill Stits	54-61	49	165	3.4	0	8	69	8.6	0
Ed Sutton	57-60	282	1109	3.9	9	14	237	16.9	1
Carl Taseff	51,53-62	60	283	4.7	3	19	193	10.2	1
Hugh Taylor	47-54	1	7	7.0	0	272	5233	19.2	58
Y.A. Tittle	48-64	372	1245	3.3	39	1	4	4.0	0
Mel Triplett	55-62	685	2856	4.2	14	43	439	10.2	4
Norm Van Brocklin	49-60	105	40	0.4	11				
Ron Waller	55-58,60	294	1569	5.3	8	44	443	10.1	1
Bobby Walson	51-62	4	12	3.0	0	311	5363	17.2	46
Bob Waterfield	45-52	75	21	0.3	13	3	19	6.3	0
Alex Webster	55-64	1196	4638	3.9	39	240	2679	11.2	7
Ted Wegert	55-56,60	109	408	3.7	4	14	131	9.4	1
Billy Wells	54,56-58,60	361	1384	3.8	5	57	725	12.7	2
Jerry Williams	49-54	172	910	5.3	10	91	1278	14.0	5
Billy Wilson	51-60					407	5902	14.5	49
George Wilson	37-46					111	1342	12.1	15
Tom Wilson	56-63	508	2553	5.0	18	61	617	10.1	5
Royce Womble	54-57,60	91	266	2.9	0	79	917	11.6	9

Name	Years	PUNT RETURNS No.	Yards	Avg.	TD	KICKOFF RETURNS No.	Yards	Avg.	TD
Frank Bernardi	55-57,60	39	392	10.1	1	4	101	25.3	0
Fred Bruney	53,56-62	53	265	5.0	0	18	421	23.4	0
Al Carmichael	53-58,60-61	122	912	7.5	0	191	4798	25.1	2
Ken Carpenter	50-53,60	34	370	10.9	1	41	895	21.8	0
Lew Carpenter	53-55,57-63	28	339	12.1	0	34	686	20.2	1
Hopalong Cassady	56-63	43	341	7.9	0	77	1594	20.7	0
Jack Christiansen	51-58	85	1084	12.8	8	59	1329	22.5	0
Lindon Crow	55-64	25	134	5.4	0				
Frank Gifford	52-60,62-64	25	121	4.8	0	23	594	25.8	0
Yale Lary	52-53,56-64	126	758	6.0	3	22	495	22.5	0
Woodley Lewis	50-60	138	1026	7.4	3	137	3325	24.3	1
Ray Matthews	51-60	61	779	12.8	3	42	1069	25.5	0
Ollie Matson	52,54-66	65	595	9.2	3	144	3746	26.0	6
Hugh McElhenny	52-64	126	920	7.3	2	83	1921	23.1	0
Don McIlhenny	56-61	1	0	0.0	0	30	747	24.9	0
Jerry Norton	54-64	46	147	3.2	0	14	415	29.6	1
Joe Perry	48-63					33	758	23.0	1
Bert Rechichar	52-61	85	311	3.7	0	23	448	19.5	0
Billy Reynolds	53-54,57-58,60	99	530	5.4	0	40	985	24.6	0
Lee Riley	55-56,58-61	48	249	5.2	0	32	764	23.9	0
Scooter Scudero	54-58,60	68	458	6.7	1	44	1143	26.0	1
Jimmy Sears	54,57-58,60-61	24	195	8.1	0	50	1169	23.4	0
Bill Stits	54-61	40	305	7.6	0	27	621	23.0	0
Carl Taseff	51,53-62	117	850	7.3	2	45	1019	22.6	0
Em Tunnell	48-61	258	2209	8.6	5	46	1215	26.4	1
Ron Waller	55-58,60	57	165	2.9	0	48	1146	23.9	0
Billy Wells	54,56-58,60	57	427	7.5	0	55	1267	23.0	0
Jerry Williams	49-54	51	277	5.4	0	20	476	23.8	0
Tom Wilson	56-63	3	28	9.3	0	62	1689	27.2	1
Vic Zucco	57-60	37	176	4.8	0	12	304	25.3	0

Name	Years	No.	Avg.
Sammy Baugh	39-52	338	44.9
Ed Brown	54-65	493	40.5
Ray Brown	58-60	95	39.2
L.G. Dupre	55-61	29	35.4
Bobby Gordon	58-60	55	38.0
Bill Jessup	51-52,54,56-58,60	75	41.0
Jack Johnson	57-61	30	35.2
Tom Landry	49-55	389	40.9
Yale Lary	52-53,56-64	503	44.3
Eddie LeBaron	52-53,55-63	171	40.9
Jerry Norton	54-64	358	43.8
Bert Rechichar	52-61	38	37.7
Clive Rush	53	60	37.7
Norm Van Brocklin	49-60	523	42.9
Bob Waterfield	45-52	315	42.4
Junior Wren	56-61	36	36.3

Name	Years	PAT	PAT Att.	PAT Pct.	FG	FG Att.	FG Pct.
Ben Agajanian	45,47-49,53-57,60-62,64	343	351	98	104	204	51
Larry Barnes	57,60	37	39	95	6	25	24
Dick Bielski	55-63	58	62	94	26	65	40
Hardy Brown	48-56,60	25	30	83	0	1	0
Fred Cone	51-57,60	221	237	93	59	102	58
Tom Fears	48-56	12	14	86	1	4	25
Ralph Felton	54-62	16	17	94	1	2	50
Bill George	52-66	14	15	93	4	8	50
Frank Gifford	52-60,62-64	10	11	91	2	7	29
Gary Glick	56-61,63	26	29	90	9	25	36
Lou Groza	46-59,61-67	810	834	97	264	481	55
Harvey Johnson	46-49,51	178	180	99	28	52	54
Joe Kuharich	40-41,45	12	13	92	0	4	0
Bobby Layne	48-62	120	124	97	34	50	68
Jim Martin	50-61,63-64	158	169	93	92	192	48
Jack Morris	58-61	15	15	100	3	8	38
Steve Myhra	57-61	180	189	95	44	91	48
Jerry Perry	54,56-62	92	96	96	32	58	55
Bert Rechichar	52-61	62	68	91	31	78	40
Les Richter	54-62	106	109	97	27	55	53
Lou Saban	46-49	21	22	95	0	2	0
Pat Sumerall	52-61	257	265	97	100	212	47
Bobby Walston	51-62	365	384	95	80	157	51
Bob Waterfield	42-52	315	336	94	60	110	55

1960-1969
From 12 to 26

The established National Football League faced yet another challenge from a rival league in the 1960's, but unlike the previous tests, this one produced far-reaching changes in the NFL. It eventually resulted in a two-fold increase in the number of teams, the adoption of many innovations to attract new fans, much-improved salaries and retirement benefits for the players, a big expansion of television coverage and the establishment of a Super Bowl championship game which attracted as much attention as baseball's World Series. Inevitably, these changes turned professional football into a big business for owners and players alike.

Having survived the challenge from the All-American Football Conference in the late 1940's, the NFL prepared to do battle with the new American Football League. The first step was to find a new commissioner to replace Bert Bell, under whose leadership the NFL had prospered for 13 years. When the owners reached a stalemate between the two primary candidates, 33-year-old Alvin (Peter) Rozelle was accepted by both factions as a compromise. In 1957 Rozelle had been named general manager of the Los Angeles Rams and one of his more noteworthy trades during the three-year stint was the acquisition of four-time All-Pro halfback Ollie Matson from the Chicago Cardinals in exchange for the rights to nine Ram players.

In an effort to head off the AFL's colonization of virgin football territory, the NFL decided to test two of the more promising areas by placing a club in Dallas beginning in 1960 and another in Minnesota to begin play in 1961. In addition, the desperate financial condition of the Cardinals and the desirability of St. Louis as an NFL city persuaded chairman of the board Violet Bidwill Wolfner and her husband, managing director Walter Wolfner, to move the team after 62 years in Chicago.

Meanwhile, the AFL laid plans for starting play in 1960, trying to avoid the pitfalls which caused the demise of three separate leagues using the same name earlier in the century. The AFL representatives and their cities were chief organizer Lamar Hunt, Dallas; William H. Sullivan, Boston; Ralph C. Wilson, Buffalo; Bob Howsam, Denver; K.S. (Bud) Adams, Houston; Barron Hilton, Los Angeles; Max Winter and William Boyer, Minneapolis-St. Paul; and Harry Wismer, New York City. Several of these men had been frustrated in attempts to buy NFL franchises previously.

When Minnesota was granted an NFL franchise, Winter and Boyer decided they had a better future in the more established league and thus withdrew from the AFL. The vacancy opened the door for an Oakland group headed by Y.C. (Chet) Soda and it included Ed McGah, Robert Osborne and Wayne Valley. The Raiders became the last of the original eight AFL teams to begin play in 1960 and eventually one of the more successful ones. Despite competition from NFL teams in Dallas, Los Angeles and New York, the AFL owners decided to stay in those cities, although the former two were later abandoned in favor of untested cities.

The AFL set out to differentiate its games from the NFL contests by adding several innovations. The new league adopted a rule for conversions whereby a team could elect to run or pass the ball across the goal line for two points as an alternative to the traditional one-point placekick used in the NFL. This added a new dimension of excitement and strategy to a play which had become nearly automatic. The AFL owners also decided to put the players' names on the backs of the jerseys and to make the scoreboard clock official, instead of having an official on the field keep the correct time as was done in the NFL. Both of these rules made the game more accessible to the average fan.

Joe Foss, a former pilot and South Dakota governor, was appointed as the first commissioner of the AFL, and a draft of college players similar to the one held annually by the NFL was

scheduled. The competition for players was expected to cause sharp increases in player salaries, just as it had done during the previous challenge from the AAFC. Because of the tempting offers made to college seniors, several players signed contracts with both leagues and soon found themselves as subjects of court battles.

The AFL won its first court cast over a player when a Los Angeles court declared Billy Cannon's contract with the Rams invalid, freeing him to sign with Houston. The Louisiana State University halfback had been the first player selected in the 1960 NFL draft, and his defection to the upstart AFL signalled the beginning of a long and costly bidding war between the two leagues. In the same year, however, Southern Methodist quarterback Don Meredith signed with the NFL's new entry in Dallas, the Cowboys, instead of with Hunt's Dallas Texans. In 1961 end Willard Dewveall became the first player to voluntarily switch leagues when he joined Houston of the AFL after playing out his option with the Chicago Bears.

The AFL received its biggest shot in the arm in 1965 when Sonny Werblin, who had taken over a shaky New York franchise from the league after Wismer had gone bankrupt in 1963, signed quarterbacks Joe Namath and John Huarte to sizeable contracts. Namath received a $225,000 bonus, an annual salary of $25,000 for three years, and no-cut and no-trade clauses in his contract, as the bidding war reached new heights. Although the cost seemed high at the time, Werblin proved himself to be a shrewd businessman, because Namath provided the charisma which made the important New York franchise a financial success and gave the league a degree of legitimacy previously unattained in th eyes of the New York media and many of the football fans across the country. As a measure of Namath's appeal, his first regular-season appearance in a Jet uniform attracted a crowd of 52,680 to Rice Stadium, where the Oilers were playing their first regular-season game after attracting an average of only 20,000 the previous year at Jeppeson Stadium. Three years later, Namath struck another blow for AFL pride when he predicted an AFL victory in Super Bowl III and then proceeded to direct the Jets to a win over the heavily favored Colts, giving the AFL its first Super Bowl triumph.

Although the New York franchise had floundered in its early years under the leadership of Wismer, Werblin wasted little time in upgrading the team. He hired Weeb Ewbank, a former Baltimore head coach, as his field boss in 1963 and the following year moved the team from the rundown Polo Grounds to new Shea Stadium, where it immediately set AFL attendance records. Werblin had a show-business background and he proved adept at utilizing that experience to attract new fans. Commissioner Foss also played a key role in preserving the franchise when he decided to have the league run the operation until the syndicate headed by Werblin came on the scene.

Another major reason behind the AFL's success was its ability to sell itself to a major television network at its inception. Under a contract signed with the American Broadcasting company, each AFL team received $150,000, and this needed revenue kept the league afloat when it otherwise might have folded. During the early years of its existence, the AFL suffered from a lack of superstars, poor attendance, the high cost of signing top draft choices and, in some cases, inadequate stadia. Attendance in the first year averaged only 16,500 but by 1962 began to climb steadily.

While the AFL may have had a shortage of quality players in its initial years, the games didn't lack for excitement or unpredictability. Most AFL teams used a wide-open, passing style which produced a lot of scoring. Although the defenses sometime seemed invisible, the style of play appealed immensely to the average fan. In the very first year Denver's Lionel Taylor caught 92 passes, and in 1964 George Blanda attempted 505 passes and Houston Teammate Charley Hennigan caught 101 of them for a total of 1,546 yards. Although Johnny Morris of the NFL's Chicago Bears caught 93 passes that same year, the older league with its stronger defenses couldn't quite match its young challenger when it came to high-scoring football.

When the Dallas Texans found their future growth limited by the presence of the NFL Cowboys and attendance figures below expectations, Hunt moved them to Kansas City after winning the 1962 AFL championship. As an inducement, Kansas City mayor H. Roe Bartle offered to enlarge Municipal Stadium and rent it to the team at $1 per year for the first two seasons, in addition to promising three times as many season tickets as the Texans sold in Dallas. With St. Louis the nearest competitor 250 miles away, Hunt saw a much brighter future in Kansas City, which became the AFL's first team in the Midwest.

The Los Angeles Chargers were actually the first AFL franchise to move to a new city, heading south for San Diego after their first year of play, in which they won the AFL's Western Division. Only 9,928 fans witnessed their title-clinching victory over Denver in 1960, and the club lost a total of $900,000 that first year. Those figures, combined with an enthusiastic appeal by San Diego officials, convinced Hilton to move the team without delay to the 34,000-seat Balboa Stadium.

Unknown to Commissioner Foss, AFL owners held a secret draft in 1961, hoping to sign the premium college players before the NFL teams held their draft. But when Foss learned of the plan, he declared the secret draft void and insisted another one be held. This infuriated Wismer, who had drafted Syracuse fullback Ernie Davis at the secret draft but saw Buffalo pick him at the official draft. Wismer tried to effect Foss' ouster but a majority of the owners backed the commissioner. While the competition for college seniors was fierce, the AFL refrained from signing established players currently under contract to NFL teams.

Rozelle convinced NFL owners that their interests would be better served if they united and sold the television rights to their games to one network in a single package. Such a plan brought added stability to the league, because the weaker clubs were able to share equally in the television revenue. Rozelle went before Congress in 1961 and convinced that body to pass a bill legalizing single-network contracts by professional sports leagues. He was rewarded the next year by being given a new five-year contract.

In 1962 a U.S. District judge ruled against the AFL's charges of monopoly by the NFL in the areas of expansion, player signings and television contracts, and the U.S. Fourth Circuit Court of Appeals refused to overturn that decision a year later. Meanwhile, both leagues competed for the spectators' dollars, the AFL instituting in 1961 a post-season All-Star game which got television exposure and the NFL experimenting in 1962 with a pre-season doubleheader involving four teams that drew a capacity house at Cleveland. The AFL had an all-Texas championship game in 1962 that went into a second overtime period before the Texans finally beat the Oilers in front of a full house of 37,981.

In 1963 the NFL was rocked by a gambling scandal which threatened the credibility of the entire league. Acting decisively, Rozelle suspended Green Bay's "Golden Boy" Paul Hornung and Detroit's defensive star Alex Karras for betting on football games in which they were not involved. In addition, five Detroit players — Joe Schmidt, Wayne Walker, John Gordy, Gary Lowe and Sam Williams — were fined $2,000 each for betting and the Lions' management was fined $4,000. Both players were reinstated 11 months later, but Rozelle's action served to maintain the public's faith in the integrity of the sport.

While Werblin was taking control of the AFL's New York franchise (changing its name from Titans to Jets) and Hunt was moving his team to Kansas City (changing its name from Texans to Chiefs), Al Davis left his job as an assistant coach at San Diego at age 33 to become the general manager and head coach at Oakland. With the Raiders finishing 2-12 and 1-13 in the

previous two seasons, Davis' task seemed formidable, but·he somehow blended several free agents and rookies with the holdovers and produced a team which went 10-4 and fell only one game short of the Western Division title. That season was only the beginning of what would prove to be a very successful career for Davis.

The survival of the AFL took a giant step in 1964 when Foss signed a five-year television contract with NBC for $36 million, guaranteeing each team $900,000 per year from television rights alone. The NFL also signed a new television contract, getting $14.1 million from CBS for the next two years of regular-season games. The new contract also permitted for the first time the telecasts of several games during prime time and also the telecasts of other games in the area of a team playing at home on a given Sunday.

With both leagues now having a measure of security because of the television revenue, they looked toward opening up new markets. They expanded into the Deep South for the first time in 1965, the NFL awarding a franchise to Atlanta and the AFL adding Miami, with both teams scheduled to begin league play in 1966. Following the same trend, New Orleans was slated to join the NFL in 1967.

While Kansas City's Hunt and Dallas' Tex Schramm were secretly discussing a merger, the war between the two leagues over signing players escalated in 1966 when placekicker Pete Gogolak played out his option with the Buffalo Bills and then signed with the NFL's New York Giants. The AFL interpreted this move as a deliberate attempt to lure away its top players, and Davis, who had replaced Foss as AFL commissioner in April 1966 after three impressive years at Oakland, set out to retaliate. The agressive 36-year-old league boss began efforts to sign top NFL players, forcing the NFL owners to seriously consider a truce in the war. The two leagues spent an estimated $7 million on draft choices alone in 1966, including $1 million by Green Bay for running backs Donny Anderson and Jim Grabowski.

To the surprise of nearly everyone, Rozelle announced on June 8, 1966 a merger agreement between the two leagues, with the AFL paying $26 million for the added financial security of joining the stable NFL. The two sides agreed to a championship game between the two leagues beginning with the 1966 season. Starting in 1967, a common draft and inter-league pre-season games were scheduled. Expansion to 26 teams by 1968 and a total merger of the two leagues into one unit by 1970 was planned. Rozelle was chosen as commissioner of the two leagues and, with the goal of a merger agreement behind him, Davis resigned his post with the AFL and returned to Oakland as managing general partner. Milt Woodward was appointed AFL president until the two leagues realigned under one banner.

At the first common draft in 1967, the AFL demonstrated its uncanny ability to assess young talent — an ability that would later prove to be a major factor in its quick rise to equality with the NFL teams. The AFL drafted such future stars as Bob Griese, Gene Upshaw, George Webster and Floyd Little, while the best the NFL could do was Mel Farr and Charles (Bubba) Smith, the No. 1 choice in the entire draft. Rozelle announced at that draft that "futures" (players whose college class had graduated but who still had a year of eligibility left) no longer could be drafted.

The AFL also had some success in inter-league games during the 1967 pre-season, Denver beating Detroit 13-7 for the first AFL triumph and defending AFL champion Kansas City embarrassing Chicago 66-27. The regular season started on an explosive note, as four kickoffs were returned for touchdowns on the opening weekend. For the season, 14 touchdowns were scored on kickoff returns, including a record four by Green Bay rookie Travis Williams and three by Chicago's Gale Sayers. Both players had record-breaking kickoff return averages — Williams 41.1 and Sayers 37.7. There also was a single-season record of nine ties during that exciting 1967 season.

Cincinnati was granted a franchise to join the AFL in 1968, and the team chose the same nickname (Bengals) that was used by the Cincinnati team in the old AFL of 1941. Former Cleveland coach Paul Brown was the leader of a group which bought the franchise, and he became its first head coach. Although his fellow owners weren't overly generous in the veteran allocation draft which supplied 40 players to the Bengals, Brown and player personnel director Al LoCasale used the draft wisely, building the Bengals into the first expansion team ever to win a division title in its third year of existence.

Two of the greatest names in NFL coaching annals retired in early 1968 — George Halas and Vince Lombardi. For Halas, 73, it was the fourth and final retirement after 40 years of professional coaching in Chicago, where he had owned a team since 1921. His coaching record was an impressive 320-147-30, giving him the most victories of any coach in NFL history. Lombardi resigned at the pinnacle of his career, having won five NFL championships during his nine-year reign at Green Bay and the frist two Super Bowls during his last two years. After one year in the sole capacity of general manager of the Packers, Lombardi took up a new challenge as part-owner, general manager and head coach of Washington in 1969 — a challenge that would be cut short by cancer after one season.

While AFL owners and players had agreed upon a pension increase in early 1968, the NFL was less sucessful. The resulting dispute prompted the NFL Players Association to declare a strike in July, and a compromise was reached only a few days before training camps were scheduled to open. The television networks learned just how powerful the influence of the football viewers had become when NBC switched at the appointed hour from its coverage of a close game between the Jets and the Raiders to begin a dramatic special of "Heidi." Enraged football fans jammed the network's switchboard, becoming even more upset when they learned that Oakland had scored two touchdowns in 17 seconds during the final minute of the game. Television had indeed created a "monster" that would have to be accommodated even further in the near future.

The AFL gained in respectability by leaps and bounds after the 1968 regular season had ended. PRO FOOTBALL WEEKLY announced the first-ever All-Pro team combining AFL and NFL players, and the AFL captured 10 of 22 positions. While Earl Morrall led the Baltimore Colts to an NFL title as a replacement for the injured Johnny Unitas, a young Joe Namath was making headlines with three touchdown passes in a 27-23 win over Oakland for the AFL championship. Because the AFL hadn't come close in either of the first two Super Bowl games, nobody gave the brash, young Jets much of a chance against the once-beaten Colts. When Namath was quoted a few days before the game as saying that the Jets would beat Baltimore, the statement was interpreted as a typical example of Super bowl "hype." Namath fulfilled his promise on Super Bowl Sunday, however, completing 17 of 28 passes for 206 yards as the Jets defeated the Colts 16-7. It was a momentous day for the AFL, and four underdogs everywhere.

When the excitement surrounding Super Bowl III began to subside, the NFL and AFL owners began deliberations on the realignment of the two leagues under one roof. The procedure wasn't as simple as some owners had expected. Many NFL owners were determined to maintain the separate identities of the two leagues within one organization. Some AFL owners also were willing to accept this plan, until Paul Brown and several other owners (New York's Phil Iselin, Denver's Gerald Phipps and Miami's Joe Robbie insisted that the AFL could never achieve parity with the NFL as long as the teams in the NFL outnumbered their AFL counterparts 16 to 10.

Once the NFL owners realized that a 16-10 split of the teams would not be approved, they had to decide which three teams would move to the AFL. At first, none of the owners wanted to move, fearing that their reputation and attendance would suffer and that they would lose important rivalries. The New York Giants and the San Francisco 49ers were exempted from switching to the AFL by the terms of the original merger agreement, because it was deemed essential that they be in a different conference from their next-door neighbors, the New

York Jets and the Oakland Raiders. Reasons for not joining the AFL seemed to be numerous, while reasons for switching were hard to find.

In a non-stop meeting that lasted nearly 36 hours, the owners finally agreed on a new alignment, with Baltimore, Cleveland and Pittsburgh moving to the AFL. Baltimore owner Carroll Rosenbloom had taken the initiative, agreeing to move his Colts to the AFL, and Cleveland's Art Modell followed Rosenbloom's lead. Modell wanted Pittsburgh to join him in a new division of the realigned American Conference and, after some hesitation, Steeler bosses Art and Dan Rooney agreed. The move by Baltimore and Cleveland came as a surprise to many fans because the clubs were two of the NFL's better teams at that time. While Pittsburgh had been a member of the NFL since 1933, its switch was less surprising in light of its five consecutive losing seasons.

Al Davis, who had been a thorn in the sides of NFL owners during his two-month tenure as AFL commissioner prior to the merger agreement, didn't win any new friends when he prolonged the marathon realignment session an additional 12 hours by insisting upon knowing the exact alignment of the 13 remaining NFL teams before giving his ratification vote. Nevertheless, the meeting adjourned without an agreement on the new setup of the 13 NFL teams, forcing the approval of the overall realignment plan to be postponed.

Two divisional arrangements came within one vote of the unanimous approval needed at that May 9-10 meeting in 1969. The first had the Vikings, Redskins, Cardinals, Giants and Eagles in the Eastern Division; the Cowboys, Packers, Bears and Lions in the Central; the Rams, 49ers, Saints and Falcons in the Western. The second plan had the Cowboys, Redskins, Cardinals and Giants in the East; the Packers, Bears, Lions and Saints in the Central; the Vikings, Rams, 49ers, Falcons And Eagles in the West. The First proposal was closer to the alignment eventually adopted, needing only a reversal of the Vikings' and Cowboys' positions.

Because the NFL owners never were able to agree on an equitable divisional setup for their 13 teams, Rozelle eventually submitted five plans and had one drawn in a lottery.

The financial aspects of the merger agreement included an $18 million indemnity payment by the AFL, which also gave the NFL an $8 million franchise fee paid by the Cincinnati owners to join the league. On the other hand, the AFL was getting assets estimated at a value of $55 million in the form of the three NFL teams which joined the AFL teams. In addition, the 13 NFL clubs agreed to pay each of the three teams who switched to the AFL approximately $2.5 million as compensation for the move.

The persistence of the AFL owners in demanding an equal share of the pie virtually guaranteed the equality of the two factions within a relatively short period of time. While the existence of the AFL vanished along with the decade, just as it had arisen from nowhere at the beginning of the 1960's, the memory of the league lingered on. The rivalry between the NFL and AFL was continued as an NFC-AFC rivalry, although the divisions had been blurred by the realignment. More than a decade after the initial merger agreement, the controversy between NFC and AFC factions continued to rage. The spirit and innovations of the American Football League pervaded professional football long after its disappearance, making the sport a more popular attraction than ever.

The end of the decade also provided some touchy decisions for Rozelle. The commissioner signed a three-year contract with the ABC television network for weekly telecasts of Monday night football games, while some observers feared that overexposure might result. Whereas the armchair quarterback had previously been limited to weekends for most of his football viewing, he now would have the opportunity to witness a football game as a prime-time "production." More importantly, the move of pro football to prime-time television meant large-scale advertising revenue and, as a result, more money in the coffers of the individual teams. Inevitably, this increase in revenue would be reflected in the salary demands of the players. Taken to its conclusion, the rapid spread in television exposure meant that the networks would have more control and the average fan less influence over the development of the sport.

Having dealt decisively with the gambling scandal in 1963, Rozelle faced a lesser but still noteworthy decision in 1969 when Namath was reportedly linked to several underworld figures through his part-ownership of a New York City nightclub. When Rozelle gave Namath the ultimatum of either selling his interest in the business or being suspended, Namath "retired" from football in a fit of pique. Although Namath was charged with "guilt by association" rather than any illegal activities, Rozelle was clearly within his broad authority as outlined in the league's constitution and by-laws and the standard player contract. Faced with the prospect of losing a substantial sum of money through a forfeited football contract and the possible loss of endorsements, Namath reconsidered his "retirement," choosing instead to sell his interest in Bachelors III and return to football.

Progress in the area of racial equality was achieved more quickly in professional football circles than in the surrounding environment, but some vestiges of foot-dragging were evident during the 1960's. Washington became the last NFL team to end the color barrier when it drafted Heisman Trophy winner Ernie Davis of Syracuse in 1962. Before the season started, the Redskins traded Davis to Cleveland for Bobby Mitchell, a black who became one of the league's leading receivers. Other blacks signed by the Redskins that year where Ron Hatcher, Leroy Jackson and John Nisby. After the 1965 season, several players in New Orleans for the AFL All-Star game charged that they were discriminated against, so the game was moved to Houston. In 1968 Merlin Briscoe of the Denver Broncos became the first black in pro football history to play regularly at quarterback, when an injury to the regular quarterback forced the rookie from Omaha to take over. Briscoe was traded to Buffalo the following year and he became a wide receiver.

A number of rule changes were adopted during the 1960's many of which made the game easier for the average fan to follow. The color of the officials' penalty flags was changed from white to gold, the uprights of the goal post were lengthened to a minimum of 20 feet above the crossbar and were painted gold, and the playing field was rimmed with a white border six feet wide. The major rule changes affecting the conduct of the game made it illegal for a player to grab the facemask of an opponent and required kicking shoes to be of standard production and not modified in any manner.

As the 1960's drew to a close, the emphasis on wide-open offensive football was beginning to change to a more conservative style of ball-control offense and short passes, as zone defenses became increasingly effective. While the influx of soccer-style kickers had accompanied a surge in the number of field goals, the number of touchdowns per game dropped significantly near the end of the decade. With 26 teams united under one organization and attendance booming, pro football was ready to begin a new era.

ALL-NFL TEAM OF THE 1960's

OFFENSE

Name	Position
Del Shofner	Split End
Charley Taylor	Split End
Gary Collins	Flanker
Boyd Dowler	Flanker
John Mackey	Tight End
Bob Brown	Tackle
Forrest Gregg	Tackle
Ralph Neely	Tackle
Gene Hickerson	Guard
Jerry Kramer	Guard
Howard Mudd	Guard
Jim Ringo	Center
Sonny Jurgensen	Quarterback
Bart Starr	Quarterback
Johnny Unitas	Quarterback
John David Crow	Halfback
Paul Hornung	Halfback
Leroy Kelly	Halfback
Gale Sayers	Halfback
Jim Brown	Fullback
Jim Taylor	Fullback
Jim Bakken	Kicker
Don Chandler	Punter

DEFENSE

Name	Position
Doug Atkins	End
Willie Davis	End
David (Deacon) Jones	End
Alex Karras	Tackle
Bob Lilly	Tackle
Merlin Olsen	Tackle
Dick Butkus	Linebacker
Larry Morris	Linebacker
Ray Nitschke	Linebacker
Tommy Nobis	Linebacker
Dave Robinson	Linebacker
Herb Adderley	Cornerback
Lem Barney	Cornerback
Bobby Boyd	Cornerback
Eddie Meador	Safety
Larry Wilson	Safety
Willy Wood	Safety

ALL-AFL TEAM OF THE 1960's

OFFENSE

Name	Position
Lance Alworth	Flanker
Don Maynard	End
Fred Arbanas	Tight End
Ron Mix	Tackle
Jim Tyrer	Tackle
Ed Budde	Guard
Billy Shaw	Guard
Jim Otto	Center
Joe Namath	Quarterback
Clem Daniels	Running Back
Paul Lowe	Running Back
George Blanda	Kicker
Jarrel Wilson	Punter

DEFENSE

Name	Position
Jerry Mays	End
Gerry Philbin	End
Houston Antwine	Tackle
Tom Sestak	Tackle
Bobby Bell	Linebacker
George Webster	Linebacker
Nick Buoniconti	Linebacker
Willie Brown	Cornerback
Dave Grayson	Cornerback
Johnny Robinson	Safety
George Saimes	Safety

(Both teams were chosen by the Pro Football Hall of Fame Selection Committee).

1960 N.F.L. Mara's Compromise

After four days of meetings and twenty-one deadlocked ballots, the league owners had still not elected a new commissioner to succeed the late Bert Bell. With the older owners supporting acting commissioner Austin Gunsel and the young owners supporting San Francisco attorney Marshall Leahy, New York Giant vice-president Wellington Mara presented an acceptable compromise candidate. He nominated Pete Rozelle, thirty-three-year-old general manager of the Los Angeles Rams. and the other owners quickly confirmed the young man as commissioner. Like Bell, Rozelle faced the challenge of a new league, the American Football League, at the start of his administration, but the NFL was strong enough at this time also to expand, shifting the Cardinals to St. Louis, putting a new team in Dallas this year, and granting Minneapolis-St. Paul a franchise for 1961. The new league would drive player salaries up, but the NFL owners had no worries about their league surviving.

EASTERN CONFERENCE

Philadelphia Eagles—The Eagles hardly looked like champions when they lost to Cleveland on opening day and barely beat the new Dallas team 27-25 the next week. But the club slowly gained momentum and by mid-season was battling the Giants and Browns for the Eastern lead. They eliminated the Giants by beating them 17-10 and 31-23 in back-to-back games, while the Browns eliminated themselves with three mid-season losses. Quarterback Norm Van Brocklin moved the team with his passes, but reserve depth was the key to the title drive. When fullback Clarence Peaks was sidelined, rookie Ted Dean filled in splendidly, and when injuries depleted the linebacking corps, center Chuck Bednarik moved over to defense. The thirty-five-year-old Bednarik was the story of the year, playing most of the game while starring at center and middle linebacker.

Cleveland Browns—The Browns opened their year with an impressive 41-24 rout of the Eagles, but the Philadelphia club evened the score three weeks later with a 31-29 squeaker. Then, while the Eagles went on a hot streak, the Browns ran into trouble in mid-season. The Giants came to Cleveland in early November and held Jimmy Brown and Bobby Mitchell to a total of six yards rushing. The 17-13 New York victory was their sixth in a row over the Browns. After the Browns edged the Cards 28-27, a 14-10 loss to Pittsburgh and a 17-17 tie with the Cards put them too far behind the Eagles to catch up. But one element of satisfaction did come from the strong finale, a 48-34 victory over the Giants at Yankee Stadium.

New York Giants—A good early-season showing kept the Giants in the Eastern race into November, but the aging New York squad was barely holding together with paste and string. A bad knee sidelined Alex Webster for most of the year, elbow and leg troubles made Chuck Conerly's availability a week-to-week affair, and an injured shoulder put Jim Katcavage out of action for the last half of the season. The Eagles, holding a slim half-game lead, came to Yankee Stadium in mid-November and beat the New Yorkers 17-10. The biggest loss of the day, however, was halfback Frank Gifford, knocked unconscious with a concussion by Chuck Bednarik's vicious tackle. Another loss in Philadelphia made the Giants' chances slim, and a tie with the fledgling Cowboys ended their hopes completely.

St. Louis Cardinals—The team's move to St. Louis had an immediate effect, as the Cards beat the Rams 43-21 to open their new history. Long-time losers in Chicago, these new Cardinals moved up to fourth place in the East behind an improved defense and versatile offense. The defensive line, led by Frank Fuller, put strong pressure on enemy passers, while the mobile linebacking crew of Bill Koman, Dale Meinert, and Ted Bates improved with experience. In the secondary, Jerry Norton starred at safety, while rookie Larry Wilson broke into the lineup as a cornerback. John Roach was the third new starting quarterback in three years, but the main forces in the offensive resurgence were end Sonny Randle and halfback John David Crow.

Pittsburgh Steelers—After beating the new Dallas Cowboys to start the season, the Steelers won only once in their next seven games, with only a matching effort by the Redskins keeping them from dropping to the bottom of the East. Injuries plagued the Steelers along the way. Bobby Layne hurt his throwing hand, a bad leg slowed John Henry Johnson, and various physical ills bothered Jimmy Orr, Mike Sandusky, and Mike Henry. Flanker Buddy Dial stayed healthy and was the main offensive threat with his speed on long passes. The defense slacked off a bit, due partly to the retirement of All-Pro cornerback Jack Butler, but still was no pushover. Starting in late November, the Steelers drove back to respectability with a three-game win streak, crippling the Browns' title hopes 14-10, locking Washington into the basement 22-10, and ending the Eagles' nine-game win streak 27-21.

Washington Redskins—The Redskin defense sprang some major leaks in the secondary, but they were nothing compared to the leaks in the offensive line. Quarterback Ralph Guglielmi watched a flood of defensive linemen pour in on him every Sunday, forcing him either to hurry his pass or hang onto the ball and get smashed to the ground. The ends he was throwing to, Bill Anderson and Joe Walton, did not have good speed, and fullback Don Bosseler, the leading rusher, was no sprinter, so the Redskins scored 16 points or less in eight of their nine losses.

WESTERN CONFERENCE

Green Bay Packers—After a close five-team race, the Packers emerged from the fray with their first Western title since 1944. They did not back into the crown but won it by taking their last three contests, two of which included head-to-head victories over the Bears and the '49ers. The Packers again were national news, and their biggest star was halfback Paul Hornung, who grabbed headlines with his unprecedented point production. As a runner, he had a nose for the end zone; as a kicker, his toe churned out points with field goals and extra points. After twelve games Hornung had set a new season's scoring record of 176 points.

Detroit Lions—With their defense jelling into a top unit, the Lions won their last four games to capture second place in the West. Rookie tackle Roger Brown joined Alex Karras, Darris McCord, and Bill Glass in a powerful front line, while Carl Brettschneider came from the Cardinals to complete the linebacking trio with Joe Schmidt and Wayne Walker. Another ex-Card, Night Train Lane, tightened up a secondary that already featured Yale Lary, Dick LeBeau, and Gary Lowe. Newcomers also helped the offense, as ex-Cleveland quarterback Jim Ninowski and freshman end Gail Cogdill made the pass a vital weapon in the Detroit attack again.

San Francisco '49ers—In a turn-about in the club's image, the defense carried the '49ers through the season. The young secondary of Abe Woodson, Jerry Mertens, Eddie Dove, and Dave Baker had meshed into a fine unit, while veterans Matt Hazeltine and Leo Nomellini anchored the linebacking front line units. The offense, however, bucked and sputtered, relying more than usual on Tommy Davis' field goals to bail it out. Head coach Red Hickey did experiment with the shotgun formation, with both ends split, a flanker and two wingbacks up near the line of scrimmage, and a quarterback all alone in the backfield, five yards back from the center. With the mobile John Brodie beating out Y. A. Tittle for the quarterback slot, the new formation often caught enemy defenses by surprise.

Baltimore Colts—Playing with a fractured vertebra in his back, Johnny Unitas still had his Colts at the head of the West. In mid-November, Baltimore held a one-game lead over Green Bay and had just won three straight games, apparently on the way to a third straight Western title. But when a torn Achilles tendon ended fullback Alan Ameche's career in mid-season, the Colt running game withered away and died. With only Unitas' passing to Ray Berry and Lenny Moore to worry about, enemy defenses concentrated solely on rushing the fragile Unitas and blanketing his receivers.

Chicago Bears—Neither Zeke Bratkowski nor Ed Brown had impressed at quarterback, fullback Rick Casares was slowing up, and the ends had no speed, but the Bears had scrapped their way to a 5-3-1 record, a half game behind the first-place Colts, by late November. The defense, led by Bill George and Doug Atkins, had kept the Bears in the race with several strong efforts through the fall. But the visions of championships dancing in George Halas' head were just so many sugar plums. The Packers just about killed any Bear hopes with a 41-13 drubbing two weeks from the end of the year, and the last two games turned into a nightmare, with a 42-0 beating by Cleveland and a 36-0 loss to Detroit.

Los Angeles Rams—It would have made great newspaper copy for new head coach Bob Waterfield and new general manager Elroy "Crazy Legs" Hirsch, great players in the salad days of the early 1950s, to lead the Rams back to glory, but it wasn't to be. Four losses right at the start established the Rams as also-rans in the West and prompted Waterfield to shake his club up. Young Frank Ryan began sharing the quarterback job with Billy Wade, Ollie Matson was shifted to a flanker position where his main duties were blocking and receiving, and Del Shofner became a defensive back after losing his offensive end job to rookie Carroll Dale. Although the Rams did beat the Packers and Colts down the stretch, the season was a troubled one all around.

Dallas Cowboys—Former New York assistant Tom Landry came in as head coach and tried to combine young talent with a coating of experienced players. For quarterbacks, Landry traded for little Eddie LeBaron and got rookie Don Meredith in the expansion draft, but the offense they commanded was practically invisible. Of the other players, end Jim Doran and linebacker Jerry Tubbs showed the most, with the roster in general an arid stretch of mediocrity. A perfect record of losses seemed inevitable for the Cowboys until they visited New York in December and gained a 31-31 tie with the Giants.

FINAL TEAM STATISTICS

OFFENSE / DEFENSE

BALT.	CHI.	CLEVE.	DALL.	DET.	G.BAY	L.A.	N.Y.	PHIL.	PITT.	ST.L.	S.F.	WASH.	STAT	BALT.	CHI.	CLEVE.	DALL.	DET.	G.BAY	L.A.	N.Y.	PHIL.	PITT.	ST.L.	S.F.	WASH.
													FIRST DOWNS:													
227	183	219	180	192	237	194	202	190	198	229	201	166	Total	195	202	208	216	204	199	221	183	205	224	158	180	223
64	83	107	57	89	135	76	81	54	81	127	90	83	by Rushing	86	94	92	106	87	74	87	79	117	90	56	82	77
143	90	96	105	88	86	101	107	121	104	89	96	71	by Passing	98	84	102	97	94	110	114	89	81	120	93	89	126
20	10	16	18	15	16	17	14	15	13	13	15	12	by Penalty	11	24	14	13	23	15	20	15	7	14	9	9	20
													RUSHING:													
345	373	383	312	392	463	343	406	351	411	484	413	415	Number	379	403	405	447	360	350	419	396	449	414	344	363	362
1289	1639	1930	1049	1714	2150	1449	1440	1134	1623	2356	1681	1313	Yards	1591	1679	1643	2242	1348	1285	1718	1267	2200	1493	1212	1587	1502
3.7	4.4	5.0	3.4	4.4	4.6	4.2	3.5	3.2	3.9	4.9	4.1	3.2	Average Yards	4.2	4.2	4.1	5.0	3.7	3.7	4.1	3.2	4.9	3.6	3.5	4.4	4.1
10	11	18	6	19	29	9	10	9	9	13	9	9	Touchdowns	17	17	10	20	8	7	16	8	14	13	8	13	9
													PASSING:													
392	324	264	354	333	279	335	322	331	285	285	336	274	Attempts	298	291	319	293	354	365	339	297	283	361	300	293	321
196	146	160	163	166	137	156	177	177	126	126	174	147	Completions	144	246	163	146	175	192	168	142	139	184	156	140	169
50.0	45.1	60.6	46.0	49.8	49.1	52.8	48.4	53.5	44.2	44.2	51.8	53.6	Completion Pct.	48.3	50.2	51.1	49.8	49.4	52.6	49.6	47.8	49.1	51.0	52.0	47.8	52.6
3164	2130	2343	2388	2022	1993	2385	2385	2957	2511	1990	1866	1816	Gross Yards	2068	1808	2370	2305	2275	2432	2010	1984	3075	2147	2001	1818	2768
208	304	299	284	344	118	366	131	141	89	179	287	385	Yards Lost Tackled	342	420	207	175	226	275	155	177	157	284	330	183	204
2956	1826	2044	2104	1678	1875	1822	2254	2816	2422	1811	1579	1431	Net Yards	1726	1388	2163	2130	2049	2157	2355	1833	1827	2791	1817	1818	2564
8.1	6.6	8.9	6.7	6.1	7.1	6.5	7.4	8.9	8.8	7.0	5.6	6.6	Avg. Yds per Att (Gs)	6.9	6.2	7.4	7.9	6.4	6.7	7.4	6.8	7.0	8.5	7.2	6.8	8.6
16.1	14.6	14.6	14.7	12.2	14.5	12.4	15.3	16.7	18.1	15.8	10.7	12.4	Avg. Yds per Com (Gs)	14.4	12.4	14.5	15.8	13.0	12.7	14.9	14.2	14.3	16.7	13.8	14.3	16.4
26	13	22	17	6	9	20	20	29	20	20	11	9	Touchdowns	8	14	15	22	17	19	18	19	14	20	20	11	24
24	32	5	33	21	13	22	23	20	21	25	12	23	Interceptions	30	10	31	15	19	22	23	22	30	16	21	20	15
6.1	9.9	1.9	9.3	6.3	4.7	6.6	7.1	6.0	7.4	8.8	3.6	8.4	Percent Intercepted	10.1	3.4	9.7	5.1	5.4	6.0	6.8	7.4	10.6	4.4	7.0	6.8	4.7
													PUNTING:													
52	64	55	60	64	49	64	49	60	64	44	65	60	Number	54	72	46	50	69	66	50	66	48	54	63	62	50
38.5	39.7	42.0	42.0	43.8	41.2	42.3	39.2	43.1	44.2	44.9	44.3	42.1	Average Distance	46.4	41.3	45.5	42.1	39.0	39.4	43.8	40.8	43.6	43.4	44.3	41.2	39.5
													PUNT RETURNS:													
23	27	21	23	31	26	25	31	28	30	30	24	15	Number	15	35	24	20	34	22	27	17	34	21	26	28	31
127	182	208	175	227	172	129	209	119	183	232	217	65	Yards	48	249	168	91	296	144	199	100	166	198	162	182	242
5.5	6.7	9.9	7.6	7.3	6.6	5.2	6.7	4.3	6.1	7.7	9.0	4.3	Average Yards	3.2	7.1	7.0	4.6	8.7	6.5	7.4	5.9	4.9	9.4	6.2	6.5	7.8
0	0	0	0	0	0	1	0	0	0	0	0	0	Touchdowns	0	0	0	0	0	0	0	0	0	0	0	0	0
													KICKOFF RETURNS:													
47	47	45	69	43	35	40	41	52	44	45	43	62	Number	44	37	62	31	45	57	52	47	53	48	57	38	42
1030	1055	900	1264	916	852	941	894	973	964	1045	1167	1363	Yards	1253	1029	1177	803	979	1158	1083	995	1076	1078	1245	769	719
21.9	22.4	20.0	18.3	21.3	24.3	23.5	21.8	18.7	21.9	23.2	27.1	22.0	Average Yards	28.5	27.8	19.0	25.9	21.8	20.3	20.8	21.2	20.3	22.5	21.8	20.2	17.1
1	0	1	0	0	0	0	0	0	0	0	1	0	Touchdowns	1	1	0	1	0	0	2	0	0	1	0	0	0
													INTERCEPTION RETURNS:													
30	10	31	15	19	22	23	22	30	16	21	20	15	Number	24	32	5	33	21	13	22	23	20	21	25	12	23
297	111	624	97	385	358	362	294	341	130	178	141	189	Yards	272	627	58	366	314	185	182	253	277	165	419	159	210
9.9	11.1	20.1	6.5	19.2	16.3	15.7	13.4	11.4	8.1	8.5	7.1	12.6	Average Yards	11.3	19.6	11.6	11.1	15.0	14.2	8.3	11.0	13.9	7.9	16.8	13.3	9.1
0	0	6	0	2	1	3	2	0	0	0	0	0	Touchdowns	1	4	0	2	0	0	2	0	1	0	2	0	1
													PENALTIES:													
51	83	49	62	68	64	64	48	57	61	46	63	69	Number	59	75	48	72	60	61	59	55	54	58	52	64	68
504	707	534	600	726	578	625	460	544	606	456	604	713	Yards	538	704	526	671	637	636	517	532	597	565	500	580	654
													FUMBLES:													
24	18	20	22	13	18	17	49	24	27	42	14	29	Number	20	13	27	21	19	23	29	28	31	25	35	15	31
12	10	12	17	9	12	9	26	10	14	22	4	15	Number Lost	9	9	14	11	11	15	13	12	15	13	23	8	19
													POINTS:													
288	194	362	177	239	332	265	271	321	240	288	208	178	Total	234	299	217	369	212	209	297	261	246	275	230	205	309
37	25	46	23	28	41	31	32	40	28	34	21	19	PAT Attempts	27	38	26	45	28	25	35	32	27	33	30	25	34
35	23	44	21	26	41	31	32	39	27	33	21	19	PAT Made	27	37	25	44	27	24	34	31	24	33	29	23	34
19	16	20	13	24	28	22	26	20	19	25	35	23	FG Attempts	30	20	21	25	12	13	29	23	28	21	16	20	32
9	7	12	6	13	15	14	13	14	11	15	19	15	FG Made	15	8	12	17	5	9	17	12	16	14	7	10	21
47.4	43.8	60.0	46.2	54.2	53.6	63.6	50.0	70.0	57.9	60.0	54.3	65.2	Percent FG Made	50.0	40.0	57.1	68.0	41.7	69.2	58.6	52.2	57.1	66.7	43.8	50.0	65.6
2	0	0	0	3	0	0	0	2	0	2	0	0	Safeties	0	2	0	2	1	1	1	1	1	0	0	1	1

1960 NFL CHAMPIONSHIP GAME

December 26, at Philadelphia
(Attendance 67,325)

Start with Hornung, End with Dean

The Green Bay Packers, a tough, young team built by coach Vince Lombardi, came to Franklin Field to face the Eagles, a veteran team centering around Norm Van Brocklin and Chuck Bednarik, for the NFL title. The Packers got the first break of the game by recovering an Eagle fumble on the Philadelphia 14-yard line on the first play from scrimmage, but four Green Bay running plays gained only nine yards. The Eagles took the ball on downs but fumbled it away three plays later on the 22-yard line. Again the Packers couldn't move the ball, and they had to settle for a Paul Hornung field goal. The quarter ended with the score 3-0, as both defenses played well against the enemy's strength. The Eagles shut off the Green Bay running game; the Packers stopped Van Brocklin's passes. The halftime score was Philadelphia 10, Green Bay 6, and neither team scored in the third quarter. Within two minutes of the fourth period, however, Green Bay capped an 80-yard drive with a Bart Starr-to-Max McGee touchdown pass to give the Packers a 13-10 lead. On the kickoff following the touchdown, Ted Dean brought the Eagles back into the game by returning the ball to the Green Bay 39. Seven plays later, Dean carried the ball over from the 5-yard line. The Packers drove downfield in the waning minutes, but time ran out with the ball on the Philadelphia 9-yard line and the score 17-13 in favor of the Eagles.

SCORING

PHILADELPHIA   0   10   0   7—17
GREEN BAY   3   3   0   7—13

First Quarter
G. B. Hornung, 20 yard field goal   6:20

Second Quarter
G. B. Hornung, 23 yard field goal   1:44
PHI. McDonald, 35 yard pass from Van Brocklin   8:08
    PAT — Walston (kick)
PHI. Walston, 15 yard field goal   11:48

Fourth Quarter
G. B. McGee, 7 yard pass from Starr   1:53
    PAT — Hornung (kick)
PHI. Dean, 5 yard rush   5:21
    PAT — Walston (kick)

TEAM STATISTICS

PHI.		G.B.
13	First Downs — Total	22
5	First Downs — Rushing	14
6	First Downs — Passing	8
2	First Downs — Penalty	0
99	Rushing Yardage	223
20	Pass Attempts	35
9	Pass Completions	21
45.0	Completion Percentage	60.0
204	Passing Yardage	178
10.2	Avg. Yards per Attempt	5.1
22.7	Avg. Yards per Completion	8.5
7	Yards Lost Tackled	0
197	Net Passing Yardage	178
0	Interceptions By	1
0	Interception Return Yardage	0
3	Fumbles — Number	1
2	Fumbles — Lost Ball	1
0	Penalties — Number	4
0	Yards Penalized	27
0	Missed Field Goals	1

INDIVIDUAL STATISTICS

PHILADELPHIA	No.	Yds.	Avg.	GREEN BAY	No.	Yds.	Avg.
PUNTING							
Van Brocklin	6		39.5	McGee	5		45.2
PUNT RETURNS							
Dean	1	10	10.0	Wood	2	11	5.5
				Carpenter	2	7	3.5
					4	18	4.5
KICKOFF RETURNS							
Dean	1	58	58.0	Symank	2	49	24.5
Brown	1	20	20.0				
Lucas	1	9	9.0				
Robb	1	4	4.0				
	4	91	22.8				

1960 N.F.L. — Eastern Conference

PHILADELPHIA EAGLES 10-2-0 Buck Shaw

Scores of Each Game		
24	CLEVELAND	41
27	Dallas	25
31	ST. LOUIS	27
28	DETROIT	10
31	Cleveland	29
34	PITTSBURGH	7
19	WASHINGTON	13
17	New York	10
31	NEW YORK	23
20	St. Louis	6
21	Pittsburgh	27
38	Washington	28

Use Name	Pos.	Hgt	Wgt	Age	Int	Pts
Jim McCusker	OT	6'2"	245	24		
J. D. Smith	OT	6'5"	250	24		6
Howard Keys	C-OT	6'3"	235	25		
John Wilcox	DE-OT	6'5"	230	22		
Stan Campbell	OG	6'	230	30		
Jerry Huth	OG	6'	228	27		
John Wittenborn (from SF)	OG	6'2"	230	24		
Bill Lapham	C	6'3"	250	26		
Marion Campbell	DE	6'3"	250	31		
Joe Robb	LB-DE	6'3"	225	23		
Gene Gossage	DT-DE	6'3"	236	25		
Riley Gunnels	DT	6'3"	240	23		
Jess Richardson	DT	6'2"	262	30		
Ed Khayat	DE-DT	6'3"	240	25		
Maxie Baughan	LB	6'1"	220	22	3	
John Nocera	LB	6'1"	215	26		
Chuck Weber	LB	6'1"	235	31	6	
Bob Pellegrini	OG-LB	6'2"	235	25		
Chuck Bednarik	C-LB	6'3"	235	35	2	
Tom Brookshier	DB	6'	198	28	1	
Don Burroughs	DB	6'4"	186	29	9	
Jimmy Carr	DB	6'1"	198	27	2	6
Bobby Freeman	DB	6'1"	200	27	4	
Bobby Jackson	DB	6'1"	190	24		
Gene Johnson	DB	6'	190	25	3	
Sonny Jurgensen	QB	5'11"	200	26		
Norm Van Brocklin	QB	6'1"	202	34		
Jerry Reichow	OE-QB	6'2"	220	25		
Billy Barnes	HB	5'11"	198	25		36
Timmy Brown	HB	5'10"	195	23		24
Theron Sapp	HB	6'1"	200	25		
Ted Dean	FB-HB	6'2"	210	22		18
Clarence Peaks	FB	6'1"	220	24		18
Tommy McDonald	FL	5'10"	182	26		78
Dick Lucas	OE	6'2"	210	26		
Pete Retzlaff	OE	6'1"	210	29		30
Bobby Walston	FL-OE	6'	190	31		105

CLEVELAND BROWNS 8-3-1 Paul Brown

Scores of Each Game		
41	Philadelphia	24
28	PITTSBURGH	20
48	Dallas	7
29	PHILADELPHIA	31
31	Washington	10
13	NEW YORK	17
28	ST. LOUIS	27
10	Pittsburgh	14
17	St. Louis	17
27	WASHINGTON	16
42	CHICAGO	0
48	New York	34

Use Name	Pos.	Hgt	Wgt	Age	Int	Pts
Bob Denton	OT	6'4"	240	26		
Mike McCormack	OT	6'4"	247	33		
Dick Schafrath	OT	6'3"	245	24		
Gene Selawski	OT	6'4"	252	24		
Gene Hickerson	OG	6'3"	248	25		
Jim Ray Smith	OG	6'3"	245	29		
John Wooten	OG	6'2"	248	25		
John Morrow	C	6'3"	240	27		
Jim Houston	DE	6'2"	230	23		
Jim Marshall	DE	6'3"	220	23		
Paul Wiggin	DE	6'3"	240	26	1	6
Bob Gain	DT	6'3"	260	32	1	6
Floyd Peters	DT	6'4"	250	25		
Jim Prestel	DT	6'5"	250	23		
Larry Stephens	DT	6'4"	248	22	1	6
Vince Costello	LB	6'	225	28		
Galen Fiss	LB	6'	227	30	1	
Walt Michaels	LB	6'	237	31		
Dave Lloyd	C-LB	6'3"	248	24		
Ross Fichtner	DB	6'	185	22		
Don Fleming	DB	6'	185	23	5	
Bobby Franklin	DB	5'11"	180	24	8	12
Rich Mostardi	DB	5'11"	188	22		
Bernie Parrish	DB	5'11"	195	25	6	6
Jim Shofner	DB	6'2"	190	24	8	
Lou Groza – Voluntarily Retired						
Len Dawson	QB	6'	195	26		
Milt Plum	QB	6'1"	205	26		12
Prentice Gautt	HB	6'	195	22		6
Bobby Mitchell	HB	6'	188	25		72
Jamie Caleb	FB-HB	6'1"	210	23		6
Jimmy Brown	FB	6'2"	228	24		66
Ray Renfro	FL	6'1"	192	29		24
A. D. Williams	OE-FL	6'2"	210	27		
Leon Clarke	OE	6'4"	234	27		24
Rich Kreitling	OE	6'2"	208	25		18
Fred Murphy	OE	6'3"	205	22		
Gern Nagler	OE	6'2"	190	27		18
Sam Baker	K	6'2"	217	28		80

NEW YORK GIANTS 6-4-2 Jim Lee Howell

Scores of Each Game		
21	San Francisco	19
35	St. Louis	14
19	Pittsburgh	17
24	WASHINGTON	24
13	ST. LOUIS	20
17	Cleveland	13
27	PITTSBURGH	24
10	PHILADELPHIA	17
23	Philadelphia	31
31	DALLAS	31
17	Washington	3
34	CLEVELAND	48

Use Name	Pos.	Hgt	Wgt	Age	Int	Pts
Don Boll	OT	6'2"	270	33		
Rosey Brown	OT	6'3"	245	27		
Frank Youso	OT	6'4"	260	24		
Lou Cordileone	OG	6'	240	23		
Bill Crawford	OG	6'1"	235	23		
Darrell Dess	OG	6'	235	24		
Jack Stroud	OG	6'1"	235	31		
Ray Wietecha	C	6'1"	225	31		
Bob Schmidt	OT-OG-C	6'4"	245	24		
Jim Katcavage	DE	6'3"	230	25		
Andy Robustelli	DE	6'1"	230	34		
Tom Scott	LB-DE	6'2"	220	30	1	6
Rosey Grier	DT	6'5"	285	27		2
Proverb Jacobs	DT	6'4"	255	25		
Dick Modzelewski	DT	6'	260	29		
Sam Huff	LB	6'1"	230	25	3	
Jim Leo	LB	6'1"	215	22		
Cliff Livingston	LB	6'3"	215	30	1	
Harland Svare	LB	6'	215	29	1	
Lindon Crow	DB	6'1"	205	27	3	6
Dick Lynch	DB	6'1"	200	24	3	6
Dick Nolan	DB	6'1"	185	28	3	
Jimmy Patton	DB	6'	180	28	6	
Lee Riley	DB	6'1"	190	28	1	
Bill Stits	DB	6'	195	29		
Chuck Conerly	QB	6'1"	185	36		
Lee Grosscup	QB	6'1"	185	23		
George Shaw	QB	6'1"	180	27		
Don Chandler	HB	6'2"	205	25		
Frank Gifford	HB	6'1"	200	30		42
Joe Morrison	HB	6'1"	195	22		30
Ed Sutton	HB	6'1"	207	25		
Alex Webster	HB	6'3"	220	29		
Mel Triplett	FB	6'1"	215	28		36
Phil King	HB-FB	6'4"	225	24		
Bill Kimber	OE	6'2"	190	24		
Kyle Rote	OE	6'	200	31		60
Bob Schnelker	OE	6'3"	215	30		12
Pat Summerall	OE	6'4"	235	30		71
Bob Simms	DE-LB-OE	6'1"	210	22		

ST. LOUIS CARDINALS 6-5-1 Pop Ivy

Scores of Each Game		
43	Los Angeles	21
14	NEW YORK	35
27	Philadelphia	31
14	Pittsburgh	27
12	DALLAS	10
20	New York	13
44	WASHINGTON	7
27	Cleveland	28
26	Washington	14
17	CLEVELAND	17
6	PHILADELPHIA	20
38	PITTSBURGH	7

Use Name	Pos.	Hgt	Wgt	Age	Int	Pts
Ed Cook	OT	6'2"	245	28		
Dale Memmelaar	OT	6'2"	265	23		
Ken Panfil	OT	6'6"	265	29		
Tom Day	OG-OT	6'2"	240	25		
Ken Gray	OG	6'2"	245	24		
Mike McGee	OG	6'1"	230	22		
Mike Rabold	OG	6'2"	235	23		
Don Gillis	C	6'3"	250	25		
Ernie Fritsch	LB-C	6'	230	23		
Luke Owens	DE	6'2"	255	27		2
Jerry Perry	DE	6'4"	240	29		44
Leo Sugar	DE	6'1"	220	31		
Ed Culpepper	DT	6'1"	255	26		
Frank Fuller	DT	6'4"	245	31		2
Don Owens (from PHI)	DT	6'5"	255	28		
Tom Redmond	DT	6'5"	250	23		
Ted Bates	LB	6'3"	220	23		
Bill Koman	LB	6'2"	230	26	1	
Dale Meinert	LB	6'2"	218	27	3	
John Tracey	LB	6'3"	228	26	1	2
Charley Ellzey	C-LB	6'3"	245	22		
Joe Driskill	DB	6'1"	195	23		
Freddy Glick	DB	6'1"	185	23		
Jimmy Hill	DB	6'2"	190	31		
Billy Stacy	DB	6'1"	195	24	4	6
Larry Wilson	DB	6'	187	22	2	
Jerry Norton	DB	5'11"	195	30	10	
Bobby Towns	HB-OE-DB	6'1"	180	22		
King Hill	QB	6'3"	207	24		6
George Izo	QB	6'3"	230	23		
John Roach	QB	6'4"	195	27		6
Joe Childress	HB	6'	200	26		12
Bobby Joe Conrad	HB	6'	195	25		34
John David Crow	HB	6'2"	215	25		54
Willie West	HB	5'10"	185	22		
Mal Hammack	FB	6'2"	205	27		12
Frank Mestnik	FB	6'2"	200	22		18
Hugh McInnis	OE	6'3"	215	22		
Sonny Randle	OE	6'2"	187	24		90
Perry Richards	OE	6'2"	205	26		

PITTSBURGH STEELERS 5-6-1 Buddy Parker

Scores of Each Game		
35	Dallas	28
20	Cleveland	28
17	NEW YORK	19
27	ST. LOUIS	14
27	Washington	27
13	GREEN BAY	19
7	Philadelphia	34
24	New York	27
14	CLEVELAND	10
22	WASHINGTON	10
27	PHILADELPHIA	21
7	St. Louis	38

Use Name	Pos.	Hgt	Wgt	Age	Int	Pts
Byron Beams	OT	6'6"	248	26		
John Kapele	OT	6'	240	23		
Frank Varrichione	OT	6'1"	230	28		
Dan James	C-OT	6'4"	275	23		
John Nisby	OG	6'1"	230	27		
Mike Sandusky	OG	6'	230	27		
Ron Stehouwer	OT-OG	6'2"	240	23		
Ed Beatty	C	6'3"	225	28		
Billy Ray Smith	DE	6'4"	230	25		
George Tarasovic	DE	6'4"	245	31	1	
Ernie Stautner	DT-DE	6'1"	230	35		
Joe Krupa	DT	6'2"	225	27		
Joe Lewis	DT	6'2"	260	25		6
Ken Longenecker	DT	6'4"	285	22		
Will Renfro	DE-DT	6'5"	220	28		
Dick Campbell	LB	6'1"	225	24	1	
Rudy Hayes	LB	6'	215	25		
Mike Henry	LB	6'2"	215	24		
John Reger	LB	6'	230	29	1	
Dean Derby	DB	6'	185	26	3	
Dick Moegle	DB	6'	195	26	6	
Jack Morris (from LA)	DB	6'	190	28		
Bert Rechichar	DB	6'1"	210	30	1	15
Scooter Scudero	DB	5'10"	174	30		
Don Sutherin	DB	5'10"	190	24	1	
Fred Williamson	DB	6'2"	205	22		
Junior Wren	DB	6'	205	30	2	
Ron Hall – Military Service						
Rudy Bukich	QB	6'1"	200	29		
Bobby Layne	QB	6'1"	210	33		48
Rex Johnston	HB	6'1"	195	22		
Tom Tracy	FB-HB	5'9"	205	28		63
Tom Barnett	DB-HB	5'11"	190	23		
John Henry Johnson	FB	6'2"	215	30		18
Larry Krutko	FB	6'	225	25		
Charlie Scales	FB	5'11"	210	21		
Buddy Dial	FL	6'1"	195	23		54
Darrell Brewster	OE	6'3"	210	30		
Jack McClairen	OE	6'4"	215	29		
Preston Carpenter	HB-OE	6'2"	205	26		12
Jimmy Orr	FL-OE	5'11"	200	24		24
Bobby Joe Green	K	5'11"	175	22		

WASHINGTON REDSKINS 1-9-2 Mike Nixon

Scores of Each Game		
0	Baltimore	20
26	DALLAS	14
24	New York	24
27	PITTSBURGH	27
10	CLEVELAND	31
7	St. Louis	44
13	Philadelphia	19
14	ST. LOUIS	26
10	Pittsburgh	22
16	Cleveland	27
3	NEW YORK	17
28	PHILADELPHIA	38

Use Name	Pos.	Hgt	Wgt	Age	Int	Pts
Ray Lemek	OT	6'	240	26		
Don Lawrence	DT-OT	6'1"	245	23		
Don Stallings	DE-DT-OT	6'4"	250	21		
Fran O'Brien	OG	6'1"	240	25		
Vince Promuto	OG	6'1"	240	22		
Red Stephens	OG	6'	232	30		
Bob Whitlow	OG	6'1"	232	24		
Jim Schrader	C	6'2"	252	28		
Bob Khayat	OG-C	6'2"	230	22		64
John Paluck	DE	6'2"	235	27		
Art Gob (to LA-A)	DE	6'4"	230	23		
Andy Stynchula	C-DE	6'3"	255	21		
Ray Krouse	DT	6'3"	270	33		
Bob Toneff	DT	6'3"	265	30		
Rod Breedlove	LB	6'2"	220	22	3	
Ralph Felton	LB	5'11"	210	28		
Dick Lasse	LB	6'2"	225	24	3	
Bill Roehnelt	LB	6'1"	230	24		
Roy Wilkins	LB	6'3"	223	26		
Billy Brewer	DB	6'	190	25		
Jim Crotty	DB	5'11"	195	22	1	
Ben Scotti	DB	6'1"	185	23	4	
Jim Wulff	DB	5'11"	185	24		
Gary Glick	HB-DB	6'2"	200	29	3	6
Pat Heenan	OE-DB	6'1"	190	22	1	
Eagle Day	QB	6'	185	28		
Ralph Guglielmi	QB	6'1"	195	27		
M. C. Reynolds	QB	6'	195	25		
Dick Haley	HB	5'10"	195	23		
Ed Vereb	HB	6'	190	26		
Sam Horner	DB-HB	6'	195	22		
Dick James	DB-HB	5'9"	180	26		36
Jim Podoley	OE-HB	6'2"	205	27		6
Don Bosseler	FB	6'1"	212	24		12
Johnny Olszewski	FB	5'11"	202	29		18
Bill Anderson	OE	6'3"	210	24		18
Tom Osborne	OE	6'3"	190	23		
Joe Walton	OE	5'11"	205	25		18

PHILADELPHIA EAGLES

Rushing

Last Name	No.	Yds	Avg	TD
Peaks	86	465	5.4	3
Barnes	117	315	2.7	4
Dean	113	304	2.7	0
Brown	9	35	3.2	2
Sapp	9	20	2.2	0
Jurgensen	4	5	1.3	0
Retzlaff	2	3	1.5	0
Van Brocklin	11	−13	−1.2	0

Receiving

Last Name	No.	Yds	Avg	TD
Retzlaff	46	826	18	5
McDonald	39	801	21	13
Walston	30	563	19	4
Barnes	19	132	7	2
Dean	15	218	15	3
Peaks	14	116	8	0
Brown	9	247	27	2
Lucas	3	34	11	0
Sapp	2	20	10	0

Punt Returns

Last Name	No.	Yds	Avg	TD
Dean	16	65	4	0
Brown	10	47	5	0
Jackson	1	5	5	0
McDonald	1	2	2	0

Kickoff Returns

Last Name	No.	Yds	Avg	TD
Dean	26	533	21	0
Brown	11	295	27	0
McDonald	2	45	23	0
Robb	4	44	11	0
Reichow	4	28	7	0
Baughan	2	18	9	0
Carr	1	5	5	0
Lucas	1	5	5	0

Passing – Punting – Kicking

PASSING	Att	Comp	%	Yds	Yd/Att	TD	Int-%	RK
Van Brocklin	284	153	54	2471	8.7	24	17- 6	2
Jurgensen	44	24	55	486	11.0	5	1- 2	
Barnes	3	0	0	0	0.0	0	2- 67	

PUNTING	No	Avg
Van Brocklin	60	43.1

KICKING	XP	Att	%	FG	Att	%
Walston	39	40	98	14	20	70
Wittenborn	0	0	0	0	3	0

CLEVELAND BROWNS

Rushing

Last Name	No.	Yds	Avg	TD
Brown	215	1257	5.8	9
Mitchell	111	506	4.6	5
Gautt	28	159	5.7	1
Caleb	8	60	7.5	1
Dawson	1	0	0.0	0
Baker	1	−11	−11.0	0
Kreitling	2	−17	−8.5	0
Plum	17	−24	−1.4	2

Receiving

Last Name	No.	Yds	Avg	TD
Mitchell	45	612	14	6
Nagler	36	616	17	3
Renfro	24	378	16	4
Brown	19	204	11	2
Kreitling	16	316	20	3
Clarke	11	184	17	4
Caleb	5	−18	−4	0
Murphy	2	36	18	0
Gautt	1	10	10	0
Williams	1	5	5	0

Punt Returns

Last Name	No.	Yds	Avg	TD
Shofner	11	105	10	0
Mitchell	9	101	11	0
Franklin	1	2	2	0

Kickoff Returns

Last Name	No.	Yds	Avg	TD
Mitchell	17	432	25	1
Brown	14	300	21	0
Caleb	5	90	18	0
Gautt	3	47	16	0
Franklin	1	23	23	0
Fleming	1	8	8	0
Parrish	2	0	0	0
Fichtner	1	0	0	0
Stephens	1	0	0	0

Passing – Punting – Kicking

PASSING	Att	Comp	%	Yds	Yd/Att	TD	Int-%	RK
Plum	250	151	60	2297	9.2	21	5- 2	1
Dawson	13	8	62	23	1.8	0	0- 0	
Mitchell	1	1	100	23	23.0	1	0- 0	

PUNTING	No	Avg
Baker	55	42.0

KICKING	XP	Att	%	FG	Att	%
Baker	44	46	96	12	20	60

NEW YORK GIANTS

Rushing

Last Name	No.	Yds	Avg	TD
Triplett	124	573	4.6	4
Morrison	103	346	3.4	2
Gifford	77	232	3.0	4
Sutton	20	135	6.8	0
King	26	97	3.7	0
Webster	22	48	2.2	0
Chandler	2	19	9.5	0
Conerly	14	1	0.1	0
Grosscup	3	1	0.3	0
Shaw	15	−12	−0.8	0

Receiving

Last Name	No.	Yds	Avg	TD
Rote	42	750	18	10
Schnelker	38	610	16	2
Morrison	29	367	13	3
Gifford	24	344	14	3
Webster	8	106	13	0
Triplett	5	48	10	2
King	3	6	2	0
Kimber	2	48	24	0
Sutton	2	30	15	0
Simms	1	58	58	0
Summerall	1	15	15	0
Dess	1	3	3	0

Punt Returns

Last Name	No.	Yds	Avg	TD
Stits	18	166	9	0
Riley	10	42	4	0
Crow	2	1	1	0
Patton	1	0	0	0

Kickoff Returns

Last Name	No.	Yds	Avg	TD
Stits	20	486	24	0
Sutton	12	223	19	0
King	2	73	37	0
Riley	3	67	22	0
Triplett	2	38	19	0
Youso	1	7	7	0
Brown	1	0	0	0

Passing – Punting – Kicking

PASSING	Att	Comp	%	Yds	Yd/Att	TD	Int-%	RK
Shaw	155	76	49	1263	8.1	11	13- 8	9
Conerly	134	66	49	954	7.1	8	7- 5	7
Grosscup	25	11	44	144	5.8	1	1- 4	
Gifford	6	3	50	24	4.0	0	1- 17	
Morrison	1	0	0	0	0.0	0	1-100	
Summerall	1	0	0	0	0.0	0	0- 0	

PUNTING	No	Avg
Chandler	31	40.5
Conerly	18	36.9

KICKING	XP	Att	%	FG	Att	%
Summerall	32	32	100	13	26	50

ST. LOUIS CARDINALS

Rushing

Last Name	No.	Yds	Avg	TD
Crow	183	1071	5.9	6
Mestnick	104	429	4.1	3
Hammack	96	347	3.6	2
Childress	34	240	7.5	0
Conrad	23	91	4.0	0
Hill	16	47	2.9	1
Norton	2	47	23.5	0
West	7	45	6.4	0
Roach	19	39	2.1	1

Receiving

Last Name	No.	Yds	Avg	TD
Randle	62	893	14	15
Crow	25	462	18	3
McInnis	13	260	20	0
Childress	11	202	18	2
Conrad	7	103	15	0
Hammack	4	36	9	0
Mestrick	3	24	8	0
Richards	1	10	10	0

Punt Returns

Last Name	No.	Yds	Avg	TD
Conrad	8	86	11	0
Stacy	14	62	4	0
West	5	58	12	0
Wilson	3	26	9	0

Kickoff Returns

Last Name	No.	Yds	Avg	TD
West	13	370	28	0
Conrad	12	338	28	0
Stacy	6	146	24	0
Wilson	6	115	19	0
Mestnick	3	39	13	0
Hammack	2	23	12	0
Memmelaar	1	8	8	0
Bates	1	6	6	0
Driskill	1	0	0	0

Passing – Punting – Kicking

PASSING	Att	Comp	%	Yds	Yd/Att	TD	Int-%	RK
Roach	188	87	46	1423	7.6	17	19- 10	13
K. Hill	55	20	36	205	3.7	1	5- 9	
Izo	24	10	42	115	4.8	0	0- 0	
Crow	18	9	50	247	13.7	2	1- 6	

PUNTING	No	Avg
Norton	39	45.6
Hill	5	39.6

KICKING	XP	Att	%	FG	Att	%
Conrad	28	29	97	2	5	40
Perry	5	5	100	13	20	65

PITTSBURGH STEELERS

Rushing

Last Name	No.	Yds	Avg	TD
Tracy	192	680	3.5	5
Johnson	118	621	5.3	2
Krutko	17	99	5.8	0
Scales	26	81	3.1	0
Orr	8	57	7.1	0
Carpenter	17	36	2.1	0
Barnett	6	25	4.2	0
Layne	19	12	0.6	2
Johnston	4	12	3.0	0
Dial	1	8	8.0	0
Bukich	3	−8	−2.7	0

Receiving

Last Name	No.	Yds	Avg	TD
Dial	40	972	24	9
Orr	29	541	19	4
Carpenter	29	495	17	2
Tracy	24	349	15	4
Johnson	12	112	9	1
Brewster	2	26	13	0
McClairen	1	17	17	0
Krutko	1	8	8	0
Scales	1	−2	−2	0
Varrichione	0	−7	0	0

Punt Returns

Last Name	No.	Yds	Avg	TD
Carpenter	13	120	9	0
Johnston	12	45	4	0
Moegle	3	15	5	0
Scudero	2	3	2	0

Kickoff Returns

Last Name	No.	Yds	Avg	TD
Johnston	18	393	22	0
Carpenter	10	255	26	0
Moegle	7	174	25	0
Scales	5	100	20	0
Tracy	1	30	30	0
Hayes	1	11	11	0
McClairen	1	1	1	0
Varrichione	1	0	0	0

Passing – Punting – Kicking

PASSING	Att	Comp	%	Yds	Yd/Att	TD	Int-%	RK
Layne	209	103	49	1814	8.7	13	17- 8	6
Bukich	51	25	49	358	7.0	2	3- 6	
Tracy	22	9	41	322	14.6	4	1- 5	
Carpenter	2	1	50	2	1.0	0	0- 0	
Johnson	1	1	100	15	15.0	1	0- 0	

PUNTING	No	Avg
Green	64	44.2

KICKING	XP	Att	%	FG	Att	%
Layne	21	22	95	5	6	83
Rechichar	6	6	100	3	7	43
Tracy	0	0	0	3	6	50

WASHINGTON REDSKINS

Rushing

Last Name	No.	Yds	Avg	TD
Bosseler	109	428	3.9	2
Guglielmi	79	247	3.1	0
Olszewski	75	227	3.0	3
James	73	199	2.7	4
Horner	22	80	3.6	0
Podoley	29	52	1.8	0
Vereb	19	38	2.0	0
Reynolds	4	20	5.0	0
Glick	1	15	15.0	0
Anderson	1	6	6.0	0
Day	3	1	0.3	0

Receiving

Last Name	No.	Yds	Avg	TD
Anderson	38	488	1?	
Walton	27	401		
Podoley	17	244		1
James	16	24?		2
Bosseler	13	6?		
Olszewski	10	62	6	0
Vereb	9	119	13	0
Horner	7	106	15	0
Osborne	7	46	7	0
Haley	3	21	7	0

Punt Returns

Last Name	No.	Yds	Avg	TD
James	7	46	7	0
Horner	3	16	5	0
Podoley	3	11	3	0
Olszewski	1	0	0	0
Vereb	1	0	0	0

Kickoff Returns

Last Name	No.	Yds	Avg	TD
Horner	24	511	21	0
James	19	458	24	0
Olszewski	5	119	24	0
Vereb	5	119	24	0
Podoley	4	87	22	0
Wilkins	2	24	12	0
Stallings	1	19	19	0
O'Brien	1	16	16	0
Lawrence	1	10	10	0

Passing – Punting – Kicking

PASSING	Att	Comp	%	Yds	Yd/Att	TD	Int-%	RK
Guglielmi	223	125	56	1547	6.9	9	19- 9	9
Reynolds	30	13	44	154	5.1	0	3- 10	
Day	19	9	47	115	6.1	0	1- 5	
James	1	0	0	0	0.0	0	0- 0	
Vereb	1	0	0	0	0.0	0	0- 0	

PUNTING	No	Avg
Day	59	42.0
Horner	1	48.0

KICKING	XP	Att	%	FG	Att	%
Khayat	19	19	100	15	23	65

1960 N.F.L. — Western Conference

GREEN BAY PACKERS 8-4-0 Vince Lombardi

Scores of Each Game		
14	CHICAGO	17
28	DETROIT	9
35	BALTIMORE	21
41	SAN FRANCISCO	14
19	Pittsburgh	13
24	Baltimore	38
41	DALLAS	7
31	LOS ANGELES	33
10	Detroit	23
41	Chicago	13
13	San Francisco	0
35	Los Angeles	21

Use Name	Pos.	Hgt	Wgt	Age	Int	Pts
Forrest Gregg	OT	6'4"	250	27		
Norm Masters	OT	6'2"	250	27		
Bob Skoronski	OT	6'3"	250	27		
Andy Cvercko	OG	6'	240	23		
Jerry Kramer	OG	6'3"	250	25		
Fuzzy Thurston	OG	6'1"	250	27		
Ken Iman	C	6'1"	230	21		
Jim Ringo	C	6'1"	235	29		
Willie Davis	DE	6'3"	240	27		6
Bill Quinlan	DE	6'3"	250	28		
Jim Temp	DE	6'4"	250	27		
Dave Hanner	DT	6'2"	260	31		
Henry Jordan	DT	6'3"	250	25		
Ken Beck	DE-DT	6'2"	250	25		
Johnny Miller	DE-DT	6'5"	260	26		
Tom Bettis	LB	6'2"	225	27		
Dan Currie	LB	6'3"	240	26	4	
Bill Forester	LB	6'3"	240	29	2	
Ray Nitschke	LB	6'3"	235	24	3	6
Hank Gremminger	DB	6'1"	205	27	3	
Dale Hackbart	DB	6'3"	200	24		
Dick Pesonen	DB	6'	190	22		
Johnny Symank	DB	5'11"	180	25	1	
Em Tunnell	DB	6'1"	210	38	3	
Jesse Whittenton	DB	6'	195	26	6	
Willie Wood	DB	5'10"	185	24		
Lamar McHan	QB	6'1"	210	28		6
Bart Starr	QB	6'1"	200	27		
Paul Hornung	HB	6'2"	215	24		176
Tom Moore	HB	6'2"	215	22		30
Paul Winslow	HB	5'11"	200	22		6
Larry Hickman	FB	6'2"	230	24		
Jim Taylor	FB	6'	215	25		66
Boyd Dowler	FL	6'5"	220	23		12
Lew Carpenter	OE-FL	6'1"	215	28		
Gary Knafelc	OE	6'4"	220	28		
Ron Kramer	OE	6'3"	230	25		
Max McGee	OE	6'3"	205	28		24
Steve Meilinger	OE	6'2"	230	30		

DETROIT LIONS 7-5-0 George Wilson

Scores of Each Game		
9	Green Bay	28
10	SAN FRANCISCO	14
10	Philadelphia	28
30	BALTIMORE	17
35	Los Angeles	48
24	San Francisco	0
12	LOS ANGELES	10
7	Chicago	28
23	GREEN BAY	10
20	Baltimore	15
23	DALLAS	14
36	CHICAGO	0

Use Name	Pos.	Hgt	Wgt	Age	Int	Pts
Ollie Spencer	C-OT	6'2"	250	29		
John Gordy	OG-OT	6'3"	250	24		
Willie McClung	DT-OT	6'2"	260	31		
Grady Alderman	OG	6'2"	230	21		
Bob Grottkau	OG	6'4"	235	23		
Harley Sewell	OG	6'1"	230	29		
Bob Scholtz	C	6'4"	250	22		
Bill Glass	DE	6'5"	255	24		
Gil Mains	DE	6'2"	250	30		
Darris McCord	OT-DE	6'4"	250	27		
Sam Williams	LB-DE	6'5"	235	29		
Roger Brown	DT	6'5"	290	23		
Alex Karras	DT	6'2"	245	24		
Jim Weatherall	DT	6'4"	250	30		
Carl Brettschneider	LB	6'1"	225	28		
Jim Martin	LB	6'2"	230	36		65
Max Messner	LB	6'3"	225	22	1	
Joe Schmidt	LB	6'1"	220	28	2	12
Wayne Walker	LB	6'2"	225	23	1	2
Night Train Lane	DB	6'1"	195	32	5	6
Dick LeBeau	DB	6'1"	185	23	4	
Gary Lowe	DB	5'11"	195	26	2	
Bruce Maher	DB	5'11"	190	23	1	2
Jim Steffen	DB	6'	195	23		
Dave Whitsell	DB	6'	190	24		
Yale Lary	DB	6'	190	29	3	
Earl Morrall	QB	6'1"	206	26		6
Jim Ninowski	QB	6'1"	200	24		30
Warren Rabb	QB	6'1"	196	23		
Terry Barr	HB	6'	190	25		12
Dan Lewis	HB	6'1"	200	24		12
Ken Webb	FB-HB	5'11"	210	25		12
Nick Pietrosante	FB	6'2"	225	23		48
Hopalong Cassady	HB-FL	5'10"	185	26		12
Dave Middleton	OE-FL	6'1"	195	27		
Gail Cogdill	OE	6'2"	195	23		6
Glenn Davis	OE	6'	180	26		
Jim Gibbons	OE	6'2"	220	24		12
Steve Junker	OE	6'3"	220	25		

SAN FRANCISCO FORTY NINERS 7-5-0 Red Hickey

Scores of Each Game		
19	NEW YORK	21
13	LOS ANGELES	9
14	Detroit	10
10	Chicago	27
14	Green Bay	41
25	CHICAGO	7
0	DETROIT	24
26	Dallas	14
30	Baltimore	22
23	Los Angeles	7
0	GREEN BAY	13
34	BALTIMORE	10

Use Name	Pos.	Hgt	Wgt	Age	Int	Pts
Len Rohde	OT	6'4"	240	22		
Bob St. Clair	OT	6'9"	265	29		
John Thomas	OT	6'4"	246	25		
Bruce Bosley	OG	6'2"	240	26		
Ted Connolly	OG	6'3"	242	28		
Mike Magac	OG	6'3"	240	22		
Karl Rubke	C	6'4"	240	24		
Frank Morze	DT-C	6'4"	264	26		
Dan Colchico	DE	6'4"	236	23		
Ed Henke	DE	6'3"	227	32		
Charlie Krueger	DE	6'4"	245	24		2
Monte Clark	DT	6'6"	260	23		
Leo Nomellini	DT	6'3"	262	35		2
Henry Schmidt	DT	6'4"	260	23		
Bob Harrison	LB	6'2"	220	23	1	
Matt Hazeltine	LB	6'1"	220	27		
Gorden Kelley	LB	6'3"	230	22	2	
Clancy Osborne	LB	6'3"	218	25		
Jerry Wilson (from PHI)	LB	6'2"	235	23		
Dave Baker	DB	6'	193	23	10	
Eddie Dove	DB	6'2"	180	23	3	
Lenny Lyles	DB	6'2"	202	24		6
Jerry Mertens	DB	6'	183	24	2	
Jimmy Ridlon	DB	6'1"	177	25		
Abe Woodson	HB-DB	5'11"	188	25	2	
John Brodie	QB	6'1"	186	25		6
Y. A. Tittle	QB	6'	195	33		
Bob Waters	QB	6'2"	184	22		
Hugh McElhenny	HB	6'1"	198	31		6
Ray Norton	HB	6'2"	184	23		
J. D. Smith	FB-HB	6'1"	200	27		36
Joe Perry	FB	6'	206	33		6
C. R. Roberts	FB	6'3"	197	24		12
R. C. Owens	OE-FL	6'3"	190	25		36
Clyde Conner	OE	6'2"	190	27		12
Dee Mackey	OE	6'5"	236	24		
Monte Stickles	OE	6'4"	230	22		
Billy Wilson	FL-OE	6'3"	190	33		6
Tommy Davis	K	6'	212	25		78

BALTIMORE COLTS 6-6-0 Weeb Ewbank

Scores of Each Game		
20	WASHINGTON	0
42	CHICAGO	7
21	Green Bay	35
31	LOS ANGELES	17
17	DETROIT	30
45	Dallas	7
38	GREEN BAY	24
24	Chicago	20
22	SAN FRANCISCO	30
15	DETROIT	20
3	Los Angeles	10
10	San Francisco	34

Use Name	Pos.	Hgt	Wgt	Age	Int	Pts
Jim Parker	OT	6'3"	275	26		
Sherman Plunkett	OT	6'4"	270	26		
George Preas	OT	6'2"	255	28		
Lebron Shields	DE-OT	6'4"	240	23		2
Steve Myhra	OG	6'1"	240	26		62
Palmer Pyle	OG	6'2"	240	23		
Alex Sandusky	OG	6'1"	238	28		
Art Spinney	OG	6'	236	33		
Buzz Nutter	C	6'4"	240	29		
Ordell Braase	DE	6'4"	242	28		
Gino Marchetti	DE	6'4"	245	34		
Jim Colvin	OG-DE	6'2"	240	23		
Don Joyce	DT-DE	6'3"	250	30		
Art Donovan	DT	6'2"	270	35		
Big Daddy Lipscomb	DT	6'6"	288	29		2
Marv Matuszak	LB	6'3"	228	29		
Bill Pellington	LB	6'2"	238	31	1	
Don Shinnick	LB	6'	235	25	5	
Dick Szymanski	LB	6'3"	235	28	1	
Zeke Smith	DE-LB	6'2"	230	24		
Bobby Boyd	DB	5'10"	190	22	7	
Milt Davis	DB	6'1"	180	31	6	
Andy Nelson	DB	6'1"	180	27	6	
Jackie Simpson	DB	5'10"	185	26		
Johnny Sample	HB-DB	6'1"	203	23	4	6
Carl Taseff	HB-DB	5'11"	194	31		
Ray Brown	QB	6'2"	195	24		
Johnny Unitas	QB	6'1"	194	27		
Alex Hawkins	HB	6'1"	190	23		30
Ed Kovac	HB	6'	197	22		
Lenny Moore	HB	6'1"	190	27		78
Mike Sommer	HB	5'11"	190	25		
Jim Welch	HB	6'	190	22		
Alan Ameche	FB	6'	220	27		18
Billy Pricer	FB	5'10"	210	25		12
Ray Berry	OE	6'2"	190	27		60
Jim Mutscheller	OE	6'1"	204	30		12
Art DeCarlo	DB-OE	6'2"	202	30		
Jerry Richardson	HB-OE	6'3"	185	24		6

CHICAGO BEARS 5-6-1 George Halas

Scores of Each Game		
17	Green Bay	14
7	Baltimore	42
34	LOS ANGELES	27
27	SAN FRANCISCO	10
24	Los Angeles	24
7	San Francisco	25
20	BALTIMORE	24
28	DETROIT	7
17	DALLAS	7
13	GREEN BAY	41
0	Cleveland	42
0	Detroit	36

Use Name	Pos.	Hgt	Wgt	Age	Int	Pts
Stan Fanning	OT	6'6"	252	22		
Bob Kilcullen	OT	6'3"	245	24		
Herm Lee	OT	6'4"	247	29		
Bob Wetoska	OT	6'3"	250	22		
Roger Davis	OG	6'3"	235	22		
Stan Jones	OG	6'1"	250	29		
Ted Karras	OG	6'1"	235	27		
Bob Konovsky	OG	6'2"	245	26		
John Mellekas	C	6'3"	255	27		
Doug Atkins	DE	6'8"	255	30		
Maury Youmans	OT-DE	6'6"	230	23		
Fred Williams	DT	6'4"	248	30		
Bill Bishop	OT-DT	6'4"	248	29		
Earl Leggett	DE-DT	6'3"	250	26	1	
Joe Fortunato	LB	6'	225	30		
Bill George	LB	6'2"	235	29	1	
Ken Kirk	LB	6'2"	230	22		
Larry Morris	LB	6'2"	230	25	1	
Roger LeClerc	C-DT-LB	6'3"	235	22		
Erich Barnes	DB	6'2"	198	25		
J. C. Caroline	DB	6'1"	190	27	3	6
Pete Manning	DB	6'3"	208	24		
Richie Petitbon	DB	6'3"	205	22	2	
Justin Rowland	DB	6'2"	188	22		
Charlie Sumner	DB	6'1"	195	30		
Vic Zucco	DB	6'	187	25	2	
Zeke Bratkowski	QB	6'2"	203	28		
Ed Brown	QB	6'2"	208	31		12
Charlie Bivins	HB	6'2"	212	21		
Willie Galimore	HB	6'1"	187	25		6
Johnny Morris	HB	5'10"	180	25		36
Glen Shaw	HB	6'1"	217	21		
John Adams	FB	6'3"	235	23		
Rick Casares	FB	6'2"	225	29		30
Merrill Douglas	FB	6'	204	24		
Angie Coia	OE	6'2"	211	22		24
Willard Dewveall	OE	6'4"	218	23		30
Jim Dooley	OE	6'4"	198	30		6
Bo Farrington	OE	6'3"	217	24		
Harlon Hill	OE	6'3"	200	28		
John Aveni	K	6'3"	210	25		44

LOS ANGELES RAMS 4-7-1 Bob Waterfield

Scores of Each Game		
21	ST. LOUIS	43
9	San Francisco	13
27	Chicago	34
17	Baltimore	31
24	CHICAGO	24
48	DETROIT	35
38	Dallas	13
10	Detroit	12
33	Green Bay	31
7	SAN FRANCISCO	23
10	BALTIMORE	3
21	GREEN BAY	35

Use Name	Pos.	Hgt	Wgt	Age	Int	Pts
Jim Boeke	OT	6'5"	230	21		
Charlie Bradshaw	OT	6'6"	255	24		
John Guzik	OG	6'3"	236	23		
Roy Hord	OG	6'4"	232	25		
Chuck Janerette	OG	6'3"	240	21		
Buck Lansford	OG	6'2"	232	27		
Art Hunter	C	6'4"	248	27		
Gene Brito	DE	6'1"	230	34		
Lamar Lundy	DE	6'7"	235	25	1	6
Lou Michaels	DE	6'2"	248	24		7
John Baker	DT-DE	6'6"	290	25	1	
John Lovetere	DT	6'4"	280	24		6
George Strugar	DT	6'5"	260	25		
John Kennerson	DE-DT	6'3"	255			
Bill Jobko	LB	6'2"	218	24	1	
Bob Long	LB	6'3"	234	26	1	
Jack Pardee	LB	6'2"	220	24	1	
Les Richter	LB	6'3"	232	29	2	2
Jerry Stalcup	OG-LB	6'	220	22	1	
Charley Britt	DB	6'2"	180	22	5	6
Don Ellersick	DB	6'1"	193	22	2	
Carl Karilivacz	DB	6'	190	29		
Ed Meador	DB	5'11"	185	23	4	6
Will Sherman	DB	6'2"	197	31	1	
Vern Valdez	DB	5'11"	190	24	1	
Buddy Humphrey	QB	6'1"	200	24		
Frank Ryan	QB	6'3"	195	24		12
Billy Wade	QB	6'2"	203	29		12
Jon Arnett	HB	5'11"	193	25		24
Dick Bass	HB	5'10"	190	23		
Tom Wilson	HB	6'	204	27		12
Clendon Thomas	DB-FL-HB	6'2"	190	23	1	12
Joe Marconi	FB	6'2"	220	26		18
Ollie Matson	FL-FB	6'2"	210	30		6
Carroll Dale	OE	6'1"	194	22		18
Jim Phillips	OE	6'1"	200	23		48
Del Shofner	DB-OE	6'3"	192	24	1	6
Danny Villanueva	K	5'11"	200	22		64

DALLAS COWBOYS 0-11-1 Tom Landry

Scores of Each Game		
28	PITTSBURGH	35
25	PHILADELPHIA	27
14	Washington	26
7	CLEVELAND	48
10	St. Louis	12
7	BALTIMORE	45
13	LOS ANGELES	38
7	Green Bay	41
14	SAN FRANCISCO	26
7	Chicago	17
31	New York	31
14	Detroit	23

Use Name	Pos.	Hgt	Wgt	Age	Int	Pts
Byron Bradfute	OT	6'3"	243	22		
Paul Dickson	OT	6'5"	250	23		
Bob Fry	OT	6'4"	240	29		
Dick Klein	OT	6'4"	255	26		
Mike Falls	OG	6'1"	240	26		
Buzz Guy	OG	6'3"	247	25		
Duane Putnam	OG	6'	233	32		
Mike Connelly	C	6'3"	235	24		
John Houser	C	6'3"	238	24		
Nate Borden	DE	6'	240	28		
Gene Cronin	DE	6'2"	232	27	1	
John Gonzaga	DE	6'3"	244	27		
Don Healy	DT	6'3"	264	24		
Bill Herchman	DT	6'2"	245	27		
Ed Husmann	DT	6'	238	29		
Tom Braatz	LB	6'1"	220	27	1	
Wayne Hansen	LB	6'2"	228	32	2	
Jack Patera	LB	6'1"	240	28	1	
Jerry Tubbs	LB	6'2"	220	25	1	
Bob Bercich	DB	6'1"	198	23	2	
Don Bishop	DB	6'2"	204	25	3	
Bill Butler	DB	5'10"	182	23	1	
Fred Doelling	DB	5'10"	190	21		
Tom Franckhauser	DB	6'	196	23	3	
Jim Mooty	DB	5'11"	177	22		
Gary Wisener	OE-DB	6'1"	206	22		
Ray Fisher — Injury						
Chuck Howley — Injury						
Don Heinrich	QB	6'	182	28		
Eddie LeBaron	QB	5'9"	166	30		6
Don Meredith	QB	6'2"	198	22		
L. G. Dupre	HB	5'11"	190	28		30
Don McIlhenny	HB	6'	204	25		12
Gene Babb	FB	6'3"	218	25		6
Mike Dowdle	FB	6'3"	210	22		
Walt Kowalczyk	FB	6'	205	25		12
Ray Mathews	FL	6'	200	31		
Dick Bielski	OE	6'1"	227	28		6
Frank Clarke	OE	6'	215	27		18
Jim Doran	OE	6'2"	211	32		18
Fred Dugan	OE	6'3"	200	26		6
Billy Howton	OE	6'2"	195	30		24
Woodley Lewis	OE	6'	195	35		
Dave Sherer	OE	6'3"	225	23		
Fred Cone	K	5'11"	198	34		39

GREEN BAY PACKERS

RUSHING

Last Name	No.	Yds	Avg	TD
Taylor	230	1101	4.8	11
Hornung	160	671	4.2	13
Moore	45	237	5.3	4
McHan	8	67	8.4	1
Carpenter	1	24	24.0	0
Hickman	7	22	3.1	0
Starr	7	12	1.7	0
McGee	2	11	5.5	0
Dowler	1	8	8.0	0
Winslow	2	−3	−1.5	0

RECEIVING

Last Name	No.	Yds	Avg	TD
McGee	38	787	21	4
Dowler	30	505	17	2
Hornung	28	257	9	2
Taylor	15	121	8	0
Knafelc	14	164	12	0
Moore	5	40	8	1
R. Kramer	4	55	14	0
Meilinger	2	43	22	0
Carpenter	1	21	21	0

PUNT RETURNS

Last Name	No.	Yds	Avg	TD
Wood	16	106	7	0
Carpenter	9	59	7	0
Forester	1	7	7	0

KICKOFF RETURNS

Last Name	No.	Yds	Avg	TD
Moore	12	397	33	0
Carpenter	12	249	21	0
Symank	4	103	26	0
Hickman	3	54	18	0
Nitschke	2	33	17	0
Temp	1	16	16	0
Meilinger	1	0	0	0

PASSING – PUNTING – KICKING

PASSING	Att	Comp	%	Yds	Yd/Att	TD	Int−%		RK
Starr	172	98	57	1358	7.9	4	8−	5	5
McHan	91	33	36	517	5.7	3	5−	5	
Hornung	16	6	38	118	7.4	2	0−	0	

PUNTING	No	Avg
McGee	31	41.6
Dowler	18	40.5

KICKING	XP	Att	%	FG	Att	%
Hornung	41	41	100	15	28	54

DETROIT LIONS

RUSHING

Last Name	No.	Yds	Avg	TD
Pietrosante	161	872	5.4	8
Lewis	92	438	4.8	1
Webb	59	166	2.8	2
Ninowski	32	81	2.5	5
Barr	17	74	4.4	1
Morrall	10	37	3.7	1
Cassady	17	28	1.6	1
Lary	1	19	19.0	0
Middleton	3	−1	−0.3	0

RECEIVING

Last Name	No.	Yds	Avg	TD
Gibbons	51	604	12	2
Cogdill	43	642	15	1
Cassady	20	238	12	1
Pietrosante	13	129	10	0
Lewis	12	192	16	1
Webb	10	68	7	0
Junker	6	55	9	0
Middleton	5	51	10	0
Barr	5	26	5	1
Davis	1	17	17	0

PUNT RETURNS

Last Name	No.	Yds	Avg	TD
Barr	14	104	7	0
Steffen	14	83	6	0
Cassady	1	25	25	0
Maher	1	10	10	0
Lary	1	5	5	0

KICKOFF RETURNS

Last Name	No.	Yds	Avg	TD
Steffen	8	225	28	0
Maher	10	214	21	0
Lewis	10	202	20	0
Cassady	4	82	21	0
Barr	4	81	20	0
Pietrosante	2	58	29	0
Webb	3	38	13	0
LeBeau	2	16	8	0

PASSING – PUNTING – KICKING

PASSING	Att	Comp	%	Yds	Yd/Att	TD	Int−%		RK
Ninowski	283	134	47	1599	5.7	2	18−	6	17
Morrall	49	32	65	423	8.6	4	3−	6	
Barr	1	0	0	0	0.0	0	0−	0	

PUNTING	No	Avg
Lary	64	43.8

KICKING	XP	Att	%	FG	Att	%
Martin	26	28	93	13	24	54

SAN FRANCISCO FORTY NINERS

RUSHING

Last Name	No.	Yds	Avg	TD
Smith	174	780	4.5	5
McElhenny	95	347	3.7	0
Roberts	73	213	2.9	2
Brodie	18	171	9.5	1
Perry	36	95	2.6	1
Tittle	10	61	6.1	0
Waters	1	8	8.0	0
Woodson	4	4	1.0	0
Norton	2	2	1.0	0

RECEIVING

Last Name	No.	Yds	Avg	TD
Connor	38	531	14	2
Owens	37	532	14	6
Smith	36	181	5	1
Stickles	22	252	11	0
McElhenny	14	114	8	1
Mackey	12	159	13	0
Roberts	9	49	5	0
Wilson	3	51	17	1
Perry	3	−3	−1	0

PUNT RETURNS

Last Name	No.	Yds	Avg	TD
Woodson	13	174	13	0
Dove	11	43	4	0

KICKOFF RETURNS

Last Name	No.	Yds	Avg	TD
Lyles	17	526	31	1
Woodson	17	498	29	0
Colchico	5	68	14	0
Roberts	3	60	20	0
Clark	1	15	15	0
J. Wilson	1	0	0	0

PASSING – PUNTING – KICKING

PASSING	Att	Comp	%	Yds	Yd/Att	TD	Int−%		RK
Brodie	207	103	50	1111	5.4	6	9−	4	12
Tittle	127	69	54	694	5.5	4	3−	2	8
Waters	2	2	100	61	30.5	1	0−	0	

PUNTING	No	Avg
Davis	62	44.1
Baker	3	47.7

KICKING	XP	Att	%	FG	Att	%
Davis	21	21	100	19	32	59

BALTIMORE COLTS

RUSHING

Last Name	No.	Yds	Avg	TD
Moore	91	374	4.1	4
Hawkins	76	267	3.5	2
Ameche	80	263	3.3	3
Unitas	36	195	5.4	0
Pricer	46	131	2.8	1
Brown	2	25	12.5	0
Welch	5	23	4.6	0
Sample	1	7	7.0	0
Taseff	4	3	0.8	0
Kovac	4	1	0.3	0

RECEIVING

Last Name	No.	Yds	Avg	TD
Berry	74	1298	18	10
Moore	45	936	21	9
Hawkins	25	280	11	3
Mutscheller	18	271	15	2
DeCarlo	8	116	15	0
Richardson	8	90	11	1
Pricer	8	77	10	1
Ameche	7	56	8	0
Kovac	2	27	14	0
Taseff	1	13	13	0

PUNT RETURNS

Last Name	No.	Yds	Avg	TD
Sample	14	101	7	0
Taseff	6	25	4	0
Nelson	3	1	0	0

KICKOFF RETURNS

Last Name	No.	Yds	Avg	TD
Sample	18	519	29	1
Taseff	14	291	21	0
Pricer	6	88	15	0
Welch	4	80	20	0
Moore	1	23	23	0
Pellington	2	11	6	0
Sommer	1	10	10	0
Kovac	1	8	8	0

PASSING – PUNTING – KICKING

PASSING	Att	Comp	%	Yds	Yd/Att	TD	Int−%		RK
Unitas	378	190	50	3099	8.2	25	24−	6	3
Brown	13	6	46	65	5.0	1	0−	0	
Moore	1	0	0	0	0.0	0	0−	0	

PUNTING	No	Avg
Brown	52	38.5

KICKING	XP	Att	%	FG	Att	%
Myhra	35	37	95	9	19	47

CHICAGO BEARS

RUSHING

Last Name	No.	Yds	Avg	TD
Casares	160	566	3.5	5
J. Morris	73	417	5.7	3
Galimore	74	368	5.0	1
Adams	23	114	5.0	0
Brown	19	89	4.7	2
Douglas	11	82	7.5	0
Bratkowski	8	20	2.5	0
Farrington	1	−2	−2.0	0
Coia	3	−4	−1.3	0
Bivens	1	−11	−11.0	0

RECEIVING

Last Name	No.	Yds	Avg	TD
Dewveall	43	804	19	5
Dooley	36	426	12	1
Coia	25	478	19	4
J. Morris	20	224	11	3
Casares	8	64	8	0
Hill	5	98	20	0
Galimore	3	35	12	0
Douglas	2	11	6	0
Adams	2	−20	−10	0
Lee	1	16	16	0
Brown	1	−6	0	0

PUNT RETURNS

Last Name	No.	Yds	Avg	TD
Zucco	10	83	8	0
J. Morris	13	75	6	0
Petitbon	2	22	11	0
Coia	2	2	1	0

KICKOFF RETURNS

Last Name	No.	Yds	Avg	TD
J. Morris	19	384	20	0
Bivens	15	362	24	0
Galimore	12	292	24	0
Zucco	1	17	17	0

PASSING – PUNTING – KICKING

PASSING	Att	Comp	%	Yds	Yd/Att	TD	Int−%		RK
Bratkowski	175	87	50	1051	6.0	6	21−	12	16
Brown	149	59	40	1079	7.2	7	11−	7	14

PUNTING	No	Avg
Brown	56	39.8
Bratkowski	7	36.0
Casares	1	60.0

KICKING	XP	Att	%	FG	Att	%
Aveni	23	25	92	7	16	44

LOS ANGELES RAMS

RUSHING

Last Name	No.	Yds	Avg	TD
Arnett	104	436	4.2	2
Marconi	42	240	5.7	3
Wade	26	171	6.6	2
Matson	61	170	2.9	1
Bass	31	153	4.9	0
Wilson	41	139	3.4	0
Ryan	19	85	4.5	1
Thomas	16	63	3.9	0
Humphrey	2	7	3.5	0
Shofner	1	−15	−15.0	0

RECEIVING

Last Name	No.	Yds	Avg	TD
Phillips	52	883	17	8
Arnett	29	226	8	2
Dale	19	336	18	3
Thomas	17	275	16	2
Matson	15	98	7	0
Bass	13	92	7	0
Shofner	12	122	10	1
Wilson	11	82	7	2
Marconi	9	32	4	0
Ryan	0	32	0	1
Wade	0	10	0	0

PUNT RETURNS

Last Name	No.	Yds	Avg	TD
Bass	11	62	6	0
Arnett	10	60	6	0
Lovetere	1	6	6	1
Sherman	1	1	1	0
Matson	1	0	0	0
Meador	1	0	0	0

KICKOFF RETURNS

Last Name	No.	Yds	Avg	TD
Arnett	17	416	24	0
Bass	11	246	22	0
Matson	9	216	24	0
Wilson	2	48	24	0
Michaels	1	15	15	0

PASSING – PUNTING – KICKING

PASSING	Att	Comp	%	Yds	Yd/Att	TD	Int−%		RK
Wade	182	106	58	1294	7.1	12	11−	6	4
Ryan	128	62	48	816	6.4	7	9−	7	14
Humphrey	24	9	38	78	3.3	0	2−	8	
Arnett	1	0	0	0	0.0	0	0−	0	

PUNTING	No	Avg
Shofner	54	42.6
Marconi	10	40.8

KICKING	XP	Att	%	FG	Att	%
Villaneuva	28	28	100	12	19	63
Richter	2	2	100	0	0	0
Michaels	1	1	100	2	3	67

DALLAS COWBOYS

RUSHING

Last Name	No.	Yds	Avg	TD
Dupre	104	362	3.5	3
McIlhenny	96	321	3.3	1
Kowalczyk	50	156	3.1	1
Babb	39	115	2.9	0
LeBaron	17	94	5.5	1
Meredith	3	4	1.3	0
Heinrich	2	3	1.5	0
Clarke	1	−6	−6.0	0

RECEIVING

Last Name	No.	Yds	Avg	TD
Doran	31	554	18	3
Dugan	29	461	16	1
Howton	23	363	16	4
Dupre	21	216	10	2
McIlhenny	15	120	8	1
Kowalczyk	14	143	10	1
Babb	13	140	11	1
Clarke	9	290	32	3
Bielski	4	38	10	1
Mathews	3	44	15	0
Lewis	1	19	19	0

PUNT RETURNS

Last Name	No.	Yds	Avg	TD
Butler	13	131	10	0
Mooty	8	37	5	0
Franckhauser	2	7	4	0

KICKOFF RETURNS

Last Name	No.	Yds	Avg	TD
Franckhauser	26	526	20	0
Butler	20	399	20	0
Mooty	12	210	18	0
Babb	3	46	15	0
Dupre	2	44	22	0
Dowdle	2	22	11	0
Putnam	1	13	13	0
Bielski	1	4	4	0
Kowalczyk	1	0	0	0
Sherer	1	0	0	0

PASSING – PUNTING – KICKING

PASSING	Att	Comp	%	Yds	Yd/Att	TD	Int−%		RK
LeBaron	225	111	49	1736	7.7	12	25−	11	9
Meredith	68	29	43	281	4.1	2	5−	7	
Heinrich	61	23	38	371	6.1	3	3−	5	

PUNTING	No	Avg
Sherer	57	42.5
LeBaron	3	33.0

KICKING	XP	Att	%	FG	Att	%
Cone	21	23	91	6	13	46

1960 A.F.L. A New Competitor

Even before the first game was played the new American Football League was a flurry of activity. Commissioner Joe Foss, the former South Dakota governor chosen by the team owners to run the league, faced a major problem when the Minneapolis owners quit the circuit in January to accept an NFL team in 1961. This strategic move by the NFL shut the new circuit out of the Midwest and almost killed it in the cradle, but the upstarts did not give up. After several days of discussion the league owners turned down a bid from an Atlanta group and instead granted the eighth franchise to a syndicate from Oakland, California. The AFL finally had its full contingent of cities—Boston, New York, Buffalo, Houston, Dallas, Denver, Los Angeles, and Oakland. In New York, Dallas, and Los Angeles, the new league would be bucking NFL teams. Oakland in reality would have to compete with the NFL San Francisco '49ers. Buffalo and Boston were both graveyards for previous pro-football failures, while Denver and Houston were virgin territory.

Work went on during the summer, when players had to be signed. The AFL honored existing NFL contracts with players and lured away no players from the established league. The new teams picked up experience by signing NFL rejects and oldsters. Most of the AFL quarterbacks had NFL credits, such as George Blanda, Jack Kemp, Babe Parilli, Tom O'Connell, Al Dorow, and Cotton Davidson. Some players from the Canadian League seized upon the AFL as a chance to play again in the United States. Frank Tripuka, Dave Kocourek, Goose Gonsoulin, Butch Songin, Al Jamison, and Sherrill Headrick all had been playing north of the border before signing with the AFL. And a flock of unknown rookies and free agents were signing, hard-working if unspectacular football players with a desire to play football for a living. Such unheralded names as Charley Hennigan, Abner Haynes, Jim Otto, and Larry Grantham went unnoticed by pro scouts until turning up in AFL training camps.

But the most spectacular aspect of the player recruiting was the bidding war with NFL teams over well-known college players. The new league wanted to build its image by signing the cream of the graduating college class, and some clubs engaged in financial combat with an NFL team to woo an All-American collegian. Some young men found this courtship so intoxicating that they signed contracts with both contestants. A series of court battles ensued that gave the AFL such dual signers as Heisman Trophy winner Billy Cannon, Johnny Robinson, and Charlie Flowers.

Another item on the agenda was finding a place to play. New York and Oakland fared the worst in the stadium hunt, with New York having to settle for the grimy old Polo Grounds, while Oakland had to play its home games in San Francisco because there was no stadium in Oakland. Houston played its games in a high-school facility and Denver used a minor-league baseball field.

A fourteen-game schedule was adopted for the league, and the two-point conversion rule, where the team may run or pass for two points after a touchdown, was put into effect for all games. But the most important move by Commissioner Foss was the signing of a national television contract with the American Broadcasting System which provided a needed $150,000 to each team.

After all this, play was ready to begin. Although average attendance per game was only 16,000, the AFL would survive 1960 and be back for more.

EASTERN DIVISION

Houston Oilers—The players came from all over. Billy Cannon, the Heisman Trophy halfback from Louisiana State, had signed a three-year contract for $100,000, one of the richest pacts in pro history. George Blanda had come out off a year's retirement after a ten-year career with the Chicago Bears. Charley Hennigan had been teaching high-school biology, and he taped his final paycheck from the school inside his helmet for inspiration in dull moments. Bill Groman was an unknown rookie from Heidelberg. Al Jamison came down from the Canadian League. Coach Lou Rymkus blended all the parts together into a high-scoring machine which took command in the Eastern Division right from the start. The Oilers at first relied on Blanda's long bombs to Groman and Hennigan, but Cannon recovered from a slow start to give the ground game some punch and the Oilers won the first AFL Eastern crown.

New York Titans—The drab old Polo Grounds, abandoned since 1957, was dusted off to serve as home for the Titans. While Titan games were played in virtual anonymity (with highly inflated announced attendance figures), the NFL Giants were playing to a packed house week after week within walking distance at Yankee Stadium. The Titans admittedly were no match for the Giants yet, but they did play interesting, wide-open football. Although fullback Bill Mathis showed promise as a runner after winning a job in mid-season, the attack lived on quarterback Al Dorow's scrambling runs and long passes to speedsters Art Powell and Don Maynard. The Titan defense was virtually nonexistent, although young Larry Grantham showed well at linebacker. The Titans won interesting games, as when they beat Denver 28-24 by blocking a punt with twenty seconds left in the game, and they lost interesting games, like a 50-43 shootout with the Chargers. But the death of guard Howard Glenn with a broken neck after the October 9 game with Houston and the dearth of paying fans cast a deep shadow over this debut season.

Buffalo Bills—The Bills were an early-AFL rarity, a team trying to

live on its defense. They had two tough linemen in Lavern Torczon and Chuck McMurtry, a mobile, hard-hitting middle linebacker in Archie Matsos, and one of the league's better secondaries, headed by NFL veterans Richie McCabe and Jim Wagstaff. But the offense couldn't launch an effective passing attack, the staple of most AFL clubs this year. Tom O'Connell, the old Cleveland quarterback, could not hold the starting passer's job given to him at the outset of the season, and Penn State All-American Rickie Lucas flopped both at quarterback and halfback. Johnny Green, an unheralded rookie, eventually took charge of the offense, whose main weapons were runner Wray Carlton and flanker Elbert Dubenion. The high point of the year was a 32-3 upset of the Los Angeles Chargers, but the Buffalo attack stalled too often to do any better than third place in the East.

Boston Patriots—The AFL broke into the box scores in Boston on Friday night, September 9. A crowd of 21,597 fans turned out at Boston University Field to watch the first regular-season AFL game ever, between the Patriots and the Denver Broncos. The Patriots displayed their weak attack right from the start by losing 13-10 to the Broncos. Coach Lou Saban had little speed on an offense led by quarterback Butch Songin, a thirty-six-year-old veteran of the Canadian League who doubled as a local high-school coach, but the defense held together well around a nucleus of Bob Dee, Tom Addison, Fred Bruney, and Ross O'Hanley. With a 35-0 trouncing of the Chargers and a 42-14 beating of the Texans to their credit, the Patriots stayed at the break-even point until losing all four of their final games. In the season's finale, before a sell-out Boston crowd of 27,123, the Pats lost 37-21 to Houston. More importantly, coach Saban shifted Gino Cappelletti from defensive back to split end for this game and discovered Boston's top receiver for the next few years.

WESTERN DIVISION

Los Angeles Chargers—The eeriest sight in pro football was the Los Angeles Chargers playing to vast stretches of empty seats in the huge Memorial Coliseum. But despite the sparse fan support, coach Sid Gillman, who had coached the Rams last season, built a high-scoring outfit which took the Western Division crown in this first AFL season. The Chargers dropped three of their first five contests before hitting their stride, losing only once in their last nine games. The offense led this second-half charge, scoring 41 or more points in each of the last four games. Although the Chargers had shelled out a lot of money for Mississippi fullback Charlie Flowers, the offensive stars were quarterback Jack Kemp, rejected by the Steelers, Giants, and '49ers in the NFL; halfback Paul Lowe, an unknown rookie from Oregon State; and tackle Ron Mix, a first-draft choice of the NFL Colts. Tragedy hit the club when end Ralph Anderson, the team's leading receiver, died of a diabetes attack in November. But in general the Chargers were an artistic if not a financial success.

Dallas Texans—The Texans had the league's best runner, best defense, and worst luck. Halfback Abner Haynes, a speedster from North Texas State, was the AFL's first running star, carrying the ball for 875 yards, catching passes out of the backfield, and running back kicks with an exciting flair. The defense posted three shutouts and allowed a grand total of seven points in its last three games, the stingiest unit in this offense-oriented season. End Mel Branch, tackle Paul Rochester, middle linebacker Sherrill Headrick, and backs Dave Webster and Johnny Bookman were the main pillars of coach Hank Stram's defense. Only a couple of heartbreaking losses kept the Texans from challenging for the Western crown, as they lost 21-20 to the Chargers, 37-35 to the Titans, and 20-19 to the Raiders. But after the season the Texans could look back on a 17-0 victory over the Chargers and a 24-0 victory over the Oilers, shutouts over both divisional champions.

Oakland Raiders—Because of the problem of getting a late start, due to Oakland replacing Minneapolis as the eighth club in the new circuit, businessman Chet Soda, who headed the group granted the Oakland franchise, did not have an easy time when it came to signing players. But coach Ernie Erdelatz weeded through the available talent and built a surprisingly respectable team. He found two quarterbacks in rookie Tom Flores and NFL veteran Babe Parilli and three hard-working runners in Tony Teresa, Billy Lott, and Jack Larscheid. From this quickly organized squad, two players would stick with the Raiders through the entire ten-year life of the AFL—center Jim Otto and guard Wayne Hawkins.

Denver Broncos—With Gene Mingo returning a punt 76 yards for a touchdown, the Broncos beat the Boston Patriots 13-10 in the first regular-season AFL game. But Denver's main offensive weapon didn't join the team until the third week of the season. End Lionel Taylor, a slow-footed but sure-handed receiver, practiced with the Broncos for four days before catching eleven passes against the Titans on September 25, and he went on to catch enough passes in twelve games to lead the league in receiving. The Broncos lived on the pass, with thirty-two-year-old Frank Tripuka throwing 478 passes all year, including fifty-two against the Oilers on November 6. The airborne Denver attack boasted the league's top point producer in halfback and kicker Gene Mingo, but the defense leaked profusely despite fine seasons by tackle Bud McFadin and safety Goose Gonsoulin. With opposing teams scoring freely, the Broncos went winless in their last eight games, salvaging only a 38-38 tie with Boston by coming back from a 38-7 deficit in the third quarter.

FINAL TEAM STATISTICS

OFFENSE

Statistic	BOSTON	BUFFALO	DALLAS	DENVER	HOUSTON	L.A.	NEW YORK	OAKLAND
FIRST DOWNS:								
Total	234	211	272	248	262	263	286	254
by Rushing	86	77	119	84	83	96	111	98
by Passing	126	109	136	141	153	141	152	138
by Penalty	22	25	17	23	26	26	23	18
RUSHING:								
Number	401	462	483	440	474	437	485	475
Yards	1218	1211	1814	1195	1565	1536	1460	1785
Average Yards	3.0	2.6	3.8	2.7	3.3	3.5	3.0	3.7
Touchdowns	11	15	24	10	15	24	14	23
PASSING:								
Attempts	475	447	435	508	456	441	474	463
Completions	223	184	209	259	218	229	236	235
Completion Percentage	46.9	41.2	48.0	51.0	47.8	51.9	49.8	50.8
Yards	2865	2689	2831	3247	3371	3177	3334	2923
Average Yards per Attempt	6.0	6.0	6.5	6.4	7.4	7.2	7.0	6.3
Average Yards per Completion	12.8	14.6	13.5	12.5	15.5	13.9	14.1	12.4
Touchdowns	25	19	16	24	31	21	32	18
Interceptions	23	29	19	35	28	29	28	28
Percent Intercepted	4.8	6.5	4.4	6.9	6.1	6.6	5.9	6.0
PUNTING:								
Number	78	89	61	70	72	58	62	76
Average Distance	35.8	39.0	39.3	37.3	35.8	39.7	37.1	38.9
PUNT RETURNS:								
Number	28	27	33	29	15	32	17	26
Yards	203	185	496	261	208	301	120	151
Average Yards	7.3	6.9	15.0	9.0	13.9	9.4	7.1	5.8
Touchdowns	0	0	1	1	0	1	1	0
KICKOFF RETURNS:								
Number	60	47	40	67	48	58	62	63
Yards	1421	945	845	1547	1225	1213	1580	1504
Average Yards	23.7	20.1	21.1	23.1	25.5	20.9	25.5	23.9
Touchdowns	0	0	0	0	2	0	2	1
INTERCEPTION RETURNS:								
Number	25	33	32	27	25	28	24	25
Yards	312	356	410	417	190	317	201	278
Average Yards	12.5	10.8	12.8	15.4	7.6	11.3	8.4	11.1
Touchdowns	0	4	4	2	0	2	1	1
PENALTIES:								
Number	69	57	80	54	75	70	53	71
Yards	730.5	615	753	501	750	648	672	718
FUMBLES:								
Number	36	30	30	32	36	36	36	41
Number Lost	22	15	18	17	17	16	20	18
POINTS:								
Total	286	296	362	309	379	373	382	319
PAT (Kick) Attempts	32	34	44	36	47	47	50	39
PAT (Kick) Made	30	28	42	33	46	46	47	37
PAT (Rush or Pass) Attempts	5	3	2	1	0	0	1	4
PAT (Rush or Pass) Made	4	2	1	0	0	0	1	2
FG Attempts	23	26	34	28	34	24	21	25
FG Made	8	12	14	18	15	13	9	6
Percent FG Made	34.8	46.2	41.2	64.3	44.1	54.2	42.9	24.0
Safeties	1	0	0	0	0	0	0	1

DEFENSE

Statistic	BOSTON	BUFFALO	DALLAS	DENVER	HOUSTON	L.A.	NEW YORK	OAKLAND
FIRST DOWNS:								
Total	237	225	253	254	282	259	252	268
by Rushing	78	103	76	112	90	97	99	99
by Passing	135	109	148	123	164	138	133	146
by Penalty	24	13	29	19	28	24	20	23
RUSHING:								
Number	477	474	422	541	438	414	449	442
Yards	1513	1393	980	2145	1027	1750	1378	1598
Average Yards	3.2	2.9	2.3	4.0	2.3	4.2	3.1	3.6
Touchdowns	21	15	14	19	6	24	20	17
PASSING:								
Attempts	429	429	503	387	557	467	450	477
Completions	210	185	261	189	271	227	216	234
Completion Percentage	49.0	43.1	51.2	48.8	48.7	48.6	48.0	49.1
Yards	2958	2461	3002	2987	3874	2851	2919	3385
Average Yards per Attempt	6.9	5.7	6.0	7.7	7.0	6.1	6.5	7.1
Average Yards per Completion	14.1	13.3	11.5	15.8	14.3	12.6	13.5	14.5
Touchdowns	19	19	19	25	28	21	27	28
Interceptions	25	33	32	27	25	28	24	25
Percent Intercepted	5.8	7.7	6.4	7.0	4.5	6.0	5.3	5.2
PUNTING:								
Number	74	77	78	67	68	62	65	75
Average Distance	37.2	37.6	37.5	39.0	37.1	40.2	37.0	37.5
PUNT RETURNS:								
Number	21	33	27	20	28	17	31	30
Yards	361	232	157	149	258	197	342	229
Average Yards	17.2	7.0	5.8	7.5	9.2	11.6	11.0	7.6
Touchdowns	3	0	0	1	0	0	0	0
KICKOFF RETURNS:								
Number	50	55	57	54	46	70	70	43
Yards	1123	1402	1347	1087	1096	1481	1785	959
Average Yards	22.5	25.5	23.6	20.1	23.8	21.2	25.5	22.3
Touchdowns	1	0	1	1	0	0	0	1
INTERCEPTION RETURNS:								
Number	23	29	19	35	28	29	28	28
Yards	336	422	171	343	316	284	228	381
Average Yards	14.6	14.6	9.0	9.8	11.3	9.8	8.1	13.6
Touchdowns	3	2	0	3	2	1	0	3
PENALTIES:								
Number	77	62	59	62	74	59	77	59
Yards	825	608.5	579	633	664	569	911	598
FUMBLES:								
Number	41	27	34	26	42	39	27	36
Number Lost	20	16	16	17	26	17	16	15
POINTS:								
Total	349	303	253	393	285	336	399	388
PAT (Kick) Attempts								
PAT (Kick) Made	43	37	31	48	33	40	51	46
PAT (Rush or Pass) Attempts								
PAT (Rush or Pass) Made								
FG Attempts	27	27	23	28	27	28	25	30
FG Made	10	14	4	17	12	14	10	14
Percent FG Made	37.0	51.9	17.4	60.7	44.4	50.0	40.0	46.7
Safeties	0	1	0	0	0	0	0	0

1960 AFL CHAMPIONSHIP GAME
January 1, at Houston
(Attendance 32,183)

Age and Blanda and a Crown

The Oilers and Chargers met on New Year's Day to decide the first AFL championship. Both clubs had high scoring offenses, but the defensive units turned in surprisingly strong performances. The only scoring of the first quarter came on a pair of field goals by Ben Agajanian, Los Angeles' forty-one-year-old kicking specialist. George Blanda, the old man in the Houston lineup, put the Oilers ahead early in the second period with a 17-yard touchdown pass to fullback Dave Smith and the successful conversion. Blanda and Agajanian both added three-pointers late in the quarter to make the score 10-9 Houston at the half. The offenses moved better in the second half, with the Oilers relying on Blanda's passing and the Chargers on Paul Lowe's running. Houston upped its lead to eight points with a seven-yard Blanda-to-Bill Groman touchdown pass, but the Chargers came right back on a long drive culminating in Lowe's two-yard dash into the end zone. Leading 17-16 after three quarters, the Oilers broke open a long pass play, a very common occurrence in the early AFL. Billy Cannon came out of the backfield and took a George Blanda pass 88 yards to a touchdown, with the extra point running the score to 24-16. The Oilers led by eight points, but the Chargers could tie the game in one swoop with a touchdown and a two-point conversion. Twice the Chargers drove deep into Houston territory only to lose the ball on downs on the 35-yard line and on the 22-yard line. The final Los Angeles drive died with one minute left, turning the ball and the league championship over to the Oilers.

SCORING

HOUSTON	0	10	7	7—24
LOS ANGELES	6	3	7	0—16

First Quarter
L.A. Agajanian, 38 yard field goal 4:02
L.A. Agajanian, 22 yard field goal 8:16

Second Quarter
Hous. Smith, 17 yard pass from Blanda 3:51
   PAT—Blanda (kick)
Hous. Blanda, 18 yard field goal 8:45
L.A. Agajanian, 27 yard field goal 14:55

Third Quarter
Hous. Groman, 7 yard pass from Blanda
   PAT—Blanda (kick)
L.A. Lowe, 2 yard rush
   PAT—Agajanian (kick)

Fourth Quarter
Hous. Cannon, 88 yard pass from Blanda
   PAT—Blanda (kick)

TEAM STATISTICS

HOUS.		L.A.
17	First Downs—Total	21
4	First Downs—Rushing	11
13	First Downs—Passing	9
0	First Downs—Penalty	1
0	Fumbles—Number	2
0	Fumbles—Lost Ball	0
4	Penalties—Number	3
54	Yards Penalized	15
0	Giveaways	2
2	Takeaways	0
+2	Difference	-2

INDIVIDUAL STATISTICS

RUSHING

HOUSTON	No.	Yds.	Avg.	LOS ANGELES	No.	Yds.	Avg.
Cannon	18	50	2.8	Lowe	21	165	7.9
Smith	19	45	2.4	Ferguson	4	11	2.8
Hall	3	5	1.6	Ford	2	-5	-2.5
	40	100	2.5	Kemp	6	-9	-1.5
					33	162	4.9

RECEIVING

HOUSTON	No.	Yds.	Avg.	LOS ANGELES	No.	Yds.	Avg.
Smith	5	52	10.4	Norton	6	55	9.2
Hennigan	4	71	17.8	Womble	2	9	4.8
Cannon	3	128	42.7	Kocourek	3	57	19.0
Groman	3	37	12.3	Lowe	3	5	1.7
Carson	1	13	13.0	Ferguson	2	19	9.5
	16	301	18.8	Flowers	1	6	6.0
					21	171	8.1

PUNTING

HOUSTON	No.		Avg.	LOS ANGELES	No.		Avg.
Milstead	5		34.0	Laraba	4		41.0

PUNT RETURNS

HOUSTON				LOS ANGELES	No.	Yds.	Avg.
None				Harris	1	27	27.0
				Sears	1	15	15.0
					2	42	21.0

KICKOFF RETURNS

HOUSTON	No.	Yds.	Avg.	LOS ANGELES	No.	Yds.	Avg.
Cannon	3	81	27.0	Lowe	4	101	25.3
Hall	2	47	23.5	Ford	1	22	22.0
	5	128	25.6		5	123	24.6

INTERCEPTION RETURNS

HOUSTON	No.	Yds.	Avg.	LOS ANGELES			
Gordon	1	27	27.0	None			
Dukes	1	8	8.0				
	2	35	17.5				

PASSING

HOUSTON	Att.	Comp.	Comp. Pct.	Yds.	Int.	Yds/Att.	Yds/Comp.
Blanda	31	16	51.6	301	0	9.7	18.8
Cannon	1	0	0.0	—	—	—	—
	32	16	50.0	301	0	9.4	18.8

LOS ANGELES	Att.	Comp.	Comp. Pct.	Yds.	Int.	Yds/Att.	Yds/Comp.
Kemp	41	21	51.2	171	2	4.2	8.1

HOUSTON OILERS 10-4-0 Lou Rymkus

Scores of Each Game		
37	Oakland	22
38	LOS ANGELES	28
13	OAKLAND	14
27	NEW YORK	21
20	DALLAS	10
42	New York	28
24	Buffalo	25
45	Denver	25
21	Los Angeles	24
20	DENVER	10
24	Boston	10
0	Dallas	24
31	BUFFALO	23
37	BOSTON	21

Use Name	Pos.	Hgt	Wgt	Age	Int	Pts
Gary Greaves	OT	6'3"	235	24		
Al Jamison	OT	6'5"	240	23		
Rich Michael	OT	6'3"	230	21		
Fred Wallner	OG	6'2"	235	31		
Hogan Wharton	OG	6'2"	245	24		
Wahoo McDaniel	OG	6'	230	23		
Bob Talamini	OG	6'1"	230	21		
George Belotti	C	6'4"	255	25		
John Simerson	C	6'3"	255	25		
Dalva Allen	DE	6'5"	245	24	1	
Don Floyd	DE	6'4"	230	21		
Dan Lanphear	DE	6'2"	220	22		
Pete Davidson	DT	6'5"	255	26		
Jerry Helluin	DT	6'2"	260	30		
George Shirkey	DT	6'4"	260	23		
Orville Trask	DT	6'4"	260	25		

Use Name	Pos.	Hgt	Wgt	Age	Int	Pts
Mike Dukes	LB	6'3"	225	24	2	
Dennit Morris	LB	6'1"	225	24	4	
Phil Perlo	LB	6'	220	24		
Hugh Pitts	LB	6'2"	225	26		
Tony Banfield	DB	6'1"	185	21	3	
Bobby Gordon	DB	6'	195	24	3	
Mark Johnston	DB	6'	203	22	4	
Charlie Kendall	DB	6'2"	185	25	2	
Jim Norton	DB	6'3"	182	21	1	
Julian Spence	DB	5'11"	170	31	4	

Use Name	Pos.	Hgt	Wgt	Age	Int	Pts
George Blanda	QB	6'1"	210	32		115
Jacky Lee	QB	6'1"	185	21		
Charley Milstead	QB	6'2"	190	22		
Don Brown	HB	6'1"	205	23		
Billy Cannon	HB	6'1"	210	23		42
Ken Hall	HB	6'1"	200	24		6
Charley Tolar	HB	5'7"	195	22		18
Doug Cline	FB	6'2"	210	21		12
Dave Smith	FB	6'1"	205	23		42
Bob White	FB	6'2"	220	22		
Jack Atchason (from BOS)	OE	6'4"	215	23		6
Johnny Carson	OE	6'3"	205	30		24
Bill Groman	OE	6'	194	24		72
Charley Hennigan	OE	6'	190	24		36
John White	OE	6'4"	230	22		
Al Witcher	DE-OE	6'1"	200	23	1	6

NEW YORK TITANS 7-7-0 Sammy Baugh

Scores of Each Game		
27	BUFFALO	3
24	BOSTON	28
28	DENVER	24
37	Dallas	35
21	Houston	27
17	Buffalo	13
28	HOUSTON	42
27	OAKLAND	28
7	LOS ANGELES	21
21	Boston	38
41	DALLAS	35
30	Denver	27
31	Oakland	28
43	Los Angeles	50

Use Name	Pos.	Hgt	Wgt	Age	Int	Pts
Larry Baker	OT	6'2"	240	23		
Ernie Barnes	OT	6'3"	257	21		
Gene Cockrell	OT	6'3"	247	27		
Jack Klotz	OT	6'5"	260	26		
Dan Callahan	OG	6'	230	22		
Frank D'Agostino	OG	6'1"	245	26		
Howard Glenn (died Oct. 9)	OG	6'	235	25		
John McMullan	OG	6'	244	25		
Bob Mischak	OG	6'	238	27		
Mike Hudock	C	6'2"	245	25		
Ed Cooke	DE	6'4"	245	25		
Bob Reifsnyder	DE	6'2"	250	23		
Joe Ryan	DE	6'2"	235	26		
Nick Mumley	OT-DE	6'6"	245	24	1	6
Dick Guesman	DT	6'4"	255	24		
Joe Katchik	DT	6'9"	290	26		
Tom Saidock	DT	6'5"	260	28		
Sid Youngelman	DT	6'3"	265	28		

Use Name	Pos.	Hgt	Wgt	Age	Int	Pts
Leon Dumbrowski	LB	6'	215	22		
Roger Ellis	LB	6'3"	233	22	1	
Larry Grantham	LB	6'	195	21	5	
Bob Marques	LB	6'	220	23		
Hall Whitley	LB	6'2"	225	25		
Eddie Bell	DB	6'1"	215	29	2	
Roger Donnahoo	DB	6'	185	22	5	12
Charlie Dupre	DB	6'1"	195	24		
Dick Felt	DB	6'	180	27	2	
Fred Julian	DB	5'9"	185	22	6	
Corky Tharp	DB	5'10"	180	27	2	
Rick Sapienza	HB-DB	5'11"	185	24		

Use Name	Pos.	Hgt	Wgt	Age	Int	Pts
Al Dorow	QB	6'	195	30		42
Dick Jamieson	QB	6'1"	190	24		
Bob Scrabis	QB	6'3"	220	24		
Dewey Bohling	HB	5'11"	190	21		36
Leon Burton	HB	5'9"	172	25		18
Don Herndon	HB	6'	195	26		6
Bill Shockley	HB	6'	185	22		86
Pete Hart	FB	5'9"	190	22		
Bill Mathis	FB	6'1"	205	21		12
Joe Pagliei	FB	6'	220	26		6
Ken Campbell	OE	6'1"	213	21		
Don Maynard	OE	6'	185	24		36
Art Powell	OE	6'3"	210	23		84
Dave Ross	OE	6'3"	210	22		6
Thurlow Cooper	DE-OE	6'4"	228	27		20

BUFFALO BILLS 5-8-1 Buster Ramsey

Scores of Each Game		
3	New York	27
21	DENVER	27
13	Boston	0
10	LOS ANGELES	24
13	NEW YORK	17
38	OAKLAND	9
25	HOUSTON	24
28	DALLAS	45
7	Oakland	20
32	Los Angeles	3
38	Denver	38
38	BOSTON	14
23	Houston	31
7	Dallas	24

Use Name	Pos.	Hgt	Wgt	Age	Int	Pts
Tony Discenzo (from BOS)	OT	6'5"	240	24		
Ed Meyer	OT	6'2"	240	23		
Harold Olson	OT	6'3"	266	21		
Bob Sedlock	OT	6'4"	295	23		
Phil Blazer	OG	6'1"	235	24		
Don Chelf	OG	6'3"	235	25		
Ed Muelhaupt	OG	6'3"	230	24		
Dan McGrew	C	6'2"	250	22		
Leroy Moore	DE	6'	230	24		
Charlie Rutkowski	DE	6'3"	248	22		
Lavern Torczon	DE	6'2"	240	24		
Mack Yoho	DE	6'2"	240	24	1	12
Gene Grabosky	DT	6'5"	275	23		
Chuck McMurtry	DT	6'	310	22		
John Scott	DT	6'4"	260	24		
Jim Sorey	DT	6'4"	270	23		

Use Name	Pos.	Hgt	Wgt	Age	Int	Pts
Bernie Buzynski	LB	6'3"	228	22	1	
Joe Hergert	LB	6'1"	217	24	1	12
Jack Laraway	LB	6'1"	220	24		
Archie Matsos	LB	6'	220	25	8	6
Sam Palumbo	LB	6'2"	230	29		
Dennis Remmert	LB	6'3"	215	21		
Joe Schaffer	LB	6'	210	22	1	
Jack Johnson	DB	6'3"	195	26	2	
Billy Kinard	DB	6'	185	26	4	
Richie McCabe	DB	6'1"	185	26	4	
Jim Wagstaff	DB	6'2"	190	24	6	6
Billy Atkins	HB-DB	6'1"	195	25	5	45

Use Name	Pos.	Hgt	Wgt	Age	Int	Pts
Bob Brodhead	QB	6'2"	207	23		2
Johnny Green	QB	6'3"	198	23		12
Tom O'Connell	QB	5'11"	190	28		8
Richie Lucas	HB-QB	6'	190	21		18
Elbert Dubenion	HB	6'	190	25		48
Willmer Fowler	HB	5'11"	185	23		6
Darrell Harper	HB	6'1"	195	21		7
Joe Kulbacki	HB	6'	185	22		6
Harold Lewis	HB	6'	200	24		
Wray Carlton	FB	6'2"	210	22		66
Carl Smith	FB	6'	200	24		6
Bob Barrett	OE	6'3"	200	24		
Dick Brubaker	OE	6'1"	195	28		6
Dan Chamberlain	OE	6'4"	200	23		24
Monte Crockett	OE	6'3"	210	21		6
Al Hoisington (from OAK)	OE	6'3"	200	25		12
Tom Rychlec	OE	6'3"	220	26		

BOSTON PATRIOTS 5-9-0 Lou Saban

Scores of Each Game		
10	DENVER	13
28	New York	24
0	BUFFALO	13
35	Los Angeles	0
14	Oakland	27
24	Denver	31
16	LOS ANGELES	45
34	OAKLAND	28
38	NEW YORK	21
42	DALLAS	14
10	HOUSTON	24
14	Buffalo	38
0	Dallas	34
21	Houston	37

Use Name	Pos.	Hgt	Wgt	Age	Int	Pts
Bob Cross	OT	6'4"	245	29		
Jerry DeLucca	OT	6'3"	250	24		
George McGee	OT	6'2"	255	24		
Abe Cohen	OG	5'11"	230	26		
Jack Davis	OG	6'	226	27		
Bob Lee	OG	6'1"	245	24		
Charlie Leo	OG	6'	233	25		
Walt Cudzik	C	6'2"	226	27		
Bill Danenhauer (from DEN)	DE	6'4"	245	25		
Bob Dee	DE	6'3"	234	27	1	
Harry Jacobs	DE	6'2"	235	23	4	
Don McComb	DE	6'4"	240	26		
Al Richardson	DE	6'3"	245	23		
Al Crow	DT	6'6"	260	27		
Art Hauser	DT	6'	243	29		
Jim Hunt	DT	5'11"	245	21		
Harry Jagielski	DT	6'	260	28		
Bob Yates	DT	6'3"	250	21		

Use Name	Pos.	Hgt	Wgt	Age	Int	Pts
Tom Addison	LB	6'3"	230	24		
Phil Bennett	LB	6'3"	225	24		
Bill Brown	LB	6'1"	230	23	1	
Jack Rudolph	LB	6'3"	225	22	2	
Tony Sardisco	LB	6'2"	225	27		
Fred Bruney	DB	5'10"	188	29	3	
Ross O'Hanley	DB	6'	185	21	3	
Chuck Shonta	DB	6'	190	22	2	6
Bob Soltis	DB	6'2"	205	23	2	
Clyde Washington	DB	6'	195	22	3	
Gino Cappelletti	OE-DB	6'	190	26	4	60

Use Name	Pos.	Hgt	Wgt	Age	Int	Pts
Tom Dimitroff	QB	5'11"	200	25		
Tom Greene	QB	6'1"	190	22		
Butch Songin	QB	6'2"	190	36		12
Harvey White	QB	6'1"	190	22		
Walter Beach	HB	6'	180	25		6
Ron Burton	HB	5'10"	190	23		6
Dick Christy	HB	5'10"	192	24		36
Jake Crouthamel	HB	5'11"	195	22		
Larry Garron	HB	6'	185	23		
Jerry Green	HB	6'	190	23		
Walt Livingston	HB	6'	195	22		6
Ger Schwedes	HB	6'1"	205	21		
Billy Wells	HB	5'9"	175	28		6
Jim Crawford	FB	6'1"	205	24		14
Bill Larson	FB	5'10"	190	21		
Alan Miller	FB	6'	195	22		18
Joe Biscaha	OE	6'1"	190	23		
Jim Colclough	OE	6'	185	24		54
Joe Johnson	OE	6'	185	30		18
Oscar Lofton	OE	6'6"	218	22		24
Mike Long	OE	6'	188	21		
Tom Stephens	OE	6'1"	190	24		18

HOUSTON OILERS

RUSHING
Last Name	No.	Yds	Avg	TD
Cannon	152	644	4.2	1
Smith	154	643	4.2	5
Tolar	54	179	3.3	3
Hall	30	118	3.9	0
Cline	37	105	2.8	2
Talamini	0	14	0.0	0
Milstead	6	−21	−3.5	0
Lee	16	−57	−3.6	0
Blanda	25	−60	−2.4	4

RECEIVING
Last Name	No.	Yds	Avg	TD
Groman	72	1473	20	12
Carson	45	604	13	4
Hennigan	44	722	16	6
Smith	22	216	10	2
Cannon	15	187	12	5
Tolar	7	71	10	0
Atchason	5	48	10	1
Witcher	4	34	9	1
Cline	4	15	4	0
J. White	1	18	18	0
Norton	1	5	5	0

PUNT RETURNS
Last Name	No.	Yds	Avg	TD
Cannon	4	96	24	0
Hall	6	72	12	0
Tolar	5	40	8	0

KICKOFF RETURNS
Last Name	No.	Yds	Avg	TD
Hall	19	594	31	1
Cannon	8	266	33	1
Tolar	13	249	19	0
Dukes	4	58	15	0
Cline	3	42	14	0
Jamison	1	5	5	0
J. White	0	11	11	0

PASSING – PUNTING – KICKING
PASSING

Last Name	Att	Comp	%	Yds	Yd/Att	TD	Int-%		RK
Blanda	363	169	47	2413	6.6	24	22−	6	5
Lee	77	41	53	842	10.9	5	6−	8	
Milstead	7	4	57	43	6.1	0	0−	0	
Smith	5	3	60	70	14.0	1	0−	0	
Cannon	3	0	0	0	0.0	0	0−	0	
Groman	1	1	100	3	3.0	1	0−	0	

PUNTING

Last Name	No	Avg
Milstead	66	35.8
Hall	6	35.0

KICKING

Last Name	XP	Att	%	FG	Att	%
Blanda	46	47	98	15	34	44

NEW YORK TITANS

RUSHING
Last Name	No.	Yds	Avg	TD
Bohling	123	431	3.5	2
Mathis	92	307	3.3	2
Dorow	124	167	1.3	7
Shockley	37	156	4.2	0
Burton	16	119	7.4	2
Hart	25	113	4.5	0
Pagliei	17	69	4.1	1
Jamieson	8	−61	−7.6	0

RECEIVING
Last Name	No.	Yds	Avg	TD
Maynard	72	1265	18	6
Powell	69	1167	17	14
Bohling	30	268	9	4
Mathis	18	103	6	0
Ross	10	122	12	1
Cooper	9	161	18	3
Shockley	8	69	9	2
Herndon	5	57	11	1
Hart	3	19	6	0
Burton	3	8	3	0
Pagliei	1	13	13	0
Sapienza	1	4	4	0
Klotz	0	5	0	0

PUNT RETURNS
Last Name	No.	Yds	Avg	TD
Burton	12	93	8	0
Donnahoo	1	15	15	1
Shockley	3	12	4	0
Tharp	1	0	0	0

KICKOFF RETURNS
Last Name	No.	Yds	Avg	TD
Burton	31	897	29	2
Shockley	17	411	24	0
Herndon	5	114	23	0
Powell	2	63	32	0
Maynard	3	59	20	0
Baker	1	18	18	0
Reifsnyder	1	16	16	0
Klotz	1	8	8	0
Cooper	1	0	0	0

PASSING – PUNTING – KICKING
PASSING

Last Name	Att	Comp	%	Yds	Yd/Att	TD	Int-%		RK
Dorow	396	201	51	2748	6.9	26	26−	7	2
Jamieson	70	35	50	586	8.4	6	2−	3	
Bohling	5	0	0	0	0.0	0	0−	0	
Scrabis	3	0	0	0	0.0	0	0−	0	

PUNTING

Last Name	No	Avg
Pagliei	48	37.1
Sapienza	8	32.4
Dorow	6	44.0

KICKING

Last Name	XP	Att	%	FG	Att	%
Shockley	47	50	94	9	21	43

2 POINT XP
Cooper (1)

BUFFALO BILLS

RUSHING
Last Name	No.	Yds	Avg	TD
Carlton	137	533	3.9	7
Fowler	93	370	4.0	1
Kulbacki	41	108	2.6	1
Dubenion	16	94	5.9	1
Lucas	46	90	1.9	2
Smith	19	61	3.2	0
Atkins	2	47	23.5	0
Brodhead	21	45	2.1	0
Harper	1	3	3.0	0
O'Connell	22	−24	−1.0	0
Green	46	−156	−3.4	2

RECEIVING
Last Name	No.	Yds	Avg	TD
Rychlec	45	590	13	0
Dubenion	42	752	18	7
Carlton	29	477	16	4
Chamberlain	17	279	16	4
Crockett	14	173	12	1
Fowler	10	99	10	0
Hoisington	8	141	18	2
Smith	7	127	18	1
Brubaker	7	75	11	1
Lucas	5	58	12	1
Kulbacki	2	9	5	0
Green	1	0	0	0

PUNT RETURNS
Last Name	No.	Yds	Avg	TD
Kulbacki	12	100	8	0
Kinard	2	24	12	0
Matsos	1	20	20	0
Dubenion	2	6	3	0
Crockett	1	5	5	0
Lucas	4	3	1	0
Lewis	1	2	2	0

KICKOFF RETURNS
Last Name	No.	Yds	Avg	TD
Kulbacki	13	226	17	0
Fowler	12	201	17	0
Lewis	4	97	24	0
Smith	2	72	36	0
Dubenion	4	68	17	0
Kinard	1	39	39	0
Hoisington	2	25	13	0
Chamberlain	1	24	24	0
Rychlec	1	3	3	0

PASSING – PUNTING – KICKING
PASSING

Last Name	Att	Comp	%	Yds	Yd/Att	TD	Int-%		RK
Green	228	89	39	1267	5.6	10	10−	4	8
O'Connell	145	65	45	1033	7.1	7	13−	9	8
Lucas	49	23	47	314	6.4	2	3−	6	
Brodhead	25	7	28	75	3.0	0	3−	12	

PUNTING

Last Name	No	Avg
Atkins	89	39.0

KICKING

Last Name	XP	Att	%	FG	Att	%
Atkins	27	32	84	6	13	46
Harper	1	2	50	3	6	67
Hergert	0	0	0	2	4	50
Yoho	0	0	0	2	5	40
O'Connell	0	0	0	1	0	

2 POINT XP
Brodhead (1)
O'Connell (1)

BOSTON PATRIOTS

RUSHING
Last Name	No.	Yds	Avg	TD
Miller	101	416	4.2	1
Christy	78	363	4.7	4
Burton	66	280	4.3	1
Crawford	51	238	4.7	2
Wells	14	59	4.2	0
Garron	8	27	3.4	0
Crouthamel	4	16	4.0	0
Livingston	10	16	1.6	1
Washington	2	10	5.0	0
White	5	7	1.4	0
Beach	6	−4	−0.7	0
Dimitroff	2	−10	−5.0	0
Greene	16	−27	−1.7	0
Songin	36	−140	−3.9	2

RECEIVING
Last Name	No.	Yds	Avg	TD
Colclough	49	666	14	9
Miller	29	284	10	2
Christy	26	268	10	2
Stephens	22	320	15	3
Burton	21	196	9	0
Lofton	19	360	19	4
Wells	14	206	15	1
Johnson	11	186	17	3
Crawford	10	92	9	0
Beach	9	132	15	0
Green	3	52	17	0
White	2	24	12	0
Long	2	10	5	0
Cappelletti	1	28	28	0
Cudzik	1	11	11	0
Garron	1	8	8	0
Livingston	1	0	0	0

PUNT RETURNS
Last Name	No.	Yds	Avg	TD
Christy	8	73	9	0
Wells	12	66	6	0
Bruney	4	31	8	0
Beach	1	21	21	0
Cohen	1	9	9	0
Cappelletti	1	3	3	0
Burton	1	0	0	0

KICKOFF RETURNS
Last Name	No.	Yds	Avg	TD
Christy	24	617	26	0
Wells	11	275	25	0
Burton	4	161	40	0
Beach	7	146	21	0
Cappelletti	4	100	25	0
Bruney	2	39	20	0
Crouthamel	2	27	14	0
Garron	1	21	21	0
Hunt	1	8	8	0
Team	1	8	8	0
Greene	1	3	3	0
Livingston	1	3	3	0

PASSING – PUNTING – KICKING
PASSING

Last Name	Att	Comp	%	Yds	Yd/Att	TD	Int-%		RK
Songin	392	187	48	2476	6.3	22	15−	4	4
Greene	63	27	43	251	4.0	1	6−	10	
Christy	11	6	55	94	8.5	2	2−	18	
White	7	3	43	44	6.3	0	0−	0	
Dimitroff	2	0	0	0	0.0	0	0−	0	

PUNTING

Last Name	No	Avg
Greene	59	37.9
Washington	17	31.7

KICKING

Last Name	XP	Att	%	FG	Att	%
Cappelletti	30	32	94	8	21	38
Crawford	0	0	0	0	1	0
Cudzik	0	0	0	0	1	0

2 POINT XP
Cappelletti (3)
Crawford (1)

LOS ANGELES 10-4-0 Sid Gillman

Scores of Each Game

21	DALLAS	20
28	Houston	38
0	Dallas	17
24	Buffalo	10
0	BOSTON	35
23	Denver	19
45	Boston	16
21	New York	7
24	HOUSTON	21
3	BUFFALO	32
52	OAKLAND	28
41	Oakland	17
41	DENVER	33
50	NEW YORK	43

Use Name	Pos.	Hgt	Wgt	Age	Int	Pts
Dick Chorovich	OT	6'4"	260	27		
Sam DeLuca	OT	6'2"	245	24		
Ron Mix	OT	6'4"	245	22		
Ernie Wright	OT	6'4"	270	21		
Al Barry	OG	6'2"	235	29		
Fred Cole	OG	5'11"	226	23		
Orlando Ferrante	OG	6'	230	27		
Charlie Kempinski	OG	6'	235	21		
Don Rogers	C	6'2"	235	23		
Ben Donnell	DE	6'5"	248	23		
Art Gob (from WAS-N)	DE	6'4"	230	23		
Ron Nery	DE	6'6"	226	25		
Maury Schleicher	DE	6'3"	240	23	1	
Paul Maguire	OE-DE	6'	210	22	3	6
Gary Finneran	DT	6'3"	240	26		
John Kompara	DT	6'2"	245	23		
Volney Peters	DT	6'4"	240	31		
Al Bansavage	LB	6'2"	230	22		
Hubert Bobo	LB	6'1"	214	25		
Ron Botcham	LB	6'1"	238	25	2	
Charlie Brueckman	LB	6'2"	225	24		
Emil Karas	LB	6'3"	225	26		
Rommie Loudd	LB	6'3"	226	26	3	
Bob Garner	DB	5'10"	190	25	2	
Dick Harris	DB	5'11"	174	23	5	6
Charley McNeil	DB	5'11"	178	24	3	
Doyle Nix	DB	6'1"	195	27	4	6
Jesse Thomas	DB	5'10"	180	31		
Henry Wallace	DB	6'	195	22		
Bob Zeman	DB	6'1"	203	23	2	
Jimmy Sears	HB-DB	5'11"	187	29	2	
Bobby Clatterbuck	QB	6'3"	196	28		
Jack Kemp	QB	6'1"	200	26		48
Bob Laraba	LB-QB	6'3"	194	27	1	
Fred Ford (from BUF)	HB	5'8"	180	22		12
Paul Lowe	HB	6'	180	23		66
Ron Waller	HB	5'11"	184	27		
Howie Ferguson	FB	6'2"	217	30		36
Charlie Flowers	FB	6'1"	207	23		12
Blanche Martin (from NY)	FB	6'	195	23		6
Royce Womble	FL	6'	184	28		24
Ralph Anderson*	OE	6'4"	225	23		30
Howard Clark	OE	6'2"	204	25		
Dave Kocourek	OE	6'5"	225	23		6
Trusse Norris	OE	6'1"	190	23		
Don Norton	OE	6'1"	180	24		30
Ben Agajanian	K	6'	220	41		85

* died Nov. 26 of diabetes

DALLAS TEXANS 8-6-0 Hank Stram

20	Los Angeles	21
34	Oakland	16
17	LOS ANGELES	0
35	NEW YORK	37
19	OAKLAND	20
10	Houston	20
17	Denver	14
45	Buffalo	28
34	DENVER	7
14	Boston	42
35	New York	41
24	HOUSTON	0
34	BOSTON	0
24	BUFFALO	7

Use Name	Pos.	Hgt	Wgt	Age	Int	Pts
Jerry Cornelison	OT	6'3"	250	23		
Charley Diamond	OT	6'2"	235	24		
R. B. Nunnery	OT	6'4"	275	26		
Jack Stone	OT	6'2"	245	23		
Sid Fournet	OG	6'	245	27		
Billy Krisher	OG	6'1"	235	24		
Al Reynolds	OG	6'3"	225	22		
Marvin Terrell	OG	6'1"	235	22		
Jim Barton	C	6'5"	250	25		
Tom Dimmick	C	6'6"	255	29		
Mel Branch	DE	6'2"	220	23		
Dick Frey	DE	6'2"	230	29		
Paul Miller	DE	6'2"	235	28		
Ray Collins	DT	5'11"	250	32		
Rufus Granderson	DT	6'5"	277	23		
Walter Napier	DT	6'4"	280	24		
Paul Rochester	DT	6'2"	250	23		
Walt Corey	LB	6'	215	22	3	
Ted Greene	LB	6'1"	230	26	3	
Sherrill Headrick	LB	6'2"	215	23	2	
Bob Hudson (to DEN)	LB	6'4"	230	30	1	
Smokey Stover	LB	6'	215	21	1	
Johnny Bookman	DB	5'11"	185	25	4	
Don Flynn	DB	6'	205	25	3	6
Jimmy Harris	DB	6'1"	175	25	2	
Charlie Jackson	DB	5'11"	180	24		
Dave Webster	DB	6'4"	215	22	6	18
Duane Wood	DB	6'1"	190	24	4	6
Carroll Zaruba	DB	5'9"	210	26		
Clem Daniels	HB-DB	6'1"	220	23	3	
Cotton Davidson	QB	6'1"	180	28		17
Hunter Enis	QB	6'2"	190	23		18
Abner Haynes	HB	6'	185	22		72
Curley Johnson	HB	6'	215	25		14
Johnny Robinson	HB	6'	195	21		54
Jim Swink	HB	6'1"	185	24		
Bo Dickinson	FB	6'2"	220	25		6
Jack Spikes	FB	6'2"	220	22		103
Ed Bernet	OE	6'3"	205	27		
Max Boydston	OE	6'2"	215	27		18
Bob Bryant	OE	6'5"	230	23		
Chris Burford	OE	6'3"	210	22		30

OAKLAND RAIDERS 6-8-0 Eddie Erdalatz

22	HOUSTON	37
16	DALLAS	34
14	Houston	13
14	Denver	31
20	Dallas	19
27	BOSTON	14
9	Buffalo	38
28	Boston	34
28	New York	27
20	BUFFALO	7
17	LOS ANGELES	41
28	NEW YORK	31
48	DENVER	10

Use Name	Pos.	Hgt	Wgt	Age	Int	Pts
Don Churchwell	OT	6'1"	255	23		
Bill Striegel (from BOS)	OT	6'2"	240	24		
Dalton Truax	OT	6'2"	235	25		
Don Deskins	OG	6'3"	240	27		
John Dittrich	OG	6'1"	240	27		
Wayne Hawkins	OG	6'	235	22		
Don Manoukian	OG	5'9"	242	25		
Ron Sabal	OG	6'2"	230	23		
Jim Otto	C	6'2"	227	22		
Larry Barnes	DE	6'1"	230	27		55
Carmen Cavalli	DE	6'4"	245	22		
George Fields	DE	6'3"	245	24	2	
Charley Powell	DE	6'2"	227	28		
Ray Armstrong	DT	6'1"	235	22		
Joe Barbee	DT	6'3"	250	25		
Paul Oglesby	DT	6'4"	235	20		
Ron Warzeka	DT	6'4"	250	29		
Bob Dougherty	LB	6'1"	240	26		
Billy Locklin	LB	6'2"	225	22		
Tom Louderback	LB	6'2"	235	26	2	
Riley Morris	LB	6'2"	230	23		
Alex Bravo	DB	6'	190	28	4	
Joe Cannavino	DB	5'11"	185	24	4	
Wayne Crow	DB	6'	205	22	4	
L. C. Joyner	DB	6'1"	187	25		
Eddie Macon	DB	6'	180	32	9	6
John Harris	HB-DB	6'1"	195	27		
Tom Flores	QB	6'1"	190	23		18
Paul Larson	QB	5'11"	180	28		
Babe Parilli	QB	6'1"	190	30		6
Bob Keyes	HB	5'10"	183	24		
Jack Larscheid	HB	5'6"	162	26		12
Nyle McFarlane	HB	6'2"	205	24		12
Billy Reynolds	HB	5'10"	200	28		
Tony Teresa	HB	5'9"	185	25		60
Billy Lott	FB	6'	205	25		38
J. D. Smith	FB	6'	220	25		12
Doug Asad	OE	6'3"	200	22		6
Al Goldstein	OE	6'	204	24		12
Charley Hardy	OE	6'	183	26		18
Gene Prebola	OE	6'3"	215	22		6

DENVER BRONCOS 4-9-1 Frankie Filchock

13	Boston	10
27	Buffalo	21
24	New York	28
31	OAKLAND	14
19	LOS ANGELES	23
31	BOSTON	24
14	DALLAS	17
25	HOUSTON	45
7	Dallas	34
10	Houston	20
38	BUFFALO	38
27	NEW YORK	30
33	Los Angeles	41
10	Oakland	48

Use Name	Pos.	Hgt	Wgt	Age	Int	Pts
Eldon Danenhauer	OT	6'4"	235	24		
Gordy Holz	OT	6'4"	270	26		
Willie Smith	OT	6'2"	255	22		
Ken Adamson	OG	6'2"	215	21		
Jack Davis	OG	6'2"	235	23		
Carl Larpenter	OG	6'4"	235	23		
Dave Strickland	OG	6'	220	28		
Frank Kuchta	C	6'2"	235	24		
Mike Nichols	C	6'3"	225	21		
Chuck Gavin	DE	6'1"	235	26		
Bill Yelverton	DE	6'4"	220	26	1	6
Joe Young	DE	6'3"	245	25		
John Hatley	DT	6'3"	260	29		
Bud McFadin	DT	6'3"	260	32		
Hal Smith (from BOS)	DT	6'5"	250	25		
Don King	OT-DT	6'3"	255	30	2	
Vaughan Alliston	LB	6'	218	26	1	
Hardy Brown	LB	6'	190	36		
Al Day	LB	6'2"	216	22		
Pete Mangum	LB	6'	220	28		
Frank Bernardi	DB	5'9"	185	27		
Dick Doyle	DB	6'	190	29	1	
Goose Gonsoulin	DB	6'3"	205	22	11	
John Pyeatt	DB	6'3"	204	26	4	6
Al Romine	DB	6'2"	195	27	3	
Bob McNamara	HB-DB	6'	188	26	4	12
Tom Dublinski	QB	6'2"	205	30		
George Herring	QB	6'2"	200	25		
Frank Tripucka	QB	6'2"	205	32		
Henry Bell	HB	5'10"	210	23		
Al Carmichael	HB	6'1"	195	30		42
Gene Mingo	HB	6'1"	200	21		123
Bob Stransky	HB	6'1"	180	24		
Ted Wegert (from NY-to BUF)	HB	5'11"	200	28		12
Don Allen	FB	6'	200	23		6
J. W. Brodnax	FB	6'	208	23		6
Dave Rolle	FB	6'	215	22		18
Don Carothers	OE	6'5"	225	24		
Pat Epperson	OE	6'3"	225	24		
Jim Greer	OE	6'3"	215	26		6
Bill Jessup	OE	6'1"	195	31		6
Lionel Taylor	OE	6'2"	214	24		72
Ken Carpenter	HB-OE	6'	212	34		6

LOS ANGELES CHARGERS

RUSHING

Last Name	No.	Yds	Avg	TD
Lowe	136	855	6.3	9
Ferguson	126	438	3.5	4
Ford	38	194	5.1	2
Flowers	39	161	4.1	1
Martin	18	58	3.2	0
Laraba	4	7	1.8	0
Waller	9	5	0.6	0
Norton	1	2	2.0	0
Clatterbuck	6	−6	−1.0	0
Kemp	90	−103	−1.1	8

RECEIVING

Last Name	No.	Yds	Avg	TD
Anderson	44	614	14	5
Kocourek	40	662	17	1
Womble	32	316	10	4
Clark	27	431	16	0
Norton	25	414	17	5
Lowe	23	377	16	2
Ferguson	21	168	8	2
Flowers	12	153	13	1
Martin	4	23	6	1
Waller	3	24	8	0
Ford	1	5	5	0

PUNT RETURNS

Last Name	No.	Yds	Avg	TD
Harris	13	105	8	0
Sears	9	101	11	0
Garner	6	85	14	0
Ford	2	6	3	0
Maguire	1	4	4	1
Lowe	1	0	0	0

KICKOFF RETURNS

Last Name	No.	Yds	Avg	TD
Lowe	28	611	22	0
Ford	18	400	22	0
Sears	8	155	19	0
Norton	8	153	19	0
DeLuca	1	0	0	0

PASSING – PUNTING – KICKING

PASSING

Last Name	Att	Comp	%	Yds	Yd/Att	TD	Int–%	RK
Kemp	406	211	52	3018	7.4	20	25– 6	1
Clatterbuck	23	15	65	112	4.9	1	1– 4	
Laraba	7	2	29	23	3.3	0	2– 29	
Lowe	3	1	33	24	8.0	0	0– 0	
Ford	1	0	0	0	0.0	0	0– 0	
Waller	1	0	0	0	0.0	0	1–100	

PUNTING

Last Name	No	Avg
Maguire	43	40.5
Laraba	15	37.2

KICKING

Last Name	XP	Att	%	FG	Att	%
Agajanian	46	47	98	13	24	54

DALLAS TEXANS

RUSHING

Last Name	No.	Yds	Avg	TD
Haynes	156	875	5.6	9
Robinson	98	458	4.8	4
Spikes	115	457	4.0	1
Dickinson	35	143	4.1	1
Johnson	23	43	1.9	1
Swink	10	15	1.5	0
Daniels	1	−2	−2.0	0
Enis	12	−12	−1.0	3
Davidson	31	−122	−3.9	1

RECEIVING

Last Name	No.	Yds	Avg	TD
Haynes	55	576	10	3
Burford	46	789	17	5
Robinson	41	611	15	4
Boydston	29	357	12	3
Spikes	11	158	14	0
Johnson	10	174	17	1
Bryant	5	43	9	0
Bernet	4	49	12	0
Swink	4	37	9	0
Dickinson	3	38	13	0
Davidson	1	−1	−1	0

PUNT RETURNS

Last Name	No.	Yds	Avg	TD
Haynes	14	215	15	0
Robinson	14	207	15	1
Daniels	3	69	23	0
Harris	1	5	5	0
Rochester	1	0	0	0

KICKOFF RETURNS

Last Name	No.	Yds	Avg	TD
Haynes	19	434	23	0
Daniels	9	162	18	0
Harris	5	117	23	0
Robinson	3	54	18	0
Swink	1	36	36	0
Dickinson	2	29	15	0
Johnson	1	13	13	0

PASSING – PUNTING – KICKING

PASSING

Last Name	Att	Comp	%	Yds	Yd/Att	TD	Int–%	RK
Davidson	379	179	47	2474	6.5	15	16– 4	5
Enis	54	30	56	357	6.6	1	2– 4	
Haynes	1	0	0	0	0.0	0	0– 0	
Robinson	1	0	0	0	0.0	0	1–100	

PUNTING

Last Name	No	Avg
Davidson	58	39.4
Johnson	3	36.7

KICKING

Last Name	XP	Att	%	FG	Att	%
Spikes	34	36	94	13	31	42
Davidson	8	8	100	1	1	100
Flynn	0	0	0	0	1	0
Johnson	0	0	0	0	1	0

2 POINT XP
Johnson (1)

OAKLAND RAIDERS

RUSHING

Last Name	No.	Yds	Avg	TD
Teresa	139	608	4.4	6
Lott	99	520	5.3	5
Larscheid	94	397	4.2	1
Smith	63	214	3.4	6
McFarlane	4	52	13.0	0
Parilli	32	25	0.8	1
Keyes	1	7	7.0	0
Reynolds	1	6	6.0	0
Goldstein	3	−2	−0.7	1
Flores	39	−42	−1.1	3

RECEIVING

Last Name	No.	Yds	Avg	TD
Lott	49	524	11	1
Teresa	35	393	11	4
Prebola	33	404	12	2
Goldstein	27	354	13	1
Hardy	24	423	18	3
Larscheid	22	187	9	1
Smith	17	194	11	1
Asad	14	197	14	1
McFarlane	5	89	18	2
Reynolds	3	43	14	0
Keyes	1	19	19	0
Parilli	1	0	0	0

PUNT RETURNS

Last Name	No.	Yds	Avg	TD
Larscheid	12	106	9	0
Reynolds	7	24	3	0
Teresa	5	12	2	0
Keyes	1	5	5	0
Cannavino	1	4	4	0

KICKOFF RETURNS

Last Name	No.	Yds	Avg	TD
Larscheid	30	852	28	0
Smith	14	373	27	1
McFarlane	5	71	14	0
Asad	3	66	22	0
Teresa	4	61	15	0
Harris	3	38	13	0
Deskins	1	15	15	0
Morris	1	3	3	0

PASSING – PUNTING – KICKING

PASSING

Last Name	Att	Comp	%	Yds	Yd/Att	TD	Int–%	RK
Flores	252	136	54	1738	6.9	12	12– 5	2
Parilli	187	87	47	1003	5.4	5	11– 6	10
Teresa	18	9	50	111	6.2	1	3– 17	
Larscheid	6	3	50	71	11.8	0	2– 33	

PUNTING

Last Name	No	Avg
Crow	76	38.9

KICKING

Last Name	XP	Att	%	FG	Att	%
Barnes	37	39	95	6	25	24

2 POINT XP
Lott (1)
Smith (1)

DENVER BRONCOS

RUSHING

Last Name	No.	Yds	Avg	TD
Rolle	130	501	3.9	2
Mingo	83	323	3.9	4
Bell	43	238	5.5	0
Carmichael	41	211	5.1	2
Wegert	36	161	4.5	1
Stransky	28	78	2.8	0
McNamara	17	33	1.9	1
Brodnax	15	18	1.2	0
Allen	30	18	0.6	1
Carpenter	4	13	3.3	0
Nichols	0	3	0.0	0
Taylor	2	−6	−3.0	0
Herring	5	−46	−9.2	0
Tripucka	37	−226	−6.1	0

RECEIVING

Last Name	No.	Yds	Avg	TD
Taylor	92	1235	13	12
Carmichael	32	616	19	5
Carpenter	29	350	12	1
Greer	22	284	13	2
Rolle	21	122	6	1
Mingo	19	156	8	1
Epperson	11	99	9	0
Jessup	9	120	13	1
McNamara	7	143	20	1
Wegert	5	68	14	1
Brodnax	5	39	8	1
Allen	5	34	7	0
Stransky	3	11	4	0
Carothers	2	25	13	0
Bell	2	13	7	0

PUNT RETURNS

Last Name	No.	Yds	Avg	TD
Carmichael	15	101	7	0
Mingo	3	92	31	1
McNamara	11	68	6	0
Wegert	4	25	6	0

KICKOFF RETURNS

Last Name	No.	Yds	Avg	TD
Carmichael	22	581	26	0
Wegert	10	252	25	0
Mingo	9	209	23	0
McNamara	9	192	21	0
Stransky	7	153	22	0
Brodnax	5	117	23	0
Allen	5	72	14	0
Bell	2	60	30	0
W. Smith	1	13	13	0
Greer	1	11	11	0
Strickland	1	9	9	0

PASSING – PUNTING – KICKING

PASSING

Last Name	Att	Comp	%	Yds	Yd/Att	TD	Int–%	RK
Tripucka	478	248	52	3038	6.4	24	34– 7	7
Herring	22	9	41	137	6.2	0	1– 5	
Mingo	7	1	14	46	6.6	0	0– 0	
Carmichael	1	1	100	26	26.0	0	0– 0	

PUNTING

Last Name	No	Avg
Herring	70	37.3

KICKING

Last Name	XP	Att	%	FG	Att	%
Mingo	33	36	92	18	28	64

1961 N.F.L. Bypassing the Crisis

For some teams, the forward pass became less important than the weekend pass. President Kennedy's activation of reserve units because of the Berlin crisis drafted many players into active military duty, among them Paul Hornung, Bobby Mitchell, Ray Nitschke, Boyd Dowler, Dick Schafrath, Bob DeMarco, John Gordy, and John Paluck. Since all of the reservists were stationed within the continental United States, most of the affected players could get back to their teams on a weekend pass, then return to their military base on Monday morning. Commissioner Pete Rozelle also had contact with the federal government, but not as a soldier. He successfully persuaded Congress to pass a bill officially exempting the NFL's package TV deal with CBS from anti-trust legislation.

EASTERN CONFERENCE

New York Giants—After the Giants lost to the Cards on opening day and looked sluggish in the first half against the Steelers, Giant coach Allie Sherman yanked quarterback Chuck Conerly and replaced him with newly acquired Y. A. Tittle. The bald-headed Tittle won the first-string job by pulling out a victory over the Steelers and flawlessly directed the New York attack through the season. With Del Shofner, Joe Walton, and Erich Barnes—all, like Tittle, acquired in off-season trades—blending in with the holdover Giant stars, New York climbed into a first-place tie with Philadelphia by beating the Eagles 38-21 in Yankee Stadium on November 12 and took sole possession of the top spot by knocking off the Eagles 28-24 in Philadelphia on December 10. Needing at least a tie to clinch the title, the Giants played Cleveland to a 7-7 deadlock to end the season.

Philadelphia Eagles—Starting with Timmy Brown's 105-yard kickoff return on the first play of the season, the Eagles displayed the league's most explosive offense. Sonny Jurgensen replaced the retired Norm Van Brocklin at quarterback and surpassed all expectations by throwing thirty-two touchdown passes in a superior air attack featuring receivers Tommy McDonald and Pete Retzlaff. But two flaws sabotaged the Eagles' title chances—a weak running game and a thin defensive secondary. Cornerback Tom Brookshier broke a leg in a 16-14 victory over the Bears, and the Giants exploited substitute Glen Amerson's inexperience the next week in a 38-21 New York win.

Cleveland Browns—Paul Brown may have been the coach of the 1950s, but a storm was gathering against him in the 1960s. Several Cleveland players, including Jimmy Brown, found the coach's stern way of dealing with his men increasingly hard to take, and quarterback Milt Plum was openly critical of Brown's system of sending every play in via alternating messenger guards. But despite the growing dissension and a disappointing defensive secondary, the Browns again were in the thick of the Eastern title chase. They trailed New York by only one game until a 37-21 Giant win on November 26 ended their hopes.

St. Louis Cardinals—Injuries crippled the Cardinal offense even before the season started. Halfback John David Crow broke an ankle, and quarterback Sam Etcheverry, debuting in the NFL after a great nine-year career in Canada, came up with a sore arm to put a dent in the running and passing attacks. Coach Pop Ivy kept his team together, throwing Prentice Gautt into Crow's spot and spelling Etcheverry with Ralph Guglielmi, and the Cards came up with upset wins over New York and Philadelphia. But more injuries, such as Ken Panfil's bad knee, dropped the club into the lower ranks in the East and prompted coach Ivy to resign with two games left.

Pittsburgh Steelers—Old age was catching up with the Steelers. Bobby Layne spent several weeks in drydock with a bad shoulder, ends Preston Carpenter and Bob Schnelker had lost their speed, and defensive linemen Ernie Stautner, Big Daddy Lipscomb, and Joe Krupa all were on the decline. With Layne out, Rudy Bukich, who had done more sitting than playing in his past six seasons, took over at quarterback and showed a good arm and no consistency. Only fullback John Henry Johnson, flanker Buddy Dial, defensive back Johnny Sample, and linebackers John Reger and Myron Pottios had top-notch seasons.

Dallas Cowboys—After going winless through their inaugural 1960 season, the Cowboys quickly picked up their first victory by beating Pittsburgh 27-24 on opening day. After four weeks, the Cowboys had also beaten Minnesota twice to climb to a 3-1 record before the league caught up with them. Two blue-chip rookies made the Cowboys a much improved team. Halfback Don Perkins, who missed the 1960 season with a broken foot, raced to 815 yards rushing with a fine showing late in the season. The defensive addition was Bob Lilly, a quick and strong defensive end who put heavy pressure on enemy passers. Veterans Eddie LeBaron and Billy Howton combined for many short pass completions, while Frank Clarke suddenly developed into a dangerous deep receiver.

Washington Redskins—Rookie head coach Bill McPeak and rookie quarterback Norm Snead both suffered through a frightening debut. McPeak found himself in charge of a club with no runners, no blockers, and a porous defensive secondary. Snead learned quickly how to throw under pressure, with his line giving him no protection from swarms of defenders clawing and thrashing him. After thirteen losses and heavy underdogs against the Dallas Cowboys, the Redskins won 34-24 to avert the stigma of a victoryless season.

WESTERN CONFERENCE

Green Bay Packers—Coach Vince Lombardi had built his team around good blocking and good tackling. His offense had the league's best running attack, with two superb guards in Jerry Kramer and Fuzzy Thurston escorting runners Jim Taylor, Paul Hornung, and Tommy Moore around end in the famous Green Bay power sweep. Against the run the Packers defense was murder, with a quick forward wall of Bill Quinlan, Henry Jordan, Dave Hanner, and Willie Davis perfectly complemented by smart linebackers Bill Forester, Ray Nitschke, and Dan Currie. The Packers were a brutally physical team, with quarterback Bart Starr directing the violence with pinpoint passing and a knack for picking apart enemy defenses. After losing to the Lions on opening day, Green Bay won its next six games and had the Western title sewed up with two weeks left in the season.

Detroit Lions—Detroit fans found it hard to believe that the Lions were NFL powers. Five times the Lions lost at home, with a 49-0 pasting by the '49ers the ultimate humiliation. But the Lions saved their best for the road by going undefeated. Coach George Wilson had built a defense to match Green Bay's, a unit with size, speed, and experience in all sectors. No other team could match tackles Alex Karras and Roger Brown, Joe Schmidt had no peer as a middle linebacker, and Yale Lary and Night Train Lane had a world of savvy in the secondary.

Baltimore Colts—Johnny Unitas' passes still packed the Baltimore attack with explosives, but the Colt defense no longer could defuse enemy offenses. With Big Daddy Lipscomb and Johnny Sample traded to Pittsburgh and Art Donovan at the end of his career, opponents found it easier to move the ball against the Colts than it had been in the late 1950s. A slow start of two wins in the first five games made any title hopes seem very slim, and even a 45-21 mid-season ambush of the Packers couldn't halt the Colts' decline into mediocrity. But the colts still showcased several fine individual performances, such as the explosive running and receiving of Lenny Moore, the continued superb pass-catching of Ray Berry, and All-Pro seasons from Jim Parker and Gino Marchetti.

Chicago Bears—First place in the West rode on the November 12 meeting of the Bears and Packers in Wrigley Field. Green Bay's record was 6-2, coming off a 45-21 pasting by the Colts; the Bears' record was 5-3, fresh from a close 16-14 loss to the Eagles. Although the Packers had shut the Bears out 24-0 in an earlier meeting, Chicago fans whipped themselves into a fury over the game. They saw a good game, as the Packers ran out to a 28-7 lead and then barely held on for a 31-28 triumph. The Bears did not recapture first place, but they did refurbish their passing attack this year. The main addition was rookie Mike Ditka, the first tight end to win a national following for his devastating blocking and effective receiving.

San Francisco '49ers—The shotgun formation burned the league up for five weeks. Using this pass-oriented formation, the '49ers won four of their first five games, including triumphs of 35-3 over Washington, 49-0 over Detroit, and 35-0 over Los Angeles. Coach Red Hickey was alternating John Brodie, rookie Bill Kilmer, and Bobby Waters at the quarterback slot on alternate plays, loading the shotgun with quarterback plunges, halfback reverses, and a spate of passes. But the dream ended on October 22 in Chicago. Knowing that a center could not block well while looking between his legs to hike a ball back to a tailback, Bear defensive coach Clark Shaughnessy put middle linebacker Bill George right over the center and had him charge straight through to the quarterback on every play. By halftime, the Bears had demoralized the '49ers; by the final gun, the Bears had won 31-0. Thus exposed, the shotgun never again exploded.

Los Angeles Rams—The Rams had a lot of offensive talent for a sixth-place team. Jon Arnett and Dick Bass were top-notch runners, Ollie Matson a multitalented back, and both Jim Phillips and Carroll Dale fine receivers. There was no fuse at quarterback, however, to start the machine rolling, as neither Zeke Bratkowski nor Frank Ryan showed any consistency in running the attack. The porous offensive line helped neither passers nor runners, and outside of rookie end Deacon Jones, bright spots were scarce for the defensive unit.

Minnesota Vikings—The Vikings, this year's expansion team, quickly surpassed Dallas' 1960 record as a new team by beating the Chicago Bears 37-13 in their first league game. The three wins the Vikes captured for the season surprised most experts and made Norm Van Brocklin's coaching debut a success. Van Brocklin stepped right from the playing ranks as quarterback with the Eagles into the head coach's job at Minnesota, and his quarterback was one with a style most unlike his own. While Van Brocklin was a pocket passer whom only a tidal wave could force to run, rookie Fran Tarkenton became the talk of the league with his scrambling.

FINAL STATISTICS

OFFENSE

	BALT.	CHI.	CLEVE.	DALLAS	DET.	G.BAY	L.A.	MINN.	N.Y.	PHIL.	PITT.	ST.L.	S.F.	WASH.
FIRST DOWNS:														
Total	274	239	246	239	233	274	236	236	**275**	252	239	202	258	193
by Rushing	124	103	116	100	96	**142**	109	104	99	78	102	83	116	55
by Passing	135	113	120	130	122	115	111	123	**160**	158	123	110	132	124
by Penalty	15	**23**	10	9	15	17	16	9	16	16	14	9	10	14
RUSHING:														
Number	456	436	476	416	439	474	415	419	464	373	**543**	386	448	361
Yards	2119	1890	2163	1819	1868	**2350**	1958	1897	1857	1507	1761	1405	2100	1072
Average Yards	4.6	4.3	4.5	4.4	4.3	**5.0**	4.7	4.5	4.0	4.0	3.2	3.6	4.7	3.0
Touchdowns	17	16	15	6	16	**27**	17	14	13	10	10	8	**27**	9
PASSING:														
Attempts	**438**	349	320	422	398	306	386	377	416	429	334	351	346	420
Completions	232	186	185	215	186	177	199	203	215	**241**	176	168	187	189
Completion Pct.	53.0	53.3	57.8	50.9	46.7	**57.8**	51.6	53.8	51.7	56.2	52.7	47.9	54.0	45.0
Passing Yards (Gross)	3018	3011	2538	2918	2830	2502	2709	2527	3035	**3824**	2622	2434	3057	2566
Yards Lost Tackled	215	339	164	257	286	**138**	372	538	295	219	290	461	253	391
Net Yards	2803	2672	2374	2661	2544	2364	2337	1989	2740	**3605**	2332	1973	2804	2175
Yds. per Att (Gross)	6.9	8.6	7.9	6.9	7.1	8.2	7.0	6.7	7.3	**8.9**	7.9	6.9	8.8	6.1
Yds. per Comp (Gross)	13.0	16.2	13.7	13.6	15.2	14.1	13.6	12.4	14.1	15.9	14.9	14.5	**16.3**	13.6
Touchdowns	17	26	20	23	14	18	13	22	27	**34**	23	21	15	12
Interceptions	29	24	**13**	27	27	16	21	22	23	26	34	23	19	28
Pct. Intercepted	6.6	6.9	**4.1**	6.4	6.8	5.2	5.4	5.8	5.5	6.1	10.2	6.6	5.5	6.7
PUNTING:														
Number	42	60	53	61	56	51	64	63	68	55	73	**85**	59	70
Average Distance	43.0	41.7	43.3	36.7	**47.6**	43.0	40.1	39.0	43.9	43.7	47.0	44.7	44.6	38.1
PUNT RETURNS:														
Number	33	27	28	23	38	20	14	23	**42**	34	40	26	24	28
Yards	269	170	283	103	357	355	184	309	289	353	**447**	236	232	197
Average Yards	8.2	6.3	10.1	4.5	9.4	**17.8**	13.1	13.4	6.9	10.4	11.2	9.1	9.7	7.0
Touchdowns	0	0	1	0	0	**2**	1	1	0	1	1	1	1	0
KICKOFF RETURNS:														
Number	53	51	50	64	50	41	56	**72**	38	53	49	47	49	64
Yards	1182	1247	1115	1345	1097	1077	1463	**1568**	850	1313	1020	992	1302	1661
Average Yards	22.3	24.5	22.3	21.0	21.9	26.3	26.1	21.8	22.4	24.8	20.8	21.1	**26.6**	26.0
Touchdowns	0	0	**1**	0	**1**	0	**1**	0	0	**1**	0	0	**1**	0
INTERCEPTION RETURNS:														
Number	16	24	20	25	29	29	23	22	**33**	17	25	24	19	26
Yards	123	371	160	374	312	446	277	356	**526**	239	498	459	322	325
Average Yards	7.7	15.5	8.0	15.0	10.8	15.4	12.0	16.2	15.9	14.1	**19.9**	19.1	16.9	12.5
Touchdowns	0	0	0	0	1	2	0	0	4	0	2	**5**	0	2
PENALTIES:														
Number	69	**81**	47	47	69	66	63	36	59	42	52	57	65	70
Yards	589	**719.5**	455	427	678	647	599	375	629	500	486	535	635	651
FUMBLES:														
Number	21	23	28	46	25	**18**	21	36	40	25	34	39	25	18
Number Lost	13	14	20	21	15	**10**	11	22	20	14	22	18	17	12
POINTS:														
Total	302	326	319	236	270	**391**	263	285	368	361	295	279	346	174
PAT Attempts	34	42	39	29	32	**49**	32	37	46	46	36	37	44	23
PAT Made	33	41	37	29	31	**49**	32	36	46	43	34	34	44	21
FG Attempts	**39**	27	23	24	33	24	27	21	34	25	28	17	22	28
FG Made	**21**	11	16	11	15	16	13	9	14	14	15	7	12	5
Percent FG Made	53.8	40.7	**69.6**	45.8	45.5	66.7	48.1	42.9	41.2	56.0	53.6	41.2	54.5	17.9
Safeties	1	0	0	0	1	0	0	0	**2**	0	0	1	1	0

DEFENSE

	BALT.	CHI.	CLEVE.	DALLAS	DET.	G. BAY	L.A.	MINN.	N.Y.	PHIL.	PITT.	ST.L.	S.F.	WASH.
FIRST DOWNS:														
Total	232	223	243	254	222	245	279	291	**212**	267	218	215	234	261
by Rushing	108	80	87	122	89	110	136	147	86	116	**71**	91	90	94
by Passing	**110**	124	146	120	121	117	121	132	**110**	145	132	112	132	154
by Penalty	14	19	10	12	12	18	22	12	16	**6**	15	12	12	13
RUSHING:														
Number	418	401	411	454	412	412	508	493	419	474	**396**	477	419	412
Yards	1869	1652	1605	2161	1520	1694	2440	2667	1761	2007	**1463**	1676	1701	1550
Average Yards	4.5	4.1	3.9	4.8	3.7	4.1	4.8	5.4	4.2	4.2	3.7	**3.5**	4.1	3.8
Touchdowns	17	10	16	20	14	12	26	29	**6**	12	11	9	13	10
PASSING:														
Attempts	351	398	358	**326**	385	414	328	365	386	383	420	389	380	409
Completions	**161**	209	200	168	203	218	184	194	176	224	201	187	196	238
Completion Pct.	45.9	52.5	55.9	51.5	52.7	52.7	56.1	53.2	**45.6**	58.5	47.9	48.1	51.6	58.2
Passing Yards (Gross)	**2320**	3164	2831	2635	2744	2630	2642	3051	2600	3183	2780	2644	2874	3493
Yards Lost Tackled	**407**	367	305	204	326	273	269	125	399	263	334	334	394	218
Net Yards	**1913**	2797	2526	2431	2418	2357	2373	2926	2201	2920	2446	2310	2480	3275
Yds. per Att (Gross)	6.6	7.9	7.9	8.1	7.1	**6.4**	8.1	8.4	6.7	8.3	6.6	6.8	7.6	8.5
Yds. per Comp (Gross)	14.4	15.1	14.2	15.7	13.5	**12.1**	14.4	15.7	14.8	14.2	13.8	14.1	14.7	14.7
Touchdowns	18	27	16	21	**11**	13	19	21	21	23	22	18	18	37
Interceptions	16	24	20	25	29	29	23	22	**33**	17	25	24	19	26
Pct. Intercepted	4.6	6.0	5.6	7.7	7.5	7.0	7.0	6.0	**8.5**	4.4	6.0	6.2	5.0	6.4
PUNTING:														
Number	64	66	54	43	67	49	51	46	83	64	**86**	67	62	58
Average Distance	41.4	42.7	42.9	45.5	43.0	**37.8**	43.3	41.4	42.4	41.8	43.8	42.0	44.0	44.2
PUNT RETURNS:														
Number	18	24	27	**17**	21	25	36	23	32	30	32	53	32	30
Yards	248	302	213	193	273	313	384	**138**	247	235	251	438	269	280
Average Yards	13.8	12.6	7.9	11.4	13.0	12.5	10.7	**6.0**	7.7	7.8	7.8	8.3	8.4	9.3
Touchdowns	1	1	**0**	**0**	1	1	**0**	**0**	**0**	1	1	1	1	1
KICKOFF RETURNS:														
Number	57	55	56	43	49	69	53	51	59	58	50	50	58	**29**
Yards	1552	1219	1465	978	1184	1597	1380	1148	1288	1224	1156	1007	1368	**666**
Average Yards	27.2	22.2	26.2	22.7	24.2	23.1	26.0	22.5	21.8	21.1	23.1	**20.1**	23.6	23.0
Touchdowns	**0**	1	1	**0**	2	**0**	**0**	**0**	**0**	1	**0**	**0**	**0**	**0**
INTERCEPTION RETURNS:														
Number	29	24	**13**	27	27	16	21	22	23	26	34	23	19	28
Yards	406	346	302	589	314	**238**	280	219	246	294	510	318	249	477
Average Yards	14.0	14.4	23.2	21.8	11.6	14.9	13.3	**10.0**	10.7	11.3	15.0	13.8	13.1	17.0
Touchdowns	1	**0**	1	6	**0**	**0**	**0**	2	1	1	2	**0**	**0**	2
PENALTIES:														
Number	66	**86**	38	38	39	52	75	65	67	62	57	59	56	63
Yards	547.5	**860**	367	362	381	609	662	638	677	684	533	546	456	603
FUMBLES:														
Number	19	22	23	30	21	30	27	31	**43**	27	36	36	21	33
Number Lost	8	13	18	18	12	17	16	**23**	21	16	20	20	12	15
POINTS:														
Total	307	302	270	380	258	223	333	407	**220**	297	287	267	272	392
PAT Attempts	37	39	34	49	28	**26**	45	52	29	38	37	30	32	50
PAT Made	37	36	33	44	28	**26**	45	50	29	36	35	30	32	49
FG Attempts	26	27	28	28	34	21	21	26	**20**	24	26	38	29	24
FG Made	16	10	11	14	20	13	6	15	**5**	11	10	19	16	13
Percent FG Made	61.5	37.0	39.3	50.0	58.8	61.9	28.6	57.7	**25.0**	45.8	38.5	50.0	55.2	54.2
Safeties	**0**	1	**0**	**0**	1	1	**0**	**0**	1	**0**	**0**	**0**	**0**	2

1961 NFL CHAMPIONSHIP GAME

December 31, at Green Bay
(Attendance 39,029)

SCORING

GREEN BAY	0	24	10	3–37
NEW YORK	0	0	0	0– 0

Second Quarter

G.B.	Hornung, 6 yard rush PAT – Hornung (kick)	0:04
G.B.	Dowler, 13 yard pass from Starr PAT – Hornung (kick)	4:19
G.B.	R. Kramer, 14 yard pass from Starr PAT – Hornung (kick)	10:04
G.B.	Hornung, 17 yard field goal	15:00

Third Quarter

G.B.	Hornung, 22 yard field goal	9:55
G.B.	R. Kramer, 13 yard pass from Starr PAT – Hornung (kick)	12:12

Fourth Quarter

G.B.	Hornung, 19 yard field goal	6:48

TEAM STATISTICS

G.B.		N.Y.
19	First Downs – Total	6
10	First Downs – Rushing	1
8	First Downs – Passing	4
1	First Downs – Penalty	1
1	Fumbles – Number	5
0	Fumbles – Number Lost	1
4	Penalties – Number	4
16	Yards Penalized	38
0	Giveaways	5
5	Takeaways	0
+5	Difference	–5

New York's Cold Reception

Although the Packers had won five Western titles before this year, this was the first NFL championship game ever staged in Green Bay. The sub-freezing Wisconsin weather suited the Packers fine as they easily rolled over the Giants. The first quarter was scoreless, but New York's Kyle Rote dropped a sure touchdown pass deep in Green Bay territory. The Giants blew another touchdown in the second quarter when halfback Bob Gaiters overthrew Rote in the end zone. The Packers, meanwhile, took a comfortable lead by scoring three touchdowns in the quarter. Paul Hornung, on leave from the Army, scored from the 6-yard line after an 80-yard Packer drive, Boyd Dowler scored on a Bart Starr pass after a Ray Nitschke interception, and a Starr-to-Ron Kramer touchdown pass followed another Packer interception. Hornung added all the extra points and a 17-yard field goal to run the halftime score to 24-0. With their running game ineffective, the Giants turned to the pass, but Green Bay's Jess Whittenton blanketed top receiver Del Shofner like a shadow. While their defense continued to thwart the Giants, the Packers added ten more points in the third quarter to put the game on ice. The Packers turned a fumbled punt by Joe Morrison into a Hornung field goal, and another sustained drive resulted in Ron Kramer's second touchdown catch. A fourth-quarter Hornung field goal made the final score 37-0 and gave Hornung a record 19 points for the championship game.

INDIVIDUAL STATISTICS

GREEN BAY	No	Yds	Avg.	NEW YORK	No	Yds	Avg.
RUSHING							
Hornung	20	89	4.5	Webster	7	19	2.7
Taylor	14	69	4.9	Wells	3	9	3.0
Moore	6	25	4.2	King	2	5	2.5
Roach	1	0	0.0	Gaiters	1	2	2.0
Pitts	3	–2	–0.7	Tittle	1	–4	–4.0
	44	181	4.1		14	31	2.2
RECEIVING							
R. Kramer	4	80	20.0	Rote	3	54	18.0
Hornung	3	47	15.7	Shofner	3	41	13.7
Dowler	3	37	12.3	Webster	3	5	1.7
	10	164	16.4	Walton	1	19	19.0
					10	119	11.9
PUNTING							
Dowler	5		42.0	Chandler	5		39.2
PUNT RETURNS							
Wood	1	4	4.0	Morrison	2	10	5.0
KICKOFF RETURNS							
Nitschke	1	18	18.0	Wells	5	98	19.6
				Gaiters	1	21	21.0
					6	119	19.8
INTERCEPTION RETURNS							
Adderley	1	14	14.0				
Gremminger	1	13	13.0	None			
Nitschke	1	9	9.0				
Whittenton	1	0	0.0				
	4	36	9.0				

PASSING

GREEN BAY	Att	Comp	Comp Pct.	Yds	Int	Yds/ Att.	Yds/ Comp	Yards Lost Tackled
Starr	17	10	58.8	164	0	9.6	16.4	0
Hornung	2	0	0.0	0	0	–	–	0
	19	10	52.6	164	0	8.6	16.4	0
NEW YORK								
Tittle	20	6	30.0	65	4	3.3	10.8	2–15
Conerly	8	4	50.0	54	0	6.8	13.5	1– 5
Gaiters	1	0	0.0	0	0	–	–	0
	29	10	34.5	119	4	4.1	11.9	3–20

NEW YORK GIANTS 10-3-1 Allie Sherman

Scores of Each Game		
10	ST. LOUIS	21
17	Pittsburgh	14
24	Washington	21
24	St. Louis	9
31	Dallas	10
24	LOS ANGELES	14
16	DALLAS	17
53	WASHINGTON	0
38	PHILADELPHIA	21
42	PITTSBURGH	21
37	Cleveland	21
17	GREEN BAY	20
28	Philadelphia	24
7	CLEVELAND	7

Use Name	Pos.	Hgt	Wgt	Age	Int	Pts
Rosey Brown	OT	6'3"	255	28		
Chuck Janerette	OT	6'3"	250	22		
Darrell Dess	OG	6'	245	25		
Zeke Smith	OG	6'2"	235	25		
Jack Stroud	OG	6'1"	250	32		
Mickey Walker	OG	6'	230	21		
Ray Wietecha	C	6'1"	230	32		
Greg Larson	OT-C	6'2"	245	22		
Jim Katcavage	DE	6'3"	240	26		2
Andy Robustelli	DE	6'1"	235	35		
Rosey Grier	DT	6'5"	290	28		
Dick Modzelewski	DT	6'	260	30		2
Larry Hayes	LB	6'3"	230	26		6
Sam Huff	LB	6'1"	230	26	3	6
Cliff Livingston	LB	6'3"	215	31	3	
Tom Scott	LB	6'2"	220	31	1	6
Bob Simms	LB	6'1"	230	23		
Gene Johnson (from MIN)	DB	6'	180	26		
Dick Lynch	DB	6'1"	205	25	9	
Dick Nolan	DB	6'1"	185	29		
Jimmy Patton	DB	6'	185	29	8	6
Bill Stits	DB	6'	195	30		
Erich Barnes	HB-DB	6'2"	198	26	7	18
Allan Webb	HB-DB	5'11"	180	26		
Chuck Conerly	QB	6'1"	185	37		
Lee Grosscup	QB	6'1"	185	24		
Y. A. Tittle	QB	6'	195	34		18
Don Chandler	HB	6'2"	210	26		
Bob Gaiters	HB	5'11"	210	23		42
Phil King	HB	6'4"	225	25		
Joel Wells	HB	6'1"	198	20		12
Joe Morrison	DB-HB	6'1"	212	23	2	12
Alex Webster	FB	6'3"	225	30		30
Pete Hall	OE	6'2"	200	23		
Kyle Rote	OE	6'	200	32		42
Del Shofner	OE	6'3"	185	25		66
Joe Walton	OE	5'11"	200	26		12
Pat Summerall	K	6'4"	235	31		88

Frank Gifford – Voluntarily Retired

Jim Podoley – Injury

PHILADELPHIA EAGLES 10-4-0 Nick Skorich

Scores of Each Game		
27	CLEVELAND	20
14	WASHINGTON	7
27	ST. LOUIS	30
21	PITTSBURGH	16
20	St. Louis	7
43	Dallas	7
27	Washington	24
16	CHICAGO	14
21	New York	38
24	Cleveland	45
35	DALLAS	13
35	Pittsburgh	24
24	NEW YORK	28
27	Detroit	24

Use Name	Pos.	Hgt	Wgt	Age	Int	Pts
Jim McCusker	OT	6'2"	245	25		
Don Oakes	OT	6'3"	245	23		
J. D. Smith	OT	6'5"	250	25		
Stan Campbell	OG	6'	230	31		
John Wittenborn	OG	6'2"	240	25		
Howard Keys	C	6'3"	240	26		
Gene Gossage	DE	6'3"	240	26		
Will Renfro	DE	6'5"	235	29		
Leo Sugar	DE	6'1"	230	32		
Marion Campbell	DT	6'3"	250	32		
Riley Gunnels	DT	6'3"	250	24		
Ed Khayat	DT	6'3"	248	26		
Jess Richardson	DT	6'2"	265	31		
Maxie Baughan	LB	6'1"	226	23	1	
Chuck Bednarik	LB	6'3"	235	36	2	
John Nocera	LB	6'1"	220	27		
Bob Pellegrini	LB	6'2"	225	26		
Chuck Weber	LB	6'1"	235	32	1	
Glen Amerson	DB	6'1"	186	22		
Tom Brookshier	DB	6'	198	29	2	
Don Burroughs	DB	6'4"	190	30	7	
Jimmy Carr	DB	6'1"	210	28	2	
Irv Cross	DB	6'1"	190	22	2	
Bobby Freeman	DB	6'1"	200	28		
King Hill	QB	6'3"	213	25		
Sonny Jurgensen	QB	5'11"	200	27		
Billy Barnes	HB	5'11"	202	26		24
Timmy Brown	HB	5'10"	190	24		30
Ted Dean	HB	6'2"	210	23		18
Clarence Peaks	FB	6'1"	220	25		30
Theron Sapp	FB	6'1"	205	26		6
Tommy McDonald	FL	5'10"	172	27		78
Dick Lucas	OE	6'2"	216	27		30
Pete Retzlaff	OE	6'1"	212	30		48
John Tracey	OE	6'3"	225	28		
Bobby Walston	OE	6'	195	32		97

CLEVELAND BROWNS 8-5-1 Paul Brown

Scores of Each Game		
20	Philadelphia	27
20	ST. LOUIS	17
25	DALLAS	7
31	WASHINGTON	7
17	GREEN BAY	49
30	Pittsburgh	28
21	St. Louis	10
13	PITTSBURGH	17
17	Washington	6
45	PHILADELPHIA	24
21	NEW YORK	37
38	Dallas	17
14	Chicago	17
7	New York	7

Use Name	Pos.	Hgt	Wgt	Age	Int	Pts
Lou Groza	OT	6'3"	248	37		85
Errol Linden	OT	6'5"	260	24		
Mike McCormack	OT	6'4"	250	34		
Ed Nutting	OT	6'4"	246	22		
Dick Schafrath	OT	6'3"	255	25		
Duane Putnam	OG	6'	233	33		
Jim Ray Smith	OG	6'3"	245	30		
John Wooten	OG	6'2"	250	26		
John Morrow	C	6'3"	248	28		
Jim Houston	DE	6'2"	235	24		
Paul Wiggin	DE	6'3"	245	27		
Johnny Brewer	DE	6'4"	225	24		
Bob Gain	DT	6'3"	260	33		
Floyd Peters	DT	6'4"	255	26		
Larry Stephens	DT	6'4"	260	23		
Vince Costello	LB	6'	232	29		6
Galen Fiss	LB	6'	227	31	1	
Walt Michaels	LB	6'	237	32	2	
Dave Lloyd	C-LB	6'3"	248	25		
Ross Fichtner	DB	6'	185	23		
Don Fleming	DB	6'	188	24	3	
Bernie Parrish	DB	5'11"	195	26	7	6
Jim Shofner	DB	6'2"	190	25	5	
Bobby Franklin	DB	5'11"	182	25	2	6
Len Dawson	QB	6'	195	27		
Milt Plum	QB	6'1"	205	27		6
Bobby Mitchell	HB	6'	192	26		60
Tom Watkins	HB	6'1"	195	24		6
Jimmy Brown	FB	6'2"	228	25		60
Preston Powell	FB	6'2"	225	24		
Ray Renfro	FL	6'1"	192	30		36
Leon Clarke	OE	6'4"	235	28		12
Bob Crespino	OE	6'4"	217	23		6
Charley Ferguson	OE	6'5"	217	21		6
Rich Kreitling	OE	6'2"	208	26		18
Gern Nagler	OE	6'2"	190	28		6
Sam Baker	K	6'2"	217	29		

Gene Hickerson – Broken Leg

ST. LOUIS CARDINALS 7-7-0 Pop Ivy Chuck Drulis Ray Prochaska Ray Willsey

Scores of Each Game		
21	New York	10
17	Cleveland	20
30	Philadelphia	27
9	NEW YORK	24
7	PHILADELPHIA	20
24	Washington	0
10	CLEVELAND	21
31	Dallas	17
14	DETROIT	45
0	Baltimore	16
27	Pittsburgh	30
38	WASHINGTON	24
31	DALLAS	13
20	PITTSBURGH	0

Use Name	Pos.	Hgt	Wgt	Age	Int	Pts
Ed Cook	OT	6'2"	240	29		
Charley Granger (from DAL)	OT	6'2"	240	23		
Ernie McMillan	OT	6'6"	255	23		
Dale Memmelaar	OT	6'2"	245	24		
Ken Panfil	OT	6'6"	255	30		
Jerry Perry	OT	6'4"	240	30		51
Bob DeMarco	OG	6'3"	240	23		
Ken Gray	OG	6'2"	240	25		
Mike McGee	OG	6'1"	230	23		
Tom Redmond	OG	6'5"	240	24		
Charley Ellzey	C	6'3"	240	23		
Don Gillis	C	6'3"	250	26		
Bob Griffin (from DEN-A)	LB-C	6'3"	250	32		
Ed Henke	DE	6'3"	230	33		
Luke Owens	DE	6'2"	255	28		
Joe Robb	DE	6'3"	230	24	1	
Frank Fuller	DT	6'4"	245	32		
Ron McDole	DT	6'3"	250	21		
Don Owens	DT	6'5"	255	29		
Ted Bates	LB	6'3"	220	24		
Bill Koman	LB	6'2"	230	27	1	
Monte Lee	LB	6'4"	225	23	1	
Dale Meinert	LB	6'2"	220	28	2	
Joe Driskill	DB	6'1"	195	24		
Jimmy Hill	DB	6'2"	190	32	4	6
Jerry Norton	DB	5'11"	195	31	7	12
Willie West	DB	5'10"	185	23	1	6
Larry Wilson	DB	6'	187	23	3	2
Pat Fischer	HB-DB	5'10"	165	21		
Billy Stacy	HB-DB	6'1"	190	25	4	24
Sam Etcheverry	QB	5'11"	190	31		
Ralph Guglielmi	QB	6'1"	195	28		6
Charley Johnson	QB	6'	190	24		
Bobby Joe Conrad	HB	6'	195	26		22
John David Crow	HB	6'2"	215	26		24
Prentice Gautt	HB	6'	200	23		36
Ken Hall (from HOU-A)	HB	6'1"	210	25		
Mal Hammack	FB	6'2"	205	28		6
Frank Mestnik	FB	6'2"	200	23		12
Taz Anderson	OE	6'2"	200	22		18
Dick Lage	OE	6'4"	228	21		
Hugh McInnis	OE	6'3"	220	23		
Sonny Randle	OE	6'2"	187	25		54

Joe Childress – Injury

PITTSBURGH STEELERS 6-8-0 Buddy Parker

Scores of Each Game		
24	Dallas	27
14	NEW YORK	17
14	Los Angeles	24
16	Philadelphia	21
20	WASHINGTON	0
28	CLEVELAND	30
20	SAN FRANCISCO	10
17	Cleveland	13
37	DALLAS	7
21	New York	42
30	ST. LOUIS	27
24	PHILADELPHIA	35
30	Washington	14
0	St. Louis	20

Use Name	Pos.	Hgt	Wgt	Age	Int	Pts
Charlie Bradshaw	OT	6'6"	255	25		
Dan James	OT	6'4"	280	24		
Dick Klein (to BOS-A)	OT	6'4"	255	27		
John Nisby	OG	6'1"	230	28		
Mike Sandusky	OG	6'	230	28		
Ron Stehouwer	OG	6'2"	230	24		
Buzz Nutter	C	6'4"	230	30		
George Demko	DE	6'3"	240	26		
John Kapele	DE	6'	240	24		
Lou Michaels	DE	6'2"	235	25	1	72
Ernie Stautner	DT-DE	6'1"	230	36		
Joe Krupa	DT	6'2"	225	28		
Big Daddy Lipscomb	DT	6'6"	288	30		
Mike Henry	LB	6'2"	215	25	1	
Myron Pottios	LB	6'2"	240	22	2	
John Reger	LB	6'	230	30	1	
Bob Schmitz	LB	6'1"	235	23		
Wilbert Scott	LB	6'	215	22		
George Tarasovic	LB	6'4"	245	32	1	
Len Burnett	DB	6'1"	195	22		
Bill Butler	DB	5'10"	185	24	3	6
Willie Daniel	DB	5'11"	185	23	3	
Johnny Sample	DB	6'1"	200	24	8	12
Jackie Simpson	DB	5'10"	185	27	2	
Brady Keys	HB-DB	6'	185	25	2	
Dick Haley (from MIN)	FL-DB	5'10"	195	24	1	
Rudy Bukich	QB	6'1"	205	30		12
Bobby Layne	QB	6'1"	210	34		5
Terry Nofsinger	QB	6'4"	205	23		
Dick Hoak	HB	5'11"	190	22		
Jack Stanton	HB	6'1"	190	23		
Tom Tracy	HB	5'9"	205	29		20
John Henry Johnson	FB	6'2"	215	31		42
Charlie Scales	FB	5'11"	215	22		
Buddy Dial	FL	6'1"	195	24		72
Red Mack	HB-FL	5'10"	185	24		12
Preston Carpenter	OE	6'2"	190	27		24
Henry Clement	OE	6'2"	200	21		
Bob Coronado	OE	6'1"	195	25		
Steve Meilinger (to STL)	OE	6'2"	230	31		
Bob Schnelker (from MIN)	OE	6'3"	215	31		24
Bobby Joe Green	K	5'11"	175	23		

NEW YORK GIANTS

RUSHING

Last Name	No.	Yds	Avg	TD
Webster	196	928	4.7	2
Gaiters	116	460	4.0	6
Wells	65	216	3.3	1
Tittle	25	85	3.4	3
Webb	6	51	8.5	0
Morrison	33	48	1.5	1
Chandler	3	30	10.0	0
Conerly	13	16	1.2	0
Grosscup	2	10	5.0	0
King	4	7	1.8	0
Shofner	1	6	6.0	0

RECEIVING

Last Name	No.	Yds	Avg	TD
Shofner	68	1125	17	11
Rote	53	805	15	7
Walton	36	544	15	2
Webster	26	313	12	3
Morrison	11	67	6	1
Gaiters	11	54	5	1
Wells	6	31	5	1
Barnes	2	74	37	1
Hall	2	22	11	0

PUNT RETURNS

Last Name	No.	Yds	Avg	TD
Stits	17	132	8	0
Wells	17	90	5	0
Webb	5	61	12	0
Morrison	3	6	2	0

KICKOFF RETURNS

Last Name	No.	Yds	Avg	TD
Gaiters	11	288	26	0
Wells	12	273	23	0
Webb	8	156	20	0
Stits	4	87	22	0
Morrison	2	32	16	0
Simms	1	14	14	0

PASSING – PUNTING – KICKING

PASSING	Att	Comp	%	Yds	Yd/Att	TD	Int–	%	RK
Tittle	285	163	57	2272	8.0	17	12–	4	3
Conerly	106	44	42	634	6.0	7	8–	8	
Grosscup	22	5	23	87	4.0	1	3–	14	
Gaiters	3	3	100	42	14.0	2	0–	0	

PUNTING	No	Avg
Chandler	68	43.9

KICKING	XP	Att	%	FG	Att	%
Summerall	46	46	100	14	34	41

PHILADELPHIA EAGLES

RUSHING

Last Name	No.	Yds	Avg	TD
Peaks	135	471	3.5	5
Brown	50	338	6.8	1
Dean	66	321	4.9	2
Barnes	92	309	3.4	1
Jurgensen	20	27	1.4	0
Sapp	7	24	3.4	1
Hill	2	9	4.5	0
Retzlaff	1	8	8.0	0

RECEIVING

Last Name	No.	Yds	Avg	TD
McDonald	64	1144	18	13
Retzlaff	50	769	15	8
Walston	34	569	17	2
Peaks	32	472	15	0
Dean	21	335	16	1
Barnes	15	194	13	3
Brown	14	264	19	2
Lucas	8	67	8	5
Sapp	3	10	3	0

PUNT RETURNS

Last Name	No.	Yds	Avg	TD
Dean	18	140	8	0
Brown	8	125	16	1
Cross	7	77	11	0
Baughan	1	11	11	0

KICKOFF RETURNS

Last Name	No.	Yds	Avg	TD
Brown	29	811	28	1
Dean	21	462	22	0
Peaks	2	29	15	0
Cross	1	11	11	0

PASSING – PUNTING – KICKING

PASSING	Att	Comp	%	Yds	Yd/Att	TD	Int–	%	RK
Jurgensen	416	235	56	3723	8.9	32	24–	6	5
Hill	12	6	50	101	8.4	2	2–	17	
Peaks	1	0	0	0	0.0	0	0–	0	

PUNTING	No	Avg
Hill	55	43.7

KICKING	XP	Att	%	FG	Att	%
Walston	43	46	93	14	25	56

CLEVELAND BROWNS

RUSHING

Last Name	No.	Yds	Avg	TD
Brown	305	1408	4.6	8
Mitchell	101	548	5.4	5
Watkins	43	209	4.9	0
Franklin	1	12	12.0	1
Powell	1	5	5.0	0
Kreitling	0	4	0.0	0
McCormack	0	4	0.0	0
Dawson	1	–10	–10.0	0
Plum	24	–17	–0.7	1

RECEIVING

Last Name	No.	Yds	Avg	TD
Renfro	48	834	17	6
Brown	46	459	10	2
Mitchell	32	368	12	3
Kreitling	21	229	11	3
Nagler	19	241	13	1
Clarke	11	211	19	2
Watkins	4	66	17	1
Ferguson	2	68	34	1
Crespino	2	62	31	1

PUNT RETURNS

Last Name	No.	Yds	Avg	TD
Mitchell	14	164	12	1
Shofner	14	119	9	0

KICKOFF RETURNS

Last Name	No.	Yds	Avg	TD
Mitchell	16	428	27	1
Powell	16	321	20	0
Watkins	9	226	25	0
Baker	3	57	19	0
Brown	2	50	25	0
Stephens	1	15	15	0
Fichtner	1	11	11	0
Linden	1	5	5	0
Brewer	1	2	2	0

PASSING – PUNTING – KICKING

PASSING	Att	Comp	%	Yds	Yd/Att	TD	Int–	%	RK
Plum	302	177	59	2416	8.0	18	10–	3	1
Dawson	15	7	47	85	5.7	1	3–	20	
Brown	3	1	33	37	12.3	1	0–	0	

PUNTING	No	Avg
Baker	53	43.3

KICKING	XP	Att	%	FG	Att	%
Groza	37	38	97	16	23	70

ST. LOUIS CARDINALS

RUSHING

Last Name	No.	Yds	Avg	TD
Gautt	129	523	4.1	3
Mestnik	95	334	3.5	1
Crow	48	192	4.0	1
Guglielmi	22	101	4.6	1
Hammack	18	79	4.4	1
Etcheverry	33	73	2.2	0
Anderson	15	39	2.6	1
McInnis	4	30	7.5	0
Conrad	20	22	1.1	0
Norton	1	15	15.0	0
Johnson	1	–3	–3.0	0

RECEIVING

Last Name	No.	Yds	Avg	TD
Randle	44	591	13	9
Conrad	30	499	17	2
Anderson	22	399	18	2
Crow	20	306	15	3
Stacy	12	241	20	1
Gautt	12	132	11	3
Mestnik	12	29	2	1
McInnis	7	107	15	0
Hammack	5	70	14	0
Hall	3	38	13	0
Fischer	1	22	22	0

PUNT RETURNS

Last Name	No.	Yds	Avg	TD
Conrad	5	103	21	1
West	11	98	9	0
Fischer	4	18	5	0
Stacy	5	9	2	0
Driskill	1	8	8	0

KICKOFF RETURNS

Last Name	No.	Yds	Avg	TD
Fischer	17	426	25	0
West	16	340	21	0
Wilson	4	83	21	0
Stacy	3	60	20	0
Conrad	1	28	28	0
Mestnik	2	27	14	0
Lee	1	12	12	0
Driskill	2	8	4	0
Hammack	1	8	8	0

PASSING – PUNTING – KICKING

PASSING	Att	Comp	%	Yds	Yd/Att	TD	Int–	%	RK
Etcheverry	196	96	49	1275	6.5	14	11–	6	11
Guglielmi	116	56	48	927	8.0	5	8–	7	
Crow	14	4	29	76	5.4	1	1–	7	
Johnson	13	5	38	51	4.0	0	2–	15	
Gautt	11	6	55	100	9.1	1	1–	9	
Conrad	1	1	100	5	5.0	0	0–	0	

PUNTING	No	Avg
Norton	85	44.7

KICKING	XP	Att	%	FG	Att	%
Perry	30	33	91	7	16	44
Conrad	4	4	100	0	1	0

PITTSBURGH STEELERS

RUSHING

Last Name	No.	Yds	Avg	TD
Johnson	213	787	3.7	6
Tracy	147	402	2.7	2
Hoak	85	302	3.6	0
Scales	50	184	3.7	0
Green	2	37	18.5	0
Keys	6	14	2.3	0
Layne	8	11	1.4	0
Carpenter	7	9	1.3	0
Meilinger	1	6	6.0	0
Dial	3	6	2.0	0
Nofsinger	6	6	1.0	0
Bukich	14	4	0.3	2
Coronado	1	–7	–7.0	0

RECEIVING

Last Name	No.	Yds	Avg	TD
Dial	53	1047	20	12
Carpenter	33	460	14	4
Schnelker	24	401	17	4
Johnson	24	262	11	0
Tracy	14	133	10	1
Mack	8	128	16	2
Meilinger	8	103	13	0
Scales	7	43	6	0
Clement	5	65	13	0
Haley	3	43	14	0
Coronado	3	32	11	0
Hoak	3	18	6	0

PUNT RETURNS

Last Name	No.	Yds	Avg	TD
Sample	26	283	11	1
Keys	9	135	15	0
Carpenter	3	18	6	0
Butler	2	11	6	0

KICKOFF RETURNS

Last Name	No.	Yds	Avg	TD
Sample	23	532	23	0
Haley	13	278	21	0
Butler	6	117	20	0
Scales	3	41	14	0
Keys	2	41	21	0
Johnson	1	11	11	0
Schmitz	1	0	0	0

PASSING – PUNTING – KICKING

PASSING	Att	Comp	%	Yds	Yd/Att	TD	Int–	%	RK
Bukich	156	89	57	1253	8.0	11	16–	10	9
Layne	149	75	50	1205	8.1	11	16–	11	14
Tracy	12	4	33	73	6.1	0	0–	0	
Nofsinger	11	7	64	78	7.1	0	0–	0	
Hoak	3	1	33	13	4.3	1	1–	33	
Johnson	2	0	0	0	0.0	0	1–	50	
Green	1	0	0	0	0.0	0	0–	0	

PUNTING	No	Avg
Green	73	47.0

KICKING	XP	Att	%	FG	Att	%
Michaels	27	29	93	15	26	58
Layne	5	5	100	0	0	0
Tracy	2	2	100	0	1	0
Green	0	0	0	0	1	0

| Scores of Each Game | Use Name | Pos. | Hgt | Wgt | Age | Int | Pts | Use Name | Pos. | Hgt | Wgt | Age | Int | Pts | Use Name | Pos. | Hgt | Wgt | Age | Int | Pts |

EASTERN CONFERENCE — Continued

DALLAS COWBOYS 4-9-1 Tom Landry

Scores of Each Game
27 PITTSBURGH 24
21 MINNESOTA 7
7 Cleveland 25
28 Minnesota 0
10 NEW YORK 31
7 PHILADELPHIA 43
17 New York 16
17 ST. LOUIS 31
7 Pittsburgh 37
28 WASHINGTON 28
13 Philadelphia 35
17 CLEVELAND 38
13 St. Louis 31
24 Washington 34

Use Name	Pos.	Hgt	Wgt	Age	Int	Pts
Byron Bradfute	OT	6'3"	243	23		
Bob Fry	OT	6'4"	240	30		
Bob McCreary	OT	6'5"	256	22		
Andy Cvercko	OG	6'	240	24		
Mike Falls	OG	6'1"	240	27		
Bob Grottkau	OG	6'4"	230	24		
John Houser	OG	6'3"	242	25		
Mike Connelly	C	6'3"	235	25		
Nate Borden	DE	6'	240	29		
Ken Frost	DT	6'4"	245	22	1	
Don Healy	DT	6'3"	264	25	1	
Bill Herchman	DT	6'2"	250	28		
Sonny Davis	LB	6'2"	220	22		
Mike Dowdle	LB	6'3"	210	23	1	
Chuck Howley	LB	6'3"	230	25	1	
Jack Patera	LB	6'1"	240	29		
Jerry Tubbs	LB	6'2"	220	26	3	
Gene Babb	FB-LB	6'3"	218	26		
Bob Bercich	DB	6'1"	198	24	3	
Don Bishop	DB	6'2"	204	26	8	
Tom Franckhauser	DB	6'	196	24	1	
Jimmy Harris	DB	6'1"	180	26	2	
Warren Livingston	DB	5'10"	180	23	1	
Dick Moegle	DB	6'	195	27	2	
Buddy Humphrey	QB	6'1"	200	25		
Eddie LeBaron	QB	5'9"	160	31		
Don Meredith	QB	6'2"	198	23		6
L. G. Dupre	HB	5'11"	190	29		
Don Perkins	HB	5'10"	198	23		30
J. W. Lockett (from SF)	FB	6'2"	230	24		18
Amos Marsh	FB	6'1"	208	22		18
Merrill Douglas	HB-FB	6'	204	25		
Dick Bielski	OE	6'1"	227	29		46
Frank Clarke	OE	6'	215	28		54
Jim Doran	OE	6'2"	211	33		12
Billy Howton	OE	6'2"	185	31		24
Lee Murchison	OE	6'3"	205	23		
Glynn Gregory	DB-OE	6'2"	200	22	1	
Allen Green	K	6'2"	215	23		34

WASHINGTON REDSKINS 1-12-1 Bill McPeak

Scores of Each Game
3 San Francisco 35
7 Philadelphia 14
21 NEW YORK 24
7 Cleveland 31
0 Pittsburgh 20
0 ST. LOUIS 24
24 PHILADELPHIA 27
6 New York 53
6 CLEVELAND 17
28 Dallas 28
6 BALTIMORE 27
24 St. Louis 38
14 PITTSBURGH 30
34 DALLAS 24

Use Name	Pos.	Hgt	Wgt	Age	Int	Pts
Ray Lemek	OT	6'	240	27		
Riley Mattson	OT	6'4"	248	22		
Fran O'Brien	OT	6'1"	250	26		
Bernie Darre	OG	6'2"	230	21		
Vince Promuto	OG	6'1"	243	23		
Ed Beatty (from PIT)	C	6'1"	230	29		
Fred Hageman	C	6'4"	244	23		
Jim Schrader	C	6'2"	252	29		
John Paluck	DE	6'2"	240	28	1	
Andy Stynchula	DE	6'3"	250	22		
Gene Cronin	LB-DE	6'2"	228	28		
Don Lawrence	DT	6'1"	245	24		
Joe Rutgens	DT	6'2"	265	22		
Bob Toneff	DT	6'3"	270	31		
Rod Breedlove	LB	6'2"	225	23	2	
Dick Lasse	LB	6'2"	225	25		
Doyle Schick	LB	6'1"	210	22		
Roy Wilkins	LB	6'3"	228	27		
Jim Crotty (to BUF-A)	DB	5'11"	190	23		
Dale Hackbart	DB	6'3"	210	25	6	12
Jim Kerr	DB	6'	195	22	7	
Joe Krakoski	DB	6'2"	200	24	4	
Ben Scotti	DB	6'1"	186	24	3	
Jim Steffen (from DET)	DB	6'	195	24	1	
Jim Wulff	HB-DB	5'11"	184	25	3	
George Izo	QB	6'3"	214	24		
Norm Snead	QB	6'4"	215	21		18
Lew Luce	HB	6'	187	23		
Mike Sommer (from BAL)	HB	5'11"	190	26		
Sam Horner	DB-HB	6'	198	23		6
Dick James	DB-HB	5'9"	175	27	1	30
Don Bosseler	FB	6'1"	212	25		18
Jim Cunningham	FB	5'11"	220	22		12
Bill Anderson	OE	6'3"	214	25		
John Aveni	OE	6'3"	215	26		42
Fred Dugan	OE	6'3"	198	27		24
Steve Junker	OE	6'3"	217	26		
Tom Osborne	OE	6'3"	190	24		12

WESTERN CONFERENCE

GREEN BAY PACKERS 11-3-0 Vince Lombardi

Scores of Each Game
13 DETROIT 17
30 SAN FRANCISCO 10
24 CHICAGO 0
45 BALTIMORE 7
49 Cleveland 17
33 Minnesota 7
28 MINNESOTA 10
21 Baltimore 45
31 Chicago 28
35 LOS ANGELES 17
17 Detroit 9
20 NEW YORK 17
21 San Francisco 22
24 Los Angeles 17

Use Name	Pos.	Hgt	Wgt	Age	Int	Pts
Forrest Gregg	OT	6'4"	250	28		
Norm Masters	OT	6'2"	250	28		
Bob Skoronski	OT	6'3"	250	28		
Jerry Kramer	OG	6'3"	250	28		
Fuzzy Thurston	OG	6'1"	250	28		
Ken Iman	C	6'1"	230	22		
Jim Ringo	C	6'1"	235	30		
Ben Davidson	DE	6'8"	275	21		
Willie Davis	DE	6'3"	240	28		
Bill Quinlan	DE	6'3"	250	29		
Dave Hanner	DT	6'2"	260	32	1	
Henry Jordan	DT	6'3"	250	26		
Ron Kostelnik	DT	6'4"	260	21		
Tom Bettis	LB	6'2"	225	28		
Dan Currie	LB	6'3"	240	27	3	6
Bill Forester	LB	6'3"	240	30	2	
Ray Nitschke	LB	6'3"	235	25	2	
Nelson Toburen	LB	6'3"	235	22		
Herb Adderley	DB	6'1"	205	22	1	
Hank Gremminger	DB	6'1"	205	28	5	
Johnny Symank	DB	5'11"	180	26	5	
Em Tunnell	DB	6'1"	210	39		
Jesse Whittenton	DB	6'	195	27	5	6
Willie Wood	DB	5'10"	185	25	5	12
John Roach	QB	6'4"	200	28		6
Bart Starr	QB	6'1"	200	28		6
Lew Carpenter	HB	6'1"	215	29		
Paul Hornung	HB	6'2"	215	25		146
Tom Moore	HB	6'2"	215	23		12
Elijah Pitts	HB	6'1"	200	22		6
Jim Taylor	FB	6'	215	26		96
Boyd Dowler	FL	6'5"	220	24		18
Lee Folkins	OE	6'5"	220	22		
Gary Knafelc	OE	6'4"	220	29		24
Ron Kramer	OE	6'3"	230	26		24
Max McGee	OE	6'3"	205	29		42
Ben Agajanian (from DAL-A)	K	6'	220	42		11

DETROIT LIONS 8-5-1 George Wilson

Scores of Each Game
17 Green Bay 13
16 Baltimore 15
0 SAN FRANCISCO 49
17 CHICAGO 31
14 LOS ANGELES 13
14 BALTIMORE 21
28 Los Angeles 10
20 San Francisco 20
45 St. Louis 14
37 Minnesota 10
9 GREEN BAY 17
16 Chicago 15
13 MINNESOTA 7
24 PHILADELPHIA 27

Use Name	Pos.	Hgt	Wgt	Age	Int	Pts
Dan LaRose	OT	6'5"	250	21		
Willie McClung	OT	6'2"	260	32		
Ollie Spencer	OG-OT	6'2"	250	30		
Harley Sewell	OG	6'1"	230	30		
Dick Mills	OG	6'3"	240	21		
John Gordy	OT-OG	6'3"	250	25		
Bob Scholtz	C	6'4"	250	25		
Bob Whitlow (from WAS)	OG-C	6'1"	236	25		
Bill Glass	DE	6'5"	255	25		
Darris McCord	DE	6'4"	250	28	1	
Sam Williams	OE-DE	6'5"	235	30		
Roger Brown	DT	6'5"	300	24	1	
John Gonzaga	DT	6'5"	250	28		
Alex Karras	DT	6'2"	245	25		
Gil Mains	DT	6'2"	250	31		
Paul Ward	DT	6'3"	247	24		
Carl Brettschneider	LB	6'1"	225	29		
Jim Martin	LB	6'2"	230	37		70
Max Messner	LB	6'3"	225	23		
Joe Schmidt	LB	6'1"	220	29	4	6
Wayne Walker	LB	6'2"	225	24	2	6
Night Train Lane	DB	6'1"	200	33	6	
Dick LeBeau	DB	6'1"	185	24	3	
Gary Lowe	DB	5'11"	195	27	5	2
Bruce Maher	DB	5'11"	190	24	1	
Yale Lary	DB	6'	190	30	6	
Earl Morrall	QB	6'1"	206	27		
Jim Ninowski	QB	6'1"	200	25		30
Hopalong Cassady	HB	5'10"	185	27		12
Dan Lewis	HB	6'1"	200	25		24
Johnny Olszewski	FB	5'11"	202	30		
Nick Pietrosante	FB	6'2"	225	24		30
Ken Webb	FB	5'11"	205	26		
Terry Barr	FL	6'	190	26		36
Pat Studstill	FL	6'1"	180	23		
Gail Cogdill	OE	6'2"	195	24		36
Glenn Davis	OE	6'	180	27		
Jim Gibbons	OE	6'2"	220	25		6

BALTIMORE COLTS 8-6-0 Weeb Ewbank

Scores of Each Game
27 LOS ANGELES 24
15 DETROIT 16
34 MINNESOTA 33
7 Green Bay 45
10 Chicago 24
17 Detroit 14
20 CHICAGO 21
45 GREEN BAY 21
20 Minnesota 28
16 ST. LOUIS 0
27 Washington 6
20 SAN FRANCISCO 17
17 Los Angeles 34
27 San Francisco 24

Use Name	Pos.	Hgt	Wgt	Age	Int	Pts
Tom Gilburg	OT	6'5"	245	22		
Jim Parker	OT	6'3"	275	27		
George Preas	OT	6'2"	250	29		
Wiley Feagin	OG	6'2"	235	24		
Alex Sandusky	OG	6'1"	242	29		
Palmer Pyle	OG	6'2"	250	24		
Dick Szymanski	C	6'3"	235	28		
Ordell Braase	DE	6'4"	242	29		
Gino Marchetti	DE	6'4"	245	35	2	
John Diehl	DT	6'7"	285	25		
Art Donovan	DT	6'2"	265	36		
Joe Lewis	DT	6'2"	250	28		
Jim Colvin	DE-DT	6'2"	250	24		
Billy Ray Smith	DE-DT	6'4"	235	26		
Marv Matuszak	LB	6'3"	230	32		
Bill Pellington	LB	6'2"	238	32	3	
Don Shinnick	LB	6'	235	26	2	
Steve Myhra	OG-LB	6'1"	240	27		96
Jackie Burkett	C-LB	6'4"	230	24	1	
Bobby Boyd	DB	5'10"	190	23	2	
Gary Glick (from WAS)	DB	6'2"	200	30	4	
Bob Harrison	DB	5'11"	187	22	3	
Lenny Lyles	DB	6'2"	202	25		
Andy Nelson	DB	6'1"	180	28		
Carl Taseff (to PHI)	DB	5'11"	194	32	1	
Jim Welch	HB-DB	6'	190	23		6
Lamar McHan	QB	6'1"	205	29		
Johnny Unitas	QB	6'1"	194	28		12
Alex Hawkins	HB	6'1"	190	24		30
Jerry Hill	HB	5'11"	210	21		
Tom Matte	HB	6'	192	22		
Lenny Moore	HB	6'1"	190	28		90
Joe Perry	FB	6'	195	34		24
Mark Smolinski	FB	6'	222	22		6
Ray Berry	OE	6'2"	190	28		
Ken Gregory	OE	6'	190	24		
Aubrey Linne	OE	6'7"	235	22		
Dee Mackey	OE	6'5"	236	25		
Jim Mutscheller	OE	6'2"	205	31		12
Jimmy Orr	OE	5'11"	180	25		24

EASTERN CONFERENCE—Continued

DALLAS COWBOYS

RUSHING

Last Name	No.	Yds	Avg	TD
Perkins	200	815	4.1	4
Marsh	84	379	4.5	1
Lockett	77	298	3.9	1
Meredith	22	176	8.0	1
LeBaron	20	72	3.6	0
Dupre	16	60	3.8	0
Douglas	5	24	4.8	0
Howton	1	9	9.0	0

RECEIVING

Last Name	No.	Yds	Avg	TD
Howton	56	785	14	4
Clarke	41	919	22	9
Perkins	32	298	9	1
Bielski	26	377	15	3
Marsh	21	189	9	2
Lockett	19	149	8	2
Doran	13	153	12	2
Dupre	6	49	8	0
Gregory	3	30	10	0
Douglas	1	−2	−2	0

PUNT RETURNS

Last Name	No.	Yds	Avg	TD
Marsh	14	71	5	0
Livingston	6	20	3	0
Perkins	1	8	8	0
Dupre	2	4	2	0

KICKOFF RETURNS

Last Name	No.	Yds	Avg	TD
Marsh	26	667	26	0
Perkins	22	443	20	0
Dupre	6	110	18	0
Lockett	5	61	12	0
Babb	2	34	17	0
Dowdle	2	33	17	0
Douglas	1	12	12	0
Doran	1	0	0	0

PASSING — PUNTING — KICKING

PASSING

Last Name	Att	Comp	%	Yds	Yd/Att	TD	Int−	%	RK
LeBaron	236	120	51	1741	7.4	14	16−	7	12
Meredith	182	94	52	1161	6.4	9	11−	6	15
Humphrey	2	1	50	16	8.0	0	0−	0	
Lockett	2	0	0	0	0.0	0	0−	0	

PUNTING

Last Name	No	Avg
Green	61	36.7

KICKING

Last Name	XP	Att	%	FG	Att	%
Green	19	19	100	5	15	33
Bielski	10	10	100	6	9	67

WASHINGTON REDSKINS

RUSHING

Last Name	No.	Yds	Avg	TD
James	71	374	5.3	3
Horner	96	275	2.9	0
Bosseler	77	220	2.9	2
Cunningham	69	160	2.3	1
Snead	34	47	1.4	3
Anderson	3	5	1.7	0
Luce	3	1	0.3	0
Sommer	11	1	0.9	0
Izo	3	−1	−0.3	0

RECEIVING

Last Name	No.	Yds	Avg	TD
Dugan	53	817	15	4
Anderson	40	637	16	0
Osborne	22	297	14	2
James	20	298	15	2
Bosseler	16	94	6	1
Cunningham	12	90	8	1
Horner	10	113	11	1
Junker	9	130	14	0
Aveni	6	84	14	1
Sommer	1	31	31	0
Wulff	1	6	6	0

PUNT RETURNS

Last Name	No.	Yds	Avg	TD
Steffen	19	153	8	0
James	12	90	8	0
Sommer	2	26	13	0
Kerr	5	23	5	0
Luce	1	0	0	0

KICKOFF RETURNS

Last Name	No.	Yds	Avg	TD
Steffen	29	691	24	0
James	21	617	29	0
Kerr	14	385	28	0
Sommer	4	98	25	0
Cunningham	4	80	20	0
Luce	4	77	19	0
Horner	4	75	19	0
Stynchula	2	73	37	0
Junker	1	0	0	0

PASSING — PUNTING — KICKING

PASSING

Last Name	Att	Comp	%	Yds	Yd/Att	TD	Int−	%	RK
Snead	375	172	46	2337	6.2	11	22−	6	16
Izo	40	16	40	214	5.4	1	6−	15	
James	4	1	25	15	3.8	0	0−	0	
Aveni	1	0	0	0	0.0	0	0−	0	

PUNTING

Last Name	No	Avg
Horner	63	38.2
James	6	35.0
Cunningham	1	46.0

KICKING

Last Name	XP	Att	%	FG	Att	%
Aveni	21	23	91	5	28	18

WESTERN CONFERENCE

GREEN BAY PACKERS

RUSHING

Last Name	No.	Yds	Avg	TD
Taylor	243	1307	5.4	15
Hornung	127	597	4.7	8
Moore	61	302	5.0	1
Pitts	23	75	3.3	1
Starr	12	56	4.7	1
R. Kramer	5	13	2.6	0
Carpenter	1	5	5.0	0
Roach	2	−5	−2.5	1

RECEIVING

Last Name	No.	Yds	Avg	TD
McGee	51	883	17	7
Dowler	36	633	18	3
R. Kramer	35	559	16	4
Taylor	25	175	7	1
Hornung	15	145	10	2
Moore	8	41	5	1
Knafelc	3	32	11	0
Carpenter	3	29	10	0
Pitts	1	5	5	0

PUNT RETURNS

Last Name	No.	Yds	Avg	TD
Wood	14	225	16	2
Carpenter	6	130	22	0

KICKOFF RETURNS

Last Name	No.	Yds	Avg	TD
Adderley	18	478	27	0
Moore	15	409	27	0
Symank	4	121	30	0
Forester	3	55	18	0
Pitts	1	14	14	0

PASSING — PUNTING — KICKING

PASSING

Last Name	Att	Comp	%	Yds	Yd/Att	TD	Int−	%	RK
Starr	295	172	58	2418	8.2	16	16−	5	3
Hornung	5	3	60	42	8.4	1	0−	0	
Roach	4	0	0	0	0.0	0	0−	0	
Moore	2	2	100	42	21.0	1	0−	0	

PUNTING

Last Name	No	Avg
Dowler	38	44.1
McGee	13	40.0

KICKING

Last Name	XP	Att	%	FG	Att	%
Hornung	41	41	100	15	22	68
Agajanian	8	8	100	1	2	50

DETROIT LIONS

RUSHING

Last Name	No.	Yds	Avg	TD
Pietrosante	201	841	4.2	5
Lewis	110	451	4.1	4
Ninowski	33	238	7.2	5
Cassady	31	131	4.2	1
Olszewski	30	109	3.6	0
Morrall	20	86	4.3	0
Lary	1	14	14.0	0
Webb	7	6	0.9	1
Barr	6	−8	−1.3	0

RECEIVING

Last Name	No.	Yds	Avg	TD
Cogdill	45	956	21	6
Gibbons	45	566	13	1
Barr	40	630	16	6
Peitrosante	26	315	12	0
Davis	9	115	13	0
Lewis	8	118	15	0
Studstill	5	54	11	0
Cassady	5	45	9	1
Olszewski	1	14	14	0
Williams	1	10	10	0
Webb	1	7	7	0

PUNT RETURNS

Last Name	No.	Yds	Avg	TD
Cassady	16	159	10	0
Studstill	8	75	9	0
Gibbons	1	14	14	0
Lary	1	8	8	0
Lane	1	6	6	0

KICKOFF RETURNS

Last Name	No.	Yds	Avg	TD
Studstill	16	448	28	1
Cassady	9	127	14	0
Olszewski	4	59	15	0
Maher	1	19	19	0
Williams	1	4	4	0
Webb	0	5	0	0

PASSING — PUNTING — KICKING

PASSING

Last Name	Att	Comp	%	Yds	Yd/Att	TD	Int−	%	RK
Ninowski	247	117	47	1921	7.8	7	18−	7	17
Morrall	150	69	46	909	6.1	7	9−	6	18
Cassady	1	0	0	0	0.0	0	0−	0	

PUNTING

Last Name	No	Avg
Lary	52	48.4
Morrall	3	37.7
Studstill	1	32.0

KICKING

Last Name	XP	Att	%	FG	Att	%
Martin	25	26	96	15	30	50
Walker	6	6	100	0	3	0

BALTIMORE COLTS

RUSHING

Last Name	No.	Yds	Avg	TD
Perry	168	675	4.0	3
Moore	92	648	7.0	7
Hawkins	86	379	4.4	4
Unitas	54	190	3.5	2
Smolinski	31	98	3.2	0
Welch	1	60	60.0	1
Matte	13	54	4.2	0
Hill	1	4	4.0	0
McHan	4	1	0.3	0

RECEIVING

Last Name	No.	Yds	Avg	TD
Berry	75	873	12	0
Moore	49	728	15	8
Perry	34	322	9	1
Mutscheller	20	370	19	2
Hawkins	20	158	8	1
Orr	18	357	20	4
Smolinski	9	100	11	1
Mackey	4	66	17	0
Matte	1	8	8	0
Szymanski	1	5	5	0

PUNT RETURNS

Last Name	No.	Yds	Avg	TD
Boyd	18	173	10	0
Taseff	5	39	8	0
Welch	5	146	29	0
Nelson	4	19	5	0
Harrison	1	16	16	0
Smolinski	1	2	2	0

KICKOFF RETURNS

Last Name	No.	Yds	Avg	TD
Lyles	28	672	24	0
Harrison	11	250	23	0
Welch	5	146	29	0
Matte	2	50	25	0
Smolinski	3	27	9	0
Lewis	1	14	14	0
Matuszak	1	14	14	0
Mackey	1	6	6	0
Gregory	1	3	3	0

PASSING — PUNTING — KICKING

PASSING

Last Name	Att	Comp	%	Yds	Yd/Att	TD	Int−	%	RK
Unitas	420	229	55	2990	7.1	16	24−	6	8
McHan	15	3	20	28	1.9	1	4−	27	
Moore	2	0	0	0	0.0	0	1−	50	
Boyd	1	0	0	0	0.0	0	0−	0	

PUNTING

Last Name	No	Avg
Gilburg	42	43.0

KICKING

Last Name	XP	Att	%	FG	Att	%
Myhra	33	34	97	21	39	54

Scores of Each Game		Use Name	Pos.	Hgt	Wgt	Age	Int	Pts

WESTERN CONFERENCE — Continued

CHICAGO BEARS 8-6-0 George Halas

Scores		Use Name	Pos.	Hgt	Wgt	Age	Int	Pts
13	Minnesota 37	Art Anderson	OT	6'3"	244	24		
21	Los Angeles 17	Herm Lee	OT	6'4"	247	30		
0	Green Bay 24	Stan Fanning	OT	6'6"	270	23		
31	Detroit 17	Roger Davis	OG	6'3"	235	23		
24	BALTIMORE 10	Stan Jones	OG	6'1"	250	30		
31	SAN FRANCISCO 0	Ted Karras	OG	6'1"	243	28		
21	Baltimore 20	Bob Wetoska	OG	6'3"	240	23		
14	Philadelphia 16	Roger LeClerc	C	6'3"	235	23		70
28	GREEN BAY 31	Mike Pyle	C	6'3"	240	22		
31	San Francisco 41	Doug Atkins	DE	6'8"	255	31		
28	LOS ANGELES 24	Bob Kilcullen	DE	6'3"	245	25		
15	DETROIT 16	Maury Youmans	DE	6'6"	260	24		
17	CLEVELAND 14	John Mellekas	DT	6'3"	255	28		
52	MINNESOTA 35	Fred Williams	DT	6'4"	248	31		

Use Name	Pos.	Hgt	Wgt	Age	Int	Pts
Joe Fortunato	LB	6'	225	31	3	
Bill George	LB	6'2"	235	30	3	
Larry Morris	LB	6'2"	230	26	1	
Ken Kirk	C-LB	6'2"	230	23		
J.C. Caroline	DB	6'1"	190	28	3	
Bobby Jackson	DB	6'1"	190	25		
Pete Manning	DB	6'3"	208	25		
Don Mullins	DB	6'1"	195	22		
Richie Petitbon	DB	6'3"	205	23	5	
Rosey Taylor	DB	5'11"	186	22		
Dave Whitsell	DB	6'	190	25	6	

Earl Leggett — Knee Injury

Use Name	Pos.	Hgt	Wgt	Age	Int	Pts
Ed Brown	QB	6'2"	210	32		4
Dick Norman	QB	6'3"	210	23		
Billy Wade	QB	6'2"	210	30		12
Charlie Bivins	HB	6'2"	212	22		6
Willie Galimore	HB	6'1"	187	26		42
J. D. Smith	HB	6'	210	26		
John Adams	FB	6'3"	235	24		6
Bill Brown	FB	5'11"	218	23		
Rick Casares	FB	6'2"	225	30		48
Johnny Morris	FL	5'10"	180	26		24
Angie Coia	OE	6'2"	202	23		18
Mike Ditka	OE	6'3"	230	21		72
Jim Dooley	OE	6'4"	198	31		
Bo Farrington	OE	6'3"	217	25		24
Harlon Hill	DB-OE	6'3"	200	29	3	

SAN FRANCISCO FORTY NINERS 7-6-1 Red Hickey

Scores		Use Name	Pos.	Hgt	Wgt	Age	Int	Pts
35	WASHINGTON 3	Len Rohde	OT	6'4"	240	23		
10	Green Bay 30	Bob St. Clair	OT	6'9"	265	30		
49	Detroit 0	John Thomas	LB-OT	6'4"	246	26		
35	LOS ANGELES 0	Bruce Bosley	OG	6'2"	240	27		
38	Minnesota 24	Ted Connolly	OG	6'3"	242	29		
0	Chicago 31	Bill Lopasky	OG	6'2"	235	24		
10	Pittsburgh 20	Mike Magac	OG	6'3"	240	23		
20	DETROIT 20	Frank Morze	C	6'4"	264	27		
7	Los Angeles 17	Dan Colchico	DE	6'4"	236	24		
41	CHICAGO 31	Lou Cordileone	DE	6'	245	24		
38	MINNESOTA 28	Charlie Krueger	DE	6'4"	245	25	2	
17	Baltimore 20	Roland Lakes	OT-DE	6'4"	247	21		
22	GREEN BAY 21	Monte Clark	DT	6'6"	260	24		
24	BALTIMORE 27	Leo Nomellini	DT	6'3"	262	36		

Use Name	Pos.	Hgt	Wgt	Age	Int	Pts
Bob Harrison	LB	6'2"	220	24	2	
Matt Hazeltine	LB	6'1"	220	28	1	
Carl Kammerer	LB	6'3"	237	24		
Gorden Kelley	LB	6'3"	230	23	1	
Dave Baker	DB	6'2"	193	24	6	
Eddie Dove	DB	6'2"	180	24	3	
Jim Johnson	DB	6'2"	190	23	5	
Jerry Mertens	DB	6'	183	25		
Jimmy Ridlon	DB	6'1"	177	26		
Abe Woodson	HB-DB	5'11"	188	26	1	12

Use Name	Pos.	Hgt	Wgt	Age	Int	Pts
John Brodie	QB	6'1"	186	26		12
Billy Kilmer	QB	6'	190	21		60
Bob Waters	QB	6'2"	190	23		18
Don McIlhenny	HB	6'	185	26		
Dale Messer	HB	5'10"	175	24		
Ray Norton	HB	6'2"	184	24		
J. D. Smith	FB-HB	6'1"	200	28		54
Bill Cooper	FB	6'1"	215	22		6
C. R. Roberts	FB	6'1"	197	25		6
Bernie Casey	OE	6'4"	215	22		6
Clyde Conner	OE	6'2"	190	28		6
R. C. Owens	OE	6'3"	195	26		36
Monte Stickles	OE	6'4"	230	23		30
Aaron Thomas	OE	6'3"	208	23		12
Tommy Davis	K	6'	212	26		80

LOS ANGELES RAMS 4-10-0 Bob Waterfield

Scores		Use Name	Pos.	Hgt	Wgt	Age	Int	Pts
24	Baltimore 27	Jim Boeke	OT	6'5"	245	22		
17	CHICAGO 21	Willie Hector	OT	6'2"	220	21		
24	PITTSBURGH 14	Frank Varrichione	OT	6'1"	235	29		
0	San Francisco 35	Charley Cowan	OG	6'4"	250	23		
13	Detroit 14	Roy Hord	OG	6'4"	250	26		
14	New York 24	Joe Scibelli	OG	6'1"	250	22		
10	DETROIT 28	Bruce Tarbox	OG	6'2"	230	22		
31	MINNESOTA 17	Art Hunter	C	6'4"	248	28		
17	SAN FRANCISCO 7	Deacon Jones	DE	6'5"	240	22		
17	Green Bay 35	Lamar Lundy	DE	6'7"	235	26		
24	Chicago 28	John Baker	DT-DE	6'6"	290	26		
21	Minnesota 42	Urban Henry	DT	6'4"	265	26		
34	BALTIMORE 17	John Lovetere	DT	6'4"	280	25		
17	GREEN BAY 24	George Strugar	DT	6'5"	258	26	1	

Use Name	Pos.	Hgt	Wgt	Age	Int	Pts
Bill Jobko	LB	6'2"	220	25	1	
Bob Long	LB	6'3"	235	27	1	
Marlin McKeever	LB	6'1"	230	21		
Jack Pardee	LB	6'2"	225	25	1	
Les Richter	LB	6'3"	235	30	4	
Charley Britt	DB	6'2"	185	23	5	
Ross Coyle	DB	6'2"	195	25		
Lindon Crow	DB	6'2"	200	28	6	
Alvin Hall	DB	6'	193	28		
Elbert Kimbrough	DB	5'11"	195	22		
Ed Meador	DB	5'11"	185	24	1	
Clendon Thomas	DB	6'2"	192	24	3	

Gene Brito — Illness

Use Name	Pos.	Hgt	Wgt	Age	Int	Pts
Zeke Bratkowski	QB	6'2"	203	29		18
Frank Ryan	QB	6'3"	200	25		
Jon Arnett	HB	5'11"	194	26		30
Pervis Atkins	HB	6'2"	195	25		
Ollie Matson	HB	6'2"	210	31		30
Tom Wilson	HB	6'	204	28		6
Dick Bass	FB	5'10"	200	24		30
Joe Marconi	FB	6'2"	225	27		24
Frank Williams	FB	6'2"	215	29		
Duane Allen	OE	6'4"	210	23		12
Carroll Dale	OE	6'1"	195	23		12
Jim Phillips	OE	6'1"	198	24		30
Danny Villanueva	K	5'11"	200	23		71

MINNESOTA VIKINGS 3-11-0 Norm Van Brocklin

Scores		Use Name	Pos.	Hgt	Wgt	Age	Int	Pts
37	CHICAGO 13	Bob Denton	OT	6'4"	240	27		
7	Dallas 21	Frank Youso	OT	6'4"	260	25		
33	Baltimore 34	Paul Dickson	DT-OT	6'5"	250	24		
0	DALLAS 28	Grady Alderman	OG	6'2"	235	22		
24	SAN FRANCISCO 38	Jerry Huth	OG	6'	228	28		
7	GREEN BAY 33	Ken Petersen	OG	6'2"	235	22		
10	Green Bay 28	Mike Rabold	OG	6'2"	238	24		
17	Los Angeles 31	Bill Lapham	C	6'3"	250	27		
28	BALTIMORE 20	Don Joyce	DE	6'3"	250	31		
10	DETROIT 37	Jim Leo	DE	6'1"	225	23		
28	San Francisco 38	Jim Marshall	DE	6'3"	230	23		
42	LOS ANGELES 21	Lebron Shields	DE	6'4"	245	24		
7	Detroit 13	Bill Bishop	DT	6'4"	248	30		
35	Chicago 52	Ed Culpepper	DT	6'1"	255	27		
		Jim Prestel	DT	6'5"	250	24		

Use Name	Pos.	Hgt	Wgt	Age	Int	Pts
Dick Grechi	LB	6'1"	230	23	1	
Rip Hawkins	LB	6'3"	230	22	5	
Clancy Osborne	LB	6'3"	217	26	4	
Karl Rubke	C-LB	6'4"	240	25	1	
Dean Derby (from PIT)	DB	6'	190	27	3	
Jack Morris	DB	6'	190	29	2	
Rich Mostardi	DB	5'11"	188	23	2	
Dick Pesonen	DB	6'	190	23	1	
Justin Rowland	DB	6'2"	188	23	1	
Charlie Sumner	DB	6'1"	195	31	2	
Will Sherman	HB-DB	6'2"	197	32		

Use Name	Pos.	Hgt	Wgt	Age	Int	Pts
George Shaw	QB	6'1"	180	28		
Fran Tarkenton	QB	6'1"	190	21		30
Jamie Caleb	HB	6'1"	210	24		
Billy Gault	HB	6'1"	185	24		
Tommy Mason	HB	6'	195	22		18
Hugh McElhenny	HB	6'1"	198	32		42
Ray Hayes	FB	6'3"	235	26		12
Doug Mayberry	FB	6'1"	225	24		
Mel Triplett	FB	6'1"	215	29		6
Dave Middleton	OE	6'1"	190	28		12
Fred Murphy	OE	6'3"	205	23		
Jerry Reichow	OE	6'2"	220	26		66
Gordon Smith	OE	6'2"	200	22		24
A. D. Williams	OE	6'2"	210	28		6
Mike Mercer	K	6'	220	25		63

WESTERN CONFERENCE – Continued

CHICAGO BEARS

RUSHING

Last Name	No.	Yds	Avg	TD
Galimore	153	707	4.6	4
Casares	135	588	4.4	8
Wade	45	255	5.7	2
Bivins	43	188	4.4	1
B. Brown	22	81	3.7	0
J. Morris	8	49	6.1	0
E. Brown	13	18	1.4	0
Smith	3	6	2.0	0
Adams	14	-2	-0.1	1

RECEIVING

Last Name	No.	Yds	Avg	TD
Ditka	56	1076	19	12
J. Morris	36	548	15	4
Galimore	33	502	15	3
Farrington	21	349	17	4
Coia	12	249	21	3
Casares	8	69	9	0
Dooley	6	90	15	0
Adams	5	80	16	0
Bivins	4	-9	-2	0
Hill	3	51	17	0
B. Brown	2	6	3	0

PUNT RETURNS

Last Name	No.	Yds	Avg	TD
J. Morris	23	155	7	0
Petitbon	2	9	5	0
Taylor	1	4	4	0
L. Morris	1	2	2	0

KICKOFF RETURNS

Last Name	No.	Yds	Avg	TD
Bivins	25	668	27	0
Taylor	14	379	27	0
Galimore	5	82	16	0
B. Brown	4	54	14	0
J. Morris	2	46	23	0
Smith	1	18	18	0

PASSING – PUNTING – KICKING

Last Name	Att	Comp	%	Yds	Yd/Att	TD	Int–	%	RK
PASSING									
Wade	250	139	56	2258	9.0	22	13–	5	2
E. Brown	98	46	47	742	7.6	4	11–	11	
Adams	1	1	100	11	11.0	0	0–	0	

Last Name	No	Avg						
PUNTING								
E. Brown	58	42.2						
Adams	2	28.0						

Last Name	XP	Att	%	FG	Att	%
KICKING						
LeClerc	40	41	98	10	24	42
E. Brown	1	1	100	1	2	50
George	0	0		0	1	0

SAN FRANCISCO FORTY NINERS

RUSHING

Last Name	No.	Yds	Avg	TD
Smith	167	823	4.9	8
Kilmer	96	509	5.3	10
Roberts	63	338	5.4	1
Waters	47	233	5.0	1
Brodie	28	90	3.2	2
McIlhenny	10	34	3.4	0
Woodson	14	23	1.6	0
Cooper	8	17	2.1	1
Messer	3	13	4.3	0
Norton	2	-2	-1.0	0
A. Thomas	1	-15	-15.0	0
Owens	0	23	0.0	1

RECEIVING

Last Name	No.	Yds	Avg	TD
Owens	55	1032	19	5
Stickles	43	794	18	5
Smith	28	343	12	1
A. Thomas	15	301	20	1
Conner	11	177	16	2
Casey	10	185	19	1
Roberts	10	83	8	0
Woodson	8	74	9	0
Messer	3	33	11	0
McIlhenny	1	6	6	0

PUNT RETURNS

Last Name	No.	Yds	Avg	TD
Woodson	16	172	11	1
Dove	6	49	8	0
Messer	2	11	6	0

KICKOFF RETURNS

Last Name	No.	Yds	Avg	TD
Woodson	27	782	29	1
McIlhenny	6	189	32	0
Smith	7	158	23	0
Norton	1	60	60	0
Cooper	3	44	15	0
Messer	3	36	12	0
Kammerer	1	18	18	0

PASSING – PUNTING – KICKING

Last Name	Att	Comp	%	Yds	Yd/Att	TD	Int–	%	RK
PASSING									
Brodie	283	155	55	2588	9.1	14	12–	4	5
Kilmer	34	19	56	286	8.4	0	4–	12	
Waters	28	13	46	183	6.5	1	2–	7	
Smith	1	0	0	0	0.0	0	1–	100	

Last Name	No	Avg
PUNTING		
Davis	50	45.4
Kilmer	9	40.4

Last Name	XP	Att	%	FG	Att	%
KICKING						
Davis	44	44	100	12	22	55

LOS ANGELES RAMS

RUSHING

Last Name	No.	Yds	Avg	TD
Arnett	158	609	3.9	4
Bass	98	608	6.2	4
Wilson	44	220	5.0	1
Matson	24	181	7.5	2
Marconi	36	146	4.1	3
Ryan	38	139	3.7	0
Bratkowski	12	36	3.0	3
Atkins	5	19	3.8	0

RECEIVING

Last Name	No.	Yds	Avg	TD
Phillips	78	1092	14	5
Dale	35	561	16	2
Matson	29	537	19	3
Arnett	28	194	7	0
Bass	16	145	9	0
Atkins	5	67	13	0
Marconi	4	20	5	1
Allen	2	80	40	2
Wilson	1	12	12	0
Scibelli	1	1	1	0

PUNT RETURNS

Last Name	No.	Yds	Avg	TD
Bass	4	109	27	1
Arnett	10	75	8	0

KICKOFF RETURNS

Last Name	No.	Yds	Avg	TD
Bass	23	698	30	0
Arnett	25	653	26	1
Atkins	4	77	19	0
Varrichione	3	23	8	0
Jones	1	12	12	0

PASSING – PUNTING – KICKING

Last Name	Att	Comp	%	Yds	Yd/Att	TD	Int–	%	RK
PASSING									
Bratkowski	230	124	54	1547	6.7	8	13–	6	13
Ryan	142	72	51	1115	7.9	5	7–	5	10
Arnett	13	3	23	47	3.6	0	1–	8	
Villanueva	1	0	0	0	0.0	0	0–	0	

Last Name	No	Avg
PUNTING		
Villanueva	46	40.1
Bratkowski	12	38.2
Marconi	6	44.2

Last Name	XP	Att	%	FG	Att	%
KICKING						
Villanueva	32	32	100	13	27	48

MINNESOTA VIKINGS

RUSHING

Last Name	No.	Yds	Avg	TD
McElhenny	120	570	4.8	3
Triplett	80	407	5.1	1
Hayes	73	319	4.4	2
Tarkenton	56	308	5.5	5
Mason	60	226	3.8	3
Mayberry	13	40	3.1	0
Shaw	10	39	3.9	0
Caleb	3	11	3.7	0
Reichow	3	9	3.0	0
Mercer	1	-32	-32.0	0

RECEIVING

Last Name	No.	Yds	Avg	TD
Reichow	50	859	17	11
McElhenny	37	283	8	3
Middleton	30	444	15	2
Mason	20	122	6	0
Hayes	16	121	8	0
Williams	13	174	13	1
Smith	12	320	27	4
Triplett	10	41	4	0
Sherman	2	40	20	0
Mayberry	2	18	9	0
Caleb	2	-8	-4	0

PUNT RETURNS

Last Name	No.	Yds	Avg	TD
McElhenny	8	155	19	1
Mason	14	146	10	0
Caleb	1	8	8	0

KICKOFF RETURNS

Last Name	No.	Yds	Avg	TD
Mason	25	603	24	0
Caleb	22	504	23	0
Rowland	8	175	22	0
Pesonen	6	136	23	0
McElhenny	2	59	30	0
Triplett	3	41	14	0
Gault	2	41	21	0
Leo	3	9	3	0
Hayes	1	0	0	0

PASSING – PUNTING – KICKING

Last Name	Att	Comp	%	Yds	Yd/Att	TD	Int–	%	RK
PASSING									
Tarkenton	280	157	56	1997	7.1	18	17–	6	7
Shaw	91	46	51	530	5.8	4	4–	4	
Reichow	3	0	0	0	0	0	1–	33	
Caleb	1	0	0	0	0.0	0	0–	0	
Mason	1	0	0	0	0.0	0	0–	0	
McElhenny	1	0	0	0	0.0	0	0–	0	

Last Name	No	Avg
PUNTING		
Mercer	63	39.0

Last Name	XP	Att	%	FG	Att	%
KICKING						
Mercer	36	37	97	9	21	43

1961 A.F.L. The Feuding Ends at the Altar

Commissioner Joe Foss had enough problems to keep him busy this year. His authority to govern the league was actually at stake in one incident. To get a jump on the NFL in signing rookies, the team owners conducted a secret draft of college seniors in November, with each club taking six name players. Foss, who set the date for the draft in December, was not informed of this draft, and when he found out about it he declared it invalid. A potential revolt of the owners narrowed down to a public feud between Foss and New York Titan owner Harry Wismer. The Titans had selected Syracuse runner Ernie Davis in the November draft that Foss nullified, and when Buffalo picked Davis in the official December draft Wismer let loose his full vocal fury on Foss. Despite Wismer's calls for Foss's ouster, the commissioner stayed in office, directed the official draft, and won a five-year renewal of his contract from the owners when the season ended. The most amazing development came in the spring of 1962 when Foss was Wismer's best man at his wedding.

Attendance around the league also troubled Foss. League attendance rose a slight amount, up to 17,000, and Houston, Buffalo, Boston, and San Diego showed increases in home attendance. In these cases, though, it was generally a case of going from horrible to merely bad. The AFL was providing exciting, wide-open games for television, but fans did not yet think it reasonable to pay to see these new teams play.

The anti-trust suit filed by the AFL against the NFL was still going through the judicial process, so the main confrontation between the two leagues was still taking place at the box office and in the signing of rookie players. The NFL was winning on all fronts in the attendance war, and the old league also grabbed off the lion's share of graduating seniors from the class of 1961. With the element of surprise gone, the AFL signed only a handful of name collegians, among them Ken Rice, Art Baker, E. J. Holub, and Earl Faison.

The league also signed a new player from a different route, one who had played out his option in the NFL. Willard Dewveall, an offensive end with the Chicago Bears, played through 1960 without signing a new contract and agreed to terms with the Houston Oilers for the 1961 season. Dewveall thus became the first player to jump to the AFL from the active ranks of the NFL.

While new players were coming into the league, some of the old ones were lost to the federal activation of Reserve units in response to the Berlin crisis. The activated players all were stationed in the continental United States, and most were able to make the league games on weekend passes. These weekday soldiers and weekend football warriors included Ron Mix, Larry Grantham, Ross O'Hanley, Proverb Jacobs, Richie Lucas, Bill Roehnelt, George McGee, Oscar Lofton, John Jelacik, and Herm Urenda.

A new city also joined the circuit as owner Barron Hilton picked up his Los Angeles Chargers and transplanted them in the virgin soil of San Diego. Attendance in San Diego topped that of Los Angeles, but the Chargers still lost money while winning on the field.

One innovation by the league this season was the scheduling of an All-Star Game after the season to showcase the league's talent. Although some NFL boosters snickered at the contest, it provided one more television date for the league to win new fans.

EASTERN DIVISION

Houston Oilers—The Oilers were mired in last place with a 1-3-1 record when owner Bud Adams canned head coach Lou Rymkus and replaced him with assistant Wally Lemm. The club's fortunes immediately turned around, as the Oilers won all their remaining nine games with a blistering offensive blitzkrieg. Lemm gave the quarterback job back to George Blanda, whom Rymkus had benched in favor of Jacky Lee, and Blanda responded with a pro record of thirty-six touchdown passes, a pair of 400 passing-yards games, and reliable long-range place-kicking, including boots of 55 and 53 yards. Charley Hennigan and Bill Groman were Blanda's deep targets, while Billy Cannon and Charley Tolar punched out yardage on the ground at a steady clip. The Oilers took over first place by beating Boston 27-15 on November 12, and they kept on wining right to the end. Coach Lemm summed up his perfect relief job by saying, "I feel like someone who inherited a million dollars in tarnished silverware. All I did was polish it."

Boston Patriots—Like the Oilers, the Patriots profited from a mid-season switch in coaches. After Mike Holovak succeeded Lou Saban as head coach, the Patriots won seven of nine games to streak into first place, only to have the Oilers win nine out of nine over the same span to win the title. The Boston attack featured no stars but still was second in the league in points scored. Butch Songin and Babe Parilli, a pair of senior citizens, shared the quarterback job and found converted defensive back Gino Cappelletti their favorite receiver. Cappelletti's kicking, however, was the spearhead of the Boston attack and won him the AFL scoring title. The Pats lost only to Houston over the last eight games, but that one loss was enough to foil the late-season drive.

New York Titans—Owner Harry Wismer made news this year. He made news with his feud with coach Sammy Baugh. He made news by publicly calling for Commissioner Joe Foss's ouster and more news when they finally made up. And he made news by announcing that his losses for 1960 and 1961 totaled $1.2 million. Wismer made more news than his football team, which played its games in virtual privacy. Three wins in the first four games got the Titans out to an early lead in the East, but a rash of injuries plus hot streaks by Houston and Boston pushed New York back into third place. Although fullback Billy Mathis developed into a bruising runner, the Titans still relied on Al Dorow's passes to Don Maynard and Art Powell for most of the offense. But while the Titans moved well through the air, enemy passers found the New York secondary easy pickings in return.

Buffalo Bills—In a league not known for great quarterbacks, the Bills had the worst quarterback situation. Ex-Redskin M. C. Reynolds, sophomore Johnny Green, and ex-Lion Warren Raab were uniformly unimpressive, and the offense sputtered despite some fine rookies in the lineup. Fullback Art Baker contributed power running, end Glenn Bass injected speed into the attack after being cut by San Diego, and Al Bemiller, Billy Shaw, Stew Barber, and Ken Rice all won jobs in the offensive line. But without a competent quarterback, the Bills had to rely on the defense to stay competitive. Lavern Torczon, Chuck McMurtry, Archie Matsos, and Billy Atkins stood out as defenders, but the unbalanced team effort cost head coach Buster Ramsey his job at the end of the season.

WESTERN DIVISION

San Diego Chargers—The Chargers celebrated their move to San Diego by winning their first eleven games to make a shambles out of the Western Division race. Head coach and general manager Sid Gillman built his defensive unit into the league's best with the addition of three excellent rookies. End Earl Faison put steady pressure on enemy passers, tackle Ernie Ladd contributed 315 pounds of muscle to the center of the line, and middle linebacker Chuck Allen, a lightly regarded twenty-eighth draft choice, was a sensation until breaking his ankle late in the year. With Dick Harris and Charley McNeil heading up a solid secondary, the San Diego defense had no weak spots. The offense held up its end of the bargain, with Jack Kemp, Paul Lowe, Dave Kocourek, and Ron Mix starring. But the team's real star was Gillman, one of the few AFL general managers who successfully signing most of the rookies on his draft list.

Dallas Texans—The Texans matched the Chargers in signing blue-chip rookies but fell farther behind them in the standings. Professional debuts by Jim Tyrer, Jerry Mays, E. J. Holub, and Dave Grayson did not prevent a slump by the defense and the team's dropping below .500 for the season. After winning three of their first four games, the Texans went into a six-game losing streak that ended the Western Division race. The team's passing attack did not live up to expectations, as quarterback Cotton Davidson was very erratic, but the running corps of Abner Haynes, Jack Spikes, Frank Jackson, and Bo Dickinson led the league in rushing yardage. Both lines had weak links, though, and suffered periodic breakdowns, throwing a mid-season monkey wrench into high pre-season hopes.

Denver Broncos—Without a balanced offensive diet, the Broncos grew weaker as the season progressed. The Denver running attack was dead last in the league, with the offense totally dependent on the passing of Frank Tripuka and George Herring. The Broncos threw the ball so often that split end Lionel Taylor set a new professional record with 100 catches for the season, not bad for a man the Chicago Bears had cut two years ago. Taylor's strong suit was his glue-fingered hands, but his lack of speed was underlined by his scoring only four touchdowns on the 100 receptions. After seven games, the Broncos had a respectable 3-4 record, but by then enemy defenses had wised up to the Denver air show. The Broncos lost their last seven games, and coach Frankie Filchock lost his job in the process.

Oakland Raiders—When the Raiders lost their first game 55-0 to Houston and their second game 44-0 to San Diego, the tone for a disastrous season was set. Coach Ernie Erdelatz was fired after the two opening massacres, but replacement Marty Feldman couldn't do much better with this squad. The Raiders scored the fewest points in the league, allowed the most points, and attracted minuscule crowds to their home games on the foreign turf of San Francisco's Candlestick Park. Not all the Raider players were inept, only most of them. Center Jim Otto won praise as the league's best at his position, Fred Williamson played well at cornerback, and halfback Clem Daniels showed promise after being picked up as a free agent. But a pair of mid-season victories over Denver and Buffalo was the best the Raiders could do as they lost their last six games of the season.

FINAL TEAM STATISTICS

OFFENSE

Category	BOSTON	BUFFALO	DALLAS	DENVER	HOUSTON	NEW YORK	OAKLAND	SAN DIEGO
FIRST DOWNS:								
Total	238	243	247	219	293	247	200	208
by Rushing	93	92	112	66	97	100	65	81
by Passing	120	128	122	127	182	126	116	110
by Penalty	25	23	13	26	14	21	19	17
RUSHING:								
Number	389	438	439	333	452	426	350	391
Yards	1675	1606	2183	1091	1896	1678	1234	1466
Average Yards	4.3	3.7	5.0	3.3	4.2	3.9	3.5	3.7
Touchdowns	15	18	23	11	15	17	10	24
PASSING:								
Attempts	420	439	399	568	498	460	423	423
Completions	206	194	177	265	254	204	209	190
Completion Percentage	49.0	44.2	44.4	46.7	51.0	44.3	49.4	44.9
Passing Yards	2795	2786	2815	3004	4568	2733	2514	3121
Average Yards per Attempt	6.7	6.3	7.1	5.3	9.2	5.9	5.9	7.4
Average Yards per Completion	13.6	14.4	15.9	11.3	18.0	13.4	12.0	16.4
Times Tackled Attempting to Pass	33	63	24	33	14	41	45	28
Yards Lost Attempting to Pass	256	442	239	284	176	346	463	274
Net Yards	2539	2344	2576	2720	4392	2387	2051	2847
Touchdowns	29	15	18	18	48	20	17	17
Interceptions	21	25	27	45	29	32	28	25
Percent Intercepted	5.0	5.7	6.8	7.9	5.8	7.0	6.6	5.9
PUNTING:								
Number	62	85	62	80	56	74	75	63
Average Distance	38.8	44.5	39.9	39.4	39.1	41.8	39.0	41.5
PUNT RETURNS:								
Number	35	19	26	33	19	26	15	29
Yards	288	187	219	369	118	463	117	458
Average Yards	8.2	9.8	8.4	11.2	6.2	17.8	7.8	15.8
Touchdowns	2	0	0	2	0	2	0	2
KICKOFF RETURNS:								
Number	49	57	53	66	43	66	68	39
Yards	1136	1208	1465	1501	940	1213	1383	642
Average Yards	23.2	21.2	27.6	22.7	21.9	18.4	20.3	16.5
Touchdowns	2	1	1	2	0	0	0	0
INTERCEPTION RETURNS:								
Number	22	29	25	26	33	25	23	49
Yards	326	311	418	355	528	315	285	929
Average Yards	14.8	10.7	16.7	13.7	16.0	12.6	12.4	19.0
Touchdowns	2	1	3	0	0	1	2	9
PENALTIES:								
Number	64	65	89	60	83	60	53	88
Yards	659	549	874.5	560	889	585	456	682.5
FUMBLES:								
Number	24	32	32	40	21	32	28	32
Number Lost	9	17	18	23	10	20	16	19
POINTS:								
Total	413	294	334	251	513	301	237	396
PAT (kick) Attempts	50	31	40	27	66	39	25	50
PAT (kick) Made	48	29	37	27	65	37	24	43
PAT (Rush or Pass) Attempts	2	7	4	5	0	1	4	2
PAT (Rush or Pass) Made	1	4	3	3	0	0	2	1
FG Attempts	32	26	24	25	26	23	26	27
FG Made	17	9	7	8	16	8	11	13
Percent FG Made	53.1	34.6	29.2	32.0	61.5	34.8	42.3	48.1
Safeties	0	1	0	1	2	0	1	0

DEFENSE

Category	BOSTON	BUFFALO	DALLAS	DENVER	HOUSTON	NEW YORK	OAKLAND	SAN DIEGO
FIRST DOWNS:								
Total	243	200	238	233	235	242	280	224
by Rushing	72	61	89	83	87	100	135	79
by Passing	151	124	129	127	126	121	129	124
by Penalty	20	15	20	23	22	21	16	21
RUSHING:								
Number	350	349	410	435	365	414	494	401
Yards	1041	1377	1525	1633	1634	1880	2382	1357
Average Yards	3.0	3.9	3.7	3.8	4.5	4.5	4.8	3.4
Touchdowns	9	9	18	17	17	20	36	7
PASSING:								
Attempts	479	430	439	433	493	462	409	485
Completions	241	206	219	194	212	211	192	224
Completion Percentage	50.3	47.9	49.9	44.8	43.0	45.7	46.9	46.2
Passing Yards	3490	3237	3077	3060	2750	3044	2942	2736
Average Yards per Attempt	7.3	7.5	7.0	7.1	5.6	6.6	7.2	5.6
Average Yards per Completion	14.5	15.7	14.1	15.8	13.0	14.4	15.3	12.2
Times Tackled Attempting to Pass	44	36	34	33	41	31	20	42
Yards Lost Attempting to Pass	408	350	300	275	359	247	168	373
Net Yards	3082	2887	2777	2785	2391	2797	2774	2363
Touchdowns	27	28	20	30	13	26	22	16
Interceptions	22	29	25	26	33	25	23	49
Percent Intercepted	4.6	6.7	5.7	6.0	6.7	5.4	5.6	10.1
PUNTING:								
Number	71	75	63	77	81	70	50	70
Average Distance	40.7	38.7	41.7	40.8	40.7	42.4	40.4	40.1
PUNT RETURNS:								
Number	15	45	20	26	20	20	34	22
Yards	245	291	216	368	271	284	352	192
Average Yards	16.3	6.5	10.8	14.2	13.6	14.2	10.4	8.7
Touchdowns	2	1	1	0	0	1	1	1
KICKOFF RETURNS:								
Number	53	54	65	42	66	51	45	65
Yards	1255	1112	1249	720	1481	1084	1066	1521
Average Yards	23.7	20.6	19.2	17.1	22.4	21.3	23.7	23.4
Touchdowns	1	1	1	0	1	0	0	1
INTERCEPTION RETURNS:								
Number	21	25	27	45	29	32	28	25
Yards	198	398	424	818	407	670	280	272
Average Yards	9.4	15.9	15.7	18.2	14.0	20.9	10.0	10.9
Touchdowns	1	4	1	5	2	3	1	1
PENALTIES:								
Number	67	76	62	98	57	86	62	54
Yards	661.5	693	619	799	588	869.5	524	501
FUMBLES:								
Number	36	20	31	25	31	36	29	33
Number Lost	20	15	18	14	15	21	12	17
POINTS:								
Total	313	342	343	432	242	390	458	219
PAT (kick) Attempts	40	42	38	55	26	48	53	26
PAT (kick) Made	40	41	37	51	22	46	50	23
PAT (Rush or Pass) Attempts	1	1	6	1	7	2	6	1
PAT (Rush or Pass) Made	0	1	3	1	2	1	5	1
FG Attempts	23	28	31	26	24	27	27	23
FG Made	9	13	12	13	6	14	12	10
Percent FG Made	39.1	46.4	38.7	50.0	25.0	51.9	44.4	43.5
Safeties	0	1	0	2	0	0	1	

SCORING

SAN DIEGO	0	0	0	3 – 3
HOUSTON	0	3	7	0 – 10

Second Quarter
Hous.   Blanda, 46 yard field goal   8:06

Third Quarter
Hous.   Cannon, 35 yard pass from Blanda   11:39
PAT—Blanda (kick)

Fourth Quarter
S.D.   Blair, 12 yard field goal   0:39

TEAM STATISTICS

S.D.		HOUS.
15	First Downs—Total	18
6	First Downs—Rushing	6
8	First Downs—Passing	8
1	First Downs—Penalty	4
2	Fumbles—Number	5
2	Fumbles—Number Lost	1
10	Penalties—Number	5
106	Yards Penalized	68
6	Giveaways	7
7	Takeaways	6
+1	Difference	−1

1961 AFL CHAMPIONSHIP GAME

December 24, at San Diego
(Attendance 29,556)

Oiling the Defense

For a second straight year, the defensive units excelled in the AFL championship game. The Chargers and Oilers, repeat winners of their divisional races, both found interceptions easy to come by, the Chargers picking off six passes and the Oilers four. Played on a sunny, 59-degree Christmas Eve, the game was a showcase for turnovers, with seven fumbles plus all the interceptions thwarting most offensive drives. Neither club generated much offense in the first half, with the only score coming on a 46-yard field goal by George Blanda late in the second quarter. The Oilers, who hadn't lost a game since Wally Lemm took over as head coach three months back, stubbornly defended their 3-0 lead throughout the third quarter and added to it late in the period. The Oilers had the ball on the San Diego 35-yard line with a third-and-five situation when a strong Charger pass rush forced Blanda out of his protective pocket. Rolling to his right, Blanda saw halfback Billy Cannon open down the middle and hit him with a pass on the 17-yard line. Cannon made a leaping catch, sidestepped a defender, and raced into the end zone. Blanda's extra point made the score 10-0 and put a heavy load of pressure on the San Diego offense. With Jack Kemp throwing freely, the Chargers broke the ice with a 12-yard George Blair field goal in the first minute of the fourth quarter, but a final San Diego bid fell short when Houston's Julian Spence picked off a Kemp pass on the Oiler 30-yard line with under two minutes left in the game.

INDIVIDUAL STATISTICS

RUSHING

SAN DIEGO	No.	Yds.	Avg.	HOUSTON	No.	Yds.	Avg.
Roberson	8	37	4.6	Tolar	16	52	3.3
Lowe	5	30	6.0	Cannon	15	48	3.2
Lincoln	3	7	2.3	Blanda	2	−4	−2.0
Kemp	4	5	1.3		33	96	2.9
	20	79	4.0				

RECEIVING

SAN DIEGO	No.	Yds.	Avg.	HOUSTON	No.	Yds.	Avg.
Kocourek	7	123	17.6	Cannon	5	53	10.6
D. Norton	3	48	16.0	Hennigan	5	43	8.6
Flowers	2	17	8.5	Groman	3	32	10.7
Roberson	1	11	11.0	Dewveall	2	10	5.0
Lowe	1	10	10.0	Tolar	2	2	1.0
Scarpitto	1	9	9.0	McLeod	1	20	20.0
Hayes	1	5	5.0		18	160	8.9
Lincoln	1	3	3.0				
	17	226	13.3				

PUNTING

SAN DIEGO	No.		Avg.	HOUSTON	No.		Avg.
Maguire	6		33.3	J. Norton	4		41.5

PUNT RETURNS

SAN DIEGO	No.	Yds.	Avg.	HOUSTON			
Lincoln	1	16	16.0	None			

KICKOFF RETURNS

SAN DIEGO	No.	Yds.	Avg.	HOUSTON			
Lowe	1	27	27.0	None			
Roberson	1	23	23.0				
	2	50	25.0				

INTERCEPTION RETURNS

SAN DIEGO	No.	Yds.	Avg.	HOUSTON	No.	Yds.	Avg.
Whitehead	2	45	15.0	Cline	1	7	7.0
McNeil	2	15	7.5	Glick	1	0	0.0
Zeman	2	0	0.0	Johnston	1	0	0.0
	6	60	10.0	Spence	1	0	0.0
					4	7	1.8

PASSING

	Att.	Comp.	Comp. Pct.	Yds.	Int.	Yds/Att.	Yds/Comp.	Yards Lost Tackled
SAN DIEGO								
Kemp	32	17	53.1	226	4	7.1	13.3	6-49
HOUSTON								
Blanda	40	18	45.0	160	5	4.0	8.9	0
Gorman	1	0	0.0	0	1	—	—	0
	41	18	43.9	160	6	3.9	8.9	0

HOUSTON OILERS 10-3-1 Lou Rymkus Wally Lemm

Scores of Each Game			Use Name	Pos.	Hgt	Wgt	Age	Int	Pts
55	OAKLAND	0	Al Jamison	OT	6'5"	245	24		
24	San Diego	34	Bob Kelly	OT	6'3"	250	21		
21	Dallas	26	Rich Michael	OT	6'3"	230	22		
12	BUFFALO	22	Leo Reed (to DEN)	OG	6'4"	240	21		
31	Boston	31	Bob Talamini	OG	6'1"	230	22		
38	DALLAS	7	Hogan Wharton	OG	6'2"	245	25		
28	Buffalo	16	Bob Schmidt	C	6'4"	245	25		
28	Denver	14	Dalva Allen	DE	6'5"	245	25		
27	BOSTON	15	Don Floyd	DE	6'4"	225	22		
49	NEW YORK	13	Dick Frey	OG-DE	6'2"	235	30		
45	DENVER	14	Byron Beams	DT	6'6"	250	27		
33	SAN DIEGO	13	Ed Husmann	DT	6'	238	30		
48	New York	21	George Shirkey	DT	6'4"	240	24		
47	Oakland	16	Orville Trask	DT	6'4"	260	26	1	

Use Name	Pos.	Hgt	Wgt	Age	Int	Pts
Ron Botcham	LB	6'1"	230	26		
Doug Cline	LB	6'2"	220	22	1	12
Mike Dukes	LB	6'3"	230	25	2	
John Guzik	LB	6'3"	228	24		
Gene Jones	LB	6'	200	24		
Jack Laraway	LB	6'1"	215	25	1	
Dennit Morris	LB	6'1"	225	25	1	
Tony Banfield	DB	6'1"	185	22	8	
Freddy Glick	DB	6'1"	190	24		
Mark Johnston	DB	6'	200	23	3	6
Charley Milstead	DB	6'2"	190	23	2	1
Jim Norton	DB	6'3"	190	22	9	
Gary Wisener	DB	6'	205	23		
Julian Spence	FL-DB	5'11"	158	32	1	

Use Name	Pos.	Hgt	Wgt	Age	Int	Pts
George Blanda	QB	6'1"	210	33		112
Jacky Lee	QB	6'1"	185	22		
Billy Cannon	HB	6'1"	212	24		90
Ken Hall (to STL-N)	HB	6'1"	210	25		6
Claude King	HB	5'11"	185	22		18
Dave Smith	FB	6'1"	210	24		18
Charley Tolar	FB	5'7"	200	23		30
Charley Hennigan	FL	6'	185	25		72
Willard Dewveall	OE	6'4"	220	24		18
Bill Groman	OE	6'	195	25		108
Bob McLeod	OE	6'5"	225	22		12
John White	OE	6'4"	230	23		6

BOSTON PATRIOTS 9-4-1 Lou Saban Mike Holovak

Scores of Each Game			Use Name	Pos.	Hgt	Wgt	Age	Int	Pts
20	NEW YORK	21	Jerry DeLucca	OT	6'3"	250	25		
45	DENVER	17	Milt Graham	OT	6'6"	235	27		
23	Buffalo	21	Dick Klein (from PIT-N)	OT	6'4"	255	27		
30	New York	37	Charley Long	OT	6'3"	240	23		
27	SAN DIEGO	38	John Simerson	OT	6'3"	255	26		
31	HOUSTON	31	Charlie Leo	OG	6'	240	26		
52	BUFFALO	21	Willis Perkins (from HOU)	OG	6'	240	24		
18	Dallas	17	Tony Sardisco	OG	6'2"	235	28		
28	DALLAS	21	Walt Cudzik	C	6'2"	235	28		
15	Houston	27	Bob Yates	C	6'3"	230	22		
20	OAKLAND	17	Bob Dee	DE	6'3"	240	28		
28	Denver	24	Larry Eisenhauer	DE	6'5"	235	21		
35	Oakland	21	Leroy Moore	DE	6'	232	25		
41	San Diego	0	Houston Antwine	DT	6'	250	22		
			Jim Hunt	DT	5'11"	245	22		
			Paul Lindquist	DT	6'3"	265	23		

Use Name	Pos.	Hgt	Wgt	Age	Int	Pts
Tom Addison	LB	6'3"	235	25	4	
Harry Jacobs	LB	6'2"	235	24		
Rommie Loudd	LB	6'3"	230	27	1	
Frank Robotti	LB	6'	220	22	2	
Walter Beach	DB	6'	185	26	1	
Fred Bruney	DB	5'10"	190	30	2	
Ron Hall	DB	6'	190	24	2	
Ross O'Hanley	DB	6'	175	22		
Al Romine	DB	6'2"	195	28		
Chuck Shonta	DB	6'	190	23	1	
Bob Soltis	DB	6'2"	205	24		
Bobby Towns	DB	6'1"	180	23		
Don Webb	DB	5'10"	180	22	5	24
Clyde Washington	HB-DB	6'	195	23	4	
Oscar Lofton — Military Service						

Use Name	Pos.	Hgt	Wgt	Age	Int	Pts
Babe Parilli	QB	6'1"	190	31		32
Butch Songin	QB	6'2"	205	37		6
Tom Yewcic	HB-QB	5'11"	185	29		6
Ron Burton	HB	6'	200	24		18
Larry Garron	HB	6'	200	24		36
Ray Ratkowski	HB	6'	195	21		
Ger Schwedes	HB	6'1"	205	22		
Jim Crawford	FB	6'1"	205	25		
Billy Lott	FB	6'	205	26		66
Gino Cappelletti	FL	6'	190	27		147
Jim Colclough	OE	6'	185	25		54
Joe Johnson	OE	6'	195	31		6
Bill Kimber	OE	6'2"	190	25		
Tom Stephens	OE	6'1"	195	25		18
George McGee — Military Service						

NEW YORK TITANS 7-7-0 Sammy Baugh

Scores of Each Game			Use Name	Pos.	Hgt	Wgt	Age	Int	Pts
21	Boston	20	Gene Cockrell	OT	6'3"	247	28		
31	Buffalo	41	Moses Gray	OT	6'3"	260	23		
35	DENVER	28	Jack Klotz	OT	6'5"	260	27		
37	BOSTON	30	Ed Walsh	OT	6'4"	243	25		
10	SAN DIEGO	25	Tom Budrewicz	OG	6'2"	245	24		
10	Denver	27	John McMullan	OG	6'	244	26		
14	Oakland	6	Bob Mischak	OG	6'	240	28		
13	San Diego	48	Bob O'Neil	OG	6'1"	238	28		
23	OAKLAND	12	Roger Ellis	C	6'3"	233	23		
13	Houston	49	Mike Hudock	C	6'2"	245	26		
21	BUFFALO	14	Ed Cooke	DE	6'4"	250	26	3	
28	DALLAS	7	Nick Mumley	DE	6'6"	255	25		
21	HOUSTON	48	Bob Reifsnyder	DE	6'2"	260	24		
24	Dallas	35	Dick Guesman	DT	6'4"	255	25	39	
			Proverb Jacobs	DT	6'4"	255	26		
			Tom Saidock	DT	6'5"	260	29		
			Sid Youngelman	DE-DT	6'3"	265	29		

Use Name	Pos.	Hgt	Wgt	Age	Int	Pts
Hubert Bobo	LB	6'1"	218	26	4	
Jerry Fields	LB	6'1"	222	22		
Jim Furey	LB	6'2"	228	27		
Larry Grantham	LB	6'	205	22	1	
Johnny Bookman	DB	5'11"	185	26	6	
Dick Felt	DB	6'	180	28	4	6
Don Flynn (from DAL)	DB	6'	205	24	2	
Paul Hynes (from DAL)	DB	6'1"	210	21		
Dainard Paulson	DB	5'11"	190	24	1	
Bert Rechichar	DB	6'1"	210	31		
Lee Riley	DB	6'1"	190	29	4	
Junior Wren	DB	6'	192	31	1	

Use Name	Pos.	Hgt	Wgt	Age	Int	Pts
Don Allard	QB	6'	190	25		
Al Dorow	QB	6'	195	31		24
Dick Jamieson	QB	6'1"	192	25		
Bob Scrabis	QB	6'3"	225	25		6
Jim Apple	HB	6'	200	22		
Dick Christy	HB	5'10"	195	25		30
Bob Renn	HB	6'	180	27		6
Bill Shockley (to BUF)	HB	6'	185	23		25
Mel West (from BOS)	HB	5'9"	190	22		18
Bob Brooks	FB	6'	215	21		
Bill Mathis	FB	6'1"	220	22		48
Don Maynard	FL	6'	185	25		48
Thurlow Cooper	OE	6'4"	228	28		24
Curley Johnson	OE	6'	215	26		
Art Powell	OE	6'3"	212	24		30

BUFFALO BILLS 6-8-0 Buster Ramsey

Scores of Each Game			Use Name	Pos.	Hgt	Wgt	Age	Int	Pts
10	DENVER	22	Don Chelf	OT	6'3"	235	26		
41	NEW YORK	31	Harold Olson	OT	6'3"	260	22		
21	BOSTON	23	Ken Rice	OT	6'2"	250	21		
11	SAN DIEGO	19	John Dittrich	OG	6'1"	240	28		
22	Houston	12	Ed Muelhaupt	OG	6'3"	230	25	6	
27	DALLAS	24	Billy Shaw	OG	6'3"	240	21		
21	Boston	52	Wayne Wolf	OG	6'2"	243	22		
16	HOUSTON	28	Al Bemiller	C	6'3"	225	22		
22	OAKLAND	31	Lavern Torczon	DE	6'2"	235	25		
30	Dallas	20	Mack Yoho	DE	6'2"	240	25	1	
23	Denver	10	Tom Day	DE	6'2"	245	26		
14	New York	21	Chuck McMurtry	DT	6'	285	23		
26	Oakland	21	John Scott	DT	6'4"	260	25		
10	San Diego	28	Jim Sorey	DT	6'4"	280	24		

Use Name	Pos.	Hgt	Wgt	Age	Int	Pts
Stew Barber	OT-LB	6'3"	235	22	3	6
Ralph Felton	LB	5'11"	210	29	2	
Joe Hergert	LB	6'1"	215	25	1	18
Cotton Letner	LB	6'1"	215	24		
Archie Matsos	LB	6'	215	26	2	
Billy Atkins	DB	6'1"	195	26	10	41
Jim Crotty (from WAS -N)	DB	5'11"	190	23	2	
Jack Johnson (to DAL)	DB	6'3"	200	27		
Billy Majors	DB	6'	175	22		
Richie McCabe	DB	6'1"	187	27	1	
Don McDonald	DB	5'11"	185	24		6
Vern Valdez	DB	5'11"	190	25	2	
Jim Wagstaff	DB	6'2"	190	25	3	

Use Name	Pos.	Hgt	Wgt	Age	Int	Pts
Johnny Green	QB	6'3"	198	24		6
Tom O'Connell	QB	5'11"	180	29		
Warren Rabb	QB	6'1"	204	24		2
M. C. Reynolds	QB	6'	195	26		24
Richie Lucas	DB-HB-QB	6'	190	22	2	12
Dewey Bohling (from NY)	HB	5'11"	190	22		18
Fred Brown	HB	5'11"	187	21		12
Wray Carlton	HB	6'2"	210	23		24
Dan Chamberlain	HB	6'4"	200	24		
Elbert Dubenion	HB	6'	190	26		48
Willmer Fowler	HB	5'11"	185	24		
Art Baker	FB	6'	220	23		18
Glenn Bass	OE	6'2"	190	22		18
Monte Crockett	OE	6'3"	210	22		
Perry Richards	OE	6'2"	205	27		18
Tom Rychlec	OE	6'3"	220	27		12

HOUSTON OILERS

RUSHING
Last Name	No.	Yds	Avg	TD
Cannon	200	948	4.7	6
Tolar	157	577	3.7	4
Smith	60	258	4.3	2
King	12	50	4.2	2
Lee	8	36	4.5	0
Hall	7	13	1.9	0
Blanda	7	12	1.7	0
Groman	1	2	2.0	1

RECEIVING
Last Name	No.	Yds	Avg	TD
Hennigan	82	1746	21	12
Groman	50	1175	24	17
Cannon	43	586	14	9
Tolar	24	219	9	1
McLeod	14	172	12	2
White	13	238	18	1
Dewveall	12	200	17	3
Smith	10	131	13	1
King	3	83	28	1
Hall	1	20	20	1
Spence	1	14	14	0
Blanda	1	-16	-16	0

PUNT RETURNS
Last Name	No.	Yds	Avg	TD
Cannon	9	70	8	0
King	7	32	5	0
Smith	1	15	15	0
Hall	2	1	1	0

KICKOFF RETURNS
Last Name	No.	Yds	Avg	TD
Cannon	18	439	24	0
King	8	190	24	0
Hall	6	140	23	0
Dukes	4	57	14	0
Tolar	2	42	21	0
Cline	1	24	24	0
Laraway	1	22	22	0
McLeod	1	13	13	0
Wharton	1	8	8	0
Smith	1	5	5	0

PASSING – PUNTING – KICKING
PASSING	Att	Comp	%	Yds	Yd/Att	TD	Int–%	RK
Blanda	362	187	52	3330	9.2	36	22– 6	1
Lee	127	66	52	1205	9.4	12	6– 5	
Cannon	5					0	1– 20	
Smith	2	1	50	33	16.5	0	0– 0	
Groman	1	0	0	0	0.0	0	0– 0	
Tolar	1	0	0	0	0.0	0	0– 0	

PUNTING	No	Avg
Norton	48	40.7
Hall	8	29.8

KICKING	XP	Att	%	FG	Att	%
Blanda	64	65	98	16	26	62
Milstead	1	1	100	0	0	0

BOSTON PATRIOTS

RUSHING
Last Name	No.	Yds	Avg	TD
Lott	100	461	4.7	5
Garron	69	389	5.6	2
Burton	82	260	3.2	2
Parilli	38	183	4.8	5
Crawford	41	148	3.6	0
Yewcic	11	51	4.6	1
Songin	8	39	4.9	0
Colclough	3	37	12.3	0
Schwedes	10	14	1.4	0
Washington	1	3	3.0	0

RECEIVING
Last Name	No.	Yds	Avg	TD
Cappelletti	45	768	17	8
Colclough	42	757	18	9
Lott	32	333	10	6
Garron	24	341	14	3
Stephens	19	186	10	2
Burton	13	115	9	0
Crawford	9	85	9	0
Johnson	9	82	9	1
Yewcic	6	56	9	0
Schwedes	1	21	21	0
Shonta	1	9	9	0

PUNT RETURNS
Last Name	No.	Yds	Avg	TD
Burton	8	128	16	0
Bruney	23	109	5	0
Klein	1	23	23	0
Webb	1	20	20	1
Lott	1	8	8	0
Moore	1	0	0	0

KICKOFF RETURNS
Last Name	No.	Yds	Avg	TD
Garron	16	438	27	1
Burton	15	401	27	1
Beach	2	38	19	0
Long	4	24	6	0
Webb	1	21	21	0
Ratkowski	1	17	17	0
Stephens	1	6	6	0
Schwedes	1	0	0	0
Cudzik	1	0	0	0

PASSING – PUNTING – KICKING
PASSING	Att	Comp	%	Yds	Yd/Att	TD	Int–%	RK
Songin	212	98	46	1429	6.7	14	9– 4	3
Parilli	198	104	53	1314	6.7	13	9– 5	2
Yewcic	8	3	38	25	3.1	1	2– 25	
Burton	1	0	0	0	0.0	0	1–100	
Cappelletti	1	1	100	27	27.0	1	0– 0	

PUNTING	No	Avg
Yewcic	62	38.8

KICKING	XP	Att	%	FG	Att	%
Cappelletti	48	50	96	17	32	53

2 POINT XP
Parilli (1)

NEW YORK TITANS

RUSHING
Last Name	No.	Yds	Avg	TD
Mathis	202	846	4.2	7
West	72	322	4.5	3
Dorow	54	317	5.9	4
Christy	81	180	2.2	2
Brooks	15	55	3.7	0
Renn	1	14	14.0	0
Shockley	5	9	1.8	0
Johnson	1	3	3.0	0
Apple	7	2	0.3	0
Scrabis	1	1	1.0	1

RECEIVING
Last Name	No.	Yds	Avg	TD
Powell	71	881	12	5
Maynard	43	629	15	8
Christy	29	521	18	1
Renn	18	268	15	1
Cooper	15	208	14	4
West	13	146	11	0
Mathis	12	42	4	1
Shockley	3	27	9	0
Johnson	1	32	32	0
O'Neil	1	-13	-13	0

PUNT RETURNS
Last Name	No.	Yds	Avg	TD
Christy	18	383	21	2
West	2	51	26	0
Apple	2	12	6	0
Maynard	1	9	9	0
Shockley	2	6	3	0
Cockrell	1	2	2	0

KICKOFF RETURNS
Last Name	No.	Yds	Avg	TD
Christy	15	360	24	0
West	13	306	24	0
Shockley	12	261	22	0
Renn	10	201	20	0
Brooks	8	111	14	0
Johnson	5	84	17	0
Hynes	2	45	23	0
Saidock	2	26	13	0
Ellis	3	25	8	0
Fields	1	19	19	0
Apple	1	16	16	0
Walsh	2	15	8	0
Budrewicz	1	0	0	0
Cooper	1	0	0	0

PASSING – PUNTING – KICKING
PASSING	Att	Comp	%	Yds	Yd/Att	TD	Int–%	RK
Dorow	438	197	45	2651	6.1	19	30– 7	7
Scrabis	21	7	33	82	3.9	1	2– 10	
Christy	1	0	0	0	0.0	0	0– 0	

PUNTING	No	Avg
Johnson	66	42.7
Wren	8	33.9

KICKING	XP	Att	%	FG	Att	%
Guesman	24	26	92	5	15	33
Shockley	13	13	100	4	9	44
Cooper	0	0	0	0	1	0

BUFFALO BILLS

RUSHING
Last Name	No.	Yds	Avg	TD
Baker	152	498	3.3	3
Carlton	101	311	3.1	4
Brown	53	192	3.6	1
Dubenion	17	173	10.2	2
Bohling	55	153	2.8	2
Reynolds	30	142	4.7	4
Atkins	2	87	43.5	1
Rabb	13	47	3.6	0
Lucas	10	15	1.5	0
Green	14	15	1.1	0
Bass	2	8	4.0	0
Fowler	1	2	2.0	0
Rychlec	1	-18	-18.0	0

RECEIVING
Last Name	No.	Yds	Avg	TD
Bass	50	765	15	3
Rychlec	33	405	12	2
Dubenion	31	461	15	6
Crockett	20	325	16	0
Richards	19	285	15	3
Carlton	17	193	11	0
Bohling	13	217	17	1
Baker	6	73	12	0
Lucas	6	69	12	0
Chamberlain	1	16	16	0
Brown	1	11	11	0

PUNT RETURNS
Last Name	No.	Yds	Avg	TD
Bass	8	75	9	0
Wagstaff	1	35	35	0
Valdez	1	30	30	0
Atkins	2	30	15	0
Brown	2	14	7	0
Dubenion	1	3	3	0
Bohling	4	0	0	0

KICKOFF RETURNS
Last Name	No.	Yds	Avg	TD
Dubenion	16	329	21	0
Baker	12	281	23	0
Bohling	10	246	25	0
Lucas	7	126	18	0
Brown	2	105	53	1
Carlton	4	60	15	0
Rice	2	13	7	0
Richards	1	10	10	0
Crockett	1	0	0	0

PASSING – PUNTING – KICKING
PASSING	Att	Comp	%	Yds	Yd/Att	TD	Int–%	RK
Reynolds	181	83	46	1004	5.6	6	13– 7	9
Green	126	56	44	903	7.2	6	5– 4	
Rabb	74	34	46	586	7.9	5	2– 3	
Lucas	50	20	40	282	5.6	2	4– 8	
O'Connell	5	1	20	11	2.2	0	1– 20	
Carlton	2	0	0	0	0.0	0	0– 0	
Bohling	1	0	0	0	0.0	0	0– 0	

PUNTING	No	Avg
Atkins	84	45.0

KICKING	XP	Att	%	FG	Att	%
Atkins	29	31	94	2	6	33
Hergert	0	0	0	6	14	43
Yoho	0	0	0	4	0	

2 POINT XP
Lucas (3)
Rabb (1)

SAN DIEGO CHARGERS 12-2-0 Sid Gillman

Scores of Each Game		
26	Dallas	10
44	OAKLAND	0
34	HOUSTON	24
19	Buffalo	11
38	Boston	27
25	New York	10
41	Oakland	10
37	DENVER	0
48	NEW YORK	13
19	Denver	16
24	DALLAS	14
13	Houston	33
28	BUFFALO	10
0	BOSTON	41

Use Name	Pos.	Hgt	Wgt	Age	Int	Pts
Sam DeLuca	OT	6'2"	245	25		
Ron Mix	OT	6'4"	245	23		
Sherman Plunkett	OT	6'4"	285	27		
Ernie Wright	OT	6'4"	270	20		
Ernie Barnes	OG	6'3"	260	22		
Orlando Ferrante	OG	6'	230	28		
Gene Selawski	OT-OG	6'4"	252	25		
Geroge Belotti (from HOU)	C	6'4"	250	26		
Don Rogers	C	6'2"	250	24		
Earl Faison	DE	6'5"	256	22	2	
Ron Nery	DE	6'6"	230	26		
Bill Hudson	DT	6'4"	270	25	1	6
Ernie Ladd	DT	6'9"	315	22		
Henry Schmidt	DT	6'4"	260	24		

Use Name	Pos.	Hgt	Wgt	Age	Int	Pts
Chuck Allen	LB	6'1"	218	21	5	6
Emil Karas	LB	6'3"	230	27	3	
Paul Maguire	LB	6'	215	23	1	
Maury Schleicher	LB	6'3"	240	24		
Bob Laraba	HB-LB	6'3"	195	28	5	19
George Blair	DB	5'11"	190	23	2	81
Claude Gibson	DB	6'1"	190	22	5	2
Dick Harris	DB	5'11"	175	24	7	18
Charley McNeil	DB	5'11"	175	25	9	12
Bud Whitehead	DB	6'	180	22	1	
Bob Zeman	DB	6'1"	203	24	8	6

Use Name	Pos.	Hgt	Wgt	Age	Int	Pts
Hunter Enis	QB	6'2"	190	24		12
Jack Kemp	QB	6'1"	200	27		36
Keith Lincoln	HB	6'2"	205	22		18
Paul Lowe	HB	6'	180	24		54
Bo Roberson	HB	6'1"	185	26		18
Charlie Flowers	FB	6'1"	220	24		18
Bob Scarpitto	FL	5'11"	185	22		12
Howard Clark	OE	6'2"	215	26		
Luther Hayes	OF	6'4"	200	22		18
Dave Kocourek	OE	6'5"	230	24		24
Don Norton	OE	6'1"	185	23		36
Jacque Mackinnon	OG-OE	6'4"	240	22		

DALLAS TEXANS 6-8-0 Hank Stram

Scores of Each Game		
10	SAN DIEGO	26
42	Oakland	35
26	HOUSTON	21
19	Denver	12
24	Buffalo	27
7	Houston	38
17	BOSTON	18
21	Boston	28
20	BUFFALO	30
14	San Diego	24
43	OAKLAND	11
7	New York	28
49	DENVER	21
35	NEW YORK	24

Use Name	Pos.	Hgt	Wgt	Age	Int	Pts
Jerry Cornelison	OT	6'3"	250	24		
Charley Diamond	OT	6'2"	235	25		
Jim Tyrer	OT	6'6"	292	22		
John Cadwell	OG	6'3"	230	22		
Sid Fournet	OG	6'	240	28		
Billy Krisher	OG	6'1"	235	25		
Al Reynolds	OG	6'3"	235	23		
Marvin Terrell	OG	6'1"	235	23		
Jon Gilliam	C	6'2"	225	22		
Mel Branch	DE	6'2"	230	24		
Luther Jeralds	DE	6'3"	235	23		
Paul Miller	DE	6'2"	240	29		
Ray Collins	DT	5'11"	250	33		
Jerry Mays	DT	6'4"	245	21	1	
Walter Napier	DT	6'4"	270	25		
Paul Rochester	DT	6'2"	250	24		

Use Name	Pos.	Hgt	Wgt	Age	Int	Pts
Ted Greene	LB	6'1"	230	27	1	
Sherrill Headrick	LB	6'2"	215	24	2	12
E. J. Holub	LB	6'4"	230	23	1	
Smokey Stover	LB	6'	230	22	2	
Dave Grayson	DB	5'10"	180	22	4	6
Ed Kelley	DB	6'2"	195	26		
Doyle Nix	DB	6'1"	195	28	3	
Dave Webster	DB	6'4"	220	23	5	
Duane Wood	DB	6'1"	190	25	4	

Use Name	Pos.	Hgt	Wgt	Age	Int	Pts
Cotton Davidson	QB	6'1"	185	28		26
Randy Duncan	QB	6'	185	23		
Tom Greene	QB	6'1"	190	23		
Abner Haynes	HB	6'	180	23		78
Frank Jackson	HB	6'1"	182	21		30
Johnny Robinson	HB	6'	195	22		42
Bo Dickenson	FB	6'2"	210	26		34
Billy Pricer	FB	5'10"	215	26		
Jack Spikes	FB	6'2"	225	23		54
Charley Barnes	OE	6'5"	230	24		
Max Boydston	OE	6'2"	210	28		6
Chris Burford	OE	6'3"	210	23		30
Tony Romeo	OE	6'2"	215	22		
Ben Agajanian (to GB-N)	K	6'	220	42		16

DENVER BRONCOS 3-11-0 Frankie Filchock

Scores of Each Game		
22	Buffalo	10
17	Boston	45
28	New York	35
19	Oakland	33
12	DALLAS	19
27	OAKLAND	24
27	NEW YORK	10
0	San Diego	37
14	HOUSTON	55
16	SAN DIEGO	19
10	BUFFALO	23
14	Houston	45
24	BOSTON	28
21	Dallas	49

Use Name	Pos.	Hgt	Wgt	Age	Int	Pts
Eldon Danenhauer	OT	6'4"	235	25		
Jerry Sturm	FB-OT	6'3"	235	24		
Ken Adamson	OG	6'2"	225	22		
Buzz Guy (from HOU)	OG	6'3"	250	26		
Carl Larpenter	OG	6'4"	235	24		
Jim Barton	C	6'5"	250	26		
Mike Nichols	C	6'3"	225	24		
John Cash	DE	6'3"	230	25		
Chuck Gavin	DE	6'1"	240	27	6	
Bob Konovsky	DE	6'2"	250	27		
Joe Young	DE	6'3"	245	26		
Art Hauser	DT	6'	240	30		
Gordy Holz	DT	6'4"	270	27		
Jack Mattox	DT	6'4"	240	22		
Bud McFadin	DT	6'3"	280	33		

Use Name	Pos.	Hgt	Wgt	Age	Int	Pts
Jim Eifrid	LB	6'1"	240	23		
Bob Griffin (to STL-N)	LB	6'3"	250	32		
Bob Hudson	LB	6'4"	235	31	3	
Pat Lamberti (from NY)	LB	6'2"	225	23	1	
Wahoo McDaniel	LB	6'	240	24		
Bill Roehnelt	LB	6'1"	225	25		
Jackie Simpson	LB	6'1"	230	24		
Jerry Stalcup	LB	6'	240	23		
Goose Gonsoulin	DB	6'3"	205	23	6	
Jim McMillin	DB	5'11"	180	23	5	
Bob McNamara	DB	6'	190	27	3	
Phil Nugent	DB	6'2"	195	22	7	
John Pyeatt	DB	6'3"	204	27		
Jimmy Sears	DB	5'11"	187	30		
Dan Smith	DB	5'10"	180	26		

Use Name	Pos.	Hgt	Wgt	Age	Int	Pts
George Herring	QB	6'2"	200	26		12
Frank Tripucka	QB	6'2"	205	33		
Buddy Allen	HB	5'10"	190	23		
Al Carmichael	HB	6'1"	195	31		
Dale Evans	HB	6'3"	210	22		
Al Frazier	HB	5'11"	180	26		50
Jack Hill	HB	6'1"	185	27		31
Gene Mingo	HB	6'	200	22		32
Donnie Stone	HB	6'2"	205	24		48
Jerry Traynham	HB	5'10"	190	22		
Dave Ames (from NY)	DB-HB	6'	185	24	1	
Fred Bukaty	FB	5'11"	195	22		32
Jim Stinnette	LB-FB	6'1"	230	23	1	6
Gene Prebola	OE	6'3"	215	23		8
Lionel Taylor	OE	6'2"	214	25		24

OAKLAND RAIDERS 2-12-0 Marty Feldman

Scores of Each Game		
0	Houston	55
0	San Diego	44
35	DALLAS	42
33	DENVER	19
24	Denver	27
10	SAN DIEGO	41
6	NEW YORK	14
31	Buffalo	22
12	New York	23
17	Boston	20
11	Dallas	43
21	BUFFALO	26
21	BOSTON	35
16	HOUSTON	47

Use Name	Pos.	Hgt	Wgt	Age	Int	Pts
Jim Brewington	OT	6'6"	280	22		
Cliff Roberts	OT	6'3"	260	26		
Ron Sabal	OT	6'2"	245	24		
Jack Stone	OT	6'2"	245	24		
Wayne Hawkins	OG	6'	235	23		
Herb Roedel	OG	6'3"	230	22		
Willie Smith	OG	6'2"	255	23		
Jim Otto	C	6'2"	240	23		
Jon Jelacic	DE	6'3"	255	24		
Charley Powell	DE	6'2"	245	29		
George Fields	DT	6'3"	245	25		
Gary Finneran	DT	6'3"	245	26		
Harry Jagielski (from BOS)	DT	6'	260	29	1	
Volney Peters	DT	6'4"	245	32		
Hal Smith	DT	6'5"	250	26		
Bob Voight	DT	6'5"	265	24		

Use Name	Pos.	Hgt	Wgt	Age	Int	Pts
Al Bansavage	LB	6'2"	220	23		
Bob Dougherty	LB	6'	240	27	2	
Tom Louderback	LB	6'2"	235	27	1	6
Riley Morris	LB	6'2"	230	24	3	6
Alex Bravo	DB	6'	190	29	2	
Joe Cannavino	DB	5'11"	185	25	5	
Bob Garner	DB	5'10"	190	26	2	
John Harris	DB	6'1"	195	28	3	
Fred Williamson	DB	6'2"	205	23	4	

Use Name	Pos.	Hgt	Wgt	Age	Int	Pts
Tom Flores	QB	6'1"	190	24		6
Nick Papac	QB	5'11"	190	26		6
Wayne Crow	HB	6'	205	23		14
Clem Daniels	HB	6'1"	220	24		12
George Fleming	HB	5'11"	188	22		63
Charley Fuller	HB	5'11"	176	22		12
Jack Larscheid	HB	5'6"	162	27		
Jim Jones	FB	6'1"	212	25		
Walt Kowalczyk	FB	6'	216	26		
Alan Miller	FB	6'	197	23		42
Doug Asad	OE	6'3"	205	23		12
Jerry Burch	OE	6'1"	195	21		6
Bob Coolbaugh	OE	6'3"	200	21		26
Charley Hardy	OE	6'	185	27		24

SAN DIEGO CHARGERS

RUSHING

Last Name	No.	Yds	Avg	TD
Lowe	175	767	4.4	9
Roberson	58	275	4.7	3
Flowers	51	177	3.5	3
Lincoln	41	150	3.7	0
Kemp	43	105	2.4	6
Enis	16	13	0.8	2
Laraba	5	5	1.0	1

RECEIVING

Last Name	No.	Yds	Avg	TD
Kocourek	55	1055	19	4
Norton	47	816	17	6
Lowe	17	103	6	0
Flowers	16	175	11	0
Hayes	14	280	20	3
Lincoln	12	208	17	2
Clark	11	182	17	0
Scarpitto	9	163	18	2
Roberson	6	81	14	0
MacKinnon	3	58	19	0

PUNT RETURNS

Last Name	No.	Yds	Avg	TD
Gibson	14	209	15	0
Lincoln	7	150	21	1
Scarpitto	4	47	12	0
Zeman	2	47	24	1
Selawski	1	5	5	0
Lowe	1	0	0	0

KICKOFF RETURNS

Last Name	No.	Yds	Avg	TD
Lowe	10	240	24	0
Roberson	13	207	16	0
Lincoln	4	98	25	0
Scarpitto	3	50	17	0
Schmidt	1	22	22	0
Gibson	3	17	6	0
Karas	1	5	5	0
Blair	1	2	2	0
Selawski	1	1	1	0
Mix	1	0	0	0
Ferrante	1	0	0	0

PASSING – PUNTING – KICKING

PASSING	Att	Comp	%	Yds	Yd/Att	TD	Int–%	RK
Kemp	364	165	45	2686	7.4	15	22– 6	5
Enis	55	23	42	365	6.6	2	3– 5	
Lowe	4	2	50	70	17.5	0	0– 0	

PUNTING	No	Avg
Maguire	62	42.2

KICKING	XP	Att	%	FG	Att	%
Blair	42	47	89	13	27	48
Laraba	1	2	50	0	0	0
Lincoln	0	1	0	0	0	0

2 POINT XP
Gibson (1)

DALLAS TEXANS

RUSHING

Last Name	No.	Yds	Avg	TD
Haynes	179	841	4.7	9
Jackson	65	386	5.9	3
Spikes	39	334	8.6	5
Dickinson	71	263	3.7	3
Robinson	52	200	3.9	2
Davidson	21	123	5.9	1
Duncan	5	42	8.5	0
Pricer	5	13	2.6	0
Gilliam	1	−6	−6.0	0
Burford	1	−13	−13.0	0

RECEIVING

Last Name	No.	Yds	Avg	TD
Burford	51	850	17	5
Robinson	35	601	17	5
Haynes	34	558	16	3
Dickinson	14	209	15	2
Jackson	13	171	13	2
Boydston	12	167	14	1
Spikes	8	136	17	0
Romeo	7	89	13	0
Pricer	2	21	11	0
Barnes	1	13	13	0

PUNT RETURNS

Last Name	No.	Yds	Avg	TD
Haynes	19	196	10	0
Mays	1	12	12	0
Headrick	2	5	3	0
Robinson	2	4	2	0
Jackson	1	2	2	0
Miller	1	0	0	0

KICKOFF RETURNS

Last Name	No.	Yds	Avg	TD
Grayson	16	453	28	0
Jackson	24	645	27	0
Haynes	8	270	34	1
Gilliam	1	23	23	0
Pricer	1	19	19	0
Stover	1	15	15	0
Mays	1	13	13	0

PASSING – PUNTING – KICKING

PASSING	Att	Comp	%	Yds	Yd/Att	TD	Int–%	RK
Davidson	330	151	46	2445	7.4	17	23– 7	5
Duncan	67	25	37	361	5.4	1	3– 4	
Jackson	2	1	50	9	4.5	0	1– 50	

PUNTING	No	Avg
Davidson	61	40.6

KICKING	XP	Att	%	FG	Att	%
Davidson	20	20	100	0	2	0
Spikes	10	13	77	4	13	31
Agajanian	7	7	100	3	9	33

2 POINT XP
Dickinson (2)
Spikes (1)

DENVER BRONCOS

RUSHING

Last Name	No.	Yds	Avg	TD
Stone	127	505	4.0	4
Bukaty	76	187	2.5	5
Ames	19	114	6.0	0
Frazier	23	110	4.8	0
Herring	15	74	4.9	2
Mingo	18	51	2.8	0
Sturm	8	31	3.9	0
Carmichael	15	24	1.6	0
Traynham	6	12	2.0	0
Stinnette	19	8	0.4	0
Allen	3	−4	−1.3	0
Tripucka	4	−8	−2.0	0

RECEIVING

Last Name	No.	Yds	Avg	TD
Taylor	100	1176	13	4
Frazier	47	799	17	6
Stone	38	344	9	4
Prebola	29	349	12	1
Bukaty	14	94	7	0
Stinnette	11	58	5	1
Mingo	8	110	14	2
Ames	6	20	3	0
Carmichael	5	23	5	0
Hill	4	33	8	0
Sturm	2	−1	−1	0
Traynham	1	−1	−1	0

PUNT RETURNS

Last Name	No.	Yds	Avg	TD
Frazier	18	231	13	1
Carmichael	7	58	8	0
Gavin	1	45	45	1
McNamara	4	17	4	0
Ames	2	17	9	0
Mingo	1	1	1	0

KICKOFF RETURNS

Last Name	No.	Yds	Avg	TD
Frazier	18	504	28	1
Carmichael	16	310	19	0
Ames	12	240	20	0
Stone	9	215	24	0
Mingo	4	120	30	0
Bukaty	3	41	14	0
Gonsoulin	1	34	34	0
Hill	1	23	23	0
Prebola	1	8	8	0
Stinnette	1	6	6	0

PASSING – PUNTING – KICKING

PASSING	Att	Comp	%	Yds	Yd/Att	TD	Int–%	RK
Tripucka	344	167	49	1690	4.9	10	21– 6	8
Herring	211	93	44	1160	5.5	5	22– 10	10
Mingo	8	4	50	136	17.0	2	0– 0	
Stone	2	1	50	18	9.0	0	0– 0	
Taylor	2	0	0	0	0.0	0	1– 50	
Frazier	1	0	0	0	0.0	0	1–100	

PUNTING	No	Avg
Herring	80	39.4

KICKING	XP	Att	%	FG	Att	%
Hill	16	16	100	5	15	33
Mingo	11	11	100	3	10	30

2 POINT XP
Bukaty (1)
Frazier (1)
Prebola (1)

OAKLAND RAIDERS

RUSHING

Last Name	No.	Yds	Avg	TD
Crow	119	490	4.1	2
Miller	85	255	3.0	3
Daniels	31	154	5.1	2
Fuller	38	134	3.5	0
Fleming	31	112	3.6	1
Flores	23	36	1.6	1
Papac	6	28	4.7	1
Kowalczyk	10	28	2.8	0
Larschied	6	3	0.5	0

RECEIVING

Last Name	No.	Yds	Avg	TD
Asad	36	501	14	2
Miller	36	315	9	4
Coolbaugh	32	435	14	4
Hardy	24	337	14	4
Crow	23	196	9	0
Burch	18	235	13	1
Daniels	13	150	12	0
Fuller	12	277	23	2
Fleming	10	49	5	0
Kowalczyk	3	8	3	0
Larschied	2	11	6	0

PUNT RETURNS

Last Name	No.	Yds	Avg	TD
Fuller	4	52	13	0
Daniels	5	34	7	0
Fleming	3	24	8	0
Garner	2	5	3	0
H. Smith	1	2	2	0

KICKOFF RETURNS

Last Name	No.	Yds	Avg	TD
Fleming	29	588	20	0
Daniels	13	276	21	0
Larschied	9	254	28	0
Fuller	8	155	19	0
Miller	6	66	11	0
Kowalczyk	1	19	19	0
Coolbaugh	1	15	15	0
Asad	1	10	10	0

PASSING – PUNTING – KICKING

PASSING	Att	Comp	%	Yds	Yd/Att	TD	Int–%	RK
Flores	366	190	52	2176	6.0	15	19– 5	3
Papac	44	13	30	173	3.9	2	7– 16	
Crow	10	6	60	165	16.5	0	0– 0	
Fleming	1	0	0	0	0.0	0	1–100	
Fuller	1	0	0	0	0.0	0	0– 0	
Larschied	1	0	0	0	0.0	0	1–100	

PUNTING	No	Avg
Crow	61	42.8
Burch	11	28.6

KICKING	XP	Att	%	FG	Att	%
Fleming	24	25	96	11	26	42

2 POINT XP
Coolbaugh (1)
Crow (1)

1962 N.F.L. Millions from the Stay-at-Homes

It was a year of renewal, consolidation, innovation, and departures. Commissioner Pete Rozelle renewed the NFL's television contract with CBS at a new rate of $4.65 million per year, and the club owners rewarded Rozelle with a new five-year contract with a hefty raise. The consolidation took place in Los Angeles, where full control of the Rams was reacquired by Dan Reeves. After taking in Edwin Pauley and Fred Levy as partners, Reeves fell to feuding with his co-owners in recent years, so Rozelle arranged for the submission of secret bids for the controlling interest in the team, which Reeves won. Innovation brought the league a new rule against grabbing another player's face mask, ground-breaking for a Hall of Fame in Canton, Ohio, and a fabulously popular pre-season doubleheader in Cleveland. And leaving the NFL stage this year, by death, were Mrs. Violet Bidwill Wolfner and James Clark, owners of the Cardinals and Eagles, and, by pink slips, long-time coaches Paul Brown and Weeb Ewbank.

EASTERN CONFERENCE

New York Giants—After fourteen years of professional football, thirty-five-year-old Y. A. Tittle became an overnight sensation as the Giant quarterback. Tittle set a new NFL record of thirty-three touchdown passes in a season, including seven in one game against the Redskins, but his style captivated New York fans more than his passing. He would retreat to his protective pocket and calmly survey the field, a thin, middle-aged man defying the behemoths rushing at him. He would back-pedal with tacklers closing in on him and flip an unexpected screen pass to Alex Webster behind a covey of blockers. Near the goal line he often ran the ball in on the bootleg play, outsprinting the deceived defenders on his aged legs. With a strong cast of players surrounding Tittle, the Giants got to the championship game by winning their last nine games.

Pittsburgh Steelers—Bobby Layne had reason to smile after his final NFL season. He wound up his career with 196 touchdown passes, surpassing Sammy Baugh's old mark of 186, and he led the Steelers to three straight wins at the end of the year to capture second place in the East. Other oldsters besides Layne turned in key performances, such as John Henry Johnson, Ernie Stautner, and Big Daddy Lipscomb. Holdover receiver Buddy Dial starred as a deep threat, and newcomer Lou Michaels excelled as a place-kicker. Perhaps the most important job was coach Buddy Parker's patch-up of the defense after injuries wiped out all his linebackers and personal differences elbowed Johnny Sample into disfavor.

Cleveland Browns—The Paul Brown era crashed to an end in a year of disappointment and tragedy. Brown had traded fleet Bobby Mitchell to Washington for the draft rights to Heisman Trophy winner Ernie Davis of Syracuse. Davis, a powerful halfback, was expected to team with Jimmy Brown in a strong running duo, but leukemia struck the rookie down before he ever played a professional game. With no good running halfbacks to divert the enemy's forces, fullback Brown for the first time ever failed to win the league rushing crown. After a lackluster campaign in which the Browns were never contenders, owner Art Modell shocked the football world by firing the most successful coach in pro-football history.

Washington Redskins—The Redskins fielded their first black players this year in Bobby Mitchell, John Nisby, Leroy Jackson, and Ron Hatcher, and the club's fortunes immediately rocketed upward. Mitchell, obtained from Cleveland for the draft rights to Ernie Davis, set the league on fire with his spectacular receiving from his new flanker position, and with quarterback Norm Snead getting good protection from the bolstered offensive line, an all-out passing attack brought the Skins four wins and two ties in their first six contests before their running game and loose pass defense caught up with them.

Dallas Cowboys—Coach Tom Landry had been a great defensive player, but his coaching genius was in a different direction. The Dallas offense was the second best in the league, trailing only the Packers in points scored, but the Dallas defense was the second worst in the league, with only Minnesota allowing more points. Landry got good mileage out of quarterbacks Eddie LeBaron and Don Meredith by shuffling them in and out of the lineup on every play. But once LeBaron was injured in mid-season and Meredith had to go it alone at quarterback, the attack slipped and the Cowboys dropped five of their last six matches.

St. Louis Cardinals—Although Wally Lemm turned out a losing squad in his first year on the job, he did uncover a fine young passer in Charley Johnson. After sitting on the bench last year and beginning this season as Sam Etcheverry's back-up, Johnson won the quarterback job four games into the season. During the remaining stretch he learned by experience and threw a lot of passes to his complementary receivers, speedster Sonny Randle and sure-handed Bobby Joe Conrad. But even with strong running from John David Crow, the attack never caught fire, due to a mediocre line.

Philadelphia Eagles—The fair Philadelphia defense had sufficed when the offense was churning out points at a furious pace, but injuries this year crippled the attack and sent the Eagles tumbling into last place. Quarterback Sonny Jurgensen, still bothered by a shoulder separation suffered in last season's Playoff Bowl, found himself throwing the ball to a bunch of strangers. Only Tommy McDonald stayed healthy among the receivers, as Pete Retzlaff, Bobby Walston, and Dick Lucas all broke arms and Hopalong Cassady broke a leg, while runner Ted Dean joined the parade with a broken foot.

WESTERN CONFERENCE

Green Bay Packers—Even with Paul Hornung below par physically, the Packers overwhelmed the league with All-Pro performances. Fullback Jim Taylor, whose strong point was neither size nor speed but meanness, took the rushing title away from Jimmy Brown and also led the league in scoring with nineteen touchdowns. Bart Starr compiled the best passing record in the circuit, while Willie Wood intercepted the most aerials. The wire service All-Pro teams were overloaded with Packers as fullback Taylor, end Ron Kramer, offensive linemen Forrest Gregg, Jerry Kramer, Fuzzy Thurston, and Jim Ringo, defensive linemen Willie Davis and Henry Jordan, linebackers Bill Forester and Dan Currie, and cornerback Herb Adderley all won honors.

Detroit Lions—Eleven wins are usually good enough for a championship, but the Lions had to settle for second place in the West behind the stampeding Green Bay Packers. The Lions did expose Vince Lombardi's supermen as mere mortals, however, in their Thanksgiving Day meeting in Detroit. The unbeaten Packers that day ran up against a fired-up Detroit defense that turned in an almost perfect performance. Tackle Roger Brown constantly blasted into the Green Bay backfield, linebacker Joe Schmidt blitzed Packer quarterback Bart Starr into the ground, and the defensive unit kept the Packers scoreless until late in the 26-14 upset victory.

Chicago Bears—Like the Packers and Lions, the Bears had a tough defense at the core of the team. The front four and secondary were solid if not spectacular, but the linebacking corps of Joe Fortunato, Bill George, and Larry Morris ranked with the NFL's best. Offensively, coach George Halas had to scramble around for runners when injuries sidelined Rick Casares and Willie Galimore. Ex-Ram Joe Marconi did a yeoman's job at fullback, while freshman Ronnie Bull hustled enough to win Rookie of the Year honors. The air attack moved well on Billy Wade's passes to Mike Ditka and Johnny Morris, but the defense dominated the Bears, as a bruising 3-0 victory over the Lions to close the season underlined.

Baltimore Colts—The last few seasons had been lackluster, and a 7-7 record this season brought coach Weeb Ewbank's regime to an end. Quarterback Johnny Unitas still was the consummate passer and signal-caller, but his supporting cast was looking slightly worn. The running attack was weak, the offensive line was aging, and the place-kicking was unsure. Strong points included a competent defense and a pair of good receivers in Jimmy Orr and Ray Berry, but not enough to save coach Ewbank's job.

San Francisco '49ers—Before the season started, coach Red Hickey called this club the best football team he had ever coached. But once the schedule began, injuries turned the '49ers into a very ordinary team. Tackle Bob St. Clair, the team's best offensive lineman, went to the sidelines with an injured Achilles tendon, and halfback Billy Kilmer, an exciting runner, passer, and blocker, missed the final three games after breaking a leg in a car accident. The defense also slipped a notch, as too much youth subverted the secondary and too much age cut down on tackle Leo Nomellini's quickness.

Minnesota Vikings—The Vikings couldn't match the three wins of their first campaign, but coach Norm Van Brocklin was gathering good young players who would later make Minnesota a title contender. Free agent Mick Tingelhoff won the center's job, rookie linebacker Roy Winston showed promise, and cornerback Ed Sharockman had a good NFL debut after missing 1961 with a broken leg. Aside from these three freshmen, improvement came from youngsters already on the roster, such as quarterback Fran Tarkenton, halfback Tommy Mason, tackle Grady Alderman, defensive end Jim Marshall, and middle linebacker Rip Hawkins.

Los Angeles Rams—Dan Reeves bought out partners Edwin Pauley and Fred Levy, thus ending the front-office bickering that had plagued the team in recent years. But while the ownership picture cleared up, the squad on the field collapsed in a wreck. The Rams won only one game all season, with their offense the worst in the league. Head coach Bob Waterfield tired of all the losing and quit after eight games, leaving the battered team to assistant Harland Svare. But even this season, the worst in Ram history, turned up two bright spots in rookies Merlin Olsen and Roman Gabriel.

FINAL TEAM STATISTICS

OFFENSE

	BALT.	CHI.	CLEVE.	DALLAS	DET.	G.BAY	L.A.	MINN.	N.Y.	PHIL.	PITT.	ST.L.	S.F.	WASH.
FIRST DOWNS:														
Total	251	228	252	246	243	281	201	223	267	235	261	268	239	241
by Rushing	94	88	105	101	103	145	84	102	92	76	133	109	112	59
by Passing	145	128	133	136	124	120	107	107	150	146	112	138	112	156
by Penalty	12	12	14	9	16	16	10	14	25	13	16	21	15	26
RUSHING:														
Numbers	448	386	414	434	489	518	376	426	430	324	572	416	460	371
Yards	1601	1489	1772	2040	1922	2460	1689	1864	1698	1155	2333	1698	1873	1088
Average Yards	3.6	3.9	4.3	4.7	3.9	4.7	4.5	4.4	3.9	3.6	4.1	4.1	4.1	2.9
Touchdowns	9	17	18	16	14	36	10	7	11	13	17	20	15	10
PASSING:														
Attempts	423	430	370	380	379	311	372	348	411	428	319	434	323	428
Completions	237	229	200	200	211	187	189	170	215	228	160	220	185	223
Completion Pct.	56.0	53.3	54.1	52.6	55.7	60.1	50.8	48.9	52.3	53.3	50.2	50.7	57.3	52.1
Passing Yardage	3330	3286	2747	3115	2827	2621	2524	2699	3446	3632	2419	3388	2491	3532
Avg. Yds per Att.	7.9	7.6	7.4	8.2	7.5	8.4	6.8	7.8	8.4	8.5	7.6	7.8	7.7	8.3
Avg. Yds per Comp.	14.1	14.3	13.7	15.6	13.4	14.0	13.4	15.9	16.0	15.9	15.1	15.4	13.5	15.8
Yards Lost Tackled	265	226	213	243	246	290	348	483	139	247	350	288	423	309
Net Yards	3065	3060	2534	2872	2581	2331	2176	2216	3307	3385	2069	3100	2068	3223
Touchdowns	27	20	17	31	19	14	14	22	35	23	14	18	19	27
Interceptions	25	28	16	17	24	13	19	31	22	31	23	30	19	27
Pct. Intercepted	5.9	6.5	4.3	4.5	6.3	4.2	5.1	8.9	5.4	7.2	7.2	6.9	5.9	6.3
PUNTING:														
Number	58	69	45	57	53	50	87	65	55	64	60	59	48	63
Average Distance	41.5	43.7	42.8	45.4	45.3	40.9	45.5	40.3	40.6	42.9	40.0	38.3	45.6	34.5
PUNT RETURNS:														
Number	34	39	20	17	39	31	27	34	17	14	19	20	27	29
Yards	272	281	111	81	502	290	252	374	58	95	169	134	207	184
Average Yards	8.0	7.2	5.6	4.8	12.9	9.4	9.3	11.0	3.4	6.8	8.9	6.7	7.7	6.3
Touchdowns	0	1	0	0	0	0	0	0	0	0	0	0	1	0
KICKOFF RETURNS:														
Number	55	53	46	59	46	30	60	67	54	61	62	64	62	61
Yards	1263	1129	983	1207	1124	716	1447	1522	1405	1385	1350	1495	1739	1720
Average Yards	23.0	21.3	21.4	20.5	24.4	23.9	24.1	22.7	26.0	22.7	21.8	23.4	28.0	28.2
Touchdowns	0	0	0	1	0	1	0	0	1	1	0	0	0	1
INTERCEPTION RETURNS:														
Number	23	23	24	20	24	31	19	25	26	26	28	16	12	28
Yards	331	468	352	366	269	452	261	280	332	289	318	229	127	285
Average Yards	14.4	20.3	14.7	18.3	11.2	14.6	13.7	11.2	12.8	11.1	11.4	14.3	10.6	10.2
Touchdowns	0	2	0	1	2	1	2	1	0	0	2	1	0	0
PENALTIES:														
Number	63	69	56	62	62	59	71	44	62	58	45	56	63	62
Yards	675	776	600	639	624	617	704	447	601	619	427	655	636	663
FUMBLES:														
Number	26	29	24	32	26	29	26	37	24	25	24	36	24	31
Number Lost	19	16	17	19	18	15	16	23	14	13	13	21	14	17
POINTS:														
Total	293	321	291	398	315	415	220	254	398	282	312	287	282	305
PAT Attempts	37	41	36	51	38	53	27	31	49	38	33	39	36	39
PAT Made	31	36	33	50	37	52	26	31	47	36	32	38	36	38
FG Attempts	28	27	31	27	34	21	20	25	28	19	42	14	23	25
FG Made	12	13	14	14	14	15	10	11	19	6	26	5	10	11
Percent FG Made	42.9	48.1	45.2	51.9	41.2	71.4	50.0	44.0	67.9	31.6	61.9	35.7	43.5	44.0
Safeties	2	0	0	0	4	0	1	2	0	0	2	0	0	0

DEFENSE

	BALT.	CHI.	CLEVE.	DALLAS	DET.	G.BAY	L.A.	MINN.	N.Y.	PHIL.	PITT.	ST.L.	S.F.	WASH.
FIRST DOWNS:														
Total	226	228	263	274	180	191	256	266	256	275	250	251	240	280
by Rushing	91	108	122	93	62	88	119	119	100	128	78	93	107	95
by Passing	119	101	125	166	105	94	124	139	136	129	157	141	113	165
by Penalty	16	19	16	15	13	9	13	8	20	18	15	17	20	20
RUSHING:														
Numbers	423	438	466	387	353	404	501	463	413	526	363	452	464	411
Yards	1504	2073	1940	1510	1231	1531	2092	1978	1677	2126	1419	1724	2241	1636
Average Yards	3.6	4.7	4.2	3.9	3.5	3.8	4.2	4.3	4.1	4.0	3.9	3.8	4.8	4.0
Touchdowns	17	17	17	17	6	4	14	20	13	23	13	18	22	12
PASSING:														
Attempts	381	363	341	437	367	355	379	397	450	363	438	377	296	412
Completions	206	170	189	233	187	187	217	214	223	198	223	196	164	247
Completion Pct.	54.1	46.8	55.4	53.3	51.0	52.7	57.3	53.9	49.6	54.5	50.9	52.0	55.4	60.0
Passing Yardage	2975	2460	2277	3904	2441	2084	3144	3365	3238	3023	3490	3302	2494	3860
Avg. Yds per Att.	7.8	6.8	6.7	8.9	6.7	5.9	8.3	8.5	7.2	8.3	8.0	8.8	8.4	9.4
Avg. Yds per Comp.	14.4	14.5	12.0	16.8	13.1	11.1	14.5	15.7	14.5	15.3	15.7	16.8	15.2	15.6
Yards Lost Tackled	356	386	293	230	455	338	255	242	369	103	284	315	186	258
Net Yards	2619	2074	1984	3674	1986	1746	2889	3123	2869	2920	3206	2987	2308	3602
Touchdowns	19	14	15	33	11	20	25	29	21	16	34	21	17	35
Interceptions	23	23	24	20	24	31	19	25	26	26	28	16	12	28
Pct. Intercepted	6.0	6.3	7.0	4.6	6.5	8.7	5.0	6.3	5.8	7.2	6.4	4.2	4.1	6.8
PUNTING:														
Number	67	71	56	63	70	58	56	52	65	42	62	61	61	49
Average Distance	42.7	41.8	40.6	40.6	44.1	43.2	45.5	43.3	38.8	38.2	40.7	40.6	44.6	42.4
PUNT RETURNS:														
Number	23	32	15	28	31	20	55	32	24	24	18	26	32	7
Yards	182	308	121	190	326	183	567	261	138	174	119	122	285	34
Average Yards	7.9	9.6	8.1	6.8	10.5	9.2	10.3	8.2	5.8	7.3	6.6	4.7	8.9	4.9
Touchdowns	0	0	0	0	0	1	1	0	0	0	0	0	0	0
KICKOFF RETURNS:														
Number	52	60	49	63	55	76	50	52	63	56	54	41	51	58
Yards	1433	1514	1098	1604	1379	1524	1211	1149	1700	1459	1151	870	1140	1253
Average Yards	27.6	25.2	22.4	25.5	25.1	20.1	24.2	22.1	27.0	26.1	21.3	21.2	22.4	21.6
Touchdowns	1	0	0	1	0	0	0	0	0	1	0	0	0	2
INTERCEPTION RETURNS:														
Number	25	28	16	17	24	13	19	31	22	31	23	30	19	27
Yards	386	328	161	263	352	122	293	445	182	555	257	389	334	292
Average Yards	15.4	11.7	10.1	15.5	14.7	9.4	15.4	14.4	8.3	17.9	11.2	13.0	17.6	10.8
Touchdowns	0	1	0	1	0	1	2	1	0	2	0	1	3	0
PENALTIES:														
Number	71	65	53	56	51	54	52	68	58	48	53	63	57	83
Yards	792	643	547	569	527	611	592	633	636	479	581	584	626	863
FUMBLES:														
Number	32	37	23	33	34	28	30	30	30	22	21	23	22	28
Number Lost	19	24	13	16	23	19	18	18	13	13	10	15	14	20
POINTS:														
Total	288	287	257	402	177	148	334	410	283	356	363	361	331	376
PAT Attempts	37	34	34	52	19	17	42	52	35	43	48	44	42	49
PAT Made	35	31	32	49	19	17	38	51	34	41	48	43	39	46
FG Attempts	22	31	14	25	25	22	33	30	27	37	19	33	20	26
FG Made	9	16	7	13	14	9	14	15	13	19	9	18	12	12
Percent FG Made	40.9	51.6	50.0	52.0	56.0	40.9	42.4	50.0	48.1	51.4	47.4	54.5	60.0	46.2
Safeties	2	2	0	1	1	1	1	1	0	0	0	0	2	0

1962 NFL
CHAMPIONSHIP GAME
December 30, at New York
(Attendance 64,892)

A Dismal Homecoming

A bone-chilling thirty-five-mile-per-hour wind lanced through Yankee Stadium, where the temperature was 20 degrees at game time and dropped steadily all afternoon. The Giants were out to avenge last year's loss to the Packers but fell short in a bitterly contested, hard-hitting ground game. The wind and cold made passing close to impossible, so the game was fought out primarily between the opposing lines and power runners. One particularly brutal pairing was Packer fullback Jim Taylor and Giant linebacker Sam Huff, the two of them butting heads constantly all game long. The Packers punched out yardage behind the crisp blocking of their offensive line and scored in the opening period on a 26-yard Jerry Kramer field goal. The Packers got a break in the second quarter when Dan Currie's hard tackle knocked the football loose from Phil King on the Giant 28-yard line. On the first play after the recovery, Paul Hornung passed 21 yards to Boyd Dowler on the halfback option, and Jim Taylor blasted through the line for the last seven yards on the next play. The Packers led 10-0 at halftime, but the Giants finally scored in the third period when Erich Barnes blocked Max McGee's punt and Jim Collier fell on it in the end zone for a touchdown. On the next series of downs, the Packers again punted, but New York's Sam Horner fumbled the ball and Green Bay recovered on the Giant 40-yard line. After that, the Packers never lost momentum, and two more Kramer field goals made the final score 16-7.

TEAM STATISTICS

N. Y.		G. B.
18	First Downs – Total	18
5	First Downs – Rushing	11
11	First Downs – Passing	6
2	First Downs – Penalty	1
7	Punts – Number	6
42.0	Punts – Average Distance	25.5
0	Punt Return Yardage	36
0	Interception Returns – Number	1
0	Interception Return – Yards	30
3	Fumbles – Number	2
2	Fumbles – Number Lost	0
4	Penalties – Number	5
62	Yards – Penalized	44
3	Giveaways	0
0	Takeaways	3
–3	Difference	+3

SCORING

NEW YORK	0	0	7	0– 7
GREEN BAY	3	7	3	3–16

First Quarter
G.B. J. Kramer, 26 yard field goal 7:11

Second Quarter
G.B. Taylor, 7 yard rush 12:21
PAT – J. Kramer (kick)

Third Quarter
N.Y. Collier, recovered blocked punt in the end zone. 7:26
PAT – Chandler (kick)
G.B. J. Kramer, 29 yard field goal 11:00

Fourth Quarter
G.B. J. Kramer, 30 yard field goal 13:10

INDIVIDUAL STATISTICS

RUSHING

NEW YORK	No	Yds	Avg.	GREEN BAY	No	Yds	Avg.
Webster	15	56	3.7	Taylor	31	85	2.7
King	11	38	3.5	Hornung	8	35	4.4
	26	94	3.6	Moore	6	24	4.0
				Starr	1	4	4.0
					46	148	3.2

RECEIVING

NEW YORK	No	Yds	Avg.	GREEN BAY	No	Yds	Avg.
Walton	5	75	15.0	Dowler	4	48	12.0
Shofner	5	69	13.8	Taylor	3	20	6.7
Gifford	4	34	8.5	R. Kramer	2	25	12.5
King	2	14	7.0	McGee	1	13	13.0
Webster	1	5	5.0		10	106	10.6
Morrison	1	0	0.0				
	18	197	10.9				

PASSING

NEW YORK	Att	Comp	Comp Pct.	Yds	Int	Yds/ Att.	Yds/ Comp
Tittle	41	18	43.9	197	1	4.8	10.9
GREEN BAY							
Starr	21	9	42.9	85	0	4.0	9.4
Hornung	1	1	100.0	21	0	21.0	21.0
	22	10	45.5	106	0	4.8	10.6

NEW YORK GIANTS 12-2-0 Allie Sherman

Scores of Each Game

7	Cleveland	17
29	Philadelphia	13
31	Pittsburgh	27
31	St. Louis	14
17	PITTSBURGH	20
17	DETROIT	14
49	WASHINGTON	34
31	ST. LOUIS	28
41	Dallas	10
42	Washington	24
19	PHILADELPHIA	14
26	Chicago	24
17	CLEVELAND	13
41	DALLAS	31

Use Name	Pos.	Hgt	Wgt	Age	Int	Pts
Rosey Brown	OT	6'3"	255	29		
Jack Stroud	OT	6'1"	250	33		
Reed Bohovich	OG-OT	6'3"	260	21		
Bookie Bolin	OG	6'2"	235	22		
Darrell Dess	OG	6'	245	26		
Greg Larson	C-OG	6'2"	245	23		
Ray Wietecha	C	6'1"	230	33		
Ken Byers	DE	6'1"	240	22		
Jim Katcavage	DE	6'3"	240	27	1	
Andy Robustelli	DE	6'1"	235	36		
Rosey Grier	DT	6'5"	290	29		
Chuck Janerette	DT	6'3"	250	23		
Dick Modzelewski	DT	6'	260	31		
Sam Huff	LB	6'1"	230	27	1	
Dick Lasse	LB	6'2"	225	26		
Tom Scott	LB	6'2"	220	32	1	
Mickey Walker	LB	6'	230	22		
Bill Winter	LB	6'3"	220	22		
Erich Barnes	DB	6'2"	198	27	6	
Sam Horner	DB	6'	198	24		
Dick Lynch	DB	6'1"	205	26	5	12
Jimmy Patton	DB	6'	185	30	7	
Dick Pesonen	DB	6'	190	24	2	
Allan Webb	DB	5'11"	180	24		
Ralph Gugliemi	QB	6'1"	195	29		
Y. A. Tittle	QB	6'	195	35		12
Johnny Counts	HB	5'10"	170	23		6
Paul Dudley	HB	6'	185	22		6
Phil King	HB	6'4"	225	26		12
Joe Morrison	DB-HB	6'1"	212	24		18
Alex Webster	FB	6'3"	225	31		54
Frank Gifford	FL	6'1"	190	32		48
Jim Collier	OE	6'2"	195	23		
Del Shofner	OE	6'3"	185	26		72
Aaron Thomas (from SF)	OE	6'3"	208	24		
Joe Walton	OE	5'11"	200	27		54
Don Chandler	K	6'2"	210	27		104

PITTSBURGH STEELERS 9-5-0 Buddy Parker

Scores of Each Game

7	Detroit	45
30	Dallas	28
27	NEW YORK	31
13	PHILADELPHIA	7
20	New York	17
27	DALLAS	42
14	CLEVELAND	41
39	MINNESOTA	31
26	St. Louis	17
23	WASHINGTON	21
14	Cleveland	35
19	ST. LOUIS	7
26	Philadelphia	17
27	Washington	24

Use Name	Pos.	Hgt	Wgt	Age	Int	Pts
Charlie Bradshaw	OT	6'6"	255	26		
Dan James	OT	6'4"	280	25		
Ray Lemek	OG	6'	240	28		
Mike Sandusky	OG	6'	230	29		
Ron Stehouwer	OG	6'2"	240	26		
Buzz Nutter	C	6'4"	230	31		
Lou Michaels	DE	6'2"	235	26		110
Ernie Stautner	DE	6'1"	230	37	1	2
John Kenerson (to NY-A)	DT	6'3"	255	23		
Joe Krupa	DT	6'2"	225	29		
Big Daddy Lipscomb	DT	6'6"	288	31		
George Strugar (to NY-A)	DT	6'5"	258	27		
Lou Cordileone (from LA)	DE-DT	6'	245	25		
Tom Bettis	LB	6'2"	225	29		
Rudy Hayes	LB	6'	215	27		
Ken Kirk	LB	6'2"	230	24		
John Reger	LB	6'	230	31	1	
Bob Schmitz	LB	6'1"	235	24	3	6
Bob Simms (from NY)	LB	6'1"	230	24		
George Tarasovic	LB	6'4"	245	33	4	
Willie Daniel	DB	5'11"	185	24	5	6
Glenn Glass	DB	6'	190	25		
Dick Haley	DB	5'10"	195	26	4	
Brady Keys	DB	6'	185	26	3	
Johnny Sample	DB	6'1"	200	25		
Jackie Simpson	DB	5'10"	185	28		
Clendon Thomas	DB	6'2"	192	25	7	
Ed Brown	QB	6'2"	210	33		
Bobby Layne	QB	6'1"	210	35		6
Terry Nofsinger	QB	6'4"	205	24		
Gary Ballman	HB	6'	190	22		
Dick Hoak	HB	5'11"	190	23		24
Tom Tracy	HB	5'9"	205	30		
Joe Womack	HB	5'9"	210	25		30
Bob Ferguson	FB	5'11"	220	21		
John Henry Johnson	FB	6'2"	215	32		54
Buddy Dial	FL	6'1"	195	25		36
Red Mack	FL	5'10"	185	25		12
John Burrell	OE	6'2"	188	22		
Preston Carpenter	OE	6'2"	190	28		24
Harlon Hill (to DET)	OE	6'3"	200	30		
John Powers	OE	6'2"	215	21		

Myron Pottios - Broken Arm

CLEVELAND BROWNS 7-6-1 Paul Brown

Scores of Each Game

17	NEW YORK	7
16	WASHINGTON	17
7	Philadelphia	35
19	DALLAS	10
14	BALTIMORE	36
34	St. Louis	7
41	Pittsburgh	14
14	PHILADELPHIA	17
9	Washington	17
38	ST. LOUIS	14
35	PITTSBURGH	14
21	Dallas	45
13	New York	17
13	San Francisco	10

Use Name	Pos.	Hgt	Wgt	Age	Int	Pts
John Brown	OT	6'2"	245	23		
Mike McCormack	OT	6'4"	250	35		
Dick Schafrath	OT	6'3"	255	26		
Gene Hickerson	OG	6'3"	248	27		
Jim Ray Smith	OG	6'3"	245	31		
John Wooten	OG	6'2"	250	27		
John Morrow	C	6'3"	248	29		
Frank Morze	C	6'4"	264	28		
Bill Glass	DE	6'5"	255	26		
Jim Houston	DE	6'2"	235	25		
Paul Wiggin	DE	6'3"	245	28		
Bob Gain	DT	6'3"	260	34		
Frank Parker	DT	6'5"	250	22		
Floyd Peters	DT	6'4"	255	27	1	
Vince Costello	LB	6'	232	30	3	6
Galen Fiss	LB	6'	227	32	4	
Mike Lucci	LB	6'2"	220	22		
Sam Tidmore	LB	6'1"	220	23		
Ross Fichtner	DB	6'	185	24	4	
Don Fleming	DB	6'	188	25	2	
Bobby Franklin	DB	5'11"	182	26	1	
Bernie Parrish	DB	5'11"	195	27	2	
Jim Shofner	DB	6'2"	190	26	4	
Jim Shorter	DB	5'11"	180	21		
John Furman	QB	6'4"	205	22		
Jim Ninowski	QB	6'1"	200	26		
Frank Ryan	QB	6'3"	200	26		6
Ernie Green	HB	6'2"	205	23		6
Charlie Scales	HB	5'11"	215	23		18
Tom Wilson	FB-HB	6'	204	29		6
Jimmy Brown	FB	6'2"	228	26		108
Ray Renfro	FL	6'1"	192	31		24
Johnny Brewer	OE	6'4"	225	25		12
Leon Clarke	OE	6'4"	235	29		
Gary Collins	OE	6'4"	208	21		12
Bob Crespino	OE	6'4"	217	24		
Rich Kreitling	OE	6'2"	208	27		18
Lou Groza	K	6'3"	248	38		75

WASHINGTON REDSKINS 5-7-2 Bill McPeak

Scores of Each Game

35	Dallas	35
17	Cleveland	16
24	ST. LOUIS	14
20	LOS ANGELES	14
17	St. Louis	17
27	Philadelphia	21
34	New York	49
10	DALLAS	38
17	CLEVELAND	9
21	Pittsburgh	23
24	NEW YORK	42
14	PHILADELPHIA	37
21	Baltimore	34
24	PITTSBURGH	27

Use Name	Pos.	Hgt	Wgt	Age	Int	Pts
Fran O'Brien	OT	6'1"	250	27		
Riley Mattson	OT	6'4"	248	23		
Bob Khayat	OG	6'2	230	24		71
Charlie Moore	OG	6'5"	230	22		
John Nisby	OG	6'1"	247	29		
Vince Promuto	OG	6'1"	243	24		
Fred Hageman	C	6'4"	244	24		
Gene Cronin	DE	6'2"	228	29		
Ed Khayat	DE	6'3"	248	27		
John Paluck	DE	6'2"	240	29		
Andy Stynchula	DE	6'3"	257	23		
Ben Davidson	DT	6'8"	275	22		
Joe Rutgens	DT	6'2"	265	23		
Bob Toneff	DT	6'3"	275	32		
Rod Breedlove	LB	6'2"	225	24	3	
Gorden Kelley	LB	6'3"	230	24	2	
Al Miller	LB	6'	220	22		
Bob Pellegrini	LB	6'2"	225	27	4	
Claude Crabb	DB	6'	190	22	6	
Doug Elmore	DB	6'	188	22	2	
Bobby Freeman	DB	6'1"	200	29	3	
Dale Hackbart	DB	6'3"	210	26	3	
Jim Kerr	DB	6'1"	195	23	1	
Jim Steffen	DB	6'	195	25	4	6
Ron Hatcher	FB-DB	5'11"	215	23		
Galen Hall	QB	5'10"	205	23	6	
George Izo	QB	6'3"	214	25		
Norm Snead	QB	6'4"	215	22		18
Billy Barnes	HB	5'11"	202	27		18
Leroy Jackson	HB	6'	190	22		6
Dick James	HB	5'9"	175	28		30
Don Bosseler	FB	6'1"	212	26		12
Jim Cunningham	FB	5'11"	220	23		12
Bobby Mitchell	FL	6'	192	27		72
Bill Anderson	OE	6'2"	214	26		12
Fred Dugan	OE	6'3"	198	28		30
Steve Junker	OE	6'3"	217	27		12
Hugh Smith	OE	6'4"	215	24		

DALLAS COWBOYS 5-8-1 Tom Landry

Scores of Each Game

35	WASHINGTON	35
28	PITTSBURGH	30
27	Los Angeles	17
10	Cleveland	19
41	PHILADELPHIA	19
42	Pittsburgh	27
24	ST. LOUIS	28
38	Washington	10
10	NEW YORK	41
33	CHICAGO	34
14	Philadelphia	28
45	CLEVELAND	21
20	St. Louis	52
31	New York	41

Use Name	Pos.	Hgt	Wgt	Age	Int	Pts
Clyde Brock	OT	6'5"	268	22		
Monte Clark	OT	6'6"	260	25		
Bob Fry	OT	6'4"	240	31		
Dale Memmelaar	OT	6'2"	245	25		
Andy Cvercko	OG	6'	243	25		
Joe Bob Isbell	OG	6'1"	225	22		
Mike Connelly	C	6'3"	235	26		
Lynn Hoyem	C	6'4"	225	22		
George Andrie	DE	6'7"	247	22		
Bob Lilly	DE	6'4"	248	23		
Ken Frost	DT	6'4"	245	23		
John Meyers	DT	6'6"	267	22		
Guy Reese	DT	6'5"	238	22		
Mike Dowdle	LB	6'3"	210	24	1	
Chuck Howley	LB	6'3"	230	26	2	
Bob Lang	LB	6'3"	235	28		
Don Talbert	LB	6'5"	225	22		
Jerry Tubbs	LB	6'2"	220	27	4	
Don Bishop	DB	6'2"	204	27	6	6
Mike Gaechter	DB	6'	190	22	5	6
Cornell Green	DB	6'4"	210	22		
Warren Livingston	DB	5'10"	180	24		
Dick Nolan	DB	6'1"	185	30		
Jerry Norton	DB	5'11"	195	32	2	6
Buddy Humphrey	QB	6'1"	200	26		
Eddie LeBaron	QB	5'9"	160	32		
Don Meredith	QB	6'2"	198	24		
Amos Bullocks	HB	6'1"	197	23		18
Don Perkins	HB	5'10"	198	24		42
J. W. Lockett	FB	6'2"	230	25		18
Amos Marsh	FB	6'1"	208	23		54
Frank Clarke	FL	6'	215	29		84
Donnie Davis	FL	6'4"	214	22		
Lee Folkins	OE	6'5"	220	23		36
Billy Howton	OE	6'2"	194	32		36
Pettis Norman	OE	6'3"	215	22		
Glynn Gregory	DB-OE	6'2"	200	23		
Sam Baker	K	6'2"	217	30		92

John Houser — Injury
Ed Nutting — Injury

NEW YORK GIANTS

RUSHING

Last Name	No.	Yds	Avg	TD
Webster	207	743	3.6	5
King	108	460	4.3	2
Morrison	35	146	4.2	1
Tittle	17	108	6.4	2
Dudley	27	100	3.7	0
Counts	14	55	3.9	0
Guglielmi	11	40	3.6	0
Gifford	2	18	9.0	1
Shofner	1	4	4.0	0
Thomas	1	−9	−9.0	0
Chandler	1	−11	−11.0	0

RECEIVING

Last Name	No.	Yds	Avg	TD
Shofner	53	1133	21	12
Webster	47	477	10	4
Gifford	39	796	20	7
Walton	33	406	12	9
King	15	186	12	0
Dudley	9	112	12	1
Morrison	6	107	18	2
Thomas	4	80	20	0
Counts	4	62	16	0
Collier	1	27	27	0
Robustelli	1	26	26	0

PUNT RETURNS

Last Name	No.	Yds	Avg	TD
Counts	8	33	4	0
Morrison	5	22	4	0
Horner	3	3	1	0
Patton	1	0	0	0

KICKOFF RETURNS

Last Name	No.	Yds	Avg	TD
Counts	26	784	30	1
Horner	11	242	22	0
Dudley	8	229	29	0
Morrison	5	113	23	0
King	2	37	19	0
Collier	1	0	0	0
Walker	1	0	0	0

PASSING – PUNTING – KICKING

PASSING	Att	Comp	%	Yds	Yd/Att	TD	Int–	%	RK
Tittle	375	200	53	3224	8.6	33	20–	5	2
Guglielmi	31	14	45	210	6.8	2	1–	3	
Gifford	2	1	50	12	6.0	0	0–	0	
Dudley	1	0		0	0.0	0	1–	100	

PUNTING	No	Avg
Chandler	55	40.6

KICKING	XP	Att	%	FG	Att	%
Chandler	47	48	98	19	28	68

PITTSBURGH STEELERS

RUSHING

Last Name	No.	Yds	Avg	TD
Johnson	251	1141	4.5	7
Womack	128	468	3.7	5
Hoak	117	442	3.8	4
Tracy	20	116	5.8	0
Hill	7	72	10.3	0
Burrell	6	38	6.3	0
Ferguson	20	37	1.9	0
Layne	15	25	1.7	1
Ballman	3	7	2.3	0
Mack	2	−2	−1.0	0
Carpenter	1	−3	−3.0	0
Brown	2	−8	−4.0	0

RECEIVING

Last Name	No.	Yds	Avg	TD
Dial	50	981	20	6
Carpenter	36	492	14	4
Johnson	32	226	7	2
Hoak	9	133	15	0
Mack	8	203	25	2
Burrell	8	193	24	0
Hill	7	101	14	0
Womack	6	57	10	0
Tracy	2	11	6	0
Powers	1	16	16	0
Ferguson	1	6	6	0

PUNT RETURNS

Last Name	No.	Yds	Avg	TD
Carpenter	7	109	16	0
Keys	7	46	7	0
Haley	1	13	13	0
Sample	4	1		0

KICKOFF RETURNS

Last Name	No.	Yds	Avg	TD
Keys	28	667	24	0
Glass	16	396	25	0
Haley	7	105	15	0
Sample	2	52	26	0
Hoak	2	40	20	0
Ferguson	2	30	15	0
Carpenter	1	29	29	0
Womack	1	16	16	0
Michaels	2	15	8	0
Sandusky	1	0	0	0

PASSING – PUNTING – KICKING

PASSING	Att	Comp	%	Yds	Yd/Att	TD	Int–	%	RK
Layne	233	116	50	1686	7.2	9	17–	7	15
Brown	84	43	51	726	8.6	5	6–	7	
Hoak	1	0	0	0	0.0	0	0–	0	
Tracy	1	1	100	7	7.0	0	0–	0	

PUNTING	No	Avg
Brown	60	40.0

KICKING	XP	Att	%	FG	Att	%
Michaels	32	33	97	26	42	62

CLEVELAND BROWNS

RUSHING

Last Name	No.	Yds	Avg	TD
Jimmy Brown	230	996	4.3	13
Ryan	42	242	5.8	1
Scales	56	239	4.3	3
Wilson	46	141	3.1	1
Green	31	139	4.5	0
Ninowski	9	15	1.7	0

RECEIVING

Last Name	No.	Yds	Avg	TD
Jimmy Brown	47	517	11	5
Kreitling	44	659	15	3
Renfro	31	638	21	4
Brewer	22	290	13	2
Green	17	194	11	1
Collins	11	153	14	2
Clarke	10	106	11	0
Wilson	8	110	14	0
Scales	8	67	8	0
Crespino	2	13	7	0

PUNT RETURNS

Last Name	No.	Yds	Avg	TD
Shofner	8	33	4	0
Green	5	31	6	0

KICKOFF RETURNS

Last Name	No.	Yds	Avg	TD
Wilson	11	307	28	0
Green	13	250	19	0
Scales	9	154	17	0
Tidmore	2	39	20	0
Collins	1	0	0	0

PASSING – PUNTING – KICKING

PASSING	Att	Comp	%	Yds	Yd/Att	TD	Int–	%	RK
Ryan	194	112	58	1541	7.9	10	7–	4	4
Ninowski	173	87	50	1178	6.8	7	8–	5	14
Jimmy Brown	2	1	50	28	14.0	0	0–	0	
Scales	1	0	0	0	0.0	0	1–	100	

PUNTING	No	Avg
Collins	45	42.8

KICKING	XP	Att	%	FG	Att	%
Groza	33	35	94	14	31	45

WASHINGTON REDSKINS

RUSHING

Last Name	No.	Yds	Avg	TD
Barnes	159	492	3.1	3
Bosseler	93	336	3.6	2
Cunningham	35	144	4.1	1
Jackson	49	112	2.3	0
James	9	13	1.4	0
Snead	20	10	0.5	3
Mitchell	1	5	5.0	0
Hall	2	2	1.0	0
Izo	1	−3	−3.0	0
Dugan	1	−9	−9.0	0
Elmore	1	−14	−14	0

RECEIVING

Last Name	No.	Yds	Avg	TD
Mitchell	72	1384	19	11
Dugan	36	466	13	5
Bosseler	32	258	8	0
Anderson	23	386	17	2
James	19	373	20	5
Barnes	14	220	16	0
Junker	11	149	14	2
Jackson	10	253	25	1
Cunningham	6	43	7	1

PUNT RETURNS

Last Name	No.	Yds	Avg	TD
James	19	145	8	0
Steffen	6	30	5	0
Mitchell	3	7	2	0
Kerr	1	2	2	0

KICKOFF RETURNS

Last Name	No.	Yds	Avg	TD
James	32	889	28	0
Mitchell	12	398	33	1
Jackson	10	272	27	0
Steffen	4	107	27	0
Cunningham	2	54	27	0
Miller	1	0	0	0

PASSING – PUNTING – KICKING

PASSING	Att	Comp	%	Yds	Yd/Att	TD	Int–	%	RK
Snead	354	184	52	2926	8.3	22	22–	6	8
Izo	37	17	46	284	7.7	3	4–	11	
Hall	32	19	59	274	8.6	2	1–	3	
Barnes	4	3	75	48	12.0	0	0–	0	
Elmore	1	0		0	0.0	0	0–	0	

PUNTING	No	Avg
Elmore	54	34.4
Anderson	7	33.6
Hackbart	2	39.0

KICKING	XP	Att	%	FG	Att	%
B. Khayat	38	38	100	11	25	44

DALLAS COWBOYS

RUSHING

Last Name	No.	Yds	Avg	TD
Perkins	222	945	4.3	7
Marsh	144	802	5.6	1
Bullocks	33	196	5.9	2
Meredith	21	74	3.5	0
Lockett	8	24	3.0	1
LeBaron	6	−1	−0.2	0

RECEIVING

Last Name	No.	Yds	Avg	TD
Howton	49	706	14	6
Clarke	47	1043	22	14
Folkins	39	536	14	6
Marsh	35	467	13	2
Perkins	13	104	8	0
Lockett	7	78	11	2
Gregory	3	70	23	0
Bullocks	3	46	15	1
Norman	2	34	17	0
Davis	2	31	16	0

PUNT RETURNS

Last Name	No.	Yds	Avg	TD
Lockett	8	45	6	0
Gaechter	6	32	5	0
Marsh	3	4	1	0

KICKOFF RETURNS

Last Name	No.	Yds	Avg	TD
Marsh	29	725	25	1
Bullocks	14	265	19	0
Lockett	6	130	22	0
Davis	4	66	17	0
Gaechter	1	16	16	0
Norman	2	5	3	0
Cverko	1	0	0	0
Memmalaar	1	0	0	0
Talbert	1	0	0	0

PASSING – PUNTING – KICKING

PASSING	Att	Comp	%	Yds	Yd/Att	TD	Int–	%	RK
Meredith	212	105	50	1679	7.9	15	8–	4	10
LeBaron	166	95	57	1436	8.7	16	9–	5	3
Baker	1	0		0	0.0	0	0–	0	
Lockett	1	0	0	0	0.0	0	0–	0	

PUNTING	No	Avg
Baker	57	45.4

KICKING	XP	Att	%	FG	Att	%
Baker	50	51	98	14	27	52

EASTERN CONFERENCE – Continued

ST. LOUIS CARDINALS 4-9-1 Wally Lemm

Scores of Each Game		
27	Philadelphia	21
0	Green Bay	17
14	Washington	24
14	NEW YORK	31
17	WASHINGTON	17
7	CLEVELAND	34
28	Dallas	24
28	New York	31
17	PITTSBURGH	26
14	Cleveland	38
17	SAN FRANCISCO	24
7	Pittsburgh	19
52	DALLAS	20
45	PHILADELPHIA	35

Use Name	Pos.	Hgt	Wgt	Age	Int	Pts
Ed Cook	OT	6'2"	240	30		
Fate Echols	OT	6'1"	255	23		
Irv Goode	OT	6'4"	235	21		
Ernie McMillan	OT	6'6"	255	24		
Ken Panfil	OT	6'6"	255	31		
Ken Gray	OG	6'2"	240	26		
Mike McGee	OG	6'1"	230	24		
Jerry Perry	OG	6'4"	240	31		53
Tom Redmond	OG	6'5"	240	25		
Bob DeMarco	C	6'3"	240	24		
Ed Henke	DE	6'3"	230	34		
Luke Owens	DE	6'2"	255	29		
Joe Robb	DE	6'3"	230	25		
Frank Fuller	DT	6'4"	245	33		
George Hultz	DT	6'4"	250	23		
Don Owens	DT	6'5"	255	30		

Use Name	Pos.	Hgt	Wgt	Age	Int	Pts
Ted Bates	LB	6'3"	220	26		
Garland Boyette	LB	6'1"	225	22		
Bill Koman	LB	6'2"	230	28		
Dale Meinert	LB	6'2"	220	29	1	
Marion Rushing	LB	6'2"	210	25		
Roland Jackson	FB-LB	6'	210	22		
Norm Beal	DB	5'11"	170	22		
Pat Fischer	DB	5'10"	165	22	3	
Jimmy Hill	DB	6'2"	190	33	2	
Billy Stacy	DB	6'1"	190	26	6	
Larry Wilson	DB	6'	187	24	2	6

Don Gillis – Injury
Monte Lee – Military Service

Use Name	Pos.	Hgt	Wgt	Age	Int	Pts
Sam Etcheverry	QB	5'11"	190	32		
Charley Johnson	QB	6'	190	25		18
Joe Childress	HB	6'	200	28		6
John David Crow	HB	6'2"	215	27		102
Prentice Gautt	FB	6'	200	24		12
Bill Triplett	DB-HB	6'2"	212	23	1	
Mal Hammack	FB	6'2"	205	29		6
Bobby Joe Conrad	FL	6'	195	27		24
Taz Anderson	OE	6'2"	200	23		18
Chuck Bryant	OE	6'2"	220	21		
Jack Elwell	OE	6'3"	200	22		
Hugh McInnis	OE	6'3"	220	24		
Sonny Randle	OE	6'2"	187	26		42
Jim Bakken	K	6'	200	21		

PHILADELPHIA EAGLES 3-10-1 Nick Skorich

Scores of Each Game		
21	ST. LOUIS	27
13	NEW YORK	29
35	CLEVELAND	7
7	Pittsburgh	13
19	Dallas	41
21	WASHINGTON	27
21	Minnesota	31
14	Cleveland	14
0	GREEN BAY	49
14	New York	19
28	DALLAS	14
37	Washington	14
17	PITTSBURGH	26
35	St. Louis	45

Use Name	Pos.	Hgt	Wgt	Age	Int	Pts
Jim McCusker	OT	6'2"	245	26		
J. D. Smith	OT	6'5"	250	26		
Bob Butler	OG	6'1"	235	21		
Pete Case	OG	6'3"	230	21		
Roy Hord (from LA)	OG	6'4"	250	27		
John Wittenborn	OG	6'2"	240	26		6
Jim Schrader	C	6'2"	252	30		
Howard Keys	OT-OG-C	6'3"	240	27		
John Baker	DE	6'6"	290	27		
Bobby Richards	DE	6'2"	225	23		
Gene Gossage	OG-DE	6'3"	240	27		
Dick Stafford	DT-DE	6'4"	235	22		
Jim Beaver	DT	6'1"	235	23		
Riley Gunnels	DT	6'3"	250	25		
John Kapele (from PIT)	DT	6'	240	25		
Joe Lewis	DT	6'2"	250	27		
Dan Oakes	DT	6'3"	245	24		

Use Name	Pos.	Hgt	Wgt	Age	Int	Pts
Maxie Baughan	LB	6'1"	226	24	1	
Chuck Bednarik	LB	6'3"	235	37		
Bob Harrison	LB	6'2"	220	25	2	
John Nocera	LB	6'1"	220	28	1	
Mike Woulfe	LB	6'2"	225	23		
Don Burroughs	DB	6'4"	190	31	7	
Jimmy Carr	DB	6'1"	210	29	3	
Irv Cross	DB	6'1"	190	23	5	
Mike McClellan	DB	6'1"	185	23	3	
Ben Scotti	DB	6'1"	186	25	4	

Use Name	Pos.	Hgt	Wgt	Age	Int	Pts
King Hill	QB	6'3"	213	26		6
Sonny Jurgensen	QB	5'11"	200	28		12
Timmy Brown	HB	5'10"	190	25		78
Ted Dean	HB	6'2"	210	24		
Don Jonas	HB	5'11"	195	23		
Theron Sapp	HB	6'1"	205	27		12
Clarence Peaks	FB	6'1"	220	26		18
Merrill Douglas	HB-FB	6'	204	26		
Frank Budd	FL	5'10"	187	23		6
Hopalong Cassady (from CLE)	FL	5'10"	185	28		12
Tommy McDonald	FL	5'10"	172	28		60
Ken Gregory	OE	6'	190	25		
Dick Lucas	OE	6'2"	216	28		6
Pete Retzlaff	OE	6'1"	210	31		18
Ralph Smith	OE	6'2"	205	23		
Bobby Walston	OE	6'	195	33		48

WESTERN CONFERENCE

GREEN BAY PACKERS 13-1-0 Vince Lombardi

Scores of Each Game		
34	MINNESOTA	7
17	ST. LOUIS	0
49	CHICAGO	0
9	DETROIT	7
48	Minnesota	21
31	SAN FRANCISCO	13
17	Baltimore	6
38	Chicago	7
49	Philadelphia	0
17	BALTIMORE	13
14	Detroit	26
41	LOS ANGELES	10
31	San Francisco	21
20	Los Angeles	17

Use Name	Pos.	Hgt	Wgt	Age	Int	Pts
Forrest Gregg	OT	6'4"	250	29		
Norm Masters	OT	6'2"	250	29		
Bob Skoronski	OT	6'3"	250	29		
Ed Blaine	OG	6'2"	240	22		
Jerry Kramer	OG	6'3"	250	27		65
Fuzzy Thurston	OG	6'1"	250	29		
Ken Iman	C	6'1"	230	23		
Jim Ringo	C	6'1"	235	31		
Willie Davis	DE	6'3"	240	29		6
Bill Quinlan	DE	6'3"	250	30	1	
Ron Gassert	DT	6'3"	250	22		
Dave Hanner	DT	6'2"	260	33	1	
Henry Jordan	DT	6'3"	250	27	1	
Ron Kostelnik	DT	6'4"	260	22		

Use Name	Pos.	Hgt	Wgt	Age	Int	Pts
Dan Currie	LB	6'3"	240	28		
Bill Forester	LB	6'3"	240	31		
Ray Nitschke	LB	6'3"	235	26	4	
Nelson Toburen	LB	6'3"	235	23		
Herb Adderley	DB	6'1"	205	23	7	12
Hank Gremminger	DB	6'1"	205	29	5	
Johnny Symank	DB	5'11"	180	27		
Jesse Whittenton	DB	6'1"	195	28	3	
Howie Williams	DB	6'2"	190	25		
Willie Wood	DB	5'10"	185	26	9	

Use Name	Pos.	Hgt	Wgt	Age	Int	Pts
John Roach	QB	6'4"	200	29		
Bart Starr	QB	6'1"	200	29		6
Paul Hornung	HB	6'2"	215	26		74
Tom Moore	HB	6'2"	215	24		42
Elijah Pitts	HB	6'1"	200	23		12
Earl Gros	FB	6'3"	220	21		12
Jim Taylor	FB	6'	215	30		**114**
Lew Carpenter	FL	6'1"	215	30		
Boyd Dowler	FL	6'5"	220	25		12
Gary Barnes	OE	6'4"	210	27		
Gary Knafelc	OE	6'4"	220	30		
Ron Kramer	OE	6'3"	230	27		42
Max McGee	OE	6'3"	205	30		18

DETROIT LIONS 11-3-0 George Wilson

Scores of Each Game		
45	PITTSBURGH	7
45	SAN FRANCISCO	24
29	Baltimore	20
7	Green Bay	9
13	LOS ANGELES	10
14	New York	17
11	CHICAGO	3
12	Los Angeles	3
38	San Francisco	24
17	Minnesota	6
26	GREEN BAY	14
21	BALTIMORE	14
37	MINNESOTA	23
0	Chicago	3

Use Name	Pos.	Hgt	Wgt	Age	Int	Pts
Dan LaRose	OT	6'5"	250	22		
John Lomakoski	OT	6'4"	250	21		
Dick Mills	OG	6'3"	240	22		
Harley Sewell	OG	6'1"	230	31		
John Gordy	OT-OG	6'3"	250	26		
Bob Whitlow	C	6'1"	236	26		
Bob Scholtz	OT-C	6'4"	250	24		
Darris McCord	DE	6'4"	250	29		2
Leo Sugar	DE	6'1"	230	33		
Sam Williams	DE	6'5"	235	31	1	12
Roger Brown	DT	6'5"	300	25		4
Mike Bundra	DT	6'3"	250	23		
John Gonzaga	DT	6'3"	250	29		
Alex Karras	DT	6'2"	245	26	1	2
Paul Ward	DT	6'3"	247	25		

Use Name	Pos.	Hgt	Wgt	Age	Int	Pts
Carl Brettschneider	LB	6'1"	225	30	2	
Max Messner	LB	6'3"	225	24		
Joe Schmidt	LB	6'1"	220	30	1	
Wayne Walker	LB	6'2"	225	25	1	64
Dave Lloyd	C-LB	6'3"	248	26		
Night Train Lane	DB	6'1"	200	34	4	
Dick LeBeau	DB	6'1"	185	25	4	12
Gary Lowe	DB	5'11"	195	28	2	
Yale Lary	DB	6'	190	31	8	
Bruce Maner	HB-DB	5'11"	190	25		
Tom Hall	OE-DB	6'1"	195	21		

Jim Martin – Voluntarily Retired

Use Name	Pos.	Hgt	Wgt	Age	Int	Pts
Earl Morrall	QB	6'1"	206	28		6
Milt Plum	QB	6'1"	205	28		21
Dick Compton	HB	6'1"	190	22		
Dan Lewis	HB	6'1"	200	26		42
Tom Watkins	HB	6'1"	195	25		18
Nick Pietrosante	FB	6'2"	225	25		24
Ken Webb	FB	5'11"	205	27		6
Terry Barr	FL	6'	190	27		18
Pat Studstill	FL	6'1"	180	24		24
Gail Cogdill	OE	6'2"	195	25		48
Jim Gibbons	OE	6'2"	220	26		12
Larry Vargo	OE	6'3"	200	22		

CHICAGO BEARS 9-5-0 George Halas

Scores of Each Game		
30	San Francisco	14
27	Los Angeles	23
0	Green Bay	49
13	Minnesota	0
27	SAN FRANCISCO	34
35	BALTIMORE	15
3	Detroit	11
7	GREEN BAY	38
31	MINNESOTA	30
34	Dallas	33
57	Baltimore	0
24	NEW YORK	26
30	LOS ANGELES	14
3	DETROIT	0

Use Name	Pos.	Hgt	Wgt	Age	Int	Pts
Art Anderson	OT	6'3"	244	25		
Jim Cadile	OT	6'3"	230	21		
Herm Lee	OT	6'4"	247	31		
Bob Wetoska	OT	6'3"	240	24		
Roger Davis	OG	6'3"	235	24		
Stan Jones	OG	6'1"	250	31		
Ted Karras	OG	6'1"	243	29		
Mike Pyle	C	6'3"	240	23		
Doug Atkins	DE	6'8"	255	32		
Ed O'Bradovich	DE	6'3"	255	22		
Maury Youmans	DE	6'6"	260	25		
Stan Fanning	DT	6'6"	270	24		
Bob Kilcullen	DT	6'3"	245	26		
Earl Leggett	DT	6'3"	250	28		
Fred Williams	DT	6'4"	248	32		

Use Name	Pos.	Hgt	Wgt	Age	Int	Pts
Joe Fortunato	LB	6'	225	32	3	
Bill George	LB	6'2"	235	31	2	
Roger LeClerc	LB	6'3"	235	24		75
Larry Morris	LB	6'2"	230	27	2	
J. C. Caroline	DB	6'1"	190	29	2	
Bennie McRae	DB	6'1"	180	21	1	
Don Mullins	DB	6'1	195	23		
Tommy Neck	DB	5'11"	190	23		
Richie Petitbon	DB	6'3"	205	24	6	6
Rosey Taylor	DB	5'11"	186	23	2	12
Dave Whitsell	DB	6'	190	26	5	

Use Name	Pos.	Hgt	Wgt	Age	Int	Pts
Rudy Bukich	QB	6'1"	205	31		
Billy Wade	QB	6'2"	210	31		30
Charlie Bivins	HB	6'2"	212	23		6
Ronnie Bull	HB	6'	200	22		6
Willie Galimore	HB	6'1"	187	27		12
Billy Martin	HB	5'11"	197	24		6
Rick Casares	FB	6'2"	225	31		18
Joe Marconi	FB	6'2"	225	28		36
Johnny Morris	FL	5'10	180	27		30
John Adams	OE	6'3"	235	25		18
Angie Coia	OE	6'2"	202	24		24
Mike Ditka	OE	6'3"	230	22		36
Jim Dooley	OE	6'4"	198	32		
Bo Farrington	OE	6'3"	217	26		6
Bobby Joe Green	K	5'11"	175	24		

RUSHING				
Last Name	No.	Yds	Avg	TD

EASTERN CONFERENCE—Continued

ST. LOUIS CARDINALS

Last Name	No.	Yds	Avg	TD
Crow	192	751	3.9	14
Gautt	114	470	4.1	2
Childress	37	162	4.4	0
Hammack	38	160	4.2	1
Johnson	25	138	5.5	3
Triplett	2	12	6.0	0
Etcheverry	8	5	0.6	0

PHILADELPHIA EAGLES

Last Name	No.	Yds	Avg	TD
Brown	137	545	4.0	5
Peaks	137	447	3.3	3
Sapp	23	53	2.3	2
Jurgensen	17	44	2.6	2
Hill	4	40	10.0	1
Smith	1	13	13.0	0
Douglas	4	7	1.8	0
Cassady	1	6	6.0	0

WESTERN CONFERENCE

GREEN BAY PACKERS

Last Name	No.	Yds	Avg	TD
Taylor	272	1474	5.4	19
Moore	112	377	3.4	7
Hornung	57	219	3.8	5
Gros	29	155	5.3	2
Pitts	22	110	5.0	2
Starr	21	72	3.4	1
McGee	3	52	17.3	0
Roach	1	5	5.0	0
R. Kramer	1	−4	−4.0	0

DETROIT LIONS

Last Name	No.	Yds	Avg	TD
Lewis	120	488	4.1	6
Watkins	113	485	4.3	3
Pietrosante	134	445	3.3	2
Webb	70	267	3.8	1
Plum	29	170	5.9	1
Morrall	17	65	3.8	1
Maher	3	8	2.7	0
Compton	1	3	3.0	0
Cogdill	1	2	2.0	0
Studstill	1	−11	−11.0	0

CHICAGO BEARS

Last Name	No.	Yds	Avg	TD
Marconi	89	406	4.6	5
Bull	113	363	3.2	1
Casares	75	255	3.4	2
Galimore	43	233	5.4	2
Wade	40	146	3.7	5
Bivins	14	44	3.1	1
Martin	9	28	3.1	1
Anderson	1	7	7.0	0
J. Morris	2	7	3.5	0

RECEIVING				
Last Name	No.	Yds	Avg	TD

ST. LOUIS CARDINALS

Last Name	No.	Yds	Avg	TD
Randle	63	1158	18	7
Conrad	62	954	15	4
Anderson	35	535	15	3
Crow	23	246	11	3
Gautt	16	240	15	0
Childress	15	207	14	1
Hammack	4	27	7	0
Elwell	1	11	11	0
McInnis	1	10	10	0

PHILADELPHIA EAGLES

Last Name	No.	Yds	Avg	TD
McDonald	58	1146	20	10
Brown	52	849	16	6
Peaks	39	347	9	0
Retzlaff	30	584	19	3
Lucas	19	236	12	1
Cassady	14	188	13	2
Sapp	6	80	13	0
Budd	5	130	26	1
Walston	4	43	11	0
Smith	1	29	29	0

GREEN BAY PACKERS

Last Name	No.	Yds	Avg	TD
McGee	49	820	17	3
Dowler	49	724	15	2
R. Kramer	37	555	15	7
Taylor	22	106	5	0
Moore	11	100	9	0
Hornung	9	168	19	2
Carpenter	7	104	15	0
Pitts	3	44	15	0

DETROIT LIONS

Last Name	No.	Yds	Avg	TD
Cogdill	53	991	19	7
Studstill	36	479	13	4
Gibbons	33	318	10	2
Pietrosante	26	251	10	2
Barr	25	425	17	3
Lewis	16	158	10	1
Watkins	12	85	7	0
Webb	10	120	12	0

CHICAGO BEARS

Last Name	No.	Yds	Avg	TD
Ditka	58	904	16	5
J. Morris	58	889	15	5
Bull	31	331	11	0
Marconi	23	306	13	1
Coia	22	361	16	4
Farrington	13	197	15	1
Casares	10	71	7	1
Adams	5	111	22	3
Galimore	5	56	11	0
Bivins	3	52	17	0
Martin	1	8	8	0

PUNT RETURNS				
Last Name	No.	Yds	Avg	TD

ST. LOUIS CARDINALS

Last Name	No.	Yds	Avg	TD
Beal	7	46	7	0
Fischer	4	37	9	0
Stacy	5	35	7	0
Conrad	2	10	5	0
Crow	2	6	3	0

PHILADELPHIA EAGLES

Last Name	No.	Yds	Avg	TD
Brown	6	81	14	0
Cassady	8	49	6	0
McDonald	5	8	2	0
Cross	1	2	2	0
Smith	1	2	2	0

GREEN BAY PACKERS

Last Name	No.	Yds	Avg	TD
Wood	23	273	12	0
Pitts	7	17	2	0
Kostelnik	1	0	0	0

DETROIT LIONS

Last Name	No.	Yds	Avg	TD
Studstill	29	457	16	0
Watkins	8	42	5	0
Maher	2	3	2	0

CHICAGO BEARS

Last Name	No.	Yds	Avg	TD
J. Morris	20	208	10	0
Martin	17	62	4	0
Taylor	2	11	6	1

KICKOFF RETURNS				
Last Name	No.	Yds	Avg	TD

ST. LOUIS CARDINALS

Last Name	No.	Yds	Avg	TD
Triplett	24	608	25	0
Beal	16	394	25	0
Fischer	7	187	27	0
Gautt	6	124	21	0
Stacy	5	121	24	0
Hammack	2	36	18	0
Childress	3	19	6	0
Anderson	1	6	6	0

PHILADELPHIA EAGLES

Last Name	No.	Yds	Avg	TD
Brown	30	831	28	1
Cassady	24	482	20	0
Douglas	6	136	23	0
Dean	4	83	21	0
Cross	2	72	36	0
Baughan	3	9	3	0
Woulfe	2	5	3	0

GREEN BAY PACKERS

Last Name	No.	Yds	Avg	TD
Adderley	15	418	28	1
Moore	13	284	22	0
Gros	1	7	7	0
Nitschke	1	7	7	0

DETROIT LIONS

Last Name	No.	Yds	Avg	TD
Studstill	20	511	26	0
Watkins	17	452	27	0
Maher	7	141	20	0
Hall	1	16	16	0
Cogdill	1	4	4	0

CHICAGO BEARS

Last Name	No.	Yds	Avg	TD
Martin	25	515	21	0
Bivins	12	243	20	0
Bull	9	235	26	0
Taylor	4	98	25	0
Marconi	2	30	15	0
O'Bradovich	1	8	8	0

PASSING — PUNTING — KICKING	
Last Name	Statistics

ST. LOUIS CARDINALS

PASSING	Att	Comp	%	Yds	Yd/Att	TD	Int—	%	RK
Johnson	308	150	49	2440	7.9	16	20—	7	13
Etcheverry	106	58	55	707	6.7	2	10—	9	
Crow	20	12	60	241	12.1	0	0—	0	

PUNTING	No	Avg
Etcheverry	59	38.3

KICKING	XP	Att	%	FG	Att	%
Perry	38	39	97	5	12	42
Bakken	0	0	0	0	1	0
Conrad	0	0	0	0	1	0

PHILADELPHIA EAGLES

PASSING	Att	Comp	%	Yds	Yd/Att	TD	Int—	%	RK
Jurgensen	366	196	54	3261	8.9	22	26—	7	5
Hill	61	31	51	361	5.9	0	5—	8	
McDonald	1	1	100	10	10.0	1	0—	0	

PUNTING	No	Avg
Hill	64	42.9

KICKING	XP	Att	%	FG	Att	%
Walston	36	38	95	4	15	27
Wittenborn	0	0	0	2	4	50

GREEN BAY PACKERS

PASSING	Att	Comp	%	Yds	Yd/Att	TD	Int—	%	RK
Starr	285	178	62	2438	8.6	12	9—	3	1
Roach	12	3	25	33	2.8	0	0—	0	
Hornung	6	4	67	80	13.3	0	2—	33	
Moore	5	2	40	70	14.0	2	1—	20	
Pitts	2	0	0	0	0.0	0	0—	0	
McGee	1	0	0	0	0.0	0	1—	100	

PUNTING	No	Avg
Dowler	36	43.1
McGee	14	35.4

KICKING	XP	Att	%	FG	Att	%
J. Kramer	38	39	97	9	11	82
Hornung	14	14	100	6	10	60

DETROIT LIONS

PASSING	Att	Comp	%	Yds	Yd/Att	TD	Int—	%	RK
Plum	325	179	55	2378	7.3	15	20—	6	11
Morrall	52	32	62	449	8.6	4	4—	8	
Lary	1	0	0	0	0.0	0	0—	0	
Lewis	1	0	0	0	0.0	0	0—	0	

PUNTING	No	Avg
Lary	52	45.3
Morrall	1	48.0

KICKING	XP	Att	%	FG	Att	%
Walker	37	37	100	9	22	41
Plum	0	0	0	5	12	42

CHICAGO BEARS

PASSING	Att	Comp	%	Yds	Yd/Att	TD	Int—	%	RK
Wade	412	225	55	3172	7.7	18	24—	6	9
Bukich	13	3	23	79	6.1	1	4—	31	
Bull	3	0	0	0	0.0	0	0—	0	
Casares	2	1	50	35	17.5	1	0—	0	

PUNTING	No	Avg
Green	69	43.7

KICKING	XP	Att	%	FG	Att	%
Leclerc	36	40	90	13	27	48

Scores of Each Game		Use Name	Pos.	Hgt	Wgt	Age	Int	Pts

WESTERN CONFERENCE – Continued

BALTIMORE COLTS 7-7-0 Weeb Ewbank

Score	Opponent	Opp	Use Name	Pos.	Hgt	Wgt	Age	Int	Pts
30	LOS ANGELES	27	Tom Gilburg	OT	6'5"	245	23		
34	Minnesota	7	George Preas	OT	6'2"	250	30		
20	DETROIT	29	Dan Sullivan	OT	6'3"	250	23		
13	SAN FRANCISCO	21	Jim Parker	OG-OT	6'3"	275	28		
36	Cleveland	14	Wiley Feagin	OG	6'2"	235	25		
15	Chicago	35	Bill Kirchiro	OG	6'1"	235	21		
6	GREEN BAY	17	Palmer Pyle	OG	6'2"	250	25		
22	San Francisco	3	Alex Sandusky	OG	6'1"	242	30		
14	Los Angeles	2	Dick Szymanski	C	6'3"	235	30		
13	Green Bay	17	Ordell Braase	DE	6'4"	242	30		
0	CHICAGO	57	Gino Marchetti	DE	6'4"	245	36		
14	Detroit	21	Don Thompson	DE	6'4"	225	23		
34	WASHINGTON	21	Jim Colvin	DT	6'2"	250	25		
42	MINNESOTA	17	John Diehl	DT	6'7"	285	26		
			Billy Ray Smith	DT	6'4"	235	27		

Use Name	Pos.	Hgt	Wgt	Age	Int	Pts
Jackie Burkett	LB	6'4"	230	25	2	
Bill Pellington	LB	6'2"	238	33	2	
Bill Saul	LB	6'4"	225	21		2
Don Shinnick	LB	6'	235	27	5	
Dave Yohn	LB	6'	220	24		
Wendell Harris	DB	5'11"	190	21	2	9
Lenny Lyles	DB	6'2"	202	26		
Andy Nelson	DB	6'1"	180	29	4	
Jim Welch	DB	6'	190	24	1	
Bobby Boyd	HB-DB	5'10"	190	24	7	
Jerry Hill – Injury						

Use Name	Pos.	Hgt	Wgt	Age	Int	Pts
Lamar McHan	QB	6'1"	205	30		
Johnny Unitas	QB	6'1"	194	29		
Bob Clemens	HB	6'1"	208	23		
Alex Hawkins	HB	6'1"	190	25		24
Tom Matte	HB	6'	192	23		18
Lenny Moore	HB	6'1"	190	29		24
Joe Perry	FB	6'	195	35		
Mark Smolinski	FB	6'	222	23		12
Jimmy Orr	FL	5'11"	180	26		66
Bake Turner	FL	6'	180	22		6
Ray Berry	OE	6'2"	190	29		18
Dick Bielski	OE	6'1"	227	30		70
Dee Mackey	OE	6'5"	236	26		24
R. C. Owens	OE	6'3"	195	27		12

SAN FRANCISCO FORTY NINERS 6-8-0 Red Hickey

Score	Opponent	Opp	Use Name	Pos.	Hgt	Wgt	Age	Int	Pts
14	CHICAGO	30	Leon Donahue	OT	6'4"	245	23		
24	Detroit	45	Roland Lakes	OT	6'4"	247	22		
21	MINNESOTA	7	Bob St. Clair	OT	6'9"	265	31		
21	BALTIMORE	13	John Sutro	OT	6'4"	245	21		
34	Chicago	27	Bruce Bosley	OG	6'2"	240	28		
13	Green Bay	31	Ted Connolly	OG	6'3"	242	30		
14	LOS ANGELES	28	Mike Magac	OG	6'3"	240	24		
3	Baltimore	22	John Mellekas	C	6'3"	255	29		
24	DETROIT	38	Dan Colchico	DE	6'4"	236	25		
35	Los Angeles	17	Clark Miller	DE	6'5"	245	23		
24	St. Louis	17	Len Rohde	DE	6'4"	240	24		
24	Minnesota	12	Charlie Krueger	DT	6'4"	245	26		
21	GREEN BAY	31	Leo Nomellini	DT	6'3"	262	37		
10	CLEVELAND	13							

Use Name	Pos.	Hgt	Wgt	Age	Int	Pts
Matt Hazeltine	LB	6'1"	220	29	2	
Carl Kammerer	LB	6'3"	237	25	1	
Ed Pine	LB	6'4"	230	22	2	
Karl Rubke	LB	6'4"	240	26		
John Thomas	LB	6'4"	246	27		
Eddie Dove	DB	6'2"	180	25	1	
Elbert Kimbrough	DB	5'11"	195	23		
Jerry Mertens	DB	6'	183	26	2	
Jimmy Ridlon	DB	6'1"	177	27	1	
Abe Woodson	DB	5'11"	188	27	2	12
Dave Baker – Military Service						

Use Name	Pos.	Hgt	Wgt	Age	Int	Pts
John Brodie	QB	6'1"	186	27		24
Bob Waters	QB	6'2"	184	24		
Billy Kilmer	HB-QB	6'	190	23		36
Bob Gaiters (from NY)	HB	5'11"	210	24		
J. D. Smith	FB-HB	6'1"	200	29		42
Dale Messer	DB-HB	5'10"	175	25	1	
Bill Cooper	FB	6'1"	215	23		
C. R. Roberts	FB	6'3"	197	26		
Jim Vollenweider	FB	6'1"	210	22		
Lloyd Winston	FB	6'2"	215	22		
Bernie Casey	FL	6'4"	215	23		36
Jim Johnson	FL	6'2"	190	24		24
Kay McFarland	FL	6'2"	180	23		
Clyde Conner	OE	6'2"	190	29		24
Monte Stickles	OE	6'4"	230	24		18
Tommy Davis	K	6'	212	27		66

MINNESOTA VIKINGS 2-11-1 Norm Van Brocklin

Score	Opponent	Opp	Use Name	Pos.	Hgt	Wgt	Age	Int	Pts
7	Green Bay	34	Grady Alderman	OT	6'2"	235	23		
7	BALTIMORE	34	Errol Linden	OT	6'5"	260	25		
7	San Francisco	21	Frank Youso	OT	6'4"	260	26		
0	CHICAGO	13	Larry Bowie	OG	6'2"	235	22		
21	GREEN BAY	48	Jerry Huth	OG	6'	228	29		
38	Los Angeles	14	Mike Rabold	OG	6'2"	238	25		
31	PHILADELPHIA	21	Mick Tingelhoff	C	6'1"	230	22		
31	Pittsburgh	39	Bob Denton	DE	6'4"	240	28		
30	Chicago	31	Jim Leo	DE	6'1"	225	24	2	
6	DETROIT	17	Jim Marshall	DE	6'3"	230	24		
24	LOS ANGELES	24	Paul Dickson	DT	6'5"	250	25		
12	SAN FRANCISCO	35	Jim Prestel	DT	6'5"	250	25		
23	Detroit	37							
17	Baltimore	42							

Use Name	Pos.	Hgt	Wgt	Age	Int	Pts
Jim Christopherson	LB	6'	215	24	1	61
Rip Hawkins	LB	6'3"	230	23	1	2
Cliff Livingston	LB	6'3"	215	32		
Clancy Osborne	LB	6'3"	217	27		
Roy Winston	LB	6'1"	225	22		
Bill Butler	DB	5'10"	194	25	5	6
Dean Derby	DB	6'	190	28	4	
Tom Franckhauser	DB	6'	196	25	4	
Chuck Lamson	DB	6'	185	23	1	
Ed Sharockman	DB	6'	195	24	6	6
Charlie Sumner	DB	6'1"	195	32	3	

Use Name	Pos.	Hgt	Wgt	Age	Int	Pts
John McCormick	QB	6'1"	210	26		
Fran Tarkenton	QB	6'1"	190	22		12
Tommy Mason	HB	6'	195	23		48
Hugh McElhenny	HB	6'1"	198	33		
Bob Reed	HB	5'11"	187	22		6
Bill Brown	FB	5'11"	218	24		6
Doug Mayberry	FB	6'1"	225	25		12
Mel Triplett	FB	6'1"	215	30		18
Oscar Donahue	FL	6'3"	195	24		6
Tom Adams	OE	6'5"	210	22		
Charley Ferguson	OE	6'5"	212	22		36
Jerry Reichow	OE	6'2"	220	27		18
Gordon Smith	OE	6'2"	200	23		6
Steve Stonebreaker	OE	6'3"	220	24		6
Mike Mercer	K	6'	220	26		3

LOS ANGELES RAMS 1-12-1 Bob Waterfield Harland Svare

Score	Opponent	Opp	Use Name	Pos.	Hgt	Wgt	Age	Int	Pts
27	Baltimore	30	Jim Boeke	OT	6'5"	245	23		
23	CHICAGO	27	Joe Carollo	OT	6'2"	258	22		
17	DALLAS	27	Frank Varrichione	OT	6'1"	235	30		
14	Washington	20	Charley Cowan	OG	6'4"	250	24		
10	Detroit	13	Duane Putnam	OG	6'	233	34		
14	MINNESOTA	38	Joe Scibelli	OG	6'1"	250	23		
28	San Francisco	14	Art Hunter	C	6'4"	248	29		
3	DETROIT	12	Deacon Jones	DE	6'5"	240	23		
2	BALTIMORE	14	Lamar Lundy	DE	6'7"	235	27		
17	SAN FRANCISCO	24	Larry Stephens	DE	6'4"	260	24		
24	Minnesota	24	John Lovetere	DT	6'4"	280	26		
10	Green Bay	41	Merlin Olsen	DT	6'5"	265	21	1	6
14	Chicago	30							
17	GREEN BAY	20							

Use Name	Pos.	Hgt	Wgt	Age	Int	Pts
Mike Henry	LB	6'2"	215	26	1	
Bill Jobko	LB	6'2"	220	26		
Marlin McKeever	LB	6'1"	230	22	2	
Jack Pardee	LB	6'2"	225	26	8	
Les Richter	LB	6'3"	235	31		
Larry Hayes	C-LB	6'3"	230	27		
Charley Britt	DB	6'2"	185	24	3	
Lindon Crow	DB	6'1"	200	29	5	6
Alvin Hall	DB	6'1"	193	29	1	
Ed Meador	DB	5'11"	185	25	1	
Carver Shannon	DB	6'1"	198	24	4	
Bobby Smith	DB	6'	185	24	1	

Use Name	Pos.	Hgt	Wgt	Age	Int	Pts
Zeke Bratkowski	QB	6'2"	203	30		
Roman Gabriel	QB	6'4"	220	22		
Ron Miller	QB	6'	190	23		
Jon Arnett	HB	5'11"	194	27		12
Dick Bass	FB-HB	5'10"	200	25		48
Ollie Matson	FB	6'2"	210	32		6
Art Perkins	FB	6'	220	22		12
Glen Shaw	FB	6'1"	217	23		
Pervis Atkins	HB-FL	6'1"	195	26		6
Duane Allen	OE	6'4"	210	24		12
Carroll Dale	OE	6'1"	195	24		18
Karl Finch	OE	6'3"	195	23		
Jim Phillips	OE	6'1"	198	25		30
Danny Villanueva	K	5'11"	200	24		56

WESTERN CONFERENCE—Continued

BALTIMORE COLTS

RUSHING

Last Name	No.	Yds	Avg	TD
Moore	106	470	4.4	2
Perry	94	359	3.8	0
Smolinski	85	265	3.1	1
Matte	74	226	3.1	2
Unitas	50	137	2.7	0
Hawkins	29	87	3.0	4
Turner	1	17	17.0	0
Orr	1	14	14.0	0
Boyd	2	13	6.5	0
Clemens	2	9	4.5	0
McHan	4	4	1.0	0

RECEIVING

Last Name	No.	Yds	Avg	TD
Orr	55	974	18	11
Berry	51	687	13	3
Mackey	25	396	16	4
Owens	25	307	12	2
Perry	22	194	9	0
Moore	18	215	12	2
Bielski	15	200	13	2
Smolinski	13	128	10	1
Matte	8	81	10	1
Hawkins	4	37	9	0
Turner	1	*111	111	1

*Includes lateral

PUNT RETURNS

Last Name	No.	Yds	Avg	TD
Turner	10	95	10	0
Harris	8	61	8	0
Hawkins	11	42	4	0
Boyd	3	23	8	0
Nelson	2	22	11	0
Shinnick	0	29	0	0

KICKOFF RETURNS

Last Name	No.	Yds	Avg	TD
Matte	27	613	23	0
Turner	20	504	25	0
Harris	3	86	29	0
Hawkins	2	35	18	0
Smolinski	2	20	10	0
Diehl	1	5	5	0

PASSING — PUNTING — KICKING

Last Name	Att	Comp	%	Yds	Yd/Att	TD	Int—	%	RK
PASSING									
Unitas	389	222	57	2967	7.6	23	23—	6	7
McHan	20	10	50	278	13.9	3	2—	10	
Matte	13	5	38	85	6.5	1	0—	0	
Hawkins	1	0	0	0	0.0	0	0—	0	

Last Name	No.	Avg							
PUNTING									
Gilburg	57	41.8							
McHan	1	22.0							

Last Name	XP	Att	%	FG	Att	%			
KICKING									
Bielski	25	28	89	11	25	44			
Harris	6	9	67	1	3	33			

SAN FRANCISCO FORTY NINERS

RUSHING

Last Name	No.	Yds	Avg	TD
Smith	258	907	3.5	6
Kilmer	93	478	5.1	5
Brodie	37	258	7.0	4
Gaiters	43	193	4.5	0
Waters	12	42	3.5	0
Vollenweider	11	37	3.4	0
Roberts	9	19	2.1	0
Cooper	2	−2	−1.0	0
Winston	1	−15	−15.0	0

RECEIVING

Last Name	No.	Yds	Avg	TD
Casey	53	819	15	6
Johnson	34	627	18	4
Conner	24	240	10	4
Stickles	22	366	17	3
Smith	21	197	9	1
Kilmer	16	152	10	1
Gaiters	5	47	9	0
Vollenweider	4	21	5	0
Messer	3	30	10	0
McFarland	3	24	8	0
Roberts	2	0	0	0
Winston	1	2	2	0

PUNT RETURNS

Last Name	No.	Yds	Avg	TD
Woodson	19	179	9	1
Dove	5	21	4	0
Messer	3	7	2	0

KICKOFF RETURNS

Last Name	No.	Yds	Avg	TD
Woodson	37	1157	31	0
Gaiters	11	273	25	0
Vollenweider	6	113	19	0
Messer	4	112	28	0
Winston	3	67	22	0
Cooper	1	17	17	0

PASSING — PUNTING — KICKING

Last Name	Att	Comp	%	Yds	Yd/Att	TD	Int—	%	RK
PASSING									
Brodie	304	175	58	2272	7.5	18	16—	5	6
Kilmer	13	8	62	191	14.7	1	3—	23	
Waters	6	2	33	28	4.7	0	0—	0	
Gaiters	2	0	0	0	0.0	0	0—	0	

Last Name	No.	Avg							
PUNTING									
Davis	48	45.6							

Last Name	XP	Att	%	FG	Att	%			
KICKING									
Davis	36	36	100	10	23	43			

MINNESOTA VIKINGS

RUSHING

Last Name	No.	Yds	Avg	TD
Mason	167	740	4.4	2
Tarkenton	41	361	8.8	2
Mayberry	74	274	3.7	1
McElhenny	50	200	4.0	0
Triplett	52	160	3.1	2
Brown	34	103	3.0	0
Reed	6	22	3.7	0
McCormick	2	4	2.0	0

RECEIVING

Last Name	No.	Yds	Avg	TD
Reichow	39	561	14	3
Mason	36	603	17	6
Donahue	16	285	18	1
McElhenny	16	191	12	0
Ferguson	14	364	26	6
Stonebreaker	12	227	19	1
Mayberry	11	100	9	1
Brown	10	124	12	1
Smith	7	138	20	1
Reed	4	37	9	1
Adams	3	51	17	0
Triplett	2	30	15	1
Tarkenton	0	−12	0	0

PUNT RETURNS

Last Name	No.	Yds	Avg	TD
Butler	12	169	14	0
Reed	9	82	9	0
Mason	6	52	9	0
McElhenny	5	43	9	0
Sharockman	1	16	16	0
Franckhauser	1	12	12	0

KICKOFF RETURNS

Last Name	No.	Yds	Avg	TD
Butler	26	588	23	0
Reed	13	337	26	0
Mason	12	301	25	0
McElhenny	7	160	23	0
Sharockman	3	71	24	0
Prestel	2	29	15	0
Denton	1	17	17	0
Stonebreaker	1	12	12	0
Bowie	2	7	4	0

PASSING — PUNTING — KICKING

Last Name	Att	Comp	%	Yds	Yd/Att	TD	Int—	%	RK
PASSING									
Tarkenton	329	163	50	2595	7.9	22	25—	8	12
McCormick	18	7	39	104	5.8	0	5—	28	
Mason	1	0	0	0	0.0	0	1—	100	

Last Name	No.	Avg							
PUNTING									
McCormick	46	39.0							
Mercer	19	43.5							

Last Name	XP	Att	%	FG	Att	%			
KICKING									
Christopherson	28	28	100	11	20	55			
Mercer	3	3	100	0	5	0			

LOS ANGELES RAMS

RUSHING

Last Name	No.	Yds	Avg	TD
Bass	196	1033	5.3	6
Arnett	76	238	3.1	2
Perkins	48	181	3.8	2
Gabriel	18	93	5.2	0
Shaw	18	76	4.2	0
Miller	3	27	9.0	0
Atkins	7	19	2.7	0
Bratkowski	7	14	2.0	0
Richter	0	8	0.0	0
Matson	3	0	0.0	0

RECEIVING

Last Name	No.	Yds	Avg	TD
Phillips	60	875	15	5
Atkins	35	393	11	1
Bass	30	262	9	2
Dale	29	584	20	3
Perkins	14	83	6	0
Arnett	12	137	11	0
Allen	3	90	30	2
Shaw	3	51	17	0
Matson	3	49	16	1

PUNT RETURNS

Last Name	No.	Yds	Avg	TD
Atkins	11	94	9	0
Bass	6	81	14	0
Arnett	5	49	10	0
Hall	4	21	5	0
Smith	1	7	7	0

KICKOFF RETURNS

Last Name	No.	Yds	Avg	TD
Atkins	28	676	24	0
Bass	19	446	23	0
Hall	8	178	22	0
Arnett	2	87	44	0
Smith	2	60	30	0
Jones	1	0	0	0

PASSING — PUNTING — KICKING

Last Name	Att	Comp	%	Yds	Yd/Att	TD	Int—	%	RK
PASSING									
Bratkowski	219	110	50	1541	7.0	9	16—	7	16
Gabriel	101	57	56	670	6.6	3	2—	2	
Miller	43	17	40	250	5.8	1	1—	2	
Arnett	5	3	60	28	5.6	1	0—	0	
Bass	3	1	33	22	7.3	0	0—	0	
Matson	1	1	100	13	13.0	0	0—	0	

Last Name	No.	Avg							
PUNTING									
Villanueva	87	45.5							

Last Name	XP	Att	%	FG	Att	%			
KICKING									
Villanueva	26	27	96	10	20	50			

1962 A.F.L. Wismer's Rubbery Titans

The near collapse of the New York franchise was the league's biggest headache this year. A sports truism says that no circuit can be big league without a healthy New York franchise, but the media there had practically ignored the Titans. Owner Harry Wismer's boisterous outbursts against Commissioner Joe Foss, head coach Sammy Baugh, and the NFL Giants had stripped the club of most of its dignity and left it a local joke in New York. The Titans became a ghost team, playing its games before empty stands in the shadows of the old, decrepit Polo Grounds. But Wismer's verbal antics paled in the face of his financial ills, and the joke almost turned into an obituary. Wismer had been losing money in a steady outflow since the league began, and the till finally ran dry in November. When the players' paychecks bounced, the word was out that Wismer was broke. To keep the Titans going, Commissioner Foss stepped in and ran the club with league funds, thus averting the embarrassment of the New York franchise folding in mid-season. While league intervention kept the ship from sinking this year, new skippers for the franchise would be needed for next year.

Dallas owner Lamar Hunt was far from broke, but the situation in that city was a failing one for the AFL. Hunt had been an original founder of the new league when his bid for an NFL franchise for Dallas was turned down in the late 1950s. Once it was certain that the AFL would get off the ground, the NFL had put an expansion team in Dallas. Fans flocked to see the NFL Cowboys play, while the AFL Texans starved in a land full of football fans. Even with the team on the road to a championship this season, attendance stayed low, so Hunt started shopping around for a new place to settle his team.

But attendance in general around the circuit took a sharp turn upward. The number of paid fans at league games increased 20 percent over last year, filling both the stands and the team's coffers very pleasantly. Seats with fans in them looked much better than empty bleachers on ABC's national broadcasts, which still provided the league with enough money to keep the circuit solvent.

A less favorable development was the decision against the anti-trust suit against the NFL. The United States District Court in Baltimore ruled against the suit, and the team owners voted to appeal the decision and keep the legal process moving.

But fans are concerned less with lawsuits, attendance figures, and league maneuvering than with the playing on the field. The Dallas Texans blossomed into the league's top team, a colorful bunch of youngsters who swept through the league behind Len Dawson, a cool quarterback with six years of non-activity in the NFL behind him. The Eastern Division race came down to a tight struggle between the Houston Oilers and the Boston Patriots that kept interest in the league alive through the end of the schedule. The clubs in New York, Oakland, and Denver faired very poorly and definitely needed help to become competitive in the near future, but the level of competition in general was markedly improved over the past. The crowning achievement of the season was the championship game between the Texans and Oilers, played before a full house in Houston. The game ran into the second overtime period before Dallas' Tommy Brooker won it on a field goal. The longest game ever played up until then, this match kept television viewers glued to their TV sets well into the evening, convincing some of them that perhaps the AFL had something going for itself.

EASTERN DIVISION

Houston Oilers—When Oiler coach Wally Lemm resigned to head up the NFL St. Louis Cardinals, Houston owner Bud Adams replied by hiring deposed St. Louis coach Pop Ivy. Although Ivy was reputed to be an offensive genius, the Houston attack bogged down in the early part of the season. A bad back made Billy Cannon a shadow of his former self, quarterback George Blanda started serving up interceptions at a generous rate, and end Bill Groman suddenly wasn't getting open for passes any more. But like last year, the Oilers caught fire after a slow start. With squat Charley Tolar leading the way with his running, the Oilers won their last seven games, sweeping into first place by beating Boston on November 18 and winning every game the rest of the way.

Boston Patriots—Coach Mike Holovak's collection of unknown veterans and youngsters from local colleges battled Houston tooth and nail for the Eastern crown. The defense, led by Larry Eisenhauer, Houston Antwine, and rookie Nick Buoniconti, was more impressive as a unit than as individuals, while the offense scratched out points on Babe Parilli's passing, Ron Burton's running, and Gino Cappelletti's kicking. The Oilers recovered from a slow start to climb right behind the first-place Patriots, and the top spot rode on their November 18 meeting in Houston. Boston not only lost the game 21-17 and first place; they also lost quarterback Parilli with a broken collarbone. Reserve passer Tom Yewcic led the Pats to victories the rest of the way until stumbling 20-0 in the final game against Oakland and thus conceding the Eastern crown to Houston.

Buffalo Bills—The Bills had always had a tough defense, and now

coach Lou Saban was building an offense that could score points. The main addition was fullback Cookie Gilchrist, a Canadian League veteran who turned out to be the best power runner in the league. Saban also picked up a fine quarterback when he claimed Jack Kemp off the San Diego waiver list. Kemp had a broken hand at the time, but Saban carried him on the roster until he healed in time to star in the last three games of the year. The defense also got an injection of new blood when rookies Tom Sestak, Mike Stratton, Ray Abruzzese, Booker Edgerson, and Carl Charon all won starting positions. The new players needed time to jell, as the Bills lost their first five games, but seven wins and a tie in the last nine games showed Buffalo fans and coach Saban that he had built a winner.

New York Titans—The front-office situation was so chaotic that the Titans were lucky to finish out the year. Owner Harry Wismer was broke by November, no longer able even to pay his players. With attendance microscopic, the team's image laughable, and the players clamoring for money, the league office stepped in and ran the team the rest of the year. The Titans stayed surprisingly competitive on the field through all the commotion. Coach Bulldog Turner discovered a good quarterback in ex-giant Lee Grosscup, and when injuries kayoed Grosscup, Turner came up with another passer in ex-Bill Johnny Green. Art Powell, Dick Christy, and Don Maynard were the principal targets for these passers, and with fullback Bill Mathis injured most of the season, the pass again was New York's sole offensive threat. Even with good seasons from Larry Grantham and Lee Riley, the defense leaked profusely and condemned the Titans to last place in the East.

WESTERN DIVISION

Dallas Texans—Hank Stram had coached Len Dawson when both were at Purdue, and when the Cleveland Browns cut the quarterback before the season started, Stram immediately invited him to join the Texans. Dawson made up for the six years he sat on NFL benches by passing for twenty-nine touchdowns and leading the Texans to the AFL championship. Runners-up to San Diego the past two years, the Texans dethroned the Chargers by adding Dawson and key rookies Curtis McClinton, Fred Arbanas, Bobby Hunt, Bill Hull, Bill Miller, Bobby Ply, and Tommy Brooker. Stram got All-Pro performances from holdovers Abner Haynes, Chris Burford, Jim Tyrer, Mel Branch, Jerry Mays, E. J. Holub, and Sherrill Headrick, and the Texans swept to the Western crown while the stands stayed clean of paying customers.

Denver Broncos—The Broncos put all their chips on their passing attack and got away with it for two months. With ancient quarterback Frank Tripuka throwing bushels of passes to Lionel Taylor, Bo Dickinson, Gene Prebola, and Bob Scarpitto, the Broncos won seven of their first nine contests to contend for the Western title for the first time ever. But since Denver had no running game and a mediocre defense, the rest of the league wised up to its unbalanced attack over the second half of the season. The Broncos lost their last five games and wound up at a 7-7 mark, but the season was an exciting one for Denver fans and new coach Jack Faulkner. Three of the Broncos won individual league titles, Lionel Taylor in receiving, Gene Mingo in scoring and field goals, and Jim Fraser in punting.

San Diego Chargers—After two years as champs in the West, the Chargers suddenly had problems fielding a healthy team. Linebacker Bob Laraba was killed in an off-season car accident, and an amazing string of injuries left the Chargers an empty shell of their winning teams. Halfback Paul Lowe started the parade by breaking his arm in a pre-season game, and a string of teammates fell in line behind him. Rookie flanker Lance Alworth, linebacker Chuck Allen, defensive back Charley McNeil, and center Wayne Frazier all missed large portions of the schedule with various ailments, and a total of eleven starters were knocked out for seven or more games. To make this season a total loss, quarterback Jack Kemp broke his hand, and when coach Sid Gillman tried to slip him through on waivers to the reserve list, Buffalo claimed him for the $100 waiver price. With rookies and substitutes playing out the schedule, the Chargers lost eight of their last nine games to sink out of contention in the West.

Oakland Raiders—The Raiders were no great football team, as the six-game losing streak left over from last year testified, but the lung infection that sidelined quarterback Tom Flores for the season left the Raiders in desperate straits. They began the year with M. C. Reynolds and Don Heinrich, a pair of old NFL rejects, as passers, but coach Marty Feldman decided to go shopping for another quarterback after only one game. He bought Cotton Davidson from Dallas, and Davidson played out the Oakland schedule with a bad shoulder. The rest of the Raider squad contained little quality outside of Jim Otto, Clem Daniels, and Fred Williamson, and the team proceeded to lose its first thirteen games to run its losing streak to a record nineteen games. On the last day of the season they treated their fans in Frank Youell Field, their temporary home in Oakland, to a 20-0 victory over Boston, their first triumph in over a year.

FINAL TEAM STATISTICS

OFFENSE

Category	BOSTON	BUFFALO	DALLAS	DENVER	HOUSTON	NEW YORK	OAKLAND	SAN DIEGO
FIRST DOWNS:								
Total	230	238	259	**270**	266	206	187	217
by Rushing	100	**119**	**119**	72	95	60	72	82
by Passing	114	96	125	**177**	157	131	100	113
by Penalty	16	**23**	15	21	14	15	15	22
RUSHING:								
Number	432	**501**	479	322	457	317	367	410
Yards	1970	**2480**	2407	1298	1742	1213	1392	1647
Average Yards	4.6	**5.0**	**5.0**	4.0	3.8	3.8	3.8	4.0
Touchdowns	11	20	**21**	15	15	9	14	13
PASSING:								
Attempts	382	351	322	**559**	475	505	446	416
Completions	195	150	195	**292**	227	242	175	168
Completion Percentage	51.0	42.7	**60.6**	52.2	47.8	47.9	39.2	40.4
Passing Yards	2930	2181	2824	**3739**	3323	3161	2671	2686
Average Yards per Attempt	7.7	6.2	**8.8**	6.7	7.0	6.3	6.0	6.5
Average Yards per Completion	15.0	14.5	14.5	12.8	14.6	13.1	15.3	**16.0**
Times Tackled Attempting to Pass	23	23	41	30	**11**	54	44	28
Yards Lost Attempting to Pass	164	197	369	335	**94**	419	376	252
Net Yards	2766	1984	2455	**3404**	3229	2742	2295	2434
Touchdowns	25	15	29	21	**32**	20	11	23
Interceptions	**13**	26	17	40	48	35	29	34
Percent Intercepted	**3.4**	7.4	5.3	7.2	10.1	6.9	6.5	8.2
PUNTING:								
Number	69	76	54	60	56	78	**83**	79
Average Distance	38.5	38.8	35.8	**42.9**	41.0	41.0	37.4	41.6
PUNT RETURNS:								
Number	26	28	27	19	28	25	**34**	29
Yards	138	196	236	128	**314**	308	257	278
Average Yards	5.3	7.0	8.7	6.7	11.2	**12.3**	7.6	9.6
Touchdowns	0	1	0	0	1	**3**	0	1
KICKOFF RETURNS:								
Number	53	52	37	57	48	**73**	65	67
Yards	1200	1176	955	1210	1245	1579	1425	**1585**
Average Yards	22.6	22.6	25.8	21.2	**25.9**	21.6	21.9	23.7
Touchdowns	1	**2**	0	0	0	0	1	1
INTERCEPTION RETURNS:								
Number	25	**36**	32	27	35	29	29	29
Yards	365	**505**	395	483	340	356	390	340
Average Yards	14.6	14.0	12.3	**17.9**	9.7	12.3	13.4	11.7
Touchdowns	3	3	0	**4**	2	1	1	1
PENALTIES:								
Number	52	74	66	64	63	84	69	**88**
Yards	456	**797**	644	613	633	771	695	768
FUMBLES:								
Number	37	27	26	28	**17**	35	31	24
Number Lost	20	12	14	14	**9**	20	20	14
POINTS:								
Total	346	309	**389**	353	387	278	213	314
PAT (kick) Attempts	40	40	**49**	36	**49**	32	23	35
PAT (kick) Made	38	34	47	34	**48**	31	20	31
PAT (Rush or Pass) Attempts	1	1	1	3	1	2	4	3
PAT (Rush or Pass) Made	1	1	0	1	1	1	2	2
FG Attempts	37	23	27	**39**	26	27	27	20
FG Made	20	9	14	**27**	11	13	9	17
Percent FG Made	54.1	39.1	51.9	69.2	42.3	48.1	33.3	**85.0**
Safeties	0	0	0	1	**2**	1	0	0

DEFENSE

Category	BOSTON	BUFFALO	DALLAS	DENVER	HOUSTON	NEW YORK	OAKLAND	SAN DIEGO
FIRST DOWNS:								
Total	220	229	234	234	**217**	253	233	248
by Rushing	**68**	89	76	88	75	103	115	105
by Passing	136	129	143	131	126	122	**106**	120
by Penalty	16	**11**	20	15	16	28	12	23
RUSHING:								
Number	393	373	**351**	439	362	453	477	437
Yards	1426	1687	**1250**	1868	1569	2049	2397	1903
Average Yards	**3.6**	4.5	**3.6**	4.3	4.3	4.5	5.0	5.0
Touchdowns	14	**10**	14	11	**10**	19	21	16
PASSING:								
Attempts	450	440	467	423	486	417	**371**	402
Completions	216	215	239	202	213	194	**169**	196
Completion Percentage	48.0	48.9	51.2	47.8	**43.8**	46.5	45.6	48.8
Passing Yards	3435	2996	2953	2894	2865	2929	**2517**	2926
Average Yards per Attempt	7.6	6.8	6.3	6.8	**5.9**	7.0	6.8	7.3
Average Yards per Completion	15.9	13.9	**12.4**	14.3	13.5	15.1	14.9	14.9
Times Tackled Attempting to Pass	34	32	28	25	32	36	23	44
Yards Lost Attempting to Pass	327	254	252	224	304	323	211	311
Net Yards	3108	2742	2701	2670	2561	2606	**2306**	2615
Touchdowns	19	24	**13**	24	18	28	21	29
Interceptions	25	**36**	32	27	35	29	29	29
Percent Intercepted	5.6	**8.2**	6.9	6.4	7.2	7.0	7.8	7.2
PUNTING:								
Number	**79**	70	63	66	72	70	67	68
Average Distance	38.5	38.1	41.2	41.5	38.9	**37.9**	40.9	40.7
PUNT RETURNS:								
Number	**11**	33	26	27	28	31	34	26
Yards	**54**	202	219	245	259	295	352	229
Average Yards	**4.9**	6.1	8.4	9.1	9.3	9.5	10.4	8.8
Touchdowns	0	1	0	2	0	0	1	1
KICKOFF RETURNS:								
Number	64	56	72	64	55	46	**39**	56
Yards	1697	1177	1559	1401	1155	1194	**961**	1231
Average Yards	26.5	21.0	21.7	21.9	21.0	26.0	24.6	22.0
Touchdowns	1	1	0	0	1	3	0	1
INTERCEPTION RETURNS:								
Number	**13**	26	17	40	48	35	29	34
Yards	55	299	113	421	**725**	544	509	508
Average Yards	4.2	11.5	6.6	10.5	15.1	15.5	17.6	14.9
Touchdowns	1	0	0	5	2	3	3	1
PENALTIES:								
Number	62	**80**	64	76	65	73	75	65
Yards	554	**786**	660	678	559	711	720	709
FUMBLES:								
Number	26	26	29	**34**	25	30	25	30
Number Lost	10	14	16	**19**	17	16	18	13
POINTS:								
Total	295	272	**233**	334	270	423	370	392
PAT (kick) Attempts	33	33	**27**	38	32	51	46	44
PAT (kick) Made	32	30	**24**	36	30	46	44	41
PAT (Rush or Pass) Attempts	3	2	1	3	1	1	0	4
PAT (Rush or Pass) Made	1	1	1	1	**0**	1	0	4
FG Attempts	26	20	28	27	31	31	32	31
FG Made	15	10	11	16	14	21	16	17
Percent FG Made	57.7	50.0	**39.3**	59.3	45.2	67.7	50.0	54.8
Safeties	**0**	**0**	**0**	**0**	**0**	**0**	1	2

SCORING

HOUSTON	0	0	7	10	0–17
DALLAS	3	14	0	0	3–20

First Quarter
Dall. Brooker, 16 yard field goal 10:32

Second Quarter
Dall. Haynes, 28 yard pass from Dawson 0:27
        PAT—Brooker (kick)
Dall. Haynes, 2 yard rush 11:21
        PAT—Brooker (kick)

Third Quarter
Hous. Dewveall, 15 yard pass from Blanda 3:10
        PAT—Blanda (kick)

Fourth Quarter
Hous. Blanda, 31 yard field goal 3:53
Hous. Tolar, 1 yard rush 9:22
        PAT—Blanda (kick)

Second Overtime (Sixth Quarter)
Dall. Brooker, 25 yard field goal 2:54

TEAM STATISTICS

DALLAS		HOUSTON
19	First Downs—Total	21
10	First Downs—Rushing	6
5	First Downs—Passing	15
4	First Downs—Penalty	0
2	Fumbles—Number	0
1	Fumbles—Number Lost	0
6	Penalties—Number	6
42	Yards Penalized	50
1	Giveaways	5
5	Takeaways	1
+4	Difference	−4

1962 AFL CHAMPIONSHIP GAME
December 23, at Houston
(Attendance 37,981)

The Longest Afternoon

Houston had won its third straight Eastern title, but the Dallas Texans, making their first title-game appearance, almost blew the Oilers off the field in the first half, running up a 17-0 score on two Abner Haynes touchdowns and a Tommy Brooker field goal. The Oilers came out for the second half in top gear, however, and quickly fought back into the game. George Blanda passed to Willard Dewveall for 15 yards and Houston's first points early in the third quarter. With their backs against the wall, the Oilers rallied to tie the score in the fourth period. Blanda kicked a 31-yard field goal early in the period, and Charley Tolar scored on a one-yard plunge with five minutes left in the game. Blanda's extra point tied the score at 17-17, and regulation time ran out without any further scoring. As the teams readied for overtime, the captains met at mid-field for the coin toss for the next periods. Instructed to take advantage of the wind, Dallas' Abner Haynes blundered by electing to kick off, thus giving the Oilers the advantage of both receiving and having the wind at their backs. The Oilers couldn't score, however, and the Texans took the ball at mid-field near the end of the first overtime period on a Bill Hull interception. With Jack Spikes carrying and receiving the ball on key plays, the Texans moved down to the Houston 19-yard line. Tommy Brooker then booted a 25-yard field goal which ended Houston's championship reign and pro football's longest game.

INDIVIDUAL STATISTICS

RUSHING

HOUSTON	No.	Yds.	Avg.
Tolar	17	58	3.4
Cannon	11	37	3.4
Smith	2	3	1.5
	30	98	3.3

DALLAS	No.	Yds.	Avg.
Spikes	11	77	7.0
McClinton	24	70	2.9
Dawson	5	26	5.2
Haynes	14	26	1.9
	54	199	3.7

RECEIVING

HOUSTON	No.	Yds.	Avg.
Dewveall	6	95	15.8
Cannon	6	54	9.0
McLeod	5	70	14.0
Hennigan	3	37	11.3
Tolar	1	8	8.0
Smith	1	6	6.0
Jamison	1	-9	-9.0
	23	261	11.3

DALLAS	No.	Yds.	Avg.
Haynes	3	45	15.0
Spikes	2	24	12.0
Arbanas	2	21	10.5
McClinton	1	4	4.0
Bishop	1	-6	-6.0
	9	88	9.8

PUNTING

HOUSTON	No.		Avg.
Norton	3		39.3

DALLAS	No.	Yds.	Avg.
Wilson	6		32.0
Saxton	2		29.0
	8		31.2

PUNT RETURNS

HOUSTON	No.	Yds.	Avg.
Jancik	1	0	0.0

DALLAS	No.	Yds.	Avg.
Jackson	1	0	0.0

KICKOFF RETURNS

HOUSTON	No.	Yds.	Avg.
Jancik	5	139	27.8

DALLAS	No.	Yds.	Avg.
Grayson	3	64	21.3
Haynes	1	22	22.0
	4	86	21.5

INTERCEPTION RETURNS

HOUSTON	No.	Yds.	Avg.
None			

DALLAS	No.	Yds.	Avg.
Robinson	2	50	25.0
Holub	1	43	43.0
Hull	1	23	23.0
Grayson	1	20	20.0
	5	136	27.2

PASSING

	Att.	Comp.	Comp. Pct.	Yds.	Int.	Yds/Att.	Yds/Comp.	Yards Lost Tackled
HOUSTON								
Blanda	46	23	50.0	261	5	5.7	11.3	0
DALLAS								
Dawson	14	9	64.3	88		6.3	9.8	6-50

HOUSTON OILERS 11-3-0 Pop Ivy

Score	Opponent		Use Name	Pos.	Hgt	Wgt	Age	Int	Pts
28	Buffalo	23	Al Jamison	OT	6'5"	250	25		
21	Boston	34	Rich Michael	OT	6'3"	242	23		
42	San Diego	17	Walt Suggs	OT	6'5"	245	23		
17	BUFFALO	14	John Frongillo	OG	6'3"	250	22		
56	NEW YORK	17	Bob Talamini	OG	6'1"	255	23		
10	Denver	20	Bill Wegener	OG	5'10"	245	21		
7	DALLAS	31	Hogan Wharton	OG	6'2"	250	26		
14	Dallas	6	Bob Schmidt	C	6'4"	250	26		
28	Oakland	20	Gary Cutsinger	DE	6'4"	240	21	1	
21	BOSTON	17	Don Floyd	DE	6'4"	247	23	4	6
33	SAN DIEGO	27	Dan Lanphear	DE	6'2"	230	24		
34	DENVER	17	Ron McDole	DE	6'3"	255	23		
32	OAKLAND	17	Ed Culpepper	DT	6'1"	260	28		
44	New York	10	Bill Herchman	DT	6'2"	255	29		
			Ed Husmann	DT	6'	245	31		
			Bob Kelly	DT	6'3"	250	22		
			Bill Miller	DT	6'4"	270	24		

Use Name	Pos.	Hgt	Wgt	Age	Int	Pts
Doug Cline	LB	6'2"	230	23	2	
Mike Dukes	LB	6'3"	230	26	2	
Tom Goode	LB	6'3"	235	23		
Larry Onesti	LB	6'	205	23		
Gene Babb	FB-LB	6'3"	220	27	2	6
Tony Banfield	DB	6'1"	185	23	6	6
Freddy Glick	DB	6'1"	190	25	3	
Bobby Jancik	DB	5'11"	178	22	2	
Mark Johnston	DB	6'2"	200	24	4	
Jim Norton	DB	6'3"	195	23	8	
Bob Suci	DB	5'10"	178	24	1	

Use Name	Pos.	Hgt	Wgt	Age	Int	Pts
George Blanda	QB	6'1"	212	34		81
Jacky Lee	QB	6'1"	185	23		
Billy Cannon	HB	6'1"	215	25		80
Dave Smith	FB	6'1"	210	25		18
Charley Tolar	HB-FB	5'7"	198	24		48
Charley Hennigan	FL	6'	187	26		48
Willard Dewveall	OE	6'4"	230	25		30
Charley Frazier	OE	6'	160	23		6
Bill Groman	OE	6'	200	26		18
Bob McCleod	OE	6'5"	240	23		36

BOSTON PATRIOTS 9-4-1 Mike Holovak

Score	Opponent		Use Name	Pos.	Hgt	Wgt	Age	Int	Pts
28	Dallas	42	Milt Graham	OT	6'6"	235	28		
21	HOUSTON	21	Dick Klein	OT	6'4"	254	28		
41	DENVER	16	Charley Long	OT	6'3"	230	24		
43	New York	14	Charlie Leo	OG	6'	240	27		
7	DALLAS	27	Billy Neighbors	OG	5'11"	240	22		
24	San Diego	20	Tony Sardisco	OG	6'2"	230	29		
26	OAKLAND	16	Walt Cudzik	C	6'2"	235	29		
28	Buffalo	28	Bob Yates	C	6'3"	230	23		
33	Denver	29	Bob Dee	DE	6'3"	240	29		
17	Houston	21	Larry Eisenhauer	DE	6'5"	230	22		
21	BUFFALO	10	Jim Hunt	DE	5'11"	245	23		
24	NEW YORK	17	Houston Antwine	DT	6'	250	23		
20	San Diego	14	Jess Richardson	DT	6'2"	265	32		
0	Oakland	20							

Use Name	Pos.	Hgt	Wgt	Age	Int	Pts
Tom Addison	LB	6'3"	230	26	5	6
Nick Buoniconti	LB	5'11"	220	21	2	
Harry Jacobs	LB	6'2"	235	25		
Rommie Loudd	LB	6'3"	225	28		
Jack Rudolph	LB	6'3"	230	24		
Fred Bruney	DB	5'10"	190	31	3	6
Dick Felt	DB	6'	185	29	5	
Ron Hall	DB	6'	190	25	3	6
Ross O'Hanley	DB	6'	185	23	5	
Chuck Shonta	DB	6'	190	24	4	
Don Webb	HB-DB	5'10"	200	23		
Oscar Lofton — Military Service						
George McGee — Military Service						

Use Name	Pos.	Hgt	Wgt	Age	Int	Pts
Don Allard	QB	6'	188	26		
Babe Parilli	QB	6'1"	190	32		12
Tom Yewcic	QB	5'11"	185	30		12
Ron Burton	HB	5'10"	190	25		42
Jim Crawford	HB	6'1"	200	26		26
Claude King	HB	5'11"	195	23		6
Larry Garron	FB	6'	215	25		36
Billy Lott	FB	6'	205	27		
Gino Capelletti	FL	6'	190	28		128
Jim Colclough	OE	6'	185	26		60
Tony Romeo	OE	6'2"	220	23		6
Tom Stephens	OE	6'1"	220	26		

BUFFALO BILLS 7-6-1 Lou Saban

Score	Opponent		Use Name	Pos.	Hgt	Wgt	Age	Int	Pts
23	HOUSTON	28	Stew Barber	OT	6'3"	242	23		
20	DENVER	23	Jerry DeLucca	OT	6'3"	250	26		
6	NEW YORK	17	Harold Olson	OT	6'3"	258	23		
21	Dallas	41	Tom Day	OG	6'2"	245	27		
14	Houston	17	George Flint	OG	6'4"	245	24		
35	SAN DIEGO	10	Billy Shaw	OG	6'3"	240	22		
14	OAKLAND	6	Al Bemiller	C	6'3"	238	23		
45	Denver	38	Frank Jackunas	C	6'3"	225	21		
28	BOSTON	28	Nate Borden	DE	6'	238	30		
40	San Diego	20	Leroy Moore (from BOS)	DE	6'	232	26	1	6
10	Oakland	6	Mack Yoho	DE	6'2"	238	26	23	
10	Boston	21	Don Healy	DT	6'3"	264	26		
23	DALLAS	14	Tom Saidock	DT	6'5"	260	30		
20	New York	3	Tom Sestak	DT	6'5"	267	26	1	6
			Jim Sorey	DT	6'4"	285	25		
			Sid Youngelman	DT	6'3"	256	30		

Use Name	Pos.	Hgt	Wgt	Age	Int	Pts
Ralph Felton	LB	5'11"	210	30		
Tom Louderback	LB	6'2"	235	28		
Archie Matsos	LB	6'	220	27		
Marv Matuszak	LB	6'3"	230	31	6	
Mike Stratton	LB	6'3"	225	20	6	
John Tracey	OE-LB	6'3"	225	28		
Ray Abruzzese	DB	6'1"	190	24	3	
Joe Cannavino	DB	5'11"	187	26	1	
Carl Charon	DB	5'10"	185	21	7	12
Jim Crotty	DB	5'11"	190	24		
Booker Edgerson	DB	5'10"	178	23	6	
Carl Taseff	DB	5'11"	193	33	2	
Willie West	DB	5'10"	193	24	3	
John Yaccino	DB	6'	190	24		
Ken Rice — Knee Injury						

Use Name	Pos.	Hgt	Wgt	Age	Int	Pts
Al Dorow	QB	6'	195	32		
Jack Kemp (from SD)	QB	6'1"	205	28		12
Warren Rabb	QB	6'1"	205	25		20
Manch Wheeler	QB	6'	190	23		
Wayne Crow	HB	6'	205	24		12
Elbert Dubenion	HB	6'	197	27		36
Carey Henley	HB	5'10"	200	23		
Art Baker	FB	6'	220	24		6
Wray Carlton	HB-FB	6'2"	220	24		12
Cookie Gilchrist	FB	6'3"	246	27		128
Willie Jones	FB	5'11"	208	22		
Glenn Bass	OE	6'2"	197	23		24
Monte Crockett	OE	6'3"	218	23		
Tom Rychlec	OE	6'3"	220	28		6
Ernie Warlick	OE	6'4"	235	30		12

NEW YORK TITANS 5-9-0 Bulldog Turner

Score	Opponent		Use Name	Pos.	Hgt	Wgt	Age	Int	Pts
28	Oakland	17	Fran Morelli	OT	6'2"	258	23		
14	San Diego	40	Alex Kroll	C-OT	6'3"	230	24		
17	Buffalo	6	Moses Gray	DT-OT	6'3"	260	24		
10	DENVER	32	Gene Cockrell	DE-OT	6'3"	247	29		
14	BOSTON	43	Sid Fournet	OG	6'	240	29		
17	Houston	56	Bob Mischak	OG	6'	240	29		
17	Dallas	20	Mike Hudock	C	6'2"	245	27		
23	SAN DIEGO	3	Karl Kaimer	DE	6'3"	230	23		
31	OAKLAND	21	John Kenerson (from PIT-N)	DE	6'3"	255	23		
31	DALLAS	52	Nick Mumley	DE	6'6"	255	26		
46	Denver	45	Lavern Torczon (from BUF)	DE	6'2"	235	26		
17	Boston	24	Bob Watters	DE	6'4"	250	26		
3	BUFFALO	20	Dick Guesman	DT	6'4"	255	26	2	
10	HOUSTON	44	Proverb Jacobs	DT	6'4"	260	27		
			George Strugar (from PIT-N)	DT	6'5"	258	27		

Use Name	Pos.	Hgt	Wgt	Age	Int	Pts
Hubert Bobo	LB	6'1"	220	27	1	
Ed Cooke	LB	6'4"	250	27	1	6
Roger Ellis	LB	6'3"	233	24		
Jerry Fields	LB	6'1"	222	23		
Larry Grantham	LB	6'	200	23	2	6
Billy Atkins	DB	6'	196	27	4	
Wayne Fontes	DB	6'	190	22	4	6
Paul Hynes	DB	6'1"	210	22	2	
Dainard Paulson	DB	5'11"	190	25	3	
Lee Riley	DB	6'1"	195	30	11	
Ed Kovac	HB-DB	6'	200	24	1	

Use Name	Pos.	Hgt	Wgt	Age	Int	Pts
Johnny Green	QB	6'3"	208	25		18
Lee Grosscup	QB	6'1"	187	25		
Dean Look	QB	5'11"	185	25		
Bob Scrabis	QB	6'3"	225	26		
Butch Songin	QB	6'2"	205	38		
Harold Stephens	QB	5'11"	175	23		
Dick Christy	HB	5'10"	192	26		48
Curley Johnson	HB	6'	215	27		
Bill Shockley	HB	6'	185	24		68
Jim Tiller	HB	5'9"	165	23		
Mel West	HB	5'9"	190	23		
Charlie Flowers	FB	6'1"	217	25		
Bobby Fowler	FB	5'11"	212	26		
Bill Mathis	FB	6'1"	220	23		18
Don Maynard	FL	6'	185	26		48
Thurlow Cooper	OE	6'4"	228	29		
Art Powell	OE	6'3"	212	25		48
Perry Richards	OE	6'2"	205	28		

HOUSTON OILERS

RUSHING

Last Name	No.	Yds	Avg	TD
Tolar	244	1012	4.1	7
Cannon	147	474	3.2	7
Smith	56	249	4.4	1
Blanda	3	6	2.0	0
Lee	4	1	0.3	0
Babb	3	0	0.0	0

RECEIVING

Last Name	No.	Yds	Avg	TD
Hennigan	54	867	16	8
McLeod	33	578	18	6
Dewveall	33	576	17	5
Cannon	32	451	14	6
Tolar	30	251	8	1
Groman	21	328	16	3
Smith	17	117	7	2
Frazier	7	155	22	1

PUNT RETURNS

Last Name	No.	Yds	Avg	TD
Jancik	14	164	12	0
Glick	12	79	7	0
Banfield	2	71	36	1

KICKOFF RETURNS

Last Name	No.	Yds	Avg	TD
Jancik	24	726	30	0
Cannon	18	442	25	0
Smith	2	37	19	0
Glick	1	22	22	0
Tolar	2	18	9	0
McLeod	1	0	0	0

PASSING – PUNTING – KICKING Statistics

PASSING

Last Name	Att	Comp	%	Yds	Yd/Att	TD	Int–%	RK
Blanda	418	197	47	2810	6.7	27	42– 10	5
Lee	50	26	52	433	8.7	4	5– 10	
Cannon	3	2	67	46	15.3	1	0– 0	
Smith	3	2	67	34	11.3	0	0– 0	
Tolar	1	0	0	0	0.0	0	1–100	

PUNTING

	No	Avg
Norton	55	41.7

KICKING

	XP	Att	%	FG	Att	%
Blanda	48	49	98	11	26	42

2 POINT XP
Cannon (1)

BOSTON PATRIOTS

RUSHING

Last Name	No.	Yds	Avg	TD
Burton	134	548	4.0	2
Crawford	139	459	3.3	2
Garron	67	392	5.8	2
Yewcic	33	215	6.5	2
Parilli	28	169	6.0	2
King	21	144	6.8	1
Lott	8	34	4.2	0
Colclough	1	14	14.0	0
Cappelletti	1	–5	–5.0	0

RECEIVING

Last Name	No.	Yds	Avg	TD
Colclough	40	868	22	10
Burton	40	461	12	4
Romeo	34	608	18	1
Cappelletti	34	479	14	5
Crawford	22	224	10	2
Garron	18	236	13	0
King	5	42	8	0
Webb	1	11	11	0
Lott	1	1	1	0

PUNT RETURNS

Last Name	No.	Yds	Avg	TD
Burton	21	122	6	0
Bruney	3	8	3	0
Buoniconti	1	8	8	0
Hall	1	0	0	0

KICKOFF RETURNS

Last Name	No.	Yds	Avg	TD
Garron	24	686	29	1
Burton	13	238	18	0
King	9	177	20	0
Stephens	2	46	23	0
Crawford	2	24	12	0
Loudd	1	15	15	0
Dee	1	14	14	0
Jacobs	1	0	0	0

PASSING – PUNTING – KICKING

PASSING

Last Name	Att	Comp	%	Yds	Yd/Att	TD	Int–%	RK
Parilli	253	140	55	1988	7.9	18	8–	3	2
Yewcic	126	54	43	903	7.2	7	5–	4
Garron	3	1	33	39	13.0	0	0– 0	

PUNTING

	No	Avg
Yewcic	68	38.7

KICKING

	XP	Att	%	FG	Att	%
Cappelletti	38	40	95	20	37	54

2 POINT XP
Crawford (1)

BUFFALO BILLS

RUSHING

Last Name	No.	Yds	Avg	TD
Gilchrist	214	1096	5.1	13
Crow	110	589	5.4	1
Carlton	94	530	5.6	2
Kemp	20	84	4.2	2
Rabb	37	77	2.1	3
Dorow	15	57	3.8	0
Dubenion	7	40	5.7	0
Jones	4	17	4.2	0
Baker	2	9	4.5	0
Wheeler	3	7	2.3	0
Henley	3	2	0.6	0

RECEIVING

Last Name	No.	Yds	Avg	TD
Warlick	35	482	14	2
Dubenion	33	571	17	5
Bass	32	555	17	4
Gilchrist	24	319	13	2
Crow	8	80	10	1
Carlton	7	54	8	0
Rychlec	6	66	11	1
Baker	3	12	4	0
Tracey	1	28	28	0
Crockett	1	14	14	0

PUNT RETURNS

Last Name	No.	Yds	Avg	TD
West	14	112	8	0
Rychlec	1	24	24	0
Taseff	4	18	5	0
Abruzzese	3	17	6	0
Moore	2	12	6	0
Sestak	2	6	3	0
Cannavino	1	3	3	0
Edgerson	1	1	1	0
Charon	0	3	0	1

KICKOFF RETURNS

Last Name	No.	Yds	Avg	TD
Jones	14	287	21	0
Dubenion	7	231	33	1
Baker	7	220	31	1
Abruzzese	10	194	19	0
Gilchrist	7	150	21	0
Henley	5	90	18	0
Flint	1	4	4	0
DeLucca	1	0	0	0

PASSING – PUNTING – KICKING

PASSING

Last Name	Att	Comp	%	Yds	Yd/Att	TD	Int–%	RK
Rabb	177	67	38	1196	6.8	10	14–	8	6
Kemp	139	64	46	928	6.7	5	6–	4
Dorow	75	30	40	333	4.4	2	7–	9
Crow	4	2	50	16	4.0	0	1– 25	
Taseff	1	0	0	0	0.0	0	0– 0	

PUNTING

	No	Avg
Crow	75	39.0

KICKING

	XP	Att	%	FG	Att	%
Yoho	20	24	83	1	3	33
Gilchrist	14	16	88	8	20	40

2 POINT XP
Rabb (1)

NEW YORK TITANS

RUSHING

Last Name	No.	Yds	Avg	TD
Christy	114	535	4.6	3
Mathis	71	245	3.4	3
Johnson	26	114	4.3	0
Flowers	21	78	3.7	0
Grosscup	8	62	7.7	0
Tiller	31	43	1.3	0
Green	17	35	2.1	0
Stephens	6	33	5.5	0
Fowler	5	27	5.4	0
West	9	16	1.7	0
Songin	4	11	2.7	0
Look	2	9	4.5	0
Kovac	3	5	1.6	0

RECEIVING

Last Name	No.	Yds	Avg	TD
Powell	64	1130	18	8
Christy	62	538	9	3
Maynard	56	1041	19	8
Johnson	14	62	4	0
Tiller	13	108	8	0
Cooper	12	122	10	1
Flowers	7	55	8	0
Richards	6	69	12	0
Mathis	6	32	5	0
Kovac	1	3	3	0
West	1	1	1	0

PUNT RETURNS

Last Name	No.	Yds	Avg	TD
Christy	15	250	17	2
Tiller	9	47	5	0
Cooke	1	11	11	1

KICKOFF RETURNS

Last Name	No.	Yds	Avg	TD
Christy	38	824	22	0
Tiller	22	462	21	0
West	3	131	44	0
Shockley	3	73	24	0
Kovac	4	72	18	0
Johnson	1	14	14	0
Cooper	1	3	3	0
Fournet	1	0	0	0

PASSING – PUNTING – KICKING

PASSING

Last Name	Att	Comp	%	Yds	Yd/Att	TD	Int–%	RK
Green	258	128	50	1741	6.8	10	18–	7	4
Grosscup	126	57	45	855	6.8	8	8–	6
Songin	90	42	47	442	4.9	2	7–	8
Stephens	22	15	68	123	5.6	0	0–	0
Christy	6	0	0	0	0.0	0	0–	0
Scrabis	2	0	0	0	0.0	0	1– 50	
Look	1	0	0	0	0.0	0	1–100	

PUNTING

	No	Avg
Johnson	50	39.9
Atkins	21	46.1
Green	3	40.3
Paulson	3	37.7

KICKING

	XP	Att	%	FG	Att	%
Shockley	29	29	100	13	26	50
Guesman	2	3	67	0	1	0

2 POINT XP
Cooper (1)

DALLAS TEXANS 11-3-0 Hank Stram

Scores of Each Game

42	BOSTON	28
26	Oakland	16
41	BUFFALO	21
28	San Diego	32
27	Boston	7
20	NEW YORK	17
31	Houston	7
6	HOUSTON	14
52	New York	31
24	Denver	3
35	OAKLAND	7
14	Buffalo	23
17	DENVER	10
26	SAN DIEGO	17

Use Name	Pos.	Hgt	Wgt	Age	Int	Pts
Jerry Cornelison	OT	6'3"	250	25		
Charley Diamond	OT	6'2"	262	26		
Jim Tyrer	OT	6'6"	290	23		
Carl Larpenter	OG-OT	6'4"	240	25		
Sonny Bishop	OG	6'2"	235	22		
Curt Merz	OG	6'4"	250	24		
Al Reynolds	OG	6'3"	235	24		
Marvin Terrell	OG	6'1"	235	24		
Jon Gilliam	C	6'2"	240	23		
Mel Branch	DE	6'2"	230	25		
Dick Davis	DE	6'2"	230	23		
Bill Hull	DE	6'6"	245	21		
Paul Rochester	DT	6'2"	260	25		
Jerry Mays	DE-DT	6'4"	247	22		

Use Name	Pos.	Hgt	Wgt	Age	Int	Pts
Walt Corey	LB	6'	220	24		
Ted Greene	LB	6'1"	230	28		
Sherrill Headrick	LB	6'2"	215	25	3	
Smokey Stover	LB	6'	235	23		
E. J. Holub	C-LB	6'4"	225	24	2	
Dave Grayson	DB	5'10"	180	23	4	
Bobby Hunt	DB	6'1"	180	22	8	
Ed Kelley	DB	6'2"	195	27		
Bobby Ply	DB	6'1"	190	21	7	
Duane Wood	DB	6'1"	200	26	4	
Johnny Robinson	HB-DB	6'	198	23	4	

Dave Webster — Injury

Use Name	Pos.	Hgt	Wgt	Age	Int	Pts
Len Dawson	QB	6'	190	28		18
Eddie Wilson	QB	6'	190	22		
Abner Haynes	HB	6'	190	24		114
Frank Jackson	HB	6'1"	182	22		24
Jimmy Saxton	HB	5'11"	173	21		
Curtis McClinton	FB	6'3"	232	23		12
Jack Spikes	FB	6'2"	220	24		7
Fred Arbanas	OE	6'3"	236	23		36
Tommy Brooker	OE	6'2"	225	22		87
Chris Burford	OE	6'3"	215	24		72
Bill Miller	OE	6'	190	20		
Tom Pennington	K	6'2"	210	22		19

DENVER BRONCOS 7-7-0 Jack Faulkner

Scores of Each Game

30	SAN DIEGO	21
23	Buffalo	20
16	Boston	41
32	New York	10
44	OAKLAND	7
23	Oakland	6
20	HOUSTON	10
38	BUFFALO	45
23	San Diego	20
29	BOSTON	33
3	DALLAS	24
45	NEW YORK	46
17	Houston	34
10	Dallas	17

Use Name	Pos.	Hgt	Wgt	Age	Int	Pts
Eldon Danenhauer	OT	6'4"	245	26		
Jim Perkins	OT	6'5"	250	23		
Jerry Sturm	OT	6'3"	245	25		
Ken Adamson	OG	6'2"	225	23		
John Denvir	OG	6'4"	245	24		
Bob McCullough	OG	6'2"	240	21		
Jim Barton	C	6'5"	250	27		
John Cash	DE	6'3"	240	26	1	
Chuck Gavin	DE	6'1"	245	28	1	
Larry Jordan	DE	6'6"	230	24		
Don Joyce	DE	6'3"	260	32		
Gordy Holz	DT	6'4"	260	28		
Ike Lassiter	DE-DT	6'5"	270	21		
Bud McFadin	DG	6'3"	270	34	6	

Use Name	Pos.	Hgt	Wgt	Age	Int	Pts
Tom Erlandson	LB	6'3"	220	22	1	
Jim Fraser	LB	6'2"	240	26	1	2
Wahoo McDaniel	LB	6'	240	25	4	
Bill Roehnelt	LB	6'1"	230	26		
Jerry Stalcup	LB	6'	230	24		
Goose Gonsoulin	DB	6'3"	210	24	7	6
Chuck Marshall	DB	6'	180	23		
John McGeever	DB	6'1"	195	23	2	6
Jim McMillin	DB	5'11"	190	24	4	12
Tom Minter (to BUF)	DB	5'10"	178	22		
Justin Rowland	DB	6'2"	190	24		
Bob Zeman	DB	6'1"	203	25	6	6

Use Name	Pos.	Hgt	Wgt	Age	Int	Pts
George Shaw	QB	6'1"	185	29		6
Frank Tripucka	QB	6'2"	208	34		6
Al Frazier	HB	5'11"	180	27		18
Gene Mingo	HB	6'1"	200	23		137
Donnie Stone	HB	6'2"	205	25		30
Jerry Tarr	HB	6'	190	22		12
Bo Dickinson	FB	6'2"	220	27		24
Johnny Olszewski	FB	5'11"	202	31		6
Jim Stinnette	FB	6'1"	230	24		6
Bob Scarpitto	FL	5'11"	195	23		36
Gene Prebola	OE	6'3"	225	24		8
Lionel Taylor	OE	6'2"	215	26		24

SAN DIEGO CHARGERS 4-10-0 Sid Gillman

Scores of Each Game

21	Denver	30
40	NEW YORK	14
17	HOUSTON	42
42	Oakland	33
32	DALLAS	28
10	Buffalo	35
20	Boston	24
3	New York	23
20	DENVER	23
20	BUFFALO	40
27	Houston	33
31	OAKLAND	21
14	BOSTON	20
17	Dallas	26

Use Name	Pos.	Hgt	Wgt	Age	Int	Pts
Jack Klotz (from NY)	OT	6'5"	260	28		
Sherman Plunkett	OT	6'4"	297	28		
Ernie Wright	OT	6'4"	265	21		
Ron Mix	OG-OT	6'4"	245	24		
Ernie Barnes	OG	6'3"	247	23		
Pat Shea	OG	6'1"	230	23		
Dick Hudson	OT-OG	6'4"	260	22		
Sam Gruneisen	LB-OG	6'1"	232	21		
Don Rogers	OG-C	6'2"	250	25		
Wayne Frazier	LB-C	6'2"	235	22		
Earl Faison	DE	6'5"	256	23	1	
Paul Miller	DE	6'2"	240	30		
Ron Nery	DE	6'6"	244	27		
Bill Hudson	DT	6'4"	277	26		
Ernie Ladd	DT	6'9"	317	23		
Henry Schmidt	DE-DT	6'4"	246	25		

Use Name	Pos.	Hgt	Wgt	Age	Int	Pts
Chuck Allen	LB	6'1"	220	22	1	
Frank Buncom	LB	6'2"	225	22	4	
Emil Karas	LB	6'3"	230	28	2	
Paul Maguire	LB	6'	223	24	1	
Bob Mitinger	LB	6'2"	222	22		
Maury Schleicher	LB	6'3"	240	25		
Bob Bethune	DB	5'11"	190	23	3	
George Blair	DB	5'11"	197	24	2	82
Claude Gibson	DB	6'1"	193	23	8	6
Dick Harris	DB	5'11"	175	25	5	
Charley McNeil	DB	5'11"	184	26	1	
Bud Whitehead	DB	6'	180	23	1	

Bob Laraba — died Feb. 16, 1962 — auto accident
Sam DeLuca — Voluntarily Retired
Paul Lowe — Broken Arm

Use Name	Pos.	Hgt	Wgt	Age	Int	Pts
John Hadl	QB	6'2"	205	22		6
Val Keckin	QB	6'4"	215	25		
Dick Wood (to DEN)	QB	6'5"	200	26		
Keith Lincoln	HB	6'2"	205	23		24
Bert Coan	HB	6'4"	215	22		
Fred Gillett	HB	6'3"	225	24		
Hez Braxton	FB	6'2"	227	26		8
Bobby Jackson	FB	6'3"	227	22		42
Jacque Mackinnon	FB	6'4"	240	23		12
Gerry McDougall	FB	6'2"	225	27		18
Lance Alworth	OE	6'	183	22		18
Reg Carolan	OE	6'6"	225	22		6
Dave Kocourek	OE	6'5"	230	25		26
Don Norton	OE	6'1"	185	24		42
Jerry Robinson	OE	5'11"	190	23		18

OAKLAND RAIDERS 1-13-0 Marty Feldman   Red Conkright

Scores of Each Game

17	NEW YORK	28
16	DALLAS	26
33	SAN DIEGO	42
7	Denver	44
6	DENVER	23
6	Buffalo	14
16	Boston	26
21	New York	31
20	HOUSTON	28
6	BUFFALO	10
7	Dallas	35
21	San Diego	31
17	Houston	32
20	BOSTON	0

Use Name	Pos.	Hgt	Wgt	Age	Int	Pts
Charley Brown	OT	6'4"	245	25		
Pete Nicklas	OT	6'4"	240	22		
Jim Norris	OT	6'4"	235	22		
Jack Stone	OT	6'2"	245	25		
Stan Campbell	OG	6'	230	32		
Dan Ficca	OG	6'1"	230	23		
Wayne Hawkins	OG	6'	235	24		
Jim Otto	C	6'2"	240	24		
Dalva Allen	DE	6'5"	245	26		
Dan Birdwell	DE	6'4"	232	21		
Jon Jelacic	DE	6'3"	255	25	1	
Riley Morris	DE	6'2"	230	25		
Joe Novsek	DE	6'4"	237	22		
Chuck McMurtry	DT	6'	280	24		
George Shirkey	DT	6'4"	255	25		
Orville Trask	DT	6'4"	260	27		

Use Name	Pos.	Hgt	Wgt	Age	Int	Pts
Bob Dougherty	LB	6'	240	28		
Charley Rieves	LB	5'11"	215	23		
Jackie Simpson	LB	6'1"	225	25	3	15
George Boynton	DB	5'11"	190	24		
Bob Garner	DB	5'10"	175	27	3	
Mel Montalbo	DB	6'1"	190	23		
Tom Morrow	DB	5'11"	180	24	10	
Rich Mostardi	DB	5'11"	188	24		
Henry Rivera	DB	5'11"	180	22		
Vern Valdez	DB	5'11"	190	26	4	
Fred Williamson	DB	6'2"	208	24	8	6

Tom Flores — Illness

Use Name	Pos.	Hgt	Wgt	Age	Int	Pts
Cotton Davidson (from DAL)	QB	6'1"	187	29		25
Hunter Enis (from DEN)	QB	6'2"	195	25		
Chan Gallegos	QB	5'9"	175	22		
Don Heinrich	QB	6'	180	30		
M. C. Reynolds	QB	6'	195	27		
Dobie Craig	HB	6'4"	200	23		24
Clem Daniels	HB	6'1"	220	25		48
Charley Fuller	HB	5'11"	175	23		
Harold Lewis	HB	6'	204	26		
Bo Roberson	HB	6'1"	197	27		44
Gene White	HB	6'1"	197	22		6
Alan Miller	FB	6'	205	24		
Willie Simpson	FB	6'	218	23		
Max Boydston	OE	6'2"	220	29		
Dick Dorsey	OE	6'3"	200	24		12
Charley Hardy	OE	6'	185	28		
Ben Agajanian	K	6'	220	43		25

DALLAS TEXANS

RUSHING

Last Name	No.	Yds	Avg	TD
Haynes	221	1049	4.7	13
McClinton	111	604	5.4	2
Dawson	38	252	6.6	3
Jackson	47	251	5.3	3
Spikes	57	232	4.0	0
Burford	1	13	13.0	0
Wilson	1	5	5.0	0
Saxton	3	1	0.3	0

RECEIVING

Last Name	No.	Yds	Avg	TD
Burford	45	645	14	12
Haynes	39	573	15	6
Arbanas	29	469	16	6
McClinton	29	333	11	0
Miller	23	277	12	0
Jackson	10	177	18	1
Spikes	10	132	13	1
Saxton	5	64	13	0
Brooker	4	138	35	3
Robinson	1	16	16	0

PUNT RETURNS

Last Name	No.	Yds	Avg	TD
Haynes	15	119	8	0
Jackson	11	117	11	0
Grayson	1	0	0	0

KICKOFF RETURNS

Last Name	No.	Yds	Avg	TD
Grayson	18	535	30	0
Jackson	10	254	25	0
Saxton	4	77	19	0
McClinton	2	32	16	0
Spikes	2	30	15	0
Haynes	1	27	27	0

PASSING – PUNTING – KICKING Statistics

PASSING

Last Name	Att	Comp	%	Yds	Yd/Att	TD	Int–%	RK
Dawson	310	189	61	2759	8.9	29	17– 5	1
Wilson	11	6	55	65	5.9	0	0– 0	
Haynes	1	0	0	0	0.0	0	0– 0	

PUNTING

Last Name	No	Avg
Wilson	47	35.8
Saxton	3	46.3

KICKING

Last Name	XP	Att	%	FG	Att	%
Brooker	33	33	100	12	22	55
Pennington	13	15	87	2	5	40
Spikes	1	1	100	0	0	0

DENVER BRONCOS

RUSHING

Last Name	No.	Yds	Avg	TD
Stone	94	360	3.8	3
Mingo	43	287	5.3	4
Dickinson	73	247	3.3	0
Frazier	39	168	4.2	2
Olszewski	33	114	3.4	0
Stinnette	21	87	4.1	1
Taylor	2	26	13.0	0
Shaw	4	10	2.5	1
Tripucka	2	−1	−0.5	1

RECEIVING

Last Name	No.	Yds	Avg	TD
Taylor	77	908	12	4
Dickinson	60	554	9	4
Prebola	41	599	15	1
Scarpitto	35	667	19	6
Stone	20	223	11	2
Mingo	14	107	8	0
Olszewski	13	150	12	1
Stinnette	13	109	8	0
Frazier	11	211	19	1
Tarr	8	211	26	2

PUNT RETURNS

Last Name	No.	Yds	Avg	TD
Zeman	5	59	12	0
Mingo	7	36	5	0
Frazier	5	32	6	0
Minter	2	1	1	0

KICKOFF RETURNS

Last Name	No.	Yds	Avg	TD
Frazier	19	388	20	0
Minter	10	227	23	0
Tarr	8	217	27	0
McGeever	5	143	29	0
Mingo	6	99	17	0
Olszewski	3	66	22	0
Stinnette	2	27	14	0
Dickinson	2	26	13	0
Danenhauer	1	11	11	0
McMillin	1	6	6	0

PASSING

Last Name	Att	Comp	%	Yds	Yd/Att	TD	Int–%	RK
Tripucka	440	240	55	2917	6.6	17	25– 6	3
Shaw	110	49	45	783	7.1	4	14– 13	
Stone	3	1	33	13	4.3	0	0– 0	
Mingo	2	1	50	18	9.0	0	1– 50	
Taylor	2	0	0	0	0.0	0	0– 0	

PUNTING

Last Name	No	Avg
Fraser	54	44.4
McDaniel	5	34.6

KICKING

Last Name	XP	Att	%	FG	Att	%
Mingo	32	34	94	27	39	69
Fraser	2	2	100	0	0	0

2 POINT XP
Prebola (1)

SAN DIEGO CHARGERS

RUSHING

Last Name	No.	Yds	Avg	TD
Lincoln	117	574	4.8	2
Jackson	106	411	3.8	5
MacKinnon	59	240	4.0	0
McDougall	43	197	4.5	3
Hadl	40	139	3.4	1
Braxton	17	35	2.1	1
Alworth	1	17	17.0	0
Robinson	2	10	5.0	0
Coan	12	10	0.8	0
Gillett	2	8	4.0	0
Keckin	1	3	3.0	0
Wood	1	0	0.0	0

RECEIVING

Last Name	No.	Yds	Avg	TD
Norton	48	771	16	7
Kocourek	39	688	18	4
Robinson	21	391	19	3
Lincoln	16	214	13	1
Jackson	13	136	10	2
Alworth	10	226	23	3
MacKinnon	9	125	14	2
McDougall	4	27	7	0
Braxton	4	17	4	0
Carolan	3	39	13	1
Coan	1	52	52	0

PUNT RETURNS

Last Name	No.	Yds	Avg	TD
Harris	7	95	14	0
Lincoln	11	94	9	0
Gibson	10	89	9	0
Braxton	1	0	0	0

KICKOFF RETURNS

Last Name	No.	Yds	Avg	TD
Robinson	32	748	23	0
Lincoln	14	398	28	1
Bethune	12	251	21	0
McDougall	3	71	24	0
Gibson	2	55	28	0
Coan	2	31	16	0
Jackson	1	16	16	0
Klotz	1	15	15	0

PASSING

Last Name	Att	Comp	%	Yds	Yd/Att	TD	Int–%	RK
Hadl	260	107	41	1632	6.3	15	24– 9	7
Wood	97	41	42	655	6.8	4	7– 7	
Keckin	9	5	56	64	7.1	0	1– 11	
Lincoln	5	2	40	43	8.6	2	0– 0	

PUNTING

Last Name	No	Avg
Maguire	79	41.6

KICKING

Last Name	XP	Att	%	FG	Att	%
Blair	31	35	89	17	20	85

2 POINT XP
Braxton (1)
Kocourek (1)

OAKLAND RAIDERS

RUSHING

Last Name	No.	Yds	Avg	TD
Daniels	161	766	4.7	7
Roberson	89	270	3.0	3
Miller	65	182	2.8	1
Davidson	25	54	2.1	3
W. Simpson	10	32	3.2	0
Gallegos	3	25	8.3	0
Enis	2	24	12.0	0
Lewis	9	18	2.0	0
Reynolds	1	9	9.0	0
Craig	1	8	8.0	0
Heinrich	1	4	4.0	0

RECEIVING

Last Name	No.	Yds	Avg	TD
Boydston	30	374	12	0
Roberson	29	583	20	3
Craig	27	492	18	4
Daniels	24	318	13	1
Dorsey	21	344	16	2
Miller	20	259	13	0
Lewis	7	53	8	0
White	6	101	17	1
Hardy	6	80	13	0
Fuller	5	67	13	0

PUNT RETURNS

Last Name	No.	Yds	Avg	TD
Garner	20	162	8	0
Lewis	9	65	7	0
Valdez	2	14	7	0
Morrow	2	13	7	0
Williamson	1	3	3	0

KICKOFF RETURNS

Last Name	No.	Yds	Avg	TD
Roberson	27	748	28	1
Daniels	24	530	22	0
Lewis	3	65	22	0
Miller	6	45	8	0
Dougherty	1	20	20	0
Garner	1	8	8	0
W. Simpson	1	7	7	0
Norris	1	2	2	0
Novsek	1	0	0	0

PASSING

Last Name	Att	Comp	%	Yds	Yd/Att	TD	Int–%	RK
Davidson	321	119	37	1977	6.2	7	23– 7	8
Enis	51	27	53	225	4.4	1	1– 2	
Gallegos	35	18	51	298	8.5	2	3– 9	
Heinrich	29	10	34	156	5.4	1	2– 7	
Roberson	6	0	0	0	0.0	0	0– 0	
Reynolds	5	2	40	23	4.6	0	0– 0	
Daniels	1	0	0	0	0.0	0	0– 0	

PUNTING

Last Name	No	Avg
Morrow	45	36.7
Davidson	40	39.2

KICKING

Last Name	XP	Att	%	FG	Att	%
Agajanian	10	11	91	5	14	36
J. Simpson	6	6	100	3	10	30
Davidson	4	5	80	1	2	50
Birdwell	0	0	0	0	1	0

2 POINTS XP
Roberson (1)
White (1)

1963 N.F.L. The Best Bet: No Bet

Commissioner Pete Rozelle dropped a bombshell when he announced that certain players had been betting on NFL games. Although none of the men had bet against their own teams, Rozelle decided that players must be above suspicion. Stars Paul Hornung of Green Bay and Alex Karras of Detroit were suspended indefinitely by Rozelle for placing a series of bets on league games, while five other members of the Detroit club were fined $2,000 apiece for betting on the championship game. Another touchy decision by Rozelle was to play the regular slate of games on November 24, a day of mourning for the assassinated President John F. Kennedy. Another tragedy was the death on May 10 of "Big Daddy" Lipscomb, one of the greatest defensive tackles of all time. He was found dead of an overdose of heroin, although many people believe that Lipscomb was drunk and was given the fatal dose after being knocked out in a robbery attempt. On the plus side, though, was the opening of the Hall of Fame in Canton, with seventeen charter members inducted.

EASTERN CONFERENCE

New York Giants—Two losses in the first five games created doubts over the aging Giants, but the team looked pleasantly ripe rather than overage by the end of the season. Winning nine of their last ten games, the Giants captured the Eastern crown for the third straight time. The New York offense, relying heavily on Y. A. Tittle's passes to split end Del Shofner, included such aged stars as Tittle, Frank Gifford, Rosey Brown, and Jack Stroud, while the defense numbered gaffers like Andy Robustelli, Dick Modzelewski, and Tom Scott as starters. But the Giants were old pros, winning all the games they needed to win and keeping their mistakes to a minimum.

Cleveland Browns—With Blanton Collier now the head coach, fullback Jimmy Brown came to camp in a much better state of mind. Brown ran wild once the regular season began, carrying the ball like a workhorse without ever looking tired. After eight games he was already over 1,000 yards for the campaign, and by the end of the season he had set a new record of 1,863 yards. Brown's running kept the Browns in the Eastern race until the Lions knocked them out one week from the end of the season. But in falling short of the title, the Browns did uncover in Frank Ryan their best quarterback since Otto Graham.

St. Louis Cardinals—Young Charley Johnson's passing was the spectacular element in the Cardinal attack, but the running game showed the greatest versatility and depth. Both John David Crow and Prentice Gautt went out with injuries, leaving the Cards without their regular running backs. To replace the injured men, coach Wally Lemm shifted Bill Triplett from defensive back to offensive halfback, and he promoted veteran Joe Childress to a starter's position after several seasons of sitting on the bench. Both runners placed in the top ten in the NFL rushing statistics and provided a fine complement to Johnson's passes to Sonny Randle and Bobby Joe Conrad.

Pittsburgh Steelers—The Steelers had played three ties during the season, so that they could win the title with the best percentage although winning fewer games than the Giants. This constitutional crisis of sorts was averted when the Giants crushed Pittsburgh 33-17. Still, the Steelers surprised most observers by getting as far as they did, relying on players whose futures seemed behind them. The attack depended on power running from John Henry Johnson and Dick Hoak, while the defense was a hardnosed outfit that compensated well for the absence of Big Daddy Lipscomb, who died tragically before the season began.

Dallas Cowboys—Although considered an outside contender for the Eastern crown, the Cowboys never got off the ground after losing their first two games. But although the defense still needed major work and the offensive line needed some shoring up, the Cowboys were still adding good young players to their core. Two rookies made good impressions, Lee Roy Jordan at outside linebacker and Tony Liscio at offensive tackle. In addition, Don Meredith assumed full-time duties at quarterback while Bob Lilly blossomed into a great defensive lineman after being shifted from end to tackle.

Washington Redskins—The long suit in the Redskin attack was the passing game, headed up by young quarterback Norm Snead. Better at the long pass than the short pass, Snead operated a long-range attack with passes to Bobby Mitchell, Fred Dugan, Bill Anderson, and rookie Pat Richter. Mitchell remained the star of the team, the most dangerous receiver in the league after he caught the ball. The running backs were slow and brittle, however, and the defense needed patching up.

Philadelphia Eagles—Winless in their last nine games, the Eagles did not even have injuries as an excuse for their last-place finish. What they could blame was poor morale on a team with better talent than the record indicated. The problems began in training camp when both Sonny Jurgensen and King Hill walked out in a joint holdout for more money. Left without a quarterback, the Eagles gave in to their demands, only to have Jurgensen bothered by various injuries during the season. Coach Nick Skorich got no production out of his fullbacks, had problems in the offensive line, and lost several mediocre defensive linemen with leg problems.

WESTERN CONFERENCE

Chicago Bears—A brutally effective defense brought coach George Halas his first championship in seventeen years. Assistant coach George Allen had installed a zone pass defense that made the Chicago unit the toughest in the league. Allowing only 10 points per game, the Bear defense grew famous around the league as it began to win games with minimal help from the offense. Doug Atkins, Ed O'Bradovich, Bill George, Joe Fortunato, Larry Morris, Richie Petitbon, and Rosey Taylor shone the brightest on defense, while the offense, led by Billy Wade, Johnny Morris, and Mike Ditka, was programmed to stick with safe running plays and short passes without any probability of interception.

Green Bay Packers—Paul Hornung was hardly missed, but the loss of quarterback Bart Starr for four games with a broken hand cost the Packers dearly. Tommy Moore and Elijah Pitts filled in admirably for Hornung at halfback, and guard Jerry Kramer handled the place-kicking duties with style. An opening 10-3 loss to the Bears was written off as a fluke, but when Chicago kept winning, first place in the West was on the line in the November 17 rematch at Chicago. By that time, however, Starr was out of action, and Zeke Bratkowski was running the Packer attack. The Bears swept the Pack out of Wrigley Field in taking a 26-7 victory, thus ending Green Bay domination.

Baltimore Colts—New coach Don Shula's regime began with five losses in the first eight games, hardly a reason for enthusiasm, but a fine stretch run served notice that the Colts were still title contenders. Shula had Johnny Unitas, Jim Parker, Ray Berry, Gino Marchetti, and some other veterans of the 1958-59 championship squads, but he also started blending in new talent of his own. Jerry Hill was promoted to starting fullback, and Tom Matte took over at halfback when Lenny Moore missed most of the campaign with an appendectomy and a head injury. Two future stars joined the offensive line when tight end John Mackey and tackle Bob Vogel, both rookies, won starting jobs in the forward wall, and two more freshmen, Fred Miller and Johnny Logan, made the defensive unit.

Detroit Lions—The suspension of Alex Karras by Commissioner Rozelle sorely hurt the defensive line, and injuries further ripped up the once impregnable Detroit defense. Three starting defensive backs went out of the lineup with injuries, Yale Lary and Night Train Lane with bad knees and Gary Lowe with a sheared tendon, and Darris McCord and Joe Schmidt stayed on the field even though below par physically. The offense received an unexpected boost when Earl Morrall developed into a first-class quarterback in beating Milt Plum out of the starting job. But the Detroit attack was not strong enough to carry the club, while the defense was no longer healthy enough to lead the way.

Minnesota Vikings—The three-year-old Vikings were quickly losing their image as an expansion club as the young men in the lineup began maturing and blending together. The Vikings won five games and tied one, with the tie coming against the bruising Chicago Bears in a key December contest. Two other games resulted in near misses for the Vikings. They had the Packers beat with under two minutes left in the game, but a ten-yard field goal was blocked by Green Bay's Herb Adderley to thwart Minnesota's bid. The Vikings also had the Colts licked until Johnny Unitas drove his team 88 yards in forty-five seconds to a winning touchdown.

Los Angeles Rams—When the Rams dropped their first five games, fans expected a repeat of last year's disastrous season. Starting in mid-season, however, the team put together an improved offense with a sturdy defense to win five of its last nine games. The offensive upswing came from the confident play of quarterback Roman Gabriel, the fine running and blocking of rookie fullback Ben Wilson, and an improved offensive line. The defensive front four of Deacon Jones, Lamar Lundy, Merlin Olsen, and Roosevelt Grier combined size and quickness, while linebacker Jack Pardee and cornerback Eddie Meador held the back lines of the defense together.

San Francisco '49ers—Abe Woodson brought three kickoffs back for touchdowns and caused so much commotion with his speed that opposing teams resorted to squib kickoffs late in the year. Woodson was the only offense the '49ers had, as the attack lost quarterback John Brodie with a broken arm, leaving the signal-calling up to journeyman Lamar McHan. The defense also suffered losses, as Charlie Krueger, Jerry Mertens, Walt Rock, and Floyd Dean all missed most of the season with knee injuries. When the team went completely flat, dissension spread through the club, and coach Red Hickey was fired in mid-season in favor of the younger Jack Christiansen.

FINAL TEAM STATISTICS

OFFENSE

	BALT.	CHI.	CLEVE.	DALLAS	DET.	G.BAY	L.A.	MINN.	N.Y.	PHIL.	PITT.	ST.L.	S.F.	WASH.
FIRST DOWNS:														
Total	257	257	252	248	230	258	209	223	**278**	203	272	254	183	244
by Rushing	95	108	**135**	105	91	114	80	97	95	78	122	105	87	81
by Passing	149	117	100	132	124	126	117	112	**164**	114	129	134	87	140
by Penalty	13	**32**	17	11	15	18	12	14	19	11	21	15	9	23
RUSHING:														
Number	396	487	460	420	415	504	405	445	453	376	**578**	423	406	344
Yards	1642	1679	**2639**	1795	1601	2248	1393	1842	1777	1438	2136	1839	1454	1289
Average Yards	4.1	3.4	**5.7**	4.3	3.9	4.5	3.4	4.1	3.9	3.8	3.7	4.3	3.6	3.7
Touchdowns	11	15	15	18	11	**22**	14	17	12	8	14	10	8	15
PASSING:														
Attempts	433	404	322	375	406	345	384	355	426	380	368	**438**	349	430
Completions	**248**	221	164	200	202	179	186	197	243	193	170	228	156	204
Completion Pct.	**57.3**	54.7	50.9	53.3	49.8	51.9	48.4	55.5	57.0	50.8	46.2	52.1	44.7	47.4
Passing Yards	**3605**	2670	2449	2799	2997	2711	2558	2687	3558	2666	3028	3403	2090	3525
Avg. Yds per Att.	8.3	6.6	7.6	7.5	7.4	7.9	6.7	7.6	**8.4**	7.0	8.2	7.8	6.0	8.2
Avg. Yds. per Comp.	14.5	12.1	14.9	14.0	14.8	15.1	13.8	13.6	14.6	13.8	**17.8**	14.9	13.4	17.3
Times Tackled	44	**20**	25	43	33	**20**	59	51	35	27	30	40	35	43
Yds. Lost Tackled	309	**177**	232	331	274	178	481	518	311	252	251	372	263	391
Net Yards	**3296**	2493	2217	2468	2723	2533	2077	2169	3247	2414	2777	3031	1827	3134
Touchdowns	20	18	27	20	26	22	11	16	**39**	22	21	30	13	17
Interceptions	**12**	14	20	21	26	21	22	17	21	31	20	21	22	34
Pct. Intercepted	**2.8**	3.5	6.2	5.6	6.4	6.1	5.7	4.8	4.9	8.2	5.4	4.8	6.3	7.9
PUNTING:														
Number	56	64	54	71	66	51	**85**	70	59	69	59	65	73	53
Average Distance	41.0	**46.5**	40.0	44.2	44.6	44.7	44.7	38.7	44.9	43.1	39.4	40.7	45.4	41.7
PUNT RETURNS:														
Number	53	30	25	23	**57**	26	31	35	40	26	31	26	18	30
Yards	485	277	285	177	**635**	229	206	405	364	226	281	166	99	391
Average Yards	9.2	9.2	11.4	7.7	11.1	8.8	6.6	11.6	9.1	8.7	9.1	6.4	5.5	**13.0**
Touchdowns	0	0	0	0	**1**	0	0	**1**	0	0	0	0	0	0
KICKOFF RETURNS:														
Number	52	26	50	48	45	46	**70**	69	46	61	49	52	62	64
Yards	1114	424	1099	1100	949	1122	1651	1556	1018	1527	1312	1070	1659	**1718**
Average Yards	21.4	16.3	22.0	22.9	21.1	24.4	23.6	22.6	22.1	25.0	26.8	20.6	26.8	**26.8**
Touchdowns	0	0	0	0	0	1	1	1	0	1	1	0	**3**	1
INTERCEPTION RETURNS:														
Number	15	**36**	22	26	24	22	19	11	34	15	25	18	14	21
Yards	174	537	343	**549**	470	312	182	200	546	210	330	383	221	357
Average Yards	11.6	14.9	15.6	21.1	19.6	14.2	9.6	18.2	16.1	14.0	13.2	**21.3**	15.8	17.0
Touchdowns	2	4	1	0	3	0	0	2	**5**	1	1	2	0	2
PENALTIES:														
Number	77	**92**	52	67	60	53	70	58	67	53	51	69	51	74
Yards	**823**	804	609	627	531	517	788	627	755	558	495	692	439	736
FUMBLES:														
Number	35	**16**	25	29	26	30	30	45	28	30	25	29	25	32
Number Lost	25	**11**	17	15	14	20	17	18	13	16	13	18	8	19
POINTS:														
Total	316	301	343	305	326	369	210	309	**448**	242	321	341	198	279
PAT Attempts	35	37	43	40	42	46	26	39	**57**	32	37	44	24	35
PAT Made	32	35	40	38	42	43	25	39	**52**	29	34	44	24	33
FG Attempts	39	33	23	20	26	34	17	24	29	15	**41**	21	31	26
FG Made	**24**	14	15	9	10	16	9	12	18	7	21	11	10	12
Percent FG Made	61.5	42.4	65.2	45.0	38.5	47.1	52.9	50.0	62.1	46.7	51.2	52.4	32.3	46.2
Safeties	**1**	**1**	0	0	**1**	**1**	**1**	0	0	0	**1**	0	0	0

DEFENSE

	BALT.	CHI.	CLEVE.	DALLAS	DET.	G.BAY	L.A.	MINN.	N.Y.	PHIL.	PITT.	ST.L.	S.F.	WASH.
FIRST DOWNS:														
Total	228	196	242	266	194	**193**	244	258	213	266	244	235	304	285
by Rushing	89	**82**	99	114	74	92	100	103	89	125	90	105	121	110
by Passing	118	96	129	139	109	**87**	126	143	106	131	132	107	168	154
by Penalty	21	18	14	13	11	14	18	12	18	**10**	22	23	15	21
RUSHING:														
Number	434	412	423	455	**405**	428	431	410	411	466	419	461	488	469
Yards	1794	**1442**	1651	2094	1564	1586	1785	1733	1669	1985	1728	1802	2076	1863
Average Yards	4.1	**3.5**	3.9	4.6	3.9	3.7	4.1	4.2	4.1	4.3	4.1	3.9	4.3	4.0
Touchdowns	16	**7**	10	12	12	11	14	12	14	17	14	19	20	12
PASSING:														
Attempts	**348**	353	408	403	378	378	379	404	368	375	384	370	450	417
Completions	181	**164**	208	202	183	180	208	233	176	211	191	180	244	230
Completion Pct.	52.0	**46.5**	51.0	50.1	48.4	47.6	54.9	57.7	47.8	56.3	49.7	48.6	54.2	55.2
Passing Yards	2589	**2045**	2718	3392	2597	2340	3025	3362	2588	3106	3400	2519	3581	3484
Avg. Yds per Att.	7.4	**5.8**	6.7	8.4	6.9	6.2	8.0	8.3	7.0	8.3	8.9	6.8	8.0	8.4
Avg. Yds. per Comp.	14.3	**12.5**	13.1	16.8	14.2	13.0	14.5	14.4	14.7	14.7	17.8	14.0	14.7	15.1
Times Tackled	45	36	29	20	45	39	27	45	**57**	29	34	41	25	33
Yds. Lost Tackled	347	311	243	161	400	327	272	364	**499**	270	299	367	210	270
Net Yards	2242	**1734**	2475	3231	2197	2013	2753	2998	2089	2836	3101	2152	3371	3214
Touchdowns	19	10	16	31	17	**9**	25	31	22	28	21	13	27	33
Interceptions	15	**36**	22	26	24	22	19	11	34	15	25	18	14	21
Pct. Intercepted	4.3	**10.2**	5.4	6.5	6.3	5.8	5.0	2.7	9.2	4.0	6.5	4.9	3.1	5.0
PUNTING:														
Number	72	73	57	50	**83**	59	61	60	71	57	66	74	55	57
Average Distance	43.5	43.2	43.7	43.2	45.5	43.4	42.5	43.9	40.4	**39.1**	44.5	40.1	43.1	44.5
PUNT RETURNS:														
Number	**19**	34	22	36	29	29	60	27	32	34	29	25	50	25
Yards	**119**	277	216	176	319	220	681	155	283	451	287	294	587	161
Average Yards	6.3	8.1	9.8	**4.9**	11.0	7.6	11.4	5.7	8.8	13.3	9.9	11.8	11.7	6.4
Touchdowns	**0**	**0**	**0**	**0**	**0**	**0**	**0**	**0**	**0**	**0**	**0**	**0**	2	**0**
KICKOFF RETURNS:														
Number	66	52	58	47	56	69	44	48	69	**31**	53	51	37	59
Yards	1520	1261	1424	1125	1206	1331	1076	1342	1816	**727**	1133	1279	816	1263
Average Yards	23.0	24.3	24.6	23.9	21.5	**19.3**	24.5	28.0	26.3	23.5	21.4	25.1	22.1	21.4
Touchdowns	**0**	**0**	1	**0**	**0**	**0**	2	3	1	**0**	**0**	1	**0**	1
INTERCEPTION RETURNS:														
Number	**12**	14	20	21	26	21	22	17	21	31	20	21	22	34
Yards	**161**	216	317	437	393	297	369	168	379	516	316	284	283	678
Average Yards	13.4	15.4	15.9	20.8	15.1	14.1	16.8	**9.9**	18.0	16.6	15.8	13.5	12.9	19.9
Touchdowns	1	1	1	5	3	1	2	2	1	1	1	**0**	1	3
PENALTIES:														
Number	58	78	63	52	57	59	63	59	66	54	78	51	73	**83**
Yards	685	718	592	479	624	568	558	621	617	598	780	577	667	**917**
FUMBLES:														
Number	32	36	13	23	24	31	25	**50**	38	23	31	32	27	20
Number Lost	17	18	10	11	11	21	13	**31**	16	15	19	19	13	10
POINTS:														
Total	285	**144**	262	378	265	206	350	390	280	381	295	285	391	398
PAT Attempts	36	**18**	30	48	32	23	43	50	39	47	36	34	51	50
PAT Made	33	**18**	29	45	30	23	39	49	37	42	34	34	50	47
FG Attempts	27	17	35	33	24	33	35	22	**14**	31	22	26	27	33
FG Made	12	6	17	15	13	15	17	13	**3**	19	15	15	11	17
Percent FG Made	44.4	35.3	48.6	45.5	54.2	45.5	48.6	59.1	**21.4**	61.3	68.2	57.7	40.7	51.1
Safeties	**0**	**0**	1	**0**	2	**0**	1	1	**0**	**0**	**0**	**0**	1	**0**

1963 NFL CHAMPIONSHIP GAME
December 29, at Chicago
(Attendance 45,801)

Shofner's Hands and Tittle's Knee

The Bears and Giants, long-time rivals in the NFL, met in the eight-degree cold of Wrigley Field to decide the league championship. The two clubs played with contrasting styles, as the Giants depended heavily on Y. A. Tittle's passes, while the Bears relied on a fierce defense to force the enemy into mistakes. The Bears, however, made the first mistake when quarterback Billy Wade fumbled the ball away on the New York 17-yard line. The Giants then marched 83 yards, with a Tittle-to-Gifford pass counting for six points. After Don Chandler added the extra point, neither team could move the ball until Chicago's Willie Galimore fumbled on his own 31. On the next play, Del Shofner got free in the end zone but had a perfect Tittle pass bounce off his frigid hands. The Bear defense then took matters into hand, as Larry Morris picked off a Tittle screen pass and ran the ball back to the New York 5. Two plays later, Wade's quarterback sneak tied the score. The Giants added three points on a Chandler field goal to make the halftime score 10-7, New York. Tittle had twisted his knee in the second quarter, and he had trouble planting his feet while throwing after that. Late in the third period Ed O'Bradovich intercepted another Tittle screen pass, bringing it back to the New York 14. Three plays later, Wade snuck across the goal line to put the Bears ahead for the first time in the game. Tittle kept throwing the ball through the fourth quarter, but the Chicago defense intercepted two passes and protected the 14-10 margin of victory.

TEAM STATISTICS

CHIC.		N.Y.
14	First Downs – Total	17
6	First Downs – Rushing	8
7	First Downs – Passing	9
1	First Downs – Penalty	0
7	Punts – Number	4
41.0	Punts – Average Distance	43.3
5	Punt Return – Yards	21
5	Interception Returns – Number	0
71	Interception Return – Yards	0
2	Fumbles – Number	2
2	Fumbles – Lost Ball	1
5	Penalties – Number	3
35	Yards Penalized	25
2	Giveaways	6
6	Takeaways	2
+4	Difference	4

SCORING

CHICAGO	7	0	7	0–14
NEW YORK	7	3	0	0–10

First Quarter

N.Y.	Gifford, 14 yard pass from Tittle PAT – Chandler (kick)	7:22
CHI.	Wade, 2 yard rush PAT – Jencks (kick)	14:44

Second Quarter

N.Y.	Chandler, 13 yard field goal	5:11

Third Quarter

CHI.	Wade, 1 yard rush PAT – Jencks (kick)	12:48

INDIVIDUAL STATISTICS

RUSHING

CHICAGO	No	Yds	Avg.	NEW YORK	No	Yds	Avg.
Bull	13	42	3.2	Morrison	18	61	3.4
Wade	8	34	4.5	King	9	39	4.3
Galimore	7	12	1.7	McElhenny	7	19	2.7
Marconi	3	5	1.7	Webster	3	7	2.3
	31	93	3.0	Tittle	1	2	2.0
					38	128	3.4

RECEIVING

CHICAGO	No	Yds	Avg.	NEW YORK	No	Yds	Avg.
Marconi	3	64	21.3	Gifford	3	45	15.0
Ditka	3	38	12.7	Morrison	3	18	6.0
J. Morris	2	19	9.5	Thomas	2	46	23.0
Coia	1	22	22.0	McElhenny	2	20	10.0
Bull	1	–5	–5.0	Webster	1	18	18.0
	10	138	13.8		11	147	13.4

PASSING

	Att	Comp	Comp Pct.	Yds	Int	Yds/ Att.	Yds/ Comp	Yards Lost Tackled
CHICAGO								
Wade	28	10	35.7	138	0	4.9	13.4	9
NEW YORK								
Tittle	29	11	37.9	147	5	5.1	13.4	7
Griffing	1	0	0.0	0	0	–	–	0
	30	11	36.7	147	5	4.9	13.4	7

1963 N.F.L. — Eastern Conference

NEW YORK GIANTS 11-3-0 Allie Sherman

Scores of Each Game		
37	Baltimore	28
0	Pittsburgh	31
37	Philadelphia	14
24	Washington	14
24	CLEVELAND	35
37	DALLAS	21
33	Cleveland	6
38	St. Louis	21
42	PHILADELPHIA	14
48	SAN FRANCISCO	14
17	ST. LOUIS	24
34	Dallas	27
44	WASHINGTON	14
33	PITTSBURGH	17

Use Name	Pos.	Hgt	Wgt	Age	Int	Pts
Rosey Brown	OT	6'3"	255	30		
Lou Kirouac	OT	6'3"	230	23		
Jack Stroud	OT	6'1"	250	34		
Lane Howell	DT-OT	6'5"	255	22		
Bookie Bolin	OG	6'2"	235	23		
Darrell Dess	OG	6'	245	27		
Ken Byers	DE-OG	6'1"	240	23		
Greg Larson	C	6'2"	245	24		
Jim Katcavage	DE	6'3"	240	28		6
Andy Robustelli	DE	6'1"	235	37		
John Lovetere	DT	6'4"	283	27		
Dick Modzelewski	DT	6'	260	32		
Bob Taylor	DE-DT	6'3"	235	23		
Al Gursky	LB	6'1"	210	22		
Jerry Hillebrand	LB	6'3"	240	23	5	6
Sam Huff	LB	6'1"	230	28	4	6
Tom Scott	LB	6'2"	220	33		
Mickey Walker	LB	6'	230	23		
Bill Winter	LB	6'3"	220	23	1	
Erich Barnes	DB	6'2"	198	28	3	
Eddie Dove (from SF)	DB	6'2"	180	26	2	
Dick Lynch	DB	6'1"	205	27	9	18
Jimmy Patton	DB	6'	185	31	6	
Dick Pesonen	DB	6'	190	25	1	
Allan Webb	DB	5'11"	180	28	3	
Louis Guy	FL-DB	6'	185	22		
Glynn Griffing	QB	6'1"	200	21		
Y. A. Tittle	QB	6'	195	36		12
Bob Anderson	HB	6'2"	210	26		
Johnny Counts	HB	5'10"	170	24		
Charlie Killett	HB	6'1"	205	22		
Phil King	HB	6'4"	225	27		48
Hugh McElhenny	HB	6'1"	190	34		12
Joe Morrison	FL-HB	6'1"	212	25		60
Alex Webster	FB	6'3"	225	32		24
Frank Gifford	FL	6'1"	190	33		42
Aaron Thomas	OE-FL	6'3"	208	25		18
Del Shofner	OE	6'3"	185	27		54
Joe Walton	OE	5'11"	200	28		36
Don Chandler	K	6'2"	210	28		106

CLEVELAND BROWNS 10-4-0 Blanton Collier

Scores of Each Game		
37	WASHINGTON	14
41	Dallas	24
20	LOS ANGELES	6
35	PITTSBURGH	23
35	New York	24
37	PHILADELPHIA	7
6	NEW YORK	33
23	Philadelphia	17
7	Pittsburgh	9
14	St. Louis	20
27	DALLAS	17
24	St. Louis	10
10	Detroit	38
27	Washington	20

Use Name	Pos.	Hgt	Wgt	Age	Int	Pts
John Brown	OT	6'2"	248	24		
Monte Clark	OT	6'6"	265	26		
Jim McCusker	OT	6'2"	245	27		
Dick Schafrath	OT	6'3"	255	27		
Roger Shoals	OT	6'4"	255	24		
Ted Connolly	OG	6'3"	242	31		
Gene Hickerson	OG	6'3"	248	28		
John Wooten	OG	6'2"	250	28		
John Morrow	C	6'3"	248	30		
Frank Morze	C	6'4"	280	29		
Bill Glass	DE	6'5"	255	27		
Paul Wiggin	DE	6'3"	245	29	1	
Bob Gain	DT	6'3"	260	35		
Jim Kanicki	DT	6'4"	270	21		
Frank Parker	DT	6'5"	255	23		
Vince Costello	LB	6'	228	31	7	
Galen Fiss	LB	6'	227	33	2	
Tom Goosby	LB	6'	235	24		
Jim Houston	LB	6'2"	240	26	1	
Mike Lucci	LB	6'2"	223	23		
Stan Sczurek	LB	5'11"	225	24		
Sam Tidmore	LB	6'1"	225	24		
Walter Beach	DB	6'	185	28		
Larry Benz	DB	5'11"	185	22	7	
Ross Fichtner	DB	6'	185	25	2	6
Bernie Parrish	DB	5'11"	195	28		
Jim Shofner	DB	6'2"	192	27		
Jim Shorter	DB	5'11"	186	22		
Bobby Franklin	HB-DB	5'11"	182	27	2	
Jim Ninowski	QB	6'1"	207	27		
Frank Ryan	QB	6'3"	200	27		12
Ernie Green	HB	6'2"	205	24		18
Charlie Scales	HB	5'11"	215	24		6
Ken Webb	HB	5'11"	205	28		
Jimmy Brown	FB	6'2"	228	27		90
Gary Collins	FL	6'4"	208	22		78
Ray Renfro	FL	6'1"	192	32		6
Johnny Brewer	OE	6'4"	235	26		
Bob Crespino	OE	6'4"	225	25		6
Tom Hutchinson	OE	6'1"	190	22		
Rich Kreitling	OE	6'2"	208	28		36
Lou Groza	K	6'3"	250	39		85

Don Fleming – killed in construction accident, June 4, 1963

ST. LOUIS CARDINALS 9-5-0 Wally Lemm

Scores of Each Game		
34	Dallas	7
28	Philadelphia	24
10	Pittsburgh	23
56	Minnesota	14
24	PITTSBURGH	23
7	GREEN BAY	30
21	Washington	7
21	NEW YORK	38
24	WASHINGTON	20
20	Cleveland	14
24	New York	17
10	CLEVELAND	24
38	PHILADELPHIA	14
24	DALLAS	28

Use Name	Pos.	Hgt	Wgt	Age	Int	Pts
Irv Goode	OT	6'4"	245	22		
Ernie McMillan	OT	6'6"	255	25		
Bob Reynolds	OT	6'6"	256	22		
Ed Cook	OG-OT	6'2"	240	31		
Ken Gray	OG	6'2"	240	27		
John Houser	OG	6'3"	242	27		
Bob DeMarco	C	6'3"	240	25		
Don Brumm	DE	6'3"	225	20		
Ed Henke	DE	6'3"	230	35		
Tom Redmond	DE	6'5"	240	26		
Joe Robb	DE	6'3"	230	26		
Fate Echols	DT	6'1"	260	24		
Don Owens	DT	6'5"	255	31		
Luke Owens	DT	6'2"	255	30		
Sam Silas	DT	6'4"	250	20		
Garland Boyette	LB	6'1"	225	23		
Bill Koman	LB	6'2"	230	29		
Dave Meggyesy	LB	6'1"	215	21		
Dale Meinert	LB	6'2"	220	30		
Marion Rushing	LB	6'2"	210	26		
Larry Stallings	LB	6'2"	225	21		
Jimmy Burson	DB	6'	180	21		
Pat Fischer	DB	5'10"	165	23	8	
Jimmy Hill	DB	6'2"	190	34	3	6
Billy Stacy	DB	6'1"	190	27	1	
Johnny Symank	DB	5'11"	180	28	1	6
Jerry Stovall	DB	6'2"	195	21	1	
Larry Wilson	DB	6'	185	25	4	12
Buddy Humphrey	QB	6'1"	197	27		
Charley Johnson	QB	6'	190	26		6
John David Crow	HB	6'2"	215	28		
Bob Paremore	HB	5'11"	190	23		12
Bill Triplett	HB	6'2"	210	24		48
Joe Childress	FB-HB	6'	200	29		24
Prentice Gautt	FB	6'	200	25		
Bill Thornton	FB	6'1"	205	23		6
Mal Hammack	OE-FB	6'2"	205	30		
Bobby Joe Conrad	FL	6'	195	28		60
Taz Anderson	OE	6'2"	200	24		
Billy Gambrell	OE	5'10"	175	21		
Sonny Randle	OE	6'2"	187	27		72
Jackie Smith	OE	6'4"	205	22		12
Jim Bakken	K	6'	200	22		77

John Wittenborn – Injury

PITTSBURGH STEELERS 7-4-3 Buddy Parker

Scores of Each Game		
21	Philadelphia	21
31	NEW YORK	0
23	ST. LOUIS	10
23	Cleveland	35
23	St. Louis	24
38	WASHINGTON	27
27	DALLAS	21
14	Green Bay	33
9	CLEVELAND	7
34	Washington	28
17	CHICAGO	17
20	PHILADELPHIA	20
24	Dallas	19
17	New York	33

Use Name	Pos.	Hgt	Wgt	Age	Int	Pts
Art Anderson	OT	6'3"	244	26		
Charlie Bradshaw	OT	6'6"	255	27		
Dan James	OT	6'4"	260	26		
Ray Lemek	OG	6'	240	29		
Mike Sandusky	OG	6'	230	30		
Ron Stehouwer	OG	6'2"	230	26		
Buzz Nutter	C	6'4"	230	32		
John Baker	DE	6'6"	270	28		
Lou Michaels	DE	6'2"	235	27	1	95
Ernie Stautner	DT-DE	6'1"	230	38		
Frank Atkinson	DT	6'3"	240	22		
Lou Cordileone	DT	6'	250	26		
Joe Krupa	DT	6'2"	235	30		
Myron Pottios	LB	6'2"	240	23	4	
John Reger	LB	6'	230	32	1	
Bob Rowley	LB	6'2"	225	21		
Andy Russell	LB	6'3"	210	21	3	
Bob Schmitz	LB	6'1"	230	25		2
George Tarasovic (to PHI)	LB	6'4"	245	34		
Jim Bradshaw	DB	6'1"	190	24	1	
Willie Daniel	DB	5'11"	185	25		
Glenn Glass	DB	6'	190	26	1	
Dick Haley	DB	5'10"	190	27	6	6
Brady Keys	DB	6'	185	27		
Clendon Thomas	DB	6'2"	195	26	8	
Ed Brown	QB	6'2"	210	34		12
Bill Nelsen	QB	6'	195	22		
Terry Nofsinger	QB	6'4"	205	25		
Dick Hoak	HB	5'11"	190	24		42
Theron Sapp (from PHI)	HB	6'1"	200	28		6
Tom Tracy (to WAS)	HB	5'9"	205	31		8
Bob Ferguson (to MIN)	FB	5'11"	220	22		6
John Henry Johnson	FB	6'2"	215	33		30
Gary Ballman	FL	6"	195	23		36
Roy Curry	FL	6'1"	195	23		6
John Burrell	OE	6'3"	188	23		
Preston Carpenter	OE	6'2"	190	29		6
Buddy Dial	OE	6'1"	195	26		54
Red Mack	OE	5'10"	185	26		18
John Powers	OE	6'2"	210	22		

Big Daddy Lipscomb – died May 10

DALLAS COWBOYS 4-10-0 Tom Landry

Scores of Each Game		
7	ST. LOUIS	34
24	CLEVELAND	41
17	Washington	21
21	Philadelphia	24
17	DETROIT	14
21	New York	37
21	Pittsburgh	27
35	WASHINGTON	20
24	San Francisco	31
27	PHILADELPHIA	20
17	Cleveland	27
27	NEW YORK	34
19	PITTSBURGH	24
28	St. Louis	24

Use Name	Pos.	Hgt	Wgt	Age	Int	Pts
Bob Fry	OT	6'4"	232	32		
Tony Liscio	OT	6'5"	240	23		
Ed Nutting	OT	6'4"	246	24		
Ray Schoenke	OT	6'3"	234	21		
Joe Bob Isbell	OG	6'1"	225	23		
Dale Memmelaar	OG	6'2"	245	26		
Lance Poimbeouf	OG	6'3"	225	23		
Jim Ray Smith	OT-OG	6'3"	245	32		
Mike Connelly	C	6'3"	242	27		
Lynn Hoyem	OG-C	6'4"	240	23		
George Andrie	DE	6'7"	248	23		
Larry Stephens	DE	6'4"	260	25		
Bob Lilly	DT-DE	6'4"	250	24		6
John Meyers	DT	6'6"	267	23		
Guy Reese	DT	6'5"	258	23		
Dave Edwards	LB	6'3"	215	24	1	
Harold Hays	LB	6'3"	235	22		
Chuck Howley	LB	6'3"	223	27	2	
Lee Roy Jordan	LB	6'2"	210	22	3	
Jerry Tubbs	LB	6'2"	215	28	2	
Don Bishop	DB	6'2"	210	28	5	
Mike Gaechter	DB	6'	196	23	3	
Cornell Green	DB	6'4"	216	23	7	6
Warren Livingston	DB	5'10"	185	25	3	
Jerry Overton	DB	6'2"	190	22		
Jimmy Ridlon	DB	6'1"	177	28		
Eddie LeBaron	QB	5'9"	170	33		
Don Meredith	QB	6'2"	200	25		18
Amos Bullocks	HB	6'1"	202	24		12
Wendell Hays	HB	6'2"	210	22		
Amos Marsh	HB	6'1"	223	24		30
Jim Stiger	HB	5'11"	190	22		6
Don Perkins	FB	5'10"	196	25		42
Frank Clarke	FL	6'	215	30		60
Gary Barnes	OE	6'4"	210	23		
Lee Folkins	OE	6'5"	220	24		24
Billy Howton	OE	6'2"	194	33		18
Pettis Norman	OE	6'3"	210	23		18
Sam Baker	K	6'2"	220	31		65

Maury Youmans – Injury
Dan Talbert – Military Service

NEW YORK GIANTS

RUSHING
Last Name	No.	Yds	Avg	TD
King	161	613	3.8	3
Morrison	119	568	4.8	3
Webster	75	255	3.4	4
McElhenny	55	175	3.2	0
Tittle	18	99	5.5	2
Killett	11	36	3.3	0
Griffing	5	20	4.0	0
Gifford	4	10	2.5	0
Chandler	1	0	0.0	0
Anderson	1	−2	−2.0	0

RECEIVING
Last Name	No.	Yds	Avg	TD
Shofner	64	1181	18	9
Gifford	42	657	16	7
King	32	377	12	5
Morrison	31	284	9	7
Walton	26	371	14	6
Thomas	22	469	21	3
Webster	15	128	9	0
McElhenny	11	91	8	2

PUNT RETURNS
Last Name	No.	Yds	Avg	TD
Dove	17	198	12	0
McElhenny	13	74	6	0
Pesonen	7	47	7	0
Webb	3	45	15	0

KICKOFF RETURNS
Last Name	No.	Yds	Avg	TD
Killett	14	332	24	0
Pesonen	8	197	25	0
McElhenny	6	136	23	0
Counts	5	107	21	0
Morrison	4	75	19	0
Webb	3	62	21	0
Dove	3	56	19	0
Guy	3	44	15	0
Scott	0	9	0	0

PASSING – PUNTING – KICKING
PASSING	Att	Comp	%	Yds	Yd/Att	TD	Int–	%	RK
Tittle	367	221	60	3145	8.6	36	14–	4	1
Griffing	40	16	40	306	7.7	3	4–	10	
Morrison	2	1	50	18	9.0	0	0–	0	

PUNTING	No	Avg
Chandler	59	44.9

KICKING	XP	Att	%	FG	Att	%
Chandler	52	56	93	18	29	62

CLEVELAND BROWNS

RUSHING
Last Name	No.	Yds	Avg	TD
Jim Brown	291	1863	6.4	12
Green	87	526	6.0	0
Ryan	62	224	3.6	2
Webb	12	58	4.8	0
Scales	2	−3	−1.5	0
Franklin	1	−10	−10.0	0
Ninowski	5	−19	−3.8	0

RECEIVING
Last Name	No.	Yds	Avg	TD
Collins	43	674	16	13
Brewer	29	454	16	0
Green	28	305	11	3
Jim Brown	24	268	11	3
Kreitling	22	386	18	6
Hutchinson	9	244	27	0
Renfro	4	82	21	1
Crespino	2	22	11	1
Webb	2	2	1	0
Scales	1	13	13	0
Ryan	0	−1	0	0

PUNT RETURNS
Last Name	No.	Yds	Avg	TD
Shorter	7	134	19	0
Green	6	79	13	0
Shofner	9	41	5	0
Parrish	3	31	10	0

KICKOFF RETURNS
Last Name	No.	Yds	Avg	TD
Scales	16	432	27	0
Green	18	394	22	0
Shorter	9	219	24	0
Franklin	2	33	17	0
Webb	1	12	12	0
Tidmore	1	5	5	0
Morrow	1	4	4	0
Benz	1	0	0	0
Shofner	1	0	0	0

PASSING – PUNTING – KICKING
PASSING	Att	Comp	%	Yds	Yd/Att	TD	Int–	%	RK
Ryan	256	135	53	2026	7.9	25	13–	5	4
Ninowski	61	29	48	423	6.9	2	6–	10	
Jim Brown	4	0	0	0	0.0	0	0–	0	
Groza	1	0	0	0	0.0	0	1–	100	

PUNTING	No	Avg
Collins	54	40.0

KICKING	XP	Att	%	FG	Att	%
Groza	40	43	93	15	23	65

ST. LOUIS CARDINALS

RUSHING
Last Name	No.	Yds	Avg	TD
Childress	174	701	4.0	2
Triplett	134	652	4.9	5
Johnson	41	143	3.5	1
Thornton	19	111	5.8	1
Paremore	36	107	3.0	0
Wilson	2	38	19.0	1
Crow	9	34	3.8	0
Stovall	1	32	32.0	0
Hammack	3	16	5.3	0
Gautt	3	5	1.7	0
Conrad	1	0	0.0	0

RECEIVING
Last Name	No.	Yds	Avg	TD
Conrad	73	967	13	10
Randle	51	1014	20	12
Triplett	31	396	13	3
Smith	28	445	16	2
Childress	25	354	14	2
Paremore	6	89	15	1
Anderson	5	47	9	0
Thornton	4	10	3	0
Gambrell	3	63	21	0
Hammack	1	15	15	0
Gautt	1	3	3	0

PUNT RETURNS
Last Name	No.	Yds	Avg	TD
Gambrell	11	111	10	0
Fischer	9	25	3	0
Paremore	4	23	6	0
Stacy	1	6	6	0
Conrad	1	1	1	0

KICKOFF RETURNS
Last Name	No.	Yds	Avg	TD
Stovall	15	419	28	0
Paremore	12	292	24	0
Triplett	14	229	16	0
Thornton	4	70	18	0
Hammack	4	60	15	0
Goode	1	0	0	0
Gray	1	0	0	0
Redmond	1	0	0	0

PASSING – PUNTING – KICKING
PASSING	Att	Comp	%	Yds	Yd/Att	TD	Int–	%	RK
Johnson	423	222	52	3280	7.8	28	21–	5	5
Humphrey	11	4	36	96	8.7	1	0–	0	
Crow	3	2	67	27	9.0	1	0–	0	
Gautt	1	0	0	0	0.0	0	0–	0	

PUNTING	No	Avg
Stovall	65	40.7

KICKING	XP	Att	%	FG	Att	%
Bakken	44	44	100	11	21	52

PITTSBURGH STEELERS

RUSHING
Last Name	No.	Yds	Avg	TD
Johnson	186	773	4.2	4
Hoak	216	679	3.1	6
Sapp	104	452	4.3	1
Ferguson	46	172	3.7	1
Tracy	29	61	2.1	1
Ballman	8	59	7.4	0
Brown	15	20	1.3	2
Mack	2	1	0.5	0
Carpenter	1	−3	−3.0	0
Nelsen	1	−6	−6.0	0

RECEIVING
Last Name	No.	Yds	Avg	TD
Dial	60	1295	22	9
Ballman	26	492	19	5
Mack	25	618	25	3
Johnson	21	145	7	1
Carpenter	17	233	14	1
Hoak	11	118	11	1
Tracy	7	112	16	0
Sapp	4	36	9	0
Ferguson	3	7	2	0
Burrell	2	27	14	0
Curry	1	31	31	1

PUNT RETURNS
Last Name	No.	Yds	Avg	TD
Keys	13	198	15	0
Haley	12	59	5	0
Thomas	6	24	4	0

KICKOFF RETURNS
Last Name	No.	Yds	Avg	TD
Ballman	22	698	32	1
Thomas	12	286	24	0
Keys	9	219	24	0
Sapp	5	58	12	0
Glass	2	46	23	0
Curry	1	27	27	0
Cordileone	1	18	18	0

PASSING – PUNTING – KICKING
PASSING	Att	Comp	%	Yds	Yd/Att	TD	Int–	%	RK
Brown	362	168	46	2982	8.2	21	20–	6	9
Tracy	4	1	25	23	5.8	0	0–	0	
Nofsinger	3	2	67	46	15.3	0	0–	0	
Nelsen	2	0	0	0	0.0	0	0–	0	

PUNTING	No	Avg
Brown	57	39.6
J. Bradshaw	2	35.0

KICKING	XP	Att	%	FG	Att	%
Michaels	32	35	91	21	41	51
Tracy	2	2	100	0	0	

DALLAS COWBOYS

RUSHING
Last Name	No.	Yds	Avg	TD
Perkins	149	614	4.1	7
Marsh	99	483	4.9	5
Bullocks	96	341	3.5	2
Meredith	41	185	4.5	3
Stiger	31	140	4.5	1
Baker	1	15	15.0	0
Clarke	1	12	12.0	0
LeBaron	2	5	2.5	0

RECEIVING
Last Name	No.	Yds	Avg	TD
Clarke	43	833	19	10
Howton	33	514	16	3
Folkins	31	407	13	4
Marsh	26	224	9	0
Norman	18	341	19	3
Barnes	15	195	13	0
Perkins	14	84	6	0
Stiger	13	131	10	0
Bullocks	7	70	10	0

PUNT RETURNS
Last Name	No.	Yds	Avg	TD
Stiger	14	141	10	0
Overton	5	32	6	0
Gaechter	2	2	1	0
Howley	1	2	2	0
Norman	1	0	0	0

KICKOFF RETURNS
Last Name	No.	Yds	Avg	TD
Bullocks	19	453	24	0
Stiger	18	432	24	0
Marsh	9	167	19	0
Hays	2	48	24	0

PASSING – PUNTING – KICKING
PASSING	Att	Comp	%	Yds	Yd/Att	TD	Int–	%	RK
Meredith	310	167	54	2381	7.7	17	18–	6	10
LeBaron	65	33	51	418	6.4	3	3–	5	

PUNTING	No	Avg
Baker	71	44.2

KICKING	XP	Att	%	FG	Att	%
Baker	38	38	100	9	20	45

EASTERN CONFERENCE – Continued

WASHINGTON REDSKINS 3-11-0 Bill McPeak

Scores of Each Game		
14	Cleveland	37
37	Los Angeles	14
21	DALLAS	17
14	NEW YORK	24
24	PHILADELPHIA	37
27	Pittsburgh	38
7	ST. LOUIS	21
20	Dallas	35
20	St. Louis	24
28	PITTSBURGH	34
13	Philadelphia	10
20	BALTIMORE	36
14	New York	44
20	CLEVELAND	27

Use Name	Pos.	Hgt	Wgt	Age	Int	Pts
Fran O'Brien	OT	6'1"	260	28		
Riley Mattson	OT	6'4"	257	24		
Andy Cvercko (from CLE)	OG	6'	243	26		
Wiley Feagin	OG	6'2"	235	26		
John Nisby	OG	6'1"	247	30		
Vince Promuto	OG	6'1"	240	25		
Fred Hageman	C	6'4"	242	25		
John Paluck	DE	6'2"	252	30	1	
Ron Snidow	DE	6'4"	245	21		
Andy Stynchula	DE	6'3"	257	24		
Ben Davidson	DT	6'8"	275	23		
Ed Khayat	DT	6'3"	245	28		
Joe Rutgens	DT	6'2"	265	24		
Bob Toneff	DT	6'3"	275	33		
Rod Breedlove	LB	6'2"	227	25	1	
Harry Butsko	LB	6'3"	220	22		
Carl Kammerer	LB	6'3"	237	26	2	
Gorden Kelley	LB	6'3"	230	25		
Al Miller	LB	6'	228	23		
Bob Pellegrini	LB	6'2"	235	28	2	
Claude Crabb	DB	6'	197	23	3	6
Dale Hackbart	DB	6'3"	208	27	1	
Ted Rzempoluch	DB	6'1"	195	22		
Johnny Sample	DB	6'1"	200	26	1	
Lonnie Sanders	DB	6'3"	200	21	3	
Jim Steffen	DB	6'	200	26	5	6
George Izo	QB	6'3"	214	26		
Norm Snead	QB	6'4"	215	23		12
Billy Barnes	HB	5'11"	195	28		36
Leroy Jackson	HB	6'	190	23		
Dick James	DB-HB	5'9"	180	29	2	36
Don Bosseler	FB	6'1"	212	27		12
Jim Cunningham	FB	5'11"	224	24		6
Dave Francis	FB	6'1"	210	22		
Frank Budd	FL	5'10"	187	24		
Bobby Mitchell	FL	6'	195	28		48
Bill Anderson	OE	6'3"	215	27		6
Jim Collier	OE	6'2"	195	24		
Fred Dugan	OE	6'3"	194	29		18
Pat Richter	OE	6'5"	230	22		18
Bob Khayat	K	6'2"	230	25		69

PHILADELPHIA EAGLES 2-10-2 Nick Skorich

Scores of Each Game		
21	PITTSBURGH	21
24	ST. LOUIS	28
14	NEW YORK	37
24	DALLAS	21
37	Washington	24
7	Cleveland	37
7	Chicago	16
17	CLEVELAND	23
14	New York	42
20	Dallas	27
10	WASHINGTON	13
20	Pittsburgh	20
14	St. Louis	38
13	MINNESOTA	34

Use Name	Pos.	Hgt	Wgt	Age	Int	Pts
Dave Graham	OT	6'3"	240	24		
J. D. Smith	OT	6'5"	250	27		
Howard Keys	OG-C-OT	6'3"	240	28		
Ed Blaine	OG	6'2"	240	23		
Bill Byrne	OG	6'	240	22		
Pete Case	OG	6'3"	237	22		
Jim Skaggs	OG	6'2"	230	23		
Jim Schrader	C	6'2"	250	31		
Jerry Mazzanti	DE	6'3"	240	23		
Bill Quinlan	DE	6'3"	250	31		
Bobby Richards	DE	6'2"	240	24		
Dick Stafford	DE	6'4"	270	23		
Frank Fuller	DT	6'4"	250	34		
Riley Gunnels	DT	6'3"	250	26		
Ray Mansfield	DT	6'3"	250	22		
John Mellekas	DT	6'3"	255	30		
Maxie Baughan	LB	6'1"	226	25	1	
Lee Roy Caffey	LB	6'3"	230	23	1	6
Bob Harrison	LB	6'2"	220	26		
Ralph Heck	LB	6'2"	220	22		
Dave Lloyd	LB	6'3"	248	27	3	
Don Burroughs	DB	6'4"	190	32	4	
Jimmy Carr	DB	6'1"	205	30	1	
Irv Cross	DB	6'1"	192	24	2	
Mike McClellan	DB	6'1"	185	24	1	
Nate Ramsey	DB	6'1"	195	22	1	
Ben Scotti	DB	6'1"	186	26	1	
Ralph Guglielmi (from NY)	QB	6'1"	195	30		
King Hill	QB	6'3"	213	27		
Sonny Jurgensen	QB	5'11"	200	29		6
Timmy Brown	HB	5'10"	190	26		66
Paul Dudley	HB	6'	185	23		
Tom Woodeshick	HB	6'	210	21		
Ted Dean	FB-HB	6'2"	210	25		
Clarence Peaks	FB	6'1"	220	27		12
Ron Goodwin	FL	6'	170	21		24
Tommy McDonald	FL	5'10"	172	29		48
Gary Henson	OE	6'3"	200	23		
Dick Lucas	OE	6'2"	215	29		
Pete Retzlaff	OE	6'1"	210	32		24
Ralph Smith	OE	6'2"	203	24		6
Mike Clark	K	6'1"	200	22		50

Mike Woulfe – Injury
Gene Gossage – Canadian Football League

WESTERN CONFERENCE

CHICAGO BEARS 11-1-2 George Halas

Scores of Each Game		
10	Green Bay	3
28	Minnesota	7
37	Detroit	21
10	BALTIMORE	3
52	Los Angeles	14
14	San Francisco	20
16	PHILADELPHIA	7
17	Baltimore	7
6	LOS ANGELES	0
26	GREEN BAY	7
17	Pittsburgh	17
17	MINNESOTA	17
27	SAN FRANCISCO	7
24	DETROIT	14

Use Name	Pos.	Hgt	Wgt	Age	Int	Pts
Steve Barnett	OT	6'1"	255	22		
Herm Lee	OT	6'4"	247	32		
Bob Wetoska	OT	6'3"	240	25		
Jim Cadile	OG	6'3"	230	22		
Roger Davis	OG	6'3"	235	25		
Ted Karras	OG	6'1"	243	30		
Mike Pyle	C	6'3"	245	24		
Doug Atkins	DE	6'8"	255	33	1	2
Bob Kilcullen	DE	6'3"	245	27		
Ed O'Bradovich	DE	6'3"	255	23		
John Johnson	DT	6'5"	260	22		
Stan Jones	DT	6'1"	250	32		
Earl Leggett	DT	6'3"	250	29		
Fred Williams	DT	6'4"	248	33		
Tom Bettis	LB	6'2"	235	30		
Joe Fortunato	LB	6'	225	33	2	
Bill George	LB	6'2"	235	32	1	
Roger LeClerc	LB	6'3"	235	25	1	39
Larry Morris	LB	6'2"	230	28		
J. C. Caroline	DB	6'1"	190	30	1	
Larry Glueck	DB	6'	190	21	1	
Bennie McRae	DB	6'1"	180	22	6	6
Richie Petitbon	DB	6'3"	205	25	8	6
Rosey Taylor	DB	5'11"	186	24	9	6
Dave Whitsell	DB	6'	190	27	6	6
Rudy Bukich	QB	6'1"	205	32		6
Billy Wade	QB	6'2"	205	32		36
Charlie Bivins	HB	6'2"	212	24		
Ronnie Bull	HB	6'	200	23		18
Willie Galimore	HB	6'1"	187	28		30
Billy Martin	HB	5'11"	196	25		
Rick Casares	FB	6'2"	225	32		6
Joe Marconi	FB	6'2"	225	29		24
Johnny Morris	FL	5'10"	180	28		12
Angie Coia	OE	6'2"	202	25		6
Mike Ditka	OE	6'3"	230	23		48
Bo Farrington	OE	6'3"	217	27		12
Bob Jencks	OE	6'5"	227	22		38
Bobby Joe Green	K	5'11"	175	25		

GREEN BAY PACKERS 11-2-1 Vince Lombardi

Scores of Each Game		
3	CHICAGO	10
31	DETROIT	10
31	BALTIMORE	20
42	LOS ANGELES	10
37	Minnesota	28
30	St. Louis	7
34	Baltimore	20
33	PITTSBURGH	14
28	MINNESOTA	7
7	Chicago	26
28	SAN FRANCISCO	10
13	Detroit	13
31	Los Angeles	14
21	San Francisco	17

Use Name	Pos.	Hgt	Wgt	Age	Int	Pts
Forrest Gregg	OT	6'4"	250	30		
Norm Masters	OT	6'2"	250	30		
Bob Skoronski	C-OT	6'3"	250	30		
Dan Grimm	OG	6'3"	240	22		
Jerry Kramer	OG	6'3"	255	28		91
Fuzzy Thurston	OG	6'1"	250	30		
Ken Iman	C	6'1"	230	24		
Jim Ringo	C	6'1"	235	32		
Lionel Aldridge	DE	6'4"	240	21		
Willie Davis	DE	6'3"	240	30		2
Urban Henry	DT-DE	6'4"	265	28		
Dave Hanner	DT	6'2"	260	34	1	
Ron Kostelnik	DT	6'4"	260	23		
Henry Jordan	DE-DT	6'3"	250	28		
Dan Currie	LB	6'3"	240	29	1	
Bill Forester	LB	6'3"	240	32	1	
Ed Holler	LB	6'2"	230	23		
Ray Nitschke	LB	6'3"	235	27	2	
Dave Robinson	LB	6'3"	240	22		
Herb Adderley	DB	6'1"	205	24	5	6
Hank Gremminger	DB	6'1"	205	30	3	6
Jerry Norton	DB	5'11"	195	33		
Jesse Whittenton	DB	6'	195	29	4	
Willie Wood	DB	5'10"	190	27	5	
John Roach	QB	6'4"	200	30		
Bart Starr	QB	6'1"	200	30		
Lew Carpenter	HB	6'1"	215	31		
Tom Moore	HB	6'2"	215	25		48
Elijah Pitts	HB	6'1"	200	24		36
Earl Gros	FB	6'3"	230	22		12
Frank Mestnik	FB	6'2"	220	25		
Jim Taylor	FB	6'	215	28		60
Boyd Dowler	FL	6'5"	225	26		36
Bob Jeter	FL	6'1"	190	25		
Jan Barrett (to OAK-A)	OE	6'3"	230	22		
Marv Fleming	OE	6'4"	225	21		12
Ron Kramer	OE	6'3"	240	28		24
Max McGee	OE	6'3"	205	31		36

Paul Hornung – Suspended by commissioner

BALTIMORE COLTS 8-6-0 Don Shula

Scores of Each Game		
28	NEW YORK	37
20	San Francisco	14
20	Green Bay	31
3	Chicago	10
20	SAN FRANCISCO	3
25	Detroit	21
20	GREEN BAY	34
7	CHICAGO	17
24	DETROIT	21
37	Minnesota	34
16	Los Angeles	17
36	Washington	20
41	MINNESOTA	10
19	LOS ANGELES	16

Use Name	Pos.	Hgt	Wgt	Age	Int	Pts
Tom Gilburg	OT	6'5"	245	24		
George Preas	OT	6'2"	250	31		
Bob Vogel	OT	6'5"	232	21		
Dan Sullivan	OG-OT	6'3"	250	24		
Jim Parker	OG	6'3"	275	29		
Palmer Pyle	OG	6'2"	250	26		
Alex Sandusky	OG	6'1"	242	31		
Dick Szymanski	C	6'3"	235	31		
Ordell Braase	DE	6'4"	242	31		
Gino Marchetti	DE	6'4"	245	37		6
Don Thompson	DE	6'4"	225	24		
Jim Colvin	DT	6'2"	255	26		2
John Diehl	DT	6'7"	285	27		
Fred Miller	DT	6'3"	240	22		
Jackie Burkett	LB	6'4"	230	26		
Jim Maples	LB	6'4"	225	22		
Bill Pellington	LB	6'2"	238	34		
Bill Saul	LB	6'4"	225	22		
Don Shinnick	LB	6'	235	28	2	
Bobby Boyd	DB	5'10"	190	25	3	6
Wendell Harris	DB	5'11"	190	22		
Jerry Logan	DB	6'1"	185	22	1	
Lenny Lyles	DB	6'2"	202	27	2	6
Andy Nelson	DB	6'1"	180	30	3	6
Jim Welch	DB	6'	190	25	4	
Gary Cuozzo	QB	6'1"	190	22		
Johnny Unitas	QB	6'1"	194	30		
Tom Matte	HB	6'	195	24		30
Lenny Moore	HB	6'1"	190	30		24
Alex Hawkins	OE-HB	6'1"	190	26		
Nate Craddock	FB	6'	220	20		
Jerry Hill	FB	5'11"	210	23		36
J. W. Lockett	FB	6'2"	230	26		6
Jimmy Orr	FL	5'11"	175	27		30
Willie Richardson	FL	6'2"	198	23		
Ray Berry	OE	6'2"	190	30		18
Dick Bielski	OE	6'1"	225	31		
John Mackey	OE	6'3"	220	21		42
R. C. Owens	OE	6'3"	195	28		
Butch Wilson	OE	6'2"	210	21		
Jim Martin	K	6'2"	230	39		104

Billy Ray Smith – Injury

EASTERN CONFERENCE—Continued

WASHINGTON REDSKINS

RUSHING

Last Name	No.	Yds	Avg	TD
James	105	384	3.7	4
Barnes	93	374	4.0	5
Bosseler	79	290	3.7	2
Snead	23	100	4.3	2
Cunningham	16	33	2.1	1
Jackson	3	30	10.0	0
Mitchell	3	24	8.0	0
Izo	3	4	1.3	0

RECEIVING

Last Name	No.	Yds	Avg	TD
Mitchell	69	1436	21	7
Richter	27	383	14	3
Bosseler	25	289	12	0
Dugan	20	288	14	3
James	15	302	20	2
Barnes	15	256	17	1
Anderson	14	288	21	1
Cunningham	8	86	11	0
Budd	5	106	21	0

PUNT RETURNS

Last Name	No.	Yds	Avg	TD
James	16	214	13	0
Steffen	5	83	17	0
Mitchell	6	49	8	0
Sample	2	45	23	0
Barnes	1	0	0	0

KICKOFF RETURNS

Last Name	No.	Yds	Avg	TD
James	30	830	28	0
Mitchell	9	343	38	0
Budd	10	252	25	0
Jackson	5	113	23	0
Cunningham	6	96	16	0
Steffen	3	84	28	0
Snidow	1	0	0	0

PASSING – PUNTING – KICKING

Last Name	Att	Comp	%	Yds	Yd/Att	TD	Int–	%	RK
PASSING									
Snead	363	175	48	3043	8.4	13	27–	7	11
Izo	58	25	43	378	6.5	3	6–	10	
Barnes	4	3	75	81	20.3	1	0–	0	
Anderson	1	0	0	0	0.0	0	1–	100	
James	1	0	0	0	0.0	0	0–	0	

Last Name	No	Avg
PUNTING		
Richter	53	41.7

Last Name	XP	Att	%	FG	Att	%
KICKING						
B. Khayat	33	35	94	12	26	46

PHILADELPHIA EAGLES

RUSHING

Last Name	No.	Yds	Avg	TD
Brown	192	841	4.4	6
Dean	79	268	3.4	0
Peaks	64	212	3.3	1
Jurgensen	13	38	2.9	1
Guglielmi	4	23	5.8	0
Dudley	11	21	1.9	0
Woodeshick	5	18	3.6	0
Hill	3	–1	–0.3	0

RECEIVING

Last Name	No.	Yds	Avg	TD
Retzlaff	57	895	16	4
McDonald	41	731	18	8
Brown	36	487	14	4
Peaks	22	167	8	1
Goodwin	15	215	14	4
Dean	14	108	8	0
R. Smith	5	63	13	1
Dudley	1	8	8	0
Woodeshick	1	–3	–3	0

PUNT RETURNS

Last Name	No.	Yds	Avg	TD
Brown	16	152	10	0
Dean	10	74	7	0

KICKOFF RETURNS

Last Name	No.	Yds	Avg	TD
Brown	33	945	29	1
Dean	16	425	27	0
Woodeshick	3	72	24	0
Henson	3	21	7	0
R. Smith	2	18	9	0
Caffey	1	6	6	0

PASSING – PUNTING – KICKING

Last Name	Att	Comp	%	Yds	Yd/Att	TD	Int–	%	RK
PASSING									
Hill	186	91	49	1213	6.5	10	17–	9	14
Jurgensen	184	99	54	1413	7.7	11	13–	7	12
Guglielmi	24	7	29	118	4.9	0	3–	13	
Brown	3	1	33	11	3.7	1	1–	33	

Last Name	No	Avg
PUNTING		
Hill	69	43.1

Last Name	XP	Att	%	FG	Att	%
KICKING						
Clark	29	32	91	7	15	47

WESTERN CONFERENCE

CHICAGO BEARS

RUSHING

Last Name	No.	Yds	Avg	TD
Marconi	118	446	3.8	2
Bull	117	404	3.5	1
Galimore	85	321	3.8	5
Casares	65	277	4.3	0
Wade	45	132	2.9	6
Bivins	44	104	2.4	0
J. Morris	1	10	10.0	0
Coia	2	2	1.0	0
Bukich	7	1	0.1	1
Whitsell	1	–8	–8.0	0
Green	2	–10	–5.0	0

RECEIVING

Last Name	No.	Yds	Avg	TD
Ditka	59	794	13	8
J. Morris	47	705	15	2
Marconi	28	335	12	2
Farrington	21	335	16	2
Bull	19	132	7	2
Casares	19	94	5	1
Galimore	13	131	10	0
Coia	11	116	11	1
Bivins	3	22	7	0
Jencks	1	6	6	0

PUNT RETURNS

Last Name	No.	Yds	Avg	TD
J. Morris	16	164	10	0
Martin	2	62	31	0
Taylor	12	51	4	0

KICKOFF RETURNS

Last Name	No.	Yds	Avg	TD
Taylor	6	118	20	0
Bull	7	105	15	0
Martin	4	99	25	0
Bivins	2	40	20	0
Galimore	1	19	19	0
Casares	2	18	9	0
Marconi	2	15	8	0
Johnson	1	10	10	0
Pyle	1	0	0	0

PASSING – PUNTING – KICKING

Last Name	Att	Comp	%	Yds	Yd/Att	TD	Int–	%	RK
PASSING									
Wade	356	192	54	2301	6.5	15	12–	3	8
Bukich	43	29	67	369	8.6	3	2–	5	
Bull	3	0	0	0	0.0	0	0–	0	
Green	1	0	0	0	0.0	0	0–	0	
LeClerc	1	0	0	0	0.0	0	0–	0	

Last Name	No	Avg
PUNTING		
Green	64	46.5

Last Name	XP	Att	%	FG	Att	%
KICKING						
Jencks	35	37	95	1	10	10
LeClerc	0	0	0	13	23	57

GREEN BAY PACKERS

RUSHING

Last Name	No.	Yds	Avg	TD
Taylor	248	1018	4.1	9
Moore	132	658	5.0	6
Pitts	54	212	3.9	5
Gros	48	203	4.2	2
Starr	13	116	8.9	0
Roach	3	31	10.3	0
Carpenter	2	8	4.0	0
Mestnik	1	4	4.0	0
Norton	2	0	0.0	0

RECEIVING

Last Name	No.	Yds	Avg	TD
Dowler	53	901	17	6
McGee	39	749	19	6
R. Kramer	32	537	17	4
Moore	23	237	10	2
Taylor	13	68	5	1
Pitts	9	54	6	1
Fleming	7	132	19	2
Gros	1	19	19	0
Carpenter	1	12	12	0
Jeter	1	2	2	0

PUNT RETURNS

Last Name	No.	Yds	Avg	TD
Wood	19	169	9	0
Pitts	7	60	9	0

KICKOFF RETURNS

Last Name	No.	Yds	Avg	TD
Adderley	20	597	30	1
Gros	17	430	25	0
Carpenter	5	75	15	0
Wood	1	20	20	0
Fleming	1	0	0	0
J. Kramer	1	0	0	0
Mestnik	1	0	0	0

PASSING – PUNTING – KICKING

Last Name	Att	Comp	%	Yds	Yd/Att	TD	Int–	%	RK
PASSING									
Starr	244	132	54	1855	7.6	15	10–	4	7
Roach	84	38	45	620	7.4	4	8–	10	
Moore	4	3	75	99	24.8	1	0–	0	
Pitts	2	2	100	41	20.5	1	0–	0	

Last Name	No	Avg
PUNTING		
Norton	51	44.7

Last Name	XP	Att	%	FG	Att	%
KICKING						
J. Kramer	43	46	93	16	34	47

BALTIMORE COLTS

RUSHING

Last Name	No.	Yds	Avg	TD
Matte	133	541	4.1	4
Bill	100	440	4.4	5
Lockett	81	273	3.4	0
Unitas	47	224	4.8	0
Moore	27	136	5.0	2
Cuozzo	3	26	8.7	0
Mackey	1	3	3.0	0
Maddock	1	1	1.0	0
Hawkins	3	–2	–0.7	0

RECEIVING

Last Name	No.	Yds	Avg	TD
Matte	48	466	10	1
Berry	44	703	16	3
Orr	41	708	17	5
Mackey	35	726	21	7
Hill	22	304	14	1
Moore	21	288	14	2
Richardson	17	204	12	0
Lockett	16	158	10	1
Hawkins	3	41	14	0
Owens	1	7	7	0

PUNT RETURNS

Last Name	No.	Yds	Avg	TD
Logan	28	279	10	0
Hawkins	17	156	9	0
Richardson	5	43	9	0
Moore	2	7	4	0
Hill	1	0	0	0

KICKOFF RETURNS

Last Name	No.	Yds	Avg	TD
Matte	16	331	21	0
Mackey	9	271	30	0
Harris	8	198	25	0
Logan	8	170	21	0
Lockett	3	52	17	0
Hill	2	32	16	0
Gilburg	3	29	10	0
Richardson	1	16	16	0
Parker	1	15	15	0
Bielski	1	0	0	0

PASSING – PUNTING – KICKING

Last Name	Att	Comp	%	Yds	Yd/Att	TD	Int–	%	RK
PASSING									
Unitas	410	237	58	3481	8.5	20	12–	3	2
Cuozzo	17	10	59	104	6.1	0	0–	0	
Matte	5	1	20	20	4.0	0	0–	0	

Last Name	No	Avg
PUNTING		
Gilburg	52	41.8
Logan	4	30.3

Last Name	XP	Att	%	FG	Att	%
KICKING						
Martin	32	35	91	24	39	62

WESTERN CONFERENCE — Continued

DETROIT LIONS 5-8-1 George Wilson

Scores of Each Game

23	Los Angeles	2
10	Green Bay	31
21	CHICAGO	37
26	SAN FRANCISCO	3
14	Dallas	17
21	BALTIMORE	25
28	MINNESOTA	10
45	San Francisco	7
21	Baltimore	24
21	LOS ANGELES	28
31	Minnesota	34
13	GREEN BAY	13
38	CLEVELAND	10
14	Chicago	24

Use Name	Pos.	Hgt	Wgt	Age	Int	Pts
Daryl Sanders	OT	6'5"	240	21		
Lucien Reeberg	OT	6'4"	308	22		
Dan LaRose	OG-OT	6'5"	250	23		
John Gordy	OG	6'3"	250	27		
John Gonzaga	OT-OG	6'3"	250	30		
Bob Whitlow	C	6'1"	236	27		
Bob Scholtz	OT-C	6'4"	250	25		
Darris McCord	DE	6'4"	250	30	1	6
Sam Williams	DE	6'5"	235	32		
Jim Simon	LB-DE	6'5"	225	22		
Roger Brown	DT	6'5"	300	26	1	
Mike Bundra	DT	6'3"	260	24		
Floyd Peters	DT	6'4"	255	28		

Alex Karras — Suspended by commissioner

Use Name	Pos.	Hgt	Wgt	Age	Int	Pts
Carl Brettschneider	LB	6'1"	225	31		
Ernie Clark	LB	6'1"	220	25		
Dennis Gaubatz	LB	6'2"	205	22	1	
Monte Lee	LB	6'4"	220	25		
Max Messner	LB	6'3"	225	25		
Joe Schmidt	LB	6'1"	220	31		
Larry Vargo	OE-LB	6'3"	215	23	1	6
Night Train Lane	DB	6'1"	200	35	5	
Dick LeBeau	DB	6'1"	185	26	5	6
Gary Lowe	DB	5'11"	195	29	2	
Bruce Maher	DB	5'11"	190	26	1	2
Dick Compton	HB-DB	6'1"	195	23	1	
Yale Lary	DB	6'	190	32	2	6
Tom Hall	OE-DB	6'1"	195	22	3	6

Use Name	Pos.	Hgt	Wgt	Age	Int	Pts
Earl Morrall	QB	6'1"	206	29		6
Milt Plum	QB	6'1"	205	29		16
Hopalong Cassady	HB	5'10"	185	29		
Larry Ferguson	HB	5'10"	185	22		
Dan Lewis	HB	6'1"	200	27		12
Tom Watkins	HB	6'1"	195	26		24
Nick Pietrosante	FB	6'2"	225	26		30
Nick Ryder	FB	6'	205	22		6
Ollie Matson	HB-FB	6'2"	210	33		
Terry Barr	FL	6'	190	28		78
Gail Cogdill	OE	6'2"	195	26		60
Jim Gibbons	OE	6'2"	220	27		6
Al Greer	OE	6'4"	190	22		

Pat Studstill — Injury

MINNESOTA VIKINGS 5-8-1 Norm Van Brocklin

Scores of Each Game

24	San Francisco	20
7	CHICAGO	28
45	SAN FRANCISCO	14
14	ST. LOUIS	56
28	GREEN BAY	37
24	Los Angeles	27
10	Detroit	28
21	LOS ANGELES	13
7	Green Bay	28
34	BALTIMORE	37
34	DETROIT	31
17	Chicago	17
10	Baltimore	41
34	Philadelphia	13

Use Name	Pos.	Hgt	Wgt	Age	Int	Pts
Grady Alderman	OT	6'2"	245	24		
Errol Linden	OT	6'5"	260	26		
Jim Battle	OG	6'2"	245	23		
Larry Bowie	OG	6'2"	245	23		
Jerry Huth	OG	6'	228	30		
Dave O'Brien	OG	6'3"	235	22		
Mick Tingelhoff	C	6'1"	235	23		
Bob Denton	DE	6'4"	240	23		
Don Hultz	DE	6'3"	220	22	1	6
Jim Marshall	DE	6'3"	235	25		6
Paul Dickson	DT	6'5"	255	26		
Jim Prestel	DT	6'5"	260	26		
Pat Russ	DT	6'4"	255	23		

Use Name	Pos.	Hgt	Wgt	Age	Int	Pts
John Campbell	LB	6'3"	215	24		
Rip Hawkins	LB	6'3"	230	24	1	
Bill Jobko	LB	6'2"	220	27		
Steve Stonebreaker	LB	6'3"	220	25		
Roy Winston	LB	6'1"	225	23	1	6
Lee Calland	DB	6'	190	22		
Terry Dillon	DB	6'	193	22		
Tom Franckhauser	DB	6'	196	26	2	
Karl Kassulke	DB	6'	193	21		
Terry Kosens	DB	6'3"	195	21		
Chuck Lamson	DB	6'	185	24	1	
Ed Sharockman	DB	6'	200	23	5	6

Use Name	Pos.	Hgt	Wgt	Age	Int	Pts
Fran Tarkenton	QB	6'1"	190	23		6
Ron Vander Kelen	QB	6'1"	185	23		
Bill Butler	HB	5'10"	194	26		6
Tommy Mason	HB	6'	196	24		54
Bob Reed	HB	5'11"	187	23		
Tom Wilson	HB	6'	204	30		24
Bill Brown	FB	5'11"	218	25		48
Jim Boylan	FL	6'1"	185	24		6
Leon Clarke	FL	6'4"	235	30		
Ray Poage	FL	6'4"	203	22		12
Paul Flatley	OE	6'1"	187	22		24
Jerry Reichow	OE	6'2"	220	28		18
Gordon Smith	OE	6'2"	215	24		12
Fred Cox	K	5'10"	205	24		75

LOS ANGELES RAMS 5-9-0 Harland Svare

Scores of Each Game

2	DETROIT	23
14	WASHINGTON	37
6	Cleveland	20
10	Green Bay	42
14	CHICAGO	52
27	MINNESOTA	24
28	SAN FRANCISCO	21
13	Minnesota	21
0	Chicago	6
28	Detroit	21
17	BALTIMORE	16
21	San Francisco	17
14	GREEN BAY	31
16	Baltimore	19

Use Name	Pos.	Hgt	Wgt	Age	Int	Pts
Jim Baeke	OT	6'5"	245	24		
Joe Carollo	OT	6'2"	260	23		
Frank Varrichione	OT	6'1"	237	31		
Don Chuy	OG	6'1"	255	22		
Charley Cowan	OG	6'4"	255	25		
Joe Scibelli	OG	6'1"	250	24		
Harley Sewell	OG	6'1"	230	32		
Larry Hayes	C	6'3"	230	28		
Art Hunter	C	6'4"	248	30		
Stan Fanning	DE	6'6"	270	25		
Deacon Jones	DE	6'5"	250	24	1	
Lamar Lundy	DE	6'7"	235	28		
Rosey Grier	DT	6'5"	290	30		
Merlin Olsen	DT	6'5"	265	22		

Use Name	Pos.	Hgt	Wgt	Age	Int	Pts
Mike Henry	LB	6'2"	220	27	5	
Cliff Livingston	LB	6'2"	215	33	1	
Jack Pardee	LB	6'2"	225	27	2	
Bill Swain	LB	6'2"	228	22		
Ken Kirk	C-LB	6'2"	225	25		
Charley Britt	DB	6'2"	185	23	1	
Lindon Crow	DB	6'1"	200	30		2
John Griffin	DB	6'1"	190	23		
Alvin Hall	DB	6'	198	30		
Bobby Smith	DB	6'	190	25	2	
Nat Whitmyer	DB	6'	183	22	1	
Ed Meador	DB	5'11"	193	26	6	
Carver Shannon	HB-DB	6'1"	198	25		6

Use Name	Pos.	Hgt	Wgt	Age	Int	Pts
Terry Baker	QB	6'3"	195	22		
Zeke Bratkowski (to GB)	QB	6'2"	203	31		
Roman Gabriel	QB	6'4"	255	23		18
Jon Arnett	HB	5'11"	194	27		12
Pervis Atkins	HB	6'1"	195	27		6
Dick Bass	HB	5'10"	200	26		30
Art Perkins	FB	6'	225	23		6
Ben Wilson	FB	6'	225	23		12
Jim Phillips	FL	6'1"	198	26		6
John Adams	OE	6'3"	235	26		
Duane Allen	OE	6'4"	225	25		
Carroll Dale	OE	6'1"	195	25		42
Marlin McKeever	OE	6'1"	235	23		
Danny Villanueva	K	5'11"	200	25		52

SAN FRANCISCO FORTY NINERS 2-12-0 Red Hickey Jack Christiansen

Scores of Each Game

20	MINNESOTA	24
14	BALTIMORE	20
14	Minnesota	45
3	Detroit	26
3	Baltimore	20
20	CHICAGO	14
21	Los Angeles	28
7	DETROIT	45
31	DALLAS	24
14	New York	48
10	Green Bay	28
17	LOS ANGELES	21
7	Chicago	27
17	GREEN BAY	21

Use Name	Pos.	Hgt	Wgt	Age	Int	Pts
Clyde Brock (from DAL)	OT	6'5"	268	23		
Len Rohde	OT	6'4"	240	25		
Bob St. Clair	OT	6'9"	265	32		
Leon Donahue	OG	6'4"	245	24		
Mike Magac	OG	6'3"	240	25		
John Thomas	OG	6'4"	246	28		
Bruce Bosley	OG-C	6'2"	240	29		
Karl Rubke	DE-C	6'4"	240	27		
Clark Miller	DE	6'5"	245	24		
Dan Colchico	DE	6'4"	236	26		
Roland Lakes	DT-DE	6'4"	273	23		
Charlie Krueger	DT	6'4"	245	27		
Leo Nomellini	DT	6'3"	262	38		
Walt Rock	DT	6'5"	240	22		
Chuck Sieminski	DT	6'4"	245	23		
Roy Williams	DT	6'7"	265	25		

Use Name	Pos.	Hgt	Wgt	Age	Int	Pts
Bill Cooper	LB	6'1"	215	24		
Mike Dowdle	LB	6'3"	237	25	2	
Matt Hazeltine	LB	6'1"	220	30		
Ed Pine	LB	6'4"	230	23	1	
Kermit Alexander	DB	5'11"	186	22	5	
Elbert Kimbrough	DB	5'11"	190	24	1	
Howie Williams (from GB)	DB	6'2"	190	26		
Abe Woodson	DB	5'11"	188	28	3	18
Jim Johnson	FL-HB	6'2"	190	25	2	

Billy Kilmer — Broken Leg
Jerry Mertens — Knee Injury
Dave Baker — Military Service

Use Name	Pos.	Hgt	Wgt	Age	Int	Pts
John Brodie	QB	6'1"	186	28		
Lamar McHan (from BAL)	QB	6'1"	205	31		
Bob Waters	QB	6'2"	184	25		
Don Lisbon	HB	6'	190	22		
Dale Messer	HB	5'10"	175	26		
Jim Vollenweider	FB	6'1"	210	23		12
Mike Lind	FB	6'2"	215	23		
Joe Perry	FB	6'	200	36		
J. D. Smith	FB	6'1"	200	30		36
Lloyd Winston	FB	6'2"	215	23		6
Bernie Casey	FL	6'4"	215	24		42
Kay McFarland	FL	6'2"	180	24		6
Clyde Conner	OE	6'2"	190	30		
Gary Knafelc	OE	6'4"	220	31		12
Monte Stickles	OE	6'4"	230	25		
Tommy Davis	K	6'	212	28		54

WESTERN CONFERENCE—Continued

DETROIT LIONS

RUSHING

Last Name	No.	Yds	Avg	TD
Lewis	133	528	4.0	2
Watkins	97	423	4.4	2
Pietrosante	112	418	3.7	5
Morrall	26	105	4.0	1
Lary	1	26	26.0	0
Plum	9	26	2.9	0
Ryder	10	23	2.3	1
Ferguson	13	23	1.8	0
Matson	13	20	1.5	0
Barr	1	9	9.0	0

RECEIVING

Last Name	No.	Yds	Avg	TD
Barr	66	1086	16	13
Cogdill	48	945	20	10
Gibbons	32	412	13	1
Pietrosante	16	173	11	0
Watkins	16	168	11	1
Lewis	15	115	8	0
Hall	3	29	10	1
Compton	2	41	21	0
Matson	2	20	10	0
Ferguson	2	8	4	0

PUNT RETURNS

Last Name	No.	Yds	Avg	TD
Watkins	32	399	12	1
Ferguson	11	108	10	0
Hall	10	107	11	0
Compton	2	11	6	0
Cassady	1	7	7	0
Maher	1	3	3	0

KICKOFF RETURNS

Last Name	No.	Yds	Avg	TD
Watkins	21	447	21	0
Ferguson	9	231	26	0
Hall	6	143	24	0
Matson	3	61	20	0
Ryder	3	33	11	0
Clark	1	13	13	0
Compton	1	13	13	0
Vargo	1	8	8	0

PASSING

Last Name	Att	Comp	%	Yds	Yd/Att	TD	Int–	%	RK
Morrall	328	174	53	2621	8.0	24	14–	4	3
Plum	77	27	35	339	4.4	2	12–	16	
Pietrosante	1	1	100	37	37.0	0	0–	0	

PUNTING

Last Name	No	Avg
Lary	35	48.9
Morrall	29	39.4
Compton	2	42.5

KICKING

Last Name	XP	Att	%	FG	Att	%
Walker	29	29	100	9	22	41
Plum	13	13	100	1	4	25

MINNESOTA VIKINGS

RUSHING

Last Name	No.	Yds	Avg	TD
Mason	166	763	4.6	7
Brown	128	445	3.5	5
Wilson	73	282	3.9	4
Tarkenton	28	162	5.8	1
Reed	21	88	4.2	0
Vander Kelen	8	65	8.1	0
Butler	17	48	2.8	0
Reichow	1	−12	−12.0	0

RECEIVING

Last Name	No.	Yds	Avg	TD
Flatley	51	867	17	4
Mason	40	365	9	2
Reichow	35	479	14	3
Brown	17	109	6	2
Poage	15	354	24	2
Reed	13	137	11	0
Wilson	7	48	7	0
Smith	6	177	30	2
Boylan	6	78	13	1
Butler	4	39	10	0
Clarke	3	34	11	0

PUNT RETURNS

Last Name	No.	Yds	Avg	TD
Butler	21	220	10	1
Reed	9	91	10	0
Mason	4	63	16	0
Kassulke	1	31	31	0

KICKOFF RETURNS

Last Name	No.	Yds	Avg	TD
Butler	33	713	22	0
Reed	13	367	28	0
Sharockman	7	139	20	0
Brown	3	105	35	1
Franckhauser	4	94	24	0
Mason	3	61	20	0
Calland	2	45	23	0
Smith	2	24	12	0
Campbell	1	8	8	0
Bowie	1	0	0	0

PASSING

Last Name	Att	Comp	%	Yds	Yd/Att	TD	Int–	%	RK
Tarkenton	297	170	57	2311	7.8	15	15–	5	6
Vander Kelen	58	27	47	376	6.5	1	2–	3	

PUNTING

Last Name	No	Avg
Cox	70	38.7

KICKING

Last Name	XP	Att	%	FG	Att	%
Cox	39	39	100	12	24	50

LOS ANGELES RAMS

RUSHING

Last Name	No.	Yds	Avg	TD
Bass	143	520	3.6	5
Wilson	109	394	3.6	1
Arnett	58	208	3.6	1
Gabriel	39	132	3.4	3
Perkins	37	70	1.9	4
Baker	9	46	5.1	0
Dale	1	12	12.0	0
Atkins	5	11	2.2	0
Meador	1	1	1.0	0
Bratkowski	4	−3	−0.8	0

RECEIVING

Last Name	No.	Yds	Avg	TD
Phillips	54	793	15	1
Dale	34	638	19	7
Bass	30	348	12	0
Arnett	15	119	8	1
Atkins	14	174	12	1
McKeever	11	152	14	0
Wilson	9	173	19	1
Adams	9	93	10	0
Perkins	8	61	8	0
Shannon	2	7	4	0

PUNT RETURNS

Last Name	No.	Yds	Avg	TD
Shannon	15	132	9	0
Atkins	12	36	3	0
Smith	2	20	10	0
Bass	1	11	11	0
Arnett	1	7	7	0

KICKOFF RETURNS

Last Name	No.	Yds	Avg	TD
Shannon	28	823	29	1
Atkins	19	429	23	0
Arnett	12	279	23	0
Whitmyer	3	80	27	0
Wilson	1	17	17	0
Perkins	1	15	15	0
McKeever	2	8	4	0
Cowan	2	0	0	0
Hall	1	0	0	0
Olsen	1	0	0	0

PASSING

Last Name	Att	Comp	%	Yds	Yd/Att	TD	Int–	%	RK
Gabriel	281	130	46	1947	6.9	8	11–	4	13
Bratkowski	93	49	53	567	6.1	4	9–	10	
Baker	19	11	58	140	7.4	0	4–	21	
Arnett	1	0	0	0	0.0	0	1–	100	
Bass	1	0	0	0	0.0	0	0–	0	

PUNTING

Last Name	No	Avg
Villanueva	81	45.4
Adams	4	30.3

KICKING

Last Name	XP	Att	%	FG	Att	%
Villanueva	25	26	96	9	17	53

SAN FRANCISCO FORTY NINERS

RUSHING

Last Name	No.	Yds	Avg	TD
Smith	162	560	3.5	5
Lisbon	109	399	3.7	0
Winston	27	127	4.7	1
Vollenweider	47	124	2.6	2
Perry	24	98	4.1	0
Brodie	7	63	9.0	0
McHan	17	59	3.5	0
Lind	8	26	3.3	0
Waters	5	−2	−0.4	0

RECEIVING

Last Name	No.	Yds	Avg	TD
Casey	47	762	16	7
Lisbon	21	259	12	2
Knafelc	18	221	12	2
Smith	17	196	12	1
Conner	16	247	15	0
Stickles	11	152	14	0
McFarland	11	126	11	1
Johnson	6	63	11	0
Perry	4	12	3	0
Lind	2	13	7	0
Winston	2	13	7	0
Vollenweider	1	26	26	0

PUNT RETURNS

Last Name	No.	Yds	Avg	TD
Woodson	13	95	7	0
Messer	5	4	1	0

KICKOFF RETURNS

Last Name	No.	Yds	Avg	TD
Woodson	29	935	32	3
Alexander	24	638	27	0
Vollenweider	4	75	19	0
Cooper	2	8	4	0
St. Clair	2	3	2	0
Stickles	1	0	0	0

PASSING

Last Name	Att	Comp	%	Yds	Yd/Att	TD	Int–	%	RK
McHan	196	83	42	1243	6.3	8	11–	6	15
Waters	88	42	48	435	4.9	1	6–	7	
Brodie	61	30	49	367	6.0	3	4–	7	
Lisbon	2	1	50	45	22.5	1	0–	0	
Davis	1	0	0	0	0.0	0	0–	0	
Perry	1	0	0	0	0.0	0	0–	0	
Vollenweider	1	0	0	0	0.0	0	1–	100	

PUNTING

Last Name	No	Avg
Davis	73	45.4

KICKING

Last Name	XP	Att	%	FG	Att	%
Davis	24	24	100	10	31	32

1963 A.F.L. Approaching Pay Dirt

Three AFL franchises found secure footing this season after three years of tenuous existence. The Dallas Texans, the 1962 league champions, defended their title as the Kansas City Chiefs, as owner Lamar Hunt tired of losing money and playing second banana to the Cowboys in Dallas. With an attractive young team, the Chiefs sold 15,000 season tickets and made money in their first season in the Midwest. On the East Coast, the New York Titans became the New York Jets and left behind the laughable image of the Harry Wismer years. New owner Sonny Werblin and new coach Weeb Ewbank could not immediately produce a winning club, but they did give the AFL a major-league operation in New York. On the West Coast, young Al Davis took charge of the Oakland Raiders and built them from doormats into an exciting club that barely missed a divisional crown. All three of these clubs enjoyed big increases in attendance, and each of them would use their new revenues to sign top rookies for next year—a cycle that could only lead upward for the league.

EASTERN DIVISION

Boston Patriots—When the television coverage of the Eastern Division playoff between the Patriots and Bills began, viewers saw not players warming up but bulldozers scraping Buffalo's War Memorial Stadium clear of snow. The Patriots had made it to this frigid showdown with a solid defense, a scrappy offense, and a clutch field-goal kicker in Gino Cappelletti. Larry Eisenhauer, Houston Antwine, and Tom Addison steadied the defense, while middle linebacker Nick Buoniconti added the spice with his frequent blitzes. Don Webb, the team's best defensive back, sat out the whole season on the disabled list, but his platoon covered for him better than the offense covered for Ron Burton. With Burton sidelined for the entire schedule with a bad back, the Patriot attack lost most of its speed. But the collapse of the Oilers, the reorganization of the Jets, and the poor start by the Bills kept the Patriots in the divisional race all season. The Patriots and Bills finished in a tie for first place, and in the winter cold of Buffalo the Patriots' old pros won the title 26-8.

Buffalo Bills—Favored by many experts to win the Eastern Division, the Bills fell flat on their face in September. Their first four games netted them three losses and a tie, dropping them into last place before they finally jelled in the month of October. Showing an ability to win close games, the Bills then took seven of their last ten games to catch Boston in a tie for the Eastern title. Quarterback Jack Kemp hit Elbert Dubenion and Bill Miller with pinpoint passes, while Cookie Gilchrist carried the running chores without much help from the halfbacks. The two leading halfbacks were knocked out with hurts, Wray Carolton with a groin injury and Roger Kochman with a leg injury that ended his career after only eight professional games. Gilchrist kept plowing ahead despite little injuries, and he set a new record of 243 yards rushing in one game, on December 8 against New York. The defense was strong up front but vulnerable in the backfield.

Houston Oilers—After three years atop the Eastern Division, the Oilers learned the hard reality of how the other half lives by falling to third place. The defending champs lost their last four straight and five of their last six games, looking more often like a routed army than like a respected football team. Injuries took a hand in the collapse, as a bad back forced tackle Al Jamison into retirement, a pulled thigh muscle kept halfback Billy Cannon on the bench most of the season, and a broken jaw sidelined defensive end Don Floyd for half the schedule. Without Jamison and Cannon, the Houston pass blocking was atrocious, subjecting thirty-six-year-old George Blanda to a rush unfit for a man his age. Cannon's absence also put the whole rushing load on fullback Charley Tolar, who got little help from rookie halfback Bill Tobin. The defense put up no pass rush without Floyd, leaving enemy passers free to spot their receivers in leisure. With all their wounded, the Oilers still managed to stay in the Eastern race until the Patriots demolished them 45-3 on November 1.

New York Jets—New general manager and head coach Weeb Ewbank completely overhauled the team, shuffling players in and out of the pre-season training camp in a steady flow. Looking to shore up the barren New York roster, Ewbank signed free agents cut loose by NFL teams. He especially pounced on players cut from his old Baltimore team, picking up from this source Dee Mackey, Mark Smolinski, Bake Turner, Dave Yohn, and rookies Winston Hill and Bill Baird. For a quarterback, Ewbank discovered Dick Wood, a strong-armed young passer cut loose most recently by the Denver Broncos. Although Wood could throw perfect long passes, his bad knees made him totally immobile, so Ewbank tailored his blocking solely to protect his passer. Billy Mathis and Mark Smolinski won starting backfield jobs on their ability

to block, and the offensive line, led by 297-pound Sherman Plunkett, shielded Wood from most enemy interference.

WESTERN DIVISION

San Diego Chargers—In winning their third Western title in four years, the Chargers fielded a backfield as exciting as any in pro football. They had a good veteran quarterback in Tobin Rote, back in the United States after three seasons in the Canadian League, and a good young quarterback in John Hadl. For runners they had Paul Lowe and Keith Lincoln, both quick, slashing runners who could get through the smallest openings in the line. The flanker was Lance Alworth, who came back from an injury-plagued rookie season to tantalize crowds with his leaping grabs and streaking deep patterns. With these talents operating behind a solid line, the San Diego offense put more points on the board than any other attack in the league, but coach Sid Gillman's riches did not end there. The defense also was both colorful and efficient, with Earl Faison, Ernie Ladd, Chuck Allen, and Dick Harris the stars of the unit. Avoiding the string of injuries that ruined the past season, the Chargers found their greatest challenge for the divisional crown not from the defending champion Kansas City team but instead from the surprising Oakland Raiders. Twice the Raiders beat the Chargers, pulling within one game of the top with a 41-27 victory with two weeks left in the season, but the Chargers won both their remaining contests to salt away the championship.

Oakland Raiders—Leaving a comfortable assistantship in San Diego to take over as head coach in Oakland, Al Davis blended holdovers from the disastrous 1962 season with free agents cut loose by other clubs and came up with an exciting team. Davis signed split end Art Powell, who had played out his option in New York, got Tom Flores back from illness, and coaxed several useful players away from other teams at a minimal cost. The offense relied on the passing of quarterbacks Flores and Cotton Davidson to receivers Powell and Bo Roberson and on the running of Clem Daniels to pile up points. Daniels combined speed and power to set a new AFL rushing record with 1,099 yards, and he was also a dangerous deep pass receiving threat coming out of the backfield. The defense had few recognizable names, but terrorized opponents with a dazzling array of blitzes. End Dalva Allen and rookie tackle Dave Costa anchored the forward wall, ex-Bill Archie Matsos starred at middle linebacker, and holdover backs Fred Williamson and Tom Morrow prospered in Davis' new setup. After starting out the season with two wins, the Raiders lost four straight games to Eastern opponents, but then the miracle began. Oakland started winning and never stopped, taking their last eight contests to finish one game behind the Chargers.

Kansas City Chiefs—A fatal injury to rookie Stone Johnson in a pre-season game started the Chiefs' season on a foreboding note and dampened the club's enthusiasm. After beating Denver 59-7 to open the season, the Chiefs then won only once in their next ten games. The defense, bolstered by rookies Buck Buchanan and Bobby Bell, stayed tough, but a breakdown in blocking short-circuited the offense. Enemy defenses constantly rushed quarterback Len Dawson with blitzes that his blockers could not pick up, and backs Curtis McClinton and Abner Haynes both fell off from their 1963 performances. Haynes, the AFL's first star, slipped so much that he was restricted to returning kicks for a time. The mid-season drought ended any hopes of repeating as Western champions, and the Chiefs hit the bottom when the New York Jets shut them out 17-0 in a November meeting in New York. After that point, however, the Chiefs put the abundant talent on their roster to full use as they won their last three games.

Denver Broncos—When the Broncos at last uncovered a major-league runner, their passing attack fell apart. The Broncos had always lived and died on the passing of Frank Tripuka, relying on the air game to overcome the lack of any ground attack. Rookie fullback Billy Joe gave the club its first running threat, someone who could break tackles and pick up vital first-down yardage, but Tripuka's arm was no longer up to the weekly strain. After two games, both of which the Broncos lost, Tripuka quit, leaving rookie Mickey Slaughter the only quarterback on the roster. Coach Jack Faulkner then signed ex-Viking John McCormick, and after only four days of practice with the team McCormick led the Broncs to a 14-0 victory over Boston. Next came a 50-34 ambushing of the San Diego Chargers, in which McCormick directed the Denver offense with the precision of a surgeon. With better days obviously on the way, the Broncos suffered a loss from which they never recovered when the Houston Oilers tore up McCormick's knee on the way to a 33-24 victory.

FINAL TEAM STATISTICS
Note: Only offensive totals are available

	BOSTON	BUFFALO	DENVER	HOUSTON	KANSAS CITY	NEW YORK	OAKLAND	SAN DIEGO
FIRST DOWNS:								
by Rushing	100	107	84	68	94	52	85	112
by Passing	107	147	133	169	141	121	142	124
RUSHING:								
Number	437	455	384	341	400	306	359	395
Yards	1618	1838	1508	1209	1697	969	1595	2201
Average Yards	3.7	4.0	3.9	3.5	4.2	3.2	4.4	5.6
Touchdowns	17	21	10	11	12	8	11	20
PASSING:								
Attempts	410	457	453	501	439	480	442	358
Completions	184	228	217	261	231	209	191	202
Percentage	44.9	49.9	47.9	52.1	52.6	43.5	43.2	56.4
Net Yards	2547	3057	2487	3210	2651	2530	2926	2950
Touchdowns	17	16	23	26	30	21	31	28
Interceptions	29	24	28	33	22	29	24	24
Percent Intercepted	7.1	5.3	6.2	6.6	5.0	6.0	5.4	6.7
PUNTING:								
Number	75	62	81	65	62	72	76	61
Average Distance	38.4	40.2	44.3	42.9	43.1	42.1	39.5	37.9
PUNT RETURNS:								
Number	40	37	30	36	26	17	36	22
Yards	373	316	387	339	259	202	395	261
Average Yards	9.3	8.5	12.9	9.4	10.0	11.9	11.0	11.9
Touchdowns	0	0	0	0	0	1	2	0
KICKOFF RETURNS:								
Number	52	52	78	69	47	74	53	52
Yards	1109	1133	1801	1821	1172	1463	1008	1168
Average Yards	21.3	21.8	23.1	26.4	24.9	19.8	19.0	22.5
Touchdowns	0	0	0	1	0	0	0	0
INTERCEPTION RETURNS:								
Number	30	22	15	36	26	21	35	29
Yards	662	156	170	453	450	284	389	316
Average Yards	22.1	7.1	11.3	12.6	17.3	13.5	11.1	10.9
Touchdowns	3	1	1	2	1	0	2	1
POINTS:								
Total	327	304	301	302	347	249	363	399
PAT (kick) Attempts	36	37	35	39	44	30	47	48
PAT (kick) Made	35	32	35	39	43	30	47	44
PAT (2-pt) Attempts	1	2	1	0	1	2	1	2
PAT (2-pt) Made	0	2	1	0	1	0	0	2
FG Attempts	38	23	30	22	28	24	19	27
FG Made	22	10	16	9	8	9	8	17
Percent FG Made	57.9	43.5	53.3	40.9	28.6	37.5	42.1	63.0
Safeties	2	2	0	0	1	0	2	0

1963 AFL CHAMPIONSHIP GAME
January 5, at San Diego
(Attendance 30,127)

Boston's Buttery Defense

SCORING

```
SAN DIEGO   21  10   7  13—51
BOSTON       7   3   0   0—10
```

First Quarter
S.D. Rote, 2 yard rush
      PAT—Blair (kick)
S.D. Lincoln, 67 yard rush
      PAT—Blair (kick)
Bos. Garron, 7 yard rush
      PAT—Cappelletti (kick)
S.D. Lowe, 58 yard rush
      PAT—Blair (kick)

Second Quarter
S.D. Blair, 11 yard field goal
Bos. Cappelletti, 15 yard field goal
S.D. Norton, 14 yard pass from Rote
      PAT—Blair (kick)

Third Quarter
S.D. Alworth, 48 yard pass from Rote
      PAT—Blair (kick)

Fourth Quarter
S.D. Lincoln, 25 yard pass from Hadl
      PAT—Pass (No Good)
S.D. Hadl, 1 yard rush
      PAT—Blair (kick)

TEAM STATISTICS

S.D.		BOS.
21	First Downs—Total	14
11	First Downs—Rushing	6
9	First Downs—Passing	8
1	First Downs—Penalty	0
1	Fumbles—Number	1
1	Fumbles—Lost Ball	0
6	Penalties—Number	1
30	Yards Penalized	18
1	Giveaways	2
2	Takeaways	1
+1	Difference	—1

In the fourth AFL championship game, San Diego's famous offense made mincemeat out of Boston's heralded defense. On the second play from scrimmage of the game, Keith Lincoln took a handoff and burst through the middle of the Boston defense for a 56-yard gain; Tobin Rote's quarterback sneak seven plays later gave San Diego a quick 7-0 lead. As soon as the Chargers got the ball back, Lincoln headed around end for a 67-yard touchdown run, making the score 14-0. The Patriots came back with a quick touchdown, but a 58-yard touchdown run by Paul Lowe, the third long run of the first quarter for the Chargers, made the score 21-7. George Blair and Gino Cappelletti exchanged field goals early in the second quarter, but Don Norton scored on a 14-yard pass play to give the Chargers a 31-10 lead at halftime. The Patriot attack got nowhere in the second half, as the San Diego line rushed quarterback Babe Parilli ferociously every time he dropped back to pass. The Chargers, however, kept adding points against the Boston defense. Lance Alworth, the Chargers' chief pass receiver, scored in the third period on a 48-yard pass from Rote, and Lincoln added his third touchdown on a 25-yard pass from reserve quarterback John Hadl in the fourth quarter. Hadl then scored on a one-yard plunge with less than two minutes remaining in the game, and George Blair's kick made the final score a lopsided 51-10. Although not even close, the game helped the AFL by showcasing an exciting offensive team in the Chargers, a direct contrast with the defense-oriented NFL champions, the Chicago Bears.

INDIVIDUAL STATISTICS

RUSHING

SAN DIEGO	No	Yds	Avg.	BOSTON	No	Yds	Avg.
Lincoln	13	206	15.8	Crump	7	18	2.6
Lowe	12	94	7.8	Garron	3	15	5.0
Rote	4	15	3.8	Lott	3	15	5.0
McDougall	1	2	2.0	Yewcic	1	14	14.0
Hadl	1	1	1.0	Parilli	1	10	10.0
Jackson	1	0	0.0	Burton	3	3	3.0
	32	218	6.8		16	75	4.7

RECEIVING

SAN DIEGO	No	Yds	Avg.	BOSTON	No	Yds	Avg.
Lincoln	7	123	17.6	Burton	4	12	3.0
Alworth	4	77	19.3	Colclough	3	26	8.7
MacKinnon	2	52	26.0	Cappelletti	2	72	36.0
Norton	2	44	22.0	Graham	2	68	34.0
Kocourek	1	5	5.0	Crump	2	28	14.0
McDougall	1	4	4.0	Lott	2	16	8.0
	17	305	17.9	Garron	2	6	3.0
					17	228	13.4

PUNTING

SAN DIEGO	No	Yds	Avg.	BOSTON	No	Yds	Avg.
Maguire	2		43.5	Yewcic	7		46.9

KICKOFF RETURNS

SAN DIEGO	No	Yds	Avg.	BOSTON	No	Yds	Avg.
Alworth	2	47	23.5	Crump	2	31	15.5
Lowe	1	23	23.0	Burton	2	27	13.5
	3	70	23.3	Garron	2	22	11.0
				Suci	1	18	18.0
				Romeo	1	9	9.0
				Yates	1	5	5.0
					9	112	12.4

INTERCEPTION RETURNS

SAN DIEGO	No	Yds	Avg.	BOSTON	
Maguire	1	10	10.0	None	
Mitinger	1	5	5.0		
	2	15	7.5		

PASSING

SAN DIEGO	Att.	Comp.	Comp. Pct.	Yds.	Int.	Yds/ Att.	Yds/ Comp.
Rote	15	10	66.7	173	0	11.5	17.3
Hadl	10	6	60.0	112	0	11.2	18.7
Lincoln	1	1	100.0	20	0	20.0	20.0
	26	17	65.4	305	0	11.7	17.9

BOSTON	Att.	Comp.	Comp. Pct.	Yds.	Int.	Yds/ Att.	Yds/ Comp.
Parilli	29	14	48.3	189	1	6.5	13.5
Yewcic	8	3	37.5	39	1	4.9	13.0
	37	17	45.9	228	2	6.2	13.4

BOSTON PATRIOTS 7-6-1 Mike Holovak

Scores of Each Game

38	NEW YORK	14
13	San Diego	17
20	Oakland	14
10	Denver	14
24	New York	31
20	OAKLAND	14
40	DENVER	21
21	Buffalo	28
45	HOUSTON	3
6	SAN DIEGO	7
24	KANSAS CITY	24
17	BUFFALO	7
46	Houston	28
3	Kansas City	35
	EAST Playoff	
26	Buffalo	8

Use Name	Pos.	Hgt	Wgt	Age	Int	Pts
Don Oakes	OT	6'3"	255	25		
Bob Yates	OT	6'3"	230	24		
Charley Long	OG	6'3"	250	25		
Billy Neighbors	OG	5'11"	240	23		
Dave Watson	OG	6'1"	220	22		
Walt Cudzik	C	6'2"	235	30		
Bob Dee	DE	6'3"	240	30		
Larry Eisenhauer	DE	6'5"	245	23	1	
Jim Hunt	DE	5'11"	245	24	1	6
Houston Antwine	DT	6'	250	24		
Jerry DeLucca (from BUF)	DT	6'3"	250	27		
Milt Graham	DT	6'6"	235	29		
Bill Hudson	DT	6'4"	255	27		
Jess Richardson	DT	6'2"	265	33		

Use Name	Pos.	Hgt	Wgt	Age	Int	Pts
Tom Addison	LB	6'3"	230	27	4	
Nick Buoniconti	LB	5'11"	220	22	3	
Don McKinnon	LB	6'3"	215	21		
Jack Rudolph	LB	6'3"	230	25		
Dick Felt	DB	6'	185	30	3	
Ron Hall	DB	6'	190	26	3	
Ross O'Hanley	DB	6'	185	24	3	
Chuck Shonta	DB	6'	200	25	3	
Bob Suci	DB	5'10"	185	25	8	12
Tom Stephens	OE-DB	6'1"	215	27	1	

Don Webb — Injury

Use Name	Pos.	Hgt	Wgt	Age	Int	Pts
Babe Parilli	QB	6'1"	190	33		30
Tom Yewcic	QB	5'11"	185	31		6
*Ron Burton	HB	5'10"	190	26		
Jim Crawford	HB	6'1"	200	27		6
Tom Neumann	HB	5'11"	205	22		6
Harry Crump	FB	6'	205	22		30
Larry Garron	FB	6'	215	26		24
Billy Lott	FB	6'	205	28		24
Jim Colclough	FL	6'	185	27		18
Gino Cappelletti	OE	6'	190	29		113
Art Graham	OE	6'1"	205	22		30
Tony Romeo	OE	6'2"	220	24		18

*Played only in playoffs

BUFFALO BILLS 7-6-1 Lou Saban

Scores of Each Game

10	San Diego	14
17	Oakland	35
27	KANSAS CITY	27
20	HOUSTON	31
12	OAKLAND	0
35	Kansas City	26
14	Houston	28
28	BOSTON	21
30	Denver	28
27	DENVER	17
13	SAN DIEGO	23
7	Boston	17
45	NEW YORK	14
19	New York	10
	EAST Playoff	
8	BOSTON	26

Use Name	Pos.	Hgt	Wgt	Age	Int	Pts
Stew Barber	OT	6'3"	250	24		
Dave Behrman	OT	6'5"	260	21		
Ken Rice	OG-OT	6'2"	250	23		
Tom Day	OG	6'2"	262	28		
George Flint	OG	6'4"	246	25		
Dick Hudson	OG	6'4"	264	23		
Charlie Leo	OG	6'	240	28		
Billy Shaw	OG	6'3"	250	23		
Al Bemiller	C	6'3"	235	24		
Ron McDole	DE	6'3"	250	23		
Leroy Moore	DE	6'	232	27		
Mack Yoho	DE	6'2"	238	27		62
Jim Dunaway	DT	6'4"	270	21		
Tom Sestak	DT	6'4"	270	27		
Sid Youngelman	DT	6'3"	260	31		

Use Name	Pos.	Hgt	Wgt	Age	Int	Pts
Harry Jacobs	LB	6'2"	230	26	1	
Marv Matuszak	LB	6'3"	230	32		
Herb Paterra	LB	6'1"	222	22		
Mike Stratton	LB	6'3"	230	21	3	6
John Tracey	LB	6'3"	225	29	5	2
Ray Abruzzese	DB	5'10"	194	22		6
Carl Charon	DB	6'1"	194	25	3	
Booker Edgerson	DB	5'10"	177	24	1	
Henry Rivera	DB	5'11"	180	23		
Gene Sykes	DB	6'1"	200	22		
Willie West	DB	6'	193	25	5	
George Saimes	HB-DB	5'10"	192	21	4	

Use Name	Pos.	Hgt	Wgt	Age	Int	Pts
Jack Kemp	QB	6'1"	200	29		48
Daryle Lamonica	QB	6'2"	216	22		2
Glenn Bass	HB	6'2"	195	24		6
Hez Braxton	HB	6'2"	227	27		
Fred Brown	HB	5'11"	190	23		6
Wray Carlton	HB	6'2"	220	25		
Wayne Crow	HB	6'	205	25		
Roger Kochman	HB	6'2"	205	24		6
Ed Rutkowski	HB	6'1"	200	22		6
Cookie Gilchrist	FB	6'3"	250	28		84
Jesse Murdock (from OAK)	FB	6'2"	203	24		
Elbert Dubenion	FL	6'	188	28		24
Charley Ferguson	OE	6'5"	215	23		18
Bill Miller	OE	6'	200	21		18
Ernie Warlick	OE	6'4"	232	31		6

HOUSTON OILERS 6-8-0 Pop Ivy

Scores of Each Game

13	OAKLAND	24
20	DENVER	14
17	New York	24
31	Buffalo	20
7	Kansas City	28
33	Denver	24
28	BUFFALO	14
28	KANSAS CITY	7
3	Boston	45
31	NEW YORK	27
0	San Diego	27
28	BOSTON	46
14	SAN DIEGO	20
49	Oakland	52

Use Name	Pos.	Hgt	Wgt	Age	Int	Pts
Bob Kelly	OT	6'3"	260	23		
Rich Michael	OT	6'3"	238	24		
Walt Suggs	OT	6'5"	255	24		
Bob Talamini	OG	6'1"	245	22		
Bill Wegener	OG	5'10"	245	22		
Hogan Wharton	OG	6'2"	250	27		
John Frongillo	C	6'3"	255	23		
Bob Schmidt	C	6'4"	250	27		
Gary Cutsinger	DE	6'4"	245	22		
Don Floyd	DE	6'4"	245	24		
Willis Perkins	DE	6'	260	26		
Ed Culpepper	DT	6'1"	250	29		
Ed Husmann	DT	6'	245	32		
Dudley Meredith	DT	6'4"	275	28		

Use Name	Pos.	Hgt	Wgt	Age	Int	Pts
Johnny Baker	LB	6'3"	220	22		
Danny Brabham	LB	6'4"	235	22	1	
Doug Cline	LB	6'2"	227	24	3	
Mike Dukes	LB	6'3"	230	27	1	
Tom Goode	LB	6'3"	235	24		
Larry Onesti	LB	6'	195	24		
Gene Babb	FB-LB	6'3"	220	28	2	
Tony Banfield	DB	6'	185	24	7	
Freddy Glick	DB	6'1"	190	26	12	6
Bobby Jancik	DB	5'11"	178	23	3	
Mark Johnston	DB	6'	200	25	1	6
Jim Norton	DB	6'3"	190	24	6	

Use Name	Pos.	Hgt	Wgt	Age	Int	Pts
George Blanda	QB	6'1"	215	35		64
Jacky Lee	QB	6'1"	187	24		
Bobby Brezina	HB	6'	200	21		
Billy Cannon	HB	6'1"	210	26		
Bill Tobin	HB	5'11"	210	21		32
Dave Smith	FB	6'1"	210	26		30
Charley Tolar	FB	5'7"	200	25		18
Charley Hennigan	FL	6'	187	27		60
Randy Kerbow	FL	6'1"	190	21		
Willard Dewveall	OE	6'4"	225	26		42
Charley Frazier	OE	6'	162	24		6
Bob McLeod	OE	6'5"	230	24		30

NEW YORK JETS 5-8-1 Weeb Ewbank

Scores of Each Game

14	Boston	38
24	HOUSTON	17
10	OAKLAND	7
31	BOSTON	24
20	San Diego	24
26	Oakland	49
35	DENVER	35
7	SAN DIEGO	53
27	Houston	31
14	Denver	9
17	KANSAS CITY	0
14	Buffalo	45
10	BUFFALO	19
0	Kansas City	48

Use Name	Pos.	Hgt	Wgt	Age	Int	Pts
Winston Hill	OT	6'4"	275	21		
Jack Klotz	OT	6'5"	250	29		
Sherman Plunkett	OT	6'4"	297	29		
Bob Butler	OG	6'1"	230	22		
Dan Ficca	OG	6'1"	245	24		
Sid Fournet	OG	6'	240	30		
Roy Hord	OG	6'4"	245	28		
Pete Perreault	OG	6'3"	245	28		
Mike Hudock	C	6'2"	245	28		
Lavern Torczon	DE	6'2"	238	27	1	
Bob Watters	DE	6'4"	245	27		
Ed Cooke	LB-DE	6'4"	250	28		
Dick Guesman	DT	6'4"	255	27		57
Chuck Janerette	DT	6'3"	250	24	1	
Bob McAdams	DT	6'3"	250	23		
George Strugar	DT	6'5"	260	28		

Use Name	Pos.	Hgt	Wgt	Age	Int	Pts
Ted Bates	LB	6'3"	220	26		
Roger Ellis	LB	6'3"	233	25		
Larry Grantham	LB	6'	200	24	3	6
Walt Michaels	LB	6'	240	34		
Jim Price	LB	6'2"	225	22	1	
Dave Yohn	LB	6'	225	25		
Billy Atkins (to BUF)	DB	6'1"	196	28		
Bill Baird	DB	5'10"	182	24	6	6
Dainard Paulson	DB	5'11"	190	26	6	
Marsh Starks	DB	6'	190	24	6	
Tony Stricker	DB	6'	185	22	1	
Clyde Washington	DB	6'	206	25	2	
Dave West	DB	6'3"	190	25		
Bill Wood	DB	5'11"	190	24		

Use Name	Pos.	Hgt	Wgt	Age	Int	Pts
Ed Chlebek	QB	5'11"	175	22		
Johnny Green	QB	6'3"	208	26		
Galen Hall	QB	5'10"	205	23		6
Dick Wood	QB	6'5"	205	27		6
Dick Christy	HB	5'10"	195	27		6
Bill Mathis	HB	6'1"	220	24		6
Bill Perkins	HB	6'2"	225	22		
Curley Johnson	FB	6'	210	28		
Mark Smolinski	FB	6'	222	24		30
Don Maynard	FL	6'	185	27		54
Ken Gregory	OE	6'	190	26		
Gene Heeter	OE	6'4"	235	22		6
Dee Mackey	OE	6'5"	236	27		18
Bake Turner	OE	6'	180	23		36

BOSTON PATRIOTS

RUSHING

Last Name	No.	Yds	Avg	TD
Garron	179	750	4.1	2
Crawford	71	233	3.3	1
Yewcic	22	161	7.3	1
Neumann	44	148	3.4	0
Parilli	36	126	3.5	5
Crump	49	120	2.5	5
Lott	35	78	2.2	3
Cappelletti	1	2	2.0	0

RECEIVING

Last Name	No.	Yds	Avg	TD
Colclough	42	793	19	3
Cappelletti	34	493	15	2
Romeo	31	438	14	3
Garron	26	418	16	2
A. Graham	21	550	26	5
Crawford	10	84	8	0
Neumann	10	48	5	1
Lott	3	61	20	1
Crump	3	19	6	0

PUNT RETURNS

Last Name	No.	Yds	Avg	TD
Suci	25	233	9	0
Stephens	14	117	8	0
Garron	1	23	23	0

KICKOFF RETURNS

Last Name	No.	Yds	Avg	TD
Garron	28	693	25	0
Suci	17	360	21	0
Crump	3	33	11	0
Romeo	1	9	9	0
Watson	1	9	9	0
Yates	2	5	3	0

PASSING – PUNTING – KICKING

PASSING

Last Name	Att	Comp	%	Yds	Yd/Att	TD	Int–%	RK
Parilli	337	153	45	2335	6.9	13	24– 7	9
Yewcic	70	29	41	444	6.3	4	5– 7	
Crawford	2	2	100	27	13.5	0	0– 0	
Garron	1	0	0	0	0.0	0	0– 0	

PUNTING

Last Name	No	Avg
Yewcic	73	39.4

KICKING

Last Name	XP	Att	%	FG	Att	%
Cappelletti	35	36	97	22	38	58

BUFFALO BILLS

RUSHING

Last Name	No.	Yds	Avg	TD
Gilchrist	232	979	4.2	12
Kochman	47	232	4.9	0
Kemp	52	226	4.3	8
Rutowski	48	144	3.0	0
Carlton	29	125	4.3	0
Bass	14	59	4.2	0
Saimes	12	41	3.4	0
Brown	6	18	3.0	1
Lamonica	9	8	0.9	0
Crow	6	6	1.0	0

RECEIVING

Last Name	No.	Yds	Avg	TD
Miller	69	860	12	3
Dubenion	55	974	18	4
Warlick	24	479	20	1
Gilchrist	24	211	9	2
Rutkowski	19	264	14	1
Ferguson	9	181	20	3
Bass	9	153	17	1
Saimes	6	12	2	0
Crow	5	69	14	0
Kochman	4	148	37	1
Brown	2	7	4	0
Stratton	1	19	19	0
Carlton	1	9	9	0

PUNT RETURNS

Last Name	No.	Yds	Avg	TD
Abruzzese	17	152	9	0
West	11	86	8	0
Rutkowski	8	67	8	0
Kochman	1	11	11	0

KICKOFF RETURNS

Last Name	No.	Yds	Avg	TD
Rutkowski	13	396	30	0
Dubenion	13	333	26	0
Saimes	7	140	20	0
Abruzzese	6	118	20	0
West	6	56	9	0
Brown	2	40	20	0
Tracey	1	21	21	0
Rivera	1	20	20	0
Murdock	1	17	17	0
Barber	1	9	9	0
Paterra	1	0	0	0
Matuszak	1	17	17	0

PASSING – PUNTING – KICKING

PASSING

Last Name	Att	Comp	%	Yds	Yd/Att	TD	Int–%	RK
Kemp	384	194	51	2914	7.5	13	20– 5	4
Lamonica	71	33	46	437	6.1	3	4– 6	
Gilchrist	1	1	100	35	35.0	0	0– 0	
Rutkowski	1	0	0	0	0.0	0	0– 0	

PUNTING

Last Name	No	Avg
Lamonica	51	40.6
Crow	10	42.4

KICKING

Last Name	XP	Att	%	FG	Att	%
Yoho	32	37	86	10	23	43

2 POINT XP

Lamonica
Tracey

HOUSTON OILERS

RUSHING

Last Name	No.	Yds	Avg	TD
Tolar	194	659	3.4	3
Tobin	75	270	3.6	4
Smith	50	202	4.0	3
Cannon	13	45	3.4	0
Norton	1	15	15.0	0
Lee	2	9	4.5	0
Babb	1	7	7.0	0
Blanda	4	1	0.2	0

RECEIVING

Last Name	No.	Yds	Avg	TD
Hennigan	61	1051	17	10
Dewveall	58	752	13	7
Tolar	41	275	7	0
McLeod	33	530	16	5
Smith	24	270	11	2
Frazier	16	269	17	1
Tobin	13	272	13	1
Kerbow	5	61	12	0
Cannon	5	39	8	0

PUNT RETURNS

Last Name	No.	Yds	Avg	TD
Glick	19	171	9	0
Jancik	13	145	11	0
Norton	4	23	6	0

KICKOFF RETURNS

Last Name	No.	Yds	Avg	TD
Jancik	45	1317	29	0
Glick	20	451	23	0
Cannon	2	39	20	0
Tobin	1	10	10	0
Tolar	1	4	4	0

PASSING – PUNTING – KICKING

PASSING

Last Name	Att	Comp	%	Yds	Yd/Att	TD	Int–%	RK
Blanda	423	224	53	3003	7.0	24	25– 6	4
Lee	75	37	49	475	6.3	2	8–11	
Smith	2	0	0	0	0.0	0	0– 0	
Cannon	1	0	0	0	0.0	0	0– 0	

PUNTING

Last Name	No	Avg
Norton	65	42.9

KICKING

Last Name	XP	Att	%	FG	Att	%
Blanda	37	37	100	9	22	41

2 POINT XP

Tobin

NEW YORK JETS

RUSHING

Last Name	No.	Yds	Avg	TD
Smolinski	150	561	3.7	4
Mathis	107	268	2.5	1
Christy	26	88	3.4	1
Hall	9	24	2.7	1
D. Wood	7	17	2.4	1
Perkins	3	8	2.6	0
Maynard	2	6	3.0	0
Johnson	2	6	3.0	0

RECEIVING

Last Name	No.	Yds	Avg	TD
Turner	71	1007	14	6
Maynard	38	780	21	9
Smolinski	34	278	8	1
Mackey	23	263	11	3
Mathis	18	177	10	1
Gregory	9	90	10	0
Heeter	8	160	20	1
Christy	8	73	9	0

PUNT RETURNS

Last Name	No.	Yds	Avg	TD
Baird	4	143	36	1
Christy	9	46	5	0
Starks	3	7	2	0
Maynard	1	6	6	0

KICKOFF RETURNS

Last Name	No.	Yds	Avg	TD
Christy	24	585	24	0
Starks	19	336	18	0
Turner	14	299	21	0
Stricker	4	90	23	0
Johnson	6	77	13	0
Perkins	4	55	14	0
Mathis	1	11	11	0
Smolinski	1	10	10	0
Mackey	1	0	0	0

PASSING – PUNTING – KICKING

PASSING

Last Name	Att	Comp	%	Yds	Yd/Att	TD	Int–%	RK
D. Wood	351	160	46	2202	6.3	18	18– 5	6
Hall	118	45	38	611	5.2	3	9– 8	
Green	6	2	33	10	1.7	0	1– 17	
Chlebek	4	2	50	5	1.3	0	0– 0	
Mathis	1	0	0	0	0.0	0	1–100	

PUNTING

Last Name	No	Avg
Johnson	71	42.6

KICKING

Last Name	XP	Att	%	FG	Att	%
Guesman	30	30	100	9	24	31

SAN DIEGO CHARGERS 11-3-0 Sid Gillman

Scores of Each Game			Use Name	Pos.	Hgt	Wgt	Age	Int	Pts	Use Name	Pos.	Hgt	Wgt	Age	Int	Pts	Use Name	Pos.	Hgt	Wgt	Age	Int	Pts
14	BUFFALO	10	Ron Mix	OT	6'4"	250	25			Chuck Allen	LB	6'1"	225	23	5	6	John Hadl	QB	6'2"	205	23		
17	BOSTON	14	Ernie Park	OT	6'3"	240	21			Frank Buncom	LB	6'1"	235	23			Tobin Rote	QB	6'3"	220	35		12
24	KANSAS CITY	10	Ernie Wright	OT	6'4"	265	22			Emil Karas	LB	6'3"	235	29	2		Paul Lowe	HB	6'	205	26		60
34	Denver	50	Sam DeLuca	OG	6'2"	242	27			Bobby Lane	LB	6'2"	222	23			Bobby Jackson	FB	6'3"	238	23		24
24	NEW YORK	20	Sam Gruneisen	OG	6'1"	252	22			Paul Maguire	LB	6'	225	25	4		Keith Lincoln	FB	6'2"	212	24		48
38	Kansas City	17	Pat Shea	OG	6'1"	243	24			Bob Mitinger	LB	6'2"	235	23	3		Gerry McDougall	FB	6'2"	225	28		6
33	OAKLAND	34	Walt Sweeney	OG	6'3"	260	22			George Blair	DB	5'11"	195	25	1	95	Lance Alworth	FL	6'	185	23		66
53	New York	7	Don Rogers	C	6'2"	245	26			Gary Glick	DB	6'2"	200	32	1		Reg Carolan	OE	6'6"	235	23		
7	Boston	6	Earl Faison	DE	6'5"	262	24		2	Dick Harris	DB	5'11"	187	26	8	6	Dave Kocourek	OE	6'5"	245	26		32
23	Buffalo	13	Bob Petrich	DE	6'4"	252	22			Charley McNeil	DB	5'11"	180	27	4		Jacque MacKinnon	OE	6'4"	250	24		24
27	HOUSTON	0	George Gross	DT	6'3"	260	22			Dick Westmoreland	DB	6'1"	180	22			Don Norton	OE	6'1"	195	25		6
27	Oakland	41	Ernie Ladd	DT	6'9"	321	24			Bud Whitehead	DB	6'	185	24	1		Jerry Robinson	OE	5'11"	190	24		12
20	Houston	14	Henry Schmidt	DT	6'4"	254	26			Keith Kinderman	FB-DB	6'	208	23									
58	DENVER	20																				

OAKLAND RAIDERS 10-4-0 Al Davis

Scores of Each Game			Use Name	Pos.	Hgt	Wgt	Age	Int	Pts	Use Name	Pos.	Hgt	Wgt	Age	Int	Pts	Use Name	Pos.	Hgt	Wgt	Age	Int	Pts
24	Houston	19	Proverb Jacobs	OT	6'4"	260	28			Bob Dougherty	LB	6'	240	29			Cotton Davidson	QB	6'1"	180	30		24
35	BUFFALO	17	Dick Klein	OT	6'4"	255	29			Archie Matsos	LB	6'	212	28	4		Tom Flores	QB	6'1"	196	26		
14	BOSTON	20	Frank Youso	OT	6'4"	255	27			Clancy Osborne	LB	6'3"	218	28	2		Clem Daniels	HB	6'1"	220	26		48
7	New York	10	Sonny Bishop	OG	6'2"	240	23			Charley Rieves	LB	5'11"	218	24			Mike Somner	HB	5'11"	192	28		
0	Buffalo	12	Wayne Hawkins	OG	6'	240	25			Jackie Simpson	LB	6'1"	225	26	2		Doug Mayberry	FB	6'1"	220	26		
14	Boston	20	Ollie Spencer	OG	6'2"	240	32			Claude Gibson	DB	6'1"	190	24	3	12	Alan Miller	FB	6'	205	25		30
49	NEW YORK	26	Bob Mischak	OE-OG	6'	240	30			Joe Krakoski	DB	6'2"	195	26	4		Glen Shaw	FB	6'1"	225	24		12
34	San Diego	33	Jim Otto	C	6'2"	240	25			Jim McMillin	DB	5'11"	190	25	4	6	Bo Roberson	HB-FL	6'1"	197	28		18
10	KANSAS CITY	7	Dalva Allen	DE	6'5"	240	27			Tom Morrow	DB	5'11"	187	25	9		Jan Barrett (from GB-N)	OE	6'3"	230	22		
22	Kansas City	7	Dan Birdwell	DE	6'4"	240	22			Warren Powers	DB	6'	188	22			Dobie Craig	OE	6'4"	200	24		12
26	Denver	10	Jon Jelacic	DE	6'3"	255	26	1	12	Fred Williamson	DB	6'2"	215	25	6		Ken Herock	OE	6'2"	230	22		18
41	SAN DIEGO	27	Dave Costa	DT	6'3"	245	21			Herm Urenda	OE-DB	5'11"	170	23			Art Powell	OE	6'3"	212	26		96
35	DENVER	31	Chuck McMurtry	DT	6'	270	25										Mike Mercer	K	6'	200	27		71
52	HOUSTON	49	Jim Norris	DT	6'4"	235	23																

KANSAS CITY CHIEFS 5-7-2 Hank Stram

Scores of Each Game			Use Name	Pos.	Hgt	Wgt	Age	Int	Pts	Use Name	Pos.	Hgt	Wgt	Age	Int	Pts	Use Name	Pos.	Hgt	Wgt	Age	Int	Pts
59	Denver	7	Charley Diamond	OT	6'2"	262	27			Bobby Bell	LB	6'4"	228	23	1		Len Dawson	QB	6'	190	29		12
27	Buffalo	27	Dave Hill	OT	6'5"	255	22			Walt Corey	LB	6'	220	25			Eddie Wilson	QB	6'	190	23		
10	San Diego	24	Jim Tyrer	OT	6'6"	290	24			Sherrill Headrick	LB	6'2"	215	26	2	6	Bert Coan	HB	6'4"	220	23		
28	HOUSTON	7	Denny Biodrowski	OG	6'1"	255	23			Smokey Stover	LB	6'	235	24			Abner Haynes	HB	6'	190	25		36
26	BUFFALO	35	Ed Budde	OG	6'5"	260	22			E. J. Holub	C-LB	6'4"	225	25	5		Jerrel Wilson	LB-HB	6'4"	225	22		
17	SAN DIEGO	38	Bill Diamond	OG	6'	240	23			Dave Grayson	DB	5'10"	184	24	5	6	Curtis McClinton	FB	6'3"	232	24		36
7	Houston	28	Al Reynolds	OG	6'3"	235	25			Bobby Hunt	DB	6'1"	180	23	6		Jack Spikes	FB	6'2"	220	25		47
7	Oakland	10	Marvin Terrell	OG	6'1"	240	25			Bobby Ply	DB	6'1"	190	22			Frank Jackson	FL	6'1"	210	23		54
7	OAKLAND	22	Jon Gilliam	C	6'2"	240	24			Johnny Robinson	DB	6'	195	24	3		Fred Arbanas	OE	6'3"	240	24		36
24	Boston	24	Mel Branch	DE	6'2"	230	26			Charley Warner	DB	5'11"	180	23	1		Tommy Brooker	OE	6'2"	230	23		38
0	New York	17	Jerry Mays	DE	6'4"	247	23		6	Duane Wood	DB	6'1"	200	27	3	6	Chris Burford	OE	6'3"	210	25		56
52	DENVER	21	Curt Merz	OG-DE	6'4"	250	25										Dick Johnson	OE	6'4"	220	24		6
35	BOSTON	3	Buck Buchanan	DT	6'7"	276	23																
48	NEW YORK	0	Curt Farrier	DT	6'6"	270	22																
			Paul Rochester (to NY)	DT	6'2"	260	26																

DENVER BRONCOS 2-11-1 Jack Faulkner

Scores of Each Game			Use Name	Pos.	Hgt	Wgt	Age	Int	Pts	Use Name	Pos.	Hgt	Wgt	Age	Int	Pts	Use Name	Pos.	Hgt	Wgt	Age	Int	Pts
7	KANSAS CITY	59	Eldon Danenhauer	OT	6'4"	245	27			Tom Erlandson	LB	6'3"	235	23			Don Breaux	QB	6'1"	205	23		
14	Houston	20	Harold Olson	OT	6'3"	255	24			Jim Fraser	LB	6'3"	236	27			John McCormick	QB	6'1"	210	26		
14	BOSTON	10	Jim Perkins	OT	6'5"	250	24			Jerry Hopkins	LB	6'2"	235	22	1		Mickey Slaughter	QB	6'	190	21		6
50	SAN DIEGO	34	Ernie Barnes	OG	6'3"	243	24			Wahoo McDaniel	LB	6'	238	26	2		Frank Tripucka	QB	6'2"	208	35		
24	HOUSTON	33	Bob McCullough	OG	6'2"	245	22			John Nocera	LB	6'1"	230	29			Hewritt Dixon	HB	6'2"	215	23		12
21	Boston	40	Tom Nomina	OG	6'5"	270	21			Leon Simmons	LB	6'	225	24			Bob Gaiters	HB	5'11"	210	25		6
35	New York	35	Frank Jackunas	C	6'3"	225	22			Willie Brown	DB	6'1"	190	22	1		Gene Mingo	HB	6'	200	24		83
28	BUFFALO	30	Jerry Sturm	C	6'3"	245	26			Goose Gonsoulin	DB	6'3"	210	25	6	6	Donnie Stone	HB	6'2"	205	24		24
17	Buffalo	27	Chuck Gavin	DE	6'1"	250	29			Tom Janik	DB	6'3"	200	22	2		Clarence Walker	HB	6'1"	205	24		
9	NEW YORK	14	Ray Jacobs	DE	6'3"	275	23			John McGeever	DB	6'1"	195	24			Charley Mitchell	DB-HB	5'11"	185	23	1	6
10	OAKLAND	26	Ike Lassiter	DE	6'5"	270	22			John Sklopan	DB	5'11"	190	22			Bo Dickinson (to HOU)	FB	6'2"	220	28		6
21	Kansas City	52	Ron Nery (to HOU)	DE	6'6"	244	28			Bruce Starling	DB	6'1"	186	21			Billy Joe	FB	6'2"	250	22		30
31	Oakland	35	Gordy Holz	DT	6'4"	260	29	1		Bob Zeman	DB	6'1"	203	26	1		Don Coffey	FL	6'3"	190	23		
20	San Diego	58	Bud McFadin	DT	6'3"	280	35		6								Al Frazier	FL	5'11"	180	28		
			Anton Peters	DT	6'3"	250	21										Bill Groman	FL	6'	190	27		18
																	Bob Scarpitto	FL	5'11"	196	24		30
																	Gene Prebola	OE	6'3"	225	25		14
																	Tom Rychlec	OE	6'3"	225	29		
																	Lionel Taylor	OE	6'2"	215	27		60

SAN DIEGO CHARGERS

RUSHING

Last Name	No.	Yds	Avg	TD
Lowe	177	1010	5.7	8
Lincoln	128	826	6.5	5
McDougall	38	199	5.2	1
Jackson	18	64	3.6	4
Rote	24	62	2.6	2
Hadl	8	26	3.3	0
Alworth	2	14	7.0	0

RECEIVING

Last Name	No.	Yds	Avg	TD
Alworth	61	1206	20	11
Lowe	26	191	7	2
Lincoln	24	325	14	3
Kocourek	23	359	16	5
Norton	21	281	13	1
Robinson	18	315	18	1
MacKinnon	11	262	24	4
McDougall	10	115	12	0
Jackson	8	85	11	0

PUNT RETURNS

Last Name	No.	Yds	Avg	TD
Alworth	11	120	11	0
Lincoln	7	98	14	0
Harris	4	43	11	0

KICKOFF RETURNS

Last Name	No.	Yds	Avg	TD
Lincoln	17	439	26	0
Alworth	10	216	22	0
Westmoreland	10	204	20	0
Lowe	5	132	26	0
McDougall	3	77	26	0
Harris	2	34	17	0
Robinson	2	27	14	0
Sweeney	1	18	18	0
Jackson	1	16	16	0
Maguire	1	5	5	0

PASSING – PUNTING – KICKING Statistics

PASSING	Att	Comp.	%	Yds	Yd/Att	TD	Int–%	RK
Rote	286	170	59	2510	8.7	20	17– 6	1
Hadl	65	28	43	502	7.7	6	6– 9	
Lowe	4	2	50	100	25.0	1	1– 25	
Lincoln	1	0	0	0	0.0	0	0– 0	
McDougall	1	1	100	11	11.0	0	0– 0	
Norton	1	1	100	15	15.0	0	0– 0	

PUNTING	No	Avg.
Maguire	58	38.6
Hadl	2	37.5

KICKING	XP	Att	%	FG	Att	%
Blair	44	48	92	17	27	63

2 POINT XP
Faison
Kocourek

OAKLAND RAIDERS

RUSHING

Last Name	No.	Yds	Avg	TD
Daniels	214	1099	5.1	3
Miller	62	270	4.4	3
Davidson	26	115	4.4	4
Roberson	19	47	2.2	0
Shaw	20	46	2.3	1
Sommer	5	21	4.2	0
Flores	11	2	0.2	0
Mercer	1	-5	-5.0	0

RECEIVING

Last Name	No.	Yds	Avg	TD
Powell	73	1304	18	16
Miller	34	404	12	2
Daniels	30	685	23	5
Roberson	25	407	16	3
Herock	15	269	18	2
Craig	7	205	29	2
Shaw	2	64	32	1
Mischak	2	25	13	0
Sommer	1	24	24	0
Barrett	1	9	9	0

PUNT RETURNS

Last Name	No.	Yds	Avg	TD
Gibson	26	307	12	2
Sommer	4	44	11	0
Roberson	2	34	17	0
Krakoski	4	10	3	0

KICKOFF RETURNS

Last Name	No.	Yds	Avg	TD
Roberson	38	809	21	0
Sommer	5	102	20	0
McMillin	1	23	23	0
Shaw	2	19	10	0
Simpson	1	11	11	0
Gibson	2	10	5	0
Klein	1	7	7	0
Birdwell	1	7	7	0
Herock	1	3	3	0

PASSING – PUNTING – KICKING

PASSING	Att	Comp	%	Yds	Yd/Att	TD	Int–%	RK
Flores	247	113	46	2101	8.5	20	13– 5	2
Davidson	194	77	40	1276	6.5	11	10– 5	8
Daniels	1	1	100	10	10.0	0	0– 0	

PUNTING	No	Avg
Mercer	75	40.0

KICKING	XP	Att	%	FG	Att	%
Mercer	47	47	100	8	21	38

KANSAS CITY CHIEFS

RUSHING

Last Name	No.	Yds	Avg	TD
McClinton	142	568	4.0	3
Haynes	99	352	3.6	4
Dawson	37	272	7.4	2
Spikes	84	257	3.1	2
Coan	17	100	5.9	0
Jackson	3	52	17.3	1
E. Wilson	8	45	5.6	0
J. Wilson	9	41	4.6	0
Burford	1	10	10.0	0

RECEIVING

Last Name	No.	Yds	Avg	TD
Burford	68	824	12	9
Jackson	50	785	16	8
Arbanas	34	373	11	6
Haynes	33	470	14	2
McClinton	27	301	11	3
Spikes	11	125	11	1
Coan	2	35	18	0
Brooker	2	32	16	0
J. Wilson	2	21	11	0
Johnson	2	17	9	1

PUNT RETURNS

Last Name	No.	Yds	Avg	TD
Jackson	11	95	9	0
Haynes	6	57	10	0
Grayson	2	39	20	0
Warner	4	25	6	0
Wood	1	18	18	0
Robinson	1	16	16	0
Headrick	1	9	9	0

KICKOFF RETURNS

Last Name	No.	Yds	Avg	TD
Grayson	20	570	29	1
Haynes	12	317	26	0
Warner	9	215	24	0
Jackson	1	20	20	0
J. Wilson	1	20	20	0
Stover	2	18	9	0
Spikes	2	12	6	0

PASSING – PUNTING – KICKING

PASSING	Att	Comp	%	Yds	Yd/Att	TD	Int–%	RK
Dawson	352	190	54	2389	6.7	26	19– 5	3
E. Wilson	82	39	48	537	6.5	3	2– 2	
Haynes	2	1	50	24	12.0	0	0– 0	
McClinton	2	1	50	33	16.5	1	0– 0	
Spikes	1	0	0	0	0.0	0	1–100	

PUNTING	No	Avg
J. Wilson	60	43.8
E. Wilson	1	43.0

KICKING	XP	Att	%	FG	Att	%
Spikes	23	24	96	2	13	15
Brooker	20	20	100	6	15	40

2 POINT XP
Burford

DENVER BRONCOS

RUSHING

Last Name	No.	Yds	Avg	TD
Joe	154	649	4.2	4
Stone	96	382	3.9	3
Slaughter	32	124	3.9	1
Dixon	23	105	4.5	2
Mingo	24	90	3.7	0
Breaux	10	51	5.1	0
Mitchell	23	45	2.0	0
Dickinson	6	32	5.3	0
Gaiters	9	20	2.2	0
Walker	2	14	7.0	0
Barnes	0	2	0.0	0
McCormick	3	-5	-1.7	0

RECEIVING

Last Name	No.	Yds	Avg	TD
Taylor	78	1101	14	10
Prebola	30	471	16	2
Groman	27	437	16	3
Stone	22	208	9	1
Scarpitto	21	463	22	5
Joe	15	90	6	1
Dixon	10	132	13	0
Mitchell	8	71	9	0
Dickinson	6	57	10	0
Mingo	3	11	4	0
Gaiters	1	74	74	1
Rychlec	1	9	9	0

PUNT RETURNS

Last Name	No.	Yds	Avg	TD
Mitchell	12	141	12	0
Mingo	7	85	12	0
Dixon	3	58	19	0
Frazier	3	42	14	0
Zeman	2	32	16	0
Brown	3	29	10	0

KICKOFF RETURNS

Last Name	No.	Yds	Avg	TD
Mitchell	37	954	26	1
Gaiters	11	225	20	0
Dixon	9	195	22	0
Frazier	7	185	24	0
Mingo	7	151	22	0
Brown	3	70	23	0
Scarpitto	1	8	8	0
Olson	2	0	0	0
Fraser	1	0	0	0
Groman	0	9	0	0
Gonsoulin	0	4	0	0

PASSING – PUNTING – KICKING

PASSING	Att	Comp	%	Yds	Yd/Att	TD	Int–%	RK
Slaughter	223	112	50	1689	7.5	12	14– 6	7
Breaux	138	70	51	935	6.7	7	6– 4	
McCormick	72	28	39	417	5.1	4	3– 4	
Tripucka	15	7	47	31	2.1	0	5– 33	
Stone	3	0	0	0	0.0	0	0– 0	
Mingo	1	0	0	0	0.0	0	0– 0	
Taylor	1	0	0	0	0.0	0	0– 0	

PUNTING	No	Avg
Fraser	78	46.1

KICKING	XP	Att	%	FG	Att	%
Mingo	35	35	100	16	30	53

2 POINT XP
Prebola

1964 N.F.L. A Blue-Chip Business

The war between the leagues was going nicely for the NFL, as all but two NFL teams made a profit during 1964. Only St. Louis and Dallas lost money, and neither had the excuse of direct AFL competition. Franchises now were blue-chip investments, with price tags well into the millions of dollars. Two of the franchises changed hands this year: William Clay Ford purchased the Detroit Lions and Jerry Wolman headed a syndicate that bought the Philadelphia Eagles. The leagues were still at war, but the NFL owners worried very little at this point.

EASTERN CONFERENCE

Cleveland Browns—The Browns added a little variety to their attack to win their first conference title since 1957. Jimmy Brown still was the ultimate runner, but he got some help in the ball-carrying department from halfback Ernie Green. For the first time in years the Browns also launched a dangerous passing game, with Gary Collins and rookie Paul Warfield providing quarterback Frank Ryan with two fine receivers. Led by tackle Dick Schafrath, the offensive line both cleared paths for the runners and protected quarterback Ryan with equal expertise. The defense had problems defending against the pass, but ex-Giant Dick Modzelewski made the line very tough against the run.

St. Louis Cardinals—Coach Wally Lemm put together a marvelously balanced team, only to have it fall apart on three embarrassing occasions. In a four-week span in mid-season, the Cards lost 47-27 to Baltimore, dropped a 31-13 decision to Dallas, and were beaten 34-17 by the collapsing New York Giants. But before and after this cold spell, the Cardinals showed a versatile offense and spirited defense. Quarterback Charley Johnson had a propensity for throwing interceptions, but he usually made up for his errant tosses with long gainers. The strong offensive line cleared the way for runners John David Crow, Joe Childress, and Willie Crenshaw, while the defense combined a small but quick line with steady linebackers and an aggressive secondary featuring Pat Fischer and Larry Wilson.

Washington Redskins—Quarterback Sonny Jurgensen, obtained in a trade with the Eagles, had few peers as a passer, and receivers Bobby Mitchell, Angelo Coia, and Preston Carpenter gave him an abundance of open receivers. Rookie halfback Charley Taylor injected speed into the running attack. But the Washington offense also had a big hole at fullback and a spotty front line of blockers, making it difficult for Jurgensen, Taylor, and Mitchell to shine their brightest. Even with a defense bolstered by ex-Giant Sam Huff and rookie Paul Krause, the Redskins lost their first four games with poor offensive performances. But after rookies Len Hauss and George Seals were thrust into the offensive line, the Skins revived and won six of their next eight games.

Philadelphia Eagles—Joe Kuharich signed a fifteen-year contract as coach and general manager and immediately dived into the trading market to rebuild the Eagles. In a blinding series of deals, he obtained Norm Snead from Washington, Earl Gros and Jim Ringo from Green Bay, Ollie Matson and Floyd Peters from Detroit, Sam Baker from Dallas, and Ray Poage and Don Hultz from Minnesota. Add three good rookies in Bob Brown, Mike Morgan, and Joe Scarpati, and solid holdovers like Pete Retzlaff, Maxie Baughan, Don Burroughs, and Irv Cross, and the Eagles had the makings of a good football team.

Dallas Cowboys—Even after the Cowboys obtained star wide receivers Tommy McDonald and Buddy Dial, the offense had problems scoring points. One cause of the trouble was Don Meredith's leg injury, which had him hobbling through a sub-par season, and another was the erratic kicking of rookie Dick Van Raaphorst. Given the field-goal kicking job after Sam Baker was dealt to Philadelphia, Van Raaphorst cost the Cowboys several games by blowing easy kicks. Although Don Perkins and Frank Clarke kept up their good work, the Dallas offense fell off from its 1963 performance. The defense, however, suddenly blended together into a strong unit.

Pittsburgh Steelers—Coach Buddy Parker had an intricate plan to improve the Steelers this year. He drafted University of Pittsburgh star Paul Martha as a flanker, and then traded incumbent flanker Buddy Dial to Dallas for the draft rights to All-American defensive lineman Scott Appleton from the University of Texas. The whole maneuver failed miserably when Appleton signed with the AFL Houston Oilers, and Martha was a king-sized bust as a pass receiver. Rookies Ben McGee and Chuck Hinton took up the slack in the defensive line, but no one could fill Dial's vacated receiver spot opposite Gary Ballman.

New York Giants—The New York dynasty crashed heavily to pieces this season. Coach Allie Sherman had traded off Sam Huff and Dick Modzelewski during the off season, hoping to fill their spots with younger men, but none of the replacements came close to the steadiness of the two departed defenders. To add to Sherman's headaches, veterans Y. A. Tittle, Alex Webster, Frank Gifford, Del Shofner, Jack Stroud, and Andy Robustelli all showed signs of advanced old age.

WESTERN CONFERENCE

Baltimore Colts—Coach Don Shula had tried to trade Lenny Moore all summer but had found no takers. Moore had lost his halfback job to Tom Matte and was coming off two injury-plagued seasons which cut his market value down to nothing. Once the regular season started, though, Moore won back his job and set a new NFL record with twenty touchdowns. Moore, Tony Lorick, and Jerry Hill provided tough running, and the Baltimore passing attack was even more effective than usual. The defense responded to the offensive improvement by playing better than anyone could expect, with veterans Gino Marchetti, Bill Pellington, and Bob Boyd the core around which a group of average defenders clustered into a solid unit. With a proper mixture of veterans and youngsters, the Colts captured the conference crown.

Green Bay Packers—Paul Hornung rejoined the Packers after his year's suspension but left his kicking eye behind. The Pack lost three games because of easy kicks Hornung missed, such as the 21-20 loss to the Colts in which Hornung missed an extra point. Outside of this one serious flaw, the Packers still were a solid, precise football team. Bart Starr and Jim Taylor starred in the backfield, and the offensive line graded out well despite the trading of Jim Ringo to Philadelphia and the loss of Jerry Kramer to stomach surgery. No one moved the ball easily against the Green Bay defense, which boasted of four All-Pros in Willie Davis, Henry Jordan, Ray Nitschke, and Willie Wood.

Minnesota Vikings—With three straight wins to end the year, the Vikings jumped up into a second-place tie in the West with the Packers. The Vikings had caught up with Green Bay after only four years in existence, and the main stepladder to progress was the Minnesota offense. At quarterback the Vikings had Fran Tarkenton, the original and best scrambler in the league. The halfback was Tommy Mason, the team's breakaway threat, and the fullback was Bill Brown, a squat young man equally adept at running, receiving, and blocking. The offensive line was not spectacular but good enough to allow the backs to star, while the Minnesota defense was making slower but sure progress.

Detroit Lions—Age was cutting heavily into the vaunted Detroit defense. Night Train Lane was thirty-six and bothered by a bad knee, Yale Lary was thirty-three, Joe Schmidt was thirty-two with a bad shoulder, and Sam Williams was thirty-three. When all these veterans could play at top form, the Lion defense still was one of the league's best, but the days where one or more of them had to sit the game out were growing more frequent. The offense was still a rather plodding unit, with flanker Terry Barr the only speedster on the attack. With neither Milt Plum nor Earl Morrall able to take over at quarterback, the offense was far from ready to pick up the slack left by the aging defense.

Los Angeles Rams—Despite a late-season slump which saw them go winless in their last five games, the Rams developed two solid lines this year. The offensive line of Joe Wendryhoski, Joe Scibelli, Don Chuy, Joe Carollo, and Frank Varricheone was quietly efficient, while the defensive front four of Deacon Jones, Merlin Olsen, Roosevelt Grier, and Lamar Lundy won attention for their speed and violence. The backfields were less settled, as two rookies started in the defensive secondary and three freshman won jobs in the offensive backfield. Bucky Pope surprised everyone with his deep pass receiving as a flanker, and Les Josephson filled in well for the sore-kneed Dick Bass. Rookie Bill Munson won the quarterback job, giving the Rams a second good young quarterback to go along with Roman Gabriel.

Chicago Bears—The Chicago offense had been nothing to write home about last year, but when injuries cut the marvelous defense down to life size, the Bears plummeted into the depths of the Western Conference. When the Bears lost three of their first four games, one of them to the Colts by 52-0, hopes for a repeat championship fluttered away. To get some additional punch from the offense, which had been crippled by the pre-season deaths of Willie Galimore and Bo Farrington in an auto accident, coach George Halas used strong-armed Rudy Bukich more often at quarterback and geared his attack around passes to Johnny Morris and Mike Ditka. Although the passes were successful often enough to place Morris and Ditka one-two in the league receiving statistics and to give Morris a new NFL season's record of ninety-three receptions, the Bear season was a huge disappointment.

San Francisco '49ers—When all their running backs were knocked out with injuries, the '49ers couldn't find enough offensive dynamite in the rest of the lineup to ignite the attack. Although Bernie Casey, Monte Stickles, and rookie Dave Parks were a fine trio of receivers, quarterback John Brodie was not a great enough passer to overcome the lack of any ground attack. The defense gave up no easy yardage, with Charlie Krueger, Clark Miller, Matt Hazeltine, rookie Dave Wilcox, and converted flanker Jim Johnson the main ribs of the unit.

FINAL TEAM STATISTICS

OFFENSE

	BALT.	CHI.	CLEVE.	DALLAS	DET.	G.BAY	L.A.	MINN.	N.Y.	PHIL.	PITT.	ST.L.	S.F.	WASH.
FIRST DOWNS:														
Total	245	248	255	230	221	250	208	258	240	243	233	275	233	193
by Rushing	100	83	119	89	87	133	78	124	81	100	110	95	76	70
by Passing	129	141	118	119	115	106	104	115	140	126	105	152	136	116
by Penalty	16	24	18	22	19	11	26	19	19	17	18	28	21	7
RUSHING:														
Number	456	356	435	421	412	495	400	519	435	430	516	456	383	366
Yards	2007	1166	2163	1691	1414	2276	1629	2183	1404	1922	2102	1770	1332	1237
Average Yards	4.4	3.3	5.0	4.0	3.4	4.6	4.1	4.2	3.2	4.5	4.1	3.9	3.5	3.4
Touchdowns	29	5	14	15	7	23	11	14	12	16	14	12	11	11
PASSING:														
Attempts	345	494	344	404	386	321	368	326	431	397	323	422	461	415
Completions	176	282	181	192	206	186	173	179	217	199	141	223	225	214
Completion Pct.	51.0	57.1	52.6	47.5	53.4	57.9	47.0	54.9	50.3	50.1	43.7	52.8	48.8	51.6
Passing Yards	3045	3056	2542	2516	2890	2474	2769	2614	2848	2746	2308	3045	2990	3071
Avg. Yds per Att.	8.8	6.2	7.4	6.2	7.5	7.7	7.5	8.0	6.6	6.9	7.2	7.2	6.5	7.4
Avg. Yds per Comp.	17.3	10.8	14.0	13.1	14.0	13.3	16.0	14.6	13.1	13.8	16.4	13.7	13.3	14.4
Times Tackled	39	30	28	68	37	47	65	48	45	35	51	37	27	44
Yards Lost Tackled	273	215	219	503	332	369	490	491	373	268	450	298	249	350
Net Yards	2772	2841	2323	2013	2558	2105	2279	2123	2475	2478	1858	2747	2741	2721
Touchdowns	22	25	28	10	23	16	18	23	16	19	14	21	18	25
Interceptions	9	21	19	24	21	6	20	12	26	18	24	24	22	16
Pct. Intercepted	2.6	4.3	5.5	5.9	5.4	1.9	5.4	3.7	6.0	4.5	7.4	5.7	4.8	3.9
PUNTING:														
Number	59	71	49	78	68	56	82	72	74	73	62	56	79	91
Average Distance	41.8	44.5	41.9	38.9	45.7	42.2	44.1	46.4	45.4	41.7	43.2	40.9	45.6	41.2
PUNT RETURNS:														
Number	48	30	20	40	35	34	34	35	28	28	30	24	43	32
Yards	453	219	303	459	411	443	181	306	193	201	238	251	322	230
Average Yards	9.4	7.3	15.2	11.5	11.7	13.0	5.3	8.7	6.9	7.2	7.9	10.5	7.5	7.2
Touchdowns	0	0	1	1	2	1	0	0	0	0	0	1	1	0
KICKOFF RETURNS:														
Number	39	58	57	46	57	45	56	53	67	59	56	63	57	52
Yards	926	1314	1323	1102	1327	1160	1258	1130	1688	1365	1356	1424	1393	1097
Average Yards	23.7	22.7	23.2	24.0	23.3	25.8	22.5	21.3	25.2	23.1	24.2	22.6	24.4	21.1
Touchdowns	0	1	0	0	0	0	0	0	1	0	0	0	0	0
INTERCEPTION RETURNS:														
Number	23	10	19	18	22	16	17	19	15	17	12	25	15	34
Yards	366	258	444	316	267	263	487	224	179	272	96	388	155	317
Average Yards	15.9	25.8	23.4	17.6	12.1	16.4	28.6	11.8	11.9	16.0	8.0	15.5	10.3	9.3
Touchdowns	1	0	3	2	0	1	3	4	1	2	1	5	0	3
PENALTIES:														
Number	74	96	60	97	75	50	76	71	65	42	59	64	79	87
Yards	785	817	611	952	674	576	803	787	532	450	615	579	741	825
FUMBLES:														
Number	31	19	15	38	23	25	40	37	44	33	28	29	42	27
Number Lost	10	12	7	19	13	17	19	18	23	22	17	16	24	17
POINTS:														
Total	428	260	415	250	280	342	283	355	241	312	253	357	236	307
PAT Attempts	54	32	50	30	34	44	33	42	30	38	31	40	30	39
PAT Made	53	29	49	28	32	42	31	40	28	36	28	40	30	35
FG Attempts	35	23	33	29	25	39	24	33	20	26	25	38	25	28
FG Made	17	13	22	14	14	12	18	21	9	16	13	25	8	12
Pct. FG Made	48.6	56.5	66.7	48.3	56.0	30.8	75.0	63.6	45.0	61.5	52.0	65.8	32.0	42.9
Safeties	0	0	0	0	1	0	0	0	0	0	0	1	1	1

DEFENSE

	BALT.	CHI.	CLEVE.	DALLAS	DET.	G.BAY	L.A.	MINN.	N.Y.	PHIL.	PITT.	ST.L.	S.F.	WASH.
FIRST DOWNS:														
Total	242	248	275	211	241	197	235	216	247	234	253	235	255	243
by Rushing	93	99	119	71	92	95	92	94	101	93	109	96	90	101
by Passing	121	121	137	121	128	91	131	105	127	128	121	128	138	125
by Penalty	28	28	19	19	21	11	12	17	19	13	23	11	27	17
RUSHING:														
Number	422	436	465	439	429	417	419	389	468	445	454	414	443	440
Yards	1798	1863	2012	1504	1638	1532	1501	1616	1919	1746	1994	1800	1560	1813
Average Yards	4.3	4.3	4.3	3.4	3.8	3.7	3.6	4.2	4.1	3.9	4.4	4.0	3.5	4.1
Touchdowns	13	19	18	6	10	15	14	10	15	15	15	13	11	20
PASSING:														
Attempts	385	366	401	377	406	318	435	375	361	406	378	389	434	406
Completions	217	188	230	172	226	173	213	182	188	202	185	193	232	193
Completion Pct.	56.4	51.4	57.4	45.6	55.7	54.4	49.0	48.5	52.1	49.8	48.9	49.6	53.5	47.5
Passing Yards	2621	2897	2932	2571	2906	1980	3094	2993	2799	2950	2582	2848	3141	2600
Avg. Yds per Att.	6.8	7.9	7.3	6.8	7.2	6.2	7.1	8.0	7.8	7.3	6.8	7.3	7.2	6.4
Avg. Yds per Comp.	12.1	15.4	12.7	14.9	12.9	11.4	14.5	16.4	14.9	14.6	14.0	14.8	13.5	13.5
Times Tackled	57	30	28	45	50	45	49	36	44	47	42	42	43	43
Yards Lost Tackled	489	275	222	325	482	333	400	269	355	379	345	356	297	353
Net Yards	2132	2622	2710	2246	2424	1647	2694	2724	2444	2571	2237	2492	2844	2247
Touchdowns	14	27	18	22	14	11	27	23	28	18	16	21	23	16
Interceptions	23	10	19	18	22	16	17	19	15	17	12	25	15	34
Pct. Intercepted	6.0	2.7	4.7	4.8	5.4	5.0	3.9	5.1	4.2	4.2	3.2	6.4	3.5	8.4
PUNTING:														
Number	73	62	57	80	66	72	73	71	59	80	67	67	76	67
Average Distance	44.0	46.6	39.7	43.5	44.0	43.5	45.1	43.8	42.2	40.5	39.5	43.5	45.8	42.1
PUNT RETURNS:														
Number	25	35	20	19	33	31	43	30	40	35	24	26	50	50
Yards	175	436	183	52	243	397	360	247	559	333	172	151	540	362
Average Yards	7.0	12.5	15.3	2.7	7.4	12.8	8.4	8.2	14.0	9.5	7.2	5.8	10.8	7.2
Touchdowns	1	0	0	0	0	2	0	0	2	0	0	0	2	0
KICKOFF RETURNS:														
Number	70	47	75	50	48	60	58	57	45	55	40	63	37	60
Yards	1490	1183	1517	1090	1052	1320	1544	1324	990	1319	989	1663	883	1499
Average Yards	21.3	25.2	20.2	21.8	21.9	22.0	26.6	23.2	22.0	24.0	24.7	26.4	23.9	25.0
Touchdowns	0	0	0	0	0	0	0	2	0	0	0	0	0	0
INTERCEPTION RETURNS:														
Number	9	21	19	24	21	6	20	12	26	18	24	24	22	16
Yards	119	260	154	370	247	58	452	149	332	273	465	302	530	321
Average Yards	13.2	12.4	8.1	15.4	11.8	9.7	22.6	10.6	12.8	15.2	19.4	12.6	24.1	20.1
Touchdowns	0	1	0	4	3	0	2	0	2	3	6	0	2	3
PENALTIES:														
Number	59	84	64	75	83	56	70	70	75	71	81	71	76	60
Yards	641	743	643	781	805	521	675	708	674	748	706	695	783	624
FUMBLES:														
Number	28	32	30	26	29	34	28	32	42	27	24	24	33	42
Number Lost	18	20	21	20	8	25	13	16	18	12	14	14	14	21
POINTS:														
Total	225	379	293	289	260	245	339	296	399	313	315	331	330	305
PAT Attempts	28	47	36	34	29	30	44	36	49	40	39	36	40	39
PAT Made	27	46	32	32	29	29	42	33	46	40	36	34	39	36
FG Attempts	24	26	23	29	38	23	27	28	39	26	25	34	34	27
FG Made	10	17	15	17	19	12	11	13	19	11	15	27	17	11
Pct. FG Made	41.7	65.4	65.2	58.6	50.0	52.2	40.7	46.4	48.7	42.3	60.0	79.4	50.0	40.7
Safeties	0	0	0	1	0	0	0	1	1	0	0	0	0	1

1964 NFL CHAMPIONSHIP GAME

December 27, at Cleveland
(Attendance 79,544)

Whitewashing the Aerialists

The Colts came into the game as heavy favorites, but the Cleveland defense effectively shut off the famous Baltimore passing attack as the Browns themselves made several big plays through the air. Neither club scored in the first half, as quarterbacks Johnny Unitas and Frank Ryan both used conservative plays to feel out the enemy. Early in the third quarter, however, a 29-yard punt by Baltimore's Tom Gilburg gave the Browns good field position and led to Lou Groza's 43-yard field goal, which finally broke the scoreless deadlock. As soon as the Browns got the ball back, they sprang Jimmy Brown loose on a pitchout good for 46 yards; in short order, Ryan hit Gary Collins with an 18-yard scoring pass. Then, just before the end of the quarter, Ryan stunned the Colts by throwing a 42-yard bomb to Collins, which, along with the extra point, ran the score up to 17-0. The Colts, in a state of shock over this sudden Cleveland outburst, tried to fight their way back into the game but could make no headway against the charged-up Brown defense. The Browns added a nine-yard Groza field goal early in the final period to run their lead to 20-0, and Ryan threw a 51-yard scoring pass to Gary Collins, the third touchdown of the afternoon for the tall flanker, to make the final score a decisive 27-0 to give Cleveland their first championship since 1955.

TEAM STATISTICS

CLEVE.		BALT.
20	First Downs – Total	11
8	First Downs – Rushing	5
9	First Downs – Passing	4
3	First Downs – Penalty	2
3	Punts – Number	4
44.0	Punts – Average Distance	33.8
1	Punt Returns – Number	2
13	Punt Returns – Yards	18
2	Interception Returns – Number	1
10	Interception Returns – Yards	14
0	Fumbles – Number	2
0	Fumbles – Lost Ball	2
7	Penalties – Number	5
59	Yards Penalized	48
1	Giveaways	4
4	Takeaways	1
+3	Difference	–3

SCORING

CLEVELAND	0	0	17	10	–27
BALTIMORE	0	0	0	0	– 0

Third Quarter
Cle. Groza, 43 yard field goal
Cle. Collins, 18 yard pass from Ryan
PAT – Groza (kick)
Cle. Collins, 42 yard pass from Ryan
PAT – Groza (kick)

Fourth Quarter
Cle. Groza, 9 yard field goal
Cle. Collins, 51 yard pass from Ryan
PAT – Groza (kick)

INDIVIDUAL STATISTICS

CLEVELAND	No	Yds	Avg.	BALTIMORE	No	Yds	Avg.
RUSHING							
Brown	27	114	4.2	Moore	9	40	4.4
Green	10	29	2.9	Hill	9	31	3.4
Ryan	3	2	0.7	Unitas	6	30	5.0
Warfield	1	–3	–3.0	Boyd	1	–9	–9.0
	41	142	3.5		25	92	3.7
RECEIVING							
Collins	5	130	26.0	Berry	3	38	12.7
Brown	3	37	12.3	Lorick	3	18	6.0
Brewer	2	26	13.0	Orr	2	31	15.5
Warfield	1	13	13.0	Moore	2	4	2.0
	11	206	18.7	Mackey	1	2	2.0
				Hill	1	2	2.0
					12	95	7.9

PASSING

	Att	Comp	Comp Pct.	Yds	Int	Yds/ Att.	Yds/ Comp	Yards Lost Tackled
CLEVELAND								
Ryan	18	11	61.6	206	1	11.4	18.7	9
BALTIMORE								
Unitas	20	12	60.0	95	2	4.8	7.9	6

1964 N.F.L. — Eastern Conference

CLEVELAND BROWNS 10-3-1 Blanton Collier

Scores of Each Game		
27	Washington	13
33	ST. LOUIS	33
28	Philadelphia	20
27	DALLAS	6
7	PITTSBURGH	23
20	Dallas	16
42	NEW YORK	20
30	Pittsburgh	17
34	WASHINGTON	24
37	DETROIT	21
21	Green Bay	28
38	PHILADELPHIA	24
19	St. Louis	28
52	New York	20

Use Name	Pos.	Hgt	Wgt	Age	Int	Pts
John Brown	OT	6'2"	248	25		
Monte Clark	OT	6'6"	265	27		
Dick Schafrath	OT	6'3"	255	28		
Roger Shoals	OG-OT	6'4"	255	25		6
Gene Hickerson	OG	6'3"	248	29		
Dale Memmelaar	OG	6'2"	248	27		
John Wooten	OG	6'2"	250	29		
John Morrow	C	6'3"	248	31		
Bill Glass	DE	6'5"	255	28		
Paul Wiggin	DE	6'3"	245	30		6
Sid Williams	DE	6'2"	235	22		6
Mike Bundra (from MIN)	DT	6'3"	260	25		
Bob Gain	DT	6'3"	260	36		
Jim Kanicki	DT	6'4"	270	22		
Dick Modzelewski	DT	6'	260	33		
Frank Parker	DT	6'5"	255	24		
Ed Bettridge	LB	6'1"	235	24		
Vince Costello	LB	6'	228	32	2	
Galen Fiss	LB	6'	227	34	1	
Jim Houston	LB	6'2"	240	27	2	6
Mike Lucci	LB	6'2"	233	24		
Stan Sczurek	LB	5'11"	230	25		
Walter Beach	DB	6'	185	29	4	6
Larry Benz	DB	5'11"	185	23	4	
Lowell Caylor	DB	6'3"	205	23		
Ross Fichtner	DB	6'	185	26	2	
Bobby Franklin	DB	5'11"	182	28		
Bernie Parrish	DB	5'11"	195	29	4	6
Dave Raimey	DB	5'10"	195	23		
Jim Ninowski	QB	6'1"	207	28		
Frank Ryan	QB	6'3"	200	28		6
Ernie Green	HB	6'2"	205	25		60
Leroy Kelly	HB	6'	195	22		6
Jimmy Brown	FB	6'2"	228	28		54
Charlie Scales	FB	5'11"	215	25		6
Gary Collins	FL	6'4"	208	23		48
Clifton McNeil	FL	6'2"	185	24		6
Walter Roberts	FL	5'10"	175	22		6
Johnny Brewer	OE	6'4"	235	27		18
Tom Hutchinson	OE	6'1"	190	23		
Paul Warfield	OE	6'	188	21		54
Lou Groza	K	6'3"	250	40		115

ST. LOUIS CARDINALS 9-3-2 Wally Lemm

Scores of Each Game		
16	Dallas	6
33	Cleveland	33
23	San Francisco	13
23	Washington	17
27	Baltimore	47
38	WASHINGTON	24
13	DALLAS	31
17	New York	34
34	PITTSBURGH	30
10	NEW YORK	10
38	Philadelphia	13
21	Pittsburgh	20
28	CLEVELAND	19
36	PHILADELPHIA	34

Use Name	Pos.	Hgt	Wgt	Age	Int	Pts
Ernie McMillan	OT	6'6"	255	26		
Bob Reynolds	OT	6'6"	265	23		
Ed Cook	OG-OT	6'2"	250	32		
Irv Goode	OG	6'4"	250	23		
Ken Gray	OG	6'2"	250	28		
Rick Sortun	OG	6'2"	225	21		
Herschel Turner	OT-OG	6'3"	230	22		
Bob DeMarco	C	6'3"	240	26		
Don Brumm	DE	6'3"	245	21		
Tom Redmond	DE	6'5"	240	27		
Joe Robb	DE	6'3"	245	27		
Chuck Walker	DE	6'2"	235	23		
Ken Kortas	DT	6'2"	290	22		
Luke Owens	DT	6'2"	260	31		
Sam Silas	DT	6'4"	250	21		
Bill Koman	LB	6'2"	230	30	2	
Dave Meggyesy	LB	6'1"	220	22		
Dale Meinert	LB	6'2"	220	31	2	6
Marion Rushing	LB	6'2"	230	27		2
Larry Stallings	LB	6'2"	230	22	2	
Monk Bailey	DB	6'	175	26		
Jimmy Burson	DB	6'	180	22	3	6
Pat Fischer	DB	5'10"	180	24	10	18
Jimmy Hill	DB	6'2"	195	35		
Jerry Stovall	DB	6'2"	205	22	3	6
Larry Wilson	DB	6'	190	26	3	6
Buddy Humphrey	QB	6'1"	200	28		
Charley Johnson	QB	6'	190	27		12
Joe Childress	HB	6'	210	30		12
Bob Paremore	HB	5'11"	190	24		
John David Crow	FB-HB	6'2"	220	29		48
Willie Crenshaw	FB	6'2"	215	23		6
Prentice Gautt	FB	6'	205	26		12
Bill Thornton	FB	6'1"	220	24		6
Bobby Joe Conrad	FL	6'	195	29		36
Taz Anderson	OE	6'2"	215	25		
Billy Gambrell	OE	5'10"	175	22		12
Sonny Randle	OE	6'2"	190	28		30
Jackie Smith	OE	6'4"	210	23		24
Mal Hammack	LB-OE	6'2"	210	31		
Jim Bakken	K	6'	200	23		115

Bill Triplett – Illness

PHILADELPHIA EAGLES 6-8-0 Joe Kuharich

Scores of Each Game		
38	NEW YORK	7
24	SAN FRANCISCO	28
20	CLEVELAND	28
21	PITTSBURGH	7
20	Washington	35
23	New York	17
34	Pittsburgh	10
10	WASHINGTON	21
10	Los Angeles	20
17	Dallas	14
13	ST. LOUIS	38
24	Cleveland	38
24	DALLAS	14
34	St. Louis	36

Use Name	Pos.	Hgt	Wgt	Age	Int	Pts
Bob Brown	OT	6'4"	280	21		
Dave Graham	OT	6'3"	250	25		
Jim Skaggs	OT	6'2"	230	24		
Ed Blaine	OG	6'2"	240	24		
Pete Case	OG	6'3"	243	23		
Lynn Hoyem	C	6'4"	240	24		
Jim Ringo	C	6'1"	230	33		
Jim Schrader	C	6'2"	250	32		
Riley Gunnels	DE	6'3"	253	27		
Don Hultz	DE	6'3"	235	23		
Bobby Richards	DE	6'2"	245	25		
George Tarasovic	DE	6'4"	245	35		
Don Thompson	DE	6'4"	240	25		
Ed Khayat	DT	6'3"	245	29		
John Meyers	DT	6'6"	267	24		
Floyd Peters	DT	6'4"	255	29		
Maxie Baughan	LB	6'1"	230	26		
Ralph Heck	LB	6'2"	224	23		
Dave Lloyd	LB	6'3"	248	28	3	
Mike Morgan	LB	6'4"	232	22		6
Don Burroughs	DB	6'4"	187	33	2	
Irv Cross	DB	6'1"	195	25	3	6
Glenn Glass	DB	6'	190	27	1	
Nate Ramsey	DB	6'1"	200	23	5	
Joe Scarpati	DB	5'10"	185	22	3	6
Claude Crabb	FL-DB	6'	197	24		
Jack Concannon	QB	6'3"	195	21		6
King Hill	QB	6'3"	213	28		
Norm Snead	QB	6'4"	215	24		12
Timmy Brown	HB	5'10"	200	27		60
Roger Gill	HB	6'1"	200	23		
Ollie Matson	HB	6'2"	210	34		30
Earl Gros	FB	6'3"	230	23		12
Izzy Lang	FB	6'1"	230	21		
Tom Woodeshick	FB	6'	205	22		12
Red Mack	FL	5'10"	185	27		6
Ron Goodwin	OE-FL	6'	184	22		18
Ray Poage	OE	6'4"	203	23		6
Pete Retzlaff	OE	6'1"	214	33		48
Ralph Smith	DB-OE	6'2"	213	25		
Sam Baker	K	6'2"	220	32		84

Jerry Mazzanti – Military Service
Mike McClellan – Military Service
Fate Echols – Canadian Football League

WASHINGTON REDSKINS 6-8-0 Bill McPeak

Scores of Each Game		
13	CLEVELAND	27
18	Dallas	24
10	New York	13
17	ST. LOUIS	23
35	PHILADELPHIA	20
24	St. Louis	38
27	CHICAGO	20
21	Philadelphia	10
24	Cleveland	34
30	Pittsburgh	0
28	DALLAS	16
36	NEW YORK	21
7	PITTSBURGH	14
17	Baltimore	45

Use Name	Pos.	Hgt	Wgt	Age	Int	Pts
Steve Barnett	OT	6'1"	255	23		
Riley Mattson	OT	6'4"	254	25		
Fran O'Brien	OT	6'1"	255	29		
John Nisby	OG	6'1"	238	31		
Vince Promuto	OG	6'1"	245	26		
George Seals	OG	6'2"	250	21		
Fred Hageman	C	6'4"	242	26		
Len Hauss	C	6'2"	220	22		
Carl Kammerer	DE	6'3"	237	27		
John Paluck	DE	6'2"	245	32		2
Ron Snidow	DE	6'4"	250	22		
Joe Rutgens	DT	6'2"	255	25		
Bob Toneff	DT	6'3"	257	34		
Fred Williams	DT	6'4"	248	34		
Rod Breedlove	LB	6'2"	227	26		
Jimmy Carr	LB	6'1"	210	31	2	
Sam Huff	LB	6'1"	230	29	4	
Bob Pellegrini	LB	6'2"	237	29		
John Reger	LB	6'	230	33	3	6
Paul Krause	DB	6'3"	198	22	12	6
Johnny Sample	DB	6'1"	200	27	4	6
Lonnie Sanders	DB	6'3"	210	22	2	
Jim Shorter	DB	5'11"	186	23	1	
Jim Steffen	DB	6'	196	27	4	
Tom Walters	DB	6'2"	195	22	2	
George Izo	QB	6'3"	218	27		
Sonny Jurgensen	QB	5'11"	200	30		18
Dick Shiner	QB	6'	190	22		
Pervis Atkins	HB	6'1"	217	28		6
Charley Taylor	HB	6'3"	215	23		60
Tom Tracy	HB	5'9"	205	32		6
Don Bosseler	FB	6'1"	214	28		
J.W. Lockett	FB	6'2"	226	27		18
Ozzie Clay	FL	6'	190	22		
Joe Hernandez	FL	6'2"	180	24		
Bobby Mitchell	FL	6'	196	29		60
Preston Carpenter	OE	6'2"	190	30		18
Angie Coia	OE	6'2"	202	26		30
Pat Richter	OE	6'5"	230	23		
Jim Martin	K	6'2"	238	40		71

DALLAS COWBOYS 5-8-1 Tom Landry

Scores of Each Game		
6	ST. LOUIS	16
24	WASHINGTON	18
17	Pittsburgh	23
6	Cleveland	27
13	NEW YORK	13
16	CLEVELAND	20
31	St. Louis	13
24	Chicago	10
31	New York	21
14	PHILADELPHIA	17
16	Washington	28
21	GREEN BAY	45
14	Philadelphia	24
17	PITTSBURGH	14

Use Name	Pos.	Hgt	Wgt	Age	Int	Pts
Jim Boeke	OT	6'5"	255	25		
Bill Frank	OT	6'5"	255	26		
Bob Fry	OT	6'4"	238	33		
Tony Liscio	OT	6'5"	240	24		
Ray Schoenke	OT	6'3"	234	22		
Jim Ray Smith	OG-OT	6'3"	245	33		
Joe Bob Isbell	OG	6'1"	250	24		
Jake Kupp	OG	6'3"	215	22		
Mike Connelly	C	6'3"	242	28		
Dave Manders	C	6'2"	240	22		
George Andrie	DE	6'7"	264	24		
Larry Stephens	DE	6'4"	260	26		
Maury Youmans	DE	6'6"	260	27		
Jim Colvin	DT	6'2"	253	27		
Bob Lilly	DT	6'4"	250	25		
Dave Edwards	LB	6'3"	213	25	1	
Harold Hays	LB	6'3"	235	23		
Chuck Howley	LB	6'3"	223	28	2	
Lee Roy Jordon	LB	6'2"	215	23	1	
Jerry Tubbs	LB	6'2"	215	29	2	
Don Bishop	DB	6'2"	215	29		
Mike Gaechter	DB	6'	196	24		
Cornell Green	DB	6'4"	220	24		
Warren Livingston	DB	5'10"	185	26	1	6
Mel Renfro	DB	6'	190	22	7	12
Jimmy Ridlon	DB	6'1"	180	29	4	12
Billy Lothridge	QB	6'1"	185	20		6
Don Meredith	QB	6'2"	205	26		24
John Roach	QB	6'4"	200	31		
Amos Bullocks	HB	6'1"	202	25		
Perry Lee Dunn	HB	6'2"	200	21		6
Amos Marsh	HB	6'1"	225	25		12
Jim Stiger	FB-HB	5'11"	190	23		12
Don Perkins	FB	5'10"	196	26		36
Frank Clarke	FL	6'	215	31		30
Buddy Dial	FL	6'1"	195	27		
Tommy McDonald	FL	5'10"	172	30		12
Lee Folkins	OE	6'5"	220	25		
Pete Gent	OE	6'4"	215	21		
Pettis Norman	OE	6'3"	223	24		12
Dick Van Raaphorst	K	5'11"	215	21		70

Jerry Overton – Off-season accident
Don Talbert – Military Service

CLEVELAND BROWNS

RUSHING
Last Name	No.	Yds	Avg	TD
Jimmy Brown	280	1446	5.2	7
Green	109	491	4.5	6
Ryan	37	217	5.9	1
Kelly	6	12	2.0	0
Scales	2	5	2.5	0
Ninowski	1	−8	−8.0	0

RECEIVING
Last Name	No.	Yds	Avg	TD
Warfield	52	920	18	9
Jimmy Brown	36	340	9	2
Collins	35	544	16	8
Brewer	25	338	14	3
Green	25	283	11	4
McNeil	4	69	17	1
Hutchinson	3	24	8	0
Roberts	1	24	24	1

PUNT RETURNS
Last Name	No.	Yds	Avg	TD
Kelly	9	171	19	1
Roberts	10	132	13	0
Williams	1	0	0	0

KICKOFF RETURNS
Last Name	No.	Yds	Avg	TD
Roberts	24	661	28	0
Kelly	24	582	24	0
Scales	5	75	15	0
Warfield	1	4	4	0
Franklin	1	1	1	0
Clark	1	0	0	0
Williams	1	0	0	0

PASSING – PUNTING – KICKING
PASSING
Last Name	Att	Comp	%	Yds	Yd/Att	TD	Int−	%	RK
Ryan	334	174	52	2404	7.2	25	19−	6	6
Ninowski	9	6	67	125	13.9	2	0−	0	
Jimmy Brown	1	1	100	13	13.0	1	0−	0	

PUNTING
Last Name	No	Avg
Collins	48	42.0
Franklin	1	36.0

KICKING
Last Name	XP	Att	%	FG	Att	%
Groza	49	50	98	22	33	67

ST. LOUIS CARDINALS

RUSHING
Last Name	No.	Yds	Avg	TD
Crow	163	554	3.4	7
Childress	102	413	4.0	0
Crenshaw	60	297	5.0	1
Thornton	39	236	6.1	1
Gautt	59	191	3.2	1
Johnson	31	93	3.0	2
Wilson	2	−14	−7.0	0

RECEIVING
Last Name	No.	Yds	Avg	TD
Conrad	61	780	13	6
Smith	47	657	14	4
Randle	25	517	21	5
Gambrell	24	398	17	2
Crow	23	257	11	1
Childress	12	203	17	2
Gautt	9	72	8	1
Crenshaw	8	58	7	0
Anderson	7	60	9	0
Thornton	7	43	6	0

PUNT RETURNS
Last Name	No.	Yds	Avg	TD
Gambrell	12	126	11	0
Bruson	12	125	10	1

KICKOFF RETURNS
Last Name	No.	Yds	Avg	TD
Stovall	24	566	24	0
Crenshaw	13	340	26	0
Paremore	9	192	21	0
Gautt	5	104	21	0
Gambrell	4	92	23	0
Hammack	2	61	31	0
Burson	2	38	19	0
Conrad	1	26	26	0
Thornton	1	5	5	0
Gray	2	0	0	0

PASSING – PUNTING – KICKING
PASSING
Last Name	Att	Comp	%	Yds	Yd/Att	TD	Int−	%	RK
Johnson	420	223	53	3045	7.3	21	24−	6	7
Crow	1	0	0	0	0.0	0	0−	0	
Humphrey	1	0	0	0	0.0	0.	0−	0	

PUNTING
Last Name	No	Avg
Smith	41	40.4
Stovall	15	42.1

KICKING
Last Name	XP	Att	%	FG	Att	%
Bakken	40	40	100	25	38	66

PHILADELPHIA EAGLES

RUSHING
Last Name	No.	Yds	Avg	TD
Gros	154	748	4.9	2
Matson	96	404	4.2	4
T. Brown	90	356	4.0	5
Woodeshick	37	180	4.9	2
Concannon	16	134	8.4	1
Snead	16	59	3.7	2
Lang	12	37	3.1	0
Hill	8	27	3.4	0
Goodwin	1	−23	−23.0	0

RECEIVING
Last Name	No.	Yds	Avg	TD
Retzlaff	51	855	17	8
Poage	37	479	13	1
Gros	29	234	8	0
Goodwin	23	335	15	3
Matson	17	242	14	1
T. Brown	15	244	16	5
Mack	8	169	21	0
Lang	6	69	12	0
Gill	4	58	15	0
Smith	4	35	9	0
Woodeshick	4	12	3	0
Crabb	1	14	14	0

PUNT RETURNS
Last Name	No.	Yds	Avg	TD
T. Brown	10	96	10	0
Gill	6	61	10	0
Lang	6	26	4	0
Matson	2	10	5	0
Scarpati	1	6	6	0
Hultz	1	2	2	0
Glass	1	0	0	0
Mack	1	0	0	0

KICKOFF RETURNS
Last Name	No.	Yds	Avg	TD
T. Brown	30	692	23	0
Lang	13	352	27	0
Gill	7	167	24	0
Matson	3	104	35	0
Gros	2	38	19	0
Glass	1	12	12	0
Morgan	2	0	0	0
Thompson	1	0	0	0

PASSING – PUNTING – KICKING
PASSING
Last Name	Att	Comp	%	Yds	Yd/Att	TD	Int−	%	RK
Snead	283	138	49	1906	6.7	14	12−	4	11
Hill	88	49	56	641	7.3	3	4−	5	
Concannon	23	12	52	199	8.7	2	1−	4	
T. Brown	2	0	0	0	0.0	0	1−	50	
Gros	1	0	0	0	0.0	0	0−	0	

PUNTING
Last Name	No	Avg
Baker	49	42.3
Hill	24	40.3

KICKING
Last Name	XP	Att	%	FG	Att	%
Baker	36	37	97	16	26	62

WASHINGTON REDSKINS

RUSHING
Last Name	No.	Yds	Avg	TD
Taylor	199	755	3.8	5
Lockett	63	175	2.8	1
Atkins	25	98	3.9	1
Tracy	24	67	2.8	1
Jurgensen	27	57	2.1	3
Bosseler	22	46	2.1	0
Mitchell	2	33	16.5	0
Shiner	2	8	4.0	0
Carpenter	1	7	7.0	0
Richter	1	−9	−9.0	0

RECEIVING
Last Name	No.	Yds	Avg	TD
Mitchell	60	904	15	10
Taylor	53	814	15	5
Carpenter	31	466	15	3
Coia	29	500	17	5
Lockett	20	204	10	2
Atkins	8	35	4	0
Bosseler	6	56	9	0
Richter	4	49	12	0
Tracy	2	25	13	0
Hernandez	1	18	18	0

PUNT RETURNS
Last Name	No.	Yds	Avg	TD
Atkins	13	138	11	0
Hernandez	5	49	10	0
Shorter	6	19	3	0
Carpenter	2	19	10	0
Clay	4	5	1	0
Carr	1	0	0	0
Kammerer	1	0	0	0

KICKOFF RETURNS
Last Name	No.	Yds	Avg	TD
Clay	19	482	25	0
Atkins	14	319	23	0
Shorter	5	81	16	0
Lockett	3	72	24	0
Mitchell	3	58	19	0
Mattson	3	30	10	0
Taylor	1	20	20	0
Hernandez	1	19	19	0
Snidow	1	16	16	0
Carr	1	0	0	0
Pellegrini	1	0	0	0

PASSING – PUNTING – KICKING
PASSING
Last Name	Att	Comp	%	Yds	Yd/Att	TD	Int−	%	RK
Jurgensen	385	207	54	2934	7.6	24	13−	3	3
Izo	18	5	28	83	4.6	1	2−	11	
Taylor	10	2	20	54	5.4	0	1−	10	
Carpenter	1	0	0	0	0.0	0	0−	0	
Shiner	1	0	0	0	0.0	0	0−	0	

PUNTING
Last Name	No	Avg
Richter	91	41.2

KICKING
Last Name	XP	Att	%	FG	Att	%
Martin	35	39	90	12	28	43

DALLAS COWBOYS

RUSHING
Last Name	No.	Yds	Avg	TD
Perkins	174	768	4.4	6
Marsh	100	401	4.0	2
Stiger	68	280	4.1	1
Dunn	26	103	4.0	1
Meredith	32	81	2.5	4
Clarke	10	46	4.6	0
Roach	8	9	1.1	0
Folkins	1	9	9.0	0
Lothridge	2	−6	−3.0	1

RECEIVING
Last Name	No.	Yds	Avg	TD
Clarke	65	973	15	5
McDonald	46	612	13	2
Norman	24	311	13	2
Perkins	15	155	10	0
Marsh	15	131	9	0
Dial	11	178	16	0
Stiger	9	85	9	1
Folkins	5	41	8	0
Dunn	2	30	15	0

PUNT RETURNS
Last Name	No.	Yds	Avg	TD
Renfro	32	418	13	1
Gaechter	5	24	5	0
McDonald	2	17	9	0
Stiger	1	0	0	0

KICKOFF RETURNS
Last Name	No.	Yds	Avg	TD
Renfro	40	1017	25	0
Dunn	2	333	17	0
Gaechter	1	31	31	0
Bullocks	1	19	19	0
Marsh	1	2	2	0
Folkins	1	0	0	0

PASSING – PUNTING – KICKING
PASSING
Last Name	Att	Comp	%	Yds	Yd/Att	TD	Int−	%	RK
Meredith	323	158	49	2143	6.6	9	16−	5	15
Roach	68	32	47	349	5.1	1	6−	9	
Lothridge	9	2	22	24	2.7	0	2−	22	
Dunn	2	0	0	0	0.0	0	0−	0	
Clarke	1	0	0	0	0.0	0	0−	0	
Stiger	1	0	0	0	0.0	0	0−	0	

PUNTING
Last Name	No	Avg
Lothridge	62	40.3
Folkins	15	33.1
Howley	1	37.0

KICKING
Last Name	XP	Att	%	FG	Att	%
Van Raaphorst	28	29	97	14	29	48

EASTERN CONFERENCE – Continued

PITTSBURGH STEELERS 5-9-0 Buddy Parker

Scores of Each Game		
14	LOS ANGELES	26
27	NEW YORK	24
23	DALLAS	17
7	Philadelphia	21
23	Cleveland	7
10	Minnesota	30
10	PHILADELPHIA	34
17	CLEVELAND	30
30	St. Louis	34
0	WASHINGTON	30
44	New York	17
20	ST. LOUIS	21
14	Washington	7
14	Dallas	17

Use Name	Pos.	Hgt	Wgt	Age	Int	Pts
Charlie Bradshaw	OT	6'6"	255	28		
Dan James	OT	6'4"	250	27		
Ray Lemek	OG	6'	240	30		
Mike Sandusky	OG	6'	230	31		
Ron Stehouwer	OG	6'2"	230	27		
Buzz Nutter	C	6'4"	230	33		
John Baker	DE	6'6"	270	29		
Dan LaRose	DE	6'5"	250	24		
Ben McGee	DE	6'2"	250	22		
Urban Henry	DT	6'4"	265	29		
Chuck Hinton	DT	6'5"	235	25	1	6
Joe Krupa	DT	6'2"	235	31		
Ray Mansfield	DT	6'3"	255	23		
Bob Harrison	LB	6'2"	225	27		
Max Messner (from NY)	LB	6'3"	225	26		
Myron Pottios	LB	6'2"	240	24	1	
Bill Saul	LB	6'4"	225	23	1	
Bob Schmitz	LB	6'1"	230	26		
Bob Soleau	LB	6'2"	235	23		
Ed Holler	LB	6'2"	235	24	1	
Jim Bradshaw	DB	6'1"	190	25	1	12
Willie Daniel	DB	5'11"	185	26	2	
Dick Haley	DB	5'10"	190	28	2	
Brady Keys	DB	6'	190	28	2	
Bob Sherman	DB	6'2"	195	22		
Ed Brown	QB	6'2"	210	35		12
Bill Nelsen	QB	6'	195	23		
Terry Nofsinger	QB	6'4"	205	26		
Tom Wade	QB	6'2"	195	22		
Dick Hoak	HB	5'11"	190	25		30
Phil King	HB	6'4"	218	28		12
Theron Sapp	HB	6'1"	200	29		
Marv Woodson	HB	6'	195	21		
John Henry Johnson	FB	6'2"	215	34		48
Clarence Peaks	FB	6'1"	212	28		12
Gary Ballman	OE-FL	6'	195	24		42
Paul Martha	OE-FL	6'	185	21		
John Burrell	OE	6'3"	190	24		
Jim Kelly	OE	6'2"	215	22		6
Chuck Logan	OE	6'4"	210	21		
John Powers	OE	6'2"	210	23		
Clendon Thomas	DB-OE	6'2"	195	27	1	6
Mike Clark	K	6'1"	200	23		67

Andy Russell – Military Service

NEW YORK GIANTS 2-10-2 Allie Sherman

Scores of Each Game		
7	Philadelphia	38
24	Pittsburgh	27
13	WASHINGTON	10
3	Detroit	26
13	Dallas	13
17	PHILADELPHIA	23
20	Cleveland	42
34	ST. LOUIS	17
21	DALLAS	31
10	St. Louis	10
17	PITTSBURGH	44
21	Washington	36
21	MINNESOTA	30
20	CLEVELAND	52

Use Name	Pos.	Hgt	Wgt	Age	Int	Pts
Roger Anderson	OT	6'5"	255	21		
Rosey Brown	OT	6'3"	255	31		
Lane Howell	OT	6'5"	255	23		
Frank Lasky	OT	6'2"	265	22		
Jack Stroud	OT	6'1"	250	35		
Bookie Bolin	OG	6'2"	240	24		
Ken Byers (to MIN)	OG	6'1"	240	24		
Darrell Dess	OG	6'	245	28		
Mickey Walker	C-OG	6'	235	24		
Greg Larson	C	6'2"	250	25		
Jim Katcavage	DE	6'3"	240	29		
Andy Robustelli	DE	6'1"	235	38		
Andy Stynchula	DT	6'3"	250	25		1
Bob Taylor	DE	6'3"	240	24		
John Contoulis	DT	6'4"	260	23		
John Lovetere	DT	6'4"	285	28		
Jim Moran	DT	6'5"	255	21		
Tom Costello	LB	6'3"	220	23		
Jerry Hillebrand	LB	6'3"	240	24	1	
Tom Scott	LB	6'2"	220	34	2	
Lou Slaby	LB	6'3"	235	22	2	
Bill Winter	LB	6'3"	220	24		
Erich Barnes	DB	6'2"	198	29	2	12
Dick Lynch	DB	6'1"	205	28	4	
Andy Nelson	DB	6'1"	180	31	1	
Jimmy Patton	DB	6'	185	32	2	
Dick Pesonen	DB	6'	190	26		
Allan Webb	DB	5'11"	180	29	1	
Y.A. Tittle	QB	6'	195	37		6
Gary Wood	QB	5'11"	188	21		18
Dick James	DB-HB	5'9"	182	30		24
Steve Thurlow	HB	6'3"	210	21		6
Clarence Childs	HB	6'	180	25		6
Alex Webster	FB	6'3"	220	33		18
Ernie Wheelwright	FB	6'3"	220	27		18
Frank Gifford	FL	6'1"	190	34		24
Homer Jones	FL	6'2"	205	23		
R. C. Owens	FL	6'3"	195	29		
Joe Morrison	HB-FL-OE	6'1"	212	26		18
Bob Crespino	OE	6'4"	225	26		
Del Shofner	OE	6'3"	185	28		
Aaron Thomas	FL-OE	6'3"	210	26		36
Don Chandler	K	6'2"	210	29		54

Joe Walton – Injury

WESTERN CONFERENCE

BALTIMORE COLTS 12-2-0 Don Shula

Scores of Each Game		
24	Minnesota	34
21	Green Bay	20
52	CHICAGO	0
35	LOS ANGELES	20
47	ST. LOUIS	27
24	GREEN BAY	21
34	Detroit	0
37	SAN FRANCISCO	7
40	Chicago	24
17	MINNESOTA	14
24	Los Angeles	7
14	San Francisco	3
14	DETROIT	31
45	WASHINGTON	17

Use Name	Pos.	Hgt	Wgt	Age	Int	Pts
George Preas	OT	6'2"	250	32		
Tom Gilburg	OT	6'5"	245	25		
Lou Kirouac	OT	6'3"	240	24		
Bob Vogel	OT	6'5"	250	22		
Jim Parker	OG	6'3"	275	30		
Alex Sandusky	OG	6'1"	242	32		
Dan Sullivan	OT-OG	6'3"	250	25		
Dick Szymanski	C	6'3"	235	32		
Ordell Braase	DE	6'4"	242	32		
Gino Marchetti	DE	6'4"	245	38		
Lou Michaels	DE	6'2"	235	28		104
John Diehl	DT	6'7"	275	28		
Fred Miller	DT	6'3"	245	23		
Guy Reese	DT	6'5"	258	24		
Billy Ray Smith	DT	6'4"	240	29		
Jackie Burkett	LB	6'4"	228	27		
Ted Davis	LB	6'1"	225	22		
Bill Pellington	LB	6'2"	238	35	2	
Don Shinnick	LB	6'	235	29	3	
Steve Stonebreaker	LB	6'3"	220	26		6
Wendell Harris	DB	5'11"	190	23	1	
Alvin Haymond	DB	6'	190	22		
Jerry Logan	DB	6'1"	185	23	6	6
Lenny Lyles	DB	6'2"	202	28	2	
Jim Welch	DB	6'	190	26		
Bobby Boyd	HB-DB	5'10"	190	26	9	
Gary Cuozzo	QB	6'1"	195	23		
Johnny Unitas	QB	6'1"	194	31		12
Tom Matte	HB	6'	205	25		6
Lenny Moore	HB	6'1"	190	31		**120**
Jerry Hill	FB	5'11"	210	24		36
Joe Don Looney	FB	6'1"	230	21		12
Tony Lorick	FB	6'1"	203	22		24
Jimmy Orr	FL	5'11"	175	28		36
Willie Richardson	FL	6'2"	198	24		
Ray Berry	OE	6'2"	187	31		36
Alex Hawkins	OE	6'1"	190	27		6
John Mackey	OE	6'3"	217	22		12
Neal Petties	OE	6'2"	198	23		6
Butch Wilson	OE	6'2"	218	22		6

GREEN BAY PACKERS 8-5-1 Vince Lombardi

Scores of Each Game		
23	CHICAGO	12
20	BALTIMORE	21
14	Detroit	10
23	MINNESOTA	24
24	SAN FRANCISCO	14
21	Baltimore	24
17	LOS ANGELES	27
42	Minnesota	13
30	DETROIT	7
14	San Francisco	24
28	CLEVELAND	21
45	Dallas	21
17	Chicago	3
24	Los Angeles	24

Use Name	Pos.	Hgt	Wgt	Age	Int	Pts
Forrest Gregg	OT	6'4"	250	31		
Steve Wright	OT	6'6"	250	22		
Norm Masters	OT	6'2"	250	31		
Bob Skoronski	C-OT	6'3"	250	31		
Dan Grimm	OG	6'3"	245	23		
Fuzzy Thurston	OG	6'1"	245	31		
Jerry Kramer	OG	6'3"	245	29		
John McDowell	OT-OG	6'3"	260	21		
Ken Bowman	C	6'3"	230	21		
Lionel Aldridge	DE	6'4"	245	22		6
Willie Davis	DE	6'3"	245	31		
Lloyd Voss	DE	6'4"	245	22		
Dave Hanner	DT	6'2"	260	35		
Henry Jordan	DT	6'3"	250	29		6
Ron Kostelnik	DT	6'4"	260	24		
Gene Breen	LB	6'2"	225	23		
Lee Roy Caffey	LB	6'3"	240	24	1	
Dan Currie	LB	6'3"	240	30	2	
Ray Nitschke	LB	6'3"	240	28	2	
Dave Robinson	LB	6'3"	245	23		
Tommy Crutcher	FB-LB	6'3"	220	22		
Herb Adderley	DB	6'1"	210	25	4	
Tom Brown	DB	6'1"	190	23	1	
Hank Gremminger	DB	6'1"	200	31	1	
Doug Hart	DB	6'	190	25	1	
Jerry Norton	DB	5'11"	195	34		
Jesse Whittenton	DB	6'	195	30	1	
Willie Wood	DB	5'10"	190	28	3	7
Zeke Bratkowski	QB	6'2"	200	32		
Dennis Claridge	QB	6'3"	225	22		
Bart Starr	QB	6'1"	200	31		18
Paul Hornung	HB	6'2"	215	27		107
Tom Moore	HB	6'2"	210	26		24
Elijah Pitts	HB	6'1"	205	25		12
Jim Taylor	FB	6'	215	29		90
Boyd Dowler	FL	6'5"	225	27		30
Bob Long	FL	6'3"	190	23		
Bob Jeter	OE-FL	6'1"	205	26		
Marv Fleming	OE	6'4"	230	22		
Ron Kramer	OE	6'3"	240	29		
Max McGee	OE	6'3"	205	32		42

Ken Iman – Broken Hand

MINNESOTA VIKINGS 8-5-1 Norm Van Brocklin

Scores of Each Game		
34	BALTIMORE	24
28	CHICAGO	34
13	Los Angeles	22
24	Green Bay	23
20	DETROIT	24
30	PITTSBURGH	10
27	San Francisco	22
13	GREEN BAY	42
24	SAN FRANCISCO	7
14	Baltimore	17
23	Detroit	23
34	LOS ANGELES	13
30	New York	21
41	Chicago	14

Use Name	Pos.	Hgt	Wgt	Age	Int	Pts
Grady Alderman	OT	6'2"	245	25		
Errol Linden	OT	6'5"	260	27		
Larry Bowie	OG	6'2"	245	24		
Palmer Pyle	OG	6'2"	250	27		
Milt Sunde	OG	6'2"	222	21		
Mick Tingelhoff	C	6'1"	235	24		
Bob Denton	DE	6'4"	244	30		
Carl Eller	DE	6'6"	247	22		6
Jim Marshall	DE	6'3"	235	26		
Howard Simpson	DE	6'5"	230	21		
Paul Dickson	DT	6'5"	255	27		
Dave O'Brien	DT	6'3"	247	23		
Jim Prestel	DT	6'5"	275	27	1	6
John Campbell	LB	6'3"	215	25		
Rip Hawkins	LB	6'3"	230	25	2	12
Bill Jobko	LB	6'2"	225	28		
John Kirby	LB	6'3"	222	22		
Bill Swain	LB	6'2"	228	23		
Roy Winston	LB	6'1"	230	24	3	
Lee Calland	DB	6'	190	23		
Karl Kassulke	DB	6'	193	22	3	
George Rose	DB	5'11"	190	21	6	6
Ed Sharockman	DB	6'	200	24	1	
Bill Butler	HB-DB	5'10"	200	27	2	
Larry Vargo	OE-DB	6'3"	215	24	1	
Fran Tarkenton	QB	6'1"	190	24		12
Ron Vander Kelen	QB	6'1"	185	24		
Ted Dean	HB	6'2"	213	26		
Tommy Mason	HB	6'	196	25		30
Tom Michel	HB	6'	210	23		
Bill Brown	FB	5'11"	220	26		96
Darrell Lester	FB	6'2"	225	23		
Bill McWatters	FB	6'	225	22		6
Tom Hall	FL	6'1"	195	23		12
Hal Bedsole	OE	6'4"	230	22		30
Paul Flatley	OE	6'1"	187	23		18
Bob Lacey	OE	6'3"	205	22		
Jerry Reichow	OE	6'2"	220	29		12
Gordon Smith	OE	6'2"	220	25		6
Fred Cox	K	5'10"	200	25		103
Bobby Walden	K	6'	195	26		

Chuck Lamson – Injury
Terry Dillon – Accidentally Drowned in May

EASTERN CONFERENCE—Continued

PITTSBURGH STEELERS

RUSHING

Last Name	No.	Yds	Avg	TD
Johnson	235	1048	4.5	7
Peaks	118	503	4.3	2
Hoak	84	258	3.1	2
Brown	26	110	4.2	2
King	26	71	2.7	1
Ballman	11	43	3.9	0
Nelsen	3	17	5.7	0
Sapp	4	15	3.8	0
Martha	4	12	3.0	0
Powers	2	10	5.0	0
Holler	1	8	8.0	0
Thomas	2	7	3.5	0

RECEIVING

Last Name	No.	Yds	Avg	TD
Ballman	47	935	20	7
Thomas	17	334	20	1
Johnson	17	69	4	1
Hoak	12	137	11	3
Peaks	12	113	9	0
Kelly	10	186	19	1
Powers	8	193	24	0
Martha	6	145	24	0
Burrell	6	113	19	0
King	4	32	8	1
Sapp	1	44	44	0
Logan	1	7	7	0

PUNT RETURNS

Last Name	No.	Yds	Avg	TD
Keys	14	172	12	0
Martha	13	64	5	0
J. Bradshaw	1	2	2	0
Baker	1	0	0	0
Woodson	1	0	0	0

KICKOFF RETURNS

Last Name	No.	Yds	Avg	TD
Ballman	14	386	28	0
Peaks	12	326	27	0
Woodson	5	178	36	0
Thomas	7	171	24	0
Keys	7	168	24	0
Sapp	4	43	11	0
King	2	27	14	0
Martha	1	26	26	0
Lemek	1	19	19	0
Kelly	1	12	12	0
Burrell	2	0	0	0

PASSING

Last Name	Att	Comp	%	Yds	Yd/Att	TD	Int-	%	RK
Brown	272	121	44	1990	7.3	12	19-	7	14
Nelsen	42	16	38	276	6.6	2	3-	7	
Nofsinger	4	3	75	35	8.8	0	1-	25	
Wade	3	1	33	7	2.3	0	0-	0	
Ballman	1	0	0	0	0.0	0	1-100		
Hoak	1	0	0	0	0.0	0	0-	0	

PUNTING

Last Name	No	Avg
Brown	31	43.4
Holler	31	43.0

KICKING

Last Name	XP	Att	%	FG	Att	%
Clark	28	31	90	13	25	52

NEW YORK GIANTS

RUSHING

Last Name	No.	Yds	Avg	TD
Wheelwright	100	402	4.0	0
Webster	76	210	2.8	3
Thurlow	64	210	3.3	0
James	55	189	3.4	3
Wood	39	158	4.1	3
Morrison	45	138	3.1	1
Childs	40	102	2.6	0
Gifford	1	2	2.0	1
Tittle	15	-7	-0.5	1

RECEIVING

Last Name	No.	Yds	Avg	TD
Thomas	43	624	15	6
Morrison	40	505	13	2
Gifford	29	429	15	3
Shofner	22	323	15	0
Webster	19	199	10	0
Wheelwright	14	204	15	3
Crespino	12	165	14	0
James	12	101	8	1
Childs	11	97	9	0
Thurlow	7	74	11	1
Jones	4	82	21	1
Owens	4	45	11	0

PUNT RETURNS

Last Name	No.	Yds	Avg	TD
James	21	153	7	0
Childs	6	40	7	0
Barnes	1	0	0	0

KICKOFF RETURNS

Last Name	No.	Yds	Avg	TD
Childs	34	987	29	1
James	23	515	22	0
Jones	6	111	19	0
Morrison	4	75	19	0

PASSING

Last Name	Att	Comp	%	Yds	Yd/Att	TD	Int-	%	RK
Tittle	281	147	52	1798	6.4	10	22-	8	16
Wood	143	66	46	952	6.7	6	3-	2	13
Thurlow	5	3	60	65	13.0	0	0-	0	
Gifford	1	1	100	33	33.0	0	0-	0	
James	1	0	0	0	0	0	1-100		

PUNTING

Last Name	No	Avg
Chandler	73	45.6
James	1	35.0

KICKING

Last Name	XP	Att	%	FG	Att	%
Chandler	27	29	93	9	20	45
Stynchula	1	1	100	0	0	0

WESTERN CONFERENCE

BALTIMORE COLTS

RUSHING

Last Name	No.	Yds	Avg	TD
Moore	157	584	3.7	16
Lorick	100	513	5.1	4
Hill	88	384	4.4	5
Matte	42	215	5.1	1
Unitas	37	162	4.4	2
Looney	23	127	5.5	1
Boyd	1	25	25.0	0
Mackey	1	-1	-1.0	0
Cuozzo	7	-2	-0.3	0

RECEIVING

Last Name	No.	Yds	Avg	TD
Berry	43	663	15	6
Orr	40	867	22	6
Mackey	22	406	18	2
Moore	21	472	22	3
Hill	14	113	8	1
Lorick	11	164	15	0
Matte	10	169	17	0
Wilson	7	86	12	1
Richardson	3	42	14	0
Hawkins	2	42	21	1
Petties	2	20	10	1
Looney	1	1	1	0

PUNT RETURNS

Last Name	No.	Yds	Avg	TD
Harris	17	214	13	0
Hawkins	16	122	8	0
Logan	13	111	9	0
Haymond	1	6	6	0
Davis	1	0	0	0

KICKOFF RETURNS

Last Name	No.	Yds	Avg	TD
Lorick	13	385	30	0
Looney	14	345	25	0
Hill	4	85	21	0
Matte	3	71	24	0
Gilburg	1	19	19	0
Davis	1	12	12	0
Petties	1	9	9	0
Boyd	1	0	0	0
Haymond	1	0	0	0

PASSING

Last Name	Att	Comp	%	Yds	Yd/Att	TD	Int-	%	RK
Unitas	305	158	52	2824	9.3	19	6-	2	4
Cuozzo	36	15	42	163	4.5	2	3-	8	
Matte	4	3	75	58	14.5	1	0-	0	

PUNTING

Last Name	No	Avg
Looney	32	42.4
Gilburg	27	41.0

KICKING

Last Name	XP	Att	%	FG	Att	%
Michaels	53	54	98	17	35	49

GREEN BAY PACKERS

RUSHING

Last Name	No.	Yds	Avg	TD
Taylor	235	1169	5.0	12
Hornung	103	415	4.0	5
Moore	102	371	3.6	2
Starr	24	165	6.9	3
Pitts	27	127	4.7	1
Norton	1	24	24.0	0
Crutcher	1	5	5.0	0
Bratkowski	2	0	0.0	0

RECEIVING

Last Name	No.	Yds	Avg	TD
Dowler	45	623	14	5
Taylor	38	354	9	3
R. Kramer	34	551	16	0
McGee	31	592	19	6
Moore	17	140	8	2
Hornung	9	98	11	0
Pitts	6	38	6	0
Fleming	4	36	9	0
Jeter	1	23	23	0
Long	1	19	19	0

PUNT RETURNS

Last Name	No.	Yds	Avg	TD
Wood	19	252	13	0
Pitts	15	191	13	1

KICKOFF RETURNS

Last Name	No.	Yds	Avg	TD
Adderly	19	508	27	0
Moore	16	431	27	0
Brown	7	167	24	0
Crutcher	2	54	27	0
Caffey	1	0	0	0

PASSING

Last Name	Att	Comp	%	Yds	Yd/Att	TD	Int-	%	RK
Starr	272	163	60	2144	7.9	15	4-	1	1
Bratkowski	36	19	53	277	7.7	1	1-	3	
Hornung	10	3	30	25	2.5	0	1-	10	
Moore	3	1	33	28	9.3	0	0-	0	

PUNTING

Last Name	No	Avg
Norton	56	42.2

KICKING

Last Name	XP	Att	%	FG	Att	%
Hornung	41	43	95	12	38	32
Wood	1	1	100	0	1	0

MINNESOTA VIKINGS

RUSHING

Last Name	No.	Yds	Avg	TD
Brown	226	866	3.8	7
Mason	169	691	4.1	4
Tarkenton	50	330	6.6	2
Michel	39	129	3.3	0
McWatters	14	60	4.3	1
Dean	5	30	6.0	0
Lester	4	18	4.5	0
Walden	1	18	18.0	0
Butler	5	11	2.2	0
Vander Kelen	1	10	10.0	0
Smith	1	2	2.0	0
Hall	4	-4	-1.0	0
Alderman	0	22	0.0	0

RECEIVING

Last Name	No.	Yds	Avg	TD
Brown	48	703	15	9
Flatley	28	450	16	3
Mason	26	239	9	1
Hall	23	325	14	2
Reichow	20	284	14	2
Bedsole	18	295	16	5
Smith	10	211	21	1
McWatters	2	-1	-1	0
Butler	1	58	58	0
Dean	1	23	23	0
Michel	1	14	14	0
Vargo	1	13	13	0

PUNT RETURNS

Last Name	No.	Yds	Avg	TD
Butler	22	156	7	0
Mason	10	150	15	0
Dean	2	0	0	0
Kassulke	1	0	0	0

KICKOFF RETURNS

Last Name	No.	Yds	Avg	TD
Butler	26	597	23	0
Michel	8	192	24	0
Rose	8	180	23	0
Brown	5	68	14	0
Dean	3	50	17	0
Mason	2	36	18	0
McWatters	1	7	7	0

PASSING

Last Name	Att	Comp	%	Yds	Yd/Att	TD	Int-	%	RK
Tarkenton	306	171	56	2506	8.2	22	11-	4	2
Vander Kelen	19	7	37	78	4.1	0	1-	5	
Mason	1	1	100	30	30.0	1	0-	0	

PUNTING

Last Name	No	Avg
Walden	72	46.4

KICKING

Last Name	XP	Att	%	FG	Att	%
Cox	40	42	95	21	33	64

WESTERN CONFERENCE—Continued

DETROIT LIONS 7-5-2 George Wilson

Scores of Each Game		Use Name	Pos.	Hgt	Wgt	Age	Int	Pts
26 San Francisco	17	Daryl Sanders	OT	6'5"	250	22		
17 Los Angeles	17	J. D. Smith	OT	6'5"	250	28		
10 GREEN BAY	14	John Gonzaga	OG-OT	6'3"	250	31		
26 NEW YORK	3	John Gordy	OG	6'3"	250	28		
24 Minnesota	20	Jim Simon	OG	6'5"	235	23		
10 Chicago	0	Wally Hilgenberg	LB-OG	6'3"	225	21		
0 BALTIMORE	34	Bob Whitlow	C	6'1"	236	28		
37 LOS ANGELES	17	Bob Schlotz	OT-C	6'4"	250	26		
7 Green Bay	30	Darris McCord	DE	6'4"	250	31		
21 Cleveland	37	Bill Quinlan	DE	6'3"	240	32	1	
23 MINNESOTA	23	Sam Williams	DE	6'5"	235	33		6
24 CHICAGO	27	Roger Brown	DT	6'5"	300	27		
31 Baltimore	14	Alex Karras	DT	6'2"	245	28	2	
24 SAN FRANCISCO	7	Roger LaLonde	DT	6'3"	255	22		

Use Name	Pos.	Hgt	Wgt	Age	Int	Pts
Ernie Clark	LB	6'1"	220	26		
Dennis Gaubatz	LB	6'2"	220	23	1	2
Monte Lee	LB	6'4"	220	26		
Joe Schmidt	LB	6'1"	220	32		
Wayne Walker	LB	6'2"	225	27	1	74
Night Train Lane	DB	6'1"	200	36	1	
Dick LeBeau	DB	6'1"	185	27	5	
Bruce Maher	DB	5'11"	190	27	2	
Wayne Rasmussen	DB	6'2"	180	22		
Bobby Thompson	DB	5'10"	175	24	3	
Dick Compton	HB-DB	6'1"	195	24		
Yale Lary	DB	6'	190	33	6	
Gary Lowe	HB-DB	5'11"	195	30		

Lucian Reeberg—Died Jan. 31, 1964 of Uremia

Use Name	Pos.	Hgt	Wgt	Age	Int	Pts
Sonny Gibbs	QB	6'7"	230	23		
Earl Morrall	QB	6'1"	206	30		
Milt Plum	QB	6'1"	205	30		6
Dan Lewis	HB	6'1"	200	28		12
Hugh McElhenny	HB	6'1"	190	35		
Tom Watkins	HB	6'1"	195	27		24
Pat Batten	FB	6'2"	225	22		
Nick Pietrosante	FB	6'2"	225	27		24
Nick Ryder	FB	6'	210	23		6
Terry Barr	FL	6'	190	29		54
Pat Studstill	FL	6'1"	175	26		6
Gail Cogdill	OE	6'2"	195	27		18
Jim Gibbons	OE	6'2"	220	28		48
Hugh McInnis	OE	6'3"	220	26		
Warren Wells	OE	6'1"	195	21		

LOS ANGELES RAMS 5-7-2 Harland Svare

Scores of Each Game		Use Name	Pos.	Hgt	Wgt	Age	Int	Pts
26 Pittsburgh	14	Joe Carollo	OT	6'2"	262	24		
17 DETROIT	17	Frank Varrichione	OT	6'1"	237	32		
22 MINNESOTA	13	Charley Cowan	OG-OT	6'4"	267	26		
20 Baltimore	35	Don Chuy	OG	6'1"	255	23		
17 Chicago	38	Roger Davis	OG	6'3"	235	26		
42 SAN FRANCISCO	14	Joe Scibelli	OG	6'1"	260	25		
27 Green Bay	17	Fred Whittingham	OG	6'2"	240	25		
17 Detroit	37	Art Hunter	C	6'4"	248	31		
20 PHILADELPHIA	10	Joe Wendryhoski	C	6'2"	245	25		
24 CHICAGO	34	Deacon Jones	DE	6'5"	267	25		
7 BALTIMORE	24	Lamar Lundy	DE	6'7"	250	29	1	6
13 Minnesota	34	Rosey Grier	DT	6'5"	290	31		
7 San Francisco	28	Gary Larsen	DT	6'5"	245	24		
24 GREEN BAY	24	Merlin Olsen	DT	6'5"	275	23		

Use Name	Pos.	Hgt	Wgt	Age	Int	Pts
Marv Harris	LB	6'1"	225	22		
Mike Henry	LB	6'1"	237	28		
Cliff Livingston	LB	6'3"	215	34		
Jack Pardee	LB	6'2"	230	28	1	
Andy Von Sonn	LB	6'2"	223	23		
Frank Budka	DB	6'	195	22	2	
Lindon Crow	DB	6'	200	31	1	
Aaron Martin	DB	6'	185	23	2	6
Ed Meador	DB	5'11"	198	27	3	
Jerry Richardson	DB	6'3"	190	21	5	
Bobby Smith	DB	6'	197	26	2	12

Use Name	Pos.	Hgt	Wgt	Age	Int	Pts
Roman Gabriel	QB	6'4"	220	24		6
Bill Munson	QB	6'2"	187	22		
Terry Baker	HB	6'3"	200	23		
Carver Shannon	HB	6'1"	206	26		
Ben Wilson	HB	6'	225	24		36
Dick Bass	FB	5'10"	200	27		12
Les Josephson	FB	6'	210	22		24
Willie Brown	FL	6'	186	21		
Jim Phillips	FL	6'1"	195	27		12
Duane Allen	OE	6'4"	225	26		6
Carroll Dale	OE	6'1"	195	26		12
Marlin McKeever	OE	6'1"	235	24		6
Bucky Pope	FL	6'5"	195	21		60
Billy Truax	OE	6'5"	240	21		
Bruce Gossett	K	6'2"	225	21		85
Danny Villanueva	K	5'11"	213	26		

CHICAGO BEARS 5-9-0 George Halas

Scores of Each Game		Use Name	Pos.	Hgt	Wgt	Age	Int	Pts
12 Green Bay	23	George Burman	OT	6'3"	240	21		
34 Minnesota	28	Herm Lee	OT	6'4"	247	33		
0 Baltimore	52	Bob Wetoska	OT	6'3"	240	26		
21 San Francisco	31	Jim Cadile	OG	6'3"	240	23		
38 LOS ANGELES	17	Dick Evey	OG	6'2"	225	23		
0 DETROIT	10	Ted Karras	OG	6'1"	243	31		
20 Washington	27	Mike Rabold	OG	6'2"	238	27		
10 DALLAS	24	Mike Pyle	C	6'3"	245	25		
24 BALTIMORE	40	Doug Atkins	DE	6'8"	255	34		
34 Los Angeles	24	Bob Kilcullen	DE	6'3"	245	28		
23 SAN FRANCISCO	21	Ed O'Bradovich	DE	6'3"	255	24		
27 Detroit	24	John Johnson	DT	6'5"	260	23		
3 GREEN BAY	17	Stan Jones	DT	6'1"	250	33		
14 MINNESOTA	41	Earl Leggett	DT	6'3"	250	30		

Use Name	Pos.	Hgt	Wgt	Age	Int	Pts
Joe Fortunato	LB	6'	225	34		
Bill George	LB	6'2"	235	33	2	
Roger LeClerc	LB	6'3"	235	26		30
Larry Morris	LB	6'2"	230	29		
Jim Purnell	LB	6'2"	205	22		
Mike Reilly	LB	6'2"	210	21		
J. C. Caroline	DB	6'1"	190	31	2	
Larry Glueck	DB	6'	190	22		
Bennie McRae	DB	6'1"	180	23	2	
Richie Petitbon	DB	6'3"	205	26	3	
John Sisk	DB	6'3"	195	22		
Rosey Taylor	DB	5'11"	186	25	2	
Dave Whitsell	HB-DB	6'	190	28	2	

Bo Farrington } Died in auto accident during
Willie Galimore } training camp, July 26, 1964

Use Name	Pos.	Hgt	Wgt	Age	Int	Pts
Rudy Bukich	QB	6'1"	205	33		
Larry Rakestraw	QB	6'2"	195	22		
Billy Wade	QB	6'2"	205	33		6
Jon Arnett	HB	5'11"	203	29		18
Charlie Bivins	HB	6'2"	212	25		6
Ronnie Bull	HB	6'	200	24		6
Andy Livingston	HB	6'	234	19		6
Billy Martin	HB	5'11"	196	26		
Rick Casares	FB	6'2"	225	33		12
Joe Marconi	FB	6'2"	225	30		30
Johnny Morris	FL	5'10"	180	29		60
Gary Barnes	OE-FL	6'4"	210	24		
Mike Ditka	OE	6'3"	230	24		36
Bob Jencks	OE	6'5"	227	23		38
Rich Kreitling	OE	6'2"	208	29		6
Bill Martin	OE	6'4"	240	21		
Bobby Joe Green	K	5'11"	175	26		

SAN FRANCISCO FORTY NINERS 4-10-0 Jack Christiansen

Scores of Each Game		Use Name	Pos.	Hgt	Wgt	Age	Int	Pts
17 DETROIT	26	Walt Rock	OT	6'5"	245	23		
28 Philadelphia	24	Len Rohde	OT	6'4"	240	26		
13 ST. LOUIS	23	Leon Donahue	OG	6'4"	245	25		
31 CHICAGO	21	Mike Magac	OG	6'3"	240	26		
14 Green Bay	24	Howard Mudd	OG	6'3"	240	22		
14 Los Angeles	42	John Thomas	OG	6'4"	240	29		
22 MINNESOTA	27	Bruce Bosley	C	6'2"	240	30		
7 Baltimore	37	Frank Morze	C	6'4"	280	30		
7 Minnesota	24	Dan Colchico	DE	6'2"	245	25		
24 GREEN BAY	14	Clark Miller	DE	6'5"	245	25		
21 Chicago	23	Karl Rubke	DE	6'4"	240	28		
3 BALTIMORE	14	Charlie Krueger	DT	6'4"	250	28		
28 LOS ANGELES	7	Roland Lakes	DT	6'4"	263	24		
7 Detroit	24	Chuck Sieminski	DT	6'4"	255	24		

Use Name	Pos.	Hgt	Wgt	Age	Int	Pts
Bill Cooper	LB	6'1"	215	25		
Floyd Dean	LB	6'4"	245	24		
Mike Dowdle	LB	6'3"	230	26	1	
Matt Hazeltine	LB	6'1"	230	31	1	
Ed Pine	LB	6'4"	235	24		
Dave Wilcox	LB	6'3"	230	21	1	
Kermit Alexander	DB	5'11"	186	23	5	6
Charley Britt (from MIN)	DB	6'2"	180	26		
Jim Johnson	DB	6'2"	190	26	3	
Elbert Kimbrough	DB	5'11"	190	25	2	
Jerry Mertens	DB	6'	185	28		
Ben Scotti	DB	6'1"	181	27		
Abe Woodson	DB	5'11"	188	29	2	

Bob St. Clair — Heel Injury

Use Name	Pos.	Hgt	Wgt	Age	Int	Pts
John Brodie	QB	6'1"	200	29		12
George Mira	QB	5'11"	183	22		
Billy Kilmer	HB-QB	6'	190	24		
Rudy Johnson	HB	5'1"	190	22		6
Dave Kopay	HB	6'2"	206	22		12
Don Lisbon	HB	6'	197	23		6
Gary Lewis	FB	6'3"	215	22		6
Mike Lind	FB	6'2"	215	24		42
J. D. Smith	FB	6'1"	210	31		
Bernie Casey	FL	6'4"	215	25		24
Dale Messer	FL	5'10"	175	27		
Kay McFarland	OE	6'2"	180	25		
Dave Parks	OE	6'2"	195	22		48
Bob Poole	OE	6'4"	216	22		
Monte Stickles	OE	6'4"	230	26		18
Tommy Davis	K	6'	212	29		54

WESTERN CONFERENCE—Continued

DETROIT LIONS

RUSHING

Last Name	No.	Yds	Avg	TD
Pietrosante	147	536	3.6	4
Lewis	122	463	3.8	1
Watkins	80	218	2.7	1
Morrall	10	70	7.0	0
McElhenny	22	48	2.2	0
Barr	2	31	15.5	0
Plum	12	28	2.3	1
Lary	2	11	5.5	0
Ryder	11	11	1.0	0
Compton	3	2	0.7	0
Cogdill	1	−4	−4.0	0

RECEIVING

Last Name	No.	Yds	Avg	TD
Barr	57	1030	18	9
Cogdill	45	665	15	2
Gibbons	45	605	13	8
Pietrosante	19	152	8	0
Lewis	11	129	12	1
Watkins	10	125	13	1
Studstill	7	102	15	1
McElhenny	5	16	3	0
Ryder	4	30	8	1
Wells	2	21	11	0
McInnis	1	15	15	0

PUNT RETURNS

Last Name	No.	Yds	Avg	TD
Watkins	16	238	15	2
Studstill	17	137	8	0
Thompson	1	27	27	0
McElhenny	1	0	0	0
Maher	0	9	0	0

KICKOFF RETURNS

Last Name	No.	Yds	Avg	TD
Studstill	29	708	24	0
Watkins	16	368	23	0
McElhenny	3	72	24	0
Ryder	2	37	19	0
Clark	2	29	15	0
Lee	1	25	25	0
Thompson	1	24	24	0
Rasmussen	1	20	20	0
Hilgenberg	1	2	2	0
Simon	1	0	0	0
Compton	0	42	0	0

PASSING — PUNTING — KICKING

PASSING

Last Name	Att	Comp	%	Yds	Yd/Att	TD	Int–	%	RK
Plum	287	154	54	2241	7.8	18	15–	5	5
Morrall	91	50	55	588	6.5	4	3–	3	
Gibbs	3	1	33	3	1.0	0	1–	33	
Barr	1	0	0	0	0.0	0	0–	0	
Lewis	1	0	0	0	0.0	0	0–	0	
Lowe	1	0	0	0	0.0	0	1–	100	
Pietrosante	1	0	0	0	0.0	0	1–	100	
Watkins	1	1	100	58	58.0	1	0–	0	

PUNTING

Last Name	No	Avg
Lary	67	46.3
Morrall	1	8.0

KICKING

Last Name	XP	Att	%	FG	Att	%
Walker	32	34	94	14	25	56

LOS ANGELES RAMS

RUSHING

Last Name	No.	Yds	Avg	TD
Wilson	159	553	3.5	5
Josephson	96	451	4.7	3
Bass	72	342	4.8	2
Munson	19	150	7.9	0
Baker	24	82	3.4	0
Shannon	17	35	2.1	0
Pope	2	11	5.5	0
Gabriel	11	5	0.5	1

RECEIVING

Last Name	No.	Yds	Avg	TD
McKeever	41	582	14	1
Dale	32	544	17	2
Pope	25	786	31	10
Josephson	21	269	13	1
Phillips	17	245	14	2
Wilson	15	116	8	1
Bass	9	83	9	0
Baker	8	92	12	0
Allen	2	29	15	1
Shannon	2	4	2	0
Brown	1	19	19	0

PUNT RETURNS

Last Name	No.	Yds	Avg	TD
Shannon	15	81	5	0
Smith	12	68	6	0
Brown	4	23	6	0
Meador	2	9	5	0
Bass	1	0	0	0

KICKOFF RETURNS

Last Name	No.	Yds	Avg	TD
Smith	20	489	24	0
Shannon	18	442	25	0
Meador	6	148	25	0
Brown	6	122	20	0
Bass	1	25	25	0
Martin	2	18	9	0
Larsen	2	14	7	0
Harris	1	0	0	0

PASSING — PUNTING — KICKING

PASSING

Last Name	Att	Comp	%	Yds	Yd/Att	TD	Int–	%	RK
Munson	223	108	48	1533	6.9	9	15–	7	17
Gabriel	143	65	45	1236	8.6	9	5–	3	9
Baker	1	0	0	0	0.0	0	0–	0	
Meador	1	0	0	0	0.0	0	0–	0	

PUNTING

Last Name	No	Avg
Villanueva	82	44.1

KICKING

Last Name	XP	Att	%	FG	Att	%
Gossett	31	33	94	18	24	75

CHICAGO BEARS

RUSHING

Last Name	No.	Yds	Avg	TD
Arnett	119	400	3.4	1
Bull	86	320	3.7	1
Casares	35	123	3.5	0
Marconi	46	98	2.1	2
Wade	24	96	4.0	1
Bivins	29	92	3.2	0
Bukich	12	28	2.3	0
Whitsell	1	14	14.0	0
Green	2	−2	−1.0	0
Livingston	2	−3	−1.5	0

RECEIVING

Last Name	No.	Yds	Avg	TD
J. Morris	93	1200	13	10
Ditka	75	897	12	5
Arnett	25	223	9	2
Kreitling	20	185	9	2
Marconi	20	181	9	3
Bull	15	35	2	0
Casares	14	113	8	2
Bivins	11	59	5	1
Barnes	4	61	15	0
Bill Martin	3	93	31	0
Billy Martin	1	9	9	0
Livingston	1	0	0	0

PUNT RETURNS

Last Name	No.	Yds	Avg	TD
Arnett	19	188	10	0
Billy Martin	11	31	3	0

KICKOFF RETURNS

Last Name	No.	Yds	Avg	TD
Billy Martin	24	534	22	0
Arnett	15	331	22	0
Bivins	8	218	27	0
Livingston	6	167	28	1
Bull	2	44	22	0
Marconi	2	12	6	0
Purnell	1	8	8	0

PASSING — PUNTING — KICKING

PASSING

Last Name	Att	Comp	%	Yds	Yd/Att	TD	Int–	%	RK
Wade	327	182	56	1944	5.9	13	14–	4	10
Bukich	160	99	62	1099	6.8	12	7–	4	8
Arnett	4	0	0	0	0.0	0	0–	0	
Bull	3	1	33	13	4.3	0	0–	0	

PUNTING

Last Name	No	Avg
Green	71	44.5

KICKING

Last Name	XP	Att	%	FG	Att	%
Jencks	29	32	91	3	7	43
LeClerc	0	0	0	10	16	63

SAN FRANCISCO FORTY NINERS

RUSHING

Last Name	No.	Yds	Avg	TD
Kopay	75	271	3.6	0
Lind	100	256	2.6	7
Mira	18	177	9.8	0
Lisbon	55	162	2.9	0
Brodie	27	135	5.0	2
Lewis	43	115	2.7	1
Kilmer	36	113	3.1	0
Smith	13	55	4.2	0
R. Johnson	16	48	3.0	1

RECEIVING

Last Name	No.	Yds	Avg	TD
Casey	58	808	14	4
Stickles	40	685	17	3
Parks	36	703	20	8
Lind	25	178	7	0
Kopay	20	135	7	2
Lisbon	13	104	8	1
Kilmer	11	136	12	0
Lewis	7	73	10	0
McFarland	5	67	13	0
R. Johnson	5	21	4	0
Messer	4	72	18	0
Poole	1	8	8	0

PUNT RETURNS

Last Name	No.	Yds	Avg	TD
Alexander	21	189	9	1
Woodson	22	133	6	0

KICKOFF RETURNS

Last Name	No.	Yds	Avg	TD
Woodson	32	880	28	0
Alexander	20	483	24	0
Kopay	2	30	15	0
Lewis	1	0	0	0
Pine	1	0	0	0
Thomas	1	0	0	0

PASSING — PUNTING — KICKING

PASSING

Last Name	Att	Comp	%	Yds	Yd/Att	TD	Int–	%	RK
Brodie	392	193	49	2498	6.4	14	16–	4	12
Mira	53	23	43	331	6.3	2	5–	9	
Kilmer	14	8	57	92	6.6	1	1–	7	
Kopay	1	0	0	0	0.0	0	0–	0	
Lind	1	1	100	69	69.0	1	0–	0	

PUNTING

Last Name	No	Avg
Davis	79	45.6

KICKING

Last Name	XP	Att	%	FG	Att	%
Davis	30	30	100	8	25	32

1964 A.F.L. TV and New York, An Unbeatable Combination

"People have now stopped asking me if we are going to make it," said Commissioner Joe Foss after signing a new television contract with the National Broadcasting Company. Starting in 1965, NBC would handle the national TV coverage of AFL games and pay the league $36 million for five seasons from 1965 to 1969. With all clubs sharing equally in the television pot, Foss no longer had any worries about any teams going bankrupt. He also had no worries over job security, as the team owners extended him a new three-year contract with a sizable raise in salary.

One of the most gratifying developments for Foss was the sudden popularity of the New York Jets. Only two years before they were the bankrupt Titans, playing in an ancient ball park and living off league funds. Now they played in the new Shea Stadium, set a single-game attendance record three times during this season, and had solid ownership led by Sonny Werblin. With the New York team healthy and strong, the whole league found new respect coming from the East Coast media.

EASTERN DIVISION

Buffalo Bills—The heart of the Bills, the AFL's first great ball-control team, was a powerful fullback and a bruising defensive line. Cookie Gilchrist as usual took care of the heavy-duty running chores, leading the league in rushing despite the lack of an accomplished running mate at halfback. The Bills passed the ball less frequently than the other AFL clubs, as Jack Kemp ran the offense quite conservatively. But when the attack bogged down, coach Lou Saban could send young Daryle Lamonica in at quarterback. A second-year pro with a liking for the long pass, Lamonica relieved Kemp in several games and pulled out victories with deep bombs to Elbert Dubenion and Glenn Bass. Supporting the offense was a strong line featuring Billy Shaw and Stew Barber. The defensive unit also boasted of a strong line, as Ron McDole, Jim Dunaway, Tom Sestak, and Tom Day jelled into the league's best front four, and a tight group of linebackers and backs played well enough behind this line to make the Buffalo defense the stingiest in allowing points. The Bills won games by outplaying opponents in the line, by blocking and tackling better, and if the offense ever needed a three-point boost, coach Saban unveiled pro football's first soccer-style place-kicker in Pete Gogolak, a Hungarian refugee who kicked the ball sideways accurately enough to score 102 points. With a full pantry of hard-nosed ball players, the Bills swept their first nine games and put down a late Boston challenge to win the Eastern crown.

Boston Patriots—Closing with a rush, the Patriots just missed repeating as Eastern champion. Starting with a November 6 win over Houston, they won five straight games to pull within a half game of the first-place Bills before their season-closing showdown on December 20. The Pats had won last year's playoff game in frigid Buffalo, but the Bills turned the tables this year by winning this key game 24-14 in a snowstorm in Boston. The Patriots got as far as they did with little help from rookies, as coach Mike Holovak continued to depend on his shopworn veterans. Thirty-three-year-old Babe Parilli won his first All-Pro honors by passing for thirty-one touchdowns, while slow-footed Gino Cappelletti caught seven TD passes and scored a league-leading 155 points on his receiving and kicking. The defense was still the Patriots' long suit, bailing the team out in victories of 17-14 over Oakland and 12-7 over Denver. The front four of Larry Eisenhauer, Bob Dee, Houston Antwine, and Jim Hunt stood firm against enemy runners, while linebacker Nick Buoniconti blitzed opposing quarterbacks to distraction. But time was growing short for the Patriots, who would soon have to replace such oldsters as Parilli, Cappelletti, and Dee.

New York Jets—With their move into spanking new Shea Stadium, the Jets immediately became the attendance sensation of the league. Their first game in the new park drew an AFL record crowd of 45,665, the second game attracted 47,746, and the November 8 match with Buffalo brought out 60,300 fans. Several factors contributed to the Jets' sudden popularity, such as the new stadium, the scarcity of available tickets for Giant games, the scheduling of games on Saturday nights, and a close identification with the colorful baseball Mets. The fans who did come out saw a team rapidly improving with good young talent. This year's rich rookie class included Matt Snell, a talented all-around fullback; Gerry Philbin and Bert Wilder, a pair of strong defensive ends; Ralph Baker, who won a starting linebacker spot; John Schmitt and Dave Herman, two reserve offensive linemen who would star in later years; and place-kicker Jim Turner. Another newcomer won a large following, as middle linebacker Wahoo McDaniel became a folk hero with New York fans with his violent tackles. Holdovers such as Larry Grantham, Bill Mathis, Don Maynard, Bake Turner, Winston Hill, and Dainard Paulson formed the nucleus of a good club, but any championships would have to wait until a top quarterback was acquired.

Houston Oilers—Hopes that 1963 was just an isolated bad year for the Oilers faded as they lost nine straight games in the center of the schedule. Sammy Baugh was this year's head coach, with Pop Ivy disposed of for not winning a championship last season, and Baugh would get the ax after this losing campaign. The Oiler roster carried heavy doses of both rookies and aging veterans. Of the several freshmen to make the squad, Sid Blanks, Scott Appleton, Pete Jacquess, W. K. Hicks, Benny Nelson, and Willie Frazier saw considerable action. At the other end of the spectrum, thirty-six-year-old George Blanda, thirty-six-year-old Bud McFadin, and thirty-four-year-old Ed Hussman held down starting posts in the Houston lineup. In between the two extremes of age came players in their prime—Charley Hennigan, Freddy Glick, Bob Talamini, and Doug Cline. Hennigan, who was Blanda's favorite pass receiver, hauled in 101 passes to set a new professional record. But not enough Oiler players were at the peak of their powers, and the team hung all its hopes on this year's youngsters improving in the near future.

WESTERN DIVISION

San Diego Chargers—Tobin Rote's old arm had few passes left in it, so John Hadl assumed the bulk of the quarterbacking duties and took the Chargers back to the championship game. The road was a little rockier this year, though. After beating Houston to open the season, the Chargers lost to Boston and Buffalo and just managed a tie with New York. With none of the Western teams very hot in the early going, San Diego then rocketed out to a comfortable lead by winning their next six games. Even a late-season slump, in which they lost three of their last four games, could not bring the Chargers back to the pack. But despite their streaky play, the Chargers boasted of one of the deepest squads in the league. They had good runners in Keith Lincoln and Paul Lowe, pro football's most exciting receiver in Lance Alworth, fine offensive linemen in Ron Mix and Walt Sweeney, and good defenders in Earl Faison, Ernie Ladd, Chuck Allen, Frank Buncom, and Dick Westmoreland. The only thing missing from the San Diego arsenal was a consistent field-goal kicker. The Chargers tried Keith Lincoln, Herb Travenio, Ben Agajanian, and George Blair at the spot during the season. But that lack was not enough to keep the Chargers away from their fourth Western crown in five years.

Kansas City Chiefs—On paper, the Chiefs looked unbeatable; on the field, the Chiefs were a .500 club. They looked like the best team in the league when they beat the Chargers 49-6 and dismantled the Jets 24-7, but they looked like scrubs while losing 33-27 to the lowly Broncos. No one could figure out how a team with good offensive and defensive units could lose seven games, but the Chiefs complicated coach Hank Stram's life by doing that. Len Dawson sparked the attack with thirty touchdown passes despite a trio of slow receivers, while the Kansas City running corps was brimming with talent. Abner Haynes was less consistent but still dangerous at halfback, rookie Mack Lee Hill bulled his way into the starting lineup, and Curtis McClinton, Jack Spikes, and Bert Coan provided unheard-of depth. The defense was one of the league's best, with two superb linemen in Jerry Mays and Buck Buchanan, a trio of fine linebackers in E. J. Holub, Sherrill Headrick, and Bobby Bell, and top backs in Dave Grayson, Duane Wood, Bobby Hunt, and Johnny Robinson. But the Chiefs found ways to lose that defied the heavy weight of their roster.

Oakland Raiders—The miraculous finish of 1963 wore off as the Raiders lost their first five games, but Al Davis' men came back in the second half of the schedule to prove that they were indeed a solid football team. The final five games brought four wins and a tie to Oakland, and among the defeated teams were San Diego and Buffalo, the teams headed for the championship game. The Raiders no longer had the element of surprise on their side, as the rest of the league had seen their blitzes last year and no longer took them lightly, but they resorted to a more settled style of play with fine results in the back stretch. Clem Daniels got off to a slow start, but the powerful halfback recovered to star during the Raiders' late drive. Helping Daniels with strong blocking was Billy Cannon, obtained from Houston to fill the gap at fullback. The defense was strengthened by the addition of end Ben Davidson, a huge lineman cut by the NFL Washington Redskins, and rookie linebacker Dan Conners—and despite the disappointing third-place finish, coach Davis was happy about adding new talent to his future champions.

Denver Broncos—Coach Jack Faulkner resorted to lend lease to get himself a quarterback, sending defensive tackle Bud McFadin to Houston in exchange for quarterback Jacky Lee, who was to return to Houston after two seasons. The deal won press space but few ball games, as Lee was a distinct disappointment in leading the attack. The offensive line was a shambles, however, and few passers could have accomplished much behind it. The poor blocking wasted some good offensive talent, such as split end Lionel Taylor, tight end Hewritt Dixon, halfback Charley Mitchell, and fullback Billy Joe. The defense was easy to march through but did cause enemy quarterbacks some pain with a late-season blitzing campaign; the best performances were turned in by Ray Jacobs, Jerry Hopkins, Willie Brown, and Goose Gonsoulin. The Broncos went into the season with no title hopes, but when they were massacred in the first four games, coach Faulkner got the ax and assistant Mac Speedie took over as head man.

FINAL TEAM STATISTICS

OFFENSE

	BOSTON	BUFFALO	DENVER	HOUSTON	K. CITY	NEW YORK	OAKLAND	SAN DIEGO
FIRST DOWNS:								
Total	226	255	207	284	250	209	270	254
by Rushing	66	114	78	80	90	79	63	85
by Passing	144	130	116	186	148	108	186	156
by Penalty	16	11	13	18	12	22	21	13
RUSHING:								
Number	381	492	391	327	415	384	331	392
Yards	1361	2040	1311	1347	1825	1457	1480	1522
Average Yards	3.6	4.1	3.4	4.1	4.4	3.8	4.5	3.9
Touchdowns	9	25	10	14	14	11	9	14
PASSING:								
Attempts	476	397	456	592	412	451	521	445
Completions	229	174	230	299	228	201	253	224
Completion Percentage	48.1	43.8	50.4	50.5	55.3	44.6	48.6	50.3
Passing Yardage	3467	3422	2541	3734	3321	2694	3886	3363
Average Yards per Attempt	7.3	8.6	5.6	6.3	8.1	6.0	7.5	7.6
Average Yards per Completion	15.1	19.7	11.0	12.5	14.6	13.4	15.4	15.0
Times Tackled Attempting to Pass	29	35	61	23	44	27	56	22
Yards Lost Attempting to Pass	301	256	520	207	446	262	464	221
Net Yards	3166	3166	2021	3527	2875	2432	3422	3142
Touchdowns	31	19	14	19	32	19	28	28
Interceptions	27	34	32	29	21	33	33	30
Percent Intercepted	5.7	8.6	7.0	4.9	5.1	7.3	6.3	6.7
PUNTING:								
Number	78	65	83	55	79	79	59	63
Average Distance	38.0	42.7	43.4	41.2	42.5	41.3	41.5	39.3
PUNT RETURNS:								
Number	38	46	25	19	40	38	33	34
Yards	276	421	259	252	400	283	447	283
Average Yards	7.3	9.2	10.4	13.3	10.0	7.4	13.5	8.3
Touchdowns	0	1	1	1	0	0	0	0
KICKOFF RETURNS:								
Number	58	48	76	66	57	54	61	53
Yards	1167	1018	1758	1559	1261	1088	1525	1288
Average Yards	20.1	21.2	23.1	23.6	22.1	20.1	25.0	24.3
Touchdowns	0	0	0	1	0	0	0	0
INTERCEPTION RETURNS:								
Number	31	28	32	30	28	34	26	30
Yards	427	470	459	437	408	477	430	487
Average Yards	13.8	16.8	14.3	14.6	14.6	14.0	16.5	16.2
Touchdowns	1	2	1	3	1	4	0	2
PENALTIES:				Not Available				
Number								
Yards								
FUMBLES:								
Number	23	32	27	24	36	15	30	30
Number Lost	12	18	8	15	20	7	18	16
POINTS:								
Total	365	400	240	310	366	278	303	341
PAT (kick) Attempts	36	46	25	38	46	33	34	43
PAT (kick) Made	36	45	22	37	46	33	34	39
PAT (Rush or Pass) Attempts	5	2	3	1	3	1	2	1
PAT (Rush or Pass) Made	3	2	3	0	1	0	0	1
FG Attempts	39	29	34	29	17	27	24	26
FG Made	25	19	14	13	8	13	15	12
Percent FG Made	64.1	65.5	41.2	44.8	47.1	48.1	62.5	46.2
Safeties		3	1	0	1	1	0	1

DEFENSE

	BOSTON	BUFFALO	DENVER	HOUSTON	K. CITY	NEW YORK	OAKLAND	SAN DIEGO
FIRST DOWNS:								
Total	243	206	271	276	211	245	255	248
by Rushing	63	48	100	103	77	79	103	82
by Passing	165	145	148	159	124	152	134	147
by Penalty	15	13	23	14	10	14	18	19
RUSHING:								
Number	356	300	424	438	390	410	396	399
Yards	1143	913	2064	1961	1315	1675	1750	1522
Average Yards	3.2	3.0	4.9	4.5	3.4	4.1	4.4	3.8
Touchdowns	10	4	21	18	9	14	20	10
PASSING:								
Attempts	530	517	440	433	440	473	433	484
Completions	261	241	215	229	218	228	206	240
Completion Percentage	49.2	46.6	48.9	52.9	49.5	48.2	47.6	49.6
Passing Yardage	3645	3361	3353	3469	2910	3472	3292	2926
Average Yards per Attempt	6.9	6.5	7.6	8.0	6.6	7.3	7.6	6.0
Average Yards per Completion	14.0	13.9	15.6	15.1	13.3	15.2	16.0	12.2
Times Tackled Attempting to Pass	47	50	44	25	28	28	37	38
Yards Lost Attempting to Pass	428	396	447	189	279	231	299	408
Net Yards	3217	2965	2906	3280	2631	3241	2993	2518
Touchdowns	23	24	29	24	25	22	21	22
Interceptions	31	28	32	30	28	34	26	30
Percent Intercepted	5.8	5.4	7.3	6.9	6.4	7.2	6.0	6.2
PUNTING:								
Number	82	87	59	56	78	71	66	62
Average Distance	41.5	41.9	41.4	39.1	40.7	40.5	41.7	41.3
PUNT RETURNS:								
Number	24	24	40	33	36	43	41	32
Yards	185	250	526	295	251	426	272	416
Average Yards	7.7	10.4	13.2	8.9	7.0	9.9	6.6	13.0
Touchdowns	0	0	1	0	0	1	0	1
KICKOFF RETURNS:								
Number	70	59	44	53	64	53	64	66
Yards	1637	1385	1166	978	1459	1236	1239	1564
Average Yards	23.4	23.5	26.5	18.5	22.8	23.3	19.4	23.7
Touchdowns	1	0	0	0	0	0	0	0
INTERCEPTION RETURNS:								
Number	27	34	32	29	21	33	33	30
Yards	485	406	441	496	228	448	713	378
Average Yards	18.0	11.9	13.8	17.1	10.9	13.6	21.6	12.6
Touchdowns	1	0	1	3	3	1	4	1
PENALTIES:				Not Available				
Number								
Yards								
FUMBLES:								
Number	33	24	40	21	29	19	19	32
Number Lost	17	15	21	8	18	10	10	15
POINTS:								
Total	297	242	438	355	306	315	350	300
PAT (kick) Attempts	33	23	52	43	36	38	43	33
PAT (kick) Made	32	22	52	41	34	36	43	32
PAT (Rush or Pass) Attempts	3	5	0	2	2	1	2	3
PAT (Rush or Pass) Made	2	2	0	1	0	1	1	3
FG Attempts	27	27	25	30	20	27	34	32
FG Made	15	14	22	14	14	15	11	14
Percent FG Made	50.0	51.9	88.0	46.7	70.0	55.6	32.3	43.8
Safeties	0	4	0	0	0	0	0	0

1964 AFL CHAMPIONSHIP GAME
December 26, at Buffalo
(Attendance 40,242)

No Instant Replay

The San Diego Chargers started fast in defending their AFL title, but the sturdy Buffalo defense caught up and turned the game around before the first half ended. The first time the Chargers got their hands on the ball they drove 80 yards in four plays; Keith Lincoln, the star of last year's championship game, ran 38 yards on one play, and Tobin Rote found Dave Kocourek with a pass good for 26 yards and the first touchdown of the game. Lincoln's extra point made the score 7-0, and some fans expected the Chargers to turn the game into a rout as they had the year before. On the Chargers' next drive, however, the Bills made the key play of the game. When Lincoln caught a short pass in the flat, Buffalo linebacker Mike Stratton leveled him with a crunching tackle that knocked the ball loose and broke one of Lincoln's ribs. With their star back out of action, the Chargers never again could move the ball against the Buffalo defense. Pete Gogolak scored the Bills' first three points on a 12-yard field goal, and 10 second-quarter points gave Buffalo a 13-7 lead at halftime. The third period was scoreless, but the differences in the teams showed through clearly. The San Diego running attack missed the injured Lincoln dearly, while Cookie Gilchrist blasted into the Chargers' line with jackhammer force and regularity. While the San Diego attack withered in the face of the Buffalo pass rush, the Bills added a final touchdown when a Jack Kemp-to-Glenn Bass pass covering 48 yards brought the ball down to the one-yard line before Kemp went over for the 20-7 victory and Buffalo's first major-league sports championship.

SCORING

	1	2	3	4	
BUFFALO	3	10	0	7	20
SAN DIEGO	7	0	0	0	7

First Quarter
S.D. Kocourek, 26 yard pass from Rote
PAT—Lincoln (kick)
BUF. Gogolak, 12 yard field goal

Second Quarter
BUF. Carlton, 4 yard rush
PAT—Gogolak (kick)
BUF. Gogolak, 17 yard field goal

Fourth Quarter
BUF. Kemp, 1 yard rush
PAT—Gogolak (kick)

TEAM STATISTICS

BUFF.		S.D.
21	First Downs—Total	15
12	First Downs—Rushing	7
8	First Downs—Passing	7
1	First Downs—Penalty	1
0	Fumbles—Number	1
0	Fumbles—Number Lost	0
3	Penalties—Number	3
45	Yards Penalized	20
0	Missed Field Goals	0

INDIVIDUAL STATISTICS

BUFFALO	No	Yds	Avg.	SAN DIEGO	No	Yds	Avg.
RUSHING							
Gilchrist	16	122	7.6	Lincoln	3	47	15.7
Carlton	18	70	3.9	Lowe	7	34	4.9
Kemp	5	16	3.2	MacKinnon	1	17	17.0
Dubenion	1	9	9.0	Kinderman	4	14	3.5
Lamonica	1	2	2.0	Hadl	1	13	13.0
	41	219	5.3	Rote	1	6	6.0
				Norton	1	−7	−7.0
					18	124	6.9
RECEIVING							
Dubenion	3	36	12.0	Kinderman	4	52	13.0
Bass	2	70	35.0	MacKinnon	3	12	4.0
Warlick	2	41	20.5	Kocourek	2	52	26.0
Gilchrist	2	22	11.0	Lowe	2	9	4.5
Ross	1	−1	−1.0	Norton	1	13	13.0
	10	168	16.8	Lincoln	1	11	11.0
					13	149	11.5
PUNTING							
Maguire	5		46.8	Hadl	5		36.4
PUNT RETURNS							
Clarke	1	6	6.0	Robinson	1	30	30.0
				Duncan	1	28	28.0
					2	58	29.0
KICKOFF RETURNS							
Rutkowski	1	27	27.0	Duncan	3	147	49.0
Warner	1	17	17.0	Warren	1	28	28.0
	2	44	22.0		4	175	43.8
INTERCEPTION RETURNS							
Warner	1	8	8.0	None			
Byrd	1	0	0.0				
Stratton	1	0	0.0				
	3	8	2.7				

PASSING

BUFFALO	Att.	Comp.	Comp. Pct.	Yds.	Int.	Yds/ Att.	Yds/ Comp.
Kemp	20	10	50.0	168	0	8.4	16.8
SAN DIEGO							
Rote	26	10	38.5	118	2	4.5	11.8
Hadl	10	3	30.0	31	1	3.1	10.3
	36	13	36.1	149	3	4.1	11.5

BUFFALO BILLS 12-2-0 Lou Saban

Scores of Each Game

34	KANSAS CITY	17
30	DENVER	13
30	SAN DIEGO	3
23	OAKLAND	20
48	Houston	17
35	Kansas City	22
34	NEW YORK	24
24	HOUSTON	10
20	New York	7
28	BOSTON	36
27	San Diego	24
13	Oakland	16
30	Denver	19
24	Boston	14

Use Name	Pos.	Hgt	Wgt	Age	Int	Pts
Stew Barber	OT	6'3"	250	25		
Dick Hudson	OT	6'4"	272	24		
Joe O'Donnell	OT	6'2"	246	22		
Al Bemiller	OG	6'3"	260	25		
George Flint	OG	6'4"	244	26		
Billy Shaw	OG	6'3"	248	24		
Walt Cudzik	C	6'2"	240	31		
Tom Day	DE	6'2"	250	29		
Ron McDole	DE	6'3"	264	24	1	
Jim Dunaway	DT	6'4"	276	22		
Tom Keating	DT	6'3"	242	21		
Dudley Meredith	DT	6'4"	275	29		
Tom Sestak	DT	6'5"	270	28	1	6
Harry Jacobs	LB	6'2"	225	27	2	
Paul Maguire	LB	6'	220	26		
Mike Stratton	LB	6'3"	240	22	1	
John Tracey	LB	6'3"	225	30	3	
Ray Abbruzzese	DB	6'1"	194	26		
Butch Byrd	DB	6'	211	22	7	6
Hagood Clarke	DB	6'	188	22		6
Ollie Dobbins	DB	5'11"	185	22		
Booker Edgerson	DB	5'10"	180	25	4	
George Saimes	DB	5'10"	195	22	6	
Gene Sykes	DB	6'1"	195	23	2	
Jack Kemp	QB	6'1"	200	30		30
Daryle Lamonica	QB	6'2"	215	23		40
Joe Auer	HB	6'1"	205	22		18
Wray Carlton	HB	6'2"	216	26		6
Bobby Smith	HB	6'	203	22		24
Cookie Gilchrist	FB	6'3"	250	29		36
Willie Ross	FB	5'10"	200	23		6
Elbert Dubenion	FL	6'	187	29		60
Ed Rutkowski	FL	6'1"	208	23		6
Glenn Bass	OE	6'2"	206	25		42
Bill Groman	OE	6'	195	28		6
Ernie Warlick	OE	6'4"	235	32		
Pete Gogolak	K	6'2"	200	22		102

Charley Ferguson – Injury

BOSTON PATRIOTS 10-3-1 Mike Holovak

Scores of Each Game

17	Oakland	14
33	San Diego	28
26	NEW YORK	10
39	Denver	10
17	SAN DIEGO	26
43	OAKLAND	43
24	KANSAS CITY	7
14	New York	35
25	HOUSTON	24
36	Buffalo	28
12	DENVER	7
34	Houston	17
31	Kansas City	24
14	BUFFALO	24

Use Name	Pos.	Hgt	Wgt	Age	Int	Pts
Don Oakes	OT	6'3"	255	26		
Bob Schmidt	OT	6'4"	250	28		
Bob Yates	OT	6'3"	230	25		
Charley Long	OG	6'3"	250	26		
Billy Neighbors	OG	5'11"	240	24		
Dave Watson	OG	6'1"	230	23		
Jon Morris	C	6'4"	240	21		
Bob Dee	DE	6'3"	240	31		
Larry Eisenhauer	DE	6'5"	250	24		
Jim Hunt	DE-DT	5'11"	245	25		
Len St. Jean	DE	6'1"	240	22		
Houston Antwine	DT	6'	270	25		
Jerry DeLucca	DT	6'3"	250	28		
Jess Richardson	DT	6'2"	265	34		
Tom Addison	LB	6'3"	230	28	2	
Nick Buoniconti	LB	5'11"	220	23	5	
Mike Dukes	LB	6'3"	235	28	1	
Lonnie Farmer	LB	6'	220	23		
Jack Rudolph	LB	6'3"	230	26		
Don McKinnon	C-LB	6'3"	230	22		
Dave Cloutier	DB	6'	195	25		
Dick Felt	DB	6'	185	31	2	
Ron Hall	DB	6'	190	27	11	
Ross O'Hanley	DB	6'	185	25	3	6
Chuck Shonta	DB	6'	200	26	1	
Don Webb	DB	5'10"	200	25		6
Tom Stephens	OE-DB	6'1"	215	28		
Babe Parilli	QB	6'1"	190	34		12
Tom Yewcic	QB	5'11"	185	32		
Ron Burton	HB	5'10"	190	27		30
J. D. Garrett	HB	5'11"	195	22		12
Jim Crawford	FB	6'1"	205	28		
Larry Garron	FB	6'	195	27		54
Jim Colclough	FL	6'	185	28		34
Al Snyder	FL	6'	195	22		
Gino Cappelletti	OE	6'	190	30		155
Art Graham	OE	6'1"	205	23		36
Tony Romeo	OE	6'2"	230	25		24

NEW YORK JETS 5-8-1 Weeb Ewbank

Scores of Each Game

30	DENVER	6
10	Boston	26
17	SAN DIEGO	17
35	OAKLAND	13
24	HOUSTON	21
24	Buffalo	34
35	BOSTON	14
7	BUFFALO	20
16	Denver	20
26	Oakland	35
27	KANSAS CITY	14
3	San Diego	38
17	Houston	33
7	Kansas City	24

Use Name	Pos.	Hgt	Wgt	Age	Int	Pts
Winston Hill	OT	6'4"	275	22		
Jim McCusker	OT	6'2"	250	28		
Sherman Plunkett	OT	6'4"	295	30		
Sam DeLuca	OG	6'2"	250	28		
Dan Ficca	OG	6'1"	250	25		
Dave Herman	OG	6'2"	255	22		
Pete Perreault	OG	6'3"	245	25		
Mike Hudock	C	6'2"	245	29		
John Schmitt	C	6'4"	265	21		
Gerry Philbin	DE	6'2"	245	23		
Lavern Torczon	DE	6'2"	250	28	1	6
Bob Watters	DE	6'4"	245	28		
Bert Wilder	DE	6'3"	245	24		
Gordy Holz	DT	6'4"	260	30		
Bob McAdams	DT	6'3"	250	24		
Paul Rochester	DT	6'2"	250	27		
Ralph Baker	LB	6'3"	235	22	2	
Ed Cummings	LB	6'2"	232	23	1	
Larry Grantham	LB	6'	206	25	2	
Wahoo McDaniel	LB	6'	240	27	3	6
Bob Rowley	LB	6'2"	225	22		
Mark Johnston (from OAK)	DB	6'	200	26	1	
Bill Pashe	DB	5'11"	185	23		
Dainard Paulson	DB	5'11"	190	27	12	6
Bill Rademacher	DB	6'1"	190	22	1	
Marsh Starks	DB	6'	190	25	1	
Vince Turner	DB	5'11"	190	21	1	
Clyde Washington	DB	6'	206	26		
Bill Baird	HB-DB	5'10"	180	25	8	6
Mike Taliaferro	QB	6'2"	210	22		
Dick Wood	QB	6'5"	205	28		6
Pete Liske	DB-QB	6'2"	195	23		
Curley Johnson	HB	6'	215	29		
Bill Mathis	HB	6'1"	220	25		24
Mark Smolinski	FB	6'	215	25		6
Matt Snell	FB	6'2"	220	22		36
Jim Evans	FL	6'1"	190	24		
Al Lawson	FL	5'11"	190	22		
Don Maynard	FL	6'	185	28		48
Gene Heeter	OE	6'4"	235	23		6
Dee Mackey	OE	6'5"	225	28		
Bake Turner	OE	6'	185	24		54
Jim Turner	K	6'2"	205	23		72

HOUSTON OILERS 4-10-0 Sammy Baugh

Scores of Each Game

21	San Diego	27
42	OAKLAND	28
38	Denver	17
7	Kansas City	28
17	BUFFALO	48
21	New York	24
17	SAN DIEGO	20
10	Buffalo	24
24	Boston	25
10	Oakland	20
19	KANSAS CITY	28
17	BOSTON	34
33	NEW YORK	17
34	DENVER	15

Use Name	Pos.	Hgt	Wgt	Age	Int	Pts
Staley Faulkner	OT	6'3"	245	23		
Jerry Fowler	OT	6'3"	255	23		
Bob Kelly	OT	6'3"	260	24		
Jack Klotz	OT	6'5"	250	30		
Walt Suggs	OT	6'5"	260	25		
Sonny Bishop	OG	6'2"	250	24		
John Frongillo	OG	6'3"	250	24		
John Talamini	OG	6'1"	255	25		
John Wittenborn	OG	6'2"	240	28		
Tom Goode	C	6'3"	250	28		
Gary Cutsinger	DE	6'4"	245	23		
Don Floyd	DE	6'4"	247	25		6
Scott Appleton	DT	6'3"	250	22	2	
Ed Husmann	DT	6'	245	34		
Bud McFadin	DT	6'3"	270	36		
Danny Brabham	LB	6'4"	240	23		
Doug Cline	LB	6'2"	230	25		
Sammy Odom	LB	6'2"	235	22	2	
Larry Onesti	LB	6'	200	25		
Charley Rieves	LB	5'11"	218	25	1	
Johnny Baker	OE-LB	6'3"	225	23	1	6
Freddy Glick	DB	6'1"	190	27	5	
W. K. Hicks	DB	6'1"	185	25	5	
Pete Jaquess	DB	6'	180	22	8	6
Benny Nelson	DB	6'	185	22	1	6
Jim Norton	DB	6'3"	190	25	1	
Bobby Jancik	FL-DB	5'11"	178	24	3	6
George Blanda	QB	6'1"	215	36		76
Don Trull	QB	6'1"	180	22		
Sid Blanks	HB	6'	198	23		42
Ode Burrell	HB	6'	185	24		6
Dalton Hoffman	FB	6'	207	24		
Dave Smith	FB	6'1"	210	27		
Charley Tolar	FB	5'7"	200	26		24
Charley Hennigan	FL	6'	187	28		48
Dobie Craig	OE	6'4"	200	25		6
Willard Dewveall	OE	6'4"	230	27		24
Charley Frazier	OE	6'	175	25		12
Willie Frazier	OE	6'4"	225	21		6
Bob McLeod	OE	6'5"	230	25		12

Rich Michael – Injury

BUFFALO BILLS

RUSHING
Last Name	No.	Yds	Avg	TD
Gilchrist	230	981	4.3	6
Smith	62	306	4.9	4
Lamonica	55	289	5.3	6
Auer	63	191	3.0	2
Kemp	37	124	3.4	5
Carlton	39	114	2.9	1
Dubenion	1	20	20.0	0
Ross	4	14	3.5	0
Hudson	1	1	1.0	0

RECEIVING
Last Name	No.	Yds	Avg	TD
Bass	43	897	21	7
Dubenion	42	1139	27	10
Gilchrist	30	345	12	0
Warlick	23	478	21	0
Rutkowski	13	234	18	1
Auer	11	166	15	0
Smith	6	72	12	0
Groman	4	68	17	1
Carlton	2	23	12	0

PUNT RETURNS
Last Name	No.	Yds	Avg	TD
Clarke	33	317	10	1
Rutkowski	8	45	6	0
Byrd	2	4	2	0

KICKOFF RETURNS
Last Name	No.	Yds	Avg	TD
Rutkowski	21	498	24	0
Clarke	16	330	21	0
Smith	3	68	23	0
Barber	2	0	0	0
Maguire	1	0	0	0
Auer	0	1	0	0

PASSING – PUNTING – KICKING
PASSING
Last Name	Att	Comp	%	Yds	Yd/Att	TD	Int—%	RK
Kemp	269	119	44	2285	8.5	13	26— 10	6
Lamonica	128	55	43	1137	8.9	6	8— 6	

PUNTING
Last Name	No	Avg
Maguire	65	42.7

KICKING
Last Name	XP	Att	%	FG	Att	%
Gogolak	45	46	98	19	29	66

2 POINT XP
Lamonica (2)

BOSTON PATRIOTS

RUSHING
Last Name	No.	Yds	Avg	TD
Garron	183	585	3.2	2
Burton	102	340	3.3	3
Garrett	56	259	4.6	2
Parilli	34	168	4.9	2
Cappelletti	1	7	7.0	0
Yewcic	5	2	0.4	0

RECEIVING
Last Name	No.	Yds	Avg	TD
Cappelletti	49	865	18	7
Graham	45	720	16	6
Garron	40	547	14	2
Colclough	32	657	21	5
Burton	27	306	11	2
Romeo	26	445	17	4
Garrett	8	101	13	0
Snyder	1	12	12	0
Crawford	1	11	11	0

PUNT RETURNS
Last Name	No.	Yds	Avg	TD
Cloutier	20	136	7	0
Burton	11	78	7	0
Stephens	5	34	7	0
Garrett	2	28	14	0

KICKOFF RETURNS
Last Name	No.	Yds	Avg	TD
Garrett	32	749	23	0
Garron	10	198	20	0
Burton	7	131	19	0
Cloutier	1	46	46	0
Dukes	2	33	17	0
Stephens	2	5	3	0
Romeo	1	5	5	0
Oakes	1	0	0	0
Watson	1	0	0	0
Yates	1	0	0	0

PASSING – PUNTING – KICKING
PASSING
Last Name	Att	Comp	%	Yds	Yd/Att	TD	Int—%	RK
Parilli	473	228	48	3465	7.3	31	27— 6	3
Garron	2	0	0	0	0.0	0	0— 0	
Yewcic	1	1	100	2	2.0	0	0— 0	

PUNTING
Last Name	No	Avg
Yewcic	72	38.7
Parilli	5	36.0

KICKING
Last Name	XP	Att	%	FG	Att	%
Cappelletti	36	36	100	25	39	64

2 POINT XP
Cappelletti
Colclough (2)

NEW YORK JETS

RUSHING
Last Name	No.	Yds	Avg	TD
Snell	215	948	4.4	5
Mathis	105	305	2.9	4
Smolinski	34	117	3.4	1
Taliaferro	9	45	5.0	0
Johnson	6	22	3.7	0
Baird	1	8	8.0	0
Wood	9	6	0.7	1
Maynard	3	3	1.0	0
J. Turner	1	3	3.0	0
Liske	1	0	0.0	0

RECEIVING
Last Name	No.	Yds	Avg	TD
B. Turner	58	974	17	9
Snell	56	393	7	1
Maynard	46	847	18	8
Mackey	14	213	15	0
Heeter	13	153	12	1
Evans	7	56	8	0
Mathis	4	39	10	0
Smolinski	3	19	6	0

PUNT RETURNS
Last Name	No.	Yds	Avg	TD
Baird	18	170	9	0
Starks	5	36	7	0
Paulson	8	34	4	0
Pashe	4	28	7	0
Rademacher	1	3	3	0
V. Turner	2	2	1	0
Rowley	0	10	0	0

KICKOFF RETURNS
Last Name	No.	Yds	Avg	TD
Evans	13	259	20	0
Baird	11	240	22	0
Starks	7	183	26	0
Snell	7	158	23	0
Johnson	4	62	16	0
V. Turner	1	25	25	0
Smolinski	2	19	10	0
Heeter	1	0	0	0
Mathis	1	0	0	0
McCusker	1	0	0	0
Perreault	1	0	0	0

PASSING – PUNTING – KICKING
PASSING
Last Name	Att	Comp	%	Yds	Yd/Att	TD	Int—%	RK
Wood	358	169	47	2298	6.4	17	25— 7	6
Taliaferro	73	23	32	341	4.7	2	5— 7	
Liske	18	9	50	55	3.1	0	2— 11	
Johnson	1	0	0	0	0.0	0	0— 0	
Snell	1	0	0	0	0.0	0	1— 100	

PUNTING
Last Name	No	Avg
Johnson	77	42.4

KICKING
Last Name	XP	Att	%	FG	Att	%
J. Turner	33	33	100	13	27	48

HOUSTON OILERS

RUSHING
Last Name	No.	Yds	Avg	TD
Blanks	145	756	5.2	6
Tolar	139	515	3.7	4
Trull	12	42	3.5	0
Smith	8	16	2.0	0
Burrell	8	10	1.3	0
Hoffman	2	3	1.5	1
Blanda	4	-2	-0.5	0
C. Frazier	1	-4	-4.0	0

RECEIVING
Last Name	No.	Yds	Avg	TD
Hennigan	101	1546	15	8
Blanks	56	497	9	1
Dewveall	38	552	15	4
Tolar	35	244	7	0
C. Frazier	31	423	14	2
W. Frazier	9	208	23	1
McLeod	8	81	10	2
Smith	7	38	5	0
Burrell	5	73	15	0
Craig	4	46	12	1
Baker	2	18	9	0
Jancik	1	14	14	0
Hoffman	1	1	1	0
Bishop	1	0	0	0
Blanda	0	-7	0	0

PUNT RETURNS
Last Name	No.	Yds	Avg	TD
Jancik	12	220	18	1
Glick	6	32	5	0
Burrell	1	0	0	0

KICKOFF RETURNS
Last Name	No.	Yds	Avg	TD
Jancik	21	488	23	0
Burrell	17	449	26	1
Nelson	13	304	23	0
Blanks	9	207	23	0
Hoffman	2	52	26	0
Glick	1	27	27	0
W. Frazier	1	0	0	0

PASSING – PUNTING – KICKING
PASSING
Last Name	Att	Comp	%	Yds	Yd/Att	TD	Int—%	RK
Blanda	505	262	52	3287	6.5	17	27— 5	3
Trull	86	36	42	439	5.1	1	2— 2	
Blanks	1	1	100	8	8.0	1	0— 0	

PUNTING
Last Name	No	Avg
Norton	53	42.8

KICKING
Last Name	XP	Att	%	FG	Att	%
Blanda	37	38	97	13	29	45

SAN DIEGO CHARGERS 8-5-1 Sid Gillman

Scores of Each Game			Use Name	Pos.	Hgt	Wgt	Age	Int	Pts
27	HOUSTON	21	Gary Kirner	OT	6'3"	245	22		
28	BOSTON	33	Ron Mix	OT	6'4"	250	26		
3	Buffalo	30	Ernie Park	OT	6'3"	253	22		
17	New York	17	Ernie Wright	OT	6'4"	265	24		
26	Boston	17	Sam Gruneisen	OG	6'1"	255	23		
42	DENVER	14	Lloyd McCoy	OG	6'1"	245	22		
20	Houston	17	Pat Shea	OG	6'1"	245	25		
31	OAKLAND	17	Walt Sweeney	OG	6'3"	255	23		
31	Denver	20	Don Rogers	C	6'2"	245	27		
28	Kansas City	14	Earl Faison	DE	6'5"	270	25	1	6
24	BUFFALO	27	Bob Mitinger	DE	6'2"	245	24		
38	NEW YORK	3	Bob Petrich	DE	6'4"	257	23	1	
6	KANSAS CITY	49	George Gross	DT	6'3"	270	23		
20	Oakland	21	Ernie Ladd	DT	6'9"	295	25		
			Fred Moore	DT	6'3"	255	24		
			Henry Schmidt	DT	6'4"	270	27	1	6

Use Name	Pos.	Hgt	Wgt	Age	Int	Pts
Chuck Allen	LB	6'1"	225	24	4	
Frank Buncom	LB	6'1"	235	24	1	
Ron Carpenter	LB	6'2"	230	23	1	
Bob Horton	LB	6'2"	230	21		
Emil Karas	LB	6'3"	235	30		
Bobby Lane	LB	6'2"	222	24		
George Blair	DB	5'11"	195	26		14
Speedy Duncan	DB	5'10"	180	21	1	
Kenny Graham	DB	6'	200	22	4	
Dick Harris	DB	5'11"	187	27	3	
Charley McNeil	DB	5'11"	180	28	2	
Jimmy Warren	DB	5'11"	185	25	2	
Dick Westmoreland	DB	6'1"	190	23	6	
Bud Whitehead	FL-DB	6'	185	25	3	

Use Name	Pos.	Hgt	Wgt	Age	Int	Pts
John Hadl	QB	6'2"	210	24		6
Tobin Rote	QB	6'3"	220	36		
Paul Lowe	HB	6'	205	27		30
Mario Mendez	HB	5'11"	200	22		
Keith Kinderman	FB	6'	215	24		
Keith Lincoln	FB	6'2"	213	25		67
Gerry McDougall	FB	6'2"	225	29		14
Lance Alworth	FL	6'	185	24		90
Dave Kocourek	OE	6'5"	245	27		30
Don Norton	OE	6'1"	195	26		36
Jerry Robinson	OE	5'11"	200	25		
Jacque MacKinnon	FB-OE	6'4"	250	25		12
Ben Agajanian	K	6'	225	45		14
Herb Travenio	K	6'	218	33		16

KANSAS CITY CHIEFS 7-7-0 Hank Stram

Scores of Each Game			Use Name	Pos.	Hgt	Wgt	Age	Int	Pts
17	Buffalo	34	Jerry Cornelison	OT	6'3"	250	27		
21	Oakland	9	Dave Hill	OT	6'5"	260	23		
28	HOUSTON	7	Jim Tyrer	OT	6'6"	292	25		
27	Denver	33	Denny Biodrowski	OG	6'1"	255	24		
22	BUFFALO	35	Ed Budd	OG	6'5"	260	23		
7	Boston	24	Curt Merz	OG	6'4"	250	26		
49	DENVER	39	Al Reynolds	OG	6'3"	235	26		
42	OAKLAND	7	Jon Gilliam	C	6'2"	240	25		
14	SAN DIEGO	28	Mel Branch	DE	6'2"	230	27		
28	Houston	19	Ed Lothamer	DE	6'5"	240	21		
14	New York	27	Jerry Mays	DT-DE	6'4"	250	24		
24	BOSTON	31	Buck Buchanan	DT	6'7"	280	24		
49	San Diego	6	Curt Farrier	DT	6'6"	245	23		
24	NEW YORK	7	John Maczuzak	DT	6'5"	250	21		
			Hatch Rosdahl (from BUF)	DT	6'5"	250	21		

Use Name	Pos.	Hgt	Wgt	Age	Int	Pts
Walt Corey	LB	6'	242	26	1	
Sherrill Headrick	LB	6'2"	215	27	1	
E. J. Holub	LB	6'4"	225	26		
Smokey Stover	LB	6'2"	232	25	2	
Bobby Bell	DE-LB	6'4"	228	24	1	6
Dave Grayson	DB	5'10"	184	25	7	
Bobby Hunt	DB	6'1"	190	24	7	6
Willie Mitchell	DB	6'1"	185	22	1	
Bobby Ply	DB	6'1"	190	23	1	
Johnny Robinson	DB	6'	195	25	2	
Charley Warner (to BUF)	DB	5'11"	180	24	1	
Duane Wood	DB	6'1"	200	28	5	

Use Name	Pos.	Hgt	Wgt	Age	Int	Pts
Pete Beathard	QB	6'2"	205	22		
Len Dawson	QB	6'	190	30		12
Eddie Wilson	QB	6'	190	24		6
Bert Coan	HB	6'4"	220	24		12
Abner Haynes	HB	6'	190	26		48
Jerrel Wilson	HB	6'4"	225	23		
Mack Lee Hill	FB	5'11"	225	22		36
Curtis McClinton	FB	6'3"	232	25		20
Jack Spikes (to SD)	FB	6'2"	220	26		
Frank Jackson	FL	6'1"	190	24		54
Fred Arbanas	OE	6'3"	240	25		48
Tommy Brooker	OE	6'2"	230	24		70
Chris Burford	OE	6'3"	210	26		42
Reg Carolan	OE	6'6"	232	24		6

OAKLAND RAIDERS 5-7-2 Al Davis

Scores of Each Game			Use Name	Pos.	Hgt	Wgt	Age	Int	Pts
14	BOSTON	17	Proverb Jacobs	OT	6'4"	260	29		
28	Houston	42	Dick Klein	OT	6'4"	250	30		
9	KANSAS CITY	21	Ken Rice	OT	6'2"	240	24		
20	Buffalo	23	Frank Youso	OT	6'4"	250	28		
13	New York	35	Wayne Hawkins	OG	6'	240	26		
43	Boston	43	Bob Mischak	OG	6'	230	31		
40	DENVER	7	Jim Otto	C	6'2"	240	26		
17	San Diego	31	Dalva Allen	DE	6'5"	245	28		
7	Kansas City	42	Ben Davidson	DE	6'8"	265	24		
20	HOUSTON	10	Jon Jelacic	DE	6'3"	255	27		
35	NEW YORK	26	Dan Birdwell	DT	6'4"	250	23	2	
20	Denver	20	Doug Brown	DT	6'4"	250	24		
16	BUFFALO	13	Dave Costa	DT	6'2"	250	22		
21	SAN DIEGO	20	Rex Mirich	DT	6'4"	250	23		
			Jim Norris	DT	6'4"	235	24	2	

Use Name	Pos.	Hgt	Wgt	Age	Int	Pts
Bill Budness	LB	6'1"	215	21	2	
Dan Conners	LB	6'1"	230	22		
Archie Matsos	LB	6'	212	29	2	
Clancy Osborne	LB	6'3"	220	29		
Jackie Simpson	LB	6'1"	225	27		
J. R. Williamson	LB	6'2"	220	22		
Claude Gibson	DB	6'1"	190	25	2	
Louis Guy	DB	6'	190	23		
Joe Krakoski	DB	6'2"	195	27		
Tom Morrow	DB	5'11"	187	26	4	
Warren Powers	DB	6'	185	23	5	
Howie Williams	DB	6'2"	185	27	1	
Fred Williamson	DB	6'2"	215	26	6	
Alan Miller — Injury						

Use Name	Pos.	Hgt	Wgt	Age	Int	Pts
Cotton Davidson	QB	6'1"	180	32		12
Tom Flores	QB	6'1"	190	27		
Billy Cannon	FB-HB	6'1"	225	27		48
Clem Daniels	HB	6'1"	220	27		48
Bo Dickinson	FB	6'2"	220	29		
Bobby Jackson (from HOU)	FB	6'3"	225	24		18
Glen Shaw	FB	6'1"	225	25		12
Bo Roberson	FL	6'1"	190	29		6
Jan Barrett	OE	6'3"	222	23		12
Fred Gillett	OE	6'3"	220	26		
Ken Herock	OE	6'2"	230	23		12
Bill Miller	OE	6'	190	22		
Art Powell	OE	6'3"	212	27		66
Mike Mercer	K	6'	200	28		79

DENVER BRONCOS 2-11-1 Jack Faulkner Mac Speedie

Scores of Each Game			Use Name	Pos.	Hgt	Wgt	Age	Int	Pts
6	New York	30	Eldon Danenhauer	OT	6'4"	245	28		
13	Buffalo	30	Harold Olson	OT	6'3"	255	25		
17	HOUSTON	38	Jim Perkins	OT	6'5"	250	25		
10	BOSTON	39	Ernie Barnes	OG	6'2"	243	25		
33	KANSAS CITY	27	Bob McCullough	OG	6'2"	245	23		
14	San Diego	42	Tom Nomina	OG	6'5"	270	22		
7	Oakland	40	Don Shackleford	OG	6'4"	255	21		
39	Kansas City	49	Jerry Sturm	C-OG	6'3"	260	27		
20	SAN DIEGO	31	Ray Kubala	C	6'4"	245	22		
20	NEW YORK	16	Ed Cooke	DE	6'4"	250	29	6	
7	Boston	12	Stan Fanning (from HOU)	DE	6'6"	270	26		
20	OAKLAND	20	Ike Lassiter	DE	6'5"	270	23		
19	BUFFALO	30	Leroy Moore	DE	6'	230	28	1	
15	Houston	34	Dick Guesman	DT	6'4"	255	28	31	
			Ray Jacobs	DT	6'3"	265	24		
			Chuck Janerette	DT	6'3"	265	25		

Use Name	Pos.	Hgt	Wgt	Age	Int	Pts
Tom Erlandson	LB	6'3"	235	24		
Jim Fraser	LB	6'3"	236	28	1	
Jerry Hopkins	LB	6'2"	235	23	2	
Larry Jordan	LB	6'6"	230	26		
Marv Matuszak	LB	6'3"	240	33	2	
Jim Price	LB	6'2"	230	23		
Billy Atkins	DB	6'1"	195	29		
Norm Bass	DB	6'3"	210	25		
Willie Brown	DB	6'1"	190	23	9	
Goose Gonsoulin	DB	6'3"	210	26	7	
John Griffin	DB	6'1"	190	24		
Tom Janik	DB	6'3"	200	23	1	6
John McGeever	DB	6'1"	195	25	6	
Jim McMillin (from OAK)	DB	5'11"	195	26	1	6
Willie West (to NY)	DB	5'10"	193	26	2	
Jim Wright	DB	5'11"	190	25	1	

Use Name	Pos.	Hgt	Wgt	Age	Int	Pts
Jacky Lee	QB	6'1"	187	25		18
Mickey Slaughter	QB	6'	190	22		2
Gene Mingo (to OAK)	HB	6'1"	190	25		39
Charley Mitchell	HB	5'11"	185	24		36
Billy Joe	FB	6'2"	250	23		14
Donnie Stone	FB	6'2"	205	27		
Al Denson	FL	6'2"	208	22		8
Bob Scarpitto	FL	5'11"	196	25		24
Odell Barry	OE	5'10"	180	22		6
Matt Snorton	OE	6'5"	250	21		
Lionel Taylor	OE	6'2"	215	28		42
Hewritt Dixon	HB-OE	6'2"	217	24		6

John McCormick — Knee Injury
Bob Zeman — Injury

SAN DIEGO CHARGERS

RUSHING

Last Name	No.	Yds	Avg	TD
Lincoln	155	632	4.1	4
Lowe	130	496	3.8	3
MacKinnon	24	124	5.2	2
Kinderman	24	111	4.6	0
McDougall	23	73	3.2	2
Hadl	20	70	3.5	1
Alworth	3	60	20.0	2
Robinson	1	10	10.0	0
Rote	10	−12	−1.2	0

RECEIVING

Last Name	No.	Yds	Avg	TD
Alworth	61	1235	20	13
Norton	49	669	14	6
Lincoln	34	302	9	2
Kocourek	33	593	18	5
Lowe	14	182	13	2
MacKinnon	10	177	18	0
Robinson	10	93	9	0
McDougall	8	106	13	0
Kinderman	3	21	7	0
Whitehead	1	−4	−4	0
Rote	1	−11	−11	0

PUNT RETURNS

Last Name	No.	Yds	Avg	TD
Alworth	18	189	11	0
Robinson	7	41	6	0
Graham	2	24	12	0
Duncan	4	19	5	0
Westmoreland	2	10	5	0
Warren	1	0	0	0

KICKOFF RETURNS

Last Name	No.	Yds	Avg	TD
Westmoreland	18	360	20	0
Warren	13	353	27	0
Duncan	9	318	35	0
Graham	7	172	25	0
Robinson	3	70	23	0
Carpenter	1	15	15	0
Norton	1	0	0	0
Wright	1	0	0	0

PASSING – PUNTING – KICKING

PASSING

Last Name	Att	Comp	%	Yds	Yd/Att	TD	Int−%	RK
Hadl	274	147	54	2157	7.9	18	15− 6	2
Rote	163	74	45	1156	7.1	9	15− 9	11
Lincoln	4	2	50	61	15.3	1	0− 0	
Lowe	2	0	0	0	0.0	0	0− 0	
Alworth	1	1	100	−11	−11.0	0	0− 0	
Kinderman	1	0	0	0	0.0	0	0− 0	

PUNTING

Last Name	No	Avg
Hadl	62	39.5
Whitehead	1	30.0

KICKING

Last Name	XP	Att	%	FG	Att	%
Lincoln	16	17	94	5	12	42
Travenio	10	12	83	2	5	40
Agajanian	8	8	100	2	4	50
Blair	5	6	83	3	5	60

2 POINT XP
McDougall

KANSAS CITY CHIEFS

RUSHING

Last Name	No.	Yds	Avg	TD
Haynes	139	697	5.0	4
M. Hill	105	576	5.5	4
McClinton	73	252	3.5	1
Spikes	34	114	3.3	0
Dawson	40	89	2.2	0
Coan	11	56	5.1	2
Beathard	4	43	10.8	0
E. Wilson	6	5	0.8	1
Jackson	2	5	2.5	0
J. Wilson	1	−10	−10.0	0

RECEIVING

Last Name	No.	Yds	Avg	TD
Jackson	62	943	15	9
Burford	51	675	13	7
Haynes	38	562	15	3
Arbanas	34	686	20	8
M. Hill	19	144	8	2
McClinton	13	221	17	2
Spikes	5	17	3	0
Carolan	3	54	18	1
Coan	2	8	4	0
J. Wilson	1	11	11	0

PUNT RETURNS

Last Name	No.	Yds	Avg	TD
Warner	12	165	14	0
Mitchell	18	160	9	0
Jackson	11	103	9	0
Robinson	1	16	16	0
Haynes	1	11	11	0

KICKOFF RETURNS

Last Name	No.	Yds	Avg	TD
Grayson	30	679	23	0
Warner	12	301	25	0
Haynes	12	278	23	0
Coan	5	124	25	0
Lothamer	1	0	0	0
Rosdahl	1	0	0	0
Stover	1	0	0	0

PASSING – PUNTING – KICKING

PASSING

Last Name	Att	Comp	%	Yds	Yd/Att	TD	Int−%	RK
Dawson	354	199	56	2879	8.1	30	18− 5	1
E. Wilson	47	25	53	392	8.3	1	1− 2	2
Beathard	9	4	44	50	5.6	1	2− 22	
Haynes	1	0	0	0	0.0	0	0− 0	
Spikes	1	0	0	0	0.0	0	0− 0	

PUNTING

Last Name	No	Avg
J. Wilson	78	42.6
E. Wilson	1	32.0

KICKING

Last Name	XP	Att	%	FG	Att	%
Brooker	46	46	100	8	17	47

2 POINT XP
McClinton

OAKLAND RAIDERS

RUSHING

Last Name	No.	Yds	Avg	TD
Daniels	173	824	4.8	2
Cannon	89	338	3.8	3
C. Davidson	29	167	5.8	2
Jackson	23	64	2.8	3
Flores	11	64	5.8	0
Shaw	9	26	2.9	2
Dickinson	4	8	2.0	0
Roberson	1	−4	−4.0	0
Youso	0	4	0.0	0

RECEIVING

Last Name	No.	Yds	Avg	TD
Powell	76	1361	18	11
Roberson	44	624	14	1
Daniels	42	696	17	6
Cannon	37	454	12	5
Herock	23	360	16	2
Barrett	12	212	18	2
Jackson	10	81	8	0
Shaw	3	31	10	0
Dickinson	3	28	9	0
Miller	2	29	15	0

PUNT RETURNS

Last Name	No.	Yds	Avg	TD
Gibson	29	419	14	0
Roberson	1	20	20	0
Krakoski	1	8	8	0
Morrow	1	0	0	0

KICKOFF RETURNS

Last Name	No.	Yds	Avg	TD
Roberson	36	975	27	0
Cannon	21	518	25	0
Jackson	2	32	16	0
Daniels	1	32	32	0
Conners	1	0	0	0
Dickinson	1	0	0	0
Klein	1	0	0	0

PASSING – PUNTING – KICKING

PASSING

Last Name	Att	Comp	%	Yds	Yd/Att	TD	Int−%	RK
C. Davidson	320	155	48	2497	7.8	21	19− 6	5
Flores	200	98	49	1389	7.0	7	14− 7	6
Daniels	1	0	0	0	0.0	0	0− 0	

PUNTING

Last Name	No	Avg
Mercer	58	42.1

KICKING

Last Name	XP	Att	%	FG	Att	%
Mercer	34	34	100	15	24	63

DENVER BRONCOS

RUSHING

Last Name	No.	Yds	Avg	TD
Mitchell	177	590	3.3	5
Joe	112	415	3.7	2
Lee	42	163	3.9	3
Slaughter	20	54	2.7	0
Stone	12	26	2.2	0
Mingo	6	26	4.3	0
Dixon	18	25	1.4	0
Barry	3	7	2.3	0
Scarpitto	1	5	5.0	0

RECEIVING

Last Name	No.	Yds	Avg	TD
Taylor	76	873	11	7
Dixon	38	585	15	1
Scarpitto	35	375	11	4
Mitchell	33	225	7	1
Denson	25	383	15	1
Joe	12	16	1	0
Stone	4	38	10	0
Barry	4	31	8	0
Mingo	4	25	6	1

PUNT RETURNS

Last Name	No.	Yds	Avg	TD
Barry	16	149	9	1
Mitchell	9	110	12	0

KICKOFF RETURNS

Last Name	No.	Yds	Avg	TD
Barry	47	1245	27	0
Mitchell	10	221	22	0
Mingo	8	163	20	0
West	5	142	28	0
Dixon	6	89	15	0
Olson	2	27	14	0
Shackleford	1	13	13	0
Jordan	1	0	0	0
Sturm	1	0	0	0

PASSING – PUNTING – KICKING

PASSING

Last Name	Att	Comp	%	Yds	Yd/Att	TD	Int−%	RK
Lee	265	133	50	1611	6.1	11	20− 8	10
Slaughter	189	97	51	930	4.9	3	11− 6	9
Mitchell	1	0	0	0	0.0	0	0− 0	
Taylor	1	0	0	0	0.0	0	1−100	

PUNTING

Last Name	No	Avg
Fraser	72	44.7
Janik	10	37.4

KICKING

Last Name	XP	Att	%	FG	Att	%
Guesman	13	15	87	6	22	27
Mingo	9	10	90	8	12	67

2 POINT XP
Denson
Joe
Slaughter

1965 N.F.L. Passing Pioneers and Hello, Dixie

The league lost two long-standing members when Curly Lambeau and Jack Mara died in June. Lambeau had founded the Green Bay Packers in 1919 and coached them through 1949, molding them into NFL powers until a postwar slump set in. Mara had for years run the New York Giants, founded by his father Tim Mara, and his death put his younger brother Wellington at the head of the New York organization. But life went on as usual in the league, with a hot Western Division race, new stars in Gale Sayers, Bob Hayes, and Dick Butkus, and the usual assortment of injuries, errors, and great plays. To spread the riches around—and also rake in some more money—the league voted to expand into Atlanta starting in 1966, reaching into the Deep South for the first time.

EASTERN CONFERENCE

Cleveland Browns—Even with Paul Warfield sidelined for most of the year by a shoulder injury and the defense saddled with the weight of advancing years, the Browns still ran away with the Eastern crown. Coach Blanton Collier had some of the finest offensive assets in the division, including a solid line, a reliable flanker in Gary Collins, a steady quarterback in Frank Ryan, and the incomparable Jimmy Brown at fullback, and the patchwork defense held up well enough to win eleven games. The Browns counted their riches even in the specialists' department, with forty-one-year-old Lou Groza an accurate place-kicker, Leroy Kelly a good punt returner, Walter Roberts a dangerous kickoff returner, and Gary Collins a fine punter in addition to his pass-catching chores.

Dallas Cowboys—The Cowboys failed to break the .500 barrier, but they did uncover one of the league's most exciting performers in rookie end Bob Hayes. A world-record-holding sprinter, Hayes terrorized defensive backs with his pure speed, streaking away from them with no possibility of being caught from behind once in the clear. While Hayes scored thirteen touchdowns, tackle Ralph Neely went unnoticed by all but the coaches with a fine rookie season. Coach Tom Landry added several other freshmen who would contribute to the strong Dallas teams of the next few years in Dan Reeves, Jethro Pugh, Craig Morton, and Obert Logan.

New York Giants—After losing all five of their pre-season games, the Giants obtained quarterback Earl Morrall from Detroit and finished in a surprising tie for second place in the East. Morrall gave the team a steady hand at the head of the offense and threw for twenty-two touchdowns. Joining Morrall in the backfield was a collection of young runners known collectively in the press as the Baby Bulls. Tucker Frederickson, Steve Thurlow, Ernie Koy, and Chuck Mercein all ground out hard overland yardage despite a lack of speed, and split end Homer Jones gave the Giants all the speed they needed in a pass receiver. Even with only a faint knowledge of pass patterns, Jones picked up over 700 yards as a receiver on only twenty-six catches after breaking into the starting lineup in mid-season.

Washington Redskins—The Redskins lost their first five games with a poor offensive show that improved only a little over the season. The Washington running attack was the league's worst, as there still was no full-time fullback, and halfback Charley Taylor came nowhere near duplicating his fine rookie season. The passing offense also slumped, as Bobby Mitchell alone among the receivers consistently got open for Sonny Jurgensen's passes. The Washington defense was a competent unit but was hurt when cornerback Johnny Sample was suspended late in the season for insubordination.

Philadelphia Eagles—Joe Kuharich had traded the Eagles into respectability last year, but progress came more slowly this season. The big trouble spot was the defensive line, which put no pressure at all on enemy passers. The Eagles resorted to frequent blitzing to compensate for the weak line, but this just made them vulnerable to quick passes. The offense was sound throughout, starting with the Bob Brown-led line. Timmy Brown starred at halfback, using his quickness to best advantage on runs and passes, Earl Gros complemented Brown with his power at fullback, and Norm Snead showed progress at quarterback.

St. Louis Cardinals—Tied with the Browns for first place in the East on October 17, the Cards swan-dived out of contention by losing eight of the next nine games and their last six contests straight. Injuries to Charley Johnson, Larry Wilson, and Jerry Stovall contributed to the collapse, and the trading of John David Crow to San Francisco hurt the club more than had been expected. Crow had been a clutch runner, the man to give the ball to when vital yardage was needed, and his departure left the Cards without a leader in the backfield.

Pittsburgh Steelers—Head coach Buddy Parker quit two weeks before the season opener, saying, "I can't win with this bunch of stiffs." On that pleasant note, assistant Mike Nixon took over as head man for a brutal 2-12 season. Nixon benched veteran quarterback Ed Brown and replaced him with Bill Nelsen, who played most of the season on a bad knee, which made him a sitting duck for enemy pass-rushers. The running attack lost its best man when John Henry Johnson was sidelined by a bad knee, and the receiving corps was so thin that the starting split end, Clendon Thomas, was a converted defensive

back. When Parker had quit as coach of the Detroit Lions before the 1957 season, the Lions went on to win the championship. This time, Parker knew what he was doing.

WESTERN CONFERENCE

Green Bay Packers—The return of guard Jerry Kramer from stomach surgery, the purchase of kicker Don Chandler from New York, and the development of Marv Fleming, Doug Hart, and Tom Brown into starters plastered over the few cracks in the Packers' solid front. After battling the Colts all season for the Western Conference lead, the Packers blew a chance to clinch the championship by managing only a tie with San Francisco in the final regular-season game. Baltimore and Green Bay finished with identical 10-3-1 records and squared off in a playoff for the Western crown. The Colts came into the playoff game with no experienced quarterback, but their fired-up defense knocked the ball loose from Bill Anderson on the first play from scrimmage, and Don Shinnick ran the fumble 25 yards for a Baltimore touchdown. Quarterback Bart Starr was shaken up on the play and missed most of the game, but the Packers fought back against the spirited Colts to tie the score at 10-10 with a Chandler field goal late in the game. For the second time in history, a pro-football game went into overtime, and another Chandler field goal, which the Colts and many observers claimed went wide, gave the Packers the victory after 13:39 of overtime play.

Baltimore Colts—Driving along to a repeat Western championship, the Colts suddenly lost both their quarterbacks, with Johnny Unitas ripping up a knee in the twelfth game and Gary Cuozzo dislocating a shoulder one week later. Coach Don Shula put halfback Tom Matte into the signal caller's spot, equiping him with a wrist band with some basic plays written on it. Relying on roll-out passes, quarterback keepers, pitchouts, and a fanatical defense, the Colts beat the Rams 20-17 in their final game to get into a Western Conference playoff with the Packers.

Chicago Bears—One of the Bears' three first-round draft picks, defensive end Steve DeLong got away to the AFL, but George Halas opened his wallet wide to sign the other two. Halfback Gale Sayers and linebacker Dick Butkus immediately rewarded Halas' generosity with All-Pro rookie seasons. Sayers burst on the national consciousness like a comet, slamming through holes at top speed and eluding defensive backs by outdodging and outrunning them. Starring as a kick returner and pass receiver as well as a runner, Sayers scored a record twenty-two touchdowns in the season. While Sayers souped up the Bear offense, Butkus helped return the defense to a high peak with his ferocity at middle linebacker.

San Francisco '49ers—With John Brodie suddenly putting all his talent together in a marvelous season, the '49er offense suddenly blossomed into the league's most explosive. Wide receivers Bernie Casey and Dave Parks gave Brodie two fine targets to hit, and the offensive line gave him good protection against enemy pass rushes. The running game improved immensely over last year with the addition of two new hard-chargers, rookie fullback Ken Willand and ex-Cardinal halfback John David Crow. The defense, however, was as undistinguished as the attack was dynamic.

Minnesota Vikings—The Viking offense still put on a good show, but the defense failed to show the expected progress, seven times getting burned for 35 or more points. This so frustrated head coach Norm Van Brocklin that he resigned in mid-season, only to be talked out of it after a couple of days by the front office. One of Van Brocklin's biggest problems was a growing tension between himself and quarterback Fran Tarkenton. The coach kept trying to make a strict pocket passer out of Tarkenton, while the quarterback stuck to his free-wheeling, scrambling style.

Detroit Lions—Owner William Clay Ford started the year by firing all of head coach George Wilson's assistants, a warning to Wilson to win or face the same fate. Wilson throught it over for a couple of days and handed in his resignation. Harry Gilmer took over as head man and ran into a flood of injuries that weighted the club down in sixth place. One of Gilmer's first decisions was to rely on one quarterback, so he kept Milt Plum and traded Earl Morrall to New York. The only problem was, Plum had a poor year, while Morrall rejuvenated the Giants with his fine passing. With the offense erratic, the Detroit defense no longer was strong enough to carry the team.

Los Angeles Rams—The front four of Deacon Jones, Merlin Olsen, Rosie Grier, and Lamar Lundy became the league's most famous defensive line and often carried the rest of the Los Angeles defense, which was ladened with as many as five rookie starters at one point. The running attack was weak, but the blocking and receiving gave quarterbacks Bill Munson and Roman Gabriel something to work with. Munson started the first ten games and led the club to only one win despite frequent flashes of talent, and Gabriel headed the attack for the final four games after Munson hurt a knee.

FINAL TEAM STATISTICS

OFFENSE

	BALT.	CHI.	CLEVE.	DALLAS	DET.	G.BAY	L.A.	MINN.	N.Y.	PHIL.	PITT.	ST.L.	S.F.	WASH.
FIRST DOWNS:														
Total	266	257	257	211	204	201	251	277	230	267	194	251	292	210
by Rushing	94	132	133	87	93	85	76	130	91	94	71	90	97	69
by Passing	144	110	97	108	93	103	153	126	112	149	104	143	172	125
by Penalty	28	15	27	16	18	13	22	21	27	24	19	18	23	16
RUSHING:														
Number	445	479	476	416	453	432	378	505	423	404	407	431	428	354
Yards	1593	2131	2331	1608	1469	1488	1464	2278	1651	1824	1378	1619	1783	1037
Average Yards	3.6	4.4	4.9	3.9	3.2	3.4	3.9	4.5	3.9	4.5	3.4	3.8	4.2	2.9
Touchdowns	13	27	19	8	16	14	8	19	12	21	10	10	13	7
PASSING:														
Attempts	399	361	329	362	374	306	445	372	342	434	354	448	454	427
Completions	222	201	160	168	170	166	230	189	171	223	161	221	272	220
Completion Pct.	55.6	55.7	48.6	46.4	45.5	54.2	51.7	50.8	50.0	51.4	45.5	49.3	59.9	51.5
Passing Yards	3330	3020	2339	2756	2083	2508	3059	2861	2685	3442	2503	3222	3633	2908
Avg. Yds per Att.	8.3	8.4	7.1	7.6	5.6	8.2	6.9	7.7	7.9	7.9	7.1	7.2	8.0	6.8
Avg. Yds per Comp.	15.0	15.0	14.6	16.4	12.3	15.1	13.3	15.1	15.7	15.4	15.5	14.6	13.4	13.2
Tackled Att. to Pass	43	30	31	55	26	43	45	35	31	33	62	30	19	39
Yards Lost Tackled	325	254	272	369	249	395	344	315	255	254	527	279	146	337
Net Yards	3005	2766	2067	2387	1834	2113	2715	2546	2430	3188	1976	2943	3487	2571
Touchdowns	31	22	23	25	14	19	22	21	23	22	10	20	35	20
Interceptions	17	12	16	18	26	14	19	12	16	26	35	25	21	20
Pct. Intercepted	4.3	3.3	4.9	5.0	7.0	4.6	4.3	3.2	4.7	6.0	9.9	5.6	4.6	4.7
PUNTS:														
Number	56	58	69	73	78	74	66	51	61	56	78	67	54	70
Average Distance	39.6	42.7	45.7	41.3	42.8	42.9	39.7	42.1	41.6	42.2	45.1	40.4	45.8	42.1
PUNT RETURNS:														
Number	45	29	36	39	34	22	32	22	24	21	33	23	38	39
Yards	421	289	427	312	358	65	225	115	35	183	259	27	283	415
Average Yards	9.4	10.0	11.9	8.0	10.5	3.0	7.0	5.2	1.5	8.7	7.8	1.2	7.4	10.6
Touchdowns	0	1	2	0	0	0	0	1	0	1	0	0	0	1
KICKOFF RETURNS:														
Number	52	45	53	44	52	50	53	67	60	60	61	55	59	49
Yards	1242	1146	1209	1166	1416	1040	1351	1524	1303	1438	1238	1287	1276	1011
Average Yards	23.9	25.5	22.8	26.5	27.2	20.8	25.5	22.7	21.7	24.0	20.3	23.4	21.6	20.6
Touchdowns	0	1	0	1	0	0	0	1	0	0	0	0	0	0
INTERCEPTION RETURNS:														
Number	22	20	24	18	26	27	11	19	16	25	12	17	13	27
Yards	318	307	349	198	343	561	224	286	249	313	282	328	97	535
Average Yards	14.5	15.4	14.5	11.0	13.2	20.8	20.4	15.1	15.6	12.5	23.5	19.3	7.5	19.8
Touchdowns	4	2	1	2	3	4	1	2	1	3	2	1	0	2
PENALTIES:														
Number	69	96	84	68	77	48	61	76	61	61	40	45	79	81
Yards	616	826	976	710	767	529	560	771	618	686	326	458	785	692
FUMBLES:														
Number	31	33	20	31	27	18	40	41	31	21	42	15	33	41
Number Lost	19	16	9	17	15	12	22	25	14	10	22	7	19	21
POINTS:														
Total	389	409	363	325	257	316	269	383	270	363	202	296	421	257
PAT Attempts	48	54	45	40	33	38	32	44	37	48	25	33	53	33
PAT Made	48	52	45	37	33	37	30	44	34	45	19	33	52	29
FG Attempte	28	26	25	27	22	26	26	35	25	25	19	31	27	22
FG Made	17	11	16	16	8	17	15	23	4	10	11	21	17	10
Percent FG Made	60.7	42.3	64.0	59.3	36.4	65.4	57.7	65.7	16.0	40.0	57.9	67.7	63.0	45.5
Safeties	1	0	0	0	1	0	1	3	1	0	0	1	0	0

DEFENSE

	BALT.	CHI.	CLEVE.	DALLAS	DET.	G.BAY	L.A.	MINN.	N.Y.	PHIL.	PITT.	ST.L.	S.F.	WASH.
FIRST DOWNS:														
Total	233	244	265	240	210	240	208	242	266	243	243	238	259	237
by Rushing	78	87	104	80	84	115	82	99	108	100	122	89	94	100
by Passing	131	136	135	138	104	111	113	120	140	129	109	133	139	101
by Penalty	24	21	26	22	22	14	13	23	18	14	12	16	26	36
RUSHING:														
Number	410	400	412	422	409	480	417	408	447	419	483	433	405	486
Yards	1483	1530	1866	1444	1460	1988	1409	1755	1956	1582	2080	1813	1535	1753
Average Yards	3.6	3.8	4.5	3.4	3.6	4.1	3.4	4.3	4.4	3.8	4.3	4.2	3.8	3.6
Touchdowns	11	11	11	13	9	10	16	17	20	11	19	11	20	18
PASSING:														
Attempts	400	444	419	426	344	383	349	357	393	393	353	380	448	318
Completions	213	217	204	205	190	187	205	187	208	215	173	184	225	161
Completion Pct.	53.3	48.9	48.7	48.1	55.2	48.8	58.7	52.4	52.9	54.7	49.0	48.4	50.2	50.6
Passing Yards	2903	3086	3153	3063	2508	2316	2884	2692	3251	3123	2703	2826	3302	2539
Avg. Yds per Att.	7.3	7.0	7.5	7.2	7.3	6.0	8.3	7.5	8.3	7.9	7.7	7.4	7.4	8.0
Avg. Yds per Comp.	13.6	14.2	15.5	14.9	13.2	12.4	14.1	14.4	15.6	14.5	15.6	15.4	14.7	15.8
Tackled Att. to Pass	39	40	38	39	49	44	32	23	39	37	33	39	25	45
Yards Lost Tackled	341	348	307	315	411	335	270	199	294	287	253	342	197	422
Net Yards	2562	2738	2846	2748	2097	1981	2614	2493	2957	2836	2450	2484	3105	2117
Touchdowns	22	18	31	17	21	11	22	31	18	28	25	24	24	15
Interceptions	22	20	24	18	26	27	11	19	16	25	12	17	13	27
Pct. Intercepted	5.5	4.5	5.7	4.2	7.6	7.0	3.2	5.3	4.1	6.4	3.4	4.5	2.9	8.5
PUNTS:														
Number	71	65	69	71	74	60	66	64	45	54	76	65	62	69
Average Distance	43.9	42.3	41.1	42.9	42.9	42.1	45.4	38.4	42.7	41.8	42.2	43.3	41.9	43.4
PUNT RETURNS:														
Number	26	22	36	26	39	36	25	29	22	37	44	32	33	30
Yards	198	123	259	139	318	290	176	261	137	263	437	267	408	138
Average Yards	7.6	5.6	7.2	5.3	8.2	8.1	7.0	9.0	6.2	7.1	9.9	8.3	12.4	4.6
Touchdowns	0	0	0	1	1	0	1	0	0	0	2	0	1	0
KICKOFF RETURNS:														
Number	63	72	58	63	43	52	54	62	54	58	30	50	59	42
Yards	1346	1583	1334	1229	858	1216	1364	1557	1175	1531	684	1228	1566	976
Average Yards	21.4	22.0	23.0	19.5	20.0	23.4	25.3	25.1	21.8	26.4	22.8	24.6	26.5	23.2
Touchdowns	1	0	0	0	0	0	0	1	0	0	0	0	1	0
INTERCEPTION RETURNS:														
Number	17	12	16	18	26	14	19	12	16	26	35	25	21	20
Yards	341	219	275	268	515	209	156	215	182	476	646	465	232	191
Average Yards	20.1	18.3	17.2	14.9	19.8	14.9	8.2	17.9	11.4	18.3	18.5	18.6	11.0	9.6
Touchdowns	1	3	1	0	2	1	0	1	1	6	6	1	3	2
PENALTIES:														
Number	80	68	62	50	61	67	70	66	83	66	58	70	71	74
Yards	786	611	586	483	637	677	566	643	848	653	615	750	727	738
FUMBLES:														
Number	33	33	13	37	33	37	27	25	32	32	28	29	34	31
Number Lost	14	24	8	20	20	23	15	11	20	11	15	15	17	15
POINTS:														
Total	284	275	325	280	295	224	328	403	338	359	397	309	402	301
PAT Attempts	35	33	43	33	36	22	40	53	41	47	53	37	52	38
PAT Made	35	30	40	29	36	22	40	52	40	44	49	36	48	37
FG Attempte	23	24	18	30	22	33	32	20	29	26	26	32	27	22
FG Made	13	15	9	17	13	22	16	11	16	11	10	17	14	12
Percent FG Made	56.5	62.5	50.0	56.7	59.1	66.7	50.0	55.0	55.2	42.3	38.5	53.1	51.9	54.5
Safeties	0	1	0	1	2	2	0	0	2	0	0	0	0	0

1965 NFL CHAMPIONSHIP GAME
January 2, at Green Bay
(Attendance 50,777)

Bulldozing the Defense

After two years as Western Division runners-up, the Green Bay Packers returned to the NFL championship game they had won in 1961 and 1962. The Cleveland Browns, the defending NFL champions, came into Lambeau Field to furnish the opposition. The playing field was muddy and footing uncertain, making straight-ahead running plays the best bets of the afternoon. The Packer defense gave Green Bay a decisive edge by dogging Cleveland fullback Jimmy Brown all afternoon, while Packer runners Jim Taylor and Paul Hornung followed strong blocking to eat up yardage on the ground. Packer quarterback Bart Starr crossed up the Browns on the first series of downs by throwing the ball; he hit Carroll Dale with a long pass that gave the Packers a quick 7-0 lead. The Browns retaliated by moving steadily downfield and scoring on a Frank Ryan-to-Gary Collins pass. The extra point went awry, however, and the Packers still led 7-6. A Lou Groza field goal gave the Browns a 9-7 lead at the end of the first quarter, and three second-period field goals, one by Groza and two by Green Bay's Don Chandler, made the halftime score 13-12 in favor of the Packers. Coach Vince Lombardi stressed ball control to his players, and the Packer offense came out for the second half ready to grind out difficult yardage. Using off-tackle blasts and power sweeps with Taylor and Hornung carrying the ball, the Packers drove 90 yards on 11 plays in the third quarter, eating up seven minutes of the clock while putting seven more points on the scoreboard. Whenever the Browns got the ball in the second half, they couldn't move against the Green Bay defense; whenever the Packers had the ball, they would hold onto it for several precious minutes before giving it up. In all, the Green Bay offensive line contributed the most to the Packer victory by constantly knocking the Cleveland defenders back to make room for Taylor and Hornung in the 20-12 victory.

SCORING

GREEN BAY	7	6	7	3–23
CLEVELAND	9	3	0	0–12

First Quarter
- G.B. Dale, 47 yard pass from Starr
  - PAT – Chandler (kick)
- Cle. Collins, 17 yard pass from Ryan
  - PAT – No Good
- Cle. Groza, 24 yard field goal

Second Quarter
- G.B. Chandler, 15 yard field goal
- G.B. Chandler, 23 yard field goal
- Cle. Groza, 28 yard field goal

Third Quarter
- G.B. Hornung, 13 yard rush
  - PAT – Chandler (kick)

Fourth Quarter
- G.B. Chandler, 29 yard field goal

TEAM STATISTICS

G. B.		CLEVE.
21	First Downs – Total	8
10	First Downs – Rushing	2
9	First Downs – Passing	5
2	First Downs – Penalty	1
3	Punts – Number	4
38.3	Punts – Average Distance	46.0
2	Punt Returns – Number	1
–10	Punt Returns – Yards	11
2	Interception Returns – Number	1
15	Interception Returns – Yards	0
0	Fumbles – Number	0
3	Penalties – Number	2
35	Yards Penalized	20
1	Giveaways	2
2	Takeaways	1
+1	Difference	–1

INDIVIDUAL STATISTICS

RUSHING

GREEN BAY	No.	Yds.	Avg.	CLEVELAND	No.	Yds.	Avg.
Hornung	18	105	5.8	Brown	12	50	4.2
Taylor	27	96	3.6	Ryan	3	9	3.0
Moore	2	3	1.5	Green	3	5	1.7
	47	204	4.3		18	64	3.6

RECEIVING

GREEN BAY	No.	Yds.	Avg.	CLEVELAND	No.	Yds.	Avg.
Dowler	5	59	11.8	Brown	3	44	14.7
Dale	2	60	30.0	Collins	3	41	13.7
Taylor	2	20	10.0	Warfield	2	30	15.0
Hornung	1	8	8.0		8	115	14.4
	10	147	14.7				

PASSING

	Att	Comp	Comp Pct.	Yds	Int	Yds/ Att.	Yds/ Comp	Yards Lost Tackled
GREEN BAY								
Starr	18	10	55.6	147	1	8.2	14.7	
Hornung	1	0	0.0	0	0	–	–	
	19	10	52.6	147	1	7.7	14.7	19
CLEVELAND								
Ryan	18	8	44.4	115	2	6.4	14.4	18

1965 N.F.L. — Eastern Conference

CLEVELAND BROWNS 11-3-0 Blanton Collier

Scores of Each Game			
17	Washington	7	
13	ST. LOUIS	49	
35	Philadelphia	17	
24	PITTSBURGH	19	
23	DALLAS	17	
38	New York	14	
17	MINNESOTA	27	
38	PHILADELPHIA	34	
34	NEW YORK	21	
24	Dallas	17	
42	Pittsburgh	21	
24	WASHINGTON	16	
7	Los Angeles	42	
27	St. Louis	24	

Use Name	Pos.	Hgt	Wgt	Age	Int	Pts
John Brown	OT	6'2"	248	26		
Monte Clark	OT	6'6"	265	28		
Dick Schafrath	OT	6'3"	255	29		
Gene Hickerson	OG	6'3"	248	30		
Dale Memmelaar	OG	6'2"	248	28		
John Wooten	OG	6'2"	250	30		
John Morrow	C	6'3"	248	32		
Jim Garcia	DE	6'4"	240	21		
Bill Glass	DE	6'5"	255	29	1	
Paul Wiggin	DE	6'3"	245	31		
Walter Johnson	DT	6'3"	265	22		
Jim Kanicki	DT	6'4"	270	23		
Dick Modzelewski	DT	6'	260	34		
Vince Costello	LB	6'	228	33	3	
Galen Fiss	LB	6'	227	35	1	
Jim Houston	LB	6'2"	240	28	2	
Dale Lindsey	LB	6'3"	220	22	1	
Stan Sczurek	LB	5'11"	230	26	1	
Sid Williams	LB	6'2"	235	23	1	
Erich Barnes	DB	6'2"	198	30	1	
Walter Beach	DB	6'	185	30		
Larry Benz	DB	5'11"	185	24	5	
Ross Fichtner	DB	6'	185	27	4	6
Bobby Franklin	DB	5'11"	182	29		
Mike Howell	DB	6'1"	187	22		
Bernie Parrish	DB	5'11"	195	30	4	
Jim Ninowski	QB	6'1"	207	29		
Frank Ryan	QB	6'3"	200	29		
Ernie Green	HB	6'2"	205	26		24
Leroy Kelly	HB	6'	195	23		12
Jimmy Brown	FB	6'2"	228	29		126
Jamie Caleb	FB	6'1"	210	28		
Charlie Scales	FB	5'11"	215	26		
Gary Collins	FL	6'4"	208	24		60
Clifton McNeil	FL	6'2"	185	25		
Johnny Brewer	TE	6'4"	235	28		6
Ralph Smith	TE	6'2"	215	26		
Tom Hutchinson	OE	6'1"	190	24		12
Walter Roberts	OE	5'10"	175	23		24
Paul Warfield	OE	6'	188	22		
Lou Groza	K	6'3"	250	41		93

Frank Parker – Operation

DALLAS COWBOYS 7-7-0 Tom Landry

Scores of Each Game			
31	NEW YORK	2	
27	WASHINGTON	7	
13	St. Louis	20	
24	PHILADELPHIA	35	
17	Cleveland	23	
3	Green Bay	13	
13	Pittsburgh	22	
39	SAN FRANCISCO	31	
24	PITTSBURGH	17	
17	CLEVELAND	24	
31	Washington	34	
21	Philadelphia	19	
27	ST. LOUIS	13	
38	New York	20	

Use Name	Pos.	Hgt	Wgt	Age	Int	Pts
Jim Boeke	OT	6'5"	255	26		
Ralph Neely	OT	6'5"	257	21		
Don Talbert	OT	6'5"	240	25		
Mike Connelly	OG	6'3"	248	29		
Leon Donahue (from SF)	OG	6'4"	245	26		
Mitch Johnson	OG	6'4"	245	23		
Jake Kupp	OG	6'3"	233	23		
Dave Manders	C	6'2"	240	23		
George Andrie	DE	6'7"	255	25		6
Garry Porterfield	DE	6'3"	223	22		
Jethro Pugh	DE	6'6"	255	21		
Maury Youmans	DE	6'6"	253	28		
Larry Stephens	DT-DE	6'4"	250	27		
Jim Colvin	DT	6'2"	255	28		
John Diehl (to OAK-A)	DT	6'7"	250	29		
Bob Lilly	DT	6'4"	255	26	1	6
Dave Edwards	LB	6'3"	226	26	2	
Harold Hays	LB	6'3"	223	24		
Chuck Howley	LB	6'3"	223	29		
Lee Roy Jordan	LB	6'2"	216	24		
Jerry Tubbs	LB	6'2"	222	30	2	
Russell Wayt	LB	6'4"	235	22		
Don Bishop	DB	6'2"	216	30		
Mike Gaechter	DB	6'	190	25	2	6
Cornell Green	DB	6'4"	215	25	3	6
Warren Livingston	DB	5'10"	190	27	3	
Obert Logan	DB	5'10"	180	23	3	6
Mel Renfro	HB-DB	6'	195	23	2	12
Don Meredith	QB	6'2"	206	27		6
Craig Morton	QB	6'4"	216	22		
Jerry Rhome	QB	6'	180	23		
Perry Lee Dunn	HB	6'2"	200	22		18
Dan Reeves	HB	6'1"	203	21		18
Don Perkins	FB	5'10"	206	27		
J. D. Smith	FB	6'1"	210	32		18
A. D. Whitfield	FB	5'10"	200	21		
Buddy Dial	FL	6'1"	195	28		6
Pete Gent	FL	6'4"	210	22		12
Pettis Norman	TE	6'3"	223	25		18
Frank Clarke	OE	6'	210	32		24
Bob Hayes	OE	6'	190	22		78
Colin Ridgway	K	6'5"	211	26		
Danny Villanueva	K	5'11"	200	27		85

Joe Bob Isbell – Injury
Tony Liscio – Injury

NEW YORK GIANTS 7-7-0 Allie Sherman

Scores of Each Game			
2	Dallas	31	
16	Philadelphia	14	
23	Pittsburgh	13	
14	Minnesota	40	
35	PHILADELPHIA	27	
14	CLEVELAND	38	
14	ST. LOUIS	10	
7	WASHINGTON	23	
21	Cleveland	34	
28	St. Louis	15	
14	CHICAGO	35	
35	PITTSBURGH	10	
27	Washington	10	
20	DALLAS	38	

Use Name	Pos.	Hgt	Wgt	Age	Int	Pts
Rosey Brown	OT	6'3"	255	32		
Frank Lasky	OT	6'2"	265	23		
John McDowell	OT	6'3"	260	22		
Bookie Bolin	OG	6'2"	240	25		
Pete Case	OG	6'3"	243	24		
Roger Davis	OG	6'3"	240	27		
Mickey Walker	OG	6'	235	25		
Greg Larson	C	6'2"	250	26		
Bob Scholtz	C	6'4"	250	27		
Glen Condren	DE	6'2"	225	23		
Rosey Davis	DE	6'5"	260	23		
Jim Katcavage	DE	6'3"	240	30		2
Andy Stynchula	DE	6'3"	250	26		21
Roger Anderson	DT	6'5"	265	22		
Mike Bundra	DT	6'3"	260	26		
Roger LaLonde	DT	6'3"	255	23		
John Lovetere	DT	6'4"	285	29		
Dave O'Brien	DT	6'3"	247	24		
Jim Carroll	LB	6'1"	225	22	1	
Tom Costello	LB	6'3"	220	24		
Jerry Hillebrand	LB	6'3"	240	25	2	6
Bill Swain	LB	6'2"	228	24		
Olen Underwood	LB	6'1"	210	23	1	
Lou Slaby	DT-LB	6'3"	235	23		
Henry Carr	DB	6'3"	205	22	2	
Clarence Childs	DB	6'	180	26		
Spider Lockhart	DB	6'2"	185	22	4	
Dick Lynch	DB	6'1"	198	29	4	6
Jimmy Patton	DB	6'	185	33	1	
Allan Webb	DB	5'11"	180	30		
Willie Williams	DB	6'	190	22	1	
Earl Morrall	QB	6'1"	206	31		
Bob Timberlake	QB	6'4"	220	22		24
Gary Wood	QB	5'11"	188	22		1
Tucker Frederickson	FB-HB	6'3"	220	22		36
Ernie Koy	HB	6'2"	225	22		
Smith Reed	HB	6'	215	23		
Steve Thurlow	HB	6'3"	216	22		30
Chuck Mercein	FB	6'3"	230	22		12
Ernie Wheelwright	FB	6'3"	240	28		
Bob Crespino	TE	6'4"	225	27		24
Aaron Thomas	FL-TE	6'3"	210	27		30
Homer Jones	FL	6'2"	205	24		36
Joe Morrison	FL	6'1"	212	27		30
Bob Lacey	OE	6'3"	205	23		
Del Shofner	OE	6'3"	185	29		12

Jim Moran – Broken Leg

WASHINGTON REDSKINS 6-8-0 Bill McPeak

Scores of Each Game			
7	CLEVELAND	17	
7	Dallas	27	
10	Detroit	14	
16	ST. LOUIS	37	
7	BALTIMORE	38	
24	St. Louis	20	
23	PHILADELPHIA	21	
23	New York	7	
14	Philadelphia	21	
31	Pittsburgh	3	
34	DALLAS	31	
16	Cleveland	24	
10	NEW YORK	27	
35	PITTSBURGH	14	

Use Name	Pos.	Hgt	Wgt	Age	Int	Pts
Fran O'Brien	OT	6'1"	255	30		
Jim Snowden	DE-OT	6'3"	255	23		
Don Croftcheck	OG	6'1"	230	22		
Darrell Dess	OG	6'	245	29		
Vince Promuto	OG	6'1"	245	27		
Robert Reed	OG	6'1"	250	22		
Dave Crossan	C	6'3"	245	25		
Len Hauss	C	6'2"	235	23		
Carl Kammerer	DE	6'3"	243	28		
John Paluck	DE	6'2"	245	32		
Bill Quinlan	DE	6'3"	250	33		
Ron Snidow	DE	6'4"	250	23	1	
Joe Rutgens	DT	6'2"	255	26		
Fred Williams	DT	6'4"	256	35		
Willie Adams	LB	6'2"	235	23		
Jimmy Carr	LB	6'1"	225	32		
Chris Hanburger	LB	6'2"	218	24	1	
Sam Huff	LB	6'1"	230	30	2	
Bob Pellegrini	LB	6'2"	242	30		6
John Reger	LB	6'	220	34		
Rickie Harris	DB	6'	182	22	1	12
Johnny Sample	DB	6'1"	205	28	6	
Lonnie Sanders	DB	6'3"	207	23	4	
Jim Shorter	DB	5'11"	185	24	2	6
Jim Steffen	DB	6'	196	28	3	
Tom Walters	DB	6'2"	195	23	1	6
Paul Krause	FL-DB	6'3"	195	23	6	6
Sonny Jurgensen	QB	5'11"	205	31		12
Dick Shiner	QB	6'	197	23		
Pervis Atkins (to OAK-A)	HB	6'1"	210	29		
George Hughley	HB	6'2"	223	26		6
Dan Lewis	HB	6'1"	200	29		24
Charley Taylor	HB	6'3"	210	24		36
Bob Briggs	FB	6'1"	228	22		
Rick Casares	FB	6'2"	225	34		
Bobby Mitchell	FL	6'	196	30		36
Bill Hunter	DB-FL	6'1"	185	22		6
Fred Mazurek	DB-FL	5'11"	192	22		
Jerry Smith	TE	6'2"	208	22		12
Preston Carpenter	OE	6'2"	208	31		
Angie Coia	OE	6'2"	196	27		18
Bob Jencks	OE	6'5"	227	24		59
Pat Richter	OE	6'5"	230	24		12
John Seedborg	K	6'	227	22		

PHILADELPHIA EAGLES 5-9-0 Joe Kuharich

Scores of Each Game			
34	ST. LOUIS	27	
14	NEW YORK	16	
17	CLEVELAND	35	
35	Dallas	24	
27	New York	35	
14	PITTSBURGH	20	
21	Washington	23	
34	Cleveland	38	
21	WASHINGTON	14	
24	Baltimore	34	
28	St. Louis	24	
19	DALLAS	21	
47	Pittsburgh	13	
28	DETROIT	35	

Use Name	Pos.	Hgt	Wgt	Age	Int	Pts
Bob Brown	OT	6'4"	276	22		
Dave Graham	OT	6'3"	250	26		
Lane Howell	OT	6'5"	255	24		
Ed Blaine	OG	6'2"	240	25		
Jim Skaggs	OT-OG	6'2"	250	25		
Lynn Hoyem	C-OG	6'4"	253	25		
Dave Recher	C	6'1"	240	22		
Jim Ringo	C	6'1"	230	34		
Bobby Richards	DE	6'2"	245	26		
George Tarasovic	DE	6'4"	248	36	1	12
Don Hultz	LB-DE	6'3"	235	24	1	
Ed Khayat	DT	6'3"	250	30		
John Meyers	DT	6'6"	276	25	2	
Floyd Peters	DT	6'4"	255	30		
Erwin Will	DT	6'5"	270	22		
Maxie Baughan	LB	6'1"	227	27	1	6
Ralph Heck	LB	6'2"	230	24		
Dave Lloyd	LB	6'3"	248	29	2	10
Mike Morgan	LB	6'4"	242	23	1	
Harold Wells	LB	6'2"	223	26		
Irv Cross	DB	6'1"	190	26	3	
Al Nelson	DB	5'11"	180	21	2	
Jim Nettles	DB	5'9"	175	23	3	6
Nate Ramsey	DB	6'1"	200	24	6	
Bob Shann	DB	6'1"	187	22		6
Joe Scarpati	HB-DB	5'10"	185	23	3	
Claude Crabb	FL-DB	6'	190	25		
Jack Concannon	QB	6'3"	195	22		
King Hill	QB	6'3"	213	29		12
Norm Snead	QB	6'4"	205	25		18
Timmy Brown	HB	5'10"	198	28		54
Ollie Matson	HB	6'2"	210	35		18
Earl Gros	FB	6'3"	220	24		54
Izzy Lang	FB	6'1"	230	22		6
Tom Woodeshick	FB	6'	220	23		
Glenn Glass	FL	6'	203	28		
Ron Goodwin	OE-FL	6'	180	23		6
Roger Gill	TE	6'1"	200	24		
Bill Cronin	TE	6'4"	220	22		
Jim Kelly	TE	6'2"	215	23		
Pete Retzlaff	TE	6'1"	214	34		60
Fred Hill	OE	6'2"	215	22		
Ray Poage	OE	6'4"	200	24		30
Sam Baker	K	6'2"	218	33		65

Jerry Mazzanti – Military Service
Mike McClellan – Military Service

CLEVELAND BROWNS

RUSHING

Last Name	No.	Yds	Avg	TD
Jimmy Brown	289	1544	5.3	17
Green	111	436	3.9	2
Kelly	37	139	3.8	0
Ryan	19	72	3.8	0
Scales	11	59	5.4	0
Ninowski	4	46	11.5	0
Roberts	3	30	10.0	0
Collins	1	16	16.0	0
Franklin	1	−11	−11.0	0

RECEIVING

Last Name	No.	Yds	Avg	TD
Collins	50	884	18	10
Jimmy Brown	34	328	10	4
Green	25	298	12	2
Roberts	16	314	20	4
Brewer	13	174	13	1
Kelly	9	122	14	0
Hutchinson	6	113	19	2
McNeil	3	69	23	0
Warfield	3	30	10	0
Scales	1	7	7	0

PUNT RETURNS

Last Name	No.	Yds	Avg	TD
Kelly	17	265	16	2
Roberts	18	162	9	0
Scales	1	0	0	0

KICKOFF RETURNS

Last Name	No.	Yds	Avg	TD
Kelly	24	621	26	0
Roberts	18	493	27	0
Scales	4	88	22	0
Green	1	4	4	0
Howell	2	3	2	0
Hutchinson	2	0	0	0
Franklin	1	0	0	0
Lindsey	1	0	0	0

PASSING – PUNTING – KICKING

PASSING

Last Name	Att	Comp	%	Yds	Yd/Att	TD	Int–%	RK
Ryan	243	119	49	1751	7.2	18	13– 5	12
Ninowski	83	40	48	549	6.6	4	3– 4	
Jimmy Brown	2	1	50	39	19.5	1	0– 0	
Groza	1	0	0	0	0.0	0	0– 0	

PUNTING

Last Name	No	Avg
Collins	65	46.7
Franklin	4	29.5

KICKING

Last Name	XP	Att	%	FG	Att	%
Groza	45	45	100	16	25	64

DALLAS COWBOYS

RUSHING

Last Name	No.	Yds	Avg	TD
Perkins	177	690	3.9	0
Smith	86	295	3.4	2
Meredith	35	247	7.1	1
Dunn	54	171	3.2	2
Reeves	33	102	3.1	2
Clarke	8	58	7.3	0
Rhome	4	11	2.8	0
Whitfield	1	0	0.0	0
Hayes	4	−8	−2.0	1
Morton	3	−8	−2.7	0

RECEIVING

Last Name	No.	Yds	Avg	TD
Hayes	46	1003	22	12
Clarke	41	682	17	4
Dial	17	283	17	1
Gent	16	233	15	2
Perkins	14	142	10	0
Norman	11	110	10	3
Reeves	9	210	23	1
Dunn	8	74	9	1
Smith	5	10	2	1

PUNT RETURNS

Last Name	No.	Yds	Avg	TD
Hayes	12	153	13	0
Renfro	24	145	6	0

KICKOFF RETURNS

Last Name	No.	Yds	Avg	TD
Renfro	21	630	30	1
Hayes	17	450	26	0
Reeves	2	45	23	0
Neely	2	13	7	0

PASSING – PUNTING – KICKING

PASSING

Last Name	Att	Comp	%	Yds	Yd/Att	TD	Int–%	RK
Meredith	305	141	46	2415	7.9	22	13– 4	8
Morton	34	17	50	173	5.1	2	4– 12	
Rhome	21	9	43	157	7.5	1	1– 5	
Reeves	2	1	50	11	5.5	0	0– 0	

PUNTING

Last Name	No	Avg
Villanueva	60	41.8
Ridgway	13	39.2

KICKING

Last Name	XP	Att	%	FG	Att	%
Villanueva	37	38	97	16	27	59

NEW YORK GIANTS

RUSHING

Last Name	No.	Yds	Avg	TD
Frederickson	195	659	3.4	5
Thurlow	106	440	4.2	4
Koy	35	174	5.0	0
Wheelwright	24	96	4.0	0
Reed	19	70	3.7	0
Wood	5	68	13.6	0
Mercein	18	55	3.1	2
Morrall	17	52	3.1	0
Morrison	3	20	6.7	1
Jones	1	17	17.0	0

RECEIVING

Last Name	No.	Yds	Avg	TD
Morrison	41	574	14	4
Thomas	27	631	23	5
Jones	26	709	27	6
Frederickson	24	177	7	1
Shofner	22	388	18	2
Thurlow	9	54	6	1
Crespino	7	57	8	4
Reed	6	42	7	0
Koy	4	22	6	0
Mercein	3	14	5	0
Wheelwright	2	17	9	0

PUNT RETURNS

Last Name	No.	Yds	Avg	TD
Williams	18	28	2	0
Carr	4	13	3	0
Lockhart	2	−6	−3	0

KICKOFF RETURNS

Last Name	No.	Yds	Avg	TD
Childs	29	718	25	0
Koy	21	401	19	0
Williams	5	113	23	0
Webb	2	48	24	0
Thurlow	1	19	19	0
Mercein	1	4	4	0
Brown	1	0	0	0

PASSING – PUNTING – KICKING

PASSING

Last Name	Att	Comp	%	Yds	Yd/Att	TD	Int–%	RK
Morrall	302	155	51	2446	8.1	22	12– 4	5
Wood	36	15	42	190	5.3	1	2– 6	
Koy	2	0	0	0	0.0	0	1– 50	
Frederickson	1	0	0	0	0.0	0	1–100	
Thurlow	1	1	100	49	49.0	0	0– 0	

PUNTING

Last Name	No	Avg
Koy	55	41.2
Lockhart	6	44.5

KICKING

Last Name	XP	Att	%	FG	Att	%
Timberlake	21	22	95	1	15	7
Stynchula	12	13	92	3	7	43
Wood	1	1	100	0	0	0
Hillebrand	0	0	0	0	1	0
Mercein	0	0	0	0	2	0

WASHINGTON REDSKINS

RUSHING

Last Name	No.	Yds	Avg	TD
Taylor	145	402	2.8	3
Lewis	117	343	2.9	2
Hughley	37	175	4.7	0
Atkins	18	44	2.4	0
Shiner	12	35	2.9	0
Jurgensen	17	23	1.4	2
Briggs	6	10	1.7	0
Casares	2	5	2.5	0

RECEIVING

Last Name	No.	Yds	Avg	TD
Mitchell	60	867	14	6
Taylor	40	577	14	3
Lewis	25	276	11	2
Carpenter	23	298	13	0
Smith	19	257	14	2
Coia	18	240	13	3
Richter	16	189	12	2
Hughley	9	93	10	1
Briggs	3	40	13	0
Jencks	2	20	10	0
Krause	2	17	9	0
Hunter	1	29	29	1
Casares	1	5	5	0
Atkins	1	0	0	0

PUNT RETURNS

Last Name	No.	Yds	Avg	TD
Harris	31	377	12	1
Mitchell	1	15	15	0
Hughley	2	12	6	0
Atkins	3	11	4	0
Mazurek	1	0	0	0
Pellegrini	1	0	0	0

KICKOFF RETURNS

Last Name	No.	Yds	Avg	TD
Hunter	18	432	24	0
Hughley	13	295	23	0
Mitchell	5	106	21	0
Harris	5	96	19	0
Walters	2	30	15	0
Atkins	1	15	15	0
Taylor	1	15	15	0
Kammerer	1	14	14	0
Briggs	2	8	4	0
Hanburger	1	0	0	0

PASSING – PUNTING – KICKING

PASSING

Last Name	Att	Comp	%	Yds	Yd/Att	TD	Int–%	RK
Jurgensen	356	190	53	2367	6.7	15	16– 5	10
Shiner	65	28	43	470	7.2	3	4– 6	
Taylor	4	1	25	45	11.3	1	0– 0	
Lewis	2	1	50	26	13.0	1	0– 0	

PUNTING

Last Name	No	Avg
Richter	54	43.8
Snidow	9	37.3
Seedburg	7	35.3

KICKING

Last Name	XP	Att	%	FG	Att	%
Jencks	29	33	88	10	22	46

PHILADELPHIA EAGLES

RUSHING

Last Name	No.	Yds	Avg	TD
T. Brown	158	861	5.4	6
Gros	145	479	3.3	7
Woodshick	28	145	5.2	0
Concannon	9	104	11.6	0
Matson	22	103	4.7	2
Snead	24	81	3.4	3
Lang	10	25	2.5	1
K. Hill	7	20	2.9	2
Scarpati	1	6	6.0	0

RECEIVING

Last Name	No.	Yds	Avg	TD
Retzlaff	66	1190	18	10
T. Brown	50	682	14	3
Poage	31	612	20	5
Gros	29	271	9	2
Goodwin	18	252	14	1
Glass	15	201	13	0
Woodshick	6	86	14	0
Crabb	2	41	21	0
Lang	2	30	15	0
Matson	2	29	15	1
Gill	1	27	27	0
F. Hill	1	21	21	0

PUNT RETURNS

Last Name	No.	Yds	Avg	TD
Cross	14	79	6	0
Shann	1	63	63	1
Gill	2	28	14	0
T. Brown	4	13	3	0

KICKOFF RETURNS

Last Name	No.	Yds	Avg	TD
Nelson	26	683	26	0
Cross	25	662	26	0
T. Brown	3	46	15	0
Lang	3	36	12	0
Wells	1	8	8	0
Morgan	1	3	3	0
Gill	1	0	0	0

PASSING – PUNTING – KICKING

PASSING

Last Name	Att	Comp	%	Yds	Yd/Att	TD	Int–%	RK
Snead	288	150	52	2346	8.2	15	13– 5	7
K. Hill	113	60	53	857	7.6	5	10– 9	
Concannon	29	12	41	176	6.1	1	3– 10	
Gros	2	1	50	63	31.5	1	0– 0	
T. Brown	1	0	0	0	0.0	0	0– 0	
Poage	1	0	0	0	0.0	0	0– 0	

PUNTING

Last Name	No	Avg
Baker	37	41.9
K. Hill	19	42.8

KICKING

Last Name	XP	Att	%	FG	Att	%
Baker	38	40	95	9	23	39
Lloyd	7	7	100	1	2	50

EASTERN CONFERENCE – Continued

ST. LOUIS CARDINALS 5-9-0 Wally Lemm

Scores of Each Game		
27	Philadelphia	34
49	Cleveland	13
20	DALLAS	13
37	Washington	16
20	Pittsburgh	7
20	WASHINGTON	24
10	New York	14
21	PITTSBURGH	17
13	Chicago	34
15	NEW YORK	28
24	PHILADELPHIA	28
3	LOS ANGELES	27
13	Dallas	27
24	CLEVELAND	27

Use Name	Pos.	Hgt	Wgt	Age	Int	Pts
Ernie McMillan	OT	6'6"	260	27		
Bob Reynolds	OT	6'6"	265	24		
Ed Cook	OG-OT	6'2"	250	33		
Irv Goode	OG	6'4"	250	24		
Ken Gray	OG	6'2"	250	29		
Rick Sortun	OG	6'2"	235	22		
Herschel Turner	OT-OG	6'3"	230	23		
Mike Alford	C	6'3"	230	22		
Bob DeMarco	C	6'3"	240	27		
Don Brumm	DE	6'3"	245	22		6
Mike Melinkovich	DE	6'4"	240	23		
Tom Redmond	DE	6'5"	250	28		
Joe Robb	DE	6'3"	245	28		
Ed McQuarters	DT	6'1"	250	22		
Luke Owens	DT	6'2"	255	32		
Sam Silas	DT	6'4"	250	22		
Chuck Walker	DT	6'2"	245	24		

Use Name	Pos.	Hgt	Wgt	Age	Int	Pts
Bill Koman	LB	6'2"	230	31	1	
Dave Meggyesy	LB	6'1"	220	23		
Dale Meinert	LB	6'2"	220	32		
Marion Rushing	LB	6'2"	230	28		
Dave Simmons	LB	6'4"	245	22		
Larry Stallings	LB	6'2"	230	23		6
Monk Bailey	DB	6'	180	27		
Jimmy Burson	DB	6'	180	23	5	
Pat Fischer	DB	5'10"	170	25	3	
Carl Silvestri	DB	6'	195	22		
Jerry Stovall	DB	6'2"	205	23	2	
Larry Wilson	DB	6'	190	27	6	6
Abe Woodson	DB	5'11"	190	30		

Use Name	Pos.	Hgt	Wgt	Age	Int	Pts
Buddy Humphrey	QB	6'1"	200	29		
Charley Johnson	QB	6'	190	28		6
Terry Nofsinger	QB	6'4"	215	27		6
Prentice Gautt	HB	6'	210	27		12
Bill Triplett	HB	6'2"	210	26		42
Joe Childress	FB	6'	210	31		
Willie Crenshaw	FB	6'2"	230	24		6
Bill Thornton	FB	6'1"	215	25		
Bobby Joe Conrad	FL	6'	195	30		30
Mal Hammack	TE	6'2"	210	32		
Chuck Logan	TE	6'4"	210	22		
Jackie Smith	TE	6'4"	215	24		12
Billy Gambrell	OE	5'10"	175	23		12
Ray Ogden	OE	6'5"	225	22		
Sonny Randle	OE	6'2"	190	29		54
Jim Bakken	K	6'	200	24		96

PITTSBURGH STEELERS 2-12-0 Mike Nixon

Scores of Each Game		
9	GREEN BAY	41
17	San Francisco	27
13	NEW YORK	23
19	Cleveland	24
7	ST. LOUIS	20
20	Philadelphia	14
22	DALLAS	13
17	St. Louis	21
17	Dallas	24
3	WASHINGTON	31
21	CLEVELAND	42
10	New York	35
13	PHILADELPHIA	47
14	Washington	35

Use Name	Pos.	Hgt	Wgt	Age	Int	Pts
Charlie Bradshaw	OT	6'6"	260	29		
Dan James	OT	6'4"	250	28		
Bob Nichols	OT	6'3"	250	22		
Ray Lemek	OG	6'	240	31		
Mike Magac	OG	6'3"	240	27		
Mike Sandusky	OG	6'	235	32		
Ed Adamchik (from NY)	C	6'2"	235	23		
Ken Henson	C	6'6"	260	22		
Art Hunter	C	6'4"	247	32		
John Baker	DE	6'6"	270	30		
Ben McGee	DE	6'2"	225	23		
Fran Mallick	DT-DE	6'3"	245	24		
Riley Gunnels	DT	6'3"	253	28		
Chuck Hinton	DT	6'5"	260	26		
Ken Kortas	DT	6'2"	280	23		
Ray Mansfield	DT	6'3"	250	24		

Use Name	Pos.	Hgt	Wgt	Age	Int	Pts
Rod Breedlove	LB	6'2"	227	27		
Gene Breen	LB	6'2"	230	24		
John Campbell	LB	6'3"	225	26		6
Max Messner	LB	6'3"	225	27	1	
Ed Pine	LB	6'4"	235	25		
Myron Pottios	LB	6'2"	240	25		
Bob Schmitz	LB	6'1"	240	27		
Jim Bradshaw	DB	6'1"	205	26	5	6
Willie Daniel	DB	5'11"	185	27	1	6
Bob Hohn	DB	6'	190	24		
Brady Keys	DB	6'	198	29	1	
Bob Sherman	DB	6'2"	195	23	1	
Marv Woodson	DB	6'	195	22	3	6

Andy Russell – Military Service

Use Name	Pos.	Hgt	Wgt	Age	Int	Pts
Ed Brown (to BAL)	QB	6'2"	220	36		
Bill Nelsen	QB	6'	195	24		6
Tom Wade	QB	6'2"	195	23		
Cannonball Butler	HB	5'10"	195	22		6
Dick Hoak	HB	5'11"	190	26		36
John Henry Johnson	FB	6'2"	205	35		
Mike Lind	FB	6'2"	225	25		12
Clarence Peaks	FB	6'1"	215	29		
Theron Sapp	FB	6'1"	210	30		
Red Mack	FL	5'10"	185	28		
Paul Martha	HB-FL	6'	185	22		
Gary Ballman	OE-FL	6'	200	25		48
John Hilton	TE	6'5"	220	23		
John Powers	LB-TE	6'2"	210	24		
Duane Allen (to BAL)	OE	6'4"	225	27		
Lee Folkins	TE	6'5"	215	26		6
Roy Jefferson	OE	6'2"	195	21		6
Jerry Simmons	OE	6'1"	190	22		
Clendon Thomas	DB-OE	6'2"	205	28		6
Mike Clark	K	6'1"	205	24		52
Frank Lambert	K	6'3"	200	22		

WESTERN CONFERENCE

GREEN BAY PACKERS 10-3-1 Vince Lombardi

Scores of Each Game		
41	Pittsburgh	9
20	BALTIMORE	17
23	CHICAGO	14
27	SAN FRANCISCO	10
31	Detroit	21
13	DALLAS	3
10	Chicago	31
7	DETROIT	12
6	LOS ANGELES	3
38	Minnesota	13
10	Los Angeles	21
24	MINNESOTA	19
42	Baltimore	27
24	San Francisco	24
	Playoff	
13	BALTIMORE	10

Use Name	Pos.	Hgt	Wgt	Age	Int	Pts
Steve Wright	OT	6'6"	250	23		
Bob Skoronski	OT	6'3"	250	32		
Forrest Gregg	OG-OT	6'4"	250	32		
Dan Grimm	OG	6'3"	245	24		
Jerry Kramer	OG	6'3"	245	30		
Fuzzy Thurston	OG	6'1"	245	32		
Ken Bowman	C	6'3"	230	22		
Bill Curry	C	6'2"	235	22		
Lionel Aldridge	DE	6'4"	245	23		
Willie Davis	DE	6'3"	245	32	1	
Lloyd Voss	DE	6'4"	260	23		
Henry Jordan	DT	6'3"	250	30		
Ron Kostelnik	DT	6'4"	260	25		
Bud Marshall	DT	6'5"	270	23		

Use Name	Pos.	Hgt	Wgt	Age	Int	Pts
Lee Roy Caffey	LB	6'3"	250	25	1	6
Tommy Crutcher	LB	6'3"	230	23	1	
Ray Nitschke	LB	6'3"	240	29	1	
Dave Robinson	LB	6'3"	245	24	3	
Herb Adderley	DB	6'1"	210	26	6	18
Tom Brown	DB	6'1"	190	24	3	
Hank Gremminger	DB	6'1"	200	32		
Doug Hart	DB	6'	190	26	4	6
Bob Jeter	DB	6'1"	205	27	1	
Willie Wood	DB	5'10"	190	29	6	

Use Name	Pos.	Hgt	Wgt	Age	Int	Pts
Zeke Bratkowski	QB	6'2"	200	33		
Dennis Claridge	QB	6'3"	225	23		
Bart Starr	QB	6'1"	200	32		6
Junior Coffey	HB	6'1"	210	23		
Paul Hornung	HB	6'2"	215	28		48
Allen Jacobs	FB	6'1"	215	24		
Tom Moore	HB	6'2"	210	27		6
Elijah Pitts	HB	6'1"	205	26		30
Jim Taylor	FB	6'	215	30		24
Carroll Dale	FL	6'1"	200	27		12
Bob Long	FL	6'3"	190	24		24
Bill Anderson	TE	6'3"	215	29		6
Marv Fleming	TE	6'4"	235	23		12
Boyd Dowler	OE	6'5"	225	28		24
Max McGee	OE	6'3"	205	33		6
Don Chandler	K	6'2"	210	30		88

BALTIMORE COLTS 10-3-1 Don Shula

Scores of Each Game		
35	MINNESOTA	16
17	Green Bay	20
27	SAN FRANCISCO	24
31	DETROIT	7
38	Washington	7
35	LOS ANGELES	20
34	San Francisco	28
26	Chicago	21
41	Minnesota	21
34	PHILADELPHIA	24
24	Detroit	24
0	CHICAGO	13
27	GREEN BAY	42
20	Los Angeles	17
	Playoff	
10	Green Bay	13

Use Name	Pos.	Hgt	Wgt	Age	Int	Pts
Tom Gilburg	OT	6'5"	245	26		
George Preas	OT	6'2"	250	33		
Bob Vogel	OT	6'5"	250	23		
Jim Parker	OG	6'3"	275	31		
Alex Sandusky	OG	6'1"	242	33		
Dan Sullivan	OG	6'3"	250	26		
Buzz Nutter	C	6'4"	240	34		
Dick Szymanski	C	6'3"	235	33		
Ordell Braase	DE	6'4"	242	33		
Roy Hilton	DE	6'6"	225	20		
Lou Michaels	DE	6'2"	240	29		101
Fred Miller	DT	6'3"	245	24		
Guy Reese	DT	6'5"	260	25		
Billy Ray Smith	DT	6'4"	240	30	1	
Glenn Ressler	C-DT	6'3"	235	21		

Use Name	Pos.	Hgt	Wgt	Age	Int	Pts
Jackie Burkett	LB	6'4"	228	28		
Ted Davis	LB	6'1"	225	23		
Dennis Gaubatz	LB	6'2"	220	24	1	
Monte Lee	LB	6'4"	220	27		
Don Shinnick	LB	6'	235	30	1	
Steve Stonebreaker	LB	6'3"	222	27	1	
Mike Curtis	FB-LB	6'2"	225	22		
Bobby Boyd	DB	5'10"	190	27	9	6
Wendell Harris	DB	5'11"	185	24	3	
Alvin Haymond	DB	6'	190	23	3	6
Jerry Logan	DB	6'1"	185	24	2	12
Lenny Lyles	DB	6'2"	202	29	1	
Jim Welch	DB	6'	190	27		

Lou Kirouac – Injury

Use Name	Pos.	Hgt	Wgt	Age	Int	Pts
Gary Cuozzo	QB	6'1"	195	24		
Johnny Unitas	QB	6'1"	194	32		6
Lenny Moore	HB	6'1"	190	32		48
Tom Matte	QB-HB	6'	205	26		6
Jerry Hill	FB	5'11"	210	25		30
Tony Lorick	FB	6'1"	215	23		18
Jimmy Orr	FL	5'11"	175	29		60
Willie Richardson	FL	6'2"	198	25		6
John Mackey	TE	6'3"	217	23		42
Butch Wilson	TE	6'2"	218	23		
Ray Berry	OE	6'2"	187	32		42
Alex Hawkins	FL-OE	6'1"	186	28		6
Neal Petties	FL-OE	6'2"	198	24		

Gino Marchetti – Voluntarily Retired

CHICAGO BEARS 9-5-0 George Halas

Scores of Each Game		
24	San Francisco	52
28	Los Angeles	30
14	Green Bay	23
31	LOS ANGELES	6
45	Minnesota	37
38	DETROIT	10
31	GREEN BAY	10
21	BALTIMORE	26
34	ST. LOUIS	13
17	Detroit	10
35	New York	14
13	Baltimore	0
61	SAN FRANCISCO	20
17	MINNESOTA	24

Use Name	Pos.	Hgt	Wgt	Age	Int	Pts
Herm Lee	OT	6'4"	247	34		
Dick Leeuwenberg	OT	6'5"	242	21		
Bob Wetoska	OT	6'3"	240	27		
Jim Cadile	OG	6'3"	240	24		
Mike Rabold	OG	6'2"	238	28		
George Seals	DT-OG	6'2"	260	22		
Mike Pyle	C	6'3"	250	26		
Doug Atkins	DE	6'8"	255	35	1	
Dick Evey	DE	6'2"	225	24	1	
Bob Kilcullen	DE	6'3"	245	29		
Ed O'Bradovich	DE	6'3"	255	25		
John Johnson	DT	6'5"	260	24		
Stan Jones	DT	6'1"	250	34		
Earl Leggett	DT	6'3"	265	31		
Dennis Murphy	DT	6'1"	250	21		

Use Name	Pos.	Hgt	Wgt	Age	Int	Pts
Dick Butkus	LB	6'3"	240	21	5	
Joe Fortunato	LB	6'	225	35	2	
Bill George	LB	6'2"	235	34		
Roger LeClerc	LB	6'3"	235	27		85
Larry Morris	LB	6'2"	230	30		
Jim Purnell	LB	6'2"	205	23		
Mike Reilly	LB	6'2"	238	22		
J. C. Caroline	DB	6'1"	190	32		
Larry Glueck	DB	6'	190	23		
Bennie McRae	DB	6'1"	180	24	4	6
Richie Petitbon	DB	6'3"	205	27	2	
Ron Smith	DB	6'1"	185	22		
Rosey Taylor	DB	5'11"	186	26	1	6
Dave Whitsell	DB	6'	190	29	4	6

Riley Mattson – Injury
Palmer Pyle – Injury

Use Name	Pos.	Hgt	Wgt	Age	Int	Pts
Rudy Bukich	QB	6'1"	205	34		18
Billy Wade	QB	6'2"	205	34		
Jon Arnett	HB	5'11"	203	30		30
Charlie Bivins	HB	6'2"	212	26		12
Ronnie Bull	HB	6'	200	25		24
Gale Sayers	HB	6'	198	22		132
Ralph Kurek	FB	6'2"	210	22		
Andy Livingston	FB	6'	234	20		12
Joe Marconi	FB	6'2"	225	31		
Johnny Morris	FL	5'10"	180	30		24
Mike Ditka	TE	6'3"	230	25		12
Billy Martin	TE	6'4"	240	22		
Dick Gordon	OE	5'11"	190	20		18
Jim Jones	OE	6'2"	187	21		24
Bobby Joe Green	K	5'11"	175	27		

EASTERN CONFERENCE – Continued

ST. LOUIS CARDINALS

RUSHING Last Name	No.	Yds	Avg	TD
Triplett	174	617	3.5	6
Crenshaw	127	437	3.4	0
Thornton	31	188	6.1	0
Gautt	44	175	4.0	2
Childress	19	94	4.9	0
Johnson	25	60	2.4	1
Bakken	1	28	28.0	0
Gambrell	4	15	3.8	0
Humphrey	2	4	2.0	0
Nofsinger	4	1	0.3	1

RECEIVING Last Name	No.	Yds	Avg	TD
Conrad	58	909	16	5
Randle	51	845	17	9
Smith	41	648	16	2
Triplett	26	256	10	1
Crenshaw	23	232	10	1
Gambrell	9	171	19	2
Gautt	9	128	14	0
Childress	3	27	9	0
Thornton	1	6	6	0

PUNT RETURNS Last Name	No.	Yds	Avg	TD
Silvestri	3	21	7	0
Woodson	18	7	0	0
Burson	1	0	0	0
Gambrell	1	−1	−1	0

KICKOFF RETURNS Last Name	No.	Yds	Avg	TD
Woodson	27	665	25	0
Gambrell	9	216	24	0
Stovall	7	198	28	0
Silvestri	4	96	24	0
Ogden	2	55	28	0
Hammack	3	34	11	0
Crenshaw	2	23	12	0
Koman	1	0	0	0

PASSING – PUNTING – KICKING

PASSING Last Name	Att	Comp	%	Yds	Yd/Att	TD	Int–%	RK
Johnson	322	155	48	2439	7.6	18	15– 5	11
Humphrey	105	58	55	736	7.0	1	9– 9	
Nofsinger	20	8	40	47	2.4	1	1– 5	
Gautt	1	0	0	0	0.0	0	0– 0	

PUNTING Last Name	No	Avg
Smith	39	39.3
Bakken	26	42.2
Stovall	2	40.0

KICKING Last Name	XP	Att	%	FG	Att	%
Bakken	33	33	100	21	31	68

PITTSBURGH STEELERS

RUSHING Last Name	No.	Yds	Avg	TD
Hoak	131	426	3.3	5
Lind	111	375	3.4	1
Peaks	47	230	4.9	0
Butler	46	108	2.3	0
Nelsen	26	84	3.2	1
Sapp	14	54	3.9	0
Ballman	17	46	2.7	3
Wade	8	43	5.4	0
Johnson	3	11	3.7	0
Martha	2	3	1.5	0
Jefferson	1	−1	−1.0	0
Brown	2	−3	−1.5	0

RECEIVING Last Name	No.	Yds	Avg	TD
Ballman	40	859	21	5
Thomas	25	431	17	1
Lind	25	236	9	1
Hoak	19	228	12	1
Jefferson	13	287	22	1
Martha	11	171	16	0
Butler	9	117	13	1
Folkins	5	58	12	0
Hilton	4	32	8	0
Mack	3	41	14	0
Peaks	3	22	7	0
Simmons	2	16	8	0
Sapp	1	10	10	0
Nelsen	1	−5	−5	0

PUNT RETURNS Last Name	No.	Yds	Avg	TD
Jefferson	13	100	8	0
Keys	10	77	8	0
J. Bradshaw	5	73	15	0
Thomas	5	9	2	0

KICKOFF RETURNS Last Name	No.	Yds	Avg	TD
Butler	25	509	20	0
Peaks	20	429	21	0
Ballman	8	150	19	0
Sapp	5	77	15	0
Woodson	2	45	23	0
Simmons	1	28	28	0

PASSING Last Name	Att	Comp	%	Yds	Yd/Att	TD	Int–%	RK
Nelsen	270	121	45	1917	7.1	8	17– 6	15
Wade	66	33	50	463	7.0	2	13– 20	
Brown	23	10	44	204	8.9	1	5– 22	

PUNTING Last Name	No	Avg
Lambert	78	45.1
Brown	2	40.0

KICKING Last Name	XP	Att	%	FG	Att	%
Clark	19	24	79	11	19	58

WESTERN CONFERENCE

GREEN BAY PACKERS

RUSHING Last Name	No.	Yds	Avg	TD
Taylor	207	734	3.5	4
Hornung	89	299	3.4	5
Starr	18	169	9.4	1
Moore	51	124	2.4	0
Pitts	54	122	2.3	4
Chandler	1	27	27.0	0
Coffey	3	12	4.0	0
Jacobs	3	5	1.7	0
Bratkowski	4	−1	−0.3	0
Claridge	2	−3	−1.5	0

RECEIVING Last Name	No.	Yds	Avg	TD
Dowler	44	610	14	4
Dale	20	382	19	2
Taylor	20	207	10	0
Hornung	19	336	18	3
Fleming	14	141	10	2
Long	13	304	23	4
Pitts	11	182	17	1
McGee	10	154	15	1
Anderson	8	105	13	1
Moore	7	87	12	1

PUNT RETURNS Last Name	No.	Yds	Avg	TD
Wood	13	38	3	0
Pitts	8	27	3	0
Adderley	1	0	0	0

KICKOFF RETURNS Last Name	No.	Yds	Avg	TD
Pitts	20	396	20	0
Moore	15	361	24	0
Adderley	10	221	22	0
Crutcher	3	53	18	0
Coffey	1	9	9	0
Grimm	1	0	0	0

PASSING Last Name	Att	Comp	%	Yds	Yd/Att	TD	Int–%	RK
Starr	251	140	56	2055	8.2	16	9– 4	4
Bratkowski	48	21	44	348	7.3	3	4– 8	
Moore	2	2	100	22	11.0	0	0– 0	
Hornung	2	1	50	19	9.5	0	1– 50	
Pitts	2	1	50	51	25.5	0	0– 0	
Claridge	1	1	100	13	13.0	0	0– 0	

PUNTING Last Name	No	Avg
Chandler	74	42.9

KICKING Last Name	XP	Att	%	FG	Att	%
Chandler	37	38	97	17	26	65

BALTIMORE COLTS

RUSHING Last Name	No.	Yds	Avg	TD
Hill	147	516	3.5	5
Moore	133	464	3.5	5
Lorick	63	296	4.7	1
Matte	69	235	3.4	1
Unitas	17	68	4.0	1
Cuozzo	6	8	1.3	0
Mackey	1	7	7.0	0
Curtis	6	1	0.2	0

RECEIVING Last Name	No.	Yds	Avg	TD
Berry	58	739	13	7
Orr	45	847	19	10
Mackey	40	814	20	7
Moore	27	414	15	3
Hill	20	112	6	0
Lorick	15	184	12	2
Matte	12	131	11	0
Hawkins	2	32	16	1
Wilson	1	38	38	0
Richardson	1	14	14	1
Curtis	1	5	5	0

PUNT RETURNS Last Name	No.	Yds	Avg	TD
Haymond	41	403	10	0
Hawkins	4	18	5	0

KICKOFF RETURNS Last Name	No.	Yds	Avg	TD
Haymond	20	614	31	0
Lorick	9	211	23	0
Matte	8	211	26	0
Curtis	2	10	5	0
Hill	1	3	3	0
Hawkins	2	0	0	0

PASSING Last Name	Att	Comp	%	Yds	Yd/Att	TD	Int–%	RK
Unitas	282	164	58	2530	9.0	23	12– 4	2
Cuozzo	105	54	51	700	6.7	7	4– 4	
Matte	7	1	14	19	2.7	0	1– 14	

PUNTING Last Name	No	Avg
Gilburg	54	39.6

KICKING Last Name	XP	Att	%	FG	Att	%
Michaels	48	48	100	17	28	61

CHICAGO BEARS

RUSHING Last Name	No.	Yds	Avg	TD
Sayers	166	867	5.2	14
Bull	91	417	4.6	3
Livingston	63	363	5.8	2
Arnett	102	363	3.6	5
Marconi	19	47	2.5	0
Bukich	28	33	1.2	3
Wade	5	18	3.6	0
J. Jones	2	13	6.5	0
Gordon	2	10	5.0	0
Kurek	1	0	0.0	0

RECEIVING Last Name	No.	Yds	Avg	TD
J. Morris	53	846	16	4
Ditka	36	454	13	2
Sayers	29	507	17	6
J. Jones	21	350	17	4
Bull	16	186	12	1
Gordon	13	279	21	3
Livingston	12	134	11	0
Arnett	12	114	10	0
Bivins	4	108	27	2
Marconi	4	43	11	0
Martin	1	−1	−1	0

PUNT RETURNS Last Name	No.	Yds	Avg	TD
Sayers	16	238	15	1
Arnett	11	52	5	0
Smith	1	2	2	0
Gordon	1	−3	−3	0

KICKOFF RETURNS Last Name	No.	Yds	Avg	TD
Sayers	21	660	31	1
Gordon	14	242	17	0
Arnett	5	150	30	0
Livingston	2	66	33	0
Smith	1	17	17	0
Kurek	1	11	11	0
LeClerc	1	0	0	0

PASSING Last Name	Att	Comp	%	Yds	Yd/Att	TD	Int–%	RK
Bukich	312	176	56	2641	8.5	20	9– 3	1
Wade	41	20	49	204	5.0	0	2– 5	
Bull	3	2	67	63	21.0	0	0– 0	
Sayers	3	2	67	53	17.7	1	1– 33	
Arnett	2	1	50	59	29.5	1	0– 0	

PUNTING Last Name	No	Avg
Green	58	42.7

KICKING Last Name	XP	Att	%	FG	Att	%
LeClerc	52	52	100	11	26	42

WESTERN CONFERENCE – Continued

SAN FRANCISCO FORTY NINERS 7-6-1 Jack Christiansen

Scores of Each Game

52	CHICAGO	24
27	PITTSBURGH	17
24	Baltimore	27
10	Green Bay	27
45	Los Angeles	21
41	MINNESOTA	42
28	BALTIMORE	34
31	Dallas	39
27	Detroit	21
30	LOS ANGELES	27
45	Minnesota	24
17	DETROIT	14
20	Chicago	61
24	GREEN BAY	24

Use Name	Pos.	Hgt	Wgt	Age	Int	Pts
Jim Norton	OT	6'4"	255	22		
Walt Rock	OT	6'5"	245	24		
Len Rohde	OT	6'4"	245	27		
Howard Mudd	OG	6'3"	240	23		
John Thomas	OG	6'4"	246	30		
Jim Wilson	OG	6'3"	255	24		
Bruce Bosley	C	6'2"	240	31		
Joe Cerne	C	6'2"	235	22		
Dan Colchico	DE	6'4"	245	28		
Dan LaRose	DE	6'5"	250	25		
Clark Miller	DE	6'5"	245	26		6
Karl Rubke	DE	6'4"	240	29		
Charlie Krueger	DT	6'4"	254	29		6
Roland Lakes	DT	6'4"	263	26		
Chuck Sieminski	DT	6'4"	265	25		

Use Name	Pos.	Hgt	Wgt	Age	Int	Pts
Ed Beard	LB	6'2"	245	25		
Jack Chapple	LB	6'2"	227	22		6
Floyd Dean	LB	6'4"	245	25		
Mike Dowdle	LB	6'3"	235	27		
Bob Harrison	LB	6'2"	225	28		
Matt Hazeltine	LB	6'1"	230	32	1	
Dave Wilcox	LB	6'3"	230	22	1	6
Kermit Alexander	DB	5'11"	186	24	3	
George Donnelly	DB	6'3"	205	22		
Jim Johnson	DB	6'2"	190	27	6	
Elbert Kimbrough	DB	5'11"	190	26	2	
Jerry Mertens	DB	6'	185	29		
Wayne Swinford	DB	6'	190	22		

Use Name	Pos.	Hgt	Wgt	Age	Int	Pts
John Brodie	QB	6'1"	200	30		6
George Mira	QB	5'11"	190	23		
John David Crow	HB	6'2"	215	30		54
Rudy Johnson	HB	5'11"	190	23		24
Dave Kopay	HB	6'2"	217	23		
Gary Lewis	FB	6'3"	230	23		18
Ken Willard	FB	6'2"	230	22		54
Bernie Casey	FL	6'4"	215	26		48
Dale Messer	FL	5'10"	175	28		
Bob Poole	TE	6'4"	216	23		
Monte Stickles	TE	6'4"	230	27		6
Vern Burke	OE	6'4"	200	24		6
Kay McFarland	OE	6'2"	180	26		6
Dave Parks	OE	6'2"	195	23		72
Tommy Davis	K	6'	212	30		103

MINNESOTA VIKINGS 7-7-0 Norm Van Brocklin

Scores of Each Game

16	Baltimore	35
29	DETROIT	31
38	Los Angeles	35
40	NEW YORK	14
37	CHICAGO	45
42	San Francisco	41
27	Cleveland	17
24	LOS ANGELES	13
21	BALTIMORE	41
13	GREEN BAY	38
24	SAN FRANCISCO	45
19	Green Bay	24
29	Detroit	7
24	Chicago	17

Use Name	Pos.	Hgt	Wgt	Age	Int	Pts
Grady Alderman	OT	6'2"	240	26		
Errol Linden	OT	6'5"	260	28		
Archie Sutton	OT	6'2"	262	22		
Larry Bowie	OG	6'2"	250	25		
Ken Byers	OG	6'1"	240	25		
Milt Sunde	C-OG	6'2"	234	22		
Mick Tingelhoff	C	6'1"	237	25		
Carl Eller	DE	6'6"	255	23		2
Jim Marshall	DE	6'3"	235	27		
Paul Dickson	DT	6'5"	255	28		
Gary Larsen	DT	6'5"	250	25		
Jim Prestel	DT	6'5"	275	28		2

Use Name	Pos.	Hgt	Wgt	Age	Int	Pts
Rip Hawkins	LB	6'3"	235	26	3	6
Bill Jobko	LB	6'2"	235	29		
John Kirby	LB	6'3"	222	23		
Lonnie Warwick	LB	6'3"	225	23		6
Roy Winston	LB	6'1"	230	25		
Lee Calland	DB	6'	190	24		
Gary Hill	DB	6'	200	21		
Jeff Jordan	DB	6'4"	190	21	4	
Karl Kassulke	DB	6'	193	23	2	
Earsell Mackbee	DB	6'1"	195	24		
George Rose	DB	5'11"	190	22	1	
Ed Sharockman	DB	6'	200	25	6	6
Larry Vargo	DB	6'3"	215	25	3	

Use Name	Pos.	Hgt	Wgt	Age	Int	Pts
Bob Berry	QB	5'11"	190	23		
Fran Tarkenton	QB	6'1"	190	25		6
Ron Vander Kelen	QB	6'1"	185	25		
Billy Barnes	HB	5'11"	202	30		
Dick James	HB	5'9"	185	31		
Phil King	HB	6'4"	220	29		6
Tommy Mason	HB	6'	196	26		66
Dave Osborn	HB	6'	205	22		12
Jim Young	HB	6'	205	22		
Bill Brown	FB	5'11"	230	27		42
Jim Phillips	FL	6'1"	195	28		6
Lance Rentzel	HB-FL	6'2"	210	21		6
Tom Hall	OE-FL	6'1"	195	26		6
Hal Bedsole	TE	6'4"	230	23		18
Paul Flatley	OE	6'1"	187	24		42
Gordon Smith	OE	6'2"	205	23		30
Fred Cox	K	5'10"	200	26		113
Bobby Walden	K	6'	195	27		

DETROIT LIONS 6-7-1 Harry Gilmer

Scores of Each Game

20	LOS ANGELES	0
31	Minnesota	29
14	WASHINGTON	10
7	Baltimore	31
21	GREEN BAY	31
10	Chicago	38
31	Los Angeles	7
12	Green Bay	7
21	SAN FRANCISCO	27
10	CHICAGO	17
24	BALTIMORE	24
14	San Francisco	17
7	MINNESOTA	29
35	Philadelphia	28

Use Name	Pos.	Hgt	Wgt	Age	Int	Pts
Daryl Sanders	OT	6'5"	250	23		
Roger Shoals	OT	6'4"	255	26		
John Gonzaga	OG-OT	6'3"	250	32		
John Gordy	OG	6'3"	250	29		
Ted Karras	OG	6'1"	243	32		
Jim Simon	OG	6'5"	235	24		
Ed Flanagan	C	6'3"	250	21		
Bob Whitlow	C	6'1"	236	29		
Larry Hand	DE	6'4"	245	25		
Darris McCord	DE	6'4"	250	32		
Sam Williams	DE	6'5"	235	34		
Roger Brown	DT	6'5"	300	28		2
Alex Karras	DT	6'2"	245	29		
Jerry Rush	DT	6'4"	255	33		

Use Name	Pos.	Hgt	Wgt	Age	Int	Pts
Ernie Clark	LB	6'1"	220	27	1	
Wally Hilgenburg	LB	6'3"	225	22		
Mike Lucci	LB	6'2"	223	25		
Joe Schmidt	LB	6'1"	220	33	4	
Wayne Walker	LB	6'2"	225	28	2	57
Jimmy Hill	DB	6'2"	195	36	1	
Jim Kearney	DB	6'2"	200	22		
Night Train Lane	DB	6'1"	200	37		
Dick LeBeau	DB	6'1"	185	28	7	6
Bruce Maher	DB	5'11"	190	28	4	
Wayne Rasmussen	DB	6'2"	180	23	5	12
Bobby Thompson	DB	5'10"	175	25	2	
Tom Vaughn	DB	5'11"	195	22		

J. D. Smith — Injury
Warren Wells — Military Service

Use Name	Pos.	Hgt	Wgt	Age	Int	Pts
George Izo	QB	6'3"	218	28		
Tom Myers	QB	6'	188	21		
Milt Plum	QB	6'1"	205	31		18
Bobby Felts (from BAL)	HB	6'2"	205	22		
Joe Don Looney	HB	6'1"	230	22		36
Amos Marsh	HB	6'1"	220	26		36
Tom Watkins	HB	6'1"	195	28		
Tom Nowatzke	FB	6'3"	228	22		12
Nick Pietrosante	FB	6'2"	225	28		6
Terry Barr	FL	6'	190	30		18
Pat Studstill	FL	6'1"	175	27		18
Jim Gibbons	TE	6'3"	228	22		12
Ron Kramer	TE	6'3"	240	30		6
Gail Cogdill	OE	6'2"	195	28		
John Henderson	OE	6'3"	190	22		6

LOS ANGELES RAMS 4-10-0 Harland Svare

Scores of Each Game

0	Detroit	20
30	CHICAGO	28
35	MINNESOTA	38
6	Chicago	31
21	SAN FRANCISCO	45
20	Baltimore	35
7	DETROIT	31
13	Minnesota	24
3	Green Bay	6
27	San Francisco	30
21	GREEN BAY	10
27	St. Louis	3
42	CLEVELAND	7
17	BALTIMORE	20

Use Name	Pos.	Hgt	Wgt	Age	Int	Pts
Joe Carollo	OT	6'2"	263	25		
Charley Cowan	OT	6'4"	275	27		
Roger Pillath	OT	6'4"	255	23		
Frank Varrichione	OT	6'1"	237	33		
Don Chuy	OG	6'1"	256	24		
Joe Scibelli	OG	6'1"	264	26		
Joe Wendryhoski	C-OG	6'2"	245	26		
Ken Iman	C	6'1"	235	26		
Frank Marchlewski	C	6'2"	226	21		
Deacon Jones	DE	6'5"	260	26		2
Lamar Lundy	DE	6'7"	260	30		
Tim Powell	DE	6'4"	248	21		
Rosey Grier	DT	6'5"	290	32		
Frank Molden	DT	6'5"	285	23	1	6
Merlin Olsen	DT	6'5"	276	24		

Use Name	Pos.	Hgt	Wgt	Age	Int	Pts
Fred Brown	LB	6'5"	223	22		
Mack Byrd	LB	6'	215	22		
Dan Currie	LB	6'3"	240	31		
Tony Guillory	LB	6'4"	220	22		
Cliff Livingston	LB	6'3"	212	35	1	
Mike Strofolino (to BAL)	LB	6'2"	240	21		
Doug Woodlief	LB	6'3"	235	21		
Chuck Lamson	DB	6'	190	26	2	
Aaron Martin	DB	6'	185	24	2	6
Dan McIlhany	DB	6'1"	195	22		
Jerry Richardson	DB	6'3"	190	22	1	
Bobby Smith (to DET)	DB	6'	197	27		
Ed Meador	DB	5'11"	203	28	2	6
Clancy Williams	HB-DB	6'2"	198	22		

Bucky Pope — Knee Injury
Jack Pardee — Voluntarily Retired

Use Name	Pos.	Hgt	Wgt	Age	Int	Pts
Roman Gabriel	QB	6'4"	225	25		12
Bill Munson	QB	6'2"	197	23		6
Ron Smith	QB	6'5"	220	23		
Terry Baker	HB	6'3"	200	24		18
Les Josephson	HB	6'	210	23		
Willie Brown	FL-HB	6'	185	22		
Dick Bass	FB	5'10"	198	28		24
Jim Stiger (from DAL)	FB	5'11"	214	24		
Ben Wilson	FB	6'	225	25		6
Tommy McDonald	FL	5'10"	175	31		54
Marlin McKeever	TE	6'1"	227	25		24
Billy Truax	TE	6'5"	240	22		6
Steve Heckard	OE	6'1"	195	22		
Jack Snow	OE	6'2"	210	22		18
Jon Kilgore	K	6'1"	200	21		
Bruce Gossett	K	6'2"	230	22		75
Billy Lothridge	K	6'1"	194	21		

WESTERN CONFERENCE – Continued

SAN FRANCISCO FORTY NINERS

RUSHING

Last Name	No.	Yds	Avg	TD
Willard	189	778	4.1	5
Crow	132	514	3.9	2
Lewis	52	256	4.9	3
Kopay	28	81	2.9	2
Mira	5	64	12.8	0
Brodie	15	60	4.0	1
Davis	1	21	21.0	0
R. Johnson	6	9	1.5	0

RECEIVING

Last Name	No.	Yds	Avg	TD
Parks	80	1344	17	12
Casey	59	765	13	8
Stickles	35	343	10	1
Willard	32	253	8	4
Crow	28	493	18	7
Kopay	11	147	13	1
Lewis	10	25	3	0
McFarland	8	106	13	1
R. Johnson	3	49	16	0
Messer	2	41	21	0
Burke	2	38	19	1
Poole	2	29	15	0

PUNT RETURNS

Last Name	No.	Yds	Avg	TD
Alexander	35	262	7	0
Swinford	2	18	9	0
Lewis	1	3	3	0

KICKOFF RETURNS

Last Name	No.	Yds	Avg	TD
Alexander	32	741	23	0
Lewis	15	355	24	0
R. Johnson	4	71	18	0
Swinford	4	61	15	0
Messer	1	27	27	0
Kopay	1	21	21	0
Cerne	1	0	0	0
Rubke	1	0	0	0

PASSING – PUNTING – KICKING

PASSING

Last Name	Att	Comp	%	Yds	Yd/Att	TD	Int–%	RK
Brodie	391	242	62	3112	8.0	30	16– 4	3
Mira	58	28	48	460	7.9	4	3– 5	
Crow	4	2	50	61	15.3	1	1– 25	
Willard	1	0	0	0	0.0	0	1–100	

PUNTING

Last Name	No	Avg
Davis	54	45.8

KICKING

Last Name	XP	Att	%	FG	Att	%
Davis	52	53	98	17	27	63

MINNESOTA VIKINGS

RUSHING

Last Name	No.	Yds	Avg	TD
Brown	160	699	4.4	6
Mason	141	597	4.2	10
Tarkenton	56	356	6.4	1
King	72	356	4.9	6
Barnes	48	148	3.1	0
Osborn	20	106	5.3	2
Vander Kelen	4	13	3.3	0
Young	3	4	1.3	0
Rentzel	1	−1	−1.0	0

RECEIVING

Last Name	No.	Yds	Avg	TD
Flatley	50	896	18	7
Brown	41	503	12	1
Smith	22	431	20	5
Mason	22	321	15	1
Hall	15	287	19	2
Phillips	15	185	12	1
King	12	96	8	1
Bedsole	8	123	15	3
Barnes	3	15	5	0
Osborn	1	4	4	0

PUNT RETURNS

Last Name	No.	Yds	Avg	TD
Mason	9	63	7	0
Hall	3	21	7	0
Warwick	1	10	10	1
Rentzel	4	9	2	0
Young	4	7	2	0
James	1	5	5	0

KICKOFF RETURNS

Last Name	No.	Yds	Avg	TD
Rentzel	23	602	26	1
Osborn	18	422	23	0
James	11	212	19	0
Hall	4	93	23	0
Young	4	78	20	0
Mason	3	66	22	0
Barnes	3	37	12	0
King	1	14	14	0

PASSING – PUNTING – KICKING

PASSING

Last Name	Att	Comp	%	Yds	Yd/Att	TD	Int–%	RK
Tarkenton	329	171	52	2609	7.9	19	11– 3	6
Vander Kelen	40	18	45	252	6.3	2	0– 0	
Berry	2	0	0	0	0.0	0	0– 0	
Mason	1	0	0	0	0.0	0	1–100	

PUNTING

Last Name	No	Avg
Walden	51	42.1

KICKING

Last Name	XP	Att	%	FG	Att	%
Cox	44	44	100	23	35	66

DETROIT LIONS

RUSHING

Last Name	No.	Yds	Avg	TD
Marsh	131	495	3.8	6
Pietrosante	107	374	3.5	1
Looney	114	356	3.1	5
Watkins	29	95	3.3	0
Nowatzke	27	73	2.7	1
Felts	22	58	2.6	0
Plum	21	37	1.8	3
Sanders	1	2	2.0	0
Studstill	1	−4	−4.0	0
Izo	1	−5	−5.0	0
Barr	1	−12	−12.0	0

RECEIVING

Last Name	No.	Yds	Avg	TD
Studstill	28	389	14	3
Barr	24	433	18	3
Cogdill	20	247	12	0
Kramer	18	206	11	1
Pietrosante	18	163	9	0
Marsh	17	159	9	2
Gibbons	12	111	9	2
Looney	12	109	9	1
Henderson	8	140	18	1
Watkins	5	53	11	0
Nowatzke	5	45	9	1
Felts	3	28	9	0

PUNT RETURNS

Last Name	No.	Yds	Avg	TD
Watkins	23	234	10	0
Vaughn	2	50	25	0
Studstill	5	47	9	0
Felts	3	27	9	0

KICKOFF RETURNS

Last Name	No.	Yds	Avg	TD
Watkins	17	584	34	0
Felts	18	422	23	0
Vaughn	13	316	24	0
Studstill	10	257	26	0
Nowatzke	2	12	6	0
Lucci	1	0	0	0

PASSING – PUNTING – KICKING

PASSING

Last Name	Att	Comp	%	Yds	Yd/Att	TD	Int–%	RK
Plum	308	143	46	1710	5.6	12	19– 6	14
Izo	59	24	41	357	6.1	2	6– 10	
Myers	5	3	60	16	3.2	0	1– 20	
Felts	1	0	0	0	0.0	0	0– 0	
Marsh	1	0	0	0	0.0	0	0– 0	

PUNTING

Last Name	No	Avg
Studstill	78	42.8

KICKING

Last Name	XP	Att	%	FG	Att	%
Walker	33	33	100	8	22	36

LOS ANGELES RAMS

RUSHING

Last Name	No.	Yds	Avg	TD
Bass	121	549	4.5	2
Josephson	71	225	3.2	0
Wilson	60	189	3.2	1
Munson	26	157	6.0	1
W. Brown	44	133	3.0	0
Baker	25	82	3.3	1
Gabriel	23	79	3.4	2
Stiger	14	62	4.4	0
Meador	2	35	17.5	1
Williams	3	3	1.0	0

RECEIVING

Last Name	No.	Yds	Avg	TD
McDonald	67	1036	15	9
McKeever	44	542	12	4
Snow	38	559	15	3
Baker	22	210	10	2
Bass	21	230	11	2
Josephson	18	169	9	0
Wilson	9	110	12	0
Truax	6	108	18	1
W. Brown	4	91	23	1
Stiger	1	9	9	0
Heckard	1	4	4	0

PUNT RETURNS

Last Name	No.	Yds	Avg	TD
Stiger	16	120	8	0
W. Brown	9	63	7	0
B. Smith	10	56	6	0
Bass	1	0	0	0

KICKOFF RETURNS

Last Name	No.	Yds	Avg	TD
W. Brown	24	615	26	0
B. Smith	18	475	26	0
Williams	9	213	24	0
Wilson	3	66	22	0
Stiger	2	28	14	0

PASSING – PUNTING – KICKING

PASSING

Last Name	Att	Comp	%	Yds	Yd/Att	TD	Int–%	RK
Munson	267	144	54	1701	6.4	10	14– 5	13
Gabriel	173	83	48	1321	7.6	11	5– 3	9
Josephson	2	1	50	15	7.5	1	0– 0	
Baker	1	1	100	14	14.0	0	0– 0	
Meador	1	0	0	0	0.0	0	0– 0	
Wilson	1	1	100	8	8.0	0	0– 0	

PUNTING

Last Name	No	Avg
Lothridge	42	38.5
Kilgore	24	41.6

KICKING

Last Name	XP	Att	%	FG	Att	%
Gossett	30	32	94	15	26	58

1965 A.F.L. Sonny and Joe and John

After years in show business, New York Jet owner Sonny Werblin was a firm believer in the star system, of the gate pull of a big-name star. Werblin set out with checkbook in hand and bagged two of college football's biggest names, Alabama's Joe Namath and Notre Dame's John Huarte, with astronomical contracts that dwarfed the pacts of even the biggest veteran stars. Some people talked about the two fine young quarterbacks Werblin had signed, some talked about the misplaced values of a society that rewarded football players with small fortunes while grossly underpaying schoolteachers, but the important thing was that they talked. They talked about Joe Namath, they talked about the New York Jets, and they talked about the AFL. They stopped talking about whether the AFL would survive; they talked more now of when the leagues would be on a par.

When the league schedule started, a lot of those talking people came out to the games. Opening day in Houston saw a crowd of 52,680 turn out to see the lowly Oilers beat the Jets, with Joe Namath glued to the bench all afternoon. One week later, 53,658 fans filled Shea Stadium in New York to welcome Namath to the big city. Namath's development into a fine passer by mid-season furthered his publicity value and made Werblin's move look like a stroke of genius.

The league was feeling confident enough to vote for expansion in 1966, setting up a new team in Miami, which had flopped as a pro-football town in 1946 but was now a fast-growing metropolis. Only a few years ago, the league had been more worried about franchises folding than in creating new outposts for the AFL.

EASTERN DIVISION

Buffalo Bills—The trade of Cookie Gilchrist to Denver took most of the punch out of the running game, and injuries to Elbert Dubenion and Glenn Bass robbed the team of its starting wide receivers, but the Bills coasted to another Eastern title on a stone-wall defense and Pete Gogolak's strong right leg. Anonymous people manned the defense, but although Ron McDole, Tom Day, Tom Sestak, Jim Dunaway, Mike Stratton, Harry Jacobs, John Tracey, Butch Byrd, Hagood Clarke, George Saimes, and Charley Warner were short on reputation as individuals, respect for them as a unit was universal. The offense began with a strong line but lacked the backs and ends to take full advantage of the blocking. Gilchrist had been dealt off because of recurring feuds with coach Lou Saban, but replacement Billy Joe was no match for Cookie as a runner, receiver, or blocker. The other runners—Wray Carlton, Bobby Smith, and Donnie Stone—were pedestrian pluggers. With Dubenion and Bass sidelined, journeymen Bo Roberson and Charley Ferguson filled the wide receiver spots, but quarterback Jack Kemp orchestrated this collection of odds and ends into a steady unit which headed for their third straight championship game in Lou Saban's last year before returning to college coaching.

New York Jets—Owner Sonny Werblin set the football world on its ear by signing the two most glamorous rookie quarterbacks to expensive contracts, Joe Namath at a $400,000 pact and Heisman Trophy winner John Huarte to a $200,000 pact. Huarte missed training camp because of the College All-Star Game and spent the year on the taxi squad, but Namath made a big splash right from the start. After sitting out the first few games, Namath took over the quarterback job and showed a quick release that triggered a strong passing arm. In addition, his sudden affluence and swinging bachelor's lifestyle made the newspapers constantly and proved to be a bonanza of publicity for the Jets and the AFL. But if Namath and Huarte attracted all the attention, other rookies made the Jets a stronger club down the second half of the season. George Sauer, playing tight end out of necessity, middle linebacker Al Atkinson, defensive end Verlon Biggs, defensive tackle Jim Harris, and defensive backs Jim Hudson and Cornell Gordon all put in solid freshman years for the improved New Yorkers who won five of their last eight games.

Boston Patriots—Head coach Mike Holovak had never paid much attention to pre-season games, expecting his team to start playing for real once the starting bell rang. The Patriots lost all five of their exhibition games this year, but then kept losing right into October. Winless in the first seven games, the Pats made a comeback in the second half of the schedule, but their horrid start killed any chances of challenging Buffalo for first place. Holovak had never gone all out to sign prestigious college seniors, relying instead on veterans and rookies from small and local schools, and now this policy was showing up in the deterioration of the team. The defense, long the club's strong point, began to creak with age, while the offense suffered because of Babe Parilli's off season. The thirty-four-year-old Parilli gave up twenty-six interceptions, a sign that his arm was losing its old zip. The Pats did sign two big-name rookie runners, Jim Nance and Joe Bellino, but neither had a good freshman season. Nance played overweight all year, while Bellino, making his pro debut after three years in the Navy, did not have the size to be a consistent ground-gainer.

Houston Oilers—With the exception of W. K. Hicks, the Oilers were using the same men in the defensive secondary that staffed the championship Houston teams in the early years of the AFL. Enemy passers burned the Oiler secondary for twenty-seven touchdown passes, a sign of the improvement in AFL play and of the lack of foresight in the Houston management. With the worst defense in the league, head coach Hugh Taylor was fortunate to pick up four wins in his year at the helm. The offense was in no shape to carry the team, as it had weaknesses in all sectors. The offensive line needed help, and the receiving fell off because of Charley Hennigan's bad knee. Halfback Sid Blanks missed the season with a knee injury, and fullback Charley Tolar had slowed up considerably, throwing the brunt of the running chores on 185-pound Ode Burrell. At quarterback, thirty-seven-year-old George Blanda was plagued with a flood of interceptions, but young Don Trull still saw little action. But even with all their problems, the Oilers did put together some good games, like a 19-17 upset of Buffalo and a 31-10 pasting of Boston.

WESTERN DIVISION

San Diego Chargers—Although the San Diego defense ranked with Buffalo's at the top of the league, the offense still won most of the headlines for the Chargers. The versatile attack boasted of stars in all quarters. Linemen Ron Mix and Walt Sweeney were among the AFL's best, and flanker Lance Alworth gained a phenomenal 1,602 yards with a variety of leaping, diving, and streaking catches which netted him fourteen touchdowns. Quarterback John Hadl developed into a top-flight pro as a passer and play-caller. Halfback Paul Lowe hustled his way to a new league rushing record of 1,121 yards, and Keith Lincoln combined with rookie Gene Foster to provide punch at the fullback slot. But the San Diego defense bailed out the offense on its rare off days, as in a 13-13 tie with Boston and a 10-10 tie with the Chiefs. Earl Faison and Ernie Ladd still stacked up runners and passers, but both star linemen expressed dissatisfaction with the organization and were playing out their option. Fitting right in with the veterans were several newcomers to the unit, rookies Rick Redman, Steve DeLong, Dick Degan, and Speedy Duncan—enough to give the Chargers their fifth Western crown in six years.

Oakland Raiders—Head coach and general manager Al Davis kept building the Raiders with top rookie talent. This year's batch of Oakland freshmen included wide receiver Fred Biletnikoff, cornerback Kent McCloughan, linebacker Gus Otto, and offensive tackles Bob Svihus and Harry Schuh. The Raiders now had sufficient depth to compensate for injuries, as Tom Flores and Dick Wood handled the quarterbacking in fine fashion with Cotton Davidson out for most of the year with an injury. The offense, with Clem Daniels and Art Powell the main guns, performed quite well, and the defense had two solid rookie starters in Otto and McCloughan and an All-Pro cornerback in Dave Grayson. An inability to beat San Diego and Buffalo killed the Oakland title chances, as the Raiders dropped all four of their contests with the divisional champions-to-be.

Kansas City Chiefs—With one of the deepest rosters in pro football, the Chiefs seemed to be playing in the shadow of an evil star. Since the team moved to Kansas City in 1963, serious injury or death struck four Chief players. Stone Johnson suffered a fatal neck injury in a 1963 pre-season game, Ed Budde almost died from a blow on the head when attacked on the street in 1964, Fred Arbanas lost most of the vision in his left eye from an off-the-field altercation, and fullback Mack Lee Hill died on the operating table of complications following knee surgery midway through this season. On the field, the Chiefs had a habit of winning some games in impressive fashion, then going flat and losing to a weaker team. The Kansas City offense still was a top-flight unit, with the receiving strengthened by rookie Otis Taylor and the running game weakened by the trade of Abner Haynes and the tragic death of Hill. The defense had no problems with men like Jerry Mays, Buck Buchanan, E. J. Holub, Sherrill Headrick, Bobby Bell, Fred Williamson, and Johnny Robinson in the lineup.

Denver Broncos—For the first time in their history, the Broncos relied on the running game as their main offensive threat. Trades brought fullback Cookie Gilchrist and halfback Abner Haynes, both legendary AFL runners, to Denver during the summer, and while Gilchrist still bulled over tackles at peak form, Haynes lost his starting job to rookie Wendell Hayes. At any rate, the depth in the running-back slots kept the attack alive despite severe uncertainty at quarterback. Coach Mac Speedie used John McCormick, Mickey Slaughter, and Jacky Lee in the passer's spot and was satisfied with none of them. Lionel Taylor got open for enough passes from the three quarterbacks to lead the league in receiving, his fifth pass-catching title in the AFL's six years of play, but none of the other receivers on the team made much of a dent on enemy defenses.

FINAL TEAM STATISTICS

OFFENSE

	BOSTON	BUFFALO	DENVER	HOUSTON	K. CITY	NEW YORK	OAKLAND	SAN DIEGO
FIRST DOWNS:								
Total	214	206	255	227	232	213	225	**268**
by Rushing	55	69	111	63	101	77	72	**127**
by Passing	130	119	117	**140**	121	121	134	127
by Penalty	**29**	18	27	24	10	15	19	14
RUSHING:								
Number	373	392	453	324	418	367	390	**486**
Yards	1117	1288	1829	1175	1752	1476	1538	**1998**
Average Yards	3.0	3.3	4.0	3.6	**4.2**	4.0	3.9	4.1
Touchdowns	8	**16**	14	10	15	11	8	13
PASSING:								
Attempts	473	461	482	**550**	395	459	431	401
Completions	193	208	222	**224**	199	209	195	203
Completion Percentage	40.8	45.1	46.1	40.7	50.4	45.5	45.2	**50.6**
Passing Yards	2854	2744	2848	3070	2894	2751	2713	**3379**
Average Yards Per Attempt	6.0	6.0	5.9	5.6	7.3	6.0	6.3	**8.4**
Average Yards Per Completion	14.8	13.2	12.8	13.7	14.5	13.2	13.9	**16.6**
Times Tackled Attempting to Pass	37	29	24	31	37	**17**	33	27
Yards Lost Attempting to Pass	347	283	208	257	351	**162**	253	276
Net Yards	2507	2461	2640	2813	2543	2589	2460	**3103**
Touchdowns	19	13	18	**25**	22	21	22	23
Interceptions	29	24	30	35	20	22	**17**	26
Percent Intercepted	6.1	5.2	6.2	6.4	5.1	4.8	**3.9**	6.5
PUNTING:								
Number	82	80	68	**85**	72	72	75	70
Average Distance	40.1	43.0	42.3	43.7	44.6	**45.3**	41.1	40.0
PUNT RETURNS:								
Number	27	36	37	28	**38**	29	34	**38**
Yards	152	389	355	189	419	166	365	**508**
Average Yards	5.6	10.8	9.6	6.8	11.0	5.7	10.7	**13.4**
Touchdowns	0	0	1	0	1	0	1	**2**
KICKOFF RETURNS:								
Number	60	45	71	**77**	48	54	46	50
Yards	1191	1022	**1731**	1669	1080	1107	990	1028
Average Yards	19.9	22.7	**24.4**	21.7	22.5	20.5	21.5	20.6
Touchdowns	0	**2**	0	0	0	0	0	0
INTERCEPTION RETURNS:								
Number	21	**32**	25	27	20	26	24	28
Yards	233	393	465	416	342	235	**482**	377
Average Yards	11.1	12.3	18.6	15.4	17.1	9.0	**20.1**	13.5
Touchdowns	0	1	3	0	2	0	**4**	3
PENALTIES:								
Number	58	78	69	76	70	58	69	**84**
Yards	537	685	750	856	744	684	661	**929**
FUMBLES:								
Number	24	28	29	23	34	27	**17**	22
Number Lost	12	14	16	11	20	18	**9**	13
POINTS:								
Total	244	313	303	298	322	285	298	**340**
PAT (Kick) Attempts	27	31	32	34	37	31	35	**40**
PAT (Kick) Made	27	31	32	34	37	31	35	**40**
PAT (Rush or Pass) Attempts	0	2	**6**	3	3	1	0	1
PAT (Rush or Pass) Made	0	0	2	2	**3**	1	0	0
FG Attempts	27	**46**	29	23	30	34	34	30
FG Made	17	**28**	13	12	13	20	17	18
Percent FG Made	**63.0**	60.9	44.8	52.2	43.3	58.8	50.0	60.0
Safeties	**2**	0	0	1	0	0	1	0

DEFENSE

	BOSTON	BUFFALO	DENVER	HOUSTON	K. CITY	NEW YORK	OAKLAND	SAN DIEGO
FIRST DOWNS:								
Total	232	226	244	271	207	235	235	**190**
by Rushing	92	65	87	132	69	85	90	**55**
by Passing	127	141	138	**111**	113	136	125	118
by Penalty	**13**	20	19	28	25	14	20	17
RUSHING:								
Number	425	360	384	508	381	432	407	**306**
Yards	1531	1114	1337	2683	1376	1551	1487	**1094**
Average Yards	3.6	**3.1**	3.5	5.3	3.6	3.6	3.7	3.6
Touchdowns	10	**5**	24	17	12	10	10	7
PASSING:								
Attempts	431	502	440	**416**	451	472	466	474
Completions	206	227	202	**177**	216	220	199	206
Completion Percentage	47.8	45.2	45.9	**42.5**	47.9	46.6	42.7	43.5
Passing Yards	2891	3416	3265	2643	2711	2900	2947	**2480**
Average Yards Per Attempt	6.7	6.8	7.4	6.4	6.0	6.1	6.3	**5.2**
Average Yards Per Completion	14.0	15.0	16.2	14.9	12.6	13.2	14.8	**12.0**
Times Tackled Attempting to Pass	30	28	26	22	**39**	22	30	38
Yards Lost Attempting to Pass	291	246	305	173	**326**	238	246	312
Net Yards	2600	3170	2960	2470	2385	2662	2701	**2168**
Touchdowns	**17**	19	23	27	18	22	27	**17**
Interceptions	21	**32**	25	27	20	26	24	28
Percent Intercepted	4.9	6.4	5.7	**6.5**	4.4	5.5	5.2	5.9
PUNTING:								
Number	78	76	73	59	**83**	78	77	80
Average Distance	42.1	40.2	45.9	42.5	44.1	**39.8**	42.1	43.4
PUNT RETURNS:								
Number	33	30	**26**	48	29	40	34	27
Yards	232	**222**	343	494	401	352	257	242
Average Yards	**7.0**	7.4	13.2	10.3	13.8	8.8	7.6	9.0
Touchdowns	**0**	**0**	1	2	2	**0**	**0**	**0**
KICKOFF RETURNS:								
Number	**41**	60	58	48	56	60	62	66
Yards	**946**	1449	1197	995	1173	1421	1227	1410
Average Yards	23.1	24.2	20.6	20.7	20.9	23.7	**19.8**	21.4
Touchdowns	1	**0**	**0**	**0**	**0**	1	**0**	**0**
INTERCEPTION RETURNS:								
Number	29	24	30	35	20	22	**17**	26
Yards	365	467	426	471	238	339	**186**	451
Average Yards	12.6	19.5	14.2	13.5	11.9	15.4	**10.9**	17.3
Touchdowns	4	1	2	3	**0**	2	**0**	1
PENALTIES:								
Number	72	69	**86**	67	60	77	69	62
Yards	658	832	836	701	623	**865**	666	665
FUMBLES:								
Number	17	**33**	27	31	24	25	23	24
Number Lost	9	**25**	14	13	13	12	14	13
POINTS:								
Total	302	**226**	392	429	285	303	239	227
PAT (Kick) Attempts	28	**21**	50	48	33	33	29	25
PAT (Kick) Made	28	**21**	50	48	33	33	29	25
PAT (Rush or Pass) Attempts	6	4	**0**	2	1	2	1	**0**
PAT (Rush or Pass) Made	2	4	**0**	2	**0**	**0**	**0**	**0**
FG Attempts	40	30	24	43	28	34	**20**	34
FG Made	22	15	14	25	16	20	**10**	16
Percent FG Made	55.0	50.0	58.3	58.1	57.1	58.8	50.0	**47.1**
Safeties	**0**	1	**0**	1	**0**	**0**	**0**	2

1965 AFL CHAMPIONSHIP GAME

December 26, at San Diego
(Attendance 30,361)

Stubbornly Brilliant

The San Diego weather was mild compared with last year's chill in Buffalo, but the Bills' defense played the same hard-hitting game and again would up as victors. Buffalo's strong front four and tight pass defense completely handcuffed the favored Chargers, as they never could get past the Buffalo 24-yard line. Through the first quarter and the first ten minutes of the second quarter, both defenses kept the scoreboard empty, but the Bills scored on a Jack Kemp-to-Ernie Warlick pass with five minutes left before intermission. The Chargers then punted the ball back to the Bills, and Butch Byrd returned the kick 74 yards down the sideline for another Buffalo score. The two quick touchdowns gave the Bills a 14-0 lead to take into the clubhouse at halftime, while the Chargers had to ponder on the goose egg on their side of the scoreboard. Going back to last year's championship game, the Chargers now were scoreless in their last five quarters against the Buffalo defense. The second half proved no more pleasant for the Chargers, as John Hadl, Keith Lincoln, Paul Lowe, and Lance Alworth could not get the ball across the Buffalo goal line. Jack Kemp, meanwhile, guided the Bills' offense steadily against the stubborn San Diego defense. Pete Gogolak booted a pair of field goals in the third quarter to give the Bills some breathing room, and his 32-yarder in the fourth quarter ran the final score to 23-0. Quarterback Kemp, a former Charger, won the game MVP award for his surgical precision in running the attack.

SCORING

SAN DIEGO	0	0	0	0– 0
BUFFALO	0	14	6	3–23

Second Quarter
- Buf. Warlick, 18 yard pass from Kemp
  PAT—Gogolak (kick)
- Buf. Byrd, 74 yard punt return
  PAT—Gogolak (kick)

Third Quarter
- Buf. Gogolak, 11 yard field goal
- Buf. Gogolak, 39 yard field goal

Fourth Quarter
- Buf. Gogolak, 32 yard field goal

TEAM STATISTICS

S.D.		BUF.
12	First Downs—Total	23
5	First Downs—Rushing	13
7	First Downs—Passing	9
0	First Downs—Penalty	1
7	Punts—Number	4
40.7	Punts—Average Distance	46.3
3	Penalties—Number	2
41	Yards—Penalized	21
2	Missed Field Goals	2

INDIVIDUAL STATISTICS

SAN DIEGO	No.	Yds.	Avg.	BUFFALO	No.	Yds.	Avg.
RUSHING							
Lowe	12	57	4.8	Carlton	16	63	3.9
Hadl	8	24	3.0	Joe	16	35	2.2
Lincoln	4	16	4.0	Stone	3	5	1.7
Foster	2	9	4.5	Smith	1	5	5.0
Breaux	1	–2	–2.0		36	108	3.0
	27	104	3.9				
RECEIVING							
Alworth	4	82	20.5	Roberson	3	88	29.3
Lowe	3	3	1.0	Warlick	3	35	11.7
Norton	1	35	35.0	Costa	2	32	16.0
Farr	1	24	24.0	Tracy	1	12	12.0
MacKinnon	1	10	10.0		9	167	18.6
Lincoln	1	7	7.0				
Kocourek	1	3	3.0				
	12	164	13.7				
PUNT RETURNS							
Duncan	1	12	12.0	Byrd	3	87	29.0
KICKOFF RETURNS							
Duncan	2	62	31.0	Warner	1	17	17.0
Farr	1	35	35.0				
	3	97	32.3				
INTERCEPTION RETURNS							
Warren	1	0	0.0	Byrd	1	24	24.0
				Jacobs	1	12	12.0
					2	36	18.0

PASSING

	Att.	Comp.	Comp. Pct.	Yds.	Int.	Yds/ Att.	Yds/ Comp.	Yards Lost Tackled
SAN DIEGO								
Hadl	23	11	47.8	140	2	6.1	12.7	
Breaux	2	1	50.0	24	0	12.0	24.0	
	25	12	48.0	164	2	6.6	13.7	45
BUFFALO								
Kemp	19	8	42.1	155	1	8.2	19.4	
Lamonica	1	1	100.0	12	0	12.0	12.0	
	20	9	45.0	167	1	8.4	18.6	15

BUFFALO BILLS 10-3-1 Lou Saban

Scores of Each Game

	Opponent	
24	BOSTON	7
30	Denver	15
33	NEW YORK	21
17	OAKLAND	12
3	SAN DIEGO	34
23	Kansas City	7
31	DENVER	13
17	HOUSTON	19
23	Boston	7
17	Oakland	14
20	San Diego	20
29	Houston	18
34	KANSAS CITY	25
12	New York	14

Use Name	Pos.	Hgt	Wgt	Age	Int	Pts
Stew Barber	OT	6'3"	250	26		
Dick Hudson	OT	6'4"	272	25		
Joe O'Donnell	OT	6'2"	246	23		
Al Bemiller	OG	6'3"	260	26		
George Flint	OG	6'4"	244	27		
Billy Shaw	OG	6'3"	248	25		
Dave Behrman	C	6'5"	260	23		
Tom Day	DE	6'2"	250	30	1	
Ron McDole	DE	6'3"	264	25	1	
Jim Dunaway	DT	6'4"	276	23		
Tom Keating	DT	6'3"	242	22		
Dudley Meredith	DT	6'4"	275	30		
Henry Schmidt	DT	6'4"	270	28		
Tom Sestak	OT-DT	6'5"	270	29		

Use Name	Pos.	Hgt	Wgt	Age	Int	Pts
Harry Jacobs	LB	6'2"	225	28	1	
Bill Laskey	LB	6'2"	250	22		
Paul Maguire	LB	6'	220	27		
Marty Schottenheimer	LB	6'3"	225	22		
Mike Stratton	LB	6'3"	240	23	2	
John Tracey	OE-LB	6'3"	225	31	1	
Butch Byrd	DB	6'	211	23	5	
Hagood Clarke	DB	6'	188	23	7	
Booker Edgerson	DB	5'10"	180	26	5	
Tom Janik	DB	6'3"	200	24		
George Saimes	DB	5'10"	195	23	4	6
Gene Sykes	DB	6'1"	195	24		
Charley Warner	HB-DB	5'11"	180	25	5	24

Use Name	Pos.	Hgt	Wgt	Age	Int	Pts
Jack Kemp	QB	6'1"	200	31		24
Daryle Lamonica	QB	6'2"	215	24		6
Joe Auer	HB	6'1"	205	23		
Wray Carlton	HB	6'2"	216	27		42
Bobby Smith	HB	6'	203	24		6
Billy Joe	FB	6'2"	250	24		36
Donnie Stone	FB	6'2"	205	28		
Elbert Dubenion	FL	6'	187	30		6
Floyd Hudlow	FL	5'11"	185	21		
Bo Roberson (from OAK)	FL	6'1"	190	30		18
Ed Rutkowski	FL	6'1"	208	24		6
Glenn Bass	OE	6'4"	240	23		
Paul Costa	OE	6'5"	215	25		12
Charley Ferguson	OE	6'	195	29		
Bill Groman	OE	5'11"	180	22		
Pete Mills	OE	5'11"	180	22		
Ernie Warlick	OE	6'4"	235	33		6
Pete Gogolak	K	6'2"	200	23		115

NEW YORK JETS 5-8-1 Weeb Ewbank

Scores of Each Game

	Opponent	
21	Houston	27
10	KANSAS CITY	14
21	Buffalo	33
13	Denver	16
24	OAKLAND	24
9	SAN DIEGO	34
45	DENVER	10
13	Kansas City	10
30	Boston	20
41	HOUSTON	14
23	BOSTON	27
7	San Diego	38
14	Oakland	24
14	BUFFALO	12

Use Name	Pos.	Hgt	Wgt	Age	Int	Pts
Nick DeFelice	OT	6'3"	250	25		
Winston Hill	OT	6'4"	275	23		
Sherman Plunkett	OT	6'4"	295	31		
Sam DeLuca	OG	6'2"	250	29		
Dan Ficca	OG	6'1"	250	26		
Dave Herman	OG	6'2"	255	23		
Pete Perreault	OG	6'3"	245	26		
Mike Hudock	C	6'2"	245	30		
John Schmitt	C	6'4"	265	22		
Gerry Philbin	DE	6'2"	245	24		
Lavern Torczon	DE	6'2"	250	29		
Bert Wilder	DE	6'3"	245	25		
Verlon Biggs	DT-DE	6'4"	250	22	1	
Jim Harris	DT	6'4"	265	21		
Paul Rochester	DT	6'2"	250	28		
Arnie Simkus	DT	6'4"	240	22		

Use Name	Pos.	Hgt	Wgt	Age	Int	Pts
Al Atkinson	LB	6'1"	225	22	1	
Ralph Baker	LB	6'3"	235	23	2	
Larry Grantham	LB	6'	206	26	1	
Wahoo McDaniel	LB	6'	240	28	1	
Jim O'Mahoney	LB	6'1"	233	24		
Ray Abbruzzese	DB	6'1"	200	27	2	
Bill Baird	DB	5'10"	180	26	3	
Cornell Gordon	DB	6'	185	24	2	
Dainard Paulson	DB	5'11"	190	28	7	
Bill Rademacher	DB	6'1"	190	23		
Clyde Washington	DB	6'	206	27		
Willie West	DB	5'10"	185	27	6	
Jim Hudson	HB-DB	6'2"	210	22		

Use Name	Pos.	Hgt	Wgt	Age	Int	Pts
Joe Namath	QB	6'2"	194	22		
Mike Taliaferro	QB	6'2"	210	23		
Charley Browning	HB	6'	220	22		
Kern Carson (from SD)	HB	6'2"	202	23		12
Cosmo Iacavazzi	HB	6'	215	30		
Curley Johnson	HB	6'1"	215	30		6
Bill Mathis	HB	6'1"	220	26		36
Bob Schweickert	HB	6'1"	195	22		
Mark Smolinski	FB	6'	215	26		
Matt Snell	FB	6'2"	220	23		24
Jim Evans	FL	6'1"	190	31		
Don Maynard	FL	6'	185	29		84
Gene Heeter	OE	6'4"	235	24		
Dee Mackey	OE	6'5"	225	29		8
Jerry Robinson	OE	5'11"	200	22		
George Sauer	OE	6'1"	206	21		12
Bake Turner	OE	6'	185	25		12
Jim Turner	K	6'2"	205	24		91

BOSTON PATRIOTS 4-8-2 Mike Holovak

Scores of Each Game

	Opponent	
7	Buffalo	24
10	Houston	31
10	DENVER	27
17	Kansas City	27
10	OAKLAND	24
13	SAN DIEGO	13
21	Oakland	30
22	San Diego	6
7	BUFFALO	23
20	NEW YORK	30
10	KANSAS CITY	10
27	New York	23
28	Denver	20
42	HOUSTON	14

Use Name	Pos.	Hgt	Wgt	Age	Int	Pts
Tom Neville	OT	6'4"	230	22		
Don Oakes	OT	6'3"	255	27		
Bob Schmidt	OT	6'4"	250	29		
Bob Yates	OT	6'3"	230	26		
Justin Canale	OG	6'2"	230	21		
Billy Neighbors	OG	6'3"	250	27		
Jon Morris	C	6'4"	240	22		
Bob Dee	DE	6'3"	240	32		
Larry Eisenhauer	DE	6'5"	250	25		
Jim Hunt	DE	5'11"	245	26		
Len St. Jean	DE	6'1"	240	23		
Bill Dawson	OE-DE	6'3"	240	21		
Houston Antwine	DT	6'	270	26	1	
George Pyne	DT	6'4"	285	22		

Use Name	Pos.	Hgt	Wgt	Age	Int	Pts
Tom Addison	LB	6'3"	230	29	1	
Nick Buoniconti	LB	5'11"	220	24	3	
Mike Dukes (to NY)	LB	6'3"	235	29	1	
Lonnie Farmer	LB	6'	220	24	1	
Ed Meixler	LB	6'2"	245	22		
Jack Rudolph	LB	6'3"	230	27		
Jay Cunningham	DB	6'	185	32		
Dick Felt	DB	6'	185	32		
White Graves	DB	6'	185	22	2	
Ron Hall	DB	6'	190	28	3	
Tom Hennessey	DB	6'	180	25	2	
Ross O'Hanley	DB	6'	185	26	1	
Chuck Shonta	DB	6'	200	27	2	
Don Webb	DB	5'10"	200	26	2	

Use Name	Pos.	Hgt	Wgt	Age	Int	Pts
Babe Parilli	QB	6'1"	190	35		
Eddie Wilson	QB	6'	190	23		
Tom Yewcic	QB	5'11"	185	33		
Joe Bellino	HB	5'9"	187	27		
Ron Burton	HB	5'10"	190	28		18
J. D. Garrett	HB	5'11"	195	23		18
Larry Garron	FB	6'	195	28		12
Jim Nance	FB	6'1"	250	22		30
Jim Colclough	HB-FL	6'2"	190	21		12
Ellis Johnson	HB-FL	6'2"	190	21		
Gino Cappelletti	OE	6'	190	31		132
Art Graham	OE	6'1"	205	24		
Tony Romeo	OE	6'2"	230	26		12
Jim Whalen	OE	6'2"	210	21		

HOUSTON OILERS 4-10-0 Hugh Taylor

Scores of Each Game

	Opponent	
27	NEW YORK	21
31	BOSTON	10
17	Oakland	21
14	San Diego	31
17	Denver	28
38	KANSAS CITY	36
19	Buffalo	17
21	OAKLAND	33
21	DENVER	31
14	New York	41
21	Kansas City	52
18	BUFFALO	29
26	SAN DIEGO	37
14	Boston	42

Use Name	Pos.	Hgt	Wgt	Age	Int	Pts
Norm Evans	OT	6'5"	235	22		
Rich Michael	OT	6'3"	245	26		
Walt Suggs	OT	6'5"	260	26		
Maxie Williams	OT	6'4"	242	25		
Sonny Bishop	OG	6'2"	245	25		
John Frongillo	OG	6'3"	250	25		
Bob Talamini	OG	6'1"	255	26		
John Wittenborn	OG	6'2"	240	29		
Wayne Frazier	C	6'2"	245	25		
Tom Goode	C	6'3"	250	26		
Gary Cutsinger	DE	6'4"	245	24	1	
Bob Evans	DE	6'3"	250	23		6
Don Floyd	DE	6'4"	247	26		
George Kinney	DE	6'4"	250	22		
Ray Straham	DT	6'3"	250	23		
Scott Appleton	DT	6'3"	250	23		
Jim Hayes	DT	6'4"	265	24		
Ed Husmann	DT	6'	245	34		
Bud McFadin	DT	6'3"	270	37		

Use Name	Pos.	Hgt	Wgt	Age	Int	Pts
Johnny Baker	LB	6'3"	225	24		
Danny Brabham	LB	6'4"	240	24		
Doug Cline	LB	6'2"	230	26		
Bobby Maples	LB	6'2"	230	22	1	
Larry Onesti	LB	6'	200	26		6
Charley Rieves	LB	5'11"	218	26		
Tony Banfield	DB	6'1"	185	26	3	
Freddy Glick	DB	6'1"	190	28	2	
W. K. Hicks	DB	6'1"	185	22	9	
Bobby Jancik	DB	5'11"	178	25	4	
Pete Jaquess	DB	6'	180	23		
Jim Norton	DB	6'3"	190	26	7	

Sid Blanks — Knee Injury

Use Name	Pos.	Hgt	Wgt	Age	Int	Pts
George Blanda	QB	6'1"	215	37		61
Don Trull	QB	6'1"	180	23		12
Ode Burrell	HB	6'	185	25		46
B. W. Cheeks	HB	6'1"	230	23		
Dalton Hoffman	FB	6'	207	23		
Harry Hooligan	FB	6'2"	225	27		
Bobby Jackson	FB	6'3"	238	25		12
Keith Kinderman	FB	6'	215	25		
Jack Spikes	FB	6'2"	220	27		27
Charley Tolar	FB	5'7"	200	27		
Charley Hennigan	FL	6'	187	29		24
Sammy Weir	FL	5'9"	170	23		
Dick Compton	OE	6'1"	195	25		12
Charley Frazier	OE	6'	175	26		36
Willie Frazier	OE	6'4"	225	22		48
Bob McLeod	OE	6'5"	230	26		

BUFFALO BILLS

RUSHING
Last Name	No.	Yds	Avg	TD
Carlton	156	592	3.8	6
Joe	123	377	3.1	4
Smith	43	137	3.2	1
Stone	19	61	3.2	0
Kemp	36	49	1.4	4
Lamonica	10	30	3.0	1
Maguire	1	21	21.0	0
Auer	3	19	6.3	0
Warner	1	2	2.0	0
Roberson	1	−4	−4.0	0

RECEIVING
Last Name	No.	Yds	Avg	TD
Roberson	46	703	15	3
Joe	27	271	10	2
Carlton	24	196	8	1
Costa	21	401	19	0
Ferguson	21	262	12	2
Bass	18	299	17	1
Dubenion	18	281	16	1
Rutkowski	18	247	14	1
Smith	12	116	10	0
Warlick	8	112	14	1
Stone	6	29	5	0
Mills	1	43	43	0
Warner	1	11	11	1
Tracey	1	2	2	0
Kemp	1	−9	−9	0

PUNT RETURNS
Last Name	No.	Yds	Avg	TD
Byrd	22	220	10	0
Rutkowski	11	127	12	0
Warner	1	16	16	0
Clarke	1	13	13	0
Hudlow	1	12	12	0
Saimes	0	1	0	0

KICKOFF RETURNS
Last Name	No.	Yds	Avg	TD
Warner	32	825	26	2
Roberson	16	318	20	0
Rutkowski	5	97	19	0
Hudlow	2	36	18	0
Maguire	1	5	5	0
Dunaway	1	0	0	0

PASSING – PUNTING – KICKING
PASSING
Last Name	Att	Comp	%	Yds	Yd/Att	TD	Int–%		RK
Kemp	391	179	46	2368	6.1	10	18–	5	6
Lamonica	70	29	41	376	5.4	3	6–	9	

PUNTING
Last Name	No	Avg
Maguire	80	43.0

KICKING
Last Name	XP	Att	%	FG	Att	%
Gogolak	31	31	100	28	46	61

NEW YORK JETS

RUSHING
Last Name	No.	Yds	Avg	TD
Snell	169	763	4.5	4
Mathis	147	604	4.1	5
Smolinski	24	59	2.5	0
Carson	7	25	3.6	2
Namath	8	19	2.4	0
McDaniel	1	13	13.0	0
Taliaferro	7	4	0.6	0
Johnson	2	3	1.5	0
Maynard	1	2	2.0	0

RECEIVING
Last Name	No.	Yds	Avg	TD
Maynard	68	1218	18	14
Snell	38	264	7	0
B. Turner	31	402	13	2
Sauer	29	301	10	2
Mathis	17	242	14	1
Mackey	16	255	16	1
Smolinski	6	25	4	0
Evans	2	24	12	0
Heeter	1	14	14	0
Johnson	1	6	6	1

PUNT RETURNS
Last Name	No.	Yds	Avg	TD
Baird	14	88	6	0
Robinson	3	36	12	0
West	10	34	3	0
Carson	1	7	7	0
B. Turner	1	1	1	0

KICKOFF RETURNS
Last Name	No.	Yds	Avg	TD
B. Turner	18	402	22	0
Carson	17	355	21	0
Robinson	7	164	23	0
Smolinski	6	98	16	0
Baird	2	50	25	0
Browning	1	31	31	0
Sauer	1	20	20	0
Abruzzese	1	16	16	0
O'Mahoney	1	15	15	0
DeFelice	1	0	0	0
Hudson	1	0	0	0
Paulson	1	0	0	0

PASSING – PUNTING – KICKING
PASSING
Last Name	Att	Comp	%	Yds	Yd/Att	TD	Int–%		RK
Namath	340	164	48	2220	6.5	18	15–	4	3
Taliaferro	119	45	38	531	4.5	3	7–	6	

PUNTING
Last Name	No	Avg
Johnson	72	45.3

KICKING
Last Name	XP	Att	%	FG	Att	%
J. Turner	31	31	100	20	34	59

2 POINT XP
Mackey

BOSTON PATRIOTS

RUSHING
Last Name	No.	Yds	Avg	TD
Nance	111	321	2.9	5
Garron	74	259	3.5	1
Parilli	50	200	4.0	0
Garrett	42	147	3.5	1
Burton	45	108	2.4	1
Bellino	24	49	2.0	0
Johnson	19	29	1.5	0
Wilson	8	4	0.5	0

RECEIVING
Last Name	No.	Yds	Avg	TD
Colclough	40	677	17	3
Cappelletti	37	680	18	9
Graham	25	316	13	0
Whalen	22	381	17	0
Garron	15	222	15	1
Romeo	15	203	14	2
Nance	12	83	7	0
Burton	10	127	13	2
Garrett	7	49	7	2
Bellino	5	74	15	0
Johnson	4	29	7	0
Yewcic	1	13	13	0

PUNT RETURNS
Last Name	No.	Yds	Avg	TD
Burton	15	61	4	0
Cunningham	5	35	7	0
Hennessey	5	21	4	0
Garrett	1	19	19	0
Nance	1	16	16	0

KICKOFF RETURNS
Last Name	No.	Yds	Avg	TD
Cunningham	17	374	22	0
Garrett	12	232	19	0
Burton	7	188	27	0
Garron	5	141	28	0
Bellino	7	138	20	0
Dukes	3	45	15	0
Nance	3	40	13	0
Johnson	2	29	15	0
Rudolph	1	4	4	0
Canale	2	0	0	0
Pyne	1	0	0	0

PASSING – PUNTING – KICKING
PASSING
Last Name	Att	Comp	%	Yds	Yd/Att	TD	Int–%		RK
Parilli	426	173	41	2597	6.1	18	26–	6	7
Wilson	46	20	44	257	5.6	1	3–	7	
Yewcic	1	0	0	0	0.0	0	0–	0	

PUNTING
Last Name	No	Avg
Yewcic	74	41.8
E. Wilson	5	38.8

KICKING
Last Name	XP	Att	%	FG	Att	%
Cappelletti	27	27	100	17	27	63

HOUSTON OILERS

RUSHING
Last Name	No.	Yds	Avg	TD
Burrell	130	528	4.1	3
Tolar	73	230	3.2	0
Spikes	47	173	3.7	3
Trull	29	145	5.0	2
Jackson	37	85	2.3	0
Hoffman	1	11	11.0	0
C. Frazier	1	10	10.0	0
Compton	1	2	2.0	0
Blanda	4	−6	−1.5	0

RECEIVING
Last Name	No.	Yds	Avg	TD
Burrell	55	650	12	4
Hennigan	41	578	14	4
C. Frazier	38	717	19	6
Wil. Frazier	37	521	14	8
Tolar	25	138	6	0
McLeod	15	226	15	1
Spikes	8	57	7	0
Compton	3	140	47	2
Jackson	1	31	31	0
Weir	1	12	12	0

PUNT RETURNS
Last Name	No.	Yds	Avg	TD
Jancik	12	85	7	0
Glick	7	44	6	0
Burrell	3	39	13	0
Jaquess	4	17	4	0
Hicks	1	4	4	0
Weir	1	0	0	0

KICKOFF RETURNS
Last Name	No.	Yds	Avg	TD
Jancik	18	430	24	0
Jaquess	13	280	22	0
Weir	10	215	22	0
Burrell	8	202	25	0
Hicks	7	181	26	0
Glick	4	84	21	0
Kinderman	4	72	18	0
Compton	4	68	17	0
Spikes	4	41	10	0
Jackson	2	39	20	0
Williams	1	23	23	0
Cheeks	1	19	19	0
Maples	1	15	15	0

PASSING – PUNTING – KICKING
PASSING
Last Name	Att	Comp	%	Yds	Yd/Att	TD	Int–%		RK
Blanda	442	186	42	2542	5.8	20	30–	7	8
Trull	107	38	36	528	4.9	5	5–	5	
Tolar	1	0	0	0	0.0	0	0–	0	

PUNTING
Last Name	No	Avg
Norton	84	44.2

KICKING
Last Name	XP	Att	%	FG	Att	%
Blanda	28	28	100	11	21	52
Spikes	6	6	100	1	2	50

2 POINT XP
Burrell (2)

SAN DIEGO CHARGERS 9-2-3 Sid Gillman

Scores of Each Game

34	DENVER	31
17	Oakland	6
10	KANSAS CITY	10
31	HOUSTON	14
34	Buffalo	3
13	Boston	13
34	New York	9
6	BOSTON	22
35	Denver	21
7	Kansas City	31
20	BUFFALO	20
38	NEW YORK	7
37	Houston	26
24	OAKLAND	14

Use Name	Pos.	Hgt	Wgt	Age	Int	Pts
Gary Kirner	OT	6'3"	245	23		
Ron Mix	OT	6'4"	250	27		
Ernie Park	OT	6'3"	253	25		
Ernie Wright	OT	6'4"	265	26		
John Farris	OG	6'4"	245	24		
Ed Mitchell	OG	6'2"	265	23		
Pat Shea	OG	6'1"	245	26		
Walt Sweeney	OG	6'3"	255	24		
Sam Gruneisen	C	6'1"	255	24		
Steve DeLong	DE	6'3"	245	22		
Earl Faison	DE	6'5"	270	26	1	6
Howard Kindig	DE	6'6"	250	24		
Bob Petrich	DE	6'4"	257	24		
George Gross	DT	6'3"	270	24		
Ernie Ladd	DT	6'9"	295	26		
Fred Moore	DT	6'3"	255	25		

Use Name	Pos.	Hgt	Wgt	Age	Int	Pts
Chuck Allen	LB	6'1"	225	25	1	
Frank Buncom	LB	6'1"	235	25		
Ron Carpenter	LB	6'2"	230	24		
Dick Degen	LB	6'1"	225	23	2	
Bob Horton	LB	6'2"	230	22		
Rick Redman	LB	5'11"	220	22	1	
Speedy Duncan	DB	5'10"	180	22	4	12
Kenny Graham	DB	6'	200	23	5	6
Dick Harris	DB	5'11"	187	28	1	
Jack Jacobson	DB	6'2"	200	24		
Jimmy Warren	DB	5'11"	185	26	5	
Dick Westmoreland	DB	6'1"	190	24	1	
Bud Whitehead	DB	6'	185	26	7	6
Bob Zeman	DB	6'1"	195	28		

Use Name	Pos.	Hgt	Wgt	Age	Int	Pts
Don Breaux	QB	6'1"	200	25		
John Hadl	QB	6'2"	210	25		6
Steve Tensi	QB	6'5"	207	22		
Gene Foster	FB-HB	5'11"	200	22		12
Paul Lowe	HB	6'	205	28		48
Jim Allison	FB	6'	225	22		
Keith Lincoln	FB	6'2"	212	26		42
Lance Alworth	FL	6'	185	25		84
Sammy Taylor	FL	6'	190	25		
Dave Kocourek	OE	6'5"	245	28		12
Jacque MacKinnon	OE	6'4"	250	26		
Don Norton	OE	6'1"	195	27		12
Herb Travenio	K	6'	218	34		94

OAKLAND RAIDERS 8-5-1 Al Davis

Scores of Each Game

37	KANSAS CITY	10
6	SAN DIEGO	17
21	HOUSTON	17
12	Buffalo	17
24	Boston	10
24	New York	24
30	BOSTON	21
7	Kansas City	14
33	Houston	21
14	BUFFALO	17
28	Denver	20
24	DENVER	13
24	NEW YORK	14
14	San Diego	24

Use Name	Pos.	Hgt	Wgt	Age	Int	Pts
Harry Schuh	OG-OT	6'2"	260	22		
Bob Svihus	OT	6'4"	245	22		
Frank Youso	OT	6'4"	250	29		
Rich Zecher	OT	6'2"	240	22		
Wayne Hawkins	OG	6'	240	27		
Marv Marinovich	OG	6'3"	250	26		
Bob Mischak	OG	6'	230	32		
Ken Rice	CG	6'2"	240	25		
Jim Otto	C	6'2"	240	27		
Ben Davidson	DE	6'8"	265	25		
Ike Lassiter	DE	6'5"	270	24		
Carleton Oats	DE	6'2"	235	22		
Dan Birdwell	DT	6'4"	250	24		
Dave Costa	DT	6'2"	250	23		
John Diehl (from DAL-N)	DT	6'7"	250	29		
Rex Mirich	DT	6'4"	250	24		

Use Name	Pos.	Hgt	Wgt	Age	Int	Pts
Bill Budness	LB	6'1"	215	22	1	
Dan Conners	LB	6'1"	230	23		
Dick Herman	LB	6'2"	215	22		
Archie Matsos	LB	6'	212	30	3	
Gus Otto	LB	6'2"	220	22	3	12
J. R. Williamson	LB	6'2"	220	23		
Dave Grayson	DB	5'10"	185	26	3	12
Claude Gibson	DB	6'1"	190	26	4	6
Joe Krakoski	DB	6'2"	195	28		
Kent McCloughan	DB	6'1"	190	22	3	
Warren Powers	DB	6'	185	24	5	
Howie Williams	DB	6'2"	185	28	2	

Use Name	Pos.	Hgt	Wgt	Age	Int	Pts
Cotton Davidson	QB	6'1"	180	33		
Tom Flores	QB	6'1"	190	28		
Dick Wood	QB	6'5"	200	29		6
Clem Daniels	HB	6'1"	220	28		72
Gene Mingo	HB	6'1"	190	26		24
Larry Todd	HB	6'1"	185	22		
Roger Hagberg	FB	6'2"	220	26		6
Alan Miller	FB	6'	210	27		24
Fred Biletnikoff	FL	6'1"	190	22		
Pervis Atkins (from WAS-N)	OE	6'1"	195	29		
Billy Cannon	OE	6'1"	225	28		
Ken Herock	OE	6'2"	230	24		
Art Powell	OE	6'3"	212	28		72
Mike Mercer	K	6'	200	29		62

KANSAS CITY CHIEFS 7-5-2 Hank Stram

Scores of Each Game

10	Oakland	37
14	New York	10
10	San Diego	10
27	BOSTON	17
31	Denver	23
7	BUFFALO	23
36	Houston	38
10	OAKLAND	7
10	NEW YORK	13
31	SAN DIEGO	7
10	Boston	10
52	HOUSTON	21
25	Buffalo	34
45	DENVER	35

Use Name	Pos.	Hgt	Wgt	Age	Int	Pts
Jerry Cornelison	OT	6'3"	250	28		
Dave Hill	OT	6'5"	260	24		
Jim Tyrer	OT	6'6"	292	26		
Denny Biodrowski	OG	6'1"	255	25		
Ed Budde	OG	6'5"	260	24		
Curt Merz	OG	6'4"	250	27		
Al Reynolds	OG	6'3"	235	27		
Jon Gilliam	C	6'2"	240	26		
Mel Branch	DE	6'2"	230	28		
Chuck Hurston	DE	6'6"	227	22		
Ed Lothamer	DE	6'5"	240	22		
Buck Buchanan	DT	6'7"	280	25		
Al Dotson	DT	6'4"	255	22		
Curt Farrier	DT	6'6"	245	24		
Jerry Mays	DT	6'4"	250	25		
Hatch Rosdahl	DT	6'5"	250	22		

Use Name	Pos.	Hgt	Wgt	Age	Int	Pts
Ronnie Caveness	LB	6'1"	215	22		
Walt Corey	LB	6'	242	27		
Jim Fraser	LB	6'3"	236	29		
Sherrill Headrick	LB	6'2"	215	28	1	
E. J. Holub	LB	6'4"	225	27	1	
Smokey Stover	LB	6'	232	26		
Bobby Bell	DE-LB	6'4"	228	25	4	6
Bobby Hunt	DB	6'1"	190	25	1	
Willie Mitchell	DB	6'1"	185	23	2	12
Bobby Ply	DB	6'1"	190	24		
Johnny Robinson	DB	6'	195	26	5	
Fred Williamson	DB	6'2"	215	27	6	

Use Name	Pos.	Hgt	Wgt	Age	Int	Pts
Pete Beathard	QB	6'2"	205	23		26
Len Dawson	QB	6'	190	31		12
Soloman Brannan	HB	6'1"	188	23		
Bert Coan	HB	6'4"	220	25		18
*Mack Lee Hill	HB	5'11"	225	23		18
Jerrel Wilson	HB	6'4"	225	24		2
Curtis McClinton	FB	6'3"	232	26		54
Frank Jackson	FL	6'1"	190	25		6
Frank Pitts	FL	6'2"	190	21		
Fred Arbanas	OE	6'2"	240	26		24
Tommy Brooker	OE	6'3"	230	25		76
Chris Burford	OE	6'3"	210	27		36
Reg Carolan	OE	6'6"	232	25		2
Otis Taylor	OE	6'2"	215	22		30

*Died Dec. 14, 1965 after knee surgery

DENVER BRONCOS 4-10-0 Mac Speedie

Scores of Each Game

31	San Diego	34
15	BUFFALO	30
27	Boston	10
16	NEW YORK	13
23	KANSAS CITY	31
28	HOUSTON	17
13	Buffalo	31
10	New York	45
21	SAN DIEGO	35
31	Houston	21
20	OAKLAND	28
13	Oakland	24
20	BOSTON	28
35	Kansas City	45

Use Name	Pos.	Hgt	Wgt	Age	Int	Pts
Lee Bernet	OT	6'2"	245	21		
Bob Breitenstein	OT	6'3"	250	22		
Eldon Danenhauer	OT	6'4"	245	29		
Jon Hohman	OG	6'1"	245	24		
Bob McCullough	OG	6'2"	245	24		
Tom Nomina	OG	6'5"	270	23		
Charlie Parker	OG	6'1"	245	24		
Jerry Sturm	OG	6'3"	260	28		
Ray Kubala	C	6'4"	245	24		
Ed Cooke	DE	6'4"	250	30	3	
Leroy Moore	DE	6'	230	29		
Ray Jacobs	DT	6'3"	265	25		
Chuck Janerette	DT	6'3"	265	26	1	
Max Leetzow	DT	6'4"	240	24		
Jim Thompson	DT	6'3"	255	24		

Use Name	Pos.	Hgt	Wgt	Age	Int	Pts
John Bramlett	LB	6'2"	210	24	1	12
Ed Cummings	LB	6'2"	228	24		
Tom Erlandson	LB	6'3"	235	25	1	
Jerry Hopkins	LB	6'2"	235	24	1	
Gene Jeter	LB	6'3"	230	23		
Jim Thibert	LB	6'3"	230	23		
Willie Brown	DB	6'1"	190	24	2	
Gerry Bussell	DB	6'	185	22		
Miller Farr (to SD)	DB	6'1"	188	22	2	
Goose Gonsoulin	DB	6'3"	210	27	6	2
John Griffin	DB	6'1"	190	25	4	12
Gary Kroner	DB	6'1"	200	24		71
John McGeever	DB	6'1"	195	26	1	
Jim McMillin	DB	5'11"	195	27		
Nemiah Wilson	DB	6'	180	22	3	6

Use Name	Pos.	Hgt	Wgt	Age	Int	Pts
Jacky Lee	QB	6'1"	187	26		
John McCormick	QB	6'1"	210	28		
Mickey Slaughter	QB	6'	190	23		
Paul Carmichael	HB	6'	200	20		
Wendell Hayes	HB	6'2"	195	24		44
Abner Haynes	HB	6'	190	27		36
Charley Mitchell	HB	5'11"	185	25		
Cookie Gilchrist	FB	6'3"	250	30		42
Darrell Lester	FB	6'2"	225	24		
Al Denson	FL	6'2"	208	23		
Bob Scarpitto	FL	5'11"	196	26		30
Odell Barry	OE	5'10"	180	23		
Hewritt Dixon	OE	6'2"	217	25		12
Lionel Taylor	OE	6'2"	215	29		36

SAN DIEGO CHARGERS

RUSHING
Last Name	No.	Yds	Avg	TD
Lowe	222	1121	5.1	7
Foster	121	469	3.9	2
Lincoln	75	302	4.1	3
Allison	29	100	3.5	0
Hadl	28	91	3.3	1
MacKinnon	3	17	5.7	0
Breaux	1	−1	−1.0	0
Shea	1	−5	−5.0	0
Norton	1	−5	−5.0	0
Alworth	3	−12	−4.0	0
Sweeney	0	8	0.0	0

RECEIVING
Last Name	No.	Yds	Avg	TD
Alworth	69	1602	23	14
Norton	34	485	14	2
Kocourek	28	363	13	2
Lincoln	23	376	16	4
Foster	17	199	12	0
Lowe	17	126	7	1
Allison	8	109	13	0
Mackinnon	6	106	18	0
Taylor	1	13	13	0

PUNT RETURNS
Last Name	No.	Yds	Avg	TD
Duncan	30	464	15	2
Graham	5	36	7	0
Harris	3	8	3	0

KICKOFF RETURNS
Last Name	No.	Yds	Avg	TD
Duncan	26	612	24	0
Foster	5	108	22	0
Allison	4	80	20	0
Lincoln	2	46	23	0
Harris	1	15	15	0
Kirner	1	0	0	0
Mackinnon	1	0	0	0

PASSING — PUNTING — KICKING
PASSING
Last Name	Att	Comp	%	Yds	Yd/Att	TD	Int−%	RK
Hadl	348	174	50	2798	8.0	20	21− 6	2
Breaux	43	22	51	404	9.4	2	4− 9	
Lowe	4	3	75	81	20.3	0	0− 0	
Foster	3	2	67	31	10.3	0	0− 0	
Lincoln	3	2	67	65	21.7	1	1− 33	

PUNTING
Last Name	No	Avg
Hadl	38	40.7
Redman	29	39.5
Allison	2	36.0
Whitehead	1	40.0

KICKING
Last Name	XP	Att	%	FG	Att	%
Travenio	40	40	100	18	30	60

OAKLAND RAIDERS

RUSHING
Last Name	No.	Yds	Avg	TD
Daniels	219	884	4.0	5
Miller	73	272	3.7	1
Todd	32	183	5.7	0
Hagberg	48	171	3.6	1
Flores	11	32	2.9	0
Wood	4	16	4.0	1
Mercer	1	−1	−1.0	0

RECEIVING
Last Name	No.	Yds	Avg	TD
Powell	52	800	15	12
Daniels	36	568	16	7
Biletnikoff	24	331	14	0
Miller	21	208	10	3
Herock	18	221	12	0
Hagberg	12	121	10	0
Todd	8	106	13	0
Cannon	7	127	18	0
Atkins	1	6	6	0
Mingo	1	5	5	0

PUNT RETURNS
Last Name	No.	Yds	Avg	TD
Gibson	31	357	12	1
Krakoski	2	5	3	0
Hagberg	1	3	3	0

KICKOFF RETURNS
Last Name	No.	Yds	Avg	TD
Todd	20	461	23	0
Gibson	9	186	21	0
Hagberg	3	50	17	0
Grayson	1	34	34	0
Herman	1	0	0	0

PASSING — PUNTING — KICKING
PASSING
Last Name	Att	Comp	%	Yds	Yd/Att	TD	Int−%	RK
Flores	269	122	45	1593	5.9	14	11− 4	5
Wood	157	69	44	1003	6.4	8	6− 4	4
Daniels	2	2	100	95	47.5	0	0− 0	
C. Davidson	1	1	100	8	8.0	0	0− 0	
Mercer	1	1	100	14	14.0	0	0− 0	
Todd	1	0	0	0	0.0	0	0− 0	

PUNTING
Last Name	No	Avg
Mercer	75	41.1

KICKING
Last Name	XP	Att	%	FG	Att	%
Mercer	35	35	100	9	15	60
Mingo	0	0	0	8	19	42

KANSAS CITY CHIEFS

RUSHING
Last Name	No.	Yds	Avg	TD
McClinton	175	661	3.8	6
M. Hill	125	627	5.0	2
Dawson	43	142	3.3	2
Beathard	25	138	5.5	4
Coan	45	137	3.0	1
Jackson	1	26	26.0	0
Taylor	2	17	8.5	0
Wilson	2	4	2.0	0

RECEIVING
Last Name	No.	Yds	Avg	TD
Burford	47	575	12	6
McClinton	37	590	16	3
Jackson	28	440	16	1
Taylor	26	446	17	5
Arbanas	24	418	17	4
M. Hill	21	264	13	1
Coan	9	85	9	2
Carolan	6	65	11	0
Pitts	1	11	11	0

PUNT RETURNS
Last Name	No.	Yds	Avg	TD
Mitchell	19	242	13	1
Jackson	13	163	13	0
Brannan	5	10	2	0
Pitts	1	4	4	0

KICKOFF RETURNS
Last Name	No.	Yds	Avg	TD
Coan	19	479	25	0
Jackson	9	260	29	0
Brannan	9	226	25	0
Pitts	5	100	20	0
Stover	3	7	2	0
Fraser	1	5	5	0
Mays	2	3	2	0

PASSING — PUNTING — KICKING
PASSING
Last Name	Att	Comp	%	Yds	Yd/Att	TD	Int−%	RK
Dawson	305	163	53	2262	7.4	21	14− 5	1
Beathard	89	36	41	632	7.1	1	6− 7	
McClinton	1	0	0	0	0.0	0	0− 0	

PUNTING
Last Name	No	Avg
Wilson	68	46.1
Fraser	3	27.0

KICKING
Last Name	XP	Att	%	FG	Att	%
Brooker	37	37	100	13	30	43

2 POINT XP
Beathard
Carolan
Wilson

DENVER BRONCOS

RUSHING
Last Name	No.	Yds	Avg	TD
Gilchrist	252	954	3.8	6
Hayes	130	526	4.1	5
Haynes	41	166	4.1	3
Scarpitto	4	94	23.5	0
Slaughter	20	75	3.8	0
Barry	2	19	9.5	0
Lee	2	1	0.5	0
McCormick	1	−2	−2.0	0
Denson	1	−4	−4.0	0

RECEIVING
Last Name	No.	Yds	Avg	TD
Taylor	85	1131	13	6
Scarpitto	32	585	18	5
Haynes	26	216	8	2
Dixon	25	354	14	2
Hayes	24	294	12	2
Gilchrist	18	154	9	1
Denson	9	102	11	0
Barry	2	11	6	0
McCullough	1	1	1	0

PUNT RETURNS
Last Name	No.	Yds	Avg	TD
Barry	21	210	10	0
Haynes	14	121	9	1
Bussell	2	24	12	0

KICKOFF RETURNS
Last Name	No.	Yds	Avg	TD
Haynes	34	901	27	0
Barry	26	611	24	0
Farr	7	123	18	0
Bussell	5	103	21	0
Hayes	4	93	23	0
Carmichael	1	15	15	0
Dixon	1	8	8	0

PASSING — PUNTING — KICKING
PASSING
Last Name	Att	Comp	%	Yds	Yd/Att	TD	Int−%	RK
McCormick	253	103	41	1292	5.1	7	14− 6	10
Slaughter	147	75	51	864	5.9	6	12− 8	9
Lee	80	44	55	692	8.7	5	3− 4	
Hayes	1	0	0	0	0.0	0	1−100	
Haynes	1	0	0	0	0.0	0	0− 0	

PUNTING
Last Name	No	Avg
Scarpitto	67	42.3
McCormick	1	45.0

KICKING
Last Name	XP	Att	%	FG	Att	%
Kroner	32	32	100	13	29	45

2 POINT XP
Gunsoulin
Hayes

1966 N.F.L. Closing the Checkbook

The war between the two leagues was getting very expensive. To sign heralded rookies Donny Anderson, Jim Grabowski, and Tommy Nobis, NFL clubs had to give each of them contracts more lucrative than that given to Joe Namath by the AFL Jets last year. But after the New York Giants signed kicker Pete Gogolak away from the AFL Buffalo Bills, the heat of battle became unbearable. Considering the signing of Gogolak as a direct slap, the AFL owners went all out to pirate away established NFL stars. With John Brodie, Roman Gabriel, and Mike Ditka on the verge of jumping and other NFL stars thinking it over, the established league sat down with the upstarts to discuss terms of peace. In June, officials of both leagues announced a merger that would change the organizational set-up of pro football. With Pete Rozelle as Commissioner over both leagues, the NFL and AFL would conduct a common draft of college players starting next year and would finish this season with the first Super Bowl between the two league champions.

EASTERN CONFERENCE

Dallas Cowboys—With Don Meredith at quarterback, the Dallas offense was the league's most versatile and explosive. Bob Hayes used his sprinter's speed to gain 1,232 yards on passes, while Dan Reeves succeeded at halfback despite his slowness afoot. Signed two years ago as a free agent, Reeves hustled his way to sixteen touchdowns, eight each by running and receiving, and was a threat to throw the option pass on sweeps. Ralph Neely led the blocking in a strong offensive line. The defense, loaded with quality players, led the league in sacking enemy quarterbacks and gave up yardage with extreme reluctance. Coach Tom Landry had been collecting talent for years, and now all the pieces had fit together.

Cleveland Browns—Jimmy Brown had retired to become an actor, but no one could blame replacement Leroy Kelly for Cleveland's slip to second place. Kelly had distinguished himself for two years as a kick returner, and when he was thrust into Brown's vacant shoes at fullback, he surprised the league by rushing for 1,141 yards, second only to Gale Sayers in the NFL. Kelly relied more on speed than did Brown, leaving the power running to Ernie Green. Paul Warfield returned from last year's shoulder injury to join Gary Collins in the wide receiving duo, and Frank Ryan found his targets often enough to throw for twenty-nine touchdowns. The Browns' fatal flaw this season was a slow start in which they lost two of their first three games.

Philadelphia Eagles—Despite a weak passing attack, the Eagles reached third place with their best record in five years. Behind a good offensive line, the running corps of Timmy Brown, Earl Gros, Tom Woodeshick, and Izzy Lang ate up large chunks of yardage, and Brown also doubled as the team's top kickoff returner, bringing two kickoffs back for touchdowns in one game against the Cowboys. The lack of quality receivers and Norm Snead's poor season hurt the attack, but the defense showed enough strength to carry the team.

St. Louis Cardinals—The Cards had a new coach in Charley Winner but the same old problem with injuries. Battling with Dallas for first place in the East, the Cards lost quarterback Charley Johnson with a knee injury and they scored only fifty-two points in their last five games, losing four of them, to fall to fourth place. Injuries also stripped end Sonny Randle, offensive linemen Bob DeMarco, Ken Gray, and Irv Goode, and cornerback Pat Fischer from the active rolls for varying lengths of time.

Washington Redskins—The Redskins brought former Cleveland great Otto Graham back to pro football as head coach, and Graham as expected put the emphasis on the pass in the Washington attack. The air game worked fine, with Sonny Jurgensen doing the pitching and Charley Taylor, converted from halfback to end in mid-season, Bobby Mitchell, and Jerry Smith doing most of the catching. Even without a legitimate running attack, the Redskins could put points on the scoreboard. But the defense needed time to jell, with seven new faces in the starting lineup.

Pittsburgh Steelers—Coach Bill Austin took the Steelers to five wins despite some severe problems on offense. The line blocked poorly, rookie Willie Asbury was the only effective runner, and the quarterback situation was unstable. Bill Nelsen hurt his knee in the second game of the year, and Ron Smith, let go by the Packers, filled in at quarterback for most of the season. The defense carried the club through the body of the schedule, but Nelsen returned to action for the last three games and beat New York 47-28 and Atlanta 57-33 to end the year.

Atlanta Falcons—The Falcons lost their first nine NFL games but came back to win three of their last five contests to escape the cellar in their first season in the league. Junior Coffey, obtained from Green Bay in the expansion draft, developed into a fine runner, but most of the impressive performances were turned in by rookies such as linebacker Tommy Nobis, quarterback Randy Johnson, and defensive backs Bob Riggle, Nick Rassas, and Ken Reaves.

New York Giants—With Tucker Frederickson out all year with a bad knee, Earl Morrall sidelined for the last half of the schedule with a broken wrist, and the defense a horrendous hodgepodge of journeymen and youth, the Giants suffered through the worst season in their history. They beat the Redskins 13-10 in mid-October for their only win of the year, and the rematch in late November resulted in a 72-41 embarrassment.

WESTERN CONFERENCE

Green Bay Packers—The Packers shelled out about $1,000,000 to sign All-American runners Donny Anderson and Jim Grabowski, but Vince Lombardi kept his Green Bay machine running with old pros and a few key replacement parts. With Paul Hornung bothered by a neck injury, Elijah Pitts did most of the playing at halfback, while ex-Ram Carroll Dale slipped past Max McGee into the starting lineup as a wide receiver. On defense, quick Bob Jeter switched from offensive end to capture a cornerback slot. The heart of the Packers, however, was still the troop of seasoned veterans who had grown used to the taste of winning, and that was good enough to bring the Packers home first in the West.

Baltimore Colts—The Colts lost the opening game of the season to the Packers and struggled futilely to catch up the rest of the year. With a veteran team that was approaching old age all at once, the Colts had solid units both on defense and offense. The defensive line relied on quickness and got some size late in the year when Gino Marchetti came out of retirement; the linebacking was strengthened by the conversion of Mike Curtis from fullback to a corner linebacker; and Bobby Boyd, Lenny Lyles, Alvin Haymond, Jerry Logan, and Jim Welch blanketed enemy pass receivers from their deep spots. The offense moved on the arm of Johnny Unitas, but the Colts lost twice to the Packers and had to settle for second place behind them.

Los Angeles Rams—The Rams had to go to court to get George Allen to be their head coach, but the results proved well worth the trouble. Allen rebuilt the Los Angeles defense into one of the league's best. He inherited a great front four in Deacon Jones, Lamar Lundy, Merlin Olsen, and Rosie Grier, but he completely overhauled the linebacking. He talked Jack Pardee out of retirement, signed Bill George as a free agent after the Bears cut him, and traded for Maxie Baughan from the Eagles and Myron Pottios from the Steelers. To tighten up the secondary, he brought in Irv Cross from Philadelphia. Although the offense lacked flair, the improved defense carried the club to its first winning season since 1958.

San Francisco '49ers—With the Houston Oilers trying to lure him into the AFL, John Brodie bargained himself into a multiyear contract worth over $900,000. With his financial future secure, Brodie did nothing to show that he could lead a team to a championship. With a good line, punishing runners in Ken Willard and John David Crow, and fine wide receivers like Bernie Casey and Dave Parks, the San Francisco attack ran in spurts, running up big scores against Detroit, Chicago, and Atlanta and losing 28-3 to Minnesota and 34-3 to Los Angeles.

Chicago Bears—With George Halas taking George Allen into court to keep him from resigning as an assistant coach, with Doug Atkins and Mike Ditka openly critical of Halas, with Rudy Bukich suffering through a miserable campaign, and with Johnny Morris sidelined with a bad knee, Bear fans found Gale Sayers' superb season a pleasant diversion from the Bears' problems. Sayers improved on his rookie season by leading the NFL in rushing, catching thirty-four passes and breaking off two touchdowns in pacing the league in kickoff returning. Adding together his rushing, receiving, and returning totals, Sayers gained 2,440 yards, a new record.

Detroit Lions—Problems at quarterback made the Detroit offense a plodding affair. Milt Plum began the year as signal-caller but went out of service with a mid-season injury. Karl Sweetan, who had spent last season with the semi-pro Pontiac Arrows, stepped in and did a creditable job as a passer but could not ignite the attack into steady fireworks. On one play, however, Sweetan got the offense moving, passing to Pat Studstill for a 99-yard touchdown against the Colts on October 16. Studstill was one of the league's sensations, developing into a dangerous pass receiver despite his small size and very ordinary speed. Another player to attract attention was Garo Yepremian, a soccer-style place-kicker from Cyprus who was signed in mid-season and booted a record six field goals against the Vikings on November 13.

Minnesota Vikings—Expecting to move up into championship status for the last few seasons, the Vikings simply were not improving with their current team. The defense was not getting much better, halfback Tommy Mason was spending more time hurt than healthy, and quarterback Fran Tarkenton was hardly on speaking terms with coach Norm Van Brocklin. Once in a while the potential would show through in big victories such as the 20-17 triumph over Green Bay, but this promising team kept losing without much promise of winning.

FINAL TEAM STATISTICS

OFFENSE

	ATL.	BALT.	CHI.	CLEV.	DALL.	DET.	G.B.	L.A.	MINN.	N.Y.	PHIL.	PITT.	ST.L.	S.F.	WASH.
FIRST DOWNS:															
Total	211	237	196	278	287	216	231	255	279	236	231	207	212	282	225
by Rushing	85	82	96	117	124	73	98	103	126	80	112	65	88	101	78
by Passing	104	142	85	142	139	126	115	133	132	129	104	117	108	153	130
by Penalty	22	13	15	19	24	17	18	19	21	27	15	25	16	28	17
RUSHING:															
Number	405	418	463	415	471	394	475	448	551	380	478	375	458	422	356
Yards	1519	1556	1927	2166	2122	1429	1673	1742	2091	1457	1859	1092	1601	1790	1377
Average Yards	3.8	3.7	4.2	5.2	4.5	3.6	3.5	3.9	3.8	3.8	3.9	2.9	3.5	4.2	3.9
Touchdowns	11	7	12	18	24	13	18	12	15	7	19	13	10	12	9
PASSING:															
Attempts	381	401	338	402	413	456	318	450	417	424	378	401	386	500	443
Completions	175	221	159	212	214	239	193	249	216	208	179	188	180	261	255
Completion Percentage	45.9	55.1	47.0	52.7	51.8	52.4	60.7	55.3	51.8	49.1	47.4	46.9	46.6	52.2	57.6
Passing Yards	2362	3172	2016	3142	3331	2752	2831	2891	2932	2999	2159	2877	2292	3239	3230
Average Yards per Attempt	6.2	7.9	5.0	7.8	8.1	6.0	8.9	6.4	7.0	7.1	5.7	7.2	5.9	6.5	7.3
Average Yards per Completion	13.5	14.4	12.7	14.8	15.6	11.5	14.7	11.6	13.6	14.4	12.1	15.3	12.7	12.4	12.7
Times Tackled Attempting to Pass	38	30	29	29	42	35	31	54	45	62	35	66	38	30	27
Yards Lost Tackled Attempting to Pass	345	242	244	237	308	328	229	351	384	524	259	523	352	247	216
Net Yards	2017	2930	1772	2905	3023	2424	2602	2540	2548	2475	1900	2354	1940	2992	3014
Touchdowns	14	26	10	33	27	8	18	12	18	20	14	18	13	21	28
Interceptions	27	27	23	15	14	28	5	17	22	31	22	22	19	26	20
Percent Intercepted	7.1	6.7	6.8	3.7	3.4	6.1	1.6	3.8	5.3	7.3	5.8	5.5	4.9	5.2	4.5
PUNTS:															
Number	73	49	80	57	65	72	62	71	60	53	65	78	81	70	68
Average Distance	40.7	45.6	42.0	39.0	39.2	41.1	41.0	42.8	41.1	38.9	39.8	42.1	35.6	40.6	42.4
PUNT RETURNS:															
Number	18	45	25	24	41	38	37	45	31	22	31	21	40	45	29
Yards	100	357	97	146	258	396	215	341	129	120	162	43	316	238	201
Average Yards	5.6	7.9	3.9	6.1	6.3	10.4	5.8	7.6	4.2	5.5	5.2	2.0	7.9	5.3	6.9
Touchdowns	0	0	0	0	0	1	1	0	0	0	1	0	1	1	1
KICKOFF RETURNS:															
Number	82	51	48	54	44	58	42	42	52	80	64	64	57	56	69
Yards	1737	1094	1341	1111	1006	1316	903	1015	987	1616	1419	1384	1348	1326	1435
Average	21.2	21.5	27.9	20.6	22.9	22.7	21.5	24.2	19.0	20.2	22.2	21.6	23.6	23.7	20.8
Touchdowns	0	0	2	0	1	0	0	0	0	1	2	1	1	0	0
INTERCEPTION RETURNS:															
Number	19	22	15	30	17	24	28	26	14	17	20	24	21	18	23
Yards	177	267	155	408	303	366	547	362	230	217	345	280	330	379	369
Average Yards	9.3	12.1	10.3	13.6	17.8	15.3	19.5	13.9	16.4	12.8	17.3	11.7	15.7	21.1	16.0
Touchdowns	1	2	0	1	3	1	6	4	1	2	1	2	3	3	1
PENALTIES:															
Number	79	64	80	69	83	82	57	72	67	57	63	75	67	86	64
Yards	753	617	714	747	824	931	544	651	787	602	666	768	586	819	591
FUMBLES:															
Number	30	19	26	17	23	33	23	25	33	29	32	34	26	26	27
Number Lost	17	12	12	10	10	21	19	12	14	13	17	17	18	12	15
POINTS:															
Total	204	314	234	403	445	206	335	289	292	263	326	316	264	320	351
PAT Attempts	26	36	26	54	56	23	43	29	34	31	39	36	28	39	41
PAT Made	21	35	24	52	56	23	41	29	34	29	38	35	27	38	39
FG Attempts	19	39	30	23	31	30	28	49	33	28	25	32	40	31	34
FG Made	9	21	18	9	17	15	12	28	18	16	18	21	23	16	22
Percent FG Made	47.4	53.8	60.0	39.1	54.8	50.0	42.9	57.1	54.5	57.1	72.0	65.6	57.5	51.6	64.7
Safeties	0	0	0	0	1	0	0	1	0	0	0	1	0	0	0

DEFENSE

	ATL.	BALT.	CHI.	CLEV.	DALL.	DET.	G.B.	L.A.	MINN.	N.Y.	PHIL.	PITT.	ST.L	S.F.	WASH.
FIRST DOWNS:															
Total	295	245	239	255	221	240	211	196	213	273	249	238	209	238	261
by Rushing	126	94	102	113	64	109	90	64	85	122	90	107	68	88	106
by Passing	151	134	116	124	140	108	106	114	116	137	139	105	109	126	134
by Penalty	18	17	21	18	17	23	15	18	12	14	20	26	32	24	21
RUSHING:															
Number	472	460	466	450	356	479	446	401	412	480	390	468	377	414	438
Yards	2172	1733	1604	1894	1176	2006	1644	1302	1686	2053	1693	1786	1192	1629	1831
Average Yards	4.6	3.8	3.4	4.2	3.3	4.2	3.7	3.2	4.1	4.3	4.3	3.8	3.2	3.9	4.2
Touchdowns	20	7	13	12	6	16	9	10	15	23	13	11	11	15	19
PASSING:															
Attempts	396	425	406	406	457	363	390	406	391	357	446	397	443	414	411
Completions	227	240	202	221	212	210	202	190	206	194	226	192	197	206	224
Completion Percentage	57.3	56.5	49.8	54.4	46.4	57.9	51.8	46.8	52.7	54.3	50.7	48.4	44.5	49.8	54.5
Passing Yards	3376	2759	2600	2650	2802	2702	2316	2830	2426	3086	2964	2849	2733	2895	3237
Average Yards per Attempt	8.5	6.5	6.4	6.5	6.1	7.4	5.9	7.0	6.2	8.6	6.6	7.2	6.2	7.0	7.9
Average Yards per Completion	14.9	11.5	12.9	12.0	13.2	12.9	11.5	14.9	11.8	15.9	13.1	14.8	13.9	14.1	14.5
Times Tackled Attempting to Pass	34	47	29	35	60	34	47	45	25	26	34	38	52	40	45
Yards Lost Tackled Attempting to Pass	276	401	233	278	420	294	357	361	190	194	287	344	433	345	376
Net Yards	3100	2358	2367	2372	2382	2408	1959	2469	2236	2892	2677	2505	2300	2550	2861
Touchdowns	26	14	13	14	17	19	7	13	13	36	23	27	15	22	21
Interceptions	19	22	15	30	17	24	28	26	14	17	20	24	21	18	23
Percent Intercepted	4.8	5.2	3.7	7.4	3.7	6.6	7.2	6.4	3.6	4.8	4.5	6.0	4.7	4.3	5.6
PUNTS:															
Number	38	71	71	56	79	71	69	73	72	58	60	64	85	76	61
Average Distance	38.6	40.6	42.4	39.7	42.4	41.1	41.3	43.8	40.6	39.8	39.9	37.8	40.7	41.2	38.4
PUNT RETURNS:															
Number	35	30	46	23	26	27	30	49	28	27	31	42	25	33	40
Yards	197	130	250	111	108	98	171	269	250	218	300	242	159	368	248
Average Yards	5.6	4.3	5.4	4.8	4.2	3.6	5.7	5.5	8.9	8.1	9.7	5.8	6.4	11.2	6.2
Touchdowns	1	0	1	0	1	0	0	0	0	1	1	0	0	1	0
KICKOFF RETURNS:															
Number	44	63	49	68	78	45	52	58	50	49	65	63	50	59	70
Yards	962	1320	1055	1501	1699	1004	1213	1329	1203	1085	1330	1485	1021	1343	1488
Average	21.9	21.0	21.5	22.1	21.8	22.3	23.3	22.9	24.1	22.1	20.5	23.6	20.4	22.8	21.3
Touchdowns	0	0	0	2	3	0	0	0	0	1	1	0	0	1	0
INTERCEPTION RETURNS:															
Number	27	27	23	15	14	28	5	17	22	31	22	22	19	26	20
Yards	385	438	426	68	274	409	75	338	337	465	380	319	236	334	251
Average Yards	14.3	16.2	18.5	4.5	19.6	14.7	15.0	19.9	15.3	15.0	17.3	14.5	12.4	12.8	12.6
Touchdowns	3	3	6	0	1	3	0	2	2	4	3	1	1	1	1
PENALTIES:															
Number	66	69	71	61	63	61	67	76	67	83	63	82	83	91	62
Yards	588	704	636	563	778	564	745	704	667	788	703	835	761	938	626
FUMBLES:															
Number	24	25	35	24	23	19	26	37	24	19	30	37	20	24	36
Number Lost	13	18	23	19	14	11	14	20	8	7	15	16	10	11	20
POINTS:															
Total	437	226	272	259	239	317	163	212	304	501	340	347	265	325	355
PAT Attempts	52	25	34	29	29	38	17	26	33	66	40	42	28	40	42
PAT Made	48	25	32	28	29	38	16	26	32	64	40	38	28	37	40
FG Attempts	41	33	29	28	31	31	27	22	41	23	30	33	41	31	31
FG Made	25	17	12	19	12	17	15	10	24	13	20	19	23	16	21
Percent FG Made	61.0	51.5	41.4	67.9	38.7	54.8	55.6	45.5	58.5	56.5	66.7	57.6	56.1	51.6	67.7
Safeties	1	0	0	0	0	0	0	0	1	1	0	0	0	0	0

Super-bound

A trip to the first Super Bowl awaited the winner of this NFL championship game, which featured the Packers and the Cowboys. The Packers took an early lead on a Bart Starr-to-Elijah Pitts touchdown pass and immediately added on another touchdown when Mel Renfro fumbled the kickoff and Jim Grabowski ran the recovery in from 17 yards out. The Cowboys, one of pro football's exciting young teams, came right back with two touchdowns to tie the score, 14-14, at the end of one quarter. The Packers scored in the second period on a long Bart Starr-to-Carroll Dale pass, while the Cowboys answered only with a Danny Villanueva field goal. Another Villanueva three-pointer lowered the Packer lead to 21-20 in the third quarter, but touchdown passes to Boyd Dowler and Max McGee ran the score to 34-20 and seemingly put the game on ice. The Cowboys fought back, however, scoring on a long pass from Don Meredith to Frank Clarke. In the final minutes, Dallas drove for the winning touchdown, only to fall short when Meredith's fourth-down pass was intercepted in the end zone by Tom Brown

1966 NFL CHAMPIONSHIP GAME

January 1, at Dallas (Attendance 74,152)

SCORING

DALLAS	14	3	3	7	–27
GREEN BAY	14	7	7	6	–34

First Quarter
- GB Pitts, 17 yd pass by Starr (Chandler – kick)
- GB Grabowski, 18 yd Fumble recovery return (Chandler – kick)
- DA Reeves, 3 yd rush (Villanueva – kick)
- DA Perkins, 23 yd rush (Villanueva – kick)

Second Quarter
- GB Dale, 51 yd pass by Starr (Chandler – kick)
- DA Villanueva, 11 yd field goal

Third Quarter
- DA Villanueva, 32 yd field goal
- GB Dowler, 16 yd pass by Starr (Chandler – kick)

Fourth Quarter
- GB McGee, 28 yd pass by Starr (Kick Blocked)
- DA Clarke, 68 yd pass by Meredith (Villanueva – kick)

TEAM STATISTICS

DALL.		G.B.
23	First Downs – Total	19
12	First Downs – Rushing	3
10	First Downs – Passing	14
1	First Downs – Penalty	2
4	Punts – Number	4
32.2	Punts – Average Distance	40.0
3	Punt Returns – Number	0
–9	Punt Returns – Yards	0
0	Interception Ret – Number	1
0	Interception Ret – Yards	0
3	Fumbles – Number	1
1	Fumbles – Lost Ball	1
6	Penalties – Number	2
29	Yards Penalized	23
73	Offensive Plays	57
231	Net Yards	367
3.2	Average Gain	6.4
2	Giveaways	1
1	Takeaways	2
–1	Difference	+1

INDIVIDUAL STATISTICS

RUSHING

DALLAS	No	Yds	Avg.	GREEN BAY	No	Yds	Avg.
Perkins	17	108	6.4	Pitts	12	66	5.5
Reeves	17	47	2.8	Taylor	10	37	3.7
Meredith	4	22	5.5	Starr	2	–1	–0.5
Norman	2	10	5.0		24	102	4.3
	40	187	4.7				

RECEIVING

DALLAS	No	Yds	Avg.	GREEN BAY	No	Yds	Avg.
Reeves	4	77	19.3	Dale	5	128	25.6
Norman	4	30	7.5	Taylor	5	23	4.6
Clarke	3	102	34.0	Fleming	3	50	16.7
Gent	3	28	9.3	Dowler	3	49	16.3
Hayes	1	1	3.0	McGee	1	28	28.0
	15	238	15.9	Pitts	1	17	17.0
				Long	1	9	9.0
					19	304	16.0

PASSING

	Att	Comp	Comp Pct.	Yds	Int	Yds/ Att.	Yds/ Comp	Yds Lost Tackled
DALLAS								
Meredith	31	15	48.4	238	1	7.7	15.9	2– 7
GREEN BAY								
Starr	28	19	67.9	304	0	10.9	16.0	5–39

DALLAS COWBOYS 10-3-1 Tom Landry

Scores of Each Game		
52	NEW YORK	7
28	MINNESOTA	17
47	Atlanta	14
56	PHILADELPHIA	7
10	St. Louis	10
21	Cleveland	30
52	PITTSBURGH	21
23	Philadelphia	24
31	Washington	30
20	Pittsburgh	7
26	CLEVELAND	14
31	ST. LOUIS	17
31	WASHINGTON	34
17	New York	7

Use Name	Pos.	Hgt	Wgt	Age	Int	Pts
Jim Boeke	OT	6'5"	255	27		
Ralph Neely	OT	6'5"	257	22		
Tony Liscio	OG-OT	6'5"	255	26		
Leon Donahue	OG	6'4"	245	27		
John Niland	OG	6'4"	250	22		
Mike Connelly	OT-OG	6'3"	248	30		
Dave Manders	C	6'2"	240	24		
Malcolm Walker	OT-C	6'4"	245	23		
George Andrie	DE	6'7"	255	26	1	6
Larry Stephens	DE	6'4"	250	28		
Jethro Pugh	DT-DE	6'6"	250	22		
John Wilbur	DT-DE	6'3"	250	23		
Jim Colvin	DT	6'2"	255	29		
Bob Lilly	DT	6'4"	255	27		
Bill Sandeman	DT	6'6"	250	23		
Willie Townes	DE-DT	6'5"	265	23		2

Use Name	Pos.	Hgt	Wgt	Age	Int	Pts
Dave Edwards	LB	6'3"	226	27	1	
Harold Hays	LB	6'3"	223	25		
Chuck Howley	LB	6'3"	223	30		6
Lee Roy Jordan	LB	6'2"	216	25	1	6
Jerry Tubbs	LB	6'2"	222	31	1	
Dick Daniels	DB	5'9"	180	20		
Mike Gaechter	DB	6'	190	26	3	
Cornell Green	DB	6'4"	215	26	4	6
Mike Johnson	DB	5'10"	186	22		
Warren Livingston	DB	5'10"	190	28	2	
Obert Logan	DB	5'10"	180	24	2	
Mel Renfro	HB-DB	6'	195	24	2	6
Jim Steffen – Injury						

Use Name	Pos.	Hgt	Wgt	Age	Int	Pts
Don Meredith	QB	6'2"	206	28		30
Craig Morton	QB	6'4"	216	23		
Jerry Rhome	QB	6'	187	24		
Dan Reeves	HB	6'1"	203	22		96
Les Shy	HB	6'1"	210	22		6
Walt Garrison	FB-HB	6'	200	22		6
Don Perkins	FB	5'10"	206	28		48
J. D. Smith	FB	6'1"	210	33		6
Buddy Dial	FL	6'1"	195	29		6
Pete Gent	FL	6'4"	210	23		6
Frank Clarke	TE	6'	210	33		24
Pettis Norman	TE	6'3"	223	26		
Bob Hayes	OE	6'	190	23		78
Danny Villanueva	K	5'11"	200	28		107

CLEVELAND BROWNS 9-5-0 Blanton Collier

Scores of Each Game		
38	Washington	14
20	GREEN BAY	21
28	ST. LOUIS	34
28	New York	7
41	PITTSBURGH	10
30	DALLAS	21
49	Atlanta	17
6	Pittsburgh	16
27	PHILADELPHIA	7
14	WASHINGTON	3
14	Dallas	26
49	NEW YORK	40
21	Philadelphia	33
38	St. Louis	10

Use Name	Pos.	Hgt	Wgt	Age	Int	Pts
Jim Battle	OT	6'4"	235	25		
John Brown	OT	6'2"	248	27		
Monte Clark	OT	6'6"	265	29		
Dick Schafrath	OT	6'3"	255	30		
Gene Hickerson	OG	6'3"	248	31		
Joe Bob Isbell	OG	6'1"	250	26		
John Wooten	OG	6'2"	250	31		
Fred Hoaglin	C	6'4"	240	22		
John Morrow	C	6'3"	248	33		
Bill Glass	DE	6'5"	255	30		6
Paul Wiggin	DE	6'3"	245	32	1	
Walter Johnson	DT	6'3"	265	23		
Jim Kanicki	DT	6'4"	270	24		
Dick Modzelewski	DT	6'	260	35		
Frank Parker	DT	6'5"	270	26		

Use Name	Pos.	Hgt	Wgt	Age	Int	Pts
Johnny Brewer	LB	6'4"	235	29	1	
Vince Costello	LB	6'	228	34	1	
Galen Fiss	LB	6'	227	36		
Dale Lindsey	LB	6'3"	220	23		
Sid Williams	LB	6'2"	235	24		
Jim Houston	TE-LB	6'2"	240	29	2	7
Erich Barnes	DB	6'2"	198	31	4	
Walter Beach	DB	6'	185	31	1	
Ross Fichtner	DB	6'	185	28	8	6
Bobby Franklin	DB	5'11"	182	30		
Mike Howell	DB	6'1"	187	23	8	
Ernie Kellerman	DB	6'	183	22	3	
Bernie Parrish (to HOU-A)	DB	5'11"	195	31	1	

Use Name	Pos.	Hgt	Wgt	Age	Int	Pts
Gary Lane	QB	6'1"	210	23		
Jim Ninowski	QB	6'1"	207	30		
Frank Ryan	QB	6'3"	200	30		
Leroy Kelly	HB	6'	195	24		96
Randy Schultz	FB-HB	5'11"	210	22		
Ernie Green	FB	6'2"	205	27		54
Charlie Harraway	FB	6'2"	230	21		
Nick Pietrosante	FB	6'2"	225	29		
Gary Collins	FL	6'4"	208	25		72
Clifton McNeil	FL	6'2"	185	26		12
Milt Morin	TE	6'4"	250	24		18
Ralph Smith	TE	6'2"	215	27		18
Paul Warfield	OE	6'	188	23		36
Walter Roberts	FL-OE	5'10"	163	24		
Lou Groza	K	6'3"	250	42		78

PHILADELPHIA EAGLES 9-5-0 Joe Kuharich

Scores of Each Game		
13	St. Louis	16
23	ATLANTA	10
35	NEW YORK	17
10	ST. LOUIS	41
7	Dallas	56
31	Pittsburgh	14
31	New York	3
13	WASHINGTON	27
24	DALLAS	23
7	Cleveland	27
35	San Francisco	34
27	PITTSBURGH	23
33	CLEVELAND	21
37	Washington	28

Use Name	Pos.	Hgt	Wgt	Age	Int	Pts
Bob Brown	OT	6'4"	276	23		
Dave Graham	OT	6'3"	250	27		
Lane Howell	OT	6'5"	270	25		
Ray Rissmiller	OT	6'4"	250	24		
Ed Blaine	OG	6'2"	240	26		
Jim Skaggs	OG	6'2"	250	26		
Bruce Van Dyke	OG	6'2"	235	22		
Lynn Hoyem	C-OG	6'4"	253	26		
Dave Recher	C	6'1"	245	23		
Jim Ringo	C	6'1"	230	35		
Randy Beisler	DE	6'4"	245	21		
Don Hultz	DE	6'3"	235	25		
Gary Pettigrew	DE	6'4"	245	21		
Dave Cahill	DT	6'3"	238	24		
John Meyers	DT	6'6"	276	26		
Floyd Peters	DT	6'4"	255	31		

Use Name	Pos.	Hgt	Wgt	Age	Int	Pts
Ike Kelley	LB	5'11"	225	22		
Dave Lloyd	LB	6'3"	248	30	3	
Mike Morgan	LB	6'4"	242	24	1	
Arunas Vasys	LB	6'2"	225	23		
Harold Wells	LB	6'2"	220	27	1	6
Fred Whittingham	LB	6'1"	240	27	1	
Aaron Martin	DB	6'	185	25	1	6
Ron Medved	DB	6'1"	210	22		
Al Nelson	DB	5'11"	186	22	1	6
Jim Nettles	DB	5'9"	180	24	3	6
Nate Ramsey	DB	6'1"	200	25	1	
Joe Scarpati	DB	5'10"	185	24	8	
Fred Brown – Knee Injury						
Frank Molden – Knee Injury						
Ray Poage – Knee Injury						
Bob Shann – Injury						

Use Name	Pos.	Hgt	Wgt	Age	Int	Pts
Jack Concannon	QB	6'3"	195	23		12
King Hill	QB	6'3"	213	30		
Norm Snead	QB	6'4"	205	26		6
Timmy Brown	HB	5'10"	198	29		48
Ollie Matson	HB	6'2"	210	36		12
Earl Gros	FB	6'3"	220	25		54
Izzy Lang	FB	6'1"	230	23		6
Tom Woodeshick	HB-FB	6'	220	24		30
Willie Brown	FL	6'	185	23		
T.J. Jackson	FL	6'	180	23		
Ron Goodwin	OE-FL	6'	180	24		6
Pete Retzlaff	TE	6'1"	214	35		36
Dave Lince	TE	6'6"	250	22		
Fred Hill	OE	6'2"	215	23		
Ben Hawkins	FL-OE	6'	180	22		
Sam Baker	K	6'2"	218	34		92

ST. LOUIS CARDINALS 8-5-1 Charley Winner

Scores of Each Game		
16	PHILADELPHIA	13
23	WASHINGTON	7
34	Cleveland	28
41	Philadelphia	10
24	NEW YORK	19
10	DALLAS	10
20	Washington	26
24	CHICAGO	17
20	New York	17
9	Pittsburgh	30
6	PITTSBURGH	3
17	Dallas	31
10	Atlanta	16
10	CLEVELAND	38

Use Name	Pos.	Hgt	Wgt	Age	Int	Pts
John McDowell	OT	6'3"	260	23		
Ernie McMillan	OT	6'6"	260	28		
Bob Reynolds	OT	6'6"	265	25		
Dave O'Brien	OG-OT	6'3"	247	25		
Ken Gray	OG	6'2"	250	30		
Frank Roy	OG	6'2"	230	23		
Rick Sortun	OG	6'2"	235	23		
Irv Goode	C-OG	6'4"	250	25		
Bob DeMarco	C	6'3"	240	28		
Dick Kasperek	C	6'3"	225	22		
Don Brumm	DE	6'3"	245	23		
Mike Melinkovich	DE	6'4"	245	24		
Joe Robb	DE	6'3"	245	29		
Dave Long	DT-DE	6'4"	235	21		
Sam Silas	DT	6'4"	250	23		
Chuck Walker	DT	6'2"	245	25		
Fred Heron	DE-DT	6'4"	250	21		

Use Name	Pos.	Hgt	Wgt	Age	Int	Pts
Bill Koman	LB	6'2"	230	32		
Dave Meggyesy	LB	6'1"	220	24		
Dale Meinert	LB	6'2"	220	33		
Dave Simmons	LB	6'4"	245	23		
Larry Stallings	LB	6'2"	230	24	1	
Mike Strofolino	LB	6'2"	230	22		
Jimmy Burson	DB	6'	180	24	2	
Pat Fischer	DB	5'10"	170	26	1	
Jim Heidel	DB	6'1"	185	22		
Jerry Stovall	DB	6'2"	205	24	3	6
Bobby Williams	DB	6'1"	185	24		
Larry Wilson	DB	6'	190	28	10	12
Abe Woodson	DB	5'11"	190	31	4	
Bill Thornton – Injury						

Use Name	Pos.	Hgt	Wgt	Age	Int	Pts
Jim Hart	QB	6'2"	195	22		
Charley Johnson	QB	6'	190	29		12
Terry Nofsinger	QB	6'4"	215	28		12
Charlie Bryant	HB	6'1"	207	25		
Roy Shivers	HB	6'	200	24		6
Bill Triplett	HB	6'2"	210	27		
Johnny Roland	FB-HB	6'2"	207	23		36
Willie Crenshaw	FB	6'2"	230	25		
Prentice Gautt	HB-FB	6'1"	210	28		12
Bobby Joe Conrad	FL	6'	195	31		12
Mal Hammack	FB	6'2"	210	33		
Ray Ogden	TE	6'5"	225	23		
Jackie Smith	TE	6'4"	215	25		18
Sonny Randle	OE	6'2"	190	30		12
Billy Gambrell	FL-OE	5'10"	175	24		30
Jim Bakken	K	6'	200	25		96

WASHINGTON REDSKINS 7-7-0 Otto Graham

Scores of Each Game		
14	CLEVELAND	38
7	St. Louis	23
33	Pittsburgh	27
24	PITTSBURGH	10
33	ATLANTA	20
10	New York	13
26	ST. LOUIS	20
27	Philadelphia	13
10	Blatimore	37
30	DALLAS	31
3	Cleveland	14
72	NEW YORK	41
34	Dallas	31
28	PHILADELPHIA	37

Use Name	Pos.	Hgt	Wgt	Age	Int	Pts
Mitch Johnson	OT	6'4"	245	24		
John Kelly	OT	6'3"	256	22		
Jim Snowden	OT	6'3"	255	24		
Tom Goosby	OG	6'	235	27		
Jake Kupp	OG	6'3"	233	24		
Vince Promuto	OG	6'1"	245	28		
Ray Schoenke	OG	6'3"	234	24		
Don Croftcheck	LB-OG	6'1"	230	23		
Dave Crossan	C	6'3"	245	26		
Len Hauss	C	6'2"	235	24		
Willie Adams	DE	6'2"	235	24		
Bill Briggs	DE	6'3"	250	22		
Carl Kammerer	DE	6'3"	243	29		
Ron Snidow	DE	6'4"	250	24		
Walt Barnes	DT	6'3"	250	22		
Stan Jones	DT	6'1"	250	35		
Joe Rutgens	DT	6'2"	255	27		

Use Name	Pos.	Hgt	Wgt	Age	Int	Pts
Jim Carroll (from NY)	LB	6'1"	230	23	1	
Chris Hanburger	LB	6'2"	218	25	1	
Sam Huff	LB	6'1"	230	31	1	
Steve Jackson	LB	6'1"	225	23	1	
John Reger	LB	6'	220	35	3	6
Billy Clay	DB	6'1"	192	22	1	
Rickie Harris	DB	6'	182	23	1	6
Paul Krause	DB	6'3"	195	24	2	
Brig Owens	DB	5'11"	190	23	7	12
Lonnie Sanders	DB	6'3"	207	24		
Jim Shorter	DB	5'11"	185	25	5	
Tom Walters	DB	6'2"	195	24		
John Seedborg – Military Service						

Use Name	Pos.	Hgt	Wgt	Age	Int	Pts
Sonny Jurgensen	QB	5'11"	205	32		
Dick Shiner	QB	6'	197	24		
Ron Rector (to ATL)	HB	6'	200	22		
Steve Thurlow (from NY)	HB	6'3"	216	23		
Tom Barrington	FB-HB	6'1"	218	22		
Joe Kantor	FB	6'1"	217	23		
A. D. Whitfield	FB	5'10"	200	22		18
Joe Don Looney (fron DET)	HB-FB	6'1"	230	23		24
John Burrell	FL	6'3"	195	26		
Fred Mazurek	FL	5'11"	192	23		
Bobby Mitchell	FL	6'	196	31		60
Jim Avery	TE	6'2"	235	22		
Pat Richter	TE	6'5"	230	25		
Jerry Smith	TE	6'2"	208	23		36
Pat Hodgson	OE	6'2"	190	22		
Charley Taylor	HB-OE	6'3"	210	25		90
Charlie Gogolak	K	5'10"	165	21		105

DALLAS COWBOYS

RUSHING

Last Name	No.	Yds	Avg	TD
Reeves	175	757	4.3	8
Perkins	186	726	3.9	8
Meredith	38	242	6.4	5
Shy	17	118	6.9	1
Garrison	16	62	3.9	1
Renfro	8	52	6.5	0
Morton	7	50	7.1	0
Clarke	8	49	6.1	0
Rhome	7	37	5.3	0
Villanueva	1	23	23.0	0
Smith	7	7	1.0	1
Hayes	1	−1	−1.0	0

RECEIVING

Last Name	No.	Yds	Avg	TD
Hayes	64	1232	19	13
Reeves	41	557	14	8
Gent	27	474	18	1
Clarke	26	355	14	4
Perkins	23	231	10	0
Dial	14	252	18	1
Norman	12	144	12	0
Renfro	4	65	16	0
Garrison	2	18	9	0
Smith	1	3	3	0

PUNT RETURNS

Last Name	No.	Yds	Avg	TD
Renfro	21	123	6	0
Hayes	17	106	6	0
Howley	1	30	30	0
Reeves	2	−1	−1	0

KICKOFF RETURNS

Last Name	No.	Yds	Avg	TD
Renfro	19	487	26	1
Garrison	20	445	22	0
Reeves	3	56	19	0
Neely	2	18	9	0

PASSING – PUNTING – KICKING

PASSING	Att	Comp	%	Yds	Yd/Att	TD	Int–%	RK
Meredith	344	177	51	2805	8.2	24	12– 3	4
Rhome	36	21	58	253	7.0	0	1– 3	
Morton	27	13	48	225	8.3	3	1– 4	
Reeves	6	3	50	48	8.0	0	0– 0	

PUNTING	No	Avg
Villanueva	65	39.2

KICKING	XP	Att	%	FG	Att	%
Villanueva	56	56	100	17	31	55

CLEVELAND BROWNS

RUSHING

Last Name	No.	Yds	Avg	TD
Kelly	209	1141	5.5	15
Green	144	750	5.2	3
Ryan	36	156	4.3	0
Harraway	7	40	5.7	0
Collins	2	38	19.0	0
Schultz	7	32	4.6	0
Pietrosante	7	20	2.9	0
Ninowski	3	−11	−3.7	0

RECEIVING

Last Name	No.	Yds	Avg	TD
Collins	56	946	17	12
Green	45	445	10	6
Warfield	36	741	21	5
Kelly	32	366	11	1
Morin	23	333	14	3
Smith	13	183	14	3
McNeil	2	94	47	2
Roberts	2	19	10	0
Pietrosante	1	12	12	0
Houston	1	10	10	1
Costello	1	−7	−7	0

PUNT RETURNS

Last Name	No.	Yds	Avg	TD
Kelly	13	104	8	0
Roberts	11	42	4	0

KICKOFF RETURNS

Last Name	No.	Yds	Avg	TD
Roberts	20	454	23	0
Kelly	19	403	21	0
Harraway	9	193	21	0
Schultz	3	52	17	0
Pietrosante	2	9	5	0
Smith	1	0	0	0

PASSING – PUNTING – KICKING

PASSING	Att	Comp	%	Yds	Yd/Att	TD	Int–%	RK
Ryan	382	200	52	2974	7.8	29	14– 4	3
Ninowski	18	11	61	175	9.7	4	1– 6	
Groza	1	1	100	−7	−7.0	0	0– 0	
Kelly	1	0	0	0	0.0	0	0– 0	

PUNTING	No	Avg
Collins	57	39.0

KICKING	XP	Att	%	FG	Att	%
Groza	51	52	98	9	23	39
Houston	1	1	100	0	0	0

PHILADELPHIA EAGLES

RUSHING

Last Name	No.	Yds	Avg	TD
T. Brown	161	548	3.4	3
Gros	102	396	3.9	7
Woodeshick	85	330	3.9	4
Lang	52	239	4.6	1
Concannon	25	195	7.8	2
Matson	29	101	3.5	1
Snead	15	32	2.1	1
Baker	1	15	15.0	0
F. Hill	1	5	5.0	0
K. Hill	7	−2	−0.3	0

RECEIVING

Last Name	No.	Yds	Avg	TD
Retzlaff	40	653	16	6
T. Brown	33	371	11	3
F. Hill	29	304	10	0
Gros	18	214	12	2
Goodwin	16	212	13	1
Hawkins	14	143	10	0
Lang	12	107	9	0
Woodeshick	10	118	12	1
Matson	6	30	5	1
Concannon	1	7	7	0

PUNT RETURNS

Last Name	No.	Yds	Avg	TD
Martin	11	118	11	1
Hawkins	9	47	5	0
Concannon	2	3	2	0
Nelson	1	3	3	0
T. Brown	1	0	0	0
W. Brown	5	−1	0	0
Scarpati	2	−8	−4	0

KICKOFF RETURNS

Last Name	No.	Yds	Avg	TD
T. Brown	20	562	28	2
Matson	26	544	21	0
Martin	4	132	33	0
W. Brown	4	58	15	0
Nelson	2	34	17	0
Whittingham	2	33	17	0
Beisler	1	17	17	0
Jackson	1	16	16	0
Lince	1	13	13	0
Medved	2	10	5	0
Hawkins	1	0	0	0

PASSING – PUNTING – KICKING

PASSING	Att	Comp	%	Yds	Yd/Att	TD	Int–%	RK
Snead	226	103	46	1275	5.6	8	11– 5	16
K. Hill	97	53	55	571	5.9	5	7– 7	
Concannon	51	21	41	262	5.1	1	4– 8	
Lang	3	2	67	51	17.0	0	0– 0	
Gros	1	0	0	0	0.0	0	0– 0	

PUNTING	No	Avg
Baker	42	41.1
K. Hill	23	37.5

KICKING	XP	Att	%	FG	Att	%
Baker	38	39	97	18	25	72

ST. LOUIS CARDINALS

RUSHING

Last Name	No.	Yds	Avg	TD
Roland	192	695	3.6	5
Gautt	110	370	3.4	1
Crenshaw	94	360	3.8	0
Johnson	20	39	2.0	2
Bryant	5	31	6.2	0
Gambrell	3	26	8.7	0
Nofsinger	18	25	1.4	2
Triplett	13	25	1.9	0
Stovall	1	17	17.0	0
Smith	1	8	8.0	0
Shivers	1	5	5.0	0

RECEIVING

Last Name	No.	Yds	Avg	TD
Smith	45	810	18	3
Conrad	34	388	11	2
Gambrell	24	409	17	5
Roland	21	213	10	0
Randle	17	218	13	2
Gautt	16	114	7	1
Crenshaw	15	46	3	0
Shivers	5	81	16	0
Triplett	2	6	3	0
Sortun	1	7	7	0

PUNT RETURNS

Last Name	No.	Yds	Avg	TD
Roland	20	221	11	1
Shivers	16	49	3	0
Gambrell	4	46	12	0

KICKOFF RETURNS

Last Name	No.	Yds	Avg	TD
Shivers	27	762	28	1
Roland	15	347	23	0
Williams	7	132	19	0
Bryant	2	70	35	0
Gambrell	1	16	16	0
Roy	2	10	5	0
Long	1	9	9	0
Melinkovich	1	2	2	0
Ogden	1	0	0	0

PASSING – PUNTING – KICKING

PASSING	Att	Comp	%	Yds	Yd/Att	TD	Int–%	RK
Johnson	205	103	50	1334	6.5	10	11– 5	9
Nofsinger	162	68	42	799	4.9	2	8– 5	18
Hart	11	4	36	29	2.6	0	0– 0	
Roland	8	5	63	130	16.3	1	0– 0	

PUNTING	No	Avg
Smith	47	37.9
Bakken	29	33.1
Stovall	5	27.8

KICKING	XP	Att	%	FG	Att	%
Bakken	27	28	96	23	40	58

WASHINGTON REDSKINS

RUSHING

Last Name	No.	Yds	Avg	TD
Whitfield	93	472	5.1	2
Taylor	87	262	3.0	3
Thurlow	80	260	3.3	0
Looney	63	220	3.5	4
Mitchell	13	141	10.8	0
Rector	9	40	4.4	0
Barrington	10	37	3.7	0
Jurgensen	12	14	1.2	0
Shiner	1	10	10.0	0
Kantor	1	2	2.0	0

RECEIVING

Last Name	No.	Yds	Avg	TD
Taylor	72	1119	16	12
Mitchell	58	905	16	9
Smith	54	686	13	6
Thurlow	23	165	7	0
Whitfield	18	101	6	1
Looney	12	49	4	0
Richter	7	100	14	0
Kupp	4	28	7	0
Mazurek	2	28	14	0
Barrington	2	23	12	0
Rector	2	9	5	0
Burrell	1	9	9	0
Johnson	1	1	1	0

PUNT RETURNS

Last Name	No.	Yds	Avg	TD
Harris	18	108	6	1
Taylor	5	63	13	0
Mitchell	4	21	5	0
Mazurek	2	9	5	0

KICKOFF RETURNS

Last Name	No.	Yds	Avg	TD
Mazurek	21	505	24	0
Harris	20	405	20	0
Looney	13	265	20	0
Taylor	3	98	33	0
Rector	3	65	22	0
Barrington	2	39	20	0
Croftcheck	2	36	18	0
Kantor	2	35	18	0
Jackson	2	26	13	0
Johnson	2	22	11	0
Barnes	1	14	14	0
Goosby	1	0	0	0

PASSING – PUNTING – KICKING

PASSING	Att	Comp	%	Yds	Yd/Att	TD	Int–%	RK
Jurgensen	436	254	58	3209	7.4	28	19– 4	2
Shiner	5	0	0	0	0.0	0	1– 20	
Barrington	1	0	0	0	0.0	0	0– 0	
Mitchell	1	1	100	21	21.0	0	0– 0	

PUNTING	No	Avg
Richter	68	42.4

KICKING	XP	Att	%	FG	Att	%
Gogolak	39	41	95	22	34	65

EASTERN CONFERENCE – Continued

PITTSBURGH STEELERS 5-8-1 Bill Austin

Scores of Each Game		
34	NEW YORK	34
17	DETROIT	3
27	WASHINGTON	33
10	Washington	24
10	Cleveland	41
14	PHILADELPHIA	31
21	Dallas	52
16	CLEVELAND	6
20	ST. LOUIS	9
7	DALLAS	20
3	St. Louis	6
23	Philadelphia	27
47	New York	28
57	Atlanta	33

Use Name	Pos.	Hgt	Wgt	Age	Int	Pts
Charlie Bradshaw	OT	6'6"	260	30		
Dan James	OT	6'4"	250	29		
Fran O'Brien (from WAS)	OT	6'1"	255	30		
Roger Pillath	OT	6'4"	242	24		
Larry Gagner	OG	6'3"	240	22		
Mike Magac	OG	6'3"	240	28		
Eli Strand	OG	6'2"	250	23		
Ralph Wenzel	OG	6'3"	240	23		
Pat Killorin	C	6'2"	220	22		
Ray Mansfield	C	6'3"	250	25		
John Baker	DE	6'6"	270	31		
Ben McGee	DE	6'2"	225	24		
Tim Powell	DE	6'4"	248	22		
Riley Gunnels	DT	6'3"	253	29	1	
Chuck Hinton	DT	6'5"	260	27		
Ken Kortas	DT	6'2"	280	24		
Lloyd Voss	DT	6'4"	260	24		
Rod Breedlove	LB	6'2"	227	28	2	
Gene Breen	LB	6'2"	230	25		
John Campbell	LB	6'3"	225	27	2	
Andy Russell	LB	6'3"	215	24		7
Bill Saul	LB	6'4"	225	25	2	
Bob Schmitz (to MIN)	LB	6'1"	240	28		
Jim Bradshaw	DB	6'1"	205	27	4	6
Willie Daniel	DB	5'11"	185	28		
Bob Hohn	DB	6'	190	25		
Brady Keys	DB	6'	198	30	4	
Paul Martha	DB	6'	185	23	3	
Clendon Thomas	DB	6'2"	205	29	2	6
Marv Woodson	DB	6'	195	23	4	6
Theron Sapp – Injury						
George Izo	QB	6'3"	218	29		
Ron Meyer	QB	6'4"	205	22		
Bill Nelsen	QB	6'	195	25		
Ron Smith	QB	6'5"	220	24		
Amos Bullocks	HB	6'1"	202	27		12
Cannonball Butler	HB	5'10"	185	23		24
Dick Hoak	HB	5'11"	190	27		6
Bobby Smith	HB	6'	203	24		
Dick Leftridge	FB	6'2"	240	21		12
Mike Lind	FB	6'2"	225	26		
Willie Asbury	FB	6'1"	230	23		54
Roy Jefferson	FL	6'2"	195	22		24
John Hilton	TE	6'5"	220	24		24
Tony Jeter	TE	6'3"	220	22		
Steve Smith	TE	6'5"	240	22		
Jerry Simmons	OE	6'1"	190	23		6
J. R. Wilburn	OE	6'2"	190	23		
Gary Ballman	FL-OE	6'	200	26		30
Mike Clark	K	6'1"	205	25		97
Frank Lambert	K	6'3"	200	23		

ATLANTA FALCONS 3-11-0 Norb Hecker

Scores of Each Game		
14	LOS ANGELES	19
10	Philadelphia	23
10	Detroit	28
14	DALLAS	47
20	Washington	33
7	SAN FRANCISCO	44
3	Green Bay	56
17	CLEVELAND	49
7	BALTIMORE	19
27	New York	16
6	Chicago	23
20	Minnesota	13
16	ST. LOUIS	10
33	PITTSBURGH	57

Use Name	Pos.	Hgt	Wgt	Age	Int	Pts
Rich Koeper	OT	6'4"	245	23		
Errol Linden	OT	6'5"	260	29		
Jim Simon	OT	6'5"	235	25		
Don Talbert	OT	6'5"	240	26		
Lou Kirouac	OG	6'3"	240	25		46
Ed Cook	OG	6'2"	250	34		
Dan Grimm	OG	6'3"	245	25		
Frank Marchlewski	C	6'2"	238	22		
Bob Whitlow	C	6'1"	236	30		
Bobby Richards	DE	6'2"	247	27		
Sam Williams	DE	6'5"	235	35		
Karl Rubke	DE	6'4"	244	30		
Jerry Jones	DT-DE	6'3"	277	22		
Bud Marshall (from WAS)	DT	6'5"	270	24		
Guy Reese	DT	6'5"	260	26		
Chuck Sieminski	DT	6'4"	265	26		
Joe Szczercko	DT	6'	245	24		
Ralph Heck	LB	6'2"	230	25		
Bill Jobko	LB	6'2"	235	30	2	
Larry Morris	LB	6'2"	230	31		
Tommy Nobis	LB	6'2"	230	22		
Marion Rushing	LB	6'2"	230	29	3	
Lee Calland	DB	6'	190	25	3	
Nick Rassas	DB	6'	190	22		
Ken Reaves	DB	6'3"	200	21	1	
Jerry Richardson	DB	6'3"	190	23	5	
Bob Riggle	DB	6'1"	200	22	3	6
Carl Silvestri	DB	6'	195	23		
Tommy Tolleson	DB	6'	185	23		
Ron Smith	HB-DB	6'1"	180	23	2	
Dennis Claridge	QB	6'3"	225	24		
Randy Johnson	QB	6'3"	195	22		24
Steve Sloan	QB	6'1"	185	22		
Junior Coffey	HB	6'1"	210	24		30
Perry Lee Dunn	HB	6'2"	200	23		
Rudy Johnson	HB	5'11"	190	24		
Preston Ridlehuber	HB	6'2"	215	22		12
Jimmy Sidle	TE-HB	6'2"	215	23		
Charlie Scales	FB	5'11"	215	27		
Ernie Wheelwright	FB	6'3"	240	29		36
Bill Wolski	FB	5'11"	203	22		
Glenn Glass (to DEN-A)	FL	6'	203	29		
Bob Sherlag	FL	6'	197	23		6
Gary Barnes	OE-FL	6'4"	210	26		6
Alex Hawkins	OE-FL	6'1"	186	29		12
Taz Anderson	TE	6'2"	215	27		18
Billy Martin	TE	6'4"	240	23		
Hugh McInnis	TE	6'3"	220	28		
Vern Burke	OE	6'4"	202	25		6
Angie Coia	OE	6'2"	196	28		
Tom Hutchinson	OE	6'1"	190	25		
Billy Lothridge	K	6'1"	194	22		
Wade Traynham	K	6'2"	218	24		2

NEW YORK GIANTS 1-12-1 Allie Sherman

Scores of Each Game		
34	Pittsburgh	34
7	Dallas	52
17	Philadelphia	35
7	CLEVELAND	28
19	St. Louis	24
13	WASHINGTON	10
3	PHILADELPHIA	31
17	ST. LOUIS	20
14	Los Angeles	55
16	ATLANTA	27
41	Washington	72
40	Cleveland	49
28	PITTSBURGH	47
7	DALLAS	17

Use Name	Pos.	Hgt	Wgt	Age	Int	Pts
Roger Davis	OT	6'3"	240	28		
Francis Peay	OT	6'5"	250	22		
Willie Young	OT	6'	247	23		
Bob Scholtz	C-OT	6'4"	250	28		
Bookie Bolin	OG	6'2"	240	26		
Pete Case	OG	6'3"	245	25		
Darrell Dess (from WAS)	OG	6'	245	30		
Charlie Harper	OG	6'2"	248	22		
Greg Larson	C	6'2"	250	27		
Joe Wellborn	C	6'2"	215	20		
Glen Condren	DE	6'2"	250	24		
Rosey Davis	DE	6'5"	260	24		
Jim Garcia	DE	6'4"	250	22		
Jim Katcavage	DE	6'3"	240	31		
Bill Matan	DE	6'4"	240	22		
Don Davis	DT	6'6"	260	22		
Jim Moran	DT	6'5"	270	23		
Jim Prestel	DT	6'5"	275	29		
Mike Ciccolella	LB	6'1"	235	22		
Jerry Hillebrand	LB	6'3"	240	26	1	6
Stan Sczurek	LB	5'11"	230	27		
Jeff Smith	LB	6'	237	22	1	
Larry Vargo	LB	6'3"	215	26	1	
Henry Carr	DB	6'3"	195	23	4	6
Clarence Childs	DB	6'	180	27	2	6
Phil Harris	DB	6'	195	21		
Wendell Harris	DB	5'11"	185	25	1	6
Spider Lockhart	DB	6'2"	175	23	6	
Dick Lynch	DB	6'1"	198	30		
Jimmy Patton	DB	6'	185	34	1	
Tucker Frederickson – Knee Injury						
Bill Swain – Knee Injury						
Tom Kennedy	QB	6'1"	200	27		
Earl Morrall	QB	6'1"	206	32		
Gary Wood	QB	5'11"	188	23		18
Steve Bowman	HB	6'	195	21		
Allen Jacobs	FB	6'1"	215	25		6
Dan Lewis	HB	6'1"	200	30		6
Smith Reed	HB	6'	215	24		
Ernie Koy	FB-HB	6'2"	230	23		
Chuck Mercein	FB	6'3"	230	23		
Pep Menefee	FL	6'1"	198	24		
Joe Morrison	HB-FB-FL	6'1"	212	28		48
Bob Crespino	TE	6'4"	225	28		12
Aaron Thomas	TE	6'3"	210	28		24
Freeman White	LB-TE	6'5"	225	22		
Del Shofner	OE	6'3"	185	30		
Homer Jones	FL-OE	6'2"	205	25		48
Pete Gogolak	K	6'2"	200	24		77

WESTERN CONFERENCE

GREEN BAY PACKERS 12-2-0 Vince Lombardi

Scores of Each Game		
24	BALTIMORE	3
21	Cleveland	20
24	LOS ANGELES	13
23	DETROIT	14
20	San Francisco	21
17	Chicago	0
56	ATLANTA	3
31	Detroit	7
17	MINNESOTA	20
13	CHICAGO	6
28	Minnesota	16
20	SAN FRANCISCO	7
14	Baltimore	10
27	Los Angeles	23

Use Name	Pos.	Hgt	Wgt	Age	Int	Pts
Bob Skoronski	OT	6'3"	250	33		
Steve Wright	OT	6'6"	250	24		
Forrest Gregg	OG-OT	6'4"	250	33		
Gale Gillingham	OG	6'3"	250	22		
Jerry Kramer	OG	6'3"	245	31		
Fuzzy Thurston	OG	6'1"	245	33		
Ken Bowman	C	6'3"	230	23		
Bill Curry	C	6'2"	235	23		
Lionel Aldridge	DE	6'4"	245	24		
Bob Brown	DE	6'5"	270	26		
Willie Davis	DE	6'3"	245	33		
Henry Jordan	DT	6'3"	250	31		
Ron Kostelnik	DT	6'4"	260	26		
Jim Weatherwax	DT	6'7"	275	23		
Lee Roy Caffey	LB	6'3"	250	26	3	6
Tommy Crutcher	LB	6'3"	230	24	1	
Ray Nitschke	LB	6'3"	240	30	2	
Dave Robinson	LB	6'3"	245	25	5	
Phil Vandersea	LB	6'3"	225	23		
Herb Adderley	DB	6'1"	210	27	4	6
Tom Brown	DB	6'1"	190	25	4	
Doug Hart	DB	6'	190	27	1	6
Dave Hathcock	DB	6'	190	23		
Bob Jeter	DB	6'1"	205	28	5	12
Willie Wood	DB	5'10"	190	30	3	6
Zeke Bratkowski	QB	6'2"	200	34		
Bart Starr	QB	6'1"	200	33		12
Donny Anderson	HB	6'3"	220	23		18
Paul Hornung	HB	6'2"	215	29		30
Elijah Pitts	HB	6'1"	205	27		60
Jim Grabowski	FB	6'2"	225	22		6
Jim Taylor	FB	6'	215	31		36
Carroll Dale	FL	6'1"	200	28		42
Bob Long	FL	6'3"	190	25		
Red Mack (from ATL)	FL	5'10"	185	29		
Bill Anderson	TE	6'3"	216	30		
Allen Brown	TE	6'5"	240	23		
Marv Fleming	TE	6'4"	235	24		12
Boyd Dowler	OE	6'5"	225	29		
Max McGee	OE	6'3"	205	34		6
Don Chandler	K	6'2"	210	31		77

BALTIMORE COLTS 9-5-0 Don Shula

Scores of Each Game		
3	Green Bay	24
38	Minnesota	23
36	SAN FRANCISCO	14
17	Chicago	27
45	DETROIT	14
20	MINNESOTA	17
17	Los Angeles	3
37	WASHINGTON	10
19	Atlanta	7
14	Detroit	20
7	LOS ANGELES	23
21	CHICAGO	16
10	GREEN BAY	14
30	San Francisco	14

Use Name	Pos.	Hgt	Wgt	Age	Int	Pts
Sam Ball	OT	6'4"	240	22		
Jim Parker	OT	6'3"	275	32		
Bob Vogel	OT	6'5"	250	24		
Glenn Ressler	C-OT	6'3"	235	22		
Dale Memmelaar	OG	6'2"	248	29		
Alex Sandusky	OG	6'1"	242	34		
Dan Sullivan	OG	6'3"	250	27		
Dick Szymanski	C	6'3"	235	34		
Ordell Braase	DE	6'4"	242	34		
Roy Hilton	DE	6'6"	240	21		
Gino Marchetti	DE	6'4"	245	40		
Lou Michaels	DE	6'2"	250	30		98
Fred Miller	DT	6'3"	245	25		
Billy Ray Smith	DT	6'4"	250	31		
Andy Stynchula	DE-DT	6'3"	250	27		
Barry Brown	LB	6'3"	230	23	1	
Jackie Burkett	LB	6'4"	228	29		
Mike Curtis	LB	6'2"	232	23		6
Ted Davis	LB	6'11"	232	24	1	
Dennis Gaubatz	LB	6'2"	232	25	2	
Don Shinnick	LB	6'	228	31	3	
Steve Stonebreaker	LB	6'3"	228	28	1	
Tom Bleick	DB	6'2"	200	23		
Bobby Boyd	DB	5'10"	190	28	6	6
George Harold	DB	6'3"	205	24		
Alvin Haymond	DB	6'	190	24	4	6
Jerry Logan	DB	6'1"	185	25	3	
Lenny Lyles	DB	6'2"	202	30	1	
Jim Welch	DB	6'	190	28		
Gary Cuozzo	QB	6'1"	195	25		
Johnny Unitas	QB	6'1"	194	33		6
Jerry Allen	HB	6'1"	205	25		
Tom Matte	HB	6'	205	27		18
Lenny Moore	FL-HB	6'1"	190	33		18
Bob Baldwin	FB-HB	6'1"	225	23		
Jerry Hill	FB	5'11"	210	26		
Tony Lorick	FB	6'1"	215	24		18
Jimmy Orr	FL	5'11"	185	30		18
Willie Richardson	FL	6'2"	198	26		12
John Mackey	TE	6'3"	217	24		54
Butch Wilson	TE	6'2"	228	24		12
Ray Berry	OE	6'2"	187	33		42
Neal Petties	OE	6'2"	198	25		
David Lee	K	6'4"	215	22		

EASTERN CONFERENCE—Continued

PITTSBURGH STEELERS

RUSHING

Last Name	No.	Yds	Avg	TD
Asbury	169	544	3.2	7
Hoak	81	212	2.6	1
Butler	46	114	2.5	2
B. Smith	24	93	3.9	0
Bullocks	29	83	2.9	1
Jefferson	2	36	18.0	0
Nelsen	6	18	3.0	0
Leftridge	8	17	2.1	2
Lind	3	4	1.3	0
Meyer	1	-2	-2.0	0
R. Smith	4	-9	-2.3	0
Izo	2	-18	-9.0	0

RECEIVING

Last Name	No.	Yds	Avg	TD
Hilton	46	603	13	4
Ballman	41	663	16	5
Jefferson	32	772	24	4
Hoak	23	239	10	0
Asbury	19	228	12	2
Wilburn	7	103	15	0
Simmons	6	68	11	1
Bullocks	5	64	13	1
Butler	4	93	23	1
B. Smith	3	26	9	0
Jeter	2	18	9	0

PUNT RETURNS

Last Name	No.	Yds	Avg	TD
Jefferson	12	29	2	0
Keys	5	11	2	0
J. Bradshaw	2	3	2	0
Simmons	2	0	0	0

KICKOFF RETURNS

Last Name	No.	Yds	Avg	TD
Ballman	20	477	24	0
Butler	17	454	27	1
Simmons	10	196	20	0
Woodson	6	113	19	0
Martha	2	39	20	0
Saul	2	35	18	0
Keys	1	18	18	0
Campbell	1	15	15	0
Lind	1	15	15	0
Russell	2	12	6	0
Leftridge	1	10	10	0
Hilton	1	0	0	0

PASSING — PUNTING — KICKING

PASSING	Att	Comp	%	Yds	Yd/Att	TD	Int-%	RK
R. Smith	181	79	44	1249	6.9	8	12- 7	12
Nelsen	112	63	56	1122	10.0	7	1- 1	
Izo	81	35	43	360	4.4	2	8- 10	
Meyer	19	7	37	59	3.1	0	1- 5	
Hoak	6	4	67	87	14.5	1	0- 0	
Asbury	1	0	0	0	0.0	0	0- 0	
Bullocks	1	0	0	0	0.0	0	0- 0	

PUNTING	No	Avg
Lambert	78	42.1

KICKING	XP	Att	%	FG	Att	%
Clark	34	34	100	21	32	66
Russell	1	1	100	0	0	0

ATLANTA FALCONS

RUSHING

Last Name	No.	Yds	Avg	TD
Coffey	199	722	3.6	4
Wheelwright	121	458	3.8	3
Ran. Johnson	35	142	4.1	4
Dunn	22	52	2.4	0
Scales	10	38	3.8	0
Ridlehuber	4	23	5.8	0
Lothridge	1	22	22.0	0
Claridge	5	15	3.0	0
Sidle	1	12	12.0	0
Rud. Johnson	3	3	1.0	0

RECEIVING

Last Name	No.	Yds	Avg	TD
Hawkins	44	661	15	2
Martin	29	330	11	0
Burke	28	348	12	1
Coffey	15	182	12	1
Wheelwright	15	137	9	3
Barnes	12	173	14	1
Anderson	10	195	20	3
Dunn	5	45	9	0
Coia	4	93	23	0
Ridlehuber	4	84	21	2
Sherlag	4	53	13	1
Scales	3	16	5	0
Hutchinson	1	28	28	0
Sidle	1	16	16	0
Marchlewski	0	1	0	0

PUNT RETURNS

Last Name	No.	Yds	Avg	TD
Smith	11	80	7	0
Rassas	4	10	3	0
Sherlag	2	8	4	0
Reaves	1	2	2	0

KICKOFF RETURNS

Last Name	No.	Yds	Avg	TD
Smith	43	1013	24	0
Rassas	8	203	25	0
Sidle	6	117	20	0
Scales	5	101	20	0
Reaves	4	85	21	0
Rushing	2	52	26	0
Morris	5	50	10	0
Dunn	2	36	18	0
Hawkins	1	30	30	0
Wolski	1	21	21	0
Coffey	1	18	18	0
Glass	1	11	11	0
Heck	1	0	0	0
Martin	1	0	0	0
Sherlag	1	0	0	0

PASSING — PUNTING — KICKING

PASSING	Att	Comp	%	Yds	Yd/Att	TD	Int-%	RK
Ran. Johnson	295	129	44	1795	6.1	12	21- 7	17
Claridge	70	40	57	471	6.7	2	2- 3	
Sloan	13	6	46	96	7.4	0	2- 15	
Dunn	2	0	0	0	0.0	0	2-100	
Lothridge	1	0	0	0	0.0	0	0- 0	

PUNTING	No	Avg
Lothridge	73	40.7

KICKING	XP	Att	%	FG	Att	%
Kirouac	19	24	79	9	18	50
Traynham	2	2	100	0	1	0

NEW YORK GIANTS

RUSHING

Last Name	No.	Yds	Avg	TD
Mercein	94	327	3.5	0
Morrison	67	275	4.1	2
Jacobs	77	273	3.5	1
Wood	28	196	7.0	3
Lewis	32	164	5.1	1
Koy	66	146	2.2	0
Jones	5	43	8.6	0
Kennedy	5	16	3.2	0
Morrall	5	12	2.4	0
Larson	0	-2	0.0	0

RECEIVING

Last Name	No.	Yds	Avg	TD
Jones	48	1044	22	8
Morrison	46	724	16	6
Thomas	43	683	16	4
Mercein	27	152	6	0
Crespino	16	167	10	2
Jacobs	10	69	7	0
Koy	8	43	5	0
Lewis	6	87	15	0
Shofner	3	19	6	0
Menefee	1	11	11	0

PUNT RETURNS

Last Name	No.	Yds	Avg	TD
Lockhart	17	113	7	0
P. Harris	5	7	1	0

KICKOFF RETURNS

Last Name	No.	Yds	Avg	TD
Childs	34	855	25	1
P. Harris	22	480	22	0
Lewis	13	214	16	0
Koy	3	20	7	0
Jacobs	2	18	9	0
White	2	14	7	0
W. Harris	1	9	9	0
Young	2	6	3	0
Rog. Davis	1	0	0	0

PASSING — PUNTING — KICKING

PASSING	Att	Comp	%	Yds	Yd/Att	TD	Int-%	RK
Wood	170	81	48	1142	6.7	6	13- 8	15
Morrall	151	71	47	1105	7.3	7	12- 8	14
Kennedy	100	55	55	748	7.5	7	6- 6	
Koy	2	0	0	0	0.0	0	0- 0	
Lewis	1	1	100	4	4.0	0	0- 0	

PUNTING	No	Avg
Koy	49	39.4
Lockhart	4	32.8

KICKING	XP	Att	%	FG	Att	%
Gogolak	29	31	94	16	28	57

WESTERN CONFERENCE

GREEN BAY PACKERS

RUSHING

Last Name	No.	Yds	Avg	TD
Taylor	204	705	3.5	4
Pitts	115	393	3.4	7
Hornung	76	200	2.6	2
Grabowski	29	127	4.4	1
Starr	21	104	5.0	2
D. Anderson	25	104	4.2	2
Chandler	1	33	33.0	0
Bratkowski	4	7	1.8	0

RECEIVING

Last Name	No.	Yds	Avg	TD
Taylor	41	331	8	2
Dale	37	876	24	7
Fleming	31	361	12	2
Dowler	29	392	14	0
Pitts	26	460	18	3
Hornung	14	192	14	3
McGee	4	91	23	1
Grabowski	4	13	3	0
Long	3	68	23	0
D. Anderson	2	33	17	0
B. Anderson	2	14	7	0

PUNT RETURNS

Last Name	No.	Yds	Avg	TD
D. Anderson	6	124	21	1
Wood	22	82	4	0
Pitts	7	9	1	0
T. Brown	2	0	0	0

KICKOFF RETURNS

Last Name	No.	Yds	Avg	TD
D. Anderson	23	533	23	0
Adderley	14	320	23	0
Vandersea	3	50	17	0
Pitts	1	0	0	0
Wood	1	0	0	0

PASSING — PUNTING — KICKING

PASSING	Att	Comp	%	Yds	Yd/Att	TD	Int-%	RK
Starr	251	156	62	2257	9.0	14	3- 1	1
Bratkowski	64	36	56	569	8.9	4	2- 3	
Pitts	2	0	0	0	0.0	0	0- 0	
Hornung	1	1	100	5	5.0	0	0- 0	

PUNTING	No	Avg
Chandler	60	40.9
D. Anderson	2	44.5

KICKING	XP	Att	%	FG	Att	%
Chandler	41	43	95	12	28	43

BALTIMORE COLTS

RUSHING

Last Name	No.	Yds	Avg	TD
Lorick	143	524	3.7	3
Hill	104	395	3.8	0
Matte	86	381	4.4	0
Moore	63	209	3.3	3
Unitas	20	44	2.2	1
Cuozzo	1	9	9.0	0
Mackey	1	-6	-6.0	0

RECEIVING

Last Name	No.	Yds	Avg	TD
Berry	56	786	14	7
Mackey	50	829	17	9
Orr	37	618	17	3
Matte	23	307	13	3
Moore	21	260	12	0
Richardson	14	246	18	2
Lorick	12	81	7	0
Hill	5	18	4	0
Wilson	3	27	9	2

PUNT RETURNS

Last Name	No.	Yds	Avg	TD
Haymond	40	347	9	0
Davis	2	7	4	0
Logan	1	3	3	0
Allen	1	0	0	0
Matte	1	0	0	0

KICKOFF RETURNS

Last Name	No.	Yds	Avg	TD
Moore	18	453	25	0
Haymond	10	223	22	0
Lorick	10	214	21	0
Curtis	3	64	21	0
Matte	3	55	18	0
Allen	3	53	18	0
Baldwin	2	18	9	0
Brown	2	14	7	0

PASSING — PUNTING — KICKING

PASSING	Att	Comp	%	Yds	Yd/Att	TD	Int-%	RK
Unitas	348	195	56	2748	7.9	22	24- 7	5
Cuozzo	50	26	52	424	8.5	4	2- 4	
Matte	3	0	0	0	0.0	0	1- 33	

PUNTING	No	Avg
Lee	49	45.6

KICKING	XP	Att	%	FG	Att	%
Michaels	35	36	97	21	39	54

WESTERN CONFERENCE – Continued

LOS ANGELES RAMS 8-6-0 George Allen

Scores of Each Game		
19	Atlanta	14
31	CHICAGO	17
13	Green Bay	24
34	SAN FRANCISCO	3
14	Detroit	7
7	Minnesota	35
10	Chicago	17
3	BALTIMORE	17
13	San Francisco	21
55	NEW YORK	14
21	MINNESOTA	6
23	Baltimore	7
23	DETROIT	3
23	GREEN BAY	27

Use Name	Pos.	Hgt	Wgt	Age	Int	Pts
Joe Carollo	OT	6'2"	263	26		
Charley Cowan	OT	6'4"	275	28		
Bob Nichols	OT	6'3"	250	23		
Don Chuy	OG	6'1"	256	25		
Ted Karras	OG	6'1"	243	33		
Joe Scibelli	OG	6'1"	264	27		
Tom Mack	OG	6'3"	245	22		
Ken Iman	C	6'1"	235	27		
Joe Wendryhoski	C	6'2"	245	27		
Bruce Anderson	DE	6'4"	230	22		
Deacon Jones	DE	6'5"	260	27	1	
Lamar Lundy	DE	6'7"	260	31	1	6
Rosey Grier	DT	6'5"	290	33		2
Earl Leggett	DT	6'3"	265	32		
Merlin Olsen	DT	6'5"	276	25		
Maxie Baughan	LB	6'1"	227	28	2	
Dan Currie	LB	6'3"	240	32		
Bill George	LB	6'2"	235	35		
Jack Pardee	LB	6'2"	230	30	2	
Myron Pottios	LB	6'2"	240	26		
Doug Woodlief	LB	6'3"	235	22		
Irv Cross	DB	6'1"	190	27	1	6
Hank Gremminger	DB	6'1"	200	33	1	
Chuck Lamson	DB	6'	190	27	5	6
Clancy Williams	DB	6'2"	198	23	8	6
George Youngblood	DB	6'3"	200	21		
Ed Meador	DB	5'11"	203	29	5	
Claude Crabb	FL-DB	6'	190	26		
Tony Guillory – Injury						
Roman Gabriel	QB	6'4"	225	26		18
Bill Munson	QB	6'2"	197	24		
Tom Moore	HB	6'	210	28		24
Les Josephson	HB	6'	210	24		6
Jim Stiger	FB-HB	5'11"	214	25		6
Dick Bass	FB	5'10"	198	29		48
Henry Dyer	FB	6'2"	225	21		
Tommy McDonald	FL	5'10"	175	32		12
Marlin McKeever	TE	6'1"	227	26		6
Dave Pivec	TE	6'3"	240	22		
Billy Truax	TE	6'5"	240	23		6
Steve Heckard	OE	6'1"	195	23		
Bucky Pope	FL-OE	6'5"	195	23		6
Jack Snow	OE	6'2"	212	23		18
Bruce Gossett	K	6'2"	230	23		113
Jon Kilgore	K	6'1"	200	22		

SAN FRANCISCO FORTY NINERS 6-6-2 Jack Christiansen

Scores of Each Game		
20	MINNESOTA	20
14	Baltimore	36
3	Los Angeles	34
21	GREEN BAY	20
44	Atlanta	7
27	DETROIT	24
3	Minnesota	28
21	LOS ANGELES	13
30	Chicago	30
34	PHILADELPHIA	35
41	Detroit	14
7	Green Bay	20
41	CHICAGO	14
14	BALTIMORE	30

Use Name	Pos.	Hgt	Wgt	Age	Int	Pts
Dave McCormick	OT	6'6"	250	23		
Walt Rock	OT	6'5"	257	25		
Len Rohde	OT	6'4"	255	28		
Howard Mudd	OG	6'3"	263	24		
John Thomas	OG	6'4"	250	31		
Jim Wilson	OG	6'3"	255	25		
Bruce Bosley	C	6'2"	246	32		
Joe Cerne	C	6'2"	235	23		
Stan Hindman	DE	6'3"	232	22		
Clark Miller	DE	6'5"	245	27		
Jim Norton	DT-DE	6'4"	255	23		
Charlie Johnson	DT	6'2"	266	22		
Charlie Krueger	DT	6'4"	267	30		
Roland Lakes	DT	6'4"	285	26		
Ed Beard	LB	6'2"	225	26		
Mike Dowdle	LB	6'3"	248	28	1	6
Bob Harrison	LB	6'2"	225	29		
Matt Hazeltine	LB	6'1"	230	33	1	6
Dave Wilcox	LB	6'3"	234	23		
Kermit Alexander	DB	5'11"	186	25	4	12
George Donnelly	DB	6'3"	205	23	2	
Jim Johnson	DB	6'2"	187	28	4	6
Elbert Kimbrough	DB	5'11"	196	27	3	
Mel Phillips	DB	6'	188	24		
Al Randolph	DB	6'2"	190	22	3	6
John Brodie	QB	6'1"	210	31		18
Billy Kilmer	QB	6'	204	26		
George Mira	QB	5'11"	192	24		
John David Crow	HB	6'2"	224	31		24
Bob Daugherty	HB	6'2"	205	24		
Jim Jackson	HB	6'	180	22		6
Dave Kopay	HB	6'2"	225	24		12
Gary Lewis	FB	6'3"	230	24		18
Ken Willard	FB	6'2"	230	23		42
Bernie Casey	FL	6'4"	210	27		6
Kay McFarland	FL	6'2"	186	27		6
Dick Witcher	FL	6'3"	210	21		6
Kent Kramer	TE	6'5"	230	22		18
Monte Stickles	TE	6'4"	235	28		12
Dave Parks	OE	6'2"	207	24		30
Wayne Swinford	OE	6'	200	23		
Tommy Davis	K	6'	220	31		86

CHICAGO BEARS 5-7-2 George Halas

Scores of Each Game		
3	Detroit	14
17	Los Angeles	31
13	Minnesota	10
27	BALTIMORE	17
0	GREEN BAY	17
17	LOS ANGELES	10
17	St. Louis	24
10	DETROIT	10
30	SAN FRANCISCO	30
6	Green Bay	13
23	ATLANTA	6
16	Baltimore	21
14	San Francisco	41
41	MINNESOTA	28

Use Name	Pos.	Hgt	Wgt	Age	Int	Pts
Herm Lee	OT	6'4"	247	35		
Riley Mattson	OT	6'4"	255	27		
Bob Wetoska	OT	6'3"	240	28		
Jim Cadile	OG	6'3"	240	25		
Mike Rabold	OG	6'2"	238	29		
George Seals	OT-OG	6'2"	260	23		
Roger LeClerc	C	6'3"	235	28		78
Mike Pyle	C	6'3"	250	27		
Doug Atkins	DE	6'8"	255	36	1	
Ed O'Bradovich	DE	6'3"	255	26		6
Brian Schweda	DE	6'3"	240	23		
Frank Cornish	DT	6'6"	285	22		
Dick Evey	DT	6'2"	225	25		
John Johnson	DT	6'5"	260	25		
Bob Kilcullen	DT	6'3"	245	30		
Doug Buffone	LB	6'1"	218	22		
Dick Butkus	LB	6'3"	245	22	1	
Joe Fortunato	LB	6'	225	36	1	6
Jim Purnell	LB	6'2"	225	24		
Mike Reilly	LB	6'2"	238	23		
Charlie Brown	DB	6'1"	193	23		
Curtis Gentry	DB	6'	187	25	1	
Benny McRae	DB	6'1"	180	25	3	
Richie Petitbon	DB	6'3"	205	28	4	
Rosey Taylor	DB	5'11"	186	27	1	
Dave Whitsell	DB	6'	190	30	3	
Andy Livingston - Knee Injury						
Rudy Bukich	QB	6'1"	205	35		12
Larry Rakestraw	QB	6'2"	195	24		
Billy Wade	QB	6'2"	205	35		
Jon Arnett	HB	5'11"	203	31		6
Gale Sayers	HB	6'	198	23		72
Brian Piccolo	FB-HB	6'	205	22		
Ralph Kurek	FB	6'2"	210	23		6
Joe Marconi	FB	6'2"	225	32		
Ronnie Bull	HB-FB	6'	200	26		
Johnny Morris	FL	5'10"	180	31		
Duane Allen	TE	6'4"	225	28		
Charlie Bivins	TE	6'2"	212	27		
Mike Ditka	TE	6'3"	230	26		12
Dick Gordon	OE	5'11"	190	21		6
Jim Jones	OE	6'2"	187	22		30
Bobby Joe Green	K	5'11"	175	28		

DETROIT LIONS 4-9-1 Harry Gilmer

Scores of Each Game		
14	CHICAGO	3
3	Pittsburgh	17
28	ATLANTA	10
14	Green Bay	23
7	LOS ANGELES	14
14	Baltimore	45
24	San Francisco	27
7	GREEN BAY	31
10	Chicago	10
32	Minnesota	31
20	BALTIMORE	14
14	SAN FRANCISCO	41
3	Los Angeles	23
16	MINNESOTA	28

Use Name	Pos.	Hgt	Wgt	Age	Int	Pts
Daryl Sanders	OT	6'5"	250	24		
Roger Shoals	OT	6'4"	255	27		
J. D. Smith	OT	6'5"	250	30		
John Gordy	OG	6'3"	250	30		
Bob Kowalkowski	OG	6'3"	245	22		
Doug Van Horn	OG	6'2"	245	22		
Mike Alford	C	6'3"	235	23		
Ed Flanagan	C	6'3"	250	22		
Larry Hand	DE	6'4"	245	26		
Jerry Mazzanti	DE	6'3"	240	26		
Darris McCord	DE	6'4"	250	33		
Roger Brown	DT	6'5"	300	29		
Alex Karras	DT	6'2"	245	30		
Jerry Rush	DT	6'4"	270	24		
Ernie Clark	LB	6'1"	220	28	1	
Bill Cody	LB	6'1"	220	22		
Wally Hilgenberg	LB	6'3"	225	23		
Mike Lucci	LB	6'2"	223	26	5	6
Lou Slaby	LB	6'3"	235	24		
Wayne Walker	LB	6'2"	225	29	1	17
Jim Kearney	DB	6'2"	200	23		
Dick LeBeau	DB	6'1"	185	29	4	
Bruce Maher	DB	5'11"	190	29	5	
Wayne Rasmussen	DB	6'2"	180	24	3	
Bobby Smith	DB	6'	197	28		
Bobby Thompson	DB	5'10"	175	26	4	
Tom Vaughn	DB	5'11"	195	23	1	
Tom Watkins – Operation						
Warren Wells – Military Service						
Tom Myers	QB	6'	188	22		
Milt Plum	QB	6'1"	205	32		1
Karl Sweetan	QB	6'1"	210	23		6
Bobby Felts	HB	6'2"	202	23		12
Amos Marsh	HB	6'1"	220	27		18
Bruce McLenna	HB	6'3"	225	24		
Jim Todd	HB	5'11"	195	23		
Tom Nowatzke	FB	6'3"	233	23		42
Pat Studstill	FL	6'1"	175	28		30
Willie Walker	FL	6'3"	200	23		
Johnnie Robinson	DB-FL	6'3"	205	21		6
Jim Gibbons	TE	6'2"	220	30		6
Ron Kramer	TE	6'3"	240	31		
Gail Cogdill	OE	6'2"	195	29		6
Bill Malinchak	OE	6'1"	190	22		
John Henderson	FL-OE	6'3"	190	23		
Garo Yepremian	K	5'8"	160	22		50

MINNESOTA VIKINGS 4-9-1 Norm Van Brocklin

Scores of Each Game		
20	San Francisco	20
23	BALTIMORE	38
17	Dallas	28
10	CHICAGO	13
35	LOS ANGELES	7
17	Baltimore	20
28	SAN FRANCISCO	3
20	Green Bay	17
31	DETROIT	32
6	Los Angeles	21
16	GREEN BAY	28
13	ATLANTA	20
28	Detroit	16
28	Chicago	41

Use Name	Pos.	Hgt	Wgt	Age	Int	Pts
Doug Davis	OT	6'4"	240	22		
Chuck Arrobio	OT	6'4"	250	22		
Grady Alderman	OT	6'2"	240	27		
Archie Sutton	OT	6'4"	262	23		
Larry Bowie	OG	6'2"	250	26		
Milt Sunde	OG	6'2"	234	23		
Jim Vellone	OG	6'2"	255	22		
Mick Tinglehoff	C	6'1"	237	26		
Carl Eller	DE	6'6"	255	24		
Jim Marshall	DE	6'3"	235	28		
Paul Dickson	DT	6'5"	255	29		
Gary Larsen	DT	6'5"	250	26		
Jerry Shay	DT	6'3"	240	22		
Mike Tilleman	DT	6'5"	260	22		
Don Hansen	LB	6'3"	226	22		
John Kirby	LB	6'3"	222	24		
Dave Tobey	LB	6'3"	230	23		
Lonnie Warwick	LB	6'3"	225	24	2	
Roy Winston	LB	6'1"	230	26		
Mike Fitzgerald	DB	5'10"	180	25	1	
Dale Hackbart	DB	6'3"	210	30	5	6
Jeff Jordan	DB	6'4"	190	22		
Karl Kassulke	DB	6'	193	24	2	
Earsell Mackbee	DB	6'1"	195	25	2	
George Rose	DB	5'11"	190	23	1	
Ed Sharockman	DB	6'	200	26	1	
Ken Byers – Injury						
Bob Berry	QB	5'11"	190	24		
Fran Tarkenton	QB	6'1"	190	26		24
Ron Vander Kelen	QB	6'1"	185	26		
Billy Barnes	HB	5'11"	202	31		6
Jim Lindsey	HB	6'2"	200	21		18
Tommy Mason	HB	6'	196	27		18
Dave Osborn	HB	6'	205	23		18
Jeff Williams	HB	6'1"	210	22		
Jim Young	HB	6'	205	23		
Bill Brown	FB	5'11"	230	28		36
Phil King	HB-FB	6'4"	220	30		6
Jim Phillips	FL	6'1"	195	29		18
Lance Rentzel	OE-FL	6'2"	210	22		
Hal Bedsole	TE	6'4"	230	24		
Preston Carpenter (from WAS)	TE	6'2"	208	32		24
John Powers	TE	6'2"	210	25		
Paul Flatley	OE	6'1"	187	25		18
Tom Hall	FL-OE	6'1"	195	25		12
Fred Cox	K	5'10"	200	27		88
Bobby Walden	K	6'	195	28		

WESTERN CONFERENCE — Continued

LOS ANGELES RAMS

RUSHING

Last Name	No.	Yds	Avg	TD
Bass	248	1090	4.4	8
Moore	104	272	2.6	1
Gabriel	52	179	3.4	3
Josephson	14	97	6.9	0
Stiger	24	95	4.0	0
Meador	1	7	7.0	0
Munson	4	3	0.8	0
Iman	1	2	2.0	0

RECEIVING

Last Name	No.	Yds	Avg	TD
Moore	60	433	7	3
McDonald	55	714	13	2
Snow	34	634	19	3
Bass	31	274	9	0
Truax	29	314	11	0
McKeever	23	277	12	1
Stiger	8	72	9	1
Heckard	5	102	20	0
Josephson	2	10	5	1
Crabb	1	47	47	0
Pope	1	14	14	1

PUNT RETURNS

Last Name	No.	Yds	Avg	TD
Stiger	33	259	8	0
Cross	12	82	7	0

KICKOFF RETURNS

Last Name	No.	Yds	Avg	TD
Williams	15	420	28	0
Cross	12	348	29	0
Stiger	7	150	21	0
Dyer	5	61	12	0
Currie	1	25	25	0
McKeever	1	8	8	0
Lamson	1	3	3	0

PASSING — PUNTING — KICKING

PASSING	Att	Comp	%	Yds	Yd/Att	TD	Int–%	RK
Gabriel	397	217	55	2540	6.4	10	16– 4	7
Munson	50	30	60	284	5.7	2	1– 2	
Kilgore	1	1	100	47	47.0	0	0– 0	
Meador	1	0	0	0	0.0	0	0– 0	
Moore	1	1	100	20	20.0	0	0– 0	

PUNTING	No	Avg
Kilgore	71	42.8

KICKING	XP	Att	%	FG	Att	%
Gossett	29	29	100	28	49	57

SAN FRANCISCO FORTY NINERS

RUSHING

Last Name	No.	Yds	Avg	TD
Willard	191	763	4.0	5
Crow	121	477	3.9	1
Kopay	47	204	4.3	1
Lewis	36	130	3.6	2
Mira	10	103	10.3	0
Davis	3	43	14.3	0
Casey	1	23	23.0	0
Kilmer	3	23	7.7	0
Brodie	5	18	3.6	3
Jackson	4	7	1.8	0
Parks	1	−1	−1.0	0

RECEIVING

Last Name	No.	Yds	Avg	TD
Parks	66	974	15	5
Casey	50	669	13	1
Willard	42	351	8	2
Crow	30	341	11	3
Stickles	27	315	12	2
McFarland	13	219	17	1
Witcher	10	115	12	1
Kopay	10	67	7	1
Lewis	7	44	6	1
Kramer	5	81	16	3
Jackson	1	63	63	1

PUNT RETURNS

Last Name	No.	Yds	Avg	TD
Alexander	30	198	7	1
Kopay	4	28	7	0
Swinford	8	12	2	0
Jackson	2	0	0	0
Donnelly	1	0	0	0

KICKOFF RETURNS

Last Name	No.	Yds	Avg	TD
Alexander	37	984	27	0
Jackson	8	162	20	0
Swinford	4	73	18	0
Lewis	3	65	22	0
Kopay	2	20	10	0
Phillips	1	20	20	0
Hindman	1	2	2	0

PASSING — PUNTING — KICKING

PASSING	Att	Comp	%	Yds	Yd/Att	TD	Int–%	RK
Brodie	427	232	54	2810	6.6	16	22– 5	8
Mira	53	22	42	284	5.4	5	2– 4	
Kilmer	16	5	31	84	5.3	0	1– 6	
Crow	4	2	50	61	15.3	0	1– 25	

PUNTING	No	Avg
Davis	63	41.4
Kilmer	7	33.4

KICKING	XP	Att	%	FG	Att	%
Davis	38	39	97	16	31	52

CHICAGO BEARS

RUSHING

Last Name	No.	Yds	Avg	TD
Sayers	229	1231	5.4	8
Bull	100	318	3.2	0
Kurek	52	179	3.4	3
Arnett	55	178	3.2	1
Bukich	18	14	0.8	2
Piccolo	3	12	4.0	0
Marconi	3	5	1.7	0
Gordon	1	2	2.0	0
Rakestraw	1	−5	−5.0	0
Jones	1	−7	−7.0	0

RECEIVING

Last Name	No.	Yds	Avg	TD
Sayers	34	447	13	2
Ditka	32	378	12	2
Jones	28	504	18	5
Bull	20	174	9	0
Gordon	15	210	14	1
Kurek	10	178	18	0
Arnett	10	42	4	0
Morris	5	49	10	0
Allen	3	28	9	0
Bivins	2	6	3	0

PUNT RETURNS

Last Name	No.	Yds	Avg	TD
Arnett	15	58	4	0
Sayers	6	44	7	0
Gordon	4	−5	−1	0

KICKOFF RETURNS

Last Name	No.	Yds	Avg	TD
Sayers	23	718	31	2
Gordon	19	521	27	0
Arnett	2	39	20	0
Butkus	3	32	11	0
Taylor	1	3	3	0
Brown	0	28	0	0

PASSING — PUNTING — KICKING

PASSING	Att	Comp	%	Yds	Yd/Att	TD	Int–%	RK
Bukich	309	147	48	1858	6.0	10	21– 7	13
Wade	21	9	43	79	3.8	0	1– 5	
Sayers	6	2	33	58	9.7	0	1– 17	
Arnett	1	0	0	0	0	0	0– 0	
Bull	1	1	100	21	21.0	0	0– 0	

PUNTING	No	Avg
Green	80	42.0

KICKING	XP	Att	%	FG	Att	%
Leclerc	24	25	96	18	30	60

DETROIT LIONS

RUSHING

Last Name	No.	Yds	Avg	TD
Nowatzke	151	512	3.4	6
Marsh	134	433	3.2	3
Sweetan	34	219	6.4	1
Felts	34	83	2.4	2
Plum	12	59	4.9	0
McLenna	16	51	3.2	0
Studstill	2	20	10.0	0
Todd	2	6	3.0	0
Wil. Walker	1	4	4.0	0

RECEIVING

Last Name	No.	Yds	Avg	TD
Studstill	67	1266	19	5
Nowatzke	54	316	6	1
Cogdill	47	411	9	1
Kramer	37	432	12	0
Marsh	12	111	9	0
Henderson	6	121	20	0
Malinchak	5	34	7	0
McLenna	3	13	4	0
Felts	2	1	1	0
Wil. Walker	1	21	21	0
Gibbons	1	2	2	1

PUNT RETURNS

Last Name	No.	Yds	Avg	TD
Robinson	13	185	14	1
Vaughn	18	179	10	0
Felts	2	20	10	0
Todd	5	12	2	0

KICKOFF RETURNS

Last Name	No.	Yds	Avg	TD
Vaughn	23	595	26	0
Felts	20	392	20	0
Robinson	6	127	21	0
Todd	3	105	35	0
Slaby	1	14	14	0
Mazzanti	1	8	8	0
Alford	1	0	0	0

PASSING — PUNTING — KICKING

PASSING	Att	Comp	%	Yds	Yd/Att	TD	Int–%	RK
Sweetan	309	157	51	1809	5.9	4	14– 5	11
Plum	146	82	56	943	6.5	4	13– 9	10
Myers	1	0	0	0	0.0	0	1–100	

PUNTING	No	Avg
Studstill	72	41.1

KICKING	XP	Att	%	FG	Att	%
Yepremian	11	11	100	13	22	59
Way. Walker	11	11	100	2	8	25
Plum	1	1	100	0	0	0

MINNESOTA VIKINGS

RUSHING

Last Name	No.	Yds	Avg	TD
Brown	251	829	3.3	6
Tarkenton	62	376	6.1	4
Osborn	87	344	4.0	1
Mason	58	235	4.1	2
Lindsey	57	146	2.6	1
Walden	5	82	16.4	0
King	17	40	2.4	0
Vender Kelen	4	19	4.8	0
Barnes	5	16	3.2	1
Berry	3	12	4.0	0
Williams	1	2	2.0	0
Carpenter	1	−10	−10.0	0

RECEIVING

Last Name	No.	Yds	Avg	TD
Flatley	50	777	16	3
Brown	37	359	10	0
Phillips	32	554	17	3
Carpenter	30	518	17	4
Hall	23	271	12	2
Lindsey	20	250	13	2
Osborn	15	141	9	2
Mason	7	39	6	1
King	2	24	12	1
Rentzel	2	10	5	0
Barnes	1	20	20	0

PUNT RETURNS

Last Name	No.	Yds	Avg	TD
Sharockman	9	95	11	0
Rentzel	11	16	1	0
Mason	3	9	3	0
Young	2	7	4	0
Lindsey	2	4	2	0
Williams	4	−2	−1	0

KICKOFF RETURNS

Last Name	No.	Yds	Avg	TD
Fitzgerald	14	301	22	0
Rentzel	9	181	20	0
Hall	7	141	20	0
Young	5	105	21	0
Lindsey	4	79	20	0
King	6	78	13	0
Williams	3	61	20	0
Rose	1	20	20	0
Osborn	1	19	19	0
Winston	1	2	2	0
Sunde	1	0	0	0

PASSING — PUNTING — KICKING

PASSING	Att	Comp	%	Yds	Yd/Att	TD	Int–%	RK
Tarkenton	358	192	54	2561	7.2	17	16– 4	6
Berry	37	13	35	215	5.8	1	5– 14	
Vander Kelen	20	10	50	147	7.4	0	1– 5	
Brown	1	0	0	0	0.0	0	0– 0	
King	1	1	100	9	9.0	0	0– 0	

PUNTING	No	Avg
Walden	60	41.1

KICKING	XP	Att	%	FG	Att	%
Cox	34	34	100	18	33	55

1966 A.F.L. Peace and the Super Bowl

After the New York Giants signed kicker Pete Gogolak away from the Buffalo Bills, the AFL owners decided to declare full-scale war against the NFL. Al Davis, the energetic young leader of the Oakland franchise, was put in charge of the war effort as Commissioner of the League, replacing Joe Foss in April, and an all-out effort was launched to steal star NFL players. Quarterbacks were special targets, with John Brodie and Roman Gabriel considered likely candidates to jump. With the bidding war for graduating collegians already costing clubs heavily, financial competition for established players would make bankruptcy a possibility for some teams. The two leagues sat down to put an end to the suicidal war, and the merger agreement was unveiled in June. Pete Rozelle became Commissioner over both leagues, the AFL agreed to pay reparations to the NFL teams, and a championship game—soon dubbed the Super Bowl—was arranged for the two league champions. By 1970, the AFL would be absorbed into the NFL, with all franchises to remain intact in their present locations. With peace at hand, Al Davis left the AFL office to return to Oakland as managing partner, just in time to preside over the opening of the new Oakland-Alameda County Coliseum. Milt Woodard took over as league president and would guide the league well up until its absorption into the NFL in 1970.

EASTERN DIVISION

Buffalo Bills—Head coach Lou Saban was looking for new challenges after winning two straight AFL championships, so he resigned to become top man at the University of Maryland. Assistant Coach Joe Collier took over the top spot and kept the Bills exactly as Saban had molded them, a tough defensive team with a ball-control offense. With a bad knee bothering Tom Sestak, Jim Dunaway and Ron McDole provided leadership in the defensive line, while the tight linebacking crew of Mike Stratton, Harry Jacobs, and John Tracey held the defense together. In the secondary, Butch Byrd, George Saimes, Hagood Clarke, and Tom Janik strangled enemy passing attacks. The Buffalo offense got help from rookies Bobby Burnett and Bobby Crockett. Burnett joined with Wray Carlton in providing the running necessary for the methodical Buffalo attack, while Crockett won the starting split-end job. The team surpassed last year's squad on paper, but lost twice to Boston during the season and headed into the final weekend a half game behind the Patriots. The Jets did their part by beating the Pats 38-28, and the Bills capitalized by defeating Denver to take their third straight Eastern title.

Boston Patriots—Jim Nance cut down on his weight and set the league on fire with his rushing in his second pro year. Using pure power plus surprising speed, Nance pounded away at defenses in work-horse fashion, gaining an AFL record 1,458 yards and eleven touchdowns for his troubles. Quarterback Babe Parilli used Nance to set up his passes, and receivers Art Graham, Gino Cappelletti, and Jim Whalen gave him targets to hit when not handing off to Nance. Parilli ran the attack so well that John Huarte, the Heisman Trophy winner obtained from the New York Jets, rarely took his warm-up wraps off. The Boston defense stuck to the same lines as in recent years, with a strong front four, a lot of blitzing from middle linebacker Nick Buoniconti, and a lukewarm secondary. With Cappelletti in top form as a place-kicker, the Pats had a final ace whenever their offense stalled in enemy territory. Coach Mike Holovak prepared his team well for the schedule, and the team twice beat the Bills during the year to take a slight lead into the final game of the year against New York, but dropped a 38-28 decision as Parilli passed for 379 yards.

New York Jets—With a wealth of young offensive talent, the Jets made an early run at the Eastern title with four straight wins to open the season. Joe Namath, Matt Snell, George Sauer, Emerson Boozer, Pete Lammons, Winston Hill, Dave Herman, and John Schmitt were all twenty-five years old or less, and veterans like Billy Mathis, Sherman Plunkett, Don Maynard, and Sam DeLuca added stability to this dynamic attack. The defense contained players of widely varied talents. Verlon Biggs, Gerry Philbin, and Al Atkinson were good young talents, but only Larry Grantham had a good season among the veterans. After the good start, several factors caught up with the Jets and dragged them back into third place. The defense had problems stopping enemy passers, Namath had problems with interceptions, and the Jets had problems winning away from Shea Stadium, beating only weak Denver and Miami teams on the road.

Houston Oilers—After losing his job with the St. Louis Cardinals, Wally Lemm returned to the Oilers as head coach for the second time. In his previous term in Texas he had taken the Oilers to a divisional crown in 1961 after being promoted to the top spot in mid-season. This year he went along mostly with the same veterans who had won for him five years ago, but the results were different, only three wins and a tie for fourth place with the fledgling Dolphins. George Blanda, Charley Hennigan, Rich Michael, Don Floyd, Freddy Glick, Bob McLeod, Jim Norton, and Bob Talamini started this year after starting for Lemm in his first regime. Veteran NFL players such as John Henry Johnson and Bernie Parrish further added to the age on the team but contributed little on the field. After opening the

season with a 45-7 win over Denver and a 31-0 thumping of Oakland, the Oilers lost most of their games the rest of the way.

Miami Dolphins—The Dolphins had problems at almost every position in their first year, but nowhere more than at quarterback. Of the two passers taken in the expansion draft, Eddie Wilson hurt a knee in training camp and missed the season, while Dick Wood had very little left in his arm. Rookie Rick Norton went out with a fractured jaw in mid-season, leaving coach George Wilson with George Wilson, Jr., his son, as the starting quarterback. Not one to be accused of nepotism, coach Wilson promoted John Stofa from the North American Football League for the last few games, and Stofa came through with four touchdown passes in the season-ending victory over Houston. Stocked mostly with over-the-hill veterans, the Dolphins got their existence off to an auspicious start when Joe Auer returned the opening kickoff of their first game all the way for a touchdown.

WESTERN DIVISION

Kansas City Chiefs—The first AFL Super Bowl representatives swept through their schedule with a powerful offense and well-coordinated defense. The Chiefs had shelled out a lot of money to halfback Mike Garrett in a pre-merger signing, and the short halfback gave the Chiefs a dangerous breakaway runner in the backfield. Curtis McClinton and Bert Coan also pitched in with hard work as ball carriers, making it hard for defenses to watch for Len Dawson passes. Chris Burford continued to run his precise patterns from the split end position, and Otis Taylor provided a deep threat at flanker with a fine sophomore season. Jim Tyrer and Ed Budde starred in the offensive line, but their comrades there showed considerably less consistency. The attack got by on the brilliance of the backs and ends, but the defense got by with a few stars and some mediocre talents.

Oakland Raiders—During Al Davis' two-month term as AFL Commissioner, the Raiders hired Johnny Rauch as their new head coach, and when Davis returned to Oakland as managing partner, some observers expected a conflict between the two men. Davis and Rauch got along well, but the Raiders finished in second place for the third time in four years. The Raiders won four of six meetings with Western opponents but lost three times to Eastern teams to kill their title chances. Despite top performances from Clem Daniels and Art Powell, the attack was a mediocre unit, but the defense played consistently well with flashes of brilliance. Tom Keating, obtained from the Buffalo Bills, used his extraordinary quickness to put a strong rush on enemy passers, and defensive ends Ben Davidson and Ike Lassiter added size to the line. The linebacking showed improvement as the young starters gained experience. The secondary was perhaps the league's best, with Dave Grayson, Kent McCloughan, and Rodger Bird each an individual star. Still, the Raiders needed a little more experience on defense and a little more punch on offense.

San Diego Chargers—The Chargers underwent a lot of changes this year, including a drop out of first place. The team's ownership changed hands in August when Barron Hilton sold the club to a group headed by Eugene Klein and Sam Schulman, and head coach Sid Gillman also sent a group of veteran players into exile. Salary disputes sent defensive linemen Ernie Ladd to Houston and Earl Faison to Miami, and the expansion draft to stock the Dolphins siphoned off defensive backs Jim Warren and Dick Westmoreland. A broken ankle sidelined middle linebacker Chuck Allen for most of the campaign, making the defense a patchwork quilt. Two veterans on offense, halfback Paul Lowe and tackle Ron Mix, suffered through off seasons, but a strong passing attack kept the Chargers rolling. Rookie Gary Garrison joined flanker Lance Alworth in a devastating receiving combo, giving quarterback John Hadl many opportunities to throw the ball. Even with all their problems, the Chargers kept the winning habit by taking their first four games, but once enemy offenses learned they could run on the San Diego line, the Chargers limped home to third place.

Denver Broncos—The Broncos scored the fewest points of any team in pro football, with problems in all sectors of the offense. Quarterbacks came and went on the Denver roster all season. John McCormick started for most of the campaign but showed very little; Mickey Slaughter, an occasional starter for the last three years, rarely got off the bench; veteran Tobin Rote came out of retirement, threw eight passes, and went right back into retirement; and rookies Max Chaboian and Scotty Glacken got late-season starting shots. With the revolving door at quarterback, end Lionel Taylor's catches fell off to thirty-five, his lowest since the AFL began. The running corps was hurt by the absence of Cookie Gilchrist, who held out into the season and was dealt to Miami, and Eldon Danehauer's injury took the best blocker out of the line. The best offense for the Broncos this year came from the kick returners, as Goldie Sellers and Nemiah Wilson scored three times on kickoff returns and Abner Haynes had the second highest average in the league for punt returns. The defense changed personnel less often than the offense but got little better results. The whole situation prompted head coach Mac Speedie to quit after two games, and assistant Ray Malavasi guided the team the rest of the way.

FINAL TEAM STATISTICS

OFFENSE

Category	BOSTON	BUFFALO	DENVER	HOUSTON	K. CITY	MIAMI	NEW YORK	OAKLAND	SAN DIEGO
FIRST DOWNS:									
Total	243	255	171	246	266	200	254	226	230
by Rushing	100	110	61	76	106	75	81	70	77
by Passing	121	126	95	144	140	103	145	144	137
by Penalty	22	19	15	26	20	22	28	12	16
RUSHING:									
Number	471	455	376	413	439	394	376	363	361
Yards	1963	1892	1173	1515	2274	1410	1442	1427	1537
Average Yards	4.2	4.2	3.1	3.7	5.2	3.6	3.8	3.9	4.3
Touchdowns	17	19	6	11	19	5	15	13	9
PASSING:									
Attempts	393	473	402	485	377	454	514	450	434
Completions	186	199	166	226	199	179	251	212	224
Completion Percentage	47.3	42.1	41.3	46.6	52.8	39.4	48.8	47.1	51.6
Passing Yards	2784	3000	2351	3168	3123	2374	3556	3425	3347
Avg. Yards per Attempt	7.1	6.3	5.8	6.5	8.3	5.2	6.9	7.6	7.7
Avg. Yards per Completion	15.0	15.1	14.2	14.0	15.7	13.3	14.2	16.2	14.9
Times Tackled Att. to Pass	25	16	37	28	30	36	9	34	32
Yards Lost Tackled	211	144	356	271	283	326	92	281	331
Net Yards	2573	2856	1995	2897	2840	2048	3464	3144	3016
Touchdowns	20	15	12	29	31	16	21	26	29
Interceptions	21	21	30	28	15	32	29	26	15
Percent Intercepted	5.3	4.4	7.5	5.8	4.0	7.0	5.6	5.8	3.5
PUNTING:									
Number	76	69	77	69	62	82	62	74	66
Average Distance	36.5	41.2	45.2	42.2	43.8	39.4	42.5	41.6	37.0
PUNT RETURNS:									
Number	24	43	26	23	31	21	36	41	21
Yards	143	411	235	159	276	204	260	367	257
Average Yards	6.0	9.6	9.0	6.9	8.9	9.7	7.2	9.0	12.2
Touchdowns	0	2	0	0	2	0	0	0	0
KICKOFF RETURNS:									
Number	54	51	58	64	54	65	62	60	55
Yards	1145	1064	1558	1514	1148	1507	1300	1191	1282
Average Yards	21.2	20.9	26.9	23.7	21.3	23.2	21.0	19.9	23.3
Touchdowns	0	1	3	0	0	1	1	0	0
INTERCEPTION RETURNS:									
Number	22	29	13	18	33	31	21	23	27
Yards	348	472	109	259	408	522	218	380	359
Average Yards	15.8	16.3	8.4	14.4	12.4	16.8	10.4	16.5	13.3
Touchdowns	0	4	0	0	0	4	1	1	1
PENALTIES:									
Number	64	62	66	71	61	73	64	80	68
Yards	601	637	771	682	680	660	682	752	667
FUMBLES:									
Number	25	27	36	19	21	29	19	22	17
Number Lost	13	15	17	12	16	10	9	12	7
POINTS:									
Total	315	358	196	335	448	213	322	315	335
PAT (kick) Attempts	36	42	20	40	52	23	35	40	40
PAT (kick) Made	35	41	20	39	48	23	34	39	39
PAT (Rush or Pass) Attempts	2	1	2	1	3	3	3	0	1
PAT (Rush or Pass) Made	2	0	1	0	2	2	2	0	0
FG Attempts	32	38	25	30	28	22	35	30	31
FG Made	16	19	14	16	22	10	18	12	16
Percent FG Made	50.0	50.0	56.0	53.3	78.6	45.5	51.4	40.0	51.6
Safeties	0	1	0	1	0	0	1	0	0

DEFENSE

Category	BOSTON	BUFFALO	DENVER	HOUSTON	K. CITY	MIAMI	NEW YORK	OAKLAND	SAN DIEGO
FIRST DOWNS:									
Total	243	192	251	244	222	237	231	211	260
by Rushing	68	49	101	88	75	83	81	84	127
by Passing	153	131	122	131	125	140	131	106	116
by Penalty	22	12	28	25	22	14	19	21	17
RUSHING:									
Number	369	344	441	422	353	416	388	418	497
Yards	1135	1051	2029	1833	1356	1510	1524	1792	2403
Average Yards	3.1	3.1	4.6	4.3	3.8	3.6	3.9	4.3	4.8
Touchdowns	7	6	17	10	14	15	14	16	19
PASSING:									
Attempts	509	466	396	438	494	425	467	405	382
Completions	247	205	192	209	226	198	212	183	170
Completion Percentage	48.5	44.0	48.5	47.7	45.8	46.6	45.4	45.2	44.5
Passing Yards	3565	3307	2819	3390	2876	3281	3064	2440	2386
Avg. Yards per Attempt	7.0	7.1	7.1	7.7	5.8	7.7	6.6	6.0	6.2
Avg. Yards per Completion	14.4	16.1	14.7	16.2	12.7	16.6	14.5	13.3	14.0
Times Tackled Att. to Pass	22	32	33	21	26	16	35	36	26
Yards Lost Tackled	209	249	304	228	262	180	310	322	231
Net Yards	3356	3058	2515	3162	2614	3101	2754	2118	2155
Touchdowns	26	22	26	35	18	25	19	15	13
Interceptions	22	29	13	18	33	31	21	23	27
Percent Intercepted	4.3	6.2	3.3	4.1	6.7	7.3	4.5	5.7	7.1
PUNTING:									
Number	86	84	60	68	69	64	81	73	52
Average Distance	38.5	39.6	42.7	40.0	41.3	43.9	40.4	41.3	43.0
PUNT RETURNS:									
Number	20	20	38	37	36	40	24	35	16
Yards	127	301	296	269	359	412	121	343	84
Average Yards	6.4	15.1	7.8	7.3	10.0	10.3	5.0	9.8	5.3
Touchdowns	1	2	0	0	1	1	0	0	0
KICKOFF RETURNS:									
Number	46	65	43	60	84	46	57	56	66
Yards	988	1329	1000	1385	2045	939	1368	1268	1387
Average Yards	21.5	20.4	23.3	23.1	24.3	20.4	24.0	22.6	21.0
Touchdowns	0	0	0	1	1	0	1	1	0
INTERCEPTION RETURNS:									
Number	21	21	30	28	15	32	29	26	15
Yards	204	303	545	448	225	370	297	405	278
Average Yards	9.7	14.4	18.2	16.0	15.0	11.6	10.2	15.6	18.5
Touchdowns	2	1	2	3	2	2	2	0	1
PENALTIES:									
Number	76	55	75	69	56	79	85	54	60
Yards	757	546	576	725	592	852	883	614	527
FUMBLES:									
Number	30	19	35	25	21	25	15	28	17
Number Lost	15	9	18	13	8	15	8	17	8
POINTS:									
Total	283	225	381	396	276	362	312	288	284
PAT (kick) Attempts	36	28	46	49	28	42	36	31	32
PAT (kick) Made	34	28	46	49	28	38	34	30	31
PAT (Rush or Pass) Attempts	0	3	1	1	4	2	1	3	1
PAT (Rush or Pass) Made	0	1	1	1	1	1	1	2	1
FG Attempts	26	22	40	30	28	36	28	30	31
FG Made	11	13	17	15	18	18	18	16	17
Percent FG Made	42.3	59.1	42.5	50.0	64.3	50.0	64.3	53.3	54.8
Safeties	0	0	0	0	2	0	0	1	1

1966 AFL CHAMPIONSHIP GAME
January 1, at Buffalo
(Attendance 42,080)

Super Reps

This year's AFL title was the most desirable in the league's short history, for this year's champion would get the chance to play the NFL champion in the first Super Bowl. The Buffalo Bills had won the last two AFL titles, but the Kansas City Chiefs solved the tough Buffalo defense and scored a decisive 31-7 victory. Len Dawson passed the Chiefs into a quick 7-0 lead with a 29-yard pass to Fred Arbanas early in the game. The Bills came back to tie the score on a surprise long pass to Elbert Dubenion from Jack Kemp, but the Chiefs moved ahead 14-7 with a second-quarter touchdown pass from Dawson to Otis Taylor. Toward the end of the first half Buffalo appeared on the verge of tying the game, but a key interception spelled disaster for the Bills. With Buffalo driving and but ten yards from a touchdown, Kemp's pass was intercepted in the end zone by Johnny Robinson, who ran the ball back 72 yards to set up a 32-yard field goal by Mike Mercer and run the score to 17-7 at halftime. The third quarter passed without any scoring, and the Chiefs put the game out of reach with a pair of fourth-quarter touchdowns. Mike Garrett, the star rookie halfback, scored from the one-yard line and the 18-yard line on running plays. The Bills remained scoreless and as a result of the Kansas City defense outshining the more famous Buffalo unit, the front four completely stifling the Bills' running game and putting a strong rush on Kemp when he dropped back to pass, the Chiefs became the AFL's first Super Bowl representatives.

SCORING

BUFFALO	7 0 0	0—	7
KANSAS CITY	7 10 0	14—	31

First Quarter
K.C. Arbanas, 29 yard pass from Dawson
    PAT — Mercer (kick)
BUFF. Dubenion, 69 yard pass from Kemp
    PAT — Lusteg (kick)

Second Quarter
K.C. Taylor, 29 yard pass from Dawson
    PAT — Mercer (kick)
K.C. Mercer, 32 yard Field goal

Fourth Quarter
K.C. Garrett, 1 yard rush
    PAT — Mercer (kick)
K.C. Garrett, 18 yard rush
    PAT — Mercer (kick)

TEAM STATISTICS

BUFF.		K.C.
9	First Downs — Total	14
2	First Downs — Rushing	6
7	First Downs — Passing	8
0	First Downs — Penalty	0
8	Punts — Number	6
39.3	Punts — Average Distance	42.3
3	Penalties — Number	4
23	Yards Penalized	40
0	Missed Field Goals	1

INDIVIDUAL STATISTICS

RUSHING

BUFFALO	No	Yds	Avg.	KANSAS CITY	No	Yds	Avg.
Carlton	9	31	3.4	Garrett	13	39	3.0
Burnett	3	6	2.0	McClinton	11	38	3.5
Kemp	1	3	3.0	Dawson	5	28	5.6
	13	40	3.1	Coan	2	6	3.0
				Eu. Thomas	2	2	1.0
					33	113	3.4

RECEIVING

BUFFALO	No	Yds	Avg.	KANSAS CITY	No	Yds	Avg.
Burnett	6	127	21.2	Taylor	5	78	15.6
Dubenion	2	79	39.5	Burford	4	76	19.0
Bass	2	26	13.0	Garrett	4	16	4.0
Crockett	1	16	16.0	Arbanas	2	44	22.0
Carlton	1	5	5.0	McClinton	1	13	13.0
	12	253	21.1		16	227	14.2

PUNT RETURNS

BUFFALO	No	Yds	Avg.	KANSAS CITY	No	Yds	Avg.
Byrd	3	0	0	Garrett	3	37	12.3
Rutkowski	2	16	8.0				
	5	16	3.2				

KICKOFF RETURNS

BUFFALO	No	Yds	Avg.	KANSAS CITY	No	Yds	Avg.
Warner	5	91	18.2	Coan	1	35	35.0
Meredith	1	8	8.0	Garrett	1	3	3.0
	6	99	16.5		2	38	19.0

INTERCEPTION RETURNS

BUFFALO	No	Yds	Avg.	KANSAS CITY	No	Yds	Avg.
None				Robinson	1	72	72.0
				Em. Thomas	1	26	26.0
					2	98	49.0

PASSING

BUFFALO	Att	Comp	Comp Pct.	Yds	Int	Yds/Att	Yds/Comp	Yards Lost Tackled
Kemp	27	12	44.4	253	2	9.4	21.1	38
KANSAS CITY								
Dawson	24	16	66.7	227	0	9.5	14.2	63

BUFFALO BILLS 9-4-1 Joe Collier

Scores of Each Game			Use Name	Pos.	Hgt	Wgt	Age	Int	Pts	Use Name	Pos.	Hgt	Wgt	Age	Int	Pts	Use Name	Pos.	Hgt	Wgt	Age	Int	Pts
7	San Diego	27	Stew Barber	OT	6'3"	250	27			Paul Guidry	LB	6'3"	225	22			Jack Kemp	QB	6'1"	200	32		30
20	KANSAS CITY	42	Wayne DeSutter	OT	6'4"	250	22			Harry Jacobs	LB	6'2"	226	29	2		Daryle Lamonica	QB	6'2"	218	25		6
58	MIAMI	24	Dick Hudson	OT	6'4"	265	26			Paul Maguire	LB	6'	228	28			Bobby Burnett	HB	6'2"	208	23		48
27	HOUSTON	20	Joe O'Donnell	OG	6'2"	252	24			Marty Schottenheimer	LB	6'3"	225	23	1		Allen Smith	HB	6'	200	23		
29	Kansas City	14	Remi Prudhomme	OG	6'4"	240	24			Mike Stratton	LB	6'3"	235	24	3	6	Wray Carlton	FB	6'2"	230	28		36
10	BOSTON	20	Billy Shaw	OG	6'3"	260	26			John Tracey	LB	6'3"	228	32	1		Doug Goodwin	FB	6'2"	228	24		
17	SAN DIEGO	17	Bob Schmidt	OT-C	6'4"	250	30			Butch Byrd	DB	6'	211	24	6	12	Jack Spikes	FB	6'2"	220	28		24
33	New York	23	Al Bemiller	OG-C	6'3"	240	27			Hagood Clarke	DB	6'	203	24	5	6	Elbert Dubenion	FL	6'	190	31		12
29	Miami	0	Tom Day	DE	6'2"	250	31			Booker Edgerson	DB	5'10"	188	27			Paul Costa	TE	6'4"	255	24		18
14	NEW YORK	3	Ron McDole	DE	6'3"	275	26	1		Tom Janik	DB	6'3"	200	25	8	12	Glenn Bass	OE	6'2"	206	27		
42	Houston	20	Dave Costa	DT	6'2"	250	24			Charlie King	DB	6'	185	23	1		Bobby Crockett	OE	6'	195	23		18
31	Oakland	10	Jim Dunaway	DT	6'4"	280	24		6	George Saimes	DB	5'10"	185	24	1		Charley Ferguson	OE	6'5"	224	26		6
3	Boston	14	Dudley Meredith	DT	6'4"	285	31			Charley Warner	DB	5'11"	170	26		6	Pete Mills	OE	5'11"	180	23		
38	DENVER	21	Tom Sestak	DT	6'5"	270	30										Ed Rutkowski	OE	6'1"	208	25		12
																	Booth Lusteg	K	5'11"	190	25		98

BOSTON PATRIOTS 8-4-2 Mike Holovak

Scores of Each Game			Use Name	Pos.	Hgt	Wgt	Age	Int	Pts	Use Name	Pos.	Hgt	Wgt	Age	Int	Pts	Use Name	Pos.	Hgt	Wgt	Age	Int	Pts
0	San Diego	24	Tom Neville	OT	6'4"	230	23			Tom Addison	LB	6'3"	230	30			John Huarte	QB	6'	190	22		
24	Denver	10	Don Oakes	OT	6'3"	255	28			Nick Buoniconti	LB	5'11"	220	25	4		Babe Parilli	QB	6'1"	190	36		6
24	KANSAS CITY	43	Karl Singer	OT	6'3"	245	22			Lonnie Farmer	LB	6'	220	25			Tom Yewcic	QB	5'11"	185	34		
24	NEW YORK	24	Justin Canale	OG	6'2"	230	22			Jim Fraser	LB	6'3"	235	30	1		J. D. Garrett	HB	5'11"	195	24		
20	Buffalo	10	Charley Long	OG	6'3"	250	28			Doug Satcher	LB	6'	222	21			Larry Garron	HB	6'	195	29		54
35	SAN DIEGO	17	Len St. Jean	OG	6'1"	240	24			Jay Cunningham	DB	5'10"	180	23			Bob Cappadonna	FB	6'1"	230	22		8
24	OAKLAND	21	Joe Avezzano	C	6'2"	235	22			Dick Felt	DB	6'	185	33	2		Jim Nance	FB	6'1"	235	23		66
10	DENVER	17	Jon Morris	C	6'4"	240	23			White Graves	DB	6'	185	23	1		Joe Bellino	FL	5'9"	185	28		6
27	HOUSTON	21	Jim Boudreaux	DE	6'4"	245	21			Ron Hall	DB	6'	190	29	6		Gino Cappelletti	FL	6'	190	32		119
27	Kansas City	27	Bob Dee	DE	6'3"	240	33			Tom Hennessey	DB	6'	185	26	6		Tony Romeo	TE	6'2"	230	27		2
20	Miami	14	Larry Eisenhauer	DE	6'5"	250	26			Billy Johnson	DB	5'11"	180	23			Jim Whalen	TE	6'2"	210	22		24
14	BUFFALO	3	Houstine Antwine	DT	6'	270	27			Vic Purvis	DB	5'11"	200	22			Jim Colclough	OE	6'	185	30		
38	Houston	14	Jim Hunt	DT	5'11"	245	27		6	Chuck Shonta	DB	6'	200	28	1		Art Graham	OE	6'1"	205	25		24
28	New York	38	Ed Khayat	DT	6'3"	250	31			Don Webb	DB	5'10"	200	27	1		Ellis Johnson	OE	6'2"	190	22		
			John Mangum	DT	6'3"	275	22																

NEW YORK JETS 6-6-2 Weeb Ewbank

Scores of Each Game			Use Name	Pos.	Hgt	Wgt	Age	Int	Pts	Use Name	Pos.	Hgt	Wgt	Age	Int	Pts	Use Name	Pos.	Hgt	Wgt	Age	Int	Pts
19	Miami	14	Nick DeFelice	OT	6'3"	250	26			Al Atkinson	LB	6'1"	230	23	4		Joe Namath	QB	6'2"	190	23		12
52	HOUSTON	13	Mitch Dudek	OT	6'4"	245	22			Ralph Baker	LB	6'3"	228	24			Mike Taliaferro	QB	6'2"	205	24		2
16	Denver	7	Winston Hill	OT	6'4"	274	24			Paul Crane	LB	6'2"	205	22			Emerson Boozer	HB	5'11"	215	23		36
24	Boston	24	Sherman Plunkett	OT	6'4"	300	32			Larry Grantham	LB	6'	206	27	1		Earl Christy	HB	5'11"	190	23		
17	SAN DIEGO	16	Steve Chomyszak	C-OT	6'5"	265	21			Jim O'Mahoney	LB	6'1"	228	25			Bill Mathis	HB	6'1"	220	27		18
0	Houston	24	Sam DeLuca	OG	6'2"	250	30			Ray Abruzzese	DB	6'1"	194	28	2		Allen Smith	HB	5'11"	195	22		
21	OAKLAND	24	Dan Ficca	OG	6'1"	245	27			Bill Baird	DB	5'10"	180	27	5	6	Mark Smolinski	FB	6'	215	27		18
23	BUFFALO	33	Dave Herman	OG	6'2"	255	24			Cornell Gordon	DB	6'	185	25			Matt Snell	FB	6'2"	220	24		48
3	Buffalo	14	Pete Perreault	OG	6'3"	245	27			Jim Gray	DB	6'	180	24			Don Maynard	FL	6'	180	30		30
30	MIAMI	13	John Schmitt	C	6'4"	265	23			Pat Gucciardo	DB	5'11"	185	22			Sammy Weir	FL	5'9"	170	24		
24	KANSAS CITY	32	Jim Waskiewicz	C	6'4"	227	22			Sherman Lewis	DB	5'10"	180	24			Pete Lammons	TE	6'3"	235	22		24
28	Oakland	28	Verlon Biggs	DE	6'4"	253	23			Dainard Paulson	DB	5'11"	190	29			Bill Rademacher	OE	6'1"	190	24		
27	San Diego	42	Gerry Philbin	DE	6'2"	245	25			Johnny Sample	DB	6'1"	205	29	6		George Sauer	OE	6'1"	206	22		32
38	BOSTON	28	Bill Yearby	DE	6'3"	235	22			Jim Hudson	DB	6'2"	210	23	3		Bake Turner	OE	6'	180	26		
			Bert Wilder	DT-DE	6'3"	245	26										Curley Johnson	K	6'	215	31		6
			Bob Werl	OG-DE	6'3"	240	23			Dee Mackey — Injury							Jim Turner	K	6'2"	205	25		88
			Jim Harris	DT	6'4"	280	22																
			Paul Rochester	DT	6'2"	250	29																
			Henry Schmidt	DT	6'4"	255	29																

HOUSTON OILERS 3-11-0 Wally Lemm

Scores of Each Game			Use Name	Pos.	Hgt	Wgt	Age	Int	Pts	Use Name	Pos.	Hgt	Wgt	Age	Int	Pts	Use Name	Pos.	Hgt	Wgt	Age	Int	Pts
45	DENVER	7	George Allen	OT	6'7"	270	22			Johnny Baker	LB	6'3"	238	25	1		George Blanda	QB	6'1"	220	38		87
31	OAKLAND	0	Glen Ray Hines	OT	6'5"	255	22			Garland Boyette	LB	6'1"	238	26			Buddy Humphrey	QB	6'1"	200	30		
13	New York	52	Rich Michael	OT	6'3"	242	27			Danny Brabham	LB	6'4"	233	25			Jacky Lee	QB	6'1"	190	27		
20	Buffalo	27	Walt Suggs	OT	6'5"	245	27			John Carrell	LB	6'3"	227	23			Don Trull	QB	6'1"	190	24		42
38	Denver	40	Sonny Bishop	OG	6'2"	245	26			Ronnie Caveness	LB	6'1"	225	23	1		Sid Blanks	HB	6'	205	25		12
24	NEW YORK	0	Bob Talamini	OG	6'1"	255	27			Doug Cline (to SD)	LB	6'2"	230	27	1	6	Ode Burrell	HB	6'	185	26		30
13	MIAMI	20	John Wittenborn	OG	6'2"	240	30			Bobby Maples	LB	6'3"	245	23			Hoyle Granger	FB-HB	6'1"	225	22		12
23	Kansas City	48	John Frongillo	C	6'3"	255	26			John Meyer	LB	6'1"	225	24			John Henry Johnson	FB	6'2"	225	36		18
23	Oakland	38	Gary Cutsinger	DE	6'4"	245	25			Olen Underwood	LB	6'1"	230	24			Donnie Stone	FB	6'2"	205	29		
21	Boston	27	Don Floyd	DE	6'4"	250	27			Freddy Glick	DB	6'1"	190	29	4		Charley Tolar	FB	5'7"	200	28		
20	BUFFALO	42	Ed Scrutchins	DE	6'3"	260	25			W. K. Hicks	DB	6'1"	185	23	3		Larry Elkins	FL	6'1"	190	23		18
22	SAN DIEGO	28	Scott Appleton	DT	6'3"	255	24			Bobby Jancik	DB	5'11"	178	26	2		Charley Hennigan	FL	6'	187	30		18
14	BOSTON	38	Jim Hayes	DT	6'4"	260	25			Jim Norton	DB	6'3"	190	27	4		Bob McLeod	TE	6'5"	230	27		18
28	Miami	29	Pat Holmes	DT	6'5"	270	26			Bernie Parrish	DB	5'11"	195	31	2		Bob Poole	TE	6'4"	215	24		
			Ernie Ladd	DT	6'9"	295	27			Mickey Sutton	DB	6'	190	23			Charley Frazier	OE	6'	175	27		72
			George Rice	OG-DT	6'3"	267	22			Allen Trammell	DB	6'	190	24									
										Theo Viltz	DB	6'2"	190	23									

MIAMI DOLPHINS 3-11-0 George Wilson

Scores of Each Game			Use Name	Pos.	Hgt	Wgt	Age	Int	Pts	Use Name	Pos.	Hgt	Wgt	Age	Int	Pts	Use Name	Pos.	Hgt	Wgt	Age	Int	Pts
14	OAKLAND	23	Norm Evans	OT	6'5"	235	23			Bob Bruggers	LB	6'1"	225	22			Rick Norton	QB	6'1"	198	22		
14	NEW YORK	19	Ernie Park	OT	6'3"	253	24			Frank Emanuel	LB	6'3"	225	23	1		John Stofa	QB	6'3"	210	24		
24	Buffalo	58	Maxie Williams	OT	6'4"	240	26			Tom Erlandson	LB	6'3"	235	26	3	6	George Wilson	QB	6'1"	190	23		2
10	San Diego	44	Billy Neighbors	OG	5'11"	245	26			Wahoo McDaniel	LB	6'	230	29	2		Dick Wood	QB	6'5"	200	30		6
10	Oakland	21	Ken Rice	OG	6'2"	240	26			Jack Rudolph	LB	6'3"	225	28	1		Joe Auer	HB	6'1"	200	24		54
24	DENVER	7	Jim Higgins	OT-OG	6'1"	250	24			Jack Thornton	LB	6'1"	230	21			Bill Hunter	HB	6'1"	180	23		
20	Houston	13	Tom Goode	C	6'3"	240	27			Pete Jaquess	DB	6'	185	24	3	6	Gene Mingo	HB	6'1"	190	27		53
0	BUFFALO	29	Mike Hudock	C	6'2"	245	31			John McGeever	DB	6'1"	195	27	2		Sam Price	FB-HB	5'11"	215	22		
16	Kansas City	34	Mel Branch	DE	6'2"	230	29			Bob Neff	DB	6'1"	185	22	1		Rick Casares	FB	6'2"	233	35		6
13	New York	30	Whit Canale	DE	6'3"	245	24			Bob Petrella	DB	6'	185	21			George Chesser	FB	6'2"	225	23		
14	BOSTON	20	Ed Cooke	DE	6'4"	250	31			Hal Wantland	DB	6'	195	22			Cookie Gilchrist	FB	6'3"	250	31		6
7	Denver	17	Earl Faison (from SD)	DE	6'5"	265	27	1		Jimmy Warren	DB	5'11"	185	27	5	6	Billy Joe	FB	6'2"	236	25		8
18	KANSAS CITY	19	John Holmes	DE	6'2"	248	22			Willie West	DB	5'10"	187	28	8		Frank Jackson	FL	6'1"	190	26		12
29	HOUSTON	28	Lavern Torczon	DE	6'2"	250	30			Dick Westmoreland	DB	6'1"	195	25	4	6	Bo Roberson	FL	6'1"	190	31		12
			Al Dotson	DT	6'4"	255	23										John Roderick	FL	6'1"	180	22		6
			Tom Nomina	DT	6'5"	270	24			Ross O'Hanley — Injury							Bill Cronin	TE	6'4"	230	23		6
			Rich Zecher	DT	6'2"	240	23			Eddie Wilson — Knee Injury							Dave Kocourek	TE	6'5"	240	29		12
																	Wes Mathews	OE	5'10"	180	22		
																	Stan Mitchell	OE	6'2"	220	22		
																	Doug Moreau	OE	6'2"	193	21		
																	Karl Noonan	OE	6'3"	185	22		6
																	Howard Twilley	OE	5'10"	180	22		

BUFFALO BILLS

Rushing
Last Name	No.	Yds	Avg	TD
Burnett	187	766	4.1	4
Carlton	156	696	4.5	6
Smith	31	148	4.8	0
Kemp	40	130	3.3	5
Spikes	28	119	4.3	3
Dubenion	3	16	5.3	0
Rutkowski	1	10	10.0	0
Lamonica	9	6	0.7	1
P. Costa	0	1	0.0	0

Receiving
Last Name	No.	Yds	Avg	TD
Dubenion	50	747	15	2
Burnett	34	419	12	4
Crockett	31	533	17	3
P. Costa	27	400	15	3
Carlton	21	280	13	0
Ferguson	16	293	18	1
Bass	10	130	13	0
Rutkowski	6	150	25	1
Spikes	2	45	23	1
O'Donnell	1	2	2	0
Smith	1	1	1	0

Punt Returns
Last Name	No.	Yds	Avg	TD
Rutkowski	18	209	12	1
Byrd	23	186	8	1
Clarke	2	12	6	0
Stratton	0	4	0	0

Kickoff Returns
Last Name	No.	Yds	Avg	TD
Warner	33	846	26	1
Rutkowski	6	121	20	0
Mills	4	76	19	0
Prudhomme	1	16	16	0
Schmidt	1	2	2	0
DeSutter	2	0	0	0
Ferguson	2	0	0	0
D. Costa	1	0	0	0
Maguire	1	0	0	0
O'Donnell	0	3	0	0

Passing – Punting – Kicking
PASSING	Att	Comp	%	Yds	Yd/Att	TD	Int—%		RK
Kemp	389	166	43	2451	6.3	11	16—	4	7
Lamonica	84	33	39	549	6.5	4	5—	6	

PUNTING	No	Avg
Maguire	69	41.2

KICKING	XP	Att	%	FG	Att	%
Lusteg	41	42	98	19	38	50

BOSTON PATRIOTS

Rushing
Last Name	No.	Yds	Avg	TD
Nance	299	1458	4.9	11
Garron	101	319	3.2	4
Cappadonna	22	88	4.0	1
Parilli	28	42	1.5	1
Huarte	7	40	5.7	0
Garrett	13	21	1.6	0
Yewcic	1	−5	−5.0	0

Receiving
Last Name	No.	Yds	Avg	TD
Graham	51	673	13	4
Cappelletti	43	676	16	6
Garron	30	416	14	5
Whalen	29	502	17	4
Colclough	16	284	18	0
Nance	8	103	13	0
Bellino	6	77	13	1
Romeo	2	46	23	0
Garrett	1	7	7	0

Punt Returns
Last Name	No.	Yds	Avg	TD
Purvis	5	43	9	0
Hennessey	7	39	6	0
B. Johnson	7	37	5	0
Bellino	4	19	5	0
Graves	1	5	5	0

Kickoff Returns
Last Name	No.	Yds	Avg	TD
Bellino	18	410	23	0
Cunningham	17	371	22	0
Purvis	8	185	23	0
Garron	2	49	25	0
Cappadonna	3	46	15	0
E. Johnson	2	45	23	0
Singer	1	27	27	0
Mangum	1	8	8	0
Colclough	1	2	2	0
B. Johnson	1	2	2	0

Passing – Punting – Kicking
PASSING	Att	Comp	%	Yds	Yd/Att	TD	Int—%		RK
Parilli	382	181	47	2721	7.1	20	20—	5	6
Huarte	11	5	46	63	5.7	0	1—	9	

PUNTING	No	Avg
Fraser	53	38.6
Yewcic	20	36.6

KICKING	XP	Att	%	FG	Att	%
Cappelletti	35	36	97	16	32	50

2 POINT XP
Cappadonna
Romeo

NEW YORK JETS

Rushing
Last Name	No.	Yds	Avg	TD
Snell	178	644	3.6	4
Boozer	97	455	4.7	5
Mathis	72	208	2.9	2
Smolinski	21	69	3.3	2
Namath	6	42	7.0	2
Johnson	2	24	12.0	0

Receiving
Last Name	No.	Yds	Avg	TD
Sauer	63	1079	17	5
Maynard	48	840	18	5
Snell	48	346	7	4
Lammons	31	565	14	4
Mathis	22	379	17	1
Smolinski	11	74	7	1
Boozer	8	133	17	0
B. Turner	7	115	16	0
Johnson	1	18	18	1
Weir	1	4	4	0
Rademacher	1	3	3	0

Punt Returns
Last Name	No.	Yds	Avg	TD
Lewis	7	76	11	0
B. Turner	10	60	6	0
Weir	8	48	6	0
Baird	5	35	7	0
Christy	5	23	5	0
Hudson	1	18	18	0

Kickoff Returns
Last Name	No.	Yds	Avg	TD
Boozer	26	659	25	1
Christy	10	203	20	0
Weir	6	121	20	0
Lewis	5	121	24	0
Gray	5	77	15	0
Smolinski	6	59	10	0
B. Turner	2	50	25	0
Wilder	1	6	6	0
Johnson	1	4	4	0

Passing – Punting – Kicking
PASSING	Att	Comp	%	Yds	Yd/Att	TD	Int—%		RK
Namath	471	232	49	3379	7.2	19	27—	6	4
Taliaferro	41	19	46	177	4.3	2	5—	5	
Hudson	1	0	0	0	0.0	0	0—	0	
Snell	1	0	0	0	0.0	0	0—	0	

PUNTING	No	Avg
Johnson	62	42.5

KICKING	XP	Att	%	FG	Att	%
J. Turner	34	35	97	18	35	51

2 POINT XP
Sauer
Taliaferro

HOUSTON OILERS

Rushing
Last Name	No.	Yds	Avg	TD
Burrell	122	406	3.3	0
Granger	56	388	6.9	1
Blanks	71	235	3.3	0
Johnson	70	226	3.2	3
Trull	38	139	3.7	7
Tolar	46	105	2.3	0
Stone ·	6	18	3.0	0
Blanda	3	1	0.3	0
Lee	1	−3	−3.0	0

Receiving
Last Name	No.	Yds	Avg	TD
Frazier	57	1129	20	12
Burrell	33	400	12	5
Hennigan	27	313	12	3
McLeod	23	339	15	3
Elkins	21	283	13	3
Blanks	19	234	12	2
Tolar	13	68	5	0
Poole	12	131	11	0
Granger	12	104	9	1
Johnson	8	150	19	0
Stone	1	17	17	0

Punt Returns
Last Name	No.	Yds	Avg	TD
Burrell	8	78	10	0
Jancik	10	62	6	0
Trammell	5	19	4	0

Kickoff Returns
Last Name	No.	Yds	Avg	TD
Jancik	34	875	26	0
Blanks	21	487	23	0
Trammell	3	63	21	0
Boyette	3	42	14	0
Hayes	2	31	16	0
Burrell	1	16	16	0

Passing – Punting – Kicking
PASSING	Att	Comp	%	Yds	Yd/Att	TD	Int—%		RK
Blanda	271	122	45	1764	6.5	17	21—	8	9
Trull	172	84	49	1200	7.0	10	5—	3	4
Humphrey	32	15	47	168	5.3	2	1—	3	
Lee	8	4	50	27	3.4	0	1—	13	
Burrell	1	1	100	9	9.0	0	0—	0	
Tolar	1	0	0	0	0.0	0	0—	0	

PUNTING	No	Avg
Norton	69	42.2

KICKING	XP	Att	%	FG	Att	%
Blanda	39	40	98	16	30	53

MIAMI DOLPHINS

Rushing
Last Name	No.	Yds	Avg	TD
Auer	121	416	3.4	4
Gilchrist	72	262	3.6	0
Joe	71	232	3.3	0
Wilson	27	137	5.1	0
Casares	43	135	3.1	0
Price	31	107	3.5	0
Chesser	16	74	4.6	0
Jackson	2	22	11.0	0
Stofa	3	17	5.7	0
Wood	5	6	1.2	1
Norton	3	2	0.7	0

Receiving
Last Name	No.	Yds	Avg	TD
Kocourek	27	320	12	2
Roberson	26	519	20	2
Auer	22	263	12	4
Noonan	17	224	13	1
Jackson	16	317	20	2
Joe	13	116	9	1
Gilchrist	13	110	8	1
Roderick	11	156	14	1
Twilley	10	128	13	0
Casares	8	45	6	1
Cronin	7	83	12	1
Mingo	3	40	13	0
Moreau	2	15	8	0
Price	2	14	7	0
Matthews	1	20	20	0
Chesser	1	4	4	0

Punt Returns
Last Name	No.	Yds	Avg	TD
Auer	5	99	20	0
Neff	10	60	6	0
Matthews	4	38	10	0
Jackson	2	7	4	0

Kickoff Returns
Last Name	No.	Yds	Avg	TD
Auer	28	698	25	1
Neff	15	376	25	0
Matthews	5	109	22	0
Jackson	4	105	26	0
Hunter	5	84	17	0
Jaquess	5	77	15	0
Roderick	1	17	17	0
Branch	1	15	15	0
Bruggers	1	3	3	0
Noonan	0	23	0	0

Passing – Punting – Kicking
PASSING	Att	Comp	%	Yds	Yd/Att	TD	Int—%		RK
Wood	230	83	36	993	4.3	4	14—	6	10
Wilson	112	46	41	764	6.8	5	10—	9	
Stofa	57	29	51	425	7.5	4	3—	11	
Norton	55	21	38	192	3.5	3	6—	11	

PUNTING	No	Avg
Wilson	42	42.1
McDaniel	32	38.2
Chesser	7	33.3

KICKING	XP	Att	%	FG	Att	%
Mingo	23	23	100	10	22	46

2 POINT XP
Joe
Wilson

KANSAS CITY CHIEFS 11-2-1 Hank Stram

Scores of Each Game			Use Name	Pos.	Hgt	Wgt	Age	Int	Pts
42	Buffalo	20	Tony DiMidio	OT	6'3"	250	24		
32	Oakland	10	Dave Hill	OT	6'5"	254	25		
43	Boston	24	Jim Tyrer	OT	6'6"	292	27		
14	BUFFALO	29	Denny Biodrowski	OG	6'1"	255	26		
37	DENVER	10	Ed Budde	OG	6'5"	260	25		
13	OAKLAND	34	Curt Merz	OG	6'4"	267	28		
56	Denver	10	Al Reynolds	OG	6'3"	250	28		
48	HOUSTON	23	Hatch Rosdahl	OG	6'5"	250	23		
24	SAN DIEGO	14	Wayne Frazier	C	6'2"	245	26		
34	MIAMI	16	Jon Gilliam	C	6'2"	240	27		
27	BOSTON	27	Aaron Brown	DE	6'5"	250	22		
32	New York	24	Chuck Hurston	DE	6'6"	230	23		
19	Miami	18	Jerry Mays	DE	6'4"	252	26		
27	San Diego	17	Buck Buchanan	DT	6'7"	287	26		
			Ed Lothamer	DT	6'5"	270	23		
			Andy Rice	DT	6'3"	266	24		

Use Name	Pos.	Hgt	Wgt	Age	Int	Pts
Bud Abell	LB	6'3"	220	25		
Bobby Bell	LB	6'4"	228	26	2	6
Walt Corey	LB	6'	233	28		
Sherrill Headrick	LB	6'2"	240	29	2	
E. J. Holub	LB	6'4"	236	28		
Smokey Stover	LB	6'	227	27	1	
Solomon Brannan	DB	6'1"	188	24		
Jimmy Hill	DB	6'2"	198	37		
Bobby Hunt	DB	6'1"	193	26	10	
Willie Mitchell	DB	6'1"	185	24	3	6
Bobby Ply	DB	6'1"	190	25	1	
Johnny Robinson	DB	6'	205	27	10	6
Fletcher Smith	DB	6'2"	188	22	2	
Emmitt Thomas	DB	6'2"	190	23		
Fred Williamson	DB	6'2"	210	28	4	

Use Name	Pos.	Hgt	Wgt	Age	Int	Pts
Pete Beathard	QB	6'2"	210	24		6
Len Dawson	QB	6'	190	32		
Bert Coan	HB	6'4"	220	26		54
Mike Garrett	HB	5'9"	195	22		48
Gene Thomas	HB	6'1"	210	23		6
Curtis McClinton	FB	6'3"	227	28		54
Jerrel Wilson	FB	6'4"	222	25		2
Otis Taylor	FL	6'2"	211	23		48
Fred Arbanas	TE	6'3"	240	27		26
Chris Burford	OE	6'3"	210	28		48
Reg Carolan	OE	6'6"	238	26		18
Frank Pitts	OE	6'2"	190	22		6
Tommy Brooker	K	6'2"	235	26		19
Mike Mercer (from OAK)	K	6'	210	30		98

Curt Farrier — Injury

OAKLAND RAIDERS 8-5-1 Johnny Rauch

Scores of Each Game			Use Name	Pos.	Hgt	Wgt	Age	Int	Pts
23	Miami	14	Jim Harvey	OT	6'5"	245	23		
0	Houston	31	Harry Schuh	OT	6'2"	260	23		
10	KANSAS CITY	32	Bob Svihus	OT	6'4"	245	23		
20	SAN DIEGO	29	Wayne Hawkins	OG	6'	240	28		
21	MIAMI	10	Palmer Pyle	OG	6'2"	245	29		
34	Kansas City	13	Dick Tyson	OG	6'2"	245	22		
24	New York	21	Jim Otto	C	6'2"	240	28		
21	Boston	24	Ben Davidson	DE	6'8"	265	26		
38	HOUSTON	23	Greg Kent	DE	6'6"	275	23		
41	San Diego	19	Ike Lassiter	DE	6'5"	270	25	1	
17	Denver	3	Carleton Oats	DT-DE	6'2"	235	23		
10	BUFFALO	31	Dan Birdwell	DT	6'4"	250	25	1	
28	NEW YORK	28	Dave Daniels	DT	6'3"	245	25		
28	DENVER	10	Tom Keating	DT	6'3"	247	23		
			Rex Mirich	DT	6'4"	250	25		

Use Name	Pos.	Hgt	Wgt	Age	Int	Pts
Bill Budness	LB	6'1"	215	23		
Dan Conners	LB	6'1"	240	24	2	6
Rich Jackson	LB	6'2"	230	25		
Bill Laskey	LB	6'2"	240	23		
Gus Otto	LB	6'2"	220	23		
Ray Schmautz	LB	6'1"	225	23		
J. R. Williamson	LB	6'2"	220	24		
Rodger Bird	DB	5'11"	195	23	4	
Dave Grayson	DB	5'10"	185	27	3	
Joe Krakoski	DB	6'2"	195	29		
Kent McCloughan	DB	6'1"	190	23	4	
Warren Powers	DB	6'	190	25	5	
Howie Williams	DB	6'2"	187	29	3	
Willie Williams	DB	6'	190	23		

George Flint — Injury

Use Name	Pos.	Hgt	Wgt	Age	Int	Pts
Cotton Davidson	QB	6'1"	180	34		
Tom Flores	QB	6'1"	190	29		6
Charlie Green	QB	6'	190	23		
Pervis Atkins	HB	6'1"	195	30		
Pete Banaszak	HB	5'11"	200	22		
Clem Daniels	HB	6'1"	218	29		60
Roger Hagberg	FB	6'2"	215	27		6
Hewritt Dixon	HB-FB	6'2"	225	26		54
Fred Biletnikoff	FL	6'1"	190	23		18
Billy Cannon	TE	6'1"	215	29		12
Tom Mitchell	TE	6'2"	235	22		6
Bill Miller	OE	6'	190	24		
Art Powell	OE	6'3"	212	29		66
Larry Todd	OE	6'1"	185	23		6
Mike Eischeid	K	6'	190	25		70

SAN DIEGO CHARGERS 7-6-1 Sid Gillman

Scores of Each Game			Use Name	Pos.	Hgt	Wgt	Age	Int	Pts
27	BUFFALO	7	Gary Kirner	OT	6'3"	248	24		
24	BOSTON	0	Ron Mix	OT	6'4"	250	28		
29	Oakland	20	Terry Owens	OT	6'6"	240	24		
44	MIAMI	10	Ernie Wright	OT	6'4"	265	26		
16	New York	17	Don Estes	OG	6'2"	250	23		
17	Buffalo	17	John Farris	OG	6'4"	245	25		
17	Boston	35	Ed Mitchell	OG	6'2"	280	24		
24	DENVER	17	Walt Sweeney	OG	6'3"	250	25		
14	Kansas City	24	Sam Gruneisen	C	6'1"	240	25		
19	OAKLAND	41	Paul Latzke	C	6'4"	245	24		
17	Denver	20	Jim Griffin	DE	6'5"	255	24		
28	Houston	22	Howard Kindig	DE	6'6"	255	25	1	
42	NEW YORK	27	Fred Moore	DE	6'3"	255	26		
17	KANSAS CITY	27	Bob Petrich	DE	6'4"	250	25		
			Houston Ridge	DE	6'4"	232	22		
			Steve DeLong	DT	6'3"	252	23		
			George Gross	DT	6'3"	258	25		
			Larry Martin	DT	6'2"	270	24		

Use Name	Pos.	Hgt	Wgt	Age	Int	Pts
Chuck Allen	LB	6'1"	225	26	1	
Frank Buncom	LB	6'1"	230	26		
Dick Degen	LB	6'1"	220	24	1	
Tom Good	LB	6'	230	22		
Emil Karas	LB	6'3"	230	32		
Mike London	LB	6'2"	230	21		
John Milks	LB	6'	222	22	1	
Bob Mitinger	LB	6'2"	230	26		
Rick Redman	LB	5'11"	225	23	2	6
Joe Beauchamp	DB	6'	185	22	2	
Speedy Duncan	DB	5'10"	175	23	7	6
Miller Farr	DB	6'1"	192	23	3	
Kenny Graham	DB	6'	195	24	5	6
Dave Plump	DB	6'1"	195	23		
Jim Tolbert	DB	6'3"	207	22	1	
Bud Whitehead	DB	6'	185	27	2	
Nat Whitmyer	DB	6'	180	25		
Bob Zeman	DB	6'1"	205	29		

Use Name	Pos.	Hgt	Wgt	Age	Int	Pts
John Hadl	QB	6'2"	215	26		12
Dan Henning	QB	6'	195	24		
Steve Tensi	QB	6'5"	215	23		
Paul Lowe	HB	6'	205	29		18
Gene Foster	FB-HB	5'11"	212	23		18
Jim Allison	FB	6'	220	23		12
Keith Lincoln	FB	6'2"	215	27		18
John Travis	FB	6'1"	216	23		
Lance Alworth	FL	6'	180	26		78
Willie Frazier	TE	6'4"	235	23		12
Jacque MacKinnon	TE	6'4"	250	27		36
Gary Garrison	OE	6'1"	195	22		24
Don Norton	OE	6'1"	195	28		
Dick Van Raaphorst	K	5'11"	215	23		87

Pat Shea — Injury

DENVER BRONCOS 4-10-0 Mac Speedie Ray Malavasi

Scores of Each Game			Use Name	Pos.	Hgt	Wgt	Age	Int	Pts
7	Houston	45	Lee Bernet	OT	6'2"	245	22		
10	BOSTON	24	Bob Breitenstein	OT	6'3"	270	23		
7	NEW YORK	16	Sam Brunelli	OG	6'1"	240	23		
40	HOUSTON	38	John Gonzaga	OG	6'3"	250	33		
10	Kansas City	37	Jon Hohman	OG	6'1"	245	23		
7	Miami	24	Bill Keating	OG	6'2"	236	21		
10	KANSAS CITY	56	Pat Matson	OG	6'1"	250	24		
17	San Diego	24	Jerry Sturm	OG	6'3"	260	29		
17	Boston	10	Larry Kaminski	C	6'2"	240	21		
3	OAKLAND	17	Ray Kubala	C	6'4"	245	24		
20	SAN DIEGO	17	Marvin Davis	DE	6'4"	252	22		
17	MIAMI	7	Dan LaRose	DE	6'5"	250	26		
10	Oakland	28	Max Leetzow	DE	6'4"	240	23		
21	Buffalo	38	George Tarasovic	DE	6'4"	250	37		
			Larry Cox	DT	6'2"	255	22		
			Jerry Inman	DT	6'3"	255	26		
			Ray Jacobs	DT	6'3"	275	26		
			Bob Young	DT	6'2"	275	23		

Use Name	Pos.	Hgt	Wgt	Age	Int	Pts
John Bramlett	LB	6'2"	220	25	1	6
Don Gulseth	LB	6'1"	240	24		
Jerry Hopkins	LB	6'2"	235	25	2	
Gene Jeter	LB	6'3"	230	24		
Archie Matsos (to SD)	LB	6'	212	31	3	
Ron Sbranti	LB	6'2"	230	21		
Willie Brown	DB	6'1"	190	25	3	
Billy Fletcher	DB	5'10"	190	22		
Goose Gonsoulin	DB	6'3"	210	28		
John Griffin	DB	6'1"	190	26		
Bob Richardson	DB	6'1"	180	22		
Lew Scott	DB	5'10"	173	23		
Goldie Sellers	DB	6'2"	198	24	3	12
Nemiah Wilson	DB	6'	165	23	1	6
Lonnie Wright	DB	6'2"	205	22	1	
Eric Crabtree	OE-DB	5'11"	190	21		

Eldon Danenhauer — Injury

Use Name	Pos.	Hgt	Wgt	Age	Int	Pts
Max Choboian	QB	6'4"	205	24		12
Scotty Glacken	QB	6'	190	21		
John McCormick	QB	6'1"	190	29		
Tobin Rote	QB	6'3"	220	38		
Mickey Slaughter	QB	6'	190	25		
Abner Haynes	HB	6'	190	28		18
Charley Mitchell	HB	5'11"	185	26		
Mike Kellogg	FB	6'	220	23		
Darrell Lester	FB	6'2"	220	25		6
Wendell Hayes	HB-FB	6'2"	195	25		6
Bob Scarpitto	FL	5'11"	196	27		32
Al Denson	TE	6'2"	208	24		18
Max Wettstein	TE	6'3"	217	22		
Jason Franci	OE	6'1"	210	22		
Glenn Glass	OE	6'	203	29		
Lionel Taylor	OE	6'2"	215	30		6
Gary Kroner	K	6'1"	200	25		62

KANSAS CITY CHIEFS

RUSHING

Last Name	No.	Yds	Avg	TD
Garrett	147	801	5.5	6
McClinton	140	540	3.9	4
Coan	96	521	5.4	7
Dawson	24	167	7.0	0
Beathard	20	152	7.6	1
G. Thomas	7	53	7.6	1
Taylor	2	33	16.5	0
Wilson	3	7	2.3	0

RECEIVING

Last Name	No.	Yds	Avg	TD
Taylor	58	1297	22	8
Burford	58	758	13	8
Arbanas	22	305	14	4
McClinton	19	285	15	5
Coan	18	131	7	2
Garrett	15	175	12	1
Carolan	7	154	22	3
Pitts	1	11	11	0
Wilson	1	7	7	0

PUNT RETURNS

Last Name	No.	Yds	Avg	TD
Garrett	17	139	8	1
E. Thomas	9	56	6	0
Brown	1	43	43	0
Pitts	1	21	21	1
Williamson	1	10	10	0
Mitchell	1	7	7	0
Ply	1	0	0	0

KICKOFF RETURNS

Last Name	No.	Yds	Avg	TD
E. Thomas	29	673	23	0
Garrett	14	323	23	0
G. Thomas	3	62	21	0
Brannan	1	24	24	0
Coan	1	22	22	0
Brown	1	6	6	0
Stover	3	0	0	0
Taylor	2	0	0	0
Pitts	0	38	0	0

PASSING – PUNTING – KICKING

PASSING

Last Name	Att	Comp	%	Yds	Yd/Att	TD	Int–%	RK
Dawson	284	159	56	2527	8.9	26	10– 4	1
Beathard	90	39	43	578	6.4	4	4– 4	
Coan	1	1	100	18	18.0	1	0– 0	
Garrett	1	0	0	0	0.0	0	0– 0	
Taylor	1	0	0	0	0.0	0	1–100	

PUNTING

Last Name	No	Avg
Wilson	61	44.5
Mercer	9	41.4

KICKING

Last Name	XP	Att	%	FG	Att	%
Mercer	35	38	92	21	30	70
Brooker	13	13	100	2	2	100
Smith	2	4	50	0	0	0

2 POINT XP
Arbanas
Wilson

OAKLAND RAIDERS

RUSHING

Last Name	No.	Yds	Avg	TD
C. Daniels	204	801	3.9	7
Hagberg	62	282	4.6	0
Dixon	68	277	4.1	5
Flores	5	50	10.0	1
Banaszak	4	18	4.5	0
Atkins	14	10	0.7	0
C. Davidson	6	–11	–1.8	0

RECEIVING

Last Name	No.	Yds	Avg	TD
Powell	53	1026	19	11
C. Daniels	40	652	16	3
Dixon	29	345	12	4
Mitchell	23	301	13	1
Hagberg	21	248	12	1
Biletnikoff	17	272	16	3
Cannon	14	436	31	2
Todd	14	134	10	1
Banaszak	1	11	11	0

PUNT RETURNS

Last Name	No.	Yds	Avg	TD
Bird	37	323	9	0
Krakoski	2	19	10	0
Atkins	1	13	13	0
Cannon	1	12	12	0

KICKOFF RETURNS

Last Name	No.	Yds	Avg	TD
Atkins	29	608	21	0
Bird	19	390	21	0
Grayson	6	128	21	0
W. Williams	2	52	26	0
Hagberg	1	13	13	0
Mirich	2	0	0	0
Powers	1	0	0	0

PASSING – PUNTING – KICKING

PASSING

Last Name	Att	Comp	%	Yds	Yd/Att	TD	Int–%	RK
Flores	306	151	49	2638	8.6	24	14– 5	3
C. Davidson	139	59	42	770	5.5	2	11– 8	
C. Daniels	3	0	0	0	0.0	0	1– 33	
Green	2	2	100	17	8.5	0	0– 0	

PUNTING

Last Name	No	Avg
Eischeid	64	42.3

KICKING

Last Name	XP	Att	%	FG	Att	%
Eischeid	37	37	100	11	26	42

SAN DIEGO CHARGERS

RUSHING

Last Name	No.	Yds	Avg	TD
Lowe	146	643	4.4	3
Foster	81	352	4.4	4
Lincoln	58	214	3.7	1
Allison	31	213	6.9	2
Hadl	38	95	2.5	2
Redman	2	14	7.0	0
Alworth	3	10	3.3	0
Tensi	1	–1	–1.0	0
Garrison	1	–3	–3.0	0

RECEIVING

Last Name	No.	Yds	Avg	TD
Alworth	73	1383	19	13
Garrison	46	642	14	4
MacKinnon	26	477	18	6
Foster	26	260	10	2
Lincoln	14	264	19	2
Allison	12	99	8	0
Lowe	12	41	3	0
Frazier	9	144	16	2
Norton	4	50	13	0
Hadl	2	–13	–7	0

PUNT RETURNS

Last Name	No.	Yds	Avg	TD
Duncan	18	238	13	1
Graham	2	15	8	0
Plump	1	4	4	0

KICKOFF RETURNS

Last Name	No.	Yds	Avg	TD
Duncan	25	642	26	0
Plump	15	345	23	0
Lowe	7	167	24	0
Beauchamp	4	64	16	0
Farr	2	54	27	0
Whitmyer	1	10	10	0
Gruneisen	1	0	0	0

PASSING – PUNTING – KICKING

PASSING

Last Name	Att	Comp	%	Yds	Yd/Att	TD	Int–%	RK
Hadl	375	200	53	2846	7.6	23	14– 4	2
Tensi	52	21	40	405	7.8	5	1– 2	
Lincoln	4	2	50	71	17.8	1	0– 0	
Lowe	3	1	33	25	8.3	0	0– 0	

PUNTING

Last Name	No	Avg
Redman	66	37.0

KICKING

Last Name	XP	Att	%	FG	Att	%
Van Raaphorst	29	40	98	14	31	52

DENVER BRONCOS

RUSHING

Last Name	No.	Yds	Avg	TD
Hayes	105	417	4.0	1
Haynes	129	304	2.4	2
Mitchell	70	199	2.8	0
Scarpitto	4	110	27.5	1
Lester	34	84	2.5	0
Choboian	21	45	2.1	2
Slaughter	1	10	10.0	0
Kellogg	6	3	0.5	0
McCormick	4	2	0.5	0
Glacken	2	–1	–0.5	0

RECEIVING

Last Name	No.	Yds	Avg	TD
Haynes	46	480	10	1
Denson	36	725	20	3
Taylor	35	448	13	1
Scarpitto	21	335	16	4
Mitchell	14	239	17	2
Hayes	8	49	6	0
Lester	2	26	13	1
Crabtree	1	38	38	0
Franci	1	8	8	0
Kellogg	1	5	5	0
Wright	1	–2	–2	0

PUNT RETURNS

Last Name	No.	Yds	Avg	TD
Haynes	10	119	12	0
Scott	7	56	8	0
Sellers	6	49	8	0
Wilson	2	10	5	0
Lester	1	1	1	0

KICKOFF RETURNS

Last Name	No.	Yds	Avg	TD
Sellers	19	541	28	2
Wilson	10	309	31	1
Scott	9	282	31	0
Haynes	9	229	25	0
Crabtree	5	129	26	0
Mitchell	3	55	18	0
Lester	1	11	11	0
Sturm	1	2	2	0
Inman	1	0	0	0

PASSING – PUNTING – KICKING

PASSING

Last Name	Att	Comp	%	Yds	Yd/Att	TD	Int–%	RK
McCormick	193	68	35	993	5.1	6	15– 8	11
Choboian	163	82	50	1110	6.8	4	12– 7	8
Slaughter	25	7	28	124	5.0	1	0– 0	
Glacken	11	6	55	84	7.6	1	0– 0	
Rote	8	3	38	40	5.0	0	1– 13	
Haynes	2	0	0	0	0.0	0	2–100	

PUNTING

Last Name	No	Avg
Scarpitto	76	45.8

KICKING

Last Name	XP	Att	%	FG	Att	%
Kroner	20	20	100	14	25	56

2 POINT XP
Scarpitto

Super Bowl I

January 15, at Los Angeles
(Attendance 61,946)

Thirty Minutes of Equality

It seemed somehow unreal. The Green Bay Packers and the Kansas City Chiefs had always been parts of different universes in the world of sports. But here they were, the champions of the NFL and the AFL, meeting on the field in a confrontation many thought was years away.

Until recently, the NFL had not even recognized that the AFL was there. The established league considered the newer league an inferior and annoying upstart, worthy only of contempt when it first began. But while AFL scores were never posted in NFL stadia, NFL owners felt the AFL's presence directly when the new league began signing a fair share of top players and driving player salaries up in general. Despite the icy external show, fans knew that the NFL people wanted nothing better than the death of the AFL.

The AFL people, however, had never denied the NFL's existence; in fact, they used the older league as an open measure of their own league. NFL games were reported right along with AFL games on the scoreboard, as if both belonged on an equal footing, and AFL clubs were measured by the hypothetical situation of how they would do against a good NFL team. Ultimate success for the AFL would be standing shoulder to shoulder with the NFL.

The war between the leagues had been fought in courtrooms and the press, with subpoenas and checkbooks. The NFL looked down on the new league with utter disdain at first, but as the rich men who owned AFL clubs bid up player salaries and threatened to lure away established NFL stars, the officials of the older league decided to swallow some pride and look for a way to end the war between the circuits.

Negotiations in the spring brought about a peace agreement between the leagues that changed the structure of pro football as it had been in the 1960s. The NFL and AFL agreed to end their financial war by holding a common draft of college seniors and respecting each other's player contracts, and although the AFL clubs had to pay reparations, the clubs of both leagues now were coequal members of a joint structure. By the end of the decade, the AFL would be absorbed completely into an expanded NFL.

But the biggest dividend for the football fan was the establishment of an NFL-AFL championship game between the two league champions. Unofficially dubbed "The Super Bowl" by the media, this game would bring together the top teams in two leagues which had never played each other. This year's game would be unprecedented.

Older fans, of course, remembered the startling entry of the Cleveland Browns into the NFL in 1950. The Browns had completely dominated the AAFC during its four-year existence, but many fans and reporters looked on that circuit as an inferior league. The Browns relished the chance to prove that *they* were not inferior, and they decisively defeated the defending champion Philadelphia Eagles in their first confrontation with NFL competition. The Browns went on to take the league title in that first season, and some fans liked the chances of the AFL team in the Super Bowl because of the Browns' example.

Emerging as the AFL champion and Super Bowl representative were the Kansas City Chiefs, a team which had played three years in Dallas before moving to Missouri. Owned by Lamar Hunt and coached from the beginning by Hank Stram, the Chiefs had compiled an 11-2-1 record during the season and dissected a strong Buffalo team in the AFL championship game. Len Dawson, who had been waived out of the NFL after five years of bench-sitting, had found himself as a quarterback in the AFL, excelling both as a passer and a play-caller. Otis Taylor, Mike Garrett, Ed Budde, Jim Tyrer, and Buck Buchanan were all talented young pros who obviously could make most teams in the NFL. For the rest of the Kansas City offense and most of the defense, a lingering doubt remained. How well would these men, all solid AFL players, make out against the best the NFL could offer?

That best, for the fourth time in the last six years, was the Green Bay Packers, that hard-hitting precision machine hand-built by coach Vince Lombardi. Although the parts were aging, Lombardi's machine still was a multifaceted wonder. His offensive line was quietly but constantly effective in moving people aside, and the running backs were the hard-nosed types who thrived on power sweeps and off-tackle smashes. At the heart of the attack was quarterback Bart Starr, a marvelous football tactician with a penchant for throwing very few interceptions. The Packer defense had set standards for all pro-football teams. Green Bay's mobile front four, big yet fast linebackers, and ball-hawking man-to-man pass defenders had written the book on modern defense. Presiding over it all and adding the special edge was coach Lombardi, the inspirational leader, the tough disciplinarian, the devout Catholic and family man, and a football theorist who set a tone for pro football which still is strong. Lombardi believed that the team that blocks and tackles best wins, and he drilled his teams to block crisply, to tackle hard, and to win.

So, on a warm January day in Los Angeles, the champions of two different leagues who played the same game but had never met came together on the same field. At first it was strange to see these two teams at the same time, but the fans and teams themselves soon settled into a very important football game for a lot of money plus the title of champion of all professional football.

The Chiefs fought the Packers to a standstill for most of the first period, but Green Bay got onto the scoreboard with a 37-yard pass from Bart Starr to Max McGee. Filling in for the injured Boyd Dowler, the thirty-four-year-old McGee would haul in seven passes today; eased out of the starting lineup this past season, he had caught only three passes during the regular campaign.

The Packers, however, were giving the Chiefs their first taste of what NFL teams had had to put up with for years. The only AFL fullback who had ever run with the ferocity of Jim Taylor was Cookie Gilchrist, who now was past his prime. The AFL had never produced as violent and perceptive a middle linebacker as Ray Nitschke, or as devastating a pair of corner linebackers as Dave Robinson and Lee Roy Caffey. The first quarter ended with the score only 7-0, but the Packers seemed to be on the verge of blowing the game wide open.

Far from folding, however, the Chiefs played their best football of the afternoon in the second period. Dawson's passes seemingly were finding gaps in the Packers' pass defense. Throwing both to his ends and backs, Dawson methodically moved the Chiefs downfield until they had the ball on the Green Bay seven-yard line. A short pass to fullback Curtis McClinton carried the ball into the end zone and marked the first time an AFL team had scored on an NFL team; some experts had freely predicted a Green Bay shutout in this contest. Seconds after the touchdown, Mike Mercer's extra-point kick knotted the score at 7-7.

With all expectations of an easy rout laid to rest, the Packers went to work on the next series of downs. Mixing passes and running plays, Starr drove the Packers deep into Kansas City territory, keying on several weak points he had discovered in the Chiefs' defense. He found that the Packers could run at end Chuck Hurston and tackle Andy Rice and throw against Sherrill Headrick, Fred Williamson, and Willie Mitchell; these men had held up against AFL competition but seemed out of their depth against the Packers. Green Bay especially enjoyed throwing against Williamson, since he had bragged that his hammer tackle, which was really only a forearm smash, would wreak havoc with the Packers. In the second half, Williamson himself would be carried from the field unconscious, the victim of a Green Bay "hammer tackle" of sorts.

Moving fairly easy through the Chiefs, the Packers scored their second touchdown on a 14-yard run by Jim Taylor, who simply ran over several Chiefs on the way to the end zone. Don Chandler's kick made the score 14-7, but the Chiefs were not yet ready to give up. Dawson responded with his own passing attack, and a 31-yard Mercer field goal cut the Green Bay lead to 14-10 at halftime.

The Chiefs had stayed surprisingly close to the Packers in the first half, and a good final thirty minutes of play could have brought them an upset victory. Beginning the second half with high hopes, the Chiefs quickly met with a misfortune which let all the air out of them. Dawson dropped back to pass but was surrounded by a strong Green Bay pass rush; instead of eating the ball and taking the loss, he heaved the ball downfield. Willie Wood of the Packers picked it off and brought it back all the way to the Kansas City five-yard line. Elijah Pitts carried it over from there, and the game was never the same afterward. The Packers oozed confidence the rest of the afternoon, while the Chiefs simply looked outmanned.

Dawson found it much harder to move the ball in the second half, and the Chiefs never threatened to score in the final two periods. The Packers, meanwhile, took firm control of the game with good blocking and tackling. Max McGee's second touchdown catch of the day built the Packer lead up to 28-10 after three quarters, and Elijah Pitts' second touchdown run made the final score 35-10.

The Chiefs came away beaten but not disgraced. Although the Green Bay steamroller eventually ground them down, the Chiefs never gave up, and their first-half showing proved that an AFL club could hold its own with a top NFL club—at least for thirty minutes. Coach Stram did learn from the game which of his players could be exploited by a strong club, and he was making plans to replace certain men before a week had passed after the game.

For Vince Lombardi and the Packers, the victory added one more trophy to their collection. Green Bay had won several NFL titles in the 1960s, and now they had won the Super Bowl, a distinct product of this decade.

Some people claimed that Super Bowl I proved the inferiority of the AFL. Probably closer to the truth was the statement that the Chiefs were not inferior to the NFL, only to the Green Bay Packers.

KANSAS CITY		GREEN BAY
	OFFENSE	
Burford	LE	Dale
Tyrer	LT	Skoronski
Budde	LG	Thurston
Frazier	C	Curry
Merz	RG	Kramer
Hill	RT	Gregg
Arbanas	RE	Fleming
Dawson	QB	Starr
O. Taylor	FL	Dowler
Garrett	HB	E. Pitts
McClinton	FB	J. Taylor
	DEFENSE	
Mays	LE	Davis
Rice	LT	Kostelnik
Buchanan	RT	Jordan
Hurston	RE	Aldridge
Bell	LLB	D. Robinson
Headrick	MLB	Nitschke
Holub	RLB	Coffey
Williamson	LCB	Adderley
Mitchell	RCB	Jeter
Hunt	LS	T. Brown
J. Robinson	RS	Wood

SUBSTITUTES
KANSAS CITY
Offense
Beathard, Gilliam
Biodrowski, F. Pitts
Carolan, Reynolds
Coan, G. Thomas
DiMidio
Defense
Abell, Smith
A. Brown, Stover
Corey, E. Thomas
Ply
Kickers
Mercer, Wilson

GREEN BAY
Offense
B. Anderson, Long
D. Anderson, Mack
Bowman, McGee
Bratkowski, Vandersea
Gillingham, Wright
Grabowski
Defense
B. Brown, Heathcock
Crutcher, Weatherwax
Hart
Kicker
Chandler

SCORING

KANSAS CITY	0	10	0	0—10
GREEN BAY	7	7	14	7—35

First Quarter
G.B. McGee, 37 yard pass from Starr
PAT — Chandler (kick)

Second Quarter
K.C. McClinton, 17 yard pass from Dawson PAT — Mercer (kick)
G.B. Taylor, 14 yard rush PAT — Chandler (kick)
K.C. Mercer, 31 yard field goal

Third Quarter
G.B. Pitts, 5 yard rush PAT — Chandler (kick)
G.B. McGee, 13 yard pass from Starr PAT — Chandler (kick)

Fourth Quarter
G.B. Pitts, 1 yard rush PAT — Chandler (kick)

TEAM STATISTICS

K.C.		G.B.
17	First Downs — Total	21
4	First Downs — Rushing	10
12	First Downs — Passing	11
1	First Downs — Penalty	0
1	Fumbles — Number	1
0	Fumbles — Lost Ball	0
4	Penalties — Number	4
26	Yards Penalized	40
64	Total Offensive Plays	64
239	Total Net Yards	358
3.7	Average Gain	5.6
1	Missed Field Goals	0
1	Giveaways	1
1	Takeaways	1
0	Difference	0

* includes Punts

INDIVIDUAL STATISTICS

KANSAS CITY / GREEN BAY

RUSHING

KANSAS CITY	No	Yds	Avg.	GREEN BAY	No	Yds	Avg.
Dawson	3	24	8.0	Taylor	16	53	3.3
Garrett	6	17	2.8	Pitts	11	45	4.1
McClinton	6	16	2.7	D. Anderson	4	30	7.5
Beathard	1	14	14.0	Grabowski	2	2	1.0
Coan	3	1	0.3		33	130	3.9
	19	72	3.8				

RECEIVING

	No	Yds	Avg.		No	Yds	Avg.
Burford	4	67	16.8	McGee	7	138	19.7
Taylor	4	57	14.3	Dale	4	59	14.8
Garrett	3	28	9.3	Pitts	2	32	16.0
McClinton	2	34	17.0	Fleming	2	22	11.0
Arbanas	2	30	15.0	Taylor	1	−1	−1.0
Carolan	1	7	7.0		16	250	15.6
Coan	1	5	5.0				
	17	228	13.4				

PUNTING

	No	Yds	Avg.		No	Yds	Avg.
Wilson	7		45.3	Chandler	3		43.3
				D. Anderson	1		43.0
					4		43.3

PUNT RETURNS

	No	Yds	Avg.		No	Yds	Avg.
Garrett	2	17	9.5	D. Anderson	3	25	8.3
E. Thomas	1	2	2.0	Wood	1	−2	−2.0
	3	19	6.3		4	23	5.8

KICKOFF RETURNS

	No	Yds	Avg.		No	Yds	Avg.
Coan	4	87	21.8	Adderley	2	40	20.0
Garrett	2	43	21.5	D. Anderson	1	25	25.0
	6	130	21.7		3	65	21.7

INTERCEPTION RETURNS

	No	Yds	Avg.		No	Yds	Avg.
Mitchell	1	0	0.0	Wood	1	50	50.0

PASSING

KANSAS CITY	Att	Comp	Comp Pct.	Yds	Int	Yds/ Att.	Yds/ Comp	Yards Lost Tackled
Dawson	27	16	59.3	211	1	7.8	13.2	43
Beathard	5	1	20.0	17	0	3.4	17.0	18
	32	17	53.1	228	1	7.1	13.4	6—61

GREEN BAY	Att	Comp	Comp Pct.	Yds	Int	Yds/ Att.	Yds/ Comp	Yards Lost Tackled
Starr	23	16	69.6	250	1	10.9	15.6	3—22
Bratkowski	1	0	0.0	0	0	—	—	0
	24	16	66.7	250	1	10.4	15.6	3—22

1967 N.F.L.   Four Crowns and Then Some

With expansion to New Orleans bringing league membership to sixteen clubs, the NFL revamped its post-season playoff system by dividing the Eastern and Western conferences into four four-team divisions. The champions of the Coastal and Central divisions would meet for the Western crown, and the champions of the Capitol and Century divisions would meet for the Eastern crown; the winners of these matches then would clash for the NFL championship. This new arrangement expanded post-season title play to three weeks, with conference championships, the league championship, and the Super Bowl.

EASTERN CONFERENCE — CAPITOL DIVISION

Dallas Cowboys—Injuries to Don Meredith, Dan Reeves, and Dave Manders slowed the offense up, but the Cowboys still had more than enough power to take the Capitol Division crown. The Cowboys had depth few teams could match, so that coach Tom Landry could find adequate replacements for his wounded troops. When quarterback Meredith missed three games, young Craig Morton filled in well, and Mike Connelly took over for Manders at center. The Dallas defense kept its fine edge, with Bob Lilly, Chuck Howley, and Cornell Green winning All-Pro honors.

Philadelphia Eagles—A disappointing season had fans calling for coach Joe Kuharich's ouster at the end of the year. The Eagles hoped to challenge the Cowboys after obtaining receivers Gary Ballman and Mike Ditka, but with their rash of injuries the Eagles were lucky to hold onto second place. Timmy Brown, Bob Brown, Lane Howell, Al Nelson, Ditka, and Ballman all missed stretches of the schedule. Despite poor protection, quarterback Norm Snead had a good year, with flanker Ben Hawkins his chief pass receiver. The Eagle defense, however, could be blamed more on a lack of talent in the line than on injuries.

Washington Redskins—Three Redskin receivers finished in the top four in the receiving statistics, and Sonny Jurgensen won the league passing title, yet the Skins finished in third place in the Capitol Division. The running and kicking games gave the passing attack little support, so opposing defenses knew the Redskins would come out throwing. Coach Otto Graham thought he had found a good fullback in first-draft choice Ray McDonald, but the big freshman was a big disappointment.

New Orleans Saints—Coach Tom Fears stocked his team liberally with veterans, with Billy Kilmer, Jim Taylor, Ray Poage, Dough Atkins, Earl Leggett, Lou Cordileone, Jackie Burkett, and Dave Whitsell all key men. The Saints did uncover two good rookies in Dan Abramowicz, a slow-footed receiver with good moves, and defensive tackle Dave Rowe, but the team relied mostly on oldsters whose best days were behind them.

CENTURY DIVISION

Cleveland Browns—A bad arm troubled quarterback Frank Ryan, defensive ends Paul Wiggin and Bill Glass slumped off in their early thirties, Erich Barnes was slowing up at cornerback, and forty-three-year-old Lou Groza was not getting the old zip into his kicks. The Browns still had top performers in Leroy Kelly, Paul Warfield, Gary Collins, Dick Schafrath, Gene Hickerson, Jim Houston and other veterans at their peak, and with the other clubs in the Century Division experiencing problems, the Browns coasted to the title without much of a challenge.

New York Giants—The Giants sent a bundle of draft choices to Minnesota for quarterback Fran Tarkenton, and the scrambling quarterback immediately injected an element of excitement back into the team. Tarkenton found a kindred spirit in split end Homer Jones, a fast receiver who ran around until he got open rather than execute precise pass patterns; Tarkenton found Jones in the open often enough for Jones to gain 1,209 yards and score thirteen touchdowns.

St. Louis Cardinals—The Cards had some of the league's best talent, a flashy blitzing defense, and a top place-kicker in Jim Bakken, but head coach Charlie Winner had his hands full of problems this season. Before the regular season even started, quarterback Charley Johnson was drafted into the Army, leaving inexperienced Jim Hart at the throttle; the youngster showed a strong arm and a tendency to throw interceptions. By the end of the year, racial tension burst into the open, with black players claiming that not enough of them were used on defense.

Pittsburgh Steelers—Bill Nelsen's bad knees again forced the Steelers to field a substitute quarterback for part of the season, and this year's emergency passer was Kent Nix, former Green Bay taxi-squader. The Pittsburgh offense frightened few opponents, but the defense was a solid, hard-working unit that kept the Steelers in most of their games. The club won only four games, but their losses included a 27-24 decision to New York and a 15-10 defeat by Washington.

WESTERN CONFERENCE — CENTRAL DIVISION

Green Bay Packers—Coach Vince Lombardi thought he was well covered at running back despite the departure of both Jim Taylor and Paul Hornung from the roster, but injuries sent him scurrying in all directions for healthy ball-carriers. Elijah Pitts and Jim Grabowski missed the late-season games with physical ills, leaving Lombardi with only Donny Anderson from the regular runners. To flesh out the backfield, Lombardi picked up journeymen Ben Wilson and Chuck Mercein and started playing rookie Travis Williams at halfback. Williams was the talk of the league with his blistering kickoff returning, and now he combined with the other substitute Packer ball-carriers in a backfield that didn't look good but punched out the necessary yardage to win.

Chicago Bears—The Bear defense regularly held opponents under 20 points, but the offense rarely capitalized on this during the first half of the schedule. Over the last seven games, the offense generated enough points to win five and tie one. Gale Sayers shone as usual throughout the year, but other players helped him move the ball down the stretch. Jack Concannon, the scrambling quarterback obtained from Philadelphia for Mike Ditka, settled comfortably into the Chicago system after October, hustling Brian Piccolo provided a running threat besides Sayers, and Dick Gordon developed into a dangerous receiver. After this flourishing finish, seventy-three-year-old George Halas called it quits as a coach.

Detroit Lions—The team had problems in the passing and kicking departments, but two gilt-edge rookies entertained fans all season. Halfback Mel Farr ran for 860 yards to give the Lions their first running threat in years. In the defensive secondary, rookie Lem Barney covered the league's best receivers without giving anything away, and once he got his hands on an errant enemy pass he threatened to sprint away to a touchdown.

Minnesota Vikings—Gone were coach Norm Van Brocklin, Fran Tarkenton, and Tommy Mason, and coming down from Canada were new head coach Bud Grant and quarterback Joe Kapp. The trade of Tarkenton to New York gave the Vikings some extra high draft choices, so their rookie class was a rich one, including Alan Page, Gene Washington, Clint Jones, John Beasley, and Bob Grim.

COASTAL DIVISION

Los Angeles Rams—Myron Pottios took over for the retired Bill George at middle linebacker, and big Roger Brown was purchased from Detroit to replace the injured Rosie Grier, but the defense continued to play with an almost perfect teamwork. Quarterback Roman Gabriel ran a ball-control offense that scored enough points to win eleven games and lose only one during the season. The Baltimore Colts stayed right with the Rams in the standings, but Los Angeles took the Coastal title by outscoring Baltimore in their two meetings.

Baltimore Colts—Even while replacing some old veterans, the Colts still swept to a 11-1-2 record. Receivers Ray Berry and Jimmy Orr went out with injuries, and subs Willie Richardson and Alex Hawkins filled in in fine fashion. Offensive tackle Jim Parker retired in mid-season with physical ills, and Sam Ball effectively plugged the hole in the line. Two rookies, huge tackle Bubba Smith and safety Rick Volk, saved a lot of action on defense. But Johnny Unitas and the tough Colt defense kept the Colts strong during all the changes.

San Francisco '49ers—Quarterback John Brodie was inconsistent, split end Dave Parks was hurt, and the team lost three of four games with the Rams and Colts. The defense developed into a solid unit, with a strong pass rush, a top linebacker in Dave Wilcox, and two good cornerbacks in Jim Johnson and Kermit Alexander, but the offense lacked the firepower to move the club above the .500 mark.

Atlanta Falcons—The rookie crop brought little help, leaving the Falcons with the same top men as last year. Tommy Nobis, Randy Johnson, and Junior Coffey continued the strong play of their rookie seasons, but coach Norb Hecker could augment his squad only with castoffs from other clubs as defensive tackle Jim Norton, split end Jerry Simmons, and veteran flanker Tommy McDonald helped out among the bargain acquisitions.

OFFENSE

	ATL.	BALT.	CHI.	CLEV.	DALL.	DET.	G.B.	L.A.	MINN.	N.O.	N.Y.	PHIL.	PITT.	ST.L.	S.F.	WASH.
FIRST DOWNS:																
Total	180	**289**	175	238	261	215	243	262	199	220	274	239	252	248	242	280
by Rushing	68	105	98	**119**	109	104	115	106	91	67	115	69	83	97	101	82
by Passing	95	159	62	102	141	92	112	133	85	135	135	146	145	131	121	**177**
by Penalty	17	**25**	15	17	11	19	16	23	23	18	24	24	24	20	20	21
RUSHING:																
Number	344	443	489	444	477	473	474	**490**	454	334	436	328	431	472	434	345
Yards	1303	1645	1852	**2139**	1900	1907	1915	1906	1811	1192	1864	1250	1397	1839	1764	1247
Average Yards	3.8	3.7	3.8	**4.8**	4.0	4.0	4.0	3.9	4.0	3.6	4.3	3.8	3.2	3.9	4.1	3.6
Touchdowns	6	**21**	12	15	13	14	18	16	10	9	16	12	13	15	16	13
PASSING:																
Attempts	370	457	268	333	417	351	331	390	336	478	406	445	442	431	469	**527**
Completions	179	265	131	160	210	160	182	206	150	237	221	244	214	204	228	**301**
Completion Percentage	48.4	**58.0**	48.9	48.0	50.4	45.6	55.0	52.8	44.6	49.6	54.4	54.8	48.4	47.3	48.6	57.1
Passing Yards	2144	3561	1673	2314	3093	1826	2758	2947	1951	2989	3382	3463	2781	3170	2862	**3887**
Average Yards per Attempt (Gross)	5.8	7.8	6.2	6.9	7.4	5.2	**8.3**	7.6	5.8	6.3	8.3	7.8	6.3	7.4	6.1	7.4
Average Yards per Completion (Gross)	12.0	13.4	12.8	14.5	14.7	11.4	15.2	14.3	13.0	12.6	15.3	14.2	13.0	**15.5**	12.6	12.9
Times Tackled Attempting to Pass	49	25	27	44	42	24	41	25	35	52	37	49	30	24	26	**19**
Yards Lost Tackled Attempting to Pass	434	198	232	372	294	195	394	213	284	391	342	369	270	229	208	**157**
Net Yards	1710	3363	1441	1942	2799	1631	2364	2734	1667	2598	3040	3094	2511	2941	2654	**3730**
Touchdowns	13	22	9	22	28	14	15	28	11	13	**33**	30	19	20	16	31
Interceptions	25	17	18	18	28	19	27	**16**	24	23	20	24	29	35	26	17
Percent Intercepted	6.8	3.7	6.7	5.4	6.7	5.4	8.2	4.1	7.1	4.8	4.9	5.4	6.6	8.1	5.5	**3.2**
PUNTS:																
Number	**87**	49	79	67	67	83	66	68	75	74	55	61	72	62	73	72
Average Distance	**43.7**	42.3	42.9	37.1	40.4	40.5	36.5	42.2	41.6	42.9	36.0	38.3	38.1	40.8	37.6	41.3
PUNT RETURNS:																
Number	25	42	22	35	33	34	39	**50**	35	23	22	29	30	34	35	34
Yards	94	323	194	**357**	320	97	157	328	107	79	102	158	143	198	314	203
Average Yards	3.8	7.7	8.8	**10.2**	9.7	2.9	4.0	6.6	3.1	3.4	4.6	5.4	4.8	5.8	9.0	6.0
Touchdowns	0	**1**	**1**	**1**	**1**	0	0	0	0	0	0	0	0	0	0	0
KICKOFF RETURNS:																
Number	69	42	47	55	48	50	46	43	53	**72**	69	62	58	66	56	61
Yards	1471	988	1157	1396	1014	1145	1241	1033	1215	**1739**	1363	1246	1221	1372	1326	1330
Average Yards	21.3	23.5	24.6	25.4	21.1	22.9	**27.0**	24.0	22.9	24.2	19.8	20.1	21.1	20.8	23.7	21.8
Touchdowns	1	0	3	1	0	0	**4**	0	1	2	0	0	0	0	0	1
INTERCEPTION RETURNS:																
Number	17	**32**	28	22	29	23	26	**32**	16	22	17	21	26	19	16	20
Yards	343	453	334	375	331	343	284	**476**	316	333	209	274	264	205	198	183
Average Yards	**20.2**	14.2	11.9	17.0	11.4	14.9	10.9	14.9	19.8	15.1	12.3	13.0	10.2	10.8	12.4	9.2
Touchdowns	2	3	2	3	3	**6**	2	4	2	2	0	2	1	1	0	1
PENALTIES:																
Number	88	52	98	72	81	65	48	85	**100**	76	80	77	68	65	89	67
Yards	866	458	953	773	785	712	531	854	**1075**	785	842	830	759	720	931	588
FUMBLES:																
Number	20	**13**	25	24	26	32	19	32	23	21	21	22	33	23	20	26
Number Lost	14	**8**	14	17	14	21	10	13	13	14	10	16	16	11	10	14
POINTS:																
Total	175	394	239	334	342	260	332	**398**	233	233	369	351	281	333	273	347
PAT Attempts	22	48	29	43	45	34	39	48	26	27	**49**	45	35	36	33	47
PAT Made	22	46	26	43	41	33	39	**48**	26	27	45	45	35	36	33	42
FG Attempts	18	37	26	23	23	21	29	**43**	33	32	21	19	22	39	33	26
FG Made	7	20	13	11	9	7	19	20	17	14	10	12	12	**27**	14	7
Percent FG Made	38.9	54.1	50.0	47.8	39.1	33.3	65.5	46.5	51.5	43.8	47.6	63.2	54.5	**69.2**	42.4	26.9
Safeties	0	0	0	0	**2**	1	1	1	0	1	0	0	0	0	0	1

DEFENSE

	ATL.	BALT.	CHI.	CLEV.	DALL.	DET.	G.B.	L.A.	MINN.	N.O.	N.Y.	PHIL.	PITT.	ST.L.	S.F.	WASH.
FIRST DOWNS:																
Total	294	208	215	281	236	205	**183**	200	217	276	261	286	228	216	237	274
by Rushing	124	78	91	115	**64**	98	98	75	105	114	113	105	80	79	92	98
by Passing	152	116	98	153	145	85	**78**	104	90	138	125	161	128	117	128	153
by Penalty	18	14	26	13	27	22	**7**	21	22	24	23	20	20	20	17	23
RUSHING:																
Number	504	387	419	459	**339**	471	443	361	500	469	416	434	418	410	407	431
Yards	2139	1411	1531	1767	**1081**	1795	1923	1119	2104	2092	1799	1741	1377	1502	1698	1852
Average Yards	4.2	3.6	3.7	3.8	3.2	3.8	4.3	**3.1**	4.2	4.5	4.3	4.0	3.3	3.7	4.2	4.3
Touchdowns	18	**5**	11	15	11	15	7	6	12	22	20	16	12	13	17	19
PASSING:																
Attempts	421	395	384	454	482	**312**	337	445	314	410	389	480	397	360	403	468
Completions	238	221	164	250	260	**143**	155	212	149	207	195	255	201	169	212	261
Completion Percentage	56.5	55.9	**42.7**	55.1	53.9	45.8	46.0	47.6	47.5	50.5	50.1	53.1	50.6	46.9	52.6	55.8
Passing Yards	3588	2678	2146	3231	3167	2089	**1644**	2694	2071	3035	2731	3382	2854	3023	2755	3713
Average Yards per Attempt (Gross)	8.5	6.8	5.6	7.1	6.6	6.7	**4.9**	6.1	6.6	7.4	7.0	7.0	7.2	8.4	6.8	7.9
Average Yards per Completion (Gross)	15.1	12.1	13.1	12.9	12.2	14.6	**10.6**	12.7	13.9	14.7	14.0	13.3	14.2	17.9	13.0	14.2
Times Tackled Attempting to Pass	21	36	30	41	45	39	29	43	36	23	31	23	29	37	**48**	38
Yards Lost Tackled Attempting to Pass	196	246	271	332	377	356	267	287	319	199	246	151	276	340	**409**	310
Net Yards	3392	2432	1875	2899	2790	1733	**1377**	2407	1752	2836	2485	3231	2578	2683	2346	3403
Touchdowns	31	13	14	19	21	**11**	13	14	17	25	25	29	22	26	19	25
Interceptions	17	**32**	28	22	29	23	26	**32**	16	22	17	21	26	19	16	20
Percent Intercepted	4.0	**8.1**	7.3	4.8	6.0	7.4	7.7	7.2	5.1	5.4	4.4	4.4	6.5	5.3	4.0	4.3
PUNTS:																
Number	49	69	77	62	72	79	75	**86**	79	63	56	50	70	81	70	72
Average Distance	39.9	39.4	41.3	39.9	42.5	39.3	41.6	40.8	38.9	39.9	39.7	**38.8**	38.9	39.0	43.8	40.1
PUNT RETURNS:																
Number	54	21	41	29	37	38	**13**	33	39	35	21	33	39	24	29	36
Yards	408	144	168	70	266	323	**22**	240	163	261	214	130	277	79	175	234
Average Yards	7.6	6.9	4.1	2.4	7.2	8.5	**1.7**	7.3	4.2	7.5	10.2	3.9	7.1	3.3	6.0	6.5
Touchdowns	**0**	**0**	**0**	**0**	**0**	1	**0**	**0**	**0**	**0**	**0**	**0**	1	1	1	**0**
KICKOFF RETURNS:																
Number	**38**	65	52	59	59	43	59	66	48	51	69	59	56	65	54	54
Yards	**889**	1483	1064	1288	1350	959	1276	1414	1076	1166	1511	1466	1300	1481	1311	1223
Average Yards	23.4	22.8	**20.5**	21.8	22.9	22.3	21.6	21.4	22.4	22.9	21.9	24.8	23.2	22.8	24.3	22.6
Touchdowns	**0**	1	**0**	2	**0**	1	**0**	2	**0**	**0**	1	2	1	1	1	1
INTERCEPTION RETURNS:																
Number	25	17	18	18	28	19	27	**16**	24	23	20	24	29	35	26	17
Yards	326	272	246	290	353	235	370	**186**	315	303	216	429	368	469	292	251
Average Yards	13.0	16.0	13.7	16.1	12.6	12.4	13.7	11.6	13.1	13.2	**10.8**	17.9	12.7	13.4	11.2	14.8
Touchdowns	4	2	1	1	3	2	3	**0**	4	**0**	1	3	1	5	3	1
PENALTIES:																
Number	87	82	82	57	64	73	55	**91**	90	83	68	67	73	89	64	86
Yards	853	**927**	782	655	717	822	482	912	906	824	774	715	833	782	596	882
FUMBLES:																
Number	26	17	23	28	27	13	23	18	**38**	21	28	28	26	19	24	21
Number Lost	10	8	16	14	**19**	10	14	13	**19**	10	15	14	13	13	13	14
POINTS:																
Total	422	198	218	297	268	259	209	**196**	294	379	379	409	320	356	337	353
PAT Attempts	53	**21**	27	37	35	32	24	23	34	48	48	52	39	46	41	46
PAT Made	52	**21**	26	36	34	31	23	22	34	46	47	52	36	42	40	45
FG Attempts	39	28	26	25	23	29	28	26	31	29	21	32	30	**19**	35	24
FG Made	16	17	10	13	**8**	12	14	12	18	15	14	15	16	12	17	10
Percent FG Made	41.0	60.7	38.5	52.0	**34.8**	41.4	50.0	46.2	58.1	51.7	66.7	46.9	53.3	63.2	48.6	41.7
Safeties	2	**0**	**0**	**0**	**0**	**0**	**0**	**0**	1	**0**	1	**0**	1	1	**0**	1

CONFERENCE PLAYOFFS

December 23, at Milwaukee (Attendance 49,861)

at Milwaukee (Attendance 49,861)

SCORING

GREEN BAY	0	14	7	7–28
LOS ANGELES	7	0	0	0– 7

First Quarter
L.A. Casey, 28 yard pass from Gabriel
PAT—Gossett (kick)

Second Quarter
G.B. Williams, 46 yard rush
PAT—Chandler (kick)
G.B. Dale, 18 yard pass from Starr
PAT—Chandler (kick)

Third Quarter
G.B. Mercein, 6 yard rush
PAT—Chandler (kick)

Fourth Quarter
G.B. Williams, 2 yard rush
PAT—Chandler (kick)

TEAM STATISTICS

G.B.		L.A.
20	First Downs—Total	12
11	First Downs—Rushing	2
8	First Downs—Passing	9
1	First Downs—Penalty	1
1	Times Tackled Passing	5
11	Yards Lost—Tackled	44
3	Fumbles—Number	0
3	Fumbles—Lost Ball	0
7	Penalties—Number	3
44	Yards Penalized	25
5	Punts—Number	6
32.6	Punts—Average Distance	39.3
3	Punt Returns—Number	1
44	Punt Returns—Yards	0
2	Kickoff Returns—Number	4
19	Kickoff Returns—Yards	80
1	Interception Returns—Number	1
20	Interception Returns—Yards	24
4	Giveaways	1
1	Takeaways	4
−3	Difference	+3

INDIVIDUAL STATISTICS

GREEN BAY	No	Yds	Avg.	LOS ANGELES	No	Yds	Avg.
RUSHING							
Williams	18	88	4.9	Bass	14	40	2.9
Anderson	12	52	4.3	Jo'phson	9	16	1.8
Mercein	12	13	1.1	Gabriel	3	6	2.0
Starr	2	8	4.0	Mason	2	13	6.5
Wilson	1	2	2.0		28	75	2.7
	45	163	3.6				
RECEIVING							
Dale	6	109	18.2	Casey	5	82	16.4
Dowler	3	35	11.7	Traux	2	45	22.5
Fleming	3	30	10.0	Jo'phson	2	30	15.0
Anderson	2	30	15.0	Snow	1	17	17.0
Mercein	2	10	5.0	Pope	1	12	12.0
Williams	1	8	8.0		11	186	16.9
	17	222	13.1				

PASSING

G.B.	Att.	Cmp.	Comp. Pct.	Yds.	Int.	Yds/ Att.	Yds/ Comp.
Starr	23	17	73.9	222	1	9.7	13.1
L.A.							
Gabriel	31	11	35.5	186	1	6.0	16.9

DALLAS	14	10	21	7–52
CLEVELAND	0	7	0	7–14

First Quarter
Dal. Baynham, 3 yard pass from Meredith
PAT—Villanueva (kick)
Dal. Perkins, 4 yard rush
PAT—Villanueva (kick)

Second Quarter
Dal. Hayes, 86 yard pass from Meredith
PAT—Villanueva (kick)
Dal. Villanueva, 10 yard field goal
Cle. Morin, 13 yard pass from Ryan
PAT—Groza (kick)

Third Quarter
Dal. Baynham, 1 yard rush
PAT—Villanueva (kick)
Dal. Perkins, 1 yard rush
PAT—Villanueva (kick)
Dal. Green, 60 yard interception return
PAT—Villanueva (kick)

Fourth Quarter
Dal. Baynham, 1 yard rush
PAT—Villanueva (kick)
Cle. Warfield, 75 yard pass from Ryan
PAT—Groza (kick)

December 24, at Dallas (Attendance 70,786)

TEAM STATISTICS

DAL.		CLE.
22	First Downs—Total	15
13	First Downs—Rushing	4
7	First Downs—Passing	10
2	First Downs—Penalty	1
1	Times Tackled Passing	5
2	Yards Lost Tackled	31
2	Fumbles—Number	0
1	Fumbles—Lost Ball	0
2	Penalties—Number	2
10	Yards Penalized	18
2	Punts—Number	7
44.5	Punts—Average Distance	39.8
4	Punt Returns—Number	2
155	Punt Returns—Yards	11
1	Kickoff Returns—Number	7
4	Kickoff Returns—Yards	112
1	Interception Returns—Number	1
60	Interception Returns—Yards	0
2	Giveaways	1
1	Takeaways	2
−1	Difference	+1

INDIVIDUAL STATISTICS

DALLAS	No	Yds	Avg.	CLEVELAND	No	Yds	Avg.
RUSHING							
Perkins	18	74	4.1	Kelly	15	96	6.4
Baynham	13	50	3.8	Green	10	49	4.9
Garrison	9	33	3.6	Ryan	2	14	7.0
Clarke	1	8	8.0		27	159	5.9
Reeves	3	7	2.3				
Meredith	2	6	3.0				
	46	178	3.9				
RECEIVING							
Hayes	5	144	28.8	Kelly	4	39	9.8
Rentzel	3	65	21.7	Warf'ld	3	99	33.9
Reeves	1	9	9.0	Morin	3	35	11.7
Perkins	1	4	4.0	Green	3	18	6.0
Baynham	1	3	3.0	Collins	1	3	3.0
	11	225	20.5		14	194	13.9

PASSING

DALL.	Att	Cmp	Pct	Yds	Int	Yd/A	Yd/C
Meredith	12	10	83.3	212	0	17.7	21.2
Morton	3	1	33.3	13	1	4.3	13.0
	15	11	73.3	225	1	15.0	20.5
CLEVE.							
Ryan	30	14	46.7	194	1	6.5	13.9

CAPITOL DIVISION

DALLAS COWBOYS 9-5-0 Tom Landry

Scores of Each Game			Use Name	Pos.	Hgt	Wgt	Age	Int	Pts
21	Cleveland	14	Jim Boeke	OT	6'5"	260	28		
38	NEW YORK	24	Ralph Neely	OT	6'5"	265	23		
13	LOS ANGELES	35	Tony Liscio	OT	6'5"	255	27		
17	Washington	14	Leon Donahue	OG	6'4"	245	28		
14	NEW ORLEANS	10	John Niland	OG	6'4"	245	23		
24	Pittsburgh	21	John Wilbur	OG	6'3"	240	24		
14	Philadelphia	21	Mike Connelly	C	6'3"	248	31		
37	ATLANTA	7	Malcolm Walker	OT-C	6'4"	250	24		
27	New Orleans	10	George Andrie	DE	6'7"	250	27		
20	WASHINGTON	27	Larry Stephens	DE	6'4"	250	29		
46	ST. LOUIS	21	Willie Townes	DE	6'5"	260	24		
17	Baltimore	23	Ron East	DT	6'4"	242	24		
38	PHILADELPHIA	17	Bob Lilly	DT	6'4"	260	28		
16	San Francisco	24	Jethro Pugh	DT	6'6"	260	23		2

Use Name	Pos.	Hgt	Wgt	Age	Int	Pts
Dave Edwards	LB	6'3"	228	28	3	6
Harold Hays	LB	6'3"	225	26		
Chuck Howley	LB	6'3"	225	31	1	6
Lee Roy Jordan	LB	6'2"	225	26	3	8
Phil Clark	DB	6'2"	207	22	1	
Dick Daniels	DB	5'9"	180	21		
Mike Gaechter	DB	6'	190	27	2	
Cornell Green	DB	6'4"	208	27	7	
Mike Johnson	DB	5'10"	184	23	5	
Mel Renfro	DB	6'	190	25	7	
Buddy Dial — Injury						
Dave Manders — Injury						

Use Name	Pos.	Hgt	Wgt	Age	Int	Pts
Don Meredith	QB	6'2"	205	29		
Craig Morton	QB	6'4"	216	24		
Jerry Rhome	QB	6'	185	25		
Craig Baynham	HB	6'1"	200	23		6
Dan Reeves	HB	6'1"	200	23		66
Les Shy	HB	6'1"	200	23		
Don Perkins	FB	5'10"	200	29		36
Walt Garrison	HB-FB	6'	205	23		
Pete Gent	FL	6'4"	205	24		
Lance Rentzel	OE-FL	6'2"	200	23		48
Frank Clarke	TE	6'	210	34		12
Pettis Norman	TE	6'3"	225	27		12
Rayfield Wright	TE	6'7"	235	22		
Bob Hayes	OE	6'	185	24		66
Sims Stokes	OE	6'1"	198	23		
Harold Deters	K	6'	200	23		12
Danny Villanueva	K	5'11"	200	29		56

PHILADELPHIA EAGLES 6-7-1 Joe Kuharich

Scores of Each Game			Use Name	Pos.	Hgt	Wgt	Age	Int	Pts
35	WASHINGTON	24	Bob Brown	OT	6'4"	295	24		
6	BALTIMORE	38	Lane Howell	OT	6'5"	272	26		
34	PITTSBURGH	24	Randy Beisler	DE-OT	6'4"	245	22		
38	Atlanta	7	Dick Hart	OG	6'2"	250	24		
27	SAN FRANCISCO	28	Jim Skaggs	OG	6'2"	252	27		
14	St. Louis	48	Bill Stetz	OG	6'3"	250	23		
21	DALLAS	14	Gordon Wright	OG	6'3"	245	23		
24	New Orleans	31	Lynn Hoyem	C-OG	6'4"	253	27		
17	Los Angeles	33	Dave Recher	C	6'1"	246	24		
48	NEW ORLEANS	21	Jim Ringo	C	6'1"	230	36		
7	New York	44	Don Hultz	DE	6'3"	242	26	1	6
35	Washington	35	Gary Pettigrew	DE	6'4"	245	22		
17	Dallas	38	Mel Tom	DE	6'4"	243	26		
28	CLEVELAND	24	Dean Wink	DE	6'4"	246	24		
			John Meyers	DT	6'6"	276	27		
			Floyd Peters	DT	6'4"	255	32	1	

Use Name	Pos.	Hgt	Wgt	Age	Int	Pts
Fred Brown	LB	6'5"	232	24	2	
Ike Kelley	LB	5'11"	225	23	1	
Dave Lloyd	LB	6'3"	248	31	1	
Mike Morgan	LB	6'4"	242	25	1	
Arunas Vasys	LB	6'2"	235	24		
Harold Wells	LB	6'2"	220	28	1	
Jim Gray	DB	6'	182	25		
Aaron Martin	DB	6'	190	26	2	
Ron Medved	DB	6'1"	210	23	2	
Jim Nettles	DB	5'9"	177	25	4	6
Al Nelson	DB	5'11"	186	23	1	
Nate Ramsey	DB	6'1"	200	26		
Taft Reed	DB	6'2"	200	25		
Joe Scarpati	DB	5'10"	185	25	4	6
Bob Shann	DB	6'1"	190	24	1	
Dave Graham — Injury						
Frank Molden — Knee Injury						

Use Name	Pos.	Hgt	Wgt	Age	Int	Pts
Benjy Dial	QB	6'1"	185	24		
King Hill	QB	6'3"	216	31		
Norm Snead	QB	6'4"	215	27		12
Timmy Brown	HB	5'10"	198	30		12
Harry Jones	HB	6'2"	205	22		
Harry Wilson	HB	5'11"	204	22		
Izzy Lang	FB	6'1"	232	24		30
Tom Woodeshick	HB-FB	6'	220	25		60
Chuck Hughes	FL	5'11"	172	24		
Ron Goodwin	OE-FL	6'	180	25		
Ben Hawkins	OE-FL	5'11"	180	23		60
Mike Ditka	TE	6'3"	235	27		
Pete Emelianchik	TE	6'2"	220	24		
Jim Kelly	TE	6'2"	218	25		24
Dave Lince	TE	6'6"	265	23		
Fred Hill						
Gary Ballman	FL-OE	6'	205	27		42
Sam Baker	K	6'2"	218	35		81

WASHINGTON REDSKINS 5-6-3 Otto Graham

Scores of Each Game			Use Name	Pos.	Hgt	Wgt	Age	Int	Pts
24	Philadelphia	35	Mitch Johnson	OT	6'4"	250	25		
30	New Orleans	10	John Kelly	OT	6'3"	250	23		
38	NEW YORK	34	Jim Snowden	OT	6'3"	255	25		
14	DALLAS	17	Don Bandy	OG	6'3"	250	22		
20	Atlanta	20	Vince Promuto	OG	6'1"	245	29		
28	Los Angeles	28	Ray Schoenke	OG	6'3"	250	25		
13	BALTIMORE	17	Dave Crossan	C	6'3"	245	27		
21	ST. LOUIS	27	Len Hauss	C	6'2"	235	25		
31	SAN FRANCISCO	28	Heath Wingate	C	6'2"	240	25		
27	Dallas	20	Bill Briggs	DE	6'3"	250	23		
37	Cleveland	42	Carl Kammerer	DE	6'3"	243	25		
35	PHILADELPHIA	35	Ron Snidow	DE	6'4"	250	25		
15	Pittsburgh	10	Walt Barnes	DT	6'3"	250	23		
14	NEW ORLEANS	30	Spain Musgrave	DT	6'4"	275	22		
			Jim Prestel	DT	6'5"	275	30		
			Joe Rutgens	DT	6'2"	255	28		

Use Name	Pos.	Hgt	Wgt	Age	Int	Pts
Ed Breding	LB	6'4"	235	22		2
Jim Carroll	LB	6'1"	230	24	1	
Chris Hanburger	LB	6'2"	218	26		
Larry Hendershot	LB	6'3"	240	22		
Sam Huff	LB	6'1"	230	32	2	
Steve Jackson	LB	6'1"	225	24		
Sid Williams	LB	6'2"	235	25		
Rickie Harris	DB	6'	182	24	1	
Paul Krause	DB	6'3"	195	25	8	
Brig Owens	DB	5'11"	190	24	1	8
Lonnie Sanders	DB	6'3"	207	25		
Jim Shorter	DB	5'11"	185	26	4	
Tom Walters	DB	6'2"	195	25		
Dick Smith	OE-DB	6'	205	23	3	

Use Name	Pos.	Hgt	Wgt	Age	Int	Pts
Sonny Jurgensen	QB	5'11"	203	33		12
Jim Ninowski	QB	6'1"	207	31		
Jerry Allen	HB	6'1"	205	26		24
Pete Larson	HB	6'1"	200	23		6
Steve Thurlow	HB	6'3"	222	24		
Joe Don Looney	FB-HB	6'1"	230	24		6
Ray McDonald	FB	6'4"	248	23		
A. D. Whitfield	FB	5'10"	200	23		18
John Burrell	FL	6'3"	195	27		
T. J. Jackson	DB-FL	6'	180	24		
John Love	DB-FL	5'11"	185	22		24
Bobby Mitchell	HB-FL	6'	196	32		42
Pat Richter	TE	6'5"	230	26		
Jerry Smith	TE	6'2"	208	24		72
Charley Taylor	OE	6'3"	210	26		54
Bruce Alford	K	6'	185	22		
Charlie Gogolak	K	5'10"	165	22		6
Gene Mingo (from MIA-A)	K	6'1"	190	28		32

NEW ORLEANS 3-11-0 Tom Fears

Scores of Each Game			Use Name	Pos.	Hgt	Wgt	Age	Int	Pts
13	LOS ANGELES	27	Dick Anderson	OT	6'5"	245	22		2
10	WASHINGTON	30	George Harvey	OT	6'4"	245	21		
7	CLEVELAND	42	Jerry Jones	OT	6'3"	270	23		
21	New York	27	Dave McCormick	OT	6'6"	250	24		
10	Dallas	14	Ray Rissmiller	OT	6'4"	250	25		
13	San Francisco	27	Jerry Sturm	OT	6'3"	260	30		
10	PITTSBURGH	14	Roy Schmidt	OG	6'3"	250	25		
31	PHILADELPHIA	24	Eli Strand	OG	6'2"	250	24		
10	DALLAS	27	Del Williams	OG	6'2"	245	21		
21	Philadelphia	48	Joe Wendryhoski	C	6'2"	245	28		
27	ATLANTA	24	Doug Atkins	DE	6'8"	270	37		
20	St. Louis	31	Jim Garcia	DE	6'4"	250	23		
10	Baltimore	30	Brian Schweda	DE	6'3"	240	24		
30	Washington	14	Lou Cordileone	DT	6'	250	30		
			Earl Leggett	DT	6'3"	265	33		
			Dave Rowe	DT	6'6"	265	22		
			Mike Tilleman	DT	6'5"	260	23		

Use Name	Pos.	Hgt	Wgt	Age	Int	Pts
Jackie Burkett	LB	6'4"	228	30	3	
Bill Cody	LB	6'1"	220	23		
Ted Davis	LB	6'1"	232	25		
Les Kelley	LB	6'3"	233	22		
Dave Simmons	LB	6'4"	245	24	1	
Steve Stonebreaker	LB	6'3"	228	29		
Phil Vandersea	LB	6'3"	225	24		
Bo Burris	DB	6'3"	195	22		
Bruce Cortez	DB	6'	175	21		
John Douglas	DB	6'1"	195	22	1	
Ben Hart	DB	6'2"	205	21	1	
Jim Heidel	DB	6'1"	185	23	1	
Obert Logan	DB	5'10"	180	25	3	
George Rose	DB	5'11"	190	24	1	
Dave Whitsell	DB	6'	190	31	10	12

Use Name	Pos.	Hgt	Wgt	Age	Int	Pts
Gary Cuozzo	QB	6'1"	195	26		6
Billy Kilmer	QB	6'	204	27		6
Gary Wood	QB	5'11"	188	24		
Tom Barrington	HB	6'1"	213	23		
Charlie Brown	HB	5'10"	187	21		12
John Gilliam	HB	6'1"	190	22		12
Jimmy Jordan	HB	6'1"	200	23		
Don McCall	HB	5'11"	195	22		12
Randy Schultz	FB-HB	6'1"	210	23		12
Jim Taylor	FB	6'	215	32		12
Ernie Wheelwright (from ATL)	FB	6'3"	236	30		6
Elijah Nevett	FL	6'	185	23		
Walter Roberts	FL	5'10"	163	25		30
Tom Hall	OE-FL	6'1"	195	26		
Vern Burke	TE	6'4"	202	26		
Jim Hester	TE	6'4"	225	22		12
Kent Kramer	TE	6'5"	235	23		
Dan Abramowicz	OE	6'1"	197	22		36
Ray Poage	OE	6'4"	205	26		
Charlie Durkee	K	5'11"	165	23		69
Tom McNeill	K	6'1"	195	25		

CAPITOL DIVISION

DALLAS COWBOYS

RUSHING

Last Name	No.	Yds	Avg	TD
Perkins	201	823	4.1	6
Reeves	173	603	3.5	5
Garrison	24	146	6.1	0
Norman	9	91	10.1	0
Meredith	28	84	3.0	0
Clarke	4	72	18.0	0
Shy	17	59	3.5	0
Morton	15	42	2.8	0
Baynham	3	6	2.0	1
Rhome	2	−11	−5.5	0
Villanueva	1	−15	−15.0	0

RECEIVING

Last Name	No.	Yds	Avg	TD
Rentzel	58	996	17	8
Hayes	49	998	20	10
Reeves	39	490	13	6
Norman	20	220	11	2
Perkins	18	116	6	0
Clarke	9	119	13	1
Gent	9	88	10	1
Shy	3	36	12	0
Baynham	3	13	4	0
Garrison	2	17	9	0

PUNT RETURNS

Last Name	No.	Yds	Avg	TD
Hayes	24	276	12	1
Rentzel	6	45	18	0
Renfro	3	−1	0	0

KICKOFF RETURNS

Last Name	No.	Yds	Avg	TD
Garrison	20	366	18	0
Baynham	12	331	28	0
Renfro	5	112	22	0
Shy	5	96	19	0
Stokes	4	92	23	0
Hayes	1	17	17	0
East	1	0	0	0

PASSING — PUNTING — KICKING

PASSING	Att	Comp	%	Yds	Yd/Att	TD	Int−%	RK
Meredith	255	128	50	1834	7.2	16	16−6	8
Morton	137	69	50	978	7.1	10	10−7	
Rhome	18	9	50	86	4.8	0	1−6	
Reeves	7	4	57	195	27.9	2	1−14	

PUNTING	No	Avg
Villanueva	67	40.4

KICKING	XP	Att	%	FG	Att	%
Villanueva	32	34	94	8	19	42
Deters	9	10	90	1	4	25

PHILADELPHIA EAGLES

RUSHING

Last Name	No.	Yds	Avg	TD
Woodeshick	155	670	4.3	6
Lang	101	336	3.3	2
T. Brown	53	179	3.4	1
Snead	9	30	3.3	2
Jones	8	17	2.1	0
Ballman	1	17	17.0	1
Goodwin	1	1	1.0	0

RECEIVING

Last Name	No.	Yds	Avg	TD
Hawkins	59	1265	21	10
Ballman	36	524	15	6
Woodeshick	34	391	12	4
Ditka	26	274	11	2
Lang	26	201	8	3
T. Brown	22	202	9	1
Kelly	21	345	16	4
F. Hill	9	144	16	0
Goodwin	6	65	11	0
Jones	3	32	11	0
Wilson	2	20	10	0

PUNT RETURNS

Last Name	No.	Yds	Avg	TD
Martin	20	128	6	0
Shann	3	17	6	0
Hughes	3	11	4	0
Scarpati	1	2	2	0
Lince	1	0	0	0
Reed	1	0	0	0

KICKOFF RETURNS

Last Name	No.	Yds	Avg	TD
T. Brown	13	301	23	0
Hawkins	10	250	25	0
Wilson	7	150	21	0
Hughes	7	126	18	0
Shann	6	133	22	0
Reed	5	111	22	0
Lince	3	46	15	0
Ballman	2	43	22	0
Jones	2	32	16	0
Gray	1	30	30	0
F. Brown	1	17	17	0
Medved	1	7	7	0
Beisler	1	0	0	0
Kelley	1	0	0	0
Ramsey	1	0	0	0
Vasys	1	0	0	0

PASSING — PUNTING — KICKING

PASSING	Att	Comp	%	Yds	Yd/Att	TD	Int−%	RK
Snead	434	240	55	3399	7.8	29	24−6	5
K. Hill	7	2	29	33	4.7	1	0−0	
Dial	3	1	33	5	1.7	0	0−0	
Lang	1	1	100	26	26.0	0	0−0	

PUNTING	No	Avg
Baker	61	38.3

KICKING	XP	Att	%	FG	Att	%
Baker	45	45	100	12	19	63

WASHINGTON REDSKINS

RUSHING

Last Name	No.	Yds	Avg	TD
Whitfield	91	384	4.2	1
Allen	77	262	3.4	1
McDonald	52	223	4.3	4
Mitchell	61	189	3.1	1
Larson	25	84	3.4	1
Jurgensen	15	46	3.1	2
Thurlow	13	33	2.5	0
Looney	11	26	2.4	1

RECEIVING

Last Name	No.	Yds	Avg	TD
Taylor	70	990	14	9
J. Smith	67	849	13	12
Mitchell	60	866	14	6
Whitfield	36	494	14	2
Love	17	248	15	1
Allen	11	101	9	1
Thurlow	10	95	10	0
McDonald	10	60	6	0
Burrell	9	95	11	0
Larson	8	45	6	0
Richter	1	31	31	0
Looney	1	12	12	0
Hanburger	1	1	1	0

PUNT RETURNS

Last Name	No.	Yds	Avg	TD
Harris	23	208	9	0
Love	11	−5	−1	0

KICKOFF RETURNS

Last Name	No.	Yds	Avg	TD
Harris	25	580	23	0
Love	17	422	25	1
T. Jackson	7	131	19	0
D. Smith	4	120	30	0
Looney	2	42	21	0
Kelly	2	19	10	0
Allen	1	13	13	0
Burrell	1	2	2	0
Briggs	1	1	1	0
McDonald	1	0	0	0

PASSING — PUNTING — KICKING

PASSING	Att	Comp	%	Yds	Yd/Att	TD	Int−%	RK
Jurgenson	508	288	57	3747	7.4	31	16−3	1
Ninowski	18	12	67	123	6.8	0	1−6	
Mitchell	1	1	100	17	17.0	0	0−0	

PUNTING	No	Avg
Richter	72	41.3

KICKING	XP	Att	%	FG	Att	%
Mingo	20	22	91	4	10	40
Love	10	11	91	2	7	29
Alford	3	4	75	0	2	0
Gogolak	3	3	100	1	4	25
Owens	2	3	67	0	2	0

NEW ORLEANS SAINTS

RUSHING

Last Name	No.	Yds	Avg	TD
Taylor	130	390	3.0	2
Wheelwright	80	241	3.0	1
Kilmer	20	142	7.1	1
Barrington	34	121	3.6	0
Schultz	32	117	3.7	2
McCall	21	86	4.1	1
Cuozzo	19	43	2.3	1
Gilliam	7	41	5.9	0
McNeill	4	38	9.5	0
Brown	8	16	2.0	2

RECEIVING

Last Name	No.	Yds	Avg	TD
Abramowicz	50	721	14	6
Taylor	38	251	7	0
Poage	24	380	16	0
Gilliam	22	264	12	1
Kramer	20	207	10	2
Hall	19	249	13	0
Roberts	17	384	23	3
Schultz	14	186	13	0
Wheelwright	13	107	8	0
Burke	8	84	11	0
McCall	4	75	19	1
Barrington	4	50	13	0
Brown	3	23	8	0
Hester	2	10	5	0

PUNT RETURNS

Last Name	No.	Yds	Avg	TD
Roberts	11	50	5	0
Douglas	2	15	8	0
Gilliam	7	13	2	0
Brown	3	1	0	0

KICKOFF RETURNS

Last Name	No.	Yds	Avg	TD
Roberts	28	737	26	1
Gilliam	16	481	30	1
McCall	7	198	28	0
Barrington	7	113	16	0
Brown	5	103	21	0
Jordan	3	56	19	0
Rose	2	21	21	0
Douglas	1	17	17	0
Vandersea	1	13	13	0
Logan	1	0	0	0
Nevett	1	0	0	0
Sturm	1	0	0	0

PASSING — PUNTING — KICKING

PASSING	Att	Comp	%	Yds	Yd/Att	TD	Int−%	RK
Cuozzo	260	134	52	1562	6.0	7	12−5	9
Kilmer	204	97	48	1341	6.6	6	11−5	15
Wood	11	5	46	62	5.6	0	0−0	
Barrington	2	0	0	0	0.0	0	0−0	
McNeill	1	1	100	24	24.0	0	0−0	

PUNTING	No	Avg
McNeill	74	42.9

KICKING	XP	Att	%	FG	Att	%
Durkee	27	27	100	14	32	44

	Scores of Each Game		Use Name	Pos.	Hgt	Wgt	Age	Int	Pts

CENTURY DIVISION

CLEVELAND BROWNS 9-5-0 Blanton Collier

Scores of Each Game			Use Name	Pos.	Hgt	Wgt	Age	Int	Pts
14	DALLAS	21	Monte Clark	OT	6'6"	255	30		
14	Detroit	31	John Demarie	OT	6'3"	250	22		
42	New Orleans	7	Dick Schafrath	OT	6'3"	255	31		
21	PITTSBURGH	10	Jim Copeland	OG	6'2"	230	22		
20	ST. LOUIS	16	Gene Hickerson	OG	6'3"	248	32		
24	CHICAGO	0	Joe Taffoni	OG	6'3"	245	22		
34	New York	38	John Wooten	OG	6'2"	250	32		
34	Pittsburgh	14	Fred Hoaglin	C	6'4"	240	23		
7	Green Bay	55	Bill Glass	DE	6'5"	255	31	1	
14	MINNESOTA	10	Jack Gregory	DE	6'6"	245	22		
42	WASHINGTON	37	Paul Wiggin	DE	6'3"	245	33		
24	NEW YORK	14	Walter Johnson	DT	6'3"	270	24		
20	St. Louis	16	Jim Kanicki	DT	6'4"	270	25		
24	Philadelphia	28	Frank Parker	DT	6'5"	270	27		

Use Name	Pos.	Hgt	Wgt	Age	Int	Pts
Billy Andrews	LB	6'	225	22		
Johnny Brewer	LB	6'4"	235	30	2	6
Jim Houston	LB	6'2"	245	30	3	12
Dale Lindsey	LB	6'3"	225	24	1	
Bob Matheson	LB	6'4"	240	22	1	
Erich Barnes	DB	6'2"	198	32	4	
Ben Davis	DB	5'11"	185	21	1	6
Ross Fichtner	DB	6'	185	29	4	
Mike Howell	DB	6'1"	187	24	3	
Ernie Kellerman	DB	6'	183	23	1	
Carl Ward	DB	5'9"	180	23	1	6
George Youngblood (to NO)	DB	6'3"	205	22		

Use Name	Pos.	Hgt	Wgt	Age	Int	Pts
Gary Lane	QB	6'1"	210	24		
Frank Ryan	QB	6'3"	200	31		
Dick Shiner	QB	6'	197	25		
Leroy Kelly	HB	6'	202	25		78
Larry Conjar	FB	6'	215	21		
Ernie Green	FB	6'2"	205	28		36
Charlie Harraway	FB	6'2"	230	22		
Nick Pietrosante	FB	6'2"	225	30		
Eppie Barney	FL	6'	198	23		
Gary Collins	FL	6'4"	215	26		42
Ron Green	FL	6'1"	200	23		
Clifton McNeil	FL	6'2"	185	27		12
Ron Duncan	TE	6'6"	255	24		
Milt Morin	TE	6'4"	250	25		
Ralph Smith	TE	6'2"	220	28		12
Paul Warfield	OE	6'	188	24		48
Lou Groza	K	6'3"	250	43		76

NEW YORK GIANTS 7-7-0 Allie Sherman

Scores of Each Game			Use Name	Pos.	Hgt	Wgt	Age	Int	Pts
37	St. Louis	20	Francis Peay	OT	6'5"	250	23		
24	Dallas	38	Willie Young	OT	6'	250	24		
34	Washington	38	Bookie Bolin	OG	6'2"	240	27		
27	NEW ORLEANS	21	Pete Case	OG	6'3"	245	26		
27	Pittsburgh	24	Darrell Dess	OG	6'	245	31	6	
21	GREEN BAY	48	Andy Gross	OG	6'	230	21		
38	CLEVELAND	34	Charlie Harper	OG	6'2"	250	23		
24	Minnesota	27	Chuck Hinton	C	6'2"	235	24		
7	Chicago	34	Greg Larson	C	6'2"	250	28		
28	PITTSBURGH	20	Glen Condren	DE	6'2"	250	25		
44	PHILADELPHIA	7	Rosey Davis	DE	6'5"	260	25		
14	Cleveland	24	Jim Katcavage	DE	6'3"	240	32		
7	DETROIT	30	Randy Staten	DE	6'1"	225	23		
37	ST. LOUIS	14	Bruce Anderson	DT	6'4"	250	23		
			Roger Anderson	DT	6'5"	265	24		
			Jim Colvin	DT	6'2"	245	30		
			Bob Lurtsema	DT	6'6"	250	25		
			Jim Moran	DT	6'5"	275	24		

Use Name	Pos.	Hgt	Wgt	Age	Int	Pts
Ken Avery	LB	6'1"	220	23		
Mike Ciccolella	LB	6'1"	235	23		
Vince Costello	LB	6'	228	35	4	
Dick Kotite	LB	6'3"	234	24		
Bill Swain	LB	6'2"	230	26	1	
Ed Weisacosky	LB	6'	236	23		
Freeman White	DB-LB	6'5"	225	23	2	
Henry Carr	DB	6'3"	195	24	1	
Clarence Childs	DB	6'	180	28		
Wendell Harris	DB	5'11"	185	26	1	2
Dave Hathcock	DB	6'	195	24		
Spider Lockhart	DB	6'2"	175	24	5	
Bobby Post	DB	6'1"	195	22		
Willie Williams	DB	6'	190	24	1	
Scott Eaton	DB	6'3"	195	23	2	

Don Davis — Injury
Tom Kennedy — Injury

Use Name	Pos.	Hgt	Wgt	Age	Int	Pts
Earl Morrall	QB	6'1"	206	33		6
Fran Tarkenton	QB	6'	190	27		12
Allen Jacobs	HB	6'1"	215	26		
Randy Minniear	HB	6'	200	23		12
Bill Triplett	HB	6'2"	210	28		12
Ernie Koy	FB-HB	6'2"	230	24		30
Tucker Frederickson	FB	6'3"	230	24		
Joe Morrison	HB-FB-FL	6'1"	212	29		54
Bob Crespino	TE	6'4"	225	29		6
Aaron Thomas	TE	6'3"	210	29		54
Del Shofner	OE	6'3"	190	31		6
Homer Jones	FL-OE	6'2"	215	26		84
Pete Gogolak	K	6'2"	200	25		46
Les Murdock	K	6'3"	245	23		6

Jeff Smith — Knee Injury
Larry Vargo — Knee Injury
Smith Reed — Military Service

ST. LOUIS CARDINALS 6-7-1 Charlie Winner

Scores of Each Game			Use Name	Pos.	Hgt	Wgt	Age	Int	Pts
20	NEW YORK	37	Ernie McMillan	OT	6'6"	260	29		
28	Pittsburgh	14	Bob Reynolds	OT	6'6"	265	26		
38	DETROIT	28	Clyde Williams	OT	6'2"	255	27		
34	Minnesota	24	Dave O'Brien	OG-OT	6'3"	245	26		
16	Cleveland	20	Ken Gray	OG	6'2"	250	31		
48	PHILADELPHIA	14	Ed Marcontell (to HOU-A)	OG	6'	260	23		
23	GREEN BAY	31	Rick Sortun	OG	6'2"	235	24		
27	Washington	21	Irv Goode	C-OG	6'4"	250	26		
14	PITTSBURGH	14	Bob DeMarco	C	6'2"	240	29		
3	Chicago	30	Dick Kasperek	C	6'3"	225	23		
21	Dallas	46	Don Brumm	DE	6'3"	245	24		
31	NEW ORLEANS	20	Joe Robb	DE	6'3"	245	30		
16	CLEVELAND	20	Bob Rowe	DE	6'4"	255	22		
14	New York	37	Dave Long	DT-DE	6'4"	235	22		
			Sam Silas	DT	6'4"	250	24		
			Chuck Walker	DT	6'2"	245	26		
			Fred Heron	DE-DT	6'4"	250	22		

Use Name	Pos.	Hgt	Wgt	Age	Int	Pts
Jerry Hillebrand	LB	6'3"	240	27		
Bill Koman	LB	6'2"	230	33		
Dave Meggyesy	LB	6'1"	220	25		
Dale Meinert	LB	6'2"	220	34	1	
Larry Stallings	LB	6'2"	230	25		
Mike Strofolino	LB	6'2"	230	23		
Mike Barnes	DB	6'3"	205	22		
Jimmy Burson	DB	6'	180	25	2	
Pat Fischer	DB	5'10"	170	27	4	6
Chuck Latourette	DB	6'	190	22		
Phil Spiller	DB	6'	195	22		
Jerry Stovall	DB	6'2"	205	25	4	
Bobby Williams	DB	6'1"	185	25	2	
Larry Wilson	DB	6'	190	29	4	

Use Name	Pos.	Hgt	Wgt	Age	Int	Pts
Jim Hart	QB	6'2"	195	23		18
Charley Johnson	QB	6'	195	26		
Charlie Bryant	HB	6'1"	207	26		
Roy Shivers	HB	6'	200	25		6
Johnny Roland	FB-HB	6'2"	207	24		66
Willie Crenshaw	FB	6'2"	230	26		
Bill Thornton	FB	6'1"	215	27		
Prentice Gautt	HB-FB	6'	210	29		12
Bobby Joe Conrad	FL	6'	195	32		12
Dave Williams	FL	6'2"	205	22		30
Chuck Logan	TE	6'4"	220	24		
Jackie Smith	TE	6'4"	215	26		54
Ted Wheeler	TE	6'3"	230	21		
Billy Gambrell	FL-OE	5'10"	175	25		12
Jim Bakken	K	6'	200	26		117

PITTSBURGH STEELERS 4-9-1 Bill Austin

Scores of Each Game			Use Name	Pos.	Hgt	Wgt	Age	Int	Pts
41	CHICAGO	13	John Brown	OT	6'2"	248	28		
14	ST. LOUIS	28	Mike Haggerty	OT	6'4"	230	21		
24	Philadelphia	34	Fran O'Brien	OT	6'1"	265	31		
10	Cleveland	21	Larry Gagner	OG	6'3"	240	23		
24	NEW YORK	27	Bruce Van Dyke	OG	6'2"	235	23		
21	DALLAS	24	Ralph Wenzel	OG	6'3"	240	24		
14	New Orleans	10	Sam Davis	OT-OG	6'1"	245	23		
14	CLEVELAND	34	Ray Mansfield	C	6'3"	250	26		
14	St. Louis	14	John Baker	DE	6'6"	270	32	1	
20	New York	28	Jerry Mazzanti	DE	6'3"	240	27		
27	MINNESOTA	41	Ben McGee	DE	6'2"	260	25	1	6
24	Detroit	14	Lloyd Voss	DE	6'4"	260	25	1	
10	WASHINGTON	15	Dick Arndt	DT	6'5"	265	23		
24	Green Bay	17	Chuck Hinton	DT	6'5"	260	28	6	
			Ken Kortas	DT	6'2"	280	25	6	

Use Name	Pos.	Hgt	Wgt	Age	Int	Pts
Rod Breedlove	LB	6'2"	225	29		
John Campbell	LB	6'3"	225	28	2	
Ray May	LB	6'1"	230	22		
Andy Russell	LB	6'3"	215	25	3	
Bill Saul	LB	6'4"	225	26	1	
Jim Bradshaw	DB	6'2"	205	28		
John Foruria	DB	6'2"	205	22		
Bob Hohn	DB	6'	185	26	2	
Paul Martha	DB	6'	185	24	4	
Bobby Morgan	DB	6'	205	27		
Clendon Thomas	DB	6'2"	200	30	2	
Marv Woodson	DB	6'	195	24	7	

Wally Hilgenburg — Injury

Use Name	Pos.	Hgt	Wgt	Age	Int	Pts
Rich Bader	QB	6'1"	190	24		
Bill Nelsen	QB	6'	195	26		
Kent Nix	QB	6'1"	195	23		12
Charlie Bivins (to BUF-A)	HB	6'2"	212	28		6
Cannonball Butler	HB	5'10"	185	24		
Dick Hoak	HB	5'11"	190	28		12
Don Shy	HB	6'1"	215	21		30
Willie Asbury	FB	6'1"	230	24		24
Earl Gros	FB	6'3"	230	26		6
Roy Jefferson	FL	6'2"	195	23		24
Jerry Marion	FL	5'10"	175	22		
Chet Anderson	TE	6'3"	245	22		12
John Hilton	TE	6'5"	220	25		30
Dick Compton	OE	6'1"	195	27		6
Marshall Cropper	OE	6'2"	210	23		
J. R. Wilburn	OE	6'2"	190	24		30
Mike Clark	K	6'1"	200	26		71
Jim Elliott	K	5'11"	184	24		

CENTURY DIVISION

CLEVELAND BROWNS

RUSHING

Last Name	No.	Yds	Avg	TD
Kelly	235	1205	5.1	11
E. Green	145	710	4.9	4
Conjar	20	78	3.9	0
Pietrosante	10	73	7.3	0
Ryan	22	57	2.6	0
Lane	2	21	10.5	0
Warfield	2	10	5.0	0
Collins	1	6	6.0	0
Shiner	2	−7	−3.5	0
Harraway	5	−14	−2.8	0

RECEIVING

Last Name	No.	Yds	Avg	TD
E. Green	39	369	9	2
Warfield	32	702	22	8
Collins	32	500	16	7
Kelly	20	282	14	2
Smith	14	211	15	1
Morin	7	90	13	0
Conjar	6	68	11	0
Pietrosante	6	56	9	0
McNeil	3	33	11	2
Barney	1	3	3	0

PUNT RETURNS

Last Name	No.	Yds	Avg	TD
Davis	18	229	13	1
Ward	6	62	10	0
Kelly	9	59	7	0
Harraway	1	7	7	0
Youngblood	1	0	0	0

KICKOFF RETURNS

Last Name	No.	Yds	Avg	TD
Davis	27	708	26	0
Ward	22	546	25	1
Kelly	5	131	26	0
Barney	1	11	11	0

PASSING – PUNTING – KICKING

PASSING

Last Name	Att	Comp	%	Yds	Yd/Att	TD	Int–%	RK
Ryan	280	136	49	2026	7.2	20	16– 6	7
Lane	43	21	49	254	5.9	2	1– 2	
Shiner	9	3	33	34	3.8	0	1–11	
Kelly	1	0	0	0	0.0	0	0– 0	

PUNTING

Last Name	No	Avg
Collins	57	36.5
Kelly	10	40.7

KICKING

Last Name	XP	Att	%	FG	Att	%
Groza	43	43	100	11	23	48

NEW YORK GIANTS

RUSHING

Last Name	No.	Yds	Avg	TD
Koy	146	704	4.8	4
Frederickson	97	311	3.2	2
Tarkenton	44	306	7.0	2
Triplett	58	161	2.9	2
Morrison	36	161	4.5	2
Minniear	35	98	2.8	1
Jones	5	60	12.0	1
Jacobs	11	23	2.1	0
Morrall	4	11	2.8	1
Case	0	16	0.0	0
Young	0	2	0.0	0
Dess	0	1	0.0	1

RECEIVING

Last Name	No.	Yds	Avg	TD
Thomas	51	877	17	9
Jones	49	1209	25	13
Morrison	37	524	14	7
Koy	32	212	7	1
Frederickson	19	153	8	0
Crespino	10	125	13	1
Minniear	8	49	6	1
Shofner	7	146	21	1
Triplett	7	69	10	0
Eaton	1	18	18	0

PUNT RETURNS

Last Name	No.	Yds	Avg	TD
Lockhart	7	54	8	0
Williams	6	28	5	0
Minniear	4	13	3	0
Hathcock	3	7	2	0
Harris	2	0	0	0

KICKOFF RETURNS

Last Name	No.	Yds	Avg	TD
Childs	29	603	21	0
Hathcock	14	315	23	0
Triplett	7	139	20	0
Minniear	6	98	16	0
Jones	2	38	19	0
Frederickson	1	19	19	0
Koy	1	18	18	0
Crespino	1	7	7	0
Lurtsema	1	7	7	0
Post	1	0	0	0

PASSING – PUNTING – KICKING

PASSING

Last Name	Att	Comp	%	Yds	Yd/Att	TD	Int–%	RK
Tarkenton	377	204	54	3088	8.2	29	19– 5	3
Morrall	24	13	54	181	7.5	3	1– 4	
Koy	4	3	75	101	25.3	1	0– 0	
Morrison	1	1	100	12	12.0	0	0– 0	

PUNTING

Last Name	No	Avg
Koy	40	37.7
Morrall	15	31.5

KICKING

Last Name	XP	Att	%	FG	Att	%
Gogolak	28	29	97	6	10	60
Murdock	13	15	87	4	9	44
Harris	2	2	100	0	1	0

ST. LOUIS CARDINALS

RUSHING

Last Name	No.	Yds	Avg	TD
Roland	234	876	3.7	10
Gautt	142	573	4.0	1
Crenshaw	44	149	3.4	0
Smith	9	86	9.6	0
Shivers	20	64	3.2	1
Hart	13	36	2.8	3
Latourette	2	23	11.5	0
Bryant	3	16	5.3	0
Thornton	4	9	2.3	0
D. Williams	1	7	7.0	0

RECEIVING

Last Name	No.	Yds	Avg	TD
Smith	56	1205	22	9
Conrad	47	637	14	2
D. Williams	28	405	14	5
Gambrell	28	398	14	2
Roland	20	269	13	1
Gautt	15	202	13	1
Crenshaw	6	30	5	0
Shivers	3	15	5	0
Thornton	1	9	9	0

PUNT RETURNS

Last Name	No.	Yds	Avg	TD
Spiller	15	124	8	0
Shivers	9	36	4	0
Latourette	6	21	4	0
Roland	3	17	6	0
C. Williams	1	0	0	0

KICKOFF RETURNS

Last Name	No.	Yds	Avg	TD
B. Williams	24	583	24	0
Bryant	14	324	23	0
Spiller	10	219	22	0
Shivers	9	160	18	0
Stallings	2	39	20	0
Roland	2	33	17	0
Crenshaw	2	14	7	0
Barnes	1	0	0	0
Fischer	1	0	0	0
Sortun	1	0	0	0

PASSING – PUNTING – KICKING

PASSING

Last Name	Att	Comp	%	Yds	Yd/Att	TD	Int–%	RK
Hart	397	192	48	3008	7.6	19	30– 8	10
Johnson	29	12	41	162	5.6	1	3– 10	
Roland	4	0	0	0	0.0	0	1– 25	
Smith	1	0	0	0	0.0	0	1–100	

PUNTING

Last Name	No	Avg
Latourette	62	40.8

KICKING

Last Name	XP	Att	%	FG	Att	%
Bakken	36	36	100	27	39	69

PITTSBURGH STEELERS

RUSHING

Last Name	No.	Yds	Avg	TD
Shy	99	341	3.4	4
Asbury	80	315	3.9	4
Butler	90	293	3.3	0
Gros	72	252	3.5	1
Hoak	52	142	2.7	1
Nix	15	45	3.0	2
Bivins	7	23	3.3	1
Hilton	1	15	15.0	0
Compton	1	1	1.0	0
Jefferson	5	−11	−2.2	0
Nelsen	9	−19	−2.1	0

RECEIVING

Last Name	No.	Yds	Avg	TD
Wilburn	51	767	15	5
Compton	42	507	12	1
Jefferson	29	459	16	4
Hilton	26	343	13	5
Gros	19	175	9	0
Hoak	17	111	7	1
Shy	12	152	13	1
Anderson	8	141	18	2
Butler	4	23	6	0
Asbury	3	52	17	0
Bivins	1	24	24	0
Marion	1	16	16	0
Cropper	1	11	11	0

PUNT RETURNS

Last Name	No.	Yds	Avg	TD
Bradshaw	16	97	6	0
Thomas	9	34	4	0
Jefferson	1	10	10	0
Marion	1	2	2	0
Shy	1	−5	−5	0

KICKOFF RETURNS

Last Name	No.	Yds	Avg	TD
Shy	21	473	23	0
Martha	18	403	22	0
Butler	10	223	22	0
Russell	6	97	16	0
Campbell	1	25	25	0
Hilton	1	0	0	0
May	1	0	0	0

PASSING – PUNTING – KICKING

PASSING

Last Name	Att	Comp	%	Yds	Yd/Att	TD	Int–%	RK
Nix	268	136	51	1587	5.9	8	19– 7	13
Nelsen	165	74	45	1125	6.8	10	9– 5	12
Hoak	8	4	50	69	8.6	1	1–13	
Clark	1	0	0	0	0.0	0	0– 0	

PUNTING

Last Name	No	Avg
Elliott	72	38.1

KICKING

Last Name	XP	Att	%	FG	Att	%
Clark	35	35	100	12	22	55

Scores of Each Game			Use Name	Pos.	Hgt	Wgt	Age	Int	Pts	Use Name	Pos.	Hgt	Wgt	Age	Int	Pts	Use Name	Pos.	Hgt	Wgt	Age	Int	Pts

CENTRAL DIVISION

GREEN BAY PACKERS 9-4-1 Vince Lombardi

Score	Opponent	Opp	Use Name	Pos.	Hgt	Wgt	Age	Int	Pts	Use Name	Pos.	Hgt	Wgt	Age	Int	Pts	Use Name	Pos.	Hgt	Wgt	Age	Int	Pts
17	DETROIT	17	Forest Gregg	OT	6'4"	250	34			Lee Roy Caffey	LB	6'3"	250	27		2	Zeke Bratkowski	QB	6'2"	210	35		
13	CHICAGO	10	Bob Skoronski	OT	6'3"	245	34			Tommy Crutcher	LB	6'3"	230	25			Don Horn	QB	6'2"	195	22		
23	ATLANTA	0	Steve Wright	OT	6'6"	250	25			Jim Flanigan	LB	6'3"	230	22			Bart Starr	QB	6'1"	190	34		
27	Detroit	17	Gale Gillingham	OG	6'3"	255	23			Ray Nitschke	LB	6'3"	240	31	3	6	Donny Anderson	HB	6'3"	210	24		54
7	MINNESOTA	10	Jerry Kramer	OG	6'3"	245	32			Dave Robinson	LB	6'3"	240	26	4		Elijah Pitts	HB	6'1"	205	28		36
48	New York	21	Fuzzy Thurston	OG	6'1"	245	34			Herb Adderley	DB	6'1"	200	28	4	6	Travis Williams	HB	6'1"	210	21		36
31	St. Louis	23	Ken Bowman	C	6'3"	230	24			Tom Brown	DB	6'1"	190	26	1		Jim Grabowski	FB	6'2"	220	23		18
10	Baltimore	13	Bob Hyland	OG-C	6'5"	250	22			Doug Hart	DB	6'	190	28			Chuck Mercein (from NY)	FB	6'3"	230	24		8
55	CLEVELAND	7	Lionel Aldridge	DE	6'4"	245	25			Bob Jeter	DB	6'1"	205	29	8		Ben Wilson	FB	6'	225	27		12
13	SAN FRANCISCO	0	Bob Brown	DE	6'5"	260	27			John Rowser	DB	6'1"	180	23			Carroll Dale	FL	6'1"	200	29		30
17	Chicago	13	Willie Davis	DE	6'3"	245	34		2	Willie Wood	DB	5'10"	190	31	4		Bob Long	FL	6'3"	205	26		
30	Minnesota	27	Henry Jordan	DT	6'3"	250	32										Claudis James	HB-FL	6'2"	190	23		
24	Los Angeles	27	Ron Kostelnik	DT	6'4"	260	27										Allen Brown	TE	6'5"	235	24		
17	PITTSBURGH	24	Jim Weatherwax	DT	6'7"	260	24										Dick Capp	TE	6'3"	235	23		
																	Marv Fleming	TE	6'4"	235	25		6
																	Boyd Dowler	OE	6'5"	225	30		24
																	Max McGee	OE	6'3"	210	35		
																	Don Chandler	K	6'2"	210	32		96

CHICAGO BEARS 7-6-1 George Halas

Score	Opponent	Opp	Use Name	Pos.	Hgt	Wgt	Age	Int	Pts	Use Name	Pos.	Hgt	Wgt	Age	Int	Pts	Use Name	Pos.	Hgt	Wgt	Age	Int	Pts
13	Pittsburgh	41	Randy Jackson	OT	6'5"	245	23			Doug Buffone	LB	6'1"	230	23	3	6	Rudy Bukich	QB	6'1"	205	36		
10	Green Bay	13	Dan James	OT	6'4"	250	30			Dick Butkus	LB	6'3"	245	23	1		Jack Concannon	QB	6'3"	205	24		18
17	Minnesota	7	Bob Pickens	OT	6'4"	258	24			Rudy Kuechenberg	LB	6'2"	215	24			Larry Rakestraw	QB	6'2"	195	25		12
3	BALTIMORE	24	George Seals	OG	6'2"	260	24			Jim Purnell	LB	6'2"	238	25			Gale Sayers	HB	6'	198	24		72
14	DETROIT	3	Bob Wetoska	OT	6'3"	240	29			Mike Reilly	LB	6'2"	230	24			Ronnie Bull	FB-HB	6'	200	27		6
0	Cleveland	24	Jim Cadile	OG	6'3"	240	26			Charlie Brown	DB	6'	193	24	1		Ralph Kurek	FB	6'2"	210	24		
17	LOS ANGELES	28	Don Croftcheck	OG	6'1"	230	24			Al Dodd	DB	6'	180	22			Andy Livingston	FB	6'	234	22		
27	Detroit	13	Doug Kriewald	OG	6'4"	245	23			Curtis Gentry	DB	6'	185	26	4		Brian Piccolo	HB-FB	6'	205	23		
34	NEW YORK	7	Mike Rabold	OG	6'2"	250	30			Bennie McRae	DB	6'1"	180	26	5	12	Johnny Morris	FL	5'10"	180	32		6
30	ST. LOUIS	3	Mike Pyle	C	6'3"	250	28			Richie Petitbon	DB	6'3"	205	29	5		Duane Allen	TE	6'4"	225	29		
13	GREEN BAY	17	Marty Amsler	DE	6'5"	260	24	1		Joe Taylor	DB	6'2"	195	26	1		Austin Denney	TE	6'2"	230	23		
28	San Francisco	14	Ed O'Bradovich	DE	6'3"	255	27			Rosey Taylor	DB	5'11"	186	28	5	6	Terry Stoepel	TE	6'4"	235	22		
10	MINNESOTA	10	Loyd Phillips	DE	6'3"	230	22										Dick Gordon	OE	5'11"	190	22		30
23	Atlanta	14	Frank Cornish	DT	6'6"	270	23		2								Bob Jones	OE	6'4"	195	22		6
			Dick Evey	DT	6'2"	245	26										Jim Jones	OE	6'2"	187	23		
			John Johnson	DT	6'5"	260	26										Bobby Joe Green	K	5'11"	175	29		
			Frank McRae	DT	6'7"	270	23										Mac Percival	K	6'4"	217	27		65

DETROIT LIONS 5-7-2 Joe Schmidt

Score	Opponent	Opp	Use Name	Pos.	Hgt	Wgt	Age	Int	Pts	Use Name	Pos.	Hgt	Wgt	Age	Int	Pts	Use Name	Pos.	Hgt	Wgt	Age	Int	Pts
17	Green Bay	17	Charlie Bradshaw	OT	6'6"	260	31			Ernie Clark	LB	6'1"	220	29	1		Milt Plum	QB	6'1"	205	33		
31	CLEVELAND	14	Bill Cottrell	OT	6'3"	265	22			Ron Goovert	LB	5'11"	225	23			Karl Sweetan	QB	6'2"	200	24		6
28	St. Louis	38	Roger Shoals	OT	6'4"	255	28			Mike Lucci	LB	6'2"	230	27	2	6	Mel Farr	HB	6'2"	208	22		36
17	GREEN BAY	27	Randy Winkler	OT	6'5"	260	24			Paul Naumoff	LB	6'1"	210	22			Bobby Felts	HB	6'2"	202	24		
3	Chicago	14	Frank Gallagher	OG	6'2"	240	24			Wayne Walker	LB	6'2"	225	30		26	Tom Watkins	HB	6'1"	195	30		30
24	ATLANTA	3	John Gordy	OG	6'3"	250	31			Lem Barney	DB	6'	202	21	10	18	Amos Marsh	FB	6'1"	220	28		18
45	San Francisco	3	Bob Kowalkowski	OG	6'3"	245	23			Mike Bass	DB	6'	190	22			Tom Nowatzke	FB	6'3"	222	24		36
13	CHICAGO	27	Chuck Walton	OG	6'3"	250	26			Dick LeBeau	DB	6'1"	185	30	4		Pat Studstill	FL	6'1"	175	29		12
10	Minnesota	10	Ed Flanagan	C	6'3"	250	23			Bruce Maher	DB	5'11"	190	30	2	2	John Henderson	OE-FL	6'3"	190	24		
7	Baltimore	41	Larry Hand	DE	6'4"	245	27	2	12	Wayne Rasmussen	DB	6'2"	180	25			Jim Gibbons	TE	6'2"	220	31		
7	LOS ANGELES	31	Lew Kamanu	DE	6'4"	245	23			Bobby Thompson	DB	5'10"	175	27			Ron Kramer	TE	6'3"	240	32		
14	PITTSBURGH	24	John McCambridge	DE	6'4"	245	21			Tom Vaughn	DB	5'11"	195	24	1		Jerry Zawadzkas	TE	6'4"	220	24		
30	New York	7	Darris McCord	DE	6'4"	250	34	1		Mike Weger	DB	6'2"	195	21			Gail Cogdill	OE	6'2"	195	30		6
14	MINNESOTA	3	Mike Melinkovich	DE	6'4"	245	25										Bill Malinchak	OE	6'1"	190	23		24
			Alex Karras	DT	6'2"	245	31			Johnnie Robinson — Injury							Garo Yepremian	K	5'8"	160	23		28
			Denis Moore	DT	6'5"	230	23																
			Jerry Rush	DT	6'4"	270	25																

MINNESOTA VIKINGS 3-8-3 Bud Grant

Score	Opponent	Opp	Use Name	Pos.	Hgt	Wgt	Age	Int	Pts	Use Name	Pos.	Hgt	Wgt	Age	Int	Pts	Use Name	Pos.	Hgt	Wgt	Age	Int	Pts
21	SAN FRANCISCO	27	Grady Alderman	OT	6'2"	240	28			Paul Faust	LB	6'	220	23			Bob Berry	QB	5'11"	190	25		
3	Los Angeles	39	Bob Breitenstein (from DEN)	OT	6'3"	267	24			Don Hansen	LB	6'3"	228	23			Joe Kapp	QB	6'2"	212	29		12
7	CHICAGO	17	Doug Davis	OT	6'4"	250	23			Jim Hargrove	LB	6'3"	230	22	1	6	Ron Vander Kelen	QB	6'1"	190	27		6
24	ST. LOUIS	34	Archie Sutton	OT	6'4"	265	24			John Kirby	LB	6'3"	235	25			Earl Denny	HB	6'1"	200	22		
10	Green Bay	7	Larry Bowie	OG	6'2"	255	27			Dave Tobey	LB	6'3"	230	24			Clint Jones	HB	6'	206	22		6
20	BALTIMORE	20	John Pentecost	OG	6'2"	250	23			Lonnie Warwick	LB	6'2"	235	25	2		Jim Lindsey	HB	6'2"	200	22		
20	Atlanta	21	Milt Sunde	OG	6'2"	250	24			Roy Winston	LB	6'1"	230	27			Dave Osborn	HB	6'	205	24		18
27	NEW YORK	24	Jim Vellone	OT-OG	6'2"	255	23			Al Coleman	DB	6'1"	195	22			Pete Tatman	HB	6'1"	220	22		
10	DETROIT	10	Mick Tingelhoff	C	6'1"	237	27			Mike Fitzgerald (to NY-ATL)	DB	5'10"	180	26			Bill Brown	FB	5'11"	230	29		30
10	Cleveland	14	Carl Eller	DE	6'6"	265	25			Dale Hackbart	DB	6'3"	210	31	2	6	Jim Phillips	FL	6'1"	195	30		18
41	Pittsburgh	27	Jim Marshall	DE	6'3"	235	29			Jeff Jordan	DB	6'4"	190	23			Bob Grim	DB-FL	6'	197	22		6
27	GREEN BAY	30	Archie Simkus	DE	6'4"	250	24			Karl Kassulke	DB	6'	195	25	2		John Beasley	TE	6'3"	228	22		24
10	Chicago	10	Paul Dickson	DT	6'5"	255	30			Brady Keys (from PIT)	DB	6'	185	31	3		Marlin McKeever	TE	6'1"	235	27		
3	Detroit	14	Gary Larsen	DT	6'5"	255	27			Earsell Mackbee	DB	6'1"	195	26	5	12	Paul Flatley	OE	6'1"	187	26		
			Alan Page	DT	6'5"	255	22			Ed Sharockman	DB	6'	200	27	3		Gene Washington	OE	6'3"	216	23		12
			Jerry Shay	DT	6'3"	245	23										Fred Cox	K	5'10"	200	28		77
																	Bobby Walden	K	6'	190	29		

CENTRAL DIVISION

GREEN BAY PACKERS

RUSHING

Last Name	No.	Yds	Avg	TD
Grabowski	120	466	3.9	2
Wilson	103	453	4.4	2
Anderson	97	402	4.1	6
Pitts	77	247	3.2	6
Williams	35	188	5.4	1
Starr	21	90	4.3	0
Mercein	14	46	4.0	1
Dale	1	9	9.0	0
Bratkowski	5	6	1.2	0
Horn	1	−2	−2.0	0

RECEIVING

Last Name	No.	Yds	Avg	TD
Dowler	54	836	15	4
Dale	35	738	21	5
Anderson	22	331	15	3
Pitts	15	210	14	0
Wilson	14	88	6	0
Grabowski	12	171	14	1
Fleming	10	126	13	1
Long	8	96	12	0
Williams	5	80	16	1
A. Brown	3	43	14	0
McGee	3	33	11	0
Mercein	1	6	6	0

PUNT RETURNS

Last Name	No.	Yds	Avg	TD
Anderson	9	98	11	0
T. Brown	9	40	4	0
Pitts	9	16	2	0
Wood	12	3	0	0

KICKOFF RETURNS

Last Name	No.	Yds	Avg	TD
Williams	18	739	41	4
Anderson	11	226	21	0
Adderley	10	207	21	0
Crutcher	3	48	16	0
A. Brown	1	13	13	0
Hart	1	8	8	0
Robinson	1	0	0	0
Wood	1	0	0	0

PASSING – PUNTING – KICKING

PASSING

Last Name	Att	Comp	%	Yds	Yd/Att	TD	Int–%	RK
Starr	210	115	55	1823	8.7	9	17– 8	6
Bratkowski	94	53	56	724	7.7	5	9–10	
Horn	24	12	50	171	7.1	1	1– 4	
Anderson	2	1	50	19	9.5	0	0– 0	
Pitts	1	1	100	21	21.0	0	0– 0	

PUNTING

Last Name	No	Avg
Anderson	65	36.6
Chandler	1	31.0

KICKING

Last Name	XP	Att	%	FG	Att	%
Chandler	39	39	100	19	29	66
Mercein	2	3	67	0	1	0

CHICAGO BEARS

RUSHING

Last Name	No.	Yds	Avg	TD
Sayers	186	880	4.7	7
Piccolo	87	317	3.6	0
Concannon	67	279	4.2	3
Bull	61	176	2.9	0
Kurek	37	112	3.0	0
Rakestraw	11	42	3.8	2
Livingston	28	41	1.5	0
J. Jones	4	19	4.8	0
Morris	1	6	6.0	0
Gordon	3	−7	−2.3	0
Bukich	4	−13	−3.3	0

RECEIVING

Last Name	No.	Yds	Avg	TD
Gordon	31	534	17	5
Morris	20	231	12	1
Bull	18	250	14	1
Sayers	16	126	8	1
Piccolo	13	103	8	0
Denny	12	113	9	0
J. Jones	7	138	20	0
Livingston	5	62	12	0
Kurek	5	30	6	0
B. Jones	3	80	27	1
Stoepel	1	6	6	0

PUNT RETURNS

Last Name	No.	Yds	Avg	TD
Gordon	12	82	7	0
Sayers	3	80	27	1
Morris	4	24	6	0
Dodd	3	8	3	0

KICKOFF RETURNS

Last Name	No.	Yds	Avg	TD
Sayers	16	603	38	3
Gordon	16	397	25	0
Kurek	5	81	16	0
Dodd	3	34	11	0
Brown	2	34	17	0
J. Taylor	1	8	8	0
Jackson	1	0	0	0
Kriewald	1	0	0	0
Kuechenberg	1	0	0	0
Stoepel	1	0	0	0

PASSING – PUNTING – KICKING

PASSING

Last Name	Att	Comp	%	Yds	Yd/Att	TD	Int–%	RK
Concannon	186	92	49	1260	6.8	6	14– 8	17
Rakestraw	44	21	48	228	5.2	3	2– 5	
Bukich	33	18	55	185	5.6	0	2– 6	
Sayers	5	0	0	0	0.0	0	0– 0	

PUNTING

Last Name	No	Avg
Green	79	42.9

KICKING

Last Name	XP	Att	%	FG	Att	%
Percival	26	29	90	13	26	50

DETROIT LIONS

RUSHING

Last Name	No.	Yds	Avg	TD
Farr	206	860	4.2	3
Watkins	106	361	3.4	4
Nowatzke	70	288	4.1	4
Marsh	58	229	3.9	2
Sweetan	17	93	5.5	1
Felts	10	66	6.6	0
Plum	6	5	0.8	0
Flanagan	0	5	0.0	0

RECEIVING

Last Name	No.	Yds	Avg	TD
Farr	39	317	8	3
Malinchak	26	397	15	4
Cogdill	21	322	15	1
Nowatzke	21	145	7	2
Henderson	13	144	11	0
Studstill	10	162	16	2
Gibbons	10	107	11	0
Watkins	8	93	12	1
Marsh	7	103	15	1
Kramer	4	40	10	0
Walton	1	−4	−4	0

PUNT RETURNS

Last Name	No.	Yds	Avg	TD
Watkins	15	57	4	0
Thompson	9	20	2	0
Barney	4	14	4	0
Vaughn	4	7	2	0
Weger	1	0	0	0
Felts	1	−1	−1	0

KICKOFF RETURNS

Last Name	No.	Yds	Avg	TD
Vaughn	16	446	28	0
Watkins	20	411	21	0
Thompson	4	134	34	0
Barney	5	87	17	0
Goovert	2	40	20	0
Weger	2	27	14	0
Zawadzkas	1	0	0	0

PASSING – PUNTING – KICKING

PASSING

Last Name	Att	Comp	%	Yds	Yd/Att	TD	Int–%	RK
Sweetan	177	74	42	901	5.1	10	11– 6	18
Plum	172	86	50	925	5.4	4	8– 5	14
Farr	2	0	0	0	0	0	0– 0	

PUNTING

Last Name	No	Avg
Barney	47	37.4
Studstill	36	44.5

KICKING

Last Name	XP	Att	%	FG	Att	%
Yepremian	22	23	96	2	6	33
Walker	11	11	100	5	15	33

MINNESOTA VIKINGS

RUSHING

Last Name	No.	Yds	Avg	TD
Osborn	215	972	4.5	2
Brown	185	610	3.3	5
Kapp	27	167	6.2	2
Jones	13	23	1.8	0
Grim	1	20	20.0	0
Lindsey	4	10	2.5	0
Vander Kelen	9	9	1.0	1

RECEIVING

Last Name	No.	Yds	Avg	TD
Osborn	34	272	8	1
Flatley	23	232	10	0
Brown	22	263	12	0
Phillips	21	352	17	3
McKeever	14	184	13	0
Washington	13	384	30	2
Beasley	13	120	9	4
Grim	6	108	18	1
Lindsey	4	36	9	0

PUNT RETURNS

Last Name	No.	Yds	Avg	TD
Grim	25	101	4	0
Keys	7	7	1	0
Fitzgerald	2	4	2	0
Sharockman	4	0	0	0

KICKOFF RETURNS

Last Name	No.	Yds	Avg	TD
Jones	25	597	24	1
Grim	22	493	22	0
Fitzgerald	12	240	20	0
Lindsey	3	71	24	0
Sharockman	1	22	22	0
Denny	1	18	18	0
Tatman	1	14	14	0

PASSING – PUNTING – KICKING

PASSING

Last Name	Att	Comp	%	Yds	Yd/Att	TD	Int–%	RK
Kapp	214	102	48	1386	6.5	8	17– 8	19
Vander Kelen	115	45	39	522	4.5	3	7– 6	
Berry	7	3	43	43	6.1	0	0– 0	

PUNTING

Last Name	No	Avg
Walden	75	41.6

KICKING

Last Name	XP	Att	%	FG	Att	%
Cox	26	26	100	17	33	52

COASTAL DIVISION

LOS ANGELES RAMS 11-1-2 George Allen

Scores of Each Game

27	New Orleans	13	28	Chicago 17
39	MINNESOTA	3	17	San Francisco 7
35	Dallas	13	33	PHILADELPHIA 17
24	SAN FRANCISCO	27	31	Atlanta 3
24	Baltimore	24	31	Detroit 7
28	WASHINGTON	28	20	ATLANTA 3
			27	GREEN BAY 24
			34	BALTIMORE 10

Use Name	Pos.	Hgt	Wgt	Age	Int	Pts
Joe Carollo	OT	6'2"	258	27		
Charley Cowan	OT	6'4"	265	29		
Bob Nichols	OT	6'3"	250	24		
Don Chuy	OG	6'1"	255	26		
Tom Mack	OG	6'3"	245	23		
Joe Scibelli	OG	6'1"	255	28		
Ken Iman	C	6'1"	240	28		
George Burman	OG-C	6'3"	255	24		
Deacon Jones	DE	6'5"	260	28		2
Lamar Lundy	DE	6'7"	260	32		
Gregg Schumacher	DE	6'2"	240	25		
Roger Brown	DT	6'5"	300	30		
Merlin Olsen	DT	6'5"	276	26		
Diron Talbert	DE	6'5"	238	23		
Dave Cahill	DE-DT	6'3"	238	25		
Maxie Baughan	LB	6'1"	230	29	4	
Gene Breen	LB	6'2"	230	26		
Tony Guillory	LB	6'4"	236	24		
Jack Pardee	LB	6'2"	230	31	6	12
Myron Pottios	LB	6'2"	240	27	1	
Doug Woodlief	LB	6'3"	230	23	2	
Claude Crabb	DB	6'	192	27	1	
Irv Cross	DB	6'1"	195	28	2	
Willie Daniel	DB	5'11"	190	29	2	
Chuck Lamson	DB	6'	195	28	2	
Ed Meador	DB	5'11"	200	30	8	12
Clancy Williams	DB	6'2"	198	24	4	
Kelton Winston	DB	6'	195	26		
Roman Gabriel	QB	6'4"	230	27		3
Bill Munson	QB	6'2"	200	25		
Willie Ellison	HB	6'1"	207	22		
Les Josephson	HB	6'	220	25		4
Tommy Mason	HB	6'	190	28		
Dick Bass	FB	5'10"	195	30		4
Jim Stiger	FB	5'11"	214	26		
Bernie Casey	FL	6'4"	210	28		4
Billy Truax	TE	6'5"	235	24		2
Dave Pivec	LB-TE	6'3"	240	23		
Bucky Pope	OE	6'5"	205	24		1
Jack Snow	OE	6'2"	195	24		4
Wendell Tucker	OE	5'10"	185	23		
Bruce Gossett	K	6'2"	230	24		10
Jon Kilgore	K	6'1"	205	23		

Hal Bedsole — Injury
Henry Dyer — Injury
Rosey Grier — Injury

BALTIMORE COLTS 11-1-2 Don Shula

Scores of Each Game

38	ATLANTA	31
38	Philadelphia	6
41	SAN FRANCISCO	7
24	Chicago	3
24	LOS ANGELES	24
20	Minnesota	20
17	Washington	13
13	GREEN BAY	10
49	Atlanta	7
41	DETROIT	7
26	San Francisco	9
23	DALLAS	17
30	NEW ORLEANS	10
10	Los Angeles	34

Use Name	Pos.	Hgt	Wgt	Age	Int	Pts
Sam Ball	OT	6'4"	240	23		
Jim Parker	OT	6'3"	275	33		
Bob Vogel	OT	6'5"	250	25		
Norman Davis	OG	6'3"	250	22		
Dale Memmelaar	OG	6'2"	246	30		
Glenn Ressler	OG	6'3"	250	23		
Dan Sullivan	OG	6'3"	250	28		
Dick Szymanski	C	6'3"	235	35		
Bill Curry	LB-C	6'2"	235	24		
Ordell Braase	DE	6'4"	245	35		6
Roy Hilton	DE	6'6"	240	22		
Lou Michaels	DE	6'2"	250	31		106
Bubba Smith	DE	6'7"	295	22		
Fred Miller	DT	6'3"	250	26		
Billy Ray Smith	DT	6'4"	250	32		
Andy Stynchula	DE-DT	6'3"	250	28		
Barry Brown	LB	6'3"	235	24		
Mike Curtis	LB	6'2"	232	24	1	
Dennis Gaubatz	LB	6'2"	232	26	2	
Ron Porter	LB	6'3"	230	22	1	
Don Shinnick	LB	6'	228	32	3	
Bobby Boyd	DB	5'10"	192	29	6	6
George Harold	DB	6'3"	194	25		
Alvin Haymond	DB	6'	194	25	2	
Jerry Logan	DB	6'1"	190	26	4	6
Lenny Lyles	DB	6'2"	204	31	5	6
Preston Pearson	DB	6'1"	190	23	1	
Charlie Stukes	DB	6'3"	212	23	2	
Rick Volk	DB	6'3"	195	22	6	6
Jim Welch	HB-DB	6'	196	29		
Johnny Unitas	QB	6'1"	196	34		
Jim Ward	QB	6'2"	195	23		
Tom Matte	HB	6'	214	28		7
Lenny Moore	HB	6'1"	198	34		
Jerry Hill	FB	5'11"	215	27		1
Tony Lorick	FB	6'1"	217	25		3
Don Alley	FL	6'2"	200	21		
Jimmy Orr	FL	5'11"	185	31		
Willie Richardson	FL	6'2"	198	27		4
John Mackey	TE	6'3"	224	25		
Butch Wilson	TE	6'2"	228	25		
Ray Berry	OE	6'2"	190	34		
Ray Perkins	OE	6'	183	25		1
Alex Hawkins (from ATL)	FL-OE	6'1"	186	30		2
David Lee	K	6'4"	215	28		

SAN FRANCISCO FORTY-NINERS 7-7-0 Jack Christiansen

Scores of Each Game

27	Minnesota	21
38	ATLANTA	7
7	Baltimore	41
27	Los Angeles	24
28	Philadelphia	27
27	NEW ORLEANS	13
3	DETROIT	45
7	LOS ANGELES	17
28	Washington	31
0	Green Bay	13
9	BALTIMORE	26
14	CHICAGO	28
34	Atlanta	28
24	DALLAS	16

Use Name	Pos.	Hgt	Wgt	Age	Int	Pts
Dave Hettema	OT	6'4"	247	25		
Walt Rock	OT	6'5"	255	26		
Len Rohde	OT	6'4"	250	29		
Elmer Collett	OG	6'4"	230	22		
Howard Mudd	OG	6'3"	254	25		
Don Parker	OG	6'3"	235	22		
John Thomas	OG	6'4"	250	32		
Bruce Bosley	C	6'2"	244	33		
Joe Cerne	C	6'2"	240	24		
Stan Hindman	DE	6'3"	232	23		
Tom Holzer	DE	6'4"	240	22		
Walter Johnson	DE	6'4"	225	23		
Clark Miller	DE	6'5"	247	28	1	
Charlie Johnson	DT	6'2"	265	23		
Charlie Krueger	DT	6'4"	260	31		
Roland Lakes	DT	6'4"	280	27		
Ed Beard	LB	6'2"	226	27		
Bob Harrison	LB	6'2"	228	30		
Matt Hazeltine	LB	6'1"	230	34		
Frank Nunley	LB	6'2"	220	21	1	
Dave Wilcox	LB	6'3"	234	24	2	
Kermit Alexander	DB	5'11"	180	26	5	
George Donnelly	DB	6'3"	210	24		
Goose Gonsoulin	DB	6'3"	210	29	3	
Jim Jackson	DB	6'	193	23	1	
Jim Johnson	DB	6'2"	187	29	2	
Mel Phillips	DB	6'	192	25	1	
Al Randolph	DB	6'2"	192	23		
Wayne Trimble	DB	6'3"	203	21		
John Brodie	QB	6'1"	210	32		
George Mira	QB	5'11"	190	25		
Steve Spurrier	QB	6'2"	203	22		
John David Crow	HB	6'2"	224	32		3
Doug Cunningham	HB	5'11"	185	21		
Dave Kopay	HB	6'2"	218	25		
Bill Tucker	FB-HB	6'2"	222	23		
Gary Lewis	FB	6'3"	230	25		4
Ken Willard	FB	6'2"	230	24		3
Chip Myers	FL	6'4"	185	22		
Wayne Swinford	FL	6'	192	24		
Dick Witcher	TE-FL	6'3"	204	22		1
Dave Olerich	TE	6'1"	220	22		
Monte Stickles	TE	6'4"	235	29		
Bob Windsor	TE	6'4"	223	24		1
Dave Parks	OE	6'2"	207	25		1
Sonny Randle	OE	6'2"	190	31		2
Tommy Davis	K	6'	220	32		7

Kay McFarland — Injury

ATLANTA FALCONS 1-12-1 Norb Hecker

Scores of Each Game

31	Baltimore	38
7	San Francisco	38
0	Green Bay	23
7	PHILADELPHIA	38
20	WASHINGTON	20
3	Detroit	24
21	MINNESOTA	20
7	Dallas	37
7	BALTIMORE	49
3	LOS ANGELES	31
24	New Orleans	27
3	Los Angeles	20
28	SAN FRANCISCO	34
14	CHICAGO	23

Use Name	Pos.	Hgt	Wgt	Age	Int	Pts
Errol Linden	OT	6'5"	260	30		
Bill Sandeman (from NO)	OT	6'6"	250	24		
Don Talbert	OT	6'5"	255	27		
Jim Simon	OG-OT	6'5"	240	26		
Ed Cook	OG	6'2"	250	35		
Dan Grimm	OG	6'3"	245	26		
Tom Harmon	OG	6'4"	238	25		
Lou Kirouac	OG	6'3"	240	26		
Jake Kupp (to NO)	OG	6'3"	233	25		
Jim Wilson	OG	6'3"	258	26		
Frank Marchlewski	C	6'2"	238	23		
Karl Rubke	DT-C	6'4"	244	31		
Bob Hughes	DE	6'4"	255	22		
Bobby Richards	DE	6'2"	245	28		
Sam Williams	DE	6'4"	245	36		
Bo Wood	DE	6'3"	225	21		
Jim Norton	DT	6'4"	254	24	1	
Chuck Sieminski	DT	6'4"	270	27		
Joe Szczecko	DT	6'	245	25		
Dick Absher (from WAS)	LB	6'4"	227	23		4
Andy Bowling	LB	6'2"	235	22		
Ralph Heck	LB	6'2"	230	26		
Tommy Nobis	LB	6'2"	235	23	3	6
Marion Rushing	LB	6'2"	230	30	1	
Bob Sanders	LB	6'3"	235	24		
Tom Bleick	DB	6'2"	200	24		
Lee Calland	DB	6'	190	26	3	6
Floyd Hudlow	DB	5'11"	195	23	2	
Nick Rassas	DB	6'	190	23		
Ken Reaves	DB	6'3"	205	22	7	
Jerry Richardson	DB	6'3"	190	24		
Bob Riggle	DB	6'1"	200	23		
Randy Johnson	QB	6'3"	196	23		
Terry Nofsinger	QB	6'4"	215	29		
Steve Sloan	QB	6'	185	23		
Perry Lee Dunn	HB	6'2"	215	24		
Tom Moore	HB	6'2"	210	29		
Ron Rector	HB	6'	200	23		
Junior Coffey	FB	6'1"	210	25		3
Jim Mankins	FB	6'1"	216	23		
Tommy McDonald	FL	5'10"	175	33		4
Ron Smith	DB-FL	6'1"	192	24		
Taz Anderson	TE	6'2"	215	28		
Billy Martin	TE	6'4"	235	24		1
Ray Ogden (from NO)	TE	6'5"	225	24		
Gary Barnes	OE	6'4"	210	27		
Jerry Simmons (from NO)	OE	6'1"	190	24		1
Billy Lothridge	K	6'1"	195	23		
Wade Traynham	K	6'2"	218	25		4

COASTAL DIVISION

LOS ANGELES RAMS

RUSHING

Last Name	No.	Yds	Avg	TD
Josephson	178	800	4.5	4
Bass	187	627	3.4	6
Mason	63	213	3.4	0
Gabriel	43	198	4.6	6
Ellison	14	84	6.0	0
Stiger	3	6	2.0	0
Munson	2	−22	−11.0	0

RECEIVING

Last Name	No.	Yds	Avg	TD
Casey	53	871	16	8
Truax	37	487	13	4
Josephson	37	400	11	4
Snow	28	735	26	8
Bass	27	212	8	1
Mason	13	70	5	0
Pope	8	152	19	2
Pivec	2	2	1	1
Ellison	1	18	18	0

PUNT RETURNS

Last Name	No.	Yds	Avg	TD
Cross	17	136	8	0
Meador	21	131	6	0
Tucker	6	40	7	0
Winston	1	12	12	0
Stiger	4	9	2	0
Crabb	1	0	0	0

KICKOFF RETURNS

Last Name	No.	Yds	Avg	TD
Ellison	13	340	26	0
Tucker	11	242	22	0
Williams	7	161	23	0
Cross	4	134	34	0
Josephson	5	91	18	0
Winston	3	65	22	0

PASSING – PUNTING – KICKING

PASSING

Last Name	Att	Comp	%	Yds	Yd/Att	TD	Int−%	RK
Gabriel	371	196	53	2779	7.5	25	13− 4	4
Munson	10	5	50	38	3.8	1	2−20	
Josephson	5	2	40	47	9.4	0	1−20	
Mason	3	2	67	65	21.7	1	0− 0	
Meador	1	1	100	18	18.0	1	0− 0	

PUNTING

Last Name	No	Avg
Kilgore	68	42.2

KICKING

Last Name	XP	Att	%	FG	Att	%
Gossett	48	48	100	20	43	47

BALTIMORE COLTS

RUSHING

Last Name	No.	Yds	Avg	TD
Matte	147	636	4.3	9
Lorick	133	436	3.3	6
Hill	90	311	3.5	2
Moore	42	132	3.1	4
Unitas	22	89	4.0	0
Ward	5	23	4.6	0
Hawkins	2	12	6.0	0
Welch	2	6	3.0	0

RECEIVING

Last Name	No.	Yds	Avg	TD
Richardson	63	860	14	8
Mackey	55	686	12	3
Matte	35	496	14	3
Hawkins	27	469	17	4
Lorick	22	189	9	0
Hill	19	156	8	0
Perkins	16	302	19	2
Moore	13	153	12	0
Berry	11	167	15	1
Orr	3	72	24	1
Alley	1	11	11	0

PUNT RETURNS

Last Name	No.	Yds	Avg	TD
Haymond	26	155	6	0
Volk	11	88	8	0
Logan	5	80	16	1

KICKOFF RETURNS

Last Name	No.	Yds	Avg	TD
Moore	16	392	25	0
Haymond	13	326	25	0
Lorick	8	212	27	0
Stukes	1	19	19	0
Logan	2	17	9	0
Matte	1	14	14	0
Davis	1	8	8	0

PASSING

Last Name	Att	Comp	%	Yds	Yd/Att	TD	Int−%	RK
Unitas	436	255	58	3428	7.9	20	16− 4	2
Ward	16	9	56	115	7.2	2	1− 6	
Matte	5	1	20	18	3.6	0	0− 0	

PUNTING

Last Name	No	Avg
Lee	49	42.3

KICKING

Last Name	XP	Att	%	FG	Att	%
Michaels	46	48	96	20	37	54

SAN FRANCISCO FORTY NINERS

RUSHING

Last Name	No.	Yds	Avg	TD
Willard	169	510	3.0	5
Crow	113	479	4.2	2
Lewis	67	342	5.1	6
Cunningham	43	212	4.9	2
Brodie	20	147	7.4	1
Mira	7	23	3.3	0
Kopay	6	21	3.5	0
Spurrier	5	18	3.6	0
Windsor	1	7	7.0	0
Tucker	3	5	1.7	0

RECEIVING

Last Name	No.	Yds	Avg	TD
Witcher	46	705	15	3
Randle	33	502	15	4
Crow	31	373	12	3
Parks	26	313	12	2
Willard	23	242	11	1
Windsor	21	254	12	2
Lewis	21	218	10	1
Cunningham	13	121	9	0
Stickles	7	86	12	0
Tucker	2	22	11	0
Myers	2	13	7	0
Kopay	2	11	6	0
Olerich	1	2	2	0

PUNT RETURNS

Last Name	No.	Yds	Avg	TD
Cunningham	27	249	9	0
Alexander	6	64	11	0
Tucker	1	1	1	0
Gonsoulin	1	0	0	0

KICKOFF RETURNS

Last Name	No.	Yds	Avg	TD
Cunningham	31	826	27	0
Tucker	9	199	22	0
Lewis	9	190	21	0
Swinford	2	51	26	0
Kopay	1	21	21	0
Windsor	1	21	21	0
Alexander	1	18	18	0
Nunley	2	0	0	0

PASSING

Last Name	Att	Comp	%	Yds	Yd/Att	TD	Int−%	RK
Brodie	349	168	48	2013	5.8	11	16− 5	11
Mira	65	35	54	592	9.1	5	3− 5	
Spurrier	50	23	46	211	4.2	0	7−14	
Crow	5	2	40	46	9.2	0	0− 0	

PUNTING

Last Name	No	Avg
Spurrier	73	37.6

KICKING

Last Name	XP	Att	%	FG	Att	%
Davis	33	33	100	14	33	42

ATLANTA FALCONS

RUSHING

Last Name	No.	Yds	Avg	TD
Coffey	180	722	4.0	4
Johnson	24	144	6.0	1
Rector	24	127	5.3	0
Moore	53	104	2.0	0
Dunn	27	63	2.3	0
Smith	8	42	5.3	0
Nofsinger	3	33	11.0	0
Lothridge	1	16	16.0	0
Mankins	2	7	3.5	0
Sloan	1	2	2.0	0

RECEIVING

Last Name	No.	Yds	Avg	TD
McDonald	33	436	13	4
Coffey	30	196	7	1
Simmons	23	312	14	2
Ogden	20	327	16	1
Martin	15	182	12	3
Dunn	13	111	9	0
Smith	11	227	21	0
Barnes	10	154	15	1
Moore	10	74	7	0
Anderson	8	99	12	1
Rector	4	13	3	0
Mankins	1	11	11	0

PUNT RETURNS

Last Name	No.	Yds	Avg	TD
Smith	20	92	5	0
Hudlow	1	2	2	0
Simmons	3	0	0	0

KICKOFF RETURNS

Last Name	No.	Yds	Avg	TD
Smith	39	976	25	1
Dunn	7	128	18	0
Hudlow	2	56	28	0
Rassas	2	51	26	0
Ogden	3	41	14	0
Simmons	2	38	19	0
Linden	3	37	12	0
Mankins	1	12	12	0
Wood	1	9	9	0
Talbert	1	2	2	0
Martin	1	0	0	0
Sandeman	1	0	0	0

PASSING

Last Name	Att	Comp	%	Yds	Yd/Att	TD	Int−%	RK
Johnson	288	142	49	1620	5.6	10	21− 7	16
Nofsinger	60	30	50	352	5.9	1	2− 3	
Sloan	18	4	22	38	2.1	0	2−11	
Dunn	2	1	50	32	16.0	1	0− 0	
Moore	2	2	100	102	51.0	1	0− 0	

PUNTING

Last Name	No	Avg
Lothridge	87	43.7

KICKING

Last Name	XP	Att	%	FG	Att	%
Traynham	22	22	100	7	18	39
Absher	4	4	100	0	1	0

1967 A.F.L. Coming Up to Equal Footing

The AFL wasn't ready yet to win a Super Bowl, but the clubs in the newer league won some respect with their showing in interleague pre-season games. The games were far more competitive than had been expected, and the AFL drew first blood when the Denver Broncos beat the Detroit Lions 13-7 in the first interleague contest. The two leagues battled on even lines through the late-summer games, but the AFL administered the worst beating when the Chiefs, still smarting from their Super Bowl loss to Green Bay, crushed the Chicago Bears 66-27. The pre-season series seemed to prove that AFL teams could play on a par with average NFL teams but that time was needed to catch up with NFL powers like the Packers.

Time was on the AFL's side, however, as the common draft assured a steady flow of young talent into the league. Teams like Boston and Denver, which had never done well in signing its draft choices, now had an easier time coming to terms with graduating collegiate talent. The AFL teams also were moving into better stadia, with the San Diego Chargers this year setting up shop in a new municipal stadium.

EASTERN DIVISION

Houston Oilers—A 3-11 team only a year ago, the Oilers used a fine rookie class and a revitalized defense to capture their first divisional crown since 1962. Every adjustment head coach Wally Lemm made in the defense worked out splendidly; he moved veterans around and inserted rookies with the touch of a chess grandmaster. Pat Holmes, a disappointment last year as a tackle, caught fire as an end. Second-year man George Rice took over a tackle spot and drew compliments around the league. Rookie linebacker George Webster combined size, speed, and sound football sense in an All-Pro freshman season, and his linebacking mates were Garland Boyette, playing the middle for the first time, and Olen Underwood. W. K. Hicks and Jim Norton held onto their secondary posts, but joining them were newcomers Miller Farr, a quick cornerback picked up in a trade from San Diego, and rookie strong safety Ken Houston. This rebuilt unit allowed only eighteen touchdowns all year. The leading lights of the offense were fullback Hoyle Granger, quarterback Pete Beathard, who was picked up in mid-season from Kansas City, and star guard Bob Talamini.

New York Jets—As usual, the Jets looked like a sure title winner until December, and then, as usual, they fell apart. Ending November with a 7-2-1 record and a one-game lead over the coming Houston Oilers, the Jets started December by losing to Denver, Kansas City, and Oakland. They straightened out in time to beat San Diego in the season's finale, but by then the Oilers had locked up first place. The Jet pass defense contributed heavily to this year's late slump, as the line failed to rush enemy passers consistently and the secondary was not airtight. The Jets also had offensive problems, although Joe Namath and receivers George Sauer and Don Maynard bombed enemy defenses regularly. Fullback Matt Snell, the team's workhorse, ripped up a knee in the opening game and didn't return to action until mid-November; by then, halfback Emerson Boozer had gone out with an injured knee of his own.

Buffalo Bills—The Buffalo defensive unit stayed strong despite the loss of middle linebacker Harry Jacobs for the last seven games with a broken elbow, but the offense, never too robust to begin with, broke down completely under a rash of knee injuries. Bobby Crockett, last year's rookie receiving threat, sat out the entire year with a bad knee, while running back Bobby Burnett, veteran guard Billy Shaw, and split end Art Powell missed at least half the schedule with their knee injuries. Quarterback Jack Kemp's bad season further hurt the attack, and only newcomer Keith Lincoln, picked up in a swap with San Diego, kept the offense alive with his running and receiving. With all the injuries, the Bills scored more than 20 points in only three games all year—not nearly enough for a fourth straight championship.

Miami Dolphins—By mid-season rookie Bob Griese had taken over as the starting quarterback. Showing a strong arm and unshakable poise, Griese hooked up with rookie split end Jack Clancy in an effective passing combination. Outside of these two rookies, however, the Miami offense gave fans little to cheer about. Halfback Abner Haynes was long past his prime and was shipped out to New York before the year ended. The line had huge gaps, and flanker Howard Twilley had neither size nor speed. The defense, though not one of the league's best, did field several representative ball players.

Boston Patriots—Jim Nance still dominated the team with his powerful ball-carrying, but the supporting cast on the Patriots slipped, and they fell to last place in the East. With no speed at halfback or in the receivers, and with Babe Parilli showing advanced symptoms of old age, defenses waited for Nance's smashes into the line, yet the big fullback from Syracuse still bowled over the expectant defenders for 1,216 yards.

WESTERN DIVISION

Oakland Raiders—In a daring trade, the Raiders sent quarterback Tom Flores and split end Art Powell, both established starters, to Buffalo for quarterback Daryle Lamonica and Glenn Bass. Bass didn't make the team, but Lamonica developed into a fine long passer. End Bill Miller came from Buffalo at little cost and gave Lamonica a steady target. Willie Brown came over from Denver and beat All-Pro Dave Grayson out of a cornerback position. Thirty-nine-year-old George Blanda signed aboard after being released by Houston; the old-timer backed up Lamonica and led the league in scoring with his steady place-kicking. The rookie crop turned up guard Gene Upshaw, who immediately ranked among the league's best offensive linemen, and linebacker Duane Benson, who played on the special teams with zeal. Of course, the Raiders already had some top-notch players, with Billy Cannon, Jim Otto, Ben Davidson, Tom Keating, and Kent McCloughan winning All-League honors among the returning veterans. The Raiders' depth showed when halfback Clem Daniels broke his ankle late in the year and Pete Banaszak filled in with no noticeable drop in quality. Thus, the Raiders easily swept the Western Division title.

Kansas City Chiefs—AFL clubs learned well the lesson taught by the Green Bay Packers in the first Super Bowl. The Packers had singled out certain weak links in the Kansas City defense and ruthlessly exploited them, and now the AFL clubs found success in directing their attacks right at the same people. Enemy offenses singled out for special treatment, linebackers Chuck Hurston and Sherrill Headrick and cornerbacks Fred Williamson and Willie Mitchell, and by the time coach Hank Stram could readjust his defense the Chiefs had lost all four of their meetings with Oakland and San Diego and all chances for a repeat title in the West. But Stram did substitute some young talent into the lineup, and after Bud Abell, Emmitt Thomas, Fletcher Smith, and rookies Jim Lynch and Willie Lanier got their bearings, the Kansas City linebacking and secondary were a lot tougher. Aside from closing out the season with three straight wins, the high point of the year was the unveiling of two spectacular special team rookies: Norwegian place-kicker Jan Stenerud, and kick returner Noland Smith.

San Diego Chargers—The Chargers got off to a fast start and had high hopes of regaining the Western Division title, only to lose their last four games and slip back into a third-place finish. Coach Sid Gillman's biggest headache was his defense, which disintegrated down the stretch. Despite high-priced talents like Scott Appleton and Steve DeLong, the line put practically no pressure at all on enemy passers, and, given time, opposing quarterbacks found the San Diego secondary easy to pick apart. The offense kept the title drive alive until late in the season and kept the fans filing into the new San Diego Stadium. Enemy defenses had to worry first about flanker Lance Alworth, pro football's premier deep pass receiver, but if they paid too much attention to him, quarterback John Hadl simply threw to ends Gary Garrison and Willie Frazier, both fine pass catchers in their own right. The line was one of the best in pro football, especially at protecting the passer, and the San Diego running attack got a quick shot of energy in the form of Dickie Post and Brad Hubbert, a pair of rookie backs.

Denver Broncos—Lou Saban returned to pro football as head coach and general manager of the Broncos and immediately ripped the club apart to get a fresh start in building a winner. At times during the season Saban was starting fifteen rookies on the two platoons, a sign of his willingness to go with youth now to build a winner later. The team's biggest problems came in pass defense, where a rookie-laden secondary and linebacking corps could not handle good air attacks. The defensive line showed more stability as veteran Dave Costa, obtained from Buffalo for a draft pick, starred at a tackle post and youngsters Rich Jackson and Pete Duranko showed promise at the ends. Saban rebuilt the offense into a creditable unit, although the line was manned by and large with inexperienced or mediocre players. Saban got himself a quarterback by trading two first-round draft choices to San Diego for Steve Tensi, a promising young passer who learned as he played in Denver. Two fine wide receivers surfaced in Al Denson, last year's tight end, and Eric Crabtree, one of last year's bench warmers, while the running game improved immensely with the arrival of rookie halfback Floyd Little.

FINAL TEAM STATISTICS

	BOSTON	BUFFALO	DENVER	HOUSTON	K.CITY	MIAMI	NEW YORK	OAKLAND	SAN DIEGO	Category	BOSTON	BUFFALO	DENVER	HOUSTON	K.CITY	MIAMI	NEW YORK	OAKLAND	SAN DIEGO
										FIRST DOWNS:									
Total	219	203	172	207	251	212	282	250	259	Total	219	201	276	233	221	269	203	182	251
by Rushing	80	65	65	111	116	65	82	79	88	by Rushing	61	73	115	86	73	115	80	60	88
by Passing	120	119	91	86	117	123	180	154	150	by Passing	138	106	143	126	132	133	111	103	148
by Penalty	19	19	16	10	18	24	20	17	21	by Penalty	20	22	18	21	16	21	12	19	15
										RUSHING									
Number	391	371	420	476	462	326	389	458	417	Number	417	437	444	424	343	466	386	352	441
Yards	1604	1271	1265	2122	2018	1323	1307	1928	1715	Yards	1350	1622	2076	1637	1408	2145	1633	1129	1553
Average Yards	4.1	3.4	3.0	4.5	4.4	4.1	3.4	4.2	4.1	Average Yards	3.2	3.7	4.7	3.9	4.1	4.6	4.2	3.2	3.5
Touchdowns	10	9	10	12	18	10	17	19	14	Touchdowns	12	11	21	7	10	18	14	9	17
										PASSING:									
Attempts	434	434	374	332	382	480	515	464	463	Attempts	423	377	459	461	462	349	424	459	464
Completions	191	183	150	143	213	229	271	236	230	Completions	211	162	214	228	229	188	195	189	230
Completion Percentage	44.0	42.2	40.1	43.1	55.8	47.7	52.6	50.9	49.7	Completion Percentage	49.9	43.0	46.6	49.5	49.6	53.9	46.0	41.2	49.6
Passing Yards	2784	2763	2190	1532	2773	2741	4128	3541	3517	Passing Yards	3123	2191	3289	2619	2890	3082	2489	2831	3455
Avg. Yards per Attempt	6.4	6.4	5.9	4.6	7.3	5.7	8.0	7.6	7.6	Avg. Yards per Attempt	7.4	5.8	7.2	5.7	6.3	8.8	5.9	6.2	7.5
Avg. Yards per Completion	14.6	15.1	14.6	10.7	13.0	12.0	15.2	15.0	15.3	Avg. Yards per Completion	14.8	13.5	15.4	11.5	12.6	16.4	12.8	15.0	15.0
Time Tackled Att. to Pass	45	45	58	20	32	41	28	40	11	Time Tackled Att. to Pass	31	43	18	25	38	28	39	67	31
Yards Lost Tackled	361	446	508	151	301	405	283	353	107	Yards Lost Tackled	267	366	164	201	354	247	347	666	303
Net Yards	2423	2317	1682	1381	2472	2336	3845	3188	3410	Net Yards	2856	1825	3125	2418	2536	2835	2142	2165	3152
Touchdowns	20	14	17	11	26	16	27	33	26	Touchdowns	28	17	27	10	13	31	20	18	26
Interceptions	32	34	18	20	19	28	29	23	24	Interceptions	17	27	28	26	31	28	27	30	13
Percent Intercepted	7.4	7.8	4.8	6.0	5.0	5.8	5.6	5.0	5.2	Percent Intercepted	4.0	7.2	6.1	5.6	6.7	8.0	6.4	6.5	2.8
										PUNTS:									
Number	65	77	105	71	61	70	65	76	63	Number	73	74	65	63	64	52	79	111	72
Average Distance	40.5	43.1	44.9	42.6	41.3	41.6	42.1	44.3	37.5	Average Distance	41.9	41.0	41.5	41.0	43.0	41.1	43.2	41.9	45.2
										PUNT RETURNS:									
Number	43	47	26	20	33	25	48	51	39	Number	31	33	61	41	31	41	36	37	21
Yards	412	199	351	255	245	128	326	642	480	Yards	252	301	718	383	331	268	311	250	224
Average Yards	9.6	4.2	13.5	12.8	7.4	5.1	6.8	12.6	12.3	Average Yards	8.1	9.1	11.8	9.3	10.7	6.5	8.6	6.8	10.7
Touchdowns	0	1	1	0	0	0	0	0	0	Touchdowns	0	0	0	0	0	0	1	0	0
										KICKOFF RETURNS:									
Number	73	51	60	44	53	67	57	45	54	Number	45	56	42	51	55	46	64	82	63
Yards	1436	1113	1518	1020	1245	1443	1144	962	1239	Yards	946	1292	1046	950	1207	1079	1387	1707	1506
Average Yards	19.7	21.8	25.3	23.2	23.5	21.5	20.1	21.4	22.9	Average Yards	21.0	23.1	24.9	18.6	21.9	23.5	21.7	20.8	23.9
Touchdowns	0	0	0	1	1	0	0	0	0	Touchdowns	0	0	1	0	1	0	0	0	0
										INTERCEPTION RETURNS:									
Number	17	27	28	26	31	28	27	30	13	Number	32	34	18	20	19	28	29	23	24
Yards	257	401	413	676	578	402	322	404	274	Yards	640	554	262	156	471	395	711	209	329
Average Yards	15.1	14.9	14.8	26.0	18.6	14.4	11.9	13.5	21.1	Average Yards	20.0	16.3	14.6	7.8	24.8	14.1	24.5	9.1	13.7
Touchdowns	2	3	3	6	4	1	1	4	2	Touchdowns	7	2	2	1	5	3	5	0	1
										PENALTIES:									
Number	59	74	48	61	68	53	64	71	72	Number	70	51	58	59	76	59	67	69	61
Yards	520	828	512	698	680	490	691	768	817	Yards	722	507	628	614	757	691	717	702	666
										FUMBLES:									
Number	37	32	30	17	28	36	15	19	18	Number	26	26	23	29	34	19	24	29	22
Number Lost	22	13	12	7	8	16	8	13	10	Number Lost	17	9	13	13	18	8	6	15	10
										POINTS:									
Total	280	237	256	258	408	219	371	468	360	Total	389	285	409	199	254	407	329	233	352
PAT (kick) Attempts	31	26	30	30	45	28	40	57	45	PAT (kick) Attempts	46	33	50	14	28	50	40	27	44
PAT (kick) Made	30	25	28	30	45	27	36	56	45	PAT (kick) Made	44	32	48	14	28	47	39	26	44
PAT (2 Point) Attempts	2	1	1	1	4	0	6	1	0	PAT (2 Point) Attempts	2	0	2	4	2	3	1	2	0
PAT (2 Point) Made	0	1	1	0	2	0	4	1	0	PAT (2 Point) Made	0	0	2	3	1	0	1	2	0
FG Attempts	31	27	28	28	36	18	32	30	30	FG Attempts	31	38	31	42	25	26	26	14	27
FG Made	16	16	12	14	21	8	17	20	15	FG Made	19	17	15	23	14	14	14	9	14
Percent	51.6	59.3	42.9	50.0	58.3	44.4	53.1	66.7	50.0	Percent	61.3	44.7	48.4	54.8	56.0	53.8	53.8	64.3	51.9
Safeties	2	0	2	0	1	0	0	1	0	Safeties	0	2	0	1	1	0	0	1	1

OFFENSE (left) — DEFENSE (right)

HOUSTON OILERS 9-4-1 — Wally Lemm

Scores of Each Game

20	KANSAS CITY	25
20	Buffalo	3
3	San Diego	13
10	DENVER	6
28	New York	28
24	Kansas City	19
10	BUFFALO	3
7	Boston	18
20	Denver	18
27	BOSTON	6
17	MIAMI	14
7	OAKLAND	19
24	SAN DIEGO	17
41	Miami	10

Use Name	Pos.	Hgt	Wgt	Age	Int	Pts
Glen Ray Hines	OT	6'5"	270	23		
Walt Suggs	OT	6'5"	265	28		
Sonny Bishop	OG	6'2"	245	27		
Ed Marcontell (from StL-N)	OG	6'	260	23		
Tom Regner	OG	6'1"	255	23		
Bob Talamini	OG	6'1"	255	28		
Bobby Maples	C	6'3"	245	24		
Don Floyd	DE	6'4"	245	28		
Pat Holmes	DE	6'5"	260	27		
Willie Jones	DE	6'2"	260	25		
Carel Stith	DE	6'5"	270	22		
Bud Marshall	DT	6'5"	270	25		
Willie Parker	DT	6'2"	270	22		
Andy Rice (from KC)	DT	6'3"	266	25		
George Rice	DT	6'3"	260	23		
Pete Barnes	LB	6'3"	245	22		
Garland Boyette	LB	6'1"	240	27		
Danny Brabham	LB	6'4"	233	26		
Ronnie Caveness	LB	6'1"	225	24		
Olen Underwood	LB	6'1"	230	25	1	
George Webster	LB	6'4"	223	21	1	
Larry Carwell	DB	6'1"	187	23		
Miller Farr	DB	6'1"	188	24	10	18
W. K. Hicks	DB	6'1"	190	24	3	
Ken Houston	DB	6'3"	190	22	4	18
Bobby Jancik	DB	5'11"	178	27	1	
Pete Johns	DB	6'3"	188	22		
Zeke Moore	DB	6'2"	190	23		6
Jim Norton	DB	6'3"	180	28	6	6
Billy Anderson	QB	6'1"	195	26		
Pete Beathard (from KC)	QB	6'2"	210	25		
Bob Davis	QB	6'3"	202	21		
Jacky Lee (to KC)	QB	6'1"	188	28		
Sid Blanks	HB	6'	208	26		
Woody Campbell	HB	5'11"	205	22		
Hoyle Granger	FB	6'1"	225	23		
Roy Hopkins	FB	6'1"	227	22		
Glenn Bass	FL	6'2"	206	28		
Ode Burrell	FL	6'	195	27		
Larry Elkins	FL	6'1"	195	24		
Bob Poole	TE	6'4"	215	25		
Alvin Reed	TE	6'5"	228	23		
Charley Frazier	OE	6'	188	28		
Lionel Taylor	OE	6'2"	215	31		
John Wittenborn	K	6'2"	240	31		

Gary Cutsinger — Back Injury

NEW YORK JETS 8-5-1 — Weeb Ewbank

Scores of Each Game

17	Buffalo	20
38	Denver	24
29	MIAMI	7
27	OAKLAND	14
28	HOUSTON	28
33	Miami	14
30	BOSTON	23
18	Kansas City	42
20	BUFFALO	10
29	Boston	24
24	DENVER	33
7	KANSAS CITY	21
29	Oakland	38
42	San Diego	31

Use Name	Pos.	Hgt	Wgt	Age	Int	Pts
Winston Hill	OT	6'4"	275	25		
Sherman Plunkett	OT	6'4"	330	33		
Jim Harris	OT	6'4"	280	23		
Paul Seiler	OG-OT	6'4"	255	21		
Dave Herman	OG	6'2"	255	25		
Pete Perreault	OG	6'3"	245	28		
Randy Rasmussen	OG	6'2"	255	22		
Jeff Richardson	OG	6'3"	260	22		
John Matlock	C	6'4"	246	22		
John Schmitt	C	6'4"	245	24		
Verlon Biggs	DE	6'4"	260	24		
Gerry Philbin	DE	6'2"	248	26		
Bert Wilder	DT-DE	6'3"	245	27		
Dennis Randall	DT	6'6"	245	21		
Paul Rochester	DT	6'2"	255	30		
John Elliott	LB-DE-DT	6'4"	245	22		
Al Atkinson	LB	6'1"	228	24	5	
Ralph Baker	LB	6'3"	228	25	1	
Paul Crane	LB	6'2"	205	23		
Larry Grantham	LB	6'	206	28	5	
Carl McAdams	LB	6'3"	240	23		
Jim Waskiewicz	OT-LB	6'4"	235	23		
Bill Baird	DB	5'10"	180	28	3	
Randy Beverly	DB	5'11"	185	23	4	
Solomon Brannan	DB	6'1"	185	25		
Cornell Gordon	DB	6'	187	26	1	
Jim Hudson	DB	6'2"	210	24	4	
Henry King	DB	6'4"	205	22		
Sherman Lewis	DB	5'10"	180	25		
Bill Rademacher	DB	6'1"	190	25		
Johnny Sample	DB	6'1"	208	30	4	6
Joe Namath	QB	6'2"	195	24		
Mike Taliaferro	QB	6'2"	205	25		
Jim Turner	QB	6'2"	205	26		
Emerson Boozer	HB	5'11"	207	24		
Earl Christy	HB	5'11"	195	24		
Bill Mathis	HB	6'1"	220	28		
Billy Joe	FB	6'2"	236	26		
Mark Smolinski	FB	6'	215	28		
Matt Snell	FB	6'2"	220	25		
Don Maynard	FL	6'	180	31		
Bob Schweickert	FL	6'1"	190	24		
Curley Johnson	TE	6'	215	32		
Pete Lammons	TE	6'3"	228	23		
George Sauer	OE	6'1"	195	23		
Bake Turner	OE	6'	180	27		

BUFFALO BILLS 4-10-0 — Joe Collier

Scores of Each Game

20	NEW YORK	17
3	HOUSTON	20
0	BOSTON	23
17	SAN DIEGO	37
17	Denver	16
20	OAKLAND	24
3	Houston	10
35	MIAMI	13
10	New York	20
20	DENVER	21
14	Miami	17
13	Kansas City	23
44	Boston	16
21	Oakland	28

Use Name	Pos.	Hgt	Wgt	Age	Int	Pts
Stew Barber	OT	6'3"	252	28		
Dick Cunningham	OT	6'2"	242	22		
Dick Hudson	OT	6'4"	265	27		
Gary Bugenhagen	OG	6'2"	248	22		
Joe O'Donnell	OG	6'2"	252	25		
Billy Shaw	OG	6'3"	258	27		
Al Bemiller	C	6'3"	246	28		
Bob Schmidt	C	6'4"	250	31		
Ron McDole	DE	6'4"	270	27	1	
Bob Petrich	DE	6'4"	250	26		
Remi Prudhomme	DE	6'4"	263	25		
Jim Dunaway	DT	6'4"	280	25	1	
Dudley Meredith	DT	6'4"	285	32	1	
Tom Sestak	DT	6'5"	260	31		6
Paul Guidry	LB	6'3"	234	23		
Harry Jacobs	LB	6'2"	244	30		
Jim LeMoine	LB	6'2"	245	22		
Paul Maguire	LB	6'	230	29		
Marty Schottenheimer	LB	6'3"	225	24	3	6
Mike Stratton	LB	6'3"	244	25	1	
John Tracey	TE-LB	6'3"	228	33	1	
Butch Byrd	DB	6'	208	25	5	
Hagood Clarke	DB	6'	195	25		
Booker Edgerson	DB	5'10"	183	28	2	
Tom Janik	DB	6'3"	190	26	10	12
Charlie King	DB	6'	185	24		
John Pitts	DB	6'4"	218	22		
George Saimes	DB	5'10"	188	25	2	
Tom Flores	QB	6'1"	200	30		
Jack Kemp	QB	6'1"	204	33		
Teddy Bailey	HB	6'	220	23		
Charlie Bivins (from PIT-N)	HB	6'2"	212	28		
Bobby Burnett	HB	6'2"	208	24		
Gene Donaldson	HB	6'2"	225	25		
Allen Smith	HB	6'	200	24		
Keith Lincoln	FB-HB	6'2"	216	28		
Jack Spikes	FB	6'2"	220	29		
Wray Carlton	HB-FB	6'2"	224	29		
Elbert Dubenion	FL	6'	187	32		
Tony King	FL	6'1"	194	23		
Monte Ledbetter (from HOU)	FL	6'2"	185	24		
Ed Rutkowski	FL	6'1"	198	26		
Paul Costa	TE	6'4"	246	25		
Bill Masters	TE	6'5"	235	23		
Art Powell	OE	6'3"	214	30		
Mike Mercer	K	6'	217	31		

Bobby Crockett — Knee Injury
Charley Ferguson — Injury
George Flint — Injury

MIAMI DOLPHINS 4-10-0 — George Wilson

Scores of Each Game

35	DENVER	21
0	KANSAS CITY	24
7	New York	29
0	Kansas City	41
10	Boston	41
14	NEW YORK	33
13	Buffalo	35
0	San Diego	24
17	Oakland	31
17	BUFFALO	14
14	Houston	17
41	SAN DIEGO	24
41	BOSTON	32
10	HOUSTON	41

Use Name	Pos.	Hgt	Wgt	Age	Int	Pts
Norm Evans	OT	6'5"	250	24		
Jack Pyburn	OT	6'6"	240	22		
Charlie Fowler	OG-OT	6'2"	260	23		
Billy Neighbors	OG	5'11"	250	27		
Ken Rice	OG	6'2"	240	27		
Freddie Woodson	OG	6'2"	250	23		
Maxie Williams	OT-OG	6'4"	250	27		
Tom Goode	C	6'3"	245	28		
Mel Branch	DE	6'	235	30		
Ed Cooke	DE	6'4"	250	32		
Jim Riley	DE	6'4"	240	22		
Claude Brownlee	DT	6'4"	265	23		
Ray Jacobs	DT	6'3"	285	27		
Tom Nomina	DT	6'5"	260	25		
John Richardson	DT	6'2"	250	22		
Rich Zecher (to BUF)	DT	6'2"	240	24		
John Bramlett	LB	6'2"	220	26	4	
Bob Bruggers	LB	6'1"	225	23	1	
Frank Emanuel	LB	6'3"	225	24	1	
Tom Erlandson	LB	6'3"	220	27	1	
Jerry Hopkins	LB	6'2"	235	26		
Wahoo McDaniel	LB	6'	230	30	1	
Pete Jaquess (to DEN)	DB	6'	184	25		
Mack Lamb	DB	6'1"	183	23		
Bob Neff	DB	6'	180	23	1	
Bob Petrella	DB	6'	185	22	3	
Jimmy Warren	DB	5'11"	175	28	4	6
Willie West	DB	5'10"	187	29	1	
Dick Westmoreland	DB	6'1"	190	26	10	6
Tom Beier	FL-DB	5'11"	198	22	1	
Bob Griese	QB	6'1"	190	22		
Rick Norton	QB	6'1"	190	23		
Archie Roberts	QB	6'	193	24		
John Stofa	QB	6'3"	210	25		
Joe Auer	HB	6'1"	205	25		
Jack Harper	HB	5'11"	190	22		
Abner Haynes (to NY)	HB	6'	190	29		
Larry Seiple	HB	6'	200	22		
George Chesser	FB	6'2"	220	24		
Stan Mitchell	FB	6'2"	220	23		
Sam Price	HB-FB	5'11"	215	23		
Jack Clancy	FL	6'1"	195	23		
Frank Jackson	FL	6'1"	185	27		
John Roderick	FL	6'1"	180	23		
Preston Carpenter	TE	6'2"	208	33		
Doug Moreau	TE	6'2"	205	22		
Karl Noonan	OE	6'3"	190	23		
Howard Twilley	OE	5'10"	180	23		
Booth Lusteg	K	5'11"	190	26		
Gene Mingo (to WAS-N)	K	6'1"	190	28		

BOSTON PATRIOTS 3-10-1 — Mike Holovak

Scores of Each Game

21	Denver	26
14	San Diego	28
7	Oakland	35
23	Buffalo	0
31	SAN DIEGO	31
41	MIAMI	10
14	OAKLAND	48
23	New York	30
18	HOUSTON	7
10	KANSAS CITY	33
24	NEW YORK	29
6	Houston	27
16	BUFFALO	44
32	Miami	41

Use Name	Pos.	Hgt	Wgt	Age	Int	Pts
Jim Boudreaux	OT	6'4"	245	22		
Tom Neville	OT	6'4"	255	24		
Don Oakes	OT	6'3"	255	29		
Karl Singer	OT	6'3"	250	23		
Justin Canale	OG	6'2"	250	23	1	
Charley Long	OG	6'3"	250	29		
Len St. Jean	OG	6'1"	240	25		
Jon Morris	C	6'4"	240	24		
Bob Dee	DE	6'3"	250	34		
Larry Eisenhauer	DE	6'5"	255	27		
Tom Fussell	DE	6'3"	245	21		
Houston Antwine	DT	6'	270	28		
Jim Hunt	DT	5'11"	255	28	2	
John Mangum	DT	6'3"	270	23		
Mel Witt	DT	6'3"	265	21		
Ed Toner	LB-DT	6'3"	250	22		
Tom Addison	LB	6'3"	230	31		
Nick Buoniconti	LB	5'11"	220	26	4	2
Ray Ilg	LB	6'1"	220	21		
Ed Philpott	LB	6'3"	240	21		
Doug Satcher	LB	6'	220	22		
John Charles	DB	6'	200	23	1	6
Jay Cunningham	DB	5'10"	180	24	1	6
White Graves	DB	6'	185	24		
Ron Hall	DB	6'	190	30	1	
Billy Johnson	DB	5'11"	175	24		
Leroy Mitchell	DB	6'2"	200	23		
Vic Purvis	DB	5'11"	200	23		
Chuck Shonta	DB	6'	200	29	3	
Don Webb	DB	5'10"	200	28	4	
John Huarte	QB	6'	190	23		
Babe Parilli	QB	6'1"	190	37		
Don Trull (from HOU)	QB	6'1"	190	25		
Joe Bellino	HB	5'9"	185	29		
J. D. Garrett	HB	5'11"	195	25		
Larry Garron	HB	6'	195	30		
Bobby Leo	HB	5'10"	180	22		
Jim Nance	FB	6'1"	240	24		
Bob Cappadona	FB	6'1"	230	23		
Gino Cappelletti	FL	6'	190	33		
Bobby Nichols	TE	6'2"	220	23		
Tony Romeo	TE	6'2"	230	28		
Jim Whalen	TE	6'2"	210	23		
Jim Colclough	OE	6'	185	31		
Art Graham	OE	6'1"	205	26		
Terry Swanson	K	6'	210	22		

HOUSTON OILERS

RUSHING

Last Name	No.	Yds	Avg	TD
Granger	236	1194	5.1	6
Campbell	110	511	4.6	4
Blanks	66	206	3.1	1
Beathard	32	133	4.2	1
Hopkins	13	42	3.2	0
Davis	5	32	6.4	0
Elkins	2	19	9.5	0
Lee	6	-3	-0.5	0
Burrell	3	-3	-1.0	0
Norton	1	-7	-7.0	0

RECEIVING

Last Name	No.	Yds	Avg	TD
Granger	31	300	10	3
Frazier	23	253	11	1
Taylor	18	233	13	1
Campbell	17	136	8	2
Burrell	12	193	16	0
Reed	11	144	13	1
Blanks	11	93	8	1
Bass	5	42	8	1
Poole	4	55	14	0
Elkins	3	32	11	0
Hopkins	3	9	3	0
Lee	1	-1	-1	0

PUNT RETURNS

Last Name	No.	Yds	Avg	TD
Carwell	9	154	17	0
Moore	5	82	16	0
Jancik	6	19	3	0

KICKOFF RETURNS

Last Name	No.	Yds	Avg	TD
Moore	14	405	29	1
Jancik	16	349	22	0
Carwell	8	164	21	0
Houston	2	40	20	0
Hopkins	1	26	26	0
Campbell	1	19	19	0
Farr	1	17	17	0
Reed	1	0	0	0

PASSING – PUNTING – KICKING

PASSING	Att	Comp	%	Yds	Yd/Att	TD	Int-%	RK
Beathard	231	94	41	1114	4.8	9	14- 6	9
Lee	91	42	46	414	4.6	3	6- 7	
Davis	19	9	47	71	3.7	0	2-11	
Campbell	1	0	0	0	0.0	0	0- 0	

PUNTING	No	Avg
Norton	71	42.6

KICKING	XP	Att	%	FG	Att	%
Wittenborn	30	30	100	14	28	50

NEW YORK JETS

RUSHING

Last Name	No.	Yds	Avg	TD
Boozer	119	442	3.7	10
Mathis	78	243	3.1	4
Snell	61	207	3.4	0
Joe	37	154	4.2	2
Smolinski	64	139	2.2	1
Taliaferro	2	20	10.0	0
Maynard	4	18	4.5	0
Namath	6	14	2.3	0
Schweickert	1	1	1.0	0
Sauer	1	-3	-3.0	0

RECEIVING

Last Name	No.	Yds	Avg	TD
Sauer	75	1189	16	6
Maynard	71	1434	20	10
Lammons	45	515	11	2
Mathis	25	429	17	3
Smolinski	21	177	8	3
Boozer	12	205	17	3
Snell	11	54	5	0
Joe	8	85	11	0
B. Turner	3	40	13	0

PUNT RETURNS

Last Name	No.	Yds	Avg	TD
Baird	25	219	9	0
Christy	16	83	5	0
Lewis	7	24	3	0

KICKOFF RETURNS

Last Name	No.	Yds	Avg	TD
Christy	23	521	23	0
Boozer	11	213	19	0
Brannan	9	204	23	0
B. Turner	4	40	10	0
Lewis	1	22	22	0
McAdams	1	16	16	0
Smolinski	1	3	3	0
Waskiewicz	2	0	0	0
Wilder	1	0	0	0

PASSING – PUNTING – KICKING

PASSING	Att	Comp	%	Yds	Yd/Att	TD	Int-%	RK
Namath	491	258	53	4007	8.2	26	28- 6	3
Taliaferro	20	11	55	96	4.8	1	1- 5	
J. Turner	4	2	50	25	6.3	0	0- 0	

PUNTING	No	Avg
Johnson	65	42.1

KICKING	XP	Att	%	FG	Att	%
J. Turner	36	39	92	17	32	53

2 POINT XP
Mathis (2)
Maynard
Sauer

BUFFALO BILLS

RUSHING

Last Name	No.	Yds	Avg	TD
Lincoln	159	601	3.8	4
Carlton	107	467	4.4	3
Burnett	45	96	2.1	0
Bivins	15	58	3.9	0
Kemp	36	58	1.6	2
Spikes	4	9	2.3	0
Donaldson	3	-1	-0.3	0
Dubenion	2	-17	-8.5	0

RECEIVING

Last Name	No.	Yds	Avg	TD
Lincoln	41	558	14	5
Costa	39	726	19	2
Dubenion	25	384	15	0
Powell	20	346	17	4
Masters	20	274	14	2
Ledbetter	13	204	16	2
Burnett	11	114	10	0
Carlton	9	97	11	0
Rutkowski	6	59	10	0
Donaldson	1	20	20	0
Tracey	1	15	15	0
Spikes	1	9	9	0

PUNT RETURNS

Last Name	No.	Yds	Avg	TD
Byrd	30	142	5	0
Rutkowski	15	43	3	0
C. King	1	12	12	0
Edgerson	1	2	2	0

KICKOFF RETURNS

Last Name	No.	Yds	Avg	TD
Bivins	16	380	24	0
Smith	16	346	22	0
C. King	12	316	26	0
Rutkowski	3	71	24	0
Meredith	3	0	0	0
Guidry	1	0	0	0

PASSING – PUNTING – KICKING

PASSING	Att	Comp	%	Yds	Yd/Att	TD	Int-%	RK
Kemp	369	161	44	2503	6.8	14	26- 7	8
Flores	64	22	34	260	4.1	0	8-13	
Rutkowski	1	0	0	0	0.0	0	0- 0	

PUNTING	No	Avg
Maguire	77	43.1

KICKING	XP	Att	%	FG	Att	%
Mercer	25	25	100	16	27	59

2 POINT XP
Kemp

MIAMI DOLPHINS

RUSHING

Last Name	No.	Yds	Avg	TD
Haynes	72	346	4.8	2
Mitchell	83	269	3.2	3
Harper	41	197	4.8	1
Price	46	179	3.9	1
Griese	37	157	4.2	1
Auer	44	128	2.9	1
Seiple	3	58	19.3	0
Jackson	1	48	48.0	0
Norton	7	14	2.0	0
Chesser	2	3	1.5	0
Stofa	2	2	1.0	1
Moreau	1	-2	-2.0	0
Clancy	3	-4	-1.3	0

RECEIVING

Last Name	No.	Yds	Avg	TD
Clancy	67	868	13	2
Moreau	34	410	12	3
Twilley	24	314	13	2
Auer	18	218	12	2
Mitchell	18	133	7	1
Haynes	16	100	6	0
Noonan	12	141	12	1
Harper	11	212	19	3
Carpenter	10	127	13	0
Jackson	9	122	14	1
Price	8	56	7	1
Seiple	1	21	21	0
Beier	1	19	19	0

PUNT RETURNS

Last Name	No.	Yds	Avg	TD
Auer	9	42	5	0
Haynes	6	37	6	0
Neff	6	34	6	0
Harper	4	15	4	0

KICKOFF RETURNS

Last Name	No.	Yds	Avg	TD
Haynes	26	569	22	0
Auer	21	441	21	0
Neff	15	351	23	0
Carpenter	3	87	29	0
Roderick	4	63	16	0
Mitchell	2	57	29	0

PASSING – PUNTING – KICKING

PASSING	Att	Comp	%	Yds	Yd/Att	TD	Int-%	RK
Griese	331	166	50	2005	6.1	15	18- 5	5
Norton	133	53	40	596	4.5	1	9- 7	
Roberts	10	5	50	11	1.1	0	1-10	
Seiple	2	2	100	61	30.5	0	0- 0	
Stofa	2	2	100	51	25.5	0	0- 0	
Clancy	1	1	100	17	17.0	0	0- 0	
Lusteg	1	0	0	0	0.0	0	0- 0	

PUNTING	No	Avg
Seiple	70	41.6

KICKING	XP	Att	%	FG	Att	%
Lusteg	18	18	100	7	12	58
Mingo	9	9	100	1	6	17

BOSTON PATRIOTS

RUSHING

Last Name	No.	Yds	Avg	TD
Nance	269	1216	4.5	7
Garron	46	163	3.5	0
Cappadona	28	100	3.6	0
Parilli	14	61	4.4	0
Trull	22	30	1.4	3
Bellino	6	15	2.5	0
Garrett	5	7	1.4	0
Leo	1	7	7.0	0
Huarte	2	5	2.5	0
Graham	1	-5	-5.0	0

RECEIVING

Last Name	No.	Yds	Avg	TD
Graham	41	606	15	4
Whalen	39	651	17	5
Cappelletti	35	397	11	3
Garron	30	507	17	5
Nance	22	196	9	1
Colclough	14	263	19	0
Cappadona	6	104	17	1
Leo	1	25	25	1
Nichols	1	19	19	0
Garrett	1	12	12	0
Romeo	1	4	4	0

PUNT RETURNS

Last Name	No.	Yds	Avg	TD
Bellino	15	129	9	0
Johnson	6	124	21	0
Cunningham	17	105	6	0
Leo	5	54	11	0

KICKOFF RETURNS

Last Name	No.	Yds	Avg	TD
Cunningham	30	627	21	0
Bellino	18	357	20	0
Leo	11	232	21	0
Garrett	4	73	18	0
Garron	3	73	24	0
Singer	2	29	15	0
Cappadona	3	26	9	0
Ilg	1	10	10	0
Johnson	1	9	9	0

PASSING – PUNTING – KICKING

PASSING	Att	Comp	%	Yds	Yd/Att	TD	Int-%	RK
Parilli	344	161	47	2317	6.7	19	24- 7	6
Trull	92	31	34	480	5.2	1	7- 8	
Huarte	9	3	33	25	2.8	0	1-11	

PUNTING	No	Avg
Swanson	65	40.5

KICKING	XP	Att	%	FG	Att	%
Cappelletti	29	30	97	16	31	52
Canale	1	1	100	0	0	0

OAKLAND RAIDERS 13-1-0 — Johnny Rauch

Scores of Each Game

	Opponent	
51	DENVER	0
35	BOSTON	7
23	KANSAS CITY	21
14	New York	27
24	Buffalo	20
48	Boston	14
51	SAN DIEGO	10
21	Denver	17
31	MIAMI	17
44	Kansas City	22
41	San Diego	21
19	Houston	7
38	NEW YORK	29
28	BUFFALO	21

Use Name	Pos.	Hgt	Wgt	Age	Int	Pts
Harry Schuh	OT	6'2"	260	24		
Bob Svihus	OT	6'4"	245	24		
Dan Archer	OG-OT	6'5"	245	22		
Jim Harvey	OG	6'5"	245	24		
Wayne Hawkins	OG	6'	240	29		
Bob Kruse	OG	6'2"	250	25		
Gene Upshaw	OT-OG	6'5"	255	22		
Jim Otto	C	6'2"	240	29		
Ben Davidson	DE	6'8"	265	27		
Ike Lassiter	DE	6'5"	270	26		
Carleton Oats	DE	6'2"	235	24		6
Dan Birdwell	DT	6'4"	250	26	1	2
Tom Keating	DT	6'3"	247	24		
Richard Sligh	DT	7'	300	22		
Duane Benson	LB	6'2"	215	22		
Bill Budness	LB	6'1"	215	24		
Dan Conners	LB	6'1"	230	25	3	12
Bill Fairband	LB	6'3"	228	21		
Bill Laskey	LB	6'2"	235	24		
Gus Otto	LB	6'2"	220	24	1	
J. R. Williamson	LB	6'2"	220	25	2	
Rodger Bird	DB	5'11"	195	24		
Willie Brown	DB	6'1"	190	26	7	6
Dave Grayson	DB	5'10"	185	28	4	
Kent McCloughan	DB	6'1"	190	24	2	
Warren Powers	DB	6'	190	26	6	12
Howie Williams	DB	6'2"	186	30	4	
George Blanda	QB	6'1"	215	39		116
Daryle Lamonica	QB	6'1"	215	26		
Pete Banaszak	HB	5'11"	200	23		12
Estes Banks	HB	6'1"	200	22		
Clem Daniels	HB	6'1"	218	30		36
Larry Todd	HB	6'1"	185	24		12
Roger Hagberg	FB	6'2"	215	28		18
Hewritt Dixon	HB-FB	6'2"	220	27		42
Fred Biletnikoff	FL	6'1"	190	24		30
Rod Sherman	FL	6'	190	22		6
Billy Cannon	TE	6'1"	215	30		60
Dave Kocourek	TE	6'5"	240	30		2
Ken Herock	OE	6'2"	230	26		
Bill Miller	OE	6'	190	29		36
Warren Wells	OE	6'1"	190	24		36
Mike Eischeid	K	6'	190	26		

Charley Warner — Injury

KANSAS CITY CHIEFS 9-5-0 — Hank Stram

	Opponent	
25	Houston	20
24	Miami	0
21	Oakland	23
41	MIAMI	0
31	San Diego	45
19	HOUSTON	24
52	DENVER	9
42	NEW YORK	18
33	Boston	10
16	SAN DIEGO	17
22	OAKLAND	44
23	BUFFALO	13
21	New York	7
38	Denver	24

Use Name	Pos.	Hgt	Wgt	Age	Int	Pts
Dave Hill	OT	6'5"	260	26		
Bob Kelly	OT	6'3"	265	27		
Jim Tyrer	OT	6'6"	292	28		
Tony DiMidio	C-OT	6'3"	250	25		
Denny Biodrowski	OG	6'1"	255	27		
Ed Budde	OG	6'2"	260	26		
Curt Merz	OG	6'4"	267	29		
Al Reynolds	OG	6'3"	250	29		
Wayne Frazier (to BUF)	C	6'2"	245	27		
Jon Gilliam	C	6'2"	240	28		
Mike Hudock	C	6'2"	245	32		
Jerry Mays	DE	6'4"	252	27		
Gene Trosch	DT-DE	6'7"	277	22		
Buck Buchanan	DT	6'7"	287	27		
Ernie Ladd (from HOU)	DT	6'9"	292	28		
Ed Lothamer	DE-DT	6'5"	260	24		
Bud Abell	LB	6'3"	220	26		
Bobby Bell	LB	6'4"	228	27	4	6
Sherrill Headrick	LB	6'2"	240	30	1	
Chuck Hurston	LB	6'6"	240	24		
Willie Lanier	LB	6'1"	245	22		
Jim Lynch	LB	6'1"	235	22	1	
E. J. Holub	C-LB	6'4"	236	29		
Bobby Hunt	DB	6'1"	193	27	5	
Jim Kearney	DB	6'2"	206	24		
Sam Longmire	DB	6'3"	195	24		
Willie Mitchell	DB	6'1"	185	25	4	6
Johnny Robinson	DB	6'	205	28	5	
Fletcher Smith	DB	6'2"	188	23	6	
Emmitt Thomas	DB	6'2"	192	24	4	6
Fred Williamson	DB	6'2"	210	29	1	6
Len Dawson	QB	6'	190	33		
Bert Coan	HB	6'4"	220	27		24
Mike Garrett	HB	5'9"	200	23		60
Gene Thomas	HB	6'1"	210	24		18
Curtis McClinton	FB	6'3"	227	29		20
Jerrel Wilson	FB	6'4"	222	26		
Gloster Richardson	FL	6'	200	24		12
Noland Smith	FL	5'6"	154	23		6
Otis Taylor	FL	6'3"	215	24		72
Fred Arbanas	TE	6'3"	240	28		30
Reg Carolan	TE	6'6"	240	27		2
Chris Burford	OE	6'3"	210	29		18
Frank Pitts	OE	6'2"	205	24		12
Jan Stenerud	K	6'2"	187	24		108
Wayne Walker	K	6'2"	215	22		

Aaron Brown — Thigh Injury

SAN DIEGO CHARGERS 8-5-1 — Sid Gillman

	Opponent	
28	BOSTON	14
13	HOUSTON	3
37	Buffalo	17
31	Boston	31
45	KANSAS CITY	31
38	Denver	21
10	Oakland	51
24	MIAMI	0
17	Kansas City	16
24	DENVER	20
21	OAKLAND	41
24	Miami	41
17	Houston	24
31	NEW YORK	42

Use Name	Pos.	Hgt	Wgt	Age	Int	Pts
Harold Akin	OT	6'5"	262	22		
Gary Kirner	OT	6'3"	248	25		
Ron Mix	OT	6'4"	250	29		
Terry Owens	OT	6'6"	240	23		
Ernie Wright	OT	6'4"	265	27		
Ed Mitchell	OG	6'2"	280	25		
Walt Sweeney	OG	6'3"	255	26		
Larry Little	DT-OG	6'1"	265	21		
Sam Gruneisen	C	6'1"	240	26		
Paul Latzke	C	6'4"	240	25		
Tom Day	DE	6'2"	262	32		
Jim Griffin	DE	6'3"	255	25		
Howard Kindig (to BUF)	DE	6'6"	255	26		
Scott Appleton	DT	6'3"	256	25		6
Ron Billingsley	DT	6'8"	265	22		
Steve DeLong	DT	6'3"	252	24		
George Gross	DT	6'3"	258	26		
Houston Ridge	DT	6'4"	235	23		
Chuck Allen	LB	6'1"	225	27	2	
Johnny Baker	LB	6'3"	238	26		
Frank Buncom	LB	6'1"	240	27		
Bernie Erickson	LB	6'2"	238	22	1	
Ron McCall	LB	6'2"	245	22		
Bob Print	LB	6'	220	23		
Rick Redman	LB	5'11"	225	24	2	
Jeff Staggs	LB	6'2"	248	23		
Joe Beauchamp	DB	6'1"	185	23	3	
Speedy Duncan	DB	5'10"	175	24	2	18
Kenny Graham	DB	6'1"	195	25	2	6
Bob Howard	DB	6'1"	190	22		
Frank Marsh	DB	6'2"	205	26		
Jim Tolbert	DB	6'3"	207	23	1	
Bud Whitehead	HB-DB	6'	185	28		
John Hadl	QB	6'2"	215	27		18
Kay Stephenson	QB	6'1"	205	22		
Gene Foster	HB	5'11"	212	24		
Paul Lowe	HB	6'	205	30		6
Dickie Post	HB	5'9"	190	21		48
Jim Allison	FB	6'	220	24		
Brad Hubbert	FB	6'1"	227	26		24
Russ Smith	HB-FB	6'1"	225	23		6
Lance Alworth	FL	6'	184	27		54
Willie Frazier	TE	6'4"	225	24		60
Jacque MacKinnon	TE	6'4"	250	28		12
Ollie Cordill	OE	6'2"	180	24		
Gary Garrison	OE	6'1"	195	23		12
Steve Newell	OE	6'1"	186	22		
Dick Van Raaphorst	K	5'11"	215	24		90

Nat Whitmyer — Injury

DENVER BRONCOS 3-11-0 — Lou Saban

	Opponent	
26	BOSTON	21
0	Oakland	51
21	Miami	35
24	NEW YORK	38
6	Houston	10
16	BUFFALO	17
21	SAN DIEGO	38
9	Kansas City	52
17	OAKLAND	21
18	HOUSTON	20
21	Buffalo	20
20	San Diego	24
33	New York	24
24	KANSAS CITY	38

Use Name	Pos.	Hgt	Wgt	Age	Int	Pts
Dave Behrman	OT	6'5"	260	25		
Bob Breitenstein (to MIN-N)	OT	6'3"	267	24		
Sam Brunelli	OT	6'1"	255	24		
Tom Cichowski	OT	6'4"	250	22		
Mike Current (from MIA)	OT	6'4"	250	21		
Pat Matson	OG	6'1"	250	23		
Ernie Park	OG	6'3"	240	25		
Don Smith	OG	6'4"	240	24		
Dick Tyson	OG	6'2"	245	23		
Bob Young	OG	6'2"	260	24		
George Goeddeke	C-OG	6'3"	240	22		
Larry Kaminski	C	6'2"	240	22		
Ray Kubala	C	6'4"	245	25		
Roger LeClerc	C	6'3"	245	29	5	
Pete Duranko	DE	6'2"	240	23		
Rich Jackson	DE	6'2"	255	26	2	
Rex Mirich	DE	6'4"	250	26		
Dave Costa	DT	6'2"	265	25		
Larry Cox	DT	6'2"	250	23		
Jerry Inman	DT	6'3"	255	27		
Bill Keating (to MIA)	DT	6'2"	236	22		
Lou Andrus	LB	6'6"	255	24		
Carl Cunningham	LB	6'2"	230	23	1	
John Huard	LB	6'	220	23	2	
Gene Jeter	LB	6'3"	230	25		
Chip Myrtle	LB	6'2"	215	22	1	
Frank Richter	LB	6'3"	230	22	2	
Henry Sorrell	LB	6'1"	215	23		
Jack Lentz	DB	6'	195	22	4	
Bobby Ply (from KC-BUF)	DB	6'1"	190	26		
Errol Prisby	DB	5'10"	184	24		
Goldie Sellers	DB	6'2"	198	25	7	6
Jim Summers	DB	5'10"	175	24		
Gene Sykes	DB	6'1"	195	26	2	
Nemiah Wilson	DB	6'	165	24	4	12
Lonnie Wright	DB	6'2"	205	23	4	
Tom Cassese	HB-DB	6'1"	197	21	1	
Scotty Glacken	QB	6'	190	22		
Jim LeClair	QB	6'1"	208	25		6
Steve Tensi	QB	6'5"	215	24		
Floyd Little	HB	5'10"	195	25		12
Fran Lynch	HB	6'1"	210	21		
Charley Mitchell	HB	5'11"	185	27		
Cookie Gilchrist	FB	6'3"	250	32		
Wendell Hayes	FB	6'2"	220	26		26
Bo Hickey	FB	5'11"	205	24		30
Mike Kellogg	FB	6'	220	24		
Al Denson	FL	6'2"	208	25		66
Bob Scarpitto	FL	5'11"	196	28		
Tom Beer	TE	6'4"	235	22		
Andre White	TE	6'5"	225	22		2
Eric Crabtree	OE	5'11"	182	22		30
Neal Sweeney	OE	6'2"	170	22		
Rick Duncan	K	6'	208	26		9
Dick Humphreys	K	6'1"	240	27		39
Gary Kroner	K	6'1"	200	26		11

Max Leetzow — Injury

OAKLAND RAIDERS

RUSHING

Last Name	No.	Yds	Avg	TD
Daniels	130	575	4.4	4
Dixon	153	559	3.7	5
Banaszak	68	376	5.5	1
Hagberg	44	146	3.3	2
Todd	29	116	4.0	2
Lamonica	22	110	5.0	4
Banks	10	26	2.6	0
Sherman	1	13	13.0	1
Wells	1	7	7.0	0

RECEIVING

Last Name	No.	Yds	Avg	TD
Dixon	59	563	10	2
Biletnikoff	40	876	22	5
Miller	38	537	14	6
Cannon	32	629	20	10
Daniels	16	222	14	2
Banaszak	16	192	12	1
Wells	13	302	23	6
Hagberg	11	114	10	1
Sherman	5	61	12	0
Todd	4	42	11	0
Kocourek	1	4	4	0
Herock	1	−1	−1	0

PUNT RETURNS

Last Name	No.	Yds	Avg	TD
Bird	46	612	13	0
Powers	2	19	10	0
Grayson	3	11	4	0

KICKOFF RETURNS

Last Name	No.	Yds	Avg	TD
Grayson	19	405	21	0
Sherman	12	279	23	0
Bird	6	143	24	0
Todd	5	123	25	0
Hagberg	2	12	6	0
Benson	1	0	0	0

PASSING – PUNTING – KICKING

PASSING

Last Name	Att	Comp	%	Yds	Yd/Att	TD	Int–%	RK
Lamonica	425	220	52	3228	7.6	30	20– 5	1
Blanda	38	15	39	285	7.5	3	3– 8	
Daniels	1	1	100	28	28.0	0	0– 0	

PUNTING

Last Name	No	Avg
Eischeid	76	44.3

KICKING

Last Name	XP	Att	%	FG	Att	%
Blanda	56	57	98	20	30	67

2 POINT XP
Kocourek

KANSAS CITY CHIEFS

RUSHING

Last Name	No.	Yds	Avg	TD
Garrett	236	1087	4.6	9
McClinton	97	392	4.0	2
Coan	63	275	4.4	4
G. Thomas	35	133	3.8	1
Dawson	20	68	3.4	0
Taylor	5	29	5.8	1
Pitts	3	19	6.3	1
Wilson	1	10	10.0	0
N. Smith	1	8	8.0	0

RECEIVING

Last Name	No.	Yds	Avg	TD
Taylor	59	958	16	11
Garrett	46	261	6	1
McClinton	26	219	8	1
Burford	25	389	16	3
Arbanas	20	295	15	5
G. Thomas	13	99	8	2
Richardson	12	312	26	2
Coan	5	41	8	0
Pitts	4	131	33	1
Carolan	2	26	13	0
N. Smith	1	42	42	0

PUNT RETURNS

Last Name	No.	Yds	Avg	TD
N. Smith	26	212	8	0
Garrett	4	22	6	0
E. Thomas	2	8	4	0
Robinson	1	3	3	0

KICKOFF RETURNS

Last Name	No.	Yds	Avg	TD
N. Smith	41	1148	28	0
G. Thomas	6	56	9	0
Coan	1	29	29	0
Carolan	1	2	2	0
Lanier	1	1	1	0
Buchanan	1	0	0	0
Hill	1	0	0	0
Lothamer	1	0	0	0
Pitts	0	9	0	0

PASSING – PUNTING – KICKING

PASSING

Last Name	Att	Comp	%	Yds	Yd/Att	TD	Int–%	RK
Dawson	357	206	58	2651	7.4	24	17– 5	2
Garrett	4	1	25	17	4.3	1	0– 0	

PUNTING

Last Name	No	Avg
Wilson	41	42.4
Walker	19	38.7
Carolan	1	42.0

KICKING

Last Name	XP	Att	%	FG	Att	%
Stenerud	45	45	100	21	36	58

2 POINT XP
Carolan
McClinton

SAN DIEGO CHARGERS

RUSHING

Last Name	No.	Yds	Avg	TD
Post	161	663	4.1	7
Hubbert	116	643	5.5	2
Smith	22	115	5.2	1
Hadl	37	107	2.9	3
Foster	38	78	2.1	0
Lowe	28	71	2.5	1
Allison	10	34	3.4	0
Stephenson	2	11	5.5	0
Alworth	1	5	5.0	0
Garrison	1	1	1.0	0
Redman	1	−13	−13.0	0

RECEIVING

Last Name	No.	Yds	Avg	TD
Frazier	57	922	16	10
Alworth	52	1010	19	9
Garrison	44	772	18	2
Post	32	278	9	1
Hubbert	19	214	11	2
Foster	9	46	5	0
Mackinnon	7	176	25	2
Newell	7	68	10	0
Lowe	2	25	13	0
Smith	1	6	6	0

PUNT RETURNS

Last Name	No.	Yds	Avg	TD
Duncan	36	434	12	0
Graham	3	46	15	0

KICKOFF RETURNS

Last Name	No.	Yds	Avg	TD
Tolbert	18	441	25	0
Post	15	371	25	0
Duncan	9	231	26	0
Lowe	8	145	18	0
Smith	3	51	17	0
Erickson	1	0	0	0

PASSING – PUNTING – KICKING

PASSING

Last Name	Att	Comp	%	Yds	Yd/Att	TD	Int–%	RK
Hadl	427	217	51	3365	7.9	24	22– 5	4
Stephenson	26	11	42	117	4.5	2	2– 8	
Post	6	1	17	9	1.5	0	0– 0	
Alworth	1	0	0	0	0.0	0	0– 0	
Foster	1	0	0	0	0.0	0	0– 0	
Lowe	1	1	100	26	26.0	0	0– 0	
Whitehead	1	0	0	0	0.0	0	0– 0	

PUNTING

Last Name	No	Avg
Redman	58	37.0
Cordill	3	48.3
Hadl	2	35.0

KICKING

Last Name	XP	Att	%	FG	Att	%
Van Raaphorst	45	45	100	15	30	50

DENVER BRONCOS

RUSHING

Last Name	No.	Yds	Avg	TD
Little	130	381	2.9	1
Mitchell	82	308	3.8	0
Hickey	73	263	3.6	4
Hayes	85	255	3.0	4
Gilchrist	10	21	2.1	0
Glacken	1	10	10.0	0
Lynch	2	7	3.5	0
LeClair	8	6	0.8	1
Cassese	1	5	5.0	0
Scarpitto	1	5	5.0	0
Tensi	24	4	0.2	0
Crabtree	2	2	1.0	0
Denson	1	−2	−2.0	0

RECEIVING

Last Name	No.	Yds	Avg	TD
Denson	46	899	20	11
Crabtree	46	716	16	5
Hayes	13	125	10	0
Beer	11	155	14	0
Hickey	7	36	5	1
Mitchell	7	15	2	0
Little	7	11	2	0
Sweeney	6	136	23	0
White	5	87	17	0
Scarpitto	1	14	14	0
Gilchrist	1	−4	−4	0

PUNT RETURNS

Last Name	No.	Yds	Avg	TD
Little	16	270	17	1
Sellers	4	24	6	0
Crabtree	2	24	12	0
Huard	1	19	19	0
Cassese	3	14	5	0

KICKOFF RETURNS

Last Name	No.	Yds	Avg	TD
Little	35	942	27	0
Mitchell	8	164	21	0
Sellers	6	120	20	0
Wilson	4	106	27	0
Hayes	3	104	35	0
Lynch	1	27	27	0
Crabtree	1	26	26	0
Cassese	1	19	19	0
Beer	1	10	10	0

PASSING – PUNTING – KICKING

PASSING

Last Name	Att	Comp	%	Yds	Yd/Att	TD	Int–%	RK
Tensi	325	131	40	1915	5.9	16	17– 5	7
LeClair	45	19	42	275	6.1	1	1– 2	
Glacken	4	0	0	0	0.0	0	0– 0	

PUNTING

Last Name	No	Avg
Scarpitto	105	44.9

KICKING

Last Name	XP	Att	%	FG	Att	%
Humphreys	18	19	95	7	15	47
Kroner	5	6	83	2	2	100
Duncan	3	3	100	2	5	40
LeClerc	2	2	100	1	6	17

2 POINT XP
Hayes

1967 Championship Games

NFL CHAMPIONSHIP GAME
December 31, at Green Bay
(Attendance 50,861)

Green Bay's Golden Gamble

Last year's game between the Packers and Cowboys had been an NFL classic, but their rematch this season ranked among the most memorable football games of all time. Both clubs had won conference playoffs to get this far, with Green Bay beating the Rams 28-7 and Dallas clobbering the Browns 52-14, and they clashed for the NFL title in a titanic struggle under nightmarish conditions.

At game time the temperature in Green Bay was 13 degrees below zero, and a fifteen-mile-per-hour wind made it almost unbearable for player and spectator alike. Somewhat better acclimated to the cold than the Cowboys, the Packers mounted a 14-0 lead by early in the second quarter. The Dallas defense, however, took matters into its own hands. Willie Townes hit Starr attempting to pass, and when the ball squirted loose George Andrie picked it up and ran it into the end zone. When Willie Wood fumbled a punt a short time later, the Cowboys added a field goal to cut the score to 14-10 at halftime.

In the fourth period, the Cowboys went ahead on the first play when halfback Dan Reeves surprised the Packer secondary by throwing a long option pass to Lance Rentzel. With their backs to the wall, the Pack still trailed 17-14 when they took over the ball on their own 31-yard line with 4:50 left in the game. Mixing running plays and passes to his backs, Starr moved the Packers quickly downfield until they had a first down on the Dallas one-yard line with under a minute left on the clock. Twice Donny Anderson tried to run it in, twice he failed, and twice Starr called time out. With no time outs remaining and twenty seconds on the clock, the Packers snubbed a field-goal try and put all their chips on one last running play. At the snap, guard Jerry Kramer pushed Jethro Pugh out of the way, and Starr plunged through the gap for the winning touchdown.

SCORING

GREEN BAY	7	7	0	7—21
DALLAS	0	10	0	7—17

First Quarter
G.B.   Dowler, 8 yard pass from Starr
　　　 PAT — Chandler (kick)

Second Quarter
G.B.   Dowler, 43 yard pass from Starr
　　　 PAT — Chandler (kick)
Dal.   Andrie, 7 yard fumble return (by Starr)
　　　 PAT — Villanueva (kick)
Dal.   Villanueva, 21 yard field goal

Fourth Quarter
Dal.   Rentzel, 50 yard pass from Reeves
　　　 PAT — Villanueva (kick)
G.B.   Starr, 1 yard rush
　　　 PAT — Chandler (kick)

TEAM STATISTICS

G.B.		DAL.
18	First Downs — Total	11
5	First Downs — Rushing	4
10	First Downs — Passing	6
3	First Downs — Penalty	1
1	Interception Returns — Number	0
15	Interception Returns — Yards	0
3	Fumbles — Number	3
2	Fumbles — Lost Ball	1
2	Penalties — Number	7
10	Yards Penalized	58
2	Giveaways	2
2	Takeaways	2
0	Difference	0

INDIVIDUAL STATISTICS

RUSHING

GREEN BAY	No	Yds	Avg.	DALLAS	No	Yds	Avg.
Anderson	18	35	1.9	Perkins	17	51	3.0
Mercein	6	20	3.3	Reeves	13	42	3.2
Williams	4	13	3.3	Meredith	1	9	9.0
Wilson	3	11	3.7	Baynham	1	−2	−2.0
Starr	1	1	1.0	Clarke	1	−8	−8.0
	32	80	2.5		33	92	2.8

RECEIVING

GREEN BAY	No	Yds	Avg.	DALLAS	No	Yds	Avg.
Dowler	4	77	19.3	Hayes	3	16	5.3
Anderson	4	44	11.0	Reeves	3	11	3.7
Dale	3	44	14.7	Rentzel	2	61	30.5
Mercein	2	22	11.0	Clarke	2	24	12.0
Williams	1	4	4.0	Baynham	1	−3	−3.0
	14	191	13.6		11	109	9.9

PUNTING

	No	Yds	Avg.		No	Yds	Avg.
Anderson	8		29.0	Villanueva	8		39.1

PUNT RETURNS

	No	Yds	Avg.		
Wood	4	21	5.3	None	
Brown	1	−2	−2.0		
	5	19	3.8		

KICKOFF RETURNS

	No	Yds	Avg.		No	Yds	Avg.
Caffey	1	7	7.0	Stevens	2	15	7.5
Crutcher	1	3	3.0	Stokes	1	28	28.0
Weatherwax	1	0	0.0		3	43	14.3
	3	10	3.3				

PASSING

GREEN BAY	Att	Comp	Comp Pct.	Yds	Int	Yds/ Att.	Yds/ Comp	Yards Lost Tackled
Starr	24	14	58.3	191	0	8.0	13.6	8—76

DALLAS	Att	Comp	Comp Pct.	Yds	Int	Yds/ Att.	Yds/ Comp	Yards Lost Tackled
Meredith	25	10	40.0	59	1	2.4	5.9	1— 9
Reeves	1	1	100.0	50	0	50.0	50.0	0— 0
	26	11	42.3	109	1	4.2	9.9	1— 9

AFL CHAMPIONSHIP GAME
December 31, at Oakland
(Attendance 53,330)

Lamonica's Field-Goal Touchdown

The Oilers had won the Eastern Division title because of their strong defense, but the Raiders had no problems moving the ball in this championship game. With guard Gene Upshaw leading a fired-up Oakland offensive line, the Raiders attacked the Oilers on the ground, with Hewritt Dixon and Pete Banaszak steadily eating up the yardage all afternoon. George Blanda, whom the Oilers had put on waivers before the season, opened the scoring with a 37-yard field goal, and a 69-yard touchdown run around left end by Dixon gave Oakland more momentum. With eighteen seconds left in the half, the Raiders lined up for a close field-goal attempt, only to have holder Daryle Lamonica jump up and throw a touchdown pass to tight end Dave Kocourek.

Trailing 17-0 and getting nowhere against the Oakland defense, the Oilers needed some fireworks at the start of the second half to get back into the game. Instead, Zeke Moore fumbled the kickoff and gave the ball back to the Raiders deep in Houston territory. The Raiders needed seven plays to reach the end zone, with Lamonica sneaking over from the 1 for the score.

Once the score reached 24-0, all the steam leaked out of the Oilers. Fullback Hoyle Granger, the key to the Houston ground attack, never got untracked all day, and quarterback Pete Beathard had no success passing against the swarming Oakland secondary.

After three periods, the score had risen to 27-0, but the Oilers finally got on the scoreboard with a touchdown pass from Beathard to Charley Frazier plus John Whittenborn's extra point. That was the only Houston score of the day, however, and before the final gun sounded, the Raiders added ten points on a Blanda field goal and a scoring pass from Lamonica to Bill Miller. The 40-7 victory put the Raiders into the Super Bowl, but an Achilles tendon injury suffered by defensive tackle Tom Keating would hobble him for that upcoming match.

SCORING

OAKLAND	3	14	10	13—40
HOUSTON	0	0	0	7— 7

First Quarter
Oak.   Blanda, 37 yard field goal

Second Quarter
Oak.   Dixon, 69 yard rush
　　　 PAT — Blanda (kick)
Oak.   Kocourek, 17 yard pass from Lamonica
　　　 PAT — Blanda (kick)

Third Quarter
Oak.   Lamonica, 1 yard rush
　　　 PAT — Blanda (kick)
Oak.   Blanda, 40 yard field goal

Fourth Quarter
Oak.   Blanda, 42 yard field goal
Hous. Frazier, 5 yard pass from Beathard
　　　 PAT — Wittenborn (kick)
Oak.   Blanda, 36 yard field goal
Oak.   Miller, 12 yard pass from Lamonica
　　　 PAT — Blanda (kick)

TEAM STATISTICS

OAK.		HOUS.
18	First Downs — Total	11
11	First Downs — Rushing	4
6	First Downs — Passing	6
1	First Downs — Penalty	1
0	Fumbles — Number	4
0	Fumbles — Lost Ball	2
4	Penalties — Number	7
69	Yards Penalized	45
2	Missed Field Goals	0
0	Giveaways	3
3	Takeaways	0
+3	Difference	−3

INDIVIDUAL STATISTICS

RUSHING

OAKLAND	No	Yds	Avg.	HOUSTON	No	Yds	Avg.
Dixon	21	144	6.9	Granger	14	19	1.4
Banaszak	15	116	7.7	Campbell	6	15	2.5
Lamonica	5	22	4.4	Blanks	1	6	6.0
Hagberg	2	−1	−0.5	Beathard	1	−2	−2.0
Todd	4	−8	−2.0		22	38	1.7
Biletnikoff	1	−10	−10.0				
	48	263	5.5				

RECEIVING

OAKLAND	No	Yds	Avg.	HOUSTON	No	Yds	Avg.
Miller	3	32	10.7	Frazier	7	81	11.6
Cannon	2	31	15.5	Reed	4	60	15.0
Biletnikoff	2	19	9.5	Campbell	2	5	2.5
Kocourek	1	17	17.0	Taylor	1	6	6.0
Dixon	1	8	8.0	Granger	1	−10	−10.0
Banaszak	1	4	4.0		15	142	9.5
	10	111	11.1				

PUNTING

	No	Yds	Avg.		No	Yds	Avg.
Eischeid	4		44.3	Norton	11		38.5

PUNT RETURNS

	No	Yds	Avg.		
Bird	5	49	9.8	None	
Sherman	1	−2	−2.0		
	6	47	7.8		

KICKOFF RETURNS

	No	Yds	Avg.		No	Yds	Avg.
Grayson	1	47	47.0	Jancik	4	100	25.0
Todd	1	32	32.0	Moore	3	87	29.0
	2	79	39.5	Burrell	1	28	28.0
				Suggs	1	0	0.0
					9	215	23.9

INTERCEPTION RETURNS

	No	Yds	Avg.		
Brown	1	2	2.0	None	

PASSING

OAKLAND	Att	Comp	Comp Pct.	Yds	Int	Yds/ Att.	Yds/ Comp	Yards Lost Tackled
Lamonica	24	10	41.7	111	0	4.6	11.1	
Blanda	2	0	0.0	0	0	0	0	
	26	10	38.5	111	0	4.3	11.1	10

HOUSTON	Att	Comp	Comp Pct.	Yds	Int	Yds/ Att.	Yds/ Comp	Yards Lost Tackled
Beathard	35	15	40.5	142	1	4.1	9.5	34

The Errors of Youth

The Packers might naturally have suffered a mental letdown after their cliff-hanging NFL championship match with the Dallas Cowboys, but the knowledge that this was Vince Lombardi's last game as head coach gave the team all the incentive it needed against the AFL champion Oakland Raiders. In his nine seasons at Green Bay, Lombardi had turned the Packers from chronic losers to perennial champions, and his players were determined that he go out a winner.

The Oakland Raiders, on the other hand, had just won their first AFL crown by severely thrashing the Houston Oilers in the championship game. Like the Kansas City Chiefs last year, the Raiders had several players obviously good enough for any league, but other Oakland players would have to prove themselves against the Packers. They did, but what hurt the Raiders this day were mistakes, the sort of errors that plague young teams in any league.

The first quarter went fairly evenly, with the only scoring coming on Don Chandler's 39-yard field goal. Another Chandler three-pointer upped the score to 6-0 in the second quarter, and then the Raiders made their first costly mistake. The Packers had the ball on their own 38-yard line when Bart Starr dropped back to pass. Someone in the Raider secondary missed his assignment and left Boyd Dowler all alone downfield; Starr hit him with a perfect pass, which he carried to the end zone. With the extra point making the score 13-0, the Raiders seemed close to early death in this contest.

Daryle Lamonica revived his team's failing spirits, however, by driving the Raiders downfield and hitting Bill Miller with a 23-yard touchdown pass. The Oakland defense then stopped the Packer offense, but Rodger Bird, normally a sure-handed punt returner, called for a fair catch and fumbled the ball. The Packers recovered near mid-field and converted the break into another Chandler field goal and a 16-7 halftime lead.

Using their ball-control offense, the Packers nursed their lead through the second half and built it up to 33-14 on a Donny Anderson touchdown, a Chandler field goal, and Herb Adderley's return of an interception for a touchdown. Lamonica threw another touchdown pass to Miller in the fourth quarter, but that only made the final score a clear-cut 33-14. Vince Lombardi, retiring to the front office, was going out a winner.

Line-ups

GREEN BAY		OAKLAND
OFFENSE		
Dowler	LE	Miller
Skoronski	LT	Svihus
Gillingham	LG	Upshaw
Bowman	C	J. Otto
Kramer	RG	Hawkins
Gregg	RT	Schuh
Fleming	RE	Cannon
Starr	QB	Lamonica
Dale	FL	Biletnikoff
Anderson	HB	Banaszak
Wilson	FB	Dixon
DEFENSE		
Davis	LE	Lassiter
Kostelnik	LT	Birdwell
Jordan	RT	Keating
Aldridge	RE	Davidson
Robinson	LLB	Laskey
Nitschke	MLB	Connors
Caffey	RLB	G. Otto
Adderley	LCB	McCloughan
Jeter	RCB	W. Brown
T. Brown	LS	Powers
Wood	RS	H. Williams

SUBSTITUTES

GREEN BAY
Offense
Bratkowski	McGee
Capp	Mercein
Hyland	Thurston
Long	T. Williams

Defense
B. Brown	Hart
Crutcher	Rowser
Flanigan	Weatherwax

Kicker
Chandler

OAKLAND
Offense
Archer	Kocourek
Hagberg	Kruse
Harvey	Todd
Herock	Wells

Defense
Bird	Oates
Benson	Sligh
Budness	Williamson
Grayson	

Kickers
Blanda	Eischeid

SCORING

GREEN BAY	3	13	10	7	33
OAKLAND	0	7	0	7	14

First Quarter
G.B. Chandler, 39 yard field goal

Second Quarter
G.B. Chandler, 20 yard field goal
G.B. Dowler, 62 yard pass from Starr PAT — Chandler (kick)
Oak. Miller, 23 yard pass from Lamonica PAT — Blanda (kick)
G.B. Chandler, 43 yard field goal

Third Quarter
G.B. Anderson, 2 yard rush PAT — Chandler (kick)
G.B. Chandler, 31 yard field goal

Fourth Quarter
G.B. Adderley, 60 yard interception return PAT — Chandler (kick)
Oak. Miller, 23 yard pass from Lamonica PAT — Blanda (kick)

TEAM STATISTICS

G.B.		OAK.
19	First Downs — Total	16
11	First Downs — Rushing	5
7	First Downs — Passing	10
1	First Downs — Penalties	1
0	Fumbles — Number	3
0	Fumbles — Lost Ball	2
1	Penalties — Number	4
12	Yards Penalized	31
69	Total Offensive Plays	57
322	Total Net Yards	293
4.7	Average Gain	5.1
0	Missed Field Goals	1
0	Giveaways	3
3	Takeaways	0
+3	Difference	−3

INDIVIDUAL STATISTICS

RUSHING

GREEN BAY	No	Yds	Avg.	OAKLAND	No	Yds	Avg.
Wilson	17	62	3.6	Dixon	12	54	4.5
Anderson	14	48	3.4	Todd	2	37	18.5
Williams	8	36	4.5	Banaszak	6	16	2.7
Starr	1	14	14.0		20	107	5.4
Mercein	1	0	0.0				
	41	160	3.9				

RECEIVING

GREEN BAY	No	Yds	Avg.	OAKLAND	No	Yds	Avg.
Dale	4	43	10.8	Miller	5	84	16.8
Fleming	4	35	8.8	Banaszak	4	69	17.3
Dowler	2	71	35.5	Cannon	2	25	12.5
Anderson	2	18	9.0	Biletnikoff	2	10	5.0
McGee	1	35	35.0	Wells	1	17	17.0
	13	202	15.5	Dixon	1	3	3.0
					15	208	13.9

PUNTING

GREEN BAY	No	Yds	Avg.	OAKLAND	No	Yds	Avg.
Anderson	6		39.0	Eischeid	6		44.0

PUNT RETURNS

GREEN BAY	No	Yds	Avg.	OAKLAND	No	Yds	Avg.
Wood	5	35	7.0	Bird	2	12	6.0

KICKOFF RETURNS

GREEN BAY	No	Yds	Avg.	OAKLAND	No	Yds	Avg.
Adderley	1	24	14.0	Todd	3	63	21.0
Williams	1	18	18.0	Grayson	2	61	30.5
Crutcher	1	7	7.0	Hawkins	1	3	3.0
	3	49	16.3	Kocourek	1	0	0.0
					7	127	18.1

INTERCEPTION RETURNS

GREEN BAY	No	Yds	Avg.	OAKLAND	
Adderley	1	60	60.0	None	

PASSING

GREEN BAY	Att	Comp	Comp Pct.	Yds	Int	Yds/ Att.	Yds/ Comp	Yards Lost Tackled
Starr	24	13	54.2	202	0	8.4	15.5	4—30
OAKLAND								
Lamonica	34	15	44.1	208	1	6.1	13.9	3—22

1968 N.F.L. Eleven Missing Monuments

A lot of familiar faces were missing from NFL playing fields this season. Retired from active duty were Ray Berry, Jim Parker, Lenny Moore, Lou Groza, Sam Huff, Del Shofner, Jim Ringo, Jim Taylor, and Don Chandler, all of them top-notch performers in the league since the 1950s. Berry left with a record 631 lifetime receptions, Groza with records of twenty-one active professional seasons and 1,608 points scored, and Ringo left with an appearance record streak of 182 consecutive games, a streak still running at his retirement. Also tucked away in front-office positions out of the public's eye were George Halas and Vince Lombardi, two of the most famous coaches in pro-football history. Age prompted Halas to leave the sidelines, while Lombardi quit because he had accomplished everything in his nine years as Packer head coach.

EASTERN CONFERENCE — CAPITOL DIVISION

Dallas Cowboys—Depth was the key to the Cowboys' continued stay atop the Capitol Division. When quarterback Don Meredith needed a rest, young Craig Morton filled in and kept the offense rolling smoothly. When halfback Dan Reeves hurt his knee in the season's fourth game, substitute runners Craig Baynham and Walt Garrison filled the breach. Other top reserves on this team were Malcolm Walker, Rayfield Wright, Larry Cole, and Blaine Nye, each of whom could have started on most NFL teams.

New York Giants—The aerial circus of Fran Tarkenton to Homer Jones kept the attack alive, but the rest of the team needed shoring up. The running backs were slow, the defensive line couldn't mount an effective pass rush, and the linebacking was inexperienced and easily fooled. They did beat Dallas, but that was more a fluke than a true reading of the team.

Washington Redskins—Combined with the retirement of Sam Huff, a pair of decisions that backfired helped bring Otto Graham's pro coaching career to an end. Graham sent a first-draft pick to Los Angeles for rookie quarterback Gary Beban, last year's Heisman Trophy winner at UCLA. After signing with the Redskins for a lucrative salary, Beban flopped in training camp as a quarterback, spent most of the year on the taxi squad, and flopped late in the season as a running back. Another Graham move that didn't work out was the trading of safety Paul Krause to Minnesota.

Philadelphia Eagles—Norm Snead broke his leg in the first pre-season game, the Eagles lost their first eleven regular season games, owner Jerry Wolman went bankrupt, and coach Joe Kuharich heard hometown crowds screaming for his head. The Eagles ended their losing streak by beating Detroit 12-0 on four Sam Baker field goals, and a second win one week later gave the club some dignity but removed all chances of landing O. J. Simpson next year. At the end of the year, Leonard Tose bought the team from Wolman and canned Kuharich, fifteen-year contract and all.

CENTURY DIVISION

Cleveland Browns—When the Browns dropped two of their first three games with a meager offensive output, coach Blanton Collier benched quarterback Frank Ryan in favor of ex-Steeler Bill Nelsen. Playing behind the solid Cleveland line, Nelsen stayed healthy all season and put some life in the Browns' attack. With Nelsen, Leroy Kelly, and Paul Warfield leading the way, the Browns began an eight-game winning streak on October 20 by beating the undefeated Colts. The streak came to an end only on the final Sunday of the season, when a meaningless loss to St. Louis tightened the final standings.

St. Louis Cardinals—The Cards beat the Browns twice, but Cleveland finished ahead by half a game. With a strong, balanced squad, the Cards had severe problems with Western opponents, losing to the Rams, Colts, and 49ers and just barely beating the Falcons 17-12. Despite the near miss at the title, several developments pleased coach Charley Winner. Quarterback Jim Hart improved considerably in his second year at the helm, cutting his interceptions from 30 down to 18. The defense replaced retired linebackers Dale Meinert and Bill Koman without a hitch, and rookie Chuck Latourette put on a good show as a kick returner, punter and sometimes defensive back.

New Orleans Saints—Although the Saints won four games, their move up to third place was due more to the Steelers' deterioration than to their own improvement. Coach Tom Fears improved his offense by signing end Dave Parks after he played out his option at San Francisco. He had to pay a steep price, however, when Commissioner Pete Rozelle deemed rookie tackle Kevin Hardy and next year's number-one draft pick as San Francisco's just renumeration.

Pittsburgh Steelers—The Steelers combined a poor offense with a limp defense in an irresistible combination for defeat, and head coach

Bill Austin found himself discharged after the debacle ended. Dick Hoak and Roy Jefferson turned in good offensive performances, but they were hardly noticeable admidst the mediocrity.

WESTERN CONFERENCE — CENTRAL DIVISION

Minnesota Vikings—The Vikings won the Central Division title with a defense as rugged as the Minnesota weather in December. The front line of Carl Eller, Jim Marshall, Alan Page, and Gary Larsen now ranked with Los Angeles' Fearsome Foursome as the top defensive lines in the league, and the linebacking and secondary were without weakness. The acquisition of safety Paul Krause from the Redskins was the knot that tied the Vikings' pass defense together. Although the offense ranked fourteenth in the league in total yardage and dead last in passing, quarterback Joe Kapp won as many headlines as the defensive people with his intense competitiveness and wobbling passes which often hit their mark in clutch situations.

Chicago Bears—Head coach Jim Dooley lost his first two games and then beat the Vikings at a terrible cost. In that game, Jack Concannon went out with a fractured collarbone and Rudy Bukich with a shoulder separation. After third-stringer Larry Rakestraw failed to move the team, Dooley gave rookie Virgil Carter a shot at quarterback. Carter drove the Bears to four straight wins before more injuries ended the team's title hopes. In the victory over San Francisco, a tackle by Kermit Alexander ripped ligaments and cartilage in Gale Sayers' right knee. One week later, a broken ankle ended Carter's fine rookie season.

Green Bay Packers—Vince Lombardi had quit as head coach, confining himself to the general manager's desk, and the Packers, under Phil Bengston, dropped to a 6-7-1 mark. Age was catching up on the players of the championship teams of the early 1960s, and replacements were not turning up. A bad arm kept quarterback Bart Starr out of action for almost half the season, and Don Chandler retired, leaving the Packers with no reliable place-kicker.

Detroit Lions—Last year's top newcomers had been Mel Farr and Lem Barney; this year's pair were wide receiver Earl McCullough and tight end Charlie Sanders. These two rookies joined with newcomers Bill Munson and Billy Gambrell to make the Detroit passing game a genuine threat to enemy defenses. Injuries plagued the running corps, however, and the reconstructed Lions needed more time together to play as a team.

COASTAL DIVISION

Baltimore Colts—A few weeks before their season's opener, the Colts had a solid team everywhere but at quarterback. Johnny Unitas was bothered by a bad elbow, so coach Don Shula sent a fourth-round draft pick and reserve end Butch Wilson to New York for journeyman quarterback Earl Morrall. Shula expected Morrall to fill in while Unitas recuperated, but while Unitas sat out most of the season, Morrall used his pinpoint passing and poised signal calling to lead the Colts to a 13-1 season. Morrall's job was made easier by the running of Tom Matte, the blocking and receiving of John Mackey, and the line play of Bob Vogel, while the defense made life miserable for heralded enemy quarterbacks.

Los Angeles Rams—Despite a string of injuries, the Rams fought their way to a 10-3-1 record. But after the season ended, owner Dan Reeves fired George Allen. Personality differences and Allen's practice of trading off draft picks for older pros convinced Reeves that he'd be better off with a different coach, but the Ram players immediately raised an outcry in favor of their deposed coach. The protests had some effect, because when Reeves held a press conference to name the new coach, he announced the return of Allen.

San Francisco '49ers—New head coach Dick Nolan took over a talent squad in his first head assignment, but he couldn't get his team past the Colts and Rams in the Coastal Division. With three losses and a tie against these two rivals, the '49ers had the misfortune of playing in pro football's strongest division. The '49ers did well against the rest of the league, with a steady attack their chief weapon. Bolstered by Nolan's confidence in him, quarterback John Brodie took firm charge of the offense, finding ex-Brown Clifton McNeil a most congenial pass receiver.

Atlanta Falcons—When the Falcons lost their first three games of the season, coach Norb Hecker was canned and ex-Viking head man Norm Van Brocklin given the job, and he tore the club apart in search of a winning combination. After a 30-7 loss to Cleveland, he put five starting players on waivers. He gave a starting safetyman's job to Billy Lothridge, a punting specialist with only one kidney. He dropped promising Randy Johnson from the starting lineup and promoted Bob Berry, whom he had coached in Minnesota to starting quarterback.

FINAL TEAM STATISTICS

OFFENSE

	ATL.	BALT.	CHI.	CLEV.	DALL.	DET.	G.B.	L.A.	MINN.	N.O.	N.Y.	PHIL.	PITT.	ST.L.	S.F.	WASH.
FIRST DOWNS:																
Total	174	258	219	248	**297**	221	240	245	223	224	256	197	245	245	260	223
by Rushing	71	110	121	104	**135**	87	96	111	114	80	119	78	91	117	98	67
by Passing	94	131	78	123	**143**	119	130	115	89	122	114	100	137	107	141	132
by Penalty	9	17	20	21	19	15	14	19	20	22	23	19	17	21	21	**24**
RUSHING:																
Number	366	463	500	447	480	433	450	**503**	500	409	474	369	399	463	443	360
Yards	1305	1809	**2377**	2031	2091	1702	1749	1932	1921	1527	1882	1411	1721	1996	1784	1164
Average Yards	3.6	3.9	**4.8**	4.5	4.4	3.9	3.9	3.8	3.8	3.7	4.0	3.8	4.3	4.3	4.0	3.2
Touchdowns	9	16	14	20	**22**	6	12	14	19	7	13	3	7	**22**	11	6
PASSING:																
Attempts	326	359	343	363	399	377	318	384	282	439	366	380	**451**	385	417	408
Completions	158	196	158	184	217	204	188	189	154	210	195	194	211	169	**239**	227
Completion Percentage	48.5	54.6	46.1	50.7	54.4	54.1	**59.1**	49.2	54.6	47.8	53.3	51.1	46.8	43.9	57.3	55.6
Passing Yards	2386	3094	1868	3039	**3295**	2649	2651	2413	1995	2549	2715	2357	2764	2389	3107	2824
Average Yards per Attempt	7.3	**8.6**	5.4	8.4	8.3	7.0	8.3	6.3	7.1	5.8	7.4	6.2	6.1	6.2	7.5	6.9
Average Yards per Completion	15.1	15.8	11.8	**16.5**	15.2	13.0	14.1	12.8	13.0	12.1	13.9	12.1	13.1	14.1	13.0	12.4
Times Tackled Attempting to Pass	70	29	24	**21**	34	45	41	28	35	33	30	26	41	23	27	37
Yards Lost Tackled Attempting to Pass	527	222	187	**181**	269	329	376	241	310	213	273	207	285	202	182	340
Net Yards	1859	2872	1681	2858	**3026**	2320	2275	2172	1685	2336	2442	2150	2479	2187	2925	2484
Touchdowns	9	**28**	10	27	25	17	21	20	11	17	21	16	22	16	24	23
Interceptions	24	22	21	16	18	**15**	**15**	17	17	29	17	29	26	20	23	18
Percent Intercepted	7.4	6.1	6.1	4.4	4.5	**4.0**	4.7	4.4	6.0	6.6	4.6	7.6	5.8	5.2	5.5	4.4
PUNTS:																
Number	75	49	66	63	59	71	59	**81**	61	75	57	60	68	65	68	76
Average Distance	**44.3**	39.5	38.0	37.3	40.9	40.4	40.0	39.6	39.3	37.6	36.0	41.3	40.4	41.6	39.0	43.3
PUNT RETURNS:																
Number	16	42	19	24	30	19	43	**44**	30	34	20	24	38	31	36	29
Yards	66	350	81	96	**405**	89	238	307	250	153	101	264	308	356	120	194
Average Yards	4.1	8.3	4.3	4.0	**13.5**	4.7	5.5	7.0	8.3	4.5	5.1	11.0	8.1	11.5	3.3	6.7
Touchdowns	0	0	0	0	**2**	0	1	0	1	1	0	1	1	1	0	0
KICKOFF RETURNS:																
Number	68	38	58	54	39	54	48	45	52	53	62	61	**70**	56	60	64
Yards	1273	1003	1370	974	841	1247	1007	1024	1049	1149	1110	1379	**1502**	1404	1064	1410
Average Yards	18.7	**26.4**	23.6	18.0	21.6	23.1	21.0	22.8	20.2	21.7	17.9	22.6	21.5	25.1	17.7	22.0
Touchdowns	0	**2**	0	0	0	1	0	1	0	0	0	1	0	0	0	0
INTERCEPTION RETURNS:																
Number	14	29	18	**32**	26	24	17	25	16	16	26	13	17	13	20	21
Yards	330	**483**	226	386	275	242	244	220	267	268	388	51	151	65	367	225
Average Yards	**23.6**	16.7	12.6	12.1	10.6	10.1	14.4	8.8	16.7	16.8	14.9	3.9	8.9	5.0	18.4	10.7
Touchdowns	2	**4**	1	2	3	1	0	2	1	1	2	0	1	0	3	1
PENALTIES:																
Number	63	75	**113**	74	77	70	64	74	65	82	67	63	46	66	90	65
Yards	659	655	**1194**	841	751	810	653	760	692	843	608	666	479	708	794	643
FUMBLES:																
Number	26	23	28	23	21	26	31	21	22	19	**17**	19	26	24	26	29
Number Lost	15	12	16	14	15	17	18	12	14	**11**	13	13	14	**11**	14	19
POINTS:																
Total	170	402	250	394	**431**	207	281	312	282	246	294	202	244	325	303	249
PAT Attempts	20	50	25	49	**54**	26	35	37	32	27	36	21	32	40	39	32
PAT Made	17	48	25	46	**54**	24	32	37	31	27	36	17	28	40	36	30
FG Attempts	21	28	36	24	29	29	29	31	29	**37**	24	30	21	24	24	19
FG Made	11	18	**25**	18	17	9	13	17	19	19	14	19	8	15	11	9
Percent FG Made	52.4	64.3	69.4	**75.0**	58.6	31.0	44.8	54.8	65.5	51.4	58.3	63.3	38.1	62.5	45.8	47.4
Safeties	0	0	0	0	**1**	0	0	**1**	**1**	0	0	**1**	0	0	0	0

DEFENSE

	ATL.	BALT.	CHI.	CLEV.	DALL.	DET.	G.B.	L.A.	MINN.	N.O.	N.Y.	PHIL.	PITT.	ST.L.	S.F.	WASH.
FIRST DOWNS:																
Total	302	207	240	259	202	214	213	**190**	210	228	263	256	244	238	250	259
by Rushing	129	71	102	110	**61**	92	105	66	98	97	125	128	92	90	111	122
by Passing	157	119	102	130	123	105	**92**	104	98	109	121	111	131	131	124	118
by Penalty	16	17	36	19	18	17	16	20	**14**	22	17	17	21	17	15	19
RUSHING:																
Number	518	375	427	423	**369**	457	476	397	432	439	425	515	441	423	445	497
Yards	3235	1339	1704	1842	**1195**	1680	1800	1305	1903	2105	2001	2141	1624	1558	1776	2194
Average Yards	4.3	3.6	4.0	4.4	**3.2**	3.7	3.8	3.3	4.4	4.8	4.7	4.2	3.7	3.7	4.0	4.4
Touchdowns	17	6	17	11	**2**	13	11	9	8	13	22	18	14	10	12	18
PASSING:																
Attempts	389	432	333	439	428	337	327	353	**315**	366	364	327	413	399	416	359
Completions	248	224	172	213	220	157	157	158	185	**153**	191	182	220	210	201	202
Completion Percentage	63.8	51.9	51.7	48.5	51.4	46.6	48.0	44.8	58.7	**41.8**	52.5	55.7	53.3	52.6	48.3	56.3
Passing Yards	3306	2405	2893	2447	2838	2448	**2031**	2196	2162	2483	2498	2557	3360	3261	2548	2662
Average Yards per Attempt	8.5	**5.6**	8.7	5.6	6.6	7.3	6.2	6.2	6.9	6.8	6.9	7.8	8.1	8.2	6.1	7.4
Average Yards per Completion	13.3	**10.7**	16.8	11.5	12.9	15.6	12.9	13.9	11.7	16.2	13.1	14.0	15.3	15.5	12.7	13.2
Times Tackled Attempting to Pass	29	45	30	26	**51**	36	28	**51**	44	34	21	21	28	44	35	21
Yards Lost Tackled Attempting to Pass	221	367	226	199	**400**	291	235	383	307	297	158	184	199	**400**	304	173
Net Yards	3085	2038	2667	2248	2438	2157	**1796**	1813	1855	2186	2340	2373	3161	2861	2244	2489
Touchdowns	30	**9**	25	19	20	12	14	12	16	25	18	20	29	23	19	16
Interceptions	14	29	18	**32**	26	24	17	25	16	16	26	13	17	13	20	21
Percent Intercepted	3.6	6.7	5.4	**7.3**	6.1	7.1	5.2	7.1	5.1	4.4	7.1	4.0	4.1	3.3	4.8	5.8
PUNTS:																
Number	45	78	66	60	77	66	77	**88**	64	69	47	55	66	70	68	57
Average Distance	41.5	40.8	40.1	39.9	40.4	40.7	39.6	40.0	38.4	40.8	40.0	38.9	40.0	**38.1**	40.9	39.6
PUNT RETURNS:																
Number	46	**19**	28	21	25	32	**19**	30	29	30	23	33	32	36	31	45
Yards	286	**62**	120	120	125	139	66	206	204	320	174	270	297	266	238	485
Average Yards	6.2	**3.3**	4.3	5.7	5.0	4.3	3.5	6.9	7.1	10.7	7.6	8.2	9.3	7.4	7.7	10.8
Touchdowns	**0**	**0**	**0**	**0**	**0**	**0**	**0**	1	**0**	1	1	**0**	2	1	**0**	2
KICKOFF RETURNS:																
Number	**42**	71	54	64	68	44	56	62	56	57	51	45	49	56	56	51
Yards	**799**	1391	968	1417	1326	1017	1211	1262	1291	1134	1344	1030	1154	1303	1163	996
Average Yards	19.0	19.6	**17.9**	22.1	19.5	23.1	21.6	20.4	23.1	19.9	26.4	22.9	23.6	23.3	20.8	19.5
Touchdowns	**0**	**0**	**0**	**0**	**0**	1	**0**	1	**0**	**0**	1	**0**	**0**	1	1	**0**
INTERCEPTION RETURNS:																
Number	24	22	21	16	18	**15**	**15**	17	17	29	17	29	26	20	23	18
Yards	326	192	260	152	331	150	150	286	360	294	**120**	408	404	173	390	192
Average Yards	13.6	8.7	12.4	9.5	18.4	10.0	10.0	16.8	21.2	10.1	**7.1**	14.1	15.5	8.7	17.0	10.7
Touchdowns	2	1	1	1	1	1	**0**	2	2	2	**0**	2	5	**0**	1	3
PENALTIES:																
Number	63	72	**91**	61	54	76	60	88	74	74	62	76	79	71	71	82
Yards	628	799	**896**	620	657	658	541	806	875	757	579	843	844	728	646	879
FUMBLES:																
Number	30	29	20	20	21	22	28	31	29	**33**	21	18	16	19	22	22
Number Lost	16	12	12	14	15	12	17	19	22	**26**	14	7	9	8	11	14
POINTS:																
Total	389	**144**	333	273	186	241	227	200	242	327	325	351	397	289	310	358
PAT Attempts	49	**16**	43	33	23	28	25	25	27	42	43	40	50	35	35	41
PAT Made	47	**15**	40	33	21	28	24	23	26	37	37	39	49	34	34	41
FG Attempts	30	19	31	26	22	29	26	**17**	27	27	23	35	26	33	32	32
FG Made	16	11	11	14	**9**	15	17	**9**	18	12	10	24	16	15	22	23
Percent FG Made	53.3	57.9	**35.5**	53.8	40.9	51.7	65.4	52.9	66.7	44.4	43.5	68.6	61.5	45.5	68.8	71.9
Safeties	**0**	**0**	1	**0**	**0**	**0**	1	**0**	**0**	1	**0**	**0**	**0**	**0**	**0**	1

CONFERENCE PLAYOFFS

EASTERN—December 21, at Cleveland (Attendance 81,497)

SCORING

CLEVELAND	3	7	14	7	–31
DALLAS	7	3	3	7	–20

First Quarter
- Cle. Cockroft, 38 yard field goal
- Dal. Howley, 44 yard fumble return
  - PAT – Clark (kick)

Second Quarter
- Dal. Clark, 16 yard field goal
- Cle. Kelly, 46 yard pass from Nelsen
  - PAT – Cockroft (kick)

Third Quarter
- Cle. Lindsey, 27 yd interception return
  - PAT – Cockroft (kick)
- Cle. Kelly, 35 yard run
  - PAT – Cockroft (kick)
- Dal. Clark, 47 yard field goal

Fourth Quarter
- Cle. E.Green, 2 yard rush
  - PAT – Cockroft (kick)
- Dal. Garrison, 2 yard pass from Morton
  - PAT – Clark (kick)

TEAM STATISTICS

CLE.		DAL.
12	First Downs – Total	13
4	First Downs – Rushing	5
8	First Downs – Passing	8
0	First Downs – Penalty	0
1	Times Tackled Passing	2
5	Yards Lost – Tackled	25
1	Fumbles – Number	1
1	Fumbles – Lost Ball	0
6	Penalties – Number	4
40	Yards Penalized	20
7	Punts – Number	5
36.1	Punts – Average Distance	41.0
3	Punt Returns – Number	0
6	Punt Returns – Yards	0
4	Kickoff Returns – Number	5
67	Kickoff Returns – Yards	72
4	Interception Returns – Number	1
52	Interception Returns – Yards	6
0	Missed Field Goals	2
2	Giveaways	4
4	Takeaways	2
+2	Difference	–2

INDIVIDUAL STATISTICS

RUSHING

CLEVELAND	No	Yds	Avg.	DALLAS	No	Yds	Avg.
Kelly	20	87	4.4	Perkins	14	51	3.6
Harraway	5	12	2.4	Morton	2	14	7.0
E.Green	3	5	1.7	Baynham	10	7	0.7
Nelsen	2	–2	–1.0	Garrison	1	6	6.0
				Meredith	1	5	5.0
				Shy	2	3	1.5
	30	102	3.4		30	86	2.9

RECEIVING

CLEVELAND	No	Yds	Avg.	DALLAS	No	Yds	Avg.
Warfield	4	86	21.5	Hayes	5	83	16.6
Morin	4	47	11.8	Rentzel	3	75	25.0
Kelly	2	46	23.0	Garrison	2	8	4.0
Collins	2	26	13.0	Baynham	1	34	34.0
Harraway	1	–2	–2.0	Norman	1	5	5.0
	13	203	15.6		12	205	17.1

PASSING

	Att	Cmp	Pct.	Yds	Int	Yd/A	Yd/C
Nelsen	25	13	52.0	203	1	8.1	15.6
Morton	23	9	39.1	163	1	7.1	18.1
Meredith	9	3	33.3	42	3	4.7	14.0
	32	12	37.5	205	4	6.4	17.1

WESTERN—December 22, at Baltimore (Attendance 60,238)

SCORING

BALTIMORE	0	7	14	3	–24
MINNESOTA	0	0	0	14	–14

Second Quarter
- Bal. Mitchell, 3 yd pass from Morrall
  - PAT – Michaels (kick)

Third Quarter
- Bal. Mackey, 49 yard pass from Morrall
  - PAT – Michaels (kick)
- Bal. Curtis, 60 yard fumble return
  - PAT – Michaels (kick)

Fourth Quarter
- Min. Martin, 1 yard pass from Kapp
  - PAT – Cox (kick)
- Bal. Michaels, 33 yard field goal
- Min. Brown, 7 yard pass from Kapp
  - PAT – Cox (kick)

TEAM STATISTICS

BAL.		MIN.
15	First Downs – Total	22
2	First Downs – Rushing	4
12	First Downs – Passing	17
1	First Downs – Penalty	1
4	Times Tackled Passing	3
35	Yards Lost – Tackled	21
1	Fumbles – Number	2
1	Fumbles – Lost Ball	1
2	Penalties – Number	4
38	Yards Penalized	30
5	Punts – Number	6
40.4	Punts – Average Distance	39.6
2	Punt Returns – Number	3
11	Punt Returns – Yards	7
3	Kickoff Returns – Number	5
54	Kickoff Returns – Yards	113
2	Interception Returns – Number	1
44	Interception Returns – Yards	21
1	Missed Field Goals	0
2	Giveaways	3
3	Takeaways	2
+1	Difference	–1

INDIVIDUAL STATISTICS

RUSHING

BALTIMORE	No	Yds	Avg.	MINNESOTA	No	Yds	Avg.
Matte	14	31	2.2	Kapp	10	52	5.2
J. Hill	8	10	1.3	Brown	10	30	3.0
Mackey	1	9	9.0	Osborn	5	4	0.8
Pearson	4	0	0.0	Jones	2	0	0.0
				Lindsey	1	–1	–1.0
	27	50	1.9		28	85	3.0

RECEIVING

BALTIMORE	No	Yds	Avg.	MINNESOTA	No	Yds	Avg.
Rich'son	6	148	24.7	Brown	8	82	10.3
Mackey	2	92	46.0	Wash'ton	5	95	19.0
Orr	2	36	18.0	Beasley	5	69	13.8
Mitchell	1	3	3.0	Henderson	5	33	6.6
Pearson	1	1	1.0	Lindsey	1	9	9.0
				Martin	1	1	1.0
				Osborn	1	–2	–2.0
	12	180	23.3		26	287	11.0

PASSING

	Att	Cmp	Pct.	Yds	Int	Yd/A	Yd/C
Morrall	22	13	59.1	280	1	12.7	21.5
Kapp	44	26	59.1	287	2	6.5	11.0

Scores of Each Game		Use Name	Pos.	Hgt	Wgt	Age	Int	Pts

CAPITOL DIVISION

DALLAS COWBOYS 12-2-0 Tom Landry

Scores of Each Game			Use Name	Pos.	Hgt	Wgt	Age	Int	Pts
59	DETROIT	13	Tony Liscio	OT	6'5"	255	28		
28	CLEVELAND	7	Ralph Neely	OT	6'5"	265	24		
45	Philadelphia	13	Rayfield Wright	TE-OT	6'7"	243	23		6
27	St. Louis	10	John Niland	OG	6'4"	245	24		
34	PHILADELPHIA	14	Blaine Nye	OG	6'4"	255	22		
20	Minnesota	7	John Wilbur	OG	6'3"	240	25		
17	GREEN BAY	28	Dave Manders	C	6'2"	250	26		
17	New Orleans	3	Malcolm Walker	OT-C	6'4"	250	25		
21	NEW YORK	27	George Andrie	DE	6'7"	250	28		
44	Washington	24	Larry Cole	DE	6'4"	230	21	1	12
34	Chicago	3	Willie Townes	DE	6'5"	260	25		6
29	WASHINGTON	20	Andy Stynchula	DT-DE	6'3"	250	29		
28	PITTSBURGH	7	Ron East	DT	6'4"	242	25		
28	New York	10	Bob Lilly	DT	6'4"	260	29		
			Jethro Pugh	DT	6'6"	260	24		2

Use Name	Pos.	Hgt	Wgt	Age	Int	Pts
Jackie Burkett	LB	6'4"	228	31		
Dave Edwards	LB	6'3"	228	29		
Chuck Howley	LB	6'3"	225	32	6	6
Lee Roy Jordan	LB	6'2"	225	27	3	
D. D. Lewis	LB	6'2"	210	22		
Dave Simmons	LB	6'4"	245	25	1	
Phil Clark	DB	6'2"	210	23		
Dick Daniels	DB	5'9"	180	22	2	
Mike Gaechter	DB	6'	190	28	3	
Cornell Green	DB	6'4"	208	28	4	6
Mike Johnson	DB	5'10"	184	24	3	
Mel Renfro	DB	6'	190	26	3	
Buddy Dial — Injury						
Leon Donohue — Injury						

Use Name	Pos.	Hgt	Wgt	Age	Int	Pts
Don Meredith	QB	6'2"	205	30		6
Craig Morton	QB	6'4"	216	25		12
Craig Baynham	HB	6'1"	206	24		48
Dan Reeves	HB	6'1"	200	24		30
Les Shy	HB	6'1"	200	24		6
Walt Garrison	FB	6'	205	24		30
Don Perkins	FB	5'10"	200	30		36
Bob Hayes	WR	6'	185	25		72
Dennis Homan	WR	6'1"	180	22		6
Dave McDaniels	WR	6'4"	200	23		
Sonny Randle (from SF)	WR	6'2"	190	32		6
Lance Rentzel	WR	6'2"	200	24		36
Pete Gent	TE	6'4"	205	25		
Pettis Norman	TE	6'3"	225	28		6
Mike Clark	K	6'1"	200	27		105
Ron Widby	K	6'4"	210	23		

NEW YORK GIANTS 7-7-0 Allie Sherman

Scores of Each Game			Use Name	Pos.	Hgt	Wgt	Age	Int	Pts
34	Pittsburgh	20	Rich Buzin	OT	6'4"	250	22		
34	Philadelphia	25	Charlie Harper	OT	6'2"	250	26		
48	WASHINGTON	21	Steve Wright	OT	6'6"	250	26		
33	NEW ORLEANS	21	Willie Young	OT	6'	250	25		
21	Atlanta	24	Pete Case	OG	6'3"	245	27		
10	SAN FRANCISCO	26	Darrell Dess	OG	6'	245	32		
13	Washington	10	Andy Gross	OG	6'	230	22		
0	BALTIMORE	26	Doug Van Horn	OG	6'2"	245	24		
27	Dallas	21	Chuck Hinton	C	6'2"	235	25		
7	PHILADELPHIA	6	Greg Larson	C	6'2"	250	29		
21	Los Angeles	24	Bruce Anderson	DE	6'4"	250	24		
10	Cleveland	45	McKinley Boston	DE	6'2"	245	22		
21	ST. LOUIS	28	Jim Katcavage	DE	6'3"	240	33		
10	DALLAS	28	Roger Anderson	DT	6'5"	265	25	1	
			Bob Lurtsema	DT	6'6"	250	26	1	
			Sam Silas	DT	6'4"	250	25		

Use Name	Pos.	Hgt	Wgt	Age	Int	Pts
Ken Avery	LB	6'1"	220	24		
Barry Brown	LB	6'3"	235	25		
Mike Ciccolella	LB	6'1"	235	24	1	
Vince Costello	LB	6'	228	36		
Tommy Crutcher	LB	6'3"	230	26		
Henry Davis	LB	6'3"	235	25		
Scott Eaton	DB	6'3"	195	24	4	
Jim Holifield	DB	6'3"	195	22		
Spider Lockhart	DB	6'2"	175	25	8	12
Bruce Maher	DB	5'11"	190	31	1	
Willie Williams	DB	6'	190	25	10	
Freeman White	TE-DB	6'5"	225	24		
Smith Reed — Military Service						

Use Name	Pos.	Hgt	Wgt	Age	Int	Pts
Gary Lane	QB	6'1"	210	25		
Fran Tarkenton	QB	6'1"	190	28		18
Gary Wood	QB	5'11"	188	25		
Ronnie Blye	HB	5'11"	185	24		6
Bobby Duhon	HB	6'	190	21		24
Randy Minniear	HB	6'	200	24		12
Ernie Koy	FB-HB	6'2"	230	25		24
Tucker Frederickson	FB	6'3"	230	24		18
Homer Jones	WR	6'2"	220	27		42
Joe Koontz	WR	6'1"	192	23		
Joe Morrison	WR	6'1"	212	30		36
Bob Crespino	TE-WR	6'4"	225	30		
Butch Wilson	WR	6'2"	228	26		
Aaron Thomas	WR-TE	6'3"	210	30		24
Pete Gogolak	K	6'2"	185	26		78

WASHINGTON REDSKINS 5-9-0 Otto Graham

Scores of Each Game			Use Name	Pos.	Hgt	Wgt	Age	Int	Pts
38	Chicago	28	Walt Rock	OT	6'5"	255	27		
17	New Orleans	37	Jim Snowden	OT	6'3"	255	26		
21	New York	48	Fred Washington	OT	6'5"	268	23		
17	PHILADELPHIA	14	Ray Schoenke	OG-OT	6'3"	250	26		
16	PITTSBURGH	13	Don Bandy	OG	6'3"	250	23		
14	St. Louis	41	Willie Banks	OG	6'2"	237	22		
10	NEW YORK	13	Vince Promuto	OG	6'1"	245	30		
14	Minnesota	27	John Wooten	OG	6'2"	250	33		
16	Philadelphia	10	Dave Crossan	C	6'3"	245	28		
24	DALLAS	44	Len Hauss	C	6'2"	235	26		
7	GREEN BAY	27	Carl Kammerer	DE	6'3"	243	31		
20	Dallas	29	Spain Musgrove	DT-DE	6'4"	275	23		
21	CLEVELAND	24	Walt Barnes	DT	6'3"	250	24		
14	DETROIT	3	Frank Bosch	DT	6'4"	246	22		
			Dennis Crane	DT	6'6"	260	23		
			Joe Rutgens	DT	6'2"	255	29		

Use Name	Pos.	Hgt	Wgt	Age	Int	Pts
Ed Breding	LB	6'4"	235	23		
Jim Carroll	LB	6'1"	207	32		
Chris Hanburger	LB	6'2"	218	27	2	6
Mike Morgan	LB	6'4"	242	26	2	
Tom Roussel	LB	6'3"	235	23		
Pat Fischer	DB	5'10"	170	28	2	
George Harold	DB	6'3"	194	26		
Rickie Harris	DB	6'	182	25	2	
Aaron Martin	DB	6'	190	27	4	
Brig Owens	DB	5'11"	190	25	8	
Jim Smith	DB	6'3"	195	21		6
Dick Smith	HB-DB	6'	205	24	1	
John Love — Military Service						
Sam Huff — Voluntarily Retired						
Joe Don Looney — Military Service						

Use Name	Pos.	Hgt	Wgt	Age	Int	Pts
Sonny Jurgensen	QB	5'11"	203	34		6
Jim Ninowski	QB	6'1"	207	32		
Harry Theofiledes	QB	5'10"	180	24		
Gary Beban	HB-QB	6'1"	195	22		
Jerry Allen	HB	6'1"	205	27		30
Bob Brunet	HB	6'1"	205	22		6
Pete Larson	FB	6'1"	200	24		12
Ray McDonald	FB	6'4"	248	24		
Steve Thurlow	FB	6'3"	222	25		
A. D. Whitfield	FB	5'10"	200	24		
Charley Taylor	WR	6'3"	210	27		30
Bobby Mitchell	WR	6'	196	33		
Jerry Smith	TE-WR	6'2"	208	25		36
Ken Barefoot	TE	6'5"	228	22		6
Marlin McKeever	TE	6'1"	235	28		
Pat Richter	TE	6'5"	230	27		54
Mike Bragg	K	5'11"	186	21		
Charlie Gogolak	K	5'10"	165	23		57

PHILADELPHIA EAGLES 2-12-0 Joe Kuharich

Scores of Each Game			Use Name	Pos.	Hgt	Wgt	Age	Int	Pts
13	Green Bay	30	Bob Brown	OT	6'4"	295	25		
25	NEW YORK	34	Dave Graham	OT	6'3"	250	29		
13	DALLAS	45	Lane Howell	OT	6'5"	272	27		
14	Washington	17	Mike Dirks	OG	6'2"	250	22		
14	Dallas	34	Dick Hart	OG	6'2"	250	25		
16	CHICAGO	29	Mark Nordquist	OG	6'4"	235	22		
3	Pittsburgh	6	Gene Ceppetelli	C	6'2"	247	26		
17	ST. LOUIS	45	Mike Evans	C	6'5"	250	21		
10	WASHINGTON	16	Dave Recher	C	6'1"	245	26		
6	New York	7	Don Hultz	DE	6'3"	242	27		
13	Cleveland	47	Gary Pettigrew	DE	6'4"	245	23		
12	Detroit	0	Tim Rossovich	DE	6'4"	245	22		
29	NEW ORLEANS	17	Mel Tom	DE	6'4"	248	27		
17	MINNESOTA	24	Frank Molden	DT	6'5"	280	26		
			Floyd Peters	DT	6'4"	255	33	1	
			Dean Wink	DT	6'4"	246	23		
			Randy Beisler	DE-DT	6'4"	245	23	1	

Use Name	Pos.	Hgt	Wgt	Age	Int	Pts
Fred Brown	LB	6'5"	232	25		
Wayne Colman	LB	6'1"	230	22		
Dave Lloyd	LB	6'3"	248	32		
Arunas Vasys	LB	6'2"	235	25		
Harold Wells	LB	6'2"	220	29	2	
Adrian Young	LB	6'1"	225	22		
Alvin Haymond	DB	6'	194	26	1	12
John Mallory	DB	6'	180	22		6
Ron Medved	DB	6'1"	210	24	1	
Al Nelson	DB	5'11"	186	24	3	
Jim Nettles	DB	5'9"	177	26		
Nate Ramsey	DB	6'1"	200	27	2	
Joe Scarpati	HB-DB	5'10"	185	26	2	
Ike Kelley — Knee Injury						
Jim Skaggs — Knee Injury						
Harry Wilson — Injury						

Use Name	Pos.	Hgt	Wgt	Age	Int	Pts
John Huarte	QB	6'	190	24		
Norm Snead	QB	6'4"	215	28		
Izzy Lang	HB	6'1"	232	25		6
Harry Jones	HB	6'2"	205	23		
Cyril Pinder	HB	6'2"	222	21		
Larry Conjar	FB	6'	214	22		2
Tom Woodeshick	FB	6'	220	26		18
Gary Ballman	WR	6'	205	28		24
Ron Goodwin	WR	6'	180	26		
Ben Hawkins	WR	6'	180	24		30
Chuck Hughes	WR	5'11"	170	25		
Mike Ditka	TE	6'3"	235	28		12
Fred Hill	TE	6'2"	215	25		18
Sam Baker	K	6'2"	218	36		74
Rick Duncan	K	6'	208	27		

CAPITOL DIVISION

DALLAS COWBOYS

RUSHING

Last Name	No.	Yds	Avg	TD
Perkins	191	836	4.4	4
Baynham	103	438	4.3	5
Garrison	45	271	6.0	5
Shy	64	179	2.8	1
Reeves	40	178	4.5	4
Meredith	22	123	5.6	1
Norman	4	51	12.8	0
Morton	4	28	7.0	2
Hayes	4	2	0.5	0
Gent	2	−5	−2.5	0
Wright	1	−10	−10.0	0

RECEIVING

Last Name	No.	Yds	Avg	TD
Rentzel	54	1009	19	6
Hayes	53	909	17	10
Baynham	29	380	13	3
Norman	18	204	11	1
Perkins	17	180	11	2
Gent	16	194	12	0
Shy	10	105	11	0
Garrison	7	111	16	0
Reeves	7	84	12	1
Homan	4	92	23	1
Randle	4	56	14	1
Wright	1	15	15	1

PUNT RETURNS

Last Name	No.	Yds	Avg	TD
Hayes	15	312	21	2
Rentzel	14	93	7	0
Homan	1	0	0	0

KICKOFF RETURNS

Last Name	No.	Yds	Avg	TD
Baynham	23	590	26	0
Daniels	9	193	21	0
Homan	2	21	11	0
Hayes	1	20	20	0
Neely	3	17	6	0
Norman	1	0	0	0

PASSING

Last Name	Att	Comp	%	Yds	Yd/Att	TD	Int−	%	RK
Meredith	309	171	55	2500	8.1	21	12−	4	2
Morton	85	44	52	752	8.9	4	6−	7	
Reeves	4	2	50	43	10.8	0	0−	0	
Baynham	1	0	0	0	0.0	0	0−	0	

PUNTING

Last Name	No	Avg
Widby	59	40.9

KICKING

Last Name	XP	Att	%	FG	Att	%
M. Clark	54	54	100	17	29	59

NEW YORK GIANTS

RUSHING

Last Name	No.	Yds	Avg	TD
Frederickson	142	486	3.4	1
Koy	89	394	4.4	3
Duhon	101	362	3.6	3
Tarkenton	57	301	5.3	1
Blye	53	243	4.6	1
Minniear	14	38	2.7	2
Morrison	9	28	3.1	0
Jones	3	18	6.0	0
Thomas	2	14	7.0	0
Wood	2	0	0.0	0
Young	2	−2	−1.0	0

RECEIVING

Last Name	No.	Yds	Avg	TD
Jones	45	1057	23	7
Morrison	37	425	11	6
Duhon	37	373	10	1
Thomas	29	449	15	4
Koy	12	59	5	1
Blye	10	91	9	0
Frederickson	10	64	6	2
Crespino	7	130	19	0
Wilson	4	34	9	0
Minniear	4	32	8	0
Larson	0	1	0	0

PUNT RETURNS

Last Name	No.	Yds	Avg	TD
Lockhart	13	69	5	0
Duhon	7	32	5	0

KICKOFF RETURNS

Last Name	No.	Yds	Avg	TD
Blye	35	734	21	0
Duhon	13	214	16	0
Holifield	7	111	16	0
Frederickson	2	13	7	0
Koontz	1	13	13	0
Hinton	1	12	12	0
Lurtsema	1	11	11	0
Eaton	1	2	2	0
Williams	1	0	0	0

PASSING

Last Name	Att	Comp	%	Yds	Yd/Att	TD	Int−	%	RK
Tarkenton	337	182	54	2555	7.6	21	12−	4	5
Wood	24	9	38	123	5.1	0	5−	21	
Koy	3	2	67	13	4.3	0	0−	0	
Duhon	2	2	100	24	12.0	0	0−	0	

PUNTING

Last Name	No	Avg
Koy	44	37.5
Williams	10	29.1
Lockhart	3	36.7

KICKING

Last Name	XP	Att	%	FG	Att	%
Gogolak	36	36	100	14	24	58

WASHINGTON REDSKINS

RUSHING

Last Name	No.	Yds	Avg	TD
Allen	123	399	3.2	4
Brunet	71	227	3.2	0
Thurlow	51	184	3.6	0
Larson	44	132	3.0	1
Whitfield	37	125	3.4	0
Mitchell	10	46	4.6	0
Jurgensen	8	21	2.6	1
Beban	5	18	3.6	0
Ninowski	2	13	6.5	0
D. Smith	3	5	1.7	0
Theofiledes	3	0	0.0	0
Taylor	2	−3	−1.5	0
Bragg	1	−3	−3.0	0

RECEIVING

Last Name	No.	Yds	Avg	TD
Taylor	48	650	14	5
Jerry Smith	45	626	14	6
Richter	42	533	13	9
Allen	21	294	14	1
Brunet	18	160	9	1
Mitchell	14	130	9	0
Whitfield	13	107	8	0
Thurlow	12	151	13	0
Larson	12	146	12	1
D. Smith	1	15	15	0
Beban	1	12	12	0

PUNT RETURNS

Last Name	No.	Yds	Avg	TD
Harris	19	144	8	0
Jim Smith	6	38	6	0
Martin	2	12	6	0
Mitchell	1	0	0	0
Owens	1	0	0	0

KICKOFF RETURNS

Last Name	No.	Yds	Avg	TD
Harris	23	579	25	0
Mitchell	11	235	21	0
D. Smith	10	228	23	0
Larson	6	151	25	0
Martin	7	146	21	0
Jim Smith	3	61	20	0
Rock	2	10	5	0
Barnes	1	0	0	0
McKeever	1	0	0	0

PASSING

Last Name	Att	Comp	%	Yds	Yd/Att	TD	Int−	%	RK
Jurgensen	292	167	57	1980	6.8	17	11−	4	8
Ninowski	95	49	52	633	6.7	4	6−	6	
Theofiledes	20	11	55	211	10.6	2	1−	5	
Beban	1	0	0	0	0.0	0	0−	0	

PUNTING

Last Name	No	Avg
Bragg	76	43.3

KICKING

Last Name	XP	Att	%	FG	Att	%
Gogolak	30	31	97	9	19	47

PHILADELPHIA EAGLES

RUSHING

Last Name	No.	Yds	Avg	TD
Woodeshick	217	947	4.4	3
Lang	69	235	3.4	0
Pinder	40	117	2.9	0
Ballman	1	30	30.0	0
Snead	9	27	3.0	0
Jones	22	24	1.1	0
Conjar	8	21	2.6	0
Huarte	2	9	4.5	0

RECEIVING

Last Name	No.	Yds	Avg	TD
Hawkins	42	707	17	5
Woodeshick	36	328	9	0
F. Hill	30	370	12	3
Ballman	30	341	11	4
Lang	17	147	9	1
Pinder	16	166	10	0
Ditka	13	111	9	2
Jones	5	87	17	0
Hughes	3	39	13	0
Mallory	1	58	58	1
Baker	1	3	3	0

PUNT RETURNS

Last Name	No.	Yds	Avg	TD
Haymond	15	201	13	1
Mallory	4	46	12	0
Scarpati	5	17	3	0

KICKOFF RETURNS

Last Name	No.	Yds	Avg	TD
Haymond	28	677	24	1
Nelson	11	308	28	0
Hawkins	12	254	21	0
Mallory	6	94	16	0
Rossovich	2	20	10	0
Jones	1	18	18	0
Graham	1	8	8	0

PASSING

Last Name	Att	Comp	%	Yds	Yd/Att	TD	Int−	%	RK
Snead	291	152	52	1655	5.7	11	21−	7	15
Huarte	15	7	47	110	7.3	1	2−	13	
Scarpati	2	1	50	3	1.5	0	0−	0	
Baker	1	1	100	58	58.0	1	0−	0	

PUNTING

Last Name	No	Avg
Baker	55	40.9
Duncan	5	45.6

KICKING

Last Name	XP	Att	%	FG	Att	%
Baker	17	21	81	19	30	63

Scores of Each Game		Use Name	Pos.	Hgt	Wgt	Age	Int	Pts

CENTURY DIVISION

CLEVELAND BROWNS 10-4-0 Blanton Collier

		Use Name	Pos.	Hgt	Wgt	Age	Int	Pts
24	New Orleans	10	Monte Clark	OT	6'6"	255	31		
7	Dallas	28	Dick Schafrath	OT	6'3"	255	32		
6	LOS ANGELES	24	Joe Taffoni	OT	6'3"	250	23		
31	PITTSBURGH	24	Jim Copeland	OG	6'2"	245	23		
21	ST. LOUIS	27	John Demarie	OG	6'3"	255	23		
30	Baltimore	20	Gene Hickerson	OG	6'3"	248	33		
30	ATLANTA	7	Fred Hoaglin	C	6'4"	240	24		
33	San Francisco	21	Bob Whitlow	C	6'1"	236	32		
35	NEW ORLEANS	17	Bill Glass	DE	6'5"	255	32	2	6
45	Pittsburgh	24	Jack Gregory	DE	6'6"	250	23		
47	PHILADELPHIA	13	Ron Snidow	DE	6'4"	250	26		
45	NEW YORK	10	Marv Upshaw	DE	6'3"	245	21		
24	Washington	21	Walter Johnson	DT	6'3"	270	25		
16	St. Louis	27	Jim Kanicki	DT	6'4"	270	26		
			Bill Sabatino	DT	6'3"	245	23		

Use Name	Pos.	Hgt	Wgt	Age	Int	Pts
Billy Andrews	LB	6'	225	23		
John Garlington	LB	6'1"	225	22	1	
Jim Houston	LB	6'2"	245	31	3	
Dale Lindsey	LB	6'3"	225	25	1	
Bob Matheson	LB	6'4"	240	23	2	
Wayne Meylan	LB	6'1"	240	22		
Erich Barnes	DB	6'2"	198	33	3	6
Ben Davis	DB	5'11"	185	22	8	
Mike Howell	DB	6'1"	187	25	6	
Nate James	DB	6'	195	23		
Ernie Kellerman	DB	6'	183	24	6	
Alvin Mitchell	DB	6'3"	195	24		
Carl Ward	DB	5'9"	180	24		

Use Name	Pos.	Hgt	Wgt	Age	Int	Pts
Bill Nelsen	QB	6'	195	27		6
Frank Ryan	QB	6'3"	200	32		
Leroy Kelly	HB	6'	200	26		120
Reece Morrison	HB	6'	205	22		12
Ernie Green	FB	6'2"	205	29		12
Charlie Harraway	FB	6'2"	230	23		6
Charlie Leigh	FB	5'11"	205	22		6
Eppie Barney	WR	6'	204	24		12
Gary Collins	WR	6'4"	215	27		
Ron Green	WR	6'1"	200	24		
Tommy McDonald	WR	5'10"	175	34		6
Paul Warfield	WR	6'	188	25		72
Milt Morin	TE	6'4"	250	26		30
Ralph Smith	TE	6'2"	220	29		
Don Cockroft	K	6'1"	185	23		100

ST. LOUIS CARDINALS 9-4-1 Charlie Winner

		Use Name	Pos.	Hgt	Wgt	Age	Int	Pts
13	LOS ANGELES	24	Bob Duncan	OT	6'3"	250	24		
17	San Francisco	35	Ernie McMillan	OT	6'6"	260	30		
21	New Orleans	20	Bob Reynolds	OT	6'6"	265	27		
10	DALLAS	27	Clyde Williams	OG-OT	6'2"	255	28		
27	Cleveland	21	Ken Gray	OG	6'2"	250	32		
41	WASHINGTON	14	Rick Sortun	OG	6'2"	235	25		
31	NEW ORLEANS	17	Ted Wheeler	OG	6'3"	245	22		
45	Philadelphia	17	Irv Goode	C-OG	6'4"	250	27		
28	PITTSBURGH	28	Bob DeMarco	C	6'3"	240	30		
0	Baltimore	27	Dick Kasperek	C	6'3"	225	24		
17	ATLANTA	12	Don Brumm	DE	6'3"	245	25	6	
20	Pittsburgh	10	Dave Long	DE	6'4"	235	23		
28	New York	21	Chuck Walker	DE	6'2"	245	27		
27	CLEVELAND	16	Fred Heron	DT	6'4"	250	23		
			Bob Rowe	DT	6'4"	260	23		
			Joe Schmiesing	DE-DT	6'4"	243	23		

Use Name	Pos.	Hgt	Wgt	Age	Int	Pts
Ernie Clark	LB	6'1"	230	30	1	
Dave Meggyesy	LB	6'1"	220	26		
Jamie Rivers	LB	6'2"	235	22	2	
Rocky Rosema	LB	6'2"	220	22		
Larry Stallings	LB	6'2"	230	26		
Mike Strofolino	LB	6'2"	230	24		
Bob Atkins	DB	6'3"	212	22	2	
Mike Barnes	DB	6'3"	205	23		
Brady Keys	DB	6'	185	32	1	
Chuck Latourette	DB	6'	190	23		6
Lonnie Sanders	DB	6'3"	207	26	3	
Mac Sauls	DB	6'	185	23		
Jerry Stovall	DB	6'2"	205	26		
Larry Wilson	DB	6'	190	30	4	

Use Name	Pos.	Hgt	Wgt	Age	Int	Pts
Jim Hart	QB	6'2"	195	24		36
Charley Johnson	QB	6'	190	31		
MacArthur Lane	HB	6'	220	26		
Johnny Roland	HB	6'2"	207	25		12
Roy Shivers	HB	6'	200	26		42
Willie Crenshaw	FB	6'2"	230	27		42
Cid Edwards	FB	6'2"	230	24		6
Bobby Joe Conrad	WR	6'	195	33		24
Jerry Daanen	WR	6'	190	23		
Freddie Hyatt	WR	6'3"	212	22		
Bob Lee	WR	6'3"	200	23		
Dave Williams	WR	6'2"	205	23		36
Chuck Logan	TE	6'4"	220	25		
Jackie Smith	TE	6'4"	215	27		30
Jim Bakken	K	6'	200	27		85

NEW ORLEANS SAINTS 4-9-1 Tom Fears

		Use Name	Pos.	Hgt	Wgt	Age	Int	Pts
10	CLEVELAND	24	Jim Boeke	OT	6'5"	260	29		
37	WASHINGTON	17	Jerry Jones	OT	6'3"	265	24		
20	ST. LOUIS	21	Dave McCormick	OT	6'6"	250	25		
21	New York	38	Jerry Sturm	OT	6'3"	260	31		
20	MINNESOTA	17	Jake Kupp	OG	6'3"	233	26		
16	Pittsburgh	12	Ross Gwinn	OG	6'3"	273	24		
17	St. Louis	31	Roy Schmidt	OG	6'3"	250	26		
3	DALLAS	17	Del Williams	OG	6'2"	245	22		
17	Cleveland	35	Joe Wendryhoski	C	6'2"	245	29		
7	Green Bay	29	Doug Atkins	DE	6'8"	270	38		
20	Detroit	20	Brian Schweda	DE	6'3"	240	25		
17	CHICAGO	23	Tom Carr	DT	6'3"	267	26		
17	Philadelphia	29	Lou Cordileone	DT	6'	250	31	1	
24	PITTSBURGH	14	Earl Leggett	DT	6'3"	265	34		
			Dave Rowe	DT	6'6"	265	23		
			Mike Tilleman	DE-DT	6'5"	280	24		

Use Name	Pos.	Hgt	Wgt	Age	Int	Pts
Johnny Brewer	LB	6'4"	235	31		
Bill Cody	LB	6'1"	220	24		
Ted Davis	LB	6'1"	232	26		
Jim Ferguson	LB	6'4"	240	25		
Les Kelley	LB	6'3"	233	23	1	
Steve Stonebreaker	LB	6'3"	225	30		
Fred Whittingham	LB	6'1"	240	29	1	
Bo Burris	DB	6'3"	195	23	3	6
John Douglas	DB	6'1"	195	23		
Ross Fichtner	DB	6'	195	30		
Gene Howard	DB	6'	190	21	3	
Elbert Kimbrough	DB	5'11"	197	29	1	
Elijah Nevett	DB	6'	185	24		
Dave Whitsell	DB	6'	190	32	6	6
George Youngblood	DB	6'3"	205	23		

Use Name	Pos.	Hgt	Wgt	Age	Int	Pts
Billy Kilmer	QB	6'	204	28		12
Ronnie South	QB	6'1"	195	23		
Karl Sweetan	QB	6'1"	200	25		
Charlie Brown	HB	5'10"	187	22		6
Don McCall	HB	5'11"	195	23		36
Tom Barrington	FB-HB	6'1"	213	24		
Tony Baker	FB	5'11"	230	23		
Tony Lorick	FB	6'1"	217	26		18
Ernie Wheelwright	FB	6'3"	236	31		6
Randy Schultz	HB-FB	6'1"	215	25		
Dan Abramowicz	WR	6'1"	195	23		42
John Gilliam	WR	6'1"	190	23		
Dave Parks	WR	6'2"	203	26		
Dave Szymakowski	WR	6'2"	198	22		
Jim Hester	TE	6'4"	225	23		12
Ray Poage	TE	6'4"	205	27		
Monte Stickles	TE	6'4"	235	30		12
Charlie Durkee	K	5'11"	165	24		84
Jim Fraser	K	6'3"	235	32		
Tom McNeill	K	6'1"	195	26		

PITTSBURGH STEELERS 2-11-1 Bill Austin

		Use Name	Pos.	Hgt	Wgt	Age	Int	Pts
20	NEW YORK	34	John Brown	OT	6'2"	248	29		
10	Los Angeles	45	Mike Haggerty	OT	6'4"	230	22		
7	BALTIMORE	41	Fran O'Brien	OT	6'1"	265	32		
24	Cleveland	31	Ernie Ruple	OT	6'4"	256	22		
13	Washington	16	Mike Taylor	OT	6'4"	247	23		
12	NEW ORLEANS	16	Sam Davis	OG	6'1"	245	24		
6	PHILADELPHIA	3	Larry Gagner	OG	6'3"	240	24		
41	Atlanta	21	Bruce Van Dyke	OG	6'2"	235	24		
28	St. Louis	28	Ralph Wenzel	OG	6'3"	240	25		
24	CLEVELAND	45	Mike Connelly	C	6'3"	235	24		
28	SAN FRANCISCO	45	Ray Mansfield	C	6'3"	250	27		
10	ST. LOUIS	20	Ben McGee	DE	6'4"	260	26		
7	Dallas	28	Lloyd Voss	DE	6'4"	260	26		
14	New Orleans	24	Dick Arndt	DT	6'5"	265	24		
			Chuck Hinton	DT	6'5"	260	29		
			Ken Kortas	DT	6'2"	280	26		
			Frank Parker	DT	6'5"	270	28		

Use Name	Pos.	Hgt	Wgt	Age	Int	Pts
John Campbell	LB	6'3"	225	29	1	
Dick Capp	LB	6'3"	235	24		
John Foruria	LB	6'2"	205	23		
Jerry Hillebrand	LB	6'3"	240	28	2	
Ray May	LB	6'1"	230	23	3	6
Andy Russell	LB	6'2"	215	26	2	
Bill Saul	LB	6'4"	225	27		
Lou Harris	DB	6'	180	22		
Bob Hohn	DB	6'	185	27		
Paul Martha	DB	6'	185	25	3	6
Clendon Thomas	DB	6'2"	200	31	3	
Bob Wade	DB	6'2"	200	23		
Marv Woodson	DB	6'	195	25	3	

Use Name	Pos.	Hgt	Wgt	Age	Int	Pts
Kent Nix	QB	6'1"	195	24		
Dick Shiner	QB	6'	197	26		
Rocky Bleier	HB	5'11"	190	22		
Dick Hoak	HB	5'11"	190	29	24	
Don Shy	HB	6'1"	210	22		6
Tom Watkins	HB	6'1"	195	31		
Willie Asbury	FB	6'1"	230	25		
Earl Gros	FB	6'3"	220	27		36
Dick Compton	WR	6'1"	200	28		6
Marshall Cropper	WR	6'3"	210	24		
Ken Hebert	WR	6'	200	23		
Roy Jefferson	WR	6'2"	195	24		72
J. R. Wilburn	WR	6'1"	190	25		18
Jon Henderson	DB-WR	6'	195	23		
John Hilton	TE	6'5"	220	26		6
Tony Jeter	TE	6'3"	223	21		
Dick Kotite	TE	6'3"	235	25		12
Booth Lusteg	K	5'11"	190	27		50
Bill Shockley	K	6'	185	30		2
Bobby Walden	K	6'	190	30		

CENTURY DIVISION

CLEVELAND BROWNS

RUSHING

Last Name	No.	Yds	Avg	TD
Kelly	248	1239	5.0	16
Harraway	91	334	3.7	0
E. Green	41	152	3.7	0
Leigh	23	144	6.3	1
Ryan	11	64	5.8	0
Morrison	18	39	2.2	1
Nelsen	13	30	2.3	1
Smith	1	13	13.0	0
Morin	1	8	8.0	0
Barney	0	8	0.0	1

RECEIVING

Last Name	No.	Yds	Avg	TD
Warfield	50	1067	21	12
Morin	43	792	18	5
Kelly	22	297	14	4
Barney	18	189	11	1
E. Green	16	142	9	2
Harraway	12	162	14	1
Collins	9	230	26	0
McDonald	7	113	16	1
Leigh	3	−4	−1	0
Morrison	2	40	20	1
Smith	2	11	6	0

PUNT RETURNS

Last Name	No.	Yds	Avg	TD
Leigh	14	76	5	0
Davis	9	11	1	0
Kelly	1	9	9	0

KICKOFF RETURNS

Last Name	No.	Yds	Avg	TD
Leigh	14	322	23	0
Ward	13	236	18	0
James	8	166	21	0
Davis	8	152	19	0
Morrison	4	85	21	0
Kelly	1	10	10	0
Smith	1	3	3	0
Andrews	1	0	0	0
Barnes	1	0	0	0
Copeland	1	0	0	0
Houston	1	0	0	0
Howell	1	0	0	0

PASSING – PUNTING – KICKING

PASSING

Last Name	Att	Comp	%	Yds	Yd/Att	TD	Int−%	RK
Nelsen	293	152	52	2366	8.1	19	10− 3	6
Ryan	66	31	47	639	9.7	7	6−	9
Kelly	4	1	25	34	8.5	1	0−	0

PUNTING

Last Name	No	Avg
Cockroft	61	37.7
Collins	2	26.0

KICKING

Last Name	XP	Att	%	FG	Att	%
Cockroft	46	48	96	18	24	75

ST. LOUIS CARDINALS

RUSHING

Last Name	No.	Yds	Avg	TD
Crenshaw	203	813	4.0	6
Roland	121	455	3.8	2
Edwards	31	214	6.9	1
Shivers	44	184	4.2	4
Smith	12	163	13.6	3
Lane	23	74	3.2	0
D. Williams	3	47	15.7	0
Hart	19	20	1.1	6
Latourette	1	15	15.0	0
Wilson	1	12	12.0	0
Johnson	5	−1	−0.2	0

RECEIVING

Last Name	No.	Yds	Avg	TD
Smith	49	789	16	2
D. Williams	43	682	16	6
Conrad	32	449	14	4
Crenshaw	23	232	10	1
Shivers	9	103	11	3
Roland	8	97	12	0
Daanen	4	35	9	0
Edwards	1	2	2	0

PUNT RETURNS

Last Name	No.	Yds	Avg	TD
Latourette	28	345	12	1
Roland	3	11	4	0

KICKOFF RETURNS

Last Name	No.	Yds	Avg	TD
Latourette	46	1237	27	0
Crenshaw	6	104	17	0
Roland	3	63	21	0
Long	1	0	0	0

PASSING – PUNTING – KICKING

PASSING

Last Name	Att	Comp	%	Yds	Yd/Att	TD	Int−%	RK
Hart	316	140	44	2059	6.5	15	18− 6	14
Johnson	67	29	43	330	4.9	1	1−	1
Latourette	1	0	0	0	0.0	0	0−	0
Roland	1	0	0	0	0.0	0	1−100	

PUNTING

Last Name	No	Avg
Latourette	65	41.6

KICKING

Last Name	XP	Att	%	FG	Att	%
Bakken	40	40	100	15	24	63

NEW ORLEANS SAINTS

RUSHING

Last Name	No.	Yds	Avg	TD
McCall	155	637	4.1	4
Lorick	104	344	3.3	0
Schultz	43	152	3.5	0
Barrington	45	111	2.5	0
Wheelwright	21	99	4.7	1
Kilmer	21	97	4.6	2
Gilliam	2	36	18.0	0
Abramowicz	2	27	13.5	0
Poage	1	22	22.0	0
South	4	5	1.3	0
Baker	4	2	0.5	0
McNeill	2	1	0.5	0
Whitsell	1	−1	−1.0	0
Sweetan	4	−5	−1.3	0

RECEIVING

Last Name	No.	Yds	Avg	TD
Abramowicz	54	890	16	7
Lorick	26	272	10	3
McCall	26	270	10	2
Parks	25	258	10	0
Gilliam	24	284	11	0
Hester	17	300	18	2
Stickles	15	206	14	2
Schultz	12	34	3	0
Barrington	9	33	4	1
Poage	1	11	11	0
Wheelwright	1	−9	−9	0

PUNT RETURNS

Last Name	No.	Yds	Avg	TD
Gilliam	15	60	4	0
Brown	8	60	8	1
Howard	8	42	5	0
Nevett	3	−9	−3	0

KICKOFF RETURNS

Last Name	No.	Yds	Avg	TD
Howard	23	533	23	0
Gilliam	15	328	22	0
Brown	8	137	17	0
Nevett	2	94	47	0
Stonebreaker	1	22	22	0
Kelley	1	20	20	0
Douglas	1	10	10	0
Jones	1	5	5	0
Whitsell	1	0	0	0

PASSING – PUNTING – KICKING

PASSING

Last Name	Att	Comp	%	Yds	Yd/Att	TD	Int−%	RK
Kilmer	315	167	53	2060	6.5	15	17− 5	10
Sweetan	78	27	35	318	4.1	1	9−	12
South	38	14	37	129	3.4	1	3−	8
Barrington	6	2	33	42	7.0	0	0−	0
McCall	1	0	0	0	0.0	0	0−	0
Parks	1	0	0	0	0.0	0	0−	0

PUNTING

Last Name	No	Avg
McNeill	49	41.0
South	14	27.6
Fraser	11	35.5
Lorick	1	36.0

KICKING

Last Name	XP	Att	%	FG	Att	%
Durkee	27	27	100	19	37	51

PITTSBURGH STEELERS

RUSHING

Last Name	No.	Yds	Avg	TD
Hoak	175	858	4.9	3
Gros	151	579	3.8	3
Shy	35	106	3.0	1
Jefferson	6	57	9.5	0
Shiner	14	53	3.8	0
Bleier	6	39	6.5	0
Nix	6	15	2.5	0
Asbury	4	9	2.3	0
Walden	2	5	2.5	0

RECEIVING

Last Name	No.	Yds	Avg	TD
Jefferson	58	1074	19	11
Wilburn	39	514	13	3
Hoak	28	253	9	1
Gros	27	211	8	3
Hilton	20	285	14	1
Shy	13	106	8	0
Kotite	6	65	11	2
Compton	5	45	9	1
Cropper	4	54	14	0
Bleier	3	68	23	0
Asbury	3	27	9	0
Henderson	3	26	9	0
Hillebrand	1	27	27	0
Jeter	1	9	9	0

PUNT RETURNS

Last Name	No.	Yds	Avg	TD
Jefferson	28	274	10	1
Harris	6	21	4	0
Bleier	2	13	7	0
Watkins	2	0	0	0

KICKOFF RETURNS

Last Name	No.	Yds	Avg	TD
Shy	28	682	24	0
Henderson	29	589	20	0
Bleier	6	119	20	0
Cropper	3	53	8	0
Watkins	1	22	22	0
Harris	1	19	19	0
Hilton	1	9	9	0
Taylor	1	9	9	0

PASSING – PUNTING – KICKING

PASSING

Last Name	Att	Comp	%	Yds	Yd/Att	TD	Int−%	RK
Shiner	304	148	49	1856	6.1	18	17− 6	12
Nix	130	56	43	720	5.5	4	8−	6
Hoak	16	7	44	188	11.8	0	1−	6
Walden	1	0	0	0	0.0	0	0−	0

PUNTING

Last Name	No	Avg
Walden	68	40.4

KICKING

Last Name	XP	Att	%	FG	Att	%
Lusteg	26	29	90	8	20	40
Shockley	2	3	67	0	1	0

CENTRAL DIVISION

MINNESOTA VIKINGS 8-6-0 Bud Grant

Scores of Each Game		
47	ATLANTA	7
26	Green Bay	13
17	CHICAGO	27
24	DETROIT	10
17	New Orleans	20
7	DALLAS	20
24	Chicago	26
27	WASHINGTON	14
14	GREEN BAY	10
13	Detroit	6
9	Baltimore	21
3	LOS ANGELES	31
30	San Francisco	20
24	Philadelphia	17

Use Name	Pos.	Hgt	Wgt	Age	Int	Pts
Grady Alderman	OT	6'2"	240	29		
Doug Davis	OT	6'4"	250	24		
Ron Yary	OT	6'6"	265	22		
Bookie Bolin	OG	6'2"	240	28		
Larry Bowie	OG	6'2"	255	28		
Milt Sunde	OG	6'2"	250	25		
Jim Vellone	OG	6'2"	255	24		
Mick Tingelhoff	C	6'1"	237	28		
Carl Eller	DE	6'6"	265	26		
Jim Marshall	DE	6'3"	235	30		2
Steve Smith	DE	6'5"	240	24		
Paul Dickson	DT	6'5"	255	31		
Gary Larsen	DT	6'5"	255	28		
Alan Page	DT	6'5"	265	23		

Use Name	Pos.	Hgt	Wgt	Age	Int	Pts
Jim Hargrove	LB	6'3"	230	22		
Wally Hilgenberg	LB	6'3"	225	25		
John Kirby	LB	6'3"	235	26		
Mike McGill	LB	6'2"	237	21		
Lonnie Warwick	LB	6'3"	235	26		
Roy Winston	LB	6'1"	230	28		
Bobby Bryant	DB	6'	175	24	2	6
Dale Hackbart	DB	6'3"	210	32		
Karl Kassulke	DB	6'	195	26	1	
Paul Krause	DB	6'3"	195	26	7	
Earsell Mackbee	DB	6'1"	195	27	2	
Ed Sharockman	DB	6'	200	28	4	
Charlie West	DB	6'1"	190	22		6

Don Hansen — Knee Injury

Use Name	Pos.	Hgt	Wgt	Age	Int	Pts
Gary Cuozzo	QB	6'1"	198	27		
King Hill (from PHI)	QB	6'3"	216	32		
Joe Kapp	QB	6'2"	212	30		18
Earl Denny	HB	6'1"	200	23		
Clint Jones	HB	6'	206	23		6
Dave Osborn	HB	6'	205	25		
Jim Lindsey	FB-HB	6'2"	200	23		24
Bill Brown	FB	5'11"	230	30		84
Oscar Reed	HB-FB	5'11"	220	24		
Bob Goodridge	WR	6'2"	202	22		
Bob Grim	WR	6'	197	23		
Tom Hall	WR	6'1"	195	27		6
John Henderson	WR	6'3"	190	25		
Art Powell	WR	6'3"	214	31		
Gene Washington	WR	6'3"	218	24		36
John Beasley	TE	6'3"	228	23		
Billy Martin	TE	6'4"	235	25		6
Fred Cox	K	5'10"	200	29		88

CHICAGO BEARS 7-7-0 Jim Dooley

Scores of Each Game		
28	WASHINGTON	38
0	Detroit	42
27	Minnesota	17
7	Baltimore	28
10	DETROIT	28
29	Philadelphia	16
26	MINNESOTA	24
13	Green Bay	10
27	SAN FRANCISCO	19
13	ATLANTA	16
3	DALLAS	34
23	New Orleans	17
17	Los Angeles	16
27	GREEN BAY	28

Use Name	Pos.	Hgt	Wgt	Age	Int	Pts
Randy Jackson	OT	6'5"	245	24		
Wayne Mass	OT	6'4"	245	22		
Bob Pickens	OT	6'4"	258	23		
Bob Wetoska	C-OT	6'3"	240	30		
Jim Cadile	OG	6'3"	240	27		
Doug Kriewald	OG	6'4"	245	23		
George Seals	OG	6'2"	260	25		
Mike Pyle	C	6'3"	250	29		
Ed O'Bradovich	DE	6'3"	255	28		
Loyd Phillips	DE	6'3"	240	23		2
Willie Holman	DT-DE	6'4"	250	23		
Frank Cornish	DT	6'6"	285	24		
Dick Evey	DT	6'2"	245	27	1	
John Johnson	DT	6'5"	260	27		

Use Name	Pos.	Hgt	Wgt	Age	Int	Pts
Doug Buffone	LB	6'1"	230	24	1	
Dick Butkus	LB	6'3"	245	24	3	
Rudy Kuechenberg	LB	6'2"	215	25		
Dan Pride	LB	6'3"	225	26		
Jim Purnell	LB	6'2"	238	26		
Mike Reilly	LB	6'2"	230	25		
Clarence Childs	DB	6'	180	29		
Curtis Gentry	DB	6'1"	185	27	1	
Major Hazelton	DB	6'1"	185	23		
Bennie McRae	DB	6'1"	180	27	4	
Richie Petitbon	DB	6'3"	205	30	2	
Joe Taylor	DB	6'2"	200	27	1	
Rosey Taylor	DB	5'11"	186	29	3	6

Marty Amsler — Injury
Terry Stoepel — Military Service

Use Name	Pos.	Hgt	Wgt	Age	Int	Pts
Rudy Bukich	QB	6'1"	205	37		
Virgil Carter	QB	6'1"	185	22		24
Jack Concannon	QB	6'3"	205	25		12
Larry Rakestraw	QB	6'2"	195	26		
Garry Lyle	HB	6'2"	198	22		
Gale Sayers	HB	6'1"	200	25		12
Brian Piccolo	HB	6'	205	24		12
Ralph Kurek	FB	6'2"	210	25		6
Andy Livingston	FB	6'	234	23		
Ronnie Bull	HB-FB	6'	200	28		18
Mike Hull	TE-FB	6'3"	220	23		
Dick Gordon	WR	5'11"	190	23		24
Bob Jones	WR	6'4"	196	23		
Cecil Turner	WR	5'10"	170	24		12
Bob Wallace	WR	6'3"	211	22		12
Austin Denney	TE	6'2"	230	24		12
Emilio Vallez	TE	6'2"	210	22		
Bobby Joe Green	K	5'11"	175	30		
Jon Kilgore	K	6'1"	205	24		
Mac Percival	K	6'4"	217	28		100

GREEN BAY PACKERS 6-7-1 Phil Bengtson

Scores of Each Game		
30	PHILADELPHIA	13
13	MINNESOTA	26
17	DETROIT	23
38	Atlanta	7
14	LOS ANGELES	16
14	Detroit	14
28	Dallas	17
10	CHICAGO	13
10	Minnesota	14
29	NEW ORLEANS	7
20	Washington	7
27	San Francisco	27
3	BALTIMORE	16
28	Chicago	27

Use Name	Pos.	Hgt	Wgt	Age	Int	Pts
Forrest Gregg	OT	6'4"	250	35		
Dick Himes	OT	6'4"	244	22		
Francis Peay	OT	6'5"	250	24		
Bob Skoronski	OT	6'3"	245	35		
Gale Gillingham	OG	6'3"	255	24		
Jerry Kramer	OG	6'3"	245	33		21
Bill Lueck	OG	6'3"	235	22		
Ken Bowman	C	6'3"	230	25		
Bob Hyland	OG-C	6'5"	250	23		
Lionel Aldridge	DE	6'4"	245	26		
Leo Carroll	DE	6'7"	250	24		
Willie Davis	DE	6'3"	245	35		
Francis Winkler	DE	6'3"	230	21		
Leon Crenshaw	DT	6'6"	280	25		
Henry Jordan	DT	6'3"	250	33		
Ron Kostelnik	DT	6'4"	260	28		
Bob Brown	DE-DT	6'5"	260	28		

Use Name	Pos.	Hgt	Wgt	Age	Int	Pts
Lee Roy Caffey	LB	6'3"	250	28		
Fred Carr	LB	6'5"	238	22		
Jim Flanigan	LB	6'3"	240	23		
Ray Nitschke	LB	6'3"	240	32	2	
Dave Robinson	LB	6'3"	240	27	2	
Phil Vandersea	TE-LB	6'3"	225	25		
Herb Adderley	DB	6'1"	200	29	3	
Tom Brown	DB	6'1"	190	27	4	12
Doug Hart	DB	6'1"	190	29	1	
Bob Jeter	DB	6'1"	205	30	3	
John Rowser	DB	6'1"	180	24		
Gordon Rule	DB	6'2"	180	22		
Willie Wood	DB	5'10"	190	32	2	

Jim Weatherwax — Knee Injury
Ben Wilson — Knee Injury

Use Name	Pos.	Hgt	Wgt	Age	Int	Pts
Zeke Bratkowski	QB	6'2"	210	36		
Don Horn	QB	6'2"	195	23		
Bart Starr	QB	6'1"	190	34		6
Bill Stevens	QB	6'3"	195	23		
Donny Anderson	HB	6'3"	210	25		36
Elijah Pitts	HB	6'1"	205	29		12
Travis Williams	HB	6'1"	210	22		
Jim Grabowski	FB	6'2"	220	24		24
Chuck Mercein	FB	6'3"	230	25		19
Carroll Dale	WR	6'1"	200	30		48
Boyd Dowler	WR	6'5"	225	31		36
Claudis James	WR	6'2"	190	24		12
Bucky Pope	WR	6'5"	200	25		
Marv Fleming	TE	6'4"	235	26		18
Errol Mann	K	6'	203	27		4
Mike Mercer (from BUF-A)	K	6'	217	32		33

DETROIT LIONS 4-8-2 Joe Schmidt

Scores of Each Game		
13	Dallas	59
42	CHICAGO	0
23	Green Bay	17
10	Minnesota	24
28	Chicago	10
14	GREEN BAY	14
7	SAN FRANCISCO	14
7	Los Angeles	10
10	BALTIMORE	27
6	MINNESOTA	13
20	NEW ORLEANS	20
0	PHILADELPHIA	12
24	Atlanta	7
3	Washington	14

Use Name	Pos.	Hgt	Wgt	Age	Int	Pts
Charlie Bradshaw	OT	6'6"	260	32		
Bill Cottrell	OT	6'3"	255	23		
Rocky Freitas	OT	6'3"	258	22		
Greg Kent	OT	6'6"	265	25		
Roger Shoals	OT	6'4"	255	29		
Frank Gallagher	OG	6'2"	240	25		
Bob Kowalkowski	OG	6'3"	245	24		
Chuck Walton	OG	6'3"	250	27		
Ed Flanagan	C	6'3"	250	24		
John Baker	DE	6'6"	270	33		
Larry Hand	DE	6'4"	245	28		
Lew Kamanu	DE	6'4"	245	24		
Joe Robb	DE	6'3"	245	31		
Alex Karras	DT	6'2"	255	32		
Denis Moore	DT	6'5"	255	25		
Jerry Rush	DT	6'4"	260	26		
Chuck Sieminski	DT	6'4"	270	28		

Use Name	Pos.	Hgt	Wgt	Age	Int	Pts
Mike Lucci	LB	6'2"	230	28	1	
Ed Mooney	LB	6'2"	238	23		
Paul Naumoff	LB	6'1"	225	23	1	
Bill Swain	LB	6'2"	230	27	1	6
Wayne Walker	LB	6'2"	225	31	1	24
Lem Barney	DB	6'	185	22	7	12
Dick LeBeau	DB	6'1"	185	31	5	
Wayne Rasmussen	DB	6'2"	175	26		
Bobby Rasmussen	DB	5'10"	185	28		
Tom Vaughn	DB	5'11"	190	25	3	
Mike Weger	DB	6'2"	185	22	5	
Jim Welch	HB-DB	6'	196	30		

Use Name	Pos.	Hgt	Wgt	Age	Int	Pts
Greg Landry	QB	6'4"	205	21		6
Bill Munson	QB	6'2"	200	26		6
Mike Campbell	HB	5'11"	200	23		
Nick Eddy	HB	6'1"	205	24		
Mel Farr	HB	6'2"	205	23		42
Dave Kopay	FB-HB	6'2"	225	26		
Tom Nowatzke	FB	6'3"	230	25		6
Bill Triplett	HB-FB	6'2"	210	29		
Billy Gambrell	WR	5'10"	175	26		42
Bill Malinchak	WR	6'1"	200	24		
Earl McCullouch	WR	5'11"	172	22		30
Phil Odle	WR	5'11"	187	25		
Jim Gibbons	TE	6'2"	230	32		
Charlie Sanders	TE	6'4"	215	22		6
Jerry DePoyster	K	6'1"	200	22		27

CENTRAL DIVISION

MINNESOTA VIKINGS

RUSHING

Last Name	No.	Yds	Avg	TD
Brown	222	805	3.6	11
Jones	128	536	4.2	1
Kapp	50	269	5.4	3
Lindsey	53	152	2.9	4
Osborn	42	140	3.3	0
Denny	2	9	4.5	0
Reed	2	6	3.0	0
Cuozzo	1	4	4.0	0
Hill	1	1	1.0	0

RECEIVING

Last Name	No.	Yds	Avg	TD
Washington	46	756	16	6
Brown	31	329	11	3
Beasley	23	289	13	0
Hall	19	268	14	1
Lindsey	15	148	10	0
Martin	10	101	10	1
Henderson	4	42	11	0
Jones	4	26	7	0
Powell	1	31	31	0
Goodridge	1	5	5	0

PUNT RETURNS

Last Name	No.	Yds	Avg	TD
West	20	201	10	1
Bryant	10	49	5	0

KICKOFF RETURNS

Last Name	No.	Yds	Avg	TD
West	22	576	26	0
Bryant	19	373	20	0
Jones	4	60	15	0
Denny	3	19	6	0
Sharockman	1	14	14	0
Lindsey	1	7	7	0
Alderman	1	0	0	0
Martin	1	0	0	0

PASSING – PUNTING – KICKING — Statistics

PASSING	Att	Comp	%	Yds	Yd/Att	TD	Int–	%	RK
Kapp	248	129	52	1695	6.8	10	17–	7	13
Hill	71	33	47	531	7.5	3	6–	8	
Cuozzo	33	24	73	297	9.0	1	0–	0	
Brown	1	1	100	3	3.0	0	0–	0	

PUNTING	No	Avg
Hill	33	41.0
Martin	28	37.4

KICKING	XP	Att	%	FG	Att	%
Cox	31	32	97	19	29	66

CHICAGO BEARS

RUSHING

Last Name	No.	Yds	Avg	TD
Sayers	138	856	6.2	2
Bull	107	472	4.4	3
Piccolo	123	450	3.7	2
Carter	48	265	5.5	4
Concannon	28	104	3.7	2
Kurek	17	95	5.6	1
Wallace	3	29	9.7	0
Lyle	4	28	7.0	0
Livingston	7	25	3.6	0
Hull	12	22	1.8	0
Turner	2	16	8.0	0
Rakestraw	9	12	1.3	0
Green	1	4	4.0	0
Denney	1	-1	-1.0	0

RECEIVING

Last Name	No.	Yds	Avg	TD
Gordon	29	477	16	4
Piccolo	28	291	10	0
Denney	23	247	11	2
Wallace	19	281	15	2
Bull	17	145	9	0
Sayers	15	117	8	0
Turner	14	208	15	2
Lyle	5	32	6	0
Kurek	4	50	13	0
Hull	4	20	5	0

PUNT RETURNS

Last Name	No.	Yds	Avg	TD
Sayers	2	29	15	0
Wallace	6	27	5	0
Turner	9	19	2	0
Gordon	1	5	5	0
Hazelton	1	1	1	0

KICKOFF RETURNS

Last Name	No.	Yds	Avg	TD
Sayers	17	461	27	0
Turner	20	363	18	0
Childs	8	291	36	0
Gordon	3	97	32	0
Wallace	3	80	27	0
Kurek	4	48	12	0
Butkus	2	30	15	0
Kuechenburg	1	0	0	0

PASSING – PUNTING – KICKING — Statistics

PASSING	Att	Comp	%	Yds	Yd/Att	TD	Int–	%	RK
Concannon	143	71	50	715	5.0	10	17–	6	16
Carter	122	55	45	769	6.3	4	5–	4	
Rakestraw	67	30	45	361	5.4	1	7–	10	
Bukich	7	2	29	23	3.3	0	0–	0	
Sayers	2	0	0	0	0.0	0	0–	0	
Bull	1	0	0	0	0.0	0	0–	0	
Kilgore	1	0	0	0	0.0	0	0–	0	

PUNTING	No	Avg
Kilgore	35	35.2
Green	27	42.3
Lyle	4	33.5

KICKING	XP	Att	%	FG	Att	%
Percival	25	25	100	25	36	69

GREEN BAY PACKERS

RUSHING

Last Name	No.	Yds	Avg	TD
Anderson	170	761	4.5	5
Grabowski	135	518	3.8	3
Pitts	72	264	3.7	2
Williams	33	63	1.9	0
Starr	11	62	5.6	1
Mercein	17	49	2.9	1
Bratkowski	8	24	3.0	0
James	1	15	15.0	0
Horn	3	-7	-2.3	0

RECEIVING

Last Name	No.	Yds	Avg	TD
Dowler	45	668	15	6
Dale	42	818	19	8
Anderson	25	333	13	1
Fleming	25	278	11	3
Grabowski	18	210	12	0
Pitts	17	142	8	0
James	8	148	19	2
Williams	5	48	10	0
Mercein	3	6	2	0

PUNT RETURNS

Last Name	No.	Yds	Avg	TD
Wood	26	126	5	0
T. Brown	16	111	7	1
Pitts	1	1	1	0

KICKOFF RETURNS

Last Name	No.	Yds	Avg	TD
Williams	28	599	21	0
Adderley	14	331	24	0
Pitts	2	40	20	0
Robinson	2	29	15	0
Vandersea	1	8	8	0
Winkler	1	0	0	0

PASSING – PUNTING – KICKING — Statistics

PASSING	Att	Comp	%	Yds	Yd/Att	TD	Int–	%	RK
Starr	171	109	64	1617	9.5	15	8–	5	4
Bratkowski	126	68	54	835	6.6	3	7–	6	
Horn	16	10	63	187	11.7	2	0–	0	
Anderson	3	1	33	12	4.0	1	0–	0	
Stevens	2	0	0	0	0.0	0	0–	0	

PUNTING	No	Avg
Anderson	59	40.0

KICKING	XP	Att	%	FG	Att	%
Mercer	12	14	86	7	12	58
Kramer	9	9	100	4	9	44
Mercein	7	7	100	2	5	40
Mann	4	4	100	0	3	0

DETROIT LIONS

RUSHING

Last Name	No.	Yds	Avg	TD
Farr	128	597	4.7	3
Triplett	120	384	3.2	0
Kopay	53	207	3.9	0
Eddy	48	176	3.7	0
Nowatzke	36	116	3.2	1
Munson	25	109	4.4	1
Landry	7	39	5.6	1
Campbell	7	24	3.4	0
DePoyster	1	20	20.0	0
Welch	3	14	4.7	0
McCullouch	3	13	4.3	0
Sanders	2	3	1.5	0

RECEIVING

Last Name	No.	Yds	Avg	TD
McCullouch	40	680	17	5
Sanders	40	533	13	1
Gambrell	28	492	18	7
Triplett	28	135	5	0
Farr	24	375	16	4
Kopay	18	130	7	0
Eddy	8	91	11	0
Odle	6	71	12	0
Nowatzke	4	6	2	0
Gibbons	2	38	19	0
Campbell	2	15	8	0
Malinchak	1	41	41	0

PUNT RETURNS

Last Name	No.	Yds	Avg	TD
Barney	13	79	6	0
Eddy	4	10	3	0
Vaughn	2	0	0	0

KICKOFF RETURNS

Last Name	No.	Yds	Avg	TD
Barney	25	670	27	1
Thompson	17	363	21	0
Vaughn	5	128	26	0
Nowatzke	3	34	11	0
Kopay	2	29	15	0
Gambrell	1	12	12	0
Mooney	1	11	11	0

PASSING – PUNTING – KICKING — Statistics

PASSING	Att	Comp	%	Yds	Yd/Att	TD	Int–	%	RK
Munson	329	181	55	2311	7.0	15	8–	2	7
Landry	48	23	48	338	7.0	2	7–	15	

PUNTING	No	Avg
DePoyster	71	40.4

KICKING	XP	Att	%	FG	Att	%
DePoyster	18	20	90	3	15	20
Walker	6	6	100	6	14	43

Scores of Each Game

COASTAL DIVISION

BALTIMORE COLTS 13-1-0 Don Shula

	Scores	
27	SAN FRANCISCO	10
28	Atlanta	20
41	Pittsburgh	7
28	CHICAGO	7
42	San Francisco	14
20	CLEVELAND	30
27	LOS ANGELES	10
26	New York	0
27	Detroit	10
27	ST. LOUIS	0
21	MINNESOTA	9
44	ATLANTA	0
16	Green Bay	3
28	Los Angeles	24

Use Name	Pos.	Hgt	Wgt	Age	Int	Pts
Sam Ball	OT	6'4"	240	24		
Bob Vogel	OT	6'5"	250	26		
Cornelius Johnson	OG	6'2"	245	25		
Glen Ressler	OG	6'3"	250	24		
Dan Sullivan	OG	6'3"	250	24		
Bill Curry	C	6'2"	235	25		
Dick Szymanski	C	6'3"	235	36		
Ordell Braase	DE	6'4"	245	36		
Roy Hilton	DE	6'6"	240	23	1	6
Lou Michaels	DE	6'2"	250	32		102
John Williams	DE	6'3"	256	22		
Fred Miller	DT	6'3"	250	27		
Billy Ray Smith	DT	6'4"	250	33		
Bubba Smith	DE-DT	6'7"	295	23		

Use Name	Pos.	Hgt	Wgt	Age	Int	Pts
Mike Curtis	LB	6'2"	232	25	2	6
Dennis Gaubatz	LB	6'2"	232	27	2	
Bob Grant	LB	6'2"	225	21		
Ron Porter	LB	6'3"	232	23		
Don Shinnick	LB	6'	228	33	1	
Sid Williams	LB	6'2"	235	26		
Ocie Austin	DB	6'3"	200	21		
Bobby Boyd	DB	5'10"	192	30	8	6
Jerry Logan	DB	6'1"	190	27	3	
Lenny Lyles	DB	6'2"	204	32	5	
Charlie Stukes	DB	6'3"	212	24	1	6
Rick Volk	DB	6'3"	195	23	6	

Use Name	Pos.	Hgt	Wgt	Age	Int	Pts
Earl Morrall	QB	6'1"	206	34		6
Johnny Unitas	QB	6'1"	196	35		
Jim Ward	QB	6'2"	195	24		
Timmy Brown	HB	5'10"	198	31		12
Tom Matte	HB	6'	214	29		60
Preston Pearson	HB	6'1"	190	23		24
Terry Cole	FB	6'1"	220	23		18
Jerry Hill	FB	5'11"	215	28		12
Gail Cogdill (from DET)	WR	6'1"	195	31		
Alex Hawkins	WR	6'1"	186	31		
Jimmy Orr	WR	5'11"	185	32		36
Ray Perkins	WR	6'	183	26		6
Willie Richardson	WR	6'2"	198	28		48
John Mackey	TE	6'3"	224	26		30
Tom Mitchell	TE	6'2"	215	24		24
David Lee	K	6'4"	215	24		

LOS ANGELES RAMS 10-3-1 George Allen

24	St. Louis	13
45	PITTSBURGH	10
24	Cleveland	6
24	SAN FRANCISCO	10
16	Green Bay	14
27	ATLANTA	14
10	Baltimore	27
10	DETROIT	7
17	Atlanta	10
20	San Francisco	20
31	Minnesota	3
16	CHICAGO	17
24	BALTIMORE	28

Use Name	Pos.	Hgt	Wgt	Age	Int	Pts
Joe Carollo	OT	6'2"	258	28		
Charley Cowan	OT	6'4"	265	30		
Jim Wilson	OT	6'3"	258	27		
Don Chuy	OG	6'1"	255	27		
Tom Mack	OG	6'3"	250	24		
Joe Scibelli	OG	6'1"	255	29		
George Burman	C-OG	6'3"	255	25		
Ken Iman	C	6'1"	240	29		
Frank Marchlewski (from ATL)	C	6'2"	238	24		
Deacon Jones	DE	6'5"	260	29		
Lamar Lundy	DE	6'7"	260	33		
Gregg Schumacher	DE	6'2"	240	26		
Coy Bacon	DT	6'4"	270	26		
Roger Brown	DT	6'5"	300	31		
Merlin Olsen	DT	6'5"	276	27		
Diron Talbert	DT	6'5"	238	24		

Use Name	Pos.	Hgt	Wgt	Age	Int	Pts
Maxie Baughan	LB	6'1"	230	30	4	
Gene Breen	LB	6'2"	230	27		
Tony Guillory	LB	6'4"	236	25		
Dean Halverson	LB	6'2"	220	22		
Jack Pardee	LB	6'2"	230	32	2	12
Myron Pottios	LB	6'2"	235	28		
Doug Woodlief	LB	6'3"	230	24		
Claude Crabb	DB	6'	192	28		
Irv Cross	DB	6'1"	195	29	3	
Willie Daniel	DB	5'11"	190	30		
Ed Meador	DB	5'11"	200	31	6	
Ron Smith	DB	6'1"	192	25	3	6
Clancy Williams	DB	6'2"	203	25	7	
Kelton Winston	DB	6'	195	27		

Dave Cahill — Knee Injury
Chuck Lamson — Injury
Les Josephson — Foot Injury

Use Name	Pos.	Hgt	Wgt	Age	Int	Pts
Roman Gabriel	QB	6'4"	230	28		24
Milt Plum	QB	6'1"	205	34		
Mike Dennis	HB	6'1"	207	24		
Willie Ellison	HB	6'1"	207	23		42
Vilnis Ezerins	FB-HB	6'1"	217	23		
Tommy Mason	FB-HB	6'	200	29		18
Dick Bass	FB	5'10"	195	31		18
Henry Dyer	FB	6'2"	235	23		6
Bernie Casey	WR	6'4"	212	29		30
Harold Jackson	WR	5'10"	175	22		
Jack Snow	WR	6'2"	195	25		18
Pat Studstill	WR	6'1"	175	30		6
Wendell Tucker	WR	5'10"	185	24		24
Dave Pivic	TE	6'2"	240	24		2
Billy Truax	TE	6'5"	235	25		18
Bruce Gossett	K	6'2"	230	25		88

SAN FRANCISCO FORTY NINERS 7-6-1 Dick Nolan

10	Baltimore	27
35	ST. LOUIS	17
28	ATLANTA	13
10	Los Angeles	24
14	BALTIMORE	42
26	New York	10
14	Detroit	7
21	CLEVELAND	33
19	Chicago	27
20	LOS ANGELES	20
45	Pittsburgh	28
27	GREEN BAY	20
20	MINNESOTA	30
14	Atlanta	12

Use Name	Pos.	Hgt	Wgt	Age	Int	Pts
Cas Banaszek	OT	6'3"	235	22		
Forrest Blue	OT	6'5"	248	22		
Lance Olssen	OT	6'5"	257	21		
Len Rohde	OT	6'4"	250	30		
Elmer Collett	OG	6'4"	244	23		
Howard Mudd	OG	6'3"	254	26		
Woody Peoples	OG	6'2"	247	25		
Bruce Bosley	C	6'2"	244	34		
Bill Belk	DE	6'3"	242	22	1	6
Stan Hindman	DE	6'3"	232	24	1	6
Clark Miller	DE	6'5"	247	29		
Charlie Johnson	DT	6'2"	265	24		
Charlie Krueger	DT	6'4"	260	32		
Roland Lakes	DT	6'4"	280	28		
Kevin Hardy	DE-DT	6'5"	287	23		

George Donnelly — Injury

Use Name	Pos.	Hgt	Wgt	Age	Int	Pts
Ed Beard	LB	6'2"	226	28	2	
Tommy Hart	LB	6'3"	212	23		
Harold Hays	LB	6'3"	225	27		
Matt Hazeltine	LB	6'1"	230	35		
Frank Nunley	LB	6'2"	230	22		
Dave Wilcox	LB	6'3"	234	25		
Kermit Alexander	DB	5'11"	180	27	9	6
Johnny Fuller	DB	6'	175	22	2	
Jim Johnson	DB	6'2"	187	30	1	
Mel Phillips	DB	6'	192	26		
Al Randolph	DB	6'2"	192	24	4	
John Woitt	DB	5'11"	174	22		

Tom Holzer — Injury
George Rose — Injury
Don Parker — Knee Injury
John Thomas — Knee Injury
Dave Hettema — Military Service

Use Name	Pos.	Hgt	Wgt	Age	Int	Pts
John Brodie	QB	6'1"	210	33		
George Mira	QB	5'11"	190	26		
Steve Spurrier	QB	6'2"	203	23		
Doug Cunningham	HB	5'11"	193	22		
Clem Daniels	HB	6'1"	218	31		
Gary Lewis	HB	6'3"	230	26		24
Ken Willard	FB	6'2"	230	25		42
Bill Tucker	TE-FB	6'2"	220	24		42
Kay McFarland	WR	6'2"	186	29		6
Clifton McNeil	WR	6'2"	185	28		42
Dick Witcher	WR	6'2"	204	23		12
Dave Olerich	TE	6'1"	220	23		
Bob Windsor	TE	6'4"	224	25		12
John David Crow	HB-TE	6'2"	224	33		30
Tommy Davis	K	6'	220	33		53
Dennis Patera	K	6'	225	22		16

ATLANTA FALCONS 2-12-0 Norb Hecker Norm Van Brocklin

7	Minnesota	47
20	BALTIMORE	28
13	San Francisco	28
7	GREEN BAY	38
24	NEW YORK	21
14	Los Angeles	27
7	Cleveland	30
21	PITTSBURGH	41
10	LOS ANGELES	17
16	Chicago	13
12	St. Louis	17
0	Baltimore	44
7	DETROIT	24
12	SAN FRANCISCO	14

Use Name	Pos.	Hgt	Wgt	Age	Int	Pts
Errol Linden	OT	6'5"	260	31		
Bill Sandeman	OT	6'6"	250	25		
Don Talbert	OT	6'5"	255	28		
Steve Duich	OG	6'3"	248	22		
Dan Grimm	OG	6'3"	245	27		
Jim Simon	OG	6'5"	240	27		
Randy Winkler	OT-OG	6'5"	255	25		
Joe Cerne	C	6'2"	240	25		
Phil Sobocinski	C	6'3"	235	22		
Rick Cash	DE	6'5"	260	23		
Claude Humphrey	DE	6'5"	255	24		
Jim Garcia	DT-DE	6'4"	250	24		
Carlton Dabney	DT	6'5"	250	21	1	
Jim Norton (to PHI)	DT	6'4"	254	25		
Jerry Shay	DT	6'3"	245	24		
Art Strahan	DT	6'5"	266	25		
Joe Szczecko	DT	6'	245	26		

Junior Coffey — Knee Injury

Use Name	Pos.	Hgt	Wgt	Age	Int	Pts
Dick Absher	LB	6'4"	227	24		
Ron Acks	LB	6'2"	225	23		
Grady Allen	LB	6'3"	215	22		
Greg Brezina	LB	6'2"	220	22		
Ralph Heck	LB	6'2"	230	27	1	
Tommy Nobis	LB	6'2"	235	24	1	
Marion Rushing (to HOU-A)	LB	6'3"	230	31		
Jimmy Burson	DB	6'	185	26	4	6
Lee Calland	DB	6'	190	27	2	
Ollie Cordill	DB	6'2"	180	25		
Mike Freeman	DB	5'11"	190	24		
Floyd Hudlow	DB	5'11"	195	24		
Billy Lothridge	DB	6'1"	195	24	3	
Nick Rassas	DB	6'	190	24	1	
Ken Reaves	DB	6'3"	205	23	1	6
Phil Spiller (to CIN-A)	DB	6'	195	23		
Larry Suchy	DB	5'11"	180	22		

Bob Sanders — Injury

Use Name	Pos.	Hgt	Wgt	Age	Int	Pts
Bob Berry	QB	5'11"	190	26		12
Randy Johnson	QB	6'3"	196	24		6
Bruce Lemmerman	QB	6'1"	196	22		
Joe Auer	HB	6'1"	205	26		
Charlie Bryant	HB	6'1"	207	27		
Cannonball Butler	HB	5'10"	185	25		12
Perry Lee Dunn	HB	6'2"	215	25		18
Billy Harris	HB	6'	195	22		6
Dwight Lee (from SF)	HB	6'2"	198	22		
Doug Goodwin	FB	6'2"	228	26		
Brendan McCarthy (to DEN-A)	FB	6'3"	220	23		
Harmon Wages	HB-FB	6'1"	210	22		6
Dave Dunaway (from GB)	WR	6'2"	205	23		
Rick Eber	WR	6'	173	23		
Paul Flatley	WR	6'1"	187	27		
Bob Long	WR	6'3"	205	27		24
Jerry Simmons	WR	6'1"	190	25		
John Wright	WR	6'	195	22		
Mike Donohoe	TE	6'3"	227	23		6
Ray Ogden	TE	6'5"	225	25		12
Bob Etter	K	5'11"	152	23		50

COASTAL DIVISION

BALTIMORE COLTS

RUSHING

Last Name	No.	Yds	Avg	TD
Matte	183	662	3.6	9
Cole	104	418	4.0	3
Hill	91	360	4.0	1
Brown	39	159	4.1	2
MacKey	10	103	10.3	0
Pearson	19	78	4.1	0
Morrall	11	18	1.6	1
Lee	3	12	4.0	0
Unitas	3	−1	−0.3	0

RECEIVING

Last Name	No.	Yds	Avg	TD
Mackey	45	644	14	5
Richardson	37	698	19	8
Orr	29	743	26	6
Matte	25	275	11	1
Hill	18	161	9	1
Perkins	15	227	15	1
Cole	13	75	6	0
Mitchell	6	117	20	4
Brown	4	53	13	0
Cogdill	3	42	14	0
Pearson	2	70	35	2
Hawkins	2	31	16	0

PUNT RETURNS

Last Name	No.	Yds	Avg	TD
Volk	25	198	8	0
Brown	16	125	8	0
Logan	1	27	27	0

KICKOFF RETURNS

Last Name	No.	Yds	Avg	TD
Pearson	15	527	35	2
Brown	15	298	20	0
Cole	5	123	25	0
Matte	1	22	22	0
Porter	1	19	19	0
Logan	1	14	14	0

PASSING

Last Name	Att	Comp	%	Yds	Yd/Att	TD	Int−	%	RK
Morrall	317	182	57	2909	9.2	26	17−	5	1
Unitas	32	11	34	139	4.3	2	4	13	
Ward	9	3	33	46	5.1	0	1−	11	
Matte	1	0	0	0	0.0	0	0−	0	

PUNTING

Last Name	No	Avg
Lee	49	39.5

KICKING

Last Name	XP	Att	%	FG	Att	%
Michaels	48	50	96	18	28	64

LOS ANGELES RAMS

RUSHING

Last Name	No.	Yds	Avg	TD
Ellison	151	616	4.1	5
Bass	121	494	4.1	1
Mason	108	395	3.7	3
Gabriel	34	139	4.1	4
Dennis	29	136	4.7	0
Dyer	55	136	2.5	1
Meador	1	11	11.0	0
Plum	2	3	1.5	0
Ezerins	2	2	1.0	0

RECEIVING

Last Name	No.	Yds	Avg	TD
Truax	35	417	12	3
Casey	29	565	19	5
Snow	29	500	17	3
Bass	27	195	7	2
Ellison	20	248	12	2
Mason	15	144	10	0
Dennis	8	53	7	0
Dyer	8	37	5	0
Tucker	7	124	18	4
Studstill	7	108	15	1
Pivec	3	27	9	0
Gabriel	1	−5	−5	0

PUNT RETURNS

Last Name	No.	Yds	Avg	TD
Smith	27	171	6	0
Meador	17	136	8	0

KICKOFF RETURNS

Last Name	No.	Yds	Avg	TD
Smith	26	718	28	1
Ellison	12	268	22	0
Meador	1	20	20	0
Williams	1	16	16	0
Dennis	2	2	1	0
Pivec	2	0	0	0
Ezerins	1	0	0	0

PASSING

Last Name	Att	Comp	%	Yds	Yd/Att	TD	Int−	%	RK
Gabriel	366	184	50	3020	8.2	19	16−	4	9
Plum	12	5	42	49	4.1	1	1−	8	
Dennis	2	0	0	0	0.0	0	0−	0	
Mason	2	0	0	0	0.0	0	0−	0	
Ellison	1	0	0	0	0.0	0	0−	0	
Studstill	1	0	0	0	0.0	0	0−	0	

PUNTING

Last Name	No	Avg
Studstill	81	39.6

KICKING

Last Name	XP	Att	%	FG	Att	%
Gossett	37	37	100	17	31	55

SAN FRANCISCO FORTY NINERS

RUSHING

Last Name	No.	Yds	Avg	TD
Willard	227	967	4.3	7
Lewis	141	573	4.1	1
Tucker	30	135	4.5	3
Brodie	18	71	3.9	0
Daniels	12	37	3.1	0
Cunningham	6	7	1.2	0
Mira	1	5	5.0	0
Crow	4	4	1.0	0
McNeil	1	−1	−1.0	0
Spurrier	1	−15	−15.0	0

RECEIVING

Last Name	No.	Yds	Avg	TD
McNeil	71	994	14	7
Witcher	39	531	14	1
Willard	36	232	6	0
Crow	31	531	17	5
Lewis	27	244	9	3
Tucker	15	197	13	4
Windsor	8	146	18	2
McFarland	5	140	28	1
Cunningham	2	25	13	0
Daniels	2	23	12	0

PUNT RETURNS

Last Name	No.	Yds	Avg	TD
Alexander	24	87	4	0
Fuller	12	33	3	0

KICKOFF RETURNS

Last Name	No.	Yds	Avg	TD
Alexander	20	360	18	0
Cunningham	14	286	20	0
Daniels	10	206	21	0
Tucker	5	103	21	0
Fuller	1	23	23	0
Hays	2	21	11	0
Banaszek	1	15	15	0
Olerich	1	4	4	0
Hart	1	3	3	0
Nunley	2	0	0	0
Peoples	1	0	0	0

PASSING

Last Name	Att	Comp	%	Yds	Yd/Att	TD	Int−	%	RK
Brodie	404	234	58	3020	7.5	22	21−	5	3
Mira	11	4	36	44	4.0	1	1−	9	
McNeil	2	1	50	43	21.5	1	1−	50	

PUNTING

Last Name	No	Avg
Spurrier	68	39.0

KICKING

Last Name	XP	Att	%	FG	Att	%
Davis	26	26	100	9	16	56
Patera	10	12	83	2	8	25

ATLANTA FALCONS

RUSHING

Last Name	No.	Yds	Avg	TD
Butler	94	365	3.9	2
Dunn	72	219	3.0	3
Wages	59	211	3.6	0
Harris	53	144	2.7	0
Berry	26	139	5.3	2
Johnson	11	97	8.8	1
McCarthy	31	86	2.8	1
Bryant	9	29	3.2	0
Auer	3	19	6.3	0
Ogden	1	12	12.0	0
Lee	6	7	1.2	0
Lemmerman	1	0	0.0	0
Simmons	1	−6	−6.0	0
Lothridge	1	−16	−16.0	0

RECEIVING

Last Name	No.	Yds	Avg	TD
Simmons	28	479	17	0
Ogden	25	452	18	2
Long	22	484	22	4
Flatley	20	305	15	0
Wages	16	121	8	1
Butler	15	127	8	0
McCarthy	13	119	9	0
Dunn	9	118	13	0
Donohoe	6	52	9	1
Harris	3	118	39	1
Bryant	1	11	11	0

PUNT RETURNS

Last Name	No.	Yds	Avg	TD
Burson	11	56	5	0
Rassas	4	10	3	0
Spiller	1	0	0	0

KICKOFF RETURNS

Last Name	No.	Yds	Avg	TD
Butler	37	799	22	0
Rassas	10	180	18	0
Bryant	5	112	22	0
Lee	3	63	21	0
Auer	2	31	16	0
Talbert	3	30	10	0
Wages	1	23	23	0
Donohoe	1	22	22	0
Szczecko	3	18	6	0
Spiller	1	18	18	0
Harris	1	16	16	0
Grimm	1	4	4	0
Allen	1	0	0	0
Cerne	1	0	0	0

PASSING

Last Name	Att	Comp	%	Yds	Yd/Att	TD	Int−	%	RK
Johnson	156	73	47	892	5.7	2	10−	6	17
Berry	153	81	53	1433	9.4	7	13−	8	11
Lemmerman	15	3	20	40	2.7	0	1−	7	
Wages	2	1	50	21	10.5	0	0−	0	

PUNTING

Last Name	No	Avg
Lothridge	75	44.3

KICKING

Last Name	XP	Att	%	FG	Att	%
Etter	17	19	89	11	21	52

1968 A.F.L. The Jets, Heidi, and Howls

Heidi, the Swiss mountain girl from the storybooks, had football fans flooding telephone lines with cries of protest on November 17. With the Jets beating Oakland 32-29 with two minutes left in the game, NBC television was faced with a dilemma; it could either continue coverage of the football game to its conclusion or it could broadcast a special dramatization of "Heidi" at its scheduled hour and leave the football game before time ran out. NBC opted for "Heidi," and football fans poured calls of protest into the television station for taking the game off the air. To add fuel to the fire, the Raiders scored two touchdowns in those last minutes to take the game 43-32. NBC tried to make amends by showing films of the final two minutes of action on the late news shows, and the network promised never again to get burned with such a decision.

EASTERN DIVISION

New York Jets—There was no December collapse for the Jets this year, as they won their last three games from Miami, Cincinnati, and Miami, both easy marks. In first place heading into the final month, the Jets this year held onto the top spot right to the end. The New York offense was too much for the rest of the Eastern Division, with Joe Namath riding herd on one of pro football's most explosive attacks. Continuing to hit George Sauer and Don Maynard with bullet passes at regular intervals, Namath also blossomed into a top diagnostician, deftly sending runners Matt Snell and Emerson Boozer into the line at the right time more often than not. Much had been expected of the New York offense, and it delivered in style; but the New York defense, consistently downgraded by opponents and the press, hung together in a unit which jumped on every enemy mistake. Even place-kicker Jim Turner, aided by new holder Babe Parilli, had a good year. With the Eastern title in their pockets, the Jets headed for a post-season date with destiny.

Houston Oilers—The Oilers caught lightning in a bottle in their surprise 1967 Eastern title, but they dropped this year to a 7-7 mark more typical of a young club still in the midst of rebuilding. Paced by two of the league's top defensive players in George Webster and Miller Farr, the Oilers still surrendered points grudgingly, but the Houston attack frightened few opponents. Fullback Hoyle Granger ran well behind a strong line, but neither he nor Woody Campbell had game-breaking speed. The receiving was strengthened by rookies Mac Haik and Jim Beirne and the development of Alvin Reed into a top tight end, but quarterback problems made the Oiler passing game extremely erratic. Pete Beathard displayed a strong arm and periods of inaccuracy before an appendectomy shelved him late in the year, and Don Trull, picked up after the Patriots cut him, was not a permanent answer.

Miami Dolphins—Fullback Larry Csonka needed time to get used to pro football but showed unmistakable power as a runner. Catching on more quickly was halfback Jim Kiick, a fifth-round draft pick who was a reliable runner and receiver. The defense was shored up by freshmen Manny Fernandez and Dick Anderson; Fernandez, signed as a free agent, provided the team's only pass-rushing, while safetyman Anderson had a flair for both tackling and intercepting. Another rookie, tackle Doug Crusan, won a starting job in the offensive line. Of course, some of the veterans also turned in good performances, with quarterback Bob Griese leading the way. The second-year passer had a good season despite poor protection and the loss of Jack Clancy, his favorite receiver, to knee surgery. Split end Karl Noonan, a slow but meticulous receiver, filled in for Clancy and hauled in fifty-eight passes.

Boston Patriots—Coach Mike Holovak made a break with the past by trading veteran quarterback Babe Parilli to New York for young Mike Taliaferro, but the Boston attack suffered for the change. Taliaferro could not ignite the offense and lost his job to rookie Tom Sherman. Other veteran Patriot players endured poor seasons. A bad ankle robbed Jim Nance of much of his effectiveness, and bad knees put defensive end Larry Eisenhauer and middle linebacker Nick Buoniconti out of action for several games. Coach Holovak got good work from cornerback Leroy Mitchell, tight end Jim Whalen, center Jon Morris, and defensive tackle Houston Antwine, but the Patriots needed a complete overhauling.

Buffalo Bills—The Bills' quarterback ills started when veterans Jack Kemp and Tom Flores were both injured before the regular season began. Coach Joel Collier started the year with rookie Dan Darragh as the signal-caller, but with the offensive line thinned out by injuries and age, Darragh soon was racked up enough by enemy defenses that his knee gave out. Next on the firing line was Kay Stephenson, a young man picked up from San Diego, and he lasted a couple of games before going out with a broken collarbone. Ed Rutkowski, a veteran utility man who had last played quarterback at Notre Dame six years ago, then stepped in and stayed healthy while guiding the Bills to the end of the season. The team scored the least points in the league but did have the satisfaction of beating the Jets 37-35 for their only victory of the season. The Bills had been a championship team only two years before, so coach Collier paid with his head two games into the campaign.

WESTERN DIVISION

Oakland Raiders—The Raiders were hit with a long string of injuries, yet still charged to a 12-2 record and a tie for the Western title. Defensive tackle Tom Keating missed the entire season with an Achilles-tendon injury suffered in last year's AFL championship game, but Carleton Oats filled in competently and Dan Birdwell compensated with his best year ever. When linebacker Bill Laskey also hurt his Achilles tendon, rookie Chip Oliver stepped into the starting lineup with a fine performance. When a knee injury shelved cornerback Kent McCloughan in mid-season, the Raiders had an exciting substitute in rookie Butch Atkinson. The offense avoided injuries but found two new starters in wide receiver Warren Wells and halfback Charlie Smith. With the title on the line, Daryle Lamonica threw five touchdown passes to win the playoff game 41-6.

Kansas City Chiefs—The Chiefs came back from last year's poor season to tie for first place in the West with a 12-2 record. The Kansas City defense allowed the fewest points in the league, with top players in all departments. Jerry Mays and Buck Buchanan starred in the line, the linebacking trio of Bobby Bell, Willie Lanier, and Jim Lynch was tops in the league, and safety Johnny Robinson steadied a secondary with several new starters. The offense matched the defense in efficiency, although an injury to Otis Taylor put more emphasis on a ball-control attack. Rookie fullback Robert Holmes, an unknown fourteenth-round draft pick, surprised everyone with his dogged ball-carrying, while veterans Mike Garrett and Curtis McClinton were bothered by injuries.

San Diego Chargers—The Chargers made the Western pennant race a three-way affair until dropping three of their last four games. Before home-town audiences, the Chargers lost 37-15 to New York, 40-3 to Kansas City, and 34-27 to Oakland, shooting all their title hopes to pieces. The Chargers had to be ranked among the league powers, but they could not beat the other top teams like the Jets, Chiefs, and Raiders. The biggest problem for coach Sid Gillman was his defense. The front four of Steve DeLong, Scott Appleton, Russ Washington, and Houston Ridge had good college press clippings but rarely got to the enemy passer, the linebacking was no better than adequate, and the secondary was solid only at Kenny Graham's strong safety spot. The San Diego attack as always found ways to put points on the scoreboard regularly. Quarterback John Hadl, operating behind an excellent offensive line, kept receivers Lance Alworth and Gary Garrison busy catching passes, and although fullback Brad Hubbert missed most of the season with a knee injury, halfback Dickie Post kept up the fine running of his rookie year.

Denver Broncos—The Broncos embarrassed themselves by losing 24-10 to the new Cincinnati Bengals on opening day, but they jelled into a respectable team after losing their first three games. In a five-week stretch from October 6 to November 3, Denver beat the Bengals, Jets, Dolphins, and Patriots while losing only to the Chargers. The key to this hot streak was the heavy pressure put on opposing passers by the Bronco defensive line, with end Rich Jackson developing into an All-Pro performer and tackle Dave Costa providing steady play against the run. The linebacking and secondary still was in a state of flux, but the strong pressure exerted by the line prevented passers from exploiting these weak spots. The Denver attack moved the ball well until quarterback Steve Tensi and split end Al Denson both went out in mid-season with broken collarbones, but rookie Marlin Briscoe, the first black ever to play regularly at T-formation quarterback in the pro ranks, kept the club interesting to the end with his scrambling and clutch passing.

Cincinnati Bengals—Paul Brown had built the Cleveland Browns into a powerhouse by signing poised players returning from World War II, but he set a different course for the new Cincinnati Bengals. Brown threw his lineup open to rookies and young players who had not fit in elsewhere. With so many inexperienced players in the lineup, most clubs would have suffered through a dismal season of hard learning, but Brown drilled his young Bengals so that they learned and played competitive football right from the start.

FINAL TEAM STATISTICS

OFFENSE

	BOSTON	BUFFALO	CIN.	DENVER	HOUSTON	K.C.	MIAMI	N.Y.	OAKLAND	S.D.
FIRST DOWNS:										
Total	181	159	171	217	240	223	247	249	287	270
by Rushing	69	71	85	75	99	123	78	80	97	93
by Passing	94	72	73	124	128	89	144	144	162	164
by Penalty	18	16	13	18	13	11	25	25	28	13
RUSHING:										
Number	421	400	421	411	462	537	417	467	471	428
Yards	1362	1527	1807	1614	1804	2227	1704	1608	2168	1765
Average Yards	3.1	3.8	4.3	3.9	3.9	4.1	4.1	3.4	4.6	4.1
Touchdowns	8	9	14	11	16	16	12	22	16	12
PASSING:										
Attempts	409	405	313	427	414	270	423	436	468	472
Completions	160	168	167	179	191	156	216	237	237	225
Completion Percentage	39.1	41.5	53.4	41.9	46.1	57.8	51.1	49.8	50.6	47.7
Passing Yards	2121	1714	1896	2826	2864	2492	2843	3574	3771	3813
Average Yards per Att.	5.2	4.2	6.1	6.6	6.9	9.2	6.7	8.2	8.1	8.1
Average Yards per Comp.	13.3	10.2	11.4	15.8	15.0	16.0	13.2	16.5	15.9	16.9
Tackled Att. to pass	38	39	38	51	29	24	52	18	29	18
Yards Lost Tackled	356	371	277	469	316	216	441	135	243	190
Net Yards	1765	1343	1619	2357	2548	2276	2402	3439	3528	3623
Touchdowns	16	7	8	20	17	20	21	20	31	29
Interceptions	33	28	11	27	25	11	22	19	18	33
Percent Intercepted	8.1	6.9	3.5	6.3	6.0	4.1	5.2	4.4	3.8	7.0
PUNTS:										
Number	96	100	84	96	73	65	75	68	64	56
Average Distance	39.9	41.8	40.9	42.7	41.2	45.3	40.6	43.8	43.6	40.7
PUNT RETURNS:										
Number	37	44	30	38	52	31	28	36	55	39
Yards	197	301	196	332	443	450	205	286	666	292
Average Yards	5.3	6.8	6.5	8.7	8.5	14.5	7.3	7.9	12.1	7.5
Touchdowns	0	1	0	1	0	2	0	0	2	1
KICKOFF RETURNS:										
Number	71	69	54	60	53	38	50	46	49	51
Yards	1442	1537	1068	1361	1235	736	1134	995	1092	1065
Average Yards	20.3	22.3	19.8	22.7	23.3	19.9	22.7	21.6	22.3	20.9
Touchdowns	0	1	0	0	0	0	0	0	0	0
INTERCEPTION RETURNS:										
Number	23	22	10	20	20	37	22	28	25	20
Yards	220	475	144	165	396	469	386	456	424	275
Average Yards	9.6	21.6	14.4	8.3	19.8	12.7	17.5	16.3	17.0	13.8
Touchdowns	1	4	2	0	5	2	1	2	4	2
PENALTIES:										
Number	67	67	55	73	61	66	48	76	81	72
Yards	682	687	586	772	644	650	485	742	958	654
FUMBLES:										
Number	28	23	27	28	28	26	17	19	34	20
Number Lost	20	14	10	13	13	16	8	9	21	12
POINTS:										
Total	229	199	215	255	303	371	276	419	453	382
PAT (kick) Attempts	26	19	24	32	38	40	36	43	54	43
PAT (kick) Made	26	19	24	31	37	39	36	43	54	40
PAT (2-Point) Attempts	0	3	1	0	0	0	0	2	1	2
PAT (2-Point) Made	0	2	0	0	0	0	0	1	1	2
FG Attempts	27	28	27	23	29	40	19	46	34	32
FG Made	15	14	13	10	12	30	8	34	21	22
Percent FG Made	55.6	50.0	48.1	43.5	41.4	75.0	42.1	73.9	61.8	68.8
Safeties	1	1	1	1	0	1	0	1	2	1

DEFENSE

	BOSTON	BUFFALO	CIN.	DENVER	HOUSTON	K.C.	MIAMI	N.Y.	OAKLAND	S.D.
FIRST DOWNS:										
Total	237	210	275	251	198	215	240	178	215	225
by Rushing	86	85	116	94	89	52	116	59	83	90
by Passing	123	103	140	145	96	140	112	104	113	118
by Penalty	28	22	19	12	13	23	12	15	19	17
RUSHING:										
Number	479	505	473	457	462	365	445	368	442	439
Yards	1825	2021	2097	1861	1704	1266	2172	1195	1804	1641
Average Yards	3.8	4.0	4.4	4.1	3.7	3.5	4.9	3.2	4.1	3.7
Touchdowns	22	15	13	20	9	4	19	9	12	13
PASSING:										
Attempts	416	340	411	429	359	461	342	403	446	430
Completions	200	143	212	217	158	214	179	187	189	217
Completion Percentage	48.1	42.1	51.6	50.6	44.0	46.4	52.3	46.4	42.4	50.5
Passing Yards	2826	2477	2903	3419	2003	3262	2904	2567	2657	2896
Average Yards per Att.	6.8	7.3	7.1	8.0	5.6	7.1	8.5	6.4	6.0	6.7
Average Yards per Comp.	14.1	17.3	13.7	15.8	12.7	15.2	16.2	13.7	14.1	13.3
Tackled Att. to pass	27	31	32	31	33	45	21	43	49	24
Yards Lost Tackled	236	273	283	256	332	439	192	399	400	204
Net Yards	2590	2204	2620	3163	1671	2823	2712	2168	2257	2692
Touchdowns	20	19	25	25	13	14	23	17	13	20
Interceptions	23	22	10	20	20	37	22	18	25	20
Percent Intercepted	5.5	6.5	2.4	4.7	5.6	8.0	6.4	6.9	5.6	4.7
PUNTS:										
Number	81	75	63	76	88	73	55	98	94	74
Average Distance	40.5	39.7	44.2	43.0	44.1	42.8	43.4	38.4	42.3	42.3
PUNT RETURNS:										
Number	59	45	41	46	40	31	28	39	40	21
Yards	502	521	252	282	379	220	250	531	211	220
Average Yards	8.5	11.6	6.1	6.1	9.5	7.1	8.9	13.6	5.3	10.5
Touchdowns	1	1	0	1	0	0	0	3	0	1
KICKOFF RETURNS:										
Number	40	49	40	29	58	54	54	82	75	60
Yards	901	1062	977	704	1302	1044	1108	1664	1652	1251
Average Yards	22.5	21.7	24.4	24.3	22.4	19.3	20.5	20.3	22.0	20.9
Touchdowns	0	0	1	0	0	0	0	0	0	0
INTERCEPTION RETURNS:										
Number	33	28	11	27	25	11	22	19	18	33
Yards	510	472	79	328	326	119	432	455	155	534
Average Yards	15.5	16.9	7.2	12.1	13.0	10.8	19.6	23.9	8.6	16.2
Touchdowns	3	6	0	3	2	0	3	0	0	2
PENALTIES:										
Number	70	66	62	64	54	62	70	65	90	63
Yards	874	540	632	750	526	564	655	695	932	692
FUMBLES:										
Number	37	24	19	24	17	22	28	29	24	26
Number Lost	17	13	9	12	10	12	18	15	15	15
POINTS:										
Total	406	367	329	404	248	170	355	280	233	310
PAT (kick) Attempts	49	41	39	47	25	18	44	34	23	35
PAT (kick) Made	49	40	37	47	25	18	43	33	22	35
PAT (2-Point) Attempts	0	0	0	1	1	0	1	2	3	1
PAT (2-Point) Made	0	0	0	1	1	0	1	2	1	0
FG Attempts	31	48	35	34	30	27	24	17	28	31
FG Made	21	27	18	21	21	14	12	9	17	19
Percent FG Made	67.7	56.3	51.4	61.8	70.0	51.9	50.0	52.9	60.7	61.3
Safeties	0	0	2	0	1	2	0	1	1	0

WESTERN DIVISION PLAYOFF
December 22 at Oakland
(Attendance 53,605)

SCORING

OAKLAND	21	7	0	13—41
KANSAS CITY	0	6	0	0— 6

First Quarter
Oak. Biletnikoff, 24 yard pass from Lamonica
　　　PAT—Blanda (kick)
Oak. Wells, 23 yard pass from Lamonica
　　　PAT—Blanda (kick)
Oak. Biletnikoff, 44 yard pass from Lamonica
　　　PAT—Blanda (kick)

Second Quarter
K.C. Stenerud, 10 yard field goal
K.C. Stenerud, 8 yard field goal
Oak. Biletnikoff, 54 yard pass from Lamonica
　　　PAT—Blanda (kick)

Fourth Quarter
Oak. Wells, 35 yard pass from Lamonica
　　　PAT—Blanda (kick)
Oak. Blanda, 41 yard field goal
Oak. Blanda, 40 yard field goal

TEAM STATISTICS

OAK.		K.C.
22	First Downs—Total	13
7	First Downs—Rushing	3
14	First Downs—Passing	9
1	First Downs—Penalty	1
1	Fumbles—Number	2
0	Fumbles—Lost Ball	0
1	Penalties—Number	2
2	Yards Penalized	20
0	Missed Field Goals	1
70	Offensive Plays—Total	61
454	Net Yards	312
6.5	Average Gain	5.1
0	Giveaways	4
4	Takeaways	0
+4	Difference	-4

INDIVIDUAL STATISTICS

RUSHING

OAKLAND	No.	Yds.	Avg.	KANSAS CITY	No.	Yds.	Avg.
Smith	13	74	5.7	Holmes	13	46	3.5
Banaszak	3	19	6.3	Hayes	3	10	3.3
Dixon	10	13	1.3	Dawson	2	9	4.5
Hagberg	4	12	3.0	Garrett	6	5	0.8
	30	118	3.9		24	70	2.9

RECEIVING

OAKLAND	No.	Yds.	Avg.	KANSAS CITY	No.	Yds.	Avg.
Biletnikoff	7	180	25.7	Pitts	5	56	11.2
Smith	5	52	10.4	Taylor	4	117	29.3
Wells	4	93	23.3	Garrett	4	31	7.8
Cannon	2	15	7.5	Richardson	3	57	19.0
Dixon	1	7	7.0	Holmes	1	-8	-8.0
	19	347	18.3		17	253	14.9

PUNTING

OAKLAND	No.	Yds.	Avg.	KANSAS CITY	No.	Yds.	Avg.
Eischeid	5		45.4	Wilson	6		50.3

PUNT RETURNS

OAKLAND	No.	Yds.	Avg.	KANSAS CITY	No.	Yds.	Avg.
Bird	3	29	9.7	Smith	2	-9	-4.5

KICKOFF RETURNS

OAKLAND	No.	Yds.	Avg.	KANSAS CITY	No.	Yds.	Avg.
Atkinson	1	34	34.0	Smith	5	73	14.6
				Mitchell	2	46	23.0
				Lanier	1	0	0.0
					8	119	14.9

INTERCEPTION RETURNS

OAKLAND	No.	Yds.	Avg.	KANSAS CITY	No.	Yds.	Avg.
Wilson	1	14	14.0	None			
Hopkins	1	7	7.0				
Connors	1	5	5.0				
Brown	1	0	0.0				
	4	26	6.5				

PASSING

	Att.	Comp.	Comp. Pct.	Yds.	Int.	Yds/ Att.	Yds/ Comp.	Yards Lost Tackled
OAKLAND								
Lamonica	39	19	48.7	347		8.9	18.3	1—11
KANSAS CITY								
Dawson	36	17	47.2	253	4	7.0	14.9	1—11

1968 A.F.L. — Eastern Division

NEW YORK JETS 11-3-0 Weeb Ewbank

Scores of Each Game		
20	Kansas City	19
47	Boston	31
35	Buffalo	37
23	SAN DIEGO	20
13	DENVER	21
20	Houston	14
48	BOSTON	14
25	BUFFALO	21
26	HOUSTON	7
32	Oakland	43
37	San Diego	15
35	MIAMI	17
27	CINCINNATI	14
31	Miami	7

Use Name	Pos.	Hgt	Wgt	Age	Int	Pts
Winston Hill	OT	6'4"	280	26		
Sam Walton	OT	6'5"	270	25		
Jeff Richardson	C-OT	6'3"	250	23		
Randy Rasmussen	OG	6'2"	255	23		
Bob Talamini	OG	6'1"	255	29		
Dave Herman	OT-OG	6'2"	255	26		
John Schmitt	C	6'4"	245	25		
Paul Crane	LB-C	6'2"	205	24		2
Verlon Biggs	DE	6'4"	270	25		
Gerry Philbin	DE	6'2"	245	27		
Steve Thompson	DE	6'5"	245	23		
John Elliott	DT	6'4"	245	23		
Ray Hayes	DT	6'5"	245	21		
Karl Henke	DT	6'4"	245	23		
Paul Rochester	DT	6'2"	255	31		
Carl McAdams	DE-DT	6'3"	240	24		
Al Atkinson	LB	6'1"	230	25	2	
Ralph Baker	LB	6'3"	235	26	3	
Larry Grantham	LB	6'	210	29		
Mike Stromberg	LB	6'2"	235	23		
Bill Baird	DB	5'10"	180	29	4	
Randy Beverly	DB	5'11"	185	24	4	6
Earl Christy	DB	5'11"	195	25	1	
Mike D'Amato	DB	6'2"	204	25		
John Dockery	DB	6'	186	23		
Cornell Gordon	DB	6'	187	27	2	
Jim Hudson	DB	6'2"	210	25	5	
Jim Richards	DB	6'1"	180	21		
Johnny Sample	DB	6'1"	208	31	7	6
Joe Namath	QB	6'2"	195	25		12
Babe Parilli	QB	6'1"	190	38		6
Jim Turner	QB	6'2"	205	27		145
Emerson Boozer	HB	5'11"	204	25		30
Bill Mathis	HB	6'1"	220	29		38
Billy Joe	FB	6'2"	236	27		18
Matt Snell	FB	6'2"	220	26		42
Lee White	FB	6'4"	240	22		
Mark Smolinski	TE-FB	6'	215	29		6
Don Maynard	WR	6'	180	32		60
Harvey Nairn	WR	6'1"	178	22		
Bill Rademacher	WR	6'1"	190	26		
George Sauer	WR	6'1"	195	24		18
Bake Turner	WR	6'	180	28		12
Curley Johnson	TE	6'	215	33		
Pete Lammons	TE	6'3"	228	24		18

Paul Seiler – Military Service

HOUSTON OILERS 7-7-0 Wally Lemm

Scores of Each Game		
21	KANSAS CITY	26
24	Miami	10
14	San Diego	30
15	OAKLAND	24
7	MIAMI	24
16	Boston	0
14	NEW YORK	20
30	Buffalo	7
27	Cincinnati	17
7	New York	26
38	DENVER	17
10	Kansas City	24
35	BUFFALO	6
45	BOSTON	17

Use Name	Pos.	Hgt	Wgt	Age	Int	Pts
Glen Ray Hines	OT	6'5"	265	24		
Bob Robertson	OT	6'4"	246	21		
Walt Suggs	OT	6'5"	265	29		
Sonny Bishop	OG	6'2"	245	28		
Tom Regner	OG	6'1"	255	24		
Dick Swatland	OG	6'3"	245	22		
Bobby Maples	C	6'3"	245	25		
Steve Quinn	C	6'1"	225	22		
Elvin Bethea	DE	6'3"	250	22		
Gary Cutsinger	DE	6'4"	245	27		
Pat Holmes	DE	6'5"	250	28		
Bud Marshall	DT	6'5"	275	26		
Dudley Meredith (from BUF)	DT	6'4"	285	33		
Willie Parker	DT	6'2"	265	23		
George Rice	DT	6'3"	260	24		
Carel Stith	DT	6'5"	265	23		
Tom Domres	DE-DT	6'3"	255	21		
Pete Barnes	LB	6'3"	245	23		
Garland Boyette	LB	6'1"	245	28	1	
Ronnie Caveness	LB	6'1"	225	25		
Marion Rushing (from ATL-N)	LB	6'2"	230	31		
Rich Stotter	LB	6'	225	23		
Olen Underwood	LB	6'1"	230	26	1	2
George Webster	LB	6'4"	223	22	1	
Larry Carwell	DB	6'1"	190	24	4	6
Miller Farr	DB	6'1"	190	25	3	12
W. K. Hicks	DB	6'1"	195	25	3	
Ken Houston	DB	6'3"	192	23	5	12
Pete Johns	DB	6'3"	190	23		
Zeke Moore	DB	6'2"	198	24		
Jim Norton	DB	6'3"	180	29	2	
Bob Smith	DB	6'	180	23		
Pete Beathard	QB	6'2"	207	26		12
Bob Davis	QB	6'3"	208	22		6
Don Trull	QB	6'1"	196	26		
Sid Blanks	HB	6'	210	27		
Ode Burrell	HB	6'	192	28		
Woody Campbell	HB	5'11"	202	23		36
Hoyle Granger	FB	6'1"	225	24		42
Roy Hopkins	FB	6'1"	225	23		
Glenn Bass	WR	6'2"	210	29		
Jim Beirne	WR	6'2"	196	21		24
Charley Frazier	WR	6'	184	29		
Mac Haik	WR	6'1"	196	22		48
Lionel Taylor	WR	6'2"	215	32		
Jim LeMoine	TE	6'2"	245	23		
Alvin Reed	TE	6'5"	230	24		30
Wayne Walker	K	6'2"	215	23		50
John Wittenborn	K	6'2"	240	32		23

MIAMI DOLPHINS 5-8-1 George Wilson

Scores of Each Game		
10	HOUSTON	24
21	OAKLAND	47
3	KANSAS CITY	48
24	Houston	7
14	BUFFALO	14
24	Cincinnati	22
14	Denver	21
28	San Diego	34
21	Buffalo	17
21	CINCINNATI	38
34	Boston	10
17	New York	35
38	BOSTON	7
7	NEW YORK	31

Use Name	Pos.	Hgt	Wgt	Age	Int	Pts
Doug Crusan	OT	6'5"	255	22		
Norm Evans	OT	6'5"	250	25		
Jack Pyburn	OT	6'6"	250	23		
Charlie Fowler	OG	6'2"	260	24		
Billy Neighbors	OG	5'11"	250	28		
Maxie Williams	OG	6'4"	250	28		
Freddie Woodson	DE-OG	6'2"	255	24		
Tom Goode	C	6'3"	250	29		
Mel Branch	DE	6'2"	235	31		
Manny Fernandez	DE	6'2"	250	22		
Bob Joswick	DE	6'5"	250	22		
Jim Riley	DE	6'4"	255	23		
Ray Jacobs	DT	6'3"	285	28		
Tom Nomina	DT	6'5"	260	26		
John Richardson	DT	6'2"	260	23		
Jim Urbanek	DT	6'4"	270	23		
Rudy Barber	LB	6'1"	255	23		
John Bramlett	LB	6'2"	210	27	2	
Bob Bruggers (to SD)	LB	6'1"	230	24		
Randy Edmunds	LB	6'2"	220	22	1	
Frank Emanuel	LB	6'3"	225	25	2	6
Jimmy Keyes	LB	6'2"	225	24		51
Wahoo McDaniel	LB	6'	230	31		
Ed Weisacosky	LB	6'	230	24		
Dick Anderson	DB	6'2"	205	22	8	6
Mack Lamb	DB	6'1"	188	24	1	
Bob Neff	DB	6'	180	24		
Bob Petrella	DB	6'	185	23	1	
Jimmy Warren	DB	5'11"	175	29	2	
Dick Washington	DB	6'1"	205	23		
Willie West	DB	5'10"	187	30	4	6
Dick Westmoreland	DB	6'1"	195	27	1	
Bob Griese	QB	6'1"	190	23		6
Kim Hammond	QB	6'1"	192	23		
Rick Norton	QB	6'1"	190	24		
Jack Harper	HB	5'11"	190	23		
Jim Kiick	HB	5'11"	215	22		24
Sam Price	HB	5'11"	215	24		
Gary Tucker	HB	5'11"	195	23		
Larry Seiple	TE-HB	6'	213	23		6
Larry Csonka	FB	6'3"	240	21		42
Stan Mitchell	HB-FB	6'2"	225	24		24
Bill Darnall	WR	6'2"	197	24		
Gene Milton	WR	5'10"	170	23		6
Karl Noonan	WR	6'3"	190	24		66
Howard Twilley	WR	5'10"	180	24		6
Jim Cox	TE	6'2"	227	24		
Doug Moreau	TE	6'2"	215	23		27

Jack Clancy – Knee Injury

BOSTON PATRIOTS 4-10-0 Mike Holovak

Scores of Each Game		
16	Buffalo	7
31	NEW YORK	47
20	Denver	17
10	Oakland	41
0	HOUSTON	16
23	BUFFALO	6
14	New York	48
14	DENVER	35
17	SAN DIEGO	27
17	Kansas City	31
10	MIAMI	34
33	CINCINNATI	14
7	Miami	38
17	Houston	45

Use Name	Pos.	Hgt	Wgt	Age	Int	Pts
Jim Boudreaux	OT	6'4"	245	23		
Paul Feldhausen	OT	6'6"	270	22		
Tom Funchess	OT	6'5"	260	23		
Tom Neville	OT	6'4"	255	25		
Don Oakes	OT	6'3"	255	30		
Karl Singer	OT	6'3"	255	24		
Justin Canale	OG	6'2"	250	24		
Charley Long	OG	6'3"	250	30		
Len St. Jean	OG	6'1"	245	26		
Jon Morris	C	6'4"	240	25		
J. R. Williamson	LB-C	6'2"	220	26		
Dennis Byrd	DE	6'4"	260	21		
Larry Eisenhauer	DE	6'5"	255	28		
Mel Witt	DE	6'3"	265	22	1	6
Houston Antwine	DT	6'	270	29		
Whit Canale	DT	6'3"	245	26		
Jim Hunt	DT	5'11"	255	29		
Ed Toner	DT	6'3"	250	23		
Nick Buoniconti	LB	5'11"	220	27	3	
Jim Cheyunski	LB	6'2"	225	22	1	
Ray Ilg	LB	6'1"	220	22		
Ed Koontz	LB	6'2"	230	21		
Ed Philpott	LB	6'3"	240	22	4	6
Doug Satcher	LB	6'	220	23	1	2
John Charles	DB	6'1"	200	24	1	
Billy Johnson	DB	5'11"	180	25	2	
Daryle Johnson	DB	5'11"	190	22	1	
Art McMahon	DB	5'11"	185	22	2	
Leroy Mitchell	DB	6'2"	190	23	7	
Willie Porter	DB	5'11"	195	22		
Don Webb	DB	5'10"	195	29		
King Corcoran	QB	6'	200	26		
Tom Sherman	QB	6'	190	22		
Mike Taliaferro	QB	6'2"	205	26		
Larry Garron	HB	6'	195	31		6
Gene Thomas (to OAK)	HB	6'1"	210	25		12
R. C. Gamble	FB-HB	6'3"	220	21		12
Preston Johnson	FB	6'2"	230	23		
Jim Nance	FB	6'1"	240	25		24
Gino Cappelletti	WR	6'	190	34		83
Jim Colclough	WR	6'	185	32		
Art Graham	WR	6'1"	205	27		6
Bobby Leo	WR	5'10"	180	23		
Aaron Marsh	WR	6'1"	190	23		24
Bill Murphy	WR	6'1"	185	21		
Bob Scarpitto	WR	5'11"	190	29		6
Bobby Nichols	TE	6'2"	220	24		
Jim Whalen	TE	6'2"	210	24		42
Terry Swanson	K	6'	210	23		

BUFFALO BILLS 1-12-1 Joe Collier

Scores of Each Game		
7	BOSTON	16
6	OAKLAND	48
23	Cincinnati	34
37	NEW YORK	35
7	KANSAS CITY	18
14	Miami	14
6	Boston	23
7	HOUSTON	30
21	New York	25
17	MIAMI	21
6	SAN DIEGO	21
32	Denver	34
10	Oakland	13
6	Houston	35

Use Name	Pos.	Hgt	Wgt	Age	Int	Pts
Stew Barber	OT	6'3"	248	29		
Dick Cunningham	OT	6'2"	244	23		
Ray Rissmiller	OT	6'4"	250	26		
Mike McBath	DE-OT	6'4"	248	22		
George Flint	OG	6'4"	240	30		
Bob Kalsu	OG	6'3"	235	23		
Billy Shaw	OG	6'3"	252	28		
Al Bemiller	C	6'3"	243	29		
Jack Frantz	C	6'3"	230	21		
Tom Day	DE	6'2"	265	33		
Ron McDole	DE	6'3"	270	28	2	
Howard Kindig	C-DE	6'6"	264	27		
Jim Dunaway	DT	6'4"	282	26		
Tom Sestak	DT	6'5"	262	32		
Bob Tatarek	DT	6'4"	255	22		
Edgar Chandler	LB	6'3"	222	22		
Paul Guidry	LB	6'3"	228	24	1	
Harry Jacobs	LB	6'2"	226	31		
Paul Maguire	LB	6'	228	30		
Marty Schottenheimer	LB	6'3"	224	25	1	
Mike Stratton	LB	6'3"	230	26	1	
Butch Byrd	DB	6'	196	26	6	6
Hagood Clarke	DB	6'	192	26		6
Booker Edgerson	DB	5'10"	183	29	4	12
Tom Janik	DB	6'3"	195	27	3	6
Jerry Lawson	DB	5'11"	192	23		
John Pitts	DB	6'4"	215	23	2	
George Saimes	DB	5'10"	185	26	2	
Charlie Brown	HB-DB	6'1"	195	25		
Dan Darragh	QB	6'3"	196	21		
Tom Flores	QB	6'1"	202	31		
Benny Russell	QB	6'1"	190	24		
Kay Stephenson	QB	6'1"	210	23		
Ed Rutkowski	WR-QB	6'1"	200	27		6
Max Anderson	HB	5'8"	180	23		18
Gary McDermott	HB	6'1"	211	22		26
Charley Mitchell	HB	5'11"	185	28		
Ben Gregory	FB-HB	6'3"	220	21		6
Bob Cappadonna	FB	6'1"	230	24		20
Wayne Patrick	FB	6'2"	225	22		
Keith Lincoln (to SD)	HB-FB	6'2"	216	29		
Bobby Crockett	WR	6'	200	25		
Elbert Dubenion	WR	6'	187	33		
Monte Ledbetter	WR	6'2"	185	25		6
Haven Moses	WR	6'3"	200	22		12
Richard Trapp	WR	6'1"	174	21		
Bill Masters	TE	6'5"	225	24		
Paul Costa	OT-TE	6'4"	248	26		12
Bruce Alford	K	6'	185	23		57
Mike Mercer (to GB-N)	K	6'	217	32		4

Jack Kemp – Knee Injury
Joe O'Donnell – Knee Injury
Charley Ferguson – Injury

NEW YORK JETS

RUSHING
Last Name	No.	Yds	Avg	TD
Snell	179	747	4.2	6
Boozer	143	441	3.1	5
Mathis	74	208	2.8	5
Joe	42	186	4.4	3
Sauer	2	21	10.5	0
Smolinski	12	15	1.3	0
Namath	5	11	2.2	2
Parilli	7	-2	-0.3	1
Johnson	2	-6	-3.0	0
Rademacher	1	-13	-13.0	0

RECEIVING
Last Name	No.	Yds	Avg	TD
Sauer	66	1141	17	3
Maynard	57	1297	23	10
Lammons	32	400	13	3
Snell	16	105	7	1
Boozer	12	101	8	0
B. Turner	10	241	24	2
Mathis	9	149	17	1
Smolinski	6	40	7	0
Johnson	5	78	16	0
Joe	2	11	6	0
Rademacher	2	11	6	0

PUNT RETURNS
Last Name	No.	Yds	Avg	TD
Christy	13	116	9	0
Baird	18	111	6	0
Richards	4	57	14	0
Philbin	1	2	2	0

KICKOFF RETURNS
Last Name	No.	Yds	Avg	TD
Christy	25	599	24	0
B. Turner	14	319	23	0
D'Amato	1	32	32	0
Snell	3	28	9	0
Smolinski	1	17	17	0
Rademacher	1	0	0	0

PASSING – PUNTING – KICKING
PASSING

Last Name	Att	Comp	%	Yds	Yd/Att	TD	Int-%		RK
Namath	380	187	49	3147	8.3	15	17—	4	3
Parilli	55	29	53	401	7.3	5	2—	4	
Snell	1	1	100	26	26.0	0	0—	0	

PUNTING

Last Name	No	Avg
Johnson	68	43.8

KICKING

Last Name	XP	Att	%	FG	Att	%
J. Turner	43	43	100	34	46	74

2 POINT XP
Mathis

HOUSTON OILERS

RUSHING
Last Name	No.	Yds	Avg	TD
Granger	202	848	4.2	7
Campbell	115	436	3.8	6
Blanks	63	169	2.7	0
Hopkins	31	104	3.4	0
Davis	15	91	6.1	1
Beathard	18	79	4.4	2
Trull	14	47	3.4	0
Norton	1	20	20.0	0
Haik	2	7	3.5	0
Beirne	1	3	3.0	0

RECEIVING
Last Name	No.	Yds	Avg	TD
Reed	46	747	16	5
Haik	32	584	18	8
Beirne	31	474	15	4
Granger	26	361	14	0
Campbell	21	234	11	0
Blanks	13	184	14	0
Frazier	9	123	14	0
Taylor	6	90	15	0
Hopkins	4	40	10	0
Burrell	2	35	18	0
Wittenborn	1	-8	-8	0

PUNT RETURNS
Last Name	No.	Yds	Avg	TD
Carwell	27	227	8	0
Blanks	22	179	8	0
Burrell	2	26	13	0
Moore	1	11	11	0

KICKOFF RETURNS
Last Name	No.	Yds	Avg	TD
Moore	32	787	25	0
Carwell	15	335	22	0
Burrell	2	70	35	0
Hopkins	1	21	21	0
Houston	1	13	13	0
Robertson	2	9	5	0

PASSING – PUNTING – KICKING
PASSING

Last Name	Att	Comp	%	Yds	Yd/Att	TD	Int-%		RK
Beathard	223	105	47	1559	7.0	7	16—	7	4
Trull	105	53	50	864	8.2	10	3—	3	
Davis	86	33	38	441	5.1	0	6—	7	

PUNTING

Last Name	No	Avg
Norton	73	41.2

KICKING

Last Name	XP	Att	%	FG	Att	%
Walker	26	26	100	8	16	50
Wittenborn	11	11	100	4	13	31

MIAMI DOLPHINS

RUSHING
Last Name	No.	Yds	Avg	TD
Kiick	165	621	3.8	4
Csonka	138	540	3.9	6
Griese	42	230	5.5	1
Mitchell	54	176	3.3	1
Milton	2	46	23.0	0
Seiple	5	42	8.4	0
Price	5	27	5.4	0
Tucker	4	13	3.3	0
Norton	1	9	9.0	0
Hammond	1	0	0.0	0

RECEIVING
Last Name	No.	Yds	Avg	TD
Noonan	58	760	13	11
Kiick	44	422	10	0
Twilley	39	604	15	1
Moreau	27	365	14	3
Cox	11	147	13	0
Csonka	11	118	11	1
Milton	9	143	16	1
Mitchell	8	190	24	3
Seiple	7	69	10	1
Darnall	2	25	13	0

PUNT RETURNS
Last Name	No.	Yds	Avg	TD
Neff	8	71	9	0
Milton	6	55	9	0
Tucker	5	40	8	0
Anderson	5	18	4	0
Washington	1	15	15	0
Harper	1	7	7	0
Warren	2	-1	-1	0

KICKOFF RETURNS
Last Name	No.	Yds	Avg	TD
Milton	18	408	23	0
Warren	10	227	23	0
Neff	5	190	38	0
Anderson	6	106	18	0
Tucker	3	54	18	0
Kiick	1	28	28	0
Price	1	22	22	0
Harper	1	18	18	0
Urbanek	2	15	8	0
Richardson	1	1	1	0
Woodson	1	0	0	0
Cox	0	41	0	0

PASSING – PUNTING – KICKING
PASSING

Last Name	Att	Comp	%	Yds	Yd/Att	TD	Int-%		RK
Griese	355	186	52	2473	7.0	21	16—	5	4
Norton	41	17	41	254	6.2	0	4—	10	
Hammond	26	13	50	116	4.5	0	2—	8	
Kiick	1	0	0	0	0.0	0	0—	0	

PUNTING

Last Name	No	Avg
Seiple	75	40.6

KICKING

Last Name	XP	Att	%	FG	Att	%
Keyes	30	30	100	7	16	44
Moreau	6	6	100	1	3	33

BOSTON PATRIOTS

RUSHING
Last Name	No.	Yds	Avg	TD
Nance	177	593	3.4	4
Gamble	78	311	4.0	1
Thomas	88	215	2.4	2
Garron	36	97	2.7	1
Sherman	25	80	3.2	0
Taliaferro	8	51	6.4	0
Marsh	4	8	2.0	0
P. Johnson	2	6	3.0	0
Cappelletti	1	2	2.0	0
Whalen	1	0	0.0	0
Corcoran	1	-1	-1.0	0

RECEIVING
Last Name	No.	Yds	Avg	TD
Whalen	47	718	15	7
Marsh	19	331	17	4
Murphy	18	268	15	0
Graham	16	242	15	1
Nance	14	51	4	0
Cappelletti	13	182	14	2
Gamble	11	55	5	1
Thomas	10	85	9	0
Colclough	8	136	17	0
Scarpitto	2	49	25	1
Garron	1	4	4	0
J. Canale	1	0	0	0

PUNT RETURNS
Last Name	No.	Yds	Avg	TD
Porter	22	135	6	0
B. Johnson	10	34	3	0
Leo	2	12	6	0
Graham	2	11	6	0
D. Johnson	1	5	5	0

KICKOFF RETURNS
Last Name	No.	Yds	Avg	TD
Porter	36	812	23	0
B. Johnson	22	442	20	0
Marsh	4	74	19	0
D. Johnson	3	63	21	0
Thomas	1	22	22	0
Long	2	20	10	0
Graham	1	9	9	0
Cheyunski	1	0	0	0
Gamble	1	0	0	0

PASSING – PUNTING – KICKING
PASSING

Last Name	Att	Comp	%	Yds	Yd/Att	TD	Int-%		RK
Sherman	226	90	40	1199	5.3	12	16—	7	9
Taliaferro	176	67	38	889	5.1	4	15—	9	11
Corcoran	7	3	43	33	4.7	0	2—	29	

PUNTING

Last Name	No	Avg
Swanson	62	39.5
Scarpitto	34	40.6

KICKING

Last Name	XP	Att	%	FG	Att	%
Cappelletti	26	26	100	15	27	56

BUFFALO BILLS

RUSHING
Last Name	No.	Yds	Avg	TD
Anderson	147	525	3.6	2
Gregory	52	283	5.4	1
Cappadona	73	272	3.7	1
McDermott	47	102	2.2	3
Rutkowski	20	96	4.8	1
Lincoln	26	84	3.2	0
Masters	6	70	11.7	0
Brown	3	39	13.0	0
Stephenson	4	30	7.5	0
Costa	2	11	5.5	1
Darragh	13	11	0.8	0
Maguire	1	6	6.0	0
Patrick	1	2	2.0	0
Moses	5	-4	-0.8	0

RECEIVING
Last Name	No.	Yds	Avg	TD
Moses	42	633	15	2
Trapp	24	235	10	0
Anderson	22	140	6	0
McDermott	20	115	6	1
Cappadona	18	92	5	2
Costa	15	172	11	1
Masters	8	101	13	0
Crockett	6	76	13	0
Gregory	5	21	4	0
Ledbetter	4	94	24	1
Rutkowski	1	27	27	0
Patrick	1	5	5	0
Lincoln	1	3	3	0
Bemiller	1	0	0	0

PUNT RETURNS
Last Name	No.	Yds	Avg	TD
Clarke	29	241	8	1
Trapp	5	26	5	0
Rutkowski	8	23	3	0
Byrd	2	11	6	0

KICKOFF RETURNS
Last Name	No.	Yds	Avg	TD
Anderson	39	971	25	1
Brown	12	274	23	0
Mitchell	5	98	20	0
Rutkowski	5	87	17	0
Costa	5	68	14	0
Lincoln	2	37	19	0
McDermott	1	16	16	0
Maguire	1	5	5	0
Barber	1	0	0	0
Ledbetter	0	18	0	0

PASSING – PUNTING – KICKING
PASSING

Last Name	Att	Comp	%	Yds	Yd/Att	TD	Int-%		RK
Darragh	215	92	43	917	4.3	3	14—	7	10
Rutkowski	100	41	41	380	3.8	0	6—	6	
Stephenson	79	29	37	364	4.6	4	7—	9	
Flores	5	3	60	15	3.0	0	1—	20	
McDermott	3	2	67	35	11.7	0	0—	0	
Russell	2	1	50	3	1.5	0	0—	0	
Anderson	1	0	0	0	0.0	0	0—	0	

PUNTING

Last Name	No	Avg
Maguire	100	41.8

KICKING

Last Name	XP	Att	%	FG	Att	%
Alford	15	15	100	14	24	58
Mercer	4	4	100	0	4	0

2 POINT XP
Cappadona
McDermott

OAKLAND RAIDERS 12-2-0 Johnny Rauch

Scores of Each Game		
48	Buffalo	6
47	Miami	21
24	Houston	15
41	BOSTON	10
14	SAN DIEGO	23
10	Kansas City	24
31	CINCINNATI	10
38	KANSAS CITY	21
43	Denver	7
43	NEW YORK	32
34	Cincinnati	0
13	BUFFALO	10
33	DENVER	27
34	San Diego	27
	Playoff	
41	KANSAS CITY	6

Use Name	Pos.	Hgt	Wgt	Age	Int	Pts
Harry Schuh	OT	6'2"	260	25		
Art Shell	OT	6'5"	255	21		
Bob Svihus	OT	6'4"	245	25		
Jim Harvey	OG-OT	6'5"	245	25		
Wayne Hawkins	OG	6'	240	30		
Bob Kruse	OG	6'2"	250	26		
Gene Upshaw	OG	6'5"	255	23		
Jim Otto	C	6'2"	248	30		
Ben Davidson	DE	6'8"	275	28		
Ike Lassiter	DE	6'5"	270	27		
Carleton Oats	DE	6'2"	260	25		
Dan Birdwell	DT	6'4"	250	27		
Al Dotson	DT	6'4"	260	25		
Karl Rubke	C-DT	6'4"	234	32		
Tom Keating – Foot Injury						
Bill Laskey – Foot Injury						
Duane Benson	LB	6'2"	215	23		
Bill Budness	LB	6'1"	215	25		
Dan Conners	LB	6'1"	230	26	2	
Bill Fairband	LB	6'3"	228	22		
Jerry Hopkins	LB	6'2"	238	27		
Dave Ogas	LB	6'3"	240	22		
Chip Oliver	LB	6'2"	220	22		
Gus Otto	LB	6'2"	220	25		
Butch Atkinson	DB	6'	180	21	4	18
Rodger Bird	DB	5'11"	195	25	3	6
Willie Brown	DB	6'1"	190	27	2	6
Dave Grayson	DB	5'10"	185	29	10	6
Kent McCloughan	DB	6'1"	190	25	1	
Warren Powers	DB	6'	190	27	1	
Howie Williams	DB	6'2"	190	31	2	
Nemiah Wilson	DB	6'	165	25		
George Blanda	QB	6'1"	215	40		117
Cotton Davidson	QB	6'1"	180	36		
Daryle Lamonica	QB	6'2"	215	27		6
Pete Banaszak	HB	5'11"	200	24		30
Preston Ridlehuber	HB	6'2"	215	24		6
Charlie Smith	HB	6'1"	205	22		42
Larry Todd	HB	6'1"	185	25		12
Hewritt Dixon	FB	6'2"	230	28		26
Roger Hagberg	FB	6'2"	215	29		12
Fred Biletnikoff	WR	6'1"	190	25		42
Eldridge Dickey	WR	6'2"	198	22		
John Eason	WR	6'2"	220	23		
Bill Miller	WR	6'	190	26		6
John Roderick	WR	6'1"	180	24		
Warren Wells	WR	6'1"	190	25		72
Billy Cannon	TE	6'1"	215	31		36
Dave Kocourek	TE	6'5"	235	31		6
Mike Eischeid	K	6'	190	27		

KANSAS CITY CHIEFS 12-2-0 Hank Stram

Scores of Each Game		
26	Houston	21
19	NEW YORK	20
34	DENVER	2
48	Miami	3
18	Buffalo	7
13	CINCINNATI	3
24	OAKLAND	10
27	SAN DIEGO	20
21	Oakland	38
16	Cincinnati	9
31	BOSTON	17
24	HOUSTON	10
40	San Diego	3
30	Denver	7
	Playoff	
6	Oakland	41

Use Name	Pos.	Hgt	Wgt	Age	Int	Pts
Dave Hill	OT	6'5"	260	27		
Jim Tyrer	OT	6'6"	275	29		
Ed Budde	OG	6'5"	260	27		
George Daney	OG	6'3"	240	32		
Curt Merz	OG	6'4"	267	30		
Mo Moorman	OG	6'5"	252	24		
E. J. Holub	C	6'4"	236	30		
Aaron Brown	DE	6'5"	265	24		
Jerry Mays	DE	6'4"	252	28		
Remi Prudhomme	DT-DE	6'4"	250	26		
Buck Buchanan	DT	6'7"	287	28	1	2
Ernie Ladd	DT	6'9"	290	29	1	
Ed Lothamer	DT	6'5"	270	25		
Curley Culp	OG-DT	6'1"	265	22		
Bud Abell	LB	6'3"	220	27	2	
Bobby Bell	LB	6'4"	228	28	5	
Chuck Hurston	LB	6'6"	240	25		
Willie Lanier	LB	6'1"	245	23	4	6
Jim Lynch	LB	6'1"	235	23	3	6
Dave Martin	LB	6'	215	21		
Caesar Belser	DB	6'	212	23		
Jim Kearney	DB	6'2"	206	25	3	
Willie Mitchell	DB	6'1"	185	26	5	
Johnny Robinson	DB	6'	205	29	6	
Goldie Sellers	DB	6'2"	198	26	3	6
Emmitt Thomas	DB	6'2"	192	25	4	
Gene Trosch – Injury						
Len Dawson	QB	6'	190	34		
Jacky Lee	QB	6'1"	185	29		
Mike Livingston	QB	6'3"	205	22		
Bert Coan	HB	6'4"	220	28		6
Mike Garrett	HB	5'9"	200	24		36
Paul Lowe (from SD)	HB	6'	205	31		
Wendell Hayes	FB-HB	6'2"	220	27		30
Robert Holmes	FB	5'9"	220	22		42
Curtis McClinton	FB	6'3"	227	30		
Jack Gehrke	WR	6'	178	22		
Sam Longmire	WR	6'3"	195	25		
Frank Pitts	WR	6'2"	200	24		36
Gloster Richardson	WR	6'	200	25		36
Noland Smith	WR	5'6"	154	24		6
Otis Taylor	WR	6'2"	215	25		30
Fred Arbanas	TE	6'3"	240	29		
Reg Carolan	TE	6'6"	240	28		
Jan Stenerud	K	6'2"	187	25		129
Jerrel Wilson	K	6'4"	222	27		

SAN DIEGO CHARGERS 9-5-0 Sid Gillman

Scores of Each Game		
29	CINCINNATI	13
30	HOUSTON	14
31	Cincinnati	10
20	New York	23
23	Oakland	14
55	DENVER	24
20	Kansas City	27
34	MIAMI	28
27	Boston	17
21	Buffalo	6
15	NEW YORK	37
47	Denver	23
3	KANSAS CITY	40
27	OAKLAND	34

Use Name	Pos.	Hgt	Wgt	Age	Int	Pts
Harold Akin	OT	6'5"	260	23		
Ron Mix	OT	6'4"	250	30		
Terry Owens	OT	6'6"	270	24		
Bob Wells	OT	6'4"	270	23		
Gary Kirner	OG	6'3"	255	26		
Larry Little	OG	6'1"	270	22		
Jim Schmedding	OG	6'2"	250	22		
Walt Sweeney	OG	6'3"	260	27		
Sam Gruneisen	C	6'1"	250	27		
Paul Latzke	C	6'4"	240	26		
Bill Lenkaitis	C	6'3"	250	22		
Marty Baccaglio (to CIN)	DE	6'3"	245	23		
Steve DeLong	DE	6'3"	252	25		
Houston Ridge	DE	6'4"	245	24		
Ron Billingsley	DT-DE	6'8"	265	23		
Scott Appleton	DT	6'3"	260	26		
Bob Briggs	DT	6'4"	270	23		
Russ Washington	DT	6'6"	290	21		
Chuck Allen	LB	6'1"	225	28	1	
Bernie Erickson (to CIN)	LB	6'2"	240	23		
Tom Erlandson	LB	6'3"	220	28	2	
Jim Fetherston	LB	6'2"	225	23	1	
Curtis Jones	LB	6'2"	245	25		
Ron McCall	LB	6'2"	245	23		
Bob Mitinger	LB	6'2"	230	28		
Bob Print	LB	6'	220	24		
Rick Redman	LB	5'11"	225	25		
Jeff Staggs	LB	6'2"	240	24	2	
Joe Beauchamp	DB	6'	185	24	5	12
Speedy Duncan	DB	5'10"	175	25	1	6
Dick Farley	DB	6'	185	22		
Kenny Graham	DB	6'	205	26	5	
Bob Howard	DB	6'1"	190	23	1	
Dick Speights	DB	5'11"	175	22		
Jim Tolbert	DB	6'3"	207	24	2	
Bud Whitehead	DB	6'	185	29		
Ken Dyer	WR-DB	6'3"	185	22		6
Jon Brittenum	QB	6'	185	24		
John Hadl	QB	6'2"	215	28		12
Dickie Post	HB	5'9"	190	22		18
Russ Smith	HB	6'1"	209	24		24
Jim Allison	FB	6'	215	25		
Gene Foster	FB	5'11"	220	25		6
Brad Hubbert	FB	6'1"	227	27		12
Gerry McDougall	FB	6'2"	225	33		
Lance Alworth	WR	6'	180	28		62
Lane Fenner	WR	6'5"	210	23		
Gary Garrison	WR	6'1"	195	24		60
Phil Tuckett	WR	6'	180	23		
Willie Frazier	TE	6'4"	235	25		18
Jacque MacKinnon	TE	6'4"	240	29		38
Andre White (from CIN)	TE	6'5"	225	23		
Dennis Partee	K	6'2"	208	22		106

DENVER BRONCOS 5-9-0 Lou Saban

Scores of Each Game		
10	Cincinnati	24
2	Kansas City	34
17	BOSTON	20
10	CINCINNATI	7
21	New York	13
24	San Diego	55
21	MIAMI	14
35	Boston	14
7	OAKLAND	43
17	Houston	38
34	BUFFALO	32
23	SAN DIEGO	47
27	Oakland	33
7	KANSAS CITY	30

Use Name	Pos.	Hgt	Wgt	Age	Int	Pts
Sam Brunelli	OT	6'1"	270	25		
Tom Cichowski	OT	6'4"	250	24		
Mike Current	OT	6'4"	260	22		
Wallace Dickey	OT	6'3"	260	27		
George Gaiser	OT	6'4"	255	23		
George Goeddeke	OG	6'3"	245	23		
Buzz Highsmith	OG	6'4"	230	25		
Bob Vaughn	OG	6'4"	240	23		
Bob Young	OG	6'2"	260	25		
Jay Bachman	C	6'3"	250	22		
Larry Kaminski	C	6'2"	245	23		
Pete Duranko	DE	6'2"	252	24		
Rich Jackson	DE	6'2"	255	27		
Paul Smith	DE	6'3"	245	23		
Dave Costa	DT	6'2"	265	26		
Larry Cox	DT	6'2"	250	24		
Jerry Inman	DT	6'3"	255	28		
Rex Mirich	DT	6'4"	250	27		
Carl Cunningham	LB	6'3"	240	24	1	
Fred Forsberg	LB	6'1"	235	24	1	
John Huard	LB	6'	220	24	2	
Gordon Lambert	LB	6'5"	245	23		
Frank Richter	LB	6'3"	230	23		
Dave Tobey	LB	6'3"	230	25		
Chip Myrtle	TE-LB	6'2"	225	23		2
Drake Garrett	DB	5'9"	183	23	2	
Charlie Greer	DB	6'	205	22	4	
Gus Holloman	DB	6'3"	195	22	1	
Pete Jaquess	DB	6'	182	26	5	
Jack Lentz	DB	6'	195	23	1	
Hal Lewis	DB	6'2"	188	25		
Tommy Luke	DB	6'	190	26		
Alex Moore	DB	6'	195	23		
Tom Oberg	DB	6'	185	23	3	
Jesse Stokes	DB	6'	190	24		
Marlin Briscoe	QB	5'10"	177	22		18
Joe DiVito	QB	6'2"	205	22		
Jim LeClair	QB	6'1"	208	24		
John McCormick	QB	6'1"	190	31		
Steve Tensi	QB	6'5"	215	25		
Terry Erwin	HB	6'	190	21		
Hub Lindsey	HB	5'11"	196	22		
Floyd Little	HB	5'10"	195	26		30
Fran Lynch	HB	6'1"	194	22		24
Garrett Ford	FB	6'2"	230	22		6
Brendan McCarthy (from ATL-N)	FB	6'3"	220	23		12
Eric Crabtree	WR	5'11"	182	23		30
Al Denson	WR	6'2"	208	26		30
Mike Haffner	WR	6'2"	205	26		6
Jim Jones	WR	6'2"	195	24		12
Bobby Moten	WR	6'4"	212	25		
Bill Van Heusen	WR	6'1"	200	22		18
Tom Beer	TE	6'4"	230	23		6
Dave Washington	TE	6'4"	228	27		
Bobby Howfield	K	5'9"	180	31		57
Bob Humphreys	K	6'1"	240	28		4

CINCINNATI BENGALS 3-11-0 Paul Brown

Scores of Each Game		
13	San Diego	29
24	DENVER	10
34	BUFFALO	23
10	SAN DIEGO	31
7	Denver	10
3	Kansas City	13
22	MIAMI	24
10	Oakland	31
17	HOUSTON	27
9	KANSAS CITY	16
38	Miami	21
0	OAKLAND	34
14	Boston	33
14	New York	27

Use Name	Pos.	Hgt	Wgt	Age	Int	Pts
Howard Fest	OT	6'6"	265	22		
Bob Kelly	OT	6'3"	270	28		
Ernie Wright	OT	6'4"	270	28		
Dan Archer	OG-OT	6'5"	245	23		
Pat Matson	OG	6'1"	245	24		
Dave Middendorf	OG	6'3"	260	22		
Pete Perreault	OG	6'3"	248	29		
Bob Johnson	C	6'5"	260	22		
John Matlock	OT-C	6'4"	255	23		
Jim Griffin	DE	6'3"	265	26		6
Harry Gunner	DE	6'6"	250	23	1	2
Willie Jones	DE	6'2"	260	26		
Dennis Randall	DE	6'6"	240	22		
Steve Chomyszak	DT	6'5"	280	23		
Bill Kindricks	DT	6'3"	268	22		
Andy Rice	DT	6'3"	268	26		
Bill Staley	DT	6'3"	250	21		
Al Beauchamp	LB	6'2"	236	24	2	6
Danny Brabham	LB	6'4"	233	27		
Frank Buncom	LB	6'1"	245	28		
Paul Elzey	LB	6'3"	235	22		
Sherrill Headrick	LB	6'2"	240	31	1	
Mike Hibler	LB	6'1"	235	22		
Wayne McClure	LB	6'1"	225	22		
John Neidert (to NY)	LB	6'2"	230	22		
Curt Frazier	DB	5'11"	193	23		
White Graves	DB	6'	185	25		
Rex Keeling	DB	6'3"	220	24		
Charlie King	DB	6'	184	25	1	6
Bill Scott	DB	6'	188	24		
Fletcher Smith	DB	6'2"	178	24	1	
Phil Spiller (from ATL-N)	DB	6'	195	23		
Bobby Hunt	HB-DB	6'1"	190	28	1	6
Jess Phillips	HB-DB	6'1"	205	21	3	
John Stofa	QB	6'3"	210	26		
Dewey Warren	QB	6'	205	23		
Sam Wyche	QB	6'4"	210	23		
Essex Johnson	HB	5'9"	190	21		18
Paul Robinson	HB	6'	200	23		54
Ted Washington	HB	5'11"	210	22		
Estes Banks	FB	6'1"	220	23		6
Ron Lamb (from DEN)	FB	6'2"	225	24		
Tom Smiley	FB	6'1"	235	24		6
Saint Saffold	WR	6'4"	202	24		
Rod Sherman	WR	6'	190	23		10
Monk Williams	WR	5'7"	155	23		
Warren McVea	HB-WR	5'10"	182	22		18
Ken Herock	TE	6'2"	230	27		
Bill Peterson	TE	6'3"	230	23		
Bob Trumpy	WR-TE	6'6"	220	23		18
Dale Livingston	K	6'	210	23		59

OAKLAND RAIDERS

Rushing
Last Name	No.	Yds	Avg	TD
Dixon	206	865	4.2	2
Smith	95	504	3.6	5
Banaszak	91	362	4.0	4
Hagberg	39	164	4.2	1
Lamonica	19	98	5.2	1
Todd	13	89	6.8	2
Eischeid	2	41	20.5	0
Wells	2	38	19.0	1
Ridlehuber	4	7	1.8	0

Receiving
Last Name	No.	Yds	Avg	TD
Biletnikoff	61	1037	17	6
Wells	53	1137	21	11
Dixon	38	360	9	2
Cannon	23	360	16	6
Smith	22	321	15	2
Banaszak	15	182	12	1
Miller	9	176	20	1
Hagberg	8	78	10	1
Todd	4	40	10	0
Kocourek	3	46	15	1
Dickey	1	34	34	0

Punt Returns
Last Name	No.	Yds	Avg	TD
Atkinson	36	490	14	2
Bird	11	128	12	0
Dickey	6	48	8	0
Shell	1	0	0	0
Wilson	1	0	0	0

Kickoff Returns
Last Name	No.	Yds	Avg	TD
Atkinson	32	802	25	0
Smith	8	167	21	0
Wilson	4	84	21	0
Hagberg	1	21	21	0
Dickey	1	17	17	0
Kruse	1	1	1	0
Hopkins	1	0	0	0
G. Otto	1	0	0	0

Passing – Punting – Kicking
PASSING	Att	Comp	%	Yds	Yd/Att	TD	Int–%	RK
Lamonica	416	206	50	3245	7.8	25	15– 4	2
Blanda	49	30	61	522	10.7	6	2– 4	
C. Davidson	2	1	50	4	2.0	0	0– 0	
Banaszak	1	0	0	0	0.0	0	1–100	

PUNTING	No	Avg
Eischeid	64	43.6

KICKING	XP	Att	%	FG	Att	%
Blanda	54	54	100	21	34	62

2 POINT XP
Dixon

KANSAS CITY CHIEFS

Rushing
Last Name	No.	Yds	Avg	TD
Holmes	174	866	5.0	7
Garrett	164	564	3.4	3
Hayes	85	340	4.0	4
Coan	40	160	4.0	1
McClinton	24	107	4.5	0
Pitts	11	107	9.7	0
Taylor	5	41	8.2	1
Dawson	20	40	2.0	0
Arbanas	3	14	4.7	0
Livingston	2	2	1.0	0
Wilson	5	1	0.2	0
Lowe	2	-1	-0.5	0
Smith	2	-2	-1.0	0
Richardson	1	-3	-3.0	0

Receiving
Last Name	No.	Yds	Avg	TD
Garrett	33	359	11	3
Pitts	30	655	22	6
Richardson	22	494	22	6
Taylor	20	420	21	4
Holmes	19	201	11	0
Hayes	12	108	9	1
Arbanas	11	189	17	0
McClinton	3	-4	-1	0
Carolan	2	26	13	0
Coan	2	15	8	0
Smith	1	15	15	0
Wilson	1	14	14	0

Punt Returns
Last Name	No.	Yds	Avg	TD
Smith	18	270	15	1
Sellers	7	129	18	1
Robinson	2	26	13	0
Mitchell	1	21	21	0
Garrett	2	4	2	0
Belser	1	0	0	0

Kickoff Returns
Last Name	No.	Yds	Avg	TD
Smith	23	549	24	0
Coan	5	100	20	0
Sellers	2	40	20	0
Belser	4	38	10	0
Kearney	1	9	9	0
Abell	1	0	0	0
Daney	1	0	0	0
Prudhomme	1	0	0	0

Passing – Punting – Kicking
PASSING	Att	Comp	%	Yds	Yd/Att	TD	Int–%	RK
Dawson	224	131	59	2109	9.4	17	9– 4	1
Lee	45	25	56	383	8.5	3	1– 2	
Garrett	1	0	0	0	0.0	0	1–100	

PUNTING	No	Avg
Wilson	63	45.1
Carolan	2	50.5

KICKING	XP	Att	%	FG	Att	%
Stenerud	39	40	98	30	40	75

SAN DIEGO CHARGERS

Rushing
Last Name	No.	Yds	Avg	TD
Post	151	758	5.0	3
Smith	88	426	4.8	4
Foster	109	394	3.6	1
Hubbert	28	119	4.3	2
Allison	23	31	1.3	0
Alworth	3	18	6.0	0
Hadl	23	14	0.6	2
Brittenum	2	-4	-2.0	0

Receiving
Last Name	No.	Yds	Avg	TD
Alworth	68	1312	19	10
Garrison	52	1103	21	10
MacKinnon	33	646	20	6
Foster	23	224	10	0
Post	18	165	9	0
Frazier	16	237	15	3
Smith	7	71	10	0
Hubbert	5	11	2	0
Allison	2	22	11	0
White	2	18	9	0
Dyer	1	22	22	0

Punt Returns
Last Name	No.	Yds	Avg	TD
Duncan	18	206	11	1
Graham	13	61	5	0
Smith	8	25	3	0

Kickoff Returns
Last Name	No.	Yds	Avg	TD
Duncan	25	586	23	0
Post	10	199	20	0
Allison	7	121	17	0
Whitehead	2	81	41	0
Speights	1	21	21	0
Smith	1	20	20	0
Baccaglio	2	0	0	0
Latzke	1	0	0	0

Passing – Punting – Kicking
PASSING	Att	Comp	%	Yds	Yd/Att	TD	Int–%	RK
Hadl	440	208	47	3473	7.9	27	32– 7	5
Brittenum	17	9	53	125	7.4	1	1– 6	
Foster	7	6	86	169	24.1	0	0– 0	
Post	4	1	25	23	5.8	0	0– 0	
Smith	3	0	0	0	0.0	1	0– 0	
Allison	1	1	100	23	23.0	1	0– 0	

PUNTING	No	Avg
Partee	56	40.7

KICKING	XP	Att	%	FG	Att	%
Partee	40	43	93	22	32	69

2 POINT XP
Alworth
MacKinnon

DENVER BRONCOS

Rushing
Last Name	No.	Yds	Avg	TD
Little	158	584	3.7	3
Briscoe	41	308	7.5	3
Lynch	66	221	3.3	4
Ford	41	186	4.5	1
McCarthy	28	89	3.2	0
Erwin	24	76	3.2	0
LeClair	12	40	3.3	0
Moore	4	22	5.5	0
Lindsey	4	17	4.3	0
Van Heusen	1	6	6.0	0
Tensi	6	2	0.3	0
Haffner	2	2	1.0	0
DiVito	1	-1	-1.0	0
Jones	1	-1	-1.0	0

Receiving
Last Name	No.	Yds	Avg	TD
Crabtree	35	601	17	5
Denson	34	586	17	5
Beer	20	276	14	1
Van Heusen	19	353	19	3
Little	19	331	17	1
Jones	13	190	15	2
Haffner	12	232	19	1
McCarthy	7	69	10	2
Ford	6	40	7	0
Lynch	4	52	13	0
Moore	3	35	12	0
Erwin	2	21	11	0
Myrtle	1	18	18	0
Washington	1	12	12	0

Punt Returns
Last Name	No.	Yds	Avg	TD
Little	24	261	11	1
Greer	9	53	6	0
Luke	3	13	4	0
Jaquess	2	5	3	0

Kickoff Returns
Last Name	No.	Yds	Avg	TD
Little	26	649	25	0
Holloman	7	194	28	0
Stokes	5	106	21	0
Garrett	3	77	26	0
Moore	4	74	19	0
Lindsey	3	72	24	0
Erwin	3	55	18	0
Greer	2	41	21	0
Luke	2	34	17	0
Crabtree	1	30	30	0
Forsberg	2	16	8	0
Dickey	1	13	13	0
Jaquess	1	0	0	0

Passing – Punting – Kicking
PASSING	Att	Comp	%	Yds	Yd/Att	TD	Int–%	RK
Briscoe	224	93	42	1589	7.1	14	13– 6	7
Tensi	119	48	40	709	6.0	5	8– 7	
LeClair	54	27	50	401	7.4	1	5– 7	
McCormick	19	8	42	89	4.7	0	1– 5	
DiVito	6	1	17	16	2.7	0	0–	
Little	2	0	0	0	0.0	0	0–	
Lynch	2	1	50	4	2.0	0	0–	
Haffner	1	1	100	18	18.0	0	0–	

PUNTING	No	Avg
Van Heusen	88	43.8
DiVito	8	30.3

KICKING	XP	Att	%	FG	Att	%
Howfield	30	30	100	9	18	50
Humphreys	1	1	100	1	5	20

CINCINNATI BENGALS

Rushing
Last Name	No.	Yds	Avg	TD
Robinson	238	1023	4.3	8
E. Johnson	26	178	6.8	3
Smiley	63	146	2.3	1
McVea	9	133	14.8	1
Banks	34	131	3.9	0
Lamp	39	107	2.7	0
Wyche	12	74	6.2	0
Saffold	1	21	21.0	0
Warren	4	17	4.3	0
Livingston	1	11	11.0	0
Keeling	1	10	10.0	0
Phillips	1	7	7.0	0
Hunt	1	5	5.0	1
Washington	1	4	4.0	0
Sherman	1	3	3.0	0
Stofa	10	1	0.1	0
Trumpy	1	-1	-1.0	0

Receiving
Last Name	No.	Yds	Avg	TD
Trumpy	37	639	17	3
Sherman	31	374	12	1
Robinson	24	128	5	1
McVea	21	264	13	2
Smiley	19	86	5	0
Saffold	16	172	11	0
Lamb	7	87	12	0
Herock	6	75	13	0
Banks	4	15	4	1
E. Johnson	1	33	33	0
Peterson	1	10	10	0
Wyche	1	5	5	0

Punt Returns
Last Name	No.	Yds	Avg	TD
E. Johnson	22	111	5	0
Spiller	2	51	26	0
Phillips	2	16	8	0
Williams	2	14	7	0
King	1	3	3	0
Robinson	1	1	1	0

Kickoff Returns
Last Name	No.	Yds	Avg	TD
McVea	14	310	22	0
E. Johnson	14	266	19	0
Banks	6	106	18	0
Williams	5	112	22	0
Spiller	5	91	18	0
Peterson	3	80	27	0
Robinson	3	58	19	0
Lamb	1	24	24	0
Phillips	1	23	23	0
McClure	1	11	11	0
Randall	1	11	11	0
Neidert	1	0	0	0
Saffold	1	0	0	0

Passing – Punting – Kicking
PASSING	Att	Comp	%	Yds	Yd/Att	TD	Int–%	RK
Stofa	177	85	48	896	5.1	5	5– 3	6
Warren	80	47	59	506	6.3	1	4– 5	
Wyche	55	35	64	494	9.0	2	2– 4	
Keeling	1	0	0	0	0.0	0	0– 0	

PUNTING	No	Avg
Livingston	70	43.4
Smith	8	28.8
Keeling	6	28.3

KICKING	XP	Att	%	FG	Att	%
Livingston	20	20	100	13	26	50
Sherman	4	4	100	0	1	0

1968 Championship Games

NFL CHAMPIONSHIP GAME
December 29, at Cleveland
(Attendance 80,628)

Evening a Past Account

The conference playoffs had produced one expected result and one upset. The Baltimore Colts beat the Minnesota Vikings 24-14 as they had been picked to do, but the Cleveland Browns had surprised the Dallas Cowboys by knocking them off 31-20 in Don Meredith's playing farewell.

The Colts and Browns had met for the NFL title four years ago, with the Browns stunning Baltimore with a 27-0 upset. The Colts again were favored this year, but their stifling defense smothered the Cleveland attack and evened the score from 1964.

The Browns had the first scoring opportunity of the game when Don Cockroft attempted a 41-yard field goal, but Bubba Smith blocked the kick. With Bill Nelsen rushed incessantly and Leroy Kelly hounded every time he touched the ball, the Browns rarely crossed into Baltimore territory all afternoon.

The first period ended without a score, but a Lou Michaels field goal gave Baltimore a 3-0 lead early in the second period. With the Colt blockers beating the Cleveland front four regularly, the Colts put together a sixty-yard, ten-play drive which ended in Tom Matte's plunge into the end zone. When the Browns tried to come back with a pass, Mike Curtis intercepted and gave the ball to his offense on the Cleveland 33. Matte ran for twelve yards on the first play, then Jerry Hill carried for nine, and Matte finally covered the last twelve yards with a dodging run through the Cleveland secondary. The halftime score was 17-0, and the Browns looked like a beaten team.

The Colts stuck to the ground in the second half, eating up yardage and time with Matte and Hill running the ball. A time-consuming drive led to Matte's third touchdown of the day in the third quarter, and ten more points in the final period ran the final score up to 34-0. After this one-sided affair ended a quick survey of the press box uncovered not one writer who gave the New York Jets a chance against the Colts in the Super Bowl.

SCORING

CLEVELAND	0	0	0	0—	0
BALTIMORE	0	17	7	10—	34

Second Quarter
Bal.   Michaels, 28 yard field goal
Bal.   Matte, 1 yard rush
        PAT—Michaels (kick)
Bal.   Matte, 12 yard rush
        PAT—Michaels (kick)

Third Quarter
Bal.   Matte, 2 yard rush
        PAT—Michaels (kick)

Fourth Quarter
Bal.   Michaels, 10 yard field goal
Bal.   Brown, 4 yard run
        PAT—Michaels (Kick)

TEAM STATISTICS

CLE.		BAL.
12	First Downs—Total	22
2	First Downs—Rushing	13
8	First Downs—Passing	8
2	First Downs—Penalty	1
2	Fumbles—Number	2
1	Fumbles—Lost Ball	1
7	Penalties—Number	3
54	Yards Penalized	15
2	Missed Field Goals	0
3	Giveaways	2
2	Takeaways	3
−1	Difference	+1

INDIVIDUAL STATISTICS

CLEVELAND	No	Yds	Avg.	BALTIMORE	No	Yds	Avg.
RUSHING							
Kelly	13	28	2.2	Matte	17	88	5.2
Harraway	6	26	4.3	Hill	11	60	5.5
Green	1	2	2.0	Brown	5	18	3.6
	20	56	2.8	Cole	3	14	4.7
				Mackey	2	4	2.0
				Morrall	1	0	0.0
					39	184	4.7
RECEIVING							
Harraway	4	40	10.0	Richardson	3	78	26.0
Morin	3	41	13.7	Mackey	2	34	17.0
Kelly	3	27	9.0	Orr	2	33	16.5
Warfield	2	30	15.0	Matte	2	15	7.5
Collins	1	13	13.0	Mitchell	1	7	7.0
	13	151	11.6	Cole	1	2	2.0
					11	169	15.4
PUNTING							
Cockroft	5		33.4	Lee	2		37.0
PUNT RETURNS							
Davis	1	4	4.0	Brown	1	0	0.0
KICKOFF RETURNS							
Morrison	3	51	19.0	Pearson	1	21	21.0
Davis	3	40	13.3				
	6	91	15.2				
INTERCEPTION RETURNS							
Davis	1	0	0.0	Volk	1	26	26.0
				Curtis	1	0	0.0
					2	26	13.0

CLEVELAND	Att.	Comp.	Comp. Pct.	Yds.	Int.	Yds/ Att.	Yds/ Comp.	Yards Lost Tackled
PASSING								
Nelsen	26	11	42.3	132	2	5.1	12.0	
Ryan	6	2	33.3	19	0	3.3	8.5	
	32	13	40.6	151	2	4.7	11.6	4—34
BALTIMORE								
Morrall	25	11	44.4	169	1	6.8	15.4	0— 0

AFL CHAMPIONSHIP GAME
December 29, at New York
(Attendance 62,627)

Down and Up, but Never Sideways

After beating the Chiefs in a Western Division playoff, the Oakland Raiders came to New York to face the brash, young New York Jets for the AFL title. Joe Namath came out throwing, and after only 3:39 of the opening period, the Jets had scored on a Namath-to-Don Maynard pass. Jim Turner later added a field goal to give the Jets a 10-0 lead after one quarter. Oakland wide receiver Fred Biletnikoff started getting open in the second quarter, however, and Daryle Lamonica hit him with a touchdown pass early in the period. Before the half ended, Jim Turner and George Blanda each kicked a three-pointer to make the score 13-10 in favor of the Jets.

Early in the second half, Lamonica's long bombs to Biletnikoff and Warren Wells gave the Raiders a first down on the New York 6-yard line. Three plays moved the ball only to the 1-yard line, so Blanda kicked a short field goal to knot the score at 13-13.

Late in the third period it was New York's turn to move. Namath mixed his plays well in driving the Jets 80 yards to a touchdown, with the final 20 yards coming on a pass to tight end Pete Lammons. Turner's kick made the count 20-13 with one period left.

The Raiders struck deep into New York territory early in the quarter, but had to settle for another Blanda field goal. Trailing 20-16, the Raiders turned the game around when George Atkinson picked off a Namath pass and returned it 32 yards to the New York 5. Pete Banaszak scored on the next play to put the Raiders ahead for the first time. Less than a minute later, a 52-yard pass play from Namath to Maynard brought the Jets into striking range of the Oakland end zone, and another pass to Maynard took the ball across the goal line and put New York on top 27-23. The Raiders drove right back into New York territory, but the Jets got the ball by recovering a loose lateral pass which the Raiders thought was an incomplete forward pass. After that, the Jets just hung on for their Super Bowl destiny.

SCORING

NEW YORK	10	3	7	7—	27
OAKLAND	0	10	3	10—	23

First Quarter
N.Y.   Maynard, 14 yard pass from Namath
        PAT—J. Turner (kick)
N.Y.   J. Turner, 33 yard field goal

Second Quarter
Oak.   Biletnikoff, 29 yard pass from Lamonica
        PAT—Blanda (kick)
N.Y.   J. Turner, 36 yard field goal
Oak.   Blanda, 26 yard field goal

Third Quarter
Oak.   Blanda, 9 yard field goal
N.Y.   Lammons, 20 yard pass from Namath
        PAT—J. Turner (kick)

Fourth Quarter
Oak.   Blanda, 20 yard field goal
Oak.   Banaszak, 4 yard rush
        PAT—Blanda (kick)
N.Y.   Maynard, 6 yard pass from Namath
        PAT—J. Turner (kick)

TEAM STATISTICS

N.Y.		OAK.
25	First Downs—Total	18
9	First Downs—Rushing	3
15	First Downs—Passing	14
1	First Downs—Penalty	1
1	Fumbles—Number	2
1	Fumbles—Lost Ball	0
4	Penalties—Number	2
26	Yards Penalized	23
1	Missed Field Goals	1
2	Giveaways	0
0	Takeaways	2
−2	Difference	+2

INDIVIDUAL STATISTICS

NEW YORK	No	Yds	Avg.	OAKLAND	No	Yds	Avg.
RUSHING							
Snell	19	71	3.7	Dixon	8	42	5.3
Boozer	11	51	4.6	Banaszak	3	6	2.0
Namath	1	14	14.0	Lamonica	3	1	0.3
Mathis	3	8	2.7	Smith	5	1	0.2
	34	144	4.2		19	50	2.6
RECEIVING							
Sauer	7	70	10.0	Biletnikoff	7	190	11.2
Maynard	6	118	19.7	Dixon	5	48	9.6
Lammons	4	52	13.0	Cannon	4	69	17.3
Snell	1	15	15.0	Wells	3	83	27.7
Boozer	1	11	11.0	Banaszak	1	11	11.0
	19	266	14.0		20	401	20.1
PUNTING							
Johnson	10		41.5	Eischeid	7		42.7
PUNT RETURNS							
Baird	2	8	4.0	Atkinson	2	11	5.5
Christy	1	0	0.0	Bird	2	6	3.0
	3	8	2.7		4	17	4.3
KICKOFF RETURNS							
Christy	3	86	28.7	Atkinson	4	112	28.0
B. Turner	1	24	24.0	Smith	1	17	17.0
	4	110	27.5		5	129	25.8
INTERCEPTION RETURNS							
None				Atkinson	1	32	32.0

NEW YORK	Att.	Comp.	Comp. Pct.	Yds.	Int.	Yds/ Att.	Yds/ Comp.	Yards Lost Tackled
PASSING								
Namath	49	19	38.8	266	1	5.4	14.0	10
OAKLAND								
Lamonica	47	20	42.6	401	0	8.5	20.1	8

The Ironclad Guarantee

When Joe Namath, three days before the game, said, "I think we'll win it; in fact, I'll guarantee it," people snickered. The New York Jets were close to three-touchdown underdogs against the Baltimore Colts, and everyone expected to see the Colts, an establishment NFL team, clobber the long-haired Jets and shut the mouth of their free-spirit quarterback. Coached by Don Shula, the Colts had a feared defense that mixed zone pass coverage and frequent blitzes and a poised offense led by quarterback Earl Morrall, who had substituted spectacularly during the season for the sore-armed Johnny Unitas.

On offense, the Colts did everything in the first half except score. They drove to the New York 20-yard line only to lose the ball on an interception. They recovered a fumble on the New York 12 only to have Lou Michaels miss a close-range field goal. They sprang Tom Matte loose on a 58-yard run only to suffer another interception to kill the drive. The play that typified the Colts' frustration the best came in the second quarter. On a razzle-dazzle play, Earl Morrall handed the ball off, got it back on a lateral, and looked downfield for a receiver. He never noticed Jimmy Orr free in the end zone, so alone that he was jumping up and down

and waving his arms to get attention. Morrall instead threw the ball down the middle right into the arms of New York's Jim Hudson.

The Jets, meanwhile, unexpectedly used the off-tackle smash as their main offensive weapon. With Winston Hill leading the way, fullback Matt Snell repeatedly picked up five and six yards through the right side of the Colt line. Whenever the Colts threw their blitz at Namath, he somehow smelled it out and beat it by shooting a quick pass to George Sauer. Mixing his plays well, Namath led the Jets on an 80-yard drive in twelve plays, with Snell carrying the ball into the end zone from the four-yard line. At halftime, the Jets were ahead 7-0.

The script stayed the same in the second half. The Jets ground out the yardage slowly, scoring on three Jim Turner field goals, while Morrall could not get the Colts on the scoreboard. Johnny Unitas, sore arm and all, took over at quarterback in the final period, and although he drove the Colts to a touchdown, it was too little too late. The Jets had won the Super Bowl 16-7; the AFL had finally triumphed.

Lineups

NEW YORK JETS		BALTIMORE
OFFENSE		
Sauer	LE	Orr
W. Hill	LT	Vogel
Talamini	LG	Ressler
Schmitt	C	Curry
Rasmussen	RG	Sullivan
Herman	RT	Ball
Lammons	TE	Mackey
Namath	QB	Morrall
Maynard	FL	W. Richardson
Boozer	RB	Matte
Snell	RB	J. Hill
DEFENSE		
Philbin	LE	B. Smith
Rochester	LT	B. R. Smith
Elliot	RT	Miller
Biggs	RE	Braase
Baker	LLB	Curtis
Atkinson	MLB	Gaubatz
Grantham	RLB	Shinnick
Sample	LHB	Boyd
Beverly	RHB	Lyles
Hudson	LS	Logan
Baird	FS	Volk

SUBSTITUTES

NEW YORK
Offense
Crane	J. Richardson
Mathis	Smolinski
Parilli	B. Turner
Rademacher	Walton

Defense
Christy	McAdams
D'Amato	Neidert
Dockery	Richards
Gordon	Thompson

Kickers
| Johnson | J. Turner |

BALTIMORE
Offense
Brown	Pearson
Cole	Perkins
Hawkins	Szymanski
Johnson	Unitas
Mitchell	J. Williams

Defense
Austin	Porter
Hilton	Stukes
Michaels	S. Williams

Kicker
Lee

SCORING

NEW YORK JETS	0 7 6	3—16	
BALTIMORE	0 0 0	7— 7	

Second Quarter
N.Y.	Snell, 4 yard rush	5:57
	PAT — Turner (kick)	

Third Quarter
N.Y.	Turner, 32 yd field goal	4:52
N.Y.	Turner, 30 yd field goal	11:02

Fourth Quarter
N.Y.	Turner, 9 yard field goal	1:34
Balt.	Hill, 1 yard rush	11:41
	PAT — Michaels (kick)	

TEAM STATISTICS

N.Y.		BALT.
21	First Downs — Total	18
10	First Downs — Rushing	7
10	First Downs — Passing	9
1	First Downs — Penalty	2
1	Fumbles — Number	1
1	Fumbles — Lost Ball	1
5	Penalties — Number	3
28	Yards Penalized	23
74	Total Offensive Plays	64
337	Total Net Yards	324
4.6	Average Gain	5.1
2	Field Goals Missed	2
1	Giveaways	5
5	Takeaways	1
+4	Difference	−4

INDIVIDUAL STATISTICS

NEW YORK JETS	No	Yds	Avg.	BALTIMORE	No	Yds	Avg.
RUSHING							
Snell	30	121	4.0	Matte	11	116	10.5
Boozer	10	19	1.9	Hill	9	29	3.2
Mathis	3	2	0.7	Unitas	1	0	0.0
	43	142	3.3	Morrall	2	−2	−1.0
					23	143	6.2
RECEIVING							
Sauer	8	133	16.6	Richardson	6	58	9.7
Snell	4	40	10.0	Orr	3	42	14.0
Mathis	3	20	6.7	Mackey	3	35	11.7
Lammons	2	13	6.5	Matte	2	30	15.0
	17	206	12.1	Hill	2	1	0.5
				Mitchell	1	15	15.0
					17	181	10.6
PUNTING							
Johnson	4		38.8	Lee	3		44.3
PUNT RETURNS							
Baird	1	0	0.0	Brown	4	34	8.5
KICKOFF RETURNS							
Christy	1	25	25.0	Pearson	2	59	29.5
				Brown	2	45	22.5
					4	104	26.0
INTERCEPTION RETURNS							
Beverly	2	0	0.0	None			
Hudson	1	9	9.0				
Sample	1	0	0.0				
	4	9	2.3				

NEW YORK	Att	Comp	Comp Pct.	Yds	Int	Yds/ Att.	Yds/ Comp	Yards Lost Tackled
PASSING								
Namath	28	17	60.7	206	0	7.4	12.1	2—11
Parilli	1	0	0.0	0	0	—	—	0
	29	17	58.6	206	0	7.1	12.1	2—11
BALTIMORE								
Morrall	17	6	35.3	71	3	4.2	11.8	0
Unitas	24	11	45.8	110	1	4.6	10.0	0
	41	17	41.5	181	4	4.4	10.6	0

1969 N.F.L. Equalizing the Competition

It took a thirty-five-hour, forty-five minute meeting to do it, but the NFL came up with a blueprint for next year's merger of the two leagues. Commissioner Pete Rozelle announced on May 17 that both leagues would be part of the NFL next year and that the Baltimore Colts, Cleveland Browns, and Pittsburgh Steelers had agreed to join the present ten AFL clubs in the American Conference, while the thirteen remaining old-line NFL clubs would form the National Conference. Each conference would be parted into Eastern, Central, and Western divisions, and interconference play would begin in the regular season. In other words, this would be the last year in which the NFL and AFL would be separate, distinctive entries.

EASTERN CONFERENCE—CAPITAL DIVISION

Dallas Cowboys— Don Meredith and Don Perkins both retired this year, but the Cowboys came up with an entire new backfield and kept on winning without a hitch. Craig Morton moved up into the starting quarterback spot, Walt Garrison, a rodeo cowboy in the summer, took over at fullback, and rookie Calvin Hill, a product of the Ivy League, led the league in rushing all season only to lose the title when sidelined with an injury for the final game of the year. All the other parts of the Cowboy machine were in fine order. Bob Hayes and Lance Rentzel provided speed at wide receiver, the offensive line was both strong and deep, and the defense pressured quarterbacks unmercifully whenever they attempted to pass.

Washington Redskins—In search of new challenges, Vince Lombardi packed his bags and moved to Washington as the head coach and general manager of the Redskins. The results were immediate, as the Skins had their first winning season since 1955. Lombardi had a good passing attack left over from the previous regime, and he constructed a solid running game with rookie halfback Larry Brown and ex-Brown fullback Charlie Harraway. On defense, Lombardi concentrated on the pass defense, rigging up a tight secondary of Pat Fischer, Mike Bass, Brig Owens, and Rickie Harris.

New Orleans Saints—Billy Kilmer was no glamorous quarterback, but he was a fine leader who moved the team well. The strength of the attack was the stable of receivers; Dan Abramowicz, Al Dodd, and Dave Parks had few peers as a group. Coach Tom Fears added a running game to the offense by coming up with Andy Livingston and Tony Baker as his new running backs. Livingston came over from the Bears, and Baker came off of last year's taxi squad; both ran with power and speed. The defense was a trouble area, although tackles Dave Rowe and Mike Tilleman played well.

Philadelphia Eagles—The Eagles began a rebuilding program under the new leadership of general manager Pete Retzlaff and head coach Jerry Williams this year. The team still finished in last place, but emphasis was placed on developing young players for the future. Williams gave plenty of playing time to rookies Leroy Keyes, Ernie Calloway, and Bill Bradley, and young veterans like Ben Hawkins, Harold Jackson, Mike Evans, Gary Pettigrew, and Tim Rossovich all were handed full-time starting jobs.

CENTURY DIVISION

Cleveland Browns—The Browns were loaded with offensive talent, such as quarterback Bill Nelsen, runner Leroy Kelly, receivers Gary Collins, Paul Warfield, and Milt Morin, and blockers Dick Schafrath and Gene Hickerson. The defense, however, featured several young Turks amidst some overage and mediocre players. Jack Gregory developed into a strong pass-rusher toward the end of the season, rookie Walt Sumner filled in well for the injured Ben Davis at cornerback, and Ernie Kellerman kept up his good work at strong safety, but problems arose at middle linebacker, where Dale Lindsey was barely adequate, and cornerback, where thirty-four-year-old Erich Barnes was playing on borrowed time.

New York Giants—When the Giants lost all their pre-season games, owner Wellington Mara canned coach Allie Sherman, long-term contract and all, and elevated assistant Alex Webster. The Giants responded to the switch by beating the Vikings. Things leveled off after that, with the Giants winning some and losing some as befits a mediocre team. One of the biggest enigmas of the year was Homer Jones, who found his way into the end zone only once all year.

St. Louis Cardinals—Injuries to Jerry Stovall, Bob Atkins, and Jamie Rivers made the Cards vulnerable to the pass; the New Orleans Saints exploited this weakness to win a 52-41 decision. The offense could produce points in a hurry, with a good line, good receivers in John Gilliam, Dave Williams, and Jackie Smith and powerful runners in Cid Edwards and Johnny Roland. Charley Johnson and Jim Hart split the quarterbacking chores, but neither could provide leadership.

Pittsburgh Steelers—New head coach Chuck Noll won only one game all year but still felt that progress was made in several areas. The defensive line was upgraded by ferocious rookie tackle Joe Greene, the secondary found a hard-hitting safety in Chuck Beatty, and the offensive line improved with the development of young veterans Larry Gagner, Bruce Van Dyke, and Ray Mansfield. Noll also got good seasons out of veterans Roy Jefferson, Ben McGee, and Andy Russell but was disappointed by a poor rookie season for Terry Hanratty.

WESTERN CONFERENCE — CENTRAL DIVISION

Minnesota Vikings—Although the heart of the Vikings was their defense, the biggest star on the team was a quarterback who had problems passing. Joe Kapp, whose passes wobbled ominously but often found the mark, set the tone of the Vikings with actions, such as his scrambling runs which included hurdling over defenders and bulling through tacklers. The Viking attack was unrelenting but unspectacular, leading the league in points scored primarily because the defense kept giving it the ball.

Detroit Lions—Just as when he had played, coach Joe Schmidt's Lions relied on the defense to carry the club. The front four was anchored by Alex Karras, the linebacking trio of Paul Naumoff, Mike Lucci, and Wayne Walker combined mobility and strength, and cornerbacks Lem Barney and Dick LeBeau made passing a difficult task for enemy quarterbacks. The Lion quarterback situation was unsettled, however, as Bill Munson and Greg Landry split the job with indifferent results, and injuries to Mel Farr and Nick Eddy hurt the running game.

Green Bay Packers—The Packers remained a tough team despite several problems. Bart Starr missed the last four games with a shoulder injury, Jerry Kramer and Bob Skoronski retired, and age was creeping up on the defensive line. The most damaging deficiency, however, was the lack of a reliable place-kicker. Coach Phil Bengtson started the year with Mike Mercer, who hit on only five of seventeen field-goal attempts, and then switched to Booth Lusteg, whose one-for-five record was no improvement.

Chicago Bears—Gale Sayers recaptured his old form after a hesitant start and rocketed to the NFL rushing crown. Outside of that, the Bears endured a campaign of unbroken gloom. The team lost its first seven games, beat the just as miserable Pittsburgh Steelers, then went on to lose their last six games. Coach Jim Dooley juggled his quarterbacks to get some life into the passing attack, but all he got for his troubles were some unhappy passers. Jack Concannon started the year at the controls, but when he couldn't move the team, Dooley put rookie Bobby Douglass into the lineup.

COASTAL DIVISION

Los Angeles Rams—Old pros like Deacon Jones, Merlin Olsen, Jack Pardee, Maxie Baughan, Clancy Williams, and Eddie Meador made few errors on defense, the hallmark of a George Allen team, and the Roman Gabriel-led offense rarely turned the ball over without holding onto it for a stretch. Operating behind a superb line of Bob Brown, Charlie Cowan, Tom Mack, Joe Scibelli, and Ken Iman, Gabriel ground out yardage with handoffs to rookie Larry Smith, Les Josephson, and Tommy Mason and with quick passes to Jack Snow, Wendell Tucker, and Billy Truax. The Rams' ball-control tactics worked so well that they won their first eleven games.

Baltimore Colts—The ill omen of their Super Bowl defeat followed the Colts through this season. Ordell Braase, Don Shinnick, and Bobby Boyd retired after the loss to the Jets, and Jerry Hill, Terry Cole, Willie Richardson, John Mackey, Lou Michaels, Dennis Gaubatz, and Lenny Lyles suffered through sub-par seasons. Thus, one year after winning the NFL championship, the Colts had a completely different look. Ted Hendricks, Roy Hilton, Bob Grant, Charlie Stukes, and Tommy Maxwell were new starters on defense, with Mike Curtis having to learn the middle linebacker spot. Johnny Unitas reclaimed the quarterback position but showed little fire.

Atlanta Falcons—Coach Norm Van Brocklin fielded two strong defensive ends in Claude Humphrey and John Zook, a top cornerback in Ken Reaves, a good tight end in Jim Mitchell, and a potential All-Pro tackle in George Kunz. One of Van Brocklin's biggest problems, however, was that his offensive line, with four rookie starters, could not pass-block.

San Francisco '49ers—Injuries cut down Kevin Hardy, John Brodie, Stan Hindman, Ed Beard, and Johnny Fuller, retirement erased Matt Hazeltine, and the '49ers fell back into the basement in the Coastal Division. Coach Dick Nolan had veteran talent in such as Ken Willard, Elmer Collett, Charlie Krueger, Dave Wilcox, Jim Johnson, and mid-season pickup Rosey Taylor, and he had rookie talent in Gene Washington, Skip Vanderbundt, Ted Kwalick, and Earl Edwards, but the '49ers persisted as one of pro football's top enigmas.

FINAL TEAM STATISTICS

OFFENSE

	ATL.	BALT.	CHI.	CLEV.	DALL.	DET.	G.B.	L.A.	MINN.	N.O.	N.Y.	PHIL.	PITT.	ST.L.	S.F.	WASH.
FIRST DOWNS:																
Total	209	255	237	250	275	198	242	209	239	**282**	235	231	210	224	253	256
by Rushing	97	99	120	97	**133**	83	95	75	102	93	91	83	81	83	84	84
by Passing	89	140	97	138	125	93	122	114	117	**158**	133	132	115	125	153	149
by Penalty	23	16	20	15	17	22	25	20	20	**31**	11	16	14	16	16	23
RUSHING:																
Number	455	417	462	447	**532**	474	432	382	489	399	397	395	400	382	391	377
Yards	2058	1490	2078	1788	**2276**	1755	1692	1413	1850	1705	1593	1563	1542	1446	1536	1532
Average Yards	**4.5**	3.6	4.5	4.0	4.3	3.7	3.9	3.7	3.8	4.3	4.0	4.0	3.9	3.8	3.9	4.1
Touchdowns	9	16	14	**17**	**17**	11	11	8	15	12	8	10	8	**17**	13	11
PASSING:																
Attempts	282	429	384	378	355	329	319	416	346	453	435	458	391	430	**496**	444
Completions	149	225	193	199	189	165	182	222	176	245	234	216	176	216	**278**	275
Completion Percentage	52.8	52.4	50.3	52.6	53.2	50.2	57.1	53.4	50.9	54.1	53.8	47.2	45.0	50.2	56.0	**61.9**
Passing Yards	2230	3143	1929	2830	3212	1958	2678	2650	2498	3215	3076	3022	2458	2940	**3379**	3106
Average Yards per Attempt	7.9	7.3	5.0	7.5	**9.0**	6.0	8.4	6.4	7.2	7.1	7.1	6.6	6.3	6.8	6.8	7.0
Average Yards per Completion	15.0	14.0	10.0	14.2	**17.0**	11.9	14.7	11.9	14.2	13.1	13.1	14.0	14.0	13.6	12.2	11.3
Times Tackled Attempting to Pass	63	19	55	20	44	42	34	**17**	34	27	37	29	52	21	27	40
Yards Lost Tackled Attempting to Pass	477	156	439	190	366	358	302	**129**	252	241	301	240	374	201	221	322
Net Yards	1753	2987	1490	2640	2846	1600	2376	2521	2246	2974	2775	2782	2084	2739	**3158**	2784
Touchdowns	20	17	11	24	24	12	20	**25**	24	22	24	20	17	19	22	22
Interceptions	12	27	21	21	18	18	17	**7**	18	20	8	28	29	25	26	16
Percent Intercepted	4.3	6.3	5.5	5.6	5.1	5.5	5.3	**1.7**	5.2	4.4	1.8	6.1	7.4	5.8	5.2	3.6
PUNTS:																
Number	69	57	76	60	63	74	59	**80**	67	49	73	74	77	73	71	70
Average Distance	41.2	**45.3**	39.0	37.5	43.3	33.9	40.1	40.7	40.0	41.4	37.6	39.8	42.3	37.6	40.5	42.2
PUNT RETURNS:																
Number	26	37	30	32	38	21	32	**58**	45	30	15	36	37	38	22	26
Yards	82	192	164	183	273	230	287	**556**	266	217	50	219	165	201	63	190
Average Yards	3.2	5.2	5.5	5.7	7.2	**11.0**	9.0	9.6	5.9	7.2	3.3	6.1	4.5	5.3	2.9	7.3
Touchdowns	0	0	0	0	0	**1**	**1**	0	0	0	0	0	0	0	0	**1**
KICKOFF RETURNS:																
Number	52	51	52	46	36	42	50	53	33	62	56	63	60	**68**	47	60
Yards	1104	1290	1132	985	718	1017	1165	1107	774	1455	1075	1258	1241	**1507**	908	1268
Average Yards	21.2	**25.3**	21.8	21.4	19.9	24.2	23.3	20.9	23.5	23.5	19.2	20.0	20.7	22.2	19.3	21.1
Touchdowns	1	1	0	0	0	1	**2**	0	0	0	0	0	1	1	0	0
INTERCEPTION RETURNS:																
Number	19	15	16	19	24	21	19	26	**30**	12	19	15	25	15	20	16
Yards	200	106	132	217	339	207	428	424	**459**	73	221	179	257	245	194	246
Average Yards	10.5	7.1	8.3	11.4	14.1	9.9	**22.5**	16.3	15.3	6.1	11.6	11.9	10.3	16.3	9.7	15.4
Touchdowns	0	0	1	**3**	1	0	2	**3**	2	0	1	**3**	0	1	1	1
PENALTIES:																
Number	63	62	89	58	81	71	63	**95**	67	83	70	80	67	72	85	74
Yards	601	561	940	603	840	734	602	**994**	744	943	777	843	659	765	845	756
FUMBLES:																
Number	37	23	27	26	28	18	31	23	**17**	20	22	18	36	24	25	23
Number Lost	19	12	17	14	12	12	21	11	12	12	15	11	20	**10**	12	**10**
POINTS:																
Total	276	279	210	351	369	259	269	320	**379**	311	264	279	218	314	277	307
PAT Attempts	33	34	26	**45**	44	26	36	36	43	35	33	33	26	40	37	37
PAT Made	33	33	26	**45**	43	26	35	36	43	33	33	31	26	38	35	35
FG Attempts	30	31	21	23	36	37	22	34	37	**41**	21	30	26	24	21	27
FG Made	15	14	8	12	20	25	6	22	**26**	22	11	16	12	12	6	16
Percent FG Made	50.0	45.2	38.1	52.2	55.6	67.6	27.3	64.7	**70.3**	53.7	52.4	53.3	46.2	50.0	28.6	59.3
Safeties	0	0	**2**	0	1	1	0	1	0	1	0	1	0	0	1	1

DEFENSE

	ATL.	BALT.	CHI.	CLEV.	DALL.	DET.	G.B.	L.A.	MINN.	N.O.	N.Y.	PHIL.	PITT.	ST.L.	S.F.	WASH.
FIRST DOWNS:																
Total	254	256	208	257	203	182	224	242	**158**	242	243	268	260	289	242	277
by Rushing	120	70	89	120	**52**	64	103	84	55	88	120	111	101	83	91	149
by Passing	120	164	98	121	141	101	107	125	**88**	131	103	136	142	185	128	110
by Penalty	14	22	21	16	**10**	17	14	33	15	23	20	21	17	21	23	18
RUSHING:																
Number	475	399	440	417	**313**	372	485	415	337	419	466	467	455	438	422	511
Yards	2032	1400	1900	1990	**1050**	1223	1982	1475	1089	1835	2053	1909	1732	1644	1704	2299
Average Yards	4.3	3.5	4.3	4.8	3.4	3.3	4.1	3.6	**3.2**	4.4	4.4	4.1	3.8	3.8	4.0	4.5
Touchdowns	14	8	17	18	**3**	7	7	8	4	15	14	15	17	10	14	26
PASSING:																
Attempts	383	459	**296**	387	458	350	360	430	410	382	340	444	410	465	402	369
Completions	225	271	**150**	202	235	167	177	202	213	200	171	243	227	260	205	192
Completion Percentage	58.7	59.0	50.7	52.2	51.3	47.7	49.2	**47.0**	52.0	52.4	50.3	54.7	55.4	55.9	51.0	52.0
Passing Yards	2536	3499	2239	2787	3109	2238	2133	2919	**2035**	3382	2430	3250	2973	3752	2726	2316
Average Yards per Attempt	6.6	7.6	7.6	7.2	6.8	6.4	5.9	6.8	**5.0**	8.9	7.1	7.3	7.3	8.1	6.8	6.3
Average Yards per Completion	11.3	12.9	14.9	13.8	13.2	13.4	12.1	14.5	**9.6**	16.9	14.2	13.4	13.1	14.4	13.3	12.1
Times Tackled Attempting to Pass	30	33	33	37	**55**	46	36	50	49	21	32	25	33	33	30	18
Yards Lost Tackled Attempting to Pass	251	250	258	323	**452**	377	288	393	404	199	275	181	304	220	255	139
Net Yards	2285	3249	1981	2464	2657	1861	1845	2526	**1631**	3183	2155	3069	2669	3532	2471	2177
Touchdowns	13	20	23	19	23	15	13	18	**8**	32	18	23	27	38	22	11
Interceptions	19	15	16	19	24	21	19	26	**30**	12	19	15	25	15	20	16
Percent Intercepted	5.0	3.3	5.4	4.9	5.5	6.0	5.3	6.0	**7.3**	3.1	5.6	3.4	6.1	3.2	5.0	4.3
PUNTS:																
Number	56	69	63	64	82	70	72	77	**100**	58	53	69	65	67	65	62
Average Distance	38.8	38.4	41.4	40.5	42.2	40.0	39.7	41.0	**36.8**	41.6	38.9	40.9	40.1	40.4	40.4	40.7
PUNT RETURNS:																
Number	38	35	28	20	43	31	**18**	36	34	27	41	21	41	35	39	36
Yards	171	182	106	72	305	133	**62**	181	237	176	449	93	396	158	293	324
Average Yards	4.5	5.2	3.8	3.6	7.1	4.3	**3.4**	5.0	7.0	6.5	11.0	4.4	9.7	4.5	7.5	9.0
Touchdowns	0	0	0	0	0	0	0	0	0	0	2	0	1	0	0	0
KICKOFF RETURNS:																
Number	52	55	**38**	56	64	59	51	56	70	48	45	51	46	49	43	48
Yards	1132	1135	**917**	1166	1242	1242	1078	1208	1453	935	1100	1043	962	1007	1186	1198
Average Yards	21.8	20.6	24.1	20.8	**19.4**	21.1	21.1	21.6	20.8	19.5	24.4	20.5	20.9	20.6	27.6	25.0
Touchdowns	2	**0**	1	**0**	**0**	**0**	1	**0**	1	**0**	**0**	**0**	1	**0**	1	**0**
INTERCEPTION RETURNS:																
Number	12	27	21	21	18	18	17	**7**	18	20	8	28	29	25	26	16
Yards	233	394	271	275	167	168	256	**40**	208	265	78	343	535	202	304	188
Average Yards	19.4	14.6	12.9	13.1	9.3	9.3	15.1	**5.7**	11.6	13.3	9.8	12.3	18.4	8.1	11.7	11.8
Touchdowns	2	3	**0**	1	1	1	1	**0**	2	**0**	**0**	3	3	**0**	1	1
PENALTIES:																
Number	73	74	66	72	58	**90**	65	88	69	81	62	79	79	71	70	83
Yards	762	848	612	746	680	857	733	709	795	773	601	**950**	793	773	671	904
FUMBLES:																
Number	**37**	18	21	32	23	24	23	33	24	20	23	31	25	19	26	19
Number Lost	**27**	10	11	22	11	21	7	12	12	10	14	14	16	12	11	10
POINTS:																
Total	268	268	339	300	223	188	221	243	**133**	393	298	377	404	389	319	319
PAT Attempts	32	32	43	38	28	23	23	26	**16**	49	35	44	50	48	39	38
PAT Made	32	31	42	36	28	23	23	25	**16**	47	32	44	49	47	38	38
FG Attempts	27	34	31	22	25	29	34	26	**18**	29	29	37	26	31	36	27
FG Made	14	15	13	12	9	9	20	20	**7**	16	18	23	17	18	15	17
Percent FG Made	51.9	44.1	41.9	54.5	36.0	**31.0**	58.8	76.9	38.9	55.2	62.1	62.2	65.4	58.1	41.7	63.0
Safeties	1	**0**	**0**	**0**	**0**	**0**	**0**	1	**0**	2	1	**0**	2	**0**	1	1

CONFERENCE PLAYOFFS

SCORING

MINNESOTA	7	0	7	9–23
LOS ANGELES	7	10	0	3–20

First Quarter
- LA Klein, 3 yard pass from Gabriel — PAT–Gossett (kick)
- Mn. Osborn, 1 yard rush — PAT–Cox (kick)

Second Quarter
- LA Gossett, 20 yard field goal
- LA Truax, 2 yard pass from Gabriel — PAT–Gossett (kick)

Third Quarter
- Mn. Osborn, 1 yard rush — PAT–Cox (kick)

Fourth Quarter
- LA Gossett, 27 yard field goal
- Mn. Kapp, 2 yard rush — PAT–Cox (kick)
- Mn. Eller, Safety-tackled Gabriel in end zone.

TEAM STATISTICS

MINN.		L.A.
18	First Downs–Total	19
7	First Downs–Rushing	10
10	First Downs–Passing	9
1	First Downs–Penalty	0
2	Times Tackled Passing	3
18	Yards Lost–Tackled	21
3	Fumbles–Number	1
1	Fumbles–Lost Ball	0
4	Penalties–Number	4
36	Yards Penalized	37
3	Punts–Number	3
39.3	Punts–Average Distance	36.3
1	Punt Returns–Number	2
6	Punt Returns–Yards	8
6	Kickoff Returns–Number	4
111	Kickoff Returns–Yards	69
1	Interception Returns–Number	2
29	Interception Returns–Yards	19
0	Missed Field Goals	1
3	Giveaways	1
1	Takeaways	3
–2	Difference	+2

INDIVIDUAL STATISTICS

MINNESOTA	No	Yds	Avg.	LOS ANGELES	No	Yds	Avg.
RUSHING							
Kapp	7	42	6.0	Smith	11	60	5.5
Osborn	13	30	2.3	Gabriel	4	26	6.5
Brown	8	22	2.8	Ellison	4	22	5.5
Reed	1	3	3.0	Josephson	10	16	1.6
	29	97	3.3	Mason	1	2	2.0
					30	126	4.2
RECEIVING							
Washington	4	90	22.5	Josephson	7	41	5.9
Henderson	4	68	17.0	Smith	6	36	6.0
Brown	2	20	10.0	Truax	5	47	9.4
Reed	2	18	9.0	Tucker	3	23	7.7
	12	196	16.3	Klein	1	3	3.0
					22	150	6.8

PASSING

	Att.	Cmp.	Pct.	Yds.	Int.	Yd/A	Yd/C
MINN.							
Kapp	19	12	63.2	196	2	10.3	16.3
L.A.							
Gabriel	32	22	62.5	150	1	4.7	6.8

December 28, at Dallas (Attendance 69,321)

SCORING

DALLAS	0	0	7	7–14
CLEVELAND	7	10	7	14–38

First Quarter
- Cle Scott, 2 yard rush — PAT–Cockroft (kick)

Second Quarter
- Cle. Morin, 6 yard pass from Nelsen — PAT–Cockroft (kick)
- Cle. Cockroft, 29 field goal

Third Quarter
- Cle. Scott, 2 yard rush — PAT–Cockroft (kick)
- Dal. Morton, 2 yard rush — PAT–Clark (kick)

Fourth Quarter
- Cle. Kelly, 1 yard rush — PAT–Cockroft (kick)
- Cle. Sumner, 88 yard interception return — PAT–Cockroft (kick)
- Dal. Rentzel, 5 yard pass from Staubach — PAT–Clark (kick)

TEAM STATISTICS

DAL.		CLE.
17	First Downs–Total	22.
9	First Downs–Rushing	4
6	First Downs–Passing	17
2	First Downs–Penalty	1
3	Times Tackled Passing	1
19	Yards Lost–Tackled	7
2	Fumbles–Number	1
1	Fumbles–Lost Ball	0
6	Penalties–Number	6
51	Yards Penalized	50
5	Punts–Number	1
36.2	Punts–Average Distance	34.0
1	Punt Returns–Number	2
0	Punt Returns–Yards	11
5	Kickoff Returns–Number	3
106	Kickoff Returns–Yards	56
0	Interception Returns–Number	2
0	Interception Returns–Yards	123
0	Missed Field Goals	1
3	Giveaways	0
0	Takeaways	3
–3	Difference	+3

INDIVIDUAL

DALLAS				CLEVELAND			
RUSHING							
Garrison	9	49	5.4	Kelly	19	66	3.5
Staubach	3	22	7.3	Scott	11	33	3.0
Hill	8	17	2.1	Morrison	2	3	1.5
Morton	4	12	3.0	Cockroft	1	0	0.0
Shy	1	0	0.0	Johnson	2	–5	–2.5
	25	100	4.0		35	97	2.8
RECEIVING							
Hayes	4	44	11.0	Warfield	8	99	11.4
Rentzel	3	41	13.7	Morin	4	52	13.0
Garrison	2	15	7.5	Scott	2	39	19.5
Norman	1	26	26.0	Collins	2	19	9.5
Hill	1	7	7.0	Kelly	2	10	5.0
Reeves	1	3	3.0	Morrison	1	18	18.0
	12	136	11.3	Jones	1	17	17.0
					20	254	12.7

PASSING

	Att.	Cmp.	Pct.	Yds.	Int.	Yd/A	Yd/C
DALLAS							
Morton	24	8	33.3	92	2	3.8	11.5
Staubach	5	4	80.0	44	0	8.8	11.0
	29	12	41.4	136	2	4.7	11.3
CLEVE.							
Nelsen	27	18	66.7	219	0	8.1	12.2
Rhome	2	2	100.0	35	0	17.5	17.5
	29	20	69.0	254	0	8.8	12.7

CAPITOL DIVISION

DALLAS COWBOYS 11-2-1 Tom Landry

Scores of Each Game

24	ST. LOUIS	3
21	New Orleans	17
38	Philadelphia	7
24	Atlanta	17
49	PHILADELPHIA	14
25	NEW YORK	3
10	Cleveland	42
33	NEW ORLEANS	17
41	Washington	28
23	Los Angeles	24
24	SAN FRANCISCO	24
10	Pittsburgh	7
27	BALTIMORE	10
20	WASHINGTON	10

Use Name	Pos.	Hgt	Wgt	Age	Int	Pts
Tony Liscio	OT	6'5"	255	29		
Ralph Neely	OT	6'5"	265	25		
Rayfield Wright	TE-OT	6'7"	250	24		
John Niland	OG	6'4"	245	25		
Blaine Nye	OG	6'4"	250	23		
John Wilbur	OG	6'3"	240	26		
Dave Manders	C	6'2"	250	27		
Malcolm Walker	C	6'4"	250	26		
George Andrie	DE	6'7"	250	29		2
Larry Cole	DE	6'4"	255	22	1	6
Halvor Hagen	OT-DE	6'5"	250	22		
Ron East	DT	6'4"	242	26		
Bob Lilly	DT	6'4"	260	30		6
Jethro Pugh	DT	6'6"	260	25		

Use Name	Pos.	Hgt	Wgt	Age	Int	Pts
Jackie Burkett	LB	6'4"	228	32		
Dave Edwards	LB	6'3"	228	30	1	
Chuck Howley	LB	6'3"	225	33	2	
Lee Roy Jordan	LB	6'2"	220	28	2	
Tom Stincic	LB	6'2"	226	22		
Fred Whittingham	LB	6'1"	240	30		
Otto Brown	DB	6'1"	188	22	1	
Phil Clark	DB	6'2"	210	24	2	
Mike Gaechter	DB	6'	190	29	3	
Cornell Green	DB	6'4"	208	29	2	
Mike Johnson	DB	5'10"	184	25		
Mel Renfro	DB	6'	190	27	10	

D. D. Lewis — Military Service
Willie Townes — Injury

Use Name	Pos.	Hgt	Wgt	Age	Int	Pts
Bob Belden	QB	6'2"	210	22		
Craig Morton	QB	6'4"	214	26		6
Roger Staubach	QB	6'2"	195	27		6
Craig Baynham	HB	6'1"	206	25		
Calvin Hill	HB	6'3"	230	22		48
Les Shy	HB	6'1"	200	25		12
Dan Reeves	FB-HB	6'1"	200	25		30
Walt Garrison	FB	6'	205	25		12
Claxton Welch	HB-FB	5'11"	200	22		
Bobby Joe Conrad	WR	6'	195	34		
Richmond Flowers	WR	6'	183	22		
Bob Hayes	WR	6'	185	26		24
Dennis Homan	WR	6'1"	180	23		
Lance Rentzel	WR	6'2"	202	25		78
Mike Ditka	TE	6'3"	225	29		18
Pettis Norman	TE	6'3"	220	29		18
Mike Clark	K	6'1"	205	28		103
Ron Widby	K	6'4"	210	24		

WASHINGTON REDSKINS 7-5-2 Vince Lombardi

Scores of Each Game

26	New Orleans	20
23	Cleveland	27
17	San Francisco	17
33	ST. LOUIS	17
20	NEW YORK	14
14	Pittsburgh	7
17	Baltimore	41
28	PHILADELPHIA	28
28	DALLAS	41
27	ATLANTA	20
13	LOS ANGELES	24
34	Philadelphia	29
17	NEW ORLEANS	14
10	Dallas	20

Use Name	Pos.	Hgt	Wgt	Age	Int	Pts
Walt Rock	OT	6'5"	255	28		
Jim Snowden	OT	6'3"	255	27		
Ray Schoenke	C-OT	6'3"	250	27		
Willie Banks	OG	6'2"	237	23		
Steve Duich	OG	6'3"	248	23		
Vince Promuto	OG	6'1"	245	31		
Dave Crossan	C	6'3"	245	29		
Len Hauss	C	6'2"	235	27		
Leo Carroll	DE	6'7"	250	25		
John Hoffman	DE	6'7"	260	26		6
Carl Kammerer	DE	6'3"	243	32		
Clark Miller	DE	6'5"	246	30		
Frank Bosch	DT	6'4"	246	23		
Dennis Crane	DT	6'6"	260	24		
Spain Musgrave	DT	6'4"	275	24		
Jim Norton	DT	6'4"	254	26		
Joe Rutgens	DT	6'2"	255	30		

Use Name	Pos.	Hgt	Wgt	Age	Int	Pts
Chris Hanburger	LB	6'2"	218	28		6
Sam Huff	LB	6'1"	230	34	3	6
Marlin McKeever	LB	6'1"	235	29	1	
Harold McLinton	LB	6'2"	235	22		
Tom Roussel	LB	6'2"	226	22		
John Didion	C-LB	6'4"	245	21		
Mike Bass	DB	6'	190	24	3	
Tom Brown	DB	6'1"	195	28		
Pat Fischer	DB	5'10"	170	29	3	
Rickie Harris	DB	6'	182	26	4	6
Brig Owens	DB	5'11"	190	26	3	
Ted Vactor	DB	6'	185	25		
Bob Wade	DB	6'2"	200	24		

Use Name	Pos.	Hgt	Wgt	Age	Int	Pts
Sonny Jurgensen	QB	5'11"	203	35		6
Frank Ryan	QB	6'3"	207	33		
Jerry Allen	HB	6'1"	200	28		
Larry Brown	HB	5'11"	195	21		24
Dave Kopay	FB-HB	6'2"	225	27		
Henry Dyer	FB	6'2"	230	24		6
Charlie Harraway	FB	6'2"	215	24		54
Chuck Mercein	FB	6'3"	220	26		
Gary Beban	WR	6'1"	195	23		
Bob Long	WR	6'3"	205	28		6
Walter Roberts	WR	5'10"	163	27		
Charley Taylor	WR	6'3"	210	28		48
Pat Richter	TE	6'5"	230	28		
Jerry Smith	TE	6'2"	208	26		54
Mike Bragg	K	5'11"	186	22		
Curt Knight	K	6'1"	190	26		83

NEW ORLEANS SAINTS 5-9-0 Tom Fears

Scores of Each Game

20	WASHINGTON	26
17	DALLAS	21
17	Los Angeles	36
17	CLEVELAND	27
10	BALTIMORE	30
10	Philadelphia	13
51	St. Louis	42
17	Dallas	33
25	New York	38
43	SAN FRANCISCO	38
26	PHILADELPHIA	17
17	Atlanta	45
14	Washington	17
27	PITTSBURGH	24

Use Name	Pos.	Hgt	Wgt	Age	Int	Pts
Jerry Jones	OT	6'3"	265	25		
Errol Linden	OT	6'5"	250	32		
Don Talbert	OT	6'5"	255	29		
Norman Davis	OG	6'3"	245	24		
Jake Kupp	OG	6'3"	246	27		
John Shinners	OG	6'2"	254	22		
Del Williams	OG	6'3"	245	23		
Jerry Sturm	C	6'3"	265	32		
Doug Atkins	DE	6'8"	275	39		
Dan Colchico	DE	6'4"	245	32		
Dave Long	DE	6'4"	245	24		
Richard Neal	DE	6'3"	254	21		
Mike Rengel	DT	6'5"	260	22		
Dave Rowe	DT	6'6"	280	24		
Mike Tilleman	DT	6'5"	280	25		

Use Name	Pos.	Hgt	Wgt	Age	Int	Pts
Dick Absher	LB	6'4"	227	25	1	
Johnny Brewer	LB	6'4"	235	32		
Bill Cody	LB	6'1"	227	25		
Ted Davis	LB	6'1"	232	27		
Les Kelley	LB	6'3"	233	24		
Mike Morgan	LB	6'4"	242	27		
Bill Saul	LB	6'4"	225	28		
Bo Burris	DB	6'3"	195	24	1	
Ollie Cordill	DB	6'2"	180	26		
Gene Howard	DB	6'	190	22	2	
Elijah Nevett	DB	6'	185	25	3	
Steve Preece	DB	6'1"	195	22	1	6
Bobby Thompson	DB	5'10"	188	29	1	
Carl Ward	DB	5'9"	180	25		
Dave Whitsell	DB	6'	185	33	3	

Lou Cordileone — Knee Injury

Use Name	Pos.	Hgt	Wgt	Age	Int	Pts
Edd Hargett	QB	5'11"	186	22		
Billy Kilmer	QB	6'	204	29		
Jim Ninowski	QB	6'1"	207	33		
Joe Don Looney	HB	6'1"	230	26		
Don Shy	HB	6'1"	205	23		12
Tony Baker	FB-HB	5'11"	230	24		12
Tom Barrington	FB-HB	6'1"	213	25		6
Andy Livingston	FB	6'	234	24		48
Tony Lorick	FB	6'1"	217	27		
Ernie Wheelwright	FB	6'3"	236	32		30
Dan Abramowicz	WR	6'	195	24		42
Al Dodd	WR	6'	180	24		
Dave Parks	TE-WR	6'2"	203	27		18
Jim Hester	TE	6'4"	250	24		6
Ray Poage	TE	6'4"	215	28		24
Tom Dempsey	K	6'1"	264	28		99
Tom McNeill	K	6'1"	195	27		

PHILADELPHIA EAGLES 4-9-1 Jerry Williams

Scores of Each Game

20	CLEVELAND	27
41	PITTSBURGH	27
7	DALLAS	38
20	Baltimore	24
14	Dallas	49
13	NEW ORLEANS	10
23	New York	20
28	Washington	28
17	LOS ANGELES	23
34	St. Louis	30
17	New Orleans	26
29	WASHINGTON	34
3	ATLANTA	27
13	San Francisco	14

Use Name	Pos.	Hgt	Wgt	Age	Int	Pts
Joe Carollo	OT	6'2"	258	29		
Dave Graham	OT	6'3"	250	30		
Lane Howell	OT	6'5"	272	28		
Don Chuy	OG	6'1"	255	28		
Dick Hart	OG	6'2"	255	26		
Jim Skaggs	OG	6'2"	252	29		
Mark Nordquist	C-OG	6'4"	242	24		
Gene Ceppetelli (to NY)	C	6'2"	247	27		
Mike Evans	C	6'5"	250	22		
Don Hultz	DE	6'3"	242	28		
Tim Rossovich	DE	6'4"	260	23		
Mel Tom	DE	6'4"	250	28		2
Ernie Calloway	DT	6'6"	240	21		
Mike Dirks	DT	6'2"	246	24		
Floyd Peters	DT	6'4"	255	34		
Gary Pettigrew	DE-DT	6'4"	255	24		

Use Name	Pos.	Hgt	Wgt	Age	Int	Pts
Wayne Colman (to NO)	LB	6'1"	230	23	1	
Tony Guillory	LB	6'4"	235	26		
Bill Hobbs	LB	6'	213	23		
Jay Johnson	'LB	6'3"	230	23		
Ike Kelley	LB	5'11"	222	25		
Dave Lloyd	LB	6'3"	248	33	2	
Ron Porter (from BAL)	LB	6'3"	232	24		
Adrian Young	LB	6'1"	225	23	1	
Bill Bradley	DB	5'11"	190	22	1	6
Irv Cross	DB	6'1"	195	30	1	
Ron Medved	DB	6'1"	195	25		
Al Nelson	DB	5'11"	186	25	3	
Nate Ramsey	DB	6'1"	200	28	2	6
Jimmy Raye	DB	6'	185	23		
Joe Scarpati	DB	5'10"	185	27	4	6

Use Name	Pos.	Hgt	Wgt	Age	Int	Pts
George Mira	QB	5'11"	190	27		
Norm Snead	QB	6'4"	215	29		12
Ronnie Blye	HB	5'11"	185	25		
Harry Jones	HB	6'2"	205	24		
Leroy Keyes	HB	6'3"	208	22		18
Harry Wilson	HB	5'11"	204	24		
Cyril Pinder	FB-HB	6'2"	222	22		6
Tom Woodeschick	FB	6'	225	27		24
Gary Ballman	WR	6'	205	29		12
Ben Hawkins	WR	6'	180	25		48
Chuck Hughes	WR	5'11"	175	26		
Harold Jackson	WR	5'10"	175	23		54
Kent Lawrence	WR	5'11"	175	22		
Fred Brown	TE	6'5"	237	26		
Fred Hill	TE	6'2"	215	26		6
Sam Baker	K	6'2"	218	37		79

CAPITOL DIVISION

DALLAS COWBOYS

RUSHING

Last Name	No.	Yds	Avg	TD
Hill	204	942	4.6	8
Garrison	176	818	4.6	2
Reeves	59	173	2.9	4
Shy	42	154	3.7	1
Morton	16	62	3.9	1
Staubach	15	60	4.0	1
Welch	6	21	3.5	0
Norman	5	20	4.0	0
Hayes	4	17	4.3	0
Rentzel	2	11	5.5	0
Baynham	3	−2	−0.7	0

RECEIVING

Last Name	No.	Yds	Avg	TD
Rentzel	43	960	22	12
Hayes	40	746	19	4
Hill	20	232	12	0
Reeves	18	187	10	1
Ditka	17	268	16	3
Norman	13	238	18	3
Garrison	13	131	10	0
Homan	12	240	20	0
Shy	8	124	16	1
Conrad	4	74	19	0
Wright	1	12	12	0

PUNT RETURNS

Last Name	No.	Yds	Avg	TD
Hayes	18	179	10	0
Renfro	15	80	5	0
Rentzel	4	14	4	0
Johnson	1	0	0	0

KICKOFF RETURNS

Last Name	No.	Yds	Avg	TD
Flowers	11	238	22	0
Hill	4	125	31	0
Baynham	6	114	19	0
Welch	5	112	22	0
Hayes	3	80	27	0
Shy	3	47	16	0
Garrison	1	2	2	0
Green	2	0	0	0
Johnson	1	0	0	0

PASSING – PUNTING – KICKING

PASSING

Last Name	Att	Comp	%	Yds	Yd/Att	TD	Int−	%	RK
Morton	302	162	54	2619	8.7	21	15−	5	5
Staubach	47	23	49	421	9.0	1	2−	4	
Hill	3	3	100	137	45.7	2	0−	0	
Reeves	3	1	33	35	11.7	0	1−	33	

PUNTING

Last Name	No	Avg
Widby	63	43.3

KICKING

Last Name	XP	Att	%	FG	Att	%
M. Clark	43	44	98	20	36	56

WASHINGTON REDSKINS

RUSHING

Last Name	No.	Yds	Avg	TD
L. Brown	202	888	4.4	4
Harraway	141	428	3.0	6
Jurgensen	17	156	9.2	1
Taylor	3	24	8.0	0
Dyer	6	18	3.0	0
Smith	3	8	2.7	0
Kopay	3	4	1.3	0
Allen	1	3	3.0	0
Bragg	1	3	3.0	0

RECEIVING

Last Name	No.	Yds	Avg	TD
Taylor	71	883	12	8
Harraway	55	489	9	3
Smith	54	682	13	9
Long	48	533	11	1
L. Brown	34	302	9	0
Kopay	6	60	10	0
Roberts	4	66	17	0
Dyer	2	86	43	1
Allen	1	5	5	0

PUNT RETURNS

Last Name	No.	Yds	Avg	TD
Harris	14	158	11	1
Roberts	12	32	3	0

KICKOFF RETURNS

Last Name	No.	Yds	Avg	TD
Harris	19	458	24	0
Roberts	17	383	23	0
Dyer	11	207	19	0
Kopay	9	187	21	0
McKeever	2	31	16	0
Snowden	1	2	2	0
Richter	1	0	0	0

PASSING – PUNTING – KICKING

PASSING

Last Name	Att	Comp	%	Yds	Yd/Att	TD	Int−	%	RK
Jurgensen	442	274	62	3102	7.0	22	15−	3	1
Ryan	1	1	100	4	4.0	0	0−	0	
Knight	1	0	0	0	0.0	0	1−100		

PUNTING

Last Name	No	Avg
Bragg	70	42.2

KICKING

Last Name	XP	Att	%	FG	Att	%
Knight	35	36	97	16	27	59

NEW ORLEANS SAINTS

RUSHING

Last Name	No.	Yds	Avg	TD
Livingston	181	761	4.2	5
Baker	134	642	4.8	1
Wheelright	25	85	3.4	4
Shy	21	75	3.6	1
Abramowicz	3	61	20.3	0
Barrington	7	33	4.7	1
Kilmer	11	18	1.6	0
Hargett	5	15	3.0	0
Dodd	3	12	4.0	0
Lorick	5	11	2.2	0
Poage	1	−3	−3.0	0
Looney	3	−5	−1.7	0

RECEIVING

Last Name	No.	Yds	Avg	TD
Abramowicz	73	1015	14	7
Dodd	37	600	16	1
Baker	34	352	10	1
Parks	31	439	14	3
Livingston	28	278	10	3
Poage	18	236	13	4
Shy	9	141	16	1
Wheelwright	8	68	9	1
Barrington	4	42	11	0
Hester	3	44	15	1

PUNT RETURNS

Last Name	No.	Yds	Avg	TD
Dodd	15	106	7	0
Howard	9	73	8	0
Thompson	4	25	6	0
Barrington	1	8	8	0
Ward	1	5	5	0

KICKOFF RETURNS

Last Name	No.	Yds	Avg	TD
Shy	16	447	28	0
Barrington	17	394	23	0
Howard	9	227	25	0
Dodd	8	171	21	0
Thompson	5	101	20	0
Ward	3	58	19	0
Nevett	2	53	27	0
Hester	1	4	4	0
Preece	1	0	0	0

PASSING – PUNTING – KICKING

PASSING

Last Name	Att	Comp	%	Yds	Yd/Att	TD	Int−	%	RK
Kilmer	360	193	54	2532	7.0	20	17−	5	8
Hargett	52	31	60	403	7.8	0	0−	0	
Ninowski	34	17	50	227	6.7	1	2−	6	
Livingston	4	3	75	38	9.5	1	1−	25	
Barrington	2	1	50	15	7.5	0	0−	0	
Looney	1	0	0	0	0.0	0	0−	0	

PUNTING

Last Name	No	Avg
Cordill	42	40.9
McNeill	7	44.6

KICKING

Last Name	XP	Att	%	FG	Att	%
Dempsey	33	35	94	22	41	54

PHILADELPHIA EAGLES

RUSHING

Last Name	No.	Yds	Avg	TD
Woodeshick	186	831	4.5	4
Keyes	121	361	3.0	3
Pinder	60	309	5.2	4
Blye	8	25	3.1	0
Mira	3	16	5.3	0
Jackson	2	10	5.0	0
Wilson	4	7	1.8	0
Bradley	1	5	5.0	0
Snead	8	2	0.3	2
Jones	1	0	0.0	0
Hawkins	1	−3	−3.0	0

RECEIVING

Last Name	No.	Yds	Avg	TD
Jackson	65	1116	17	9
Hawkins	43	761	18	8
Ballman	31	492	16	2
Keyes	29	276	10	0
Woodeshick	22	177	8	0
Pinder	12	77	6	0
Hill	6	64	11	1
Hughes	3	29	10	0
Blye	2	−6	−3	0
Brown	1	20	20	0
Lawrence	1	10	10	0
Wilson	1	6	6	0

PUNT RETURNS

Last Name	No.	Yds	Avg	TD
Bradley	28	181	6	0
Lawrence	2	26	13	0
Scarpati	4	6	2	0
Hawkins	1	6	6	0
Hughes	1	0	0	0

KICKOFF RETURNS

Last Name	No.	Yds	Avg	TD
Bradley	21	467	22	0
Blye	19	370	19	0
Keyes	9	200	22	0
Lawrence	5	97	19	0
Nelson	3	63	21	0
Pinder	4	56	14	0
Graham	2	5	3	0

PASSING – PUNTING – KICKING

PASSING

Last Name	Att	Comp	%	Yds	Yd/Att	TD	Int−	%	RK
Snead	379	190	50	2768	7.3	19	23−	6	12
Mira	76	25	33	240	3.2	1	5−	7	
Keyes	2	1	50	14	7.0	0	0−	0	
Bradley	1	0	0	0	0.0	0	0−	0	

PUNTING

Last Name	No	Avg
Bradley	74	39.8

KICKING

Last Name	XP	Att	%	FG	Att	%
Baker	31	31	100	16	30	53

Scores of Each Game		Use Name	Pos.	Hgt	Wgt	Age	Int	Pts

CENTURY DIVISION

CLEVELAND BROWNS 10-3-1 Blanton Collier

Scores of Each Game		Use Name	Pos.	Hgt	Wgt	Age	Int	Pts
27	Philadelphia 20	Monte Clark	OT	6'6"	250	32		
27	WASHINGTON 23	Bob Oliver	OT	6'3"	240	22		
21	DETROIT 28	Dick Schafrath	OT	6'3"	248	33		
27	New Orleans 17	Joe Taffoni	OT	6'3"	250	24		
42	PITTSBURGH 31	Jim Copeland	OG	6'2"	245	24		
21	ST. LOUIS 21	John Demarie	OG	6'3"	255	24		
42	DALLAS 10	Gene Hickerson	OG	6'3"	248	34		
3	Minnesota 51	Chuck Reynolds	OG	6'2"	240	22		
24	Pittsburgh 3	Fred Hoaglin	C	6'4"	250	25		
28	NEW YORK 17	Jack Gregory	DE	6'6"	250	24	1	
28	Chicago 24	Ron Snidow	DE	6'4"	250	27		
20	GREEN BAY 7	Marv Upshaw	DT-DE	6'3"	245	22	1	
27	St. Louis 21	Walter Johnson	DT	6'3"	275	26		6
14	New York 27	Jim Kanicki	DT	6'4"	270	27		
		Joe Righetti	DT	6'3"	253	21		
		Al Jenkins	DE-DT	6'2"	255	23		

Use Name	Pos.	Hgt	Wgt	Age	Int	Pts
Billy Andrews	LB	6'	225	24		
John Garlington	LB	6'1"	225	23	2	
Jim Houston	LB	6'2"	240	32		
Dale Lindsey	LB	6'3"	225	26	1	
Bob Matheson	LB	6'4"	240	24		
Wayne Meylan	LB	6'1"	235	23		
Erich Barnes	DB	6'2"	212	34	1	6
Dean Brown	DB	5'10"	170	22		
Mike Howell	DB	6'1"	190	26	6	
Ernie Kellerman	DB	6'	185	25	3	6
Alvin Mitchell	DB	6'3"	195	25		
Freddie Summers	DB	6'1"	180	22		
Walt Sumner	DB	6'1"	180	22	4	6
Ben Davis — Knee Injury						

Use Name	Pos.	Hgt	Wgt	Age	Int	Pts
Bill Nelsen	QB	6'	195	28		
Jerry Rhome	QB	6'	185	27		
Ron Johnson	HB	6'1"	205	21		42
Reece Morrison	HB	6'	205	23		6
Bo Scott	FB	6'3"	210	26		
Charlie Leigh	FB	5'11"	205	23		
Leroy Kelly	HB-FB	6'	200	27		60
Gary Collins	WR	6'4"	220	28		66
Fair Hooker	WR	6'1"	193	22		
Dave Jones	WR	6'2"	185	22		
Paul Warfield	WR	6'	188	26		60
Chip Glass	TE	6'4"	236	22		12
Milt Morin	TE	6'4"	250	27		
Don Cockroft	K	6'1"	185	24		81

NEW YORK GIANTS 6-8-0 Allie Sherman

Scores of Each Game		Use Name	Pos.	Hgt	Wgt	Age	Int	Pts
24	MINNESOTA 23	Rich Buzin	OT	6'4"	250	23		
0	Detroit 24	Steve Wright	OT	6'6"	250	27		
28	CHICAGO 24	Willie Young	OT	6'	265	26		
10	PITTSBURGH 7	Pete Case	OG	6'3"	245	28		
14	Washington 20	Darrell Dess	OG	6'	245	33		
3	Dallas 25	Doug Van Horn	OG	6'2"	245	25		
20	PHILADELPHIA 23	Charlie Harper	OT-OG	6'2"	250	25		
17	St. Louis 42	Chuck Hinton	C	6'2"	235	26		
24	NEW ORLEANS 25	Greg Larson	C	6'2"	250	30		
17	Cleveland 28	Bruce Anderson	DE	6'4"	260	25		
17	Green Bay 20	Fred Dryer	DE	6'6"	235	23		
10	Green Bay 20	John Johnson	DT	6'5"	260	28		
49	ST. LOUIS 6	Tim McCann	DT	6'5"	265	22		
21	Pittsburgh 17	Frank Molden	DT	6'5"	280	27		
27	CLEVELAND 14	Frank Parker	DT	6'5"	270	29		
		Joe Szczecko	DT	6'	245	27		
		Bob Lurtsema	DE-DT	6'6"	250	27		

Use Name	Pos.	Hgt	Wgt	Age	Int	Pts
McKinley Boston	LB	6'2"	245	23		
Tommy Crutcher	LB	6'3"	230	27	1	
Henry Davis	LB	6'3"	235	26		
Ralph Heck	LB	6'2"	230	28	2	
Ray Hickl	LB	6'2"	210	22		
John Kirby (from MIN)	LB	6'3"	235	27		
Harold Wells	LB	6'2"	220	30		
Al Brenner	DB	6'1"	200	21		
Scott Eaton	DB	6'3"	195	25	2	6
Jim Holifield	DB	6'3"	195	23	1	
Spider Lockhart	DB	6'2"	175	26	2	
Tom Longo	DB	6'2"	198	25	2	
Bruce Maher	DB	5'11"	185	32	5	
Willie Williams	DB	6'	190	26	4	
Bobby Duhon — Injury						

Use Name	Pos.	Hgt	Wgt	Age	Int	Pts
Milt Plum	QB	6'1"	205	35		
Frank Tarkenton	QB	6'1"	190	29		
Gary Wood	QB	5'11"	188	26		
John Fuqua	HB	5'11"	200	22		
Randy Minniear	HB	6'	210	25		6
Ernie Koy	FB-HB	6'2"	230	26		36
Joe Morrison	WR-HB	6'1"	212	31		66
Junior Coffey (from ATL)	FB	6'1"	210	27		30
Tucker Frederickson	FB	6'3"	220	26		6
Dave Dunaway	WR	6'2"	205	24		
Don Herrmann	WR	6'2"	195	22		30
Rich Houston	WR	6'2"	197	23		
Homer Jones	WR	6'2"	215	28		6
Dick Kotite	TE	6'3"	235	26		6
Freeman White	TE	6'5"	225	25		6
Butch Wilson	TE	6'2"	228	27		
Aaron Thomas	WR-TE	6'3"	210	31		18
Pete Gogolak	K	6'2"	185	27		66
Curley Johnson	K	6'	215	34		

ST. LOUIS CARDINALS 4-9-1 Charlie Winner

Scores of Each Game		Use Name	Pos.	Hgt	Wgt	Age	Int	Pts
3	Dallas 24	Vern Emerson	OT	6'5"	260	23		
20	CHICAGO 17	Ernie McMillan	OT	6'6"	260	31		
27	Pittsburgh 14	Bob Reynolds	OT	6'6"	265	28		
17	Washington 33	Clyde Williams	OT	6'2"	250	29		
10	MINNESOTA 27	Irv Goode	OG	6'4"	250	27		
21	Cleveland 21	Ken Gray	OG	6'2"	250	33		
42	NEW ORLEANS 51	Rick Sortun	OG	6'2"	240	26		
42	New York 17	Bob DeMarco	C	6'3"	245	31		
0	Detroit 20	Wayne Mulligan	C	6'2"	245	22		
30	PHILADELPHIA 34	Don Brumm	DE	6'4"	245	26		
47	PITTSBURGH 10	Rolf Krueger	DE	6'4"	245	22		
6	New York 49	Cal Snowden	DE	6'4"	235	22		
21	CLEVELAND 27	Chuck Walker	DE	6'2"	250	28		
28	Green Bay 45	Fred Heron	DT	6'4"	255	24		
		Bob Rowe	DT	6'4"	255	24	2	6
		Joe Schmiesing	DT	6'4"	245	24		

Use Name	Pos.	Hgt	Wgt	Age	Int	Pts
Chip Healy	LB	6'3"	230	22		
Dave Meggyesy	LB	6'1"	230	27		
Dave Olerich	LB	6'1"	220	24		
Jamie Rivers	LB	6'2"	235	23		
Rocky Rosema	LB	6'2"	230	23	1	
Larry Stallings	LB	6'2"	230	27		6
Bob Atkins	DB	6'3"	212	23	3	
Lonnie Sanders	DB	6'3"	205	27		
Mac Sauls	DB	6'	185	24		
Jerry Stovall	DB	6'2"	195	27	1	
Roger Wehrli	DB	6'1"	185	21	3	
Larry Wilson	DB	6'	190	31	2	6
Mike Wilson	DB	5'11"	185	22		
Terry Brown	WR-DB	6'1"	205	22	1	

Use Name	Pos.	Hgt	Wgt	Age	Int	Pts
Jim Hart	QB	6'2"	205	25		12
King Hill	QB	6'3"	216	33		
Charley Johnson	QB	6'	190	32		6
MacArthur Lane	HB	6'	220	27		6
Johnny Roland	HB	6'2"	215	26		36
Roy Shivers	HB	6'	200	27		18
Willie Crenshaw	FB	6'2"	230	28		18
Cid Edwards	FB	6'2"	230	25		18
Jerry Daanen	WR	6'	190	24		
John Gilliam	WR	6'1"	190	24		60
Freddie Hyatt	WR	6'3"	212	23		
Dave Williams	WR	6'2"	205	24		42
Bob Brown	TE	6'3"	225	26		
Jackie Smith	TE	6'4"	230	28		6
Jim Bakken	K	6'	200	28		74

PITTSBURGH STEELERS 1-13-0 Chuck Noll

Scores of Each Game		Use Name	Pos.	Hgt	Wgt	Age	Int	Pts
16	DETROIT 13	John Brown	OT	6'2"	255	30		
27	Philadelphia 41	Mike Haggerty	OT	6'4"	240	23		
14	ST. LOUIS 27	Mike Taylor (to NO)	OT	6'	245	24		
7	New York 10	Sam Davis	OG	6'1"	245	25		
31	Cleveland 42	Larry Gagner	OG	6'3"	240	25		
7	WASHINGTON 14	Bruce Van Dyke	OG	6'2"	246	25		
34	GREEN BAY 38	Ralph Wenzel	OG	6'3"	236	26		
7	Chicago 38	Jon Kolb	C	6'2"	220	22		
3	CLEVELAND 24	Ray Mansfield	C	6'3"	240	28		
14	Minnesota 52	L. C. Greenwood	DE	6'5"	240	22		
10	St. Louis 47	Ben McGee	DE	6'2"	250	27		
7	DALLAS 10	Lloyd Voss	DE	6'4"	256	27		
17	NEW YORK 21	Dick Arndt	DT	6'5"	265	25		
24	New Orleans 27	Joe Greene	DT	6'4"	270	22		
		Chuck Hinton	DT	6'5"	258	30	1	
		Clarence Washington	DT	6'3"	265	22		

Use Name	Pos.	Hgt	Wgt	Age	Int	Pts
John Campbell (to BAL)	LB	6'3"	225	30		
Doug Fisher	LB	6'1"	225	22		
Jerry Hillebrand	LB	6'3"	240	29	1	
Ray May	LB	6'1"	230	24	2	
Andy Russell	LB	6'3"	225	27	2	
Brian Stenger	LB	6'4"	220	22	3	
Sid Williams	LB	6'2"	235	27		
Chuck Beatty	DB	6'2"	207	23		
Lee Calland (from CHI)	DB	6'	190	28	2	
Bob Hohn	DB	6'	185	28	5	
Paul Martha	DB	6'	187	26	5	
Clancy Oliver	DB	6'1"	180	21		
Jim Shorter	DB	5'11"	180	28	3	
Marv Woodson (to NO)	DB	6'	195	26	1	
Rocky Bleier — Military Service						

Use Name	Pos.	Hgt	Wgt	Age	Int	Pts
Terry Hanratty	QB	6'1"	200	21		
Kent Nix	QB	6'1"	195	25		
Dick Shiner	QB	6'	197	27		6
Bob Campbell	HB	6'	195	22		
Dick Hoak	HB	5'11"	195	30		18
Don McCall	HB	5'11"	195	24		6
Warren Bankston	FB	6'4"	226	22		6
Earl Gros	FB	6'3"	220	28		42
Don Alley	WR	6'2"	200	23		
Marshall Cropper	WR	6'3"	200	25		
Jon Henderson	WR	6'	195	24		18
Roy Jefferson	WR	6'2"	190	25		54
J. R. Wilburn	WR	6'2"	190	26		
Erwin Williams	WR	6'5"	215	22		6
Bob Adams	TE	6'2"	225	23		
John Hilton	TE	6'5"	222	27		
Gene Mingo	K	6'1"	216	30		62
Bobby Walden	K	6'	190	30		

CENTURY DIVISION

CLEVELAND BROWNS

RUSHING

Last Name	No.	Yds	Avg	TD
Kelly	196	817	4.2	9
R. Johnson	137	471	3.4	7
Morrison	60	301	5.0	1
Scott	44	157	3.6	0
Morin	2	30	15.0	0
Warfield	2	23	11.5	0
Rhome	1	0	0.0	0
Nelsen	5	-11	-2.2	0

RECEIVING

Last Name	No.	Yds	Avg	TD
Collins	54	786	15	11
Warfield	42	886	21	10
Morin	37	495	13	0
R. Johnson	24	164	7	0
Kelly	20	267	13	1
Morrison	6	71	12	0
Scott	6	25	4	0
Glass	4	91	23	2
Jones	2	33	17	0
Hooker	2	21	11	0
Leigh	2	-9	-5	0

PUNT RETURNS

Last Name	No.	Yds	Avg	TD
Sumner	9	88	10	0
Morrison	11	49	4	0
Kelly	7	28	4	0
Leigh	5	18	4	0

KICKOFF RETURNS

Last Name	No.	Yds	Avg	TD
Scott	25	722	29	0
Morrison	9	155	17	0
Brown	2	45	23	0
R. Johnson	1	31	31	0
Kelly	2	26	13	0
Leigh	2	6	3	0
Howell	1	0	0	0
Jenkins	1	0	0	0
Kanicki	1	0	0	0
Mathesen	1	0	0	0
Mitchell	1	0	0	0

PASSING

Last Name	Att	Comp	%	Yds	Yd/Att	TD	Int-	%	RK
Nelson	352	190	54	2743	7.8	23	19-	5	6
Rhome	19	7	37	35	1.8	0	2-	11	
Kelly	5	1	20	36	7.2	1	0-	0	
Morrison	1	1	100	16	16.0	0	0-	0	
R. Johnson	1	0	0	0	0.0	0	0-	0	

PUNTING

Last Name	No	Avg
Cockroft	57	37.5
Collins	3	37.3

KICKING

Last Name	XP	Att	%	FG	Att	%
Cockroft	45	45	100	12	23	52

NEW YORK GIANTS

RUSHING

Last Name	No.	Yds	Avg	TD
Coffey	131	511	3.9	2
Morrison	107	387	3.6	4
Koy	76	300	3.9	2
Tarkenton	37	172	4.6	0
Minniear	35	141	4.0	1
Frederickson	33	136	4.1	0
Fuqua	20	89	4.5	0
Houston	1	11	11.0	0
Jones	3	8	2.7	0
Dunaway	1	4	4.0	0
Wood	1	3	3.0	0
Plum	1	-1	-1.0	0

RECEIVING

Last Name	No.	Yds	Avg	TD
Morrison	44	647	15	7
Jones	42	744	18	1
Herrmann	33	423	13	5
White	29	315	11	1
Thomas	22	348	16	3
Koy	19	152	8	4
Frederickson	14	95	7	0
Coffey	14	89	6	3
Wilson	10	132	13	0
Minniear	6	68	11	0
Fuqua	3	11	4	0
Houston	2	69	35	0
Dunaway	2	37	19	0
Young	1	8	8	0
Kotite	1	2	2	1

PUNT RETURNS

Last Name	No.	Yds	Avg	TD
Lockhart	10	29	3	0
Minniear	3	15	5	0
Brenner	2	6	3	0

KICKOFF RETURNS

Last Name	No.	Yds	Avg	TD
Fuqua	20	399	20	0
Houston	12	252	21	0
Holifield	8	156	20	0
Williams	6	96	16	0
Minniear	5	83	17	0
Brenner	2	39	20	0
Longo	2	31	16	0
Lockhart	1	19	19	0

PASSING

Last Name	Att	Comp	%	Yds	Yd/Att	TD	Int-	%	RK
Tarkenton	409	220	54	2918	7.1	23	8-	2	3
Wood	16	10	63	106	6.6	1	0-	0	
Plum	9	3	33	37	4.1	0	0-	0	
Koy	1	1	100	15	15.0	0	0-	0	

PUNTING

Last Name	No	Avg
Koy	26	35.9
C. Johnson	22	37.4
Dunaway	13	38.2
Gogolak	12	40.9

KICKING

Last Name	XP	Att	%	FG	Att	%
Gogolak	33	33	100	11	21	52

ST. LOUIS CARDINALS

RUSHING

Last Name	No.	Yds	Avg	TD
Edwards	107	504	4.7	3
Roland	138	498	3.6	5
Crenshaw	55	172	3.1	3
Shivers	27	115	4.3	2
Lane	25	93	3.7	1
Johnson	17	51	3.0	1
Hart	7	16	2.3	2
D. Williams	1	1	1.0	0
Smith	4	0	0.0	0
Gilliam	1	-4	-4.0	0

RECEIVING

Last Name	No.	Yds	Avg	TD
D. Williams	56	702	13	7
Gilliam	52	997	19	9
Smith	43	561	13	1
Edwards	23	309	13	0
Roland	12	136	11	1
Crenshaw	11	94	9	0
Lane	9	61	7	0
Shivers	7	61	9	1
Daanen	2	12	6	0
T. Brown	1	7	7	0

PUNT RETURNS

Last Name	No.	Yds	Avg	TD
Wehrli	13	65	5	0
Roland	10	53	5	0
Shivers	9	44	5	0
T. Brown	6	39	7	0

KICKOFF RETURNS

Last Name	No.	Yds	Avg	TD
Lane	20	523	26	0
Gilliam	11	339	31	1
T. Brown	15	320	21	0
Shivers	10	205	21	0
M. Wilson	4	66	17	0
Crenshaw	4	34	9	0
Wehrli	1	18	18	0
Olerich	2	2	1	0
C. Williams	1	0	0	0

PASSING

Last Name	Att	Comp	%	Yds	Yd/Att	TD	Int-	%	RK
Johnson	260	131	50	1847	7.1	13	13-	5	13
Hart	169	84	50	1086	6.4	6	12-	7	18
Hill	1	1	100	7	7.0	0	0-	0	

PUNTING

Last Name	No	Avg
Hill	73	37.6

KICKING

Last Name	XP	Att	%	FG	Att	%
Bakken	38	40	95	12	24	50

PITTSBURGH STEELERS

RUSHING

Last Name	No.	Yds	Avg	TD
Hoak	151	531	3.5	2
Gros	116	343	3.0	4
Bankston	62	259	4.2	1
Hanratty	10	106	10.6	0
McCall	30	98	3.3	0
Nix	10	70	7.0	0
Shiner	14	55	3.9	1
Jefferson	4	46	11.5	0
Wilburn	2	29	14.5	0
B. Campbell	1	5	5.0	0

RECEIVING

Last Name	No.	Yds	Avg	TD
Jefferson	67	1079	16	9
Wilburn	20	373	19	0
Hoak	20	190	10	1
Gros	17	131	8	3
Hilton	12	231	19	0
Henderson	12	188	16	3
Cropper	9	116	13	0
Adams	6	80	13	0
Bankston	6	6	1	0
E. Williams	3	14	5	1
McCall	2	2	1	0
B. Campbell	1	32	32	0
Alley	1	16	16	0

PUNT RETURNS

Last Name	No.	Yds	Avg	TD
B. Campbell	28	133	5	0
Jefferson	4	23	6	0
Hoak	1	9	9	0
Martha	3	0	0	0
Davis	1	0	0	0

KICKOFF RETURNS

Last Name	No.	Yds	Avg	TD
McCall	21	532	25	1
B. Campbell	26	522	20	0
Bankston	4	89	22	0
Jefferson	4	80	20	0
Woodson	1	18	18	0
Davis	3	0	0	0
Kolb	1	0	0	0

PASSING

Last Name	Att	Comp	%	Yds	Yd/Att	TF	Int-	%	RK
Shiner	209	97	46	1422	6.8	7	10-	5	15
Hanratty	126	52	41	716	5.7	8	13-	10	
Nix	53	25	47	290	5.5	2	6-	11	
Hoak	3	2	67	30	10.0	0	0-	0	

PUNTING

Last Name	No	Avg
Walden	77	42.3

KICKING

Last Name	XP	Att	%	FG	Att	%
Mingo	26	26	100	12	26	46

Scores of Each Game

CENTRAL DIVISION

MINNESOTA VIKINGS 12-2-0 Bud Grant

			Use Name	Pos.	Hgt	Wgt	Age	Int	Pts
23	New York	24	Grady Alderman	OT	6'2"	242	30		
52	BALTIMORE	14	Doug Davis	OT	6'4"	255	25		
19	GREEN BAY	7	Ron Yary	OT	6'6"	265	23		
31	Chicago	0	Bookie Bolin	OG	6'2"	250	29		
27	St. Louis	10	Milt Sunde	OG	6'2"	250	26		
24	DETROIT	10	Jim Vellone	OG	6'2"	255	25		
31	CHICAGO	14	Ed White	OG	6'2"	252	22		
51	CLEVELAND	3	Mick Tingelhoff	C	6'1"	237	29		
9	Green Bay	7	Carl Eller	DE	6'6"	265	27		
52	PITTSBURGH	14	Jim Marshall	DE	6'3"	260	31	1	
27	Detroit	0	Steve Smith	DE	6'5"	240	25		
20	Los Angeles	13	Paul Dickson	DT	6'5"	257	32		
10	SAN FRANCISCO	7	Gary Larsen	DT	6'5"	260	29		
3	Atlanta	10	Alan Page	DT	6'5"	260	24		6

Use Name	Pos.	Hgt	Wgt	Age	Int	Pts
Jim Hargrove	LB	6'3"	232	24		
Wally Hilgenberg	LB	6'3"	235	26		
Mike McGill	LB	6'2"	237	22		
Mike Reilly	LB	6'2"	235	26		6
Lonnie Warwick	LB	6'3"	237	27	4	
Roy Winston	LB	6'1"	230	29	3	
Bobby Bryant	DB	6'	175	25	8	
Karl Kassulke	DB	6'	195	27	2	
Paul Krause	DB	6'3"	195	27	5	6
Earsell Mackbee	DB	6'1"	195	28	6	
Ed Sharockman	DB	6'	200	29	1	
Charlie West	DB	6'1"	190	23		
Dale Hackbart	LB-DB	6'3"	214	33		

Use Name	Pos.	Hgt	Wgt	Age	Int	Pts
Gary Cuozzo	QB	6'1"	195	28		
Joe Kapp	QB	6'2"	215	31		
Bob Lee	QB	6'2"	195	24		
Billy Harris	HB	6'	190	23		
Clint Jones	HB	6'	206	24		18
Dave Osborn	HB	6'	205	26		48
Bill Brown	FB	5'11"	230	31		18
Jim Lindsey	HB-FB	6'2"	212	24		12
Oscar Reed	HB-FB	5'11"	222	25		18
Bob Grim	WR	6'	197	24		6
Tom Hall	WR	6'1"	195	28		
John Henderson	WR	6'3"	190	26		30
Gene Washington	WR	6'3"	218	25		54
John Beasley	TE	6'3"	230	24		30
Kent Kramer	TE	6'5"	235	25		6
Fred Cox	K	5'10"	200	30		121

DETROIT LIONS 9-4-1 Joe Schmidt

			Use Name	Pos.	Hgt	Wgt	Age	Int	Pts
13	Pittsburgh	16	Rocky Freitas	OT	6'6"	260	23		
24	NEW YORK	0	Roger Shoals	OT	6'4"	255	30		
28	Cleveland	21	Jim Yarbrough	OT	6'5"	250	22		
17	GREEN BAY	28	Frank Gallagher	OG	6'2"	240	26		
13	CHICAGO	7	Bob Kowalkowski	OG	6'3"	245	25		
10	Minnesota	24	Rocky Rasley	OG	6'3"	248	22		
26	San Francisco	14	Chuck Walton	OG	6'3"	250	28		
27	ATLANTA	21	Ed Flanagan	C	6'3"	250	25		
20	ST. LOUIS	0	Bill Cottrell	OG-C	6'3"	250	24		
16	Green Bay	10	Larry Hand	DE	6'4"	245	29		
0	MINNESOTA	27	Joe Robb	DE	6'3"	245	32		
17	Baltimore	17	Denis Moore	DT-DE	6'5"	250	26		
28	LOS ANGELES	0	Alex Karras	DT	6'2"	255	33	1	
20	Chicago	3	Jerry Rush	DT	6'4"	260	27		
			Dan Goich	DE-DT	6'4"	265	25		

Use Name	Pos.	Hgt	Wgt	Age	Int	Pts
Mike Lucci	LB	6'2"	230	29		
Ed Mooney	LB	6'2"	240	24		
Paul Naumoff	LB	6'1"	225	24		
Tom Nowatzke	LB	6'3"	230	26		
Bill Swain	LB	6'2"	230	28		
Wayne Walker	LB	6'2"	225	32	1	
Lem Barney	DB	6'	185	23	8	6
Dick LeBeau	DB	6'1"	185	32	6	
Wayne Rasmussen	DB	6'2"	175	27		
Tom Vaughn	DB	5'11"	190	26	2	
Mike Weger	DB	6'2"	185	23	3	
Bobby Williams	DB	6'1"	205	27		

Use Name	Pos.	Hgt	Wgt	Age	Int	Pts
Greg Barton	QB	6'2"	195	23		
Greg Landry	QB	6'4"	205	22		6
Bill Munson	QB	6'2"	200	27		
Nick Eddy	HB	6'1"	205	25		18
Mel Farr	HB	6'2"	205	24		24
Altie Taylor	HB	5'10"	196	21		
Bill Triplett	FB	6'2"	210	30		24
Larry Watkins	FB	6'2"	215	22		6
Bill Malinchak	WR	6'1"	200	25		
Earl McCullouch	WR	5'11"	180	23		30
Phil Odle	WR	5'11"	190	26		
Larry Walton	WR	5'11"	180	22		
John Wright	WR	6'	197	23		18
Craig Cotton	TE	6'4"	222	22		
Charlie Sanders	TE	6'4"	215	23		18
Rick Duncan	K	6'	208	28		
Errol Mann	K	6'	200	28		101

GREEN BAY PACKERS 8-6-0 Phil Bengtson

			Use Name	Pos.	Hgt	Wgt	Age	Int	Pts
17	CHICAGO	0	Forrest Gregg	OT	6'4"	250	36		
14	SAN FRANCISCO	7	Bill Hayhoe	OT	6'8"	258	22		
7	Minnesota	19	Dick Himes	OT	6'4"	244	23		
28	Detroit	17	Francis Peay	OT	6'5"	250	25		
21	Los Angeles	34	Dave Bradley	OG	6'4"	250	25		
28	ATLANTA	10	Gale Gillingham	OG	6'3"	255	25		
38	Pittsburgh	34	Bill Lueck	OG	6'3"	235	23		
6	Baltimore	14	Ken Bowman	C	6'3"	230	26		
7	MINNESOTA	9	Bob Hyland	OG-C	6'5"	250	24		
10	DETROIT	16	Lionel Aldridge	DE	6'4"	245	28		
20	NEW YORK	10	Willie Davis	DE	6'3"	245	36	1	
7	Cleveland	20	Phil Vandersea	DE	6'3"	235	26		
21	Chicago	3	Francis Winkler	DE	6'3"	230	22		
45	ST. LOUIS	28	Bob Brown	DT	6'5"	260	29		
			Henry Jordan	DT	6'3"	250	34		
			Rich Moore	DT	6'6"	285	22		
			Jim Weatherwax	DT	6'7"	260	26		

Use Name	Pos.	Hgt	Wgt	Age	Int	Pts
Lee Roy Caffey	LB	6'3"	250	29	2	
Fred Carr	LB	6'5"	238	23		
Jim Flanigan	LB	6'3"	240	24		
Ray Nitschke	LB	6'3"	235	33	2	
Dave Robinson	LB	6'3"	240	28		
Herb Adderley	DB	6'1"	200	30	5	6
Doug Hart	DB	6'	190	30	3	6
Bob Jeter	DB	6'1"	205	31	3	
John Rowser	DB	6'1"	180	25		
Gordon Rule	DB	6'2"	180	23		
Willie Wood	DB	5'10"	190	33	3	

Zeke Bratkowski — Voluntarily Retired

Use Name	Pos.	Hgt	Wgt	Age	Int	Pts
Don Horn	QB	6'2"	195	24		6
Bart Starr	QB	6'1"	190	36		
Bill Stevens	QB	6'3"	195	24		
Donny Anderson	HB	6'3"	210	26		12
Elijah Pitts	HB	6'1"	205	30		6
Travis Williams	HB	6'1"	210	23		54
Jim Grabowski	FB	6'2"	220	25		12
Perry Williams	FB	6'2"	220	22		
Dave Hampton	HB-FB	6'	210	22		42
Carroll Dale	WR	6'1"	200	31		36
Boyd Dowler	WR	6'5"	225	32		24
John Spilis	WR	6'3"	205	21		
Marv Fleming	TE	6'4"	235	27		12
Ron Jones	TE	6'3"	220	22		
Booth Lusteg	K	5'11"	190	28		15
Mike Mercer	K	6'	217	33		38

CHICAGO BEARS 1-13-0 Jim Dooley

			Use Name	Pos.	Hgt	Wgt	Age	Int	Pts
0	Green Bay	17	Randy Jackson	OT	6'5"	245	25		
17	St. Louis	20	Wayne Mass	OT	6'4"	245	23		
24	New York	28	Rufus Mayes	OT	6'5"	255	21		
0	MINNESOTA	31	Bob Pickens	OT	6'4"	258	26		
7	Detroit	13	Bob Wetoska	C-OT	6'3"	240	31		
14	LOS ANGELES	9	Jim Cadile	OG	6'3"	240	28		
14	Minnesota	31	Howard Mudd (from SF)	OG	6'3"	252	27		
38	PITTSBURGH	7	George Seals	OG	6'2"	260	26		
31	Atlanta	48	Jim Ferguson (from ATL)	C	6'4"	240	26		
21	BALTIMORE	24	Mike Pyle	C	6'3"	250	30		
24	CLEVELAND	28	Marty Amsler	DE	6'5"	255	26		
21	San Francisco	42	Dave Hale	DE	6'7"	230	22		
3	GREEN BAY	21	Willie Holman	DE	6'4"	250	24		
3	DETROIT	20	Ed O'Bradovich	DE	6'3"	255	29	2	
			Loyd Phillips	DE	6'3"	240	24		
			Frank Cornish	DT	6'6"	300	25		
			Dick Evey	DT	6'2"	245	28	2	
			Ken Kortas	DT	6'5"	280	27		

Use Name	Pos.	Hgt	Wgt	Age	Int	Pts
Doug Buffone	LB	6'1"	230	25	2	
Dick Butkus	LB	6'3"	245	25	2	2
Tim Casey (to DEN-A)	LB	6'1"	225	25		
Rudy Kuechenberg	LB	6'2"	215	26		
Dave Martin	LB	6'1"	225	22		
Dan Pride	LB	6'3"	225	27	1	
Dick Daniels	DB	5'9"	180	23	3	
Major Hazelton	DB	6'1"	185	24		
Bennie McRae	DB	6'1"	180	28	1	
Joe Taylor	DB	6'2"	200	28	3	
George Youngblood	DB	6'3"	205	24	3	6
Garry Lyle	HB-DB	6'2"	198	23	1	

Terry Stoepel — Military Service

Use Name	Pos.	Hgt	Wgt	Age	Int	Pts
Virgil Carter	QB	6'1"	185	23		
Jack Concannon	QB	6'3"	205	26		6
Bobby Douglass	QB	6'3"	215	22		12
Gale Sayers	HB	6'	198	26		48
Brian Piccolo	FB-HB	6'	200	29		18
Ronnie Bull	FB	6'	205	30		
Mike Hull	FB	6'3"	220	24		
Ralph Kurek	FB	6'2"	210	26		
Ross Montgomery	FB	6'3"	220	22		
Ron Copeland	WR	6'4"	196	22		
Dick Gordon	WR	5'11"	190	24		24
Bob Jones	WR	6'1"	190	26		
Jerry Simmons (from ATL)	WR	6'3"	180	22		
Cecil Turner	WR	5'10"	170	25		
Bob Wallace	WR	6'3"	211	23		30
Austin Denney	TE	6'2"	230	25		6
Emilio Vallez	TE	6'2"	210	23		
Ray Odgen	WR-TE	6'5"	225	26		
Bobby Joe Green	K	5'11"	175	31		
Mac Percival	K	6'4"	220	29		50

CENTRAL DIVISION

MINNESOTA VIKINGS

RUSHING

Last Name	No.	Yds	Avg	TD
Osborn	186	643	3.5	7
Brown	126	430	3.4	3
Reed	83	393	4.7	1
Jones	54	241	4.5	3
Kapp	22	104	4.7	0
Lindsey	6	21	3.5	1
Harris	6	13	2.2	0
Lee	3	9	3.0	0
Cuozzo	3	-4	-1.3	0

RECEIVING

Last Name	No.	Yds	Avg	TD
Washington	39	821	21	9
Henderson	34	553	16	5
Beasley	33	361	11	4
Osborn	22	236	11	1
Brown	21	183	9	0
Grim	10	155	16	1
Reed	7	59	8	2
Jones	3	23	8	0
Lindsey	2	45	23	1
Kramer	2	37	19	1
Harris	2	13	7	0
Hall	1	12	12	0

PUNT RETURNS

Last Name	No.	Yds	Avg	TD
West	39	245	6	0
Grim	4	12	3	0
Bryant	2	9	5	0

KICKOFF RETURNS

Last Name	No.	Yds	Avg	TD
Jones	17	444	26	0
West	9	240	27	0
Reed	1	38	38	0
Lindsey	2	26	13	0
Harris	1	23	23	0
Smith	1	3	3	0
Alderman	1	0	0	0
Sunde	1	0	0	0

PASSING – PUNTING – KICKING

PASSING

Last Name	Att	Comp	%	Yds	Yd/Att	TD	Int—	%	RK
Kapp	237	120	51	1726	7.3	19	13—	5	10
Cuozzo	98	49	50	693	7.1	4	5—	5	
Lee	11	7	64	79	7.2	1	0—	0	

PUNTING

Last Name	No	Avg
Lee	67	40.0

KICKING

Last Name	XP	Att	%	FG	Att	%
Cox	43	43	100	26	37	70

DETROIT LIONS

RUSHING

Last Name	No.	Yds	Avg	TD
Triplett	111	377	3.4	3
Taylor	118	348	2.9	0
Eddy	78	272	3.5	2
Farr	58	245	4.2	4
Landry	33	243	7.4	1
Watkins	62	201	3.2	1
Barney	3	36	12.0	0
Munson	7	31	4.4	0
L. Walton	2	6	3.0	0
McCullouch	1	4	4.0	0
Sanders	1	-8	-8.0	0

RECEIVING

Last Name	No.	Yds	Avg	TD
Sanders	42	656	16	3
McCullouch	33	529	16	5
Triplett	13	141	11	1
Farr	13	94	7	0
Watkins	13	87	7	0
Taylor	13	86	7	0
Wright	12	130	11	2
L. Walton	12	109	9	0
Eddy	10	78	8	1
Malinchak	2	24	12	0
Odle	2	24	12	0

PUNT RETURNS

Last Name	No.	Yds	Avg	TD
Barney	9	191	21	1
L. Walton	9	24	3	0
Vaughn	2	10	5	0
Eddy	1	5	5	0

KICKOFF RETURNS

Last Name	No.	Yds	Avg	TD
Williams	17	563	33	1
L. Walton	12	230	19	0
Barney	7	154	22	0
Vaughn	2	44	22	0
Nowatzke	1	14	14	0
Mooney	2	12	6	0
Yarbrough	1	0	0	0

PASSING – PUNTING – KICKING

PASSING

Last Name	Att	Comp	%	Yds	Yd/Att	TD	Int—	%	RK
Munson	166	84	51	1062	6.4	7	8—	5	14
Landry	160	80	50	853	5.3	4	10—	6	20
Barton	1	0	0	0	0.0	0	0—	0	
Farr	1	0	0	0	0.0	0	0—	0	
L. Walton	1	1	100	43	43.0	1	0—	0	

PUNTING

Last Name	No	Avg
Barney	66	34.1
Malinchak	5	36.8
Duncan	3	25.7

KICKING

Last Name	XP	Att	%	FG	Att	%
Mann	26	26	100	25	37	68

GREEN BAY PACKERS

RUSHING

Last Name	No.	Yds	Avg	TD
T. Williams	129	536	4.2	4
Hampton	80	365	4.6	4
Anderson	87	288	3.3	1
Grabowski	73	261	3.6	1
Pitts	35	134	3.8	0
Starr	7	60	8.6	0
P. Williams	18	55	3.1	0
Horn	3	-7	-2.3	1

RECEIVING

Last Name	No.	Yds	Avg	TD
Dale	45	879	20	6
Dowler	31	477	15	4
T. Williams	27	275	10	3
Fleming	18	226	13	2
Hampton	15	216	14	2
Anderson	14	308	22	1
Grabowski	12	98	8	1
Pitts	9	47	5	1
Spilis	7	89	13	0
P. Williams	4	63	16	0

PUNT RETURNS

Last Name	No.	Yds	Avg	TD
T. Williams	8	189	24	1
Pitts	16	60	4	0
Wood	8	38	5	0

KICKOFF RETURNS

Last Name	No.	Yds	Avg	TD
Hampton	22	582	26	1
T. Williams	21	517	25	1
Robinson	3	31	10	0
Pitts	1	22	22	0
Gillingham	1	13	13	0
Hyland	1	0	0	0
P. Williams	1	0	0	0

PASSING – PUNTING – KICKING

PASSING

Last Name	Att	Comp	%	Yds	Yd/Att	TD	Int—	%	RK
Horn	168	89	53	1505	9.0	11	11—	7	11
Starr	148	92	62	1161	7.8	9	6—	4	2
Stevens	3	1	33	12	4.0	0	0—	0	

PUNTING

Last Name	No	Avg
Anderson	58	40.2
Dowler	1	34.0

KICKING

Last Name	XP	Att	%	FG	Att	%
Mercer	23	23	100	5	17	29
Lusteg	12	12	100	1	5	20

CHICAGO BEARS

RUSHING

Last Name	No.	Yds	Avg	TD
Sayers	236	1032	4.4	8
Douglass	51	408	8.0	2
Bull	44	187	4.3	0
Piccolo	45	148	3.3	2
Hull	29	81	2.8	1
Concannon	22	62	2.8	1
Montgomery	15	52	3.5	0
Gordon	2	28	14.0	0
Kurek	8	24	3.0	0
Carter	4	19	4.8	0
Green	1	17	17.0	0
Wallace	4	16	4.0	0
Denney	1	4	4.0	0

RECEIVING

Last Name	No.	Yds	Avg	TD
Wallace	47	553	12	5
Gordon	36	414	12	4
Denney	22	203	9	1
Piccolo	17	143	8	1
Sayers	17	116	7	0
Simmons	14	182	13	0
Bull	14	91	7	0
Hull	12	63	5	0
Ogden	7	100	14	0
Kurek	4	30	8	0
Montgomery	2	8	4	0
Turner	1	19	19	0
Lyle	1	11	11	0

PUNT RETURNS

Last Name	No.	Yds	Avg	TD
Lyle	12	78	7	0
Piccolo	9	43	5	0
Turner	8	32	4	0
Gordon	1	11	11	0

KICKOFF RETURNS

Last Name	No.	Yds	Avg	TD
Sayers	14	339	24	0
Turner	10	326	33	0
Lyle	11	248	23	0
Gordon	6	105	18	0
Kurek	4	66	17	0
Butkus	3	28	9	0
Seals	2	20	10	0
Holman	1	0	0	0
Kuechenberg	1	0	0	0

PASSING – PUNTING – KICKING

PASSING

Last Name	Att	Comp	%	Yds	Yd/Att	TD	Int—	%	RK
Concannon	160	87	54	783	4.9	4	8—	5	16
Douglass	148	68	46	773	5.2	5	8—	5	19
Carter	71	36	51	343	4.8	2	5—	7	
Green	2	2	100	30	15.0	0	0—	0	
Sayers	2	0	0	0	0.0	0	0—	0	
Bull	1	0	0	0	0.0	0	0—	0	

PUNTING

Last Name	No	Avg
Green	76	39.0

KICKING

Last Name	XP	Att	%	FG	Att	%
Percival	26	26	100	8	21	38

COASTAL DIVISION

LOS ANGELES RAMS 11-3-0 George Allen

Scores of Each Game

27	Baltimore	20
17	ATLANTA	7
36	NEW ORLEANS	17
27	San Francisco	21
34	GREEN BAY	21
9	Chicago	7
38	Atlanta	6
41	SAN FRANCISCO	30
23	Philadelphia	17
24	DALLAS	23
24	Washington	13
13	MINNESOTA	20
0	Detroit	28
7	BALTIMORE	13

Use Name	Pos.	Hgt	Wgt	Age	Int	Pts
Bob Brown	OT	6'4"	275	26		
Charley Cowan	OT	6'4"	265	31		
Mitch Johnson	OT	6'4"	250	27		
Mike LaHood	OG	6'3"	248	24		
Tom Mack	OG	6'3"	250	25		
George Burman	C-OG	6'3"	255	26		
Ken Iman	C	6'1"	240	30		
Frank Marchlewski	C	6'2"	240	25		
Rick Cash	DE	6'5"	260	24		
Deacon Jones	DE	6'5"	250	30		
Lamar Lundy	DE	6'7"	250	34		
Diron Talbert	DE	6'5"	245	25		
Coy Bacon	DT	6'4"	270	27		
Roger Brown	DT	6'5"	285	32		
Merlin Olsen	DT	6'5"	270	28		

Use Name	Pos.	Hgt	Wgt	Age	Int	Pts
Maxie Gaughan	LB	6'1"	230	31		
Jack Pardee	LB	6'2"	225	33	1	
John Pergine	LB	6'1"	225	22		
Myron Pottios	LB	6'2"	232	29	1	
Jim Purnell	LB	6'2"	238	27		
Doug Woodlief	LB	6'3"	225	25	4	
Willie Daniel	DB	5'11"	190	31	1	
Alvin Haymond	DB	6'	194	27		
Ed Meador	DB	5'11"	190	32	5	12
Jim Nettles	DB	5'9"	177	27	2	
Richie Petitbon	DB	6'3"	208	31	5	
Nate Shaw	DB	6'2"	205	24		
Ron Smith	DB	6'1"	192	26	3	6
Clancy Williams	DB	6'2"	194	26	4	

Jim Wilson — Injury

Use Name	Pos.	Hgt	Wgt	Age	Int	Pts
Roman Gabriel	QB	6'4"	220	29		30
Karl Sweetan	QB	6'1"	200	26		
Mike Dennis	HB	6'1"	207	25		
Willie Ellison	HB	6'1"	200	24		12
Larry Smith	HB	6'3"	220	21		18
Dick Bass	FB	5'10"	195	32		
Les Josephson	FB	6'	207	26		12
Izzy Lang	FB	6'1"	232	26		
Tommy Mason	HB-FB	6'	195	30		12
David Ray	WR	6'	195	24		
Jack Snow	WR	6'2"	190	26		36
Pat Studstill	WR	6'1"	175	31		
Wendell Tucker	WR	5'10"	185	25		42
Pat Curran	TE	6'3"	238	23		
Bob Klein	TE	6'5"	235	22		6
Billy Truax	TE	6'5"	235	26		30
Bruce Gossett	K	6'2"	230	26		102

BALTIMORE COLTS 8-5-1 Don Shula

Scores of Each Game

20	LOS ANGELES	27
14	Minnesota	52
21	Atlanta	14
24	PHILADELPHIA	20
30	New Orleans	10
21	SAN FRANCISCO	24
41	WASHINGTON	17
14	GREEN BAY	6
17	San Francisco	20
24	Chicago	21
13	ATLANTA	6
17	DETROIT	17
10	Dallas	27
13	Los Angeles	7

Use Name	Pos.	Hgt	Wgt	Age	Int	Pts
Sam Ball	OT	6'4"	240	25		
Bob Vogel	OT	6'5"	250	27		
Dan Grimm (to WAS)	OG	6'3"	245	28		
Cornelius Johnson	OG	6'2"	245	26		
Glenn Ressler	OG	6'3"	250	25		
Dan Sullivan	OG	6'3"	250	30		
John Williams	OG	6'3"	256	23		
Bill Curry	C	6'2"	235	26		
Carl Mauck	C	6'3"	240	22		
Roy Hilton	DE	6'6"	240	24		
Lou Michaels	DE	6'2"	250	33		75
Bubba Smith	DE	6'7"	295	24		
Ron Kostelnik	DT	6'4"	260	29		
Fred Miller	DT	6'3"	250	28		
Billy Ray Smith	DT	6'4"	250	34		

Use Name	Pos.	Hgt	Wgt	Age	Int	Pts
Mike Curtis	LB	6'2"	232	26		
Dennis Gaubatz	LB	6'2"	232	28	1	
Bob Grant	LB	6'2"	225	23	3	
Ted Hendricks	LB	6'7"	215	21		
Butch Riley	LB	6'2"	220	22		
Don Shinnick	LB	6'	228	34		
Ocie Austin	DB	6'3"	200	22	2	
Jim Duncan	DB	6'2"	200	23		6
Jerry Logan	DB	6'1"	190	28	1	
Lenny Lyles	DB	6'2"	204	33		
Tommy Maxwell	DB	6'2"	195	22		
Charlie Stukes	DB	6'3"	212	25	1	
Rick Volk	DB	6'3"	195	24	4	

Use Name	Pos.	Hgt	Wgt	Age	Int	Pts
Earl Morrall	QB	6'1"	206	35		
Johnny Unitas	QB	6'1"	196	36		
Tom Matte	HB	6'	214	30		78
Preston Pearson	HB	6'1"	190	24		
Terry Cole	FB	6'2"	220	24		18
Larry Conjar	FB	6'	214	23		
Perry Lee Dunn	FB	6'2"	215	26		
Jerry Hill	FB	5'11"	215	29		12
Eddie Hinton	WR	6'	200	22		
Jimmy Orr	WR	5'11"	185	33		12
Ray Perkins	WR	6'	183	27		12
Willie Richardson	WR	6'2"	198	29		12
Sam Havrilak	DB-WR	6'2"	195	21		
John Mackey	TE	6'2"	224	27		12
Tom Mitchell	TE	6'2"	215	25		
Roland Moss	TE	6'3"	215	22		
David Lee	K	6'4"	230	25		

ATLANTA FALCONS 6-8-0 Norm Van Brocklin

Scores of Each Game

24	SAN FRANCISCO	12
7	Los Angeles	17
14	BALTIMORE	21
17	DALLAS	24
21	San Francsico	7
10	Green Bay	28
6	LOS ANGELES	38
21	Detroit	27
48	CHICAGO	31
20	Washington	27
6	Baltimore	13
45	NEW ORLEANS	17
27	Philadelphia	3
10	MINNESOTA	3

Use Name	Pos.	Hgt	Wgt	Age	Int	Pts
Bob Kelly	OT	6'3"	270	29		
George Kunz	OT	6'5"	245	22		
Bill Sandeman	OT	6'6"	250	26		
Bob Breitenstein	OG-OT	6'3"	267	26		
Dick Enderle	OG	6'1"	247	21		
Mal Snider	OG	6'4"	235	22		6
Roy Schmidt	OT-OG	6'3"	250	27		
Bruce Bosley	C	6'2"	244	35		
Jim Waskiewicz	C	6'4"	240	25		
Bob Hughes	DE	6'4"	250	24		
Claude Humphrey	DE	6'5"	255	25		6
John Zook	DE	6'5"	240	21	2	
Dave Cahill	DT	6'3"	245	27		
Glen Condren	DT	6'2"	250	27		
Bill Sabatino	DT	6'3"	245	24		
Jerry Shay	DT	6'3"	245	25		

Use Name	Pos.	Hgt	Wgt	Age	Int	Pts
Ron Acks	LB	6'2"	225	24		6
Grady Allen	LB	6'3"	225	23	1	
Greg Brezina	LB	6'1"	220	23		
Ted Cottrell	LB	6'1"	232	22		
Fritz Greenlee	LB	6'2"	230	25		
Don Hansen	LB	6'3"	228	25	2	
Tommy Nobis	LB	6'2"	235	25	1	
Jeff Van Note	LB	6'2"	230	23		
Mike Freeman	DB	5'11"	190	25		
Al Lavan	DB	6'1"	194	22	2	
John Mallory	DB	6'	190	23	1	
Ken Reaves	DB	6'3"	205	24	3	
Rudy Redmond	DB	6'	185	22	5	
Jim Weatherford	DB	5'10"	180	23	1	6
Nate Wright (to STL)	DB	5'11"	180	22	2	

Randy Winkler — Military Service

Use Name	Pos.	Hgt	Wgt	Age	Int	Pts
Bob Berry	QB	5'11"	190	27		
Randy Johnson	QB	6'3"	196	25		
Bruce Lemmerman	QB	6'1"	190	23		
Cannonball Butler	HB	5'10"	185	26		3
Gary McDermott	HB	6'1"	211	23		
Jeff Stanceil	HB	6'	192	22		
Paul Gipson	FB-HB	6'	205	23		
Harmon Wages	FB	6'1"	210	23		
Charlie Bryant	HB-FB	6'1"	207	28		
Gail Cogdill	WR	6'2"	200	32		3
Paul Flatley	WR	6'1"	187	28		
Bob Lee	WR	6'3"	200	24		
Monte Ledbetter (From BUF-A)	WR	6'2"	185	26		
Tom McCauley	WR	6'3"	184	22		
Jim Mitchell	TE	6'2"	224	21		
Ralph Smith	TE	6'2"	220	30		
Bob Etter	K	5'11"	152	24		
Billy Lothridge	K	6'1"	190	25		

SAN FRANCISCO FORTY NINERS 4-8-2 Dick Nolan

Scores of Each Game

12	Atlanta	24
7	Green Bay	14
17	WASHINGTON	17
21	LOS ANGELES	27
7	ATLANTA	21
24	Baltimore	21
14	DETROIT	26
30	Los Angeles	41
20	BALTIMORE	17
38	New Orleans	43
24	Dallas	24
42	CHICAGO	21
7	Minnesota	10
14	PHILADELPHIA	13

Use Name	Pos.	Hgt	Wgt	Age	Int	Pts
Cas Banaszek	OT	6'3"	240	23		
Lance Olssen	OT	6'5"	267	22		
Len Rohde	OT	6'4"	250	31		
Elmer Collett	OG	6'4"	244	24		
Woody Peoples	OG	6'2"	247	26		
Randy Beisler	OT-OG	6'4"	255	24		
Forrest Blue	C	6'5"	248	23		
Bill Belk	DE	6'3"	242	23		
Tommy Hart	DE	6'3"	235	24		
Stan Hindman	DE	6'3"	237	25		
Earl Edwards	DT-DE	6'6"	276	23		
Charlie Krueger	DT	6'4"	270	33	1	
Roland Lakes	DT	6'4"	265	29		6
Sam Silas	DE-DT	6'4"	255	28		

Use Name	Pos.	Hgt	Wgt	Age	Int	Pts
Ed Beard	LB	6'2"	220	29		
Harold Hays	LB	6'3"	225	28		
Frank Nunley	LB	6'2"	230	23	1	
Jim Sniadecki	LB	6'2"	220	22		
Skip Vanderbundt	LB	6'3"	240	22		
Dave Wilcox	LB	6'3"	237	26	2	
Kermit Alexander	DB	5'11"	186	28	5	
Johnny Fuller	DB	6'	175	23	1	
Jim Johnson	DB	6'2"	187	31	5	
Mel Phillips	DB	6'	192	27		
Al Randolph	DB	6'2"	204	25	2	
Rosey Taylor (from CHI)	DB	5'11"	186	30	2	
John Woitt	DB	5'11"	170	23	1	6

Kevin Hardy — Knee Injury
Dave Hettema — Military Service
Matt Hazeltine — Voluntary Retirement

Use Name	Pos.	Hgt	Wgt	Age	Int	Pts
John Brodie	QB	6'1"	204	34		
Steve Spurrier	QB	6'2"	203	24		
Doug Cunningham	HB	5'11"	190	23		
Gene Moore	HB	6'	208	22		
Noland Smith (From KC-A)	HB	5'6"	156	25		
Jimmy Thomas	HB	6'1"	216	22		
Gary Lewis	FB-HB	6'2"	225	26		
Ken Willard	FB	6'2"	225	26		
Bill Tucker	FB	6'2"	225	25		
Lee Johnson	WR	6'1"	204	24		
Clifton McNeil	WR	6'2"	185	29		
Gene Washington	WR	6'1"	186	22		
Dick Witcher	WR	6'3"	204	24		
Bill Wondolowski	WR	5'11"	168	22		
Ted Kwalick	TE	6'4"	230	22		
Bob Windsor	TE	6'4"	230	26		
Tommy Davis	K	6'	225	34		
Momcilo Gavric	K	5'10"	167	31		
Jon Kilgore	K	6'1"	205	25		

COASTAL DIVISION

LOS ANGELES RAMS

RUSHING

Last Name	No.	Yds	Avg	TD
L. Smith	166	599	3.6	1
Josephson	124	461	3.7	0
Gabriel	35	156	4.5	5
Mason	33	135	4.1	1
Ellison	20	56	2.8	1
Meador	1	5	5.0	0
Bass	1	1	1.0	0
Lang	1	1	1.0	0
Sweetan	1	−1	−1.0	0

RECEIVING

Last Name	No.	Yds	Avg	TD
Snow	49	734	15	6
L. Smith	46	300	7	2
Tucker	38	629	17	7
Truax	37	431	12	5
Josephson	32	295	9	2
Mason	11	185	17	1
Ellison	4	31	8	1
Studstill	3	28	9	0
Klein	2	17	9	1

PUNT RETURNS

Last Name	No.	Yds	Avg	TD
Haymond	33	435	13	0
R. Smith	23	122	5	0
Pergine	1	0	0	0
Meador	1	−1	−1	0

KICKOFF RETURNS

Last Name	No.	Yds	Avg	TD
R. Smith	27	585	22	0
Haymond	16	375	23	0
Lang	4	70	18	0
Ellison	2	38	19	0
Curran	2	28	14	0
Burman	1	11	11	0
Klein	1	0	0	0

PASSING – PUNTING – KICKING

PASSING

Last Name	Att	Comp	%	Yds	Yd/Att	TD	Int−	%	RK
Gabriel	399	217	54	2549	6.4	24	7−	2	4
Sweetan	13	5	38	101	7.8	1	0−	0	
Ellison	2	0	0	0	0.0	0	0−	0	
Meador	1	0	0	0	0.0	0	0−	0	
L. Smith	1	0	0	0	0.0	0	0−	0	

PUNTING

Last Name	No	Avg
Studstill	80	40.7

KICKING

Last Name	XP	Att	%	FG	Att	%
Gossett	36	36	100	22	34	65

BALTIMORE COLTS

RUSHING

Last Name	No.	Yds	Avg	TD
Matte	235	909	3.9	11
Cole	73	375	5.2	2
Hill	49	143	2.9	2
Pearson	24	81	3.4	0
Havrilak	5	49	9.8	1
Dunn	13	45	3.5	0
Perkins	3	36	12.0	0
Unitas	11	23	2.1	0
Mackey	2	3	1.5	0
Conjar	1	0	0.0	0
Hinton	1	−3	−3.0	0

RECEIVING

Last Name	No.	Yds	Avg	TD
Richardson	43	646	15	3
Matte	43	513	12	2
Mackey	34	443	13	2
Perkins	28	391	14	5
Orr	25	474	19	2
Hinton	13	269	21	1
Hill	11	44	4	0
Mitchell	9	199	22	3
Cole	9	65	7	1
Dunn	5	30	6	0
Pearson	4	64	16	0
Havrilak	1	5	5	0

PUNT RETURNS

Last Name	No.	Yds	Avg	TD
Volk	10	58	6	0
Havrilak	13	56	4	0
Logan	8	41	5	0
Pearson	6	37	6	0

KICKOFF RETURNS

Last Name	No.	Yds	Avg	TD
Pearson	31	706	23	0
Duncan	19	560	29	1
Hinton	1	24	24	0

PASSING – PUNTING – KICKING

PASSING

Last Name	Att	Comp	%	Yds	Yd/Att	TD	Int−	%	RK
Unitas	327	178	54	2342	7.2	12	20−	6	9
Morrall	99	46	46	755	7.6	5	7−	7	
Matte	3	1	33	46	15.3	0	0−	0	

PUNTING

Last Name	No	Avg
Lee	57	45.3

KICKING

Last Name	XP	Att	%	FG	Att	%
Michaels	33	34	97	14	31	45

ATLANTA FALCONS

RUSHING

Last Name	No.	Yds	Avg	TD
Butler	163	655	4.0	3
Wages	72	375	5.2	3
Gipson	62	303	4.9	1
Bryant	50	246	4.9	0
Mitchell	5	77	15.4	0
Berry	20	68	3.4	0
Lemmerman	10	57	5.7	1
Johnson	11	55	5.0	1
McCauley	2	49	24.5	0
McDermott	7	6	0.9	0
Stanceil	4	−1	−0.3	0

RECEIVING

Last Name	No.	Yds	Avg	TD
Flatley	45	834	19	6
Cogdill	24	374	16	5
Mitchell	22	339	15	4
Wages	22	228	10	1
Butler	17	297	17	2
Gipson	4	33	8	0
Smith	2	17	9	0
Bryant	2	15	8	0
Ledbetter	1	16	16	0
Brezina	1	9	9	0

PUNT RETURNS

Last Name	No.	Yds	Avg	TD
Mallory	13	42	3	0
Freeman	4	30	8	0
Wright	4	21	5	0
Cahill	1	0	0	0
McCauley	4	−11	−3	0

KICKOFF RETURNS

Last Name	No.	Yds	Avg	TD
Bryant	21	407	19	0
Butler	13	405	31	0
Gipson	9	145	16	0
Wages	6	76	13	0
Snider	1	48	48	1
Kunz	1	13	13	0
Stanceil	1	10	10	0

PASSING – PUNTING – KICKING

PASSING

Last Name	Att	Comp	%	Yds	Yd/Att	TD	Int−	%	RK
Berry	124	71	57	1087	8.8	10	2−	2	
Johnson	93	51	55	788	8.5	8	5−	5	
Lemmerman	62	25	40	330	5.3	1	4−	6	
Gipson	1	0	0	0	0.0	0	1−100		
Lothridge	1	1	100	9	9.0	0	0−	0	
Wages	1	1	100	16	16.0	1	0−	0	

PUNTING

Last Name	No	Avg
Lothridge	69	41.2

KICKING

Last Name	XP	Att	%	FG	Att	%
Etter	33	33	100	15	30	50

SAN FRANCISCO FORTY NINERS

RUSHING

Last Name	No.	Yds	Avg	TD
Willard	171	557	3.3	7
Cunningham	147	541	3.7	3
Thomas	23	190	8.3	1
Tucker	20	72	3.6	2
Brodie	11	62	5.6	0
Spurrier	5	49	9.8	0
Windsor	5	39	7.8	0
Davis	2	21	10.5	0
Lewis	4	5	1.3	0
Moore	2	4	2.0	0
Washington	1	−4	−4.0	0

RECEIVING

Last Name	No.	Yds	Avg	TD
Washington	51	711	14	3
Cunningham	51	484	9	0
Windsor	49	597	12	2
Willard	36	326	9	3
Witcher	33	435	13	3
Thomas	18	364	20	5
McNeil	17	255	15	3
Tucker	14	104	7	2
L. Johnson	4	42	11	0
Kwalick	2	32	16	1
Moore	2	28	14	0
Edwards	1	1	1	0

PUNT RETURNS

Last Name	No.	Yds	Avg	TD
Smith	10	46	5	0
Cunningham	3	23	8	0
Fuller	5	12	2	0
Alexander	4	−18	−5	0

KICKOFF RETURNS

Last Name	No.	Yds	Avg	TD
Smith	14	315	23	0
Cunningham	9	207	23	0
Fuller	8	155	19	0
Lewis	5	155	31	0
Alexander	3	47	16	0
Taylor	1	16	16	0
Wilcox	1	10	10	0
Edwards	3	3	1	0
Kwalick	1	0	0	0
Sniadecki	1	0	0	0
Tucker	1	0	0	0

PASSING – PUNTING – KICKING

PASSING

Last Name	Att	Comp	%	Yds	Yd/Att	TD	Int−	%	RK
Brodie	347	194	56	2405	6.9	16	15−	4	7
Spurrier	146	81	55	926	6.3	5	11−	8	17
Cunningham	3	3	100	48	16.0	1	0−	0	

PUNTING

Last Name	No	Avg
Kilgore	36	40.3
Davis	23	41.5
Spurrier	12	39.0

KICKING

Last Name	XP	Att	%	FG	Att	%
Gavric	22	24	92	3	11	27
Davis	13	13	100	3	10	30

1969 A.F.L. Losing One Status to Gain Another

With the announcement of the realignment of pro football for 1970, the AFL learned that this was its last season in existence. None of the league officials grieved very heavily, since all ten clubs would be part of the NFL's American Conference next year, but some fans and players openly mourned the passing of the AFL as a separate organization. With two distinct leagues, the Super Bowl had much of the flavor of baseball's World Series, but some people expected the excitement to pale with the amalgamation into one league.

Twenty players from the premier season of 1960 still were active in 1969. George Blanda, Billy Cannon, Gino Cappelletti, Tom Flores, Larry Grantham, Wayne Hawkins, Jim Hunt, Harry Jacobs, Jack Kemp, Jacky Lee, Paul Lowe, Paul Maguire, Billy Mathis, Don Maynard, Ron Mix, Jim Otto, Babe Parilli, Johnny Robinson, Paul Rochester, and Ernie Wright all followed different paths into the new league, and each of them stuck around for ten years to watch the AFL progress from an inferior product in fancy settings to a top-notch league on a par with the long-established NFL.

The AFL went out not with a whisper but with the trumpets of victory. The Kansas City Chiefs, who won the league championship in a new playoff setup which pitted first- and second-place finishers in the opposite divisions against each other in an opening round before the championship game, won a final triumph for the AFL by beating the Minnesota Vikings 23-7 in the Super Bowl.

EASTERN DIVISION

New York Jets—The Jets coasted to another divisional title, beating every Eastern opponent they met during the season. Their four losses to Western teams, however, pointed out weak spots in the defending champions' club. The New York secondary folded against a good passing attack. Last year's starting cornerbacks, Johnny Sample and Randy Beverly, both fell out of favor with coach Weeb Ewbank, and the younger replacements couldn't handle top-notch receivers. A strong pass rush and good linebacking compensated for the leaky secondary to some extent, with Gerry Philbin, John Elliott, and Larry Grantham key men in the front lines. The Jet offense still put a lot of points on the scoreboard, with Joe Namath, Matt Snell, Emerson Boozer, Don Maynard, George Sauer, and Pete Lammons moving the ball against the best of defenses.

Houston Oilers—The Houston defense played so well that the team won half its games with little help from the offense. Elvin Bethea, George Webster, Miller Farr, and Ken Houston all ranked with the AFL's top defenders, and Zeke Moore, Garland Boyette, and W. K. Hicks were quality players who stood up to any attack in the league. Not even the absence of Leroy Mitchell, the fine cornerback obtained from Boston who suffered a broken neck in training camp, seriously hurt the Oilers' defense. The offense, however, creaked and groaned with pain in several spots. Hoyle Granger and Roy Hopkins, the starting runners, both were fullback types, strong on straight-ahead plays but not fast enough to make outside plays work. Pete Beathard compounded the unit's problems by failing to ignite an effective passing attack; after leading the club to a divisional crown in 1967, the twenty-seven-year-old passer had made little progress since.

Boston Patriots—New head coach Clive Rush found instant unpopularity with the fans and press when the Patriots lost their first seven games of the season, but his charges found themselves and won four of their next five matches. They shut out Houston 24-0, beat Cincinnati, Buffalo, and Miami, and lost to Miami 17-16 when Rush elected to gamble for a two-point conversion which failed. The Boston defense, stripped of stars Nick Buoniconti and Leroy Mitchell in off-season trades, had no charismatic players or exciting standouts, but the unit grew tighter with each game. The offense got a boost from rookies Carl Garrett, Ron Sellers, and Mike Montler and veterans Mike Taliaferro and Jim Nance, both rebounding from off-seasons.

Buffalo Bills—Head coach Johnny Rauch quit the Oakland Raiders to come to Buffalo, and he lost more games in this one year than he had in three years in Oakland. But the big story of the season was the arrival of O. J. Simpson. The Heisman Trophy winner from USC had openly expressed reluctance about playing in Buffalo, but once he signed with the Bills, he gave the team a much-needed running threat in the backfield. Simpson gained 697 yards rushing despite playing behind a porous line and under a head coach who built his offense around passing.

Miami Dolphins—The Dolphins slipped back into last place in the East, and head coach George Wilson paid for it with his job. Wilson, however, left behind a solid core of quality players for the next regime. Guard Larry Little and linebacker Nick Buoniconti had joined the team this year in trades which cost Miami very little, and rookies Lloyd

Mumford, Bill Stanfill, and Mercury Morris further swelled the ranks of top players on the team. Already on the Miami scene were Bob Griese, Larry Csonka, Jim Kiick, Manny Fernandez, and Howard Twilley—enough talent to change Miami's future fortunes.

WESTERN DIVISION

Oakland Raiders—Throwing for thirty-four touchdowns, Lamonica won the league MVP award for the second time in the past three seasons. On the other end of Lamonica's passes were two complementary wide receivers, Warren Wells, whose strong point was speed, and Fred Biletnikoff, who relied on good moves and sure hands to make fifty-four catches. With the running attack a secondary feature, the offensive line spent most of its time expertly shielding Lamonica from enemy rushers. On defense, the Raiders got better the farther back you went. The line was adequate; Tom Keating recovered from his Achilles tendon injury, but Dan Birdwell missed most of the season with a bad knee. The linebacking corps of Dan Conners, Gus Otto, and Chip Oliver used the excellent mobility to fine advantage, and the secondary of Willie Brown, Nemiah Wilson, Dave Grayson, and George Atkinson had few peers in the pro ranks. With new coach John Madden blending all the pieces together into a harmonious whole, the Raiders edged the Chiefs out for first place in the West by beating them twice during the season.

Kansas City Chiefs—While the Raiders moved the ball primarily on passes, the Chiefs stuck to the ground on offense. Quarterbacks Len Dawson and Mike Livingston had a deep contingent of running backs to call on; Mike Garrett and Warren McVea provided speed from the halfback slot, and Robert Holmes and Wendell Hayes gave the Chiefs power at fullback. These four handled the running chores so well that coach Hank Stram moved Curtis McClinton to tight end and used rookie Ed Podolak exclusively as a kick returner. The Chiefs reversed Oakland's strategy and used the pass only to loosen enemy defenses for the run. The Kansas City defensive unit was brimming with talented players. Jerry Mays and Buck Buchanan had long starred in the line, and Aaron Brown and Curley Culp had fit in since the championship season of 1966. The linebacking trio of Bobby Bell, Willie Lanier, and Jim Lynch had everything. The secondary of Emmitt Thomas, rookie Jim Marsalis, Johnny Robinson, and Jim Kearney left few enemy receivers unattended.

San Diego Chargers—Five games from the end of the season, a bad case of ulcers forced Sid Gillman to give up the coaching reign and concentrate on his general manager's duties. Of course, the Chargers' 4-5-0 record at the time may have contributed to Gillman's decision and to his ulcers. Assistant Charlie Waller moved up to head coach, and after the Chargers lost their first game for him, the team won its last four outings. The talent on the roster was deep enough to make winning an expected event, not just a late-season occurrence. Halfback Dickie Post, receivers Lance Alworth and Gary Garrison, and guard Walt Sweeney all stood out for excellence, but the Chargers were let down by John Hadl's poor season and Ron Mix's injury-plagued campaign. The defense got good years out of Steve DeLong, Pete Barnes, Rick Redman, Jim Hill, Bob Howard, and Kenny Graham, but the rest of the unit needed patching up.

Denver Broncos—The Broncos began the season with impressive victories over the Patriots and Jets, but injuries took most of the steam out of the offense by mid-season. Quarterback Steve Tensi was bothered by a bad knee, receivers Mike Haffner and Bill Van Heusen missed the last month of the season with injured knees, and runner Floyd Little missed five games with shoulder and knee problems. Little's absence particularly hurt the team, as he had developed into a top runner before getting hurt. Inexperience rather than injuries troubled the defense, but this young unit came up with occasional sterling performances like a 13-0 shutout of the Chargers. The strength of the defense lay up front, where Rich Jackson and Dave Costa were two of the league's top linemen. The linebackers and deep backs all were young players, with speedy rookie cornerback Bill Thompson one of the most exciting newcomers in the AFL.

Cincinnati Bengals—Paul Brown's youth parade brought Greg Cook, Speedy Thomas, Horst Muhlmann, Bill Bergey, Royce Berry, and Ken Riley to Cincinnati as freshman starters this year, with Cook an immediate sensation at quarterback. After starring in the College All-Star game, the blond, handsome Cook reported to the Bengal's training camp and took right over as the offensive leader. On opening day, he threw two touchdown passes in leading the team to a victory over Miami. One week later, he threw three scoring passes and ran for another six points in engineering an upset over San Diego, and he helped beat the Chiefs in their third game. Cook then sat out a month of action with a sore passing arm, but he returned to beat Oakland.

FINAL TEAM STATISTICS

OFFENSE

	BOSTON	BUFFALO	CIN.	DENVER	HOUSTON	K.C.	MIAMI	NEW YORK	OAKLAND	S.D.
FIRST DOWNS:										
Total	166	224	172	243	256	258	224	252	261	275
by Rushing	64	83	66	87	95	129	73	98	84	119
by Passing	87	122	95	130	146	125	131	130	153	131
by Penalty	15	19	11	26	15	4	20	24	24	25
RUSHING:										
Number	367	384	363	394	440	522	401	469	459	455
Yards	1489	1522	1523	1637	1706	2220	1513	1782	1765	1985
Average Yards	4.1	4.0	4.2	4.2	3.9	4.3	3.8	3.8	3.8	4.4
Touchdowns	11	7	10	12	12	19	12	14	4	18
PASSING:										
Attempts	338	442	308	403	489	351	424	394	439	444
Completions	162	215	163	192	239	196	201	203	227	208
Completion Percentage	47.9	48.6	52.9	47.6	48.9	55.8	47.4	51.5	51.7	46.8
Passing Yards	2191	2716	2720	2835	3147	2638	2558	2939	3375	2927
Average Yards per Att.	6.5	6.1	8.8	7.0	6.4	7.5	6.0	7.5	7.7	6.6
Average Yards per Comp.	13.5	12.6	16.7	14.8	13.2	13.5	12.7	14.5	14.9	14.1
Tackled Att. to Pass	24	42	57	44	36	26	53	16	12	33
Yards Lost Tackled	261	371	375	311	322	251	481	138	104	301
Net Yards	1930	2345	2345	2524	2825	2387	2077	2801	3271	2626
Touchdowns	19	17	22	23	15	16	12	21	36	13
Interceptions	18	30	15	23	31	20	29	20	26	21
Percent Intercepted	5.3	6.8	4.9	5.7	6.3	5.7	6.8	5.1	5.9	4.7
PUNTS:										
Number	70	78	85	72	70	68	85	56	69	71
Average Distance	41.5	44.5	38.8	40.1	38.9	44.4	40.6	44.3	42.7	44.6
PUNT RETURNS:										
Number	23	31	23	37	43	32	45	39	39	31
Yards	212	187	135	450	391	251	266	256	225	300
Average Yards	9.2	6.0	5.9	12.2	9.1	7.8	5.9	6.6	5.8	9.7
Touchdowns	0	0	0	0	0	0	0	0	0	0
KICKOFF RETURNS:										
Number	54	62	55	56	49	41	60	46	42	39
Yards	1247	1475	1165	1323	1141	1090	1383	985	996	842
Average Yards	23.1	23.8	21.2	23.6	23.3	26.6	23.1	21.4	23.7	21.6
Touchdowns	0	0	0	0	0	1	1	0	0	0
INTERCEPTION RETURNS:										
Number	20	19	21	14	23	32	18	29	26	31
Yards	326	251	362	228	335	595	317	348	484	444
Average Yards	16.3	13.2	17.2	16.3	14.6	18.6	17.6	12.0	18.6	14.3
Touchdowns	1	1	1	2	2	2	2	1	4	3
PENALTIES:										
Number	77	67	50	80	70	62	53	61	100	63
Yards	837	632	556	753	730	757	631	725	1274	731
FUMBLES:										
Number	15	35	30	15	24	34	27	19	17	27
Number Lost	10	21	23	8	17	19	13	13	7	13
POINTS:										
Total	266	230	280	297	278	359	233	353	377	288
PAT (kick) Attempts	29	24	33	37	29	38	27	33	45	34
PAT (kick) Made	26	23	32	36	29	38	26	33	45	33
PAT (2–Point) Attempts	3	2	0	0	2	2	1	4	0	1
PAT (2–Point) Made	1	0	0	0	2	0	0	1	0	0
FG Attempts	34	26	24	29	40	35	22	47	37	28
FG Made	14	17	16	13	19	27	13	32	20	15
Percent FG Made	41.2	65.4	66.7	44.8	47.5	77.1	59.1	68.1	54.1	53.6
Safeties	2	0	1	0	1	0	0	0	1	0

DEFENSE

	BOSTON	BUFFALO	CIN.	DENVER	HOUSTON	K.C.	MIAMI	NEW YORK	OAKLAND	S.D.
FIRST DOWNS:										
Total	278	236	278	276	183	181	206	229	232	232
by Rushing	142	106	135	95	77	53	66	63	90	71
by Passing	115	118	130	151	93	111	126	151	107	148
by Penalty	21	12	13	30	13	17	14	15	35	13
RUSHING:										
Number	528	454	523	436	430	314	422	343	438	366
Yards	2359	1858	2651	1709	1556	1091	1489	1326	1661	1442
Average Yards	4.5	4.1	5.1	3.9	3.6	3.5	3.5	3.9	3.8	3.9
Touchdowns	18	17	13	15	10	6	9	7	13	11
PASSING:										
Attempts	348	368	396	437	371	426	404	437	422	423
Completions	203	175	205	223	167	200	196	232	164	241
Completion Percentage	58.3	47.6	51.8	51.0	45.0	46.9	48.5	53.1	38.9	57.0
Passing Yards	2610	2772	2866	3295	2495	2491	2845	3086	2511	3075
Average Yards per Att.	7.5	7.5	7.2	7.5	6.7	5.8	7.0	7.1	6.0	7.3
Average Yards per Comp.	12.9	15.8	14.0	14.8	14.9	12.5	14.5	13.3	15.3	12.8
Tackled Att. to Pass	22	31	16	45	32	48	25	42	47	35
Yards Lost Tackled	159	296	180	363	278	419	208	330	402	280
Net Yards	2451	2476	2686	2932	2217	2072	2637	2756	2109	2795
Touchdowns	18	21	24	19	18	10	25	22	15	22
Interceptions	20	19	21	14	23	32	18	29	26	31
Percent Intercepted	5.7	5.2	5.3	3.2	6.2	7.5	4.5	6.6	6.2	7.3
PUNTS:										
Number	55	62	55	71	85	84	80	69	87	76
Average Distance	38.6	42.7	41.4	43.1	43.1	43.0	44.1	39.8	41.8	40.3
PUNT RETURNS:										
Number	19	45	39	35	37	43	30	28	37	30
Yards	114	466	297	246	196	502	130	280	151	291
Average Yards	6.0	10.4	7.6	7.0	5.3	11.7	4.3	10.0	4.1	9.7
Touchdowns	0	0	0	0	0	0	0	0	0	0
KICKOFF RETURNS:										
Number	56	55	39	21	38	59	47	72	64	53
Yards	1068	1322	1065	471	792	1431	1073	1669	1518	1238
Average Yards	19.1	24.0	27.3	22.4	20.8	24.3	22.8	23.2	23.7	23.4
Touchdowns	0	0	1	1	0	0	0	0	0	0
INTERCEPTION RETURNS:										
Number	18	30	15	23	31	20	29	20	26	21
Yards	225	449	239	421	441	325	596	380	349	265
Average Yards	12.5	15.0	15.9	18.3	14.2	16.3	20.6	19.0	13.4	12.6
Touchdowns	1	2	0	4	3	3	3	2	1	0
PENALTIES:										
Number	69	71	72	84	61	39	66	69	81	71
Yards	810	719	824	901	592	443	840	788	918	791
FUMBLES:										
Number	33	25	19	24	27	25	27	25	25	13
Number Lost	14	18	15	14	17	15	13	16	16	6
POINTS:										
Total	316	359	367	344	279	177	332	269	242	276
PAT (kick) Attempts	38	40	42	38	33	17	33	28	27	33
PAT (kick) Made	37	39	41	38	33	16	32	28	26	31
PAT (2–Point) Attempts	0	0	0	2	0	2	4	4	2	1
PAT (2–Point) Made	0	0	0	0	0	0	1	2	0	1
FG Attempts	28	41	46	32	30	27	36	27	30	25
FG Made	17	26	24	22	16	15	24	15	14	13
Percent FG Made	60.7	63.4	52.2	68.8	53.3	55.6	66.7	55.6	46.7	52.0
Safeties	0	1	1	0	0	1	2	0	0	0

INTER–DIVISIONAL PLAYOFFS

December 20, at New York (Attendance 62,977)

SCORING

NEW YORK	3	0	0	3–6
KANSAS CITY	0	3	3	7–13

First Quarter
N.Y. J. Turner, 27 yard field goal

Second Quarter
K.C. Stenerud, 23 yard field goal

Third Quarter
K.C. Stenerud, 25 yard field goal

Fourth Quarter
N.Y. J. Turner, 7 yard field goal
K.C. Richardson, 19 yard pass from Dawson PAT–Stenerud (kick)

TEAM STATISTICS

N.Y.		K.C.
19	First Downs–Total	14
5	First Downs–Rushing	3
11	First Downs–Passing	9
3	First Downs–Penalty	2
1	Fumbles–Number	0
1	Fumbles–Lost Ball	0
3	Penalties–Number	5
15	Yards Penalized	63
0	Missed Field Goals	3
64	Offensive Plays–Total	59
235	Net Yards	276
3.7	Average Gain	4.7
4	Giveaways	0
0	Takeaways	4
–4	Difference	+4

INDIVIDUAL STATISTICS

NEW YORK	No	Yds	Avg.	KANSAS CITY	No	Yds	Avg.
RUSHING							
Snell	12	61	5.1	Garrett	18	67	3.7
Boozer	3	14	4.7	Hayes	10	32	3.2
Mathis	6	11	1.8	Holmes	1	0	0.0
Namath	1	1	1.0	McVea	1	0	0.0
	22	87	4.0		30	99	3.3
RECEIVING							
Sauer	5	61	12.2	Hayes	5	46	9.2
Lammons	3	37	12.3	Taylor	2	74	37.0
B. Turner	2	25	12.5	Arbanas	2	39	19.5
Maynard	1	18	18.0	Holmes	1	29	29.0
Boozer	1	10	10.0	Richardson	1	19	19.0
Snell	1	9	9.0	Pitts	1	–6	–6.0
Mathis	1	4	4.0		12	201	16.8
	14	164	11.7				
PUNTING							
O'Neal	5		37.2	Wilson	6		33.5
PUNT RETURNS							
Battle	2	10	5.0	Garrett	1	10	10.0
				Mitchell	1	4	4.0
					2	14	7.0
KICKOFF RETURNS							
Battle	3	64	21.3	Holmes	2	33	16.5
Nock	1	33	33.0	Hayes	1	31	31.0
	4	97	24.3		3	64	21.3
INTERCEPTION RETURNS							
None				Marsalis	2	42	21.0
				Thomas	1	0	0.0
					3	42	14.0

PASSING

	Att.	Comp.	Comp. Pct.	Yds.	Int.	Yds/ Att.	Yds/ Comp.	Yds Lost Tkld.
NEW YORK								
Namath	40	14	35.0	164	3	4.1	11.7	2–16
KANSAS CITY								
Dawson	27	12	44.4	201	0	7.4	16.8	2–24

December 21, at Oakland (Attendance 53,539)

SCORING

OAKLAND	28	7	14	7–56
HOUSTON	0	0	0	7– 7

First Quarter
Oak. Biletnikoff, 13 yard pass from Lamonica PAT–Blanda (kick)
Oak. Atkinson, 57 yard interception return PAT–Blanda (kick)
Oak. Sherman, 24 yard pass from Lamonica PAT–Blanda (kick)
Oak. Biletnikoff, 31 yard pass from Lamonica PAT–Blanda (kick)

Second Quarter
Oak. Smith, 60 yard pass from Lamonica PAT–Blanda (kick)

Third Quarter
Oak. Sherman, 23 yard pass from Lamonica PAT–Blanda (kick)
Oak. Gannon, 3 yard pass from Lamonica PAT–Blanda (kick)

Fourth Quarter
Hou. Reed, 8 yard pass from Beathard PAT–Gerela (kick)
Oak. Hubbard, 4 yard rush PAT–Blanda (kick)

TEAM STATISTICS

OAK.		HOUS.
17	First Downs–Total	14
5	First Downs–Rushing	1
11	First Downs–Passing	10
1	First Downs–Penalty	3
3	Fumbles–Number	3
1	Fumbles–Lost Ball	2
7	Penalties–Number	3
63	Yards Penalized	48
0	Missed Field Goals	0
60	Offensive Plays–Total	71
412	Net Yards	197
6.9	Average Gain	2.8
4	Giveaways	5
5	Takeaways	4
+1	Difference	–1

INDIVIDUAL STATISTICS

OAKLAND	No	Yds	Avg.	HOUSTON	No	Yds	Avg.
RUSHING							
Dixon	13	48	3.7	Granger	14	29	2.1
Todd	8	31	3.9	LeVias	1	4	4.0
Hubbard	6	19	3.2	Campbell	1	0	0.0
Hagberg	2	9	4.5	Beathard	3	–5	–1.7
Smith	8	3	0.4		19	28	1.5
	37	110	3.0				
RECEIVING							
Smith	4	103	25.8	Reed	7	81	11.6
Sherman	4	60	15.0	Beirne	5	48	9.6
Biletnikoff	3	70	23.3	Granger	3	31	10.3
Todd	1	40	40.0	Haik	2	42	21.0
Hubbard	1	33	33.0	LeVias	1	7	7.0
Cannon	1	3	3.0		18	209	11.6
	14	309	22.1				
PUNTING							
Eischeid	5		42.0	Burrell	11		41.4
PUNT RETURNS							
Atkinson	2	19	9.5	LeVias	2	4	2.0
Sherman	1	8	8.0				
	3	27	9.0				
KICKOFF RETURNS							
Atkinson	1	38	38.0	LeVias	4	69	17.3
Sherman	1	26	26.0	Burrell	3	61	20.3
	2	64	32.0		7	130	18.6
INTERCEPTION RETURNS							
Atkinson	1	57	57.0	Farr	1	0	0.0
Brown	1	15	15.0	Moore	1	0	0.0
Wilson	1	0	0.0	Peacock	1	0	0.0
	3	72	24.0		3	0	0.0

PASSING

	Att.	Cmp.	Comp. Pct.	Yds.	Int.	Yds/ Att.	Yds/ Comp.	Lost Tkld.
OAKLAND								
Lamonica	17	13	76.5	276	1	16.2	21.2	
Blanda	5	1	20.0	33	2	6.6	33.0	
	22	14	63.6	309	3	14.0	22.1	1– 7
HOUSTON								
Beathard	46	18	39.1	209	3	4.5	11.6	6–40

NEW YORK JETS 10-4-0 Weeb Ewbank

Scores of Each Game		
33	Buffalo	19
19	Denver	21
27	San Diego	34
23	Boston	14
21	Cincinnati	7
26	HOUSTON	17
23	BOSTON	17
34	MIAMI	31
16	BUFFALO	6
16	KANSAS CITY	34
40	CINCINNATI	7
14	OAKLAND	27
34	Houston	26
27	Miami	9

Use Name	Pos.	Hgt	Wgt	Age	Int	Pts
Winston Hill	OT	6'4"	280	27		
Sam Walton	OT	6'5"	270	26		
Roger Finnie	OT	6'3"	245	22		
Paul Seiler	C-OT	6'4"	255	23		
Dave Herman	OG	6'2"	255	27		
Pete Perreault	OG	6'3"	248	30		
Randy Rasmussen	OG	6'2"	255	24		
Gordon Wright	OG	6'3"	245	25		
John Schmitt	C	6'4"	245	26		
Paul Crane	LB-C	6'2"	205	25	3	12
Verlon Biggs	DE	6'4"	270	26		
Jimmie Jones	DE	6'3"	215	22		
Gerry Philbin	DE	6'2"	245	28	1	
John Elliott	DT	6'4"	245	24		
Carl McAdams	DT	6'3"	240	25		
Paul Rochester	DT	6'2"	255	32		
Steve Thompson	DT	6'5"	245	24		

Use Name	Pos.	Hgt	Wgt	Age	Int	Pts
Al Atkinson	LB	6'1"	230	26	2	
Ralph Baker	LB	6'3"	235	27	1	
Jim Carroll	LB	6'1"	230	26		
Larry Grantham	LB	6'	210	30		
John Neidert	LB	6'2"	230	23		
Bill Baird	DB	5'10"	180	30	5	
Mike Battle	DB	6'1"	175	23	1	
Randy Beverly	DB	5'11"	185	25	2	
John Dockery	DB	6'	186	24	5	
Cornell Gordon	DB	6'	187	28	4	
Jim Hudson	DB	6'2"	210	26	2	
Cecil Leonard	DB	5'11"	170	23		
Jim Richards	DB	6'1"	180	22	3	

Harvey Nairn – Military Service

Use Name	Pos.	Hgt	Wgt	Age	Int	Pts
Joe Namath	QB	6'2"	195	26		12
Babe Parilli	QB	6'1"	190	39		
Jim Turner	QB	6'2"	205	28		129
Al Woodall	QB	6'5"	210	23		
Emerson Boozer	HB	5'11"	204	26		24
Bill Mathis	HB	6'1"	220	30		30
George Nock	HB	5'10"	200	23		
Matt Snell	FB	6'2"	220	27		30
Lee White	FB	6'4"	240	23		
Don Maynard	WR	6'	180	33		38
Steve O'Neal	WR	6'3"	185	23		
George Sauer	WR	6'1"	195	25		48
Bake Turner	WR	6'	180	29		18
Pete Lammons	TE	6'3"	228	25		12
Wayne Stewart	TE	6'7"	202	22		

HOUSTON OILERS 6-6-2 Wally Lemm

Scores of Each Game		
17	Oakland	21
17	Buffalo	3
22	MIAMI	10
28	BUFFALO	14
0	Kansas City	24
17	New York	26
24	DENVER	21
0	Boston	24
31	CINCINNATI	31
20	Denver	20
32	Miami	7
17	SAN DIEGO	21
26	NEW YORK	34
27	BOSTON	23

Use Name	Pos.	Hgt	Wgt	Age	Int	Pts
Elbert Drungo	OT	6'5"	250	26		
Glen Ray Hines	OT	6'5"	265	25		
Walt Suggs	OT	6'5"	260	30		
Sonny Bishop	OG	6'2"	245	29		
Jim LeMoine	OG	6'2"	245	24		
Tom Regner	OG	6'1"	255	25		
Hank Autry	C	6'3"	230	22		
Bobby Maples	C	6'3"	245	26		
Elvin Bethea	DE	6'3"	250	23		2
Pat Holmes	DE	6'5"	250	29		
Glenn Woods	DE	6'4"	250	23		
Ben Mayes	DT-DE	6'5"	265	24		
Tom Domres	DT	6'3"	255	22		6
Willie Parker	DT	6'2"	265	24		
George Rice	DT	6'3"	260	25		
Carel Stith	DT	6'5"	265	24		

Use Name	Pos.	Hgt	Wgt	Age	Int	Pts
Garland Boyette	LB	6'1"	245	29		
Ron Pritchard	LB	6'1"	222	22		
Olen Underwood	LB	6'1"	230	27	1	
Loyd Wainscott	LB	6'1"	235	22		
Ed Watson	LB	6'2"	222	24		
George Webster	LB	6'4"	223	23	2	
John Douglas	DB	6'1"	195	24		
Miller Farr	DB	6'1"	190	26	6	
W. K. Hicks	DB	6'1"	195	26	4	
Ken Houston	DB	6'3"	192	24	4	6
Zeke Moore	DB	6'2"	198	25	4	6
Johnny Peacock	DB	6'2"	205	22	2	6

Leroy Mitchell – Broken Neck

Use Name	Pos.	Hgt	Wgt	Age	Int	Pts
Pete Beathard	QB	6'2"	207	27		12
Bob Davis	QB	6'3"	208	23		
Don Trull	QB	6'1"	196	27		12
Ode Burrell	HB	6'	192	29		
Woody Campbell	HB	5'11"	202	24		6
Mike Richardson	HB	5'11"	185	22		2
Hoyle Granger	FB-HB	6'1"	225	25		24
Roy Hopkins	FB	6'1"	225	24		30
Rich Johnson	HB-FB	6'1"	210	22		6
Jim Beirne	WR	6'2"	196	22		26
Mac Haik	WR	6'1"	196	23		6
Charlie Joiner	WR	5'11"	185	21		
Jerry LeVias	WR	5'10"	175	22		30
Paul Zaeske	WR	6'2"	200	23		
Ed Carrington	TE	6'4"	225	25		
Alvin Reed	TE	6'5"	230	25		12
Roy Gerela	K	5'10"	185	21		86

BOSTON PATRIOTS 4-10-0 Clive Rush

Scores of Each Game		
7	Denver	35
0	KANSAS CITY	31
23	OAKLAND	38
14	NEW YORK	23
16	Buffalo	23
10	SAN DIEGO	13
17	New York	23
24	HOUSTON	0
16	MIAMI	17
25	Cincinnati	14
35	BUFFALO	21
38	Miami	23
18	San Diego	28
23	Houston	27

Use Name	Pos.	Hgt	Wgt	Age	Int	Pts
Tom Funchess	OT	6'5"	260	24		
Ezell Jones	OT	6'4"	255	22		2
Tom Neville	OT	6'4"	255	26		
Charley Long	OG	6'3"	250	31		
Len St. Jean	OG	6'1"	245	27		
Mike Montler	C-OG	6'4"	270	25		
Jon Morris	C	6'4"	240	26		
J. R. Williamson	LB-C	6'2"	220	27		
Ron Berger	DE	6'8"	275	25		
Johnny Cagle	DE	6'3"	260	22		
Larry Eisenhauer	DE	6'5"	255	29		
Mel Witt	DE	6'3"	265	23		
Karl Henke	DT-DE	6'4"	245	24		
Houston Antwine	DT	6'	270	30		
Jim Hunt	DT	5'11"	255	30		
Ray Jacobs	DT	6'3"	285	29		
Ed Toner	DT	6'3"	250	24		

Use Name	Pos.	Hgt	Wgt	Age	Int	Pts
John Bramlett	LB	6'2"	210	28	1	
Jim Cheyunski	LB	6'2"	220	23	1	
Ed Philpott	LB	6'3"	240	23	4	
Marty Schottenheimer	LB	6'3"	224	26	1	
Larry Carwell	DB	6'1"	190	25	4	
John Charles	DB	6'1"	200	25	4	6
Tom Janik	DB	6'3"	195	28	1	
Daryle Johnson	DB	5'11"	190	23	2	8
Art McMahon	DB	5'11"	185	23		
John Outlaw	DB	5'10"	180	24		
Clarence Scott	DB	6'2"	205	25		
Don Webb	DB	5'10"	195	30	2	

Use Name	Pos.	Hgt	Wgt	Age	Int	Pts
Kim Hammond	QB	6'1"	192	24		2
Mike Taliaferro	QB	6'2"	205	27		
Teddy Bailey	HB	6'	200	25		
Sid Blanks	HB	6'	210	28		
Carl Garrett	HB	5'11"	210	22		42
Bob Gladieux	HB	5'11"	190	22		
Jim Nance	FB	6'1"	240	26		36
R. C. Gamble	HB-FB	6'3"	220	22		
Gino Cappelletti	WR	6'	190	35		68
Charley Frazier	WR	6'	184	30		42
Aaron Marsh	WR	6'1"	190	24		
Bill Rademacher	WR	6'1"	190	27		18
Tom Richardson	WR	6'2"	195	24		
Ron Sellers	WR	6'4"	198	22		36
Ken Herock	TE	6'2"	230	28		
Jim Whalen	TE	6'2"	210	25		6
Barry Brown	LB-TE	6'3"	220	26		

BUFFALO BILLS 4-10-0 Johnny Rauch

Scores of Each Game		
19	NEW YORK	33
3	HOUSTON	17
41	DENVER	28
14	Houston	28
23	BOSTON	16
21	Oakland	50
6	Miami	24
7	KANSAS CITY	29
6	New York	16
28	MIAMI	3
21	Boston	35
16	CINCINNATI	13
19	Kansas City	22
6	San Diego	45

Use Name	Pos.	Hgt	Wgt	Age	Int	Pts
Stew Barber	OT	6'3"	248	30		
Paul Costa	OT	6'4"	248	27		
Howard Kindig	OT	6'6"	264	28		
Mike Richey	OT	6'5"	250	22		
George Flint	OG	6'4"	240	31		
Billy Shaw	OG	6'3"	252	29		
Angelo Loukas	OG	6'3"	250	22		
Joe O'Donnell	OG	6'2"	252	26		
Al Bemiller	C	6'3"	243	30		
Mike McBath	DE	6'4"	248	23		
Ron McDole	DE	6'3"	270	29		
Julian Nunamaker	DE	6'3"	250	23		
Chuck DeVleigher	DT	6'4"	265	22		
Jim Dunaway	DT	6'4"	282	27		
Waddey Harvey	DT	6'4"	270	22		
Bob Kruse	DT	6'2"	250	27		
Bob Tatarek	DT	6'4"	255	23		

Use Name	Pos.	Hgt	Wgt	Age	Int	Pts
Edgar Chandler	LB	6'3"	222	23		
Jerald Collins	LB	6'1"	220	22		
Paul Guidry	LB	6'3"	228	25	2	
Harry Jacobs	LB	6'2"	226	32	2	
Paul Maguire	LB	6'	228	31		
Dave Ogas	LB	6'3"	240	23		
Mike Stratton	LB	6'3"	230	27		
Butch Byrd	DB	6'	196	27	7	6
Hilton Crawford	DB	6'	198	24		
Booker Edgerson	DB	5'10"	183	30	1	6
John Pitts	DB	6'4"	215	24	2	
Pete Richardson	DB	6'1"	205	22	2	
George Saimes	DB	5'10"	185	27	3	
Robert James	WR-DB	6'1"	177	22		

Bob Kalsu – Military Service

Use Name	Pos.	Hgt	Wgt	Age	Int	Pts
Dan Darragh	QB	6'3"	196	22		
James Harris	QB	6'3"	215	22		
Jack Kemp	QB	6'1"	204	35		
Tom Sherman (from BOS)	QB	6'	190	23		
Max Anderson	HB	5'8"	180	24		6
Preston Ridlehuber	HB	6'2"	215	25		
O. J. Simpson	HB	6'2"	204	22		30
Bill Enyart	FB	6'4"	236	22		18
Wayne Patrick	FB	6'2"	225	23		18
Marlin Briscoe	WR	5'10"	177	23		30
Bobby Crockett	WR	6'	200	26		
Monte Ledbetter (to ATL-N)	WR	6'2"	185	26		
Haven Moses	WR	6'3"	200	23		30
Roy Reeves	WR	5'11"	182	23		
Bubba Thornton	WR	6'	175	22		
Charley Ferguson	TE	6'5"	224	29		
Willie Grate	TE	6'4"	225	23		6
Bill Masters	TE	6'5"	225	25		6
Bruce Alford	K	6'	185	24		74

MIAMI DOLPHINS 3-10-1 George Wilson

Scores of Each Game		
21	Cincinnati	27
17	Oakland	20
10	Houston	22
20	OAKLAND	20
14	SAN DIEGO	21
10	Kansas City	17
24	BUFFALO	6
31	New York	34
17	Boston	16
3	Buffalo	28
7	HOUSTON	32
23	BOSTON	38
27	DENVER	24
9	NEW YORK	27

Use Name	Pos.	Hgt	Wgt	Age	Int	Pts
John Boynton	OT	6'4"	255	23		
Doug Crusan	OT	6'5"	255	23		
Norm Evans	OT	6'5"	250	26		
Billy Neighbors	OG	5'11"	250	29		
Maxie Williams	OG	6'4"	250	29		
Larry Little	OT-OG	6'1"	270	23		
Tom Goode	C	6'3"	250	30		
Jeff Richardson	OT-C	6'3"	250	24		
Norm McBride	DE	6'3"	235	22		
Jim Riley	DE	6'4"	255	24		
Bill Stanfill	DE	6'5"	250	22	2	12
Bob Joswick	DT-DE	6'5"	250	23		
Manny Fernandez	DT	6'2"	250	23		
Bob Heinz	DT	6'6"	265	22		
John Richardson	DT	6'2"	260	24		
Freddie Woodson	OG-DT	6'2"	255	25		

Use Name	Pos.	Hgt	Wgt	Age	Int	Pts
Nick Buoniconti	LB	5'11"	220	28	3	
Randy Edmunds	LB	6'2"	220	23		
Frank Emanuel	LB	6'3"	225	26		
Jimmy Keyes	LB	6'2"	225	25		
Dale McCullers	LB	6'1"	215	21		
Jesse Powell	LB	6'1"	212	22		
Ed Weisacosky	LB	6'	230	25	3	
Dick Anderson	DB	6'2"	205	23	3	
Tom Beier	DB	5'11"	198	24	1	
Garry Grady	DB	5'11"	180	22		
Lloyd Mumphord	DB	5'11"	180	22	5	
Willie Pearson	DB	6'	190	22		
Bob Petralla	DB	6'	185	24	1	
Jimmy Warren	DB	5'11"	175	30		
Dick Westmoreland	DB	6'1"	195	28		

Use Name	Pos.	Hgt	Wgt	Age	Int	Pts
Bob Griese	QB	6'1"	190	24		
Rick Norton	QB	6'1"	190	25		
John Stofa (From CIN)	QB	6'3"	210	27		
Jim Kiick	HB	5'11"	215	23		60
Mercury Morris	HB	5'10"	185	22		12
Barry Pryor	HB	6'	215	23		
Larry Csonka	FB	6'3"	240	22		18
Stan Mitchell	FB	6'2"	225	25		
Jack Clancy	WR	6'1"	195	25		6
Bill Darnall	WR	6'2"	197	25		
Jimmy Hines	WR	6'	175	22		
Gene Milton	WR	5'10"	170	24		6
Karl Noonan	WR	6'3"	190	25		18
Howard Twilley	WR	5'10"	180	25		6
Tommy Boutwell	QB-WR	6'2"	205	22		
Jim Mertens	TE	6'3"	235	22		
Doug Moreau	TE	6'2"	215	24		
Larry Seiple	TE	6'	213	24		30
Karl Kremser	K	6'	180	24		65

NEW YORK JETS

RUSHING

Last Name	No.	Yds	Avg	TD
Snell	191	695	3.6	4
Boozer	130	604	4.6	4
Mathis	96	355	3.7	4
White	28	88	3.1	0
Namath	11	33	3.0	2
Woodall	4	13	3.3	0
Sauer	1	5	5.0	0
Parilli	3	4	1.3	0
B. Turner	1	−4	−4.0	0
Nock	3	−5	−1.7	0
Maynard	1	−6	−6.0	0

RECEIVING

Last Name	No.	Yds	Avg	TD
Maynard	47	938	20	6
Sauer	45	745	17	8
Lammons	33	400	12	2
Snell	22	187	9	1
Boozer	20	222	11	0
Mathis	18	183	10	1
B. Turner	11	221	20	3
Stewart	5	39	8	0
Dockery	1	6	6	0
White	1	−2	−2	0

PUNT RETURNS

Last Name	No.	Yds	Avg	TD
Battle	34	235	7	0
Baird	4	21	5	0
Leonard	1	0	0	0

KICKOFF RETURNS

Last Name	No.	Yds	Avg	TD
Battle	31	750	24	0
Leonard	7	120	17	0
B. Turner	3	74	25	0
Richards	2	36	18	0
White	1	5	5	0
Carroll	1	0	0	0
Sauer	1	0	0	0

PASSING – PUNTING – KICKING

Last Name	Att	Comp	%	Yds	Yd/Att	TD	Int—	%	RK
PASSING									
Namath	361	185	51	2734	7.6	19	17—	5	2
Parilli	24	14	58	138	5.8	2	1—	4	
Woodall	9	4	44	67	7.4	0	2—	22	

Last Name	No	Avg							
PUNTING									
O'Neal	54	44.3							
B. Turner	2	44.5							

Last Name	XP	Att	%	FG	Att	%			
KICKING									
J. Turner	33	33	100	32	47	68			

2 POINT XP
Maynard

HOUSTON OILERS

RUSHING

Last Name	No.	Yds	Avg	TD
Granger	186	740	4.0	3
Hopkins	131	473	3.6	4
Burrell	41	147	3.6	0
Campbell	28	98	3.5	1
Beathard	19	89	4.7	2
Richardson	5	51	10.2	0
Johnson	11	42	3.8	0
Trull	8	25	3.1	2
Haik	2	21	10.5	0
LeVias	6	18	3.0	0
Davis	3	2	0.7	0

RECEIVING

Last Name	No.	Yds	Avg	TD
Reed	51	664	13	2
LeVias	42	696	17	5
Beirne	42	540	13	4
Hopkins	29	338	12	1
Haik	27	375	14	1
Granger	27	330	12	1
Campbell	7	82	12	0
Joiner	7	77	11	0
Burrell	5	28	6	0
Johnson	2	17	9	1

PUNT RETURNS

Last Name	No.	Yds	Avg	TD
LeVias	35	292	8	0
Richardson	7	93	13	0
Burrell	1	6	6	0

KICKOFF RETURNS

Last Name	No.	Yds	Avg	TD
LeVias	38	940	25	0
Burrell	5	101	20	0
Joiner	3	73	24	0
Reed	3	0	0	0
Houston	0	27	0	0

PASSING – PUNTING – KICKING

Last Name	Att	Comp	%	Yds	Yd/Att	TD	Int—	%	RK
PASSING									
Beathard	370	180	49	2455	6.6	10	21—	6	8
Trull	75	34	45	469	6.3	3	6—	8	
Davis	42	25	60	223	5.3	2	4—	10	
LeVias	2	0	0	0	0.0	0	0—	0	

Last Name	No	Avg							
PUNTING									
Gerela	41	40.4							
Burrell	29	36.8							

Last Name	XP	Att	%	FG	Att	%			
KICKING									
Gerela	29	29	100	19	40	48			

2 POINT XP
Beirne
Richardson

BOSTON PATRIOTS

RUSHING

Last Name	No.	Yds	Avg	TD
Nance	193	750	3.9	6
Garrett	137	691	5.0	5
Gamble	16	35	2.2	0
Blanks	7	30	4.3	0
Frazier	2	−1	−0.5	0
Taliaferro	12	−16	−1.3	0

RECEIVING

Last Name	No.	Yds	Avg	TD
Garrett	29	267	9	2
Nance	29	168	6	0
Sellers	27	705	26	6
Frazier	19	306	16	7
Rademacher	17	217	13	3
Whalen	16	235	15	1
Marsh	8	108	14	0
Gamble	7	74	11	0
Brown	6	69	12	0
Blanks	2	16	8	0
Cappelletti	1	21	21	0
Richardson	1	5	5	0

PUNT RETURNS

Last Name	No.	Yds	Avg	TD
Garrett	12	159	13	0
Carwell	5	43	9	0
Blanks	5	10	2	0
Janik	1	0	0	0

KICKOFF RETURNS

Last Name	No.	Yds	Avg	TD
Garrett	28	792	28	0
Marsh	6	136	23	0
Blanks	6	131	22	0
Gladieux	4	61	15	0
Scott	6	43	7	0
Carwell	1	28	28	0
Gamble	1	23	23	0
Berger	1	20	20	0
Schott'nhmer	1	13	13	0

PASSING – PUNTING – KICKING

Last Name	Att	Comp	%	Yds	Yd/Att	TD	Int—	%	RK
PASSING									
Taliaferro	331	160	48	2160	6.5	19	18—	5	11
Hammond	6	2	33	31	5.2	0	0—	0	
Garrett	1	0	0	0	0.0	0	0—	0	

Last Name	No	Avg							
PUNTING									
Janik	70	41.5							

Last Name	XP	Att	%	FG	Att	%			
KICKING									
Cappelletti	26	27	96	14	34	41			

2 POINT XP
Hammond

BUFFALO BILLS

RUSHING

Last Name	No.	Yds	Avg	TD
Simpson	181	697	3.9	2
Patrick	83	361	4.3	3
Enyart	47	191	4.1	1
Kemp	37	124	3.4	0
Anderson	13	74	5.7	1
Ridlehuber	4	25	6.3	0
Harris	10	25	2.5	0
Sherman	2	14	7.0	0
Darragh	6	14	2.3	0
Masters	1	−3	−3.0	0

RECEIVING

Last Name	No.	Yds	Avg	TD
Moses	39	752	19	5
Patrick	35	229	7	0
Masters	33	387	12	1
Briscoe	32	532	17	5
Simpson	30	343	11	3
Enyart	19	186	10	2
Thornton	14	134	10	0
Anderson	7	65	9	0
Crockett	4	50	13	0
Grate	1	19	19	1
James	1	19	19	0

PUNT RETURNS

Last Name	No.	Yds	Avg	TD
Anderson	19	142	7	0
Byrd	7	37	5	0
Reeves	2	3	2	0
Ridlehuber	1	3	3	0
James	1	2	2	0
Richardson	1	0	0	0

KICKOFF RETURNS

Last Name	No.	Yds	Avg	TD
Thornton	30	749	25	0
Simpson	21	529	25	0
Anderson	4	86	22	0
Crawford	3	74	25	0
Collins	2	14	7	0
Enyart	1	12	12	0
Harvey	1	11	11	0

PASSING – PUNTING – KICKING

Last Name	Att	Comp	%	Yds	Yd/Att	TD	Int—	RK	
PASSING									
Kemp	344	170	49	1981	5.8	13	22—	6	9
Darragh	52	24	46	365	7.0	1	6—	12	
Harris	36	15	42	270	7.5	1	1—	3	
Sherman	2	2	100	20	10.0	1	0—	0	
Briscoe	1	0	0	0.0		0	1—	100	
Maguire	1	1	100	19	19.0	0	0—	0	
Ridlehuber	1	1	100	45	45.0	1	0—	0	

Last Name	No	Avg							
PUNTING									
Maguire	78	44.5							

Last Name	XP	Att	%	FG	Att	%			
KICKING									
Alford	23	24	96	17	26	65			

MIAMI DOLPHINS

RUSHING

Last Name	No.	Yds	Avg	TD
Kiick	180	575	3.2	9
Csonka	131	566	4.3	2
Morris	23	110	4.8	1
Griese	21	102	4.9	0
Mitchell	28	80	2.9	0
Milton	7	62	8.9	0
Norton	8	16	2.0	0
Hines	1	7	7.0	0
Seiple	1	6	6.0	0
Noonan	1	−11	−11.0	0

RECEIVING

Last Name	No.	Yds	Avg	TD
Seiple	41	577	14	5
Kiick	29	443	15	1
Noonan	29	307	11	3
Clancy	21	289	14	1
Csonka	21	183	9	1
Milton	12	179	15	0
Twilley	10	158	16	1
Mitchell	10	125	13	0
Moreau	10	136	14	0
Morris	6	65	11	0
Boutwell	4	29	7	0
Mertens	2	26	13	0
Hines	2	23	12	0
Pryor	2	−3	−2	0
Darnall	1	13	13	0
Anderson	1	8	8	0

PUNT RETURNS

Last Name	No.	Yds	Avg	TD
Morris	25	172	7	0
Anderson	12	82	7	0
Beier	5	8	2	0
Milton	1	4	4	0
McCullers	1	0	0	0
Twilley	1	0	0	0

KICKOFF RETURNS

Last Name	No.	Yds	Avg	TD
Morris	43	1136	26	1
Milton	8	166	21	0
Beier	4	58	15	0
Hines	1	22	22	0
Mertens	2	1	1	0
Mumphord	1	0	0	0
Warren	1	0	0	0

PASSING – PUNTING – KICKING

Last Name	Att	Comp	%	Yds	Yd/Att	TD	Int—	%	RK
PASSING									
Griese	252	121	48	1695	6.7	10	16—	6	10
Norton	148	65	44	709	4.8	2	11—	7	12
Stofa	23	14	61	146	6.4	0	2—	9	
Seiple	1	1	100	8	8.0	0	0—	0	

Last Name	No	Avg							
PUNTING									
Seiple	80	40.8							
Anderson	5	37.6							

Last Name	XP	Att	%	FG	Att	%			
KICKING									
Kremser	26	27	96	13	22	59			

OAKLAND RAIDERS 12-1-1 John Madden

Scores of Each Game

21	HOUSTON	17
20	MIAMI	17
38	Boston	23
20	Miami	20
24	Denver	14
50	BUFFALO	21
24	San Diego	12
17	Cincinnati	31
41	DENVER	10
21	SAN DIEGO	16
27	Kansas City	24
27	New York	14
37	CINCINNATI	17
10	KANSAS CITY	6

Use Name	Pos.	Hgt	Wgt	Age	Int	Pts
Harry Schuh	OT	6'2"	260	26		
Art Shell	OT	6'5"	255	22		
Bob Svihus	OT	6'4"	245	26		
George Buehler	OG	6'2"	260	22		
Jim Harvey	OG	6'5"	245	26		
Wayne Hawkins	OG	6'	240	31		
Gene Upshaw	OG	6'5"	255	24		
Jim Otto	C	6'2"	248	31		
Ben Davidson	DE	6'8"	275	29		
Ike Lassiter	DE	6'5"	270	28		
Carleton Oats	DT-DE	6'2"	260	26		
Dan Birdwell	DT	6'4"	250	28		
Al Dotson	DT	6'4"	260	26		2
Tom Keating	DT	6'3"	247	26		
Art Thoms	DT	6'5"	250	22		
Duane Benson	LB	6'2"	215	24		
Bill Budness	LB	6'1"	215	26		
Dan Conners	LB	6'1	230	27	1	12
Bill Laskey	LB	6'2"	235	26	3	
Chip Oliver	LB	6'2"	220	23	1	6
Gus Otto	LB	6'2"	220	26	2	
Jackie Allen	DB	6'1"	187	21		
Butch Atkinson	DB	6'	180	22	2	6
Willie Brown	DB	6'1"	190	28	5	
Dave Grayson	DB	5'10"	185	30	8	6
Kent McCloughan	DB	6'1"	190	26		
Howie Williams	DB	6'2"	190	32	2	
Nemiah Wilson	DB	6'	165	26	2	
George Blanda	QB	6'1"	215	41		105
Daryle Lamonica	QB	6'2"	215	28		6
Charlie Smith	HB	6'1"	205	23		24
Larry Todd	HB	6'1"	185	26		12
Pete Banaszak	FB-HB	5'11"	200	25		18
Hewritt Dixon	FB	6'2"	230	29		6
Marv Hubbard	FB	6'1"	215	23		
Fred Biletnikoff	WR	6'1"	190	26		72
Drew Buie	WR	6'2"	178	22		
Rod Sherman	WR	6'	190	24		
Warren Wells	WR	6'1"	190	26		84
Billy Cannon	TE	6'1"	215	32		12
Lloyd Edwards	TE	6'3"	248	22		
Roger Hagberg	TE	6'2"	215	30		6
Mike Eischeid	K	6'	190	28		

KANSAS CITY CHIEFS 11-2-0 Hank Stram

Scores of Each Game

27	San Diego	9
31	Boston	0
19	Cincinnati	24
26	Denver	13
24	HOUSTON	0
17	MIAMI	10
42	CINCINNATI	22
29	Buffalo	7
27	SAN DIEGO	3
34	New York	16
24	OAKLAND	27
31	DENVER	17
22	BUFFALO	19
6	Oakland	10

Use Name	Pos.	Hgt	Wgt	Age	Int	Pts
Dave Hill	OT	6'5"	260	28		
Jim Tyrer	OT	6'6"	275	30		
Ed Budde	OG	6'5"	260	28		
George Daney	OG	6'3"	240	22		6
Mo Moorman	OG	6'5"	252	25		
E. J. Holub	C	6'4"	236	31		
Remi Prudhomme	C	6'4"	250	27		
Aaron Brown	DE	6'5"	265	25		
Jerry Mays	DE	6'4"	252	29		
Gene Trosch	DE	6'7"	277	24		
Buck Buchanan	DT	6'7"	287	29		
Curley Culp	DT	6'1"	265	23		
Ed Lothamer	DT	6'5"	270	26		
Bobby Bell	LB	6'4"	228	29		6
Chuck Hurston	LB	6'6"	240	26		
Willie Lanier	LB	6'1"	245	24	4	
Jim Lynch	LB	6'1"	235	24	3	
Bob Stein	LB	6'2"	235	21		
Caesar Belser	DB	6'	212	24		
Jim Kearney	DB	6'2"	206	26	5	6
Jim Marsalis	DB	5'11"	194	23	2	
Willie Mitchell	DB	6'1"	185	27	1	
Johnny Robinson	DB	6'	205	30	8	
Goldie Sellers	DB	6'2"	198	27		6
Emmitt Thomas	DB	6'2"	192	26	9	6
Len Dawson	QB	6'	190	35		
Tom Flores (from BUF)	QB	6'1"	202	32		
Jacky Lee	QB	6'1"	185	30		
Mike Livingston	QB	6'3"	205	23		
Mike Garrett	HB	5'9"	200	25		48
Paul Lowe	HB	6'	205	32		
Warren McVea	HB	5'10"	182	23		42
Ed Podolak	HB	6'1"	204	22		
Noland Smith (to SF-N)	HB	5'6"	156	25		
Wendell Hayes	FB	6'2"	220	28		24
Robert Holmes	FB	5'9"	220	23		30
Frank Pitts	WR	6'2"	200	25		12
Gloster Richardson	WR	6'	200	26		12
Otis Taylor	WR	6'2"	215	26		42
Mickey McCarty	TE	6'5"	255	22		
Curtis McClinton	TE	6'3"	227	31		
Morris Stroud	TE	6'10"	235	23		
Fred Arbanas	OT-TE	6'3"	240	30		
Jan Stenerud	K	6'2"	187	26		119
Jerrel Wilson	K	6'4"	222	28		

SAN DIEGO CHARGERS 8-6-0 Sid Gillman Charlie Waller

Scores of Each Game

9	KANSAS CITY	27
20	Cincinnati	34
34	NEW YORK	27
21	CINCINNATI	14
21	Miami	14
13	Boston	10
12	OAKLAND	24
0	Denver	13
3	Kansas City	27
16	Oakland	21
45	DENVER	24
21	Houston	17
28	BOSTON	18
45	BUFFALO	6

Use Name	Pos.	Hgt	Wgt	Age	Int	Pts
Gene Ferguson	OT	6'7"	306	21		6
Ron Mix	OT	6'4"	250	31		
Terry Owens	OT	6'6"	270	25		
Bob Wells	OT	6'4"	270	24		
Gary Kirner	OG	6'3"	255	27		
Jim Schmedding	OG	6'2"	250	23		
Walt Sweeney	OG	6'3"	260	28		
Sam Gruneisen	C	6'1"	250	28		
Bill Lenkaitis	OG-C	6'3"	250	23		
Ron Billingsley	DE	6'8"	265	24		
Steve DeLong	DE	6'3"	252	26		
Houston Ridge	DE	6'4"	245	25		
Bob Briggs	DT	6'4"	270	24		
LevertCarr	DT	6'5"	250	25		
Dan Sartin	DT	6'1"	245	23		
Russ Washington	DT	6'6"	290	22		
Chuck Allen	LB	6'1"	225	29		
Pete Barnes	LB	6'3"	245	24	5	
Bob Bruggers	LB	6'1"	230	25	1	
Jim Campbell	LB	6'3"	218	23	1	
Jim Fetherston	LB	6'2"	225	24		
Rick Redman	LB	5'11"	225	26	1	
Jeff Staggs	LB	6'2"	240	25		
Joe Beauchamp	DB	6'	185	25		
Speedy Duncan	DB	5'10"	175	26	6	6
Dick Farley	DB	6'	185	23		
Kenny Graham	DB	6'	205	27	4	12
Jim Hill	DB	6'2"	192	22	7	
Bob Howard	DB	6'1"	190	24	6	
Gene Huey	DB	5'11"	190	22		
Larry Rentz	DB	6'1"	170	22		
Jim Tolbert	DB	6'3"	207	25		
Marty Domres	QB	6'3"	212	22		24
John Hadl	QB	6'2"	215	29		12
Dickie Post	HB	5'9"	190	23		36
Ron Sayers	HB	6'1"	202	22		
Russ Smith	FB-HB	6'1"	209	25		12
Gene Foster	FB	5'11"	220	26		6
Brad Hubbert	FB	6'1"	227	28		24
Lance Alworth	WR	6'	180	29		24
Rick Eber	WR	6'	185	24		6
Gary Garrison	WR	6'1"	195	25		42
Richard Trapp	WR	6'1"	174	22		
Willie Frazier	TE	6'4"	235	26		
Jacque MacKinnon	TE	6'4"	240	30		
Jeff Queen	TE	6'1"	230	23		
Dennis Partee	K	6'2"	208	23		78

DENVER BRONCOS 5-8-1 Lou Saban

Scores of Each Game

35	BOSTON	7
21	NEW YORK	19
28	Buffalo	41
13	KANSAS CITY	26
14	OAKLAND	24
30	Cincinnati	23
21	Houston	24
13	SAN DIEGO	0
10	Oakland	41
20	HOUSTON	20
24	San Diego	45
17	Kansas City	31
24	Miami	27
27	CINCINNATI	16

Use Name	Pos.	Hgt	Wgt	Age	Int	Pts
Sam Brunelli	OT	6'1"	270	26		
Mike Current	OT	6'4"	260	23		
Wallace Dickey	OT	6'3"	260	28		
George Goeddeke	OG	6'3"	253	24		
Buzz Highsmith	OG	6'4"	230	26		
Mike Schnitker	OG	6'3"	235	22		
Bob Young	OG	6'2"	260	26		
Jay Bachman	C	6'3"	250	23		
Larry Kaminski	C	6'2"	245	24		
Walt Barnes	DE	6'3"	250	25		
Pete Duranko	DE	6'2"	252	25		
Rich Jackson	DE	6'2"	255	28		
Dave Costa	DT	6'2"	265	27		
Jerry Inman	DT	6'3"	255	29		
Rex Mirich	DT	6'4"	250	28		
Paul Smith	DT	6'3"	245	24		
Tim Casey (from CHI-N)	LB	6'1"	225	25		
Gary Crane	LB	6'4"	230	22		
Ken Criter	LB	5'11"	223	22		
Carl Cunningham	LB	6'3"	240	25	2	
John Huard	LB	6'	220	25	2	
Gordon Lambert	LB	6'5"	245	24		
Chip Myrtle	LB	6'2"	225	24		
Frank Richter	LB	6'3"	230	24		
Phil Brady	DB	6'2"	211	26		
George Burrell	DB	5'10"	180	21	2	6
Grady Cavness	DB	5'11"	187	22	2	
Charlie Greer	DB	6'	205	23	2	
Gus Holloman	DB	6'3"	195	23	1	
Pete Jaquess	DB	6'	182	27		
Tom Oberg	DB	6'	185	24		
Jimmy Smith	DB	6'3"	190	24		
Bill Thompson	DB	6'1"	200	22	3	6
Ted Alfen	HB-DB	6'	195	22		
Pete Liske	QB	6'2"	185	28		
Al Pastrana	QB	6'1"	190	24		
Steve Tensi	QB	6'5"	215	26		
Bobby Burnett	HB	6'2"	208	26		
Floyd Little	HB	5'10"	195	27		42
Frank Quayle	HB	5'10"	195	22		
Wandy Williams	HB	6'1"	193	23		6
Henry Jones	FB	6'2"	235	23		
Brendan McCarthy	FB	6'3"	220	24		
Tom Smiley	FB	6'1"	235	25		24
Fran Lynch	HB-FB	6'1"	194	23		12
Al Denson	WR	6'2"	208	27		60
John Embree	WR	6'4"	207	25		30
Mike Haffner	WR	6'2"	205	27		30
Bill Van Heusen	WR	6'1"	200	23		
Tom Beer	TE	6'4"	230	24		
Tom Buckman	TE	6'4"	230	22		6
Dave Pivec	TE	6'3"	240	25		
Bobby Howfield	K	5'9"	180	32		75

CINCINNATI BENGALS 4-9-1 Paul Brown

Scores of Each Game

27	MIAMI	21
34	SAN DIEGO	20
24	KANSAS CITY	19
14	San Diego	21
7	NEW YORK	21
23	DENVER	30
22	Kansas City	42
31	OAKLAND	17
31	Houston	31
14	BOSTON	25
7	New York	40
13	Buffalo	16
17	Oakland	37
16	Denver	27

Use Name	Pos.	Hgt	Wgt	Age	Int	Pts
Howard Fest	OT	6'6"	265	23		
Frank Peters	OT	6'4"	250	21		
Ernie Wright	OT	6'4"	270	29		
Ernie Park	OG-OT	6'3"	240	27		
Justin Canale	OG	6'2"	250	25		
Guy Dennis	OG	6'2"	255	22		
Pat Matson	OG	6'1"	245	25		
Dave Middendorf	OG	6'3"	260	23		
Mike Wilson	OG	6'1"	240	21		
Bob Johnson	C	6'5"	260	23		
Marty Baccaglio	DE	6'3"	245	24		
Royce Berry	DE	6'3"	242	23		
Harry Gunner	DE	6'6"	250	24	1	6
Steve Chomyszak	DT	6'5"	280	24		
Andy Rice	DT	6'3"	268	27		
Bill Staley	DT	6'3"	250	22		
Ken Avery	LB	6'1"	225	25		
Al Beauchamp	LB	6'2"	236	25	1	
Bill Bergey	LB	6'2"	240	24	2	
Tim Buchanan	LB	6'	233	23		
Ed Harmon	LB	6'4"	230	22		
Bill Peterson	LB	6'3"	230	24	4	
Al Coleman	DB	6'1"	183	24		
Ken Dyer	DB	6'3"	185	23		
John Guillory	DB	5'10"	190	24	1	
Bobby Hunt	DB	6'1"	190	29	4	
Charlie King	DB	6'	184	26		
Ken Riley	DB	6'	182	22	4	
Fletcher Smith	DB	6'2"	178	25	4	
Jim Williams	DB	6'1"	190	23		
Greg Cook	QB	6'3"	212	22		6
Sam Wyche	QB	6'4"	210	24		6
Essex Johnson	HB	5'9"	190	22		
Paul Robinson	HB	6'	200	24		24
Ron Lamb	FB	6'2"	225	25		
Clem Turner	FB	6'1"	245	24		
Jess Phillips	HB-FB	6'1"	205	22		18
Eric Crabtree	WR	5'11"	182	24		42
Jack Gehrke	WR	6'	178	23		
Chip Myers	WR	6'4"	200	24		12
Tommie Smith	WR	6'4"	190	25		
Speedy Thomas	WR	6'1"	175	22		24
Bruce Coslet	TE	6'3"	225	23		6
Bob Trumpy	WR-TE	6'6"	220	24		54
Dale Livingston	K	6'	210	24		
Horst Muhlman	K	6'1"	210	29		80
Terry Swanson	K	6'	210	24		

Frank Buncom —Died Sept. 14, 1969 from pulmonary embolism

OAKLAND RAIDERS

RUSHING

Last Name	No.	Yds	Avg	TD
Smith	177	600	3.4	2
Dixon	107	398	3.7	0
Banaszak	88	377	4.3	0
Todd	47	198	4.2	1
Hubbard	21	119	5.7	0
Lamonica	13	36	2.8	1
Wells	3	24	8.0	0
Eischeid	1	10	10.0	0
Hagberg	1	3	3.0	0
Blanda	1	0	0.0	0

RECEIVING

Last Name	No.	Yds	Avg	TD
Biletnikoff	54	837	15	12
Wells	47	1260	27	14
Dixon	33	275	8	1
Smith	30	322	11	2
Cannon	21	262	12	2
Banaszak	17	119	7	3
Todd	16	149	9	1
Hagberg	6	84	14	1
Hubbard	2	30	15	0
Buie	1	37	37	0

PUNT RETURNS

Last Name	No.	Yds	Avg	TD
Atkinson	25	153	6	0
Sherman	9	46	5	0
Grayson	4	28	7	0
Allen	1	−2	−2	0

KICKOFF RETURNS

Last Name	No.	Yds	Avg	TD
Atkinson	16	382	24	0
Sherman	12	300	25	0
Smith	10	247	25	0
Allen	3	67	22	0
Benson	1	0	0	0

PASSING – PUNTING – KICKING

PASSING	Att	Comp	%	Yds	Yd/Att	TD	Int−	%	RK
Lamonica	426	221	52	3302	7.8	34	25−	6	3
Blanda	13	6	46	73	5.6	2	1−	8	

PUNTING	No	Avg
Eischeid	69	42.7

KICKING	XP	Att	%	FG	Att	%
Blanda	45	45	100	20	37	54

KANSAS CITY CHIEFS

RUSHING

Last Name	No.	Yds	Avg	TD
Garrett	168	732	4.4	6
Holmes	150	612	4.1	2
McVea	106	500	4.7	7
Hayes	62	208	3.4	4
Livingston	15	102	6.8	0
Lowe	10	33	3.3	0
Pitts	5	28	5.6	0
Dawson	1	3	3.0	0
Lee	1	3	3.0	0
Arbanas	1	1	1.0	0
Flores	1	0	0.0	0
Taylor	2	−2	−1.0	0

RECEIVING

Last Name	No.	Yds	Avg	TD
Garrett	43	432	10	2
Taylor	41	696	17	7
Pitts	31	470	15	2
Holmes	26	266	10	3
Richardson	23	381	17	2
Arbanas	16	258	16	0
Hayes	9	64	7	0
McVea	7	71	10	0

PUNT RETURNS

Last Name	No.	Yds	Avg	TD
Smith	9	107	12	0
Mitchell	13	101	8	0
Garrett	8	28	4	0
Sellers	2	15	8	0

KICKOFF RETURNS

Last Name	No.	Yds	Avg	TD
McVea	13	318	24	0
Mitchell	7	178	25	0
Podolak	7	165	24	0
Smith	4	125	31	0
Lowe	5	116	23	0
Hayes	2	81	41	0
Holmes	2	54	27	0
Bell	1	53	53	1

PASSING – PUNTING – KICKING

PASSING	Att	Comp	%	Yds	Yd/Att	TD	Int−	%	RK
Dawson	166	98	59	1323	8.0	9	13−	8	6
Livingston	161	84	52	1123	7.0	4	6−	4	4
Lee	20	12	60	109	5.5	1	1−	5	
Flores	6	3	50	49	8.2	1	0−	0	
McVea	3	1	33	50	16.7	1	0−	0	

PUNTING	No	Avg
Wilson	68	44.4

KICKING	XP	Att	%	FG	Att	%
Stenerud	38	38	100	27	35	77

SAN DIEGO CHARGERS

RUSHING

Last Name	No.	Yds	Avg	TD
Post	182	873	4.8	6
Hubbert	94	333	3.5	4
Foster	64	236	3.7	0
Smith	51	211	4.1	2
Domres	19	145	7.6	4
Hadl	26	109	4.2	2
Sayers	14	53	3.8	0
Alworth	5	25	5.0	0

RECEIVING

Last Name	No.	Yds	Avg	TD
Alworth	64	1003	16	4
Garrison	40	804	20	7
Post	24	235	10	0
Frazier	17	205	12	0
Foster	14	83	6	1
Hubbert	11	43	4	0
Queen	10	148	15	0
Smith	10	144	14	0
Eber	9	141	16	1
MacKinnon	7	82	12	0
Trapp	2	39	20	0

PUNT RETURNS

Last Name	No.	Yds	Avg	TD
Duncan	27	280	10	0
Graham	3	15	5	0
Smith	1	5	5	0

KICKOFF RETURNS

Last Name	No.	Yds	Avg	TD
Duncan	21	587	28	0
Smith	6	138	23	0
Post	4	74	19	0
Sayers	2	42	21	0
Foster	1	1	1	0
Fetherston	3	0	0	0
Briggs	1	0	0	0
Huey	1	0	0	0

PASSING – PUNTING – KICKING

PASSING	Att	Comp	%	Yds	Yd/Att	TD	Int−	%	RK
Hadl	324	158	49	2253	7.0	10	11−	3	5
Domres	112	47	42	631	5.6	2	10−	9	
Foster	5	2	40	39	7.8	1	0−	0	
Post	2	1	50	4	2.0	0	0−	0	
Hubbert	1	0	0	0	0.0	0	0−	0	

PUNTING	No	Avg
Partee	71	44.6

KICKING	XP	Att	%	FG	Att	%
Partee	33	33	100	15	28	54

DENVER BRONCOS

RUSHING

Last Name	No.	Yds	Avg	TD
Little	146	729	5.0	6
Lynch	96	407	4.2	2
Quayle	57	183	3.2	0
Smiley	56	166	3.0	3
Tensi	12	63	5.3	0
Liske	10	50	5.0	0
Williams	10	18	1.8	1
Denson	1	9	9.0	0
Burnett	5	9	1.8	0
Jones	1	3	3.0	0

RECEIVING

Last Name	No.	Yds	Avg	TD
Denson	53	809	15	10
Haffner	35	563	16	5
Embree	29	469	16	5
Little	19	218	11	1
Quayle	11	167	15	0
Beer	9	200	22	0
Pivic	9	117	13	0
Lynch	9	86	10	0
Williams	5	56	11	0
Smiley	5	23	5	1
Buckman	4	48	12	1
Van Heusen	3	64	21	0
Pastrana	1	15	15	0

PUNT RETURNS

Last Name	No.	Yds	Avg	TD
Thompson	25	288	12	0
Little	6	70	12	0
Burrell	5	56	11	0
Greer	1	36	36	0

KICKOFF RETURNS

Last Name	No.	Yds	Avg	TD
Williams	23	574	25	0
Thompson	18	513	29	0
Burrell	6	108	18	0
Little	3	81	27	0
Criter	3	31	10	0
Barnes	1	16	16	0
Hollomon	1	0	0	0
Myrtle	1	0	0	0

PASSING – PUNTING – KICKING

PASSING	Att	Comp	%	Yds	Yd/Att	TD	Int−	%	RK
Tensi	286	131	46	1990	7.0	14	12−	4	7
Liske	115	61	53	845	7.4	9	11−	10	
Little	2	0	0	0	0.0	0	0−	0	

PUNTING	No	Avg
Holloman	47	39.7
Van Heusen	25	40.8

KICKING	XP	Att	%	FG	Att	%
Howfield	36	37	97	13	29	45

CINCINNATI BENGALS

RUSHING

Last Name	No.	Yds	Avg	TD
Phillips	118	578	4.9	3
Robinson	160	489	3.1	4
Cook	25	148	5.9	1
Wyche	12	107	8.9	1
Turner	23	105	4.6	0
E. Johnson	15	54	3.6	0
Livingston	1	18	18.0	0
Thomas	4	16	4.0	1
Lamb	5	8	1.6	0

RECEIVING

Last Name	No.	Yds	Avg	TD
Crabtree	40	855	21	7
Trumpy	37	835	23	9
Thomas	33	481	15	3
Robinson	20	104	5	0
Phillips	13	128	10	0
Myers	10	205	21	2
Turner	5	14	3	0
Riley	2	15	8	0
T. Smith	1	41	41	0
Coslet	1	39	39	1
E. Johnson	1	3	3	0

PUNT RETURNS

Last Name	No.	Yds	Avg	TD
E. Johnson	17	85	5	0
Thomas	4	15	4	0
Coleman	1	0	0	0
Guillory	1	0	0	0
King	0	35	0	0

KICKOFF RETURNS

Last Name	No.	Yds	Avg	TD
E. Johnson	16	362	23	0
Riley	14	334	24	0
Guillory	8	170	21	0
Robinson	5	168	34	0
Lamb	5	64	13	0
Phillips	3	52	17	0
Turner	3	15	15	0
Gunner	1	0	0	0

PASSING – PUNTING – KICKING

PASSING	Att	Comp	%	Yds	Yd/Att	TD	Int−	%	RK
Cook	197	106	54	1854	9.4	15	11−	6	1
Wyche	108	54	50	838	7.8	7	4−	4	
Livingston	2	1	50	15	7.5	0	0−	0	
Gehrke	1	1	100	13	13.0	0	0−	0	

PUNTING	No	Avg
Livingston	70	39.6
Swanson	12	38.3
Muhlmann	2	19.0
Lamb	1	29.0

KICKING	XP	Att	%	FG	Att	%
Muhlmann	32	33	97	16	24	67

1969 NFL CHAMPIONSHIP GAME
January 4, 1970 at Minnesota
(Attendance 46,503)

SCORING

MINNESOTA	14 10 3 0—27	
CLEVELAND	0 0 0 7— 7	

First Quarter
Min. Kapp, 7 yard rush   3:48
    PAT—Cox (kick)
Min. Washington, 75 yard pass from Kapp   7:07
    PAT—Cox (kick)

Second Quarter
Min. Cox, 30 yard field goal   1:07
Min. Osborn, 20 yard rush   10:15
    PAT—Cox (kick)

Third Quarter
Min. Cox, 32 yard field goal   11:18

Fourth Quarter
Cle. Collins, 3 yard pass from Nelsen   1:24
    PAT—Cockroft (kick)

TEAM STATISTICS

MINN.		CLEVE.
18	First Downs—Total	14
13	First Downs—Rushing	4
5	First Downs—Passing	10
0	First Downs—Penalty	0
0	Fumbles—Number	2
0	Fumbles—Lost Ball	1
3	Penalties—Number	1
33	Yards Penalized	5
0	Giveaways	3
3	Takeaways	0
+3	Difference	−3

Viking Heat

The Browns had beaten the Cowboys 38-14 in the first round of the playoffs with a tight pass defense and sharp passing by Bill Nelsen, and they hoped to pull another upset over the Vikings in the NFL title match. The Vikings had crushed the Browns 51-3 in a regular-season meeting and had disposed of the powerful Los Angeles Rams 23-20 with a fourth-quarter rally in last week's opening playoff game, and their superb defense made them favorites for this game.

Conditions for the game were typical of Minnesota in January. Snow ringed the field, and 8-degree temperature chilled the spectators through their layers of clothing. The Browns suffered from the cold, resorting to heaters and special footgear to combat it, but the Vikings used no heaters at all. Coach Bud Grant said, "we generate our own heat."

On the first series of the game, the Browns showed their discomfort in this weather. Cornerback Walt Sumner slipped and fell while covering Viking receiver Gene Washington, and Joe Kapp hit his man with a pass good for 33 yards down to the Cleveland 24-yard line. The Vikings moved down to the 7-yard line, and Kapp scored on a play characteristic of his rough style. He bumped into fullback Bill Brown in his backfield, then stormed straight ahead and broke several tackles on his way to the end zone. Several minutes later, Cleveland cornerback Erich Barnes lost his footing and fell while covering Washington, and Kapp whipped a pass which he end carried 75 yards for a second Minnesota touchdown. Trailing 14-0 and fully aware that the Minnesota defense allowed its opponents an average of only ten points a game, the Browns looked like a beaten team before the first quarter had ended. With the Viking defense keeping the Cleveland attack bottled up all afternoon, Minnesota won the game 27-7 and the NFL championship in the team's ninth year of operation.

INDIVIDUAL STATISTICS

MINNESOTA	No	Yds	Avg.	CLEVELAND	No	Yds	Avg.
RUSHING							
Osborn	18	108	6.0	Kelly	15	80	5.3
Kapp	8	57	7.1	Scott	6	17	2.8
Brown	12	43	3.6		21	97	4.6
Reed	5	7	1.4				
Jones	2	7	3.5				
	45	222	4.9				
RECEIVING							
Washington	3	120	40.0	Scott	5	56	11.2
Henderson	2	17	8.5	Collins	5	43	8.6
Brown	1	20	20.0	Warfield	4	47	11.8
Beasley	1	12	12.0	Kelly	2	17	8.5
	7	169	24.1	Morin	1	18	18.0
					17	181	10.6
PUNTING							
Lee	3		41.0	Cockroft	3		33.0
PUNT RETURNS							
West	1	1	1.0	Kelly	2	10	5.0
				Morrison	1	11	11.0
					3	21	7.0
KICKOFF RETURNS							
West	1	22	22.0	Scott	4	60	15.0
Jones	1	20	20.0	Morrison	1	23	23.0
	2	42	21.0		5	83	16.6
INTERCEPTION RETURNS							
Hilgenberg	1	0	0.0	None			
Krause	1	0	0.0				
	2	0	0.0				

MINNESOTA	Att.	Comp.	Comp. Pct.	Yds.	Int.	Yds/ Att.	Yds/ Comp.	Yards Lost Tackled
Kapp	13	7	53.8	169	0	13.0	24.1	1— 8
CLEVELAND								
Nelsen	33	17	51.5	181	2	5.5	10.6	2—10

1969 AFL CHAMPIONSHIP GAME
January 4, 1970 at Oakland
(Attendance 53,564)

SCORING

OAKLAND	7 0 0 0— 7	
KANSAS CITY	0 7 7 3—17	

First Quarter
Oak. Smith, 3 yard rush   14:14
    PAT—Blanda (kick)

Second Quarter
K.C. Hayes, 1 yard rush   13:10
    PAT—Stenerud (kick)

Third Quarter
K.C. Holmes, 5 yard rush   11:17
    PAT—Stenerud (kick)

Fourth Quarter
K.C. Stenerud, 22 yard field goal   10:12

TEAM STATISTICS

OAK.		K.C.
18	First Downs—Total	13
6	First Downs—Rushing	5
10	First Downs—Passing	6
2	First Downs—Penalty	2
1	Fumbles—Number	5
0	Fumbles—Lost Ball	4
5	Penalties—Number	5
45	Yards Penalized	43
4	Giveaways	4
4	Takeaways	4
0	Difference	0

Finishing First When It Counts

The AFL installed a new playoff system for its final season, pitting the first-place finishers against the runners-up in the opposite division, with the winners playing for the league crown. The result was that two Western clubs met in the title game, as the first-place Raiders clobbered Houston 56-7 while the second-place Chiefs upset the New York Jets 13-6.

While the Raiders took a 7-0 lead on Charlie Smith's touchdown late in the first period, Kansas City passer Len Dawson found the Oakland defense hard to crack, as he missed on seven straight passes. Late in the second quarter, however, he hit Frank Pitts with a 41-yard bomb which brought the ball to the Oakland 1-yard line. From there, Wendell Hayes smashed over, and the Chiefs took a 7-7 tie into the locker room at halftime.

Early in the second half, Lamonica hurt his passing hand against the helmet of Aaron Brown and could not grip the ball properly for the rest of the game. George Blanda relieved Lamonica at quarterback but had no miracles up his sleeve today. In addition to missing three field-goal attempts, he could not stand up under the Kansas City pass rush and saw one of his passes intercepted in the end zone. After intercepting Blanda's pass, Emmitt Thomas had run it out to the 6-yard line. Dawson then moved his team downfield through the air. Otis Taylor and Robert Holmes caught passes for long gains, and a pass interference penalty on the Raiders gave the Chiefs a first down on the Oakland 7. Holmes carried the ball three straight times to reach the end zone and put the Chiefs ahead 14-7.

Sore hand and all, Lamonica returned to the lineup in the final period, but three of his crippled passes were picked off by the Chiefs, who won the game 17-7 and headed off to the Super Bowl despite finishing second behind the Raiders in the regular season.

INDIVIDUAL STATISTICS

OAKLAND	No	Yds	Avg.	KANSAS CITY	No	Yds	Avg.
RUSHING							
Dixon	12	36	3.0	Hayes	8	35	4.4
Smith	12	31	2.6	Garrett	7	19	2.7
Banaszak	2	8	4.0	Holmes	18	14	0.8
Todd	2	4	2.0	McVea	3	13	4.3
	28	79	2.8	Dawson	3	5	1.7
					39	86	2.2
RECEIVING							
Smith	8	86	10.8	Taylor	3	62	20.7
Sherman	3	45	15.0	Holmes	2	16	8.0
Cannon	2	22	11.0	Pitts	1	41	41.0
Banaszak	2	13	6.5	Arbanas	1	10	10.0
Wells	1	24	24.0		7	129	18.4
Dixon	1	1	1.0				
	17	191	11.2				
PUNTING							
Eischeid	6		48.5	Wilson	8		42.9
PUNT RETURNS							
Atkinson	2	−1	−0.5	Garrett	4	9	2.3
KICKOFF RETURNS							
Atkinson	3	95	31.7	Holmes	1	26	26.0
Sherman	1	17	17.0	Hill	1	0	0.0
	4	112	28.0	Hayes	Lat	17	—
					2	43	21.5
INTERCEPTION RETURNS							
None				Thomas	2	69	34.5
				Marsalis	1	23	23.0
				Kearney	1	17	17.0
					4	109	27.3

OAKLAND	Att.	Comp.	Comp. Pct.	Yds.	Int.	Yds/ Att.	Yds/ Comp.	Yards Lost Tackled
Lamonica	39	15	38.5	167	3	4.3	11.1	
Blanda	6	2	33.3	24	1	4.0	12.0	
	45	17	37.8	191	4	4.2	11.2	4—37
KANSAS CITY								
Dawson	17	7	41.2	129	0	7.6	18.4	1— 8

An Upsetting Farewell

All of the Kansas City Chiefs wore a patch on their jerseys saying "AFL-10." This referred to the ten-year existence of the AFL, which would fade into oblivion after this game and the AFL All-Star Game a week later. As things turned out, the Chiefs took the AFL out in style by handily beating the NFL champion Minnesota Vikings.

It didn't figure. The Vikings had bullied their way through the NFL with a frightening defense, led by the front four of Jim Marshall, Carl Eller, Alan Page, and Gary Larsen and a ball-control attack paced by tough quarterback Joe Kapp. Odds-makers branded the Vikings as two-touchdown favorites to return the Super Bowl title to the NFL after a year in the possession of the AFL New York Jets.

The Chiefs had been to the Super Bowl before, however, and knew how to prepare better for the fanfare. While the Vikings were awed by the hubbub in New Orleans during the week before the game, the Chiefs seriously set about to avenge their loss to Green Bay in Super Bowl I.

The "I" formation that Kansas City used, concealing the position of their backs until the last moment before the play, gave the Minnesota defense some problems right from the start. The Chiefs assigned two men each to block Marshall and Eller, and this move gave the Kansas City backs room to run. Quarterback Len Dawson also found the Viking zone pass coverage less difficult than had been imagined, and he would complete twelve of seventeen passes through the afternoon.

The Kansas City defensive linemen, meanwhile, were putting hot pressure on Joe Kapp, forcing him to hurry his passes. While the defense harassed Kapp in the first period, the Chiefs got close enough to the goal line for Jan Stenerud to boot a 32-yard field goal to put the Chiefs ahead 3-0.

The second quarter went no better for the Viking attack as the Chiefs scored 13 points to break the game open. Stenerud kicked another field goal, Mike Garrett scored a touchdown after the Vikings had fumbled deep in their own territory, and Stenerud's third field goal made the score 16-0 at halftime.

The Vikings came out for the second half ready to climb back into the game, and Kapp immediately led them on a 69-yard drive that led to the Vikings' first touchdown. But the Vikes could not score again, and Otis Taylor's brilliant 46-yard run with a short pass made the final score only a little worse, 23-7, in favor of the Chiefs and, for the final time, the AFL.

KANSAS CITY / MINNESOTA

KANSAS CITY	OFFENSE	MINNESOTA
Pitts	WR	Washington
Tyrer	LT	Alderman
Budde	LG	Vellone
Holub	C	Tingelhoff
Moorman	RG	Sunde
Hill	RT	Yary
Arbanas	TE	Beasley
Taylor	WR	Henderson
Dawson	QB	Kapp
Garrett	RB	Osborn
Holmes	RB	B. Brown

	DEFENSE	
Mays	LE	Eller
Culp	LT	Larsen
Buchanan	RT	Page
A. Brown	RE	Marshall
Bell	LLB	Winston
Lanier	MLB	Warwick
Lynch	RLB	Hilgenberg
Marsalis	LCB	Mackbee
Thomas	RCB	Sharockman
Kearney	LS	Kassulke
Robinson	RS	Krause

SUBSTITUTES

KANSAS CITY
Offense
Daney McVea
Hayes Podolak
Livingston Prudhomme
McClinton Richardson
Defense
Belser Sellers
Hurston Stein
Lothamer Trosch
Mitchell
Kickers
Stenerud Wilson

MINNESOTA
Offense
Cuozzo Lee
Grim Lindsey
Harris Reed
Jones Smith
Kramer White
Defense
Dickson McGill
Hackbart West
Hargrove
Kicker
Cox

SCORING

KANSAS CITY	3	13	7	0—23	
MINNESOTA	0	0	7	0— 7	

First Quarter
K.C.　Stenerud, 48 yard field goal

Second Quarter
K.C.　Stenerud, 32 yard field goal
K.C.　Stenerud, 25 yard field goal
K.C.　Garrett, 5 yard rush
　　　PAT — Stenerud (kick)

Third Quarter
Minn.　Osborn, 4 yard rush
　　　PAT — Cox (kick)
K.C.　Taylor, 46 yard pass from Dawson
　　　PAT — Stenerud (kick)

TEAM STATISTICS

K.C.		MINN.
18	First Downs — Total	13
8	First Downs — Rushing	2
7	First Downs — Passing	10
3	First Downs — Penalty	1
0	Fumbles — Number	3
0	Fumbles — Lost Ball	2
4	Penalties — Number	6
47	Yards Penalized	67
62	Total Offensive Plays	50
273	Total Net Yards	239
4.4	Average Gain	4.8
0	Missed Field Goals	1
1	Giveaways	5
5	Takeaways	1
+4	Difference	−4

INDIVIDUAL STATISTICS

RUSHING

KANSAS CITY	No	Yds	Avg.	MINNESOTA	No	Yds	Avg.
Garrett	11	39	3.5	Brown	6	26	4.3
Pitts	3	37	12.3	Reed	4	17	4.3
Hayes	8	31	3.9	Osborn	7	15	2.1
McVea	12	26	2.2	Kapp	2	9	4.5
Dawson	3	11	3.7		19	67	3.5
Holmes	5	7	1.4				
	42	151	3.6				

RECEIVING

KANSAS CITY	No	Yds	Avg.	MINNESOTA	No	Yds	Avg.
Taylor	6	81	13.5	Henderson	7	111	15.9
Pitts	3	33	11.0	Brown	3	11	3.7
Garrett	2	25	12.5	Beasley	2	41	20.5
Hayes	1	3	3.0	Reed	2	16	8.0
	12	142	11.8	Osborn	2	11	5.5
				Washington	1	9	9.0
					17	199	11.7

PUNTING

KANSAS CITY	No		Avg.	MINNESOTA	No		Avg.
Wilson	4		48.5	Lee	3		37.0

PUNT RETURNS

KANSAS CITY	No	Yds	Avg.	MINNESOTA	No	Yds	Avg.
Garrett	1	0	0.0	West	2	18	9.0

KICKOFF RETURNS

KANSAS CITY	No	Yds	Avg.	MINNESOTA	No	Yds	Avg.
Hayes	2	36	18.0	West	3	46	15.3
				Jones	1	33	33.0
					4	79	19.8

INTERCEPTION RETURNS

KANSAS CITY	No	Yds	Avg.	MINNESOTA	No	Yds	Avg.
Lanier	1	9	9.0	Krause	1	0	0.0
Robinson	1	9	9.0				
Thomas	1	6	6.0				
	3	24	8.0				

PASSING

KANSAS CITY	Att	Comp	Comp Pct.	Yds	Int	Yds/ Att.	Yds/ Comp	Yards Lost Tackled
Dawson	17	12	70.6	142	1	8.4	11.8	3—20

MINNESOTA	Att	Comp	Comp Pct.	Yds	Int	Yds/ Att.	Yds/ Comp	Yards Lost Tackled
Kapp	25	16	64.0	183	2	7.3	11.4	
Cuozzo	3	1	33.3	16	1	5.3	16.0	
	28	17	60.7	199	3	7.1	11.7	3—27

Use Name (Nicknames) – Positions	Team by Year	See Section	Hgt	Wgt	College	Int	Pts
Abell, Bud LB	66-68KC-A		6'3"	220	Missouri	2	
Abruzzese, Ray DB	62-64BufA 65-66NY-A		6'1"	194	Alabama	10	
Absher, Dick LB	67Was 67-68Atl 69-71NO 72Phi		6'4"	231	Maryland	3	4
Adamchik, Ed C	65NYG 65Pit		6'2"	235	Pittsburgh		
Adams, John FB-OE	59-62ChiB 63LA	2	6'3"	235	Los Angeles State		24
Adams, Tom OE	62Min		6'5"	210	Minnesota-Duluth		
Adams, Willie LB-DE	65-66Was		6'2"	235	New Mexico State		
Adamson, Ken OG	60-62DenA		6'2"	222	Notre Dame		
Adderly, Herb DB	61-69GB 70-72Dal	3	6'1"	204	Michigan State	48	54
Addison, Tom LB	60-67BosA		6'3"	231	South Carolina	16	6
Akin, Howard OT	67-68SD-A		6'5"	261	Oklahoma State		
Alderman, Grady OT-OG	60Det 61-74Min		6'2"	242	Detroit		
Aldridge, Lionel DE	63-71GB 72-73SD		6'4"	245	Utah State		6
Alexander, Kermit DB	63-69SF 70-71LA 72-73Phi	3	5'11"	185	U.C.L.A.	43	36
Alfen, Ted HB	69DenA		6'	195	Springfield		
Alford, Bruce K	67Was 68-69BufA	5	6'	185	Texas Christian		134
Alford, Mike C	65StL 66Det		6'3"	233	Auburn		
Allard, Don QB	61NY-A 61BosA		6'	189	Boston College		
Allen, Buddy HB	61DenA		5'10"	190	Utah State		
Allen, Chuck LB	61-69SD-A 70-71Pit 72Phi		6'1"	224	Washington	28	12
Allen, Dalva DE	60-61HouA 62-64OakA		6'5"	224	Houston	1	
Allen, Don FB	60DenA	2	6'	200	Texas		6
Allen, Duane OE-TE	61-64LA 65Pit 65Bal 66-67ChiB	2	6'4"	221	Santa Ana J.C.		30
Allen, George OT	66HouA		6'7"	270	West Texas State		
Allen, Jerry HB	66Bal 67-69Was	2	6'1"	204	Nebraska-Omaha		54
Alley, Don WR-FL	67Bal 69Pit		6'2"	200	Adams State		
Allison, Jim FB	65-68SD-A	2	6'	220	San Diego State		12
Alliston, Vaughan LB	60DenA		6'	218	Mississippi	1	
Alworth, Lance FL-WR-OE	62-70SD-A 71-72Dal	23	6'	182	Arkansas		524
Amerson, Glen DB	61Phi		6'1"	186	Texas Tech		
Ames, Dave HB-DB	61NY-A 61DenA		6'	185	Richmond	1	
Amsler, Marty DE	67ChiB 68JJ 69ChiB 70GB		6'5"	257	Indiana, Evansville	1	
Anderson, Art OT	61-62ChiB 63Pit		6'3"	244	Idaho		
Anderson, Bill OE-TE	58-63Was 65-66GB	2	6'3"	211	Tennessee		90
Anderson, Billy QB	67HouA		6'1"	195	Tulsa		
Anderson, Bob HB	63NYG		6'2"	210	Army		
Anderson, Bruce DE-DT	66LA 67-69NYG 70Was		6'4"	246	Williamette		
Anderson, Chet TE	67Pit		6'3"	245	Minnesota		12
Anderson, Dick OT	67NO		6'5"	245	Ohio State		2
Anderson, Max HB	68-69BufA 70KJ 71Buf	23	5'8"	180	Arizona State		24
Anderson, Ralph OE	58ChiB 60LA-A	2	6'4"	223	Los Angeles State		36
died Nov. 26, 1960—diabetes							
Anderson, Roger DT-OT	64-65NYG 66CFL 67-68NYG		6'5"	263	Virginia Union	1	
Anderson, Taz OE-TE	61-64StL 66-67Atl	2	6'2"	208	Georgia Tech		60
Andrie, George DE	62-72Dal		6'7"	252	Marquette	1	14
Andrus, Lou LB	67DenA		6'6"	255	Brigham Young		
Antwine, Houston DT	61-69BosA 70Bos 71NE 72Phi		6'	265	Southern Illinois	1	
Apple, Jim HB	61NY-A		6'	200	Upsala		
Appleton, Scott DT	64-66HouA 67-68SD-A		6'3"	254	Texas	2	6
Arbanas, Fred TE-OE	61XJ 62DalA 63-69KC-A 70KC	2	6'3"	240	Michigan State		206
Archer, Dan OG-OT	67OakA 68CinA		6'5"	245	Oregon		
Armstrong, Ray DT	60OakA		6'1"	235	Texas Christian		
Arndt, Dick DT	67-70Pit		6'5"	265	Idaho		
Arnett, Jon HB-FL-OE	57-63LA 64-66ChiB	123	5'11"	197	Southern Calif.		234
Arrobio, Chuck OT	66Min		6'4"	250	Southern Calif.		
Asad, Doug OE	60-61OakA	2	6'3"	203	Northwestern		18
Asbury, Willie FB	66-68Pit	2	6'1"	230	Kent State		78
Atchason, Jack OE	60BosA 60HouA		6'4"	215	Western Illinois		6
Atkins, Billy DB-HB	58-59SF 60-61BufA 62-63NY-A 63BufA 64DenA	45	6'1"	196	Auburn	20	86
Atkins, Doug DE	53-54Cle 55-66ChiB 67-69NO		6'8"	257	Tennessee	3	2
Atkins, Pervis HB-FL-OE	61-63LA 64-65Was 65-66OakA	23	6'1"	200	New Mexico State		18
Atkinson, Frank DT	63Pit		6'3"	240	Stanford		
Auer, Joe HB	64-65BufA 66-67MiaA 68Atl	23	6'1"	204	Georgia Tech		
Autry, Hank C	69HouA 70Hou		6'3"	233	Southern Miss.		
Aveni, John OE-K	59-60ChiB 61Was	5	6'3"	212	Indiana		144
Avery, Jim TE	66Was		6'2"	235	Northern Illinois		
Avezzano, Joe C	66BosA		6'2"	235	Florida State		
Babb, Gene FB-LB	57-58SF 60-61Dal 62-63HouA	2	6'3"	216	Austin	4	30
Baccaglio, Marty DE	68SD-A 68-69CinA 70Cin		6'3"	245	San Jose State		
Bachman, Jay C	68-69DenA 70-71Den		6'3"	250	Cincinnati		
Badar, Rich QB	67Pit		6'1"	190	Indiana		
Bailey, Monk DB	64-65StL		6'	178	Utah		
Bailey, Teddy HB	67BufA 69BosA		6'	210	Cincinnati		
Baird, Bill DB-HB	63-69NY-A	3	5'10"	180	San Fran. State	34	18
Baker, Art FB	61-62BufA	2	6'	220	Syracuse		24
Baker, Dave DB	59-61SF 62-63MS		6'	192	Oklahoma	21	
Baker, John DE-DT-OT	58-61LA 62Phi 63-67Pit 68Det		6'6"	279	N. Car. Central	2	
Baker, Johnny LB-DE	63-69HouA 67SD-A		6'3"	229	Mississippi State	2	6
Baker, Larry OT	60NY-A		6'2"	240	Bowling Green		
Baker, Ralph LB	64-69NY-A 70-74NYJ		6'3"	232	Penn State	19	13
Baker, Sam FB-K	53Was 54-55MS 56-59Was 60-61Cle 62-63Dal 64-69Phi	2 45	6'2"	217	Oregon State		977
Baker, Terry HB-QB	63-65LA	2	6'3"	198	Oregon State		18
Bakken, Jim K	62-77StL	45	6'	199	Wisconsin		1320
Baldwin, Bob HB-FB	66Bal		6'1"	225	Clemson		
Ball, Sam OT	66-70Bal		6'4"	240	Kentucky		
Ballman, Gary WR-FL-OE-TE-HB	62-66Pit 67-72Phi 72NYG 73Min	23	6'	203	Michigan State		252
Bandy, Don OG	67-68Was		6'3"	250	Tulsa		
Banfield, Tony DB	60-63,65HouA		6'1"	185	Oklahoma State	27	6
Banks, Estes FB-HB	67OakA 68CinA	2	6'1"	210	Colorado		
Bansavage, Al LB	60LA-A 61OakA		6'2"	225	Southern Calif.		
Barbee, Joe DT	60OakA		6'3"	250	Kent State		
Barber, Rudy LB	68MiaA		6'1"	255	Bethune-Cookman		
Barber, Stew OT-LB	61-69BufA		6'3"	247	Penn State	3	6
Barefoot, Ken TE	68Was		6'5"	228	Virginia Tech		6
Barnes, Billy HB	57-61Phi 62-63Was 65-66Min	12	5'11"	201	Wake Forest		228
Barnes, Charlie OE	61DalA		6'5"	230	Northeast La.		
Barnes, Erich DB	58-60ChiB 61-64NYG 65-71Cle		6'2"	201	Purdue	45	60
Barnes, Ernie OG-OT	60NY-A 61-62SD-A 63-64DenA		6'3"	250	N. Car. Central		
Barnes, Gary OE-FL	62GB 63Dal 64ChiB 66-67Atl	2	6'4"	210	Clemson		12
Barnes, Mike DB	67-68StL		6'3"	205	Texas-Arlington		

Use Name (Nicknames) – Positions	Team by Year	See Section	Hgt	Wgt	College	Int	Pts
Barnes, Walt DE-DT	66-68Was 69DenA 70-71Den 72JJ		6'3"	250	Nebraska		
Barnett, Steve OT	63ChiB 64Was		6'1"	255	Oregon		
Barney, Eppie WR-FL	67-68Cle	2	6'	201	Iowa State		12
Barr, Terry FL-DB-HB	57-65Det	23	6'	189	Michigan	5	228
Barrett, Bob OE	60BufA		6'3"	200	Baldwin-Wallace		
Barrett, Jan OE	63GB 63-64OakA	2	6'3"	226	Fresno State		12
Barrington, Tom HB-FB	66Was 67-70NO	23	6'1"	214	Ohio State		24
Barry, Odell OE	64-65DenA	3	5'10"	180	Findlay		6
Barton, Greg QB	69Det 71CFL		6'2"	195	Tulsa		
Barton, Jim C	60DalA 61-62DenA		6'5"	250	Marshall		
Bass, Dick FB-HB	60-69LA	23	5'10"	197	U. of Pacific		252
Bass, Glenn OE-HB-FL-WR	61-66BufA 67-68HouA	2	6'2"	202	East Carolina		102
Bass, Norm DB	64DenA		6'3"	210	U. of Pacific		
61-63 played major league baseball							
Bates, Ted LB	59ChiC 60-62StL 63NY-A		6'3"	219	Oregon State		
Batten, Pat FB	64Det		6'2"	225	Hardin-Simmons		
Battle, Jim OG	63Min		6'1"	240	Southern Illinois		
Battle, Jim OT	66Cle		6'4"	235	Southern U.		
Battle, Mike DB	69NY-A 70NYJ	3	6'1"	175	Southern Calif.	1	
Baughan, Maxie LB	60-65Phi 66-70LA		6'1"	227	Georgia Tech	18	6
Baynham, Craig HB	67-69Dal 70ChiB 71JJ 72StL	23	6'1"	204	Georgia Tech		54
Beach, Walter DB	60-61BosA 63-66Cle		6'	184	Central Michigan	6	12
Beal, Norm DB	62StL		5'11"	170	Missouri		
Beans, Byron OT-DT	59-60Pit 61HouA		6'6"	249	Notre Dame		
Beard, Ed LB	65-72SF		6'2"	225	Tennessee	3	
Beathard, Pete QB	64-67KC-A 67-69HouA 70-71StL 72LA 73KC 74WFL 75Oak	12	6'2"	205	Southern Calif.		68
Beaver, Jim DT	62Phi		6'1"	235	Florida		
Beban, Gary QB-HB-WR	68-69Was		6'1"	195	U.C.L.A.		
Bedsole, Hal TE-OE	64-66Min 67JJ	2	6'4"	230	Southern Calif.		48
Beer, Tom TE-OG	67-69DenA 70Bos 71-72NE	2	6'4"	232	Houston		24
Behrman, Dave OT-C	63,65BufA 67DenA		6'5"	260	Michigan State		
Beier, Tom DB-FL	67,69MiaA		5'11"	198	Georgia Tech	2	
Beldon, Bob QB	69-70Dal		6'2"	208	Notre Dame		
Bell, Bobby LB-DE	63-69KC-A 70-74KC		6'4"	228	Minnesota	26	54
Bell Henry HB	60DenA	2	5'10"	210	none		
Bellino, Joe HB-FL	65-67BosA	23	5'9"	186	Navy		
Belotti, George C	60-61HouA 61SD-A		6'4"	253	Southern Calif.		
Bemiller, Al C-OG	61-69BufA		6'3"	243	Syracuse		
Bengston, Phil	HC68-70GB				Minnesota		
Bennett, Phil LB	60BosA		6'3"	225	Miami (Fla.)		
Benz, Larry DB	63-65Cle		5'11"	185	Northwestern	16	
Bercich, Bob DB	60-61Dal		6'1"	198	Michigan State	5	
Bernet, Lee OT	65-66DenA		6'2"	245	Wisconsin		
Berry, Ray OE	55-67Bal	2	6'2"	189	S.M.U.		408
Bethune, Bob DB	62SD-A		5'11"	190	Mississippi State	3	
Bettridge, Ed LB	64Cle		6'1"	235	Bowling Green		
Beverly, Randy DB	67-69NY-A 70Bos 71NE		5'11"	189	Colorado State	12	6
Biodrowski, Denny OG	63-67KC-A		6'1"	255	Memphis State		
Bird, Rodger DB	66-68OakA	3	5'11"	195	Kentucky	7	6
Birdwell, Dan DT-DE	62-69OakA		6'4"	247	Houston	4	2
Bishop, Don DB-FL-HB	58-59Pit 59ChiB 60-65Dal		6'2"	209	Los Angeles City C.	22	6
Bishop, Sonny OG	62DalA 63OakA 64-69HouA		6'2"	243	Fresno State		
Bivins, Charlie HB-TE	60-66ChiB 67Pit 67BufA	23	6'2"	212	Morris Brown		36
Blaine, Ed OG	62GB 63-66Phi		6'2"	240	Missouri		
Blair, George DB	61-64SD-A	5	5'11"	194	Mississippi	5	272
Blanda, George QB-DB-LB-K	49-58ChiB 60-66HouA 67-69OakA 70-75Oak	12 5	6'1"	210	Kentucky	1	2000
Blanks, Sid HB	64HouA 65KJ 66-68HouA 69BosA 70Bos	23	6'	206	Texas A & I		66
Blazer, Phil OG	60BufA		6'1"	235	North Carolina		
Bleick, Tom DB	66Bal 67Atl		6'2"	200	Georgia Tech		
Blye (born Bliey), Ronnie HB	68NYG 69Phi	23	5'11"	185	Notre Dame, Florida A&M		6
Bobo, Hubert LB	60LA-A 61-62NY-A		6'1"	217	Ohio State		5
Boeke, Jim OT	60-63LA 64-67Dal 68NO		6'5"	250	Heidelberg		
Bohling, Dewey HB	60-61NY-A 61BufA	2	5'11"	190	Hardin-Simmons		54
Bohovich, Reed OG-OT	62NYG		6'3"	260	Lehigh		
Bolin, Bookie OG	62-67NYG 68-69Min		6'2"	240	Mississippi		
Bookman, Johnny DB	57NYG 60DalA 61NY-A		5'11"	182	Miami (Fla.)	13	6
Bosch, Frank DT	68-70Was		6'4"	246	Colorado		
Bosely, Bruce OG-C-DE	56-68SF 69Atl		6'2"	241	West Virginia		
Bosseler, Don FB	57-64Was	2	6'1"	212	Miami (Fla.)		138
Boston, McKinley DE-LB	68-69NYG		6'2"	245	Minnesota		
Botchan, Ron LB	60LA-A 61HouA		6'1"	234	Occidental	2	
Boudreaux, Jim OT-DE	66-68BosA		6'4"	245	Louisiana Tech		
Boutwell, Tommy WR-QB	69MiaA		6'2"	205	Southern Miss.		
Bowie, Larry OG	62-68Min		6'2"	247	Purdue		
Bowling, Andy LB	67Atl		6'3"	235	Virginia Tech		
Bowman, Ken C	64-73GB 74XJ		6'3"	230	Wisconsin		
Bowman, Steve HB	66NYG		6'	195	Alabama		
Boyd, Bobby DB-HB	60-68Bal		5'10"	190	Oklahoma	57	30
Boyette, Garland LB	62-63StL 66-69HouA 70-72Hou		6'1"	237	Grambling	2	6
Boylan, Jim FL	63Min		6'1"	185	Washington State		6
Boynton, George DB	62OakA		5'11"	190	East Texas State		
Boynton, John OT	69MiaA		6'4"	255	Tennessee		
Braase, Ordell DE	57-68Bal		6'4"	240	South Dakota		
Brabham, Danny LB	63-67HouA, 68CinA		6'4"	236	Arkansas	1	
Bradfute, Byron OT	60-61Dal		6'3"	243	Southern Miss.		
Bradshaw, Charlie OT	58-60LA 61-66Pit 67-68Det		6'6"	255	Baylor		
Bradshaw, Jim DB	63-67Pit		6'1"	199	Tenn.-Chatanooga	11	24
Brady, Phil DB	69DenA		6'2"	211	Brigham Young		
Bramlett, John LB	65-66DenA 67-68MiaA 69BosA 70Bos 71Atl		6'2"	216	Memphis State	10	18
Branch, Mel DE	60-62DalA 63-65KC-A 66-68MiaA		6'2"	231	Louisiana State		
Brannen, Solomon DB-HB	65-66KC-A 67NY-A		6'1"	188	Morris Brown		
Bratkowski, Zeke QB	54ChiB 55-56MS 57-60ChiB 61-63LA 64-68GB 69-70VR 71GB	12 4	6'4"	204	Georgia		30
Bravo, Alex DB	57-58LA 60-61OakA		6'	190	Cal. St. Polytech	6	
Braxton, Hez FB-HB	62SD-A 63BufA		6'2"	227	Virginia Union		8
Breaux, Don QB	63DenA 65SD-A	1	6'1"	203	McNeese State		
Breding, Ed LB	67-68Was		6'4"	235	Texas A&M		2
Breedlove, Rod LB	65-67Pit		6'2"	225	Maryland	11	
Breen, Gene LB	64GB 65-66Pit 67-68LA		6'2"	229	Virginia Tech		

Use Name (Nicknames) – Positions	Team by Year	See Section	Hgt	Wgt	College	Int	Pts
Breitenstein, Bob OT-OG	65-67DenA 67Min 69-70Atl		6'3"	264	Tulsa		
Brenner, Al DB	69-70NYG		6'1"	200	Michigan State		
Brewer, Billy DB	60Was		6'	190	Mississippi		
Brewer, Johnny LB-OE-TE-DE	61-67Cle 68-70NO	2	6'4"	233	Mississippi	3	42
Brewington, Jim OT	61OakA		6'6"	280	N. Car. Central		
Brezina, Bobby HB	63HouA		6'	200	Houston		
Briggs, Bill DE	66-67Was		6'3"	250	Iowa		
Briggs, Bob FB	65Was		6'1"	228	Central St.-Okla.		
Britt, Charley DB	60-63LA 64Min 64SF		6'2"	183	Georgia	14	6
Brittenum, Jon QB	68SD-A		6'	185	Arkansas		
Brock, Clyde OT	62-63Dal 63SF		6'5"	268	Utah State		
Brodhead, Bob QB	60BufA	1	6'2"	207	Duke		2
Brodie, John QB	57-73SF	12	6'1"	198	Stanford		132
Brodnax, J. W. FB	60DenA		6'	208	Louisiana State		6
Brooker, Tommy OE-K	63DalA 63-66KC-A	5	6'2"	230	Alabama		290
Brooks, Bob FB	61NY-A		6'	215	Ohio U.		
Brown, Allen TE	66-67GB		6'5"	238	Mississippi		
Brown, Barry LB-TE	66-67Bal 68NYG 69BosA 70Bos	2	6'3"	228	Florida	1	
Brown, Bill LB	60BosA		6'1"	230	Syracuse	1	
Brown, Bill FB	61ChiB 62-74Min	2	5'11"	225	Illinois		456
Brown, Bob OT	64-68Phi 69-70LA 71-73Oak		6'4"	284	Nebraska		
Brown, Charley OT	62OakA		6'4"	245	Houston		
Brown, Charlie DB-HB	66-67ChiB 68BufA		6'1"	194	Syracuse	1	
Brown, Charlie HB	67-68NO		5'10"	187	Missouri		18
Brown, Don HB	60HouA		6'1"	205	Houston		
Brown, Doug DT	64OakA		6'4"	250	Fresno State		
Brown, Fred HB	61,63BufA	2	5'11"	189	Georgia		18
Brown, Fred LB-TE	65LA 66KJ 67-69Phi		6'5"	231	Miami (Fla.)	2	
Brown, Jimmie FB	56-65Cle	23	6'2"	228	Syracuse		756
Brown, John OT	62-66Cle 67-71Pit 72JJ		6'2"	250	Syracuse		
Brown, Roger DT	60-66Det 67-69LA		6'5"	298	Md. Eastern Shore	2	6
Brown, Timmy HB	59GB 60-67Phi 68Bal	23	5'10"	195	Ball State		384
Brown, Tom DB	64-68GB 69Was	3	6'1"	191	Maryland	13	12
63 played major league baseball							
Brown, Willie FL-HB	64-65LA 66Phi		6'	185	Souther Calif.		
Brown, Willie DB	63-66DenA 67-69OakA 70-77Oak		6'1"	194	Grambling	53	12
Browning, Charley HB	65NY-A		6'	220	Washington		
Brownlee, Claude DT	67MiaA		6'4"	265	Benedict		
Bruggers, Bob LB	66-68MiaA 68-69SD-A 70-71SD		6'1"	226	Minnesota	2	
Brumm, Don DE	63-69StL 70-71Phi 72StL		6'3"	243	Purdue		
Brunelli, Sam OT-OG	66-69DenA 70-71Den 72JJ		6'1"	263	Colorado State		
Bryant, Bob OE	60DalA		6'5"	230	Texas		
Bryant, Charlie HB-FB	66-67StL 68-69Atl	23	6'1"	207	Allen		
Bryant, Chuck OE	62StL		6'2"	220	Ohio State		
Buchanan, Buck DT	63-69KC-A 70-75KC		6'7"	279	Grambling	3	2
Buchanan, Tim LB	69CinA		6'	233	Hawaii		
Buckman, Tom TE	69DenA 71JJ		6'4"	230	Texas A&M		6
Budd, Frank FL	62Phi 63Was	2	5'10"	187	Villanova		6
Budde, Ed OG	63-69KC-A 70-76 KC		6'5"	261	Michigan State		
Budka, Frank DB	64LA		6'	195	Notre Dame	2	
Budness, Bill LB	62-69OakA 70Oak		6'1"	215	Boston U.	3	
Budrewicz, Tom OG	61NY-A		6'2"	245	Brown		
Bugenhagen, Gary OG-OT	67BufA 70Bos		6'2"	249	Syracuse		
Bukaty, Fred FB	61DenA	2	5'11"	195	Kansas		32
Bukich, Rudy QB	53LA 54-55MS 56LA 57-58Was	12	6'1"	202	Southern Calif.		54
	58-59ChiB 60-61Pit 62-68ChiB						
Bull, Ronnie HB-FB	62-70ChiB 71Phi	2	6'	200	Baylor		84
Bullocks, Amos HB	62-64Dal 66Pit	23	6'1"	201	Southern Illinois		42
Buncom, Frank LB	62-67SD-A 68CinA		6'1"	236	Southern Calif.	5	
died Sept. 14, 1969 – pulmonary embolism							
Bundra, Mike DT	62-63Det 64Min 64Cle 65Bal		6'3"	258	Southern Calif.		
Buoniconti, Nick LB	62-68BosA 69MiaA 70-74Mia 75BG		5'11"	220	Notre Dame	32	8
	76Mia						
Burch, Jerry OE	61OakA	2	6'1"	195	Georgia Tech		6
Burford, Chris OE	60-62DalA 63-67KC-A	2	6'3"	211	Stanford		332
Burke, Vern OE	65SF 66Atl 67NO	2	6'4"	201	Oregon State		12
Burkett, Jackie LB-C	61-66Bal 67NO 68-69Dal 70NO		6'4"	229	Auburn	10	
Burman, George C-OG-OT	64ChiB 67-70LA 71-72Was		6'3"	253	Northwestern		
Burnett, Bobby HB	66-67BufA 68JJ 69DenA	2	6'2"	208	Arkansas		48
Burnett, Len DB	61Pit		6'1"	195	Oregon		
Burrell, George DB	69DenA		5'10"	180	Pennsylvania	2	6
Burrell, John OE-FL	62-64Pit 66-67Was	2	6'3"	191	Rice		
Burrell, Ode HB-FL	64-69HouA	234	6'	189	Mississippi State		82
Burris, Bo DB	67-69NO		6'3"	195	Houston	4	6
Burroughs, Don DB	55-59LA 60-64Phi		6'4"	185	Colorado State	50	
Burson, Jimmy DB	63-67StL 68Atl		6'	181	Auburn	16	12
Burton, Leon HB	60NY-A	3	5'9"	172	Arizona		18
Burton, Ron HB	60-65BosA	23	5'10"	190	Northwestern		114
Bussell, Jerry DB	65DenA		6'	185	Georgia Tech		
Butkus, Dick LB-C	65-73ChiB		6'3"	244	Illinois	22	10
Butler, Bill DB-HB	59GB 60Dal 61Pit 62-64Min	23	5'10"	189	Tenn.-Chatanooga	11	24
Butler, Bob OG	62Phi 63NY-A		6'1"	233	Kentucky		
Butler, Cannonball HB	65-67Pit 68-71Atl 72StL 73JJ	23	5'10"	191	Edward Waters		102
Butsko, Harry LB	63Was		6'3"	220	Maryland		
Buzyniski, Bernie LB	60BufA		6'3"	228	Holy Cross	1	
Byers, Ken OG-DE	62-63NYG 64-65Min 66JJ		6'1"	240	Cincinnati		
Byrd, Butch DB	63-69BufA 70Buf 71Den	3	6'	203	Boston U.	40	36
Byrd, Dennis DE	68BosA		6'4"	260	N. Carolina State		
Byrd, Mack LB	65LA		6'	215	Southern Calif.		
Byrne, Bill OG	63Phi		6'	240	Boston College		
Cadile, Jim OG-OT	62-72ChiB		6'3"	239	San Jose State		
Cadwell, John OG	61DalA		6'3"	230	Oregon State		
Caffey, Lee Roy LB	63Phi 64-69GB 70ChiB 71Dal 72SD		6'3"	247	Texas A&M	11	18
Cagle, Johnny DE	69BosA		6'3"	260	Clemson		
Cahill, Dave DT-DE	66Phi 67LA 68KJ 69Atl		6'3"	240	Arizona State		
Caleb, Jamie HB-FB	60Cle 61Min 62CFL 65Cle	3	6'1"	210	Grambling		6
Callahan, Dan OG	60NY-A		6'	230	Wooster		
Calland, Lee DB	63-65Min 66-68Atl 69ChiB 69-72Pit		6'	190	Louisville	19	6
Campbell, Bob HB	69Pit	3	6'	195	Penn State		
Campbell, Jim LB	69SD-A		6'3"	218	West Texas State	1	
Campbell, John LB	63-64Min 65-69Pit 69Bal		6'3"	222	Minnesota	5	6
Campbell, Ken OE	60NY-A		6'1"	213	West Chester St.		
Campbell, Mike HB	68Det		5'11"	200	Lenoir Rhyne		

Use Name (Nicknames) – Positions	Team by Year	See Section	Hgt	Wgt	College	Int	Pts
Campbell, Woody HB	67-69HouA 70-71Hou	2	5'1"	205	Northwestern		90
Canale, Justin OG	65-68BosA 69CinA		6'2"	242	Mississippi State		1
Canale, Whit DE-DT	66MiaA 68BosA		6'3"	245	Tennessee		
Cannavino, Joe DB	60-61OakA 62BufA		5'11"	186	Ohio State	10	
Cannon, Billy TE-HB-FB-OE	60-63HouA 64-69OakA 70KC	23	6'1"	216	Louisiana State		392
Capp, Dick LB-TE	67GB 68Pit		6'3"	235	Boston College		
Cappadonna, Bob FB	66-67BosA 68BufA	2	6'1"	230	Northeastern		34
Cappelletti, Gino FL-WR-OE-DB	60-69BosA 70Bos	2 5	6'	190	Minnesota	4	1130
Carlton, Wray HB-FB	60-67BufA	2	6'2"	218	Duke		204
Carmichael, Paul HB	65DenA		6'	200	El Camino J.C.		
Carolan, Reg OE-TE	62-63SD-A 64-68KC-A	2	6'6"	235	Toledo		34
Caroline, J. C. DB-HB	56-65ChiB	2	6'1"	190	Illinois	24	36
Carollo, Joe OT	62-68LA 69-70Phi 71LA 72-73Cle		6'2"	262	Notre Dame		
Carothers, Don OE	60DenA		6'5"	225	Bradley		
Carpenter, Preston OE-TE-HB	56-59Cle 60-63Pit	23	6'2"	197	Arkansas		144
Carpenter, Ron LB	64-65SD-A		6'2"	230	Texas A&M	1	
Carr, Henry DB	65-67NYG		6'3"	198	Arizona State	7	6
Carr, Jimmy DB-LB-HB	55,57ChiC 59-63Phi 64-65Was	2	6'1"	206	Morris Harvey	15	6
Carr, Tom DT	68NO		6'3"	267	Morgan State		
Carrell, John LB	66HouA		6'3"	227	Texas Tech		
Carrington, Ed TE	68KJ 69HouA		6'4"	225	Virginia		
Carroll, Jim LB	65-66NYG 66-68Was 69NY-A		6'1"	229	Notre Dame	3	
Carroll, Leo DE	67KJ 68GB 69-70Was 71JJ		6'7"	250	San Diego State		
Carson, Kern HB	65SD-A 65NY-A			202	San Diego State		12
Carwell, Larry DB	67-68HouA 69BosA 70Bos 71-72NE	3		191	Iowa State	14	18
Casares, Rick FB	55-64ChiB 65Was 66MiaA	2	6'2	226	Florida		360
Case, Pete OG	62-64Phi 65-70NYG		6'3"	242	Georgia		
Casey, Bernie FL-WR-OE	61-66SF 67-68LA	2	6'4"	213	Bowling Green		240
Casey, Tim LB	69ChiB 69DenA		6'1"	225	Oregon		
Cash, John DE	61-62DenA		6'3"	235	Allen	1	
Cassesse, Tom DB-HB	67DenA		6'1"	197	C. W. Post	1	
Cavalli, Carmen DE	60OakA		6'4"	245	Richmond		
Caveness, Ronnie LB	65KC-A 66-68HouA		6'1"	223	Arkansas	1	
Cavness, Grady DB	69DenA 70Atl		5'11"	190	Texas-El Paso	2	
Caylor, Lowell DB	64Cle		6'3"	205	Miami-Ohio		
Ceppetelli, Gene C	68-69Phi 69NYG		6'2"	247	Villanova		
Cernel, Joe C	65-67SF 68Atl		6'2"	238	Northwestern		
Chamberlain, Dan OE-HB	60-61BufA	2	6'4"	200	Sacramento State		24
Chandler, Don HB-K	56-64NYG 65-67GB	45	6'2"	208	Florida		530
Chapple, Jack LB	65SF		6'2"	227	Stanford		6
Charon, Carl DB	62-63BufA		5'10"	190	Michigan State	7	18
Cheeks, B. W. HB	65HouA		6'1"	230	Texas Southern		
Chelf, Don OG-OT	60-61BufA		6'3"	235	Iowa		
Chesser, George FB	66-67MiaA		6'2"	223	Delta State		
Childress, Joe HB-FB	56-59ChiC 60StL	2	6'	202	Auburn		96
	61JJ 62-65StL						
Childs, Clarence DB-HB	64-67NYG 68ChiB	23	6'	180	Florida A&M	2	12
Chlebek, Ed QB	63NY-A		5'11"	175	Western Michigan		
Choboian, Max QB	66DenA	1	6'4"	205	San Fran. State		12
Christopherson, Jim LB	62Min	5	6'	215	Concordia-Moor.	1	61
Christy, Dick HB	58Pit 60BosA 61-63NY-A	23	5'10"	191	N. Carolina State		120
Christy, Earl HB-DB	66-68NY-A	3	5'11"	193	Md. Eastern Shore	1	1
Chuy, Don OG	63-68LA 69Phi		6'1"	255	Clemson		
Ciccolella, Mike LB	66-68NYG		6'1"	235	Dayton	1	
Cichowski, Tom OT	67-68DenA		6'4"	250	Maryland		
Clancy, Jack WR-FL	67MiaA 68KJ 69MiaA 70GB	2	6'1"	295	Michigan		30
Claridge, Dennis QB	64-65GB 66Atl	1	6'3"	225	Nebraska		
Clark, Ernie LB	63-67Det 68StL		6'1"	222	Michigan State	4	
Clark, Howard DE	60LA-A 61SD-A	2	6'2"	210	Tenn.-Chattanooga		
Clark, Mike K	63Phi 64-67Pit 68-71Dal 72JJ 73Dal	5	6'1"	203	Texas A&M		724
Clark, Monte OT-DT-DE	59-61SF 62Dal 63-69Cle HC76SF		6'6"	260	Southern Calif.		
Clark, Phil DB	67-69Dal 70ChiB 71NE		6'2"	209	Northwestern	4	
Clarke, Frank OE-FL-TE	57-59Cle 60-67Dal	2	6'	211	Colorado		306
Clarke, Hagood DB	64-68BufA	3	6'	193	Florida	12	18
Clay, Billy DB	66Was		6'1"	192	Mississippi	1	
Clay, Ozzie FL	64Was		6'	190	Iowa State		
Clemens, Bob HB	62Bal		6'1"	208	Pittsburgh		
Clemens, Henry OE	61Pit		6'2"	200	North Carolina		
Cline, Doug LB-FB	60-66HouA 66SD-A	2	6'2"	225	Clemson	7	30
Cloutier, Dave DB	64BosA		6'	195	Maine		
Coan, Bert HB	62SD-A 63-68KC-A	23	6'4"	219	Kansas		114
Cockrell, Gene OT-DE	60-62NY-A		6'3"	247	Hardin-Simmons		
Cody, Bill LB	66Det 67-70NO 72Phi		6'1"	225	Auburn		
Coffey, Don FL	63DenA		6'3"	190	Memphis State		
Coffey, Junior FB-HB	65GB 66-67Atl 68KJ	2	6'1"	211	Washington		90
	69Atl 69NYG 70KJ 71NYG						
Cogdill, Gail OE-WR	60-68Det 68Bal 69-70Atl	2	6'2"	195	Washington State		216
Cohen, Abe OG	60BosA		5'11"	230	Tenn.-Chattanooga		
Coia, Angie OE	60-63ChiB 64-65Was 66Atl	2	6'2"	202	Southern Calif.		120
Colchico, Dan DE	60-65SF 69NO		6'4"	240	San Jose State		
Colclough, Jim OE-FL-WR	60-68BosA	2	6'	185	Boston College		238
Cole, Fred OG	60LA-A		5'11"	226	Maryland		
Cole, Terry FB	68-69Bal 70Pit 71Mia	2	6'1"	220	Indiana		36
Collier, Blanton	HC63-70Cle				Georgetown (Ky.)		
Collier, Jim OE	62NYG 63Was		6'2"	195	Arkansas		
Collier, Joel	HC66-68BufA				Northwestern		
Collins, Gary FL-WR-OE	62-71Cle	2 4	6'4"	211	Maryland		420
Colvin, Jim DT-DE-OG	60-63Bal 64-66Dal 67NYG		6'2"	250	Houston		2
Compton, Dick OE-DB-HB-WR	62-64Det 65HouA 67-68Pit	2	6'1"	195	McMurry	1	24
Concannon, Jack QB	64-66Phi 67-71ChiB 74GB 75Det	12	6'3"	201	Boston College		72
Condren, Glen DT-DE	65-67NYG 69-72Atl		6'2"	246	Oklahoma		
Conjar, Larry FB	65Cle 68Phi 69-70Bal	2	6'	214	Notre Dame		2
Connelly, Mike C-OG-OT	60-67Dal 68Pit		6'3"	242	Utah State		
Conners, Dan LB	64-69OakA 70-74Oak		6'1"	231	Miami (Fla.)	15	30
Conrad, Bobby Joe FL-HB-WR-DB	58-59ChiC	23 5	6'	194	Texas A&M	4	389
	60-68StL 69Dal						
Contoulis, John DT	64NYG		6'4"	260	Connecticut		
Cook, Ed OT-OG	58-59ChiC 60-65StL 66-67Atl		6'2"	245	Notre Dame		
Cook, Greg QB	69CinA 70-72SJ 73Cin	12	6'3"	214	Cincinnati		6
Cooke, Ed DE-LB	58ChiB 58Phi 60-63NY-A		6'4"	248	Maryland	7	12
	64-65DenA 66-67MiaA						
Coolbaugh, Bob OE	61OakA	2	6'3"	200	Richmond		26
Cooper, Bill FB-LB	61-64SF		6'1"	215	Muskingum		6

Use Name (Nicknames) – Positions	Team by Year	See Section	Hgt	Wgt	College	Int	Pts
Cooper, Thurlow OE-DE	60-62NY-A	2	6'4"	228	Maine		52
Copeland, Ron WR	69ChiB		6'4"	196	U.C.L.A.		
Corcoran, King QB	68BosA		6'	200	Maryland		
Cordileone, Lou DT-DE-OG	60NYG 61SF 62LA		6'	247	Clemson	1	
	62-63Pit 67-68NO 69KJ						
Cordill, Ollie DB-OE	67SD-A 68Atl 69NO	4	6'2"	180	Memphis State		
Corey, Walt LB	60,62DalA 63-66KC-A		6'	229	Miami (Fla.)	4	
Cornelison, Jerry OT	60-62DalA 64-65KC-A		6'3"	250	S.M.U.		
Cornish, Frank DT	66-70ChiB 70-71Mia 72Buf		6'6"	285	Grambling	2	
Coronado, Bob OE	61Pit		6'1"	195	U. of Pacific		
Cortez, Bruce DB	67NO		6'	175	Parsons		
Costa, Dave DT-DE	63-65OakA 66BufA 67-69DenA		6'2"	257	Utah		2
	70-71Den 72-73SD 74Buf						
Costa, Paul OT-TE-OE	65-69BufA 70-72Buf	2	6'4"	252	Notre Dame		42
Costello, Tom LB	64-65NYG		6'3"	220	Dayton		
Costello, Vince LB	57-66Cle 67-68NYG		6'	228	Ohio U.	22	12
Cottrell, Bill OT-C-OG	67-70Det 71JJ 72Den		6'3"	255	Delaware Valley		
Cottrell, Ted LB	69-70AtL		6'1"	233	Delaware Valley		
Counts, Johnny HB	62-63NYG	3	5'10"	170	Illinois		6
Cowan, Charley OT-OG	61-75LA		6'4"	264	N. Mex. Highlands		
Cox, Jim TE	68MiaA	2	6'2"	227	Miami (Fla.)		
Cox, Larry DT	66-68DenA		6'2"	250	Abilene Christian		
Coyle, Russ DB	61LA		6'2"	195	Oklahoma		
Crabb, Claude DB-FL	62-63Was 64-65Phi 66-68LA		6'	193	Colorado	10	6
Crabtree, Eric WR-OE-DB	66-68DenA 69CinA	2	5'11"	184	Pittsburgh		132
	70-71Cin 71NE						
Craddock, Nate FB	63Bal		6'	220	Parsons		
Craig, Dobie OE-HB	62-63OakA 64HouA	2	6'4"	200	Howard Payne		42
Crane, Dennis DT-OT	68-69Was 70NYG		6'6"	260	Southern Calif.		
Crane, Gary LB	69DenA		6'4"	230	Arkansas State		
Crane, Paul LB-C	66-69NY-A 70-72NYJ		6'2"	208	Alabama	5	14
Crawford, Bill OG	60NYG		6'1"	235	British Columbia		
Crawford, Hilton DB	69BufA		6'	198	Grambling		
Crawford, Jim FB-HB	60-64BosA	2	6'1"	203	Wyoming		46
Crenshaw, Leon DT	68GB		6'6"	280	Tuskegee		
Crenshaw, Willie FB	64-69StL 70Den	23	6'2"	228	Kansas State		108
Crespino, Bob OE-TE-WR	61-64Cle 64-68NYG	2	6'4"	223	Mississippi		54
Crockett, Bobby WR-OE	66BufA 67KJ 68-69BufA	2	6'	198	Arkansas		18
Crockett, Monte OE	60-62BufA	2	6'3"	213	N. Mex. Highlands		6
Croftcheck, Don OG-LB	65-66Was 67ChiB		6'1"	230	Indiana		
Cronin, Bill TE	65Phi 66MiaA		6'4"	225	Boston College		6
Cropper, Marshall WR-OE	67-69Pit	2	6'3"	207	Md. Eastern Shore		
Cross, Irv DB	61-65Phi 66-68LA 69Phi	3	6'1"	192	Northwestern	22	12
Crossan, Dave C	65-69Was		6'3"	245	Maryland		
Crotty, Jim DB	60-61Was 61-62BufA		5'11"	192	Notre Dame	3	
Crouthamel, Jake HB	60BosA		5'11"	195	Dartmouth		
Crow, Al DT	60BosA		6'6"	260	William & Mary		
Crow, John David HB-FB-TE	58-59ChiC	12	6'2"	218	Texas A&M		444
	60-64StL 65-68SF						
Crow, Wayne HB-DB	60-61OakA 62-63BufA	2 4	6'	205	California	4	26
Crump, Harry FB	63BosA	2	6'	205	Boston College		30
Crutcher, Tommy LB-FB	64-67GB 68-69NYG		6'3"	229	Texas Christian	3	
	70KJ 71-72GB						
Cudzik, Walt C-LB	54Was 60-63BosA 64BufA		6'2"	231	Purdue		
Culpepper, Ed DT	58-59ChiC 60StL 61Min 62-63HouA		6'1"	255	Alabama		
Cummings, Ed LB	64NY-A 65DenA		6'2"	230	Stanford	1	
Cunningham, Carl LB	67-69DenA 70Den 71NO		6'3"	240	Houston	4	
Cunningham, Jay DB	65-67BosA	3	5'10"	180	Bowling Green	3	6
Cunningham, Jim FB	61-63Was	2	5'11"	221	Pittsburgh		30
Cuozzo, Gary QB	63-66Bal 67NO 68-71Min 72StL	12	6'1"	195	Virginia		6
Currie, Dan LB	58-64GB 65-66LA		6'3"	239	Michigan State	11	6
Curry, Bill C-LB	65-66GB 67-72Bal 73Hou 74LA		6'2"	235	Georgia Tech		
Curry, Ray FL	63Pit		6'1"	195	Jackson State		6
Cutsinger, Gary DE	62-66HouA 67XJ 68HouA		6'4"	244	Oklahoma State		
Cvercko, Andy OG	60GB 61-62Dal 63Cle 63Was		6'	242	Northwestern		
Daanen, Jerry WR	68-70StL		6'	190	Miami (Fla.)		
Dabney, Carlton DT	68Atl 69-70XJ		6'5"	250	Morgan State	1	
Dale, Carroll WR-OE-FL	60-64LA 65-72GB 73Min	2	6'1"	198	Virginia Tech.		312
D'Amato, Mike DB	68NY-A		6'2"	204	Hofstra		
Danenhauer, Bill DE	60DenA 60BosA		6'4"	245	Kansas St. Teachers		
Danenhauer, Eldon OT	60-65DenA 66KJ		6'4"	242	Pittsburgh State		
Daniel, Willie DB	61-66Pit 67-69LA		5'11"	187	Mississippi State	14	12
Daniels, Clem HB-DB	60DalA 61-67OakA 68SF	23	6'1"	219	Prairie View	3	324
Daniels, Dave DT	66OakA		6'3"	245	Florida A&M		
Daniels, Dick DB	66-68Dal 69-60ChiB 71JJ		5'9"	180	Pacific (Ore.)	7	
Darnall, Bill WR	68-69MiaA 70JJ		6'2"	197	North Carolina		
Darragh, Dan QB	68-69BufA 70Buf	1	6'3"	196	William & Mary		
Darre, Bernie OG	61Was		6'2"	230	Tulane		
Daugherty, Bob HB	66SF		6'2"	205	Tulsa		
Davidson, Ben DE-DT	61GB 62-63Was 64-69OakA		6'8"	272	Washington		
	70-71Oak 72FJ						
Davidson, Cotton QB	54Bal 55-56MS 57Bal 58CFL	12 45	6'1"	182	Baylor		104
	60-62DalA 62-66OakA 67JJ 68OakA						
Davidson, Pete DT	60HouA		6'5"	255	The Citadel		
Davis, Al	HC63-65OakA				Syracuse		
Davis, Dick DE	62DalA		6'2"	230	Kansas		
Davis, Don DT	66NYG 67JJ		6'6"	260	Los Angeles State		
Davis, Donnie FL-TE	62Dal 70Hou		6'4"	220	Southern U.		
Davis, Doug OT	66-72Min		6'4"	250	Kentucky		
Davis, Glenn OE	60-61Det	2	6'	180	Ohio State		
Davis, Jack OG	60BosA		6'	226	Maryland		
Davis, Jack OG	60DenA		6'2"	235	Arizona		
Davis, Marvin DE	66DenA		6'4"	252	Wichita State		
Davis, Norman OG	67Bal 69NO 70Phi		6'3"	247	Grambling		
Davis, Roger OG-OT	60-63ChiB 64LA 65-66NYG		6'3"	236	Syracuse		
Davis, Rosey DE	65-67NYG		6'5"	260	Tennessee State		
Davis, Sonny LB	61Dal		6'2"	220	Baylor		
Davis, Ted LB	64-66Bal 67-69NO 70Mia		6'1"	230	Georgia Tech	2	
Davis, Tommy K	59-69SF	45	6'	215	Louisiana State		738
Davis, Willie DE-OT	58-59Cle 60-69GB		6'3"	243	Grambling	2	16
Dawson, Bill DE-OE	65BosA		6'3"	240	Florida State		
Dawson, Len QB	57-59Pit 60-61Cle 62DalA	12	6'	190	Purdue		54
	63-69KC-A 70-75KC						
Day, Al LB	60DenA		6'2"	216	Eastern Michigan		
Day, Eagle QB	59-60Was	1 4	6'	183	Mississippi		
Day, Tom DE-OG-DT-OT	60StL 61-66BufA 67SD-A 68BufA		6'2"	252	N. Carolina A&T	1	
Dean, Floyd LB	64-65SF		6'4"	245	Florida		
Dean, Ted HB-FB	60-63Phi 64Min	23	6'2"	211	Wichita State		36
Dee, Bob DE-DT	57-58Was 60-67BosA		6'3"	248	Holy Cross	1	
DeFelice, Mick OT	65-66NY-A		6'3"	250	Southern Conn. St.		
Degen, Dick LB	65-66SD-A		6'1"	223	Long Beach State	3	
DeLong, Steve DT-DE	65-69SD-A 70-71SD 72ChiB		6'3"	251	Tennessee	1	
DeLuca, Sam OG-OT	61LA-A 61SD-A 62VR		6'2"	247	South Carolina		
	63SD-A 64-66NY-A						
DeLuca, Jerry OT-DT	59Phi 60-61BosA 62-63BufA		6'3"	249	Middle Tennessee		
	63-64BosA						
DeMarco, Bob C-OG	61-69StL 70-71Mia 72-74Cle 75LA		6'3"	243	Dayton		
Demko, George DE	61Pit		6'3"	240	Appalachian State		
Denney, Austin TE	67-69ChiB 70-71 Buf	2	6'2"	230	Tennessee		18
Dennis, Mike HB	68-69LA	2	6'1"	207	Mississippi		
Denny, Earl HB	67-68Min		6'1"	200	Missouri		
Denson, Al WR-FL-TE	64-69DenA 70Den 71Min	2	6'2"	208	Florida A&M		194
Denton, Bob DE-OT	60Cle 61-64Min		6'4"	241	U. of Pacific		
Denvir, John OG	62DenA		6'4"	245	Colorado		
Deskins, Don OG	60OakA		6'3"	240	Michigan		
Dess, Darrell OG-OT	58Pit 59-64NYG 65-66Was		6'	243	N. Carolina State		6
	66-69NYG						
DeSutter, Wayne OT	66BufA		6'4"	250	Western Illinois		
Deters, Harold K	67Dal	5	6'	200	N. Carolina State		12
DeVleigher, Chuck DT	69BufA		6'4"	265	Memphis State		
Dewveall, Willard OE	59-60ChiB 61-64HouA	2	6'4"	224	S.M.U.		162
Dial, Benjy QB	67Phi		6'1"	185	Eastern New Mex.		
Dial, Buddy FL-OE	59-63Pit 64-66Dal 67-68JJ	2	6'1"	194	Rice		264
Diamond, Bill OG	63KC-A		6'	240	Miami (Fla.)		
Diamond, Charley OT	60-62DalA 63KC-A		6'2"	249	Miami (Fla.)		
Dickey, Eldridge WR	68OakA 71Oak		6'2"	198	Tennessee State		6
Dickey, Wallace OT	68-69DenA		6'3"	260	SW Texas State		
Dickinson, Bo FB	60-61DalA 62-63DenA	2	6'2"	218	Southern Miss.		70
	63HouA 64OakA						
Dickson, Paul DT-OT	59LA 60Dal 61-70Min 71StL		6'5"	252	Baylor		
Diehl, John DT	61-64Bal 65Dal 65OakA		6'7"	276	Virginia		
Dillon, Terry DB	63Min		6'	193	Montana		
died May, 1964 – accidental drowing							
DiMidio, Tony OT-C	66-67KC-A		6'3"	250	West Chester St.		
Dimitroff, Tom QB	60BosA		5'11"	200	Miami - Ohio		
Dirks, Mike DT-OG	68-71Phi		6'2"	247	Wyoming		6
Discenzo, Tony OT	60BosA 60BufA		6'5"	240	Michigan State		
Ditka, Mike TE-OE	61-66ChiB 67-68Phi 69-72Dal	2	6'3"	229	Pittsburgh		270
DiVito, Joe QB	68DenA		6'2"	205	Boston College		
Dixon, Hewritt FB-HB-OE	63-65DenA 66-69OakA	2	6'2"	223	Florida A&M		170
	70Oak 71JJ						
Dobbins, Ollie DB	64BufA		5'11"	185	Morgan State		
Doelling, Fred DB	60Dal		5'10"	190	Pennsylvania		
Donahue, Oscar FL	62Min	2	6'3"	195	San Jose State		
Donaldson, Gene FB	67BufA		6'2"	225	Purdue		
Donnahoo, Roger DB	60NY-A		6'	185	Michigan State	5	12
Donnell, Ben DE	60LA-A		6'5"	248	Vanderbilt		
Donnelly, George DB	65-67SF 68JJ		6'3"	207	Illinois	2	
Donahue, Leon OG-OT	62-65SF 65-67Dal 68JJ		6'4"	245	San Jose State		
Dorsey, Dick OE	62OakA	2	6'3"	200	Southern Calif., Oklahoma		12
Dotson, Al DT	65KC-A 66MiaA 68-69OakA 70Oak		6'4"	258	Grambling		2
Dougherty, Bob LB	57LA 58Pit 60-63OakA		6'	238	Cincinnati, Kentucky	3	
Douglas, John DB	67-68NO 69HouA 70JJ		6'1"	195	Texas Southern	1	
Douglas, Merrill FB-HB	58-60ChiB 61Dal 62Phi	2	6'	204	Utah		12
Dove, Eddie DB	59-63SF 63NYG	3	6'2"	181	Colorado	10	
Dowdle, Mike LB-FB	60-62Dal 63-66SF		6'3"	226	Texas	6	6
Dowler, Boyd FL-OE-WR	59-69GB 70VR 71Was	2 4	6'5"	224	Colorado		240
Driskill, Joe DB	60-61StL		6'1"	195	Northeast La.		
Dubenion, Elbert FL-HB-WR	60-68BufA	23	6'	189	Bluffton		234
Dudek, Mitch OT	66NY-A		6'4"	245	Xavier - Ohio		
Dudley, Paul HB	62NYG 63Phi	2	6'	185	Arkansas		6
Dugan, Fred OE	58-59SF 60Dal 61-63Was	2	6'3"	197	Dayton		78
Duich, Steve OG	68Atl 69Was		6'3"	248	San Diego State		
Dukes, Mike LB	60-63HouA 64-65BosA 65NY-A		6'3"	231	Clemson	9	
Dumbrowski, Leon LB	60NY-A		6'	215	Delaware		
Dunaway, Dave WR	68GB 68Atl 69NYG		6'2"	205	Duke		
Dunaway, Jim DT	63-69BufA 70-71Buf 72Mia 73JJ		6'4"	278	Mississippi	1	6
Duncan, Randy QB	61DalA	1	6'	185	Iowa		
Duncan, Rick K	67DenA 68Phi 69Det		6'	208	Eastern Montana		9
Duncan, Ron TE	67Cle		6'6"	255	Wittenberg		
Duncan, Speedy DB	64-69SD-A 70SD 71-74Was	3	5'10"	177	Jackson State	24	54
Duncom, Bob OT	68StL		6'3"	250	West Texas State		
Dunn, Perry Lee HB-FB	64-65Dal 66-68Atl 69Bal	2	6'2"	208	Mississippi		42
Dupre, Charlie DB	60NY-A		6'1"	195	Baylor		
Durkee, Charlie K	67-68,71-72NO	5	5'11'	165	Oklahoma State		243
Dyer, Henry FB	66LA 67JJ 68LA 69-70Was	2	6'2"	230	Grambling		12
Dyer, Ken DB-WR	68SD-A 69CinA 70-71Cin		6'3"	187	Arizona State	3	6
Eason, John WR	68OakA		6'2"	220	Florida A&M		
Eaton, Scott DB	67-71NYG 72JJ		6'3"	199	Oregon State	11	6
Eber, Rick WR	68Atl 69SD-A 70SD 71JJ	2	6'	181	Tulsa		6
Echols, Fate OT-DT	62-63StL 64CFL		6'1"	258	Northwestern		
Eddy, Nick HB	67JJ 68-70Det 71KJ 72Det	2	6'1"	207	Notre Dame		
Edgerson, Booker DB	62-69BufA 70Den		5'10"	182	Western Illinois	23	2
Edmunds, Randy LB	68-69MiaA 71NE 72Bal		6'2"	223	Georgia Tech	1	
Edwards, Dave LB	63-75Dal		6'3"	224	Auburn	13	6
Edwards, Lloyd TE	69OakA		6'3"	248	San Diego State		
Eifrid, Jim LB	61DenA		6'	240	Colorado State		
Eisenhauer, Larry DE	61-69BosA		6'5"	247	Boston College	1	
Elkins, Larry FL	66-67HouA 69JJ	2	6'1"	193	Baylor		18
Ellersick, Don DB	60LA		6'1"	193	Washington State	2	
Elliott, Jim K	67Pit	4	5'11"	184	Presbyterian		
Ellis, Roger LB-C	60-63NY-A		6'3"	233	Maine	1	
Ellzey, Charley C-LB	60-61StL		6'3"	243	Southern Miss.		
Elmore, Doug DB	62Was	4	6'	188	Mississippi	2	
Elwell, Jack OE	62StL		6'3"	200	Purdue		
Elzey, Paul LB	68CinA		6'3"	235	Toledo		
Emanuel, Frank LB	66-69MiaA 70NO		6'3"	225	Tennessee	4	6
Embree, John WR	69DenA 70Den 71JJ	2	6'4"	201	Compton J.C.		30

Use Name (Nicknames) – Positions	Team by Year	See Section	Hgt	Wgt	College	Int	Pts
Emelianchik, Pete TE	67Phi		6'2"	220	Richmond		
Enis, Hunter QB	60DalA 61SD-A 62DenA 62OakA	12	6'2"	192	Texas Christian		30
Epperson, Pat OE	60DenA	2	6'3"	225	Adams State		
Erdelatz, Eddie	HC60OakA				St. Mary's		
Erickson, Bernie LB	67-68SD-A 68CinA		6'2"	239	Abilene Christian	1	
Erlandson, Tom LB	62-65DenA 66-67MiaA 68SD-A		6'3"	229	Washington State	8	6
Erwin, Terry HB	68DenA		6'	190	Boston College		
Estes, Don OG	66SD-A		6'2"	250	Louisiana State		
Etcheverry, Sam QB	61-62StL	12 4	5'11"	190	Denver		
Etter, Bob K	68-69Atl	5	5'11"	152	Georgia		128
Evans, Bob DE	65HouA		6'3"	250	Texas A&M		
Evans, Dale HB	61DenA		6'3"	210	Kansas State		
Evans, Jim FL	64-65NY-A		6'1"	190	Texas-El Paso		
Evey, Dick DT-DE-OG	64-69ChiB 70LA 71Det		6'2"	238	Tennessee	2	
Ewbank, Weeb	HC54-62Bal HC63-69NY-A HC70-73NYJ				Miami-Ohio		
Ezerins, Vilnis HB-FB	68LA		6'1"	217	Whitewater		
Fairband, Bill LB	67-68OakA		6'3"	228	Colorado		
Faison, Earl DE	61-66SD-A 66MiaA		6'5"	263	Indiana	6	14
Falls, Mike OG	60-61Dal		6'1"	240	Minnesota		
Fanning, Stan OT-DE-DT	60-62ChiB 63LA 64HouA 64DenA		6'6"	267	Idaho		
Farley, Dick DB	68-69SD-A		6'	185	Boston U.		
Farmer, Lonnie LB	64-66BosA		6'	220	Tenn.-Chatanooga	1	
Farr, Miller DB	65DenA 65-66SD-A 67-69HouA		6'1"	190	Wichita	35	36
	70-72StL 73Det						
Farrier, Curt DT	63-65KC-A 66JJ		6'6"	253	Montana State		
Farrington, Bo OE	60-63ChiB	2	6'3"	217	Prairie View		42
killed in auto accident at 1964 training camp							
Farris, John OG	65-66SD-A		6'4"	245	San Diego State		
Faulkner, Jack	HC62-64DenA				Miami (Fla.)		
Faulkner, Staley OT	64HouA		6'3"	245	Texas		
Faust, Paul LB	67Min		6'	220	Minnesota		
Feagin, Wiley OG	61-62Bal 63Was		6'2"	236	Houston		
Feldhausen, Paul OT	68BosA		6'6"	270	Northland		
Feldman, Marty	HC61-62OakA				Stanford		
Felt, Dick DB	60-61NY-A 62-66BosA		6'	184	Brigham Young	18	6
Felts, Bobby HB	65Bal 65-67Det	23	6'2"	203	Florida A&M		12
Fenner, Lane WR	68SD-A		6'5"	210	Florida State		
Ferguson, Bob FB	62-63Pit 63Min	2	5'11"	220	Ohio State		6
Ferguson, Charley OE-TE	61Cle 62Min 63BufA	2	6'5"	218	Tennessee State		78
	64JJ 65-66BufA 67-68JJ 69BufA						
Ferguson, Jim C-LB	68NO 69Atl 69ChiB 71JJ		6'4"	240	Southern Calif.		
Ferguson, Larry HB	63Det		5'10"	185	Iowa		
Ferrante, Orlando OG	60LA-A 61SD-A		6'	230	Southern Calif.		
Fetherston, Jim LB	68-69SD-A		6'2"	225	California	1	
Ficca, Dan OG	62Oak-A 63-66NY-A		6'1"	244	Southern Calif.		
Fichtner, Ross DB	60-67Cle 68NO		6'	186	Purdue	27	18
Fields, George DE-DT	60-61OakA		6'3"	245	Cal. St. Bakersfield	2	
Fields, Jerry LB	61-62NY-A		6'1"	222	Ohio State		
Finch, Karl OE	62LA		6'3"	195	Cal. St. Polytech		
Finneran, Gary DT	60LA-A 61OakA		6'3"	240	Southern Calif.		
Fischer, Pat (Mouse) DB-HB	61-67StL 68-77Was	3	5'10"	170	Nebraska	56	30
Fisher, Doug LB	69-70Pit		6'1"	225	San Diego State		
Fiss, Galen LB	56-66Cle		6'	226	Kansas	13	
Fitzgerald, Mike DB	66-67Min 67NYG 67Atl	3	5'10"	180	Iowa State	1	
Flanigan, Jim LB	67-70GB 71NO		6'3"	238	Pittsburgh	1	
Flatley, Paul OE-WR	63-67Min 68-70Atl	2	6'1"	187	Northwestern		144
Fleming, Don DB	60-62Cle		6'	187	Florida	10	
died June 4, 1963 – construction accident							
Fleming, George HB	61OakA	23 5	5'11"	188	Washington		63
Fleming, Marv TE-OE	63-69GB 70-74Mia	2	6'4"	233	Utah		96
Fletcher, Billy DB	66DenA		5'10"	190	Memphis State		
Flint, George OG	62-65BufA 66JJ 67-69BufA		6'4"	243	Arizona State		
Flores, Tom QB	60-61OakA 62IL 63-66OakA	12	6'1"	194	U. of Pacific		30
	67-69BufA 69KC-A						
Flowers, Charlie FB	60LA-A 61SD-A 62NY-A	2	6'1"	215	Mississippi		30
Floyd, Don DE	60-67HouA		6'4"	242	Texas Christian	4	12
Flynn, Don DB	60-61DalA 61NY-A		6'	205	Houston	5	6
Folkins, Lee TE-DE	61GB 62-64Dal 65Pit	2	6'5"	219	Washington		66
Fontes, Wayne DB	62NY-A		6'	190	Michigan State	4	6
Ford, Fred HB	60BufA 60LA-A	2	5'8"	180	Cal. St. Polytech		12
Ford, Garrett FB	68DenA	2	6'2"	230	West Virginia		6
Fortunato, Joe LB-FB	55-66ChiB		6'	225	Mississippi State	16	18
Foruria, John DB-HB	67-68Pit		6'2"	205	Idaho		
Foster, Gene FB-HB	65-69SD-A 70SD	2	5'11"	214	Arizona State		46
Fournet, Sid OG-LB-DE	55-56LA 57Pit		6'	235	Louisiana State	1	
	60-61DalA 62-63NY-A						
Fowler, Bobby FB	62NY-A		5'11"	212	Martin J.C.		
Fowler, Charlie OG-OT	67-68MiaA		6'2"	260	Houston		
Fowler, Jerry OT	64HouA		6'3"	255	NW State-La.		
Fowler, Willmer HB	60-61BufA	2	5'11"	185	Northwestern		6
Franci, Jason OE	66DenA		6'1"	210	Cal.-Santa Barbara		
Francis, Dave FB	63Was		6'1"	210	Ohio State		
Frankhauser, Tom DB	59LA 60-61Dal 62-63Min	3	6'	195	Purdue	13	
Frank, Bill OT	64Dal		6'5"	255	Colorado		
Franklin, Bobby DB-HB	60-66Cle		5'11"	182	Mississippi	13	18
Frantz, Jack C	68BufA		6'3"	230	California		
Fraser, Jim LB-K	62-64DenA 65KC-A 66BosA 68NO	4	6'3"	236	Wisconsin	3	2
Frazier, Al HB-FL	61-63DenA	23	5'11"	180	Florida A&M		68
Frazier, Charley OE-WR	62-68HouA 69BosA 70Bos	2	6'	177	Texas Southern		180
Frazier, Curt DB	68CinA		5'11"	183	Fresno State		
Frazier, Wayne C-LB	62SD-A 65HouA		6'2"	243	Auburn		
	66-67KC-A 67BufA						
Frazier, Willie TE-OE	64-66HouA 66-69SD-A 70SD	2	6'4"	235	Ark.-Pine Bluff		222
	71Hou 71-72KC 74WFL 75Hou 76KJ						
Fredrickson, Tucker FB-HB	65NYG 66KJ 67-71NYG	2	6'3"	233	Auburn		102
Freeman, Bobby DB-HB	57-58Cle 59GB 60-61Phi 62Was		6'1"	202	Auburn	15	
Freeman, Mike DB	68-70Atl		5'11"	187	Fresno State	1	
Frey, Dick DE-OG	60DalA 61HouA		6'2"	233	Texas A&M		
Fritsch, Ernie C-LB	60StL		6'	230	Detroit		
Frongillo, John OG-C	62-66HouA		6'3"	252	Baylor		
Frost, Ken DT	61-62Dal		6'4"	245	Tennessee	1	
Fuller, Charley HB	61-62OakA	2	5'11"	176	San Fran. State		12
Furey, Jim LB	60NY-A		6'	228	Kansas State		
Furman, John QB	62Cle		6'4"	205	Texas-El Paso		
Fussell, Tom DE	67BosA		6'3"	245	Louisiana State		

Use Name (Nicknames) – Positions	Team by Year	See Section	Hgt	Wgt	College	Int	Pts
Gabriel, Roman QB	62-72LA 73-77Phi	12	6'4"	225	N. Carolina State		180
Gaechter, Mike DB	62-69Dal		6'	192	Oregon	21	12
Gagner, Larry OG	66-69Pit 70JJ 72KC		6'3"	246	Florida		
Gaiser, George OT	68DenA		6'4"	255	S.M.U.		
Gaiters, Bob HB	61-62NYG 62SF 63DenA	23	5'11"	210	New Mexico State		48
Galimore, Willie HB	57-63ChiB	23	6'1"	187	Florida A&M		222
killed in auto accident at 1964 training camp							
Gamble, R. C. HB-FB	68-69BosA	2	6'3"	220	S. Carolina State		12
Gambrell, Billy OE-FL-WR	63-67StL 68Det	23	5'10"	175	South Carolina		105
Garcia, Jim DE-DT	65Cle 66NYG 67NO 68Atl		6'4"	248	Purdue		
Garner, Bob DB	60LA-A 61-62OakA	3	5'10"	185	Fresno State	7	
Garrett, Drake QB	68DenA 70Den		5'9"	183	Michigan State	2	
Garrett, J.D. HB	64-67DenA	23	5'11"	195	Grambling		36
Garrett, Mike HB	66-69KC-A 70KC 70-73SD	23	5'9"	199	Southern Calif.		294
Garron, Larry HB-FB	60-68BosA	23	6'	199	Western Illinois		252
Gassert, Ron DT	62GB		6'3"	250	Virginia		
Gaubatz, Dennis LB	63-64Det 65-69Bal		6'2"	225	Louisiana State	10	2
Gault, Billy LB	61Min		6'1"	185	Texas Christian		
Gault, Prentice HB-FB-LB	60Cle 61-67StL	2	6'	204	Oklahoma		102
Gavin, Chuck DE	60-63DenA		6'1"	243	Tennessee State	1	6
Gavric, Momcilo K	69SF	5	5'10"	167	none		31
Gehrke, Jack WR	68KC-A 69CinC 71Den 72JJ	2	6'	178	Utah		
Gent, Pete FL-TE-OE	64-68Dal	2	6'4"	209	Michigan State		24
Gentry, Curtis DB	66-68ChiB		6'	186	Md. Eastern Shore	6	
Gibbons, Jim OE-TE	58-68Det	2	6'2"	220	Iowa		120
Gibbs, Sonny QB	64Det		6'7"	230	Texas Christian		
Gibson, Claude DB	61-62SD-A 63-65OakA	3	6'1"	191	N. Carolina State	22	26
Gilburg, Tom OT	61-65Bal	4	6'5"	245	Syracuse		
Gilchrist, Cookie FB	62-64BufA 65DenA	2 5	6'3"	249	none		296
	66MiaA 67DenA						
Gill, Roger HB-TE	64-65Phi		6'1"	200	Texas Tech		
Gillett, Fred HB-OE	62SD-A 64OakA		6'3"	228	Los Angeles State		
Gilliam, Jon C	61-62DalA 63-67KC-A		6'2"	238	East Texas State		
Gillis, Don C	58-59ChiC 60-61StL 62JJ		6'3"	245	Rice		
Gillman, Sid	HC55-59LA HC60LA-A HC61-69SD-A				Ohio State		
	HC71SD HC73-74Hou						
Glacken, Scotty QB	66-67DenA		6'	190	Duke		
Glass, Bill DE-C-OT	58-61Det 62-68Cle		6'5"	252	Baylor	4	12
Glass, Glenn DB-FL-OE	62-63Pit 64-65Phi	2	6'	197	Tennessee	2	
	66Atl 66DenA						
Glenn, Howard OG	60NY-A		6'	235	Linfield		
died Oct. 9, 1960 – broken neck							
Glick, Freddie DB	59ChiC 60StL 61-66HouA	3	6'1"	189	Colorado State	31	6
Glueck, Larry DB	63-65ChiB		6'	190	Villanova	1	
Goeddeke, George OG-OT-C	67-69DenA 70-72Den 73JJ		6'3"	250	Notre Dame		
Gogolak, Charlie K	66-68Was 70Bos 71-72NE	5	5'10"	168	Princeton		270
Gogolak, Pete K	64-65BufA 66-74NYG	5	6'2"	193	Cornell		863
Goldstein, Al OE	60OakA	2	6'	204	North Carolina		12
Gonsoulin, Goose DB	60-66DenA 67SF		6'3"	209	Baylor	46	14
Gonzaga, John OT-OG-DT-DE	56-59SF 60Dal		6'3"	247	none		
	61-65Det 66DenA						
Good, Tom LB	66SD-A		6'	230	Marshall		
Goode, Tom C-LB	62-65HouA 66-69MiaA 70Bal		6'3"	244	Mississippi State		
Goodridge, Bob WR	68Min		6'2"	202	Vanderbilt		
Goodwin, Doug FB	65KJ 66BufA 68Atl		6'2"	228	Md. Eastern Shore		
Goodwin, Ron OE-FL-WR	63-68Phi	2	6'	180	Baylor		54
Goosby, Tom OG-LB	63Cle 66Was		6'	235	Baldwin-Wallace		
Goovert, Ron LB	67Det		5'11"	225	Michigan State		
Gordon, Cornell DB	65-69NY-A 70-72Den		6'	187	N. Carolina A&T	14	
Gordy, John OG-OT	57Det 58VR 59-67Det		6'3"	248	Tennessee		
Gossage, Gene DE-OG-DT	60-62Phi 63CFL		6'3"	239	Northwestern		
Gossett, Bruce K	64-69LA 70-74SF	5	6'2"	229	Richmond		1031
Grabosky, Gene DT	60BufA		6'5"	275	Syracuse		
Grabowski, Jim FB	66-70GB 71ChiB	2	6'2"	221	Illinois		66
Grady, Garry DB	69MiaA		5'11"	180	Eastern Michigan		
Graham, Art OE-WR	63-68BosA	2	6'1"	205	Boston College		120
Graham, Dave OT	63-66Phi 67JJ 68-69Phi 70JJ		6'3"	248	Virginia		
Graham, Kenny DB	64-69SD-A 70Cin 70Pit	3	6'	201	Washington State	28	30
Graham, Milt OT-DT	61-63BosA		6'6"	235	Colgate		
Granderson, Rufus DT	60DalA		6'5"	277	Prairie View		
Granger, Charley OT	61Dal 61StL		6'2"	240	Southern U.		
Granger, Hoyle FB-HB	66-69HouA 70Hou 71NO 72Hou	2	6'1"	225	Mississippi State		144
Grantham, Larry LB	60-69NY-A 70-73NYJ		6'	204	Mississippi	24	18
Grate, Willie TE	69BufA 70Buf		6'4"	225	S. Carolina State		18
Graves, White DB	65-67BosA 68CinA		6'	185	Louisiana State	3	
Gray, Jim DB	66NY-A 67Phi		6'	181	Toledo		
Gray, Ken OG-LB	58-59ChiC 60-69StL 70Hou		6'2"	245	Howard Payne		
Gray, Moses OT-DT	61-62NY-A		6'3"	260	Indiana		
Grayson, Dave DB	61-62DalA 63-64KC-A	3	5'10"	184	Oregon	49	36
	65-69OakA 70Oak						
Greaves, Gary OT	60HouA		6'3"	235	Miami (Fla.)		
Grecni, Dick LB	61Min		6'1"	230	Ohio U.	1	
Green, Allen K	61Dal	45	6'2"	215	Mississippi		34
Green, Bobby Joe K	60-61Pit 62-73ChiB		5'11"	175	Florida		
Green, Charlie QB	66OakA		6'	190	Wittenberg		
Green, Cornell DB	62-74Dal		6'4"	211	Utah State	34	24
Green, Ernie HB-FB	62-68Cle	23	6'2"	205	Louisville		210
Green, Jerry HB	68BosA		6'	190	Georgia Tech		
Green, Johnny QB	60-61BufA 62-63NY-A	12	6'3"	203	Tenn.-Chatanooga		36
Green, Ron FL-WR	67-68Cle		6'1"	200	North Dakota		
Greene, Ted LB	60-62DalA		6'1"	230	Tampa	4	
Greene, Tom QB	60BosA 61DalA	12 4	6'1"	190	Holy Cross		
Greenlee, Fritz LB	69SF		6'2"	230	Arizona State		
Greer, Al OE	63Det		6'4"	190	Jackson State		
Green, Jim OE	60DenA		6'3"	215	Elizabeth City St.		6
Gregg, Forrest OT-OG-DT	56GB 57MS 58-70GB		6'4"	249	S.M.U.		
	71Dal HC75-77Cle						
Gregory, Ben HB-FB	68BufA	2	6'3"	220	Nebraska		6
Gregory, Glynn OE-DB	61-62Dal		6'2"	200	S.M.U.	1	
Gregory, Ken OE	61Bal 62Phi 63NY-A		6'	190	Whittier		
Gremminger, Hank DB	56-65GB 66LA		6'1"	201	Baylor	29	6
Grier, Rosey DT-DE	55-56NYG 57MS 58-62NYG		6'5"	284	Penn State		4
	63-66LA 67JJ						
Griffin, Jim DE	66-67SD-A 68CinA		6'3"	258	Grambling		6
Griffin, John DB	63LA 64-66DenA		6'1"	190	Memphis State	4	12
Griffing, Glynn QB	63NYG	1	6'1"	200	Mississippi		
Grimm, Dan OG	63-65GB 66-68Atl 69Bal 69Was		6'3"	244	Colorado		

Use Name (Nicknames) – Positions	Team by Year	See Section	Hgt	Wgt	College	Int	Pts
Groman, Bill OE-FL	60-62HouA 63DenA 64-65BufA	2	6'	195	Heidelberg		222
Gros, Earl FB	62-63GB 64-66Phi 67-69Pit 70NO	2	6'3"	224	Louisiana State		228
Grosscup, Lee QB	60-61NYG 62NY-A	1	6'1"	186	Utah		
Grottkau, Bob OG	59-60Det 61Dal		6'4"	228	Oregon		
Gruneisen, Sam C-OG-LB	62-69SD-A 70-72SD 73Hou		6'1"	248	Villanova		
Gucciardo, Pat DB	66NY-A		5'11"	185	Kent State		
Guesman, Dick DT	62-63NY-A 64DenA	5	6'4"	255	West Virginia		129
Gugliemi, Ralph QB	55Was 56-57MS 58-60Was 61StL 62-63NYG 63Phi	12	6'1"	196	Notre Dame		12
Guidry, Paul LB	66-69BufA 70-72Buf 73Hou		6'3"	229	McNeese State	5	
Guillory, John DB	69CinA 70Cin		5'10"	190	Stanford	1	
Guillory, Tony LB	65LA 66JJ 67-68LA 69Phi		6'4"	232	Nebraska, Lamar Tech		
Gulseth, Don LB	66DenA		6'1"	240	North Dakota		
Gunnels, Riley DT-DE	60-64Phi 65-66Pit		6'3"	250	Georgia		
Gunner, Harry DE	68-69CinA 70ChiB		6'6"	250	Oregon State	2	8
Gursky, Al LB	63NYG		6'1"	210	Penn State		
Guy, Louis DB-FL	63NYG 64OakA		6'	188	Mississippi		
Guzik, John LB-OG	59-60LA 61HouA		6'3"	231	Pittsburgh		
Gwinn, Ross OG	68NO		6'3"	273	NW State-La.		
Hackbart, Dale DB	60GB 61-63Was 64-65CFL 66-70Min 71-72StL 73Den		6'3"	210	Minnesota	19	24
Hadl, John QB	62-69SD-A 70-72SD 73-74LA 74-75GB 76-77Hou	12 4	6'2"	213	Kansas		96
Haffner, Mike WR	68-69DenA 70Den 71Cin	2	6'2"	205	U.C.L.A.		42
Hagberg, Roger FB-TE	65-69OakA	2	6'2"	216	Minnesota		48
Hageman, Fred C	61-64Was		6'4"	243	Kansas		
Haggerty, Mike OT	67-70Pit 71NE 72Det		6'4"	239	Miami (Fla.)		
Haik, Mac WR	68-69HouA 70-71Hou	2	6'1"	195	Mississippi		54
Hale, Dave DT-DE	67-71ChiB 72JJ 73ChiB		6'7"	251	Ottawa (Kans.)		
Haley, Dick DB-HB-FL-OE	59-60Was 61Min 61-64Pit	3	5'10"	193	Pittsburgh	14	12
Hall, Alvin DB	61-63LA		6'	195	none	1	
Hall, Galen QB	62Was 63NY-A	1	5'10"	200	Penn State		12
Hall, Ken HB	59ChiC 60-61HouA 61StL	23	6'1"	205	Texas A&M		24
Hall, Pete OE	61NYG		6'2"	200	Marquette		
Hall, Ron DB	59Pit 60MS 61-67BosA		6'	190	Missouri Valley	30	6
Hall, Tom FL-OE-WR-DB	62-63Det 64-66Min 67NO 68-69Min	2	6'1"	195	Minnesota	3	48
Hammack, Mal FB-OE-TE-LB	55ChiB 56MS 57-59ChiB 60-66StL	2	6'2"	205	Florida		48
Hammond, Kim QB	68MiaA 69BosA	1	6'1"	192	Florida State		2
Hardy, Charley OE	60-62OakA	2	6'	184	San Jose State		42
Harmon, Ed LB	69CinA		6'4"	230	Louisville		
Harmon, Tom OG	67Atl		6'4"	238	Gustavus Adolphus		
Harold, George DB	66-67Bal 68Was		6'3"	198	Allen		
Harper, Charlie OG-OT-DT	66-72NYG		6'2"	250	Oklahoma State		
Harper, Darrell HB	60BufA		6'1"	195	Michigan		7
Harper, Jack HB	67-68MiaA	2	5'11"	190	Florida		24
Harris, Billy HB	68Atl 69Min 70JJ 71NO	2	6'	196	Colorado		6
Harris, Dick DB	60LA-A 61-65SD-A	3	6'	185	Quachita Baptist	12	
Harris, Jim DT	65-67NY-A		6'4"	275	Utah State		
Harris, John DB-HB	60-61OakA		6'1"	195	Santa Monica J.C.	3	
Harris, Lou DB	68Pit		6'	180	Kent State		
Harris, Marv LB	64LA		6'1"	225	Stanford		
Harris, Phil DB	66NYG		6'	195	Texas		
Harris, Rickie DB	65-70Was 71-72NE	3	6'	182	Arizona	15	24
Harris, Wendell DB	62-65Bal 66-67NYG	3 5	5'11"	188	Louisiana State	8	17
Harrison, Bob LB	59-61SF 62-63Phi 64Pit 65-67SF		6'2"	223	Oklahoma	5	
Harrison, Bob DB	61Bal		5'11"	187	Ohio U.	3	
Hart, Ben DB	67NO		6'2"	205	Oklahoma	1	
Hart, Dick OG	67-70Phi 71JJ 72Buf		6'2"	250	none		
Hart, Doug DB	64-71GB		6'	190	Texas-Arlington	15	32
Hart, Pete FB	60NY-A	2	5'9"	190	Hardin-Simmons		
Harvey, George OT	67NO		6'4"	245	Kansas		
Harvey, Jim OG-OT	66-69OakA 70-71Oak		6'5"	247	Mississippi		
Harvey, Waddey DT	69BufA 70Buf		6'4"	276	Virginia Tech		
Hatcher, Ron DB-FB	62Was		5'11"	215	Michigan State		
Hathcock, Dave DB	66GB 67NYG		6'	193	Memphis State		
Hawkins, Alex HB-OE-FL-WR	59-65Bal 66-67Atl 67-68Bal	23	6'1"	188	South Carolina		132
Hawkins, Ben WR-FL-OE	66-73Phi 74Cle	2	6'	180	Arizona State		198
Hawkins, Rip LB	65-65Min		6'3"	231	North Carolina	12	20
Hawkins, Wayne OG	60-69OakA		6'	239	U. of Pacific		
Hayes, Jim DT	65-66HouA		6'4"	263	Jackson State		
Hayes, Larry C-LB	61NYG 62-63LA		6'3"	230	Vanderbilt		6
Hayes, Luther DE	61SD-A	2	6'4"	200	Southern Calif.		18
Hayes, Ray FB	61Min	2	6'3"	235	Central St.-Okla.		12
Hayes, Ray DT	68NY-A		6'5"	248	Toledo		
Hayes, Rudy LB	59-60,62Pit		6'	217	Clemson		
Hayes, Wendell FB-HB	63Dal 65-67DenA 68-69KC-A 70-74KC	2	6'2"	215	Humboldt State		214
Haymond, Alvin DB	64-67Bal 68Phi 69-71LA 72Was 73Hou	3	6'	193	Southern U.	10	30
Haynes, Abner HB	60-62DalA 63-64KC-A 65-66DenA 67MiaA 67NY-A	23	6'	188	North Texas State		414
Hays, Harold LB	68-69SF		6'3"	227	Southern Miss.		
Hazeltine, Matt LB	55-68SF 69VR 70NYG		6'1"	220	California	13	18
Hazelton, Major DB	68-69ChiB 70NO		6'1"	185	Florida A&M		
Headrick, Sherrill LB	60-62DalA 63-67KC-A 68CinA		6'2"	223	Texas Christian	15	18
Healy, Chip LB	69-70StL		6'3"	233	Vanderbilt		
Healy, Don DT-OG	58-59ChiB 60-61Dal 62BufA		6'3"	259	Maryland	1	
Hebert, Ken WR	68Pit		6'	200	Houston		
Heck, Ralph LB	63-65Phi 66-68Atl 69-71NYG		6'2"	228	Colorado	5	6
Heckard, Steve OE	65-66LA		6'1"	195	Davidson		
Hector, Willie OT	61LA		6'2"	220	U. of Pacific		
Heenan, Pat DB-OE	60Was		6'1"	190	Notre Dame	1	
Heeter, Gene OE	63-65NY-A	2	6'4"	235	West Virginia		12
Heidel, Jim DB	66StL 67NO		6'1"	185	Mississippi	1	
Hendershot, Larry LB	67Was		6'3"	240	Arizona State		
Henderson, John WR-OE-FL	65-67Det 68-72Min	2	6'3"	191	Michigan		60
Henderson, Jon WR-DB	68-69Pit 70Was	23	6'	198	Colorado State		36
Henke, Karl DT-DE	68NY-A 69BosA		6'4"	245	Tulsa		
Henley, Carey HB	62BufA		5'10"	200	Tenn.-Chatanooga		
Hennessey, Tom DB	65-66BosA		6'	183	Holy Cross	8	
Hennigan, Charley FL-OE	60-66HouA	2	6'	187	NW State-La.		306
Henning, Dan QB	66SD-A		6'	195	William & Mary		

Use Name (Nicknames) – Positions	Team by Year	See Section	Hgt	Wgt	College	Int	Pts
Henry, Mike LB	59-61Pit 62-64LA		6'2"	220	Southern Calif.		
Henry, Urban DT-DE	61LA 63GB 64Pit		6'4"	265	Georgia Tech		
Henson, Gary DE	63Phi		6'3"	200	Colorado		
Henson, Ken C	65Pit		6'6"	260	Texas Christian		
Hergert, Joe LB	60-61BufA	5	6'1"	216	Florida	2	30
Herman, Dave OG-OT	64-69NY-A 70-73NYJ		6'2"	255	Michigan State		
Herman, Dick LB	65OakA		6'2"	215	Florida State		
Hernandez, Joe FL	64Was		6'2"	180	Arizona		
Herndon, Don HB	60NY-A		6'	195	Tampa		6
Herock, Ken OE-TE	63-65,67OakA 68CinA 69BosA	2	6'2"	230	West Virginia		30
Heron, Fred DT-DE	66-72StL		6'4"	255	San Jose State		
Herring, George QB	60-61DenA	1 4	6'2"	200	Southern Miss.		12
Hester, Jim TE	67-69NO 70ChiB		6'4"	238	North Dakota		18
Hettema, Dave OT	67SF 68-69MS 70Atl		6'4"	249	New Mexico		
Hibler, Mike LB	68CinA		6'1"	235	Stanford		
Hickerson, Gene OG	58-60Cle 61BL 62-73Cle		6'3"	248	Mississippi		
Hickey, Bo FB	67DenA	2	5'11"	225	Maryland		30
Hickl, Ray LB	69-70NYG		6'2"	215	Texas A&I		
Hickman, Harry FB	59ChiC 60GB		6'2"	227	Baylor		
Hicks, W. K. DB	64-69HouA 70-72NYJ		6'1"	191	Texas Southern	40	
Higgins, Jim OG	66MiaA		6'1"	250	Xavier-Ohio		
Highsmith, Buzz OG-OT-C	68-69DenA 72Hou		6'4"	238	Florida A&M		
Hill, Dave OT	63-69KC-A 70-74KC		6'5"	259	Auburn		
Hill, Fred TE-OE-WR	65-71Phi	2	6'2"	215	Southern Calif.		30
Hill, Gary DB	65Mia		6'	200	Southern Calif.		
Hill, Jack HB	61DenA	5	6'1"	185	Utah State		31
Hill, Jerry FB-HB	61Bal 62JJ 63-70Bal	2	5'11"	212	Wyoming		150
Hill, Jimmy DB	55-57ChiC 58AJ 59ChiC 60-64StL 65Det 66KC-A		6'2"	192	Sam Houston St.	20	18
Hill, King QB	58-59ChiC 60StL 61-68Phi 68Min 69StL	12 4	6'3"	212	Rice		54
Hill, Mack Lee HB-FB	64-65KC-A	2	5'11"	225	Southern U.		54
died Dec. 14, 1965 after knee surgery							
Hill, Winston OT	63-69NY-A 70-76NYJ 77LA		6'4"	278	Texas Southern		
Hillebrand, Jerry LB	63-66NYG 67StL 68-70Pit		6'3"	240	Colorado	14	18
Hilton, John TE	65-69Pit 70GB 71Min 72-73Det 74WFL	2	6'5"	222	Richmond		96
Hindman, Stan DE-DT	66-71,74SF		6'3"	236	Mississippi	1	6
Hines, Glen Ray OT	66-69HouA 71-72NO 73Pit		6'5"	264	Arkansas		
Hines, Jimmy WR	69MiaA		6'	175	Texas Southern		
Hinton, Chuck DT	64-71Pit 71NYJ 72Bal		6'5"	257	N. Car. Central	2	12
Hinton, Chuck C	67-69NYG		6'2"	235	Mississippi		
Hoak, Dick HB	61-70Pit	12	5'11"	191	Penn State		198
Hodgson, Pat OE	66Was		6'2"	190	Georgia		
Hoffman, Dalton FB	64-65HouA		6'	207	Baylor		6
Hohman, John OG	65-66DenA		6'1"	243	Wisconsin		
Hohn, Bob DB	65-69Pit		6'	187	Nebraska	7	
Hoisington, Al OE	60OakA 60BufA		6'3"	200	Pasadena City		12
Holifield, Jim DB	68-69NYG		6'3"	195	Jackson State	1	
Holler, Ed LB	63GB 64Pit	4	6'2"	233	South Carolina	1	
Holmes, John DE	66MiaA		6'2"	248	Florida A&M		
Holmes, Pat DE-DT	66-69HouA 70-72Hou 73KC		6'5"	254	Texas Tech	1	
Holub, E. J. LB-C	61-62DalA 63-69KC-A 70KC		6'4"	231	Texas Tech	9	
Holz, Gordy DT-OT	60-63DenA 64NY-A		6'4"	264	Minnesota	1	
Holzer, Tom DE	67SF 68JJ		6'4"	250	Louisville		
Hooligan, Harry FB	65HouA		6'2"	225	Bishop		
Hopkins, Jerry LB	63-66DenA 67MiaA 68OakA		6'2"	236	Texas A&M	6	
Hopkins, Roy FB	67-69HouA 70Hou 71JJ	2	6'1"	233	Texas Southern		48
Hord, Roy OG	60-62LA 62Phi 63NY-A		6'4"	244	Duke		
Horner, Sam HB-DB	60-61Was 62NYG	234	6'	197	V.M.I.		6
Hornung, Paul (The Golden Boy) HB-FB	57-62GB 63SL 64-66GB	12 5	6'2"	215	Notre Dame		760
Horton, Bob LB	64-65SD-A		6'2"	230	Boston U.		
Houser, John OG-C	57-59LA 60-61Dal 62JJ 63StL		6'3"	239	Redlands		
Houston, Jim LB-DE-TE	60-72Cle		6'2"	239	Ohio State	14	25
Howell, Lane OT-DT	63-64NYG 65-69Phi		6'5"	264	Grambling		
Howell, Mike DB	65-72Cle 72Mia		6'1"	189	Grambling	27	
Howley, Chuck LB	58-59ChiB 60JJ 61-73Dal		6'3"	228	West Virginia	25	
Hoyem, Lynn C-OG	62-63Dal 64-67Phi		6'4"	244	Long Beach State		
Huard, John LB	67-69DenA 70-71JJ		6'	220	Maine	6	
Huarte, John QB	66-67BosA 68Phi 70-71KC 72ChiB	1	6'	188	Notre Dame		
Hubbert, Brad FB	67-69SD-A 70SD	2	6'1"	230	Arizona		66
Hudlow, Floyd DB-FL	65BufA 67-68Atl		5'11"	192	Arizona	2	
Hudock, Mike C	60-65NY-A 66MiaA 67KC-A		6'1"	245	Miami (Fla.)		
Hudson, Bill DT	61-62SD-A 63BosA		6'4"	267	Clemson	1	6
Hudson, Dick OT-OG	62SD-A 63-67BufA		6'4"	266	Memphis State		
Hudson, Jim DB	65-69NY-A 70NYJ		6'2"	210	Texas	14	
Huey, Gene DB	69SD-A		5'11"	190	Wyoming		
Huff, Sam LB	56-63NYG 64-67Was 68VR 69Was		6'1"	230	West Virginia	30	30
Hughes, Bob DE	67,69Atl		6'4"	253	Jackson State		
Hughes, Chuck WR	67-69Phi 70-71Det	2	5'11"	173	Texas-El Paso		
died Oct. 24, 1971 – heart attack							
Hughley, George HB	65Was	2	6'2"	223	Central St.-Okla.		6
Hull, Bill DE	62DalA		6'6"	245	Wake Forest		
Hultz, Don DE-DT-LB	63Min 64-73Phi 74ChiB		6'3"	238	Southern Miss.	4	12
Hultz, George DT	62StL		6'4"	250	Southern Miss.		
Humphrey, Buddy QB	59-60LA 61-62Dal 63-65StL 66HouA	1	6'1"	198	Baylor		
Humphreys, Bob K	67-68DenA	5	6'1"	240	Wichita State		43
Hunt, Bobby DB-HB	62DalA 63-67KC-A 68-69CinA		6'1"	188	Auburn	42	12
Hunt, Jim (Earthquake) DT-DE	60-69BosA 70Bos		5'11"	249	Prairie View	1	14
Hunter, Art C-OT-DT-DE	54GB 55MS 56-59Cle 60-64LA 65Pit		6'4"	243	Notre Dame		
Hunter, Bill FL-HB-DB	65Was 66MiaA		6'1"	183	Syracuse		6
Hurston, Chuck LB-DE	65-69KC-A 70KC 71Buf		6'6"	237	Auburn		
Husmann, Ed DT-OG-LB-DE	53ChiC 54-55MS 56-59ChiC 60Dal 61-65HouA		6'	235	Nebraska		
Hutchinson, Tom OE	66Atl	2	6'1"	190	Kentucky		12
Huth, Jerry OG	56NYG 57-58MS 59-60Phi 61-63Min		6'	226	Wake Forest		6
Hynes, Paul DB	61DalA 61-62NY-A		6'1"	210	Louisiana Tech	2	
Iacovazzi, Cosmo HB	65NY-A		5'11"	200	Princeton		
Ilg, Ray LB	67-68BosA		6'1"	220	Colgate		
Iman, Ken C	60-63GB 64BH 65-74LA		6'1"	236	SE Missouri St.		
Inman, Jerry DT	66-69DenA 70-71Den 72JJ 73Den		6'3"	255	Oregon		
Isbell, Joe Bob OG	62-64Dal 65JJ 66Cle		6'1"	238	Houston		
Izo, George QB	60StL 61-64Was 65Det 66Pit	1	6'3"	218	Notre Dame		

Use Name (Nicknames) – Positions	Team by Year	See Section	Hgt	Wgt	College	Int	Pts
Jackson, Bobby DB	60Phi 61ChiB		6'1"	190	Alabama		
Jackson, Bobby FB	62-63SD-A 64HouA 64OakA 65HouA	2	6'3"	232	New Mexico State		96
Jackson, Frank FL-HB	61-62DalA 63-65KC-A 66-67MiaA	23	6'1"	187	S.M.U.		186
Jackson, Jim DB-HB	66-67SF		6'	187	Western Illinois	1	6
Jackson, Leroy HB	62-63Was	2	6'	190	Western Illinois		6
Jackson, Rich DE-LB	66OakA 67-69DenA 70-72Den 72Cle		6'2"	252	Southern U.		2
Jackson, Roland FB-LB	62StL		6'	210	Rice		
Jackson, Steve LB	66-67Was		6'1"	225	Texas-Arlington	1	
Jackson, T. J. FL-DB	66Phi 67Was		6'	180	none		
Jackunas, Frank C	62BufA 63DenA		6'3"	225	Detroit		
Jacobs, Allen FB-HB	65GB 66-67NYG	2	6'1"	215	Utah		6
Jacobs, Harry LB-DE	60-62BosA 63-69BufA 72NO		6'2"	228	Bradley	12	
Jacobs, Proverb DT-OT	58Phi 61NYG 61-62NY-A 63-64OakA		6'4"	258	California		
Jacobs, Ray DT-DE	63-66DenA 67-68MiaA 69BosA		6'3"	276	Howard Payne		
Jacobson, Jack DB	65SD-A		6'2"	200	Oklahoma State		
Jagielski, Harry DT-OT	56ChiC 56Was 60-61BosA 61OakA		6'	257	Indiana	1	
James, Claudis WR-HB-FL	67-68GB		6'2"	190	Jackson State		
James, Dan OT-C	60-66Pit 67ChiB		6'4"	262	Ohio State		
James, Dick HB-DB	56-63Was 64NYG 65Min	23	5'9"	179	Oregon	12	204
James, Nate DB	68Cle		6'1"	195	Florida A&M		
Jamieson, Al OT	60-62HouA		6'5"	245	Colgate		
Jamieson, Dick QB	60-61NY-A	1	6'1"	191	Bradley		
Janick, Bobby DB-FL	62-67HouA	3	5'11"	178	Lamar Tech	15	6
Janerette, Chuck DT-OT-OG	60LA 61-62NYG 63NY-A 64-65DenA		6'3"	253	Penn State	2	
Janik, Tom DB	63-64DenA 65-68BufA 69BosA 70Bos 71NE	4	6'3"	198	Texas A&I	25	36
Jaquess, Pete DB	64-65HouA 66-71MiaA 67-69DenA 70Den		6'	182	Eastern New Mex.	16	12
Jelacic, Jon DE-OG	58NYG 61-64OakA		6'3"	250	Minnesota	2	12
Jencks, Bob OE	63-64ChiB 65Was	5	6'5"	227	Miami-Ohio		135
Jeralds, Luther DE	61DalA		6'3"	235	N. Car. Central		
Jeter, Bob DB-FL-OE	63-70GB 71-73ChiB		6'1"	203	Iowa	26	12
Jeter, Gene LB	65-67DenA		6'3"	230	Ark.-Pine Bluff		
Jeter, Tony TE	66,68Pit		6'3"	222	Nebraska		
Jobko, Bill LB	58-62LA 63-65Min 66Atl		6'2"	224	Ohio State	5	
Joe, Billy FB	63-64DenA 65BufA 66MiaA 67-68NY-A	2	6'2"	243	Villanova		118
Johns, Pete DB	67-68HouA		6'3"	189	Tulane		
Johnson, Billy DB	66-68BosA		5'11"	178	Nebraska	2	
Johnson, Charley QB	61-69StL 70-71Hou 72-75Den	12	6'	191	New Mexico State		60
Johnson, Charlie DT	66-68SF		6'2"	265	Louisville		
Johnson, Cornelius OG	68-73Dal		6'2"	245	Virginia Union		
Johnson, Curley HB-TE-OE-FB-K	60DalA 61-68NY-A 69NYG	2 4	6'	215	Houston		26
Johnson, Daryle DB	68-69BosA 70Bos		5'11"	190	Morgan State	5	8
Johnson, Dick OE	63KC-A		6'4"	220	Minnesota		6
Johnson, Ellis HB-FL-OE	65-66BosA		6'2"	190	Southeastern La.		
Johnson, Gene DB	59-60Phi 61Min 61NYG		6'	187	Cincinnati	4	
Johnson, Jay LB	69-70Phi		6'3"	230	East Texas State		
Johnson, Jim DB-FL	61-76SF	2	6'2"	188	U.C.L.A.	47	38
Johnson, John DT	63-68ChiB 69NYG		6'5"	260	Indiana		
Johnson, John Henry FB-HB-DB	54-56SF 57-59Det 60-65Pit 66HouA	2	6'2"	210	St. Mary's, Arizona State		330
Johnson, Lee WR	69-70SF		6'1"	204	Tennessee State		
Johnson, Mike DB	66-69Dal		5'10"	185	Kansas	8	
Johnson, Mitch OT-OG	65Dal 66-67Was 69-70LA 71Cle 72Was		6'4"	249	U.C.L.A.		
Johnson, Preston FB	68BosA		6'2"	230	Florida A&M		
Johnson, Rich HB-FB	69HouA		6'1"	210	Illinois		6
Johnson, Rudy HB	64-65SF 66Atl	2	5'11"	190	Nebraska		6
Johnson, Walter DE	67SF		6'4"	225	Tuskegee		
Johnston, Mark DB	60-63HouA 64OakA 64NY-A		6'	201	Northwestern	13	12
Johnston, Rex HB	60Pit		6'1"	195	Southern Calif.		
64 played major league baseball							
Jonas, Don HB	62Phi		5'11"	195	Penn State		
Jones, Bob WR-OE	67-69ChiB		6'1"	194	Virginia Union		
Jones, Curtis LB	68SD-A		6'2"	245	Missouri		
Jones, Dave WR	69-71Cle		6'2"	185	Kansas State		
Jones, Deacon DE	61-71LA 72-73SD 74Was		6'5"	254	S. Carolina State	2	3
Jones, Ezell OT	69BosA 70Bos		6'4"	255	Minnesota		
Jones, Gene LB	61HouA		6'	200	Rice		
Jones, Harry HB	67-70Phi 71JJ	2	6'2"	205	Arkansas		
Jones, Henry FB	69DenA		6'2"	235	Grambling		
Jones, Homer WR-FL-OE	64-69NYG 70Cle	23	6'2"	211	Texas Southern		228
Jones, Jerry OT-DT-DE	66Atl 67-69NO		6'3"	269	Bowling Green		
Jones, Jim OE-WR	65-67ChiB 68DenA	2	6'2"	189	Wisconsin		66
Jones, Ron TE	69GB		6'3"	220	Texas-El Paso		
Jones, Stan OG-DT-OT	54-65ChiB 66Was		6'1"	252	Maryland		
Jones, Willie FB	62BufA		5'11"	208	Purdue		
Jones, Willie DT-DE	67HouA 68CinA 70-71Cin		6'2"	260	Kansas State		
Jordan, Henry DT-DE	57-58Cle 59-69GB		6'3"	249	Virginia	1	6
Jordan, Jeff DB	65-67Min		6'4"	190	Tulsa	4	
Jordan, Jimmy HB	67NO		6'1"	200	Florida		
Jordan, Larry LB-DE	62,64DenA		6'6"	230	Youngstown		
Jordan, Lee Roy LB	63-76Dal		6'2"	219	Alabama	32	20
Josephson, Les FB-HB	64-67LA 68FJ 69-74LA	2	6'	209	Augustana (S.D.)		168
Joswick, Bob DE-DT	68-69MiaA		6'5"	250	Tulsa		
Joyner, L. C. DB	60OakA		6'1"	197	none		
Julian, Fred DB	60NY-A		5'9"	185	Michigan	6	
Junker, Steve OE	57Det 58KJ 59-60Det 61-62Was	2	6'3"	217	Xavier-Ohio		36
Jurgensen, Sonny QB	57-63Phi 64-74Was	12	5'11"	202	Duke		90
Kaimer, Karl DE	62NY-A		6'3"	230	Boston U.		
Kalsu, Bob OG	68BufA 69MS		6'3"	235	Oklahoma		
Killed in action in Viet Nam 1970							
Kamanu, Lew DE	67-68Det		6'4"	245	Weber State		
Kammerer, Carl DE-LB	61-62SF 63-69Was		6'3"	240	U. of Pacific	3	
Kanicki, Jim DT	63-69Cle 70-71NYG 72KJ		6'4"	270	Michigan State		
Kantor, Joe FB	66Was		6'1"	217	Notre Dame		
Kapele, John DE-OT-DT	60-62Pit 62Phi		6'	240	Brigham Young		
Kapp, Joe QB	67-69Min 70Bos 71HO	12	6'2"	214	California		30
Karas, Emil LB-DE	59Was 60LA-A 61-64, 66SD-A		6'3"	230	Dayton	8	
Karras, Alex DT	58-62Det 63SL 64-70Det		6'2"	248	Iowa	4	2

Use Name (Nicknames) – Positions	Team by Year	See Section	Hgt	Wgt	College	Int	Pts
Karras, Ted OG-OT-LB	58-59Pit 60-64ChiB 65Det 66LA		6'1"	240	Indiana		
Kasperek, Dick C	66-68StL		6'3"	225	Iowa State		
Kassulke, Karl DB	63-72Min		6'	194	Drake	19	
1973 paralyzed in motorcycle accident							
Katcavage, Jim DE-DT	56-68NYG		6'3"	237	Dayton	1	12
Katcik, Joe DT	60NY-A		6'9"	290	Notre Dame		
Keating, Bill OG-OT	66-67DenA 67MiaA		6'2"	236	Michigan		
Keckin, Val QB	62SD-A		6'4"	215	Southern Miss.		
Keeling, Rex DB	68CinA		6'3"	220	Sanford		
Kellerman, Ernie DB	66-71Cle 72Cin 73Buf		6'	184	Miami-Ohio	19	6
Kelley, Ed DB	61-62DalA		6'2"	195	Texas		
Kelley, Gordon LB	60-61SF 62-63Was		6'3"	230	Georgia	5	
Kelley, Ike LB	66-67Phi 68KJ 69-71Phi 72JJ		5'11"	224	Ohio State	1	
Kelley, Les LB	67-69NO		6'3"	233	Alabama	1	
Kellogg, Mike FB	66-67DenA		6'	220	Santa Clara		
Kelly, Bob OT-DT	61-64HouA 67KC-A 68CinA 69Atl		6'3"	261	New Mexico State		
Kelly, Leroy HB-FB	64-73Cle	23	6'	199	Morgan State		540
Kemp, Jack QB	57Pit 58CFL 60LA-A 61-62SD-A 62-67BufA 68KJ 69BufA	12	6'1"	201	Occidental		242
Kempinski, Charlie OG	60LA-A		6'	235	Mississippi		
Kendall, Charlie DB	60HouA		6'2"	185	U.C.L.A.	2	
Kennerson, John DE-OT	60LA 62Pit 62NY-A		6'3"	255	Kentucky State		
Kennedy, Tom QB	66NYG 67JJ	1	6'1"	200	Los Angeles State		
Kent, Greg OT-DE	66OakA 67CFL 68Det		6'6"	270	Utah		
Kerbow, Randy FL	63HouA		6'1"	190	Rice		
Kerr, Jim DB	61-62Was		6'	195	Penn State	8	
Keyes, Bob HB	60OakA		5'10"	183	San Diego State		
Keyes, Jimmy LB	68-69MiaA	5	6'2"	225	Mississippi		51
Keys, Brady DB-HB	61-67Pit 67Min 68StL	3	6'	189	Colorado State	16	
Keys, Howard C-OT-OG	60-63Phi		6'3"	239	Oklahoma State		
Khayat, Bob OG-C-K	60,62-63Was	5	6'2"	230	Mississippi		204
Khayat, Ed DT-DE-OT	57Was 58-61Phi 62-63Was 64-65Phi 66BosA HC71-72Phi		6'3"	240	Tulane	1	
Kilcullen, Bob DE-OT-DT	57-58ChiB 59MS 60-66ChiB		6'3"	245	Texas Tech		
Kilgore, John K	65-67LA 68ChiB 69SF	4	6'1"	203	Auburn		
Killett, Charlie HB	63NYG		6'1"	205	Memphis State		
Killorin, Pat C	66Pit		6'2"	220	Syracuse		
Kilmer, Billy QB	61-62SF 63BL 64,66SF 67-70NO 71-77Was	12	6'	201	U.C.L.A.		132
Kimber, Bill OE	59-60NYG 61BosA		6'2"	192	Florida State		
Kimbrough, Elbert DB	61LA 62-66SF 68NO		5'11"	193	Northwestern	9	
Kinderman, Keith FB-DB	63-64SD-A 65HouA		6'	213	Florida State		
Kindig, Howard DE-OT-C	65-66SD-A 67-69BufA 70-71Buf 72Mia 73JJ 74NYJ		6'6"	260	Los Angeles State	1	
Kindricks, Bill DT	68CinA		6'3"	268	Alabama A&M		
King, Charlie DB	66-67BufA 68-69CinA		6'	185	Purdue	2	6
King, Claude HB	61HouA 62BosA	2	5'11"	190	Houston		24
King, Henry DB	67NY-A		6'4"	205	Utah State		
King, Phil (Chief) HB-FB	58-63NYG 64Pit 65-66Min	23	6'4"	223	Vanderbilt		96
King, Tony FL	67BufA		6'1"	194	Findlay		
Kinney, George DE	65HouA		6'4"	250	Wiley		
Kirby, John LB	64-69Min 69-70NYG		6'3"	229	Nebraska		
Kirchiro, Bill OG	62Bal		6'1"	235	Maryland		
Kirk, Len LB-C	60-61ChiB 62Pit 63LA		6'2"	229	Mississippi		
Kirner, Gary OT-OG	64-69SD-A		6'3"	249	Southern Calif.		
Kirouac, Lou OG-OT	63NYG 64Bal 65JJ 66-67Atl	5	6'3"	238	Boston College		46
Klein, Dick OT	58-59ChiB 60Dal 61Pit 61-62BosA 63-64OakA		6'4"	254	Iowa		
Klotz, Jack OT	60-62NY-A 62SD-A 63NY-A 64HouA		6'5"	256	Widener		
Kochman, Roger HB	63BufA	2	6'2"	205	Penn State		6
Kocourek, Dave OE-TE	60LA-A 61-65SD-A 66MiaA 67-68OakA	2	6'5"	237	Wisconsin		150
Koeper, Rich OT	66Atl		6'4"	245	Oregon State		
Koman, Bill LB	56Bal 57-58Phi 59ChiC 60-67StL		6'2"	229	North Carolina	7	
Kompara, John DT	60LA-A		6'2"	245	South Carolina		
Koontz, Ed LB	68BosA		6'2"	230	Catawba		
Koontz, Joe WR	68NYG		6'1"	192	San Fran. State		
Kopay, Dave HB-FB	64-67SF 68Det 69-70Was 72NO 72GB	2	6'2"	220	Washington		48
Kortas, Ken DT	64StL 65-68Pit 69ChiB		6'2"	282	Louisville		6
Kosens, Terry DB	63Min		6'3"	195	Hofstra		
Kostelnik, Ron DT	61-68GB 69Bal		6'4"	260	Cincinnati		
Kctite, Dick TE-LB	67NYG 68Pit 69,71-72NYG	2	6'3"	233	Wagner		30
Kovac, Ed HB-DB	60Bal 62NY-A		6'	199	Cincinnati	1	
Kowalczyk, Walt FB-DB	58-59Phi 60Dal 61OakA	2	6'	208	Michigan State	1	18
Koy, Ernie HB-FB	65-70NYG	234	6'2"	228	Texas		90
Krakoski, Joe DB	61Was 63-66OakA		6'2"	196	Illinois	8	
Kramer, Jerry OG	58-68GB	5	6'3"	246	Idaho		177
Kramer, Ron OE-TE	57GB 58MS 59-64GB 65-67Det	2	6'3"	234	Michigan		96
Kreitling, Rich OE	59-63Cle 64ChiB	2	6'2"	208	Illinois		102
Kremser, Karl K	69MiaA 70Mia	5	6'	178	Army, Tennessee		67
Kriewald, Doug OG	67-68ChiB		6'4"	245	West Texas State		
Krisher, Billy OG	58Pit 60-61DalA		6'1"	233	Oklahoma		
Kroll, Alex C-OT	62NY-A		6'3"	230	Rutgers		
Kroner, Gary DB-K	65-67DenA	5	6'1"	200	Wisconsin		144
Krueger, Charlie DT-DE	59-73SF		6'4"	256	Texas A&M	1	12
Krupa, Joe DT	56-64Pit		6'2"	232	Purdue		
Kruse, Bob OG-OT	67-68OakA 69BufA		6'2"	250	Colorado State, Wayne State-Neb.		
Kubala, Ray C	64-67DenA		6'4"	245	Texas A&M		
Kuechenberg, Rudy LB	67-69ChiB 70GB 71Atl		6'2"	215	Indiana		
Kulbachi, Joe HB	60BufA	2	6'	185	Purdue		6
Kurek, Ralph FB	65-70ChiB	2	6'2"	210	Wisconsin		12
Lacey, Bob OE	64Min 65NYG		6'3"	205	North Carolina		
Ladd, Ernie DT	61-65SD-A 66-67HouA 67-68KC-A		6'9"	302	Grambling	1	
Lage, Dick OE	61StL		6'4"	222	Lenoir Rhyne		
Lakes, Roland DT-OT-DE	61-70SF 71NYG		6'4"	267	Wichita State		6
LaLonde, Roger DT	64Det 65NYG		6'3"	255	Muskingum		
Lamb, Mack DB	67-68MiaA		6'1"	188	Tennessee State	1	
Lambert, Frank K	65-66Pit	4	6'3"	200	Mississippi		
Lambert, Gordon LB	68-69DenA		6'5"	245	West Virginia, Tennessee-Martin		
Lamberti, Pat LB	61NY-A 61DenA		6'2"	225	Richmond	1	
Lammans, Pete TE	67-69NY-A 70-71NYJ 72GB	2	6'3"	229	Texas		84
Lamonica, Daryle QB	63-66BufA 67-69OakA 70-74Oak	12 4	6'2"	215	Notre Dame		90
Lamson, Chuck DB	62-63Min 64JJ 65-67LA 68JJ		6'	189	Wyoming	11	6
Lane, Bobby LB	63-64SD-A		6'2"	222	Baylor		
Lane, Gary QB	66-67Cle 68NYG	1	6'1"	210	Missouri		

Use Name (Nicknames) – Positions	Team by Year	See Section	Hgt	Wgt	College	Int	Pts
Lang, Izzy FB-HB	64-68Phi 69LA	2	6'1"	231	Tennessee State		48
Lanphear, Dan DE	60,62HouA		6'2"	225	Wisconsin		
Laphan, Bill C	60Phi 61Min		6'3"	250	Iowa		
Laraba, Bob LB-QB-HB died Feb. 16, 1962 auto accident	60LA-A 61SD-A		6'3"	195	Texas-El Paso	6	19
Laraway, Jack LB	60BufA 61HouA		6'1"	218	Purdue	1	
LaRose, Dan DE-OT-OG	61-63Det 64Pit 65SF 66DenA		6'5"	250	Missouri		
Larpenter, Carl OG-OT	61-62DenA 62DalA		6'4"	237	Texas		
Larscheid, Jack HB	60-61OakA	23	5'6"	162	U. of Pacific		12
Larsen, Gary DT	64LA 65-74Min		6'5"	256	Concordia-Moor.		
Larson, Bill FB	60BosA		5'10"	190	Illinois Wesleyan		
Larson, Greg C-OG-OT	61-73NYG		6'2"	249	Minnesota		
Larson, Pete HB	67-68Was	2	6'1"	200	Cornell		18
Lasky, Frank OT	64-65NYG		6'2"	265	Florida		
Lasse, Dick LB	58-59Pit 60-61Was 62NYG		6'2"	222	Syracuse	3	
Lassiter, Ike DE-DT	62-64DenA 65-69OakA 70Bos 71NE		6'5"	270	St. Augustine	1	
Latourette, Chuck DB-WR	67-68,70-71StL	34	6'	190	Rice		12
Latzke, Paul C	66-68SD-A		6'4"	242	U. of Pacific		
Lavan, Al DB	69-70Atl		6'1"	194	Colorado State	5	
Lawrence, Don DT-OG-OT	59-61Was		6'1"	245	Notre Dame		
Lawrence, Kent WR	69Phi 70Atl		5'11"	175	Georgia		
Lawson, Al FL	64NY-A		5'11"	190	Delaware State		
Lawson, Jerry DB	68BufA		5'11"	192	Utah		
LeBeau, Dick DB	59-72Det		6'1"	185	Ohio State	62	14
LeClair, Jim QB	67-68DenA	1	6'1"	208	C. W. Post		6
LeClerc, Roger LB-C-DT	60-66ChiB 67DenA	5	6'3"	236	Trinity (Conn.)		382
Ledbetter, Monte WR-FL	67HouA 67-69BufA 69Atl	2	6'2"	185	NW State-La.		18
Lee, Bob OG	60BosA		6'1"	245	Missouri		
Lee, Bob WR	68StL 69Atl		6'3"	200	Minnesota		
Lee, Dwight HB	68SF 68Atl		6'2"	198	Michigan State		
Lee, Herm OT-OG	57Pit 58-66ChiB		6'4"	244	Florida A&M		
Lee, Jacky QB	60-63HouA 64-65DenA 66-67HouA 67-69KC-A	12	6'1"	186	Cincinnati		18
Lee, Monte LB	61StL 62MS 63-64Det 65Bal		6'4"	221	Texas	1	
Leetzow, Max DE-DT	65-66DenA 67JJ		6'4"	240	Idaho		
Leeuwenberg, Dick OT	65ChiB		6'5"	242	Stanford		
Leftridge, Dick FB	66Pit		6'2"	240	West Virginia		12
Leggett, Earl DT-DE	57-60ChiB 61KJ 62-65ChiB 66LA 67-68NO		6'3"	254	Louisiana State	1	2
Lemek, Ray OT-OG	57-61Was 62-65Pit		6'	238	Notre Dame		
Lemm, Wally	HC61HouA HC62-65StL HC66-69HouA HC70Hou				Carroll (Wisc.)		
Lemmerman, Bruce QB	68-69Atl	1	6'1"	196	San Fern. Valley		
LeMoine, Jim OG-LB-TE	67BufA 68-69HouA		6'2"	245	Utah State		
Lentz, Jack DB	67-68DenA		6'	195	Holy Cross	5	
Leo Bobby HB-WR	67-68BosA		5'10"	180	Harvard		6
Leo, Charlie OG	60-62BosA 63BufA		6'	238	Indiana		
Leo, Jim DE-LB	60NYG 61-62Min		6'1"	222	Cincinnati		2
Lester, Darrell FB	64Min 65-66DenA	2	6'2"	223	McNeese State		6
Letner, Cotton LB	61BufA		6'1"	215	Tennessee		
Lewis, Dan HB	58-64Det 65Was 66NYG	23	6'1"	199	Wisconsin		144
Lewis, Gary FB-HB	64-69SF 70NO	23	6'3"	228	Arizona State		108
Lewis, Hal DB	68DenA		6'2"	188	Arizona State		
Lewis, Harold HB-DB	59Bal 60BufA 62OakA		6'	200	Houston		
Lewis, Joe DT	58-60Pit 61Bal 62Phi		6'2"	256	Compton J.C.	1	6
Lewis, Sherman DB	66-67NY-A		5'10"	180	Michigan State		
Lilly, Bob DT-DE	61-74Dal		6'4"	256	Texas Christian	1	24
Lince, Dave TE	66-67Phi		6'6"	258	North Dakota		
Lincoln, Keith HB-FB	61-66SD-A 67-68BufA 68SD-A	23 5	6'2"	212	Washington State		271
Lind, Mike DB	63-64SF 65-66Pit	2	6'2"	220	Notre Dame		54
Linden, Errol OT	61Cle 62-65Min 66-68Atl 69-70NO		6'5"	258	Houston		
Lindquist, Paul DT	61BosA		6'3"	265	New Hampshire		
Lindsey, Dale LB	65-72Cle 73NO		6'3"	224	Western Kentucky	8	6
Lindsey, Hub HB	68DenA		5'11"	196	Wyoming		
Lindsey, Jim HB-FB	66-72Min	2	6'2"	206	Arkansas		66
Linne, Aubrey OE	61Bal		6'7"	235	Texas Christian		
Lisbon, Don HB	63-64SF	2	6'	194	Bowling Green		18
Liscio, Tony OT-OG	63-64Dal 65JJ 66-71Dal		6'5"	251	Tulsa		
Liske, Pete QB	64NY-A 65-68CFL 69DenA 70Den 71-72Phi	12	6'2"	199	Penn State		12
Livingston, Andy FB-HB	64-65ChiB 66KJ 67-68ChiB 69-70NO	2	6'	234	none		66
Livingston, Cliff LB-DE	54-61NYG 62Min 63-65LA		6'3"	212	U.C.L.A.	8	6
Livingston, Dale K	68-69CinA 70GB	45	6'	210	Western Michigan		123
Livingston, Walt HB	60BosA		6'	185	Heidelberg		
Livingston, Warren DB	61-66Dal		5'10"	185	Arizona	10	6
Lloyd, Dave LB-C	59-61Cle 62Det 63-70Phi		6'3"	247	Georgia	14	10
Lockett, J. W. FB	61SF 61-62Dal 63Bal 64Was	2	6'2"	229	Central St.-Okla.		60
Locklin, Billy LB	60OakA		6'2"	225	New Mexico State		
Lofton, Oscar OE	60BosA 61-62MS	2	6'6"	218	Southeastern La.		24
Logan, Chuck TE-OE	64Pit 65,67-68StL		6'4"	215	Northwestern		
Logan, Jerry DB	63-72Bal	3	6'1"	188	West Texas State	34	36
Logan, Obert DB	65-66Dal 67NO		5'10"	180	Trinity (Texas)	8	6
Lomakoski, John OT	62Det		6'4"	250	Western Michigan		
Lombardi, Vince died Sept. 3, 1970 – cancer	HC59-67GB HC69-70Was				Fordham		
London, Mike LB	66SD-A		6'2"	230	Wisconsin		
Long, Bob FL-WR	64-67GB 68Atl 69Was 70LA	2	6'3"	199	Wichita State		60
Long, Charley OG-OT	61-69BosA		6'3"	247	Tenn.-Chattanooga		
Long, Dave DE-DT	66-68StL 69-72NO		6'4"	241	Iowa		
Long, Mike OE	60BosA		6'	188	Brandeis		
Longenecker, Ken DT	60Pit		6'4"	285	Lebanon Valley		
Longmire, Sam DB-WR	67-68KC-A		6'3"	195	Purdue		
Look, Dean QB 61 played major league baseball	62NY-A		5'11"	185	Michigan State		
Looney, Joe Don FB-HB	64Bal 65-66Det 66-67Was 68MS 69NO	234	6'1"	230	Oklahoma		78
Lopasky, Bill OG	61SF		6'2"	235	West Virginia		
Lorick, Tony FB	64-67Bal 68-69NO	23	6'1"	214	Arizona State		114
Lothamer, Ed DT-DE	64-69KC-A 71-72KC		6'5"	261	Michigan State		
Lothridge, Billy QB-DB-K	64Dal 65LA 66-71Atl 72Mia	4	6'1"	194	Georgia Tech	3	6
Lott, Billy FB-HB-DB	58NYG 60OakA 61-63BosA	2	6'	203	Mississippi		128
Loudd, Rommie LB	60LA-A 61-62BosA		6'3"	227	U.C.L.A.	4	
Louderback, Tom LB-C-OG	58-59Phi 60-61OakA 62BufA		6'2"	235	San Jose State	3	6
Loukas, Angelo OG-OT	69BufA 70Bos		6'3"	250	Northwestern		
Love, John FL-WR-DB	67Was 68MS 72LA	23 5	5'11"	185	North Texas State		40

Use Name (Nicknames) – Positions	Team by Year	See Section	Hgt	Wgt	College	Int	Pts
Lovetere, John DT	59-62LA 63-65NYG		6'4"	280	Compton J.C.		6
Lowe, Gary DB-HB	56-57Was 57-64Det		5'11"	196	Michigan State	20	2
Lowe, Paul HB	60LA-A 61SD-A 62BA 63-67SD-A 68-69KC-A	23	6'	200	Oregon State		282
Lucas, Dick OE	58Pit 60-63Phi	2	6'2"	213	Boston College		36
Lucas, Richie QB-HB-DB	60-61BufA	12	6'	190	Penn State	2	30
Lucci, Mike LB	62-64Cle 65-73Det		6'2"	230	Tennessee	21	24
Luce, Lew HB	61Was		6'	187	Penn State		
Luke, Tommy DB	68DenA		6'	190	Mississippi		
Lundy, Lamar DE-OE	57-69LA	2	6'7"	245	Purdue	3	54
Lusteg, Booth K	66BufA 67MiaA 68Pit 69GB	5	5'11"	190	Connecticut		202
Lyles, Lenny DB-HB	58Bal 59-60SF 61-69Bal	23	6'2"	202	Louisville	16	48
Lynch, Dick DB	58Was 59-66NYG		6'1"	202	Notre Dame	37	42
Mack, Red FL-OE-HB	61-63Pit 64Phi 65Pit 66Atl 66GB	2	5'10"	185	Notre Dame		48
Mackbee, Earsell DB	65-69Min		6'1"	195	Utah State	15	12
Mackey, Dee OE	60SF 61-62Bal 63-66NY-A	2	6'5"	232	East Texas State		50
Mackey, John TE-OE	63-71Bal 72SD	2	6'3"	222	Syracuse		228
MacKinnon, Jacque TE-OE-FB-OG	61-69SD-A 70Oak	2	6'4"	245	Colgate		134
Maczuzak, John DT	64KC-A		6'5"	250	Pittsburgh		
Magac, Mike OG	60-64SF 65-66Pit		6'3"	240	Missouri		
Maguire, Paul LB-DE-OE-K	60LA-A 61-63SD-A 64-69BufA 70Buf	4	6'	224	The Citadel	9	6
Maher, Bruce DB-HB	60-67Det 68-69NYG		5'11"	190	Detroit	22	6
Majors, Billy DB	61BufA		6'	175	Tennessee		
Malavasi, Ray	HC66DenA				Army, Mississippi St.		
Mallick, Fran DE-DT	65Pit		6'3"	245	none		
Mallory, John DB	68Phi 69-71Atl	3	6'	188	West Virginia	2	24
Manders, Dave C	64-66Dal 67JJ 68-74Dall		6'2"	247	Michigan State		
Mangum, John DT	66-67BosA		6'3"	273	Southern Miss.		
Mankins, Jim FB	67Atl		6'1"	235	Florida State		
Manning, Pete DB	60-61ChiB		6'3"	208	Wake Forest		
Manoukian, Don OG	60OakA		5'9"	242	Stanford		
Maples, Jim LB	63Bal		6'4"	225	Baylor		
Marchlewski, Frank C	65LA 66-68Atl 68-69LA 70Buf		6'2"	237	Minnesota		
Marconi, Joe FB-HB	56-61LA 62-66ChiB	2	6'2"	225	West Virginia		234
Marcontell, Ed OG	67StL 67HouA		6'	220	Lamar Tech		
Marinovich, Marv OG	65OakA		6'3"	250	Southern Calif.		
Marion, Jerry FL	67Pit		5'10"	175	Wyoming		
Marques, Bob LB	60NY-A		6'	220	Boston U.		
Marsh, Aaron WR	68-69BosA	2	6'	190	Eastern Kentucky		24
Marsh, Amos HB-FB	61-64Dal 65-67Det	23	6'	218	Oregon State		198
Marsh, Frank DB	67SD-A		6'2"	205	Oregon State		
Marshall, Bud DT	65GB 66Was 66Atl 67-68HouA		6'5"	271	S.F. Austin State		
Marshall, Chuck DB	62DenA		6'	180	Oregon State		
Marshall, Jim DE	60Cle 61-77Min		6'3"	239	Ohio State	1	8
Martha, Paul DB-FL-OE-HB	64-69Pit 70Den	2	6'	186	Pittsburgh	21	6
Martin, Aaron DB	64-65LA 66-67Phi 68Was	3	6'	187	N. Car. Central		
Martin, Billy (Bill) TE-OE	64-65ChiB 66-67Atl 68Min	2 4	6'4"	238	Georgia Tech		24
Martin, Billy HB	62-64ChiB	3	5'11"	196	Minnesota		6
Martin, Blanche FB	60NY-A 60LA-A		6'	195	Michigan State		6
Martin, Dave LB	68KC-A 69Cin		6'	220	Notre Dame		
Martin, Larry DT	66SD-A		6'2"	270	San Diego State		
Mason, Tommy HB-FB	61-66Min 67-70LA 71Was 72JJ	23	6'	195	Tulane		270
Masters, Norm OT	57-64GB		6'2"	249	Michigan State		
Matan, Bill DE	66NYG		6'4"	240	Kansas State		
Mathis, Bill HB-FB	60-69NY-A	2	6'1"	219	Clemson		282
Matsos, Archie LB	60-62BufA 63-65OakA 66DenA 66SD-A		6'	215	Michigan State	22	6
Matte, Tom HB-QB	61-72Bal	123	6'	207	Ohio State		342
Matthews, Wes OE	66MiaA		5'10"	180	NE State-Okla.		
Mattox, Jack DT	61DenA		6'4"	240	Fresno State		
Matson, Riley OT	61-64Was 65JJ 66ChiB		6'4"	252	Oregon		
Mayberry, Doug FB	61-62Min 63OakA	2	6'1"	223	Utah State		12
Mayes, Ben DE-DT	69HouA		6'5"	265	Duke		
Maynard, Don FL-WR-OE-HB	58NYG 60-69NY-A 70-72NYJ 73StL	23	6'	180	Texas-El Paso		532
Mays, Jerry DE-DT	61-62DalA 63-69KC-A 70KC		6'4"	250	S.M.U.	1	6
Mazurek, Fred FL-DB	65-66Was		5'11"	192	Pittsburgh		
Mazzanti, Jerry DE	63Phi 64-65MS 66Det 67Pit		6'3"	240	Arkansas		
McAdams, Bob DT	63-64NY-A		6'3"	250	N. Car. Central		
McAdams, Carl LB-DT-DE	66BN 67-69NY-A		6'3"	240	Oklahoma		
McBride, Norm DE	69MiaA 70Mia		6'3"	240	Utah		
McCall, Don HB	67-68NO 69Pit 70NO	23	5'11"	195	Southern Calif.		60
McCall, Ron LB	67-68SD-A		6'2"	245	Weber State		
McCambridge, John DE	67Det		6'4"	245	Northwestern		
McCann, Tim DT	69NYG		6'5"	265	Princeton		
McCarthy, Brendan FB	68Atl 68-69DenA	2	6'3"	220	Boston College		18
McCarty, Mickey TE	69KC-A		6'5"	255	Texas Christian		
McClellan, Mike DB	62-63Phi 64-65MS		6'1"	185	Oklahoma	4	
McClinton, Curtis FB-TE	62DalA 63-69KC-A	2	6'3"	230	Kansas		196
McCloughan, Kent DB	65-69OakA 70Oak		6'1"	190	Nebraska	15	
McClure, Wayne LB	68CinA 70Cin		6'1"	225	Mississippi		
McComb, Don DE	60BosA		6'4"	240	Villanova		
McCord, Darris DE-DT-OT	55-67Det		6'4"	247	Tennessee	3	8
McCormick, Dave OT	66SF 67-68NO		6'6"	250	Louisiana State		
McCormick, John QB	62Min 63DenA 64KJ 65-66,68DenA	1 4	6'1"	201	Massachusetts		
McCoy, Lloyd OG	64SD-A		6'1"	245	San Diego State		
McCreary, Bob OT	61Dal		6'5"	256	Wake Forest		
McCullers, Dale LB	69MiaA		6'1"	215	Florida State		
McCullough, Bob OG	62-65DenA		6'5"	244	Colorado		
McCuster, Jim OT	58ChiC 59-62Phi 63Cle 64NY-A		6'2"	246	Pittsburgh		
McDaniel, Wahoo LB-OG	60HouA 61-63DenA 64-65NY-A 66-68MiaA	4	6'	235	Oklahoma	13	6
McDaniels, Dave WR	68Dal		6'4"	200	Miss. Valley St.		
McDermott, Gary HB	68BufA 69Atl	2	6'1"	211	Tulsa		26
McDole, Ron DE-DT	61StL 62HouA 63-69BufA 70Buf 71-77Was		6'3"	266	Nebraska	11	14
McDonald, Don DB	61BufA		5'11"	185	Houston		
McDonald, Ray FB	67-68Was	2	6'4"	248	Idaho		24
McDonald, Tommy FL-HB-WR	57-63Phi 64Dal 65-66LA 67Atl 68Cle	23	5'10"	176	Oklahoma		510
McDougall, Gerry FB	62-64,68SD-A	2	6'2"	225	U.C.L.A.		38
McDowell, John OT-OG	64GB 65NYG 66StL		6'3"	260	St. John's-Minn.		
McFadin, Bud DT-DG-OG-LB	52-56LA 60-63DenA 64-65HouA		6'3"	260	Texas	1	24

Use Name (Nicknames) – Positions	Team by Year	See Section	Hgt	Wgt	College	Int	Pts
McFarland, Kay FL-OE-WR	62-66SF 67JJ 68SF	2	6'2"	182	Colorado State		24
McFarlane, Nyle HB	60OakA		6'2"	205	Brigham Young		12
McGee, Ben DE-DT	64-72Pit		6'2"	255	Jackson State	1	6
McGee, George OT	60BosA 61-62MS		6'2"	259	Southern U.		
McGee, Max OE	54GB 55-56MS 57-67GB	2 4	6'3"	205	Tulane		306
McGee, Mike OG	60-62StL		6'1"	230	Duke		
McGeever, John DB	62-65DenA 66MiaA		6'1"	195	Auburn	11	6
McGrew, Dan C	60BufA		6'2"	250	Purdue		
McIlhany, Dan DB	65LA		6'1"	195	Texas A&M	2	
McInnis, Hugh OE-TE	60-62StL 64Det 66Atl	2	6'3"	219	Southern Miss.		
McKeever, Marlin LB-TE-OE	61-66LA 67Min	2	6'1"	233	Southern Calif.	9	36
	68-70Was 71-72LA 73Phi						
McKinnon, Don LB-C	63-64BosA		6'3"	223	Dartmouth		
McLenna, Bruce HB	66Det		6'3"	225	Hillsdale		
McLeod, Bob OE-TE	61-66HouA	2	6'5"	231	Abilene Christian		114
McMahon, Art DB	68-69BosA 70Bos 72NE		5'11"	188	N. Carolina State	3	
McMillan, Ernie OT	61-74StL 75GB		6'6"	258	Illinois		
McMillan, Jim DB	61-62DenA 63-64OakA 64-65DenA		5'11"	190	Colorado State	14	24
McMullen, John OG	60-61NY-A		6'	244	Notre Dame		
McMurty, Chuck DT	60-61BufA 62-63OakA		6'	286	Whittier		
McNamara, Bob DB-HB	60-61DenA		6'	189	Minnesota	7	12
McNeil, Charley DB	60LA-A 61-64SD-A		5'11"	179	Compton J.C.	19	12
McNeil, Clifton WR-FL	64-67Cle 68-69SF 70-71NYG	2	6'2"	186	Grambling		138
	71-72Was 73Hou						
McQuarters, Ed DT	65StL		6'1"	250	Oklahoma		
McRae, Bennie DB	62-70ChiB 71NYG		6'1"	180	Michigan	27	24
McRae, Frank DT	67ChiB		6'7"	270	Tennessee State		
McWaters, Bill FB	64Min		6'	225	North Texas State		
Meador, Ed DB	59-70LA	3	5'11"	193	Arkansas Tech	46	36
Medved, Ron DB	66-70Phi		6'1"	205	Washington	3	
Meggysey, Dave LB	63-69StL		6'1"	221	Syracuse		
Meinert, Dale LB-OG-OT	58-59ChiC 60-67StL		6'2"	219	Oklahoma State	9	6
Meixler, Ed LB	65BosA		6'3"	245	Boston U.		
Melinkovich, Mike DE	65-66StL 67Det		6'4"	243	Grays Harbor J.C.		
Mellekas, John C-DT-OT	56ChiB 57MS 58-61ChiB		6'3"	255	Arizona		
	62SF 63Phi						
Memmelaar, Dale OG-OT	59ChiC 60-61StL 62-63Dal		6'2"	247	Wyoming		
	64-65Cle 66-67Dal						
Mendez, Mario HB	64SD-A		5'11"	200	San Diego State		
Menefee, Pep FL	66NYG		6'1"	198	New Mexico State		
Mercein, Chuck FB	65-67NYG 67-68GB 69Was 70NYJ	2 5	6'3"	227	Yale		45
Mercer, Mike K	61-62Min 63-66OakA 66KC-A	45	6'	208	Arizona State		594
	67-68BufA 68-69GB 70SD						
Meredith, Don (Dandy Don) QB	60-68Dal	12	6'2"	202	S.M.U.		
Meredith, Dudley DT	63HouA 64-68BufA 68HouA		6'4"	280	Lamar Tech	1	
Mertens, Jerry DB	58-62SF 63KJ 64-65SF		6'	184	Drake	8	6
Mertens, Jim TE	69MiaA		6'3"	235	Fairmont State		
Merz, Curt OG-DE	62DalA 63-68KC-A		6'4"	257	Iowa		
Messer, Dale HB-FL-DB	61-65SF	2	5'10"	175	Fresno State	1	
Messner, Max LB	60-63Det 64NYG 64-65Pit		6'3"	225	Cincinnati	2	
Mestnik, Frank FB	60-61StL 63GB	2	6'2"	200	Marquette		30
Meyer, Ed OT	60BufA		6'2"	240	West Texas State		
Meyer, John LB	66HouA		6'1"	225	Notre Dame		
Meyer, Ron QB	66Pit		6'4"	205	S. Dakota State		
Meyers, John DT	62-63Dal 64-67Phi		6'6"	272	Washington	2	
Meylan, Wayne LB	68-69Cle 70Min		6'1"	237	Nebraska		
Michael, Rich OT	60-63HouA 64JJ 65-66HouA		6'3"	238	Ohio State		
Michaels, Lou DE-K	58-60LA 61-63Pit	5	6'2"	243	Kentucky		955
	64-69Bal 71GB						
Michel, Tom HB	64Min	2	6'	210	East Carolina		
Middendorf, Dave OG	68-69CinA 70NYJ		6'3"	260	Washington State		
Milks, John LB	66SD-A		6'	222	San Diego State	1	
Miller, Al LB	62-63Was		6'	224	Ohio U.		
Miller, Alan FB	60BosA 61-63OakA 64JJ 65OakA	2	6'	202	Boston College		120
Miller, Bill DT	62HouA		6'4"	270	N. Mex. Highlands		
Miller, Bill OE-WR	62DalA 63BufA 64,66-68OakA	2	6'	192	Miami (Fla.)		60
Miller, Clark DE	62-68SF 69Was 70LA		6'5"	246	Utah State	1	6
Miller, Fred DT	63-72Bal		6'3"	248	Louisiana State		
Miller, Ron QB	62LA	1	6'	190	Wisconsin		
Mills, Dick OG	61-62Det		6'3"	240	Pittsburgh		
Mills, Pete OE	65-66BufA		5'11"	180	Wichita State		
Milstead, Charlie QB-DB	60-61HouA	4	6'2"	190	Texas A&M	2	1
Milton, Gene WR	68-69MiaA	23	5'10"	170	Florida A&M		12
Mingo, Gene HB-K	60-63DenA 64-65OakA	23 5	6'1"	199	none		629
	66-67MiaA 67Was 69-70Pit						
Minnicar, Randy HB	66BL 67-69NYG 70Cle	2	6'	205	Purdue		36
Minter, Tom DB	62DenA 62BufA		5'10"	178	Baylor		
Mira, George QB	64-68SF 69Phi 71Mia	12	5'11"	190	Miami (Fla.)		
Mirich, Rex DT-DE	64-66OakA 67-69DenA 70Bos		6'4"	251	Arizona State		
Mischak, Bob OG	58NYG 60-62NY-A 63-65OakA		6'	237	Army		
Mitchell, Alvin DB-WR	68-69Cle 70Den		6'3"	195	Morgan State		
Mitchell, Bobby FL-HB-WR	58-61Cle 62-68Was	23	6'	192	Illinois		546
Mitchell, Charley HB-DB	63-67DenA 68BufA	23	5'11"	185	Washington	1	54
Mitchell, Ed OG	65-67SD-A		6'2"	275	Southern U.		
Mitchell, Stan FB-HB-OE	66-69MiaA 70Mia 71JJ	2	6'2"	220	Tennessee		54
Mitchell, Willie DB	64-69KC-A 70KC	3	6'1"	185	Tennessee State	16	24
Mitinger, Bob LB-DE	62-64,66,68SD-A		6'2"	232	Penn State	3	
Mix, Ron OT-OG	60LA-A 61-69SD-A 70VR 71Oak		6'4"	249	Southern Calif.		
Molden, Frank DT	65LA 66-67KJ 68Phi 69NYG		6'5"	282	Jackson State	1	6
Montalbo, Mel DB	62OakA		6'1"	190	Utah State		
Moore, Alex DB	68DenA		6'	195	Norfolk State		
Moore, Charlie OG	62Was		6'5"	230	Arkansas		
Moore, Denis DT-DE	67-69Det		6'5"	247	Southern Calif.		
Moore, Fred DT-DE	64-66SD-A		6'4"	260	Oklahoma	1	
Moore, Gene HB	69SF		6'	208	Occidental		
Moore, Lenny HB-FL	56-67Bal	23	6'1"	191	Penn State		678
Moore, Leroy DE	60BufA 61-62BosA 62-63BufA		6'	231	Ft. Valley State	2	6
	64-65DenA						
Moore, Rich DT	69-70GB		6'6"	285	Villanova		
Moore, Tom HB	60-65GB 66LA 67Atl	23	6'2"	213	Vanderbilt		186
Mooty, Jim DB	60Dal		5'11"	177	Arkansas		
Moran, Jim DT	64NYG 65BL 66-67NYG		6'5"	260	Idaho		
Moreau, Doug TE-OE	66-69MiaA	2	6'2"	207	Louisiana State		45
Morelli, Fran OT	62NY-A		6'2"	258	Colgate		
Morgan, Bobby DB	67Pit		6'	205	New Mexico		

Use Name (Nicknames) – Positions	Team by Year	See Section	Hgt	Wgt	College	Int	Pts
Morgan, Mike LB	64-67Phi 68Was 69-70NO 71JJ		6'4"	241	Louisiana State	6	12
Morrall, Earl QB	56SF 57-58Pit 58-64Det	12 4	6'1"	205	Michigan State		48
	65-67NYG 68-71Bal 72-76Mia						
Morris, Dennit LB	58SF 60-61HouA		6'1"	228	Oklahoma	5	
Morris, Johnny FL-HB	58-67ChiB	23	5'10"	180	Cal.-Santa Barbara		222
Morris, Larry LB-HB	55-57LA 59-64ChiB 66Atl	2	6'2"	226	Georgia Tech	6	12
Morris, Riley LB-DE	60-62OakA		6'2"	230	Florida A&M	3	6
Morrison, Joe HB-FL-WR-FB-DB-OE	59-72NYG	23	6'1"	210	Cincinnati		390
Morrow, John C-OG-DE	56LA 57MS 58-59LA 60-66Cle		6'3"	244	Michigan		
Morrow, Tom DB	62-64OakA	4	5'11"	185	Southern Miss.	23	
Morze, Frank C-DT	57-61SF 62-63Cle 64SF		6'4"	272	Boston College		
Mostardi, Rich DB	60Cle 61Min 62OakA		5'11"	188	Kent State	2	
Moten, Bobby WR	68DenA		6'4"	212	Bishop		
Mudd, Howard OG	64-69SF 69-70ChiB		6'3"	251	Hillsdale		
Muelhaupt, Ed OG	60-61BufA		6'3"	230	Iowa State		
Mullins, Don DB	61-62ChiB		6'1"	195	Houston		
Mumley, Nick DE-OT	60-62NY-A		6'6"	252	Purdue	1	6
Murchison, Lee OE	61Dal		6'3"	205	U. of Pacific		
Murdock, Jesse HB-FB	63OakA 63BufA		6'2"	203	Calif. Western		
Murdock, Les K	67NYG	5	6'3"	245	Florida State		25
Murphy, Bill WR	68BosA	2	6'1"	185	Cornell		
Murphy, Dennis DT	65ChiB		6'1"	250	Florida		
Murphy, Fred OE	60Cle 61Min		6'3"	205	Georgia Tech		
Musgrove, Spain DT-DE	67-69Was 70Hou		6'4"	275	Utah State		
Myers, Tom QB	65-66Det		6'	188	Northwestern		
Nairn, Harvey WR	68NY-A 69MS		6'1"	178	Southern U.		
Nance, Jim FB	65-69Bos A 70Bos 71NE 73NYJ	2	6'1"	241	Syracuse		276
Napier, Walter DT	60-61DalA		6'4"	275	Paul Quinn		
Neck, Tommy DB	62ChiB		5'11"	190	Louisiana State		
Neff, Bob DB	66-68MiaA	3	6'	182	S.F. Austin State	2	
Neidert, John (J.T.) LB	68CinA 68-69NY-A 70ChiB		6'2"	230	Louisville		
Neighbors, Billy OG	62-65BosA 66-69MiaA		5'11"	244	Alabama		
Nelsen, Bill QB	63-67Pit 68-72Cle	12	6'	195	Southern Calif.		12
Nelson, Al DB	65-73Phi	3	5'11"	185	Cincinnati	13	18
Nelson, Andy (Bones) DB	57-63Bal 64NYG		6'1"	180	Memphis State	33	18
Nelson, Benny DB	64HouA		6'	185	Alabama	1	6
Nery, Ron DE	60LA-A 61-62SD-A 63DenA 63HouA		6'6"	236	Kansas State		
Nettles, Jim DB	65-68Phi 69-72LA		5'9"	177	Wisconsin	26	24
Neumann, Tom HB	63BosA	2	5'11"	205	Northern Michigan		6
Nevett, Elijah DB-FL	67-70NO		6'	185	Clark-Ga.	6	
Newell, Steve OE	67SD-A		6'1"	186	Long Beach State		
Nichols, Bob OT	65Pit 66-67LA		6'3"	250	Stanford		
Nichols, Bobby TE	66-67BosA		6'2"	220	Boston U.		
Nichols, Mike C	60-61DenA		6'3"	225	Ark.-Pine Bluff		
Nicklas, Pete OT	62OakA		6'4"	240	Baylor		
Ninowski, Jim QB	58-59Cle 60-61Det 62-66Cle	12	6'1"	206	Michigan State		60
	67-68Was 69NO						
Nisby, John OG	57-61Pit 62-64Was		6'1"	235	Pacific (Ore.)		
Nitschke, Ray LB	58-72GB		6'3"	235	Illinois	25	12
Nocera, John LB	59-62Phi 63DenA		6'1"	220	Iowa	1	
Nofsinger, Terry QB	61-64Pit 65-66StL 67Atl	12	6'4"	209	Utah		18
Nomina, Tom DT-OG	63-65DenA 66-68MiaA		6'5"	267	Miami-Ohio		
Noonan, Karl WR-OE	66-69MiaA 70-71Mia 72KJ	2	6'3"	193	Iowa		102
Norman, Dick QB	61ChiB		6'3"	210	Stanford		
Norman, Pettis TE-OE	62-70Dal 71-73SD	2	6'3"	220	Johnson C. Smith		90
Norris, Jim DT-OT	62-64OakA		6'4"	235	Houston	2	
Norris, Trusse OE	69LA-A		6'1"	190	U.C.L.A.		
Norton, Don OE	60LA-A 61-66SD-A	2	6'1"	190	Iowa		162
Norton, Jim DB	60-68HouA	4	6'3"	187	Idaho	45	
Norton, Jim DT-OT-OE	65-66SF 67-68Atl 68Phi		6'4"	254	Washington	1	
	69Was 70NYG						
Norton, Ray HB	60-61SF		6'2"	184	San Jose State		
Norton, Rick QB	66-69MiaA 70GB	1	6'1"	192	Kentucky		
Novsek, Joe DE	62OakA		6'4"	237	Tulsa		
Nowatzke, Tom FB-LB	65-69Det 70-72Bal	2	6'3"	229	Indiana	1	102
Nugent, Phil DB	61DenA		6'2"	195	Tulane	7	
Nunnery, R. B. OT	60DalA		6'4"	275	Louisiana State		
Nutting, Ed OT	61Cle 62JJ 63Dal		6'4"	246	Georgia Tech		
Oakes, Don OT-DT	61-62Phi 63-68BosA		6'3"	253	Virginia Tech		
Oates, Carlton DE-DT	65-69OakA 70-72Oak 73GB		6'2"	252	Florida A&M		6
Oberg, Tom DB	68-69DenA		6'	185	Portland State	3	
O'Bradovich, Ed DE	62-71ChiB		6'3"	255	Illinois		8
O'Brien, Dave DT-OT-OG	63-64Min 65NYG 66-67StL		6'3"	244	Boston College		
O'Brien, Fran OT-OG-DE	59Cle 60-66Was 66-68Pit		6'1"	253	Michigan State		
Odle, Phil WR	68-70Det		5'11"	191	Brigham Young		
Odom, Sammy LB	64HouA		6'2"	235	NW State-La.	2	
O'Donnell, Joe OG-OT	64-67BufA 68KJ 69BufA 70-71Buf		6'2"	253	Michigan		
Ogas, Dave LB	68OakA 69BufA		6'3"	240	San Diego State		
Ogden, Ray TE-WR-OE	65-66StL 67NO	2	6'5"	225	Alabama		24
	67-68Atl 69-71ChiB						
Oglesby, Paul DT	60OakA		6'4"	235	U.C.L.A.		
O'Hanley, Ross DB	60-65BosA 66JJ		6'	183	Boston College	15	6
Oliver, Bob OT	69Cle		6'3"	240	Abilene Christian		
Oliver, Chip LB	68-69OakA		6'2"	220	Southern Calif.	1	6
Oliver, Clancy DB	69-70Pit		6'1"	180	San Diego State		
Olsen, Merlin DT	62-76LA		6'5"	270	Utah State	1	6
Olson, Harold OT	60-62BufA 63-64DenA		6'3"	259	Clemson		
Olssen, Lance OT	68-69SF		6'5"	262	Purdue		
O'Mahoney, Jim LB	65-66NY-A		6'1"	231	Miami (Fla.)		
Onesti, Larry LB	62-65HouA		6'	200	Northwestern		6
Orr, Jimmy FL-OE-WR	58-60Pit 61-70Bal	2 4	5'11"	185	Georgia		396
Osborne, Clancy LB	59-60SF 61-62Min 63-64OakA		6'3"	218	Arizona State	6	
Osborne, Tom OE	60-61Was	2	6'3"	190	Hastings		12
Otto, Gus LB	65-69OakA 70-73Oak		6'2"	220	Missouri	6	12
Otto, Jim C	60-69OakA 70-74Oak		6'2"	244	Miami (Fla.)		
Overton, Jerry DB	63Dal		6'2"	190	Utah		
	injured in accident before 1964 season						
Owens, Don OT-DT	57Was 58-60Phi 60-63StL		6'5"	255	Southern Miss.		6
Owens, Luke DE-DT-OT	57Bal 58-59ChiC 60-65StL		6'2"	254	Kent State		2
Owens, R. C. (Alley Oop) OE-FL	57-61SF 62-63Bal 64NYG	2	6'3"	197	Coll. of Idaho		138
Pagliei, Joe FB	59Phi 60NY-A	4	6'	220	Clemson		6
Paluck, John DE-DT	56Was 57-58MS 59-65Was		6'2"	241	Pittsburgh	2	8
Papac, Nick QB	61OakA	1	5'11"	190	Fresno State		6

Use Name (Nicknames) – Positions	Team by Year	See Section	Hgt	Wgt	College	Int	Pts
Pardee, Jack LB	57-64LA 65VR 66-70LA 71-72Was HC75-77ChiB		6'2"	224	Texas A&M	22	38
Paremore, Bob HB	63-64StL	2	5'11"	190	Florida A&M		12
Parilli, Babe QB	52-53GB 54-55MS 56Cle 57-58GB 59CFL 60OakA 61-67BosA 68-69NY-A	12	6'1"	190	Kentucky		146
Park, Ernie OT-OG	63-65SD-A 66MiaA 67DenA 69CinA		6'3"	247	McMurray		
Parker, Charlie OG	65DenA		6'1"	245	Southern Miss.		
Parker, Don OG	67SF 68KJ		6'3"	235	Virginia		
Parker, Frank DT	62-64Cle 65IL 66-67Cle 68Pit 69NYG		6'5"	263	Oklahoma State		
Parker, Jim OT-OG	57-67Bal		6'3"	273	Ohio State		
Parker, Willie DT	68-69HouA 70Hou		6'2"	266	Ark.—Pine Bluff		
Parks, Dave OE-TE-WR	64-67SF 68-72NO 73Hou	2	6'2"	202	Texas Tech		264
Parrish, Bernie DB	59-66Cle 66HouA		5'11"	194	Florida	31	24
Pashe, Bill DB	64NY-A		5'11"	185	George Washington		
Patera, Dennis K	68SF	5	6'	225	Brigham Young		16
Patera, Herb LB	63BufA		6'1"	222	Michigan State		
Patton, Jimmy DB	55-66NYG	3	6'	183	Mississippi	52	24
Paulson, Dainard DB	61-66NY-A		5'11"	190	Oregon State	29	6
Peacock, Johnny DB	69HouA 70Hou		6'2"	203	Houston	5	12
Peaks, Clarence FB	57-63Phi 64-65Pit	23	6'1"	218	Michigan State		144
Pearson, Willie DB	69MiaA		6'	190	N. Carolina A&T		
Pellegrini, Bob LB-OG	56, 58-61Phi 62-65Was		6'2"	233	Maryland	13	6
Pennington, Tom K	62DalA	5	6'2"	210	Georgia		19
Pentecost, John OG	67 Min		6'2"	250	U.C.L.A.		
Perkins, Art FB	62-63LA	2	6'	223	North Texas State		36
Perkins, Bill HB	63NY-A		6'2"	225	Iowa		
Perkins, Don FB-HB	61-68Dal	2	5'10"	200	New Mexico		270
Perkins, Jim OT	6[illegible] 64DenA		6'5"	250	Colorado		
Perkins, Ray WR-OE	67-71Dal	2	6'	183	Alabama		66
Perkins, Willis OG-DE	61HouA 61BosA 63HouA		6'	250	Texas Southern		
Perlo, Phil LB	60 HouA		6'	220	Maryland		
Perreault, Pete OG-OT	63-67NY-A 68CinA 69NY-A 70NYJ 71Min		6'3"	246	Boston U.		
Pesonen, Dick DB	60GB 61Min 62-64NYG		6'	190	Minnesota-Duluth	4	
Peters, Anton DT	63DenA		6'3"	250	Florida		
Peters, Floyd DT	59-62Cle 63Det 64-69Phi 70Was		6'4"	254	San Fran. State	3	
Peters, Frank OT	69CinA		6'4"	250	Ohio U.		
Peterson, Ken OG	61 Min		6'2"	235	Utah		
Petitbon, Richie LB	59-68ChiB 69-70LA 71-73Was		6'3"	206	Tulane	48	18
Petrella, Bob DB	66-69MiaA 70-71Mia		6'	186	Tennessee	5	
Petrich, Bob DE	63-66SD-A 67BufA		6'4"	253	West Texas State	1	
Petties, Neal OE-FL	64-66Bal		6'2"	198	San Diego State		6
Philbin, Gerry DE	64-69NY-A 70-72NYJ 73Phi 74WFL		6'2"	245	Buffalo	1	
Phillips Jim (Red) OE-FL	58-64LA 65-67Min	2	6'1"	197	Auburn		204
Phillips, Loyd DE	67-69ChiB		6'3"	237	Arkansas	3	
Philpott, Ed LB	67-69BosA 70Bos 71NE		6'3"	240	Miami-Ohio	9	6
Piccolo, Brian HB-FB	66-69ChiB	2	6'	205	Wake Forest		30
died June 16, 1970-cancer							
Pickens, Bob OT	67-69ChiB		6'4"	258	Nebraska		
Pietrosante, Nick FB	59-65Det 66-67Cle	2	6'2"	225	Notre Dame		180
Pillath, Roger OT	65LA 66Pit		6'4"	249	Wisconsin		
Pine, Ed LB	62-64SF 65Pit		6'4"	233	Utah	3	
Pitts, Elijah HB	61-69GB 70LA 70NO 71GB	23	6'1"	204	Philander Smith		210
Pivec, Dave TE-LB	66-68LA 69DenA	2	6'3"	240	Notre Dame		8
Plum, Milt QB	57-61Cle 62-67Det 68LA 69NYG	12 5	6'1"	205	Penn State		112
Plump, Dave DB	66SD-A		6'1"	195	Fresno State		
Plunkett, Sherman (Tank) OT	58-60Bal 61-62SD-A 63-67NY-A		6'4"	290	Md. Eastern Shore		
Ply, Bobby DB	62DalA 63-67KC-A 67BufA 67DenA		6'1"	190	Baylor	9	
Poage, Ray TE-OE-FL	63Min 64-65Phi 66KJ 67-70NO 71Atl	2	6'4"	208	Texas		78
Poimbeouf, Lance OG	63Dal		6'3"	225	Southwestern La.		
Poole, Bob TE-OE-FL	64-65SF 66-67HouA	2	6'4"	216	Clemson		
Pope, Bucky OE-WR	64LA 65KJ 66-67LA 68GB	2	6'5"	199	Catawba		78
Porter, Willie DB	68BosA	3	5'11"	195	Texas Southern		
Porterfield, Garry DE	65Dal		6'3"	223	Tulsa		
Post, Bobby DB	67NYG		6'1"	195	Kings Point		
Post, Dickie HB	67-69SD-A 70SD 71Den 71Hou	23	5'9"	190	Houston		114
Pottios, Myron LB	61Pit 62BA 63-65Pit 66-70LA 71-73Was		6'2"	236	Notre Dame	12	
Powell, Art OE-DB-WR	59Phi 60-62NY-A 63-66OakA 67BufA 68Min	2	6'3"	211	San Jose State	3	492
Powell, Preston FB	61Cle		6'2"	225	Grambling		
Powell, Tim DE	65LA 66Pit		6'4"	248	Northwestern		
Powers, John OE-TE-LB	62-65Pit 66Min		6'2"	211	Notre Dame		
Powers, Warren DB	63-68OakA		6'	188	Nebraska	22	12
Preas, George OT-OG-LB	55-65Bal		6'2"	244	Virginia Tech		
Prebola, Gene OE	60OakA 61-63DenA	2	6'3"	220	Boston U.		42
Prestell, Jim DT	60Cle 61-66Min 66NYG 67Was		6'5"	264	Idaho	1	8
Price, Jim LB	63NY-A 64DenA		6'2"	228	Auburn	1	
Price, Sam HB-FB	66-68MiaA	2	5'11"	215	Illinois		12
Pride, Dan LB	68-69ChiB		6'3"	225	Jackson State	1	
Print, Bob LB	67-68SD-A		6'	220	Dayton		
Prisby, Errol DB	67DenA		5'10"	184	Cincinnati		
Promuto, Vince OG	60-70 Was		6'1"	244	Holy Cross		
Prudhomme, Remi C-OG-DE-DT	66-67BufA 68-69KC-A 70JJ 71-72NO 72Buf		6'4"	251	Louisiana State		
Pryor, Barry HB	69MiaA 70Mia		6'1"	215	Boston U.		
Purnell, Jim LB	64-68ChiB 69-72GB		6'2"	229	Wisconsin	3	
Purvis, Vic DB	66-67BosA		5'11"	200	Southern Miss.		
Pyburn, Jack OT	67-68MiaA		6'6"	245	Texas A&M		
Pyeatt, John DB	60-61DenA		6'3"	204	none	4	6
Pyle, Mike C	61-69ChiB		6'3"	247	Yale		
Pyle, Palmer OG	60-63Bal 64Min 65JJ 66OakA		6'2"	248	Michigan State		
Pyne, George DT	65BosA		6'4"	285	Olivet		
Quayle, Frank HB	69DenA	2	5'10"	195	Virginia		
Quinlan, Bill DE	57-58Cle 59-62GB 63Phi 64Det 65Was		6'3"	248	Michigan	3	
Quinn, Steve C	68HouA		6'1"	225	Notre Dame		
Rabb, Warren QB	60Det 61-62BufA	12	6'1"	202	Louisiana State		22
Rabald, Mike OG	59Det 60StL 61-62Min 64-67ChiB		6'2"	239	Indiana		
Rademacher, Bill WR-DB-OE	64-68NY-A 69BosA 70Bos	2	6'1"	190	Northern Michigan	1	18
Raimey, Dave DB	64Cle		5'10"	195	Michigan		
Rakestraw, Larry QB	64, 66-68ChiB	1	6'2"	195	Georgia		12
Ramsey, Nate DB	63-72Phi 73NO		6'1"	200	Indiana	21	6
Randall, Dennis DE-DT	67NY-A 68CinA		6'6"	243	Oklahoma State		

Use Name (Nicknames) – Positions	Team by Year	See Section	Hgt	Wgt	College	Int	Pts
Randle, Sonny OE-WR	59ChiC 60-66StL 67-68SF 68Dal	2	6'2"	189	Virginia		390
Rasmussen, Wayne DB	64-72Det 73JJ		6'2"	179	S. Dakota State	16	12
Rassas, Nick DB	66-68Atl		6'	190	Notre Dame	1	
Ratkowski, Ray HB	61BosA		6'	195	Notre Dame		
Raye, Jimmy DB	69Phi		6'	185	Michigan State		
Recher, Dave C	65-68Phi		6'1"	244	Iowa		
Rector, Ron HB	66Was 66-67Atl	2	6'	200	Northwestern		
Redman, Rick LB	65-69SD-A 70-73SD	4	5'11"	225	Washington	9	6
Redmond, Tom DE-OG-OT	60-65StL		6'5"	243	Vanderbilt		
Reeberg, Lucian OT	63Det		6'4"	308	Hampton Institute		
died Jan. 31, 1964—uremia							
Reed, Bob HB	62-63Min	23	5'11"	187	U. of Pacific		6
Reed, Leo OG-OT	61HouA 61DenA		6'4"	240	Colorado State		
Reed, Robert OG	65Was		6'1"	250	Tennessee State		
Reed, Smith HB	65-66NYG 67-68MS		6'	215	Alcorn A&M		
Reed, Taft DB	67Phi		6'2"	200	Jackson State		
Reese, Guy DT	62-63Dal 64-65Bal 66Atl		6'5"	255	S.M.U.		
Reeves, Dan HB-FB	65-72Dal	12	6'1"	201	South Carolina		253
Reeves, Roy WR	69BufA		5'11"	182	South Carolina		
Reger, John LB-OG	55-63 Pit 64-66 Was		6'	225	Pittsburgh	15	18
Regner, Tom OG	67-69HouA 70-72Hou		6'1"	255	Notre Dame		
Reichow, Jerry OE-QB	56-57Det 58KJ 59Det 60Phi 61-64Min	12	6'2"	217	Iowa		144
Reifsnyder, Bob DE	60-61NY-A		6'2"	255	Navy		
Reilly, Mike LB	64-68ChiB 69Min		6'2"	230	Iowa		6
Remmert, Dennis LB	60BufA		6'3"	215	Iowa State		
Rengel, Mike DT	69NO 70JJ		6'5"	260	Hawaii		
Renn, Bob HB	61NY-A	2	6'	180	Florida State		6
Rentz, Larry DB	69SD-A		6'1"	170	Florida		
Rentzel, Lance WR-FL-OE-HB	65-66Min 67-70Dal 71-72LA 73SL 74LA	23	6'2"	203	Oklahoma		248
Retzlaff, Pete OE-TE-FL	56-66Phi	2	6'1"	211	S. Dakota State		282
Reynolds, Al OG	60-62DalA 63-67KC-A		6'3"	238	Tarkio		
Reynolds, Bob OT	63-71StL 72-73NE 73StL		6'6"	264	Bowling Green		
Reynolds, Chuck C-OG	69-70Cle		6'2"	240	Tulsa		2
Reynolds, M.C. (Chief) QB	58-59ChiC 60Was 61BufA 62OakA	12	6'	193	Louisiana State		24
Rhome, Jerry QB	65-67Dal 69Cle 70Hou 71LA	12	6'	186	Tulsa		6
Rice, George DT-OG	66-69HouA		6'3"	262	Louisiana State		
Rice, Ken OG-OT	61BufA 62KJ 63BufA 64-65OakA 66-67MiaA		6'2"	243	Auburn		
Richards, Bobby DE	62-65 Phi 66-67Atl		6'2"	241	Louisiana State		
Richards, Jim DB	68-69NY-A 70-71MS		6'1"	180	Virginia Tech	3	
Richards, Perry OE	57Pit 58Det 59ChiC 60StL 61BufA 62NY-A	2	6'2"	205	Detroit		24
Richardson, Al DE	60BosA		6'3"	250	Grambling		
Richardson, Bob (Red) DB	66DenA		6'1"	180	U.C.L.A.		
Richardson, Jeff OT-C-OG	67-68NY-A 69MiaA		6'3"	253	Michigan State		
Richardson, Jerry (The Razor) FL-OE-HB	59-60Bal	2	6'3"	185	Wofford		24
Richardson, Jerry DB	64-65LA 66-67Atl		6'3"	190	West Texas State	11	
Richardson, Tom WR	69BosA 70Bos		6'2"	195	Jackson State		
Richardson, Willie FL-WR	63-69Bal 70Mia 71Bal	2	6'2"	198	Jackson State		150
Richey, Mike OT	69BufA 70NO		6'5"	257	North Carolina		
Richter, Frank LB	67-69DenA		6'3"	230	Georgia	2	
Richter, Pat OE-TE	63-70Was	2 4	6'5"	230	Wisconsin		84
Ridge, Houston DE-DT	66-69SD-A 70JJ		6'4"	239	San Diego State		
Ridgeway, Colin K	65 Dal		6'5"	211	Lamar Tech		
Ridlehuber, Preston HB	66Atl 68OakA 69BufA		6'2"	215	Georgia		18
Ridlon, Jimmy DB	57-62SF 63-64Dal		6'1"	181	Syracuse	9	12
Rieves, Charley LB	62-63OakA 64-65HouA		5'11"	217	Houston	1	
Riggle, Bob DB	66-67Atl 68JJ		6'1"	200	Penn State	3	6
Righetti, Joe DT	69-70Cle		6'3"	253	Waynesburg		
Riley, Butch LB	69Bal		6'2"	220	Texas A&I		
Riley, Jim DE	67-69MiaA 70-71Mia 72KJ		6'4"	252	Oklahoma		
Ringo, Jim C	53-63GB 64-67Phi HC76-77Buf		6'1"	232	Syracuse		
Rissmiller, Ray OT	66Phi 67NO 68BufA		6'4"	250	Georgia		
Rivera, Henry DB	62OakA 63BufA		5'11"	180	Oregon State		
Roach, Johnny QB-DB	56ChiC 57-58MS 59ChicC 60StL 61-63GB 64Dal	12	6'4"	197	S.M.U.		12
Robb, Joe DE- LB	59-60Phi 61-67StL 68-71Det		6'3"	238	Texas Christian	1	
Roberson, Bo FL-HB	61SD-A 62-65OakA 65BufA 66MiaA	23	6'1"	192	Cornell		116
Roberts, Archie QB	67MiaA		6'1"	193	Columbia		
Roberts, Cliff OT	61OakA		6'3"	260	Illinois		
Roberts, C. R. FB	59-62SF	2	6'3"	202	Southern Calif.		24
Roberts, Walter (The Flea) FL-WR-OE	64-66Cle 67NO 69-70Was	23	5'10"	167	San Jose State		66
Robertson, Bob OT	68HouA		6'4"	246	Illinois		
Robinson, Dave LB	63-72GB 73-74Was		6'3"	243	Penn State	27	6
Robinson, Jerry OE	62-64SD-A 65NY-A	23	5'11"	195	Grambling		30
Robinson, Johnnie DB-FL	66Det 67JJ		6'3"	205	Tennessee State		6
Robinson, Johnny DB-HB	60-62DalA 63-69KC-A 70-71KC	2	6'	200	Louisiana State	57	108
Robotti, Frank LB	61BosA		6'	220	Boston College	2	
Rochester, Paul DT	60-62DalA 63KC-A 63-69NY-A		6'2"	254	Michigan State		
Rock, Walt OT-DT	63-67SF 68-73Was		6'5"	252	Maryland		
Roderick, John FL-WR	66-67MiaA 68OakA	2	6'1"	180	S.M.U.		6
Roedel, Herb OG	61OakA		6'3"	230	Marquette		
Roehnelt, Bill LB	58-59ChiB 60Was 61-62DenA		6'1"	227	Bradley		
Rogers, Don C-OG	60LA-A 61-64SD-A		6'2"	245	South Carolina		
Rohde, Len OT-DE	60-74SF		6'4"	246	Utah State		
Roland, Johnny HB-FB	66-72StL 73NYG	23	6'2"	213	Missouri		216
Rolle, Dave FB	60DenA	2	6'	215	Oklahoma		18
Romeo, Tony OE-TE	61DalA 62-67BosA	2	6'2"	225	Florida State		62
Rosdahl, Hatch DT-OG-DE	64BufA 64-66KC-A		6'5"	250	Penn State		
Rose, George DB	64-66Min 67NO 68JJ		5'11"	190	Auburn	9	6
Rosema, Rocky LB	68-71StL		6'2"	228	Michigan	1	
Ross, Dave OE	60NY-A	2	6'3"	210	Los Angeles State		6
Ross, Willie FB	64BufA		5'10"	200	Nebraska		6
Rowland, Justin DB	60ChiB 61Min 62DenA		6'2"	189	Texas Christian	1	
Rowley, Bob LB	63Pit 64NY-A		6'2"	225	Virginia		
Roy, Frank OG	66StL		6'2"	230	Utah		
Rubke, Karl LB-DE-C-DT	57-60SF 61Min 62-65SF 66-67Atl 68OakA		6'4"	240	Southern Calif.	2	
Rudolph, Jack LB	60, 62-65BosA 66MiaA		6'3"	228	Georgia Tech	3	
Rule, Gordon DB	68-69GB		6'2"	180	Dartmouth		
Ruple, Ernie DT	68Pit		6'4"	256	Arkansas		
Rush, Jerry DT	65-71Det		6'4"	264	Michigan State		
Rushing, Marion LB	59ChicC 62-65StL 66-68Atl 68HouA		6'2"	223	Southern Illinois	4	2

Use Name (Nicknames) – Positions	Team by Year	See Section	Hgt	Wgt	College	Int	Pts
Russ, Pat DT	63Min		6'4"	255	Purdue		
Russell, Benny QB	68BufA		6'1"	190	Louisville		
Rutgens, Joe DT	61-69Was		6'2"	258	Illinois		
Rutkowski, Charlie DE	60BufA		6'3"	248	Ripon		
Rutkowski, Ed FL-HB-OE-QB-WR	63-68BufA	123	6'1"	204	Notre Dame		36
Ryan, Frank QB	58-61LA 62-68Cle 69-70Was	12	6'3"	199	Rice		42
Ryan, Joe DE	60NY-A		6'2"	235	Villanova		
Rychlec, Tom OE	58Det 60-62BufA 63DenA	2	6'3"	220	American Inter.		18
Ryder, Nick FB	63-64Det		6'	208	Miami (Fla.)		12
Rzempolich, Ted DB	63Was		6'1"	195	Virginia		
Sabel, Ron OT-OG	60-61OakA		6'2"	238	Purdue		
Sabatino, Bill DT	68Cle 69Atl		6'3"	245	Colorado		
Safford, Saint WR	68CinA	2	6'4"	202	San Jose State		
Saidock, Tom DT	59Phi 58JJ 60-61NY-A 62BufA		6'5"	261	Michigan State		
Saimes, George DB-HB	63-69BufA 70-72Den		5'10"	188	Michigan State	22	6
St. Jean, Len OG-DE	64-69BosA 70Bos 71-73NE		6'1"	244	Northern Michigan		
Sample, Johnny DB-HB	58-60Bal 61-62Pit 63-65Was 63-68NY-A	3	6'1"	203	Md. Eastern Shore	41	36
Sandeman, Bill OT-DT	65KJ 66Dal 67NO 67-73Atl		6'6"	254	U. of Pacific		
Sanders, Bob LB	67Atl 68JJ		6'3"	235	North Texas State		
Sanders, Daryl OT	63-63Det		6'5"	248	Ohio State		
Sanders, Lonnie DB	63-67Was 68-69StL		6'3"	206	Michigan State	12	
Sandusky, Alex OG	54-66Bal		6'1"	235	Clarion St. (Pa.)		
Sandusky, Mike OG	57-65Pit		6'	231	Maryland		
Sapienza, Rick DB-HB	60NY-A		5'11"	185	Villanova		
Sapp, Theron HB-FB	59-63Phi 63-65Pit 66JJ	2	6'1"	203	Georgia		30
Sardisco, Tony OG-LB	56Was 56SF 60-62BosA		6'2"	226	Tulane		
Sartin, Dan DT	69SD-A		6'1"	245	Mississippi		
Satcher, Doug LB	66-68BosA		6'	221	Southern Miss.	1	2
Sauer, George WR-OE	65-69NY-A 70NYJ	2	6'1"	199	Texas		172
Saul, Bill LB	62-63Bal 64,66-68Pit 69NO 70Det		6'4"	225	Penn State	4	2
Sauls, Mac DB	68-69Atl		6'	185	SW Texas State		
Saxton, Jimmy HB	62DalA		5'11"	173	Texas		
Sayers, Gale HB	65-71ChiB	23	6'	199	Kansas		336
Sayers, Ron HB	69SD-A		6'1"	202	Nebraska-Omaha		
Sbranti, Ron LB	66DenA		6'2"	230	Utah State		
Scales, Charlie FB-HB	60-61Pit 62-65Cle 66Atl	23	5'11"	214	Indiana		30
Scarpati, Joe DB-HB	64-69Phi 70NO 71JJ		5'10"	185	N. Carolina State	25	18
Scarpitto, Bob FL-WR	61SD-A 62-67DenA 68BosA	2 4	5'11"	194	Notre Dame		170
Schaffer, Joe LB	60BufA		6'	210	Tennessee	1	
Schafrath, Dick OT-OG-DE	57-71Cle		6'3"	253	Ohio State		
Schick, Doyle LB	61Was		6'1"	210	Kansas		
Schleicher, Maury LB-DE	59ChiC 60LA-A 61-62SD-A		6'3"	238	Penn State	1	
Schmautz, Ray LB	66OakA		6'1"	225	San Diego State		
Schmedding, Jim OG	68-69SD-A 70SD		6'2"	250	Weber State		
Schmidt, Bob C-OT-OG	59-60NYG 61-63HouA 64-65BosA 66-67BufA		6'4"	248	Minnesota		
Schmidt, Henry DT-DE	59-60SF 61-64SD-A 65BufA 66NY-A		6'4"	258	Southern Calif., Trinity (Texas)	1	6
Schmidt, Roy OG-OT	67-68NO 69Atl 70Was 71Min		6'3"	250	Long Beach State		
Schmitt, John C	64-69NY-A 70-73NYJ 74GB		6'4"	253	Hofstra		
Schmitz, Bob LB	61-66Pit 66Min		6'1"	235	Montana State	3	8
Schoenke, Ray OG-OT-C	63-64Dal 66-75Was		6'3"	246	S.M.U.		
Scholtz, Bob C-OG	60-64Det 65-66NYG		6'4"	250	Notre Dame		
Schottenheimer, Marty LB	65-68BufA 69BosA 70Bos		6'3"	225	Pittsburgh	6	6
Schuh, Harry OT-OG	65-69OakA 70Oak 71-73LA 74GB		6'2"	260	Memphis State		
Schultz, Randy HB-FB	66Cle 67-68NO	2	5'11"	210	Iowa State		12
Schumacher, Gregg DE	67-68LA		6'2"	240	Illinois		
Schweda, Brian DE	65HJ 66ChiB 67-68NO		6'3"	240	Kansas		
Schwedes, Ger HB	60-61BosA		6'1"	205	Syracuse		
Schweickert, Bob HB-FL	65,67NY-A		6'1"	193	Virginia Tech		
Scibelli, Joe OG	61-75LA		6'1"	256	Notre Dame		
Scott, Bill DB	68DenA		6'	188	Idaho		
Scott, John DT	60-61BufA		6'4"	260	Ohio State		
Scott, Lew DB	66DenA		5'10"	173	Oregon State		
Scott, Wilbert LB	61Pit		6'	215	Indiana		
Scotti, Ben DB	59-61Was 62-63Phi 64SF		6'1"	185	Maryland	10	
Scrabis, Bob QB	60-62NY-A	1	6'3"	223	Penn State		6
Scrutchins, Ed DE	66HouA		6'3"	260	Toledo		
Sczurek, Stan LB	63-65Cle 66NYG		5'11"	229	Purdue	1	
Seals, George DT-OG-OT	64Was 65-71ChiB 72-73KC		6'2"	259	Missouri	1	6
Sedlock, Bob OT	60BufA		6'4"	295	Georgia		
Seedborg, John K	65Was 66MS		6'	227	Arizona State		
Selawski, Gene OT-OG	59LA 60Cle 61SD-A		6'4"	252	Purdue		
Sellers, Goldie DB	66-67DenA 68-69KC-A 70LJ	3	6'2"	198	Grambling	13	30
Sestak, Tom DT-OT	62-68BufA		6'5"	267	McNeese State	2	18
Shackleford, Don OG	64DenA		6'4"	255	U. of Pacific		
Shann, Bob DB	65Phi 66JJ 67Phi		6'1"	189	Boston College	1	6
Shannon, Carver DB-HB	62-64LA	3	6'1"	201	Southern Illinois	4	6
Sharockman, Ed DB	61BN 62-72Min		6'	200	Pittsburgh	40	36
Shaw, Billy OG	61-69BufA		6'3"	250	Georgia Tech		
Shaw, Glen FB-HB	60ChiB 62LA 63-64OakA	2	6'1"	221	Kentucky		24
Shaw, Nate LB	69-70LA		6'2"	205	Southern Calif.		
Shaw, Jerry DT	66-67Min 68-69Atl 70-71NYG		6'3"	244	Purdue		
Shea, Pat OG	62-65SD-A 66JJ		6'1"	241	Southern Calif.		
Sherer, Dave OE	59Bal 60Dal	4	6'3"	218	S.M.U.		
Sherlag, Bob FL	66Atl		6'	197	Memphis State		6
Sherman, Bob DB	64-65Pit		6'2"	195	Iowa	1	
Sherman, Tom QB	68-69BosA 69BufA	12	6'	190	Penn State		
Shields, Lebron DE-OT	60Bal 61Min		6'4"	243	Tennessee		2
Shiner, Dick QB	64-66Was 67Cle 68-69Pit 70NYG 71,73Atl 73-74NE	12	6'	197	Maryland		12
Shinnick, Don LB	57-69Bal		6'	232	U.C.L.A.	37	
Shirkey, George DT	60-61HouA 62OakA		6'4"	252	Austin		
Shivers, Roy HB	66-72StL	23	6'	200	Utah State		90
Shoals, Roger OT-OG	63-64Cle 65-70Det 71Den		6'4"	256	Maryland		6
Shockley, Bill HB-K	60-61NY-A 61BufA 62NY-A 68Pit	23 5	6'	185	West Chester St.		181
Shofner, Del OE-DB	57-60LA 61-67NYG	2 4	6'3"	186	Baylor	3	306
Shofner, Jim DB	58-63Cle	3	6'2"	191	Texas Christian	20	
Shonta, Chuck DB	60-67BosA		6'	196	Eastern Michigan	15	6
Shorter, Jim DB	62-63Cle 64-67Was 69Pit		5'11"	184	Detroit	15	6

Use Name (Nicknames) – Positions	Team by Year	See Section	Hgt	Wgt	College	Int	Pts
Shy, Les HB	68-69Dal 70NYG	23	6'1"	202	Long Beach State		24
Sidle, Jimmy TE-HB	66Atl		6'2"	215	Auburn		
Sieminski, Chuck DT	63-65SF 66-67Atl 68Det		6'4"	262	Penn State		
Silas, Sam DT-DE	63-67StL 68NYG 69-70SF		6'4"	251	Southern Illinois		
Silvestri, Carl DB	65StL 66Atl		6'	195	Wisconsin		
Simkus, Arnie DT-DE	65NY-A 67Min		6'4"	245	Michigan		
Simmons, Dave LB	65-66StL 67NO 68Dal		6'4"	245	Georgia Tech	2	
Simmons, Jerry WR-OE	65-67Pit 67NO 67-69Atl 69ChiB 71-74Den	2	6'1"	190	Bethune-Cookman		54
Simmons, Leon LB	63DenA		6'	225	Grambling		
Simms, Bob LB-OE-DE	60-61NYG 62Pit		6'1"	223	Rutgers		
Simon, Jim OG-OT-DE-LB	63-65Det 66-68Atl		6'5"	235	Miami (Fla.)		
Simpson, Howard DE	64Min		6'5"	230	Auburn		
Simpson, Jackie DB	58-60Bal 61-62Pit		5'10"	183	Florida	2	
Simpson, Jackie LB	61DenA 62-64OakA	5	6'1"	226	Mississippi	5	15
Simpson, Willie FB	62OakA		6'	218	San Fran. State		
Singer, Karl OT	66-68BosA		6'3"	250	Purdue		
Sisk, John DB	64ChiB		6'3"	195	Miami (Fla.)		
Skaggs, Jim OG-OT	62BN 63-67Phi 68KJ 69-72Phi		6'2"	246	Washington		
Sklopan, John DB	63DenA		5'11"	190	Southern Miss.		
Skoronski, Bob OT-C	56GB 57-58MS 59-69GB		6'3"	249	Indiana		
Slaby, Lou LB-DT	64-65NYG 66Det		6'3"	235	Pittsburgh		
Slaughter, Mickey QB	63-66DenA	12	6'	190	Louisiana Tech.		8
Sligh, Richard DT	67OakA		7'	300	N.Car. Central		
Sloan, Steve QB	66-67Atl	1	6'	185	Alabama		
Smiley, Tom FB	68CinA 69DenA 70Hou	2	6'1"	235	Lamar Tech		30
Smith, Allen HB	66NY-A		5'11"	195	Findlay		
Smith, Allen HB	66-67BufA	2	6'	200	Ft. Valley State		
Smith, Billy Ray DT-DE	57LA 58-60Pit 61-62Bal 63JJ 64-70Bal		6'4"	240	Arkansas	1	
Smith, Bob DB	68HouA		6'	180	Miami-Ohio		
Smith, Bobby DB	62-65LA 65-66Det	3	6'	193	U.C.L.A.	5	12
Smith, Bobby HB	64-65BufA 66Pit	2	6'	203	North Texas State		30
Smith, Carl FB	60BufA		6'	200	Tennessee		6
Smith, Dan DB	61DenA		5'10"	180	NE State-Okla.		
Smith, Dave FB	60-64HouA		6'1"	209	Ripon		108
Smith, Dick DB-HB-OE	67-68Was		6'	205	Northwestern	4	
Smith, Don OG	67DenA		6'4"	240	Florida A&M		
Smith, Fletcher DB	66-67KC-A 68-69CinA 70-71Cin		6'2"	182	Tennessee State	15	2
Smith, Gordon OE	61-65Min	2	6'2"	211	Missouri		78
Smith, Hal DT	60BosA 60DenA 61OakA		6'5"	250	U.C.L.A.		
Smith, Hugh OE	62Was		6'4"	215	Kansas		
Smith, Jackie TE-OE	63-77StL	2 4	6'4"	225	NW State-La.		258
Smith, J. D. FB-HB-DB	56ChiB 56-64SF 65-66Dal	2	6'1"	205	N. Carolina A&T	2	276
Smith, J. D. OT	59-63Phi 64Det 65JJ 66Det		6'5"	250	Rice		6
Smith, J. D. (Jet Stream) FB-HB	60OakA 61ChiB	2	6'	215	Compton J.C.		
Smith, Jeff LB	66NYG 67KJ		6'	237	Southern Calif.	1	
Smith, Jim DB	68Was		6'3"	195	Oregon		6
Smith, Jimmy DB	69DenA		6'3"	190	Utah State		
Smith, Jim Ray OG-OT-DE	56-62Cle 63-64Dal		6'3"	241	Baylor		
Smith, Noland (Super Gnat) WR-FL-HB	67-69KC-A 69SF	3	5'6"	155	Tennessee State		12
Smith, Ralph (Catfish) TE-OE-DB	62-64Phi 65-68Cle 69Atl	2	6'2"	214	Missipi		36
Smith, Ron QB	65LA 66Pit	1	6'5"	220	Richmond		
Smith, Russ HB-FB	67-69SD-A 70SD	2	6'1"	214	Miami (Fla.)		60
Smith, Tommie WR	69CinA		6'4"	190	San Jose State		
Smith, Willie OG-OT	60DenA 61OakA		6'2"	255	Michigan		
Smith, Zeke OG-DE-LB	60Bal 61NYG		6'2"	233	Auburn		
Smolinski, Mark FB-TE	61-62Bal 63-68NY-A	2	6'	218	Wyoming		102
Snead, Norm QB	61-63Was 64-70Phi 71Min 72-74NYG 74-75SF 76NYG	12	6'4"	215	Wake Forest		138
Snell, Matt FB	64-69NY-A 70-72NYJ	2	6'2"	220	Ohio State		186
Snidow, Ron DE-DT	63-67Was 68-72Cle		6'4"	249	Oregon	1	2
Snorton, Matt OE	64DenA		6'5"	250	Michigan State		
Snowden, Jim OT-DE	65-71Was 72JJ		6'3"	255	Notre Dame		
Snyder, Al FL	64BosA		6'	195	Holy Cross		
Soborinski, Phil C	68Atl		6'3"	235	Wisconsin		
Soleau, Bob LB	64Pit		6'2"	235	William & Mary		
Soltis, Bob DB	60-61BosA		6'2"	205	Minnesota	2	
Sommer, Mike HB-DB	58-59Was 59-61Bal 61Was 63OakA	2	5'11"	190	George Washington		12
Songin, Butch QB	60-61BosA 62NY-A	12	6'2"	200	Boston College		18
Sorey, Jim DT	60-62BufA		6'4"	278	Texas Southern		
Sorrell, Henry LB	67DenA		6'1"	215	Tenn.-Chattanooga		
Sortun, Rick OG	64-69StL		6'2"	234	Washington		
South, Ronnie QB	68NO	1	6'1"	195	Arkansas		
Speights, Dick DB	68SD-A		5'11"	175	Wyoming		
Spence, Julian (Sus) DB-FL	56ChiC 57SF 60-61HouA		5'11"	170	Sam Houston St.	6	
Spikes, Jack FB	60-62DalA 63-64KC-A 64SD-A 65HouA 66-67BufA	2 5	6'2"	221	Texas Christian		262
Spiller, Phil DB	67StL 68Atl 68CinA		6'	195	Los Angeles State	2	
Stacy, Billy DB-HB	59ChiC 60-63StL	23	6'1"	191	Mississippi State	20	42
Stafford, Dick DE-DT	62-63Phi		6'4"	253	Texas Tech		
Stalcup, Jerry LB-OG	60LA 61-62DenA		6'	230	Wisconsin	1	
Stallings, Don DT-DE-OT	60Was		6'4"	250	North Carolina		
Stallings, Larry LB	63-76StL		6'2"	230	Georgia Tech	9	18
Stanciel, Jeff HB	69Atl		6'	192	Miss. Valley St.		
Stanton, Jack HB	61Pit		6'1"	190	N. Carolina State		
Starks, Marsh DB	63-64NY-A	3	6'	190	Illinois	1	6
Starling, Bruce DB	63DenA		6'1"	186	Florida		
Starr, Bart QB	56-71GB HC75-77GB	12	6'1"	197	Alabama		90
Staten, Randy DE	67NYG		6'1"	225	Minnesota		
Steffen, Jim DB	59-61Det 61-65Was 66JJ	3	6'	196	U.C.L.A.	17	12
Stenhouwer, Ron OG-OT	60-64Pit		6'2"	232	Colorado State		
Stephens, Harold QB	62NY-A		5'11"	175	Hardin-Simmons		
Stephens, Larry DE-DT	60-61Cle 62LA 63-67Dal		6'4"	245	Texas	1	6
Stephens, Tom OE-DB	60-64BosA	2	6'1"	207	Syracuse	1	36
Stephenson, Kay QB	67SD-A 68BufA	1	6'1"	208	Florida		
Stetz, Bill OG	67Phi		6'3"	250	Boston College		
Stevens, Bill QB	68-69GB		6'3"	195	Texas-El Paso		
Stickles, Monte OE-TE	60-67SF 68NO	2	6'4"	232	Notre Dame		96
Stiger, Jim HB-FB	63-65Dal 65-67LA	23	5'11"	204	Washington		24
Stinnette, Jim FB-LB	61-62DenA	2	6'1"	230	Oregon State	1	12
Stith, Carel DT-DE	67-69HouA		6'5"	267	Nebraska		

Use Name (Nicknames) – Positions	Team by Year	See Section	Hgt	Wgt	College	Int	Pts
Stoepel, Terry TE	67ChiB 68-69MS 70Hou		6'4"	235	Tulsa		
Stofa, John QB	66-67MiaA 68-69CinA 69MiaA 70Mia	1	6'3"	210	Buffalo		6
Stokes, Jesse DB	68DenA		6'	190	Corpus Christi		
Stokes, Sims OE	67Dal		6'1"	198	Northern Arizona		
Stone, Donnie HB-FB	61-64DenA 65BufA 66HouA	2	6'2"	205	Arkansas		102
Stone, Jack OT	60DalA 61-62OakA		6'2"	245	Oregon		
Stonebraker, Steve LB-OE	62-63Min 64-66Bal 67-68NO	2	6'3"	223	Detroit	2	12
Stotter, Rich LB	68HouA		6'	225	Houston		
Stovall, Jerry DB	63-71StL	34	6'2"	201	Louisiana State	18	12
Stover, Smokey LB	60-62DalA 63-66KC-A		6'	229	Northeast La.	6	
Strahan, Art DT	68Atl		6'5"	266	Texas Southern		
Strahan, Ray DE	65HouA		6'6"	250	Texas Southern		
Stram, Hank	HC60-62DalA HC63-69KC-A HC70-74KC HC76-77NO				Purdue		
Strand, Eli OG	66Pit 67NO		6'2"	250	Iowa State		
Stransky, Bob HB	60DenA	2	6'1"	180	Colorado		
Stratton, Mike LB	62-69BufA 70-72Buf 73SD		6'3"	236	Tennessee	21	12
Stricker, Tony DB	63NY-A		6'	185	Colorado	1	
Strickland, Dave OG	60DenA		6'	220	Memphis State		
Strofolino, Mike LB	65LA 65Bal 66-68StL		6'2"	223	Villanova		
Stromberg, Mike LB	68NY-A		6'2"	235	Temple		
Struger, George DT	57-61LA 62Pit 62-63NY-A		6'5"	259	Washington	1	
Studstill, Pat FL-WR	61-62Det 63JJ 64-67Det 68-71LA 72NE	234	6'1"	176	Houston		114
Sturm, Jerry C-OT-OG-FB	61-66DenA 67-70NO 71Hou 72Phi		6'3"	257	Illinois		
Stynchula, Andy DE-DT-C	60-63Was 64-65NYG 66-67Bal 68Dal	5	6'3"	252	Penn State		22
Suchy, Larry DB	68Atl		5'11"	180	Mississippi Coll.		
Suci, Bob DB	62HouA 63BosA	3	5'10'	182	Michigan State	9	12
Suggs, Walt OT-C	62-69HouA 70-71Hou		6'5"	257	Mississippi State		
Sullivan, Dan OG-OT	62-72Bal		6'3"	250	Boston College		
Sommers, Jim DB	67DenA		5'10"	175	Michigan State		
Sunde, Milt OG-C	64-74Min		6'2"	245	Minnesota		
Sutro, John OT	62SF		6'4"	245	San Jose State		
Sutton, Archie OT	65-67Min		6'4"	263	Illinois		
Sutton, Mickey DB	66HouA		6'	190	Auburn		
Svihus, Bob OT-OG	65-69OakA 70Oak 71-73NYJ		6'4"	245	Southern Calif.		
Swain, Bill LB	63LA 64Min 65NYG 66KJ 67 NYG 68-69Det		6'2"	229	Oregon	2	6
Swanson, Terry K	67-68BosA 69CinA	4	6'	210	Massachusetts		
Swatland, Dick OG	68HouA		6'3"	245	Notre Dame		
Sweeney, Neal OE	67DenA		6'2"	170	Tulsa		
Sweeney, Walt OG	63-69SD-A 70-73SD 74-75Was 76KJ		6'3"	256	Syracuse		
Sweetan, Karl QB	66-67Det 68NO 69-70LA	12	6'1"	203	Wake Forest		12
Swinford, Wayne DB-OE-FL	65-67SF		6'	194	Georgia		
Swink, Jim HB	60DalA		6'1"	185	Texas Christian		
Sykes, Gene DB	63-65BufA 67DenA		6'1"	196	Louisiana State	4	
Symand, Johnny DB	57-62GB 63StL		5'11"	180	Florida	19	6
Szczecko, Joe DT	66-68Atl 69NYG		6'	245	Northwestern		
Szymakowski, Dave WR	68NO		6'2"	198	West Texas State		
Szymanski, Dick C-LB	55Bal 56MS 57-68Bal		6'3"	233	Notre Dame	6	6
Talamini, Bob OG	60-67HouA 68NY-A		6'1"	249	Kentucky		
Talbert, Don OT-LB	62Dal 63-64MS 65Dal 66-68Atl 69-70NO 71Dal		6'5"	248	Texas		
Taliferro, Mike QB	64-67NY-A 68-69BosA 70Bos 71NE 72Buf	12	6'2"	206	Illinois		2
Tarasovic, George DE-LB-C	52-53Pit 54-55MS 56-63Pit 63-65Phi 66DenA		6'4"	245	Lousiana State	7	18
Tarbox, Bruce OG	61LA		6'2"	230	Syracuse		
Tarkenton, Fran QB	61-66Min 67-71NYG 72-77Min	12	6'1"	190	Georgia		186
Tarr, Jerry HB	62DenA		6'	190	Oregon		12
Tatman, Pete HB	67Min		6'1"	220	Nebraska		
Taylor, Bob DE-DT	63-64NYG		6'3"	238	Md. Eastern Shore		
Taylor, Jim FB	58-66GB 67NO	2	6'	214	Louisiana State		558
Taylor, Lionel OE-WR-FL	59ChiB 60-66DenA 67-68HouA	2	6'2"	215	N. Mex. Highlands		270
Taylor, Rosey DB	61-69ChiB 69-71SF 72Was 73JJ	3	5'11"	186	Grambling	32	36
Taylor, Sammy FL	65SD-A		6'	190	Grambling		
Tensi, Steve QB	65-66SD-A 67-69DenA 70Den	12	6'5"	213	Florida State		
Teresa, Tony HB	58SF 60OakA	2	5'9"	188	San Jose State		60
Terrell, Marvin OG	60-62DalA 63KC-A		6'1"	236	Mississippi		
Tharp, Corky DB	60NY-A		5'10"	180	Alabama	2	
Theofiledes, Harry QB	68Was		5'10"	180	Waynesberg		
Thibert, Jim LB	65DenA		6'3"	230	Toledo		
Thomas, Aaron TE-OE-FL-WR	61-62SF 62-70NYG	2	6'3"	209	Oregon State		222
Thomas, Clendon DB-OE-FL-HB	58-61LA 62-68Pit	2	6'2"	196	Oklahoma	27	30
Thomas, Gene HB	66-67KC-A 68BosA 68OakA	2	6'1"	210	Florida A&M		36
Thomas, John OG-OT-LB	58-67SF 68JJ		6'4"	246	U. of Pacific		
Thompson, Bobby DB	64-68Det 69NO	3	5'10"	179	Arizona	10	
Thompson, Don DE	62-63Bal 64Phi		6'4"	230	Richmond		
Thompson, Jim DT	65DenA		6'3"	255	Southern Illinois		
Thornton, Bill FB	63-65StL 66JJ 67StL	2	6'1"	214	Nebraska		12
Thornton, Bubba WR	69BufA	23	6'	175	Texas Christian		
Thornton, Jack LB	66MiaA		6'1"	230	Auburn		
Thurlow, Steve HB-FB	64-66NYG 66-68Was	2	6'3"	217	Stanford		36
Thurston, Fuzzy OG	58Bal 59-67GB		6'1"	247	Valparaiso		
Tidmore, Sam LB	62-63Cle		6'1"	223	Ohio State		
Tiller, Jim HB	62NY-A	2	5'9"	165	Purdue		
Timberlake, Bob QB	65NYG	5	6'4"	220	Michigan		24
Tingelhoff, Mike C	62-77Min		6'1"	237	Nebraska		
Tobey, Dave LB	66-67Min 68DenA		6'3"	230	Oregon		
Tobin, Bill HB	63HouA	2	5'11"	210	Missouri		32
Toburen, Nelson LB	61-62GB		6'3"	235	Wichita State		
Todd, Jim HB	66Det		5'11"	195	Ball State		
Todd, Larry HB	65-69OakA 70Oak	23	6'1"	185	Arizona State		42
Tolar, Charley FB-HB	60-66HouA	2	5'7"	199	NW State-La.		138
Tolleson, Tommy DB	66Atl		6'	185	Alabama		
Toner, Ed DT-LB	67-69BosA 70JJ		6'3"	250	Massachusetts		
Torczon, Lavern DE	60-62BufA 62-65NY-A 66MiaA		6'2"	243	Nebraska	2	6
Townes, Willie DE-DT	66-68Dal 69JJ 70NO		6'5"	263	Tulsa		8
Towns, Bobby DB-DE-HB	60StL 61BosA		6'1"	180	Georgia		
Tracey, John (Jack) LB-OE-TE	59ChiC 60StL 61Phi 62-67BufA	2	6'3"	225	Texas A&M	12	4
Tracy, Tom (Tom the Bomb) HB-FB	56-57Det 58-63Pit 63-64Was	12	5'9"	205	Tennessee		199

Use Name (Nicknames) – Positions	Team by Year	See Section	Hgt	Wgt	College	Int	Pts
Trammell, Allen DB	66HouA		6'	190	Florida		
Trapp, Richard WR	68BufA 69SD-A	2	6'1"	174	Florida		
Trask, Orville DT	60-61HouA 62OakA		6'4"	260	Rice	1	
Travenio, Herb K	64-65SD-A	5	6'	218	none		110
Travis, John FB	66SD-A		6'1"	216	San Jose State		
Traynham, Jerry HB	61DenA		5'10"	190	Southern Calif.		
Traynham, Wade K	66-67Atl	5	6'2"	218	Frederick		45
Trimble, Wayne DB	67SF		6'3"	203	Alabama		
Triplett, Bill HB-FB-DB	62-63StL 64IL 65-66StL 67NYG 68-72Det	23	6'2"	212	Miami-Ohio	1	132
Tripucka, Frank QB	49Det 50-52ChiC 52Dal 53-59CFL 60-63DenA	12 4	6'2"	192	Notre Dame		36
Trosch, Gene DE-DT	67KC-A 68JJ 69KC-A 70LJ		6'7"	277	Miami (Fla.)		
Truax, Billy TE-OE	64-70LA 71-73Dal	2	6'5"	238	Louisiana State		108
Truax, Dalton OT	60OakA		6'2"	235	Tulane		
Trull, Don QB	64-67HouA 67BosA 68-69HouA	12	6'1"	189	Baylor		84
Tubbs, Jerry LB-C	57-58ChiC 56-59SF 60-66Dal		6'2"	221	Oklahoma	17	
Tucker, Bill FB-HB-TE	67-70SF 71ChiB	23	6'2"	221	Tennessee State		78
Tucker, Gary HB	68MiaA		5'11"	195	Tenn.-Chatanooga		
Tucker, Wendell WR-OE	67-70LA	2	5'10"	185	S. Carolina State		66
Tuckett, Phil WR	68SD-A		6'	180	Weber State		
Turner, Bake OE-WR-FL	62Bal 63-69NY-A 70Bos	23	6'	180	Texas Tech		150
Turner, Herschel OG-OT	64-65StL		6'3"	230	Kentucky		
Turner, Vince DB	64NY-A		5'11"	190	Missouri	1	
Tyrer, Jim OT	61-62DalA 63-69KC-A 70-73KC 74Was		6'6"	283	Ohio State		
Tyson, Dick OG	66OakA 67DenA		6'2"	245	Tulsa		
Underwood, Olen LB	65NYG 66-69HouA 70Hou 71Den		6'1"	224	Texas	5	2
Unitas, Johnny QB	56-72Bal 73SD	12	6'1"	194	Louisville		78
Urbanek, Jim DT	68MiaA		6'4"	270	Mississippi		
Urenda, Herm DB-OE	63OakA		5'11"	170	U. of Pacific		
Valdez, Vern DB	60LA 61BufA 62OakA		5'11"	190	San Diego	7	
Vallez, Emilio TE	68-69ChiB		6'2"	210	New Mexico		
Vander Kelen, Ron QB	63-67Min	12	6'1"	186	Wisconsin		6
Vandersea, Phil LB-DE-TE	66GB 67NO 68-69GB		6'3"	228	Massachusetts		
Van Raaphorst, Dick K	64Dal 66-67SD-A	5	5'11"	215	Ohio State		247
Vargo, Larry DB-OE-LB	62-63Det 64-65Min 66NYG 67KJ		6'3"	212	Detroit	6	6
Varrichione, Frank OT	55-60Pit 61-65LA		6'1"	234	Notre Dame		
Vasys, Aruras HB	66-68Phi		6'2"	232	Notre Dame		
Vaughn, Bob OG	68DenA		6'4"	240	Mississippi		
Vaughn, Tom DB	65-71Det	3	5'11"	192	Iowa State	9	
Vellone, Jim OG-OT	66-70Min 71IL		6'2"	255	Southern Calif.		
Vereb, Ed HB	60Was		6'	190	Maryland		
Villanueva, Danny K	60-64LA 65-67Dal	45	5'11"	202	New Mexico State		491
Viltz, Theo DB	66HouA		6'2"	190	Southern Calif.		
Vogel, Bob OT	63-72Bal		6'5"	248	Ohio State		
Voight, Bob DT	61OakA		6'5"	265	Los Angeles State		
Vollenweider, Jim HB-FB	62-63SF	2	6'1"	210	Miami (Fla.)		12
Von Sonn, Andy LB	64LA		6'2"	223	U.C.L.A.		
Voss, Lloyd DE-DT-OT	64-65GB 66-71Pit 72Den		6'4"	256	Nebraska	1	
Wade, Billy QB	54-60LA 61-66ChiB	12	6'2"	204	Vanderbilt		144
Wade, Bob DB	68Pit 69Was 70Den		6'2"	200	Morgan State	1	
Wade, Tom QB	64-65Pit	1	6'2"	195	Texas		
Wagstaff, Jim DB	59ChiC 60-61BufA		6'2"	192	Idaho State	9	6
Wainscott, Loyd LB	69HouA 70Hou		6'1"	235	Texas-Austin		
Walker, Clarence HB	63DenA		6'1"	205	Southern Illinois		
Walter, Malcolm C-OT	65KJ 66-69Dal 70GB		6'4"	249	Rice		
Walker, Mickey OG-LB-C	61-65NYG		6'	232	Michigan State		
Walker, Wayne LB	58-72Det	5	6'2"	225	Idaho	14	345
Walker, Wayne K	67KC-A 68HouA	5	6'2"	215	NW State-La.		50
Walker, Willie FL	66Det		6'3"	200	Tennessee State		
Wallace, Henry DB	60LA-A		6'	195	U. of Pacific		
Waller, Charlie	HC69SD-A HC70SD				Georgia		
Walsh, Ed OT	61NY-A		6'4"	243	Widener		
Walters, Tom DB	64-67Was		6'2"	195	Southern Miss.	3	6
Walton, Joe OE-DE	57-60Was 61-63NYG 64XJ	2	5'11"	202	Pittsburgh	1	168
Walton, Sam OT	68-69NY-A 71Hou		6'5"	270	East Texas State		
Wantland, Hal DB	66MiaA		6'	195	Tennessee		
Ward, Carl DB	67-68Cle 69NO	3	5'9"	180	Michigan	1	6
Ward, Jim QB	67-68Bal 71Phi 72JJ	1	6'2"	197	Gettysburg		
Ward, Paul DT	61-62Det		6'3"	247	Whitworth		
Warlick, Ernie DE	62-65BufA	2	6'4"	234	N. Carolina Central		24
Warner, Charley DB-HB	63-64KC-A 64-66BufA 67JJ	3	5'11"	178	Prairie View	7	30
Warren, Dewey QB	68CinA	1	6'	205	Tennessee		
Warren, Jimmy DB	64-65SD-A 66-69MiaA 70-74,77Oak	3	5'11"	178	Illinois	25	24
Warwick, Lonnie LB	65-72Min 73-74Atl 75WFL		6'3"	235	Tennessee Tech	12	6
Warzeka, Ron DT	60OakA		6'4"	250	Montana State		
Washington, Clarence DT	69-70Pit 71JJ		6'3"	265	Ark.-Pine Bluff		
Washington, Clyde DB-HB	60-61BosA 63-65NY-A		6'	202	Purdue	9	
Washington, Dave TE	68DenA		6'4"	228	Southern Calif.		
Washington, Dick DB	68MiaA		6'1"	205	Bethune-Cookman		
Washington, Fred OT	68Was		6'5"	268	North Texas State		
Washington, Ted HB	68CinA		5'11"	210	San Diego State		
Waskiewicz, Jim C-OT-LB	66-67NY-A 69Atl		6'4"	237	Wichita State		
Waters, Bob QB	60-63SF	12	6'2"	184	Presbyterian		18
Watkins, Tom HB	61Cle 62-65Det 66JJ 67Det 68Pit	23	6'1"	195	Iowa State		102
Watson, Dave OG	63-64BosA		6'1"	225	Georgia Tech		
Watson, Ed LB	69HouA		6'2"	222	Grambling		
Watters, Bob DE	62-64NY-A		6'4"	247	Lincoln (Mo.)		
Wayt, Russell LB	65Dal		6'4"	235	Rice		
Weatherford, Jim DB	69Atl		5'10"	180	Tennessee	1	6
Weatherwax, Jim DT	66-67GB 68KJ 69GB		6'7"	265	Los Angeles State		
Webb, Allan DB-HB	61-65NYG		5'11"	180	Arnold	7	
Webb, Bob HB-DB	61-62BosA 63JJ 64-69BosA 70Bos 71NE		5'10"	196	Iowa State	21	24
Webb, Ken HB-FB	58-62Det 63Cle	23	5'11"	207	Presbyterian		54
Webster, Dave DB	60-61DalA 62JJ		6'4"	218	Prairie View	11	18
Wegener, Bill OG	62-63HouA		5'10"	245	Missouri		
Weir, Sammy FL	65HouA 66NY-A		5'9"	170	Arkansas State		
Weisacosky, Ed LB	67NYG 68-69MiaA 70Mia 71-72NE		6'	228	Miami (Fla.)	3	

Use Name (Nicknames) – Positions	Team by Year	See Section	Hgt	Wgt	College	Int	Pts
Welch, Jim DB-HB	60-67Bal 68Det		6'	191	S.M.U.	5	6
Wellborn, Joe C	66NYG		6'2"	215	Texas A&M		
Wells, Bob OT	68-69SD-A 70SD		6'4"	273	Johnson C. Smith		
Wells, Harold LB	65-68Phi 69NYG		6'2"	221	Purdue	4	6
Wells, Joel HB	61NYG	2	6'1"	198	Clemson		12
Wells, Warren WR-OE	64Det 65-66MS 67-69OakA 70Oak	2	6'1"	191	Texas Southern		258
71—Declared ineligible to play pro football							
Wendryhoski, Joe C-OG	64-66LA 67-68NO		6'2"	245	Illinois		
Wenzel, Ralph OG	66-70Pit 72-73SD		6'3"	244	San Diego State		
Werl, Bob OG-DE	66NY-A		6'3"	240	Miami (Fla.)		
West, Dave DB	63NY-A		6'3"	190	Central St.-Ohio		
West, Mel HB	61BosA 61-62NY-A	2	5'9"	190	Missouri		18
West, Willie DB-HB	60-61StL 62-63BufA 64DenA 64-65NY-A 66-68MiaA	3	5'10"	188	Oregon	30	12
Westmoreland, Dick DB	63-65SD-A 66-69MiaA	3	6'1"	191	N. Carolina A&T	22	12
Wetoska, Bob OT-OG-C	60-69ChiB		6'3"	241	Notre Dame		
Wettstein, Max TE	66DenA		6'3"	217	Florida State		
Whalen, Jim TE-OE	65-69BosA 70-71Den 71Phi	2	6'2"	210	Boston College		120
Wharton, Hogan OG	60-63HouA		6'2"	248	Houston		
Wheeler, Manuch QB	62BufA		6'	190	Maine		
Wheeler, Ted OG-TE	67-68StL 70ChiB		6'3"	240	West Texas State		
Wheelwright, Ernie FB	64-65NYG 66-67Atl 67-70NO	2	6'3"	235	Southern Illinois		96
White, Andre TE	67DenA 68CinA 68SD-A		6'5"	225	Florida A&M		2
White, Bob FB	60HouA		6'2"	220	Ohio State		
White, Freeman TE-DB-LB	66-69NYG	2	6'5"	225	Nebraska	2	6
White, Gene HB	62OakA		6'1"	197	Florida A&M		8
White, Harvey QB	60BosA		6'1"	190	Clemson		
White, John OE	60-61HouA		6'4"	230	Texas Southern		6
Whitehead, Bud DB-FL-HB	61-68SD-A		6'	184	Florida State	15	6
Whitfield, A.D. FB	65Dal 66-68Was	2	5'10"	200	North Texas State		36
Whitley, Hall LB	60NY-A		6'2"	225	Texas A&I		
Whitlow, Bob C-OG	60-61Was 61-65Det 66Atl 68Cle		6'1"	236	Arizona		
Whitmyer, Nat DB	63LA 66SD-A 67JJ		6'	182	Washington	1	
Whitsell, Dave DB-HB	58-60Det 61-66ChiB 67-69NO		6'	189	Indiana	46	30
Whittenton, Jesse DB	56-57LA 58-64GB		6'	193	Texas El-Paso	24	12
Whittingham, Fred LB-OG	63JJ 64LA 66Phi 67-68NO 69Dal 70Bos 71Phi		6'1"	240	Cal. St. Polytech	3	
Wiggin, Paul DE	57-67Cle HC75-77KC		6'3"	242	Stanford	3	12
Wilbur, John OG-DE-DT	66-69Dal 70LA 71-73Was		6'3"	245	Stanford		
Wilburn, J. R. WR-OE	66-70Pit	2	6'2"	190	South Carolina		48
Wilcox, Dave LB	64-74SF		6'3"	235	Oregon	14	12
Wilcox, John OT-DE	60Phi		6'5"	230	Oregon		
Wilder, Bert DE-DT	64-67NY-A		6'3"	245	N. Carolina State		
Will, Erwin DT	65Phi		6'5"	270	Dayton		
Willard, Ken FB	65-73SF 74StL	2	6'2"	225	North Carolina		372
Williams, Bobby DB	59GB 60Cle 61Min	2	6'2"	210	U. of Pacific		6
Williams, Bobby DB	66-67StL 69-71Det	3	6'1"	195	Central State-Okla.	3	12
Williams, Clancy DB-HB	65-72LA	3	6'2"	197	Washington State	28	12
Williams, Clyde OT-OG	67-71StL		6'2"	252	Southern U.		
Williams, Erwin WR	69Pit		6'5"	215	Md. Eastern Shore		6
Williams, Frank FB	61LA		6'2"	215	Pepperdine		
Williams, Howie DB	62-63GB 63SF 64-69OakA		6'2"	188	Howard J.C.	14	
Williams, Jeff HB	66Min		6'1"	210	Oklahoma State		
Williams, Jim DB	69CinA		6'1"	190	Alcorn A&M		
Williams, Maxie OG-OT	65HouA 66-69MiaA 70Mia		6'4"	247	Southeastern La.		
Williams, Monk WR	68CinA		5'7"	155	Ark.-Pine Bluff		
Williams, Ray DT	63StL		6'7"	265	U. of Pacific		
Williams, Sam DE-OE-LB	59LA 60-65Det 66-67Atl		6'5"	235	Michigan State	1	20
Williams, Sid LB-DE	64-66Cle 67Was 68Bal 69Pit		6'2"	235	Southern U.	1	6
Williams, Travis HB	67-70GB 71LA 72KJ	23	6'1"	210	Arizona State		108
Williams, Wandy HB	69DenA 70Den		6'	192	Kansas, Hofstra		6
Williams, Willie DB	65NYG 66OakA 67-73NYG		6'	190	Grambling	35	
Williamson, Fred (The Hammer) DB	60Pit 61-64OakA 65-67KC-A		6'2"	210	Northwestern	35	12
Williamson, J. R. LB-C	64-67OakA 68-69BosA 70Bos 71JJ		6'2"	220	Louisiana Tech	3	
Willsey, Ray	HC61StL				California		
Wilson, Ben FB-HB	63-65LA 67GB 68KJ	2	6'	225	Southern Calif.		66
Wilson, Butch TE-OE	63-67Bal 68-69NYG	2	6'2"	223	Alabama		18
Wilson, Eddie QB	62DalA 63-64KC-A 65BosA 66KJ	1 4	6'	190	Arizona		6
Wilson, George QB	66MiaA	12 4	6'1"	190	Xavier-Ohio		2
Wilson, Harry HB	67Phi 68JJ 69Phi		5'11"	204	Nebraska		
Wilson, Jerrel HB-FB-LB-K	63-69KC-A 70-77KC	4	6'4"	222	Southern Miss.	4	
Wilson, Jim OG-OT	65-66SF 67Atl 68LA 69-71JJ		6'3"	257	Georgia		
Wilson, Larry DB	60-72StL		6'	190	Utah	52	50
Wilson, Mike DB	69StL		5'11"	185	Western Illinois		
Wingate, Heath C	67Was		6'2"	240	Bowling Green		
Wink, Dean DE-DT	67-68Phi		6'4"	246	Yankton		
Winkler, Francis DE	68-69GB		6'3"	230	Memphis State		
Winkler, Randy OG-OT	67Det 68Atl 69-70MS 71GB		6'5"	258	Tarleton State		
Winner, Charlie	HC66-70StL HC74-75NYJ				SE Missouri St., Washington-St.L		
Winslow, Paul HB	60GB		5'11"	200	N. Car. Central		6
Winslow, Kelton DB	67-68LA		6'	195	Wiley		
Winston, Lloyd FB	62-63SF	2	6'2"	215	Southern Calif.		6
Winston, Roy LB	62-76Min		6'1"	226	Louisiana State	12	20
Winter, Bill LB	62-64NYG		6'4"	220	St. Olaf		
Wisener, Gary DB-OE	60Dal 61HouA		6'1"	206	Baylor		
Witcher, Al OE-DE	60HouA		6'1"	200	Baylor	1	6
Witcher, Dick WR-TE-FL	66-73SF	2	6'3"	205	U.C.L.A.		90
Witt, Mel DE-DT	67-69BosA 70Bos		6'3"	261	Texas-Arlington	1	6
Wittenborn, John OG-K	58-60SF 60-62Phi 63JJ	5	6'2"	238	SE Missouri State		101
Woitt, John DB	68-69SF		5'11"	172	Mississippi State	1	6
Wolff, Wayne OG	61BufA		6'2"	243	Wake Forest		
Wolski, Bill FB	66Atl		5'11"	203	Notre Dame		
Womack, Joe HB	62Pit		5'9"	210	Los Angeles State		30
Wondolowski, Bill WR	69SF		5'10"	168	Eastern Montana		
Wood, Bill DB	63NY-A		5'11"	190	West Va. Wesleyan		
Wood, Bo DE	67Atl		6'3"	225	North Carolina		
Wood, Dick QB	62SD-A 62DenA 63-64NY-A 65OakA 66MiaA	12	6'5"	202	Auburn		24
Wood, Duane DB	60-62DalA 63-64KC-A		6'1"	196	Oklahoma State	20	12
Wood, Gary QB	64-66NYG 67NO 68-69NYG	12	5'11"	188	Cornell		37
Wood, Willie DB	60-71GB		5'10"	189	Southern Calif.	48	25
Woodeshick, Tom FB-HB	63-71Phi 72StL	2	6'	219	West Virginia		162
Woodlief, Doug LB	65-69LA 70JJ		6'3"	231	Memphis State	6	
Woods, Glenn DE	69HouA		6'4"	250	Prairie View		
Woodson, Abe DB-HB	58-64SF 65-66StL	3	5'11"	188	Illinois	19	48
Woodson, Freddie OG-DE-DT	67-69MiaA		6'2"	253	Florida A&M		
Woodson, Marv DB-HB	64-69Pit 69NO		6'	195	Indiana	18	12
Woulfe, Mike LB	62Phi 63JJ		6'2"	225	Colorado		
Wright, Ernie OT	60LA-A 61-67SD-A 68-69CinA 70-71Cin 72SD		6'4"	268	Ohio State		
Wright, Gordon OG	67Phi 69NY-A		6'3"	245	Delaware State		
Wright, Jim DB	64DenA		5'11"	190	Memphis State	1	
Wright, John WR	68Atl 69Det 70JJ	2	6'	196	Illinois		18
Wright, Lonnie DB	66-67DenA		6'2"	205	Colorado State	5	
67-72 played in A.B.A.							
Wright, Steve OT-OG	64-67GB 68-69NYG 70Was 71ChiB 72StL		6'6"	250	Alabama		
Wulff, Jim DB-HB	60-61Was		6'1"	185	Michigan State	3	
Yaccino, John DB	62BufA		6'	190	Pittsburgh		
Yates, Bob OT-C-DT	60-65BosA		6'3"	233	Syracuse		
Yearby, Bill DE	66NY-A		6'3"	235	Michigan		
Yelverton, Bill DE	60DenA		6'4"	220	Mississippi	1	6
Yewcic, Tom QB-HB	61-66BosA	12 4	5'11"	185	Michigan State		24
57 played major league baseball							
Yohn, Dave LB	62Bal 63NY-A		6'	223	Gettysburg		
Yoho, Mack DE	60-63BufA	5	6'2"	239	Miami-Ohio	2	97
Youmans, Maury DE-DT	60-62ChiB 63JJ 64-65Dal		6'6"	253	Syracuse		
Young, Jim HB	65-66Min		6'	205	Queens (Ont.)		
Young, Joe DE	60-61DenA		6'3"	245	Arizona		
Youngblood, George DB	66LA 67Cle 67-68NO 69ChiB 63-65OakA		6'3"	204	Los Angeles State	3	6
Youso, Frank OT	58-60NYG 61-62Min 63-65OakA		6'4"	257	Minnesota		
Zaeske, Paul WR	69HouA 70Hou		6'2"	200	North Park		
Zaruba, Carroll DB	60DalA		5'9"	210	Nebraska		
Zawadzkas, Jerry TE	67Det		6'4"	220	Columbia		
Zecher, Rich DT-OT	65OakA 66-67MiaA 67BufA		6'2"	240	Utah State		
Zeman, Bob DB	60LA-A 61SD-A 62-63DenA 64JJ 65-66SD-A		6'1"	202	Wisconsin	17	12

Lifetime Statistics - 1960-1969 Players Section 1 - PASSING
(All men with 25 or more passing attempts)

Name	Years	Att.	Comp.	Comp. Pct.	Yards	Yds./ Att.	TD	Int.	Pct. Int.
Jon Arnett	57-66	33	8	24.2	147	4.5	2	2	6.1
Billy Barnes	57-63,65-66	25	10	40.0	233	9.3	4	4	16.0
Pete Beathard	64-73,75	1282	575	44.9	8176	6.4	43	84	6.6
George Blanda	49-58,60-74	4007	1911	47.7	26920	6.7	236	277	6.9
Zeke Bratkowski	54,57-68,71	1484	762	51.3	10345	7.0	65	122	8.2
Don Breaux	63,65	181	92	50.8	1339	7.4	9	10	5.5
Marlin Briscoe	68-75	233	97	41.6	1697	7.2	14	14	6.0
Bob Brodhead	60	25	7	28.0	75	3.0	0	3	12.0
John Brodie	57-73	4491	2469	55.0	31548	7.0	214	224	5.0
Rudy Bukich	53,56-68	1190	626	52.6	8433	7.1	61	74	6.2
Max Chaboian	66	163	82	50.3	1110	6.8	4	12	7.4
Dennis Claridge	64-66	71	41	57.7	484	6.8	2	2	2.8
Jack Concannon	64-71,74-75	1110	560	50.5	6270	5.6	36	63	5.7
Greg Cook	69,73	200	107	53.5	1865	9.3	15	11	5.5
John David Crow	58-68	70	33	47.1	759	10.8	5	5	7.1
Garry Cuozzo	63-72	1182	584	49.4	7402	6.3	43	55	4.7
Dan Darragh	68-70	296	127	42.9	1352	4.6	4	22	7.4
Cotton Davidson	54,57,60-66,68	1752	770	43.9	11760	6.7	73	108	6.2
Len Dawson	57-75	3741	2136	57.1	28711	7.7	239	183	4.9
Eagle Day	59-60	32	15	46.9	194	6.1	0	2	6.2
Randy Duncan	61	67	25	37.3	361	5.4	1	3	4.5
Hunter Enis	60-62	160	80	50.0	947	5.9	4	6	3.7
Sam Etcheverry	61-62	302	154	51.0	1982	6.6	16	21	7.0
Tom Flores	60-61,63-69	1715	838	48.9	11959	7.0	93	92	5.4
Roman Gabriel	62-77	4498	2366	52.6	29444	6.5	201	149	3.3
Chan Gallegos	62	35	18	51.4	298	8.5	2	3	8.6
Johnny Green	60-63	618	275	44.5	3921	6.3	26	34	5.5
Tom Greene	60-61	63	27	42.9	251	4.0	1	6	9.5
Glynn Griffing	63	40	16	40.0	306	7.7	3	4	10.0
Lee Grosscup	60-62	173	73	42.2	1086	6.3	10	12	6.9
Ralph Gugliemi	55,58-63	626	292	46.6	4119	6.6	24	52	8.3
John Hadl	62-77	4688	2363	50.4	30503	7.1	244	268	5.7
Galen Hall	62-63	150	64	42.7	885	5.9	5	10	6.7
Kim Hammond	68-69	32	15	46.9	147	4.6	0	2	6.3
George Herring	60-61	233	102	43.8	1297	5.6	5	23	9.9
King Hill	58-69	881	429	48.7	5553	6.3	37	71	8.1
Dick Hoak	61-70	40	20	50.0	427	10.7	4	3	7.5
Paul Hornung	57-62,64-66	55	24	43.6	383	7.0	5	4	7.3
John Huarte	66-68,70-72	48	19	39.6	230	4.8	1	5	10.4
Buddy Humphrey	59-66	175	87	49.7	1094	6.3	4	12	6.9
George Izo	60-66	317	132	41.6	1791	5.6	12	32	10.1
Dick Jamieson	60-61	70	35	50.0	586	8.4	6	2	2.9
Charley Johnson	61-75	3392	1737	51.2	24510	7.2	170	181	5.3
Sonny Jurgensen	57-74	4292	2433	57.1	32224	7.6	255	189	4.4
Joe Kapp	67-70	918	449	48.9	5911	6.4	40	64	7.0
Jack Kemp	57,60-67,69	2973	1437	48.3	21222	7.1	114	183	6.2
Tom Kennedy	66	100	55	55.0	748	7.5	7	6	6.0
Billy Kilmer	61-62,64,66-77	2939	1512	53.1	20179	6.9	148	143	4.9
Daryle Lamonica	63-74	2601	1288	49.5	19154	7.4	164	138	5.3
Gary Lane	66-68	43	21	48.8	254	5.9	2	1	2.3
Jim LeClair	67-68	99	46	46.5	678	6.8	2	6	6.1
Jacky Lee	60-69	838	430	51.3	6191	7.4	46	57	6.8
Bruce Lemmerman	68-69	77	28	36.4	370	4.8	1	5	6.5
Pete Liske	64,69-72	778	396	50.9	5170	6.6	30	46	5.9
Richie Lucas	60-61	99	43	43.4	496	5.0	4	7	7.1
Tom Matte	61-72	42	12	28.6	246	5.9	2	2	4.8
John McCormick	62-63,65-66,68	555	214	38.6	2895	5.2	17	38	6.8
Don Meredith	60-68	2308	1170	50.7	17199	7.5	135	111	4.8
Ron Miller	62	43	17	39.5	250	5.8	1	1	2.3
George Mira	64-69,71	346	148	42.8	2110	6.1	19	20	5.8
Earl Morrall	56-76	2689	1379	51.3	20809	7.7	161	148	5.5
Bill Nelsen	63-72	1905	963	50.6	14165	7.4	99	101	5.3
Jim Ninowski	58-69	1048	513	49.0	7133	6.8	34	67	6.4
Terry Nofsinger	61-67	260	118	45.4	1357	5.2	4	12	4.6
Rick Norton	66-70	382	159	41.6	1815	4.8	7	30	7.9
Nick Papac	61	44	13	29.5	173	3.9	2	7	15.8
Babe Parilli	52-53,56-58,60-69	3330	1552	46.6	22671	6.8	178	220	6.6
Milt Plum	57-69	2419	1306	54.0	17536	7.2	132	127	5.3
Warren Rabb	60-62	251	101	40.2	1782	7.1	15	16	6.4
Larry Rakestraw	64,66-68	111	51	45.9	589	5.3	4	9	8.1
Dan Reeves	65-72	32	14	43.8	370	11.6	2	4	12.5
Jerry Reichow	56-57,59-64	38	12	31.6	187	4.9	0	4	10.5
M. C. Reynolds	58-62	450	222	49.3	2932	6.5	17	28	6.2
Jerry Rhome	65-67,69-71	280	139	49.6	1628	5.8	7	14	5.0
Johnny Roach	56,59-64	413	182	44.1	2765	6.7	24	37	9.0
Ed Rutkowski	63-68	102	41	40.2	380	3.7	0	6	5.9
Frank Ryan	58-70	2133	1090	51.1	16042	7.5	149	111	5.2
Bob Scrabis	60-62	26	7	26.9	82	3.2	1	3	11.5
Tom Sherman	68-69	228	92	40.4	1219	5.3	16	16	7.0
Dick Shiner	64-71,73-74	736	354	48.1	4801	6.5	36	43	5.8
Mickey Slaughter	63-66	584	291	49.8	3607	6.3	22	37	6.3
Steve Sloan	66-67	31	10	32.3	134	4.3	0	4	12.9
Ron Smith	65-66	181	79	43.6	1249	6.9	8	12	6.6
Norm Snead	61-76	4353	2276	52.2	30797	7.1	196	257	5.9
Butch Songin	60-62	694	327	47.1	4347	6.3	38	31	4.5
Ronnie South	68	38	14	36.8	129	3.4	1	3	7.9
Bart Starr	56-71	3149	1808	57.4	24718	7.8	152	138	4.4
Kay Stephenson	67-68	105	40	38.1	481	4.6	6	9	8.6
John Stofa	66-70	312	146	46.8	1758	5.6	12	11	3.5
Karl Sweetan	66-70	590	269	45.6	3210	5.4	17	34	5.8
Mike Taliaferro	64-72	966	419	43.4	5241	5.4	36	63	6.5
Fran Tarkenton	61-77	5895	3341	56.8	43535	7.4	317	234	4.0
Steve Tensi	65-70	862	369	42.8	5558	6.4	43	46	5.3
Tom Tracy	56-64	67	24	35.8	854	12.7	6	5	7.5
Frank Tripucka	49-52,60-63	1745	879	50.4	10282	5.9	59	124	7.1
Don Trull	64-69	617	276	44.7	3980	6.5	30	28	4.5
Johnny Unitas	56-73	5186	2830	54.6	40239	7.8	290	253	4.9
Ron Vander Kelen	63-67	252	107	42.5	1375	5.5	6	11	4.4
Billy Wade	54-66	2523	1370	54.3	18530	7.3	124	134	5.3
Tom Wade	64-65	69	34	49.3	470	6.8	2	13	18.8
Jim Ward	67-68,71	26	13	50.0	165	6.3	2	2	7.7
Dewey Warren	68	80	47	58.8	506	6.3	1	4	5.0
Bob Waters	60-63	124	59	47.6	707	5.7	3	8	6.5
Eddie Wilson	62-65	186	90	48.4	1251	6.7	5	6	3.2
George Wilson	66	112	46	41.1	764	6.8	5	10	8.9
Dick Wood	62-66	1193	522	43.8	7151	6.0	51	70	5.9
Gary Wood	64-69	400	186	46.5	2575	6.4	14	23	5.7
Tom Yewcic	61-66	206	87	42.2	1374	6.7	12	12	5.8

Lifetime Statistics - 1960-1969 Players Section 2 - RUSHING and RECEIVING
(All men with 25 or more rushing attempts or 10 or more receptions)

		RUSHING				RECEIVING			
Name	Years	Att.	Yards	Avg.	TD	Rec.	Yards	Avg.	TD
John Adams	59-63	41	99	2.4	1	21	264	12.6	3
Don Allen	60	30	18	0.6	1	5	34	6.8	0
Duane Allen	61-67					10	227	22.7	5
Jerry Allen	66-69	201	664	3.3	7	33	400	12.1	2
Jim Allison	65-68	93	378	4.1	2	22	230	10.5	0
Lance Alworth	62-72	24	129	5.4	2	542	10267	18.9	85
Bill Anderson	58-63,65-66	4	11	2.8	0	168	3048	18.1	15
Max Anderson	68-69,71	160	599	3.7	3	29	205	7.1	0
Ralph Anderson	58,60					55	791	14.4	6
Taz Anderson	61-64,66-67					87	1335	15.3	9
Fred Arbanas	62-70	4	15	3.8	0	218	3101	14.2	34
Jon Arnett	57-66	964	3833	4.0	26	222	2290	10.3	10
Doug Asad	60-61					50	698	14.0	3
Willie Asbury	66-68	253	868	3.4	11	25	307	12.2	2
Pervis Atkins	61-66	74	201	2.7	1	64	675	10.5	2
Joe Auer	64-68	234	773	3.3	7	51	647	12.7	6
Gene Babb	57-58,60-63	152	461	3.0	3	33	281	8.5	1
Art Baker	61-62	154	507	3.3	3	9	85	9.4	0
Sam Baker	53,56-69	49	234	4.8	2	7	59	8.4	0
Terry Baker	63-65	58	210	3.6	1	30	302	10.1	2
Gary Ballman	62-73	41	202	4.9	4	323	5366	16.6	37
Estes Banks	67-68	44	157	3.6	0	4	15	3.8	1
Billy Barnes	57-63,65-66	994	3421	3.4	29	153	1786	11.7	9
Gary Barnes	62-64,66-67					41	583	14.2	2
Eppie Barney	67-68	0	8	–	1	19	192	10.1	1
Terry Barr	57-65	32	151	4.7	2	227	3810	16.8	35
Jan Barrett	63-64					13	221	17.0	2
Tom Barrrington	66-70	168	530	3.2	3	41	278	6.8	1
Dick Bass	60-69	1218	5417	4.4	34	204	1841	9.0	7
Glenn Bass	60-68	16	67	4.2	0	167	2841	17.0	17
Craig Baynham	67-70,72	152	553	3.6	6	45	466	10.4	3
Pete Beathard	64-73,75	131	680	5.2	11				
Hal Bedsole	64-66					26	418	16.1	8
Harry Bell	60	42	238	5.5	0	2	13	6.5	0
Joe Bellino	65-67	30	64	2.1	0	11	153	13.9	1
Ray Berry	55-67					631	9275	14.7	68
Charles Bivins	60-67	153	498	3.3	3	28	262	9.4	3
George Blanda	49-58,60-75	144	268	1.9	9	1	-16	-16.0	0
Sid Blanks	64-70	365	1440	3.9	7	106	1073	10.1	4
Ronnie Blye	68-69	61	268	4.4	1	12	85	7.1	0
Dewey Bohling	60-61	178	584	3.3	4	43	485	11.3	5
Don Bosseler	57-64	775	3112	4.0	22	136	1083	8.0	1
Zeke Bratkowski	54,57-68,71	92	308	3.3	5				
Johnny Brewer	61-70					89	1256	14.1	6
John Brodie	57-73	235	1167	5.0	22				
Barry Brown	66-70					21	214	10.2	0
Bill Brown	61-74	1649	5838	3.5	52	286	3183	11.1	23
Fred Brown	61,63	59	210	3.6	2	3	18	6.0	0
Jimmy Brown	57-65	2359	12312	5.2	106	262	2499	9.5	20
Timmy Brown	59-68	889	3862	4.3	31	235	3399	14.5	26
Willie Brown	64-66	44	133	3.0	0	5	110	22.0	1
Charlie Bryant	66-69	67	322	4.8	0	3	26	8.7	0
Frank Budd	62-63					10	236	23.6	1
Fred Bukaty	61	76	187	2.5	5	15	94	6.7	0
Rudy Bukich	53,56-68	112	109	1.0	9				
Ronnie Bull	62-71	881	3222	3.7	9	172	1479	8.6	5
Amos Bullocks	62-64,66	158	620	3.9	5	15	180	12.0	2
Jerry Burch	61					18	235	13.1	1
Chris Burford	60-67	3	10	3.3	0	391	5505	14.1	55
Vern Burke	65-67					38	470	12.4	2

Lifetime Statistics - 1960-1969 Players Section 2 - **RUSHING AND RECEIVING** (continued)
(All men with 25 or more rushing attempts or 10 or more receptions)

		RUSHING				RECEIVING			
Name	**Years**	**Att.**	**Yards**	**Avg.**	**TD**	**Rec.**	**Yards**	**Avg.**	**TD**
Bobby Burnett	66-67,69	237	871	3.7	4	45	533	11.8	4
John Burrell	62-64,66-67	6	38	6.3	0	26	437	16.8	0
Ode Burrell	64-69	304	1088	3.6	3	112	1379	12.3	9
Ron Burton	60-65	429	1536	3.6	9	111	1205	10.9	8
Bill Butler	59-64	29	108	3.7	0	6	95	15.8	0
Cannonball Butler	65-72	797	2768	3.5	9	89	959	10.8	7
Woody Campbell	67-71	408	1493	3.7	13	80	709	8.9	2
Billy Cannon	60-70	602	2455	4.1	17	236	3656	15.5	47
Bob Cappadonna	66-68	123	460	3.7	2	24	196	8.2	3
Gino Cappelletti	60-70	4	6	1.5	0	292	4589	15.7	42
Wray Carlton	60-67	819	3368	4.1	29	110	1329	12.1	5
Reg Carolan	62-68					23	364	15.8	5
J.C. Caroline	56-65	68	263	3.9	2	6	111	18.5	1
Preston Carpenter	56-67	223	884	4.0	1	305	4457	14.6	23
Jimmy Carr	55,57,59-65	30	115	3.8	0	9	157	17.4	0
Rick Casares	55-66	1431	5787	4.0	49	191	1588	8.3	11
Bernie Casey	61-68	1	23	23.0	0	359	5444	15.2	40
Dan Chamberlain	60-61					18	295	16.4	4
Joe Childress	56-60,62-65	530	2210	4.2	3	121	1700	14.0	13
Clarence Childs	64-68	40	102	2.6	0	11	97	8.8	0
Dick Christy	58,60-63	337	1267	3.8	10	132	1473	11.2	6
Jack Clancy	67,69-70	3	–4	–1.3	0	104	1401	13.5	5
Howard Clark	60-61					38	613	16.1	0
Franke Clarke	57-67	32	231	7.2	1	291	5426	18.6	50
Doug Cline	60-66	37	105	2.8	2	4	15	3.8	0
Bert Coan	62-68	284	1259	4.4	15	39	367	9.4	4
Junior Coffey	65-67,69,71	535	2037	3.8	10	64	487	7.6	5
Gail Cogdill	60-70	2	–2	–1.0	0	356	5696	16.0	34
Angie Coia	60-66	5	–2	–0.4	0	121	2037	16.8	20
Jim Colclough	60-68	4	51	12.8	0	283	5101	18.0	39
Terry Cole	68-71	189	641	3.4	5	25	171	6.8	1
Gary Collins	62-71	8	60	15.0	0	331	5299	16.0	70
Dick Compton	62-65,67-68	6	8	1.3	0	52	733	14.1	14
Jack Concannon	64-71,74-75	217	1026	4.7	12				
Larry Conjar	67-70	30	102	3.4	0	6	68	11.3	0
Bobby Joe Conrad	58-69	118	441	3.7	2	422	5902	14.0	38
Greg Cook	69,73	25	148	5.9	1				
Bob Coolbaugh	61					32	435	13.6	4
Thurlow Cooper	60-62					36	491	13.6	8
Paul Costa	65-72	2	12	6.0	1	102	1699	16.7	6
Jim Cox	68					11	147	13.4	0
Eric Crabtree	66-71	8	37	4.6	0	164	2663	16.2	22
Dobie Craig	62-64	1	8	8.0	0	38	743	19.6	7
Jim Crawford	60-64	302	1078	3.6	5	52	496	9.5	2
Willie Crenshaw	64-70	652	2428	3.7	15	104	797	7.7	3
Bob Crespino	61-68					58	741	12.8	9
Bobby Crockett	66,68-69					41	659	16.1	3
Monte Crockett	60-62					35	512	14.6	1
Marshall Cropper	67-69					14	181	12.9	0
John David Crow	58-68	1157	4963	4.3	38	258	3699	14.3	35
Wayne Crow	60-63	235	1085	4.6	3	36	345	9.6	1
Harry Crump	63	49	120	2.5	5	3	19	6.3	0
Jim Cunningham	61-63	120	337	2.8	3	26	219	8.4	2
Gary Cuozzo	63-72	16	176	2.3	1				
Carroll Dale	60-73	4	30	7.5	0	438	8277	18.9	52
Clem Daniels	60-68	1146	5138	4.5	30	203	3314	16.3	24
Cotton Davidson	54,57,60-66,68	149	357	2.4	11				
Glenn Davis	60-61					10	132	13.2	0
Len Dawson	57-75	294	1293	4.4	9				
Ted Dean	60-64	263	923	3.5	2	51	684	13.4	4
Austin Denney	67-71	2	3	1.5	0	71	764	10.8	3
Mike Dennis	68-69	29	136	4.7	0	8	53	6.6	0
Al Denson	64-71	4	3	0.8	0	260	4275	16.4	32
Willard Dewveall	59-64					204	3304	16.2	27
Buddy Dial	59-66	4	14	3.5	0	261	5436	20.8	44
Bo Dickinson	60-64	189	693	3.7	4	86	886	10.3	6
Mike Ditka	61-62	2	2	1.0	0	427	5812	13.6	43
Hewitt Dixon	63-70	772	3090	4.0	15	263	2821	10.7	13
Oscar Donahue	62					16	285	17.8	1
Mike Dorsey	62					21	344	16.4	2
Merrill Douglas	58-62	54	213	3.9	2	4	26	6.5	0
Boyd Dowler	59-69,71	2	28	14.0	0	474	7270	15.3	40
Elbert Dubenion	60-68	46	326	7.1	3	296	5309	17.9	35
Paul Dudley	62-63	38	121	3.2	0	10	120	12.0	1
Fred Dugan	58-63	1	–9	–9	0	153	2226	14.5	13
Perry Lee Dunn	64-69	214	653	3.1	6	42	408	9.7	1
Henry Dyer	66,68-70	82	256	3.1	1	14	160	11.4	1
Rick Eder	68-70					11	184	16.7	1
Nick Eddy	68-70,72	152	523	3.4	3	24	237	9.9	2
Larry Elkins	66-67	2	19	9.5	0	24	315	13.1	3
John Embree	69-70					33	519	15.7	5
Hunter Enis	60-62	30	25	0.8	5				
Pat Epperson	60					11	99	9.0	0
Sam Etcheverry	61-62	41	78	1.9	0				
Bo Farrington	60-63	1	–2	–2.0	0	55	881	16.0	7
Bobby Felts	65-67	66	207	3.1	2	5	29	5.8	0
Bob Ferguson	62-63	66	209	3.2	1	4	13	3.3	0
Charley Ferguson	61-63,65-66,68-69					62	1168	18.8	13
Paul Flatley	63-70					306	4905	16.0	24
George Fleming	61	31	112	3.6	1	10	49	4.9	0
Marv Fleming	63-74					157	1823	11.6	16
Tom Flores	60-61,63-69	101	142	1.4	5				
Charlie Flowers	60-62	111	416	3.7	4	35	383	10.9	1
Lee Folkins	61-65	1	9	9.0	0	80	1042	13.0	10
Fred Ford	60	38	194	5.1	2	1	5	5.0	0
Garrett Ford	68	41	186	4.5	1	6	40	6.7	0
Gene Foster	65-70	445	1613	3.6	4	99	904	9.1	3
Willmer Fowler	60-61	94	372	4.0	1	10	99	9.9	0
Al Frazier	61-63	62	278	4.5	2	58	1010	17.4	7
Charley Frazier	62-70	4	5	1.3	0	209	3461	16.6	30
Willie Frazier	64-72,75	6	118	19.7	1	207	3069	14.8	35
Tucker Frederickson	65,67-71	651	2209	3.4	9	128	1011	7.9	8
Charley Fuller	61-62	38	134	3.5	0	17	344	20.2	2
Roman Gabriel	62-77	354	1302	3.7	30	1	–5	–5.0	0
Bob Gaiters	61-63	168	673	4.0	6	17	175	10.3	2
Willie Galimore	57-63	670	2985	4.5	26	87	1201	13.8	10
R.C. Gamble	68-69	94	346	3.7	1	18	129	7.2	1
Billy Gambrell	63-68	7	41	5.9	0	116	1931	16.6	18
J.D. Garrett	64-67	116	434	3.7	3	17	169	9.9	2
Mike Garrett	66-73	1308	5481	4.2	35	238	2010	8.4	13
Larry Garron	60-68	763	2981	3.9	14	185	2502	13.5	26
Prentice Gault	60-67	629	2466	3.9	11	79	901	11.4	6
Jack Gehrke	68-69,71-72	1	2	2.0	0	14	254	18.1	0
Pete Gent	64-68	2	–5	–2.5	0	68	989	14.5	4
Jim Gibbons	58-68					287	3561	12.4	20
Cookie Gilchrist	62-67	1010	4293	4.3	37	110	1135	10.3	6
Glenn Glass	62-66					15	201	13.4	0
Al Goldstein	60	3	–2	–0.7	1	27	354	13.1	1
Ron Goodwin	63-68	2	–22	–11.0	0	78	1079	13.8	9
Jim Grabowski	66-71	475	1731	3.6	8	82	675	8.2	3
Art Graham	63-68	1	–5	–5.0	0	199	3107	15.6	20
Hoyle Granger	66-72	805	3653	4.5	19	134	1339	10.0	5
Ernie Green	62-68	668	3204	4.8	15	195	2036	10.4	20
Johnny Green	60-63	77	–106	–1.4	6	1	0	0.0	0
Tom Greene	60-61	16	–27	–1.7	0				
Jim Greer	60					22	284	12.9	1
Ben Gregory	68	52	283	5.4	1	5	21	4.2	0
Bill Groman	60-65	1	2	2.0	1	174	3481	20.0	36
Earl Gros	62-70	821	3157	3.8	28	142	1255	8.8	10
Ralph Gugliemi	55,58-63	177	633	3.6	2				
John Hadl	62-77	351	1112	3.2	16	3	–9	–3.0	0
Mike Haffner	68-71	3	3	1.0	0	59	991	16.8	7
Roger Hagberg	65-69	194	766	3.9	4	58	645	11.1	4
Mac Haik	67-71	4	28	7.0	0	76	1149	15.1	9
Ken Hall	59-61	51	212	4.2	0	8	118	14.8	2
Tom Hall	62-69	4	–4	–1.0	0	103	1441	14.0	8
Mal Hammack	55,57-66	320	1278	4.0	7	27	255	9.4	0
Charley Hardy	60-62					54	840	15.6	7
Jack Harper	67-68	41	197	4.8	1	11	212	19.3	3
Billy Harris	68-69,71	60	158	2.6	0	5	131	26.2	1
Pete Hart	60	25	113	4.5	0	3	19	6.3	0
Alex Hawkins	59-68	208	787	3.8	10	129	1751	13.6	12
Ben Hawkins	66-73	10	8	0.8	0	261	4764	18.3	32
Luther Hayes	61					14	280	20.0	3
Ray Hayes	61	73	319	4.4	2	16	121	8.1	0
Wendell Hayes	63,65-74	988	3758	3.8	28	161	1461	9.1	7
Abner Haynes	60-67	1036	4630	4.5	46	287	3538	12.3	20
Gene Heeter	63-65					22	327	14.9	2
John Henderson	65-72					108	1735	16.1	10
Jon Henderson	68-70					28	390	13.9	6
Charley Hennigan	60-66					410	6823	16.6	51
Ken Herock	63-69					63	924	14.7	4
Bo Hickey	67	73	263	3.6	4	7	36	5.1	1
Fred Hill	65-71	1	5	5.0	0	85	1005	11.8	5
Jerry Hill	61,63-70	606	2668	4.4	22	117	970	8.3	3
King Hill	58-69	88	306	3.5	9				
Mack Lee Hill	64-65	230	1203	5.2	6	40	408	10.2	3
John Hilton	65-73	1	15	15.0	0	144	2047	14.2	16
Dick Hoak	61-70	1132	3965	3.5	25	146	1452	9.9	8
Roy Hopkins	67-70	232	826	3.6	7	50	529	10.6	1
Sam Horner	60-62	118	355	3.0	0	17	219	12.9	1
Paul Hornung	57-62,64-66	893	3711	4.2	50	130	1480	11.4	12
Brad Hubbert	67-70	287	1270	4.4	9	42	312	7.4	2
Chuck Hughes	67-71					15	262	17.5	0
George Hughley	65	37	175	4.7	0	9	93	10.3	1
Tom Hutchinson	63-66					19	409	21.5	2
Bobby Jackson	62-65	184	624	3.4	14	32	333	10.4	2
Frank Jackson	61-67	121	790	6.5	7	188	2955	15.7	24
Leroy Jackson	62-63	52	142	2.7	0	10	253	25.3	0
Allen Jacobs	65-67	91	301	3.3	1	10	69	6.9	0
Dick James	56-65	502	1930	3.8	19	104	1669	16.0	15
Billy Joe	63-68	539	2013	3.7	15	77	589	7.6	4
Charley Johnson	61-75	196	539	2.8	10				
Curley Johnson	60-69	64	209	3.3	1	32	370	11.6	3
Jim Johnson	61-75					40	690	17.3	4
John Henry Johnson	54-66	1571	6803	4.3	48	186	1478	7.9	7
Rudy Johnson	64-66	25	60	2.4	1	8	70	8.8	0
Harry Jones	67-70	44	85	1.9	0	9	131	14.6	0
Homer Jones	64-70	17	146	8.6	1	224	4986	22.3	36
Jim Jones	65-68	8	24	3.0	0	69	1182	17.1	11
Les Josephson	64-67,69-74	797	3407	4.3	17	194	1970	10.2	11
Steve Junker	57,59-62					48	639	13.3	6
Sonny Jurgensen	57-74	181	493	2.7	15	1	–3	–3.0	0
Joe Kapp	67-70	119	611	5.1	5				
Jim Kelly	64-65,67					31	531	17.1	5
Leroy Kelly	64-73	1727	7274	4.2	74	190	2281	12.0	13
Jack Kemp	57,60-67,69	394	796	2.0	40				
Billy Kilmer	61-62,64,66-75	361	1508	4.2	21	27	288	10.7	1
Claude King	61-62	33	194	5.9	3	8	125	15.6	1
Phil King	58-66	569	2192	3.9	7	86	951	11.1	9

Lifetime Statistics - 1960-1969 Players Section 2 - **RUSHING AND RECEIVING** (continued)
(All men with 25 or more rushing attempts or 10 or more receptions)

		RUSHING				RECEIVING			
Name	**Years**	**Att.**	**Yards**	**Avg.**	**TD**	**Rec.**	**Yards**	**Avg.**	**TD**
Roger Kochman	63	47	232	4.9	0	4	148	37.0	1
Dave Kocourek	60-68					249	4090	16.4	24
Dave Kopay	64-72	235	876	3.7	3	77	593	7.7	4
Dick Kotite	67-69,71-72					17	213	12.5	5
Walt Kowalczyk	58-61	103	264	2.6	2	34	256	7.5	1
Ernie Koy	65-70	414	1723	4.2	9	76	498	6.6	6
Ron Kramer	57,59-67	6	9	1.5	0	229	3272	14.3	16
Rich Kreitling	59-64	2	−13	−6.5	0	123	1775	14.4	17
Joe Kulbacki	60	41	108	2.6	1	2	9	4.5	0
Ralph Kurek	65-70	121	434	3.6	2	26	299	11.5	0
Pete Lammons	66-72	0	3	–	0	185	2364	12.8	14
Daryle Lamonica	63-74	166	640	3.9	14				
Izzy Lang	64-69	245	873	3.6	4	63	554	8.8	4
Jack Larscheid	60-61	100	400	4.0	1	24	198	8.3	1
Pete Larson	67-68					20	191	9.6	1
Monte Ledbetter	67-69					18	314	17.4	3
Jacky Lee	60-69	82	150	1.8	3	1	−1	−1.0	0
Darrell Lester	64-66	38	102	2.7	0	2	26	13.0	1
Dan Lewis	58-66	800	3205	4.0	19	99	1162	11.7	5
Gary Lewis	64-70	343	1421	4.1	13	72	604	8.4	5
Keith Lincoln	61-68	759	3383	4.5	19	165	2250	13.6	19
Mike Lind	63-66	222	661	3.0	8	52	427	8.2	1
Jim Lindsey	66-72	178	566	3.2	6	56	632	11.3	4
Don Lisbon	63-64	164	561	3.4	0	34	363	10.7	3
Pete Liske	64,69-72	38	141	3.7	2				
Andy Livingston	64-65,67-70	291	1216	4.2	7	46	474	10.3	3
J.W. Lockett	61-64	229	170	3.4	3	62	589	9.5	7
Oscar Lofton	60					19	360	18.9	4
Bob Long	64-70					98	1539	15.7	10
Joe Don Looney	64-67,69	214	724	3.4	11	26	171	6.6	2
Tony Lorick	64-69	548	2124	3.9	14	86	890	10.3	5
Billy Lott	58,60-63	246	1123	4.6	13	85	919	10.8	8
John Love	67,72					18	267	14.8	2
Paul Lowe	60-61,63-69	1026	4995	4.9	40	111	1045	9.4	7
Dick Lucas	58,60-63					34	384	11.3	6
Richie Lucas	60-61	56	105	1.9	2	11	127	11.5	1
Lamar Lundy	57-69					35	584	16.7	6
Lenny Lyles	58-69	35	69	2.0	2	8	57	7.1	1
Red Mack	61-66	4	−1	−0.3	0	52	1159	22.3	8
Dee Mackey	60-65					94	1352	14.4	8
John Mackey	63-72	19	127	6.7	0	331	5236	15.8	38
Jacques MacKinnon	61-70	86	377	4.4	2	112	2109	18.8	20
Joe Marconi	56-66	673	2771	4.1	30	136	1326	9.8	9
Aaron Marsh	68-69	4	8	2.0	0	27	439	16.3	4
Amos Marsh	61-67	750	3222	4.3	25	133	1384	10.4	7
Paul Martha	64-70	6	15	2.5	0	17	316	18.6	0
Billy Martin	64-68					58	705	12.2	4
Tommy Mason	61-71	1040	4203	4.0	32	214	2324	10.9	13
Bill Mathis	60-69	1044	3589	3.4	37	149	1775	11.9	9
Tom Matte	61-72	1200	4646	3.9	45	249	2869	11.5	12
Doug Mayberry	61-63	87	314	3.6	1	13	118	9.1	1
Don Maynard	58,60-73	24	70	2.9	0	633	11834	18.7	88
Don McCall	67-70	229	884	3.9	6	37	390	10.5	3
Brendan McCarthy	68-69	59	175	3.0	1	20	184	9.2	2
Curtis McClinton	62-69	762	3124	4.1	18	154	1945	12.6	14
Gary McDermott	68-69	54	108	2.0	3	20	115	5.8	1
Roy McDonald	67-68	52	223	4.3	4	10	60	6.0	0
Tommy McDonald	57-68	17	22	1.3	0	495	8380	16.9	84
Gerry McDougall	62-64,68	104	469	4.5	6	22	248	11.3	0
Kay McFarland	62-66,68					45	682	15.2	4
Max McGee	54,57-67	12	121	10.1	0	345	6346	18.4	50
Hugh McInnis	60-62,64,66	4	30	7.5	0	22	392	17.8	0
Marlin McKeever	61-73					133	1737	13.1	6
Bob McLeod	61-66					126	1926	15.3	19
Clifton McNeil	64-73	5	6	1.2	0	181	2734	15.1	22
Chuck Mercein	65-70	163	531	3.3	4	37	205	5.5	1
Don Meredith	60-68	242	1216	5.0	15				
Dale Messer	61-65					12	176	14.7	0
Frank Mestnik	60-61,63	200	767	3.8	4	15	53	3.5	1
Tom Michel	64	39	129	3.3	0	1	14	14.0	0
Alan Miller	60-63,65	386	1395	3.6	9	130	1470	11.3	11
Bill Miller	62-64,66-68					141	1879	13.3	10
Gene Milton	68-69	9	108	12.0	0	21	322	15.3	1
Gene Mingo	60-70	185	777	4.2	8	52	454	8.7	4
Randy Minniear	67-70	96	316	3.3	5	19	148	7.8	1
George Mira	60-64,71	50	379	7.6	0				
Bobby Mitchell	58-68	513	2735	5.3	18	521	7954	15.3	65
Charley Mitchell	63-68	352	1142	3.2	5	62	650	8.9	3
Stan Mitchell	60-70	173	548	3.2	4	42	533	12.7	5
Lenny Moore	56-67	1069	5174	4.8	63	363	6039	16.6	48
Tom Moore	60-67	660	2445	3.7	21	141	1152	8.2	10
Doug Moreau	66-69	1	−2	−2.0	0	73	926	12.7	6
Earl Morrall	56-75	235	878	3.7	8				
Johnny Morris	58-67	224	1040	4.6	5	356	5059	14.2	31
Larry Morris	55-57,59-66	40	148	3.7	1				
Joe Morrison	59-72	677	2474	3.7	18	395	4993	12.6	47
Bill Murphy	68					18	268	14.9	0
Jim Nance	65-71,73	1341	5401	4.0	45	133	870	6.5	1
Bill Nelsen	63-72	84	89	1.1	2	1	−5	−5.0	0
Tom Neumann	63	44	148	3.4	0	10	48	4.8	0
Jim Ninowski	58-69	92	367	4.0	10				
Terry Nofsinger	61-67	31	65	2.1	3				
Karl Noonan	66-71	2	−20	−10.0	0	136	1798	13.2	17
Pettis Norman	62-73	23	198	8.6	0	183	2492	13.6	15
Don Norton	60-66	2	−3	−1.5	0	228	3486	15.3	27
Tom Nowatzke	65-72	361	1249	3.5	13	100	605	6.1	4

		RUSHING				RECEIVING			
Name	**Years**	**Att.**	**Yards**	**Avg.**	**TD**	**Rec.**	**Yards**	**Avg.**	**TD**
Ray Ogden	65-73	1	12	12.0	0	53	885	16.7	4
Jimmy Orr	58-70	15	122	8.1	0	400	7914	19.8	66
Tom Osborne	60-61					29	343	11.8	2
R.C. Owens	57-64	1	23	23.0	1	206	3285	15.9	22
Bob Paremore	63-64	36	107	3.0	0	6	89	14.8	1
Babe Parilli	52-53,56-58,60-69	394	1416	3.6	24				
Dave Parks	64-73	4	−10	−2.5	0	360	5619	15.6	44
Clarence Peaks	57-65	951	3660	3.8	21	190	1793	9.4	3
Art Perkins	62-63	85	251	3.0	6	22	144	6.5	0
Don Perkins	61-68	1500	6217	4.1	42	146	1310	9.0	3
Ray Perkins	67-71	10	77	7.7	0	93	1538	16.5	11
Jim Phillips	58-67					401	6044	15.1	34
Brian Piccolo	66-69	258	927	3.6	4	58	537	9.3	1
Nick Pietrosante	59-67	955	4026	4.2	28	131	1391	10.6	2
Elijah Pitts	61-71	514	1788	3.5	28	104	1265	12.0	6
Dave Pivec	66-69					14	146	10.4	1
Milt Plum	57-69	217	531	2.4	13	1	20	20.0	0
Ray Poage	63-65,67-71	3	32	10.7	0	145	2309	15.9	13
Bob Poole	64-67					19	223	11.7	0
Bucky Pope	64,66-68	2	11	5.5	0	34	952	28.0	13
Dickie Post	67-71	608	2605	4.3	17	96	903	9.4	2
Art Powell	59-68					479	8046	16.8	81
Gene Prebola	60-63					133	1823	13.7	6
Sam Price	66-68	82	213	3.8	1	10	70	7.0	1
Frank Quayle	69	57	183	3.2	0	11	167	15.2	0
Warren Rabb	60-62	50	124	2.5	3				
Bill Rademacher	64-70	1	−13	−13.0	0	24	282	11.8	3
Sonny Randle	59-68					365	5996	16.4	65
Ron Rector	66-67	33	167	5.1	0	6	22	3.7	0
Bob Reed	62-63	27	110	4.1	0	17	174	10.2	1
Dan Reeves	65-72	535	1990	3.7	25	129	1693	13.1	17
Jerry Reichow	56-57,59-64	20	105	5.3	0	172	2579	15.0	24
Bob Renn	61	1	14	14.0	0	18	268	14.9	1
Lance Rentzel	65-72,74	26	196	7.5	2	268	4826	18.0	38
Pete Retzlaff	56-66	6	−4	−0.7	0	452	7412	16.4	47
M.C. Reynolds	58-62	88	419	4.8	4				
Jerry Rhome	65-67,69-71	26	91	3.5	1				
Perry Richards	57-62					39	558	14.3	4
Jerry Richardson	59-60					15	171	11.4	4
Willie Richardson	63-71	2	27	13.5	0	195	2950	15.1	25
Pat Richter	63-70	1	−9	−9.0	0	99	1315	13.3	14
Johnny Roach	56,59-64	42	99	2.4	2				
Bo Roberson	61-66	168	584	3.5	6	176	2917	16.6	12
C.R. Roberts	59-62	155	637	4.1	4	21	132	6.3	0
Walter Roberts	64-67,69-70	5	45	9.0	0	67	1218	18.2	9
Jerry Robinson	62-65	3	20	6.7	0	49	799	16.3	4
Johnny Robinson	60-71	150	658	4.4	6	77	1228	15.9	9
John Roderick	66-68					11	156	14.2	1
Johnny Roland	66-74	1015	3750	3.7	28	153	1430	9.3	6
Dave Rolle	60	130	501	3.9	2	21	122	5.8	1
Tony Romeo	61-67					116	1833	15.8	10
Dave Ross	60					10	122	12.2	1
Ed Rutkowski	63-68	69	250	3.6	1	63	981	15.6	4
Frank Ryan	58-70	310	1358	4.4	6	0	31	–	1
Tom Rychlec	58,60-63	1	−18	−18.0	0	87	1091	12.5	3
Saint Saffold	68	1	21	21.0	0	16	172	10.8	0
Theron Sapp	59-65	202	763	3.8	5	23	247	10.7	0
George Sauer	65-70	4	23	5.8	0	309	4965	16.1	28
Gale Sayers	65-71	1001	4956	5.0	39	112	1307	11.7	9
Charlie Scales	60-66	157	603	3.8	4	21	144	6.9	0
Bob Scarpitto	61-68	10	214	21.4	1	156	2651	17.0	27
Randy Schultz	66-68	82	301	3.7	2	26	220	8.5	0
Glen Shaw	60,62-64	47	148	3.1	3	8	146	18.3	1
Tom Sherman	68-69	27	94	3.5	0				
Dick Shiner	64-71,73-74	58	161	2.8	2				
Roy Shivers	66-72	176	680	3.9	10	38	400	10.5	4
Bill Shockley	60-62,68	42	165	3.9	0	31	96	8.7	2
Del Shofner	57-67	4	1	0.3	0	349	6470	18.5	51
Les Shy	66-70	144	523	3.6	3	23	273	11.9	1
Jerry Simmons	65-69,71-74	3	−3	−1.0	0	138	2105	15.3	9
Mickey Slaughter	63-66	73	263	3.6	1				
Tom Smiley	68-70	120	312	2.6	4	24	109	4.5	1
Allen Smith	66-67	31	148	4.8	0	1	1	1.0	0
Bobby Smith	64-66	129	536	4.2	5	21	214	10.2	0
Dave Smith	60-64	328	1368	4.2	11	80	772	9.7	7
Gordon Smith	61-65	1	2	2.0	0	57	1277	22.4	13
Jackie Smith	63-75	38	327	8.6	3	472	7847	16.6	39
J.D. Smith	56-66	1100	4672	4.2	40	127	1122	8.8	6
J.D. Smith	60-61	66	220	3.3	6	17	194	11.4	1
Ralph Smith	62-69	2	26	13.0	0	41	549	13.4	5
Russ Smith	67-70	213	915	4.3	10	23	265	11.5	0
Mark Smolinski	61-68	421	1323	3.1	9	103	841	8.2	7
Norm Snead	61-75	209	522	2.5	23				
Matt Snell	64-72	1057	4285	4.1	24	193	1375	7.1	7
Mike Sommer	58-61,63	78	253	3.2	2	9	166	18.4	0
Butch Songin	60-62	48	−90	−1.9	2				
Jack Spikes	60-67	408	1693	4.1	18	56	679	12.1	3
Billy Stacy	59-63					12	241	20.1	1
Bart Starr	56-71	247	1308	5.3	15				
Tom Stephens	60-64					41	506	12.3	5
Monte Stickles	60-68					222	3199	14.4	16
Jim Stiger	63-67	140	583	4.2	2	31	297	9.6	2
Jim Stinnette	61-62	40	95	2.4	1	24	167	7.0	1
Donnie Stone	61-66	354	1352	3.8	10	91	859	9.4	7
Steve Stonebraker	62-68					12	227	18.9	1

Lifetime Statistics - 1960-1969 Players   Section 2 - RUSHING and RECEIVING (continued)
(All men with 25 or more rushing attempts or 10 or more receptions)

Name	Years	Att.	Yards	Avg.	TD	Rec.	Yards	Avg.	TD
Bob Stransky	60	28	78	2.8	0	3	11	3.7	0
Pat Studstill	61-62,64-72	6	39	6.5	0	181	2840	15.7	18
Kark Sweetan	66-70	56	307	5.5	2				
Mike Taliaferro	64-72	46	134	2.9	0				
Fran Tarkenton	61-77	651	3680	5.7	31	0	-12	—	0
Jim Taylor	58-67	1941	8597	4.4	83	225	1756	7.8	10
Lionel Taylor	59-68	4	20	5.0	0	567	7195	12.7	45
Steve Tensi	65-70	47	82	1.7	0				
Tony Teresa	58,60	139	608	4.4	6	35	393	11.2	4
Aaron Thomas	61-70	4	-10	-2.5	0	262	4554	17.4	37
Clendon Thomas	58-68	18	70	3.9	0	60	1046	17.4	4
Gene Thomas	66-68	130	401	3.1	4	23	184	8.0	2
Bill Thornton	63-65,67	93	544	5.8	2	13	68	5.2	0
Bubba Thornton	69					14	134	9.6	0
Steve Thurlow	64-68	314	1127	3.6	4	61	539	8.8	2
Jim Tiller	62	31	43	1.3	0	13	108	8.3	0
Bill Tobin	63	75	270	3.6	4	13	172	13.2	1
Larry Todd	65-70	138	625	4.5	5	51	522	10.2	2
Charley Tolar	60-66	907	3277	3.6	21	175	1266	7.2	2
John Tracey	59-67					20	303	15.2	0
Tom Tracy	56-64	808	2912	3.6	17	113	1468	13.0	14
Richard Trapp	68-69					26	274	10.5	0
Bill Triplett	62-63,65-72	681	2446	3.6	17	113	1055	9.3	5
Frank Tripucka	49-52,60-63	70	-125	-1.8	6				
Billy Truax	64-73					199	2458	12.4	17
Don Trull	64-69	123	428	3.5	14				
Bill Tucker	67-71	127	431	3.4	6	59	496	8.4	7
Wendell Tucker	67-70					57	983	17.2	11
Bake Turner	62-70	2	13	6.5	0	220	3539	16.1	25
Johnny Unitas	56-73	450	1777	3.9	13	1	1	1.0	0
Ron Vander Kelen	63-67	26	116	4.5	1				
Jim Vollenweider	62-63	58	161	2.8	2	5	47	9.4	0
Billy Wade	54-66	318	1334	4.2	24	0	10	—	0
Joe Walton	57-63					178	2628	14.8	28
Ernie Warlick	62-65					90	1551	17.2	4
Bob Waters	60-63	65	281	4.3	3				
Tom Watkins	61-65,67-68	468	1791	3.8	10	55	590	10.7	4
Ken Webb	58-63	264	891	3.4	8	46	483	10.5	1
Joel Wells	61	65	216	3.3	1	6	31	5.2	1
Warren Wells	64,67-70	9	103	11.4	1	158	3655	23.1	42
Mel West	61-62	81	338	4.2	3	14	147	10.5	0
Jim Whelan	65-71	1	0	0.0	0	197	3155	16.0	20
Ernie Wheelwright	64-70	387	1426	3.7	9	54	531	9.8	7
Freeman White	66-69					29	315	10.9	1
John White	60-61					14	256	18.3	1
A. D. Whitfield	65-68	222	981	4.4	3	67	702	10.5	3
J. R. Wilburn	66-70	7	54	7.7	0	123	1834	14.9	8
Ken Willard	65-74	1622	6105	3.8	45	277	2184	7.9	17
A. D. Williams	59-61					15	190	12.7	1
Travis Williams	67-71	289	1166	4.0	6	52	598	11.5	5
Ben Wilson	63-65,67	431	1589	3.7	9	47	487	10.4	2
Butch Wilson	63-69					25	317	12.7	3
George Wilson	66	27	137	5.1	0				
Lloyd Winston	62-63	28	112	4.0	1	3	15	5.0	0
Dick Witcher	66-73					172	2359	13.7	14
Joe Womack	62	128	468	3.7	5	6	57	9.5	0
Dick Wood	61-66	26	45	1.7	4				
Gary Wood	64-69	75	419	5.6	6				
Tom Woodeshick	63-72	836	3577	4.3	21	126	1175	9.3	6
John Wright	68-69					12	130	10.8	2
Tom Yewcic	61-66	72	424	5.9	4	7	69	9.9	0

Lifetime Statistics - 1960-1969 Players   Section 3 - PUNT RETURNS and KICKOFF RETURNS
(All men with 25 or more Punt Returns or 25 or more Kickoff Returns)

Name	Year(s)	No.	Yards	Avg.	TD	No.	Yards	Avg.	TD
Herb Adderley	61-72	1	0	0.0	0	120	3080	25.7	2
Kermit Alexander	63-73	133	835	6.3	2	153	3586	23.4	0
Lance Alworth	62-72	29	309	10.7	0	10	216	21.6	0
Max Anderson	68-69,71	19	142	7.5	0	43	1057	24.6	1
Jon Arnett	57-66	120	981	8.2	1	126	3110	24.7	2
Pervis Atkins	61-66	40	292	7.3	0	95	2124	22.4	0
Joe Auer	64-68	14	141	10.1	0	51	1171	23.0	1
Bill Baird	63-69	88	787	8.9	1	13	290	22.3	0
Gary Ballman	62-73					66	1754	26.6	1
Terry Barr	57-65	50	262	5.2	0	26	655	25.2	1
Tom Barrington	66-70	1	8	8.0	0	32	675	21.1	0
Odell Barry	64-65	37	359	9.7	1	73	1856	25.4	0
Dick Bass	60-69	24	263	11.0	1	54	1415	26.2	0
Mike Battle	69-70	53	352	6.6	0	71	1641	23.1	0
Craig Baynham	67-70,72					41	1035	25.2	0
Joe Bellino	65-67	19	148	7.8	0	43	905	21.0	0
Roger Bird	66-68	94	283	5.4	0	25	533	21.3	0
Charlie Bivins	60-67					78	1911	24.5	0
Sid Blanks	64-70	36	272	7.6	0	43	977	22.7	0
Ronnie Blye	68-69					54	1104	20.4	0
Jimmie Brown	57-65					29	648	22.3	0
Timmy Brown	59-68	71	639	9.0	1	184	4781	26.0	5
Tom Brown	64-69	27	151	5.6	1	7	167	23.9	0
Willie Brown	64-66	18	85	4.7	0	34	795	23.4	0
Charlie Bryant	66-69					42	913	21.7	0
Amos Bullocks	62-64,66					34	737	21.7	0
Ode Burrell	64-69	15	149	9.9	0	33	838	25.4	1
Leon Burton	60	12	93	7.8	0	31	897	28.9	2
Ron Burton	60-65	56	389	6.9	0	46	1119	24.3	1
Bill Butler	59-64	88	850	9.7	2	132	2886	21.9	0
Cannonball Butler	65-72					133	2931	22.0	1
Butch Byrd	64-71					86	600	7.0	1
Jamie Caleb	60-61,65	1	8	8.0	0	27	594	22.0	0
Bob Campbell	69	28	133	4.8	0	26	522	20.1	0
Billy Cannon	60-70	14	178	12.7	0	67	1704	25.4	1
Preston Carpenter	56-67	26	284	10.9	0	29	752	25.9	0
Larry Carwell	67-72	49	474	9.7	0	25	557	22.3	0
Clarence Childs	64-68	6	40	6.7	0	134	3454	25.8	2
Dick Christy	58,60-65	67	905	13.5	4	117	2770	23.7	0
Earl Christy	66-68	34	222	6.5	0	58	1323	22.8	0
Hagood Clarke	64-68	65	583	9.0	2	16	330	20.6	0
Bert Coan	62-68					33	785	23.9	0
Bobby Joe Conrad	58-69	51	462	9.1	2	33	813	24.6	0
Johnny Counts	62-63	8	33	4.1	0	31	891	28.7	1
Willie Crenshaw	64-70					27	515	19.1	0
Irv Cross	61-69	51	376	7.4	0	44	1227	27.9	0
Jay Cunningham	65-67	22	140	6.4	0	64	1372	21.4	0
Clem Daniels	60-68	8	103	12.9	0	57	1206	21.2	0
Ted Dean	60-64	46	279	6.1	0	70	1553	22.2	0
Eddie Dove	59-63	61	437	7.2	0	3	56	18.7	0
Elbert Dubenion	60-68	3	9	3.0	0	40	961	24.0	1
Speedy Duncan	64-74	202	2201	10.9	4	180	4539	25.2	0
Bobby Felts	65-67	6	46	7.7	0	38	814	21.4	0
Pat Fischer	61-77	17	80	4.7	0	26	613	24.5	0
Mike Fitzgerald	66-67	2	4	2.0	0	26	541	20.8	0
George Fleming	61	3	24	8.0	0	60	1634	27.2	0
Tom Frankhauser	59-63	3	19	6.3	0	30	620	20.7	0
Al Frazier	61-63	26	305	11.7	1	44	1077	24.5	1
Bob Gaiters	61-63					33	786	23.8	0
Willie Galimore	57-63					43	1100	25.6	1
Billy Gambrell	63-68	28	282	10.1	0	15	336	22.4	0
Bob Garner	60-63	28	252	9.0	0	1	8	8.0	0
J. D. Garrett	64-67	3	47	15.7	0	48	1054	22.0	0
Mike Garrett	66-73	39	235	6.0	1	14	323	23.1	0
Larry Garron	60-68	1	23	23.0	0	89	2299	25.8	2
Claude Gibson	61-65	110	1381	12.6	3	17	268	15.8	0
Freddie Glick	59-66	44	326	7.4	0	26	584	22.5	0
Kenny Graham	64-70	29	238	8.2	0	7	172	24.6	0
Dave Grayson	61-70	10	78	7.8	0	110	2804	25.5	1
Ernie Green	62-68	11	110	10.0	0	32	648	20.3	0
Dick Haley	59-64	20	87	4.4	0	37	729	19.7	0
Ken Hall	59-61	11	164	14.9	1	31	833	26.9	1
Dick Harris	60-65	27	251	9.3	0	3	49	16.3	0
Rickie Harris	65-72	128	1029	8.0	3	102	2326	22.8	0
Wendell Harris	62-67	27	275	10.2	0	12	293	24.4	0
Alex Hawkins	59-68	52	358	6.9	0	6	86	14.3	0
Alvin Haymond	64-73	253	2148	8.5	1	170	4438	26.1	2
Abner Haynes	60-67	85	875	10.3	1	121	3025	25.0	1
Jon Henderson	68-70					30	589	19.6	0
Sam Horner	60-62	6	19	3.2	0	39	828	21.2	0
Frank Jackson	61-67	49	487	9.9	0	48	1284	26.8	0
Dick James	56-65	120	952	7.9	0	189	4676	24.7	0
Bobby Jancik	62-67	67	695	10.4	1	158	4185	26.5	0
Homer Jones	64-70					37	888	24.0	1
Leroy Kelly	64-73	94	990	10.5	3	76	1784	23.5	0
Brady Keys	61-68	65	646	9.9	0	47	1113	23.7	0
Phil King	58-66					30	592	19.7	0
Ernie Koy	65-70					25	439	17.6	0
Jack Larscheid	60-61	12	106	8.8	0	39	1106	28.4	0
Chuck Latourette	67-68,70-71	64	537	8.4	1	59	1491	25.3	1
Dan Lewis	58-66					30	535	17.8	0
Gary Lewis	64-70	1	3	3.0	0	32	784	24.5	0
Keith Lincoln	61-68	25	342	13.7	1	39	1018	26.1	0
Jerry Logan	63-72	62	577	9.3	1	12	217	18.1	0
Joe Don Looney	64-67,69					29	652	22.5	0
Tony Lorick	64-69					40	1022	25.6	0
John Love	67,72	21	34	1.6	0	25	589	23.6	1
Paul Lowe	60-61,63-69	2	0	0.0	0	63	1411	22.4	0
Lenny Lyles	58-69					81	2161	26.7	3
John Mallory	68-71	39	294	7.5	1	6	94	15.7	0
Amos Marsh	61-67	17	75	4.4	0	65	1561	24.0	1
Aaron Martin	64-68	33	258	7.8	0	13	296	22.8	0
Billy Martin	62-64	30	155	5.2	0	53	1148	21.7	0
Tommy Mason	61-71	46	483	10.5	0	45	1067	23.7	0
Tom Matte	61-72	1	0	0.0	0	62	1367	22.0	0
Don Maynard	58,60-73	26	132	5.1	0	14	343	24.5	0
Don McCall	67-70					29	756	26.1	0
Tommy McDonald	57-68	73	404	5.5	1	51	1055	20.7	0
Ed Meador	59-70	43	275	6.4	0	7	168	24.0	0
Gene Milton	68-69	7	59	8.4	0	26	574	22.1	0

Lifetime Statistics — 1960-1969 Players Section 3 — PUNT RETURNS and KICKOFF RETURNS (continued)
(All men with 25 or more Punt Returns or 25 or more Kickoff Returns)

Name	Years	PUNT RETURNS No.	Yards	Avg.	TD	KICKOFF RETURNS No.	Yards	Avg.	TD
Gene Mingo	60-70	18	214	11.9	1	34	742	21.8	0
Bobby Mitchell	58-68	69	699	10.1	3	102	2690	26.4	5
Charley Mitchell	63-68	21	251	12.0	0	63	1492	23.7	1
Willie Mitchell	64-70	56	564	10.1	1	7	178	25.4	0
Lenny Moore	56-67	14	56	4.0	0	49	1088	22.2	0
Tom Moore	60-67					71	1882	26.5	0
Johnny Morris	58-67	104	893	8.6	0	54	1267	23.5	0
Joe Morrison	59-72	23	79	3.4	0	30	640	21.3	0
Bob Neff	66-68	24	165	6.9	0	35	917	26.2	0
Al Nelson	65-73	1	3	3.0	0	101	2625	26.0	0
Jimmy Patton	55-66	27	143	5.3	1	28	735	26.3	1
Clarence Peaks	57-65					39	882	22.6	0
Elijah Pitts	61-71	75	394	5.3	1	28	535	19.1	0
Willie Porter	68	22	135	6.1	0	36	812	22.6	0
Dickie Post	67-71					34	760	22.4	0
Bob Reed	62-63	18	173	9.6	0	26	704	27.1	0
Lance Rentzel	65-72,74	48	217	4.5	0	32	783	24.5	1
Bo Roberson	61-66	3	54	18.0	0	130	3057	23.5	1
Walter Roberts	64-67,69-70	72	446	6.2	0	107	2728	25.5	1
Jerry Robinson	62-65	10	77	7.7	0	44	1009	22.9	0
Johnny Roland	66-73	49	452	9.2	2	25	507	20.3	0
Ed Rutkowski	63-68	68	514	7.6	1	53	1270	24.0	0
Johnny Sample	58-68	68	559	8.2	1	60	1560	26.0	1
Gale Sayers	65-71	27	391	14.5	2	91	2781	30.6	6
Charlie Scales	60-66	1	0	0.0	0	46	991	21.5	0
Goldie Sellers	66-69	19	217	11.4	1	27	701	26.0	2
Carver Shannon	62-64	30	213	7.1	0	46	1265	27.5	1
Roy Shivers	66-72	34	129	3.8	0	48	1162	24.2	1
Bill Shockley	60-62,68	5	18	3.6	0	32	745	23.3	0
Jim Shofner	58-63	46	308	6.7	0	1	0	0.0	0
Les Shy	66-70					29	687	23.7	0
Bobby Smith	62-66	25	151	6.0	0	40	1024	25.6	0
Noland Smith	67-69	63	635	10.1	1	82	2137	26.1	1
Billy Stacy	59-63	54	393	7.3	2	26	607	23.3	0
Marsh Starks	63-64	8	43	5.4	0	26	519	20.0	0
Jim Steffen	59-66	47	349	7.4	0	44	1107	25.2	0
Jim Stiger	63-67	68	529	7.8	0	27	610	22.6	0
Jerry Stovall	63-71					46	1183	25.7	0
Pat Studstill	61-62,64-72	59	716	12.1	0	75	1924	25.7	1
Bob Suci	62-63	25	233	9.3	0	17	360	21.2	0
Rosey Taylor	61-72	15	66	4.4	1	26	614	23.6	0
Bobby Thompson	64-69	14	72	5.1	0	27	622	23.0	0
Bubba Thornton	69					30	749	25.0	0
Larry Todd	65-70					25	584	23.3	0
Bill Triplett	62-63,65-72					49	1058	21.6	0
Bill Tucker	67-71	1	1	1.0	0	40	879	22.0	0
Bake Turner	62-70	21	156	7.4	0	75	1688	22.5	0
Tom Vaughn	65-71	33	298	9.0	0	62	1595	25.7	0
Carl Ward	67-69	7	67	9.6	0	38	840	22.1	1
Charley Warner	63-66	17	206	12.1	0	86	2187	25.4	3
Jimmy Warren	64-74,77	4	-1	-0.3	0	30	684	22.8	0
Tom Watkins	61-65,67-68	96	970	10.1	3	101	2510	24.9	0
Ken Webb	58-63					27	561	20.8	0
Willie West	60-68	51	388	7.6	0	40	908	22.7	0
Dick Westmoreland	63-69	2	10	5.0	0	28	564	20.1	0
Bobby Williams	66-67,69-71					77	1934	25.1	2
Clancy Williams	65-72					32	810	25.3	0
Travis Williams	67-71	13	213	16.4	1	102	2801	27.5	6
Willie Wood	60-71	187	1391	7.4	2	3	20	6.7	0
Abe Woodson	58-66	123	956	7.8	2	193	5538	28.7	5

Lifetime Statistics — 1960-1969 Players Section 4 — PUNTING
(All men with 25 or more Punts)

Name	Years	No.	Avg.
Billy Atkins	58-64	219	42.0
Sam Baker	53,56-69	701	42.7
Jim Bakken	62-77	61	37.5
Zeke Bratkowski	54,57-68,71	90	38.7
Ode Burrell	64-69	29	36.8
Don Chandler	56-67	660	43.5
Gary Collins	62-71	336	41.0
Ollie Cordill	67-69	45	41.4
Wayne Crow	60-63	222	40.2
Cotton Davidson	54,57,60-66,68	278	38.4
Tommy Davis	56-69	511	44.7
Eagle Day	59-60	59	42.0
Boyd Dowler	59-69,71	93	42.9
Jim Elliott	67	72	38.1
Doug Elmore	62	54	34.4
Sam Etcheverry	61-62	59	38.3
Jim Fraser	62-66,68	271	43.3
Tom Gilburg	61-65	232	41.4
Allen Green	61	61	36.7
Bobby Joe Green	60-73	970	42.6
Tom Greene	60-61	59	37.9
John Hadl	62-77	105	39.7
George Herring	60-61	150	38.4
King Hill	58-69	368	41.3
Ed Holler	63-64	31	43.0
Sam Horner	60-62	64	38.4
Tom Janik	63-71	253	39.1
Curley Johnson	60-69	556	42.5
John Kilgore	65-69	234	41.0
Ernie Koy	65-70	225	38.5
Frank Lambert	65-66	156	43.6
Daryle Lamonica	63-74	51	40.6
Chuck Latourette	67-68,70-71	248	40.5
Dale Livingston	68-70	146	41.1
Joe Don Looney	64-67,69	32	42.4
Billy Lothridge	64-72	532	41.0
Paul Maguire	60-70	794	41.7
Billy Martin	64-68	28	37.4
John McCormick	62-63,65-66,68	47	39.1
Wahoo McDaniel	60-68	37	37.7
Max McGee	54,57-67	256	41.6
Mike Mercer	61-70	307	40.6
Charley Milstead	60-61	66	35.8
Earl Morrall	56-76	106	37.7
Tom Morrow	62-64	45	36.9
Jim Norton	60-68	518	42.4
Jimmy Orr	58-70	59	39.4
Joe Paglieri	59-60	49	37.3
Rick Redman	65-73	153	37.5
Pat Richter	63-70	338	42.0
Bob Scarpito	61-68	282	44.0
Dave Sherer	59-60	102	42.2
Del Shofner	57-67	153	42.0
Jackie Smith	63-77	86	38.5
Jerry Stovall	63-71	87	40.2
Pat Studstill	61-62,64-72	560	40.7
Terry Swanson	67-69	139	39.8
Frank Tripucka	49-52,60-63	93	38.8
Danny Villanueva	60-67	488	42.7
Eddie Wilson	62-65	54	36.1
George Wilson	66	42	42.1
Jerrel Wilson	63-77	1009	43.8
Tom Yewcic	61-66	369	39.4

Lifetime Statistics — 1960-1969 Players Section 5 — KICKING
(All men with 10 or more PAT or Field Goal attempts)

Name	Years	PAT	PAT Att.	PAT Pct.	FG	FG Att.	FG Pct.
Bruce Alford	67-69	41	43	95	31	52	60
Billy Atkins	58-64	56	63	89	8	19	42
John Aveni	59-61	72	80	90	22	63	35
Sam Baker	53,56-69	428	444	96	179	316	57
Jim Bakken	62-77	507	523	97	267	419	64
George Blair	61-64	122	136	90	50	79	63
George Blanda	49-58,60-75	941	957	98	335	638	53
Tommy Brooker	62-66	149	149	100	41	86	48
Gino Cappelletti	60-70	342	353	97	172	333	51
Don Chandler	56-67	248	258	96	94	161	58
Jim Christopherson	62	28	28	100	11	20	55
Mike Clark	63-71,73	325	338	96	133	232	57
Bobby Joe Conrad	58-69	95	99	96	14	33	42
Cotton Davidson	54,57,60-66,68	32	33	97	2	5	40
Tommy Davis	59-69	348	350	97	130	276	47
Harold Deters	67	9	10	90	1	4	25
Charlie Durkee	67-68,71-72	87	88	99	52	101	51
Bob Etter	68-69	50	52	96	26	51	51
George Fleming	61	24	25	96	11	26	42
Momcilo Gavric	69	22	24	92	3	11	27
Cookie Gilchrist	62-67	14	16	88	8	20	40
Charlie Gogolak	66-68,70-72	114	117	97	52	93	56
Pete Gogolak	64-74	344	354	97	173	294	59
Bruce Gossett	64-74	374	383	98	219	360	61
Allen Green	61	19	19	100	5	15	33
Dick Guesman	60-64	69	74	93	20	62	32
Wendell Harris	60-67	8	11	73	1	4	25
Joe Hergert	60-61				8	18	44
Jack Hill	61	16	16	100	5	15	23
Paul Hornung	57-62,64-66	190	194	98	66	140	47
Bob Humphreys	67-68	19	20	95	8	20	40
Bob Jencks	63-65	93	102	91	14	39	36
Jimmy Keyes	68-69	30	30	100	7	16	44
Bob Khayat	60,62-63	90	92	98	38	74	51
Lou Kirouac	63-64,66-67	19	24	79	9	18	50
Jerry Kramer	58-68	90	94	96	29	54	54
Karl Kremser	69-70	28	29	97	13	23	57
Gary Kroner	65-67	57	58	98	29	56	52
Roger LeClerc	60-67	154	160	96	76	152	50
Keith Lincoln	61-68	16	18	89	5	12	42
Dale Livingston	68-70	39	41	95	28	54	52
John Love	67,72	10	11	91	2	7	29
Booth Lusteg	66-69	97	101	96	35	75	47
Chuck Mercein	65-70	9	10	90	2	8	25
Mike Mercer	61-70	288	295	98	102	195	52
Lou Michaels	58-69,71	386	402	96	187	341	55
Gene Mingo	60-70	215	223	96	112	220	51
Les Murdock	67	13	15	87	4	9	44
Dennis Patera	68	10	12	83	2	8	25
Tom Pennington	62	13	15	87	2	5	40
Milt Plum	57-69	16	16	100	6	16	38
Bill Shockley	60-62,68	91	95	96	26	57	46
Jackie Simpson	61-64	6	6	100	3	10	30
Jack Spikes	60-67	74	80	93	20	59	34
Andy Stynchula	60-68	13	14	93	3	7	43
Bob Timberlake	65	21	22	95	1	15	7
Herb Travenio	64-65	50	52	96	20	35	57
Wade Traynham	66-67	24	24	100	7	19	37
Dick Van Raaphorst	64,66-67	112	114	98	45	90	50
Danny Villanueva	60-67	236	241	98	85	160	53
Wayne Walker	67-68	26	26	100	8	16	50
Wayne Walker	58-72	172	175	98	53	131	40
John Wittenborn	58-62,64-68	41	41	100	20	45	44
Mack Yoho	60-63	52	61	85	13	35	37

1960-1969:
Emergence of the AFL

New York Jets . . . 1968 Super Bowl champs celebrate

JOE NAMATH

WEEB EWBANK

VINCE LOMBARDI (left) and GEORGE HALAS . . .
two of the greatest quit.

Y.A. TITTLE . . . '60's "Comeback Kid"

JOE NAMATH . . . Pete Rozelle
helps with press

HANK STRAM (left) and Sid Gillman . . .
big AFL winners

AL DAVIS . . . AFL's "boy commissioner"

ALEX KARRAS . . . before suspension   GALE SAYERS . . . after operation

Kansas City Chiefs hoist Coach Stram during glory days.

THE DECADE'S GREATEST QUARTERBACKS . . . Bart Starr (left) and Johnny Unitas.

LAMAR HUNT . . . chief AFL organizer   **JIM BROWN . . . decade's greatest runner**

1970-1977:
The Dolphin Domination

Garo Yepremian (1) leaps with joy after his field goal beat Kansas City in AFC playoff to end NFL longest game ever and start Miami's domination of professional football.

JIM MANDICH . . . after Super Bowl TD

DON SHULA . . .
after first Super Bowl win.

BOB GRIESE (left) and DON SHULA . . .
Dolphin directors

TERRY BRADSHAW . . .
No. 1 in famed draft

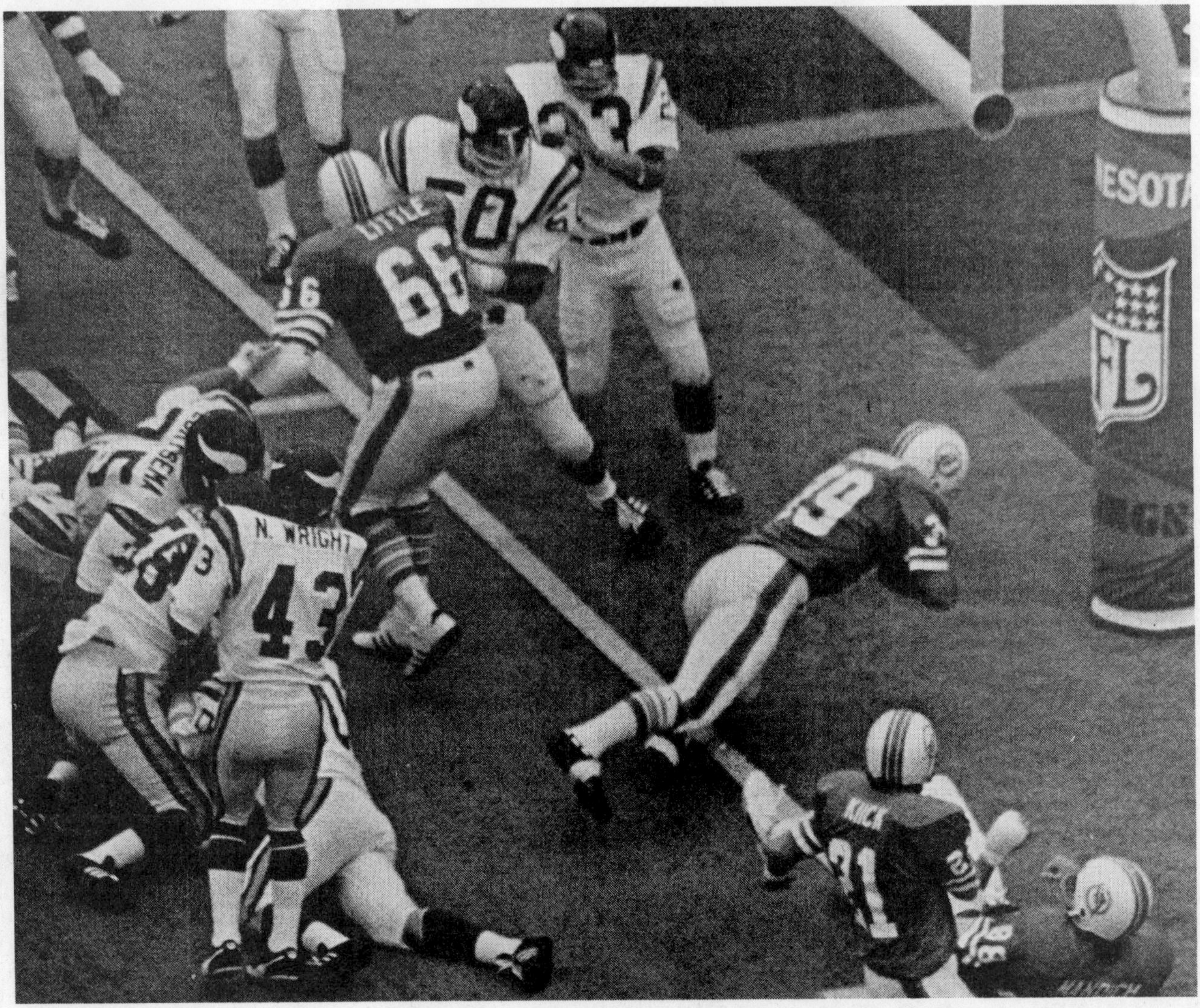

LARRY CSONKA scores for Dolphins against Vikings in 24-7 Super Bowl VIII victory.

WORLD FOOTBALL LEAGUE

KICKOFF: JULY 10

WFL

GARY DAVIDSON . . .
WFL leader

WFL action between Chicago Fire and visiting Houston Texans

LARRY CSONKA (left) and JIM KIICK . . . before WFL jump

PAUL WARFIELD . . made WFL jump

DUANE THOMAS (33). . . star of Cowboys' Super VI win over Dolphins.

Ed Garvey . . .
NFLPA leader

Two unmistakable Dallas sights . . . Roger Staubach and Cowgirls take over center stage in NFL.

1970 - 1977
BIG DOLLARS - TV
The Players Association and the WFL

On February 1, 1970 they made it official. As agreed upon three years and eight months before, the National and American Football Leagues entered into marriage. Their courtship was rocky to the very end. As late as January, the important matter of the older NFL's divisional realignment remained - unsettled. But by March 16, the biggest problem faced by a "competition committee" of Tex Schramm, Vince Lombardi, Paul Brown and Al Davis upon convening in Honolulu was whether or not to allow the two-point play option after touchdowns as was the case in the AFL. After settling that issue—deciding to stick to the NFL rule of a single point after touchdowns—all that was left for the committee to take care of were relatively minor matters regarding things like jerseys and the type of football that would be used.

Enhancing the union of the two leagues was a splendid wedding present from the American Broadcasting Company. For slightly more than $8 million each season, ABC agreed to telecast 13 prime-time games on Monday night. The risk of professional football over-exposing itself the way boxing did was offset by an over-all TV bill to the three major networks that came to about $150 million, including the three-year Monday night package. Divided out, it meant each of the 26 teams would receive approximately $1.7 million in 1970—$500,000 more than what each NFL team was getting and $800,000 more than the eight charter AFL franchises were receiving.

Before too long the two leagues officially became the American and National Football Conferences of the National Football League, with Kansas City Chief Owner Lamar Hunt and Chicago Bear Owner George Halas selected as their respective figurehead presidents. In their first draft under one roof in February, the first player chosen was Terry Bradshaw, a strong-armed signal caller from Louisiana Tech, by Pittsburgh. Bradshaw went on to live up to his high rating and was the first of many wise draft selections enabling the Steelers to become an AFC powerhouse after years of mediocrity in the old NFL. The first "shocker" pick of the '70's was Texas A & M running back Larry Stegent, selected by St. Louis over such well-publicized runners as Heisman Trophy winner Steve Owens of Oklahoma and Colorado's Bob Anderson. Recurring leg ailments forced Stegent to spend practically his whole pro career limping on the sidelines.

Armed with the largest TV contract in the history of professional sports and delighted by the news that '69 attendance figures had also reached record-breaking proportions, the NFL prepared for the '70 season with unabashed enthusiasm. Before it got underway, however, NFL players rallied together in early July and displayed surprisingly strong union strength by threatening to sit out the season unless management could settle a list of grievances, the biggest of which had to do with their pension fund. Peace was assured in August as the players received a pension fund increase of roughly $11 million, and although neither side was entirely satisfied with the settlement, a contract agreement that extended to the 1974 season enabled the emphasis in the decade's first three years to be placed mainly on the game itself.

In September, just a few weeks before the regular season began, Lombardi, a dominant force in the '60's as head coach of the mighty Green Bay Packers, died of stomach cancer. His influence lived on, however, as bone-crunching defenses and conservative but powerful running attacks were what most head coaches felt they needed to win games. In the very first inter-conference struggle on the first week of the '70 season, Bud Grant's Minnesota Vikings avenged their Super Bowl loss to Hank Stram's Kansas City Chiefs the previous year, defeating them 27-10 with a heavy dependence on ball control and an opportunistic defense that quickly capitalized on Chief mistakes. After the game Grant said, "We proved that the defense of the 1960's can beat the offense of the '70's." Further proof was provided by Don Shula's Miami Dolphins, a team that went on to become the '70's first true dynasty, with three successive Super Bowl trips beginning in 1971.

After losing 24-3 to the Dallas Cowboys and Duane Thomas that year, the stage was set for professional football's most impressive team performance, a perfect 17-0 season. Behind the unspectacular but effective power running of Larry Csonka, Jim Kiick and Mercury Morris, the smooth, calculated quarter-backing of Bob Griese and Earl Morrall and a defense that had "no names" but plenty of quickness and savvy, the Dolphins wrote 1972's biggest and most colorful story. And while at first it appeared the flamboyant Stram would replace Lombardi as the '70's dominant coaching figure, the genius Shula exhibited through the decade as the Miami mentor resulted in his No. 1 ranking with two years left in the decade. After Miami Owner Joe Robbie lured him away from Baltimore in May of 1970, offering him a piece of the team to sweeten the pot, Colt Owner Carroll Rosenbloom leveled tampering charges. Commissioner Peter Rozelle agreed and Rosenbloom received the Dolphins' No. 1 draft pick in 1971. Shula quickly made up for the loss of that draft choice with an unexpected 10-4 record and the Dolphins' first playoff berth in his rookie year at the helm. The next year Miami won its first of four consecutive AFC East Championship with a 10-3-1 mark. Their opening-round 27-24 playoff victory in '71 over Kansas City was one of pro football's most memorable contests—an 82 minute, 40 second thriller on Christmas Day that substantiated the increasing importance of the field goal kicker in pro football. After usually reliable Chief PK Jan Stenerud missed two "gimmee" three-pointers (four altogether), the last one a 31-yard attempt with 35 seconds left in regulation that would have given his team the victory, little Garo Yepremian finally ended the NFL's longest game ever with a dramatic 37-yarder with 7:20 remaining in the sixth quarter.

Visions of Yepremian's kick in the Kansas City twilight still burned brightly when Shula's troops began their march toward perfection the next year. Before the season began a seemingly unimportant league ruling to move the hashmarks closer to the middle of the field resulted in much greater success for "outside" running attacks. This trend provided the perfect complement to Csonka's inside strength, and by the time the '72 season was over, the Dolphins had rewritten the NFL rushing record (2,960 yards), and Shula had become the first NFL coach to win 100 games in his first decade. In '73 the Dolphins picked up where they left off, crushing three playoff opponents 85-33, including a 24-7 rout of Minnesota in Super Bowl VII. In an effort to curb the Dolphins' seemingly unyielding dominance in the NFL, defensive masterminds like Grant, Dallas' Tom Landry and San Francisco's Dick Nolan tried to emulate Shula and Miami defensive coordinator Bill Arnsparger's winning formula with increasingly complicated strategies that continued to take the game away from the offense. High-scoring, pass-laden games, the kind that epitomized the AFL in its salad years, were few and far between. Field position, zone defenses and cautious play selection that guaranteed a cutdown in turnovers tended to eliminate some of the game's most exciting elements.

Meanwhile, the NFL's viewing audience was multiplying rapidly every week. Before the '73 season began, Congress lifted the TV blackout on games sold out 72 hours in advance, thanks mainly to the efforts of Massachusetts Senator Torbert MacDonald. Rozelle, adhering to his claim that only seven NFL teams were assured of sellouts on a weekly basis, gloomily predicted that the game would suffer greatly as a result. But the Capitol Hill politicians saw the bill's passing as an overwhelmingly popular victory for the average fan at a time when the Watergate controversy was tarnishing their image. The real victors were the TV people, and a situation was developing wherby future TV contracts would provide the game's biggest meal ticket—not the ticket-paying customers. The number of "no shows" at each game became a meaningful statistic, but the game didn't suffer enough at the gate to bring back the blackout.

However, because enough people were hooked by the convenience of lounging in their easy chairs while watching their favorite teams, TV ratings became healthier than ever before. Media hype reached new heights, especially for post-season games headed by the annual Super Bowl. Fortunately, the powers of the league realized there was nothing overly exciting about games like the '73 Super Bowl in which Miami lulled the Vikings—and numerous fans everywhere—to sleep. They were astute enough to sense a staleness had seeped deep enough into their product to warrant a change in its makeup before the '74 season began. Pressure produced by the formation of the World Football League that same year further necessitated a new look. At a meeting in New York, concerned and worried over the growing number of stars who were planning to defect to the new league, NFL owners laid down the following rule changes:

• Overtime—In an effort to do away with ties, an alternative to a loss that had become more and more acceptable by coaches wishing to play it safe, a sudden-death, 15-minute extra period was introduced for pre-season and regular-season games. If a score remained even at the completion of the added session, the game would still be declared a tie.

• Kicking—The goal posts were moved back 10 yards from the goal line to the end line to do away with an over-reliance on the easy three-pointer. In addition, kickoffs were moved back five yards to the 35-yard line while missed field goals would be returned to the line of scrimmage or 20-yard line, whichever was further from the goal line. What this meant most of all was that the punter would become more important, with his placement and coffin-corner kicking ability outweighting the distance he kicked the ball. Finally, players on a team kicking for a field goal or punting could not cross the line of scrimmage until the ball was kicked. This meant a punter's "hang time" would also become especially significant.

• Passing—Roll blocking and the cutting down of wide receivers were eliminated to take away what had become a distinct advantage for defenses. Also, downfield blockers were allowed to make contact only once with potential receivers, and wide receivers blocking back toward the ball three yards from the line of scrimmage could not block below the waist.

• Penalties—Infractions for offensive holding, illegal use of hands and tripping were reduced from 15 to 10 yards when they occurred in the area of the line of scrimmage to three yards beyond it.

The WFL, meanwhile, was shooting for a July 10 opening with 12 franchises, six of them in cities already occupied by NFL teams, preparing for 20 regular-season weeks of what was being billed as a wide-open brand of football with 10 "revolutionary" rule changes (kickoffs from the 30-yard line to insure more runbacks, goal posts moved back to the rear of the endzone, missed field goals to be returned to the line of scrimmage except when attempted inside the 20-yard line, an optional two-point conversion attempt, receivers needing just one foot in bounds for a completion, a fifth quarter split into two 7½-minute segments to break ties, a restriction on the fair catches of punts, motion permitted by an offensive back toward the line of scrimmage before the snapping of the ball, hash marks moved in toward the center of the field and the return of any incompleted pass into the endzone on fourth down to the previous line of scrimmage instead of being automatically returned to the 20-yard line).

The commissioner of the WFL was Gary L. Davidson, an attorney who founded the American Basketball Association and co-founded the World Hockey Association. He resigned in '73 as president of the WHA to devote his full time and energy to the organization of the WFL. The 12 initial franchises were the Birmingham Americans, Chicago Fire, Detroit Wheels, the Hawaiians, Houston Texans, Jacksonville Sharks, Memphis Southmen, New York Stars, Philadelphia Bell, Portland Storm, Southern California Sun and Florida Blazers. Games were scheduled primarily on Wednesdays and Thursdays, and a TV package with the independent TVS network was hoped to net in excess of $1 million for WFL clubs, with weekly telecasts aired live on Thursday nights on more than 135 stations across the country.

Skeptics quickly painted gloomy forecasts based on anticipated TV revenue that would return $100,000 to each team at best, and they cast doubts over the projected $2.2 million operating budget for the first season. Davidson was shooting for average crowds of about 28,000 to 30,000 per game, with an average ticket price of about $7.50. These figures instantly made professional sports followers in New York laugh, considering that the Stars would be playing their games in Dowing Stadium on Randall's Island, a worn out facility with a well-documented history of sports fatalities. But early indications showed that the Fire could offer an attractive alternative to the NFL Bears in win-starved Chicago, and untapped locations like Birmingham and Memphis (switched from Toronto to avoid a conflict with the Canadian Football League before the season began) could garner commendable attendance figures.

But what really made the NFL and sports fans everywhere stand up and take notice was the shocking announcement in the spring of '74 that three of pro football's biggest individual attractions—Miami's Csonka, Kiick and WR Paul Warfield—planned to leave the team they helped make a dynasty and jump to the WFL Toronto franchise - after fulfilling the final year of their contracts with the Dolphins. The combined offer to the trio from Toronto millionaire owner John Bassett came to $3.5 million. Csonka, the Dolphins' offensive pillar of strength, was offered the largest share of the Toronto package—$1 million up front and $2 million to be insured by Lloyds of London as compared to the estimated $65,000 the final year of his Miami contract was worth. The three players' agent, Ed Keating, demanded a $3.5 million counter offer from the Dolphins, plus a deposit of $3 million in the bank to accompany a three-year no-cut, no-trade agreement and a provision the money be payable to their heirs if anything should happen to them. While Robbie and Shula lividly blasted the proposal, Dolphin teammates and other players around the league couldn't hold back their envy.

Miami TE Jim Mandich quickly announced he had a contract offer from the Birmingham franchise for three years at $225,000 and would sign with the Americans if the Dolphs couldn't match it. Other big-name stars didn't hesitate to jump on the bandwagon. Running backs Charley Harraway and Paul Robinson from Washington and Houston, respectively, agreed to play for Birmingham immediately. The list of star players planning to defect in '75 along with the Miami trio included QB Craig Morton (from Dallas to the Houston Texans), WR Ron Jessie (from Detroit to Birmingham), RB Calvin Hill (from Dallas to the Hawaiians), TE Ted Kwalick (from San Francisco to the Hawaiians) and QB Daryl Lamonica (from Oakland to Southern California). Ken Stabler, the passing ace who had more than adequately replaced Lamonica as Oakland's No. 1 signal caller, planned a move back to his native Alabama in 1976 to play with Birmingham when his Raider contract ran out.

But the WFL would have to depend on lesser-known players for the most part in its first year. On July 24, the Americans pleased a legitimately large home-town crowd with a 58-33 victory over Memphis that was just what the doctor ordered. NFL reject QB's George Mira (Birmingham) and John Huarte (Memphis) engaged in the kind of barn-burning passing battle that any football fan would savor in his memory bank for a long time to come. But in Philadelphia, doctored attendance figures gave the league its first real dose of adverse publicity. It was reported in mid-August that the Bell's actual paid attendance at its first home game was only 13,800—a far cry from the 55,534 figure it threw out for public consumption. After the announced attendance of 64,719 for its second home game turned out to be a paltry 6,200 paid, Bell President John B. Kelly, jr., abruptly resigned from his post. As August drew to a close, one of the league's best teams after six regular-season weeks, the Florida Blazers coached by Jack Pardee, was threatening to move to Atlanta because it was so badly under-capitalized. Six weeks later, the Houston Texans were quickly transferred to Louisiana the day before a game with first-place Birmingham and as a result, the team's coach, Jim Garrett, and first-string QB, Mike Taliaferro, quit the squad in a huff. The next week the Stars were swept away from Randall's Island and moved to Charlotte. In Jacksonville, it was announced the Shark players hadn't been paid in five weeks and that the team's ownership was being taken over by the league. In Detroit, the Wheels were declared legally bankrupt after no one among their reported 33 co-owners could clean up debts exceeding $2.5 million.

Fifteen weeks into the season the Wheels and Sharks were disbanded, and it was announced teams originally scheduled to play those clubs the rest of the year would play each other instead. Discouraging reports that players in Orlando, Southern California, Portland and Hawaii weren't getting paid as was the case with the defunct Jacksonville franchise - began to cast very real doubts about the league's future. In early November an emergency session was called in Chicago that ended with Davidson resigning as commissioner. Facing over-all debts reported as high as $20 million in its first season, the WFL no longer posed a serious threat to the NFL.

Under the direction of Chris Hemmeter, the original owner of the Hawaiian franchise, the league attempted to play the '75 season with the hope a clever reorganizational plan that was built around shared profits would keep it afloat. But even with the "Hemmeter Plan," a new $12 million deficit was incurred by the time the season was 10 weeks old, and in late October of '75 the league officially went under. Besides providing tragi-comic memories of players drinking water and eating biscuits before the '74 championship game, and uniforms being literally ripped off the backs of some of them by a local sheriff afterward, the WFL's main legacy was a crop of decent players like QB's Pat Haden and Danny White that would become valuable members of NFL teams, and coaches like Jack Pardee and John McVay who would eventually become respectable NFL field bosses. What had been at one time a major thorn in the NFL's side was now eliminated, but there were still big problems that needed solving, particularly the renegotiation of a new contract with the National Football League Players' Association. Renewed strike threats and legal hassles began early in 1974 and continued right up to the night of February 16, 1977 when NFLPA executive director Ed Garvey and Sargent Karch, management's main negotiator, finally reached a new contract agreement.

When the '74 contract renegotiation talks began, dissatisfaction among players was never so obvious, and in Garvey, they had a sharp, acid-tongued spokesman who seemed to have a special talent for turning off the owners. At the core of their unhappiness was the overwhelming power they felt Commissioner Rozelle exercised in decision covering a broad range of issues. After Los Angeles WR Lance Rentzel was arrested on drug charges, a majority of players fumed when Rozelle suspended him for the entire '73 season. The commissioner had concluded that Rentzel's actions were severely detrimental to the

league, and players questioned his right to make such reaching moral decision that ran the risk of ruining a play career. Equally unpopular was the commissioner's power decide on the type of compensation a team was allowed after losing a free agent (the Rozelle Rule). Such a power, they argued, was an illegal restriction designed to minimize player movement, while Rozelle and the owners contended that the Rozelle Rule was essential in maintaining competitive balance in the NFL. Both sides drifted further apart, and the result of their inability to bargain in good faith resulted in pre-season strikes in '74 and '75 that left a bad taste in the public's mouth. Making matters worse were growing differences of opinion among the players that seriously threatened to destroy the union in '75.

But after three years of continued bitterness, both sides made great strides toward peace by changing their stances early in '76. Garvey projected a much-needed mellowness that made it easier for him to deal face-to-face with management. Helping along in this regard was federal judge Earl R. Larson's court decision the previous winter that confirmed Garvey's claim that the Rozelle Rule was indeed illegal. He knew the decision gave him new-found leverage in confrontations with the owners, but he also knew there was no longer a need for abrasive rehetoric because the proof was in the ruling itself. Furthermore, not long after the Larson ruling, the courts upheld the need for college and expansion drafts for the 1977 season, a decision which resulted in a judicial compromise of sorts. And if compromise had been deemed good enough for the courts, it certainly was a strong enough measure to bring about a settlement. Karch followed the same line of reasoning and a new agreement was reached that offered the following highlights:

• The union was assured of survival, since all the players joining the pros after February 1, 1974 would have to pay the equivalent of annual union dues even if they declined to sign up as members.

• The owners gained restoration of a modified draft and compensation system for free agents, as well as assurance that there would be no strike for five years and an end to costly litigation initiated by the players.

• Rozelle lost his one-man authority over player-club disputes unless they involved conduct detrimental to the integrity of professional football. He also lost his authority to set compensation for a free-agent veteran switching to another team. A specific set of draft choices would be given in payment, depending upon the new salary of the player. Two impartial arbitrators-James Scearce, former head of the Fereral Mediation Service, and Paul Martha, a formal player-would decide non-playing field controversies.

• Veterans were to receive higher pre-season pay and biger pay-offs for post-season playoffs. A player released because of injury the previous season must be paid half his salary up to $37,500. After four years, no option clause would be allowed in any player's contract without his permission and he would be paid 110 per cent of his salary while playing out his option year. If waived, a veteran with four years in the NFL could declare himself a free agent and try to sign on with any team that wants him.

The new contract agreement undoubtedly still contained some flaws. Player movement during the '77 offseason appeared to be stymied by the teams' collective reluctance to make offers to free agents for fear of losing high draft choices. But for the most part professional football was enjoying greater prosperity than ever before. Expansion teams in Seattle and Tampa Bay were flourishing, and the number of nationally televised games for the '78 season was expanded to include three Sunday nights and one Thursday night offering. Two more teams would be added to the playoffs while the schedule format was changed to hopefully put teams on a more equal footing. The AFC was clearly the strongest of the two conferences, but the NFC's Dallas franchise was beginning to be thought of in the same terms as the great Miami teams of the early '70's. The emphasis was once again on the game itself.

N.F.C. 1970 The Monday-Night Circus

fan found a new addiction this season: Monday-... American Broadcasting Company telecast a game ... of the season, with Howard Cosell, Don Meredith ... men behind the mikes. For the first time ever, ... secondary to the show put on by the announcers ...osell, the verbose ex-labor lawyer who had built a reputation by being highly critical of almost everything, commented on each game in highly dramatic tones, while ex-Dallas Cowboy quarterback Don Meredith, dubbed "Dandy Don" by Cosell, mixed his analysis with homespun country witticisms. The interplay between these two, sometimes veering off into mutual needling, delighted some and drove others to turn the sound off on their sets. Jackson, the member of the trio who concentrated on reporting the game, was rewarded after the season by being dropped from the series.

EASTERN DIVISION

Dallas Cowboys—The Cowboys had so much talent, some coaches would have been delighted to trade their starters for the Dallas second-stringers. With two good running backs already in the fold in Calvin Hill and Walt Garrison, the Cowboys this year added rookie Duane Thomas, an uncommunicative man who did his talking by running over people while carrying a football. Herb Adderley was obtained from Green Bay to further strengthen the secondary, and when Lance Rentzel sat out the last weeks of the season with personal problems, rookie Reggie Rucker filled in capably. Although the offensive line had always been strong, Dave Manders, Blaine Nye, and Rayfield Wright all rose up from the second string to win starting jobs. Even at quarterback, coach Tom Landry had his pick of a good pocket passer in Craig Morton or a top roll-out passer in Roger Staubach.

New York Giants—Quarterback Fran Tarkenton ran the attack with imagination, Ron Johnson developed into a superb runner and receiver after coming over from Cleveland, Tucker Frederickson shook the injury hex for this year, Clifton McNeil grabbed Tarkenton's passes, and the offensive line matured into a sturdy unit. The defense was less impressive, but aces Fred Dryer, Jim Files, and Spider Lockhart held the platoon together. After beating St. Louis one week from the end, the Giants held a share of first place with Dallas heading into their final game before losing 31-3 to the Rams.

St. Louis Cardinals—The Cards sailed into December with an 8-2-1 record and first place in the East was theirs for the taking. Twice during the year the Cards had beaten the Cowboys, laying a 38-0 drubbing on them in their meeting in Dallas. MacArthur Lane, Ernie McMillan, Larry Stallings, Roger Wehrli, and Larry Wilson all turned in All-Pro performances, while a host of other Cards all enjoyed good seasons. But just when the team seemed about to capture its first title since moving to St. Louis in 1960, the roof caved in. First the Detroit Lions beat them, then the New York Giants clubbed them 34-17 to knock them out of first place. Then, with the title a fleeting dream, the Cards dropped their finale 28-27 to the Redskins.

Washington Redskins—When training camp opened, head coach Vince Lombardi wasn't there; he was in the hospital, terminally ill with cancer. Assistant Bill Austin took over as head man until Lombardi got out of the hospital, but the all-time great coach died on September 3, two weeks before the start of the regular season. Austin guided the club through the season, but the team never really recovered from Lombardi's death. The only bright spot of the year was the development of runner Larry Brown into a star. Using his blockers well and fighting for every yard, Brown became the first Redskin to rush 1,000 yards.

Philadelphia Eagles—A flabby defense and an injury to fullback Tom Woodeshick shackled the Eagles into last place in the Eastern Division, but the team did have talent in several areas. The trio of Gary Ballman, Harold Jackson, and Ben Hawkins provided top-notch receiving, and Cyril Pinder ran well at halfback. The linebacking corps had three solid players in Adrian Young, Tim Rossovich, and Ron Porter; Rossovich had other skills in addition to his talents on the field. The curly-haired, mustachioed Rossovich would occasionally do unusual things, such as walking into a party with his hair on fire.

CENTRAL DIVISION

Minnesota Vikings—The Vikings still had that marvelous defense, but they lacked that extra inspirational spark when quarterback Joe Kapp sat out the early games over a salary dispute and then was sold to Boston. Carl Eller, Alan Page, Paul Krause, and the other members of the defense smothered enough enemy offenses to win twelve games, while the offense operated just enough under Gary Cuozzo to make it back to first place this year. Place kicker Fred Cox could be counted on to make good on three-pointers within the 40-yard line to bail out the offense. But although Cuozzo passed the ball better than Kapp, the fanatical leadership Kapp provided was missing.

Detroit Lions—Even without a clear-cut starter at quarterback, the Lion attack still blossomed into a steady point-producing outfit. Bill Munson and Greg Landry split the passer's spot, although Landry played more as the season went on, and both found good runners in Mel Farr and Altie Taylor and good receivers in Earl McCullough, Larry Walton, and Charlie Sanders. The line gave both quarterbacks good protection and figured highly in the offense's performance. On defense, the linebacking and secondary corps were full with top players, with Dick LeBeau and Paul Naumoff of All-Pro quality, but the front four needed some new blood, as Alex Karras no longer was rushing quarterbacks as he once had.

Chicago Bears—Gale Sayers, the once incomparable runner, hurt his knee and went out of action early in the season for surgery. Brian Piccolo fell fatally ill with cancer. Quarterback Bobby Douglass threw four touchdown passes in his first starting assignment of the year, but broke his wrist late in the game and missed the rest of the year. Pre-season trades for Elijah Pitts, Lee Roy Caffey, and Craig Baynham didn't work out. But the Bears did win six games, and did uncover an exciting player in little Cecil Turner, who returned four kickoffs all the way to tie the NFL record.

Green Bay Packers—The Packers kept dropping veterans of the Lombardi years and suffered through another losing season. Willie Davis, Henry Jordan, and Boyd Dowler all retired, Elijah Pitts, Lee Roy Caffey, and Bob Hyland were dealt to Chicago, and Herb Adderley and Marv Fleming went to Dallas and Miami in trades. Of those staying on the scene, a sore arm hampered quarterback Bart Starr, a torn Achilles tendon sidelined linebacker Dave Robinson, and age started catching up on middle linebacker Ray Nitschke.

WESTERN DIVISION

San Francisco '49ers—After years of near misses and disappointing finishes, the '49ers finally put everything together and won the Western crown. The offense, always respected, blossomed into one of pro football's best with fine seasons from John Brodie, Gene Washington, Forrest Blue, and Cas Banaszek. The entire front line had a good year, allowing Brodie to be dropped only eight times all season. The defense, however, surprised most experts by turning in a superb performance. Coach Dick Nolan rotated the front four spots and thus kept fresh men in the game at all times. Dave Wilcox starred at linebacker, and the secondary of Jim Johnson, rookie Bruce Taylor, Rosey Taylor, and Al Randolph discouraged enemy passers. The acquisition of place kicker Bruce Gossett from Los Angeles nicely rounded out the picture.

Los Angeles Rams—Coach George Allen kept adding veterans to the squad, this year bringing in Kermit Alexander, but the Rams fell just short of the Western title. The defense as usual made life difficult for enemy offenses, and the Los Angeles attack again moved slowly but surely under the direction of Roman Gabriel. The rise of the '49ers gave the Rams competition for the divisional crown, however, and a 28-23 loss to Detroit on the final Monday-night game of the year knocked the Rams out of first place for good. The team recovered to beat New York to end the season, but that was to be George Allen's last game with the Rams. Owner Dan Reeves, already dying with cancer, fired Allen after the season despite his 49-17-4 record.

Atlanta Falcons—After improving for several seasons, the Falcons fell back for the first time under coach Norm Van Brocklin's regime. One weight on the team's progress was a remarkably unexciting offense, with an unsettled quarterback situation, no speed in the running back and receiving spots, and chaos in the front line. The defense had three star players in end Claude Humphrey, middle linebacker Tommy Nobis, and cornerback Ken Reaves, but most of the other positions lacked a quality occupant.

New Orleans Saints—The Saints' roster was like a revolving door, with players joining and leaving the squad in steady flows all season. Head coach Tom Fears was one of the mid-season departures, with J. D. Roberts promoted from a minor-league team to take charge of the Saints. The Saints had a few good players who put out consistently good performances, but they were almost buried amidst the chaos and mediocrity which ruined the season for the team. Flanker Dan Abramowicz and defensive tackle Dave Rowe played well, but the hero of the club was place kicker Tom Dempsey, a man born without a right hand and without toes on his right foot. Using a special kicking shoe, Dempsey was an erratic kicker but made the record books by booting a 63-yard three-pointer to beat the Detroit Lions.

FINAL TEAM STATISTICS

OFFENSE

	ATL.	CHI.	DALL.	DET.	G.B.	L.A.	MINN.	N.O.	N.Y.G.	PHIL.	ST.L.	S.F.	WASH.
FIRST DOWNS:													
Total	199	179	229	243	194	224	225	183	257	229	226	237	249
by Rushing	76	55	119	113	69	93	98	55	94	81	110	86	122
by Passing	110	104	95	107	110	120	111	112	150	126	104	125	100
by Penalty	13	20	15	23	15	11	16	16	13	22	12	26	27
RUSHING:													
Number	431	353	522	514	453	430	508	371	465	450	429	471	444
Yards	1600	1092	2300	2127	1595	1763	1634	1215	1799	1539	1998	1580	2021
Average Yards	3.7	3.1	4.4	4.1	3.5	4.1	3.2	3.3	3.9	3.4	4.7	3.4	4.6
Touchdowns	4	3	16	16	8	12	16	4	11	11	18	13	11
PASSING:													
Attempts	342	422	297	294	351	426	344	415	403	410	390	383	342
Completions	197	210	149	167	177	218	173	213	230	218	178	226	203
Completion Percentage	57.6	49.8	50.2	56.8	50.4	51.2	50.3	51.3	57.1	53.2	45.6	59.0	59.4
Passing Yards	2262	2431	2445	2121	2196	2658	2378	2690	2892	2651	2689	2990	2357
Avg. Yards per Attempt	6.6	5.8	8.2	7.2	6.3	6.2	6.9	6.5	7.2	6.5	6.9	7.8	6.9
Avg. Yards per Complet.	11.5	11.6	16.4	12.7	12.4	12.2	13.7	12.6	12.6	12.2	15.1	13.2	11.6
Times Tackled Passing	53	33	39	36	43	23	29	28	37	23	26	8	29
Yards Lost Tackled	431	258	296	264	382	150	197	232	258	200	216	67	249
Net Yards	1831	2173	2149	1857	1814	2508	2181	2458	2634	2451	2473	2923	2108
Touchdowns	18	21	18	19	11	17	12	11	19	16	16	25	23
Interceptions	21	22	16	12	24	13	15	22	12	23	19	10	10
Percent Intercepted	6.1	5.2	5.4	4.1	6.8	3.1	4.4	5.3	3.0	5.6	4.9	2.6	2.9
PUNTS:													
Number	76	84	69	62	87	67	61	77	54	71	65	75	61
Average Distance	38.7	40.8	41.3	40.0	40.2	39.1	37.9	42.5	38.3	36.6	40.9	38.4	40.9
PUNT RETURNS:													
Number	34	57	32	34	25	62	35	29	29	32	41	48	27
Yards	356	246	237	306	98	418	216	214	193	100	315	550	45
Average Yards	10.5	4.3	7.4	9.0	3.9	6.7	6.2	7.4	6.7	3.1	7.7	11.5	1.7
Touchdowns	2	0	0	1	0	0	0	0	1	0	1	0	0
KICKOFF RETURNS:													
Number	47	56	37	43	63	47	36	53	52	59	47	49	61
Yards	916	1472	888	959	1422	1236	842	1044	1157	1252	926	967	1223
Average Yards	19.5	26.3	24.0	22.3	22.6	26.3	23.4	19.7	22.3	21.2	19.7	19.7	20.0
Touchdowns	0	4	1	1	2	1	0	0	0	0	0	0	0
INTERCEPTION RETURNS:													
Number	19	17	24	28	20	19	28	22	17	10	21	22	15
Yards	191	129	307	417	398	280	412	260	223	102	255	308	240
Average Yards	10.1	7.6	12.8	14.9	19.9	14.7	14.7	11.8	13.1	10.2	12.1	14.0	16.0
Touchdowns	0	0	0	4	1	2	2	0	0	0	2	2	0
PENALTIES:													
Number	76	94	87	58	76	88	60	91	71	73	84	88	65
Yards	807	853	934	659	691	959	631	1029	641	799	896	997	613
FUMBLES:													
Number	24	29	29	26	34	27	25	27	29	26	24	24	26
Number Lost	17	13	12	15	17	17	16	18	14	16	14	15	14
POINTS:													
Total	206	256	299	347	196	325	335	172	301	241	325	352	297
PAT Attempts	26	28	35	41	22	34	35	17	32	29	38	41	34
PAT Made	23	28	35	41	19	34	35	16	32	25	37	39	33
FG Attempts	25	34	27	29	28	45	46	34	41	25	32	31	27
FG Made	9	20	18	20	15	29	30	18	25	14	20	21	20
Percent FG Made	36.0	58.8	66.7	69.0	53.6	64.4	65.2	52.9	61.0	56.0	62.5	67.7	74.1
Safeties	0	0	0	0	0	0	0	0	1	0	0	2	0

DEFENSE

	ATL.	CHI.	DALL.	DET.	G.B.	L.A.	MINN.	N.O.	N.Y.G.	PHIL.	ST.L.	S.F.	WASH.
FIRST DOWNS:													
Total	211	234	205	186	202	195	168	263	223	213	242	213	266
by Rushing	93	83	87	61	88	64	68	100	98	102	96	81	125
by Passing	98	133	105	112	102	113	89	150	110	95	116	110	125
by Penalty	20	18	13	13	12	18	11	13	15	16	30	22	16
RUSHING:													
Number	479	459	415	362	453	395	398	469	419	457	472	425	468
Yards	1722	1471	1656	1152	1829	1359	1365	1891	1692	2064	1762	1799	2068
Average Yards	3.6	3.2	4.0	3.2	4.0	3.4	3.4	4.0	4.0	4.5	3.7	4.2	4.4
Touchdowns	14	11	10	7	14	6	4	15	11	16	10	12	19
PASSING:													
Attempts	348	394	399	371	369	378	367	430	364	313	382	384	374
Completions	191	233	193	194	177	196	195	238	186	161	183	185	205
Completion Percentage	54.9	59.1	48.4	52.3	48.0	51.9	53.1	55.3	51.1	51.4	47.9	48.2	54.8
Passing Yards	2397	2925	2226	2491	2496	2615	1798	3197	2650	2176	2416	2434	2434
Avg. Yards per Attempt	6.9	7.4	5.6	6.7	6.8	6.9	4.9	7.4	7.3	7.0	6.3	6.3	6.5
Avg. Yards per Complet.	12.5	12.6	11.5	12.8	14.1	13.3	9.2	13.4	14.2	13.5	13.2	13.2	11.9
Times Tackled Passing	30	42	41	23	32	53	49	17	35	34	40	30	24
Yards Lost Tackled	243	329	313	195	270	426	360	136	279	287	309	261	169
Net Yards	2154	2596	1913	2296	2226	2189	1438	3061	2371	1889	2107	2173	2265
Touchdowns	11	18	10	14	13	15	6	19	19	16	16	19	14
Interceptions	19	17	24	28	20	19	28	22	17	10	21	22	15
Percent Intercepted	5.5	4.3	6.0	7.5	5.4	5.0	7.6	5.1	4.7	3.2	5.5	5.7	4.0
PUNTS:													
Number	60	87	74	70	71	88	84	56	62	62	80	82	56
Average Distance	41.2	37.6	41.1	39.1	40.1	37.8	37.5	40.4	39.7	39.1	40.0	40.4	39.3
PUNT RETURNS:													
Number	40	40	38	29	40	32	38	41	21	22	26	38	35
Yards	267	268	281	113	338	181	322	434	61	163	90	180	259
Average Yards	6.7	6.7	7.4	3.9	8.5	5.7	8.5	10.6	2.9	7.4	3.5	4.7	7.4
Touchdowns	0	0	1	0	0	0	1	1	0	1	0	0	0
KICKOFF RETURNS:													
Number	41	47	60	67	36	71	69	35	57	50	54	58	49
Yards	983	935	1142	1427	888	1278	1514	735	1359	1030	1262	1362	1181
Average Yards	24.0	19.9	19.0	21.3	24.7	18.0	21.9	21.0	23.8	20.6	23.4	23.5	24.1
Touchdowns	1	0	0	0	0	0	3	0	1	1	1	0	1
INTERCEPTION RETURNS:													
Number	21	22	16	12	24	13	15	22	12	23	19	10	10
Yards	283	251	259	174	421	92	175	256	172	461	276	95	181
Average Yards	13.5	11.4	16.2	14.5	17.5	7.1	11.7	11.6	14.3	20.0	14.5	9.5	18.1
Touchdowns	1	1	1	1	3	0	0	1	0	2	0	0	1
PENALTIES:													
Number	93	76	70	90	63	77	58	79	71	90	68	87	87
Yards	897	826	732	805	686	825	586	875	675	991	659	965	930
FUMBLES:													
Number	22	27	25	30	29	28	27	26	31	25	20	35	22
Number Lost	16	14	15	16	17	16	16	16	13	18	14	20	13
POINTS:													
Total	261	261	221	202	293	202	143	347	270	332	228	267	314
PAT Attempts	29	31	24	22	30	22	14	40	32	36	27	32	37
PAT Made	27	27	24	22	29	22	14	38	30	35	27	30	36
FG Attempts	40	29	26	26	42	25	27	34	29	39	26	24	26
FG Made	20	16	17	16	28	16	15	23	16	27	13	15	18
Percent FG Made	50.0	55.2	65.4	61.5	66.7	64.0	55.6	67.6	55.2	69.2	50.0	62.5	69.2
Safeties	0	0	1	0	0	0	0	0	0	0	0	0	1

CONFERENCE PLAYOFFS

December 26, at Dallas (Attendance 69,613)

SCORING

DALLAS	3	0	0	2	–5
DETROIT	0	0	0	0	–0

First Quarter
Dal. Clark, 26 yard field goal

Fourth Quarter
Dal. Andrie, Safety-tackled Landry

TEAM STATISTICS

DALLAS		DETR.
19	First Downs–Total	7
11	First Downs–Rushing	2
8	First Downs–Passing	5
0	First Downs–Penalty	0
0	Fumbles–Number	3
0	Fumbles–Lost Ball	2
6	Penalties–Number	0
47	Yards Penalized	0
0	Missed Field Goals	0
69	Offensive Plays–Total	50
231	Net Yards	156
3.3	Average Gain	3.1
1	Giveaways	3
3	Takeaways	1
+2	Difference	–2

INDIVIDUAL STATISTICS

DALLAS	No.	Yds.	Avg.	DETROIT	No.	Yds.	Avg.
RUSHING							
Thomas	30	135	4.5	Farr	12	31	2.6
Garrison	17	72	4.2	Taylor	9	16	1.8
Morton	3	2	0.7	Landry	3	15	5.0
	50	209	4.2	Owens	2	9	4.5
				Walton	1	5	5.0
					27	76	2.8
RECEIVING							
Garrison	2	8	4.0	Walton	3	39	13.0
Hayes	1	20	20.0	Taylor	2	7	3.5
Norman	1	10	10.0	McCullough	1	39	39.0
	4	38	9.5	Owens	1	7	7.0
					7	92	13.1
PUNTING							
Widby	8		44.7	Weaver	8		48.8
PUNT RETURNS							
Renfro	4	23	5.8	Barney	5	20	4.0
				Vaughan	1	1	1.0
					6	21	3.5
KICKOFF RETURNS							
Hayes	1	16	16.0	Williams	1	24	24.0
Waters	1	9	9.0	Maxwell	1	13	13.0
	2	25	12.5		2	37	18.5
INTERCEPTION RETURNS							
Renfro	1	13	13.0	Weger	1	31	31.0

PASSING

	Att.	Comp.	Comp. Pct.	Yds.	Int.	Yds/ Att.	Yds/ Comp.	Yds Lost Tkld.
DALLAS								
Morton	18	4	22.2	38	1	2.1	9.5	1–16
DETROIT								
Landry	12	5	41.7	48	0	4.0	9.6	
Munson	8	2	25.0	44	1	5.5	22.0	
	20	7	35.0	92	1	4.8	13.1	3–12

December 27, at Bloomington (Attendance 45,103)

SCORING

MINNESOTA	7	0	0	7	–14
SAN FRANCISCO	7	3	0	7	–17

First Quarter
Min. Krause, 22 yard fumble return
PAT–Cox (kick)
S.F. Witcher, 24 yard pass from Brodie
PAT–Gossett (kick)

Second Quarter
S.F. Gossett, 40 yard field goal

Fourth Quarter
S.F. Brodie, 1 yard rush
PAT–Gossett (kick)
Min. Washington, 24 yard pass from Cuozzo
PAT–Cox (kick)

TEAM STATISTICS

MINN.		S.F.
14	First Downs–Total	14
7	First Downs–Rushing	5
6	First Downs–Passing	8
1	First Downs–Penalty	1
3	Fumbles–Number	5
2	Fumbles–Lost Ball	3
1	Penalties–Number	3
5	Yards Penalized	37
2	Missed Field Goals	1
60	Offensive Plays–Total	71
241	Net Yards	289
4.1	Average Gain	4.1
4	Giveaways	3
3	Takeaways	4
–1	Difference	+1

INDIVIDUAL STATISTICS

MINNESOTA	No.	Yds.	Avg.	SAN FRANCISCO	No	Yds	Avg.
RUSHING							
Jones	15	60	4.0	Willard	27	85	3.1
Osborn	12	41	3.4	Tucker	7	5	0.7
Cuozzo	1	11	11.0	Brodie	2	3	1.5
Brown	2	5	2.5	Kwalick	1	2	2.0
	30	117	3.9	Cunningham	1	0	0.0
					38	95	2.5
RECEIVING							
Henderson	5	80	16.0	Tucker	6	48	8.0
Grim	2	37	18.5	Witcher	4	45	11.3
Washington	1	24	24.0	Kwalick	3	45	15.0
Jones	1	5	5.0	Washington	2	45	22.5
	9	146	16.2	Willard	1	18	18.0
					16	201	12.6
PUNTING							
McNeill	7		39.4	Spurrier	8		33.8
PUNT RETURNS							
None				B. Taylor	5	69	13.8
KICKOFF RETURNS							
Jones	3	49	16.3	Beard	1	17	17.0
Brown	1	23	23.0	Tucker	1	13	13.0
	4	72	18.0	Hoskins	1	0	0.0
					3	30	10.0
INTERCEPTION RETURNS							
None				Sniadecki	1	5	5.0
				B. Taylor	1	0	0.0
					2	5	2.5

PASSING

	Att.	Comp.	Comp. Pct.	Yds.	Int.	Yds/ Att.	Yds/ Comp.	Yds Lost Tkld.
MINNESOTA								
Cuozzo	27	9	33.3	146	2	5.4	16.2	3–22
SAN FRANCISCO								
Brodie	32	16	50.0	201	0	6.3	12.6	1– 8

1970 N.F.C. — Eastern Division

DALLAS COWBOYS 10-4-0 Tom Landry

Scores of Each Game		
17	Philadelphia	7
28	N. Y. GIANTS	10
7	St. Louis	20
13	ATLANTA	0
13	Minnesota	54
27	Kansas City	16
21	PHILADELPHIA	17
20	N. Y. Giants	23
0	ST. LOUIS	38
45	Washington	21
16	GREEN BAY	3
34	WASHINGTON	0
6	Cleveland	2
52	HOUSTON	10

Use Name	Pos.	Hgt	Wgt	Age	Int	Pts
Bob Asher	OT	6'5"	250	22		
Tony Liscio	OT	6'5"	255	30		
Ralph Neely	OT	6'5"	265	26		
Rayfield Wright	OT	6'7"	255	25		
John Niland	OG	6'4"	245	26		
Blaine Nye	OG	6'4"	250	24		
Halvor Hagen	C-OG	6'5"	253	23		
Dave Manders	C	6'2"	250	28		
George Andrie	DE	6'7"	250	30		
Larry Cole	DE	6'4"	255	23		
Pat Toomay	DE	6'5"	244	25		
Ron East	DT	6'4"	242	27		
Bob Lilly	DT	6'4"	260	31		
Jethro Pugh	DT	6'6"	260	26	1	
Dave Edwards	LB	6'3"	225	31	2	
Chuck Howley	LB	6'3"	225	34	2	
Lee Roy Jordan	LB	6'2"	220	29	1	
Steve Kiner	LB	6'	218	23	1	
D. D. Lewis	LB	6'2"	225	24		
Tom Stincic	LB	6'2"	230	23	1	
Herb Adderley	DB	6'1"	200	31	3	
Richmond Flowers	DB	6'	180	23		
Cornell Green	DB	6'4"	208	30	1	
Cliff Harris	DB	6'	184	21	2	
Mel Renfro	DB	6'	190	28	4	
Mark Washington	DB	5'10"	188	22	1	6
Charlie Waters	DB	6'1"	193	21	5	
Bob Belden	QB	6'2"	205	23		
Craig Morton	QB	6'4"	214	27		
Roger Staubach	QB	6'2"	197	28		
Dan Reeves	HB	6'1"	200	26		12
Claxton Welch	HB	5'11"	203	23		6
Calvin Hill	FB-HB	6'3"	227	23		24
Duane Thomas	FB-HB	6'1"	220	23		30
Walt Garrison	FB	6'	205	26		30
Margene Atkins	WR	5'10"	183	23		
Bob Hayes	WR	6'	185	27		66
Dennis Homan	WR	6'1"	180	24		
Lance Rentzel	WR	6'2"	202	26		30
Reggie Rucker	WR	6'2"	190	22		6
Mike Ditka	TE	6'3"	225	30		
Pettis Norman	TE	6'3"	220	30		
Mike Clark	K	6'1"	205	29		89
Ron Widby	K	6'4"	210	25		

NEW YORK GIANTS 9-5-0 Alex Webster

Scores of Each Game		
16	CHICAGO	24
10	Dallas	28
10	New Orleans	14
30	PHILADELPHIA	23
16	Boston	0
35	ST. LOUIS	17
22	N. Y. Jets	10
23	DALLAS	20
35	WASHINGTON	33
20	Philadelphia	23
27	Washington	24
20	BUFFALO	6
34	St. Louis	17
3	LOS ANGELES	31

Use Name	Pos.	Hgt	Wgt	Age	Int	Pts
Rich Buzin	OT	6'4"	250	24		
Dennis Crane	OT	6'6"	260	25		
Willie Young	OT	6'	265	27		
Charlie Harper	OG-OT	6'2"	250	26		
Willie Banks	OG	6'2"	237	24		
Pete Case	OG	6'3"	245	29		
Doug Van Horn	OG	6'2"	245	26		
Len Johnson	C-OG	6'2"	250	24		
Pat Hughes	C	6'2"	240	23		
Greg Larson	C	6'2"	250	31		
John Baker	DE	6'5"	260	28		
Fred Dryer	DE	6'6"	240	24		
Bob Lurtsema	DE	6'6"	250	28		
Jim Kanicki	DT	6'4"	270	28		
Jim Norton	DT	6'4"	254	27		
Jerry Shay	DT	6'3"	245	26		
John Douglas	LB	6'2"	225	25		
Jim Files	LB	6'4"	240	22	1	2
Matt Hazeltine	LB	6'1"	225	37	1	
Ralph Heck	LB	6'2"	230	29	1	
Ray Hickl	LB	6'2"	220	23		
John Kirby	LB	6'3"	232	28		
Al Brenner	DB	6'1"	200	22		
Otto Brown	DB	6'1"	188	23		
Scott Eaton	DB	6'3"	205	26	2	
Joe Green	DB	5'11"	195	23		
Spider Lockhart	DB	6'2"	175	27	4	
Tom Longo	DB	6'1"	200	26	2	
Kenny Parker	DB	6'1"	190	24		
Willie Williams	DB	6'	190	27	6	
Dick Shiner	QB	6'	197	28		
Fran Tarkenton	QB	6'1"	190	30		12
Bobby Duhon	HB	6'	195	23		6
Ron Johnson	HB	6'1"	205	22		72
Les Shy	HB	6'1"	200	26		
Joe Morrison	FB-WR-HB	6'1"	212	32		
Tucker Frederickson	FB	6'3"	220	27		24
Ernie Koy	HB-FB	6'2"	225	27		
Don Herrmann	WR	6'2"	195	23		12
Rich Houston	WR	6'2"	197	24		
Clifton McNeil	WR	6'2"	187	30		30
Bob Tucker	TE	6'3"	230	25		30
Aaron Thomas	WR-TE	6'3"	210	32		6
Pete Gogolak	K	6'2"	190	28		107
Bill Johnson	K	6'2"	208	26		

Junior Coffey – Knee Injury
Tommy Crutcher – Knee Injury

ST. LOUIS CARDINALS 8-5-1 Charlie Winner

Scores of Each Game		
13	Los Angeles	34
27	WASHINGTON	17
20	DALLAS	7
24	NEW ORLEANS	17
35	Philadelphia	20
17	N. Y. Giants	35
44	HOUSTON	0
31	BOSTON	0
38	Dallas	0
6	Kansas City	6
23	PHILADELPHIA	14
3	Detroit	16
17	N. Y. GIANTS	34
27	Washington	28

Use Name	Pos.	Hgt	Wgt	Age	Int	Pts
Vern Emerson	OT	6'5"	260	24		
Ernie McMillan	OT	6'6"	255	32		
Bob Reynolds	OT	6'6"	265	29		
Clyde Williams	OG-OT	6'2"	250	30		
Irv Goode	OG	6'4"	255	29		
Chuck Hutchison	OG	6'3"	240	21		
Mike LaHood	OG	6'3"	250	25		
Wayne Mulligan	C	6'2"	245	23		
Rolf Krueger	DE	6'4"	250	23		
Cal Snowden	DE	6'4"	250	23		
Chuck Walker	DE	6'2"	250	29		
Joe Schmiesing	DT-DE	6'4"	250	25		
Fred Heron	DT	6'4"	260	25		
Bob Rowe	DT	6'4"	255	25		
Mike Siwok	DT	6'3"	260	22		
Chip Healy	LB	6'3"	235	23		
Dave Olerich	LB	6'1"	225	25		
Don Parish	LB	6'1"	220	22	1	6
Jamie Rivers	LB	6'2"	235	24		
Rocky Romesa	LB	6'2"	230	24		
Larry Stallings	LB	6'2"	230	28	1	
Terry Brown	DB	6'1"	210	23		
Miller Farr	DB	6'1"	190	27	5	6
Chuck Latourette	DB	6'	190	25		6
Tony Plummer	DB	5'11"	190	23		
Jerry Stovall	DB	6'2"	195	28	2	
Roger Wehrli	DB	6'1"	195	22	6	
Larry Wilson	DB	6'	195	32	5	
Nate Wright	DB	5'11"	180	23	1	
Pete Beathard	QB	6'2"	210	28		
Jim Hart	QB	6'2"	205	26		
Charlie Pittman	HB	6'1"	200	22		
Roy Shivers	HB	6'	200	28		12
Paul White	HB	6'	200	22		
MacArthur Lane	FB-HB	6'	220	28		78
Cid Edwards	FB	6'2"	230	26		12
Johnny Roland	HB-FB	6'2"	215	27		30
Jerry Daanen	WR	6'	190	25		
John Gilliam	WR	6'1"	195	25		36
Freddie Hyatt	WR	6'3"	210	24		
Dave Williams•	WR	6'2"	210	25		18
Bob Brown	TE	6'3"	225	27		
Jim McFarland	TE	6'5"	225	22		
Jackie Smith	TE	6'4"	235	29		24
Jim Bakken	K	6'	195	29		97

WASHINGTON REDSKINS 6-8-0 Bill Austin

Scores of Each Game		
17	San Francisco	26
17	St. Louis	27
33	Philadelphia	21
31	DETROIT	10
20	Oakland	34
20	CINCINNATI	0
19	Denver	3
10	MINNESOTA	19
33	N. Y. Giants	35
21	DALLAS	45
24	N. Y. GIANTS	27
0	Dallas	34
24	PHILADELPHIA	6
28	ST. LOUIS	27

Use Name	Pos.	Hgt	Wgt	Age	Int	Pts
Walt Rock	OT	6'5"	255	29		
Jim Snowden	OT	6'3"	255	28		
Steve Wright	OT	6'6"	250	28		
Paul Laaveg	OG	6'4"	245	21		
Vince Promuto	OG	6'1"	245	32		
Roy Schmidt	OG	6'3"	250	28		
Ray Schoenke	OG	6'3"	250	28		
Gene Hamlin	C	6'3"	245	24		
Len Hauss	C	6'2"	235	28		
Bruce Anderson	DE	6'4"	250	26		
Bill Brundige	DE	6'5"	270	21		
Leo Carroll	DE	6'7"	250	26		
Terry Hermeling	DE	6'5"	255	24		
John Hoffman	DE	6'7"	260	27		
Frank Bosch	DT	6'4"	246	24		
Floyd Peters	DT	6'4"	255	35		
Manny Sistrunk	DT	6'5"	265	23		
Chris Hanburger	LB	6'2"	218	29	1	
Marlin McKeever	LB	6'1"	235	30		
Harold McLinton	LB	6'2"	235	23		
Tom Roussel	LB	6'3"	235	25		
Rusty Tillman	LB	6'2"	230	24		
John Didion	C-LB	6'4"	245	22		
Mike Bass	DB	6'	190	25	4	
Pat Fischer	DB	5'10"	170	30	2	
Jim Harris	DB	5'11"	173	24		
Rickie Harris	DB	6'	182	27	3	
Jon Jaqua	DB	6'	190	22	1	
Brig Owens	DB	5'11"	190	27	4	
Ted Vactor	DB	6'	185	26		
Sonny Jurgensen	QB	5'11"	203	36		6
Frank Ryan	QB	6'3"	207	34		
Larry Brown	HB	5'11"	195	22		42
Bob Brunet	HB	6'1"	205	24		
Danny Pierce	FB-HB	6'3"	216	22		
Henry Dyer	FB	6'2"	230	25		
Charlie Harraway	FB	6'2"	215	25		30
Dave Kopay	HB-FB	6'2"	225	28		
Jon Henderson	WR	6'	200	25		18
Bill Malinchak	WR	6'1"	200	26		
Walter Roberts	WR	5'10"	163	28		6
Charley Taylor	WR	6'3"	210	29		48
Mack Alston	TE	6'2"	230	23		
Pat Richter	TE	6'5"	230	29		
Jerry Smith	TE	6'2"	208	27		54
Mike Bragg	K	5'11"	186	23		
Curt Knight	K	6'1"	190	27		93

PHILADELPHIA EAGLES 3-10-1 Jerry Williams

Scores of Each Game		
7	DALLAS	17
16	Chicago	20
21	WASHINGTON	33
23	N. Y. Giants	30
20	ST. LOUIS	35
17	Green Bay	30
17	Dallas	21
24	MIAMI	17
13	ATLANTA	13
23	N. Y. GIANTS	20
14	St. Louis	23
10	Baltimore	29
6	Washington	24
30	PITTSBURGH	20

Use Name	Pos.	Hgt	Wgt	Age	Int	Pts
Joe Carollo	OT	6'2"	265	30		
Wade Key	OT	6'4"	245	23		
Dick Stevens	OT	6'4"	240	22		
Norman Davis	OG	6'3"	245	25		
Dick Hart	OG	6'2"	250	27		
Jim Skaggs	OG	6'2"	250	30		
Mark Nordquist	C-OG	6'4"	246	24		
Mike Evans	C	6'5"	250	23		
Calvin Hunt	C	6'3"	243	22		
Don Brumm	DE	6'3"	245	27		
Ernie Calloway	DE	6'6"	240	22		
Mel Tom	DE	6'4"	250	29		
Mike Dirks	DT	6'2"	246	24		6
Gary Pettigrew	DT	6'4"	255	25		
Don Hultz	DE-DT	6'3"	240	29		
Carl Gersbach	LB	6'1"	230	23		
Bill Hobbs	LB	6'	220	24		
Jay Johnson	LB	6'3"	230	24		
Ike Kelley	LB	5'11"	224	26		
Dave Lloyd	LB	6'3"	248	34		
Ron Porter	LB	6'3"	232	25		
Tim Rossovich	LB	6'4"	250	24		
Adrian Young	LB	6'1"	232	24	2	
Bill Bradley	DB	5'11"	190	23		
Richard Harvey	DB	6'2"	190	24		
Ed Hayes	DB	6'1"	185	24	1	
Ray Jones	DB	6'	187	22	2	
Ron Medved	DB	6'1"	200	26		
Al Nelson	DB	5'11"	186	26	2	
Steve Preece	DB	6'1"	195	23	2	6
Nate Ramsey	DB	6'1"	200	29	1	
Jim Throner	DB	6'2"	194	21		
Rick Arrington	QB	6'2"	185	23		6
Norm Snead	QB	6'4"	215	30		18
Harry Jones	HB	6'2"	205	25		
Leroy Keyes	HB	6'3"	208	23		
Cyril Pinder	HB	6'2"	222	23		12
Larry Watkins	FB-HB	6'2"	215	23		6
Lee Bougess	FB	6'2"	210	22		24
Tom Woodeshick	FB	6'	222	28		12
Ben Hawkins	WR	6'	180	26		24
Harold Jackson	WR	5'10"	175	24		30
Billy Walik	WR	5'11"	180	22		
Steve Zabel	TE	6'4"	235	22		6
Gary Ballman	WR-TE	6'	205	30		18
Fred Hill	WR-TE	6'2"	215	27		6
Mark Moseley	K	5'11"	182	22		67

Dave Graham – Injury

DALLAS COWBOYS

RUSHING

Last Name	No.	Yds	Avg	TD
Thomas	151	803	5.3	5
Hill	153	577	3.8	4
Garrison	126	507	4.0	3
Staubach	27	221	8.2	0
Reeves	35	84	2.4	2
Morton	16	37	2.3	0
Hayes	4	34	8.5	0
Norman	2	16	8.0	0
Welch	5	13	2.6	1
Rentzel	1	11	11.0	0
Homan	2	-3	-1.5	0

RECEIVING

Last Name	No.	Yds	Avg	TD
Hayes	34	889	26	10
Rentzel	28	556	20	5
Garrison	21	205	10	2
Hill	13	95	7	0
Reeves	12	140	12	0
Thomas	10	73	7	0
Rucker	9	200	22	1
Ditka	8	98	12	0
Homan	7	105	15	0
Norman	6	70	12	0
Kiner	1	14	14	0

PUNT RETURNS

Last Name	No.	Yds	Avg	TD
Hayes	15	116	8	0
Renfro	13	77	6	0
Adkins	4	44	11	0

KICKOFF RETURNS

Last Name	No.	Yds	Avg	TD
Thomas	19	416	22	0
Washington	5	242	48	1
Adkins	7	149	21	0
Kiner	3	50	17	0
Harris	1	22	22	0
Waters	1	6	6	0
Flowers	1	3	3	0

PASSING – PUNTING – KICKING

Last Name	Att	Comp	%	Yds	Yd/Att	TD	Int–	%	RK
PASSING									
Morton	207	102	49	1819	8.8	15	7–	3	5
Staubach	82	44	54	542	6.6	2	8–	10	
Hill	4	1	25	12	3.0	0	0–	0	
Reeves	3	1	33	14	4.7	0	1–	33	
Rentzel	1	1	100	58	58.0	1	0–	0	

Last Name	No	Avg
PUNTING		
Widby	69	41.3

Last Name	XP	Att	%	FG	Att	%
KICKING						
Clark	35	35	100	18	27	67

NEW YORK GIANTS

RUSHING

Last Name	No.	Yds	Avg	TD
R. Johnson	263	1027	3.9	8
Frederickson	120	375	3.1	1
Tarkenton	43	236	5.5	2
Duhon	18	111	6.2	0
Morrison	11	25	2.3	0
Shy	4	13	3.3	0
McNeil	4	7	1.8	0
Koy	2	5	2.5	0

RECEIVING

Last Name	No.	Yds	Avg	TD
McNeil	50	764	15	4
R. Johnson	48	487	10	4
Tucker	40	571	14	5
Frederickson	40	408	10	3
Herrmann	24	290	12	2
Morrison	11	136	12	0
Thomas	6	92	15	1
Houston	4	68	17	0
Duhon	4	58	15	0
Shy	2	8	4	0
Koy	1	10	10	0

PUNT RETURNS

Last Name	No.	Yds	Avg	TD
Duhon	19	157	8	1
Lockhart	9	31	3	0
Brenner	1	5	5	0

KICKOFF RETURNS

Last Name	No.	Yds	Avg	TD
Shy	21	544	26	0
Duhon	14	255	18	0
Houston	8	173	22	0
R. Johnson	5	140	28	0
Green	2	26	13	0
Douglas	1	16	16	0
Hughes	1	3	3	0

PASSING – PUNTING – KICKING

Last Name	Att	Comp	%	Yds	Yd/Att	TD	Int–	%	RK
PASSING									
Tarkenton	389	219	56	2777	7.1	19	12–	3	3
Shiner	12	9	75	87	7.3	0	0–	0	
Duhon	2	2	100	28	14.0	0	0–	0	

Last Name	No	Avg
PUNTING		
B. Johnson	43	39.5
Koy	11	33.5

Last Name	XP	Att	%	FG	Att	%
KICKING						
Gogalak	32	32	100	25	41	61

ST. LOUIS CARDINALS

RUSHING

Last Name	No.	Yds	Avg	TD
Lane	206	977	4.7	11
Roland	94	392	4.2	3
Edwards	70	350	5.0	1
Shivers	24	98	4.1	2
Gilliam	5	68	13.6	1
Smith	5	43	8.6	0
Latourette	2	38	19.0	0
Hart	18	18	1.0	0
B. Brown	1	8	8.0	0
Pittman	2	4	2.0	0
Beathard	2	2	1.0	0

RECEIVING

Last Name	No.	Yds	Avg	TD
Gilliam	45	952	21	5
Smith	37	687	19	4
Lane	32	365	11	2
D. Williams	23	364	16	3
Edwards	19	150	8	1
Roland	17	96	6	1
Shivers	3	44	15	0
Daanen	2	31	16	0

PUNT RETURNS

Last Name	No.	Yds	Avg	TD
Latourette	30	171	6	0
Roland	10	140	14	1
Wehrli	1	4	4	0

KICKOFF RETURNS

Last Name	No.	Yds	Avg	TD
Latourette	13	254	20	0
Pittman	10	237	24	0
Wright	8	156	20	0
Gilliam	5	107	21	0
White	3	65	22	0
Roland	3	40	13	0
Shivers	2	35	18	0
T. Brown	2	32	16	0
Wilson	1	0	0	0

PASSING – PUNTING – KICKING

Last Name	Att	Comp	%	Yds	Yd/Att	TD	Int–	%	RK
PASSING									
Hart	373	171	46	2575	6.9	14	18–	5	9
Beathard	17	7	41	114	6.7	2	1–	6	

Last Name	No	Avg
PUNTING		
Latourette	65	40.9

Last Name	XP	Att	%	FG	Att	%
KICKING						
Bakken	37	38	97	20	32	63

WASHINGTON REDSKINS

RUSHING

Last Name	No.	Yds	Avg	TD
Brown	237	1125	4.7	5
Harraway	146	577	4.0	5
Dyer	21	102	4.9	0
Kopay	13	49	3.8	0
Jurgensen	6	39	6.5	1
Brunet	9	37	4.1	0
Smith	2	29	14.5	0
Bragg	2	25	12.5	0
Taylor	1	17	17.0	0
Roberts	2	15	7.5	0
Pierce	5	6	1.2	0

RECEIVING

Last Name	No.	Yds	Avg	TD
Smith	43	575	13	9
Taylor	42	593	14	8
Brown	37	341	9	2
Roberts	27	411	15	1
Harraway	24	136	6	0
Henderson	13	176	14	3
Kopay	7	24	3	0
Dyer	4	37	9	0
Brunet	3	28	9	0
Richter	2	30	15	0
Pierce	1	6	6	0

PUNT RETURNS

Last Name	No.	Yds	Avg	TD
Roberts	10	28	3	0
R. Harris	14	10	1	0
Vactor	2	7	4	0
Kopay	1	0	0	0

KICKOFF RETURNS

Last Name	No.	Yds	Avg	TD
Vactor	28	700	25	0
R. Harris	10	208	21	0
J. Harris	9	172	19	0
Dyer	5	78	16	0
Hanburger	2	33	17	0
McKeever	1	21	21	0
Tillman	1	10	10	0
Brundige	1	1	1	0
Richter	2	0	0	0
Bass	1	0	0	0
Henderson	1	0	0	0

PASSING – PUNTING – KICKING

Last Name	Att	Comp	%	Yds	Yd/Att	TD	Int–	%	RK
PASSING									
Jurgensen	337	202	60	2354	7.0	23	10–	3	2
Ryan	4	1	25	3	0.8	0	0–	0	
Bragg	1	0	0	0	0.0	0	0–	0	

Last Name	No	Avg
PUNTING		
Bragg	61	40.9

Last Name	XP	Att	%	FG	Att	%
KICKING						
Knight	33	34	97	20	27	74

PHILADELPHIA EAGLES

RUSHING

Last Name	No.	Yds	Avg	TD
Pinder	166	657	4.0	2
Bouggess	159	401	2.5	2
Woodeshick	52	254	4.9	2
Watkins	32	96	3.0	1
H. Jones	13	44	3.4	0
Snead	18	35	1.9	3
Arrington	4	33	8.3	1
Bradley	1	14	14.0	0
Keyes	2	7	3.5	0
Hawkins	2	3	1.5	0
Jackson	1	-5	-5.0	0

RECEIVING

Last Name	No.	Yds	Avg	TD
Bouggess	50	401	8	2
Ballman	47	601	13	3
Jackson	41	613	15	5
Hawkins	30	612	20	4
Pinder	28	249	9	0
Zabel	8	119	15	1
Woodeshick	6	28	5	0
Hill	3	10	3	1
Watkins	3	6	2	0
H. Jones	1	12	12	0
Walik	1	0	0	0

PUNT RETURNS

Last Name	No.	Yds	Avg	TD
Walik	20	78	4	0
Hawkins	10	16	2	0
Hayes	2	6	3	0

KICKOFF RETURNS

Last Name	No.	Yds	Avg	TD
Walik	32	805	25	0
Nelson	10	187	19	0
Hayes	6	107	18	0
R. Jones	6	97	16	0
H. Jones	2	23	12	0
Rossovich	1	22	22	0
Pettigrew	1	11	11	0
Hawkins	1	0	0	0

PASSING – PUNTING – KICKING

Last Name	Att	Comp	%	Yds	Yd/Att	TD	Int–	%	RK
PASSING									
Snead	335	181	54	2323	6.9	15	20–	6	7
Arrington	73	37	51	328	4.5	1	3–	4	
Ballman	1	0	0	0	0.0	0	0–	0	
Bouggess	1	0	0	0	0.0	0	0–	0	

Last Name	No	Avg
PUNTING		
Bradley	61	36.8
Moseley	10	35.0

Last Name	XP	Att	%	FG	Att	%
KICKING						
Moseley	25	28	89	14	25	56

MINNESOTA VIKINGS 12-2-0 Bud Grant

Scores of Each Game			Use Name	Pos.	Hgt	Wgt	Age	Int	Pts
27	KANSAS CITY	10	Grady Alderman	OT	6'2"	245	31		
26	NEW ORLEANS	0	Doug Davis	OT	6'4"	255	26		
10	Green Bay	13	Steve Smith	OT	6'5"	250	26		
24	Chicago	0	Ron Yary	OT	6'6"	255	24		
54	DALLAS	13	Milt Sunde	OG	6'2"	250	27		
13	LOS ANGELES	3	Jim Vellone	OG	6'2"	255	26		
30	Detroit	17	Ed White	OG	6'2"	260	23		
19	Washington	10	Mick Tingelhoff	C	6'1"	237	30		
24	DETROIT	20	Carl Eller	DE	6'6"	250	28		
10	GREEN BAY	3	Jim Marshall	DE	6'3"	248	32		
10	N. Y. Jets	20	John Ward	DE	6'4"	260	22		
16	CHICAGO	13	Paul Dickson	DT	6'5"	250	33		
35	Boston	14	Gary Larsen	DT	6'5"	260	30		
37	Atlanta	7	Alan Page	DT	6'5"	245	25	1	6

Use Name	Pos.	Hgt	Wgt	Age	Int	Pts
Jim Hargrove	LB	6'3"	235	25		
Wally Hilgenberg	LB	6'3"	230	27	2	
Mike McGill	LB	6'2"	235	23		6
Wayne Meylan	LB	6'1"	235	24		
Lonnie Warwick	LB	6'3"	237	28	3	
Roy Winston	LB	6'1"	228	30	1	6
Bobby Bryant	DB	6'	170	26	3	6
John Charles	DB	6'1"	200	26	1	
Dale Hackbart	DB	6'3"	205	34		
Karl Kassulke	DB	6'	195	28	3	
Paul Krause	DB	6'3"	188	28	6	
Ted Provost	DB	6'2"	195	22		
Ed Sharockman	DB	6'	200	30	7	18
Charlie West	DB	6'1"	190	24	1	
Billy Harris — Injury						

Use Name	Pos.	Hgt	Wgt	Age	Int	Pts
Bill Cappleman	QB	6'3"	210	23		
Gary Cuozzo	QB	6'1"	195	29		
Bob Lee	QB	6'2"	195	25		6
Clint Jones	HB	6'	206	25		54
Dave Osborn	HB	6'	205	27		36
Bill Brown	FB	5'11"	230	32		12
Jim Lindsey	HB-FB	6'2"	210	25		6
Oscar Reed	HB-FB	5'11"	222	26		6
Bob Grim	WR	6'	200	25		
John Henderson	WR	6'3"	190	27		12
Gene Washington	WR	6'3"	208	26		24
John Beasley	TE	6'3"	233	25		12
Kent Kramer	TE	6'5"	235	26		
Stu Voigt	TE	6'1"	220	22		
Fred Cox	K	5'10"	200	31		125
Tom McNeill	K	6'1"	195	28		

DETROIT LIONS 10-4-0 Joe Schmidt

Scores of Each Game			Use Name	Pos.	Hgt	Wgt	Age	Int	Pts
40	Green Bay	0	Rocky Freitas	OT	6'6"	280	24		
38	CINCINNATI	3	Roger Shoals	OT	6'4"	260	31		
28	CHICAGO	14	Jim Yarbrough	OT	6'6"	250	23		
10	Washington	31	Frank Gallagher	OG	6'2"	245	27		
41	Cleveland	24	Bob Kowalkowski	OG	6'3"	240	26		
16	Chicago	10	Rocky Rasley	OG	6'3"	250	23		
17	MINNESOTA	30	Chuck Walton	OG	6'3"	255	29		
17	New Orleans	19	Bill Cottrell	C	6'3"	255	25		
20	Minnesota	24	Ed Flanagan	C	6'3"	245	26		
28	SAN FRANCISCO	7	Larry Hand	DE	6'4"	250	30	1	6
28	OAKLAND	14	Jim Mitchell	DE	6'3"	245	21		
16	ST. LOUIS	3	Joe Robb	DE	6'4"	245	33		
28	Los Angeles	23	Dan Goich	DT	6'4"	265	26		
20	GREEN BAY	0	Dave Haverdick	DT	6'4"	245	22		
			Alex Karras	DT	6'2"	245	34		
			Jerry Rush	DT	6'4"	265	28		

Use Name	Pos.	Hgt	Wgt	Age	Int	Pts
Mike Lucci	LB	6'2"	230	30	2	
Ed Mooney	LB	6'2"	225	25		
Paul Naumoff	LB	6'1"	215	25		
Bill Saul	LB	6'4"	225	29		
Wayne Walker	LB	6'2"	228	33		
Lem Barney	DB	6'	188	24	7	18
Dick LeBeau	DB	6'1"	185	33	9	
Wayne Rasmussen	DB	6'2"	180	28	2	
Tom Vaughn	DB	5'11"	190	27	1	
Mike Weger	DB	6'2"	200	24	5	6
Bobby Williams	DB	6'1"	200	28	1	6

Use Name	Pos.	Hgt	Wgt	Age	Int	Pts
Greg Landry	QB	6'4"	205	23		6
Bill Munson	QB	6'2"	210	28		
Nick Eddy	HB	6'	207	26		6
Altie Taylor	HB	5'10"	196	22		24
Mel Farr	FB-HB	6'2"	210	25		66
Steve Owens	FB	6'2"	220	22		12
Bill Triplett	FB	6'2"	215	31		6
Bruce Maxwell	HB-FB	6'1"	222	23		
Charlie Brown	WR	6'2"	195	21		
Chuck Hughes	WR	5'11"	175	27		
Earl McCullouch	WR	5'11"	175	24		24
Phil Odle	WR	5'11"	195	27		
Larry Walton	WR	5'11"	180	23		30
John Wright	WR	6'	197	23		
Craig Cotton	TE	6'4"	222	23		
Charlie Sanders	TE	6'4"	235	24		36
Errol Mann	K	6'	200	29		101
Herman Weaver	K	6'4"	210	21		

CHICAGO BEARS 6-8-0 Jim Dooley

Scores of Each Game			Use Name	Pos.	Hgt	Wgt	Age	Int	Pts
24	N. Y. Giants	16	Jeff Curchin	OT	6'6"	265	22		
20	PHILADELPHIA	16	Randy Jackson	OT	6'5"	245	26		
14	Detroit	28	Wayne Mass	OT	6'4"	240	24		
0	MINNESOTA	24	Jim Cadile	OG	6'3"	240	29		
7	SAN DIEGO	20	Glenn Holloway	OG	6'3"	245	21		
10	DETROIT	16	Howard Mudd	OG	6'3"	252	28		
23	Atlanta	14	Ted Wheeler	OG	6'3"	245	24		
16	SAN FRANCISCO	37	Bob Hyland	C	6'5"	250	25		
19	Green Bay	20	Harry Gunner	DE	6'6"	250	25		
31	BUFFALO	13	Ed O'Bradovich	DE	6'3"	255	26		
20	Baltimore	21	Willie Holman	DT-DE	6'4"	250	25		
13	Minnesota	16	Dave Hale	DT	6'7"	260	23		
35	GREEN BAY	17	George Seals	DT	6'2"	260	27	1	
24	New Orleans	3	Bill Staley	DT	6'3"	248	23		

Use Name	Pos.	Hgt	Wgt	Age	Int	Pts
Ross Brupbacher	LB	6'3"	215	22	2	
Doug Buffone	LB	6'1"	225	26	4	
Dick Butkus	LB	6'3"	245	26	3	
Lee Roy Caffey	LB	6'3"	250	30		
Jimmy Gunn	LB	6'1"	220	21		
John Neidert	LB	6'2"	230	24		
Phil Clark	DB	6'2"	208	25	1	
Dick Daniels	DB	5'9"	180	24	2	
Butch Davis	DB	5'11"	183	22	1	
Bennie McRae	DB	6'1"	180	29	1	
Ron Smith	DB	6'1"	192	27		
Joe Tayler	DB	6'2"	200	29	2	
Garry Lyle	HB-DB	6'2"	198	24		
Brian Piccolo — Died 6-16-70 — cancer						

Use Name	Pos.	Hgt	Wgt	Age	Int	Pts
Jack Concannon	QB	6'3"	205	27		12
Bobby Douglass	QB	6'3"	215	23		
Kent Nix	QB	6'1"	195	26		
Craig Baynham	HB	6'1"	203	26		
Gale Sayers	HB	6'	198	27		
Don Shy (from NO)	HB	6'1"	205	24		6
Ronnie Bull	FB-HB	6'	200	30		
Mike Hull	FB	6'3"	220	25		
Ralph Kurek	FB	6'2"	210	27		
Ross Montgomery	FB	6'3"	220	23		
Linzy Cole	WR	5'11"	170	22		
George Farmer	WR	6'4"	210	22		12
Dick Gordon	WR	5'11"	190	25		78
Jim Seymour	WR	6'4"	210	23		24
Cecil Turner	WR	5'10"	170	26		24
Jim Hester	TE	6'4"	250	25		
Ray Ogden	TE	6'5"	225	27		6
Bob Wallace	TE	6'3"	211	24		
Rich Coady	C-TE	6'3"	238	25		6
Bobby Joe Green	K	5'11"	175	32		
Mac Percival	K	6'4"	220	30		88

GREEN BAY PACKERS 6-8-0 Phil Bengtson

Scores of Each Game			Use Name	Pos.	Hgt	Wgt	Age	Int	Pts
0	DETROIT	40	Forrest Gregg	OT	6'4"	250	37		
27	ATLANTA	24	Bill Hayhoe	OT	6'8"	258	23		
13	MINNESOTA	10	Dick Himes	OT	6'4"	244	24		
22	San Diego	20	Francis Peay	OT	6'5"	250	26		
21	LOS ANGELES	31	Dave Bradley	OG	6'4"	245	23		
30	PHILADELPHIA	17	Gale Gillingham	OG	6'3"	255	26		
10	San Francisco	26	Bill Lueck	OG	6'3"	235	24		
10	BALTIMORE	13	Ken Bowman	C	6'3"	230	27		
20	CHICAGO	19	Malcolm Walker	OT-C	6'4"	250	27		
3	Minnesota	10	Lionel Aldridge	DE	6'4"	245	28		
3	Dallas	16	Marty Amsler	DE	6'5"	255	25		
20	Pittsburgh	12	Bob Brown	DE	6'5"	260	30		
17	Chicago	35	Clarence Williams	DE	6'5"	255	23		
0	Detroit	20	Kevin Hardy	DT	6'5"	260	25		
			Mike McCoy	DT	6'5"	284	21		
			Rich Moore	DT	6'6"	285	23		

Use Name	Pos.	Hgt	Wgt	Age	Int	Pts
Fred Carr	LB	6'5"	238	24	2	
Jim Carter	LB	6'3"	235	21		
Jim Flanigan	LB	6'3"	240	25		
Rudy Kuechenberg	LB	6'2"	215	27		
Ray Nitschke	LB	6'3"	235	34		
Dave Robinson	LB	6'3"	240	29	2	
Cleo Walker	C-LB	6'3"	220	22		
Ken Ellis	DB	5'10"	190	22	3	
Lee Harden	DB	5'11"	195	23		
Doug Hart	DB	6'	190	31	3	6
Ervin Hunt	DB	6'2"	190	23		
Bob Jeter	DB	6'1"	205	32	3	
Al Matthews	DB	5'11"	190	22		
Willie Wood	DB	5'10"	190	34	1	
Zeke Bratkowski — Voluntarily Retired						
Boyd Dowler — Voluntarily Retired						

Use Name	Pos.	Hgt	Wgt	Age	Int	Pts
Don Horn	QB	6'2"	195	25		
Rick Norton	QB	6'1"	190	26		
Frank Patrick	QB	6'7"	225	23		
Bart Starr	QB	6'1"	190	37		6
Donny Anderson	HB	6'3"	210	27		30
Larry Krause	HB	6'	208	22		
Travis Williams	HB	6'1"	210	24		12
Jim Grabowski	FB	6'2"	220	26		
Perry Williams	FB	6'2"	220	23		
Dave Hampton	HB-FB	6'	210	23		6
Mike Carter	WR	6'1"	210	22		
Jack Clancy	WR	6'1"	195	26		12
Carroll Dale	WR	6'1"	200	32		12
John Spilis	WR	6'3"	205	22		
John Hilton	TE	6'5"	225	28		24
Rich McGeorge	TE	6'4"	235	21		12
Dale Livingston	K	6'	210	25		64

MINNESOTA VIKINGS

RUSHING

Last Name	No.	Yds	Avg	TD
Osborn	207	681	3.3	5
Jones	120	369	3.1	9
Brown	101	324	3.2	0
Reed	42	132	3.1	1
Cuozzo	17	61	3.6	0
Lindsey	11	47	4.3	0
Lee	10	20	2.0	1

RECEIVING

Last Name	No.	Yds	Avg	TD
Washington	44	702	16	4
Henderson	31	527	17	2
Grim	23	287	12	0
Osborn	23	202	9	1
Beasley	17	237	14	2
Brown	15	149	10	2
Jones	9	117	13	0
Reed	6	53	9	0
Lindsey	4	94	24	1
Kramer	1	10	10	0

PUNT RETURNS

Last Name	No.	Yds	Avg	TD
West	29	169	6	0
Grim	5	46	9	0
Dickson	1	1	1	0

KICKOFF RETURNS

Last Name	No.	Yds	Avg	TD
Jones	19	452	24	0
West	11	319	29	0
Reed	5	71	14	0
Smith	1	0	0	0

PASSING – PUNTING – KICKING

PASSING	Att	Comp	%	Yds	Yd/Att	TD	Int–	%	RK
Cuozzo	257	128	50	1720	6.7	7	10–	4	9
Lee	79	40	51	610	7.7	5	5–	6	
Cappleman	7	4	57	49	7.0	0	0–	0	
Cox	1	1	100	–1	–1.0	0	0–	0	

PUNTING	No	Avg
McNeill	61	37.9

KICKING	XP	Att	%	FG	Att	%
Cox	35	35	100	30	46	65

DETROIT LIONS

RUSHING

Last Name	No.	Yds	Avg	TD
Farr	166	717	4.3	9
Taylor	198	666	3.4	2
Landry	35	350	10.0	1
Triplett	48	156	3.3	1
Owens	36	122	3.4	2
Eddy	18	47	2.6	1
Munson	9	33	3.7	0
L. Walton	2	20	10.0	0
Maxwell	1	9	9.0	0
McCullouch	1	7	7.0	0

RECEIVING

Last Name	No.	Yds	Avg	TD
Sanders	40	544	14	6
L. Walton	30	532	18	5
Farr	29	213	7	2
Taylor	27	261	10	2
McCullouch	15	278	19	4
Hughes	8	162	20	0
Triplett	6	52	9	0
Eddy	4	22	6	0
Owens	4	21	5	0
Brown	2	38	19	0
Cotton	1	6	6	0
Freitas	1	–8	–8	0

PUNT RETURNS

Last Name	No.	Yds	Avg	TD
Barney	25	259	10	1
Eddy	4	25	6	0
Vaughn	3	22	7	0
L. Walton	2	0	0	0

KICKOFF RETURNS

Last Name	No.	Yds	Avg	TD
Williams	25	544	22	1
Eddy	7	168	24	0
Barney	2	96	48	0
Vaughn	3	66	22	0
Owens	1	26	26	0
L. Walton	1	21	21	0
Maxwell	1	20	20	0
Mooney	1	12	12	0
Naumoff	2	6	3	0

PASSING – PUNTING – KICKING

PASSING	Att	Comp	%	Yds	Yd/Att	TD	Int–	%	RK
Munson	158	84	53	1049	6.6	10	7–	4	8
Landry	136	83	61	1072	7.9	9	5–	4	

PUNTING	No	Avg
Weaver	62	40.0

KICKING	XP	Att	%	FG	Att	%
Mann	41	41	100	20	29	69

CHICAGO BEARS

RUSHING

Last Name	No.	Yds	Avg	TD
Montgomery	62	229	3.7	0
Shy	79	227	2.9	1
Bull	68	214	3.1	0
Concannon	42	136	3.2	2
Hull	32	99	3.1	0
Baynham	26	68	2.6	0
Sayers	23	52	2.3	0
Kurek	6	24	4.0	0
Douglass	7	22	3.1	0
Gordon	4	17	4.3	0
Green	1	7	7.0	0
Turner	3	–3	–1.0	0

RECEIVING

Last Name	No.	Yds	Avg	TD
Gordon	71	1026	14	13
Farmer	31	496	16	2
Wallace	15	160	11	0
Montgomery	14	75	5	0
Bull	13	60	5	0
Hull	13	44	3	0
Baynham	12	43	4	0
Shy	10	149	15	0
Hester	7	54	8	0
Seymour	6	145	24	4
Coady	6	44	7	1
Cole	3	47	16	0
Kurek	3	11	4	0
Turner	2	53	27	0
Percival	1	19	19	0
Ogden	1	6	6	1
Lyle	1	5	5	0
Sayers	1	–6	–6	0

PUNT RETURNS

Last Name	No.	Yds	Avg	TD
Smith	33	126	4	0
Cole	14	83	6	0
Lyle	9	37	4	0
Turner	1	0	0	0

KICKOFF RETURNS

Last Name	No.	Yds	Avg	TD
Turner	23	752	33	4
Smith	28	651	23	0
Montgomery	4	69	17	0
Butkus	1	0	0	0

PASSING – PUNTING – KICKING

PASSING	Att	Comp	%	Yds	Yd/Att	TD	Int–	%	RK
Concannon	385	194	50	2130	5.5	16	18–	5	9
Douglass	30	12	40	218	7.3	4	3–	10	
Bull	4	2	50	46	11.5	1	1–	25	
Green	2	2	100	37	18.5	0	0–	0	
Nix	1	0	0	0	0.0	0	0–	0	

PUNTING	No	Avg
Green	83	40.9
Lyle	1	29.0

KICKING	XP	Att	%	FG	Att	%
Percival	28	28	100	20	34	59

GREEN BAY PACKERS

RUSHING

Last Name	No.	Yds	Avg	TD
Anderson	222	853	3.8	5
T. Williams	74	276	3.7	1
Grabowski	67	210	3.1	1
Hampton	48	115	2.4	0
Starr	12	62	5.2	1
P. Williams	17	44	2.6	0
Krause	2	13	6.5	0
Dale	2	9	4.5	0
Patrick	2	5	2.5	0
Horn	5	4	0.8	0
McGeorge	1	3	3.0	0
Livingston	1	1	1.0	0

RECEIVING

Last Name	No.	Yds	Avg	TD
Dale	49	814	17	2
Anderson	36	414	12	0
Hilton	25	350	14	4
Grabowski	19	83	4	0
Clancy	16	244	15	2
T. Williams	12	127	11	1
Hampton	7	23	3	0
Spilis	6	76	13	0
P. Williams	3	11	4	0
McGeorge	2	32	16	2
Krause	2	22	11	0

PUNT RETURNS

Last Name	No.	Yds	Avg	TD
Wood	11	58	5	0
Ellis	7	27	4	0
T. Williams	4	20	5	0
C. Williams	1	0	0	0
Harden	2	–7	–4	0

KICKOFF RETURNS

Last Name	No.	Yds	Avg	TD
Krause	18	513	29	1
Ellis	22	451	21	0
T. Williams	10	203	20	0
Hampton	6	188	31	1
McCoy	3	22	7	0
Gregg	2	21	11	0
P. Williams	1	20	20	0
Himes	1	4	4	0

PASSING – PUNTING – KICKING

PASSING	Att	Comp	%	Yds	Yd/Att	TD	Int–	%	RK
Starr	255	140	55	1645	6.5	3	13–	5	1
Horn	76	28	37	428	5.6	2	10–	13	
Patrick	14	6	43	59	4.2	0	1–	7	
Norton	5	3	60	64	12.8	1	0–	0	
Anderson	1	0	0	0	0.0	0	0–	0	

PUNTING	No	Avg
Anderson	81	40.8
Livingston	6	33.2

KICKING	XP	Att	%	FG	Att	%
Livingston	19	21	90	15	28	54

SAN FRANCISCO FORTY NINERS 10-3-1 Dick Nolan

Scores of Each Game

	Opponent	
26	WASHINGTON	17
34	CLEVELAND	31
20	Atlanta	21
20	Los Angeles	6
20	NEW ORLEANS	20
19	DENVER	14
26	GREEN BAY	10
30	Chicago	16
30	Houston	20
7	Detroit	28
13	LOS ANGELES	30
24	ATLANTA	20
38	New Orleans	27
38	Oakland	7

Use Name	Pos.	Hgt	Wgt	Age	Int	Pts
Cas Banaszek	OT	6'3"	250	24		
Len Rohde	OT	6'4"	250	32		
Randy Beisler	OG-OT	6'4"	255	25		
Elmer Collett	OG	6'4"	240	25		
Bob Hoskins	OG	6'2"	235	24		
Woody Peoples	OG	6'2"	247	27		
Forrest Blue	C	6'5"	260	24		
Bill Belk	DE	6'3"	254	24		
Cedrick Hardman	DE	6'3"	255	21		
Tommy Hart	DE	6'3"	250	25	1	
Stan Hindman	DE	6'3"	235	26		
Earl Edwards	DT	6'6"	265	24		
Charlie Krueger	DT	6'4"	270	34		
Roland Lakes	DT	6'4"	268	30		
Sam Silas	DE-DT	6'4"	255	27		

Use Name	Pos.	Hgt	Wgt	Age	Int	Pts
Ed Beard	LB	6'2"	220	30		
Carter Campbell	LB	6'3"	214	22		
Frank Nunley	LB	6'2"	230	24	3	
Jim Sniadecki	LB	6'2"	220	23		
Skip Vanderbundt	LB	6'3"	234	23	3	
Dave Wilcox	LB	6'3"	237	27	2	
Johnny Fuller	DB	6'	175	24	1	
Jim Johnson	DB	6'2"	184	32	2	8
Mel Phillips	DB	6'	192	28	3	6
Al Randolph	DB	6'2"	200	26	1	2
Mike Simpson	DB	5'11"	175	23		
Bruce Taylor	DB	6'	180	22	3	6
Rosey Taylor	DB	5'11"	186	31	3	

Use Name	Pos.	Hgt	Wgt	Age	Int	Pts
John Brodie	QB	6'1"	203	35		12
Steve Spurrier	QB	6'2"	203	25		
Doug Cunningham	HB	5'11"	190	24		18
John Isenbarger	HB	6'3"	205	22		6
Jim Strong	HB	6'1"	204	23		
Jimmy Thomas	WR-HB	6'1"	216	23		18
Ken Willard	FB	6'2"	225	27		60
Bill Tucker	HB-FB	6'2"	216	26		12
Lee Johnson	WR	6'1"	204	25		
Preston Riley	WR	6'	180	22		
Gene Washington	WR	6'1"	186	23		72
Dick Witcher	WR	6'3"	204	25		12
Ted Kwalick	TE	6'4"	230	23		6
Bob Windsor	TE	6'4"	230	27		12
Bruce Gossett	K	6'2"	225	27		102

LOS ANGELES RAMS 9-4-1 George Allen

	Opponent	
34	ST. LOUIS	13
19	Buffalo	0
37	SAN DIEGO	10
6	SAN FRANCISCO	20
31	Green Bay	21
3	Minnesota	13
30	New Orleans	17
10	ATLANTA	10
20	N.Y. JETS	31
17	Atlanta	7
30	San Francisco	13
34	NEW ORLEANS	16
23	DETROIT	28
31	N.Y. Giants	3

Use Name	Pos.	Hgt	Wgt	Age	Int	Pts
Bob Brown	OT	6'4"	290	27		
Charley Cowan	OT	6'4"	265	32		
Mitch Johnson	OT	6'4"	250	28		
Tom Mack	OG	6'3"	250	26		
Joe Scibelli	OG	6'1"	255	31		
John Wilbur	OG	6'3"	240	27		
Ken Iman	C	6'1"	240	31		
George Burman	OG-C	6'3"	255	27		
Coy Bacon	DE	6'4"	270	28	6	
Rick Cash	DE	6'5"	260	25		
Deacon Jones	DE	6'5"	250	31		
Clark Miller	DE	6'5"	246	31		
Dick Evey	DT	6'2"	245	29		
Merlin Olsen	DT	6'5"	270	29		
Diron Talbert	DT	6'5"	255	26		

Use Name	Pos.	Hgt	Wgt	Age	Int	Pts
Maxie Baughan	LB	6'1"	230	32	1	
Jack Pardee	LB	6'2"	225	34	1	
John Pergine	LB	6'1"	225	23		
Myron Pottios	LB	6'2"	232	30	2	
Jim Purnell	LB	6'2"	238	28		
Jack Reynolds	LB	6'1"	232	22		
Rich Saul	LB	6'3"	235	22		
Kermit Alexander	DB	5'11"	186	29	4	6
Alvin Haymond	DB	6'	194	28		6
Ed Meador	DB	5'11"	190	33	2	
Jim Nettles	DB	5'9"	177	28	3	
Richie Petitbon	DB	6'3"	208	32	1	
Nate Shaw	DB	6'2"	205	25		
Clancy Williams	DB	6'2"	194	27	5	6

Doug Woodlief — Injury
Jim Wilson — Injury

Use Name	Pos.	Hgt	Wgt	Age	Int	Pts
Roman Gabriel	QB	6'4"	220	30		6
Karl Sweetan	QB	6'1"	205	27		
Willie Ellison	HB	6'1"	200	25		42
Larry Smith	HB	6'3"	220	22		12
Tommy Mason	FB-HB	6'	195	31		6
Pat Curran	FB	6'3"	238	24		6
Les Josephson	HB-FB	6'1"	215	25		30
Jeff Jordan						
Bob Long	WR	6'3"	205	29		
David Ray	WR	6'	195	25		121
Jack Snow	WR	6'2"	190	27		42
Pat Studstill	WR	6'1"	175	32		12
Wendell Tucker	WR	5'10"	185	26		
Donnie Williams	WR	6'3"	210	22		
Bob Klein	TE	6'5"	235	23		
Billy Truax	TE	6'5"	235	27		18

ATLANTA FALCONS 4-8-2 Norm Van Brocklin

	Opponent	
14	New Orleans	3
24	Green Bay	27
21	SAN FRANCISCO	20
0	Dallas	13
10	Denver	24
32	NEW ORLEANS	14
14	CHICAGO	23
10	Los Angeles	10
13	Philadelphia	13
7	LOS ANGELES	17
7	MIAMI	20
20	San Francisco	24
27	PITTSBURGH	16
7	MINNESOTA	37

Use Name	Pos.	Hgt	Wgt	Age	Int	Pts
Dave Hettema	OT	6'4"	250	28		
George Kunz	OT	6'5"	245	23		
Bill Sandeman	OT	6'6"	260	27		
Mal Snider	OT	6'4"	250	23		
Dick Enderle	OG	6'1"	258	22		
Andy Mauer	OG	6'3"	257	21		
Gary Roberts	OG	6'2"	242	23		
Bob Breitenstein	OT-OG	6'3"	267	27		
John Matlock	C	6'4"	250	25		
Jeff Van Note	C	6'2"	244	24		
Claude Humphrey	DE	6'5"	244	26	1	
Randy Marshall	DE	6'5"	237	23		6
John Zook	DE	6'5"	240	22	1	
Glen Condren	DT	6'2"	247	28		
Greg Lens	DT	6'5"	260	25		
Jim Sullivan	DE-DT	6'4"	240	26		

Greg Brezina — Injury

Use Name	Pos.	Hgt	Wgt	Age	Int	Pts
Ron Acks	LB	6'2"	225	25		
Grady Allen	LB	6'3"	230	24	1	
Ted Cottrell	LB	6'1"	233	23		
Dean Halverson	LB	6'2"	220	24		
Don Hansen	LB	6'3"	220	26	1	
Tommy Nobis	LB	6'2"	237	26	2	
John Small	LB	6'5"	254	23		
Grady Cavness	DB	5'11"	192	23		
Mike Freeman	DB	5'11"	180	26	1	
Al Lavan	DB	6'1"	194	23	3	
John Mallory	DB	6'	198	24	1	12
Tom McCauley	DB	6'3"	184	23	1	6
Ken Reaves	DB	6'3"	202	25	6	
Rudy Redmond	DB	6'	190	23	1	

Carlton Dabney — Back Injury
Randy Winkler — Military Service

Use Name	Pos.	Hgt	Wgt	Age	Int	Pts
Bob Berry	QB	5'11"	190	28		
Randy Johnson	QB	6'3"	210	26		
Cannonball Butler	HB	5'10"	195	27		6
Sonny Campbell	HB	5'11"	192	22		12
Paul Gipson	FB-HB	6'	205	24		18
Harmon Wages	FB	6'1"	216	24		18
Art Malone	HB-FB	5'11"	209	22		6
Mike Brunson	WR	6'1"	187	23		
Gail Cogdill	WR	6'2"	200	33		6
Paul Flatley	WR	6'1"	190	29		6
Kent Lawrence	WR	5'11"	175	23		
Todd Snyder	WR	6'2"	184	21		12
Mike Donohoe	TE	6'3"	227	25		6
Jim Mitchell	TE	6'2"	235	22		42
Billy Lothridge	K	6'1"	190	26		
Kenny Vinyard	K	5'10"	190	23		50

NEW ORLEANS SAINTS 2-11-1 Tom Fears J. D. Roberts

	Opponent	
3	ATLANTA	14
0	Minnesota	26
14	N.Y. GIANTS	10
17	St. Louis	24
20	San Francisco	20
14	Atlanta	32
17	LOS ANGELES	30
19	DETROIT	17
10	Miami	21
14	DENVER	31
6	Cincinnati	26
16	Los Angeles	34
27	SAN FRANCISCO	38
3	CHICAGO	24

Use Name	Pos.	Hgt	Wgt	Age	Int	Pts
Errol Linden	OT	6'5"	250	33		
Mike Richey	OT	6'5"	263	23		
Don Talbert	OT	6'5"	255	30		
Mike Taylor	OT	6'4"	245	25		
Jake Kupp	OG	6'3"	248	28		
John Shinners	OG	6'2"	254	23		
Doug Sutherland	OG	6'3"	250	22		
Jerry Sturm	C-OT-OG	6'3"	265	33		
Del Williams	C	6'2"	240	24		
Larry Estes	DE	6'6"	260	23		
Dave Long	DE	6'4"	245	25		
Richard Neal	DE	6'3"	254	22		
Willie Townes	DT-DE	6'5"	265	27		
Dave Rowe	DT	6'6"	280	25		
Clovis Swinney	DT	6'3"	240	25		
Mike Tilleman	DT	6'5"	280	26		

Use Name	Pos.	Hgt	Wgt	Age	Int	Pts
Dick Absher	LB	6'4"	235	26		
Johnny Brewer	LB	6'4"	235	33		
Jackie Burkett	LB	6'4"	228	33	4	
Bill Cody	LB	6'1"	230	26		
Wayne Colman	LB	6'1"	230	24		
Frank Emanuel	LB	6'3"	225	27		
Hap Farber (from MIN)	LB	6'1"	220	22		
Harry Jacobs	LB	6'2"	226	33		
Mike Morgan	LB	6'4"	242	28	1	6
Major Hazelton	DB	6'1"	185	25		
Hugo Hollas	DB	6'1"	190	25	5	
Gene Howard	DB	6'	190	23		
Delles Howell	DB	6'3"	195	23	3	
Dicky Lyons	DB	6'	190	23	1	
Elijah Nevett	DB	6'	185	26	3	
Joe Scarpati	DB	5'10"	185	28	1	
Doug Wyatt	DB	6'1"	195	23	4	

Mike Rengel — Injury

Use Name	Pos.	Hgt	Wgt	Age	Int	Pts
Edd Hargett	QB	5'11"	185	23		
Billy Kilmer	QB	6'	204	30		
Steve Ramsey	QB	6'2"	210	22		
Bill Dusenbery	HB	6'2"	198	21		
Don McCall	HB	5'11"	195	25		6
Vic Nyvall	HB	5'10"	185	22		
Elijah Pitts (from LA)	HB	6'1"	205	31		
Tony Baker	FB-HB	5'11"	225	25		6
Tom Barrington	FB-HB	6'1"	213	26		12
Dick Davis (from DEN)	FB-HB	5'11"	215	23		
Earl Gros	FB	6'3"	220	29		
Andy Livingston	FB	6'	235	25		
Jim Otis	FB	6'	220	22		
Ernie Wheelwright	FB	6'3"	235	33		
Gary Lewis	HB-FB	6'3"	230	28		
Dan Abramowicz	WR	6'1"	195	25		30
Ken Burrough	WR	6'4"	212	22		12
Al Dodd	WR	6'	180	25		12
Bob Shaw	WR	6'	194	21		
Dave Parks	TE	6'2"	203	28		12
Ray Poage	WR	6'4"	215	29		
Tom Dempsey	K	6'1"	264	29		70
Julian Fagan	K	6'3"	205	22		

SAN FRANCISCO FORTY NINERS

RUSHING

Last Name	No.	Yds	Avg	TD
Willard	236	789	3.3	7
Cunningham	128	443	3.5	3
Tucker	42	137	3.3	1
Thomas	31	89	2.9	0
Kwalick	3	65	21.7	0
Isenbarger	18	43	2.4	0
Brodie	9	29	3.2	2
Strong	2	3	1.5	0
Spurrier	2	−18	−9.0	0

RECEIVING

Last Name	No.	Yds	Avg	TD
Washington	53	1100	21	12
Cunningham	35	209	6	0
Windsor	31	363	12	2
Willard	31	259	8	3
Witcher	22	288	13	2
Tucker	17	108	6	1
Thomas	12	221	18	3
Kwalick	10	148	15	1
Isenbarger	8	158	20	1
Riley	7	136	19	0

PUNT RETURNS

Last Name	No.	Yds	Avg	TD
B. Taylor	43	516	12	0
Fuller	4	29	7	0
Riley	1	5	5	0

KICKOFF RETURNS

Last Name	No.	Yds	Avg	TD
Tucker	25	577	23	0
B. Taylor	12	190	16	0
Thomas	6	177	30	0
Beard	2	8	4	0
Fuller	1	8	8	0
Belk	1	7	7	0
Riley	1	0	0	0
Windsor	1	0	0	0

PASSING - PUNTING - KICKING

PASSING	Att	Comp	%	Yds	Yd/Att	TD	Int−	%	RK
Brodie	378	223	59	2941	7.8	24	10−	3	1
Spurrier	4	3	75	49	12.3	1	0−	0	
Isenbarger	1	0	0	0	0.0	0	0−	0	

PUNTING	No	Avg
Spurrier	75	38.4

KICKING	XP	Att	%	FG	Att	%
Gossett	39	41	95	21	31	68

LOS ANGELES RAMS

RUSHING

Last Name	No.	Yds	Avg	TD
Josephson	150	640	4.3	5
Ellison	90	381	4.2	5
Smith	77	338	4.4	1
Mason	44	123	2.8	0
Gabriel	28	104	3.7	1
Curran	25	92	3.7	0
Jordan	10	50	5.0	0
Studstill	1	23	23.0	0
Petitbon	1	3	3.0	0
Johnson	1	1	1.0	0

RECEIVING

Last Name	No.	Yds	Avg	TD
Snow	51	859	17	7
Josephson	44	427	10	0
Truax	36	420	12	3
Smith	24	164	7	1
Studstill	18	252	14	2
Tucker	12	230	19	0
Mason	12	127	11	1
Ellison	10	84	8	2
Long	3	35	12	1
Curran	3	25	8	0
Klein	2	20	10	0
Ray	1	11	11	0
D. Williams	1	9	9	0
Jordan	1	−5	−5	0

PUNT RETURNS

Last Name	No.	Yds	Avg	TD
Haymond	53	376	7	0
Alexander	7	38	5	0
Nettles	2	4	2	0

KICKOFF RETURNS

Last Name	No.	Yds	Avg	TD
Haymond	35	1022	29	1
Alexander	7	126	18	0
Curran	3	51	17	0
Ellison	1	20	20	0
Johnson	1	17	17	0

PASSING - PUNTING - KICKING

PASSING	Att	Comp	%	Yds	Yd/Att	TD	Int−	%	RK
Gabriel	407	211	52	2552	6.3	16	12−	3	6
Sweetan	13	6	46	81	6.2	1	0−	0	
Curran	2	0	0	0	0.0	0	1−	50	
Smith	2	0	0	0	0.0	0	0−	0	
Josephson	1	1	100	25	25.0	0	0−	0	
Studstill	1	0	0	0	0.0	0	0−	0	

PUNTING	No	Avg
Studstill	67	39.1

KICKING	XP	Att	%	FG	Att	%
Ray	34	34	100	29	45	64

ATLANTA FALCONS

RUSHING

Last Name	No.	Yds	Avg	TD
Butler	166	636	3.8	0
Wages	119	228	3.5	1
Gipson	52	177	3.4	0
Malone	40	136	3.4	0
Campbell	28	116	4.1	2
Berry	13	60	4.6	0
Mitchell	5	23	4.6	1
Johnson	7	21	3.0	0
Brunson	1	9	9.0	0

RECEIVING

Last Name	No.	Yds	Avg	TD
Mitchell	44	650	15	6
Flatley	39	544	14	1
Wages	26	153	6	2
Butler	24	151	6	1
Snyder	23	311	14	2
Gipson	16	186	12	3
Malone	9	38	4	0
Cogdill	7	101	14	1
Campbell	7	92	13	0
Donohoe	2	36	18	1

PUNT RETURNS

Last Name	No.	Yds	Avg	TD
Mallory	17	203	12	1
McCauley	14	138	10	1
Freeman	3	15	5	0

KICKOFF RETURNS

Last Name	No.	Yds	Avg	TD
Butler	14	284	20	0
Campbell	10	230	23	0
Gipson	8	189	24	0
Malone	5	66	13	0
Cavness	3	61	20	0
Brunson	4	54	14	0
Wages	1	22	22	0
Lavan	1	10	10	0
Freeman	1	0	0	0

PASSING - PUNTING - KICKING

PASSING	Att	Comp	%	Yds	Yd/Att	TD	Int−	%	RK
Berry	269	156	58	1806	6.7	16	13−	5	4
Johnson	72	40	56	443	6.2	2	8−	11	
Wages	1	1	100	13	13.0	0	0−	0	

PUNTING	No	Avg
Lothridge	76	38.7

KICKING	XP	Att	%	FG	Att	%
Vinyard	23	26	88	9	25	36

NEW ORLEANS SAINTS

RUSHING

Last Name	No.	Yds	Avg	TD
Baker	82	337	4.1	1
Barrington	72	228	3.2	2
Otis	71	211	3.0	0
Pitts	35	104	3.0	0
Davis	27	94	3.5	0
McCall	23	63	2.7	1
Wheelwright	16	45	2.8	0
Kilmer	12	42	3.5	0
Dodd	5	31	6.2	0
Livingston	10	29	2.9	0
Poage	1	13	13.0	0
Abramowicz	1	7	7.0	0
Hargett	4	7	1.8	0
Dusenbery	4	6	1.5	0
Nyvall	5	6	1.2	0
Burrough	1	4	4.0	0
Gros	4	2	0.5	0
Fagan	1	−6	−6.0	0

RECEIVING

Last Name	No.	Yds	Avg	TD
Abramowicz	55	906	16	5
Dodd	28	484	17	1
Parks	26	447	17	2
Barrington	22	130	6	0
Otis	20	124	6	0
Poage	15	166	11	1
Burrough	13	196	15	2
Baker	12	47	4	0
Pitts	7	63	9	0
McCall	5	43	9	0
Davis	4	29	7	0
Gros	2	0	0	0
Nyvall	2	−1	−1	0
Shaw	1	49	49	0
Wheelwright	1	7	7	0

PUNT RETURNS

Last Name	No.	Yds	Avg	TD
Dodd	14	129	9	0
Lyons	5	34	7	0
Hollas	4	22	6	0
Wyatt	1	15	15	0
Howard	5	14	3	0

KICKOFF RETURNS

Last Name	No.	Yds	Avg	TD
Dodd	15	319	21	0
Burrough	15	298	20	0
Dusenbery	10	183	18	0
Barrington	6	129	22	0
McCall	1	26	26	0
Otis	2	22	11	0
Pitts	1	22	22	0
Lyons	1	20	20	0
Lewis	1	19	19	0
Poage	1	6	6	0

PASSING - PUNTING - KICKING

PASSING	Att	Comp	%	Yds	Yd/Att	TD	Int−	%	RK
Kilmer	237	135	57	1557	6.6	6	17−	7	12
Hargett	175	78	45	1133	6.5	5	5−	3	12
Ramsey	2	0	0	0	0.0	0	0−	0	
Dodd	1	0	0	0	0.0	0	0−	0	

PUNTING	No	Avg
Fagan	77	42.5

KICKING	XP	Att	%	FG	Att	%
Dempsey	16	17	94	18	34	53

1970 A.F.C. New League, Old Faces

In their first season in the NFL, the old AFL clubs found things rougher than they expected. In interconference games, the NFC came out on top in two thirds of them. An AFC team did win the Super Bowl, but that was the Baltimore Colts, an old-line NFL club which had moved over to the AFC this season along with Cleveland and Pittsburgh. Nevertheless, the ten clubs which had made up the AFL placed a good share of players on all All-Pro teams, and the two expansion teams which came out of the AFL gave good reason for the former members to be proud. The Miami Dolphins and Cincinnati Bengals, both created in the mid 1960s, each made the playoffs. The Atlanta Falcons and New Orleans Saints, NFL expansion teams from the same period, came nowhere near matching the record of these two.

EASTERN DIVISION

Baltimore Colts—Soft-Spoken Don McCafferty took over as head coach after Don Shula quit to go to Miami, and the Colts rewarded him with a championship in his first season on the job. The Baltimore offense scored the most points in the conference, yet went through some mid-season changes. John Williams moved into the starting lineup at guard after an embarrassing 44-24 loss to Kansas City, hustling Tom Nowatzke filled in as running back when injuries kayoed Tom Matte, and oldsters Johnny Unitas and Earl Morrall occasionally relieved each other at quarterback. The defense, however, was a picture of stability, with stars Bubba Smith, Mike Curtis, Ted Hendricks, Rick Volk, and Jerry Logan leading a quick and mobile unit.

Miami Dolphins—The Dolphins had to pay highly to get Don Shula, including a first-draft choice which went to Baltimore as compensation, but the results proved the new coach's worth. Under Shula's direction, Bob Griese matured as a quarterback, Larry Csonka, Jim Kiick, and Mercury Morris developed into top runners, and the offensive line meshed into a fine unit, with Larry Little blossoming into a star. On defense, however, Shula did his best job, turning an indifferent unit into the conference's best. Five rookies started on defense, Mike Kolen, Doug Swift, Tim Foley, Curtis Johnson, and Jake Scott. The veteran pillars on the platoon were Manny Fernandez, Nick Buoniconti, and Dick Anderson.

New York Jets—Injuries destroyed the Jets' chances of defending their divisional title. Joe Namath's broken wrist robbed the offense of its leader, and a torn Achilles tendon took fullback Matt Snell out of the lineup just when he was running better than at any time in his career. Emerson Boozer, Don Maynard, and Roger Finnie also missed a lot of time in sick bay, forcing wholesale replacements on the offensive unit. Although Al Woodall, George Nock, and Rich Caster were capable substitutes, they could not replace the firepower lost in Namath, Snell, and Maynard. Injuries also hurt the defense, with Steve Thompson and Jim Hudson the major casualties, but that unit held together well and kept the Jets respectable in their worst moments.

Buffalo Bills—Rookie Dennis Shaw won the starting quarterback job and showed the potential to become a fine passer, while receiver Marlin Briscoe caught enough Shaw passes to lead the league in receiving. On the defensive unit, Al Cowlings, Edgar Chandler, and Bobby James showed talent and enthusiasm to make up for their inexperience. Unfortunate events of the year included O. J. Simpson's knee injury which sidelined him for the second half of the season, Mike Stratton's Achilles tendon injury, and Wayne Patrick's separated shoulder.

Boston Patriots—The Patriots shelled out a bundle to pick up quarterback Joe Kapp from Minnesota in mid-season, but Kapp was out of shape and unfamiliar with the Boston system; the result was a season in which he threw three touchdown passes and seventeen interceptions. Kapp's poor season fit in well with the entire situation on the Patriots. Running backs Jim Nance and Carl Garrett seemed apathetic at times, Gino Cappelletti continued to regress as a place kicker, the offensive line never lived up to its potential, and the defense lost Jim Cheyunski and rookie Phil Olsen to injuries. By mid-season, John Mazur had replaced Clive Rush as head coach.

CENTRAL DIVISION

Cincinnati Bengals—Even with quarterback Greg Cook out of action with a bad shoulder, the Bengals still stormed into the playoffs and delighted coach 'Paul Brown by beating the Browns out for first place in the Central Division. The Cincinnati defense had been strengthened by rookies Mike Reid, Ron Carpenter, and Lemar Parrish, but the offense started out slowly under new quarterback Virgil Carter. After

losing six of their first seven games, the Bengals suddenly jelled; they beat Buffalo, Cleveland, Pittsburgh, and their other four remaining opponents to streak past the rival Browns from upstate. Starring along the way were runners Jess Phillips and Paul Robinson, receiver Chip Myers, center Bob Johnson, kicker Horst Muhlmann, linebacker Bill Bergey, and rookies Reid, Carpenter, and Parrish.

Cleveland Browns—Aside from Leroy Kelly's bad season and a chaotic linebacking situation, two off-season trades contributed the most to Cleveland's slump this year. With Bill Nelsen's bad knees making him a constant question mark, the Browns traded star receiver Paul Warfield to Miami for their first-draft pick, which Cleveland used to take Purdue quarterback Mike Phipps. Then the Browns shipped Ron Johnson, Jim Kanicki, and Wayne Meylan to New York for receiver Homer Jones. While Warfield and Johnson starred in their new surroundings, Phipps showed that he needed plenty more seasoning and Jones failed to even win a starting job.

Pittsburgh Steelers—Even with Terry Bradshaw not delivering as expected, the Steelers did make a mid-season run at the Central Division crown before slumping off into five losses in their last six games. The big improvement in the Steelers came on defense, where Mean Joe Greene and Andy Russell stood out on a unit with eleven solid starters. Less impressive was the offense, where coach Chuck Noll fielded a complete new set of runners and receivers to go with his rookie quarterback.

Houston Oilers—Coach Wally Lemm announced before the season that this was his final year with the Oilers, but his team gave him very little in the way of a going-away gift, as they dropped into last place in the AFC Central Division. Injuries hurt the team, as quarterback Charley Johnson, newly acquired from St. Louis, linebacker George Webster, guard Tom Regner, and fullback Hoyle Granger all suffered disabling wounds. But even without the injuries, the Oilers had too few good players to challenge seriously for the title in their weak division.

WESTERN DIVISION

Oakland Raiders—Old George Blanda, playing his twenty-first season of pro football, made a specialty out of pulling games out of the fire at the last second as he saved five games in a row with late heroics. He filled in for the injured Daryle Lamonica and threw a pair of touchdown passes to beat Pittsburgh 31-14, he kicked a 48-yard field goal with three seconds left to tie Kansas City 17-17, he kicked a 52-yarder to beat Cleveland 23-20 in the last three seconds, he came off the bench to drive the Raiders to the winning touchdown in a 24-19 victory over Denver, and he kicked a field goal with four seconds left to beat San Diego 20-17—all of which helped Oakland to take first place in the West.

Kansas City Chiefs—The spark which had moved the club last year was missing, especially on offense; the Kansas City attack virtually ignored long-gaining plays and confined itself to short passes and inside running plays. The overconservative offense wasted the talents of Otis Taylor, who scored only three touchdowns all year, and Ed Podolak, who scored only four times after breaking into the starting lineup. Coach Hank Stram made only two substitutions in last year's lineup, replacing Mike Garrett at halfback with Podolak and promoting Jack Rudnay to starting center over sore-kneed E. J. Holub.

San Diego Chargers—With a flabby pass rush and a secondary that picked off only five enemy passes all year, the defense gave head coach Charlie Walker his biggest headache in his first full season on the job. The front four contained heralded ex-collegians in Steve DeLong, Ron Billingsley, and Gene Ferguson, but the best work came from unknown rookie Joe Owens. While Pete Barnes and Bob Babich solidified the linebacking, the secondary of Bob Howard, Joe Beauchamp, Jim Hill, and Jim Tolbert was remarkably undistinguished. Injuries to Dickie Post and Brad Hubbert hurt the running attack, but a strong passing game kept the offense in business.

Denver Broncos—The Broncos charged out of the starting gate with a 4-1 record, but problems at quarterback eventually caught up with the team. Steve Tensi missed most of the campaign with injuries and Pete Liske played quarterback most of the way. Although Liske had leadership ability and skill at reading defenses, the ex-Canadian League star did not have a strong enough arm to hold the job. By the end of the year, coach Lou Saban was playing rookie Al Pastrana at the spot with dismal results. The high point of the season for Saban was the development of Floyd Little into an All-Pro workhorse runner and the good showing of rookie Bobby Anderson.

FINAL TEAM STATISTICS

OFFENSE

	BALT.	BOS.	BUFF.	CIN.	CLEV.	DENV.	HOUS.	K.C.	MIAMI	N.Y.J.	OAK.	PITT.	S.D.
FIRST DOWNS:													
Total	**242**	184	203	210	239	217	232	183	228	230	**270**	206	231
by Rushing	70	63	71	100	87	84	88	83	106	90	**107**	84	83
by Passing	**148**	98	120	97	134	112	126	86	100	122	139	97	119
by Penalty	24	23	12	13	18	21	18	14	22	18	24	25	**29**
RUSHING:													
Number	411	334	367	461	462	436	419	448	**492**	463	471	432	395
Yards	1336	1040	1465	2057	1579	1802	1556	1858	**2082**	1653	1964	1715	1450
Average Yards	3.3	3.1	4.0	**4.5**	3.4	4.1	3.7	4.1	4.2	3.6	4.2	4.0	3.7
Touchdowns	9	11	8	16	14	**17**	10	11	14	11	7	13	9
PASSING:													
Attempts	416	392	402	339	392	403	**470**	289	299	386	418	384	387
Completions	219	176	213	172	190	183	**238**	154	159	193	210	150	192
Completion Percentage	52.6	44.9	53.0	50.7	48.5	45.4	50.6	**53.3**	53.2	50.0	50.2	39.1	49.6
Passing Yards	**3087**	1975	2916	2097	2752	2358	2768	2038	2284	2592	3029	2312	2936
Avg. Yards per Attempt	7.4	5.0	7.3	6.2	7.0	5.9	5.9	7.1	**7.6**	6.7	7.2	6.0	7.6
Avg. Yards per Complet.	14.1	11.2	13.7	12.2	14.5	12.9	11.6	13.2	14.4	13.4	14.4	**15.4**	15.3
Times Tackled Passing	33	42	53	31	**16**	44	33	38	36	35	19	28	57
Yards Lost Tackled	289	389	486	227	170	333	262	319	327	285	**164**	275	433
Net Yards	2798	1586	2430	1870	2582	2025	2506	1719	1957	2307	**2865**	2037	2503
Touchdowns	23	7	13	12	17	11	12	13	15	14	**28**	12	24
Interceptions	22	28	26	**11**	24	28	23	16	19	22	21	32	19
Percent Intercepted	5.3	7.1	6.5	**3.2**	6.1	6.9	4.9	5.5	6.4	5.7	5.0	8.3	4.9
PUNTS:													
Number	63	86	83	79	71	**87**	84	76	58	73	79	78	74
Average Distance	44.7	39.1	38.9	**46.2**	42.6	42.9	42.4	44.9	41.2	40.1	39.5	44.2	42.8
PUNT RETURNS:													
Number	36	32	45	37	34	**63**	41	31	30	26	37	51	31
Yards	351	305	298	327	236	**556**	257	371	295	150	308	281	173
Average Yards	9.8	9.5	6.6	8.8	6.9	8.8	6.3	**12.0**	9.8	5.8	8.3	5.5	5.6
Touchdowns	**1**	0	0	**1**	0	0	0	0	**1**	0	**1**	0	0
KICKOFF RETURNS:													
Number	45	**62**	**62**	39	44	49	55	44	48	56	44	40	42
Yards	1161	**1275**	1244	1002	1001	1114	1168	997	1036	1106	1017	997	813
Average Yards	**25.8**	20.6	20.1	25.7	22.8	22.7	21.2	22.7	21.6	19.8	23.1	24.9	19.4
Touchdowns	1	0	**2**	1	1	0	0	0	1	0	0	0	0
INTERCEPTION RETURNS:													
Number	25	8	11	23	19	16	18	**31**	23	23	19	23	9
Yards	408	184	179	180	324	220	242	395	**414**	281	112	266	90
Average Yards	16.3	**23.0**	16.3	7.8	17.1	13.8	13.4	12.7	18.0	12.2	5.9	11.6	10.0
Touchdowns	**3**	0	2	0	**3**	0	0	1	1	2	0	1	0
PENALTIES:													
Number	71	88	**99**	71	65	94	78	83	77	88	92	82	79
Yards	708	849	**1108**	831	634	887	833	888	834	1022	1021	835	852
FUMBLES:													
Number	25	**18**	37	22	24	23	26	26	24	20	21	30	19
Number Lost	14	13	26	12	14	13	15	15	11	11	9	16	**6**
POINTS:													
Total	**321**	149	204	312	286	253	217	272	297	255	300	210	282
PAT Attempts	**38**	18	25	34	35	28	23	26	33	28	36	26	35
PAT Made	**36**	17	24	33	34	27	23	26	33	28	**36**	24	34
FG Attempts	34	22	19	37	22	32	32	**42**	30	35	29	28	19
FG Made	19	8	10	25	12	18	18	**30**	22	19	16	10	12
Percent FG Made	55.9	36.4	52.6	67.6	54.5	56.3	56.3	71.4	**73.3**	54.3	55.2	35.7	63.2
Safeties	0	0	0	0	**3**	2	1	0	0	1	0	0	1

DEFENSE

	BALT.	BOS.	BUFF.	CIN.	CLEVE	DENV.	HOUS.	K.C.	MIAMI	N.Y.J.	OAK.	PITT.	S.D.
FIRST DOWNS:													
Total	214	242	213	236	236	**199**	227	226	226	216	223	225	245
by Rushing	79	115	87	87	104	67	85	83	82	**65**	90	91	106
by Passing	120	105	**103**	131	120	118	115	111	128	122	104	120	117
by Penalty	15	22	23	18	**12**	14	27	32	16	29	29	14	22
RUSHING:													
Number	390	503	484	418	451	409	466	418	**387**	408	460	487	480
Yards	1439	2074	1718	1543	2006	1351	1793	1657	1453	**1283**	2027	1679	1967
Average Yards	3.7	4.1	3.5	3.7	4.4	3.3	3.8	4.0	3.8	**3.1**	4.4	3.4	4.1
Touchdowns	**6**	20	16	11	10	7	16	10	8	7	10	8	15
PASSING:													
Attempts	452	**334**	338	428	357	379	344	408	403	383	339	393	365
Completions	238	177	**157**	209	186	191	164	195	234	165	**157**	191	207
Completion Percentage	52.7	53.0	46.4	48.8	52.1	50.4	47.7	47.8	58.1	**43.1**	46.3	48.6	56.7
Passing Yards	2780	2430	2334	2885	2528	2810	2851	**2280**	2708	2680	2386	2555	2422
Avg. Yards per Attempt	6.2	7.3	6.9	6.7	7.1	7.4	8.3	**5.6**	6.7	7.0	7.0	6.5	6.6
Avg. Yards per Complet.	11.7	13.7	14.9	13.8	13.6	14.7	17.4	11.7	**11.6**	16.2	15.2	13.4	11.7
Times Tackled Passing	41	28	31	28	34	**50**	30	35	18	35	39	26	27
Yards Lost Tackled	374	243	246	250	290	**456**	246	270	157	308	297	238	207
Net Yards	2406	2187	2088	2635	2238	2354	2605	**2010**	2551	2372	2089	2317	2215
Touchdowns	16	19	15	18	16	20	25	15	17	20	22	21	13
Interceptions	25	8	11	23	19	16	18	**31**	23	23	19	23	9
Percent Intercepted	5.5	2.4	3.3	5.4	5.3	4.2	5.2	**7.6**	5.7	6.0	5.6	5.9	2.5
PUNTS:													
Number	78	63	76	80	66	**89**	77	79	63	68	80	85	64
Average Distance	**38.4**	43.8	44.0	43.8	42.4	44.9	44.4	43.4	41.7	38.9	41.6	41.9	44.1
PUNT RETURNS:													
Number	38	42	42	48	23	56	52	51	**20**	42	40	51	34
Yards	365	303	291	392	83	416	441	414	**241**	380	303	304	312
Average Yards	9.6	7.2	6.9	8.2	**3.6**	7.4	8.5	8.1	12.1	9.0	7.6	6.0	9.2
Touchdowns	1	1	2	2	**0**	**0**	**0**	**0**	1	1	**0**	1	**0**
KICKOFF RETURNS:													
Number	58	41	46	33	39	**24**	32	45	55	58	54	49	52
Yards	1237	841	1112	774	956	**544**	741	1128	1142	1210	1233	1068	1153
Average Yards	21.3	**20.5**	24.2	23.5	24.5	22.7	23.2	25.1	20.8	20.9	22.8	21.8	22.2
Touchdowns	**0**	2	1	**0**	**0**	**0**	**0**	**0**	1	2	**0**	1	**0**
INTERCEPTION RETURNS:													
Number	22	28	26	**11**	24	28	23	16	19	22	21	32	19
Yards	283	302	334	**150**	399	213	334	195	258	397	303	318	235
Average Yards	12.9	10.8	12.8	13.6	16.6	**7.6**	14.5	12.2	13.6	18.0	14.4	9.9	12.4
Touchdowns	1	2	**0**	**0**	4	**0**	2	**0**	1	3	1	1	**0**
PENALTIES:													
Number	**101**	**101**	73	81	88	82	76	77	68	70	87	76	89
Yards	1032	1096	814	784	871	817	833	817	704	655	**1148**	790	998
FUMBLES:													
Number	14	33	23	28	28	**35**	22	22	24	22	17	29	21
Number Lost	9	**17**	15	16	12	16	8	12	15	11	8	15	15
POINTS:													
Total	234	361	337	255	265	264	352	244	**228**	286	293	272	278
PAT Attempts	**25**	44	35	31	32	28	44	26	28	33	33	32	30
PAT Made	**25**	44	35	31	31	27	44	**25**	27	32	32	29	29
FG Attempts	37	28	46	24	26	36	30	28	**22**	32	31	32	40
FG Made	19	17	30	12	14	23	14	21	**11**	18	21	15	23
Percent FG Made	51.4	60.7	65.2	50.0	53.8	63.9	**46.7**	75.0	50.0	56.3	67.7	46.9	57.5
Safeties	1	1	1	1	**0**	**0**	1	**0**	**0**	1	**0**	3	**0**

CONFERENCE PLAYOFFS

December 27, at Oakland (Attendance 52,594)

SCORING

OAKLAND	**0**	**7**	**7**	**7–21**
MIAMI	**0**	**7**	**0**	**7–14**

Second Quarter
Mia. Warfield, 16 yard pass from Griese PAT—Yepremian (kick)
Oak. Biletnikoff, 22 yard pass from Lamonica PAT—Blanda (kick)

Third Quarter
Oak. Brown, 50 yard interception return PAT—Blanda (kick)

Fourth Quarter
Oak. Sherman, 82 yard pass from Lamonica PAT—Blanda (kick)
Mia. Richardson, 7 yard pass from Griese PAT—Yepremian (kick)

TEAM STATISTICS

OAK.		MIAMI
12	First Downs—Total	16
5	First Downs—Rushing	5
7	First Downs—Passing	9
0	First Downs—Penalty	2
4	Fumbles—Number	2
2	Fumbles—Lost Ball	0
4	Penalties—Number	0
30	Yards Penalized	0
1	Missed Field Goals	2
52	Offensive Plays—Total	63
301	Net Yards	242
5.8	Average Gain	3.8
2	Giveaways	1
1	Takeaways	2
−1	Difference	+1

INDIVIDUAL STATISTICS

OAKLAND	No.	Yds.	Avg.	MIAMI	No.	Yds.	Avg.
RUSHING							
Hubbard	18	58	3.2	Kiick	14	64	6.0
Smith	9	37	4.1	Morris	8	29	3.6
Dixon	8	31	3.9	Csonka	10	23	2.3
Banaszak	1	−6	−6.0	Griese	1	2	2.0
	36	120	3.3		33	118	3.6
RECEIVING							
Biletnikoff	3	46	15.3	Warfield	4	62	15.5
Chester	2	47	23.5	Kiick	4	34	8.5
Sherman	1	82	82.0	Richardson	2	30	15.0
Smith	1	9	9.0	Morris	2	15	7.5
Dixon	1	3	3.0	Twilley	1	14	14.0
	8	187	23.4		13	155	11.9
PUNTING							
Eischeid	4		32.2	Seiple	5		39.2
PUNT RETURNS							
Atkinson	1	−1	−1.0	Scott	1	−1	−1.0
				Anderson	1	−4	−4.0
					2	−5	−2.5
KICKOFF RETURNS							
Sherman	1	22	22.0	Ginn	2	27	13.5
Atkinson	1	19	19.0	Morris	1	21	21.0
Budness	1	0	0.0	Seiple	1	8	8.0
	3	41	13.7		4	56	14.0

PASSING

OAKLAND	Att.	Comp.	Comp. Pct.	Yds.	Int.	Yds/ Att.	Yds/ Comp.	Yards Lost Tkld.
Lamonica	16	8	50.0	187	0	11.7	23.4	0– 0
MIAMI								
Griese	27	13	48.1	155	1	5.7	11.9	3–31

December 26, at Baltimore (Attendance 49,694)

SCORING

BALTIMORE	**7**	**3**	**0**	**7–17**
CINCINNATI	**0**	**0**	**0**	**0– 0**

First Quarter
Bal. Jefferson, 45 yard pass from Unitas PAT—O'Brien (kick)

Second Quarter
Bal. O'Brien, 44 yard field goal

Fourth Quarter
Bal. Hinton, 53 yard pass from Unitas PAT—O'Brien (kick)

TEAM STATISTICS

BALT.		CIN.
15	First Downs—Total	7
12	First Downs—Rushing	2
3	First Downs—Passing	5
0	First Downs—Penalty	0
0	Fumbles—Number	1
0	Fumbles—Lost Ball	0
6	Penalties—Number	1
63	Yards Penalized	5
2	Missed Field Goals	1
66	Offensive Plays—Total	46
299	Net Yards	139
4.5	Average Gain	3.0
0	Giveaways	1
1	Takeaways	0
+1	Difference	−1

INDIVIDUAL STATISTICS

BALTIMORE	No.	Yds.	Avg.	CINCINNATI	No.	Yds.	Avg.
RUSHING							
Bulaich	25	116	4.6	Robinson	5	25	5.0
Nowatzke	10	25	2.5	Carter	2	16	8.0
Unitas	2	18	9.0	Phillips	10	12	1.2
Hill	3	11	3.7	Lewis	3	10	3.3
Jefferson	3	5	1.7	Johnson	2	0	0.0
Havrilak	3	0	0.0		22	63	2.9
Hinton	1	−5	−5.0				
	47	170	3.6				
RECEIVING							
Hinton	3	86	28.7	Myers	4	66	16.5
Jefferson	2	51	25.5	Phillips	2	12	6.0
Mackey	1	8	8.0	Thomas	1	9	9.0
	6	145	24.2	Johnson	1	6	6.0
					8	93	11.6
PUNTING							
Lee	6		38.3	Lewis	8		39.1
PUNT RETURNS							
Gardin	7	28	4.0	Parrish	2	6	3.0
KICKOFF RETURNS							
Nowatzke	1	0	0.0	Robinson	2	29	14.5
				Lamb	1	17	17.0
					3	46	15.3
INTERCEPTION RETURNS							
M. Curtis	1	0	0.0	None			

PASSING

BALTIMORE	Att.	Comp.	Comp. Pct.	Yds.	Int.	Yds/ Att.	Yds/ Comp.	Yds Lost Tkld
Unitas	17	6	35.3	145	0	8.5	24.2	2–16
CINCINNATI								
Carter	20	7	35.0	64	1	3.2	9.1	
Wyche	1	1	100.0	29	0	29.0	29.0	
	21	8	38.1	93	1	4.4	11.6	3–17

BALTIMORE COLTS 11-2-1 Don McCafferty

Scores of Each Game		
16	San Diego	14
24	KANSAS CITY	44
14	Boston	6
24	Houston	20
29	N.Y. Jets	22
27	BOSTON	3
35	MIAMI	0
13	Green Bay	10
17	BUFFALO	17
17	Miami	34
21	CHICAGO	20
29	PHILADELPHIA	10
20	Buffalo	14
35	N.Y. JETS	20

Use Name	Pos.	Hgt	Wgt	Age	Int	Pts
Sam Ball	OT	6'4"	240	26		
Dennis Nelson	OT	6'5"	260	24		
Bob Vogel	OT	6'5"	250	28		
Cornelius Johnson	OG	6'2"	245	27		
Glenn Ressler	OG	6'3"	250	26		
Dan Sullivan	OG	6'3"	250	31		
John Williams	OG	6'3"	256	24		
Bill Curry	C	6'2"	235	27		
Tom Goode	C	6'3"	245	31		
Roy Hilton	DE	6'6"	240	25		
Billy Newsome	DE	6'4"	240	22		
Bubba Smith	DE	6'7"	295	25		
Jim Bailey	DT	6'4"	245	22		
Fred Miller	DT	6'3"	250	29		
Billy Ray Smith	DT	6'4"	250	35		
George Wright	DT	6'3"	260	23		
Mike Curtis	LB	6'2"	232	27	5	
Bob Grant	LB	6'2"	225	24	2	6
Ted Hendricks	LB	6'7"	215	22	1	6
Ray May	LB	6'1"	230	25	1	
Robbie Nichols	LB	6'3"	220	23		
Tom Curtis	DB	6'1"	196	22	1	
Jim Duncan	DB	6'2"	220	24	2	6
Ron Gardin	DB	5'11"	180	25		6
Jerry Logan	DB	6'1"	190	29	6	12
Tommy Maxwell	DB	6'2"	195	23		
Charlie Stukes	DB	6'3"	212	26	3	
Rick Volk	DB	6'3"	195	25	4	
Earl Morrall	QB	6'1"	206	36		
Johnny Unitas	QB	6'1"	196	37		
Sam Havrilak	HB	6'2"	195	22		
Jack Maitland	HB	6'1"	210	22		12
Tom Matte	HB	6'	214	31		
Norm Bulaich	FB-HB	6'1"	218	23		18
Larry Conjar	FB	6'	214	24		
Jerry Hill	FB	5'11"	217	30		12
Tom Nowatzke	FB	6'3"	230	27		6
Eddie Hinton	WR	6'	200	23		42
Roy Jefferson	WR	6'2"	190	26		42
Jim O'Brien	WR	6'	195	23		93
Jimmy Orr	WR	5'11"	185	34		12
Ray Perkins	WR	6'	183	28		6
John Mackey	TE	6'3"	224	28		18
Tom Mitchell	TE	6'2"	215	26		24
David Lee	K	6'4"	230	26		

MIAMI DOLPHINS 10-4-0 Don Shula

Scores of Each Game		
14	Boston	27
20	Houston	10
20	OAKLAND	13
20	N.Y. Jets	6
33	Buffalo	14
0	CLEVELAND	28
0	Baltimore	35
17	Philadelphia	24
21	NEW ORLEANS	10
34	BALTIMORE	17
20	Atlanta	7
37	BOSTON	20
16	N.Y. JETS	10
45	BUFFALO	7

Use Name	Pos.	Hgt	Wgt	Age	Int	Pts
Doug Crusan	OT	6'5"	260	24		
Norm Evans	OT	6'5"	250	27		
Wayne Moore	OT	6'6"	265	25		
Bob Kuechenberg	OG	6'3"	255	22		
Jim Langer	OG	6'2"	240	22		
Larry Little	OG	6'1"	270	24		
Maxie Williams	OG	6'4"	250	30		
Bob DeMarco	C	6'3"	245	32		
Carl Mauck	C	6'3"	240	23		
Norm McBride	DE	6'3"	245	23		
Jim Riley	DE	6'4"	260	25		
Bill Stanfill	DE	6'5"	250	23		
Frank Cornish (from CHI)	DT	6'6"	285	26		
Manny Fernandez	DT	6'2"	250	24		
Bob Heinz	DT	6'6"	290	23		
John Richardson	DT	6'2"	260	25		
Nick Buoniconti	LB	5'11"	220	29		
Ted Davis	LB	6'1"	232	28	1	
Mike Kolen	LB	6'2"	215	22		
Dick Palmer	LB	6'2"	220	22		
Jesse Powell	LB	6'1"	215	23		
Doug Swift	LB	6'3"	230	21		
Ed Weisacosky	LB	6'	230	26		
Dick Anderson	DB	6'2"	200	24	8	
Dean Brown	DB	5'10"	170	23	1	
Tim Foley	DB	6'	195	22		
Curtis Johnson	DB	6'2"	200	22	3	
Lloyd Mumphord	DB	5'11"	180	23	5	12
Bob Petrella	DB	6'	185	25		
Jake Scott	DB	6'	188	25	5	6
Bill Darnall—Injury						
Bob Griese	QB	6'1"	190	25		12
John Stofa	QB	6'3"	210	28		
Hubert Ginn	HB	5'11"	190	23		
Jim Kiick	HB	5'11"	220	24		36
Mercury Morris	HB	5'10"	190	23		6
Barry Pryor	HB	6'	215	24		
Larry Csonka	FB	6'3"	250	23		36
Stan Mitchell	FB	6'2"	210	26		6
Karl Noonan	WR	6'3"	205	26		6
Willie Richardson	WR	6'2"	198	30		6
Howard Twilley	WR	5'10"	180	26		30
Paul Warfield	WR	6'	190	27		36
Marv Fleming	TE	6'4"	235	28		
Jim Mandich	TE	6'3"	225	21		6
Larry Seiple	TE	6'	220	25		
Karl Kremser	K	6'	175	25		2
Garo Yepremian	K	5'8"	172	26		97

NEW YORK JETS 4-10-0 Weeb Ewbank

Scores of Each Game		
21	Cleveland	31
31	Boston	21
31	Buffalo	34
6	MIAMI	20
22	BALTIMORE	29
6	BUFFALO	10
10	N.Y. GIANTS	22
17	Pittsburgh	21
31	Los Angeles	20
17	BOSTON	3
20	MINNESOTA	10
13	OAKLAND	14
10	Miami	16
20	Baltimore	35

Use Name	Pos.	Hgt	Wgt	Age	Int	Pts
Dave Foley	OT	6'5"	255	22		
Winston Hill	OT	6'4"	285	28		
Roger Finnie	OG-OT	6'3"	245	23		
Tom Bayless	OG	6'3"	240	22		
Dave Herman	OG	6'2"	255	28		
Dave Middendorf	OG	6'3"	260	24		
Randy Rasmussen	OG	6'2"	255	25		
Pete Perreault	OT-OG	6'3"	248	31		
John Schmitt	C	6'4"	250	27		
Paul Crane	LB-C	6'2"	212	26		
Verlon Biggs	DE	6'4"	270	27		
Jimmie Jones	DE	6'3"	215	23		
Gerry Philbin	DE	6'2'	245	29		
Mark Lomas	DT-DE	6'4'	230	22		
John Elliott	DT	6'4"	244	25		2
John Little	DE-DT	6'3"	220	23		
Steve Thompson	DE-DT	6'5"	245	25		
Al Atkinson	LB	6'1"	230	27	3	
Ralph Baker	LB	6'3"	235	28	2	
John Ebersole	LB	6'3"	240	21		
Larry Grantham	LB	6'	210	31	3	6
Dennis Onkotz	LB	6'1"	220	22		
Mike Battle	DB	6'1"	175	24		
John Dockery	DB	6'	186	25		
W.K. Hicks	DB	6'1"	195	27	8	
Gus Holloman	DB	6'3"	195	24	3	
Jim Hudson	DB	6'2"	210	27		
Cecil Leonard	DB	5'11"	160	24		
Steve Tannen	DB	6'1"	194	22	2	6
Earlie Thomas	DB	6'1"	190	24	2	6
Jim Richards—Military Service						
Paul Seiler—Injury						
Bob Davis	QB	6'3"	205	25		
Joe Namath	QB	6'2"	200	27		
Jim Turner	QB	6'2"	215	29		85
Al Woodall	QB	6'5"	205	24		
Emerson Boozer	HB	5'11"	195	27		30
Cliff McClain	HB	6'	217	22		
George Nock	HB	5'10"	200	24		36
Chuck Mercein	FB	6'3"	222	27		6
Matt Snell	FB	6'2"	220	28		6
Lee White	FB	6'4"	235	24		6
Eddie Bell	WR	5'10"	160	22		12
Rich Caster	WR	6'5"	222	21		18
Don Maynard	WR	6'	180	34		
Steve O'Neal	WR	6'3"	185	24		
George Sauer	WR	6'1"	195	26		24
Gary Arthur	TE	6'5"	230	22		
Pete Lammons	TE	6'3"	230	26		12
Wayne Stewart	TE	6'7"	213	23		

BUFFALO BILLS 3-10-1 Johnny Rauch

Scores of Each Game		
10	DENVER	25
0	LOS ANGELES	19
34	N.Y. JETS	31
10	Pittsburgh	23
14	MIAMI	33
10	N.Y. Jets	6
45	Boston	10
14	CINCINNATI	43
17	Baltimore	17
13	Chicago	31
10	BOSTON	14
6	N.Y. Giants	20
14	BALTIMORE	20
7	Miami	45

Use Name	Pos.	Hgt	Wgt	Age	Int	Pts
Levert Carr	OT	6'5"	260	26		
Paul Costa	OT	6'4"	255	28		
Jerry Gantt	OT	6'4"	266	21		
Art Laster	OT	6'4"	280	22		
Howard Kindig	C-OT	6'6"	264	29		
Richard Cheek	OG	6'3"	266	22		
Joe O'Donnell	OG	6'2"	262	27		
Jim Reilly	OG	6'2"	260	22		
Wayne Fowler	C	6'3"	260	21		
Frank Marchlewski	C	6'2"	240	26		
Al Cowlings	DE	6'5"	258	23		
Mike McBath	DE	6'4"	248	24		
Ron McDole	DE	6'3"	288	30		
Jim Dunaway	DT	6'4"	277	28		
Waddey Harvey	DT	6'4"	282	23		
Julian Nunamaker	DT	6'3"	252	24		
Bob Tatarek	DT	6'4"	260	24		
Al Andrews	LB	6'3"	216	26		
Edgar Chandler	LB	6'3"	235	24	1	6
Jerald Collins	LB	6'1"	220	23		
Dick Cunningham	LB	6'2"	244	25		
Paul Guidry	LB	6'3"	233	26		
Mike McCaffrey	LB	6'3"	235	24		
Mike Stratton	LB	6'3"	240	28		
Jackie Allen	DB	6'1"	187	22		
Butch Byrd	DB	6'	196	28	4	6
Ike Hill	DB	5'10"	180	23		
Robert James	DB	6'1"	177	23		
Tommy Pharr	DB	5'10"	187	23		
John Pitts	DB	6'4"	223	25	1	
Pete Richardson	DB	6'1"	193	23	5	
Max Anderson — Knee Injury						
Dan Darragh	QB	6'3"	196	23		
James Harris	QB	6'3"	215	23		
Dennis Shaw	QB	6'2"	210	23		
Greg Jones	HB	6'1"	200	22		12
Lloyd Pate	HB	6'1"	205	24		6
O. J. Simpson	HB	6'2"	204	23		36
Bill Enyart	FB	6'4"	236	23		6
Wayne Patrick	FB	6'2"	254	24		6
Glenn Alexander	WR	6'3"	205	23		
Marlin Briscoe	WR	5'10"	177	24		48
Clyde Glosson	WR	5'11"	175	23		
Haven Moses	WR	6'3"	205	24		12
Austin Denney	TE	6'2"	230	26		
Willie Grate	TE	6'4"	225	24		12
Roland Moss (from SD)	HB-TE	6'3"	215	23		
Grant Guthrie	K	6'	210	22		54
Paul Maguire	K	6'	232	32		

BOSTON PATRIOTS 2-12-0 Clive Rush John Mazur

Scores of Each Game		
27	MIAMI	14
21	N.Y. JETS	31
6	Baltimore	14
10	Kansas City	23
0	N.Y. GIANTS	16
3	BALTIMORE	27
10	BUFFALO	45
0	St. Louis	31
14	SAN DIEGO	16
3	N.Y. Jets	17
14	Buffalo	10
20	Miami	37
14	MINNESOTA	35
7	Cincinnati	45

Use Name	Pos.	Hgt	Wgt	Age	Int	Pts
Tom Funchess	OT	6'5"	260	25		
Ezell Jones	OT	6'4"	255	23		
Tom Neville	OT	6'4"	255	27		
Len St. Jean	OG	6'1"	245	28		
Gary Bugenhagen	OT-OG	6'2"	250	25		
Angelo Loukas	OT-OG	6'3"	250	23		
Jon Morris	C	6'4"	255	27		
Mike Montler	OG-C	6'4"	270	26		
Ron Berger	DE	6'8"	275	26		
Ike Lassiter	DE	6'5"	270	29		
Dennis Wirgowski	DE	6'5"	255	22		
Mel Witt	DE	6'3"	250	24		
Houston Antwine	DT	6'	270	31		
Jim Hunt	DT	5'11"	255	31		
Rex Mirich	DT	6'4"	258	29		
Mike Ballou	LB	6'3"	235	22		
John Bramlett	LB	6'2"	220	29	1	
Jim Cheyunski	LB	6'2"	220	24		
Ed Philpott	LB	6'3"	240	24	1	
Marty Schottenheimer	LB	6'3"	225	27		
Fred Whittingham	LB	6'1"	240	31		
J.R. Williamson	LB	6'2"	220	28	1	
Randy Beverly	DB	5'11"	185	26		
Larry Carwell	DB	6'1"	190	26		
Tom Janik	DB	6'3"	200	29		
Daryle Johnson	DB	5'11"	190	24	2	
Art McMahon	DB	6'1"	190	24	1	
John Outlaw	DB	5'10"	180	25		
Clarence Scott	DB	6'2"	205	26	1	
Don Webb	DB	5'10"	195	31	1	
Ed Toner — Injury						
Joe Kapp	QB	6'2"	215	32		
Mike Taliaferro	QB	6'2"	205	28		
Sid Blanks	HB	6'	205	29		
Carl Garrett	HB	5'11"	210	23		24
Bob Gladieux (to BUF)	HB	5'11"	190	23		
Odell Lawson	HB	6'2"	218	22		
Jim Nance	FB	6'1"	240	27		42
Eddie Ray	TE-FB	6'1"	230	23		
Ginn Cappelletti	WR	6'	190	36		30
Charley Frazier	WR	6'	190	31		
Gayle Knief	WR	6'3"	205	23		6
Bill Rademacher	WR	6'1"	190	28		
Tom Richardson	WR	6'2"	195	25		
Ron Sellers	WR	6'4"	195	23		24
Bake Turner	WR	6'	180	30		12
Tom Beer	TE	6'4"	228	25		
Barry Brown	TE	6'3"	220	27		
Charlie Gogolak	K	5'10"	170	25		11

BALTIMORE COLTS

RUSHING

Last Name	No.	Yds	Avg	TD
Bulaich	139	426	3.1	3
Nowatzke	73	248	3.4	1
Maitland	74	209	2.8	1
Havrilak	54	159	2.9	0
Hill	36	115	3.2	2
Hinton	5	58	11.6	2
Jefferson	4	47	11.8	0
Matte	12	43	3.6	0
Unitas	9	16	1.8	0
Morrall	2	6	3.0	0
Perkins	2	6	3.0	0
Conjar	1	3	3.0	0

RECEIVING

Last Name	No.	Yds	Avg	TD
Hinton	47	733	16	5
Jefferson	44	749	17	7
Mackey	28	435	16	3
Mitchell	20	261	13	4
Nowatzke	16	93	6	0
Havrilak	14	141	10	0
Bulaich	11	123	11	0
Orr	10	199	20	2
Perkins	10	194	19	1
Maitland	9	67	7	1
Hill	8	62	8	0
O'Brien	1	28	28	0
Matte	1	2	2	0

PUNT RETURNS

Last Name	No.	Yds	Avg	TD
Gardin	28	330	12	1
Volk	3	15	5	0
Logan	2	4	2	0
T. Curtis	3	2	1	0

KICKOFF RETURNS

Last Name	No.	Yds	Avg	TD
Duncan	20	707	35	1
Gardin	11	265	24	0
Nowatzke	7	93	13	0
Havrilak	2	36	18	0
Maitland	1	28	28	0
Grant	1	21	21	0
Jefferson	1	11	11	0
Newsome	1	0	0	0
Stukes	1	0	0	0

PASSING – PUNTING – KICKING

PASSING	Att	Comp	%	Yds	Yd/Att	TD	Int–	%	RK
Unitas	321	166	52	2213	6.9	14	18–	6	6
Morrall	93	51	55	792	8.5	9	4–	4	
Havrilak	2	2	100	82	41.0	0	0–	0	

PUNTING	No	Avg
Lee	63	44.7

KICKING	XP	Att	%	FG	Att	%
O'Brien	36	38	95	19	34	56

MIAMI DOLPHINS

RUSHING

Last Name	No.	Yds	Avg	TD
Csonka	193	874	4.5	6
Kiick	191	658	3.4	5
Morris	60	409	6.8	0
Griese	26	89	3.4	2
Mitchell	8	23	2.9	0
Seiple	2	21	10.5	0
Warfield	2	13	6.5	0
Stofa	2	5	2.5	0
Pryor	2	0	0.0	0
Ginn	5	-1	-0.2	0
Noonan	1	-9	-9.0	0

RECEIVING

Last Name	No.	Yds	Avg	TD
Kiick	42	497	12	0
Warfield	28	703	25	6
Twilley	22	281	13	5
Fleming	18	205	11	0
Morris	12	149	12	0
Csonka	11	94	9	0
Noonan	10	186	19	1
W. Richardson	7	67	10	1
Mitchell	6	85	14	1
Seiple	2	14	7	0
Mandich	1	3	3	1

PUNT RETURNS

Last Name	No.	Yds	Avg	TD
Scott	27	290	11	1
Anderson	1	6	6	0
Morris	2	-1	-1	0

KICKOFF RETURNS

Last Name	No.	Yds	Avg	TD
Morris	28	812	29	1
Scott	4	117	29	0
Ginn	5	59	12	0
Mitchell	4	35	9	0
Anderson	1	8	8	0
Seiple	2	5	3	0
Mandich	2	0	0	0
Brown	1	0	0	0
Foley	1	0	0	0

PASSING – PUNTING – KICKING

PASSING	Att	Comp	%	Yds	Yd/Att	TD	Int–	%	RK
Griese	245	142	58	2019	8.2	12	17–	7	4
Stofa	53	16	30	240	4.5	3	2–	4	
Kiick	1	1	100	25	25.0	0	0–	0	

PUNTING	No	Avg
Seiple	58	41.2

KICKING	XP	Att	%	FG	Att	%
Yepremian	31	31	100	22	29	76
Kremser	2	2	100	0	1	0

NEW YORK JETS

RUSHING

Last Name	No.	Yds	Avg	TD
Boozer	139	581	4.2	5
Nock	135	402	3.0	5
Snell	64	281	4.4	1
White	70	215	3.1	0
Woodall	28	110	3.9	0
Mercein	20	44	2.2	0
O'Neal	1	16	16.0	0
Davis	2	11	5.5	0
Turner	1	1	1.0	0
Namath	1	-1	-1.0	0
Bell	2	-7	-3.5	0

RECEIVING

Last Name	No.	Yds	Avg	TD
Maynard	31	525	17	0
Sauer	31	510	16	4
Boozer	28	258	9	0
Lammons	25	316	13	2
Bell	21	246	12	2
Caster	19	393	21	3
Nock	18	146	8	1
White	12	125	10	1
Mercein	3	27	9	1
Snell	2	26	13	0
McClain	1	11	11	0
Stewart	1	7	7	0
Battle	1	2	2	0

PUNT RETURNS

Last Name	No.	Yds	Avg	TD
Battle	19	117	6	0
Bell	7	33	5	0

KICKOFF RETURNS

Last Name	No.	Yds	Avg	TD
Battle	40	891	22	0
McClain	4	70	18	0
Bell	3	61	20	0
Leonard	1	35	35	0
Mercein	4	32	8	0
Nock	1	18	18	0
Caster	1	0	0	0
Onkotz	1	0	0	0
Tannen	1	-1	-1	0

PASSING – PUNTING – KICKING

PASSING	Att	Comp	%	Yds	Yd/Att	TD	Int–	%	RK
Woodall	188	96	51	1265	6.7	9	9–	5	9
Namath	179	90	50	1259	7.0	5	12–	7	13
Davis	17	6	35	66	3.9	0	0–	0	
Bell	1	0	0	0	0.0	0	1–	100	
O'Neal	1	1	100	2	2.0	0	0–	0	

PUNTING	No	Avg
O'Neal	73	40.1

KICKING	XP	Att	%	FG	Att	%
Turner	28	28	100	19	35	54

BUFFALO BILLS

RUSHING

Last Name	No.	Yds	Avg	TD
Simpson	120	488	4.1	5
Patrick	66	259	3.9	1
Shaw	39	210	5.4	0
Enyart	58	196	3.4	0
Pate	46	162	3.5	1
Jones	31	113	3.6	1
Darragh	1	26	26.0	0
Briscoe	3	19	6.3	0
Harris	3	-8	-2.7	0

RECEIVING

Last Name	No.	Yds	Avg	TD
Briscoe	57	1036	18	8
Moses	39	726	19	2
Enyart	35	235	7	1
Pate	19	103	5	0
Patrick	16	142	9	0
Denney	14	201	14	0
Simpson	10	139	14	0
Jones	8	89	11	0
Grate	7	147	21	2
Alexander	4	51	13	0
Moss	2	31	16	0
Glosson	2	16	8	0

PUNT RETURNS

Last Name	No.	Yds	Avg	TD
Pharr	23	184	8	0
Hill	19	102	5	0
Allen	2	10	5	0
Alexander	1	2	2	0

KICKOFF RETURNS

Last Name	No.	Yds	Avg	TD
Simpson	7	333	48	1
Alexander	12	204	17	0
Hill	9	165	18	0
Jones	7	162	23	1
Moss	7	131	19	0
Glosson	4	61	15	0
Enyart	3	60	20	0
Patrick	3	38	13	0
Pate	1	21	21	0
Collins	2	17	9	0
Andrews	1	16	16	0
McCaffrey	2	15	8	0
Laster	2	8	4	0
McBath	1	7	7	0
Pharr	1	6	6	0
Costa	1	0	0	0

PASSING – PUNTING – KICKING

PASSING	Att	Comp	%	Yds	Yd/Att	TD	Int–	%	RK
Shaw	321	178	55	2507	7.8	10	20–	6	4
Harris	50	24	48	338	6.8	3	4–	8	
Darragh	29	11	38	71	2.5	0	2–	7	
Simpson	2	0	0	0	0.0	0	0–	0	

PUNTING	No	Avg
Maguire	83	38.9

KICKING	XP	Att	%	FG	Att	%
Guthrie	24	25	96	10	19	53

BOSTON PATRIOTS

RUSHING

Last Name	No.	Yds	Avg	TD
Nance	145	522	3.6	7
Garrett	88	272	3.1	4
Lawson	56	99	1.8	0
Kapp	20	71	3.6	0
Blanks	13	44	3.4	0
Ray	5	13	2.6	0
Taliaferro	3	11	3.7	0
Gladieux	4	8	2.0	0

RECEIVING

Last Name	No.	Yds	Avg	TD
Sellers	38	550	14	4
Turner	28	428	15	2
Garrett	26	216	8	0
Nance	26	148	6	0
Brown	15	145	10	0
Beer	11	150	14	0
Lawson	11	113	10	0
Frazier	9	86	10	0
Blanks	5	49	10	0
Rademacher	4	51	13	0
Knief	3	39	13	1

PUNT RETURNS

Last Name	No.	Yds	Avg	TD
Garrett	17	168	10	0
Blanks	9	83	9	0
Carwell	3	48	16	0
Johnson	2	6	3	0
Lawson	1	0	0	0

KICKOFF RETURNS

Last Name	No.	Yds	Avg	TD
Lawson	25	546	22	0
Garrett	24	511	21	0
Blanks	7	152	22	0
Carwell	1	30	30	0
Whittingham	1	24	24	0
Schottenheimer	1	8	8	0
Beer	1	4	4	0
Beverly	1	0	0	0
Brown	1	0	0	0

PASSING – PUNTING – KICKING

PASSING	Att	Comp	%	Yds	Yd/Att	TD	Int–	%	RK
Kapp	219	98	45	1104	5.0	3	17–	8	17
Taliaferro	173	78	45	871	5.0	4	11–	6	16

PUNTING	No	Avg
Janik	86	39.1

KICKING	XP	Att	%	FG	Att	%
Cappelletti	12	13	92	6	15	40
Gogolak	5	5	100	2	7	29

CINCINNATI BENGALS 8-6-0 Paul Brown

Scores of Each Game

31	OAKLAND	21
3	Detroit	38
13	HOUSTON	20
27	Cleveland	30
19	KANSAS CITY	27
0	Washington	20
10	Pittsburgh	21
43	Buffalo	14
14	CLEVELAND	10
34	PITTSBURGH	7
26	NEW ORLEANS	6
17	San Diego	14
30	Houston	20
45	BOSTON	7

Use Name	Pos.	Hgt	Wgt	Age	Int	Pts
Howard Fest	OT	6'6"	268	24		
Rufus Mayes	OT	6'5"	255	22		
Ernie Wright	OT	6'4"	270	30		
Guy Dennis	OG	6'2"	255	23		
Pat Matson	OG	6'1"	245	26		
Mike Wilson	OT-OG	6'1"	240	22		
Bob Johnson	C	6'5"	265	24		
Marty Baccaglio	DE	6'3"	245	25		
Royce Berry	DE	6'3"	248	24		12
Ron Carpenter	DE	6'4"	260	22		
Nick Roman	DE	6'3"	230	22		
Steve Chomyszak	DT	6'5"	265	25		
Willie Jones	DT	6'2"	260	28		
Mike Reid	DT	6'3"	258	23		

Use Name	Pos.	Hgt	Wgt	Age	Int	Pts
Ken Avery	LB	6'1"	225	26	1	
Al Beauchamp	LB	6'2"	236	26	1	6
Bill Bergey	LB	6'2"	240	25	3	
Larry Ely	LB	6'1"	230	22		
Wayne McClure	LB	6'1"	225	24		
Bill Peterson	LB	6'3"	230	25		
Al Coleman	DB	6'1"	183	25		
Sandy Durko	DB	6'1"	185	22		
Ken Dyer	DB	6'3"	186	24	3	
Kenny Graham (to PIT)	DB	6'	205	28	3	
John Guillory	DB	5'10"	190	25		
Lemar Parrish	DB	5'11"	185	22	5	18
Ken Riley	DB	6'	184	23	4	
Fletcher Smith	DB	6'2"	180	26	3	

Greg Cook—Shoulder Injury

Use Name	Pos.	Hgt	Wgt	Age	Int	Pts
Virgil Carter	QB	6'1"	200	24		12
Dave Lewis	QB	6'2"	210	24		
Sam Wyche	QB	6'4"	210	25		12
Essex Johnson	HB	5'9"	200	23		24
Paul Robinson	HB	6'	200	25		42
Paul Dunn	FB-HB	6'	210	22		
Doug Dressler	FB	6'3"	220	22		
Ron Lamb	FB	6'2"	230	26		
Jess Phillips	HB-FB	6'1"	210	23		30
Eric Crabtree	WR	5'11"	182	25		12
Chip Myers	WR	6'4"	200	25		6
Speedy Thomas	WR	5'11"	178	23		12
Bruce Coslet	TE	6'3"	230	24		6
Mike Kelly	TE	6'4"	215	22		
Bob Trumpy	TE	6'6"	225	25		12
Horst Muhlmann	K	6'1"	210	30		108

CLEVELAND BROWNS 7-7-0 Blanton Collier

Scores of Each Game

31	N.Y. JETS	21
31	San Francisco	34
15	PITTSBURGH	7
30	CINCINNATI	27
24	DETROIT	41
28	Miami	0
10	SAN DIEGO	27
20	Oakland	23
10	Cincinnati	14
28	HOUSTON	14
9	Pittsburgh	28
21	Houston	10
2	DALLAS	6
27	Denver	13

Use Name	Pos.	Hgt	Wgt	Age	Int	Pts
Al Jenkins	OT	6'2"	255	24		
Bob McKay	OT	6'5"	260	22		
Dick Schafrath	OT	6'3"	258	34		
Joe Taffoni	OT	6'3"	250	25		
Jim Copeland	OG	6'2"	245	25		
John Demarie	OG	6'3"	255	25		
Gene Hickerson	OG	6'3"	248	35		
Fred Hoaglin	C	6'4"	250	26		
Chuck Reynolds	C	6'2"	240	23		2
Jack Gregory	DE	6'6"	250	25		
Joe Jones	DE	6'6"	246	22		
Ron Snidow	DE	6'4"	250	28		2
Walter Johnson	DT	6'3"	275	27	1	2
Joel Righetti	DT	6'3"	253	22		
Jerry Sherk	DT	6'4"	253	22		
Bill Yanchar	DT	6'3"	250	22		

Use Name	Pos.	Hgt	Wgt	Age	Int	Pts
Billy Andrews	LB	6'	225	25	1	6
Tom Beutler	LB	6'1"	232	23		
John Garlington	LB	6'1"	225	24	1	
Jim Houston	LB	6'2"	240	33	1	
Dale Lindsey	LB	6'3"	225	27	2	6
Bob Matheson	LB	6'4"	240	25	1	
Erich Barnes	DB	6'2"	212	35	5	6
Ben Davis	DB	5'11"	185	24	1	
Mike Howell	DB	6'1"	190	27	1	
Ernie Kellerman	DB	6'	185	26	1	
Tom Schoen	DB	5'11"	185	24		
Rickey Stevenson	DB	5'11"	188	22		
Freddie Summers	DB	6'1"	180	23		
Walt Sumner	DB	6'1"	180	23	4	

Use Name	Pos.	Hgt	Wgt	Age	Int	Pts
Don Gault	QB	6'2"	190	24		
Bill Nelsen	QB	6'	195	29		
Mike Phipps	QB	6'2"	207	22		
Ken Brown	HB	5'10"	205	24		
Leroy Kelly	HB	6'	200	28		48
Randy Minniear	HB	6'	210	26		6
Reece Morrison	HB	6'	205	24		6
Bo Scott	FB	6'3"	210	27		66
Steve Engel	HB-FB	6'1"	218	22		
Gary Collins	WR	6'4"	210	29		24
Fair Hooker	WR	6'1"	193	23		12
Dave Jones	WR	6'2"	185	23		
Homer Jones	WR	6'2"	215	29		12
Chip Glass	TE	6'4"	236	23		12
Milt Morin	TE	6'4"	240	28		6
Don Cockroft	K	6'1"	190	25		70

PITTSBURGH STEELERS 5-9-0 Chuck Noll

Scores of Each Game

7	HOUSTON	19
13	Denver	16
7	Cleveland	15
23	BUFFALO	10
7	Houston	3
14	Oakland	31
21	CINCINNATI	10
21	N.Y. JETS	17
14	KANSAS CITY	31
7	Cincinnati	34
28	CLEVELAND	9
12	GREEN BAY	20
16	Atlanta	27
20	Philadelphia	30

Use Name	Pos.	Hgt	Wgt	Age	Int	Pts
John Brown	OT	6'2"	255	31		
Mike Haggerty	OT	6'4"	240	24		
Rick Sharp	OT	6'3"	262	22		
Sam Davis	OG	6'1"	245	26		
Bruce Van Dyke	OG	6'2"	225	26		
Ralph Wenzel	OG	6'3"	250	27		
Ray Mansfield	C	6'3"	240	29		
Jon Kolb	OT-C	6'2"	220	23		
L. C. Greenwood	DE	6'5"	240	23		
Ben McGee	DE	6'2"	250	28		
Lloyd Voss	DE	6'4"	256	28		
Dick Arndt	DT	6'5"	265	26		
Joe Greene	DT	6'4"	270	23		
Chuck Hinton	DT	6'5"	248	31		
Clarence Washington	DT	6'3"	265	23		

Rocky Bleier — Wounded in Military Service

Use Name	Pos.	Hgt	Wgt	Age	Int	Pts
Chuck Allen	LB	6'1"	225	30	4	
Carl Crennel	LB	6'1"	230	21		
Henry Davis	LB	6'3"	235	27		
Doug Fisher	LB	6'1"	225	23		
Jerry Hillebrand	LB	6'3"	240	30	2	
Andy Russell	LB	6'3"	225	28	3	
Brian Stenger	LB	6'4"	220	23		
Ocie Austin	DB	6'3"	200	23	1	
Fred Barry	DB	5'10"	184	22		
Chuck Beatty	DB	6'2"	200	24	2	6
Mel Blount	DB	6'3"	205	22	1	
Lee Calland	DB	6'	185	29	7	
Clancy Oliver	DB	6'1"	180	22		
John Rowser	DB	6'1"	180	26	3	
John Sodaski	DB	6'1"	197	22		

Larry Gagner—Injury from automobile accident

Use Name	Pos.	Hgt	Wgt	Age	Int	Pts
Terry Bradshaw	QB	6'3"	218	21		6
Terry Hanratty	QB	6'1"	200	22		
Dick Hoak	HB	5'11"	190	31		6
Preston Pearson	HB	6'1"	190	25		12
John Fuqua	FB-HB	6'	200	23		54
Warren Bankston	FB	6'4"	225	23		12
Terry Cole	FB	6'1"	220	25		
Hubie Bryant	WR	5'10"	175	24		
Dave Kalina	WR	6'3"	205	23		
Ron Shanklin	WR	6'1"	180	23		24
Dave Smith	WR	6'2"	205	23		12
Jon Staggers	WR	5'10"	186	21		6
J. R. Wilburn	WR	6'2"	190	27		
Bob Adams	TE	6'2"	225	24		
Dennis Hughes	TE	6'1"	220	22		18
Gene Mingo	K	6'1"	210	31		32
Bobby Walden	K	6'	190	32		
Allen Watson	K	5'10"	165	25		22

HOUSTON OILERS 3-10-1 Wally Lemm

Scores of Each Game

19	Pittsburgh	7
10	MIAMI	20
20	Cincinnati	13
20	BALTIMORE	24
3	PITTSBURGH	7
31	San Diego	31
0	St. Louis	44
9	Kansas City	24
20	SAN FRANCISCO	30
14	Cleveland	28
31	DENVER	21
10	CLEVELAND	21
20	CINCINNATI	30
10	Dallas	52

Use Name	Pos.	Hgt	Wgt	Age	Int	Pts
Elbert Drungo	OT	6'5"	250	27		
Glen Ray Hines	OT	6'5"	265	26		
Walt Suggs	OT	6'5"	260	31		
Ken Gray	OG	6'2"	250	34		
Tom Regner	OG	6'1"	255	26		
Ron Saul	OG	6'2"	255	22		
Doug Wilkerson	OG	6'2"	245	23		
Hank Autry	C	6'3"	235	23		
Bobby Maples	C	6'3"	245	27		
Elvin Bethea	DE	6'3"	255	24		
Pat Holmes	DE	6'5"	250	30		
Spain Musgrove	DT-DE	6'4"	275	25		
Lee Brooks	DT	6'5"	266	22		
Tom Domres	DT	6'3"	255	23		
Willie Parker	DT	6'2"	265	25		

Use Name	Pos.	Hgt	Wgt	Age	Int	Pts
Garland Boyette	LB	6'1"	245	30	1	
Claude Harvey	LB	6'4"	225	22		
Jess Lewis	LB	6'3"	230	23		
Ron Pritchard	LB	6'1"	235	23	2	2
Olen Underwood	LB	6'1"	220	28		
Loyd Wainscott	LB	6'1"	235	23		
George Webster	LB	6'4"	223	24		
Bob Atkins	DB	6'3"	215	24	1	
Ken Houston	DB	6'3"	195	25	3	
Benny Johnson	DB	5'11"	178	22		
Leroy Mitchell	DB	6'2"	190	25	2	
Zeke Moore	DB	6'2"	198	26	6	
Johnny Peacock	DB	6'2"	200	23	3	6

John Douglas—Injury

Use Name	Pos.	Hgt	Wgt	Age	Int	Pts
Charley Johnson	QB	6'	190	33		
Bob Naponic	QB	6'	190	23		
Jerry Rhome	QB	6'	188	28		6
Woody Campbell	HB	5'11"	208	25		6
Mike Richardson	HB	5'11"	198	23		18
Joe Dawkins	FB-HB	5'11"	220	22		12
Hoyle Granger	FB	6'1"	225	26		6
Roy Hopkins	FB	6'1"	215	25		18
Tom Smiley	FB	6'1"	235	26		
Jim Beirne	WR	6'1"	196	23		6
Mac Haik	WR	6'1"	196	24		
Charlie Joiner	WR	5'11"	185	22		18
Jerry LeVias	WR	5'10"	175	23		30
Paul Zaeske	WR	6'2"	200	24		
Donnie Davis	TE	6'4"	225	30		
Alvin Reed	TE	6'5"	230	26		12
Terry Stoepel	TE	6'4"	235	23		
Roy Gerela	K	5'10"	185	22		77
Spike Jones	K	6'2"	190	23		

CINCINNATI BENGALS

RUSHING
Last Name	No.	Yds	Avg	TD
Phillips	163	648	4.0	4
Robinson	149	622	4.2	6
E. Johnson	65	273	4.2	2
Carter	34	246	7.2	2
Wyche	19	118	6.2	2
Dressler	18	77	4.3	0
Lamb	6	35	5.8	0
Crabtree	3	23	7.7	0
Lewis	2	8	4.0	0
Thomas	2	7	3.5	0

RECEIVING
Last Name	No.	Yds	Avg	TD
Myers	32	542	17	1
Phillips	31	124	4	1
Trumpy	29	480	17	2
Thomas	21	257	12	2
Crabtree	19	231	12	2
Robinson	17	175	10	1
E. Johnson	15	190	13	2
Coslet	8	98	12	1

PUNT RETURNS
Last Name	No.	Yds	Avg	TD
Parrish	23	194	8	1

KICKOFF RETURNS
Last Name	No.	Yds	Avg	TD
Parrish	16	482	30	1
Robinson	14	363	26	0
E. Johnson	3	68	23	0
Dressler	4	48	12	0
Lamb	2	41	21	0

PASSING – PUNTING – KICKING

PASSING
Last Name	Att	Comp	%	Yds	Yd/Att	TD	Int–	%	RK
Carter	278	143	51	1647	5.9	9	9–	3	7
Wyche	57	26	46	411	7.2	3	2–	4	
Lewis	4	3	75	39	9.8	0	0–	0	

PUNTING
Last Name	No	Avg
Lewis	79	46.2

KICKING
Last Name	XP	Att	%	FG	ATT	%
Muhlman	33	33	100	25	37	68

CLEVELAND BROWNS

RUSHING
Last Name	No.	Yds	Avg	TD
Kelly	206	656	3.2	6
Scott	151	503	2.9	2
Morrison	73	175	2.4	0
Phipps	11	94	8.5	0
Minniear	12	39	3.3	1
Morin	1	2	2.0	0
Nelsen	7	–4	–0.6	0
Brown	1	–8	–8.0	0

RECEIVING
Last Name	No.	Yds	Avg	TD
Scott	40	351	9	4
Morin	37	611	17	1
Hooker	28	490	18	2
Collins	26	351	14	4
Kelly	24	311	13	2
Glass	19	403	21	2
H. Jones	10	141	14	1
Morrison	5	95	19	1
Minniear	1	–1	–1	0

PUNT RETURNS
Last Name	No.	Yds	Avg	TD
Morrison	15	133	9	0
Sumner	8	70	9	0
Schoen	8	18	2	0
Kelly	2	15	8	0
Jenkins	1	0	0	0

KICKOFF RETURNS
Last Name	No.	Yds	Avg	TD
H. Jones	29	739	25	1
Morrison	7	153	22	0
Brown	2	44	22	0
Schoen	1	27	27	0
Matheson	2	21	11	0
Righetti	1	17	17	0
Glass	1	0	0	0
Morin	1	0	0	0

PASSING – PUNTING – KICKING

PASSING
Last Name	Att	Comp	%	Yds	Yd/Att	TD	Int–	%	RK
Nelsen	313	159	51	2156	6.9	16	16–	5	8
Phipps	60	29	48	529	8.8	1	5–	8	
Gault	19	2	11	67	3.5	0	3–	16	

PUNTING
Last Name	No	Avg
Cockroft	71	42.6

KICKING
Last Name	XP	Att	%	FG	ATT	%
Cockroft	34	35	97	12	22	55

PITTSBURGH STEELERS

RUSHING
Last Name	No.	Yds	Avg	TD
Fuqua	138	691	5.0	7
Pearson	173	503	2.9	2
Bradshaw	32	233	7.3	1
Bankston	26	122	4.7	2
Hoak	40	115	2.9	1
Bryant	3	25	8.3	0
Wilburn	5	25	5.0	0
Cole	9	8	0.9	0
Smith	1	6	6.0	0
Hanratty	4	–5	–1.3	0
Hughes	1	–8	–8.0	0

RECEIVING
Last Name	No.	Yds	Avg	TD
Shanklin	30	691	23	4
Smith	30	458	15	2
Hughes	24	332	14	3
Fuqua	23	289	13	2
Bryant	8	154	19	0
Bankston	7	30	4	0
Staggers	6	118	20	1
Wilburn	6	77	13	0
Pearson	6	71	12	0
Hoak	4	25	6	0
Adams	3	36	12	0
Cole	3	31	10	0

PUNT RETURNS
Last Name	No.	Yds	Avg	TD
Bryant	37	159	4	0
Staggers	13	70	5	0
Blount	1	52	52	0

KICKOFF RETURNS
Last Name	No.	Yds	Avg	TD
Blount	18	535	30	0
Staggers	14	333	24	0
Pearson	4	114	29	0
Sharp	1	9	9	0
Wenzel	1	6	6	0
Calland	1	0	0	0
Washington	1	0	0	0

PASSING – PUNTING – KICKING

PASSING
Last Name	Att	Comp	%	Yds	Yd/Att	TD	Int–	%	RK
Bradshaw	218	83	38	1410	6.5	6	24–	11	15
Hanratty	163	64	39	842	5.2	5	8–	5	14
Hoak	2	2	100	40	20.0	1	0–	0	
Walden	1	1	100	20	20.0	0	0–	0	

PUNTING
Last Name	No	Avg
Walden	75	45.2
Bradshaw	3	17.3

KICKING
Last Name	XP	Att	%	FG	ATT	%
Mingo	17	17	100	5	18	28
Watson	7	8	88	5	10	50

HOUSTON OILERS

RUSHING
Last Name	No.	Yds	Avg	TD
Dawkins	124	517	4.2	2
Richardson	103	368	3.6	2
Hopkins	57	207	3.6	3
Campbell	59	189	3.2	1
Granger	51	169	3.3	1
Rhome	9	54	6.0	1
LeVias	7	37	5.3	0
Naponic	3	12	4.0	0
C. Johnson	5	3	0.6	0
Smiley	1	0	0.0	0

RECEIVING
Last Name	No.	Yds	Avg	TD
Reed	47	604	13	2
LeVias	41	529	13	5
Richardson	34	381	11	0
Joiner	28	416	15	3
Haik	17	190	11	0
Beirne	16	216	14	1
Dawkins	15	94	6	0
Campbell	15	78	5	0
Hopkins	14	142	10	0
Granger	11	118	11	0

PUNT RETURNS
Last Name	No.	Yds	Avg	TD
LeVias	25	213	9	0
Richardson	10	30	3	0
Houston	4	13	3	0
Beirne	1	1	1	0
Dawkins	1	0	0	0

KICKOFF RETURNS
Last Name	No.	Yds	Avg	TD
LeVias	26	598	23	0
B. Johnson	15	320	21	0
Moore	7	190	27	0
Drungo	1	25	25	0
Hopkins	1	20	20	0
Lewis	1	15	15	0
Davis	2	0	0	0
Granger	1	0	0	0
Reed	1	0	0	0

PASSING – PUNTING – KICKING

PASSING
Last Name	Att	Comp	%	Yds	Yd/Att	TD	Int–	%	RK
C. Johnson	281	144	51	1652	5.9	7	12–	4	10
Rhome	168	88	52	1031	6.1	5	8–	5	11
Naponic	20	6	30	85	4.3	0	2–	10	
LeVias	1	0	0	0	0.0	0	1–	100	

PUNTING
Last Name	No	Avg
Jones	84	42.4

KICKING
Last Name	XP	Att	%	FG	ATT	%
Gerela	23	23	100	18	32	56

Scores of Each Game			Use Name	Pos.	Hgt	Wgt	Age	Int	Pts	Use Name	Pos.	Hgt	Wgt	Age	Int	Pts	Use Name	Pos.	Hgt	Wgt	Age	Int	Pts

OAKLAND RAIDERS 8-4-2 John Madden

			Use Name	Pos.	Hgt	Wgt	Age	Int	Pts
21	Cincinnati	31	Harry Schuh	OT	6'2"	260	27		
27	San Diego	27	Art Shell	OT	6'5"	255	23		
13	Miami	20	Bob Svihus	OT	6'4"	245	27		
35	DENVER	23	George Buehler	OG	6'2"	260	23		
34	WASHINGTON	20	Jim Harvey	OG	6'5"	250	27		
31	PITTSBURGH	14	Gene Upshaw	OG	6'5"	255	25		
17	Kansas City	17	Jim Otto	C	6'2"	248	32		
23	CLEVELAND	20	Tony Cline	DE	6'2"	230	22	1	
24	Denver	19	Ben Davidson	DE	6'8"	280	30		
20	SAN DIEGO	17	Carleton Oats	DT-DE	6'2"	260	27		
14	Detroit	28	Al Dotson	DT	6'4"	260	27		
14	N.Y. Jets	13	Tom Keating	DT	6'2"	247	27		
20	KANSAS CITY	6	Art Thoms	DT	6'5"	250	23		
7	SAN FRANCISCO	38							

Use Name	Pos.	Hgt	Wgt	Age	Int	Pts
Duane Benson	LB	6'2"	215	25	1	
Bill Budness	LB	6'1"	215	27		
Dan Conners	LB	6'1"	230	28		
Gerald Irons	LB	6'2"	230	23		
Bill Laskey	LB	6'2"	235	27	1	
Gus Otto	LB	6'2"	220	27		
Carl Weathers	LB	6'2"	220	22		
Butch Atkinson	DB	6'	180	23	3	
Willie Brown	DB	6'1"	190	29	3	
Dave Grayson	DB	5'10"	187	31	1	
Kent McCloughan	DB	6'1"	190	27	5	
Jimmy Warren	DB	5'11"	175	31	2	
Nemiah Wilson	DB	6'	160	27	2	
Alvin Wyatt	DB	5'10"	185	22		6

Roger Hagberg — died April 15, 1970 Auto Accident

Use Name	Pos.	Hgt	Wgt	Age	Int	Pts
George Blanda	QB	6'1"	215	42		84
Daryle Lamonica	QB	6'2"	215	29		
Ken Stabler	QB	6'3"	194	24		
Pete Banaszak	HB	5'11"	200	26		12
Don Highsmith	HB	6'	200	22		
Charlie Smith	HB	6'1"	205	24		30
Larry Todd	HB	6'1"	185	27		
Hewritt Dixon	FB	6'2"	230	30		12
Marv Hubbard	FB	6'1"	215	24		6
Fred Biletnikoff	WR	6'1"	190	27		42
Drew Buie	WR	6'2"	178	23		
Rod Sherman	WR	6'	190	25		
Warren Wells	WR	6'1"	190	27		66
Ray Chester	TE	6'2"	220	22		42
Ted Koy	TE	6'1"	210	22		
Jacque MacKinnon	TE	6'4"	240	31		
Mike Eischeid	K	6'	190	29		

KANSAS CITY CHIEFS 7-5-2 Hank Stram

			Use Name	Pos.	Hgt	Wgt	Age	Int	Pts
10	Minnesota	27	Dave Hill	OT	6'5"	260	29		
44	Baltimore	24	Sid Smith	OT	6'4"	260	22		
13	Denver	26	Jim Tyrer	OT	6'6"	270	31		
23	BOSTON	10	Ed Budde	OG	6'5"	260	29		
27	Cincinnati	19	George Daney	OG	6'3"	240	23		
16	DALLAS	27	Mo Moorman	OG	6'5"	252	26		
17	OAKLAND	17	E. J. Holub	C	6'4"	236	32		
24	HOUSTON	9	Mike Oriard	C	6'4"	223	22		
31	Pittsburgh	14	Jack Rudnay	C	6'3"	240	22		
6	ST. LOUIS	6	Aaron Brown	DE	6'5"	265	26		
26	SAN DIEGO	14	Jerry Mays	DE	6'4"	250	30		
16	DENVER	0	Marv Upshaw	DE	6'3"	245	23		
6	Oakland	20	Buck Buchanan	DT	6'7"	275	30		
13	San Diego	31	Curley Culp	DT	6'1"	265	24		
			Bob Liggett	DT	6'2"	255	23		

Use Name	Pos.	Hgt	Wgt	Age	Int	Pts
Bobby Bell	LB	6'4"	228	30	3	6
Chuck Hurston	LB	6'6"	240	27		
Willie Lanier	LB	6'1"	245	25	2	
Jim Lynch	LB	6'1"	235	25	3	
Bob Stein	LB	6'2"	235	22		
Clyde Werner	LB	6'4"	225	22		
Ceasar Belser	DB	6'	212	25		
Dave Hadley	DB	5'9"	186	21		
Jim Kearney	DB	6'2"	206	27	4	
Jim Marsalis	DB	5'11"	194	24	4	
Willie Mitchell	DB	6'1"	185	28		
Johnny Robinson	DB	6'	205	31	10	6
Emmitt Thomas	DB	6'2"	192	27	5	

Remi Prudhomme — Injury
Goldie Sellers — Thigh Injury
Gene Trosch — Thigh Injury

Use Name	Pos.	Hgt	Wgt	Age	Int	Pts
Len Dawson	QB	6'	190	36		
John Huarte	QB	6'	185	26		
Mike Livingston	QB	6'3"	212	24		
Warren McVea	HB	5'10"	182	24		24
Ed Podolak	HB	6'1"	204	23		24
Wendell Hayes	FB	6'2"	220	29		30
Robert Holmes	FB	5'9"	220	24		24
Frank Pitts	WR	6'2"	200	26		12
Otis Taylor	WR	6'2"	215	27		18
Lewis Porter	WR	5'11"	178	23		
Gloster Richardson	WR	6'	200	27		12
Fred Arbanas	TE	6'3"	245	31		6
Billy Cannon	TE	6'1"	215	33		12
Morris Stroud	TE	6'10"	245	24		6
Jan Stenerud	K	6'2"	187	27		116
Jerrel Wilson	K	6'4"	222	29		

SAN DIEGO CHARGERS 5-6-3 Charlie Waller

			Use Name	Pos.	Hgt	Wgt	Age	Int	Pts
14	BALTIMORE	16	Terry Owens	OT	6'6"	275	26		
27	OAKLAND	27	Russ Washington	OT	6'6"	295	23		
10	Los Angeles	37	Bob Wells	OT	6'4"	280	25		
20	GREEN BAY	22	Ira Gordon	OG	6'3"	268	22		
20	Chicago	7	Bill Lenkaitis	OG	6'3"	265	24		
31	HOUSTON	31	Jim Schmedding	OG	6'2"	250	24		
27	Cleveland	10	Walt Sweeney	OG	6'3"	256	29		
24	DENVER	21	Sam Gruneisen	C	6'1"	250	29		
16	Boston	14	Cal Withrow	C	6'	240	25		
17	Oakland	20	Bob Briggs	DE	6'4"	276	25		
14	Kansas City	26	Joe Owens	DE	6'2"	235	23	2	
14	CINCINNATI	17	Jeff Staggs	DE	6'2"	246	26		
17	Denver	17	Ron Billingsley	DT	6'8"	290	25		
31	KANSAS CITY	13	Steve DeLong	DT	6'3"	252	27	1	
			Gene Ferguson	DT	6'7"	300	22		
			Andy Rice	DT	6'3"	268	28		
			Tom Williams	DT	6'4"	250	22		

Use Name	Pos.	Hgt	Wgt	Age	Int	Pts
Bob Babich	LB	6'2"	230	23		
Pete Barnes	LB	6'3"	247	25	3	
Bob Bruggers	LB	6'1"	224	26		
Jack Protz	LB	6'1"	218	22		
Rick Redman	LB	5'11"	230	27		
Joe Beauchamp	DB	6'	185	26	1	
Chuck Detwiler	DB	6'	185	23	6	
Speedy Duncan	DB	5'10"	175	27		
Chris Fletcher	DB	5'11"	185	21		
Jim Hill	DB	6'2"	190	23		
Bob Howard	DB	6'1"	190	25	2	
Jim Tolbert	DB	6'3"	207	26	2	

Ron Mix — Voluntarily Retired
Houston Ridge — Injury

Use Name	Pos.	Hgt	Wgt	Age	Int	Pts
Wayne Clark	QB	6'2"	200	23		
Marty Domres	QB	6'3"	215	23		
John Hadl	QB	6'2"	218	30		6
Mike Garrett (from KC)	HB	5'9"	200	26		12
Dickie Post	HB	5'9"	190	24		6
Dave Smith	HB	6'1"	210	22		
Russ Smith	FB-HB	6'1"	212	26		18
Brad Hubbert	FB	6'1"	240	29		6
Jeff Queen	FB	6'1"	220	24		12
Gene Foster	HB-FB	5'11"	220	27		
Lance Alworth	WR	6'	180	30		24
Rick Eber	WR	6'1"	185	25		
Gary Garrison	WR	6'1"	193	26		72
Walker Gillette	WR	6'5"	198	23		
Willie Frazier	TE	6'4"	250	27		48
Art Strozier	TE	6'3"	220	22		
Mike Mercer	K	6'	215	34		70
Dennis Partee	K	6'2"	218	24		

DENVER BRONCOS 5-8-1 Lou Saban

			Use Name	Pos.	Hgt	Wgt	Age	Int	Pts
25	Buffalo	10	Sam Brunelli	OT	6'1"	270	27		
16	PITTSBURGH	13	Mike Current	OT	6'4"	274	24		
26	KANSAS CITY	13	Steve Alexakos	OG	6'2"	260	23		
23	Oakland	35	George Goeddeke	OG	6'3"	253	25		
24	ATLANTA	10	Mike Schnitker	OG	6'3"	245	23		
14	San Francisco	19	Bob Young	OG	6'2"	256	27		
3	WASHINGTON	19	Jay Bachman	C	6'3"	250	24		
21	San Diego	24	Larry Kaminski	C	6'2"	245	25		
19	OAKLAND	24	Walt Barnes	DE	6'3"	250	26		
31	New Orleans	6	Pete Duranko	DE	6'2"	250	26		
21	Houston	31	Rich Jackson	DE	6'2"	255	29		
0	Kansas City	16	Alden Roche	DE	6'4"	255	25		
17	SAN DIEGO	17	Dave Costa	DT	6'2"	260	28		
13	CLEVELAND	27	Jerry Inman	DT	6'3"	256	30		
			Paul Smith	DT	6'3"	256	25		

John Huard — Injury

Use Name	Pos.	Hgt	Wgt	Age	Int	Pts
Bill Butler	LB	6'4"	226	26		
Ken Criter	LB	5'11"	223	23		
Carl Cunningham	LB	6'3"	240	26		
Fred Forsberg	LB	6'1"	235	26		
Bill McKoy	LB	6'3"	235	22		
Chip Myrtle	LB	6'2"	225	25		
Dave Washington	LB	6'5"	215	22	2	
Booker Edgerson	DB	5'10"	183	31		
Drake Garrett	DB	5'9"	181	24		
Cornell Gordon	DB	6'	187	29	3	
Charlie Greer	DB	6'	205	24	4	
Pete Jaquess	DB	6'	182	28		
Paul Martha	DB	6'	187	27	6	
George Saimes	DB	5'10"	185	28		
Bill Thompson	DB	6'1"	200	23	2	
Bob Wade	DB	6'2"	200	25	1	
Alvin Mitchell	WR-DB	6'3"	195	26		

Use Name	Pos.	Hgt	Wgt	Age	Int	Pts
Pete Liske	QB	6'2"	206	29		6
Al Pastrana	QB	6'1"	190	25		6
Steve Tensi	QB	6'5"	210	27		
Floyd Little	HB	5'10"	196	28		18
Wandy Williams	HB	6'1"	190	24		
Bobby Anderson	FB-HB	6'	208	22		24
Willie Crenshaw	FB	6'2"	230	29		36
Clem Turner	FB	6'1"	236	25		12
Fran Lynch	HB-FB	6'1"	205	24		6
Al Denson	WR	6'2"	208	28		12
John Embree	WR	6'4"	194	26		
Mike Haffner	WR	6'2"	205	28		6
Jerry Hendren	WR	6'2"	187	22		
Bill Van Heusen	WR	6'1"	200	24		12
Bill Masters	TE	6'5"	240	26		12
Jim Whalen	TE	6'2"	210	26		18
Bobby Howfield	K	5'9"	180	33		81

OAKLAND RAIDERS

RUSHING
Last Name	No.	Yds	Avg	TD
Dixon	197	861	4.4	1
Smith	168	681	4.1	3
Hubbard	51	246	4.8	1
Banaszak	21	75	3.6	2
Todd	17	39	2.3	0
Wells	3	34	11.3	0
Lamonica	8	24	3.0	0
Blanda	2	4	2.0	0
Sherman	1	2	2.0	0
Highsmith	2	2	1.0	0
Stabler	1	-4	-4.0	0

RECEIVING
Last Name	No.	Yds	Avg	TD
Biletnikoff	45	768	17	7
Wells	43	935	22	11
Chester	42	556	13	7
Dixon	31	207	7	1
Smith	23	173	8	2
Sherman	18	285	16	0
Todd	5	51	10	0
Buie	2	52	26	0
Banaszak	1	2	2	0

PUNT RETURNS
Last Name	No.	Yds	Avg	TD
Wyatt	25	231	9	1
Sherman	8	65	8	0
Atkinson	4	12	3	0

KICKOFF RETURNS
Last Name	No.	Yds	Avg	TD
Atkinson	23	574	25	0
Wyatt	13	286	22	0
Warren	2	47	24	0
Hubbard	2	41	21	0
Sherman	2	39	20	0
Thoms	2	30	15	0

PASSING – PUNTING – KICKING
PASSING
Last Name	Att	Comp	%	Yds	Yd/Att	TD	Int—	%	RK
Lamonica	356	179	50	2516	7.1	22	15-	4	1
Blanda	55	29	53	461	8.4	6	5-	9	
Stabler	7	2	29	52	7.4	0	1-	14	

PUNTING
Last Name	No	Avg
Eischeid	79	39.5

KICKING
Last Name	XP	Att	%	FG	Att	%
Blanda	36	36	100	16	29	55

KANSAS CITY CHIEFS

RUSHING
Last Name	No.	Yds	Avg	TD
Podolak	168	749	4.5	3
Hayes	109	381	3.5	5
McVea	61	260	4.3	0
Holmes	63	206	3.3	3
Pitts	5	84	16.8	0
Dawson	11	46	4.2	0
Livingston	3	26	8.7	0
Porter	2	21	10.5	0
Taylor	3	13	4.3	0
Cannon	1	6	6.0	0
Richardson	1	4	4.0	0

RECEIVING
Last Name	No.	Yds	Avg	TD
Taylor	34	618	18	3
Podolak	26	307	12	1
Hayes	26	219	8	0
Holmes	23	173	8	1
Pitts	11	172	16	2
Arbanas	8	108	14	1
Cannon	7	125	18	2
Richardson	5	171	34	2
McVea	5	26	5	0
Stroud	4	86	22	1
Porter	1	29	29	0

PUNT RETURNS
Last Name	No.	Yds	Avg	TD
Podolak	23	311	14	0
Mitchell	4	33	8	0
Porter	1	-3	-3	0

KICKOFF RETURNS
Last Name	No.	Yds	Avg	TD
Holmes	19	535	28	0
Podolak	17	348	20	0
McVea	3	57	19	0
Stein	3	23	8	0
Porter	1	22	22	0
Smith	1	12	12	0

PASSING – PUNTING – KICKING
PASSING
Last Name	Att	Comp	%	Yds	Yd/Att	TD	Int—	%	RK
Dawson	262	141	54	1876	7.2	13	14-	5	3
Livingston	22	11	50	122	5.6	0	1-	5	
Huarte	2	0	0	0	0.0	0	1-	50	
Podolak	2	2	100	40	20.0	0	0-	0	
McVea	1	0	0	0	0.0	0	0-	0	

PUNTING
Last Name	No	Avg
Wilson	76	44.9

KICKING
Last Name	XP	Att	%	FG	Att	%
Stenerud	26	26	100	30	42	71

SAN DIEGO CHARGERS

RUSHING
Last Name	No.	Yds	Avg	TD
Queen	77	261	3.4	1
Post	74	225	3.0	1
Garrett	67	208	3.1	1
Hadl	28	188	6.7	1
Hubbert	49	175	3.6	1
R. Smith	52	163	3.1	3
Frazier	5	120	24.0	1
Foster	32	84	2.6	0
D. Smith	14	42	3.0	0
Domres	14	39	2.8	0
Garrison	4	7	1.8	0

RECEIVING
Last Name	No.	Yds	Avg	TD
Garrison	44	1006	23	12
Frazier	38	497	13	6
Alworth	35	608	17	4
Queen	20	236	12	1
Garrett	14	131	9	1
Post	13	113	9	0
Foster	10	92	9	0
Hubbert	7	44	6	0
R. Smith	5	44	9	0
D. Smith	4	65	16	0
Eber	2	43	22	0
Strozier	2	40	20	0
Gillette	2	21	11	0

PUNT RETURNS
Last Name	No.	Yds	Avg	TD
Fletcher	16	137	9	0
R. Smith	9	31	3	0
Garrett	3	30	10	0
Duncan	5	10	2	0
Detwiler	1	-5	-5	0

KICKOFF RETURNS
Last Name	No.	Yds	Avg	TD
Duncan	19	410	22	0
Fletcher	17	382	22	0
Queen	1	12	12	0
R. Smith	1	9	9	0
Beauchamp	1	0	0	0
Hill	1	0	0	0
T. Owens	1	0	0	0

PASSING – PUNTING – KICKING
PASSING
Last Name	Att	Comp	%	Yds	Yd/Att	TD	Int—	%	RK
Hadl	327	162	50	2388	7.3	22	15-	5	2
Domres	55	28	51	491	8.9	2	4-	7	
Foster	3	1	33	9	3.0	0	0-	0	
Clark	2	1	50	48	24.0	0	0-	0	

PUNTING
Last Name	No	Avg
Partee	65	43.9
Mercer	8	35.4
Hadl	1	30.0

KICKING
Last Name	XP	Att	%	FG	Att	%
Mercer	34	35	97	12	19	63

DENVER BRONCOS

RUSHING
Last Name	No.	Yds	Avg	TD
Little	209	901	4.3	3
Anderson	83	368	4.4	4
Crenshaw	69	200	2.9	5
Turner	29	106	3.7	2
Pastrana	14	89	6.4	1
Lynch	20	81	4.1	1
Liske	7	42	6.0	1
Tensi	4	14	3.5	0
Haffner	1	1	1.0	0

RECEIVING
Last Name	No.	Yds	Avg	TD
Denson	47	646	14	2
Whalen	36	503	14	3
Crenshaw	18	105	6	1
Little	17	161	9	0
Van Heusen	16	382	24	2
Haffner	12	196	16	1
Anderson	9	140	16	0
Masters	9	83	9	2
Turner	8	23	3	0
Lynch	7	69	10	0
Embree	4	50	13	0

PUNT RETURNS
Last Name	No.	Yds	Avg	TD
Thompson	23	233	10	0
Little	22	187	9	0
Greer	14	123	9	0
Jaquess	4	13	3	0

KICKOFF RETURNS
Last Name	No.	Yds	Avg	TD
Anderson	21	520	25	0
Hendren	8	197	25	0
Thompson	9	188	21	0
Little	6	126	21	0
Turner	1	31	31	0
Criter	2	20	10	0
Washington	1	20	20	0
Myrtle	1	1	1	0
Lynch	0	11	0	0

PASSING – PUNTING – KICKING
PASSING
Last Name	Att	Comp	%	Yds	Yd/Att	TD	Int—	%	RK
Liske	238	112	47	1340	5.6	7	11-	5	12
Tensi	80	38	48	539	6.7	3	8-	10	
Pastrana	75	29	39	420	5.6	1	9-	12	
Anderson	7	4	57	59	8.4	0	0-	0	
Little	2	0	0	0	0.0	0	0-	0	
Van Heusen	1	0	0	0	0.0	0	0-	0	

PUNTING
Last Name	No	Avg
Van Heusen	87	42.9

KICKING
Last Name	XP	Att	%	FG	Att	%
Howfield	27	28	96	18	32	56

1970 Championship Games

NFC CHAMPIONSHIP GAME
January 3, at San Francisco
(Attendance 59,364)

Two Interceptions Too Many

The opening round of the first NFC playoffs had produced two interesting games, as the Cowboys had beaten the Lions 5-0 on a field as muddy as a pigsty and the '49ers had edged the tough Vikings 17-14. In the conference championship, the Cowboys and '49ers would use different offensive styles with different results.

Dallas quarterback Craig Morton had a sore arm and could not match the passing ability of San Francisco's John Brodie, but the Cowboys did have two strong runners in rookie Duane Thomas and Walt Garrison, plus a top-notch offensive line to block for them. Neither offense did much in the first quarter, as Bruce Gossett of San Francisco booted a 16-yard field goal while Dallas' Mike Clark missed from the 40. The defensive deadlock continued into the second period, with Clark hitting on a 21 yard field goal to knot the first half score at 3-3.

The Cowboys got the first big break of the game in the third period. With Dallas end Larry Cole putting heavy pressure on him, Brodie rushed a pass over the middle which Lee Roy Jordan picked off at the San Francisco 13-yard line. Duane Thomas covered the ground to the end zone on the very next play, and Clark's extra point made the score 10-3. The '49ers drove right back into Dallas territory, but Mel Renfro intercepted a Brodie pass on the 18-yard line to extinguish that threat. The Cowboys then pounded their way downfield on the running of Thomas and Garrison, with a swing pass from Morton to Garrison covering the final five yards to the goal line.

Brodie then led his team on a 73-yard drive capped by a 26-yard scoring pitch to Dick Witcher; with Gossett's extra point, the '49ers trailed 17-10 with fifteen minutes left to play. The Dallas defense stood firm for the rest of the day, however, and the Cowboys headed off to the Super Bowl after failing in four previous playoff tries.

SCORING

SAN FRANCISCO	3	0	7	0—10
DALLAS	0	3	14	0—17

First Quarter
S.F. Gossett, 16 yard field goal

Second Quarter
Dal. Clark, 21 yard field goal

Third Quarter
Dal. Thomas, 13 yard rush
PAT—Clark (kick)
Dal. Garrison, 5 yard pass from Morton
PAT—Clark (kick)
S.F. Witcher, 26 yard pass from Brodie
PAT—Gossett (kick)

TEAM STATISTICS

S.F.		DALLAS
15	First Downs—Total	22
2	First Downs—Rushing	16
12	First Downs—Passing	5
1	First Downs—Penalty	1
1	Fumbles—Number	4
0	Fumbles—Lost Ball	1
5	Penalties—Number	7
51	Yards Penalized	75
1	Missed Field Goals	2
61	Offensive Plays—Total	75
307	Net Yards	319
5.0	Average Gain	4.3
2	Giveaways	1
1	Takeaways	2
-1	Difference	+1

INDIVIDUAL STATISTICS

SAN FRANCISCO	No	Yds	Avg	DALLAS	No	Yds	Avg
RUSHING							
Willard	13	42	3.2	Thomas	27	143	5.3
Cunningham	5	14	2.8	Garrison	17	71	4.2
Thomas	1	5	5.0	Welch	5	27	5.4
				Reeves	2	-12	-6.0
	19	61	3.2		51	229	4.5
RECEIVING							
Washington	6	88	14.7	Garrison	3	51	17.0
Cunningham	4	34	8.5	Thomas	2	24	12.0
Windsor	3	70	23.3	Rucker	1	21	21.0
Witcher	3	41	13.7	Ditka	1	5	5.0
Willard	2	22	11.0		7	101	14.4
Kwalick	1	7	7.0				
	19	262	13.8				
PUNTING							
Spurrier	5		41.0	Widby	6		40.2
PUNT RETURNS							
B. Taylor	2	5	2.5	Hayes	1	8	8.0
				Reeves	1	0	0.0
					2	8	4.0
KICKOFF RETURNS							
Thomas	3	66	22.0	Washington	1	20	20.0
Tucker	1	23	23.0	Waters	1	16	16.0
	4	89	22.3	Kiner	1	10	10.0
					3	46	15.3
INTERCEPTION RETURNS							
None				Renfro	1	19	19.0
				Jordan	1	4	4.0
					2	23	11.5

PASSING

SAN FRANCISCO	Att.	Comp.	Comp. Pct.	Yds.	Int.	Yds/ Att.	Yds/ Comp.	Yards Lost Tackled
Brodie	30	19	47.5	262	2	6.6	13.8	2—16
DALLAS								
Morton	22	7	31.8	101	0	4.6	14.4	2—11

AFC CHAMPIONSHIP GAME
January 3, at Baltimore
(Attendance 54,799)

Two Old Men and One Crown

One old AFL team and one old NFL team squared off in the first AFC championship match. The Oakland Raiders got this far by beating the upcoming Miami Dolphins 21-14 in the first playoff round, while the Baltimore Colts arrived at this game fresh from a 17-0 whitewash of the Cincinnati Bengals. Before the game was over, it had developed into a duel of two of pro football's oldest quarterbacks, Johnny Unitas and George Blanda.

Baltimore scored the only points of the first quarter on Jim O'Brien's 16-yard field goal, as neither Unitas nor Oakland's Daryle Lamonica could spark the offense. Early in the second quarter, Lamonica pulled a thigh muscle when hit by Bubba Smith, so the forty-three-year-old Blanda had to take over at quarterback. By the time he entered the game, Baltimore had run its lead to 10-0 on a Norm Bulaich touchdown that Unitas had set up with a key pass to Eddie Hinton. When Blanda could drive his team only to the Baltimore 40-yard line, he simply kicked a field goal to net three points and drop the halftime score to 10-3.

The Raiders tied the score in the third quarter when Blanda hit Fred Biletnikoff with a 38-yard touchdown pass. Coolly directing his offense, Unitas brought the Colts back close enough for O'Brien to kick a field goal, and he engineered another long drive late in the period which Bulaich capped with his second touchdown.

Blanda responded in the final period by driving the Raiders 80 yards, with the final 15 yards coming on a pass to Warren Wells. The Raiders now trailed 20-17, but the Baltimore defense came through with clutch plays when needed. The Raiders twice were in scoring range of the Baltimore goal line, but both drives ended with Blanda passes getting intercepted in the end zone. The Colts finally iced the victory away when Unitas hit Ray Perkins, one of four wide receivers in on the play, with a 68-yard scoring pass which lengthened the final score to 27-17.

SCORING

BALTIMORE	3	7	10	7—27
OAKLAND	0	3	7	7—17

First Quarter
Balt. O'Brien, 16 yard field goal

Second Quarter
Balt. Bulaich, 2 yard rush
PAT—O'Brien (kick)
Oak. Blanda, 48 yard field goal

Third Quarter
Oak. Biletnikoff, 38 yard pass from Blanda
PAT—Blanda (kick)
Balt. O'Brien, 23 yard field goal
Balt. Bulaich, 11 yard rush
PAT—O'Brien (kick)

Fourth Quarter
Oak. Wells, 15 yard pass from Blanda
PAT—Blanda (kick)
Balt. Perkins, 68 yard pass from Unitas
PAT—O'Brien (kick)

TEAM STATISTICS

BALT.		OAK.
18	First Downs—Total	16
7	First Downs—Rushing	5
11	First Downs—Passing	10
0	First Downs—Penalty	1
0	Fumbles—Number	1
0	Fumbles—Lost Ball	1
2	Penalties—Number	2
10	Yards Penalized	20
2	Missed Field Goals	0
71	Offensive Plays—Total	63
363	Net Yards	336
5.1	Average Gain	5.3
0	Giveaways	4
4	Takeaways	0
+4	Difference	-4

INDIVIDUAL STATISTICS

BALTIMORE	No	Yds	Avg	OAKLAND	No	Yds	Avg
RUSHING							
Bulaich	22	71	3.2	Dixon	10	51	5.1
Nowatzke	8	32	4.0	Smith	9	44	4.9
Hill	5	12	2.4	Hubbard	3	12	4.0
Unitas	2	9	4.5		22	107	4.9
Havrilak	1	2	2.0				
	38	126	3.3				
RECEIVING							
Hinton	5	115	23.0	Wells	5	108	21.6
Jefferson	3	36	12.0	Biletnikoff	5	92	18.4
Perkins	2	80	40.0	Dixon	3	15	5.0
Mackey	1	14	14.0	Chester	2	36	18.0
	11	245	22.3	Smith	2	21	10.5
				Hubbard	1	5	5.0
					18	277	15.4
PUNTING							
Lee	6		45.3	Eischeid	5		40.0
PUNT RETURNS							
Gardin	2	1	0.5	Atkinson	2	10	5.0
KICKOFF RETURNS							
Duncan	4	105	26.3	Atkinson	2	37	18.5
				Sherman	1	23	23.0
					3	60	20.0
INTERCEPTION RETURNS							
Logan	1	16	16.0	None			
May	1	0	0.0				
Volk	1	0	0.0				
	3	16	5.3				

PASSING

BALTIMORE	Att.	Comp.	Comp. Pct.	Yds.	Int.	Yds/ Att.	Yds/ Comp.	Yards Lost Tackled
Unitas	30	11	36.7	245	0	8.2	22.3	3— 8
OAKLAND								
Blanda	32	17	53.0	271	3	8.5	15.9	
Lamonica	4	1	25.0	6	0	1.5	6.0	
	36	18	50.0	277	3	7.7	15.4	5—48

Follow the Bouncing Ball

The first Super Bowl under the new merger arrangement ended in high drama after being, for most of the afternoon, a comedy of errors. Both the Dallas Cowboys and Baltimore Colts took turns giving the game away, but neither team would take it until the final seconds of play.

The strong defenses of both clubs dominated the first-quarter action, although the Cowboys did score on a 14-yard Mike Clark field goal. Another Clark field goal made the score 6-0 in the second quarter when the Colts tied the score on a fluke play. Baltimore quarterback Johnny Unitas threw a long pass down the center of the field to wide receiver Eddie Hinton; the ball bounced off Hinton's hands, back up into the air, grazed the fingertips of Dallas cornerback Mel Renfro, and came right down to the surprised John Mackey. Taking the ball around mid-field, Mackey sprinted the rest of the way to the end zone. The Cowboys blocked the Baltimore extra point, however, so the score remained tied at 6-6.

On the next Baltimore offensive series, a hard tackle by George Andrie forced Unitas to fumble the ball on his own 29-yard line and sent him out of the game with bruised ribs. Cowboy quarterback Craig Morton, operating with a sore arm, then moved his team down to the 7-yard line, from where a short pass to Duane Thomas scored the only Dallas touchdown of the day. Clark's conversion ran the score to 13-6, and neither offense could score again before the end of the half.

The Colts kept up the parade of mistakes when Jim Duncan fumbled the opening kickoff deep in Baltimore territory. The Cowboys then drove from the 31-yard line to the two-yard line on five plays, with Thomas' hard running the key element. With the ball in the shadows of the goal posts, Thomas took a handoff and fumbled the ball, the Colts recovering on the one-foot line.

With the threat erased, the third quarter settled into a pattern of offensive futility, with neither Morton nor Earl Morrall, filling in for the injured Unitas, able to ignite an attack. With only eight minutes left in the game, the Cowboys still clung to their 13-6 lead.

At that point, however, a Morton pass bounced off the fingers of fullback Walt Garrison into the hands of Colt safety Rick Volk, who returned the ball 17 yards to the Dallas three-yard line. In short order, Tom Nowatzke smashed over for the touchdown, and Jim O'Brien added the tying extra point.

Overtime seemed imminent late in the final quarter, but another Morton pass was intercepted with 1:09 left in the game. Mike Curtis stole the pass on the Dallas 41 and returned it to the 28. Two running plays ran the clock down, and then Jim O'Brien, Baltimore's rookie kicker, booted a 32-yard three-pointer to give the Colts an artistically flawed but nonetheless satisfying 16-13 victory.

BALTIMORE		DALLAS
	OFFENSE	
Hinton	WR	Hayes
Vogel	LT	Neely
Ressler	LG	Niland
Curry	C	Manders
Williams	RG	Nye
Sullivan	RT	Wright
Mackey	TE	Norman
Jefferson	WR	Rucker
Unitas	QB	Morton
Bulaich	RB	Thomas
Nowatzke	RB	Garrison
	DEFENSE	
Bubba Smith	LE	Cole
B. R. Smith	LT	Pugh
Miller	RT	Lilly
Hilton	RE	Andrie
May	LLB	Edwards
Curtis	MLB	Jordan
Hendricks	RLB	Howley
Stukes	LCB	Adderley
Duncan	RCB	Renfro
Logan	LS	Green
Volk	RS	Waters

SUBSTITUTES

BALTIMORE
Offense
Ball	Maitland
Goode	Mitchell
Havrilak	Morrall
J. Hill	Perkins
Johnson	

Defense
Gardin	Newsome
Grant	Nichols
Maxwell	

Kickers
| O'Brien | Lee |

DALLAS
Offense
Asher	Homan
Ditka	Reeves
C. Hill	Welch

Defense
East	Lewis
Flowers	Stincic
Harris	Toomay
Kiner	Washington

Kickers
| Clark | Widby |

SCORING

BALTIMORE	0	6	0	10—16
DALLAS	3	10	0	0—13

First Quarter
Dall.   Clark, 14 yard field goal

Second Quarter
Dall.   Clark, 30 yard field goal
Balt.   Mackey, 75 yard pass from Unitas
        PAT — O'Brien (kick—blocked)
Dall.   Thomas, 7 yard pass from Morton
        PAT — Clark (kick)

Fourth Quarter
Balt.   Nowatzke, 2 yard rush
        PAT — O'Brien (kick)
Balt.   O'Brien, 32 yard field goal

TEAM STATISTICS

BALT.		DALLAS
14	First Downs — Total	10
4	First Downs — Rushing	4
6	First Downs — Passing	5
4	First Downs — Penalty	1
5	Fumbles — Number	1
3	Fumbles — Lost Ball	1
4	Penalties — Number	10
31	Yards Penalized	133
1	Missed Field Goals	0
56	Offensive Plays	59
329	Net Yards	215
5.9	Average Gain	3.7
6	Giveaways	4
4	Takeaways	6
−2	Difference	+2

INDIVIDUAL STATISTICS

RUSHING

BALTIMORE	No	Yds	Avg.	DALLAS	No	Yds	Avg.
Nowatzke	10	33	3.3	Garrison	12	65	5.4
Bulaich	18	28	1.6	Thomas	18	35	1.9
Unitas	1	4	4.0	Morton	1	2	2.0
Havrilak	1	3	3.0		31	102	3.3
Morrall	1	1	1.0				
	31	69	2.2				

RECEIVING

BALTIMORE	No	Yds	Avg.	DALLAS	No	Yds	Avg.
Jefferson	3	52	17.3	Reeves	5	46	9.2
Mackey	2	80	40.0	Thomas	4	21	5.3
Hinton	2	51	25.5	Garrison	2	19	9.5
Havrilak	2	27	13.5	Hayes	1	41	41.0
Nowatzke	1	45	45.0		12	127	10.6
Bulaich	1	5	5.0				
	11	260	23.6				

PUNTING

	No	Yds	Avg.		No	Yds	Avg.
Lee	4		41.5	Widby	9		41.9

PUNT RETURNS

	No	Yds	Avg.		No	Yds	Avg.
Gardin	4	4	1.0	Hayes	3	9	3.0
Logan	1	8	8.0				
	5	12	2.4				

KICKOFF RETURNS

	No	Yds	Avg.		No	Yds	Avg.
Duncan	4	90	22.5	Harris	1	18	18.0
				Hill	1	14	14.0
				Lewis	1	2	2.0
					3	34	11.1

INTERCEPTION RETURNS

	No	Yds	Avg.		No	Yds	Avg.
Volk	1	30	30.0	Howley	2	22	11.0
Logan	1	14	14.0	Renfro	1	0	0.0
Curtis	1	13	13.0		3	22	7.3
	3	57	19.0				

PASSING

BALTIMORE	Att	Comp	Comp Pct.	Yds.	Int	Yds/ Att.	Yds/ Comp	Yards Lost Tackled
Morrall	15	7	46.7	147	1	9.8	21.0	0— 0
Unitas	9	3	33.3	88	2	9.8	29.3	0— 0
Havrilak	1	1	100.0	25	0	25.0	25.0	0— 0
	25	11	44.0	260	3	10.4	23.6	0— 0

DALLAS	Att	Comp	Comp Pct.	Yds.	Int	Yds/ Att.	Yds/ Comp	Yards Lost Tackled
Morton	26	12	46.2	127	3	4.9	10.6	2—14

1971 N.F.C.   With a Little Offensive Help

nd frequent passing had enlivened the game ever
nd Sammy Baugh made their debuts in the 1930s
ray of offensive life since the days of Otto Graham
l in the late 1940s. This year, however, defense
h most teams rigging up complex zone defenses
r-passing quarterbacks impotent, scoring dropped
and the field-goal kicker replaced the deep receiver as pro football's
glamorous point producer. To counter the new defenses, pro offenses
employed big, strong running backs and quarterbacks who could throw
on the roll-out play and carry the ball occasionally. But a rule of
thumb for this season was that the team with the better defense usually
won; indeed, all four teams which made the playoffs had outstanding
defenses which often overshadowed their offensive platoons.

EASTERN DIVISION

Dallas Cowboys—For the first half of the season, coach Tom Landry
alternated Craig Morton and Roger Staubach at quarterback; the Cowboys won four games and lost three. But starting with the eighth
game, Landry gave the job full time to Staubach, and the team won
its last seven games to move past the Redskins into first place. Both
Dallas quarterbacks were fine passers, but Staubach gave the defense
something extra to worry about by often running with the ball. By
mid-season, defenses also had to worry about Duane Thomas running
the ball. After sitting out the early games over a salary dispute, Thomas
returned to the team in a sullen mood, but his ball-carrying fit right
into the Dallas scheme of things.

Washington Redskins—When George Allen was hired as head coach,
he immediately set out to trade for veteran players who would make
no mistakes on the field. The resulting collection of football oldsters
became known as the Over the Hill Gang. In a dazzling array of trades,
Allen picked up Billy Kilmer, Roy Jefferson, Boyd Dowler, Clifton
McNeil, Ron McDole, Verlon Biggs, Diron Talbert, Jack Pardee, Myron
Pottios, Richie Petitbon, John Wilbur, and Speedy Duncan. Allen
rigged together a defense which indeed made no errors, which
delighted in forcing enemy offenses into fumbles and interceptions.
The Washington attack started out fast but slumped when injuries
erased Sonny Jurgensen, Charley Taylor, and Jerry Smith from the
lineup and cut down on Larry Brown's effectiveness.

Philadelphia Eagles—Apparently on the way to another dismal season
after losing their first three games, the Eagles fired head coach Jerry
Williams and replaced him with young Ed Khayat. The Eagles lost
their first two games under Khayat, but then went on to a 7-2 record.
The defense triggered the reversal by jelling into one of the league's
top units. On this surprising platoon, only Tim Rossovich and Bill
Bradley had recognizable names; the others were parts of a nameless
horde which swarmed over enemy players. The Eagles' offense, on
the other hand, was feeble.

St. Louis Cardinals—Bob Hollway's first season as head coach flattened
out into a 4-9-1 record and a disappointing fourth-place finish in
the East. Hollway had coached the magnificent Viking defense as
an assistant at Minnesota, but the St. Louis defense this season suffered
from a variety of injuries and a slow adjustment to Hollway's new
system. The Cardinal offense also sputtered, with neither Jim Hart
nor Pete Beathard taking charge at quarterback.

New York Giants—The Giants had the worst defense in the NFC,
totally unable to put pressure on enemy passers, while the secondary
suffered from injuries and Bennie McRae's advanced years. Ron
Johnson's knee injury ripped the heart out of the Giant running attack.
In the passing department, quarterback Fran Tarkenton found tight
end Bob Tucker a congenial target, but there was no deep threat
to replace the traded Homer Jones.

CENTRAL DIVISION

Minnesota Vikings—The Vikings' great defense again won first place
in the Central Division, but the Minnesota offense just didn't have
the power or direction to make the Vikings a complete team. At the
quarterback spot, Gary Cuozzo, Bob Lee, and Norm Snead all rotated
without any of them igniting a spark in the attack. Injuries to receivers
Gene Washington and John Beasley also hurt the passing game,
although Bob Grim rebounded from years of injuries to become a
legitimate deep threat. Clint Jones, Dave Osborn, Jim Lindsey, Oscar
Reed, and Bill Brown all were short-yardage runners, adept at grinding
out yards behind the strong Viking front wall.

Detroit Lions—Blossoming into stardom in his fourth pro season was
quarterback Greg Landry, a man with a strong passing arm plus the
size and strength of a fullback in carrying the ball. Landry set a record
for quarterbacks this season with 530 yards rushing. Second in the
entire NFC in rushing yardage was Lion fullback Steve Owens, the
powerful Heisman Trophy winner who had suffered through an
injury-ruined rookie season last year. With Altie Taylor also picking
up yardage on the ground, the Lions had the best running attack in
the conference. The defense held the Lions back this season, with the
front four unable to mount a pass rush now that Alex Karras had
passed his prime and was cut loose before the season started. One
tragic note of the season was the death of Chuck Hughes, who collapsed of a heart attack on the field in full view of millions.

Chicago Bears—Even with Gale Sayers still out with his bad knee,
the Bears got off to a strong start. Middle linebacker Dick Butkus held
the defense together with his outstanding play, and reserve quarterback Kent Nix was the offensive hero in the early going. After mid-
season, however, both Nix and Jack Concannon were injured, leaving
the entire quarterbacking load on Bobby Douglass' shoulders. The
Bears dropped six of their last seven, and coach Jim Dooley got the
ax at the end of the season.

Green Bay Packers—Dan Devine, who left the University of Missouri
to take over as head coach in Green Bay, suffered through a trying
professional debut as his Packers blew an early lead and lost to the
Giants 42-40 on opening day. To make matters worse, several players
smashed into Devine on an out-of-bounds play and broke his leg.
Getting through the rest of the season with the help of a crutch,
Devine found little pleasing in the Packers' drop to last place in the
Central Division. His hardest decision was to bench all-time great Ray
Nitschke, and his greatest pleasure was the play of rookie fullback
John Brockington, who led the NFC in rushing 1,105 yards.

WESTERN DIVISION

San Francisco '49ers—Even with John Brodie suffering through an
erratic season, the '49ers still had enough talent on both platoons
to beat out the surprising Los Angeles Rams for first place in the
West. Operating behind a top-notch offensive line, the '49ers running
game prospered with Ken Willard's good year and a fine rookie performance from speedster Vic Washington. This took the pressure off
Brodie, who still had Gene Washington, Ted Kwalick, and Dick Witcher
to throw to. On defense, coach Dick Nolan stuck with one set of linemen
and was rewarded with excellent seasons from Cedrick Hardman,
Charlie Krueger, Earl Edwards, and Tommy Hart.

Los Angeles Rams—Long-time UCLA coach Tommy Prothro moved
into the professional ranks by rebuilding the Rams and almost winning
a divisional title. Prothro traded away Diron Talbert, Jack Pardee,
Myron Pottios, Maxie Baughan, Richie Petitbon, Tommy Mason,
Bob Brown, Wendell Tucker, and Billy Truax from last year's team
and replaced them with younger players. The defense had eight new
starters, with only Deacon Jones, Merlin Olsen, and Coy Bacon returning, but the new unit hung together well. On the offense, key new
starters were Willie Ellison, who ran for a record 247 yards against
New Orleans on December 5, Lance Rentzel, Bob Klein, and Harry
Schuh.

Atlanta Falcons—The Falcons enjoyed their first season ever with
an aggressive defense and a patchwork offense. The front four fielded
two top linemen in Claude Humphrey and John Zook, linebacker
Don Hansen's fine season made up for the loss of Tommy Nobis
to a knee injury, and Ken Reaves starred in an underrated secondary
which allowed the least passing yards in the Conference. On offense,
the line improved into a good unit, with George Kunz and Mal Snider
the top performers. The running attack lost its speed when a knee
injury sidelined rookie Joe Profit, but Cannonball Butler, Art Malone,
Harmon Wages, and free agent rookie Willie Belton ground out the
yardage with straight-ahead power plays. Both of the wide receivers
were rookies, Ken Burrow and Wes Chesson, but at quarterback the
Falcons could field only journeymen Bob Berry and Dick Shiner.

New Orleans Saints—Rookie quarterback Archie Manning made a
fine professional debut by scoring a touchdown on the last play of
the game to beat the Rams 24-20 on opening day. Foot and leg problems
kept him on the bench for much of the campaign, but Manning did
show a strong arm and a talent for running with the ball. With Manning
or Ed Hargett at quarterback, the New Orleans offense showed new
punch. The line was improved with the addition of Glen Ray Hines,
Don Morrison, and John Didion, and the receiving corps had always
been the Saints' strongest department. At running back, second-year
man Jim Strong, picked up from San Francisco, and rookies Bob
Gresham and James Ford handled most of the running chores.

FINAL TEAM STATISTICS

OFFENSE

	ATL.	CHI.	DALL.	DET.	G.B.	L.A.	MINN.	N.O.	N.Y.G.	PHIL.	ST.L.	S.F.	WASH.
FIRST DOWNS:													
Total	221	189	**288**	269	208	234	198	242	236	201	212	257	212
by Rushing	99	75	**135**	131	115	105	89	105	86	65	86	113	77
by Passing	108	99	**144**	104	87	111	95	106	140	119	109	122	112
by Penalty	14	15	9	**34**	6	18	14	31	10	17	17	22	23
RUSHING:													
Number	494	365	512	**532**	500	460	484	452	394	407	417	498	477
Yards	1703	1434	2249	**2376**	2229	2139	1695	1711	1461	1248	1530	2129	1757
Average Yards	3.4	3.9	4.4	4.5	4.5	**4.7**	3.5	3.8	3.7	3.1	3.7	4.3	3.7
Touchdowns	12	6	**25**	15	18	15	14	18	11	6	8	12	8
PASSING:													
Attempts	285	443	361	299	254	370	334	387	**462**	390	385	391	334
Completions	167	186	206	157	121	185	157	182	**268**	200	170	209	182
Completion Percentage	**58.6**	42.0	57.1	52.5	47.6	50.0	47.0	47.0	58.0	51.3	44.2	53.5	54.5
Passing Yards	2495	2294	3037	2453	1842	2304	1910	2355	**3062**	2552	2656	2688	2391
Avg. Yards per Attempt	**8.8**	5.4	8.4	8.2	7.3	6.2	5.7	6.1	6.6	6.5	6.9	6.9	7.2
Avg. Yards per Complet.	14.9	12.3	14.7	**15.6**	15.2	12.5	12.2	12.9	11.4	12.8	15.6	12.9	13.1
Times Tackled Passing	31	49	32	31	18	26	28	50	40	26	19	**11**	17
Yards Lost Tackled	239	392	251	252	157	210	255	400	348	229	185	**111**	118
Net Yards	2256	1902	**2786**	2201	1685	2094	1655	1955	2714	2323	2471	2577	2273
Touchdowns	16	12	**22**	17	12	18	9	12	14	13	14	18	13
Interceptions	21	28	14	14	24	**11**	18	14	25	20	26	24	15
Percent Intercepted	7.4	6.3	3.9	4.7	9.4	**3.0**	5.4	3.6	5.4	5.1	6.8	6.1	4.5
PUNTS:													
Number	60	77	56	42	56	70	**89**	77	66	75	61	51	58
Average Distance	36.9	40.2	41.6	41.7	40.0	41.4	39.5	41.4	40.6	**41.9**	38.8	38.7	40.5
PUNT RETURNS:													
Number	37	36	31	23	38	35	27	16	19	24	30	39	**45**
Yards	174	262	248	194	177	172	164	100	122	172	234	268	**427**
Average Yards	4.7	7.3	8.0	8.4	4.7	4.9	6.1	6.3	6.4	7.2	7.8	6.9	**9.5**
Touchdowns	0	0	0	0	0	0	0	0	0	0	0	0	0
KICKOFF RETURNS:													
Number	59	59	50	51	58	54	41	56	**63**	49	58	46	43
Yards	1477	1325	1376	1233	**1546**	1322	960	1143	1416	1183	1363	1075	913
Average Yards	25.0	22.5	**27.5**	24.2	26.7	24.5	23.4	20.4	22.5	24.1	23.5	23.4	21.2
Touchdowns	0	0	**2**	**2**	1	1	0	0	1	0	1	0	0
INTERCEPTION RETURNS:													
Number	20	22	26	22	16	27	27	20	15	22	17	14	**29**
Yards	180	267	402	295	205	452	**572**	342	227	374	191	186	480
Average Yards	9.0	12.1	15.5	13.4	12.8	16.7	**21.2**	17.1	15.1	17.0	11.2	13.3	16.6
Touchdowns	1	0	0	3	0	2	1	1	1	1	1	0	**5**
PENALTIES:													
Number	79	78	**94**	69	61	79	70	85	77	81	66	88	80
Yards	723	746	952	738	568	642	661	869	640	838	643	**961**	801
FUMBLES:													
Number	39	28	30	35	29	32	25	29	37	**21**	35	33	32
Number Lost	15	18	21	19	20	18	12	**11**	20	15	20	18	20
POINTS:													
Total	274	185	**406**	341	274	313	245	266	228	221	231	300	276
PAT Attempts	34	20	**50**	39	33	37	25	31	30	24	24	33	27
PAT Made	29	20	**50**	39	32	37	25	29	30	23	24	33	27
FG Attempts	21	33	33	37	26	29	32	28	17	37	32	36	**49**
FG Made	13	15	18	22	14	18	22	17	6	18	21	23	**29**
Percent FG Made	61.9	45.5	54.5	59.5	53.8	62.1	**68.8**	60.7	35.3	48.6	65.6	63.9	59.2
Safeties	1	0	1	1	1	0	**2**	0	0	0	0	0	0

DEFENSE

	ATL.	CHI.	DALL.	DET.	G.B.	L.A.	MINN.	N.O.	N.Y.G.	PHIL.	ST.L.	S.F.	WASH.
FIRST DOWNS:													
Total	237	234	200	210	230	239	**194**	260	228	251	244	199	213
by Rushing	114	99	**59**	97	104	91	88	129	104	104	109	80	73
by Passing	106	117	125	99	110	129	**88**	110	112	129	120	96	119
by Penalty	17	18	16	14	16	19	18	21	**12**	18	15	23	21
RUSHING:													
Number	500	509	**353**	432	489	455	447	495	449	450	486	408	408
Yards	2149	2116	**1144**	1842	1707	1658	1600	2200	2059	1962	1985	1668	1396
Average Yards	4.3	4.2	**3.2**	4.3	3.5	3.6	3.6	4.4	4.6	4.4	4.1	4.1	3.4
Touchdowns	19	14	8	15	7	11	**2**	18	12	16	10	4	7
PASSING:													
Attempts	343	362	421	**306**	353	387	405	333	333	407	375	341	411
Completions	164	192	209	163	186	200	206	175	173	220	212	**152**	191
Completion Percentage	47.8	53.0	49.6	53.3	52.7	51.7	50.9	52.6	52.0	54.1	56.5	**44.6**	46.5
Passing Yards	**1895**	2607	2660	2163	2469	2693	2022	2472	2458	2971	2546	2309	2448
Avg. Yards per Attempt	5.5	7.2	6.3	7.1	7.0	7.0	**5.0**	7.4	7.4	7.3	6.8	6.8	6.0
Avg. Yards per Complet.	11.6	13.6	12.7	13.3	13.3	13.5	**9.8**	14.1	14.2	13.5	12.0	15.2	12.8
Times Tackled Passing	31	28	43	**18**	19	37	27	24	18	32	20	38	36
Yards Lost Tackled	257	203	336	**146**	168	314	216	234	151	311	166	298	321
Net Yards	**1638**	2404	2324	2017	2301	2379	1806	2238	2307	2660	2380	2011	2127
Touchdowns	**9**	12	15	17	21	15	10	20	25	16	12	17	11
Interceptions	20	22	26	22	16	27	27	20	15	22	17	14	**29**
Percent Intercepted	5.8	6.1	6.2	**7.2**	4.5	7.0	6.7	6.1	4.5	5.4	4.5	4.1	7.1
PUNTS:													
Number	63	67	65	58	61	66	**78**	**50**	61	57	58	73	77
Average Distance	41.4	40.2	41.5	41.2	40.1	**39.4**	40.0	41.2	39.8	40.5	40.4	39.7	41.2
PUNT RETURNS:													
Number	26	31	26	18	23	27	47	43	50	40	24	19	**17**
Yards	117	172	231	111	169	67	336	251	319	372	160	**44**	87
Average Yards	4.5	5.5	8.9	6.2	7.3	2.5	7.1	5.8	6.4	9.3	6.7	**2.3**	5.1
Touchdowns	0	0	0	0	0	0	0	0	0	0	1	0	0
KICKOFF RETURNS:													
Number	52	**32**	70	70	56	57	49	54	45	48	54	61	61
Yards	1228	**817**	1681	1627	1248	1176	1077	1326	1063	1101	1318	1467	1066
Average Yards	23.6	25.5	24.0	23.2	22.3	20.6	22.0	24.6	23.6	22.9	24.4	24.0	**17.5**
Touchdowns	1	1	**0**	**0**	**0**	1	**0**	2	**0**	1	1	**0**	**0**
INTERCEPTION RETURNS:													
Number	21	28	14	14	24	**11**	18	14	25	20	26	24	15
Yards	242	465	304	207	449	**83**	204	171	377	359	358	385	284
Average Yards	11.5	16.6	21.7	14.8	18.7	**7.5**	11.3	12.2	15.1	18.0	13.8	16.0	18.9
Touchdowns	**0**	1	1	1	2	1	1	1	4	1	**0**	1	1
PENALTIES:													
Number	61	78	61	97	60	62	57	**98**	69	94	79	75	93
Yards	614	819	647	942	514	665	615	**967**	730	908	831	610	720
FUMBLES:													
Number	32	36	**40**	23	33	22	34	39	29	34	28	31	22
Number Lost	18	23	**25**	11	16	7	18	**25**	15	**25**	16	16	12
POINTS:													
Total	277	276	222	286	298	260	**139**	347	362	302	279	216	190
PAT Attempts	31	29	25	35	34	30	**14**	44	42	36	29	23	20
PAT Made	31	28	24	35	32	29	**13**	44	42	35	28	21	19
FG Attempts	**23**	41	25	25	37	32	32	26	32	33	39	33	33
FG Made	20	24	16	**13**	20	17	14	**13**	22	17	25	19	17
Percent FG Made	87.0	58.5	64.0	52.0	54.1	53.1	**43.8**	50.0	68.8	51.5	64.1	57.6	51.5
Safeties	**0**	1	**0**	1	1	**0**	**0**	**0**	1	**0**	1	**0**	**0**

CONFERENCE PLAYOFFS

December 25 at Bloomington
(Attendance 47,307)

SCORING

MINNESOTA	**0**	**3**	**0**	**9–12**
DALLAS	**3**	**3**	**14**	**0–20**

First Quarter
Dal. Clark, 26 yard field goal

Second Quarter
Min. Cox, 27 yard field goal
Dal. Clark, 44 yard field goal

Third Quarter
Dal. Thomas, 13 yard rush
PAT–Clark (kick)
Dal. Hayes, 9 yard pass from Staubach
PAT–Clark (kick)

Fourth Quarter
Min. Page, safety tackled Staubach in end zone
Min. Voigt, 6 yard pass from Cuozzo
PAT–Cox (kick)

TEAM STATISTICS

MINN.		DALLAS
17	First Downs–Total	10
5	First Downs–Rushing	5
12	First Downs–Passing	5
0	First Downs–Penalty	0
1	Fumbles–Number	0
1	Fumbles–Lost Ball	0
2	Penalties–Number	2
18	Yards Penalized	10
2	Missed Field Goals	0
64	Offensive Plays–Total	55
311	Net Yards	183
4.9	Average Gain	3.3
5	Giveaways	0
0	Takeaways	5
–5	Difference	+5

INDIVIDUAL STATISTICS

MINNESOTA	No.	Yds.	Avg.	DALLAS	No.	Yds.	Avg.
RUSHING							
Jones	15	52	3.5	D. Thomas	21	66	3.1
Lee	3	28	9.3	Hill	14	28	2.0
Osborn	6	13	2.2	Garrison	2	2	1.0
Lindsey	1	6	6.0	Staubach	2	2	1.0
Grim	1	2	2.0		39	98	2.5
	26	101	3.9				
RECEIVING							
Washington	5	70	14.0	Hayes	3	31	10.3
Grim	4	74	18.5	Alworth	2	33	16.5
Voigt	4	46	11.5	Ditka	2	18	9.0
Reed	4	–3	–0.8	Hill	2	14	7.0
Lindsey	1	25	25.0	D. Thomas	1	3	3.0
White	1	–2	–2.0		10	99	9.9
	19	210	11.1				
PUNTING							
Lee	4		43.5	Widby	7		37.0
PUNT RETURNS							
West	2	6	3.0	Waters	2	37	18.5
KICKOFF RETURNS							
Jones	2	75	37.5	I. Thomas	2	31	15.5
West	2	74	37.0	Harris	1	21	21.0
Bryant	1	22	22.0		3	52	17.3
Brown	1	17	17.0				
	6	188	31.3				
INTERCEPTION RETURNS							
None				Harris	1	30	30.0
				Howley	1	26	26.0
				Adderly	1	8	8.0
				Jordan	1	5	5.0
					4	69	17.3

PASSING

MINNESOTA	Att.	Comp.	Comp. Pct.	Yds.	Int.	Yds/ Att.	Yds/ Comp.	Yds. Lost Tkld.
Cuozzo	22	12	54.5	124	2	5.6	10.3	0– 0
Lee	16	7	43.8	86	2	5.4	12.3	0– 0
	38	19	50.0	210	4	5.5	11.1	0– 0
DALLAS								
Staubach	14	10	71.4	99	0	7.1	9.9	2–14

December 26, at San Francisco
(Attendance 45,327)

SCORING

SAN FRANCISCO	**0**	**3**	**14**	**7–24**
WASHINGTON	**7**	**3**	**3**	**7–20**

First Quarter
Was. Smith, 5 yard pass from Kilmer
PAT–Knight (kick)

Second Quarter
S.F. Gossett, 23 yard field goal
Was. Knight, 40 yard field goal

Third Quarter
S.F. G. Washington, 78 yard pass from Brodie PAT–Gossett (kick)
S.F. Windsor, 2 yard pass from Brodie
PAT–Gossett (kick)
Was. Knight, 36 yard field goal

Fourth Quarter
S.F. Hoskins, recovered fumble in end zone
PAT–Gossett (kick)
Was. Brown, 16 yard pass from Kilmer
PAT–Knight (kick)

TEAM STATISTICS

S.F.		WASH.
11	First Downs–Total	13
2	First Downs–Rushing	6
9	First Downs–Passing	5
0	First Downs–Penalty	2
0	Fumbles – Number	3
0	Fumbles–Lost Ball	2
3	Penalties–Number	4
41	Yards Penalized	55
0	Missed Field Goals	1
59	Offensive Plays–Total	67
285	Net Yards	192
4.8	Average Gain	2.9
0	Giveaways	3
3	Takeaways	0
+3	Difference	–3

INDIVIDUAL STATISTICS

SAN FRANCISCO	No.	Yds.	Avg.	WASHINGTON	No.	Yds.	Avg.
RUSHING							
V. Washington	16	59	3.7	Brown	27	84	3.1
Willard	19	46	2.4	Harraway	10	28	2.8
Schreiber	4	7	1.8	Kilmer	1	0	0.0
	39	112	2.8	Jefferson	1	–13	–13.0
					39	99	2.5
RECEIVING							
Kwalick	3	26	8.7	Brown	6	62	10.3
Witcher	2	28	14.0	Smith	3	32	10.7
G. Washington	1	78	78.0	Mason	1	8	8.0
Schreiber	1	22	22.0	Harraway	1	4	4.0
V. Washington	1	10	10.0		11	106	9.6
Willard	1	10	10.0				
Windsor	1	2	2.0				
	10	176	17.6				
PUNTING							
Spurrier	10		33.7	Bragg	5		46.0
PUNT RETURNS							
Fuller	1	8	8.0	Duncan	2	11	5.5
Simpson	1	4	4.0	Vactor	1	47	47.0
B. Taylor	1	1	1.0		3	58	19.3
	3	13	4.3				
KICKOFF RETURNS							
V. Washington	4	79	19.8	Duncan	3	170	56.7
Cunningham	1	0	0.0	McLinton	1	19	19.0
	5	79	15.8		4	189	47.3
INTERCEPTION RETURNS							
R. Taylor	1	17	17.0	None			

PASSING

SAN FRANCISCO	Att.	Cmp.	Comp. Pct.	Yds.	Int.	Yds/ Att.	Yds/ Comp.	Yds Lost Tkld.
Brodie	19	10	52.6	176	0	9.3	17.6	1– 3
WASHINGTON								
Kilmer	27	11	40.7	106	1	3.9	9.6	1–13

1971 N.F.C. — Eastern Division

DALLAS COWBOYS 11-3-0 Tom Landry

Scores of Each Game		
49	Buffalo	37
42	Philadelphia	7
16	WASHINGTON	20
20	N.Y. GIANTS	13
14	New Orleans	24
44	NEW ENGLAND	21
19	Chicago	23
16	St. Louis	13
20	PHILADELPHIA	7
13	Washington	0
28	LOS ANGELES	21
52	N.Y. JETS	10
42	N.Y. Giants	14
31	ST. LOUIS	12

Use Name	Pos.	Hgt	Wgt	Age	Int	Pts
Forrest Gregg	OT	6'4"	250	38		
Tony Liscio	OT	6'5"	255	31		
Ralph Neely	OT	6'5"	265	27		
Don Talbert	OT	6'5"	255	31		
Rayfield Wright	OT	6'7"	255	26		
John Niland	OG	6'4"	245	27		
Blaine Nye	OG	6'4"	250	25		
Rodney Wallace	OG	6'5"	255	22		
John Fitzgerald	C	6'5"	250	23		
Dave Manders	C	6'2"	250	29		
George Andrie	DE	6'7"	250	31		
Larry Cole	DE	6'4"	255	24		
Tody Smith	DE	6'5"	245	22		
Pat Toomay	DE	6'5"	244	26		
Bill Gregory	DT	6'5"	255	21		
Bob Lilly	DT	6'4"	260	32		6
Jethro Pugh	DT	6'6"	260	27		

Use Name	Pos.	Hgt	Wgt	Age	Int	Pts
Lee Roy Caffey	LB	6'3"	250	31		
Dave Edwards	LB	6'3"	225	32	2	
Chuck Howley	LB	6'3"	225	35	5	
Lee Roy Jordan	LB	6'2"	220	30	2	
D. D. Lewis	LB	6'2"	225	25	1	
Tom Stincic	LB	6'2"	230	24		
Herb Adderley	DB	6'1"	200	32	6	
Cornell Green	DB	6'4"	208	31	2	
Cliff Harris	DB	6'	184	22	2	
Mel Renfro	DB	6'	190	29	4	
Ike Thomas	DB	6'2"	193	23		12
Mark Washington	DB	5'10"	183	23		
Charlie Waters	DB	6'1"	193	22	2	

Bob Asher – Injury

Use Name	Pos.	Hgt	Wgt	Age	Int	Pts
Craig Morton	QB	6'4"	214	28		6
Roger Staubach	QB	6'2"	197	29		12
Dan Reeves	HB	6'1"	200	27		1
Claxton Welch	HB	5'11"	203	24		8
Joe Williams	HB	6'	195	24		6
Calvin Hill	FB-HB	6'3"	235	24		66
Duane Thomas	FB-HB	6'1"	210	24		78
Walt Garrison	FB	6'	205	27		12
Margene Adkins	WR	5'10"	183	24		
Lance Alworth	WR	6'	180	31		12
Bob Hayes	WR	6'	185	28		48
Gloster Richardson	WR	6'	200	28		18
Mike Ditka	TE	6'3"	225	31		6
Billy Truax	TE	6'5"	235	28		6
Mike Clark	K	6'1"	205	30		86
Toni Fritsch	K	5'7"	185	26		17
Ron Widby	K	6'4"	210	26		

WASHINGTON REDSKINS 9-4-1 George Allen

Scores of Each Game		
24	ST. LOUIS	17
30	N.Y. Giants	3
20	Dallas	16
22	HOUSTON	13
20	ST. LOUIS	0
20	Kansas City	27
24	NEW ORLEANS	14
7	PHILADELPHIA	7
15	Chicago	16
0	DALLAS	13
20	Philadelphia	13
23	N.Y. GIANTS	7
38	Los Angeles	24
13	CLEVELAND	20

Use Name	Pos.	Hgt	Wgt	Age	Int	Pts
Terry Hermeling	OT	6'5"	255	25		
Walt Rock	OT	6'5"	255	30		
Jim Snowden	OT	6'3"	255	29		
Mike Taylor	OT	6'4"	245	26		
Paul Laaveg	OG	6'4"	245	22		
Ray Schoenke	OG	6'3"	250	29		
John Wilbur	OG	6'3"	250	28		
George Burman	C-OG	6'3"	255	28		
Len Hauss	C	6'2"	235	29		
Verlon Biggs	DE	6'4"	270	28		
Jimmie Jones	DE	6'3"	215	24		
Ron McDole	DE	6'3"	288	31	3	6
Bill Brundige	DT	6'5"	270	22		
Manny Sistrunk	DT	6'5"	265	24		
Diron Talbert	DT	6'5"	255	27		

Use Name	Pos.	Hgt	Wgt	Age	Int	Pts
Bob Grant	LB	6'2"	225	25		
Chris Hanburger	LB	6'2"	218	30	1	6
Harold McLinton	LB	6'2"	235	24		
Jack Pardee	LB	6'2"	225	35	5	6
Myron Pottios	LB	6'2"	232	31	1	
Rusty Tillman	LB	6'2"	230	25		
Mike Bass	DB	6'	190	26	8	6
Speedy Duncan	DB	5'10"	175	28	1	6
Pat Fischer	DB	5'10"	170	31	3	6
Jon Jaqua	DB	6'	190	23		
Brig Owens	DB	5'11"	190	28	2	
Richie Petitbon	DB	6'3"	208	33	5	
Ted Vactor	DB	6'	185	27		

Use Name	Pos.	Hgt	Wgt	Age	Int	Pts
Sonny Jurgensen	QB	5'11"	203	37		
Billy Kilmer	QB	6'	204	31		12
Sam Wyche	QB	6'4"	210	26		
Larry Brown	HB	5'11"	195	23		36
Bob Brunet	HB	6'1"	205	25		
Tommy Mason	FB-HB	6'	195	32		
Charlie Harraway	FB	6'2"	215	26		12
Mike Hull	FB	6'3"	220	26		
Jeff Jordan	HB-FB	6'1"	215	26		
Boyd Dowler	WR	6'5"	225	34		
Roy Jefferson	WR	6'2"	195	27		24
Bill Malinchak	WR	6'1"	200	27		
Clifton McNeil (from NYG)	WR	6'2"	187	31		18
Charley Taylor	WR	6'3"	210	30		24
Mack Alston	TE	6'2"	230	24		
Jerry Smith	TE	6'2"	208	28		6
Mike Bragg	K	5'11"	186	24		
Curt Knight	K	6'1"	190	28		114

PHILADELPHIA EAGLES 6-7-1 Jerry Williams Ed Khayat

Scores of Each Game		
14	Cincinnati	37
7	DALLAS	42
3	SAN FRANCISCO	31
0	MINNESOTA	13
10	Oakland	34
23	N.Y. GIANTS	7
17	DENVER	16
7	Washington	7
7	Dallas	20
37	St. Louis	20
13	WASHINGTON	20
23	Detroit	20
19	ST. LOUIS	7
41	N.Y. Giants	28

Use Name	Pos.	Hgt	Wgt	Age	Int	Pts
Wayde Key	OT	6'4"	245	24		
Steve Smith	OT	6'5"	250	27		6
Dick Stevens	OT	6'4"	240	23		
Henry Allison	OG	6'2"	255	24		
Jim Skaggs	OG	6'2"	250	31		
Tuufuli Uperesa	OG	6'3"	255	23		
Mike Evans	C	6'5"	250	24		
Mark Nordquist	OG-C	6'4"	245	25		
Don Brumm	DE	6'3"	245	28		
Richard Harris	DE	6'4"	260	23		
Mel Tom	DE	6'4"	250	30		
Mike Dirks	DT	6'2"	245	25		
Don Hultz	DT	6'3"	240	30	1	
Gary Pettigrew	DT	6'4"	255	26		
Ernie Calloway	DE-DT	6'6"	240	23		

Dick Hart – Injury
Harry Jones – Injury

Use Name	Pos.	Hgt	Wgt	Age	Int	Pts
Bob Creech	LB	6'3"	222	22		
Bill Hobbs	LB	6'	220	25		6
Ike Kelley	LB	5'11"	224	27		
Ron Porter	LB	6'3"	232	26		
Tim Rossovich	LB	6'4"	240	25	1	
Fred Whittingham	LB	6'1"	240	32		
Adrian Young	LB	6'1"	232	25		
Steve Zabel	TE-LB	6'4"	235	23	1	12
Bill Bradley	DB	5'11"	190	24	11	
Vern Davis	DB	6'4"	208	21		
Leroy Keyes	DB	6'3"	208	24	6	
Al Nelson	DB	5'11"	186	27	2	12
Steve Preece	DB	6'1"	195	24		
Nate Ramsey	DB	6'1"	200	30		
Jack Smith	DB	6'4"	204	23		
Jim Thrower	DB	6'2"	194	22		

Greg Barton – Canadian Football League

Use Name	Pos.	Hgt	Wgt	Age	Int	Pts
Rich Arrington	QB	6'2"	190	24		
Pete Liske	QB	6'2"	200	30		6
Jim Ward	QB	6'2"	200	27		
Tom Bailey	HB	6'2"	211	22		6
Ronnie Bull	FB-HB	6'	200	31		6
Sonny Davis	FB-HB	5'11"	215	23		6
Larry Watkins	FB-HB	6'2"	215	24		6
Lee Bouggess	FB	6'2"	210	23		18
Tom Woodeshick	FB	6'	222	29		6
Tony Baker (from NO)	FB	5'11"	225	26		6
Harold Carmichael	WR	6'7"	225	21		
Ben Hawkins	WR	6'	180	27		30
Harold Jackson	WR	5'10"	175	25		18
Billy Walik	WR	5'11"	180	23		
Kent Kramer	TE	6'5"	235	27		6
Gary Ballman	WR-TE	6'2"	210	31		
Fred Hill	WR-TE	6'2"	215	28		
Tom Dempsey	K	6'1"	264	30		49
Happy Feller	K	5'11"	185	22		28
Tom McNeill	K	6'1"	195	29		

ST. LOUIS CARDINALS 4-9-1 Bob Hollway

Scores of Each Game		
17	WASHINGTON	24
17	N.Y. JETS	10
20	N.Y. GIANTS	21
26	Atlanta	9
0	Washington	20
14	SAN FRANCISCO	26
28	Buffalo	23
13	DALLAS	16
17	San Diego	20
20	PHILADELPHIA	37
24	N.Y. Giants	7
16	GREEN BAY	16
7	Philadelphia	19
12	Dallas	31

Use Name	Pos.	Hgt	Wgt	Age	Int	Pts
Vern Emerson	OT	6'5"	260	25		
Ernie McMillan	OT	6'6"	255	33		
Bob Reynolds	OT	6'6"	265	30		
Dan Dierdorf	OG-OT	6'4"	265	22		
Irv Goode	OG	6'4"	255	30		
Chuck Hutchison	OG	6'3"	240	22		
Clyde Williams	OG	6'2"	250	31		
Tom Banks	C	6'1"	240	23		
Wayne Mulligan	C	6'2"	245	24		
Joe Schmiesing	DE	6'4"	260	26		
Chuck Walker	DE	6'2"	250	30		
Ron Yankowski	DE	6'5"	225	24		
Rolf Krueger	DT-DE	6'4"	250	24		
Paul Dickson	DT	6'5"	250	34		
Fred Heron	DT	6'4"	260	26		
Bob Rowe	DT	6'4"	260	26		

Terry Brown – Injury

Use Name	Pos.	Hgt	Wgt	Age	Int	Pts
Jim Hargrove	LB	6'3"	223	26		
Mike McGill	LB	6'2"	235	24	1	
Terry Miller	LB	6'2"	225	25		
Rick Ogle	LB	6'3"	230	22		
Jamie Rivers	LB	6'2"	235	25		
Rocky Rosema	LB	6'2"	230	25		
Larry Stallings	LB	6'2"	230	29	1	6
Jeff Allen	DB	5'11"	190	23		
Miller Farr	DB	6'1"	190	28	2	
Dale Hackbart	DB	6'3"	220	35	1	
George Hoey	DB	5'10"	170	24		6
Tom Longo	DB	6'1"	200	27		
Ted Provost	DB	6'2"	195	23		
Jerry Stovall	DB	6'2"	195	29	2	
Norm Thompson	DB	6'1"	175	23	4	
Roger Wehrli	DB	6'1"	195	23	2	
Larry Willingham	DB	6'1"	190	22		
Larry Wilson	DB	6'	195	33	4	

Use Name	Pos.	Hgt	Wgt	Age	Int	Pts
Pete Beathard	QB	6'2"	200	29		
Jim Hart	QB	6'2"	200	27		
Roy Shivers	HB	6'	200	29		6
Larry Stegent	HB	6'1"	200	23		
Paul White	HB	6'	200	23		
MacArthur Lane	FB-HB	6'	220	29		18
Cid Edwards	FB	6'2"	230	27		24
Johnny Roland	HB-FB	6'2"	215	28		
John Gilliam	WR	6'1"	195	26		18
Mel Gray	WR	5'9"	170	22		24
Freddie Hyatt	WR	6'3"	200	25		
Chuck Latourette	WR	6'	190	26		
Dave Williams	WR	6'2"	210	26		6
Jim McFarland	TE	6'5"	225	23		12
Jackie Smith	TE	6'4"	235	30		24
Jim Bakken	K	6'	195	30		87

NEW YORK GIANTS 4-10-0 Alex Webster

Scores of Each Game		
42	Green Bay	40
3	WASHINGTON	30
21	St. Louis	20
13	Dallas	20
7	BALTIMORE	31
7	Philadelphia	23
10	MINNESOTA	17
35	SAN DIEGO	17
21	Atlanta	17
13	Pittsburg	17
7	ST. LOUIS	24
7	Washington	23
14	DALLAS	42
28	PHILADELPHIA	41

Use Name	Pos.	Hgt	Wgt	Age	Int	Pts
Willie Young	OT	6'	265	28		
Charlie Harper	OG-OT	6'2"	250	27		
Bob Hyland	OG-OT	6'5"	250	26		
Steve Alexakos	OG	6'2"	260	24		
Doug Van Horn	OG	6'2"	245	27		
Wayne Walton	OG	6'5"	245	22		
Greg Larson	C	6'2"	250	32		
Fred Dryer	DE	6'6"	240	25		
Bob Lurtsema	DE	6'6"	250	29		
Henry Reed	DE	6'3"	230	22	1	
Dave Tipton	DE	6'6"	240	22		
Dick Hanson	DT	6'6"	280	22		
Jim Kanicki	DT	6'4"	270	29		
Roland Lakes	DT	6'4"	263	31		
Dave Roller	DT	6'2"	240	21		
Jerry Shay	DT	6'3"	245	27		
Vern Vanoy	DT	6'8"	270	25		

Use Name	Pos.	Hgt	Wgt	Age	Int	Pts
John Douglas	LB	6'2"	225	26		
Jim Files	LB	6'4"	240	23	1	
Ralph Heck	LB	6'2"	230	30	1	6
Ron Hornsby	LB	6'3"	232	22		
Pat Hughes	LB	6'2"	240	24		
Pete Athas	WR-DB	5'11"	185	23	2	6
Otto Brown	DB	6'1"	183	24		6
Scott Eaton	DB	6'3"	205	27	1	
Richmond Flowers (from DAL)	DB	6'	180	24	1	
Joe Green	DB	5'11"	195	24		6
Spider Lockhart	DB	6'2"	175	28	3	
Bennie McRae	DB	6'1"	180	30		
Willie Williams	DB	6'	190	28		5

Use Name	Pos.	Hgt	Wgt	Age	Int	Pts
Randy Johnson	QB	6'3"	205	27		
Fran Tarkenton	QB	6'1"	190	31		18
Bobby Duhon	HB	6'	195	24		6
Ron Johnson	HB	6'1"	205	23		6
Rocky Thompson	HB	5'11"	200	23		12
Charlie Evans	FB	6'1"	215	23		30
Tucker Fredrickson	FB	6'3"	220	28		6
Junior Coffey	HB-FB	6'1"	215	29		
Don Herrmann	WR	6'2"	195	24		6
Rich Houston	WR	6'2"	197	25		24
Coleman Zeno	WR	6'4"	210	24		
Joe Morrison	HB-FB-WR	6'1"	212	33		6
Dick Kotite	TE	6'3"	230	28		12
Bob Tucker	TE	6'3"	230	26		24
Tom Blanchard	K	6'	190	23		
Pete Gogolak	K	6'2"	190	29		48

DALLAS COWBOYS

RUSHING

Last Name	No.	Yds	Avg	TD
D. Thomas	175	793	4.5	11
Hill	106	468	4.4	8
Garrison	127	429	3.4	1
Staubach	41	343	8.4	2
Reeves	17	79	4.6	0
Williams	21	67	3.2	1
Welch	14	51	3.6	1
Hayes	3	18	6.0	0
Morton	4	9	2.3	1
Ditka	2	2	1.0	0
Alworth	2	−10	−5.0	0

RECEIVING

Last Name	No.	Yds	Avg	TD
Garrison	40	396	10	1
Hayes	35	840	24	8
Alworth	34	487	14	2
Ditka	30	360	12	1
Hill	19	244	13	3
Truax	15	232	15	1
D. Thomas	13	153	12	2
Richardson	8	170	21	3
Adkins	4	53	13	0
Williams	3	59	20	0
Reeves	3	25	8	0
Welch	1	−1	−1	0

PUNT RETURNS

Last Name	No.	Yds	Avg	TD
Harris	17	129	8	0
Waters	9	109	12	0
Adkins	4	5	1	0
Hayes	1	5	5	0

KICKOFF RETURNS

Last Name	No.	Yds	Avg	TD
Harris	29	823	28	0
I. Thomas	7	295	42	2
Welch	4	105	26	0
D. Thomas	2	64	32	0
Ditka	3	30	10	0
Waters	1	18	18	0
Lewis	1	15	15	0
Hayes	1	14	14	0
Williams	1	12	12	0
Green	1	0	0	0

PASSING

Last Name	Att	Comp	%	Yds	Yd/Att	TD	Int−	%	RK
Staubach	211	126	60	1882	8.9	15	4−	2	1
Morton	143	76	55	1131	7.9	7	8−	6	7
Reeves	5	2	40	24	4.8	0	1−	20	
Hill	1	0	0	0	0.0	0	1−	100	
D. Thomas	1	0	0	0	0.0	0	0−	0	

PUNTING

Last Name	No	Avg
Widby	56	41.6

KICKING

Last Name	XP	Att	%	FG	Att	%
Clark	47	47	100	13	25	52
Fritsch	2	2	100	5	8	63
Reeves	1	1	100	0	0	

WASHINGTON REDSKINS

RUSHING

Last Name	No.	Yds	Avg	TD
Brown	253	948	3.7	4
Harraway	156	635	4.1	2
Mason	31	85	2.7	0
Jurgensen	3	29	9.7	0
Brunet	10	27	2.7	0
Jefferson	2	13	6.5	0
Hull	2	8	4.0	0
Kilmer	17	5	0.3	2
Smith	1	5	5.0	0
Wyche	1	4	4.0	0
Petitbon	1	−2	−2.0	0

RECEIVING

Last Name	No.	Yds	Avg	TD
Jefferson	47	701	15	4
McNeil	30	453	15	3
Dowler	26	352	14	0
C. Taylor	24	370	15	4
Harraway	20	121	6	0
Smith	16	227	14	1
Brown	16	176	11	2
Mason	12	109	9	0
Alston	5	87	17	0
Brunet	2	4	2	0

PUNT RETURNS

Last Name	No.	Yds	Avg	TD
Duncan	22	233	11	0
Vactor	23	194	8	0

KICKOFF RETURNS

Last Name	No.	Yds	Avg	TD
Duncan	27	724	27	0
Jaqua	6	78	13	0
Bass	4	61	15	0
McLinton	5	46	9	0
Tillman	1	4	4	0

PASSING

Last Name	Att	Comp	%	Yds	Yd/Att	TD	Int−	%	RK
Kilmer	306	166	54	2221	7.3	13	13−	4	3
Jurgensen	28	16	57	170	7.1	0	2−	7	

PUNTING

Last Name	No	Avg
Bragg	58	40.5

KICKING

Last Name	XP	Att	%	FG	Att	%
Knight	27	27	100	29	49	59

PHILADELPHIA EAGLES

RUSHING

Last Name	No.	Yds	Avg	TD
Bull	94	351	3.7	0
Bouggess	97	262	2.7	2
Woodeshick	66	188	2.8	0
Baker	46	174	3.8	0
S. Davis	47	163	3.5	1
Watkins	35	98	2.8	1
Bailey	5	41	8.2	1
Jackson	23	41	1.8	0
Liske	13	29	2.2	1
Arrington	5	23	4.6	0
Hawkins	4	8	2.0	0
Zabel	1	−5	−5.0	0

RECEIVING

Last Name	No.	Yds	Avg	TD
Jackson	47	716	15	3
Hawkins	37	650	18	4
Bouggess	24	170	7	1
Carmichael	20	288	14	0
Ballman	13	238	18	0
S. Davis	11	46	4	0
Baker	10	80	8	1
Bull	9	75	8	1
Hill	7	92	13	0
Bailey	7	55	8	0
Kramer	6	65	11	1
Watkins	6	40	7	0
Woodeshick	6	36	6	1
Zabel	2	4	2	2

PUNT RETURNS

Last Name	No.	Yds	Avg	TD
Bradley	18	118	7	0
Walik	5	48	10	0
Hawkins	1	6	6	0

KICKOFF RETURNS

Last Name	No.	Yds	Avg	TD
Walik	14	369	26	0
Nelson	13	358	28	0
Thrower	12	299	25	0
Jackson	2	48	24	0
S. Davis	2	44	22	0
Pettigrew	2	37	19	0
Harris	2	28	14	0
Kramer	1	0	0	0
Zabel	1	0	0	0

PASSING

Last Name	Att	Comp	%	Yds	Yd/Att	TD	Int−	%	RK
Liske	269	143	53	1957	7.3	11	15−	6	9
Arrington	118	55	47	576	4.9	2	5−	4	
Bull	1	1	100	15	15.0	0	0−	0	
S. Davis	1	0	0	0	0.0	0	0−	0	
Ward	1	1	100	4	4.0	0	0−	0	

PUNTING

Last Name	No	Avg
McNeill	73	42.0
Bradley	2	38.0

KICKING

Last Name	XP	Att	%	FG	Att	%
Dempsey	13	14	93	12	17	71
Feller	10	10	100	6	20	30

ST. LOUIS CARDINALS

RUSHING

Last Name	No.	Yds	Avg	TD
Lane	150	592	3.9	3
Edwards	108	316	2.9	4
Roland	78	278	3.6	0
Shivers	55	202	3.7	1
Gray	2	56	28.0	0
Beathard	4	29	7.3	0
Latourette	3	19	6.3	0
Gilliam	2	16	8.0	0
Smith	1	10	10.0	0
Hart	13	9	0.7	0
White	1	3	3.0	0

RECEIVING

Last Name	No.	Yds	Avg	TD
Gilliam	42	837	20	3
Lane	29	298	10	0
Smith	21	379	18	4
Gray	18	534	30	4
Roland	15	108	7	0
D. Williams	12	182	15	1
Edwards	12	122	10	0
Shivers	10	76	8	0
McFarland	5	54	11	2
Hyatt	4	58	15	0
Stegent	1	12	12	0
Reynolds	1	−4	−4	0

PUNT RETURNS

Last Name	No.	Yds	Avg	TD
Willingham	10	84	8	0
Wehrli	9	84	9	0
Thompson	5	27	5	0
Gilliam	1	21	21	0
Roland	3	10	3	0
Stallings	1	8	8	0
Dickson	1	0	0	0

KICKOFF RETURNS

Last Name	No.	Yds	Avg	TD
Gray	30	740	25	0
Hoey	9	251	28	1
Thompson	7	182	26	0
Willingham	6	125	21	0
Edwards	2	41	21	0
Roland	2	24	12	0
Dierdorf	1	0	0	0
Stegent	1	0	0	0

PASSING

Last Name	Att	Comp	%	Yds	Yd/Att	TD	Int−	%	RK
Hart	243	110	45	1626	6.7	8	14−	6	13
Beathard	141	60	43	1030	7.3	6	12−	9	15
Shivers	1	0	0	0	0.0	0	0−	0	

PUNTING

Last Name	No	Avg
Latourette	56	38.5
Bakken	5	41.4

KICKING

Last Name	XP	Att	%	FG	Att	%
Bakken	24	24	100	21	32	66

NEW YORK GIANTS

RUSHING

Last Name	No.	Yds	Avg	TD
Duhon	93	344	3.7	1
Frederickson	64	242	3.8	0
Thompson	54	177	3.3	1
Evans	48	171	3.6	5
Ron Johnson	32	156	4.9	1
Morrison	38	131	3.4	0
Tarkenton	30	111	3.7	3
Coffey	22	70	3.2	0
Randy Johnson	6	29	4.8	0
Zeno	2	10	5.0	0
Athas	1	3	3.0	0
Houston	2	2	1.0	0
Tucker	1	1	1.0	0

RECEIVING

Last Name	No.	Yds	Avg	TD
Tucker	59	791	13	4
Morrison	40	411	10	1
Herrmann	27	297	11	1
Duhon	25	266	11	0
Houston	24	426	18	4
Frederickson	21	114	5	1
Thompson	16	85	5	0
Evans	13	144	11	0
Kotite	10	146	15	2
Ron Johnson	6	47	8	0
Zeno	5	97	19	0
Coffey	5	20	4	0

PUNT RETURNS

Last Name	No.	Yds	Avg	TD
Duhon	12	77	6	0
Lockhart	4	24	6	0
Athas	3	21	7	0

KICKOFF RETURNS

Last Name	No.	Yds	Avg	TD
Thompson	36	947	26	1
Duhon	11	200	18	0
Flowers	8	156	20	0
Green	5	106	21	0
Douglas	1	7	7	0
Dryer	1	0	0	0
Walton	1	0	0	0

PASSING

Last Name	Att	Comp	%	Yds	Yd/Att	TD	Int−	%	RK
Tarkenton	386	226	59	2567	6.7	11	21−	5	8
Ran. Johnson	74	41	55	477	6.5	3	3−	4	
Blanchard	1	1	100	18	18.0	0	0−	0	
Duhon	1	0	0	0	0.0	0	1−	100	

PUNTING

Last Name	No	Avg
Blanchard	66	40.6

KICKING

Last Name	XP	Att	%	FG	Att	%
Gogolak	30	30	100	6	17	35

Scores of Each Game			Use Name	Pos.	Hgt	Wgt	Age	Int	Pts

MINNESOTA VIKINGS 11-3-0 Bud Grant

	Opponent	Score	Use Name	Pos.	Hgt	Wgt	Age	Int	Pts
16	Detroit	13	Grady Alderman	OT	6'2"	247	32		
17	CHICAGO	20	Doug Davis	OT	6'4"	250	27		
19	BUFFALO	0	Ron Yary	OT	6'6"	255	25		
13	Philadelphia	0	Pete Perreault	OG-OT	6'3"	248	32		
24	Green Bay	13	Roy Schmidt	OG	6'3"	250	29		
10	BALTIMORE	3	Milt Sunde	OG	6'2"	250	28		
17	N.Y. Giants	10	Doug Sutherland	OG	6'3"	250	23		
9	SAN FRANCISCO	13	Ed White	OG	6'2"	262	24		
3	GREEN BAY	0	Mick Tingelhoff	C	6'1"	237	31		
23	New Orleans	10	Godfrey Zaunbrecher	C	6'2"	235	23		
24	ATLANTA	7	Carl Eller	DE	6'6"	247	29		
14	San Diego	30	Jim Marshall	DE	6'3"	248	33		
29	DETROIT	10	John Ward	DE	6'4"	260	23		
27	Chicago	10	Gary Larsen	DT	6'5"	260	31		
			Alan Page	DT	6'5"	245	26		
			Jerry Patton	DT	6'3"	260	25		

Use Name	Pos.	Hgt	Wgt	Age	Int	Pts
Carl Gersbach	LB	6'1"	230	24		
Wally Hilgenberg	LB	6'3"	230	28	2	
Noel Jenke	LB	6'1"	218	24		
Lonnie Warwick	LB	6'3"	238	29		
Carl Winfrey	LB	6'	230	22		
Roy Winston	LB	6'1"	222	31	1	6
Bobby Bryant	DB	6'	170	27	3	
Karl Kassulke	DB	6'	195	29	2	
Paul Krause	DB	6'3"	200	29	6	
Ed Sharockman	DB	6'	200	31	6	
Charlie West	DB	6'1"	197	25	7	
Jeff Wright	DB	5'11"	190	22		
Nate Wright	DB	5'11"	180	24		
John Beasley — Injury						
Jim Vellone — Hodgkin's Disease						

Use Name	Pos.	Hgt	Wgt	Age	Int	Pts
Gary Cuozzo	QB	6'1"	195	30		
Bob Lee	QB	6'2"	195	26		6
Norm Snead	QB	6'4"	215	31		6
Clint Jones	HB	6'	205	26		24
Dave Osborn	HB	6'	208	28		36
Bill Brown	FB	5'11"	230	33		12
Leo Hayden	HB-FB	6'	212	23		
Jim Lindsey	HB-FB	6'2"	210	26		6
Oscar Reed	HB-FB	5'11"	222	27		6
Al Denson	WR	6'2"	208	29		
Bob Grim	WR	6'	195	26		42
John Henderson	WR	6'3"	195	28		
Gene Washington	WR	6'3"	208	27		
Bob Brown	TE	6'3"	225	28		
John Hilton	TE	6'5"	225	29		
Stu Voigt	TE	6'1"	220	23		6
Fred Cox	K	5'10"	200	32		91

DETROIT LIONS 7-6-1 Joe Schmidt

	Opponent	Score	Use Name	Pos.	Hgt	Wgt	Age	Int	Pts
13	MINNESOTA	16	Rocky Freitas	OT	6'6"	280	25		
34	New England	7	Ray Parson	OT	6'4"	250	24		
41	ATLANTA	38	Jim Yarbrough	OT	6'6"	250	24		
31	GREEN BAY	28	Frank Gallagher	OG	6'2"	245	28		
31	Houston	7	Bob Kowalkowski	OG	6'3"	240	27		
23	CHICAGO	28	Chuck Walton	OG	6'3"	255	30		
14	Green Bay	14	Dave Thompson	C-OG	6'4"	275	22		
24	Denver	20	Ed Flanagan	C	6'3"	245	27		
13	LOS ANGELES	21	Larry Hand	DE	6'4"	250	31		
28	Chicago	3	Jim Mitchell	DE	6'3"	245	22		
32	KANSAS CITY	21	Joe Robb	DE	6'3"	245	34		
20	PHILADELPHIA	23	Bob Bell	DT	6'4"	250	23	6	
10	Minnesota	29	Dick Evey	DT	6'4"	245	30		
27	San Francisco	31	Jerry Rush	DT	6'4"	265	29		
			Larry Woods	DT	6'6"	260	23		

Use Name	Pos.	Hgt	Wgt	Age	Int	Pts
Ken Lee	LB	6'4"	230	22		
Mike Lucci	LB	6'2"	230	31	5	12
Ed Mooney	LB	6'2"	225	26		
Paul Naumoff	LB	6'1"	215	26		
Wayne Walker	LB	6'2"	228	34	2	2
Charlie Weaver	LB	6'2"	218	22		
Lem Barney	DB	6'	188	25	3	6
Al Clark	DB	6'	180	23		
Dick LeBeau	DB	6'1"	185	34	6	
Wayne Rasmussen	DB	6'2"	180	29	4	
Tom Vaughn	DB	5'11"	190	28	1	
Mike Weger	DB	6'2"	200	25	1	6
Bobby Williams	DB	6'1"	200	29		
Charlie Brown — Injury						
Bill Cottrell — Injury						
Nick Eddy — Knee Injury						

Use Name	Pos.	Hgt	Wgt	Age	Int	Pts
Greg Landry	QB	6'4"	205	24		18
Bill Munson	QB	6'2"	210	29		
Altie Taylor	HB	5'10"	196	23		30
Mickey Zofko	HB	6'3"	195	21		
Mel Farr	FB-HB	6'2"	210	26		6
Paul Gipson	FB-HB	6'	210	25		
Steve Owens	FB	6'2"	220	23		60
Bill Triplett	FB	6'2"	215	32		
*Chuck Hughes	WR	5'11"	175	24		
Ron Jessie	WR	6'	183	23		14
Earl McCullouch	WR	5'11"	175	25		18
Larry Walton	WR	5'11"	180	24		30
Craig Cotton	TE	6'4"	222	24		
Charlie Sanders	TE	6'4"	235	25		30
Errol Mann	K	6'	200	30		103
Herman Weaver	K	6'4"	210	22		

*Died Oct. 24, 1971 — Heart Attack

CHICAGO BEARS 6-8-0 Jim Dooley

	Opponent	Score	Use Name	Pos.	Hgt	Wgt	Age	Int	Pts
17	PITTSBURGH	15	Jeff Curchin	OT	6'6"	255	23		
20	Minnesota	17	Randy Jackson	OT	6'5"	245	27		
3	Los Angeles	17	Steve Wright	OT	6'6"	250	29		
35	NEW ORLEANS	14	Jim Cadile	OG	6'3"	240	30		
0	San Francisco	13	Glenn Holloway	OG	6'3"	245	22		
28	Detroit	23	Bob Newton	OT-OG	6'4"	250	22		
23	DALLAS	19	Rich Coady	C	6'3"	238	26		
14	GREEN BAY	17	Gene Hamlin	C	6'3"	245	25		
16	WASHINGTON	15	John Hoffman	DE	6'7"	260	28		
3	DETROIT	28	Willie Holman	DE	6'4"	250	26		
3	Miami	34	Tony McGee	DE	6'4"	250	22		
3	Denver	6	Ed O'Bradovich	DE	6'3"	255	31		
10	Green Bay	31	Dave Hale	DT	6'7"	260	24		
10	MINNESOTA	27	George Seals	DT	6'2"	260	28	6	
			Bill Staley	DT	6'3"	248	24		

Use Name	Pos.	Hgt	Wgt	Age	Int	Pts
Ross Brupbacher	LB	6'3"	215	23	2	6
Doug Buffone	LB	6'1"	225	27	2	
Dick Butkus	LB	6'3"	245	27	4	1
Jimmy Gunn	LB	6'1"	215	22	1	
Larry Rowden	LB	6'2"	220	21		
Charlie Ford	DB	6'3"	185	22	5	
Cliff Hardy	DB	6'	187	24		
Bob Jeter	DB	6'1"	205	33	1	
Garry Lyle	DB	6'2"	198	25	1	
Jerry Moore	DB	6'3"	208	21		
Ron Smith	DB	6'1"	192	28	3	
Joe Taylor	DB	6'2"	200	30	3	
Craig Baynham — Injury						

Use Name	Pos.	Hgt	Wgt	Age	Int	Pts
Jack Concannon	QB	6'3"	205	28		
Bobby Douglass	QB	6'3"	215	24		19
Kent Nix	QB	6'1"	195	27		
Joe Moore	HB	6'1"	205	22		
Cyril Pinder	HB	6'2"	222	24		6
Gale Sayers	HB	6'	198	28		
Don Shy	HB	6'1"	210	27		12
Jim Grabowski	FB	6'2"	220	27		
Jim Harrison	FB	6'4"	235	22		
Bill Tucker	FB	6'2"	220	27		
George Farmer	WR	6'4"	210	23		30
Dick Gordon	WR	5'11"	190	26		30
Jim Seymour	WR	6'4"	210	24		
Cecil Turner	WR	5'10"	170	27		
Ray Ogden	TE	6'5"	225	28		
Earl Thomas	TE	6'3"	224	22		
Bob Wallace	TE	6'3"	211	25		12
Bobby Joe Green	K	5'11"	175	34		
Mac Percival	K	6'4"	220	31		63

GREEN BAY PACKERS 4-8-2 Dan Devine

	Opponent	Score	Use Name	Pos.	Hgt	Wgt	Age	Int	Pts
40	N.Y. GIANTS	42	Bill Hayhoe	OT	6'8"	258	24		
34	DENVER	13	Dick Himes	OT	6'4"	244	25		
20	CINCINNATI	17	Francis Peay	OT	6'5"	250	27		
28	Detroit	31	Dave Bradley	OG	6'4"	245	24		
13	MINNESOTA	24	Gale Gillingham	OG	6'3"	255	27		
13	Los Angeles	30	Bill Lueck	OG	6'3"	235	25		
14	DETROIT	14	Randy Winkler	OG	6'5"	260	28		
17	Chicago	14	Ken Bowman	C	6'3"	230	28		
0	Minnesota	3	Wimpy Winther	C	6'4"	260	23		
21	Atlanta	28	Cal Withrow	C	6'	240	26		
21	NEW ORLEANS	29	Lionel Aldridge	DE	6'4"	245	30		
16	St. Louis	16	Alden Roche	DE	6'4"	255	26		
31	CHICAGO	10	Donnell Smith	DE	6'4"	245	22		
6	Miami	27	Clarence Williams	DE	6'5"	255	24		
			Bob Brown	DT	6'5"	260	31		
			Jim DeLisle	DT	6'4"	254	22		
			Mike McCoy	DT	6'5"	284	22		

Use Name	Pos.	Hgt	Wgt	Age	Int	Pts
Fred Carr	LB	6'5"	238	25		
Jim Carter	LB	6'3"	235	22	1	
Tommy Crutcher	LB	6'3"	235	29		
Ray Nitschke	LB	6'3"	235	35	1	
Dave Robinson	LB	6'3"	245	30	3	
Ken Ellis	DB	5'10"	190	23	6	6
Charlie Hall	DB	6'1"	195	22		
Doug Hart	DB	6'	190	32	2	8
Al Matthews	DB	5'11"	190	23	1	
Al Randolph	DB	6'2"	196	27	1	
Willie Wood	DB	5'10"	190	35	1	

Use Name	Pos.	Hgt	Wgt	Age	Int	Pts
Zeke Bratkowski	QB	6'2"	215	39		6
Scott Hunter	QB	6'2"	205	23		24
Frank Patrick	QB	6'7"	225	24		
Bart Starr	QB	6'1"	190	38		6
Donny Anderson	HB	6'3"	210	28		36
Larry Krause	HB	6'	208	23		
Elijah Pitts	HB	6'1"	210	32		
Dave Hampton	FB-HB	6'	210	24		30
John Brockington	FB	6'	225	22		30
Perry Williams	FB	6'2"	220	24		
Carroll Dale	WR	6'1"	200	33		24
Dave Davis	WR	6'	175	23		
John Spilis	WR	6'3"	205	23		6
Len Garrett	TE	6'3"	230	22		
Rich McGeorge	TE	6'4"	235	22		24
Dave Conway	K	6'	195	25		5
Ken Duncan	K	6'2"	210	26		
Lou Michaels	K	6'2"	250	35		43
Tim Webster	K	6'	195	21		26

MINNESOTA VIKINGS

RUSHING

Last Name	No.	Yds	Avg	TD
Jones	180	675	3.8	4
Osborn	123	349	2.8	5
Lindsey	46	182	4.0	0
Reed	50	182	3.6	1
Bill Brown	46	136	3.0	2
Grim	6	127	21.2	0
Cuozzo	15	24	1.6	0
Lee	11	14	1.3	1
Snead	6	6	1.0	1
Denson	1	0	0.0	0

RECEIVING

Last Name	No.	Yds	Avg	TD
Grim	45	691	15	7
Osborn	25	195	8	1
Voigt	15	214	14	1
Reed	15	138	9	0
Washington	12	165	14	0
Denson	10	125	13	0
Bill Brown	10	94	9	0
Jones	9	98	11	0
Lindsey	8	31	4	0
Bob Brown	6	141	24	0
Henderson	2	18	9	0

PUNT RETURNS

Last Name	No.	Yds	Avg	TD
West	18	94	5	0
Grim	7	44	6	0
Bryant	2	26	13	0

KICKOFF RETURNS

Last Name	No.	Yds	Avg	TD
West	24	556	23	0
Jones	12	329	27	0
Grim	3	52	17	0
Bryant	1	23	23	0
Voigt	1	0	0	0

PASSING – PUNTING – KICKING Statistics

PASSING

	Att	Comp	%	Yds	Yd/Att	TD	Int–	%	RK
Cuozzo	168	75	45	842	5.0	6	8–	5	14
Lee	90	45	50	598	6.6	2	4–	4	
Snead	75	37	49	470	6.3	1	6–	8	
Grim	1	0	0	0	0.0	0	0–	0	

PUNTING

	No	Avg
Lee	89	39.5

KICKING

	XP	Att	%	FG	Att	%
Cox	25	25	100	22	32	69

DETROIT LIONS

RUSHING

Last Name	No.	Yds	Avg	TD
Owens	246	1035	4.2	8
Taylor	174	736	4.2	4
Landry	76	530	7.0	3
Farr	22	64	2.9	0
Gipson	4	12	3.0	0
Munson	3	9	3.0	0
Triplett	4	4	1.0	0
Jessie	1	0	0.0	0
McCullouch	1	−7	−7.0	0
L. Walton	1	−7	−7.0	0

RECEIVING

Last Name	No.	Yds	Avg	TD
Owens	32	350	11	2
Sanders	31	502	16	5
L. Walton	30	491	16	5
Taylor	26	270	10	1
McCullouch	21	552	26	3
Cotton	6	88	15	0
Farr	5	60	12	1
Jessie	4	87	22	0
Hughes	1	32	32	0
Gipson	1	21	21	0

PUNT RETURNS

Last Name	No.	Yds	Avg	TD
Barney	14	122	9	0
L. Walton	6	38	6	0
Vaughn	2	30	15	0
Thompson	1	4	4	0

KICKOFF RETURNS

Last Name	No.	Yds	Avg	TD
Jessie	16	470	29	2
Barney	9	222	25	0
Clark	8	216	27	0
Williams	4	112	28	0
Gipson	5	105	21	0
Triplett	3	70	23	0
Parson	2	26	13	0
Mooney	2	8	4	0
Cotton	1	4	4	0
Rasmussen	1	0	0	0

PASSING – PUNTING – KICKING Statistics

PASSING

	Att	Comp	%	Yds	Yd/Att	TD	Int–	%	RK
Landry	261	136	52	2237	8.6	16	13–	5	2
Munson	38	21	55	216	5.7	1	1–	3	

PUNTING

	No	Avg
H. Weaver	42	41.7

KICKING

	XP	Att	%	FG	Att	%
Mann	37	37	100	22	37	60
Walker	2	2	100	0	0	0

CHICAGO BEARS

RUSHING

Last Name	No.	Yds	Avg	TD
Shy	116	420	3.6	2
Pinder	63	311	4.9	4
Douglass	39	284	7.3	3
Grabowski	51	149	2.9	0
Joe Moore	29	90	3.1	0
Tucker	32	82	2.6	0
Sayers	13	38	2.9	0
Buffone	1	19	19.0	0
Harrison	5	13	2.6	0
Nix	9	12	1.3	0
Farmer	1	11	11.0	0
Concannon	5	5	1.0	0
Wallace	1	0	0.0	0

RECEIVING

Last Name	No.	Yds	Avg	TD
Farmer	46	737	16	5
Gordon	43	610	14	5
Wallace	27	400	15	2
Shy	19	163	9	0
Grabowski	17	100	6	0
Tucker	11	65	6	0
Pinder	10	51	5	0
Seymour	5	75	15	0
Thomas	3	40	13	0
Joe Moore	2	22	11	0
Harrison	2	18	9	0
Turner	1	13	13	0

PUNT RETURNS

Last Name	No.	Yds	Avg	TD
Smith	26	194	7	0
Turner	9	63	7	0
Lyle	1	5	5	0

KICKOFF RETURNS

Last Name	No.	Yds	Avg	TD
Smith	26	671	26	0
Turner	31	639	21	0
Butkus	2	15	8	0

PASSING – PUNTING – KICKING Statistics

PASSING

	Att	Comp	%	Yds	Yd/Att	TD	Int–	%	RK
Douglass	225	91	40	1164	5.2	5	15–	7	16
Nix	137	51	37	760	5.6	6	10–	7	
Concannon	77	42	55	334	4.3	0	3–	4	
Green	2	1	50	13	6.5	0	0–	0	
Shy	1	1	100	23	23.0	1	0–	0	
Wallace	1	0	0	0	0.0	0	0–	0	

PUNTING

	No	Avg
Green	77	40.2

KICKING

	XP	Att	%	FG	Att	%
Percival	18	18	100	15	33	46
Butkus	1	1	100	0	0	0
Douglass	1	1	100	0	0	0

GREEN BAY PACKERS

RUSHING

Last Name	No.	Yds	Avg	TD
Brockington	216	1105	5.1	4
Anderson	186	757	4.1	5
Hampton	67	307	4.6	3
Hunter	21	50	2.4	4
Starr	3	11	3.7	1
P. Williams	3	4	1.3	0
Bratkowski	1	1	1.0	1
Krause	3	−6	−2.0	0

RECEIVING

Last Name	No.	Yds	Avg	TD
Dale	31	598	19	4
McGeorge	27	463	17	4
Anderson	26	306	12	1
Spilis	14	281	20	1
Brockington	14	98	7	1
Davis	6	59	10	0
Hampton	3	37	12	1

PUNT RETURNS

Last Name	No.	Yds	Avg	TD
Ellis	22	107	5	0
Davis	6	36	6	0
Wood	4	21	5	0
Pitts	5	13	3	0
Randolph	1	0	0	0

KICKOFF RETURNS

Last Name	No.	Yds	Avg	TD
Hampton	46	1314	29	1
Krause	5	101	20	0
Pitts	2	41	21	0
P. Williams	2	41	21	0
Davis	1	22	22	0
Ellis	1	22	22	0
Carter	1	5	5	0

PASSING – PUNTING – KICKING Statistics

PASSING

	Att	Comp	%	Yds	Yd/Att	TD	Int–	%	RK
Hunter	163	75	46	1210	7.4	7	17–	10	11
Starr	45	24	53	286	6.4	0	3–	7	
Bratkowski	37	19	51	298	8.1	4	3–	8	
Patrick	5	1	20	39	7.8	0	1–	20	
Anderson	4	2	50	9	2.3	1	0–	0	

PUNTING

	No	Avg
Anderson	50	40.4
Duncan	6	36.0

KICKING

	XP	Att	%	FG	Att	%
Michaels	19	20	95	8	14	57
Webster	8	8	100	6	11	55
Conway	5	5	100	0	1	0

SAN FRANCISCO FORTY NINERS 9-5-0 Dick Nolan

Scores of Each Game			Use Name	Pos.	Hgt	Wgt	Age	Int	Pts
17	Atlanta	20	Cas Banaszek	OT	6'3"	250	25		
38	New Orleans	20	Len Rohde	OT	6'4"	250	33		
31	Philadelphia	3	John Watson	OT	6'4"	248	22		
13	LOS ANGELES	20	Randy Beisler	OG	6'4"	255	26		
13	CHICAGO	0	Elmer Collett	OG	6'4"	240	26		
26	St. Louis	14	Bob Hoskins	OG	6'2"	235	25		
27	NEW ENGLAND	10	Woody Peoples	OG	6'2"	247	28		
13	Minnesota	9	Forrest Blue	C	6'5"	260	25		6
20	NEW ORLEANS	26	Bill Belk	DE	6'3"	258	25		
6	Los Angeles	17	Cedrick Hardman	DE	6'3"	255	22		
24	N.Y. Jets	21	Tommy Hart	DE	6'3"	257	26		6
17	KANSAS CITY	26	Earl Edwards	DT	6'6"	272	25		
24	ATLANTA	3	Charlie Krueger	DT	6'4"	260	35		
31	DETROIT	27	Stan Hindman	DE-DT	6'3"	235	27		

Use Name	Pos.	Hgt	Wgt	Age	Int	Pts
Ed Beard	LB	6'2"	220	31		
Frank Nunley	LB	6'2"	232	25	1	
Jim Sniadecki	LB	6'2"	220	24		
Skip Vanderbundt	LB	6'3"	230	24	1	
Dave Wilcox	LB	6'3"	235	28		
Johnny Fuller	DB	6'	185	25	2	
Tony Harris	DB	6'2"	190	22		
Jim Johnson	DB	6'2"	185	33	3	
Mel Phillips	DB	6'	196	29		
Mike Simpson	DB	5'11"	175	24	1	
Bruce Taylor	DB	6'	180	23	3	6
Rosey Taylor	DB	5'11"	186	32	3	

Use Name	Pos.	Hgt	Wgt	Age	Int	Pts
John Brodie	QB	6'1"	203	36		18
Steve Spurrier	QB	6'2"	200	26		
Doug Cunningham	HB	5'11"	192	25		6
John Isenbarger	HB	6'3"	205	23		
Vic Washington	HB	5'10"	196	25		42
Ken Willard	FB	6'2"	225	28		30
Larry Schreiber	HB-FB	6'	200	24		7
Preston Riley	WR	6'	180	23		
Gene Washington	WR	6'1"	185	24		24
Dick Witcher	WR	6'3"	204	26		18
Jimmy Thomas	HB-WR	6'1"	214	24		6
Ted Kwalick	TE	6'4"	220	24		30
Bob Windsor	TE	6'4"	230	28		
Bruce Gossett	K	6'2"	235	28		101
Jim McCann	K	6'2"	170	22		

LOS ANGELES RAMS 8-5-1 Tommy Prothro

Scores of Each Game			Use Name	Pos.	Hgt	Wgt	Age	Int	Pts
20	New Orleans	24	Rich Buzin	OT	6'4"	250	25		
20	ATLANTA	20	Joe Carollo	OT	6'2"	265	31		
17	CHICAGO	3	Charley Cowan	OT	6'4"	265	33		
20	San Francisco	13	Harry Schuh	OT	6'2"	260	28		
24	Atlanta	16	Mike LaHood	OG	6'3"	250	26		
30	GREEN BAY	13	Tom Mack	OG	6'3"	250	27		
14	MIAMI	20	Joe Scibelli	OG	6'1"	255	32		
17	Baltimore	24	Ken Iman	C	6'1"	240	32		
21	Detroit	13	Rich Saul	OG-C	6'3"	235	23		
17	SAN FRANSICCO	6	Deacon Jones	DE	6'5"	250	32		
21	Dallas	28	Jack Youngblood	DE	6'4"	248	21		
45	NEW ORLEANS	28	Coy Bacon	DT-DE	6'4"	270	29	1	
24	WASHINGTON	38	Bill Nelson	DT	6'7"	270	23		
23	Pittsburgh	14	Merlin Olsen	DT	6'5"	270	30		
			Phil Olsen	DT	6'5"	265	23		
			Greg Wojcik	DT	6'6"	268	25		

Use Name	Pos.	Hgt	Wgt	Age	Int	Pts
Ken Geddes	LB	6'3"	235	23		
Dean Halverson	LB	6'2"	212	25		
Marlin McKeever	LB	6'1"	235	31	4	
Don Parish (from STL)	LB	6'1"	220	23		
John Pergine	LB	6'1"	225	24		
Jim Purnell	LB	6'2"	238	29	2	
Jack Reynolds	LB	6'1"	232	23		
Isiah Robertson	LB	6'3"	225	22	4	
Kermit Alexander	DB	5'11"	186	30	3	6
Dave Elmendorf	DB	6'1"	195	22	2	
Alvin Haymond	DB	6'	194	29		
Gene Howard	DB	6'	190	24	6	6
Jim Nettles	DB	5'9"	177	29	5	6
Clancy Williams	DB	6'2"	194	28		
Jim Wilson — Injury						
Jim Ferguson — Injury						

Use Name	Pos.	Hgt	Wgt	Age	Int	Pts
Roman Gabriel	QB	6'4"	220	31		12
Jerry Rhome	QB	6'	188	29		
Willie Ellison	HB	6'1"	200	26		24
Larry Smith	HB	6'3"	220	23		30
Bob Thomas	HB	5'10"	200	22		
Travis Williams	HB	6'1"	210	25		6
Les Josephson	FB	6'	207	28		30
Lee White	FB	6'4"	235	25		
Matt Maslowski	WR	6'3"	210	21		6
David Ray	WR	6'	195	26		91
Lance Rentzel	WR	6'2"	202	27		36
Jack Snow	WR	6'2"	190	28		24
Pat Studstill	WR	6'1"	175	33		
Roger Williams	WR	5'10"	180	25		
Pat Curran	TE	6'3"	238	25		6
Bob Klein	TE	6'5"	235	24		

ATLANTA FALCONS 7-6-1 Norm Van Brocklin

Scores of Each Game			Use Name	Pos.	Hgt	Wgt	Age	Int	Pts
20	SAN FRANCISCO	17	George Kunz	OT	6'5"	256	24		
20	Los Angeles	20	Bill Sandeman	OT	6'6"	256	28		
38	Detroit	41	Mal Snider	OT	6'4"	252	24		
9	ST. LOUIS	26	Dick Enderle	OG	6'1"	248	23		
16	LOS ANGELES	24	Andy Mauer	OG	6'3"	257	22		
28	NEW ORLEANS	6	Jim Miller	OG	6'3"	240	22		
31	Cleveland	14	John Matlock	C	6'4"	250	26		
9	Cincinnati	6	Jeff Van Note	C	6'2"	244	25		
17	N.Y. GIANTS	21	Claude Humphrey	DE	6'5"	248	27		
28	GREEN BAY	21	Mike Lewis	DE	6'3"	223	22		
7	Minnesota	24	Randy Marshall	DE	6'3"	237	24		
24	OAKLAND	13	John Zook	DE	6'5"	248	23	2	
3	San Francisco	24	Glen Condren	DT	6'2"	250	29		
24	New Orleans	20	Greg Lens	DT	6'5"	260	26		
			John Small	LB-DT	6'5"	254	24		

Use Name	Pos.	Hgt	Wgt	Age	Int	Pts
Ron Acks	LB	6'2"	220	26	1	
Grady Allen	LB	6'3"	230	25		
John Bramlett	LB	6'2"	220	30		
Greg Brezina	LB	6'2"	226	25	3	
Don Hansen	LB	6'3"	220	27	3	6
Rudy Kuechenberg	LB	6'2"	215	28		
Tommy Nobis	LB	6'2"	237	27		
Cleo Walker	LB	6'3"	220	23		
Ray Brown	DB	6'2"	198	22	3	
Tom Hayes	DB	6'1"	193	25	3	18
John Mallory	DB	6'	184	25		6
Tom McCauley	DB	6'3"	193	24	1	
Tony Plummer	DB	5'11"	190	24		
Ken Reaves	DB	6'3"	203	26	6	
Rudy Redmond	DB	6'	190	24		
Larry Shears	DB	5'10"	185	22		

Use Name	Pos.	Hgt	Wgt	Age	Int	Pts
Bob Berry	QB	5'11"	190	29		
Leo Hart	QB	6'4"	203	22		
Dick Shiner	QB	6'	195	29		6
Willie Belton	HB	5'11"	196	22		6
Cannonball Butler	HB	5'10"	200	28		24
Sonny Campbell	HB	5'11"	192	23		
Joe Profit	HB	6'	204	22		6
Art Malone	FB	5'11"	209	23		48
Harmon Wages	FB	6'1"	222	25		
Ken Burrow	WR	6'	190	23		36
Wes Chesson	WR	6'2"	190	22		
Ray Jarvis	WR	5'11"	193	22		
Todd Snyder	WR	6'2"	184	22		
Mike Donohoe	TE	6'3"	228	26		
Jim Mitchell	TE	6'2"	225	23		36
Ray Poage	TE	6'4"	215	30		
Bill Bell	K	6'1"	190	23		68
Billy Lothridge	K	6'1"	200	27		

NEW ORLEANS SAINTS 4-8-2 J. D. Roberts

Scores of Each Game			Use Name	Pos.	Hgt	Wgt	Age	Int	Pts
24	LOS ANGELES	20	Glen Ray Hines	OT	6'5"	265	27		
20	SAN FRANCISCO	38	Sam Holden	OT	6'3"	258	24		
13	Houston	13	Don Morrison	OT	6'5"	255	21		
14	Chicago	35	Jake Kupp	OG	6'3"	248	29		
24	DALLAS	14	John Shinners	OG	6'2"	254	24		
6	Atlanta	28	Remi Pudhomme	C-OG	6'4"	250	29		
14	Washington	24	John Didion	C	6'4"	245	23		
21	OAKLAND	21	Del Williams	OG	6'2"	240	25		
26	San Francisco	20	Larry Estes	DE	6'6"	260	24		
10	MINNESOTA	23	Richard Neal	DE	6'3"	254	23		
29	Green Bay	21	Joe Owens	DE	6'2"	235	24		
28	Los Angeles	45	Mike Walker	DE	6'4"	235	21		
17	CLEVELAND	21	Dan Goich	DT	6'4"	267	25		
20	ATLANTA	24	Dave Long	DT	6'4"	245	26		
			Bob Pollard	DT	6'3"	245	22		
			Doug Mooers	DE-DT	6'6"	265	24		

Use Name	Pos.	Hgt	Wgt	Age	Int	Pts
Dick Absher	LB	6'4"	235	27	1	
Wayne Colman	LB	6'1"	230	25	1	
Carl Cunningham	LB	6'3"	240	27		
Jim Flanigan	LB	6'3"	240	26	1	
Ray Hester	LB	6'2"	215	22		
Tom Roussel	LB	6'3"	235	26		
Richard Harvey	DB	6'2"	190	25		
Hugo Hollas	DB	6'1"	190	26	5	
Delles Howell	DB	6'3"	195	24	5	
Bivian Lee	DB	6'3"	200	23		
Dee Martin	DB	6'1"	190	22	3	
Reynaud Moore	DB	6'2"	190	21		
Doug Wyatt	DB	6'1"	195	24	4	6
Leo Carroll — Injury						
John Huard — Injury						
Mike Morgan — Injury						
Joe Scarpati — Injury						

Use Name	Pos.	Hgt	Wgt	Age	Int	Pts
Edd Hargett	QB	5'11"	185	24		6
Archie Manning	QB	6'3"	204	22		24
Bob Gresham	HB	5'11"	193	23		36
Billy Harris	HB	6'	204	25		
Virgil Robinson	HB	5'11"	195	23		12
James Ford	FB-HB	6'	205	21		12
Hoyle Granger	FB	6'1"	225	27		6
Dave Kopay	HB-FB	6'2"	218	29		
Jim Strong	HB-FB	6'1"	204	24		18
Dan Abramowicz	WR	6'1"	195	26		30
Al Dodd	WR	6'	185	26		
Bob Newland	WR	6'2"	190	22		
Carlos Bell	TE	6'5"	238	22		
Don Burchfield	TE	6'2"	227	22		
Dave Parks	TE	6'2"	203	29		30
Skip Butler (to NYG)	K	6'2"	200	23		8
Charlie Durkee	K	5'11"	165	27		72
Julian Fagan	K	6'3"	205	23		

SAN FRANCISCO FORTY NINERS

RUSHING

Last Name	No.	Yds	Avg	TD
Willard	216	855	4.0	4
V. Washington	191	811	4.2	3
Schreiber	34	180	5.3	0
Cunningham	25	98	3.9	1
Kwalick	6	62	10.3	0
Brodie	14	45	3.2	3
Thomas	3	36	12.0	1
Isenbarger	5	34	6.8	0
Windsor	1	21	21.0	0
Spurrier	1	2	2.0	0
McCann	2	−15	−7.5	0

RECEIVING

Last Name	No.	Yds	Avg	TD
Kwalick	52	664	13	5
G. Wash'gton	46	884	19	4
V. Wash'gton	36	317	9	4
Willard	27	202	7	1
Cunningham	19	188	10	0
Witcher	18	250	14	3
Schreiber	3	79	26	1
Riley	3	39	13	0
Thomas	3	33	11	0
Windsor	2	32	16	0

PUNT RETURNS

Last Name	No.	Yds	Avg	TD
B. Taylor	34	235	7	0
Fuller	3	31	10	0
Riley	1	2	2	0
Vanderbundt	1	0	0	0

KICKOFF RETURNS

Last Name	No.	Yds	Avg	TD
V. Wash'gton	33	858	26	0
Cunningham	6	121	20	0
Windsor	4	66	17	0
Beard	1	21	21	0
Kwalick	2	9	5	0

PASSING – PUNTING – KICKING Statistics

PASSING

Last Name	Att	Comp	%	Yds	Yd/Att	TD	Int−	%	RK
Brodie	387	208	54	2642	6.8	18	24−	6	6
Spurrier	4	1	25	46	11.5	0	0−	0	

PUNTING

Last Name	No	Avg
McCann	49	38.7
Spurrier	2	38.5

KICKING

Last Name	XP	Att	%	FG	Att	%
Gossett	32	32	100	23	36	64
Schreiber	1	1	100	0	0	0

LOS ANGELES RAMS

RUSHING

Last Name	No.	Yds	Avg	TD
Ellison	211	1000	4.7	4
Josephson	99	449	4.5	3
Smith	91	404	4.4	0
Rentzel	14	113	8.1	1
T. Williams	18	103	5.7	0
Gabriel	18	48	2.7	2
Klein	3	21	7.0	0
White	2	11	5.5	0
Rhome	3	0	0.0	0
Snow	1	−10	−10.0	0

RECEIVING

Last Name	No.	Yds	Avg	TD
Rentzel	38	534	14	5
Snow	37	666	18	5
Ellison	32	238	7	0
Smith	31	324	10	0
Josephson	26	230	9	2
Klein	14	160	11	4
Maslowski	3	82	27	1
T. Williams	3	68	23	0
Curran	1	2	2	1

PUNT RETURNS

Last Name	No.	Yds	Avg	TD
Haymond	24	123	5	0
Rentzel	9	40	4	0
Alexander	1	5	5	0
T. Williams	1	4	4	0

KICKOFF RETURNS

Last Name	No.	Yds	Avg	TD
T. Williams	25	743	30	1
Haymond	9	207	23	0
Howard	7	164	23	0
R. Williams	4	100	25	0
Youngblood	2	36	18	0
Curran	3	35	12	0
LaHood	1	25	25	0
Thomas	1	12	12	0
Josephson	1	0	0	0
Saul	1	0	0	0

PASSING – PUNTING – KICKING

PASSING

Last Name	Att	Comp	%	Yds	Yd/Att	TD	Int−	%	RK
Gabriel	352	180	51	2238	6.4	17	10−	3	5
Rhome	18	5	28	66	5.6	1	1−	6	

PUNTING

Last Name	No	Avg
Studstill	70	41.4

KICKING

Last Name	XP	Att	%	FG	Att	%
Ray	37	37	100	18	29	62

ATLANTA FALCONS

RUSHING

Last Name	No.	Yds	Avg	TD
Butler	186	594	3.2	2
Malone	120	438	3.7	6
Wages	64	266	4.2	1
Belton	56	237	4.2	1
Campbell	29	79	2.7	0
Berry	19	31	1.6	0
Mitchell	4	25	6.3	0
Jarvis	1	13	13.0	0
Profit	3	10	3.3	1
Shiner	10	9	0.9	1
Burrow	1	5	5.0	0
Chesson	1	−4	−4.0	0

RECEIVING

Last Name	No.	Yds	Avg	TD
Malone	34	380	11	2
Burrow	33	741	22	6
Mitchell	33	593	18	5
Chesson	20	224	11	0
Wages	19	249	13	1
Butler	15	143	10	2
Poage	4	71	18	0
Campbell	3	40	13	0
Belton	3	22	7	0
Mallory	1	27	27	0
Brezina	1	3	3	0
Kunz	1	2	2	0

PUNT RETURNS

Last Name	No.	Yds	Avg	TD
Belton	30	163	5	0
McCauley	1	8	8	0
Mallory	5	3	1	0
Brown	1	0	0	0

KICKOFF RETURNS

Last Name	No.	Yds	Avg	TD
Belton	28	706	25	0
Butler	13	372	29	0
Profit	10	247	25	0
Campbell	4	95	24	0
Wages	1	21	21	0
Enderle	1	20	20	0
Small	1	12	12	0
Matlock	1	4	4	0

PASSING – PUNTING – KICKING

PASSING

Last Name	Att	Comp	%	Yds	Yd/Att	TD	Int−	%	RK
Berry	226	136	60	2005	8.9	11	16−	7	4
Shiner	57	30	53	463	8.1	5	5−	9	
Hart	1	0	0	0	0.0	0	0−	0	
Lothridge	1	1	100	27	27.0	0	0−	0	

PUNTING

Last Name	No	Avg
Lothridge	44	37.3
Bell	16	36.1

KICKING

Last Name	XP	Att	%	FG	Att	%
Bell	29	33	88	13	21	62

NEW ORLEANS SAINTS

RUSHING

Last Name	No.	Yds	Avg	TD
Strong	95	404	4.3	3
Gresham	127	383	3.0	6
Ford	93	379	4.1	2
Manning	33	172	5.2	4
Granger	32	139	4.3	1
Robinson	29	96	3.3	1
Hargett	9	24	2.7	1
Dodd	1	7	7.0	0
Harris	1	1	1.0	0
Parks	2	−2	−1.0	0
Fagan	1	−17	−17.0	0

RECEIVING

Last Name	No.	Yds	Avg	TD
Abramowicz	37	657	18	5
Parks	35	568	16	5
Newland	21	319	15	0
Gresham	17	203	12	0
Strong	16	78	5	0
Dodd	15	298	20	0
Robinson	12	53	4	1
Granger	12	52	4	0
Ford	7	54	8	0
Burchfield	3	36	12	0
Manning	1	−7	−7	0

PUNT RETURNS

Last Name	No.	Yds	Avg	TD
Dodd	13	88	7	0
Moore	2	12	6	0
Abramowicz	1	0	0	0

KICKOFF RETURNS

Last Name	No.	Yds	Avg	TD
Robinson	19	443	23	0
Dodd	12	252	21	0
Moore	11	246	22	0
Strong	9	134	15	0
Gresham	3	60	20	0
Burchfield	1	5	5	0
Absher	1	3	3	0

PASSING – PUNTING – KICKING

PASSING

Last Name	Att	Comp	%	Yds	Yd/Att	TD	Int−	%	RK
Hargett	210	96	46	1191	5.7	6	5−	2	10
Manning	177	86	49	1164	6.6	6	9−	5	11

PUNTING

Last Name	No	Avg
Fagan	77	41.4

KICKING

Last Name	XP	Att	%	FG	Att	%
Durkee	24	25	96	16	23	70
Butler	5	6	83	1	5	20

1971 A.F.C. Aerial Oneupmanship

The old American Football League had never had an abundant supply of good quarterbacks, but the AFC now held the edge in that department over the NFC. The AFC had good veterans like Johnny Unitas and Len Dawson, men in their peak years like Joe Namath, John Hadl, Bob Griese, and Daryle Lamonica, and promising young passers like Jim Plunkett, Terry Bradshaw, Mike Phipps, and Dan Pastorini. After five years of the common draft, the AFC had picked the quarterback plums from the college crop, while the only exciting young passers in the NFC were Roger Staubach, Greg Landry, and Archie Manning.

EASTERN DIVISION

Miami Dolphins— Although the Miami defense played surprisingly strong, the pride of the Dolphins was their versatile offense. Enemy defenses had to contend with an unheralded but solid line, a great deep receiver in Paul Warfield, a good short receiver in Howard Twilley, two relentless runners in Larry Csonka and Jim Kiick, a breakaway runner in Mercury Morris, and an enormously resourceful quarterback in young Bob Griese. Whenever the attack stalled, place kicker Garo Yepremian was deadly within the 50-yard line. With all this offensive firepower, the Dolphins raced evenly with the Colts through most of the season. Although assured of at least a wild-card berth in the playoffs, the Dolphins seemed to have conceded first place by losing to Baltimore on the next to last weekend, but a victory over Green Bay, plus the Colts' upset loss to New England, let the Dolphins slip into first place on the final day of the season.

Baltimore Colts— The Colts won the wild-card playoff spot on the strength of the conference's best defense and a strong offense. The defense had some problems at one cornerback slot, but the presence of stars Bubba Smith, Ted Hendricks, Mike Curtis, Ray May, Charlie Stukes, Rick Volk, and Jerry Logan glossed over any shortcomings in the other positions. The offense went with Earl Morrall at quarterback for the first half of the schedule, but Johnny Unitas recovered from an off-season Achilles tendon injury to reclaim the starting spot down the stretch. Although his arm was not what it once had been, Unitas still had enough guile to maneuver his way through the best defenses in the league.

New England Patriots— The Patriots had a brand-new name, a brand-new stadium in Foxboro, Massachusetts, to play in, and a talented new quarterback in rookie Jim Plunkett. In his professional debut, Plunkett threw two touchdown passes in leading the Patriots to a 20-6 upset victory over the Oakland Raiders, and the big rookie continued to impress friend and foe alike all season with his arm and poise. To catch Plunkett's passes, the Patriots signed little Randy Vataha, Plunkett's college teammate who had been cut by the Rams early in training camp. Other newcomers who made a good impression were rookie defensive tackle Julius Adams and ex-Dallas linebacker Steve Kiner.

New York Jets— The Jets again went through the season with many of their regulars missing from action. Injuries sidelined Joe Namath, Matt Snell, Gerry Philbin, and John Elliott for long stretches of time, George Sauer and Steve Thompson both quit football at their physical prime for other interests, and Verlon Biggs played out his option and signed with the Washington Redskins. Injuries so decimated the defensive line that coach Weeb Ewbank at one point talked Clovis Swinney out of his job selling cars to help the Jets out.

Buffalo Bills— For the second time in the last four years, scout Harvey Johnson stepped in as interim head coach under dismal conditions. This year, Johnny Rauch resigned before the season began, leaving Johnson to guide the dispirited Bills through a horrendous 1-13-0 campaign. Major problems during the year were injuries in the offensive line, where Johnson was forced to start five rookies and a second-year man, quarterback Dennis Shaw's serious regression from his good rookie showing, and a disorganized defense.

CENTRAL DIVISION

Cleveland Browns— With Mike Phipps still not ready to take over as starting quarterback, Bill Nelsen took his aching knees into battle once more and took the Browns to the championship of the NFL's weakest division. The road to first place was a rocky one, with the Browns losing four straight mid-season games before going on a five-game winning streak. On paper, the Browns looked like a team evenly balanced between strengths and weaknesses. Leroy Kelly, Bo Scott, Milt Morin, Clarence Scott, Jack Gregory, and Walter Johnson fit comfortably into the asset column, but under the deficit heading were listed disorganization in the linebacking and secondary, advanced age in several offensive linemen, and the lack of a clutch wide receiver.

Pittsburgh Steelers— Dave Smith won a place on the roster of famous bloopers with his bonehead play of October 18. Sprinting to the end zone with a pass, Smith mistook the 5-yard line for the goal line and slammed the ball down on the ground, thinking that he had scored a touchdown. The referee noticed full well that Smith had never carried the ball across the goal line, and when the ball rolled through the end zone, he ruled it a touchback, gave the ball to Kansas City, and erased six points that Smith and the Steelers were already counting. But aside from that play, Smith enjoyed a fine season, as did fellow wide receiver Ron Shanklin and quarterback Terry Bradshaw.

Houston Oilers— Owner Bud Adams hired Ed Hughes, a man highly respected around the league, as his new head coach, but Adams quickly lost confidence in the coach and put him on the spot by firing one of his assistants in mid-season with no notice. The players rallied around Hughes late in the year and won their final three games after a very slow start. One of Hughes' moves during the season was to bench quarterback Charley Johnson and try rookies Lynn Dickey and Dan Pastorini at the position. Pastorini finally nailed down the starting job, showing good potential despite taking a steady pounding from defenders who sliced right through the porous Houston front wall.

Cincinnati Bengals— The Bengals slumped back into last place in the Central Division. Six of those losses, however, were by four points or less, so the Bengals were not nearly as lame as their record indicated. The Cincinnati attack again relied heavily on the run, with rookie Fred Willis and Essex Johnson taking over from Jess Phillips and Paul Robinson as the heavy-duty ball carriers. The need for a strong ground game was underlined by the weakened situation at quarterback. Greg Cook, the rookie marvel of 1970, still was out of action with a bad shoulder, and Virgil Carter missed several games with injuries.

WESTERN DIVISION

Kansas City Chiefs— The Chiefs opened up their offense and won first place in the Western Division. Morris Stroud and rookie Elmo Wright developed into good receivers, giving Len Dawson two new targets to throw at and also taking some of the defense's attention away from Otis Taylor. No longer the only receiving threat on the team, Taylor enjoyed his best year as a pro, leading the NFL in yards gained on receptions. Ed Podolak spearheaded the running game and also contributed in the receiving and kick-returning departments. On defense, Jerry Mays' retirement weakened the front four, but the linebacking trio of Bobby Bell, Willie Lanier, and Jim Lynch plus the talented secondary kept the unit in fine condition.

Oakland Raiders— The Raiders finished out of first place for the first time in five years, but they still compiled a winning record despite several sizable difficulties. First of all, Warren Wells, who was Daryle Lamonica's favorite deep receiver, ran afoul of the law and had to sit the season out. Then Hewitt Dixon and Charlie Smith, both starting running backs, went out of action with injuries, and the advancing years of Tom Keating's and Ben Davidson's started cutting down in Tom Keating's and Ben Davidson's effectiveness in the defensive line. To remedy all these problems, Madden inserted rookie receiver Mike Siani into the lineup to team up with Fred Biletnikoff on the flanks, he promoted subs Marv Hubbard and Pete Banaszak to starters with fine results, and he rejuvenated the defense by giving lots of playing time to youngsters Tony Cline, Art Thoms, Harold Rice, Horace Jones, and Phil Villapiano.

San Diego Chargers— The San Diego management had a new look at the start of the season as Sid Gillman decided to resume his coaching duties and Harland Svare came in as general manager. By mid-season, however, Gillman got into a disagreement with owner Eugene Klein and found himself out of work. Svare, meanwhile, found himself back on the field as head coach for the final four games. As usual, the San Diego defense leaked profusely, while the offense cranked out points at a rapid clip. The trade of Lance Alworth to Dallas gave the attack a new look, with rookie Billy Parks filling in with great results until he broke his arm late in the year.

Denver Broncos— Floyd Little's strong running cheered Lou Saban somewhat, but assorted other troubles made the coach's final half season a vexing one. Injuries erased starters Rich Jackson, Pete Duranko, Larry Kaminski, and Sam Brunelli and exposed the thinness of the Denver bench. None of the wide receivers on the team took up the slack left by the trade of Al Denson to Minnesota, and the quarterback situation was a highly unhealthy one. After several injury-filled seasons, quarterback Steve Tensi packed it all in, leaving ex-Packer Don Horn at the starting quarterback. After a lackluster first half, Horn went out with an injury, leaving only inexperienced Steve Ramsey as a passer. Nine games were enough for Saban this year, and assistant Jerry Smith took over as head man for the final five games.

FINAL TEAM STATISTICS

OFFENSE

	BALT.	BUFF.	CIN.	CLEV.	DENV.	HOUS.	K.C.	MIAMI	N.ENG.	N.Y.J.	OAK.	PITT.	S.D.
FIRST DOWNS:													
Total	242	185	236	231	217	201	240	232	190	202	258	226	**264**
by Rushing	123	68	109	89	102	62	108	121	85	115	**128**	98	86
by Passing	104	96	115	127	105	117	119	94	94	67	110	111	**147**
by Penalty	15	21	12	15	10	22	13	17	11	20	20	17	**31**
RUSHING:													
Number	**512**	320	462	461	**512**	361	487	486	419	485	473	416	390
Yards	2149	1337	2142	1558	2093	1106	1843	**2429**	1669	1888	2130	1758	1604
Average Yards	4.2	4.2	4.6	3.4	4.1	3.1	3.8	**5.0**	4.0	3.9	4.5	4.2	4.1
Touchdowns	**23**	6	14	19	9	10	14	11	7	12	19	10	11
PASSING:													
Attempts	344	401	365	376	358	423	337	293	330	278	348	414	**450**
Completions	176	202	214	188	175	194	183	156	159	119	174	214	**244**
Completion Percentage	51.2	50.4	**58.6**	50.0	48.9	45.9	54.3	53.2	48.2	42.8	50.0	51.7	54.2
Passing Yards	2152	2410	2427	2521	2243	2643	2694	2248	2206	1556	2363	2446	**3305**
Avg. Yards per Attempt	6.3	6.0	6.6	6.7	6.3	6.2	**8.0**	7.7	6.7	5.6	6.8	5.9	7.3
Avg. Yards per Complet.	12.2	11.9	11.3	13.4	12.8	13.6	**14.7**	14.4	13.9	13.1	13.6	11.4	13.5
Times Tackled Passing	27	49	40	22	22	31	35	25	36	23	24	37	**19**
Yards Lost Tackled	230	421	303	222	178	234	347	265	319	177	235	322	**171**
Net Yards	1922	1989	2124	2299	2065	2409	2347	1983	1887	1379	2128	2124	**3134**
Touchdowns	10	12	15	14	8	12	15	20	19	15	21	15	**23**
Interceptions	21	32	11	27	27	37	13	**10**	16	16	26	26	28
Percent Intercepted	6.1	8.0	**3.0**	7.2	7.5	8.7	3.9	3.4	4.8	5.8	7.5	6.3	6.2
PUNTS:													
Number	62	75	73	67	76	75	64	52	**87**	78	62	79	55
Average Distance	41.0	40.9	44.7	39.9	41.8	40.6	**44.8**	40.1	37.3	38.8	39.9	43.7	43.5
PUNT RETURNS:													
Number	43	**44**	25	40	41	32	33	41	31	25	29	35	37
Yards	351	343	145	359	320	198	150	**432**	181	155	182	264	215
Average Yards	8.2	7.8	5.8	9.0	7.8	6.2	4.5	**10.5**	5.8	6.2	6.3	7.5	5.8
Touchdowns	0	**2**	0	0	0	0	0	0	0	0	0	1	0
KICKOFF RETURNS:													
Number	32	**74**	43	46	44	59	47	32	64	55	54	49	49
Yards	679	**1673**	863	1065	960	1409	1031	806	1354	1168	1234	1120	1000
Average Yards	21.2	22.6	20.1	23.2	21.8	23.9	21.9	**25.2**	21.2	21.2	22.9	22.9	20.4
Touchdowns	0	0	0	0	0	0	0	**1**	0	0	0	0	0
INTERCEPTION RETURNS:													
Number	28	11	27	24	20	23	27	17	15	13	23	17	22
Yards	367	93	273	283	288	**456**	403	143	229	136	453	246	317
Average Yards	13.1	8.5	10.1	11.8	14.4	**19.8**	14.9	8.4	15.3	10.5	19.7	14.5	14.4
Touchdowns	1	0	2	0	1	**5**	3	0	2	0	2	1	2
PENALTIES:													
Number	57	74	82	68	67	**91**	72	65	67	70	81	88	81
Yards	529	691	**921**	612	781	856	734	632	657	672	869	898	895
FUMBLES:													
Number	26	33	29	29	25	24	23	**22**	26	30	26	37	30
Number Lost	11	16	12	18	12	14	13	13	16	**10**	13	16	15
POINTS:													
Total	313	184	284	285	203	251	302	315	238	212	**344**	246	311
PAT Attempts	36	21	32	34	18	29	32	33	29	27	**43**	28	37
PAT Made	35	20	32	34	18	26	32	33	28	26	**41**	27	36
FG Attempts	29	25	36	28	38	28	**45**	40	21	19	22	27	29
FG Made	20	12	20	15	25	17	26	**28**	12	8	15	17	17
Percent FG Made	69.0	48.0	55.6	53.6	65.8	60.7	57.8	**70.0**	57.1	42.1	68.2	63.0	58.6
Safeties	**1**	**1**	0	**1**	**1**	0	0	0	0	0	0	0	**1**

DEFENSE

	BALT.	BUFF.	CIN.	CLEV.	DENV.	HOUS.	K.C.	MIAMI	N.ENG.	N.Y.J.	OAK.	PITT.	S.D.
FIRST DOWNS:													
Total	**166**	250	213	232	206	237	223	214	237	235	242	225	272
by Rushing	**60**	135	93	115	90	117	73	93	106	118	100	81	143
by Passing	95	101	102	100	**91**	97	125	111	111	101	122	132	114
by Penalty	11	14	18	17	25	23	25	**10**	20	16	20	12	15
RUSHING:													
Number	**352**	562	446	484	426	489	367	403	481	472	480	440	493
Yards	**1113**	2496	1778	2227	1834	1723	1300	1661	1918	2302	1751	1482	2296
Average Yards	**3.2**	4.4	4.0	4.6	4.3	3.5	3.5	4.1	4.0	4.9	3.6	3.4	4.7
Touchdowns	**8**	21	11	14	11	22	9	10	14	18	14	13	25
PASSING:													
Attempts	361	**303**	335	339	356	354	418	363	350	342	359	408	347
Completions	185	157	157	156	**150**	180	209	206	170	163	184	235	193
Completion Percentage	51.2	51.8	46.9	46.0	**42.1**	50.8	50.0	56.7	48.6	47.7	51.3	57.6	55.6
Passing Yards	**2027**	2333	2382	2170	2420	2416	2703	2293	2403	2285	2609	3060	2439
Avg. Yards per Attempt	**5.6**	7.7	7.1	6.4	6.8	6.8	6.5	6.3	6.9	6.7	7.3	7.5	7.0
Avg. Yards per Complet.	**11.0**	14.9	15.2	13.9	16.1	13.4	12.9	11.1	14.1	14.0	14.2	13.0	12.6
Times Tackled Passing	33	30	30	25	**44**	37	28	34	25	27	32	33	19
Yards Lost Tackled	288	225	254	203	**435**	344	235	293	249	230	223	294	177
Net Yards	**1739**	2108	2128	1967	1985	2072	2468	2000	2154	2055	2386	2766	2262
Touchdowns	**9**	20	19	12	18	11	11	10	16	17	15	16	15
Interceptions	**28**	11	27	24	20	23	27	17	15	13	23	17	22
Percent Intercepted	7.8	3.6	**8.1**	7.1	5.6	6.5	6.5	4.7	4.3	3.8	6.4	4.2	6.3
PUNTS:													
Number	**88**	66	73	66	67	76	67	72	66	65	59	77	67
Average Distance	38.9	39.0	40.9	42.4	45.7	42.2	40.7	40.7	38.8	**38.1**	41.7	41.5	43.7
PUNT RETURNS:													
Number	40	40	41	26	45	39	40	26	36	41	26	45	**20**
Yards	267	446	304	227	468	304	286	106	279	359	168	319	**40**
Average Yards	6.7	11.2	7.4	8.7	10.4	7.8	7.2	4.1	7.8	8.8	6.5	7.1	**2.0**
Touchdowns	0	0	1	0	0	0	0	0	1	0	0	0	0
KICKOFF RETURNS:													
Number	62	42	39	55	43	41	47	59	49	**34**	55	45	55
Yards	1345	971	1024	1252	1059	**862**	1071	1180	1427	906	1155	1002	1245
Average Yards	21.7	23.1	26.3	22.8	24.6	20.8	22.8	**20.0**	29.1	26.6	21.0	22.3	22.6
Touchdowns	0	0	0	0	0	0	0	0	1	1	0	0	0
INTERCEPTION RETURNS:													
Number	21	32	11	27	27	37	13	**10**	16	16	26	26	28
Yards	220	418	219	453	432	505	167	166	**157**	279	267	350	339
Average Yards	10.5	13.1	19.9	16.8	16.0	13.6	12.8	16.6	**9.8**	17.4	10.3	13.5	12.1
Touchdowns	1	3	1	2	2	3	**0**	1	1	1	**0**	1	4
PENALTIES:													
Number	67	**89**	72	86	78	75	71	62	60	81	80	81	84
Yards	687	883	722	772	771	**916**	751	569	559	814	832	784	887
FUMBLES:													
Number	22	17	21	31	36	31	16	**38**	35	35	26	27	27
Number Lost	13	11	12	16	**20**	14	6	14	14	14	17	18	10
POINTS:													
Total	**140**	394	265	273	275	330	208	174	325	299	278	292	341
PAT Attempts	**18**	45	32	30	32	37	21	21	35	37	30	32	44
PAT Made	**17**	45	31	30	32	36	20	21	34	35	30	30	44
FG Attempts	**18**	38	22	31	35	35	32	21	36	25	34	35	24
FG Made	**5**	25	14	21	17	24	20	9	27	14	22	22	11
Percent FG Made	**27.8**	65.8	63.6	67.7	48.6	68.9	62.5	42.9	75.0	56.0	64.7	62.9	45.8
Safeties	**0**	2	**0**	**0**	**0**	**0**	1	**0**	**0**	**0**	1	2	**0**

CONFERENCE PLAYOFFS

December 25, at Kansas City
(Attendance 45,822)

SCORING

KANSAS CITY	**10**	**0**	**7**	**7**	**0**	**0–24**
MIAMI	**0**	**10**	**7**	**7**	**0**	**3–27**

First Quarter
- K.C. Stenerud, 24 yard field goal
- K.C. Podolak, 7 yard pass from Dawson
  PAT–Stenerud (kick)

Second Quarter
- Mia. Csonka, 1 yard rush
  PAT–Yepremian (kick)
- Mia. Yepremian, 14 yard field goal

Third Quarter
- K.C. Otis, 1 yard rush
  PAT–Stenerud (kick)
- Mia. Kiick, 1 yard rush
  PAT–Yepremian (kick)

Fourth Quarter
- K.C. Podolak, 3 yard rush
  PAT–Stenerud (kick)
- Mia. Fleming, 5 yard pass from Griese
  PAT–Yepremian (kick)

Second Overtime Period
- Mia. Yepremian, 37 yard field goal 7:40

TEAM STATISTICS

K.C.		MIAMI
23	First Downs–Total	22
13	First Downs–Rushing	6
10	First Downs–Passing	14
0	First Downs–Penalty	2
2	Fumbles–Number	0
2	Fumbles–Lost Ball	0
6	Penalties–Number	5
44	Yards Penalized	26
3	Missed Field Goals	1
71	Offensive Plays–Total	78
451	Net Yards	407
6.4	Average Gain	5.2
4	Giveaways	2
2	Takeaways	4
–2	Difference	+2

INDIVIDUAL STATISTICS

KANSAS CITY	No.	Yds.	Avg.	MIAMI	No.	Yds.	Avg.
RUSHING							
Hayes	22	100	4.5	Csonka	24	86	3.6
Podolak	17	85	5.0	Kiick	15	56	3.7
Wright	2	15	7.5	Griese	2	9	4.5
Otis	3	13	4.3	Warfield	2	–7	–3.5
	44	213	4.8		43	144	3.3
RECEIVING							
Podolak	8	110	13.8	Warfield	7	140	20.0
Wright	3	104	34.7	Twilley	5	58	11.6
Taylor	3	12	4.0	Fleming	4	37	9.3
Hayes	3	6	2.0	Kiick	3	24	8.0
Frazier	1	14	14.0	Mandich	1	4	4.0
	18	246	13.7		20	263	13.2
PUNTING							
Wilson	2		51.0	Seiple	6		40.0
PUNT RETURNS							
Podolak	2	1	0.5	Scott	1	18	18.0
KICKOFF RETURNS							
Podolak	3	154	52.0	Morris	2	61	30.5
INTERCEPTION RETURNS							
Lanier	1	17	17.0	Scott	1	13	13.0
Lynch	1	0	0.0	Johnson	1	0	0.0
	2	17	8.5		2	13	6.5

PASSING

KANSAS CITY	Att.	Comp.	Comp. Pct.	Yds.	Int.	Yds/ Att.	Yds/ Comp.	Yds Lost Tkld.
Dawson	26	18	69.2	246	2	9.5	13.7	1–8
Podolak	1	0	0.0	0	0	–	–	
	27	18	66.7	246	2	9.1	13.7	1–8
MIAMI								
Griese	35	20	57.1	263	2	7.5	13.2	0–0

December 26, at Cleveland
(Attendance 70,734)

SCORING

CLEVELAND	**0**	**0**	**3**	**0–**	**3**
BALTIMORE	**0**	**14**	**3**	**3–**	**20**

Second Quarter
- Balt. Nottingham, 1 yard rush
  PAT–O'Brien (kick)
- Balt. Nottingham, 7 yard rush
  PAT–O'Brien (kick)

Third Quarter
- Cle. Cockroft, 14 yard field goal
- Balt. O'Brien, 42 yard field goal

Fourth Quarter
- Balt. O'Brien, 15 yard field goal

TEAM STATISTICS

CLE.		BALT.
11	First Downs–Total	16
5	First Downs–Rushing	7
5	First Downs–Passing	8
1	First Downs–Penalty	1
6	Fumbles–Number	2
2	Fumbles–Lost Ball	2
3	Penalties–Number	5
16	Yards Penalized	43
2	Missed Field Goals	0
56	Offensive Plays–Total	64
165	Net Yards	271
2.9	Average Gain	4.2
5	Giveaways	3
3	Takeaways	5
–2	Difference	+2

INDIVIDUAL STATISTICS

CLEVELAND	No.	Yds.	Avg.	BALTIMORE	No.	Yds.	Avg.
RUSHING							
Kelly	14	49	3.5	Nottingham	23	92	4.0
Bo Scott	8	25	3.1	Matte	16	26	1.6
Nelsen	2	–5	–2.5	McCauley	3	9	3.0
	24	69	2.9	Nowatzke	1	1	1.0
					43	128	3.0
RECEIVING							
Bo Scott	5	41	8.2	Mitchell	5	73	14.6
Kelly	4	24	6.0	Matte	3	22	7.3
Hooker	1	39	39.0	Hinton	2	30	15.0
Morin	1	16	16.0	Perkins	1	10	10.0
Glass	1	11	11.0	Nottingham	1	5	5.0
	12	131	10.9	Havrilak	1	3	3.0
					13	143	11.0
PUNTING							
Cockroft	5		40.8	Lee	6		37.2
PUNT RETURNS							
Kelly	3	71	23.7	Volk	4	27	6.8
D. Jones	1	3	3.0				
	4	74	18.5				
KICKOFF RETURNS							
S. Brown	2	34	17.0	Pittman	1	25	25.0
Bo Scott	1	30	30.0				
Morrison	1	19	19.0				
Dieken	1	15	15.0				
	5	98	19.6				
INTERCEPTION RETURNS							
Snidow	1	1	1.0	Volk	2	56	28.0
C. Scott	Lat	22	–	Stukes	1	23	23.0
	1	23	23.0		3	89	29.7

PASSING

CLEVE.	Att.	Cmp.	Pct.	Yds.	Int.	Yd/A	Yd/C	Tkld
Nelsen	21	9	42.9	104	3	5.0	11.6	
Phipps	6	3	50.0	27	0	4.5	9.0	
	27	12	44.4	131	3	4.9	10.9	5–35
BALT.								
Unitas	21	13	61.9	143	1	6.8	11.0	0– 0

MIAMI DOLPHINS 10-3-1 Don Shula

Scores of Each Game		
10	Denver	10
29	Buffalo	14
10	N.Y. JETS	14
23	Cincinnati	13
41	NEW ENGLAND	3
30	N.Y. Jets	14
20	Los Angeles	14
34	BUFFALO	0
24	PITTSBURGH	21
17	BALTIMORE	14
34	CHICAGO	3
13	New England	34
3	Baltimore	14
27	GREEN BAY	6

Use Name	Pos.	Hgt	Wgt	Age	Int	Pts
Doug Crusan	OT	6'5"	250	25		
Norm Evans	OT	6'5"	252	28		
Wayne Mass	OT	6'4"	240	25		
Bob Kuechenberg	CG	6'3"	247	23		
Jim Langer	OG	6'2"	250	23		
Larry Little	OG	6'1"	265	25		
Bob DeMarco	C	6'3"	250	33		
Vern Den Herder	DE	6'6"	250	22		
Jim Riley	DE	6'4"	250	26		
Bill Stanfill	DE	6'5"	250	24		
Frank Cornish	DT	6'6"	285	27		
Manny Fernandez	DT	6'2"	248	25		
John Richardson	DT	6'2"	248	26		
Bob Heinz	DE-DT	6'6"	270	24		
Dick Palmer—Injury						

Use Name	Pos.	Hgt	Wgt	Age	Int	Pts
Nick Buoniconti	LB	5'11"	220	30	1	
Dale Farley	LB	6'3"	235	22		
Mike Kolen	LB	6'2"	220	23		
Bob Matheson	LB	6'4"	240	26		
Jesse Powell	LB	6'1"	215	24		
Doug Swift	LB	6'3"	228	22	1	
Dick Anderson	DB	6'2"	196	25	2	
Tim Foley	DB	6'	194	23	4	
Curtis Johnson	DB	6'2"	196	23	2	6
Ray Jones	DB	6'	187	23		
Lloyd Mumphord	DB	5'11"	180	24		
Bob Petrella	DB	6'	190	26		
Jake Scott	DB	6'	188	26	7	
Dean Brown—Injury						
Dick Daniels—Injury						
Stan Mitchell—Injury						

Use Name	Pos.	Hgt	Wgt	Age	Int	Pts
Bob Griese	QB	6'1"	190	26		
George Mira	QB	5'11"	192	29		
Hubert Ginn	HB	5'11"	188	24		
Jim Kiick	HB	5'11"	215	25		18
Mercury Morris	HB	5'10"	190	24		12
Terry Cole	FB	6'1"	220	26		
Larry Csonka	FB	6'3"	237	24		48
Charlie Leigh	FB	5'11"	205	25		
Karl Noonan	WR	6'3"	198	27		
Otto Stowe	WR	6'2"	188	22		6
Howard Twilley	WR	5'10"	185	27		24
Paul Warfield	WR	6'	185	28		66
Marv Fleming	TE	6'4"	235	29		12
Jim Mandich	TE	6'3"	224	23		6
Larry Seiple	TE	6'	215	26		
Garo Yepremian	K	5'8"	165	27		117

BALTIMORE COLTS 10-4-0 Don McCafferty

Scores of Each Game		
22	N.Y. JETS	0
13	CLEVELAND	14
23	New England	3
43	Buffalo	0
31	N.Y. Giants	7
3	Minnesota	10
34	PITTSBURGH	21
24	LOS ANGELES	17
14	N.Y. Jets	13
14	Miami	17
37	Oakland	14
24	BUFFALO	0
14	MIAMI	3
17	NEW ENGLAND	21

Use Name	Pos.	Hgt	Wgt	Age	Int	Pts
Lynn Larson	OT	6'4"	254	23		
Dennis Nelson	OT	6'5"	260	25		
Bob Vogel	OT	6'5"	250	29		
Cornelius Johnson	OG	6'2"	245	28		
Glenn Ressler	OG	6'3"	250	27		
Dan Sullivan	OG	6'3"	250	32		
John Williams	OG	6'3"	256	25		
Bill Curry	C	6'2"	236	28		
Ken Mendenhall	C	6'3"	235	23		
Roy Hilton	DE	6'6"	240	26		
Billy Newsome	DE	6'4"	240	23	2	6
Bubba Smith	DE	6'7"	295	26		
Jim Bailey	DT	6'4"	245	23		
Rusty Ganas	DT	6'4"	257	21		
Fred Miller	DT	6'3"	250	30		
George Wright	DT	6'3"	260	24		

Use Name	Pos.	Hgt	Wgt	Age	Int	Pts
Tom Beutler	LB	6'1"	232	24		
Mike Curtis	LB	6'2"	232	28	3	
Ted Hendricks	LB	6'7"	215	23	5	6
Bill Laskey	LB	6'2"	235	28		
Ray May	LB	6'1"	230	26	1	
Robbie Nichols	LB	6'3"	220	24		
Tom Nowatzke	FB-LB	6'3"	230	28	1	
Tom Curtis	DB	6'1"	196	23		
Jim Duncan	DB	6'2"	200	25		
Lenny Dunlap	DB	6'1"	195	22		
Lonnie Hepburn	DB	5'11"	185	22		
Rex Kern	DB	5'11"	190	22		
Jerry Logan	DB	6'1"	190	30	4	
Charlie Stukes	DB	6'3"	212	27	8	
Rick Volk	DB	6'3"	195	26	4	

Use Name	Pos.	Hgt	Wgt	Age	Int	Pts
Earl Morrall	QB	6'1"	206	37		
Johnny Unitas	QB	6'1"	196	38		
Tom Matte	HB	6'	214	32		48
Don McCauley	HB	6'1"	207	22		12
Charlie Pittman	HB	6'1"	200	23		
Don Nottingham	FB	5'10"	210	22		36
Norm Bulaich	HB-FB	6'1"	218	24		60
Sam Havrilak	WR	6'2"	195	23		
Eddie Hinton	WR	6'	200	24		12
Jim O'Brien	WR	6'	195	24		95
Ray Perkins	WR	6'	183	29		24
Willie Richardson	WR	6'2"	198	31		12
John Mackey	TE	6'3"	224	29		
Tom Mitchell	TE	6'2"	215	27		
David Lee	K	6'4"	230	27		

NEW ENGLAND PATRIOTS 6-8-0 John Mazur

Scores of Each Game		
20	OAKLAND	6
7	DETROIT	34
3	BALTIMORE	23
20	N.Y. JETS	0
3	Miami	41
21	Dallas	44
10	San Francisco	27
28	HOUSTON	20
38	BUFFALO	33
7	Cleveland	27
20	Buffalo	27
34	MIAMI	13
6	N.Y. Jets	13
21	Baltimore	17

Use Name	Pos.	Hgt	Wgt	Age	Int	Pts
Mike Haggerty	OT	6'4"	250	25		
Mike Montler	OT	6'4"	270	27		
Tom Neville	OT	6'4"	255	28		
Bill Lenkaitis	OG	6'3"	265	25		
Len St. Jean	OG	6'1"	245	29		
Halvor Hagen	C-OG	6'5"	253	24		
Jon Morris	C	6'4"	255	28		
Ike Lassiter	DE	6'5"	270	30		
Art May	DE	6'3"	245	22		
Dennis Wirgowski	DE	6'5"	255	23		
Ron Berger	DT-DE	6'8"	275	27		
Julius Adams	DT	6'3"	258	23		
Houston Antwine	DT	6'	270	32		
Dave Rowe	DT	6'6"	280	26		
Bill Atessis	DE-DT	6'3"	240	22		
Rick Cash—Injury						
Joe Kapp—Holdout						
J. R. Williamson—Injury						

Use Name	Pos.	Hgt	Wgt	Age	Int	Pts
Jim Cheyunski	LB	6'2"	220	25	1	
Dennis Coleman	LB	6'3"	225	22		
Randy Edmunds	LB	6'2"	225	25		
Steve Kiner	LB	6'	219	24	4	
Ed Philpott	LB	6'3"	240	25		
Ed Weisacosky	LB	6'	220	27		
Randy Beverly	DB	5'11"	205	27	2	
Larry Carwell	DB	6'1"	200	27	5	6
Phil Clark	DB	6'2"	208	26		
Rickie Harris	DB	6'	182	28		
Tom Janik	DB	6'3"	200	30		
Irv Mallory	DB	6'1"	196	22		
John Outlaw	DB	5'10"	175	26	3	6
Perry Pruett	DB	6'1"	190	22		
Clarence Scott	DB	6'2"	205	27		
Don Webb	DB	5'10"	185	32		
Ron Gardin (from BAL)	WR-DB	5'11"	180	26		

Use Name	Pos.	Hgt	Wgt	Age	Int	Pts
Jim Plunkett	QB	6'3"	220	23		
Mike Taliaferro	QB	6'2"	205	29		
Carl Garrett	HB	5'11"	210	24		12
Bob Gladieux	HB	5'11"	190	24		
Jack Maitland	HB	6'1"	210	23		6
Odell Lawson	FB	6'2"	218	23		
Jim Nance	FB	6'1"	240	28		30
Hubie Bryant	WR	5'10"	168	25		6
Eric Crabtree (from CIN)	WR	5'11"	185	26		18
Reggie Rucker (from DAL-NYG)	WR	6'2"	190	23		6
Ron Sellers	WR	6'4"	195	24		18
Eric Stolberg	WR	6'2"	180	22		
Al Sykes	WR	6'3"	180	24		
Randy Vataha	WR	5'10"	180	22		54
Roland Moss	TE	6'3"	215	24		12
Tom Beer	OG-TE	6'4"	235	26		18
Charlie Gogolak	K	5'10"	170	26		64

NEW YORK JETS 6-8-0 Weeb Ewbank

Scores of Each Game		
0	Baltimore	22
10	St. Louis	17
14	Miami	10
0	New England	20
28	BUFFALO	17
14	MIAMI	30
21	San Diego	49
13	KANSAS CITY	10
13	BALTIMORE	14
20	Buffalo	7
21	SAN FRANCISCO	24
10	Dallas	52
13	NEW ENGLAND	6
35	CINCINNATI	21

Use Name	Pos.	Hgt	Wgt	Age	Int	Pts
Winston Hill	OT	6'4"	285	29		
John Mooring	OT	6'6"	255	24		
Bob Svihus	OT	6'4"	245	28		
Dave Foley	C-OT	6'5"	255	23		
Dave Herman	OG	6'2"	255	29		
Roy Kirksey	OG	6'1"	265	23		
Randy Rasmussen	OG	6'2"	255	26		
John Schmitt	C	6'4"	250	28		
Paul Crane	LB-C	6'2"	212	27	1	
Mark Lomas	DE	6'4"	230	23		
Gerry Philbin	DE	6'2"	245	30		
John Little	DT-DE	6'3"	220	24		
Steve Thompson	DT-DE	6'5"	245	25		
John Elliott	DT	6'4"	244	26		
Roger Finnie	DT	6'3"	245	24		
Chuck Hinton (from PIT)	DT	6'5"	264	32		
Scott Palmer	DT	6'3"	245	23		
Clovis Swinney	DT	6'3"	240	26		

Use Name	Pos.	Hgt	Wgt	Age	Int	Pts
Al Atkinson	LB	6'1"	230	28	2	
Ralph Baker	LB	6'3"	235	29		1
Larry Grantham	LB	6'	210	32	1	
John Ebersole	LB	6'3"	240	22		
Bill Zapalac	DE-LB	6'4"	225	23		
John Dockery	DB	6'	186	26	2	
Chris Farasopoulos	DB	5'11"	190	22		
W.K. Hicks	DB	6'1"	195	28		4
Gus Holloman	DB	6'3"	195	25	2	
Rich Sowells	DB	6'	175	22		
Steve Tannen	DB	6'1"	194	23		
Earlie Thomas	DB	6'1"	190	25		
Phil Wise	DB	6'	190	22	1	
Jim Richards—Military Service						

Use Name	Pos.	Hgt	Wgt	Age	Int	Pts
Bob Davis	QB	6'3"	205	26		6
Joe Namath	QB	6'2"	200	28		
Al Woodall	QB	6'5"	205	25		
Emerson Boozer	HB	5'11"	195	28		36
George Nock	HB	5'10"	200	25		30
Cliff McClain	FB-HB	6'	217	23		12
John Riggins	FB	6'2"	237	22		18
Matt Snell	FB	6'2"	220	29		
Steve Harkey	HB-FB	6'	215	22		
Eddie Bell	WR	5'10"	160	23		6
Rich Caster	WR	6'5"	222	22		36
Don Maynard	WR	6'	180	35		12
Steve O'Neal	WR	6'3"	185	25		
Vern Studdard	WR	5'11"	175	23		
Gary Arthur	TE	6'5"	230	23		
Pete Lammons	TE	6'3"	230	27		6
Wayne Stewart	TE	6'7"	213	24		
Bobby Howfield	K	5'9"	180	34		49

BUFFALO BILLS 1-13-0 Harvey Johnson

Scores of Each Game		
37	DALLAS	49
14	MIAMI	29
0	Minnesota	19
0	BALTIMORE	43
17	N.Y. Jets	28
3	San Diego	20
23	ST. LOUIS	28
0	Miami	34
33	New England	38
7	N.Y. JETS	20
27	NEW ENGLAND	20
0	Baltimore	24
14	HOUSTON	20
9	Kansas City	22

Use Name	Pos.	Hgt	Wgt	Age	Int	Pts
Paul Costa	OT	6'4"	255	29		
Donnie Green	OT	6'7"	270	23		
Willie Young	OT	6'4"	270	23		
Bob Hews	DE-OT	6'5"	240	22		
Joe O'Donnell	OG	6'2"	262	28		
Mike Wilson	OG	6'1"	240	23		
Levert Carr	OT-OG	6'5"	260	27		
Bruce Jarvis	C	6'7"	246	22		
Howard Kindig	OT-C	6'6"	265	30		
Mike McBath	DE	6'4"	248	25		
Al Cowlings	DE	6'5"	258	24		
Louis Ross	DE	6'6"	238	24		
Cal Snowden	DE	6'4"	242	24		
Bill McKinley	LB-DE	6'3"	240	22		
Jim Dunaway	DT	6'4"	277	29		
Bob Tatarek	DT	6'4"	260	25		

Use Name	Pos.	Hgt	Wgt	Age	Int	Pts
Al Andrews	LB	6'3"	216	27	1	
Edgar Chandler	LB	6'3"	235	25	1	2
Jerald Collins	LB	6'1"	220	24		
Dick Cunningham	LB	6'2"	232	26		
Paul Guidry	LB	6'3"	233	27	1	
Mike Stratton	LB	6'3"	240	29		
Chuck Hurston	LB	6'6"	240	28		
Jackie Allen	DB	6'1"	187	23		
Tim Beamer	DB	5'11"	185	23		
Tony Greene	DB	5'10"	170	22		
Robert James	DB	6'1"	185	24	4	6
John Pitts	DB	6'4"	223	26	2	
Pete Richardson	DB	6'1"	193	24	1	
Alvin Wyatt	DB	5'10"	185	23	1	6
Richard Cheek – Knee Injury						
Julian Nunamaker – Injury						
Jim Reilly – Illness						

Use Name	Pos.	Hgt	Wgt	Age	Int	Pts
James Harris	QB	6'3"	215	24		
Dennis Shaw	QB	6'2"	210	24		
Max Anderson	HB	5'8"	180	26		
Greg Jones	HB	6'1"	200	23		6
O.J. Simpson	HB	6'2"	214	24		30
Jim Braxton	FB	6'2"	226	22		
Wayne Patrick	FB	6'2"	254	25		6
Marlin Briscoe	WR	5'10"	178	25		30
Bob Chandler	WR	6'	180	22		
J.D. Hill	WR	6'1"	193	22		12
Haven Moses	WR	6'3"	205	25		12
Ike Hill	DB-WR	5'10"	180	24		12
Austin Denney	TE	6'2"	230	27		
Ted Koy	TE	6'1"	210	23		6
Jan White	TE	6'2"	215	22		
Dave Chapple	K	6'	180	24		
Grant Guthrie	K	6'	210	23		17
Spike Jones	K	6'2"	190	24		
John Leypoldt	K	6'2"	224	25		39

MIAMI DOLPHINS

RUSHING

Last Name	No.	Yds	Avg	TD
Csonka	195	1051	5.4	7
Kiick	162	738	4.6	3
Morris	57	315	5.5	1
Warfield	9	115	12.8	0
Ginn	22	97	4.4	0
Griese	26	82	3.2	0
Leigh	5	15	3.0	0
Seiple	1	14	14.0	0
Cole	3	11	3.7	0
Mira	6	−9	−1.5	0

RECEIVING

Last Name	No.	Yds	Avg	TD
Warfield	43	996	23	11
Kiick	40	338	8	0
Twilley	23	349	15	4
Fleming	13	137	11	2
Csonka	13	113	9	1
Noonan	10	180	18	0
Stowe	5	68	14	1
Morris	5	16	3	0
Mandich	3	19	6	1
Seiple	1	32	32	0

PUNT RETURNS

Last Name	No.	Yds	Avg	TD
Scott	33	318	10	0
Anderson	8	114	14	0

KICKOFF RETURNS

Last Name	No.	Yds	Avg	TD
Morris	15	423	28	1
Ginn	10	252	25	0
Leigh	4	99	25	0
Matheson	3	32	11	0

PASSING – PUNTING – KICKING — Statistics

PASSING

Last Name	Att	Comp	%	Yds	Yd/Att	TD	Int−	%	RK
Griese	263	145	55	2089	7.9	19	9−	3	1
Mira	30	11	37	158	5.3	1	1−	3	

PUNTING

Last Name	No	Avg
Seiple	52	40.1

KICKING

Last Name	XP	Att	%	FG	Att	%
Yepremian	33	33	100	28	40	70

BALTIMORE COLTS

RUSHING

Last Name	No.	Yds	Avg	TD
Bulaich	152	741	4.9	8
Matte	173	607	3.5	8
Nottingham	95	388	4.1	5
McCauley	58	246	4.2	2
Hinton	4	56	14.0	0
Perkins	5	35	7.0	0
Richardson	2	27	13.5	0
Mackey	3	18	6.0	0
Morrall	6	13	2.2	0
Mitchell	2	9	4.5	0
Unitas	9	5	0.6	0
Pittman	2	3	1.5	0
Nowatzke	1	1	1.0	0

RECEIVING

Last Name	No.	Yds	Avg	TD
Mitchell	33	402	12	0
Matte	29	239	8	0
Hinton	25	436	17	2
Bulaich	25	229	9	2
Perkins	24	424	18	4
Nottingham	15	88	6	0
Mackey	11	143	13	0
Richardson	10	173	17	2
McCauley	3	6	2	0
Havrilak	1	12	12	0

PUNT RETURNS

Last Name	No.	Yds	Avg	TD
Volk	22	118	5	0
Dunlap	8	112	14	0
Kern	3	19	6	0
T. Curtis	7	15	2	0
Logan	1	12	12	0

KICKOFF RETURNS

Last Name	No.	Yds	Avg	TD
Pittman	14	330	24	0
McCauley	8	194	24	0
Duncan	3	102	34	0
Dunlap	1	28	28	0
Logan	1	16	16	0
Stukes	1	8	8	0
Nowatzke	1	1	1	0
T. Curtis	1	0	0	0
Matte	1	0	0	0
Mitchell	1	0	0	0

PASSING

Last Name	Att	Comp	%	Yds	Yd/Att	TD	Int−	%	RK
Unitas	176	92	52	942	5.4	3	9−	5	10
Morrall	167	84	50	1210	7.3	7	12−	7	9
Matte	1	0	0	0	0.0	0	0−	0	

PUNTING

Last Name	No	Avg
Lee	62	41.0

KICKING

Last Name	XP	Att	%	FG	Att	%
O'Brien	35	36	97	20	29	69

NEW ENGLAND PATRIOTS

RUSHING

Last Name	No.	Yds	Avg	TD
Garrett	181	784	4.3	1
Nance	129	463	3.6	5
Plunkett	45	210	4.7	0
Gladieux	37	175	4.7	0
Maitland	13	25	1.9	1
Crabtree	3	12	4.0	0
Lawson	8	8	1.0	0
Bryant	4	1	0.3	0
Rucker	1	14	14.0	0
Neville	0	−8	0.0	0

RECEIVING

Last Name	No.	Yds	Avg	TD
Vataha	51	872	17	9
Crabtree	23	222	10	3
Garrett	22	265	12	1
Nance	18	95	5	0
Sellers	14	222	16	3
Bryant	14	212	15	1
Beer	12	191	16	3
Moss	9	124	14	1
Gladieux	6	60	10	0
Rucker	4	52	13	1
Sykes	1	15	15	0
Maitland	1	6	6	0

PUNT RETURNS

Last Name	No.	Yds	Avg	TD
Garrett	8	124	16	0
Gardin	6	89	15	0
Bryant	10	24	2	0
Harris	5	19	4	0
Gladieux	4	0	0	0

KICKOFF RETURNS

Last Name	No.	Yds	Avg	TD
Garrett	24	538	22	0
Gardin	14	321	23	0
Bryant	10	252	25	0
Gladieux	6	85	14	0
Lawson	2	47	24	0
Rucker	2	45	23	0
Maitland	2	40	20	0
Mallory	1	19	19	0
Hagen	1	7	7	0
Janik	1	0	0	0
Webb	1	0	0	0

PASSING

Last Name	Att	Comp	%	Yds	Yd/Att	TD	Int−	%	RK
Plunkett	328	158	48	2158	6.6	19	16−	5	5
Gladieux	2	1	50	48	24.0	0	0−	0	

PUNTING

Last Name	No	Avg
Janik	87	37.3

KICKING

Last Name	XP	Att	%	FG	Att	%
Gogolak	28	28	100	12	21	57

NEW YORK JETS

RUSHING

Last Name	No.	Yds	Avg	TD
Riggins	180	769	4.3	1
Boozer	188	618	3.3	5
Davis	18	154	8.6	1
Nock	48	137	2.9	3
McClain	12	108	9.0	2
Harkey	20	62	3.1	0
Woodall	13	26	2.0	0
Caster	2	10	5.0	0
Maynard	1	2	2.0	0
Namath	3	−1	−0.3	0
Lammons	0	3	0.0	0

RECEIVING

Last Name	No.	Yds	Avg	TD
Riggins	36	231	6	2
Caster	26	454	17	6
Maynard	21	408	19	2
Boozer	11	120	11	1
Lammons	8	149	19	1
Nock	6	44	7	2
Bell	5	110	22	1
Harkey	5	28	6	0
Arthur	1	12	12	0

PUNT RETURNS

Last Name	No.	Yds	Avg	TD
Farasopoulos	19	155	8	0
Studdard	4	3	1	0
Hicks	1	0	0	0
Bell	1	−3	−3	0

KICKOFF RETURNS

Last Name	No.	Yds	Avg	TD
Farasopoulos	25	545	22	0
Studdard	15	329	22	0
Wise	8	210	26	0
Nock	5	71	14	0
McClain	1	11	11	0
Harkey	1	2	2	0

PASSING

Last Name	Att	Comp	%	Yds	Yd/Att	TD	Int−	%	RK
Davis	121	49	40	624	5.2	10	8−	7	
Woodall	97	42	43	395	4.1	0	2−	2	
Namath	59	28	47	537	9.1	5	6−	10	
O'Neal	1	0	0	0	0.0	0	0−	0	

PUNTING

Last Name	No	Avg
O'Neal	78	38.8

KICKING

Last Name	XP	Att	%	FG	Att	%
Howfield	25	26	96	8	19	42
Baker	1	1	100	0	0	

BUFFALO BILLS

RUSHING

Last Name	No.	Yds	Avg	TD
Simpson	183	742	4.1	5
Patrick	79	332	4.2	1
Braxton	21	84	4.0	0
Shaw	14	82	5.9	0
G. Jones	16	53	3.3	0
Harris	6	42	7.0	0
J. D. Hill	1	2	2.0	0

RECEIVING

Last Name	No.	Yds	Avg	TD
Briscoe	44	603	14	5
Patrick	36	327	9	0
Moses	23	470	20	2
Simpson	21	162	8	0
Braxton	18	141	8	0
G. Jones	16	113	7	1
White	13	130	10	0
J. D. Hill	11	216	20	2
Koy	10	133	13	1
B. Chandler	5	60	12	0
I. Hill	5	55	11	1

PUNT RETURNS

Last Name	No.	Yds	Avg	TD
Wyatt	23	188	8	1
I. Hill	14	133	10	1
Beamer	7	22	3	0

KICKOFF RETURNS

Last Name	No.	Yds	Avg	TD
Wyatt	30	762	25	0
Beamer	20	394	20	0
I. Hill	12	280	23	0
Simpson	4	107	27	0
Braxton	5	90	18	0
G. Jones	1	24	24	0
Kindig	2	16	8	0

PASSING

Last Name	Att	Comp	%	Yds	Yd/Att	TD	Int−	%	RK
Shaw	291	149	51	1813	6.2	11	26−	9	11
Harris	103	51	50	512	5.0	1	6−	6	
Braxton	3	1	33	49	16.3	0	0−	0	
Briscoe	2	1	50	36	18.0	0	0−	0	
Simpson	2	0	0	0	0.0	0	0−	0	

PUNTING

Last Name	No	Avg
S. Jones	72	41.2
Chapple	3	33.7

KICKING

Last Name	XP	Att	%	FG	Att	%
Leypoldt	12	12	100	9	15	60
Guthrie	8	9	89	3	10	30

CLEVELAND BROWNS 9-5-0 Nick Skorich

Scores of Each Game

31	HOUSTON	0
14	Baltimore	13
20	OAKLAND	34
27	PITTSBURG	17
27	Cincinnati	24
0	DENVER	27
14	ATLANTA	31
9	Pittsburgh	26
7	Kansas City	13
27	NEW ENGLAND	7
37	Houston	24
31	CINCINNATI	27
21	New Orleans	17
20	Washington	13

Use Name	Pos.	Hgt	Wgt	Age	Int	Pts
Doug Dieken	OT	6'5"	237	22		2
Mitch Johnson	OT	6'4"	250	29		
Bob McKay	OT	6'5"	260	23		
Dick Schrafrath	OT	6'3"	258	35		
Jim Copeland	OG	6'2"	245	26		
John Demarie	OG	6'3"	255	26		
Gene Hickerson	OG	6'3"	248	36		
Mike Sikich	OG	6'2"	243	22		
Fred Hoaglin	C	6'4"	250	27		
Jack Gregory	DE	6'6"	250	26		
Joe Jones	DE	6'6"	246	23		
Bob Briggs	DT-DE	6'4"	276	26		
Walter Johnson	DT	6'3"	275	28		6
Jerry Sherk	DT	6'4"	253	23	2	
Ron Snidow	DT	6'4"	250	29		

Use Name	Pos.	Hgt	Wgt	Age	Int	Pts
Billy Andrews	LB	6'	225	26	3	
John Garlington	LB	6'1"	225	25	1	
Charlie Hall	LB	6'3"	215	22		
Jim Houston	LB	6'2"	240	34		
Rick Kingrea	LB	6'1"	233	22		
Dale Lindsey	LB	6'3"	225	28	2	
Erich Barnes	DB	6'2"	212	36		
Ben Davis	DB	5'11"	186	25	2	
Mike Howell	DB	6'1"	190	28	2	
Ernie Kellerman	DB	6'	185	27	3	
Clarence Scott	DB	6'	175	22	4	
Freddie Summers	DB	6'1"	180	24		
Walt Sumner	DB	6'1"	180	24	2	

Use Name	Pos.	Hgt	Wgt	Age	Int	Pts
Bill Nelson	QB	6'	195	30		
Mike Phipps	QB	6'2"	207	23		
Ken Brown	HB	5'10"	205	24		
Leroy Kelly	HB	6'	200	29		72
Reece Morrison	HB	6'	205	25		
Bo Scott	FB	6'3"	210	28		60
Bo Cornell	FB	6'1"	217	22		
Stan Brown	WR	5'9"	184	22		
Gary Collins	WR	6'4"	210	30		18
Fair Hooker	WR	6'1"	193	24		6
Dave Jones	WR	6'2"	185	24		
Frank Pitts	WR	6'2"	200	27		24
Chip Glass	TE	6'4"	236	24		6
Milt Morin	TE	6'4"	240	29		12
Don Cockroft	K	6'1"	190	26		79

PITTSBURGH STEELERS 6-8-0 Chuck Noll

15	Chicago	17
21	CINCINNATI	10
21	SAN DIEGO	17
17	Cleveland	27
16	Kansas Ctiy	38
23	HOUSTON	16
21	Baltimore	34
26	CLEVELAND	9
21	Miami	24
17	N.Y. GIANTS	13
10	DENVER	22
3	Houston	29
21	Cincinnati	13
14	LOS ANGELES	23

Use Name	Pos.	Hgt	Wgt	Age	Int	Pts
John Brown	OT	6'2"	255	32		
Rick Sharp	OT	6'3"	265	23		
Jon Kolb	C-OT	6'2"	262	24		
Sam Davis	OG	6'1"	255	27		
Mel Holmes	OG	6'3"	250	21		
Gerry Mullins	OG	6'3"	235	22		
Bruce Van Dyke	OG	6'2"	255	27		
Jim Clack	C	6'3"	250	23		
Ray Mansfield	C	6'3"	255	30		
Bobby Maples	C	6'3"	245	28		
Bert Askson	DE	6'4"	220	25		
L.C. Greenwood	DE	6'5"	240	24		
Dwight White	DE	6'4"	250	22		
Ben McGee	DT-DE	6'2"	260	29		
Joe Greene	DT	6'4"	280	24		
Lloyd Voss	DT	6'4"	255	29		

Use Name	Pos.	Hgt	Wgt	Age	Int	Pts
Chuck Allen	LB	6'1"	227	31	3	
Henry Davis	LB	6'3"	235	28		
Jack Ham	LB	6'3"	220	22	2	
Andy Russell	LB	6'3"	225	29		
Brian Stenger	LB	6'4"	230	24		
Ralph Anderson	DB	6'2"	180	22	1	
Ocie Austin	DB	6'3"	200	24		
Chuck Beatty	DB	6'2"	200	25		
Mel Blount	DB	6'3"	205	23	2	
Lee Calland	DB	6'	190	30	2	
Glen Edwards	DB	6'	185	24	1	
John Rowser	DB	6'1"	185	27	4	6
Mike Wagner	DB	6'1"	196	22	2	

Clarence Washington—Injury

Use Name	Pos.	Hgt	Wgt	Age	Int	Pts
Terry Bradshaw	QB	6'3"	218	22		30
Terry Hanratty	QB	6'1"	210	23		6
Bob Leahy	QB	6'2"	205	25		
Rocky Bleier	HB	5'11"	205	25		
Jim Brumfield	HB	6'1"	195	24		
Preston Pearson	HB	6'1"	190	26		18
John Fuqua	FB-HB	5'11"	200	24		30
Warren Bankston	FB	6'4"	230	24		
Frank Lewis	WR	6'1"	196	24		
Ron Shanklin	WR	6'1"	180	24		36
Dave Smith	WR	6'2"	205	24		30
Jon Staggers	WR	5'10"	186	22		
Al Young	WR	6'1"	195	22		
Bob Adams	TE	6'2"	225	25		
Larry Brown	TE	6'4"	225	22		6
Dennis Hughes	TE	6'1"	220	22		
Roy Gerela	K	5'10"	185	23		78
Bobby Walden	K	6'	190	33		

HOUSTON OILERS 4-9-1 Ed Hughes

0	Cleveland	31
16	KANSAS CITY	20
13	NEW ORLEANS	13
13	Washington	22
7	DETROIT	31
16	Pittsburg	23
10	CINCINNATI	6
20	New England	28
21	Oakland	41
13	Cincinnati	28
24	CLEVELAND	37
29	PITTSBURGH	3
20	Buffalo	14
49	SAN DIEGO	33

Use Name	Pos.	Hgt	Wgt	Age	Int	Pts
Tom Funchess	OT	6'5"	260	26		
Sam Walton	OT	6'5"	270	28		
Gene Ferguson	OT	6'7"	300	23		
Walt Suggs	C-OT	6'5"	250	32		
Elbert Drungo	OG	6'5"	250	28		
Tom Regner	OG	6'1"	255	27		
Ron Saul	OG	6'2"	255	23		
Bob Young	OG	6'2"	256	28		
Jerry Sturm	C	6'3"	265	34		
Allen Aldridge	DE	6'3"	260	26		
Elvin Bethea	DE	6'3"	262	25		
Pat Holmes	DE	6'5"	250	31		
Scott Lewis	DE	6'6"	260	21		
Ron Billingsley	DT	6'8"	290	26		
Lee Brooks	DT	6'5"	266	23	1	
Tom Domres (to DEN)	DT	6'3"	260	24		
Mike Tilleman	DT	6'5"	280	27		

Use Name	Pos.	Hgt	Wgt	Age	Int	Pts
Garland Boyette	LB	6'1"	235	31		6
Phil Croyle	LB	6'3"	220	23		
Dave Olerich	LB	6'1"	225	26		
Ron Pritchard	LB	6'1"	235	24		
George Webster	LB	6'4"	223	25		
Willie Alexander	DB	6'2"	195	21	4	
Bob Atkins	DB	6'3"	210	25	1	6
John Charles	DB	6'1"	200	27	5	
Ken Houston	DB	6'3"	196	26	9	30
Leroy Howard	DB	5'11"	175	22		
Benny Johnson	DB	5'11"	178	23		
Zeke Moore	DB	6'2"	196	27	3	

Roy Hopkins – Injury

Use Name	Pos.	Hgt	Wgt	Age	Int	Pts
Lynn Dickey	QB	6'4"	218	21		
Charley Johnson	QB	6'	190	34		
Dan Pastorini	QB	6'3"	220	22		18
Woody Campbell	HB	5'11"	208	26		6
Andy Hopkins	HB	5'10"	187	22		
Dickie Post (from DEN)	HB	5'9"	190	25		6
Mike Richardson	HB	5'11"	196	24		
Ward Walsh	HB	6'	215	22		6
Robert Holmes (from KC)	FB	5'9"	220	25		24
Leroy Sledge	FB	6'3"	230	25		6
Joe Dawkins (to DEN)	HB-FB	5'11"	222	23		12
Jim Beirne	WR	6'2"	196	24		6
Ken Burrough	WR	6'4"	210	24		
Linzy Cole	WR	5'11"	170	23		
Mac Haik	WR	6'1"	195	25		
Charlie Joiner	WR	5'11"	188	23		42
Alvin Reed	TE	6'5"	230	27		6
Floyd Rice	TE	6'3"	220	22		
Braden Beck	K	6'2"	200	27		4
Mark Moseley	K	5'11"	182	23		73

CINCINNATI BENGALS 4-10-0 Paul Brown

37	PHILADELPHIA	14
10	Pittsburgh	21
17	Green Bay	20
13	MIAMI	23
24	CLEVELAND	27
27	Oakland	31
6	Houston	10
6	ATLANTA	9
24	Denver	10
28	HOUSTON	13
31	SAN DIEGO	0
27	Cleveland	31
13	PITTSBURGH	21
21	N.Y. JETS	35

Use Name	Pos.	Hgt	Wgt	Age	Int	Pts
Howard Fest	OT	6'6"	268	25		
Vern Holland	OT	6'5"	270	23		
Rufus Mayes	OT	6'5"	255	23		
Ernie Wright	OT	6'4"	270	31		
Guy Dennis	OG	6'2"	255	24		
Steve Lawson	OG	6'3"	265	22		
Pat Matson	OG	6'1"	245	27		
Bob Johnson	C	6'5"	265	25		
Royce Berry	DE	6'3"	248	25		
Ron Carpenter	DE	6'4"	260	23		
Ken Johnson	DE	6'5"	262	24		
Nick Roman	DE	6'3"	230	23		
Steve Chomyszak	DT	6'5"	265	26		
Willie Jones	DT	6'2"	260	29		
Mike Reid	DT	6'3"	258	24		

Use Name	Pos.	Hgt	Wgt	Age	Int	Pts
Doug Adams	LB	6'	223	22		
Ken Avery	LB	6'1"	225	27		
Al Beauchamp	LB	6'2"	236	27	6	6
Bill Bergey	LB	6'2"	240	26	1	
Larry Ely	LB	6'1"	230	23		
Bill Peterson	LB	6'3"	230	26	1	
Al Coleman	DB	6'1"	183	26	1	
Neal Craig	DB	6'1"	185	23	1	
Sandy Durko	DB	6'1"	185	23	4	
Ken Dyer	DB	6'3"	190	25		
Jim Harris	DB	5'11"	173	25		
Lemar Parrish	DB	5'11"	185	23	7	12
Ken Riley	DB	6'	184	24	5	
Fletcher Smith	DB	6'2"	180	27	1	

Greg Cook—Shoulder Injury

Use Name	Pos.	Hgt	Wgt	Age	Int	Pts
Ken Anderson	QB	6'1"	202	22		6
Virgil Carter	QB	6'1"	200	25		1
Dave Lewis	QB	6'2"	210	25		
Essex Johnson	HB	5'9"	195	24		36
Paul Robinson	HB	6'	200	26		6
Jess Phillips	HB	6'1"	210	24		6
Doug Dressler	FB	6'3"	220	23		6
Ron Lamb	FB	6'2"	220	23		
Fred Willis	FB	6'	215	23		42
Mike Haffner	WR	6'2"	205	29		
Ed Marshall	WR	6'5"	200	23		
Chip Myers	WR	6'4"	200	26		6
Speedy Thomas	WR	6'1"	178	24		12
Bruce Coslet	TE	6'3"	230	25		24
Mike Kelley	TE	6'4"	215	23		
Bob Trumpy	TE	6'6"	225	26		18
Horst Muhlmann	K	6'1"	210	31		91

CLEVELAND BROWNS

RUSHING

Last Name	No.	Yds	Avg	TD
Kelly	234	865	3.7	10
B. Scott	179	606	3.4	9
K. Brown	11	47	4.3	0
Phipps	6	35	5.8	0
Cornell	11	12	1.1	0
Cockroft	1	12	12.0	0
Morin	1	1	1.0	0
Morrison	5	-2	-0.4	0
Nelsen	13	-18	-1.4	0

RECEIVING

Last Name	No.	Yds	Avg	TD
Hooker	45	649	14	1
Morin	40	581	15	2
B. Scott	30	233	8	1
Pitts	27	487	18	4
Kelly	25	252	10	2
Collins	15	231	15	3
D. Jones	4	66	17	0
Cornell	1	18	18	0
Glass	1	4	4	1

PUNT RETURNS

Last Name	No.	Yds	Avg	TD
Kelly	30	292	10	0
D. Jones	9	63	7	0
Kellerman	1	4	4	0

KICKOFF RETURNS

Last Name	No.	Yds	Avg	TD
K. Brown	15	330	22	0
Morrison	9	267	30	0
Pitts	9	238	26	0
S. Brown	7	157	22	0
Houston	1	21	21	0
Cornell	1	19	19	0
Dieken	1	16	16	0
Kelly	1	11	11	0
Kellerman	1	5	5	0
Glass	1	1	1	0

PASSING – PUNTING – KICKING

PASSING	Att	Comp	%	Yds	Yd/Att	TD	Int–	%	RK
Nelsen	325	174	54	2319	7.1	13	23–	7	5
Phipps	47	13	28	179	3.8	1	4	9	
Kelly	4	1	25	23	5.8	0	0–	0	

PUNTING	No	Avg
Cockroft	62	40.5
Collins	5	32.4

KICKING	XP	Att	%	FG	Att	%
Cockroft	34	34	100	15	28	54

PITTSBURGH STEELERS

RUSHING

Last Name	No.	Yds	Avg	TD
Fuqua	155	625	4.0	4
Pearson	131	605	4.6	0
Bankston	70	274	3.9	0
Bradshaw	53	247	4.7	5
Walden	1	14	14.0	0
Staggers	1	5	5.0	0
Hanratty	1	3	3.0	1
Shanklin	2	1	0.5	0
Leahy	1	-6	-6.0	0
Smith	1	-10	-10.0	0

RECEIVING

Last Name	No.	Yds	Avg	TD
Shanklin	49	652	13	6
Fuqua	49	427	9	1
Smith	47	663	14	5
Pearson	20	246	12	2
Adams	20	160	8	0
Bankston	17	148	9	0
Staggers	8	103	13	0
Lewis	3	44	15	0
L. Brown	1	3	3	1

PUNT RETURNS

Last Name	No.	Yds	Avg	TD
Staggers	31	262	8	1
Wagner	2	2	1	0
Edwards	1	0	0	0
Fuqua	1	0	0	0

KICKOFF RETURNS

Last Name	No.	Yds	Avg	TD
Brumfield	12	271	23	0
Staggers	10	261	26	0
Pearson	7	205	29	0
Edwards	9	198	22	0
Bankston	5	76	15	0
Blount	4	76	19	0
Bleier	1	21	21	0
Clack	1	12	12	0

PASSING – PUNTING – KICKING

PASSING	Att	Comp	%	Yds	Yd/Att	TD	Int–	%	RK
Bradshaw	373	203	54	2259	6.1	13	22–	6	8
Hanratty	29	7	24	159	5.5	2	3–	10	
Leahy	11	3	27	18	1.6	0	1–	9	
Walden	1	1	100	10	10.0	0	0–	0	

PUNTING	No	Avg
Walden	79	43.7

KICKING	XP	Att	%	FG	Att	%
Gerela	27	27	100	17	27	63

HOUSTON OILERS

RUSHING

Last Name	No.	Yds	Avg	TD
R. Holmes	112	323	2.9	4
Campbell	96	259	2.7	1
Pastorini	26	140	5.4	3
Dawkins	42	135	3.2	2
Walsh	38	129	3.4	0
Post	40	86	2.2	0
Sledge	24	74	3.1	0
Richardson	17	33	1.9	0
Dickey	1	4	4.0	0
Hopkins	2	2	1.0	0
C. Johnson	2	0	0.0	0

RECEIVING

Last Name	No.	Yds	Avg	TD
Beirne	38	550	14	1
Joiner	31	681	22	7
Reed	25	408	16	1
Burrough	25	370	15	1
Campbell	20	179	9	0
R. Holmes	19	154	8	0
Post	9	112	12	1
Dawkins	9	53	6	0
Walsh	6	36	6	1
Sledge	6	32	5	1
Richardson	4	17	4	0

PUNT RETURNS

Last Name	No.	Yds	Avg	TD
Cole	14	107	8	0
Houston	16	91	6	0
Rice	2	0	0	0

KICKOFF RETURNS

Last Name	No.	Yds	Avg	TD
Cole	32	834	26	0
R. Holmes	12	300	25	0
Moore	10	214	21	0
Burrough	8	157	20	0
Post	5	116	23	0
Dawkins	2	34	17	0
Richardson	1	26	26	0
Joiner	1	25	25	0
Walsh	1	24	24	0
Rice	1	0	0	0

PASSING – PUNTING – KICKING

PASSING	Att	Comp	%	Yds	Yd/Att	TD	Int–	%	RK
Pastorini	270	127	47	1702	6.3	7	21–	8	12
C. Johnson	94	46	49	592	6.3	3	7–	7	
Dickey	57	19	33	315	5.5	0	9–	16	
Campbell	2	2	100	34	17.0	2	0–	0	

PUNTING	No	Avg
Pastorini	75	40.6

KICKING	XP	Att	%	FG	Att	%
Moseley	25	27	93	16	26	62
Beck	1	2	50	1	2	50

CINCINNATI BENGALS

RUSHING

Last Name	No.	Yds	Avg	TD
Willis	135	590	4.4	7
E. Johnson	85	522	6.1	4
Phillips	94	420	4.5	0
Robinson	49	213	4.3	1
Dressler	54	204	3.8	1
Anderson	22	125	5.7	1
Carter	8	42	5.3	0
Lamb	5	13	2.6	0
Durko	1	7	7.0	0
Lewis	6	6	1.0	0
Thomas	2	-1	-0.5	0

RECEIVING

Last Name	No.	Yds	Avg	TD
Trumpy	40	531	13	3
Myers	27	286	11	1
Willis	24	223	9	0
Thomas	22	327	15	2
Phillips	22	125	6	1
Coslet	21	356	17	4
Dressler	19	145	8	0
E. Johnson	14	258	18	2
Robinson	8	47	6	0
Marshall	2	18	9	0
Kelly	1	9	9	0

PUNT RETURNS

Last Name	No.	Yds	Avg	TD
Parrish	12	93	8	0
E. Johnson	3	28	9	0
Durko	6	14	2	0
Thomas	4	10	3	0

KICKOFF RETURNS

Last Name	No.	Yds	Avg	TD
Robinson	18	335	19	0
Parrish	13	296	23	0
Willis	4	81	20	0
Phillips	2	49	25	0
Lamb	2	42	21	0
E. Johnson	2	40	20	0
Dressler	1	20	20	0
Kelly	1	0	0	0

PASSING – PUNTING – KICKING

PASSING	Att	Comp	%	Yds	Yd/Att	TD	Int–	%	RK
Carter	222	138	62	1624	7.3	10	7–	3	3
Anderson	131	72	55	777	5.9	5	4–	3	
Lewis	10	3	30	18	1.8	0	0–	0	
Willis	2	1	50	8	4.0	0	0–	0	

PUNTING	No	Avg
Lewis	72	44.8
Dressler	1	34.0

KICKING	XP	Att	%	FG	Att	%
Muhlmann	31	31	100	20	36	56
Carter	1	1	100	0	0	0

KANSAS CITY CHIEFS 10-3-1 Hank Stram

Scores of Each Game			Use Name	Pos.	Hgt	Wgt	Age	Int	Pts
14	San Diego	21	Dave Hill	OT	6'5"	260	30		
20	Houston	16	Sid Smith	OT	6'4"	260	23		
16	Denver	3	Jim Tyrer	OT	6'6"	270	32		
31	SAN DIEGO	10	Ed Budde	OG	6'5"	260	30		
38	PITTSBURGH	16	George Daney	OG	6'3"	240	24		
27	WASHINGTON	20	Mo Moorman	OG	6'5"	252	27		
20	Oakland	20	Mike Oriard	C	6'4"	223	23		
10	N.Y. Jets	13	Jack Rudnay	C	6'3"	240	23		
13	CLEVELAND	7	Bruce Bergey	DE	6'4"	240	24		
28	DENVER	10	Aaron Brown	DE	6'5"	265	27	1	6
21	Detroit	32	Marv Upshaw	DE	6'4"	245	24		
26	San Francisco	17	Buck Buchanan	DT	6'7"	275	31	1	
16	OAKLAND	14	Curley Culp	DT	6'1"	265	25		
22	BUFFALO	9	Ed Lothamer	DT	6'5"	270	28		
			Wilbur Young	DT	6'6"	305	22	1	

Use Name	Pos.	Hgt	Wgt	Age	Int	Pts
Bobby Bell	LB	6'4"	228	31	1	6
Willie Lanier	LB	6'1"	245	26	2	
Jim Lynch	LB	6'1"	235	26	1	
Bob Stein	DE-LB	6'2"	235	23	1	
Nate Allen	DB	5'10"	170	23		
Caesar Belser	DB	6'	212	26		
Dave Hadley	DB	5'9"	186	22	1	
Jim Kearney	DB	6'2"	206	28	3	
Jim Marsalis	DB	5'11"	194	25	3	
Kerry Reardon	DB	5'11"	180	22		
Johnny Robinson	DB	6'	205	32	4	
Mike Sensibaugh	DB	5'11"	192	22		
Emmitt Thomas	DB	6'2"	192	28	8	6

Clyde Werner—Knee Injury

Use Name	Pos.	Hgt	Wgt	Age	Int	Pts
Len Dawson	QB	6'	190	37		
John Huarte	QB	6'	185	27		
Mike Livingston	QB	6'3"	212	25		
Mike Adamle	HB	5'9"	197	21		6
Warren McVea	HB	5'10"	182	25		18
Ed Podolak	HB	6'1"	202	24		54
Glenn Ellison	HB-FB	6'1"	215	22		
Wendell Hayes	FB	6'2"	220	30		12
Jim Otis	WR	6'	220	23		12
Dennis Homan	WR	6'1"	180	25		
Bruce Jankowski	WR	5'11"	185	22		
Otis Taylor	WR	6'2"	215	28		48
Elmo Wright	WR	6'	190	22		18
Willie Frazier (from HOU)	TE	6'4"	250	28		
Morris Stroud	TE	6'10"	255	25		6
Jan Stenerud	K	6'2"	187	28		110
Jerrel Wilson	K	6'4"	222	30		

OAKLAND RAIDERS 8-4-2 John Madden

Scores of Each Game			Use Name	Pos.	Hgt	Wgt	Age	Int	Pts
6	New England	20	Bob Brown	OT	6'4"	290	28		
34	San Diego	0	Ron Mix	OT	6'4"	250	33		
34	Cleveland	20	Art Shell	OT	6'5"	255	24		
27	Denver	16	Paul Seiler	C-OT	6'4"	245	25		
34	PHILADELPHIA	10	George Buehler	OG	6'2"	260	24		
31	CINCINNATI	27	Jim Harvey	OG	6'5"	250	28		
20	KANSAS CITY	20	Gene Upshaw	OG	6'5"	255	26		
21	New Orleans	21	Warren Koegel	C	6'3"	250	21		
41	HOUSTON	21	Jim Otto	C	6'2"	248	33		
34	SAN DIEGO	33	Tony Cline	DE	6'2"	230	31		
14	BALTIMORE	37	Ben Davidson	DE	6'8"	280	31		
13	Atlanta	24	Horace Jones	DE	6'3"	240	22		
14	Kansas City	16	Harold Rice	DE	6'2"	230	26		
21	DENVER	13	Tom Gibson	DT	6'6"	290	23		
			Tom Keating	DT	6'3"	247	28		
			Carleton Oats	DT	6'2"	260	28		
			Art Thomas	DT	6'5"	250	24		

Use Name	Pos.	Hgt	Wgt	Age	Int	Pts
Duane Benson	LB	6'2"	215	26		
Dan Conners	LB	6'1"	230	29	3	
Gerald Irons	LB	6'2"	230	24		
Terry Mendenhall	LB	6'1"	210	22		
Gus Otto	LB	6'2"	220	28		
Greg Slough	LB	6'3"	230	23		
Phil Villapiano	LB	6'1"	210	22	2	
Carl Weathers	LB	6'2"	220	23		
Butch Atkinson	DB	6'	180	24	4	6
Willie Brown	DB	6'1"	190	30	2	
Tommy Maxwell	DB	6'2"	195	24		
Jack Tatum	DB	5'10"	200	22	4	
Jimmy Warren	DB	5'11"	175	32	2	12
Nemiah Wilson	DB	6'	160	28	5	

Hewitt Dixon — Injury
Warren Wells — Legal probation — ineligible to play pro football.

Use Name	Pos.	Hgt	Wgt	Age	Int	Pts
George Blanda	QB	6'1"	215	43		86
Daryle Lamonica	QB	6'2"	215	30		
Ken Stabler	QB	6'3"	194	25		12
Clarence Davis	HB	5'10"	190	22		12
Don Highsmith	HB	6'	200	23		6
Charlie Smith	HB	6'1"	205	25		6
Pete Banaszak	FB-HB	5'11"	210	27		48
Bill Enyart	FB	6'4"	235	24		
Marv Hubbard	FB	6'1"	215	25		36
Fred Biletnikoff	WR	6'1"	190	28		54
Drew Buie	WR	6'2"	178	24		12
Eldridge Dickey	WR	6'2"	198	25		
Rod Sherman	WR	6'	190	26		6
Ray Chester	TE	6'3"	220	23		42
Bob Moore	TE	6'3"	220	22		
Jerry DePoyster	K	6'1"	205	25		
Mike Eischeid	K	6'	190	30		

SAN DIEGO CHARGERS 6-8-0 Sid Gillman Harland Svare

Scores of Each Game			Use Name	Pos.	Hgt	Wgt	Age	Int	Pts
21	KANSAS CITY	14	Terry Owens	OT	6'6"	275	27		
0	OAKLAND	34	Russ Washington	OT	6'6"	295	24		
17	Pittsburg	21	Ira Gordon	OG-OT	6'3"	268	23		
10	Kansas City	31	Harris Jones	OG	6'4"	233	26		
16	Denver	20	Walt Sweeney	OG	6'3"	256	30		
20	BUFFALO	3	Doug Wilkerson	OG	6'2"	245	24		
49	N.Y. JETS	21	Sam Gruneisen	C	6'1"	250	30		
17	N.Y. Giants	35	Carl Mauck	C	6'3"	234	24		
20	St. LOUIS	17	Jack Porter	C	6'4"	255	23		
33	Oakland	34	West Grant (from BUF)	DE	6'3"	245	24		
0	Cincinnati	31	Jeff Staggs	DE	6'2"	246	27		
30	MINNESOTA	14	Lee Thomas	DE	6'5"	246	24		
45	DENVER	17	Steve DeLong	DT-DE	6'3"	252	28		
33	Houston	49	Ron East	DT	6'4"	242	28		
			Kevin Hardy	DT	6'5"	260	26		
			Andy Rice	DT	6'3"	268	29		
			Gary Nowak	DT	6'5"	247	22		
			Tom Williams	DT	6'4"	250	23		

Use Name	Pos.	Hgt	Wgt	Age	Int	Pts
Bob Babich	LB	6'2"	230	24		6
Pete Barnes	LB	6'3"	247	26	2	6
Bob Bruggers	LB	6'1"	224	27		
Rick Redman	LB	5'11"	230	28	1	
Mel Rogers	LB	6'2"	230	24		
John Tanner	LB	6'4"	222	26		
Ray White	LB	6'1"	225	22	2	
Joe Beauchamp	DB	6'	185	27	4	
Chuck Detwiler	DB	6'	185	24		
Chris Fletcher	DB	5'11"	185	22	3	6
Jim Hill	DB	6'2"	190	24	2	
Bob Howard	DB	6'1"	190	26	4	
Bryant Salter	DB	6'4"	200	21	6	
Jim Tolbert	DB	6'3"	207	27		

Rick Eber—Injury

Use Name	Pos.	Hgt	Wgt	Age	Int	Pts
Marty Domres	QB	6'3"	215	24		
John Hadl	QB	6'2"	218	31		6
Mike Garrett	HB	5'9"	200	27		42
Mike Montgomery	HB	6'2"	202	22		18
Leon Burns	FB	6'2"	223	26		6
Jeff Queen	FB	6'1"	220	25		42
Eddie Ray	FB	6'1"	230	24		
Chuck Dicus	WR	6'	172	22		6
Gary Garrison	WR	6'1"	193	27		36
Walker Gillette	WR	6'5"	198	24		12
Jerry LeVias	WR	5'10"	178	24		6
Billy Parks	WR	6'1"	185	23		24
Pettis Norman	TE	6'3"	220	31		6
Art Strozier	TE	6'2"	220	25		
Dennis Partee	K	6'2"	218	25		87

DENVER BRONCOS 4-9-1 Lou Saban Jerry Smith

Scores of Each Game			Use Name	Pos.	Hgt	Wgt	Age	Int	Pts
10	MIAMI	10	Sam Brunelli	OT	6'1"	270	28		
13	Green Bay	34	Mike Current	OT	6'4"	274	25		
3	KANSAS CITY	16	Marv Montgomery	OT	6'6"	255	23		
16	OAKLAND	27	Roger Shoals	OT	6'4"	260	32		
20	SAN DIEGO	16	George Goeddeke	OG	6'3"	253	26		
27	Cleveland	0	Mike Schitkner	OG	6'3"	245	24		
16	Philadelphia	17	Larron Jackson	OT-OG	6'3"	270	22		
20	DETROIT	24	Jay Bachman	C	6'3"	250	25		
10	CINCINNATI	24	Larry Kaminski	C	6'2"	245	26		
10	Kansas City	28	Tommy Lyons	C	6'2"	228	23		
22	Pittsburg	10	Lyle Alzado	DE	6'3"	252	22		
6	CHICAGO	3	Walt Barnes	DE	6'3"	250	27		
17	San Diego	45	Rich Jackson	DE	6'2"	255	30		
13	Oakland	21	Dave Costa	DT	6'2"	260	28		
			Jerry Inman	DT	6'3"	256	31		
			Paul Smith	DT	6'3"	256	26		

Use Name	Pos.	Hgt	Wgt	Age	Int	Pts
Carter Campbell	LB	6'3"	232	23		
Ken Criter	LB	5'11"	223	24		
Fred Forsberg	LB	6'1"	235	27	3	6
Bill McKoy	LB	6'3"	235	23		
Chip Myrtle	LB	6'2"	225	26	3	
Olen Underwood	LB	6'2"	220	29	1	
Dave Washington	LB	6'5"	215	23	1	
Butch Byrd	DB	6'	196	29		
Cornell Gordon	DB	6'	187	30	2	
Charlie Greer	DB	6'	205	25	3	
Leroy Mitchell	DB	6'2"	190	26	2	
Randy Montgomery	DB	5'11"	182	24		
George Saimes	DB	5'10"	183	29		
Bill Thompson	DB	6'1"	200	24	5	

Tom Buckman — Injury
Pete Duranko — Injury

Use Name	Pos.	Hgt	Wgt	Age	Int	Pts
Don Horn	QB	6'2"	195	26		
Steve Ramsey	QB	6'2"	210	23		
Floyd Little	HB	5'10"	196	29		36
Fran Lynch	FB-HB	6'1"	205	25		8
Clem Turner	FB	6'1"	236	26		6
Bobby Anderson	HB-FB	6'	208	23		24
Gordon Bowdell	WR	6'2"	203	22		
Jack Gehrke	WR	6'	178	25		
Dwight Harrison	WR	6'1"	178	22		12
Jerry Simmons	WR	6'1"	190	28		6
Bill Van Huesen	WR	6'1"	200	25		
Bill Masters	TE	6'5"	240	27		6
John Mosier	TE	6'3"	220	23		
Jim Whalen (to PHI)	TE	6'2"	210	27		
Jim Turner	K	6'2"	205	30		93

John Embree—Injury

KANSAS CITY CHIEFS

RUSHING

Last Name	No.	Yds	Avg	TD
Podolak	184	708	3.8	9
Hayes	132	537	4.1	1
McVea	68	288	4.2	0
Otis	49	184	3.8	0
Adamle	13	43	3.3	0
Taylor	1	25	25.0	1
Dawson	12	24	2.0	0
Livingston	5	11	2.2	0
Frazier	1	−2	−2.0	0
Wright	1	−10	−10.0	0

RECEIVING

Last Name	No.	Yds	Avg	TD
Taylor	57	1110	19	7
Podolak	36	252	7	0
Wright	26	528	20	3
Stroud	22	454	21	1
Hayes	16	150	9	1
Otis	13	81	6	2
Frazier	10	154	15	0
McVea	5	−3	−1	0
Homan	2	47	24	0
Smith	1	12	12	0
Adamle	1	6	6	1

PUNT RETURNS

Last Name	No.	Yds	Avg	TD
Podolak	14	84	6	0
Homan	10	61	6	0
Reardon	3	5	2	0
Belser	1	2	2	0
Sensibaugh	5	−2	0	0

KICKOFF RETURNS

Last Name	No.	Yds	Avg	TD
Reardon	12	308	26	0
McVea	9	177	20	0
Adamle	7	149	21	0
Hayes	4	75	19	0
Sensibaugh	4	71	18	0
Podolak	3	65	22	0
Bergey	1	15	15	0

PASSING – PUNTING – KICKING

PASSING	Att	Comp	%	Yds	Yd/Att	TD	Int−	%	RK
Dawson	301	167	55	2504	8.3	15	13−	4	2
Livingston	28	12	43	130	4.6	0	0−	0	
Huarte	6	2	33	18	3.0	0	0−	0	
Podolak	2	2	100	42	21.0	0	0−	0	

PUNTING	No	Avg
Wilson	64	44.8

KICKING	XP	Att	%	FG	Att	%
Stenerud	32	32	100	26	44	59
Stein	0	0	0	0	1	0

OAKLAND RAIDERS

RUSHING

Last Name	No.	Yds	Avg	TD
Hubbard	181	867	4.8	5
Banaszak	137	563	4.1	8
Davis	54	321	5.9	2
Highsmith	76	307	4.0	1
Buie	2	32	16.0	0
Stabler	4	29	7.3	2
Lamonica	4	16	4.0	0
Chester	3	5	1.7	0
Smith	11	4	0.4	1
DePoyster	1	−14	−14.0	0

RECEIVING

Last Name	No.	Yds	Avg	TD
Biletnikoff	61	929	15	9
Chester	28	442	16	7
Hubbard	22	167	8	1
Davis	15	97	6	0
Banaszak	13	128	10	0
Sherman	12	187	16	1
Highsmith	10	109	11	0
Buie	5	133	27	2
Dickey	4	89	15	1
Smith	2	67	34	0
Moore	2	26	13	0

PUNT RETURNS

Last Name	No.	Yds	Avg	TD
Atkinson	20	159	8	0
Maxwell	6	21	4	0
Sherman	2	1	0	0
Highsmith	1	0	0	0

KICKOFF RETURNS

Last Name	No.	Yds	Avg	TD
Davis	27	734	27	0
Highsmith	21	454	22	0
Hubbard	3	46	15	0
Banaszak	1	0	0	0
Seiler	1	0	0	0
Smith	1	0	0	0

PASSING – PUNTING – KICKING

PASSING	Att	Comp	%	Yds	Yd/Att	TD	Int−	%	RK
Lamonica	242	118	49	1717	7.1	16	16−	7	7
Blanda	58	32	55	378	6.5	4	6−	10	
Stabler	48	24	50	268	5.6	1	4	8	

PUNTING	No	Avg
DePoyster	51	39.5
Eischeid	11	41.9

KICKING	XP	Att	%	FG	Att	%
Blanda	41	42	98	15	22	68

SAN DIEGO CHARGERS

RUSHING

Last Name	No.	Yds	Avg	TD
Garrett	140	591	4.2	4
Queen	95	318	3.3	4
Montgomery	60	226	3.8	1
Burns	61	223	3.7	1
Parks	5	77	15.4	0
Hadl	18	75	4.2	1
LeVias	4	73	18.3	0
Ray	2	15	7.5	0
Partee	1	7	7.0	0
Norman	1	1	1.0	0
Domres	1	0	0.0	0
Garrison	1	0	0.0	0
Dicus	1	−2	−2.0	0

RECEIVING

Last Name	No.	Yds	Avg	TD
Garrison	42	889	21	6
Parks	41	609	15	4
Garrett	41	283	7	3
Montgomery	28	361	13	2
Norman	27	358	13	1
Queen	23	270	12	3
LeVias	21	265	13	1
Gillette	10	147	15	2
Dicus	6	89	15	1
Burns	3	22	7	0
Strozier	1	6	6	0
Tanner	1	6	6	0

PUNT RETURNS

Last Name	No.	Yds	Avg	TD
LeVias	22	145	7	0
Fletcher	12	68	6	0
Garrett	3	2	1	0

KICKOFF RETURNS

Last Name	No.	Yds	Avg	TD
LeVias	24	559	23	0
Fletcher	11	217	20	0
Salter	8	172	22	0
Rogers	1	20	20	0
Burns	2	19	10	0
Sweeney	1	13	13	0
Thomas	1	0	0	0
Wilkerson	1	0	0	0

PASSING – PUNTING – KICKING

PASSING	Att	Comp	%	Yds	Yd/Att	TD	Int−	%	RK
Hadl	431	233	54	3075	7.1	21	25−	6	4
Domres	12	7	58	97	8.1	1	3−	25	
Montgomery	6	3	50	80	13.3	1	0−	0	
Garrett	1	1	100	53	53.0	0	0−	0	

PUNTING	No	Avg
Partee	55	43.5

KICKING	XP	Att	%	FG	Att	%
Partee	36	37	97	17	29	59

DENVER BRONCOS

RUSHING

Last Name	No.	Yds	Avg	TD
Little	284	1133	4.0	6
Anderson	139	533	3.8	3
Lynch	26	162	6.2	0
Masters	7	71	10.1	0
C. Turner	17	43	2.5	0
Harrison	5	36	7.2	0
Mosier	4	31	7.8	0
Horn	6	15	2.5	0
Van Heusen	1	10	10.0	0
Simmons	1	7	7.0	0
Ramsey	3	6	2.0	0
Gehrke	1	2	2.0	0

RECEIVING

Last Name	No.	Yds	Avg	TD
Anderson	37	353	10	1
Masters	27	382	14	1
Little	26	255	10	0
Simmons	25	403	16	1
Harrison	19	265	14	2
Gehrke	14	254	18	0
Whalen	8	165	21	0
C. Turner	7	65	9	1
Mosier	3	36	12	0
Lynch	2	42	21	1
Bowdell	1	19	19	0
Van Heusen	1	10	10	0
Washington	1	0	0	0
Schnitker	1	−11	−11	0

PUNT RETURNS

Last Name	No.	Yds	Avg	TD
Thompson	29	274	9	0
Greer	11	46	4	0
Mitchell	1	0	0	0

KICKOFF RETURNS

Last Name	No.	Yds	Avg	TD
Little	7	199	28	0
Anderson	8	187	23	0
Thompson	5	105	21	0
C. Turner	5	100	20	0
Criter	5	81	16	0
R. Montgomery	4	80	20	0
Bachman	2	20	10	0
Forsberg	1	19	19	0
Lynch	0	19	0	0

PASSING – PUNTING – KICKING

PASSING	Att	Comp	%	Yds	Yd/Att	TD	Int−	%	RK
Ramsey	178	84	47	1120	6.3	15	13−	7	13
Horn	173	89	51	1056	6.1	3	14−	8	14
Anderson	3	1	33	48	16.0	0	0−	0	
Gehrke	2	1	50	19	9.5	0	0−	0	
Little	1	0	0	0	0.0	0	0−	0	
Van Heusen	1	0	0	0	0.0	0	0−	0	

PUNTING	No	Avg
Van Heusen	76	41.8

KICKING	XP	Att	%	FG	Att	%
J. Turner	18	18	100	25	38	66

1971 Championship Games

Brodie's Mistake and Dallas' Defense

SCORING

DALLAS	0	7	0	7—14
SAN FRANCISCO	0	0	3	0— 3

Second Quarter
Dall.   Hill, 1 yard rush
PAT—Clark (kick)

Third Quarter
S.F.   Gossett, 28 yard field goal

Fourth Quarter
Dall.   D. Thomas, 2 yard rush
PAT—Clark (kick)

TEAM STATISTICS

DALLAS		S.F.
16	First Downs—Total	9
9	First Downs—Rushing	2
7	First Downs—Passing	7
0	First Downs—Penalty	0
2	Fumbles—Number	0
1	Fumbles—Lost Ball	0
2	Penalties—Number	1
30	Yards Penalized	12
3	Missed Field Goals	1
70	Offensive Plays—Total	47
244	Net Yards	239
3.5	Average Gain	5.1
1	Giveaways	3
3	Takeaways	1
+2	Difference	−2

The Cowboys and '49ers both won a return trip to the conference title game on the strength of a strong defense. Dallas had beaten the Vikings 20-12 to begin the playoffs, while the '49ers topped Washington 24-20 in the opening round, and the defensive units would decide the game as they had last week.

Quarterbacks Roger Staubach and John Brodie made no headway against the psyched-up defenses in the first quarter. In the second period, however, Brodie committed a fatal error that the Cowboys capitalized on. Deep in his own territory, Brodie aimed a short screen pass to fullback Ken Willard without noticing Dallas' George Andrie lurking ominously on the scene. Once the ball was in the air, Andrie stepped in front of Willard, grabbed it, and lumbered down to the 1-yard line before being stopped. Calvin Hill carried the ball in, and Mike Clark's kick gave the Cowboys a 7-0 lead. Bruce Gossett put the '49ers on the scoreboard with a 28-yard field goal late in the period that cut the halftime Dallas lead down to 7-3.

The defensive units continued to dominate in the third period, and the slender Dallas lead looked as though it might hold up. In the fourth quarter, however, Roger Staubach went to work on some insurance points. Taking over on their own 20-yard line, the Cowboys drove downfield in a drive in which they converted four third-down situations into first downs. Staubach kept the drive alive with his scrambling, often creating time for his receivers to get open or finding room to run the ball himself. One key third-down play saw coach Tom Landry send tight end Mike Ditka into the lineup after '49er safety Mel Phillips was injured; Ditka promptly caught a clutch third-down pass against substitute safety Johnny Fuller. Duane Thomas sprinted around end for the final two yards, and the Dallas defense never let up for a second in preserving the 14-3 victory.

INDIVIDUAL STATISTICS

RUSHING

DALLAS	No	Yds	Avg.	SAN FRANCISCO	No	Yds	Avg.
Staubach	8	55	6.9	V. Washington	10	58	5.8
Garrison	14	52	3.7	Willard	6	3	0.5
D. Thomas	15	44	2.9		16	61	3.8
Hill	9	21	2.3				
	46	172	3.7				

RECEIVING

	No	Yds	Avg.		No	Yds	Avg.
Truax	2	43	21.5	G. Washington	4	88	22.0
Hayes	2	22	11.0	Kwalick	4	52	13.0
Alworth	1	17	17.0	V. Washington	3	28	9.3
Reeves	1	17	17.0	Willard	1	6	6.0
D. Thomas	1	7	7.0	Witcher	1	6	6.0
Ditka	1	5	5.0	Cunningham	1	4	4.0
Garrison	1	−8	−8.0		14	184	13.1
	9	103	11.4				

PUNTING

	No		Avg.		No		Avg.
Widby	6		45.0	Spurrier	6		38.2

PUNT RETURNS

	No	Yds	Avg.		No	Yds	Avg.
Hayes	1	3	3.0	Fuller	2	10	5.0
Harris	1	1	1.0	Taylor	1	0	0.0
	2	4	2.0		3	10	3.3

KICKOFF RETURNS

	No	Yds	Avg.		No	Yds	Avg.
Harris	1	19	19.0	V. Washington	2	35	17.5
				Cunningham	1	21	21.0
					3	56	18.7

INTERCEPTION RETURNS

	No	Yds	Avg.		
Jordan	1	23	23.0	None	
Andrie	1	7	7.0		
Harris	1	2	2.0		
	3	32	10.7		

PASSING

DALLAS	Att.	Comp.	Comp. Pct.	Yds.	Int.	Yds/ Att.	Yds/ Comp.	Yards Lost Tackled
Staubach	18	9	50.0	103	0	5.7	11.4	6—31
SAN FRANCISCO								
Brodie	30	14	46.7	184	3	6.1	13.1	1— 6

Good Strategy, Wrong Target

SCORING

MIAMI	7	0	7	7—21
BALTIMORE	0	0	0	0— 0

First Quarter
Miami   Warfield, 75 yard pass from Griese
PAT—Yepremian (kick)

Third Quarter
Miami   Anderson, 62 yard interception return
PAT—Yepremian (kick)

Fourth Quarter
Miami   Csonka, 5 yard rush
PAT—Yepremian (kick)

TEAM STATISTICS

MIAMI		BALT.
13	First Downs—Total	16
8	First Downs—Rushing	6
4	First Downs—Passing	10
1	First Downs—Penalty	0
0	Fumbles—Number	1
0	Fumbles—Lost Ball	0
1	Penalties—Number	2
12	Yards Penalized	20
0	Missed Field Goals	3
45	Offensive Plays—Total	68
286	Net Yards	302
6.4	Average Gain	4.4
1	Giveaways	3
3	Takeaways	1
+2	Difference	−2

The Dolphins had to guard against a letdown in this game as they were coming off an exhausting victory in the opening round of the playoffs. The Chiefs and Dolphins had battled back and forth all afternoon, with regulation time ending in a 24-24 tie. The two clubs fought through almost eighteen minutes of overtime before Garo Yepremian ended football's longest game with a 37-yard field goal.

The Colts, on the other hand, were coming off an easy 20-3 triumph over the Browns, so they were well rested physically and emotionally. Coach Don McCafferty planned to use a ball-control offense and a tight defense to defeat the Dolphins, but a 75-yard touchdown pass from Bob Griese to Paul Warfield early in the first quarter put Miami ahead 7-0 and put the pressure on Johnny Unitas and the Baltimore offense. But with starting backs Tom Matte and Norm Bulaich out of action with injuries, the Colts could not grind the yardage out against the quick Miami defense. The Colt defense also held up after the early Miami touchdown, and the half ended with the score 7-0.

With their ground attack getting no place against the Miami defense, the Colts went to the air in the third period. But while Griese had scored on a long bomb in the opening period, Unitas met disaster when he went for the bomb in the third quarter. Throwing deep for Eddie Hinton, Unitas undershot his man and instead hit Miami safety Dick Anderson. With his mates throwing blocks like experienced offensive players, Anderson weaved 62 yards with the ball for the second Miami touchdown.

Unitas had no luck crossing the Miami goal line for the rest of the afternoon, while the Dolphins scored a third touchdown on Larry Csonka's five-yard run which had been set up by a 50-yard pass to Warfield.

INDIVIDUAL STATISTICS

RUSHING

MIAMI	No	Yds	Avg.	BALTIMORE	No	Yds	Avg.
Kiick	18	66	3.7	McCauley	15	50	3.3
Csonka	15	63	4.2	Nottingham	11	33	3.0
Griese	1	12	12.0	Nowatzke	2	5	2.5
Morris	1	3	3.0	Unitas	1	5	5.0
	35	144	4.1		29	93	3.2

RECEIVING

	No	Yds	Avg.		No	Yds	Avg.
Warfield	2	125	62.5	Hinton	6	98	16.3
Twilley	2	33	16.5	Nottingham	4	26	6.5
	4	158	39.5	Perkins	3	19	6.3
				Havrilak	2	31	15.5
				McCauley	2	24	12.0
				Mitchell	1	14	14.0
				Mackey	1	6	6.0
				Matte	1	6	6.0
					20	224	11.2

PUNTING

	No		Avg.		No		Avg.
Seiple	6		42.7	Lee	3		45.3

PUNT RETURNS

	No	Yds	Avg.		No	Yds	Avg.
Scott	2	20	10.0	Volk	5	20	4.0

KICKOFF RETURNS

	No	Yds	Avg.		No	Yds	Avg.
Morris	1	22	22.0	Pittman	2	58	29.0

INTERCEPTION RETURNS

	No	Yds	Avg.		No	Yds	Avg.
Anderson	1	62	62.0	Logan	1	0	0.0
Kolen	1	11	11.0				
Scott	1	0	0.0				
	3	73	24.3				

PASSING

MIAMI	Att.	Comp.	Comp. Pct.	Yds.	Int.	Yds/ Att.	Yds/ Comp.	Yards Lost Tackled
Griese	8	4	50.0	158	1	19.8	39.5	2—16
BALTIMORE								
Unitas	36	20	55.6	224	3	6.3	11.2	3—15

Finally Lassoing the Championship

The Cowboys had ended every season since 1966 with a loss in the playoffs, before finally losing last year in the Super Bowl to Baltimore. But now they were hopeful of kicking that habit with a new quarterback in charge of the offense. Since Roger Staubach had replaced Craig Morton as the starting passer halfway through the season, the Cowboys had won seven straight regular-season games and two playoff games. To end the doubts about their ability to win the big games, the Cowboys would have to beat the Miami Dolphins, an up-and-coming young team masterfully built by head coach Don Shula.

The young Dolphins made their first mistake in the opening period when fullback Larry Csonka muffed a handoff from quarterback Bob Griese on the Dallas 48-yard line. After Dallas recovered the fumble, Staubach led the Cowboys deep into Miami territory before settling for a Mike Clark field goal.

Even in the first quarter, Dallas consistently ate up yardage on the ground, with Duane Thomas and Walt Garrison carrying the ball through gaping holes cut open by Cowboy linemen. The Dallas defense, meanwhile, completely shut off the Miami running attack of Csonka and Jim Kiick. The Cowboys also mixed passes into their attack, and a seven-yard touchdown pass from Staubach to Lance Alworth capped a long Dallas drive in the second period. Although the Dolphins scored on a Garo Yepremian field goal, the Cowboys dominated the first half and took a 10-3 lead into the clubhouse at halftime.

After taking the second-half kickoff, the Cowboys ate up five minutes of the clock with a ball-control drive that featured strong running by Duane Thomas. A pitchout to Thomas for three yards scored the touchdown and opened the Dallas lead to 17-3.

Trailing by two touchdowns after three periods, the Dolphins desperately needed some offensive fireworks in the fourth quarter. Instead, they ran into disaster. With his team finally on the march, Griese lashed a pass at Kiick at mid-field. Cowboy linebacker Chuck Howley had been knocked down when the pass was thrown, but he jumped up and picked it off in front of Kiick. With a convoy of blockers in front of him, Howley chugged downfield with the ball before running out of gas on the Miami 9. Two running plays moved the ball to the 7, and then Staubach hit Mike Ditka in the end zone with a pass to put the game out of reach for the Dolphins. Mike Clark's extra point made the score 24-3, and although the Dolphins launched a drive deep into Dallas territory, a fumble by Griese ended the last Miami scoring threat of the day.

DALLAS		MIAMI
	OFFENSE	
Hayes	WR	Warfield
Liscio	LT	Crusan
Niland	LG	Kuechenberg
Manders	C	DeMarco
Nye	RG	Little
Wright	RT	Evans
Ditka	TE	Fleming
Alworth	WR	Twilley
Staubach	QB	Griese
D. Thomas	RB	Kiick
Garrison	RB	Csonka
	DEFENSE	
L. Cole	LE	Riley
Pugh	LT	Fernandez
Lillie	RT	Heinz
Andrie	RE	Stanfill
Edwards	LLB	Swift
Jordan	MLB	Buoniconti
Howley	RLB	Kolen
Adderley	LCB	Foley
Renfro	RCB	Johnson
Green	LS	Anderson
Harris	RS	Scott

SUBSTITUTES
DALLAS
Offense
Fitzgerald	Truax
Hill	Welch
Reeves	Williams

Defense
Gregory	I. Thomas
Lewis	Toomay
Smith	Waters
Stincic	

Kickers
Clark	Widby

MIAMI
Offense
T. Cole	Moore
Ginn	Morris
Langer	Noonan
Mandich	Stowe

Defense
Cornish	Mumphord
Den Herder	Petrella
Matheson	Powell

Kickers
Yepremian	Seiple

SCORING

DALLAS	3	7	7	7—24
MIAMI	0	3	0	0— 3

First Quarter
Dallas   Clark, 9 yard field goal

Second Quarter
Dallas   Alworth, 7 yard pass from Staubach   PAT — Clark (kick)
Miami   Yepremian, 31 yard field goal

Third Quarter
Dallas   D. Thomas, 3 yard rush
PAT — Clark (kick)

Fourth Quarter
Dallas   Ditka, 7 yard pass from Staubach   PAT — Clark (kick)

TEAM STATISTICS

DALLAS		MIAMI
23	First Downs — Total	10
15	First Downs — Rushing	3
8	First Downs — Passing	7
0	First Downs — Penalty	0
1	Fumbles — Number	2
1	Fumbles — Lost Ball	2
3	Penalties — Number	0
15	Yards Penalized	0
0	Missed Field Goals	1
69	Offensive Plays	44
352	Net Yards	185
5.1	Average Gain	4.2
1	Giveaways	3
3	Takeaways	1
+2	Difference	−2

INDIVIDUAL STATISTICS

DALLAS	No	Yds	Avg.	MIAMI	No	Yds	Avg.
RUSHING							
D. Thomas	19	95	5.0	Csonka	9	40	4.4
Garrison	14	74	5.3	Kiick	10	40	4.0
Hill	7	25	3.6	Griese	1	0	0.0
Staubach	5	18	3.6		20	80	4.0
Ditka	1	17	17.0				
Hayes	1	16	16.0				
Reeves	1	7	7.0				
	48	252	5.3				
RECEIVING							
D. Thomas	3	17	5.7	Warfield	4	39	9.8
Alworth	2	28	14.0	Kiick	3	21	7.0
Ditka	2	28	14.0	Csonka	2	18	9.0
Hayes	2	23	11.5	Fleming	1	27	27.0
Garrison	2	11	5.5	Twilley	1	20	20.0
Hill	1	12	12.0	Mandich	1	9	9.0
	12	119	9.9		12	134	11.2
PUNTING							
Widby	5		37.2	Seiple	5		40.0
PUNT RETURNS							
Hayes	1	−1	−1.0	Scott	1	21	21.0
KICKOFF RETURNS							
I. Thomas	1	32	32.0	Morris	4	90	22.5
Waters	1	11	11.0	Ginn	1	32	32.0
	2	43	21.5		5	122	24.4
INTERCEPTION RETURNS							
Howley	1	41	41.0	None			

PASSING

DALLAS	Att	Comp	Comp Pct.	Yds	Int	Yds/ Att.	Yds/ Comp	Yards Lost Tackled
Staubach	19	12	63.2	119	0	6.3	9.9	2−19
MIAMI								
Griese	23	12	52.2	134	1	5.8	11.2	1−29

1972 N.F.C. Grounded but Not Stopped

In modern offensive football, the wide receiver was fast becoming an ornamental decoy, while the quarterback's main function was no longer passing the ball but handing it off. A record number of ten rushers carried the ball for 1,000 yards this year as the running back now was pro football's chief offensive weapon. The development of zone pass defenses had cut down on the air game's potency, so clubs more and more decided to move the ball on the ground in three- and four-yard chunks rather than going for twenty or thirty yards at a time with pass plays. An ever-increasing number of teams found that the best offense against a zone defense was two strong running backs and a strong-legged place kicker. Fading away into history were the days when long bombers like Van Brocklin, Unitas, and Lamonica captivated crowds and captured headlines with spectacular heaves.

EASTERN DIVISION

Washington Redskins—George Allen's collection of misfits and rejects, known collectively as the Over the Hill Gang, stayed at a high level of enthusiasm all season and knocked the Dallas Cowboys out of first place in the Eastern Division for the first time since 1965. Allen's pride and joy was his defensive unit, which allowed the fewest points of any defense in the conference. The offense moved the ball well despite the absence of Sonny Jurgensen for most of the season with injuries; most of the time, substitute quarterback Bill Kilmer had only to hand off to halfback Larry Brown to keep the Skins on the march. Running at top speed and using his blockers well, Brown piled up a conference-leading total of 1,216 yards rushing despite sitting out the last two games of the season with an injury.

Dallas Cowboys—The Cowboys still had one of the deepest rosters in the NFL, but they dropped to second place in the East because they lacked the fine competitive edge they had last year. They lost to the Packers, Redskins, and '49ers during the season, and with a chance to take first place on the final day of the season they lost a listless 23-3 decision to New York and settled for the wild-card spot in the playoffs. The Cowboys did have several personnel problems. Duane Thomas' non-relations with his teammates forced the team to trade him to San Diego, a shoulder injury sidelined quarterback Roger Staubach for most of the season, a bad back took George Andrie out of the defensive line, and Bob Lilly's back hurt him all through the season.

New York Giants—Comebackers and newcomers led the Giants to a surprising winning season. The chief comeback was by halfback Ron Johnson, rebounding from a 1971 knee injury to carry the ball with his old authority and flair. Kicker Pete Gogolak also came back from a poor 1971 season to give the Giants a consistent three-point threat within the 40-yard line. Newcomers to the New York squad more than made up for the traded Fran Tarkenton and Fred Dryer. Quarterback Norm Snead led the NFC in passing statistics, but his main value was as a steady leader on offense. The defensive line improved immensely with the addition of end Jack Gregory from the Browns and rookie tackles John Mendenhall and Larry Jacobson.

St. Louis Cardinals—Despite top talent in some positions, the Cards stumbled through a season in which Gary Cuozzo, Tim Van Galder, and Jim Hart took turns as the starting quarterback, in which the defensive line had problems rushing opposing passers, and in which injuries sidelined linebackers Jamie Rivers, Jeff Staggs, and Mike McGill. Even though the Cards won their final two games, coach Bob Holloway got the ax after the season; departing of his own accord was safety Larry Wilson, retiring after a great thirteen-year pro career.

Philadelphia Eagles—The tough defense coach Ed Khayat had built last year was weakened by the trade of Tim Rossovich to San Diego because of a personality clash with the coach and by injuries to Ernie Calloway and Steve Zabel. The offensive had great receivers in Harold Jackson, Ben Hawkins, and Harold Carmichael but didn't have a quarterback who could consistently get the ball to them. Veteran Pete Liske had all the qualifications except a strong arm, while rookie John Reaves had a great arm but also the chronic rookie problem of inexperience. Rookie Po James played well at halfback, but the Eagles lacked the great back necessary in this era of running football.

CENTRAL DIVISION

Green Bay Packers—In his second year as coach, Dan Devine took the Packers back to the top in the Central Division with a grinding defense and a methodical ball-control offense. The pride of the defense was the secondary of Ken Ellis, rookie Willie Buchanon, Jim Hill, and Al Matthews, four young speedsters who minimized the effect of Willie Wood's retirement. The Packers didn't have any stars like Willie Davis or Henry Jordan or a younger Ray Nitschke in the front lines, but the rebuilt front four and linebacking constantly frustrated enemy running attacks. Bart Starr's retirement left Scott Hunter in charge of the offense, although Starr remained as an assistant coach and called all the plays for Hunter. Even though his arm was not strong, Hunter kept the attack moving simply by handing off to back John Brockington and MacArthur Lane.

Detroit Lions—The Detroit offense steadily turned out points, ranking second in the league in point production, but the defense could not compete with the other units in Green Bay and Minnesota. Coach Joe Schmidt was swimming in offensive talents—a fine quarterback in Greg Landry, good runners in Steve Owens and Altie Taylor, a star receiver in Charlie Sanders, and one of the best offensive lines in the NFL. The chief defensive shortcoming was the lack of a strong pass rush. Despite taking defensive linemen Bob Bell and Herb Orvis as their first draft choices the last two years, the Lions had not rebuilt their line into a top unit. At the end of the year coach Schmidt resigned and defensive stars Wayne Walker and Dick LeBeau retired.

Minnesota Vikings—The Vikings solved their quarterback problems by getting Fran Tarkenton back from the Giants in a trade, but the defense slumped off from the super level it had been playing at. Injuries nagged Carl Eller, Alan Page, and Gary Larsen and made the Minnesota front four less fearsome than usual. Middle linebacker Lonnie Warwick missed eight games on the disabled list, and rookie Jeff Siemon showed much promise and made many mistakes. On offense, Tarkenton gave the team a major-league passer, but the receiving corps suffered because of Gene Washington's second straight injury-plagued season. The Viking running backs were all good for sure short yardage, but none of them ever threatened to break loose a long run.

Chicago Bears—The Bears had a completely schizophrenic offense, first in the NFL in rushing, last in passing. Quarterback Bobby Douglass was a big, strong lad who set a new record of 968 yards gained rushing by a quarterback, but his passes came infrequently and often shot wide of the intended receiver. Douglass, fullback Jim Harrison, and halfbacks Don Shy and Cyril Pinder moved the ball well on the ground, but enemy defenses paid a minimum of attention to the Chicago air game. For a while the all-out running attack worked, but once opposing teams got wise to the Bear game plan, Chicago lost six of their last seven games. Coach Abe Gibron's first year on the job saw Gale Sayers retire with a bad knee and Dick Butkus continue to play up to All-Pro standards with a knee that hurt him more and more with each game.

WESTERN DIVISION

San Francisco '49ers—Heisman Trophy winner Steve Spurrier had done little else but punt in his past five seasons as a pro, but he stepped in for the injured John Brodie in mid-season and quarterbacked the '49ers to first place in the West. With a solid line to protect him and two great receivers in Gene Washington and Ted Kwalick to throw to, Spurrier engineered five San Francisco victories in the final six games, reaching his personal peak with five touchdown passes on November 19 against the Bears. On defense, the '49ers launched a ferocious pass rush despite disabling injuries to Cedrick Hardman and Earl Edwards; Tommy Hart and Charley Krueger responded with superior seasons to pick up the slack. The '49er playoff hopes soared in their final game when Brodie returned from the injured list to spark the team to a 20-17 victory over Minnesota.

Atlanta Falcons—The Falcons were strong at every position except quarterback, kicker, and defensive tackle, but these flaws kept the club from doing better than second place in the West. Quarterback Bob Berry had made the best of his limited talent, but coach Norm Van Brocklin had lost confidence in his ability to lead the Falcons to a title. Neither did kicker Bill Bell nor defensive tackles Glen Condren and Mike Lewis satisfy the coach. The Falcons did have a liberal supply of All-Stars in Claude Humphrey, John Zook, Tommy Nobis, Ken Reaves, George Kunz, Jim Mitchell, and Dave Hampton. Picked up from Green Bay, Hampton gained his 1,000th yard rushing of the year late in the final game. The game was stopped and the ball presented to Hampton. On his next carry Hampton lost five yards to finish at 995 yards for the year. Hampton, however, kept the ball.

Los Angeles Rams—With the death of owner Dan Reeves in April 1971, his family operated the club for a year and then sold the Rams to Robert Irsay. Before the 1972 season began, however, Irsay traded the Rams to Carroll Rosenbloom for his ownership of the Colts. Rosenbloom had grown accustomed to excellence from his Colt teams, but his first Ram squad disappointed him by finishing below .500 and in third place. Coach Tommy Prothro had daringly traded off Deacon Jones during the summer and replaced him with ex-Giant Fred Dryer, but leaks in the secondary hurt the defense more than the rebuilt front four. Quarterback Roman Gabriel's sore arm put a crimp in the offense, and five losses in the last six games cost Prothro his job.

New Orleans Saints—While the mid-1960s expansion teams in Atlanta, Miami, and Cincinnati had all achieved respectability, the Saints still had a look of a patchwork team created out of odds and ends. Coach J.D. Roberts had some topnotch players in quarterback Archie Manning, receiver Danny Abramowicz, tackle Glen Ray Hines, and rookie middle linebacker Joe Federspiel, but most of the roster was made up of journeymen and inexperienced youngsters. The distinguishing marks of the Saints this year were an uncanny ability to lose the ball on fumbles and interceptions and a morale problem in which the players expected one another to make errors and lose games.

FINAL TEAM STATISTICS

OFFENSE

	ATL.	CHI.	DALL.	DET.	G.B.	L.A.	MINN.	N.O.	N.Y.	PHIL.	ST.L.	S.F.	WASH.
FIRST DOWNS:													
Total	231	190	256	240	195	238	235	226	**265**	203	181	234	235
by Rushing	113	**124**	118	120	109	113	95	83	120	78	68	87	110
by Passing	101	54	126	97	72	108	127	123	124	110	102	**129**	106
by Penalty	17	12	12	**23**	14	17	13	20	21	15	11	18	19
RUSHING:													
Number	500	536	499	473	**544**	472	472	337	524	398	361	445	513
Yards	2092	**2360**	2124	2021	2127	2209	1740	1230	2022	1393	1229	1616	2082
Average Yards	4.2	4.4	4.3	4.3	3.9	**4.7**	3.7	3.6	3.9	3.5	3.4	3.6	4.1
Touchdowns	16	15	17	**20**	17	17	11	5	16	2	9	11	17
PASSING:													
Attempts	296	205	367	305	237	371	385	**449**	344	375	363	380	284
Completions	157	78	196	155	101	184	218	**230**	206	184	171	217	159
Completion Percentage	53.0	38.0	53.4	50.8	42.6	49.6	56.6	51.2	**59.9**	49.1	47.1	57.1	56.0
Passing Yards	2202	1283	2580	2283	1536	2282	2726	2781	2537	2527	2259	**2888**	2281
Avg. Yards per Attempt	7.4	6.3	7.0	7.5	6.5	6.2	7.1	6.2	7.4	6.7	6.2	7.6	**8.0**
Avg. Yards per Complet.	14.0	**16.4**	13.2	14.7	15.2	12.4	12.5	12.1	12.3	13.7	13.2	13.3	14.3
Times Tackled Passing	41	32	31	26	17	16	26	43	**10**	53	30	22	11
Yards Lost Tackled	283	175	238	149	124	136	203	347	**76**	457	221	153	88
Net Yards	1919	1108	2342	2134	1412	2146	2523	2434	2461	2070	2038	**2735**	2193
Touchdowns	13	9	16	19	7	13	19	18	20	10	11	**27**	21
Interceptions	15	13	23	18	**9**	22	13	21	15	20	23	24	15
Percent Intercepted	5.1	4.3	6.3	5.9	3.8	5.9	**3.4**	4.7	4.4	5.3	6.3	6.3	5.3
PUNTS:													
Number	61	67	51	43	65	53	62	71	47	63	**73**	64	59
Average Distance	42.8	41.2	38.2	40.3	41.8	**44.2**	42.8	40.8	42.7	40.3	39.4	39.7	38.5
PUNT RETURNS:													
Number	27	28	28	18	25	33	26	16	18	27	16	**44**	34
Yards	194	178	134	100	364	347	159	43	125	179	61	**373**	159
Average Yards	7.2	6.4	4.8	5.6	**14.6**	10.5	6.1	2.7	6.9	6.6	3.8	8.5	4.7
Touchdowns	0	0	0	0	**2**	0	0	0	0	0	0	0	0
KICKOFF RETURNS:													
Number	52	52	50	52	49	56	42	**62**	50	59	53	44	48
Yards	1039	**1528**	1080	1304	1141	1287	989	1312	1262	1375	1152	1041	1133
Average Yards	20.0	**29.4**	21.6	25.1	23.3	23.0	23.5	21.2	25.2	23.3	21.7	23.7	23.6
Touchdowns	0	**2**	0	0	0	0	0	0	1	0	0	1	0
INTERCEPTION RETURNS:													
Number	18	21	16	12	17	16	**26**	14	23	19	11	19	17
Yards	205	193	213	184	223	251	365	141	205	164	118	146	287
Average Yards	11.4	9.2	13.3	15.3	13.1	15.7	14.0	10.1	8.9	8.6	10.7	7.7	**16.9**
Touchdowns	1	0	1	1	1	1	2	0	2	0	0	**3**	1
PENALTIES:													
Number	73	74	**90**	48	63	78	51	69	57	76	64	73	78
Yards	650	574	**841**	417	610	648	440	585	512	690	582	664	721
FUMBLES: Number	42	40	27	**17**	22	24	32	33	32	37	43	30	27
Number Lost	19	22	15	**7**	10	9	19	16	14	18	16	13	11
POINTS:													
Total	269	225	319	339	304	291	301	215	331	145	193	**353**	336
PAT Attempts	31	27	36	40	29	31	34	26	39	12	22	**43**	42
PAT Made	31	27	36	39	29	31	34	24	34	11	19	**41**	40
FG Attempts	30	24	36	29	**48**	41	33	25	31	35	22	29	30
FG Made	16	12	21	20	**33**	24	21	11	21	20	14	18	14
Percent FG Made	53.3	50.0	58.3	**69.0**	68.8	58.5	63.6	44.0	67.7	57.1	63.6	62.1	46.7
Safeties	**2**	0	**2**	0	1	1	0	1	0	1	0	0	1

DEFENSE

	ATL.	CHI.	DALL.	DET.	G.B.	L.A.	MINN.	N.O.	N.Y.	PHIL.	ST.L.	S.F.	WASH.
FIRST DOWNS:													
Total	221	224	217	239	209	235	**200**	251	218	268	276	221	223
by Rushing	122	96	**81**	126	85	101	103	107	101	137	119	96	95
by Passing	83	108	113	103	109	110	**82**	129	111	117	138	105	108
by Penalty	16	20	23	10	15	24	15	15	**6**	14	19	20	20
RUSHING:													
Number	504	476	428	491	443	438	454	482	**402**	544	548	446	427
Yards	2063	1751	**1515**	2204	1517	1762	2002	2089	1855	2266	2189	1847	1733
Average Yards	4.1	3.7	3.5	4.5	**3.4**	4.0	4.4	4.3	4.6	4.2	4.0	4.1	4.1
Touchdowns	16	11	**7**	14	14	9	13	15	9	22	11	12	12
PASSING:													
Attempts	**301**	342	382	312	340	363	331	367	333	318	365	366	367
Completions	**137**	180	187	171	174	181	169	213	182	175	221	169	186
Completion Percentage	**45.5**	52.6	49.0	54.8	51.2	49.9	51.1	58.0	54.7	55.0	60.5	46.2	50.7
Passing Yards	1911	2345	2508	2146	2209	2472	**1791**	2596	2571	2615	2733	2582	2130
Avg. Yards per Attempt	6.3	6.9	6.6	6.9	6.5	6.8	**5.4**	7.1	7.7	8.2	7.5	7.1	5.8
Avg. Yards per Complet.	13.9	13.0	13.4	12.5	12.7	13.7	**10.6**	12.2	14.1	14.9	12.4	15.3	11.5
Times Tackled Passing	24	23	32	21	29	42	21	24	37	17	22	**46**	35
Yards Lost Tackled	207	173	268	142	252	327	92	194	232	143	183	**403**	268
Net Yards	1704	2172	2240	2004	1957	2145	**1699**	2402	2339	2472	2550	2179	1862
Touchdowns	13	16	18	18	**7**	20	13	21	19	20	15	14	10
Interceptions	18	21	16	12	17	16	**26**	14	23	19	11	19	17
Percent Intercepted	6.0	6.1	4.2	3.8	5.0	4.4	**7.9**	3.8	6.9	6.0	3.0	5.2	4.6
PUNTS:													
Number	56	62	65	46	66	71	62	52	47	54	48	**72**	69
Average Distance	41.8	43.0	40.6	38.8	41.4	41.2	41.5	39.3	**38.1**	40.5	39.4	43.4	40.1
PUNT RETURNS:													
Number	30	24	**15**	26	32	22	35	36	27	26	37	20	19
Yards	239	126	41	321	225	54	317	281	171	137	144	70	**39**
Average Yards	8.0	5.3	2.7	12.3	7.0	2.5	9.1	7.8	6.3	5.3	3.9	3.5	**2.1**
Touchdowns	0	0	0	1	0	0	0	0	0	0	0	0	0
KICKOFF RETURNS:													
Number	48	42	52	68	46	54	62	50	63	41	**40**	66	53
Yards	1076	1025	1272	1593	932	999	1373	1129	1516	**886**	1037	1530	1191
Average Yards	22.4	24.4	24.5	23.4	20.3	**18.5**	22.1	22.6	24.1	21.6	25.9	23.2	22.5
Touchdowns	1	0	0	1	0	0	0	0	0	0	1	0	0
INTERCEPTION RETURNS:													
Number	15	13	23	23	**9**	22	13	21	15	20	23	24	15
Yards	206	104	302	294	**69**	439	116	349	192	198	289	240	160
Average Yards	13.7	8.0	13.1	16.3	**7.7**	20.0	8.9	16.6	12.8	9.9	12.6	10.0	10.7
Touchdowns	1	1	1	**0**	2	3	**0**	1	**0**	**0**	3	1	1
PENALTIES:													
Number	61	69	59	**86**	50	60	47	78	66	72	68	81	64
Yards	555	644	586	703	446	553	490	**711**	641	637	645	677	568
FUMBLES: Number	23	37	**40**	32	35	25	27	27	31	30	31	**40**	28
Number Lost	15	14	17	15	**19**	11	14	13	15	8	16	17	15
POINTS:													
Total	274	275	240	290	226	286	252	361	247	352	303	249	**218**
PAT Attempts	32	31	28	34	26	34	27	38	28	43	31	28	**23**
PAT Made	31	30	27	32	25	32	24	38	25	42	31	28	**23**
FG Attempts	31	27	34	34	27	30	35	43	29	**25**	47	29	33
FG Made	17	19	**15**	18	**15**	16	22	31	18	16	28	17	19
Percent FG Made	54.8	70.4	**44.1**	52.9	55.6	53.3	62.9	72.1	62.1	64.0	59.6	58.6	57.6
Safeties	**0**	1	**0**	**0**	**0**	1	**0**	1	**0**	2	1	1	**0**

CONFERENCE PLAYOFFS

December 23, at San Francisco (Attendance 59,746)

SCORING

SAN FRANCISCO	7	14	7	0–28
DALLAS	3	10	0	17–30

First Quarter
- S.F. V. Washington, 97 yard kickoff return–PAT–Gossett (kick)
- DAL. Fritsch, 37 yard field goal

Second Quarter
- S.F. Schreiber, 1 yard rush PAT–Gossett (kick)
- S.F. Schreiber, 1 yard rush PAT–Gossett (kick)
- DAL. Fritsch, 45 yard field goal
- DAL. Alworth, 28 yard pass from Morton–PAT–Fritsch (kick)

Third Quarter
- S.F. Schreiber, 1 yard rush PAT–Gossett (kick)

Fourth Quarter
- DAL. Fritsch, 27 yard field goal
- DAL. Parks, 20 yard pass from Staubach–PAT–Fritsch (kick)
- DAL. Sellers, 10 yard pass from Staubach–PAT–Fritsch (kick)

TEAM STATISTICS

S.F.		DAL.
13	First Downs–Total	22
7	First Downs–Rushing	5
6	First Downs–Passing	15
0	First Downs–Penalty	2
5	Fumbles–Number	4
1	Fumbles–Lost Ball	3
7	Penalties–Number	3
56	Yards Penalized	35
2	Missed Field Goals	0
59	Offensive Plays	77
261	Net Yards	402
4.4	Average Gain	5.2
3	Giveaways	5
5	Takeaways	3
+2	Difference	–2

INDIVIDUAL STATISTICS

SAN FRANCISCO	No.	Yds.	Avg.	DALLAS	No.	Yds.	Avg.
RUSHING							
V. Washington	10	56	5.6	Hill	18	125	6.9
Schreiber	26	52	2.0	Staubach	3	23	7.7
Thomas	1	3	3.0	Garrison	9	15	1.7
	37	111	3.0	Morton	1	2	2.0
					31	165	5.3
RECEIVING							
Riley	4	41	10.3	Parks	7	125	16.9
G. Washington	3	76	25.3	Garrison	3	24	8.0
Schreiber	3	20	6.7	Alworth	2	50	25.0
V. Washington	1	8	8.0	Sellers	2	21	10.5
Kwalick	1	5	5.0	Montgomery	2	19	9.5
	12	150	12.5	Hayes	1	13	13.0
				Ditka	1	9	9.0
				Hill	1	6	6.0
				Truax	1	3	3.0
					20	270	13.5
PUNTING							
McCann	6		37.3	Bateman	6		41.8
PUNT RETURNS							
Taylor	1	5	5.0	Waters	1	2	2.0
KICKOFF RETURNS							
V. Washington	3	136	45.3	Harris	3	83	27.7
Beard	1	5	5.0				
McGill	1	5	5.0				
	5	146	29.2				
INTERCEPTION RETURNS							
Vanderbundt	2	4	2.0	Waters	2	12	6.0

PASSING

	Att.	Comp.	Comp. Pct.	Yds.	Int.	Yds/ Att.	Yds/ Comp.	Yards Lost Tackled
SAN FRANCISCO								
Brodie	22	12	54.5	150	2	6.8	12.5	0– 0
DALLAS								
Morton	21	8	38.1	96	2	4.6	12.0	
Staubach	20	12	60.0	174	0	8.7	14.5	
	41	20	48.8	270	2	6.6	13.5	5–33

December 24, at Washington (Attendance 52,321)

SCORING

WASHINGTON	0	10	0	6–16
GREEN BAY	0	3	0	0– 3

Second Quarter
- G.B. Marcol, 17 yard field goal
- WASH. Jefferson, 32 yard pass from Kilmer–PAT–Knight (kick)
- WASH. Knight, 42 yard field goal

Fourth Quarter
- WASH. Knight, 35 yard field goal
- WASH. Knight, 46 yard field goal

TEAM STATISTICS

WASH.		G.B.
13	First Downs–Total	10
6	First Downs–Rushing	2
4	First Downs–Passing	8
3	First Downs–Penalty	0
1	Fumbles–Number	0
1	Fumbles–Lost Ball	0
4	Penalties–Number	6
39	Yards Penalized	54
0	Missed Field Goals	1
51	Offensive Plays	55
232	Net Yards	211
4.5	Average Gain	3.8
1	Giveaways	1
1	Takeaways	1
0	Difference	0

INDIVIDUAL STATISTICS

WASHINGTON	No.	Yds.	Avg.	GREEN BAY	No.	Yds.	Avg.
RUSHING							
Brown	25	101	4.0	Lane	14	56	4.0
Harraway	10	34	3.4	Hunter	2	13	6.5
Kilmer	1	3	3.0	Brockington	13	9	0.7
	36	138	3.8		29	78	2.7
RECEIVING							
Jefferson	5	84	16.8	Lane	4	42	10.5
Taylor	2	16	8.0	Dale	2	28	14.0
	7	100	14.3	Glass	2	23	11.5
				Brockington	2	17	8.5
				Staggers	1	23	23.0
				Garrett	1	17	17.0
					12	150	12.5
PUNTING							
Bragg	6		46.5	Widby	8		36.6
PUNT RETURNS							
Haymond	2	4	2.0	Staggers	3	20	6.7
Vactor	1	15	15.0	Ellis	1	13	13.0
	3	19	6.3		4	33	8.3
KICKOFF RETURNS							
Mul-Key	2	60	30.0	Thomas	3	50	16.7
				Hudson	1	12	12.0
					4	62	15.5
INTERCEPTION RETURNS							
Hanburger	1	15	15.0	None			

PASSING

	Att.	Comp.	Comp. Pct.	Yds.	Int.	Yds/ Att.	Yds/ Comp.	Yards Lost Tackled
WASHINGTON								
Kilmer	14	7	50.0	100	0	7.1	14.3	1– 6
GREEN BAY								
Hunter	24	12	50.0	150	1	6.3	12.5	2–17

WASHINGTON REDSKINS 11-3-0 George Allen

Scores of Each Game		
24	Minnesota	21
24	ST. LOUIS	10
23	New England	24
14	PHILADELPHIA	0
33	St. Louis	3
24	DALLAS	20
23	N.Y. Giants	16
35	N.Y. Jets	17
27	N.Y. GIANTS	13
24	ATLANTA	13
21	GREEN BAY	16
23	Philadelphia	7
24	Dallas	34
17	BUFFALO	24

Use Name	Pos.	Hgt	Wgt	Age	Int	Pts
Terry Hermeling	OT	6'5"	255	26		
Mitch Johnson	OT	6'4"	250	30		
Walt Rock	OT	6'5"	255	31		
Paul Laaveg	OG	6'4"	245	23		
John Wilbur	OG	6'3"	250	29		
Ray Schoenke	OT-OG	6'3"	250	30		
Len Hauss	C	6'2"	235	30		
George Burman	OG-C	6'3"	255	29		
Verlon Biggs	DE	6'4"	275	29		6
Mike Fanucci	DE	6'4"	225	22		
Jimmie Jones	DE	6'3"	215	25		
Ron McDole	DT-DE	6'3"	265	32		
Bill Brundige	DT	6'5"	270	23		
Manny Sistrunk	DT	6'5"	265	25		
Diron Talbert	DT	6'5"	255	28		

Jim Snowden — Injury

Use Name	Pos.	Hgt	Wgt	Age	Int	Pts
Chris Hamburger	LB	6'2"	218	31	4	6
Harold McLinton	LB	6'2"	235	25	2	
Jack Pardee	LB	6'2"	225	36		
Myron Pottios	LB	6'2"	232	32		
Rusty Tillman	LB	6'2"	230	26		
Mike Bass	DB	6'	190	27	3	6
Speedy Duncan	DB	5'10"	180	29	1	
Pat Fischer	DB	5'10"	170	32	4	
Alvin Haymond	DB	6'	194	30		
Jon Jaqua	DB	6'	190	24		
Brig Owens	DB	5'11"	190	29	1	
Richie Petitbon	DB	6'3"	208	34		
Jeff Severson	DB	6'1"	180	22		
Rosey Taylor	DB	5'11"	186	33	1	
Ted Vactor	DB	6'	185	28	1	

Tommy Mason — Injury

Use Name	Pos.	Hgt	Wgt	Age	Int	Pts
Sonny Jurgensen	QB	5'11"	203	38		
Billy Kilmer	QB	6'	204	32		
Sam Wyche	QB	6'4"	218	27		
Larry Brown	HB	5'11"	195	24		72
Bob Brunet	HB	6'1"	205	26		12
Herb Mul–Key	HB	6'	190	22		6
George Nock	HB	5'10"	200	26		
Charlie Harraway	FB	6'2"	215	27		36
Mike Hull	FB	6'3"	220	27		
Jeff Jordan	HB-FB	6'1"	215	27		
Roy Jefferson	WR	6'2"	195	28		18
Bill Malinchak	WR	6'1"	200	28		8
Clifton McNeil	WR	6'2"	187	32		
Charley Taylor	WR	6'3"	210	31		42
Mack Alston	TE	6'2"	230	25		
Jerry Smith	TE	6'2"	208	29		42
Mike Bragg	K	5'11"	186	25		
Curt Knight	K	6'1"	190	29		82

DALLAS COWBOYS 10-4-0 Tom Landry

Scores of Each Game		
28	PHILADELPHIA	6
23	N.Y. Giants	14
13	Green Bay	16
17	PITTSBURGH	13
21	Baltimore	0
20	Washington	24
28	DETROIT	24
34	San Diego	28
33	ST. LOUIS	24
28	Philadelphia	7
10	SAN FRANCISCO	31
27	St. Louis	6
34	WASHINGTON	24
3	N.Y. GIANTS	23

Use Name	Pos.	Hgt	Wgt	Age	Int	Pts
Ralph Neely	OT	6'5"	265	28		
Rayfield Wright	OT	6'7"	255	27		
Rodney Wallace	OG-OT	6'5"	255	23		
John Niland	OG	6'4"	245	28		6
Blaine Nye	OG	6'4"	250	26		
John Fitzgerald	C-OG	6'5"	250	24		
Dave Manders	C	6'2"	250	30		
George Andrie	DE	6'7"	250	32		
Larry Cole	DE	6'4"	250	25		
Tody Smith	DE	6'5"	245	23		
Pat Toomay	DE	6'5"	244	27		
Bill Gregory	DE	6'5"	255	22		
Bob Lilly	DT	6'4"	260	33		
Jethro Pugh	DT	6'6"	260	28		

Use Name	Pos.	Hgt	Wgt	Age	Int	Pts
John Babinecz	LB	6'1"	222	22		
Ralph Coleman	LB	6'4"	216	22		
Dave Edwards	LB	6'3"	225	33		
Chuck Howley	LB	6'3"	225	36	1	
Lee Roy Jordan	LB	6'2"	220	31	2	
Mike Keller	LB	6'4"	220	21		
D. D. Lewis	LB	6'2"	225	26	1	
Herb Adderly	DB	6'1"	200	33		
Benny Barnes	DB	6'1"	190	21		
Cornell Green	DB	6'4"	208	32	2	
Cliff Harris	DB	6'	184	23	3	
Mel Renfro	DB	6'	190	30	1	
Mark Washington	DB	5'10"	188	24		2
Charlie Waters	DB	6'1"	193	23	6	6

Use Name	Pos.	Hgt	Wgt	Age	Int	Pts
Craig Morton	QB	6'4"	214	29		12
Roger Staubach	QB	6'2"	197	30		
Mike Montgomery	HB	6'2"	210	23		18
Dan Reeves	HB	6'1"	200	28		
Calvin Hill	FB-HB	6'3"	227	25		54
Robert Newhouse	FB-HB	5'10"	202	22		6
Walt Garrison	FB	6'	205	28		60
Bill Thomas	FB	6'2"	225	22		
Lance Alworth	WR	6'	180	32		12
Bob Hayes	WR	6'	185	29		
Billy Parks	WR	6'1"	185	24		6
Ron Sellers	WR	6'4"	195	25		30
Mike Ditka	TE	6'3"	225	32		6
Jean Fugett	TE	6'3"	220	20		
Billy Truax	TE	6'5"	240	29		
Marv Bateman	K	6'4"	213	22		
Toni Fritsch	K	5'7"	185	27		99

NEW YORK GIANTS 8-6-0 Alex Webster

Scores of Each Game		
16	Detroit	30
14	DALLAS	23
27	Philadelphia	12
45	NEW ORLEANS	21
23	San Francisco	17
27	ST. LOUIS	21
16	WASHINGTON	23
29	DENVER	17
13	Washington	27
13	St. Louis	7
62	PHILADELPHIA	10
10	Cincinnati	13
13	MIAMI	23
23	Dallas	3

Use Name	Pos.	Hgt	Wgt	Age	Int	Pts
Joe Taffoni	OT	6'3"	255	27		
Willie Young	OT	6'	265	29		
John Hill	C-OT	6'2"	245	22		
Mark Ellison	OG	6'2"	250	23		
Dick Enderle	OG	6'1"	250	24		
Doug Van Horn	OG	6'2"	245	28		
Bob Hyland	C-OT-OG	6'5"	255	27		
Greg Larson	C	6'2"	250	33		
Jack Gregory	DE	6'6"	250	27		
Henry Reed	DE	6'3"	230	23		
Larry Jacobsen	DT-DE	6'6"	260	22		
Dan Goich	DT	6'4"	250	28		
John Mendenhall	DT	6'1"	255	23		
Charlie Harper	DT	6'2"	250	28		
Dave Tipton	DE-DT	6'	240	23		

Use Name	Pos.	Hgt	Wgt	Age	Int	Pts
Carter Campbell	LB	6'3"	240	24		
John Douglas	LB	6'2"	228	27	1	
Jim Files	LB	6'4"	240	24	2	6
Ron Hornsby	LB	6'3"	232	23		
Pat Hughes	LB	6'2"	240	25	2	
Pete Athas	DB	5'11"	185	24	4	
Otto Brown	DB	6'1"	188	25	1	
Chuck Crist	DB	6'2"	205	21	1	
Richmond Flowers	DB	6'	180	25	4	
Spider Lockhart	DB	6'2"	175	29	4	6
Eldridge Small	DB	6'1"	190	22		
Willie Williams	DB	6'	190	29	4	

Scott Eaton — Injury
Jim Kanicki — Knee Injury

Use Name	Pos.	Hgt	Wgt	Age	Int	Pts
Randy Johnson	QB	6'3"	205	28		6
Norm Snead	QB	6'4"	215	32		
Bobby Duhon	HB	6'	195	25		
Ron Johnson	HB	6'1"	205	24		84
Rocky Thompson	HB	5'11"	200	24		6
Vin Clements	FB	6'3"	210	23		
Charlie Evans	FB	6'1"	220	24		30
Joe Orduna	HB-FB	6'	195	24		12
Bob Grim	WR	6'	200	27		6
Don Herrmann	WR	6'2"	205	25		30
Rich Houston	WR	6'2"	195	26		18
Joe Morrison	HB-FB-WR	6'1"	212	34		
Dick Kotite	TE	6'3"	230	29		
Bob Tucker	TE	6'3"	230	27		30
Tom Gatewood	WR-TE	6'3"	215	21		
Tom Blanchard	K	6'	190	24		
Pete Gogolak	K	6'2"	190	30		97

ST. LOUIS CARDINALS 4-9-1 Bob Holloway

Scores of Each Game		
10	Baltimore	3
10	Washington	24
19	PITTSBURGH	25
19	Minnesota	17
3	WASHINGTON	33
21	N.Y. Giants	27
10	CHICAGO	27
6	Philadelphia	6
24	Dallas	33
7	N.Y. GIANTS	13
10	Miami	31
6	DALLAS	27
24	LOS ANGELES	14
24	PHILADELPHIA	23

Use Name	Pos.	Hgt	Wgt	Age	Int	Pts
Ernie McMillan	OT	6'6"	255	34		
Steve Wright	OT	6'6"	250	30		
Dan Dierdorf	OG-OT	6'4"	265	23		
Dave Bradley	OG	6'4"	245	25		
Conrad Dobler	OG	6'3"	250	21		
Chuck Hutchison	OG	6'3"	240	23		
Bob Young	OG	6'2"	260	29		
Wayne Mulligan	C	6'2"	245	25		
Tom Banks	OG-C	6'1"	240	24		
Tom Beckman	DE	6'5"	250	21		
Don Brumm	DE	6'3"	245	29		
Martin Imhof	DE	6'6"	255	22		
Ron Yankowski	DE	6'5"	225	25		
Fred Heron	DT	6'4"	240	27		
Scott Palmer	DT	6'3"	245	24		
John Richardson	DT	6'2"	250	28		
Bob Rowe	DT	6'4"	260	27		

Use Name	Pos.	Hgt	Wgt	Age	Int	Pts
Mark Arneson	LB	6'2"	220	22		
Steve Conley (from CIN)	LB	6'2"	225	23		
Jim Hargrove	LB	6'3"	225	27		
Mike McGill	LB	6'2"	235	25	2	
Terry Miller	LB	6'2"	225	26		
Jamie Rivers	LB	6'2"	235	26		
Jeff Staggs	LB	6'2"	240	28	1	
Larry Stallings	LB	6'2"	230	30		
Miller Farr	DB	6'1"	190	29	3	
Dale Hackbart	DB	6'3"	210	36	1	
Norm Thompson	DB	6'1"	175	24	1	12
Eric Washington	DB	6'2"	190	22		
Roger Wehrli	DB	6'1"	195	24		
Larry Willingham	DB	6'1"	190	23		
Larry Wilson	DB	6'	195	34	3	

Jeff Allen — Injury
Larry Stegent — Injury

Use Name	Pos.	Hgt	Wgt	Age	Int	Pts
Gary Cuozzo	QB	6'1"	195	31		
Jim Hart	QB	6'2"	200	28		
Tim Van Galder	QB	6'1"	190	28		
Danny Anderson	HB	6'3"	210	29		36
Craig Baynham	HB	6'1"	205	28		
Cannonball Butler	HB	5'10"	200	29		
Roy Shivers	HB	6'	200	30		
Leo Hayden	FB-HB	6'	210	24		6
Don Heater	FB-HB	6'2"	205	22		
Leon Burns	FB	6'2"	235	27		12
Tom Woodeshick	FB	6'	222	30		
Johnny Roland	HB-FB	6'2"	215	29		24
Walker Gillette	WR	6'5"	200	25		12
Mel Gray	WR	5'9"	170	23		
Freddie Hyatt	WR	6'3"	200	26		
Bobby Moore	WR	6'2"	210	22		18
Bob Wicks	WR	6'3"	195	22		
Jim McFarland	TE	6'5"	225	24		
Ara Person	TE	6'2"	220	23		
Jackie Smith	TE	6'4"	235	31		12
Jim Bakken	K	6'	195	31		61

PHILADELPHIA EAGLES 2-11-1 Ed Khayat

Scores of Each Game		
6	Dallas	28
17	CLEVELAND	27
12	N.Y. GIANTS	27
0	Washington	14
3	LOS ANGELES	34
21	Kansas City	20
3	New Orleans	21
6	ST. LOUIS	6
18	Houston	17
7	DALLAS	28
10	N.Y. Giants	62
7	WASHINGTON	23
12	CHICAGO	21
23	St. Louis	24

Use Name	Pos.	Hgt	Wgt	Age	Int	Pts
Wade Key	OT	6'4"	245	25		
Wayne Mass (from NE)	OT	6'4"	245	26		
Steve Smith	OT	6'5"	250	28		
Dick Stevens	OT	6'4"	240	24		
Henry Allison	OG	6'2"	255	25		
Tom Luken	OG	6'3"	253	22		
Jim Skaggs	OG	6'2"	250	32		
Vern Winfield	OG	6'2"	248	23		
Mark Nordquist	C-OG	6'4"	246	26		
Mike Evans	C	6'5"	250	26		
Jerry Sturm	C	6'3"	260	35		
Larry Estes	DE	6'6"	250	25		
Richard Harris	DE	6'4"	260	24		
Mel Tom	DE	6'4"	250	31		
Houston Antwine	DT	6'	270	33		
Don Hultz	DT	6'3"	240	31		
Gary Pettigrew	DT	6'4"	255	27		
Ernie Calloway	DE-DT	6'6"	255	24		

Use Name	Pos.	Hgt	Wgt	Age	Int	Pts
Dick Absher	LB	6'4"	235	28	1	
Chuck Allen	LB	6'1"	225	32	1	
John Bunting	LB	6'1"	220	22	1	
Bill Cody	LB	6'1"	230	28		
Bob Creech	LB	6'3"	228	23		
Bill Overmeyer	LB	6'3"	220	23		
Ron Porter	LB	6'3"	232	27	2	
John Sodaski	LB	6'2"	222	24		
Steve Zabel	LB	6'4"	235	24		
Kermit Alexander	DB	5'11"	186	31		
Jackie Allen	DB	6'1"	187	24		
Bill Bradley	DB	5'11"	190	25	9	
Al Coleman	DB	6'1"	183	27		2
Pat Gibbs	DB	5'10"	188	22		
Leroy Keyes	DB	6'3"	208	25	2	
Al Nelson	DB	5'11"	186	28		
Nate Ramsey	DB	6'1"	200	31	3	
Jim Thrower	DB	6'2"	194	23		

Lee Bouggess — Injury
Ike Kelly — Injury

Use Name	Pos.	Hgt	Wgt	Age	Int	Pts
Rick Arrington	QB	6'2"	185	25		
Pete Liske	QB	6'2"	200	31		
John Reaves	QB	6'3"	210	22		6
Larry Crowe	HB	6'1"	198	22		
Po James	HB	6'1"	202	23		6
Tom Sullivan	HB	6'	190	22		
Sonny Davis	FB-HB	5'11"	215	24		
Tony Baker	FB	5'11"	225	27		
Larry Watkins	FB	6'2"	230	25		6
Tom Bailey	HB-FB	6'2"	211	23		
Harold Carmichael	WR	6'7"	225	22		12
Ben Hawkins	WR	6'	180	28		6
Harold Jackson	WR	5'10"	175	26		24
Billy Walik	WR	5'11"	180	24		6
Clark Hoss	TE	6'8"	235	23		
Kent Kramer	TE	6'5"	235	28		6
Gary Ballman	WR-TE	6'	215	32		
Tom Dempsey	K	6'1"	255	31		71
Tom McNeil	K	6'1"	195	30		

WASHINGTON REDSKINS

RUSHING
Last Name	No.	Yds	Avg	TD
Brown	285	1216	4.3	8
Harraway	148	567	3.8	6
Mul-Key	33	155	4.7	1
Brunet	30	82	2.7	2
C. Taylor	3	39	13.0	0
Nock	6	22	3.7	0
Smith	1	9	9.0	0
Kilmer	3	−3	−1.0	0
Jurgensen	4	−5	−1.3	0

RECEIVING
Last Name	No.	Yds	Avg	TD
C. Taylor	49	673	14	7
Jefferson	35	550	16	3
Brown	32	473	15	4
Smith	21	353	17	2
Harraway	15	105	7	0
Mul-Key	4	66	17	0
Alston	2	53	27	0
Brunet	1	8	8	0

PUNT RETURNS
Last Name	No.	Yds	Avg	TD
Vactor	17	88	5	0
Duncan	11	70	6	0
Haymond	6	1	0	0

KICKOFF RETURNS
Last Name	No.	Yds	Avg	TD
Duncan	15	364	24	0
Haymond	10	291	29	0
Mul-Key	8	209	26	0
Brunet	8	190	24	0
Bass	2	22	11	0
Vactor	1	21	21	0
Fanucci	1	15	15	0
McLinton	1	15	15	0
Tillman	2	6	3	0

PASSING – PUNTING – KICKING
PASSING	Att	Comp	%	Yds	Yd/Att	TD	Int–	%	RK
Kilmer	225	120	53	1648	7.3	19	11–	5	4
Jurgensen	59	39	66	633	10.7	2	4–	7	

PUNTING	No	Avg
Bragg	59	38.5

KICKING	XP	Att	%	FG	Att	%
Knight	40	41	98	14	30	47

DALLAS COWBOYS

RUSHING
Last Name	No.	Yds	Avg	TD
Hill	245	1036	4.2	6
Garrison	167	784	4.7	7
Newhouse	28	116	4.1	1
Montgomery	35	81	2.3	1
Staubach	6	45	7.5	0
Morton	8	26	3.3	2
Reeves	3	14	4.7	0
Neely	1	10	10.0	0
Hayes	2	8	4.0	0
Alworth	1	2	2.0	0
Fugett	3	2	0.7	0

RECEIVING
Last Name	No.	Yds	Avg	TD
Hill	43	364	8	3
Garrison	37	390	11	3
Sellers	31	653	21	5
Parks	18	298	17	1
Ditka	17	198	12	1
Hayes	15	200	13	0
Alworth	15	195	13	2
Montgomery	8	131	16	1
Fugett	7	94	13	0
Truax	4	49	12	0
Newhouse	1	8	8	0

PUNT RETURNS
Last Name	No.	Yds	Avg	TD
Harris	19	78	4	0
Waters	9	56	6	0

KICKOFF RETURNS
Last Name	No.	Yds	Avg	TD
Harris	26	615	24	0
Newhouse	18	382	21	0
Thomas	2	50	25	0
Waters	2	18	9	0
Montgomery	1	15	15	0
Fugett	1	0	0	0

PASSING – PUNTING – KICKING
PASSING	Att	Comp	%	Yds	Yd/Att	TD	Int–	%	RK
Morton	339	185	55	2396	7.1	15	21–	6	8
Staubach	20	9	45	98	4.9	0	2–	10	
Hill	3	1	33	55	18.3	1	0–	0	
Montgomery	3	1	33	31	10.3	0	0–	0	
Reeves	2	0	0	0	0.0	0	0–	0	

PUNTING	No	Avg
Bateman	51	38.2

KICKING	XP	Att	%	FG	Att	%
Fritsch	36	36	100	21	36	58

NEW YORK GIANTS

RUSHING
Last Name	No.	Yds	Avg	TD
Ron Johnson	298	1182	4.0	9
Evans	91	317	3.5	4
Clements	46	221	4.8	0
Orduna	36	129	3.6	1
Morrison	9	36	4.0	0
Thompson	9	35	3.9	0
Randy Johnson	9	26	2.9	1
Duhon	9	23	2.6	0
Snead	10	21	2.1	0
Blanchard	1	17	17.0	0
Herrmann	3	9	3.0	0
Tucker	3	6	2.0	1

RECEIVING
Last Name	No.	Yds	Avg	TD
Tucker	55	764	14	4
Ron Johnson	45	451	10	5
Herrmann	28	422	15	5
Houston	27	468	17	3
Evans	26	182	7	1
Clements	9	118	13	0
Grim	5	67	13	1
Morrison	5	39	8	0
Orduna	4	6	2	1
Duhon	2	20	10	0

PUNT RETURNS
Last Name	No.	Yds	Avg	TD
Athas	8	95	12	0
Duhon	2	20	10	0
Grim	7	10	1	0
Mendenhall	1	0	0	0

KICKOFF RETURNS
Last Name	No.	Yds	Avg	TD
Thompson	29	821	28	1
Orduna	12	244	20	0
Small	1	100	100	0
Duhon	2	47	24	0
Douglas	4	43	11	0
Crist	1	7	7	0
Enderle	1	0	0	0

PASSING – PUNTING – KICKING
PASSING	Att	Comp	%	Yds	Yd/Att	TD	Int–	%	RK
Snead	325	196	60	2307	7.1	17	12–	4	2
Ran Johnson	17	10	59	230	13.5	3	3–	18	
Blanchard	1	0	0	0	0.0	0	0–	0	
Ron Johnson	1	0	0	0	0.0	0	0–	0	

PUNTING	No	Avg
Blanchard	47	42.7

KICKING	XP	Att	%	FG	Att	%
Gogolak	34	38	89	21	31	68

ST. LOUIS CARDINALS

RUSHING
Last Name	No.	Yds	Avg	TD
Anderson	153	536	3.5	4
Roland	105	414	3.9	2
Burns	26	69	2.7	2
Moore	9	44	4.9	0
Baynham	17	43	2.5	0
Smith	5	31	6.2	0
Van Galder	9	28	3.1	0
Hart	9	17	1.9	0
Woodeshick	5	14	2.8	0
Shivers	5	12	2.4	0
Hayden	8	11	1.4	1
Cuozzo	4	7	1.8	0
Butler	6	3	0.5	0
Conley	3	8	2.7	0

RECEIVING
Last Name	No.	Yds	Avg	TD
Roland	38	321	8	0
Gillette	33	550	17	2
Moore	29	500	17	3
Anderson	28	298	11	2
Smith	26	407	16	2
Burns	6	24	4	0
Gray	3	62	21	0
Hyatt	2	32	16	0
Shivers	1	20	20	0
Hayden	1	17	17	0
Baynham	1	10	10	0
Butler	1	8	8	0
Wicks	1	8	8	0
Woodeshick	1	2	2	0

PUNT RETURNS
Last Name	No.	Yds	Avg	TD
Willingham	9	41	5	0
Wehrli	5	24	5	0
Gray	2	−4	−2	0

KICKOFF RETURNS
Last Name	No.	Yds	Avg	TD
Moore	20	437	22	0
Gray	17	378	22	0
Willingham	9	194	22	0
Butler	4	85	21	0
Hyatt	1	41	41	0
Wehrli	1	10	10	0
Burns	1	7	7	0

PASSING – PUNTING – KICKING
PASSING	Att	Comp	%	Yds	Yd/Att	TD	Int–	%	RK
Cuozzo	158	69	44	897	5.7	5	11–	7	13
Hart	119	60	50	857	7.2	5	5–	4	
Van Galder	79	40	51	434	5.5	1	7–	9	
Anderson	3	2	67	71	23.7	0	0–	0	
Smith	2	0	0	0	0.0	0	0–	0	
Wilson	2	0	0	0	0.0	0	0–	0	

PUNTING	No	Avg
Anderson	72	39.5
Bakken	1	26.0

KICKING	XP	Att	%	FG	Att	%
Bakken	19	21	90	14	22	64

PHILADELPHIA EAGLES

RUSHING
Last Name	No.	Yds	Avg	TD
James	182	565	3.1	0
Baker	90	322	3.6	0
Watkins	67	262	3.9	1
Reaves	18	109	6.1	1
Jackson	9	76	8.4	0
Bailey	7	22	3.1	0
Liske	7	20	2.9	0
Sullivan	13	13	1.0	0
Arrington	1	2	2.0	0
Crowe	1	2	2.0	0
Hawkins	3	0	0.0	0

RECEIVING
Last Name	No.	Yds	Avg	TD
Jackson	62	1048	17	4
Hawkins	30	512	17	1
Carmichael	20	276	14	2
James	20	156	8	0
Baker	16	114	7	0
Kramer	11	176	16	0
Ballman	9	183	20	0
Watkins	6	−2	0	0
Bailey	5	32	6	0
Sullivan	4	17	4	0
Walik	1	15	15	1

PUNT RETURNS
Last Name	No.	Yds	Avg	TD
Bradley	22	155	7	0
Winfield	1	12	12	0
Gibbs	1	8	8	0
Walik	3	4	1	0

KICKOFF RETURNS
Last Name	No.	Yds	Avg	TD
Nelson	25	728	29	0
Walik	21	466	22	0
Sullivan	3	72	24	0
Gibbs	3	61	20	0
Bradley	2	22	11	0
Pettigrew	1	17	17	0
Winfield	3	9	3	0
Overmyer	1	0	0	0

PASSING – PUNTING – KICKING
PASSING	Att	Comp	%	Yds	Yd/Att	TD	Int–	%	RK
Reaves	224	108	48	1508	6.7	7	12–	5	10
Liske	138	71	51	973	7.1	3	7–	5	
Arrington	13	5	38	46	3.5	0	1–	8	

PUNTING	No	Avg
Bradley	56	40.2
McNeill	7	41.4

KICKING	XP	Att	%	FG	Att	%
Dempsey	11	12	92	20	35	57

GREEN BAY PACKERS 10-4-0 Dan Devine

Scores		Use Name	Pos.	Hgt	Wgt	Age	Int	Pts
26	Cleveland 10	Bill Hayhoe	OT	6'8"	258	25		
14	OAKLAND 20	Dick Himes	OT	6'4"	244	26		
16	DALLAS 13	Kevin Hunt	OT	6'5"	260	23		
20	CHICAGO 17	Francis Peay	OT	6'5"	250	28		
24	Detroit 23	Bill Lueck	OG	6'3"	235	26		
9	ATLANTA 10	Mal Snider	OG	6'4"	250	25		
13	MINNESOTA 27	Keith Wortman	OG	6'2"	245	22		
34	SAN FRANCISCO 24	Ken Bowman	C	6'3"	230	29		
23	Chicago 17	Cal Withrow	C	6'	240	27		
23	Houston 10	Dave Pureifory	DE	6'1"	260	22		
16	Washington 21	Alden Roche	DE	6'4"	255	27		
33	DETROIT 7	Clarence Williams	DE	6'5"	255	25	6	
23	Minnesota 7	Bob Brown	DT	6'5"	260	32	2	
30	New Orleans 20	Gale Gillingham	DT	6'3"	255	28		
		Mike McCoy	DT	6'5"	284	23		
		Vern Vanoy	DT	6'8"	270	26		

Use Name	Pos.	Hgt	Wgt	Age	Int	Pts
Fred Carr	LB	6'5"	238	26		
Jim Carter	LB	6'3"	235	23	1	
Tommy Crutcher	LB	6'3"	230	30		
Larry Hefner	LB	6'2"	215	23		
Ray Nitschke	LB	6'3"	235	36		
Dave Robinson	LB	6'3"	245	31	2	
Willie Buchanon	DB	6'	190	21	4	6
Ken Ellis	DB	5'10"	190	24	4	12
Paul Gibson	DB	6'2"	195	24		
Charlie Hall	DB	6'1"	195	23		
Jim Hill	DB	6'2"	190	25	4	
Bob Kroll	DB	6'1"	195	22		
Al Matthews	DB	5'11"	190	24	2	
Ike Thomas	DB	6'2"	193	24		
Larry Krause — Injury						

Use Name	Pos.	Hgt	Wgt	Age	Int	Pts
Scott Hunter	QB	6'2"	205	24		30
Frank Patrick	QB	6'7"	225	25		
Jerry Tagge	QB	6'2"	220	22		6
Bob Hudson	HB	5'11"	210	24		
MacArthur Lane	HB	6'	220	30		18
Dave Kopay	FB-HB	6'2"	218	30		
John Brockington	FB	6'1"	225	23		54
Perry Williams	FB	6'2"	220	25		
Carroll Dale	WR	6'1"	200	34		6
Dave Davis	WR	6'	175	24		6
Leland Glass	WR	6'	185	22		6
Jon Staggers	WR	5'10"	186	23		12
Len Garrett	TE	6'3"	230	23		
Pete Lammons	TE	6'3"	228	28		
Rich McGeorge	TE	6'4"	235	23		12
Chester Marcol	K	6'	190	23		128
Ron Widby	K	6'4"	210	27		

DETROIT LIONS 8-5-1 Joe Schmidt

Scores		Use Name	Pos.	Hgt	Wgt	Age	Int	Pts
30	N.Y. GIANTS 16	Rocky Freitas	OT	6'6"	270	26		
10	MINNESOTA 34	Gordon Jolley	OT	6'5"	230	23		
38	Chicago 24	Jim Yarbrough	OT	6'6"	265	25		
26	Atlanta 23	Frank Gallagher	OG	6'2"	245	29		
23	GREEN BAY 24	Bob Kowalkowski	OG	6'3"	240	28		
34	SAN DIEGO 20	Rocky Rasley	OG	6'3"	250	25		
24	Dallas 28	Chuck Walton	OG	6'3"	255	31		
14	CHICAGO 0	Ed Flanagan	C	6'3"	245	28		
14	Minnesota 16	Dave Thompson	OT-C	6'4"	275	24		
27	NEW ORLEANS 14	Gene Hamlin	C	6'3"	245	26		
37	N.Y. JETS 20	Larry Hand	DE	6'4"	250	32		
7	Green Bay 33	Jim Mitchell	DE	6'3"	245	23	1	
21	Buffalo 21	Herb Orvis	DE	6'5"	240	25		
34	Los Angeles 17	Ken Sanders	DE	6'5"	225	22		
		Bob Bell	DT	6'4"	250	24		
		John Gordon	DT	6'6"	260	24		
		Joe Schmiesing	DT	6'4"	260	27		
		Bob Tatarek (from BUF)	DT	6'4"	270	26		
		Larry Woods	DT	6'6"	260	24		

Use Name	Pos.	Hgt	Wgt	Age	Int	Pts
Mike Lucci	LB	6'2"	230	32	2	
Paul Naumoff	LB	6'1"	215	27	1	
Rick Ogle	LB	6'3"	230	23		
Wayne Walker	LB	6'2"	228	35		
Charlie Weaver	LB	6'2"	218	23	1	
Adrian Young (from PHI)	LB	6'1"	232	26		
Lem Barney	DB	6'	188	26	3	
Leon Jenkins	DB	5'11"	165	22		
Dick LeBeau	DB	6'1"	185	35		
Charlie Potts	DB	6'3"	210	23		
Al Randolph	DB	6'2"	205	28		
Wayne Rasmussen	DB	6'2"	180	30	2	
Rudy Redmond	DB	6'	195	25	2	6
Mike Weger	DB	6'2"	200	26		
Sonny Campbell — Injury						
Ed Mooney — Injury						

Use Name	Pos.	Hgt	Wgt	Age	Int	Pts
Greg Landry	QB	6'4"	210	25		54
Bill Munson	QB	6'2"	210	30		
Nick Eddy	HB	6'1"	210	28		6
Mel Farr	HB	6'2"	210	27		18
Altie Taylor	HB	5'10"	200	24		36
Mickey Zofko	HB	6'2"	195	22		1
Steve Owens	FB	6'2"	215	24		24
Bill Triplett	FB	6'2"	215	33		
Al Barnes	WR	6'1"	170	23		6
Ron Jessie	WR	6'	183	24		24
Earl McCullouch	WR	5'11"	175	26		6
Larry Walton	WR	5'11"	180	25		36
Craig Cotton	TE	6'4"	222	25		6
John Hilton	TE	6'5"	225	30		6
Charlie Sanders	TE	6'4"	225	26		12
Errol Mann	K	6'	200	31		98
Herman Weaver	K	6'4"	210	23		

MINNESOTA VIKINGS 7-7-0 Bud Grant

Scores		Use Name	Pos.	Hgt	Wgt	Age	Int	Pts
21	WASHINGTON 24	Grady Alderman	OT	6'2"	247	33		
34	Detroit 10	Doug Davis	OT	6'4"	250	28		
14	MIAMI 16	Ron Yary	OT	6'6"	255	26		
17	ST. LOUIS 19	Ed White	OG	6'2"	262	25		
23	Denver 20	Milt Sunde	C-OG	6'2"	250	29		
10	Chicago 13	John Ward	DE-OG	6'4"	250	24		
27	Green Bay 13	Mick Tingelhoff	C	6'1"	237	32		
37	NEW ORLEANS 6	Godfrey Zaunbrecher	C	6'2"	240	24		
16	DETROIT 14	Carl Eller	DE	6'6"	247	30		
45	Los Angeles 41	Jim Marshall	DE	6'3"	248	34		
10	Pittsburgh 23	Bob Lurtsema	DT-DE	6'6"	250	30		
23	CHICAGO 10	Gary Larsen	DT	6'5"	260	32		
7	GREEN BAY 23	Alan Page	DT	6'5"	245	27		
17	San Francisco 20	Doug Sutherland	DE-DT	6'3"	250	24		

Use Name	Pos.	Hgt	Wgt	Age	Int	Pts
Carl Gersbach	LB	6'1"	230	25		
Wally Hilgenberg	LB	6'3"	230	29	1	6
Amos Martin	LB	6'3"	228	23		
Jeff Siemon	LB	6'2"	230	22	2	
Lonnie Warwick	LB	6'3"	238	30	1	
Roy Winston	LB	6'1"	222	32	3	
Terry Brown	DB	6'1"	205	25		
Bobby Bryant	DB	6'	170	28	4	6
Karl Kassulke	DB	6'	195	30	2	
Paul Krause	DB	6'3"	200	30	6	12
Ed Sharockman	DB	6'	200	32		
Charlie West	DB	6'1"	197	26	3	
Jeff Wright	DB	5'11"	190	23	2	
Nate Wright	DB	5'11"	180	25	2	

Use Name	Pos.	Hgt	Wgt	Age	Int	Pts
Bob Lee	QB	6'2"	195	27		
Fran Tarkenton	QB	6'1"	190	32		
Clint Jones	HB	6'	205	27		12
Dave Osborn	HB	6'	208	29		18
Ed Marinaro	FB-HB	6'2"	212	22		6
Bill Brown	FB	5'11"	228	34		48
Oscar Reed	HB-FB	5'11"	222	28		12
Jim Lindsey	HB-FB	6'2"	210	27		
Calvin Demery	WR	6'	190	22		
John Gilliam	WR	6'	195	27		42
John Henderson	WR	6'3"	195	29		12
Gene Washington	WR	6'3"	208	28		12
John Beasley	TE	6'3"	228	27		6
Stu Voigt	TE	6'1"	220	24		12
Fred Cox	K	5'10"	200	33		97
Mike Eischeid	K	6'	190	31		

CHICAGO BEARS 4-9-1 Abe Gibron

Scores		Use Name	Pos.	Hgt	Wgt	Age	Int	Pts
21	ATLANTA 37	Lionel Antoine	OT	6'6"	255	22		
13	LOS ANGELES 13	Rich Buzin	OT	6'4"	250	26		
24	DETROIT 38	Randy Jackson	OT	6'5"	250	28		
17	Green Bay 20	Bob Asher	OG-OT	6'5"	250	24		
17	Cleveland 0	Jim Cadile	OG	6'3"	250	31		
13	MINNESOTA 10	Glen Holloway	OG	6'3"	250	23		
27	St. Louis 10	Ernie Janet	OG	6'4"	250	23		
0	Detroit 14	Bob Newton	OG	6'4"	250	23		
17	GREEN BAY 23	Rich Coady	C	6'3"	245	27		
21	SAN FRANCISCO 34	Steve DeLong	DE	6'3"	254	29		
3	CINCINNATI 13	Willie Holman	DE	6'4"	250	27		
10	Minnesota 23	Larry Horton	DT-DE	6'4"	248	23		
21	Philadelphia 12	Bill Line	DT	6'7"	260	23		
21	Oakland 28	Jim Osborne	DT	6'3"	250	22		
		Andy Rice	DT	6'3"	268	30		
		Bill Staley	DT	6'3"	250	25		
		Tony McGee	DE-DT	6'4"	250	23		

Use Name	Pos.	Hgt	Wgt	Age	Int	Pts
Ross Brupbacher	LB	6'3"	215	24	1	6
Doug Buffone	LB	6'1"	230	28	1	
Jimmy Gunn	LB	6'1"	220	23		
Bill McKinney	LB	6'1"	226	27		
Bob Pifferini	LB	6'2"	226	22		
Larry Rowden	LB	6'2"	220	22		
Dick Butkus	C-LB	6'3"	245	28	2	1
Craig Clemons	DB	5'11"	187	23		
Charlie Ford	DB	6'3"	185	23	7	
Bob Jeter	DB	6'1"	200	34	2	
Garry Lyle	DB	6'2"	198	26	2	
Jerry Moore	DB	6'3"	208	22	1	
Ron Smith	DB	6'1"	195	29	1	6
Joe Taylor	DB	6'2"	200	31	4	
Joe Moore — Injury						
Dave Hale — Injury						

Use Name	Pos.	Hgt	Wgt	Age	Int	Pts
Bobby Douglass	QB	6'3"	225	25		48
John Huarte	QB	6'	185	28		
Cyril Pinder	HB	6'2"	210	25		18
Gary Kosins	FB-HB	6'1"	215	23		6
Don Shy	FB-HB	6'1"	210	26		6
Jim Harrison	FB	6'4"	235	23		18
Roger Lawson	HB-FB	6'2"	215	22		
George Farmer	WR	6'4"	214	24		12
Jim Seymour	WR	6'4"	210	25		6
Cecil Turner	WR	5'10"	176	28		
Bob Parsons	TE	6'4"	234	22		6
Earl Thomas	TE	6'3"	225	23		24
Bob Wallace	TE	6'3"	220	26		
Bobby Joe Green	K	5'11"	175	34		
Mac Percival	K	6'4"	220	32		62

GREEN BAY PACKERS

RUSHING

Last Name	No.	Yds	Avg	TD
Brockington	274	1027	3.7	8
Lane	177	821	4.6	3
P. Williams	33	139	4.2	0
Hudson	15	62	4.1	0
Kopay	10	39	3.9	0
Hunter	22	37	1.7	5
Glass	2	13	6.5	0
Davis	2	0	0.0	0
Tagge	8	−3	−0.4	1
Staggers	1	−8	−8.0	0

RECEIVING

Last Name	No.	Yds	Avg	TD
Lane	26	285	11	0
Brockington	19	243	13	1
Dale	16	317	20	0
Glass	15	261	17	1
Staggers	8	123	15	1
Davis	4	119	30	1
Garrett	4	66	17	0
McGeorge	4	50	13	2
Kopay	3	19	6	0
Nitschke	1	34	34	0
Lammons	1	19	19	0

PUNT RETURNS

Last Name	No.	Yds	Avg	TD
Ellis	14	215	15	1
Staggers	9	148	16	1
Glass	1	1	1	0
Hudson	1	0	0	0

KICKOFF RETURNS

Last Name	No.	Yds	Avg	TD
Thomas	21	572	27	0
Staggers	11	260	24	0
Hudson	11	247	22	0
Kroll	1	23	23	0
Robinson	1	20	20	0
Ellis	1	10	10	0
P. Williams	1	9	9	0
Garrett	1	0	0	0
Wortman	1	0	0	0

PASSING – PUNTING – KICKING

PASSING	Att	Comp	%	Yds	Yd/Att	TD	Int–	%	RK
Hunter	199	86	43	1252	6.3	6	9–	5	10
Tagge	29	10	34	154	5.3	0	0–	0	
Patrick	4	1	25	9	2.3	0	0–	0	
Lane	2	2	100	19	9.5	0	0–	0	
Widby	2	2	100	102	51.0	1	0–	0	
Staggers	1	0	0	0	0.0	0	0–	0	

PUNTING	No	Avg
Widby	65	41.8

KICKING	XP	Att	%	FG	Att	%
Marcol	29	29	100	33	48	69

DETROIT LIONS

RUSHING

Last Name	No.	Yds	Avg	TD
Taylor	154	658	4.3	4
Landry	81	524	6.5	9
Owens	143	519	3.6	4
Farr	62	216	3.5	3
Triplett	17	48	2.8	0
Zofko	7	28	4.0	0
Eddy	8	28	3.5	0
Munson	1	0	0.0	0

RECEIVING

Last Name	No.	Yds	Avg	TD
Taylor	29	250	9	2
C. Sanders	27	416	15	2
L. Walton	24	485	20	6
Jessie	24	424	18	4
Owens	15	100	7	0
Farr	10	132	13	0
Cotton	8	129	16	1
Hilton	5	133	27	1
McCullouch	5	96	19	1
Barnes	4	58	15	1
Eddy	2	46	23	1
Zofko	2	14	7	0

PUNT RETURNS

Last Name	No.	Yds	Avg	TD
Barney	15	108	7	0
L. Walton	3	−8	−3	0

KICKOFF RETURNS

Last Name	No.	Yds	Avg	TD
Zofko	26	616	24	0
Jessie	23	558	24	0
Barney	1	17	17	0
Triplett	1	12	12	0
Orvis	1	5	5	0
L. Walton	0	96	0	0

PASSING – PUNTING – KICKING

PASSING	Att	Comp	%	Yds	Yd/Att	TD	Int–	%	RK
Landry	268	134	50	2066	7.7	18	13–	6	6
Munson	35	20	57	194	5.5	1	1–	3	
Jessie	1	0	0	0	0.0	0	0–	0	
McCullouch	1	1	100	23	23.0	0	0–	0	

PUNTING	No	Avg
H. Weaver	43	40.3

KICKING	XP	Att	%	FG	Att	%
Mann	38	39	97	20	29	69
Zofko	1	1	100	0	0	0

MINNESOTA VIKINGS

RUSHING

Last Name	No.	Yds	Avg	TD
Reed	151	639	4.2	2
Bill Brown	82	263	3.2	4
Osborn	82	261	3.2	2
Marinaro	66	223	3.4	0
Tarkenton	27	180	6.7	0
Jones	52	164	3.2	2
Gilliam	8	14	1.8	0
Lindsey	1	8	8.0	0
Voigt	1	1	1.0	0
Krause	1	0	0.0	0
Eischeid	1	−13	−13.0	0

RECEIVING

Last Name	No.	Yds	Avg	TD
Gilliam	47	1035	22	7
Reed	30	205	7	0
Beasley	28	232	8	1
Marinaro	28	218	8	1
Bill Brown	22	298	14	4
Osborn	20	166	8	1
Washington	18	259	14	2
Henderson	10	190	19	2
Voigt	6	50	8	1
Jones	6	42	7	0
Lindsey	3	28	9	0
White	0	3	0	0

PUNT RETURNS

Last Name	No.	Yds	Avg	TD
West	16	111	7	0
Bryant	10	48	5	0

KICKOFF RETURNS

Last Name	No.	Yds	Avg	TD
Gilliam	14	369	26	0
Jones	12	327	27	0
West	9	196	22	0
Bryant	2	41	21	0
Bill Brown	3	37	12	0
Lindsey	1	17	17	0
Voigt	1	2	2	0

PASSING – PUNTING – KICKING

PASSING	Att	Comp	%	Yds	Yd/Att	TD	Int–	%	RK
Tarkenton	378	215	57	2651	7.0	18	13–	3	1
Lee	6	3	50	75	12.5	1	0–	0	
Krause	1	0	0	0	0.0	0	0–	0	

PUNTING	No	Avg
Eischeid	62	42.8

KICKING	XP	Att	%	FG	Att	%
Cox	34	34	100	21	33	64

CHICAGO BEARS

RUSHING

Last Name	No.	Yds	Avg	TD
Douglass	141	968	6.9	8
Harrison	167	622	3.7	2
Shy	91	342	3.8	1
Pinder	87	300	3.4	3
Lawson	33	106	3.2	1
Butkus	1	28	28.0	0
Thomas	5	13	2.6	0
Kosins	3	5	1.7	0
Parsons	1	0	0.0	0
Turner	3	0	0.0	0
Huarte	1	−2	−2.0	0
Seymour	1	−9	−9.0	0
Farmer	2	−13	−6.5	0

RECEIVING

Last Name	No.	Yds	Avg	TD
Thomas	20	365	18	3
Farmer	14	380	27	2
Seymour	10	165	17	1
Shy	10	109	11	0
Lawson	8	120	15	0
Harrison	8	30	4	1
Turner	3	71	24	0
Kosins	2	15	8	1
Pinder	1	13	13	0
Wallace	1	9	9	0
Parsons	1	6	6	1

PUNT RETURNS

Last Name	No.	Yds	Avg	TD
Smith	26	163	6	0
Clemons	2	15	8	0

KICKOFF RETURNS

Last Name	No.	Yds	Avg	TD
Smith	30	924	31	1
Turner	16	409	26	0
Clemons	2	53	27	0
Holloway	1	28	28	0
Butkus	1	15	15	0
Pinder	1	14	14	0
Horton	1	3	3	0
Thomas	0	82	0	1

PASSING – PUNTING – KICKING

PASSING	Att	Comp	%	Yds	Yd/Att	TD	Int–	%	RK
Douglass	198	75	38	1246	6.3	9	12–	6	12
Huarte	5	2	40	14	2.8	0	0–	0	
Green	2	1	50	23	11.5	0	1–	50	

PUNTING	No	Avg
Green	67	41.2

KICKING	XP	Att	%	FG	Att	%
Percival	26	26	100	12	24	50
Butkus	1	1	100	0	0	0

SAN FRANCISCO FORTY NINERS 8-5-1 Dick Nolan

Scores of Each Game		
34	SAN DIEGO	3
20	Buffalo	27
37	New Orleans	2
7	Los Angeles	31
17	N.Y. GIANTS	23
20	NEW ORLEANS	20
49	Atlanta	14
24	Green Bay	34
24	BALTIMORE	21
34	Chicago	21
31	Dallas	10
16	LOS ANGELES	26
20	ATLANTA	0
20	MINNESOTA	17

Use Name	Pos.	Hgt	Wgt	Age	Int	Pts
Len Rohde	OT	6'4"	248	34		
John Watson	OT	6'4"	248	23		
Cas Banaszek	C-OT	6'3"	250	26		
Randy Beisler	OG	6'4"	250	27		
Elmer Collett	OG	6'4"	240	27		
Woody Peoples	OG	6'2"	258	29		
Forrest Blue	C	6'5"	260	26		
Bill Belk	DE	6'3"	253	26		
Cedrick Hardman	DE	6'3"	255	23		
Tommy Hart	DE	6'3"	248	27	1	
Rolf Krueger	DT-DE	6'4"	253	25		
Earl Edwards	DT	6'6"	262	26		
Bob Hoskins	DT	6'2"	253	26		
Charlie Krueger	DT	6'4"	268	36		

Use Name	Pos.	Hgt	Wgt	Age	Int	Pts
Ed Beard	LB	6'2"	220	32	1	
Marty Huff	LB	6'2"	234	23		
Frank Nunley	LB	6'2"	230	26	1	
Dave Olerich	LB	6'1"	220	27		
Jim Sniadecki	LB	6'2"	230	25		
Skip Vanderbundt	LB	6'3"	224	25	2	18
Dave Wilcox	LB	6'3"	240	29	3	
Johnny Fuller	DB	6'	185	26	1	
Windlan Hall	DB	5'11"	178	22	1	
Jim Johnson	DB	6'2"	187	34	4	
Ralph McGill	DB	5'11"	183	22		
Mel Phillips	DB	6'	194	30	1	
Mike Simpson	DB	5'11"	168	25	2	6
Bruce Taylor	DB	6'	187	24	2	

Use Name	Pos.	Hgt	Wgt	Age	Int	Pts
John Brodie	QB	6'1"	203	37		6
Joe Reed	QB	6'1"	195	24		
Steve Spurrier	QB	6'2"	203	27		
John Isenbarger	HB	6'3"	205	24		6
Doug Cunningham	HB	5'11"	190	26		
Jimmy Thomas	HB	6'1"	214	25		6
Vic Washington	HB	5'10"	196	26		30
Ken Willard	FB	6'2"	216	29		30
Larry Schreiber	HB-FB	6'	200	25		18
Terry Beasley	WR	5'10"	184	21		
Preston Riley	WR	6'	180	24		6
Gene Washington	WR	6'1"	185	25		72
Ted Kwalick	TE	6'4"	223	25		54
Dick Witcher	TE	6'3"	204	27		6
Bruce Gossett	K	6'2"	228	29		95
Jim McCann	K	6'2"	163	23		

ATLANTA FALCONS 7-7-0 Norm Van Brocklin

Scores of Each Game		
37	Chicago	21
20	New England	21
31	LOS ANGELES	3
23	DETROIT	26
21	New Orleans	14
10	Green Bay	9
14	SAN FRANCISCO	49
7	Los Angeles	20
36	NEW ORLEANS	20
13	Washington	24
23	DENVER	20
20	HOUSTON	10
0	San Francisco	20
14	KANSAS CITY	17

Use Name	Pos.	Hgt	Wgt	Age	Int	Pts
Len Gotshalk	OT	6'4"	244	22		
George Kunz	OT	6'5"	257	25		
Bill Sandeman	OT	6'6"	252	29		
Dennis Havig	OG	6'2"	245	23		
Andy Maurer	OG	6'3"	265	23		
Jim Miller	OG	6'3"	240	23		
Ted Fritsch	C	6'2"	240	22		
Jeff Van Note	OG-C	6'2"	243	26		
Claude Humphrey	DE	6'5"	252	28		2
John Zook	DE	6'5"	243	24		6
Chuck Walker (from STL)	DT-DE	6'2"	250	31		
Glen Condren	DT	6'2"	250	30		
Rosie Manning	DT	6'5"	256	22		
John Small	DT	6'5"	270	25		
Mike Lewis	DE-DT	6'3"	244	23	1	2

Use Name	Pos.	Hgt	Wgt	Age	Int	Pts
Grady Allen	LB	6'3"	230	26		
Duane Benson	LB	6'2"	215	27		
Greg Brezina	LB	6'2"	226	26		
Don Hansen	LB	6'3"	235	28	1	
Noel Jenke	LB	6'1"	220	25		
Tommy Nobis	LB	6'2"	240	28	3	6
Ray Brown	DB	6'2"	208	23	2	
Ray Easterling	DB	6'	195	22		
Clarence Ellis	DB	5'11"	193	22	3	
Willie Germany	DB	6'	192	23		
Tom Hayes	DB	6'1"	200	26	5	
Tony Plummer	DB	5'11"	188	25		
Ken Reaves	DB	6'3"	210	27	3	
Larry Shears	DB	5'10"	185	23		

Harmon Wages — Knee Injury

Use Name	Pos.	Hgt	Wgt	Age	Int	Pts
Bob Berry	QB	5'11"	185	30		12
Pat Sullivan	QB	6'0"	198	22		
Willie Belton	HB	5'11"	207	23		
Dave Hampton	HB	6'	210	25		42
Joe Profit	HB	6'	213	23		
Ron Lamb	FB	6'2"	225	28		
Art Malone	FB	5'11"	211	24		60
Eddie Ray	FB	6'2"	240	25		
Ken Burrow	WR	6'	190	24		30
Wes Chesson	WR	6'2"	195	23		6
Ray Jarvis	WR	5'11"	200	23		
Todd Snyder	WR	6'2"	194	23		
Larry Mialik	TE	6'2"	226	22		
Jim Mitchell	TE	6'2"	234	24		24
Bill Bell	K	6'1"	192	24		79
John James	K	6'3"	197	23		

LOS ANGELES RAMS 6-7-1 Tommy Prothro

Scores of Each Game		
34	NEW ORLEANS	14
13	Chicago	13
3	Atlanta	31
31	SAN FRANCISCO	7
34	Philadelphia	3
15	CINCINNATI	12
17	Oakland	45
20	ATLANTA	7
10	DENVER	16
41	MINNESOTA	45
16	New Orleans	19
26	San Francisco	16
14	St. Louis	24
17	DETROIT	34

Use Name	Pos.	Hgt	Wgt	Age	Int	Pts
Charley Cowan	OT	6'4"	250	23		
Harry Schuh	OT	6'2"	260	29		
John Williams	OG-OT	6'3"	256	26		
Mike LaHood	OG	6'3"	250	27		
Tom Mack	OG	6'3"	250	28		
Joe Scibelli	OG	6'1"	255	33		
Ken Iman	C	6'1"	240	33		
Rich Saul	OG-C	6'3"	235	24		
Coy Bacon	DE	6'4"	270	30		
Fred Dryer	DE	6'6"	240	26		
Jack Youngblood	DE	6'4"	250	22		
Larry Brooks	DT	6'3"	255	22		
Bill Nelson	DT	6'7"	270	24		
Merlin Olsen	DT	6'5"	270	31		
Phil Olsen	DT	6'5"	265	24		

Use Name	Pos.	Hgt	Wgt	Age	Int	Pts
Ken Geddes	LB	6'3"	235	24		
Dean Halverson	LB	6'2"	212	26		
Marlin McKeever	LB	6'1"	235	32	2	
John Pergine	LB	6'1"	225	25		
Jim Purnell	LB	6'2"	238	30	1	
Jack Reynolds	LB	6'1"	232	24		
Isiah Robertson	LB	6'3"	225	23		
Al Clark	DB	6'	180	24	1	
Dave Elmendorf	DB	6'1"	195	23	3	
Gene Howard	DB	6'	190	23	6	
Jim Nettles	DB	5'9"	177	30	6	
Clancy Williams	DB	6'2"	194	29		
Roger Williams	DB	5'10"	180	26		

Travis Williams — Knee Injury

Use Name	Pos.	Hgt	Wgt	Age	Int	Pts
Pete Beathard	QB	6'2"	200	30		
Roman Gabriel	QB	6'4"	220	32		6
Jim Bertelsen	HB	5'11"	205	22		36
Lawrence McCutcheon	HB	6'1"	205	22		
Larry Smith	HB	6'3"	220	24		18
Bob Thomas	HB	5'10"	200	23		18
Les Josephson	FB	6'	207	29		6
Willie Ellison	HB-FB	6'1"	200	27		36
Dick Gordon	WR	5'11"	190	27		6
John Love	WR	5'11"	185	27		6
David Ray	WR	6'	195	27		103
Lance Rentzel	WR	6'2"	202	28		12
Jack Snow	WR	6'2"	190	29		24
Joe Sweet	WR	6'2"	196	24		8
Pat Curran	TE	6'3"	238	26		
Bob Klein	TE	6'5"	235	25		6
Dave Chapple	K	6'	180	25		

NEW ORLEANS SAINTS 2-11-1 J. D. Roberts

Scores of Each Game		
14	Los Angeles	34
17	KANSAS CITY	20
2	SAN FRANCISCO	37
21	N.Y. Giants	45
20	ATLANTA	21
20	San Francisco	20
21	PHILADELPHIA	3
6	Minnesota	37
20	Atlanta	36
14	Detroit	27
19	LOS ANGELES	16
17	N.Y. Jets	18
10	NEW ENGLAND	17
20	GREEN BAY	30

Use Name	Pos.	Hgt	Wgt	Age	Int	Pts
Glen Ray Hines	OT	6'5"	265	28		
Don Morrison	OT	6'5"	255	22		
Craig Robinson	OT	6'4"	250	23		
Carl Johnson	OG-OT	6'3"	240	22		
Jake Kupp	OG	6'3"	248	30		
Royce Smith	OG	6'3"	245	23		
Del Williams	OG	6'2"	240	26		
John Didion	C	6'4"	245	24		
Bob Kuziel	C	6'4"	255	22		
Wimpy Winther	C	6'4"	260	24		
Mike Crangle	DE	6'4"	243	25		
Richard Neal	DE	6'3"	254	24	6	
Joe Owens	DE	6'2"	245	25	2	
Faddie Tillman	DT-DE	6'5"	230	23		
Dave Long	DT	6'4"	245	27		
Doug Mooers	DT	6'6"	265	25		
Bob Pollard	DT	6'3"	245	23		

Use Name	Pos.	Hgt	Wgt	Age	Int	Pts
Wayne Coleman	LB	6'1"	230	26		
Joe Federspiel	LB	6'1"	225	22		
Willie Hall	LB	6'2"	217	22		
Ray Hester	LB	6'2"	215	23		
Bill Hobbs	LB	6'	220	26		
Dick Palmer (from BUF)	LB	6'2"	232	24		
Tom Roussel	LB	6'3"	235	27	2	
Tom Stincic	LB	6'2"	230	25		
Billy Hayes	DB	6'1"	175	25		
Hugo Hollas	DB	6'1"	190	25	1	
Delles Howell	DB	6'3"	202	25	1	
Ernie Jackson	DB	5'10"	173	22	3	6
Bivian Lee	DB	6'3"	200	24	4	
Tom Myers	DB	5'11"	184	21	3	
Doug Wyatt	DB	6'1"	195	25		6

Carlos Bell — Injury
Al Dodd — Injury
Dee Martin — Knee Injury

Use Name	Pos.	Hgt	Wgt	Age	Int	Pts
Edd Hargett	QB	5'11"	190	25		
Archie Manning	QB	6'3"	204	23		12
Bob Gresham	HB	5'11"	195	24		18
Virgil Robinson	HB	5'11"	195	24		
Joe Williams	HB	6'	193	25		
James Ford	FB-HB	6'	200	22		
Bill Butler	FB	6'	218	22		12
Jim Strong	FB	6'1"	204	25		
Arthur Green	HB-FB	5'11"	198	24		
Dan Abramowicz	WR	6'1"	195	27		42
Margene Adkins	WR	5'10"	183	25		
Bob Newland	WR	6'2"	190	23		12
Cephus Weatherspoon	WR	6'1"	182	24		
Creston Whitaker	WR	6'2"	187	24		
Bob Brown	TE	6'3"	225	29		6
Dave Parks	TE	6'2"	203	30		36
Charlie Durkee	K	5'11"	165	28		18
Julian Fagan	K	6'3"	205	24		
Happy Feller	K	5'11"	185	23		28
Toni Linhart	K	6'	170	30		11

SAN FRANCISCO FORTY NINERS

RUSHING

Last Name	No.	Yds	Avg	TD
V. Washington	141	468	3.3	3
Schreiber	118	420	3.6	2
Willard	100	345	3.5	4
Thomas	52	250	4.8	1
Spurrier	11	51	4.6	0
Cunningham	8	32	4.0	0
Reed	4	22	5.5	0
Kwalick	5	11	2.2	0
Isenbarger	3	9	3.0	0
Brodie	3	8	2.7	1

RECEIVING

Last Name	No.	Yds	Avg	TD
G. Wash'gton	46	918	20	12
V. Wash'gton	43	393	9	1
Kwalick	40	751	19	9
Schreiber	31	283	9	1
Willard	24	131	5	1
Thomas	15	148	10	0
Riley	11	156	14	1
Isenbarger	3	66	22	1
Witcher	3	22	7	1
Beasley	1	20	20	0

PUNT RETURNS

Last Name	No.	Yds	Avg	TD
McGill	22	219	10	0
Taylor	21	145	7	0
Fuller	1	9	9	0

KICKOFF RETURNS

Last Name	No.	Yds	Avg	TD
V. Washington	27	771	29	1
McGill	10	192	19	0
Schreiber	2	41	21	0
Nunley	1	21	21	0
Hoskins	2	17	9	0
Beard	2	−1	−1	0

PASSING – PUNTING – KICKING

PASSING	Att	Comp	%	Yds	Yd/Att	TD	Int−	%	RK
Spurrier	269	147	55	1983	7.4	18	16−	6	4
Brodie	110	70	64	905	8.2	9	8−	7	
Isenbarger	1	0	0	0	0.0	0	0−	0	

PUNTING	No	Avg
McCann	64	39.7

KICKING	XP	Att	%	FG	Att	%
Gossett	41	42	98	18	29	62

ATLANTA FALCONS

RUSHING

Last Name	No.	Yds	Avg	TD
Hampton	230	995	4.3	6
Malone	180	798	4.4	8
Profit	40	132	3.3	0
Berry	24	86	3.6	2
Ray	8	34	4.3	0
Belton	10	20	2.0	0
Mitchell	2	19	9.5	0
Sullivan	2	8	4.0	0
Burrow	3	3	1.0	0
Bell	1	−3	−3.0	0

RECEIVING

Last Name	No.	Yds	Avg	TD
Malone	50	585	12	2
Burrow	29	492	17	5
Mitchell	28	470	17	4
Hampton	23	244	11	1
Chesson	18	338	19	1
Profit	3	22	7	0
Snyder	1	19	19	0
Jarvis	1	18	18	0
Ray	1	14	14	0
Lamb	1	10	10	0
Belton	1	−1	−1	0
Berry	1	−9	−9	0

PUNT RETURNS

Last Name	No.	Yds	Avg	TD
Belton	17	110	6	0
Brown	8	71	9	0
Ellis	1	13	13	0
Small	1	0	0	0

KICKOFF RETURNS

Last Name	No.	Yds	Avg	TD
Hampton	25	535	21	0
Belton	21	441	21	0
Malone	2	37	19	0
Plummer	1	21	21	0
Germany	2	5	3	0
Chesson	1	0	0	0

PASSING – PUNTING – KICKING

PASSING	Att	Comp	%	Yds	Yd/Att	TD	Int−	%	RK
Berry	277	154	56	2158	7.8	13	12−	4	3
Sullivan	19	3	16	44	2.3	0	3−	16	

PUNTING	No	Avg
James	61	42.8

KICKING	XP	Att	%	FG	Att	%
Bell	31	31	100	16	30	53

LOS ANGELES RAMS

RUSHING

Last Name	No.	Yds	Avg	TD
Ellison	170	764	4.5	5
Bertelsen	123	581	4.7	5
Thomas	77	433	5.6	3
Smith	60	276	4.6	2
Josephson	18	75	4.2	0
Rentzel	7	71	10.1	1
Gabriel	14	16	1.1	1
Sweet	1	1	1.0	0
Beathard	1	−1	−1.0	0
Klein	1	−7	−7.0	0

RECEIVING

Last Name	No.	Yds	Avg	TD
Snow	30	590	20	4
Bertelsen	29	331	11	1
Klein	29	330	11	1
Rentzel	27	365	14	1
Ellison	23	141	6	1
Smith	15	186	12	1
Josephson	14	170	12	1
Thomas	11	95	9	0
Gordon	3	29	10	1
Sweet	2	26	13	1
Love	1	19	19	1

PUNT RETURNS

Last Name	No.	Yds	Avg	TD
Bertelson	16	232	15	0
Elmendorf	3	56	19	0
Love	10	39	4	0
Gordon	4	20	5	0

KICKOFF RETURNS

Last Name	No.	Yds	Avg	TD
Ellison	14	345	25	0
Thomas	8	212	27	0
Love	8	167	21	0
R. Williams	6	141	24	0
Gordon	4	141	35	0
Bertelsen	4	88	22	0
Clark	3	59	20	0
Howard	2	51	26	0
Pergine	3	46	15	0
Curran	4	37	9	0

PASSING – PUNTING – KICKING

PASSING	Att	Comp	%	Yds	Yd/Att	TD	Int−	%	RK
Gabriel	323	165	51	2027	6.3	12	15−	5	9
Beathard	48	19	40	255	5.3	1	7−	15	

PUNTING	No	Avg
Chapple	53	44.2

KICKING	XP	Att	%	FG	Att	%
Ray	31	31	100	24	41	59

NEW ORLEANS SAINTS

RUSHING

Last Name	No.	Yds	Avg	TD
Gresham	121	381	3.1	3
Manning	63	351	5.6	2
Butler	54	233	4.3	0
Strong	37	120	3.2	0
J. Williams	31	72	2.3	0
Green	14	51	3.6	0
Ford	11	28	2.5	0
V. Robinson	5	1	0.2	0
Parks	1	−7	−7.0	0

RECEIVING

Last Name	No.	Yds	Avg	TD
Newland	47	579	12	2
Abramowicz	38	668	18	7
Parks	32	542	17	6
Gresham	29	192	7	0
Butler	25	226	9	2
J. Williams	16	116	7	0
Strong	14	123	9	0
Brown	11	175	16	1
Adkins	9	96	11	0
Green	7	49	7	0
Ford	1	9	9	0
Whitaker	1	6	6	0

PUNT RETURNS

Last Name	No.	Yds	Avg	TD
Myers	9	43	5	0
Adkins	7	0	0	0

KICKOFF RETURNS

Last Name	No.	Yds	Avg	TD
Adkins	43	1020	24	0
Green	8	187	23	0
Strong	4	53	13	0
J. Williams	2	23	12	0
Butler	1	14	14	0
Hollas	2	9	5	0
Newland	1	6	6	0

PASSING – PUNTING – KICKING

PASSING	Att	Comp	%	Yds	Yd/Att	TD	Int−	%	RK
Manning	448	230	51	2781	6.2	18	21−	5	7
Gresham	1	0	0	0	0.0	0	0−	0	

PUNTING	No	Avg
Fagan	71	40.8

KICKING	XP	Att	%	FG	Att	%
Feller	10	11	91	6	11	55
Durkee	9	9	100	3	9	33
Linhart	5	5	100	2	5	40

1972 A.F.C. Perfect From Start to Finish

Vince Lombardi's Packers had never done it. George Halas' Chicago Bears had come close but always fallen short. But Don Shula's Miami Dolphins did it; they went through the season unbeaten and untied and won three more games in the playoffs to finish with a perfect 17-0-0 record. The Bears had finished the 1934 and 1942 regular seasons with unblemished records, but both squads lost in the NFL championship game. Before the NFL split up into divisions, the Canton Bulldogs had gone undefeated in 1922 and 1923 and the Green Bay Packers in 1929, but each of those teams had been tied during the season. Paul Brown's Cleveland Browns breezed through the 1948 AAFC season without a loss or tie, but they had not been able to repeat that achievement after coming over to the NFL. The Dolphins were the first NFL team to compile an absolutely perfect record for a season, and they were a young team which had still not reached full development.

EASTERN DIVISION

Miami Dolphins—Seven years ago the Dolphins had been created out of castoffs from the eight AFL teams; four years ago, they had finished on the bottom of the AFL's Eastern Division. But since Don Shula had taken over as coach in 1970, he had rebuilt, reorganized, and psyched the Dolphins into a powerhouse which rolled undefeated and untied through the 1973 season. The Miami defense was known as the "No-Name Defense," but those anonymous defenders allowed the fewest points in the NFL. After Bob Griese went out with an ankle injury in mid-season, veteran Earl Morrall stepped in at quarterback and kept the offense moving. The five Miami interior linemen—Norm Evans, Wayne Moore, Bob Keuchenberg, Larry Little, and Jim Langer—had all been cut loose by other pro teams, but the Dolphin blocking protected Morrall and cleared the way for runners Larry Csonka, Mercury Morris, and Jim Kiick. Csonka and Morris became the first teammates ever to gain 1,000 yards each in one season.

New York Jets—Quarterback Joe Namath stayed healthy all year and again wreaked havoc on defensive backs with his bullet passing, but the Jets nevertheless finished with a 7-7 record and out of the playoffs. The Jet defense unfortunately allowed points as readily as Namath and the offense could score them. None of the deep backs had a good year, while the front line was hurt by Gerry Philbin's disenchantment with coach Weeb Ewbank and John Elliott's slow recovery from knee surgery. The New York offensive cupboard was full. Running behind a line that was growing shopworn, John Riggins and Emerson Boozer balanced Namath's passing with consistently strong ball-carrying. But when Riggins and Boozer both went out of action late in the year with injuries, the Jet attack lost most of its spark.

Baltimore Colts—New owner Bob Irsay installed Joe Thomas as his general manager, and Thomas began ripping the team apart after it fell out of contention with four losses in the first five games. He fired coach Don McCafferty, ordered interim coach John Sandusky to bench veteran quarterback John Unitas in favor of younger Marty Domres, and one by one disposed of Baltimore veterans who had starred in the late 1960s and early 1970s. Before next season would begin, Thomas had traded off Unitas, Tom Matte, Dan Sullivan, Bill Curry, Bubba Smith, Fred Miller, Jerry Logan, Billy Newsome, Tom Nowatzke, and Norm Bulaich, and Bob Vogel retired.

Buffalo Bills—By the end of the opening game, starting offensive linemen Bruce Jarvis and Jim Reilly were out for the season with injuries. More blockers went onto the disabled list as the season progressed, and the Bills scoured the country for healthy offensive linemen to fill the breach. But even with the patchwork line, O. J. Simpson blossomed into stardom by running for 1,251 yards, the most in the NFL. Helping O. J. to prominence was head coach Lou Saban, who returned to the Bills with an offensive plan of going to Simpson twice as often as he had been used. Saban had quit the Bills after leading them to the AFL championship in 1965, but victories came harder with this Buffalo squad as only Walt Patulski, Don Croft, and Bobby James caused any excitement in the defensive platoon.

New England Patriots—General manager Upton Bell and head coach John Mazur battled with each other all season over how to build the Patriots. When the team won only three games all year, both Bell and Mazur were out of work by the end of the year. The biggest offensive problem was a deteriorating offensive line which exposed quarterback Jim Plunkett to severe punishment from enemy linemen. On defense, only Julius Adams and Jim Cheyunski provided any stability in the line and linebacking. Several veteran Patriots were lopped from the squad this year, as Jim Nance, Houston Antwine, Ron Sellers, and Don Webb all were casualties of a rebuilding program cursed with two dissenting architects. Before the season was over, coach Mazur had quit. In an unusual move to end an unusual season, the San Diego Chargers lent scout Phil Bengtson to the Patriots as interim head coach for the rest of the year.

CENTRAL DIVISION

Pittsburgh Steelers—Pittsburgh fans thoroughly enjoyed the Steelers' drive to their first title of any sort. One group of fans dubbed themselves "Franco's Army" and adopted rookie fullback Franco Harris as their favorite. Harris' power running had given the Pittsburgh attack a new

dimension. Another group of fans, known as "Gerela's Gorillas," took place-kicker Roy Gerela as their idol. Appreciated by all Steeler fans were quarterback Terry Bradshaw and the very strong defensive unit. With both platoons playing well, the Steelers held a share of first place until December 3, when a 30-0 thumping of the Browns gave the team complete possession of the top rung in the division.

Cleveland Browns—The Browns' greatest asset was their ability to stay cool in pressure situations. Despite injuries in the defensive line, a chaotic linebacking situation, and problems in the offensive line, the Browns calmly beat the Bengals and Jets in the final two games to win the AFC wild-card berth in the playoffs. The partial retirement of Bill Nelsen put the quarterbacking burden squarely on Mike Phipps' shoulders, and the young passer responded with a season of steady progress as a leader. The Browns had strength at running back, with Leroy Kelly and Bo Scott, and in the secondary, where youngsters Clarence Scott and Tom Darden had become instant stars.

Cincinnati Bengals—The Bengals' season unfolded in three separate stages. First came the good start of four wins in the opening five games, then a mid-season slump of four losses in five games, and finally a late spurt of three wins in the last four games. Playing consistently well throughout the season was the Cincinnati defense, a unit strengthened by the addition of two top rookies in Sherman White and Tommy Casanova. Veteran Bengal defenders Mike Reid, Ron Carpenter, Bill Bergey, and Lemar Parrish shared with the rookies a wealth of talent, but the offense lacked the polished excellence of the defense; too many holes remained to be filled in this platoon. The Bengals needed a powerful running back and a speedy wide receiver, but few people bet against Paul Brown finding them in next year's draft as he had found his defense.

Houston Oilers—Owner Bud Adams used a long-term contract to lure head coach Bill Peterson away from Rice, but the new coach could not stop the deterioration of the Oilers. Outside of an early-season upset of the Jets, the Oilers served as the NFL's punching bag. Mid-season trades brought Fred Willis, Paul Robinson, and Dave Smith to Houston, but they could not help an offense plagued with a porous line. On defense, the team's two best linemen, Elvin Bethea and Mike Tilleman, demanded to be traded; two starting linebackers, George Webster and Ron Pritchard, were traded in mid-season.

WESTERN DIVISION

Oakland Raiders—The Raiders had a knack for slipping new talent into the lineup while continuing to win without interruption. The defensive line, for instance, had been completely rebuilt in the last two seasons. Veterans like Ben Davidson, Tom Keating, and Carleton Oates had been eased aside in favor of youngsters Horace Jones, Art Thoms, Otis Sistrunk, and Tony Cline. The defense, meanwhile, suffered no letdown at all in stopping the run or pressuring the passer. At linebacker, the Raiders surrounded veteran Dan Conners with young outside men Phil Villipiano and Gerald Irons, and the secondary had veteran cornerbacks in Willie Brown and Nemiah Wilson and young safeties in George Atkinson and Jack Tatum. The offense had the same mixture of experience and youth, while the specialists ranged from rookie punt returner Cliff Branch to forty-four-year-old place-kicker George Blanda.

Kansas City Chiefs—Unable to win regularly at home, the Chiefs thus gave the Raiders only a weak challenge for the Western Division title. After years as an AFC power, the team was starting to crack under the weight of time. Safety Johnny Robinson retired, offensive linemen Ed Budde, Jim Tyrer, and Dave Hill were slowing down, and quarterback Len Dawson needed more rest. Other trouble spots for coach Hank Stram were receiver Elmo Wright's injury, a mediocre showing by the defensive ends, and a disappointing showing by rookie runner Jeff Kinney.

Denver Broncos—The Broncos followed the trend to hiring college coaches by signing John Ralston away from Stanford, but Ralston went out and traded for a veteran quarterback to lead the young Broncos on the field. Charley Johnson came over from Houston and gave the club a top passer and a poised offensive leader. With the Denver passing attack in good order, Floyd Little carried less of the offensive burden but still picked up 859 yards on the ground. Ralston traded away veteran defensive linemen Richard Jackson and Dave Costa, but the new unit of Lyle Alzado, Paul Smith, Pete Duranko, and Lloyd Voss kept pressure on opposing quarterbacks as the Broncos had their highest finish in ten years.

San Diego Chargers—Coach Harland Svare traded for some of the league's most famous oldsters and malcontents, bringing John Mackey, Deacon Jones, Lionel Aldridge, Dave Costa, Cid Edwards, Tim Rossovich, and Duane Thomas to San Diego. The Thomas deal was a complete washout, as Thomas' personal problems put him in no mood to play football. Injuries bothered Rossovich, and age had cut down on Mackey's skills, but the other acquisitions enjoyed good seasons in their new home. The defense suffered, however, when injuries decimated the secondary, and the offense was hurt by a difference in philosophy between quarterback John Hadl and offensive coach Bob Schnelker. Whereas Hadl had always run a wide-open passing attack, Schnelker insisted on a ball-control offense.

FINAL TEAM STATISTICS

OFFENSE

	BALT.	BUFF.	CIN.	CLEV.	DENV.	HOUS.	K.C.	MIAMI	N.ENG.	N.Y.	OAK.	PITT.	S.D.
FIRST DOWNS:													
Total	251	221	255	215	237	183	245	291	236	250	**297**	228	262
by Rushing	97	104	112	102	87	80	118	**170**	86	106	145	131	123
by Passing	124	98	122	101	**132**	88	116	102	126	117	122	79	116
by Penalty	**30**	19	21	12	18	15	11	19	24	27	**30**	18	23
RUSHING:													
Number	462	512	491	453	409	397	476	**613**	386	461	521	497	504
Yards	1894	2132	1996	1793	1838	1518	1915	**2960**	1532	2010	2376	2520	1995
Average Yards	4.1	4.2	4.1	4.0	4.5	3.8	4.0	4.8	4.0	4.4	4.6	**5.1**	4.0
Touchdowns	10	11	16	13	17	7	6	**26**	13	18	20	22	12
PASSING:													
Attempts	381	316	384	337	384	375	384	259	**412**	347	370	324	377
Completions	203	164	**219**	158	201	181	217	144	198	172	198	156	192
Completion Percentage	53.3	51.9	**57.0**	46.9	52.3	48.3	56.5	55.6	48.1	49.6	53.5	48.1	50.9
Passing Yards	2503	2012	2513	2135	2900	2045	2335	2235	2579	**2930**	2599	1958	2516
Avg. Yards per Attempt	6.6	6.4	6.5	6.3	7.6	5.5	6.1	**8.6**	6.3	8.4	7.0	6.0	6.7
Avg. Yards per Complet.	12.3	12.3	11.5	13.5	14.4	11.3	10.8	15.5	13.0	**17.0**	13.1	12.6	13.1
Time Tackled Passing	25	49	24	27	38	45	34	21	44	**17**	24	32	23
Yards Lost Tackled	210	411	192	219	266	372	297	159	452	**153**	230	247	212
Net Yards	2293	1601	2321	1916	2634	1673	2038	2076	2127	**2777**	2369	1711	2304
Touchdowns	15	16	10	13	19	10	20	17	10	21	**23**	12	15
Interceptions	12	24	**11**	19	23	23	20	12	28	22	15	12	28
Percent Intercepted	3.1	7.6	**2.9**	5.6	6.0	6.1	5.2	4.6	6.8	• 6.3	7.6	3.7	7.4
PUNTS:													
Number	57	80	66	81	60	**85**	66	44	75	51	55	66	45
Average Distance	42.1	38.8	42.1	43.2	40.1	41.0	**44.8**	39.4	38.1	39.3	36.9	43.6	40.3
PUNT RETURNS:													
Number	43	25	**47**	37	28	34	29	40	17	25	24	30	23
Yards	348	164	**437**	211	310	163	126	329	37	242	66	262	185
Average Yards	8.1	6.6	9.3	5.7	**11.1**	4.8	4.3	8.2	2.2	9.7	2.8	8.7	8.0
Touchdowns	0	0	**2**	0	1	0	0	0	0	1	0	0	0
KICKOFF RETURNS:													
Number	47	**60**	46	41	55	54	46	24	55	56	38	33	**60**
Yards	**1321**	1389	1018	933	1256	1093	1057	546	1293	1218	813	760	1273
Average Yards	**28.1**	23.2	22.1	22.8	22.8	20.2	23.0	22.8	23.5	21.8	21.4	23.0	21.2
Touchdowns	**1**	0	0	0	**1**	0	0	0	0	0	0	0	0
INTERCEPTION RETURNS:													
Number	23	23	20	13	10	6	24	26	10	19	25	**28**	24
Yards	331	369	326	154	109	93	**396**	286	223	282	328	395	310
Average Yards	14.4	16.0	16.3	11.8	10.9	15.5	16.5	11.0	**22.3**	14.8	13.1	14.1	12.9
Touchdowns	1	3	3	1	0	0	**5**	1	0	0	1	1	1
PENALTIES:													
Number	58	87	76	57	**89**	66	69	68	66	74	84	81	87
Yards	605	**900**	738	536	827	581	653	714	761	719	757	728	789
FUMBLES:													
Number	37	29	28	**21**	25	30	23	25	26	**21**	31	27	40
Number Lost	22	15	18	**9**	11	10	12	16	10	**9**	17	14	20
POINTS:													
Total	235	257	299	268	325	164	287	**385**	192	367	365	343	264
PAT Attempts	28	30	31	29	38	18	32	**45**	24	41	**45**	37	30
PAT Made	28	29	30	28	37	17	32	43	24	40	**44**	35	28
FG Attempts	39	24	40	27	29	21	36	37	16	37	26	**41**	31
FG Made	13	16	27	22	20	13	21	24	8	27	17	**28**	18
Percent FG Made	33.3	66.7	67.5	**81.5**	69.0	61.9	58.3	64.9	50.0	73.0	65.4	68.3	58.1
Safeties	0	0	**1**	0	0	0	0	0	0	0	0	**1**	**1**

DEFENSE

	BALT.	BUFF.	CIN.	CLEV.	DENV.	HOUS.	K.C.	MIAMI	N.ENG.	N.Y.	OAK.	PITT.	S.D.
FIRST DOWNS:													
Total	233	249	207	240	251	263	227	**186**	288	255	227	228	244
by Rushing	111	125	98	130	102	147	93	**76**	143	121	97	88	99
by Passing	109	95	92	**89**	123	100	116	96	124	118	104	116	124
by Penalty	**13**	29	17	21	26	16	18	14	21	16	26	24	21
RUSHING:													
Number	515	532	406	520	439	546	453	**389**	548	476	469	445	435
Yards	1989	2241	1815	2333	1668	2591	1805	**1548**	2717	2072	1764	1715	1673
Average Yards	3.9	4.2	4.5	4.5	3.8	4.7	4.0	4.0	5.0	4.4	**3.8**	3.9	3.8
Touchdowns	15	26	11	13	15	23	12	8	27	16	9	**6**	18
PASSING:													
Attempts	313	**308**	350	310	397	324	368	348	326	363	348	411	358
Completions	178	**131**	167	160	206	174	186	178	175	186	166	206	201
Completion Percentage	56.9	**42.5**	47.7	51.6	51.9	53.7	50.5	51.1	53.7	51.2	47.7	50.1	56.1
Passing Yards	2555	2148	2033	**1994**	2540	2315	2483	2029	2634	2888	2363	2393	2441
Avg. Yards per Attempt	8.2	7.0	**5.8**	6.4	6.4	7.1	6.7	5.8	8.1	8.0	6.8	5.8	6.8
Avg. Yards per Complet.	14.4	16.4	12.2	12.5	12.3	13.3	13.3	**11.4**	15.1	15.5	14.2	11.6	12.1
Time Tackled Passing	25	22	38	38	**41**	24	32	33	15	27	27	40	26
Yards Lost Tackled	232	197	296	258	**357**	172	261	280	101	251	211	337	233
Net Yards	2323	1951	1737	**1736**	2183	2143	2222	1749	2533	2637	2152	2056	2208
Touchdowns	15	19	11	14	19	12	17	10	24	18	14	**9**	18
Interceptions	23	23	20	13	10	6	24	26	10	19	25	**28**	24
Percent Intercepted	7.3	**7.5**	5.7	4.2	2.5	1.9	6.5	7.5	3.1	5.2	7.2	6.8	6.7
PUNTS:													
Number	71	65	**84**	74	66	61	61	68	48	56	56	74	56
Average Distance	39.0	39.5	42.4	40.9	45.2	42.1	40.3	41.1	40.4	39.4	42.5	40.3	**38.4**
PUNT RETURNS:													
Number	29	39	26	46	28	31	38	**17**	34	23	28	37	**17**
Yards	204	329	152	357	249	299	328	**67**	366	239	215	169	157
Average Yards	7.0	8.4	5.8	7.8	8.9	9.6	8.6	**3.9**	10.8	10.4	7.7	4.6	9.2
Touchdowns	**0**	1	**0**	**0**	1	1	**0**	**0**	1	**0**	**0**	**0**	1
KICKOFF RETURNS:													
Number	50	29	44	50	54	**28**	43	56	32	47	59	54	53
Yards	1091	644	984	1198	1246	**547**	1083	1283	784	1386	1393	1190	1225
Average Yards	21.8	22.2	22.4	24.0	23.1	**19.5**	25.2	22.9	24.5	29.5	23.6	22.0	23.1
Touchdowns	**0**	**0**	**0**	**0**	**0**	**0**	**0**	**0**	**0**	1	1	**0**	1
INTERCEPTION RETURNS:													
Number	12	24	**11**	19	23	23	20	12	28	22	15	12	28
Yards	169	305	**70**	145	441	319	278	249	490	271	178	195	229
Average Yards	14.1	12.7	**6.4**	7.6	19.2	13.9	13.9	20.8	17.5	12.3	11.9	16.3	8.2
Touchdowns	**0**	1	**0**	**0**	6	3	**0**	2	2	1	**0**	1	**0**
PENALTIES:													
Number	84	72	69	63	83	79	66	70	**88**	86	83	77	75
Yards	826	685	581	557	784	741	643	659	**862**	856	801	712	679
FUMBLES:													
Number	22	**20**	30	39	27	29	35	32	23	21	22	37	26
Number Lost	13	8	9	16	12	18	19	**20**	14	12	12	**20**	10
POINTS:													
Total	252	377	229	249	350	380	254	**171**	446	324	248	175	344
PAT Attempts	30	47	24	27	41	40	30	21	54	37	27	**18**	41
PAT Made	27	47	23	27	39	39	29	18	54	36	26	**17**	41
FG Attempts	24	27	29	29	33	40	31	**19**	36	33	37	27	28
FG Made	15	16	20	20	21	33	15	**9**	22	22	20	16	19
Percent FG Made	62.5	59.3	69.0	69.0	63.6	82.5	48.4	**47.4**	61.1	66.7	54.1	59.3	67.9
Safeties	**0**	**0**	1	**0**	1	1	**0**	**0**	1	**0**	**0**	1	**0**

CONFERENCE PLAYOFFS

December 23, at Pittsburgh (Attendance 50,327)

SCORING

PITTSBURGH	**0**	**0**	**3**	**10–13**
OAKLAND	**0**	**0**	**0**	**7– 7**

Third Quarter
PIT. Gerela, 18 yard field goal

Fourth Quarter
PIT. Gerela, 29 yard field goal
OAK. Stabler, 30 yard rush
PAT–Blanda (kick)
PIT. Harris, 60 yard pass from Bradshaw PAT–Gerela (kick)

TEAM STATISTICS

PITT.		OAK.
13	First Downs–Total	13
7	First Downs–Rushing	9
6	First Downs–Passing	4
0	First Downs–Penalty	0
0	Fumbles–Number	3
0	Fumbles–Lost Ball	2
1	Penalties–Number	2
5	Yards Penalized	15
1	Missed Field Goals	0
64	Offensive Plays	65
252	Net Yards	216
3.9	Average Gain	3.3
1	Giveaways	4
4	Takeaways	1
+3	Difference	–3

INDIVIDUAL STATISTICS

PITTSBURGH	No.	Yds.	Avg.	OAKLAND	No.	Yds.	Avg.
RUSHING							
Harris	18	64	3.6	Smith	14	57	4.1
Fuqua	16	25	1.6	Hubbard	14	44	3.1
Bradshaw	2	19	9.5	Stabler	1	30	30.0
	36	108	3.0	Davis	2	7	3.5
					31	138	4.5
RECEIVING							
Harris	5	96	19.2	Chester	3	40	13.3
Shanklin	3	55	18.3	Biletnikoff	3	28	9.3
Fuqua	1	11	11.0	Smith	2	8	4.0
McMakin	1	9	9.0	Banaszek	1	12	12.0
Young	1	4	4.0	Siani	1	7	7.0
	11	175	15.9	Otto	1	5	5.0
				Hubbard	1	2	2.0
					12	102	8.5
PUNTING							
Walden	6		48.2	DePoyster	7		45.1
PUNT RETURNS							
Edwards	3	39	13.0	Atkinson	1	37	37.0
KICKOFF RETURNS							
Pearson	1	21	21.0	Davis	1	26	26.0
INTERCEPTION RETURNS							
Ham	1	0	0.0	Wilson	1	7	7.0
Russell	1	0	0.0				
	2	0	0.0				

PASSING

	Att.	Comp.	Comp. Pct.	Yds.	Int.	Yds/ Att.	Yds/ Comp.	Yards Lost Tackled
PITTSBURGH								
Bradshaw	25	11	44.0	175	1	7.0	15.9	3–31
OAKLAND								
Lamonica	18	6	33.0	45	2	2.5	7.5	
Stabler	12	6	50.0	57	0	4.8	9.5	
	30	12	40.0	102	2	3.4	8.5	4–24

December 24, at Miami (Attendance 78,916)

SCORING

MIAMI	**10**	**0**	**0**	**10–20**
CLEVELAND	**0**	**0**	**7**	**7–14**

First Quarter
MIA. Babb, 6 yard return of blocked punt PAT–Yepremiam (kick)
MIA. Yepremiam, 40 yard field goal

Third Quarter
CLE. Phipps, 5 yard rush
PAT – Cockroft (kick)

Fourth Quarter
MIA. Yepremiam, 46 yard field goal
CLE. Hooker, 27 yard pass from Phipps PAT–Cockroft (kick)
MIA. Kiick, 8 yard rush
PAT–Yepremiam (kick)

TEAM STATISTICS

MIAMI		CLEVE.
17	First Downs–Total	15
11	First Downs–Rushing	9
4	First Downs–Passing	6
2	First Downs–Penalty	0
2	Fumbles–Number	2
2	Fumbles–Lost Ball	0
3	Penalties–Number	3
25	Yards Penalized	25
2	Missed Field Goals	0
64	Offensive Plays	57
272	Net Yards	283
4.3	Average Gain	5.0
2	Giveaways	5
5	Takeaways	2
+3	Difference	–3

INDIVIDUAL STATISTICS

MIAMI	No.	Yds.	Avg.	CLEVELAND	No.	Yds.	Avg.
RUSHING							
Morris	15	72	4.8	Scott	16	94	5.9
Kiick	14	50	3.6	Phipps	8	47	5.9
Warfield	2	41	20.5	Brown	4	13	3.3
Csonka	12	32	2.7	Kelly	4	11	2.8
Morrall	4	3	0.8		32	165	5.2
	47	198	4.2				
RECEIVING							
Twilley	3	33	11.0	Scott	4	30	7.5
Warfield	2	50	25.0	Hooker	3	53	17.7
Kiick	1	5	5.0	Kelly	1	27	27.0
	6	88	14.7	Morin	1	21	21.0
					9	131	14.6
PUNTING							
Seiple	5		42.0	Cockroft	6		34.7
PUNT RETURNS							
Scott	1	1	1.0	Darden	1	38	38.0
				Kelley	1	8	8.0
					2	46	23.0
KICKOFF RETURNS							
None				Lefear	3	56	18.7
INTERCEPTION RETURNS							
Swift	2	19	9.5	None			
Anderson	2	12	6.0				
Johnson	1	33	33.0				
	5	64	12.8				

PASSING

	Att.	Comp.	Comp. Pct.	Yds.	Int.	Yds/ Att.	Yds/ Comp.	Yards Lost Tackled
MIAMI								
Morrall	13	6	46.2	88	0	6.8	14.7	4–14
CLEVELAND								
Phipps	23	9	39.1	131	5	5.7	14.6	2–13

MIAMI DOLPHINS 14-0-0 Don Shula

Scores of Each Game		
20	Kansas City	10
34	HOUSTON	13
16	Minnesota	14
27	N.Y. Jets	17
24	SAN DIEGO	10
24	BUFFALO	23
23	Baltimore	0
30	Buffalo	16
52	NEW ENGLAND	0
28	N.Y. JETS	24
31	ST. LOUIS	10
37	New England	21
23	N.Y. Giants	13
16	BALTIMORE	0

Use Name	Pos.	Hgt	Wgt	Age	Int	Pts
Doug Crusan	OT	6'5"	250	26		
Norm Evans	OT	6'5"	252	29		
Wayne Moore	OT	6'6"	265	27		
Bob Kuechenberg	OG	6'3"	247	24		
Larry Little	OG	6'1"	265	26		
Al Jenkins	OT-OG	6'2"	245	26		
Jim Langer	C	6'2"	250	24		
Howard Kindig	OT-C	6'6"	260	31		
Vern Den Herder	DE	6'6"	250	23	1	
Bill Stanfill	DE	6'5"	250	25		
Bob Matheson	LB-DE	6'4"	240	27		
Jim Dunaway	DT	6'4"	277	30		
Manny Fernandez	DT	6'2"	248	26		
Baldy Moore	DT	6'5"	265	26		
Bob Heinz	DE-DT	6'6"	270	25		

Use Name	Pos.	Hgt	Wgt	Age	Int	Pts
Larry Ball	LB	6'6"	225	22		
Nick Buoniconti	LB	5'11"	220	31	2	
Mike Kolen	LB	6'2"	220	24	1	
Jesse Powell	LB	6'1"	215	25		
Doug Swift	LB	6'3"	228	23	3	
Dick Anderson	DB	6'2"	196	26	3	6
Charlie Babb	DB	6'	190	22	1	
Tim Foley	DB	6'	194	24	3	
Curtis Johnson	DB	6'2"	196	24	3	
Lloyd Mumphford	DB	5'11"	180	25	4	6
Jake Scott	DB	6'	188	27	5	

Karl Noonan — Knee Injury
Jim Riley — Knee Injury

Use Name	Pos.	Hgt	Wgt	Age	Int	Pts
Jim Del Gaizo	QB	6'1"	198	25		
Bob Griese	QB	6'1"	190	27		6
Earl Morrall	QB	6'1"	206	38		6
Hubert Ginn	HB	5'11"	188	25		6
Ed Jenkins	HB	6'2"	210	22		
Jim Kiick	HB	5'11"	215	26		36
Mercury Morris	HB	5'10"	190	25		72
Larry Csonka	FB	6'3"	237	25		36
Charlie Leigh	FB	5'11"	205	26		
Marlin Briscoe	WR	5'10"	178	26		24
Otto Stowe	WR	6'2"	188	23		12
Howard Twilley	WR	5'10"	185	28		18
Paul Warfield	WR	6'	185	29		18
Marv Fleming	TE	6'4"	235	30		6
Jim Mandich	TE	6'3"	224	24		18
Larry Seiple	TE	6'	215	27		
Billy Lothridge	K	6'1"	200	28		
Garo Yepremian	K	5'8"	172	28		115

NEW YORK JETS 7-7-0 Weeb Ewbank

Scores of Each Game		
41	Buffalo	24
44	Baltimore	34
20	Houston	26
17	MIAMI	27
41	New England	13
24	BALTIMORE	20
34	NEW ENGLAND	10
17	WASHINGTON	35
41	BUFFALO	3
24	Miami	28
20	Detroit	37
18	NEW ORLEANS	17
16	Oakland	24
10	CLEVELAND	26

Use Name	Pos.	Hgt	Wgt	Age	Int	Pts
Winston Hill	OT	6'4"	270	30		
Bob Svihus	OT	6'4"	245	29		
John Mooring	C-OT	6'6"	255	25		
Roger Finnie	OG	6'3"	245	25		
Dave Herman	OG	6'2"	255	30		
Randy Rasmussen	OG	6'2"	255	27		6
Roy Kirksey	DT-OG	6'1"	265	24		
John Schmitt	C	6'4"	250	29		
Gerry Philbin	DE	6'2"	245	31		
Joey Jackson	DT-DE	6'4"	257	23		
Mark Lomas	DT-DE	6'4"	245	24		
John Elliott	DT	6'4"	244	27		
John Little	DT	6'3"	235	25		
Steve Thompson	DT	6'5"	237	27		
Ed Galigher	DE-DT	6'4"	255	21		

Use Name	Pos.	Hgt	Wgt	Age	Int	Pts
Al Atkinson	LB	6'1"	230	29	1	
Ralph Baker	LB	6'3"	228	30	2	
John Ebersole	LB	6'3"	227	23		
Larry Grantham	LB	6'	210	33		
Mike Taylor	LB	6'1"	230	22	1	
Paul Crane	C-LB	6'2"	212	28	1	
Bill Zapalac	DE-LB	6'4"	225	24		
Chris Farasopoulos	DB	5'11"	190	23	2	6
W. K. Hicks	DB	6'1"	195	29	1	
Gus Holloman	DB	6'3"	195	26	1	
Rich Sowells	DB	6'	175	23	2	
Steve Tannen	DB	6'1"	194	24	7	
Earlie Thomas	DB	6'1"	190	26	1	
Phil Wise	DB	6'	190	23		

Use Name	Pos.	Hgt	Wgt	Age	Int	Pts
Bob Davis	QB	6'3"	205	27		
Joe Namath	QB	6'2"	200	29		
Hank Bjorklund	BH	6'1"	200	22		
Emerson Boozer	HB	5'11"	195	29		84
Cliff McClain	HB	6'	217	24		
John Riggins	FB	6'2"	233	23		48
Matt Snell	FB	6'2"	220	30		
Steve Harkey	HB-FB	6'	215	23		
Jerome Barkum	WR	6'3"	215	22		12
Eddie Bell	WR	5'10"	160	24		12
Don Maynard	WR	6'	180	36		12
Rocky Turner	WR	6'	190	22		
Rich Caster	TE	6'5"	228	23		60
Wayne Stewart	TE	6'7"	213	25		6
Bobby Howfield	K	5'9"	180	35		121
Steve O'Neal	K	6'3"	185	26		

BALTIMORE COLTS 5-9-0 Don McCafferty John Sandusky

Scores of Each Game		
3	ST. LOUIS	10
34	N.Y. JETS	44
17	Buffalo	0
20	SAN DIEGO	23
0	DALLAS	21
20	N.Y. Jets	24
0	MIAMI	23
24	New England	17
21	San Francisco	24
20	Cincinnati	19
31	NEW ENGLAND	0
35	BUFFALO	7
10	Kansas City	24
0	Miami	16

Use Name	Pos.	Hgt	Wgt	Age	Int	Pts
Tom Drougas	OT	6'4"	257	22		
Dennis Nelson	OT	6'5"	260	26		
Bob Vogel	OT	6'5"	250	30		
Cornelius Johnson	OG	6'2"	245	29		
Glenn Ressler	OG	6'3"	250	28		
John Shinners	OG	6'2"	254	25		
Dan Sullivan	OG	6'3"	250	33		
Bill Curry	C	6'2"	236	29		
Ken Mendenhall	C	6'3"	235	24		
Dick Amman	DE	6'5"	234	21		
Roy Hilton	DE	6'6"	240	27		
Billy Newsome	DE	6'4"	250	24		
Chuck Hinton	DT	6'5"	264	33		
Fred Miller	DT	6'3"	250	31		
Jim Bailey	DE-DT	6'4"	255	24		

Use Name	Pos.	Hgt	Wgt	Age	Int	Pts
Mike Curtis	LB	6'2"	232	29	4	6
Randy Edmunds	LB	6'2"	225	26		
Ted Hendricks	LB	6'7"	220	24	2	
Bill Laskey	LB	6'2"	235	29		
Ray May	LB	6'1"	230	27	2	
Stan White	LB	6'1"	225	22		
Lonnie Hepburn	DB	5'11"	180	23	1	
Rex Kern	DB	5'11"	190	23		
Bruce Laird	DB	6'	185	22	1	
Jerry Logan	DB	6'1"	190	31	4	
Jack Mildren	DB	6'1"	200	22		
Nelson Munsey	DB	6'1"	185	24		6
Charlie Stukes	DB	6'3"	212	28	5	
Rick Volk	DB	6'3"	195	27	4	

Bubba Smith — Knee Injury

Use Name	Pos.	Hgt	Wgt	Age	Int	Pts
Marty Domres	QB	6'3"	220	25		6
Johnny Unitas	QB	6'1"	196	39		
Tom Matte	HB	6'	214	33		6
Don McCauley	HB	6'1"	207	23		30
Lydell Mitchell	HB	5'11"	204	23		12
Don Nottingham	FB	5'10"	210	23		18
Tom Nowatzke	FB	6'3"	230	29		
Norm Bulaich	HB-FB	6'1"	218	25		6
Glenn Doughty	WR	6'2"	204	21		
Willie Franklin	WR	6'2"	194	22		
Sam Havrilak	WR	6'2"	195	24		36
Eddie Hinton	WR	6'	200	25		6
Jim O'Brien	WR	6'	195	25		75
Cotton Speyrer	WR	6'	175	23		
Tom Mitchell	TE	6'2"	215	28		24
John Mosier	TE	6'3"	220	24		
David Lee	K	6'4"	230	28		
Boris Shlapak	K	6'	165	22		4

BUFFALO BILLS 4-9-1 Lou Saban

Scores of Each Game		
24	N.Y. JETS	41
27	SAN FRANCISCO	20
0	BALTIMORE	17
38	NEW ENGLAND	14
16	Oakland	28
23	Miami	24
21	PITTSBURGH	38
16	MIAMI	30
3	N.Y. Jets	41
27	New England	24
10	Cleveland	27
7	Baltimore	35
21	DETROIT	21
24	Washington	17

Use Name	Pos.	Hgt	Wgt	Age	Int	Pts
Paul Costa	OT	6'4"	268	30		
Dave Foley	OT	6'5"	255	24		
Donnie Green	OT	6'7"	285	24		
Willie Young	OT	6'4"	270	29		
Bill Adams	OG	6'2"	250	22		
Dick Hart	OG	6'2"	250	29		
Reggie McKenzie	OG	6'4"	235	22		
Jeff Curchin	OT-OG	6'6"	255	24		
Remi Prudhomme (from NO)	C-OG	6'4"	250	30		
Tom Beard	C	6'6"	280	23		
Bruce Jarvis	C	6'7"	245	23		
John Matlock	C	6'4"	250	27		
Bobby Penchion	OG-C	6'5"	255	23		
Walt Patulski	DE	6'6"	252	22		
Louis Ross	DE	6'6"	242	25		
Al Cowlings	DT-DE	6'5"	250	25		
Frank Cornish	DT	6'6"	285	28		
Don Croft	DT	6'3"	252	23		
Steve Okoniewski	DT	6'3"	247	23		
Jerry Patton	DT	6'3"	250	26		
Mike McBath	DE-DT	6'4"	250	26		

Use Name	Pos.	Hgt	Wgt	Age	Int	Pts
Edgar Chandler	LB	6'3"	225	26		
Dick Cunningham	LB	6'2"	232	27		
Dale Farley	LB	6'3"	235	23	1	
Paul Guidry	LB	6'3"	233	28	1	
Ken Lee	LB	6'4"	232	23	6	6
Jeff Lyman	LB	6'2"	230	22		
Andy Selfridge	LB	6'4"	218	23		
Mike Stratton	LB	6'3"	240	30	1	
Dave Washington	TE-LB	6'5"	220	24	1	
Leon Garror	DB	6'	180	24		
Tony Greene	DB	5'10"	170	23	3	6
Robert James	DB	6'1"	185	25	1	
John Pitts	DB	6'4"	215	27	1	
John Saunders	DB	6'3"	202	22		
Maurice Tyler	DB	6'	188	22	4	
Alvin Wyatt	DB	5'10"	180	24	4	6

Mike Clark — Injury
Irv Goode — Knee Injury

Use Name	Pos.	Hgt	Wgt	Age	Int	Pts
Leo Hart	QB	6'4"	203	23		
Dennis Shaw	QB	6'2"	215	25		
Mike Taliaferro	QB	6'2"	205	30		
Randy Jackson	HB	6'	220	23		6
O. J. Simpson	HB	6'2"	214	25		36
Ted Koy	FB-HB	6'1"	215	24		
Jim Braxton	FB	6'2"	226	23		36
Wayne Patrick	FB	6'2"	245	26		6
Bob Chandler	WR	6'	180	23		30
Linzy Cole (from HOU)	WR	5'11"	170	24		
Dwight Harrison (from DEN)	WR	6'1"	178	23		
J. D. Hill	WR	6'1"	193	23		30
Bob Christiansen	TE	6'4"	230	23		
Jan White	TE	6'2"	216	23		12
Spike Jones	K	6'2"	190	25		
John Leypoldt	K	6'2"	224	26		77

Bill McKinley — Injury
Jim Reilly — Illness

NEW ENGLAND PATRIOTS 3-11-0 John Mazur Phil Bengtson

Scores of Each Game		
7	CINCINNATI	31
21	ATLANTA	20
24	WASHINGTON	23
14	Buffalo	38
13	N.Y. JETS	41
3	Pittsburgh	33
10	N.Y. Jets	34
17	BALTIMORE	24
0	Miami	52
24	BUFFALO	27
0	Baltimore	31
21	MIAMI	37
17	New Orleans	10
21	Denver	45

Use Name	Pos.	Hgt	Wgt	Age	Int	Pts
Mike Montler	OT	6'4"	255	28		
Tom Neville	OT	6'4"	255	29		
Bob Reynolds	OT	6'6"	265	31		
Sam Adams	OG	6'3"	252	23		
Halvor Hagen	OG	6'5"	253	25		
Len St. Jean	OG	6'1"	250	30		
Bill Lenkaitis	C-OG	6'3"	260	26		
Jon Morris	C	6'4"	254	29		
Ron Berger	DE	6'8"	285	28		
Jim White	DE	6'3"	256	23		
Dennis Wirgowski	DT-DE	6'5"	250	24		
Rick Cash	DT	6'5"	260	26		
Dave Rowe	DT	6'6"	280	27		
Julius Adams	DE-DT	6'3"	260	24		

Use Name	Pos.	Hgt	Wgt	Age	Int	Pts
Ron Acks	LB	6'2"	220	27		
Dick Blanchard	LB	6'3"	225	23	1	
Jim Cheyunski	LB	6'2"	225	26		
Ralph Cindrich	LB	6'1"	228	22		
Ron Kadziel	LB	6'4"	230	23		
Ed Weisacosky	LB	6'	220	28		
Ron Bolton	DB	6'2"	180	22		
Larry Carwell	DB	6'1"	190	28	1	6
Rickie Harris	DB	6'	182	29	3	
George Haey	DB	5'10"	170	25	1	
Honor Jackson	DB	6'1"	195	23	4	
Art McMahon	DB	5'11"	190	26		
John Outlaw	DB	5'10"	180	27		
Clarence Scott	DB	6'2"	200	28		

Use Name	Pos.	Hgt	Wgt	Age	Int	Pts
Brian Dowling	QB	6'2"	210	25		18
Jim Plunkett	QB	6'3"	220	24		6
Carl Garrett	HB	5'11"	215	25		30
Bob Gladieux	HB	5'11"	195	25		
Jack Maitland	HB	6'1"	210	24		
Henry Matthews	HB	6'3"	203	23		
John Tarver	FB	6'3"	227	23		12
Josh Ashton	HB-FB	6'1"	205	23		24
Hubie Bryant	WR	5'10"	168	26		
Tom Reynolds	WR	6'3"	200	23		12
Reggie Rucker	WR	6'2"	190	24		18
Pat Studstill	WR	6'1"	175	34		
Randy Vataha	WR	5'10"	175	23		12
Tom Beer	TE	6'4"	235	27		
Bob Windsor	TE	6'4"	226	29		6
Charlie Gogolak	K	5'10"	170	27		27
Mike Walker	K	6'	190	22		21

MIAMI DOLPHINS

Rushing

Last Name	No.	Yds	Avg	TD
Csonka	213	1117	5.2	6
Morris	190	1000	5.3	12
Kiick	137	521	3.8	5
Ginn	27	142	5.3	1
Leigh	21	79	3.8	0
Morrall	17	67	3.9	1
Warfield	4	23	5.8	0
Griese	3	11	3.7	1
DelGaizo	1	0	0.0	0

Receiving

Last Name	No.	Yds	Avg	TD
Warfield	29	606	21	3
Kiick	21	147	7	1
Twilley	20	364	18	3
Briscoe	16	279	17	4
Morris	15	168	11	0
Stowe	13	276	21	2
Fleming	13	156	12	1
Mandich	11	168	15	3
Csonka	5	48	10	0
Ginn	1	23	23	0

Punt Returns

Last Name	No.	Yds	Avg	TD
Leigh	22	210	10	0
Scott	13	100	8	0
Anderson	5	19	4	0

Kickoff Returns

Last Name	No.	Yds	Avg	TD
Morris	14	334	24	0
Leigh	6	153	26	0
Matheson	2	34	17	0
Ginn	1	25	25	0
Briscoe	1	0	0	0

Passing – Punting – Kicking

Passing

Last Name	Att	Comp	%	Yds	Yd/Att	TD	Int–	%	RK
Morrall	150	83	55	1360	9.1	11	7–	5	1
Griese	97	53	55	638	6.6	4	4–	4	
DelGaizo	9	5	56	165	18.3	2	1–	11	
Briscoe	3	3	100	72	24.0	0	0–	0	

Punting

Last Name	No	Avg
Seiple	36	39.9
Lothridge	4	37.5
Anderson	4	36.8

Kicking

Last Name	XP	Att	%	FG	Att	%
Yepremian	43	45	96	24	37	65

NEW YORK JETS

Rushing

Last Name	No.	Yds	Avg	TD
Riggins	207	944	4.6	7
Boozer	120	549	4.6	11
McClain	59	305	5.2	0
Harkey	45	129	2.9	0
Bjorklund	15	42	2.8	0
Davis	6	32	5.3	0
Namath	6	8	1.3	0
Caster	2	6	3.0	0
Bell	1	−5	−5.0	0

Receiving

Last Name	No.	Yds	Avg	TD
Caster	39	833	21	10
Bell	35	629	18	2
Maynard	29	510	18	2
Riggins	21	230	11	1
Barkum	16	304	19	2
Boozer	11	142	13	3
Harkey	9	114	13	0
McClain	6	88	15	0
Bjorklund	4	54	14	0
Stewart	2	26	13	1

Punt Returns

Last Name	No.	Yds	Avg	TD
Farasopoulos	17	179	11	1
Turner	5	38	8	0
Hicks	3	25	8	0

Kickoff Returns

Last Name	No.	Yds	Avg	TD
Farasopoulos	26	627	24	0
Wise	9	211	23	0
Bjorklund	7	150	21	0
Hicks	4	73	24	0
Turner	3	57	19	0
McClain	2	45	23	0
Kirksey	2	33	17	0
Snell	1	14	14	0
Zapalac	1	8	8	0
Barkum	1	0	0	0

Passing – Punting – Kicking

Passing

Last Name	Att	Comp	%	Yds	Yd/Att	TD	Int–	%	RK
Namath	324	162	50	2816	8.7	19	21–	6	8
Davis	22	10	46	114	5.2	2	1–	5	
McClain	1	0	0	0	0.0	0	0–	0	

Punting

Last Name	No	Avg
O'Neal	51	39.3

Kicking

Last Name	XP	Att	%	FG	Att	%
Howfield	40	41	98	27	37	73

BALTIMORE COLTS

Rushing

Last Name	No.	Yds	Avg	TD
McCauley	178	675	3.8	2
Nottingham	123	466	3.8	3
L. Mitchell	45	215	4.8	1
Matte	33	137	4.2	0
Domres	30	137	4.6	1
Bulaich	27	109	4.0	1
Havrilak	12	72	6.0	2
Doughty	2	33	16.5	0
Unitas	3	15	5.0	0
Nowatzke	3	11	3.7	0
O'Brien	3	9	3.0	0
Mildren	3	8	2.7	0
T. Mitchell	0	7	0.0	0

Receiving

Last Name	No.	Yds	Avg	TD
T. Mitchell	40	494	12	4
Havrilak	33	571	17	4
McCauley	30	256	9	2
Nottingham	25	191	7	0
L. Mitchell	18	147	8	1
Matte	14	182	13	1
O'Brien	11	263	24	2
Hinton	11	146	13	1
Bulaich	9	55	6	0
Speyrer	8	114	14	0
Doughty	3	31	10	0
Mosier	1	53	53	0

Punt Returns

Last Name	No.	Yds	Avg	TD
Laird	34	303	9	0
Volk	5	25	5	0
Logan	4	20	5	0

Kickoff Returns

Last Name	No.	Yds	Avg	TD
Laird	29	843	29	0
McCauley	13	377	29	1
Bulaich	1	62	62	0
Nottingham	2	38	19	0
Mildren	1	1	1	0
Hendricks	1	0	0	0

Passing – Punting – Kicking

Passing

Last Name	Att	Comp	%	Yds	Yd/Att	TD	Int–	%	RK
Domres	222	115	52	1392	6.3	11	6–	3	6
Unitas	157	88	56	1111	7.1	4	6–	4	4
Havrilak	1	0	0	0	0.0	0	0–	0	
Mildren	1	0	0	0	0.0	0	0–	0	

Punting

Last Name	No	Avg
Lee	57	42.1

Kicking

Last Name	XP	Att	%	FG	Att	%
O'Brien	24	24	100	13	31	42
Shlapak	4	4	100	0	8	0

BUFFALO BILLS

Rushing

Last Name	No.	Yds	Avg	TD
Simpson	291	1251	4.3	6
Braxton	116	453	3.9	5
Shaw	35	138	3.9	0
Patrick	35	130	3.7	0
Jackson	17	57	3.4	0
B. Chandler	3	27	9.0	0
L. Hart	5	19	3.8	0
Taliaferro	5	19	3.8	0
Jones	2	18	9.0	0
Hill	1	11	11.0	0
Harrison	1	9	9.0	0
Koy	1	9	9.0	0

Receiving

Last Name	No.	Yds	Avg	TD
Hill	52	754	15	5
B. Chandler	33	528	16	5
Simpson	27	198	7	0
Braxton	24	232	10	1
White	12	148	12	2
Patrick	8	42	5	1
Jackson	2	21	11	1
Harrison	1	16	16	0
Koy	1	9	9	0
Washington	1	4	4	0

Punt Returns

Last Name	No.	Yds	Avg	TD
Wyatt	11	85	8	0
Cole	7	35	5	0
Hill	4	24	6	0
Greene	2	18	9	0
Harrison	1	2	2	0

Kickoff Returns

Last Name	No.	Yds	Avg	TD
Cole	18	456	25	0
Wyatt	17	432	25	0
Greene	15	378	25	0
Koy	5	63	13	0
Selfridge	3	36	12	0
Hill	2	32	16	0
Simpson	1	21	21	0
Braxton	1	12	12	0
Prudhomme	1	0	0	0

Passing – Punting – Kicking

Passing

Last Name	Att	Comp	%	Yds	Yd/Att	TD	Int–	%	RK
Shaw	258	136	53	1666	6.5	14	17–	7	9
Taliaferro	33	16	48	176	5.3	1	4–	12	
L. Hart	15	6	40	53	3.5	0	3–	20	
Simpson	8	5	63	113	14.1	1	0–	0	
Jones	2	1	50	4	2.0	0	0–	0	

Punting

Last Name	No	Avg
Jones	80	38.8

Kicking

Last Name	XP	Att	%	FG	Att	%
Leypoldt	29	30	97	16	24	67

NEW ENGLAND PATRIOTS

Rushing

Last Name	No.	Yds	Avg	TD
Ashton	128	546	4.3	3
Garrett	131	488	3.7	5
Plunkett	36	230	6.4	1
Tarver	42	132	3.1	1
Gladieux	24	56	2.3	0
Dowling	7	35	5.0	3
Maitland	13	33	2.5	0
Studstill	1	11	11.0	0
Rucker	3	5	1.7	0
Windsor	1	−4	−4.0	0

Receiving

Last Name	No.	Yds	Avg	TD
Rucker	44	681	15	3
Windsor	33	383	12	1
Garrett	30	410	14	0
Vataha	25	369	15	2
Ashton	22	207	9	1
Gladieux	19	192	10	0
Tarver	11	112	10	1
T. Reynolds	8	152	19	2
Maitland	4	33	8	0
Beer	2	40	20	0

Punt Returns

Last Name	No.	Yds	Avg	TD
Garrett	6	36	6	0
Harris	4	5	1	0
Carwell	5	2	0	0
Gladieux	2	−6	−3	0

Kickoff Returns

Last Name	No.	Yds	Avg	TD
Garrett	16	410	26	0
Ashton	15	309	21	0
Rucker	8	227	28	0
Hoey	9	210	23	0
Matthews	3	74	25	0
Maitland	3	48	16	0
Beer	1	15	15	0

Passing – Punting – Kicking

Passing

Last Name	Att	Comp	%	Yds	Yd/Att	TD	Int–	%	RK
Plunkett	355	169	48	2196	6.2	8	25–	7	14
Dowling	54	29	54	383	7.1	2	1–	2	
Garrett	1	0	0	0	0.0	0	1–	100	
Gladieux	1	0	0	0	0.0	0	1–	100	
Studstill	1	0	0	0	0.0	0	0–	0	

Punting

Last Name	No	Avg
Studstill	75	38.1

Kicking

Last Name	XP	Att	%	FG	Att	%
Walker	15	15	100	2	8	25
Gogolak	9	9	100	6	8	75

PITTSBURGH STEELERS 11-3-0 — Chuck Noll

	Opponent	
34	OAKLAND	28
10	Cincinnati	15
25	St. Louis	19
13	Dallas	17
24	HOUSTON	7
33	NEW ENGLAND	3
38	Buffalo	21
40	CINCINNATI	17
16	KANSAS CITY	7
24	Cleveland	26
23	MINNESOTA	10
30	CLEVELAND	0
9	Houston	3
24	San Diego	2

Use Name	Pos.	Hgt	Wgt	Age	Int	Pts
Gordon Gravelle	OT	6'5"	250	23		
Jon Kolb	OT	6'2"	262	25		
Gerry Mullins	OG-OT	6'3"	235	23		6
Sam Davis	OG	6'1"	255	28		
Bruce Van Dyke	OG	6'2"	255	28		
Mel Holmes	OT-OG	6'3"	250	22		
Jim Clack	C	6'3"	250	24		
Ray Mansfield	C	6'3"	255	31		
L.C. Greenwood	DE	6'5"	245	25		
Craig Hanneman	DE	6'3"	240	23		
Dwight White	DE	6'4"	250	23		
Steve Furness	DT	6'4"	255	21		
Joe Greene	DT	6'4"	270	25		
Ernie Holmes	DT	6'3"	260	24		
Ben McGee	DT	6'2"	260	30		
Ed Bradley	LB	6'2"	240	22		
Henry Davis	LB	6'3"	235	29	2	6
Jack Ham	LB	6'3"	220	23	7	6
Andy Russell	LB	6'3"	225	30		
Brian Stenger	LB	6'4"	230	25		
George Webster (from HOU)	LB	6'4"	223	26		
Carl Winfrey	LB	6'	230	23		
Ralph Anderson	DB	6'2"	180	23	3	2
Chuck Beatty (to STL)	DB	6'2"	205	26	2	
Mel Blount	DB	6'3"	205	24	3	6
Lee Calland	DB	6'	190	31		
John Dockery	DB	6'	186	27		
Glen Edwards	DB	6'	185	25	1	
John Rowser	DB	6'1"	185	28	4	
Mike Wagner	DB	6'1"	196	23	6	
Terry Bradshaw	QB	6'3"	218	23		42
Joe Gilliam	QB	6'2"	187	21		
Terry Hanratty	QB	6'1"	210	24		
Rocky Bleier	HB	5'11"	205	26		
Preston Pearson	HB	6'1"	205	27		
Franco Harris	FB-HB	6'2"	230	22		66
Warren Bankston	FB	6'4"	235	25		
Steve Davis	HB-FB	6'1"	218	22		6
John Fuqua	HB-FB	5'11"	200	25		24
Frank Lewis	WR	6'1"	196	25		30
Barry Pearson	WR	5'11"	185	22		
Ron Shanklin	WR	6'1"	180	25		18
Al Young	WR	6'1"	195	23		
Larry Brown	TE	6'4"	225	23		6
John McMakin	TE	6'3"	232	21		6
Roy Gerela	K	5'10"	185	24		119
Bobby Walden	K	6'	190	34		

Bob Adams — Injury
John Brown — Injury

CLEVELAND BROWNS 10-4-0 — Nick Skorich

	Opponent	
10	GREEN BAY	26
27	Philadelphia	17
27	CINCINNATI	6
7	KANSAS CITY	31
0	CHICAGO	17
23	Houston	17
27	Denver	20
20	HOUSTON	0
21	San Diego	17
26	PITTSBURGH	24
27	BUFFALO	10
0	Pittsburgh	30
27	Cincinnati	24
26	N.Y. Jets	10

Use Name	Pos.	Hgt	Wgt	Age	Int	Pts
Joe Carollo	OT	6'2"	265	32		
Doug Dieken	OT	6'5"	237	23		
Bob McKay	OT	6'6"	260	24		
Chris Morris	OT	6'3"	250	22		
John Demarie	C-OG-OT	6'3"	246	27		
Gene Hickerson	OG	6'3"	252	37		
Bubba Pena	OG	6'2"	250	23		
Craig Wycinsky	OG	6'3"	243	24		
Jim Copeland	C-OG	6'2"	243	27		
Bob DeMarco	C	6'3"	248	34		
Fred Hoaglin	C	6'4"	246	28		
Wes Grant	DE	6'3"	245	25		
Rich Jackson (from DEN)	DE	6'2"	255	31		
Nick Roman	DE	6'3"	235	24	1	6
Ron Snidow	DE	6'4"	247	30		
Bob Briggs	DT-DE	6'4"	258	27	1	6
Cotton Fest	DT	6'2"	255	22		
Walter Johnson	DT	6'3"	263	29	1	
George Wright	DT	6'3"	265	25		
Jerry Sherk	DE-DT	6'4"	258	24		
Billy Andrews	LB	6'	220	27	1	
John Garlington	LB	6'1"	218	26	1	
Charlie Hall	LB	6'3"	220	23	1	
Rick Kingrea	LB	6'1"	233	23		
Dale Lindsey	LB	6'3"	225	29		
Mel Long	LB	6'	228	25		
Jim Houston	DE-LB	6'3"	236	35		
Cliff Brooks	DB	6'1"	190	23		
Thom Darden	DB	6'2"	195	22	3	
Ben Davis	DB	5'11"	180	26	3	
Mike Howell (to MIA)	DB	6'1"	190	29	1	
Bobby Majors	DB	6'1"	193	23		
Clarence Scott	DB	6'	180	23		6
Walt Sumner	DB	6'1"	195	25		
Don Horn	QB	6'2"	195	27		
Bill Nelsen	QB	6'	195	31		
Mike Phipps	QB	6'2"	208	24		30
Leroy Kelly	HB	6'	202	30		30
Bill LeFear	HB	5'11"	197	22		
Ken Brown	FB-HB	5'10"	203	26		12
Bo Cornell	FB	6'1"	215	23		
Bo Scott	FB	6'3"	215	29		12
Charlie Brinkman	WR	6'2"	208	23		
Fair Hooker	WR	6'1"	190	25		12
Frank Pitts	WR	6'2"	200	28		48
Gloster Richardson	WR	6'	200	29		
Paul Staroba	WR	6'3"	204	23		6
Chip Glass	TE	6'4"	235	25		
Milt Morin	TE	6'4"	236	30		6
Don Cockroft	K	6'1"	195	27		94

Joe Jones — Knee Injury

CINCINNATI BENGALS 8-6-0 — Paul Brown

	Opponent	
31	New England	7
15	PITTSBURGH	10
6	Cleveland	27
21	DENVER	10
23	Kansas City	16
12	Los Angeles	15
30	HOUSTON	7
17	Pittsburgh	40
14	OAKLAND	20
19	BALTIMORE	20
13	Chicago	3
13	N.Y. GIANTS	10
24	CLEVELAND	27
61	Houston	17

Use Name	Pos.	Hgt	Wgt	Age	Int	Pts
Vern Holland	OT	6'5"	270	24		
Stan Walters	OT	6'6"	270	24		
Rufus Mayes	OG-OT	6'5"	260	24		
Guy Dennis	OG	6'2"	255	25		
Steve Lawson	OG	6'3"	265	23		
Pat Matson	OG	6'1"	245	28		
Howard Fest	OT-OG	6'6"	262	26		
Tom DeLeone	C-OG	6'2"	252	22		
Bob Johnson	C	6'4"	260	26		
Royce Berry	DE	6'3"	250	26		
Ron Carpenter	DE	6'4"	260	24		
Sherman White	DE	6'5"	255	23		2
Steve Chomyszak	DT	6'5"	270	27		
Ken Johnson	DT	6'5"	265	24		
Mike Reid	DT	6'3"	250	25		
Doug Adams	LB	6'	227	23	3	
Ken Avery	LB	6'1"	230	28		
Al Beauchamp	LB	6'2"	237	28	1	
Bill Bergey	LB	6'2"	243	27		
Tim Kearney	LB	6'2"	227	21		
Jim LeClair	LB	6'3"	226	21		
Bill Peterson	LB	6'3"	225	22		
Ron Pritchard (from HOU)	LB	6'1"	235	25		
Tommy Casanova	DB	6'2"	202	22	5	6
Neal Craig	DB	6'1"	190	24	2	6
Bernie Jackson	DB	6'	173	22	1	
Ernie Kellerman	DB	6'	183	28		
Lemar Parrish	DB	5'11"	184	24	5	18
Ken Riley	DB	6'	180	25	3	
Ken Anderson	QB	6'1"	211	23		18
Virgil Carter	QB	6'1"	198	26		12
Dave Lewis	QB	6'2"	218	26		
Essex Johnson	HB	5'9"	197	25		36
Reece Morrison (from CLE)	HB	6'	207	26		
Doug Dressler	FB	6'3"	226	24		42
Jess Phillips	HB-FB	6'1"	205	25		6
Drew Buie	WR	6'2"	185	25		
Charlie Joiner (from HOU)	WR	5'11"	188	24		12
Chip Myers	WR	6'4"	210	27		18
Speedy Thomas	WR	6'1"	170	25		6
Bruce Coslet	TE	6'3"	220	26		6
Mike Kelly	TE	6'4"	222	24		
Bob Trumpy	TE	6'6"	228	27		12
Pete Watson	TE	6'1"	210	22		
Horst Muhlmann	K	6'1"	220	32		111

Greg Cook — Shoulder Injury
Sandy Durko — Injury

HOUSTON OILERS 1-13-0 — Bill Peterson

	Opponent	
17	Denver	30
13	Miami	34
26	N.Y. JETS	20
0	OAKLAND	34
7	Pittsburgh	24
17	CLEVELAND	23
7	Cincinnati	30
0	Cleveland	20
17	PHILADELPHIA	18
10	GREEN BAY	23
20	San Diego	34
10	Atlanta	20
3	PITTSBURGH	9
17	CINCINNATI	61

Use Name	Pos.	Hgt	Wgt	Age	Int	Pts
Lavert Carr	OT	6'5"	260	28		
Gene Ferguson	OT	6'7"	300	24		
Tom Funchess	OT	6'5"	265	27		
Buzz Highsmith	C-OT	6'4"	255	29		
Soloman Freelon	OG	6'2"	250	21		
Ralph Miller	OG	6'4"	260	23		
Tom Regner	OG	6'1"	255	28		
Ron Saul	OG	6'2"	255	24		
Calvin Hunt	C	6'1"	245	24		
Guy Murdock	C	6'2"	245	21		
Allen Aldridge	DE	6'6"	260	24		
Elvin Bethea	DE	6'3"	262	26		
Council Rudolph	DE	6'3"	260	22		
Pat Holmes	DT-DE	6'5"	250	32		
Ron Billingsley	DT	6'8"	290	27		
Lee Brooks	DT	6'5"	255	24		
Mike Tilleman	DT	6'5"	280	28		
Greg Sampson	DE-DT	6'6"	260	21		
Garland Boyette	LB	6'1"	235	32		
Phil Croyle	LB	6'3"	220	24		
Rich Lewis	LB	6'3"	220	22		
Floyd Rice	LB	6'3"	225	23		
Guy Roberts	LB	6'1"	215	22		
Willie Alexander	DB	6'2"	195	22	1	
Bob Atkins	DB	6'3"	210	26	2	
John Charles	DB	6'1"	192	28	2	
Ken Houston	DB	6'3"	195	27		
Benny Johnson	DB	5'11"	178	24	1	
Zeke Moore	DB	6'2"	196	28		
Jim Tolbert	DB	6'3"	202	28		
Ed Baker	QB	6'2"	198	23		
Kent Nix	QB	6'1"	195	28		
Dan Pastorini	QB	6'3"	215	23		12
Al Johnson	HB	6'	200	22		
Paul Robinson (from CIN)	HB	6'	198	27		
Willie Rodgers	HB	6'	210	23		6
Ward Walsh (to GB)	HB	6'	210	23		
Hoyle Granger	FB	6'1"	225	28		
Robert Holmes	FB	5'9"	220	26		
Fred Willis (from CIN)	FB	6'	212	24		12
Lewis Jolley	HB-FB	6'	210	22		
Ken Burrough	WR	6'4"	210	24		24
Rhett Dawson	WR	6'1"	185	23		6
Dave Smith (from PIT)	WR	6'2"	205	25		
Alvin Reed	TE	6'5"	235	28		
Jim Beirne	WR-TE	6'2"	196	25		6
Skip Butler	K	6'2"	200	24		51
Mark Moseley	K	5'11"	182	24		5

Lynn Dickey — Hip Injury
Elbert Drungo — Knee Injury

PITTSBURGH STEELERS

RUSHING

Last Name	No.	Yds	Avg	TD
Harris	188	1055	5.6	10
Fuqua	150	665	4.4	4
Bradshaw	58	346	6.0	7
P. Pearson	67	264	3.9	0
Steve Davis	20	85	4.3	1
Lewis	3	68	22.7	0
Bankston	7	20	2.9	0
Bleier	1	17	17.0	0
McMakin	1	0	0.0	0
Gilliam	2	0	0.0	0

RECEIVING

Last Name	No.	Yds	Avg	TD
Shanklin	38	669	18	3
Lewis	27	391	14	5
McMakin	21	277	13	1
Harris	21	180	9	1
Fuqua	18	152	8	0
P. Pearson	11	79	7	0
Young	6	86	14	0
Brown	1	13	13	1
Bankston	1	5	5	0
Steve Davis	1	5	5	0
Mullins	1	3	3	1

PUNT RETURNS

Last Name	No.	Yds	Avg	TD
Edwards	22	202	9	0
Lewis	5	56	11	0
Bleier	2	1	1	0
P. Pearson	1	3	3	0

KICKOFF RETURNS

Last Name	No.	Yds	Avg	TD
P. Pearson	13	292	22	0
Steve Davis	7	207	30	0
Harris	8	183	23	0
Bleier	2	40	20	0
Bankston	1	20	20	0
Edwards	1	18	18	0
McMakin	1	0	0	0

PASSING – PUNTING – KICKING

PASSING

Last Name	Att	Comp	%	Yds	Yd/Att	TD	Int–	%	RK
Bradshaw	308	147	48	1887	6.1	12	12–	4	12
Gilliam	11	7	64	48	4.4	0	0–	0	
Hanratty	4	2	50	23	5.8	0	0–	0	
Walden	1	0	0	0	0.0	0	0–	0	

PUNTING

Last Name	No	Avg
Walden	65	43.8
Gerela	1	29.0

KICKING

Last Name	XP	Att	%	FG	Att	%
Gerela	35	36	97	28	41	68

CLEVELAND BROWNS

RUSHING

Last Name	No.	Yds	Avg	TD
Kelly	224	811	3.6	4
B. Scott	123	571	4.6	2
Phipps	60	256	4.3	5
Brown	32	114	3.6	2
Pitts	3	29	9.7	0
Cornell	7	8	1.1	0
Lefear	3	6	2.0	0
Nelsen	1	–2	–2.0	0

RECEIVING

Last Name	No.	Yds	Avg	TD
Pitts	36	620	17	8
Hooker	32	441	14	5
Morin	30	540	18	1
Kelly	23	204	9	1
B. Scott	23	172	8	0
Brown	5	64	13	0
Glass	5	61	12	0
Cornell	2	7	4	0
Staroba	1	19	19	1
Richardson	1	7	7	0

PUNT RETURNS

Last Name	No.	Yds	Avg	TD
Majors	16	96	6	0
Darden	15	61	4	0
Kelly	5	40	8	0
Sumner	1	14	14	0

KICKOFF RETURNS

Last Name	No.	Yds	Avg	TD
Brown	20	473	24	0
Majors	10	222	22	0
Lefear	6	138	23	0
Johnson	2	33	17	0

PASSING – PUNTING – KICKING

PASSING

Last Name	Att	Comp	%	Yds	Yd/Att	TD	Int–	%	RK
Phipps	305	144	47	1994	6.5	13	16–	5	11
Nelsen	31	14	45	141	4.6	0	3–	10	
Kelly	1	0	0	0	0.0	0	0–	0	

PUNTING

Last Name	No	Avg
Cockroft	81	43.2

KICKING

Last Name	XP	Att	%	FG	Att	%
Cockroft	28	29	97	22	27	81

CINCINNATI BENGALS

RUSHING

Last Name	No.	Yds	Avg	TD
E. Johnson	212	825	3.9	4
Dressler	128	565	4.4	1
Phillips	48	207	4.3	1
Anderson	22	94	4.3	3
Carter	12	57	4.8	2
Lewis	1	15	15.0	0
Joiner	3	14	4.7	0
Morrison	1	2	2.0	0

RECEIVING

Last Name	No.	Yds	Avg	TD
Myers	57	792	14	3
Trumpy	44	500	11	2
Dressler	39	348	9	1
E. Johnson	29	420	14	2
Joiner	24	439	18	2
Thomas	17	171	10	1
Phillips	10	50	5	0
Coslet	5	48	10	1
Buie	1	5	5	0

PUNT RETURNS

Last Name	No.	Yds	Avg	TD
Casanova	30	289	10	1
Parrish	15	141	9	1
E. Johnson	2	7	4	0

KICKOFF RETURNS

Last Name	No.	Yds	Avg	TD
Jackson	21	509	24	0
Parrish	15	348	23	0
Joiner	5	88	18	0
Morrison	3	67	22	0
Casanova	1	34	34	0
Lewis	1	15	15	0
E. Johnson	1	13	13	0
Dennis	1	11	11	0
Kelly	1	0	0	0

PASSING – PUNTING – KICKING

PASSING

Last Name	Att	Comp	%	Yds	Yd/Att	Td	Int–	%	RK
Anderson	301	171	57	1918	6.4	7	7–	2	5
Carter	82	47	57	579	7.1	3	4–	5	

PUNTING

Last Name	No	Avg
Lewis	66	42.1

KICKING

Last Name	XP	Att	%	FG	Att	%
Muhlmann	30	31	97	27	40	68

HOUSTON OILERS

RUSHING

Last Name	No.	Yds	Avg	TD
Willis	134	461	3.4	0
Robinson	107	449	4.2	1
Pastorini	38	205	5.4	2
Rodgers	71	204	2.9	2
Granger	42	175	4.2	0
Holmes	43	172	4.0	0
Walsh	8	36	4.5	0
A. Johnson	11	13	1.2	0
Baker	1	9	9.0	0
Nix	3	3	1.0	0

RECEIVING

Last Name	No.	Yds	Avg	TD
Willis	45	297	7	2
Smith	30	316	11	0
Burrough	26	521	20	4
Reed	19	251	13	0
Granger	15	74	5	0
Robinson	14	112	8	0
Beirne	7	95	14	1
Dawson	6	78	13	1
Rodgers	6	61	10	0
Holmes	6	32	5	0
A. Johnson	6	24	4	0
Walsh	4	22	6	0

PUNT RETURNS

Last Name	No.	Yds	Avg	TD
Houston	25	148	6	0
Moore	7	15	2	0
A. Johnson	2	0	0	0

KICKOFF RETURNS

Last Name	No.	Yds	Avg	TD
Rodgers	17	335	20	0
B. Johnson	13	230	18	0
Jolley	11	267	24	0
A. Johnson	7	154	22	0
Holmes	2	39	20	0
Moore	1	22	22	0
Granger	1	5	5	0

PASSING – PUNTING – KICKING

PASSING

Last Name	Att	Comp	%	Yds	Yd/Att	Td	Int–	%	RK
Pastorini	299	144	48	1711	5.7	7	12–	4	13
Nix	63	33	52	287	4.6	3	6–	9	
Baker	10	4	40	47	4.7	0	4–	40	
Willis	4	1	25	16	4.0	0	1–	25	

PUNTING

Last Name	No	Avg
Pastorini	82	41.2
Butler	3	35.0

KICKING

Last Name	XP	Att	%	FG	Att	%
Butler	15	16	94	12	19	63
Moseley	2	2	100	1	2	50

Scores of Each Game			Use Name	Pos.	Hgt	Wgt	Age	Int	Pts	Use Name	Pos.	Hgt	Wgt	Age	Int	Pts	Use Name	Pos.	Hgt	Wgt	Age	Int	Pts

OAKLAND RAIDERS 10-3-1 John Madden

			Use Name	Pos.	Hgt	Wgt	Age	Int	Pts	Use Name	Pos.	Hgt	Wgt	Age	Int	Pts	Use Name	Pos.	Hgt	Wgt	Age	Int	Pts
28	Pittsburgh	34	Bob Brown	OT	6'4"	280	29			Joe Carroll	LB	6'1"	220	22			George Blanda	QB	6'1"	215	44		95
20	Green Bay	14	Art Shell	OT	6'5"	265	25			Dan Conners	LB	6'1"	230	30	1		Daryle Lamonica	QB	6'2"	215	31		
17	SAN DIEGO	17	Paul Seiler	C-OT	6'4"	260	26			Gerald Irons	LB	6'2"	230	25	2		Ken Stabler	QB	6'3"	215	26		
34	Houston	0	George Buehler	OG	6'2"	260	25			Terry Mendenhall	LB	6'1"	210	23			Clarence Davis	HB	5'10"	190	23		36
28	BUFFALO	16	Gene Upshaw	OG	6'5"	255	27			Gus Otto	LB	6'2"	220	29			Don Highsmith	HB	6'	200	24		
23	DENVER	30	John Vella	OG	6'4"	255	22			Greg Slough	LB	6'3"	230	24			Charlie Smith	HB	6'	205	26		60
45	LOS ANGELES	17	Jim Otto	C	6'2"	255	34			Phil Villapiano	LB	6'1"	222	23	3	6	Marv Hubbard	FB	6'1"	225	26		24
14	Kansas City	27	Dave Dalby	OG-C	6'2"	240	21			Butch Atkinson	DB	6'	180	25	4		Peter Banaszak	HB-FB	5'11"	180	26		6
20	Cincinnati	14	Tony Cline	DE	6'2"	240	24	1		Willie Brown	DB	6'1"	190	31	4		Jeff Queen	TE-FB	6'11"	220	26		
37	Denver	20	Horace Jones	DE	6'3"	240	23			Tommy Maxwell	DB	6'2"	195	25			Fred Biletnikoff	WR	6'1"	190	29		42
26	KANSAS CITY	3	Tom Keating	DT	6'2"	247	29			Jack Tatum	DB	5'10"	200	23	4	6	Cliff Branch	WR	5'11"	170	24		
21	San Diego	19	Carleton Oats	DT	6'2"	260	29			Skip Thomas	DB	6'1"	205	22			Mike Siani	WR	6'2"	195	22		30
24	N.Y. JETS	16	Art Thoms	DT	6'5"	250	25	1		Jimmy Warren	DB	5'11"	175	33			Ray Chester	TE	6'3"	225	24		48
28	CHICAGO	21	Otis Sistrunk	DE-DT	6'4"	255	24	1		Nemiah Wilson	DB	6'	165	29	4		Bob Moore	TE	6'3"	220	23		6
																	Jerry DePoyster	K	6'1"	200	26		
			Ben Davidson — Heel Injury							Warren Koegel — Injury													

KANSAS CITY CHIEFS 8-6-0 Hank Stram

			Use Name	Pos.	Hgt	Wgt	Age	Int	Pts	Use Name	Pos.	Hgt	Wgt	Age	Int	Pts	Use Name	Pos.	Hgt	Wgt	Age	Int	Pts
10	MIAMI	20	Dave Hill	OT	6'5"	260	31			Bobby Bell	LB	6'4"	228	32	3	6	Len Dawson	QB	6'	190	38		
20	New Orleans	17	Sid Smith	OT	6'4"	260	24			Keith Best	LB	6'3"	220	22			Mike Livingston	QB	6'3"	212	26		
45	Denver	24	Jim Tyrer	OT	6'6"	280	33			Willie Lanier	LB	6'1"	245	27	2		Mike Adamle	HB	5'9"	197	22		6
31	Cleveland	7	Ed Budde	OG	6'5"	265	31			Jim Lynch	LB	6'1"	235	27			Ed Podolak	HB	6'2"	204	25		36
16	CINCINNATI	23	George Daney	OG	6'3"	240	25			Bob Stein	LB	6'2"	235	24			Wendell Hayes	FB	6'2"	220	31		18
20	PHILADELPHIA	21	Larry Gagner	OG	6'3"	268	28			Clyde Werner	LB	6'4"	225	24	1		Jim Otis	FB	6'	220	24		
26	San Diego	14	Mo Moorman	OG	6'5"	252	28			Nate Allen	DB	5'10"	170	24	1		Jeff Kinney	HB-FB	6'2"	215	22		6
27	OAKLAND	14	Mike Oriard	C	6'4"	223	24			Jim Kearney	DB	6'2"	206	29	5	24	Dennis Homan	WR	6'1"	180	26		6
7	Pittsburgh	16	Jack Rudnay	C	6'3"	240	24			Jim Marsalis	DB	5'11"	194	26	2		Otis Taylor	WR	6'2"	215	29		36
17	SAN DIEGO	27	Aaron Brown	DE	6'5"	255	28			Larry Marshall	DB	5'10"	195	22			Bob West	WR	6'4"	218	21		18
3	Oakland	26	Marv Upshaw	DE	6'3"	260	25			Kerry Reardon	DB	5'11"	180	23			Elmo Wright	WR	6'	190	23		
24	DENVER	21	Wilbur Young	DT-DE	6'6"	285	23			Mike Sensibaugh	DB	5'11"	192	23	8		Willie Frazier	TE	6'4"	234	29		30
24	BALTIMORE	10	Buck Buchanan	DT	6'7"	270	32			Emmitt Thomas	DB	6'2"	192	29	2		Morris Stroud	TE	6'10"	255	26		6
17	Atlanta	14	Curley Culp	DT	6'1"	265	26										Jan Stenerud	K	6'2"	187	29		95
			Ed Lothamer	DT	6'5"	270	29			Warren McVea—Knee Injury							Jerrel Wilson	K	6'4"	222	31		
			George Seals	DT	6'2"	260	29																

DENVER BRONCOS 5-9-0 John Ralston

			Use Name	Pos.	Hgt	Wgt	Age	Int	Pts	Use Name	Pos.	Hgt	Wgt	Age	Int	Pts	Use Name	Pos.	Hgt	Wgt	Age	Int	Pts
30	HOUSTON	17	Mike Current	OT	6'4"	274	26			Ken Criter	LB	5'11"	223	25			Mike Ernst	QB	6'1"	190	21		
14	San Diego	37	Marv Montgomery	OT	6'6"	255	24	1		Fred Forsberg	Lb	6'1"	235	28			Charley Johnson	QB	6'	190	35		
24	KANSAS CITY	45	Rick Sharp	OT	6'3"	265	24			Bob Geddes	LB	6'2"	240	26			Steve Ramsey	QB	6'2"	210	24		12
10	Cincinnati	21	George Goeddeke	OG-OT	6'3"	253	27			Tom Graham	LB	6'2"	235	22	2		Floyd Little	FB-HB	5'10"	196	30		78
20	MINNESOTA	23	Bill Cottrell	OG	6'3"	255	27			Bill McKoy	LB	6'3"	235	24			Fran Lynch	FB	6'1"	205	26		12
30	Oakland	23	Larron Jackson	OG	6'3"	270	23			Chip Myrtle	LB	6'2"	225	27			Clem Turner	FB	6'2"	236	27		
20	CLEVELAND	27	Mike Schnitker	OG	6'3"	245	25			Don Parish	LB	6'1"	220	24			Bobby Anderson	HB-FB	6'	208	24		12
17	N.Y. Giants	29	Tommy Lyons	C-OG	6'2"	250	24			Mike Simone	LB	6'	210	22			Joe Dawkins	HB-FB	5'11"	223	24		12
16	Los Angeles	10	Larry Kaminski	C	6'2"	245	27			Cornell Gordon	DB	6'	187	31			Jim Krieg	WR	5'9"	172	23		
20	OAKLAND	37	Bobby Maples	C	6'3"	250	29			Charlie Greer	DB	6'	205	26	2	6	Haven Moses (from BUF)	WR	6'3"	205	26		36
20	Atlanta	23	Lyle Alzado	DE	6'3"	252	23			Leroy Mitchell	DB	6'2"	190	27	3		Rod Sherman	WR	6'	190	27		18
21	Kansas City	14	John Hoffman (from STL)	DE	6'7"	260	29			Randy Montgomery	DB	5'11"	182	25		6	Jerry Simmons	WR	6'1"	190	29		12
38	SAN DIEGO	13	Lloyd Voss	DT-DE	6'4"	255	30			Steve Preece (from PHI)	DB	6'1"	195	25	1		Bill Van Heusen	WR	6'1"	200	26		6
45	NEW ENGLAND	21	Tom Domres	DT	6'3"	260	25			George Saimes	DB	5'10"	188	30			Bill Masters	TE	6'5"	240	28		18
			Paul Smith	DT	6'3"	256	27			Bill Thompson	DB	6'1"	200	25	1		Riley Odoms	TE	6'4"	230	22		6
			Pete Duranko	DE-DT	6'2"	250	28			Bill West	DB	5'10"	185	24			Jim Turner	K	6'2"	205	31		97
			Walt Barnes — Injury							Sam Brunelli — Injury							Jerry Inman — Injury						
										Jack Gehrke — Injury													

SAN DIEGO CHARGERS 4-9-1 Harland Svare

			Use Name	Pos.	Hgt	Wgt	Age	Int	Pts	Use Name	Pos.	Hgt	Wgt	Age	Int	Pts	Use Name	Pos.	Hgt	Wgt	Age	Int	Pts
3	San Francisco	34	Ira Gordon	OT	6'3"	268	24			John Andrews	LB	6'3"	225	23			Wayne Clark	QB	6'2"	200	25		
37	DENVER	14	Terry Owens	OT	6'6"	268	28			Bob Babich	LB	6'2"	230	25	2		John Hadl	QB	6'2"	214	32		6
17	Oakland	17	Russ Washington	OT	6'6"	294	25			Pete Barnes	LB	6'3"	240	27	1		Mike Garrett	HB	5'9"	200	28		42
23	Baltimore	20	Ernie Wright	OT	6'4"	270	32			Lee Roy Caffey	LB	6'3"	250	32	1		John Sykes	HB	5'11"	195	23		
10	Miami	24	Walt Sweeney	OG	6'3"	256	31			Pete Lazetich	LB	6'3"	245	22			Jesse Taylor	HB	6'	200	24		6
20	Detroit	34	Ralph Wenzel	OG	6'3"	250	29			Rick Redman	LB	5'11"	222	29	1		Oscar Dragon	FB-HB	6'	214	22		
14	KANSAS CITY	26	Doug Wilkerson	OG	6'2"	250	25			Tim Rossovich	LB	6'4"	240	26	1		Cid Edwards	FB	6'2"	230	28		42
28	DALLAS	34	Sam Gruneisen	C	6'1"	250	31			Ray White	LB	6'1"	242	23			Lee White	FB	6'4"	240	26		
17	CLEVELAND	21	Carl Mauck	C	6'3"	245	25	6		Joe Beauchamp	DB	6'	182	28	6	6	Mike Carter	WR	6'1"	210	24		
27	Kansas City	17	Lionel Aldridge	DE	6'4"	245	30			Reggie Berry	DB	6'	190	23			Chuck Dicus	WR	6'	176	23		12
34	HOUSTON	20	Deacon Jones	DE	6'5"	250	33			Chuck Detwiler	DB	6'	185	24			Gary Garrison	WR	6'1"	193	28		42
19	OAKLAND	21	Cal Snowden	DE	6'4"	253	25			Lenny Dunlap	DB	6'1"	195	23	5		Jerry LeVias	WR	5'10"	178	25		
13	Denver	38	Lee Thomas	DE	6'5"	246	25			Chris Fletcher	DB	5'11"	185	23			Dave Williams	WR	6'2"	200	27		18
2	PITTSBURGH	24	Dave Costa	DT	6'2"	260	30	2		Bob Howard	DB	6'1"	175	27			John Mackey	TE	6'3"	224	30		
			Ron East	DT	6'4"	236	29			Ray Jones	DB	6'	187	24			Pettis Norman	TE	6'3"	220	32		
			Kevin Hardy	DT	6'5"	276	27			Bryant Salter	DB	6'4"	194	22	7		Bill McClard	K	5'10"	202	20		11
			Greg Wojcik	DT	6'6"	268	26										Dennis Partee	K	6'2"	230	26		71
										Harris Jones — Injury							Duane Thomas — Holdout						
										Mel Rogers — Shoulder Injury													

OAKLAND RAIDERS

RUSHING

Last Name	No.	Yds	Avg	TD
Hubbard	219	1100	5.0	4
Smith	170	686	4.0	8
Davis	71	363	5.1	6
Banaszak	30	138	4.6	1
Lamonica	10	33	3.3	0
Stabler	6	27	4.5	0
Highsmith	9	11	1.2	1
Queen	4	10	2.5	0
Branch	1	5	5.0	0
Chester	1	3	3.0	0

RECEIVING

Last Name	No.	Yds	Avg	TD
Biletnikoff	58	802	14	7
Chester	34	576	17	8
Siani	28	496	18	5
Smith	28	353	13	2
Hubbard	22	103	5	0
Banaszak	9	63	7	0
Davis	8	82	10	0
Moore	6	49	8	1
Branch	3	41	14	0
Highsmith	2	34	17	0

PUNT RETURNS

Last Name	No.	Yds	Avg	TD
Atkinson	10	33	3	0
Branch	12	21	2	0
Maxwell	2	12	6	0

KICKOFF RETURNS

Last Name	No.	Yds	Avg	TD
Davis	18	464	26	0
Branch	9	191	21	0
Atkinson	3	75	25	0
Warren	4	57	14	0
Maxwell	1	26	26	0
Seiler	1	0	0	0
Slough	1	0	0	0
Smith	1	0	0	0

PASSING – PUNTING – KICKING

PASSING	Att	Comp	%	Yds	Yd/Att	TD	Int–	%	RK
Lamonica	281	149	53	1998	7.1	18	12–	4	2
Stabler	74	44	60	524	7.1	4	3–	4	
Blanda	15	5	33	77	5.1	1	0–	0	

PUNTING	No.	Avg							
DePoyster	55	36.9							

KICKING	XP	Att	%	FG	Att	%			
Blanda	44	44	100	17	26	65			

KANSAS CITY CHIEFS

RUSHING

Last Name	No.	Yds	Avg	TD
Podolak	171	615	3.6	4
Hayes	128	536	4.2	1
Adamle	73	303	4.2	1
Livingston	14	133	9.5	0
Kinney	38	122	3.2	1
Otis	29	92	3.2	0
Dawson	15	75	5.0	0
Wright	1	24	24.0	0
Taylor	5	13	2.6	0
West	2	2	1.0	0

RECEIVING

Last Name	No.	Yds	Avg	TD
Taylor	57	821	14	6
Podolak	46	345	8	2
Hayes	31	295	9	3
Adamle	15	76	5	0
Frazier	13	172	13	5
Homan	12	135	11	1
Otis	12	76	6	0
Wright	11	81	7	0
West	9	165	18	2
Stroud	4	80	20	1
Kinney	4	45	11	0
Jankowski	2	24	12	0
Allen	1	20	20	0

PUNT RETURNS

Last Name	No.	Yds	Avg	TD
Marshall	18	103	8	0
Podolak	8	11	1	0
Homan	2	9	5	0
Reardon	1	3	3	0

KICKOFF RETURNS

Last Name	No.	Yds	Avg	TD
Marshall	23	651	28	0
Adamle	8	185	23	0
Podolak	7	119	17	0
Kinney	4	63	16	0
Reardon	2	35	18	0
Upshaw	1	4	4	0
Kearney	1	0	0	0

PASSING – PUNTING – KICKING

PASSING	Att	Comp	%	Yds	Yd/Att	TD	Int–	%	RK
Dawson	305	175	57	1835	6.0	13	12–	4	7
Livingston	78	41	53	480	6.2	7	8–	10	
Wilson	1	1	100	20	20.0	0	0–	0	

PUNTING	No.	Avg							
Wilson	66	44.8							

KICKING	XP	Att	%	FG	Att	%			
Stenerud	32	32	100	21	36	58			

DENVER BRONCOS

RUSHING

Last Name	No.	Yds	Avg	TD
Little	216	859	4.0	9
Anderson	72	319	4.4	1
Dawkins	56	243	4.3	2
Lynch	34	164	4.8	2
Van Heusen	3	76	25.3	1
Odoms	5	72	14.4	0
Krieg	1	63	63.0	0
C. Turner	5	16	3.2	0
Ramsey	6	15	2.5	2
Moses	2	11	5.5	0
Ernst	1	4	4.0	0
Sherman	1	2	2.0	0
Johnson	3	0	0.0	0
Masters	3	–15	–5.0	0

RECEIVING

Last Name	No.	Yds	Avg	TD
Sherman	38	661	17	3
Little	28	367	13	4
Masters	25	393	16	3
Anderson	23	215	9	1
Odoms	21	320	15	1
Moses	18	284	16	6
Dawkins	18	242	13	0
Simmons	17	235	14	2
Lynch	7	75	11	0
Krieg	4	99	25	0
Van Heusen	4	59	15	0
C. Turner	1	10	10	0

PUNT RETURNS

Last Name	No.	Yds	Avg	TD
Sherman	10	89	9	0
Thompson	4	82	21	0
Greer	4	67	17	1
Little	8	64	8	0
Simone	1	5	5	0
Krieg	1	3	3	0

KICKOFF RETURNS

Last Name	No.	Yds	Avg	TD
Montgomery	29	756	26	1
Dawkins	15	357	24	0
Little	3	48	16	0
Lynch	3	45	15	0
C. Turner	1	25	25	0
Krieg	1	18	18	0
Anderson	1	13	13	0
Simone	1	–6	–6	0
Preece	1	0	0	0

PASSING – PUNTING – KICKING

PASSING	Att	Comp	%	Yds	Yd/Att	TD	Int–	%	RK
Johnson	238	132	55	1783	7.5	14	14–	6	3
Ramsey	137	65	47	1050	7.7	3	9–	7	
Ernst	4	1	25	10	2.5	0	0–	0	
Anderson	3	1	33	14	4.7	1	0–	0	
Little	2	2	100	43	21.5	1	0–	0	

PUNTING	No.	Avg							
Van Heusen	60	40.1							

KICKING	XP	Att	%	FG	Att	%			
J Turner	37	37	100	20	29	69			

SAN DIEGO CHARGERS

RUSHING

Last Name	No.	Yds	Avg	TD
Garrett	272	1031	3.8	6
Anderson	157	679	4.3	5
Hadl	22	99	4.5	1
L. White	23	75	3.3	0
Taylor	13	58	4.5	0
Dragon	9	30	3.3	0
Carter	1	25	25.0	0
Williams	1	14	14.0	0
Norman	1	9	9.0	0
Garrison	2	–6	–3.0	0
Clark	2	–8	–4.0	0
Dicus	1	–11	–11.0	0

RECEIVING

Last Name	No.	Yds	Avg	TD
Garrison	52	744	14	7
Edwards	40	557	14	2
Garrett	31	245	8	1
Norman	19	262	14	0
Dicus	18	227	13	2
Williams	14	315	23	3
Mackey	11	110	10	0
L. White	3	20	7	0
Carter	2	24	12	0
LeVias	1	8	8	0
Hadl	1	4	4	0

PUNT RETURNS

Last Name	No.	Yds	Avg	TD
Dunlap	19	179	9	0
Garrett	2	10	5	0
Taylor	1	0	0	0
LeVias	1	–4	–4	0

KICKOFF RETURNS

Last Name	No.	Yds	Avg	TD
Taylor	31	676	22	0
Dunlap	12	271	23	0
Berry	7	138	20	0
Detwiler	4	94	24	0
Sykes	2	44	22	0
R. Jones	3	41	14	0
Beauchamp	1	0	0	0
Williams	0	9	0	0

PASSING – PUNTING – KICKING

PASSING	Att	Comp	%	Yds	Yd/Att	TD	Int–	%	RK
Hadl	370	190	51	2449	6.6	15	26–	7	10
Clark	6	2	33	67	11.2	0	2–	33	
Garrett	1	0	0	0	0.0	0	0–	0	

PUNTING	No.	Avg							
Partee	45	40.3							

KICKING	XP	Att	%	FG	Att	%			
Partee	26	28	93	15	25	60			
McClard	2	2	100	3	6	50			

1972 Championship Games

No Stronger Than Its Weakest Link

SCORING

WASHINGTON	0	10	0	16—26	
DALLAS	0	3	0	0— 3	

Second Quarter
Wash.   Knight, 18 yard field goal
Wash.   Taylor, 15 yard pass from Kilmer
        PAT—Knight (Kick)
Dall.   Fritsch, 35 yard field goal

Fourth Quarter
Wash.   Taylor, 45 yard pass from Kilmer
        PAT—Knight (Kick)
Wash.   Knight, 39 yard field goal
Wash.   Knight, 46 yard field goal
Wash.   Knight, 45 yard field goal

TEAM STATISTICS

WASH.		DALLAS
16	First Downs—Total	8
4	First Downs—Rushing	3
11	First Downs—Passing	3
1	First Downs—Penalty	2
2	Fumbles—Number	1
1	Fumbles—Lost Ball	1
4	Penalties—Number	4
38	Yards Penalized	30
0	Missed Field Goals	1
62	Offensive Plays—Total	45
316	Net Yards	169
5.1	Average Gain	3.8
1	Giveaways	1
1	Takeaways	1
0	Difference	0

The Cowboys and Redskins, arch-rivals in the Eastern Division, each made it to the NFC title game with a strong showing in the first round of the playoffs. The Redskins completely stifled the Packer running attack in a 16-3 triumph, while the Cowboys rallied in the fourth quarter to beat the '49ers 30-28. The two clubs had split their meetings during the regular season, and this match would decide the Super Bowl berth.

Roger Staubach, who had sat out most of the season with an injured shoulder but had returned to action in the come-from-behind victory over San Francisco the week before, started at quarterback for the Cowboys in place of Craig Morton. The Washington defense greeted him with a ferocious pass rush that kept him off balance all afternoon and prevented any second-half heroics.

The Washington offensive game plan called for attacking the Cowboys at their weak left cornerback spot, where Charley Waters, normally a safety, had beaten Herb Adderley out of a job. Leading 3-0 in the second quarter, the Redskins went to work on Waters. Charley Taylor beat him to haul in a 51-yard pass, and several plays later Kilmer hit Taylor with a 15-yard scoring pitch. The Cowboys answered with a drive deep into Washington territory, but when Calvin Hill overthrew Walt Garrison in the end zone on an option pass, they had to settle for a Toni Fritsch field goal.

Early in the third period Waters broke an arm, and coach Tom Landry put Mark Washington into the corner position and left the veteran Adderley on the bench. Taylor exploited Washington's inexperience in the fourth quarter by beating him for a 45-yard touchdown pass which gave the Redskins some breathing room. Forced to go to the air, the Cowboys could make no headway against the Redskin defense, and three Curt Knight field goals in the final quarter gave the Redskins a much savored 26-3 victory.

INDIVIDUAL STATISTICS

WASHINGTON	No	Yds	Avg.	DALLAS	No	Yds	Avg.
RUSHING							
Brown	30	88	2.9	Staubach	5	59	11.8
Harraway	11	19	1.7	Hill	9	22	2.4
Kilmer	3	15	5.0	Garrison	7	15	2.1
	44	122	2.8		21	96	4.6
RECEIVING							
Taylor	7	146	20.9	Sellers	2	29	14.5
Harraway	3	13	4.3	Garrison	2	18	9.0
Jefferson	2	19	9.5	Hill	2	11	5.5
Brown	2	16	8.0	Parks	1	21	21.0
	14	194	13.9	Alworth	1	15	15.0
				Ditka	1	4	4.0
					9	98	10.9
PUNTING							
Bragg	4		36.0	Bateman	7		43.1
PUNT RETURNS							
Haymond	4	10	2.5	Waters	3	−5	−1.7
KICKOFF RETURNS							
None				Harris	2	29	14.5
				Newhouse	1	25	25.0
					3	54	18.0

	Att.	Comp.	Comp. Pct.	Yds.	Int.	Yds/ Att.	Yds/ Comp.	Yards Lost Tackled
WASHINGTON								
Kilmer	18	14	77.8	194	0	10.8	13.9	0— 0
DALLAS								
Staubach	20	9	45.0	98	0	4.9	10.9	3—25
Hill	1	0	0.0	0	0	—	—	—
	21	9	42.9	98	0	4.7	10.9	3—25

Simply Not Enough of Bradshaw

SCORING

PITTSBURGH	7	0	3	7—17	
MIAMI	0	7	7	7—21	

First Quarter
Pitt.   Mullins, Recovery of Pitt fumble in end zone
        PAT—Gerela (kick)

Second Quarter
Miami   Csonka, 9 yard pass from Morrall
        PAT—Yepremian (kick)

Third Quarter
Pitt.   Gerela, 14 yard field goal
Miami   Kiick, 2 yard rush
        PAT—Yepremian (kick)

Fourth Quarter
Miami   Kiick, 3 yard rush
        PAT—Yepremian (kick)
Pitt.   Young, 12 yard pass from Bradshaw
        PAT—Gerela (kick)

TEAM STATISTICS

PITT.		MIAMI
13	First Downs—Total	19
6	First Downs—Rushing	11
6	First Downs—Passing	6
1	First Downs—Penalty	2
2	Fumbles—Number	0
0	Fumbles—Lost Ball	0
4	Penalties—Number	2
30	Yards Penalized	19
1	Missed Field Goals	0
48	Offensive Plays—Total	65
250	Net Yards	314
5.2	Average Gain	4.8
2	Giveaways	1
1	Takeaways	2
−1	Difference	+1

The Dolphins came into this game after a miracle season, while the Steelers came in after a miracle play. By beating Cleveland 20-14 last week in the start of the playoffs, the Dolphins ran their record to 15-0 for the season. The Steelers had a less shining record, but their spirits were high after beating the Raiders 13-7 in the opening round of the playoffs. In that game the Steelers scored the winning touchdown with five seconds left on a deflected pass which Franco Harris snagged in mid-air and carried across the goal line.

In the first quarter, after an extended drive into Miami territory, Terry Bradshaw fumbled on the three-yard line and Gerry Mullins fell on the ball as it rolled into the end zone. Although the Steelers took a 7-0 lead, the play was costly, as Bradshaw was knocked dizzy and had to be relieved by Terry Hanratty.

An alert play by punter Larry Seiple helped the Dolphins tie the score in the second quarter. Noticing that all the Steelers had dropped back to block for the return, Seiple crossed the defense up and ran with the ball, gaining 37 yards to the Pittsburgh 12-yard line. Two plays later Morrall hit Csonka with a scoring pass, and Garo Yepremian added the extra point.

As the second half began, Miami coach Don Shula put Bob Griese, out since October with a broken leg, in at quarterback to shake up his offense. The Steelers went ahead 10-7 on a Roy Gerela field goal, but Griese hit Paul Warfield with a 52-yard pass play which put the Dolphins in striking distance. Six plays later, Jim Kiick carried the ball in, and another Kiick touchdown in the fourth quarter lengthened the Miami lead to 21-10. Bradshaw returned to action for the final seven minutes of the game, but after leading the Steelers to one touchdown, he suffered two interceptions in his final three passes.

INDIVIDUAL STATISTICS

PITTSBURGH	No	Yds	Avg.	MIAMI	No	Yds	Avg.
RUSHING							
Harris	16	76	4.8	Morris	16	76	4.8
Fuqua	8	47	5.9	Csonka	24	68	2.8
Bradshaw	2	5	2.5	Seiple	1	37	37.0
	26	128	4.9	Kiick	8	12	1.5
					49	193	3.9
RECEIVING							
Young	4	54	13.5	Fleming	5	50	10.0
Shanklin	2	49	24.5	Warfield	2	63	31.5
Harris	2	3	1.5	Csonka	1	9	9.0
McMakin	1	22	22.0	Mandich	1	5	5.0
Brown	1	9	9.0	Morris	1	−6	−6.0
	10	137	13.7		10	121	12.1
PUNTING							
Walden	4		51.3	Seiple	4		35.5
PUNT RETURNS							
Edwards	1	5	5.0	None			
KICKOFF RETURNS							
P. Pearson	2	63	31.5	Morris	1	23	23.0
S. Davis	1	22	22.0				
	3	85	28.3				
INTERCEPTION RETURNS							
Edwards	1	28	28.0	Buoniconti	1	6	6.0
				Kuler	1	5	5.0
					2	11	5.5

	Att.	Comp.	Comp. Pct.	Yds.	Int.	Yds/ Att.	Yds/ Comp.	Yards Lost Tackled
PITTSBURGH								
Bradshaw	10	5	50.0	80	2	8.0	16.0	
Hanratty	10	5	50.0	57	0	5.7	11.4	
	20	10	50.0	137	2	6.9	13.7	2—15
MIAMI								
Morrall	11	7	63.6	51	1	4.6	7.3	
Griese	5	3	60.0	70	0	14.0	23.3	
	16	10	62.5	121	1	7.6	12.1	0— 0

Super Perfect

The contrasts were interesting. The Miami Dolphins had swept through fourteen regular-season games and two playoff games without a loss and now had a chance to compile a perfect 17-0 record for the year. Under the thorough leadership of head coach Don Shula, the Dolphins had rebounded from last year's Super Bowl loss to Dallas to become a cool, mature, precise club, with programmed brutality on both platoons.

The Washington Redskins had mostly veteran players, but their style was not one of coolness. Coach George Allen strove to whip his men into a frenzy before every game, and he put a fanatical emphasis on this game. A loss in this game would spoil the entire season, he said, and he drilled his troops in Spartan fashion to prepare them for the younger Dolphins.

The Miami defense scuttled the Washington running attack right from the start, a reversal from last year's dissection of the Dolphin front wall by the Cowboys. Larry Brown and Charley Harraway found Miami tackle Manny Fernandez forever in their path, and quarterback Bill Kilmer suffered through a bad afternoon with his passing. The Dolphins picked off three passes, with safety Jake Scott making two of the interceptions.

The Dolphin attack moved well against the heralded Redskin defense, but three penalties prevented any score until late in the period. Just before the end of the quarter Howard Twilley beat Pat Fischer to the outside and hauled in a 28-yard Bob Griese touchdown pass which he carried in from the 5. Leading 7-0, the Dolphins continued to paralyze the Redskin offense in the second period and scored again late in the period. One minute before halftime Jim Kiick capped a long Miami drive by going over from the one-yard line, giving the Dolphins a solid 14-0 lead at intermission.

The Redskins finally got their offense rolling after taking the second-half kickoff. With Brown gaining on the ground and Kilmer completing three passes, the Redskins drove into Miami territory before the drive stalled. Curt Knight then lined up a comparitively easy 32-yard field goal, but his kick sailed wide to the right and the Dolphins took possession.

The Miami defense re-established its superiority through the second half as the Dolphin offense held onto the ball long enough on each possession to eat up valuable time. With two minutes left in the game, Garo Yepremian attempted a 42-yard field goal, only to have it blocked. When the ball bounced back to him, he picked it up and started to run toward the sidelines. With no football experience except kicking, Yepremian then attempted to pass the ball, only to have it slip out of his hands right to Mike Bass of the Redskins. Bass ran 49 yards with the aborted pass for Washington's only score of the day, but the Dolphins hung onto the 14-7 lead the rest of the way and became the first NFL team ever to go through a complete season with all wins.

Lineups

MIAMI		WASHINGTON
OFFENSE		
Warfield	WR	C. Taylor
W. Moore	LT	Hermeling
Kuechenberg	LG	Laaveg
Langer	C	Hauss
Little	RG	Wilbur
Evans	RT	Rock
Fleming	TE	Smith
Twilley	WR	Jefferson
Griese	QB	Kilmer
Kiick	RB	Brown
Csonka	RB	Harraway
DEFENSE		
Den Herder	LE	McDole
Fernandez	LT	Brundige
Heinz	RT	Talbert
Stanfill	RE	Biggs
Swift	LLB	Pardee
Bouniconti	MLB	Pottios
Kolen	RLB	Hanburger
Mumphord	LCB	Fischer
Johnson	RCB	Bass
Anderson	LS	Owens
Scott	RS	R. Taylor

SUBSTITUTES

MIAMI
Offense
Briscoe, Leigh, Crusan, Mandich, Ginn, Morrall, Jenkins, Morris, Kindig
Defense
Babb, M. Moore, Ball, Powell, Matheson, Stuckey
Kickers
Seiple, Yepremian

WASHINGTON
Offense
Alston, McNeil, Brunet, Mul-Key, Burman, Wyche, Hull
Defense
Fanucci, Severson, Haymond, Sistrunk, Jaqua, Tillman, McLinton, Vactor
Kickers
Bragg, Knight

SCORING

MIAMI	7 7 0 0—	14
WASHINGTON	0 0 0 7—	7

First Quarter
Mia. Twilley, 28 yd pass from Griese
PAT — Yepremian (kick) 14:59

Second Quarter
Mia. Kiick, 1 yard rush
PAT — Yepremian (kick) 14:42

Fourth Quarter
Was. Bass, 49 yard fumble return
PAT — Knight 12:53

TEAM STATISTICS

MIAMI		WASH.
12	First Downs — Total	16
7	First Downs — Rushing	9
5	First Downs — Passing	7
0	First Downs — Penalty	0
2	Fumbles — Number	1
1	Fumbles — Lost Ball	0
3	Penalties — Number	3
35	Yards Penalized	25
50	Total Offensive Plays	66
253	Total Net Yards	228
5.1	Average Gain	3.5
1	Missed Field Goals	1
2	Giveaways	3
3	Takeaways	2
+1	Difference	—1

INDIVIDUAL STATISTICS

RUSHING

MIAMI	No	Yds	Avg.	WASHINGTON	No	Yds	Avg.
Csonka	15	112	7.5	Brown	22	72	3.3
Kiick	12	38	3.2	Harraway	10	37	3.7
Morris	10	34	3.4	Kilmer	2	18	9.0
	37	184	5.0	Taylor	1	8	8.0
				Smith	1	6	6.0
					36	141	3.9

RECEIVING

MIAMI	No	Yds	Avg.	WASHINGTON	No	Yds	Avg.
Warfield	3	36	12.0	Jefferson	5	50	10.0
Kiick	2	6	3.0	Brown	5	26	5.2
Twilley	1	28	28.0	Taylor	2	20	10.0
Mandich	1	19	19.0	Smith	1	11	11.0
Csonka	1	—1	-1.0	Harraway	1	—3	-3.0
	8	88	11.0		14	104	7.4

PUNTING

MIAMI	No		Avg.	WASHINGTON	No		Avg.
Seiple	7		43.0	Bragg	5		31.2

PUNT RETURNS

MIAMI	No	Yds	Avg.	WASHINGTON	No	Yds	Avg.
Scott	2	4	2.0	Haymond	4	9	2.3

KICKOFF RETURNS

MIAMI	No	Yds	Avg.	WASHINGTON	No	Yds	Avg.
Morris	2	33	16.5	Haymond	2	30	15.0
				Mul-Key	1	15	15.0
					3	45	15.0

INTERCEPTION RETURNS

MIAMI	No	Yds	Avg.	WASHINGTON	No	Yds	Avg.
Scott	2	63	31.5	Owens	1	0	0.0
Buoniconti	1	32	32.0				
	3	95	31.7				

PASSING

MIAMI	Att	Comp	Comp Pct.	Yds	Int	Yds/Att.	Yds/Comp	Yards Lost Tackled
Griese	11	8	72.7	88	1	8.0	11.0	2—19
WASHINGTON								
Kilmer	28	14	50.0	104	3	3.7	7.4	2—17

1973 N.F.C. Recession at the Concessions

When Congress passed a bill forbidding television blackouts of games sold out forty-eight hours ahead of time, the NFL reluctantly televised home games for the first time in years. This situation gave birth to a new football term, the "no-show," who was a fan holding a ticket for a sold-out game but instead watched it at home on TV. Ticket sales were not affected by the new ruling, but concession profits fell in the parks on days when unpleasant weather made the television set a much more comfortable way to view the game.

EASTERN DIVISION

Dallas Cowboys—The Cowboys had injuries at several key positions but still made the playoffs. When newly acquired flanker Otto Stowe broke an ankle in mid-season, rookie Drew Pearson stepped into the starting lineup and began grabbing passes in all kinds of situations. A bad back made defensive tackle Bob Lilly's season a miserable one, but middle linebacker Lee Roy Jordan took charge of the defense with his first All-Pro season in an eleven-year pro career. Other added assets for coach Tom Landry were quarterback Roger Staubach's staying healthy for the entire season, Bob Hayes's recovery from an off-season to reclaim his starting wide-receiver job, and tight end Billy Joe DuPree's good rookie season.

Washington Redskins—The Over the Hill Gang was far from finished. Coach George Allen added Dave Robinson, Ken Houston, Alvin Reed, and Duane Thomas to his squad through a variety of trades. Robinson and Houston replaced the retired Jack Pardee and Roosevelt Taylor on the defensive unit, while Reed and Thomas gave the Skins all-star depth on offense. Thomas left his personal problems behind him when he reported to the Redskins, working hard to regain his top form of the 1971 season, but the superb running and blocking of backs Larry Brown and Charley Harraway kept Duane on the bench for most of the season. Veteran passing ace Sonny Jurgensen stayed healthy enough to share the quarterback job with Billy Kilmer, and their collective wisdom guided the Redskins attack.

Philadelphia Eagles—New head coach Mike McCormack ripped the Eagles apart and started all over again from scratch. To run the offense, he paid a high price to the Rams for Roman Gabriel, a quarterback who was used to winning. Ex-Colt Norm Bulaich and second-year man Tom Sullivan started at running back, tall Harold Carmichael and rookie Don Zimmerman won the wide-receiver jobs, and rookie Charley Young was an instant All-Pro at tight end. Operating behind a line with two fine rookies in Jerry Sisemore and Guy Morriss, Gabriel picked enemy defenses apart with precision passing and sharp play-calling. Coach McCormack had less success in rebuilding the defense. End Mel Tom was traded to Chicago after an argument with an assistant coach, cornerback Nate Ramsey was cut in mid-season, and knee injuries kayoed linebacker Steve Zabel and cornerback Al Nelson.

St. Louis Cardinals—New head coach Don Coryell succeeded in building a fine passing attack, but injuries and a bad defense held the Cards under .500 for the third straight season. Quarterback Jim Hart won the starting position and developed into a top passer, hitting wide receivers Mel Gray and Ahmad Rashad (previously known as Bobby Moore) with long bombs which had grown infrequent in 1970s pro football. But the St. Louis defense had problems stopping even mediocre attacks, despite a good rookie season from massive end Dave Butz. Late-season injuries crippled both platoons, with Hart and most of the offensive line out for the last few games of the year.

New York Giants—A perfect 6-0 record in pre-season play inflated Giant hopes to a vibrating level, but the cruel reality which followed turned the season into a nightmare. After opening with a win and tie in Yankee Stadium, the Giants for all purposes became a road team for the rest of the season. Yankee Stadium was shut for repairs, so the Giants held their practices in Jersey City and played their "home" games in the Yale Bowl in New Haven. The gypsy life disheartened the players, and the team lost seven straight games after leaving the old ball park. Coach Alex Webster announced his resignation before the final game, not a totally unexpected move.

CENTRAL DIVISION

Minnesota Vikings—Fran Tarkenton finally began burying his image as a loser by leading the Vikings into the playoffs with a 12-2 record for the regular season. Aiding Tarkenton considerably was the front four of Carl Eller, Alan Page, Gary Larsen, and Jim Marshall, all of whom stayed healthy and gave the Minnesota defense its old devastating strength. The secondary lost safety Karl Kassulke when he was seriously hurt in a pre-season motorcycle accident, but the quartet of Bobby Bryant, Nate Wright, Paul Krause, and Jeff Wright threw an airtight cover on enemy receivers. The Viking offense had a new weapon in rookie Chuck Foreman, a slashing runner who also caught passes. At wide receiver, John Gilliam made fans forget the traded Gene Washington with his speed and sure hands. The Vikings had always had a defense, but now that they had an offense they outclassed their rivals in the Central Division.

Detroit Lions—High hopes for a divisional title flattened out into a disappointing second-place finish and bitter words from the owner and coach. The Lions compiled a 1-4-1 record in their first six games, with a 29-27 loss to Baltimore on October 21 the bitterest pill to swallow. Coach Don McCafferty said, "If we can't beat the Colts, we can't beat anybody." Owner William Clay Ford added, "I don't think they want to win—at least it doesn't look like it." The Lions responded with a 27-0 shutout of the Packers the next week, but a limp 20-0 loss to Washington on Thanksgiving Day brought another public blast from McCafferty. "We stunk out the joint," said the coach. We've got some losers on this ball club and they won't be around next year."

Green Bay Packers—The Packer defense had carried the team into the playoffs last year, but the one-dimensional Green Bay offense was too much of a load for the defense to carry this season. John Brockington and MacArthur Lane kept eating up the yardage on the ground, with Brockington gaining 1,000 yard for the third time in his three-year pro career. The Green Bay passing attack, however, was next to nonexistent. Coach Dan Devine gave youngsters Scott Hunter, Jim Del Gaizo, and Jerry Tagge each a shot at the quarterback job, but none of them took the pressure off the runners with a consistent passing game. The offensive line enjoyed its greatest success clearing the way for Brockington and Lane, with guard Gale Gillingham bouncing back from an injury-filled 1972 season to win All-Pro honors.

Chicago Bears—Dick Butkus scored the first touchdown of his pro career by falling on a Houston fumble in the end zone on October 28, but a bad knee made it increasingly hard for him to cover pass receivers coming out of the backfield. The problem with the Bears' offense had nothing to do with injuries; quarterback Bobby Douglass was a superior runner but simply could not pass well. Chicago fans singled Douglass out for insults whenever the Bears lost, calling on coach Abe Gibron to stick rookie quarterback Gary Huff into the lineup. Gibron stayed with Douglass until November 18, when he gave Huff his first extended chance. The inexperienced rookie threw four interceptions as the Lions crushed the Bears 30-7; the fans afterward booed Douglass but didn't call for Huff.

WESTERN DIVISION

Los Angeles Rams—Carroll Rosenbloom had given Weeb Ewbank, Don Shula, and Don McCafferty their first head coaching positions while he owned the Colts, and he struck gold again this year with the Rams by hiring Chuck Knox as the head man. Knox led a team supposedly in need of an overhauling to a runaway title in the Western Division and a berth in the playoffs. The Los Angeles passing attack profited from two new faces brought in by Knox. Quarterback John Hadl came over from San Diego and receiver Harold Jackson from Philadelphia in major trades, and both men starred in their new surroundings. Two strong young runners, Larry McCutcheon and Jim Bertelsen, made Hadl's signal-calling task easier, with the excellent offensive line laboring anonymously for both the runners and passers. The defensive unit played up to the standards set by George Allen, although Merlin Olsen was the only starter left from that era. With little expected of them, the Rams won their first six games of the year and ran away from the other teams in the division.

Atlanta Falcons—With solid starters at every position except quarterback, the Falcons opened the season with a smashing triumph over the Saints in which Dick Shiner masterfully engineered the Atlanta attack. Shiner soon regressed into the mediocre form he had shown all his career, and coach Norm Van Brocklin next turned to Bob Lee at the position. An ex-Viking with little experience, Lee sparked the Falcons to a 41-0 victory over San Diego and a mid-season winning streak which made the team a prime candidate for the wild-card spot in the playoffs. December, however, brought bad times to the Falcons, as they lost to Buffalo and St. Louis.

San Francisco '49ers—Disappointment colored the '49ers season as the team finished a distant third in the West. Fullback Ken Willard publicly expressed his disappointment when benched at the start of the season. Bad knees turned receiver Gene Washington and cornerback Jim Johnson into disappointing performers. Quarterback John Brodie endured the bitterest season of all, finding himself on the bench behind Steve Spurrier and Joe Reed after the team got off to a slow start. The thirty-eight-year-old Brodie announced in mid-season that this would be his last campaign, and coach Dick Nolan gave him the starting nod in the season's finale against the Steelers, but a sore arm sent him out of the game in the first half.

New Orleans Saints—John North replaced J. D. Roberts as head coach in training camp, taking over a club that looked like one of the worst in the league. An opening-day trouncing by the Falcons embarrassed the team, but North patiently developed his defense into a good unit. The Saints beat the Bears on October 7 for their first victory, and they won four other games during the season, including an upset of the Washington Redskins. Young veterans Billy Newsome, Joe Owens, Joe Federspiel, Ernie Jackson, and Bivian Lee starred on the improved defensive platoon, while quarterback Archie Manning got some help on offense from end John Beasley, runner Jess Phillips and receiver Jubilee Dunbar, all picked up in trades.

FINAL TEAM STATISTICS

(Other statistics not available at press time)

OFFENSE

	ATL.	CHI.	DALL.	DET.	G.B.	L.A.	MINN.	N.O.	N.Y.	PHIL.	ST.L.	S.F.	WASH.
FIRST DOWNS:													
Total	240	193	281	237	187	**294**	246	207	239	267	238	251	232
by Rushing	123	97	139	122	98	**177**	135	100	83	103	96	97	76
by Passing	100	77	127	104	72	101	99	88	141	**147**	111	127	131
by Penalty	17	19	15	11	17	16	12	19	15	17	**31**	27	25
RUSHING:													
Number	518	496	542	496	527	**659**	538	497	456	417	416	422	459
Yards	2037	1907	2418	2133	1973	**2925**	2275	1842	1478	1791	1671	1743	1439
Average Yards	3.9	3.8	**4.5**	4.3	3.7	4.4	4.2	3.7	3.2	4.3	4.0	4.1	3.1
Touchdowns	**18**	11	17	17	10	**18**	14	5	11	9	13	15	9
PASSING:													
Attempts	320	303	321	325	255	271	298	338	412	**479**	394	466	372
Completions	168	136	192	171	119	144	179	163	230	**275**	210	233	209
Completion Percentage	52.5	44.9	59.8	52.6	46.7	53.1	**60.1**	48.2	55.8	57.4	53.3	50.0	56.2
Passing Yards	2362	1617	2602	2105	1503	2107	2234	1901	2762	**3236**	2592	2645	2560
Avg. Yards per Attempt	7.4	5.3	**8.1**	6.4	5.9	7.8	7.5	5.6	6.7	6.8	6.6	5.7	6.9
Avg. Yards per Complet.	14.1	11.9	13.6	12.3	12.6	**14.6**	12.5	11.7	12.0	11.8	12.3	11.4	12.2
Times Tackled Passing	41	49	43	27	27	**17**	32	37	28	34	27	27	31
Yards Lost Tackled	361	395	269	192	220	**126**	278	242	201	238	209	164	202
Net Yards	2001	1222	2333	1913	1283	1981	1956	1659	2561	**2998**	2383	2481	2358
Touchdowns	14	8	**26**	12	7	22	16	11	14	23	16	9	20
Interceptions	12	16	16	19	17	11	**9**	17	30	13	15	25	14
Percent Intercepted	3.8	5.3	5.0	5.8	6.7	4.1	3.0	5.0	7.3	**2.7**	3.8	5.4	3.8
PUNTS:													
Number	63	**86**	59	54	68	51	66	81	68	64	66	79	64
Average Distance	42.6	39.8	41.5	43.2	41.0	40.8	39.8	41.7	38.8	40.9	37.5	**43.7**	40.3
PUNT RETURNS:													
Number	48	37	28	35	30	**51**	28	22	21	15	27	37	40
Yards	429	204	174	289	137	**478**	140	218	160	116	192	393	331
Average Yards	8.9	5.5	6.2	8.3	4.6	9.4	5.0	9.9	7.6	7.7	7.1	**10.6**	8.3
Touchdowns	0	**1**	0	0	0	0	0	0	0	0	0	0	0
KICKOFF RETURNS:													
Number	53	59	33	50	53	36	35	47	56	**63**	58	**63**	43
Yards	1107	1344	725	1061	1189	915	752	947	1198	**1441**	1369	1301	1118
Average Yards	20.9	22.8	22.0	21.2	22.4	25.4	21.5	20.1	21.4	22.9	23.6	20.7	**26.0**
Touchdowns	0	**1**	0	0	0	**1**	0	0	0	0	**1**	0	**1**
INTERCEPTION RETURNS:													
Number	22	14	18	22	15	20	21	16	20	15	10	17	**26**
Yards	528	176	300	522	220	300	263	126	214	120	71	134	**598**
Average Yards	**24.0**	12.6	16.7	23.7	14.7	15.0	12.5	7.9	10.7	8.0	7.1	7.9	23.0
Touchdowns	2	0	2	1	3	1	2	0	0	1	0	0	**4**
PENALTIES:													
Number	66	86	83	64	68	54	55	58	67	61	61	**93**	81
Yards	598	817	762	584	653	606	482	516	586	566	594	**903**	771
FUMBLES:													
Number	40	40	25	30	23	**21**	29	34	23	41	36	32	32
Number Lost	21	26	12	14	11	**9**	17	17	10	15	14	14	18
POINTS:													
Total	318	195	382	271	202	**388**	296	163	226	310	286	262	325
PAT Attempts	34	22	**46**	30	20	42	33	16	25	34	31	26	37
PAT Made	34	21	**45**	28	19	40	33	16	25	34	31	26	37
FG Attempts	38	24	30	33	35	**47**	35	36	28	40	32	33	42
FG Made	26	14	19	21	21	**30**	21	17	17	24	23	26	22
Percent FG Made	68.4	58.3	63.3	63.6	60.0	63.8	60.0	47.2	60.7	60.0	71.9	**78.8**	52.4
Safeties	1	0	2	0	0	**3**	1	0	0	0	0	1	0

DEFENSE

	ATL.	CHI.	DALL.	DET.	G.B.	L.A.	MINN.	N.O.	N.Y.	PHIL.	ST.L.	S.F.	WASH.
FIRST DOWNS:													
Total	212	247	208	245	230	**173**	220	271	240	286	307	242	233
by Rushing	104	138	83	127	114	**71**	105	131	126	136	135	112	89
by Passing	92	90	106	98	101	**87**	100	119	94	135	157	115	119
by Penalty	16	19	19	20	**15**	**15**	**15**	21	20	**15**	**15**	**15**	25
RUSHING:													
Number	520	563	435	501	506	**366**	450	556	497	513	504	513	480
Yards	2129	2509	1471	2117	1999	**1270**	1974	2402	2174	2423	2120	1963	1603
Average Yards	4.1	4.5	3.4	4.2	4.0	3.5	4.4	4.3	4.4	4.7	4.2	3.8	**3.3**
Touchdowns	12	19	**5**	10	13	**5**	**5**	17	21	22	16	11	8
PASSING:													
Attempts	324	303	352	332	327	328	377	337	**275**	370	417	383	406
Completions	**151**	156	187	173	180	179	198	176	161	219	252	194	203
Completion Percentage	**46.6**	51.5	53.1	52.1	55.0	54.6	52.5	52.2	58.5	59.2	60.4	50.7	50.0
Passing Yards	**1619**	1978	2301	2058	2050	2023	2124	2333	2252	2789	3226	2591	2531
Avg. Yards per Attempt	**5.0**	6.5	6.5	6.2	6.3	6.2	5.6	6.9	8.2	7.5	7.7	6.8	6.2
Avg. Yards per Complet.	10.7	12.7	12.3	11.9	11.4	11.3	**10.7**	13.3	14.0	12.7	12.8	13.4	12.5
Times Tackled Passing	29	32	40	33	25	45	30	24	35	21	29	32	**53**
Yards Lost Tackled	189	304	306	270	228	342	230	155	267	150	197	225	**355**
Net Yards	**1430**	1674	1995	1788	1822	1681	1894	2178	1985	2639	3029	2366	2176
Touchdowns	11	17	15	15	14	10	**8**	15	17	22	23	19	12
Interceptions	22	14	18	22	15	20	21	16	20	15	10	17	**26**
Percent Intercepted	6.8	4.6	5.1	6.6	4.6	6.1	5.6	4.7	**7.3**	4.1	2.4	4.4	6.4
PUNTS:													
Number	80	66	70	65	67	**81**	57	63	52	49	54	72	**81**
Average Distance	42.1	40.5	39.4	41.5	38.9	40.8	41.0	44.5	40.9	39.9	41.4	41.3	**38.4**
PUNT RETURNS:													
Number	30	40	29	30	41	24	41	49	32	35	23	46	**14**
Yards	185	294	152	166	300	261	271	587	379	376	186	367	**104**
Average Yards	6.1	7.4	5.2	5.5	7.3	10.9	6.5	11.9	11.8	10.8	8.1	8.0	7.4
Touchdowns	**0**	**0**	1	**0**	0	0	1	1	**0**	**0**	**0**	**0**	**0**
KICKOFF RETURNS:													
Number	58	**33**	53	59	40	68	58	**33**	43	55	57	52	62
Yards	1369	813	1320	1220	817	1318	1148	**724**	988	1246	1350	1151	1237
Average Yards	23.6	24.6	24.9	20.7	20.4	19.4	**19.1**	22.0	22.7	22.7	23.7	22.1	20.0
Touchdowns	**0**	**0**	**0**	**0**	**0**	**0**	**0**	**0**	**0**	1	1	1	1
INTERCEPTION RETURNS:													
Number	12	16	16	19	17	11	**9**	17	30	13	15	25	14
Yards	**83**	335	151	171	256	103	88	280	525	287	267	379	173
Average Yards	**6.9**	20.9	9.4	9.0	15.1	9.4	9.8	16.5	17.5	22.1	17.8	15.2	12.4
Touchdowns	**0**	1	1	**0**	1	1	**0**	3	3	1	2	1	**0**
PENALTIES:													
Number	58	77	52	68	54	61	58	69	58	73	**95**	77	86
Yards	562	672	516	606	483	566	633	751	484	692	**892**	754	708
FUMBLES:													
Number	29	35	**44**	31	34	29	36	32	32	31	31	23	35
Number Lost	15	19	**23**	11	18	18	15	14	12	15	17	15	18
POINTS:													
Total	224	334	203	247	259	178	**168**	312	362	393	365	319	198
PAT Attempts	24	37	23	26	28	17	**15**	36	42	47	42	32	21
PAT Made	23	35	23	25	28	16	**15**	35	42	45	41	32	21
FG Attempts	28	38	30	31	**27**	**27**	38	34	30	40	34	45	29
FG Made	19	25	**14**	22	19	20	21	19	22	22	24	31	17
Percent FG Made	67.9	65.8	**46.7**	71.0	70.4	74.1	55.3	55.9	73.3	55.0	70.6	68.9	58.6
Safeties	**0**	1	**0**	**0**	3	0	**0**	2	1	**0**	**0**	1	**0**

CONFERENCE PLAYOFFS

December 22, at Minnesota (Attendance 45,475)

SCORING

MINNESOTA	**0**	**3**	**7**	**17–27**
WASHINGTON	**0**	**7**	**3**	**10–20**

Second Quarter
- Minn. Cox, 19 yard field goal
- Wash. Brown, 3 yard rush PAT–Knight (kick)

Third Quarter
- Minn. Brown, 2 yard rush PAT–Cox (kick)
- Wash. Knight, 52 yard field goal

Fourth Quarter
- Wash. Knight, 42 yard field goal
- Minn. Gilliam, 28 yard pass from Tarkenton PAT–Cox (kick)
- Minn. Gilliam, 6 yard pass from Tarkenton PAT–Cox (kick)
- Wash. Jefferson, 28 yard pass from Kilmer PAT–Knight (kick)
- Minn. Cox, 30 yard field goal

TEAM STATISTICS

MINN.		WASH.
17	First Downs–Total	18
6	First Downs–Rushing	10
11	First Downs–Passing	7
0	First Downs–Penalty	1
2	Fumbles–Number	2
2	Fumbles–Lost Ball	1
2	Penalties–Number	0
9	Yards Penalized	0
0	Missed Field Goals	2
63	Offensive Plays	66
359	Net Yards	314
5.7	Average Gain	4.8
3	Giveaways	2
2	Takeaways	3
–1	Difference	+1

INDIVIDUAL STATISTICS

MINNESOTA	No.	Yds.	Avg.	WASHINGTON	No.	Yds.	Avg.
RUSHING							
Reed	17	95	5.6	Brown	29	115	4.0
Foreman	11	40	3.6	Harraway	13	40	3.1
Marinaro	1	3	3.0		42	155	3.7
Brown	1	2	2.0				
Tarkenton	4	1	0.3				
	34	141	4.1				
RECEIVING							
Reed	5	76	15.2	Jefferson	6	84	14.0
Voigt	3	39	13.0	Taylor	4	56	14.0
Foreman	3	23	7.7	Brown	2	13	6.5
Gilliam	2	36	18.0	Harraway	1	6	6.0
Dale	2	31	15.5		13	159	12.2
Lash	1	17	17.0				
	16	222	13.9				
PUNTING							
Eischeid	6		31.9	Bragg	4		37.3
PUNT RETURNS							
Bryant	2	3	1.5	Duncan	3	8	2.7
				Mul-Key	1	10	10.0
					4	18	4.5
KICKOFF RETURNS							
Gilliam	3	49	16.3	Mul-Key	3	69	23.0
West	2	78	39.0	Brunet	2	35	17.5
	5	127	25.4		5	104	20.8
INTERCEPTION RETURNS							
N. Wright	1	26	26.0	Bass	1	28	28.0

PASSING

MINNESOTA	Att.	Comp.	Comp. Pct.	Yds.	Int.	Yds/ Att.	Yds/ Comp.	Yards Lost Tackled
Tarkenton	28	16	57.1	222	1	7.9	13.9	1–4
WASHINGTON								
Kilmer	24	13	54.2	159	1	6.6	12.2	0–0

December 23, at Irving, Tex. (Attendance 64,291)

SCORING

DALLAS	**14**	**3**	**0**	**10–27**
LOS ANGELES	**0**	**6**	**0**	**10–16**

First Quarter
- Dall. Hill, 3 yard rush PAT–Fritsch (kick)
- Dall. Pearson, 4 yard pass from Staubach PAT–Fritsch (kick)

Second Quarter
- Dall. Fritsch, 39 yard field goal
- L.A. Ray, 33 yard field goal
- L.A. Ray, 37 yard field goal

Fourth Quarter
- L.A. Ray, 40 yard field goal
- L.A. Baker, 5 yard rush PAT–Ray (kick)
- Dall. Pearson, 83 yard pass from Staubach PAT–Fritsch (kick)
- Dall. Fritsch, 12 yard field goal

TEAM STATISTICS

DALL.		L.A.
15	First Downs–Total	11
11	First Downs–Rushing	5
4	First Downs–Passing	5
0	First Downs–Penalty	1
2	Fumbles–Number	2
2	Fumbles–Lost Ball	2
5	Penalties–Number	2
44	Yards Penalized	20
0	Missed Field Goals	3
68	Offensive Plays	58
298	Net Yards	192
4.4	Average Gain	3.3
4	Giveaways	3
3	Takeaways	4
–1	Difference	+1

INDIVIDUAL STATISTICS

DALLAS	No.	Yds.	Avg.	LOS ANGELES	No.	Yds.	Avg.
RUSHING							
Hill	25	97	3.9	McCutcheon	13	48	3.7
Staubach	4	30	7.5	Bertelsen	12	37	3.1
Garrison	10	30	3.0	Hadl	2	10	5.0
Newhouse	6	5	0.8	Baker	1	5	5.0
	45	162	3.6	Smith	2	–7	–3.5
					30	93	3.1
RECEIVING							
Pearson	2	87	43.5	Snow	3	77	25.7
Hill	2	21	10.5	Smith	2	13	6.5
Fuggett	1	38	38.0	Jackson	1	40	40.0
Hayes	1	29	29.0	McCutcheon	1	3	3.0
Garrison	1	3	3.0		7	133	19.0
DuPree	1	2	2.0				
	8	180	22.5				
PUNTING							
Bateman	7		46.7	Chapple	5		43.6
PUNT RETURNS							
Richards	2	3	1.5	Bertelsen	4	52	13.0
				Elmendorf	1	1	1.0
					5	53	10.6
KICKOFF RETURNS							
Waters	1	23	23.0	Scribner	4	106	26.5
Harris	1	19	19.0	Clark	2	49	24.5
	2	42	21.0		6	155	25.8
INTERCEPTION RETURNS							
Jordan	1	2	2.0	Reynolds	1	4	4.0
				Elmendorf	1	0	0.0
					2	4	2.0

PASSING

DALLAS	Att.	Comp.	Comp. Pct.	Yds.	Int.	Yds/ Att.	Yds/ Comp.	Yards Lost Tackled
Staubach	16	8	50.0	180	2	11.3	22.5	7–44
LOS ANGELES								
Hadl	23	7	30.4	133	1	5.8	19.0	5–34
McCutcheon	1	0	0.0	0	0	–	–	0– 0
	24	7	29.2	133	1	5.5	19.0	5–34

1973 N.F.C. — Eastern Division

DALLAS COWBOYS 10-4-0 — Tom Landry

Scores of Each Game

	Opponent	
20	Chicago	17
40	NEW ORLEANS	3
45	ST. LOUIS	10
7	Washington	14
31	Los Angeles	37
45	N. Y. GIANTS	28
16	Philadelphia	30
38	CINCINNATI	10
10	N. Y. Giants	10
31	PHILADELPHIA	10
7	MIAMI	14
22	Denver	10
27	WASHINGTON	7
30	St. Louis	3

Use Name	Pos.	Hgt	Wgt	Age	Int	Pts
Ralph Neely	OT	6'5"	265	29		
Rodney Wallace	OT	6'5"	255	24		
Rayfield Wright	OT	6'7"	255	28		
John Niland	OG	6'4"	245	29		
Blaine Nye	OG	6'4"	250	27		
Jim Arneson	C-OG	6'3"	236	22		
Bruce Walton	C-OG	6'6"	250	22		
John Fitzgerald	C	6'5"	250	25		
Dave Manders	C	6'2"	250	31		
Larry Cole	DE	6'4"	250	26		
Harvey Martin	DE	6'5"	262	22		
Pat Toomay	DE	6'5"	244	28	1	
Bill Gregory	DT	6'5"	255	23		
Bob Lilly	DT	6'4"	260	34		
Jethro Pugh	DT	6'6"	260	29		
John Babinecz	LB	6'1"	222	23		
Rodrigo Barnes	LB	6'1"	215	23		
Dave Edwards	LB	6'3"	225	34		
Chuck Howley	LB	6'3"	225	27		
Lee Roy Jordan	LB	6'2"	220	32	6	6
Mike Keller	LB	6'4"	220	22		
D. D. Lewis	LB	6'2"	225	27		6
Benny Barnes	DB	6'1"	190	22	1	4
Cornell Green	DB	6'4"	208	33		
Cliff Harris	DB	6'	184	24	2	
Mel Renfro	DB	6'	190	31	2	6
Mark Washington	DB	5'10"	188	25	1	
Charlie Waters	DB	6'1"	193	24	5	
Craig Morton	QB	6'4"	214	30		
Roger Staubach	QB	6'2"	197	31		18
Cyril Pinder	HB	6'2"	205	22		
Les Strayhorn	HB	5'10"	205	22		
Calvin Hill	FB-HB	6'3"	227	26		36
Walt Garrison	FB	6'	205	29		48
Robert Newhouse	HB-FB	5'10"	202	23		12
Larry Robinson	HB-FB	6'4"	210	22		
Bob Hayes	WR	6'	185	30		18
Mike Montgomery	WR	6'2"	210	24		
Drew Pearson	WR	6'	175	22		12
Golden Richards	WR	6'	172	22		
Otto Stowe	WR	6'2"	188	24		30
Billy Joe DuPree	TE	6'4"	225	23		36
Jean Fugett	TE	6'3"	220	21		
Billy Truax	TE	6'5"	240	30		
Marv Bateman	K	6'4"	213	23		
Mike Clark	K	6'1"	205	32		
Toni Fritsch	K	5'7"	185	28		

WASHINGTON REDSKINS 10-4-0 — George Allen

Scores of Each Game

	Opponent	
38	SAN DIEGO	0
27	St. Louis	34
28	Philadelphia	7
14	DALLAS	7
21	N. Y. Giants	3
31	ST. LOUIS	13
3	New Orleans	19
16	Pittsburgh	21
33	SAN FRANCISCO	9
22	BALTIMORE	14
20	Detroit	0
27	N. Y. GIANTS	24
7	Dallas	27
38	PHILADELPHIA	20

Use Name	Pos.	Hgt	Wgt	Age	Int	Pts
Terry Hermeling	OT	6'5"	255	27		
Walt Rock	OT	6'5"	255	32		
George Starke	OT	6'5"	250	25		
Paul Laaveg	OG	6'4"	245	24		
Ray Schoenke	OG	6'3"	250	31		
John Wilbur	OG	6'3"	250	30		
Len Hauss	C	6'2"	235	31		
Dan Ryczek	C	6'3"	250	24		
Verlon Biggs	DE	6'4"	275	30		6
Jimmie Jones	DE	6'3"	215	26		
Ron McDole	DE	6'5"	265	33		
Bill Brundige	DT	6'5"	270	24		
Manny Sistrunk	DT	6'5"	265	26		
Diron Talbert	DT	6'5"	255	29		
Jon Jaqua – Injury						
Chris Hanburger	LB	6'2"	218	32	1	
Harold McLinton	LB	6'2"	235	26		
John Pergine	LB	6'1"	225	26		
Myron Pottios	LB	6'2"	232	33		
Dave Robinson	LB	6'3"	245	32	4	6
Rusty Tillman	LB	6'2"	230	27		
Mike Bass	DB	6'	190	28	5	6
Speedy Duncan	DB	5'10"	180	30	1	
Pat Fischer	DB	5'10"	170	33	3	
Ken Houston	DB	6'3"	198	28	6	
Brig Owens	DB	5'11"	190	30	5	12
Richie Petitbon	DB	6'3"	208	35		
Ted Vactor	DB	6'	185	29	1	6
Larry Willis	DB	5'11"	170	24		
Rosey Taylor – Injury						
Sonny Jurgensen	QB	5'11"	203	39		
Billy Kilmer	QB	6'2"	204	33		
Larry Brown	HB	5'11"	195	25		8
Bob Brunet	HB	6'1"	205	27		
Herb Mul-Key	HB	6'	190	23		
Charlie Harraway	FB	6'2"	215	28		
Mike Hull	FB	6'3"	220	28		
Duane Thomas	HB-FB	6'1"	215	26		
Frank Grant	WR	5'11"	180	23		
Roy Jefferson	WR	6'2"	195	29		
Bill Malinchak	WR	6'	200	29		
Charlie Taylor	WR	6'3"	210	32		
Mike Hancock	TE	6'4"	220	23		
Alvin Reed	TE	6'5"	235	29		
Jerry Smith	TE	6'3"	208	30		
Mike Bragg	K	5'11"	186	26		
Curt Knight	K	6'1"	190	30		10

PHILADELPHIA EAGLES 5-8-1 — Mike McCormack

Scores of Each Game

	Opponent	
23	ST. LOUIS	34
23	N. Y. Giants	23
7	WASHINGTON	28
26	Buffalo	27
27	St. Louis	24
21	Minnesota	28
30	DALLAS	16
24	NEW ENGLAND	23
27	ATLANTA	44
10	Dallas	31
20	N. Y. GIANTS	16
28	San Francisco	38
24	N. Y. JETS	23
20	Washington	38

Use Name	Pos.	Hgt	Wgt	Age	Int	Pts
Jerry Sisemore	OT	6'4"	260	22		
Steve Smith	OT	6'5"	250	29		
Dick Stevens	OT	6'4"	240	25		
Wade Key	OG	6'4"	245	26		
Roy Kirksey	OG	6'1"	265	25		
Tom Luken	OG	6'3"	253	23		
Mark Nordquist	OG	6'4"	246	27		
Vern Winfield	OG	6'2"	248	24		
Mike Evans	C	6'5"	250	27		
Guy Morriss	C	6'4"	255	22		
Gerry Philbin	DE	6'2"	245	32		
Dennis Wirgowski	DE	6'5"	250	25	1	
Will Wynn	DE	6'4"	240	24		6
Bill Dunstan	DT	6'4"	250	24		
Don Hultz	DT	6'3"	240	32		
Gary Pettigrew	DT	6'4"	255	28		
Richard Harris	DE-DT	6'4"	260	25		
John Bunting	LB	6'1"	220	23		
Dick Cunningham	LB	6'2"	238	28		
Dean Halverson	LB	6'2"	225	27		
Marlin McKeever	LB	6'2"	235	33		
Kevin Reilly	LB	6'2"	220	21		
Tom Roussel	LB	6'3"	235	28		
John Sodaski	LB	6'1"	222	25	1	
Steve Zabel	LB	6'4"	235	25	2	
Kermit Alexander	DB	5'11"	186	32		
Bill Bradley	DB	5'11"	190	26	4	
Al Coleman	DB	6'1"	183	28		
Joe Lavender	DB	6'4"	190	24		
Randy Logan	DB	6'1"	195	22	5	
Al Nelson	DB	5'11"	186	29		
John Outlaw	DB	5'10"	180	28	2	
Roman Gabriel	QB	6'4"	220	33		
John Reaves	QB	6'3"	210	24		
Po James	HB	6'1"	202	24		
Greg Oliver	HB	6'	192	24		
Tom Sullivan	HB	6'	190	23		
Tom Bailey	FB-HB	6'2"	211	24		
Lee Bouggess	FB	6'2"	210	25		
Norm Bulaich	HB-FB	6'1"	218	26		
Harold Carmichael	WR	6'7"	225	23		
Stan Davis	WR	5'10"	180	23		
Ben Hawkins	WR	6'	180	29		
Bob Picard	WR	6'1"	195	23		
Don Zimmerman	WR	6'3"	195	23		
Kent Kramer	TE	6'5"	235	29		
Charlie Young	TE	6'4"	230	22		
Tom Dempsey	K	6'1"	255	32		
Tom McNeill	K	6'1"	195	31		

ST. LOUIS CARDINALS 4-9-1 — Don Coryell

Scores of Each Game

	Opponent	
34	Philadelphia	23
34	WASHINGTON	27
10	Dallas	45
10	OAKLAND	17
24	PHILADELPHIA	27
13	Washington	31
35	N. Y. GIANTS	27
17	DENVER	17
21	Green Bay	25
13	N. Y. Giants	24
24	Cincinnati	42
16	DETROIT	20
32	Atlanta	10
3	DALLAS	30

Use Name	Pos.	Hgt	Wgt	Age	Int	Pts
Dan Dierdorf	OT	6'4"	265	24		
Ernie McMillan	OT	6'6"	255	35		
Mike Taylor	OT	6'4"	255	28		
Tom Banks	OG	6'2"	235	22		
Ron Davis	OG	6'2"	235	22		
Conrad Dobler	OG	6'3"	250	22		
Roger Finnie	OG	6'3"	245	26		
Bob Young	OG	6'2"	260	30		
Tom Brahaney	C	6'2"	225	21		
Warren Koegel	C	6'3"	250	23		
Wayne Mulligan	C	6'2"	245	26		
Council Rudolph	DE	6'3"	260	23		
Ron Yankowski	DE	6'5"	240	26		
Dave Butz	DT-DE	6'7"	290	23		
Lee Brooks	DT	6'5"	265	25		
John Richardson	DT	6'2"	250	27		
Bob Rowe	DT	6'4"	260	28		
Bonnie Sloan	DT	6'5"	260	24		
Mark Arneson	LB	6'2"	220	23	1	
Pete Barnes	LB	6'3"	240	28	1	
Jack LeVeck	LB	6'	225	23		
Terry Miller	LB	6'2"	225	27		
Jamie Rivers	LB	6'2"	235	27	1	
Jeff Staggs	LB	6'2"	240	29		
Larry Stallings	LB	6'2"	230	31	1	
Dwayne Crump	DB	5'11"	180	23		
Chuck Detwiler	DB	6'	185	26	1	
Clarence Duren	DB	6'1"	190	22		
Norm Thompson	DB	6'1"	175	25		
Jim Tolbert	DB	6'1"	202	29	2	
Eric Washington	DB	6'2"	190	23		
Roger Wehrli	DB	6'1"	195	25	1	
Leon Burns – Injury						
Jim Hart	QB	6'2"	215	29		
Gary Keithley	QB	6'3"	205	22		
Donny Anderson	HB	6'3"	210	30		
Willie Belton	HB	5'11"	195	24		
Terry Metcalf	HB	5'10"	185	21		
Eddie Moss	HB	6'	215	24		
Jim Otis	FB	6'	220	25		
Leo Hayden	HB-FB	6'	210	25		
Don Shy	HB-FB	6'1"	205	28		
Walker Gillette	WR	6'5"	200	26		
Mel Gray	WR	5'9"	170	24		
Don Maynard	WR	6'	180	37		
Marv Owens	WR	6'2"	210	23		
Ahmad Rashad	WR	6'2"	210	23		
Gary Hammond	HB-WR	5'11"	180	24		
Jim McFarland	TE	6'5"	225	25		
Jackie Smith	TE	6'4"	235	32		
Jim Bakken	K	6'	200	32		

NEW YORK GIANTS 2-11-1 — Alex Webster

Scores of Each Game

	Opponent	
34	HOUSTON	14
23	PHILADELPHIA	23
10	Cleveland	12
14	GREEN BAY	16
3	WASHINGTON	21
28	Dallas	45
27	St. Louis	35
0	Oakland	42
10	DALLAS	23
24	St. Louis	13
16	Philadelphia	20
24	Washington	27
6	Los Angeles	40
7	MINNESOTA	31

Use Name	Pos.	Hgt	Wgt	Age	Int	Pts
Bart Buetow	OT	6'5"	250	22		
John Hill	OT	6'2"	245	23		
Joe Taffoni	OT	6'3"	255	28		
Willie Young	OT	6'	265	30		
Mark Ellison	OG	6'2"	245	25		
Dick Enderle	OG	6'1"	250	25		
Doug Van Horn	OG	6'2"	245	29		
Bob Hyland	OT-C	6'5"	255	28		
Greg Larson	C	6'2"	250	34		
Carter Campbell	DE	6'3"	240	25		
Jack Gregory	DE	6'5"	250	28		
Dave Tipton	DE	6'6"	240	24		
Rich Glover	DT	6'1"	240	22		
Dan Goich	DT	6'4"	250	28		
Larry Jacobson	DT	6'6"	260	23		
John Mendenhall	DT	6'1"	255	24		
John Douglas	LB	6'2"	228	28	1	
Jim Files	LB	6'4"	240	25	1	
Ron Hornsby	LB	6'3"	232	24		
Pat Hughes	LB	6'2"	240	26	3	
Brian Kelley	LB	6'3"	222	22		
Henry Reed	LB	6'3"	230	24	1	
Brad Van Pelt	LB	6'5"	235	22		
Pete Athas	DB	5'11"	185	27	5	
Otto Brown	DB	6'1"	188	25		
Chuck Crist	DB	6'2"	205	22	2	
Richmond Flowers	DB	6'	180	26	1	
Spider Lockhart	DB	6'1"	175	30	2	
Ron Lumpkin	DB	6'2"	200	22		
Eldridge Small	DB	6'1"	190	23		
Willie Williams	DB	6'	190	30	4	
Randy Johnson	QB	6'3"	205	29		
Norm Snead	QB	6'4"	215	33		
Ron Johnson	HB	6'1"	205	25		
Jack Rizzo	HB	5'10"	195	24		
Rocky Thompson	HB	5'11"	200	25		
Joe Orduna	FB-HB	6'	195	25		
Vin Clements	FB	6'3"	215	24		
Charlie Evans	FB	6'1"	220	25		
Johnny Roland	HB-FB	6'2"	220	30		
Bob Grim	WR	6'	200	28		
Don Herrmann	WR	6'2"	205	26		
Rich Houston	WR	6'2"	195	27		
Walt Love	WR	5'9"	180	22		
Gary Ballman (to MIN)	TE	6'	215	33		
Tom Gatewood	TE	6'2"	205	24		
Bob Tucker	TE	6'3"	230	28		
Tom Blanchard	K	6'	190	26		
Pete Gogolak	K	6'2"	190	31		
Jim McCann	K	6'2"	163	24		

DALLAS COWBOYS

RUSHING
Last Name	No.	Yds	Avg	TD
Hill	273	1142	4.2	6
Garrison	105	440	4.2	6
Newhouse	84	436	5.2	1
Staubach	46	250	5.4	3
Strayhorn	11	62	5.6	0
Fugett	1	34	34.0	0
Stowe	3	28	9.3	0
Robinson	2	17	8.5	0
Pinder	12	15	1.3	0
Richards	1	2	2.0	0
DuPree	2	2	1.0	0
Morton	2	0	0.0	0
Montgomery	1	−10	−10.0	0

RECEIVING
Last Name	No.	Yds	Avg	TD
Hill	32	290	9	0
DuPree	29	392	14	5
Garrison	26	273	11	2
Stowe	23	389	17	6
Pearson	22	388	18	2
Hayes	22	360	16	3
Montgomery	14	164	12	3
Fugett	9	168	19	3
Newhouse	9	87	10	1
Richards	6	91	15	1

PUNT RETURNS
Last Name	No.	Yds	Avg	TD
Richards	21	139	7	0
Harris	3	20	7	0
Pearson	2	13	7	0
Montgomery	2	2	1	0

KICKOFF RETURNS
Last Name	No.	Yds	Avg	TD
Montgomery	6	175	29	0
Pearson	7	155	22	0
Harris	6	148	25	0
Robinson	4	86	22	0
Newhouse	3	62	21	0
Richards	3	44	15	0
Strayhorn	2	44	22	0
Walton	1	11	11	0
Washington	1	0	0	0

PASSING – PUNTING – KICKING

PASSING
Last Name	Att	Comp	%	Yds	Yd/Att	TD	Int–%	RK
Staubach	286	179	63	2428	8.5	23	15– 5	2
Morton	32	13	41	174	5.4	3	1– 3	
Garrison	1	0	0	0	0.0	0	0– 0	
Hill	1	0	0	0	0.0	0	0– 0	
Montgomery	1	0	0	0	0.0	0	0– 0	

PUNTING
Last Name	No	Avg
Bateman	55	41.6
Montgomery	4	39.5

KICKING
Last Name	XP	Att	%	FG	Att	%
Fritsch	43	43	100	18	28	64
Clark	1	2	50	1	2	50
Bateman	1	1	100	0	0	

WASHINGTON REDSKINS

RUSHING
Last Name	No.	Yds	Avg	TD
Brown	273	860	3.2	8
Harraway	128	452	3.5	1
Thomas	32	95	3.0	0
Mul-Key	8	20	2.5	0
Kilmer	9	10	1.1	0
Jurgensen	3	7	2.3	0
Brunet	2	4	2.0	0
Jefferson	1	1	1.0	0
Hull	2	−3	−1.5	0
C. Taylor	1	−7	−7.0	0

RECEIVING
Last Name	No.	Yds	Avg	TD
C. Taylor	59	801	14	7
Jefferson	41	595	15	1
Brown	40	482	12	6
Harraway	32	291	9	3
Smith	19	215	11	0
Reed	9	124	14	0
Thomas	5	40	8	0
Hancock	2	3	2	1
Grant	1	12	12	0
Jurgensen	1	−3	−3	0

PUNT RETURNS
Last Name	No.	Yds	Avg	TD
Duncan	28	228	8	0
Mul-Key	11	103	9	0
Smith	1	0	0	0

KICKOFF RETURNS
Last Name	No.	Yds	Avg	TD
Mul-Key	36	1011	28	1
Duncan	4	65	16	0
Tillman	3	42	14	0

PASSING – PUNTING – KICKING

PASSING
Last Name	Att	Comp	%	Yds	Yd/Att	TD	Int–%	RK
Kilmer	227	122	54	1656	7.3	14	9– 4	6
Jurgensen	145	87	60	904	6.2	6	5– 3	

PUNTING
Last Name	No	Avg
Bragg	64	40.3

KICKING
Last Name	XP	Att	%	FG	Att	%
Knight	37	37	100	22	42	52

PHILADELPHIA EAGLES

RUSHING
Last Name	No.	Yds	Avg	TD
Sullivan	217	968	4.5	4
Bulaich	106	436	4.1	1
James	36	178	4.9	1
Bailey	20	91	4.6	0
Carmichael	3	42	14.0	0
Bouggess	15	34	2.3	1
Young	4	24	6.0	1
Gabriel	12	10	0.8	0
Oliver	1	6	6.0	0
Reaves	2	2	1.0	0
Bradley	1	0	0.0	0

RECEIVING
Last Name	No.	Yds	Avg	TD
Carmichael	67	1116	17	9
Young	55	854	16	6
Sullivan	50	322	6	1
Bulaich	42	403	10	3
Zimmerman	22	220	10	3
James	17	94	6	0
Bailey	10	80	8	1
Hawkins	6	114	19	0
Bouggess	4	18	5	0
Oliver	1	9	9	0
Davis	1	6	6	0

PUNT RETURNS
Last Name	No.	Yds	Avg	TD
Bradley	8	106	13	0
Alexander	5	10	2	0
Davis	2	0	0	0

KICKOFF RETURNS
Last Name	No.	Yds	Avg	TD
James	16	413	26	0
Sullivan	12	280	23	0
Nelson	11	264	24	0
Davis	10	236	24	0
Alexander	9	189	21	0
Coleman	2	24	12	0
Bailey	2	18	9	0
Oliver	1	17	17	0

PASSING – PUNTING – KICKING

PASSING
Last Name	Att	Comp	%	Yds	Yd/Att	TD	Int–%	RK
Gabriel	460	270	59	3219	7.0	23	12– 3	1
Reaves	19	5	26	17	0.9	0	1– 5	

PUNTING
Last Name	No	Avg
McNeill	46	40.9
Bradley	18	40.8

KICKING
Last Name	XP	Att	%	FG	Att	%
Dempsey	34	34	100	24	40	60

ST. LOUIS CARDINALS

RUSHING
Last Name	No.	Yds	Avg	TD
Anderson	167	679	4.1	10
Metcalf	148	628	4.2	2
Otis	55	234	4.3	1
Gray	16	66	4.1	0
Moss	14	41	2.9	0
Keithley	8	29	3.6	0
Hammond	4	11	2.8	0
Hart	3	−3	−1.0	0
Smith	1	−14	−14.0	0

RECEIVING
Last Name	No.	Yds	Avg	TD
Smith	41	600	15	1
Anderson	41	409	10	3
Metcalf	37	316	9	0
Rashad	30	409	14	3
Gray	29	513	18	7
Gillette	20	244	12	1
Hammond	4	39	10	0
Shy	3	15	5	1
Otis	2	19	10	0
McFarland	2	10	5	0
Maynard	1	18	18	0

PUNT RETURNS
Last Name	No.	Yds	Avg	TD
Wehrli	9	92	10	0
Hammond	11	80	7	0
Thompson	6	18	3	0
Belton	1	2	2	0

KICKOFF RETURNS
Last Name	No.	Yds	Avg	TD
Shy	16	445	28	1
Hammond	12	314	26	0
Metcalf	4	124	31	0
Hayden	5	98	20	0
Belton	3	83	28	0
Moss	4	78	20	0
Gray	4	73	18	0
McFarland	3	57	19	0
Detwiler	3	55	18	0
Butz	1	23	23	0
Owens	1	19	19	0
Wehrli	2	0	0	0

PASSING – PUNTING – KICKING

PASSING
Last Name	Att	Comp	%	Yds	Yd/Att	TD	Int–%	RK
Hart	320	178	56	2223	7.0	15	10– 3	4
Keithley	73	32	44	369	5.1	1	5– 7	
Hammond	1	0	0	0	0.0	0	0– 0	

PUNTING
Last Name	No	Avg
Keithley	66	37.5

KICKING
Last Name	XP	Att	%	FG	Att	%
Bakken	31	31	100	23	32	72

NEW YORK GIANTS

RUSHING
Last Name	No.	Yds	Avg	TD
...n Johnson	260	902	3.5	6
...ements	57	214	3.8	1
...land	53	142	2.7	1
...duna	36	104	2.9	1
...ans	34	77	2.3	1
...ndy Johnson	4	24	6.0	0
...ead	4	13	3.3	0
...ompson	5	5	1.0	0
...cker	1	4	4.0	0
...zzo	1	3	3.0	0
...m	1	−10	−10.0	0

RECEIVING
Last Name	No.	Yds	Avg	TD
Tucker	50	681	14	5
Herrmann	43	520	12	2
Grim	37	593	16	2
Ron Johnson	32	377	12	3
Roland	22	190	9	1
Clements	15	129	9	1
Evans	13	100	8	0
Houston	8	90	11	0
Orduna	6	44	7	0
Ballman	3	38	13	0
Hyland	1	16	16	0
Rizzo	1	11	11	0
Young	1	−5	−5	0

PUNT RETURNS
Last Name	No.	Yds	Avg	TD
Athas	20	153	8	0
Crist	1	7	7	0

KICKOFF RETURNS
Last Name	No.	Yds	Avg	TD
Love	18	396	22	0
Houston	15	375	25	0
Small	11	207	19	0
Orduna	6	104	17	0
Rizzo	4	86	22	0
Kelley	2	30	15	0

PASSING – PUNTING – KICKING

PASSING
Last Name	Att	Comp	%	Yds	Yd/Att	TD	Int–%	RK
Snead	235	131	56	1483	6.3	7	22– 9	11
Ran. Johnson	177	99	56	1279	7.2	7	8– 5	

PUNTING
Last Name	No	Avg
Blanchard	56	41.9
McCann	12	24.5

KICKING
Last Name	XP	Att	%	FG	Att	%
Gogolak	25	25	100	17	28	61

MINNESOTA VIKINGS 12-2-0 Bud Grant

Scores of Each Game

24	OAKLAND	16
22	Chicago	13
11	GREEN BAY	3
23	Detroit	9
17	San Francisco	13
28	PHILADELPHIA	21
10	LOS ANGELES	9
26	CLEVELAND	3
28	DETROIT	7
14	Atlanta	20
31	CHICAGO	13
0	Cincinnati	27
31	Green Bay	7
31	N. Y. Giants	7

Use Name	Pos.	Hgt	Wgt	Age	Int	Pts
Grady Alderman	OT	6'2"	247	34		
Ron Yary	OT	6'6"	255	27		
Charlie Goodrum	OG-OT	6'3"	256	23		
Frank Gallagher (from ATL)	OG	6'2"	245	30		
Steve Lawson	OG	6'3"	265	24		
Milt Sunde	OG	6'2"	250	30		
John Ward	OG	6'4"	260	25		
Ed White	OG	6'2"	262	26		
Mick Tingelhoff	C	6'1"	237	33		
Godfrey Zaunbrecher	C	6'2"	240	25		
Carl Eller	DE	6'6"	247	31		
Jim Marshall	DE	6'3"	248	35		
Bob Lurtsema	DT-DE	6'6"	250	31		
Gary Larsen	DT	6'5"	260	33		
Alan Page	DT	6'5"	245	28		
Doug Sutherland	DT	6'3"	250	25		
Wally Hilgenberg	LB	6'3"	230	30	1	6
Amos Martin	LB	6'3"	228	24		
Ron Porter	LB	6'3"	232	28		
Jeff Siemon	LB	6'2"	230	23	2	
Roy Winston	LB	6'1"	222	33		2
Terry Brown	DB	6'1"	205	26	1	6
Bobby Bryant	DB	6'	170	29	7	6
Paul Krause	DB	6'3"	200	31	4	
Al Randolph	DB	6'2"	205	29		
Charlie West	DB	6'1"	197	27		
Jeff Wright	DB	5'11"	190	24	3	
Nate Wright	DB	5'11"	180	26	3	
Bob Berry	QB	5'11"	185	31		
Fran Tarkenton	QB	6'1"	190	33		6
Brent McClanahan	HB	5'10"	202	22		
Dave Osborn	HB	6'	208	30		
Chuck Foreman	FB-HB	6'2"	216	22		36
Bill Brown	FB	5'11"	222	35		24
Ed Marinaro	HB-FB	6'2"	212	23		24
Oscar Reed	HB-FB	5'11"	222	29		18
Carroll Dale	WR	6'1"	200	35		
Rhett Dawson	WR	6'1"	185	24		
John Gilliam	WR	6'1"	195	28		54
Jim Lash	WR	6'2"	200	21		
Doug Kingsriter	TE	6'2"	222	23		
Stu Voigt	TE	6'1"	220	25		12
Fred Cox	K	5'10"	200	34		96
Mike Eischeid	K	6'	190	32		

Karl Kassulke — Paralyzed in motorcycle accident

DETROIT LIONS 6-7-1 Don McCafferty

10	Pittsburgh	24
13	Green Bay	13
31	ATLANTA	6
9	MINNESOTA	23
13	New Orleans	20
27	BALTIMORE	29
34	GREEN BAY	0
30	SAN FRANCISCO	20
7	Minnesota	28
30	Chicago	7
0	WASHINGTON	20
20	St. Louis	16
40	CHICAGO	7
7	Miami	34

Use Name	Pos.	Hgt	Wgt	Age	Int	Pts
Rocky Freitas	OT	6'6"	270	27		
Mike Haggerty	OT	6'4"	245	27		
Gordon Jolley	OT	6'5"	250	24		
Jim Yarbrough	OT	6'6"	265	26		
Guy Dennis	OG	6'2"	255	26		
Bob Kowalkowski	OG	6'3"	240	29		
Rocky Rasley	OG	6'3"	250	26		
Chuck Walton	OG	6'3"	255	32		
Ed Flanagan	C	6'3"	245	29		
Dave Thompson	OG-C	6'4"	275	24		
Larry Hand	DE	6'4"	250	33		
Jim Mitchell	DE	6'3"	245	24		
Ken Sanders	DE	6'5"	240	23		
Bob Bell	DT	6'4"	250	25		
Herb Orvis	DT	6'5"	240	26		
Ernie Price	DT	6'4"	255	22		
John Small	DT	6'5"	260	26		
Mike Hennigan	LB	6'2"	210	21		
Jim Laslavic	LB	6'2"	230	21		
Mike Lucci	LB	6'2"	230	33	4	
Paul Naumoff	LB	6'1"	215	28		
Jim Teal	LB	6'3"	225	23		
Charlie Weaver	LB	6'2"	218	24	2	
Lem Barney	DB	6'	188	27	4	
Miller Farr	DB	6'1"	190	30	1	
Willie Germany	DB	6'	192	24		
Dick Jauron	DB	6'	190	22	4	6
Levi Johnson	DB	6'2"	190	22	5	
Jim Thrower	DB	6'2"	194	24		
Mike Weger	DB	6'2"	200	27	2	
Doug Wyatt	DB	6'1"	195	26		
Bill Cappleman	QB	6'3"	210	26		
Greg Landry	QB	6'2"	210	26		12
Bill Munson	QB	6'2"	210	31		
Mel Farr	HB	6'2"	210	28		24
Altie Taylor	HB	5'10"	200	25		30
Mickey Zofko	HB	6'3"	195	23		
Leon Crosswhite	FB	5'11"	225	21		
Jim Hooks	FB	6'2"	215	22		6
Steve Owens	FB	6'2"	215	25		18
Al Barnes	WR	6'1"	170	24		6
Ron Jessie	WR	6'	183	25		24
Earl McCullouch	WR	5'11"	175	27		6
Jim O'Brien	WR	6'	195	26		38
Larry Walton	WR	5'11"	180	26		30
John Hilton	TE	6'5"	225	31		6
Charlie Sanders	TE	6'4"	225	27		12
Errol Mann	K	6'	200	32		53
Herman Weaver	K	6'4"	210	24		

Wayne Rasmussen — Injury
Rudy Redmond — Injury

GREEN BAY PACKERS 5-7-2 Dan Devine

23	N. Y. JETS	7
13	DETROIT	13
3	Minnesota	11
16	N. Y. Giants	14
10	KANSAS CITY	10
7	Los Angeles	24
0	Detroit	34
17	CHICAGO	31
25	ST. LOUIS	21
24	New England	33
6	San Francisco	20
30	NEW ORLEANS	10
7	MINNESOTA	31
21	Chicago	0

Use Name	Pos.	Hgt	Wgt	Age	Int	Pts
Kent Branstetter	OT	6'3"	260	24		
Bill Hayhoe	OT	6'8"	258	26		
Dick Himes	OT	6'4"	244	27		
Mal Snider	OG-OT	6'4"	250	26		
Gale Gillingham	OG	6'3"	255	29		
Bill Lueck	OG	6'3"	235	27		
Keith Wortman	OG	6'2"	245	23		
Ken Bowman	C	6'3"	230	30		
Larry McCarren	C	6'3"	240	22		
Cal Withrow	C	6'	240	28		
Aaron Brown	DE	6'5"	270	29		
Dave Pureifory	DE	6'1"	260	23		
Alden Roche	DE	6'4"	255	28		
Clarence Williams	DE	6'5"	255	26		
Bob Brown	DT	6'5"	260	33		
Mike McCoy	DT	6'5"	284	24		
Carleton Oats	DT	6'2"	260	30		
Fred Carr	LB	6'5"	238	27		
Jim Carter	LB	6'3"	235	24	3	6
Larry Hefner	LB	6'2"	230	24	1	
Noel Jenke	LB	6'1"	225	26		
Tom MacLeod	LB	6'3"	220	22	2	
Tom Toner	LB	6'3"	225	23	1	
Hise Austin	DB	6'4"	195	22		
Willie Buchanan	DB	6'	190	22		
Ken Ellis	DB	5'10"	190	25	3	6
Charlie Hall	DB	6'1"	195	24		
Jim Hill	DB	6'2"	190	25	3	
Al Matthews	DB	5'11"	190	25	2	6
Perry Smith	DB	6'1"	195	22		
Ike Thomas	WR-DB	6'2"	193	25		
Jim Del Gaizo	QB	6'1"	198	26		6
Scott Hunter	QB	6'2"	205	25		6
Jerry Tagge	QB	6'2"	220	23		12
Don Highsmith	HB	6'	200	25		
Larry Krause	HB	6'	208	25		
MacArthur Lane	HB	6'2"	220	31		12
Ron McBride	HB	6'	200	24		
Les Goodman	FB-HB	5'11"	206	23		6
John Brockington	FB	6'1"	225	24		18
Perry Williams	FB	6'2"	220	26		6
Leland Glass	WR	6'	185	23		
Barry Smith	WR	6'1"	185	22		12
Jon Staggers	WR	5'10"	186	24		24
Paul Staroba	WR	6'3"	204	24		
Mike Donohoe	TE	6'3"	228	28		
Rich McGeorge	TE	6'4"	235	24		6
Chester Marcol	K	6'	190	24		82
Ron Widby	K	6'4"	220	28		

Bob Kroll — Injury

CHICAGO BEARS 3-11-0 Abe Gibron

17	DALLAS	20
13	MINNESOTA	22
33	Denver	14
16	New Orleans	21
6	Atlanta	46
10	NEW ENGLAND	13
35	HOUSTON	14
31	Green Bay	17
7	Kansas City	19
7	DETROIT	30
13	Minnesota	31
0	LOS ANGELES	26
7	Detroit	40
0	GREEN BAY	21

Use Name	Pos.	Hgt	Wgt	Age	Int	Pts
Lionel Antwine	OT	6'6"	255	23		
Bob Asher	OT	6'5"	250	25		
Randy Jackson	OT	6'5"	250	29		
Steve Kinney	OT	6'5"	255	24		
Glenn Holloway	OG	6'3"	255	24		
Ernie Janet	OG	6'4"	250	24		
Bob Newton	OG	6'4"	250	24		
Rich Coady	C	6'3"	235	28		
Willie Holman (to WAS)	DE	6'4"	250	28		
Gary Hrivnak	DE	6'5"	248	22		
Tony McGee	DE	6'4"	250	25		
Mel Tom (from PHI)	DE	6'4"	250	32		
Wally Chambers	DT	6'6"	250	22		
Dave Hale	DT	6'7"	255	26		
Jim Osborne	DT	6'3"	250	23		
Andy Rice	DT	6'3"	268	31		
Doug Buffone	LB	6'1"	225	29	3	
Dick Butkus	LB	6'3"	245	29	1	6
Gail Clark	LB	6'2"	227	22		
Jimmy Gunn	LB	6'1"	220	24		
Bob Pifferini	LB	6'2"	226	23		
Don Rives	LB	6'2"	215	22		
Adrian Young	LB	6'1"	232	27		
Craig Clemons	DB	5'11"	200	24	2	
Allan Ellis	DB	5'10"	185	22	1	
Charlie Ford	DB	6'3"	185	24	2	
Bob Jeter	DB	6'1"	200	35		
Garry Lyle	DB	6'2"	198	27	5	
Willie Roberts	DB	6'1"	190	25		
Joe Taylor	DB	6'2"	200	32		
Bobby Douglass	QB	6'3"	225	26		30
Gary Huff	QB	6'1"	200	22		
Carl Garrett	HB	5'11"	215	26		30
Joe Moore	HB	6'1"	205	24		
Reggie Sanderson	HB	5'10"	206	22		
Gary Kosins	FB-HB	6'1"	220	24		
Jim Harrison	FB	6'4"	235	24		18
Roger Lawson	HB-FB	6'2"	215	23		
George Farmer	WR	6'4"	214	25		6
Ike Hill	WR	5'10"	180	26		12
Dave Juenger	WR	6'1"	195	22		
Mike Reppond	WR	6'	180	22		
Tom Reynolds	WR	6'3"	200	24		
Cecil Turner	WR	5'10"	176	29		
Craig Cotton	TE	6'4"	222	26		
Bob Parsons	TE	6'4"	234	23		6
Earl Thomas	WR-TE	6'3"	215	24		24
Bobby Joe Green	K	5'11"	175	35		
Mac Percival	K	6'4"	220	33		28
Mirro Roder	K	6'1"	218	29		35

MINNESOTA VIKINGS

RUSHING

Last Name	No.	Yds	Avg	TD
Foreman	182	801	4.4	4
Reed	100	401	4.0	3
Marinaro	95	302	3.2	2
Osborn	48	216	4.5	0
B. Brown	47	206	4.4	3
Tarkenton	41	202	4.9	1
Gilliam	5	71	14.2	1
McClanahan	17	69	4.1	0
Berry	2	5	2.5	0
Voigt	1	2	2.0	0

RECEIVING

Last Name	No.	Yds	Avg	TD
Gilliam	42	907	22	8
Foreman	37	362	10	2
Marinaro	26	196	8	2
Voigt	23	318	14	2
Reed	19	122	6	0
Dale	14	192	14	0
B. Brown	5	22	4	1
Osborn	3	4	1	0
Lash	2	34	17	0
Kingsriter	2	27	14	0
Dawson	2	24	12	0
Ward	1	1	1	0

PUNT RETURNS

Last Name	No.	Yds	Avg	TD
Bryant	25	140	6	0
J. Wright	2	0	0	0
West	1	0	0	0

KICKOFF RETURNS

Last Name	No.	Yds	Avg	TD
McClanahan	16	410	26	0
Gilliam	10	174	17	0
West	3	104	35	0
B. Brown	3	35	12	0
Reed	2	29	15	0
J. Wright	1	0	0	0

PASSING – PUNTING – KICKING

PASSING

Last Name	Att	Comp	%	Yds	Yd/Att	TD	Int–%	RK
Tarkenton	274	169	62	2113	7.7	15	7–3	3
Berry	24	10	42	121	5.0	1	2–8	

PUNTING

Last Name	No.	Avg					
Eischeid	66	39.8					

KICKING

Last Name	XP	Att	%	FG	Att	%
Cox	33	33	100	21	35	60

DETROIT LIONS

RUSHING

Last Name	No.	Yds	Avg	TD
Taylor	176	719	4.1	5
Owens	113	401	3.5	3
Mel Farr	97	373	3.8	4
Landry	42	267	6.4	2
Hooks	19	110	5.8	0
L. Walton	4	74	18.5	1
Munson	10	33	3.3	0
Zofko	11	33	3.0	0
Jessie	5	31	6.2	1
Crosswhite	11	30	2.7	1
C. Walton	1	26	26.0	0
H. Weaver	1	18	18.0	0
McCullouch	2	12	6.0	0
Barney	2	9	4.5	0
C. Sanders	1	−1	−1.0	0
Cappleman	1	−2	−2.0	0

RECEIVING

Last Name	No.	Yds	Avg	TD
C. Sanders	28	433	15	2
Taylor	27	252	9	0
Mel Farr	26	183	7	0
Owens	24	232	10	2
L. Walton	21	302	14	4
Jessie	20	364	18	3
McCullouch	9	179	20	1
Hilton	6	70	12	1
Barnes	3	43	14	1
Zofko	2	16	8	0
O'Brien	2	14	7	0
C. Walton	1	7	7	0
Hooks	1	6	6	0
Crosswhite	1	4	4	0

PUNT RETURNS

Last Name	No.	Yds	Avg	TD
Barney	27	231	9	0
Jauron	6	49	8	0
L. Walton	1	9	9	0
Teal	1	0	0	0

KICKOFF RETURNS

Last Name	No.	Yds	Avg	TD
Jauron	17	405	24	0
Taylor	12	295	25	0
Jessie	6	154	26	0
Thrower	3	54	18	0
Hooks	2	52	26	0
Johnson	3	51	17	0
Barney	1	28	28	0
Jolley	1	15	15	0
Zofko	1	7	7	0
Barnes	1	0	0	0
Dennis	1	0	0	0
Germany	1	0	0	0
C. Weaver	1	0	0	0

PASSING – PUNTING – KICKING

PASSING

Last Name	Att	Comp	%	Yds	Yd/Att	TD	Int–%	RK
Munson	187	95	51	1129	6.0	9	8–4	12
Landry	128	70	55	908	7.1	3	10–8	
Cappleman	11	5	45	33	3.0	0	1–9	
Zofko	1	1	100	35	35.0	0	0–0	

PUNTING

Last Name	No.	Avg
H. Weaver	54	43.2

KICKING

Last Name	XP	Att	%	FG	Att	%
Mann	14	14	100	13	19	68
O'Brien	14	14	100	8	14	57

GREEN BAY PACKERS

RUSHING

Last Name	No.	Yds	Avg	TD
Brockington	265	1144	4.3	3
Lane	170	528	3.1	1
Goodman	18	88	4.9	1
P. Williams	32	87	2.7	1
Tagge	15	62	4.1	2
Staggers	4	33	8.3	1
Staroba	1	11	11.0	0
Krause	1	8	8.0	0
Highsmith	7	7	1.0	0
B. Smith	1	5	5.0	0
Hunter	8	3	0.4	1
Del Gaizo	4	1	0.3	0

RECEIVING

Last Name	No.	Yds	Avg	TD
Lane	27	255	9	1
Staggers	25	412	16	3
McGeorge	16	260	16	1
Brockington	16	128	8	0
B. Smith	15	233	16	2
Glass	11	119	11	0
P. Williams	5	44	9	0
Goodman	2	19	10	0
Staroba	1	23	23	0
Donohoe	1	10	10	0

PUNT RETURNS

Last Name	No.	Yds	Avg	TD
Staggers	19	90	5	0
Ellis	11	47	4	0

KICKOFF RETURNS

Last Name	No.	Yds	Avg	TD
Thomas	23	527	23	0
Ellis	12	319	27	0
Krause	11	244	22	0
Lane	2	31	16	0
P. Williams	1	24	24	0
A. Brown	2	19	10	0
Highsmith	1	18	18	0
B. Brown	1	7	7	0

PASSING – PUNTING – KICKING

PASSING

Last Name	Att	Comp	%	Yds	Yd/Att	TD	Int–%	RK
Tagge	106	56	53	720	6.8	2	7–7	
Hunter	84	35	42	442	5.3	2	4–5	
Del Gaizo	62	27	44	318	5.1	2	6–10	
Lane	2	1	50	23	11.5	1	0–0	
Brockington	1	0	0	0	0.0	0	0–0	

PUNTING

Last Name	No.	Avg
Widby	56	43.1
Staroba	12	31.1

KICKING

Last Name	XP	Att	%	FG	Att	%
Marcol	19	20	95	21	35	60

CHICAGO BEARS

RUSHING

Last Name	No.	Yds	Avg	TD
Garrett	175	655	3.7	5
Douglass	94	525	5.6	5
Harrison	100	374	3.7	1
Moore	58	191	3.3	0
Lawson	24	70	2.9	0
Kosins	24	65	2.7	0
Huff	11	22	2.0	0
Sanderson	3	8	2.7	0
Farmer	1	8	8.0	0
Thomas	1	5	5.0	0
Parsons	2	2	1.0	0
Hill	3	−14	−4.7	0

RECEIVING

Last Name	No.	Yds	Avg	TD
Thomas	24	343	14	4
Garrett	23	292	13	0
Harrison	21	200	10	2
Farmer	15	219	15	1
Cotton	13	186	14	0
Hill	10	119	12	0
Lawson	9	60	7	0
Reynolds	7	127	18	0
Sanderson	5	23	5	0
Kosins	4	8	2	0
Moore	3	17	6	0
Parsons	2	23	12	1

PUNT RETURNS

Last Name	No.	Yds	Avg	TD
Hill	36	204	6	1
Moore	1	0	0	0

KICKOFF RETURNS

Last Name	No.	Yds	Avg	TD
Hill	27	637	24	1
Garrett	16	486	30	0
Turner	8	127	16	0
Sanderson	2	44	22	0
Cotton	2	15	8	0
Parsons	2	15	8	0
Holloway	1	8	8	0
Osborne	1	0	0	0
Thomas	0	12	0	0

PASSING – PUNTING – KICKING

PASSING

Last Name	Att	Comp	%	Yds	Yd/Att	TD	Int–%	RK
Douglass	174	81	47	1057	6.1	5	7–4	13
Huff	126	54	43	525	4.2	3	8–6	
Garrett	1	0	0	0	0.0	0	0–0	
Hill	1	1	100	35	35.0	0	0–0	
Thomas	1	0	0	0	0.0	0	1–100	

PUNTING

Last Name	No.	Avg
Green	82	40.5
Parsons	4	26.5

KICKING

Last Name	XP	Att	%	FG	Att	%
Roder	11	12	92	8	16	50
Percival	10	10	100	6	8	75

LOS ANGELES RAMS 12-2-0 Chuck Knox

Scores of Each Game		
23	Kansas City	13
31	ATLANTA	0
40	San Francisco	20
31	Houston	26
37	DALLAS	31
24	GREEN BAY	7
9	Minnesota	10
13	Atlanta	15
29	NEW ORLEANS	7
31	SAN FRANCISCO	13
24	New Orleans	13
26	Chicago	0
40	N. Y. GIANTS	6
30	CLEVELAND	17

Use Name	Pos.	Hgt	Wgt	Age	Int	Pts
Charley Cowan	OT	6'4"	265	35		
Harry Schuh	OT	6'2"	260	30		
John Williams	OT	6'3"	256	27		
Tom Mack	OG	6'3"	250	29		
Joe Scibelli	OG	6'1"	255	34		
Rich Saul	C-OG	6'3"	235	25		
Ken Iman	C	6'1"	240	34		
Fred Dryer	DE	6'6"	240	27		
Jack Youngblood	DE	6'4"	250	23		
Larry Brooks	DT	6'3"	255	23		
Bill Nelson	DT	6'7"	270	25		
Merlin Olsen	DT	6'5"	270	32		
Phil Olsen	DT	6'5"	265	25		

Use Name	Pos.	Hgt	Wgt	Age	Int	Pts
Ken Geddes	LB	6'3"	235	25		
Rick Kay	LB	6'4"	235	23		
Jack Reynolds	LB	6'1"	232	25	2	
Isiah Robertson	LB	6'3"	225	24	3	6
Bob Stein	LB	6'2"	235	25	1	
Jim Youngblood	LB	6'3"	240	23	1	
Cullen Bryant	DB	6'1"	210	22		6
Al Clark	DB	6'	180	25	1	
Dave Elmendorf	DB	6'1"	195	24	1	
Eddie McMillan	DB	6'	180	21	4	
Steve Preece	DB	6'1"	195	26	2	6
Charlie Stukes	DB	6'3"	212	29	5	
Bill Drake	WR-DB	6'1"	195	23		

Use Name	Pos.	Hgt	Wgt	Age	Int	Pts
John Hadl	QB	6'2"	214	33		
James Harris	QB	6'3"	210	26		
Jim Bertelsen	HB	5'11"	205	23		30
Lawrence McCutcheon	HB	6'1"	205	23		30
Rob Scribner	HB	6'	200	22		
Larry Smith	HB	6'3"	220	25		12
Tony Baker	FB	5'11"	225	28		42
Les Josephson	FB	6'	207	30		12
Dick Gordon (to GB)	WR	5'11"	190	28		
Harold Jackson	WR	5'10"	175	27		78
David Ray	WR	6'	195	28		130
Rod Sherman	WR	6'	190	28		
Jack Snow	WR	6'2"	190	30		12
Joe Sweet	WR	6'2"	196	25		
Pat Curran	TE	6'3"	238	27		
Bob Klein	TE	6'5"	235	26		12
Dave Chapple	K	6'	180	26		

ATLANTA FALCONS 9-5-0 Norm Van Brocklin

Scores of Each Game		
62	New Orleans	7
0	Los Angeles	31
6	Detroit	31
9	SAN FRANCISCO	13
46	CHICAGO	6
41	San Diego	0
17	San Francisco	3
15	LOS ANGELES	13
44	Philadelphia	27
20	MINNESOTA	14
28	N. Y. Jets	20
6	BUFFALO	17
10	ST. LOUIS	32
14	NEW ORLEANS	10

Use Name	Pos.	Hgt	Wgt	Age	Int	Pts
Nick Bebout	OT	6'5"	260	22		
Len Gotshalk	OT	6'2"	260	23		
George Kunz	OT	6'5"	268	26		
Bill Sandeman	OT	6'6"	265	30		
Dennis Havig	OG	6'2"	256	24		
Andy Maurer	OG	6'3"	247	24		
Ted Fritsch	C	6'2"	240	23		
Jeff Van Note	C	6'2"	247	27		
Claude Humphrey	DE	6'5"	265	29	1	
Greg Marx	DE	6'4"	260	23		
John Zook	DE	6'5"	250	25		
Mike Lewis	DT	6'3"	260	24		
Rosie Manning	DT	6'5"	256	23		
Mike Tilleman	DT	6'5"	278	29		
Chuck Walker	DT	6'2"	260	32	1	

Use Name	Pos.	Hgt	Wgt	Age	Int	Pts
Duane Benson	LB	6'2"	215	28		
Greg Brezina	LB	6'2"	226	27	3	
Don Hansen	LB	6'3"	228	29	1	
Ken Mitchell	LB	6'1"	224	25		
Tommy Nobis	LB	6'2"	243	29		
Lonnie Warwick	LB	6'2"	240	31		
Ray Brown	DB	6'2"	202	24	6	
Ray Easterling	DB	6'	195	23		
Clarence Ellis	DB	5'11"	190	23	2	
Tom Hayes	DB	6'1"	198	27	4	12
Rolland Lawrence	DB	5'10"	180	22	1	
Tony Plummer	DB	5'11"	188	26	1	6
Ken Reaves	DB	6'3"	210	28	2	

Use Name	Pos.	Hgt	Wgt	Age	Int	Pts
Bob Lee	QB	6'2"	195	28		
Dick Shiner (to NE)	QB	6'	195	31		
Pat Sullivan	QB	6'	200	23		
Dave Hampton	HB	6'	210	26		30
Joe Washington	HB	5'9"	180	22		
Eddie Ray	FB	6'1"	240	26		66
Art Malone	FB	5'11"	216	25		18
Harmon Wages	FB	6'1"	212	27		6
Ken Burrow	WR	6'	190	25		42
Wes Chesson	WR	6'2"	195	24		6
Al Dodd	WR	6'	178	28		
Tom Geredine	WR	6'2"	195	23		6
Louis Neal	WR	6'4"	215	22		6
Larry Mialik	TE	6'2"	226	23		
Jim Mitchell	TE	6'2"	236	25		
John James	K	6'3"	197	24		
Nick Mike-Mayer	K	5'8"	186	23		112

SAN FRANCISCO FORTY-NINERS 5-9-0 Dick Nolan

Scores of Each Game		
13	Miami	21
36	Denver	34
20	LOS ANGELES	40
13	Atlanta	9
13	MINNESOTA	17
40	NEW ORLEANS	0
3	ATLANTA	17
20	Detroit	30
9	Washington	33
13	Los Angeles	31
20	GREEN BAY	6
38	PHILADELPHIA	28
10	New Orleans	16
14	PITTSBURGH	37

Use Name	Pos.	Hgt	Wgt	Age	Int	Pts
Cas Banaszek	OT	6'3"	250	27		
Len Rohde	OT	6'4"	248	35		
John Watson	OG-OT	6'4"	248	24		
Randy Beisler	OG	6'4"	244	28		
Ed Hardy	OG	6'4"	242	21		
Woody Peoples	OG	6'2"	250	30		
Forrest Blue	C	6'5"	260	27		
Jean Barrett	OT-C	6'6"	254	22		
Bill Belk	DE	6'3"	242	27		
Cedrick Hardman	DE	6'3"	255	24	2	
Tommy Hart	DE	6'3"	248	28		
Bob Hoskins	DT	6'2"	250	27		
Charlie Krueger	DT	6'4"	254	37		
Rolf Krueger	DT	6'4"	253	26		

Use Name	Pos.	Hgt	Wgt	Age	Int	Pts
Willie Harper	LB	6'2"	215	23		
Charlie Hunt	LB	6'2"	212	22		
Frank Nunley	LB	6'2"	230	27	1	
Dave Olerich	LB	6'1"	220	28		
Jim Sniadecki	LB	6'2"	228	26	1	
Skip Vanderbundt	LB	6'3"	224	26	1	
Dave Wilcox	LB	6'3"	234	30	2	
Windlan Hall	DB	5'11"	175	23	1	12
Jim Johnson	DB	6'2"	188	35	4	
Ralph McGill	DB	5'11"	186	24		
Mel Phillips	DB	6'	190	31	1	
Mike Simpson	DB	5'11"	170	26		
Bruce Taylor	DB	6'	180	25	6	

Terry Beasley — Shoulder Injury

Use Name	Pos.	Hgt	Wgt	Age	Int	Pts
John Brodie	QB	6'1"	203	38		6
Joe Reed	QB	6'1"	192	25		
Steve Spurrier	QB	6'2"	200	28		12
Dave Atkins	HB	6'1"	202	24		6
Doug Cunningham	HB	5'11"	195	27		6
Jimmy Thomas	HB	6'1"	214	26		6
Vic Washington	HB	5'10"	196	27		48
Ken Willard	FB	6'2"	220	30		12
Randy Jackson	HB-FB	6'	220	24		
Larry Schreiber	HB-FB	6'	210	26		
Dan Abramowicz (from NO)	WR	6'1"	195	28		6
Ed Beverly	WR	5'11"	168	23		
John Isenbarger	WR	6'3"	196	25		
Gene Washington	WR	6'1"	185	26		12
Ted Kwalick	TE	6'4"	226	26		30
Dick Witcher	TE	6'3"	204	28		
Bruce Gossett	K	6'2"	228	30		104
Tom Wittum	K	6'1"	185	23		

NEW ORLEANS SAINTS 5-9-0 John North

Scores of Each Game		
7	ATLANTA	62
3	Dallas	40
10	Baltimore	14
21	CHICAGO	16
20	DETROIT	13
0	San Francisco	40
19	WASHINGTON	3
13	BUFFALO	0
7	Los Angeles	29
14	San Diego	17
13	LOS ANGELES	24
10	Green Bay	30
16	SAN FRANCISCO	10
10	Atlanta	14

Use Name	Pos.	Hgt	Wgt	Age	Int	Pts
Paul Ferson	OT	6'5"	260	23		
Carl Johnson	OT	6'3"	255	23		
Don Morrison	OT	6'5"	255	23		
Craig Robinson	OT	6'5"	250	24		
Jake Kupp	OG	6'3"	248	31		
Royce Smith	OG	6'3"	245	24		
Del Williams	OG	6'2"	240	27		
John Didion	C	6'4"	245	25		
Steve Baumgartner	DE	6'7"	260	22		
Andy Dorris	DE	6'4"	230	22		
Billy Newsome	DE	6'4"	250	26	1	
Joe Owens	DE	6'2"	245	25	1	
Derland Moore	DT	6'4"	260	21	1	
Bob Pollard	DT	6'3"	245	24		
Elex Price	DT	6'3"	260	23		

Use Name	Pos.	Hgt	Wgt	Age	Int	Pts
Wayne Colman	LB	6'1"	230	27		
Bob Creech	LB	6'2"	228	24		
Joe Federspiel	LB	6'1"	225	23	1	
Willie Hall	LB	6'2"	225	23		
Ray Hester	LB	6'2"	215	24		
Rick Kingrea	LB	6'1"	233	24		
Dale Lindsey	LB	6'3"	225	30		
Jim Merlo	LB	6'2"	220	21	3	
Dick Palmer	LB	6'2"	232	25		
Mike Fink	DB	5'11"	180	22		
Johnny Fuller	DB	6'	185	27	1	
Ernie Jackson	DB	5'10"	175	23	3	
Bivian Lee	DB	6'3"	200	25	3	
Jerry Moore	DB	6'3"	208	23		
Tom Myers	DB	5'11"	184	22	3	
Nate Ramsey	DB	6'1"	200	32		

Ron Billingsley — Injury
Hugo Hollas — Knee Injury

Use Name	Pos.	Hgt	Wgt	Age	Int	Pts
Bob Davis	QB	6'3"	205	27		
Archie Manning	QB	6'3"	215	24		12
Bobby Scott	QB	6'1"	200	24		
Henry Matthews	HB	6'3"	203	24		
Joe Profit (from ATL)	HB	6'	213	24		12
Howard Stevens	HB	5'5"	175	23		12
Jess Phillips	FB-HB	6'1"	210	26		
Bill Butler	FB	6'	210	23		18
Odell Lawson	FB	6'2"	205	25		
Lincoln Minor	HB-FB	6'2"	211	23		
Jubilee Dunbar	WR	6'	196	26		24
Freddie Hyatt	WR	6'3"	200	27		
Bob Newland	WR	6'2"	190	24		24
Preston Riley	WR	6'	180	25		
Speedy Thomas	WR	6'1"	170	26		
Doug Winslow	WR	5'11"	180	22		
Bert Askson	TE	6'3"	220	27		
John Beasley (from MIN)	TE	6'3"	228	28		12
Bob Brown	TE	6'3"	225	30		
Len Garrett (from GB)	TE	6'3"	230	24		
Mike Kelly	TE	6'4"	215	25		
Happy Feller	K	5'11"	185	24		19
Bill McClard	K	5'10"	202	21		48
Steve O'Neal	K	6'3"	185	27		

LOS ANGELES RAMS

RUSHING

Last Name	No.	Yds	Avg	TD
McCutcheon	210	1097	5.2	2
Bertelsen	206	854	4.1	4
Baker	85	344	4.0	7
Smith	79	291	3.7	2
Josephson	36	174	4.8	2
Scribner	20	109	5.5	0
Harris	4	29	7.3	0
Gordon	2	15	7.5	0
Preece	1	11	11.0	1
Hadl	14	5	0.4	0
Chapple	1	0	0.0	0
Jackson	2	−8	−4.0	0

RECEIVING

Last Name	No.	Yds	Avg	TD
Jackson	40	874	22	13
McCutcheon	30	289	10	3
Klein	21	277	13	2
Bertelsen	19	267	14	1
Snow	16	252	16	2
Smith	10	65	7	0
Curran	5	56	11	1
Scribner	2	19	10	0
Sherman	1	8	8	0

PUNT RETURNS

Last Name	No.	Yds	Avg	TD
Bertelsen	26	259	10	0
Elmendorf	22	187	9	0
Scribner	3	32	11	0

KICKOFF RETURNS

Last Name	No.	Yds	Avg	TD
Bryant	13	369	28	1
Scribner	11	314	29	0
Clark	2	80	40	0
Gordon	3	68	23	0
Curran	1	24	24	0
Elmendorf	2	23	12	0
Smith	1	16	16	0
Bertelsen	1	15	15	0
McCutcheon	1	6	6	0
Klein	1	0	0	0

PASSING – PUNTING – KICKING

PASSING	Att	Comp	%	Yds	Yd/Att	TD	Int−%	RK
Hadl	258	135	52	2008	7.8	22	11− 4	5
Harris	11	7	64	68	6.2	0	0 − 0	
Smith	2	2	100	31	15.5	0	0 − 0	

PUNTING	No	Avg
Chapple	51	40.8

KICKING	XP	Att	%	FG	Att	%
Ray	40	42	95	30	47	64

ATLANTA FALCONS

RUSHING

Last Name	No.	Yds	Avg	TD
Hampton	263	997	3.8	4
Ray	96	434	4.5	9
Malone	76	336	4.4	2
Lee	29	67	2.3	0
Wages	18	47	2.6	1
Washington	4	36	9.0	0
J. Mitchell	5	34	6.8	0
Sullivan	3	19	6.3	0
Burrow	2	17	8.5	0
Shiner	3	−2	−0.7	0
Geredine	1	−3	−3.0	0

RECEIVING

Last Name	No.	Yds	Avg	TD
J. Mitchell	32	420	13	0
Burrow	31	567	18	7
Hampton	25	273	11	1
Dodd	19	291	15	0
Ray	19	192	10	2
Malone	19	177	9	1
Geredine	12	231	19	1
Neal	5	131	26	1
Chesson	2	36	18	1
Mialik	2	30	15	0
Wages	2	14	7	0

PUNT RETURNS

Last Name	No.	Yds	Avg	TD
Brown	40	360	9	0
Dodd	8	69	9	0

KICKOFF RETURNS

Last Name	No.	Yds	Avg	TD
Washington	20	432	22	0
Hampton	11	258	23	0
Geredine	9	211	23	0
Plummer	5	115	23	0
Lawrence	3	71	24	0
Benson	3	20	7	0
Wages	1	0	0	0

PASSING – PUNTING – KICKING

PASSING	Att	Comp	%	Yds	Yd/Att	TD	Int−%	RK
Lee	230	120	52	1786	7.8	10	8 − 3	7
Shiner	68	36	53	432	6.4	3	4 − 6	
Sullivan	26	14	54	175	6.7	1	0 − 0	

PUNTING	No	Avg
James	63	42.6

KICKING	XP	Att	%	FG	Att	%
Mike-Mayer	34	34	100	26	38	68

SAN FRANCISCO FORTY-NINERS

RUSHING

Last Name	No.	Yds	Avg	TD
V. Washington	151	543	3.5	8
Willard	83	366	4.4	1
Thomas	56	259	4.6	1
Cunningham	44	165	3.8	1
Schreiber	42	163	3.9	0
Reed	15	85	5.7	0
Wittum	1	63	63.0	0
Kwalick	5	37	7.4	0
Spurrier	9	32	3.6	2
Atkins	4	19	4.8	1
Brodie	5	16	3.2	1
Jackson	6	10	1.7	0
Isenbarger	1	−6	−6.0	0

RECEIVING

Last Name	No.	Yds	Avg	TD
Kwalick	47	729	16	5
G. Washington	37	606	16	2
Abramowicz	37	460	12	1
V. Washington	33	238	7	0
Willard	22	160	7	1
Thomas	19	157	8	0
Cunningham	15	118	8	0
Schreiber	12	98	8	0
Isenbarger	10	67	7	0
Jackson	1	20	20	0
Witcher	1	13	13	0
Atkins	1	−3	−3	0

PUNT RETURNS

Last Name	No.	Yds	Avg	TD
Taylor	15	207	14	0
McGill	22	186	8	0

KICKOFF RETURNS

Last Name	No.	Yds	Avg	TD
V. Washington	24	549	23	0
McGill	17	374	22	0
Cunningham	8	173	22	0
Atkins	3	93	31	0
Thomas	5	81	16	0
Olerich	2	17	9	0
Hall	1	14	14	0
Simpson	1	0	0	0
Sniadecki	1	0	0	0
Willard	1	0	0	0

PASSING – PUNTING – KICKING

PASSING	Att	Comp	%	Yds	Yd/Att	TD	Int−%	RK
Brodie	194	98	51	1126	5.8	3	12− 6	15
Spurrier	157	83	53	882	5.6	4	7 − 4	14
Reed	114	51	45	589	5.2	2	6 − 5	
Isenbarger	1	1	100	48	48.0	0	0 − 0	

PUNTING	No	Avg
Wittum	79	43.7

KICKING	XP	Att	%	FG	Att	%
Gossett	26	26	100	26	33	79

NEW ORLEANS SAINTS

RUSHING

Last Name	No.	Yds	Avg	TD
Phillips	198	663	3.3	0
Butler	87	348	4.0	1
Profit	90	329	3.7	2
Manning	63	293	4.7	2
Stevens	45	183	4.1	2
Lawson	6	23	3.8	0
Scott	9	18	2.0	0
Davis	3	10	3.3	0
Minor	3	10	3.3	0
Myers	1	8	8.0	0
Newland	1	6	6.0	0
Matthews	4	4	1.0	0
Dunbar	3	3	1.0	0
O'Neal	2	−1	−0.5	0

RECEIVING

Last Name	No.	Yds	Avg	TD
Beasley	32	283	9	2
Newland	29	489	17	4
Dunbar	23	447	19	4
Phillips	22	169	8	0
Butler	19	125	7	2
Brown	11	132	12	0
Profit	11	108	10	0
Winslow	4	45	11	0
Stevens	4	39	10	0
Garrett	2	30	15	0
Matthews	2	19	10	0
Lawson	2	−5	−3	0
Minor	1	5	5	0

PUNT RETURNS

Last Name	No.	Yds	Avg	TD
Stevens	17	171	10	0
Winslow	5	47	9	0

KICKOFF RETURNS

Last Name	No.	Yds	Avg	TD
Stevens	26	590	23	0
Profit	8	144	18	0
Lawson	7	118	17	0
Fink	5	81	16	0
Moore	1	14	14	0
Jackson	1	0	0	0

PASSING – PUNTING – KICKING

PASSING	Att	Comp	%	Yds	Yd/Att	TD	Int−%	RK
Manning	267	140	52	1642	6.2	10	12− 4	10
Scott	54	18	33	245	4.5	1	3 − 6	
Davis	17	5	29	14	0.8	0	2 −12	

PUNTING	No	Avg
O'Neal	81	41.7

KICKING	XP	Att	%	FG	Att	%
McClard	9	9	100	13	24	54
Feller	7	7	100	4	12	33

1973 A.F.C. The Runningest Buffalo

Just as baseball fans had spent the year counting Hank Aaron's home runs as he closed in on Babe Ruth's one-year home run mark, football fans added up O. J. Simpson's rushing yardage week by week as he went after Jimmy Brown's one-year rushing mark of 1,863 yards. Simpson, the main ingredient in the Buffalo offense, excited the football world by running for a record 250 yards on opening day against New England. After seven games, he already had gained 1,000 yards, a goal coveted by runners for an entire season. With two games left on the schedule, O. J. had 1,584 yards and needed two good days to break the record. A good day of 219 yards against New England put him within shouting distance of the record. Needing 61 yards to set a new mark, Simpson quickly broke the record in the season's finale in cold, rainy New York. With a workhorse performance the rest of the day, he became the first runner ever to gain 2,000 yards in one season.

EASTERN DIVISION

Miami Dolphins—The Dolphins were aiming at a second perfect season, but a tough 12-7 loss to Oakland in their second game brought an end to those hopes. But the Dolphins still had the cold, hard precision and flawless execution which made them the class of professional football. The offense still had Griese, Csonka, Warfield, Little, Langer, and company; the defense boasted of Stanfill, Buoniconti, Anderson, Scott, and the rest of the No Name Defense. Coach Don Shula again made sure that his players were hungry, and except for the loss to Oakland and a 16-3 upset by the Colts after Miami had clinched the Eastern crown, the Dolphins came close to another flawless season.

Buffalo Bills—When O. J. Simpson faced the reporters after breaking Jimmy Brown's single-season rushing mark, he began the meeting by introducing the offensive linemen one by one. They included Mike Montler, Reggie MacKenzie, Donnie Green, Dave Foley, and rookies Joe DeLamielleure and Paul Seymour. They were the reasons for O. J.'s success, so he figured they deserved to share in the glory. Simpson was not the entire story of the Bills' surge to a 9-5 record and second place in the East. Rookie quarterback Joe Ferguson played well, although his main task was handing off to Simpson. J. D. Hill and Bob Chandler gave the team a pair of fine wide receivers, and another receiver, Dwight Harrison, was converted into a starter in the secondary. Earl Edwards came from the '49ers in a trade and beefed up the front line of the defense.

New England Patriots—The defense could not stop a strong running attack, and good clubs simply cranked the yardage out against the Patriots on the ground. O. J. Simpson, for instance, enjoyed his two most productive days of his record season against New England. But even with the defensive problems, coach Chuck Fairbanks' first season was successful because of the fine rookie class the Patriots fielded. Guard John Hannah strengthened the blocking, Darryl Stingley won a starting wide-receiver job, Sam Cunningham added power to the running game, and little Mack Herron excited people on kick returns. Veteran receiver Reggie Rucker provided a bonus by developing into a star, but the kicking game still bothered the Pats, as rookie Jeff White booted a punt for -6 yards in one game and missed an extra point and an 18-yard field goal in a 24-23 loss to Philadelphia.

New York Jets—Weeb Ewbank's final year as head coach before retirement degenerated into a dismal 4-10 season. The defense played well through the campaign, but the offensive unit suffered from age, injury, and turmoil. Flanker Don Maynard was cut in the pre-season, while fullback John Riggins did not sign a contract until just before opening day and never did reach his best form. The offensive line slipped in its pass protection, exposing the Jet quarterbacks to enemy tacklers. Joe Namath went out of action with an injured shoulder against the Colts on September 23, and Al Woodall followed him onto the disabled list two weeks later to leave rookie free-agent Bill Demory as the team's only quarterback.

Baltimore Colts—A thorough housecleaning had swept out many veterans of recent years, as new head coach Howard Schnellenberger suffered through a 4-10 season in which few of his personnel shifts worked out very well. Second-year runner Lydell Mitchell did star in the backfield, but the offense was hurt by ex-Raider tight end Ray Chester's poor showing and by a confused quarterback situation. Rookie Bert Jones began the year as the starter, but veteran Marty Domres took over the position over the back part of the schedule; neither name could ignite much of a passing attack. The Colts enjoyed one moment of glory by beating the Dolphins late in the year.

CENTRAL DIVISION

Cincinnati Bengals—The maturing of quarterback Ken Anderson and the addition of three talented rookies brought the Cincinnati offense up to the level of its topnotch defensive unit. With experience improving his poise, Anderson calmly executed the plays called by coach Paul Brown via messenger guards. Giving Brown and Anderson more to work with were rookies Isaac Curtis, Bobby Clark, and Lenvil Elliott, three swift and powerful freshmen. Curtis gave the Bengals a deep threat at wide receiver, while Clark provided power in the backfield

to go along with the speed of veteran Eassex Johnson. When injuries slowed up these two runners late in the season, Elliott broke into the lineup with a flair. The Bengal defense had been solid all along, so the team stormed into first place with a strong finish.

Pittsburgh Steelers—The Pittsburgh offense kept raking in points despite constant injuries to key players. Fullback Franco Harris missed the early going with a bad knee, and by the time he got back into action, halfback Frenchy Fuqua went out with a broken collarbone. Quarterback Terry Bradshaw starred until he suffered a shoulder separation in mid-season; Terry Hanratty then stepped in and kept the attack rolling until injured ribs put him out of commission. With third-stringer Joe Gilliam at quarterback, the Steelers rose up and beat the Washington Redskins 21-16. The defense turned in strong performances week after week, with Joe Greene, L. C. Greenwood, Andy Russell, Jack Ham, and Mike Wagner all candidates for All-Pro honors as the Steelers again made it to the playoffs.

Cleveland Browns—Age had turned the Browns into a mediocre team that finished third in the AFC Central Division. The Cleveland offensive unit especially creaked, with the line laboring under the weight of three thirty-three-year-old members. Fullback Bo Scott's injury and quarterback Mike Phipps' slower-than-expected development further slowed the attack, and the Browns' two first-round draft picks were of very little help. Receiver Steve Holden spent most of the season on the bench, while guard Pete Adams passed his rookie season on the disabled list. The Cleveland defense, however, held together well, aided immensely by ex-Charger Bob Babich's work at middle linebacker, and the Browns posted a winning record.

Houston Oilers—The Oilers had given coach Bill Peterson what was described as a "lifetime" pact to join the team in 1972, but his lifetime as Houston head coach ran out after five games of this season. With Peterson's two-year record at 1-18 after five straight losses this year, general manager Sid Gillman stepped out of the front office to take over as head coach. Hoping to recapture the magic of his years at San Diego, Gillman headed the Oilers for the remainder of the season, but could only manage one victory.

WESTERN DIVISION

Oakland Raiders—The Raiders failed to score a touchdown in their first three games, so coach John Madden decided to bench quarterback Daryle Lamonica and replace him with lefty Ken Stabler. Whereas Lamonica excelled at throwing the long pass, Stabler thrived on running the ball-control offense preferred by coach Madden. With two strong runners in Marv Hubbard and Charlie Smith, two sure-handed receivers in Fred Biletnikoff and Mike Siani, and a superb front line, Stabler found many assets to manipulate in the Oakland attack. The defense had lots of old assets and one big addition in ex-Colt Bubba Smith. The Raider defense kept the team in the Western race early in the year, and the offense came through in victories over Kansas City and Denver in December to win first place and a playoff berth.

Denver Broncos—Bronco fans were amazed to find their club in the fight for first place all season long. In two years on the job, coach John Ralston had built a fine offense around the passing of veteran Charley Johnson and the running of star Floyd Little, with a solid line supporting both the air and ground games. The defense added two stand-out rookies in end Barney Chavous and cornerback Calvin Jones, and veteran tackle Paul Smith sparked the squad with his All-Pro performance at rushing enemy passers. On the last day of the season the Broncos faced Oakland in a face-to-face duel for the Western title. Trailing 14-10 in the fourth quarter, the Broncos gambled on a fake punt play on fourth down. Bill Van Heusen did not gain the needed yards. The Raiders took the ball over and scored a touchdown as the Broncos had to settle for second place in their first winning season ever.

Kansas City Chiefs—After a poor pre-season, the Kansas City defense played with its accustomed vigor in the regular season, but the offense had problems generating any steam at all. Veteran quarterback Len Dawson suffered from a variety of small hurts which kept him out of the lineup much of the time, and substitute Pete Beathard, in his second tour of duty in Kansas City, could not get the attack moving in early season trials. Coach Hank Stram finally turned to Mickey Livingston, who brought the offense back to life, and the Chiefs suddenly were in first place in late November. A 14-10 loss to Denver, however, knocked them out of first place, and a 37-7 beating at the hands of the Raiders ended any playoffs hopes for this year.

San Diego Chargers—The Chargers' attempt to regain respectability by bringing in old, established players failed miserably this year. Quarterback Johnny Unitas had little zip left in his arm after seventeen years with the Colts, and he wound up on the bench watching rookie Dan Fouts lead the attack. An injury to receiver Gary Garrison further hurt the offense, and coach Harland Svare unexplainedly benched runner Mike Garrett early in the season. Morale on the club plunged, and when receiver Dave Williams was released in mid-season, he called the team "a zoo." Svare resigned as coach after eight games to concentrate on front-office duties as general manager, turning over the reigns to assistant Ron Waller.

FINAL TEAM STATISTICS

(Other statistics not available at press time)

OFFENSE

	BALT.	BUFF.	CIN.	CLEV.	DENV.	HOUS.	K.C.	MIAMI	N.ENG.	N.Y.	OAK.	PITT.	S.D.
FIRST DOWNS:													
Total	218	219	252	200	253	193	208	215	237	222	**288**	217	198
by Rushing	121	**152**	124	107	111	89	106	111	97	95	129	111	88
by Passing	79	60	108	79	127	93	93	91	122	109	**139**	89	93
by Penalty	18	7	**20**	14	15	11	9	13	18	18	**20**	17	17
RUSHING:													
Number	536	**605**	515	506	487	386	511	507	454	453	547	555	431
Yards	2031	**3088**	2236	1968	1954	1388	1793	2521	1612	1864	2510	2143	1814
Average Yards	3.8	**5.1**	4.3	3.9	4.0	3.6	3.5	5.0	3.6	4.1	4.6	3.9	4.2
Touchdowns	9	**20**	13	12	16	9	11	16	15	7	14	12	9
PASSING:													
Attempts	300	213	332	308	378	**411**	313	256	380	373	353	309	363
Completions	137	96	180	152	196	**225**	173	133	195	181	205	140	161
Completion Percentage	45.7	45.1	54.2	49.4	51.9	54.7	55.3	52.0	51.3	48.5	**58.1**	45.3	44.4
Passing Yards	1746	1236	2439	1741	**2706**	2370	2039	1675	2581	2353	2611	2157	2129
Avg. Yards per Attempt	5.8	5.8	7.3	5.7	7.2	5.8	6.5	6.5	6.8	6.3	**7.4**	7.0	5.9
Avg. Yards per Complet.	12.7	12.9	13.6	11.5	13.8	10.5	11.8	12.6	13.2	13.0	12.7	**15.4**	13.2
Times Tackled Passing	32	31	24	45	27	43	39	**13**	37	37	45	30	37
Yards Lost Tackled	271	239	163	368	187	451	296	**93**	350	297	348	230	321
Net Yards	1475	997	2276	1373	**2519**	1919	1743	1582	2231	2056	2263	1927	1808
Touchdowns	14	4	18	10	**22**	11	10	17	13	16	16	20	9
Interceptions	25	14	**12**	20	20	27	13	**12**	17	22	18	26	30
Percent Intercepted	8.3	6.6	**3.6**	6.5	5.3	6.6	4.2	4.7	4.5	5.9	5.1	8.4	8.3
PUNTS:													
Number	62	66	68	82	69	**85**	80	48	61	74	69	62	72
Average Distance	38.7	40.3	41.0	40.5	45.1	38.8	**45.5**	42.3	37.7	37.1	45.3	41.1	41.1
PUNT RETURNS:													
Number	24	32	45	36	40	30	42	37	33	27	46	**52**	33
Yards	129	279	333	308	404	227	279	382	324	165	344	**416**	408
Average Yards	5.4	8.7	7.4	8.6	10.1	7.6	6.6	10.3	9.8	6.1	7.5	8.0	**12.4**
Touchdowns	0	1	0	0	0	0	0	0	0	0	1	0	**2**
KICKOFF RETURNS:													
Number	60	42	39	49	36	**76**	31	24	57	52	39	40	70
Yards	1343	972	876	1084	793	**1799**	725	523	1372	1061	937	843	1597
Average Yards	22.4	23.1	22.5	22.1	22.0	23.7	23.4	21.8	**24.1**	20.4	24.0	21.1	22.8
Touchdowns	1	**2**	0	0	0	1	0	0	1	1	0	0	0
INTERCEPTION RETURNS:													
Number	15	14	18	12	14	17	21	21	13	19	17	**37**	16
Yards	116	224	166	202	220	298	328	335	105	288	162	**673**	205
Average Yards	7.7	16.0	9.2	16.8	15.7	17.5	15.6	16.0	8.1	15.2	9.5	**18.2**	12.8
Touchdowns	1	1	0	1	2	0	1	2	0	2	0	**3**	1
PENALTIES:													
Number	57	75	83	70	83	**95**	83	52	50	62	82	84	74
Yards	483	744	799	620	745	**900**	797	416	550	575	759	817	628
FUMBLES:													
Number	**16**	27	25	34	21	43	36	22	51	32	29	36	41
Number Lost	13	13	14	17	**9**	25	18	16	25	17	16	14	21
POINTS:													
Total	226	259	286	234	**354**	199	231	343	258	240	292	347	188
PAT Attempts	26	28	32	24	**41**	22	23	38	31	27	32	37	22
PAT Made	22	28	31	24	**40**	22	21	38	25	27	31	36	20
FG Attempts	28	30	31	31	33	24	38	37	29	24	33	**43**	27
FG Made	16	21	21	22	22	15	24	25	15	17	23	**29**	12
Percent FG Made	57.1	70.0	67.7	**71.0**	66.7	62.5	63.2	67.6	51.7	70.8	69.7	67.4	44.4
Safeties	0	0	0	0	**1**	0	0	**1**	**1**	0	0	**1**	0

DEFENSE

	BALT.	BUFF.	CIN.	CLEV.	DENV.	HOUS.	K.C.	MIAMI	N.ENG.	N.Y.	OAK.	PITT.	S.D.
FIRST DOWNS:													
Total	243	231	219	196	239	274	209	195	215	226	**194**	210	267
by Rushing	104	101	109	102	97	138	90	109	142	116	**88**	95	125
by Passing	123	112	97	79	121	114	95	78	**67**	101	92	91	124
by Penalty	16	18	13	15	21	22	24	8	**6**	9	14	24	18
RUSHING:													
Number	491	455	459	513	455	576	493	511	560	538	**435**	488	559
Yards	2089	1797	1807	2091	1795	2410	1956	1991	2850	2228	**1470**	1652	2264
Average Yards	4.3	3.9	3.9	4.1	3.9	4.2	4.0	3.9	5.1	4.1	**3.4**	3.4	4.1
Touchdowns	15	11	15	7	14	19	11	9	16	12	**5**	8	23
PASSING:													
Attempts	331	368	338	312	387	326	324	320	**240**	296	370	359	341
Completions	199	166	182	144	202	178	157	151	**134**	150	170	164	177
Completion Percentage	60.1	**45.1**	53.8	46.2	52.2	54.6	48.5	47.2	55.8	50.7	45.9	45.7	51.9
Passing Yards	2599	2394	2240	1984	2766	2466	1942	1604	**1600**	2148	1995	1923	2473
Avg. Yards per Attempt	7.9	6.5	6.6	6.4	7.1	7.6	6.0	**5.0**	6.7	7.3	5.4	5.4	7.3
Avg. Yards per Complet.	13.1	14.4	12.3	13.8	13.7	13.9	12.4	**10.6**	11.9	14.3	11.7	11.7	14.0
Times Tackled Passing	25	32	**43**	29	36	27	38	**45**	32	26	40	33	26
Yards Lost Tackled	200	276	**342**	248	326	229	323	314	262	198	305	251	219
Net Yards	2399	2118	1898	1736	2440	2237	1619	**1290**	1338	1950	1690	1672	2254
Touchdowns	16	12	9	16	15	26	11	**5**	11	18	12	11	18
Interceptions	15	14	18	12	14	17	21	21	13	19	17	**37**	16
Percent Intercepted	4.5	3.8	5.3	3.8	3.6	5.2	6.5	6.6	5.4	6.4	4.6	**10.3**	4.7
PUNTS:													
Number	47	63	77	78	69	62	84	76	62	67	**90**	75	60
Average Distance	**37.4**	39.8	41.7	40.4	43.3	39.6	42.9	38.5	40.5	40.9	43.1	42.4	43.1
PUNT RETURNS:													
Number	**27**	34	**27**	44	31	44	48	30	29	36	40	37	35
Yards	280	312	**123**	270	257	343	446	182	152	411	290	308	257
Average Yards	10.4	9.2	**4.6**	6.1	8.3	7.8	9.5	6.1	5.2	11.3	7.3	8.3	7.4
Touchdowns	**0**	1	**0**	**0**	**0**	**0**	**0**	**0**	**0**	1	**0**	**0**	**0**
KICKOFF RETURNS:													
Number	42	44	42	48	61	37	40	56	40	44	46	59	**35**
Yards	950	934	1170	1165	1244	**811**	1031	1202	963	1021	981	1357	862
Average Yards	22.6	21.2	27.9	24.3	**20.4**	21.9	25.8	21.5	24.1	23.2	21.4	23.0	24.6
Touchdowns	**0**	1	1	**0**	1	1	**0**	**0**	1	**0**	**0**	**0**	1
INTERCEPTION RETURNS:													
Number	25	14	**12**	20	20	27	13	**12**	17	22	18	26	30
Yards	336	**149**	198	271	331	357	151	190	385	296	187	512	532
Average Yards	13.4	10.6	16.5	13.6	16.6	13.2	11.6	15.8	22.6	13.5	**10.4**	19.7	17.7
Touchdowns	4	**0**	1	**0**	1	4	**0**	**0**	1	2	1	2	**0**
PENALTIES:													
Number	69	53	78	79	84	**90**	63	**61**	77	86	67	86	68
Yards	684	485	710	738	**824**	811	649	616	693	783	623	757	579
FUMBLES:													
Number	35	30	31	21	26	29	33	29	29	30	35	**41**	31
Number Lost	**22**	19	16	9	15	10	18	8	18	19	16	18	18
POINTS:													
Total	341	230	231	255	296	447	192	**150**	300	306	175	210	386
PAT Attempts	39	25	27	**24**	31	53	22	**15**	32	34	19	22	46
PAT Made	38	23	27	24	30	52	21	**13**	30	33	19	21	42
FG Attempts	33	34	**23**	46	35	42	27	27	32	34	30	29	38
FG Made	29	19	14	29	26	25	**13**	15	26	23	14	19	22
Percent FG Made	69.7	55.9	60.9	63.0	74.3	59.5	48.1	55.6	81.3	67.6	**46.7**	65.5	57.9
Safeties	**0**	**0**	**0**	**0**	1	1	**0**	1	**0**	**0**	**0**	**0**	1

CONFERENCE PLAYOFFS

December 22, at Oakland (Attendance 51,110)

SCORING

OAKLAND	7	3	13	10–33
PITTSBURGH	0	7	0	7–14

First Quarter
Oak. Hubbard, 1 yard rush PAT–Blanda (kick)

Second Quarter
Oak. Blanda, 25 yard field goal
Pitt. B. Pearson, 4 yard pass from Bradshaw PAT–Gerela (kick)

Third Quarter
Oak. Blanda, 31 yard field goal
Oak. Blanda, 22 yard field goal
Oak. W. Brown, 54 yard interception return PAT–Blanda (kick)

Fourth Quarter
Oak. Blanda, 10 yard field goal
Pitt. Lewis, 26 yard pass from Bradshaw PAT–Gerela (kick)
Oak. Hubbard, 1 yard rush PAT–Blanda (kick)

TEAM STATISTICS

OAK.		PITT.
24	First Downs–Total	15
14	First Downs–Rushing	2
8	First Downs–Passing	10
2	First Downs–Penalty	3
0	Fumbles–Number	1
0	Fumbles–Lost Ball	0
9	Penalties–Number	4
75	Yards Penalized	60
1	Missed Field Goals	0
74	Offensive Plays	46
361	Net Yards	223
4.8	Average Gain	4.8
0	Giveaways	3
3	Takeaways	0
+3	Difference	−3

INDIVIDUAL STATISTICS

OAKLAND	No	Yds	Avg.	PITTSBURGH	No	Yds	Avg.
RUSHING							
Hubbard	20	91	4.6	Harris	10	29	2.9
C. Smith	17	73	4.3	P. Pearson	4	14	3.5
C. Davis	12	48	4.0	Fuqua	3	13	4.3
Banaszak	5	17	3.4	Bradshaw	3	9	3.0
Moore	1	3	3.0		20	65	3.2
	55	232	4.2				
RECEIVING							
Siani	5	68	13.6	Lewis	4	70	17.5
Moore	3	26	8.7	Fuqua	4	52	13.0
C. Smith	2	10	5.0	B. Pearson	2	7	3.5
Hubbard	1	17	17.0	P. Pearson	1	24	24.0
Biletnikoff	1	8	8.0	Williams	1	14	14.0
Banaszak	1	5	5.0		12	167	13.9
	13	134	10.3				
PUNTING							
Guy	2		39.0	Walden	5		41.6
PUNT RETURNS							
Atkinson	2	11	5.5	Edwards	1	20	20.0
KICKOFF RETURNS							
C. Davis	3	58	19.3	P. Pearson	4	79	19.8
				Steve Davis	3	77	25.7
					7	156	22.3
INTERCEPTION RETURNS							
W. Brown	1	54	54.0				
Atkinson	1	8	8.0	None			
Villapiano	1	0	0.0				
	3	62	20.7				

PASSING

OAKLAND	Att.	Comp.	Comp. Pct.	Yds.	Int.	Yds/ Att.	Yds/ Comp.	Yards Lost Tackled
Stabler	17	14	82.4	142	0	8.4	10.1	2–13
PITTSBURGH								
Bradshaw	25	12	48.0	167	3	6.7	13.9	1– 9

December 23, at Miami (Attendance 80,047)

SCORING

MIAMI	14	7	10	3–34
CINCINNATI	3	13	0	0–16

First Quarter
Mia. Warfield, 13 yard pass from Griese PAT–Yepremian (kick)
Cin. Muhlmann, 24 yard field goal
Mia. Csonka, 1 yard rush PAT–Yepremian (kick)

Second Quarer
Mia. Morris, 4 yard rush PAT–Yepremian (kick)
Cin. Craig, 45 yard interception return PAT–Muhlmann (kick)
Cin. Muhlmann, 46 yard field goal
Cin. Muhlmann, 12 yard field goal

Third Quarter
Mia. Mandich, 7 yard pass from Griese PAT–Yepremian (kick)
Mia. Yepremian, 50 yard field goal

Fourth Quarter
Mia. Yepremian, 46 yard field goal

TEAM STATISTICS

MIAMI		CIN.
27	First Downs–Total	11
18	First Downs–Rushing	5
9	First Downs–Passing	6
0	First Downs–Penalty	0
2	Fumbles–Number	0
1	Fumbles–Lost Ball	0
1	Penalties–Number	2
5	Yards Penalized	19
0	Missed Field Goals	0
71	Offensive Plays	50
400	Net Yards	194
5.6	Average Gain	3.9
3	Giveaways	1
1	Takeaways	3
−2	Difference	+2

INDIVIDUAL STATISTICS

MIAMI	No	Yds	Avg.	CINCINNATI	No	Yds	Avg.
RUSHING							
Morris	20	106	5.3	Clark	7	40	5.7
Csonka	20	71	3.6	Anderson	3	26	8.8
Kiick	10	51	5.1	E. Johnson	2	17	8.5
Leigh	1	8	8.0	Elliott	7	15	2.1
Nottingham	1	5	5.0	Curtis	1	−1	−1.0
	52	241	4.6		20	97	4.9
RECEIVING							
Warfield	4	95	23.8	Elliott	9	53	5.9
Mandich	3	28	9.3	Joiner	2	33	16.5
Kiick	3	19	6.3	Clark	2	18	9.0
Briscoe	1	17	17.0	Curtis	1	9	9.0
	11	159	14.5		14	113	8.1
PUNTING							
Seiple	2		49.0	Lewis	7		36.3
PUNT RETURNS							
Scott	1	4	4.0	Casanova	1	15	15.0
Anderson	1	2	2.0	Parrish	1	11	11.0
	2	6	3.0		2	26	13.0
KICKOFF RETURNS							
Anderson	1	14	14.0	Parrish	1	25	25.0
Morris	1	0	0.0	Jackson	1	17	17.0
	2	14	7.0		2	42	21.0
INTERCEPTION RETURNS							
Anderson	1	19	19.0	Craig	1	45	45.0
				Casanova	1	0	0.0
					2	45	22.5

PASSING

MIAMI	Att.	Comp.	Comp. Pct.	Yds.	Int.	Yds/ Att.	Yds/ Comp.	Yards Lost Tackled
Griese	18	11	61.1	159	1	8.8	14.5	
Briscoe	1	0	0.0	0	1	–	–	
	19	11	57.9	159	2	8.4	14.5	0– 0
CINCINNATI								
Anderson	27	14	51.9	113	1	4.2	8.1	3–16

MIAMI DOLPHINS 12-2 Don Shula

Scores of Each Game		
21	SAN FRANCISCO	13
7	Oakland	12
44	NEW ENGLAND	23
31	N. Y. JETS	3
17	Cleveland	9
27	BUFFALO	6
30	New England	14
24	N. Y. Jets	14
44	BALTIMORE	0
17	Buffalo	0
14	Dallas	7
30	PITTSBURGH	26
3	Baltimore	16
34	DETROIT	7

Use Name	Pos.	Hgt	Wgt	Age	Int	Pts
Doug Crusan	OT	6'5"	250	27		
Norm Evans	OT	6'5"	252	30		
Wayne Moore	OT	6'6"	265	28		
Willie Young	OT	6'4"	270	25		
Bob Kuechenberg	OG	6'3"	247	25		
Larry Little	OG	6'1"	265	27		
Ed Newman	OG	6'2"	245	22		
Jim Langer	C	6'2"	250	25		
Irv Goode	OG-C	6'4"	252	32		
Vern Den Herder	DE	6'6"	250	24		
Bill Stanfill	DE	6'5"	250	26		
Bob Heinz	DT-DE	6'6"	270	26		
Manny Fernandez	DT	6'2"	250	27		
Baldy Moore	DT	6'2"	265	27		
Larry Woods	DT	6'6"	260	25		
Larry Ball	LB	6'6"	225	23	1	
Bruce Bannon	LB	6'3"	225	22		
Nick Buoniconti	LB	5'11"	220	32		6
Mike Kolen	LB	6'2"	220	25	2	
Bob Matheson	LB-DE	6'4"	240	28		
Jesse Powell	LB	6'1"	215	26		
Doug Swift	LB	6'3"	228	24	1	
Dick Anderson	DB	6'2"	196	27	8	12
Charlie Babb	DB	6'	190	23		
Tim Foley	DB	6'	194	25	2	12
Curtis Johnson	DB	6'2"	196	25	2	2
Lloyd Mumphord	DB	5'11"	180	26		
Jake Scott	DB	6'	188	28	4	
Henry Stuckey	DB	6'1"	190	23	1	
Bob Griese	QB	6'1"	190	28		
Earl Morrall	QB	6'1"	206	39		
Jim Kiick	HB	5'11"	215	27		
Mercury Morris	HB	5'10"	190	26		60
Charlie Leigh	FB-HB	5'11"	205	27		6
Larry Csonka	FB	6'3"	237	26		30
Don Nottingham (from BAL)	FB	5'10"	210	24		6
Marlin Briscoe	WR	5'10"	178	27		12
Bo Rather	WR	6'1"	182	22		
Ron Sellers	WR	6'4"	195	26		
Howard Twilley	WR	5'10"	185	29		
Paul Warfield	WR	6'	185	30		66
Marv Fleming	TE	6'4"	235	31		
Jim Mandich	TE	6'3"	224	25		24
Larry Seiple	TE	6'	215	28		
Garo Yepremian	K	5'8"	175	29		113

Jim Dunaway — Injury
Howard Kindig — Injury
Ed Jenkins — Injury

BUFFALO BILLS 9-5 Lou Saban

Scores of Each Game		
31	New England	13
7	San Diego	34
9	N. Y. JETS	7
27	PHILADELPHIA	26
31	BALTIMORE	13
6	Miami	27
23	KANSAS CITY	14
0	New Orleans	13
13	CINCINNATI	16
0	MIAMI	17
24	Baltimore	17
17	Atlanta	6
37	NEW ENGLAND	13
34	N. Y. Jets	14

Use Name	Pos.	Hgt	Wgt	Age	Int	Pts
Dave Foley	OT	6'5"	255	25		
Donnie Green	OT	6'7"	272	25		
Mike Montler	C-OT	6'4"	255	29		
Joe DeLamielleure	OG	6'3"	254	22		
Reggie McKenzie	OG	6'4"	235	23		
Bobby Penchion	OG	6'5"	265	24		
Bruce Jarvis	C	6'7"	250	24		
Willie Parker	OG-C	6'3"	240	24		
Earl Edwards	DE	6'6"	262	27		
Halvor Hagen	DE	6'5"	245	26		
Walt Patulski	DE	6'6"	260	23		
Mike Kadish	DT	6'5"	265	23		
Bob Kampa	DT	6'4"	252	22		
Steve Okoniewski	DT	6'3"	247	24		
Jerry Patton	DT	6'3"	265	27		
Jeff Winans	DT	6'5"	265	21		
Jim Cheyunski	LB	6'2"	225	27	3	
Phil Croyle (from HOU)	LB	6'3"	220	25		
Dale Farley	LB	6'3"	235	24		
Fred Forsberg (from DEN)	LB	6'1"	235	29	1	
Merv Krakau	LB	6'1"	242	22		
Rich Lewis	LB	6'3"	220	23		
John Skorupan	LB	6'2"	214	22		
Bill Cahill	DB	5'11"	180	22		6
Leon Garror	DB	6'	180	25	1	
Tony Greene	DB	5'10"	170	24	1	
Dwight Harrison	DB	6'1"	178	24	5	6
Robert James	DB	6'1"	185	26	1	
Ernie Kellerman	DB	6'	183	29	2	
Ken Stone (to WAS)	DB	6'1"	180	22		6
Donnie Walker	DB	6'1"	185	22	1	
Joe Ferguson	QB	6'1"	190	23		12
Dennis Shaw	QB	6'2"	215	26		
Steve Jones	HB	6'	200	22		
O. J. Simpson	HB	6'2"	214	26		72
Pete Van Valkenberg	HB	6'2"	192	23		
Jim Braxton	FB	6'2"	243	24		24
Bo Cornell	FB	6'1"	215	24		
Larry Watkins	FB	6'2"	230	26		18
Bob Chandler	WR	6'	180	24		19
Wallace Francis	WR	5'11"	188	21		12
J. D. Hill	WR	6'1"	202	24		
Ray Jarvis	WR	5'11"	193	24		
Ted Koy	TE	6'1"	212	25		
Paul Seymour	TE	6'5"	260	23		
Dave Washington	TE	6'5"	220	25		
Spike Jones	K	6'2"	190	26		
John Leypoldt	K	6'2"	230	27		90

Don Croft — Knee Injury

NEW ENGLAND PATRIOTS 5-9 Chuck Fairbanks

Scores of Each Game		
13	BUFFALO	31
7	KANSAS CITY	10
23	Miami	44
24	BALTIMORE	16
7	N. Y. JETS	9
13	Chicago	10
14	MIAMI	30
23	Philadelphia	24
13	N. Y. Jets	33
33	GREEN BAY	24
32	Houston	0
30	SAN DIEGO	14
13	Buffalo	37
13	Baltimore	18

Use Name	Pos.	Hgt	Wgt	Age	Int	Pts
Tom Neville	OT	6'4"	255	30		
Leon Gray	OT	6'3"	256	21		
Bob Reynolds (to STL)	OT	6'6"	265	32		
Willie Banks	OG	6'2"	250	27		
Sam Adams	OT-OG	6'3"	252	24		
John Hannah	OG	6'2"	265	22		
Bill Lenkaitis	OG	6'3"	260	27		
Len St. Jean	OG	6'1"	250	31		
Jon Morris	C	6'4"	254	30		
Doug Dumler	C	6'3"	242	22		
Nate Dorsey	DE	6'4"	240	23		
Ray Hamilton	DE	6'1"	232	22		
Donnell Smith	DE	6'4"	245	24		
Julius Adams	DT-DE	6'3"	257	25		
Rick Cash	DT	6'5"	260	27		
Mel Lunsford	DT	6'3"	250	23		
Art Moore	DT	6'5"	253	22		
Dave Rowe	DT	6'6"	280	28		
Ron Acks	LB	6'2"	220	28	1	
Edgar Chandler	LB	6'3"	225	27		
Will Foster	LB	6'2"	230	24		6
Bob Geddes	LB	6'2"	240	27		
Steve Kiner	LB	6'	218	26		2
Steve King	LB	6'4"	255	22		
Brian Stenger	LB	6'4"	230	26		
John Tanner	LB	6'4"	235	28		
Ralph Anderson	DB	6'2"	180	24	2	
Ron Bolton	DB	6'2"	180	23	6	
Greg Boyd	DB	6'2"	200	21		
Sandy Durko	DB	6'1"	185	25	3	
George Hoey	DB	5'10"	170	26		
Honor Jackson (to NYG)	DB	6'1"	195	24	1	
Don Martin	DB	5'11"	187	23		
Dave Mason	DB	6'	200	23		
Brian Dowling	QB	6'2"	200	26		
Jim Plunkett	QB	6'3"	220	25		30
Josh Ashton	HB	6'1"	205	24		
Mack Herron	HB	5'5"	170	25		24
Bob McCall	HB	6'	205	23		
Claxton Welch	HB	5'11"	203	26		
Paul Gipson	FB-HB	6'	210	26		
Sam Cunningham	FB	6'3"	215	23		30
John Tarver	FB	6'3"	227	24		24
Reggie Rucker	WR	6'2"	190	25		18
Darryl Stingley	WR	6'	190	21		12
Randy Vataha	WR	5'10"	175	24		12
Bob Adams	TE	6'2"	225	27		
John Mosier	TE	6'3"	220	25		
Bob Windsor	TE	6'4"	226	30		24
Bruce Barnes	K	5'11"	215	22		
Bill Bell	K	6'1"	192	25		7
Jeff White	K	5'11"	170	24		63

Wayne Patrick — Knee Injury

NEW YORK JETS 4-10 Weeb Ewbank

Scores of Each Game		
7	Green Bay	23
34	Baltimore	10
7	Buffalo	9
3	Miami	31
9	New England	7
14	Pittsburgh	26
28	DENVER	40
14	MIAMI	24
33	NEW ENGLAND	13
14	Cincinnati	20
20	ATLANTA	28
20	BALTIMORE	17
23	Philadelphia	24
14	BUFFALO	34

Use Name	Pos.	Hgt	Wgt	Age	Int	Pts
Winston Hill	OT	6'4"	280	31		
Bob Svihus	OT	6'4"	245	30		
Robert Woods	OT	6'3"	255	23		
John Mooring	C-OT	6'6"	255	26		
Dave Herman	OG	6'2"	255	31		
Randy Rasmussen	OG	6'2"	255	28		
Gary Puetz	OT-OG	6'3"	255	21		
Rick Harrell	C	6'3"	238	22		
John Schmitt	C	6'4"	250	30		
Ed Galigher	DE	6'4"	255	22		
Mark Lomas	DE	6'4"	250	25		
Joey Jackson	DT-DE	6'4"	270	24		
Richard Neal	DT-DE	6'3"	254	25		
John Little	DT	6'3"	250	26		
Steve Thompson	DT	6'5"	250	28		
John Elliott	DE-DT	6'4"	244	28		
Al Atkinson	LB	6'1"	230	30	1	
Ralph Baker	LB	6'3"	228	31	4	6
John Ebersole	LB	6'3"	235	24	1	
Bill Ferguson	LB	6'3"	225	22		
Rob Spicer	LB	6'4"	227	22		
Mike Taylor	LB	6'1"	230	23		
Bill Zapalac	LB	6'4"	225	25		
Chris Farasopoulos	DB	5'11"	190	24	1	
Delles Howell	DB	6'3"	200	26	4	
Burgess Owens	DB	6'2"	200	22	1	6
Rich Sowells	DB	6'	175	24	3	6
Steve Tannen	DB	6'1"	194	25	1	
Earlie Thomas	DB	6'1"	190	27	2	
Phil Wise	DB	6'	190	24		6
Bill Demory	QB	6'2"	195	22		
Joe Namath	QB	6'2"	200	30		
Al Woodall	QB	6'5"	194	27		
Mike Adamle	HB	5'9"	197	23		
Hank Bjorklund	HB	6'1"	200	23		
Emerson Boozer	HB	5'11"	205	30		36
Cliff McClain	HB	6'	217	25		
Jim Nance	FB	6'1"	240	30		
John Riggins	FB	6'2"	230	24		24
Margene Adkins	WR	5'10"	183	26		
Jerome Barkum	WR	6'3"	215	23		36
Eddie Bell	WR	5'10"	160	25		12
David Knight	WR	6'1"	182	22		6
Rocky Turner	DB-WR	6'	200	23		
Dennis Cambal	TE	6'3"	228	24		
Rich Caster	TE	6'5"	228	24		24
Julian Fagan	K	6'3"	205	25		
Bobby Howfield	K	5'9"	180	36		78

BALTIMORE COLTS 4-10 Howard Schnellenberger

Scores of Each Game		
14	Cleveland	24
10	N. Y. JETS	34
14	NEW ORLEANS	10
16	New England	24
13	Buffalo	31
29	Detroit	27
21	OAKLAND	34
27	HOUSTON	31
0	Miami	44
14	Washington	22
17	BUFFALO	24
17	N. Y. Jets	20
16	MIAMI	3
18	NEW ENGLAND	13

Use Name	Pos.	Hgt	Wgt	Age	Int	Pts
Tom Drougas	OT	6'4"	257	23		
Dennis Nelson	OT	6'5"	260	27		
David Taylor	OT	6'4"	254	23		
Elmer Collett	OG	6'4"	240	28		
Cornelius Johnson	OG	6'2"	245	30		
Glenn Ressler	OG	6'3"	250	29		
Fred Hoaglin	C	6'4"	246	29		
Ken Mendenhall	C	6'3"	235	25		
Dan Neal	C	6'4"	240	24		
Mike Barnes	DE	6'6"	255	22		
Roy Hilton	DE	6'6"	240	28		
Dick Amman	DT-DE	6'5"	250	22		
Jim Bailey	DT	6'4"	255	25		
Joe Ehrmann	DT	6'5"	260	24		
Joe Schmiesing	DE-DT	6'4"	260	28		
Bill Windauer	DT	6'3"	245	23		
Stan Cherry	LB	6'5"	200	22		
Mike Curtis	LB	6'2"	232	30	2	
Ted Hendricks	LB	6'7"	220	25	3	6
Mike Kaczmarek	LB	6'4"	235	22	1	
Ed Mooney	LB	6'2"	225	28		
Stan White	LB	6'1"	225	23	4	6
Brian Herosian	DB	6'3"	200	22		
Rex Kern	DB	5'11"	190	24	2	
Bruce Laird	DB	6'	185	23		
Jack Mildren	DB	6'1"	200	23		
Nelson Munsey	DB	6'1"	185	25		
Ray Oldham	DB	6'	200	22	2	
Rick Volk	DB	6'3"	195	28	1	
Marty Domres	QB	6'3"	220	26		12
Bert Jones	QB	6'3"	205	21		
Hubert Ginn (from MIA)	HB	5'11"	188	26		
Lydell Mitchell	HB	5'11"	204	24		12
Bill Olds	FB	6'1"	224	22		12
Don McCauley	HB-FB	6'1"	207	24		12
Glenn Doughty	WR	6'2"	204	22		24
Sam Havrilak	WR	6'2"	195	25		
Ollie Smith	WR	6'2"	195	24		
Cotton Speyrer	WR	6'	175	24		30
Tom Mitchell	TE-WR	6'2"	215	29		24
John Andrews	TE	6'3"	227	24		6
Ray Chester	TE	6'3"	235	25		6
George Hunt	K	6'1"	215	23		70
David Lee	K	6'4"	230	29		

MIAMI DOLPHINS

RUSHING

Last Name	No.	Yds	Avg	TD
Csonka	219	1003	4.6	5
Morris	149	954	6.4	10
Kiick	76	257	3.4	0
Nottingham	52	252	4.8	1
Leigh	22	134	6.1	1
Griese	13	20	1.5	0
Warfield	1	15	15.0	0
Morrall	1	9	9.0	0
Briscoe	2	−5	−2.5	0

RECEIVING

Last Name	No.	Yds	Avg	TD
Briscoe	30	447	15	2
Warfield	29	514	18	11
Kiick	27	208	8	0
Mandich	24	302	13	4
Csonka	7	22	3	0
Morris	4	51	13	0
Leigh	4	9	2	0
Nottingham	3	26	9	0
Fleming	3	22	7	0
Sellers	2	54	27	0
Twilley	2	30	15	0

PUNT RETURNS

Last Name	No.	Yds	Avg	TD
Scott	22	266	12	0
Leigh	9	64	7	0
Anderson	6	52	9	0

KICKOFF RETURNS

Last Name	No.	Yds	Avg	TD
Leigh	9	251	28	0
Morris	11	242	22	0
Scott	2	20	10	0
Nottingham	1	17	17	0
Bannon	1	10	10	0
Seiple	1	0	0	0

PASSING – PUNTING – KICKING Statistics

PASSING

Last Name	Att	Comp	%	Yds	Yd/Att	TD	Int–%	RK
Griese	218	116	53	1422	6.5	17	8– 4	3
Morrall	38	17	45	253	6.7	0	4–11	

PUNTING

Last Name	No.	Avg						
Seiple	48	42.3						

KICKING

Last Name	XP	Att	%	FG	Att	%		
Yepremian	38	38	100	25	37	68		

BUFFALO BILLS

RUSHING

Last Name	No.	Yds	Avg	TD
Simpson	332	2003	6.0	12
Braxton	108	494	4.6	4
Watkins	98	414	4.2	2
Ferguson	48	147	3.1	2
Van Valkenberg	2	20	10.0	0
Cornell	4	13	3.3	0
Steve Jones	4	9	2.3	0
Shaw	4	2	0.5	0
Chandler	5	−14	−2.8	0

RECEIVING

Last Name	No.	Yds	Avg	TD
Chandler	30	427	14	3
Hill	29	422	15	0
Watkins	12	86	7	1
Seymour	10	114	11	0
Braxton	6	101	17	0
Simpson	6	70	12	0
R. Jarvis	1	12	12	0
Van Valkenberg	1	7	7	0
Ferguson	1	−3	−3	0

PUNT RETURNS

Last Name	No.	Yds	Avg	TD
Walker	25	210	8	0
Cahill	4	73	18	1
Chandler	2	5	3	0
Hill	1	−9	−9	0

KICKOFF RETURNS

Last Name	No.	Yds	Avg	TD
Francis	23	687	30	2
Jones	6	116	19	0
R. Jarvis	5	84	17	0
Cahill	2	42	21	0
Watkins	1	18	18	0
Parker	1	16	16	0
T. Greene	1	7	7	0
Cornell	1	2	2	0
Braxton	1	0	0	0
Van Valkenberg	1	0	0	0

PASSING – PUNTING – KICKING Statistics

PASSING

Last Name	Att	Comp	%	Yds	Yd/Att	TD	Int–%	RK
Ferguson	164	73	45	939	5.7	4	10– 6	13
Shaw	46	22	48	300	6.5	0	4– 9	
Simpson	2	1	50	−3	−1.5	0	0– 0	
Chandler	1	0	0	0	0.0	0	0– 0	

PUNTING

Last Name	No	Avg						
Spike Jones	66	40.3						

KICKING

Last Name	XP	Att	%	FG	Att	%		
Leypoldt	27	27	100	21	30	70		
Chandler	1	1	100	0	0	0		

NEW ENGLAND PATRIOTS

RUSHING

Last Name	No.	Yds	Avg	TD
Cunningham	155	516	3.3	4
Tarver	72	321	4.5	4
Ashton	93	305	3.3	0
Plunkett	44	209	4.8	5
Herron	61	200	3.3	2
Stingley	6	64	10.7	0
McCall	10	15	1.5	0
B. Adams	2	7	3.5	0
Gipson	5	−1	−0.2	0
Rucker	2	−1	−0.5	0
Welch	1	−2	−2.0	0
Windsor	1	−6	−6.0	0
Vataha	2	−15	−7.5	0

RECEIVING

Last Name	No.	Yds	Avg	TD
Rucker	53	743	14	3
Windsor	23	348	15	4
Stingley	23	339	15	2
Vataha	20	341	17	2
Herron	18	265	15	1
Cunningham	15	144	10	1
B. Adams	14	197	14	0
Ashton	11	113	10	0
Tarver	9	41	6	0
Welch	6	22	4	0
McCall	3	18	6	0

PUNT RETURNS

Last Name	No.	Yds	Avg	TD
Herron	27	282	10	0
Durko	3	21	7	0
Stingley	3	31	7	0

KICKOFF RETURNS

Last Name	No.	Yds	Avg	TD
Herron	41	1092	27	1
Stingley	6	143	24	0
Rucker	5	103	21	0
McCall	2	17	9	0
Tarver	1	17	17	0
Hannah	1	0	0	0
Windsor	1	0	0	0

PASSING – PUNTING – KICKING Statistics

PASSING

Last Name	Att	Comp	%	Yds	Yd/Att	TD	Int–%	RK
Plunkett	376	193	51	2550	6.8	13	17– 5	5

PUNTING

Last Name	No	Avg						
Barnes	55	38.8						
White	6	27.2						

KICKING

Last Name	XP	Att	%	FG	Att	%		
White	21	25	84	14	25	56		
Bell	4	5	80	1	4	25		

NEW YORK JETS

RUSHING

Last Name	No.	Yds	Avg	TD
Boozer	182	831	4.6	3
Riggins	134	482	3.6	4
Adamle	67	264	3.9	0
Nance	18	78	4.3	0
Bjorkland	22	72	3.3	0
Woodall	13	68	5.2	0
Fagan	2	47	23.5	0
McClain	8	32	4.0	0
Barkum	1	2	2.0	0
Demory	4	−1	−0.3	0
Namath	1	−2	−2.0	0
Caster	1	−9	−9.0	0

RECEIVING

Last Name	No.	Yds	Avg	TD
Barkum	44	810	18	6
Caster	35	593	17	4
Bell	24	319	13	2
Riggins	23	158	7	0
Boozer	22	130	6	3
Adamle	9	63	7	0
Adkins	6	109	18	0
Knight	6	78	13	1
McClain	6	52	9	0
Nance	4	26	7	0
Bjorkland	2	15	8	0

PUNT RETURNS

Last Name	No.	Yds	Avg	TD
Farasopoulos	14	111	8	0
Turner	11	54	5	0
Tannen	2	0	0	0

KICKOFF RETURNS

Last Name	No.	Yds	Avg	TD
Adkins	31	615	20	0
Bjorkland	9	175	19	0
Owens	2	103	52	1
McClain	5	89	18	0
Adamle	5	79	16	0

PASSING – PUNTING – KICKING Statistics

PASSING

Last Name	Att	Comp	%	Yds	Yd/Att	TD	Int–%	RK
Woodall	201	101	50	1228	6.1	9	8– 4	6
Namath	133	68	51	966	7.3	5	6– 5	
Demory	39	12	31	159	4.1	2	8–21	

PUNTING

Last Name	No	Avg						
Fagan	74	37.1						

KICKING

Last Name	XP	Att	%	FG	Att	%		
Howfield	27	27	100	17	24	71		

BALTIMORE COLTS

RUSHING

Last Name	No.	Yds	Avg	TD
L. Mitchell	253	963	3.8	2
McCauley	144	514	3.6	2
Domres	32	126	3.9	2
Olds	26	100	3.8	2
Doughty	10	96	9.6	0
Jones	18	58	3.2	0
Ginn	16	47	2.9	0
Mildren	2	14	7.0	0
Havrilak	2	9	4.5	0
Chester	1	1	1.0	0
Speyrer	1	1	1.0	0
Smith	1	−3	−3.0	0
Lee	2	−16	−8.0	0
Nelson	0	3	0.0	0

RECEIVING

Last Name	No.	Yds	Avg	TD
Doughty	25	587	23	4
T. Mitchell	25	313	13	4
McCauley	25	186	7	0
Chester	18	181	10	1
Speyrer	17	311	18	4
L. Mitchell	17	113	7	0
Ginn	3	2	1	0
Olds	2	−4	−2	0
Smith	1	37	37	0
Havrilak	1	9	9	0
Andrews	1	1	1	1

PUNT RETURNS

Last Name	No.	Yds	Avg	TD
Laird	15	72	5	0
Volk	7	45	6	0
Kern	2	12	6	0

KICKOFF RETURNS

Last Name	No.	Yds	Avg	TD
Laird	24	547	23	0
Speyrer	17	496	29	1
Ginn	9	198	22	0
White	1	17	17	0
Volk	2	16	8	0
Olds	3	14	5	0
Andrews	1	13	13	0
Munsey	1	13	13	0
McCauley	1	12	12	0

PASSING – PUNTING – KICKING Statistics

PASSING

Last Name	Att	Comp	%	Yds	Yd/Att	TD	Int–%	RK
Domres	191	93	49	1153	6.0	9	13– 7	11
Jones	108	43	40	539	5.0	4	12–11	
Speyrer	1	1	100	54	54.0	1	0– 0	

PUNTING

Last Name	No	Avg						
Lee	62	38.7						

KICKING

Last Name	XP	Att	%	FG	Att	%		
Hunt	22	24	92	16	28	57		

CINCINNATI BENGALS 10-4-0 Paul Brown

Scores of Each Game			Use Name	Pos.	Hgt	Wgt	Age	Int	Pts
10	Denver	28	Vern Holland	OT	6'5"	270	25		
24	HOUSTON	10	Rufus Mayes	OT	6'5"	260	25		
20	San Diego	13	Stan Walters	OT	6'6"	270	25		
10	CLEVELAND	17	Howard Fest	OG-OT	6'6"	262	27		
9	PITTSBURGH	7	Pat Matson	OG	6'1"	245	29		
14	KANSAS CITY	6	John Shinners	OG	6'2"	254	26		
13	Pittsburgh	20	Tom DeLeone	C	6'2"	252	23		
10	Dallas	38	Bob Johnson	C	6'5"	260	27		
16	Buffalo	13	Royce Berry	DE	6'3"	250	27		
20	N. Y. JETS	14	Ken Johnson	DE	6'5"	256	26		
42	ST. LOUIS	24	Lee Thomas	DE	6'5"	246	26		
27	MINNESOTA	0	Sherman White	DE	6'5"	255	24		
34	Cleveland	17	Ron Carpenter	DT	6'4"	260	25		
27	Houston	24	Steve Chomyszak	DT	6'5"	265	28		
			Mike Reid	DT	6'3"	255	26		

Use Name	Pos.	Hgt	Wgt	Age	Int	Pts
Doug Adams	LB	6'	222	24		
Ken Avery	LB	6'1"	227	29	1	
Al Beauchamp	LB	6'2"	237	29	3	
Bill Bergey	LB	6'2"	243	28	3	
Tim Kearney	LB	6'2"	227	22		
Jim LeClair	LB	6'2"	226	22		
Ron Pritchard	LB	6'1"	235	26		
Lyle Blackwood	DB	6'	190	22		
Tommy Casanova	DB	6'2"	202	23	4	
Neal Craig	DB	6'1"	190	25	2	
Bernie Jackson	DB	6'	173	23	1	
Bob Jones	DB	6'1"	194	22		
Lemar Parrish	DB	5'11"	185	25	2	6
Ken Riley	DB	6'	180	26	2	

Virgil Carter — Broken Collarbone
Doug Dressler — Knee Injury

Use Name	Pos.	Hgt	Wgt	Age	Int	Pts
Ken Anderson	QB	6'1"	211	24		
Greg Cook	QB	6'3"	215	26		
Mike Ernst	QB	6'1"	190	22		
Lenvil Elliott	HB	6'	200	22		12
Essex Johnson	HB	5'9"	200	26		42
Reece Morrison	HB	6'	207	27		
Booby Clark	FB	6'2"	245	22		48
Joe Wilson	HB-FB	5'10"	210	22		
Isaac Curtis	WR	6'	190	22		54
Tim George	WR	6'5"	225	21		
Charlie Joiner	WR	5'11"	188	25		
Chip Myers	WR	6'4"	210	28		
Bruce Coslet	TE	6'3"	227	27		
Al Chandler	TE	6'2"	233	22		
Bob Trumpy	TE	6'6"	228	28		30
Dave Lewis	K	6'2"	225	27		
Horst Muhlmann	K	6'1"	220	33		94

PITTSBURGH STEELERS 10-4-0 Chuck Noll

Scores of Each Game			Use Name	Pos.	Hgt	Wgt	Age	Int	Pts
24	DETROIT	10	Gordon Gravelle	OT	6'5"	250	24		
33	CLEVELAND	6	Glen Ray Hines	OT	6'5"	265	29		
36	Houston	7	Jon Kolb	OT	6'2"	262	26		
38	SAN DIEGO	21	Sam Davis	OG	6'1"	255	29		
7	Cincinnati	19	Mel Holmes	OG	6'3"	250	23		
26	N. Y. JETS	14	Bruce Van Dyke	OG	6'2"	255	29		
20	CINCINNATI	13	Gerry Mullins	OT-OG	6'3"	244	24		
21	WASHINGTON	16	Jim Clack	C	6'3"	250	25		
17	Oakland	9	Ray Mansfield	C	6'3"	260	32		
13	DENVER	23	L. C. Greenwood	DE	6'6"	245	26		
16	Cleveland	21	Dwight White	DE	6'4"	250	24	2	2
26	Miami	30	Steve Furness	DT-DE	6'4"	255	22		
33	HOUSTON	7	Joe Greene	DT	6'4"	275	26		
37	San Francisco	14	Craig Hanneman	DT	6'3"	240	24		
			Ernie Holmes	DT	6'3"	260	25		
			Tom Keating	DT	6'3"	247	30		

Use Name	Pos.	Hgt	Wgt	Age	Int	Pts
Ed Bradley	LB	6'2"	240	23		
Henry Davis	LB	6'3"	235	30	2	
Jack Ham	LB	6'1"	225	24	2	6
Andy Russell	LB	6'3"	225	31	3	6
Loren Toews	LB	6'3"	212	21	2	
George Webster	LB	6'4"	223	27		
Mel Blount	DB	6'3"	205	25	4	
John Dockery	DB	6'	186	28	1	
Glen Edwards	DB	6'	185	26	6	6
Dennis Meyer	DB	5'11"	186	22		6
John Rowser	DB	6'1"	185	29		
J.T. Thomas	DB	6'2"	196	22	1	
Mike Wagner	DB	6'1"	196	24	8	6

Al Young — Illness

Use Name	Pos.	Hgt	Wgt	Age	Int	Pts
Terry Bradshaw	QB	6'3"	218	24		18
Joe Gilliam	QB	6'2"	187	22		
Terry Hanratty	QB	6'1"	210	25		
Rocky Bleier	HB	5'11"	205	27		
Preston Pearson	HB	6'1"	205	28		24
Franco Harris	FB-HB	6'2"	230	23		18
Steve Davis	HB-FB	6'1"	218	23		18
John Fuqua	HB-FB	5'11"	205	26		12
Dave Davis	WR	6'	175	25		
Frank Lewis	WR	6'1"	196	26		18
Barry Pearson	WR	5'11"	185	23		18
Glenn Scolnik	WR	6'3"	190	22		
Ron Shanklin	WR	6'1"	180	26		60
Larry Brown	TE	6'4"	225	24		
John McMakin	TE	6'3"	232	22		6
Roy Gerela	K	5'10"	185	25		123
Bobby Walden	K	6'	190	35		

CLEVELAND BROWNS 7-5-2 Nick Skorich

Scores of Each Game			Use Name	Pos.	Hgt	Wgt	Age	Int	Pts
24	BALTIMORE	14	Joe Carollo	OT	6'2"	265	33		
6	Pittsburgh	33	Doug Dieken	OT	6'5"	254	24		
12	N. Y. GIANTS	10	Bob McKay	OT	6'5"	260	25		
17	Cincinnati	10	Chris Morris	OT	6'3"	250	23		
9	MIAMI	17	John Demarie	OG	6'3"	246	28		
42	HOUSTON	13	Chuck Hutchison	OG	6'3"	240	24		
16	SAN DIEGO	16	Gene Hickerson	OG	6'3"	252	38		
3	Minnesota	26	Jim Copeland	C-OG	6'2"	243	28		
23	Houston	13	Bob DeMarco	C	6'3"	248	35		
7	Oakland	3	Bob Briggs	DE	6'4"	250	25		
21	PITTSBURGH	16	Joe Jones	DE	6'6"	250	25		
20	Kansas City	20	Nick Roman	DE	6'3"	244	25		
17	CINCINNATI	34	Carl Barisich	DT	6'4"	255	22		
17	Los Angeles	30	Walter Johnson	DT	6'3"	265	30		
			Jerry Sherk	DT	6'4"	255	25		

Use Name	Pos.	Hgt	Wgt	Age	Int	Pts
Billy Andrews	LB	6'	220	28		
Bob Babich	LB	6'2"	230	26	1	
John Garlington	LB	6'1"	218	27	1	
Charlie Hall	LB	6'3"	225	24		
Mel Long	LB	6'	228	26		
Jim Romaniszyn	LB	6'2"	214	21		
Cliff Brooks	DB	6'1"	190	24		
Thom Darden	DB	6'2"	195	23	1	
Ben Davis	DB	5'11"	180	27	2	
Van Green	DB	6'1"	192	22		6
Clarence Scott	DB	6'	180	24	5	6
Jim Stienke	DB	5'11"	188	22		
Walt Sumner	DB	6'1"	195	26	2	

Bubba Pena — Knee Injury

Use Name	Pos.	Hgt	Wgt	Age	Int	Pts
Don Horn	QB	6'2"	195	28		
Mike Phipps	QB	6'2"	205	25		30
Leroy Kelly	HB	6'	202	31		18
Billy LeFear	HB	5'11"	197	23		
Greg Pruitt	HB	5'10"	186	22		30
Hugh McKinnis	FB	6'	225	25		
Bo Scott	FB	6'3"	215	30		6
Ken Brown	HB-FB	5'10"	203	27		
Steve Holden	WR	6'	192	22		
Fair Hooker	WR	6'1"	195	26		12
Frank Pitts	WR	6'2"	200	29		24
Gloster Richardson	WR	6'	200	30		6
Dave Sullivan	WR	5'11"	185	22		
Chip Glass	TE	6'4"	235	26		
Milt Morin	TE	6'4"	236	31		6
Ken Smith	TE	6'4"	225	22		
Don Cockroft	K	6'1"	195	28		90

HOUSTON OILERS 1-13-0 Bill Peterson Sid Gillman

Scores of Each Game			Use Name	Pos.	Hgt	Wgt	Age	Int	Pts
14	N. Y. Giants	34	Levert Carr	OT	6'5"	260	29		
10	Cincinnati	24	Elbert Drungo	OT	6'5"	265	30		
7	PITTSBURGH	36	Tom Funchess	OT	6'5"	270	28		
26	LOS ANGELES	31	Kevin Hunt (from NE)	OT	6'5"	260	24		
20	DENVER	48	Soloman Freelon	OG	6'2"	250	22		
13	Cleveland	42	Brian Goodman	OG	6'2"	250	24		
14	Chicago	35	Al Jenkins	OG	6'2"	245	27		
31	Baltimore	27	Harris Jones	OG	6'4"	245	24		
13	CLEVELAND	23	Ralph Miller	OG	6'4"	260	24		
14	Kansas City	38	Ron Saul	OG	6'2"	255	25		
0	NEW ENGLAND	32	Bill Curry	C	6'2"	236	30		
6	OAKLAND	17	Sam Gruneisen	C	6'1"	250	32		
7	Pittsburgh	33	Calvin Hunt	C	6'3"	245	25		
24	CINCINNATI	27	Ron Lou	C	6'2"	235	22		
			Elvin Bethea	DE	6'3"	262	27		
			Mike Fanucci	DE	6'4"	240	23		
			Tody Smith	DE	6'5"	245	24		
			Wes Grant	DT-DE	6'5"	245	26		
			Al Cowlings	DT	6'5"	255	26		
			John Matuszak	DT	6'8"	290	22		
			Greg Sampson	DT	6'6"	260	22		

Use Name	Pos.	Hgt	Wgt	Age	Int	Pts
Gregg Bingham	LB	6'1"	227	22	2	
Ralph Cindrich	LB	6'1"	228	23		
Paul Guidry	LB	6'3"	233	29		
Brian McConnell	LB	6'4"	207	23		
Guy Roberts	LB	6'1"	215	23	4	
Ted Washington	LB	6'1"	240	25		
Willie Alexander	DB	6'2"	195	23	3	
Bob Atkins	DB	6'1"	210	27		
Joe Blahak	DB	5'9"	182	23	2	
John Charles	DB	6'1"	200	29		
Larry Eaglin	DB	6'3"	195	22		6
Alvin Haymond	DB	6'	194	31		
Benny Johnson	DB	5'11"	178	25		
Zeke Moore	DB	6'2"	196	29		
Jeff Severson	DB	6'1"	180	23	4	
Alvin Wyatt	DB	5'10"	180	25		

Jim Ford — Leg Injury
Willie Rogers — Knee Injury
Sid Smith — Injury

Use Name	Pos.	Hgt	Wgt	Age	Int	Pts
Lynn Dickey	QB	6'4"	218	23		24
Edd Hargett	QB	5'11"	190	26		
Dan Pastorini	QB	6'3"	215	24		
Bob Gresham	HB	5'11"	195	25		24
Al Johnson	HB	6'	200	23		
Paul Robinson	HB	6'	195	29		12
George Amundson	FB-HB	6'3"	215	23		
Lewis Jolley	FB-HB	6'	210	23		
Bill Thomas	FB	6'2"	225	23		
Fred Willis	FB	6'	212	25		30
Jim Beirne	WR	6'2"	196	26		
Ken Burrough	WR	6'4"	210	25		18
Eddie Hinton	WR	6'	200	26		
Clifton McNeil	WR	6'2"	187	33		
Billy Parks	WR	6'1"	185	25		6
Dave Parks	TE	6'2"	203	31		6
Mack Alston	TE	6'2"	230	26		24
Ron Mayo	TE	6'3"	223	22		
Skip Butler	K	6'2"	200	25		66
Dave Green (to CIN)	K	5'11"	200	23		

CINCINNATI BENGALS

RUSHING

Last Name	No.	Yds	Avg	TD
E. Johnson	195	997	5.1	4
Clark	254	988	3.9	8
Elliott	22	122	5.5	1
Anderson	26	97	3.7	0
Wilson	10	39	3.9	0
Morrison	3	11	3.7	0
Lewis	3	−7	−2.3	0
Curtis	2	−11	−5.5	0

RECEIVING

Last Name	No.	Yds	Avg	TD
Curtis	45	843	19	9
Clark	45	347	8	0
Trumpy	29	435	15	5
E. Johnson	28	356	13	3
Joiner	13	214	16	0
Coslet	9	123	14	0
Myers	7	77	11	0
George	2	28	14	0
Elliott	1	12	12	1
Morrison	1	4	4	0

PUNT RETURNS

Last Name	No.	Yds	Avg	TD
Parrish	25	200	8	0
Casanova	15	119	8	0
Blackwood	4	12	3	0
Lewis	1	2	2	0

KICKOFF RETURNS

Last Name	No.	Yds	Avg	TD
Jackson	21	520	25	0
Wilson	8	173	22	0
Parrish	7	143	20	0
Lewis	2	40	20	0
Coslet	1	0	0	0

PASSING – PUNTING – KICKING Statistics

PASSING	Att	Comp	%	Yds	Yd/Att	TD	Int−%	RK
Anderson	329	179	54	2428	7.4	18	12− 4	1
Cook	3	1	33	11	3.7	0	0− 0	

PUNTING	No	Avg
Lewis	68	41.0

KICKING	XP	Att	%	FG	Att	%
Muhlmann	31	32	97	21	31	68

PITTSBURGH STEELERS

RUSHING

Last Name	No.	Yds	Avg	TD
Harris	188	698	3.7	3
P. Pearson	132	554	4.2	2
Fuqua	117	457	3.9	2
Steve Davis	67	266	4.0	2
Bradshaw	34	145	4.3	3
Gilliam	6	23	3.8	0
Shanklin	3	1	0.3	0
Bleier	3	0	0.0	0
Hanratty	3	0	0.0	0
Walden	1	0	0.0	0
Lewis	1	−1	−1.0	0

RECEIVING

Last Name	No.	Yds	Avg	TD
Shanklin	30	711	24	10
Lewis	23	409	18	3
B. Pearson	23	317	14	3
Fuqua	17	150	9	0
McMakin	13	195	15	1
P. Pearson	11	173	16	2
Harris	10	69	7	0
Steve Davis	7	31	4	1
Brown	5	88	18	0
D. Davis	1	14	14	0

PUNT RETURNS

Last Name	No.	Yds	Avg	TD
Edwards	34	336	10	0
Meyer	18	80	4	0

KICKOFF RETURNS

Last Name	No.	Yds	Avg	TD
Steve Davis	15	404	27	0
P. Pearson	16	308	19	0
Bleier	3	47	16	0
Harris	1	23	23	0
Fuqua	1	22	22	0
Hanneman	1	20	20	0
Edwards	1	10	10	0
Webster	1	9	9	0
Mansfield	1	0	0	0

PASSING – PUNTING – KICKING Statistics

PASSING	Att	Comp	%	Yds	Yd/Att	TD	Int−%	RK
Bradshaw	180	89	49	1183	6.6	10	15− 8	8
Hanratty	69	31	45	643	9.3	8	5− 7	
Gilliam	60	20	33	331	5.5	2	6−10	

PUNTING	No	Avg
Walden	62	41.1

KICKING	XP	Att	%	FG	Att	%
Gerela	36	37	97	29	43	67

CLEVELAND BROWNS

RUSHING

Last Name	No.	Yds	Avg	TD
Brown	161	537	3.3	0
Phipps	60	395	6.6	5
Kelly	132	389	2.9	3
Pruitt	61	369	6.0	4
LeFear	26	135	5.2	0
Bo Scott	34	79	2.3	0
McKinnis	28	77	2.8	0
Cockroft	1	−3	−3.0	0
Richardson	3	−10	−3.3	0

RECEIVING

Last Name	No.	Yds	Avg	TD
Pitts	31	317	10	4
Morin	26	417	16	1
Brown	22	187	9	0
Hooker	18	196	11	2
Kelly	15	180	12	0
Richardson	12	175	15	1
Pruitt	9	110	12	1
Bo Scott	6	23	4	1
LeFear	5	38	8	0
Holden	3	27	9	0
McKinnis	3	11	4	0
Glass	2	60	30	0

PUNT RETURNS

Last Name	No.	Yds	Avg	TD
Pruitt	16	180	11	0
Darden	9	51	6	0
LeFear	7	51	7	0
Holden	2	19	10	0
Kelly	1	7	7	0
Hall	1	0	0	0

KICKOFF RETURNS

Last Name	No.	Yds	Avg	TD
Pruitt	16	453	28	0
Le Fear	15	337	22	0
Holden	8	172	22	0
Long	6	87	15	0
Romaniszyn	2	21	11	0
Dieken	2	14	7	0

PASSING – PUNTING – KICKING Statistics

PASSING	Att	Comp	%	Yds	Yd/Att	TD	Int−%	RK
Phipps	299	148	49	1719	5.8	9	20− 7	9
Horn	8	4	50	22	2.8	1	0− 0	
Pruitt	1	0	0	0	0.0	0	0− 0	

PUNTING	No	Avg
Cockroft	82	40.5

KICKING	XP	Att	%	FG	Att	%
Cockroft	24	24	100	22	31	71

HOUSTON OILERS

RUSHING

Last Name	No.	Yds	Avg	TD
Willis	171	579	3.4	4
Gresham	104	400	3.8	2
Robinson	34	151	4.4	2
Pastorini	31	102	3.3	0
Amundson	15	56	3.7	0
Thomas	10	39	3.9	0
Burrough	5	38	7.6	1
Alston	1	13	13.0	0
Dickey	6	9	1.5	0
Jolley	7	6	0.9	0
Hinton	1	−2	−2.0	0
Johnson	1	−3	−3.0	0

RECEIVING

Last Name	No.	Yds	Avg	TD
Willis	57	371	7	1
B. Parks	43	581	14	1
Burrough	43	577	13	2
Gresham	28	244	9	1
Alston	19	195	10	4
Hinton	13	202	16	1
Amundson	7	60	9	0
Robinson	7	46	7	0
Jolley	3	56	19	0
D. Parks	3	31	10	1
Thomas	1	4	4	0
McNeil	1	3	3	0

PUNT RETURNS

Last Name	No.	Yds	Avg	TD
Severson	16	126	8	0
Haymond	14	101	7	0

KICKOFF RETURNS

Last Name	No.	Yds	Avg	TD
Gresham	27	723	27	0
Haymond	28	703	25	0
Hinton	8	141	18	0
Eaglin	3	76	25	0
Blahak	2	41	21	0
Jolley	2	41	21	0
Fanucci	3	40	13	0
Severson	1	17	17	0

PASSING – PUNTING – KICKING Statistics

PASSING	Att	Comp	%	Yds	Yd/Att	TD	Int−%	RK
Pastorini	290	154	53	1482	5.1	5	17− 6	10
Dickey	120	71	59	888	7.4	6	10− 8	
Willis	1	0	0	0	0.0	0	0− 0	

PUNTING	No	Avg
Butler	36	37.3
Pastorini	27	40.3
Green	22	39.5

KICKING	XP	Att	%	FG	Att	%
Butler	21	21	100	15	24	63
Dickey	1	1	100	0	0	0

OAKLAND RAIDERS 9-4-1 John Madden

Scores of Each Game

Pts	Opponent	Pts
16	Minnesota	24
12	MIAMI	7
3	Kansas City	16
17	St. Louis	10
27	SAN DIEGO	17
23	Denver	23
34	Baltimore	21
42	N. Y. Giants	0
9	PITTSBURGH	17
3	CLEVELAND	7
31	San Diego	3
17	Houston	6
37	KANSAS CITY	7
21	DENVER	7

Use Name	Pos.	Hgt	Wgt	Age	Int	Pts
Art Shell	OT	6'5"	265	26		
John Vella	OT	6'4"	255	23		
Bob Brown	OT	6'4"	280	30		
Paul Seiler	C-OT	6'4"	260	27		
George Buehler	OG	6'2"	260	26		
Gene Upshaw	OG	6'5"	255	28		
Dave Dalby	C-OG	6'2"	240	22		
Jim Otto	C	6'2"	255	35		
Tony Cline	DE	6'2"	240	25		
Horace Jones	DE	6'3"	255	24		
Bubba Smith	DE	6'7"	265	28		
Kelvin Korver	DT	6'6"	260	24	1	
Otis Sistrunk	DT	6'4"	255	25		
Art Thoms	DT	6'5"	250	26		

Use Name	Pos.	Hgt	Wgt	Age	Int	Pts
Joe Carroll	LB	6'1"	220	23		
Dan Conners	LB	6'1"	230	31		
Gerald Irons	LB	6'2"	230	26	2	
Monte Johnson	LB	6'4"	235	21		
Phil Villapiano	LB	6'1"	222	24	1	
Gary Weaver	LB	6'1"	224	24		
Butch Atkinson	DB	6'	180	26	3	12
Willie Brown	DB	6'1"	190	32	3	
Tommy Maxwell	DB	6'2"	195	26		
Jack Tatum	DB	5'10"	200	24	1	
Skip Thomas	DB	6'1"	205	23	2	
Jimmy Warren	DB	5'11"	175	34	1	
Nemiah Wilson	DB	6'	165	30	3	

Jackie Allen — Injury

Use Name	Pos.	Hgt	Wgt	Age	Int	Pts
George Blanda	QB	6'1"	215	45		100
Daryle Lamonica	QB	6'2"	215	32		
Ken Stabler	QB	6'3"	215	29		
Clarence Davis	HB	5'10"	190	24		24
Bob Hudson	HB	5'11"	205	25		
Charlie Smith	HB	6'1"	205	27		30
Marv Hubbard	FB	6'1"	225	27		36
Pete Banaszak	HB-FB	5'11"	210	29		
Jeff Queen	TE-FB	6'1"	220	27		
Fred Biletnikoff	WR	6'1"	190	30		24
Cliff Branch	WR	5'11"	170	25		18
Mike Siani	WR	6'2"	195	23		18
Steve Sweeney	WR	6'2"	205	22		6
Warren Bankston	TE	6'4"	235	26		
Bob Moore	TE	6'3"	220	24		24
Ray Guy	K	6'3"	190	23		

DENVER BRONCOS 7-5-2 John Ralston

Pts	Opponent	Pts
28	CINCINNATI	10
34	SAN FRANCISCO	36
14	CHICAGO	33
14	Kansas City	16
48	Houston	20
23	OAKLAND	23
40	N. Y. Jets	28
17	St. Louis	17
30	SAN DIEGO	19
23	Pittsburgh	13
14	KANSAS CITY	10
10	DALLAS	22
42	San Diego	28
7	Oakland	21

Use Name	Pos.	Hgt	Wgt	Age	Int	Pts
Mike Askea	OT	6'4"	260	22		
Mike Current	OT	6'4"	274	27		
Larron Jackson	OT	6'3"	270	24		
Marv Montgomery	OT	6'6"	255	25		
Paul Howard	OG	6'3"	260	22		
Tommy Lyons	OG	6'2"	228	25		
Mike Schnitker	OG	6'3"	245	26		
Larry Kaminski	C	6'2"	245	28		
Bobby Maples	C	6'3"	250	30		
Lyle Alzado	DE	6'3"	252	24		
Barney Chavous	DE	6'3"	252	22		
John Grant	DE	6'3"	235	23		
Ed Smith	DE	6'5"	240	23		
Pete Duranko	DT	6'2"	250	29		
Jerry Inman	DT	6'3"	256	33		
Paul Smith	DT	6'3"	256	28		

Use Name	Pos.	Hgt	Wgt	Age	Int	Pts
Ken Criter	LB	5'11"	223	26		2
Tom Graham	LB	6'2"	235	23		
Tom Jackson	LB	5'11"	220	22		
Bill Laskey	LB	6'2"	235	30	2	
Ray May (from BAL)	LB	6'1"	230	28	1	
Jim O'Malley	LB	6'1"	230	22		
Mike Simone	LB	6'	210	23		
Charlie Greer	DB	6'	205	27	1	
Dale Hackbart	DB	6'3"	210	37		
Calvin Jones	DB	5'7"	170	22	4	
Leroy Mitchell	DB	6'	190	28		
Randy Montgomery	DB	5'11"	182	26		
John Pitts	DB	6'4"	218	28		
Bill Thompson	DB	6'1"	200	26	3	12
Maurice Tyler	DB	6'	188	23		

Tom Domres — Injury
George Goeddeke — Injury
Chip Myrtle — Injury

Use Name	Pos.	Hgt	Wgt	Age	Int	Pts
Charley Johnson	QB	6'	190	36		
Steve Ramsey	QB	6'2"	210	25		
Bobby Anderson	HB	6'	208	25		6
Otis Armstrong	HB	5'10"	196	22		6
Floyd Little	HB	5'10"	196	31		78
Oliver Ross	FB-HB	6'	210	23		
Joe Dawkins	FB	5'11"	223	25		12
Fran Lynch	HB-FB	6'1"	205	27		
Haven Moses	WR	6'3"	205	27		54
Jerry Simmons	WR	6'1"	190	30		6
Bill Van Heusen	WR	6'1"	200	27		6
Gene Washington	WR	6'3"	205	29		18
Bill Masters	TE	6'5"	240	29		
Riley Odoms	TE	6'4"	230	23		42
Jim Turner	K	6'2"	205	32		106

KANSAS CITY CHIEFS 7-5-2 Hank Stram

Pts	Opponent	Pts
13	LOS ANGELES	23
10	New England	7
16	OAKLAND	3
16	DENVER	14
10	Green Bay	10
6	Cincinnati	14
14	Buffalo	23
19	San Diego	0
19	CHICAGO	7
38	HOUSTON	14
10	Denver	14
20	CLEVELAND	20
7	Oakland	37
33	SAN DIEGO	6

Use Name	Pos.	Hgt	Wgt	Age	Int	Pts
Dave Hill	OT	6'5"	260	32		
Francis Peay	OT	6'5"	250	29		
Jim Tyrer	OT	6'6"	280	34		
Ed Budde	OG	6'5"	265	32		
George Daney	OG	6'3"	240	26		
Mo Moorman	OT-OG	6'5"	252	29		
Wayne Walton	OT-OG	6'5"	255	24		
Jack Rudnay	C	6'3"	240	25		
Mike Oriard	OG-C	6'4"	223	25		
Pat Holmes	DE	6'5"	250	33	1	
John Lohmeyer	DE	6'4"	230	22		6
Marv Upshaw	DE	6'3"	260	26		
Wilbur Young	DE	6'6"	285	24		
Buck Buchanan	DT	6'7"	270	33	1	
Curley Culp	DT	6'1"	265	27		
George Seals	DT	6'2"	260	30		

Use Name	Pos.	Hgt	Wgt	Age	Int	Pts
Bobby Bell	LB	6'4"	228	33	1	
Willie Lanier	LB	6'1"	245	28	3	6
Jim Lynch	LB	6'1"	235	28	1	
Al Palewicz	LB	6'1"	215	23		
Clyde Werner	LB	6'4"	225	25		
Nate Allen	DB	5'10"	170	25	1	
Doug Jones	DB	6'2"	202	23		
Jim Kearney	DB	6'2"	206	30	3	
Jim Marsalis	DB	5'11"	194	27	2	
Larry Marshall	DB	5'11"	195	23		
Kerry Reardon	DB	5'11"	180	24	2	
Mike Sensibaugh	DB	5'11"	192	24	3	
Emmitt Thomas	DB	6'2"	192	30	3	

Cannonball Butler — Injury
Ernie Calloway — Knee Injury

Use Name	Pos.	Hgt	Wgt	Age	Int	Pts
Pete Beathard	QB	6'2"	200	31		6
Len Dawson	QB	6'	190	39		
Mike Livingston	QB	6'3"	212	27		12
Leroy Keyes	HB	6'	208	26		
Warren McVea	HB	5'10"	182	27		
Ed Podolak	HB	6'1"	205	26		18
Willie Ellison	FB-HB	6'1"	210	28		12
Wendell Hayes	FB	6'2"	215	28		12
Jeff Kinney	HB-FB	6'2"	215	22		6
Andy Hamilton	WR	6'3"	190	23		
Dan Kratzer	WR	6'2"	194	24		
Dave Smith	WR	6'2"	205	26		
Otis Taylor	WR	6'3"	215	30		24
Bob West	WR	6'4"	218	22		
Elmo Wright	WR	6'	190	24		12
Gary Butler	TE	6'3"	235	22		12
Morris Stroud	TE	6'10"	255	27		12
Jan Stenerud	K	6'2"	187	30		93
Jerrel Wilson	K	6'4"	222	32		

SAN DIEGO CHARGERS 2-11-1 Harland Svare Ron Waller

Pts	Opponent	Pts
0	Washington	38
34	BUFFALO	7
13	CINCINNATI	20
21	Pittsburgh	38
17	Oakland	27
0	ATLANTA	41
16	Cleveland	16
0	KANSAS CITY	19
19	Denver	30
17	NEW ORLEANS	14
3	OAKLAND	31
14	New England	30
28	DENVER	42
6	Kansas City	33

Use Name	Pos.	Hgt	Wgt	Age	Int	Pts
Ira Gordon	OT	6'3"	268	25		
Terry Owens	OT	6'6"	268	29		
Russ Washington	OT	6'6"	290	26		
Al Dennis	OG	6'4"	250	22		
Walt Sweeney	OG	6'3"	256	32		
Ralph Wenzel	OG	6'3"	250	30		
Doug Wilkerson	OG	6'2"	256	26		
Jay Douglas	C	6'6"	242	22		
Carl Mauck	C	6'3"	243	26		
Lionel Aldridge	DE	6'4"	245	31		
Coy Bacon	DE	6'4"	270	31		6
Deacon Jones	DE	6'5"	250	34		
Pete Lazetich	DE	6'3"	225	23		
Cal Snowden	DE	6'4"	253	26		
Dave Costa	DT	6'2"	260	31		
Greg Wojcik	DT	6'4"	243	30		

Use Name	Pos.	Hgt	Wgt	Age	Int	Pts
Carl Gersbach	LB	6'1"	230	26	1	
Rick Redman	LB	5'11"	222	30	1	
Floyd Rice (from HOU)	LB	6'3"	223	24	1	6
Mel Rogers	LB	6'2"	230	26	1	
Tim Rossovich	LB	6'4"	240	27	1	
Mike Stratton	LB	6'3"	240	31	3	
Joe Beauchamp	DB	6'	188	29		
Reggie Berry	DB	6'	190	24		
Lenny Dunlap	DB	6'1"	195	24		
Chris Fletcher	DB	5'11"	185	24		
Bob Howard	DB	6'1"	177	28	5	
Willie McGee	DB	5'11"	175	23		
Bryant Salter	DB	6'4"	196	23	1	
Ron Smith	DB	6'1"	195	30	1	12

Ray White — Injury

Use Name	Pos.	Hgt	Wgt	Age	Int	Pts
Wayne Clark	QB	6'2"	205	26		
Dan Fouts	QB	6'3"	193	22		
Johnny Unitas	QB	6'1"	196	40		
Mike Garrett	HB	5'9"	200	29		6
Clint Jones	HB	6'	205	28		6
Bob Thomas	HB	5'10"	200	24		6
Cid Edwards	FB	6'2"	230	29		6
Robert Holmes	FB	5'9"	220	27		42
Gary Garrison	WR	6'1"	193	29		12
Ron Holliday	WR	5'9"	168	25	1	
Jerry LeVias	WR	5'10"	178	26		18
Dave Williams (to PIT)	WR	6'2"	200	28		
Pettis Norman	TE	6'3"	220	33		
Gary Parris	TE	6'2"	226	23		
Jim Thaxton	TE	6'2"	240	24		12
Dennis Partee	K	6'2"	230	27		7
Ray Wersching	K	5'11"	210	23		48

OAKLAND RAIDERS

RUSHING
Last Name	No.	Yds	Avg	TD
Hubbard	193	903	4.7	6
C. Smith	173	682	3.9	4
Davis	116	609	5.3	4
Banaszak	34	198	5.8	0
Stabler	21	101	4.8	0
Guy	1	21	21.0	0
Hudson	4	3	0.8	0
Lamonica	5	-7	-1.4	0

RECEIVING
Last Name	No.	Yds	Avg	TD
Biletnikoff	48	660	14	4
Siani	45	742	16	3
Moore	34	375	11	4
C. Smith	28	260	9	1
Branch	19	290	15	3
Hubbard	15	116	8	0
Davis	7	76	11	0
Banaszak	6	31	5	0
Sweeny	2	52	26	1
Hudson	1	9	9	0

PUNT RETURNS
Last Name	No.	Yds	Avg	TD
Atkinson	41	336	8	1
Maxwell	4	8	2	0
Warren	1	0	0	0

KICKOFF RETURNS
Last Name	No.	Yds	Avg	TD
Davis	19	504	27	0
Hudson	14	350	25	0
Banaszak	3	48	16	0
C. Smith	2	23	12	0
Bankston	1	12	12	0

PASSING – PUNTING – KICKING

PASSING
Last Name	Att	Comp	%	Yds	Yd/Att	TD	Int–%		RK
Stabler	260	163	63	1997	7.7	14	10–	4	2
Lamonica	93	42	45	614	6.6	2	8–	9	

PUNTING
Last Name	No	Avg
Guy	69	45.3

KICKING
Last Name	XP	Att	%	FG	Att	%
Blanda	31	31	100	23	33	70

DENVER BRONCOS

RUSHING
Last Name	No.	Yds	Avg	TD
Little	256	979	3.8	12
Dawkins	160	706	4.4	2
Armstrong	26	90	3.5	0
Anderson	19	61	3.2	0
Odoms	5	53	10.6	0
Van Heusen	4	34	8.5	0
Moses	3	25	8.3	1
Ross	5	21	4.2	0
Johnson	7	-2	-0.3	0
Simmons	1	-4	-4.0	0
Masters	1	-9	-9.0	0

RECEIVING
Last Name	No.	Yds	Avg	TD
Odoms	43	629	15	7
Little	41	423	10	1
Dawkins	30	329	11	0
Moses	28	518	19	8
Anderson	15	153	10	0
Simmons	13	249	19	1
Washington	10	150	15	3
Van Heusen	8	149	19	1
Masters	5	65	13	0
Armstrong	2	43	22	1
Jackson	1	-2	-2	0

PUNT RETURNS
Last Name	No.	Yds	Avg	TD
Thompson	30	366	12	0
Tyler	4	20	5	0
Greer	3	11	4	0
Little	1	7	7	0
Criter	1	0	0	0
Mitchell	1	0	0	0

KICKOFF RETURNS
Last Name	No.	Yds	Avg	TD
Armstrong	20	472	24	0
Dawkins	10	222	22	0
Thompson	1	25	25	0
Tyler	1	23	23	0
Montgomery	1	22	22	0
Lynch	1	14	14	0
Forsberg	1	12	12	0
Simone	1	3	3	0

PASSING – PUNTING – KICKING

PASSING
Last Name	Att	Comp	%	Yds	Yd/Att	TD	Int–%		RK
Johnson	346	184	53	2465	7.1	20	17–	5	3
Ramsey	27	10	37	194	7.2	2	2–	7	
Anderson	3	2	67	47	15.7	0	0–	0	
Turner	1	0	0	0	0.0	0	1–100		
Van Heusen	1	0	0	0	0.0	0	0–	0	

PUNTING
Last Name	No	Avg
Van Heusen	69	45.1

KICKING
Last Name	XP	Att	%	FG	Att	%
Turner	40	40	100	22	33	67

KANSAS CITY CHIEFS

RUSHING
Last Name	No.	Yds	Avg	TD
Podolak	210	721	3.4	3
Ellison	108	411	3.8	2
Hayes	95	352	3.7	2
Kinney	50	128	2.6	1
Livingston	19	94	4.9	·2
Dawson	6	40	6.7	0
Wright	5	29	5.8	0
Beathard	6	16	2.7	1
Butler	2	10	5.0	0
McVea	4	5	1.3	0
Keyes	2	1	0.5	0
Taylor	4	-14	-3.5	0

RECEIVING
Last Name	No.	Yds	Avg	TD
Podolak	55	445	8	0
Taylor	34	565	17	4
Hayes	18	134	7	0
Wright	16	252	16	2
Stroud	12	216	18	2
Kinney	11	126	11	0
Ellison	9	64	7	0
Butler	8	124	16	2
West	4	65	16	0
Hamilton	2	35	18	0
Smith	2	20	10	0
Moorman	1	-1	-1	0
Keyes	1	-6	-6	0

PUNT RETURNS
Last Name	No.	Yds	Avg	TD
Marshall	29	180	6	0
Podolak	11	90	8	0
Reardon	2	9	5	0

KICKOFF RETURNS
Last Name	No.	Yds	Avg	TD
Marshall	14	391	28	0
McVea	8	146	18	0
Kinney	5	130	26	0
Reardon	2	45	23	0
Werner	1	13	13	0
West	1	0	0	0

PASSING – PUNTING – KICKING

PASSING
Last Name	Att	Comp	%	Yds	Yd/Att	TD	Int–%		RK
Livingston	145	75	52	916	6.3	6	7–	5	7
Dawson	101	66	65	725	7.2	2	5–	5	
Beathard	64	31	48	389	6.1	2	1–	2	
Keyes	1	0	0	0	0.0	0	0–	0	
Podolak	1	0	0	0	0.0	0	0–	0	
Wilson	1	1	100	9	9.0	0	0–	0	

PUNTING
Last Name	No	Avg
Wilson	80	45.5

KICKING
Last Name	XP	Att	%	FG	Att	%
Stenerud	21	23	91	24	38	63

SAN DIEGO CHARGERS

RUSHING
Last Name	No.	Yds	Avg	TD
Edwards	133	609	4.6	1
Garrett	114	467	4.1	0
Holmes	78	289	3.7	7
C. Jones	55	170	3.1	1
Clark	13	86	6.6	0
Holliday	6	70	11.7	0
Thomas	22	48	2.2	0
LeVias	2	33	16.5	0
Fouts	7	32	4.6	0
Norman	1	10	10.0	0

RECEIVING
Last Name	No.	Yds	Avg	TD
LeVias	30	536	18	3
Edwards	25	164	7	0
Holmes	19	151	8	0
Garrett	15	124	8	1
Garrison	14	292	21	2
Holliday	14	182	13	0
Norman	13	200	15	0
C. Jones	7	126	18	0
Thaxton	7	119	17	2
Dave Williams	7	118	17	0
Thomas	7	51	7	1
McGee	3	67	22	0

PUNT RETURNS
Last Name	No.	Yds	Avg	TD
Smith	27	352	13	2
McGee	6	56	9	0

KICKOFF RETURNS
Last Name	No.	Yds	Avg	TD
Smith	36	947	26	0
McGee	20	423	21	0
C. Jones	10	217	22	0
Rice	2	17	9	0
East	1	8	8	0
Rogers	1	4	4	0
Douglas	1	0	0	0
Wenzel	1	0	0	0
Holliday	0	-2	0	0

PASSING – PUNTING – KICKING

PASSING
Last Name	Att	Comp	%	Yds	Yd/Att	TD	Int–%		RK
Fouts	194	87	45	1126	5.8	6	13–	7	12
Clark	90	40	44	532	5.9	0	9–10		
Unitas	76	34	45	471	6.2	3	7–	9	
Holliday	2	0	0	0	0.0	0	1–50		
Garrett	1	0	0	0	0.0	0	0–	0	

PUNTING
Last Name	No	Avg
Partee	72	41.1

KICKING
Last Name	XP	Att	%	FG	Att	%
Wersching	15	17	88	11	25	44
Partee	4	4	100	1	2	50
Holliday	1	1	100	0	0	0

1973 Championship Games

Tarkenton's Winning Formula

Fran Tarkenton was in his first playoffs in his thirteen-year career, and he celebrated last week by leading the Vikings to a 27-20 victory over the Redskins. Now he hoped to further destroy his image as a loser by beating the Cowboys, who had defeated the Rams 27-16 in the opening round of the playoffs.

The Vikings established a winning formula on offense in the first half by mixing unexpected passes with a strong running attack. The Minnesota blockers keyed on removing middle linebacker Lee Roy Jordan from all running plays, and with star tackle Bob Lilly out of action with a bad back, the Cowboys could not stop ball carriers Chuck Foreman and Oscar Reed. The Vikings controlled the ball for most of the first half, and their defense foiled the Cowboys whenever they got the ball.

Fred Cox scored Minnesota's first three points with a first-quarter field goal, and the Vikings added a touchdown in the second period on an 86-yard drive capped by Foreman's five-yard run.

The Dallas offense, playing without the injured Calvin Hill, could not crack the Minnesota defense until Golden Richards put the Cowboys on the scoreboard by returning a punt 63 yards for a touchdown. The Cowboys now had the momentum to take the lead, but Tarkenton deflated the Dallas hopes three plays later when he hit John Gilliam with a long bomb that went for a 54-yard touchdown. The Cowboys added a Toni Fritsch field goal late in the period to make the score 17-10 with fifteen minutes left.

Turnovers dominated the final period. The teams took turns giving the ball up until Bobby Bryant intercepted a Staubach pass and returned it 63 yards for a score. Another intercepted pass led to a Cox field goal which lengthened the Viking lead to 27-10. The Cowboys suffered the final indignity late in the game when Walt Garrison fumbled the ball away on the Minnesota two-yard line.

SCORING

DALLAS	0	0	10	0—10
MINNESOTA	3	7	7	10—27

First Quarter
Minn.   Cox, 44 yard field goal

Second Quarter
Minn.   Foreman, 5 yard rush
     PAT—Cox (kick)

Third Quarter
Dall.   Richards, 63 yard punt return
     PAT—Fritsch (kick)
Minn.   Gilliam, 54 yard pass from Tarkenton
     PAT—Cox (kick)
Dall.   Fritsch, 17 yard field goal

Fourth Quarter
Minn.   Bryant, 63 yard interception return
     PAT—Cox (kick)
Minn.   Cox, 34 yard field goal

TEAM STATISTICS

DALLAS		MINN.
9	First Downs—Total	20
3	First Downs—Rushing	14
5	First Downs—Passing	6
1	First Downs—Penalty	0
2	Fumbles—Number	4
2	Fumbles—Lost Ball	3
2	Penalties—Number	3
20	Yards Penalized	33
0	Missed Field Goals	0
49	Offensive Plays	72
153	Net Yards	306
3.1	Average Gain	4.3
6	Giveaways	4
4	Takeaways	6
−2	Difference	+2

INDIVIDUAL STATISTICS

RUSHING

DALLAS	No	Yds	Avg.	MINNESOTA	No	Yds	Avg.
Newhouse	14	40	2.9	Foreman	19	76	4.0
Staubach	5	30	6.0	Reed	18	75	4.2
Garrison	5	9	1.8	Osborn	4	27	6.8
Fugett	1	1	1.0	Tarkenton	4	16	4.0
	25	80	3.2	Brown	2	9	4.5
					47	203	4.3

RECEIVING

DALLAS	No	Yds	Avg.	MINNESOTA	No	Yds	Avg.
Hayes	2	25	12.5	Foreman	4	28	7.0
Pearson	2	24	12.0	Gilliam	2	63	31.5
Montgomery	2	15	7.5	Voigt	2	23	11.5
DuPree	1	20	20.0	Lash	1	11	11.0
Garrison	1	10	10.0	Reed	1	8	8.0
Fugett	1	−1	−1.0		10	133	13.3
Newhouse	1	−4	−4.0				
	10	89	8.9				

PUNTING

DALLAS	No	Yds	Avg.	MINNESOTA	No	Yds	Avg.
Bateman	4		39.5	Eischeid	3		43.3

PUNT RETURNS

DALLAS	No	Yds	Avg.	MINNESOTA	No	Yds	Avg.
Richards	1	63	63.0	Bryant	1	0	0.0

KICKOFF RETURNS

DALLAS	No	Yds	Avg.	MINNESOTA	No	Yds	Avg.
Harris	2	54	27.0	West	2	45	22.5
Waters	1	18	18.0	Gilliam	1	21	21.0
	3	72	24.0		3	66	22.0

INTERCEPTION RETURNS

DALLAS	No	Yds	Avg.	MINNESOTA	No	Yds	Avg.
Waters	1	1	1.0	Bryant	2	63	31.5
				J. Wright	1	13	13.0
				Siemon	1	0	0.0
					4	76	19.0

PASSING

DALLAS	Att.	Comp.	Comp. Pct.	Yds.	Int.	Yds/ Att.	Yds/ Comp.	Yards Lost Tackled
Staubach	21	10	47.6	89	4	4.2	8.9	2—26
MINNESOTA								
Tarkenton	21	10	47.6	133	1	6.3	13.3	4—30

Bringing the Raiders Down to Earth

The Raiders had used a powerful running attack to beat the Steelers 33-14 in the AFC semifinal match, but the Dolphins, coming off a 34-16 victory over the Bengals, taught the Raiders a lesson about ball control in this AFC title match. Dolphin quarterback Bob Griese passed the ball only six times all game, relying instead on his powerful running backs to grind out the yardage. Larry Csonka and Mercury Morris plowed through gaping holes in the Oakland defense cut by the Miami blockers, and the Dolphins succeeded in eating up both yardage and the clock.

On the first series of the day, the Dolphins drove 64 yards to a touchdown, with the key play of the drive a 27-yard scramble by Griese on third-and-11 on the Oakland 38-yard line. Larry Csonka plowed over from the 11-yard line for the score.

The Raiders threatened in the first period when Ken Stabler hit Mike Siani with a pass deep in Miami territory, but a holding penalty nullified the play and extinguished the threat. The Dolphins, meanwhile, put together another long drive late in the half, and Csonka scored from the 2 after Griese had frozen the Raiders by faking a roll-out.

George Blanda put the Raiders on the scoreboard early in the second half with a 21-yard field goal, but Charley Leigh's 52-yard return of the kickoff led to Garo Yepremian's 42-yard three-pointer to make the score 17-3. Stabler started clicking on short passes late in the period, and his 25-yard scoring pitch to Siani narrowed the Miami lead to 17-10.

The Dolphins gave themselves some breathing room five minutes into the fourth quarter with a Yepremian field goal, and when the defensive unit stopped the Raiders on a fourth-and-inches try, the Miami attack ground out a final touchdown to run the winning margin to 27-10.

SCORING

MIAMI	7	7	3	10—27
OAKLAND	0	0	10	0—10

First Quarter
Miami   Csonka, 11 yard rush
     PAT—Yepremian (kick)

Second Quarter
Miami   Csonka, 2 yard rush
     PAT—Yepremian (kick)

Third Quarter
Oak.   Blanda, 21 yard field goal
Miami   Yepremian, 42 yard field goal
Oak.   Siani, 25 yard pass from Stabler
     PAT—Blanda (kick)

Fourth Quarter
Miami   Yepremian, 26 yard field goal
Miami   Csonka, 2 yard rush
     PAT—Yepremian (kick)

TEAM STATISTICS

MIAMI		OAK.
21	First Downs—Total	15
18	First Downs—Rushing	4
2	First Downs—Passing	8
1	First Downs—Penalty	2
1	Fumbles—Number	1
0	Fumbles—Lost Ball	0
3	Penalties—Number	3
26	Yards Penalized	35
0	Missed Field Goals	1
60	Offensive Plays	49
292	Net Yards	236
4.9	Average Gain	4.8
1	Giveaways	1
1	Takeaways	1
0	Difference	0

INDIVIDUAL STATISTICS

RUSHING

MIAMI	No	Yds	Avg.	OAKLAND	No	Yds	Avg.
Csonka	29	117	4.0	Hubbard	10	54	5.4
Morris	14	86	6.1	C. Smith	10	35	3.5
Griese	3	39	13.0	C. Davis	4	15	3.8
Kiick	6	12	2.0	Banaszak	2	3	1.5
Nottingham	1	12	12.0		26	107	4.1
	53	266	5.0				

RECEIVING

MIAMI	No	Yds	Avg.	OAKLAND	No	Yds	Avg.
Warfield	1	27	27.0	C. Smith	5	43	8.6
Briscoe	1	6	6.0	Siani	3	45	15.0
Kiick	1	1	1.0	Biletnikoff	2	15	7.5
	3	34	11.3	Hubbard	2	11	5.5
				Moore	1	9	4.5
				C. Davis	1	6	6.0
					15	129	8.6

PUNTING

MIAMI	No	Yds	Avg.	OAKLAND	No	Yds	Avg.
Seiple	1		39.0	Guy	2		51.0

PUNT RETURNS

MIAMI	No	Yds	Avg.	OAKLAND	No	Yds	Avg.
Scott	2	10	5.0	Atkinson	1	0	0.0

KICKOFF RETURNS

MIAMI	No	Yds	Avg.	OAKLAND	No	Yds	Avg.
Leigh	1	52	52.0	C. Davis	3	68	22.7
Morris	1	19	19.0	C. Smith	1	21	21.0
Nottingham	1	19	19.0		4	89	22.3
	3	90	30.0				

INTERCEPTION RETURNS

MIAMI	No	Yds	Avg.	OAKLAND	No	Yds	Avg.
Matheson	1	29	29.0	W. Brown	1	0	0.0

PASSING

MIAMI	Att.	Comp.	Comp. Pct.	Yds.	Int.	Yds/ Att.	Yds/ Comp.	Yards Lost Tackled
Griese	6	3	50.0	34	1	5.7	11.3	1—8
OAKLAND								
Stabler	23	15	65.2	129	1	5.6	8.6	0—0

Dolphin Defense and Csonka Crashes

The Dolphins did not enjoy a perfect season this year, but they did play an almost perfect game against the Vikings in the Super Bowl. After receiving the opening kickoff, the Dolphins immediately set the tone of the day with a crunching 62-yard drive. With the Miami line ripping the famous Minnesota front four to shreds, Larry Csonka repeatedly burst through the middle for good yardage. On the tenth play of the drive, Csonka bulled into the end zone from five yards out; the Dolphins now had a 7-0 lead to nurse.

Viking quarterback Fran Tarkenton, a man eager to erase his image as a loser, could make no progress against the swarming Miami defense. The Dolphin line smothered the Minnesota running game, and the Dolphin zone defense made passing a very risky proposition. Tarkenton tried every play in the Viking playbook to no avail.

The Dolphins, meanwhile, did not stop with their seven-point lead. With Bob Griese passing very rarely, the Miami attack continued to move the ball on the ground. The Dolphin linemen habitually beat the Viking front four off the ball, slamming into them before they could react; Minnesota ends Carl Eller and Jim Marshall were taken out of almost every play. The second Dolphin touchdown came late in the opening quarter on a plunge by Jim Kiick, who had not scored all season. Garo Yepremian added the extra point, and the 14-0 lead looked close to impregnable.

Yepremian added a field goal in the second quarter to give the Dolphins a 17-0 halftime edge that understated the one-sidedness of the first half. The Vikings were not making out-and-out blunders; they simply were being beaten by better blocking and tackling. They did make a mistake on the second-half kickoff when a clipping penalty called back a long return by John Gilliam. The momentum which the return had given to the Vikings immediately shifted back to the Dolphins, and within seven minutes Csonka drove into the end zone for the third Miami touchdown.

With the decision no longer in doubt, the Vikings got onto the scoreboard in the fourth quarter on a touchdown run by Tarkenton. After Cox booted the extra point, the Vikings shocked Miami by recovering an on-side kick; once again, however, a penalty nullified the play and nipped a Minnesota rally before it could begin.

By the end of the day, the Dolphins again were undisputed champions of pro football, and Larry Csonka had set a Super Bowl rushing record with 145 hard-fought yards. With two straight championships to their credit, the Dolphins now drew comparisons with the Packers of Vince Lombardi's era. Although Marv Fleming, who played on both clubs, said, "This is the greatest team ever," the question joined the ranks of unanswerable sports fantasies.

LINEUPS

MIAMI		MINNESOTA
	OFFENSE	
Warfield	WR	Dale
W. Moore	LT	Alderman
Kuechenberg	LG	White
Langer	C	Tingelhoff
Little	RG	Gallagher
Evans	RT	Yary
Mandich	TE	Voigt
Briscoe	WR	Gilliam
Griese	QB	Tarkenton
Morris	RB	Foreman
Csonka	RB	Reed
	DEFENSE	
Den Herder	LE	Eller
Fernandez	LT	Larsen
Heinz	RT	Page
Stanfill	RE	Marshall
Swift	LLB	Winston
Buoniconti	MLB	Siemon
Kolen	RLB	Hilgenberg
Mumphord	LCB	N. Wright
Johnson	RCB	Bryant
Anderson	LS	J. Wright
Scott	RS	Krause

SUBSTITUTES

MIAMI

OFFENSE	
Crusan	Morrall
Fleming	Newman
Goode	Nottingham
Kiick	Twilley

DEFENSE	
Babb	Matheson
Ball	M. Moore
Bannon	Stuckey
Foley	

KICKERS	
Seiple	Yepremian

MINNESOTA

OFFENSE	
B. Brown	Lash
Goodrum	Marinaro
Kingsriter	Osborn

DEFENSE	
T. Brown	Porter
Lurtsema	Sutherland
Martin	West

KICKERS	
Cox	Eischeid

SCORING

MIAMI		14 3 7 0—24
MINNESOTA		0 0 0 7— 7

First Quarter
Mia. Csonka, 5 yard rush   9:33
PAT — Yepremian (kick)
Mia. Kiick, 1 yard rush   13:38
PAT — Yepremian (kick)

Second Quarter
Mia. Yepremian, 28 yard field goal
8:58

Third Quarter
Mia. Csonka, 2 yard rush   6:16
PAT — Yepremian (kick)

Fourth Quarter
Minn. Tarkenton, 4 yard rush   1:35
PAT — Cox (kick)

TEAM STATISTICS

MIAMI		MINN.
21	First Downs — Total	14
13	First Downs — Rushing	5
4	First Downs — Passing	8
4	First Downs — Penalty	1
1	Fumbles — Number	2
0	Fumbles — Lost Ball	1
1	Penalties — Number	7
4	Yards Penalized	65
0	Missed Field Goals	0
61	Offensive Plays	54
259	Net Yards	238
4.2	Average Gain	4.4
0	Giveaways	2
2	Takeaways	0
+2	Difference	−2

INDIVIDUAL STATISTICS

MIAMI	No	Yds	Avg.	MINNESOTA	No	Yds	Avg.
			RUSHING				
Csonka	33	145	4.4	Reed	11	32	2.9
Morris	11	34	3.1	Foreman	7	18	2.6
Kiick	7	10	1.4	Tarkenton	4	17	4.3
Griese	2	7	3.5	Marinaro	1	3	3.0
	53	196	3.7	B. Brown	1	2	2.0
					24	72	3.0
			RECEIVING				
Warfield	2	33	16.5	Foreman	5	27	5.4
Mandich	2	21	10.5	Gilliam	4	44	11.0
Briscoe	2	19	9.5	Voigt	3	46	15.3
	6	73	12.2	Marinaro	2	39	19.5
				B. Brown	1	9	9.0
				Kingsriter	1	9	9.0
				Lash	1	9	9.0
				Reed	1	−1	−1.0
					18	182	10.1
			PUNTING				
Seiple	3		39.6	Eischeid	5		42.2
			PUNT RETURNS				
Scott	3	20	6.7				
			KICKOFF RETURNS				
Scott	2	47	23.5	Gilliam	2	41	20.5
				West	2	28	14.0
					4	69	17.3
			INTERCEPTION RETURNS				
Johnson	1	10	10.0	None			

PASSING MIAMI	Att	Comp	Comp Pct.	Yds	Int	Yds/ Att.	Yds/ Comp	Yards Lost Tackled
Griese	7	6	85.7	73	0	10.4	12.2	1—10
MINNESOTA								
Tarkenton	28	18	64.3	182	1	6.5	10.1	2—16

1974 N.F.C. Internal and External Headaches

The summer was a troubled one for the N.F.L. The Players Association called a strike on July 1 for a variety of reasons, and veteran players spent the early part of training camp walking picket lines and working out in local playgrounds. While the early exhibition games went on with an overwhelming number of rookies and free agents, the World Football League opened shop as the newest alternative to the N.F.L. The twelve W.F.L. teams threw a lot of money around and signed to future contracts such N.F.L. stars as Larry Csonka, Paul Warfield, Jim Kiick, Calvin Hill, Kenny Stabler, Ted Kwalick, Bill Bergey, John Gilliam, Ted Hendricks, Tim Foley, Craig Morton, and Rayfield Wright, all scheduled for delivery in one to three years, after their N.F.L. contracts ran out.

The W.F.L. started play in July with mostly nondescript players and huge crowds in attendance. But by the time the N.F.L. strike ended in August, the W.F.L. was in big trouble. Those huge attendance figures turned out to be padded with thousands of freebies, and the club owners found their reserves of capital rapidly shrinking. By September, franchises were shifting cities and clubs were going bankrupt, and players were going without paychecks—strong indications that the W.F.L. was a sinking ship and no threat at all to the established league.

EASTERN DIVISION

St. Louis Cardinals—The Cards didn't figure as a contender this season, but six straight wins at the start of the schedule established them as the Cinderella club of the N.F.C. Coach Don Coryell had rigged together a potent offense last season, but his defense rebounded from a disappointed 1973 campaign to keep the Cards in every game by holding enemy scoring down. Big tackle Dave Butz missed most of the season with a knee injury, but the defense held together around an All-Pro performance by cornerback Roger Wehrli. The heart of the team, however, was the offense, which had breakaway potential both in the air and on the ground. A strong offensive line cleared the way for quick running back Terry Metcalf and protected quarterback Jim Hart while he zeroed in on speedster Mel Gray. The Cards made the playoffs for the first time since 1948, when the club was still based in Chicago.

Washington Redskins—Instead of an experienced, shopworn veteran, coach George Allen's prize acquisition this year was quarterback Joe Theismann, a star at Notre Dame seasoned by play in the Canadian Football League. But Theismann's main duty this season was running back punts, as veterans Billy Kilmer and Sonny Jurgensen continued to pilot the Redskin attack. Jurgensen particularly captured the public's fancy, as this 40-year-old passer with the protruding belly won several games in relief performances. The Redskins relied more than usual on the air game, as the running attack suffered from bad seasons by Larry Brown and Duane Thomas, plus Charlie Harraway's jump to the W.F.L. The defense was as tough as ever and brought the team home in a tie for first place.

Dallas Cowboys—After the Cowboys won their opening game and then lost four straight, fans and writers were saying prayers over the team's dead playoff chances. But the Cowboys didn't count themselves out and started the long fight back to catch the Cardinals and Redskins. One key game on that road was a November 17 confrontation in Washington, where the Redskins roared out to a 28–0 halftime lead; the Cowboys came back, 28–21, but fell short when Drew Pearson dropped a pass in the end zone late in the game. The two clubs met again on Thanksgiving Day, with the Redskins taking a 16–3 lead and knocking quarterback Roger Staubach out of action. Rookie Clint Longley then came into the fray and led the Cowboys to a 24–23 win with a 50-yard touchdown pass to Pearson with only 28 seconds left. But the Cowboys could not overcome their earlier disasters and didn't make the playoffs for the first time in nine years.

Philadelphia Eagles—Coach Mike McCormack had built the Eagles into an offensive power last year, and the addition of middle linebacker Bill Bergey from Cincinnati was expected to tighten up the defense enough to permit a shot at the playoffs. Four wins in the first five games kept the Eagles hot on the heels of first-place St. Louis, but then six straight losses ended any playoff hopes. The defense was much improved, but the offense went flat, with quarterback Roman Gabriel benched for the last three games in favor of rookie Mike Boryla.

New York Giants—The Giants had a new General Manager in former star player Andy Robustelli and a new head coach in Bill Arnsparger, who designed the famous Miami defense while an assistant under Don Shula. The new management drafted two fine rookie guards in John Hicks and Tom Mullen, and quarterback Craig Morton benefited from their pass protection after coming over from Dallas in an October trade. But despite improvements at some positions, the Giants still came up short at most positions and still had to practice in Jersey City, New Jersey and play home games in the Yale Bowl in New Haven, Connecticut. Without a real home, the Giants suffered through a 2–12 season, including a string of disheartening losses coming late in the fourth quarter.

CENTRAL DIVISION

Minnesota Vikings—The Vikings used a familiar formula to quickly take charge of the Central Division. The blend of an overwhelming defense plus a versatile offense versed at ball-control had won divisional titles before, and again propelled the Vikings into the playoffs this season. The front four of Alan Page, Carl Eller, Jim Marshall, and Doug Sutherland put unrelenting pressure on enemy offenses, and the secondary didn't lose much when cornerback Bobby Bryant broke his arm and was replaced by rookie Jackie Wallace. The Viking offense had stars in all sectors, featuring quarterback Fran Tarkenton, running back Chuck Foreman, wide receiver John Gilliam, and tackle Ron Yary.

Detroit Lions—The season got off to a depressing start when head coach Don McCafferty died of a heart attack in training camp. With assistant Rick Forzano taking over the reigns, the Lions got off to a slow start in the regular season and seemed destined to finish in the lower ranks of the league. But the club righted itself and stayed in contention for a wildcard playoff berth in December before being eliminated. Bill Munson captured the starting quarterback's job in the preseason, but Greg Landry reclaimed the position late in the year when Munson suffered a dislocated shoulder.

Green Bay Packers—The Packer defense, bolstered by the addition of All-Pro linebacker Ted Hendricks from Baltimore, was one of the N.F.L.'s best, but the offense could generate little fireworks. Runners John Brockington and MacArthur Lane punched out less yards than had been expected, and young quarterback Jerry Tagge couldn't ignite a respectable passing attack. An October trade for John Hadl helped the offense somewhat, but not enough to give the Pack a winning season. Rumors of coach Dan Devine's impending dismissal circulated all season, but Devine beat the punch by resigning after the season to become head coach at Notre Dame.

Chicago Bears—The Bears beat Detroit in their opening game, but persistent quarterback problems quickly dragged the Bears down into another losing season. Neither Gary Huff nor Bobby Douglass was successful in putting points on the scoreboard, and coach Abe Gibron was fired after the season. The Bears were such a dull show that a game against the Giants on December 1 drew a crowd of 18,802 and a no-show total of 36,951. With Dick Butkus retired, the Bears simply had no big names to draw a crowd in bad weather.

WESTERN DIVISION

Los Angeles Rams—Experts made the Rams the preseason favorite to reach the Super Bowl, but coach Chuck Knox's club never jelled into a powerhouse. They easily outdistanced the weak competition in the Western Division, but upset losses to clubs like New England and New Orleans belied the shaky base of the team's good record. One major change made by coach Knox was the trade of quarterback John Hadl to Green Bay in October and the elevation of sub James Harris to the starter's slot. The only black starting quarterback in the N.F.C., Harris had fine support from a strong offensive line, good receivers, and great running from Lawrence McCutcheon. The defense was the stingiest in the entire N.F.L. with end Jack Youngblood and tackle Larry Brooks making All-Pro, and with tackle Merlin Olsen still a formidable force.

San Francisco '49ers—The '49er offense sputtered under a veritable parade of quarterbacks. With John Brodie retired, Steve Spurrier was expected to start, but he suffered a shoulder separation in a preseason game. Joe Reed began the season in competent fashion but soon fell apart. Rookie Dennis Morrison then took his turn, and 13th-draft-choice Tom Owen got a chance and saw considerable action in the latter part of the schedule. Veteran Norm Snead came over in a mid-season trade but could accomplish little more than the others in the parade. Rookie Wilbur Jackson injected some punch into the running game, but the defense suffered from Charlie Krueger's retirement, Jim Johnson's bad toe, and Mel Phillips' broken arm.

New Orleans Saints—Another mediocre season fanned recurrent rumors that quarterback Archie Manning was going to be traded to shore up several other positions. A flurry of quarterback trading in late October in the N.F.C. saw Manning stay in New Orleans, but coach John North was evidently not completely satisfied with his young passer. North sat Manning down for several games and started subs Bobby Scott and Larry Cipa.

Atlanta Falcons—The Falcons seemed ready to move into the playoff ranks for the first time, but instead the club degenerated into a dismal also-ran. Quarterbacks Bob Lee, Pat Sullivan, and Kim McQuilken could not move the offense, and the entire squad bristled under coach Norm Van Brocklin's stern regime. Rumors of the Dutchman's imminent firing ran wild in Atlanta, and a press conference in November saw Van Brocklin challenge a reporter to a fist fight. Van Brocklin was then canned with the team record at 2–6, and Atlanta fans were so disenchanted that there were 48,830 no-shows for the season's finale on December 15 against Green Bay.

FINAL TEAM STATISTICS

OFFENSE

	ATL.	CHI.	DALL.	DET.	G.B.	L.A.	MINN.	N.O.	N.Y.	PHIL.	St.L.	S.F.	WASH.
FIRST DOWNS:													
Total	174	203	295	211	214	265	264	233	215	244	247	227	249
by Rushing	77	92	147	88	87	132	114	117	90	79	120	101	77
by Passing	86	96	129	114	108	112	136	91	107	141	117	104	156
by Penalty	11	15	19	9	19	21	14	25	18	24	10	22	16
RUSHING:													
Number	400	434	542	397	482	566	488	503	441	415	466	477	470
Yards	1493	1480	2454	1433	1571	2125	1856	1983	1496	1385	1956	1981	1443
Average Yards	3.7	3.4	4.5	3.6	3.3	3.8	3.8	3.9	3.4	3.3	4.2	4.2	3.1
Touchdowns	6	10	22	13	10	16	17	9	11	13	12	10	11
PASSING:													
Attempts	356	396	385	377	385	338	400	389	393	461	391	361	413
Completions	160	185	206	216	187	169	234	185	207	258	201	170	254
Completion Percentage	44.9	46.7	53.5	57.3	48.6	50.0	58.5	47.6	52.7	56.0	51.4	47.1	61.5
Passing Yards	1781	2079	2856	2475	2162	2368	2909	2037	2349	2531	2492	2281	2978
Avg. Yards per Attempt	5.0	5.3	7.4	6.6	5.6	7.0	7.3	5.2	6.0	5.5	6.4	6.3	7.2
Avg. Yards per Complet.	11.1	11.2	13.9	11.5	11.6	14.0	12.4	11.0	11.4	9.8	12.4	13.4	11.7
Times Tackled Passing	50	36	47	35	17	21	19	37	20	42	16	35	25
Yards Lost Passing	474	359	327	255	126	161	154	276	156	319	134	274	176
Net Yards	1307	1720	2529	2220	2036	2207	2755	1761	2193	2212	2358	2007	2802
Touchdowns	4	8	14	11	5	16	22	10	12	14	20	15	22
Interceptions	31	22	15	11	21	13	13	21	26	17	8	28	11
Percent Intercepted	8.7	5.6	3.9	2.9	5.5	3.8	3.3	5.4	6.6	3.7	2.1	7.8	2.7
PUNTS:													
Number	96	91	73	73	69	75	73	91	69	84	81	70	74
Average Distance	40.5	37.7	38.5	38.2	38.4	36.4	36.1	41.8	40.1	36.0	38.7	40.8	38.1
PUNT RETURNS:													
Number	51	44	62	34	42	53	43	43	41	37	52	44	46
Yards	635	248	573	429	416	507	320	415	408	339	512	398	453
Average Yards	12.5	5.6	9.2	12.6	9.9	9.6	7.4	9.7	10.0	9.2	9.8	9.9	9.8
Touchdowns	1	0	1	0	2	0	0	0	0	0	0	1	1
KICKOFF RETURNS:													
Number	60	57	49	62	49	40	50	53	59	48	50	51	45
Yards	1296	1256	1071	1293	1022	938	1090	1040	1458	1062	1203	1144	1166
Average Yards	21.6	22.0	21.9	20.9	20.9	23.5	21.8	19.6	24.7	22.1	24.1	22.4	25.9
Touchdowns	0	0	0	0	0	1	0	0	0	0	1	0	1
INTERCEPTION RETURNS:													
Number	17	18	13	17	23	22	22	16	15	18	16	20	26
Yards	210	293	110	266	278	340	282	179	91	176	372	247	328
Average Yards	12.4	16.3	8.5	15.6	12.1	15.5	12.8	11.2	6.1	9.8	23.3	12.4	13.1
Touchdowns	1	0	0	2	1	2	0	1	0	1	1	1	2
PENALTIES:													
Number	82	88	86	86	55	58	56	75	65	76	77	63	78
Yards	636	679	703	719	536	550	501	598	567	722	645	606	621
FUMBLES:													
Number	32	35	31	23	25	29	24	26	28	32	37	31	16
Number Lost	24	15	16	14	16	14	9	12	10	12	9	14	9
POINTS:													
Total	111	152	297	256	210	263	310	166	195	242	285	226	320
PAT Attempts	12	18	38	27	19	35	40	20	24	31	36	28	28
PAT Made	12	17	37	23	19	26	32	19	21	26	30	25	35
FG Attempts	16	13	21	32	39	16	20	16	19	16	22	24	31
FG Made	9	9	10	23	25	9	12	9	10	10	13	11	19
Percent FG Made	56.3	69.2	47.6	71.9	64.1	56.3	60.0	56.3	52.6	62.5	59.1	45.8	61.3
Safeties	0	0	1	1	1	0	1	0	0	0	0	0	0

DEFENSE

	ATL.	CHI.	DALL.	DET.	G.B.	L.A.	MINN.	N.O.	N.Y.	PHIL.	St.L.	S.F.	WASH.
FIRST DOWNS:													
Total	238	231	199	270	218	186	230	226	291	248	249	232	210
by Rushing	140	104	63	127	93	66	100	104	134	105	108	113	79
by Passing	85	102	110	124	106	109	120	105	142	129	122	101	114
by Penalty	13	25	26	19	19	11	10	17	15	14	19	18	17
RUSHING:													
Number	627	519	417	486	465	381	437	447	521	460	461	503	414
Yards	2564	1739	1344	2102	1641	1302	1605	1758	1916	1797	1888	2033	1439
Average Yards	4.1	3.4	3.2	4.3	3.5	3.4	3.7	3.9	3.7	3.9	4.1	4.0	3.5
Touchdowns	19	17	8	17	10	4	12	11	15	14	15	13	7
PASSING:													
Attempts	302	329	349	405	383	381	396	369	415	434	413	339	399
Completions	136	174	178	219	188	194	214	193	245	230	230	178	197
Completion Percentage	45.0	52.9	51.0	54.1	49.1	50.9	54.0	52.3	59.0	53.0	55.7	52.5	49.4
Passing Yards	1847	2250	2451	2423	2254	2465	2569	2330	2688	2684	2581	2178	2102
Avg. Yards per Attempt	6.1	6.8	7.0	6.0	5.9	6.7	6.5	6.3	6.5	6.2	6.2	6.5	5.3
Avg. Yards per Complet.	13.6	12.9	13.8	11.1	12.0	12.7	12.0	12.1	11.0	11.7	11.2	12.2	10.7
Times Tackled Passing	31	25	37	24	28	44	31	37	25	28	35	28	31
Yards Lost Passing	275	171	332	187	254	363	267	291	147	211	218	247	256
Net Yards	1572	2079	2119	2236	2000	2102	2302	2039	2541	2473	2363	1931	1846
Touchdowns	13	12	17	13	10	16	8	17	22	9	11	14	13
Interceptions	17	18	13	17	23	22	22	16	15	18	16	20	25
Percent Intercepted	5.6	5.5	3.7	4.2	6.0	5.8	5.6	4.3	3.6	4.1	3.9	6.0	6.4
PUNTS:													
Number	84	77	93	62	84	95	75	77	65	73	85	74	80
Average Distance	38.3	38.5	39.9	37.2	36.6	41.2	37.1	42.5	36.2	39.1	39.2	39.5	38.4
PUNT RETURNS:													
Number	59	58	31	37	48	40	45	59	43	37	56	46	50
Yards	658	633	343	275	356	453	345	906	478	252	518	491	458
Average Yards	11.2	10.9	11.1	7.4	7.4	11.3	7.7	15.4	11.0	6.8	9.3	10.7	9.2
Touchdowns	1	1	1	0	0	1	0	2	0	0	1	0	1
KICKOFF RETURNS:													
Number	33	35	61	60	55	58	64	40	45	46	54	51	64
Yards	812	700	1194	1256	1156	1232	1116	894	1154	1028	1203	1099	1379
Average Yards	24.6	20.0	19.6	20.9	21.0	21.2	17.4	22.4	25.6	22.3	22.3	21.5	21.5
Touchdowns	0	0	0	0	0	0	0	0	0	1	0	0	0
INTERCEPTION RETURNS:													
Number	31	22	15	11	21	13	13	21	26	17	8	28	11
Yards	451	225	93	149	289	92	185	258	372	362	75	409	75
Average Yards	14.5	10.2	6.2	13.5	13.8	7.1	14.2	12.3	14.3	21.3	9.4	14.6	6.8
Touchdowns	1	1	0	0	1	0	1	2	2	1	0	1	1
PENALTIES:													
Number	54	74	69	71	88	82	70	77	80	86	80	85	69
Yards	449	601	657	566	715	772	660	690	616	722	654	830	529
FUMBLES:													
Number	26	28	31	23	19	15	25	37	28	36	24	38	28
Number Lost	12	14	13	13	12	3	11	19	10	16	9	20	15
POINTS:													
Total	271	279	235	270	206	181	195	263	299	217	218	236	196
PAT Attempts	34	33	28	30	23	22	21	34	39	26	27	29	24
PAT Made	31	29	28	28	17	19	18	29	32	25	26	26	22
FG Attempts	28	23	21	32	26	14	24	17	24	26	14	19	15
FG Made	12	16	13	20	17	10	17	10	11	12	10	12	10
Percent FG Made	42.9	69.6	61.9	62.5	65.4	71.4	70.7	58.8	45.8	46.2	71.4	63.2	66.7
Safeties	0	2	0	1	0	0	0	0	0	0	0	0	0

CONFERENCE PLAYOFFS

December 21, at Minnesota (Attendance 44,626)

SCORING

MINNESOTA	0	7	16	7	– 30
ST. LOUIS	0	7	0	7	– 14

Second Quarter
- St.L. Thomas, 13 yard pass from Hart PAT–Bakken (kick)
- Minn. Gilliam, 16 yard pass from Tarkenton PAT–Cox (kick)

Third Quarter
- Minn. Cox, 37 yard field goal
- Minn. N. Wright, 20 yard fumble return PAT–Cox (kick)
- Minn. Gilliam, 38 yard pass from Tarkenton PAT-kick failed

Fourth Quarter
- Minn. Foreman, 4 yard rush PAT–Cox (kick)
- St.L. Metcalf, 11 yard rush PAT–Bakken (kick)

TEAM STATISTICS

MINN.		St.L.
19	First Downs-Total	17
12	First Downs-Rushing	6
7	First Downs-Passing	10
0	First Downs-Penalty	1
0	Fumbles-Number	2
0	Fumbles-Lost Ball	1
4	Penalties-Number	1
39	Yards Penalized	15
0	Missed Field Goals	1
66	Offensive Plays	67
363	Net Yards	284
5.5	Average Gain	4.2
2	Giveaways	2
2	Takeaways	2
0	Difference	0

INDIVIDUAL STATISTICS

MINNESOTA	No.	Yds.	Avg.	ST. LOUIS	No.	Yds.	Avg.
RUSHING							
Foreman	23	114	5.0	Metcalf	15	55	3.7
Osborn	16	67	4.2	Otis	8	35	4.4
Gilliam	1	16	16.0	Hart	1	10	10.0
Tarkenton	2	0	2.0	Willard	1	0	0.0
	42	197	4.7		25	100	4.0
RECEIVING							
Foreman	5	54	10.8	Thomas	6	64	10.7
Osborn	4	36	9.0	Gray	5	77	15.4
Gilliam	2	54	27.0	Metcalf	4	43	10.8
Voigt	2	25	12.5	Hammond	1	10	10.0
	13	169	13.0	Smith	1	7	7.0
				Otis	1	–1	–1.0
					18	200	11.1
PUNTING							
Eischeid	5		38.2	Roberts	7		36.4
PUNT RETURNS							
Wallace	1	3	3.0	Metcalf	3	18	6.0
KICKOFF RETURNS							
McCullum	2	49	24.5	Metcalf	3	85	28.3
Kingswriter	1	0	1.0	Hartle	3	14	4.7
	3	49	16.3		6	99	16.5
INTERCEPTION RETURNS							
J. Wright	1	18	18.0	Wehrli	1	10	10.0
				Arneson	1	7	7.0
					2	17	8.5

PASSING

MINNESOTA	Att.	Comp.	Comp. Pct.	Yds	Int	Yds/ Att.	Yds/ Comp.	Lost Tackled
Tarkenton	23	13	56.5	169	2	7.3	13.0	1–3
ST. LOUIS								
Hart	40	18	45.0	200	1	5.0	11.1	2-16

December 22, at Los Angeles (Attendance 80,118)

SCORING

LOS ANGELES	7	0	3	9	–19
WASHINGTON	3	7	0	0	–10

First Quarter
- L.A. Klein, 10 yard pass from Harris PAT–Ray (kick)
- Was. Bragg, 35 yard field goal

Second Quarter
- Was. Denson, 1 yard rush PAT–Bragg (kick)

Third Quarter
- L.A. Ray, 37 yard field goal

Fourth Quarter
- L.A. Ray, 26 yard field goal
- L.A. Robertson, 59 yard interception return PAT–bad center pass no attempt made

TEAM STATISTICS

L.A.		WASH.
14	First Downs-Total	13
8	First Downs-Rushing	4
6	First Downs-Passing	7
0	First Downs-Penalty	2
2	Fumbles-Number	3
0	Fumbles-Lost Ball	3
5	Penalties-Number	1
49	Yards Penalized	5
2	Missed Field Goals	0
66	Offensive Plays	58
226	Net Yards	218
3.4	Average Gain	3.8
2	Giveaways	6
6	Takeaways	2
+4	Difference	–4

INDIVIDUAL STATISTICS

LOS ANGELES	No.	Yds.	Avg.	WASHINGTON	No.	Yds.	Avg.
RUSHING							
McCutcheon	26	71	2.7	Brown	18	39	2.2
Bertelsen	6	34	5.7	Denson	7	5	0.7
Harris	6	17	2.8	Kilmer	2	5	2.5
Capelletti	1	5	2.5		27	49	1.8
Baker	2	2	1.0				
Scribner	1	2	2.0				
	42	131	3.1				
RECEIVING							
Jackson	2	35	17.5	Taylor	4	79	19.8
Klein	2	23	11.5	Evans	4	31	7.8
McCutcheon	2	20	10.0	J. Smith	2	35	17.5
Curran	1	12	12.0	Denson	2	17	8.5
Bertelsen	1	5	5.0	Grant	1	15	15.0
	8	95	11.9		13	177	13.6
PUNTING							
Burke	5		43.0	Bragg	5		45.2
PUNT RETURNS							
Bertelsen	1	10	10.0	Theismann	4	22	5.5
Bryant	1	6	6.0	L. Jones	1	9	9.0
	2	16	8.0		5	31	6.2
KICKOFF RETURNS							
Bryant	3	82	27.3	L. Jones	4	76	19.0
				Cunningham	1	19	19.0
					5	95	19.0
INTERCEPTION RETURNS							
Robertson	1	59	59.0	Fischer	1	17	17.0
Reynolds	1	12	12.0	Stone	1	7	7.0
Simpson	1	0	0.0		2	24	12.0
	3	71	23.7				

PASSING

LOS ANGELES	Att.	Comp.	Comp. Pct.	Yds.	Int.	Yds/ Att.	Yds/ Comp.	Yards Lost Tackled
Harris	24	8	33.3	95	2	4.0	11.9	0–0
WASHINGTON								
Kilmer	18	7	38.9	99	0	5.5	14.1	0–0
Jurgensen	12	6	50.0	78	3	6.5	13.0	1–8
	30	13	43.3	177	3	5.9	13.6	1–8

ST. LOUIS CARDINALS 10-4-0 Don Coryell

Scores of Each Game		
7	PHILADELPHIA	3
17	Washington	10
29	CLEVELAND	7
34	San Francisco	9
31	DALLAS	28
31	Houston	27
23	WASHINGTON	20
14	Dallas	17
24	MINNESOTA	28
13	Philadelphia	3
23	N.Y. Giants	21
13	KANSAS CITY	17
10	New Orleans	14
26	N.Y. GIANTS	14

Use Name	Pos.	Hgt	Wgt	Age	Int	Pts
Dan Dierdorf	OT	6'4"	280	25		
Greg Kindle	OT	6'4"	265	23		
Ernie McMillan	OT	6'6"	265	36		
Conrad Dobler	OG	6'3"	255	23		
Bob Young	OG	6'2"	270	31		
Roger Finnie	OT-OG	6'3"	250	27		
Tom Banks	C	6'1"	240	26		
Tom Brahaney	C	6'2"	250	22		
Cal Withrow	C	6'	240	29		
Bob Crum	DE	6'5"	240	23		
Council Rudolph	DE	6'3"	245	24		
Ron Yankowski	DE	6'5"	235	27		6
Lee Brooks	DT-DE	6'5"	240	26		
Bob Bell	DT	6'4"	250	26		
Dave Butz	DT	6'7"	290	24		
Steve George	DT	6'5"	265	23		
Bob Rowe	DT	6'4"	245	29		
Mark Arneson	LB	6'2"	220	24		
Pete Barnes	LB	6'3"	235	29		
Greg Hartle	LB	6'2"	225	23		
Jack LeVeck	LB	6'	220	24		
Terry Miller	LB	6'2"	220	28		
Steve Neils	LB	6'2"	215	23		
Larry Stallings	LB	6'2"	230	32	2	
Dwayne Crump	DB	5'11"	180	24	1	
Clarence Duren	DB	6'1"	190	23	2	
Ken Reaves (from NO)	DB	6'3"	210	29	1	
Hurles Scales (from CHI)	DB	6'1"	200	23		
Scott Stringer	DB	5'11"	180	23		
Norm Thompson	DB	6'1"	180	26	6	6
Jim Tolbert	DB	6'3"	210	30	2	
Roger Wehrli	DB	6'1"	190	26	2	6
Ron Davis – Injury						
Jim Hart	QB	6'2"	210	30		12
Dennis Shaw	QB	6'2"	210	27		
Donny Anderson	HB	6'3"	215	31		36
Willie Belton	HB	5'11"	195	25		
Steve Jones (from BUF)	HB	6'	200	23		
Terry Metcalf	HB	5'10"	185	22		48
Eddie Moss	HB	6'	215	25		
Jim Otis	FB	6'	225	26		6
Ken Willard	FB	6'2"	215	31		6
J. V. Cain	WR	6'4"	225	23		6
Mel Gray	WR	5'9"	170	25		36
Gary Hammond	WR	5'11"	185	25		
Earl Thomas	WR	6'3"	215	25		30
Jim McFarland	TE	6'5"	225	26		
Jackie Smith	TE	6'4"	230	33		18
Sergio Albert	K	6'3"	195	22		
Jim Bakken	K	6'	200	33		69
Hal Roberts	K	6'1"	180	22		

WASHINGTON REDSKINS 10-4-0 George Allen

Scores of Each Game		
13	N.Y. Giants	10
10	St. Louis	17
30	DENVER	3
17	Cincinnati	28
20	MIAMI	17
24	N.Y. GIANTS	3
20	St. Louis	23
17	Green Bay	6
27	Philadelphia	20
28	DALLAS	21
26	PHILADELPHIA	7
23	Dallas	24
23	Los Angeles	17
42	CHICAGO	0

Use Name	Pos.	Hgt	Wgt	Age	Int	Pts
George Starke	OT	6'5"	250	26		
Jim Tyrer	OT	6'6"	270	35		
Paul Laaveg	OG	6'4"	250	25		
Ray Schoenke	OG	6'3"	250	32		
Walt Sweeney	OG	6'3"	254	33		
Fred Sturt	OT-OG	6'4"	255	23		
Len Hauss	C	6'2"	235	32		
Dan Ryczek	C	6'3"	245	25		
Verlon Biggs	DE	6'4"	275	31		
Martin Imhof	DE	6'6"	256	24		
Deacon Jones	DE	6'5"	272	35		1
Ron McDole	DE	6'3"	265	34		
Bill Brundige	DT	6'5"	270	25		
Dennis Johnson	DT	6'4"	260	22		
Manny Sistrunk	DT	6'5"	265	27		
Diron Talbert	DT	6'5"	255	30		
Bob Brunet – Injury						
Terry Hermeling – Injury						
Brad Dusek	LB	6'2"	214	23		
Chris Hanburger	LB	6'2"	218	33	4	6
Harold McLinton	LB	6'2"	235	27	1	6
Stu O'Dell	LB	6'1"	220	22		
John Pergine	LB	6'1"	225	27		
Dave Robinson	LB	6'3"	245	33	2	
Russ Tillman	LB	6'2"	230	28		
Mike Varty	LB	6'1"	220	22		
Mike Bass	DB	6'	190	29	3	6
Speedy Duncan	DB	5'10"	180	31		
Pat Fischer	DB	5'10"	170	34	3	
Ken Houston	DB	6'3"	198	29	2	6
Larry Jones	DB	5'10"	170	23		6
Brig Owens	DB	5'11"	190	31	4	
Bryant Salter	DB	6'4"	196	24	1	
Ken Stone	DB	6'1"	180	23	5	
Ted Vactor – Injury						
Sonny Jurgensen	QB	5'11"	203	40		
Billy Kilmer	QB	6'	204	34		
Joe Theismann	QB	6'	184	24		6
Larry Brown	HB	5'11"	195	26		42
Doug Cunningham	HB	5'11"	195	28		
Herb Mul-Key	HB	6'	190	24		
Larry Smith	HB	6'3"	220	26		6
Moses Denson	FB-HB	6'1"	215	30		12
Charlie Evans	FB	6'1"	220	26		12
Mike Hull	FB	6'3"	220	29		
Duane Thomas	HB-FB	6'1"	215	27		36
Frank Grant	WR	5'11"	180	24		6
Roy Jefferson	WR	6'2"	195	30		24
Bill Malinchak	WR	6'1"	200	30		
Charley Taylor	WR	6'3"	210	33		30
Mike Hancock	TE	6'4"	220	24		
Alvin Reed	TE	6'5"	235	30		6
Jerry Smith	TE	6'2"	208	31		18
Mike Bragg	K	5'11"	186	27		10
Mark Moseley	K	5'11"	205	26		81

DALLAS COWBOYS 8-6-0 Tom Landry

Scores of Each Game		
24	Atlanta	0
10	Philadelphia	13
6	N.Y. GIANTS	14
21	MINNESOTA	23
28	St. Louis	31
31	PHILADELPHIA	24
21	N.Y. Giants	7
17	ST. LOUIS	14
20	SAN FRANCISCO	14
21	Washington	28
10	Houston	0
24	WASHINGTON	23
41	CLEVELAND	17
23	Oakland	27

Use Name	Pos.	Hgt	Wgt	Age	Int	Pts
Ralph Neely	OT	6'5"	255	30		
Bruce Walton	OT	6'6"	252	23		
Rayfield Wright	OT	6'7"	260	29		
Gene Killian	OG	6'4"	250	21		
John Niland	OG	6'4"	255	30		
Blaine Nye	OG	6'4"	255	28		
Jim Arneson	C-OG	6'3"	252	23		
John Fitzgerald	C	6'5"	255	26		
Dave Manders	C	6'2"	250	32		
Larry Cole	DE	6'4"	250	27		
Too Tall Jones	DE	6'9"	260	23		
Harvey Martin	DE	6'5"	252	23		
Pat Toomay	DE	6'5"	250	29		
Bill Gregory	DT	6'5"	252	24		
Bob Lilly	DT	6'4"	260	35		
Jethro Pugh	DT	6'6"	250	30		
Dave Edwards	LB	6'3"	226	35		
Ken Hutcherson	LB	6'1"	220	22		
Lee Roy Jordan	LB	6'2"	226	33	2	
D. D. Lewis	LB	6'2"	218	28	2	
Calvin Peterson	LB	6'3"	220	21		
Louie Walker	LB	6'1"	216	22		
Benny Barnes	DB	6'1"	192	23		
Cornell Green	DB	6'4"	212	34	2	
Cliff Harris	DB	6'	190	25	3	
Mel Renfro	DB	6'	192	32	1	
Mark Washington	DB	5'10"	186	26	1	
Charlie Waters	DB	6'1"	193	25	2	
Toni Fritsch – Knee Injury						
Rodney Wallace – Injury						
John Babinecz – Injury						
Clint Longley	QB	6'1"	193	22		
Roger Staubach	QB	6'2"	197	32		18
Doug Dennison	HB	6'1"	195	22		24
Dennis Morgan	HB	5'11"	200	22		6
Les Strayhorn	HB	5'10"	205	23		
Charles Young	HB	6'1"	210	21		
Calvin Hill	FB-HB	6'3"	230	27		42
Walt Garrison	FB	6'	205	30		36
Robert Newhouse	HB-FB	5'10"	205	24		18
Bob Hayes	WR	6'	190	31		6
Bill Houston	WR	6'3"	208	23		
Drew Pearson	WR	6'	183	23		18
Golden Richards	WR	6'	183	23		30
Billy Joe DuPree	TE	6'4"	228	24		24
Jean Fugett	TE	6'3"	226	22		6
Ron Howard	TE	6'4"	215	23		
Duane Carrell	K	5'10"	185	24		
Efren Herrera	K	5'9"	185	23		57
Mac Percival	K	6'4"	220	34		10

PHILADELPHIA EAGLES 7-7-0 Mike McCormack

Scores of Each Game		
3	St. Louis	7
13	DALLAS	10
30	BALTIMORE	10
13	San Diego	7
35	N.Y. GIANTS	7
24	Dallas	31
10	New Orleans	14
0	Pittsburgh	27
20	WASHINGTON	27
3	ST. LOUIS	13
7	Washington	26
36	GREEN BAY	14
20	N.Y. Giants	7
28	DETROIT	17

Use Name	Pos.	Hgt	Wgt	Age	Int	Pts
Herb Dobbins	OT	6'4"	260	23		
Jerry Sisemore	OT	6'4"	250	23		
Steve Smith	OT	6'5"	250	30		
Dick Stevens	OT	6'4"	245	26		
Wade Key	OG	6'4"	245	27		
Roy Kirksey	OG	6'1"	255	26		
Tom Luken	OG	6'3"	253	24		
Mark Nordquist	OG	6'4"	246	28		
Guy Morriss	C	6'4"	245	23		
Willie Cullars	DE	6'5"	250	23		
Joe Jones	DE	6'6"	250	26		
Will Wynn	DE	6'4"	245	25		6
Jim Cagle	DT	6'5"	255	22		
Bill Dunstan	DT	6'4"	250	25		6
Jerry Patton	DT	6'3"	265	28	1	
Mitch Sutton	DT	6'4"	265	23		
Bill Bergey	LB	6'2"	250	29	5	
John Bunting	LB	6'1"	220	24	2	
Dean Halverson	LB	6'2"	230	28	1	
Frank LeMaster	LB	6'2"	224	22		
Kevin Reilly	LB	6'2"	220	22		
Steve Zabel	LB	6'4"	234	26	2	
Bill Bradley	DB	5'11"	190	27	2	
Charlie Ford	DB	6'3"	195	25		
Joe Lavender	DB	6'4"	190	25	1	12
Randy Logan	DB	6'1"	195	23	2	
Larry Marshall (from MIN)	DB	5'10"	195	24		
John Outlaw	DB	5'10"	180	29	2	
Artimus Parker	DB	6'3"	215	22		
Marion Reeves	DB	6'1"	195	22		
Al Coleman – Injury						
Mike Boryla	QB	6'3"	200	23		
Roman Gabriel	QB	6'4"	220	34		
John Reaves	QB	6'3"	210	24		
Po James	HB	6'1"	202	25		12
Greg Oliver	HB	6'	192	25		
Tom Sullivan	HB	6'	190	24		72
Tom Bailey	FB-HB	6'2"	211	25		
Norm Bulaich	FB	6'1"	218	27		
Randy Jackson	FB	6'	220	25		
Harold Carmichael	WR	6'7"	225	24		48
Wes Chesson	WR	6'2"	190	25		
Bob Picard	WR	6'1"	195	24		
Charlie Smith	WR	6'1"	185	24		
Don Zimmerman	WR	6'3"	195	24		12
Kent Kramer	TE	6'5"	235	30		
Charlie Young	TE	6'4"	238	23		18
Tom Dempsey	K	6'1"	265	33		56
Merritt Kersey	K	6'1"	205	24		

NEW YORK GIANTS 2-12-0 Bill Arnsparger

Scores of Each Game		
10	WASHINGTON	13
20	NEW ENGLAND	28
14	Dallas	6
7	ATLANTA	14
7	Philadelphia	35
3	Washington	24
7	DALLAS	21
33	Kansas City	27
20	N.Y. JETS (OT)	26
19	Detroit	20
21	ST. LOUIS	23
13	Chicago	16
7	PHILADELPHIA	20
14	St. Louis	26

Use Name	Pos.	Hgt	Wgt	Age	Int	Pts
John Hill	OT	6'2"	245	24		
Doug Van Horn	OT	6'2"	245	30		
Willie Young	OT	6'	255	31		
Dick Enderle	OG	6'1"	250	26		
John Hicks	OG	6'2"	258	23		
Tom Mullen	OG	6'3"	245	22		
Karl Chandler	C	6'5"	250	22		
Bob Hyland	C	6'5"	255	29		
Rick Dvorak	DE	6'4"	235	22		
Jack Gregory	DE	6'6"	255	29		
Roy Hilton	DE	6'6"	240	29		6
George Hasenohrl	DT	6'1"	260	23		
Larry Jacobson	DT	6'6"	260	24		
John Mendenhall	DT	6'1"	255	25		
Gary Pettigrew	DT	6'4"	255	29		
Jim Pietrzak	DT	6'5"	260	21		
Andy Rice	DT	6'3"	268	32		
Carl Wafer	DT	6'3"	250	23		
Ron Hornsby	LB	6'3"	228	25	1	
Pat Hughes	LB	6'2"	225	27	2	
Brian Kelley	LB	6'3"	222	23	1	
Henry Reed	LB	6'3"	230	25		
Andy Selfridge	LB	6'4"	220	25	1	
Bill Singletary	LB	6'2"	230	23		
Brad Van Pelt	LB	6'5"	235	23	2	
Pete Athas	DB	5'11"	185	26	2	
Bobby Brooks	DB	6'1"	195	23		
Chuck Crist	DB	6'2"	205	23	3	
Honor Jackson	DB	6'1"	195	25		
Spider Lockhart	DB	6'2"	175	31	2	
Clyde Powers	DB	6'1"	195	23		
Eldridge Small	DB	6'1"	190	24	1	
Jim Stienke	DB	5'11"	182	23		
Jim DelGaizo	QB	6'1"	190	27		
Craig Morton (from DAL)	QB	6'4"	210	31		
Norm Snead (to SF)	QB	6'4"	215	34		
Carl Summerell	QB	6'4"	208	22		
Steve Crosby	HB	5'11"	205	24		
Ron Johnson	HB	6'1"	205	26		36
Leon McQuay	HB	5'9"	195	24		6
Mickey Zofko (from DET)	HB	6'3"	195	24		
Joe Dawkins	FB	5'11"	220	26		30
Doug Kotar	HB-FB	5'11"	205	23		24
Don Clune	WR	6'3"	195	22		
Walker Gillette	WR	6'5"	200	27		18
Bob Grim	WR	6'	200	29		12
Don Herrmann	WR	6'2"	205	27		
Ray Rhodes	WR	5'11"	185	23		
Chip Glass	TE	6'4"	235	27		
Bob Tucker	TE	6'3"	230	29		12
Pete Gogolak	K	6'2"	190	32		51
Dave Jennings	K	6'4"	205	22		

ST. LOUIS CARDINALS

RUSHING

Last Name	No.	Yds	Avg	TD
Metcalf	152	718	4.7	6
Otis	158	664	4.2	1
Anderson	90	316	3.5	3
Willard	40	175	4.4	0
Belton	12	49	4.1	0
Hart	10	21	2.1	2
Moss	4	13	3.3	0

RECEIVING

Last Name	No.	Yds	Avg	TD
Metcalf	50	377	8	1
Gray	39	770	20	6
Thomas	34	513	15	5
Smith	25	413	17	3
Otis	19	109	6	0
Anderson	15	116	8	3
Cain	13	152	12	1
Willard	4	28	7	1
Hammond	2	14	7	0

PUNT RETURNS

Last Name	No.	Yds	Avg	TD
Metcalf	26	340	13	0
Hammond	17	125	7	0
Wehrli	4	39	10	0
Belton	4	8	2	0
Tolbert	1	0	0	0

KICKOFF RETURNS

Last Name	No.	Yds	Avg	TD
Metcalf	20	623	31	1
Hammond	11	268	24	0
Moss	8	133	17	0
Belton	5	111	22	0
LeVeck	2	32	16	0
Reaves	1	22	22	0
Finnie	1	8	8	0
Cain	1	5	5	0
Crum	1	1	1	0

PASSING — PUNTING — KICKING

PASSING	Att	Comp	%	Yds	Yd/Att	TD	Int-%	RK
Hart	388	200	52	2411	6.2	20	8— 2	5
Metcalf	2	0	0	0	0.0	0	0— 0	
Hammond	1	1	100	81	81.0	0	0— 0	

PUNTING	No	Avg
Roberts	81	38.7

KICKING	XP	Att	%	FG	Att	%
Bakken	30	36	83	13	22	59

WASHINGTON REDSKINS

RUSHING

Last Name	No.	Yds	Avg	TD
Brown	163	430	2.6	3
Denson	103	391	3.8	0
Thomas	95	347	3.7	5
L. Smith	55	149	2.7	0
Evans	32	79	2.5	2
Kilmer	6	27	4.5	0
Cunningham	5	17	3.4	0
Theismann	3	12	4.0	1
J. Smith	1	5	5.0	0
Mul-Key	1	3	3.0	0
Taylor	1	−1	−1.0	0
Jurgensen	4	−6	−1.5	0
Grant	1	−10	−10.0	0

RECEIVING

Last Name	No.	Yds	Avg	TD
Taylor	54	738	14	5
J. Smith	44	554	13	3
Jefferson	43	654	15	4
Brown	37	388	11	4
Denson	26	174	7	2
L. Smith	23	137	6	0
Thomas	10	31	3	1
Grant	9	196	22	1
Reed	4	36	9	1
Evans	2	44	22	0
Cunningham	2	26	13	0

PUNT RETURNS

Last Name	No.	Yds	Avg	TD
Theismann	15	157	11	0
Mul-Key	13	140	11	0
Houston	6	81	14	1
L. Jones	8	54	7	0
Duncan	3	19	6	0
Stone	1	2	2	0

KICKOFF RETURNS

Last Name	No.	Yds	Avg	TD
L. Jones	23	672	29	1
Mul-Key	10	285	29	0
Evans	4	60	15	0
L. Smith	2	57	29	0
Denson	2	49	25	0
Bass	1	22	22	0
Ryczek	1	11	11	0
Tillman	1	10	10	0
Dusek	1	0	0	0

PASSING — PUNTING — KICKING

PASSING	Att	Comp	%	Yds	Yd/Att	TD	Int-%	RK
Kilmer	234	137	59	1632	7.0	10	6— 3	4
Jurgensen	167	107	64	1185	7.1	11	5— 3	1
Theismann	11	9	82	145	13.2	1	0— 0	
Brown	1	1	100	16	16.0	0	0— 0	

PUNTING	No	Avg
Bragg	74	38.1

KICKING	XP	Att	%	FG	Att	%
Moseley	27	29	93	18	30	60
Bragg	7	8	88	1	1	100
D. Jones	1	1	100	0	0	—

DALLAS COWBOYS

RUSHING

Last Name	No.	Yds	Avg	TD
Hill	185	844	4.6	7
Newhouse	124	501	4.0	3
Garrison	113	429	3.8	5
Staubach	47	320	6.8	3
Young	33	205	6.2	0
Strayhorn	11	66	6.0	0
Dennison	16	52	3.3	4
DuPree	4	43	10.8	0
Pearson	3	6	2.0	0
Waters	1	6	6.0	0
Richards	1	−5	−5.0	0
Longley	4	−13	−3.2	0

RECEIVING

Last Name	No.	Yds	Avg	TD
Pearson	62	**1087**	18	2
Garrison	34	253	7	1
DuPree	29	466	16	4
Richards	26	467	18	5
Hill	12	134	11	0
Young	11	73	7	0
Newhouse	9	67	7	0
Hayes	7	118	17	1
Houston	6	72	12	0
Fugett	4	60	15	1
Dennison	2	23	12	0
Strayhorn	2	12	6	0
Barnes	1	37	37	0
Staubach	1	−13	−13	0

PUNT RETURNS

Last Name	No.	Yds	Avg	TD
Morgan	19	287	15	1
Harris	26	193	7	0
Richards	13	74	6	0
Hayes	2	11	6	0
Waters	1	8	8	0
Renfro	1	0	0	0

KICKOFF RETURNS

Last Name	No.	Yds	Avg	TD
Morgan	35	823	24	0
Young	8	161	20	0
Dennison	3	54	18	0
Strayhorn	2	19	10	0
Harris	1	14	14	0

PASSING — PUNTING — KICKING

PASSING	Att	Comp	%	Yds	Yd/Att	TD	Int-%	RK
Staubach	360	190	53	2552	7.1	11	15— 4	6
Longley	21	12	57	209	10.0	2	0— 0	
Carrell	1	1	100	37	37.0	0	0— 0	
Pearson	1	1	100	46	46.0	1	0— 0	

PUNTING	No	Avg
Carrell	40	39.8

KICKING	XP	Att	%	FG	Att	%
Herrera	33	33	100	8	13	62
Percival	4	5	80	2	8	25

PHILADELPHIA EAGLES

RUSHING

Last Name	No.	Yds	Avg	TD
Sullivan	244	760	3.1	11
James	67	276	4.1	2
Bulaich	50	152	3.0	0
Gabriel	14	76	5.4	0
Young	6	38	6.3	0
Bailey	10	32	3.2	0
Boryla	6	25	4.2	0
Oliver	7	19	2.7	0
Reaves	1	8	8.0	0
Jackson	7	3	0.4	0
Kersey	1	2	2.0	0
Carmichael	2	−6	−3.0	0

RECEIVING

Last Name	No.	Yds	Avg	TD
Young	63	696	11	3
Carmichael	56	649	12	8
Sullivan	39	312	8	1
James	33	230	7	0
Zimmerman	30	368	12	2
Bulaich	28	204	7	0
Bailey	6	27	5	0
Jackson	2	17	9	0
C. Smith	1	28	28	0

PUNT RETURNS

Last Name	No.	Yds	Avg	TD
Bradley	22	248	11	0
Marshall	13	118	9	0
Reeves	3	12	4	0
C. Smith	4	7	2	0

KICKOFF RETURNS

Last Name	No.	Yds	Avg	TD
Marshall	20	468	23	0
Jackson	14	339	24	0
James	12	238	20	0
Kramer	2	39	20	0
Kirksey	1	19	19	0
Bailey	1	14	14	0
Chesson	1	1	1	0
Zimmerman	1	0	0	0

PASSING — PUNTING — KICKING

PASSING	Att	Comp	%	Yds	Yd/Att	TD	Int-%	RK
Gabriel	338	193	57	1867	5.5	9	12— 4	8
Boryla	102	60	59	580	5.7	5	3— 3	
Reaves	20	5	25	84	4.2	0	2—10	
Carmichael	1	0	0	0	0.0	0	0— 0	

PUNTING	No	Avg
Kersey	82	36.1
Bradley	2	33.5

KICKING	XP	Att	%	FG	Att	%
Dempsey	26	30	87	10	16	63

NEW YORK GIANTS

RUSHING

Last Name	No.	Yds	Avg	TD
Dawkins	156	561	3.6	2
Kotar	106	396	3.7	4
McQuay	55	240	4.4	1
Johnson	97	218	2.2	4
Crosby	14	55	3.9	0
Snead	4	29	7.3	0
Del Gaizo	3	15	5.0	0
Summerell	2	8	4.0	0
Zofko	3	6	2.0	0
Morton	4	5	1.3	0
Rhodes	1	−6	−6.0	0

RECEIVING

Last Name	No.	Yds	Avg	TD
Dawkins	46	332	7	3
Tucker	41	496	12	2
Gillette	29	466	16	3
Grim	28	466	17	2
Johnson	24	171	7	2
Herrmann	10	97	10	0
Kotar	10	57	6	0
Rhodes	9	138	15	0
McQuay	5	59	12	0
Glass	3	23	8	0
Zofko	3	15	5	0
Crosby	2	44	22	0

PUNT RETURNS

Last Name	No.	Yds	Avg	TD
Athas	20	180	9	0
Rhodes	10	124	12	0
McQuay	7	81	12	0
Kotar	3	14	5	0
Brooks	1	9	9	0

KICKOFF RETURNS

Last Name	No.	Yds	Avg	TD
McQuay	25	689	28	0
Kotar	15	350	23	0
Dawkins	4	154	39	0
Brooks	5	106	21	0
Crosby	2	47	24	0
Small	2	46	23	0
Zofko	3	33	11	0
Rhodes	1	27	27	0
Kelley	3	29	8	0
Powers	1	0	0	0

PASSING — PUNTING — KICKING

PASSING	Att	Comp	%	Yds	Yd/Att	TD	Int-%	RK
Morton	239	124	52	1522	6.4	9	13— 5	9
Snead	159	97	61	983	6.2	5	8— 5	
Del Gaizo	32	12	38	165	5.2	0	3— 9	
Summerell	13	6	46	59	4.5	0	3—23	

PUNTING	No	Avg
Jennings	68	39.8
Crosby	1	60.0

KICKING	XP	Att	%	FG	Att	%
Gogolak	21	23	91	10	19	53

MINNESOTA VIKINGS 10-4-0 Bud Grant

Scores of Each Game

32	Green Bay	17
7	Detroit	6
11	CHIGAGO	7
23	Dallas	21
51	HOUSTON	10
16	DETROIT	20
14	NEW ENGLAND	17
17	Chicago	0
28	St. Louis	24
7	GREEN BAY	19
17	Los Angeles	20
29	NEW ORLEANS	9
23	ATLANTA	10
35	Kansas City	15

Use Name	Pos.	Hgt	Wgt	Age	Int	Pts
Grady Alderman	OT	6'2"	247	35		
Charlie Goodrum	OT	6'3"	256	24		
Steve Riley	OT	6'6"	258	21		
Ron Yary	OT	6'6"	255	28		
Steve Lawson	OG	6'3"	265	25		
Andy Mauer (From NO)	OG	6'3"	275	25		
Milt Sunde	OG	6'2"	250	31		
Ed White	OG	6'2"	280	27		
Scott Anderson	C	6'4"	234	23		
Mick Tingelhoff	C	6'1"	240	34		
Dave Boone	DE	6'3"	248	23		
Carl Eller	DE	6'6"	247	32		
Jim Marshall	DE	6'3"	240	36		
Bob Lurtsema	DT-DE	6'6"	250	32		
Gary Larsen	DT	6'5"	255	34		
Alan Page	DT	6'5"	245	29		
Doug Sutherland	DT	6'3"	250	26		

Use Name	Pos.	Hgt	Wgt	Age	Int	Pts
Matt Blair	LB	6'5"	230	22		
Wally Hilgenberg	LB	6'3"	230	31		2
Amos Martin	LB	6'3"	228	25	3	6
Fred McNeill	LB	6'2"	230	22		
Jeff Sieman	LB	6'2"	230	24	2	
Roy Winston	LB	6'1"	222	34		
Joe Blahak	DB	5'9"	188	24		
Terry Brown	DB	6'1"	205	27	2	
Bobby Bryant	DB	6'	170	30		
Paul Krause	DB	6'3"	200	32	2	
Randy Poltl	DB	6'3"	190	22		
Jackie Wallace	DB	6'3"	197	23	1	
Jeff Wright	DB	5'11"	190	25	4	
Nate Wright	DB	5'11"	180	27	6	

John Ward — Injury

Use Name	Pos.	Hgt	Wgt	Age	Int	Pts
Bob Berry	QB	5'11"	185	32		
Fran Tarkenton	QB	6'1"	190	34		
Brent McClanahan	HB	5'11"	202	23		
Dave Osborn	HB	6'	208	31		
Chuck Foreman	FB-HB	6'2"	207	23		
Bill Brown	FB	5'11"	222	36		
Ed Marinaro	HB-FB	6'2"	212	24		
Oscar Reed	HB-FB	5'11"	222	30		
John Gilliam	WR	6'1"	195	29		
John Holland	WR	6'	190	22		
Jim Lash	WR	6'2"	200	22		
Sam McCullum	WR	6'2"	203	21		
Steve Craig	TE	6'3"	230	23		
Doug Kingswriter	TE	6'2"	222	24		
Stu Voigt	TE	6'1"	226	24		
Fred Cox	K	5'10"	200	35		
Mike Eischeid	K	6'	190	33		

DETROIT LIONS 7-7-0 Don McCafferty – died of heart attack July 28, 1974 Rick Forzano

Scores of Each Game

9	Chicago	17
6	MINNESOTA	7
19	Green Bay	21
13	Los Angeles	16
17	SAN FRANCISCO	14
20	Minnesota	16
19	GREEN BAY	17
19	NEW ORLEANS	14
13	Oakland	35
20	N.Y. GIANTS	19
34	CHICAGO	17
27	DENVER	31
23	Cincinnati	19
17	Philadelphia	28

Use Name	Pos.	Hgt	Wgt	Age	Int	Pts
Rocky Freitas	OT	6'6"	270	28		
Gordon Jolley	OT	6'5"	250	25		
Jim Yarbrough	OT	6'6"	265	27		
Bob Kowalkowski	OG	6'3"	240	30		
Chuck Walton	OG	6'3"	256	33		
Daryl White	OG	6'3"	250	22		
Guy Dennis	C-OG	6'2"	255	27		
Ed Flanagan	C	6'3"	245	30		
Fred Rothwell	C	6'3"	240	21		
Larry Hand	DE	6'4"	250	34		
Ken Sanders	DE	6'5"	240	24		
Ernie Price	DT-DE	6'4"	255	23		
Billy Howard	DT	6'4"	245	24		
Herb Orvis	DT	6'5"	240	27		
Jim Mitchell	DE-DT	6'3"	245	25	2	
John Small	LB-DT	6'5"	260	27		

Use Name	Pos.	Hgt	Wgt	Age	Int	Pts
Mike Hennigan	LB	6'2"	210	22		
Jim Laslavic	LB	6'2"	230	22	1	
Paul Naumoff	LB	6'1"	215	29	1	
Ed O'Neil	LB	6'3"	245	21		
Charlie Weaver	LB	6'2"	220	25	3	
Lem Barney	DB	6'	190	28	4	
Carl Capria	DB	6'3"	185	22		
Ben Davis	DB	5'11"	180	28	1	
Bill Frohbose	DB	6'	185	22		
Dick Jauron	DB	6'	190	23	4	
Levi Johnson	DB	6'3"	190	23	5	18
Jim Thrower	DB	6'2"	195	25		
Charlie West	DB	6'1"	200	28	1	
Doug Wyatt	DB	6'1"	195	27		

Dick Cunningham — Injury
Mike Weger — Knee Injury

Use Name	Pos.	Hgt	Wgt	Age	Int	Pts
Greg Landry	QB	6'4"	210	27		
Bill Munson	QB	6'2"	210	32		
Sam Wyche	QB	6'4"	220	29		
Dexter Bussey	HB	6'1"	195	22		
Jimmie Jones	HB	5'10"	205	24		
Altie Taylor	HB	5'10"	200	26		3
Leon Crosswhite	FB	6'2"	215	24		
Jim Hooks	FB	5'11"	225	22		
Steve Owens	FB	6'2"	215	26		
Ray Jarvis	WR	5'10"	195	25		
Ron Jessie	WR	6'	185	26		24
Bob Pickard	WR	6'	185	21		
Larry Walton	WR	5'11"	185	27		18
T. C. Blair	TE	6'4"	220	23		
Charlie Sanders	TE	6'4"	225	28		1
Errol Mann	K	6'	200	33		9
Herman Weaver	K	6'4"	210	25		

GREEN BAY PACKERS 6-8-0 Dan Devine

Scores of Each Game

17	MINNESOTA	32
20	Baltimore	13
21	DETROIT	19
7	BUFFALO	27
17	LOS ANGELES	6
9	Chicago	10
17	Detroit	19
6	WASHINGTON	17
20	CHICAGO	3
3	Minnesota	7
34	SAN DIEGO	0
14	Philadelphia	36
6	San Francisco	7
3	Atlanta	10

Use Name	Pos.	Hgt	Wgt	Age	Int	Pts
Dick Himes	OT	6'4"	260	28		
Lee Nystrom	OT	6'5"	260	23		
Harry Schuh	OT	6'2"	260	31		
Gale Gillingham	OG	6'3"	265	30		
Bill Lueck	OG	6'3"	250	28		
Bruce Van Dyke	OG	6'2"	255	30		
Keith Wortman	OG	6'2"	250	24		
Mal Snider	OT-OG	6'4"	250	27		
Larry McCarren	C	6'3"	248	23		
John Schmitt	C	6'4"	250	31		
Aaron Brown	DE	6'5"	270	30		
Mike Fanucci	DE	6'4"	242	24		
Dave Pureifory	DE	6'1"	255	24		
Alden Roche	DE	6'4"	255	29		
Clarence Williams	DE	6'5"	255	27	1	
Mike McCoy	DT	6'5"	275	25	1	
Steve Okoniewski	DT	6'3"	252	25		

Ken Bowman — Back Injury

Use Name	Pos.	Hgt	Wgt	Age	Int	Pts
Ron Acks	LB	6'2"	225	29		
Fred Carr	LB	6'5"	240	28	1	
Jim Carter	LB	6'3"	245	25	1	
Mark Cooney	LB	6'4"	230	22		
Larry Hefner	LB	6'2"	230	25		
Ted Hendricks	LB	6'7"	220	26	5	2
Noel Jenke	LB	6'1"	225	27		
Willie Buchanon	DB	6'	190	23	4	
Ken Ellis	DB	5'10"	195	26	3	6
Charley Hall	DB	6'1"	190	25	2	
Jim Hill	DB	6'2"	195	27	2	
Dave Mason	DB	6'	195	24		
Al Matthews	DB	5'11"	190	26	3	
Perry Smith	DB	6'1"	195	23		

Bill Hayhoe — Injury
Tom Toner — Collarbone Injury
Ron Widby — Back Injury

Use Name	Pos.	Hgt	Wgt	Age	Int	Pts
Jack Concannon	QB	6'3"	200	31		
John Hadl (from LA)	QB	6'2"	214	34		
Jerry Tagge	QB	6'2"	215	24		
Larry Krause	HB	6'	208	26		
MacArthur Lane	HB	6'	220	32		36
Eric Torkelson	HB	6'2"	194	21		6
Les Goodman	FB-HB	5'11"	206	24		
Charlie Leigh (from MIA)	FB-HB	5'11"	206	28		
John Brockington	FB	6'1"	225	25		30
Barty Smith	FB	6'4"	240	22		
Steve Odom	WR	5'8"	165	21		18
Ken Payne	WR	6'1"	185	23		
Barry Smith	WR	6'1"	190	23		6
Jon Staggers	WR	5'10"	180	25		6
Mike Donohoe	TE	6'3"	230	29		
Rich McGeorge	TE	6'4"	230	25		
Chester Marcol	K	6'	190	25		94
Randy Walker	K	5'10"	177	22		

CHICAGO BEARS 4-10-0 Abe Gibron

Scores of Each Game

17	DETROIT	9
21	N.Y. JETS	23
7	Minnesota	11
24	NEW ORLEANS	10
10	Atlanta	13
10	GREEN BAY	9
6	Buffalo	16
0	MINNESOTA	17
3	Green Bay	20
9	SAN FRANCISCO	34
17	Detroit	34
16	N.Y. GIANTS	13
21	San Diego	28
0	Washington	42

Use Name	Pos.	Hgt	Wgt	Age	Int	Pts
Lionel Antoine	OT	6'6"	263	24		
Bob Asher	OT	6'5"	260	26		
Randy Jackson	OT	6'5"	247	30		
Steve Kinney	OT	6'5"	260	25		
Tom Forrest	OG	6'2"	255	22		
Mike Hoban	OG	6'2"	235	22		
Ernie Janet	OG	6'4"	255	25		
Bob Newton	OG	6'4"	260	25		
Rich Coady	C	6'3"	246	29		
Gary Hrivnak	DE	6'5"	254	23		
Mel Tom	DE	6'4"	242	33		
Richard Harris	DT-DE	6'4"	255	26		
Wally Chambers	DT	6'6"	255	23		
Dave Gallagher	DT	6'4"	256	22		
Don Hultz	DT	6'3"	240	33		
Jim Osborne	DT	6'3"	254	24		

Use Name	Pos.	Hgt	Wgt	Age	Int	Pts
Waymond Bryant	LB	6'3"	230	22	2	
Doug Buffone	LB	6'1"	227	30	1	
Jimmy Gunn	LB	6'1"	218	25		
Bob Pifferini	LB	6'2"	226	24		
Don Rives	LB	6'2"	220	23		
Craig Clemons	DB	5'11"	200	25	4	
Allan Ellis	DB	5'10"	182	23	3	
Norm Hodgins	DB	6'1"	190	22		
Bill Knox	DB	5'9"	193	23	2	
Garry Lyle	DB	6'2"	193	28	3	
Randy Montgomery	DB	5'11"	185	27	2	
Joe Taylor	DB	6'2"	197	32	1	

Tom Reynolds – injury

Use Name	Pos.	Hgt	Wgt	Age	Int	Pts
Joe Barnes	QB	5'11"	196	22		
Bobby Douglass	QB	6'3"	228	27		6
Gary Huff	QB	6'1"	194	23		12
Dave Gagnon	HB	5'10"	210	22		
Carl Garrett	HB	5'11"	205	27		12
Ken Grandberry	HB	6'	196	22		12
Clifton Taylor	HB	5'11"	200	22		
Pete Van Valkenberg (from GB)	HB	6'2"	205	24		
Gary Kosins	FB-HB	6'1"	213	25		6
Jim Harrison	FB	6'4"	238	25		6
Perry Williams	FB	6'2"	222	27		6
George Farmer	WR	6'4"	214	26		
Ike Hill	WR	5'10"	180	27		6
Bo Rather	WR	6'1"	180	23		18
Charlie Wade	WR	5'10"	163	24		6
Wayne Wheeler	WR	6'2"	180	25		6
Jim Kelly	TE	6'4"	210	23		
Fred Pagac	TE	6'	220	22		
Bob Parsons	TE	6'4"	234	24		6
Mirro Roder	K	6'1"	228	30		44

MINNESOTA VIKINGS

RUSHING

Last Name	No.	Yds	Avg	TD
Foreman	199	777	3.9	9
Osborn	131	514	3.9	4
Reed	62	215	3.5	0
Jones	32	147	4.6	1
Marinaro	44	124	2.8	1
Tarkenton	21	120	5.7	2
B. Brown	19	41	2.2	0
McClanahan	9	41	4.6	1
Gilliam	2	16	8.0	0
Berry	1	8	8.0	0

RECEIVING

Last Name	No.	Yds	Avg	TD
Foreman	53	586	11	6
Lash	32	631	20	0
Voigt	32	268	8	5
Osborn	29	196	7	0
Gilliam	26	578	22	5
Marinaro	17	132	8	1
Reed	15	99	7	1
McCullum	7	138	20	3
Kingsriter	5	89	18	0
Holland	5	84	17	0
B. Brown	5	41	8	0
Craig	4	26	7	1
McClanahan	3	35	12	0
N. Wright	1	6	6	0

PUNT RETURNS

Last Name	No.	Yds	Avg	TD
Wallace	25	191	8	0
McCullum	12	85	7	0
Hilgenberg	1	−2	−2	0

KICKOFF RETURNS

Last Name	No.	Yds	Avg	TD
McClanahan	23	549	24	0
McCullum	12	300	25	0
Gilliam	3	86	29	0
Wallace	2	31	16	0
Foreman	1	30	30	0
B. Brown	3	19	6	0
Osborn	1	14	14	0
Marinaro	1	5	5	0

PASSING – PUNTING – KICKING

PASSING

Last Name	Att	Comp	%	Yds	Yd/Att	TD	Int−%	RK
Tarkenton	351	199	57	2598	7.4	17	12− 3	3
Berry	48	34	71	305	6.4	5	1− 2	
Eischeid	1	1	100	6	6.0	0	0− 0	

PUNTING

Last Name	No	Avg
Eischeid	73	36.1

KICKING

Last Name	XP	Att	%	FG	Att	%
Cox	32	39	82	12	20	60

DETROIT LIONS

RUSHING

Last Name	No.	Yds	Avg	TD
Taylor	150	532	3.5	5
Owens	97	374	3.9	3
Jones	32	147	4.6	1
Hooks	44	143	3.3	0
Landry	22	95	4.3	1
Crosswhite	12	49	4.1	1
Munson	18	40	2.2	1
Bussey	9	22	2.4	0
Jessie	6	17	2.8	1
Pickard	1	5	5.0	0
L. Walton	2	3	1.5	0
Wyche	1	0	0.0	0

RECEIVING

Last Name	No.	Yds	Avg	TD
Jessie	54	761	14	3
C. Sanders	42	532	13	3
L. Walton	31	404	13	3
Taylor	30	293	10	1
Owens	24	158	7	0
Hooks	9	53	6	0
Pickard	8	88	11	1
Jones	4	35	9	0
Bussey	4	24	6	0
Jarvis	3	87	29	0
Crosswhite	3	31	10	0
Munson	1	−6	−6	0

PUNT RETURNS

Last Name	No.	Yds	Avg	TD
Jauron	17	286	17	0
Jarvis	5	62	12	0
Barney	5	37	7	0
West	6	32	5	0
Capria	1	12	12	0

KICKOFF RETURNS

Last Name	No.	Yds	Avg	TD
Jones	38	927	24	0
Jarvis	5	90	18	0
West	4	71	18	0
Bussey	5	59	12	0
Jessie	2	55	28	0
L. Walton	1	22	22	0
Jauron	2	21	11	0
Dennis	1	18	18	0
Crosswhite	1	11	11	0
Johnson	1	0	0	0

PASSING – PUNTING – KICKING

PASSING

Last Name	Att	Comp	%	Yds	Yd/Att	TD	Int−%	RK
Munson	292	166	57	1874	6.4	8	7− 2	6
Landry	82	49	60	572	7.0	3	3− 4	
L. Walton	2	1	50	29	14.5	0	0− 0	
Wyche	1	0	0	0	0.0	0	1−100	

PUNTING

Last Name	No	Avg
H. Weaver	72	38.5
Mann	1	18.0

KICKING

Last Name	XP	Att	%	FG	Att	%
Mann	23	26	88	23	32	72

GREEN BAY PACKERS

RUSHING

Last Name	No.	Yds	Avg	TD
Brockington	266	883	3.3	5
Lane	137	362	2.6	3
Goodman	20	101	5.1	0
Odom	6	66	11.0	1
Torkelson	13	60	4.6	0
Tagge	18	58	3.2	0
Hadl	19	25	1.3	0
Barty Smith	9	19	2.1	0
Walker	1	18	18.0	0
Concannon	3	7	2.3	1
Leigh	1	0	0.0	0

RECEIVING

Last Name	No.	Yds	Avg	TD
Brockington	43	314	7	0
Lane	34	315	9	3
Staggers	32	450	14	0
McGeorge	30	440	15	0
Barty Smith	20	294	15	1
Odom	15	249	17	1
Payne	5	63	13	0
Goodman	5	19	4	0
Torkelson	2	10	5	0
Donohue	1	8	8	0

PUNT RETURNS

Last Name	No.	Yds	Avg	TD
Staggers	22	222	10	1
Odom	15	191	13	1
Ellis	3	3	1	0
Hefner	1	0	0	0
Torkelson	1	0	0	0

KICKOFF RETURNS

Last Name	No.	Yds	Avg	TD
Odom	31	713	23	0
Leigh	11	251	23	0
Goodman	4	49	12	0
Torkelson	1	20	20	0
Okoniewski	2	11	6	0
Krause	1	6	6	0

PASSING – PUNTING – KICKING

PASSING

Last Name	Att	Comp	%	Yds	Yd/Att	TD	Int−%	RK
Hadl	299	142	48	1752	5.9	8	14− 5	12
Tagge	146	70	48	709	4.9	1	10− 7	15
Concannon	54	28	52	381	7.1	3	3− 6	
Lane	1	0	0	0	0.0	0	0− 0	

PUNTING

Last Name	No	Avg
Walker	69	38.4

KICKING

Last Name	XP	Att	%	FG	Att	%
Marcol	19	19	100	25	39	64

CHICAGO BEARS

RUSHING

Last Name	No.	Yds	Avg	TD
Grandberry	144	475	3.3	2
Garrett	96	346	3.6	1
Douglass	36	229	6.4	1
Williams	74	218	2.9	1
Harrison	36	94	2.6	1
Huff	23	37	1.6	2
Kosins	8	30	3.8	1
Barnes	1	19	19.0	0
C. Taylor	9	18	2.0	1
Gagnon	1	15	15.0	0
Rather	2	10	5.0	0
Hodgins	1	3	3.0	0
Rives	1	2	2.0	0
Pagac	1	−1	−1.0	0
Wade	1	−15	−15.0	0

RECEIVING

Last Name	No.	Yds	Avg	TD
Wade	39	683	18	1
Grandberry	30	212	7	0
Rather	29	400	14	3
Williams	25	167	7	0
Garrett	16	132	8	1
Kelly	8	100	13	0
Hill	7	109	16	1
Pagac	6	79	13	0
Wheeler	5	59	12	1
Farmer	5	45	9	0
Harrison	5	38	8	0
Gagnon	4	20	5	0
C. Taylor	3	23	8	0
Parsons	2	9	5	1
Kosins	1	3	3	0

PUNT RETURNS

Last Name	No.	Yds	Avg	TD
Hill	33	183	6	0
Knox	5	35	7	0
Van Valkenburg	4	22	6	0
Hodgins	2	8	4	0

KICKOFF RETURNS

Last Name	No.	Yds	Avg	TD
Grandberry	22	568	26	0
C. Taylor	27	567	21	0
Pagac	3	53	18	0
Van Valkenburg	2	42	21	0
Gagnon	2	32	16	0
Gallagher	1	16	16	0
Kinney	1	0	0	0

PASSING – PUNTING – KICKING

PASSING

Last Name	Att	Comp	%	Yds	Yd/Att	TD	Int−%	RK
Huff	283	142	50	1663	5.9	6	17− 6	13
Douglass	100	41	41	387	3.9	2	4− 4	
Barnes	9	2	22	29	3.2	0	1−11	
Hill	1	0	0	0	0.0	0	0− 0	
Hodgins	1	0	0	0	0.0	0	0− 0	
Parsons	1	0	0	0	0.0	0	0− 0	
Rather	1	0	0	0	0.0	0	0− 0	

PUNTING

Last Name	No	Avg
Parsons	90	37.9
Barnes	1	27.0

KICKING

Last Name	XP	Att	%	FG	Att	%
Roder	17	17	100	9	13	69

LOS ANGELES RAMS 10-4-0 Chuck Knox

Scores of Each Game		
17	Denver	10
24	NEW ORLEANS	0
14	New England	20
16	DETROIT	13
6	Green Bay	17
37	SAN FRANCISCO	14
20	N.Y. Jets	13
15	San Francisco	13
21	ATLANTA	0
7	New Orleans	20
20	MINNESOTA	17
30	Atlanta	7
17	WASHINGTON	23
19	BUFFALO	14

Use Name	Pos.	Hgt	Wgt	Age	Int	Pts
Charlie Cowan	OT	6'4"	265	36		
Tim Stokes	OT	6'5"	252	24		
John Williams	OT	6'3"	256	28		
Tom Mack	OG	6'3"	250	30		
Joe Scibelli	OG	6'1"	255	35		
Rich Saul	C-OG	6'3"	235	26		
Bill Curry	C	6'2"	235	31		
Ken Iman	C	6'1"	240	35		
Fred Dryer	DE	6'6"	240	28		
Jack Youngblood	DE	6'4"	255	24		
Cody Jones	DT-DE	6'5"	240	23		
Larry Brooks	DT	6'3"	255	24		
Bill Nelson	DT	6'7"	270	26		
Merlin Olsen	DT	6'5"	270	33		
Phil Olsen	DT	6'5"	265	26		

Use Name	Pos.	Hgt	Wgt	Age	Int	Pts
Ken Geddes	LB	6'3"	235	26	2	
Jim Peterson	LB	6'5"	240	24		
Jack Reynolds	LB	6'1"	232	26		
Isiah Robertson	LB	6'3"	225	25	2	
Bob Stein	LB	6'2"	235	26		
Jim Youngblood	LB	6'3"	240	24		
Al Clark	DB	6'	185	26		
Bill Drake	DB	6'1"	195	24		
Dave Elmendorf	DB	6'1"	195	25	7	12
Eddie McMillan	DB	6'	190	22		
Tony Plummer	DB	5'11"	190	27		
Steve Preece	DB	6'1"	195	27	3	
Bill Simpson	DB	6'1"	180	22	1	
Charlie Stukes	DB	6'3"	212	30	7	

Rick Kay – Knee Injury

Use Name	Pos.	Hgt	Wgt	Age	Int	Pts
James Harris	QB	6'3"	210	27		30
Ron Jaworski	QB	6'2"	185	23		6
Jim Bertelsen	HB	5'11"	205	24		12
Larry McCutcheon	HB	6'1"	205	24		30
Bob Scribner	HB	6'	200	23		6
Cullen Bryant	HB	6'1"	218	23		6
Tony Baker	FB	5'11"	215	29		30
Les Josephson	FB	6'	207	31		
John Cappelletti	HB-FB	6'1"	217	22		
Harold Jackson	WR	5'10"	175	28		30
Willie McGee	WR	5'11"	178	24		
Lance Rentzel	WR	6'2"	202	30		6
Jack Snow	WR	6'2"	190	31		18
Pat Curran	TE	6'3"	238	28		
Bob Klein	TE	6'5"	235	27		24
Terry Nelson	TE	6'2"	230	23		
Mike Burke	K	5'10"	188	24		1
Dave Chapple (to NE)	K	6'	195	27		
David Ray	K	6'	195	29		52

SAN FRANCISCO FORTY-NINERS 6-8-0 Dick Nolan

Scores of Each Game		
17	New Orleans	13
16	Atlanta	10
3	CINCINNATI	21
9	ST. LOUIS	34
14	Detroit	17
14	Los Angeles	37
24	OAKLAND	35
13	LOS ANGELES	15
14	Dallas	20
34	Chicago	0
27	ATLANTA	0
0	Cleveland	7
7	GREEN BAY	6
35	NEW ORLEANS	2

Use Name	Pos.	Hgt	Wgt	Age	Int	Pts
Cas Banaszek	OT	6'3"	255	28		
Keith Fahnhorst	OT	6'6"	255	22		
Len Rohde	OT	6'4"	248	36		
Jean Barrett	C-OT	6'6"	254	23		
Bobby Penchion	OG	6'5"	252	25		
Woody Peoples	OG	6'2"	252	31		
Randy Beisler	OT-OG	6'4"	247	29		
John Watson	OT-OG	6'4"	245	25		
Forrest Blue	C	6'5"	265	28		
Cedrick Hardman	DE	6'3"	258	25		
Tommy Hart	DE	6'3"	248	29		
Bill Belk	DT-DE	6'3"	248	28		6
Rolf Krueger	DT-DE	6'4"	253	27		
Mike Raines	DT-DE	6'5"	255	20		
Stan Hindman	DT	6'3"	245	30		
Bob Hoskins	DT	6'2"	250	28		
Bill Sandifer	DT	6'6"	278	22		

Use Name	Pos.	Hgt	Wgt	Age	Int	Pts
Willie Harper	LB	6'2"	220	24		
Tom Hull	LB	6'3"	230	22		
Billy McKoy	LB	6'3"	226	26		
Frank Nunley	LB	6'2"	234	28	4	
Skip Vanderbundt	LB	6'3"	223	27	2	
Dave Wilcox	LB	6'3"	240	31	1	6
Caesar Belser	DB	6'	205	29		
Windlan Hall	DB	6'1"	190	29		
Hugo Hollas	DB	6'1"	190	29		
Mike Holmes	DB	6'2"	193	23	3	
Jim Johnson	DB	6'2"	185	36	3	
Ralph McGill	DB	5'11"	183	24	5	
Mel Phillips	DB	6'	190	32	1	
John Saunders	DB	6'3"	196	24		
Bruce Taylor	DB	6'	190	26	1	

Ed Hardy — Injury

Use Name	Pos.	Hgt	Wgt	Age	Int	Pts
Dennis Morrison	QB	6'3"	211	23		
Tom Owen	QB	6'1"	194	21		6
Joe Reed	QB	6'1"	195	26		
Steve Spurrier	QB	6'2"	198	29		
Manfred Moore	HB	6'	194	23		12
Del Williams	HB	6'	195	23		18
Wilbur Jackson	HB	6'1"	215	22		12
Sammy Johnson	FB	6'1"	223	21		12
Larry Schreiber	HB-FB	6'	210	27		24
Danny Abramowicz	WR	6'1"	193	29	6	
Terry Beasley	WR	5'10"	182	24		18
Mike Bettiga	WR	6'3"	193	24		
Gene Washington	WR	6'1"	185	27		36
Bob West	WR	6'4"	218	23		
Tom Mitchell	TE	6'2"	215	30		
Ted Kwalick	WR-TE	6'4"	228	27		12
Bruce Gossett	K	6'2"	230	31		58
Tom Wittum	K	6'1"	190	24		

NEW ORLEANS SAINTS 5-9-0 John North

Scores of Each Game		
13	SAN FRANCISCO	17
0	Los Angeles	24
10	ATLANTA	13
10	Chicago	24
17	Denver	33
13	Atlanta	3
14	PHILADELPHIA	10
14	Detroit	19
0	MIAMI	21
20	LOS ANGELES	7
7	PITTSBURGH	28
9	Minnesota	29
14	ST. LOUIS	10
2	San Francisco	35

Use Name	Pos.	Hgt	Wgt	Age	Int	Pts
Phil LaPorta	OT	6'4"	256	21		
John Mooring	OT	6'6"	255	27		
Don Morrison	OT	6'5"	260	24		
Jake Kupp	OG	6'3"	248	32		
Rocky Rasley	OG	6'3"	255	27		
Emanuel Zanders	OG	6'1"	263	23		
John Didion	C	6'4"	255	26		
Dave Thompson	OT-C	6'4"	260	25		
Steve Baumgartner	DE	6'7"	260	23		
Andy Dorris	DE	6'4"	230	23		
Billy Newsome	DE	6'4"	260	26		
Joe Owens	DE	6'2"	250	27		
Derland Moore	DT	6'4"	260	22		
Elex Price	DT	6'3"	260	24		
Bob Pollard	DE-DT	6'3"	250	25		

Use Name	Pos.	Hgt	Wgt	Age	Int	Pts
Don Coleman	LB	6'2"	222	21		
Wayne Colman	LB	6'1"	220	28	1	
Joe Federspiel	LB	6'1"	235	24	1	
Rick Kingrea	LB	6'1"	230	25		
Jim Merlo	LB	6'1"	225	22		
Rick Middleton	LB	6'2"	228	22		
Greg Boyd	DB	6'2"	200	22		
Chris Farasopolous	DB	5'11"	190	25	1	
Johnny Fuller	DB	6'	185	28	1	
Ernie Jackson	DB	5'10"	175	24	4	
Bivian Lee	DB	6'3"	200	26		
Jerry Moore	DB	6'3"	208	24	1	
Tom Myers	DB	5'11"	184	23	3	
Terry Schmidt	DB	6'	180	22	4	6
Mo Spencer	DB	6'	175	22		

Use Name	Pos.	Hgt	Wgt	Age	Int	Pts
Larry Cipa	QB	6'3"	209	21		6
Archie Manning	QB	6'3"	215	25		6
Bobby Scott	QB	6'1"	200	25		
Alvin Maxon	HB	5'11"	205	21		18
Howard Stevens	HB	5'5"	165	24		6
Bill Butler	FB-HB	6'	210	24		
Jess Phillips	FB-HB	6'1"	210	27		12
Jack DeGrenier	FB	6'1"	225	22		
Odell Lawson	FB	6'2"	205	26		
Rod McNeill	FB	6'2"	220	23		6
Dave Davis	WR	6'	175	26		
Sam Havrilak	WR	6'2"	195	25		
Earl McCullouch	WR	5'11"	175	28		
Bob Newland	WR	6'2"	190	25		12
Joel Parker	WR	6'5"	212	22		24
Speedy Thomas	WR	6'1"	170	27		
Bob Wicks	WR	6'3"	205	24		
Richard Williams	WR	5'11"	170	22		
John Beasley	TE	6'3"	228	29		
Len Garrett	TE	6'3"	230	25		
Paul Seal	TE	6'4"	222	22		24
Tom Blanchard	K	6'	190	26		
Donnie Gibbs	K	6'2"	205	28		
Bill McClard	K	5'10"	202	22		46

ATLANTA FALCONS 3-11-0 Norm Van Brocklin Marion Campbell

Scores of Each Game		
0	DALLAS	24
10	SAN FRANCISCO	16
13	New Orleans	14
14	N.Y. Giants	7
13	CHICAGO	10
3	NEW ORLEANS	13
17	Pittsburgh	24
7	Miami	42
0	Los Angeles	21
7	BALTIMORE	17
0	San Francisco	27
7	LOS ANGELES	30
10	Minnesota	23
10	GREEN BAY	3

Use Name	Pos.	Hgt	Wgt	Age	Int	Pts
Nick Bebout	OT	6'5"	260	23		
George Kunz	OT	6'5"	268	27		
Dennis Havig	OG	6'2"	256	25		
Jim Miller	OG	6'3"	240	25		
Royce Smith	OG	6'3"	250	25		
Len Gotshalk	OT-OG	6'4"	260	24		
Ted Fritsch	C	6'2"	242	24		
Paul Ryczek	C	6'2"	230	22		
Jeff Van Note	C	6'2"	247	28		
Claude Humphrey	DE	6'5"	265	30		
John Zook	DE	6'5"	250	26	1	
Larry Bailey	DT	6'4"	238	22		
Mike Lewis	DT	6'3"	260	24		
Rosie Manning	DT	6'5"	255	23		
Mike Tilleman	DT	6'5"	278	30		
Chuck Walker	DT	6'2"	260	33		

Use Name	Pos.	Hgt	Wgt	Age	Int	Pts
Greg Brezina	LB	6'2"	220	28	1	
Don Hansen	LB	6'3"	228	30	1	
Ken Mitchell	LB	6'1"	224	26		
Tommy Nobis	LB	6'2"	243	30	1	
Dick Palmer	LB	6'2"	232	28		
Lonnie Warwick	LB	6'3"	240	32		
Ray Brown	DB	6'2"	202	25	8	6
Rick Byas	DB	5'9"	180	23		
Ray Easterling	DB	6'	192	24		
Clarence Ellis	DB	5'11"	190	24	3	
Tom Hayes	DB	6'1"	198	28	1	
Rudy Holmes	DB	5'10"	178	21		
Rolland Lawrence	DB	5'10"	180	23	1	

Use Name	Pos.	Hgt	Wgt	Age	Int	Pts
Bob Lee	QB	6'2"	200	29		6
Kim McQuilken	QB	6'2"	203	23		
Pat Sullivan	QB	6'	200	24		
Dave Hampton	HB	6'	202	27		12
Molly McGee	HB	5'10"	184	21		
Haskel Stanback	HB	6'	210	22		6
Vince Kendrick	FB	6'	223	22		6
Eddie Ray	FB	6'1"	240	27		
Art Malone	HB-FB	5'11"	216	26		12
Ken Burrow	WR	6'	190	26		6
Al Dodd	WR	6'	178	29		6
Tom Geredine	WR	6'2"	190	24		
Louie Neal	WR	6'4"	215	23		
Gerald Tinker	WR	5'9"	170	23		6
Henry Childs (to NO)	TE	6'2"	223	23		
Larry Mialik	TE	6'2"	226	23		
Jim Mitchell	TE	6'2"	236	26		6
John James	K	6'3"	200	25		
Nick Mike-Mayer	K	5'8"	187	24		

LOS ANGELES RAMS

RUSHING

Last Name	No.	Yds	Avg	TD
McCutcheon	236	1109	4.7	3
Bertelsen	127	419	3.3	2
Cappelletti	55	198	3.6	0
Baker	53	135	2.5	5
Harris	42	112	2.7	5
Josephson	11	35	3.2	0
Jaworski	7	34	4.9	1
Bryant	10	24	2.4	0
Scribner	9	24	2.7	0
Snow	1	13	13.0	0
Jackson	1	4	4.0	0
T. Nelson	1	3	3.0	0
Preece	1	−4	−4.0	0
Rentzel	1	−9	−9.0	0

RECEIVING

Last Name	No.	Yds	Avg	TD
McCutcheon	39	408	11	2
Jackson	30	514	17	5
Snow	24	397	17	3
Klein	24	336	14	4
Bertelsen	20	175	9	0
Rentzel	18	396	22	1
Cappelletti	6	35	6	0
Baker	4	65	16	0
Scribner	2	28	14	1
Bryant	2	14	7	0

PUNT RETURNS

Last Name	No.	Yds	Avg	TD
Bryant	17	171	10	0
Elmendorf	17	134	8	0
Bertelsen	11	132	12	0
Scribner	8	70	9	0

KICKOFF RETURNS

Last Name	No.	Yds	Avg	TD
Bryant	23	617	27	1
McGee	12	288	24	0
Cappelletti	2	17	9	0
Curran	1	16	16	0
Scribner	1	0	0	0
Youngblood	1	0	0	0

PASSING – PUNTING – KICKING

PASSING

Last Name	Att	Comp	%	Yds	Yd/Att	TD	Int–%	RK
Harris	198	106	54	1544	7.8	11	6– 3	2
Jaworski	24	10	42	144	6.0	0	1– 4	
Burke	1	1	0	0	0.0	0	0– 0	

PUNTING

Last Name	No	Avg
Chapple	55	36.3
Burke	46	37.0

KICKING

Last Name	XP	Att	%	FG	Att	%
Ray	25	31	81	9	16	56
Burke	1	3	33	0	0	—

SAN FRANCISCO FORTY-NINERS

RUSHING

Last Name	No.	Yds	Avg	TD
Jackson	174	705	4.1	0
Schreiber	174	634	3.6	3
Johnson	44	237	5.4	2
Williams	36	201	5.6	3
Reed	16	107	6.7	0
Owen	16	36	2.3	1
Moore	10	24	2.4	1
Wittum	1	13	13.0	0
Washington	2	4	2.0	0
Morrison	1	0	0.0	0
Mitchell	1	−2	−2.0	0
Beasley	1	−3	−3.0	0

RECEIVING

Last Name	No.	Yds	Avg	TD
Schreiber	30	217	7	1
Washington	29	615	21	6
Abramowicz	25	369	15	1
Jackson	23	190	8	2
Mitchell	19	262	14	0
Beasley	17	253	15	3
Kwalick	13	231	18	2
Johnson	11	106	10	0
Moore	2	29	15	0
Williams	1	9	9	0

PUNT RETURNS

Last Name	No.	Yds	Avg	TD
McGill	20	166	8	0
Moore	5	149	30	1
Holmes	9	45	5	0
Taylor	10	38	4	0

KICKOFF RETURNS

Last Name	No.	Yds	Avg	TD
Holmes	25	612	25	0
Moore	18	398	22	0
Jackson	5	103	21	0
Johnson	2	31	16	0
West	1	0	0	0

PASSING – PUNTING – KICKING

PASSING

Last Name	Att	Comp	%	Yds	Yd/Att	TD	Int–%	RK
Owen	184	88	48	1327	7.2	10	15– 8	11
Reed	74	29	39	316	4.3	2	7–10	
Morrison	51	21	41	227	4.5	1	5–10	
Spurrier	3	1	33	2	0.7	0	0– 0	
Abramowicz	1	1	100	41	41.0	0	0– 0	

PUNTING

Last Name	No	Avg
Wittum	68	41.2
Gossett	2	28.0

KICKING

Last Name	XP	Att	%	FG	Att	%
Gossett	25	27	93	11	24	46

NEW ORLEANS SAINTS

RUSHING

Last Name	No.	Yds	Avg	TD
Maxson	165	714	4.3	2
Phillips	174	556	3.2	2
Manning	28	204	7.3	1
Stevens	43	190	4.4	1
DeGrenier	33	110	3.3	0
McNeil	22	90	4.1	1
Butler	21	74	3.5	0
Cipa	12	35	2.9	1
Seal	2	7	3.5	1
Parker	2	2	1.0	0
Scott	1	1	1.0	0

RECEIVING

Last Name	No.	Yds	Avg	TD
Maxon	42	294	7	1
Parker	41	455	11	4
Seal	32	466	15	3
Newland	27	490	18	2
Stevens	13	81	6	0
Phillips	11	55	5	0
Beasley	5	85	17	0
McNeil	5	64	13	0
DeGrenier	4	13	3	0
Butler	2	3	2	0
Havrilak	1	23	23	0
McCullouch	1	5	5	0
Thomas	1	3	3	0

PUNT RETURNS

Last Name	No.	Yds	Avg	TD
Stevens	37	376	10	0
Farasopoulos	3	36	12	0
Jackson	2	3	2	0
McNeill	1	0	0	0

KICKOFF RETURNS

Last Name	No.	Yds	Avg	TD
Stevens	33	749	23	0
Phillips	7	124	18	0
Jackson	1	27	27	0
Schmidt	1	23	23	0
Kingrea	1	22	22	0
Federspeil	2	20	10	0
Lawson	1	20	20	0
Middleton	2	18	9	0
Davis	1	14	14	0
Coleman	2	13	7	0
Butler	1	12	12	0
Spencer	1	−2	−2	0

PASSING – PUNTING – KICKING

PASSING

Last Name	Att	Comp	%	Yds	Yd/Att	TD	Int–%	RK
Manning	261	134	51	1429	5.5	6	16– 6	14
Scott	71	31	44	366	5.2	4	4– 6	
Cipa	55	20	36	242	4.4	0	0– 0	
McClard	1	0	0	0	0.0	0	1–100	
Parker	1	0	0	0	0.0	0	0– 0	

PUNTING

Last Name	No	Avg
Blanchard	88	42.1
Gibbs	3	33.0

KICKING

Last Name	XP	Att	%	FG	Att	%
McClard	19	20	95	9	16	56

ATLANTA FALCONS

RUSHING

Last Name	No.	Yds	Avg	TD
Hampton	127	464	3.7	2
Malone	116	410	3.5	2
Stanback	57	235	4.1	1
Ray	46	139	3.0	0
Lee	19	99	5.2	1
Kendrick	17	71	4.2	0
McGee	7	30	4.3	0
J. Mitchell	3	21	7.0	0
Sullivan	3	19	6.3	0
Tinker	2	5	2.5	0
McQuilken	2	1	0.5	0
Neal	1	−1	−1.0	0

RECEIVING

Last Name	No.	Yds	Avg	TD
Burrow	34	545	16	1
J. Mitchell	30	479	16	1
Malone	28	168	6	0
Hampton	13	111	9	0
Dodd	12	130	11	
Kendrick	12	86	7	
Ray	10	43	4	
Neal	8	99	12	
Stanback	8	39	5	
Geredine	4	69	1	
Tinker	1	12		

PUNT RETURNS

Last Name	No.	Yds	Avg	TD
Dodd	27	344	13	0
Tinker	14	195	14	1
Brown	9	96	11	0
Fritsch	1	0	0	0

KICKOFF RETURNS

Last Name	No.	Yds	Avg	TD
Tinker	29	704	24	0
Geredine	9	219	24	0
McGee	8	167	21	0
Byas	5	136	27	0
Mitchell	4	36	9	0
Easterling	2	34	17	0
Childs	1	0	0	0
Fritsch	1	0	0	0
Ryczek	1	0	0	0

PASSING – PUNTING – KICKING

PASSING

Last Name	Att	Comp	%	Yds	Yd/Att	TD	Int–%	RK
Lee	172	78	45	852	5.0	3	14– 8	16
Sullivan	105	48	46	556	5.3	1	8– 8	
McQuilken	79	34	43	373	4.7	0	9–11	

PUNTING

Last Name	No	Avg
James	96	40.5

KICKING

Last Name	XP	Att	%	FG	Att	%
Mike-Mayer	12	12	100	9	16	56

1974 A.F.C. Same Game, Different Rules

The N.F.L. this year took some steps to return to its games the offensive fireworks that had been so common in the 1950's and 1960's. To promote more passing, the "bump-and-run" method of pass defense was closely regulated. To cut down on the number of field goals and increase the emphasis on touchdowns, the league fathers moved the goal posts back to the rear of the end zone, where they had stood all along in college ball and where they had stood in pro ball until being moved up to the goal line in 1933. Another change brought missed field goals that travel into the end zone back out to the line of scrimmage. And an extra sudden-death period was added for all tie games during the season, a measure heretofore reserved for playoff games. All these moves did produce some additional points and a couple of overtime games, but the main shift in tactics was to a new reliance on coffin-corner punting, with an eye to keeping opponents bottled up in a poor field position all game long.

EASTERN DIVISION

Miami Dolphins—The signing of Larry Csonka, Paul Warfield, Jim Kiick, Tim Foley, and Bob Kuechenberg to future contracts with the new World Football League caused some bitterness in the Dolphin family; but coach Don Shula decided to play his best players regardless of where they might be in the future. When the Dolphins got off to a lack-lustre start, it was injuries, not dissension, at the heart of the team's problems. Csonka, Warfield, Wayne Moore, Doug Swift, Mercury Morris, and Manny Fernandez all suffered through injury-cursed seasons to throw the finely-tuned Dolphin machine out of gear. But subs like Nat Moore, Don Nottingham, and Ben Malone came through when thrown into the breach, and the Dolphins soon were playing in their usual championship style. A 35–28 victory over Buffalo on November 17 put Miami back into first place, and the Dolphins held on to it the rest of the way.

Buffalo Bills—O.J. Simpson couldn't duplicate his record-setting performance of last year, but he still raced for 1125 yards despite a sore knee. The Buffalo attack had an added dimension this season, as young quarterback Joe Ferguson passed the ball much more often to wide receivers like ex-Cardinal Ahmad Rashad. A sound defense featuring backs Bobby James and Tony Greene complemented the powerful offense and helped boost the Bills into first place with a 29–28 win over New England on October 20. Although the Dolphins knocked the Bills out of the top slot one month later, Buffalo still marched into the playoffs as the wild-card team.

New England Patriots—The Pats began the season with a reorganized defense and an almost unbelievable stretch of good football. The Patriots beat the defending champion Dolphins 34–24 on opening day, and chalked up another big upset by upending the highly-touted Rams 20–14 two weeks later. The team's opening spurt brought in four straight wins and six out of the first seven. But then injuries started decimating the New England offense. Darryl Stingley, Reggie Rucker, Bob Windsor, and Sam Cunningham all went out of the lineup, and the crippled Patriot squad faltered badly down the stretch. But aside from the steady work of quarterback Jim Plunkett and defensive tackle Julius Adams, the star of the season was Mack Herron, the diminutive halfback who set a new record for total yardage gained in all categories combined for one season.

New York Jets—Charley Winner succeeded his father-in-law Weeb Ewbank as head coach this year, but a 1–7 start made it debatable if he would be staying long in New York. But then Joe Namath led his mates to a 26–20 overtime win over the rival Giants, and the Jets suddenly came together. The team won its last six games to reach the .500 level and reclaim some of the dignity lost in the horrendous first part of the schedule.

Baltimore Colts—The year started on a down note, as All-Pro linebacker Ted Hendricks signed a future contract with the W.F.L. and was then traded at a dirt-cheap price to Green Bay by General Manager Joe Thomas. The personnel situation on the Colt roster was even worse than last season, and coach Howard Schnellenberger was fired after three games, with his fate sealed by an argument he had with owner Robert Irsay over whether Marty Domres or Bert Jones should play quarterback. Thomas doubled as coach for the rest of the year but could direct the team to only two wins.

CENTRAL DIVISION

Pittsburgh Steelers—The Steelers' strong 6–0 preseason showing was less surprising than Joe Gilliam's winning the starting quarterback job away from Terry Bradshaw. Gilliam faltered in mid-season and was benched in favor of Bradshaw, but the Steelers had so much talent that they easily captured first place in the Central Division. The Steelers had a solid offensive line, a copious supply of wide receivers, a superb fullback in Franco Harris, and a brutally effective defense featuring Mean Joe Greene, L.C. Greenwood, Andy Russell, and Jack Ham. The biggest

bonus of the year was the play of halfback Rocky Bleier, who had recovered well enough from leg injuries suffered in the Vietnam war to claim a starting job in the offensive backfield.

Cincinnati Bengals—Passer Ken Anderson enjoyed a fine season, but a variety of circumstances reduced the Bengals to a 7–7 campaign. The defense never recovered from the loss of All-Pro middle linebacker Bill Bergey, whom coach Paul Brown traded to Philadelphia after he signed a future contract with the W.F.L. Injuries did in the offense. The backfield lost Booby Clark to foot and hand injuries and Essex Johnson to a bad knee, while the line suffered from Vern Holland's broken leg and Bob Johnson's broken ankle.

Houston Oilers—Coach Sid Gillman patched up the pitiful Oilers and turned out a respectable football team. The process needed time to take effect, as the Oilers won their opening game and then dropped five straight. During the early part of the campaign, Gillman also had to endure the efforts of defensive tackle John Matuszak to jump to the W.F.L. He actually did jump to the Houston Texans of that league, but was served with a restraining order right on the field in the middle of his first game. Soon after his return to the Oilers, Gillman sent him off to Kansas City in return for Curley Culp. A defensive front three of Elvin Bethea, Culp, and Tody Smith spearheaded a much improved defense that led the Oilers to six wins in their last eight games, including upsets over the Bills and Steelers. But despite his achievement of turning the Oilers around, Gillman resigned both his coach and General Manager positions after the season in a dispute with owner Bud Adams over how freely Gillman spent the team's money on a variety of "extravagant" arrangements such as an illegally-large taxi squad.

Cleveland Browns—The once-mighty Browns tumbled to their worst season ever, a humbling 4–10 campaign which dumped them ignominiously into the cellar in the Central Division. Five losses in the first six games took the Browns out of any playoff contention, and things improved only slightly the rest of the year. Little Greg Pruitt excited the fans, but the team in general was a dull loser that cost coach Nick Skorich his job.

WESTERN DIVISION

Oakland Raiders—Quarterback Ken Stabler signed a future pact with the W.F.L., but he didn't let it cramp his style with the Raiders this year. The lefty passer guided the N.F.L.'s most explosive offense with the cool of a surgeon, throwing a league-leading 26 touchdown passes. His wide receivers were Fred Biletnikoff, with average speed but extraordinary moves, and Cliff Branch, a small sprinter who broke into the lineup when Mike Siani was injured. Power running came from big Marv Hubbard, and the versatile offensive line had All-Pro candidates in Gene Upshaw and Art Shell. With such an offense, the defense played far better than it had to for the Raiders to nail down the Western Division title. The offensive riches included 46-year-old George Blanda, whose place kicking left little to be desired and who got into the final game of the year at quarterback and threw a touchdown pass.

Denver Broncos—The Broncos hoped to challenge for a playoff berth, but they never climbed above a mediocre level during this season. A noteworthy game of this disappointing campaign was a 35–35 tie with the Pittsburgh Steelers on September 22, the first N.F.L. regular season game to go into overtime; an extra period resulted in no score, and the extra exertion may have contributed to both team's losing the next week. On the positive side for the Broncos, tight end Riley Odoms won All-Pro honors for his play, while second-year running back Otis Armstrong surprisingly blossomed into a dangerous runner, piling up a league-leading total of 1407 yards.

Kansas City Chiefs—The old Kansas City powerhouse that used to battle Oakland for the Western title every season was no more. Age was eating into the talent at almost all the positions, and only a handful of younger players showed a capacity for playing up to the standards of the old Chiefs. Rookie Woody Green did sparkle in his limited performances at running back, but his addition only balanced the mid-season loss of Ed Podolak with a thumb injury. The Chiefs endured their first losing season since 1963, but the gradual slide to this point prompted owner Lamar Hunt to fire Hank Stram, the only coach the team had had since opening shop in Dallas 15 years before.

San Diego Chargers—Preseason training camp saw all-time great quarterback Johnny Unitas come into camp, work out for a few days, and then announce his retirement. New coach Tommy Prothro manned the passer's position with youngsters Dan Fouts and Jesse Freitas, and the young quarterbacks helped the Chargers win five games in a rebuilding season. The sturdiest building block Prothro could find was rookie Don Woods, an exciting runner whom the Green Bay Packers had cut loose on waivers before the season.

FINAL TEAM STATISTICS

OFFENSE

	BALT.	BUFF.	CIN.	CLEV.	DENV	HOUS.	K.C.	MIAMI	N.ENG	N.Y.	OAK.	PITT.	S.D.
FIRST DOWNS:													
Total	244	220	260	223	258	200	224	272	255	234	**284**	251	245
by Rushing	110	118	115	104	120	76	92	134	123	96	127	**136**	113
by Passing	109	85	131	92	118	103	113	118	113	119	**137**	98	117
by Penalty	25	17	14	**27**	20	21	19	20	19	19	20	17	15
RUSHING:													
Number	450	545	445	461	486	421	469	**570**	520	444	561	546	508
Yards	1818	2094	1978	1924	2157	1361	1720	2191	2134	1625	2334	**2417**	2111
Average Yards	4.0	3.8	**4.4**	4.2	4.4	3.2	3.7	3.8	4.1	3.7	4.2	4.4	4.2
Touchdowns	13	11	14	14	20	16	10	**25**	21	12	15	19	15
PASSING:													
Attempts	**425**	251	353	367	329	363	395	283	359	369	335	386	349
Completions	221	128	**224**	179	184	203	211	171	177	194	186	166	165
Completion Percentage	52.0	51.0	**63.5**	48.8	55.9	55.9	53.4	60.4	49.3	52.6	55.5	43.0	47.3
Passing Yards	2424	1728	**2804**	2129	2660	2275	2421	2313	2514	2631	2561	2154	2479
Avg. Yards per Attempt	5.7	6.9	7.9	5.8	8.1	6.3	6.1	**8.2**	7.0	7.1	7.6	5.6	7.1
Avg. Yards per Complet.	11.0	13.5	12.5	11.9	14.5	11.2	11.5	13.5	14.2	13.6	13.8	13.0	**15.0**
Times Tackled Passing	49	33	37	48	46	33	37	31	21	19	24	**18**	23
Yards Lost Tackled	399	236	293	402	332	298	313	229	**174**	195	177	196	175
Net Yards	2025	1492	**2511**	1727	2328	1977	2108	2084	2340	2436	2384	1958	2304
Touchdowns	9	14	18	12	18	12	11	18	19	20	**28**	12	12
Interceptions	24	15	**13**	24	17	19	25	18	23	24	18	21	22
Percent Intercepted	5.7	6.0	**3.7**	6.5	5.2	5.2	6.3	6.4	6.4	6.5	5.4	5.4	6.3
PUNTS:													
Number	71	69	66	**90**	75	79	83	65	71	75	74	78	76
Average Distance	37.1	40.6	40.9	40.5	40.3	39.2	41.7	38.6	36.2	35.9	**42.2**	39.0	40.0
PUNT RETURNS:													
Number	42	56	52	52	43	41	44	46	40	53	45	**67**	37
Yards	253	460	632	523	474	495	296	520	533	425	517	**774**	287
Average Yards	6.0	8.2	12.2	10.1	11.0	12.1	6.7	11.3	**13.3**	8.0	11.5	11.6	7.8
Touchdowns	0	0	**2**	0	0	0	0	0	0	0	0	1	0
KICKOFF RETURNS:													
Number	**66**	50	54	60	54	62	56	49	58	61	50	42	55
Yards	**1489**	1128	1157	1375	1188	1419	1211	1118	1198	1307	1140	901	1142
Average Yards	22.6	22.6	21.4	**22.9**	22.0	22.9	21.6	22.8	20.7	21.4	22.8	21.5	20.8
Touchdowns	0	0	0	**1**	0	0	0	0	0	0	0	0	0
INTERCEPTION RETURNS:													
Number	10	20	9	24	22	21	**28**	16	24	17	27	25	15
Yards	87	413	110	336	311	313	**531**	139	294	278	378	320	273
Average Yards	8.7	**20.7**	12.2	14.0	14.1	14.9	19.0	8.7	12.3	16.4	14.0	12.8	18.2
Touchdowns	0	2	0	2	1	1	**5**	0	2	2	1	2	0
PENALTIES:													
Number	66	79	78	78	76	90	70	69	87	76	92	**104**	74
Yards	587	706	653	767	632	749	515	556	843	600	845	**978**	609
FUMBLES:													
Number	28	32	27	34	23	26	29	25	26	26	**22**	33	24
Number Lost	13	14	18	15	13	14	13	13	15	**8**	10	19	11
POINTS:													
Total	190	264	283	251	702	236	233	327	348	279	**355**	305	212
PAT Attempts	22	30	36	30	39	30	26	43	43	36	**46**	35	28
PAT Made	22	25	32	29	35	29	24	43	42	27	**44**	33	26
FG Attempts	20	**33**	18	16	21	19	24	15	22	18	17	29	16
FG Made	12	19	11	14	11	9	17	8	16	12	11	**20**	6
Percent FG Made	60.0	57.6	61.1	**87.5**	52.4	47.4	**70.8**	**53.3**	72.7	66.7	64.7	69.0	37.5
Safeties	0	**1**	**1**	0	0	0	**1**	**1**	0	0	**1**	**1**	0

DEFENSE

	BALT.	BUFF.	CIN.	CLEV.	DENV	HOUS	K.C.	MIAMI	N.ENG.	N.Y.	OAK.	PITT.	S.D.
FIRST DOWNS:													
Total	237	219	256	247	265	268	267	208	240	267	237	**200**	272
by Rushing	120	96	127	126	109	124	107	**83**	100	132	110	87	128
by Passing	101	97	109	95	135	129	141	117	129	112	106	**83**	127
by Penalty	16	26	20	26	21	15	19	**8**	11	23	21	30	17
RUSHING:													
Number	516	489	497	555	487	474	502	**404**	467	539	459	472	508
Yards	1961	1878	2152	2415	1808	2050	1801	1624	**1587**	2240	2108	1608	2160
Average Yards	3.8	3.8	4.3	4.4	3.7	4.3	3.6	4.0	3.4	4.2	4.6	**3.4**	4.3
Touchdowns	20	19	16	17	17	15	16	**7**	16	20	12	**7**	21
PASSING:													
Attempts	312	311	359	**308**	426	405	408	372	374	347	367	339	367
Completions	180	146	186	**139**	237	231	206	200	210	186	175	147	222
Completion Percentage	57.7	46.9	51.8	45.1	55.6	57.0	50.5	53.8	56.1	53.6	47.7	**43.4**	60.5
Passing Yards	2348	1898	2110	2259	2805	2724	2838	2452	2774	2249	2425	**1872**	2815
Avg. Yards per Attempt	7.5	6.1	5.9	7.3	6.6	6.7	7.0	6.6	7.4	6.5	6.6	**5.5**	7.7
Avg. Yards per Complet.	13.0	13.0	11.3	16.3	11.8	**11.8**	13.8	12.3	13.2	12.1	13.9	12.7	12.7
Times Tackled Passing	21	32	36	28	32	40	26	31	38	25	36	**52**	18
Yards Lost Tackled	183	287	320	234	222	349	175	270	294	192	314	**406**	145
Net Yards	2165	1611	1790	2025	2583	2375	2663	2182	2480	2057	2111	**1466**	2670
Touchdowns	16	**11**	13	22	14	19	22	14	17	14	12	14	13
Interceptions	10	20	9	24	22	21	**28**	16	24	17	27	25	15
Percent Intercepted	3.2	6.4	2.5	**7.8**	5.2	5.2	6.9	4.3	6.4	4.9	7.4	7.4	4.1
PUNTS:													
Number	67	77	81	76	70	70	80	70	75	71	73	**91**	66
Average Distance	38.4	**37.1**	37.8	38.0	42.6	39.1	40.1	39.2	38.4	37.2	39.9	41.2	40.6
PUNT RETURNS:													
Number	46	45	41	68	45	56	55	42	41	**27**	40	47	48
Yards	413	416	457	705	529	500	634	**259**	314	352	283	413	401
Average Yards	9.0	9.2	11.1	10.4	11.8	8.9	11.5	**6.2**	7.7	13.0	7.1	8.8	8.4
Touchdowns	**0**	**0**	**0**	1	**0**	**0**	**0**	**0**	**0**	**0**	**0**	**0**	**0**
KICKOFF RETURNS:													
Number	45	58	55	55	57	51	54	64	64	57	69	56	**39**
Yards	**903**	1345	1198	1345	1369	1111	1333	1222	1678	1395	1455	1275	960
Average Yards	20.1	23.2	21.8	24.5	24.0	21.8	24.7	**19.1**	26.2	24.5	21.1	22.8	24.6
Touchdowns	**0**	**0**	**0**	1	1	**0**	**0**	**0**	1	**0**	**0**	**0**	**0**
INTERCEPTION RETURNS:													
Number	24	15	**13**	24	17	19	25	18	23	24	18	21	22
Yards	384	183	**140**	423	304	238	336	320	331	452	276	222	311
Average Yards	16.0	12.2	10.8	17.6	17.9	12.5	13.4	17.8	14.4	18.8	15.3	**10.6**	14.1
Touchdowns	3	1	**0**	1	3	**0**	1	1	2	4	2	1	1
PENALTIES:													
Number	75	73	77	81	78	**94**	83	67	76	78	61	76	80
Yards	737	597	640	731	595	**872**	811	525	642	684	502	575	751
FUMBLES:													
Number	25	26	23	31	22	26	34	33	29	18	32	**38**	19
Number Lost	14	11	11	16	11	15	16	17	14	9	14	**22**	13
POINTS:													
Total	329	244	259	344	294	282	293	216	289	300	228	**189**	285
PAT Attempts	40	32	30	43	35	34	40	25	37	38	27	**22**	37
PAT Made	38	28	28	38	34	30	**33**	24	32	36	25	**21**	36
FG Attempts	27	15	22	23	24	23	**14**	21	18	24	22	17	20
FG Made	17	8	17	14	16	16	**6**	14	11	12	13	12	9
Percent FG Made	63.0	53.3	77.3	60.9	66.7	69.6	**42.9**	66.7	61.1	50.0	59.1	70.6	45.0
Safeties	**0**	**0**	**0**	3	1	**0**	1	**0**	1	**0**	1	**0**	**0**

CONFERENCE PLAYOFFS

December 21, at Oakland (Attendance 52,817)

SCORING

OAKLAND	0	7	7	14–28
MIAMI	7	3	6	10–26

First Quarter
- Mia. N. Moore, 89-yard kickoff return PAT–Yepremian (kick)

Second Quarter
- Oak. C. Smith, 31 yard pass from Stabler PAT–Blanda (kick)
- Mia. Yepremian, 33 yard field goal

Third Quarter
- Oak. Biletnikoff, 13 yard pass from Stabler PAT–Blanda (kick)
- Mia. Warfield, 16 yard pass from Griese PAT–kick missed

Fourth Quarter
- Mia. Yepremian, 46 yard field goal
- Oak. Branch, 72 yard pass from Stabler PAT–Blanda (kick)
- Mia. Malone, 23 yard rush PAT–Yepremian (kick)
- Oak. Davis, 8 yard pass from Stabler PAT–Blanda (kick)

TEAM STATISTICS

OAK.		MIAMI
19	First Downs-Total	18
8	First Downs-Rushing	10
11	First Downs-Passing	6
0	First Downs-Penalty	2
0	Fumbles-Number	0
0	Fumbles-Lost Ball	0
3	Penalties-Number	3
59	Yards Penalized	15
0	Missed Field Goals	0
64	Offensive Plays	57
411	Net Yards	294
6.4	Average Gain	5.2
1	Giveaways	1
1	Takeaways	1
0	Difference	0

INDIVIDUAL STATISTICS

OAKLAND	No.	Yds.	Avg.	MIAMI	No.	Yds.	Avg.
RUSHING							
Davis	12	59	4.9	Csonka	24	114	4.8
Hubbard	14	55	3.9	Malone	14	83	5.9
Banaszak	3	14	4.7	Griese	2	14	7.0
Stabler	3	7	2.3	Kiick	1	2	2.0
	32	135	4.2		41	213	5.2
RECEIVING							
Biletnikoff	8	122	15.3	Warfield	3	47	15.7
Branch	3	84	28.0	N. Moore	2	40	20.0
Moore	3	22	7.3	Nottingham	1	9	9.0
C. Smith	2	35	17.5	Kiick	1	5	5.0
C. Davis	2	16	8.0		7	101	14.4
Hubbard	1	9	9.0				
Pitts	1	5	5.0				
	20	293	14.7				
PUNTING							
Guy	7		42.7	Seiple	6		33.2
PUNT RETURNS							
R. Smith	3	16	5.3	N. Moore	2	5	2.5
KICKOFF RETURNS							
Hart	4	88	22.0	N. Moore	3	137	45.7
R. Smith	2	47	23.5	Ginn	2	46	23.0
	6	135	22.5		5	183	36.6
INTERCEPTION RETURNS							
Villapiano	1	5	5.0				

PASSING

OAKLAND	Att.	Comp.	Comp. Pct.	Yds.	Int.	Yds/ Att.	Yds/ Comp.	Yards Lost Tackled
Stabler	30	20	66.7	293	1	9.8	14.7	2–17
MIAMI								
Griese	14	7	50.0	101	0	7.2	14.4	2–20

December 22, at Pittsburgh (Attendance 48,321)

SCORING

PITTSBURGH	3	26	0	3–32
BUFFALO	7	0	7	0–14

First Quarter
- Pitt. Gerela, 21 yard field goal
- Buf. Seymour, 22 yard pass from Ferguson PAT–Leypoldt (kick)

Second Quarter
- Pit. Bleier, 27 yard pass from Bradshaw PAT–kick blocked
- Pit. Harris, 1 yard rush PAT–Gerela (kick)
- Pit. Harris, 4 yard rush PAT–kick blocked
- Pit. Harris, 1 yard rush PAT–Gerela (kick)

Third Quarter
- Buf. Simpson, 3 yard pass from Ferguson PAT–Leypoldt (kick)

Fourth Quarter
- Pit. Gerela, 22 yard field goal

TEAM STATISTICS

PITT.		BUF.
29	First Downs-Total	15
18	First Downs-Rushing	5
9	First Downs-Passing	10
2	First Downs-Penalty	0
2	Fumbles-Number	2
0	Fumbles-Lost Ball	1
2	Penalties-Number	3
10	Yards Penalized	15
0	Missed Field Goals	0
72	Offensive Plays	47
438	Net Yards	264
6.1	Average Gain	5.6
0	Giveaways	1
1	Takeaways	0
+1	Difference	–1

INDIVIDUAL STATISTICS

PITTSBURGH	No.	Yds.	Avg.	BUFFALO	No.	Yds.	Avg.
RUSHING							
Harris	24	74	3.1	Simpson	15	49	3.3
Bradshaw	5	48	9.6	Braxton	5	48	9.6
Bleier	14	45	3.2	Ferguson	1	3	3.0
Steve Davis	5	32	6.4		21	100	4.8
Swann	2	24	12.0				
Gilliam	1	12	12.0				
	51	235	4.6				
RECEIVING							
Swann	3	60	20.0	Hill	4	59	14.8
Bleier	3	54	18.0	Simpson	3	37	12.3
Lewis	2	18	9.0	Seymour	2	35	17.5
Brown	1	29	29.0	Rashad	1	25	25.0
McMakin	1	22	22.0	Braxton	1	8	8.0
Shanklin	1	15	15.0		11	164	14.9
Harris	1	5	5.0				
	12	203	16.9				
PUNTING							
Walden	3		38.7	Bateman	5		39.4
PUNT RETURNS							
Edwards	2	13	6.5	Walker	2	11	5.5
Swann	2	12	6.0				
	4	25	6.3				
KICKOFF RETURNS							
Blount	2	56	28.0	Francis	6	118	19.7
Steve Davis	1	30	30.0				
	3	86	28.7				

PASSING

PITTSBURGH	Att.	Comp.	Comp. Pct.	Yds	Int.	Yds/ Att.	Yds/ Comp.	Yards Lost Tackled
Bradshaw	19	12	63.2	203	0	10.7	16.9	0–0
Gilliam	2	0	00.0	0	0	–	–	0–0
	21	12	57.1	203	0	9.7	16.9	0–0
BUFFALO								
Ferguson	26	11	42.3	164	0	6.3	14.9	0–0

MIAMI DOLPHINS 11-3-0 Don Shula

Scores of Each Game		
24	New England	34
24	Buffalo	16
28	San Diego	21
21	N.Y. JETS	17
17	Washington	20
9	KANSAS CITY	3
17	BALTIMORE	7
42	ATLANTA	7
21	New Orleans	0
35	BUFFALO	28
14	N.Y. Jets	17
24	CINCINNATI	3
17	Baltimore	16
34	NEW ENGLAND	27

Use Name	Pos.	Hgt	Wgt	Age	Int	Pts
Doug Crusan	OT	6'5"	250	28		
Norm Evans	OT	6'5"	250	31		
Tom Funchess	OT	6'5"	270	29		
Wayne Moore	OT	6'6"	265	29		
Tom Wickert	OT	6'4"	246	22		
Larry Little	OG	6'1"	265	28		
Ed Newman	OG	6'2"	245	23		
Bob Kuechenberg	OT-OG	6'3"	252	26		
Jim Langer	C	6'2"	253	26		
Irv Goode	OG-C	6'4"	262	33		
Vern Den Herder	DE	6'6"	252	25		
Bill Stanfill	DE	6'5"	252	27		
Don Reese	DT-DE	6'6"	255	22		
Randy Crowder	DT	6'2"	236	22		
Manny Fernandez	DT	6'2"	250	28		
Baldy Moore	DT	6'2"	265	28		
Bob Heinz	DE-DT	6'6"	265	27		
Larry Ball	LB	6'6"	235	24		
Bruce Bannon	LB	6'3"	225	23		
Nick Buoniconti	LB	5'11"	220	33	2	
Mike Kolen	LB	6'2"	222	26	1	
Bob Matheson	LB	6'4"	235	29	1	
Doug Swift	LB	6'3"	226	25		
Dick Anderson	DB	6'2"	196	28	1	
Charlie Babb	DB	6'	190	24		
Tim Foley	DB	6'	194	26	2	2
Curtis Johnson	DB	6'2"	196	26		
Lloyd Mumphrey	DB	5'11"	176	27		
Jake Scott	DB	6'	188	29	8	
Henry Stuckey	DB	6'1"	180	24	1	
Jeris White	DB	5'11"	180	21		
Bob Griese	QB	6'1"	190	29		6
Earl Morrall	QB	6'1"	210	40		
Don Strock	QB	6'5"	216	23		
Hubert Ginn	HB	5'11"	185	27		12
Jim Kiick	HB	5'11"	214	28		12
Benny Malone	HB	5'10"	193	22		18
Mercury Morris	HB	5'10"	192	27		12
Larry Csonka	FB	6'3"	237	27		54
Don Nottingham	FB	5'10"	210	25		48
Melvin Baker	WR	6'	192	24		12
Marlin Briscoe	WR	5'10"	175	28		6
Nat Moore	WR	5'10"	180	22		12
Howard Twilley	WR	5'10"	185	30		12
Paul Warfield	WR	6'	188	31		12
Marv Fleming	TE	6'4"	230	32		6
Jim Mandich	TE	6'3"	224	26		36
Larry Seiple	TE	6'	214	29		
Garo Yepremian	K	5'8"	175	30		67

BUFFALO BILLS 9-5-0 Lou Saban

Scores of Each Game		
21	OAKLAND	20
16	MIAMI	24
16	N.Y. JETS	12
27	Green Bay	7
27	Baltimore	14
30	NEW ENGLAND	28
16	CHICAGO	6
29	New England	28
9	HOUSTON	21
28	Miami	35
15	Cleveland	10
6	BALTIMORE	0
10	N.Y. Jets	20
14	Los Angeles	19

Use Name	Pos.	Hgt	Wgt	Age	Int	Pts
Dave Foley	OT	6'5"	253	26		
Donnie Green	OT	6'7"	272	26		
Halvor Hagen	OT	6'5"	253	27		
Bill Adams	OG	6'2"	254	24		
Joe DeLamielleure	OG	6'3"	245	23		
Reggie McKenzie	OG	6'4"	242	24		
Bruce Jarvis	C	6'7"	250	25		
Nick Nighswander	C	6'	232	22		
Mike Montler	OT-C	6'4"	253	30		
Willie Parker	OG-C	6'3"	245	25		
Dave Costa	DE	6'2"	250	32		
Dave Means	DE	6'4"	235	22		
Walt Patulski	DE	6'6"	260	24		
Don Croft	DT	6'3"	254	25		
Mike Kadish	DT	6'5"	270	24		2
Jeff Yeates	DT	6'3"	240	23		
Earl Edwards	DE-DT	6'6"	256	28		
Doug Allen	LB	6'2"	228	22	1	
Jim Cheyunski	LB	6'2"	220	28	1	
Merv Krakau	LB	6'1"	237	23	1	
Rich Lewis	LB	6'3"	215	24	1	
John Skorupan	LB	6'2"	220	23		
Bo Cornell	FB-LB	6'1"	215	25		
Ted Koy	TE-LB	6'1"	210	26		
Dave Washington	TE-LB	6'5"	223	26	2	12
Bill Cahill	DB	5'11"	170	23		
Neal Craig	DB	6'1"	190	26	1	6
Tony Greene	DB	5'10"	170	25	9	
Dwight Harrison	DB	6'1"	185	25	1	
Robert James	DB	6'1"	184	27	3	
Rex Kern	DB	5'11"	190	25		
Al Randolph	DB	6'2"	205	30		
Donnie Walker	DB	6'1"	180	23		
Jeff Winans — Injury						
Joe Ferguson	QB	6'1"	180	24		12
Scott Hunter	QB	6'2"	205	26		
Gary Marangi	QB	6'1"	196	22		
Don Calhoun	HB	6'	198	22		
Clint Haserlig	HB	6'	190	22		
Gary Hayman	HB	6'1"	198	23		
Ed Jenkins (from NYG, to NE)	HB	6'2"	210	24		
Wayne Mosley	HB	6'	190	21		
O. J. Simpson	HB	6'2"	212	27		24
Jim Braxton	FB	6'2"	240	25		24
Larry Watkins	FB	6'2"	235	27		12
Bob Chandler	WR	6'	180	25		6
Wallace Francis	WR	5'11"	195	22		
J. D. Hill	WR	6'1"	190	25		36
Ahmad Rashad	WR	6'2"	200	24		36
Reuben Gant	TE	6'4"	230	22		
Paul Seymour	TE	6'5"	243	24		12
Marv Bateman (from DAL)	K	6'4"	210	24		
Spike Jones	K	6'2"	195	27		
John Leypoldt	K	6'2"	237	28		82

NEW ENGLAND PATRIOTS 7-7-0 Chuck Fairbanks

Scores of Each Game		
34	MIAMI	24
28	N.Y. Giants	20
20	LOS ANGELES	14
42	BALTIMORE	3
24	N.Y. Jets	0
28	Buffalo	30
17	Minnesota	14
28	BUFFALO	29
14	CLEVELAND	21
16	N.Y. JETS	21
27	Baltimore	17
26	Oakland	41
17	PITTSBURGH	21
27	Miami	34

Use Name	Pos.	Hgt	Wgt	Age	Int	Pts
Allen Gallaher	OT	6'3"	255	23		
Leon Gray	OT	6'3"	256	22		
Tom Neville	OT	6'4"	253	31		
Sam Adams	OG	6'3"	252	25		
Bill DuLac	OG	6'4"	260	23		
John Hannah	OG	6'2"	265	23		6
Doug Dumler	C	6'3"	242	23		
Jon Morris	C	6'4"	248	31		
Bill Lenkaitis	OG-C	6'3"	250	28		
Craig Hanneman	DE	6'3"	245	25		
Tony McGee	DE	6'4"	245	25		
Donnell Smith	DE	6'4"	252	25		
Julius Adams	DT-DE	6'3"	257	26		
Mel Lunsford	DT-DE	6'3"	260	24		
Ray Hamilton	NT	6'1"	245	23		
Art Moore	NT	6'5"	253	23		
Gail Clark	LB	6'2"	225	23		
Kent Carter	LB	6'3"	235	24		
Rodrigo Barnes (from DAL)	LB	6'1"	215	24		
Maury Damkroger	LB	6'2"	230	22		
Bob Geddes	LB	6'2"	240	28	2	6
Sam Hunt	LB	6'1"	240	23	3	
Steve King	LB	6'4"	230	23	1	
Steve Nelson	LB	6'2"	230	23		
John Tanner	TE-LB	6'4"	235	29		6
George Webster	LB	6'4"	230	28		
Ron Bolton	DB	6'2"	170	24	7	
Sandy Durko	DB	6'1"	186	26		
Prentice McCray	DB	6'1"	187	23	3	
Dave McCurry	DB	6'1"	187	23		
Jim Massey	DB	5'11"	198	26		
Jack Mildren	DB	6'1"	200	24	3	
Ken Pope	DB	5'11"	200	22		
Deac Sanders	DB	6'1"	178	24	5	6
Neil Graff	QB	6'3"	200	24		
Jim Plunkett	QB	6'3"	212	26		12
Dick Shiner	QB	6'	210	32		
Josh Ashton	HB	6'1"	202	25		
Noe Gonzalez	HB	6'	210	23		
Mack Herron	HB	5'5"	175	26		72
Andy Johnson	HB	6'	204	21		
Sam Cunningham	FB	6'3"	224	24		66
John Tarver	FB	6'3"	220	25		12
Joe Wilson	HB-FB	5'10"	210	23		
Eddie Hinton	WR	6'	200	27		
Al Marshall	WR	6'2"	190	23		6
Reggie Rucker	WR	6'2"	190	26		24
Steve Schubert	WR	5'10"	185	23		6
Darryl Stingley	WR	6'	195	22		12
Joe Sweet	WR	6'2"	196	26		
Randy Vataha	WR	5'10"	170	25		18
Bob Adams	TE	6'2"	222	28		
Bob Windsor	TE	6'4"	225	31		6
Bruce Barnes	K	5'11"	212	23		
John Smith	K	6'	185	24		90

NEW YORK JETS 7-7-0 Charley Winner

Scores of Each Game		
16	Kansas City	24
23	Chicago	21
12	Buffalo	16
17	Miami	21
0	NEW ENGLAND	24
20	BALTIMORE	35
13	LOS ANGELES	20
22	HOUSTON	27
26	N.Y. Giants (OT)	20
21	New England	16
17	MIAMI	14
27	SAN DIEGO	14
20	BUFFALO	10
45	Baltimore	38

Use Name	Pos.	Hgt	Wgt	Age	Int	Pts
Gordie Browne	OT	6'5"	265	22		
Winston Hill	OT	6'4"	280	32		
Robert Woods	OT	6'3"	255	24		
Roger Bernhardt	OG	6'4"	244	24		
Randy Rasmussen	OG	6'2"	267	29		
Travis Roach	OG	6'2"	260	24		
Gary Puetz	OT-OG	6'3"	255	22		
Howard Kindig	C	6'6"	260	33		
Warren Koegel	C	6'3"	260	24		
Wayne Mulligan	C	6'2"	250	27		
Ed Galigher	DE	6'4"	260	23		
Mark Lomas	DE	6'4"	250	26		
John Little	DT-DE	6'3"	250	27		
Carl Barzilauskas	DT	6'6"	280	23		
Larry Woods	DT	6'6"	270	26		
Richard Neal	DE-DT	6'3"	260	26		
Joe Schmiesing	DE-DT	6'4"	256	29		
Al Atkinson	LB	6'1"	230	31		
Ralph Baker	LB	6'3"	228	32	2	6
John Ebersole	LB	6'3"	235	25	3	
Bill Ferguson	LB	6'3"	225	23		
Steve Reese	LB	6'2"	232	22		
Jamie Rivers	LB	6'2"	245	28	1	
Delles Howell	DB	6'3"	200	27	2	
Burgess Owens	DB	6'2"	200	23	3	12
Rich Sowells	DB	6'	185	25	2	
Steve Tannen	DB	6'1"	194	26	2	
Earlie Thomas	DB	6'1"	190	28		
Phil Wise	DB	6'	190	25		
Roscoe Word	DB	5'11"	170	21	2	
Bill Demory	QB	6'2"	195	23		
Joe Namath	QB	6'2"	200	31		6
Al Woodall	QB	6'5"	194	28		
Mike Adamle	HB	5'9"	193	24		12
Hank Bjorklund	HB	6'1"	200	24		
Emerson Boozer	HB	5'11"	205	31		30
Jazz Jackson	HB	5'8"	167	22		12
Bob Burns	FB	6'3"	212	22		6
John Riggins	FB	6'2"	230	25		42
Jerome Barkum	WR	6'3"	212	24		18
Eddie Bell	WR	5'10"	160	26		6
Dave Knight	WR	6'1"	182	23		24
Marv Owens	WR	5'11"	205	24		
Lou Piccone	WR	5'9"	175	25		
Willie Brister	TE	6'4"	236	22		
Rich Caster	TE	6'5"	228	25		42
Greg Gantt	K	5'11"	188	22		1
Bobby Howfield	K	5'9"	180	37		26
Pat Leahy	K	6'	200	23		36

BALTIMORE COLTS 2-12-0 Howard Schnellenberger Joe Thomas

Scores of Each Game		
0	Pittsburgh	30
13	GREEN BAY	20
10	Philadelphia	30
3	New England	42
14	BUFFALO	27
35	N.Y. Jets	20
7	Miami	17
14	CINCINNATI	24
6	DENVER	17
17	Atlanta	7
17	NEW ENGLAND	27
0	Buffalo	6
16	MIAMI	17
38	N.Y. JETS	45

Use Name	Pos.	Hgt	Wgt	Age	Int	Pts
Dennis Nelson	OT	6'5"	260	28		
Dave Simonson	OT	6'6"	246	22		
David Taylor	OT	6'4"	254	24		
Elmer Collett	OG	6'4"	240	29		
Robert Pratt	OG	6'3"	255	23		
Glenn Ressler	OG	6'3"	250	30		
Bob Van Duyne	OG	6'5"	235	22		
Ken Mendenhall	C	6'3"	240	25		
Dan Neal	C	6'4"	240	25		
Mike Barnes	DE	6'6"	255	23		
Fred Cook	DE	6'4"	235	22		
John Dutton	DE	6'7"	260	23		
Steve Williams	DE	6'6"	260	23		
Jim Bailey	DT	6'4"	255	26		
Joe Ehrmann	DT	6'5"	260	25		
Bill Windauer	DT	6'3"	245	24		
Tony Bertuca	LB	6'2"	225	24		
Mike Curtis	LB	6'2"	232	31	3	
Dan Dickel	LB	6'3"	220	22	1	
Tom MacLeod	LB	6'3"	230	23		
Danny Rhodes	LB	6'2"	220	23		
Stan White	LB	6'1"	225	24	1	
Randy Hall	DB	6'3"	185	22		
Bruce Laird	DB	6'	185	24	1	
Nelson Munsey	DB	6'1"	185	26		
Doug Nettles	DB	6'	177	23	1	
Ray Oldham	DB	6'	200	23	1	
Tim Rudnick	DB	5'10"	185	22		
Rick Volk	DB	6'3"	195	29	2	
Marty Domres	QB	6'3"	222	27		12
Bert Jones	QB	6'3"	205	22		24
Bill Troup	QB	6'5"	220	23		
Lydell Mitchell	HB	5'11"	204	25		42
Joe Orduna	HB	6'	195	26		6
Bill Olds	FB	6'1"	224	23		18
Don McCauley	HB-FB	6'1"	214	25		6
Tim Berra	WR	5'11"	185	22		
Roger Carr	WR	6'3"	200	22		
Glenn Doughty	WR	6'2"	204	23		12
Freddie Scott	WR	6'2"	175	22		
Ollie Smith	WR	6'2"	195	25		
Cotton Speyrer	WR	6'	175	25		6
John Andrews	TE	6'3"	227	25		
Ray Chester	TE	6'3"	235	26		6
Ron Mayo	TE	6'3"	223	23		
David Lee	K	6'4"	230	30		
Toni Linhart	K	6'	178	32		58

MIAMI DOLPHINS

RUSHING
Last Name	No.	Yds	Avg	TD
Csonka	197	749	3.8	9
Malone	117	479	4.1	3
Kiick	86	274	3.2	1
Nottingham	66	273	4.1	8
Morris	56	214	3.8	1
Ginn	26	99	3.8	2
Griese	16	66	4.1	1
Briscoe	1	17	17.0	0
N. Moore	3	16	5.3	0
Morrall	1	11	11.0	0
Strock	1	-7	-7.0	0

RECEIVING
Last Name	No.	Yds	Avg	TD
N. Moore	37	605	16	2
Mandich	33	374	11	6
Warfield	27	536	20	2
Twilley	24	256	11	2
Kiick	18	155	9	1
Briscoe	11	132	12	1
Csonka	7	35	5	0
Baker	4	121	30	2
Nottingham	3	40	13	0
Morris	2	27	14	1
Malone	2	26	13	0
Ginn	2	3	2	0
Fleming	1	3	3	1

PUNT RETURNS
Last Name	No.	Yds	Avg	TD
Scott	31	346	11	0
N. Moore	9	136	15	0
Babb	2	29	15	0
Anderson	3	9	3	0
Stuckey	1	0	0	0

KICKOFF RETURNS
Last Name	No.	Yds	Avg	TD
N. Moore	22	587	27	0
Ginn	12	235	20	0
Malone	6	159	27	0
Matheson	5	65	13	0
Baker	1	22	22	0
Babb	1	0	0	0

PASSING
Last Name	Att	Comp	%	Yds	Yd/Att	TD	Int–%	RK
Griese	253	152	60	1968	7.8	16	15– 6	4
Morrall	27	17	63	301	11.1	2	3–11	
Kiick	1	1	100	13	13.0	0	0– 0	
Moore	1	1	100	31	31.0	0	0– 0	
Briscoe	1	0	0	0	0.0	0	0– 0	

PUNTING
Last Name	No	Avg
Seiple	65	38.6

KICKING
Last Name	XP	Att	%	FG	Att	%
Yepremian	43	43	100	8	15	53

BUFFALO BILLS

RUSHING
Last Name	No.	Yds	Avg	TD
Simpson	270	1125	4.2	3
Braxton	146	543	3.7	4
Watkins	41	170	4.1	2
Ferguson	54	111	2.1	2
Calhoun	21	88	4.2	0
Hayman	7	31	4.4	0
Marangi	4	20	5.0	0
Mosley	2	6	3.0	0

RECEIVING
Last Name	No.	Yds	Avg	TD
Rashad	36	433	12	4
Hill	32	572	18	6
Braxton	18	171	10	0
Seymour	15	246	16	2
Simpson	15	189	13	1
Chandler	7	88	13	1
Calhoun	2	10	5	0
Jenkins	1	12	12	0
Watkins	1	7	7	0
Green	1	0	0	0

PUNT RETURNS
Last Name	No.	Yds	Avg	TD
Walker	43	384	9	0
Cahill	10	62	6	0
Hayman	2	13	7	0
Kern	1	1	1	0

KICKOFF RETURNS
Last Name	No.	Yds	Avg	TD
Francis	37	947	26	0
Calhoun	6	90	15	0
Cornell	3	45	15	0
Cahill	1	26	26	0
Walker	1	20	20	0
Craig	1	0	0	0
Rashad	1	0	0	0

PASSING
Last Name	Att	Comp	%	Yds	Yd/Att	TD	Int–%	RK
Ferguson	232	119	51	1588	6.8	12	12– 5	7
Marangi	18	9	50	140	7.8	2	3–17	
Simpson	1	0	0	0	0.0	0	0– 0	

PUNTING
Last Name	No	Avg
Bateman	67	40.5
Jones	35	37.3

KICKING
Last Name	XP	Att	%	FG	Att	%
Leypoldt	25	29	86	19	33	58

NEW ENGLAND PATRIOTS

RUSHING
Last Name	No.	Yds	Avg	TD
Herron	231	824	3.6	7
Cunningham	166	811	4.9	9
Plunkett	30	161	5.4	2
Tarver	41	101	2.5	2
Ashton	26	99	3.8	0
Stingley	5	63	12.6	1
Wilson	15	57	3.8	0
Vataha	3	21	7.0	0
Hinton	1	1	1.0	0
Johnson	2	-4	-2.0	0

RECEIVING
Last Name	No.	Yds	Avg	TD
Herron	38	474	13	5
Rucker	27	436	16	4
Vataha	25	561	22	3
Cunningham	22	214	10	2
B. Adams	17	244	14	0
Windsor	12	127	11	1
Stingley	10	139	14	1
Tarver	9	37	4	0
Johnson	8	147	18	0
Wilson	3	38	13	0
Hinton	2	36	18	0
Tanner	2	23	12	1
Schubert	1	21	21	1
Marshall	1	17	17	1

PUNT RETURNS
Last Name	No.	Yds	Avg	TD
Herron	35	517	15	0
Schubert	3	15	5	0
Durko	1	1	1	0
Hinton	1	0	0	0

KICKOFF RETURNS
Last Name	No.	Yds	Avg	TD
Herron	28	629	23	0
Johnson	15	303	20	0
Schubert	5	112	22	0
Hinton	3	83	28	0
Wilson	2	33	17	0
Hunt	1	21	21	0
Tanner	2	17	9	0
Durko	1	0	0	0
D. Smith	1	0	0	0

PASSING
Last Name	Att	Comp	%	Yds	Yd/Att	TD	Int–%	RK
Plunkett	352	173	49	2457	7.0	19	22– 6	9
Shiner	6	3	50	37	6.2	0	1–17	
Graff	1	1	100	20	20.0	0	0– 0	

PUNTING
Last Name	No	Avg
B. Barnes	45	35.6

KICKING
Last Name	XP	Att	%	FG	Att	%
J. Smith	42	43	98	16	22	73

NEW YORK JETS

RUSHING
Last Name	No.	Yds	Avg	TD
Riggins	169	680	4.0	5
Boozer	153	563	3.7	4
Burns	40	158	4.0	0
Adamle	28	93	3.3	2
Jackson	20	74	3.7	0
Bjorklund	23	57	2.5	0
Barkum	1	2	2.0	1
Namath	8	1	0.1	1
Woodall	2	-3	-1.5	0

RECEIVING
Last Name	No.	Yds	Avg	TD
Barkum	41	524	13	3
Knight	40	579	15	4
Caster	38	745	20	7
Riggins	19	180	10	2
Boozer	14	161	12	1
Bell	13	126	10	1
Burns	11	83	8	1
Adamle	9	84	9	0
Brister	5	90	18	0
Jackson	2	44	22	1
Bjorklund	2	15	8	0

PUNT RETURNS
Last Name	No.	Yds	Avg	TD
Word	38	301	8	0
Piccone	9	75	8	0
Jackson	6	49	8	0

KICKOFF RETURNS
Last Name	No.	Yds	Avg	TD
Piccone	39	961	25	0
Jackson	4	100	25	0
Bjorklund	4	73	18	0
Word	4	69	17	0
Burns	3	52	17	0
B. Owens	3	35	12	0
Adamle	2	17	9	0
Knight	2	0	0	0

PASSING
Last Name	Att	Comp	%	Yds	Yd/Att	TD	Int–%	RK
Namath	361	191	53	2616	7.2	20	22– 6	5
Woodall	8	3	38	15	1.9	0	2–25	

PUNTING
Last Name	No	Avg
Gantt	75	35.9

KICKING
Last Name	XP	Att	%	FG	Att	%
Leahy	18	19	95	6	11	55
Howfield	8	12	67	6	7	86
Gantt	1	2	50	0	0	—

BALTIMORE COLTS

RUSHING
Last Name	No.	Yds	Avg	TD
Mitchell	214	757	3.5	5
Olds	129	475	3.7	1
Jones	39	279	7.2	4
Domres	22	145	6.6	2
McCauley	30	90	3.0	0
Doughty	7	51	7.3	0
Scott	2	12	6.0	0
Andrews	5	6	1.2	0
Orduna	2	3	1.5	1

RECEIVING
Last Name	No.	Yds	Avg	TD
Mitchell	72	544	8	2
Chester	37	461	13	1
Doughty	24	300	13	2
Carr	21	405	19	0
Olds	21	153	7	2
Scott	18	317	18	0
McCauley	17	112	7	1
Speyrer	9	110	12	1
Smith	1	14	14	0
Orduna	1	8	8	0

PUNT RETURNS
Last Name	No.	Yds	Avg	TD
Berra	16	114	7	0
Speyrer	8	54	7	0
Scott	3	31	10	0
Laird	11	30	3	0
Rudnick	2	23	12	0
Volk	1	1	1	0
Bertuca	1	0	0	0

KICKOFF RETURNS
Last Name	No.	Yds	Avg	TD
Speyrer	22	539	25	0
Laird	19	499	26	0
Berra	13	259	20	0
Orduna	3	68	23	0
Scott	3	61	20	0
Mayo	2	23	12	0
Andrews	1	18	18	0
McCauley	1	17	17	0
Rudnick	1	5	5	0
Oldham	1	0	0	0

PASSING
Last Name	Att	Comp	%	Yds	Yd/Att	TD	Int–%	RK
Jones	270	143	53	1610	6.0	8	12– 4	10
Domres	153	77	50	803	5.2	0	12– 8	15
McCauley	2	1	50	11	5.5	1	0– 0	

PUNTING
Last Name	No	Avg
Lee	71	37.1

KICKING
Last Name	XP	Att	%	FG	Att	%
Linhart	22	22	100	12	20	60

Scores of Each Game			Use Name	Pos.	Hgt	Wgt	Age	Int	Pts

PITTSBURGH STEELERS 10-3-1 Chuck Noll

Score	Opponent		Use Name	Pos.	Hgt	Wgt	Age	Int	Pts
30	BALTIMORE	0	Gordon Gravelle	OT	6'5"	250	25		
35	Denver (OT)	35	Jon Kolb	OT	6'2"	262	27		
0	OAKLAND	17	Dave Reavis	OT	6'5"	250	24		
13	Houston	7	Rick Druschel	OG-OT	6'2"	248	22		
34	Kansas City	24	Sam Davis	OG	6'1"	255	30		
20	CLEVELAND	16	Jim Clack	C-OG	6'3"	250	26		
24	ATLANTA	17	Gerry Mullins	OT-OG	6'3"	244	25		6
27	PHILADELPHIA	0	Ray Mansfield	C	6'3"	260	33		
10	Cincinnati	17	Mike Webster	OG-C	6'1"	232	22		
26	Cleveland	16	L. C. Greenwood	DE	6'5"	245	27		2
28	New Orleans	7	Dwight White	DE	6'4"	255	25		
10	HOUSTON	13	Jim Wolf	DE	6'2"	230	22		
21	New England	17	Charlie Davis	DT	6'1"	265	22		
27	CINCINNATI	3	Joe Greene	DT	6'4"	275	27	1	
			Ernie Holmes	DT	6'3"	260	26		
			Steve Furness	DE-DT	6'4"	255	24		

Use Name	Pos.	Hgt	Wgt	Age	Int	Pts
Ed Bradley	LB	6'2"	240	24		
Jack Ham	LB	6'3"	225	25	5	
Marv Kellum	LB	6'2"	225	22	1	
Jack Lambert	LB	6'4"	215	22	2	
Andy Russell	LB	6'3"	225	32	1	
Loren Toews	LB	6'3"	212	22		
Jimmy Allen	DB	6'2"	194	22		
Mel Blount	DB	6'3"	205	26	2	6
Dick Conn	DB	6'	185	23		
Glen Edwards	DB	6'	185	27	5	6
Donnie Shell	DB	5'11"	190	22	1	
Jim Thomas	DB	6'2"	196	23	5	6
Mike Wagner	DB	6'1"	210	25	2	
Henry Davis — Injury						

Use Name	Pos.	Hgt	Wgt	Age	Int	Pts
Terry Bradshaw	QB	6'3"	218	25		12
Joe Gilliam	QB	6'2"	187	23		6
Terry Hanratty	QB	6'1"	210	26		
Rocky Bleier	HB	5'11"	210	28		12
Preston Pearson	HB	6'1"	205	29		24
Franco Harris	FB-HB	6'2"	230	24		36
Reggie Harrison (from STL)	FB	5'11"	215	24		6
Steve Davis	HB-FB	6'1"	218	24		18
John Fuqua	HB-FB	5'11"	195	27		12
Reggie Garrett	WR	6'1"	172	22		
Frank Lewis	WR	6'1"	196	27		24
Ron Shanklin	WR	6'1"	190	27		6
John Stallworth	WR	6'2"	183	22		6
Lynn Swann	WR	5'10"	178	22		18
Larry Brown	TE	6'4"	230	25		6
Randy Grossman	TE	6'1"	215	20		
John McMakin	TE	6'3"	232	23		
Roy Gerela	K	5'10"	185	26		93
Bobby Walden	K	6'	190	26		

CINCINNATI BENGALS 7-7-0 Paul Brown

Score	Opponent		Use Name	Pos.	Hgt	Wgt	Age	Int	Pts
33	CLEVELAND	7	Vern Holland	OT	6'5"	268	26		
17	SAN DIEGO	20	Dave Lapham	OT	6'3"	255	22		
21	San Francisco	3	Rufus Mayes	OT	6'5"	258	26		
28	WASHINGTON	17	Stan Walters	OT	6'6"	262	26		
34	Cleveland	24	Howard Fest	OG-OT	6'6"	256	28		
27	Oakland	30	Pat Matson	OG	6'1"	245	30		
21	HOUSTON	34	John Shinners	OG	6'2"	255	27		
24	Baltimore	14	Bob Johnson	C	6'5"	262	28		
17	PITTSBURGH	10	Royce Berry	DE	6'3"	250	28		
3	Houston	20	Ken Johnson	DE	6'5"	256	27		
33	KANSAS CITY	6	Bob Maddox	DE	6'5"	232	25	6	
3	Miami	24	Sherman White	DE	6'5"	255	25		
19	DETROIT	23	Ron Carpenter	DT	6'4"	260	26	2	
3	Pittsburgh	27	Bill Kollar	DT	6'3"	255	21		
			Mike Reid	DT	6'3"	255	27		

Use Name	Pos.	Hgt	Wgt	Age	Int	Pts
Doug Adams	LB	6'1"	226	25		
Ken Avery	LB	6'1"	227	30		
Al Beauchamp	LB	6'2"	232	30	1	
Evan Jolitz	LB	6'2"	225	22		
Tim Kearney	LB	6'2"	230	23		
Vic Koegel	LB	6'	215	22		
Jim LeClair	LB	6'3"	235	23		
Ron Pritchard	LB	6'1"	230	27		
Lyle Blackwood	DB	6'1"	190	23		
Tommy Casanova	DB	6'2"	195	24	2	
Bernie Jackson	DB	6'	178	24	1	
Bob Jones	DB	6'1"	194	23		
Lemar Parrish	DB	5'11"	185	26		18
Ken Riley	DB	6'	182	27	5	
Ken Sawyer	DB	6'	192	22		

Use Name	Pos.	Hgt	Wgt	Age	Int	Pts
Ken Anderson	QB	6'1"	211	25		12
Wayne Clark	QB	6'2"	203	27		6
Charlie Davis	HB	5'11"	200	22		
Lenvil Elliott	HB	6'	205	23		12
Essex Johnson	HB	5'9"	200	27		6
Booby Clark	FB	6'2"	245	23		36
Doug Dressler	FB	6'3"	228	26		12
Ed Williams	FB	6'2"	245	24		24
Isaac Curtis	WR	6'	193	23		60
Charlie Joiner	WR	5'11"	188	26		6
John McDaniel	WR	6'1"	193	22		
Chip Myers	WR	6'4"	205	29		6
Al Chandler	TE	6'2"	230	23		
Bruce Coslet	TE	6'3"	227	28		
Bob Trumpy	TE	6'6"	228	29		12
Dave Green	K	5'11"	208	24		
Horst Muhlmann	K	6'1"	220	34		65

HOUSTON OILERS 7-7-0 Sid Gillman

Score	Opponent		Use Name	Pos.	Hgt	Wgt	Age	Int	Pts
21	SAN DIEGO	14	Elbert Drungo	OT	6'5"	265	31		
7	Cleveland	20	Kevin Hunt	OT	6'5"	260	25		
7	KANSAS CITY	17	Greg Sampson	OT	6'6"	260	23		
7	PITTSBURGH	13	Ronnie Carroll	OG	6'2"	265	25		
10	Minnesota	51	Curley Culp (from KC)	DT-OG	6'1"	265	28		
27	ST. LOUIS	31	Soloman Freelon	OG	6'2"	250	23		
34	Cincinnati	21	Brian Goodman	OG	6'2"	250	25		
27	N.Y. Jets	22	Harris Jones	OG	6'4"	245	29		
21	Buffalo	9	Ron Saul	OG	6'2"	255	26		
20	CINCINNATI	3	Fred Hoaglin	C	6'4"	250	30		
0	DALLAS	10	Sid Smith	OT-C	6'4"	260	26		
13	Pittsburgh	10	Elvin Bethea	DE	6'2"	255	28	6	
14	Denver	37	Ed Fisher	DE	6'3"	245	25		
28	CLEVELAND	24	Tody Smith	DE	6'5"	250	25	1	
			Jim White	DE	6'3"	255	25		
			Al Cowlings	LB-DT	6'5"	245	27		
			Bubba McCollum	DT	6'	250	22		
			Ron Lou — injury						

Use Name	Pos.	Hgt	Wgt	Age	Int	Pts
Duane Benson	LB	6'2"	215	29	2	
Greg Bingham	LB	6'1"	230	23	4	
Ralph Cindrich (to DEN)	LB	6'2"	230	24		
Marvin Davis	LB	6'4"	235	22		
Steve Kiner	LB	6'	220	27	1	
Guy Roberts	LB	6'1"	217	24		
Ted Washington	LB	6'1"	240	24		
Willie Alexander	DB	6'2"	190	24	2	
Bob Atkins	DB	6'3"	210	28	6	
John Charles	DB	6'1"	200	30		
Leonard Fairley	DB	5'11"	200	24		
Al Johnson	DB	6'	200	24		
Tommy Maxwell	DB	6'2"	195	27	2	
Zeke Moore	DB	6'2"	196	30	2	6
Jeff Severson	DB	6'1"	185	24	1	
C. L. Whittington	DB	6'1"	200	22		

Use Name	Pos.	Hgt	Wgt	Age	Int	Pts
Lynn Dickey	QB	6'4"	210	24		
James Foote	QB	6'2"	210	22		
Dan Pastorini	QB	6'3"	205	25		
Ronnie Coleman	HB	5'10"	195	23		6
Bob Gresham	HB	5'11"	200	24		
Willie Rodgers	HB	6'	210	25		30
Vic Washington	HB	5'10"	196	28		12
Terry Wells	HB	5'11"	195	23		
George Amundson	FB	6'3"	215	23		30
Fred Willis	FB	6'	205	26		24
Ken Burrough	WR	6'4"	210	26		12
Billy Johnson	WR	5'9"	170	22		18
Mike Montgomery	WR	6'2"	210	25		6
Billy Parks	WR	6'1"	190	26		6
Mack Alston	TE	6'2"	230	27		18
Jerry Broadnax	TE	6'2"	225	23		
Jeff Queen	TE	6'1"	217	28		6
David Beverly	K	6'2"	180	24		
Skip Butler	K	6'2"	200	26		56

CLEVELAND BROWNS 4-10-0 Nick Skorich

Score	Opponent		Use Name	Pos.	Hgt	Wgt	Age	Int	Pts
7	Cincinnati	33	Barry Darrow	OT	6'7"	260	24		
20	HOUSTON	7	Doug Dieken	OT	6'5"	254	25		
7	St. Louis	29	Bob McKay	OT	6'6"	260	26		
24	OAKLAND	40	Gerry Sullivan	OT	6'4"	250	22		
24	CINCINNATI	34	Pete Adams	OG	6'4"	260	23		
16	Pittsburgh	20	Jim Copeland	OG	6'2"	243	29		
23	DENVER	21	John Demarie	OG	6'3"	246	29		
25	San Diego	36	Glen Holloway	OG	6'3"	250	25		
21	New England	14	Chuck Hutchison	OG	6'3"	250	25		
16	PITTSBURGH	26	Tom DeLeone	C	6'2"	252	24		
10	BUFFALO	15	Bob DeMarco	C	6'3"	248	36		
7	SAN FRANCISCO	0	Mark Ilgenfritz	DE	6'4"	250	22		
17	Dallas	41	Mike Seifert	DE	6'3"	245	23		
24	Houston	28	Carl Barisch	DT	6'4"	255	23		
			Walter Johnson	DT	6'3"	265	31		
			Jerry Sherk	DT	6'4"	255	26		

Use Name	Pos.	Hgt	Wgt	Age	Int	Pts
Billy Andrews	LB	6'	225	29	1	
Bob Babich	LB	6'2"	230	27	1	
John Garlington	LB	6'1"	218	28	2	
Charlie Hall	LB	6'3"	225	25	3	6
Mel Long	LB	6'	228	27		
Jim Romaniszyn	LB	6'2"	224	22		
Preston Anderson	DB	6'1"	183	22		
Cliff Brooks	DB	6'1"	190	25		
Eddie Brown	DB	5'11"	180	22	2	
Thom Darden	DB	6'2"	195	24	8	6
Van Green	DB	6'1"	192	23	2	6
Clarence Scott	DB	6'	180	25	4	
Walt Sumner	DB	6'1"	195	27		
Ken Smith — Injury						

Use Name	Pos.	Hgt	Wgt	Age	Int	Pts
Mike Phipps	QB	6'2"	205	26		6
Brian Sipe	QB	6'1"	195	25		24
Ken Brown	HB	5'10"	203	28		36
Greg Pruitt	HB	5'10"	190	23		30
Billy LeFear	WR-HB	5'11"	197	24		
Hugh McKinnis	FB	6'	215	26		12
Bo Scott	FB	6'3"	215	31		
Jubilee Dunbar	WR	6'	196	27		
Tim George	WR	6'5"	180	27		
Ben Hawkins	WR	6'1"	180	30		
Steve Holden	WR	6'	198	23		18
Fair Hooker	WR	6'1"	195	27		6
Gloster Richardson	WR	6'	200	31		12
Dave Sullivan	WR	5'11"	185	23		
Milt Morin	TE	6'4"	236	32		18
Jim Thaxton (From SD)	TE	6'2"	240	25	1	
Don Cockroft	K	6'1"	195	29		71
Chris Gartner	K	6'	170	24		

PITTSBURGH STEELERS

RUSHING

Last Name	No.	Yds	Avg	TD
Harris	208	1006	4.8	5
Bleier	88	373	4.2	2
Pearson	70	317	4.5	4
Steve Davis	71	246	3.5	2
Bradshaw	34	224	6.6	2
Fuqua	50	156	3.1	2
Gilliam	14	41	2.9	1
Harrison	6	30	5.0	1
Lewis	2	25	12.5	0
Swann	1	14	14.0	0
Hanratty	1	-6	-6.0	0
Stallworth	1	-9	-9.0	0

RECEIVING

Last Name	No.	Yds	Avg	TD
Lewis	30	365	12	4
Harris	23	200	9	1
Shanklin	19	324	17	1
Brown	17	190	11	1
Stallworth	16	269	17	1
Grossman	13	164	13	0
Swann	11	208	19	2
Steve Davis	11	152	14	1
Pearson	11	118	11	0
Bleier	7	87	12	0
Fuqua	6	68	11	0
Mullins	1	7	7	1
Harrison	1	2	2	0

PUNT RETURNS

Last Name	No.	Yds	Avg	TD
Swann	41	577	14	1
Edwards	16	128	8	0
Conn	10	69	7	0

KICKOFF RETURNS

Last Name	No.	Yds	Avg	TD
Steve Davis	12	269	22	0
Pearson	12	258	22	0
Blount	5	152	30	0
Harrison	4	72	18	0
Bleier	3	67	22	0
Conn	1	34	34	0
Edwards	2	31	16	0
Swann	2	11	6	0
Allen	1	7	7	0

PASSING – PUNTING – KICKING

PASSING	Att	Comp	%	Yds	Yd/Att	TD	Int-%	RK
Gilliam	212	96	45	1274	6.0	4	8-4	12
Bradshaw	148	67	45	785	5.3	7	8-5	13
Hanratty	26	3	12	95	3.7	1	5-19	

PUNTING	No	Avg
Walden	78	39.0

KICKING	XP	Att	%	FG	Att	%
Gerela	33	35	94	20	29	69

CINCINNATI BENGALS

RUSHING

Last Name	No.	Yds	Avg	TD
Davis	72	375	5.2	0
Elliott	68	345	5.1	1
Anderson	43	314	7.3	2
B. Clark	99	312	3.2	5
Dressler	72	255	3.5	2
Williams	58	238	4.1	3
Curtis	8	62	7.8	0
E. Johnson	19	44	2.3	0
Joiner	4	20	5.0	0
W. Clark	1	8	8.0	0
McDaniel	1	5	5.0	0

RECEIVING

Last Name	No.	Yds	Avg	TD
Myers	32	383	12	1
Curtis	30	633	21	10
Dressler	29	196	7	0
Joiner	24	390	16	1
B. Clark	23	194	8	1
Trumpy	21	330	16	2
Davis	19	171	9	0
Elliott	18	187	10	1
Williams	13	98	8	1
E. Johnson	8	85	11	1
McDaniel	2	79	40	0
Coslet	2	24	12	0
Jackson	1	22	22	0
Chandler	1	9	9	0
Johnson	1	3	3	0

PUNT RETURNS

Last Name	No.	Yds	Avg	TD
Parrish	18	338	19	2
Casanova	24	265	11	0
Blackwood	10	29	3	0

KICKOFF RETURNS

Last Name	No.	Yds	Avg	TD
Jackson	29	682	24	0
Davis	12	243	20	0
McDaniel	3	64	21	0
Casanova	1	48	48	0
Parrish	2	36	18	0
Williams	2	33	17	0
Dressler	3	33	11	0
Blackwood	1	17	17	0
Elliott	1	2	2	0

PASSING – PUNTING – KICKING

PASSING	Att	Comp	%	Yds	Yd/Att	TD	Int-%	RK
Anderson	328	213	65	2667	8.1	18	10-3	1
W. Clark	22	9	41	98	4.5	0	3-14	
Green	2	1	50	22	11.0	0	0-0	
Elliott	1	1	100	17	17.0	0	0-0	

PUNTING	No	Avg
Green	66	40.9

KICKING	XP	Att	%	FG	Att	%
Muhlmann	32	35	91	11	18	61

HOUSTON OILERS

RUSHING

Last Name	No.	Yds	Avg	TD
Rodgers	122	413	3.4	5
V. Washington	74	281	3.8	2
Willis	74	239	3.2	3
Coleman	52	193	3.7	1
Amundson	59	138	2.3	4
B. Johnson	5	82	16.4	1
Dickey	3	7	2.3	0
Queen	2	7	3.5	0
Gresham	3	6	2.0	0
Beverly	1	4	4.0	0
Burrough	1	0	0.0	0
Alston	1	-3	-3.0	0
Pastorini	24	-6	-0.2	0

RECEIVING

Last Name	No.	Yds	Avg	TD
Burrough	36	492	14	2
B. Johnson	29	388	13	2
Willis	25	130	5	1
Rodgers	24	153	6	0
Parks	20	330	17	1
Amundson	18	152	8	1
Alston	17	249	15	3
V. Washington	13	92	7	0
Montgomery	9	179	20	1
Coleman	4	9	2	0
Broadnax	3	69	23	0
Gresham	3	19	6	0
Wells	1	9	9	0
Queen	1	4	4	1

PUNT RETURNS

Last Name	No.	Yds	Avg	TD
B. Johnson	30	409	14	0
Severson	11	86	8	0

KICKOFF RETURNS

Last Name	No.	Yds	Avg	TD
B. Johnson	29	785	27	0
Gresham	9	180	20	0
V. Washington	7	177	25	0
Severson	6	108	18	0
Coleman	3	91	30	0
Whittington	3	37	12	0
Amundson	2	17	9	0
A. Johnson	1	14	14	0
Saul	1	10	10	0
Jones	1	0	0	0

PASSING – PUNTING – KICKING

PASSING	Att	Comp	%	Yds	Yd/Att	TD	Int-%	RK
Pastorini	247	140	57	1571	6.4	10	10-4	5
Dickey	113	63	56	704	6.2	2	8-7	
Coleman	2	0	0	0	0.0	0	0-0	
Amundson	1	0	0	0	0.0	0	1-100	

PUNTING	No	Avg
Beverly	79	39.2

KICKING	XP	Att	%	FG	Att	%
Butler	29	29	100	9	19	47

CLEVELAND BROWNS

RUSHING

Last Name	No.	Yds	Avg	TD
Pruitt	126	540	4.3	3
McKinnis	124	519	4.2	2
K. Brown	125	458	3.7	4
Phipps	39	279	7.2	1
B. Scott	23	86	3.7	0
Sipe	16	44	2.8	4
Holden	1	6	6.0	0
LeFear	6	2	0.3	0
Thaxton	1	-10	-10.0	0

RECEIVING

Last Name	No.	Yds	Avg	TD
McKinnis	32	258	8	0
Holden	30	452	15	3
K. Brown	29	194	7	2
Morin	27	330	12	3
Pruitt	21	274	13	1
Richardson	9	266	30	2
B. Scott	7	22	3	0
Dunbar	6	74	12	0
D. Sullivan	5	92	18	0
Thaxton	4	71	18	0
Hooker	4	48	12	1
LeFear	4	21	5	0
Green	1	27	27	0

PUNT RETURNS

Last Name	No.	Yds	Avg	TD
Pruitt	27	349	13	0
Darden	21	173	8	0
LeFear	2	1	1	0
E. Brown	2	0	0	0

KICKOFF RETURNS

Last Name	No.	Yds	Avg	TD
Pruitt	22	606	28	1
LeFear	26	574	22	0
E. Brown	6	138	23	0
Romaniszyn	5	48	10	0
K. Brown	1	9	9	0

PASSING – PUNTING – KICKING

PASSING	Att	Comp	%	Yds	Yd/Att	TD	Int-%	RK
Phipps	256	117	46	1384	5.4	9	17-7	14
Sipe	108	59	55	603	5.6	1	7-7	
Pruitt	2	2	100	115	57.5	2	0-0	
Cockroft	1	1	100	27	27.0	0	0-0	

PUNTING	No	Avg
Cockroft	90	40.5

KICKING	XP	Att	%	FG	Att	%
Cockroft	29	30	97	14	16	88

OAKLAND RAIDERS 12-2-0 — John Madden

Scores of Each Game:

20	Buffalo	21
27	KANSAS CITY	7
17	Pittsburgh	0
40	Cleveland	24
14	SAN DIEGO	10
30	CINCINNATI	27
35	San Francisco	24
28	Denver	17
35	DETROIT	13
17	San Diego	10
17	DENVER	20
41	NEW ENGLAND	26
7	Kansas City	6
27	DALLAS	23

Use Name	Pos.	Hgt	Wgt	Age	Int	Pts
Henry Lawrence	OT	6'4"	268	22		
Harold Paul	OT	6'5"	245	24		
Art Shell	OT	6'5"	265	27		
John Vella	OT	6'4"	255	24		
George Buehler	OG	6'2"	260	27		
Dan Medlin	OG	6'3"	260	24		
Gene Upshaw	OG	6'5"	255	29		
Jim Otto	C	6'2"	255	36		
Dave Dalby	OG-C	6'2"	240	23		
Tony Cline	DE	6'2"	244	26		
Horace Jones	DE	6'3"	255	25		
Bubba Smith	DE	6'7"	265	29		
Kelvin Korver	DT	6'6"	270	25		
Otis Sistrunk	DT	6'4"	255	26	1	2
Art Thoms	DT	6'5"	260	27		6
Dan Conners	LB	6'1"	230	32	3	
Mike Dennery	LB	6'	222	24		
Gerald Irons	LB	6'2"	230	27	2	
Monte Johnson	LB	6'4"	235	22	1	
Phil Villapiano	LB	6'1"	222	25		
Gary Weaver	LB	6'1"	224	25		
Butch Atkinson	DB	6'	180	26	4	
Willie Brown	DB	6'1"	195	33	1	
Bob Prout	DB	6'1"	190	23		
Ron Smith	DB	6'1"	195	31		
Jack Tatum	DB	5'10"	200	25	4	
Skip Thomas	DB	6'1"	205	24	6	6
Jimmy Warren	DB	5'11"	175	35	2	
Nemiah Wilson	DB	6'	165	31	3	
George Blanda	QB	6'2"	215	46		77
Daryle Lamonica	QB	6'2"	215	33		
Larry Lawrence	QB	6'2"	208	25		
Ken Stabler	QB	6'3"	215	28		6
Clarence Davis	HB	5'10"	195	25		18
Harold Hart	HB	6'	206	21		18
Bob Hudson	HB	5'11"	205	26		
Charlie Smith	HB	6'1"	205	28		12
Mark van Eeghen	FB-HB	6'1"	215	22		
Warren Bankston	FB	6'4"	235	27		
Marv Hubbard	FB	6'1"	225	28		24
Pete Banaszak	HB-FB	5'11"	210	30		30
Fred Biletnikoff	WR	6'1"	190	31		42
Morris Bradshaw	WR	6'	198	21		
Cliff Branch	WR	5'11"	170	26		78
Frank Pitts	WR	6'2"	200	30		
Mike Siani	WR	6'2"	195	24		
Dave Casper	TE	6'4"	250	22		18
Bob Moore	TE	6'3"	220	25		12
Ray Guy	K	6'3"	190	24		
George Jakowenko	K	5'9"	170	26		

DENVER BRONCOS 7-6-1 — John Ralston

Scores of Each Game:

10	LOS ANGELES	17
35	PITTSBURGH (OT)	35
3	Washington	30
17	Kansas City	14
33	NEW ORLEANS	17
27	SAN DIEGO	7
21	Cleveland	23
17	OAKLAND	28
17	Baltimore	6
34	KANSAS CITY	42
20	Oakland	17
31	Detroit	27
37	HOUSTON	14
0	San Diego	17

Use Name	Pos.	Hgt	Wgt	Age	Int	Pts
Mike Current	OT	6'4"	270	28		
Claudie Minor	OT	6'4"	280	23		
Marv Montgomery	OT	6'6"	255	26		
LeFrancis Arnold	OG	6'3"	245	21		
Paul Howard	OG	6'3"	260	23		
Tommy Lyons	OG	6'2"	230	26		
Mike Schnitker	OG	6'3"	245	27		
Larron Jackson	OT-OG	6'3"	260	25		
Bobby Maples	C	6'3"	250	31		
Lyle Alzado	DE	6'3"	265	25		
Barney Chavous	DE	6'3"	252	23		
Steve Coleman	DE	6'4"	252	23		
John Grant	DE	6'3"	235	24		
Ed Smith	DE	6'5"	240	24	1	
Pete Duranko	DT	6'2"	250	30		
Dan Goich	DT	6'4"	250	30		
Bob Kampa (from BUF)	DT	6'4"	245	23		
Paul Smith	DT	6'3"	256	29		
Ken Criter	LB	5'11"	223	27		
Randy Gradishar	LB	6'3"	233	22		
Tom Jackson	LB	5'11"	220	23	1	
Bill Laskey	LB	6'2"	230	31	1	
Ray May	LB	6'1"	230	29	2	
Jim O'Malley	LB	6'1"	230	23		
Joe Rizzo	LB	6'1"	220	23		
Mike Simone	LB	6'	210	24		
Charlie Greer	DB	6'	205	28	1	
Lonnie Hepburn	DB	5'11"	180	25		
Calvin Jones	DB	5'7"	170	23	5	
John Pitts	DB	6'4"	218	29	1	
John Rowser	DB	6'1"	190	30	4	
Bill Thompson	DB	6'1"	200	27	5	6
Maurice Tyler	DB	6'	188	24	1	
John Hufnagel	QB	6'1"	194	23		
Charley Johnson	QB	6'	200	37		
Steve Ramsey	QB	6'2"	210	26		
Otis Armstrong	HB	5'10"	196	23		72
Floyd Little	HB	5'10"	196	32		6
Oliver Ross	HB	6'	210	24		
Jon Keyworth	HB	6'3"	230	23		60
Fran Lynch	HB-FB	6'1"	205	28		
Haven Moses	WR	6'3"	208	28		12
Jerry Simmons	WR	6'1"	190	31		12
Otto Stowe	WR	6'2"	188	25		
Bill Van Heusen	WR	6'1"	200	28		24
Boyd Brown	TE	6'4"	216	22		
Bill Masters	TE	6'5"	240	30		
Riley Odoms	TE	6'4"	230	24		30
Jim Turner	K	6'2"	205	33		68

Bobby Anderson — Broken Ankle

KANSAS CITY CHIEFS 5-9-0 — Hank Stram

Scores of Each Game:

24	N.Y. JETS	16
7	Oakland	27
7	Houston	7
14	DENVER	17
24	PITTSBURGH	34
3	Miami	9
24	San Diego	14
21	N.Y. GIANTS	33
7	SAN DIEGO	14
42	Denver	34
6	Cincinnati	33
17	St. Louis	13
6	OAKLAND	7
15	MINNESOTA	35

Use Name	Pos.	Hgt	Wgt	Age	Int	Pts
Tom Drougas (from DEN)	OT	6'4"	267	24		
Charlie Getty	OT	6'4"	260	22		
Dave Hill	OT	6'5"	260	33		
Jim Nicholson	OT	6'6"	260	24		
Francis Peay	OT	6'5"	250	30		
Wayne Walton	OG-OT	6'5"	255	25		
Ed Budde	OG	6'5"	265	33		
Tom Condon	OG	6'3"	240	21		
George Daney	OG	6'3"	240	27		
Tom Humphrey	C	6'2"	260	24		
Jack Rudnay	C	6'3"	240	26		
Bob Briggs	DE	6'4"	258	29		
Fred DeBernardi	DE	6'6"	250	25		
Marv Upshaw	DE	6'3"	260	27	1	6
Wilbur Young	DE	6'6"	285	25	1	6
Buck Buchanan	DT	6'7"	270	34		
Tom Keating	DT	6'3"	247	31		
John Matuszak	DT	6'8"	275	23		
Bobby Bell	LB	6'4"	228	34	1	6
Tom Graham (from DEN)	LB	6'2"	235	24		
Willie Lanier	LB	6'1"	245	29	2	2
Jim Lynch	LB	6'1"	235	29		
Al Palewicz	LB	6'1"	215	24		
Bob Thornbladh	LB	6'1"	220	22		
Clyde Werner	LB	6'4"	230	26	1	
Nate Allen	DB	5'10"	170	24	1	
Doug Jones	DB	6'2"	202	24	1	
Jim Kearney	DB	6'2"	206	31		
Jim Marsalis	DB	5'11"	194	28		
Willie Osley	DB	6'	195	24		
Kerry Reardon	DB	5'11"	180	25	4	
Mike Sensibaugh	DB	6'2"	192	25	4	
Emmitt Thomas	DB	6'2"	192	31	12	12
Dean Carlson	QB	6'3"	210	24		
Len Dawson	QB	6'	190	40		
David Jaynes	QB	6'2"	212	22		
Mike Livingston	QB	6'3"	212	28		
Woody Green	HB	6'1"	205	23		24
Cleo Miller	HB	5'11"	202	22		
Donnie Joe Morris	HB	5'11"	195	24		
Ed Podolak	HB	6'1"	205	27		12
Willie Ellison	FB-HB	6'1"	210	29		12
Wendell Hayes	FB	6'2"	220	33		12
Bill Thomas	FB	6'2"	225	24		
Jeff Kinney	HB-FB	6'2"	215	24		
Larry Brunson	WR	5'11"	180	25		12
Andy Hamilton	WR	6'3"	190	24		
Barry Pearson	WR	5'11"	185	24		
Otis Taylor	WR	6'2"	215	31		12
Elmo Wright	WR	6'	190	25		
John Strada	TE	6'3"	230	22		
Morris Stroud	TE	6'10"	255	28		1
Jan Stenerud	K	6'2"	187	31		7
Jerrel Wilson	K	6'4"	222	33		

Gary Butler — Knee Injury
John Lohmeyer — Injury

SAN DIEGO CHARGERS 5-9-0 — Tommy Prothro

Scores of Each Game:

14	Houston	21
20	Cincinnati	17
21	MIAMI	28
7	PHILADELPHIA	13
10	Oakland	14
7	Denver	27
14	KANSAS CITY	24
36	CLEVELAND	25
14	Kansas City	7
10	OAKLAND	17
0	Green Bay	34
14	N.Y. Jets	27
28	CHICAGO	21
17	DENVER	0

Use Name	Pos.	Hgt	Wgt	Age	Int	Pts
Terry Owens	OT	6'6"	260	30		
Brian Vertefeuille	OT	6'3"	252	23		
Russ Washington	OT	6'6"	290	27		
Mark Markovich	OG	6'5"	256	21		
Doug Wilkerson	OG	6'2"	256	27		
Ira Gordon	OT-OG	6'3"	265	26		
Jay Douglas	C	6'6"	260	23		
Carl Mauck	C	6'3"	243	27		
Coy Bacon	DE	6'4"	270	32		
Raymond Baylor	DE	6'5"	263	27		
Blenda Gay	DE	6'5"	250	24		6
Pete Lazetich	DE	6'3"	245	24		
Dave Tipton	DE	6'6"	240	25		
Bon Boatwright	DT	6'5"	262	22		
Bob Brown	DT	6'5"	290	34		
Dave Rowe	DT	6'6"	265	29		
John Teerlinck	DT	6'5"	245	23		
Charles Anthony	LB	6'1"	230	22	1	
Fred Forsberg	LB	6'1"	225	30		
Carl Gersbach	LB	6'1"	230	27	1	
Don Goode	LB	6'2"	234	23		
Mike Lee	LB	6'	232	23		
Chip Myrtle	LB	6'2"	225	29		
Floyd Rice	LB	6'3"	223	25	3	
Mel Rogers	LB	6'2"	233	27		
Jeff Staggs	LB	6'2"	240	30		
Joe Beauchamp	DB	6'	188	30	1	
Reggie Berry	DB	6'	185	25		
Danny Colbert	DB	5'11"	167	23		
Lenny Dunlap	DB	6'1"	198	25		
Chris Fletcher	DB	5'11"	182	25	4	
George Hoey	DB	5'10"	180	27	1	
Bob Howard	DB	6'1"	177	29	3	
Sam Williams	DB	6'2"	192	22	1	
Dan Fouts	QB	6'3"	193	23		
Jesse Freitas	QB	6'1"	203	22		
Don Horn	QB	6'2"	195	29		
Glen Bonner	HB	6'2"	202	22		
Bob Thomas	HB	5'10"	202	25		
Tommy Thompson	HB	6'1"	205	23		
Don Woods	HB	6'1"	210	23		6
Cid Edwards	FB	6'2"	230	30		
Bo Matthews	FB	6'4"	230	22		
Jim Beirne	WR	6'2"	206	27		
Harrison Davis	WR	6'4"	220	22		1
Gary Garrison	WR	6'1"	195	30		30
Dick Gordon	WR	5'11"	190	29		
Jerry LeVias	WR	5'10"	177	27		
Dave Grannell	TE	6'2"	230	22		
Gary Parris	TE	6'2"	226	24		
Wayne Stewart	TE	6'7"	230	27		
Dennis Partee	K	6'2"	209	28		
Ray Wersching	K	5'11"	210	24		

Clint Jones — Injury
Reece Morrison — Injury

OAKLAND RAIDERS

RUSHING

Last Name	No.	Yds	Avg	TD
Hubbard	188	865	4.6	4
Davis	129	554	4.3	2
Banaszak	80	272	3.4	5
Hart	51	268	5.3	2
C. Smith	64	194	3.0	1
van Eeghen	28	139	5.0	0
L. Lawrence	4	39	9.8	0
Hudson	1	12	12.0	0
Bankston	1	6	6.0	0
Stabler	12	−2	−0.2	1
Lamonica	2	−3	−1.5	0
Pitts	1	−10	−10.0	0

RECEIVING

Last Name	No.	Yds	Avg	TD
Branch	60	1092	18	13
Biletnikoff	42	593	14	7
Moore	30	356	12	2
Davis	11	145	13	1
Hubbard	11	95	9	0
Banaszak	9	64	7	0
C. Smith	8	100	13	1
van Eeghen	4	33	8	0
Casper	4	26	7	3
Siani	3	30	10	1
Pitts	3	23	8	0
Hart	1	4	4	0

PUNT RETURNS

Last Name	No.	Yds	Avg	TD
R. Smith	41	486	12	0
Atkinson	4	31	8	0

KICKOFF RETURNS

Last Name	No.	Yds	Avg	TD
Hart	18	466	26	0
R. Smith	19	420	22	0
Banaszak	8	137	17	0
Davis	3	107	36	0
Bankston	1	10	10	0
Bradshaw	1	0	0	0

PASSING — PUNTING — KICKING

PASSING	Att	Comp	%	Yds	Yd/Att	TD	Int−%	RK
Stabler	310	178	57	2469	8.0	26	12− 4	2
L. Lawrence	11	4	36	29	2.6	0	1− 9	
Lamonica	9	3	33	35	3.9	1	4− 44	
Blanda	4	1	25	28	7.0	1	0− 0	
Guy	1	0	0	0	0.0	0	0−100	

PUNTING	No	Avg
Guy	74	42.2

KICKING	XP	Att	%	FG	Att	%
Blanda	44	46	96	11	17	65

DENVER BRONCOS

RUSHING

Last Name	No.	Yds	Avg	TD
Armstrong	263	1407	5.3	9
Keyworth	81	374	4.6	10
Little	117	312	2.7	1
Odoms	4	25	6.3	0
Hufnagel	2	22	11.0	0
Moses	2	16	8.0	0
Ross	3	8	2.7	0
Stowe	1	1	1.0	0
Van Heusen	1	−1	−1.0	0
Ramsey	5	−2	−0.4	0
Lynch	3	−2	−0.7	0
Johnson	4	−3	−0.7	0

RECEIVING

Last Name	No.	Yds	Avg	TD
Odoms	42	639	15	6
Armstrong	38	405	11	3
Moses	34	559	16	2
Little	29	344	12	0
Van Heusen	16	421	26	4
Keyworth	12	109	9	0
Simmons	10	161	16	2
Stowe	2	9	5	0
Ross	1	13	13	0

PUNT RETURNS

Last Name	No.	Yds	Avg	TD
Thompson	26	350	14	0
Greer	13	90	7	0
Little	4	34	9	0

KICKOFF RETURNS

Last Name	No.	Yds	Avg	TD
Armstrong	16	386	24	0
Thompson	13	325	25	0
Little	8	171	21	0
Ross	7	117	17	0
Keyworth	4	85	21	0
Brown	3	56	19	0
Criter	3	48	16	0

PASSING — PUNTING — KICKING

PASSING	Att	Comp	%	Yds	Yd/Att	TD	Int−%	RK
Johnson	244	136	56	1969	8.1	13	9− 4	3
Ramsey	74	41	55	580	7.8	5	7−10	
Hufnagel	10	6	60	70	7.0	0	1−10	
Van Heusen	1	1	100	41	41.0	0	0− 0	

PUNTING	No	Avg
Van Heusen	75	40.3

KICKING	XP	Att	%	FG	Att	%
Turner	35	38	92	11	21	52

KANSAS CITY CHIEFS

RUSHING

Last Name	No.	Yds	Avg	TD
Green	135	509	3.8	3
Podolak	101	386	3.8	2
Kinney	63	249	4.0	0
Hayes	57	206	3.6	2
Miller	40	186	4.7	0
Ellison	37	114	3.1	2
Livingston	9	28	3.1	0
Dawson	11	28	2.5	0
Wright	3	26	8.7	1
Carlson	2	17	8.5	0
Taylor	1	6	6.0	0
Pearson	1	1	1.0	0
Jaynes	1	0	0.0	0
B. Thomas	3	−3	−1.0	0
Brunson	5	−33	−6.6	0

RECEIVING

Last Name	No.	Yds	Avg	TD
Podolak	43	306	7	1
Pearson	27	387	14	1
Green	26	247	10	1
Taylor	24	375	16	2
Brunson	22	374	17	2
Kinney	18	105	6	1
Miller	14	149	11	0
Wright	13	209	16	1
Stroud	12	141	12	2
Ellison	5	64	13	0
Hayes	4	23	6	0
Hamilton	2	25	13	0
Strada	1	16	16	0

PUNT RETURNS

Last Name	No.	Yds	Avg	TD
Podolak	15	134	9	0
Brunson	19	111	6	0
Reardon	4	30	8	0
Green	5	21	4	0
Morris	1	0	0	0

KICKOFF RETURNS

Last Name	No.	Yds	Avg	TD
B. Thomas	25	571	23	0
Miller	14	310	22	0
Brunson	12	280	23	0
Morris	1	17	17	0
Green	1	16	16	0
Keating	1	10	10	0
Humphrey	1	7	7	0
Jones	1	0	0	0

PASSING — PUNTING — KICKING

PASSING	Att	Comp	%	Yds	Yd/Att	TD	Int−%	RK
Dawson	235	138	59	1573	6.7	7	13− 6	8
Livingston	141	66	47	732	5.2	4	10− 7	16
Carlson	15	7	47	116	7.7	0	1− 7	
Jaynes	2	0	0	0.0	0	1−50		
Wilson	2	0	0	0	0.0	0	0− 0	

PUNTING	No	Avg
Wilson	83	41.7

KICKING	XP	Att	%	FG	Att	%
Stenerud	24	26	92	17	24	71

SAN DIEGO CHARGERS

RUSHING

Last Name	No.	Yds	Avg	TD
Woods	227	1162	5.1	7
Matthews	95	328	3.5	4
Edwards	65	261	4.0	0
Bonner	66	199	3.0	3
Fouts	19	63	3.3	1
Thomas	21	56	2.7	0
M. Gordon	1	25	25.0	0
Freitas	6	16	2.7	0
Thompson	6	8	1.3	0
Davis	2	−7	−3.5	0

RECEIVING

Last Name	No.	Yds	Avg	TD
Garrison	41	785	19	5
Woods	26	349	13	3
Stewart	19	283	15	1
Davis	18	432	24	2
Edwards	13	102	8	0
Matthews	12	90	8	0
Bonner	11	101	9	1
LeVias	9	105	12	0
Beirne	7	121	17	0
Grannell	3	51	17	0
Parris	3	36	12	0
D. Gordon	2	15	8	0
Thomas	1	9	9	0

PUNT RETURNS

Last Name	No.	Yds	Avg	TD
Colbert	15	128	9	0
LeVias	5	41	8	0
D. Gordon	8	39	5	0
Hoey	4	38	10	0
Davis	4	34	9	0
Beirne	1	7	7	0

KICKOFF RETURNS

Last Name	No.	Yds	Avg	TD
D. Gordon	14	354	25	0
Thompson	12	242	20	0
Colbert	10	215	22	0
LeVias	6	116	19	0
Hoey	3	73	24	0
Woods	3	61	20	0
Thomas	2	32	16	0
Parris	3	29	10	0
Dunlap	1	19	19	0
Stewart	1	1	1	0

PASSING — PUNTING — KICKING

PASSING	Att	Comp	%	Yds	Yd/Att	TD	Int−%	RK
Fouts	237	115	49	1732	7.3	8	13− 6	11
Freitas	109	49	45	719	6.6	3	8− 7	
Woods	3	1	33	28	9.3	1	1−33	

PUNTING	No	Avg
Partee	76	40.0

KICKING	XP	Att	%	FG	Att	%
Partee	26	28	93	1	5	20
Wersching	0	0	—	5	11	45

1974 Championship Games

Six Inches Short of Glory

The Vikings were looking for a third trip to the Super Bowl after beating the Cardinals 30–14 in the opening round of the playoffs. The Rams, on the other hand, were looking for their first Super Bowl ticket after beating the Redskins 19–10 for their first playoff victory since 1952. Both clubs rode strong defenses into this title match, but the Vikings had come through the pressure of post-season play before and for that reason were touted as the favorites in this game. Although both defensive units played up to championship standards, the offensive units looked tight under the pressure. Turnovers made the contest a sloppy affair, with the Vikings losing the ball three times and the Rams five times. Neither team could move the ball in the first period, with the Viking defense showing right from the start that it would hold Lawrence McCutcheon, the NFC's leading rusher, to way below his average yardage. The Vikings scored in the second period on a Fran Tarkenton-to-Jim Lash pass, and a David Ray field goal made the score 7–3 in favor of Minnesota at halftime. Minnesota's Mike Eischeid placed a coffin-corner punt out of bounds on the Los Angeles one-yard line early in the third period, and the Rams started a long trek upfield. Five plays later, quarterback James Harris hit Harold Jackson with a long pass that carried the ball 73 yards to the Minnesota 2-yard line, with a clutch tackle by safety Jeff Wright preventing a touchdown. John Cappelletti carried the ball to the six-inch line on the next play, but that was as close as the Rams would come. Guard Tom Mack was called for illegal motion before the next play, and the ball was moved back to around the five yard line. Harris ran for three yards on the next play, but then his pass into the end zone for tight end Pat Curran was tipped away by cornerback Jackie Wallace and picked off by linebacker Wally Hilgenberg. After their 99-yard drive had gone for naught, the Rams never again came close to taking the lead. The Vikings marched 80 yards in the fourth period, with Dave Osborn scoring from the one-yard line on a fourth-down play. A long touchdown pass from Harris to Jackson brought the Rams back to 14–10 late in the game, but the Viking pass rush crumpled the Rams' late attempts to score again.

SCORING

MINNESOTA	0	7	0	7–14
LOS ANGELES	0	3	0	7–10

Second Quarter
Minn.   Lash, 29 yard pass from Tarkenton
        PAT—Cox (kick)
L.A.   Ray, 27 yard field goal

Fourth Quarter
Minn.   Osborn, 1 yard rush
        PAT—Cox (kick)
L.A.   Jackson, 44 yard pass from Harris
        PAT—Ray (kick)

TEAM STATISTICS

MINN.		L.A.
18	First Downs—Total	15
9	First Downs—Rushing	5
7	First Downs—Passing	10
2	First Downs—Penalty	0
5	Fumbles—Number	3
2	Fumbles—Lost Ball	3
2	Penalties—Number	7
20	Yards Penalized	70
0	Missed Field Goals	0
69	Offensive Plays	58
269	Net Yards	340
3.9	Average Gain	5.9
3	Giveaways	5
5	Takeaways	3
+2	Difference	−2

INDIVIDUAL STATISTICS

RUSHING

MINNESOTA	No	Yds	Avg.	LOS ANGELES	No	Yds	Avg.
Foreman	22	80	3.6	Bertelsen	14	65	4.6
Osborn	20	76	3.8	McCutcheon	12	32	2.7
Tarkenton	4	5	1.2	Harris	3	17	5.7
Marinaro	1	3	3.0	Cappelletti	3	8	2.7
	47	164	3.5	Baker	1	−1	−1.0
					33	121	3.7

RECEIVING

MINNESOTA	No	Yds	Avg.	LOS ANGELES	No	Yds	Avg.
Voigt	4	43	10.8	Bertelsen	5	53	10.6
Lash	2	40	20.0	Jackson	3	139	46.3
Gilliam	2	33	16.5	McCutcheon	2	22	11.0
Marinaro	1	6	6.0	Snow	1	19	19.0
Osborn	1	1	1.0	Klein	1	10	10.0
	10	123	12.3	Cappelletti	1	5	5.0
					13	248	19.1

PUNTING

	No	Yds	Avg.		No	Yds	Avg.
Eischeid	6		39.2	Burke	5		43.8

PUNT RETURNS

	No	Yds	Avg.		No	Yds	Avg.
McCullum	3	20	6.7	Bryant	3	18	6.0
N. Wright	1	3	3.0	Scribner	1	1	1.0
	4	23	5.6	Bertelsen	1	0	0.0
					5	19	3.8

KICKOFF RETURNS

	No	Yds	Avg.		No	Yds	Avg.
McClanahan	2	55	27.5	Bryant	3	57	19.0
McCullum	1	23	23.0				
	3	78	26.0				

INTERCEPTION RETURNS

	No	Yds	Avg.		No	Yds	Avg.
Poltl	1	16	16.0	Stukes	1	0	0.0
Hilgenberg	1	0	0.0				
	2	16	8.0				

PASSING

MINNESOTA	Att.	Comp.	Comp. Pct.	Yds.	Int.	Yds/ Att.	Yds/ Comp.	Yards Lost Tackled
Tarkenton	20	10	50.0	123	1	6.2	12.3	2–18

LOS ANGELES	Att.	Comp.	Comp. Pct.	Yds.	Int.	Yds/ Att.	Yds/ Comp.	Yards Lost Tackled
Harris	23	13	56.5	248	2	10.8	19.1	2–29

Near, but Not Far Enough

The Raiders were the popular choice to go on to the Super Bowl, after their fine regular season and then their stirring upset of the Miami Dolphins December 21, taking a 28–26 victory with a Ken Stabler-to-Clarence Davis touchdown pass with 26 seconds left in the game. With the Dolphin dynasty ended, the Raiders seemed the logical heir apparent, but the Steelers, fresh from a 32–14 dissection of Buffalo in the opening playoff round, disputed this line of succession. The key to the game was the Steeler defense, which completely nullified the Raider offense that had led the NFL in points scored. The Raiders found some room to move in the air, but the ground lanes were totally blocked off by the Pittsburgh linemen and linebackers. Conversely, the Oakland defense shut off the Pittsburgh passing game for most of the afternoon, but Steeler runners Franco Harris and Rocky Bleier were able to steadily eat up yardage behind the fine blocking of their offensive line. The Raiders scored in the opening period with George Blanda hitting a 40-yard field goal. Roy Gerela drilled one home from 23 yards in the second period to send the clubs off at halftime tied at 3–3. The Raiders took a 10–3 lead in the third quarter when Stabler whipped a 38-yard touchdown pass to Cliff Branch, one of the swift receiver's nine receptions of the day. The Oakland defense shut the Steelers out in the third period, and the Raiders seemed on the way to their second Super Bowl appearance. The opportunistic Steelers, however, were waiting to pounce on any Oakland errors. The Steelers knotted the game at 10–10 on Franco Harris's eight-yard touchdown carry, and then the defensive unit took over. Pittsburgh linebacker Jack Ham picked off a Stabler pass on the Oakland 33-yard line and carried it back all the way down to the nine yard line. Terry Bradshaw soon capitalized on this break by tossing a six-yard scoring pass to Lynn Swann, and now the Steelers were in charge and the Raiders forced to play "catch up" football. They closed the gap to 17–13 on a Blanda field goal, but Steeler rookie Jack Lambert intercepted a Stabler pass which Franco Harris soon converted into a 22-yard touchdown run, making the final score 24–13.

The frustration for Oakland was neatly summed up by John Madden, the head coach, when he said after the game, "It's really hard to come this far and lose."

SCORING

OAKLAND	3	0	7	3–13
PITTSBURGH	0	3	0	21–24

First Quarter
Oak.   Blanda, 40 yard field goal

Second Quarter
Pitt.   Gerela, 23 yard field goal

Third Quarter
Oak.   Branch, 38 yard pass from Stabler
        PAT—Blanda (kick)

Fourth Quarter
Pitt.   Harris, 8 yard rush
        PAT—Gerela (kick)
Pitt.   Swann, 6 yard pass from Bradshaw
        PAT—Gerela (kick)
Oak.   Blanda, 24 yard field goal
Pitt.   Harris, 21 yard rush
        PAT—Gerela (kick)

TEAM STATISTICS

OAK.		PITT.
15	First Downs—Total	20
0	First Downs—Rushing	11
13	First Downs—Passing	7
2	First Downs—Penalty	2
0	Fumbles—Number	3
0	Fumbles—Lost Ball	2
5	Penalties—Number	4
60	Yards Penalized	30
1	Missed Field Goals	1
59	Offensive Plays	68
278	Net Yards	305
4.7	Average Gain	4.5
3	Giveaways	3
3	Takeaways	3
0	Difference	0

INDIVIDUAL STATISTICS

RUSHING

OAKLAND	No	Yds	Avg.	PITTSBURGH	No	Yds	Avg.
C. Davis	10	16	1.6	Harris	29	111	3.8
Banaszak	3	7	2.3	Bleier	18	98	5.4
Hubbard	7	6	0.9	Bradshaw	3	15	5.0
Stabler	1	0	0.0		50	224	4.5
	21	29	1.4				

RECEIVING

OAKLAND	No	Yds	Avg.	PITTSBURGH	No	Yds	Avg.
Branch	9	186	20.7	L. Brown	2	37	18.5
Moore	4	32	8.0	Bleier	2	25	12.5
Biletnikoff	3	45	15.0	Swann	2	17	8.5
C. Davis	2	8	4.0	Stallworth	2	16	8.0
Banaszak	1	0	0.0		8	95	11.9
	19	271	4.3				

PUNTING

OAKLAND	No	Yds	Avg.	PITTSBURGH	No	Yds	Avg.
Guy	5		43.4	Walden	4		41.0

PUNT RETURNS

	No	Yds	Avg.		No	Yds	Avg.
none				Swann	3	30	10.0
				Edwards	1	15	15.0
					4	45	11.3

KICKOFF RETURNS

	No	Yds	Avg.		No	Yds	Avg.
Hart	3	63	21.0	S. Davis	3	76	25.3
R. Smith	2	42	21.0	Pearson	1	28	28.0
	5	105	21.0		4	104	26.0

INTERCEPTION RETURNS

	No	Yds	Avg.		No	Yds	Avg.
Wilson	1	37	37.0	Ham	2	19	9.5
				Thomas	1	37	37.0
					3	56	18.7

PASSING

OAKLAND	Att.	Comp.	Comp. Pct.	Yds.	Int.	Yds/ Att.	Yds/ Comp.	Yards Lost Tackled
Stabler	36	19	52.8	271	3	7.5	14.3	2–22

PITTSBURGH	Att.	Comp.	Comp. Pct.	Yds.	Int.	Yds/ Att.	Yds/ Comp.	Yards Lost Tackled
Bradshaw	17	8	47.1	95	1	5.6	11.9	1–14

January 12, at New Orleans
(Attendance 79,065)

Rooney's 42-Year Reward

This year's Super Bowl matchups included the Minnesota Vikings, ...ce losers of the NFL's big meal ticket, and the Pittsburgh Steelers, ...o were enjoying their first trip to the post season event. For the ...kings, already branded as a club unable to win the big one, the game ...s a matter of professional pride. The Steelers motivation came from ... fact that they had finally pocketed their first conference title since ...33, the year the franchise began.

...Many of the past Super Bowls have been conservative and relatively ...ll games, Super Bowl IX was no exception as both teams continued ... same offensive pattern of trying to avoid costly mistakes rather than ...ing to break the game open. In fact, the only score of the first half ...as ...afety, with the Steelers getting two points when Viking quarterback ...an Tarkenton botched a pitch-out deep in his own territory and had ...fall on the ball in the end zone. The close 2–0 halftime score belied a ... difference in the teams; the Pittsburgh defense, led by Joe Greene, ...d successfully shut down Viking running star Chuck Foreman, while ... Steeler offensive line was opening up constant holes in the Viking ...nt four to allow Franco Harris to go rushing through.

...The break that the Steelers were waiting for came on the opening ...koff of the second half, when Minnesota's Bill Brown fumbled the

ball and Pittsburgh's Marv Kellum recovered it on the Viking 30-yard line. Harris followed his offensive line the rest of the way, covering 24 yards in one carry and finally going over for the touchdown on a nine-yard sweep around left end. The 9–0 Steeler lead held up through the third period, but the Vikings came back with a strong challenge in the final period. A pass interference call on Mike Wagner gave the Vikes the ball on the Steeler five-yard line, but Foreman fumbled on the next play and Greene recovered for Pittsburgh. Four plays later. Matt Blair blocked Bobby Walden's punt, with Terry Brown falling on it in the end zone for a Viking touchdown. Fred Cox missed the extra point, and the Steeler defense steadfastly refused to let the Vikes close enough to go for the tying field goal. A 65-yard Pittsburgh drive culminating in a four-yard scoring pass from Terry Bradshaw to Larry Brown iced the game away with 3:31 left.

By the time the final gun sounded the Vikings had their third loss in three attempts, and the Steelers had a host of triumphs which included Franco Harris and his record-setting 158 yards rushing and the happiest owner in pro football in Art Rooney who, after 42 frustrating years, finally claimed his dream—a pro football championship.

LINEUPS

...TSBURGH	OFFENSE	MINNESOTA
...is	WR	Lash
...	LT	Goodrum
...k	LG	Maurer
...sfield	C	Tingelhoff
...ins	RG	White
...velle	RT	Yary
...rown	TE	Voigt
...nklin	WR	Gilliam
...shaw	QB	Tarkenton
...r	RB	Foreman
...is	RB	Osborn
	DEFENSE	
...nwood	LE	Eller
...ne	LT	Sutherland
...nes	RT	Page
...e	RE	Marshall
...bert	LLB	Winston
...ell	MLB	Siemon
...nt	RLB	Hilgenberg
...mas	LCB	N. Wright
...ner	RCB	Wallace
...rds	LS	J. Wright
	RS	Krause

SUBSTITUTES

...TSBURGH	OFFENSE	
...am Davis		McMakin
...teve Davis		Pearson
...ruschel		Reaves
...arrett		Swann
...rossman		Stallworth
...arrison		Webster
	DEFENSE	
...llen		Furness
...radley		Kellum
...onn		Shell
...Davis		Toews
	KICKERS	
...ierela		Walden

...NNESOTA	OFFENSE	
...lderman		Marinaro
...nderson		McClanahan
...Brown		McCullum
...raig		Reed
...ingsriter		Sunde
...awson		
	DEFENSE	
...lair		Martin
...Brown		McNeill
...arsen		Poltl
...urtsema		
	KICKERS	
...ox		Eischeid

SCORING

PITTSBURGH	0 2 7 7 – 16	
MINNESOTA	0 0 0 6 – 6	

Second Quarter
Pitt. Safety – Tarkenton tackled
in end zone. 7:49

Third Quarter
Pitt. Harris, 12 yard rush 1:35
PAT – Gerela (kick

Fourth Quarter
Minn. T. Brown, Recovered 4:27
blocked punt in end zone.
Kick failed
Pitt. L. Brown, 4 yard pass 11:29
from Bradshaw
PAT – Gerela (kick)

TEAM STATISTICS

	PITT.		MINN.
17	First Downs-Total		9
11	First Downs-Rushing		2
5	First Downs-Passing		5
1	First Downs-Penalty		2
4	Fumbles-Number		3
2	Fumbles-Lost Ball		2
8	Penalties-Number		4
122	Yards Penalized		18
1	Missed Field Goals		1
73	Offensive Plays		47
333	Net Yards		119
4.6	Average Gain		2.5
2	Giveaways		5
5	Takeaways		2
+3	Difference		–3

INDIVIDUAL STATISTICS

PITTSBURGH / MINNESOTA

RUSHING

PITTSBURGH	No.	Yds.	Avg.	MINNESOTA	No.	Yds.	Avg.
Harris	34	158	4.6	Foreman	12	18	1.5
Bleier	17	65	3.8	Tarkenton	1	0	0.0
Bradshaw	5	33	6.6	Osborn	8	–1	–0.1
Swann	1	–7	–7.0		21	17	0.8
	57	249	4.4				

RECEIVING

	No.	Yds.	Avg.		No.	Yds.	Avg.
T. Brown	3	49	16.3	Foreman	5	50	10.0
Stallworth	3	24	8.0	Voigt	2	31	15.5
Bleier	2	11	5.5	Osborn	2	7	3.5
Lewis	1	12	12.0	Gilliam	1	16	16.0
	9	96	10.7	Reed	1	–2	–2.0
					11	102	9.3

PUNTING

	No.		Avg.		No.		Avg.
Walden	7		34.7	Eischeid	6		37.2

PUNT RETURNS

	No.	Yds.	Avg.		No.	Yds.	Avg.
Swann	3	34	11.3	McCullum	3	11	3.7
Edwards	2	2	1.0	N. Wright	1	1	1.0
	5	36	7.2		4	12	3.0

KICKOFF RETURNS

	No.	Yds.	Avg.		No.	Yds.	Avg.
Harrison	2	17	8.5	McCullum	1	26	26.0
Pearson	1	15	15.0	McClanahan	1	22	22.0
	3	32	10.7	B. Brown	1	2	2.0
					3	50	16.7

INTERCEPTION RETURNS

	No.	Yds.	Avg.				
Wagner	1	26	26.0	none			
Blount	1	10	10.0				
Greene	1	10	10.0				
	3	46	15.3				

PASSING

PITTSBURGH	Att.	Comp.	Comp. Pct.	Yds.	Int.	Yds/ Att.	Yds/ Comp.	Yards Lost Tackled
Bradshaw	14	9	64.3	96	0	6.9	10.7	2–12
MINNESOTA								
Tarkenton	26	11	42.3	102	3	3.9	9.3	0–0

1975 N.F.C. Striking Toward Freedom

The N.F.L. Players Association had struck during training camp in 1974 over the inability to reach agreement with the club owners on a contract, eventually going back to work without a settlement. In the training camps of 1975, the contract negotiations still dragged on, with Players Association president Ed Garvey unable to maintain a united front among his players. With the Rozelle Rule concerning free agent status the main bone of contention, the New England Patriots took the lead by striking on September 13, the Saturday before their final exhibition game. The Pats sat that game out, and by Wednesday, the Redskins, Jets, Giants, and Lions had joined them in striking. A truce was arranged on Thursday, September 18, so that the regular season got under way without a delay on Sunday. Only after the season did the players' fight to do away with the Rozelle Rule, which limited their freedom of movement in playing out their option, come to fruit. In the winter, federal judge Earl R. Larson ruled that the Rozelle Rule was an illegal monopolistic practice by the N.F.L. The lawyers' bills piled up for the league into 1976, as the owners appealed Larson's ruling and successfully beat back a legal challenge to the college and expansion drafts to be held for the upcoming season.

EASTERN DIVISION

St. Louis Cardinals—The Cards started the season in lacklustre form, with losses to the Cowboys and Redskins among their first four decisions. But quarterback Jim Hart got his explosive offense rolling thereafter and won nine of the remaining ten games on the schedule to recapture first place in the East. The Cards took the top spot directly, beating both the Redskins and Cowboys down the stretch. The Cards trailed the Redskins 17-10 with 20 seconds remaining in the game on November 16 when Hart threw a pass to Mel Gray in the end zone. Gray dropped the ball when hit, but after conferring on the field for three minutes amidst pressure from both teams and the fans, the officials ruled that he had held on to it just long enough to make it a legal catch and a touchdown. Jim Bakken kicked the extra point to send the game into overtime, and he won it 20-17 with a field goal seven minutes into the extra period.

Dallas Cowboys—This was to be a rebuilding year for the Cowboys. After all, they had not made the playoffs last season, and from that squad, Calvin Hill had jumped to the W.F.L. and Bob Lilly, Walt Garrison, and Cornell Green had retired. But the expert observers did not take note of the depth on the Dallas roster and the marvelous collection of rookies that reported to the team. With holdover stars like Roger Staubach and Drew Pearson, a blossoming star like Robert Newhouse, and a serviceable pickup in veteran Preston Pearson, the offense kept rolling along in fine fashion, even spicing things up with an occasional shift into the shotgun formation. Oldsters like Mel Renfro, Lee Roy Jordan, and Jethro Pugh anchored the defense, but youngsters like Too Tall Jones and Harvey Martin provided much of the thunder. The Cowboys got off to a quick start, hit a midseason slump, and finished strong to capture a wildcard spot in the playoffs.

Washington Redskins—The Redskin defensive unit had the same tough veteran look of recent years, but the offense took on a more youthful appearance. Sonny Jurgensen was retired, young Frank Grant took over a wide receiver spot, and rookie Mike Thomas revitalized the running attack with 919 yards. With Jurgensen gone, Billy Kilmer handled almost all the quarterbacking and came through with high grades despite some injury problems. When the Skins won six of their first eight games, including triumphs over St. Louis and Dallas, a playoff berth seemed assured. But losses to St. Louis and Oakland cast a shadow over those hopes, and with the wildcard spot on the line on December 13, the Skins were crushed by the Cowboys 31-10. The dispirited club dropped the season's finale to the Eagles and went home, out of the playoffs for the first time in George Allen's reign. One highpoint of the disappointing campaign was Charley Taylor's moving into first place in the all-time list of pass receivers, surpassing Don Maynard's old mark.

New York Giants—Moving into Shea Stadium as temporary boarders with the Jets, the Giants began their second season under Bill Arnsbarger with a promising 23-14 victory over the Eagles. But the club lapsed back into mediocrity, losing three games, upsetting Buffalo 17-14, and then losing six of the next seven, including a 40-14 humiliation to the Green Bay Packers. The offense lost much of its zip at midseason, and the defense suffered because of John Mendenhall's bad ankle.

Philadelphia Eagles—The Eagles had no draft picks in the first six rounds of the college draft, and with no new help arriving, last year's late-season slump continued into this campaign. The team had top-notch performers at several positions, with tight end Charley Young and middle linebacker Bill Bergey among the very best at their positions. A weak pass rush and other soft spots, however, sent the Eagles to the bottom of the division. They did win four games, including two over the Redskins, and they did battle Dallas and St. Louis furiously before losing close decisions, but this was not enough to save coach Mike McCormick from the chopping block after the season.

CENTRAL DIVISION

Minnesota Vikings—The only Viking weakness on paper seemed to be at wide receiver, where John Gilliam had jumped to the W.F.L.

But when Gilliam's Chicago team folded in September, he return to the Vikes in time for the opening of the N.F.L. schedule. With return, the Vikings excelled at all positions and ripped off ten straig victories at the start of the campaign to quickly ice away the Cent Division title. The defensive unit, led by Carl Eller, Alan Page, J Siemon, and Paul Krause, turned in its usual superb performan and the offense produced the most points in the N.F.C., than greatly to Fran Tarkenton and Chuck Foreman. Tarkenton led Conference in touchdown passes and moved past Johnny Unitas in first place in the all-time totals. Foreman enjoyed an exceptio season, scoring 22 touchdowns to tie Gale Sayers' old mark wh O.J. Simpson also surpassed this year.

Detroit Lions—Pre-season predictions didn't hold out much ho for the Lions. Their top receiver, Ron Jessie, had played out his opti and signed with Los Angeles, and the rest of the squad simply did measure up to the powers of the Conference. Three victories in first four games fanned some sparks of hope, but the team faded i blaze of injuries. Bill Munson and Greg Landry, the two top quart backs, both went on the shelf with injuries on October 26, and thi stringer Joe Reed filled in the rest of the way.

Chicago Bears—Jack Pardee came in as head coach, fresh from leadi the Florida Blazers into the championship game of the W.F.L. year. He promised a fresh look, but the same pale complexion show on both the offensive and defensive units. The most glaring sore s was quarterback, where Bobby Douglass started the season. He led team to a 35-7 opening game loss and was soon on waivers. Gary H handled the controls through the bulk of the schedule, but rookie B Avellini finished the season at the helm, showing promise in a 42- triumph over New Orleans. Bright spots were Wally Chambers' gr year in the defensive line and the influx of new talent in rookie runne Walter Payton and Roland Harper, rookie defensive end M Hartenstein, and tight end Greg Latta, a W.F.L. refugee.

Green Bay Packers—The naming of Bart Starr as head coa beckoned to the championship years of Vince Lombardi, but the quarterback brought no magic with him this year. The Pack lost first four games before upsetting Dallas 19-17 to get into the victo column. The Packers won three of their last five contests, but all ca over weak opponents. Starr faced the same problem that plagued departed Dan Devine—how to generate an offense. John Hadl cursed with interceptions, and fullback John Brockington slip in production.

WESTERN DIVISION

Los Angeles Rams—The Rams had never jelled into the superpo that people expected, but they still had undeniable quality and de in all sectors. The defensive unit, featuring Jack Youngblood a Isaiah Robertson, ranked next to the Minnesota outfit in frugality points allowed. The offense had a solid line led by Tom Mack, fi receivers in Harold Jackson and Ron Jessie, and a stable of ha charging runners like Larry McCutcheon, Cullen Bryant, J Bertelson, and John Cappelletti. James Harris at quarterback was j good enough to lead this club to a runaway victory in the Weste Division. Coach Chuck Knox found riches on his bench when Ha injured his shoulder on December 14 and back-up Ron Jaworski to the team to a victory in the finale.

San Francisco 49ers—The early promise of the Dick Nolan regi petered out into the frustration of a lukewarm club with some flashes. After a weak start, the 49ers came alive in mid-season three straight wins, including a 24-23 upset of the Rams. But then club dropped its last four games of the schedule to slip out of contenti for the playoffs and cost Nolan his job. The quarterback position a recurring problem, with neither Steve Spurrier nor Norm Sne taking charge. Del Williams and Gene Washington provided so offensive flair, but the 49ers needed some new direction to turn th fortunes around.

Atlanta Falcons—The Falcons traded a lot to Baltimore for the f pick in the college draft, using that pick to take quarterback St Bartkowski. Bartkowski showed good potential despite an injur elbow and a less-than-sterling offensive unit around him. The m threat was Dave Hampton, who ran for 1002 yards. The defens unit also had its problems, but had a coming star in cornerba Rolland Lawrence. The fans still seemed turned off after the ris expectations and ultimate turmoil of the Van Brocklin years, and sparse audience of 29,444 saw the Falcons beat the Saints 14-7 October 5.

New Orleans Saints—The Saints relapsed into pitifulness this seas They lost their first three games while scoring only 10 points, b Green Bay 20-19, and then lost their next two games. Coach Jo North was canned at this point, and Ernie Hefferle took over on interim basis. He made it look easy when the Saints beat Atlanta 2 in his first game in charge, but his club then found its true level a lost its last seven games. The end of the season saw Hank Stram s on as the new head coach to try to build the Saints into the sort of po that the Kansas City Chiefs had been under him.

FINAL TEAM STATISTICS

OFFENSE

	ATL.	CHI.	DALL.	DET.	G.B.	L.A.	MINN.	N.O.	N.Y.	PHIL.	ST.L.	S.F.	WASH.
FIRST DOWNS:													
Total	225	190	288	241	211	273	**314**	215	229	237	276	240	272
by Rushing	87	74	132	111	84	134	**142**	109	95	84	131	86	97
by Passing	118	99	142	111	112	120	**156**	82	105	134	128	133	150
by Penalty	20	17	14	19	15	19	16	24	**29**	19	17	21	25
RUSHING:													
Number	465	441	571	532	431	**585**	556	463	482	461	555	422	444
Yards	1794	1653	**2432**	2147	1547	2371	2094	1642	1627	1702	2402	1598	1752
Average Yards	3.9	3.7	4.3	4.0	3.6	4.1	3.8	3.5	3.4	3.7	**4.3**	3.8	3.9
Touchdowns	12	11	17	10	14	18	18	9	17	3	**19**	12	9
PASSING:													
Attempts	388	356	376	362	394	334	446	392	379	**458**	355	450	448
Completions	165	191	207	183	212	181	**281**	181	193	238	187	234	229
Completion Percentage	42.5	53.7	55.1	50.6	53.8	54.2	**63.0**	46.2	50.9	52.0	52.7	52.0	51.1
Passing Yards	2361	2169	2835	2240	2400	2450	**3121**	1961	2457	2640	2619	2806	3092
Avg. Yards per Attempt	6.1	6.1	**7.5**	6.2	6.1	7.3	7.0	5.0	6.5	5.8	7.4	6.2	6.9
Avg. Yards per Complet.	**14.3**	11.4	13.7	12.2	11.3	13.5	11.1	10.8	12.7	11.1	14.0	12.0	13.5
Times Tackled Passing	32	32	39	41	42	30	29	53	49	30	**8**	33	27
Yards Lost Passing	294	330	242	323	328	255	260	416	355	200	**66**	246	175
Net Yards	2067	1839	2593	1917	2072	2195	2861	1545	2102	2440	2553	2560	**2917**
Touchdowns	18	9	19	15	11	14	27	8	11	19	20	15	**28**
Interceptions	29	23	17	**12**	22	17	14	24	18	23	20	19	29
Percent Intercepted	7.5	6.5	4.5	3.3	5.6	5.1	**3.1**	6.1	4.8	5.0	5.9	4.2	6.5
PUNTS:													
Number	89	94	68	81	**95**	73	73	92	86	83	64	67	72
Average Distance	41.5	39.0	39.4	**41.9**	35.8	39.4	41.1	41.0	39.0	38.9	37.7	**41.9**	40.6
PUNT RETURNS:													
Number	35	51	32	36	30	55	36	47	49	35	40	**63**	61
Yards	248	512	313	328	190	517	167	372	350	299	410	**616**	464
Average Yards	7.1	10.0	9.8	9.1	6.3	9.4	4.6	9.1	7.1	8.5	**10.3**	9.8	7.6
Touchdowns	0	0	**1**	0	0	0	0	0	**1**	0	**1**	0	**1**
KICKOFF RETURNS:													
Number	66	**75**	54	52	63	34	36	62	55	59	55	60	58
Yards	1217	**1644**	1158	1114	1398	764	787	1291	1250	1388	1337	1372	1296
Average Yards	18.4	21.9	21.4	21.4	22.2	22.5	21.9	20.8	22.7	23.5	**24.3**	22.9	22.3
Touchdowns	0	0	**1**	0	**1**	0	0	0	0	0	**1**	0	0
INTERCEPTION RETURNS:													
Number	25	13	25	20	14	22	**28**	16	16	26	22	11	18
Yards	342	241	346	315	174	372	**404**	305	117	344	249	138	335
Average Yards	13.7	18.5	13.8	15.8	12.4	16.9	14.4	**19.1**	7.3	13.2	11.3	12.5	18.6
Touchdowns	2	2	**3**	1	0	2	0	0	0	2	1	1	0
PENALTIES:													
Number	78	**100**	94	95	72	73	90	71	52	81	83	89	78
Yards	635	**881**	715	838	606	746	708	527	440	744	730	693	723
FUMBLES:													
Number	37	35	**25**	28	31	26	33	33	44	29	33	44	28
Number Lost	19	17	18	18	16	**8**	12	16	19	12	19	25	17
POINTS:													
Total	240	191	350	245	226	312	**377**	165	216	225	356	255	325
PAT Attempts	33	22	41	29	27	36	**48**	19	29	24	43	31	40
PAT Made	30	18	38	25	22	31	**46**	18	24	21	41	27	37
FG Attempts	10	23	**35**	21	17	26	17	21	11	29	24	28	25
FG Made	4	13	**22**	14	12	21	13	11	6	20	19	14	16
Percent FG Made	40.0	56.5	62.9	66.7	70.6	**80.8**	76.5	52.4	54.5	69.0	79.2	50.0	64.0
Safeties	0	1	0	2	**3**	1	2	0	0	0	0	0	0

DEFENSE

	ATL.	CHI.	DALL.	DET.	G.B.	L.A.	MINN.	N.O.	N.Y.	PHIL.	ST.L.	S.F.	WASH.
FIRST DOWNS:													
Total	288	282	234	235	260	204	**190**	251	264	275	284	253	255
by Rushing	131	118	100	100	132	**77**	**77**	105	137	130	118	102	105
by Passing	142	143	113	116	112	103	**93**	125	120	123	142	130	128
by Penalty	15	21	21	19	16	24	20	21	**7**	22	24	21	22
RUSHING:													
Number	571	547	474	480	580	423	**383**	507	555	529	487	518	525
Yards	2277	2070	1699	1929	2339	1533	**1532**	1930	2422	2233	1925	1829	2047
Average Yards	4.0	3.8	3.6	4.0	4.0	3.6	4.0	3.8	4.4	4.2	4.0	**3.5**	3.9
Touchdowns	13	25	13	12	14	**4**	7	15	16	20	16	14	11
PASSING:													
Attempts	437	399	373	360	369	387	360	**354**	365	424	446	411	389
Completions	227	208	**162**	181	192	187	175	206	196	226	233	228	217
Completion Percentage	51.9	52.1	**43.4**	50.3	52.0	48.3	48.6	58.2	53.7	53.3	52.2	55.5	55.8
Passing Yards	2810	2825	2328	2377	2474	2126	**1994**	2587	2539	2658	2862	2521	2714
Avg. Yards per Attempt	6.4	7.1	6.2	6.6	6.7	**5.5**	5.5	7.3	6.6	6.3	6.4	6.1	7.0
Avg. Yards per Complet.	12.4	13.6	14.4	13.1	12.9	**11.4**	11.4	12.6	12.9	11.8	12.3	11.6	13.0
Times Tackled Passing	35	35	41	38	32	43	**46**	28	26	17	24	40	36
Yards Lost Passing	275	319	288	306	302	337	**373**	200	172	120	192	324	276
Net Yards	2535	2506	2040	2071	2172	1789	**1621**	2387	2367	2538	2670	2197	2438
Touchdowns	16	22	19	16	13	**11**	14	25	20	13	16	15	17
Interceptions	25	13	25	20	14	22	**28**	16	16	26	22	11	18
Percent Intercepted	5.7	3.0	6.6	5.6	3.8	5.7	**7.8**	4.5	4.4	6.1	5.0	2.7	4.6
PUNTS:													
Number	71	86	82	80	70	**89**	**89**	75	82	65	67	84	87
Average Distance	41.1	41.4	39.6	**36.9**	39.7	39.7	39.6	42.7	37.6	37.0	40.1	42.1	38.9
PUNT RETURNS:													
Number	52	49	37	41	45	45	51	61	39	58	**34**	43	38
Yards	389	303	261	524	**222**	401	419	679	364	530	329	490	240
Average Yards	7.5	6.2	7.1	12.8	**4.9**	8.9	8.2	11.1	9.3	9.1	9.7	11.4	6.3
Touchdowns	**0**	**0**	**0**	1	**0**	**0**	**0**	1	1	1	**0**	**0**	**0**
KICKOFF RETURNS:													
Number	45	43	66	53	49	64	69	**42**	46	51	71	48	64
Yards	1038	**893**	1576	1084	1051	1327	1345	1073	927	1149	1609	1061	1357
Average Yards	23.1	20.8	23.9	20.5	21.4	21.0	**19.5**	25.5	20.2	22.5	22.7	22.1	21.2
Touchdowns	**0**	**0**	**0**	**0**	1	**0**	**0**	1	**0**	**0**	1	**0**	1
INTERCEPTION RETURNS:													
Number	29	23	17	**12**	22	17	14	24	18	23	20	19	29
Yards	602	235	203	**82**	388	204	235	367	214	411	216	212	469
Average Yards	20.8	10.2	11.9	**6.8**	17.6	12.0	16.8	15.3	11.9	17.9	10.8	11.2	16.2
Touchdowns	1	**0**	**0**	**0**	2	**0**	**0**	2	1	2	**0**	**0**	4
PENALTIES:													
Number	78	78	63	94	73	85	91	77	**97**	**97**	82	86	89
Yards	721	723	639	**874**	544	626	681	726	755	784	679	702	772
FUMBLES:													
Number	25	29	43	30	**44**	31	29	43	22	30	26	34	27
Number Lost	12	14	19	17	**27**	18	13	22	8	18	15	16	19
POINTS:													
Total	289	379	268	262	285	**135**	180	360	306	302	276	286	276
PAT Attempts	31	48	32	31	32	**15**	21	48	39	36	33	34	33
PAT Made	28	47	31	26	30	**13**	19	44	37	32	27	31	27
FG Attempts	38	18	18	23	31	19	13	**12**	21	27	26	22	30
FG Made	25	14	13	16	21	10	9	**8**	11	18	15	17	17
Percent FG Made	65.8	77.8	72.2	69.6	67.7	52.6	69.2	66.7	**52.4**	66.7	57.7	77.3	56.7
Safeties	**0**	1	**0**	1	**0**	1	1	2	1	**0**	**0**	**0**	**0**

CONFERENCE PLAYOFFS

December 27, at Los Angeles (Attendance 72,650)

SCORING

LOS ANGELES	14	14	0	7	– 35
ST. LOUIS	0	9	7	7	– 23

First Quarter
- L.A. Jaworski, 5 yard rush PAT – Dempsey (kick)
- L.A. Youngblood, 47 yard interception return PAT – Dempsey (kick)

Second Quarter
- L.A. Simpson, 65 yard interception return PAT – Dempsey (kick)
- St.L. Otis, 3 yard rush PAT – Kick failed
- L.A. Jackson, 66 yard pass from Jaworski PAT – Dempsey (kick)
- St.L. Bakken, 29 yard field goal

Third Quarter
- St. L. M. Gray, 11 yard pass from Hart PAT – Bakken (kick)

Fourth Quarter
- L.A. Jessie, 2 yard fumble recovery PAT – Dempsey (kick)
- St.L. Jones, 3 yard rush PAT – Bakken (kick)

TEAM STATISTICS

L.A.		ST.L.
26	First Downs – Total	22
14	First Downs – Rushing	5
10	First Downs – Passing	16
2	First Downs – Penalty	1
5	Fumbles – Number	3
3	Fumbles – Lost Ball	2
5	Penalties – Number	6
38	Yards Penalized	70
1	Missed Field Goals	0
73	Offensive Plays	70
440	Net Yards	363
6.0	Average Gain	5.2
3	Giveaways	5
5	Takeaways	3
+2	Difference	-2

INDIVIDUAL STATISTICS

LOS ANGELES	No.	Yds.	Avg.	ST. LOUIS	No.	Yds.	Avg.
RUSHING							
McCutcheon	37	202	5.5	Otis	12	38	3.2
Scribner	4	16	4.0	Jones	6	28	4.7
Bryant	3	12	4.0	Metcalf	8	27	3.4
Jaworski	8	7	0.9	Latin	1	2	2.0
	52	237	4.6		27	95	3.5
RECEIVING							
Jessie	4	52	13.0	Metcalf	6	94	15.7
McCutcheon	3	8	2.7	Otis	4	52	13.0
Jackson	2	84	42.0	M. Gray	3	52	17.3
Bryant	2	26	13.0	Harris	2	33	16.5
T. Nelson	1	33	33.0	Latin	2	23	11.5
	12	203	16.9	Jones	2	19	9.5
				Cain	2	17	8.5
				Smith	1	1	1.0
					22	291	13.2
PUNTING							
Carrell	5		31.6	West	6		42.7
PUNT RETURNS							
Scribner	1	7	7.0	Metcalf	1	3	3.0
Elmendorf	1	0	0.0				
	2	7	3.5				
KICKOFF RETURNS							
Bryant	3	61	20.3	Metcalf	3	105	35.0
Jessie	1	17	17.0	Hammond	2	36	13.0
Elmendorf	1	12	12.0	Crump	1	28	28.0
	5	90	18.0	Latin	1	22	22.0
					7	191	27.3
INTERCEPTION RETURNS							
Simpson	2	83	41.5	none			
Youngblood	1	47	47.0				
	3	130	43.3				

PASSING

	Att.	Comp.	Comp. Pct.	Yds	Int	Yds/ Att.	Yds/ Comp	Yards Lost Tackled
LOS ANGELES								
Jaworski	23	12	52.2	203	0	8.8	16.9	0-0
ST. LOUIS								
Hart	41	22	53.7	291	3	7.1	13.2	2-23

December 28, at Minnesota (Attendance 46,425)

SCORING

MINNESOTA	0	7	0	7	– 14
DALLAS	0	0	7	10	– 17

Second Quarter
- Min.. Foreman, 1 yard rush PAT – Cox (kick)

Third Quarter
- Dall. Dennison, 4 yard rush PAT – Fritsch (kick)

Fourth Quarter
- Dall. Fritsch, 24 yard field goal
- Minn. McClanahan, 1 yard rush PAT – Cox (kick)
- Dall. D. Pearson, 50 yard pass from Staubach PAT – Fritsch (kick)

TEAM STATISTICS

MINN.		DALL.
12	First Downs – Total	19
6	First Downs – Rushing	7
6	First Downs – Passing	11
0	First Downs – Penalty	1
2	Fumbles – Number	3
0	Fumbles – Lost Ball	1
7	Penalties – Number	4
60	Yards Penalized	30
1	Missed Field Goals	1
58	Offensive Plays	75
215	Net Yards	356
3.1	Average Gain	4.3
1	Giveaways	1
1	Takeaways	1
0	Difference	0

INDIVIDUAL STATISTICS

MINNESOTA	No.	Yds.	Avg.	DALLAS	No.	Yds.	Avg.
RUSHING							
Foreman	18	56	3.1	Dennison	11	36	3.3
Tarkenton	3	32	10.7	P. Pearson	11	34	3.1
McClanahan	4	22	5.5	Newhouse	12	33	2.8
Marinaro	2	5	2.5	Staubach	7	24	3.4
	27	115	4.3	Fuggett	1	4	4.0
					42	131	3.1
RECEIVING							
Marinaro	5	64	12.8	P. Pearson	5	77	15.4
Foreman	4	42	10.5	D. Pearson	4	91	22.8
Gilliam	1	15	15.0	Newhouse	2	25	12.5
Lash	1	15	15.0	Richards	2	20	10.0
Voigt	1	-1	-1.0	Fuggett	2	13	6.5
	12	135	11.3	DuPree	1	17	17.0
				Dennison	1	3	3.0
					17	246	14.4
PUNTING							
Clabo	7		39.6	Hoopes	6		38.5
PUNT RETURNS							
McCullum	3	4	1.3	Richards	2	13	6.5
Bryant	1	1	1.0	Harris	2	5	2.5
	4	5	1.3		4	18	4.5
KICKOFF RETURNS							
McClanahan	2	38	19.0	P. Pearson	2	26	13.0
McCullum	1	3	3.0	Dennison	1	13	13.0
Osborn	1	0	0.0		3	39	13.0
	4	41	10.3				
INTERCEPTION RETURNS							
none				Renfro	1	0	0.0

PASSING

	Att.	Comp.	Comp. Pct.	Yds.	Int.	Yds/ Att.	Yds/ Comp	Yards Lost Tackled
MINNESOTA								
Tarkenton	26	12	46.2	135	1	15.2	11.3	4-35
DALLAS								
Staubach	29	17	58.6	256	0	8.8	15.1	5-21

ST. LOUIS CARDINALS 11-3 Don Coryell

Scores of Each Game		
23	ATLANTA	20
31	Dallas	*37
26	N.Y. GIANTS	14
17	Washington	27
31	PHILADELPHIA	20
20	N.Y. Giants	13
24	NEW ENGLAND	17
24	Philadelphia	23
20	WASHINGTON	*17
37	N.Y. Jets	6
14	BUFFALO	32
31	DALLAS	17
34	Chicago	20
24	Detroit	13

Use Name	Pos.	Hgt	Wgt	Age	Int	Pts
Dan Dierdorf	OT	6'4"	280	26		
Greg Kindle	OG-OT	6'4"	265	24		
Roger Finnie	OG-OT	6'3"	250	28		
Henry Allison	OG	6'3"	255	28		
Conrad Dobler	OG	6'3"	255	24		
Bob Young	OG	6'2"	270	32		
Tom Brahaney	C	6'2"	250	23		
Tom Banks	OG-C	6'1"	245	27		
Bob Bell	DE	6'4"	250	27		
Council Rudolph	DE	6'3"	245	25	1	
Ron Yankowski	DE	6'5"	250	28		
Lee Brooks	DT	6'5"	250	27		
Charlie Davis	DT	6'1"	265	23		
Bob Rowe	DT	6'4"	270	30		

Use Name	Pos.	Hgt	Wgt	Age	Int	Pts
Mark Arneson	LB	6'2"	220	25	1	
Pete Barnes	LB	6'3"	240	30	2	
Greg Hartle	LB	6'2"	225	24		
Steve Neils	LB	6'2"	215	24		
Larry Stallings	LB	6'2"	230	33	1	
Ray White	LB	6'1"	220	26		
Dwayne Crump	DB	5'11"	180	25		6
Clarence Duren	DB	6'1"	190	24	1	
Tim Gray	DB	6'1"	200	22		
Ken Reaves	DB	6'3"	210	30	3	
Norm Thompson	DB	6'1"	180	27	7	6
Jim Tolbert	DB	6'3"	210	31		
Roger Wehrli	DB	6'1"	190	27	6	1

Steve George — Knee Injury

Use Name	Pos.	Hgt	Wgt	Age	Int	Pts
Jim Hart	QB	6'2"	210	31		6
Gary Keithley	QB	6'3"	215	24		
Dennis Shaw	QB	6'2"	210	28		
Josh Ashton	HB	6'1"	205	26		
Steve Jones	HB	6'	200	24		18
Jerry Latin	HB	5'10"	190	22		6
Terry Metcalf	HB	5'10"	185	23		78
Eddie Moss	FB	6'	215	26		6
Jim Otis	FB	6'	225	27		36
Mel Gray	WR	5'9"	175	26		66
Gary Hammond	WR	5'11"	185	26		
Ike Harris	WR	6'3"	205	22		
Earl Thomas	WR	6'3"	220	26		12
J.V. Cain	TE	6'4"	225	24		6
Jackie Smith	TE	6'4"	230	34		12
Jeff West	TE	6'3"	220	22		
Jim Bakken	K	6'	200	34		97

DALLAS COWBOYS 10-4 Tom Landry

Scores of Each Game		
18	LOS ANGELES	7
37	ST. LOUIS	*31
36	Detroit	10
13	N.Y. Giants	7
17	GREEN BAY	19
20	Philadelphia	17
24	Washington	*30
31	KANSAS CITY	34
34	New England	31
27	PHILADELPHIA	17
14	N.Y. GIANTS	3
17	St. Louis	31
31	WASHINGTON	10
31	N.Y. Jets	21

Use Name	Pos.	Hgt	Wgt	Age	Int	Pts
Pat Donovan	OT	6'4"	250	22		
Ralph Neely	OT	6'5"	260	31		
Bruce Walton	OT	6'6"	252	24		
Rayfield Wright	OT	6'7"	260	29		
Burton Lawless	OG	6'4"	250	21		
Blaine Nye	OG	6'4"	255	29		
Herbert Scott	OG	6'2"	250	22		
Kyle Davis	C	6'4"	240	22		
John Fitzgerald	C	6'5"	255	27		
Too Tall Jones	DE	6'9"	260	24	1	
Harvey Martin	DE	6'5"	257	24		
Randy White	LB-DT-DE	6'4"	245	22		
Larry Cole	DT	6'4"	250	28		
Bill Gregory	DT	6'5"	252	25	1	
Jethro Pugh	DT	6'6"	250	31		

Use Name	Pos.	Hgt	Wgt	Age	Int	Pts
Bob Breunig	LB	6'2"	227	22		
Warren Capone	LB	6'1"	218	24		
Dave Edwards	LB	6'3"	225	36		
Thomas Henderson	LB	6'2"	220	22		6
Lee Roy Jordan	LB	6'2"	220	34	6	
D.D. Lewis	LB	6'2"	218	29		
Cal Peterson	LB	6'3"	220	22	1	
Benny Barnes	DB	6'1"	185	24		
Cliff Harris	DB	6'	190	25	3	6
Randy Hughes	DB	6'4"	200	22	2	6
Mel Renfro	DB	6'	190	33	4	
Mark Washington	DB	5'10"	186	27	4	
Charlie Waters	DB	6'1"	193	26	3	6
Roland Woolsey	DB	6'1"	182	22		

Use Name	Pos.	Hgt	Wgt	Age	Int	Pts
Clint Longley	QB	6'1"	193	23		
Roger Staubach	QB	6'2"	197	33		24
Preston Pearson	HB	6'1"	205	30		24
Charley Young	HB	6'1"	210	22		18
Doug Dennison	FB-HB	6'1"	195	23		42
Scott Laidlaw	FB	6'	206	22		
Robert Newhouse	FB	5'10"	200	25		12
Percy Howard	WR	6'4"	210	23		
Drew Pearson	WR	6'	180	24		48
Golden Richards	WR	6'	183	24		30
Billy Joe DuPree	TE	6'4"	228	25		6
Ron Howard	TE	6'4"	225	24		
Jean Fugett	WR-TE	6'3"	226	23		18
Toni Fritsch	K	5'7"	195	30		104
Mitch Hoopes	K	6'1"	210	22		

Efren Herrera — Injury

WASHINGTON REDSKINS 8-6 George Allen

Scores of Each Game		
41	NEW ORLEANS	3
49	N.Y. GIANTS	13
10	Philadelphia	26
27	St. Louis	17
10	Houston	13
23	Cleveland	7
30	DALLAS	*24
21	N.Y. Giants	13
17	St. Louis	*20
23	OAKLAND	*26
31	MINNESOTA	30
30	Atlanta	27
10	Dallas	31
3	PHILADELPHIA	26

Use Name	Pos.	Hgt	Wgt	Age	Int	Pts
Terry Hermeling	OT	6'5"	255	29		
George Starke	OT	6'5"	250	27		
Tim Stokes	OT	6'5"	250	25		
Paul Laaveg	OG	6'4"	250	26		
Walt Sweeney	OG	6'3"	254	34		
Ray Schoenke	OT-OG	6'3"	250	33		
Jim Arneson	C-OG	6'3"	252	24		
Len Hauss	C	6'2"	235	33		
Bob Kuziel	C	6'4"	255	25		
Dan Ryzcek	C	6'3"	245	26		
Dave Butz	DE	6'7"	297	25		
Ron McDole	DE	6'3"	265	35		6
Bill Brundige	DT	6'5"	270	26		
Dennis Johnson	DT	6'4"	260	23	1	
Manny Sistrunk	DT	6'5"	265	28		
Diron Talbert	DT	6'5"	255	31		

Use Name	Pos.	Hgt	Wgt	Age	Int	Pts
Brad Dusek	LB	6'2"	214	24		6
Chris Hanburger	LB	6'2"	218	33	3	
Harold McLinton	LB	6'2"	235	28		
John Pergine	LB	6'1"	225	28		6
Russ Tillman	LB	6'2"	230	29		
Pete Wysocki	LB	6'2"	225	26		
Mike Bass	DB	6'	190	30	4	
Eddie Brown (from CLE)	DB	5'11"	185	23	1	
Pat Fischer	DB	5'10"	170	35	3	
Ken Houston	DB	6'3"	198	30	4	
Brig Owens	DB	5'11"	190	32	1	
Bryant Salter	DB	6'4"	196	25	1	
Ken Stone	DB	6'1"	180	24		
Spencer Thomas	DB	6'2"	185	24		

Verlon Biggs — Knee Injury

Use Name	Pos.	Hgt	Wgt	Age	Int	Pts
Randy Johnson	QB	6'3"	205	31		
Billy Kilmer	QB	6'	204	35		6
Joe Theismann	QB	6'	184	25		
Larry Brown	HB	5'11"	195	27		30
Ralph Nelson	HB	6'2"	195	21		6
Mike Thomas	HB	5'11"	190	22		42
Bob Brunet	FB	6'1"	205	29		6
Moses Denson	FB	6'1"	215	31		
Frank Grant	WR	5'11"	180	25		48
Roy Jefferson	WR	6'2"	195	31		12
Larry Jones	WR	5'10"	170	24		6
Charley Taylor	WR	6'3"	210	34		36
Alvin Reed	TE	6'5"	235	31		12
Jerry Smith	TE	6'2"	208	32		18
Mike Bragg	K	5'11"	186	28		
Mark Moseley	K	5'11"	205	27		85

Mike Hancock — Injury
Stu O'Dell — Shoulder Injury

NEW YORK GIANTS 5-9 Bill Arnsparger

Scores of Each Game		
23	Philadelphia	14
13	Washington	49
14	St. Louis	26
7	DALLAS	13
17	Buffalo	14
13	ST. LOUIS	20
35	SAN DIEGO	24
13	WASHINGTON	21
10	PHILADELPHIA	13
14	Green Bay	40
3	Dallas	14
0	BALTIMORE	21
28	NEW ORLEANS	14
26	San Francisco	23

Use Name	Pos.	Hgt	Wgt	Age	Int	Pts
Dave Simonson	OT	6'6"	248	23		
Al Simpson	OT	6'5"	255	24		
Doug Van Horn	OT	6'2"	245	31		
Willie Young	OT	6'	255	32		
Dick Enderle	OG	6'1"	250	27		
John Hicks	OG	6'2"	258	24		
Tom Mullen	OG	6'3"	245	23		
Karl Chandler	C	6'5"	250	23		
Bob Hyland	C	6'5"	255	30		
Rick Dvorak	DE	6'4"	235	23		
Dave Gallagher	DE	6'4"	256	23		
Jack Gregory	DE	6'6"	255	30		
George Martin	DE	6'4"	245	22		
John Mendenhall	DT	6'1"	255	26		
Jim Pietrzak	DT	6'5"	260	22		
Bill Windauer (from MIA)	DT	6'3"	248	25		

Use Name	Pos.	Hgt	Wgt	Age	Int	Pts
Jimmy Gunn (from CHI)	LB	6'1"	218	26	1	
Pat Hughes	LB	6'2"	225	28		
Brian Kelley	LB	6'3"	222	24	3	
Bob Schmit	LB	6'1"	220	25		
Andy Selfridge	LB	6'4"	220	26		
Brad Van Pelt	LB	6'5"	235	24	3	
Bobby Brooks	DB	6'1"	195	24	4	
Rondy Colbert	DB	5'9"	165	21		6
Charlie Ford (from BUF)	DB	6'3"	185	26	1	
Robert Giblin	DB	6'2"	205	22		
Spider Lockhart	DB	6'2"	175	32	1	
Clyde Powers	DB	6'1"	195	24	3	
Jim Stienke	DB	5'11"	182	24	2	
Henry Stuckey	DB	6'1"	180	25		

Larry Jacobson — Broken Ankle

Use Name	Pos.	Hgt	Wgt	Age	Int	Pts
Craig Morton	QB	6'4"	210	32		
Carl Summerell	QB	6'4"	208	23		
Mike Wells	QB	6'5"	225	24		
Steve Crosby	HB	5'11"	205	23		
Ron Johnson	HB	6'1"	205	27		36
Doug Kotar	HB	5'11"	205	24		36
Joe Dawkins	FB	5'11"	220	27		12
Larry Watkins	FB	6'2"	230	28		18
Marsh White	FB	6'2"	220	22		6
Danny Buggs	WR	6'2"	185	22		
Don Clune	WR	6'3"	195	23		
Walker Gillette	WR	6'5"	200	28		12
Ray Rhodes	WR	5'11"	185	24		36
Jim O'Bradovich	TE	6'2"	225	22		6
Bob Tucker	TE	6'3"	230	30		6
George Hunt	K	6'1"	215	25		42
Dave Jennings	K	6'4"	205	23		

PHILADELPHIA EAGLES 4-10 Mike McCormack

Scores of Each Game		
14	N.Y. GIANTS	23
13	Chicago	15
26	WASHINGTON	10
16	Miami	24
20	St. Louis	31
17	DALLAS	20
3	LOS ANGELES	42
23	ST. LOUIS	24
13	N.Y. Giants	10
17	Dallas	27
27	SAN FRANCISCO	17
0	CINCINNATI	31
10	Denver	25
26	Washington	3

Use Name	Pos.	Hgt	Wgt	Age	Int	Pts
Jeff Bleamer	OT	6'4"	253	22		
Jerry Sisemore	OT	6'4"	260	24		
Stan Walters	OT	6'6"	270	27		
Ernie Janet (from GB)	OG	6'4"	255	26		
Wade Key	OG	6'4"	245	28		
Bill Lueck	OG	6'3"	250	29		
Tom Luken	OG	6'3"	253	25		
John Niland	OG	6'4"	250	31		
Ron Lou	C	6'2"	240	24		
Guy Morriss	C	6'4"	255	24		
Don Ratliff	DE	6'5"	250	25		
Blenda Gay	DE	6'5"	255	25		
Will Wynn	DE	6'4"	245	26		
Bill Dunstan	DT	6'4"	250	26		
Rich Glover	DT	6'1"	244	24		
Mitch Sutton	DT	6'4"	255	24		
Rosie Manning (from ATL)	DT	6'5"	259	24		

Use Name	Pos.	Hgt	Wgt	Age	Int	Pts
Bill Bergey	LB	6'2"	250	30	3	
John Bunting	LB	6'1"	220	25	1	
Steve Colavito	LB	6'	225	24		
Tom Ehlers	LB	6'2"	218	23		
Dean Halverson	LB	6'2"	230	29		
Frank LeMaster	LB	6'2"	230	23	4	6
Jim Opperman	LB	6'3"	220	22		
Bill Bradley	DB	5'11"	190	28	5	
Cliff Brooks	DB	6'1"	190	26		
Joe Lavender	DB	6'4"	190	26	3	6
Randy Logan	DB	6'1"	195	24	1	
Larry Marshall	DB	5'10"	195	25		
John Outlaw	DB	5'10"	180	30	5	
Artimus Parker	DB	6'3"	215	23	4	

Tom Bailey — Knee Injury

Use Name	Pos.	Hgt	Wgt	Age	Int	Pts
Mike Boryla	QB	6'3"	200	24		
Roman Gabriel	QB	6'4"	220	35		6
Bill Troup	QB	6'5"	220	24		
Po James	HB	6'1"	202	26		12
Merritt Kersey	HB	6'1"	205	25		
James McAlister	HB	6'1"	205	23		18
Dennis Morgan	HB	5'11"	195	23		
Tom Sullivan	FB-HB	6'	190	25		
Art Malone	FB	5'11"	216	27		
John Tarver	FB	6'3"	220	26		
George Amundson	HB-FB	6'3"	215	24		
Harold Carmichael	WR	6'7"	225	25		42
Bob Picard	WR	6'1"	195	25		
Charlie Smith	WR	6'1"	185	25		36
Don Zimmerman	WR	6'3"	195	25		
Keith Krepfle	TE	6'3"	225	23		
Charlie Young	TE	6'4"	238	24		18
Spike Jones	K	6'2"	185	28		
Horst Muhlmann	K	6'1"	220	35		81

*Overtime

ST. LOUIS CARDINALS

RUSHING
Last Name	No.	Yds	Avg	TD
Otis	269	1076	4.0	5
Metcalf	165	816	4.9	9
Jones	54	275	5.1	2
Latin	35	165	4.7	1
Ashton	10	44	4.4	0
Hammond	3	13	4.3	0
Moss	4	12	3.0	1
Hart	11	7	0.6	1
M. Gray	1	6	6.0	0
Shaw	3	−12	−4.0	0

RECEIVING
Last Name	No.	Yds	Avg	TD
M. Gray	48	926	19	11
Metcalf	43	378	9	2
Thomas	21	375	18	2
Jones	19	194	10	1
Harris	15	266	18	0
Smith	13	246	19	2
Cain	12	134	11	1
Otis	12	69	6	1
Latin	2	25	13	0
Hammond	2	6	3	0

PUNT RETURNS
Last Name	No.	Yds	Avg	TD
Metcalf	23	285	12	1
Hammond	9	70	8	0
M. Gray	7	53	8	0
Wehrli	1	2	2	0

KICKOFF RETURNS
Last Name	No.	Yds	Avg	TD
Metcalf	35	960	27	1
Hammond	13	254	20	0
Smith	1	25	25	0
Moss	1	21	21	0
Hartle	1	20	20	0
T. Gray	1	20	20	0
Jones	1	18	18	0
Wehrli	1	10	10	0
Reaves	1	9	9	0

PASSING – PUNTING – KICKING
PASSING	Att	Comp	%	Yds	Yd/Att	TD	Int–%	RK
Hart	345	182	53	2507	7.3	19	19– 6	6
Shaw	8	4	50	61	7.6	0	1–13	
Metcalf	2	1	50	51	25.5	1	0– 0	

PUNTING	No	Avg
West	64	37.7

KICKING	XP	Att	%	FG	Att	%
Bakken	40	41	98	19	24	82

DALLAS COWBOYS

RUSHING
Last Name	No.	Yds	Avg	TD
Newhouse	209	930	4.4	2
P. Pearson	133	509	3.8	2
Dennison	111	383	3.5	7
Staubach	55	316	5.7	4
Young	50	225	4.5	2
Richards	3	18	6.0	0
Hoopes	1	13	13.0	0
Longley	3	12	4.0	0
D. Pearson	1	11	11.0	0
Laidlaw	3	10	3.3	0
DuPree	1	3	3.0	0
Fugett	1	2	2.0	0

RECEIVING
Last Name	No.	Yds	Avg	TD
D. Pearson	46	822	18	8
Fugett	38	488	13	3
Newhouse	34	275	8	0
P. Pearson	27	353	13	2
Richards	21	451	22	4
Young	18	184	10	1
Laidlaw	11	100	9	0
DuPree	9	138	15	1
Dennison	2	5	3	0
Breunig	1	21	21	0

PUNT RETURNS
Last Name	No.	Yds	Avg	TD
Richards	28	288	10	1
Woolsey	4	25	6	0

KICKOFF RETURNS
Last Name	No.	Yds	Avg	TD
P. Pearson	16	391	24	0
Dennison	13	262	20	0
Woolsey	12	247	21	0
Henderson	4	130	33	1
Young	3	54	18	0
P. Howard	2	51	26	0
Breunig	2	13	7	0
Peterson	1	10	10	0
Waters	1	0	0	0

PASSING – PUNTING – KICKING
PASSING	Att	Comp	%	Yds	Yd/Att	TD	Int–%	RK
Staubach	348	198	57	2666	7.7	17	16– 5	2
Longley	23	7	30	102	4.4	1	1– 4	
Hoopes	3	1	33	21	7.0	0	0– 0	
Newhouse	2	1	50	46	23.0	1	0– 0	

PUNTING	No	Avg
Hoopes	68	39.4

KICKING	XP	Att	%	FG	Att	%
Fritsch	38	40	95	22	35	63

WASHINGTON REDSKINS

RUSHING
Last Name	No.	Yds	Avg	TD
M. Thomas	235	919	3.9	4
L. Brown	97	352	3.6	3
Denson	56	195	3.5	0
Nelson	31	139	4.5	0
Grant	3	46	15.3	0
Kilmer	11	34	3.1	1
Theismann	3	34	11.3	0
Brunet	6	23	3.8	1
R. Johnson	2	10	5.0	0

RECEIVING
Last Name	No.	Yds	Avg	TD
Taylor	53	744	14	6
Grant	41	776	19	8
M. Thomas	40	483	12	3
Smith	31	391	13	3
L. Brown	25	225	9	2
Jefferson	15	255	17	2
Denson	13	81	6	0
Nelson	5	58	12	1
Pergine	2	41	21	1
Jones	2	33	17	0
Reed	2	5	3	2

PUNT RETURNS
Last Name	No.	Yds	Avg	TD
Jones	53	407	8	1
E. Brown	8	68	9	0
Theismann	2	5	3	0

KICKOFF RETURNS
Last Name	No.	Yds	Avg	TD
Jones	47	1086	23	0
E. Brown	6	126	21	0
Nelson	5	107	21	0
Brunet	5	83	17	0
Tillman	1	4	4	0
Grant	0	16	0	0

PASSING – PUNTING – KICKING
PASSING	Att	Comp	%	Yds	Yd/Att	TD	Int–%	RK
Kilmer	346	178	51	2440	7.1	23	16– 5	3
Johnson	79	41	52	556	7.0	4	10–13	
Theismann	22	10	46	96	4.4	1	3–14	
Anderson	1	0	0	0	0.0	0	0– 0	

PUNTING	No	Avg
Bragg	72	40.6

KICKING	XP	Att	%	FG	Att	%
Moseley	37	39	95	16	25	64

NEW YORK GIANTS

RUSHING
Last Name	No.	Yds	Avg	TD
Dawkins	129	438	3.4	2
Kotar	122	378	3.1	6
Johnson	116	351	3.0	5
Watkins	68	303	4.5	3
White	17	90	5.3	0
Morton	22	72	3.3	0
Summerell	3	4	1.3	0
Buggs	1	0	0.0	0
Rhodes	3	−4	−1.3	0
Tucker	1	−5	−5.0	0

RECEIVING
Last Name	No.	Yds	Avg	TD
Gillette	43	600	14	2
Tucker	34	484	14	1
Johnson	34	280	8	1
Rhodes	26	537	21	6
Dawkins	24	245	10	0
Kotar	9	86	10	0
Obradovich	7	65	9	1
Watkins	7	43	6	0
Clune	5	97	19	0
White	3	15	5	0
Hicks	1	5	5	0

PUNT RETURNS
Last Name	No.	Yds	Avg	TD
Colbert	27	238	9	1
Buggs	19	93	5	0
Lockhart	2	14	7	0
Kotar	1	5	5	0

KICKOFF RETURNS
Last Name	No.	Yds	Avg	TD
Colbert	17	408	24	0
Kotar	17	405	24	0
Buggs	16	353	22	0
Obradovich	2	38	19	0
Dawkins	1	32	32	0
Crosby	1	14	14	0
Selfridge	1	0	0	0

PASSING – PUNTING – KICKING
PASSING	Att	Comp	%	Yds	Yd/Att	TD	Int–%	RK
Morton	363	186	51	2359	6.5	11	16– 4	8
Summerell	16	7	44	98	6.1	0	2–13	

PUNTING	No	Avg
Jennings	76	40.9
Hunt	9	24.2
Crosby	1	28.0

KICKING	XP	Att	%	FG	Att	%
Hunt	24	29	83	6	11	55

PHILADELPHIA EAGLES

RUSHING
Last Name	No.	Yds	Avg	TD
Sullivan	173	632	3.7	0
McAlister	103	335	3.3	1
Malone	101	325	3.2	0
James	43	196	4.6	1
Smith	9	85	9.4	0
Gabriel	13	70	5.4	0
Boryla	8	33	4.1	0
Tarver	7	20	2.9	0
Carmichael	1	6	6.0	0
Young	2	1	0.5	0
Jones	1	−1	−1.0	0

RECEIVING
Last Name	No.	Yds	Avg	TD
Young	49	659	13	3
Carmichael	49	639	13	7
Smith	37	515	14	6
James	32	267	8	1
Sullivan	28	276	10	0
Malone	20	120	6	0
McAlister	17	134	8	2
Tarver	5	14	3	0
Krepfle	1	16	16	0

PUNT RETURNS
Last Name	No.	Yds	Avg	TD
Marshall	23	235	10	0
Morgan	8	60	8	0
Bradley	4	4	1	0

KICKOFF RETURNS
Last Name	No.	Yds	Avg	TD
Marshall	22	557	25	0
James	13	311	24	0
McAlister	12	278	23	0
Morgan	7	170	24	0
Sullivan	3	42	14	0
Opperman	1	15	15	0
Sisemore	1	15	15	0

PASSING – PUNTING – KICKING
PASSING	Att	Comp	%	Yds	Yd/Att	TD	Int–%	RK
Gabriel	292	151	52	1644	5.6	13	11– 4	7
Boryla	166	87	52	996	6.0	6	12– 7	14

PUNTING	No	Avg
Jones	68	40.3
Kersey	15	32.6

KICKING	XP	Att	%	FG	Att	%
Muhlmann	21	24	88	20	29	69

MINNESOTA VIKINGS 12-2 Bud Grant

Scores of Each Game

27	SAN FRANCISCO	17
42	Cleveland	10
28	CHICAGO	3
29	N.Y. JETS	21
25	DETROIT	19
13	Chicago	9
28	Green Bay	17
38	ATLANTA	0
20	New Orleans	7
28	SAN DIEGO	13
30	Washington	31
24	GREEN BAY	3
10	Detroit	17
35	Buffalo	13

Use Name	Pos.	Hgt	Wgt	Age	Int	Pts
Charlie Goodrum	OT	6'3"	256	25		
Steve Riley	OT	6'6"	258	22		
Ron Yary	OT	6'6"	255	29		
Steve Lawson	OG	6'3"	265	26		
Andy Mauer	OG	6'3"	275	26		
Ed White	OG	6'2"	270	28		
Mick Tingelhoff	C	6'1"	240	35		
John Ward	OG-C	6'4"	250	27		
Carl Eller	DE	6'6"	247	33		1
Jim Marshall	DE	6'3"	240	37		
Mark Mullaney	DE	6'6"	242	22		
Alan Page	DT	6'5"	245	30		
Doug Sutherland	DT	6'3"	250	27		
Bob Lurtsema	DE-DT	6'6"	250	33		
Matt Blair	LB	6'5"	230	23	1	
Wally Hilgenberg	LB	6'3"	230	32	1	
Amos Martin	LB	6'3"	228	26		
Fred McNeill	LB	6'2"	230	23	1	
Jeff Siemen	LB	6'2"	237	25	3	
Bob Stein (from SD)	LB	6'2"	235	27		
Roy Winston	LB	6'1"	222	35		
Pete Athas (from CLE)	DB	5'11"	185	27	1	
Autry Beamon	DB	6'	190	21	1	2
Joe Blahak	DB	5'9"	188	24	1	2
Terry Brown	DB	6'1"	205	28	2	6
Bobby Bryant	DB	6'	170	31		6
Paul Krause	DB	6'3"	200	33	10	6
Jeff Wright	DB	5'11"	190	26		
Nate Wright	DB	5'11"	180	28		
Bob Berry	QB	5'11"	185	33		
Bob Lee	QB	6'2"	195	30		
Fran Tarkenton	QB	6'1"	190	35		12
Chuck Foreman	HB	6'2"	207	24		132
Ed Marinaro	FB-HB	6'2"	212	25		24
Brent McClanahan	FB-HB	5'10"	202	24		6
Robert Miller	FB	6'1"	204	22		6
Dave Osborn	FB	6'	208	32		6
John Gilliam	WR	6'1"	195	30		42
Clint Haslerig (from BUF)	WR	6'	194	23		
Jim Lash	WR	6'2"	200	23		24
Sam McCullum	WR	6'2"	203	22		
Steve Craig	TE	6'3"	230	24		
Doug Kingsriter	TE	6'2"	222	25		
Stu Voight	TE	6'1"	225	27		24
Neil Clabo	K	6'2"	200	22		
Fred Cox	K	5'10"	200	36		85

DETROIT LIONS 7-7 Rick Forzano

Scores of Each Game

30	GREEN BAY	16
17	Atlanta	14
10	DALLAS	36
27	CHICAGO	7
19	Minnesota	25
8	Houston	24
28	San Francisco	17
21	CLEVELAND	10
13	GREEN BAY	10
21	Kansas City	*24
0	LOS ANGELES	20
21	Chicago	25
17	MINNESOTA	10
13	ST. LOUIS	24

Use Name	Pos.	Hgt	Wgt	Age	Int	Pts
Rocky Freitas	OT	6'6"	275	29		
Craig Hertwig	OT	6'8"	270	23		
Jim Yarbrough	OT	6'6"	265	28		
Lynn Boden	OG	6'5"	270	22		
Bob Kowalkowski	OG	6'3"	245	31		
Gordon Jolley	OT-OG	6'5"	245	26		
Guy Dennis	C-OG	6'2"	250	28		
Richard Hicks	C	6'4"	250	24		
Jon Morris	C	6'4"	250	32		
Ernie Price	DE	6'4"	245	24		2
Ken Sanders	DE	6'5"	245	25		
Larry Hand	DT-DE	6'4"	245	35		1
Doug English	DT	6'5"	245	22		
Herb Orris	DT	6'4"	245	28		
Billy Howard	DE-DT	6'4"	255	25		
Jim Mitchell	DE-DT	6'3"	250	26		
Larry Ball	LB	6'6"	235	25		
Mike Hennigan	LB	6'2"	225	23		6
Jim Laslavic	LB	6'2"	240	23	2	
Paul Naumoff	LB	6'1"	215	30	2	
Ed O'Neil	LB	6'3"	235	22		6
Charlie Weaver	LB	6'2"	225	26	1	
Lem Barney	DB	6'	190	29	5	
Ben Davis	DB	5'11"	180	29	1	6
Lenny Dunlap	DB	6'1"	200	26		
Dick Jauron	DB	6'	190	24	4	
Levi Johnson	DB	6'3"	200	24	3	6
Mike Weger	DB	6'2"	200	29	1	
Charlie West	DB	6'1"	195	29		
Steve Ownes — Knee Injury						
Larry Walton — Knee Injury						
Jim Thrower — Knee Injury						
Jack Concannon	QB	6'3"	200	32		
Greg Landry	QB	6'4"	205	28		
Bill Munson	QB	6'2"	200	33		
Joe Reed	QB	6'1"	195	27		6
Dexter Bussey	HB	6'1"	210	23		24
Altie Taylor	HB	5'10"	200	27		24
Bobby Thompson	HB	5'11"	195	28		6
Jim Hooks	FB	5'11"	225	23		
Horace King	FB	6'2"	210	22		12
Marlin Briscoe (from SD)	WR	5'10"	180	29		
George Farmer (from CHI)	WR	6'4"	214	27		
Dennis Franklin	WR	6'1"	185	22		
Ray Jarvis	WR	5'11"	190	26		24
Jon Staggers	WR	5'10"	185	26		12
Leonard Thompson	WR	5'10"	190	23		
John McMakin	TE	6'3"	225	24		
Charlie Sanders	TE	6'4"	230	29		18
Errol Mann	K	6'3"	205	34		67
Alan Pringle	K	6'	195	23		
Herman Weaver	K	6'4"	210	26		

GREEN BAY PACKERS 4-10 Bart Starr

Scores of Each Game

16	DETROIT	30
13	Denver	23
7	MIAMI	31
19	New Orleans	20
19	Dallas	17
13	PITTSBURGH	16
17	MINNESOTA	28
14	Chicago	27
10	Detroit	13
40	N.Y. GIANTS	14
28	CHICAGO	7
3	Minnesota	24
5	Los Angeles	22
22	ATLANTA	13

Use Name	Pos.	Hgt	Wgt	Age	Int	Pts
Ernie McMillan	OT	6'6"	265	37		
Dick Himes	OT	6'4"	260	29		
Bill Bain	OG	6'4"	270	23		
Pat Matson	OG	6'1"	245	31		
Bruce Van Dyke	OG	6'2"	255	31		
Keith Wortman	OG	6'2"	250	25		
Robert McCaffrey	C	6'2"	245	23		
Larry McCarren	C	6'3"	248	24		
Bill Cooke	DE	6'5"	250	24		
Dave Pureifory	DE	6'1"	255	25	4	
Alden Roche	DE	6'4"	255	30		
Clarence Williams	DE	6'5"	255	28		
Mike McCoy	DT	6'5"	275	26		6
Steve Okoniewski	DT	6'3"	272	26		
Dave Roller	DT	6'2"	270	25		
Bill Hayhoe — Broken Leg						
Ron Acks	LB	6'2"	225	30		
Fred Carr	LB	6'5"	240	29	3	
Jim Carter	LB	6'3"	245	26		
Larry Hefner	LB	6'2"	230	26		
Tom Hull	LB	6'3"	230	23		
Tom Toner	LB	6'3"	235	25	1	2
Gary Weaver	LB	6'1"	224	26		
Willie Buchanon	DB	6'	190	24		
Ken Ellis	DB	5'10"	195	27	1	
Johnnie Gray	DB	5'11"	185	21	1	
Charlie Hall	DB	6'1"	190	26		
Steve Luke	DB	6'2"	205	21		
Al Matthews	DB	5'11"	190	27	2	
Hurles Scales	DB	6'1"	200	24		
Perry Smith	DB	6'1"	195	24	6	
Norm Hodgkins — Injury						
Larry Krause — Shoulder Injury						
Carlos Brown	QB	6'3"	210	23		
John Hadl	QB	6'2"	214	35		
Don Milan	QB	6'3"	196	26		
Will Harrell	HB	5'8"	182	22		18
Eric Torkelson	HB	6'2"	195	22		12
Terry Wells	HB	5'11"	195	24		
John Brockington	FB	6'1"	225	26		48
Barty Smith	FB	6'4"	240	23		30
Kent Gaydos	WR	6'6"	228	25		
Steve Odom	WR	5'8"	174	22		30
Ken Payne	WR	6'1"	185	24		
Barry Smith	WR	6'1"	190	24		6
Gerald Tinker (from ATL)	WR	5'9"	175	24		12
Charlie Wade	WR	5'10"	163	25		
Bert Askson	TE	6'3"	225	29		
Rich McGeorge	TE	6'4"	230	26		6
David Beverly (from HOU)	K	6'2"	182	25		
Steve Broussard	K	6'	200	26		
Joe Danelo	K	5'9"	166	21		53
Chester Marcol	K	6'	190	26		

CHICAGO BEARS 4-10 Jack Pardee

Scores of Each Game

7	BALTIMORE	35
15	PHILADELPHIA	13
3	Minnesota	28
7	Detroit	27
3	Pittsburgh	34
9	MINNESOTA	13
13	MIAMI	46
27	GREEN BAY	14
3	San Francisco	31
10	Los Angeles	38
7	Green Bay	28
25	DETROIT	21
20	ST. LOUIS	34
42	New Orleans	17

Use Name	Pos.	Hgt	Wgt	Age	Int	Pts
Lionel Antoine	OT	6'6"	263	25		
Bob Asher	OT	6'5"	260	27		
Jeff Sevy	OT	6'5"	250	24		
Noah Jackson	OG	6'2"	263	24		
Bob Newton	OG	6'4"	260	26		
Revie Sorey	OG	6'2"	260	21		
Mark Nordquist	C-OG	6'4"	246	29		
Dan Neal	C	6'4"	240	26		
Dan Peiffer	C	6'3"	250	24		
Richard Harris	DE	6'5"	255	27		
Mike Hartenstine	DE	6'3"	250	22	2	
Gary Hrivnak	DE	6'5"	254	24		
Mel Tom	DE	6'4"	242	34		
Wally Chambers	DT	6'6"	255	24		
Jim Osborne	DT	6'3"	254	25		
Ron Rydalch	DT	6'4"	260	23		
Roger Stillwell	DT	6'5"	265	23		
John Babinecz	LB	6'1"	222	25	1	
Waymond Bryant	LB	6'3"	230	23		
Doug Buffone	LB	6'1"	227	31	1	
Larry Ely	LB	6'1"	230	27	1	
Carl Gersbach	LB	6'1"	230	28	1	
Bob Pifferini	LB	6'2"	226	25		
Don Rives	LB	6'2"	230	24		
Craig Clemons	DB	5'11"	200	26	2	6
Earl Douthit	DB	6'2"	188	22		
Allan Ellis	DB	5'10"	182	24	2	
Bill Knox	DB	5'9"	193	24		
Virgil Livers	DB	5'8"	176	23	2	6
Doug Plank	DB	6'	197	22	2	
Ted Vactor	DB	6'	185	31		
Nemiah Wilson	DB	6'	165	32		
Bob Avellini	QB	6'	197	22		6
Virgil Carter (from SD)	QB	6'1"	185	29		
Gary Huff	QB	6'1"	194	24		
Roland Harper	HB	5'11"	194	22		
Johnny Musso	HB	5'11"	205	25		
Walter Payton	HB	5'11"	200	21		42
Mike Adamle	FB-HB	5'9"	193	25		6
Tom Donchez	FB	6'2"	216	22		
Cid Edwards	FB	6'2"	230	31		6
Bob Grim	WR	6'	200	30		12
Bo Rather	WR	6'1"	180	24		12
Steve Schubert	WR	5'10"	185	24		
Ron Shanklin	WR	6'1"	190	28		
Gary Butler	TE	6'3"	235	24		
Greg Latta	TE	6'3"	226	22		18
Bob Parsons	TE	6'4"	234	26		6
Bob Thomas	K	5'10"	178	23		57

*Overtime

MINNESOTA VIKINGS

RUSHING

Last Name	No.	Yds	Avg	TD
Foreman	280	1070	3.8	13
Marinaro	101	358	3.5	1
McClanahan	92	336	3.7	0
Tarkenton	16	108	6.8	2
Osborn	32	94	2.9	1
Miller	30	93	3.1	1
Gilliam	3	35	11.7	0
Berry	1	0	0.0	0
Lee	1	0	0.0	0

RECEIVING

Last Name	No.	Yds	Avg	TD
Foreman	73	691	10	9
Marinaro	54	462	9	3
Gilliam	50	777	16	7
Lash	37	535	15	3
Voigt	34	363	11	4
McClanahan	18	141	8	1
Craig	6	68	11	0
Miller	4	35	9	0
Haslerig	2	28	14	0
McCullum	2	25	13	0
Osborn	1	-4	-4	0

PUNT RETURNS

Last Name	No.	Yds	Avg	TD
Bryant	19	125	7	0
McCullum	12	22	2	0
J. Wright	1	22	22	0
Athas	6	37	6	0
Beamon	1	0	0	0
Blair	2	-2	-1	0

KICKOFF RETURNS

Last Name	No.	Yds	Avg	TD
McClanahan	17	360	21	0
McCullum	9	221	25	0
Athas	6	95	16	0
Miller	5	93	19	0
Marinaro	5	71	14	0
Osborn	1	38	38	0
Foreman	1	4	4	0

PASSING – PUNTING – KICKING

Last Name	Att	Comp	%	Yds	Yd/Att	TD	Int–%	RK
PASSING								
Tarkenton	425	273	64	2994	7.0	25	13– 3	1
Lee	14	5	36	103	7.4	2	1– 7	
Berry	6	3	50	24	4.0	0	0– 0	
Lash	1	0	0	0	0.0	0	0– 0	

Last Name	No.	Avg
PUNTING		
Clabo	73	41.1

Last Name	XP	Att	%	FG	Att	%
KICKING						
Cox	46	48	96	13	17	76

DETROIT LIONS

RUSHING

Last Name	No.	Yds	Avg	TD
Bussey	157	696	4.4	2
Taylor	195	638	3.3	4
B. Thompson	51	268	5.3	1
King	61	260	4.3	2
Reed	34	193	5.7	1
Landry	20	92	4.6	0
Staggers	2	26	13.0	0
Jarvis	1	0	0.0	0
Munson	4	-3	-0.8	0
Briscoe	2	-3	-1.5	0
Hooks	4	-8	-2.0	0
L. Thompson	1	-12	-12.0	0

RECEIVING

Last Name	No.	Yds	Avg	TD
Sanders	37	486	13	3
Jarvis	29	501	17	4
Briscoe	24	372	16	4
Taylor	21	111	5	0
B. Thompson	19	122	6	0
Bussey	14	175	13	2
Staggers	14	174	12	2
King	13	81	6	0
Farmer	8	118	15	0
Franklin	5	109	22	0
McMakin	2	43	22	0
Hooks	1	5	5	0

PUNT RETURNS

Last Name	No.	Yds	Avg	TD
West	22	219	10	0
Barney	8	80	10	0
Jauron	6	29	5	0

KICKOFF RETURNS

Last Name	No.	Yds	Avg	TD
B. Thompson	22	565	26	0
L. Thompson	12	271	23	0
King	6	117	20	0
Weger	3	42	14	0
West	2	41	21	0
Bussey	2	38	19	0
Hooks	2	8	4	0
Dunlap	1	19	19	0
Hennigan	1	13	13	0
Dennis	1	0	0	0

PASSING – PUNTING – KICKING

Last Name	Att	Comp	%	Yds	Yd/Att	TD	Int–%	RK
PASSING								
Reed	191	86	45	1181	6.2	9	10– 5	10
Munson	109	65	60	626	5.7	5	2– 2	
Landry	56	31	55	403	7.2	1	0– 0	
Concannon	2	1	50	30	15.0	0	0– 0	
Briscoe	2	0	0	0	0.0	0	0– 0	
King	1	0	0	0	0.0	0	0– 0	
H. Weaver	1	0	0	0	0.0	0	0– 0	

Last Name	No.	Avg
PUNTING		
H. Weaver	80	42.0
Mann	1	34.0

Last Name	XP	Att	%	FG	Att	%
KICKING						
Mann	25	29	86	14	21	67

GREEN BAY PACKERS

RUSHING

Last Name	No.	Yds	Avg	TD
Brockington	144	434	3.0	7
Harrell	121	359	3.0	1
Barty Smith	60	243	4.1	4
Torkelson	42	226	5.4	2
Wells	33	139	4.2	0
Odom	5	55	11.0	0
Hadl	20	47	2.4	0
Milan	4	41	10.3	0
Tinker	1	5	5.0	0
Payne	1	-2	-2.0	0

RECEIVING

Last Name	No.	Yds	Avg	TD
Payne	58	766	13	0
Harrell	34	261	8	2
Brockington	33	242	8	1
McGeorge	32	458	14	1
Barty Smith	16	140	9	1
Odom	15	299	20	4
Barry Smith	6	77	13	1
Torkelson	6	37	6	0
Wells	6	11	2	0
Tinker	4	84	21	1
Askson	2	25	13	0

PUNT RETURNS

Last Name	No.	Yds	Avg	TD
Harrell	21	136	7	0
Ellis	6	27	5	0
Gray	1	27	27	0
Hall	1	0	0	0
Odom	1	0	0	0

KICKOFF RETURNS

Last Name	No.	Yds	Avg	TD
Odom	42	1034	25	1
Luke	6	91	15	0
Torkelson	5	89	18	0
Harrell	3	78	26	0
Barty Smith	4	53	13	0
Wells	1	26	26	0
McGeorge	1	17	17	0
Bain	1	10	10	0

PASSING – PUNTING – KICKING

Last Name	Att	Comp	%	Yds	Yd/Att	TD	Int–%	RK
PASSING								
Hadl	353	191	54	2095	5.9	6	21– 6	13
Milan	32	15	47	181	5.7	1	1– 3	
Harrell	5	3	60	61	12.2	3	0– 0	
Brown	4	3	75	63	15.8	1	0– 0	

Last Name	No.	Avg
PUNTING		
Beverly	78	37.7
Broussard	29	31.8

Last Name	XP	Att	%	FG	Att	%
KICKING						
Danelo	20	23	87	11	16	69

CHICAGO BEARS

RUSHING

Last Name	No.	Yds	Avg	TD
Payton	196	679	3.5	7
Harper	100	453	4.5	1
Adamle	94	353	3.8	1
Edwards	27	73	2.7	0
Musso	6	33	5.5	0
Rather	4	24	6.0	0
Huff	5	7	1.4	0
Avellini	4	-3	-0.8	1

RECEIVING

Last Name	No.	Yds	Avg	TD
Rather	39	685	18	2
Payton	33	213	7	0
Grim	28	374	13	2
Harper	27	191	7	0
Latta	16	202	13	3
Adamle	15	111	7	0
Parsons	13	184	14	1
Edwards	11	86	8	1
Schubert	5	68	14	0
Jackson	1	17	17	0
Sevy	1	6	6	0

PUNT RETURNS

Last Name	No.	Yds	Avg	TD
Livers	42	**456**	11	0
Schubert	6	33	6	0
Plank	3	23	8	0
Knox	1	0	0	0

KICKOFF RETURNS

Last Name	No.	Yds	Avg	TD
Livers	26	529	20	0
Payton	14	444	**32**	0
Douthitt	13	333	26	0
Schubert	9	146	16	0
Knox	4	67	17	0
Harper	4	67	17	0
Adamle	1	27	27	0
Vactor	1	25	25	0
Rather	1	6	6	0
Osborne	1	0	0	0

PASSING – PUNTING – KICKING

Last Name	Att	Comp	%	Yds	Yd/Att	TD	Int–%	RK
PASSING								
Huff	205	114	56	1083	5.3	3	9– 4	12
Avellini	126	67	53	942	7.5	6	11– 9	
Carter	5	3	60	24	4.8	0	1– 20	
Adamle	2	2	100	57	28.5	0	0– 0	
Grim	1	0	0	0	0.0	0	0– 0	
Parsons	1	0	0	0	0.0	0	0– 0	
Payton	1	0	0	0	0.0	0	1–100	

Last Name	No.	Avg
PUNTING		
Parsons	93	39.0
Payton	1	39.0

Last Name	XP	Att	%	FG	Att	%
KICKING						
Thomas	18	22	82	13	23	57

LOS ANGELES RAMS 12-2 Chuck Knox

Scores of Each Game			Use Name	Pos.	Hgt	Wgt	Age	Int	Pts
7	Dallas	18	Charlie Cowan	OT	6'4"	265	37		
23	San Francisco	14	Doug France	OT	6'5"	260	22		
24	BALTIMORE	13	John Williams	OT	6'3"	256	29		
13	San Diego	*10	Dennis Harrah	OG	6'5"	257	22		
22	ATLANTA	7	Tom Mack	OG	6'3"	250	31		
38	NEW ORLEANS	14	Joe Scibelli	OG	6'1"	255	36		
42	Philadelphia	3	Bob DeMarco	C	6'3"	245	37		
23	SAN FRANCISCO	24	Rich Saul	C	6'3"	235	27		
16	Atlanta	7	Al Cowlings	DE	6'5"	245	28		
38	CHICAGO	10	Fred Dryer	DE	6'6"	240	29	1	6
20	Detroit	0	Mike Fanning	DE	6'6"	260	22		
14	New Orleans	7	Jack Youngblood	DE	6'4"	255	25		2
22	GREEN BAY	5	Larry Brooks	DT	6'3"	255	25		
10	PITTSBURGH	3	Cody Jones	DT	6'5"	240	24		
			Bill Nelson	DT	6'7"	270	27		
			Merlin Olsen	DT	6'5"	270	34		

Use Name	Pos.	Hgt	Wgt	Age	Int	Pts
Ken Geddes	LB	6'3"	235	27	1	
Rick Kay	LB	6'4"	235	25		
Jim Peterson	LB	6'5"	240	25		6
Jack Reynolds	LB	6'1"	232	27	1	
Isiah Robertson	LB	6'3"	225	26	4	6
Jim Youngblood	LB	6'3"	240	25		
Al Clark	DB	6'	185	26		
Dave Elmendorf	DB	6'1"	195	26	4	
Monte Jackson	DB	5'11"	190	22	2	6
Eddie McMillan	DB	6'	190	23	3	
Rod Perry	DB	5'9"	170	21		
Steve Preece	DB	6'1"	195	28		
Bill Simpson	DB	6'1"	180	23	6	

Charlie Stukes — Knee Injury

Use Name	Pos.	Hgt	Wgt	Age	Int	Pts
James Harris	QB	6'3"	210	28		6
Ron Jaworski	QB	6'2"	185	24		12
John Cappelletti	HB	6'1"	217	23		36
Larry McCutcheon	HB	6'1"	205	25		18
Rob Scribner	HB	6'	200	24		12
Jim Bertelsen	FB	5'11"	205	25		18
Cullen Bryant	FB	6'1"	240	24		12
Rod Phillips	TE-FB	6'	220	22		
Harold Jackson	WR	5'10"	175	29		42
Ron Jessie	WR	6'	185	27		18
Willie McGee	WR	5'11"	178	25		
Jack Snow	WR	6'2"	190	32		6
Bob Klein	TE	6'5"	235	28		12
Terry Nelson	TE	6'2"	230	23		
Duane Carrell	K	5'10"	185	25		
Tom Dempsey	K	6'1"	260	34		94

SAN FRANCISCO FORTY-NINERS 5-9 Dick Nolan

Scores of Each Game			Use Name	Pos.	Hgt	Wgt	Age	Int	Pts
17	Minnesota	27	Cas Banaszek	OT	6'3"	255	29		
14	LOS ANGELES	23	Keith Fahnhorst	OT	6'6"	265	23		
20	Kansas City	3	Jeff Hart	OT	6'6"	266	21		
3	ATLANTA	17	Bobby Penchion	OG	6'5"	252	26		
35	NEW ORLEANS	21	Woody Peoples	OG	6'2"	252	32		
16	New England	24	John Watson	OT-OG	6'4"	245	26		
17	DETROIT	28	Bill Reid	C	6'1"	242	23		
24	Los Angeles	23	Jean Barrett	OG-C	6'6"	254	24		
31	CHICAGO	3	Cleveland Elam	DE	6'3"	254	23		
16	New Orleans	6	Cedrick Hardman	DE	6'3"	258	26		
17	Philadelphia	27	Tommy Hart	DE	6'3"	244	30	6	
13	HOUSTON	27	Wayne Baker	DT	6'6"	270	22		
9	Atlanta	31	Bob Haskins	DT	6'2"	250	29		
23	N.Y. GIANTS	26	Bill Sandifer	DT	6'6"	278	23		
			Jimmy Webb	DT	6'5"	248	23		

Use Name	Pos.	Hgt	Wgt	Age	Int	Pts
Greg Collins	LB	6'2"	234	22		
Willie Harper	LB	6'2"	220	25		
Frank Nunley	LB	6'2"	234	29	1	
Skip Vanderbundt	LB	6'3"	223	28	2	
Dave Washington	LB	6'5"	223	27		6
Nate Allen	DB	5'10"	170	27	1	6
Tim Anderson	DB	6'	192	26		
Windlan Hall	DB	5'11"	175	25		
Jim Johnson	DB	6'2"	185	37	2	
Ralph McGill	DB	5'11"	183	25	1	
Mel Phillips	DB	6'	190	33	1	
John Saunders	DB	6'3"	196	25		
Bruce Taylor	DB	6'	190	27	3	

Use Name	Pos.	Hgt	Wgt	Age	Int	Pts
Tom Owen	QB	6'1"	194	22		
Norm Snead	QB	6'4"	215	35		6
Steve Spurrier	QB	6'2"	198	30		
Wilbur Jackson	HB	6'1"	215	23		
Kermit Johnson	HB	6'	200	23		
Del Williams	HB	6'	195	24		24
Sammy Johnson	FB	6'2"	223	22		18
Larry Schreiber	FB	6'	209	28		36
Terry Beasley	WR	5'10"	184	25		
Bob Hayes	WR	6'	185	32		
Mike Holmes	WR	6'2"	193	24		6
Gene Washington	WR	6'1"	185	28		54
Len Garrett (from NO)	TE	6'3"	230	26		
Bill Larson	TE	6'3"	225	21		
Tom Mitchell	TE	6'2"	215	31		18
Steve Mike-Mayer	K	6'	178	27		69
Tom Wittum	K	6'1"	190	25		

ATLANTA FALCONS 4-10 Marion Campbell

Scores of Each Game			Use Name	Pos.	Hgt	Wgt	Age	Int	Pts
20	St. Louis	23	Brent Adams	OT	6'5"	256	23		
14	DETROIT	17	Nick Bebout	UT	6'5"	267	24		
14	NEW ORLEANS	7	Len Gotshalk	OT	6'4"	253	25		
17	San Francisco	3	Dennis Havig	OG	6'2"	254	26		
7	Los Angeles	22	Larron Jackson	OG	6'3"	260	26		
14	CINCINNATI	21	Royce Smith	OG	6'3"	260	26		
7	New Orleans	23	Paul Ryczek	C	6'2"	238	23		
0	Minnesota	38	Jeff Van Note	C	6'2"	252	29		
7	LOS ANGELES	16	John Zook	DE	6'5"	248	27		
35	DENVER	21	Roy Hilton	DE	6'6"	250	30		
34	Oakland	*37	Mike Lewis	DT	6'3"	258	25		
27	WASHINGTON	30	Jeff Merrow	DT	6'4"	230	22		
31	SAN FRANCISCO	9	Mike Tilleman	DT	6'5"	273	31		
13	Green Bay	22	Chuck Walker	DT	6'2"	250	33		
			Claude Humphrey — Knee Injury						

Use Name	Pos.	Hgt	Wgt	Age	Int	Pts
Greg Brezina	LB	6'2"	220	29	4	
Don Hansen	LB	6'3"	226	31	1	
Fulton Kuykendall	LB	6'5"	225	22		
Tommy Nobis	LB	6'2"	232	31		
Ralph Ortega	LB	6'2"	220	22		
Carl Russ	LB	6'2"	227	22		
Ray Brown	DB	6'2"	208	26	4	6
Rick Byas	DB	5'9"	172	24		
Ray Easterling	DB	6'	186	25	3	
Tom Hayes	DB	6'1"	196	29	4	
Bob Jones	DB	6'1"	193	24		
Rolland Lawrence	DB	5'10"	174	24	9	6
Ron Mabra	DB	5'10"	164	24		

Ted Fritsch — Knee Injury
Vince Kendrick — Knee Injury
Jim Miller — Knee Injury

Use Name	Pos.	Hgt	Wgt	Age	Int	Pts
Steve Bartkowski	QB	6'4"	213	22		12
Kim McQuilken	QB	6'2"	200	24		
Pat Sullivan	QB	6'	200	25		
Larry Crowe	HB	6'1"	198	25		
Dave Hampton	HB	6'	206	28		36
Mack Herron (from NE)	HB	5'5"	175	27		
Haskel Stanback	HB	6'	210	23		30
Brad Davis	FB	5'11"	208	22		
Monroe Eley	FB	6'2"	210	23		
Woody Thompson	FB	6'1"	228	23		
Oscar Reed	HB-FB	5'11"	222	31		
Ken Burrow	WR	6'	188	27		12
Wallace Francis	WR	5'11"	185	23		24
Alfred Jenkins	WR	5'10"	155	23		
Frank Pitts	WR	6'2"	200	31		
Greg McCrary	TE	6'3"	230	23		
Jim Mitchell	TE	6'2"	235	27		30
John James	K	6'3"	197	26		
Nick Mike-Mayer	K	5'8"	185	25		42

NEW ORLEANS SAINTS 2-12 John North Ernie Hefferle

Scores of Each Game			Use Name	Pos.	Hgt	Wgt	Age	Int	Pts
3	Washington	41	John Hill	OT	6'2"	245	25		
0	CINCINNATI	21	Phil LaPorta	OT	6'4"	256	22		
7	Atlanta	14	Chris Morris	OT	6'3"	250	25		
20	GREEN BAY	19	Don Morrison	OT	6'5"	260	25		
21	San Francisco	35	Kurt Schumacher	OT	6'3"	260	23		
14	Los Angeles	38	Dave Thompson	C-OT	6'4"	260	26		
23	ATLANTA	7	Jake Kupp	OG	6'3"	248	33		
10	Oakland	48	Emanuel Zanders	OG	6'1"	260	24		
7	MINNESOTA	20	Tom Wickert	OT-OG	6'4"	246	23		
6	SAN FRANCISCO	16	Sylvester Croom	C	6'	235	20		
16	Cleveland	17	Lee Gross	C	6'3"	245	22		
7	LOS ANGELES	14	Steve Baumgartner	DE	6'7"	260	24		
14	N.Y. Giants	28	Andy Dorris	DE	6'4"	240	24		
17	CHICAGO	42	Elois Grooms	DE	6'4"	240	22		
			Joe Owens	DE	6'2"	250	28		
			Derland Moore	DT	6'4"	260	23		
			Bob Pollard	DT	6'3"	250	26		
			Elex Price	DT	6'3"	255	25		

Use Name	Pos.	Hgt	Wgt	Age	Int	Pts
Rusty Chambers	LB	6'1"	215	21		6
Don Coleman	LB	6'2"	222	22		
Joe Federspiel	LB	6'1"	235	25		
Rick Kingrea	LB	6'1"	230	26	1	
Rick Middleton	LB	6'2"	228	23	1	
Greg Westbrooks	LB	6'2"	215	22	1	
Chuck Crist	DB	6'2"	205	24	3	
Jim DeRatt	DB	6'	203	22		
Johnny Fuller	DB	6'	185	29		
Ernie Jackson	DB	5'10"	175	25	2	
Bivian Lee	DB	6'3"	200	27	2	
Tom Myers	DB	5'11"	184	24	5	6
Terry Schmidt	DB	6'	177	23	1	
Mo Spencer	DB	6'	175	23		

Wayne Colman — Broken Arm
Dave Davis — Ankle Injury
Jim Merlo — Injury
Bob Newland — Injury

Use Name	Pos.	Hgt	Wgt	Age	Int	Pts
Larry Cipa	QB	6'3"	209	22		
Archie Manning	QB	6'3"	207	26		6
Bobby Scott	QB	6'1"	200	26		
Alvin Maxson	HB	5'11"	205	22		18
Steve Rogers	HB	6'2"	200	22		
Mike Strachan	HB	6'	195	22		12
Andrew Jones	FB	6'2"	213	22		6
Morris LaGrand (from KC)	FB	6'1"	220	22		6
Rod McNeill	FB	6'2"	220	24		24
Larry Burton	WR	6'1"	190	23		12
Gil Chapman	WR	5'9"	180	22		
Andy Hamilton	WR	6'3"	190	25		
Don Herrmann	WR	6'2"	205	28		6
Joel Parker	WR	6'5"	212	23		12
Henry Childs	TE	6'2"	223	24		
Paul Seal	TE	6'4"	222	23		6
Tom Blanchard	K	6'	180	27		
Bill McClard	K	5'10"	202	23		4
Richie Szaro	K	5'11"	205	27		47

*Overtime

LOS ANGELES RAMS

RUSHING

Last Name	No.	Yds	Avg	TD
McCutcheon	213	911	4.3	2
Bryant	117	467	4.0	2
Bertelsen	116	457	3.9	3
Scribner	42	216	5.1	2
Cappelletti	48	158	3.3	6
Phillips	17	69	4.1	0
Harris	18	45	2.5	1
Jaworski	12	33	2.8	1
Jessie	2	15	7.5	0

RECEIVING

Last Name	No.	Yds	Avg	TD
H. Jackson	43	786	18	7
Jessie	41	547	13	3
McCutcheon	31	230	7	1
Bryant	20	229	12	0
Klein	16	237	15	2
Bertelsen	14	208	15	0
McGee	6	83	14	0
Snow	4	86	22	1
Scribner	2	28	14	0
Phillips	2	10	5	0
Nelson	1	5	5	0
Cowan	1	1	1	0

PUNT RETURNS

Last Name	No.	Yds	Avg	TD
Scribner	26	205	8	0
Bertelsen	11	143	13	0
Elmendorf	15	125	8	0
Bryant	2	47	24	0
Simpson	1	-3	-3	0

KICKOFF RETURNS

Last Name	No.	Yds	Avg	TD
McGee	17	404	24	0
Bryant	12	280	23	0
Cappelletti	3	39	13	0
Scribner	1	24	24	0
Bertelsen	1	17	17	0

PASSING – PUNTING – KICKING

PASSING	Att	Comp	%	Yds	Yd/Att	TD	Int–%	RK
Harris	285	157	55	2148	7.5	14	15– 5	4
Jaworski	48	24	50	302	6.3	0	2– 4	
McCutcheon	1	0	0	0	0.0	0	0– 0	

PUNTING	No	Avg
Carrell	73	39.4

KICKING	XP	Att	%	FG	Att	%
Dempsey	31	36	86	21	26	81

SAN FRANCISCO FORTY-NINERS

RUSHING

Last Name	No.	Yds	Avg	TD
D. Williams	117	631	5.4	3
Schreiber	134	337	2.5	5
Jackson	78	303	3.9	0
S. Johnson	55	185	3.4	3
Spurrier	15	91	6.1	0
Snead	9	30	3.3	1
K. Johnson	4	25	6.3	0
Moore	3	10	3.3	0
Beasley	1	5	5.0	0
Owen	1	1	1.0	0
Hayes	2	-2	-1.0	0
Holmes	1	-4	-4.0	0
Washington	1	-4	-4.0	0
Wittum	1	-10	-10.0	0

RECEIVING

Last Name	No.	Yds	Avg	TD
Washington	44	735	17	9
Schreiber	40	289	7	1
Williams	34	370	11	1
Mitchell	25	366	15	3
S. Johnson	23	177	8	0
Beasley	20	297	15	0
Jackson	17	128	8	0
Holmes	16	220	14	1
Hayes	6	119	20	0
Larson	5	64	13	0
Wittum	2	29	15	0
Moore	1	11	11	0
Fahnhorst	1	1	1	0

PUNT RETURNS

Last Name	No.	Yds	Avg	TD
McGill	31	290	9	0
Taylor	16	166	10	0
Moore	16	160	10	0

KICKOFF RETURNS

Last Name	No.	Yds	Avg	TD
Moore	26	650	25	0
S. Johnson	17	400	24	0
K. Johnson	6	135	23	0
Holmes	2	59	30	0
Baker	4	45	11	0
Hart	2	28	14	0
Williams	1	24	24	0
Hall	1	18	18	0
Fahnhorst	1	13	13	0

PASSING – PUNTING – KICKING

PASSING	Att	Comp	%	Yds	Yd/Att	TD	Int–%	RK
Spurrier	207	102	49	1151	5.6	5	7– 3	9
Snead	189	108	57	1337	7.1	9	10– 5	5
Owen	51	24	47	318	6.2	1	2– 4	
S. Johnson	2	0	0	0	0.0	0	0– 0	
Washington	1	0	0	0	0.0	0	0– 0	

PUNTING	No	Avg
Wittum	67	41.9

KICKING	XP	Att	%	FG	Att	%
Mike-Mayer	27	31	87	14	28	50

ATLANTA FALCONS

RUSHING

Last Name	No.	Yds	Avg	TD
Hampton	250	1002	4.0	5
Stanback	105	440	4.2	5
Herron	62	274	4.4	0
Thompson	68	247	3.6	0
Reed	14	40	2.9	0
McQuilken	4	26	6.5	0
Bartkowski	14	15	1.1	2
Francis	2	12	6.0	0
Sullivan	6	9	1.5	0
Tinker	1	5	5.0	0
Ely	1	3	3.0	0

RECEIVING

Last Name	No.	Yds	Avg	TD
Jenkins	38	767	20	6
J. Mitchell	34	536	16	4
Burrow	25	323	13	2
Hampton	21	195	9	1
Stanback	14	115	8	0
Thompson	14	92	7	0
Francis	13	270	21	4
Tinker	7	121	17	2
Herron	5	50	10	0
Reed	2	1	1	0
Jones	1	25	25	0

PUNT RETURNS

Last Name	No.	Yds	Avg	TD
Herron	22	183	8	0
Eley	7	61	9	0
Jenkins	6	38	6	0
Tinker	6	23	4	0
Mabra	4	20	5	0
Brown	2	12	6	0

KICKOFF RETURNS

Last Name	No.	Yds	Avg	TD
Tinker	13	307	24	0
Francis	14	265	19	0
Herron	13	264	20	0
Eley	8	131	16	0
Byas	5	94	19	0
Lawrence	4	80	20	0
Thompson	4	62	16	0
McCrary	3	48	16	0
Jenkins	1	24	24	0
Reed	2	17	9	0
Davis	1	0	0	0

PASSING – PUNTING – KICKING

PASSING	Att	Comp	%	Yds	Yd/Att	TD	Int–%	RK
Bartkowski	255	115	45	1662	6.5	13	15– 6	11
Sullivan	70	28	40	380	5.4	3	5– 7	
McQuilken	61	20	33	253	4.2	1	9–15	
James	1	1	100	25	25.0	0	0– 0	
Stanback	1	1	100	41	41.0	1	0– 0	

PUNTING	No	Avg
James	89	41.5

KICKING	XP	Att	%	FG	Att	%
Mike-Mayer	30	33	91	4	10	40

NEW ORLEANS SAINTS

RUSHING

Last Name	No.	Yds	Avg	TD
Strachan	161	668	4.1	2
Maxson	139	371	2.7	3
McNeill	61	206	3.4	2
Manning	33	186	5.6	1
Jones	42	108	2.6	1
Rogers	17	62	3.6	0
LaGrand	13	38	2.9	1
Seal	1	10	10.0	0
Burton	2	8	4.0	0
Cipa	6	2	0.3	0

RECEIVING

Last Name	No.	Yds	Avg	TD
Maxson	41	234	6	0
Strachan	30	224	8	0
Seal	28	414	15	1
McNeill	18	138	8	2
Burton	16	305	19	2
Hamilton	12	210	18	0
Childs	10	179	18	0
Jones	10	52	5	0
Parker	9	123	14	2
Herrmann	3	47	16	1
Chapman	1	7	7	0
Rogers	1	2	2	0
LaGrand	1	-1	-1	0

PUNT RETURNS

Last Name	No.	Yds	Avg	TD
Chapman	17	207	12	0
Schmidt	11	76	7	0
Myers	10	70	7	0
DeRatt	2	17	9	0
Spencer	1	0	0	0

KICKOFF RETURNS

Last Name	No.	Yds	Avg	TD
Chapman	28	614	22	0
McNeill	10	276	28	0
Maxson	6	103	17	0
Rogers	6	98	16	0
Strachan	5	91	18	0
Spencer	5	68	14	0
Schmidt	2	54	27	0
Chambers	1	15	15	0

PASSING – PUNTING – KICKING

PASSING	Att	Comp	%	Yds	Yd/Att	TD	Int–%	RK
Manning	338	159	47	1683	5.0	7	20– 6	15
Cipa	37	14	38	182	4.9	1	3– 8	
Scott	17	8	47	96	5.7	0	1– 6	

PUNTING	No	Avg
Blanchard	92	41.0

KICKING	XP	Att	%	FG	Att	%
Szaro	17	17	100	10	16	63

1975 A.F.C. Closing The Marketplace

The World Football League began its second year of play with some impressive new assets. Larry Csonka, Paul Warfield, and Jim Kiick reported to the Memphis club amidst much publicity, Calvin Hill and Ted Kwalick joined the Hawaii team, and John Gilliam played in the Chicago lineup. But other N.F.L. stars such as Kenny Stabler, L.C. Greenwood, and Curly Culp made haste to cancel their future contracts with W.F.L. clubs, and some of last year's stars of the new league, such as Tony Adams and Greg Latta, jumped at the chance to sign with N.F.L. teams. These departing players had taken an accurate reading of the league's pulse, for the massively bad publicity from last season carried over into 1975 and plunged the once-optimistic circuit into a new round of staggering debts and defaulted contracts. On October 22, 11 weeks into its 20-week schedule, the W.F.L. closed its doors and went out of business. Attendance for this second season averaged 13,371 per game and was fading, while new debts accumulated this year totaled up to about $10 million.

EASTERN DIVISION

Baltimore Colts—The Colts seemed headed for another dismal season when they dropped four of their first five games, but they then beat the Jets 45-28 and roared through the rest of the schedule with the momentum of a runaway boulder. New coach Ted Marchibroda found the young talent under his command suddenly jelling into a top-flight unit in mid-season. Quarterback Bert Jones blossomed into one of the N.F.L.'s dangerous young passers, while Lydell Mitchell starred as a runner and receiver out of the backfield. The offensive line, bolstered by All-Pro tackle George Kunz from the Falcons, played far better than expected, and the defensive front four of Fred Cook, John Dutton, Joe Ehrmann, and Mike Barnes sacked quarterbacks with amazing regularity. The turnabout was so sudden that observers had to wonder when Cinderella was going to turn back into a pumpkin. On November 10, the Colts came back from a 21-0 deficit to beat the Bills 42-35. They upset the Dolphins in Miami 33-17 on November 23, and three weeks later climbed into a first-place tie by beating the Dolphins in Baltimore 10-7 in overtime. A 34-21 victory over New England in the final game clinched a playoff spot for the surprise team of the year.

Miami Dolphins—Coach Don Shula had other worries besides the defection of Larry Csonka, Paul Warfield, and Jim Kiick to the W.F.L. Injuries played havoc with his defensive platoon, striking down Dick Anderson, Nick Buoniconti, Bob Heinz, Manny Fernandez, and Bill Stanfill. But Shula managed to plug all the holes, getting good seasons out of odds and ends like Norm Bulaich, Don Nottingham, and Charlie Babb. After beating Buffalo 35-30 on October 26, the Dolphins looked home free for another divisional title. But the Oilers upset them 20-19 on November 16, and the Colts clobbered them 33-17 the next week. But worse than losing the game to the Colts was losing Bob Griese in that contest for the rest of the season with a toe injury. Forty-one year old Earl Morrall played well in leading the Dolphins to a 20-7 decision over New England but hurt his knee in the process. That left third-stringer Don Strock at quarterback. He engineered a 31-21 victory over Buffalo, but the red-hot Colts then took the 10-7 decision in an epic overtime contest. With two losses to the Colts, the Dolphins incredibly found themselves out of the playoffs.

Buffalo Bills—O.J. Simpson had reached the stage where he was in a class only with the greats of the past. Running behind the great Buffalo offensive line, the Juice rushed for 1817 yards and set a new record with 23 touchdowns scored for the season. Quarterback Joe Ferguson found it easier to pass against defenses keying on the running of Simpson and Jim Braxton. The only fly in the ointment was a defensive backfield which was decimated by injuries. After the Bills won five of their first six games, opponents began scoring points as fast as O.J. and company could put them on the board. Midseason losses to the Colts, Bengals, and Dolphins put an end to the playoff hopes for this year.

New York Jets—Two victories in the first three games fueled hopes for the Jets, but the defensive unit suddenly fell to pieces. After the promising start, the Jets lost to the Vikings 29-21, to the Dolphins 43-0, and to the Colts 45-28. Losses to the Bills and Vikings were followed by a 52-19 slaughter at the hands of the Colts, during which two Jets players broke into a fist fight on the sidelines. Coach Charley Winner got the axe and was replaced on an interim basis by Ken Shipp. One victory in five games was all Shipp could coax out of this squad with massive defensive problems and a mediocre season out of Joe Namath.

New England Patriots—The bad vibrations started with the strike in the final week of training camp and carried throughout the season. Jim Plunkett twice separated his shoulder, robbing the attack of leadership right at the start of the campaign. After the second injury, rookie Steve Grogan played so well that fans at Schaeffer Stadium booed Plunkett when he returned to the lineup. Mack Herron symbolized the turnaround in Patriot fortunes. After setting a record last season for total yardage, Herron fell out of favor with coach Chuck Fairbanks, found himself benched, and was waived to Atlanta late in the season.

CENTRAL DIVISION

Pittsburgh Steelers—Despite a 37-0 triumph over San Diego to start the season, the Steelers looked better and better as the campaign wore on. After losing to Buffalo in their second game, the Steelers then tore through the league with 11 straight victories. The Pittsburgh defense smothered enemy attacks week after week, even while losing Joe Greene for a time with neck and groin injuries. Franco Harris led the offense with 1246 yards on the ground, but the performances of Terry Bradshaw, Lynn Swann, and the yeoman line ranked as high in excellence. The Steelers beat back challenges from the Oilers and Bengals to brand themselves the team to beat in the playoffs.

Cincinnati Bengals—Even with All-Pro defensive lineman Mike Reid retired to a career as a pianist, the Bengals had talent enough to threaten the Steelers in the Central Division. Paul Brown's men ran out to six quick wins but then lost 30-24 to the Steelers on November 2 to fall into a first place tie. They then dropped into second place by losing to the Browns the next week. Although they beat back the challenging Oilers 23-9 on November 30, the attempt to recapture first place failed by again bowing to the Steelers 35-14 on December 13. But a 47-17 shellacking of San Diego in the final game clinched a wildcard berth in the playoffs.

Houston Oilers—Bum Phillips thoroughly enjoyed his first year as head coach as the Oilers made a surprise run at a playoff berth. The Oilers won six of their first seven games, but inability to beat either the Steelers or Bengals condemned them to being an exciting also-ran. The defensive front three of Elvin Bethea, Curly Culp, and Tody Smith had new comfort in Robert Brazile, an excellent rookie linebacker. Operating behind a surprisingly strong line, quarterback Dan Pastorini got off lots of passes to Ken Burrough, while Ronnie Coleman and rookie Don Hardeman crunched out the yardage on the ground. The real star of the season, however, was Billy Johnson, a flashy little wide receiver and kick returner whose wobbly-leg victory dance after touchdowns turned on the fans and threatened spiking with extinction.

Cleveland Browns—The Browns had fallen on hardtimes, and the hiring of Forrest Gregg as head coach had no immediate effect on the situation. Nine losses at the start of the campaign horrified fans who had known only success until recently. An upset 35-23 victory over state-rival Cincinnati soothed some of the hurt, but few people would deny that the Browns were weaker at more positions than they were strong. Greg Pruitt and Reggie Rucker stood out as offensive threats among the rubble, while Jerry Sherk and rookie Mack Mitchell worked hard in the defensive line.

WESTERN DIVISION

Oakland Raiders—The depth on the Raiders was such that the second unit could probably have played winning ball in the N.F.L. Despite Jim Otto's retirement and a bad knee which hobbled Kenny Stabler, the Oakland offensive machine rolled on with a strong line, five good running backs, and a complementary set of wide receivers in Cliff Branch and Fred Biletnikoff. The defense had a new recruit in All-Pro linebacker Ted Hendricks who was so strong that Bubba Smith was cut. George Blanda and Ray Guy gave Oakland an edge in kicking, while the specialty teams sparkled with kickoff returner Harold Hart and rookie punt receiver Neal Colzie. As expected, the Raiders easily captured the Western Division crown, but their plans to go all the way through the playoffs to the Super Bowl were soon thwarted by the Steelers.

Denver Broncos—The Broncos opened the season with two victories, but then fell into a rut which sank them below the .500 level. The ground game suffered when Otis Armstrong was injured, although second-year man Jon Keyworth assumed the heavy-duty running chores with some flair. At quarterback, veteran Charley Johnson failed to ignite the offense, lost his job to Steve Ramsey, then broke his collarbone after getting back into the lineup. At the end of this disappointing campaign, Johnson and Denver favorite Floyd Little retired after distinguished careers.

Kansas City Chiefs—New coach Paul Wiggins had to suffer through three straight losses at the start of the schedule, but the 42-10 upset over Oakland on national television got the Chiefs into the win column with a vengeance. The Chiefs did make a long-shot run at a playoff berth before dropping their last four games. Without a long string of injuries, the Chiefs might have stayed in the thick of the race. The offensive line was hurt and then Otis Taylor went out with a bad knee, and both Mickey Livingston and Len Dawson were kayoed with injuries, leaving W.F.L. ex-patriot Tony Adams running the offense at the end. Wiggins could look back on good performances from Willie Lanier, Emmitt Thomas, Jack Rudnay, and Woody Green, and count on better things to come from his spirited squad.

San Diego Chargers—Experts speculated as December began whether the Chargers would complete their schedule at 0-14, the first team ever to reach that mark. With a perfect record of 11 losses, the Chargers beat the Chiefs and ruined their chance at the record book. The Chargers had no offense at all, with the running game wiped out by injuries to Don Woods and Bo Matthews and with quarterbacks Don Fouts and Jesse Freitas unable to ignite any attack. The Chargers presented such a dull show that only 24,349 fans showed up on November 9 to see them lose to New England.

FINAL TEAM STATISTICS

OFFENSE

	BALT.	BUFF.	CIN.	CLEV.	DENV.	HOUS.	K.C.	MIAMI	N.ENG.	N.Y.	OAK.	PITT.	S.D.
FIRST DOWNS:													
Total	266	318	295	247	268	234	261	266	253	266	315	288	198
by Rushing	131	162	107	109	109	121	110	136	94	126	159	149	98
by Passing	114	132	166	114	137	90	128	108	133	111	139	125	89
by Penalty	21	24	22	24	22	23	23	22	26	29	17	14	11
RUSHING:													
Number	536	588	499	440	490	526	487	594	472	501	643	581	434
Yards	2217	2974	1819	1850	1993	2068	1847	2500	1845	2079	2573	2633	1801
Average Yards	4.1	5.1	3.6	4.2	4.1	3.9	3.8	4.2	3.9	4.1	4.0	4.5	4.1
Touchdowns	28	26	20	14	9	14	14	26	14	15	28	22	14
PASSING:													
Attempts	354	354	433	437	427	347	395	279	401	384	350	337	337
Completions	211	182	255	220	210	165	217	170	193	174	196	191	165
Completion Percentage	59.6	51.4	58.9	50.3	49.2	47.6	54.9	60.9	48.1	45.3	56.0	56.7	49.0
Passing Yards	2606	2661	3497	2297	2900	2099	2785	2196	2768	2468	2625	2544	1998
Avg. Yards per Attempt	7.4	7.5	8.1	5.3	7.0	6.0	7.1	7.8	6.9	6.4	7.5	6.7	5.9
Avg. Yards per Complet.	12.4	14.6	13.7	10.4	13.7	12.7	12.8	12.9	14.3	14.2	13.4	13.3	12.1
Times Tackled Passing	38	22	34	38	47	27	53	23	39	34	26	31	50
Yards Lost Passing	325	168	256	340	359	230	425	187	330	317	234	290	388
Net Yards	2281	2493	3241	1957	2541	1869	2360	2009	2438	2151	2391	2254	1610
Touchdowns	19	28	23	7	15	14	15	19	16	16	19	21	7
Interceptions	8	19	14	23	34	17	16	17	28	33	28	12	17
Percent Intercepted	2.3	5.4	3.2	5.3	8.0	4.9	4.1	6.1	7.0	8.6	8.0	3.6	5.0
PUNTS:													
Number	86	61	68	82	63	74	72	65	83	59	68	69	79
Average Distance	39.6	41.6	39.0	40.5	39.9	39.3	39.3	38.6	38.8	36.5	43.8	39.4	36.7
PUNT RETURNS:													
Number	42	33	48	40	41	43	37	43	33	22	58	54	38
Yards	439	278	267	294	570	620	303	509	262	116	688	548	442
Average Yards	10.5	8.4	5.6	7.4	11.5	14.4	8.2	11.8	7.9	5.3	11.9	10.1	11.6
Touchdowns	0	0	0	0	0	3	0	1	0	0	0	0	1
KICKOFF RETURNS:													
Number	52	62	46	67	59	54	62	40	66	74	51	38	69
Yards	1190	1457	1042	1526	1446	1144	1350	949	1250	1704	1324	815	1482
Average Yards	22.9	23.5	22.7	22.8	24.5	21.2	21.8	23.7	23.0	23.0	26.0	21.4	21.5
Touchdowns	0	0	0	0	0	1	0	0	1	0	1	1	0
INTERCEPTION RETURNS:													
Number	29	25	22	10	16	24	20	21	13	15	35	27	20
Yards	493	376	410	107	293	425	388	183	165	98	450	421	223
Average Yards	17.0	15.0	18.6	10.7	18.3	17.7	19.4	8.7	12.7	6.5	12.9	15.6	11.2
Touchdowns	4	2	2	1	1	0	0	0	1	0	0	0	0
PENALTIES:													
Number	80	90	88	85	92	100	82	74	89	99	101	89	84
Yards	760	748	783	851	790	849	658	575	719	799	951	756	705
FUMBLES:													
Number	18	24	31	35	28	28	38	20	43	24	31	34	32
Number Lost	10	15	20	14	14	17	18	9	22	8	20	20	12
POINTS:													
Total	395	420	340	218	254	293	282	357	258	258	375	373	189
PAT Attempts	52	57	45	24	28	34	31	46	33	32	48	46	22
PAT Made	51	51	40	21	23	31	30	40	33	27	44	44	21
FG Attempts	18	16	21	23	29	30	32	16	17	21	21	21	24
FG Made	10	9	10	17	21	18	22	13	9	13	13	17	12
Percent FG Made	55.6	56.3	47.6	73.9	72.4	60.0	68.8	81.3	52.9	61.9	61.9	80.9	50.0
Safeties	1	0	0	1	0	2	0	1	0	0	2	1	0

DEFENSE

	BALT.	BUFF.	CIN.	CLEV.	DENV.	HOUS.	K.C.	MIAMI	N.ENG.	N.Y.	OAK.	PITT.	S.D.
FIRST DOWNS:													
Total	242	300	241	274	247	264	289	224	254	308	242	214	312
by Rushing	101	124	115	124	119	104	149	92	118	155	99	91	154
by Passing	124	151	107	125	106	137	121	113	120	133	113	97	139
by Penalty	17	25	19	25	22	23	19	19	16	20	30	26	19
RUSHING:													
Number	453	480	473	544	526	498	562	443	555	574	475	431	606
Yards	1821	1993	2194	2032	1974	1680	2724	1768	2220	2737	1785	1825	2442
Average Yards	4.0	4.2	4.6	3.7	3.8	3.4	4.8	4.0	4.0	4.8	3.8	4.2	4.0
Touchdowns	17	21	15	21	19	13	24	14	20	25	15	8	21
PASSING:													
Attempts	393	431	389	361	348	409	325	375	368	316	398	396	390
Completions	193	237	175	202	181	235	186	200	213	180	171	183	237
Completion Percentage	49.1	55.0	45.0	56.0	52.0	57.5	57.2	53.3	57.9	57.0	43.0	46.2	60.8
Passing Yards	2317	3355	2001	2889	2245	2800	2703	2335	2515	2860	2318	2194	2719
Avg. Yards per Attempt	5.9	7.6	5.1	8.0	6.5	6.9	8.3	6.2	6.8	9.1	5.8	5.5	7.0
Avg. Yards per Complet.	12.0	14.1	11.4	14.3	12.4	11.9	14.5	11.7	11.8	15.9	13.6	12.0	11.5
Times Tackled Passing	59	30	27	34	27	45	28	40	33	19	55	43	26
Yards Lost Passing	496	275	272	298	213	343	191	314	271	141	474	358	209
Net Yards	1821	3080	1729	2591	2032	2457	2512	2021	2244	2719	1844	1836	2510
Touchdowns	17	25	11	25	14	14	18	9	18	26	14	9	16
Interceptions	29	25	22	10	16	24	20	21	13	15	35	27	20
Percent Intercepted	7.4	5.8	5.7	2.8	4.6	5.9	6.2	5.6	3.5	4.7	8.8	6.8	5.1
PUNTS:													
Number	83	59	77	73	76	73	61	72	77	56	86	90	56
Average Distance	38.6	40.7	40.8	38.5	42.1	41.0	40.7	39.9	39.5	33.7	38.7	40.1	39.8
PUNT RETURNS:													
Number	51	29	42	45	39	47	36	34	42	22	35	36	48
Yards	513	179	386	469	534	356	503	373	513	208	265	199	373
Average Yards	10.1	6.2	9.2	10.4	13.7	7.6	14.0	11.0	12.2	9.5	7.6	5.5	7.8
Touchdowns	0	0	1	0	0	0	0	1	1	1	0	0	0
KICKOFF RETURNS:													
Number	70	64	66	48	57	61	59	65	46	52	68	64	40
Yards	1655	1496	1560	1279	1273	1355	1334	1549	1142	1203	1262	1304	1101
Average Yards	23.6	23.4	23.6	26.6	22.3	22.2	22.6	23.8	24.8	23.1	18.6	20.4	27.5
Touchdowns	1	0	0	1	0	0	0	1	0	0	0	0	0
INTERCEPTION RETURNS:													
Number	8	19	14	23	34	17	16	17	28	33	28	12	17
Yards	111	262	244	340	447	186	179	214	388	538	549	47	171
Average Yards	13.9	13.8	17.4	14.8	13.2	10.9	11.2	12.6	13.9	16.3	19.6	3.9	10.0
Touchdowns	0	0	1	1	1	0	1	1	1	4	2	0	1
PENALTIES:													
Number	79	80	91	89	88	91	99	82	103	93	63	85	81
Yards	700	651	821	735	779	892	934	716	759	798	527	700	686
FUMBLES:													
Number	29	42	40	26	37	38	40	23	31	25	14	22	34
Number Lost	12	20	22	16	16	19	22	9	16	13	6	10	14
POINTS:													
Total	269	355	246	372	307	226	341	222	358	433	255	162	345
PAT Attempts	36	47	30	48	35	27	44	27	42	57	32	19	40
PAT Made	35	46	26	45	34	21	40	25	37	53	30	15	35
FG Attempts	10	16	15	21	28	21	22	20	35	16	20	18	34
FG Made	6	9	12	13	21	13	11	11	23	12	11	11	22
Percent FG Made	60.0	56.3	80.0	61.9	75.0	61.9	50.0	55.0	65.7	75.0	55.0	61.1	64.7
Safeties	0	0	2	0	0	2	2	1	0	1	0	0	2

CONFERENCE PLAYOFFS

December 27, at Pittsburgh (Attendance 49,053)

SCORING

PITTSBURGH	7	0	7	14	— 28
BALTIMORE	0	7	3	0	— 10

First Quarter
Pitt. Harris, 8 yard rush
PAT – Gerela (kick)

Second Quarter
Balt. Doughty, 5 yard pass from Domres PAT – Linhart (kick)

Third Quarter
Balt. Linhart, 21 yard field goal
Pitt. Bleier, 7 yard rush
PAT – Gerela (kick)

Fourth Quarter
Pitt. Bradshaw, 2 yard rush
PAT – Gerela (kick)
Pitt. Russell, 93 yard fumble return
PAT – Gerela (kick)

TEAM STATISTICS

PITT.		BALT.
16	First Downs – Total	10
13	First Downs – Rushing	4
3	First Downs – Passing	4
0	First Downs – Penalty	2
3	Fumbles – Number	2
3	Fumbles – Lost Ball	1
5	Penalties – Number	6
45	Yards Penalized	53
0	Missed Field Goals	0
59	Offensive Plays	68
287	Net Yards	154
4.9	Average Gain	2.3
5	Giveaways	3
3	Takeaways	5
-2	Difference	+2

INDIVIDUAL STATISTICS

PITTSBURGH	No.	Yds.	Avg.	BALTIMORE	No.	Yds.	Avg.
RUSHING							
Harris	27	153	5.7	Mitchell	26	63	2.4
Bleier	12	28	2.3	Domres	4	17	4.3
Bradshaw	3	22	7.3	Olds	5	6	1.2
Collier	1	8	8.0	Jones	2	6	3.0
	43	211	4.9	McCauley	3	3	1.0
				Carr	1	-13	-13.0
					41	82	2.0
RECEIVING							
Lewis	3	65	31.7	Mitchell	4	20	5.0
Swann	2	15	7.5	Doughty	2	63	31.5
Bleier	2	14	7.0	McCauley	1	9	9.0
L. Brown	1	9	9.0	Kennedy	1	8	8.0
	8	103	12.9		8	100	12.5
PUNTING							
Walden	4		39.8	Lee	9		40.1
PUNT RETURNS							
Edwards	2	22	11.0	Stevens	3	30	10.0
Collier	1	17	17.0	Volk	1	0	0.0
D. Brown	1	7	7.0		4	30	7.5
	4	46	11.5				
KICKOFF RETURNS							
D. Brown	2	53	26.5	Laird	4	86	21.5
Harrison	1	21	21.0	McCauley	1	17	17.0
	3	74	24.7		5	103	20.6
INTERCEPTION RETURNS							
Blount	1	20	20.0	Mumphord	2	67	33.5
Ham	1	6	6.0				
	2	26	13.0				

PASSING

PITTSBURGH	Att.	Comp.	Comp. Pct.	Yds.	Int.	Yds/ Att.	Yds/ Comp.	Yards Lost Tackled
Bradshaw	13	8	61.6	103	2	7.9	12.9	3-27
BALTIMORE								
Jones	11	6	54.5	91	0	8.3	11.4	
Domres	11	2	18.1	9	2	0.8	4.5	
	22	8	36.4	100	2	4.5	12.5	5-28

December 28, at Oakland (Attendance 53,039)

SCORING

OAKLAND	3	14	7	7	— 31
CINCINNATI	0	7	7	14	— 28

First Quarter
Oak. Blanda, 27 yard field goal

Second Quarter
Oak. Siani, 9 yard pass from Stabler PAT – Blanda (kick)
Cin. Fritts, 1 yard rush
PAT – Green (kick)
Oak. Moore, 8 yard pass from Stabler PAT – Blanda (kick)

Third Quarter
Oak. Banaszak, 6 yard rush
PAT – Blanda (kick)
Cin. Elliott, 6 yard rush
PAT – Green (kick)

Fourth Quarter
Oak. Casper, 2 yard pass from Stabler PAT – Blanda (kick)
Cin. Joiner, 25 yard pass from Anderson PAT – Green (kick)
Cin. Curtis, 14 yard pass from Anderson PAT – Green (kick)

TEAM STATISTICS

OAK.		CIN.
27	First Downs – Total	17
9	First Downs – Rushing	8
15	First Downs – Passing	6
3	First Downs – Penalty	3
2	Fumbles – Number	1
1	Fumbles – Lost Ball	0
7	Penalties – Number	5
64	Yards Penalized	37
2	Missed Field Goals	0
75	Offensive Plays	57
358	Net Yards	258
4.8	Average Gain	4.5
2	Giveaways	0
0	Takeaways	2
-2	Difference	+2

INDIVIDUAL STATISTICS

OAKLAND	No.	Yds.	Avg.	CINCINNATI	No.	Yds.	Avg.
RUSHING							
C. Davis	16	63	3.9	B. Clark	8	46	5.8
Banaszak	17	62	3.6	Elliott	4	25	6.3
Hubbard	12	33	2.8	Fritts	6	14	2.3
J. Phillips	3	16	5.3	Anderson	3	12	4.0
van Eeghen	1	3	3.0	Johnson	3	0	0.0
Stabler	2	-4	-2.0	Williams	1	0	0.0
	51	173	3.4		25	97	3.9
RECEIVING							
Moore	6	57	9.5	B. Clark	4	38	9.5
Branch	5	89	17.8	Myers	3	67	22.3
Siani	3	35	11.7	Joiner	3	60	20.0
C. Davis	2	16	8.0	Curtis	3	20	6.7
Casper	1	2	2.0	Coslet	2	14	7.0
	17	199	11.7	Elliott	1	9	9.0
				Trumpy	1	-7	-7.0
					17	201	11.8
PUNTING							
Guy	1		38.0	D. Green	6		35.8
PUNT RETURNS							
Colzie	4	64	16.0	Blackwood	1	7	7.0
KICKOFF RETURNS							
C. Davis	4	93	23.3	B. Jackson	2	43	21.5
Hart	1	28	28.0	Elliott	1	18	18.0
	5	121	24.2	Parish	1	10	10.0
					4	71	17.8
INTERCEPTION RETURNS							
none				K. Riley	1	34	34.0

PASSING

OAKLAND	Att.	Comp.	Comp. Pct.	Yds.	Int.	Yds/ Att.	Yds/ Comp.	Yards Lost Tackled
Stabler	23	17	73.9	199	1	8.7	11.7	4-14
CINCINNATI								
Anderson	27	17	63.0	201	0	7.4	11.8	5-40

BALTIMORE COLTS 10-4 Ted Marchibroda

Scores of Each Game		
35	Chicago	7
20	OAKLAND	31
13	Los Angeles	24
31	BUFFALO	38
10	New England	21
45	N.Y. Jets	28
21	CLEVELAND	7
42	Buffalo	35
52	N.Y. JETS	19
33	Miami	17
28	KANSAS CITY	14
21	N.Y. Giants	0
10	MIAMI	7
34	NEW ENGLAND	21

Use Name	Pos.	Hgt	Wgt	Age	Int	Pts
Ed George	OT	6'4"	270	29		
George Kunz	OT	6'5"	266	28		
David Taylor	OT	6'4"	257	25		
Elmer Collett	OG	6'4"	246	30		
Ken Huff	OG	6'4"	260	22		
Robert Pratt	OG	6'3"	248	24		
Bob Van Duyne	OG	6'5"	245	23		
Forrest Blue	C	6'5"	265	29		
Ken Mendenhall	C	6'3"	250	26		
Fred Cook	DE	6'4"	247	23	1	6
John Dutton	DE	6'7"	268	23		
Glenn Robinson	DE	6'6"	236	24		
Mike Barnes	DT	6'6"	260	24		
Joe Ehrmann	DT	6'5"	254	26		
Dave Pear	DT	6'2"	242	22		
Jim Cheyunski	LB	6'2"	220	29	2	
Mike Curtis	LB	6'2"	232	32	1	
Dan Dickel	LB	6'3"	230	23		
Derrel Luce	LB	6'3"	224	22		
Tom MacLeod	LB	6'3"	228	24	1	
Mike Varty	LB	6'1"	225	23		
Stan White	LB	6'1"	220	25	8	6
Bruce Laird	DB	6'	198	25	3	2
Lloyd Mumphord	DB	5'11"	176	28	4	
Nelson Munsey	DB	6'1"	198	27	3	6
Doug Nettles	DB	6'	178	24		
Ray Oldham	DB	6'	190	24	2	
Rick Volk	DB	6'3"	195	30		
Jackie Wallace	DB	6'3"	197	24	4	12
Marty Domres	QB	6'3"	230	28		6
Bert Jones	QB	6'3"	212	23		18
Marshall Johnson	HB	6'1"	190	22		12
Lydell Mitchell	HB	5'11"	195	26		90
Howard Stevens	HB	5'5"	165	25		
Roosevelt Leaks	FB	5'10"	220	22		6
Bill Olds	FB	6'1"	222	24		24
Don McCauley	HB-FB	6'1"	216	26		66
Roger Carr	WR	6'3"	193	23		12
Glenn Doughty	WR	6'2"	202	24		24
Freddie Scott	WR	6'2"	170	23		
Ray Chester	TE	6'3"	236	27		18
Jimmie Kennedy	TE	6'3"	233	23		6
David Lee	K	6'4"	220	31		
Toni Linhart	K	6'	180	33		81

Randy Hall — Foot Injury

MIAMI DOLPHINS 10-4 Don Shula

Scores of Each Game		
21	OAKLAND	31
22	New England	14
31	Green Bay	7
24	PHILADELPHIA	16
43	N.Y. Jets	0
35	Buffalo	30
46	Chicago	13
27	N.Y. JETS	7
19	Houston	20
17	BALTIMORE	33
20	NEW ENGLAND	7
31	BUFFALO	21
7	Baltimore	10
14	DENVER	13

Use Name	Pos.	Hgt	Wgt	Age	Int	Pts
Darryl Carlton	OT	6'6"	260	22		
Norm Evans	OT	6'5"	250	32		
Wayne Moore	OT	6'6"	265	30		
Tom Drougas	OG-OT	6'4"	255	25		
Bob Kuechenberg	OG	6'3"	252	27		
Larry Little	OG	6'1"	265	29		
Ed Newman	OG	6'2"	245	24		
Jim Langer	C	6'2"	253	27		
Vern Den Herder	DE	6'6"	252	26		
Don Reese	DE	6'6"	255	23		2
Bill Stanfill	DE	6'5"	252	28		
Randy Crowder	DT	6'2"	236	23		
Manny Fernandez	DT	6'2"	250	29		
John Andrews	DE-DT	6'6"	250	23		
Rodrigo Barnes (from NE)	LB	6'1"	215	25		
Bruce Elia	LB	6'1"	222	22		
Mike Kolen	LB	6'2"	222	27	1	
Bob Matheson	LB	6'4"	235	30	3	
Earnest Rhone	LB	6'2"	212	22	2	
Doug Swift	LB	6'3"	226	26		
Steve Towle	LB	6'2"	233	21	1	
Charlie Babb	DB	6'	190	25	4	
Tim Foley	DB	6'	194	27		
Barry Hill	DB	6'3"	185	22		
Curtis Johnson	DB	6'2"	196	27	4	
Jake Scott	DB	6'	188	30	6	
Jeris White	DB	5'11"	180	22		
Jim Del Gaizo	QB	6'1"	190	28		
Bob Griese	QB	6'1"	190	30		6
Earl Morrall	QB	6'1"	210	41		
Don Strock	QB	6'5"	216	24		6
Hubert Ginn	HB	5'11"	185	28		
Benny Malone	HB	5'10"	193	23		18
Mercury Morris	HB	5'10"	192	28		24
Larry Seiple	HB	6'	214	30		
Norm Bulaich	FB	6'1"	220	28		60
Don Nottingham	FB	5'10"	210	26		72
Stan Winfrey	FB	5'11"	223	22		
Nat Moore	WR	5'10"	180	23		24
Morris Owens	WR	6'	190	22		
Cotton Speyrer	WR	6'	175	26		
Howard Twilley	WR	5'10"	185	31		24
Freddie Solomon	HB-WR	5'11"	180	22		18
Jim Mandich	TE	6'3"	224	27		24
Jim McFarland	TE	6'5"	225	27		
Andre Tillman	TE	6'5"	230	22		
Garo Yepremian	K	5'8"	175	31		79

Bob Heinz — Knee Injury
Dick Anderson — Knee Injury
Nick Buoniconti — Broken Finger

BUFFALO BILLS 8-6 Lou Saban

Scores of Each Game		
42	N.Y. JETS	14
30	Pittsburgh	21
38	DENVER	10
38	Baltimore	31
14	N.Y. GIANTS	17
30	MIAMI	35
24	N.Y. Jets	23
35	BALTIMORE	42
24	Cincinnati	33
45	NEW ENGLAND	31
32	St. Louis	14
21	Miami	31
34	New England	14
13	MINNESOTA	35

Use Name	Pos.	Hgt	Wgt	Age	Int	Pts
Dave Foley	OT	6'5"	247	27		
Donnie Green	OT	6'7"	252	27		
Halvor Hagen	OT	6'5"	260	28		
Bill Adams	OG	6'2"	246	25		
Joe DeLamielleure	OG	6'3"	248	24		
Reggie McKenzie	OG	6'4"	244	25		
Mike Montler	C	6'4"	245	31		
Willie Parker	C	6'3"	252	26		
Mark Johnson	DE	6'2"	240	22		
Dave Means	DE	6'4"	235	23		
Walt Patulski	DE	6'6"	260	25		
Pat Toomay	DE	6'5"	244	30	1	6
Jeff Winans	DE	6'5"	260	23		
Don Croft	DT	6'3"	260	26		
Earl Edwards	DT	6'6"	254	29		
Mike Kadish	DT	6'5"	270	25		6
Jeff Yeates	DT	6'3"	250	24		
Doug Allen	LB	6'2"	228	23		
Bo Cornell	LB	6'1"	222	26		
Merv Krakau	LB	6'1"	233	24	1	
John McCrumbly	LB	6'1"	245	23		
Bob Nelson	LB	6'4"	232	22		
Tom Ruud	LB	6'3"	223	22		
John Skorupan	LB	6'2"	225	24	1	
Steve Freeman	DB	5'11"	185	22	2	6
Tony Greene	DB	5'10"	170	26	6	
Dwight Harrison	DB	6'1"	186	26	8	
Ed Jones	DB	6'	185	23	3	
Royce McKinney	DB	6'1"	190	21		
Frank Oliver	DB	6'1"	189	23		
Ike Thomas	DB	6'2"	195	27	2	
Joe Ferguson	QB	6'1"	184	25		6
Gary Marangi	QB	6'1"	203	23		
Gary Hayman	HB	6'1"	202	24		
O.J. Simpson	HB	6'2"	212	28		**138**
Jim Braxton	FB	6'2"	242	26		78
Steve Schnarr	FB	6'2"	218	22		
Dan Abramowicz	WR	6'1"	193	30		
Bob Chandler	WR	6'	180	26		36
J. D. Hill	WR	6'1"	185	26		42
John Holland	WR	6'	190	23		6
Vic Washington	DB-WR	5'10"	196	29		
Reuben Gant	TE	6'4"	230	23		12
Paul Seymour	TE	6'5"	246	25		6
Marv Bateman	K	6'4"	214	25		
John Leypoldt	K	6'2"	226	29		78

Robert James — Knee Injury
Doug Jones — Knee Injury
Ahmad Rashad — Knee Injury

NEW ENGLAND PATRIOTS 3-11 Chuck Fairbanks

Scores of Each Game		
0	HOUSTON	7
14	MIAMI	22
7	N.Y. Jets	36
10	Cincinnati	27
21	BALTIMORE	10
24	SAN FRANCISCO	16
17	St. Louis	24
33	San Diego	19
31	DALLAS	34
31	Buffalo	45
7	Miami	20
28	N.Y. JETS	30
14	BUFFALO	34
21	Baltimore	34

Use Name	Pos.	Hgt	Wgt	Age	Int	Pts
Leon Gray	OT	6'3"	256	23		
Shelby Jordan	OT	6'7"	260	23		
Sam Adams	OG	6'3"	252	26		
Steve Corbett	OG	6'4"	248	24		
Bill Du Lac	OG	6'4"	260	24		
John Hannah	OG	6'2"	265	24		
Doug Dumler	C	6'3"	242	24		
Bill Lenkaitis	C	6'3"	250	29		
Julius Adams	DE	6'3"	260	27		
Craig Hanneman	DE	6'3"	245	26		
Mel Lunsford	DE	6'3"	260	25		
Tony McGee	DE	6'4"	245	26		
Martin Imhoff	DE	6'6"	256	25		
Pete Cusick	NT	6'1'	255	22		
Ray Hamilton	NT	6'1"	245	24		6
Jerry Patton	DT	6'3"	255	29		
Dave Tipton (to SD)	DT	6'1"	255	21		
Maury Damkroger	LB	6'2"	230	23		
Bob Geddes	LB	6'2"	240	29		
Sam Hunt	LB	6'1"	240	24		
Steve King	LB	6'4"	230	24		
Steve Nelson	LB	6'2"	230	24	2	
Kevin Reilly	LB	6'2"	220	23	1	
Rod Shoate	LB	6'1"	211	22		
George Webster	LB	6'4"	230	29	1	
Steve Zabel	LB	6'4"	230	27		
Ron Bolton	DB	6'2"	170	25	5	
Dick Conn	DB	6'	185	24		
Bob Howard	DB	6'1"	177	30	3	6
Durwood Keeton	DB	5'10"	180	23		
Jim Massey	DB	5'11"	198	27		
Prentice McCray	DB	6'1"	187	24		
Deac Sanders	DB	6'1"	178	25	1	
Neil Graff	QB	6'3"	200	25		
Steve Grogan	QB	6'4"	200	22		18
Jim Plunkett	QB	6'3"	212	27		6
Don Calhoun (from BUF)	HB	6'	198	23		12
Andy Johnson	HB	6'	204	22		24
Leon McQuay	HB	5'9"	195	25		
Bobby Anderson	FB-HB	6'	208	27		
Allen Carter	FB	5'11"	208	22		6
Sam Cunningham	FB	6'3"	224	25		48
Steve Burks	WR	6'5"	211	22		
Darryl Stingley	WR	6'	195	23		12
Randy Vataha	WR	5'10"	170	26		36
Elmo Wright (from HOU)	WR	6'	190	26		
Russ Francis	TE	6'6"	240	22		24
Bob Windsor	TE	6'4"	225	32		
Mike Patrick	K	6'	213	22		
John Smith	K	6'	185	25		60

Arthur Moore — Knee Injury
Joe Wilson — Ankle Injury
Al Marshall — Knee Injury
Tom Neville — Broken Leg
Leon Crosswhite — Foot Injury

NEW YORK JETS 3-11 Charley Winner Ken Shipp

Scores of Each Game		
14	Buffalo	42
30	Kansas City	24
36	NEW ENGLAND	7
21	Minnesota	29
0	MIAMI	43
28	BALTIMORE	45
23	BUFFALO	24
7	Miami	27
19	Baltimore	52
6	ST. LOUIS	37
7	PITTSBURGH	20
30	New England	28
16	San Diego	24
21	DALLAS	31

Use Name	Pos.	Hgt	Wgt	Age	Int	Pts
Gordie Browne	OT	6'5"	265	23		
Winston Hill	OT	6'4"	280	33		
Robert Woods	OT	6'3"	255	25		
Garry Puetz	OG	6'3"	265	23		
Randy Rasmussen	OG	6'2"	267	30		
Darrell Austin	OT-OG	6'4"	250	23		
Wayne Mulligan	C	6'2"	250	28		
Joe Fields	OG-C	6'2"	240	21		
Richard Neal	DE	6'3"	260	27		
Billy Newsome	DE	6'4"	246	27		
Jim Bailey	DT	6'4"	255	27	1	
Carl Barzilauskas	DT	6'6"	280	24		
Ed Galigher	DT	6'4"	253	24		
Larry Woods	DT	6'6"	270	27		
Ken Bernich	LB	6'2"	250	23		
John Ebersole	LB	6'3"	227	26	2	
Rich Lewis	LB	6'3"	215	25		
Steve Reese	LB	6'2"	232	23		
Jamie Rivers	LB	6'2"	245	29		
Godwin Turk	LB	6'3"	230	24	2	
Richard Wood	LB	6'2"	215	22		
Carl Capria	DB	6'3"	185	23		
Jerry Davis	DB	5'11"	182	24		
George Hoey (from DEN)	DB	5'10"	180	28		
Delles Howell	DB	6'3"	200	28	2	
Burgess Owens	DB	6'2"	200	24	3	
Bob Prout	DB	6'1"	183	24	1	
Rich Sowells	DB	6'	180	26	1	
Ed Taylor	DB	6'	170	22		
Donnie Walker	DB	6'1"	180	24		
Phil Wise	DB	6'	190	26	2	
Roscoe Word	DB	5'11"	170	22	1	
John Jones	QB	6'1"	180	23		
Joe Namath	QB	6'2"	200	32		
Emerson Boozer	HB	5'11"	205	32		6
Carl Garrett	HB	5'11"	205	28		36
Bob Gresham	HB	5'11"	195	27		6
Jazz Jackson	HB	5'8"	167	23		
John Riggins	FB	6'2"	225	26		54
Steve Davis	HB-FB	6'1"	218	25		6
Jerome Barkum	WR	6'3"	212	25		30
Eddie Bell	WR	5'10"	160	27		24
David Knight	WR	6'1"	175	24		
Lou Piccone	WR	5'9"	175	26		
Willie Brister	TE	6'4"	236	23		6
Rich Caster	TE	6'5"	228	26		24
Greg Gantt	K	5'11"	188	23		
Pat Leahy	K	6'	200	24		66

Al Atkinson — Knee Injury
Mark Lomas — Foot Injury
Steve Tannen — Shoulder Injury
Al Woodall — Knee Injury

BALTIMORE COLTS

Rushing

Last Name	No.	Yds	Avg	TD
Mitchell	289	1193	4.1	11
Jones	47	321	6.8	3
Olds	94	281	3.0	2
McCauley	60	196	3.3	10
Leaks	41	175	4.3	1
Domres	4	46	11.5	1
Doughty	1	5	5.0	0

Receiving

Last Name	No.	Yds	Avg	TD
Mitchell	60	544	9	4
Doughty	39	666	17	4
Chester	38	457	12	3
Olds	30	194	7	2
Carr	23	517	23	2
McCauley	14	93	7	1
Johnson	4	115	29	2
Kennedy	2	15	8	1
Leaks	1	5	5	0

Punt Returns

Last Name	No.	Yds	Avg	TD
Stevens	36	396	11	0
Wallace	6	43	7	0

Kickoff Returns

Last Name	No.	Yds	Avg	TD
Laird	31	799	26	0
Johnson	7	134	19	0
McCauley	4	86	22	0
Stevens	3	71	24	0
Pratt	4	64	16	0
Kennedy	2	36	18	0
Wallace	1	0	0	0

Passing – Punting – Kicking

PASSING	Att	Comp	%	Yds	Yd/Att	TD	Int–%	RK
Jones	344	203	59	2483	7.2	18	8– 2	3
Domres	10	8	80	123	12.3	1	0– 0	

PUNTING	No	Avg
Lee	86	39.6

KICKING	XP	Att	%	FG	Att	%
Linhart	51	52	98	10	18	56

MIAMI DOLPHINS

Rushing

Last Name	No.	Yds	Avg	TD
Morris	219	875	4.0	4
Nottingham	168	718	4.3	12
Bulaich	78	309	4.0	5
Malone	65	220	3.4	3
Solomon	4	87	21.8	0
Ginn	21	78	3.7	0
Moore	8	69	8.6	0
Griese	17	59	3.5	1
Strock	6	38	6.3	1
Morrall	4	33	8.3	0
Winfrey	3	10	3.3	0
Seiple	1	4	4.0	0

Receiving

Last Name	No.	Yds	Avg	TD
Moore	40	705	18	4
Bulaich	32	276	9	5
Twilley	24	366	15	4
Solomon	22	339	15	2
Mandich	21	217	10	4
Seiple	10	84	8	0
Nottingham	9	66	7	0
Tillman	5	60	12	0
Ginn	3	21	7	0
Malone	2	47	24	0
Morris	2	15	8	0

Punt Returns

Last Name	No.	Yds	Avg	TD
Solomon	26	320	12	1
Babb	7	95	14	0
Moore	8	80	10	0
Scott	1	10	10	0
Ginn	1	4	4	0

Kickoff Returns

Last Name	No.	Yds	Avg	TD
Solomon	17	348	21	0
Moore	9	243	27	0
Ginn	9	235	26	0
Nottingham	3	80	27	0
Winfrey	1	25	25	0
Malone	1	18	18	0

Passing – Punting – Kicking

PASSING	Att	Comp	%	Yds	Yd/Att	TD	Int–%	RK
Griese	191	118	62	1693	8.9	14	13– 7	5
Strock	45	26	58	230	5.1	2	2– 4	
Morrall	43	26	61	273	6.4	3	2– 5	

PUNTING	No	Avg
Seiple	65	38.6

KICKING	XP	Att	%	FG	Att	%
Yepremian	40	46	87	13	16	81

BUFFALO BILLS

Rushing

Last Name	No.	Yds	Avg	TD
Simpson	329	1817	5.5	16
Braxton	186	823	4.4	9
Ferguson	23	82	3.6	1
Marangi	7	78	11.1	0
Washington	9	49	5.4	0
Hayman	10	30	3.0	0
Haslerig	2	9	4.5	0
Chandler	2	5	2.5	0
Hill	1	1	1.0	0

Receiving

Last Name	No.	Yds	Avg	TD
Chandler	55	746	14	6
Hill	36	667	19	7
Simpson	28	426	15	7
Braxton	26	282	11	4
Seymour	19	268	14	1
Gant	9	107	12	2
Holland	7	144	21	1
Washington	2	21	11	0

Punt Returns

Last Name	No.	Yds	Avg	TD
Hayman	25	216	9	0
Holland	7	53	8	0
Jones	1	9	9	0

Kickoff Returns

Last Name	No.	Yds	Avg	TD
Washington	35	923	26	0
Hayman	8	179	22	0
McKinney	6	151	25	0
Schnarr	4	80	20	0
Holland	4	67	17	0
Cornell	3	38	13	0
McKenzie	1	15	15	0
Ruud	1	4	4	0

Passing – Punting – Kicking

PASSING	Att	Comp	%	Yds	Yd/Att	TD	Int–%	RK
Ferguson	321	169	53	2426	7.6	25	17– 5	6
Marangi	33	13	39	235	7.1	3	2– 6	

PUNTING	No	Avg
Bateman	61	41.6

KICKING	XP	Att	%	FG	Att	%
Leypoldt	51	57	89	9	16	56

NEW ENGLAND PATRIOTS

Rushing

Last Name	No.	Yds	Avg	TD
Cunningham	169	666	3.9	6
Johnson	117	488	4.2	3
Calhoun	42	184	4.4	1
Grogan	30	110	3.7	3
Carter	22	95	4.3	0
McQuay	33	47	1.4	0
Stingley	6	39	6.5	0
Plunkett	4	7	1.8	1
Vataha	1	4	4.0	0
Graff	2	2	1.0	0
Anderson	1	1	1.0	0

Receiving

Last Name	No.	Yds	Avg	TD
Vataha	46	720	16	6
Francis	35	636	18	4
Cunningham	32	253	8	2
Johnson	26	294	11	1
Stingley	21	378	18	2
Burks	6	158	26	0
Windsor	6	57	10	0
Calhoun	5	111	22	1
Wright	4	46	12	0
McQuay	4	27	7	0
Carter	2	39	20	0

Punt Returns

Last Name	No.	Yds	Avg	TD
Stingley	15	113	8	0
Johnson	6	60	10	0

Kickoff Returns

Last Name	No.	Yds	Avg	TD
Carter	32	879	28	1
McQuay	15	252	17	0
Johnson	10	188	19	0
Burks	4	65	16	0
Stingley	2	44	22	0
Calhoun	1	17	17	0

Passing – Punting – Kicking

PASSING	Att	Comp	%	Yds	Yd/Att	TD	Int–%	RK
Grogan	274	139	51	1976	7.2	11	18– 7	11
Plunkett	92	36	39	571	6.2	3	7– 8	
Graff	35	18	51	221	6.3	2	3– 9	

PUNTING	No	Avg
Patrick	83	38.8

KICKING	XP	Att	%	FG	Att	%
Smith	33	33	100	9	17	53

NEW YORK JETS

Rushing

Last Name	No.	Yds	Avg	TD
Riggins	238	1005	4.2	8
Garrett	122	566	4.6	5
S. Davis	70	290	4.1	1
Gresham	25	98	3.9	1
Jones	9	59	6.6	0
Boozer	20	51	2.6	0
Jackson	6	11	1.8	0
Namath	10	6	0.6	0
Barkum	1	−7	−7.0	0

Receiving

Last Name	No.	Yds	Avg	TD
Caster	47	820	17	4
Barkum	36	549	15	5
Riggins	30	363	12	1
Bell	20	344	17	4
Garrett	19	180	10	1
Piccone	7	79	11	0
S. Davis	6	56	9	0
Jackson	5	54	11	0
Gresham	2	4	2	0
Boozer	1	16	16	1
Brister	1	3	3	0

Punt Returns

Last Name	No.	Yds	Avg	TD
Piccone	18	74	4	0
Bell	2	42	21	0
Jackson	1	0	0	0
Sowells	1	0	0	0

Kickoff Returns

Last Name	No.	Yds	Avg	TD
Piccone	26	637	25	0
S. Davis	20	483	24	0
Garrett	7	159	23	0
Gresham	7	153	22	0
Taylor	7	151	22	0
Wood	3	27	9	0
Jackson	2	52	26	0
Word	1	22	22	0
Wise	1	20	20	0

Passing – Punting – Kicking

PASSING	Att	Comp	%	Yds	Yd/Att	TD	Int–%	RK
Namath	326	157	48	2286	7.0	15	28– 9	13
Jones	57	16	28	181	3.2	1	5– 9	
Gantt	1	1	100	1	1.0	0	0– 0	

PUNTING	No	Avg
Gantt	59	36.5

KICKING	XP	Att	%	FG	Att	%
Leahy	27	30	90	13	21	62

PITTSBURGH STEELERS 12-2 Chuck Noll

Scores of Each Game		
37	San Diego	0
21	BUFFALO	30
42	Cleveland	6
20	DENVER	9
34	CHICAGO	3
16	Green Bay	13
30	Cincinnati	24
24	HOUSTON	17
28	KANSAS CITY	3
32	Houston	9
20	N.Y. Jets	7
31	CLEVELAND	17
35	CINCINNATI	14
3	Los Angeles	10

Use Name	Pos.	Hgt	Wgt	Age	Int	Pts
Gordon Gravelle	OT	6'5"	255	26		
Jon Kolb	OT	6'2"	262	28		
Dave Reavis	OT	6'5"	254	25		
Sam Davis	OG	6'1"	250	31		
Gerry Mullins	OT-OG	6'3"	240	26		6
Jim Clack	C-OG	6'3"	250	27		
Ray Mansfield	C	6'3"	260	34		
Mike Webster	OG-C	6'1"	245	23		
John Banaszak	DE	6'3"	232	25		
L. C. Greenwood	DE	6'5"	245	28		
Dwight White	DE	6'4"	255	26		2
Joe Greene	DT	6'4"	275	28		
Ernie Holmes	DT	6'3"	260	27		
Steve Furness	DE-DT	6'4"	255	25		
Ed Bradley	LB	6'2"	232	25		
Jack Ham	LB	6'3"	225	26	1	
Marv Kellum	LB	6'2"	225	23		
Jack Lambert	LB	6'4"	220	23	2	
Andy Russell	LB	6'3"	220	33		
Loren Toews	LB	6'3"	222	23		
Jimmy Allen	DB	6'2"	194	23	2	
Mel Blount	DB	6'3"	200	27	11	
Dave Brown	DB	6'1"	200	22		
Glen Edwards	DB	6'1"	185	28	3	
Donnie Shell	DB	5'11"	195	23	1	
J. T. Thomas	DB	6'2"	196	24	3	6
Mike Wagner	DB	6'1"	210	26	4	
Terry Bradshaw	QB	6'3"	210	26		18
Joe Gilliam	QB	6'2"	187	24		
Terry Hanratty	QB	6'1"	205	27		
Rocky Bleier	HB	5'11"	210	29		12
Mike Collier	HB	5'11"	200	21		24
John Fuqua	HB	5'11"	200	28		6
Franco Harris	FB	6'2"	230	25		66
Reggie Harrison	FB	5'11"	215	25		18
Reggie Garrett	WR	6'1"	175	23		6
Frank Lewis	WR	6'1"	196	28		12
John Stallworth	WR	6'2"	185	23		24
Lynn Swann	WR	5'10"	180	23		66
Larry Brown	TE	6'4"	230	26		6
Randy Grossman	TE	6'1"	215	21		6
Roy Gerela	K	5'10"	190	27		95
Bobby Walden	K	6'	197	37		

CINCINNATI BENGALS 11-3 Paul Brown

Scores of Each Game		
24	CLEVELAND	17
21	New Orleans	0
21	Houston	19
27	NEW ENGLAND	10
14	OAKLAND	10
21	Atlanta	14
24	PITTSBURGH	30
17	Denver	16
33	BUFFALO	24
23	Cleveland	35
23	HOUSTON	19
31	Philadelphia	0
14	Pittsburgh	35
47	SAN DIEGO	17

Use Name	Pos.	Hgt	Wgt	Age	Int	Pts
Vern Holland	OT	6'5"	268	27		
Al Krevis	OT	6'6"	263	23		
Rufus Mayes	OT	6'5"	265	27		
Howard Fest	OG	6'6"	262	29		
Dave Lapham	OG	6'3"	258	23		
John Shinners	OG	6'2"	255	28		
Bob Johnson	C	6'5"	255	29		
Ken Johnson	DE	6'5"	260	28		
Sherman White	DE	6'5"	250	26		
Bob Brown	DT	6'5"	290	35		
Ron Carpenter	DT	6'4"	260	27		
Bill Kollar	DT	6'3"	250	22		
Baldy Moore	DT	6'5"	265	29		
Al Beauchamp	LB	6'2"	232	31		
Glenn Cameron	LB	6'2"	230	22		
Brad Cousino	LB	6'	220	22		
Chris Devlin	LB	6'2"	221	21		
Bo Harris	LB	6'3"	230	22		
Jim LeClair	LB	6'2"	235	24	3	
Ron Pritchard	LB	6'1"	230	28		
Lyle Blackwood	DB	6'	192	24	2	
Tommy Casanova	DB	6'2"	195	25		
Marvin Cobb	DB	6'	185	22	4	6
Ricky Davis	DB	6'1"	182	22	1	
Bernie Jackson	DB	6'	178	25	5	
Lemar Parrish	DB	5'11"	185	27	1	
Ken Riley	DB	6'	182	28	6	6
Ken Anderson	QB	6'1"	211	26		12
John Reaves	QB	6'3"	210	25		12
Lenvil Elliott	HB	6'	205	24		24
Stan Fritts	HB	6'1"	215	22		60
Essex Johnson	HB	5'9"	200	28		12
Booby Clark	FB	6'2"	245	24		24
Harold Henson	FB	6'3"	240	22		
Ed Williams	FB	6'2"	245	25		18
Isaac Curtis	WR	6'	193	24		42
Charlie Joiner	WR	5'11"	189	27		30
Chip Myers	WR	6'4"	205	30		18
John McDaniel	WR	6'1"	193	23		
Bruce Coslet	TE	6'3"	227	29		
Jack Novak	TE	6'4"	242	22		
Bob Trumpy	TE	6'6"	228	30		6
Dave Green	K	5'11"	208	25		70

Royce Berry — Dislocated Wrist

Charlie Davis — Knee Injury

HOUSTON OILERS 10-4 Bum Phillips

Scores of Each Game		
7	New England	0
33	SAN DIEGO	17
19	CINCINNATI	21
40	Cleveland	10
13	WASHINGTON	17
24	DETROIT	8
17	Kansas City	13
17	Pittsburgh	24
20	MIAMI	19
9	PITTSBURGH	32
19	Cincinnati	23
27	San Francisco	13
27	Oakland	26
21	CLEVELAND	10

Use Name	Pos.	Hgt	Wgt	Age	Int	Pts
Elbert Drungo	OT	6'5"	265	32		
Kevin Hunt	OT	6'5"	260	26		
Greg Sampson	OT	6'6"	270	24		
Ed Fisher	OG	6'3"	245	26		
Conway Hayman	OG	6'3"	262	22		
Ron Saul	OG	6'2"	250	27		
Fred Hoaglin	C	6'4"	250	31		
Carl Mauck	C	6'3"	248	30		
Curley Culp	DG	6'1"	265	29	6	
Elvin Bethea	DE	6'3"	250	29	2	
Tody Smith	DE	6'5"	250	26		
Jim White	DE	6'3"	255	26		
Bubba Smith	DT-DE	6'7"	265	30		
John Little	DE-DT	6'3"	250	28		
Duane Benson	LB	6'2"	220	30		
Gregg Bingham	LB	6'1"	230	24	4	
Robert Brazile	LB	6'4"	235	22		
Ralph Cindrich	LB	6'1"	230	25		
Steve Kiner	LB	6'	220	28	2	
Guy Roberts	LB	6'1"	220	25		
Ted Thompson	LB	6'1"	215	22		
Ted Washington	LB	6'1"	240	25	3	
Willie Alexander	DB	6'2"	190	25	3	
Bob Atkins	DB	6'3"	210	29	4	
Mark Cotney	DB	5'11"	200	23		
Willie Germany	DB	6'	192	26	2	6
Zeke Moore	DB	6'2"	197	31	5	
Greg Stemrick	DB	5'11"	185	23		
C. L. Whittington	DB	6'1"	200	23	1	
Lynn Dickey	QB	6'4"	210	25		
Dan Pastorini	QB	6'3"	205	26		6
Ronnie Coleman	HB	5'10"	195	24		30
Willie Rogers	HB	6'	210	26		8
Don Hardeman	FB	6'2"	235	23		30
Robert Holmes	FB	5'9"	220	29		
Fred Willis	FB	6'	205	27		12
Jim Beirne	WR	6'2"	206	28		
Ken Burrough	WR	6'4"	210	27		48
Emmett Edwards	WR	6'1"	187	23		
Nate Hawkins	WR	6'1"	190	25		
Billy Johnson	WR	5'9"	170	23		30
Billy Parks	WR	6'1"	190	27		
Mack Alston	TE	6'2"	230	28		24
Willie Frazier	TE	6'4"	235	32		
John Sawyer	TE	6'2"	230	22		6
Skip Butler	K	6'2"	200	27		85

Ronnie Carroll — Injury
Al Johnson — Ankle Injury
Lee Thomas — Injury

CLEVELAND BROWNS 3-11 Forrest Gregg

Scores of Each Game		
17	Cincinnati	24
10	MINNESOTA	42
6	PITTSBURGH	42
10	HOUSTON	40
15	Denver	16
7	WASHINGTON	23
7	Baltimore	21
10	Detroit	21
17	Oakland	38
35	CINCINNATI	23
17	NEW ORLEANS	16
17	Pittsburgh	31
40	KANSAS CITY	14
10	Houston	21

Use Name	Pos.	Hgt	Wgt	Age	Int	Pts
Barry Darrow	OT	6'7"	260	25		
Doug Dieken	OT	6'5"	252	26		
Robert Jackson	OT	6'5"	245	22		
Gerry Sullivan	OT	6'4"	250	23		
Chuck Hutchison	OG	6'3"	250	26		
Bob McKay	OG	6'5"	265	27		
Tom DeLeone	C	6'2"	248	25		
John Demarie	C	6'3"	248	30		
Joe Jones (from PHI)	DE	6'6"	250	27		
Ron East	DE	6'4"	250	32		
Mack Mitchell	DE	6'7"	245	23		
Carl Barisich	DT	6'4"	255	24		
Walter Johnson	DT	6'3"	265	32		
Jerry Sherk	DT	6'4"	250	27		
Dick Ambrose	LB	6'	235	22		
Bob Babich	LB	6'2"	230	28		
John Garlington	LB	6'1"	220	29		
Dave Graf	LB	6'2"	215	22	1	
Charlie Hall	LB	6'3"	230	26	2	6
Jack LeVeck	LB	6'	225	25		
Neal Craig	DB	6'1"	190	27	1	
Van Green	DB	6'1"	192	24	1	
Jim Hill	DB	6'2"	195	28	1	6
Tony Peters	DB	6'1"	192	22	1	
John Pitts (from DEN)	DB	6'4"	218	30	1	
Clarence Scott	DB	6'	180	26	2	
Will Cureton	QB	6'3"	200	25		
Mike Phipps	QB	6'2"	205	27		
Brian Sipe	QB	6'1"	190	26		
Ken Brown	HB	5'10"	203	29		6
Cleo Miller (from KC)	HB	5'11"	202	23		6
Larry Poole	HB	6'	195	23		
Greg Pruitt	HB	5'10"	190	24		54
Henry Hynoski	FB	6'	210	22		
Hugh McKinnis	FB	6'	220	27		24
Billy Pritchett	FB	6'3"	230	24		
Steve Holden	WR	6'	194	24		
Billy Lefear	WR	5'11"	197	25		
Willie Miller	WR	5'9"	172	28		6
Reggie Rucker	WR	6'2"	190	27		18
Milt Morin	TE	6'4"	240	33		
Garry Parris	TE	6'2"	226	25		
Oscar Roan	TE	6'6"	214	28		18
Don Cockroft	K	6'1"	195	30		72

Pete Adams — Knee Injury
Thom Darden — Knee Injury

PITTSBURGH STEELERS

Rushing

Last Name	No.	Yds	Avg	TD
Harris	262	1246	4.8	10
Bleier	140	528	3.8	2
Fuqua	74	285	3.9	1
Bradshaw	35	210	6.0	3
Harrison	43	191	4.4	3
Collier	21	124	5.9	3
Lewis	2	36	18.0	0
Swann	3	13	4.3	0
Hanratty	1	0	0.0	0

Receiving

Last Name	No.	Yds	Avg	TD
Swann	49	781	16	11
Harris	28	214	8	1
Stallworth	20	423	21	4
Fuqua	18	146	8	0
Lewis	17	308	18	2
L. Brown	16	244	15	1
Bleier	15	65	4	0
Garrett	13	178	14	1
Grossman	11	135	12	1
Shell	2	39	20	0
Collier	1	7	7	0
Harrison	1	4	4	0

Punt Returns

Last Name	No.	Yds	Avg	TD
Edwards	25	267	11	0
D. Brown	22	217	10	0
Swann	7	64	9	0

Kickoff Returns

Last Name	No.	Yds	Avg	TD
Collier	22	523	24	1
Blount	8	139	17	0
D. Brown	6	126	21	0
Harris	1	27	27	0
Fuqua	1	0	0	0

Passing – Punting – Kicking

PASSING	Att	Comp	%	Yds	Yd/Att	TD	Int–%	RK
Bradshaw	286	165	58	2055	7.2	18	9– 3	4
Gilliam	48	24	50	450	9.4	3	3– 6	
Walden	3	2	67	39	13.0	0	0– 0	

PUNTING	No	Avg
Walden	69	39.4

KICKING	XP	Att	%	FG	Att	%
Gerela	44	46	96	17	21	81

CINCINNATI BENGALS

Rushing

Last Name	No.	Yds	Avg	TD
Clark	167	594	3.6	4
Fritts	94	375	4.0	8
Elliott	71	308	4.3	1
Anderson	49	188	3.8	2
E. Johnson	58	177	3.1	1
Williams	35	136	3.9	2
Henson	11	38	3.5	0
Reaves	6	13	2.2	0
Coslet	1	1	1.0	0
McDaniel	1	–2	–2.0	0
Curtis	6	–9	–1.5	0

Receiving

Last Name	No.	Yds	Avg	TD
Curtis	44	934	21	7
Clark	42	334	8	0
Joiner	37	726	20	5
Myers	36	527	15	3
E. Johnson	25	196	8	1
Trumpy	22	276	13	1
Elliott	20	196	10	3
Coslet	10	117	12	0
Williams	10	96	10	1
Fritts	6	63	11	2
Novak	2	34	17	0
Hensen	1	–2	–2	0

Punt Returns

Last Name	No.	Yds	Avg	TD
Blackwood	23	123	5	0
Parrish	13	83	6	0
Casanova	11	60	6	0
Cobb	1	1	1	0

Kickoff Returns

Last Name	No.	Yds	Avg	TD
Jackson	25	587	24	0
Elliott	13	272	21	0
Parrish	4	114	29	0
McDaniel	3	69	23	0
Cobb	1	0	0	0
Cousino	1	0	0	0

Passing – Punting – Kicking

PASSING	Att	Comp	%	Yds	Yd/Att	TD	Int–%	RK
Anderson	377	228	61	3169	8.4	21	11– 3	1
Reaves	51	25	49	297	5.8	2	3– 6	
Fritts	4	2	50	31	7.8	0	0– 0	
Green	1	0	0	0	0.0	0	0– 0	

PUNTING	No	Avg
Green	68	39.0

KICKING	XP	Att	%	FG	Att	%
Green	40	45	89	10	21	48

HOUSTON OILERS

Rushing

Last Name	No.	Yds	Avg	TD
Coleman	175	790	4.5	5
Hardeman	166	648	3.9	5
Willis	118	420	3.6	2
Pastorini	23	97	4.2	1
Rodgers	18	55	3.1	1
Holmes	19	42	2.2	0
Johnson	5	17	3.4	0
Dickey	1	3	3.0	0
Edwards	1	–4	–4.0	0

Receiving

Last Name	No.	Yds	Avg	TD
Burrough	53	1063	20	8
Johnson	37	393	11	1
Willis	20	104	5	0
Alston	18	165	9	4
Coleman	18	129	7	0
Sawyer	7	144	21	1
Hardeman	5	10	2	0
Edwards	2	22	11	0
Hawkins	1	32	32	0
Beirne	1	15	15	0
Frazier	1	9	9	0
Parks	1	8	8	0
Holmes	1	5	5	0

Punt Returns

Last Name	No.	Yds	Avg	TD
Johnson	40	612	15	3
Cotney	2	8	4	0
Coleman	1	0	0	0

Kickoff Returns

Last Name	No.	Yds	Avg	TD
Johnson	33	798	24	1
Cotney	10	189	19	0
Coleman	8	149	19	0
Rodgers	1	13	13	0
Whittington	1	0	0	0
Thompson	1	–5	–5	0

Passing – Punting – Kicking

PASSING	Att	Comp	%	Yds	Yd/Att	TD	Int–%	RK
Pastorini	342	163	48	2053	6.0	14	16– 5	10
Dickey	4	2	50	46	11.5	0	1–25	
Coleman	1	0	0	0	0.0	0	0– 0	

PUNTING	No	Avg
Pastorini	62	39.5

KICKING	XP	Att	%	FG	Att	%
Butler	31	34	91	18	30	60

CLEVELAND BROWNS

Rushing

Last Name	No.	Yds	Avg	TD
Pruitt	217	1067	4.9	8
McKinnis	71	259	3.6	4
Pritchett	75	199	2.7	0
Poole	17	114	6.7	0
Phipps	18	70	3.9	0
Sipe	9	60	6.7	0
K. Brown	16	45	2.8	1
Hynoski	7	38	5.4	0
C. Miller	13	23	1.8	1
Cureton	1	1	1.0	0
W. Miller	1	–2	–2.0	0
Holden	2	–4	–2.0	0

Receiving

Last Name	No.	Yds	Avg	TD
Rucker	60	770	13	3
Pruitt	44	299	7	1
Roan	41	463	11	3
Holden	21	320	15	0
McKinnis	17	155	9	0
Pritchett	16	109	7	0
W. Miller	7	57	8	0
Hynoski	4	31	8	0
Brown	2	23	12	0
C. Miller	2	20	10	0
Morin	1	19	19	0
Lefear	1	14	14	0
Parris	1	12	12	0
Poole	1	5	5	0
Craig	1	1	1	0
Green	1	–1	–1	0

Punt Returns

Last Name	No.	Yds	Avg	TD
Pruitt	13	130	10	0
W. Miller	10	47	5	0
Poole	6	35	6	0
Hynoski	2	16	8	0
Lefear	1	14	14	0
Green	1	0	0	0

Kickoff Returns

Last Name	No.	Yds	Avg	TD
Lefear	13	412	32	0
Pruitt	14	302	22	0
C. Miller	12	241	20	0
Hynoski	8	194	24	0
K. Brown	7	126	18	0
W. Miller	4	94	24	0
Poole	2	65	33	0
McKinnis	3	39	13	0
Ambrose	1	3	3	0

Passing – Punting – Kicking

PASSING	Att	Comp	%	Yds	Yd/Att	TD	Int–%	RK
Phipps	313	162	52	1749	5.6	4	19– 6	14
Sipe	88	45	51	427	4.9	1	3– 3	
Cureton	32	10	31	95	3.0	1	1– 3	
Cockroft	2	2	100	0	0.0	0	0– 0	
Hynoski	1	0	0	0	0.0	0	0– 0	
W. Miller	1	1	100	26	26.0	1	0– 0	

PUNTING	No	Avg
Cockroft	82	40.5

KICKING	XP	Att	%	FG	Att	%
Cockroft	21	24	88	17	23	74

OAKLAND RAIDERS 11-3 John Madden

Scores of Each Game		
31	Miami	21
31	Baltimore	20
6	San Diego	0
10	KANSAS CITY	42
10	Cincinnati	14
25	SAN DIEGO	0
42	Denver	17
48	NEW ORLEANS	10
38	CLEVELAND	17
26	Washington	*23
37	ATLANTA	*34
17	DENVER	10
26	Houston	27
28	Kansas City	20

Use Name	Pos.	Hgt	Wgt	Age	Int	Pts
Henry Lawrence	OT	6'4"	278	23		
Art Shell	OT	6'5"	265	28		
John Vella	OT	6'4"	260	25		
George Buehler	OG	6'2"	270	28		
Dan Medlin	OG	6'3"	252	25		
Gene Upshaw	OG	6'5"	255	30		
Dave Dalby	C	6'2"	250	24		
Steve Sylvester	OG-C	6'4"	262	22		
Tony Cline	DE	6'2"	244	27		
Horace Jones	DE	6'3"	260	26		
Dave Rowe (from SD)	DT	6'6"	270	30		
Kelvin Korver	DT	6'6"	270	26		
Otis Sistrunk	DT	6'3"	273	27		
Art Thoms	DT	6'5"	250	28	1	

Use Name	Pos.	Hgt	Wgt	Age	Int	Pts
Mike Dennery	LB	6'	226	25		
Willie Hall	LB	6'2"	220	25		2
Ted Hendricks	LB	6'7"	220	27	2	2
Gerald Irons	LB	6'2"	236	28	1	
Monte Johnson	LB	6'4"	240	23	1	
Phil Villapiano	LB	6'1"	222	26	2	
Butch Atkinson	DB	6'1"	210	34	4	
Willie Brown	DB	6'1"	210	34	4	
Neal Colzie	DB	6'2"	205	22	4	
Charlie Phillips	DB	6'2"	215	22	6	
Jack Tatum	DB	5'10"	206	26	4	
Skip Thomas	DB	6'1"	205	25	6	

Use Name	Pos.	Hgt	Wgt	Age	Int	Pts
George Blanda	QB	6'2"	215	47		83
Pete Beathard	QB	6'2"	205	33		
David Humm	QB	6'2"	184	23		
Larry Lawrence	QB	6'1"	208	26		
Ken Stabler	QB	6'3"	215	29		
Pete Banaszak	HB	5'11"	210	31		96
Louis Carter	HB	5'11"	200	22		
Clarence Davis	HB	5'10"	195	26		30
Harold Hart	HB	6'	206	22		24
Jess Phillips	FB-HB	6'1"	208	28		6
Marv Hubbard	FB	6'1"	235	29		12
Mark van Eeghen	FB	6'1"	225	23		18
Fred Biletnikoff	WR	6'1"	190	32		12
Morris Bradshaw	WR	6'	195	22		24
Cliff Branch	WR	5'11"	170	27		54
Mike Siani	WR	6'2"	195	25		
Dave Casper	TE	6'4"	230	23		6
Ted Kwalick	TE	6'4"	226	28		
Bob Moore	TE	6'3"	220	26		
Warren Bankston	FB-TE	6'4"	235	28		6
Ray Guy	K	6'3"	195	25		

DENVER BRONCOS 6-8 John Ralston

Scores of Each Game		
37	KANSAS CITY	33
23	GREEN BAY	13
14	Buffalo	38
9	Pittsburgh	20
16	CLEVELAND	15
13	Kansas City	26
17	OAKLAND	42
16	CINCINNATI	17
27	San Diego	17
21	Atlanta	35
13	SAN DIEGO	*10
10	Oakland	17
25	PHILADELPHIA	10
13	Miami	14

Use Name	Pos.	Hgt	Wgt	Age	Int	Pts
Mike Current	OT	6'4"	258	29		
Claudie Minor	OT	6'4"	285	24		
Marv Montgomery	OT	6'6"	255	27		
Stan Rogers	OT	6'4"	255	23		
Brian Goodman	OG	6'2"	250	26		
Paul Howard	OG	6'3"	260	24		
Tommy Lyons	OG	6'2"	230	27		
Carl Schaukowitch	OG	6'2"	237	24		
Bobby Maples	C	6'3"	250	32		
Phil Olsen	DT-C	6'5"	260	27		
Barney Chavous	DE	6'3"	252	24		
Lyle Alzado	DT-DE	6'3"	265	26		
John Grant	DT-DE	6'3"	235	25		
Rubin Carter	DT	6'	256	22		
Paul Smith	DT	6'3"	256	30	6	

Ed Smith — Knee Injury

Use Name	Pos.	Hgt	Wgt	Age	Int	Pts
Randy Gradishar	LB	6'3"	235	23	3	6
Tom Jackson	LB	5'11"	220	24	2	
Mike Lemon (from NO)	LB	6'2"	215	24		
Ray May	LB	6'1"	230	30	1	
Jim O'Malley	LB	6'1"	230	24	1	
Joe Rizzo	LB	6'1"	220	24		
Bob Swenson	LB	6'3"	220	22	1	
Steve Haggerty	DB	5'10"	175	22		
Calvin Jones	DB	5'7"	170	24	1	
Randy Poltl	DB	6'3"	190	23		
John Rowser	DB	6'1"	190	31	1	
Jeff Severson	DB	6'1"	185	25		
Earlie Thomas	DB	6'1"	190	29	2	
Bill Thompson	DB	6'1"	200	28	2	
Louis Wright	DB	6'2"	195	22	2	

Clarence Ellis — Knee Injury

Use Name	Pos.	Hgt	Wgt	Age	Int	Pts
John Hufnagel	QB	6'1"	194	24		
Charley Johnson	QB	6'	190	38		
Steve Ramsey	QB	6'2"	210	27		
Otis Armstrong	HB	5'11"	196	24		
Floyd Little	HB	5'10"	195	33		24
Fran Lynch	FB-HB	6'1"	205	29		24
Mike Franckowiak	FB	6'3"	220	22		
Al Haywood	FB	5'11"	215	27		
Jon Keyworth	FB	6'3"	230	23		24
Oliver Ross	HB-FB	6'	210	25		
Jack Dolbin	WR	5'10"	180	26		24
Haven Moses	WR	6'3"	208	29		12
Rick Upchurch	WR	5'10"	170	23		18
Bill Van Heusen	WR	6'1"	200	29		6
Bob Adams	TE	6'2"	220	29		
Boyd Brown	TE	6'4"	216	23		
Riley Odoms	TE	6'4"	230	25		24
Jim Turner	K	6'2"	205	34		66

KANSAS CITY CHIEFS 5-9 Paul Wiggin

Scores of Each Game		
33	Denver	37
24	N.Y. JETS	30
3	SAN FRANCISCO	20
42	OAKLAND	10
12	San Diego	10
26	DENVER	13
13	HOUSTON	17
34	Dallas	31
3	Pittsburgh	28
24	DETROIT	*21
14	Baltimore	28
20	SAN DIEGO	28
14	Cleveland	40
20	Oakland	28

Use Name	Pos.	Hgt	Wgt	Age	Int	Pts
Gary Palmer	OT	6'4"	255	24		
Charlie Getty	OT	6'4"	260	23		
Jim Nicholson	OT	6'6"	260	25		
Bill Story	OT	6'3"	245	23		
Randy Beisler	OG	6'4"	244	30		
Roger Bernhardt	OG	6'4"	245	25		
Ed Budde	OG	6'5"	265	34		
Tom Condon	OG	6'3"	240	22		
Rocky Rasley	OG	6'3"	255	28		
Mike Wilson	OG	6'1"	250	27		
Charlie Ane	C	6'1"	233	23		
Jack Rudnay	C	6'3"	240	27		
John Lohmeyer	DE	6'4"	230	24		
Bob Maddox	DE	6'5"	232	26		
John Matuszak	DE	6'8"	275	24	6	
Louis Ross	DE	6'6"	265	28		
Wilbur Young	DE	6'6"	285	26		
Buck Buchanan	DT	6'7"	270	35		
Larry Estes	DT	6'6"	250	28		
Tom Keating	DT	6'3"	247	32		
Marv Upshaw	DT	6'3"	260	28		

Use Name	Pos.	Hgt	Wgt	Age	Int	Pts
Ken Avery	LB	6'1"	227	31		
Tim Kearney	LB	6'2"	230	24		
Willie Lanier	LB	6'1"	245	30	5	
Jim Lynch	LB	6'1"	225	30		
Al Palewicz	LB	6'1"	215	25		
Bill Peterson	LB	6'3"	225	30		
Hise Austin	DB	6'4"	187	24		
Jim Kearney	DB	6'2"	206	32		
Jim Marsalis	DB	5'11"	190	29	1	
Don Martin	DB	5'11"	185	25		
Kerry Reardon	DB	5'11"	180	26	3	
Mike Sensibaugh	DB	5'11"	192	26	5	
Emmitt Thomas	DB	6'2"	192	32	6	

Clyde Werner — Tendon Injury

Use Name	Pos.	Hgt	Wgt	Age	Int	Pts
Tony Adams	QB	6'	198	25		
Wayne Clark	QB	6'2"	203	28		
Len Dawson	QB	6'	190	41		
Mike Livingston	QB	6'3"	212	29		12
Woody Green	HB	6'1"	205	24		36
Ed Podolak	HB	6'1"	208	28		30
Charlie Thomas	HB	5'9"	180	24		
Doug Dressler (from NE)	FB	6'3"	228	27		6
MacArthur Lane	FB	6'	220	33		12
Jeff Kinney	HB-FB	6'2"	215	25		12
Larry Brunson	WR	5'11"	180	26		12
Reggie Craig	WR	6'	187	22		
Barry Pearson	WR	5'11"	185	25		18
Otis Taylor	WR	6'2"	215	32		
Bill Masters	TE	6'5"	240	31		18
Walter White	TE	6'3"	208	24		18
Jim McCann	K	6'2"	165	26		
Jan Stenerud	K	6'2"	187	32		96
Jerrel Wilson	K	6'4"	222	34		

SAN DIEGO CHARGERS 2-12 Tommy Prothro

Scores of Each Game		
0	PITTSBURGH	37
17	Houston	33
0	OAKLAND	6
10	LOS ANGELES	*13
10	KANSAS CITY	12
0	Oakland	25
24	N.Y. Giants	35
19	NEW ENGLAND	33
17	DENVER	27
13	Minnesota	28
10	Denver	*13
28	Kansas City	20
24	N.Y. JETS	16
17	Cincinnati	47

Use Name	Pos.	Hgt	Wgt	Age	Int	Pts
Terry Owens	OT	6'6"	264	31		
Billy Shields	OT	6'7"	260	22		
Russ Washington	OT	6'6"	285	28		
Booker Brown	OG	6'3"	257	22		
Ira Gordon	OG	6'3"	283	27		
Ralph Perretta	OG	6'2"	252	22		
Doug Wilkerson	OG	6'2"	262	28		
Ed Flanagan	C	6'3"	245	31		
Mark Markovich	C	6'5"	256	22		
Coy Bacon	DE	6'4"	278	33		
Fred Dean	DE	6'3"	220	23		
Gary Johnson	DT	6'2"	262	23		
Louie Kelcher	DT	6'5"	282	22		
John Teerlinck	DT	6'5"	250	24		
Greg Wojcik	DT	6'6"	270	32		

Use Name	Pos.	Hgt	Wgt	Age	Int	Pts
Billy Andrews	LB	6'	220	30		
Don Goode	LB	6'2"	225	24	1	
Tom Graham	LB	6'2"	235	25	2	
Drew Mahalic	LB	6'4"	225	22	1	
Floyd Rice	LB	6'3"	225	26	1	
Frank Tate	LB	6'3"	225	23		
Joe Beauchamp	DB	6'	184	31	1	
Danny Colbert	DB	5'11"	176	24	2	
Chris Fletcher	DB	5'11"	190	26	6	
Mike Fuller	DB	5'9"	195	22	1	6
Hal Stringert	DB	5'11"	180	23		
Maurice Tyler	DB	6'	190	25		
Mike Williams	DB	5'10"	180	21	4	
Sam Williams	DB	6'2"	186	23	1	

Charles Anthony — Broken Leg
Jim Harrison — Injury
Ken Hutcherson — Leg Injury

Use Name	Pos.	Hgt	Wgt	Age	Int	Pts
Dan Fouts	QB	6'3"	204	24		12
Jesse Freitas	QB	6'1"	192	23		
Bobby Douglass (from CHI)	HB-QB	6'2"	228	28		6
Dave Atkins	HB	6'1"	208	26		
Glen Bonner	HB	6'2"	202	23		
Charlie Smith	HB	6'1"	205	29		
Don Woods	HB	6'1"	214	24		12
Rickey Young	HB	6'2"	193	21		36
Tony Baker	FB	5'11"	215	30		6
Bo Matthews	FB	6'4"	230	23		18
Sam Scarber	FB	6'2"	232	27		12
Melvin Baker (from NO-NE)	WR	6'	192	25		
Gary Garrison	WR	6'1"	194	31		12
Dwight McDonald	WR	6'2"	187	24		18
Joe Sweet	WR	6'2"	196	27		
Chuck Bradley	TE	6'6"	232	24		
Craig Cotton	TE	6'4"	222	27		
Pat Curran	TE	6'3"	238	29		1
Denniss Partee	K	6'2"	225	29		
Ray Wersching	K	5'11"	222	25		56

*Overtime

OAKLAND RAIDERS

Rushing

Last Name	No.	Yds	Avg	TD
Banaszak	187	672	3.6	16
van Eeghen	136	597	4.4	2
Davis	112	486	4.3	4
J. Phillips	63	298	4.7	1
Hubbard	60	294	4.9	2
Hart	56	173	3.1	3
Carter	11	27	2.5	0
Humm	7	21	3.0	0
Branch	2	18	9.0	0
Lawrence	2	−3	−1.5	0
Stabler	6	−5	−0.8	0
Bradshaw	1	−5	−5.0	0

Receiving

Last Name	No.	Yds	Avg	TD
Branch	51	893	18	9
Biletnikoff	43	587	14	2
Moore	19	175	9	0
Siani	17	294	17	0
van Eeghen	12	42	4	1
Davis	11	126	12	1
Banaszak	10	64	6	0
Bradshaw	7	180	26	4
Hubbard	7	81	12	0
Hart	6	27	5	0
Casper	5	71	14	1
J. Phillips	4	25	6	0
Carter	2	39	20	0
Bankston	2	21	11	1

Punt Returns

Last Name	No.	Yds	Avg	TD
Colzie	48	655	14	0
Atkinson	8	33	4	0
Phillips	2	0	0	0

Kickoff Returns

Last Name	No.	Yds	Avg	TD
Hart	17	518	31	1
J. Phillips	12	310	26	0
Davis	9	268	30	0
van Eeghen	7	112	16	0
Atkinson	2	60	30	0
Banaszak	2	24	12	0
Bankston	1	19	19	0
Carter	1	13	13	0

Passing

Last Name	Att	Comp	%	Yds	Yd/Att	TD	Int−%	RK
Stabler	293	171	58	2296	7.8	16	24− 8	8
Humm	38	18	47	246	6.5	3	2− 5	
Lawrence	15	5	33	50	3.3	0	1− 7	
Blanda	3	1	33	11	3.7	0	1−33	
Guy	1	1	100	22	22.0	0	0− 0	

Punting

Last Name	No	Avg
Guy	68	43.8

Kicking

Last Name	XP	Att	%	FG	Att	%
Blanda	44	48	96	13	21	62

DENVER BRONCOS

Rushing

Last Name	No.	Yds	Avg	TD
Keyworth	182	725	4.0	3
Little	125	445	3.6	2
Lynch	57	218	3.8	3
Armstrong	31	155	5.0	0
Ross	42	121	2.9	0
Upchurch	16	97	6.1	1
Dolbin	5	72	14.4	0
Hufnagel	8	47	5.9	0
Ramsey	6	38	6.3	0
Odoms	5	27	5.4	0
Van Heusen	2	26	13.0	0
Johnson	10	21	2.1	0
Franckowiak	1	1	1.0	0

Receiving

Last Name	No.	Yds	Avg	TD
Keyworth	42	314	8	1
Odoms	40	544	14	3
Moses	29	505	17	2
Little	29	308	11	2
Dolbin	22	421	19	3
Upchurch	18	436	24	2
Van Heusen	15	246	16	1
Ross	7	69	10	0
Lynch	6	33	6	1
Brown	1	14	14	0
Armstrong	1	10	10	0

Punt Returns

Last Name	No.	Yds	Avg	TD
Upchurch	27	312	12	0
Thompson	13	158	12	0
Lynch	1	0	0	0

Kickoff Returns

Last Name	No.	Yds	Avg	TD
Upchurch	40	1084	27	0
Little	16	307	19	0
Ross	1	20	20	0
Severson	1	20	20	0
Maples	1	15	15	0

Passing

Last Name	Att	Comp	%	Yds	Yd/Att	TD	Int−%	RK
Ramsey	233	128	55	1562	6.7	9	14− 6	9
Johnson	142	65	46	1021	7.2	5	12− 9	15
Hufnagel	51	16	31	287	5.6	1	8−16	
Van Heusen	1	1	100	30	30.0	0	0− 0	

Punting

Last Name	No	Avg
Van Heusen	63	39.9

Kicking

Last Name	XP	Att	%	FG	Att	%
Turner	23	26	88	21	28	75

KANSAS CITY CHIEFS

Rushing

Last Name	No.	Yds	Avg	TD
Green	167	611	3.7	5
Podolak	102	351	3.4	3
Lane	79	311	3.9	2
Kinney	85	304	3.6	2
Brunson	2	89	44.5	0
Livingston	13	68	5.2	1
Adams	8	42	5.3	0
Dressler	6	24	4.0	0
Dawson	5	7	1.4	0
White	3	−10	−3.3	0

Receiving

Last Name	No.	Yds	Avg	TD
Podolak	37	332	9	2
Pearson	36	608	17	3
Lane	25	202	8	0
Masters	24	314	13	3
White	23	559	24	3
Brunson	23	398	17	2
Green	23	215	9	1
Kinney	21	148	7	0
Dressler	3	6	2	1
Craig	1	10	10	0
LaGrand	1	−1	−1	0
Adams	1	−7	−7	0

Punt Returns

Last Name	No.	Yds	Avg	TD
Thomas	12	112	9	0
Podolak	13	96	7	0
Reardon	5	41	8	0
Pearson	2	31	16	0
Craig	4	19	5	0
Brunson	1	4	4	0

Kickoff Returns

Last Name	No.	Yds	Avg	TD
Thomas	22	516	24	0
Green	16	343	21	0
Craig	10	247	25	0
Kinney	2	39	20	0
Dressler	1	18	18	0
Brunson	1	8	8	0
Peterson	1	8	8	0

Passing

Last Name	Att	Comp	%	Yds	Yd/Att	TD	Int−%	RK
Livingston	176	88	50	1245	7.1	8	6− 3	7
Dawson	140	93	66	1095	7.8	5	4− 3	2
Adams	77	36	47	445	5.8	2	4− 5	
Podolak	1	0	0	0	0.0	0	1−100	
White	1	0	0	0	0.0	0	1−100	

Punting

Last Name	No	Avg
Wilson	54	41.4
McCann	14	35.2
Dressler	4	25.0

Kicking

Last Name	XP	Att	%	FG	Att	%
Stenerud	30	31	97	22	32	69

SAN DIEGO CHARGERS

Rushing

Last Name	No.	Yds	Avg	TD
Young	138	577	4.2	5
Woods	87	317	3.6	2
Matthews	71	254	3.6	3
Fouts	23	170	7.4	4
T. Baker	42	131	3.1	1
Bonner	28	120	4.3	0
Scarber	15	68	4.5	1
Freitas	11	56	5.1	0
Douglass	10	42	4.2	0
Douglass	5	34	6.8	1
Garrison	3	30	10.0	0
Curran	3	21	7.0	0
Carter	2	11	5.5	0
M. Baker	1	21	21.0	0
Atkins	1	4	4.0	0

Receiving

Last Name	No.	Yds	Avg	TD
Curran	45	619	14	0
Garrison	27	438	16	2
Young	21	166	8	1
McDonald	19	298	16	3
Woods	13	101	8	0
Scarber	12	68	6	1
Matthews	9	59	7	0
Sweet	8	147	18	0
T. Baker	6	27	5	0
M. Baker	2	26	13	0
Bonner	2	8	4	0
Bradley	1	42	42	0

Punt Returns

Last Name	No.	Yds	Avg	TD
Fuller	36	410	11	1
Colbert	2	32	16	0

Kickoff Returns

Last Name	No.	Yds	Avg	TD
Fuller	31	725	23	0
Young	15	323	22	0
Smith	8	222	28	0
Andrews	6	93	16	0
Colbert	5	91	18	0
Curran	3	28	9	0
Markovich	1	0	0	0

Passing

Last Name	Att	Comp	%	Yds	Yd/Att	TD	Int−%	RK
Fouts	195	106	54	1396	7.2	2	10− 5	12
Freitas	110	49	45	525	4.8	5	5− 5	
Douglass	47	15	32	140	3.0	0	3− 6	

Punting

Last Name	No	Avg
Partee	79	36.8

Kicking

Last Name	XP	Att	%	FG	Att	%
Wersching	20	21	95	12	24	50

1975 Championship Games

NFC CHAMPIONSHIP GAME
January 4, 1976 at Los Angeles
(Attendance 84,483)

SCORING

LOS ANGELES	0	0	0	7—	7
DALLAS	7	14	13	3—	37

First Quarter
Dall. P.Pearson, 18 yard pass from Staubach
PAT—Fritsch (kick)

Second Quarter
Dall. Richards, 4 yard pass from Staubach
PAT—Fritsch (kick)
Dall. P. Pearson, 15 yard pass from Staubach
PAT—Fritsch (kick)

Third Quarter
Dall. P. Pearson, 19 yard pass from Staubach
PAT—Fritsch (kick)
Dall. Fritsch, 40 yard field goal
Dall. Fritsch, 26 yard field goal

Fourth Quarter
L.A. Cappelletti, 1 yard rush
PAT—Dempsey (kick)
Dall. Fritsch, 26 yard field goal

TEAM STATISTICS

L.A.		DALLAS
9	First Downs — Total	24
1	First Downs — Rushing	8
7	First Downs — Passing	15
1	First Downs — Penalty	1
1	Fumbles — Number	1
0	Fumbles — Lost Ball	0
4	Penalties — Number	5
25	Yards Penalized	59
2	Missed Field Goals	0
45	Offensive Plays	78
118	Net Yards	441
2.6	Average Gain	5.7
3	Giveaways	1
1	Takeaways	3
–2	Difference	+2

A Study in Contrasts

In the NFC semifinal match Los Angeles won easily over St. Louis, 35-23. By contrast, Dallas, the wild-card team, came back from a 14-10 deficit with 24 seconds left to play (a 50-yard TD bomb from Roger Staubach to Drew Pearson) to astonish Minnesota 17-14. But past performances went out the window in this championship game as the Cowboys totally humiliated the favorite Rams 37-7.

The game was one of the most lopsided ever staged in the playoffs, and represented a drastic difference in playing styles. While coach Chuck Knox's Rams played it close to the vest and suffered for it as a consequence, coach Tom Landry did just the opposite with Dallas. Leading 14-0 in the second quarter as the result of two touchdown passes by Staubach, Landry had the Cowboys go for broke rather than cautiously sit on the lead. Staubach connected to Preston Pearson on a 15-yard pass to run the score to 21-0 and then called several time outs to try and get into field goal range as the half ran out. The Rams play on the other hand was best typified by their choice on the first series of downs when the game opened. Facing third down and 15 from their 30, they elected to run a sweep. It was unsuccessful and they punted the ball away.

Dallas ran the score to 34-0 in the third quarter behind Staubach's fourth TD pass of the day, and two field goals by Toni Fritsch. In the 4th quarter the Rams scored a touchdown to avoid their first home field shutout in 30 years. Fritsch then added another field goal to make the final score 37-7.

Part of the Rams fall from grace following a 13-2 regular season was the inability of All-Pro ends Jack Youngblood and Fred Dryer to penetrate Staubach even once, and for Lawrence McCutcheon, Pro Bowl running back, to gain ten yards in 11 rushes. Also stopped cold was All-Pro wide receiver Harold Jackson, who had no completions for the day. As a final capper, last year's Pro Bowl Most Valuable Player, quarterback James Harris, suffering from an injured shoulder, was yanked early in the first quarter after throwing an interception.

INDIVIDUAL STATISTICS

RUSHING

LOS ANGELES	No.	Yds	Avg.	DALLAS	No	Yds	Avg.
Jaworski	2	12	6.0	Newhouse	16	64	4.0
McCutcheon	11	10	0.9	Staubach	7	54	7.7
Cappelletti	1	1	1.0	Dennison	13	35	2.7
Scribner	1	1	1.0	P. Pearson	7	20	2.9
Bryant	1	–2	–2.0	Young	6	17	2.8
	16	22	1.4	Fuggett	1	5	5.0
					50	195	3.9

RECEIVING

LOS ANGELES	No.	Yds	Avg.	DALLAS	No	Yds	Avg.
Jessie	4	52	13.0	P. Pearson	7	123	17.6
McCutcheon	3	39	13.0	D. Pearson	5	46	9.2
Nelson	3	28	9.3	Richards	2	46	23.0
Bryant	1	28	28.0	Fuggett	2	5	2.5
	11	147	13.4	Young	1	15	15.0
				Dennison	1	11	11.0
					18	246	13.7

PUNTING

LOS ANGELES	No.	Yds	Avg.	DALLAS	No	Yds	Avg.
Carrell	7		35.4	Hoopes	4		34.8

PUNT RETURNS

LOS ANGELES	No.	Yds	Avg.	DALLAS	No	Yds	Avg.
Scribner	2	3	1.5	Richards	3	17	5.7
				Harris	1	9	9.0
					4	26	6.5

KICKOFF RETURNS

LOS ANGELES	No.	Yds	Avg.	DALLAS	No	Yds	Avg.
McGee	5	103	20.6	Dennison	2	47	23.5
Bryant	2	49	24.5				
Jessie	1	15	15.0				
	8	167	20.9				

INTERCEPTION RETURNS

LOS ANGELES	No.	Yds	Avg.	DALLAS	No	Yds	Avg.
Simpson	1	37	37.0	Lewis	2	20	10.0
				C. Harris	1	22	22.0
					3	42	14.0

PASSING

LOS ANGELES	Att	Comp	Comp Pct.	Yds	Int	Yds/ Att.	Yds/ Comp	Yards Lost Tackled
Jaworski	22	11	50.0	147	2	6.7	13.4	5–51
J. Harris	2	0	00.0	0	1	—	—	—
	24	11	45.8	147	3	6.1	13.4	5–51
DALLAS								
Staubach	26	16	61.5	220	1	8.5	13.8	0–0
Longley	2	2	100.0	26	0	13.0	13.0	0–0
	28	18	64.3	246	1	8.8	13.7	0–0

AFC CHAMPIONSHIP GAME
January 4, 1976 at Pittsburgh
(Attendance 49,103)

SCORING

PITTSBURGH	0	3	0	13—	16
OAKLAND	0	0	0	10—	10

Second Quarter
Pit. Gerela, 36 yard field goal

Fourth Quarter
Pit. Harris, 25 yard rush
PAT—Gerela (kick)
Oak. Siani, 14 yard pass from Stabler
PAT—Blanda (kick)
Pit. Stallworth, 20 yard pass from Bradshaw
PAT—Kick no good
Oak. Blanda, 41 yard field goal.

TEAM STATISTICS

PIT.		OAK.
16	First Downs — Total	18
5	First Downs — Rushing	3
10	First Downs — Passing	13
1	First Downs — Penalty	2
5	Fumbles — Number	4
5	Fumbles — Lost Ball	3
3	Penalties — Number	4
32	Yards Penalized	40
2	Missed Field Goals	1
64	Offensive Plays	76
332	Net Yards	321
5.2	Average Gain	4.2
8	Giveaways	5
5	Takeaways	8
–3	Difference	+3

A Cold Reception

Oakland had done everything they could to prepare for Pittsburgh in the AFC Championship game. They went through the season with a 12-3 record and then held off Cincinnati 31-28 in the semifinal game. But they were met with an ice-covered and snow swept field and bone-chilling cold, plus the nearly impregnable defense of the Steelers. When the long afternoon came to a close they found themselves on the short end of a 16-10 score and another summer in which to think of the Super Bowl again.

Pittsburgh got ready for their second Super Bowl try by going through a 13-2 campaign and then stopping the Baltimore resurgence 28-10. The big plus for the Steelers was the return to fulltime duty after eight weeks of a hurting, defensive tackle Joe Greene.

When the first half came to a close, Pittsburgh led 3-0 as the result of a 36-yard field goal by Roy Gerela. In the third quarter the hard-hitting defensive battle continued with both teams unable to reach the scoreboard. Then, within a six minutes stretch of the final quarter Pittsburgh's Franco Harris bruised his way for 25 yards into the end zone, Oakland quarterback Ken Stabler hit Mike Siani with a 14-yard pass, and Terry Bradshaw, the Steeler's quarterback, hit John Stallworth with a 20-yard pass. Gerela's kick failed, and the score stood at 16:7.

By the time Oakland got on the board again there were 12 seconds left to play. Stabler had taken over the ball with 1:31 on the clock and drove his club from the Oakland 35 to the Pittsburgh 24. Ageless George Blanda, who had reached an NFL milestone during the season by scoring his 2000th career point, booted a 41-yard field goal to put the score at 16-10.

On the ensuing kickoff to Pittsburgh, Oakland went for the miracle by attempting a dribbler. Marv Hubbard recovered the ball for Oakland with seven seconds left. Stabler, at his own 45, threw a long bomb which hit Cliff Branch on the 15. But the Steelers were there to stop him as the season ran out for Oakland.

INDIVIDUAL STATISTICS

RUSHING

PITTSBURGH	No	Yds	Avg.	OAKLAND	No	Yds	Avg.
Harris	27	79	2.9	Banaszak	8	33	4.1
Bradshaw	2	22	11.0	Hubbard	10	30	3.0
Bleier	10	16	1.6	Davis	13	29	2.2
	39	117	3.0	Phillips	1	1	1.0
					32	93	2.9

RECEIVING

PITTSBURGH	No	Yds	Avg.	OAKLAND	No	Yds	Avg.
Harris	5	58	11.6	Siani	5	80	18.0
Grossman	4	36	9.0	Casper	5	67	13.4
Swann	2	45	22.5	Branch	2	56	28.0
Stallworth	2	30	15.0	Banaszak	2	12	6.0
Lewis	1	33	33.0	Moore	2	12	6.0
L. Brown	1	13	13.0	Hart	1	16	16.0
	15	215	14.3	Davis	1	3	3.0
					18	246	13.7

PUNTING

PITTSBURGH	No	Yds	Avg.	OAKLAND	No	Yds	Avg.
Walden	4		38.5	Guy	8		37.8

PUNT RETURNS

PITTSBURGH	No	Yds	Avg.	OAKLAND	No	Yds	Avg.
D. Brown	2	28	14.0	Siani	1	0	0.0
Collier	1	0	0.0				
	3	28	9.3				

KICKOFF RETURNS

PITTSBURGH	No	Yds	Avg.	OAKLAND	No	Yds	Avg.
Collier	2	57	28.5	Davis	3	56	18.7
Harrison	1	2	2.0	Banaszak	1	15	15.0
	3	59	19.7		4	71	17.8

INTERCEPTION RETURNS

PITTSBURGH	No	Yds	Avg.	OAKLAND	No	Yds	Avg.
Wagner	2	34	17.0	Tatum	2	8	4.0
				M. Johnson	1	11	11.0
					3	19	6.3

PASSING

PITTSBURGH	Att	Comp	Comp Pct.	Yds	Int	Yds/ Att.	Yds/ Comp	Yards Lost Tackled
Bradshaw	25	15	60.0	215	3	8.6	14.3	0–0
OAKLAND								
Stabler	42	18	42.9	246	2	5.9	13.7	2–18

Swann's Song

Unlike past Super Bowl efforts, which had more fanfare off the field than on, this year's edition featured enough excitement to compete with the pre-game show. Favorite Pittsburgh, returning for the second time in two years, was facing Dallas, the first wildcard team to ever reach the NFL finals.

Through the first three quarters Dallas held a 10-7 lead. Then, at 3:32 of the final quarter, Reggie Harrison, a Pittsburgh reserve running back who plays on special teams, blocked a punt by Mitch Hoopes at the Dallas 9. The ball bounced off Harrison's face hard enough to wind up in the Dallas end zone, good enough for a two-point safety and run the score to 10-9. It was a play which was considered the turning point of the game. Roy Gerela put Pittsburgh in front for the first time with a 36-yard field at 6:19. A few minutes later Mike Wagner intercepted a Roger Staubach pass and returned it 19 yards to the Dallas 7. Terry Bradshaw was unable to get the touchdown, but Gerela booted an 18-yard field goal.

With the score 15-10, the game's hero, Lynn Swann, took a 59-yard pass from Bradshaw and ran it 5 yards into the end zone at 11:58. The kick failed and the stage was set for the final dramatics. The Cowboys drove 80 yards in five plays with under two minutes to play to make the score 21-17. On the drive, two passes of 30 and 11 yards from Staubach to Drew Pearson proved the key. Terry Hanratty replaced Bradshaw, who had been shaken up on his 64-yard pass to Swann, for Pittsburgh's last offensive series and found himself with fourth down and 9 to go on the Dallas 41. Only 1:28 was left to play and coach Chuck Noll decided to gamble, owing to the fact that Dallas had no time outs left. Rather than punt and risk the run back, he had the Steelers go for the run. They got two yards and Dallas took possession. Five plays later the game was over and Pittsburgh had its second straight Super Bowl triumph.

Dallas coach Tom Landry blamed the defeat on the blocked punt by Harrison, which he said changed the momentum of the game around. He may have been right, but Swann's performance—which earned him the game's Most Valuable Player award—was momentum enough for the Steelers. Hospitalized only two weeks earlier with a concussion, and dropping passes in practice, the fleet-footed receiver returned to catch four passes for an astonishing total of 161 yards—a Super Bowl record certain to stand for many years.

LINEUPS

PITTSBURGH		DALLAS
	OFFENSE	
Stallworth	WR	Richards
Kolb	LT	Neely
Clack	LG	Lawless
Mansfield	C	Fitzgerald
Mullins	RG	Nye
Gravelle	RT	Wright
L. Brown	TE	Fugett
Swann	WR	D. Pearson
Bradshaw	QB	Staubach
Bleier	RB	P. Pearson
F. Harris	RB	Newhouse
	DEFENSE	
Greenwood	LE	Jones
Green	LT	Pugh
Holmes	RT	Cole
D. White	RE	Martin
Ham	LLB	D. Edwards
Lambert	MLB	Jordan
Russell	RLB	Lewis
Thomas	LCB	Washington
Blount	RCB	Renfro
Wagner	LS	Waters
G. Edwards	RS	C. Harris

SUBSTITUTES

PITTSBURGH

OFFENSE	
Collier	Hanratty
S. Davis	Harrison
Fuqua	Lewis
Garrett	Reavis
Grossman	Webster
DEFENSE	
Allen	Furness
Banaszak	Kellum
Bradley	Shell
D. Brown	Toews
KICKERS	
Gerela	Walden

DALLAS

OFFENSE	
K. Davis	P. Howard
Dennison	R. Howard
Donovan	Scott
DuPree	Young
DEFENSE	
Barnes	Hughes
Breunig	Peterson
Capone	R. White
Gregory	Woolsey
Henderson	
Kickers	
Fritsch	Hoopes

SCORING

PITTSBURGH	7 0 0 14	—21
DALLAS	7 3 0 7	—17

First Quarter

Dall.   D. Pearson, 29 yard pass from Staubach   4:36
PAT — Fritsch (kick)

Pitt.   Grossman, 7 yard pass from Bradshaw   3:03
PAT — Gerela (kick)

Second Quarter

Dall.   Fritsch, 36 yard field goal   0:15

Fourth Quarter

Pitt.   Safety — Harrison blocked punt out of end zone   3:32

Pitt.   Gerela, 36 yard field goal   6:19

Pitt.   Gerela, 18 yard field goal   8:23

Pitt.   Swann, 64 yard pass from Bradshaw   11:58
PAT — Gerela (kick — failed)

Dall.   P. Howard, 34 yard pass from Staubach   13:12
PAT — Fritsch (kick)

TEAM STATISTICS

PITT.		DALL.
13	First Downs — Total	14
7	First Downs — Rushing	6
6	First Downs — Passing	8
0	First Downs — Penalty	0
4	Fumbles — Number	4
0	Fumbles — Lost Ball	0
0	Penalties — Number	2
0	Yards Penalized	20
2	Missed Field Goals	0
67	Offensive Plays	62
339	Net Yards	270
5.1	Average Gain	4.4
0	Giveaways	3
3	Takeaways	0
+3	Difference	-3

INDIVIDUAL STATISTICS

RUSHING

PITTSBURGH	No	Yds	Avg.	DALLAS	No	Yds	Avg.
F. Harris	27	82	3.0	Newhouse	16	56	3.5
Bleier	15	51	3.4	Staubach	5	22	4.4
Bradshaw	4	16	4.0	Dennison	5	16	3.2
	46	149	3.2	P. Pearson	5	14	2.8
					31	108	3.5

RECEIVING

PITTSBURGH	No	Yds	Avg.	DALLAS	No	Yds	Avg.
Swann	4	161	40.3	P. Pearson	5	53	10.6
Stallworth	2	8	4.0	Young	3	31	10.3
F. Harris	1	26	26.0	D. Pearson	2	59	29.5
L. Brown	1	7	7.0	Newhouse	2	12	6.0
Grossman	1	7	7.0	P. Howard	1	34	34.0
	9	209	23.2	Fugett	1	9	9.0
				Dennison	1	6	6.0
					15	204	13.6

PUNTING

PITTSBURGH	No	Yds	Avg.	DALLAS	No	Yds	Avg.
Walden	4		39.8	Hoopes	7		35.0

PUNT RETURNS

PITTSBURGH	No	Yds	Avg.	DALLAS	No	Yds	Avg.
D. Brown	3	14	4.7	Richards	1	3	3.0
G. Edwards	2	17	8.5				
	5	31	6.2				

KICKOFF RETURNS

PITTSBURGH	No	Yds	Avg.	DALLAS	No	Yds	Avg.
Blount	3	64	21.3	P. Pearson	4	48	12.0
Collier	1	25	25.0	Henderson	*0	48	—
	4	89	22.3	* = lateral	4	96	24.0

INTERCEPTION RETURNS

PITTSBURGH	No	Yds	Avg.	DALLAS
Thomas	1	35	35.0	none
G. Edwards	1	35	35.0	
Wagner	1	19	19.0	
	3	89	29.7	

PASSING

PITTSBURGH	Att	Comp	Comp Pct.	Yds.	Int	Yds/ Att.	Comp	Yards Lost Tackled
Bradshaw	19	9	47.4	209	0	11.0	23.2	2-19
DALLAS								
Staubach	24	15	62.5	204	3	8.5	13.6	7-42

1976 N.F.C. THE VIKES — Bridesmaids, Again

EASTERN DIVISION

Dallas Cowboys — Providing themselves beyond expectations with a trip to the Super Bowl the previous year, the Pokes rung up 11 victories and eight Pro Bowl selections (more than any team except Pittsburgh) on the way to a first-place finish that was tarnished by their first-round playoff failure against Los Angeles. Dallas' offense scored just 13 TD's in its last eight games, however, as the need for a breakaway running threat became more evident. While the pass catching chores appeared to be in good hands as Drew Pearson led the NFC in receptions and Billy Joe DuPree set a club record for catches by a tight end (42), only twice did a Cowboy rusher gain over 100 yards in a game.

Washington Redskins — After making four major trades and spending a bundle on free agents John Riggins, Calvin Hill and Jean Fugett before the season began, the pressure was on Head Coach George Allen to produce a winner. The Skins squeaked past St. Louis for the NFC "Wild Card" spot before Minnesota humiliated them in the playoffs. Critics remained divided all year on the question of who between Billy Kilmer and Joe Theismann should be the starting QB, but the feisty Kilmer emerged as the No. 1 man after engineering clutch victories down the stretch. As usual, the Skins' special teams were magnificent as Eddie Brown fell just a few yards short of an NFL punt return record and PK Mark Moseley led the NFC in scoring.

St. Louis Cardinals — Despite leading the league in offense and featuring three All-Pros in their offensive line, the 10-4 Cards failed to make the playoffs because of their two losses to conference rival Washington, also 10-4 for the year. The "Cardiac" crew won eight of its 10 games by seven points or less, four of them coming after halftime deficits. Their most dramatic victory came in Week No. 10 when they rallied from 15 points behind in the second half to nip the Rams 30-28 on Jim Bakken's 25-yard FG with four seconds left. But the next week at home against the Skins, the Cards suffered a costly emotional letdown, losing 16-10 after usually reliable WR Mel Gray dropped a last-minute endzone pass that would have won the game. After losing 19-14 the next week in Dallas, one play again stood out—an apparent pass interference penalty against TE J.V. Cain in the endzone with a minute remaining that was never called.

Philadelphia Eagles — Well-aware of the long-range drafting deficiencies caused by earlier trades for Roman Gabriel, Mike Boryla and Bill Bergey, rookie Head Coach Dick Vermeil announced at the beginning of the season it would take at least five years to turn things around in Philly. After Gabriel had trouble coming back from off-season knee surgery and Boryla finished the year with the lowest passing average per play among starting NFL QB's, the stage was set for the deal with L.A. that brought in strong-armed Ron Jaworski before the '77 season began. Each of the Eagles' four wins were against losing teams, and at one point in the second half of the season, they lost five straight and scored only 17 points.

New York Giants — Equipped with a flashy new stadium in New Jersey, the Giants couldn't help but be associated with the ill-fated WFL. In April they signed FB Larry Csonka, and after an 0-7 start, they replaced Head Coach Bill Arnsparger with Zonk's WFL mentor in Memphis, John McVay. The Giants finished 3-4 under McVay, good enough to win him a two-year contract. They finally won their first game the 10th week, upsetting Washington 12-9 behind a strong defense led by LB's Brad Van Pelt and Harry Carson. The offense, particularly the line, was weak all year, however, as Craig Morton's mediocre quarterbacking signalled his departure to Denver and Csonka and OT Tom Mullen were knocked out late in the season with knee injuries.

CENTRAL DIVISION

Minnesota Vikings — Fighting off repeated claims that they were too old, the Vikes had another banner year, grabbing their eighth straight division title. After WR John Gilliam and RB Ed Marinaro became free agents and left the team, newcomer WR's Ahmad Rashad and Sammy White, the latter a brilliant rookie, picked up the slack offensively with more than 50 catches apiece. Multi-purpose RB Chuck Foreman led the team in receiving and rushing while Fran Tarkenton continued to capture all of the NFL's major passing records. But after their fourth frustrating Super Bowl loss, Foreman threatened not to return unless his salary increased and Tarkenton said he might retire to become another jock-turned-TV broadcaster.

Chicago Bears — Jack Pardee was named NFC Coach of the Year for piloting the Bears to a 7-7 finish, their best since '68. With a demanding schedule forcing them to take on six playoff qualifiers, they responded with two victories among the six—33-7 over Washington and 14-13 over Minnesota—as well as tough one-point losses to Oakland and Minnesota that would have been wins if not for faulty kicking. But aside from Walter Payton's 1,390 rushing yards, tops in the NFC, the Bears' offense remained unimaginative. The verdict was still out on second-year QB Bob Avellini, especially after he finished the season with a two-for 17 passing performance in a 28-14 loss to Denver. Sid Gillman, one of the game's great free-thinkers, was lured out of retirement after the season ended to become offensive coordinator.

Detroit Lions — Dissension and a rough 1-3 start cost Rick Forzano his head coaching job. Replacement Tommy Hudspeth got off on the right foot by opening up the offense with a double-wing, double-WR formation that shocked New England 30-10 the fifth week. But a pitiful offensive line and a dismal 1-6 road record that included losses to New Orleans and the New York Giants did little to secure Hudspeth's future. Behind OLB Charlie Weaver, the team's MVP, and linemen Jim Mitchell and Ken Sanders, the Lions' stunting defense remained strong, allowing the NFL's third lowest yardage total despite losing three tackles to surgery.

Green Bay Packers — Blessed with decent draft picks for the first time since '72, the Pack showed a very slight improvement, one more victory than '75, in Bart Starr's second season at the helm, and still needed help at almost every position when the year ended. Green Bay's five wins were all against sub-.500 teams, and it had to come from behind in the second half in four of them. QB Lynn Dickey, obtained from Houston before the season began in exchange for QB John Hadl and CB Ken Ellis, was respectable until a shoulder separation knocked him out of the last four games.

WESTERN DIVISION

Los Angeles Rams — On the way to their fourth straight division title, the Rams featured a season-long battle among James Harris, Ron Jaworski and Pat Haden for the starting QB job. While nagging injuries continually hampered his competitors, Haden finally emerged as L.A.'s No. 1 man with five regular-season games left. A bountiful rushing attack headed by Lawrence McCutcheon and John Cappelletti was the key factor in the NFC's highest-scoring offense. Defensively, CB Monte Jackson's league-leading 10 interceptions spearheaded a sterling secondary that received strong assistance from a tough defensive line anchored by LT Merlin Olsen in his last season. The team's individual highlight was Harris' fourth-week, 436-yard passing performance in a 31-28 victory over Miami, the second-best ever by a Ram QB.

San Francisco 49ers — With Monte Clark replacing Dick Nolan as head coach, the Niners were the NFL's biggest surprise the first half of the season with a 6-1 record. They fell to 2-5 the second half, but finished the year with the conference's best defense, led by All-Pro DE Tommy Hart and his sack-happy cohorts, and a productive ground game featuring Delvin Williams and Wilbur Jackson. Monday night victories over L.A. and Minnesota were the strongest indicators of what appeared to be a long and happy coaching career in S.F. for Clark, but his falling out with the team's new owners after the season cut it short and paved the way for a strife-torn '77 campaign conducted by new GM Joe Thomas.

New Orleans Saints — New Head Coach Hank Stram had "Thunder and Lightning" in his offense in the form of rookie runners Tony Galbreath and Chuck Muncie, but a porous front wall offset their effectiveness as the Saints finished 4-10, two victories better than '75. QB's Bobby Scott and Bobby Douglass took over for Archie Manning, on the sidelines all season with tendonitis in his passing shoulder.

Atlanta Falcons — The Falcs lost four of their first five games, at which point GM Pat Peppler abruptly replaced Marion Campbell as head coach. A crucial blow to their offense was the knee injury that knocked QB Steve Bartkowski out of the lineup for nine games. The high point of their dreary 4-10 season came in the 11th week when they scored 17 points in the fourth quarter to upset playoff-bound Dallas 17-10. John James provided excellent punting all season while tiny WR Alfred Jenkins remained a constant long-range threat.

Seattle Seahawks — In their first season, the Seattle expansionites fared much better than their Tampa Bay counterparts, winning two games against the Bucs and Atlanta and coming up with close calls against Minnesota, St. Louis and Green Bay. On offense, QB Jim Zorn displayed great potential at times but threw too many interceptions while Steve Largent and Sherm Smith were pleasant surprises at WR and RB, respectively. The defense was a mess, however, giving up about 400 yards and 30 points a game.

FINAL TEAM STATISTICS

OFFENSE

	ATL.	CHI.	DALL.	DET.	G.B.	L.A.	MINN.	N.O.	N.Y.	PHIL.	ST.L.	S.F.	SEA.	WASH.
FIRST DOWNS:														
Total	191	201	269	259	210	265	294	226	216	220	**307**	242	239	255
by Rushing	78	115	111	123	99	143	125	92	98	109	**140**	131	75	114
by Passing	93	67	140	120	94	111	**150**	111	97	91	142	91	141	122
by Penalty	20	19	18	16	17	11	19	23	21	20	**25**	20	23	19
RUSHING:														
Number	470	578	538	516	485	**613**	540	431	530	505	580	576	374	548
Yards	1689	2363	2147	2213	1722	**2528**	2003	1775	1904	2080	2301	2447	1416	2111
Average Yards	3.6	4.1	4.0	**4.3**	3.6	4.1	3.7	4.1	3.6	4.1	4.0	4.2	3.8	3.9
Touchdowns	10	20	16	9	15	**23**	18	16	11	8	17	14	14	10
PASSING:														
Attempts	354	278	390	356	357	315	442	403	326	369	392	306	**480**	370
Completions	157	123	222	201	164	171	**270**	206	175	182	220	155	229	187
Completion Pct.	44.4	44.2	56.9	56.5	45.9	54.3	**61.1**	51.1	53.7	49.3	56.1	50.7	47.7	50.5
Passing Yards	1809	1705	2967	2630	2105	2629	**3117**	2353	2104	1844	2967	1963	2874	2288
Avg. Yds. per Att.	5.1	6.1	7.6	7.4	5.9	**8.3**	7.1	5.8	6.5	5.0	7.6	6.4	6.0	6.2
Avg. Yds per Comp.	11.5	13.9	13.4	13.1	12.8	**15.4**	11.5	11.4	12.0	10.1	13.5	12.7	12.6	12.2
Times Tackled	44	24	30	67	41	32	31	51	44	43	**17**	34	28	38
Yds Lost Tackled	395	225	230	490	375	288	262	369	312	352	**132**	325	225	303
Net Yards	1414	1480	2737	2140	1730	2341	**2855**	1984	1792	1492	2835	1638	2649	1985
Touchdowns	10	9	17	**20**	10	17	17	8	9	11	18	15	13	**20**
Interceptions	24	15	13	12	22	15	**10**	14	24	18	13	21	30	20
Pct. Intercepted	6.8	5.4	3.3	3.4	6.2	4.8	**2.2**	3.5	7.4	4.9	3.3	6.9	6.3	5.4
PUNTS:														
Number	**101**	100	74	85	84	79	69	**101**	77	97	66	91	82	90
Average Distance	**42.1**	37.3	37.0	38.8	36.6	38.1	38.8	39.3	39.7	35.5	35.3	39.9	37.4	38.9
PUNT RETURNS:														
Number	60	43	45	31	40	52	40	42	41	41	36	**65**	37	52
Yards	385	269	489	207	300	476	271	375	197	425	350	557	246	**688**
Average Yards	6.4	6.3	10.9	6.7	7.5	9.2	6.8	8.9	4.8	10.4	9.7	8.6	6.6	**13.2**
Touchdowns	0	0	0	0	0	0	0	0	0	0	0	**2**	0	1
KICKOFF RETURNS:														
Number	60	51	42	47	65	44	42	62	53	58	54	38	**79**	50
Yards	1269	1087	1027	987	1361	1027	859	1173	1044	1148	1102	777	**1605**	1066
Average Yards	21.2	21.3	**24.5**	21.0	20.9	23.3	20.5	18.9	19.7	19.8	20.4	20.4	20.3	21.3
Touchdowns	0	0	0	0	0	**1**	0	0	0	0	0	0	0	0
INTERCEPTION RET:														
Number	18	24	16	24	11	**32**	19	12	12	9	19	9	15	26
Yards	207	215	133	**445**	197	376	213	212	62	195	243	93	218	190
Average Yards	11.5	9.0	8.3	18.5	17.9	11.8	11.2	17.7	5.2	**21.7**	12.8	10.3	14.5	7.3
Touchdowns	0	2	0	**3**	2	**3**	0	**3**	0	0	1	0	1	0
PENALTIES:														
Number	84	**114**	94	97	87	83	77	103	86	91	84	102	80	90
Yards	714	**984**	761	819	791	764	615	901	734	722	683	848	684	868
FUMBLES:														
Number	30	**24**	26	38	37	29	33	32	27	33	44	30	30	36
Number Lost	17	13	16	21	23	21	19	18	**12**	14	24	**12**	18	23
POINTS:														
Total	172	253	296	262	218	**351**	305	253	170	165	309	270	229	291
PAT Attempts	20	31	34	32	27	44	36	29	21	19	36	32	29	32
PAT Made	20	27	34	28	24	**36**	32	25	20	18	33	26	26	31
FG Attempts	21	25	23	24	19	26	31	23	21	16	27	28	16	**34**
FG Made	10	12	18	14	10	17	19	18	8	11	20	16	9	**22**
Percent FG Made	47.6	48.0	**78.3**	58.3	52.6	65.4	61.3	**78.3**	38.1	68.8	74.1	57.1	56.3	64.7
Safeties	1	**2**	**2**	0	1	0	0	0	0	0	0	**2**	1	1

DEFENSE

	ATL.	CHI.	DALL.	DET.	G.B.	L.A.	MINN.	N.O.	N.Y.	PHIL.	ST.L.	S.F.	SEA.	WASH.
FIRST DOWNS:														
Total	257	250	246	**191**	262	213	207	275	251	262	239	218	323	215
by Rushing	143	104	113	94	132	**79**	103	129	120	113	111	94	166	109
by Passing	95	128	111	**76**	107	118	91	121	119	129	105	102	136	91
by Penalty	19	18	22	21	23	16	13	25	**12**	20	23	22	21	15
RUSHING:														
Number	574	522	484	496	546	**429**	487	554	560	532	491	487	614	555
Yards	2577	1984	1821	1901	2288	**1564**	2096	2289	2203	2053	1979	1786	2876	2205
Average Yards	4.5	3.8	3.8	3.8	4.2	**3.6**	4.3	4.1	3.9	3.9	4.0	3.7	4.7	4.0
Touchdowns	22	**10**	12	13	17	1	14	22	14	16	19	**10**	20	12
PASSING:														
Attempts	340	401	391	**313**	354	397	323	367	330	404	342	374	367	354
Completions	184	200	187	**137**	196	199	158	200	189	237	176	180	223	146
Completion Pct.	54.1	49.9	47.8	43.8	55.4	50.1	48.9	54.5	57.3	58.7	51.5	48.1	60.8	**41.2**
Passing Yards	2276	2612	2236	1904	2192	2487	**1897**	2514	2230	2688	2358	2349	2770	2241
Avg. Yds. per Att.	6.7	6.5	**5.7**	6.1	6.2	6.3	5.9	6.9	6.8	6.7	6.9	6.3	7.5	6.3
Avg. Yds per Comp.	12.4	13.1	12.0	13.9	**11.2**	12.5	12.0	12.6	11.8	11.3	13.4	13.1	12.4	15.4
Times Tackled	35	49	44	28	43	45	45	39	31	19	31	**61**	27	44
Yds Lost Tackled	275	395	327	218	357	395	322	312	242	138	248	**573**	246	324
Net Yards	2001	2217	1909	1686	1835	2092	**1575**	2202	1988	2550	2110	1776	2524	1917
Touchdowns	14	15	12	11	13	11	**8**	18	11	17	13	13	27	11
Interceptions	18	24	16	24	11	**32**	19	12	12	9	19	9	15	26
Pct. Intercepted	5.3	6.0	4.1	7.7	3.1	**8.1**	5.9	3.3	3.6	2.2	5.6	2.4	4.1	7.3
PUNTS:														
Number	87	85	95	84	77	95	79	**88**	78	86	71	**108**	65	93
Average Distance	38.5	36.3	38.7	40.1	38.5	41.2	37.1	39.4	37.0	37.9	38.8	40.1	**35.0**	38.9
PUNT RETURNS:														
Number	52	44	**28**	39	48	39	40	64	45	53	33	52	56	44
Yards	360	346	**252**	278	268	281	286	742	500	405	304	351	537	323
Average Yards	6.9	7.9	9.0	7.1	**5.6**	7.2	7.2	11.6	11.1	7.6	9.2	6.8	9.6	7.3
Touchdowns	**0**	**0**	**0**	**0**	**0**	**0**	**0**	1	**0**	**0**	1	**0**	1	**0**
KICKOFF RETURNS:														
Number	**38**	54	62	55	44	70	66	54	39	44	66	46	47	63
Yards	934	969	1275	1188	784	1383	1209	1359	**725**	912	1623	924	1041	1028
Average Yards	24.6	17.9	20.6	21.6	17.8	19.8	18.3	25.2	18.6	20.7	24.6	20.1	22.1	**16.3**
Touchdowns	**0**	**0**	**0**	**0**	**0**	**0**	**0**	**0**	**0**	**0**	1	**0**	**0**	**0**
INTERCEPTION RET:														
Number	24	15	13	12	22	15	**10**	14	24	18	13	21	30	20
Yards	469	213	155	**121**	362	211	185	140	249	189	134	253	388	149
Average Yards	19.5	14.2	11.9	10.1	16.5	14.1	18.5	10.0	10.4	10.5	10.3	12.0	12.9	**7.5**
Touchdowns	4	**0**	1	**0**	3	**0**	**0**	1	1	1	**0**	2	4	**0**
PENALTIES:														
Number	102	86	71	88	104	82	76	**105**	104	105	83	94	**106**	95
Yards	868	699	643	696	914	747	653	**883**	835	907	708	906	**926**	818
FUMBLES:														
Number	30	37	32	27	27	31	24	**38**	32	31	32	37	24	**38**
Number Lost	20	23	12	15	15	16	13	**27**	15	15	20	16	11	21
POINTS:														
Total	312	216	194	220	299	190	**176**	346	250	286	267	190	429	217
PAT Attempts	40	25	25	25	34	22	22	44	27	35	34	25	53	23
PAT Made	32	25	23	25	29	20	**14**	36	26	33	31	20	51	22
FG Attempts	17	25	**12**	28	33	20	25	17	31	24	20	21	30	30
FG Made	12	13	7	15	22	12	10	14	20	13	10	**6**	20	19
Percent FG Made	70.6	52.0	58.3	53.6	66.7	60.0	40.0	82.4	64.5	54.2	50.0	**28.6**	66.7	63.3
Safeties	2	1	**0**	**0**	**0**	1	**0**	2	1	2	1	1	**0**	**0**

December 18, at Minnesota (Attendance 48,169)

SCORING

MINNESOTA	14	7	14	0–35
WASHINGTON	3	0	3	14–20

First Quarter
- Minn. — Voigt, 18 yard pass from Tarkenton PAT—Cox (kick)
- Wash. — Moseley, 47 yard field goal
- Minn. — S. White, 27 yard pass from Tarkenton PAT—Cox (kick)

Second Quarter
- Minn. — Foreman, 2 yard rush PAT—Cox (kick)

Third Quarter
- Minn. — Foreman, 30 yard rush PAT—Cox (kick)
- Wash. — Moseley, 35 yard field goal
- Minn. — S. White, 9 yard pass from Tarkenton PAT—Cox (kick)

Fourth Quarter
- Wash. — Grant, 12 yard pass from Kilmer PAT—Moseley (kick)
- Wash. — Jefferson, 3 yard pass from Kilmer PAT—Moseley (kick)

TEAM STATISTICS

MINN.		WASH.
21	First Downs-Total	19
11	First Downs-Rushing	3
9	First Downs-Passing	15
1	First Downs-Penalties	1
2	Fumbles-Number	0
0	Fumbles-Lost Ball	0
5	Penalties-Number	7
30	Yards Penalized	57
0	Missed Field Goals	1
69	Offensive Plays	68
384	Net Yards	365
5.6	Average Gain	5.4
2	Giveaways	2
2	Takeaways	2
0	Difference	0

INDIVIDUAL STATISTICS

MINNESOTA	No	Yds	Avg	WASHINGTON	No	Yds	Avg
RUSHING							
Foreman	20	105	5.3	Thomas	11	45	4.1
McClanahan	20	101	5.1	Riggins	7	30	4.3
Johnson	2	11	5.5		18	75	4.2
Tarkenton	1	3	3.0				
Miller	2	1	0.5				
Lee	1	0	1.0				
	46	221	4.8				
RECEIVING							
S. White	4	64	16.0	Grant	6	70	11.6
Voigt	4	42	10.5	Fugett	4	61	15.3
McClanahan	3	29	9.7	Jefferson	4	59	14.8
Rashad	1	35	35.0	Hill	4	31	7.8
	12	170	14.2	Riggins	4	29	7.3
				Thomas	2	18	9.0
				Smith	1	30	30.0
				L. Brown	1	0	0.0
					26	298	11.5
PUNTING							
Clabo	6		46.0	Bragg	6		32.8
PUNT RETURNS							
Willis	2	12	6.0	E. Brown	6	55	9.2
KICKOFF RETURNS							
Willis	2	25	12.5	E. Brown	6	136	22.7
Miller	1	16	16.0				
Johnson	1	0	0.0				
	4	41	10.3				
INTERCEPTION RETURNS							
Bryant	1	0	0.0	Scott	1	17	17.0
N. Wright	1	0	0.0	Houston	1	8	8.0
	2	0	0.0		2	25	12.5

PASSING

MINNESOTA	Att.	Comp.	Comp. Pct.	Yds.	Int.	Yds/ Att.	Yds. Comp.	Yards Lost Tackled
Tarkenton	21	12	57.1	170	2	8.1	14.2	1–7
Lee	1	0	00.0					
	22	12	54.5	170	2	7.7	14.2	1–7
WASHINGTON								
Kilmer	49	26	53.1	298	2	6.1	11.5	1–8

December 19, at Irving, Texas (Attendance 63,283)

SCORING

DALLAS	3	7	0	2–12
LOS ANGELES	0	7	0	7–14

First Quarter
- Dall. — Herrara, 44 yard field goal

Second Quarter
- L.A. — Haden, 4 yard rush PAT—Dempsey (kick)
- Dall. — Laidlaw, 1 yard rush PAT—Herrara (kick)

Fourth Quarter
- L.A. — McCutcheon, 1 yard rush PAT—Dempsey (kick)
- Dall. — Safety—R. Jackson, tackled in end zone

TEAM STATISTICS

DALLAS		L.A.
14	First Downs-Total	17
4	First Downs-Rushing	6
9	First Downs-Passing	8
1	First Downs-Penalty	3
3	Fumbles-Number	0
1	Fumbles-Lost Ball	0
6	Penalties-Number	8
34	Yards Penalized	94
0	Missed Field Goals	0
69	Offensive Plays	73
211	Net Yards	250
3.0	Average Gain	3.4
4	Giveaways	3
3	Takeaways	4
–1	Difference	+1

INDIVIDUAL STATISTICS

DALLAS	No	Yds	Avg.	LOS ANGELES	No	Yds	Avg.
RUSHING							
P. Pearson	13	43	3.3	McCutcheon	21	58	2.8
Newhouse	9	25	2.8	Cappelletti	19	54	2.8
Staubach	2	8	4.0	Haden	8	16	2.0
D. Pearson	1	4	4.0	R. Jackson	1	–8	–8.0
Dennison	1	3	3.0		49	120	2.4
Laidlaw	2	2	1.0				
	28	85	3.0				
RECEIVING							
P. Pearson	6	41	6.8	H. Jackson	6	116	19.3
D. Pearson	3	38	12.7	Cappelletti	2	15	7.5
DuPree	3	34	11.3	Klein	1	12	12.0
Newhouse	2	19	9.5	McCutcheon	1	9	9.0
Johnson	1	18	18.0		10	152	15.2
	15	150	10.0				
PUNTING							
D. White	6		38.6	R. Jackson	7		36.1
PUNT RETURNS							
Johnson	4	64	16	Bryant	2	23	11.5
KICKOFF RETURNS							
Johnson	2	49	24.5	Bryant	2	45	22.5
				Geredine	1	26	26.0
					3	71	23.7
INTERCEPTION RETURNS							
Barnes	2	0	0.0	Robertson	1	15	15.0
Waters	1	9	9.0	Elmendorf	1	5	5.0
	3	9	3.0	M. Jackson	1	0	0.0
					3	20	6.7

PASSING

DALLAS	Att.	Comp.	Comp. Pct.	Yds.	Int.	Yds/ Att.	Yds/ Comp.	Yards Lost Tackled
Staubach	37	15	40.5	150	3	4.1	10.0	4–24
LOS ANGELES								
Haden	21	10	47.6	152	3	7.2	15.2	3–22

DALLAS COWBOYS 11-3 Tom Landry

Scores of Each Game		
27	PHILADELPHIA	7
24	New Orleans	6
30	BALTIMORE	27
28	Seattle	13
24	N.Y. Giants	14
17	St. Louis	21
31	CHICAGO	21
20	Washington	7
9	N.Y. GIANTS	3
17	BUFFALO	10
10	Atlanta	17
19	ST. LOUIS	14
26	Philadelphia	7
14	WASHINGTON	27

Use Name	Pos.	Hgt.	Wgt.	Age	Int	Pts.
Pat Donovan	OT	6'4"	250	23		
Ralph Neely	OT	6'5"	255	32		
Rayfield Wright	OT	6'7"	255	31		
Jim Eidson	OG-C	6'3"	264	22		
Burton Lawless	OG	6'4"	250	22		
Blaine Nye	OG	6'4"	255	30		
Tom Rafferty	OG-C	6'3"	250	22		
Herbert Scott	OG	6'2"	250	23		
John Fitzgerald	C	6'5"	252	28		
Too Tall Jones	DE	6'9"	265	25		
Harvey Martin	DE	6'5"	252	25	1	
Greg Schaum	DE	6'3"	246	22		
Larry Cole	DT	6'4"	250	29		
Bill Gregory	DT	6'5"	252	26		
Jethro Pugh	DT	6'6"	248	32		
Bob Breunig	LB	6'2"	228	23		
Mike Hegman	LB	6'1"	221	23		
Tim Henderson	LB	6'2"	223	23	2	
Lee Roy Jordon	LB	6'2"	220	35		
D.D. Lewis	LB	6'2"	215	30		
Randy White	LB	6'4"	240	23		
Benny Barnes	DB	6'1"	190	25	1	
Cliff Harris	DB	6'	190	27	3	
Randy Hughes	DB	6'4"	210	23	1	
Aaron Kyle	DB	5'10"	181	22	2	
Beasley Reece	DB	6'1"	186	22		
Mel Renfro	DB	6'	190	34	3	
Mark Washington	DB	5'10"	186	28	4	
Charlie Waters	DB	6'1"	195	27	3	
Roger Staubach	QB	6'2"	197	34		18
Danny White	QB	6'2"	180	24		
Doug Dennison	HB-FB	6'1"	208	24		36
Preston Pearson	HB	6'1"	208	31		18
Charley Young	HB	6'1"	220	23		6
Jim Jensen	FB	6'3"	230	22		
Scott Laidlaw	FB	6'	206	23		24
Robert Newhouse	FB-HB	5'10"	205	26		18
Butch Johnson	WR	6'1"	187	22		12
Drew Pearson	WR	6'	185	25		42
Golden Richards	WR	6'	190	25		18
Billy Joe DuPree	TE	6'4"	230	26		12
Jay Saldi	TE	6'3"	217	21		
Efren Herrera	K	5'9"	190	25		88

Kyle Davis – Knee Injury

Percy Howard – Injured

WASHINGTON REDSKINS 10-4 George Allen

Scores of Each Game		
19	N.Y. GIANTS	17
31	SEATTLE	7
20	Philadelphia	*17
7	Chicago	33
30	KANSAS CITY	33
20	DETROIT	7
20	ST. LOUIS	10
7	DALLAS	20
24	San Francisco	21
9	N.Y. Giants	12
16	St. Louis	10
24	PHILADELPHIA	0
37	N.Y. Jets	16
27	Dallas	24

Use Name	Pos.	Hgt.	Wgt.	Age	Int	Pts.
Terry Hermeling	OT	6'5"	255	30		
George Starke	OT	6'5"	249	28		
Tim Stokes	OT	6'5"	252	26		
Dan Nugent	OG	6'3"	250	23		
Ron Saul	OG	6'2"	254	28		
Ted Fritsch	C	6'2"	242	26		
Len Hauss	C	6'2"	235	34		
Bob Kuziel	C	6'5"	255	26		
Dallas Hickman	DE	6'6"	235	24		
Karl Lorch	DE	6'3"	260	26		
Ron McDole	DE	6'3"	265	36		2
Bill Brundige	DT-DE	6'5"	270	27		
Dave Butz	DT	6'7"	285	26		
Dennis Johnson	DT	6'4"	260	24	1	
Diron Talbert	DT	6'5"	255	32		
Brad Dusek	LB	6'2"	214	25	1	6
Chris Hanburger	LB	6'2"	218	35	1	
Harold McLinton	LB	6'2"	235	29	1	
Stu O'Dell	LB	6'1"	220	24		
Russ Tillmann	LB	6'2"	230	30		
Pete Wysocki	LB	6'2"	225	27		
Eddie Brown	DB	5'11"	190	24	1	6
Pat Fischer	DB	5'10"	170	36	5	
Ken Houston	DB	6'3"	198	31	4	
Joe Lavender	DB	6'4"	190	27	8	
Brig Owens	DB	5'11"	190	33		
Jake Scott	DB	6'	188	31	4	
Gerard Williams	DB	6'1"	184	24		
Billy Kilmer	QB	6'	204	36		
Joe Theismann	QB	6'	184	26		6
Larry Brown	HB	5'11"	195	28		
Bob Brunet	HB	6'1"	205	30		
Mike Thomas	HB	5'11"	190	23		54
Calvin Hill	FB	6'3"	227	29		6
John Riggins	FB	6'2"	230	27		24
Danny Buggs (from NY GIANTS)	WR	6'2"	185	23		
Brian Fryer	WR	6'1"	185	23		
Frank Grant	WR	5'11"	181	26		30
Roy Jefferson	WR	6'2"	195	32		12
Larry Jones	WR	5'10"	170	25		
Bill Malinchak	WR	6'1"	200	32		
Doug Winslow	WR	5'11"	181	25		
Jean Fugett	TE	6'3"	226	24		36
Jerry Smith	TE	6'2"	208	33		12
Mike Bragg	K	5'11"	186	29		
Mark Moseley	K	5'11"	205	28		**97**

Paul Laaveg – Knee Injury
Ernie Janet – Groin Injury
Walt Sweeney – Knee Injury

Charley Taylor – Shoulder Injury

ST. LOUIS CARDINALS 10-4 Don Coryell

Scores of Each Game		
30	Seattle	24
29	GREEN BAY	0
24	San Diego	43
27	N.Y. GIANTS	21
33	PHILADELPHIA	14
21	DALLAS	17
10	Washington	20
23	SAN FRANCISCO	*20
17	Philadelphia	14
30	Los Angeles	28
10	WASHINGTON	16
14	Dallas	19
24	BALTIMORE	17
17	N.Y. Giants	14

Use Name	Pos.	Hgt.	Wgt.	Age	Int	Pts.
Dan Dierdorf	OT	6'4"	280	27		
Roger Finnie	OT-OG	6'3"	250	29		
Brad Oates	OT	6'6"	270	22		
Henry Allison	OG	6'3"	255	29		
Conrad Dobler	OG	6'3"	255	25		
Keith Wortman	OG	6'2"	248	26		
Bob Young	OG	6'2"	270	33		
Tom Banks	C-OG	6'1"	245	28		
Tom Brahaney	C	6'2"	250	24		
Bob Bell	DE	6'4"	250	28		
Ron Yankowski	DE	6'5"	250	29		
John Zook	DE	6'5"	250	28		
Lee Brooks	DT	6'5"	250	28		
Charlie Davis	DT	6'1"	265	24		
Mike Dawson	DT	6'4"	270	22		
Steve Okoniewski	DT-DE	6'3"	267	27		
Marv Upshaw	DT	6'3"	260	29		
Mark Arneson	LB	6'2"	220	26	1	
Al Beauchamp	LB	6'2"	235	32		
Carl Gersbach	LB	6'1"	230	29		
Greg Hartle	LB	6'2"	225	25		
Tim Kearney (from TAMPA BAY)	LB	6'2"	228	25	1	
Mike McDonald	LB	6'2"	215	23		
Mike McGraw	LB	6'2"	225	22		
Steve Neils	LB	6'2"	215	25		
Larry Stallings	LB	6'2"	230	34		
Ray White	LB	6'1"	220	27	2	
Dwayne Crump	DB	5'11"	180	26		
Clarence Duren	DB	6'1"	190	25	1	
Lee Nelson	DB	5'10"	185	22		
Ken Reaves	DB	6'3"	210	31	2	
Mike Sensibaugh	DB	5'11"	190	27	4	6
Jeff Severson	DB	6'1"	185	26		
Norm Thompson	DB	6'1"	180	28	4	
Roger Wehrli	DB	6'1"	190	28		
Billy Donckers	QB	6'1"	205	25		
Jim Hart	QB	6'2"	210	32		
Steve Jones	HB	6'	200	25		54
Jerry Latin	HB	5'10"	190	23		6
Terry Metcalf	HB	5'10"	185	24		42
Wayne Morris	HB	6'	200	22		24
Eddie Moss	FB	6'	215	27		
Jim Otis	FB	6'	225	28		12
J.V. Cain	WR	6'4"	225	25		30
Mel Gray	WR	5'9"	175	27		30
Gary Hammond	WR	5'11"	185	27		
Ike Harris	WR	6'3"	205	25		6
Pat Tilley	WR	5'10"	175	23		6
Terry Joyce	TE	6'6"	230	22		
Jackie Smith	TE	6'4"	230	35		
Jim Bakken	K	6'	200	35		93

Walt Patulski – Knee Injury
Bob Rowe – Back Injury

PHILADELPHIA EAGLES 4-10 Dick Vermeil

Scores of Each Game		
7	Dallas	27
20	N.Y. GIANTS	7
17	WASHINGTON	*20
14	Atlanta	13
14	St. Louis	33
13	Green Bay	28
12	MINNESOTA	31
10	N.Y. Giants	0
14	ST. LOUIS	17
3	Cleveland	24
7	OAKLAND	26
0	Washington	24
7	DALLAS	26
27	SEATTLE	10

Use Name	Pos.	Hgt.	Wgt.	Age	Int	Pts.
Ed George	OT	6'4"	270	30		
Dennis Nelson	OT	6'5"	260	30		
Stan Walters	OT	6'6"	270	28		
Jeff Bleamer	OG-OT	6'4"	253	23		
Wade Key	OG	6'4"	245	29		
Jerry Sisemore	OG-OT	6'4"	260	25		
Dennis Franks	C	6'1"	236	23		
Guy Morriss	C	6'4"	255	25		
Blenda Gay	DE	6'5"	255	25		
Carl Hairston	DE	6'3"	245	23		
Bill Wynn	DE	6'4"	245	27		
Bill Dunstan	DT	6'4"	250	27		
Pete Lazetich	DT	6'3"	245	26		
Manny Sistrunk	DT	6'5"	275	29		
Bill Bergey	LB	6'2"	250	31	2	
John Bunting	LB	6'1"	220	26		
Tom Ehlers	LB	6'2"	218	24	1	
Frank LeMaster	LB	6'2"	231	24		
Drew Mahalic	LB	6'4"	228	23		
Jerry Tautolo	LB	6'2"	234	22		
Bill Bradley	DB	5'11"	190	29	2	
Mark Burke	DB	6'1"	175	22		
Tommy Campbell	DB	6'	188	26		
Al Clark	DB	6'	185	28	1	
Randy Logan	DB	6'1"	195	25	1	
Larry Marshall	DB	5'10"	195	26		
John Outlaw	DB	5'10"	180	30	2	
Artimus Parker	DB	6'3"	200	24		
Mike Boryla	QB	6'3"	200	25		12
Roman Gabriel	QB	6'4"	220	36		
John Walton	QB	6'2"	210	28		
Dave Hampton (from ATLANTA)	HB	6'	202	29		6
Mike Hogan	HB-FB	6'2"	205	21		
Herb Lusk	HB	6'	190	23		
James McAlister	HB	6'1"	205	24		
Tom Sullivan	HB	6'	190	26		18
Art Malone	FB	5'11"	216	28		6
Bill Olds (from SEATTLE)	FB	6'1"	224	25		6
Harold Carmichael	WR	6'7"	225	26		30
Vince Papale	WR	6'2"	195	30		
Charlie Smith	WR	6'1"	185	26		30
Keith Krepfle	TE	6'3"	225	24		6
Charlie Young	TE	6'4"	238	25		
Spike Jones	K	6'2"	195	29		
Horst Muhlmann	K	6'1"	219	36		51

Tom Luken – Knee Injury
John Niland – Knee Injury

Dean Halverson – Injured

NEW YORK GIANTS 3-11 Bill Arnsparger (0-7), John McVay (3-4)

Scores of Each Game		
17	Washington	19
7	Philadelphia	20
10	Los Angeles	24
21	St. Louis	27
14	DALLAS	24
7	Minnesota	24
0	PITTSBURGH	27
0	PHILADELPHIA	10
3	Dallas	9
12	WASHINGTON	9
13	Denver	14
28	SEATTLE	16
24	DETROIT	10
14	ST. LOUIS	17

Use Name	Pos.	Hgt.	Wgt.	Age	Int	Pts.
Mike Gibbons	OT	6'4"	262	25		
Dick Leavitt	OT	6'3"	285	22		
Doug Van Horn	OT	6'2"	245	32		
Bill Ellenboggen	OG-OT	6'4"	260	25		
John Hicks	OG	6'2"	258	25		
Ron Mikolajczyk	OG	6'3"	275	26		
Tom Mullen	OG-OT	6'3"	250	24		
Al Simpson	OG-OT	6'5"	255	25		
Karl Chandler	C-OG	6'5"	250	24		
Ralph Hill	C	6'1"	245	26		
Troy Archer	DE	6'4"	250	21		
Rick Dvorak	DE	6'4"	245	24		
Jack Gregory	DE	6'6"	250	31		
George Martin	DE	6'4"	245	23		
Dave Gallagher	DT	6'4"	256	24	1	
John Mendenhall	DT	6'1"	255	27	1	
Harry Carson	LB	6'2"	228	22		
Brad Cousino	LB	6'	220	23		
Pat Hughes	LB	6'2"	225	29	1	
Brian Kelley	LB	6'3"	222	25		
Dan Lloyd	LB	6'2"	225	22		
Bob Schmit	LB	6'1"	220	26		
John Tate	LB	6'2"	230	23		
Brad Van Pelt	LB	6'5"	235	25	2	
Bobby Brooks	DB	6'1"	195	25	1	
Bill Bryant	DB	5'11"	195	25		
Rondy Colbert	DB	5'9"	165	22		
Larry Mallory	DB	5'11"	185	24	1	
Clyde Powers	DB	6'1"	195	25	1	
Jim Stienke	DB	5'11"	182	25	2	6
Henry Stuckey	DB	6'1"	180	26		
Rick Volk	DB	6'3"	195	31	2	
Craig Morton	QB	6'4"	210	33		
Dennis Shaw	QB	6'2"	215	29		
Norm Snead	QB	6'4"	215	36		
Gordon Bell	HB	5'9"	180	22		12
Steve Crosby	HB	5'11"	205	26		
Bob Hammond	HB	5'9"	175	24		
Doug Kotar	HB	5'11"	205	25		18
Larry Csonka	FB	6'3"	237	29		24
Larry Watkins	FB	6'2"	230	29		6
Marsh White	FB	6'2"	220	23		6
Walker Gillette	WR	6'5"	200	29		12
Ed Marshall (from NY JETS)	WR	6'4"	198	28		18
Ray Rhodes	WR	5'11"	185	25		6
Jim Robinson	WR	5'9"	170	23		6
Roger Wallace	WR	5'11"	180	24		
Gary Shirk	TE	6'1"	220	26		6
Bob Tucker	TE	6'3"	230	31		6
Joe Danelo	K	5'9"	166	22		44
Dave Jennings	K	6'4"	205	24		

Jim Pietrzak – Back Injury

Charlie Ford – Knee Injury
Robert Giblin – Shoulder Injury

* – Overtime

DALLAS COWBOYS

RUSHING

Last Name	No.	Yds	Avg	TD
ennison	153	542	3.5	6
ewhouse	116	450	3.9	3
aidlaw	94	424	4.5	3
Pearson	68	233	3.4	1
oung	48	208	4.3	0
taubach	43	184	4.3	3
uPree	7	50	7.1	0
Pearson	2	20	10.0	0
aldi	1	19	19.0	0
White	6	17	2.8	0

RECEIVING

Last Name	No.	Yds.	Avg	TD
D. Pearson	58	806	14	6
DuPree	42	680	16	2
Laidlaw	38	325	9	1
P. Pearson	23	316	14	2
Richards	19	414	22	3
Newhouse	15	86	6	0
Young	11	134	12	1
Dennison	8	67	8	0
Johnson	5	84	17	2
Barnes	1	43	43	0
Reece	1	6	6	0
Saldi	1	6	6	0

PUNT RETURNS

Last Name	No.	Yds	Avg	TD
Johnson	45	489	11	0

KICKOFF RETURNS

Last Name	No.	Yds	Avg	TD
Johnson	28	693	25	0
Jensen	13	313	24	0
Saldi	1	9	9	0
Henderson	0	12	0	0

PASSING – PUNTING – KICKING

PASSING	Att	Comp	%	Yds	Yd/Att	TD	Int–%		RK
Staubach	369	208	56	2715	7.4	14	11–	3	5
D. White	20	13	65	213	10.7	2	2–	10	
D. Pearson	1	1	100	39	39.0	1	0–	0	

PUNTING	No	Avg
D. White	70	38.4
Herrera	2	24.5

KICKING	XP	Att	%	FG	Att	%
Herrera	34	34	100	18	23	78

WASHINGTON REDSKINS

RUSHING

Last Name	No.	Yds	Avg	TD
homas	254	1101	4.3	5
iggins	162	572	3.5	3
ll	79	301	3.8	1
heismann	17	97	5.7	1
Brown	20	56	2.8	0
ugett	2	0	0.0	0
ilmer	13	-7	-0.5	0
rant	1	-9	-9.0	0

RECEIVING

Last Name	No.	Yds.	Avg	TD
Grant	50	818	16	5
Thomas	28	290	10	4
Jefferson	27	364	13	2
Fugett	27	334	12	6
Riggins	21	172	8	1
L. Brown	17	98	6	0
Hill	7	100	14	0
Smith	7	75	11	2
Buggs	2	25	13	0
Malinchak	1	12	12	0

PUNT RETURNS

Last Name	No.	Yds	Avg	TD
E. Brown	45	646	13	1
Scott	3	27	9	0
Jones	1	15	15	0

KICKOFF RETURNS

Last Name	No.	Yds	Avg	TD
E. Brown	30	738	25	0
Fryer	9	166	18	0
Brunet	4	85	21	0
Winslow	2	32	16	0
Jones	1	16	16	0
Owens	1	15	15	0
Tillman	1	14	14	0
Lorch	1	0	0	0
Wysocki	1	0	0	0

PASSING – PUNTING – KICKING

PASSING	Att	Comp	%	Yds	Yd/Att	TD	Int–%		RK
Kilmer	206	108	52	1252	6.1	12	10–	5	6
Theismann	163	79	49	1036	6.4	8	10–	6	9
Hill	1	0	0	0	0.0	0	0–	0	

PUNTING	No	Avg
Bragg	90	38.9

KICKING	XP	Att	%	FG	Att	%
Moseley	31	32	97	22	34	65

ST. LOUIS CARDINALS

RUSHING

Last Name	No.	Yds	Avg	TD
ris	233	891	3.8	2
etcalf	134	537	4.0	3
nes	113	451	4.0	8
orris	64	292	4.6	3
atin	25	115	4.6	1
ehrli	2	8	4.0	0
hart	8	7	0.9	0
oyce	1	0	0.0	0

RECEIVING

Last Name	No.	Yds.	Avg	TD
Harris	52	782	15	1
Gray	36	686	19	5
Metcalf	33	388	12	4
Jones	29	152	5	1
Tilley	26	407	16	1
Cain	26	400	15	5
Morris	8	75	9	1
Latin	4	35	9	0
Smith	3	22	7	0
Otis	2	15	8	0
Hammond	1	5	5	0

PUNT RETURNS

Last Name	No.	Yds	Avg	TD
Metcalf	17	188	11	0
Tilley	15	146	10	0
Hammond	3	16	5	0
Neils	1	0	0	0

KICKOFF RETURNS

Last Name	No.	Yds	Avg	TD
Latin	16	357	22	0
Metcalf	16	325	20	0
Morris	9	181	20	0
Smith	3	63	21	0
Crump	3	57	19	0
Hammond	2	36	18	0
Nelson	1	43	43	0
McGraw	1	13	13	0
Oates	1	12	12	0
Okoniewski	1	12	12	0
Severson	1	3	3	0

PASSING – PUNTING – KICKING

PASSING	Att	Comp	%	Yds	Yd/Att	TD	Int–%		RK
Hart	388	218	56	2946	7.6	18	13–	3	4
Donckers	1	1	100	16	16.0	0	0–	0	
Metcalf	1	0	0	0	0.0	0	0–	0	
Wehrli	1	0	0	0	0.0	0	0–	0	

PUNTING	No	Avg
Joyce	64	36.4

KICKING	XP	Att	%	FG	Att	%
Bakken	33	35	94	20	27	74

PHILADELPHIA EAGLES

RUSHING

Last Name	No.	Yds	Avg	TD
ogan	123	561	4.6	0
ullivan	99	399	4.0	2
ampton	83	291	3.5	1
cAlister	68	265	3.9	0
usk	61	254	4.2	0
oryla	29	166	5.7	2
lds	38	129	3.4	1
mith	9	25	2.8	1
alone	2	14	7.0	1
oung	1	6	6.0	0
abriel	4	2	0.5	0
alton	2	1	0.5	0

RECEIVING

Last Name	No.	Yds.	Avg	TD
Carmichael	42	503	12	5
Young	30	374	12	0
Smith	27	412	15	4
Hogan	15	89	6	0
Sullivan	14	116	8	1
Lusk	13	119	9	0
McAlister	12	72	6	0
Hampton	12	57	5	0
Olds	9	29	3	0
Krepfle	6	80	13	1
Malone	1	-3	-3	0
LeMaster	1	-4	-4	0

PUNT RETURNS

Last Name	No.	Yds	Avg	TD
Marshall	27	290	11	0
Bradley	9	64	7	0
Clark	4	57	14	0
Burke	1	14	14	0

KICKOFF RETURNS

Last Name	No.	Yds	Avg	TD
Marshall	30	651	22	0
McAlister	9	172	19	0
Lusk	7	155	22	0
Sullivan	5	108	22	0
Hampton	3	46	15	0
Olds	1	11	11	0
Ehlers	1	8	8	0
Bleamer	1	0	0	0
Smith	1	-3	-3	0

PASSING – PUNTING – KICKING

PASSING	Att	Comp	%	Yds	Yd/Att	TD	Int–%		RK
Boryla	246	123	50	1247	5.1	9	14–	6	12
Gabriel	92	46	50	476	5.2	2	2–	2	
Walton	28	12	43	125	4.5	0	2–	7	
Carmichael	2	0	0	0	0.0	0	0–	0	
Jones	1	1	100	-4	-4.0	0	0–	0	

PUNTING	No	Avg
Jones	94	36.6

KICKING	XP	Att	%	FG	Att	%
Muhlmann	18	19	95	11	16	69

NEW YORK GIANTS

RUSHING

Last Name	No.	Yds	Avg	TD
otar	185	731	4.0	3
sonka	160	569	3.6	4
ell	67	233	3.5	2
hite	69	223	3.2	1
atkins	26	96	3.7	1
orton	15	48	3.2	0
hodes	2	10	5.0	0
allory	1	0	0.0	0
nead	3	-1	-0.3	0
rosby	1	-1	-1.0	0
illette	1	-4	-4.0	0

RECEIVING

Last Name	No.	Yds.	Avg	TD
Tucker	42	498	12	1
Kotar	36	319	9	0
Bell	25	198	8	0
Robinson	18	249	14	1
Rhodes	16	305	19	1
Gillette	16	263	16	2
Marshall	8	166	21	3
Csonka	6	39	7	0
Shirk	4	52	13	1
Watkins	2	8	4	0
White	2	7	4	0

PUNT RETURNS

Last Name	No.	Yds	Avg	TD
Robinson	24	106	4	0
Colbert	13	72	6	0
Stienke	3	18	6	0
Bell	1	1	1	0

KICKOFF RETURNS

Last Name	No.	Yds	Avg	TD
Robinson	20	444	22	0
Bell	18	352	20	0
Shirk	6	109	18	0
Kotar	3	39	13	0
Hammond	2	44	22	0
Colbert	2	42	21	0
Watkins	1	9	9	0
Carson	1	5	5	0

PASSING – PUNTING – KICKING

PASSING	Att	Comp	%	Yds	Yd/Att	TD	Int–%		RK
Morton	284	153	54	1865	6.6	9	20–	7	11
Snead	42	22	52	239	5.7	0	4–	10	

PUNTING	No	Avg
Jennings	74	41.3

KICKING	XP	Att	%	FG	Att	%
Danelo	20	21	95	8	21	38

MINNESOTA VIKINGS 11-2-1 — Bud Grant

Scores of Each Game

40	New Orleans	9
10	LOS ANGELES	*10
10	Detroit	9
17	PITTSBURGH	6
20	CHICAGO	19
24	N.Y. GIANTS	7
31	Philadelphia	12
13	Chicago	14
31	DETROIT	23
27	SEATTLE	21
17	Green Bay	10
16	San Francisco	20
20	GREEN BAY	9
29	Miami	7

Use Name	Pos.	Hgt.	Wgt.	Age	Int	Pts
Bart Buetow	OT	6'5"	250	25		
Charlie Goodrum	OT	6'3"	256	26		
Steve Riley	OT	6'6"	258	23		
Ron Yary	OT	6'6"	255	30		
Wes Hamilton	OG	6'3"	255	23		
Ed White	OG	6'2"	270	29		
Mick Tingelhoff	C	6'1"	240	36		
Scott Anderson	C	6'4"	250	25		
Doug Dumler	C	6'3"	245	25		
Carl Eller	DE	6'6"	247	34		
Jim Marshall	DE	6'3"	240	39		
Mark Mullaney	DE	6'6"	242	23		
Alan Page	DT	6'5"	245	31		
Doug Sutherland	DT	6'3"	250	28		
James White	DT	6'4"	263	22		

Use Name	Pos.	Hgt.	Wgt.	Age	Int	Pts
Matt Blair	LB	6'5"	229	24	2	
Wally Hilgenberg	LB	6'3"	229	33		
Amos Martin	LB	6'3"	228	27		
Fred McNeill	LB	6'2"	229	24		
Jeff Siemon	LB	6'2"	237	26	1	
Roy Winston	LB	6'1"	222	36		
Nate Allen	DB	5'10"	174	28	3	6
Autry Beamon	DB	6'1"	190	22	1	
Bobby Bryant	DB	6'	170	32	2	
Windlan Hall	DB	5'11"	175	26		
Paul Krause	DB	6'3"	200	34	2	
Jeff Wright	DB	5'11"	190	27	1	
Nate Wright	DB	5'11"	180	29	7	

Use Name	Pos.	Hgt.	Wgt.	Age	Int	Pts
Bob Berry	QB	5'11"	185	34		
Bob Lee	QB	6'2"	195	31		
Fran Tarkenton	QB	6'1"	190	36		6
Chuck Foreman	HB	6'2"	207	25		84
Brent McClanahan	HB-FB	5'10"	202	25		30
Robert Miller	HB	5'11"	204	23		6
Bob Groce	FB	6'2"	210	22		
Sammy Johnson (from S.F.)	FB	6'	217	23		12
Mark Kellar	FB	6'	225	24		
Willie Spencer	FB	6'3"	235	23		
Bob Grim	WR	6'	188	31		
Ahmad Rashad	WR	6'2"	206	26		18
Sammie White	WR	5'11"	189	22		60
Leonard Willis	WR	5'10"	180	23		
Steve Craig	TE	6'3"	231	25		
Stu Voigt	TE	6'1"	225	28		6
Neil Clabo	K	6'2"	200	23		
Fred Cox	K	5'10"	200	37		89

CHICAGO BEARS 7-7 — Jack Pardee

Scores of Each Game

10	DETROIT	3
19	San Francisco	12
0	ATLANTA	10
33	WASHINGTON	7
19	Minnesota	20
12	Los Angeles	20
21	Dallas	31
14	MINNESOTA	13
27	OAKLAND	28
24	GREEN BAY	13
10	Detroit	14
16	Green Bay	10
34	Seattle	7
14	DENVER	28

Use Name	Pos.	Hgt.	Wgt.	Age	Int	Pts
Lionel Antoine	OT	6'6"	266	26		
Dan Jiggetts	OT	6'4"	274	22		
Dennis Lick	OT	6'3"	271	22		
Jeff Sevy	OT-OG	6'5"	260	25		
Noah Jackson	OG	6'2"	265	25		
Revie Sorey	OG	6'2"	270	22		
John Ward (from TAMPA)	OG-C	6'4"	269	28		
Dan Neal	C-OG	6'4"	257	27		
Don Peiffer	C	6'3"	254	25		
Royce Berry	DE	6'3"	239	30		
Mike Hartenstine	DE	6'3"	256	23		6
Jerry Meyers	DE	6'4"	245	22		
Roger Stillwell	DE	6'5"	254	24		
Wally Chambers	DT	6'6"	250	25	1	
Jim Osborne	DT	6'3"	248	26		
Ron Rydalch	DT	6'4"	262	24		

Gary Hrivnak — Injury

Use Name	Pos.	Hgt.	Wgt.	Age	Int	Pts
Ross Brupbacher	LB	6'3"	220	28	7	
Waymond Bryant	LB	6'3"	239	24	2	
Doug Buffore	LB	6'1"	229	32		
Tom Hicks	LB	6'4"	235	23		
Larry Muckensturm	LB	6'4"	226	22		
Dan Rives	LB	6'2"	230	25		
Craig Clemons	DB	5'11"	195	27	1	
Allan Ellis	DB	5'10"	180	25	6	6
Gary Fencik	DB	6'1"	190	22		
Bill Knox	DB	5'9"	190	25		
Virgil Livers	DB	5'9"	176	24	3	
Doug Plank	DB	6'	198	23	4	
Terry Schmidt	DB	6'	175	24		

Use Name	Pos.	Hgt.	Wgt.	Age	Int	Pts
Bob Avellini	QB	6'2"	211	23		6
Virgil Carter	QB	6'1"	190	30		
Gary Huff	QB	6'1"	199	25		
Mike Adamle	HB-FB	5'9"	198	26		8
Roland Harper	HB-FB	6'	215	23		18
Johnny Musso	HB	5'11"	201	26		26
Walter Payton	HB	5'11"	203	22		78
Larry Schreiber	FB-HB	6'	205	29		
Brian Baschnagel	WR-DB	6'	195	22		
Randy Burks	WR	5'11"	170	23		6
Bo Rather	WR	6'1"	188	25		
Steve Schubert	WR	5'10"	187	25		
James Scott	WR	6'1"	185	24		36
Ron Shanklin	WR	6'1"	187	28		
Bob Bruer	TE	6'5"	230	23		
Gary Butler	TE	6'3"	225	23		
Greg Latta	TE	6'3"	228	23		
Bob Parsons	TE	6'4"	241	26		
Bob Thomas	K	5'10"	177	24		63

DETROIT LIONS 6-8 — Rick Forzano (1-3), Tommy Hudspeth (5-5)

Scores of Each Game

3	Chicago	10
24	ATLANTA	10
9	MINNESOTA	10
14	Green Bay	24
30	NEW ENGLAND	10
7	Washington	20
41	Seattle	14
27	GREEN BAY	6
23	Minnesota	31
16	New Orleans	17
14	CHICAGO	10
27	BUFFALO	14
10	N.Y. Giants	24
17	LOS ANGELES	20

Use Name	Pos.	Hgt.	Wgt.	Age	Int	Pts
Russ Bolinger	OT	6'5"	255	21		
Rocky Freitas	OT	6'6"	275	30		
Craig Hertwig	OT	6'8"	270	24		
Jim Yarbrough	OT	6'6"	265	29		
Lynn Boden	OG	6'5"	270	23		
Bob Kowalkowski	OG	6'3"	245	32		
Ken Long	OG	6'3"	265	23		
Mark Markovich	C	6'5"	255	23		
Jon Morris	C	6'4"	250	33		
Billy Howard	DE	6'4"	255	26		
Jim Mitchell	DE	6'3"	250	27		
Ernie Price	DE	6'4"	245	25		
Ken Sanders	DE	6'5"	245	26		
Don Croft	DT	6'3"	258	27		
Doug English	DT	6'5"	245	23		
Larry Hand	DT	6'4"	245	36	1	
Herb Orvis	DT	6'5"	245	29		

Use Name	Pos.	Hgt.	Wgt.	Age	Int	Pts
Jim Laslavic	LB	6'2"	240	24	2	
Paul Naumoff	LB	6'1"	215	31		
Ed O'Neil	LB	6'3"	235	23	1	6
Garth Ten Napel	LB	6'1"	210	22		
Charlie Weaver	LB	6'2"	225	27	2	
John Woodcock	LB	6'3"	240	22		
Lem Barney	DB	6'	190	32	2	6
Ben Davis	DB	5'11"	180	30		
James Hunter	DB	6'3"	195	22	7	6
Dick Jauron	DB	6'	190	25	2	
Levi Johnson	DB	6'3"	200	25	6	6
Maurice Tyler	DB	6'	188	26		
Charlie West	DB	6'1"	190	30	1	

Use Name	Pos.	Hgt.	Wgt.	Age	Int	Pts
Gary Danielson	QB	6'2"	195	24		
Greg Landry	QB	6'4"	205	29		6
Joe Reed	QB	6'1"	195	28		6
Andy Bolton (from SEATTLE)	HB	6'1"	205	22		
Dexter Bussey	HB	6'1"	210	24		18
Bobby Thompson	HB	5'11"	195	29		
Lawrence Gaines	FB	6'1"	240	22		30
Jim Hooks	FB	5'11"	225	24		
Horace King	FB	5'10"	210	23		
Dennis Franklin	WR	6'1"	185	23		
J.D. Hill	WR	6'1"	185	27		
Ray Jarvis	WR	6'1"	190	27		30
Bob Picard (from PHI.)	WR	6'1"	198	26		
Leonard Thompson	WR	5'10"	190	24		
Larry Walton	WR	6'	185	29		18
David Hill	TE	6'2"	220	22		30
Charlie Sanders	TE	6'4"	230	30		30
Benny Ricardo (from BUFFALO)	K	5'9"	175	22		54
Herman Weaver	K	6'4"	210	27		

GREEN BAY PACKERS 5-9 — Bart Starr

Scores of Each Game

14	SAN FRANCISCO	26
0	St. Louis	29
7	Cincinnati	28
24	DETROIT	14
27	SEATTLE	20
28	PHILADELPHIA	13
14	Oakland	18
6	Detroit	27
32	NEW ORLEANS	27
13	Chicago	24
10	MINNESOTA	17
10	CHICAGO	16
9	Minnesota	20
24	Atlanta	20

Use Name	Pos.	Hgt.	Wgt.	Age	Int	Pts
Dick Himes	OT	6'4"	260	30		
Mark Koncar	OT	6'5"	271	23		
Dick Enderle (from S.F.)	OG	6'1"	250	28		
Gale Gillingham	OG	6'3"	265	32		
Melvin Jackson	OG	6'1"	267	22		
Steve Knutson	OG	6'3"	254	24		
Bruce Van Dyke	OG	6'2"	255	32		
Bob Hyland	C	6'5"	255	31		
Larry McCarren	C	6'3"	248	24		
Bob Barber	DE	6'3"	240	24		
Dave Pureifory	DE	6'1"	255	27		
Alden Roche	DE	6'4"	255	31		
Clarence Williams	DE	6'5"	255	29		
Mike McCoy	DT	6'5"	275	27		
Dave Roller	DT	6'2"	270	26		

Use Name	Pos.	Hgt.	Wgt.	Age	Int	Pts
Ron Acks	LB	6'2"	225	31		
Fred Carr	LB	6'5"	240	30	1	6
Jerry Dandridge	LB	6'1"	222	22		
Jim Gueno	LB	6'2"	220	22		
Don Hansen (from SEATTLE)	LB	6'3"	228	32		
Bob Lally	LB	6'2"	230	24		
Tom Perko	LB	6'3"	233	22		
Tom Toner	LB	6'3"	235	26	1	
Gary Weaver	LB	6'1"	225	27		
Willie Buchanan	DB	6'	190	25	2	
Jim Burrow	DB	5'11"	181	22		
Johnny Gray	DB	5'11"	185	22	4	6
Charlie Hall	DB	6'1"	190	28		
Steve Luke	DB	6'2"	205	22	2	
Mike C. McCoy	DB	5'11"	183	23		
Perry Smith	DB	6'1"	195	25	1	
Steve Wagner	DB	6'2"	198	22		

Jim Carter — Broken Arm

Use Name	Pos.	Hgt.	Wgt.	Age	Int	Pts
Carlos Brown	QB	6'3"	210	24		
Lynn Dickey	QB	6'4"	220	26		6
Randy Johnson (from WASH.)	QB	6'3"	205	32		6
Will Harrell	HB	5'9"	182	23		24
Dave Osborn	HB	6'	208	33		
Clifton Taylor	HB	6'	195	24		6
Eric Torkelson	HB	6'2"	194	24		12
John Brockington	FB	6'1"	225	27		12
Barty Smith	FB	6'4"	240	24		30
Ken Starch	FB	5'11"	210	22		
Jessie Green	WR	6'2"	185	22		
Steve Odom	WR	5'8"	174	23		12
Ken Payne	WR	6'1"	185	25		24
Ollie Smith	WR	6'2"	200	27		6
Don Zimmerman (from PHI.)	WR	6'3"	195	26		
Bert Askon	TE	6'3"	225	30		6
Rich McGeorge	TE	6'4"	230	27		6
Randy Beverly	K	6'2"	180	26		
Chester Marcol	K	6'	190	26		54

Don Milan — Broken Wrist
Gerald Tinker — Knee Injury

* — Overtime

MINNESOTA VIKINGS

RUSHING

Last Name	No.	Yds	Avg	TD
Foreman	278	1155	4.2	13
McClanahan	130	382	2.9	4
Miller	67	286	4.3	0
Johnson	41	150	3.7	2
Tarkenton	27	45	1.7	1
Kellar	7	25	3.6	0
Groce	3	18	6.0	0
Lee	2	2	1.0	0
Spencer	4	2	0.5	0
S. White	5	−10	−2.0	0

RECEIVING

Last Name	No.	Yds	Avg	TD
Foreman	55	567	10	1
Rashad	53	671	13	3
S.White	51	906	18	10
McClanahan	40	252	6	1
Voigt	28	303	11	1
Miller	23	181	8	1
Grim	9	108	12	0
Johnson	7	74	11	0
Craig	3	33	11	0
Kellar	2	22	11	0

PUNT RETURNS

Last Name	No.	Yds	Avg	TD
Willis	30	207	7	0
Beamon	7	19	3	0
S.White	3	45	15	0

KICKOFF RETURNS

Last Name	No.	Yds	Avg	TD
Willis	24	552	23	0
S. White	9	173	19	0
Miller	5	77	15	0
Johnson	2	35	18	0
Kellar	1	22	22	0
Blair	1	0	0	0

PASSING – PUNTING – KICKING

PASSING	Att	Comp	%	Yds	Yd/Att	TD	Int−%	RK
Tarkenton	412	255	62	2961	7.2	17	8− 2	3
Lee	30	15	50	156	5.2	0	2− 7	

PUNTING	No	Avg
Clabo	69	38.8

KICKING	XP	Att	%	FG	Att	%
Cox	32	36	89	19	31	61

CHICAGO BEARS

RUSHING

Last Name	No.	Yds	Avg	TD
Payton	311	1390	4.5	13
Harper	147	625	4.3	2
Musso	57	200	3.5	4
Adamle	33	93	2.8	0
Avellini	18	58	3.2	1
Schreiber	4	15	3.8	0
Rather	1	4	4.0	0
Parsons	1	2	2.0	0
Carter	1	0	0.0	0
Scott	2	−4	−2.0	0
Latta	2	−8	−4.0	0
Baschnagel	1	−12	−12.0	0

RECEIVING

Last Name	No.	Yds	Avg	TD
Harper	29	291	10	1
Scott	26	512	20	6
Latta	18	254	14	0
Payton	15	149	10	0
Baschnagel	13	226	17	0
Rather	5	33	7	0
Schubert	4	74	19	0
Adamle	4	28	7	1
Musso	4	26	7	0
Shanklin	2	32	16	0
Burks	1	55	55	1
Schreiber	1	16	16	0
Parsons	1	9	9	0

PUNT RETURNS

Last Name	No.	Yds	Avg	TD
Livers	28	205	7	0
Schubert	11	60	5	0
Baschnagel	2	2	1	0
Adamle	1	2	2	0
Knox	1	0	0	0

KICKOFF RETURNS

Last Name	No.	Yds	Avg	TD
Baschnagel	29	754	26	0
Adamle	11	179	16	0
Harper	6	119	20	0
Musso	2	18	9	0
Livers	1	14	14	0
Schubert	1	3	3	0
Payton	1	0	0	0

PASSING – PUNTING – KICKING

PASSING	Att	Comp	%	Yds	Yd/Att	TD	Int−%	RK
Avellini	271	118	44	1580	5.8	8	15− 6	14
Carter	5	3	60	77	15.4	1	0− 0	
Parsons	2	2	100	48	24.0	0	0− 0	

PUNTING	No	Avg
Parsons	99	37.6

KICKING	XP	Att	%	FG	Att	%
Thomas	27	30	90	12	25	48

DETROIT LIONS

RUSHING

Last Name	No.	Yds	Avg	TD
Bussey	196	858	4.4	3
Gaines	155	659	4.3	4
King	93	325	3.5	0
Landry	43	234	5.4	1
Bolton	15	71	4.7	0
Reed	11	63	5.7	1
B.Thompson	13	42	3.2	0
Walton	1	5	5.0	0
L.Thompaon	1	0	0.0	0
H.Weaver	1	0	0.0	0

RECEIVING

Last Name	No.	Yds	Avg	TD
Jarvis	39	822	21	5
C.Sanders	35	545	16	5
Bussey	28	218	8	0
Gaines	23	130	6	1
King	21	163	8	0
Walton	20	293	15	3
D.Hill	19	249	13	5
B.Thompson	10	108	11	0
L.Thompson	3	52	17	0
O'Neil	1	32	32	1
Franklin	1	16	16	0
J.D. Hill	1	2	2	0

PUNT RETURNS

Last Name	No.	Yds	Avg	TD
Barney	23	191	8	0
Hunter	4	7	2	0
West	3	9	3	0
Ten Napel	1	0	0	0

KICKOFF RETURNS

Last Name	No.	Yds	Avg	TD
B. Thompson	22	431	20	0
Hunter	14	375	27	0
Bolton	15	280	19	0
L.Thompson	5	86	17	0
King	3	63	21	0
Long	2	18	9	0
Bussey	1	14	14	0

PASSING – PUNTING – KICKING

PASSING	Att	Comp	%	Yds	Yd/Att	TD	Int−%	RK
Landry	291	168	58	2191	7.5	17	8− 3	2
Reed	62	32	52	425	6.9	3	3− 5	
H. Weaver	2	1	50	14	7.0	0	0− 0	
D. Hill	1	0	0	0	0.0	1	1−100	

PUNTING	No	Avg
H. Weaver	83	39.5
Ricardo	1	16.0

KICKING	XP	Att	%	FG	Att	%
Ricardo	21	23	91	11	18	61

GREEN BAY PACKERS

RUSHING

Last Name	No.	Yds	Avg	TD
Harrell	130	435	3.3	3
Brockington	117	406	3.5	2
B.Smith	97	355	3.7	5
Torkelson	88	289	3.3	2
Odom	4	78	19.5	0
Brown	12	49	4.1	0
Taylor	14	47	3.4	1
Johnson	5	25	5.0	1
Dickey	11	19	1.7	1
Osborn	6	16	2.7	0
Zimmerman	1	3	3.0	0

RECEIVING

Last Name	No.	Yds	Avg	TD
Payne	33	467	14	4
McGeorge	24	278	12	1
Odom	23	456	20	2
O.Smith	20	364	18	1
Torkelson	19	140	7	0
Harrell	17	201	12	1
B.Smith	11	88	8	0
Brockington	11	49	4	0
Taylor	2	21	11	0
Hall	1	18	18	0
Zimmerman	1	13	13	0
Jackson	1	8	8	0
Askon	1	2	2	1

PUNT RETURNS

Last Name	No.	Yds	Avg	TD
Gray	37	307	8	0
Harrell	3	−7	−2	0

KICKOFF RETURNS

Last Name	No.	Yds	Avg	TD
Odom	29	610	21	0
M.C. McCoy	18	457	25	0
Torkelson	6	123	21	0
Taylor	3	59	20	0
Hyland	3	31	10	0
Osborn	3	19	6	0
Wagner	1	27	27	0
Gray	1	23	23	0
O.Smith	1	12	12	0

PASSING – PUNTING – KICKING

PASSING	Att	Comp	%	Yds	Yd/Att	TD	Int−%	RK
Dickey	243	115	47	1465	6.0	7	14− 6	13
Brown	74	26	35	333	4.5	2	6− 8	
Johnson	35	21	60	249	7.1	0	1− 3	
Harrell	4	1	25	40	10.0	1	1− 25	
Beverly	1	1	100	18	18.0	0	0− 0	

PUNTING	No	Avg
Beverly	83	37.0

KICKING	XP	Att	%	%	Att	%
Marcol	24	27	89	10	19	53

LOS ANGELES RAMS 10-3-1 Chuck Knox

Scores of E Each Game		
30	Atlanta	14
10	Minnesota	*10
24	N.Y. GIANTS	10
31	Miami	28
0	SAN FRANCISCO	16
20	CHICAGO	12
16	New Orleans	10
45	SEATTLE	6
12	Cincinnati	20
28	ST. LOUIS	30
23	San Francisco	3
33	NEW ORLEANS	14
59	ATLANTA	0
20	Detroit	17

Use Name	Pos.	Hgt.	Wgt.	Age	Int	Pts
Doug France	OT	6'5"	260	23		
Jackie Slater	OT	6'4"	252	22		
John Williams	OT	6'3"	256	30		
Dennis Harrah	OG	6'5"	257	23		
Greg Horton	OG	6'4"	245	25		
Tom Mack	OG	6'3"	250	32		
Geoff Reece	C	6'4"	247	24		
Rich Saul	C	6'3"	250	28		
Fred Dryer	DE	6'6"	240	30		
Mike Fanning	DE	6'6"	260	23		
Jack Youngblood	DE	6'4"	255	26		
Larry Brooks	DT	6'3"	255	26		
Cody Jones	DT	6'5"	240	25		
Merlin Olsen	DT	6'5"	270	35		
Carl Ekern	LB	6'3"	220	22		
Rick Kay	LB	6'4"	235	26	1	
Kevin McClain	LB	6'2"	238	21		
Jack Reynolds	LB	6'1"	232	28		
Isiah Robertson	LB	6'3"	225	27	4	
Mel Rogers	LB	6'2"	230	29		
Jim Youngblood	LB	6'3"	239	26	2	
Dave Elmendorf	DB	6'1"	195	27	2	
Monte Jackson	DB	5'11"	189	23	10	18
Rod Perry	DB	5'9"	170	22	8	
Steve Preece	DB	6'1"	195	29	1	
Bill Simpson	DB	6'1"	180	24	4	
Pat Thomas	DB	5'9"	180	22		
Pat Haden	QB	5'11"	182	23		24
James Harris	QB	6'3"	210	29		12
Ron Jaworski	QB	6'2"	185	25		6
John Cappelletti	HB-FB	6'1"	217	24		12
Lawrence McCutcheon	HB	6'1"	205	26		66
Rob Scribner	HB	6'	200	25		6
Jim Bertelsen	FB	5'11"	205	26		12
Cullen Bryant	FB	6'1"	235	25		18
Rod Phillips	FB	6'	220	23		6
Tom Geredine	WR	6'2"	189	26		6
Harold Jackson	WR	5'10"	175	30		30
Ron Jessie	WR	6'	185	28		36
Freeman Johns	WR	6'1"	175	22		
Dwight Scales	WR	6'2"	170	23		6
Bob Klein	TE	6'5"	235	29		6
Terry Nelson	TE	6'2"	230	25		
Tom Dempsey	K	6'1"	260	35		87
Rusty Jackson	K	6'2"	190	25		

SAN FRANCISCO FORTY NINERS 8-6 Monte Clark

Scores of E Each Game		
26	Green Bay	14
12	CHICAGO	19
37	Seattle	21
17	N.Y. JETS	6
16	Los Angeles	0
33	NEW ORLEANS	3
15	ATLANTA	0
20	St. Louis	*23
21	WASHINGTON	24
16	Atlanta	21
3	LOS ANGELES	23
20	MINNESOTA	16
7	San Diego	*13
27	New Orleans	7

Use Name	Pos.	Hgt.	Wgt.	Age	Int	Pts
Cas Banaszek	OT	6'3"	247	30		
Jean Barrett	OT-C	6'6"	248	25		
Bill Cooke	OT	6'5"	250	25		
Keith Fahnhorst	OT	6'6"	256	24		
Steve Lawson	OG	6'3"	265	27		
Andy Mauer	OG	6'3"	275	27		
Mark Nordquist (from CHI.)	OG-C	6'4"	255	30		
John Watson	OG	6'4"	244	27		
Randy Cross	C	6'3"	247	22		
Tony Cline	DE	6'2"	244	28		
Cedrick Hardman	DE	6'3"	244	27		
Tommy Hart	DE	6'3"	249	31		2
Bill Sandifer	DE-DT	6'6"	260	24		
Cleveland Elam	DT	6'4"	252	24		6
Jimmy Webb	DT	6'4"	247	24		
Bruce Elia	LB	6'1"	217	23		
Willie Harper	LB	6'2"	208	26		
Dale Mitchell	LB	6'3"	223	23		
Frank Nunley	LB	6'2"	221	30	1	
Skip Vanderbundt	LB	6'3"	222	29	2	
Dave Washington	LB	6'5"	228	28		
Jim Johnson	DB	6'2"	187	38	1	
Anthony Leonard	DB	5'11"	170	23		6
Eddie Lewis	DB	6'	177	22		
Ralph McGill	DB	5'11"	178	26		6
Mel Phillips	DB	6'	184	34	2	
Bruce Rhodes	DB	6'	187	22	3	
Bruce Taylor	DB	6'	186	28		
Scott Bull	QB	6'5"	211	23		12
Marty Domres	QB	6'4"	220	29		
Jim Plunkett	QB	6'3"	219	28		
Paul Hofer	HB	6'	195	24		6
Kermit Johnson	HB	6'	202	24		6
Del Williams	HB	6'	197	25		54
Bob Ferrell	FB-HB	6'	208	23		6
Wilbur Jackson	FB	6'1"	219	24		12
Kenny Harrison	WR	6'	170	22		
Jim Lash (from MINNESOTA)	WR	6'2"	199	24		
Willie McGee	WR	5'11"	187	26		24
Steve Rivera	WR	5'11"	184	22		
Gene Washington	WR	6'1"	187	29		36
Tom Mitchell	TE	6'2"	226	32		6
Jim O'Bradovich	TE	6'2"	225	23		
Steve Mike-Mayer	K	6'	179	28		74
Tom Wittum	K	6'1"	191	26		

Bob Hoskins — Illness
Woody Peoples — Knee Injury
Bill Reid — Knee Injury

ATLANTA FALCONS 4-10 Marion Campbell (1-4) Pat Peppler (3-6)

Scores of E Each Game		
14	LOS ANGELES	30
10	Detroit	24
10	Chicago	0
13	PHILADELPHIA	14
0	New Orleans	30
17	CLEVELAND	20
0	San Francisco	15
23	NEW ORLEANS	20
13	Seattle	30
21	SAN FRANCISCO	16
17	DALLAS	10
14	Houston	20
0	Los Angeles	59
20	GREEN BAY	24

Use Name	Pos.	Hgt.	Wgt.	Age	Int	Pts
Brent Adams	OT	6'5"	256	24		
Greg Kindle	OT	6'4"	265	25		
Phil McKinnely	OT	6'4"	248	22		
Dave Scott	OT	6'4"	285	22		
Len Gotshalk	OG	6'4"	259	26		
Larron Jackson	OG	6'3"	260	27		
Royce Smith	OG	6'3"	250	27		
Paul Ryczek	C	6'2"	230	24		
Jeff Van Note	C	6'2"	247	30		
Jim Weatherly	C	6'3"	245	24		
Jim Bailey	DE	6'5"	255	28		
Claude Humphrey	DE	6'5"	265	32		2
Jeff Merrow	DE-DT	6'4"	230	23		
Ron East	DT	6'4"	250	33		
Steve George	DT	6'6"	265	25		
Mike Lewis	DT	6'3"	261	27		
Mike Tilleman	DT	6'5"	278	32		
Bill Windauer	DT	6'3"	250	26		
Greg Brezina	LB	6'1"	221	30		
Jim Cope	LB	6'1"	235	23		
Fulton Kuykendall	LB	6'5"	225	23		
Dewey McClain	LB	6'3"	236	22	1	
Tommy Nobis	LB	6'2"	243	32	1	
Ralph Ortega	LB	6'2"	220	23		
Guy Roberts	LB	6'1"	220	26	1	
Ray Brown	DB	6'2"	202	27	3	
Rick Byas	DB	5'9"	180	25		
Ray Easterling	DB	6'	192	26	3	
Bob Jones	DB	6'2"	193	25		
Rolland Lawrence	DB	5'10"	179	25	6	
Ron Mabra	DB	5'10"	170	25		
Frank Reed	DB	5'11"	193	22	3	
Steve Bartkowski	QB	6'4"	213	23		6
Scott Hunter	QB	6'2"	205	28		6
Kim McQuilken	QB	6'2"	203	25		
Bubba Bean	HB	5'11"	195	22		18
Sonny Collins	HB	6'1"	196	23		
Mike Esposito	HB	6'	185	23		
Haskel Stanback	HB	6'	210	24		24
Brad Davis	FB	5'10"	200	23		
Billy Pritchett	FB	6'3"	233	25		6
Woody Thompson	FB	6'1"	228	24		
Karl Farmer	WR	5'11"	165	22		
Wallace Francis	WR	5'11"	190	24		
John Gilliam	WR	6'1"	187	31		12
Al Jenkins	WR	5'10"	172	24		36
Scott Piper	WR	6'1"	179	22		
Bob Adams	TE	6'2"	218	30		
Jim Mitchell	TE	6'2"	236	28		
John James	K	6'3"	200	27		
Nick Mike-Mayer	K	5'8"	187	26		50

Monroe Eley — Injury
Greg McCrary — Leg Injury

NEW ORLEANS SAINTS 4-10 Hank Stram

Scores of E Each Game		
9	MINNESOTA	40
6	DALLAS	24
27	Kansas City	17
26	HOUSTON	31
30	ATLANTA	0
3	San Francisco	33
10	LOS ANGELES	16
20	Atlanta	23
27	Green Bay	32
17	DETROIT	16
51	Seattle	27
14	Los Angeles	33
6	New England	27
7	SAN FRANCISCO	27

Use Name	Pos.	Hgt.	Wgt.	Age	Int	Pts
Jeff Hart	OT	6'5"	252	22		
Marv Montgomery (from DENV.)	OT	6'6"	255	28		
Don Morrison	OT	6'5"	250	26		
Kurt Schumacher	OT	6'3"	246	23		
Terry Stieve	OG	6'2"	242	22		
Tom Wickert	OG-OT	6'4"	252	24		
Emanuel Zanders	OG	6'1"	248	25		
Lee Gross	C	6'3"	235	23		
John Hill	C	6'2"	246	26		
Steve Baumgartner	DE	6'7"	255	25		
Andy Dorris	DE	6'4"	240	25		
Elois Grooms	DE	6'4"	250	23		
Jeff Winans (from OAKLAND)	DE	6'5"	260	24		
Derland Moore	DT	6'4"	253	24		
Bob Pollard	DT	6'3"	251	27		
Elex Price	DT	6'3"	253	26	1	6
Ken Bordelon	LB	6'4"	236	22		
Warren Capone	LB	6'1"	220	25		6
Wayne Colman	LB	6'1"	215	30		
Joe Federspiel	LB	6'1"	230	26		
Rick Kingrea	LB	6'1"	222	27		
Jim Merlo	LB	6'1"	220	24	4	12
Greg Westbrooks	LB	6'2"	217	23		
Pete Athas	DB	5'11"	185	28	2	
Chuck Crist	DB	6'2"	205	25	1	
Ernie Jackson	DB	5'10"	176	26	2	
Benny Johnson	DB	5'11"	178	28		
Jim Kearney	DB	6'2"	196	33		
Tom Myers	DB	5'11"	170	25	1	6
Mo Spencer	DB	6'	176	24	1	
Bobby Douglass	QB	6'3"	228	29		12
Bobby Scott	QB	6'1"	197	27		6
Alvin Maxson	HB	5'11"	201	24		6
Leon McQuay	HB	5'9"	200	26		
Mike Strachan	HB	6'	200	23		12
Tony Galbreath	FB-HB	6'	220	22		48
Andrew Jones	FB	6'2"	218	23		
Kim Jones	FB	6'4"	238	24		
Chuck Muncie	FB	6'3"	220	23		12
Larry Burton	WR	6'1"	193	24		12
Clarence Chapman	WR	5'10"	185	22		
Don Herrmann	WR	6'2"	193	29		
Tinker Owens	WR	5'11"	170	21		6
Henry Childs	TE	6'2"	220	25		24
Paul Seal	TE	6'4"	223	24		
Jim Thaxton	TE	6'2"	240	27		6
Tom Blanchard	K	6'	187	28		
Richie Szaro	K	5'11"	204	28		79

Archie Manning — Shoulder Injury
Joel Parker — Injury
Louis Ross — Injury
Bob Stein — Injury

SEATTLE SEAHAWKS 2-12 Jack Patera

Scores of E Each Game		
24	ST. LOUIS	30
7	Washington	31
21	SAN FRANCISCO	37
13	DALLAS	28
20	Green Bay	27
13	Tampa Bay	10
14	DETROIT	41
6	Los Angeles	45
30	ATLANTA	13
21	Minnesota	27
27	NEW ORLEANS	51
16	N.Y. Giants	28
7	CHICAGO	34
10	Philadelphia	27

Use Name	Pos.	Hgt.	Wgt.	Age	Int	Pts
Nick Bebout	OT	6'5"	260	25		
Norm Evans	OT	6'5"	250	33		
Gordon Jolley	OT-OG	6'5"	245	27		
Dave Simonson (from HOUSTON)	OT	6'6"	250	24		
Ron Coder	OG	6'4"	250	22		
John Demarie	OG	6'3"	248	31		
Bob Newton	OG	6'4"	260	27		
Bobby Penchion	OG	6'5"	252	27		
Fred Hoaglin	C	6'4"	250	32		
Art Kuehn	C	6'3"	270	23		
Richard Harris	DE	6'4"	258	28		
Bob Lurtsema (from MIN.)	DE-DT	6'6"	250	34		
Dave Tipton	DE	6'6"	246	27		
Carl Barisich	DT	6'4"	255	25		
Steve Niehaus	DT	6'4"	270	21		
Larry Woods	DT	6'6"	268	28		
Ed Bradley	LB	6'2"	239	26	1	
Randy Coffield	LB	6'3"	215	22		
Greg Collins	LB	6'3"	227	23		
Mike Curtis	LB	6'2"	232	33	2	
Ken Geddes	LB	6'3"	235	28		
Sammy Green	LB	6'2"	228	21		
Lyle Blackwood	DB	6'	190	25		
Dave Brown	DB	6'1"	190	23	4	2
Don Dufek	DB	6'	195	22		
Ernie Jones	DB	6'3"	180	23		
Al Matthews	DB	5'11"	190	28	3	6
Eddie McMillan	DB	6'	190	24	1	
Roland Woolsey	DB	6'1"	182	23	4	
Bill Munson	QB	6'2"	205	34		
Steve Myer	QB	6'2"	188	22		
Jim Zorn	QB	6'2"	200	23		24
Ralph Nelson	HB	6'2"	195	22		6
Oliver Ross	HB-FB	6'	210	26		
Hugh McKinnis	FB	6'	219	28		24
Sherman Smith	FB	6'4"	217	21		30
Don Testerman	FB	6'2"	230	23		12
Don Clune	WR	6'3"	195	24		
Steve Largent	WR	5'11"	184	21		24
Sam McCullum	WR	6'2"	203	23		24
Steve Raible	WR	6'2"	195	22		12
Ron Howard	TE	6'4"	225	25		
John McMakin	TE	6'3"	225	25		12
Don Bitterlich	K	5'7"	166	22		10
Rick Engles	K	5'11"	170	22		
John Leypoldt (from BUFFALO)	K	6'2"	230	30		46

Ken Hutcherson — Injury

* — Overtime

LOS ANGELES RAMS

RUSHING

Last Name	No.	Yds	Avg	TD
McCutcheon	291	1168	4.0	9
Cappelletti	177	688	3.9	1
Phillips	34	206	6.1	1
Bertelsen	42	155	3.7	2
Haden	25	84	3.4	4
Harris	12	76	6.3	2
Bryant	21	64	3.0	2
Jessie	4	37	9.3	0
H. Jackson	1	15	15.0	0
Jaworski	2	15	7.5	1
Scribner	2	12	6.0	0
Geredine	1	8	8.0	0
Preece	1	0	0.0	0

RECEIVING

Last Name	No.	Yds	Avg	TD
H. Jackson	39	751	19	5
Jessie	34	779	23	6
Cappelletti	30	302	10	1
McCutcheon	28	305	11	2
Klein	20	229	11	1
Bertelsen	6	33	6	0
Nelson	4	48	12	0
Phillips	4	23	6	0
Scales	3	105	35	1
Bryant	2	28	14	0
Geredine	1	23	23	1
Harrah	0	3	0	0

PUNT RETURNS

Last Name	No.	Yds	Avg	TD
Bryant	29	321	11	0
Bertelsen	10	55	6	0
Scribner	8	54	7	0
Scales	4	46	12	0
Johns	1	0	0	0

KICKOFF RETURNS

Last Name	No.	Yds	Avg	TD
Bryant	16	459	29	1
Geredine	9	181	20	0
Thomas	7	140	20	0
Scales	7	136	19	0
Scribner	3	54	18	0
Johns	2	56	28	0
Nelson	0	1	0	0

PASSING – PUNTING – KICKING

PASSING	Att	Comp	%	Yds	Yd/Att	TD	Int–%		RK
Harris	158	91	58	1460	9.2	6	6–	4	1
Haden	105	60	57	896	8.5	8	4–	4	
Jaworski	52	20	39	273	5.3	1	5–	10	

PUNTING	No	Avg
R. Jackson	77	39.0

KICKING	XP	Att	%	FG	Att	%
Dempsey	36	44	82	17	26	65

SAN FRANCISCO FORTY NINERS

RUSHING

Last Name	No.	Yds	Avg	TD
Williams	248	1203	4.9	7
Jackson	200	792	4.0	1
K. Johnson	32	99	3.1	1
Plunkett	19	95	5.0	0
Hofer	18	74	4.1	0
Bull	15	66	4.4	2
Ferrell	9	28	3.1	1
Domres	4	18	4.5	0
McGee	3	12	4.0	0
Lash	3	5	1.7	0
G. Washington	1	3	3.0	0

RECEIVING

Last Name	No.	Yds	Avg	TD
G. Washington	33	457	14	6
Jackson	33	324	10	1
Williams	27	283	10	2
T. Mitchell	20	240	12	1
Lash	17	242	14	0
McGee	13	269	21	4
Hofer	4	45	11	1
Harris	3	65	22	0
K. Johnson	1	11	11	0
O'Bradovich	1	11	11	0
Ferrell	1	9	9	0
Rivera	1	7	7	0

PUNT RETURNS

Last Name	No.	Yds	Avg	TD
Anthony	35	293	8	1
Rhodes	16	142	9	0
McGill	10	103	10	1
Taylor	3	16	5	0
Rivera	1	3	3	0

KICKOFF RETURNS

Last Name	No.	Yds	Avg	TD
Leonard	26	553	21	0
Hofer	5	91	18	0
K. Johnson	4	114	29	0
T. Mitchell	2	7	4	0
Ferrell	1	12	12	0

PASSING – PUNTING – KICKING

PASSING	Att	Comp	%	Yds	Yd/Att	TD	Int–%		RK
Plunkett	243	126	52	1592	6.6	13	16–	7	8
Bull	48	21	44	252	5.3	2	4–	8	
Domres	14	7	50	101	7.2	0	1–	7	
Williams	1	1	100	18	18.0	0	0–	0	

PUNTING	No	Avg
Wittum	89	40.8

KICKING	XP	Att	%	FG	Att	%
Mike-Mayer	26	30	87	16	28	57

ATLANTA FALCONS

RUSHING

Last Name	No.	Yds	Avg	TD
Bean	124	428	3.5	2
Stanback	95	324	3.4	3
Collins	91	319	3.5	0
Esposito	60	317	5.3	2
Thompson	42	152	3.6	0
Pritchett	14	74	5.3	1
Hunter	14	41	2.9	1
McQuilken	9	26	2.9	0
Mitchell	1	–6	–6.0	0
Bartkowski	8	–10	–1.3	1

RECEIVING

Last Name	No.	Yds	Avg	TD
Jenkins	41	710	17	6
Gilliam	21	292	14	2
Stanback	21	174	8	1
Mitchell	17	209	12	0
Esposito	17	88	5	0
Bean	16	148	9	1
Thompson	16	111	7	0
Collins	4	37	9	0
Francis	2	24	12	0
Bob Adams	1	15	15	0
Pritchett	1	1	1	0

PUNT RETURNS

Last Name	No.	Yds	Avg	TD
Lawrence	54	372	7	0
Byas	1	8	8	0
Esposito	1	6	6	0
Farmer	1	0	0	0
Mabra	1	0	0	0
Roberts	1	0	0	0
Jones	1	–1	–1	0

KICKOFF RETURNS

Last Name	No.	Yds	Avg	TD
Lawrence	21	521	25	0
Byas	12	270	23	0
Francis	9	156	17	0
Collins	7	141	20	0
Mabra	3	61	20	0
Bean	2	38	19	0
Jones	1	22	22	0
Bob Adams	1	21	21	0
Stanback	1	18	18	0
Esposito	1	12	12	0
Ortega	1	9	9	0
Roberts	1	0	0	0

PASSING – PUNTING – KICKING

PASSING	Att	Comp	%	Yds	Yds/Att	TD	Int–%		RK
McQuilken	121	48	40	450	3.7	2	10–	8	
Bartkowski	120	57	48	677	5.6	2	4–	8	
Hunter	110	51	46	633	5.8	5	4–	4	
Bean	1	1	100	49	49.0	1	0–	0	
Esposito	1	0	0	0	0.0	0	0–	0	
Jenkins	1	0	0	0	0.0	0	1–100		

PUNTING	No	Avg
James	101	42.1

KICKING	XP	Att	%	FG	Att	%
Mike-Mayer	20	20	100	10	21	48

NEW ORLEANS SAINTS

RUSHING

Last Name	No.	Yds	Avg	TD
Muncie	149	659	4.4	2
Galbreath	136	570	4.2	7
Strachan	66	258	3.9	2
Maxson	34	120	3.5	1
Douglass	21	92	4.4	2
Scott	12	48	4.0	1
K. Jones	6	21	3.5	0
Childs	1	16	16.0	0
A. Jones	1	2	2.0	0
Burton	3	–4	–1.3	0
Seal	2	–7	–3.5	0

RECEIVING

Last Name	No.	Yds	Avg	TD
Galbreath	54	420	8	1
Herrmann	34	535	16	0
Muncie	31	272	9	0
Childs	26	349	13	3
Burton	18	297	17	2
Owens	12	241	20	1
Seal	9	72	8	0
Thaxton	7	112	16	1
Maxson	7	21	3	0
Strachan	6	22	4	0
K. Jones	1	14	14	0
Douglass	1	–2	–2	0

PUNT RETURNS

Last Name	No.	Yds	Avg	TD
Athas	35	332	9	0
Myers	2	22	11	0
Galbreath	2	8	4	0
McQuay	2	5	3	0
Crist	1	8	8	0

KICKOFF RETURNS

Last Name	No.	Yds	Avg	TD
Galbreath	20	399	20	0
Maxson	11	191	17	0
Thaxton	8	185	23	0
McQuay	8	151	19	0
Muncie	3	69	23	0
Chapman	3	63	21	0
Athas	2	68	34	0
Schumacher	2	17	9	0
Capone	2	0	0	0
Hart	1	12	12	0
K. Jones	1	12	12	0
Childs	1	6	6	0

PASSING – PUNTING – KICKING

PASSING	Att	Comp	%	Yds	Yd/Att	TD	Int–%		RK
Scott	190	103	54	1065	5.6	4	6–	3	7
Douglass	213	103	48	1288	6.0	4	8–	4	10

PUNTING	No	Avg
Blanchard	101	39.3

KICKING	XP	Att	%	FG	Att	%
Szaro	25	29	86	18	23	78

SEATTLE SEAHAWKS

RUSHING

Last Name	No.	Yds	Avg	TD
Smith	119	537	4.5	4
Zorn	52	246	4.7	4
Testerman	67	246	3.7	1
Nelson	52	173	3.3	1
McKinnis	46	105	2.3	4
Engles	3	37	12.3	0
Ross	13	23	1.8	0
Munson	1	6	6.0	0
Howard	1	2	2.0	0
Raible	1	2	2.0	0
Largent	4	–14	–3.5	0

RECEIVING

Last Name	No.	Yds	Avg	TD
Largent	54	705	13	4
Howard	37	422	11	0
Smith	36	384	11	1
McCullum	32	506	16	4
Testerman	25	232	9	1
McKinnis	13	148	11	0
Nelson	12	96	8	0
McMakin	9	158	18	2
Raible	4	126	32	1
Clune	4	67	17	0
Ross	2	22	11	0
Blackwood	1	8	8	0

PUNT RETURNS

Last Name	No.	Yds	Avg	TD
Blackwood	19	132	7	0
Brown	11	74	7	0
Largent	4	36	9	0
Woolsey	2	5	3	0
McMillan	1	–1	–1	0

KICKOFF RETURNS

Last Name	No.	Yds	Avg	TD
Ross	30	655	22	0
Blackwood	10	230	23	0
Dufek	9	177	20	0
Largent	8	156	20	0
Smith	5	78	16	0
Testerman	2	29	15	0

PASSING – PUNTING – KICKING

PASSING	Att	Comp	%	Yds	Yds/Att	TD	Int–%		RK
Zorn	439	208	47	2571	5.9	12	27–	6	15
Munson	37	20	54	295	8.0	1	3–	8	
Smith	2	0	0	0	0.0	0	0–	0	
Engles	1	1	100	8	8.0	0	0–	0	
Largent	1	0	0	0	0.0	0	0–	0	

PUNTING	No	Avg
Engles	80	38.3

KICKING	XP	Att	%	FG	Att	%
Leypoldt	22	25	88	8	15	53
Bitterlich	7	7	100	1	4	25

1976 A.F.C. The Pats "Cinderella team" Almost Took It All

EASTERN DIVISION

Baltimore Colts — The season started in turmoil with Coach Ted Marchibroda resigning just before the opener in a power struggle with GM Joe Thomas. When several assistants threatened to follow Marchibroda's lead and QB Bert Jones spoke publicly in his coach's defense, Thomas and Owner Bob Irsay quickly made amends with the coach. That was the beginning of the end for master builder Thomas, who was fired at the end of the season after five years at Baltimore. The Colts won eight of their first nine games and finished 11-3, edging New England for the division crown on the basis of a better intra-division record. Jones had a super year, passing for 24 TD's and a 102.6 rating. WR Roger Carr provided the deep threat, leading the league in reception yardage and average gain and ranking second in TD's. RB Lydell Mitchell placed second in AFC rushing and third in receptions. The Colts led the league in total offense, but a vulnerable defense was their undoing in the playoffs.

New England Patriots — The one-year rise from a 3-11 record to 11-3 and a "Wild Card" berth in the playoffs marked the Pats as the 1976 Cinderella team and Chuck Fairbanks as the Coach of the Year. Major reasons for the team's meteoric improvement were Steve Grogan, who proved himself an NFL-caliber QB in his first full season as a starter, and CB Mike Haynes, who was second in the AFC in punt return average and interceptions as Defensive Rookie of the Year. Led by RB's Sam Cunningham, Andy Johnson and Don Calhoun, the Pats ranked first in the league in yards per rush and second in scoring. Their 50 takeaways also were tops. After dropping their opener to Baltimore, the Pats beat overwhelming favorites Miami, Pittsburgh and Oakland in succession. Following mid-season upsets by Detroit and Miami, they won their last six games to reach the playoffs.

Miami Dolphins — After a 10-4 season in '75, Miami slipped to 6-8, Don Shula's first losing season as a head coach. A crippling series of injuries rocked the team, forcing 22 players to miss a total of 144 games. After a 6-0 preseason, Miami beat only one team above .500—a 10-3 upset of New England. The defense ranked only 26th in yards yielded, leaving too heavy a load for the offense. Rookie Duriel Harris led the NFL with a 32.9 kickoff return average.

New York Jets — Lou Holtz left North Carolina State to become the Jets' fourth head coach in four years, but his optimism turned sour and he unexpectedly resigned before the final game. Holtz inherited a sticky QB situation in which he had to choose between 33-year-old Joe Namath and rookie Richard Todd, who started six games and was the QB of record in the wins over Buffalo. Rookie free agent Clark Gaines became a starting RB in the seventh game and recorded four 100-yard games, outgaining all other NFL rookie runners and leading the club in receptions.

Buffalo Bills — O.J. Simpson's trade demands began a problem-filled year for the Bills. Simpson finally was coaxed back into the fold with a $2½ million contract over three years, but the team never recovered from the dispute. Added to the Bills' woes were the off-season departures of WR's Ahmad Rashad and J.D. Hill and defensive linemen Earl Edwards, Walt Patulski and Pat Toomay. RB Jim Braxton injured his knee in the opener and was lost for the season, as was QB Joe Ferguson, who suffered a back injury in the seventh game. A disillusioned Lou Saban resigned as head coach after five games with five years still remaining on a 10-year contract, and offensive line coach Jim Ringo replaced him. Things got even worse for Ringo. The Bills lost their last 10 games, nine under Ringo. Despite his slow start, Simpson led the NFL in rushing, but QB Gary Marangi finished last in AFC passing and the defense wasn't much better.

CENTRAL DIVISION

Pittsburgh Steelers — The two-time defending Super Bowl champs found themselves in a deep hole after losing four of their first five games, but they regrouped and won their last nine games to grab the division title for the third year in a row. The manner in which they won those last nine was awe-inspiring, as they yielded only 28 points or an average of 3.1 per game. After going 19 games without a shutout, the Steel Curtain recorded five in the last eight games. Led by All-Pro MLB Jack Lambert, the defense had a string of 15 consecutive scoreless quarters and 22 periods in a row without allowing a TD. Injuries in the fifth and 10th games sidelined QB Terry Bradshaw for two games each, but rookie Mike Kruczek filled in remarkably well, starting six games during the winning streak, including both wins over Cincinnati. RB's Franco Harris and Rocky Bleier both rushed for more than 1,000 yards behind a talented offensive line.

Cincinnati Bengals — Leading the division by two games over Pittsburgh with only three to play, the Bengals lost to the Steelers and Raiders back-to-back and watched their playoff chances go down the drain. Despite a 10-4 record, their two losses to Pittsburgh were the deciding factor. Their fine defensive showing was led by DE Coy Bacon, who recorded a league-high 26 sacks after an off-season trade from San Diego for WR Charlie Joiner. CB Ken Riley led the AFC in interceptions, and SS Tom Casanova, MLB Jim LeClair and CB Lemar Parrish were named All-Pro on defense. Offensively, QB Ken Anderson played below his league-leading pace of the previous two years but WR Isaac Curtis and TE Bob Trumpy combined for 13 TD catches.

Cleveland Browns — Forrest Gregg guided the team to a surprising 9-5 record after a 3-11 mark in his first year. Although their schedule was relatively easy, the Browns nevertheless played well. Behind a sound offensive line which allowed only 19 sacks (second in NFL), Brian Sipe developed into a respected QB. RB Greg Pruitt reached 1,000 yards for the second year in a row despite recurring ankle sprains. All-Pro DT Jerry Sherk (12 sacks) led a defense which ranked fourth in the NFL against the run. The acquisitions of LB Gerald Irons and CB Ron Bolton solidified the defense, and FS Thom Darden rebounded from knee surgery to lead the club in interceptions. After a poor 1-3 start, the Browns won eight of their next nine games before losing the finale.

Houston Oilers — Injuries and a lack of depth precipitated a fall from a 10-4 record in '75 to 5-9 in '76. After roaring to a 4-1 start, Houston lost eight of its last nine games. It lost four games by four points or less, and two of those defeats prevented it from standing 6-0 after six weeks. The running attack was far below par, and disgruntled QB Dan Pastorini asked to be traded at midseason but was injured the next week. Vet John Hadl played well as backup QB, and WR Ken Burrough had an excellent year. Despite injuries to key players, the 3-4 defense ranked high, sparked by OLB Robert Brazile (named All-Pro in his second year), MG Curley Culp and DE Elvin Bethea (14½ sacks).

WESTERN DIVISION

Oakland Raiders — Winning its fifth division title in a row, Oakland had the best record (13-1) in the NFL. Aside from a one-sided loss at New England, the defense was able to overcome a rash of injuries which sidelined three starters (Tony Cline, Horace Jones and Art Thoms) from the four-man front. Coach John Madden switched to a 3-4 alignment which gave up fewer points than in '75. Free agent John Matuszak was signed after the opener and became a starter at DE. However, the offense was primarily responsible for the team's success. QB Ken Stabler had an outstanding season, his 103.7 passer rating the sixth best of all-time. WR Cliff Branch's fine receiving stats were among the NFL's best, and RB Mark van Eeghen became only the third Raider ever to rush for 1,000 yards in a season, behind the blocking of LT Art Shell and LG Gene Upshaw.

Denver Broncos — Denver enjoyed the best season in its 17-year history but a crushing defeat at New England ended its playoff bid. Coach John Ralston, who had directed the team to its first three winning seasons during his five-year tenure, resigned under fire after the season. His successor was Red Miller, the offensive coordinator of the only team which scored more than 26 points against Denver all year. Denver ranked second in the AFC in points allowed and in rushing defense, led by LB's Tom Jackson and Randy Gradishar. The offense was less impressive, although RB Otis Armstrong gained 1,000 yards for the second time in his four-year career. Steve Ramsey held the QB job before falling into disfavor due to a poor performance in the Patriot game. Rick Upchurch averaged a league-high 13.7 yards per punt return with four TD's.

San Diego Chargers — After jumping off to a 4-2 start, the team lost six of its last eight games and finished 6-8, still a big improvement upon the 2-12 mark in '75. The defense ranked only 22nd overall, due largely to a weak pass defense. Guided by an offensive coordinator Bill Walsh, QB Dan Fouts had his best year, ranking 13th in NFL passing with more attempts than any other AFC QB. But he had only one accomplished WR in Charlie Joiner, who topped 1,000 yards in his first year as a Charger. The ground game ranked seventh in yardage per carry, with sophomore Rickey Young averaging 5.0.

Kansas City Chiefs — Four of K.C.'s five wins were against teams which finished with better records, including playoff-bound Washington. The offense ranked second in NFL passing yardage, as QB Mike Livingston finally cast aside the shadow of ex-teammate Len Dawson after eight years. Livingston had rapidly improving receivers in Walter White, Henry Marshall and Larry Brunson, and veteran RB MacArthur Lane led the NFL in receptions. The inexperienced defense was a different story, ranking 27th out of 28 teams overall.

Tampa Bay Buccaneers — The expansion team finished its first year without a win while Coach John McKay built for the future. It averaged only 8.9 points and was blanked five times, while giving up 29.4 points a game. The Bucs put a league-high 17 players on injured reserve, including six defensive starters. The play of veteran QB Steve Spurrier was so unimpressive that he was waived after the season ended. WR Morris Owens was the Bucs' most explosive offensive weapon, catching six TD passes.

FINAL TEAM STATISTICS

OFFENSE

	BALT.	BUFF.	CIN.	CLEV.	DENV.	HOUS.	K.C.	MIAMI	N.ENG.	N.Y.	OAK.	PITT.	S.D.	T.B.
FIRST DOWNS:														
Total	301	250	238	260	239	199	275	267	260	220	**303**	271	256	191
by Rushing	133	135	114	119	106	71	103	122	150	104	**137**	163	111	71
by Passing	144	102	110	112	114	110	**152**	125	95	93	146	94	127	93
by Penalty	24	13	14	**29**	19	18	20	20	15	23	20	14	18	27
RUSHING:														
Number	565	548	481	533	500	416	498	491	591	438	557	**653**	473	433
Yards	2303	2566	2109	2295	1932	1498	1873	2118	2948	1924	2285	**2971**	2040	1503
Average Yards	4.1	4.7	4.4	4.3	3.9	3.6	3.8	4.3	**5.0**	4.4	4.1	4.5	4.3	3.5
Touchdowns	26	11	15	9	14	6	18	15	24	10	14	**33**	13	5
PASSING:														
Attempts	361	383	360	373	353	**423**	419	346	309	393	361	277	388	376
Completions	215	156	187	209	168	227	229	193	146	180	**232**	143	223	181
Completion Pct.	59.6	40.7	51.9	56.0	47.6	53.7	54.7	55.8	47.2	45.8	**64.3**	51.6	57.5	48.1
Passing Yards	3221	2084	2443	2399	2510	2429	**3303**	2604	1910	1989	3195	1935	2687	1926
Avg. Yards per Att.	**8.9**	5.4	6.8	6.4	7.1	5.7	7.9	7.5	6.2	5.1	8.9	7.0	6.9	5.1
Avg. Yds per Comp.	**15.0**	13.4	13.1	11.5	14.9	10.7	14.4	13.5	13.1	11.1	13.8	13.5	12.1	10.6
Times Tackled	30	33	37	**19**	48	39	42	37	19	45	28	27	46	50
Yds Lost Tackled	288	246	252	**152**	306	357	374	336	164	383	290	269	271	423
Net Yards	**2933**	1838	2191	2247	2204	2072	2929	2268	1746	1606	1905	1666	2416	1503
Touchdowns	24	16	21	21	15	17	15	15	18	7	**33**	10	17	9
Interceptions	**10**	17	15	15	22	19	17	15	20	28	18	12	18	20
Pct. Intercepted	**2.8**	4.4	4.2	4.0	6.2	4.5	4.1	4.3	6.5	7.1	5.0	4.3	4.6	5.3
PUNTS:														
Number	59	87	76	69	84	**100**	68	62	67	81	67	76	82	92
Average Distance	39.7	**42.3**	39.5	37.4	35.1	35.3	41.1	38.2	40.1	39.7	41.6	39.2	38.7	39.3
PUNT RETURNS:														
Number	40	33	54	49	51	48	34	35	48	40	50	**71**	45	43
Yards	315	220	343	369	**640**	504	429	415	628	289	553	636	490	366
Average Yards	7.9	6.7	6.4	7.5	12.5	10.5	12.6	11.9	**13.1**	7.2	11.1	9.0	10.9	8.5
Touchdowns	0	1	0	0	**4**	1	0	1	2	1	0	0	0	0
KICKOFF RETURNS:														
Number	52	**75**	49	54	46	58	65	55	46	73	46	41	52	70
Yards	1072	1594	1046	1182	1075	1229	1538	1347	1087	**1597**	1025	855	1076	1488
Average Yards	20.6	21.3	21.3	21.9	23.4	21.2	23.7	**24.5**	23.6	21.9	22.3	20.9	20.7	21.3
Touchdowns	0	0	**1**	0	0	0	0	0	0	0	0	0	0	0
INTERCEPTION RET:														
Number	15	19	**26**	21	24	11	23	11	23	11	16	22	20	9
Yards	211	293	330	234	452	176	161	144	**505**	146	128	262	299	99
Average Yards	14.1	15.4	12.7	11.1	18.8	16.0	7.0	13.1	**22.0**	13.3	8.0	11.9	15.0	11.0
Touchdowns	0	1	3	1	**4**	0	0	0	3	0	0	0	1	0
PENALTIES:														
Number	92	91	79	107	105	99	97	70	102	71	107	**111**	78	109
Yards	786	797	700	**1037**	986	776	789	582	914	627	957	836	579	875
FUMBLES:														
Number	25	45	38	45	23	25	32	**14**	28	44	21	40	28	30
Number Lost	18	26	20	22	12	14	16	**8**	16	25	11	19	13	17
POINTS:														
Total	**417**	245	335	267	315	222	290	263	376	169	350	342	248	125
PAT Attempts	**51**	30	42	32	39	25	33	31	48	20	47	43	32	15
PAT Made	**49**	26	39	28	36	24	27	29	43	16	42	40	26	11
FG Attempts	27	24	27	28	21	27	**38**	23	25	16	19	26	20	17
FG Made	20	13	14	15	15	16	**21**	16	15	11	8	14	10	8
Percent FG Made	**74.1**	54.2	51.9	53.6	71.4	59.3	55.3	69.6	60.0	68.8	42.1	53.8	50.0	47.1
Safeties	**1**	0	**1**	**1**	0	0	**1**	0	0	0	**1**	**1**	0	0

DEFENSE

	BALT.	BUFF.	CIN.	CLEV.	DENV.	HOUS.	K.C.	MIAMI	N.ENG.	N.Y.	OAK.	PITT.	S.D.	T.B.
FIRST DOWNS:														
Total	229	262	234	244	222	226	309	268	258	277	261	**182**	259	284
by Rushing	83	128	116	109	90	117	161	125	102	135	98	**69**	113	136
by Passing	126	110	103	111	104	**90**	132	131	134	127	138	96	132	124
by Penalty	20	24	15	24	28	19	16	**12**	22	15	25	17	14	24
RUSHING:														
Number	**438**	533	520	445	496	540	555	525	462	582	478	452	516	588
Yards	1844	2465	1912	1761	1709	2072	2861	2411	1847	2592	1903	**1457**	2048	2560
Average Yards	4.2	4.6	3.7	4.0	3.4	3.8	5.2	4.6	4.0	4.5	4.0	**3.2**	4.0	4.4
Touchdowns	11	19	11	15	14	13	24	14	12	14	17	**5**	10	23
PASSING:														
Attempts	372	337	364	392	391	345	375	347	437	374	389	373	386	**321**
Completions	192	163	177	225	214	173	215	195	229	204	197	**158**	219	178
Completion Pct.	51.6	48.4	48.6	57.4	54.7	50.1	57.3	56.2	52.4	54.5	50.6	**42.4**	56.7	55.5
Passing Yards	2804	2475	2202	2353	2265	2259	2684	2863	2604	2468	2846	**2179**	2822	2142
Avg. Yards per Att.	7.5	7.3	6.0	6.0	**5.8**	6.5	7.2	8.3	6.0	6.6	7.3	5.8	7.3	7.5
Avg. Yds per Comp.	14.6	15.2	12.4	**10.5**	10.6	13.1	12.5	14.7	11.4	12.1	14.5	13.8	12.9	13.6
Times Tackled	**56**	28	46	32	32	50	22	20	47	16	46	41	23	24
Yds Lost Tackled	**461**	210	444	321	240	344	188	193	429	144	370	313	194	171
Net Yards	2343	2265	**1758**	2032	2025	1915	2496	2670	2175	2324	2476	1866	2628	2241
Touchdowns	16	18	13	18	**8**	17	25	20	16	25	13	9	21	19
Interceptions	15	19	**26**	21	24	11	23	11	23	11	16	22	20	9
Pct. Intercepted	4.0	5.6	**7.1**	5.4	6.1	3.2	6.1	3.2	5.3	2.9	4.1	5.9	5.2	2.8
PUNTS:														
Number	79	72	86	71	91	**96**	64	63	75	66	87	94	66	65
Average Distance	**36.9**	38.5	38.2	37.4	37.3	38.7	39.1	41.2	38.8	40.5	38.9	37.5	41.2	39.3
PUNT RETURNS:														
Number	**33**	52	41	45	43	60	39	34	37	55	38	36	45	71
Yards	231	878	323	517	372	659	376	272	288	458	264	**206**	601	754
Average Yards	7.0	16.9	7.9	11.5	8.7	11.0	9.6	8.0	7.8	8.3	6.9	**5.7**	13.4	10.6
Touchdowns	**0**	2	1	2	1	**0**	1	**0**	**0**	1	**0**	**0**	1	1
KICKOFF RETURNS:														
Number	77	48	66	57	50	53	55	57	71	39	61	61	49	**35**
Yards	1716	1204	1616	1347	1208	1125	1263	1246	1569	899	1123	1284	1072	**717**
Average Yards	22.3	25.1	24.5	23.6	24.2	21.2	23.0	21.9	22.1	23.1	**18.4**	21.0	21.9	20.5
Touchdowns	**0**	**0**	**0**	1	**0**	**0**	**0**	**0**	**0**	**0**	**0**	**0**	**0**	**0**
INTERCEPTION RET:														
Number	**10**	17	15	15	22	19	17	15	20	28	18	12	18	20
Yards	146	246	**102**	123	260	197	243	128	380	430	185	106	185	490
Average Yards	14.6	14.5	**6.8**	8.2	11.8	10.4	14.3	8.5	19.0	15.4	10.3	8.8	10.3	24.5
Touchdowns	1	**0**	**0**	**0**	1	**0**	1	**0**	**0**	3	**0**	**0**	1	4
PENALTIES:														
Number	89	92	90	89	88	107	88	94	83	87	96	80	92	**114**
Yards	770	704	768	711	715	**963**	762	716	715	796	918	630	823	935
FUMBLES:														
Number	32	37	34	24	23	33	35	31	37	36	26	**42**	24	33
Number Lost	21	23	15	11	13	17	20	18	**27**	21	9	24	11	19
POINTS:														
Total	246	363	210	287	206	273	376	264	236	383	237	**138**	285	412
PAT Attempts	29	41	25	37	25	31	51	34	29	45	31	**14**	34	50
PAT Made	27	39	24	32	20	29	43	30	26	42	27	**12**	30	48
FG Attempts	20	30	22	19	28	29	18	21	**17**	29	**17**	24	34	31
FG Made	15	26	12	11	12	18	9	10	12	23	**8**	14	17	20
Percent FG Made	75.0	86.7	54.5	57.9	**42.9**	62.1	50.0	47.6	70.6	79.3	47.1	58.3	50.0	64.5
Safeties	**0**	**0**	**0**	**0**	**0**	2	**0**	**0**	**0**	1	**0**	**0**	0	2

CONFERENCE PLAYOFFS

December 18, at Oakland (Attendance 53,045)

SCORING

OAKLAND	3	7	0	14–24
NEW ENGLAND	7	0	14	0–21

First Quarter
- N.E. — A. Johnson, 1 yard rush PAT–Smith (kick)
- Oak. — Mann, 40 yard field goal

Second Quarter
- Oak. — Biletnikoff, 31 yard pass from Stabler PAT–Mann (kick)

Third Quarter
- N.E. — Francis, 26 yard pass from Grogan PAT–Smith (kick)
- N.E. — J. Phillips, 3 yard rush PAT–Smith (kick)

Fourth Quarter
- Oak. — van Eeghen, 1 yard rush PAT–Mann (kick)
- Oak. — Stabler, 1 yard rush PAT–Mann (kick)

TEAM STATISTICS

Oak.		N.E.
20	First Downs-Total	23
5	First Downs-Rushing	10
13	First Downs-Passing	6
2	First Downs-Penalty	7
1	Fumbles-Number	1
1	Fumbles-Lost Ball	1
11	Penalties-Number	10
93	Yards Penalized	83
0	Missed Field Goals	1
70	Offensive Plays	73
302	Net Yards	331
4.3	Average Gain	4.5
1	Giveaways	3
3	Takeaways	1
+2	Difference	–2

INDIVIDUAL STATISTICS

OAKLAND	No	Yds	Avg.	NEW ENGLAND	No	Yds	Avg.
RUSHING							
van Eeghen	11	39	3.5	Cun'ham	20	68	3.4
C. Davis	7	29	4.1	Grogan	7	35	5.0
Banaszak	4	28	7.0	A. Johnson	14	32	2.9
Garrett	1	4	4.0	Calhoun	5	17	3.4
Stabler	1	1	1.0	J. Phillips	3	12	4.0
	24	101	4.2		49	164	3.3
RECEIVING							
Biletnikoff	9	137	15.2	Francis	4	96	24.0
Casper	4	47	11.8	Stingley	2	36	18.0
Branch	3	32	10.7	Cun'ham	2	14	7.0
van Eeghen	1	8	8.0	A. Johnson	2	13	6.5
C. Davis	1	5	5.0	Briscoe	1	7	7.0
Garrett	1	4	4.0	Chandler	1	1	1.0
	19	233	12.3		12	167	13.9
PUNTING							
Guy	5		37.8	Patrick	3		44.0
PUNT RETURNS							
Colzie	3	53	17.7	Haynes	1	13	13.0
KICKOFF RETURNS							
Garrett	4	119	29.8	J. Phillips	4	67	16.8
				Webster	1	0	0.0
					5	67	13.4
INTERCEPTION RETURNS							
Thomas	1	18	18.0	none			
Johnson	1	0	0.0				
	2	18	9.0				

PASSING

OAKLAND	Att.	Comp.	Comp. Pct.	Yds.	Int.	Yds/ Att.	Yds/ Comp.	Yards Lost Tackled
Stabler	32	19	59.4	233	0	7.3	12.3	4–32
NEW ENGLAND								
Grogan	23	12	52.2	167	1	7.3	13.9	
Francis	1	0	0.0	0	1	0.0	0.0	
	24	12	50.0	167	2	7.0	13.9	0–0

December 19, at Baltimore (Attendance 60,020)

SCORING

BALTIMORE	7	0	0	7–14
PITTSBURGH	9	17	0	14–40

First Quarter
- Pitt. — Lewis, 76 yard pass from Bradshaw PAT–No Good
- Pitt. — Gerela, 45 yard field goal
- Balt. — Carr, 17 yard pass from Jones PAT–Linhart (kick)

Second Quarter
- Pitt. — Harrison, 1 yard rush PAT–Gerela (kick)
- Pitt. — Swann, 29 yard pass from Bradshaw PAT–Gerela (kick)
- Pitt. — Gerela, 25 yard field goal

Fourth Quarter
- Pitt. — Swan, 11 yard pass from Bradshaw PAT–Gerela (kick)
- Balt. — Leaks, 1 yard rush PAT–Linhart (kick)
- Pitt. — Harrison, 10 yard rush PAT–Gerela (kick)

TEAM STATISTICS

BALT.		PITT.
16	First Downs-Total	29
4	First Downs-Rushing	12
8	First Downs-Passing	15
4	First Downs-Penalty	2
0	Fumbles-Number	2
0	Fumbles-Lost Ball	2
7	Penalties-Number	12
59	Yards Penalized	88
0	Missed Field Goals	0
53	Offensive Plays	65
170	Net Yards	526
3.2	Average Gain	8.1
2	Giveaways	2
2	Takeaways	2
0	Difference	0

INDIVIDUAL STATISTICS

BALTIMORE	No.	Yds	Avg.	PITTSBURGH	No.	Yds	Avg.
Mitchell	16	55	3.4	Harris	18	132	7.3
Leaks	4	12	3.0	Fugua	11	54	4.9
Jones	2	3	1.5	Harrison	10	40	4.0
McCauley	1	1	1.0	Bleier	1	–1	–1.0
	23	71	3.1		40	225	5.6
RECEIVING							
Mitchell	5	42	8.4	Swann	5	77	15.4
Chester	3	42	14.0	Harrison	4	37	9.3
Carr	2	35	17.5	Harris	3	24	8.0
Daughty	1	25	25.0	Lewis	2	103	51.5
	11	144	13.1	Fugua	2	34	17.0
				Bell	2	25	12.5
				Stallworth	1	8	8.0
					19	308	16.2
PUNTING							
D. Lee	4		40.5	Walden	1		33.0
PUNT RETURNS							
Stevens	1	11	11.0	Swann	3	12	4.0
KICKOFF RETURNS							
Stevens	3	66	22.0	Bell	1	60	60.0
H. Lee	3	39	13.0	Pough	1	19	19.0
Laird	1	3	3.0		2	79	39.5
	7	108	15.4				
INTERCEPTION RETURNS							
none				Edwards	1	26	26.0
				Wagner	1	12	12.0
					2	38	19.0

PASSING

BALTIMORE	Att.	Comp.	Comp. Pct.	Yds.	Int.	Yds/ Att.	Yds/ Comp.	Yards Lost Tackled
Jones	25	11	44.0	144	2	5.8	13.1	5–45
PITTSBURGH								
Bradshaw	18	14	77.7	264	0	14.7	18.9	1–1
Kruczek	6	5	83.3	44	0	7.3	8.8	
	24	19	79.2	308	0	12.8	16.2	1–1

BALTIMORE COLTS 11-3 Ted Marchibroda

Scores of Each Game

27	New England	13
28	CINCINNATI	27
27	Dallas	30
42	TAMPA BAY	17
28	MIAMI	14
31	Buffalo	13
20	N.Y. Jets	0
38	HOUSTON	14
37	San Deigo	21
14	NEW ENGLAND	21
17	Miami	16
33	N.Y. JETS	16
17	St. Louis	24
58	BUFFALO	20

Use Name	Pos.	Hgt	Wgt	Age	Int	Pts
George Kunz	OT	6'5"	261	29		
David Taylor	OT	6'4"	264	26		
Elmer Collett	OG	6'4"	246	31		
Ken Huff	OG	6'4"	257	23		
Robert Pratt	OG	6'4"	248	25		
Bob Van Duyne	OG	6'5"	249	24		
Forrest Blue	C	6'5"	260	30		
Ken Mendenhall	C	6'3"	250	28		
Fred Cook	DE	6'4"	246	24	1	
John Dutton	DE	6'7"	266	25		
Ron Fernandes	DE	6'4"	239	24	2	
Mike Barnes	DT	6'6"	256	25		
Joe Ehrmann	DT	6'5"	254	27		
Ken Novak	DT	6'7"	275	22		

Use Name	Pos.	Hgt	Wgt	Age	Int	Pts
Jim Cheyunski	LB	6'2"	220	30		
Dan Dickel	LB	6'3"	230	24		
Derrel Luce	LB	6'3"	227	23	2	6
Sanders Shiver	LB	6'2"	222	21		
Ed Simonini	LB	6'	220	22		
Stan White	LB	6'1"	223	26	3	
Tim Baylor	DB	6'6"	191	22		
Randy Hall	DB	6'3"	194	24		
Bruce Laird	DB	6'	198	26		
Lloyd Mumphord	DB	5'11"	178	29	1	
Nelson Munsey	DB	6'1"	191	28	1	
Ray Oldham	DB	6'	192	25	2	
Jackie Wallace	DB	6'3"	198	25	5	

Marshall Johnson — Knee Injury
Tom McLeod — Foot Injury
Doug Nettles — Shoulder Injury

Use Name	Pos.	Hgt	Wgt	Age	Int	Pts
Bert Jones	QB	6'3"	212	24		
Mike Kirkland	QB	6'1"	195	22		
Bill Troup	QB	6'5"	215	25		
Lydell Mitchell	HB	5'11"	195	27		
Howard Stevens	HB	5'5"	165	26		
Roosevelt Leaks	FB	6'1"	225	23		
Ron Lee	FB	6'4"	222	22		
Don McCauley	FB-HB	6'1"	215	27		
Roger Carr	WR	6'3"	196	24		
Glenn Doughty	WR	6'2"	202	25		
Freddie Scott	WR	6'2"	170	24		
Ricky Thompson	WR	6'	170	22		
Ray Chester	TE	6'3"	236	28		
Jimmie Kennedy	TE	6'3"	230	24		
David Lee	K	6'4"	224	32		
Toni Linhart	K	6'	179	34		

NEW ENGLAND PATRIOTS 11-3 Chuck Fairbanks

Scores of Each Game

13	BALTIMORE	27
30	MIAMI	14
30	Pittsburgh	27
48	OAKLAND	17
10	Detroit	30
41	N.Y. JETS	7
26	Buffalo	22
3	Miami	10
20	BUFFALO	10
21	Baltimore	14
38	N.Y. Jets	24
38	DENVER	14
27	NEW ORLEANS	6
31	Tampa Bay	14

Use Name	Pos.	Hgt	Wgt	Age	Int	Pts
Leon Gray	OT	6'3"	256	24		
Bob McKay	OT	6'5"	265	28		
Tom Neville	OT	6'4"	253	33		
Sam Adams	OG	6'3"	252	27		
John Hannah	OG	6'2"	265	25		
Fred Sturt	OG	6'4"	255	25		
Pete Brock	C-TE	6'5"	253	22	6	
Bill Lenkaitis	C	6'4"	250	30		
Julius Adams	DE	6'3"	260	28		
Mel Lunsford	DE	6'3"	250	26		
Tony McGee	DE	6'4"	245	27		
Richard Bishop	NT	6'1"	275	26		
Ray Hamilton	NT	6'1"	245	25		
Art Moore	NT	6'5"	253	25		
Dave Tipton	NT	6'1"	250	22		

Steve Corbett — Neck Injury
Pete Kusick — Knee Injury
Craig Hanneman — Injury
Shelby Jordan — Declared Ineligible

Use Name	Pos.	Hgt	Wgt	Age	Int	Pts
Pete Barnes	LB	6'3"	240	31		
Sam Hunt	LB	6'1"	240	25	2	6
Steve King	LB	6'4"	225	25		
Steve Nelson	LB	6'2"	230	25	2	
Jim Romaniszyn	LB	6'2"	220	24		
Donnie Thomas	LB	6'2"	245	23		
George Webster	LB	6'4"	230	30		
Steve Zabel	LB	6'4"	235	28	1	
Doug Beaudoin	DB	6'1"	200	22		
Joe Blahak (From TAMPA BAY)	DB	5'9"	186	25		
Dick Conn	DB	6'	180	25		
Tim Fox	DB	5'11"	186	22	3	
Willie Germany	DB	6'	192	27		
Mike Haynes	DB	6'2"	189	23	8	12
Bob Howard	DB	6'1"	177	31	3	
Prentice McCray	DB	6'1"	187	25	5	12
Deac Sanders	DB	6'1"	178	26		

Rod Shoate — Knee Injury

Use Name	Pos.	Hgt	Wgt	Age	Int	Pts
Steve Grogan	QB	6'4"	200	23		
Tom Owen	QB	6'1"	194	23		
Don Calhoun	HB	6'	198	24		
Ike Forte	HB	6'	196	22		
Andy Johnson	HB	6'	204	23		
Jess Phillips	HB-FB	6'1"	208	29		
Sam Cunningham	FB	6'3"	224	26		
Marlin Briscoe	WR	5'10"	180	30		
Steve Burks	WR	6'5"	211	23		
Darryl Stingley	WR	6'	195	24		
Randy Vataha	WR-DB	5'10"	170	27		
Al Chandler	TE	6'2"	229	25		
Russ Francis	TE	6'6"	240	23		
Mike Patrick	K	6'	213	23		
John Smith	K	6'	185	26		

MIAMI DOLPHINS 6-8 Don Shula

Scores of Each Game

30	Buffalo	21
14	New England	30
16	N.Y. JETS	0
28	LOS ANGELES	31
14	Baltimore	28
17	KANSAS CITY	*20
23	Tampa Bay	20
10	NEW ENGLAND	3
27	N.Y. Jets	7
3	Pittsburgh	14
16	BALTIMORE	17
13	Cleveland	17
45	BUFFALO	27
7	MINNESOTA	29

Use Name	Pos.	Hgt	Wgt	Age	Int	Pts
Darryl Carlton	OT	6'6"	260	23		
Tom Drougas	OT	6'4"	255	26		
Wayne Moore	OT	6'6"	265	31		
Bob Kuechenberg	OG	6'3"	252	28		
Larry Little	OG	6'1"	265	30		
Mel Mitchell	OG	6'3"	260	23		
Ed Newman	OG	6'2"	245	25		
Jim Langer	C	6'2"	253	28		
John Andrews	DE	6'6"	251	24		
Vern Den Herder	DE	6'6"	252	27		
Wally Pesuit (From ATLANTA)	DE	6'4"	260	22		
Don Reese	DE-DT	6'6"	255	24		
Bill Stanfill	DE	6'5"	252	29		
Randy Crowder	DT	6'2"	236	24		
Bob Heinz	DT	6'6"	265	29		

Manny Fernandez — Knee Injury
Mike Kolen — Knee Injury
Ernest Rhone — Knee Injury

Use Name	Pos.	Hgt	Wgt	Age	Int	Pts
Nick Buoniconti	LB	5'11"	210	35		
Rusty Chambers (From N.O.)	LB	6'1"	215	22		
Mike Dennery	LB	6'	225	26		
Larry Gordon	LB	6'4"	230	23		
Bob Matheson	LB	6'4"	235	31	2	
Andy Selfridge	LB	6'4"	220	27		
Steve Towle	LB	6'2"	233	22		
Dick Anderson	DB	6'2"	196	30	1	
Charlie Babb	DB	6'	190	26	2	
Ted Bachman (From SEATTLE)	DB	6'	190	24		
Ken Ellis (From HOUSTON)	DB	5'10"	190	28	2	
Tim Foley	DB	6'	194	28		
Barry Hill	DB	6'3"	185	23		
Mike Holmes (from BUF.)	DB-WR	6'2"	198	25		
Curtis Johnson	DB	6'2"	196	28	1	
Bryant Salter (to BALT.)	DB	6'4"	196	26	1	
Jeris White	DB	5'11"	180	23	2	

Use Name	Pos.	Hgt	Wgt	Age	Int	Pts
Bob Griese	QB	6'1"	190	31		
Earl Morrall	QB	6'1"	210	42		
Don Strock	QB	6'5"	203	25		
Gary Davis	HB	5'10"	202	21		
Clayton Heath (From BUF.)	HB	5'11"	195	25		
Benny Malone	HB	5'10"	193	24		
Norm Bulaich	FB-HB	6'1"	218	29		
Don Nottingham	FB	5'10"	210	27		
Stan Winfrey	FB	6'1"	223	23		
Duriel Harris	WR	5'11"	175	21		
Ike Hill	WR	5'10"	180	29		
Nat Moore	WR	5'10"	180	24		
Freddie Solomon	WR	5'11"	181	23		
Howard Twilley	WR	5'10"	185	32		
Jim Mandich	TE	6'3"	224	28		
Loaird McCreary	TE	6'5"	227	23		
Larry Seiple	TE	6'	214	31		
Andre Tillman	TE	6'5"	230	23		
Garo Yepremian	K	5'8"	175	32		

NEW YORK JETS 3-11 Lou Holtz

Scores of Each Game

17	Cleveland	38
3	Denver	46
0	Miami	16
6	San Francisco	17
17	BUFFALO	14
7	New England	41
0	BALTIMORE	20
19	Buffalo	14
7	MIAMI	27
34	TAMPA BAY	0
24	NEW ENGLAND	38
16	Baltimore	33
16	WASHINGTON	37
3	CINCINNATI	42

Use Name	Pos.	Hgt	Wgt	Age	Int	Pts
Winston Hill	OT	6'4"	272	34		
Al Krevis	OT	6'6"	263	24		
John Roman	OT	6'4"	248	24		
Robert Woods	OT	6'3"	259	26		
Gary Puetz	OG-OT	6'4"	267	24		
Randy Rasmussen	OG	6'2"	255	31		
Darrell Austin	C-OG	6'4"	252	24		
Joe Fields	C-OG	6'2"	245	22		
Richard Neal	DE	6'3"	263	28		
Billy Newsome	DE	6'4"	268	28		
Lawrence Pillers	DE	6'3"	250	23		
Carl Barzilauskas	DT	6'6"	265	25		
Larry Faulk	DT-DE	6'3"	249	23		
Ed Galigher	DE	6'4"	253	25		

Mark Lomas — Knee Injury
Wayne Mulligan — Knee Injury

Use Name	Pos.	Hgt	Wgt	Age	Int	Pts
Greg Buttle	LB	6'2"	235	22	2	6
John Ebersole	LB	6'3"	235	27	1	
Mike Hennigan	LB	6'2"	225	24		
Larry Keller	LB	6'2"	220	22	1	
Bob Martin	LB	6'1"	217	22	2	
Steve Poole	LB	6'1"	232	22		6
James Rosecrans	LB	6'2"	230	23		
Carl Russ	LB	6'2"	227	23		
Harry Howard	DB	6'	189	26		
Tommy Marvaso	DB	6'1"	190	24		
Burgess Owens	DB	6'2"	200	25		
Rich Sowells	DB	6'	181	27	2	
Shafer Suggs	DB	6'1"	194	23	1	
Ed Taylor	DB	6'	172	23	1	
Phil Wise	DB	6'	202	27		

Don Coleman — Knee Injury

Use Name	Pos.	Hgt	Wgt	Age	Int	Pts
Steve Joachim	QB	6'3"	215	24		
Joe Namath	QB	6'2"	200	33		
Richard Todd	QB	6'2"	210	22		
Clark Gaines	HB	6'1"	192	22		
Louie Giammona	HB	5'9"	180	24		
Bob Gresham	HB	5'11"	200	28		
Jazz Jackson	HB	5'8"	174	24		
Steve Rogers	HB	6'2"	205	23		
Allen Carter (from N. ENG.)	FB-HB	5'11"	208	23		
Steve Davis	FB-HB	6'1"	210	26		
Ed Marinaro	FB	6'2"	219	26		
Jerome Barkum	WR	6'3"	212	26		
Don Buckey	WR	5'11"	180	22		
Keith Denson	WR	5'8"	165	24		
Clint Haserlig	WR	6'	189	24		
David Knight	WR	6'1"	175	25		
Lou Piccone	WR	5'9"	184	27		
Howard Satterwhite	WR	5'11"	185	23		
Rich Caster	TE-WR	6'5"	224	27		
Richard Osborne (from PHI.)	TE	6'3"	230	24		
Duane Carrell	K	5'10"	185	26		
Pat Leahy	K	6'	200	25		

BUFFALO BILLS 2-12 Lou Saban (2-3) Jim Ringo (0-9)

Scores of Each Game

21	Miami	30
3	HOUSTON	13
14	Tampa Bay	9
50	KANSAS CITY	17
14	N.Y. Jets	17
13	BALTIMORE	31
22	NEW ENGLAND	26
14	N.Y. JETS	19
10	New England	20
10	Dallas	17
13	SAN DIEGO	34
14	Detroit	27
27	Miami	45
20	Baltimore	58

Use Name	Pos.	Hgt	Wgt	Age	Int	Pts
Joe Devlin	OT	6'4"	258	22		
Dave Foley	OT	6'5"	247	28		
Donnie Green	OT	6'7"	252	28		
Bill Adams	OG-OT	6'2"	246	26		
Joe DeLamielleure	OG	6'3"	248	25		
Reggie McKenzie	OG	6'4"	242	26		
Mike Montler	C	6'4"	245	32		
Willie Parker	C-OG	6'3"	245	27		
Bob Patton	C	6'1"	245	22		
Mark Johnson	DE	6'2"	240	23		
Ken Jones	DE	6'5"	252	23		
Jeff Lloyd	DE	6'6"	255	22		
Marty Smith	DE	6'3"	250	22		
Sherman White	DE	6'5"	245	27	1	
Mike Kadish	DT	6'5"	270	26		
Ben Williams	DT	6'2"	258	22		
Jeff Yeates (to ATLANTA)	DT	6'3"	248	25		

Use Name	Pos.	Hgt	Wgt	Age	Int	Pts
Bo Cornell	LB	6'1"	222	27		
Dan Jilek	LB	6'2"	212	22	2	
Merv Krakau	LB	6'1"	233	25	1	
Bob Nelson	LB	6'4"	232	23		
Tom Ruud	LB	6'2"	223	23		
John Skorupan	LB	6'2"	221	25	1	
Tim Anderson	DB	6'	194	27		
Cliff Brooks (from PHI & NYJ)	DB	6'1"	190	27		
Mario Clark	DB	6'2"	190	22	2	
Steve Freeman	DB	5'11"	185	23		
Van Green (from CLEVELAND)	DB	6'1"	192	25		
Tony Greene	DB	5'10"	170	27	5	6
Dwight Harrison	DB	6'1"	186	27	1	
Doug Jones	DB	6'2"	205	26	3	
Keith Moody	DB	5'11"	171	23	3	6

Ron Holliday — Knee Injury
Robert James — Knee Injury

Use Name	Pos.	Hgt	Wgt	Age	Int	Pts
Joe Ferguson	QB	6'1"	184	26		
Gary Marangi	QB	6'1"	203	24		
Sam Wyche (from ST. LOUIS)	QB	6'4"	220	30		
Roland Hooks	HB	6'	197	23		
Darnell Powell	HB	6'	197	22		
Andy Reid	HB	6'	195	22		
O.J. Simpson	HB	6'2"	212	29		
Vic Washington	HB	5'10"	195	30		
Jim Braxton	FB	6'2"	242	27		
Jeff Kinney (from K.C.)	FB-HB	6'2"	215	26		
Eddie Ray	FB	6'1"	240	29		
Bob Chandler	WR	6'	180	27		
Emmett Edwards (from HOUS.)	WR	6'1"	190	24		
Robert Gaddis	WR	5'11"	178	24		
John Holland	WR	6'	190	24		
Fred Coleman	TE	6'4"	240	23		
Reuben Gant	TE-WR	6'4"	225	24		
Paul Seymour	TE	6'5"	245	26		
Marv Bateman	K	6'4"	214	26		
George Jakowenko	K	5'9"	180	28		

* – Overtime

BALTIMORE COLTS

RUSHING

Last Name	No.	Yds	Avg	TD
Mitchell	289	1200	4.2	5
Leaks	118	445	3.8	7
McCauley	69	227	3.3	9
R. Lee	41	220	5.4	1
Jones	38	214	5.6	2
Doughty	2	7	2.3	0
Stevens	1	3	3.0	1
Troup	5	-1	0.2	1
D. Lee	1	-12	-12.0	0

RECEIVING

Last Name	No.	Yds	Avg	TD
Mitchell	60	555	9	3
Carr	43	1112	26	11
Doughty	40	628	16	5
McCauley	34	347	10	2
Chester	24	467	19	3
Leaks	8	43	5	0
Scott	3	35	12	0
Kennedy	1	32	32	0
Thompson	1	11	11	0
R. Lee	1	-9	-9	0

PUNT RETURNS

Last Name	No.	Yds	Avg	TD
Stevens	39	315	8	0
R. Lee	1	0	0	0

KICKOFF RETURNS

Last Name	No.	Yds	Avg	TD
Stevens	30	710	24	0
Laird	7	143	20	0
Kennedy	4	64	16	0
Wallace	3	61	20	0
R. Lee	3	24	8	0
Pratt	1	21	21	0
Scott	1	20	20	0
McCauley	1	17	17	0
Novak	1	12	12	0
Huff	1	0	0	0

PASSING – PUNTING – KICKING

PASSING	Att	Comp	%	Yds	Yd/Att	TD	Int–%	RK
Jones	343	207	60	3104	9.0	24	9– 3	2
Troup	18	8	44	117	6.5	0	1– 6	

PUNTING	No	Avg		
D. Lee	59	39.7		

KICKING	XP	Att	%	FG	Att	%
Linhart	49	50	98	20	27	74

NEW ENGLAND PATRIOTS

RUSHING

Last Name	No.	Yds	Avg	TD
Cunningham	172	824	4.8	3
Calhoun	129	721	5.6	1
Johnson	169	699	4.1	6
Grogan	60	397	6.6	12
Phillips	24	164	6.8	1
Forte	25	100	4.0	1
Stingley	8	45	5.6	0
Francis	2	12	6.0	0
Burks	1	2	2.0	0
Patrick	1	-16	-16.0	0

RECEIVING

Last Name	No.	Yds	Avg	TD
Johnson	29	343	12	4
Cunningham	27	299	11	0
Francis	26	367	14	3
Stingley	17	370	22	4
Calhoun	12	56	5	0
Vataha	11	192	17	1
Briscoe	10	136	14	1
Chandler	5	49	10	3
Forte	3	9	3	1
Burks	2	27	14	0
Phillips	1	18	18	0
Brock	1	6	6	1

PUNT RETURNS

Last Name	No.	Yds	Avg	TD
Haynes	45	608	14	2
Beaudoin	2	18	9	0
Stingley	1	2	2	0

KICKOFF RETURNS

Last Name	No.	Yds	Avg	TD
Phillips	14	397	28	0
Calhoun	9	183	20	0
Beaudoin	6	134	22	0
Forte	3	62	21	0
Conn	2	29	15	0
McKay	1	23	23	0

PASSING – PUNTING – KICKING

PASSING	Att	Comp	%	Yds	Yd/Att	TD	Int–%	RK
Grogan	302	145	48	1903	6.3	18	20– 7	12
Owen	5	1	20	7	1.4	0	0– 0	
Johnson	2	0	0	0	0.0	0	0– 0	

PUNTING	No	Avg		
Patrick	67	40.1		

KICKING	XP	Att	%	FG	Att	%
Smith	42	46	91	15	25	60
Zabel	1	1	100			

MIAMI DOLPHINS

RUSHING

Last Name	No.	Yds	Avg	TD
Malone	186	797	4.3	4
Bulaich	122	540	4.4	4
Winfrey	52	205	3.9	1
Nottingham	63	185	2.9	3
Davis	31	160	5.2	1
Griese	23	108	4.7	0
Solomon	4	60	15.0	1
N. Moore	4	36	9.0	0
Seiple	3	14	4.7	0
Strock	2	13	6.5	1
Heath	1	0	0.0	0

RECEIVING

Last Name	No.	Yds	Avg	TD
N. Moore	33	625	19	4
Bulaich	28	151	5	0
Solomon	27	453	17	2
Harris	22	372	17	1
Mandich	22	260	12	4
Twilley	14	214	15	1
Tillman	13	130	10	1
Seiple	10	138	14	1
Malone	9	103	11	0
Winfrey	6	55	9	1
Nottingham	4	33	8	0
McCreary	2	51	26	0
Davis	2	8	4	0
Holmes	1	11	11	0

PUNT RETURNS

Last Name	No.	Yds	Avg	TD
Solomon	13	205	16	1
Harris	9	79	9	0
N. Moore	8	72	9	0
Babb	3	38	13	0
Anderson	2	21	11	0

KICKOFF RETURNS

Last Name	No.	Yds	Avg	TD
Davis	26	617	24	0
Harris	17	559	33	0
Nottingham	6	107	18	0
Holmes	4	90	23	0
N. Moore	2	28	14	0
Winfrey	2	24	12	0
Solomon	1	12	12	0
Tillman	1	0	0	0

PASSING – PUNTING – KICKING

PASSING	Att	Comp	%	Yds	Yd/Att	TD	Int--%	RK
Griese	272	162	60	2097	7.7	11	12– 4	4
Strock	47	21	45	359	7.6	3	2– 4	
Morrall	26	10	39	148	5.7	1	1– 4	
Solomon	1	0	0	0	0.0	0	0– 0	

PUNTING	No	Avg		
Seiple	62	38.2		

KICKING	XP	Att	%	FG	Att	%
Yepremian	29	31	94	16	23	70

NEW YORK JETS

RUSHING

Last Name	No.	Yds	Avg	TD
Gaines	157	724	4.6	3
Davis	94	418	4.4	3
Marinaro	77	312	4.1	2
Giammona	39	158	3.8	1
Todd	28	107	3.8	1
Gresham	30	92	3.1	0
Caster	6	73	12.2	0
Buttle	1	26	26.0	0
Piccone	1	11	11.0	0
Jackson	1	6	6.0	0
Namath	2	5	2.5	0
Carrell	2	0	0.0	0

RECEIVING

Last Name	No.	Yds	Avg	TD
Gaines	41	400	10	2
Caster	31	391	13	1
Marinaro	21	168	8	0
Knight	20	403	20	2
Giammona	15	145	10	0
Piccone	12	147	12	0
Gresham	11	66	6	0
Davis	8	57	7	0
Satterwhite	7	110	16	0
Barkum	5	54	11	1
Buckey	5	36	7	0
Osborne	2	9	5	1
Jackson	2	3	2	0

PUNT RETURNS

Last Name	No.	Yds	Avg	TD
Piccone	21	173	8	1
Giammona	12	117	10	0
Jackson	6	-1	0	0
Marvaso	1	0	0	0

KICKOFF RETURNS

Last Name	No.	Yds	Avg	TD
Piccone	31	699	23	0
Giammona	23	527	23	0
Jackson	10	207	21	0
Denson	6	129	22	0
Hennigan	1	22	22	0
Osborne	1	8	8	0
Gaines	1	5	5	0

PASSING – PUNTING – KICKING

PASSING	Att	Comp	%	Yds	Yd/Att	TD	Int–%	RK
Namath	230	114	50	1090	4.7	4	16– 7	14
Todd	162	65	40	870	5.4	3	12– 7	15
Gresham	1	1	100	29	29.0	0	0– 0	

PUNTING	No	Avg.		
Carrell	81	39.7		

KICKING	XP	Att	%	FG	Att	%
Leahy	16	20	80	11	16	69

BUFFALO BILLS

RUSHING

Last Name	No.	Yds	Avg	TD
Simpson	290	1503	5.2	8
Kinney	118	482	4.1	1
Marangi	39	230	5.9	2
Hooks	25	116	4.6	0
Ferguson	18	81	4.5	0
Washington	22	65	3.0	0
Ray	24	56	2.3	0
Powell	11	40	3.6	0
Braxton	1	0	0.0	0
Chandler	1	0	0.0	0
Edwards	1	0	0.0	0

RECEIVING

Last Name	No.	Yds	Avg	TD
Chandler	61	824	14	10
Simpson	22	259	12	1
Seymour	16	169	11	0
Holland	15	299	20	2
Kinney	14	78	6	0
Gant	12	263	22	3
Hooks	6	72	12	0
Washington	3	29	10	0
Ray	3	26	9	0
Edwards	2	53	27	0
Montler	1	6	6	0
Powell	1	6	6	0

PUNT RETURNS

Last Name	No.	Yds	Avg	TD
Moody	16	166	10	1
Hooks	11	45	4	0
Holland	4	11	3	0
Gaddis	1	6	6	0

KICKOFF RETURNS

Last Name	No.	Yds	Avg	TD
Moody	26	605	23	0
Hooks	23	521	23	0
Ruud	6	68	11	0
Powell	4	101	25	0
Holland	4	62	16	0
Washington	3	63	21	0
Cornell	2	32	16	0
Gaddis	1	16	16	0

PASSING – PUNTING – KICKING

PASSING	Att	Comp	%	Yds	Yd/Att	TD	Int–%	RK
Ferguson	151	74	49	1086	7.2	9	1– 1	3
Marangi	232	82	35	998	4.3	7	16– 7	16
Wyche	1	1	100	5	5.0	0	0– 0	

PUNTING	No	Avg		
Bateman	86	42.8		

KICKING	XP	Att	%	FG	Att	%
Jakowenko	21	24	88	12	17	71

PITTSBURGH STEELERS 10-4 Chuck Noll

Scores of Each Game

28	Oakland	31
31	CLEVELAND	14
27	NEW ENGLAND	30
6	Minnesota	17
16	Cleveland	18
23	CINCINNATI	6
27	N.Y. Giants	0
23	SAN DIEGO	0
45	Kansas City	0
14	MIAMI	3
32	HOUSTON	16
7	Cincinnati	3
42	TAMPA BAY	0
21	Houston	0

Use Name	Pos.	Hgt	Wgt	Age	Int	Pts
Gordon Gravelle	OT	6'5"	250	27		
Jon Kolb	OT	6'2"	262	29		
Jim Clack	OG	6'3"	250	28		
Sam Davis	OG	6'1"	255	32		
Gerry Mullins	OG-OT	6'3"	244	27		
Ray Mansfield	C	6'3"	260	35		
Ray Pinney	C-OT	6'4"	240	22		
Mike Webster	C	6'1"	250	24		
John Banaszak	DE	6'3"	244	26		
L.C. Greenwood	DE	6'5"	250	29		
Dwight White	DE	6'4"	255	27		
Gary Dunn	DT	6'3"	240	23		
Steve Furness	DT-DE	6'4"	255	25		
Joe Greene	DT	6'4"	275	29		
Ernie Holmes	DT	6'3"	260	28		
Jack Ham	LB	6'3"	225	27	2	
Marv Kellum	LB	6'2"	225	24		
Jack Lambert	LB	6'4"	220	24	2	
Andy Russell	LB	6'3"	225	34	1	
Loren Toews	LB	6'3"	222	24	2	
Jim Allen	DB	6'2"	194	24		
Mel Blount	DB	6'3"	205	28	6	
Glen Edwards	DB	6'	185	29	6	
Donnie Shell	DB	5'11"	190	24	1	
J.T. Thomas	DB	6'2"	196	25	2	
Mike Wagner	DB	6'1"	200	27	2	
Terry Bradshaw	QB	6'3"	200	27		18
Neil Graff (from SEATTLE)	QB	6'3"	200	26		
Mike Kruczek	QB	6'	196	23		12
Rocky Bleier	HB	5'11"	210	30		30
Jack Deploaine	HB	5'10"	205	22		12
John Fuqua	HB	5'11"	200	29		6
Franco Harris	FB	6'2"	225	26		84
Reggie Harrison	FB	5'11"	220	26		24
Theo Bell	WR	6'	180	22		
Frank Lewis	WR	6'1"	196	29		12
Ernest Pough	WR	6'1"	174	24		6
John Stallworth	WR	6'2"	183	24		18
Lynn Swann	WR	5'10"	180	24		18
Larry Brown	TE	6'4"	229	27		
Bennie Cunningham	TE	6'4"	255	21		6
Randy Grossman	TE	6'1"	215	22		6
Roy Gerela	K	5'10"	185	28		82
Bobby Walden	K	6'	190	38		

Mike Collier — Knee Injury
Reggie Garrett — Back Injury

CINCINNATI BENGALS 10-4 Bill Johnson

Scores of Each Game

17	DENVER	7
27	Baltimore	28
28	GREEN BAY	7
45	Cleveland	24
21	TAMPA BAY	0
6	Pittsburgh	23
27	Houston	7
21	CLEVELAND	6
20	LOS ANGELES	12
31	HOUSTON	27
27	Kansas City	24
3	PITTSBURGH	7
20	Oakland	35
42	N.Y. Jets	3

Use Name	Pos.	Hgt	Wgt	Age	Int	Pts
Vern Holland	OT	6'5"	272	28		
Ron Hunt	OT	6'6"	274	21		
Rufus Mayes	OT	6'5"	268	28		
Glenn Bujnoch	OG	6'5"	260	22		
Greg Fairchild	OG-OT	6'4"	258	22		
Dave Lapham	OG	6'4"	258	24		
John Shinners	OG	6'2"	259	29		
Bob Johnson	C	6'5"	255	30		
Coy Bacon	DE	6'4"	270	34	2	
Gary Burley	DE	6'3"	262	23		
Ken Johnson	DE	6'5"	262	29		
Bob Brown	DT	6'5"	280	36		
Ron Carpenter	DT	6'4"	265	28		
Bill Kollar	DT	6'4"	256	23		
Glenn Cameron	LB	6'1"	230	23		
Chris Devlin	LB	6'3"	228	22	1	
Bo Harris	LB	6'3"	228	23	2	
Jim LeClair	LB	6'2"	237	25	1	
Ron Pritchard	LB	6'1"	226	29	1	
Reggie Williams	LB	6'1"	230	21	1	
Tommy Casanova	DB	6'2"	194	26	5	18
Marvin Cobb	DB	6'	191	23	3	
Bernie Jackson	DB	6'	179	26	1	
Melvin Morgan	DB	5'11"	175	23		6
Lemar Parrish	DB	5'11"	180	28	2	
Scott Perry	DB	6'	185	22		
Ken Riley	DB	6'	183	29	9	6
Ken Anderson	QB	6'1"	210	27		6
John Reaves	QB	6'3"	202	26		
Tony Davis	HB	5'10"	210	23		6
Lenvil Elliott	HB	6'	207	25		18
Archie Griffin	HB	5'9"	191	22		6
Willie Shelby	HB	5'10"	190	23		6
Booby Clark	FB	6'2"	245	25		48
Stan Fritts	FB-HB	6'1"	215	23		18
Billy Brooks	WR	6'4"	215	23		
Isaac Curtis	WR	6'	195	25		36
John McDaniel	WR	6'1"	194	24		6
Pat McInally	WR	6'5"	200	23		
Chip Myers	WR	6'4"	208	31		6
Bruce Coslet	TE	6'3"	225	30		12
Bob Trumpy	TE	6'6"	231	31		42
Chris Bahr	K	5'9"	170	23		81

CLEVELAND BROWNS 9-5 Forrest Gregg

Scores of Each Game

38	N.Y. JETS	17
14	Pittsburgh	31
13	Denver	44
24	CINCINNATI	45
18	PITTSBURGH	16
20	Atlanta	17
21	SAN DIEGO	17
6	Cincinnati	21
21	Houston	7
24	PHILADELPHIA	3
24	Tampa Bay	7
17	MIAMI	13
13	HOUSTON	10
14	Kansas City	39

Use Name	Pos.	Hgt	Wgt	Age	Int	Pts
Barry Darrow	OT	6'7"	260	26		
Doug Dieken	OT	6'5"	252	27		
Henry Sheppard	OT-OG	6'6"	246	23		
Pete Adams	OG	6'4"	260	25		
Al Dennis	OG	6'4"	250	25		
Bob Jackson	OG	6'5"	245	23		
Tom DeLeone	C	6'2"	248	26		
Gerry Sullivan	C-OT	6'4"	250	24		
Earl Edwards	DE-DT	6'6"	256	30		
Joe Jones	DE	6'6"	250	28		6
Mack Mitchell	DE	6'7"	245	24		
Mike St. Clair	DE	6'5"	245	22		
Walter Johnson	DT	6'3"	265	33		
Jerry Sherk	DT	6'4"	250	28	1	
Dick Ambrose	LB	6'	235	23		
Bob Babich	LB	6'2"	231	29	2	
John Garlington	LB	6'1"	221	30		
Dave Graf	LB	6'2"	215	23		
Charlie Hall	LB	6'3"	230	27	1	
Gerald Irons	LB	6'2"	230	29	1	
Ron Bolton	DB	6'2"	170	26	3	6
Terry Brown	DB	6'1"	205	29	1	
Neil Craig	DB	6'1"	190	28	1	
Bill Craven	DB	5'11"	190	24		
Thom Darden	DB	6'2"	193	26	7	
Tony Peters	DB	6'1"	192	23		
Clarence Scott	DB	6'	180	27	4	
Dave Mays	QB	6'1"	204	27		
Mike Phipps	QB	6'2"	205	28		
Brian Sipe	QB	6'1"	190	27		1
Brian Duncan	HB	6'	201	24		
Cleo Miller	HB-FB	5'11"	202	24		24
Larry Poole	HB	6'	195	24		
Greg Pruitt	HB	5'10"	190	25		30
Mike Pruitt	FB	6'	214	22		
Ricky Feacher (from N. ENG.)	WR	5'10"	174	22		
Steve Holden	WR	6'	194	25		
Dave Logan	WR	6'4"	226	22		
Willie Miller	WR	5'9"	172	29		
Reggie Rucker	WR	6'2"	190	28		48
Paul Warfield	WR	6'	188	33		36
Gary Parris	TE	6'2"	226	26		
Oscar Roan	TE	6'6"	214	24		24
Don Cockroft	K	6'1"	195	31		72

Chuck Hutchinson — Knee Injury

Billy LeFear — Injury

HOUSTON OILERS 5-9 Bum Phillips

Scores of Each Game

20	TAMPA BAY	0
13	Buffalo	3
13	OAKLAND	14
31	New Orleans	26
17	DENVER	3
27	San Diego	30
7	CINCINNATI	27
14	Baltimore	38
7	CLEVELAND	21
27	Cincinnati	31
16	Pittsburgh	32
20	ATLANTA	14
10	Cleveland	13
0	PITTSBURGH	21

Use Name	Pos.	Hgt	Wgt	Age	Int	Pts
Elbert Drungo	OT	6'5"	265	33		
Kevin Hunt	OT	6'5"	260	27		
Greg Sampson	OT	6'6"	270	25		
Bobby Simon	OT-OG	6'3"	252	23		
Ed Fisher	OG	6'3"	250	27		
Dennis Havig	OG	6'2"	256	27		
Conway Hayman	OG	6'3"	262	27		
Ron Lou	C	6'2"	242	25		
Carl Mauck	C	6'3"	250	29		
Elvin Bethea	DE	6'3"	255	30		
Albert Burton	DE	6'5"	270	24		
Joe Owens	DE	6'2"	245	29		
Bubba Smith	DE	6'7"	265	31		
Tody Smith (to BUFFALO)	DE	6'5"	250	27		
Curley Culp	MG	6'1"	265	30		
John Little	MG	6'3"	250	29		
Duane Benson	LB	6'2"	225	31		
Gregg Bingham	LB	6'1"	230	25	2	
Robert Brazile	LB	6'4"	238	23	1	
Steve Kiner	LB	6'	225	29		
Tim Rossovich	LB	6'4"	240	30		
Ted Thompson	LB	6'1"	220	23		
Ted Washington	LB	6'1"	245	28		
Willie Alexander	DB	6'2"	195	26		
Bob Atkins	DB	6'3"	210	30		
Zeke Moore	DB	6'2"	195	32	1	
Mike Reinfeldt (from OAK.)	DB	6'2"	178	23	1	
Greg Stemrick	DB	5'11"	185	24	1	
Mike Weger	DB	6'2"	200	30		
C.L. Whittington	DB	6'1"	200	24	5	6
Sam Williams	DB	6'2"	192	24		
James Foote	QB	6'2"	210	24		
John Hadl	QB	6'2"	215	36		
Don Pastorini	QB	6'3"	205	27		
Ronnie Coleman	HB	5'10"	198	25		36
Al Johnson	HB	6'	200	26		
Altie Taylor	HB	5'10"	200	28		
Joe Dawkins	FB	5'11"	220	28		
Don Hardeman	FB	6'2"	235	24		
Fred Willis	FB	6'	205	28		18
Mel Baker	WR	6'	182	26		
Mike Barber	WR-TE	6'3"	235	23		
Jim Beirne	WR	6'2"	208	29		
Ken Burrough	WR	6'4"	210	28		42
Billy Johnson	WR	5'9"	170	24		24
Earl Thomas	WR	6'3"	215	27		
Mack Alston	TE	6'2"	230	29		
Alvis Darby (from SEATTLE)	TE	6'4"	216	21		
John Sawyer	TE	6'2"	230	23		
Skip Butler	K	6'2"	200	28		72
Leroy Clark	K	5'11"	200	26		

Willie Frazier — Knee Injury
Willie Rogers — Injury

PITTSBURGH STEELERS

RUSHING

Last Name	No.	Yds	Avg	TD
Harris	289	1128	3.9	14
Bleier	220	1036	4.7	5
Harrison	54	235	4.4	4
Bradshaw	31	219	7.1	3
Kruczek	18	106	5.9	2
Deloplaine	17	91	5.4	2
Fugua	15	63	4.2	1
Stallworth	0	47	—	1
Lewis	2	24	12.0	1
Pough	2	8	4.0	0
Walden	3	7	2.3	0
Bell	1	5	5.0	0
Swann	1	2	2.0	0

RECEIVING

Last Name	No.	Yds	Avg	TD
Swann	28	516	18	3
Bleier	24	294	12	0
Harris	23	151	7	0
Lewis	17	306	18	1
Grossman	15	181	12	1
Stallworth	9	111	12	2
Pough	8	161	20	1
Brown	7	97	14	0
Cunningham	5	49	10	1
Bell	3	43	14	1
Harrison	2	19	10	0
Fugua	1	4	4	0
Deloplaine	1	3	3	0

PUNT RETURNS

Last Name	No.	Yds	Avg	TD
Bell	39	390	10	0
Deloplaine	17	150	9	0
Fugua	11	77	7	0
Swann	3	11	4	0
Edwards	1	8	8	0

KICKOFF RETURNS

Last Name	No.	Yds	Avg	TD
Pough	18	369	21	0
Deloplaine	17	385	23	0
Fugua	4	75	19	0
Harrison	1	26	26	0
Clack	1	0	0	0

PASSING — PUNTING — KICKING

PASSING

Last Name	Att	Comp	%	Yds	Yd/Att	TD	Int–%	RK
Bradshaw	192	92	48	1177	6.1	10	9– 5	10
Kruczek	85	51	60	758	8.9	0	3– 4	

PUNTING

Last Name	No	Avg
Walden	76	39.2

KICKING

Last Name	XP	Att	%	FG	Att	%
Gerella	40	43	93	14	26	54

CINCINNATI BENGALS

RUSHING

Last Name	No.	Yds	Avg	TD
Clark	151	671	4.4	7
Griffin	138	625	4.5	3
Elliott	69	276	4.0	0
Fritts	47	200	4.3	3
Davis	36	178	4.9	1
Anderson	31	134	4.3	1
Curtis	3	29	9.7	0
Shelby	5	9	1.8	0
Brooks	1	–13	–13.0	0

RECEIVING

Last Name	No.	Yds	Avg	TD
Curtis	41	766	19	6
Clark	23	158	7	1
Elliott	22	188	9	3
Trumpy	21	323	15	7
Myers	17	267	16	1
Brooks	16	191	12	0
Griffin	16	138	9	0
McDaniel	12	232	19	1
Fritts	9	75	8	0
Coslet	5	73	15	0
Davis	4	29	7	0
Shelby	1	3	3	0

PUNT RETURNS

Last Name	No.	Yds	Avg	TD
Shelby	21	162	8	0
Parrish	20	122	6	0
Casanova	10	45	5	0
Cobb	3	14	5	0

KICKOFF RETURNS

Last Name	No.	Yds	Avg	TD
Shelby	30	761	25	1
Elliott	5	98	20	0
Davis	4	21	5	0
Parrish	3	62	21	0
Griffin	3	56	19	0
Hunt	2	24	12	0
Morgan	1	14	14	0
Fritts	1	10	10	0

PASSING — PUNTING — KICKING

PASSING

Last Name	Att	Comp	%	Yds	Yd/Att	TD	Int–%	RK
Anderson	338	179	53	2367	7.0	19	14– 4	7
Reaves	22	8	36	76	3.5	2	1– 5	

PUNTING

Last Name	No	Avg
McInally	76	39.5

KICKING

Last Name	XP	Att	%	FG	Att	%
Bahr	39	42	93	14	27	52

CLEVELAND BROWNS

RUSHING

Last Name	No.	Yds	Avg	TD
M. Pruitt	209	1000	4.8	4
G. Miller	153	613	4.0	4
Poole	78	356	4.6	1
G. Pruitt	52	138	2.7	0
Sipe	18	71	3.9	0
Duncan	11	44	4.0	0
Rucker	2	30	15.0	0
Phipps	4	26	6.5	0
Mays	5	14	2.8	0
Warfield	1	3	3.0	0

RECEIVING

Last Name	No.	Yds	Avg	TD
Rucker	49	676	14	8
G. Pruitt	45	341	8	1
Warfield	38	613	16	6
C. Miller	16	145	9	0
Roan	15	174	12	4
Poole	14	70	5	0
Holden	8	128	16	1
M. Pruitt	8	26	3	0
Duncan	6	49	8	1
Logan	5	104	21	0
Parris	5	73	15	0
Feacher	2	38	19	0

PUNT RETURNS

Last Name	No.	Yds	Avg	TD
Holden	31	205	7	0
Feacher	13	142	11	0
W. Miller	5	22	4	0

KICKOFF RETURNS

Last Name	No.	Yds	Avg	TD
Feacher	24	551	23	0
Holden	19	461	24	0
Duncan	6	145	24	0
M. Pruitt	6	106	18	0
Poole	3	62	21	0
G. Pruitt	1	27	27	0
C. Miller	1	23	23	0
Ambrose	1	16	16	0
Jackson	1	16	16	0
Graf	1	15	15	0
W. Miller	1	0	0	0

PASSING — PUNTING — KICKING

PASSING

Last Name	Att	Comp	%	Yds	Yd/Att	TD	Int–%	RK
Sipe	312	178	57	2113	6.8	17	14– 4	6
Phipps	37	20	54	146	3.9	3	0– 0	
Mays	20	9	45	101	5.1	0	1– 5	
G. Pruitt	3	2	67	39	13.0	1	0– 0	
Cockroft	1	0	0	0	0.0	0	0– 0	

PUNTING

Last Name	No	Avg
Cockroft	64	38.9
Mays	2	45.5

KICKING

Last Name	XP	Att	%	FG	Att	%
Cockroft	27	30	90	15	28	54
Sipe	1	1	100			

HOUSTON OILERS

RUSHING

Last Name	No.	Yds	Avg	TD
Coleman	171	684	4.0	2
Willis	148	542	3.7	2
Hardeman	32	114	3.6	1
Hawkins	31	61	2.0	1
Pastorini	11	45	4.1	0
Burrough	3	22	7.3	0
Taylor	5	11	2.2	0
Hadl	7	11	1.6	0
A. Johnson	6	6	1.0	0
Baker	1	2	2.0	0
Butler	1	0	0.0	0

RECEIVING

Last Name	No.	Yds	Avg	TD
Burrough	51	932	18	7
B. Johnson	47	495	11	4
Coleman	40	247	6	3
Willis	32	255	8	1
Alston	19	174	9	1
Sawyer	18	208	12	1
Hardeman	7	25	4	0
Thomas	4	15	4	0
Baker	3	32	11	0
Dawkins	3	21	7	0
Taylor	2	15	8	0
Stemrick	1	10	10	0

PUNT RETURNS

Last Name	No.	Yds	Avg	TD
B. Johnson	38	403	11	0
Coleman	7	91	13	1
Whittington	3	10	3	0

KICKOFF RETURNS

Last Name	No.	Yds	Avg	TD
B. Johnson	26	579	22	0
Taylor	15	302	20	0
A. Johnson	8	150	19	0
Hardeman	7	171	24	0
Baker	1	15	15	0
Beirne	1	12	12	0

PASSING — PUNTING — KICKING

PASSING

Last Name	Att	Comp	%	Yds	Yd/Att	TD	Int–%	RK
Pastorini	309	167	54	1795	5.8	10	10– 3	9
Hadl	113	60	53	634	5.6	7	8– 7	
Coleman	1	0	0	0	0.0	0	1–100	

PUNTING

Last Name	No	Avg
Pastorini	70	36.7
Butler	11	33.6
Clark	10	33.5
Sawyer	1	32.0

KICKING

Last Name	XP	Att	%	FG	Att	%
Butler	24	24	100	16	27	59

OAKLAND RAIDERS 13-1 John Madden

Scores of Each Game		
31	PITTSBURGH	28
24	Kansas City	21
14	Houston	13
17	New England	48
27	San Diego	17
17	Denver	10
18	GREEN BAY	14
19	DENVER	6
28	Chicago	27
21	KANSAS CITY	10
26	Philadelphia	7
49	TAMPA BAY	16
35	CINCINNATI	20
24	SAN DIEGO	0

Use Name	Pos.	Hgt	Wgt	Age	Int	Pts
Henry Lawrence	OT	6'4"	273	24		
Art Shell	OT	6'5"	265	29		
John Vella	OT	6'4"	260	26		
George Buehler	OG	6'2"	270	29		
Dan Medlin	OG	6'4"	252	26		
Gene Upshaw	OG	6'5"	255	31		
Dave Dalby	C	6'2"	250	25		
Steve Sylvester	C	6'4"	262	23		
John Matuszak	DE	6'8"	275	25		
Herb McMath	DE	6'4"	245	21		
Charles Philyaw	DE	6'9"	270	22		
Dave Rowe	DT	6'6"	271	31		
Otis Sistrunk	DT	6'4"	273	28		
Rodrigo Barnes	LB	6'1"	215	26		
Greg Blankenship (to PITT.)	LB	6'1"	212	22		
Rik Bonness	LB	6'3"	220	22		
Willie Hall	LB	6'2"	225	26	2	
Ted Hendricks	LB	6'7"	220	28	1	2
Monte Johnson	LB	6'4"	240	24	4	
Floyd Rice	LB	6'3"	223	27		
Phil Villapiano	LB	6'1"	225	27	1	
Butch Atkinson	DB	6'	185	29		
Willie Brown	DB	6'1"	210	35	3	
Neal Colzie	DB	6'2"	205	23		
Charlie Phillips	DB	6'2"	215	23	1	
Jack Tatum	DB	5'10"	206	27	2	
Skip Thomas	DB	6'1"	205	26	2	
David Humm	QB	6'2"	184	24		
Mike Rae	QB	6'	190	25		6
Ken Stabler	QB	6'3"	215	30		6
Pete Banaszak	HB-FB	5'11"	210	32		30
Clarence Davis	HB	5'10"	195	27		18
Carl Garrett	HB	5'11"	205	29		6
Hubert Ginn	HB	5'11"	185	29		
Rick Jennings	HB	5'9"	180	23		
Manfred Moore (from T. BAY)	HB	6'	199	25		
Terry Kunz	FB	6'1"	215	23		
Mark van Eeghen	FB	6'2"	225	24		18
Fred Biletnikoff	WR	6'1"	190	35		42
Morris Bradshaw	WR	6'	195	23		6
Cliff Branch	WR	5'11"	170	28		72
Mike Siani	WR	6'2"	195	26		12
Warren Bankston	TE	6'4"	235	29		6
Dave Casper	TE	6'4"	228	24		60
Ted Kwalick	TE	6'4"	225	29		
Ray Guy	K	6'3"	195	26		
Errol Mann (from DETROIT)	K	6'	205	35		59
Fred Steinford	K	5'11"	180	24		28

Horace Jones — Knee Injury
Kelvin Korver — Knee Injury
Art Thoms — Knee Injury

Marv Hubbard — Shoulder Injury
Frank Tate — Injury

DENVER BRONCOS 9-5 John Ralston

Scores of Each Game		
7	Cincinnati	17
46	N.Y. JETS	3
44	CLEVELAND	13
26	SAN DIEGO	0
3	Houston	17
10	OAKLAND	17
35	Kansas City	26
6	Oakland	19
48	TAMPA BAY	13
17	San Diego	0
14	N.Y. GIANTS	13
14	New England	38
17	KANSAS CITY	16
28	Chicago	14

Use Name	Pos.	Hgt	Wgt	Age	Int	Pts
Bill Bain	OT	6'4"	270	24		
Glenn Hyde	OT	6'3"	250	25		
Claudie Minor	OT	6'4"	280	25		
Scott Parrish	OT	6'6"	270	23		
Tom Glassic	OG	6'4"	254	22		
Harvey Goodman	OG	6'4"	260	23		
Tommy Lyons	OG	6'2"	230	28		
Bobby Maples	C	6'3"	250	33		
Phil Olsen	C	6'5"	260	28		
Barney Chavous	DE	6'3"	252	25		
Paul Smith	DE	6'3"	256	31		
Jim White (from SEATTLE)	DE	6'3"	260	27		
Lyle Alzado	DT	6'3"	252	27		
Rubin Carter	DT	6'	256	23		
John Grant	DT	6'3"	235	26		
Wayne Hammond	DT	6'5"	255	23		
Martin Imhof	DT	6'6"	255	26		
Randy Moore	DT	6'2"	241	22		
Rich Baska	LB	6'3"	225	24		
Larry Evans	LB	6'2"	216	23		
Randy Gradishar	LB	6'3"	233	24	3	6
Tom Jackson	LB	5'11"	220	25	7	6
Joe Rizzo	LB	6'1"	220	25	1	
Bob Swenson	LB	6'3"	220	23	2	
Godwin Turk	LB	6'2"	230	25		
Steve Foley	DB	6'2"	181	22	4	
Billy Hardee	DB	6'	185	22		
Calvin Jones	DB	5'7"	169	25	2	6
Chris Pane	DB	5'11"	181	23		
Randy Poltl	DB	6'3"	190	24	1	6
John Rowser	DB	6'1"	190	32	4	12
Bill Thompson	DB	6'1"	200	29		
Louie Wright	DB	6'2"	195	23		
Craig Penrose	QB	6'3"	222	23		
Steve Ramsey	QB	6'2"	210	28		
Norris Weese	QB	6'1"	195	25		
Otis Armstrong	HB	5'10"	196	25		36
Jim Kiick	HB	5'11"	215	30		12
Mike Franckowiak	FB	6'3"	220	23		
Jon Keyworth	FB	6'3"	230	25		24
Lonnie Perrin	FB	6'1"	222	24		12
Jack Dolbin	WR	5'10"	180	27		6
Haven Moses	WR	6'3"	208	30		42
John Schultz	WR	5'10"	182	23		
Rich Upchurch	WR	5'10"	170	24		36
Billy VanHeusen	WR	6'1"	200	30		
Boyd Brown	TE	6'4"	216	24		
Riley Odoms	TE	6'4"	230	26		30
Jim Turner	K	6'2"	205	35		81

Paul Howard — Injury
Carl Schaukowitz — Injury

Fran Lynch — Knee Injury
Charlie Smith — Knee Injury

SAN DIEGO CHARGERS 6-8 Tommy Prothro

Scores of Each Game		
30	Kansas City	16
23	Tampa Bay	0
43	ST. LOUIS	24
0	Denver	26
17	OAKLAND	27
30	HOUSTON	27
17	Cleveland	21
0	Pittsburgh	23
21	BALTIMORE	37
0	DENVER	17
34	Buffalo	13
20	KANSAS CITY	23
13	SAN FRANCISCO	* 7
0	Oakland	24

Use Name	Pos.	Hgt	Wgt	Age	Int	Pts
Billy Shields	OT	6'7"	272	23		
Ron Singleton	OT	6'7"	245	24		
Russ Washington	OT	6'6"	290	29		
Charles Aiu	OG	6'2"	248	22		
Don Macek	OG	6'3"	253	22		
Ralph Perretta	OG-C	6'2"	252	23		
Doug Wilkerson	OG	6'2"	262	29		
Ed Flanagan	C	6'3"	245	32		
Fred Dean	DE	6'3"	226	24		
Leroy Jones	DE	6'8"	245	25	1	
John Lee	DE	6'2"	247	23		
Charles DeJurnett	DT	6'4"	270	24		
Gary Johnson	DT	6'2"	262	24		
Louie Kelcher	DT	6'5"	282	23		
Don Goode	LB	6'2"	230	25	6	
Tom Graham	LB	6'2"	235	26	3	
Bob Horn	LB	6'3"	235	22	1	
Woodrow Lowe	LB	6'	227	22	1	
Rick Middleton	LB	6'2"	234	24		
Ray Preston	LB	6'	223	22		
Danny Colbert	DB	5'11"	182	25		
Chris Fletcher	DB	5'11"	189	27		
Mike Fuller	DB	5'9"	195	23	1	1
Tom Hayes	DB	6'1"	198	30	2	6
Hal Stringert	DB	5'11"	185	24	1	
Jim Tolbert	DB	6'3"	210	32		
Mike Williams	DB	5'10"	181	22		
Dan Fouts	QB	6'3"	204	25		
Neal Jeffrey	QB	6'1"	180	23		
Clint Longley	QB	6'1"	195	24		
Mercury Morris	HB	5'10"	192	29		12
Joe Washington	HB	5'10"	184	22		
Rickey Young	HB	6'2"	193	22		30
Bo Matthews	FB	6'4"	230	24		24
Sam Scarber	FB	6'2"	232	28		12
Don Woods	FB-HB	6'1"	210	25		24
Eddie Bell	WR	5'10"	160	28		
Larry Dorsey	WR	6'1"	195	23		
Walt Garrison	WR	6'1"	190	32		6
Charlie Joiner	WR	5'11"	180	28		42
Dwight McDonald	WR	6'2"	187	25		24
Artie Owens	WR	5'10"	170	23		6
Chuck Bradley	TE	6'6"	255	25		
Pat Curran	TE	6'3"	238	30		6
Larry Mialik	TE	6'2"	226	26		
Jeff West	TE	6'3"	220	23		
Toni Fritsch	K	5'7"	195	31		29
Mitch Hoopes (to HOUSTON)	K	6'1"	210	23		
Ray Wersching	K	5'11"	222	26		26

Booker Brown — Illness
John Teerlinck — Knee Injury

KANSAS CITY CHIEFS 5-9 Paul Wiggin

Scores of Each Game		
16	SAN DIEGO	30
21	OAKLAND	24
17	NEW ORLEANS	27
17	Buffalo	50
33	Washington	30
20	Miami	*17
26	DENVER	35
28	Tampa Bay	19
0	PITTSBURGH	45
10	Oakland	21
24	CINCINNATI	27
23	San Diego	20
16	Denver	17
39	CLEVELAND	14

Use Name	Pos.	Hgt	Wgt	Age	Int	Pts
Charlie Getty	OT	6'4"	260	24		
Matt Herkenhoff	OT	6'4"	255	25		
Jim Nicholson	OT	6'6"	261	26		
Ed Budde	OG	6'5"	265	35		
Tom Condon	OG	6'3"	240	23		
Rod Walters	OG	6'3"	258	22		
Charlie Ane	C	6'1"	233	24		
Orrin Olsen	C	6'1"	245	23		
Jack Rudnay	C	6'3"	240	28		
Larry Estes	DE-DT	6'6"	250	29		
John Lohmeyer	DE	6'4"	229	25		2
Whitney Paul	DE	6'3"	220	22		
Jim Wolf	DE	6'3"	250	24		
Wilbur Young	DE	6'6"	285	27		
Willie Lee	DT	6'5"	249	26		
Bob Maddox	DT	6'5"	248	27		
Keith Simons	DT	6'3"	254	22		
Billy Andrews	LB	6'	220	31	1	
Jimbo Elrod	LB	6'	209	22	1	
Willie Lanier	LB	6'1"	245	31	3	
Jim Lynch	LB	6'1"	225	31	2	
Dave Rozumek	LB	6'2"	215	22		
Clyde Werner	LB	6'4"	230	28		
Gary Barbaro	DB	6'4"	198	22	3	
Tim Collier	DB	6'	166	22	2	
Tim Gray	DB	6'1"	200	23	4	
Kerry Reardon	DB	5'11"	180	27	5	
Steve Taylor	DB	6'3"	204	22		
Emmitt Thomas	DB	6'2"	192	33	2	
Tony Adams	QB	6'	198	26		
Mike Livingston	QB	6'3"	212	30		12
Mike Nott	QB	6'3"	203	24		
Woody Green	HB	6'1"	205	25		6
Ed Podolak	HB	6'1"	205	29		30
Tommy Reamon	HB	5'10"	192	24		30
Glynn Harrison	FB	5'11"	190	22		
MacArthur Lane	FB	6'	220	34		36
Pat McNeil	FB	5'9"	208	22		
Larry Brunson	WR	5'11"	180	27		6
Reggie Craig	WR	6'	187	23		
Henry Marshall	WR	6'2"	205	22		18
Barry Pearson	WR	5'11"	185	26		
Lawrence Williams	WR	5'10"	175	22		
Bill Masters	TE	6'5"	240	32		18
Walter White	TE	6'3"	218	25		42
Jan Stenerud	K	6'2"	187	33		90
Jerrel Wilson	K	6'4"	222	35		

Ken Avery — Injury
Randy Beisler — Injury
Roger Bernhardt — Injury

TAMPA BAY BUCCANEERS 0-14 John McKay

Scores of Each Game		
0	Houston	20
0	SAN DIEGO	23
9	BUFFALO	14
17	Baltimore	42
0	Cincinnati	21
10	SEATTLE	13
20	MIAMI	23
19	KANSAS CITY	28
13	Denver	48
0	N.Y. Jets	34
7	CLEVELAND	24
16	Oakland	49
0	Pittsburgh	42
14	NEW ENGLAND	31

Use Name	Pos.	Hgt	Wgt	Age	Int	Pts
Mike Current	OT	6'4"	270	30		
Dave Reavis	OT	6'5"	250	26		
Steve Wilson	OT	6'3"	268	22		
Randy Young	OT	6'5"	250	22		
Steve Young	OT	6'8"	272	23		
Tom Alward	OG	6'4"	255	23		
Howard Fest	OG	6'6"	263	30		
Everett Little	OG	6'4"	265	22		
Dan Ryczek	C	6'3"	250	27		
Ed McAleney (from ATLANTA)	DE	6'2"	235	22		
Council Rudolph	DE	6'3"	255	26		
Leroy Selmon	DE	6'3"	263	21		
Pat Toomay	DE	6'5"	244	31		
Larry Jameson	DT	6'7"	270	23		
Maulty Moore	DT	6'5"	265	30		
Dave Pear	DT	6'2"	248	23		
Dewey Selmon	DT	6'1"	254	22		
Larry Ball	LB	6'6"	235	26	1	
Bert Cooper	LB	6'1"	242	24		
Jimmy Gunn	LB	6'1"	231	27		
Charlie Hunt	LB	6'3"	218	25		
Mike Lemon	LB	6'2"	220	25		
Cal Peterson	LB	6'3"	213	23	1	
Jim Peterson	LB	6'5"	226	26		
Steve Reese	LB	6'2"	223	24		
Glenn Robinson	LB-DE	6'6"	245	24		
Jimmy Sims	LB	6'	195	25		
Richard Wood	LB	6'2"	215	23		
Mark Cotney	DB	6'	207	24	3	
Ricky Davis	DB	6'	178	23		
Earl Douthit	DB	6'2"	188	23		
Curtis Jordan	DB	6'2"	182	22	2	
Don Martin	DB	5'11"	185	26		
Frank Oliver	DB	6'	198	24		
Reggie Pierson (from DET.)	DB	5'11"	185	23		
Danny Reece	DB	5'11"	187	21		6
Ken Stone	DB	6'1"	180	25	2	
Mike Washington	DB	6'3"	190	23		
Roscoe Word (from NYJ & BUF)	DB	5'11"	169	24		
Parnell Dickinson	QB	6'2"	185	23		
Terry Hanratty	QB	6'1"	205	28		
Larry Lawrence	QB	6'1"	208	27		
Steve Spurrier	QB	6'2"	205	31		
Louis Carter	HB	5'11"	209	23		6
Charlie Davis	HB	5'11"	200	24		6
Essex Johnson	HB	5'9"	200	29		12
Jimmy DuBose	FB	5'11"	217	21		
Vince Kendrick	FB	6'	239	24		
Rod McNeill (from N. ORLEANS)	FB	6'2"	215	25		
Ed Williams	FB	6'2"	245	26		12
Freddie Douglass	WR	5'9"	185	22		
Isaac Hagins	WR	5'9"	179	22		
Curtis Leak	WR	5'11"	180	22		
Lee McGriff	WR	5'9"	163	22		
John McKay	WR	5'11"	175	23		6
Morris Owens (from MIAMI)	WR	6'	190	23		36
Barry Smith	WR	6'1"	195	25		
Bob Moore	TE	6'3"	229	27		
Jack Novak	TE	6'4"	242	23		6
Fred Pagac	TE	6'	220	24		
Dave Green	K	5'11"	208	26		35
Mirro Roder	K	6'1"	218	32		

Charlie Evans — Knee Injury
Kent Gaydos — Injury
Harold Hart — Injury

* — Overtime

OAKLAND RAIDERS

RUSHING

Last Name	No.	Yds.	Avg	TD
van Eeghen	233	1012	4.3	3
Davis	114	516	4.5	3
Banaszak	114	370	3.2	5
Garrett	48	220	4.6	1
Ginn	10	53	5.3	0
Rae	10	37	3.7	1
Kunz	4	33	8.3	0
Jennings	10	22	2.2	0
Branch	3	12	4.0	0
Casper	1	5	5.0	0
Bradshaw	1	4	4.0	0
Moore	7	4	0.6	0
Bankston	1	3	3.0	0
Guy	1	0	0.0	0
Stabler	7	−2	−0.3	1

RECEIVING

Last Name	No.	Yds	Avg	TD
Casper	53	691	13	10
Branch	46	1111	24	12
Biletnikoff	43	551	13	7
Davis	21	191	7	0
van Eeghen	17	173	10	0
Banaszak	15	74	5	0
Siani	11	173	16	2
Garrett	9	108	12	0
Bankston	5	73	15	1
Moore	5	46	9	0
Kwalick	4	15	4	0
Bradshaw	1	25	25	1
Jennings	1	10	10	0

PUNT RETURNS

Last Name	No.	Yds	Avg	TD
Colzie	41	448	11	0
Moore	20	184	9	0
Phillips	2	7	4	0
Jennings	1	20	20	0

KICKOFF RETURNS

Last Name	No.	Yds	Avg	TD
Garrett	18	388	22	0
Jennings	16	417	26	0
Moore	8	162	20	0
Colzie	6	115	19	0
Bankston	2	27	14	0
Banaszak	2	23	12	0
Ginn	1	27	27	0

PASSING – PUNTING – KICKING

PASSING	Att	Comp	%	Yds	Yd/Att	TD	Int–%	RK
Stabler	291	194	67	2737	9.4	27	17– 6	1
Rae	65	35	54	417	6.4	6	1– 2	
Humm	5	3	60	41	8.2	0	0– 0	

PUNTING	No	Avg
Guy	67	41.6

KICKING	XP	Att	%	FG	Att	%
Mann	35	37	95	8	21	38
Steinfort	16	19	84	4	8	50
Guy	0	1	0			

DENVER BRONCOS

RUSHING

Last Name	No.	Yds.	Avg	TD
Armstrong	247	1008	4.1	5
Keyworth	122	349	2.9	3
Weese	23	142	6.2	0
Perrin	37	118	3.2	2
Kiick	31	114	3.7	1
Upchurch	6	71	11.8	1
Ramsey	13	51	3.9	0
Odoms	3	36	12.0	2
Franckowiak	12	25	2.1	0
Van Heusen	1	20	20.0	0
Dolbin	2	5	2.5	0
Penrose	2	−3	−1.5	0
Moses	1	−4	−4.0	0

RECEIVING

Last Name	No.	Yds	Avg	TD
Armstrong	39	457	12	1
Odoms	30	477	16	3
Moses	25	498	20	7
Keyworth	22	201	9	1
Dolbin	19	354	19	1
Upchurch	12	340	28	1
Kiick	10	78	8	0
Franckowiak	4	42	11	0
Perrin	4	35	9	0
Schultz	2	29	15	0
Lyons	1	−1	−1	0

PUNT RETURNS

Last Name	No.	Yds	Avg	TD
Upchurch	39	536	14	4
Thompson	6	60	10	0
Foley	5	42	8	0
Schultz	1	2	2	0

KICKOFF RETURNS

Last Name	No.	Yds	Avg	TD
Upchurch	22	514	23	0
Perrin	14	391	28	0
Schultz	3	82	27	0
B. Brown	3	41	14	0
Franckowiak	2	22	11	0
Hyde	1	17	17	0
Goodman	1	8	8	0

PASSING – PUNTING – KICKING

PASSING	Att	Comp	%	Yds	Yd/Att	TD	Int–%	RK
Ramsey	270	128	47	1931	7.2	11	13– 5	11
Weese	47	24	51	314	6.7	1	6– 13	
Penrose	36	16	44	265	7.4	3	3– 8	

PUNTING	No	Avg
Weese	52	35.6
Van Heusen	31	35.3

KICKING	XP	Att	%	FG	Att	%
Turner	36	39	92	15	21	71

SAN DIEGO CHARGERS

RUSHING

Last Name	No.	Yds.	Avg	TD
Young	162	802	5.0	4
Woods	126	450	3.6	3
Morris	50	256	5.1	2
Scarber	61	236	3.9	1
Matthews	46	199	4.3	3
Fouts	18	65	3.6	0
Longley	4	22	5.5	0
Curran	1	12	12.0	0
Hoopes	2	10	5.0	0
Jeffrey	1	0	0.0	0
West	1	0	0.0	0
Dorsey	1	−12	−12.0	0

RECEIVING

Last Name	No.	Yds	Avg	TD
Joiner	50	1056	21	7
Young	47	441	9	1
Woods	34	224	7	1
Curran	33	349	11	1
Scarber	14	96	7	1
Matthews	12	81	7	0
McDonald	11	161	15	4
Dorsey	8	108	14	0
Morris	8	52	7	0
Owens	3	54	18	1
Garrison	2	58	29	1
Bradley	1	7	7	0

PUNT RETURNS

Last Name	No.	Yds	Avg	TD
Fuller	33	436	13	0
Bell	7	31	4	0
Williams	5	23	5	0

KICKOFF RETURNS

Last Name	No.	Yds	Avg	TD
Owens	25	551	22	0
Fuller	20	420	21	0
Perretta	2	24	12	0
Middleton	1	21	21	0
Matthews	1	19	19	0
Bell	1	18	18	0
Preston	1	16	16	0
Horn	1	7	7	0

PASSING – PUNTING – KICKING

PASSING	Att	Comp	%	Yds	Yd/Att	TD	Int–%	RK
Fouts	359	208	58	2535	7.1	14	15– 4	8
Longley	24	12	50	130	5.4	2	3– 13	
Jeffrey	2	2	100	11	5.5	0	0– 0	
Woods	2	1	50	11	5.5	1	0– 0	
Joiner	1	0	0	0	0.0	0	0– 0	

PUNTING	No	Avg
Hoopes	49	37.7
West	38	40.7

KICKING	XP	Att	%	FG	Att	%
Fritsch	11	14	79	6	12	50
Wersching	14	16	88	4	8	50
Fuller	1	1	100			

KANSAS CITY CHIEFS

RUSHING

Last Name	No.	Yds.	Avg	TD
Lane	162	542	3.3	5
Podolak	88	371	4.2	5
Green	73	322	4.4	1
Reamon	103	314	3.0	4
Marshall	5	101	20.2	1
Livingston	31	89	2.9	2
Adams	5	46	9.2	0
Harrison	16	41	2.6	0
McNeil	8	26	3.3	0
White	2	15	7.5	0
Stenerud	1	0	0.0	0
Brunson	3	−1	−0.3	0

RECEIVING

Last Name	No.	Yds	Avg	TD
Lane	66	686	10	1
White	47	808	17	7
Brunson	33	656	20	1
Marshall	28	443	16	2
Masters	18	269	15	3
Podolak	13	156	12	0
Reamon	10	136	14	1
Green	9	100	11	0
McNeil	2	33	17	0
Harrison	1	12	12	0
Williams	1	9	9	0
Getty	1	−5	−5	0

PUNT RETURNS

Last Name	No.	Yds	Avg	TD
Brunson	31	387	12	0
Andrews	1	38	38	0
Reardon	1	4	4	0
Reamon	1	0	0	0

KICKOFF RETURNS

Last Name	No.	Yds	Avg	TD
Williams	25	688	28	0
Reamon	19	424	22	0
Harrison	13	278	21	0
Green	3	82	27	0
Craig	2	45	23	0
McNeil	2	21	11	0
Marshall	1	0	0	0

PASSING – PUNTING – KICKING

PASSING	Att	Comp	%	Yds	Yd/Att	TD	Int–%	RK
Livingston	338	189	56	2682	7.9	12	13– 4	5
Adams	71	36	51	575	8.1	3	4– 6	
Nott	10	4	40	46	4.6	0	0– 0	

PUNTING	No	Avg
Wilson	65	42.0
Nott	1	35.0
Stenerud	1	28.0

KICKING	XP	Att	%	FG	Att	%
Stenerud	27	33	82	21	38	55

TAMPA BAY BUCCANEERS

RUSHING

Last Name	No.	Yds.	Avg	TD
Carter	171	521	3.0	1
Williams	87	324	3.7	2
Johnson	47	166	3.5	1
McNeill	27	135	5.0	0
C. Davis	41	107	2.6	1
Dickinson	13	103	7.9	0
DuBose	20	62	3.1	0
Spurrier	12	48	4.0	0
B. Moore	2	23	11.5	0
Pagac	1	4	4.0	0
Kendrick	1	3	3.0	0
Owens	2	2	1.0	0
Hanratty	1	1	1.0	0
Green	1	0	0.0	0

RECEIVING

Last Name	No.	Yds	Avg	TD
Owens	30	390	13	6
Johnson	25	201	8	1
B. Moore	24	289	12	0
Williams	23	166	7	0
McKay	20	302	15	1
Carter	20	135	7	0
Novak	8	130	16	1
McNeill	7	33	5	0
DuBose	5	26	5	0
Smith	4	88	22	0
Douglass	3	58	19	0
C. Davis	3	32	11	0
Pagac	2	15	8	0
Green	1	9	9	0
Ryczek	1	6	6	0

PUNT RETURNS

Last Name	No.	Yds	Avg	TD
Reece	20	143	7	0
Douglass	4	78	20	0
Cotney	3	26	9	0
Stone	1	11	11	0
Hagins	1	2	2	0
Word	1	−8	−8	0

KICKOFF RETURNS

Last Name	No.	Yds	Avg	TD
McNeil	17	384	23	0
Carter	15	300	20	0
Johnson	13	287	22	0
Douglass	7	167	24	0
C. Davis	4	73	18	0
Word	2	36	18	0
Hagins	2	35	18	0
DuBose	1	34	34	0
Reece	1	30	30	0
Cooper	1	22	22	0
Pagac	1	20	20	0
Lemon	1	2	2	0

PASSING – PUNTING – KICKING

PASSING	Att	Comp	%	Yds	Yd/Att	TD	Int–%	RK
Spurrier	311	156	50	1628	5.2	7	12– 4	13
Dickinson	39	15	38	210	5.4	1	5– 13	
Hanratty	14	6	43	32	2.3	0	1– 7	
Carter	5	2	40	24	4.8	1	0– 0	
Lawrence	5	0	0	0	0.0	0	2– 40	
McGriff	1	1	100	39	39.0	0	0– 0	
R. Davis	1	1	100	−7	−7.0	0	0– 0	

PUNTING	No	Avg
Green	92	39.3

KICKING	XP	Att	%	FG	Att	%
Green	11	14	79	8	14	57
Roder				0	3	0

1976 Championship Games

SCORING

MINNESOTA	7	3	7	7—24
LOS ANGELES	0	0	13	0—13

First Quarter
Minn. Bryant, 90 yard blocked field goal return
PAT — Cox (kick)

Second Quarter
Minn. Cox, 25 yard field goal

Third Quarter
Minn. Foreman, 1 yard rush
PAT — Cox (kick)
L.A. McCutcheon, 10 yard rush
PAT — Kick no good
L.A. H. Jackson, 5 yard pass from Haden
PAT — Dempsey (kick)

Fourth Quarter
Minn. Johnson, 12 yard rush
PAT — Cox (kick)

TEAM STATISTICS

MINN.		L.A.
13	First Downs—Total	21
6	First Downs—Rushing	14
7	First Downs—Passing	7
0	First Downs—Penalty	0
1	Fumbles— Number	4
1	Fumbles—Lost Ball	2
4	Penalty—Number	3
32	Yards Penalized	33
0	Missed Field Goals	1
60	Offensive Plays	71
267	Net Yards	336
4.5	Average Gain	4.7
2	Giveaways	4
4	Takeaways	2
+2	Difference	-2

Minnesota never looked better while bombing Washington 35-20 in an NFC semi-final playoff bout that featured two TD's apiece by RB Chuck Foreman and WR Sammy White. Los Angeles, meanwhile, just barely got by Dallas 14-12 when the Pokes failed to take advantage of a blocked punt that put the ball on L.A.'s 17-yard line with 1:59 remaining. On this frosty Sunday in Bloomington, however, the Vikes, behind sore-kneed QB Fran Tarkenton, were no match for the Rams statistically except where it counted most—on the specialty teams. The end result was a 24-13 victory for Minnesota, enabling it to make its third visit to the Super Bowl in four years.

The game's biggest play occurred early in the first quarter after the Vikings' defense put the clamps on a strong Ram drive spearheaded by the running of Lawrence McCutcheon and John Cappelletti. With the ball spotted just inches short of Minnesota's goal-line on fourth down, Ram Head Coach Chuck Knox decided to play it safe with a field goal attempt by Tom Dempsey. Earlier in the year in a 10-10 overtime tie against the same Vikings, the Rams twice failed to score from one yard out after deciding not to kick field goals. Nate Allen, who had blocked Dempsey's overtime FG attempt in that earlier game, cleanly deflected the ball after charging in from the right side, and after it took a lucky bounce in the opposite direction, Bobby Bryant picked it up and scampered 90 yards for a TD with the closest Ram 15 yards behind.

Minnesota's Matt Blair followed suit with a second-quarter block of Rusty Jackson's punt after the latter dropped the snap, and it was soon 10-0 after Fred Cox's 25-yard field goal. The Rams' special team miseries continued when Dempsey failed to convert the extra point following their first TD of the game, and when they scored again late in the third quarter, after RE Fred Dryer blindsided Tarkenton and LE Jack Youngblood recovered the subsequent fumble to set up WR Harold Jackson's TD catch, their four-point deficit (17-13) meant the Rams would have to come up with more than a field goal to overtake the Vikes.

With Pat Haden at the controls, L. A. got as far as the Viking 39 with three minutes to go before failing to convert four aerial attempts, the last one intercepted by Bryant. Tarkenton connected with Foreman on a 57-yard safety-valve pass on third down to set up Sammy Johnson's clinching 12-yard TD. Foreman accounted for 119 yards on two plays, almost half of the Vikings' total offense. His brilliant 62-yard run set up Minnesota's second TD to put it ahead 17-0 in the third quarter.

Beside Tarkenton's injury, MLB Jeff Siemon didn't start but played the last three quarters with his legs heavily taped while WR White sat out most of the game with a fever. But that wasn't enough to keep the Rams from losing their third straight NFC Championship game.

INDIVIDUAL STATISTICS

MINNESOTA	No	Yds	Avg.	LOS ANGELES	No	Yds	Avg.
RUSHING							
Foreman	15	118	7.9	McCutcheon	26	128	4.9
Miller	10	28	2.8	Cappelletti	16	59	3.7
Johnson	2	12	6.0	Haden	3	3	1.0
McClanahan	1	2	2.0	Jessie	1	3	3.0
Tarkenton	1	-2	-2.0		46	193	4.2
	29	158	5.4				
RECEIVING							
Foreman	5	81	16.2	H Jackson	4	70	17.5
Rashad	3	28	9.3	Jessie	2	60	30.0
Miller	3	24	8.0	McCutcheon	2	18	9.0
Grim	1	10	10.0	Cappelletti	1	13	13.0
	12	143	11.9		9	161	17.9
PUNTING							
Clabo	8		35.1	R. Jackson	7		29.4
PUNT RETURNS							
Willis	3	20	6.7	C. Bryant	4	31	7.8
				Bertelsen	3	19	6.3
					7	50	7.1
KICKOFF RETURNS							
Willis	3	69	23.0	Geredine	3	50	16.7
				C. Bryant	1	21	21.0
				Scribner	1	8	8.0
					5	79	15.8
INTERCEPTION RETURNS							
B. Bryant	2	17	8.5	M. Jackson	1	0	0.0

MINNESOTA	Att.	Comp.	Comp. Pct.	Yds.	Int.	Yds/ Att.	Yds/ Comp.	Yards Lost Tackled
PASSING								
Tarkenton	27	12	44.4	143	1	5.3	11.9	4—34
LOS ANGELES								
Haden	22	9	40.9	161	2	7.3	17.9	3—18

SCORING

OAKLAND	3	14	7	0—24
PITTSBURGH	0	7	0	0— 7

First Quarter
Oak. Mann, 39 yard field goal

Second Quarter
Oak. C. Davis, 1 yard rush
PAT — Mann (kick)
Pitt. Harrison, 3 yard rush
PAT — Mansfield (kick)
Oak. Bankston, 4 yard pass from Stabler
PAT — Mann (kick)

Third Quarter
Oak. Banaszak, 5 yard pass from Stabler
PAT — Mann (kick)

TEAM STATISTICS

OAK.		PITT.
15	First Downs—Total	13
7	First Downs—Rushing	3
7	First Downs—Passing	8
1	First Downs—Penalty	2
2	Fumbles—Number	1
0	Fumbles—Lost Ball	0
7	Penalty—Number	5
34	Yards Penalized	29
0	Missed Field Goals	0
69	Offensive Plays	59
220	Net Yards	237
3.2	Average Gain	4.0
0	Giveaways	1
1	Takeaways	0
+1	Difference	-1

Pittsburgh had a surprisingly easy time with Baltimore in the AFC semi-final, but its 40-14 victory proved costly as running backs Franco Harris and Rocky Bleier suffered rib and toe injuries, respectively, that kept them from playing Oakland in the AFC Championship game. The Raiders' semi-final opponent, New England, was just one controversial penalty away from upsetting Oakland. Raider QB Ken Stabler engineered two late TD drives to edge the Pats 24-21, the last drive staying alive when New England NT Ray Hamilton was called for roughing Stabler on fourth down with 57 seconds remaining. Without Harris and Bleier, the Steelers were easy pickings for the Raiders as Oakland won 24-7 to end a string of six straight AFC title losses.

Forced into installing a one-back offense featuring Reggie Harrison, Steeler Head Coach Chuck Noll tried to help his confused QB Terry Bradshaw by calling all the Steelers' plays from the sidelines. Pittsburgh didn't get a first down until midway through the second quarter, at which time Oakland already led 10-0. The Raiders' rushers had a comparatively easy time, allowing Stabler to play-pass for Oakland's last two touchdowns. Willie Hall, the linebacker Raider Head Coach John Madden inserted into the starting lineup after converting to a 3-4 defense earlier in the year, set up Oakland's first TD with a brilliant 25-yard interception return to the Steelers' one-yard line. He also knocked down a pass, forced a fumble and made five unassisted tackles along with numerous assists.

Pittsburgh got on the scoreboard after an impressive second-quarter drive kept alive with the sharp third-down passing of Bradshaw but Stabler bounced right back with a demoralizing four-yard TD score to TE Warren Bankston 19 seconds before halftime. Stabler's longest pass of the day, 28 yards to WR Cliff Branch, was completed after he detected a safety blitz which earlier had thrown him for a 17-yard loss. The completion led to the second half's only score, a five-yard toss over the middle to RB Pete Banaszak on another adjusted pattern. On the play, Steeler LB Jack Ham got to Stabler, knocking a cap off Stabler's front tooth and delivering a big welt on his back that sent him to the sidelines. It didn't make much difference for the frustrated Steelers, however. Stabler's replacement, Mike Rae, ran out the clock as the Raiders relied on defense in the final period, and with no ground game to speak of, Bradshaw resorted to desperation passes in a futile attempt to get back in the game.

INDIVIDUAL STATISTICS

OAKLAND	No	Yds	Avg.	PITTSBURGH	No	Yds	Avg.
RUSHING							
van Eeghen	22	66	3.0	Harrison	11	44	4.0
C. Davis	11	54	4.9	Fuqua	8	24	3.0
Banaszak	15	46	3.1	Bradshaw	1	4	4.0
Garrett	2	4	2.0	Cunningham	1	0	0.0
Casper	1	-13.0	-13.0		21	72	3.4
	51	157	3.1				
RECEIVING							
Branch	3	46	15.3	Cunningham	4	36	9.0
Bankston	2	11	5.5	Swann	3	58	19.3
C. Davis	2	7	3.5	Fuqua	2	11	5.5
van Eeghen	1	14	14.0	Harrison	2	10	5.0
Banaszak	1	5	5.0	Brown	1	32	32.0
Casper	1	5	5.0	Stallworth	1	18	18.0
	10	88	8.8	Lewis	1	11	11.0
					14	176	12.6
PUNTING							
Guy	7		44.0	Walden	7		37.3
PUNT RETURNS							
Colzie	2	19	8.5	Bell	2	14	7.0
				Swann	1	4	4.0
					3	18	6.0
KICKOFF RETURNS							
Garrett	2	35	17.5	Pough	3	65	21.7
				Bell	1	16	16.0
				Blount	1	16	16.0
					5	97	19.4
INTERCEPTION RETURNS							
Hall	1	25	25.0	none			

OAKLAND	Att.	Comp.	Comp. Pct.	Yds.	Int.	Yds/ Att.	Yds/ Comp.	Yards Lost Tackled
PASSING								
Stabler	16	10	62.5	88	0	5.5	8.8	2—25
PITTSBURGH								
Bradshaw	35	14	40.0	176	1	5.0	12.6	3—11

All the Silver

When the Oakland Raiders knocked off the defending NFL champion Pittsburgh Steelers, 24-7, to win the AFC, it seemed that coach John Madden and his Raiders would finally have their day in the sun. For all their frustration, the Raiders had won the Western Division title seven of eight times, but not since 1967, when they were humbled by Green Bay, have they appeared in the Super Bowl. Now all that remained in their way was Fran Tarkenton and the Minneota Vikings, three-time losers of the game's most valuable prize.

As things turned out, Minnesota proved hardly an opposition for the devastating Raiders as they rang up 266 yards on the ground and 163 yards in the air. Although the first quarter went scoreless, the Raiders were on top 16-0 at the half behind a field goal, a Ken Stabler pass, and Pete Banaszak's one-yard run. Errol Mann added another field goal in the third quarter and Tarkenton finally put Minnesota on the board to make the score 19-7 as the quarter ran out.

Whatever hopes the Vikings had for a comeback were soon dispelled as Banaszak again crossed the goal line 7:21 into the fourth quarter. A few minutes later Willie Brown intercepted a Tarkenton pass and ran the ball back 75 yards for a touchdown to make the score 32-7. With Bob Lee in the game for Tarkenton, the Vikings again got on the scoreboard, but it was simply a case of too little, too late.

Although Banaszak had scored two touchdowns and Clarence Davis rushed for a career-high 137 yards, the game's most valuable player honors went to Fred Biletnikoff, who caught four passes for 79 yards and set up three scores. The secret to the Raiders overwhelming victory was their ability to exploit the weak left side of the Vikings' line and to keep premier runner Chuck Foreman in check with only 44 yards in 17 attempts.

For the black and silver clad Raiders their dreams had finally become a reality. For the Vikings, the reality seemed more like a nightmare.

LINEUPS

OAKLAND		MINNESOTA
	OFFENSE	
Branch	WR	Rashad
Shell	LT	Riley
Upshaw	LG	Goodrum
Dalby	C	Tinglehoff
Buehler	RG	E. White
Vella	RT	Yary
Casper	TE	Voigt
Biletnikoff	WR	S. White
Stabler	QB	Tarkenton
Davis	RB	Foreman
van Eeghen	RB	McClanahan
	DEFENSE	
Matuzek	LE	Eller
Rowe	LT	Sutherland
Sistrunk	RT	Page
M. Johnson	RE	Marshall
Villapiano	LLB	Blair
Willie Hall	MLB	Siemon
Hendricks	RLB	Hilgenberg
Thomas	LCB	N. Wright
Brown	RCB	Bryant
Tatum	FS	Krause
Atkinson	SS	J. Wright

SUBSTITUTES

OAKLAND

OFFENSE	
Banaszak	Medlin
Bankston	Moore
Bradshaw	Rae
Garrett	Siani
Humm	Sylvester
Lawrence	
DEFENSE	
Barnes	McMath
Bonness	Phillips
Colzie	Philyaw
Ginn	Rice
KICKERS	
Guy	Mann

MINNESOTA

OFFENSE	
Berry	Hamilton
Bueton	S. Johnson
Craig	Lee
Dumler	Miller
Grim	Willis
Groce	
DEFENSE	
Allen	McNeil
Beamon	Mullaney
Windlan Hall	J. White
Martin	Winston
KICKERS	
Clabo	Cox

SCORING

OAKLAND	0	16	3	13—32
MINNESOTA	0	0	7	7—14

Second Quarter
Oak.	Mann, 24 yard field goal	0:48
Oak.	Casper, 1 yard pass from Stabler PAT—Mann (kick)	7:50
Oak.	Banaszak, 1 yard rush PAT — Kick (no good)	11:27

Third Quarter
Oak.	Mann, 40 yard field goal	9:44
Minn.	S. White, 8 yard pass from Tarkenton PAT—Cox (kick)	14:13

Fourth Quarter
Oak.	Banaszak, 2 yard rush PAT — Mann (kick)	7:21
Oak.	Brown, 75 yard interception return PAT—Kick (no good)	9:17
Minn.	Voigt, 13 yard pass from Lee PAT — Cox (kick)	14:35

TEAM STATISTICS

OAK.		MINN.
21	First Downs—Total	20
13	First Downs—Rushing	2
8	First Downs—Passing	15
0	First Downs—Penalty	3
0	Fumbles—Number	1
0	Fumbles—Lost Ball	1
4	Penalties—Number	2
30	Yards Penalized	25
1	Missed Field Goals	0
73	Offensive Plays	71
429	Net Yards	353
5.9	Average Gain	5.0
3	Takeaways	0
0	Giveaways	3
+3	Difference	-3

INDIVIDUAL STATISTICS

OAKLAND / MINNESOTA

RUSHING

OAKLAND	No	Yds	Avg.	MINNESOTA	No	Yds	Avg.
Davis	16	137	8.6	Foreman	17	44	2.6
van Eeghen	18	73	4.1	S. Johnson	2	9	4.5
Garrett	4	19	4.8	S. White	1	7	7.0
Banaszak	10	19	1.9	Lee	1	4	4.0
Ginn	2	9	4.5	Miller	2	4	2.0
Rae	2	9	4.5	McClanahan	3	3	1.0
	52	266	5.1		26	71	2.7

RECEIVING

	No	Yds	Avg.		No	Yds	Avg.
Biletnikoff	4	79	19.8	S. White	5	77	15.4
Casper	4	70	17.5	Foreman	5	62	12.4
Branch	3	20	6.7	Voigt	4	49	12.3
Garrett	1	11	11.0	Miller	4	19	4.8
	12	180	15.0	Rashad	3	53	17.7
				S. Johnson	3	26	8.7
					24	286	11.9

PUNTING

	No		Avg.		No		Avg.
Guy	4		40.5	Clabo	7		37.9

PUNT RETURNS

	No		Yds		No		Yds
Colzie	4		43	Willis	3		14	4.7

KICKOFF RETURNS

	No	Yds	Avg.		No	Yds	Avg.
Garrett	2	47	23.5	S. White	4	79	19.8
Siani	1	0	0.0	Willis	3	57	19.0
	3	47	15.7		7	136	19.4

INTERCEPTION RETURNS

	No	Yds	Avg.		
Brown	1	75	75.0	none	
Willie Hall	1	16	16.0		
	2	91	45.5		

PASSING

OAKLAND	Att.	Comp.	Comp Pct.	Yds.	Int.	Yds/ Att.	Yds/ Comp.	Yards Lost Tackled
Stabler	19	12	63.2	180	0	9.5	15.0	2—17
MINNESOTA								
Tarkenton	35	17	48.6	205	2	5.9	12.1	1—4
Lee	9	7	77.8	81	0	9.0	11.6	
	44	24	54.5	286	2	6.5	11.9	1—4

1977 In Review

FIRST WEEK OF REGULAR SEASON

Don Coryell tried hard to warn the rest of the NFL about the Denver Broncos after they whitewashed the St. Louis Cardinals 7-0 in Mile High Stadium on the first regular-season Sunday of 1977, but no one paid much attention—not even first-year Bronco Head Coach Red (Robert) Miller.

"That's bull," Miller said emphatically upon hearing the Cardinal head coach's suggestion after the game that the Broncs were a real title contender. "That's one of the problems this franchise has had—win one game and start talking playoffs. We've got to win a lot more before we can talk that way."

Deep down inside, however, the ex-offensive line coach of the New England Patriots knew he had a good thing going. After inheriting a squad which finished a respectable 9-5 under John Ralston in '76, Denver stormed through the '77 pre-season at a blistering 5-1 pace, scoring twice as many points as its opposition.

The Cardinals, meanwhile, looked nothing like the high-powered offensive machine that had established itself as one of the NFC's most successful and exciting teams, having finished with a dismal 1-5 pre-season record.

In the opener, both teams picked up where they left off in the preseason. Denver's defense shut down at least five excellent Cardinal scoring chances with MLB Randy Gradishar (10 tackles and a sack) leading the way. Offensively, veteran QB Craig Morton, acquired in the offseason from the New York Giants in a trade for QB Steve Ramsey, and a fourth-round draft choice directed an unspectacular but efficient attack, capping off the day with a surprising third-down bootleg dash that killed off any hopes the Cards had for one of their patented comebacks.

The Big Red sputtered badly on offense. With RB Terry Metcalf (injured hand) out of the lineup, it was held to 69 rushing yards while usually dependable PK Jim Bakken muffed four FG attempts.

"Everybody's very concerned," said TE J.V. Cain of the Cards' offensive problems. "But we'll put a few things together in the next 13 weeks."

Making matters worse for the Cardinals was the tough 16-10 overtime victory Eastern Conference rival Dallas took away from the Minnesota Vikings in Bloomington. Like the Broncos, the Dallas defense provided the key to victory, forcing five turnovers (three interceptions, two fumbles) and coming up with crucial sacks of Viking QB Fran Tarkenton.

Roger Staubach scurried around a tired Viking defense for the winner from four yards out on a pass-run option 6:14 into the overtime period. For the day, he completed 18 of 30 passes for 196 yards and one TD, a diving seven-yard stab in the endzone by dependable RB Preston Pearson (116 yards total offense—63 rushing, 53 receiving—compared to 11 yards rushing by highly-touted rookie Tony Dorsett).

In Foxboro, the New England Patriots gave their fans an opening-day scare, edging Kansas City 21-17 with the help of an 11-man blitz that smothered a Chief drive with time running out. Forced to play without offensive linemen John Hannah and Leon Gray, both holding out for more money on the advice of agent Howard Slusher, the Pats still managed 411 yards of total offense against a shaky Chief defense.

After early throwing problems, Steve Grogan completed 10 of his last 13 passes, and WR Darryl Stingley emerged from the shadow of Randy Vataha (waived to Green Bay earlier in the week) with a 34-yard end-around score as well as a 21-yard TD catch.

The Chiefs kept the verdict close with a strong offensive effort (ground game averaged 5.2 yards) but ultimately failed to match the heroics of lesser-lights New York (Giants), Atlanta and Cleveland.

Joe Danelo's 30-yard FG with three seconds left carried the Giants over the Washington Redskins 20-17 in East Rutherford and handed George Allen his first opening-game loss in 12 seasons as a head coach. A fumble by RB Mike Thomas that set up the winning FG, and poor coverage by S Ken Houston on an eight-yard TD toss from first-year QB Jerry Golsteyn to sub TE Gary Shirk nailed the Skins' coffin.

In Atlanta, rookie Head Coach Leeman Bennett turned the tables on the team for which he was sending in plays the previous year with a stunning 17-6 win over Los Angeles that featured a Claude Humphrey-led defense which yielded only 59 rushing yards and a fine QB performance by Scott Hunter - (pressed into action after Steve Bartkowski's knee gave out in

the Falcs' pre-season finale at New England).

The Rams were another team with a surprisingly poor pre-season (1-5), and with Head Coach Chuck Knox deciding to go with notable free-agent acquisition Joe Namath at quarterback instead of Pat Haden, the situation didn't change as the Falcons charged through a crippled front wall, severely hampered by OT Doug France's absence (injured leg).

In Cincinnati, the Browns - minus such stalwarts as All-Pro DT Jerry Sherk, WR Paul Warfield, and OT Doug Dieken - still managed to upset the Bengals 13-3. Cleveland QB Brian Sipe lifted the Browns out of an early hole with a 42-yard, third-and-long reception to Dave Logan that eventually resulted in the game's first score, a 41-yard FG by Don Cockroft.

The Bengals lost a home opener for the first time in their 10-year history as they ran only three first-half plays in Cleveland territory and consistently failed to capitalize on later scoring opportunities.

In the Chicago Bears' home opener, the big story was Walter Payton, slashing for 160 yards on the ground, mostly on draws, to spearhead a 30-20 victory over the Detroit Lions. The Bears led 27-7 at one point, but the Lions fought back behind their new-look, two-tight end offense. Detroit's specialty teams, however, particularly P Mitch Hoopes, were primarily responsible for negating an offensive attack that ended up outgaining the Bears by 63 yards.

While Payton was gaining eight more yards than the amount he garnered in his four previous efforts against Detroit, O.J. Simpson was being handled effectively in Buffalo by the Miami Dolphins. The Juice carried the ball 21 times for 71 yards against a four-linebacker defense that kept him from going wide as Miami wiped up the Bills 13-0. LB Steve Towle shined on defense for Miami with six solo tackles and seven assists, and the Bills helped out by fumbling the ball seven times (losing three of them) and dropping numerous Joe Ferguson passes.

Shutouts also proved to be the order of the day in Oakland, where the defending Super Bowl Champion Raiders creamed the San Diego Chargers 24-0, and in Houston, where the Oilers defeated the New York Jets 20-0.

In the Raiders' victory, a brilliant defense that held the Chargers to just 121 yards and Ray Guy's five punts for a 46.2-yard average made the difference.

The Oilers, featuring 17 new players, were led by NG Curley Culp, whose 27-yard TD scamper with a Richard Todd fumble (after the ball was knocked away by Elvin Bethea) started things off on the right foot. The Jet's defense was good enough to allow the Oilers only 138 yards on 20 passes while their offense managed only 11 first downs all day.

While Bert Jones threw mostly short passes in the Baltimore Colts' 29-14 victory in Seattle, two straight bombs to his favorite receiver Roger Carr, the latter a 21-yard TD toss, provided the clincher. For the most part, the Colts' strong running game (114 yards for Lydell Mitchell) did the damage against a Seahawk team that hung tough despite a poor day by QB Jim Zorn (14 of 34 passes).

The Philadelphia Eagles started the season on a happy note with a 13-3 win over Tampa Bay despite turning the ball over five times. Rookie RB Rickey Bell's drive-ending fumble and five sacks by an Eagle defense that kept fresh with rotating nose-guards made it a depressing day for Bucs' Head Coach John McKay.

It was like two different games in New Orleans as the Green Bay Packers jumped off to a 24-0 halftime lead but barely held on to defeat the Saints 24-20. Like the Lions, the Saints were hurt badly by their special teams as Rich Szaro missed a crucial extra point late in the game and Willard Harrell broke free for a 75-yard punt return TD in the first half.

The Pack, gaining only 28 yards in the final 30 minutes with virtually no ground game, was saved by SS Steve Luke's leaping fourth-quarter deflection of a well-thrown Archie Manning bomb intended for TE Jim Thaxton.

The first week of the season ended on a rather lackluster note as the Pittsburgh Steelers manhandled the struggling San Francisco 49ers 27-0 in the year's first Monday night showcase.

It was the Steelers' sixth shutout in their last 10 regular season games as well as their 11th straight victory. Franco Harris enjoyed his finest opening-game performance (101 yards rushing) while the Niners were blanked for the third straight time, including the last two pre-season games.

SECOND WEEK

The inherent danger of violence in the NFL made its presence felt leading up to the second regular-season weekend, particularly in Pittsburgh, where "The Game" was taking place between the Steelers and Oakland, the team that defeated them in the '76 AFC Championship Game.

Memories of that game alone would have provided more than enough advance billing, but there was also the game in Oakland on opening day the year before. A marvelously exciting contest (Oakland 31, Pittsburgh 28) was eventually overshadowed by one play—a violent collision between Pittsburgh's Lynn Swann and Oakland SS George Atkinson that knocked the brilliant wide receiver out of the game with a serious concussion.

Atkinson eventually was fined $1,500 and later filed a $2 million slander suit against Steeler Head Coach Chuck Noll for branding him as a "criminal element" in the NFL.

Atkinson lost his suit but, as a result of the trial, Pittsburgh's Mel Blount became infuriated with Noll for placing the All-Pro cornerback in the same category as Atkinson in the heat of cross-examination.

Commissioner Peter Rozelle's well-publicized warning to league owners that flagrant violence would not be tolerated in '77 further enhanced the buildup to a game that never lived up to its bloodbath potential.

The Steelers, who looked like champions the week before against San Francisco despite pre-season holdouts by Blount and MLB Jack Lambert, gift-wrapped two fumbles and three interceptions that led to a 16-7 Oakland victory, its third straight over Pittsburgh in two seasons.

The Steelers dominated the game statistically, but their mistakes and three FG's by Oakland's Errol Mann demoted them to .500 status.

A much better game, maybe the best regular-season game all year, was played one night later in Cleveland, where the upstart Browns knocked off faltering New England in overtime, 30-27.

After winning the second toin coss, Cleveland marched 10 plays to set up the winning score at 4:45 of the overtime period, a 35-yard FG by veteran Don Cockroft. New England counterpart John Smith's 34-yard shot as regulation time expired set up the fifth quarter.

The game featured many outstanding individual performances, but none was better than the one turned in by the Browns' multi-purpose RB Greg Pruitt (151 yards rushing, 51 yards receiving and a five-yard TD pass off the option).

With the Browns getting additional unexpected assistance from youngsters like P Greg Coleman - (who was helping Browns' fans forget the money holdout by second-round pick Tom Skladany), DT Mickey Sims and DB Oliver Davis, the Browns earned their 10th regular-season victory in 12 games, setting the stage for a big AFC Central matchup the next week at home against Pittsburgh.

Fine efforts by QB Steve Grogan (15 of 23 for 172 yards and two TD's) and RB Sam Cunningham (70 yards rushing, 52 receiving and one TD) were wasted as the Patriots were forced to go to the wire for the second straight week against supposedly inferior opponents.

After finding out the Browns were for real the previous week, AFC Central rival Cincinnati rebounded with a 42-20 victory over Seattle that was much closer than the score indicated.

The Bengals started out like gangbusters with 28 first-half points, but their offense suddenly stalled as Seattle stormed back to within eight points after three quarters behind the long-range passing of Jim Zorn (82-yard TD pass to rookie RB Dave Sims set a club record).

But as is often the case when the Bengals are in trouble, QB Ken Anderson teamed up with WR Isaac Curtis (three catches for 100 yards) on a 32-yard TD pass play to assure the inconsistent Bengals of a victory.

The Houston Oilers kept pace with Cleveland in the AFC Central, thanks to CB Willie Alexander's 95-yard, fourth-quarter interception return that buried Green Bay 16-10 and ruined a fine defensive effort on Oiler offensive heavyweights Billy "White Shoes" Johnson (33 yards on four punt returns) and Ken Burrough (three catches for 23 yards).

Alexander's theft also erased an impressive Packer ball-control drive (seven minutes), and it came on the first pass in eight straight plays by QB Lynn Dickey, who earlier had two passes picked off.

It took another fine individual defensive play to carry Washington past Atlanta 10-6 as LB Mike Curtis (replacing Chris Hanburger—appendectomy) sacked Scott Hunter for a 13-yard loss from the Redskins' 17 with 1:53 left to play.

Atlanta continued to look tough despite the loss, running 20 more plays than the Skins in its second-straight turnover-free game while Washington fans spent most of their time booing QB Billy Kilmer (two interceptions midway through fourth quarter).

The San Francisco 49ers started out their home season with a nice scoring drive against Miami, but the Dolphs simply had too much Nat Moore on their way to a 19-15 decision. WR Moore latched on to TD passes of 32 and 73 yards from a bespectacled Bob Griese and ran another one in on a 19-yard end-around to account for all of Miami's scoring.

Niner QB Jim Plunkett looked much better than he did against Pittsburgh (three of 13 for 30 yards), but continued to look uncomfortable with new Head Coach Ken Meyer's play-calling system from the bench.

Two of the most impressive team performances of the week were turned in by Detroit, as it treated the home fans to a 429-yard offensive outburst in defeating New Orleans 23-19, and San Diego, with Johnny Rodgers and a much-improved defense easily mopping up on the Chiefs in Kansas City, 23-7.

The Lions' defense held the Saints' solid ground game to under 100 yards, while RB Dexter Bussey's 150 rushing yards provided the offensive highlights along with TE Charlie Sanders' club record-breaking reception (surpassing Gail Cogdill's 325 career catches).

While mistakes kept the disappointing Saints close in Detroit (Wilbur Summers—the Lions' fifth punter of the year—had one blocked for a TD), there was no doubt the Chargers were in control in K.C. with Rodgers' seven punt returns for 130 yards making up for a poor debut against Oakland and Ray Guy.

In Los Angeles, Joe Namath's see-saw career appeared to be on the upswing as he called a strong game in leading the Rams past Philadelphia 20-0 with the help of RB Lawrence McCutcheon (106 yards rushing), WR Ron Jesse (five catches, 74 yards after a poor pre-season) and OT Doug France, who helped the Rams control the ball for two-thirds of the game.

The Eagles moved the ball into Ram territory only twice as ex-Ram QB Ron Jaworski was sacked twice and threw three interceptions.

Not quite as one-sided was the Cowboys' 41-21 victory over the New York Giants in Irving, featuring 31 first-half points by the Pokes against a team that had never given up more than 17 points in a game under Head Coach John McVay.

At one point Roger Staubach completed nine straight passes while Heisman Trophy winner Tony Dorsett scored two TD's and piled up 98 offensive yards (62 rushing, 36 receiving)—against a line-backer thin Giant defense (Brad Van Pelt and Harry Carson out with shoulder and back injuries, respectively).

For the second week in a row the Baltimore Colts appeared to be holding back offensively despite winning, this time 20-12 on the road over the New York Jets. Even though receivers Roger Carr, Glenn Doughty and Ray Chester (hurt early in the game) were on the sidelines, RB Lydell Mitchell still complained that his team showed "no imagination" on the way to compiling just two more yards total offense than the Jets.

Rocky Mountain fever was beginning to spread in Denver, meanwhile, as the Broncs came out smoking offensively after a close first half to maul troubled Buffalo 26-6.

Including the final pre-season game, the Broncs' defense entered the third week of the season without yielding a point (Buffalo's TD came on Bo Cornell's 22-yard fumble return) while the Bills, outgained 210-50 in the second half, had failed to score a TD on offense.

If Walter Payton had been really thinking about having an even better year in '78, he obviously was aiming to stay away from performances like the one he turned in at St. Louis the second week when his 36 rushing yards and his decision to stay inbounds on a game-ending drive helped the Cards nip Chicago 16-13.

PK Jim Bakken rebounded with three FG's for the Big Red while QB Jim Hart carried the load on offense (club-record 12-straight completions) and MLB Tim Kearney did the same on defense.

A Saturday night victory by Minnesota in Tampa (9-3) started the week off on a dull note as the Vikes' did just enough offensively on a damp field to hold back the Bucs, a fast-improving team defensively. The Bucs' only offensive thrust, however, was provided by rookie RB Ricky Bell, who outgained Minnesota's Chuck Foreman on the ground 66-58.

THIRD WEEK

Although they were separated by eight points, the New York Jets' encounter with the Baltimore Colts Sept. 25 was much closer than it looked. If jet rookie Bruce Harper's 92-yard punt return TD hadn't been nullified by a clipping penalty, and if Duane Carrell hadn't bobbled the snap on the ensuing punt attempt, the young season's biggest upset might have materialized.

But the pesky young Jets waited only one week to really make it happen. Their 30-27 victims were the unsuspecting New England Patriots, still weary from a tough Monday Night overtime defeat in Cleveland as well as the constant internal stress caused by the holdouts of offensive linemen John Hannah and Leon Gray.

In this game the Jets got most of the breaks and the Pats provided plenty of them (10 penalties for 100 yards, three interceptions, two fumbles)—especially Mike Haynes. After rookie WR Wes Walker beat him man-to-man on a 25-yard TD pass from Richard Todd to push the Jets ahead 27-20 in the fourth quarter, the usually outstanding cornerback decided not to call for a fair catch with time running out and lost a booming 47-yard punt by newcomer Chuck Ramsey when he was stripped of the ball by Billy Hardee.

The Patriots had tied the game 27-27 with 1:27 remaining on Steve Grogan's 22-yard TD toss to Darryl Stingley, but after the Jets' special teams converged on Haynes to avenge rookie Raymond Clayborn's first-quarter, 100-yard kickoff return TD, there was just enough time for PK Pat Leahy to slam home a 32-yarder that made up for the PAT he missed after Walker's TD.

Soothed by the presence of home-run threat Walker, Todd looked increasingly comfortable against N.E. (12 for 21, 154 yards, two TD's) despite three more interceptions. Meanwhile, the Pats fell two full games behind the Colts and Miami in the AFC East and continued to struggle defensively, yielding 30 points for the second straight week.

The surprising Dolphins kept pace with the Colts by displaying an explosive offense against Houston in a 27-7 home-field triumph that featured a 21-point, first-quarter outburst fueled by WR Duriel Harris (five catches, 87 yards, and a TD).

The Dolphs' rookie-laden defense helped out with a brilliant goal-line stand (Oilers had five chances to score from the Miami three) as Houston was outgained on the ground 217-68.

The Colts, meanwhile, came up with a balanced offensive attack despite numerous injuries and allowed O.J. Simpson only 58 rushing yards by playing SS Bruce Laird up close on the line in a 17-14 decision over Buffalo in Baltimore.

Bills' QB Joe Ferguson teamed up exceptionally well with WR Bob Chandler (seven catches, 78 yards, one TD) as Buffalo gained just seven fewer yards offensively than the Colts while coughing up the ball three times.

Other surprises in week No. 3 were produced by Atlanta and Washington in the NFC and San Diego in the AFC.

The Falcs swamped the Giants 17-3 behind reserve QB Kim McQuilken and remained tied with Los Angeles in the NFC West at 2-1 despite three missed FG's by Nick Mike-Mayer. Atlanta's defense continued to raise eyebrows around the league, sacking the Giants nine times (a team record) and allowing them only 72 passing yards.

In Washington, Billy Kilmer temporarily silenced his critics by throwing three TD passes in "one of the biggest wins in seven years" according to Head Coach George Allen, a 24-14 victory over mysterious St. Louis.

The Cardinals came from behind with 14 fourth-quarter points (Terry Metcalf was on the bench most of the first three quarters), but CB Joe Lavender's interception midway through the fourth quarter—followed two plays later by John Riggins' tackle-breaking, 45-yard TD reception—kept the Skins close in the NFC East.

The Chargers stayed right behind Oakland and Denver in the AFC West after totally dominating Cincinnati in San Diego, 24-3, as WR Charley Joiner got together with QB Jim Harris on two TD circus catches and the vastly-improved Charger defense sacked unimpressive Ken Anderson five times while allowing the Bengals to cross midfield only three times.

The Dallas Cowboys readied themselves for key inter-conference battles with St. Louis and Washington by blowing Tampa Bay out early in a 23-7 decision that featured a home-crowd pleasing dunk over the crossbar by LB Tom Henderson after he ran 79 yards with an interception.

After giving up only 45 points in three games despite spending an undue amount of time on the field because of their pathetic offense, the Bucs' "D" continued to carry the team, even scoring Tampa's first TD of the season on LB Richard Wood's 37-yard jaunt after scooping up Tony Dorsett's fumble.

In Cleveland, the Pittsburgh Steelers brought the Browns back to earth, brawling their way to a 28-14 victory that produced 21 yellow flags for a total of 186 yards.

The "Steel Curtain" defense hadn't yet reached its superb '76 form, but it was good enough to hold Cleveland to 165 total yards while QB Terry Bradshaw paced the offense (three TD passes, one TD run) along with Lynn Swann (seven catches for 71 yards, two TD's).

Logjams like the one in the AFC Central—with the Steelers, Browns and Oilers all knotted up at 2-1—had come to be expected in the NFL, but over in the NFC-Central, the Minnesota Vikings were finally starting to get some competition at the top of the ladder.

The Vikes kept their composure after Green Bay WR Steve Odom sprinted 95 yards with a Lynn Dickey sideliner (one yard short of a team record), and rebounded behind Fran Tarkenton's medium-range aerials to Sammy White to put down the Pack 19-7 and give Head Coach Bud Grant his 100th NFL career victory.

But the Detroit Lions also moved their record to 2-1, thanks in great part to a bad day by Philadelphia PK Horst Muhlmann, by just barely holding out 17-13 against the Eagles and the dangerous passing combination of QB Ron Jaworski and WR Harold Carmichael. In addition to the PAT and two FG's missed by Muhlmann, RB Tom Sullivan's fumble was recovered by FS Lem Barney to kill off a late Philadelphia scoring opportunity set up by Detroit RB Dexter Bussey's fumble.

The Chicago Bears fell a game behind Minnesota and Detroit after embarrassingly succumbing to New Orleans and Archie Manning, who enjoyed one of his greatest performances with three TD scrambles to go with a TD pass to Chuck Muncie.

The Bear defense, missing DT Wally Chambers and FS Doug Plank, couldn't crack a leaky New Orleans front wall (Manning was sacked 13 times in the first two games). Eleven Chicago penalties—including two that nullified TD's—overshadowed another great performance by RB Walter Payton (19 for 140, two TD's rushing; four for 53, one TD receiving).

In Los Angeles, the Rams' specialty teams made the difference in a 34-14 victory that proved costly when WR Ron Jessie was knocked out for the season on the Rams' opening series with a knee injury that required surgery.

Niners' QB Jim Plunkett again looked like a winner, directing scoring drives of 85 and 63 yards, but not enough to overcome long kickoff returns by Wendell Tyler and Cullen Bryant, a blocked punt by FS Bill Simpson and fine kicking by PK Rafael Septien and P Glen Walker.

In the Monday Night game in Kansas City, the Oakland Raiders poured it on the Chiefs with four straight second-half scoring drives and a season-high 539 offensive yards to win 37-28.

Despite a flock of injuries as a result of the Pittsburgh battle the week before—including a knee injury that knocked LB Phil Villapiano out for the season—the Raiders grabbed their 16th straight (regular and post-season) victory while QB Ken Stabler (19 of 28 for 297 yards, one TD), RB's Mark van Eeghen and Clarence Davis (both over 100 yards rushing) and TE Dave Casper (seven catches for 101 yards) compiling eye-catching individual statistics.

Rookie RB Tony Reed gained 119 yards on the ground for K.C. while S Gary Barbaro's interception (fourth of the year) and fumble recovery set up two early Chief scores.

And while the Raiders continued to look like the class of the NFL, Denver kept pace in the AFC West with a 24-13 triumph in Seattle that was keyed by QB Craig Morton's new-found bootlegging expertise.

Seattle's Steve Myer, starting his first game at quarterback in place of the injured Jim Zorn, staged a flashy debut (20 of 29 for 165 yards, one TD), but with the Broncs clinging to a 17-13 lead late in the third period, Morton kept alive a methodical TD drive with scrambles of 13 and 14 yards that complemented his fine 181-yard passing performance.

FOURTH WEEK

The Chicago Bears' 24-23 victory over disappointing Los Angeles on a rainy Monday night in the Windy City brought Week No. 4 in the NFL to an exciting climax, but the game's real significance didn't show up in the won-lost column.

It was the performances of the starting QB's, Bob Avellini for Chicago and Joe Namath for Los Angeles, that left the biggest impact. At the same time Avellini's three-year career reached new heights, after calling his own plays for the first time and proving there was more to the Bears' offense than Walter Payton, four interceptions and a devastating tackle by DT Jim Osborne marked the beginning of the end for the illustrious "Broadway Joe."

The Bears came from 13 points behind the first half to take the lead after TD bombs of 70 and 72 yards from Avellini to James Scott, a speedy WFL refugee who would go on to become the NFC's second-leading receiver. Payton's fourth-quarter, 51-yard burst after both teams exchanged FG's set up Avellini's third TD strike, a 29-yarder to Greg Latta, another former member of the WFL.

Despite working against one of the worst defenses in the league statistically, Namath had all kinds of problems with the Chicago unit led by safeties Doug Plank (two interceptions after returning from a knee injury) and Gary Fencik (45 tackles in three weeks).

And after Osborne's tackle sent Namath wobbling to the sidelines, his replacement, Pat Haden, came on to direct a crisp TD drive, culminated by a 26-yard TD pass to WR Dwight Scales. Hampered again by his famous but fragile knees as well as a bruised sternum, Namath didn't run another play for the Rams all year and retired to no one's surprise at the end of the season. Meanwhile, Haden, whom many felt should have been L.A.'s No. 1 QB in the first place, went on to become the NFC's second-leading passer.

Avellini completed 11 of 17 passes for 219 yards and rushed for 32 more on six carries to offset 15 Bear penalties as both teams evened their records at 2-2.

Four teams remained unbeaten after the fourth week: Baltimore, in first place all by itself in the AFC East after mauling Miami 45-28; Oakland, a 26-10 winner on the road over mistake-prone Cleveland; Dallas, a come-from-behind 30-24 victor in St. Louis, and Denver, setting itself up for an AFC West showdown the next weekend in Oakland after thumping Kansas City at home 23-7.

The offenses didn't waste any time in the Colt-Dolphin contest as three TD's were scored (Lydell Mitchell's 64-yard run, Freddie Solomon's 90-yard kickoff return and Benny Malone's 52-yard run) in the game's first 2½ minutes. Malone's 66-yard TD run gave Miami a 28-10 lead early in the second quarter before the Colts reeled off 35 unanswered points to temporarily silence growing criticism of their offense.

It was a defensive argument, however, that put the Colts on the winning track. By playing their linebackers wider apart, the Colts became more aggressive holding Malone to only five yards on six carries in the second half and eventually sacking Miami QB Bob Griese five times.

Oakland was the first team in 1977 not to lose a game after playng the previous Monday night as it intercepted two Brian Sipe passes and recovered a fumble (three altogether) to set up scores.

Behind Sipe, the Browns were able to convert only one of nine third downs while the Raiders, emphasizing a strong ground game that featured a 114-yard performance by Mark van Eeghen, converted seven of 16. PK Errol Mann helped out with three first-half FG's.

The Cardinals (1-3) set a club record for penalties (166 yards) in their loss to Dallas, including two pass interference calls on CB Lee Nelson (replacing injured Perry Smith) that led to Dallas' final two touchdowns in the fourth quarter.

Big Red QB Jim Hart played hurt (nine for 32 passing) after being sacked by DE Harvey Martin early in the game. The Cowboys' Tony Dorsett exploded with 141 rushing yards and two TD's, including a club-record 77-yard romp.

The Broncs didn't have much to offer offensively, hurting themselves with nine penalties, but the way their defense mopped up on the Chiefs (four interceptions, two fumble recoveries and six sacks for 52 yards), it didn't matter. Chief RB Ed Podolak's seven-yard TD run in the fourth quarter was the first rushing TD given up by the Broncs all year.

It was another big weekend in the NFL as four teams kept their opponents off the scoreboard: Atlanta, 7-0 over San Francisco; Washington, extending Tampa Bay's losing streak to 18 games with a 10-0 decision; San Diego, 14-0 over New Orleans and New England, 31-0 winners over Seattle with offensive linemen John Hannah and Leon Gray back in the fold.

There were only two plays, one after another, worth talking about in Atlanta's victory over the 49ers—Edgar Field's partial block of Tom Wittum's punt that resulted in Billy Ryckman's recovery at the S.F. 39-yard line, and Ralph McGill's deflection of a Scott Hunter pass on the next play that enabled Falcon WR Alfred Jenkins to turn it into a TD reception.

The 49ers' defense continued to work overtime as their passing offense netted only 35 yards. Falcon CB Rolland Lawrence was all over the field, scoring two TD's that were nullified by penalties after an interception and a 67-yard lateral romp resulting from Wilson Faumuina's fumble recovery.

Washington's Eddie Brown set a record with 11 punt returns in the Skins' win, two of them setting up Washington's only scores. The Redskins blew three other scoring opportunities, but 10 sacks (three by DE Dennis Johnson) of Gary Huff and Randy Hedberg helped stop the Bucs cold.

San Diego joined the sacking parade with eight on its way to blanking a Hank Stram-led team for the first time in 14 years and allowing just 10 points in three straight games. The Saints never got inside the Charger 20 and were burned on an 88-yard punt return TD by Johnny Fuller, a carbon copy of one by Willard Harrell that led to an earlier loss to Green Bay.

Seattle signal caller Steve Myer played his first game ever in the rain and his performance against the Pats was all wet (five for 23, four interceptions). His counterpart, Steve Grogan, threw three TD passes as New England gained 333 yards, including 101 on 31 carries by first-quarter workhorse Sam Cunningham.

The Steelers lost more than the AFC Central lead against Houston. After QB's Terry Bradshaw and Mike Kruczek suffered a fractured wrist and a shoulder separation, respectively, the Oilers jumped all over emergency replacement Tony Dungy to assure themselves of a 27-10 victory.

The Oilers featured a big-play offense as a 44-yard halfback option pass from Ronnie Coleman to Kenny Burrough gave them their first score and a 51-yard TD bomb to Billy "White Shoes" Johnson, his first reception of the season, gave them the lead for good.

Cincinnati, meanwhile, remained tied with Pittsburgh and Cleveland in the AFC Central with a 17-7 victory over Green Bay. The Bengals remained inconsistent on offense despite Boobie Clark's 89 rushing yards while Green Bay's offense was virtually non-existent in the second half.

A trick play carried the Vikings to a 14-7 victory over Detroit in Bloomington as Sammy White rambled 59 yards with a surprise lateral from Ahmad Rashad (six catches for 85 yards) in the first quarter. Detroit WR Luther Blue's eight-yard TD reception was the only score in the final three quarters, even though Fran Tarkenton and Greg Landry completed 46 passes for a total of 478 yards between them.

Richard Todd had the best day of his career (10 of 15 for 194 yards, one TD) as the Jets edged Buffalo 24-19. Mistakes again proved costly to Buffalo as QB Joe Ferguson's fourth-quarter fumble was recovered by Richard Neal on the Bills' 17, setting up a game-winning TD run by Clark Gaines (20 carries for 94 yards).

O.J. Simpson finally had a good day (122 yards on 23 carries) and Buffalo outgained the Jets on offense by five yards. After the game Bills' players were vocal in their support of Head Coach Jim Ringo, rumored to be on his way out if Buffalo lost to the Jets.

In East Rutherford, Herb Lusk's two TD runs, one of them for 70 yards, led the Eagles to a 28-10 victory over the Giants, losers in three straight games. Joe Pisarcik was a surprise starter in place of Jerry Golsteyn for the Giants and he was sacked four times, bringing the total to 19 in just four games.

FIFTH WEEK

Heading into their fifth-week battle in Oakland for sole possession of first place in the AFC West, the verdict was still out on the Denver Broncos. The Broncs were superb for the most part while winning their first four games, especially their speedy "Orange Crush" defense, but the combined record of those opponents the first four weeks of the '77 season was 1-15.

But after humiliating the defending Super Bowl champion Raiders 30-7 and abruptly halting Oakland's 17-game winning streak (one short of the league record), there was no doubt the men from the Mile High City were for real.

The Raiders were no match for Denver's defense as they were held to a season-low point total. Oakland chalked up eight turnovers while Denver had none, and QB Ken Stabler threw seven interceptions (one short of the single-game record), three of them to OLB Joe Rizzo.

But while four of Denver's thefts led directly to 23 points, the game's highlight came on the most unlikely play of the year. Denver PK Jim Turner, who had never before caught a pass except in practice, was on the receiving end of a shocking 25-yard TD pass from Norris Weese after a fake FG that put the Broncs ahead 21-7 at halftime. The embarrassed Raiders never recovered.

The schedule, however, provided Oakland with a quick opportunity to avenge the defeat two weeks later in Denver, where bright orange Broncomania had already infected everyone in the city to produce the season's most colorful off-the-field story. Everyone would be watching. They now knew that the Broncos were a legitimate title contender for the first time since 1962, when last they were in first place so far into the season.

Denver wasn't the only team that used razzle-dazzle to help it to victory in the fifth week. In Bloomington, on a first-down play against the Chicago Bears in overtime, Minnesota surprisingly lined up for a 21-yard FG attempt. Holder Jeff Krause took the snap, picked himself up and nonchalantly lobbed his first pass completion in 14 pro seasons to TE Stu Voigt in the endzone to beat the Bears 22-16.

Chuck Foreman rambled for 150 yards and a TD for the Vikes and blocked kicks by LB Matt Blair and DT Alan Page on Bob Thomas' extra point and 41-yard FG attempt with 1:55 left in regulation, respectively, were keys in pulling the Purple People two games in front of the Bears and a game ahead of Detroit in the NFC Central.

While free-wheeling, fancy plays made Red Miller and Bud Grant look like geniuses, questionable coaching decisions by San Diego's Tommy Prothro and Atlanta's Leeman Bennett couldn't be overlooked in the Chargers' 24-20 loss to New England and the Falcons' 3-0 loss to win-starved Buffalo.

With six minutes left to play and the Chargers down 17-13 but threatening on the Pats' 43-yard line, Prothro elected to punt on fourth and less than a yard despite N.E.'s game-long ability to control the ball (Pats outrushed S.D. by more than 200 yards).

San Diego reserve QB Bill Munson completed five straight passes on the way to a 16-yard TD toss to Charlie Joiner to make the game close, but the Pats picked up 16 first downs rushing (Sam Cunningham: 25 carries for 141 yards) to stay in contention in the AFC East against Baltimore, their opponent in Foxboro the next weekend.

In Buffalo, the Falcs trailed by three with four minutes left and faced a fourth-and-one situation after moving the ball down to the Bills' four-yard line. Instead of Atlanta tying the game with a chip-shot FG, QB Scott Hunter attempted a rollout for a first down and was stopped cold by SS Doug Jones and CB Keith Moody.

While Hunter had a poor day (nine for 29 passing, two interceptions), Buffalo Head Coach Jim Ringo finally reached the winner's circle after 13 attempts and O.J. Simpson gained 138 yards, allowing him to become only the second man in NFL history to top the 10,000-yard career rushing mark (Jim Brown is the other).

The Bears weren't the only team handicapped by faulty kicking. Detroit barely got by Green Bay 10-6 despite four missed FG's by Steve Mike-Mayer, while poor punting by Jerrell Wilson helped bury the Chiefs, 17-6 losers to Baltimore.

FS Lem Barney was the hero for the Lions, intercepting two passes and causing WR Ollie Smith's fumble late in the game to kill off a late Packer rally. The Pack lost its fourth straight as QB Lynn Dickey was sacked five times (twice by LE Ken Sanders) and Green Bay runners averaged only 2.3 yards per carry.

After erupting the week before against Miami, the Colts returned to form by doing just enough offensively to carry them past the inferior Chiefs. They scored two quick TD's as a result of Wilson's 24-yard punt and a fumbled kickoff return by Ted McKnight, and that was all they really needed.

In an NFC West shootout in Los Angeles, Chuck Knox's troops returned to their conservative, ball-control game plan, ramming the ball down the New Orleans Saints' throats 61 times on the way to a 14-7 victory to stay tied for first place with Atlanta at 3-2.

Ram QB Pat Haden threw only 16 passes, but four of them were clutch third-down conversions, and Lawrence McCutcheon came up with his 20th rushing performance over 100 yards. Still angered over what they thought were "cheap shots" by the Bears in their loss to Chicago six days earlier, the Rams' defense held the 1-4 Saints to only 77 yards.

The Houston Oilers were another angry team after Cleveland DE Mike St. Clair's late hit forced sore-ankled QB Dan Pastorini to the sidelines in the Browns' 24-23, come-from-behind victory. Pastorini had come off the bench after QB John Hadl's two early interceptions handed Cleveland 14 easy points.

Don Cockroft's game-winning, 30-yard FG as time expired was set up primarily by the gutty running of Greg Pruitt, who was in for only one play during the first 55 minutes because of an ankle injury.

But nobody played with more pain than Terry Bradshaw in Pittsburgh's 20-14 Monday night victory over Cincinnati that kept the Steelers tied for the AFC Central lead at 3-2 with Houston and Cleveland. Bradshaw, playing with his broken left wrist in a cast, threw only nine passes but completed six of them while his counterpart, Ken Anderson, left the game in the second quarter with a knee injury.

OLB Jack Ham's interception and CB Mel Blount's fumble recovery resulted in two short TD runs by Rocky Bleier to put Pitt in front early, and the Bengals kept the Steelers on their toes in the final seconds when Reggie Williams recovered a punt in the endzone and Mel Morgan recovered an onside kick moments later.

Injuries ultimately took their toll on the Washington Redskins as Dallas battered its spirited NFC East rivals 34-16 and moved two games in front of them with its fifth straight victory of the season.

Going into the second quarter, two Redskin fullbacks and two starting guards had limped off the field, including FB John Riggins with torn knee ligaments. Eight Cowboy sacks pressured QB's Billy Kilmer and Joe Theismann into a combined seven-for-25 passing performance.

Offensively, Dallas' Roger Staubach picked on a young cornerback for the second straight week, this time Gerard Williams, as he threw a 45-yard bomb past him into the arms of WR Drew Pearson for the go-ahead score. Both placekickers, Dallas' Efren Herrera and Washington's Mark Moseley, booted FG's over 50 yards.

Jim Hart didn't let a sore shoulder keep him from completing 17 of 25 passes for 209 yards and a TD in St. Louis' 21-17 victory over Philadelphia that moved the Big Red's record to 2-3. Eagle QB Ron Jaworski completed 17 passes for 264 yards and two TD's, but he also threw three interceptions while RB Mike Hogan accounted for 89 of the Eagles' 96 rushing yards.

An injury to RB Norm Bulaich (cracked rib) resulted in his replacement, Don Nottingham, receiving a game ball in Miami's too-close-for-comfort 21-17 win over the New York Jets.

Dolphin Head Coach Don Shula was disappointed at his team's continued poor second-half play as Miami almost blew a 21-0 lead. Nottingham gained 96 yards on the ground and provided excellent strongside blocking for RB Benny Malone, who gained over 100 yards for the second straight game. The Jets hurt themselves with two fumbles, two blocked punts and a holding penalty that nullified a TD pass from Richard Todd to TE Jerome Barkum.

328

In Seattle, the Tampa Bay Bucs scored more points than in their first four games combined against the Seahawks' shaky defense, but it wasn't enough as Steve Myer's four TD passes led Seattle to a 30-23 victory that featured a combined 759 yards in total offense.

The San Francisco 49ers remained winless and were off to their worst start since 1963 after losing to the New York Giants 20-17 in East Rutherford, but after the game San Francisco Owner Edward DeBartolo, Jr., said he wasn't ready to give up on Head Coach Ken Meyer.

Giant QB Joe Pisarcik played it safe with only six passes (none in the first or fourth quarter) as Niner turnovers resulted in a 17-point second quarter for the Giants and negated a 275-154 advantage in total yards.

SIXTH WEEK

Heading down the stretch in the 1977 race for playoff spots and the eventual Super Bowl crown, the decisions of league officials produced what had to be a record number of controversies. Never were crucial calls by the men in zebra shirts scrutinized so closely by coaches and the media.

The first real signs of dissatisfaction with the refs became evident as the sixth regular-season weekend drew near, and they came from the upper echelons of the AFC Central Division.

In Cincinnati, the Bengal brass was having a hard time forgetting a 20-14 Monday night loss to Pittsburgh because of a quick whistle that blew away a sure TD on a fumble recovery by SS Jerry Anderson. Responding to its complaints, assistant supervisor of officials Nick Skorich said simply, "somebody goofed," a much clearer explanation than what the league had to offer later in the season when questionable officiating soiled the playoffs.

And in Houston, Oiler Head Coach Bum Phillips was still burning over a fumble ruling in his team's 24-23 loss to Cleveland that he thought should have been ruled an incomplete pass because QB Dan Pastorini was in the act of throwing. Referee Cal LePore, however, stuck by his decision, claiming "the ball had not left Pastorini's hand." The ruling was one of the first in a series of bad-luck calls that contributed to the Oilers' absence in the playoffs despite coming up with one of the strongest performances in the NFL the second half of the '77 season.

The officiating wasn't a factor, however, in the big sixth-week matchups in Foxboro and Los Angeles, as the Pats and Rams came up with their strongest performances of the season against powerful opponents to remain in playoff contention.

The Pats moved their record to 4-2, one game behind Baltimore and Miami in the AFC East, after handing the Colts their first loss of the season, 17-3. A marvelous defense led by DE Julius Adams and CB's Mike Haynes and Bob Howard was the key as Colt QB Bert Jones was sacked five times and held to only 11 net passing yards and RB Lydell Mitchell gained only 29 yards on 13 carries and caught no passes. The offensive highlight was TE Russ Francis' 31-yard TD reception in which he weaved his way around three defenders.

The Rams, meanwhile, waited until Monday night to smother Minnesota 35-3 as they outrushed the Vikes 283-98 with the help of rookie breakaway threat Wendell Tyler's eight carries for 102 yards, including a 44-yard TD. The win enabled them to keep pace with Atlanta in the NFC West at 4-2 while the Vikes dropped to 4-2 in the NFC Central but remained in first by a game.

It was a happy week for Kansas City and San Francisco as each won its first game of the season by defeating San Diego 21-16 and Detroit 28-7, respectively.

The Chiefs staged an amazing comeback with the help of Charger miscues by scoring 14 points within 22 seconds late in the fourth quarter to overcome a 16-7 deficit. Fumbles by QB James Harris and RB Rickey Young set up the Chief's come-from-behind scores, and the strange game ended after Harris, who had misread coverage all day, threw a pass intended for RB Joe Washington that was intercepted by SS Gary Barbaro on the K.C. one to ruin a final San Diego charge.

Jim Plunkett was much better off than Harris after calling the plays himself for the first time as a 49er on the way to deflating the listless Lions with TD passes of 32 and 35 yards to WR Gene Washington. The Niners' ground game finally came to life as Delvin Williams and Wilbur Jackson combined for 182 yards, and their "Gold Rush" defense sacked Lion QB's eight times and intercepted its first pass in 10 games.

In Washington, the New York Giants whipped Washington 17-6 to move their record to 3-0 against the Skins under Head Coach John McVay. New York recovered three fumbles and intercepted a pass but nearly matched the Skins' offensive futility (Washington had only two TD's in its last 12 quarters) by striking out on three scoring chances inside the Redskins' 15-yard line.

The New York Jets just missed coming up with their second big upset of the season, but QB Ken Stabler and a strong Oakland ground game (Mark van Eeghen had 143 yards on 36 carries) overcame Richard Todd's fantastic 396-yard, four-TD passing performance in a 28-27 nail-biter.

Pat Leahy's missed PAT after an 87-yard TD bomb to rookie WR Wes Walker (four catches for 178 yards) and two unsuccessful FG attempts (26 and 32 yards) made the difference as Stabler threw fourth-quarter TD passes to WR's Fred Biletnikoff and Mike Siani to bail out the Raiders.

Blocked punts carried the Cowboys and Packers to victory against Philadelphia and Tampa Bay, respectively, as Dallas grabbed a three-game lead in the NFC Central after upending Philly 16-10 and Green Bay blitzed the Bucs 13-0.

The Eagles, mostly on the strength of their tough defense, held a 7-6 lead after three quarters against the Pokes until Jay Saldi blocked Spike Jones' punt 1:22 into the fourth quarter and SS Charlie Waters picked up the ball and raced 17 yards for the go-ahead score. Eagle signal caller Ron Jaworski unknowingly played the game with a broken thumb.

The big play that allowed the Pack to avenge a 10-7 pre-season loss to the Bucs came when LB Jim Gueno broke through the Buccaneer line and forced Dave Green's first-ever punt block. RB Eric Torkelson (73 yards) followed up with a five-yard TD run that gave Green Bay all the points it needed.

Tampa QB Gary Huff, already wearing a left knee brace, cracked a rib after DE Mike Butler's tackle in the fourth quarter. Green Bay QB Lynn Dickey, benefitting greatly from the blocking of RG Mel Jackson, completed 11 of 15 passes as the Pack moved its record to 2-4.

In other games, the Denver Broncos showed their fine depth while defeating Cincinnati 24-13 despite injuries to RB Jon Keyworth, OLB Tom Jackson, CB Louie Wright and QB Craig Morton; Atlanta's superb defense stymied the punchless Chicago Bears 16-10; quick-striking Miami took care of Seattle 31-13 before a surprisingly small crowd (29,858); the St. Louis Cardinals' offense, after averaging only 15 points a game, erupted against New Orleans in a 49-31 barn-burner; Pittsburgh managed to win two games in a row for the first time this season by dumping Houston 27-10 and the Cleveland Browns, after five consecutive back-breakers, chalked up a relatively easy victory against beleaguered Buffalo 27-16.

Denver's Larry Evans, replacing Jackson, set up the Broncs' first 10 points with a recovery of PR Willie Shelby's fumble and an interception, and Morton, who left the game later with a knee injury, broke open with an 81-yard TD bomb to WR Jack Dolbin that extended the league's longest-running win streak to eight.

Bengal QB Kenny Anderson, who came into the game with a sprained knee, injured his left thigh after knocking into RE Lyle Alzado's helmet, and for the rest of the year he remained a "questionable" starter, although not officially listed on the team's injury reports. RB Pete Johnson ran for 55 yards on the third play of the game and finished with 108 yards on 16 carries.

The Bears hurt themselves with two fumbles and three interceptions as RB Walter Payton was held to 69 yards and their only TD came with five seconds left on an 84-yard kickoff return by Brian Baschnagel.

The Falcs, who had only fumbled twice and been intercepted twice in six games, were error-free again as P John James' five boots inside the 20-yard line gave them excellent field position.

WR Nat Moore caught two TD passes and RB Don Nottingham added two more running as the Dolphs scored 10 points in the final 31 seconds of the first half against Seattle. But Head Coach Don Shula was more pleased with a fourth-quarter TD drive that lasted seven minutes.

Fifty-four first downs kept the St. Louis and New Orleans defenses busy as RB Wayne Morris scored four TD's and rushed for 95 yards for the Big Red and CB Roger Wehrli's 19-yard run on a fake FG iced the decision.

QB Bobby Scott, replacing sore-ankled Archie Manning for New Orleans, was 16 of 35 for 285 yards and three TD's. Two of them went to TE Henry Childs, whose first score of 59 yards ended with a brilliant individual effort in which he carried FS Mike Sensibaugh on his back the final 18 yards to the endzone.

Even though they lost five of seven fumbles (14 of 22 for the season), the Steelers remained tied for first in the AFC Central with Cleveland as Terry Bradshaw threw for 227 yards and two TD's and RE Dwight White came up with two of the five interceptions against Dan Pastorini, who had thrown only four interceptions all year going into the game.

The Bills piled up 256 yards in the first 30 minutes against Cleveland, but still trailed 13-10 after two fumbles, two interceptions and 108 yards in penalties. TE Reuben Gant caught five passes for 111 yards and a TD, and PR Keith Moody set a club record with his 91-yard TD return for the losers.

Cleveland came up with the most effective rushing performance against Buffalo all season (219 yards). Preferring to let RB's Cleo Miller and Greg Pruitt carry the load (207 rushing yards between them), QB Brian Sipe threw only eight passes in the second half.

SEVENTH WEEK

Nothing more needed to be said after QB Kenny Stabler's post-game explanation of the Oakland Raiders' game plan against the Denver Broncos as the '77 season reached the halfway point.

"We wanted to run the ball, play defense and let Ray Guy punt," Stabler explained after the defending Super Bowl champs waylaid the Broncs 24-14 just two weeks after being humiliated by Denver before the Oakland fans.

True to form, the Raiders pounded away at the right side of the opposition's defense on 35 of 57 rushing plays, enabling Clarence Davis (105 yards) and Mark van Eeghen (82) to pace a 200-yard rushing attack while Guy averaged 49.1 yards on eight punts, including three over 60 yards.

The Broncos turned over the ball three times with two fumbles and an interception which led to two Raider scores, and QB Craig Morton was sacked eight times for 62 yards, in four instances by DE Pat Toomay.

The victory created a tie between Oakland and Denver for first place in the AFC West and set the stage for an unforgettable AFC Championship rubber match nine weeks later.

After barely nipping the New York Jets one week earlier, Raider Head Coach John Madden couldn't have been happier with his team's convincing dominance on hostile grounds.

"It was one of our great wins," said Madden. "Today we made things happen...we have the toughest part of the schedule behind us in terms of travel, and we're 6-1 at the halfway point."

Opposing coach Red Miller remained confident in defeat. "We start all over now," he said. "We lost to a strong, strong team and I think maybe we'll meet them again. At least, I hope so."

Three thrillers also highlighted the NFL's seventh week as San Diego spanked Miami 14-13 on QB James Harris' five-yard TD sweep on fourth down with two seconds remaining, New Orleans upset Los Angeles 27-26 as Rich Szaro's 31-yard field goal bounced off and over the right upright as time was running out and Cincinnati squeaked by Houston 13-10 in overtime on Chris Bahr's 22-yarder with 9:09 left in the extra period.

Harris' heroics made up for dismal performance a week earlier against Kansas City as he continued to wreak havoc on the Dolphins, a team he destroyed with 436 passing yards as a Ram the year before.

With 2:33 remaining, it looked like the Dolphs had it made after CB Norris Thomas' interception, but moments later Charger LB Don Goode stripped RB Benny Malone of the ball and DT Gary Johnson recovered on the Miami 28 to set up the dramatic finish.

Miami dropped into a tie with New England for second in the AFC East at 5-2 as QB Bob Griese threw for only 82 yards and three interceptions, all of them in the second quarter by FS Clarence Duren.

The Saints rambled for 253 yards against the NFC's top-ranked team in defensing the run-going into the game, and QB Bobby Scott called a smart game, calling audibles 85 per cent of the time with a preponderance of pitchouts to RB's Tony Galbreath and Mike Strachan, who took turns blocking for each other.

Pat Haden continued to look good for the Rams, reeling off 261 passing yards and two TD's to WR Harold Jackson (eight catches for 127 yards), but it couldn't keep L.A. from dropping to a 4-3 mark in the NFC West to keep it tied at the top with Atlanta.

The Bengals were a disturbed team going into the battle at home against Houston after CB Mel Morgan was suspended for one game without pay by Commissioner Pete Rozelle as a result of his forearm blow to the head of Pittsburgh WR John Stallworth in a Monday night loss two weeks earlier. The Bengals wondered why Steeler CB Mel Blount wasn't assessed a similar penalty after hitting TE Bob Trumpy hard enough to cause a concussion in the same game. And second-string QB John Reaves was wondering aloud why he hadn't seen more action against Denver the previous week when starter Kenny Anderson was obviously hurting with painful knee and thigh injuries.

Reaves got a chance to start against Houston, however, and he responded with a mediocre first-half performance (five of 13 completions, two interceptions). Oiler QB John Hadl was even worse on his way to producing eight net passing yards in three quarters.

The special teams provided Cincy with its only TD of the day when Scott Perry blocked Cliff Parsley's punt and Willie Shelby recovered the ball in the endzone, but the Oilers rallied to tie the game on a five-minute, fourth-quarter TD drive in which new QB Dan Pastorini completed seven passes against a suddenly shaky secondary on the way to a three-yard TD lob to RB Ronnie Coleman.

With just 27 seconds left in regulation, Shelby was saved from wearing goat horns after what was to become another controversial officiating decision. The second-year running back had all kinds of trouble with the ensuing kickoff after Coleman's TD, and Oiler Steve Baumgartner fell on the ball in the Bengals' endzone. But instead of ruling a TD for Houston, official Vince Jacob said Shelby was standing on the sideline, making it a touchback.

After winning the coin toss, the Bengals moved the ball well behind Anderson on the way to Bahr's game-winning three-pointer, with WR Billy Brooks' 17-yard reception on third down and Pete Johnson's 11-yard run setting up the easy chip shot.

While the Raider-Bronco game accurately reflected the shape of things to come the second half of the season, some teams did not finish the season in the same way they performed in their seventh-week performances.

Cleveland's total collapse was unforseeable after it destroyed Kansas City 44-7 to move into first place all by its lonesome in the AFC Central, a game in front of Pittsburgh.

The Browns rolled up 527 yards total offense and a team-record 34 first downs, and converted six turnovers into 31 points against a team that caused one of its players, OT Jim Nicholson, to publicly question his teammates' motivation. Greg Pruitt ran for 153 yards on 18 carries and scored on the third longest TD run in Cleveland history (78 yards) while the other Pruitt, Mike, picked up 96 yards and a TD on 20 carries.

Another deceiving performance was turned in by St. Louis in its 28-0 Monday night victory over the New York Giants, although a close look at the stats (Giants outgained St. Louis 301-258) showed that it really won on the strength of a fumble recovery and three interceptions, including one by FS Mike Sensibaugh for a 79-yard TD.

Cardinal RG Conrad Dobler's fumble recovery for a TD offered comic relief as the Cards and Giants emerged from the game tied for third in the NFC Eas at 3-3, three full games behind Dallas, the only team remaining undefeated after destroying Detroit 37-0.

The Pokes didn't have to look as good as they did because the Lions were putrid while collecting only two first downs the entire first half and none in the third quarter.

Detroit QB's (Greg Landry and Joe Reed) set up Dallas scores by throwing interceptions to CB Mark Washington and LB Mike Hegman and fumbling once to set up another, but despite its downhill trek, which featured an amazing allowance of 35 QB sacks after seven games, the Lions remained in contention in the NFC Central with a 3-4 record that tied them for second with Chicago.

In Seattle, the Seahawks reached the high point of their young existence with a 56-17 rout over Buffalo that forced 13 team and eight individual records to be rewritten. While Jim Zorn wasn't much of a surprise with the second four-touchdown outing of his career (296 yards passing) and Seahawk WR's Steve Largent and Duke Fergerson continued to impress with four catches apiece for 134 yards and 114 yards, respectively, Seattle finally came up with a strong rushing output as three backs topped the 50-yard mark (Sherman Smith, David Sims and Al Hunter).

For the Bills, things couldn't have gotten any lower as the pain of their sixth loss of the season was intensified a few days later after they learned RB O.J. Simpson would have to submit to knee surgery and would be out for the rest of the season.

With the Juice on the sidelines, no one could come close to matching the rushing brilliance of Chicago's Walter Payton, a fact substantiated by his 205-yard rushing performance in the Bears' 26-0 victory in Green Bay that tied him with the great Gale Sayers for the team single-game rushing record.

With 2:02 remaining in the first quarter, Payton already had gained 111 yards on nine attempts, and he finished the day by becoming the Bears' fourth best career ground-gainer, only 58 yards short of Willie Galimore in third place.

Loud boos pervaded through Lambeau Field as Bart Starr's 2-5 Pack played a shameful game, allowing the Bears to average just short of seven yards a carry.

In other games, Baltimore took advantage of 17 Pittsburgh penalties for 122 yards, five interceptions of Terry Bradshaw and a fumble recovery to strangle the Steelers 31-21; Fran Tarkenton's six-yard TD lob to newly-acquired TE Bob Tucker was enough to carry Minnesota over Atlanta 14-7; San Francisco won its second straight after five losses by beating Tampa Bay 20-10; Joe Theismann staged a memorable '77 starting debut by producing 312 yards total offense in Washington's 23-17 victory over Philly and Darryl Stingley caught eight passes for 121 yards in New England's 24-13 victory over the New York Jets.

Pittsburgh gave Baltimore an NFL-record nine first downs on penalties as Colt QB Bert Jones rebounded from a poor performance against New England with two TD passes and a TD run.

In addition to Tarkenton's 235-yard passing performance before a record crowd of 59,257 in Atlanta, Chuck Foreman broke loose for a 51-yard run that set up the Vikes' winning score and bettered his best gain of the year by more than 30 yards.

QB Steve Bartkowski, out for eight weeks after knee surgery, replaced an ineffective Scott Hunter in the second half and did nothing to improve the Falcs' woeful 10-point-per-game scoring average. On defense, CB Rolland Lawrence intercepted two Tarkenton passes.

DT Cleveland Elam was a standout for San Francisco against the Bucs with four sacks and constant pressure administered to newcomer Jeb Blount while QB Jim Plunkett mixed another strong 49er rushing performance (over 200 yards) with short effective passes, including six for 61 yards to TE Tom Mitchell, who equaled his pass-catching production of the previous two years.

Blount, forced into action after only two days of practice when Randy Hedberg wasn't sufficiently able to recover from a concussion, managed to throw for 149 yards and just one interception despite relentless pursuit.

Theismann threw two quick 15-yard TD passes to TE Jean Fugett to give Washington an early 14-0 lead over Philadelphia, but QB Ron Jaworski's 48-yard TD pass to WR Harold Carmichael early in the fourth quarter made a game out of it. PK Mark Moseley kicked three FG's, including two for 46 and 51 yards, and the Skins' pass defense held off the late-charging Eagles by breaking up four straight passing attempts inside its 20 in the game's final 90 seconds.

With Stingley doing most of the receiving, Sam Cunningham and Don Calhoun combined for 145 yards rushing as the Pats climbed into a second-place AFC East tie with Miami. Rookie pass catchers Stanley Morgan and Don Hasselbeck were each beneficiaries of a Steve Grogan TD pass, but the game's real difference in the eyes of Jets' Head Coach Walt Michaels were "those two guys on the left side," namely OG John Hannah and OT Leon Gray.

EIGHTH WEEK

Paul Wiggin became the first NFL head coach of the season to fall by the wayside when the Kansas City Chiefs announced his dismissal the day after a 44-7 loss to Cleveland.

The Chiefs had won only one of their first seven games and were mired in the AFC West basement, trailing even second-year Seattle, However, the Chiefs had faced the most difficult first-half schedule of any team in the NFL, with each of their seven opponents posting winning records at the halfway point of the regular season.

The firing came as a surprise to nearly everyone, including Wiggin. Less than a year ago, Owner Lamar Hunt had been so impressed by Wiggin's rebuilding program that he tore up the coach's old contract and offered him a new one, estimated at $60,000 per year, for three additional years. But Hunt changed his tune, saying about the firing: "We're no longer satisfied with the progress we are making."

Wiggin succeeded Hank Stram in 1975, taking over a team which was aging and on the decline. Wiggin recorded 5-9 records in each of the next two seasons while building a youthful nucleus for the team. But Wiggin's insistence on using inexperienced players, like rookie RB's Mark Bailey and Tony Reed, led to a large number of mistakes and, eventually, caused his downfall.

The firing upset many Kansas City fans and players, including QB Mike Livingston, who said, "They should have fired us (the players) instead of him." As it turned out, the move was a forerunner of a shakeup around the league. Before 1978 was barely two months old, 10 head coaches from the start of the previous season had been replaced—marking one of the largest turnovers in coaches in recent history.

Defensive backfield coach Tom Bettis, an assistant at Kansas City since 1966, was named to replace Wiggin on an interim basis, with his future at the helm depending on the Chiefs' showing during the final seven games.

Bettis went to his veterans—namely Livingston, Ed Podolak and newcomer John Brockington in the backfield—in his head coaching debut, and the Chiefs responded with a 20-10 victory over Green Bay at Arrowhead Stadium. The 30-year-old Podolak, who is the Chiefs' all-time leading rusher despite a series of nagging injuries, carried the ball 18 times for 98 yards and caught four passes for 51 yards.

The Chiefs' usually-porous defense limited the Packers to 199 total yards, and the only touchdown Green Bay scored was a 96-yard kickoff return on a reverse, with Terdell Middleton going the final 85 yards after a handoff from Steve Odom. After the win, the Chiefs awarded the game ball to the departed Wiggin.

It was a rewarding debut for Bettis, but it was to be his last victory celebration as Kansas City head coach. Playing a second-half schedule that was somewhat easier than the first half but still tough by most standards, the Chiefs were winless the rest of the season and Bettis experienced the same fate as Wiggin.

Buffalo scored one of the bigger upsets of the season, shocking New England 24-14 at Foxboro. RB Roland Hooks, a No. 10 draft choice out of North Carolina State in 1975, erupted from O.J. Simpson's shadow by rushing for 155 yards in 27 carries against a tough Patriot defense.

QB Joe Ferguson, who had an unproductive first half of the season, completed 15 of 22 passes for 201 yards and one touchdown. TE Reuben Gant was Ferguson's primary target, catching seven passes for 97 yards. Patriot QB Steve Grogan completed only nine of 27 passes and TE Russ Francis was lost to the team due to broken ribs.

Hooks' performance came only days after it was announced that Simpson would undergo surgery on his left knee and be lost to the team for the rest of the season. Although Hooks had fewer than 50 yards rushing in the first seven games, he finished the season near 500.

The loss dropped New England's record to 5-3, two games behind front-running Baltimore and a game behind Miami. The loss to Buffalo turned out to be one of the unexpected defeats which cost the Patriots a spot in the playoffs.

The topsy-turvy AFC Central found all four of its teams within one game of each other after the weekend. Cleveland remained on top with a 5-3 record despite a 10-7 loss to Cincinnati—its third home setback of the season after losing there only once in 1976.

The game was low-scoring because of the rash of penalty flags thrown—35 in all, even though only 21 of them were actually stepped off. The officiating crew of referee Red Cashion, which had incurred threats of violence from Steeler DT Joe Greene after penalizing Pittsburgh 17 times for 122 yards the previous week, called offsides or encroachment against the Browns 11 times.

After a 7-7 first half, the Bengals' Chris Bahr provided the only scoring in the final 30 minutes, kicking a game-winning 47-yard FG early in the third quarter following the Bengals' recovery of a second Cleo Miller fumble, one of four Cleveland turnovers. The Cincinnati win avenged a 13-3 loss to the Browns in the season opener.

Pittsburgh failed to gain ground when it dropped a 21-7 decision to surprising Denver at Mile High Stadium, as the Steelers continued to make costly turnovers and lose key players due to injuries. The Steelers' two lost fumbles gave them a league-high total of 34 turnovers in eight games, and Denver punter Bucky Dilts kept them pinned deep in their end consistently.

Although the Steelers outgained the Broncos 216 to 174, Rick Upchurch's club-record 167 yards in five punt returns, including an 87-yard TD, prompted Steeler Coach Chuck Noll to say, "We're going to have to put some starters on our kicking team."

Injuries to DE's L.C. Greenwood and John Banaszak in the Denver game put them on the sidelines along with All-Pro MLB Jack Lambert, who was out with a knee injury, and S Glen Edwards, who bolted the team on Thursday because of the Steelers' refusal to renegotiate his contract. Edwards probably wouldn't have been able to play anyway because he had been listed as "doubtful" due to a hamstring injury.

Meanwhile, Greene was awaiting a hearing with Commissioner Pete Rozelle in regard to his aforementioned comments about the officiating crew headed by Cashion.

Houston broke a three-game losing streak with a 47-0 rout of Chicago at the Astrodome. The Oilers outgained the Bears 489 to 125, as their three-man front recorded six sacks and held Chicago to a net of minus-12 yards passing in their second shutout of the season.

Offensively, the Oilers stars were WR Ken Burrough, WR-KR Billy "White Shoes" Johnson and QB Dan Pastorini. Burrough caught six passes for 180 yards and two TD's, including an 85-yarder. Johnson had a 75-yard return of a free kick following a safety and a 61-yard run on a reverse, both good for TD's. Pastorini completed 11 of 18 passes for 246 yards and two TD's. Also, rookie RB Rob Carpenter gained 75 yards in 11 carries in his first NFL start.

The victory began a successful second half of the season for the Oilers, who lost only two games the rest of the way—by close margins to playoff-bound Oakland and Denver. It also marked an upturn in Houston's offensive production after the team had averaged only 16 points per game in the first half of the season and had ranked last in offensive yardage in the AFC.

The lopsided score also provided a commentary on the relative strength of the two divisions involved, not to mention the overall superiority of the AFC. The Bears' lackluster defense provoked Burrough to comment: "I'd sure like to play against that type pass defense every week. When I see what some of those NFC receivers get to go against every game, it makes me want to cry."

Minnesota did nothing but reinforce that stereotype when the Vikings were embarrassed 27-7 in front of the home folks at Bloomington by the unpredictable Cardinals.

Although the Cards' running game did most of the damage, the Vikings' pass defense was hardly guilt-free. St. Louis rushed for 316 yards, or 6.2 per carry, led by sophomore sensation Wayne Morris with 27 carries for 182 yards (the second-best rushing total in Cardinal history) and Terry Metcalf with 11 for 83. Jim Hart completed 10 of 14 passes for 143 yards and two TD's, with only his three interceptions preventing a more one-sided score.

Detroit prevented a complete loss of face by the NFC Central when the Lions upset San Diego 20-0 at the Silverdome. The win extended the Lions' unblemished home record to 4-0 and it also moved the Lions into second place in the division, one game behind Minnesota.

Gun-shy QB Greg Landry took heed of his offensive line's dubious total of 35 sacks allowed in the first seven games and chose to concentrate on the ground game, particularly against the Chargers' fine pass rush. The strategy worked, as Detroit rushed for 197 yards and Landry avoided a single sack while completing five of seven passes for 67 yards. Rookie RB Rick Kane, subbing for injured Dexter Bussey, gained 105 yards in 24 carries and Horace King added 64 yards in 16 tries.

Despite a scoreless first half, the Lions' sound defense kept them in the game until the offense gained momentum. The Detroit victory was the first by an NFC team in 11 inter-conference games this season and the Lions' first shutout since 1973.

In other games, Baltimore defeated Washington 10-3 Monday night on Bert Jones' 12-yard TD pass to WR Freddie Scott in the fourth quarter;

Miami stayed one game behind the Colts with a 14-10 win over the Jets in which Jet QB Richard Todd suffered a bruised knee after being sacked four times in the second quarter; Oakland kept pace with Denver at 7-1 by thrashing Seattle 44-7; Tampa Bay suffered its third shutout of the season in a 31-0 defeat at Lost Angeles; Dallas remained unbeaten with a 24-10 decision over the Giants; San Francisco knocked Atlanta out of a first-place tie with the Rams with a 10-3 victory aided by seven 49er sacks, and host Philadelphia coasted past New Orleans 28-7 with the aid of Spike Jones' four punts inside the Saints' 10-yard line.

NINTH WEEK

A rash of injuries in week No. 9 rocked the NFL, as five quarterbacks were lost for the remainder of the season. Minnesota's Fran Tarkenton, Green Bay's Lynn Dickey and San Diego backup Bill Munson all suffered broken legs in weekend games, while a shoulder separation by Cleveland's Brian Sipe and a sprained foot by San Diego's James Harris eventually proved to be more serious than first anticipated and brought their seasons to a premature end.

Three other QB's—Pittsburgh's Terry Bradshaw, Buffalo's Joe Ferguson and the Giants' Joe Pisarcik—suffered minor injuries which did not prevent them from returning the following week. Four others—the Jets' Richard Todd, Tampa Bay's Gary Huff and New Orleans' Archie Manning and Bobby Scott—were unable to play because of earlier injuries, making Nov. 13 a truly unlucky day for signal callers.

The "Cardiac Cards" continued their mid-season hot streak, handing Dallas its first loss of the season after eight victories in the Monday night game. The win was the Cardinals' fifth in a row since Wayne Morris joined Terry Metcalf in the starting backfield and it moved them one game ahead of Washington and within two games of the front-running Cowboys in the NFC East. It was the first time since 1970 that St. Louis defeated the Pokes in Dallas.

The Cards used the same fourth-quarter heroics which Dallas had employed in their first meeting of the season—a 30-24 Cowboy victory sparked by two fourth-quarter TD's. This time the Cards struck twice in the final period—on Jim Hart TD passes of 49 yards to speedster Mel Gray and three yards to backup TE Jackie Smith—to rally from a 17-10 deficit to a 24-17 win.

St. Louis gained 295 yards against a Dallas defense which had allowed only 185 per game, with Morris and Metcalf rushing for a combined 135 yards and the talented Cardinal offensive line permitting only one sack by a Cowboy defense which had 39 sacks in the first eight games.

Miami set the stage for an interesting Thanksgiving Day showdown in St. Louis by handing AFC East rival New England a 17-5 loss at the Orange Bowl. The victory kept Miami within one game of division-leading Baltimore and gave the Dolphins a two-game edge over the disappointing Patriots.

The Dolphins' young defense was the backbone of the win over the Pats, holding a potent New England offense without a touchdown. Dolphin rookie DE A.J. Duhe blocked a Mike Patrick punt to set up a TD which gave Miami an insurmountable 17-3 lead in the fourth quarter. The scoring play was a 26-yard pass from Bob Griese to WR Nat Moore, on which Griese detected an all-out blitz by the Pats and smartly called an audible designed to exploit the Pats' man-to-man coverage on Moore.

Although New England had controlled the ball for all but six plays of the third quarter and failed to score, the play which broke the Pats' momentum was a 73-yard kickoff return by second-year RB Gary Davis, setting up Garo Yepremian's 35-yard field goal.

Chicago needed a miracle in the final seconds to rebound from the previous week's debacle at Houston. QB Bob Avellini threw a 37-yard TD pass to TE Greg Latta with three seconds to play, giving the Bears a 28-27 triumph and keeping alive their chances for a playoff spot. Latta ran right past Chief SS Tim Gray and was all alone in the endzone when the ball arrived, much to the amazement of Avellini, who called the play a "prayer."

Incredibly, 21 points were scored in the final 2:02 of the game, starting with RB Walter Payton's 15-yard TD scamper for a 21-20 Chicago lead. Kansas City responded with a go-ahead TD with 24 seconds left on a play that took the Bears by surprise. With first-and-10 on the Chicago 14, the

Chiefs took their last timeout, causing the Bears to expect either a pass or a field goal attempt. But the Chiefs surprised them by sending RB Ed Podolak around right end for a 14-yard TD. That set the stage for the late heroics by Avellini and Latta.

Payton, a third-year sensation out of Jackson State and the heart-and-soul of the Chicago offense, finished the game with 192 yards on 33 carries, giving him 1,129 yards on 199 carries for the season. Payton went over the 1,000-yard mark in the first half on a superb 18-yard run. The play was a sweep to the right but, when Payton found the outside congested, he cut back toward the middle and broke five tackles before being stopped. That play led to the first of his three TD's.

The defeat was a particularly bitter pill for the Chiefs, who had led 17-0 at halftime. It dropped them behind Seattle into the AFC West cellar, ruining Podolak's 102-yard rushing performance and Coach Tom Bettis' return to his hometown. Both teams were bothered by numerous injuries to defensive players, as evidenced by the 789 yards of total offense amassed by the two teams.

The Chicago victory provided a psychological lift for the next game against division leader Minnesota, which also bounced back from a one-sided loss to St. Louis to blast Cincinnati 42-10, despite the injury to Tarkenton. The 37-year-old QB from Georgia completed an amazing 17 of 18 passes for 195 yards before being injured on a sack by Bengal DE Gary Burley, who had made 11 tackles and one sack the previous week. Although Tarkenton had missed only one game in his 17-year pro career due to an injury, the broken leg forced him to miss the last five regular-season games and two playoff games.

Rookie Tommy Kramer replaced Tarkenton late in the third quarter with a 21-10 lead and directed the Vikes to three more TD's, with the aid of a fumble recovery and an interception in Bengal territory. Viking RB Chuck Foreman spearheaded the ground assault with 133 yards on 29 carries, as Minnesota avenged its only shutout since 1962, a 27-0 loss to the Bengals in 1973.

Detroit dropped into a tie with Chicago at 4-5, two games behind Minnesota, by losing at Atlanta 17-6. Once again the stingy Falcon defense almost singlehandedly won the game, scoring 14 of its team's points on a 14-yard return of a fumble by LB Ralph Ortega and a 20-yard interception return by LB Robert Pennywell. Atlanta scored all of its points in the fourth quarter after spotting the Lions a 6-0 first-period lead. The Falcs have given up only 62 points in nine games, best in the NFL.

Pittsburgh moved into a first-place tie with Cleveland in the AFC Central by beating the Browns 35-31 at Three Rivers Stadium. The victory gave the Steelers a 22-2 record against division foes since the 1970 realignment, an 8-0 record against the Browns at Three Rivers and seven wins in the last eight meetings with Cleveland.

Bradshaw played an excellent game at QB for Pittsburgh, completing 13 of 21 for 283 yards and three TD's. The Steelers built a 35-10 lead early in the fourth quarter before their injury-weakened defense collapsed. Although they were playing with only four healthy defensive linemen and without MLB Jack Lambert and S Donnie Shell, the Steelers had held the Browns to only three first-half points.

QB Dave Mays, in his second season with the Browns after a stint in the World Football League, replaced the injured Sipe and completed 17 of 32 passes for 269 yards and three fourth-quarter TD's, but Cleveland ran out of time. Both teams continued to be plagued by turnovers, committing four apiece.

Houston dropped one game off the AFC Central pace by losing a high-scoring contest at Oakland, 34-29. It was the third close game between the two teams in as many years, the last two having been decided by a single point. Although the Raiders had won a '77 pre-season game 40-0 over the Oilers, the closeness of this game was a good indication of how much Houston had improved since then.

Dan Pastorini threw TD bombs of 71 yards to WR Billy "White Shoes" Johnson and 41 yards to WR Ken Burrough, but he also had four intercepted, including a crucial pickoff by FS Jack Tatum at the Raider six with 3:55 remaining. The Oilers' Rob Carpenter rushed for 120 yards on 19 carries to balance the attack. Because Oakland could average only 2.3 yards per carry against the Oilers' rugged 3-4 defense, Ken Stabler went to the air and connected on 23 of 31 attempts for 264 yards and two TD's. A total of nine turnovers marred the hard-hitting game.

Denver rallied from a 14-3 halftime deficit with two scoring passes from Craig Morton to WR Haven Moses, giving the Broncos a 17-14 win at San Diego and maintaining their first-place tie with Oakland at 8-1. The crippling injuries to Harris and Munson, the Chargers' top two QB's, occurred in the fourth quarter as the Chargers were in the process of letting their lead slip away. Harris returned for the final few plays of the game, hobbling on one leg, but those were to be his last plays of the season.

In other action, Baltimore took advantage of 10 quarterback sacks (three each by ends Fred Cook and John Dutton and strongside LB Tom MacLeod and one by tackle Mike Barnes) to flatten Buffalo 31-13; Mark Moseley booted a 54-yard FG, giving him four out of six from the 50 or beyond for the season, to propel Washington to a 17-14 win over Philadelphia and drop Eagle Coach Dick Vermeil's record against the Redskins to 0-4; San Francisco won a 10-7 overtime decision at New Orleans on Ray Wersching's 33-yard field goal after Rich Szaro's 30-yard attempt in regulation had hit the left upright and bounced back; Seattle held an opponent to under 10 points for the first time in its history with a 17-0 upset of the Jets (without Todd) at Shea Stadium behind a 445-yard offense; Los Angeles coasted past Green Bay 24-6 as Dickey broke his leg under a heavy rush on the Packers' final offensive play of the game and the Giants blanked Tampa Bay 10-0 despite being outgained 287 to 197.

TENTH WEEK

Walter Payton joined the ranks of the NFL's all-time greats with a performance that outshined all others during the 10th week of the season. Payton set a new single-game rushing record with 275 yards gained in a 10-7 win over Minnesota at Soldier Field. The victory moved the Bears just one game behind Minnesota in the NFC Central title chase.

The 5-10½, 204-pound power plant carried the ball 40 times, one shy of the league record held by Franco Harris, and surpassed O.J. Simpson's 273-yard mark set the previous Thanksgiving. The record-breaker occurred on a controversial play selection by Chicago Coach Jack Pardee, who elected to bypass a FG attempt on fourth-and-goal at the Viking six with the Bears leading 10-7 and 2½ minutes to play. Payton ran a sweep around right end on the play and gained four yards, eclipsing Simpson's record but turning the ball over to the Vikes.

Pardee later explained his decision to bypass the FG, saying he felt the only way the Bears could have lost the game was to have a FG blocked and returned by the Vikes for a TD. Considering that Minnesota's only score of the game had been set up by LB Matt Blair's blocked punt (his fourth blocked kick of the season) and that QB Bob Lee had been ineffective as a replacement for the injured Fran Tarkenton, Pardee's reasoning seemed to make sense.

The Vikings' six-point overtime victory in the first meeting of the season, coupled with the Bears' three-point win in the second meeting, gave the Vikings an edge in point differential in head-to-head competition, one of the factors used in breaking ties for playoff spots. As it turned out, both clubs finished the year at 9-5 and the tie-breaking procedure came down to the point differential, making Minnesota the division winner and renewing the controversy about the bypassed FG. Chicago made the playoffs anyway—as the NFC's "Wild Card" team.

Payton's big day boosted his season rushing total to 1,404 yards after 10 games, 81 yards ahead of Simpson's 1973 pace when the Buffalo runner totaled a single-season record of 2,003 yards. Ironically, had the Bears elected to try the FG which could have given them the NFC Central title, Payton probably wouldn't have had another chance in that game to break Simpson's single-game mark.

Another matchup of playoff contenders produced a second brilliant display of power running, as Franco Harris carried 29 times for a career-high 179 yards in Pittsburgh's 28-13 triumph over Dallas at Three Rivers Stadium. The six-year veteran from Penn State rambled for a 61-yard TD in the second quarter and provided an insurance TD in the third quarter on a two-yard run. The Steelers rolled up 228 yards on the ground and 320 total yards against a club which had started the week as the NFC's best rushing defense (114.1 yards per game) and the league's best overall defense (197.3 yards per game).

Cowboy rookie RB Tony Dorsett, returning to the city of his college triumphs, gained 73 yards on 17 carries (41 yards in the first quarter) and scored one TD in his first pro start. The defeat was Dallas' second in a row following eight consecutive victories.

San Diego sidetracked the Raiders' drive toward their sixth straight AFC West title, upsetting the 12½-point favorites 12-7. The victory was the Chargers' first in the last 19 meetings with Oakland and their first-ever over the Raiders at San Diego Stadium. Every bit as crucial to the Raiders as the defeat, which dropped them one game behind front-running Denver, was an injury to Ken Stabler's left knee which sidelined him about 10 minutes into the game. It was the same knee which had twice undergone surgery but, fortunately for Oakland, Stabler was able to play the following week.

Actually, the injury to Stabler was somewhat of an equalizer for San Diego, which had to play the entire game with rookie QB Cliff Olander, a skinny, 6-5, 196-pounder drafted out of New Mexico State in the fifth round primarily for his punting ability. Olander's starting assignment was necessitated by serious injuries the previous week to the Chargers' top two QB's, James Harris and Bill Munson.

Although San Diego's starting QB in 1976, Dan Fouts, had announced earlier in the week that he would end his option-year holdout and rejoin the team after losing his grievance against it, there was no way he could get ready in time to play against Oakland.

While Olander completed only five of 13 passes for 51 yards and had two intercepted, he did prove he can run, gaining 30 yards on seven carries. The rest of the Charges proved they could run, too, as the team rolled up 263 yards, or 4.5 per carry, against a formidable Raider defense. RB Rickey Young led the Chargers with 83 yards on 17 carries, while teammate Joe Washington added 55 yards on only six tries.

The Charger defense became No. 1 (in yards yielded) in the AFC with its strong performance, limiting Oakland to 30 yards passing, 142 total yards and only 15 offensive plays in the second half. Sensational rookie PK Rolf Benirschke provided all of the second-half scoring with field goals of 22 and 46 yards.

Another playoff contender suffered a jolting upset when Miami dropped a 23-17 decision to host Cincinnati. The difference in the game was the superb kicking of Bengal Chris Bahr and the five turnovers by the Dolphins, who slipped two games behind Baltimore. Bahr was perfect in three FG attempts from 44, 43 and 42 yards, giving him 12-of-18 accuracy for the year and four of six from 40 to 49 yards out. Miami didn't help its own cause, either, by losing two fumbles on the slippery Astro-Turf and having three Bob Griese passes intercepted. Although only 5-5, the enigmatic Bengals stayed very much alive in the AFC Central race, rebounding amazingly well from the 42-10 defeat at Minnesota the previous week.

Statistically, the game was close, except for the turnovers and the punting. The Bengals also lost two fumbles, both of which led to Miami TD's, but Ken Anderson didn't have a single pass intercepted in 26 attempts. The Bengals' Pat McInally enjoyed a huge advantage in the punting department, averaging 42.5 yards per punt compared to rookie Mike Michel's 30.8.

After Miami had taken a 17-16 lead on Garo Yepremian's 35-yard FG with 10 minutes left in the game, Cincinnati got the game-winner with a trick play. Using what they call a "triple pass," the Bengals' Anderson got the ball back following a fake reverse and tossed a 29-yard scoring pass to TE Bob Trumpy, who had beaten rookie FS Vern Roberson, a replacement for injured Charlie Babb.

Two of the few bright spots for Miami were rookies Leroy Harris and Bob Baumhower. Harris, a fifth-round RB out of Arkansas State, got his first start as a replacement for injured Norm Bulaich and responded with 108 yards on 20 carries. Baumhower, a second-round NT from Alabama, led the defense with 19 tackles, two sacks and a fumble recovery which led to a TD. At the other extreme, Griese had such a bad day (10 of 29, three interceptions) that his passing rating slipped from 87.0 to 78.6, dropping him out of the top spot into second behind Bert Jones.

Jones had a fantastic day in the Colts' 33-12 romp over the visiting Jets, who lost their second in a row without injured QB Richard Todd. Jones completed 23 of 36 passes for 322 yards and three TD's with one interception. TE Raymond Chester became the club's first 100-yard receiver of the year (five for 102 yards) and his 53-yard TD catch was the Colts' longest of the season. RB Lydell Mitchell and WR's Glenn Doughty and Roger Carr each had more than 50 yards in receptions. FS Lyle Blackwood, a still-unsigned free-agent acquisition from Seattle during the pre-season, picked off three Matt Robinson passes, giving him the league lead with eight interceptions.

Washington kept its playoff hopes alive with a 10-9 Monday night victory over Green Bay at RFK Stadium. Joe Theismann's seven-yard scoring pass to RB Mike Thomas in the fourth quarter provided the winning margin, and it was the only TD of the game, as four FG's were kicked. Chester Marcol accounted for all of the Packers' points with FG's of 40, 42 and 44 yards in three attempts, giving him five of five between the 40 and 49 and 10 of 15 overall.

Rookie QB David Whitehurst, an eighth-round pick from Furman making his first start for the injured Lynn Dickey, looked promising at times under the pressure of a nationwide TV audience. He completed 12 of 24 passes for 140 yards with three interceptions in the face of a strong Redskin pass rush which sacked him six times.

In other games, Los Angeles snapped the 49ers' four-game winning streak, 23-10, by capitalizing on its superior specialty teams for the second time in two meetings between the clubs, in front of the first sellout crowd of the season at Candlestick Park. Rob Carpenter's 97 yards rushing boosted his three-game total to 292 and sparked Houston to a 22-10 win at Seattle, as Seahawk QB Jim Zorn was so stymied by the Oilers' 3-4 defense that he completed only two of 15 passes for 19 yards and was benched in favor of Steve Myer. Cleveland broke a two-game losing streak and kept a share of the AFC Central lead with a 21-7 win over the Giants at East Rutherford, paced by LB Gerald Irons' 53-yard interception return for the go-ahead TD, two thefts by CB Oliver Davis and QB Dave Mays' respectable 13-of-24 passing in his first start for the injured Brian Sipe.

Atlanta watched its playoff hopes grow dim in a 21-20 defeat at New Orleans decided by Kim McQuilken's fumble of a snap on a 20-yard FG attempt and the ensuing 16-yard TD pass from Archie Manning to TE Henry Childs with one minute left in the game. Cardinal RB Jim Otis, who had lost his job earlier in the season to Wayne Morris, started in place of the injured Morris and gained 97 yards on 18 carries, scoring two TD's and rallying St. Louis from a 16-0 third-quarter deficit to a 21-16 win over Philadelphia.

A 256-yard running attack and a defense which sacked Joe Ferguson four times and held RB Roland Hooks to 64 yards (instead of the 155 he gained in the last meeting) propelled New England to a 20-7 win over Buffalo, keeping the Patriots three games behind Baltimore. Detroit overcame a 7-0 Tampa Bay lead at halftime and escaped becoming the Bucs' first victim, in a 16-7 victory iced by backup SS Reggie Pinkney's 48-yard interception return for a TD. Denver moved a game ahead of Oakland at 9-1 with a 14-7 triumph over Kansas City on Craig Morton's 23-yard TD pass to WR Haven Moses with 4:29 to play.

ELEVENTH WEEK

If any doubts about the AFC's dominance over the older NFC remained after the AFC had won 13 of the 16 inter-conference games during the first 10 weeks of 1977, they were put to rest in the 11th week.

In a showdown between playoff contenders from each conference, Miami of the AFC buried St. Louis of the NFC 55-14 at Busch Stadium in a nationally televised Thanksgiving Day contest which intensified Coach Don Coryell's dissatisfaction with the Cardinal organization and also heightened the club's unhappiness with All-Pro guard Conrad Dobler. Neither would return as Cardinals in 1978.

Dobler was at the center of a last-minute, bench-emptying melee which led to his ejection, and he shoved a Cardinal assistant coach in an angry display on the sidelines.

St. Louis started the game with a makeshift secondary, Jeff Severson starting for FS Mike Sensibaugh (broken arm) and rookie Carl Allen replacing CB Lee Nelson (knee surgery). Miami's veteran QB Bob Griese, quickly took advantage of the inexperience, throwing a club-record six TD passes, including three to swift WR Nat Moore. Miami led 14-0 after only 5:15 had elapsed, 28-7 at halftime and 48-7 after three quarters.

However, the Cards' inexperienced secondary was hardly the only reason for their poor showing. Miami also outrushed St. Louis (minus OT Dan Dierdorf) 295 to 54, averaging 5.4 yards per carry. Gary Davis, a second-year pro from Cal Poly (San Luis Obispo), led the Dolphin runners with 104 yards on 20 carries, while rookie Leroy Harris and Benny Malone added 76 and 64 yards, respectively.

Griese's spectacular performance improved his passing rating from 78.6 to 86.9, giving him the AFC lead over Baltimore's Bert Jones. Griese completed 15 of 23 for 207 yards with one interception, and his six TD passes represented one for every four attempts. Overall, Miami outgained the Cards 503 to 210.

Despite the one-sided defeat, St. Louis remained in the driver's seat for the NFC's "Wild Card" playoff berth, but it never materialized because the Cards went on to lose all three of their remaining games. Meanwhile, Miami moved to within one game of Baltimore in the AFC East, but at the same time the Dolphins' playoff hopes were damaged by season-ending injuries to starting DE Vern Den Herder (knee surgery) and starting FS Charlie Babb (broken collarbone), plus a less serious one to starting ILB Steve Towle (knee and ribs).

RB Terry Metcalf, another Cardinal who would leave the club during the next offseason, broke Ollie Matson's club record for career combined yardage by surpassing 8,509 in the Miami game.

With only six days of practice under his belt since ending a 125-day, self-imposed holdout, San Diego QB Dan Fouts played as if he had been around all season long in leading the Chargers to a 30-28 victory over stubborn Seattle. With rookie Cliff Olander the only other available QB after injuries sidelined James Harris and Bill Munson the previous week, Fouts was given a quick refresher course during the week, and he responded by completing 19 of 26 passes for 199 yards and one TD, with one interception.

Not to be outdone, Seahawk QB Jim Zorn became the first NFL passer to throw four TD passes on two different occasions in '77, completing 16 of 26 for 291 yards with two interceptions. One of Zorn's TD passes was a 74-yarder to WR Steve Largent, whose two TD catches moved him into second behind Miami's Nat Moore in TD receptions with eight. SS Autry Beamon set a Seattle single-season record by grabbing his fifth interception.

The Chargers' much-improved front four made a key play in the fourth quarter when DE Leroy Jones belted Zorn just as the Seahawk QB was about to release the ball, and DE Fred Dean literally grabbed the ball off Zorn's back and raced 22 yards with the interception for a TD which put San Diego out of reach at 30-21. The Chargers recorded three QB sacks, giving them 38 in 11 games—the most by a San Diego team since 1964.

The victory improved the Chargers' record to 6-5, marking the first time since '68 that they have been above .500 so late in the season. Rookie PK Rolf Benirschke also played a big role in the win, kicking field goals of 40, 26 and 39 yards in three attempts.

Another placekicker who was instrumental in his team's triumph was San Francisco's Ray Wersching, who booted a 42-yard FG as time expired to give the host 49ers a 20-17 win over New Orleans. Only two weeks earlier, Wersching had kicked a 33-yard game-winner in overtime against the Saints. The deciding FG in the second meeting was set up by a roughing-the-passer penalty against Saint rookie DT Mike Fultz on the same play on which 49er QB Jim Plunkett threw an interception that would have sent the game into overtime. Wersching also kicked a 40-yarder in the second quarter.

Niner RB Wilbur Jackson had a career-high 190 yards rushing, four short of Delvin Williams' club record, on just 16 carries. Jackson's 80-yard scamper in the second quarter was the longest of the NFL season, and he scored two TD's on runs of 34 and one yard. Although it was his second 100-yard game of the season and third of his career, the fourth-year pro from Alabama might have reached the 200-yard mark if he hadn't been forced to leave the game with six minutes left due to a pulled hamstring. One New Orleans highlight was a 92-yard kickoff return by Clarence Chapman, who broke four tackles along the way.

Denver passed a crucial test in its bid to reach the playoffs for the first time in its 18-year history, capitalizing on three interceptions for a 27-13 win over Baltimore in a battle of the NFL's two winningest teams at Mile High Stadium. After TD passes from Craig Morton to WR's Rick Upchurch (41 yards) and Jack Dolbin (19 yards) staked Denver to a 14-0 lead, the Colts cut it to 14-13 with FG's of 40 and 43 yards by Toni Linhart and a 15-yard TD pass from Bert Jones to RB Lydell Mitchell. With Baltimore driving for a go-ahead score, Bronco LB Tom Jackson made a key interception and returned it a club-record 73 yards for a TD that swung the momentum back to Denver.

The Broncos had a team-record 162 yards in interception returns, including CB Louis Wright's 59-yarder which set up the final TD and SS

Bill Thompson's 30-yarder which led to the Upchurch TD. Although the high-scoring Colt offense controlled the ball for 79 plays, it was held 11 points under its average by a Bronco defense which topped the AFC in rushing yardage given up and in points allowed.

Mitchell was held to a meager 14 yards on seven carries, forcing Jones to depend on his passing game. He completed 27 of 46 for 252 yards and one TD but the three interceptions were crucial. RB Don McCauley caught 11 passes for 112 yards and Mitchell caught nine for 74, raising his league-leading number of receptions to 51.

Although Denver ran only 47 offensive plays, it averaged 6.8 yards per play, as Morton accounted for 14 passes for 171 yards. Rookie RB Rob Lytle made his first NFL start as a replacement for injured Otis Armstrong (ankle), gaining 71 yards on 19 carries. RB Lonnie Perrin's 62-yard run was the Broncos' longest of the season. Although Denver converted only one of 11 third-down plays, its four TD drives used up only 12 plays.

Chicago kept its playoff hopes alive by drubbing Detroit 31-14 in a Thanksgiving Day game at the Pontiac Silverdome and for all practical purposes eliminated the Lions from playoff contention.

After being limited to only 20 yards on seven carries in the first half, Bear RB Walter Payton rolled up 117 yards after intermission on 13 carries, rallying the visitors from a 7-0 halftime deficit to 31 second-half points. Payton moved 94 yards ahead of O.J. Simpson's 1973 record pace with 1,541 yards, and his rushing average for the last five games was an impressive 8.8 per carry. "Sweetness" also set a club record with his eighth 100-yard game of the year, not to mention the 17th of his career.

Bear QB Bob Avellini also had an outstanding game, completing 14 of 21 for 260 yards and two TD's, including a 75-yarder to Payton, who caught four for 107 yards.

Washington's playoff bid received a jolt when the Redskins blew a 7-0 halftime lead and dropped a 14-7 decision to Dallas at RFK Stadium as the Cowboys became the first team to clinch a playoff spot. Two costly penalties against Redskin reserve LB Pete Wysocki; FG misses of 41, 40 and 43 yards by usually reliable PK Mark Moseley; 91 yards in penalties, and five dropped passes all contributed to Washington's defeat.

Pittsburgh took over sole possession of first place in the AFC Central for the first time in '77 with a 23-20 win over the Jets while Cleveland was being blanked 9-0 by Los Angeles.

The Steelers narrowly escaped a major upset, due in part to an offside penalty on Charlie White which nullified a third-quarter Jet TD on a blocked punt. Although rookie RB Scott Dierking recorded the Jets' first 100-yard rushing game of the season (23 for 107), the Jets squandered their total yardage advantage by throwing five interceptions and losing one fumble.

Meanwhile, Cleveland was held scoreless for the first time since a 30-0 loss to Pittsburgh on Dec. 3, 1972. QB Dave Mays was unable to get the Browns' offense rolling, and the limited use of RB Greg Pruitt (11 for 39) put Coach Forrest Gregg in Owner Art Modell's dog house. QB Pat Haden directed a 12-play, 86-yard scoring drive capped by RB John Cappelletti's seven-yard run on the Rams' first possession. In the second half Cleveland's defense stiffened but the offense penetrated no further than the Ram 36. CB Ron Bolton tied a Cleveland record with three interceptions.

In other games, New England used eight QB sacks to defeat Philadelphia 14-6 at Foxboro; Houston demolished Kansas City 34-20 as Rob Carpenter and Ronnie Coleman combined for 250 yards rushing; Tampa Bay suffered its fifth shutout of the year, 17-0 at the hands of Atlanta, as the Falcons intercepted four Buccaneer passes and recorded four sacks; Minnesota stayed one game ahead of Chicago by slipping past host Green Bay 13-6 on Bob Lee's 40-yard TD pass to WR Sammie White in blizzard-like conditions; Cincinnati rode three first-quarter TD's to a 30-13 conquest of the visiting Giants, and Oakland coasted past Buffalo 34-13 in the Monday night game on the strength of a 307-yard rushing attack, including Mark van Eeghen's 26 carries for 143 yards.

TWELFTH WEEK

Denver sewed up its first AFC West crown with a 24-14 victory at Houston while Oakland was upset 20-14 at Los Angeles in key games during the 12th week.

The Broncos once again relied on their rugged 3-4 defense and Craig

Morton's intelligent play-calling to win their 11th game in 12 outings. Denver converted 10 of 17 third-down plays, including eight in a row on the three drives which produced its first 17 points.

After RB Ronnie Coleman's two-yard run had given Houston a 7-0 lead, Morton threw 13-yard TD passes to TE Riley Odoms and WR Rick Upchurch for a 14-7 halftime advantage. Craig Penrose, filling in for Morton (strained shoulder) on the first series of the second half, guided Denver 40 yards into position for Jim Turner's 42-yard FG. Oiler QB Dan Pastorini cut the lead to 17-14 with a 29-yard TD pass to WR Ken Burrough late in the third quarter, but backup QB Norris Weese finished off another Morton drive with a five-yard TD on a rollout to give Denver a safe 24-14 lead in the fourth quarter.

Morton completed 13 of 22 for 187 yards with one interception, while Pastorini connected on 10 of 19 for 152 yards. Houston rookie Rob Carpenter was the only runner to gain more than 50 yards, carrying 20 times for 64 yards. Odoms had his most productive game of the year with six receptions for 86 yards and WR Haven Moses caught four for 77 yards, while Burrough gained 80 yards on just two catches.

The Bronco defense was so tough in the final three quarters that Houston had ball possession for only 13½ of the final final 45 minutes and ran only 51 offensive plays, compared to Denver's 77. In addition, Bucky Dilts' punting averaged 50 yards and effectively contained PR Billy "White Shoes" Johnson, who had only one return for minus-nine yards.

Although the Rams were underdogs for the first time in '77, they jolted the defending Super Bowl champion Raiders on Pat Haden's 43-yard TD pass to WR Harold Jackson with 2:10 left to play. The hard-hitting game was marked by eight turnovers (six by Oakland) as the Ram defense continued its late-season resurgence, having yielded only 16 points in four previous games.

Raider All-Pro QB Ken Stabler was limited to only 16 completions in 38 attempts for 194 yards and was intercepted and sacked four times each. Ram CB Monte Jackson had two interceptions for the second straight week and LB Jim Youngblood and SS Dave Elmendorf each picked off a pass. DE Jack Youngblood sacked Stabler twice and DT Mike Fanning had a key sack in the last 19 seconds.

Haden improved his league-leading passing rating by completing 13 of 22 for 186 yards, and RB Lawrence McCutcheon caught four for 63 yards. McCutcheon also gained 97 yards on 25 carries, putting him over 1,000 yards for the fourth time in five years and also bettering Dick Bass' club record of 1,218 rushing attempts. On the losing side, RB Mark van Eeghen kept his AFC rushing lead with 79 yards on 16 carries.

Facing elimination from the AFC East race if they lost to division-leading Baltimore, Don Shula's amazing Dolphins closed out the week with a convincing 17-6 triumph over the Colts at the Orange Bowl in the most important Monday night TV game of the season.

Miami rookie RB Leroy Harris broke open a tight game with seven minutes remaining when he bolted 77 yards through the line for a TD which gave the Dolphins an 11-point lead. Harris' run was the longest from scrimmage in the club's history, and his 140-yard game (17 carries) gave him a three-game average of 108 yards since his first start. Miami had taken a 10-6 lead into halftime as the result of Bob Griese's 15-yard TD pass to TE Andre Tillman, following a 27-yard FG by Garo Yepremian and FG's of 32 and 27 yards by Baltimore's Toni Linhart.

The victory was particularly satisfying to the Dolphins, not only because it moved them into a first-place tie with Baltimore, but also because it avenged a loss in the fourth week of the season in which Miami led the Colts 28-10 in the second quarter only to lose the game 45-28. In that first meeting, the Dolphin defense collapsed, but it rose to the challenge the second time, holding Baltimore scoreless for the final three quarters and without a TD for the entire game, despite the absence of two starters for the game and ILB Steve Towle (shoulder separation) for the second half. The talented replacements were DE Bob Heinz, FS Vern Roberson and ILB Rusty Chambers.

The Dolphin win also broke a string of six consecutive defeats at the hands of Baltimore, including a 17-16 loss on Monday night TV in '76 when DT Mike Barnes blocked a Dolphin PAT in the final minute.

Minnesota made the best comeback of the season on Sunday, wiping out a 24-0 deficit in the third quarter and rallying for a 28-27 win over San Francisco behind the arm of rookie QB Tommy Kramer. The No. 1 draft choice from Rice relieved veteran Bob Lee and fired three TD passes in

the fourth quarter to save the Vikings from dropping into a first-place tie with Chicago.

Kramer hit WR Ahmad Rashad with an eight-yarder and TE Bob Tucker with a nine-yarder for the first two TD's, and then he tied the game with a 69-yard bomb to former Rookie of the Year Sammy White after DT James White had recovered a 49er fumble. Veteran PK Fred Cox added the winning PAT, his fourth of the game.

Free-agent rookie Dave Williams, making his debut as a kick returner, sparked the 49ers' early surge, returning a kickoff 80 yards for a TD against the Vikes' outstanding specialty team and later returning a punt 60 yards to set up another score. But Lee threw a 15-yard TD pass to RB Brent McClanahan to cut the deficit to 24-7 before Kramer took over. After the rookie's first two TD tosses cut the margin to 24-21, a 68-yard kickoff return by 49er Tony Leonard paved the way for Ray Wersching's 31-yard FG. But Kramer quickly capitalized on the fumble recovery after a Viking punt and spotted Sammy White behind the defender.

The 49ers' total of 231 yards in punt and kickoff returns nearly matched their 247 yards in total offense, and Minnesota topped that figure in passing yardage alone (257 net). Kramer hit nine of 13 passes for 188 yards and Lee completed 11 of 19 for 94 yards with two interceptions, as the two combined for four TD passes against a 49er defense which had allowed only six aerial TD's in its first 11 games. RB Delvin Williams led the 49er offense with 107 yards on 27 carries, but QB Jim Plunkett completed only five of 13 passes for 57 yards with one interception.

New England set the stage for an important showdown against Miami by squeaking past host Atlanta 16-10 on Steve Grogan's 33-yard TD pass to rookie WR Stanley Morgan in the fourth quarter. The winning score came on a third-down play and capped an 89-yard march against the stingiest defense in the NFL (99 points in 12 games). The defeat dropped the Cinderella Falcons three games behind the Rams and all but eliminated Coach Leeman Bennett's team from "Wild Card" contention.

The winning TD was the only six-pointer yielded by Atlanta all afternoon, as the Pats had to settle for three FG's (36, 32 and 30 yards) by John Smith in mounting a 9-0 lead in the third quarter. The Falcons' unproductive offense finally put some points on the board when Steve Bartkowski (seven of 18 for 124 yards, four interceptions) threw a 15-yard TD pass to WR Wallace Francis, and Fred Steinfort added a 25-yard FG early in the fourth period for a short-lived 10-9 Falcon lead. But Morgan made the game-winning play—catching the pass, putting a move on the LB to get outside and using his blazing speed to outrun SS Ray Brown.

New England's defense was a good match for Atlanta's in this game, sacking Bartkowski eight times for losses totaling 67 yards. Patriot DE Julius Adams, a native Georgian, accounted for five of the sacks and boosted the Pats' AFC-leading sack total to 48. New England limited the Falcs to an average gain of only 2.3 yards for 54 offensive plays. Patriot CB Mike Haynes had two interceptions, including one with 56 seconds left that preserved the victory.

Atlanta picked off three passes, raising its NFC-leading total to 23, and CB Rolland Lawrence got his seventh, also an NFC high. Morgan had his best game as a pro, catching five passes for 90 yards, and Falcon WR Alfred Jenkins extended his pass-catching streak to 38 games with three receptions for 54 yards.

Dallas' rookie racehorse, RB Tony Dorsett, enjoyed his most productive game in the NFL with 206 yards rushing and two TD's in a 24-14 win over Philadelphia that clinched the Cowboys' ninth NFC East crown in 12 years.

Tony D. broke open a 17-14 game early in the fourth quarter when he bolted over RG behind Tom Rafferty's block on MLB Bill Bergey and dashed 84 yards for a TD. The run was the longest of the season in the NFL and also the longest in Cowboy annals, breaking Dorsett's mark of 77 yards set in the fourth week against St. Louis. His 206-yard effort (on 23 carries) also set a club record, wiping out Calvin Hill's mark of 153, and made him only the third rookie ever to rush for 200 yards. (The others were the Rams' Tom Wilson, 223 yards vs. Packers in '56, and Cleveland's Jim Brown, 237 vs. Rams in '57.)

The Giants avenged a 28-0 humiliation before a Monday night national TV audience in the seventh week of the season by defeating St. Louis 27-7 at East Rutherford and further disrupting the Cardinals' playoff chances. The Giants had season-high outputs of 318 yards total offense and 234 yards rushing, led by RB Doug Kotar's 18 carries for 88 yards. QB

Joe Pisarcik completed only three of 11 passes for 84 yards, but one was a 64-yarder to TE Gary Shirk that set up the final TD. The Giants' Dave Jennings broke Tom Landry's club record of 82 punts in a season.

Cincinnati got ready for a crucial meeting with Pittsburgh by pounding host Kansas City 27-7 with three TD's set up by two Chief fumbles and a 70-yard punt return by Tony Davis. San Diego guaranteed Tommy Prothro his best record in four years as Charger head coach by scoring on its first seven possessions and routing Cleveland 37-14 with a season-high 425-yard total offense and Dan Fouts fine passing (14 of 20 for 237 yards, three TD's). Pittsburgh defeated Seattle 30-20 behind RB Franco Harris' 28th career 100-yard game and QB Terry Bradshaw's two rushing TD's.

Chicago handed host Tampa Bay its fourth shutout in five games and sixth of the season, not to mention its 26th consecutive loss, in a 10-0 desision in which Buccaneer RB Ricky Bell set a club rushing record with 94 yards on 25 carries and the tough Tampa defense "held" Walter Payton to 101 yards on 33 carries (a 3.1 average). Detroit Coach Tommy Hudspeth passed up a short FG try with four minutes left in the game and, as a result, the Lions were edged 10-9 at Green Bay, snapping a five-game Packer losing streak.

The Jets squeezed past host New Orleans 16-13 on three FG's by Pat Leahy (career-long 48, 29 and 27 yards) and RB Clark Gaines' first 100-yard rushing effort of the year (22 for 103 yards). Washington stayed alive in NFC "Wild Card" chase with a 10-0 win at Buffalo witnessed by a Rich Stadium record-low crowd of 22,975 fans who saw the Bills commit three turnovers, miss two FG's and drop many catchable passes.

THIRTEENTH WEEK

The ever-changing playoff picture in the AFC East took another strange turn in the 13th week, when Baltimore actually improved its chances of reaching the playoffs by losing 13-10 to visiting Detroit. Meanwhile, a fired-up New England team defeated Miami 14-10, only to learn shortly afterward that its playoff hopes had been severely damaged by the Colt defeat.

The Patriots began the final two weeks of the season with the knowledge that they could still win the division title if they beat both of the other contenders, Miami and Baltimore, in their last two games. Such a development would have left all three teams with 10-4 final records, and the Pats would have won the tie-breaker on the basis of their 3-1 record in head-to-head competition with the Dolphins and Colts.

New England did not, however, foresee Baltimore losing at home to the 16-point underdog Lions, who had not won a single road game in six previous outings in '77 and had beaten only Seattle in seven road contests in '76. The effect of such an upset was to place the Patriots' playoffs hopes in the hands of a weak Buffalo team, which would have to win the following Saturday at Miami in order for the Pats to grab the title with a victory over Baltimore. If the 3-10 Bills failed to defeat the 9-4 Dolphins, a Patriot victory over the Colts would serve only to clinch the title for Miami, which would win the playoff tie-breaker over the Pats on the basis of its superior record in division games (6-2 to New England's 5-3).

Regardless of whether Baltimore won or lost the Detroit game, it would still have to defeat New England in the final game to reach the playoffs. However, the loss to the Lions figured to take much of the steam out of the strong-finishing Pats, whose only incentive to beat the Colts would be one of revenge—assuming Miami disposed of Buffalo on Saturday. That realization, along with the manner in which the Colts lost to Detroit, caused many fans to wonder just how hard Baltimore tried to win that game.

Surprisingly, Baltimore was the team to first come from behind and take a lead late in the game. Colt QB Bert Jones (21 of 38 for 221 yards, two interceptions) directed a 63-yard drive which culminated in a 34-yard TD pass to RB Lydell Mitchell for a 10-6 Colt lead with 4:53 remaining. FS Lyle Blackwood, the league leader with 10 interceptions, appeared to have ensured a Colt victory when he picked off a Gary Danielson pass with 1:03 left, but Baltimore was forced to punt from its 21 on fourth-and-15 with 23 seconds to play. Leonard Thompson broke through the Colt offensive line untouched, blocked David Lee's punt, picked up the loose ball and ran two yards for the winning TD.

Post-game speculation revolved around why Colt Coach Ted Marchibroda didn't have his punter run out of the endzone for a safety,

giving Baltimore a free kick from its own 20-yard line while still retaining a lead. "We didn't go for the safety because I didn't want the Lions to have the ball again," Marchibroda said later. He added that he was afraid Lee might get tackled before he reached the endzone, although such a possibility could have been eliminated by taking another delay-of-game penalty before snapping the ball.

New England extended its winning streak to four games, avenging a 17-5 loss at Miami four weeks earlier. The Pats jumped to a 14-0 lead in the first quarter on 71 and 51-yard marches capped by one-yard TD runs by Ike Forte and Sam Cunningham. Although the Pats were held scoreless the rest of the way, their defense did a remarkable job in holding down Miami. The Pats held the Dolphin running game to only 25 yards (fewest in Coach Don Shula's eight-year reign at Miami) on 19 carries—a 1.3 average—and sacked Bob Griese six times, giving the AFC's leading defense 54 sacks for the year.

Griese (22 of 38 for 260 yards, one interception), who became the NFL's 21st QB to surpass 20,000 career passing yards, cut the Pats' lead to 14-10 with a 23-yard TD pass to Nat Moore in the fourth quarter. But the Patriot defense denied him the go-ahead TD, stiffening after Miami had first-and-10 at the Pats' 27 with 1:51 left. The stubborn Patriot defense also stopped Miami twice on fourth-and-goal at the Pats' one during the third period.

New England could have built a sizable lead at halftime but twice fumbled the ball away on its 11 and four-yard lines. Two rookies led the Dolphin defense, NT Bob Baumhower making 17 tackles and recovering two fumbles and DE A.J. Duhe sacking Steve Grogan twice.

Cincinnati stepped into the driver's seat for the AFC Central title with a 17-10 victory over Pittsburgh on an icy Riverfront Stadium field in two-degree weather. The win snapped a string of six straight Bengal losses to the Steelers, and the margin of victory gave Cincinnati a one-point edge in point differential should the two teams both win their final games. With the powerhouse Steelers to contend with each year, Cincinnati hadn't won a division title since 1973.

Bengal All-Pro CB Lemar Parrish got his club off to a fast start, intercepting a Terry Bradshaw pass on the opening series and returning it 47 yards for a TD. Pittsburgh then took command for the rest of the half, scoring on RB Franco Harris' five-yard TD run and Roy Gerela's 32-yard FG for a 10-7 halftime lead.

At intermission the Steelers enjoyed statistical advantages of 14 to six in first downs, 240 to 203 in total yards and 128 to eight in rushing yardage, including 101 yards on the ground by Harris alone. Even so, the Bengals could have been ahead if they hadn't wasted a fumble recovery by DE Coy Bacon at the Steeler 12 and a drive that reached the Steeler 20 before running out of gas.

The second half was a different story. The Bengal defense came to life and limited Pittsburgh to a total of minus-five yards rushing in the second half, shutting off Harris completely and forcing him into a key fumble which ignited the Bengal resurgence.

On the first play after the turnover, Bengal QB Ken Anderson fired a 57-yard pass to WR Billy Brooks (six for 166 yards), setting up Chris Bahr's 24-yard FG for a 10-10 tie. On the ensuing kickoff, rookie SS Jerry Anderson stripped the ball from Steeler KR Jim Smith, and Bengal Lenvil Elliott recovered at the Steeler 43. Again using the quick-strike strategy, Anderson went to the air on first down and fired a 43-yard TD pass to WR Pat McInally, who beat S Glen Edwards on a deep pattern. Bahr's PAT gave Cincinnati a 17-10 cushion and, more importantly, a one-point edge in point differential over two games.

The fourth quarter was scoreless, but not for lack of scoring chances. Pittsburgh reached the Bengal 20 early in the period but Harris again fumbled and Bengal CB Ken Riley recovered. Cincinnati also had two fine opportunities but they went awry when Bahr's 24-yard FG attempt bounced off an upright after a bad snap and when RB Archie Griffin fumbled at the Steeler 21. Pittsburgh then took over with 1:51 left, needing only a FG to move ahead in point differential. Bradshaw completed three passes and then was sacked by DE Gary Burley. Three incomplete passes brought an end to the drive, although the second one nearly went for a TD but for Riley's last-second deflection.

Tampa Bay became the scene of joyous celebration as a result of the Bucs' first-ever NFL triumph after 26 consecutive defeats (three short of the NFL record set by the Chicago Cardinals, 1942-45). The victim was struggling New Orleans, which had six passes intercepted in a 33-14 embarrassment before the home folks at the Louisiana Superdome. The Bucs' point total was the highest in their history, surpassing by 10 the previous high at Seattle. In fact, the impotent Buccaneer offense had scored only 53 points in 12 previous games in '77—an average of 4.4 per game—and had been blanked six times.

To be sure, the Bucs' rapidly improving defense was more responsible for the victory than was the offense. The defensive unit held New Orleans without a single first down in the opening 24 minutes enroute to a 13-0 halftime lead, and then it returned three second-half interceptions for TD's (tying an NFL record) which turned the game into a rout. CB Mike Washington and LB Richard Wood each had two thefts, while CB Jeris White and DE Greg Johnson each had one. Washington had a 45-yard TD return, Wood a 10-yarder and Johnson intercepted one in the endzone, accounting for 18 points.

The Bucs sacked Saint QB's Archie Manning and Bobby Scott five times, three by DE Lee Roy Selmon and one each by DE's Council Rudolph and backup Greg Johnson. Anchored around NT Dave Pear and ILB's Wood and Dewey Selmon, the Buc defense limited the Saints to only 96 rushing yards.

Offensively, Buc QB Gary Huff completed seven of nine passes for 96 yards and one TD, a five-yarder to WR Morris Owens, and RB Jim DuBose gained 59 yards on 17 carries. The Bucs had gone ahead 26-0 before New Orleans finally scored its two TD's in the fourth quarter. The Saints' specialty teams also were found wanting, allowing the Bucs 75 yards on four punt returns (Danny Reece, three for 46; Isaac Hagins, one for 29).

Oakland clinched the AFC's "Wild Card" spot with a 35-13 pounding of Minnesota, as the Vikings lost the ball four times on fumbles and three times on interceptions, giving them an NFC-high 45 turnovers for the season. Viking rookie QB Tommy Kramer was unimpressive in his first NFL start and was sacked four times, as Oakland rolled to a 21-0 lead in the opening eight minutes.

Washington eliminated St. Louis from the NFC "Wild Card" chase with a 26-20 win at Busch Stadium and thereby kept the Redskins' slim playoff chances alive. Washington rode Mark Moseley's flawless FG kicking (40, 23, 37 and 42 yards) and veteran QB Bill Kilmer's short passing game to a 26-13 lead before the Cards nearly pulled the game out of the fire. A 68-yard TD pass from Jim Hart to RB Terry Metcalf cut the margin to six with 10:39 remaining. When Hart again tried to hit Metcalf in the endzone with 1:14 left, fifth DB Eddie Brown made a game-saving interception.

Kilmer, starting in place of Joe Theismann for the first time in seven games, had good protection and picked apart the Cardinal defense, throwing eight times to RB Calvin Hill for 66 yards, including a 14-yard TD. Hart (seven of 26 for 156 yards) was victimized by three interceptions and nearly six dropped passes.

Despite rushing for 119 yards on 19 carries, catching two passes for 79 yards and returning three kickoffs for 58 yards, Metcalf was booed lustily by the crowd after his 10th fumble of the season on a kickoff return, setting up Washington's final TD. (In '76 he led the NFL with 15 fumbles.) Metcalf declared after the game that he had no wish to play another year in St. Louis and, as it turned out, he left the NFL altogether after the season ended.

Houston avenged a bitter defeat at the hands of Cleveland earlier in the year by edging the Browns 19-15 on a frozen Municipal Stadium turf with the aid of Billy "White Shoes" Johnson's 72-yard punt return for a TD, despite the Browns' total yardage advantage of 400 to 167. Buffalo snapped a four-game losing streak with a 14-10 win over the host Jets on TD passes of five and 11 yards from Joe Ferguson to WR Bob Chandler, who raised his season total to 53 receptions. Seattle won the battle to stay out of the AFC West cellar with a 34-31 triumph at Kansas City sparked by a 203-yard rushing attack. Denver rallied from a 9-7 deficit in the fourth quarter to nip visiting San Diego 17-9, despite Charger rookie PK Rolf Benirschke extending his perfect FG string to 11 with three FG's (46, 32 and 27 yards).

Chicago kept its playoff drive on schedule with a 21-10 win over Green Bay paced by RB Walter Payton's 32 carries for 163 yards and two TD's. Philadelphia defeated the Giants for the second time, 17-14, although Eagle QB Ron Jaworski was sacked five times and his passing game netted minus-13 yards. Los Angeles got its revenge for a season-opening 17-6 loss at Atlanta by drubbing the Falcons 23-7 and gaining 386 yards against the NFL's top defense, including 265 on the ground (Lawrence McCutcheon, 17 for 152). In the Monday night game, San Francisco had

its best scoring output of the season but still lost 42-35 to Dallas in a game marked by superb passing (Jim Plunkett, 15 of 29 for 263 yards, four TD's; Roger Staubach, 14 of 19 for 220 yards, three TD's),

FOURTEENTH WEEK

A controversial ruling on an apparent fumble by Baltimore QB Bert Jones became the center of attention in the final week of the regular season. The Colts capitalized on the official's error to score the winning TD against New England and thereby capture the AFC East title for the third consecutive year. The Colt victory eliminated Miami from the playoffs, as the Dolphins needed a Colt defeat to finish first in the division.

The most talked-about play of the season occurred on Baltimore's game-winning, 99-yard march when Colt RB Lydell Mitchell failed to hear Jones' checkoff of the original call. Jones had no alternative but to keep the football, and he lost control of it as soon as he was hit by a wave of onrushing Patriot defenders at the six-yard line. Patriot LB Sam Hunt recovered at the 10, but referee Fred Silva, whose crew was responsible for an incorrect call which cost Houston a game earlier, ruled that he had blown the play dead before the fumble.

TV replays showed that Silva was unable to see the fumble from his angle, which was the proper position for a referee to be in at that moment. Because he couldn't see the fumble, he blew the whistle as soon as Jones fell to the turf. And because the whistle blew before Hunt recovered, the ball had to be ruled dead at that instant.

The mistake was understandable when viewed from Silva's angle, but it could not have been overruled under existing NFL rules. The "non-fumble" ruling had to stand, and it proved to be a blessing for the Colts. RB Don McCauley, the Colts' bread-and-butter man on third downs and short-yardage plays, soon followed the missed fumble with a three-yard TD run, and Toni Linhart's PAT gave the Colts their winning 30-24 margin.

Baltimore's victory climaxed an amazing comeback from a 21-3 deficit early in the third quarter. New England had taken a 14-3 halftime lead on QB Steve Grogan's five-yard TD pass to TE Russ Francis and Grogan's one-yard scoring run while the Colts could manage only a 28-yard FG by Linhart. Rookie speedster Raymond Clayborn had made it 21-3 when he returned the opening kickoff of the second half 101 yards for another TD. Jones' 14-yard TD pass to WR Glenn Doughty cut the gap to 21-10, but a 30-yard FG by John Smith boosted the Pats' lead to 14.

Perhaps the most important play in the Colt comeback was a 78-yard scoring strike from Jones to TE Raymond Chester that caught the Pats in a blitz by both safetymen. That TD seemed to wake up the Colt offense and it moved the hosts to within 24-16, despite the PAT being blocked. A 12-yard TD pass from Jones to WR Freddie Scott in the fourth quarter made it 24-23 and set the stage for the disputed fumble and McCauley's winning TD.

Baltimore outgained the Pats 483 to 270, spurred by Jones' remarkable passing (19 of 30 for 340 yards, three TD's). Chester had four receptions for 122 yards and Doughty had five for 110.

Chicago was thankful to a New Jersey sporting goods dealer who supplied 34 pairs of special-sole shoes which enabled them to win a 12-9 overtime game against the Giants and thus make the playoffs as the NFC's "Wild Card" team. The Bears came to Giants Stadium unprepared for the icy artificial turf which greeted them, and they spent the first half sliding around in a downpour of freezing rain. The new shoes, which arrived in time for the second half at a cost of about $1,000 to the Bears, provided the difference in the closely fought game.

Giant PK Joe Danelo sent the game into overtime with a 27-yard FG with 38 seconds remaining after a 14-play drive. The drive followed the only TD of the game—a four-yard run by rookie RB Robin Earl—and DE George Martin's block of Bob Thomas' low-trajectory PAT try. The only previous scoring had been FG's of 38 and 19 yards by Danelo and a 32-yarder by Thomas.

The Bears started the winning drive when Len Walterscheid returned a Dave Jennings punt 10 yards to the Giant 45, where he fumbled but Bear LB Don Rives recovered. QB Bob Avellini threw twice to TE Greg Latta for gains of two and 18 yards to the Giant 25. Then RB Walter Payton made a clutch catch of another Avellini pass and rambled to the 10.

With the clock still running and the 15-minute overtime period nearing expiration. Thomas rushed onto the field and booted a game-winning, 28-yard FG with nine seconds left, atoning for two previous misses and the blocked PAT. A tie at the end of the extra period would have given the "Wild Card" berth to Washington, which equaled Chicago's 9-5 record but had a poorer point differential in conference games.

Next to winning the game, the Bears' secondary goal was to enable Payton to break O.J. Simpson's single-season rushing record of 2,003 yards. Payton needed 199 yards to eclipse Simpson's mark, but the combination of the Giants' tough defense and the treacherous field conditions limited Payton to only 47 yards on 15 carries—his lowest output since St. Louis held him to 36 yards on 11 carries in the second week. The victory gave the Bears their best record since '65 (also 9-5) and put them in the playoffs for the first time in 14 years (they won the '63 NFL Championship 14-10 over the Giants).

After Cincinnati had pushed aside perennial nemesis Pittsburgh the previous week, all the Bengals had to do to win the division was beat Houston. But the Bengals watched their playoff dreams slip away in a 21-16 defeat at the Astrodome. For the fast-finishing Oilers, the victory avenged a 13-10 overtime defeat at Cincinnati earlier in the year, in which line judge Vince Jacob (a member of the Silva officiating crew involved in the Bert Jones "non-fumble" controversy) made an incorrect decision that wiped out an Oiler TD in the final 27 seconds of regulation time. The officiating error prompted a private apology from Commissioner Pete Rozelle to Oiler Coach Bum Phillips.

Billy "White Shoes" Johnson was the difference this time. The Oilers' speedy WR-KR accounted for 263 yards in total offense and return yardage on just 13 possessions. Johnson caught six passes for 138 yards, returned four kickoffs for 81 yards and two punts for 13 yards, and ran once for 31 yards, scoring one TD and setting up another TD and the clinching FG. Oiler QB Dan Pastorini completed 10 of 21 passes for 190 yards and one TD, while Bengal QB Ken Anderson suffered through a miserable game (eight of 23 for 97 yards, one TD). Both QB's had missed part of the previous meeting due to injuries.

Aside from Johnson, Houston's success was due largely to its strong pass rush, which had five sacks for losses totaling 37 yards. Rookie DE James Young got to Anderson three times, including one which produced a safety and a 15-6 Oiler lead in the third quarter. With injured WR Isaac Curtin (knee) out of the Bengal lineup for the sixth straight game, Houston was able to put double coverage on WR Billy Brooks, limiting him to one catch for 19 yards.

Bengal backup WR Pat McInally made two superb receptions in the fourth quarter, one an 11-yard TD from Anderson that cut Houston's lead to 15-13. Two fourth-quarter FG's from 27 and 26 yards by Tom Dempsey put the Oilers ahead 21-13, and that was too much for Cincinnati to overcome against the rugged Houston defense.

Two plays proved to be especially costly to Cincinnati. In punt formation late in the first half, McInally decided on his own to try for a first down on fourth-and-five. When he started to run and found his path blocked, he tried to kick on the run but had the punt blocked. Houston recovered on the Bengal 20 and in two plays scored a TD which gave the Oilers a 13-6 halftime lead. Another key play was veteran TE Bob Trumpy's fumble at the end of a 32-yard reception to the Oiler 34. Instead of putting Cincinnati in position for a go-ahead TD, the play enabled Oiler CB Greg Stemrick to return the fumble 36 yards and set up the FG which put the game out of reach.

Minnesota captured its fifth straight NFC Central title and ninth in 10 years with a 30-21 victory over Detroit in a nationally televised Saturday night game at the Silverdome. Coach Bud Grant switched from rookie Tommy Kramer to veteran Bob Lee as his starting QB for this important game, and Lee responded with a brilliant performance (11 of 16 for 206 yards, two TD's). Lee and All-Pro RB Chuck Foreman (33 carries for 156 yards, two TD's) spearheaded the Vikes to a 24-7 lead early in the third quarter, giving Minnesota the division crown over 9-5 Chicago on the basis of point differential in head-to-head competition (29-26).

Washington and Miami both won games on Saturday with the hope of slipping into the playoffs, but Dame Fortune passed them by.

The Redskins upset playoff-bound Los Angeles 17-14 although they nearly blew a 17-point lead in the fourth quarter. The Skins had moved in front 17-0 in the third quarter on Bill Kilmer TD passes of 59 yards to WR Frank Grant and three yards to TE Jean Fugett and a 45-yard FG by Mark Moseley which eventually proved to be the difference. Ram rookie QB Vince Ferragamo (eight of 14 for 66 yards) replaced Pat Haden in the fourth quarter and sparked a comeback, throwing TD passes of 17 yards to TE Terry Nelson and two yards to backup RB Jim Jodat.

The Rams had two opportunities to send the game into overtime, but PK Rafael Septien booted a 45 yard FG attempt wide right, got a second chance when backup LB Joe Harris was penalized for running into the kicker, and then kicked a 40-yarder wide left as time expired.

Miami shelled Buffalo 31-14 at the Orange Bowl behind Bob Griese's passing, WR Nat Moore's receiving and Gary Davis' running. Griese completed eight of 11 passes for 209 yards and two TD's in the first half alone, staking the Dolphins to a 21-0 halftime lead. Moore caught five for 144 yards, including two 67-yard dashes on sideline passes that set up first-half TD's. Davis carried 26 times for 172 yards, including a 60-yard TD jaunt in the fourth quarter. Buffalo QB Joe Ferguson had a productive day (25 of 40 for 331 yards, one TD, three interceptions) but most of the yardage was gained after Miami was well in control of the outcome.

In beating New Orleans 35-7, Atlanta broke the modern-day record for fewest points allowed in a season, the Falcons' yield of 129 surpassing the old mark of 133 set by Minnesota in 1969. Dallas held Denver without a TD in a 14-6 win at Irving that matched the eventual Super Bowl foes, as Cowboy QB Roger Staubach completed 15 of 20 passes for 160 yards and two TD's. Seattle became the winningest second-year expansion team in NFL history (5-9) by edging Cleveland 20-19 on a four-play, 80-yard drive in the final 1:36 aided by a 52-yard pass interference penalty and capped by a 15-yard TD pass from Jim Zorn to WR Steve Largent, who beat CB Oliver Davis. It was Largent's 10th TD catch of the season and gave him a total of 33 receptions for 643 yards.

Tampa Bay won for the first time at home, upsetting St. Louis (four straight losses) 17-7 behind Gary Huff's passing (seven of 12 for 171 yards, one interception), which included a 61-yard TD bomb to WR Morris Owens. Pittsburgh rallied from a 9-0 deficit to defeat host San Diego 10-9 in an inconsequential game shortly after Cincinnati had handed the division title to the Steelers. Philadelphia ended the season at 5-9 by virtue of a 27-0 triumph over the Jets, as the Eagles intercepted three passes and sacked Jet QB Richard Todd seven times.

Oakland used the week to regroup for the playoffs, as the AFC's "Wild Card" team sat out four injured regulars, including QB Ken Stabler, in a 21-20 win over Kansas City. Green Bay closed its season at 4-10 with a 16-14 victory over San Francisco sparked by rookie David Whitehurst's passing (17 of 22 for 219 yards, one TD) and CB Willie Buchanon's 29-yard interception return for a TD.

1977 In Review

WEEK 1

DARRYL STINGLEY . . . out of Vataha's shadow in N.E.

SCOTT HUNTER . . . calling signals in Falcs' upset over Rams

RED MILLER . . . senses a good thing early in Denver

WEEK 2

GREG PRUITT . . .
Brown's 151-yard rusher

ISAAC CURTIS . . .
Bengal Savior

MIKE CURTIS . . .
Skin's defensive star

GEORGE ATKINSON . . . Raiders' "criminal element?"

ERROL MANN . . . Raider kicks off great season
with 3 FG's vs. Pitt

WEEK 3

BOB CHANDLER . . . 7 catches for Bills vs. Colts

RICHARD TODD . . . guides Jets to upset

MIKE HAYNES . . . Pat CB troubled by Jets

TOM HENDERSON . . . spearheads Cowboy defense

WEEK 4

BOB AVELLINI . . . reached new heights for Bears

BENNY MALONE . . .
Dolphin dynamo

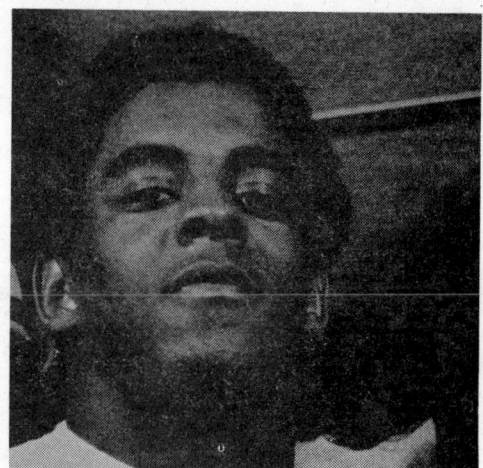

TONY DORSETT . . .
Cowboy catalyst

JOE NAMATH . . . about to call it a career

ROLLAND LAWRENCE (22) . . .
busy Falc CB

CHUCK FOREMAN . . . blasts his way to 150-yard day vs. Bears

SAM CUNNINGHAM . . . punishes Chargers with 141-yard effort

JIM TURNER . . .
Bronc's tricky kicker

WEEK 5

DAN PASTORINI . . . Oiler QB involved in controversial call

KEN ANDERSON . . . Bengal QB playing in pain

JULIUS ADAMS . . . Pat DE clobbers Colts

WENDELL TYLER . . . Rams' rookie breakaway threat

WEEK 6

RAY GUY . . . kicks 'em a mile high in Denver

JAMES HARRIS . . . Charger QB a hero in Miami

PAT HADEN . . .looking good for Rams

KEN STABLER . . . Raider QB enjoys sweet revenge

WEEK 7

WEEK 8

PAUL WIGGIN . . .
first coach to go

ED PODOLAK . . .
K.C. offensive star

ROLAND HOOKS (25) . . . O.J.'s replacement stuns Pats

KEN BURROUGH . . . six catches in Oilers' rout

RICK UPCHURCH . . . breaks Broncs'
return record

FRAN TARKENTON . . . broken leg ruins great day

LYNN DICKEY . . . Pack QB roughed up by Bengals

BRIAN SIPE . . . injured Cleveland QB

WAYNE MORRIS . . . a key to Cards' revival

A.J. DUHE . . . Miami's rookie stud

WALTER PATON . . . Bearhugs broadcaster after breaking rush record

FRANCO HARRIS . . . Steeler RB runs over Pokes

CLIFF OLANDER . . . Charger QB upsets Oakland

MATT BLAIR . . . Vike's kick-block specialist

BOB GRIESE . . . mutilates Cards

CONRAD DOBLER . . .
hastens St.L. exit

DAN FOUTS . . . stages memorable S.D. debut vs. Seattle

GARY DAVIS . . . top Dolphin rusher vs. Big Red

WEEK 12

TOM GLASSIC (62) . . . hugs Haven Moses after Denver clinches division title

TOMMY KRAMER . . .
Vike comeback artist

JACK YOUNGBLOOD . . .
Ram DE rocks Raiders

RILEY ODOMS . . .
6 catches vs. Oilers

WEEK 13

GARY HUFF . . . engineers first Buc win ever

TED MARCHIBRODA (right) . . . loss helps his Colts make playoffs

'WHITE SHOES' JOHNSON . . . trips up Browns with 72-yard punt return TD

BERT JONES . . . involved in regular season's most controversial play

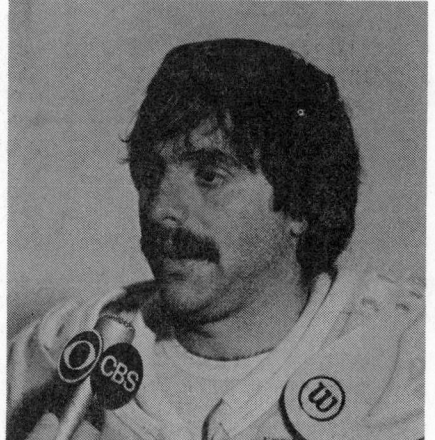

BOB THOMAS . . . Bear PK describes game-winner

RAY CHESTER . . . catch kills Pats

BILLY KILMER . . . almost gets Skins into playoffs

STEVE LARGENT . . . clutch Seahawk WR

THE PLAYOFFS

HAVEN MOSES . . . another clutch catch for Broncos

ROB LYTLE . . .
fumble or not?

TOM LANDRY . . .
after NFC title

DALLAS DEFENSE . . . crushes Chuck Foreman in NFC title game

SUPER BOWL XII

SUPER BOWL MVP's . . . Randy White (left) and Harvey Martin

DALLAS FANS . . . Cowboys grant their wish

HARVEY MARTIN . . . never stopped pressuring Craig Morton.

FINAL TEAM STATISTICS

OFFENSE

	ATL.	CHI.	DALL.	DET.	G.B.	L.A.	MINN.	N.O.	NY G	PHIL.	ST. L.	S.F.	T.B.	WASH.
FIRST DOWNS:														
Total	198	247	272	218	195	270	245	223	201	211	247	219	168	227
by Rushing	102	141	118	94	81	139	110	115	105	98	114	126	84	79
by Passing	80	94	136	103	91	112	126	96	73	100	117	81	69	134
by Penalty	16	12	18	21	23	19	9	12	23	13	16	12	15	24
RUSHING:														
Number	582	599	564	479	469	621	510	484	548	484	507	564	465	502
Yards	1890	2811	2369	1706	1464	2575	1821	2024	1897	1722	2042	2086	1424	1752
Average Yards	3.2	4.7	4.2	3.6	3.1	4.1	3.6	4.2	3.5	3.6	4.0	3.7	3.1	3.5
Touchdowns	9	18	21	11	5	19	9	14	11	10	19	16	4	4
PASSING:														
Attempts	297	305	372	384	327	339	388	321	311	349	366	277	321	383
Completions	140	161	215	191	164	182	228	166	134	167	195	136	131	183
Completion Pct.	47.1	52.8	57.8	49.7	50.2	53.7	58.8	51.7	43.1	47.9	53.3	49.1	40.8	47.8
Passing Yards	1740	2070	2689	1959	2013	2253	2692	1933	1762	2198	2608	1797	1714	2284
Avg. Yds per Att.	5.9	6.8	7.2	5.1	6.2	6.6	6.9	6.0	5.7	6.3	7.1	6.5	5.3	6.0
Avg. Yds per Comp.	12.4	12.9	12.5	10.3	12.3	12.4	11.8	11.6	13.1	13.2	13.4	13.2	13.1	12.5
Times Tackled	40	26	33	54	32	25	35	46	46	47	15	36	48	52
Yds Lost Tackled	384	226	246	441	265	237	324	360	375	342	109	289	445	421
Net Yards	1356	1844	2443	1518	1748	2016	2368	1573	1387	1856	2499	1508	1269	1863
Touchdowns	8	11	18	7	6	16	19	13	6	18	14	9	3	15
Interceptions	16	18	10	16	21	11	22	21	22	21	21	17	30	16
Pct. Intercepted	5.4	5.9	2.7	4.2	6.4	3.2	5.7	6.5	7.1	6.0	5.7	6.1	9.3	4.2
PUNTS:														
Number	106	82	83	101	86	73	83	87	100	95	72	80	99	91
Average	41.2	39.4	38.7	36.2	39.4	35.2	39.8	41.0	39.9	36.5	36.2	35.0	39.9	38.5
PUNT RETURNS:														
Number	59	47	61	42	38	51	58	37	46	50	40	48	48	57
Yards	402	471	545	345	321	360	346	281	446	518	300	292	359	452
Average Yards	6.8	10.0	8.9	8.2	8.4	7.1	6.0	7.6	9.7	10.4	7.5	6.1	7.5	7.9
Touchdowns	0	1	0	1	1	0	0	0	1	0	0	0	0	0
KICKOFF RETURNS:														
Number	34	57	44	58	51	33	45	63	54	45	59	49	43	47
Yards	621	1273	1071	1239	947	705.3	834	1355	1036	1110	1271	1174	914	1087
Average Yards	18.3	22.3	24.3	21.4	18.6	21.4	18.5	21.5	19.2	24.7	21.5	24.0	21.3	23.1
Touchdowns	0	1	0	1	1	0	0	1	0	1	0	1	0	0
INTERCEPTION RET:														
Number	26	18	21	19	13	25	16	10	12	21	19	8	23	21
Yards	462	138	229	319	89	472	109	83	179	300	267	133	368	188
Average Yards	17.8	7.7	10.9	16.8	6.8	18.9	6.8	8.3	14.9	14.3	14.1	16.6	16.0	9.0
Touchdowns	2	0	1	1	1	1	0	1	2	0	1	0	3	0
PENALTIES:														
Number	101	97	106	86	82	89	75	86	91	78	95	99	88	94
Yards	898	852	865	692	690	869	556	794	880	642	837	830	717	802
FUMBLES:														
Number	28	36	26	26	24	32	36	20	27	31	31	27	30	26
Number Lost	9	17	14	14	9	17	24	11	12	17	16	8	16	14
POINTS:														
Total	179	255	345	183	134	302	231	232	181	220	272	220	103	196
PAT Attempts	20	31	42	23	14	36	30	31	20	29	36	27	11	19
PAT Made	20	27	39	19	11	32	25	29	19	25	35	25	10	19
FG Attempts	30	27	29	19	21	30	17	12	23	15	16	19	17	37
FG Made	13	14	18	8	13	18	8	5	14	7	7	11	9	21
Percent FG Made	43.3	51.9	62.1	42.1	61.9	60.0	47.1	41.7	60.9	46.7	43.8	57.9	52.9	56.8
Safeties	0	0	0	1	0	0	1	1	0	0	0	0	0	0

DEFENSE

	ATL.	CHI.	DALL.	DET.	G.B.	L.A.	MINN.	N.O.	NY G	PHIL.	ST. L.	S.F.	T.B.	WASH.
FIRST DOWNS:														
Total	192	241	205	206	259	203	212	272	224	216	258	221	240	234
by Rushing	100	124	88	93	139	90	119	153	94	95	122	108	123	112
by Passing	76	106	94	103	105	94	80	103	109	106	120	93	106	102
by Penalty	16	11	23	10	15	19	13	16	21	15	16	20	11	20
RUSHING:														
Number	504	541	457	521	583	462	548	623	519	523	513	551	581	537
Yards	1858	2157	1651	1905	2317	1698	2222	2729	1777	1917	2235	1869	2031	2039
Average Yards	3.7	4.0	3.6	3.7	4.0	3.7	4.1	4.4	3.4	3.7	4.4	3.4	3.5	3.8
Touchdowns	5	14	9	13	16	7	11	21	16	10	11	16	13	8
PASSING:														
Attempts	320	377	371	302	319	370	312	290	328	358	376	270	337	380
Completions	141	182	154	161	186	180	149	154	185	183	198	139	190	167
Completion Pct.	44.1	48.3	41.5	53.3	58.3	48.6	47.8	53.1	56.4	51.1	52.7	51.5	56.4	43.9
Passing Yards	1775	2334	1991	2123	2042	2236	1835	2127	2399	2192	2476	1948	2141	2430
Avg. Yds per Att.	5.5	6.2	5.4	7.0	6.4	6.0	5.9	7.3	7.3	6.1	6.6	7.2	6.4	6.4
Avg. Yds per Comp.	12.6	12.8	12.9	13.2	11.0	12.4	12.3	13.8	13.0	12.0	12.5	14.0	11.3	14.6
Times Tackled	42	27	53	32	37	36	30	27	38	47	25	42	30	44
Yds Lost Tackled	391	207	429	256	323	359	254	234	303	316	209	360	246	359
Net Yards	1384	2127	1562	1867	1719	1877	1581	1893	2096	1876	2267	1588	1895	2071
Touchdowns	9	7	14	14	10	11	15	15	12	14	22	14	10	12
Interceptions	26	18	21	19	13	25	16	10	12	21	19	8	23	21
Pct. Intercepted	8.1	4.8	5.7	6.3	4.1	6.8	5.1	3.4	3.7	5.9	5.1	3.0	6.8	5.5
PUNTS:														
Number	101	93	103	87	76	89	92	75	88	91	72	86	84	95
Average	36.3	39.1	37.1	39.5	36.5	38.7	38.2	38.8	38.9	38.7	39.5	37.5	39.9	36.6
PUNT RETURNS:														
Number	58	42	36	62	53	29	42	51	67	45	33	47	71	50
Yards	519	216	280	535	311	116	507	604	680	244	157	444	469	228
Average Yards	8.9	5.1	7.8	8.6	5.9	4.0	12.1	11.8	10.1	5.4	4.8	9.4	6.6	4.6
Touchdowns	0	0	1	1	0	0	1	2	0	0	0	0	0	0
KICKOFF RETURNS:														
Number	43	52	71	33	39	53	48	45	35	46	55	48	33	54
Yards	1021	1010	1614	741	786	1156	999	1075	895	940	1104	1025	699	1033
Average Yards	23.7	19.4	22.7	22.5	20.2	21.8	20.8	23.9	25.6	20.4	20.1	21.4	21.2	19.1
Touchdowns	1	1	0	0	0	0	2	0	1	0	0	1	0	0
INTERCEPTION RET:														
Number	16	18	10	16	21	11	22	21	22	21	21	17	30	16
Yards	195	171	184	207	349	136	187	392	330	256	183	298	429	296
Average Yards	12.2	9.5	18.4	12.9	16.6	12.4	8.5	18.7	15.0	12.2	8.7	17.5	14.3	18.5
Touchdowns	0	1	0	1	1	0	0	4	2	0	1	1	3	1
PENALTIES:														
Number	99	83	78	88	101	94	82	104	106	84	82	96	87	100
Yards	860	731	731	770	799	825	688	972	886	698	817	820	714	857
FUMBLES:														
Number	35	27	22	32	27	26	23	29	47	24	19	21	34	28
Number Lost	22	13	10	16	11	16	13	15	20	13	12	10	18	12
POINTS:														
Total	129	253	212	252	219	146	227	336	265	207	287	260	223	189
PAT Attempts	15	27	26	31	27	18	30	42	33	25	34	32	26	21
PAT Made	12	26	26	28	22	17	26	39	31	24	32	29	23	21
FG Attempts	16	29	15	24	23	18	17	24	22	26	26	22	27	29
FG Made	9	21	10	12	11	7	7	15	12	11	17	13	14	14
Percent FG Made	56.3	72.4	66.7	50.0	47.8	38.9	41.2	62.5	54.5	42.3	65.4	59.1	51.9	48.3
Safeties	0	1	0	1	1	0	0	0	0	0	0	0	1	0

CONFERENCE PLAYOFFS

December 26, at Irving, Texas (Attendance 62,920)

SCORING

DALLAS	7	10	17	3	– 37
CHICAGO	0	0	0	7	– 7

First Quarter
Dall. Dennison, 2 yard rush
PAT – Herrara (kick)

Second Quarter
Dall. DuPree, 26 yard pass from Staubach PAT – Herrera (kick)
Dall. Herrera, 21 yard field goal

Third Quarter
Dall. Dorsett, 22 yard rush
PAT – Herrera (kick)
Dall. Herrera, 31 yard field goal
Dall. Dorsett, 7 yard rush
PAT – Herrera (kick)

Fourth Quarter
Dall. Herrera, 27 yard field goal
Chi. Schubert, 34 yard pass from Avellini PAT – Thomas (kick)

TEAM STATISTICS

DALLAS		CHICAGO
20	First Downs – Total	15
13	First Downs – Rushing	4
7	First Downs – Passing	9
0	First Downs – Penalty	2
2	Fumbles – Number	3
2	Fumbles – Lost Ball	3
3	Penalties – Number	4
35	Yards Penalized	43
0	Missed Field Goals	0
64	Offensive Plays	55
367	Net Yards	224
5.7	Average Gain	4.0
3	Giveaways	7
7	Takeaways	3
+4	Difference	-4

INDIVIDUAL STATISTICS

DALLAS	No	Yds	Avg.	CHICAGO	No	Yds	Avg.
RUSHING							
Dorsett	17	85	5.0	Payton	19	60	3.2
Newhouse	16	80	5.0	Harper	5	11	2.2
Dennison	8	40	5.0	Earl	2	6	3.0
Staubach	4	25	6.3	Avellini	1	4	4.0
Brinson	3	3	1.0		27	81	3.0
	48	233	4.8				
RECEIVING							
D. Pearson	2	38	19.0	Schubert	5	69	13.8
Dorsett	2	37	18.5	Payton	3	33	11.0
DuPree	1	28	28.0	Scott	3	29	9.7
Newhouse	1	15	15.0	Latta	2	25	12.5
Richards	1	12	12.0	Earl	1	15	15.0
Brinson	1	6	6.0	Harper	1	6	6.0
	8	136	17.0		15	177	11.8
PUNTING							
D. White	3		37.0	Parsons	6		43.4
PUNT RETURNS							
Johnson	3	26	8.7	Schubert	1	7	7.0
Hill	1	12	12.0				
	4	38	9.5				
KICKOFF RETURNS							
Brinson	1	28	28.0	Walterscheid	4	98	24.5
Johnson	1	16	16.0	Payton	3	57	19.0
	2	44	22.0	Musso	1	7	7.0
					8	162	20.3
INTERCEPTION RETURNS							
Waters	3	53	17.7	Livers	1	8	8.0
Lewis	1	23	23.0				
	4	76	19.0				

PASSING

DALLAS	Att.	Comp.	Comp. Pct.	Yds.	Int.	Yds/ Att.	Yds/ Comp.	Yards Lost Tackled
Staubach	13	8	61.5	136	1	10.5	17.0	2– 2
CHICAGO								
Avellini	25	15	60.0	177	4	7.1	11.8	3–34

December 26, at Los Angeles (Attendance 62,538)

SCORING

LOS ANGELES	0	0	0	7	– 7
MINNESOTA	7	0	0	7	– 14

First Quarter
Minn. Foreman, 5 yard rush
PAT – Cox (kick)

Fourth Quarter
Minn. Johnson, 1 yard rush
PAT – Cox (kick)
L.A. H. Jackson, 1 yard pass from Haden PAT – Septien (kick)

TEAM STATISTICS

L.A.		MINN.
14	First Downs – Total	14
7	First Downs – Rushing	9
6	First Downs – Passing	4
1	First Downs – Penalty	1
1	Fumbles – Number	1
0	Fumbles – Lost Ball	0
2	Penalties – Number	7
15	Yards Penalized	50
1	Missed Field Goals	0
62	Offensive Plays	60
267	Net Yards	189
4.3	Average Gain	3.2
3	Giveaways	0
0	Takeaways	3
-3	Difference	+3

INDIVIDUAL STATISTICS

LOS ANGELES	No	Yds	Avg.	MINNESOTA	No	Yds	Avg.
RUSHING							
McCutcheon	16	102	6.4	Foreman	31	101	3.3
Haden	3	27	9.0	Miller	12	52	4.3
Cappelletti	7	11	1.6	Johnson	3	1	0.3
Phillips	1	9	9.0	Lee	3	-10	-3.3
Nelson	1	0	0.0		49	144	2.9
Tyler	1	0	0.0				
	29	149	5.1				
RECEIVING							
Nelson	5	85	17.0	Rashad	2	37	18.5
H. Jackson	3	21	7.0	Miller	2	14	7.0
McCutcheon	2	15	7.5	Foreman	1	6	6.0
Phillips	2	0	0.0		5	57	11.4
Waddy	1	5	5.0				
Cappelletti	1	4	4.0				
	14	130	9.3				
PUNTING							
Walker	5		37.6	Clabo	5		40.8
PUNT RETURNS							
Waddy	3	17	5.7	Moore	2	30	15.0
Bryant	1	19	19.0				
Scales	1	2	2.0				
	5	38	7.6				
KICKOFF RETURNS							
Tyler	2	43	21.5	Moore	1	15	15.0
INTERCEPTION RETURNS							
none				Krause	1	14	14.0
				J. Wright	1	3	3.0
				Allen	1	0	0.0
					3	17	5.7

PASSING

LOS ANGELES	Att.	Comp.	Comp. Pct.	Yds.	Int.	Yds/ Att.	Yds/ Comp.	Yards Lost Tackled
Haden	32	14	43.8	130	3	4.1	9.3	1–12
MINNESOTA								
Lee	10	5	50.0	57	0	5.7	11.8	1–12

FINAL TEAM STATISTICS

OFFENSE

	BALT.	BUFF.	CIN.	CLEV.	DENV.	HOU.	K.C.	MIA.	N.E.	NY J	OAK.	PIT.	S.D.	SEA.
FIRST DOWNS:														
Total	269	246	248	271	223	228	228	267	247	195	305	266	235	251
by Rushing	111	93	110	119	101	112	95	143	132	83	156	122	93	116
by Passing	136	141	112	119	107	91	101	107	101	96	125	124	121	116
by Penalty	22	12	26	33	15	25	23	17	14	16	24	20	21	19
RUSHING:														
Number	566	450	488	510	523	509	456	519	603	437	681	581	488	461
Yards	2123	1861	1861	2200	2043	1989	1843	2366	2303	1618	2627	2258	1761	1964
Average Yards	3.8	4.1	3.8	4.3	3.9	3.9	4.0	4.6	3.8	3.7	3.9	3.9	3.6	4.3
Touchdowns	17	3	10	9	16	15	13	18	13	6	20	20	10	12
PASSING:														
Attempts	395	458	385	377	313	347	374	311	305	360	324	341	369	387
Completions	224	221	192	208	163	181	190	182	160	170	184	173	206	175
Completion Pct.	56.7	48.3	49.9	55.2	52.1	52.2	50.8	58.5	52.5	47.2	56.8	50.7	55.8	45.2
Passing Yards	2686	2803	2550	2374	2265	2107	2514	2264	2162	2286	2338	2632	2442	2459
Avg. Yds Per Att.	6.8	6.1	6.6	6.3	7.2	6.1	6.7	7.3	7.1	6.4	7.2	7.7	6.6	6.4
Avg. Yds Per Comp.	12.0	12.7	13.3	11.4	13.9	11.6	13.2	12.4	13.5	13.4	12.7	15.2	11.9	14.1
Times Tackled	26	36	31	24	50	23	48	36	14	35	25	27	24	21
Yds Lost Tackled	221	273	217	199	402	232	421	303	155	284	229	245	198	131
Net Yards	2465	2530	2333	2175	1863	1875	2093	1961	2007	2002	2109	2387	2244	2328
Touchdowns	17	12	12	19	15	14	11	22	17	14	21	17	11	23
Interceptions	12	24	16	31	12	21	26	14	21	26	24	21	20	32
Pct. Intercepted	3.0	5.2	4.2	8.2	3.8	6.1	7.0	4.5	6.9	7.2	7.4	6.2	5.4	8.3
PUNTS:														
Number	84	83	70	62	91	79	89	58	68	76	59	73	73	64
Average	37.4	38.9	41.3	39.0	39.2	38.4	39.4	36.9	34.6	37.6	43.3	36.3	37.1	38.0
PUNT RETURNS:														
Number	42	32	41	38	58	36	36	40	43	38	37	46	46	32
Yards	323	380	328	322	712	539	236	315	429	540	373	389	521	217
Average Yards	7.7	11.9	8.0	8.5	12.3	15.0	6.6	7.9	10.0	12.6	10.1	8.5	11.3	6.8
Touchdowns	0	2	0	0	1	2	0	0	0	0	0	0	1	0
KICKOFF RETURNS:														
Number	48	60	46	53	34	46	63	38	39	61	49	45	39	71
Yards	912	1238	886	1075	732	1056	1284	1011	1051	1374	909	995	734	1502
Average Yards	19.0	20.6	19.7	20.3	21.5	23.0	20.4	26.6	26.9	22.5	18.6	22.1	18.8	21.2
Touchdowns	0	0	0	0	0	1	0	1	3	0	0	0	0	0
INTERCEPTION RET:														
Number	30	21	16	23	25	26	21	15	19	11	26	31	21	25
Yards	434	329	238	430	491	429	348	124	194	153	352	374	317	356
Average Yards	14.5	15.7	14.9	18.7	19.6	16.5	16.6	8.3	10.2	13.9	13.5	12.1	15.1	14.2
Touchdowns	0	1	2	3	2	1	2	0	0	1	0	0	2	1
PENALTIES:														
Number	77	87	89	125	91	106	82	59	112	62	89	122	97	76
Yards	620	866	859	1046	883	835	706	432	931	508	747	973	813	656
FUMBLES:														
Number	24	36	37	34	28	30	33	22	28	24	22	41	29	27
Number Lost	14	20	16	22	15	17	21	13	15	14	16	28	11	14
POINTS:														
Total	295	160	238	269	274	299	225	313	278	191	351	283	222	282
PAT Attempts	35	19	26	31	34	36	29	41	33	21	42	37	25	37
PAT Made	32	17	25	30	31	29	27	37	33	18	39	34	21	33
FG Attempts	26	17	27	23	19	25	18	22	21	25	28	14	23	18
FG Made	17	9	19	17	13	16	8	10	15	15	20	9	17	9
Percent FG Made	65.4	52.9	70.4	73.9	68.4	64.0	44.4	45.5	71.4	60.0	71.4	64.3	73.9	50.0
Safeties	1	1	0	1	0	3	0	1	0	1	1	0	0	0

DEFENSE

	BALT.	BUFF.	CIN.	CLEV.	DENV.	HOU.	K.C.	MIA.	N.E.	NY J	OAK.	PIT.	S.D.	SEA.
FIRST DOWNS:														
Total	210	260	253	261	217	247	304	227	215	283	204	228	228	295
by Rushing	78	134	113	113	77	103	169	101	86	137	86	80	102	152
by Passing	116	98	113	116	234	124	113	117	111	131	105	112	105	125
by Penalty	16	28	27	32	17	20	22	9	18	15	13	36	21	18
RUSHING:														
Number	423	589	525	524	470	522	632	467	452	575	408	493	508	596
Yards	798	2405	1897	2098	1531	1815	2971	1749	1605	2245	1754	1723	1927	2485
Average Yards	4.3	4.1	3.6	4.0	3.3	3.5	4.7	3.7	3.6	3.9	4.3	3.5	3.8	4.2
Touchdowns	11	21	15	14	5	11	23	12	8	14	7	9	11	21
PASSING:														
Attempts	382	316	351	340	426	379	333	414	356	377	367	357	380	349
Completions	181	155	196	184	235	192	175	226	188	215	177	157	172	199
Completion Pct.	47.4	49.1	55.8	54.1	55.2	50.7	52.7	54.6	52.8	57.0	48.2	40.0	45.3	57.0
Passing Yards	2549	2213	2453	2298	2556	2431	2244	2393	2504	2587	2503	2254	2088	2464
Avg. Yds Per Att.	6.7	7.0	7.0	6.8	6.0	6.4	6.7	5.8	7.0	6.9	6.8	6.3	5.5	7.1
Avg. Yds Per Comp.	14.1	14.3	12.5	12.5	10.9	12.7	12.8	10.6	13.3	12.0	14.1	14.4	12.1	12.4
Times Tackled	47	17	25	31	35	32	25	20	58	26	35	32	44	18
Yds Lost Tackled	359	165	226	281	312	289	222	160	471	184	281	285	363	131
Net Yards	2190	2048	2227	2017	2244	2142	2022	2233	2033	2403	2222	1969	1725	2333
Touchdowns	10	17	14	15	11	12	15	10	16	23	17	16	14	19
Interceptions	30	21	16	23	25	26	21	15	19	11	26	31	21	25
Pct. Intercepted	7.9	6.7	4.6	6.8	5.9	6.9	6.3	3.6	5.3	2.9	7.1	8.7	5.5	7.2
PUNTS:														
Number	81	73	75	70	95	77	63	67	78	73	74	79	76	54
Average	36.2	36.2	37.6	37.7	40.7	40.8	41.0	38.5	39.1	38.2	37.6	40.3	40.6	36.0
PUNT RETURNS:														
Number	44	42	38	31	55	46	50	29	33	46	31	34	40	42
Yards	481	604	260	558	397	340	703	267	270	448	217	380	378	389
Average Yards	10.9	14.4	6.8	18.0	7.2	7.4	14.1	9.2	8.2	9.7	7.0	11.2	9.5	9.3
Touchdowns	1	0	0	3	0	0	0	0	0	0	0	1	0	0
KICKOFF RETURNS:														
Number	60	40	48	50	50	63	44	59	52	45	63	48	47	50
Yards	1514	814	1029	986	1084	1331	958	1281	1086	946	997	1080	952	1240
Average Yards	25.2	20.3	21.4	19.7	21.7	21.1	21.8	21.7	20.9	21.0	15.8	22.5	20.3	24.8
Touchdowns	2	1	0	0	0	0	1	0	0	1	0	0	0	0
INTERCEPTION RET:														
Number	12	24	16	31	12	21	26	14	21	26	24	21	20	32
Yards	298	326	192	351	172	253	390	238	279	420	373	299	109	592
Average Yards	24.8	13.6	12.0	11.3	14.3	12.0	15.0	17.0	13.3	16.2	15.5	14.2	5.5	18.5
Touchdowns	1	0	0	0	0	1	3	0	2	0	2	1	0	3
PENALTIES:														
Number	78	71	103	117	97	97	105	82	71	89	82	82	87	96
Yards	618	638	768	979	718	791	929	644	610	788	717	784	831	794
FUMBLES:														
Number	27	21	34	32	28	39	39	37	20	37	31	28	28	20
Number Lost	17	12	23	16	14	28	23	18	10	17	21	13	10	11
POINTS:														
Total	221	313	235	267	148	230	349	197	217	300	230	243	205	373
PAT Attempts	27	39	29	32	18	26	42	23	26	39	29	29	26	43
PAT Made	24	37	26	27	16	24	37	21	22	34	23	27	25	42
FG Attempts	21	21	18	22	22	22	28	20	21	21	19	21	13	31
FG Made	11	14	11	16	8	16	20	12	13	10	11	14	8	23
Percent FG Made	52.4	66.7	61.7	72.7	36.4	72.7	71.4	60.0	61.9	47.6	57.9	66.7	61.5	74.2
Safeties	1	0	1	0	0	1	0	1	0	1	0	0	0	2

CONFERENCE PLAYOFFS

December 24, at Baltimore (Attendance 60,753)

SCORING

BALT.	0	10	7	14	0	0 – 31
OAK.	7	0	14	10	0	6 – 37

First Quarter
- Oak. Davis, 30 yard rush; PAT – Mann (kick)

Second Quarter
- Balt. Laird, 61 yard interception return; PAT – Linhart (kick)
- Balt. Linhart, 35 yard field goal

Third Quarter
- Oak. Casper, 8 yard pass from Stabler; PAT – Mann (kick)
- Balt. Johnson, 87 yard kickoff return; PAT – Linhart (kick)
- Oak. Casper, 10 yard pass from Stabler; PAT – Mann (kick)

Fourth Quarter
- Balt. R. Lee, 1 yard rush; PAT – Linhart (kick)
- Oak. Banazak, 1 yard rush; PAT – Mann (kick)
- Balt. R. Lee, 13 yard rush; PAT – Linhart (kick)
- Oak. Mann, 22 yard field goal

Second Overtime
- Oak. Casper, 10 yard pass from Stabler; PAT – none attempted

TEAM STATISTICS

BALT.		OAK.
22	First Downs – Total	28
10	First Downs – Rushing	8
8	First Downs – Passing	17
4	First Downs – Penalty	3
1	Fumbles – Number	4
0	Fumbles – Lost Ball	2
8	Penalties – Number	7
82	Yards Penalized	65
0	Missed Field Goals	1
82	Offensive Plays	89
301	Net Yards	491
3.7	Average Gain	5.5
0	Giveaways	4
4	Takeaways	0
14	Difference	-4

INDIVIDUAL STATISTICS

BALTIMORE	No	Yds	Avg.	OAKLAND	No	Yds	Avg.
RUSHING							
Mitchell	23	67	2.9	v. Eeghen	19	76	4.0
R. Lee	11	46	4.2	Davis	16	48	3.0
Leaks	8	35	4.4	Banaszak	11	37	3.4
Jones	6	30	5.0	Garrett	1	6	6.0
McCauley	2	9	4.5		47	167	3.6
	50	187	3.7				
RECEIVING							
Mitchell	3	39	13.0	Biletnikoff	7	88	12.6
Scott	2	45	22.5	Branch	6	113	18.8
R. Lee	2	22	11.0	Casper	4	70	17.5
McCauley	2	11	5.5	v. Eeghen	2	39	19.5
Chester	1	30	30.0	Davis	2	35	17.5
Doughty	1	20	20.0		21	345	16.4
Pratt	1	-3	-3.0				
	12	164	13.7				
PUNTING							
D. Lee	12		36.5	Guy	8		46.8
PUNT RETURNS							
Blackwood	2	6	3.0	Colzie	5	42	8.4
Johnson	1	16	16.0	Bradshaw	1	0	0.0
	3	22	7.3		6	42	7.0
KICKOFF RETURNS							
Johnson	3	134	44.7	Garrett	5	169	33.8
McCauley	1	25	25.0	Davis	1	17	17.0
Blackwood	1	17	17.0		6	186	31.0
Nettles	1	17	17.0				
	6	193	32.2				
INTERCEPTION RETURNS							
Laird	2	61	30.5	none			

PASSING

	Att	Comp	Comp. Pct.	Yds	Int	Yds/ Att.	Yds/ Comp	Yards Lost Tackled
BALTIMORE								
Jones	26	12	46.2	164	0	6.3	13.7	6-50
OAKLAND								
Stabler	40	21	52.5	345	2	8.6	16.4	2-21

December 24, at Denver (Attendance 75,011)

SCORING

DENVER	7	7	7	13 – 34
PITTSBURGH	0	14	0	7 – 21

First Quarter
- Denv. Lytle, 7 yard rush; PAT – Turner (kick)

Second Quarter
- Pitt. Bradshaw, 1 yard rush; PAT – Gerela (kick)
- Denv. Armstong, 10 yard rush; PAT – Turner (kick)
- Pitt. Harris, 1 yard rush; PAT – Gerela (kick)

Third Quarter
- Denv. Odoms, 30 yard pass from Morton; PAT – Turner (kick)

Fourth Quarter
- Pitt. Brown, 1 yard pass from Bradshaw; PAT – Gerela (kick)
- Denv. Turner, 44 yard field goal
- Denv. Turner, 25 yard field goal
- Denv. Dolbin, 34 yard pass from Morton; PAT – Turner (kick)

TEAM STATISTICS

DENVER		PITTS.
15	First Downs – Total	18
5	First Downs – Rushing	10
9	First Downs – Passing	8
1	First Downs – Penalty	0
3	Fumbles – Number	2
1	Fumbles – Lost Ball	1
3	Penalties – Number	10
20	Yards Penalized	67
0	Missed Field Goals	0
61	Offensive Plays	76
258	Net Yards	307
4.2	Average Gain	4.0
0	Giveaways	3
3	Takeaways	0
+3	Difference	-3

INDIVIDUAL STATISTICS

DENVER	No	Yds	Avg.	PITTSBURGH	No	Yds	Avg.
RUSHING							
Armstrong	11	44	4.0	Harris	28	92	3.3
Lytle	12	26	2.2	Bradshaw	4	21	5.3
Keyworth	5	20	4.0	Bleier	7	14	2.0
Jensen	4	13	3.3		39	127	3.3
Morton	5	0	0.0				
	37	103	2.8				
RECEIVING							
Odoms	5	43	8.6	Stallworth	4	80	20.0
Moses	2	45	22.5	Harris	4	20	5.0
Jensen	2	33	16.5	Cunningham	3	42	14.0
Dolbin	1	34	34.0	Maxson	3	11	3.7
Armstrong	1	9	9.0	Bleier	2	10	5.0
	11	164	14.9	Grossman	1	10	10.0
				Swann	1	6	6.0
				Brown	1	1	1.0
					19	180	9.5
PUNTING							
Dilts	5		37.6	Engles	5		40.8
PUNT RETURNS							
Thompson	2	5	2.5	Smith	4	31	7.8
Schultz	1	4	4.0				
Upchurch	1	3	3.0				
	4	12	3.0				
KICKOFF RETURNS							
Upchurch	3	48	19.3	Smith	4	80	20.0
Schultz	1	27	27.0	Maxson	1	24	24.0
	4	85	21.3		5	104	20.8
INTERCEPTION RETURNS							
T. Jackson	2	49	24.5	none			
B. Jackson	1	15	15.0				
	3	64	31.3				

PASSING

	Att	Comp	Comp. Pct.	Yds	Int	Yds/ Att.	Yds/ Comp	Yards Lost Tackled
DENVER								
Morton	23	11	47.8	164	0	7.1	14.9	1-9
PITTSBURGH								
Bradshaw	37	19	51.4	180	3	4.9	9.5	0

1977 N.F.C. — Eastern Division

DALLAS COWBOYS 12-2 Tom Landry

Scores of Each Game		
16	Minnesota	10
41	N.Y. GIANTS	21
23	TAMPA BAY	7
30	St. Louis	24
34	WASHINGTON	16
16	Philadelphia	10
37	DETROIT	0
24	N.Y. Giants	10
17	ST. LOUIS	24
13	Pittsburgh	28
14	Washington	7
24	PHILADELPHIA	14
42	San Francisco	35
14	DENVER	6

Use Name	Pos.	Hgt	Wgt	Age	Int	Pts
Pat Donovan	OT	6'4"	255	24		
Andy Frederick	OT	6'6"	241	22		
Ralph Neely	OT	6'5"	255	33		
Rayfield Wright	OT	6'7"	260	32		
Jim Cooper	OG-C	6'5"	252	21		
Burton Lawless	OG	6'4"	250	23		
Tom Rafferty	OG-C	6'3"	250	23		
Herbert Scott	OG	6'2"	250	24		
John Fitzgerald	C	6'5"	260	29		
Too Tall Jones	DE	6'9"	265	26		
Harvey Martin	DE	6'5"	252	26		
David Stalls	DE	6'4"	236	21		
Larry Cole	DT-DE	6'4"	260	30		
Bill Gregory	DT	6'5"	260	27		
Jethro Pugh	DT	6'6"	250	33		
Randy White	DT	6'4"	245	24		

Use Name	Pos.	Hgt	Wgt	Age	Int	Pts
Bob Breunig	LB	6'2"	227	24	1	
Guy Brown	LB	6'4"	215	22		
Mike Hegman	LB	6'1"	225	24	1	
Tom Henderson	LB	6'2"	220	24	3	6
Bruce Huther	LB	6'1"	217	23		
D.D. Lewis	LB	6'2"	215	31	1	
Benny Barnes	DB	6'1"	195	26		
Cliff Harris	DB	6'	192	28	5	
Randy Hughes	DB	6'4"	208	24	2	
Aaron Kyle	DB	5'10"	185	23	1	
Mel Renfro	DB	6'	192	35	2	
Mark Washington	DB	5'10"	187	29	2	
Charlie Waters	DB	6'1"	198	28	3	6

Jim Eidson – Injury
Greg Schaum – Knee Injury
Charley Young – Knee Injury

Use Name	Pos.	Hgt	Wgt	Age	Int	Pts
Glenn Carano	QB	6'3"	195	21		
Roger Staubach	QB	6'2"	202	35		18
Danny White	QB	6'2"	192	25		
Doug Dennison	HB	6'1"	204	25		6
Tony Dorsett	HB	5'11"	192	23		78
Preston Pearson	HB	6'1"	206	32		30
Larry Brinson	FB	6'	214	23		6
Scott Laidlaw	FB	6'	205	24		6
Robert Newhouse	FB	5'10"	205	27		24
Tony Hill	WR	6'2"	196	21		
Butch Johnson	WR	6'1"	191	23		6
Drew Pearson	WR	6'	183	26		12
Golden Richards	WR	6'	180	26		18
Billy Joe DuPree	TE	6'4"	226	27		18
Jay Saldi	TE	6'3"	224	22		18
Efren Herrera	K	5'9"	190	26		93

Percy Howard – Injury

WASHINGTON REDSKINS 9-5 George Allen

Scores of Each Game		
17	N.Y. Giants	20
10	ATLANTA	6
24	ST. LOUIS	14
10	Tampa Bay	0
16	Dallas	34
6	N.Y. GIANTS	17
23	PHILADELPHIA	17
3	Baltimore	10
17	Philadelphia	14
10	GREEN BAY	9
7	DALLAS	14
10	Buffalo	0
26	St. Louis	20
17	LOS ANGELES	14

Use Name	Pos.	Hgt	Wgt	Age	Int	Pts
George Starke	OT	6'5"	249	29		
Tim Stokes	OT	6'5"	252	27		
Tony Hermeling	OG	6'5"	255	31		
Dan Nugent	OG	6'3"	250	24		
Ron Saul	OG	6'2"	254	29		
Ted Fritsch	C	6'2"	242	27		
Len Hauss	C	6'2"	235	35		
Bob Kuziel	C-OT	6'5"	255	27		
Dallas Hickman	DE	6'6"	235	25		
Dennis Johnson	DE	6'4"	260	25		
Karl Lorch	DE	6'3"	253	27		
Ron McDole	DE	6'3"	265	37	2	
Bill Wynn	DE	6'4"	245	28		
Bill Brundige	DT	6'5"	270	28		
Dave Butz	DT	6'7"	285	27		
Diron Talbert	DT	6'5"	255	33		

Use Name	Pos.	Hgt	Wgt	Age	Int	Pts
Mike Curtis	LB	6'2"	232	34	1	
Brad Dusek	LB	6'2"	214	26	1	
Chris Hanburger	LB	6'2"	218	36		
Joe Harris	LB	6'1"	225	24		
Harold McLinton	LB	6'2"	235	30		
Stu O'Dell	LB	6'1"	220	25		
Rusty Tillman	LB	6'2"	230	31		
Pete Wysocki	LB	6'2"	225	28		
Eddie Brown	DB	5'11"	190	25	1	
Pat Fischer	DB	5'10"	170	37		
Windlan Hall (from MINN.)	DB	5'11"	175	27		
Ken Houston	DB	6'3"	198	32	5	
Joe Lavender	DB	6'4"	190	28	4	
Mark Murphy	DB	6'4"	210	22		
Brig Owens	DB	5'11"	190	34		
Jake Scott	DB	6'	188	32	3	
Gerard Williams	DB	6'1"	184	25	4	

Use Name	Pos.	Hgt	Wgt	Age	Int	Pts
Billy Kilmer	QB	6'	204	37		
Joe Theismann	QB	6'	184	27		6
Bob Brunet	HB	6'1"	205	31		
Clarence Harmon	HB	5'11"	190	21		6
Mike Thomas	HB	5'11"	190	24		30
Calvin Hill	FB	6'3"	227	30		6
Eddie Moss	FB	6'	215	28		
John Riggins	FB	6'2"	230	28		12
Danny Buggs	WR	6'2"	185	24		6
Frank Grant	WR	5'11"	181	27		18
Larry Jones	WR	5'10"	170	26		
Howard Satterwhite (to BALT.)	WR	5'11"	185	24		
Charley Taylor	WR	6'3"	210	35		
Jean Fugett	TE	6'3"	226	25		30
Jerry Smith	TE	6'2"	208	34		
Mike Bragg	K	5'11"	186	30		
Mark Moseley	K	5'11"	205	29		82

Brian Fryer – Injury

ST. LOUIS CARDINALS 7-7 Don Coryell

Scores of Each Game		
0	Denver	7
16	CHICAGO	13
14	Washington	24
24	DALLAS	30
21	Philadelphia	17
49	NEW ORLEANS	31
28	N.Y. GIANTS	0
27	Minnesota	7
24	Dallas	17
21	PHILADELPHIA	16
14	MIAMI	55
7	N.Y. Giants	27
20	WASHINGTON	26
7	Tampa Bay	17

Use Name	Pos.	Hgt	Wgt	Age	Int	Pts
Dan Dierdorf	OT	6'4"	288	28		
Roger Finnie	OT	6'3"	248	30		
Brad Oates	OT	6'6"	274	23		
Dan Audick	OG	6'3"	244	22		
Conrad Dobler	OG	6'3"	253	26		6
Keith Wortman	OG-OT-C	6'2"	262	27		
Bob Young	OG	6'2"	279	34		
Tom Banks	C	6'1"	244	29		
Tom Brahaney	C	6'2"	246	25		
Bob Bell	DE	6'4"	257	29		
Ron Yankowski	DE	6'5"	258	30		
John Zook	DE	6'5"	254	29		
Charlie Davis	DT	6'1"	268	25		6
Mike Dawson	DT	6'4"	274	23		
Walt Patulski	DT	6'6"	267	27		

Ray White – Knee Injury

Use Name	Pos.	Hgt	Wgt	Age	Int	Pts
Kurt Allerman	LB	6'3"	222	22		
Mark Arneson	LB	6'2"	224	27	2	
Tim Black	LB	6'2"	215	22		
Tim Kearney	LB	6'2"	225	26		
Marv Kellum	LB	6'2"	225	25	1	
Steve Neils	LB	6'2"	218	26		
Eric Williams	LB	6'2"	217	22		
Carl Allen	DB	6'	185	21	1	
Bill Bradley	DB	5'11"	190	30		
Rondy Colbert	DB	5'9"	165	23		
Robert Giblin	DB	6'2"	210	24		
Lee Nelson	DB	5'10"	183	23	4	
Ken Reaves	DB	6'3"	208	32	2	
Mike Sensibaugh	DB	5'11"	190	28	3	6
Jeff Severson	DB	6'1"	185	27	1	
Perry Smith	DB	6'1"	198	26		
Roger Wehrli	DB	6'1"	193	29	5	

Use Name	Pos.	Hgt	Wgt	Age	Int	Pts
Billy Donckers	QB	6'1"	207	26		
Jim Hart	QB	6'2"	210	33		
Steve Pisarkiewicz	QB	6'2"	205	23		
Steve Jones	HB	6'	198	26		18
Jerry Latin	HB	5'10"	186	24		12
Terry Metcalf	HB	5'10"	185	25		36
Wayne Morris	FB	6'	208	23		54
Jim Otis	FB	6'	226	29		12
Mel Gray	WR	5'9"	178	28		30
Ike Harris	WR	6'3"	205	24		18
Ken Stone	WR-DB	6'1"	180	26		
Pat Tilley	WR	5'10"	171	24		
J.V. Cain	TE	6'4"	221	26		12
Jackie Smith	TE	6'4"	226	37		6
Jim Bakken	K	6'	198	36		56
Duane Carrell (from NY JETS)	K	5'10"	178	27		
Terry Joyce	K	6'6"	227	23		

PHILADELPHIA EAGLES 5-9 Dick Vermeil

Scores of Each Game		
13	TAMPA BAY	3
0	Los Angeles	20
13	Detroit	17
28	N.Y. Giants	10
17	ST. LOUIS	21
10	DALLAS	16
17	Washington	23
28	NEW ORLEANS	7
14	WASHINGTON	17
16	St. Louis	21
6	New England	14
14	Dallas	24
17	N.Y. GIANTS	14
27	N.Y. JETS	0

Use Name	Pos.	Hgt	Wgt	Age	Int	Pts
Ed George	OT	6'4"	270	31		
Donnie Green	OT	6'7"	261	29		
Dennis Nelson	OT	6'5"	260	31		
Stan Walters	OT	6'6"	270	29		
Wade Key	OG	6'4"	245	30		
Tom Luken	OG	6'3"	253	27		
Jerry Sisemore	OG	6'4"	260	26		
Dennis Franks	C	6'1"	236	24		
Guy Morriss	C	6'4"	255	26		
Lem Burnham	DE	6'4"	228	30		
Carl Hairston	DE	6'3"	245	24		
Manny Sistrunk	DE	6'5"	276	30		
Art Thoms	DE-MG	6'5"	250	30		
Johnny Jackson	MG	6'2"	250	24		
Charles Johnson	MG	6'3"	262	25		
Pete Lazetich	MG	6'3"	245	27		

Use Name	Pos.	Hgt	Wgt	Age	Int	Pts
Bill Bergey	LB	6'2"	245	32	2	
John Bunting	LB	6'1"	220	27		
Tom Ehlers	LB	6'2"	218	25		
Frank LeMaster	LB	6'2"	231	25		
Drew Mahalic	LB	6'4"	225	24		
James Reed	LB	6'2"	230	22		
Jerry Tautolo	LB	6'2"	235	23		
Herman Edwards	DB	6'	194	23	6	
Eric Johnson	DB	6'1"	192	25		
Randy Logan	DB	6'1"	195	26	5	
Larry Marshall	DB	5'10"	195	27		
Mark Mitchell	DB	6'1"	180	22		
John Outlaw	DB	5'10"	180	31	2	
Deac Sanders	DB	6'1"	178	27	6	

Use Name	Pos.	Hgt	Wgt	Age	Int	Pts
Roman Gabriel	QB	6'4"	225	37		
Ron Jaworski	QB	6'2"	195	26		30
John Walton	QB	6'2"	210	29		
Herb Lusk	HB	6'	190	24		18
Wilbert Montgomery	HB	5'10"	195	22		18
Tom Sullivan	HB	6'	190	27		12
James Betterson	FB	6'	210	23		6
Cleveland Franklin	FB	6'2"	216	22		
Mike Hogan	FB	6'2"	215	22		6
Harold Carmichael	WR	6'7"	225	27		42
Wally Henry	WR	5'8"	170	22		
Vince Papale	WR	6'2"	195	31		
Larry Sievers	WR	6'4"	204	23		
Charlie Smith	WR	6'1"	185	27		24
Keith Krepfle	TE	6'3"	225	25		18
Richard Osborne	TE	6'3"	230	23		
Ove Johannson	K	5'10"	175	29		4
Spike Jones	K	6'2"	195	30		
Nick Mike-Mayer (from ATL)	K	5'8"	187	27		44
Horst Muhlmann	K	6'1"	211	37		26

NEW YORK GIANTS 5-9 John McVay

Scores of Each Game		
20	WASHINGTON	17
21	Dallas	41
3	Atlanta	17
10	PHILADELPHIA	28
20	SAN FRANCISCO	17
17	Washington	6
0	St. Louis	28
13	DALLAS	24
10	Tampa Bay	0
7	CLEVELAND	21
13	Cincinnati	30
27	ST. LOUIS	7
14	Philadelphia	17
9	CHICAGO	*12

Use Name	Pos.	Hgt	Wgt	Age	Int	Pts
Mike Gibbons	OT	6'4"	262	26		
Gordon Gravelle	OT	6'5"	252	28		
Ron Mikolajczyk	OG	6'3"	275	27		
Tom Mullen	OT	6'3"	250	25		
Brad Benson	OG	6'3"	255	21		
Bill Ellenbogen	OG-OT	6'5"	255	26		
John Hicks	OG	6'2"	258	26		
Doug Van Horn	OG-OT	6'2"	243	33		
Karl Chandler	C	6'5"	250	25		
Ralph Hill	C	6'1"	245	27		
Jack Gregory	DE	6'6"	250	32		
Gary Jeter	DE	6'4"	250	22		
George Martin	DE	6'4"	245	24	1	6
Troy Archer	DT	6'4"	250	22		
John Mendenhall	DT	6'1"	255	28		
Jim Pietrzak	DT	6'5"	260	24		
J.T. Turner	DT	6'3"	250	24		

Dick Leavitt – Knee Injury

Use Name	Pos.	Hgt	Wgt	Age	Int	Pts
Harry Carson	LB	6'2"	235	23		
Brian Kelley	LB	6'3"	222	26	1	
Dan Lloyd	LB	6'2"	225	23		
Frank Marion	LB	6'3"	230	26		
Andy Selfridge	LB	6'4"	220	28		
Brad Van Pelt	LB	6'5"	235	26	2	
Bill Bryant	DB	5'11"	195	26	3	6
Ernie Jones	DB	6'3"	180	24	1	
Larry Mallory	DB	5'11"	185	25	1	
Clyde Powers	DB	6'1"	195	26	1	
Beasley Reece	DB	6'1"	186	23		
Ray Rhodes	DB	5'11"	185	26	2	
Jim Stienke	DB	5'11"	182	26		

Use Name	Pos.	Hgt	Wgt	Age	Int	Pts
Randy Dean	QB	6'3"	195	22		
Jerry Golsteyn	QB	6'4"	210	23		
Joe Pisarcik	QB	6'4"	220	25		12
Gordon Bell	HB	5'9"	180	23		
Bob Hammond	HB	5'10"	170	25		24
Harold Hart	HB	6'	211	24		
Doug Kotar	HB	5'11"	203	26		12
Larry Csonka	FB	6'3"	233	30		6
Willie Spencer	FB	6'3"	235	24		18
Larry Watkins	FB	6'2"	230	30		
Ed Marshall	WR	6'5"	200	29		
Emery Moorehead	WR	6'2"	210	23		6
Johnny Perkins	WR	6'2"	205	24		
Jim Robinson	WR	5'9"	170	24		18
Boyd Brown	TE	6'4"	216	25		
Al Dixon	TE	6'5"	220	23		
Gary Shirk	TE	6'1"	220	27		12
Joe Danelo	K	5'9"	166	23		61
Dave Jennings	K	6'4"	203	25		

Marsh White – Wrist Injury

*Overtime

DALLAS COWBOYS

RUSHING

Last Name	No	Yds	Avg	TD
Dorsett	208	1007	4.8	12
Newhouse	180	721	4.0	3
P. Pearson	89	341	3.8	1
Staubach	51	171	3.4	3
Dennison	12	60	5.0	1
Brinson	8	28	3.5	1
D. Pearson	2	22	11.0	0
Laidlaw	9	15	1.7	0
DuPree	3	9	3.0	0
D. White	1	−2	−2.0	0
Johnson	1	−3	−3.0	0

RECEIVING

Last Name	No	Yds	Avg	TD
D. Pearson	48	870	18	2
P. Pearson	46	535	12	4
Dorsett	29	273	9	1
DuPree	28	347	12	3
Richards	17	225	13	3
Newhouse	16	106	7	1
Johnson	12	135	11	1
Saldi	11	108	10	2
Laidlaw	5	60	12	1
Hill	2	21	11	0
Dennison	1	9	9	0

PUNT RETURNS

Last Name	No	Yds	Avg	TD
Johnson	50	423	8	0
Hill	10	124	12	0
Harris	1	−2	−2	0

KICKOFF RETURNS

Last Name	No	Yds	Avg	TD
Johnson	22	536	24	0
Brinson	17	409	24	0
Hill	3	64	21	0
Dennison	1	30	30	0
DuPree	0	24	—	0
Henderson	1	8	8	0

PASSING – PUNTING – KICKING

PASSING

Last Name	Att	Comp	%	Yds	Yd/Att	TD	Int–%	RK
Staubach	361	210	58	2620	7.3	18	9– 2	1
D. White	10	4	40	35	3.5	0	1– 10	
Dorsett	1	1	100	34	34.0	0	0– 0	

PUNTING

Last Name	No	Avg
D. White	80	39.6
Herrera	2	22.0

KICKING

Last Name	XP	Att	%	FG	Att	%
Herrera	39	41	95	18	29	62

WASHINGTON REDSKINS

RUSHING

Last Name	No	Yds	Avg	TD
Thomas	228	806	3.5	3
Harmon	94	310	3.3	0
Hill	69	257	3.7	0
Riggins	68	203	3.0	0
Theismann	29	149	5.1	1
Kilmer	10	20	2.0	0
Brunet	3	6	2.0	0
Jones	1	1	1.0	0

RECEIVING

Last Name	No	Yds	Avg	TD
Fuggett	36	631	17	5
Grant	34	480	14	3
Thomas	28	245	9	2
Buggs	26	341	13	1
Hill	18	154	9	1
Taylor	14	158	11	0
Harmon	14	119	9	1
Riggins	7	95	14	0
Jones	5	55	11	0
Smith	1	6	6	0

PUNT RETURNS

Last Name	No	Yds	Avg	TD
Brown	57	452	8	0

KICKOFF RETURNS

Last Name	No	Yds	Avg	TD
Brown	34	852	25	0
Murphy	3	44	15	0
Tillman	3	39	13	0
Jones	2	42	21	0
Brunet	2	40	20	0
Moss	2	35	18	0
Harmon	1	18	18	0
Buggs	0	17	—	0

PASSING – PUNTING – KICKING

PASSING

Last Name	Att	Comp	%	Yds	Yd/Att	TD	Int–%	RK
Kilmer	201	99	49	1187	5.9	8	7– 4	6
Thiesmann	182	84	46	1097	6.0	7	9– 5	11

PUNTING

Last Name	No	Avg
Bragg	91	38.5

KICKING

Last Name	XP	Att	%	FG	Att	%
Moseley	19	19	100	21	37	57

ST. LOUIS CARDINALS

RUSHING

Last Name	No	Yds	Avg	TD
Metcalf	149	739	5.0	4
Morris	165	661	4.0	8
Otis	99	334	3.4	2
Latin	56	208	3.7	2
Jones	24	77	3.2	3
Wehrli	1	19	19.0	0
Hart	11	18	1.6	0
Gray	1	−1	−1.0	0
Joyce	1	−13	−13.0	0
Carrell	2	−15	−7.5	0

RECEIVING

Last Name	No	Yds	Avg	TD
Harris	40	547	14	3
Gray	38	782	21	5
Metcalf	34	403	12	2
Cain	25	328	13	2
Morris	24	222	9	1
Jones	12	66	6	0
Latin	9	89	10	0
Tilley	5	64	13	0
J. Smith	5	49	10	1
Otis	2	18	9	0
Stone	1	40	40	0

PUNT RETURNS

Last Name	No	Yds	Avg	TD
Metcalf	14	108	8	0
Tilley	13	111	9	0
Bradley	11	77	7	0
Nelson	1	4	4	0
Severson	1	0	0	0

KICKOFF RETURNS

Last Name	No	Yds	Avg	TD
Metcalf	32	772	24	0
Jones	8	132	17	0
Bradley	7	75	19	0
Latin	3	79	26	0
Nelson	3	68	23	0
Allerman	2	39	20	0
Morris	2	39	20	0
Otis	1	16	16	0
Wortman	1	15	15	0
Oates	1	11	11	0
J. Smith	1	15	15	0
P. Smith	1	10	10	0

PASSING – PUNTING – KICKING

PASSING

Last Name	Att	Comp	%	Yds	Yd/Att	TD	Int–%	RK
Hart	355	186	52	2542	7.2	13	20– 6	7
Donckers	5	5	100	38	7.6	0	0– 0	
Metcalf	5	3	60	27	5.4	1	1– 20	
Joyce	1	1	100	1	1.0	0	0– 0	

PUNTING

Last Name	No	Avg
Carrell	63	36.7
Joyce	22	38.7

KICKING

Last Name	XP	Att	%	FG	Att	%
Bakken	35	36	97	7	16	44

PHILADELPHIA EAGLES

RUSHING

Last Name	No	Yds	Avg	TD
Hogan	155	546	3.5	0
Sullivan	125	363	2.9	0
Betterson	62	233	3.8	1
Lusk	52	229	4.4	2
Montgomery	45	183	4.1	2
Jaworski	40	127	3.2	5
Lemaster	1	30	30.0	0
Smith	2	13	6.5	0
Franklin	1	0	0.0	0
Henry	1	−2	−2.0	0

RECEIVING

Last Name	No	Yds	Avg	TD
Carmichael	46	665	15	7
Smith	33	464	14	4
Krepfle	27	530	20	3
Sullivan	26	223	9	2
Hogan	19	118	6	1
Lusk	5	102	20	1
Betterson	4	41	10	0
Montgomery	3	18	6	0
Henry	2	16	8	0
Papale	1	15	15	0
Osborne	1	6	6	0

PUNT RETURNS

Last Name	No	Yds	Avg	TD
Marshall	46	489	11	0
Henry	2	25	13	0
Mitchell	2	4	2	0

KICKOFF RETURNS

Last Name	No	Yds	Avg	TD
Montgomery	23	619	27	1
Marshall	20	455	23	0
Lusk	1	23	23	0
Betterson	1	13	13	0

PASSING – PUNTING – KICKING

PASSING

Last Name	Att	Comp	%	Yds	Yd/Att	TD	Int–%	RK
Jaworski	346	166	48	2183	6.3	18	21– 6	10
Gabriel	3	1	33	15	5.0	0	0– 0	

PUNTING

Last Name	No.	Avg.
Jones	93.	37.2
Mike-Mayer	1	23.0

KICKING

Last Name	XP	Att	%	FG	Att	%
Muhlmann	17	19	89	3	8	38
Mike-Mayer	14	14	100	10	22	45
Johansson	1	3	33	1	4	25

NEW YORK GIANTS

RUSHING

Last Name	No	Yds	Avg	TD
Hammond	154	577	3.7	3
Kotar	132	480	3.6	2
Csonka	134	464	3.5	1
Spencer	62	184	3.0	3
Watkins	19	71	3.7	0
Bell	16	63	3.9	0
Pisarcik	27	57	2.1	2
Moorehead	1	5	5.0	0
Golsteyn	3	−4	−1.3	0

RECEIVING

Last Name	No	Yds	Avg	TD
Robinson	22	422	19	3
Perkins	20	279	14	0
Hammond	19	136	7	0
Shirk	16	280	18	2
Kotar	15	73	5	0
Moorehead	12	143	12	1
Marshall	7	178	25	0
Dixon	6	78	13	0
Bell	4	33	8	0
Spencer	4	20	5	0
Csonka	2	20	10	0
Watkins	1	9	9	0

PUNT RETURNS

Last Name	No	Yds	Avg	TD
Hammond	32	334	10	1
Robinson	7	87	12	0
Steinke	5	30	6	0
Bell	1	0	0	0
Reece	1	−5	−5	0

KICKOFF RETURNS

Last Name	No	Yds	Avg	TD
Hammond	19	419	22	0
Bell	12	235	20	0
Reece	7	159	23	0
Moorehead	4	65	16	0
Spencer	3	44	15	0
Shirk	3	38	13	0
Kotar	2	36	18	0
Kelley	1	20	20	0
Hill	1	11	11	0
Selfridge	1	9	9	0
Mallory	1	0	0	0

PASSING – PUNTING – KICKING

PASSING

Last Name	Att	Comp	%	Yds	Yd/Att	TD	Int–%	RK
Pisarcik	241	103	43	1346	5.6	4	14– 6	13
Golsteyn	70	31	44	416	5.9	2	8– 11	

PUNTING

Last Name	No	Avg.
Jennings	100	39.9

KICKING

Last Name	XP	Att	%	FG	Att	%
Danelo	19	20	95	14	23	61

MINNESOTA VIKINGS 9-5 Bud Grant

Scores of Each Game		
10	DALLAS	16
9	Tampa Bay	3
19	GREEN BAY	7
14	DETROIT	7
22	CHICAGO	16
3	Los Angeles	35
14	Atlanta	7
7	ST. LOUIS	27
42	CINCINNATI	10
7	Chicago	10
13	Green Bay	6
28	SAN FRANCISCO	27
13	Oakland	35
30	Detroit	21

Use Name	Pos.	Hgt	Wgt	Age	Int	Pts
Bart Buetow	OT	6'5"	250	26		
Steve Riley	OT	6'6"	258	24		
Ron Yary	OT	6'6"	255	31		
Charlie Goodrum	OG	6'3"	256	27		
Wes Hamilton	OG	6'3"	255	24		
Dennis Swilley	OG-OT	6'4"	241	22		
Ed White	OG-OT	6'2"	270	30		
Doug Dumler	C	6'3"	242	26		
Mick Tinglehoff	C	6'1"	240	37		
Carl Eller	DE	6'6"	247	35		2
Joey Jackson	DE-DT	6'4"	262	28		
Jim Marshall	DE	6'3"	240	39		
Mark Mullaney	DE	6'6"	242	24		
Alan Page	DT	6'5"	245	32		
Doug Sutherland	DT	6'3"	250	29		
James White	DT	6'3"	263	23		
Matt Blair	LB	6'5"	229	25	1	6
Wally Hilgenberg	LB	6'3"	229	34		
Fred McNeill	LB	6'2"	229	25	1	
Jeff Siemon	LB	6'2"	237	27	1	
Scott Studwell	LB	6'2"	224	23	1	
Nate Allen	DB	5'10"	174	29	1	
Joe Blahak	DB	5'9"	185	27		
Bobby Bryant	DB	6'	170	33	4	
Tom Hannon	DB	6'	193	22		
Paul Krause	DB	6'3"	205	35	2	
Phil Wise	DB	6'	193	28	1	
Jeff Wright	DB	5'11"	190	28	1	
Nate Wright	DB	5'11"	180	30	3	6
Tommy Kramer	QB	6'1"	199	22		
Bob Lee	QB	6'2"	195	32		
Fran Tarkenton	QB	6'1"	185	37		
Chuck Foreman	HB	6'2"	207	26		54
Sammy Johnson	HB-FB	6'	226	24		12
Manfred Moore	HB	6'	200	26		
Mark Kellar	FB	6'	225	25		
Brent McClanahan	FB	5'10"	202	26		18
Robert Miller	FB	5'11"	204	24		
Bob Grim	WR	6'	188	32		
Ahmad Rashad	WR	6'2"	200	27		12
Sammy White	WR	5'11"	189	23		54
Steve Craig	TE	6'3"	231	26		
Bob Tucker (from NY GIANTS)	TE	6'3"	230	32		12
Stu Voigt	TE	6'1"	225	29		6
Neil Clabo	K	6'2"	200	24		
Fred Cox	K	5'10"	200	38		49

CHICAGO BEARS 9-5 Jack Pardee

Scores of Each Game		
30	DETROIT	20
13	St. Louis	16
24	NEW ORLEANS	42
24	LOS ANGELES	23
16	Minnesota	22
10	ATLANTA	16
26	Green Bay	0
0	Houston	47
28	KANSAS CITY	27
10	MINNESOTA	7
31	Detroit	14
10	Tampa Bay	0
21	GREEN BAY	10
12	N.Y. Giants	*9

Use Name	Pos.	Hgt	Wgt	Age	Int	Pts
Ted Albrecht	OT-OG	6'4"	253	22		
Dan Jiggetts	OT	6'4"	276	23		
Dennis Lick	OT	6'3"	268	23		
Jeff Sevy	OT-DT-DE	6'5"	261	26		
Fred Dean	OG	6'3"	253	22		
Noah Jackson	OG	6'2"	273	26		
Revie Sorey	OG	6'2"	259	23		
Dan Neal	C-OG	6'4"	248	28		
Dan Peiffer	C	6'3"	251	26		
Mike Hartenstine	DE	6'3"	257	24		
Jerry Meyers	DE-DT	6'4"	245	23		
Billy Newsome	DE	6'4"	250	29		
Wally Chambers	DT-DE	6'6"	259	26		
Jim Osborne	DT	6'3"	251	27		
Don Rydalch	DT	6'4"	257	25		
Roger Stilwell	DT-DE	6'6"	258	25		
Waymond Bryant	LB	6'3"	239	25		
Doug Buffone	LB	6'1"	227	33	1	
Gary Campbell	LB	6'1"	218	25		
Tom Hicks	LB	6'4"	225	24	1	
Jerry Muckensturm	LB	6'4"	226	23		
Don Rives	LB	6'2"	231	26		
Mel Rogers	LB	6'2"	230	30		
Craig Clemons	DB	5'11"	191	28		
Allan Ellis	DB	5'10"	175	26	6	
Gary Fencik	DB	6'1"	192	23	4	
Virgil Livers	DB	5'9"	178	25	2	
Doug Plank	DB	6'	201	24	4	
Terry Schmidt	DB	6'	176	25		
Mike Spivey	DB	6'	194	23		
Len Walterscheid	DB	5'11"	190	22		
Bob Avellini	QB	6'2"	206	24		6
Vince Evans	QB	6'2"	216	22		
Mike Phipps	QB	6'2"	211	29		
Art Best	HB	6'1"	205	24		
Johnny Musso	HB-FB	5'11"	196	27		12
Walter Payton	HB	5'11"	205	23		96
Robin Earl	FB	6'5"	247	22		6
Roland Harper	FB	6'	209	24		
Brian Baschnagel	WR	6'	193	23		6
Bo Rather	WR	6'1"	189	26		12
Steve Rivera (from SF)	WR	5'11"	183	23		
Steve Schubert	WR	5'10"	188	26		6
James Scott	WR	6'1"	191	25		18
Chuck Bradley (from SD)	TE	6'6"	239	26		
Greg Latta	TE	6'3"	230	24		24
Bob Parsons	TE	6'4"	232	27		
Bob Thomas	K	5'10"	174	25		69

Lionel Antoine — Knee Injury
Larry Schreiber — Injury

DETROIT LIONS 6-8 Tommy Hudspeth

Scores of Each Game		
20	Chicago	30
23	NEW ORLEANS	19
17	PHILADELPHIA	13
7	Minnesota	14
10	GREEN BAY	6
7	San Francisco	28
0	Dallas	37
20	SAN DIEGO	0
6	Atlanta	17
16	TAMPA BAY	7
14	CHICAGO	31
9	Green Bay	10
13	Baltimore	10
21	MINNESOTA	30

Use Name	Pos.	Hgt	Wgt	Age	Int	Pts
Rocky Freitas	OT	6'6"	275	31		
Craig Hertwig	OT	6'8"	270	25		
Dave Simonsen	OT	6'6"	248	25		
Jim Yarbrough	OT	6'6"	270	30		
Gary Anderson	OG	6'3"	250	21		
Lynn Boden	OG	6'5"	270	24		
Russ Bolinger	OG-OT	6'5"	255	22		
Mark Markovich	OG-C	6'5"	255	24		
Mel Mitchell	OG-C	6'3"	260	24		
Jon Morris	C	6'4"	250	34		
Jim Mitchell	DE	6'3"	250	28		
Ernie Price	DE	6'4"	245	26		
Ken Sanders	DE	6'5"	245	27		
John Woodcock	DE	6'3"	240	23		
Doug English	DT	6'5"	255	24		2
Larry Hand	DT	6'4"	245	37		
Herb Orvis	DT	6'5"	255	30		
Tony Daykin	LB	6'1"	215	22		
Jim Laslavic	LB	6'2"	240	25	1	
Mike McGraw	LB	6'2"	225	23		
Paul Naumoff	LB	6'1"	215	32		
Ed O'Neil	LB	6'3"	235	24		6
Garth Ten Napel	LB	6'1"	215	23		
Charlie Weaver	LB	6'2"	225	28	1	
Len Barney	DB	6'	190	31	3	
James Hunter	DB	6'3"	195	23	6	
Dick Jauron	DB	6'	190	26	3	
Levi Johnson	DB	6'3"	200	26	2	
Reggie Pinkney	DB	5'11"	190	22	2	6
Randy Rich (to DENVER)	DB	5'10"	175	23		
Charlie West	DB	6'1"	195	31	1	
Walt Williams	DB	6'	185	23		
Gary Danielson	QB	6'2"	195	25		
Greg Landry	QB	6'4"	205	30		
Joe Reed	QB	6'1"	195	29		
Andy Bolton	HB	6'1"	205	23		
Dexter Bussey	HB	6'1"	210	25		30
Rick Kane	HB	5'11"	200	22		24
Eddie Payton (from CLEVE)	HB	5'8"	175	26		12
Glenn Capriola	FB	5'11"	219	22		
Marv Hubbard	FB	6'1"	235	31		6
Horace King	FB	5'10"	210	24		6
Luther Blue	WR	5'11"	190	21		6
J.D. Hill	WR	6'1"	185	28		6
Ray Jarvis	WR	5'11"	190	28		6
Leonard Thompson	WR-HB	5'10"	190	25		12
David Hill	TE	6'2"	220	23		12
Bill Larson (from WASH)	TE	6'3"	225	23		
Charlie Sanders	TE	6'4"	230	31		6
Mitch Hoopes	K	6'1"	204	24		
Steve Mike-Mayer	K	6'	180	29		43
Wilbur Summers	K	6'4"	220	23		

Lawrence Gaines — Knee Injury
Ken Long — Injury
Benny Ricardo — Shoulder Injury

GREEN BAY PACKERS 4-10 Bart Starr

Scores of Each Game		
24	New Orleans	20
10	HOUSTON	16
7	Minnesota	19
7	CINCINNATI	17
6	Detroit	10
13	Tampa Bay	0
0	CHICAGO	26
10	Kansas City	20
6	LOS ANGELES	24
9	Washington	10
6	MINNESOTA	13
10	DETROIT	9
10	Chicago	21
16	SAN FRANCISCO	14

Use Name	Pos.	Hgt	Wgt	Age	Int	Pts
Dick Himes	OT	6'4"	260	31		
Steve Knutson	OT-OG	6'3"	254	25		
Greg Koch	OT	6'4"	265	22		
Mark Koncar	OT	6'5"	268	24		
Dennis Havig	OG	6'2"	251	28		
Melvin Jackson	OG	6'1"	267	23		
Bob Kowalkowski	OG	6'3"	245	33		
Rick Scribner	OG	6'4"	257	21		
Darrel Gofourth	C	6'3"	260	22		
Larry McCarren	C	6'3"	248	25		
Bob Barber	DE-DT	6'3"	240	25		
Mike Butler	DE	6'5"	265	23		
Ezra Johnson	DE	6'4"	240	21		
Clarence Williams	DE-DT	6'5"	255	30		
Herb McMath	DT	6'4"	250	22		
Dave Pureifory	DT	6'1"	255	28		
Dave Roller	DT	6'2"	270	27		
Fred Carr	LB	6'5"	240	31	1	
Jim Carter	LB	6'3"	245	28		
Jim Cheyunski	LB	6'2"	220	31		
Jim Gueno	LB	6'2"	220	23		
Don Hansen	LB	6'3"	228	33		
Blane Smith	LB	6'3"	238	23		
Tom Toner	LB	6'3"	235	27	1	
Gary Weaver	LB	6'1"	225	28		
Willie Buchanon	DB	6'	190	26	2	6
Johnnie Gray	DB	5'11"	185	23	1	
Steve Luke	DB	6'2"	205	23	4	
Mike McCoy	DB	5'11"	183	24	4	
Tim Moresco	DB	5'11"	176	22		
Terry Randolph	DB	6'	184	22		
Steve Wagner	DB	6'2"	208	23		
Lynn Dickey	QB	6'4"	220	27		
Brian Dowling	QB	6'2"	210	30		
David Whitehurst	QB	6'2"	204	22		6
Will Harrell	HB	5'9"	182	24		12
Terdell Middleton	HB	6'	195	22		6
Nate Simpson	HB	5'10"	176	22		
Jim Culbreath	FB	6'	209	24		
Barty Smith	FB	6'4"	240	25		18
Eric Torkelson	FB	6'2"	194	25		6
Keith Hartwig (from MINN)	WR	6'	186	23		
Steve Odom	WR	5'8"	174	24		18
Ken Payne (to PHIL)	WR	6'1"	185	26		6
Ollie Smith	WR	6'2"	200	28		
Audra Thompson	WR-HB	6'	186	25		
Randy Vataha	WR	5'10"	170	28		
Bert Askon	TE	6'3"	225	31		
Rich McGeorge	TE	6'4"	230	28		6
David Beverly	K	6'2"	180	27		
Chester Marcol	K	6'	190	27		50

TAMPA BAY BUCCANEERS 2-12 John McKay

Scores of Each Game		
3	Philadelphia	13
3	MINNESOTA	9
7	Dallas	23
0	WASHINGTON	10
23	Seattle	30
0	GREEN BAY	13
10	San Francisco	20
0	Los Angeles	31
0	N.Y. GIANTS	10
7	Detroit	16
0	ATLANTA	17
0	CHICAGO	10
33	New Orleans	14
17	ST. LOUIS	7

Use Name	Pos.	Hgt	Wgt	Age	Int	Pts
Darryl Carlton	OT	6'6"	270	24		
Blanchard Carter	OT	6'4"	250	22		
Dave Reavis	OT-OG	6'5"	250	27		
Randy Johnson	OG	6'2"	255	24		
Dan Medlin	OG	6'4"	255	27		
Steve Wilson	OG-C	6'3"	265	23		
Jeff Winans	OG-OT	6'5"	265	25		
Dan Ryczek	C	6'3"	250	28		
Charles Hannah	DE	6'5"	250	22		
Glenn Robinson	DE	6'6"	245	25		
Council Rudolph	DE	6'3"	255	27		
Leroy Selmon	DE	6'3"	260	22		
Greg Johnson (from BALT & CHI)	DT-MG-DE	6'4"	240	23	1	6
Bill Kollar	MG	6'4"	256	24		
Dave Pear	MG	6'2"	250	24		
Rik Bonness	LB	6'3"	220	23		
Paul Harris	LB	6'3"	225	22		
Cecil Johnson	LB	6'2"	220	22	1	
Mike Lemon	LB	6'2"	220	26		
Dave Lewis	LB	6'4"	230	22	2	
Dewey Selmon	LB	6'1"	250	23	2	
Richard Wood	LB	6'2"	215	24	4	12
Cedric Brown	DB	6'1"	190	23	2	
Mark Cotney	DB	6'	205	25	1	
Curtis Jordan	DB	6'2"	185	23	1	
Reggie Pierson	DB	5'11"	185	24		
Danny Reece	DB	5'11"	190	22		
Mike Washington	DB	6'3"	190	24	5	6
Jeris White	DB	5'11"	180	24	4	
Jeb Blount	QB	6'3"	200	23		
Parnell Dickinson	QB	6'2"	185	24		
Randy Hedberg	QB	6'3"	200	22		
Gary Huff	QB	6'1"	195	26		
Louis Carter	HB	5'11"	209	24		12
Anthony Davis	HB	5'10"	190	24		6
Jack Wender	HB	6'	210	23		
Ricky Bell	FB	6'2"	220	21		6
Jimmy DuBose	FB	5'11"	215	22		
Ed Williams	FB	6'2"	245	27		
Isaac Hagins	WR	5'9"	180	23		
John McKay	WR	5'11"	185	24		
Larry Mucker	WR	5'11"	190	22		
Morris Owens	WR	6'	190	24		18
George Ragsdale	WR-HB	5'11"	185	23		
Gary Butler	TE	6'3"	235	26		
Bob Moore	TE	6'3"	225	28		
Dana Nafziger	TE	6'1"	220	23		
Jack Novak	TE	6'4"	240	24		
Charles Waddell	TE	6'5"	235	24		
Dave Green	K	5'11"	205	27		17
Allan Leavitt	K	5'11"	176	21		20
Larry Swider	K	6'2"	193	22		

Howard Fest — Injury
Tody Smith — Injury
Mike Boryla — Knee Injury

*—Overtime

MINNESOTA VIKINGS

Rushing

Last Name	No.	Yds	Avg	TD
Foreman	270	1112	4.1	6
McClanahan	95	324	3.4	1
Johnson	55	217	3.9	2
Miller	46	152	3.3	0
Kellar	7	15	2.1	0
Tarkenton	15	6	0.4	0
Kramer	10	3	0.3	0
Lee	12	−8	−0.7	0

Receiving

Last Name	No.	Yds	Avg	TD
Rashad	51	681	13	2
S. White	41	760	19	9
Foreman	38	308	8	3
McClanahan	34	276	8	2
Miller	27	246	9	0
Voigt	20	212	11	1
Tucker	15	200	13	2
Johnson	4	21	5	0
Grim	3	65	22	0
Craig	1	14	14	0

Punt Returns

Last Name	No.	Yds	Avg	TD
Moore	47	277	6	0
Grim	11	69	6	0

Kickoff Returns

Last Name	No.	Yds	Avg	TD
Moore	24	524	22	0
S. White	7	113	16	0
Miller	5	66	13	0
McClanahan	4	90	23	0
Kellar	3	37	12	0
Grim	1	4	4	0
Swilley	1	0	0	0

Passing – Punting – Kicking

PASSING	Att	Comp	%	Yds	Yd/Att	TD	Int–%	RK
Tarkenton	258	155	60	1734	6.7	9	14– 5	3
Lee	72	42	58	522	7.3	4	4– 6	
Kramer	57	30	53	425	7.5	5	4– 7	
Krause	1	1	100	11	11.0	1	0– 0	

PUNTING	No	Avg
Clabo	83	39.8

KICKING	XP	Att	%	FG	Att	%
Cox	25	29	86	8	17	47

CHICAGO BEARS

Rushing

Last Name	No.	Yds	Avg	TD
Payton	339	1852	5.5	14
Harper	120	457	3.8	0
Earl	56	233	4.2	1
Musso	37	132	3.6	2
Avellini	37	109	2.9	1
Best	6	20	3.3	0
Rather	2	8	4.0	0
Baschnagel	1	0	0.0	0
Evans	1	0	0.0	0

Receiving

Last Name	No.	Yds	Avg	TD
Scott	50	809	16	3
Payton	27	269	10	2
Latta	26	335	13	4
Harper	19	142	8	0
Rather	17	294	17	2
Schubert	8	119	15	0
Earl	6	32	5	0
Baschnagel	4	50	13	0
Musso	3	13	4	0
Rivera	1	7	7	0

Punt Returns

Last Name	No.	Yds	Avg	TD
Schubert	31	291	9	1
Walterscheid	6	59	10	0
Livers	6	46	8	0
Baschnagel	3	54	18	0
Rivera	3	7	2	0
Plank	1	21	21	0

Kickoff Returns

Last Name	No.	Yds	Avg	TD
Baschnagel	23	557	24	1
Evans	13	253	19	0
Best	6	127	21	0
Musso	5	100	20	0
Walterscheid	3	59	20	0
Harper	3	44	15	0
Payton	2	95	48	0
Earl	2	38	19	0

Passing – Punting – Kicking

PASSING	Att	Comp	%	Yds	Yd/Att	TD	Int–%	RK
Avellini	293	154	53	2004	6.8	11	18– 6	9
Phipps	5	3	60	5	1.0	0	0– 0	
Parsons	4	4	100	61	15.3	0	0– 0	
Harper	2	0	0	0	0.0	0	0– 0	
Baschnagel	1	0	0	0	0.0	0	0– 0	

PUNTING	No	Avg
Parsons	80	40.4

KICKING	XP	Att	%	FG	Att	%
Thomas	27	30	90	14	27	52

DETROIT LIONS

Rushing

Last Name	No.	Yds	Avg	TD
King	155	521	3.4	1
Kane	124	421	3.4	4
Bussey	85	338	4.0	4
Hubbard	38	150	3.9	1
Landry	25	99	4.0	0
Thompson	31	91	2.9	1
Danielson	7	62	8.9	0
Payton	4	13	3.3	0
D. Hill	4	10	2.5	0
Bolton	3	4	1.3	0
Reed	1	3	3.0	0
Summers	1	0	0.0	0
Blue	1	−6	−6.0	0

Receiving

Last Name	No.	Yds	Avg	TD
King	40	238	6	0
D. Hill	32	465	14	2
Jarvis	28	353	13	1
J.D. Hill	24	247	10	1
Kane	18	186	10	0
C. Sanders	14	170	12	1
Bussey	11	116	11	1
Blue	8	90	11	1
Thompson	7	42	6	0
Hubbard	6	36	6	0
Payton	2	10	5	0
Bolton	1	6	6	0

Punt Returns

Last Name	No.	Yds	Avg	TD
Payton	30	290	10	1
Jauron	11	41	4	0
Rich	2	18	9	0
Kane	1	13	13	0
Blue	1	0	0	0

Kickoff Returns

Last Name	No.	Yds	Avg	TD
Payton	22	548	25	1
Kane	16	376	24	0
Bolton	6	86	14	0
Thompson	5	84	17	0
Rich	5	73	15	0
Hunter	4	95	24	0
Blue	1	24	24	0
Hubbard	1	18	18	0
Boden	1	14	14	0
Woodcock	1	12	12	0

Passing – Punting – Kicking

PASSING	Att	Comp	%	Yds	Yd/Att	TD	Int–%	RK
Landry	240	135	56	1359	5.7	6	7– 3	4
Danielson	100	42	42	445	4.5	1	5– 5	
Reed	40	13	33	150	3.8	0	4– 10	
Summers	1	1	100	5	5.0	0	0– 0	
Thompson	1	0	0	0	0.0	0	0– 0	
D. Hill	1	0	0	0	0.0	0	0– 0	
Payton	1	0	0	0	0.0	0	0– 0	

PUNTING	No	Avg
Summers	93	36.8
Hoopes	6	39.2

KICKING	XP	Att	%	FG	Att	%
Mike-Mayer	19	21	90	8	19	42

GREEN BAY PACKERS

Rushing

Last Name	No.	Yds	Avg	TD
Ba. Smith	166	554	3.3	2
Torkelson	103	309	3.0	1
Simpson	60	204	3.4	0
Harrell	60	140	2.3	1
Middleton	35	97	2.8	0
Whitehurst	14	55	3.9	1
Culbreath	12	53	4.4	0
Dickey	5	24	4.8	0
Odom	1	6	6.0	0
Beverly	2	−3	−1.5	0

Receiving

Last Name	No.	Yds	Avg	TD
Ba. Smith	37	340	9	1
Odom	27	549	20	3
O. Smith	22	357	16	0
Harrell	19	194	10	0
McGeorge	17	142	8	1
Torkelson	11	107	10	0
Vataha	10	109	11	0
Payne	7	99	14	1
Simpson	5	19	4	0
Askon	2	51	26	0
Thompson	2	12	6	0
Culbreath	2	6	3	0
Middleton	1	27	27	0

Punt Returns

Last Name	No.	Yds	Avg	TD
Harrell	28	253	9	1
Gray	10	68	7	0

Kickoff Returns

Last Name	No.	Yds	Avg	TD
Odom	23	468	20	0
Wagner	6	62	10	0
Culbreath	5	82	16	0
Middleton	4	141	35	1
Thompson	4	82	21	0
Harrell	3	48	16	0
Torkelson	2	36	18	0
Moresco	1	15	15	0
Gofourth	1	13	13	0
Gueno	1	0	0	0
Simpson	1	0	0	0

Passing – Punting – Kicking

PASSING	Att	Comp	%	Yds	Yd/Att	TD	Int–%	RK
Dickey	220	113	51	1346	6.1	5	14– 6	12
Whitehurst	105	50	48	634	6.0	1	7– 7	
Harrell	1	1	100	33	33.0	0	0– 0	
Dowling	1	0	0	0	0.0	0	0– 0	

PUNTING	No	Avg
Beverly	85	39.9

KICKING	XP	Att	%	FG	Att	%
Marcol	11	14	79	13	21	62

TAMPA BAY BUCCANEERS

Rushing

Last Name	No.	Yds	Avg	TD
Bell	148	436	2.9	1
Davis	95	297	3.1	1
DuBose	71	284	4.0	0
Williams	63	198	3.1	0
L. Carter	59	117	2.0	2
Hedberg	9	35	3.9	0
Blount	5	26	5.2	0
Ragsdale	3	21	7.0	0
Huff	8	10	1.3	0
Hagins	1	2	2.0	0
Green	1	0	0.0	0
Owens	2	−2	−1.0	0

Receiving

Last Name	No.	Yds	Avg	TD
Owens	34	655	19	3
Hagins	15	196	13	0
McKay	12	164	14	0
DuBose	11	89	8	0
Bell	11	88	8	0
Williams	10	67	7	0
L. Carter	10	65	7	0
Nafziger	9	119	13	0
Davis	8	91	11	0
Mucker	4	59	15	0
Reece	2	59	30	0
Novak	2	24	12	0
Ragsdale	2	17	9	0
Butler	1	21	21	0

Punt Returns

Last Name	No.	Yds	Avg	TD
Reece	31	274	9	0
Hagins	17	85	5	0

Kickoff Returns

Last Name	No.	Yds	Avg	TD
Hagins	21	493	23	0
Davis	15	277	18	0
Reece	3	72	24	0
Ragsdale	3	68	23	0
Nafziger	1	4	4	0

Passing – Punting – Kicking

PASSING	Att	Comp	%	Yds	Yd/Att	TD	Int–%	RK
Huff	138	67	49	889	6.4	3	13– 9	
Hedberg	90	25	28	244	2.7	0	10– 11	
Blount	89	37	42	522	5.9	0	7– 8	
Green	2	2	100	59	29.5	0	0– 0	
L. Carter	2	0	0	0	0.0	0	0– 0	

PUNTING	No	Avg
Green	98	40.3

KICKING	XP	Att	%	FG	Att	%
Leavitt	5	5	100	5	10	50
Green	5	6	83	4	7	71

LOS ANGELES RAMS 10-4 Chuck Knox

Scores of Each Game		
6	Atlanta	17
20	PHILADELPHIA	0
34	SAN FRANCISCO	14
23	Chicago	24
14	NEW ORLEANS	7
35	MINNESOTA	3
26	New Orleans	27
31	TAMPA BAY	0
24	Green Bay	6
23	San Francisco	10
9	Cleveland	0
20	OAKLAND	14
23	ATLANTA	7
14	Washington	17

Use Name	Pos.	Hgt	Wgt	Age	Int	Pts
Doug France	OT	6'5"	272	24		
Winston Hill	OT	6'4"	272	35		
Jeff Williams	OT	6'4"	256	22		
John Williams	OT	6'3"	265	31		
Dennis Harrah	OG	6'5"	257	24		
Greg Horton	OG	6'4"	245	26		
Tom Mack	OG	6'3"	250	33		
Jackie Slater	OG	6'4"	270	23		
Rick Nuzum	C	6'4"	238	25		
Rich Saul	C	6'3"	250	29		
Al Cowlings	DE-DT	6'5"	245	30		
Fred Dryer	DE	6'6"	240	31		
Jack Youngblood	DE	6'4"	242	27		
Larry Brooks	DT	5'3"	255	27		
Mike Fanning	DT	6'6"	260	24		
Cody Jones	DT-DE	6'5"	240	26		

Use Name	Pos.	Hgt	Wgt	Age	Int	Pts
Bob Brudzinski	LB	6'4"	230	22	2	
Carl Ekern	LB	6'3"	220	23		
Kevin McClain	LB	6'2"	227	22		
Bob Pifferini	LB	6'2"	226	27		
Jack Reynolds	LB	6'1"	232	29		
Isiah Robertson	LB	6'3"	225	28	1	
Jim Youngblood	LB	6'3"	239	27	2	6
Nolan Cromwell	DB	6'1"	196	22		
Dave Elmendorf	DB	6'1"	195	28	2	
Monte Jackson	DB	5'11"	189	24	5	
Rod Perry	DB	5'9"	170	23	1	
Bill Simpson	DB	6'1"	180	25	6	
Pat Thomas	DB	5'9"	180	23	5	
Jackie Wallace	DB	6'3"	198	26	1	

Willie Miller — Elbow Injury
Rob Scribner — Thigh Injury

Use Name	Pos.	Hgt	Wgt	Age	Int	Pts
Vince Ferragamo	QB	6'3"	208	23		
Pat Haden	QB	5'11"	182	24		12
Joe Namath	QB	6'2"	200	34		
Sonny Collins	HB	6'1"	195	24		
Lawrence McCutcheon	HB	6'1"	205	27		54
Wendell Tyler	HB	5'10"	188	22		18
Cullen Bryant	FB	6'1"	235	26		
John Cappelletti	FB-HB	6'1"	217	25		36
Jim Jodat	FB	5'11"	210	23		12
Rod Phillips	FB	6'	220	24		6
Harold Jackson	WR	5'10"	175	31		36
Ron Jessie	WR	6'	185	29		
Freeman Johns	WR	6'1"	175	23		
Dwight Scales	WR	6'2"	170	24		6
Billy Waddy	WR	5'11"	185	23		6
Terry Nelson	TE	6'2"	230	26		18
Charlie Young	TE	6'4"	235	26		6
Raphael Septien	K	5'9"	171	23		86
Glenn Walker	K	6'1"	210	25		

ATLANTA FALCONS 7-7 Leeman Bennett

Scores of Each Game		
17	LOS ANGELES	6
6	Washington	10
17	N.Y. GIANTS	3
7	San Francisco	0
0	Buffalo	3
16	Chicago	10
7	MINNESOTA	14
3	SAN FRANCISCO	10
17	DETROIT	6
20	New Orleans	21
17	Tampa Bay	0
10	NEW ENGLAND	16
7	Los Angeles	23
35	NEW ORLEANS	7

Use Name	Pos.	Hgt	Wgt	Age	Int	Pts
Bob Adams	OT	6'2"	218	31		
Warren Bryant	OT	6'6"	270	21		
Phil McKinnely	OT-TE	6'4"	248	24		
Greg Kindle	OG	6'4"	265	26		
Dave Scott	OG	6'4"	285	23		
R.C. Thielemann	OG-C	6'4"	247	22		
Paul Ryczek	C	6'2"	230	25		
Jeff Van Note	OG-C	6'2"	247	31		
Edgar Fields	DE	6'2"	255	23		
Claude Humphrey	DE	6'5"	265	33		
Jeff Merrow (to OAK)	DE-LB	6'4"	230	24		
Jeff Yeates	DE-OG	6'3"	248	26		
Jim Bailey	DT	6'5"	260	29		
Wilson Faumuina	DT	6'5"	275	23		
Bob Jordan	DT	6'6"	255	22		
Mike Lewis	DT	6'3"	261	28		
Mike Tilleman	DT	6'5"	278	32		

Use Name	Pos.	Hgt	Wgt	Age	Int	Pts
Greg Brezing	LB	6'1"	221	31		
Rick Kay (from LA)	LB	6'4"	235	27		
Fulton Kuykendall	LB	6'5"	225	24		
Ron McCartney	LB	6'1"	220	23		
Dewey McClain	LB	6'3"	236	23		
Ralph Ortega	LB	6'2"	220	24	4	6
Robert Pennywell	LB	6'1"	222	22	2	6
Andy Spivia	LB	6'2"	218	22		
Ray Brown	DB	6'1"	202	28	5	
Rick Byas	DB	5'9"	180	26	3	6
Ray Easterling	DB	6'	192	27	4	
Rolland Lawrence	DB	5'10"	179	26	7	
Tom Moriarty	DB	6'	185	24		
Frank Reed	DB	5'11"	193	23		

Len Gotshalk — Knee Injury

Use Name	Pos.	Hgt	Wgt	Age	Int	Pts
Steve Bartkowski	QB	6'4"	213	24		
Scott Hunter	QB	6'2"	205	29		6
June Jones	QB	6'4"	200	24		
Kim McQuilken	QB	6'2"	203	26		
Bubba Bean	HB	5'11"	195	22		
Mike Esposito	HB-DB	6'	183	24	1	
Secedrick McIntyre	HB	5'10"	190	23		6
Haskel Stanback	HB	6'	210	25		36
Monroe Eley	FB	6'2"	210	28		6
Billy Ray Pritchett	FB	6'3"	230	26		
Woody Thompson	FB	6'1"	228	25		6
Karl Farmer	WR	5'11"	165	23		
Wallace Francis	WR	5'11"	190	25		6
Al Jenkins	WR	5'10"	172	25		24
Billy Ryckman	WR	5'11"	172	22		6
Grey McCrary	TE	6'3"	230	25		6
Jim Mitchell	TE	6'2"	236	29		
John James	K	6'3"	200	28		
Fred Steinfort	K	5'11"	180	25		31

SAN FRANCISCO FORTY-NINERS 5-9 Ken Meyer

Scores of Each Game		
0	Pittsburgh	27
15	MIAMI	19
14	Los Angeles	34
0	ATLANTA	7
17	N.Y. Giants	20
28	DETROIT	7
20	TAMPA BAY	10
10	Atlanta	3
10	New Orleans	7
10	LOS ANGELES	23
20	NEW ORLEANS	17
27	Minnesota	28
35	DALLAS	42
14	Green Bay	16

Use Name	Pos.	Hgt	Wgt	Age	Int	Pts
John Ayers	OT-OG	6'5"	247	24		
Cas Banaszak	OT	6'3"	252	31		
Jean Barrett	OT-C	6'6"	250	26		
Keith Fahnhorst	OT	6'6"	263	25		
Ron Singleton	OT	6'7"	245	25		
Steve Lawson	OG	6'3"	257	28		
Johnny Miller	OG	6'1"	247	23		
Woody Peoples	OG	6'2"	250	34		
Randy Cross	C	6'3"	250	23		
Tony Cline	DE	6'2"	237	29		
Cedric Hardman	DE	6'3"	244	28		
Tommy Hart	DE	6'3"	246	32		
Bill Cooke	DT-DE	6'5"	243	26		
Cleveland Elam	DT	6'4"	251	25		
Ed Galigher	DT	6'4"	247	26		
Jimmy Webb	DT	6'5"	245	25		

Use Name	Pos.	Hgt	Wgt	Age	Int	Pts
Mike Baldassin	LB	6'1"	218	22		6
Ed Bradley	LB	6'2"	225	27		
Bruce Elia	LB	6'1"	220	24		
Willie Harper	LB	6'2"	205	27	1	
Dale Mitchell	LB	6'3"	225	24		
Howard Stidham	LB	6'2"	214	22		
Skip Vanderbundt	LB	6'3"	225	30	1	
Dave Washington	LB	6'5"	230	29	2	
Stan Black	DB	6'	196	21		
Mike Burns	DB	6'	181	23		
Anthony Leonard	DB	5'11"	165	24	1	
Eddie Lewis	DB	6'	174	23		
Al Matthews	DB	5'11"	190	29		
Ralph McGill	DB	5'11"	180	27	1	
Mel Phillips	DB	6'	185	35	2	
Bruce Taylor	DB	6'	178	29		

Bruce Rhodes — Injury

Use Name	Pos.	Hgt	Wgt	Age	Int	Pts
Scott Bull	QB	6'5"	215	24		
Steve DeBerg	QB	6'2"	205	23		
Jim Plunkett	QB	6'3"	207	29		6
Paul Hofer	HB	6'	193	25		
Dave Williams	HB-FB	6'2"	200	23		6
Del Williams	HB	6'	195	26		54
Bob Ferrell	FB	6'	219	24		6
Wilbur Jackson	FB	6'1"	213	25		42
Kenny Harrison	WR	6'	164	23		6
Jim Lash	WR	6'2"	200	25		
Willie McGee	WR	5'11"	178	27		
Gene Washington	WR	6'1"	180	30		30
Tom Mitchell	TE	6'2"	225	33		
Jim O'Bradovich	TE	6'2"	227	24		
Paul Seal	TE	6'4"	223	25		6
Ray Wersching	K	5'11"	210	27		53
Tom Wittum	K	6'1"	198	27		5

NEW ORLEANS SAINTS 3-11 Hank Stram

Scores of Each Game		
20	GREEN BAY	24
19	Detroit	23
42	Chicago	24
0	SAN DIEGO	14
7	Los Angeles	14
31	St. Louis	49
27	LOS ANGELES	26
7	Philadelphia	28
7	SAN FRANCISCO	10
21	ATLANTA	20
17	San Francisco	20
13	N.Y. JETS	16
14	TAMPA BAY	33
7	Atlanta	35

Use Name	Pos.	Hgt	Wgt	Age	Int	Pts
Dave Hubbard	OT	6'7"	270	21		
Dave Lafary	OT	6'7"	280	22		
Marv Montgomery	OT	6'6"	255	29		
Don Morrison	OT	6'5"	250	27		
Mike Watson	OT	6'6"	272	21		
Robert Woods (from NYJ)	OT-OG	6'5"	259	27		
Kurt Schumacher	OG	6'3"	246	24		
Terry Stieve	OG	6'2"	242	23		
Emanuel Zanders	OG	6'1"	248	26		
Lee Gross	C	6'3"	235	24		
John Hill	C	6'2"	246	27		
John Watson	C-OG	6'4"	244	28		
Joe Campbell	DE	6'6"	254	22		
Elois Grooms	DE	6'4"	250	24	6	
Bob Pollard	DE-DT	6'2"	236	28		6
Oakley Dalton	DT	6'6"	285	25		
Mike Fultz	DT	6'5"	278	23		
Derland Moore	DT	6'4"	253	25		
Elex Price	DT	6'3"	265	27		

Use Name	Pos.	Hgt	Wgt	Age	Int	Pts
Ken Bordelon	LB	6'4"	226	23		
Joe Federspiel	LB	6'1"	230	27		
Pat Hughes	LB	6'2"	225	30	1	
Rick Kingrea	LB	6'1"	222	28		
Jim Merlo	LB	6'1"	220	25	1	6
Greg Westbrooks	LB	6'2"	217	24		
Wade Bosarge	DB	5'10"	175	21		
Craig Cassady	DB	5'11"	175	23		
Clarence Chapman	DB	5'10"	185	23	1	6
Chuck Crist	DB	6'2"	205	26	4	
Ernie Jackson	DB	5'10"	176	27	1	
Jim Marsalis	DB	5'11"	190	31	1	
Tom Myers	DB	5'11"	180	26	1	6
Jimmy Stewart	DB	5'11"	190	22		

Mo Spencer — Neck Injury

Use Name	Pos.	Hgt	Wgt	Age	Int	Pts
Bobby Douglass	QB	6'3"	228	30		
Archie Manning	QB	6'3"	200	28		30
Bobby Scott	QB	6'1"	197	28		
Greg Boykin	HB	6'	225	23		
Chuck Muncie	HB-FB	6'3"	220	24		42
Mike Strachan	HB	6'	200	24		
Tony Galbreath	FB	6'1"	230	23		18
Kim Jones	FB	6'4"	243	25		
Larry Burton	WR	6'1"	193	25		
John Gilliam (from CHI)	WR	6'1"	187	32		6
Don Herrmann	WR	6'2"	193	30		
Richard Mauti	WR	6'	190	23		
Joel Parker	WR	6'5"	215	25		
Leonard Willis (to BUFF)	WR	5'10"	180	24		
Henry Childs	TE	6'2"	220	26		54
Jim Thaxton	TE-WR	6'2"	242	28		6
Tom Blanchard	K	6'	180	29		
Richie Szaro	K	5'11"	204	29		44

Tinker Owens — Injury

LOS ANGELES RAMS

RUSHING

Last Name	No.	Yds.	Avg	TD
McCutcheon	294	1238	4.2	7
Cappelletti	178	598	3.4	5
Tyler	61	317	5.2	3
Phillips	37	183	4.9	1
Haden	29	106	3.7	2
Bryant	6	42	7.0	0
Waddy	2	34	17.0	0
Nelson	3	31	10.3	0
Jodat	5	15	3.0	1
H. Jackson	1	6	6.0	0
Namath	4	5	1.3	0
Ferragamo	1	0	0.0	0

RECEIVING

Last Name	No.	Yds	Avg	TD
H. Jackson	48	666	14	6
Nelson	31	401	13	3
Cappelletti	28	228	8	1
McCutcheon	25	274	11	2
Waddy	23	355	15	1
Jessie	9	139	15	0
Scales	5	104	21	1
Young	5	35	7	1
Bryant	4	28	7	0
Wallace	1	13	13	0
Phillips	1	5	5	0
Tyler	1	3	3	0
Jodat	1	2	2	1

PUNT RETURNS

Last Name	No.	Yds	Avg	TD
Waddy	31	219	7	0
Bryant	20	141	7	0

KICKOFF RETURNS

Last Name	No.	Yds	Avg	TD
Tyler	24	523	22	0
Jodat	6	129	22	0
Bryant	2	35	18	0
Phillips	1	10	10	0
Ekern	1	8	8	0

PASSING – PUNTING – KICKING

PASSING

Last Name	Att	Comp	%	Yds	Yd/Att	TD	Int–	%	RK
Haden	215	122	56	1551	7.2	11	6–	3	2
Namath	107	50	47	606	5.7	3	5–	5	
Ferragamo	15	9	60	83	5.5	2	0–	0	
Walker	1	1	100	13	13.0	0	0–	0	

PUNTING

Last Name	No	Avg
Walker	73	35.2

KICKING

Last Name	XP	Att	%	FG	Att	%
Septien	32	35	91	18	30	60

ATLANTA FALCONS

RUSHING

Last Name	No.	Yds.	Avg	TD
Stanback	247	873	3.5	6
Thompson	132	478	3.6	1
Eley	97	273	2.8	1
Esposito	34	101	3.0	0
Hunter	28	70	2.5	1
McIntyre	13	65	5.0	0
Bartkowski	18	13	0.7	0
Jenkins	2	7	3.5	0
Pritchett	3	7	2.3	0
Francis	4	6	1.5	0
Farmer	1	4	4.0	0
McQuilken	2	–1	–0.5	0
Mitchell	1	–6	–6.0	0

RECEIVING

Last Name	No.	Yds	Avg	TD
Jenkins	39	677	17	4
Stanback	30	261	9	0
Francis	26	390	15	1
Mitchell	17	178	10	0
Thompson	12	56	5	0
Eley	9	60	7	0
McCrary	2	48	24	1
Farmer	2	39	20	0
McIntyre	1	27	27	1
Ryckman	1	5	5	0
Esposito	1	–1	–1	0

PUNT RETURNS

Last Name	No.	Yds	Avg	TD
Lawrence	51	352	7	0
Ryckman	7	40	6	0
Byas	1	10	10	0

KICKOFF RETURNS

Last Name	No.	Yds	Avg	TD
Farmer	21	419	20	0
Moriarty	8	136	17	0
Francis	1	22	22	0
Eley	1	16	16	0
McIntyre	1	15	15	0
Lawrence	1	13	13	0
Ryckman	1	0	0	0

PASSING – PUNTING – KICKING

PASSING

Last Name	Att	Comp	%	Yds	Yd/Att	TD	Int–	%	RK
Hunter	151	70	46	898	6.0	2	3–	2	
Bartkowski	136	64	47	796	5.9	5	13–	10	
McQuilkin	7	5	71	47	6.7	1	0–	0	
Jones	1	1	100	–1	–1.0	0	0–	0	
Esposito	1	0	0	0	0.0	0	0–	0	
James	1	0	0	0	0.0	0	0–	0	

PUNTING

Last Name	No	Avg
James	105	41.4

KICKING

Last Name	XP	Att	%	FG	Att	%
Steinfort	13	13	100	6	11	55

SAN FRANCISCO FORTY-NINERS

RUSHING

Last Name	No.	Yds.	Avg	TD
Del Williams	268	931	3.5	7
Jackson	179	780	4.4	7
Ferrell	41	160	3.9	1
Hofer	34	106	3.1	0
Plunkett	28	71	2.5	1
Bull	5	20	4.0	0
Harrison	6	15	2.5	0
Da. Williams	2	6	3.0	0
McGee	1	–3	–3.0	0

RECEIVING

Last Name	No.	Yds	Avg	TD
G. Washington	32	638	20	5
Jackson	22	169	8	0
Del Williams	20	179	9	2
T. Mitchell	19	226	12	0
Harrison	15	217	14	1
Seal	13	230	18	1
Hofer	5	46	9	0
Lash	3	22	7	0
McGee	2	27	14	0
O'Bradovich	2	16	8	0
Ferrell	2	12	6	0
Cline	1	15	15	0

PUNT RETURNS

Last Name	No.	Yds	Avg	TD
Leonard	22	154	7	0
Black	13	38	3	0
Da. Williams	1	60	60	0
Elia	1	1	1	0
Baldassin	1	0	0	0

KICKOFF RETURNS

Last Name	No.	Yds	Avg	TD
Hofer	36	871	24	0
Da. Williams	4	122	31	1
Ferrell	3	35	12	0
Leonard	1	68	68	0
O'Bradovich	1	9	9	0
Del Williams	1	9	9	0

PASSING – PUNTING – KICKING

PASSING

Last Name	Att	Comp	%	Yds	Yd/Att	TD	Int–	%	RK
Plunkett	248	128	52	1693	6.8	9	14–	6	8
Bull	24	7	29	89	3.7	0	2–	8	
Wittum	3	1	33	15	5.0	0	0–	0	
Harrison	1	0	0	0	0.0	0	0–	0	
Del Williams	1	0	0	0	0.0	0	1–	100	

PUNTING

Last Name	No	Avg
Wittum	77	36.4

KICKING

Last Name	XP	Att	%	FG	Att	%
Wersching	23	23	100	10	17	59
Wittum	2	4	50	1	2	50

NEW ORLEANS SAINTS

RUSHING

Last Name	No.	Yds.	Avg	TD
Muncie	201	811	4.0	6
Galbreath	168	644	3.8	3
Strachan	55	271	4.9	0
Manning	39	270	6.9	0
Douglass	2	23	11.5	0
Jones	8	23	2.9	0
Scott	4	11	2.8	0
Thaxton	1	–3	–3.0	0
Boykin	5	–9	–1.8	0
Herrmann	1	–17	–17.0	0

RECEIVING

Last Name	No.	Yds	Avg	TD
Galbreath	41	265	7	0
Childs	33	518	16	9
Herrmann	32	408	13	0
Muncie	21	248	12	1
Thaxton	14	211	15	1
Gilliam	11	133	12	1
Mauti	4	71	18	0
Strachan	3	26	9	0
Boykin	3	21	7	0
Burton	1	13	13	0
Jones	1	9	9	0
Parker	1	7	7	0
Grooms	1	3	3	1

PUNT RETURNS

Last Name	No.	Yds	Avg	TD
Mauti	37	281	8	0

KICKOFF RETURNS

Last Name	No.	Yds	Avg	TD
Mauti	27	609	23	0
Chapman	15	385	26	1
Willis	8	148	19	0
Boykin	5	76	15	0
Campbell	2	33	17	0
Jones	2	23	12	0
Kingrea	2	21	11	0
Stewart	1	33	33	0
Muncie	1	19	19	0
Thaxton	0	8	–	0

PASSING – PUNTING – KICKING

PASSING

Last Name	Att	Comp	%	Yds	Yd/Att	TD	Int–	%	RK
Manning	205	113	55	1284	6.3	8	9–	4	5
Scott	82	36	44	516	6.3	3	8–	10	
Douglass	31	16	52	130	4.2	1	3–	10	
Blanchard	3	1	33	3	1.0	1	1–	38	

PUNTING

Last Name	No	Avg
Blanchard	82	42.4
Scott	3	31.7

KICKING

Last Name	XP	Att	%	FG	Att	%
Szaro	29	31	94	5	12	42

BALTIMORE COLTS 10-4 Ted Marchibroda

Scores of Each Game		
29	Seattle	14
20	N.Y. Jets	12
17	BUFFALO	14
45	MIAMI	28
17	Kansas City	6
3	New England	17
31	PITTSBURGH	21
10	WASHINGTON	3
31	Buffalo	13
33	N.Y. JETS	12
13	Denver	27
6	Miami	17
10	DETROIT	13
30	NEW ENGLAND	24

Use Name	Pos.	Hgt	Wgt	Age	Int	Pts
Wade Griffin	OT	6'5"	231	23		
George Kunz	OT	6'5"	262	30		
David Taylor	OT	6'4"	264	27		
Elmer Collett	OG	6'4"	241	32		
Ken Huff	OG	6'4"	262	24		
Robert Pratt	OG	6'4"	248	26		6
Bob Van Duyne	OG-OT	6'5"	244	25		
Forrest Blue	C	6'5"	260	31		
Ken Mendenhall	C	6'3"	250	29		
Fred Cook	DE	6'3"	243	25		
John Dutton	DE	6'7"	266	26		
Ron Fernandes	DE	6'4"	255	25		
Mike Barnes	DT	6'6"	256	26		
Joe Ehrmann	DT	6'5"	264	28		
Ken Novak	DT	6'7"	264	23		
Dan Dickel	LB	6'3"	230	25		
Derrel Luce	LB	6'3"	227	24		
Tom McCleod	LB	6'3"	224	26	2	
Sanders Shiver	LB	6'2"	222	22		
Ed Simonini	LB	6'	210	23	1	
Stan White	LB	6'1"	223	27	7	
Tim Baylor	DB	6'6"	191	23		
Lyle Blackwood	DB	6'	190	26	10	
Bruce Laird	DB	6'	198	27	3	
Lloyd Mumphord	DB	5'11"	178	30		
Nelson Munsey	DB	6'1"	186	29	3	
Doug Nettles	DB	6'	178	26	1	2
Ray Oldham	DB	6'	192	26		
Norm Thompson	DB	6'1"	180	29	3	
Bert Jones	QB	6'3"	212	25		12
Mike Kirkland	QB	6'1"	195	23		
Bill Troup	QB	6'5"	215	26		
Don McCauley	HB-FB	6'1"	215	28		48
Lydell Mitchell	HB	5'11"	198	28		42
Howard Stevens	HB	5'5"	165	27		
Roosevelt Leaks	FB	5'10"	225	24		24
Ron Lee	FB	6'4"	228	23		18
Roger Carr	WR	6'3"	196	25		6
Glenn Doughty	WR	6'1"	205	26		24
Perry Griggs	WR	5'10"	182	23		
Marshall Johnson	WR	6'1"	190	24		
Freddie Scott	WR	6'2"	175	25		12
Ricky Thompson	WR	6'	176	23		
Mack Alston	TE	6'2"	230	30		
Ray Chester	TE	6'3"	236	29		18
Jimmie Kennedy	TE	6'3"	230	25		
David Lee	K	6'4"	216	33		
Toni Linhart	K	6'	179	35		83

Delles Howell — Injury

MIAMI DOLPHINS 10-4 Don Shula

Scores of Each Game		
13	Buffalo	0
19	San Francisco	15
27	HOUSTON	7
28	Baltimore	45
21	N.Y. JETS	17
31	SEATTLE	13
13	SAN DIEGO	14
14	N.Y. Jets	10
17	NEW ENGLAND	5
17	Cincinnati	23
55	St. Louis	14
17	BALTIMORE	6
10	New England	14
31	BUFFALO	14

Use Name	Pos.	Hgt	Wgt	Age	Int	Pts
Mike Current	OT	6'4"	270	31		
Wayne Moore	OT	6'6"	265	32		
Steve Young	OT	6'8"	270	24		
Bob Kuechenberg	OG-C	6'3"	255	29		
Larry Little	OG-OT	6'1"	265	31		
Ed Newman	OG	6'2"	245	26		
Wally Pesuit	OG-OT	6'4"	250	23		
Jim Langer	C	6'2"	253	29		
John Alexander	DE	6'2"	250	21		
Vern Den Herder	DE	6'6"	252	28		
A.J. Duhe	DE	6'4"	247	21		
Rick Dvorak (from NYG)	DE	6'4"	245	25		
Carl Barisich	NT	6'4"	255	26		
Bob Baumhower	NT	6'5"	258	22		
Bob Heinz	NT-DE	6'6"	260	30		
Bill Windauer	NT	6'3"	250	27		
Larry Ball	LB	6'6"	235	27		
Kim Bokamper	LB	6'6"	245	22		
Rusty Chambers	LB	6'1"	220	23		
Larry Gordon	LB	6'4"	230	24	1	
Mike Kolen	LB	6'2"	222	29		
Bob Matheson	LB	6'4"	235	32	1	
Ernest Rhone	LB	6'2"	212	24		
Guy Roberts	LB	6'1"	220	27		
Steve Towle	LB	6'2"	233	23		
Dick Anderson	DB	6'2"	196	31		
Charlie Babb	DB	6'	190	27	1	
Charles Cornelius	DB	5'9"	176	25		
Tim Foley	DB	6'	194	29	3	
Curtis Johnson	DB	6'2"	196	29	4	
Vern Roberson	DB	6'1"	195	25	1	
Norris Thomas	DB	5'11"	170	23	3	
Rick Volk	DB	6'3"	195	32	1	
Bob Griese	QB	6'1"	190	32		
Don Strock	QB	6'5"	203	26		
Gary Davis	HB	5'10"	202	22		18
Benny Malone	HB	5'10"	193	25		30
Nat Moore	HB-WR	5'10"	180	25		78
Norm Bulaich	FB	6'1"	218	30		24
Leroy Harris	FB	5'9"	220	23		24
Don Nottingham	FB	5'10"	210	28		12
Stan Winfrey (from T BAY, (to BUFF)	FB	5'11"	223	24		
Terry Anderson	WR	5'9"	182	22		
Duriel Harris	WR	5'11"	175	22		30
Freddie Solomon	WR	5'11"	181	24		12
Jim Mandich	TE-WR	6'3"	214	29		
Loaird McCreary	TE-WR	6'5"	227	24		6
Larry Seiple	TE-WR	6'	214	32		
Andre Tillman	TE	6'5"	230	24		12
Mike Michel	K	5'10"	177	23		
Garo Yepremian	K	5'8"	175	33		67

Manny Fernandez — Knee Injury
Bill Stanfill — Injury

NEW ENGLAND PATRIOTS 9-5 Chuck Fairbanks

Scores of Each Game		
21	KANSAS CITY	17
27	Cleveland	30
27	N.Y. Jets	30
31	SEATTLE	0
24	San Diego	20
17	BALTIMORE	3
24	N.Y. JETS	13
14	BUFFALO	24
5	Miami	17
20	Buffalo	7
14	PHILADELPHIA	6
16	Atlanta	10
14	MIAMI	10
24	Baltimore	30

Use Name	Pos.	Hgt	Wgt	Age	Int	Pts
Leon Gray	OT	6'3"	255	25		
Shelby Jordan	OT	6'7"	260	25		
Bob McKay	OT	6'5"	265	29		
Tom Neville	OT	6'4"	255	34		
Sam Adams	OG	6'3"	255	28		
Pete Brock	OG-C	6'5"	260	23		
John Hannah	OG	6'2"	265	26		
Fred Sturt	OG	6'4"	255	26		
Bob Hyland	C	6'5"	255	32		
Bill Lenkaitis	C	6'3"	252	31		
Julius Adams	DE	6'3"	260	29		
Greg Boyd	DE	6'6"	270	24		
Mel Lunsford	DE	6'3"	260	27		
Tony McGee	DE	6'4"	250	28		
Richard Bishop	NT	6'1"	260	27		
Ray Hamilton	NT	6'1"	250	26		
Art Moore	NT	6'5"	260	26		
Pete Barnes	LB	6'3"	240	32	1	
Ray Costict	LB	6'	214	22		
Sam Hunt	LB	6'1"	250	26	2	
Steve King	LB	6'4"	228	26		
Steve Nelson	LB	6'2"	228	26		
Rod Shoate	LB	6'1"	215	24		
Steve Zabel	LB	6'4"	228	29		
Doug Beaudoin	DB	6'1"	195	23		
Ray Clayborn	DB	6'1"	181	22		20
Dick Conn	DB	6'	185	26		
Tim Fox	DB	5'11"	190	23	3	
Mike Haynes	DB	6'2"	195	24	5	
Bob Howard	DB	6'1"	175	32	4	
Prentice McCray	DB	6'1"	190	24	4	
Steve Grogan	QB	6'4"	205	24		6
Tom Owen	QB	6'1"	200	24		
Don Calhoun	HB-FB	6'	215	25		24
Ike Forte	HB	6'	202	23		12
Horace Ivory	HB	6'	197	23		
Sam Cunningham	FB	6'3"	230	27		30
Jess Phillips	FB	6'1"	208	30		6
Steve Burks	WR	6'5"	210	24		
Stanley Morgan	WR	5'10"	180	22		18
Darryl Stingley	WR	6'	193	25		36
Don Westbrook	WR	5'10"	188	24		
Al Chandler	TE	6'2"	228	26		
Russ Francis	TE	6'6"	240	24		24
Don Hasselbeck	TE	6'7"	245	23		24
Mike Patrick	K	6'	195	24		
John Smith	K	6'	190	27		78

Pete Cusick — Knee Injury
Andy Johnson — Knee Injury
Jim Romaniszyn — Injury

BUFFALO BILLS 3-11 Jim Ringo

Scores of Each Game		
0	MIAMI	13
6	Denver	26
14	Baltimore	17
19	N.Y. JETS	24
3	ATLANTA	0
16	CLEVELAND	27
17	Seattle	56
24	New England	14
13	BALTIMORE	31
7	NEW ENGLAND	20
20	Oakland	14
0	WASHINGTON	10
14	N.Y. Jets	10
14	Miami	31

Use Name	Pos.	Hgt	Wgt	Age	Int	Pts
Joe Devlin	OT	6'4"	258	23		
Dave Foley	OT	6'5"	247	29		
Ken Jones	OT	6'5"	252	24		
Bill Adams	OG	6'2"	246	27		
Joe DeLamielleure	OG	6'3"	248	26		
Reggie McKenzie	OG	6'4"	242	27		
Willie Parker	C	6'3"	245	28		
Connie Zelencik	C-OG	6'4"	245	22		
Phil Dokes	DE	6'4"	258	21		
Greg Morton	DE	6'1"	230	23		
Sherman White	DE	6'5"	250	28		
Ben Williams	DE	6'2"	258	23		
Bill Dunstan	DT	6'4"	250	28		
Mike Kadish	DT	6'5"	270	27		
John Little	DT	6'3"	250	30		
Greg Collins	LB	6'3"	227	24		
Bo Cornell	LB	6'1"	222	28		6
Dan Jilek	LB	6'2"	219	23		
Merv Krakau	LB	6'2"	248	26		
Bob Nelson	LB	6'4"	232	24		
Shane Nelson	LB	6'1"	222	22		
Tom Ruud	LB	6'2"	223	24		
John Skorupan	LB	6'2"	221	26		
Mario Clark	DB	6'2"	190	23	7	
Steve Freeman	DB	5'11"	185	24	1	
Tony Greene	DB	5'10"	170	28	9	2
Dwight Harrison	DB	6'1"	186	28	2	
Doug Jones	DB	6'2"	205	27	2	6
Keith Moody	DB	5'11"	171	24		6
Charles Romes	DB	6'1"	191	23		
Fred Besana	QB	6'4"	200	23		
Joe Ferguson	QB	6'1"	184	27		12
Ken Johnson	QB	6'2"	205	26		
Curtis Brown	HB	5'10"	203	22		6
Mike Collier	HB	5'11"	200	23		
Reuben Gibson	HB	6'	196	22		
Roland Hooks	HB	6'	197	24		
O.J. Simpson	HB	6'2"	212	30		
Jim Braxton	FB	6'2"	240	28		12
Mike Franckowiak	FB	6'3"	218	24		
Mel Baker	WR	6'	190	27		
Bob Chandler	WR	6'	180	28		24
Reggie Craig (from CLE)	WR	6'	190	24		
John Holland	WR	6'	190	25		
John Kimbrough	WR	5'10"	165	23		18
Lou Piccone	WR	5'9"	184	28		12
Reuben Gant	TE	6'4"	225	25		12
Paul Seymour	TE	6'5"	245	27		
Marv Bateman	K	6'4"	215	27		
Carson Long	K	5'10"	210	22		34
Neil O'Donoghue	K	6'6"	204	24		10

NEW YORK JETS 3-11 Walt Michaels

Scores of Each Game		
0	Houston	20
12	BALTIMORE	20
30	NEW ENGLAND	27
24	Buffalo	19
17	Miami	21
27	OAKLAND	28
13	New England	24
10	MIAMI	14
0	SEATTLE	17
12	Baltimore	33
20	PITTSBURGH	23
16	New Orleans	13
10	BUFFALO	14
0	Philadelphia	27

Use Name	Pos.	Hgt	Wgt	Age	Int	Pts
Jeff Bleamer	OT-OG	6'4"	253	24		
Ken Helms	OT-C	6'4"	265	22		
Marvin Powell	OT	6'5"	264	22		
Gary Puetz	OT-OG	6'4"	265	25		
Dan Alexander	OG	6'4"	245	22		
Darrell Austin	OG-C	6'4"	252	25		
Randy Rasmussen	OG	6'2"	255	32		
John Roman	OG-OT	6'4"	251	25		
Joe Fields	C-OG	6'2"	245	23		
Al Burton	DE	6'5"	265	25		
John Hennessy	DE	6'3"	246	22		
Richard Neal	DE	6'3"	256	29		
Lawrence Pillers	DE	6'3"	257	24		
Carl Barzilauskas	DT	6'6"	270	26		
Joe Klecko	DT	6'3"	256	23		
Tank Marshall	DT	6'4"	245	22		
Abdul Salaam	DT	6'3"	260	24		
Greg Buttle	LB	6'2"	229	23	2	6
John Ebersole	LB	6'3"	235	28	1	
Mike Hennigan	LB	6'2"	215	25		
Jim Jerome	LB	6'4"	225	23		
Larry Keller	LB	6'2"	225	23	1	
Bob Martin	LB	6'1"	223	23	1	
Al Palewicz	LB	6'1"	217	27		
Carl Russ	LB	6'2"	227	24		
Billy Hardee	DB	6'	185	23	1	
Ron Mabra	DB	5'10"	164	26		
Tommy Marvaso	DB	6'1"	191	23		
Burgess Owens	DB	6'2"	195	26	3	
Artimus Parker	DB	6'3"	200	25	1	
Ken Schroy	DB	6'2"	191	24		
Shafer Suggs	DB	6'1"	200	24		
Ed Taylor	DB	6'	176	24	1	
Maurice Tyler	DB	6'	190	27		
Marty Domres	QB	6'4"	220	30		
Matt Robinson	QB	6'2"	196	22		
Richard Todd	QB	6'2"	205	23		12
Bruce Harper	HB-WR	5'8"	174	22		6
Kevin Long	HB	6'1"	205	22		
Charlie White	HB-FB	6'	222	24		12
Scott Dierking	FB	5'10"	215	22		6
Clark Gaines	FB-HB	6'1"	201	23		24
Tom Newton	FB	6'	205	23		
Rich Caster	WR	6'5"	230	28		6
Shelton Diggs	WR	6'1"	190	22		
David Knight	WR	6'1"	170	26		
Wesley Walker	WR	6'	172	22		18
Jerome Barkum	TE	6'3"	217	27		36
Bob Raba	TE	6'1"	222	22		
Pat Leahy	K	6'	190	26		63
Chuck Ramsey	K	6'2"	195	25		

Don Coleman — Knee Injury
Louie Giammona — Knee Injury

BALTIMORE COLTS

RUSHING
Last Name	No.	Yds	Avg	TD
Mitchell	301	1159	3.9	3
R. Lee	84	346	4.1	3
Leaks	59	237	4.0	3
McCauley	83	234	2.8	6
Jones	28	146	5.2	0
Doughty	2	11	5.5	0
D. Lee	2	-2	-1.0	0
Troup	7	-8	-1.1	0

RECEIVING
Last Name	No.	Yds	Avg	TD
Mitchell	71	620	9	4
McCauley	51	495	10	2
Chester	31	556	18	3
Doughty	28	435	16	4
Scott	18	267	15	2
Carr	11	199	18	1
R. Lee	10	60	6	0
Leaks	3	39	13	1
R. Thompson	1	15	15	0

PUNT RETURNS
Last Name	No.	Yds	Avg	TD
Stevens	34	301	9	0
Blackwood	7	22	3	0
Oldham	1	0	0	0

KICKOFF RETURNS
Last Name	No.	Yds	Avg	TD
Laird	24	541	23	0
Stevens	11	216	20	0
McCauley	5	67	13	0
Blackwood	1	24	24	0
Huff	1	15	15	0
Johnson	1	15	15	0
Griggs	1	12	12	0
Kennedy	1	9	9	0
Shiver	1	7	7	0
Griffin	1	6	6	0
Doughty	1	0	0	0

PASSING – PUNTING – KICKING
PASSING	Att	Comp	%	Yds	Yd/Att	TD	Int–	%	RK
Jones	393	224	57	2686	6.8	17	11–	3	3
Troup	2	0		0	0.0	0	1–	50	

PUNTING	No	Avg
D. Lee	82	38.3

KICKING	XP	Att	%	FG	Att	%
Linhart	32	35	91	17	26	65

MIAMI DOLPHINS

RUSHING
Last Name	No.	Yds	Avg	TD
Malone	129	615	4.8	5
Davis	126	533	4.2	2
L. Harris	91	417	4.6	0
Bulaich	91	416	4.6	4
Nottingham	44	214	4.9	2
N. Moore	14	89	6.4	1
Solomon	6	43	7.2	0
Griese	16	30	1.9	0
T. Anderson	1	11	11.0	0
Michel	1	-2	-2.0	0

RECEIVING
Last Name	No.	Yds	Avg	TD
N. Moore	52	765	15	12
D. Harris	34	601	18	5
Bulaich	25	180	7	0
Tillman	17	169	10	2
Davis	14	151	11	0
Solomon	12	181	15	1
Nottingham	8	58	7	0
L. Harris	7	29	4	0
Mandich	6	63	11	0
Malone	4	58	15	0
McCreary	2	10	5	1
Seiple	1	-1	-1	0

PUNT RETURNS
Last Name	No.	Yds	Avg	TD
Solomon	32	285	9	0
D. Anderson	4	3	1	0
Babb	2	10	5	0
Davis	1	11	17	0
T. Anderson	1	6	6	0

KICKOFF RETURNS
Last Name	No.	Yds	Avg	TD
Davis	14	414	30	0
Solomon	10	273	27	1
T. Anderson	7	167	24	0
D. Harris	4	91	23	0
Nottingham	2	36	18	0
McCreary	1	30	30	0

PASSING – PUNTING – KICKING
PASSING	Att	Comp	%	Yds	Yd/Att	TD	Int–	%	RK
Griese	307	180	59	2252	7.3	22	13–	4	1
Strock	4	2	50	12	3.0	0	1–	25	

PUNTING	No	Avg
Michel	35	38.2
Seiple	22	36.4

KICKING	XP	Att	%	FG	Att	%
Yepremian	37	40	93	10	22	45
Michel	0	1	0			

NEW ENGLAND PATRIOTS

RUSHING
Last Name	No.	Yds	Avg	TD
Cunningham	270	1015	3.8	4
Calhoun	198	727	3.7	4
Grogan	61	324	5.3	1
Forte	62	157	2.5	2
Stingley	3	33	11.0	1
Phillips	5	27	5.4	1
Morgan	1	10	10.0	0
Ivory	3	10	3.3	0

RECEIVING
Last Name	No.	Yds	Avg	TD
Cunningham	42	370	9	1
Stingley	39	657	17	5
Morgan	21	443	21	3
Francis	16	229	14	4
Calhoun	13	152	12	0
Hasselbeck	9	76	8	4
Forte	8	88	11	0
Chandler	7	68	10	0
Burks	5	79	16	0

PUNT RETURNS
Last Name	No.	Yds	Avg	TD
Haynes	24	200	8	0
Morgan	16	220	14	0
Forte	2	9	5	0
Beaudoin	1	0	0	0

KICKOFF RETURNS
Last Name	No.	Yds	Avg	TD
Clayborn	28	869	31	3
Phillips	6	93	16	0
Beaudoin	4	73	18	0
McKay	1	16	16	0

PASSING – PUNTING – KICKING
PASSING	Att	Comp	%	Yds	Yd/Att	TD	Int–	%	RK
Grogan	305	160	52	2162	7.1	17	21–	7	7

PUNTING	No	Avg
Patrick	65	36.2

KICKING	XP	Att	%	FG	Att	%
Smith	33	33	100	15	21	71

BUFFALO BILLS

RUSHING
Last Name	No.	Yds	Avg	TD
Simpson	126	557	4.4	0
Hooks	128	497	3.9	0
Braxton	113	372	3.3	1
Ferguson	41	279	6.8	2
Collier	31	116	3.7	0
Brown	8	34	4.3	0
Piccone	1	6	6.0	0
Franckowiak	1	0	0.0	0
Bateman	1	0	0.0	0

RECEIVING
Last Name	No.	Yds	Avg	TD
Chandler	60	745	12	4
Braxton	43	461	11	1
Gant	41	646	16	2
Piccone	17	240	14	2
Hooks	16	195	12	0
Simpson	16	138	9	0
Kimbrough	10	207	21	2
Holland	8	107	13	0
Brown	5	20	4	1
Collier	3	23	8	0
Seymour	2	21	11	0
Craig	1	5	5	0

PUNT RETURNS
Last Name	No.	Yds	Avg	TD
Moody	15	196	13	1
Kimbrough	16	184	12	1
Craig	1	0	0	0
Willis	1	0	0	0

KICKOFF RETURNS
Last Name	No.	Yds	Avg	TD
Moody	30	636	21	0
Kimbrough	15	346	23	0
Piccone	4	89	22	0
Collier	4	55	14	0
Brown	3	66	22	0
Romes	1	18	18	0
B. Nelson	1	10	10	0
Dunstan	1	9	9	0
Franckowiak	1	9	9	0

PASSING – PUNTING – KICKING
PASSING	Att	Comp	%	Yds	Yd/Att	TD	Int–	%	RK
Ferguson	457	221	48	2803	6.1	12	24–	5	13
Simpson	1	0		0	0.0	0	0–	0	

PUNTING	No	Avg
Bateman	81	39.9

KICKING	XP	Att	%	FG	Att	%
Long	13	14	93	7	11	64
O'Donoghue	4	5	80	2	6	33
Klaban		0	2		0	

NEW YORK JETS

RUSHING
Last Name	No.	Yds	Avg	TD
Gaines	158	595	3.8	3
Dierking	79	315	4.0	0
Harper	44	198	4.5	0
Long	56	170	3.0	1
White	50	151	3.0	1
Todd	24	46	1.9	2
Robinson	5	45	9.0	0
Newton	8	39	4.9	0
Keller	1	25	25.0	0
Walker	3	25	8.3	0
Domres	4	23	5.8	0
Diggs	1	16	16.0	0
Caster	2	-15	-7.5	0

RECEIVING
Last Name	No.	Yds	Avg	TD
Gaines	55	469	9	1
Walker	35	740	21	3
Barkum	26	450	17	6
Harper	21	209	10	1
Caster	10	205	21	1
Knight	7	129	18	0
Newton	5	33	7	0
Long	5	17	3	0
Dierking	4	29	7	1
White	2	5	3	1

PUNT RETURNS
Last Name	No.	Yds	Avg	TD
Harper	34	425	13	0
Schroy	3	38	13	0
Hardee	1	17	17	0

KICKOFF RETURNS
Last Name	No.	Yds	Avg	TD
Harper	42	1035	25	0
Hardee	7	148	21	0
Dierking	6	91	15	0
Raba	4	64	16	0
Marvaso	2	36	18	0

PASSING – PUNTING – KICKING
PASSING	Att	Comp	%	Yds	Yd/Att	TD	Int–	%	RK
Todd	265	133	50	1863	7.0	11	17–	6	10
Robinson	54	20	37	310	5.7	2	8–	15	
Domres	40	17	43	113	2.8	1	1–	3	
Harper	1	0		0	0.0	0	0–	0	

PUNTING	No	Avg
Ramsey	62	37.1

KICKING	XP	Att	%	FG	Att	%
Leahy	18	21	86	15	25	60

PITTSBURGH STEELERS 9-5 — Chuck Noll

Scores of Each Game

27	SAN FRANCISCO	0	
7	OAKLAND	16	
28	Cleveland	14	
10	Houston	27	
20	CINCINNATI	14	
27	HOUSTON	10	
21	Baltimore	31	
21	Denver	21	
35	CLEVELAND	31	
28	DALLAS	13	
23	N.Y. Jets	20	
30	SEATTLE	20	
10	Cincinnati	17	
10	San Diego	9	

Use Name	Pos.	Hgt	Wgt	Age	Int	Pts
Larry Brown	OT-TE	6'4"	245	28		
Jon Kolb	OT	6'2"	262	30		
Jim Clack	OG-C	6'3"	250	29		
Sam Davis	OG	6'1"	255	33		
Gerry Mullins	OG-OT	6'3"	244	28		
Ted Peterson	C-OT-OG	6'5"	244	22		
Ray Pinney	C-OT	6'4"	240	23		
Mike Webster	C	6'1"	250	25		
John Banaszak	DE	6'3"	244	27		
L.C. Greenwood	DE	6'5"	250	30		
Dwight White	DE	6'4"	255	28	2	
Steve Furness	DT-DE	6'4"	255	26		
Joe Greene	DT	6'4"	264	30		
Ernie Holmes	DT	6'3"	260	29		
Robin Cole	LB-DE	6'2"	220	21		
Brad Cousino	LB	6'	215	24		
Jack Ham	LB	6'3"	225	28	4	
Dave LaCrosse	LB	6'3"	210	21		
Jack Lambert	LB	6'4"	220	25	1	
Loren Toews	LB	6'3"	222	25	2	
Dennis Winston	LB	6'	228	21		
Jim Allen	DB	6'2"	194	25	5	
Mel Blount	DB	6'3"	205	29	6	
Tony Dungy	DB	6'	188	21	3	
Glen Edwards	DB	6'	185	30	3	
Brent Sexton	DB	6'1"	190	24		
Donnie Shell	DB	5'11"	190	25	3	
J.T. Thomas	DB	6'2"	196	26	2	
Mike Wagner	DB	6'1"	200	28		
Terry Bradshaw	QB	6'3"	215	28		18
Neil Graff	QB	6'3"	205	27		
Mike Kruczek	QB	6'	201	24		
Cliff Stoudt	QB	6'4"	218	22		
Rocky Bleier	HB	5'11"	210	31		24
Jack Deloplaine	HB	5'10"	205	23		
Alvin Mason	HB	5'11"	201	25		
Laverne Smith	HB	5'10"	193	22		
Franco Harris	FB	6'2"	225	27		66
Reggie Harrison	FB	6'3"	220	27		
Sidney Thornton	FB	5'11"	230	22		12
Frank Lewis	WR	6'1"	196	30		6
Ernest Pough	WR	6'1"	174	25		
Jim Smith	WR	6'2"	205	22		
John Stallworth	WR	6'2"	183	25		42
Lynn Swann	WR	5'10"	180	25		42
Bennie Cunningham	TE	6'4"	247	22		12
Randy Grossman	TE	6'1"	225	23		
Rick Engles (from SEATTLE)	K	5'11"	180	23		
Roy Gerela	K	5'10"	185	29		61
Bobby Walden	K	6'	197	39		

Gary Dunn — Knee Injury
Theo Bell — Foot Injury
John Fuqua — Broken Finger

CINCINNATI BENGALS 8-6 — Bill Johnson

Scores of Each Game

3	CLEVELAND	13
43	SEATTLE	20
3	San Diego	24
17	Green Bay	7
13	Pittsburgh	20
13	DENVER	24
13	HOUSTON	10
10	Cleveland	7
10	Minnesota	42
23	MIAMI	17
30	N.Y. GIANTS	13
27	Kansas City	7
17	PITTSBURGH	10
16	Houston	21

Use Name	Pos.	Hgt	Wgt	Age	Int	Pts
Vern Holland	OT	6'5"	265	29		
Ron Hunt	OT	6'6"	255	22		
Rufus Mayes	OT	6'5"	256	29		
Glenn Bujnoch	OG	6'5"	251	23		6
Greg Fairchild	OG-C	6'4"	257	23		
Dave Lapham	OG-OT-C	6'4"	259	25		
John Shinners	OG	6'2"	259	30		
Bob Johnson	C	6'5"	256	31		
Ken Johnson	DE	6'5"	258	30		
Coy Bacon	DE	6'4"	265	35		
Gary Burley	DE	6'3"	255	24		
Ron Carpenter	DT	6'4"	265	29		
Eddie Edwards	DT	6'5"	256	23		
Walter Johnson	DT	6'3"	265	34		
Wilson Whitley	DT	6'3"	264	22		
Glenn Cameron	LB	6'1"	217	24		
Bo Harris	LB	6'3"	221	24	2	
Jim LeClair	LB	6'2"	238	26	2	
Ray Phillips	LB	6'3"	221	23		
Ron Pritchard	LB	6'1"	208	30		
Reggie Williams	LB	6'1"	228	22	3	12
Jerry Anderson	DB	5'11"	198	23		
Tommy Casanova	DB	6'2"	196	27	1	
Marvin Cobb	DB	6'	191	24	2	
Melvin Morgan	DB	6'	186	24	1	
Lemar Parrish	DB	5'11"	183	29	3	6
Scott Perry	DB	6'	182	23		
Ken Riley	DB	6'	185	30	2	
Ken Anderson	QB	6'1"	212	28		12
John Reeves	QB	6'3"	210	27		
Mike Wells	QB	6'5"	225	26		
Lenvil Elliott	HB	6'	208	26		6
Archie Griffin	HB	5'9"	193	23		
Willie Shelby	HB	5'11"	198	24		6
Booby Clark	FB	6'2"	242	26		
Tony Davis	FB	5'10"	210	24		12
Pete Johnson	FB	6'	240	23		24
Billy Brooks	WR	6'4"	202	24		24
Isaac Curtis	WR	6'	192	26		12
Steve Holden (from CLE)	WR	6'	200	26		
John McDaniel	WR	6'1"	197	25		
Pat McInally	WR	6'6"	210	24		18
Mike Cobb	TE	6'5"	248	21		
Jim Corbett	TE	6'4"	214	22		6
Bob Trumpy	TE	6'5"	228	32		6
Rick Walker	TE	6'3"	237	22		
Chris Bahr	K	5'9"	168	24		82

Chris Devlin — Achilles Injury

HOUSTON OILERS 8-6 — Bum Phillips

Scores of Each Game

20	N.Y. JETS	0
16	Green Bay	10
7	Miami	27
27	PITTSBURGH	10
23	CLEVELAND	24
27	Pittsburgh	10
10	Cincinnati	13
47	CHICAGO	0
29	Oakland	34
22	Seattle	10
34	KANSAS CITY	20
14	DENVER	24
19	Cleveland	15
21	CINCINNATI	16

Use Name	Pos.	Hgt	Wgt	Age	Int	Pts
Conway Hayman	OT	6'3"	260	28		
Kevin Hunt	OT-OG	6'5"	260	28		
Greg Sampson	OT	6'6"	270	26		
Morris Towns	OT	6'4"	275	23		
Elbert Drungo	OG	6'5"	265	34		
Ed Fisher	OG-C	6'3"	250	28		
George Reihner	OG	6'4"	263	22		
David Carter	C	6'2"	225	24		
Carl Mauck	C	6'3"	250	30		
Steve Baumgartner (from NO)	DE-DT	6'7"	255	26		
Elvin Bethea	DE	6'3"	255	31		
Andy Dorris (from SEATTLE)	DE	6'4"	240	26		
Ernest Kirk	DE	6'2"	265	25	1	
James Young	DE	6'2"	260	26	4	
Curly Culp	MG	6'1"	265	31	1	
Ken Kennard	MG-DE	6'2"	245	22		2
Gregg Bingham	LB	6'1"	230	26	2	6
Robert Brazile	LB	6'4"	238	24	3	
Steve Kiner	LB	6'	225	30	1	
Art Stringer	LB	6'1"	223	23	1	
Ted Thompson	LB	6'1"	220	24		
Ted Washington	LB	6'1"	245	29	3	
Willie Alexander	DB	6'2"	195	27	3	6
Bill Currier	DB	6'	190	22	2	
Al Johnson	DB	6'2"	200	27		
Kurt Knoff	DB	6'5"	188	23		
Zeke Moore	DB	6'2"	195	33	3	6
Mike Reinfeldt	DB	6'2"	195	24	5	
Rich Sowells	DB	6'	180	28		
Greg Stemrick	DB	5'11"	185	25	1	6
Mike Weger	DB	6'2"	200	31		
Tom Dunivan	QB	6'3"	210	23		
John Hadl	QB	6'2"	215	37		6
Dan Pastorini	QB	6'3"	205	28		12
Ronnie Coleman	HB	5'10"	198	26		36
Mike Voight	HB	6'	214	23		
Rob Carpenter	FB	6'1"	214	22		6
Don Hardeman	FB	6'2"	235	25		18
Tim Wilson	FB	6'3"	220	23		18
Warren Anderson	WR	6'2"	195	22		
Ken Burrough	WR	6'4"	210	29		48
Eddie Foster	WR	5'10"	185	23		
Gary Garrison	WR	6'1"	194	33		
Billy Johnson	WR	5'9"	170	25		42
Mike Barber	TE	6'2"	235	24		6
Jim Giles	TE	6'3"	225	22		
Skip Butler	K	6'	200	29		2
Tom Dempsey	K	6'1"	260	36		20
Toni Fritsch	K	5'7"	189	32		55
Cliff Parsley	K	6'1"	211	22		

C.L. Whittington — Injury
Fred Willis — Injury

CLEVELAND BROWNS 6-8 — Forrest Gregg (6-7), Dick Modzelewski (0-1)

Scores of Each Game

13	Cincinnati	3
30	NEW ENGLAND	27
14	PITTSBURGH	28
10	OAKLAND	26
24	Houston	23
27	Buffalo	16
44	KANSAS CITY	7
7	CINCINNATI	10
7	Pittsburgh	10
21	N.Y. Giants	7
0	LOS ANGELES	9
14	San Diego	37
15	HOUSTON	19
19	Seattle	20

Use Name	Pos.	Hgt	Wgt	Age	Int	Pts
Barry Darrow	OT	6'7"	260	27		
Doug Dieken	OT	6'5"	252	28		
Bob Lingenfelter	OT	6'7"	277	23		
Al Dennis	OG	6'4"	250	26		
Bob Jackson	OG	6'5"	250	24		
Henry Sheppard	OG	6'6"	246	24		
Tom DeLeone	C	6'2"	248	27		
Gerry Sullivan	C	6'4"	250	25		
Joe Jones	DE	6'7"	250	29		
Mack Mitchell	DE	6'7"	245	25		
Mike St. Clair	DE	6'5"	245	23		
Earl Edwards	DT	6'6"	256	31		
Steve Okoniewski (from St. L.)	DT	6'3"	255	28		
Jerry Sherk	DT	6'4"	250	29		2
Robert Sims	DT	6'5"	282	22		
Dick Ambrose	LB	6'	235	24		
Bob Babich	LB	6'2"	231	30		
John Garlington	LB	6'2"	221	31		
Dave Graf	LB	6'2"	215	24		
Charlie Hall	LB	6'3"	235	28	1	
Gerald Irons	LB	6'2"	230	30	3	6
Mark Johnson	LB	6'2"	236	24		
Ron Bolton	DB	6'2"	170	27	3	
Thom Darden	DB	6'2"	193	27	6	6
Oliver Davis	DB	6'1"	200	23	3	
Ken Ellis	DB	5'10"	195	29		
Broderick Jones	DB	6'1"	195	22	1	
Tony Peters	DB	6'1"	192	24	2	
Clarence Scott	DB	6'	180	28	3	6
Roland Woolsey	DB	6'1"	182	24	1	
Terry Luck	QB	6'3"	205	23		6
Gary Marangi	QB	6'1"	203	25		
Dave Mays	QB	6'1"	204	28		
Brian Sipe	QB	6'1"	190	28		
Larry Poole	HB	6'	195	25		24
Greg Pruitt	HB	5'10"	190	26		24
Brian Duncan	FB-HB	6'	201	25		6
Cleo Miller	FB	5'11"	202	25		30
Mike Pruitt	FB	6'	214	23		6
Ricky Feacher	WR	5'10"	174	23		
Dave Logan	WR	6'4"	226	23		
Reggie Rucker	WR	6'2"	190	29		12
Paul Warfield	WR	6'	188	34		12
Lawrence Williams (from K.C.)	WR	5'10"	173	23		
Gary Parris	TE	6'2"	226	27		30
Oscar Roan	TE	6'6"	214	25		12
Don Cockroft	K	6'1"	195	32		81
Greg Coleman	K	6'	178	22		

Pete Adams — Injury
Bill Craven — Injury

PITTSBURGH STEELERS

RUSHING

Last Name	No.	Yds	Avg	TD
Harris	300	1162	3.9	11
Bleier	135	465	3.4	4
Harrison	36	175	4.9	0
Bradshaw	31	171	5.5	3
Thornton	27	103	3.8	2
Maxson	18	56	3.1	0
L. Smith	14	55	3.9	0
Stallworth	6	47	7.8	0
Dungy	3	8	2.7	0
Deloplaine	2	7	3.5	0
Swann	2	6	3.0	0
Graff	5	3	0.6	0
Kruczek	1	0	0.0	0
Walden	1	0	0.0	0

RECEIVING

Last Name	No.	Yds	Avg	TD
Swann	50	789	16	7
Stallworth	44	784	18	7
Cunningham	20	347	17	2
Bleier	18	161	9	0
Lewis	11	263	24	1
Harris	11	62	6	0
Maxson	5	70	14	0
Grossman	5	57	11	0
J. Smith	4	80	20	0
Harrison	3	11	4	0
Thornton	1	5	5	0
Pough	1	3	3	0

PUNT RETURNS

Last Name	No.	Yds	Avg	TD
J. Smith	36	294	8	0
Swann	9	88	10	0
Deloplaine	1	7	7	0

KICKOFF RETURNS

Last Name	No.	Yds	Avg	TD
J. Smith	16	381	24	0
L. Smith	16	365	23	0
Pough	7	111	16	0
Maxson	5	120	24	0
Deloplaine	1	18	18	0

PASSING – PUNTING – KICKING

PASSING	Att	Comp	%	Yds	Yd/Att	TD	Int–	%	RK
Bradshaw	314	162	52	2523	8.0	17	19–	6	5
Graff	12	6	50	47	3.9	0	0–	0	
Dungy	8	3	38	43	5.4	0	2–	25	
Kruczek	7	2	29	19	2.7	0	0–	0	

PUNTING	No	Avg
Walden	67	37.0
Engles	9	34.0

KICKING	XP	Att	%	FG	Att	%
Gerela	34	37	92	9	14	64

CINCINNATI BENGALS

RUSHING

Last Name	No.	Yds	Avg	TD
P. Johnson	153	585	3.8	4
Griffin	137	549	4.0	0
Elliott	65	269	4.1	0
Clark	68	226	3.3	1
K. Anderson	26	128	4.9	2
Davis	27	81	3.0	2
Casanova	1	20	20.0	0
Bujnoch	1	4	4.0	1
McInally	1	4	4.0	0
Ma. Cobb	1	0	0.0	0
Reaves	5	0	0.0	0
Corbett	1	−1	−1.0	0
Brooks	2	−4	−2.0	0

RECEIVING

Last Name	No.	Yds	Avg	TD
Brooks	39	772	20	4
Elliott	29	238	8	1
Griffin	28	240	9	0
Curtis	20	338	17	2
Trumpy	18	251	14	1
McInally	17	258	15	3
McDaniel	12	148	12	0
Davis	9	83	9	0
Corbett	7	127	18	1
Clark	7	33	5	0
P. Johnson	5	49	10	0
Walker	1	13	13	0

PUNT RETURNS

Last Name	No.	Yds	Avg	TD
Davis	19	220	12	0
Shelby	11	54	5	0
Parrish	4	30	8	0
Holden	3	14	5	0
Casanova	1	6	6	0
Ma. Cobb	1	4	4	0
Williams	1	0	0	0
J. Anderson	1	0	0	0

KICKOFF RETURNS

Last Name	No.	Yds	Avg	TD
Shelby	19	403	21	0
Griffin	9	192	21	0
J. Anderson	8	129	16	0
Davis	3	42	14	0
Holden	2	42	21	0
Elliott	1	23	23	0
Parrish	1	23	23	0
Ma. Cobb	1	15	15	0
P. Johnson	1	11	11	0
Fairchild	1	6	6	0

PASSING – PUNTING – KICKING

PASSING	Att	Comp	%	Yds	Yd/Att	TD	Int–	%	RK
K. Anderson	323	166	51	2145	6.6	11	11–	3	6
Reeves	59	24	41	383	6.5	0	5–	9	
Griffin	1	1	100	18	18.0	1	0–	0	
McInally	1	1	100	4	4.0	0	0–	0	
Ma. Cobb	1	0	0	0	0.0	0	0–	0	

PUNTING	No	Avg
McInally	67	41.8
Bahr	2	44.0

KICKING	XP	Att	%	FG	Att	%
Bahr	25	26	97	19	27	70

HOUSTON OILERS

RUSHING

Last Name	No.	Yds	Avg	TD
Coleman	185	660	3.6	5
Carpenter	144	652	4.5	1
Wilson	99	343	3.5	3
Hardeman	42	162	3.9	2
B. Johnson	6	102	17.0	1
Pastorini	18	39	2.2	2
Voight	7	20	2.9	0
Burrough	4	10	2.5	0
Hadl	3	11	3.7	1
Giles	1	−10	−10.0	0

RECEIVING

Last Name	No.	Yds	Avg	TD
Burrough	43	816	19	8
Carpenter	23	156	7	0
Coleman	22	115	5	1
B. Johnson	20	412	21	3
Wilson	20	107	5	0
Giles	17	147	9	0
Foster	15	208	14	0
Hardeman	11	47	4	1
Barber	9	94	10	1
Garrison	1	5	5	0

PUNT RETURNS

Last Name	No.	Yds	Avg	TD
B. Johnson	35	539	15	2
Stemrick	1	0	0	0

KICKOFF RETURNS

Last Name	No.	Yds	Avg	TD
B. Johnson	25	630	25	1
Anderson	8	182	23	0
Voight	8	156	20	0
Wilson	2	33	17	0
Foster	1	31	31	0
Stringer	1	15	15	0
Thompson	1	9	9	0

PASSING – PUNTING – KICKING

PASSING	Att	Comp	%	Yds	Yd/Att	TD	Int–	%	RK
Pastorini	319	169	53	1987	6.2	13	18–	6	8
Hadl	24	11	46	76	3.2	0	3–	13	
Coleman	3	1	33	44	14.7	1	0–	0	
Burrough	1	0	0	0	0.0	0	0–	0	

PUNTING	No	Avg
Parsley	77	39.4

KICKING	XP	Att	%	FG	Att	%
Fritsch	19	20	95	12	16	75
Dempsey	8	11	73	4	6	67
Butler	2	3	67	0	3	0
Pastorini	0	1	0			

CLEVELAND BROWNS

RUSHING

Last Name	No.	Yds	Avg	TD
G. Pruitt	236	1086	4.6	3
Miller	163	756	4.6	4
M. Pruitt	47	205	4.4	1
Poole	38	118	3.1	1
Williams	2	30	15.0	1
Duncan	5	16	3.2	0
Sipe	10	14	1.4	0
Rucker	2	6	3.0	0
Warfield	1	2	2.0	0
Mays	4	2	0.5	0
Luck	3	−2	−0.7	0
Coleman	1	−3	−3.0	0

RECEIVING

Last Name	No.	Yds	Avg	TD
Miller	41	291	7	1
G. Pruitt	37	471	13	1
Rucker	36	565	16	2
Parris	21	213	10	5
Logan	19	284	15	1
Warfield	18	251	14	2
Poole	17	137	8	3
Roan	13	136	11	2
Williams	7	94	13	0
M. Pruitt	3	12	4	0
Duncan	1	5	5	1
Luck	1	4	4	1

PUNT RETURNS

Last Name	No.	Yds	Avg	TD
Woolsey	32	290	9	0
Feacher	2	15	8	0

KICKOFF RETURNS

Last Name	No.	Yds	Avg	TD
Williams	25	518	21	0
Duncan	15	298	20	0
Feacher	11	219	20	0
M. Pruitt	6	131	22	0
Ellis	5	80	16	0
Jackson	1	21	21	0
Ambrose	1	20	20	0
Babich	1	14	14	0
Woolsey	1	2	2	0

PASSING – PUNTING – KICKING

PASSING	Att	Comp	%	Yds	Yd/Att	TD	Int–	%	RK
Sipe	195	112	57	1233	6.3	9	14–	7	9
Mays	121	67	55	797	6.6	6	10–	8	
Luck	50	25	50	316	6.3	1	7–	14	
G. Pruitt	9	4	44	28	3.1	3	0–	0	
Logan	2	0	0	0	0.0	0	0–	0	

PUNTING	No	Avg
Coleman	61	39.2
Cockroft	1	30.0

KICKING	XP	Att	%	FG	Att	%
Cockroft	30	31	97	17	23	74

DENVER BRONCOS 12-2 Red Miller

Scores of Each Game		
7	ST. LOUIS	0
26	BUFFALO	6
24	Seattle	13
23	KANSAS CITY	7
30	Oakland	7
24	Cincinnati	13
14	OAKLAND	24
21	PITTSBURGH	7
17	San Diego	14
14	Kansas City	7
27	BALTIMORE	13
24	Houston	14
17	SAN DIEGO	9
6	Dallas	14

Use Name	Pos.	Hgt	Wgt	Age	Int	Pts
Henry Allison (from St. L)	OT-OG	6'3"	263	30		
Glenn Hyde	OT	6'3"	255	26		
Andy Maurer	OT	6'3"	265	28		
Claudie Minor	OT	6'4"	280	26		
Bill Bryan	OG	6'2"	246	22		
Tom Glassic	OG	6'4"	248	23		
Paul Howard	OG	6'3"	260	26		
Steve Schindler	OG	6'3"	252	23		
Bobby Maples	C	6'3"	250	34		
Mike Montler	C	6'4"	250	33		
Lyle Alzado	DE	6'3"	250	28		
Barney Chevous	DE	6'3"	250	26		
Brian Manor	DE	6'4"	247	25		
Paul Smith	DE	6'3"	250	32	1	
Ruben Carter	NT	6'	254	24		
John Grant	NT	6'3"	246	27		
Rich Baska	LB	6'3"	224	25		
Larry Evans	LB	6'2"	218	24	1	
Randy Gradishar	LB	6'3"	231	25	3	
Tom Jackson	LB	5'11"	224	26	4	6
Rob Nairne	LB	6'4"	220	23		
Joe Rizzo	LB	6'1"	220	23	3	
Bob Swenson	LB	6'3"	223	26	1	
Goodwin Turk	LB	6'2"	230	26		
Steve Foley	DB	6'2"	190	23	3	
Bernie Jackson	DB	6'	181	27	1	
Chris Pane	DB	5'11"	185	24		
Randy Poltl	DB	6'3"	188	25		
Larry Riley	DB	5'10"	189	22		
Bill Thompson	DB	6'1"	200	30	5	
Louie Wright	DB	6'2"	195	24	3	6
Craig Morton	QB	6'4"	214	34		24
Craig Penrose	QB	6'3"	205	24		
Norris Weese	QB	6'1"	193	26		6
Otis Armstrong	HB	5'10"	197	26		24
Jim Kiick (to WASH)	HB	5'11"	215	31		
Bob Lytle	HB	6'1"	198	22		12
Jim Jensen	FB-TE	6'3"	240	23		6
Jon Keyworth	FB	6'3"	234	26		6
Lonnie Perrin	FB	6'1"	224	25		24
Jack Dolbin	WR	5'10"	183	28		18
Haven Moses	WR	6'3"	200	31		24
John Schultz	WR	5'10"	183	24		
Rick Upchurch	WR	5'10"	180	25		24
Ron Egloff	TE	6'5"	227	21		
Riley Odoms	TE	6'4"	232	27		18
Buck Dilts	K	5'9"	190	23		
Jim Turner	K	6'2"	212	36		76

Bill Bain — Knee Injury
Randy Moore — Injury

OAKLAND RAIDERS 11-3 John Madden

Scores of Each Game		
24	SAN DIEGO	0
16	Pittsburgh	7
37	Kansas City	28
26	Cleveland	10
7	DENVER	30
28	N.Y. Jets	27
24	Denver	14
44	SEATTLE	7
34	HOUSTON	29
7	San Diego	12
34	BUFFALO	13
14	Los Angeles	20
35	MINNESOTA	13
21	KANSAS CITY	20

Use Name	Pos.	Hgt	Wgt	Age	Int	Pts
Henry Lawrence	OT-OG	6'4"	270	25		
Art Shell	OT	6'5"	275	30		
John Vella	OT	6'4"	260	27		
George Buehler	OG	6'2"	270	30		
Everett Little	OG	6'4"	265	23		
Mickey Marvin	OG	6'4"	270	21		
Gene Upshaw	OG	6'5"	255	32		
Dave Dalby	C	6'2"	250	26		
Steve Sylvester	C-OT-OG	6'4"	260	24		
John Matuszak	DE	6'8"	270	26		
Charles Philyaw	DE	6'9"	270	23		
Otis Sistrunk	DE	6'4"	270	29	1	
Pat Toomay	DE	6'5"	245	32		
Mike McCoy	MG	6'5"	275	28		
Dave Rowe	MG	6'6"	270	32		
Jeff Barnes	LB	6'2"	215	22		
Willie Hall	LB	6'2"	225	27	1	6
Ted Hendricks	LB	6'7"	220	29		2
Monte Johnson	LB	6'4"	240	25	2	
Randy McClanahan	LB	6'5"	225	22		
Floyd Rice	LB	6'3"	225	28	2	
Phil Villapiano	LB	6'1"	225	28		
Butch Atkinson	DB	6'	185	30	2	
Willie Brown	DB	6'1"	210	36	4	
Neal Colzie	DB	6'2"	205	24	3	
Lester Hayes	DB	6'	208	22	1	
Steve Jackson	DB	6'1"	192	22	1	
Charlie Phillips	DB	6'2"	215	24	2	
Jack Tatum	DB	5'10"	205	28	6	
Skip Thomas	DB	6'	205	27	1	
Jimmie Warren	DB	5'11"	175	38		
David Humm	QB	6'2"	185	25		
Mike Rae	QB	6'	190	26		6
Ken Stabler	QB	6'3"	215	31		
Clarence Davis	HB	5'10"	195	28		30
Carl Garrett	HB	5'11"	205	30		18
Hubert Ginn	HB	5'11"	185	30		
Pete Banaszak	FB-HB	5'11"	210	33		30
Terry Robiskie	FB	6'1"	210	22		6
Mark van Eeghen	FB	6'2"	225	25		42
Fred Biletnikoff	WR	6'1"	190	34		30
Morris Bradshaw	WR	6'	196	24		
Cliff Branch	WR	5'11"	170	29		36
Rick Jennings (from TB, SF)	WR-HB	5'9"	180	24		
Mike Siani	WR	6'2"	195	27		12
Warren Bankston	TE	6'4"	235	30		
Dave Casper	TE	6'4"	230	25		36
Ted Kwalick	TE	6'4"	225	30		
Ray Guy	K	6'3"	195	27		
Errol Mann	K	6'	205	36		99

Kelvin Korver — Knee Injury
Terry Kunz — Injury

SAN DIEGO CHARGERS 7-7 Tommy Prothro

Scores of Each Game		
0	Oakland	24
23	Kansas City	7
24	CINCINNATI	3
14	New Orleans	0
20	NEW ENGLAND	24
16	KANSAS CITY	21
14	Miami	13
0	Detroit	20
14	DENVER	17
12	OAKLAND	7
30	Seattle	28
37	CLEVELAND	14
9	Denver	17
9	PITTSBURGH	10

Use Name	Pos.	Hgt	Wgt	Age	Int	Pts
Booker Brown	OT	6'2"	257	24		
Billy Shieds	OT	6'2"	254	24		
Russ Washington	OT	6'6"	290	30		
Charles Aiu	OG	6'2"	254	23		
Don Macek	OG-C	6'3"	253	23		
Doug Wilkerson	OG	6'2"	257	30		
Ralph Perretta	C	6'2"	250	24		
Bob Rush	C	6'5"	258	21		
Fred Dean	DE	6'3"	226	25	1	12
Leroy Jones	DE	6'8"	274	26	1	6
John Lee	DE	6'2"	253	24		
Charles DeJurnett	DT-DE	6'4"	270	25		
Gary Johnson	DT	6'2"	254	25		
Louie Kelcher	DT	6'5"	282	24		
Don Goode	LB	6'2"	231	26		
Tom Graham	LB	6'2"	235	27		
Bob Horn	LB	6'3"	237	23	1	
Woodrow Lowe	LB	6'	227	23	1	
Rick Middleton	LB	6'2"	228	25		
Ray Preston	LB	6'	215	23		
Jerome Dove	DB	6'	186	23	1	
Clarence Duren	DB	6'1"	190	26	4	
Mike Fuller	DB	5'9"	188	24	5	12
Pete Shaw	DB	5'10"	184	23		
Hal Stringert	DB	5'11"	185	25	4	
Mike Williams	DB	5'10"	180	23	3	
Dan Fouts	QB	6'3"	204	26		
James Harris	QB	6'3"	217	30		12
Neal Jeffrey	QB	6'1"	180	24		
Bill Munson	QB	6'2"	205	36		
Cliff Olander	QB	6'5"	196	22		
Hank Bauer	HB	5'10"	195	23		6
Joe Washington	HB	5'10"	182	23		
Rickey Young	HB	6'2"	198	23		24
Larry Barnes	FB-HB	5'11"	220	23		
Bo Matthews	FB	6'4"	230	25		
Clarence Williams	FB	5'9"	198	22		12
Don Woods	FB	6'1"	209	26		12
Larry Dorsey	WR	6'1"	195	24		12
Charlie Joiner	WR	5'11"	188	29		36
Dwight McDonald	WR	6'2"	187	26		
Artie Owens	WR	5'10"	174	24		
Johnnie Rodgers	WR	5'10"	180	26		
Pat Curran	TE	6'3"	238	31		
Bob Klein	TE	6'5"	245	30		6
Jeff West	TE	6'3"	211	24		
Rolf Benirschke	K	6'	165	22		72

Danny Colbert — Injury

SEATTLE SEAHAWKS 5-9 Jack Patera

Scores of Each Game		
14	BALTIMORE	29
20	Cincinnati	42
13	DENVER	24
0	New England	31
30	TAMPA BAY	23
13	Miami	31
56	BUFFALO	17
7	Oakland	44
17	N.Y. Jets	0
10	HOUSTON	22
28	SAN DIEGO	30
20	Pittsburgh	30
34	Kansas City	31
20	CLEVELAND	19

Use Name	Pos.	Hgt	Wgt	Age	Int	Pts
Steve August	OT	6'5"	254	22		
Nick Bebout	OT	6'5"	260	26		
Norm Evans	OT	6'5"	250	34		
Ron Coder	OG	6'4"	250	23		
Gordon Jolley	OG-OT	6'5"	245	28		
Tom Lynch	OG	6'5"	260	22		
Bob Newton	OG	6'4"	260	28		
Art Kuehn	C	6'3"	255	24		
Geoff Reece	C	6'4"	247	25		
John Yarno	C	6'5"	251	22		
Dennis Boyd	DE-DT	6'6"	255	21		
Richard Harris	DE	6'4"	258	29		
Horace Jones	DE	6'3"	255	28		
Alden Roche	DE	6'4"	255	32		
Ron East	DT	6'4"	248	34		
Bob Lurtsema	DT-DE	6'6"	250	35		
Steve Niehaus	DT-DE	6'4"	270	22		
Bill Sandifer	DT	6'6"	262	25		
Terry Beeson	LB	6'3"	240	21		
Pete Cronan	LB	6'2"	238	22		
Ken Geddes	LB	6'3"	235	29	3	
Sammy Green	LB	6'2"	230	22	1	
Mike Jones	LB	6'2"	214	23		
Amos Martin	LB	6'3"	228	28		
Charles McShane	LB	6'3"	230	23		
Autry Beamon	DB	6'1"	190	23	6	6
Dave Brown	DB	6'1"	190	24	4	6
Ron Dufek	DB	6'	195	23	2	
Doug Long	DB	6'	189	22		
Eddie McMillan	DB	6'	190	25	4	
Walter Packer	DB	5'10"	174	21		
Steve Preece	DB	6'1"	195	30	4	
Cornell Webster	DB	6'	180	22	1	
Sam Adkins	QB	6'2"	214	22		
Steve Myer	QB	6'2"	188	23		
Jim Zorn	QB	6'2"	200	24		6
Al Hunter	HB	5'11"	195	22		6
David Sims	HB	6'3"	216	21		48
Sherman Smith	HB-FB	6'3"	216	22		36
Tony Benjamin	FB	6'3"	225	21		
Ed Marinaro	FB-HB	6'2"	207	27		
Don Testerman	FB	6'2"	235	24		30
Duke Fergerson	WR	6'1"	193	23		12
Steve Largent	WR	5'11"	184	22		60
Sam McCullum	WR	6'2"	203	24		6
Steve Raible	WR	6'2"	195	23		
Ron Howard	TE	6'4"	240	26		6
Fred Rayhle	TE	6'5"	216	23		
John Sawyer	TE	6'2"	230	24		
John Leypoldt	K	6'2"	230	31		60
Herman Weaver	K	6'4"	210	28		

Randy Coffield — Injury

KANSAS CITY CHIEFS 2-12 Paul Wiggin (1-6), Tom Bettis (1-6)

Scores of Each Game		
17	New England	21
7	SAN DIEGO	23
28	OAKLAND	37
7	Denver	23
6	BALTIMORE	17
21	San Diego	16
7	Cleveland	44
20	GREEN BAY	10
27	Chicago	28
7	DENVER	14
2	Houston	34
7	CINCINNATI	27
31	SEATTLE	34
20	Oakland	21

Use Name	Pos.	Hgt	Wgt	Age	Int	Pts
Matt Herkenhoff	OT	6'4"	255	26		
Jim Nicholson	OT	6'6"	275	27		
Tom Wickert (from DET)	OT-OG	6'4"	248	25		
Tom Condon	OG	6'3"	240	24		
Charlie Getty	OG-OT	6'4"	260	25		
Darius Helton	OG	6'2"	260	22		
Bob Simmons	OG-OT	6'4"	260	23		
Charlie Ane	C	6'1"	233	25		
Jack Rudnay	C	6'3"	240	29		
Larry Estes	DE	6'6"	250	30		
John Lohmeyer	DE-DT	6'4"	229	26		2
Whitney Paul	DE	6'3"	220	23	1	
Wilbur Young	DE	6'6"	290	28		
Cliff Frazier	DT	6'4"	265	22		
Willie Lee	DT	6'5"	249	27		6
Keith Simons	DT	6'3"	254	23		
Billy Andrews	LB	6'	220	32		
Ray Burks	LB	6'3"	217	22		
Jimbo Elrod	LB	6'	223	23		
Tom Howard	LB	6'2"	208	23	1	
Willie Lanier	LB	6'1"	245	32		
Jim Lynch	LB	6'1"	225	32	3	
Otis Rodgers	LB	6'3"	230	23		
Dave Rozumek	LB	6'2"	212	23		
Gary Barbaro	DB	6'4"	198	23	8	6
Tim Collier	DB	6'	166	23	2	6
Ricky Davis	DB	6'1"	180	24		
Chris Golub	DB	6'2"	196	22		
Tim Gray	DB	6'1"	200	24	2	12
Gary Green	DB	5'11"	184	21	3	
Emmitt Thomas	DB	6'2"	192	34	1	
Ricky Wesson	DB	5'9"	163	22		
Tony Adams	QB	6'	198	27		
Mike Livingston	QB	6'3"	211	31		6
Mark Vitali	QB	6'5"	209	22		
Ted McNight	HB	6'1"	203	23		
Arnold Morgado	HB	6'	210	24		
Ed Podolak	HB	6'1"	205	30		30
Tony Reed	HB	5'11"	197	22		12
Mark Bailey	FB	6'3"	237	22		18
John Brockington (from GB)	FB	6'1"	225	28		12
MacArthur Lane	FB	6'	220	35		6
Pat McNeil	FB	5'9"	208	23		
Larry Brunson	WR	5'11"	180	28		
Gerald Butler	WR	6'5"	205	23		
Henry Marshall	WR	6'2"	205	23		24
Charlie Wade	WR	5'10"	163	27		
Edwin Bechman	TE	6'4"	223	22		
Andre Samuels	TE	6'4"	229	24		
Walter White	TE	6'3"	218	26		30
Jan Stenerud	K	6'2"	187	34		51
Jerrel Wilson	K	6'4"	222	36		

Rod Walters — Injury
Woody Green — Knee Injury

DENVER BRONCOS

Rushing

Last Name	No.	Yds	Avg	TD
Armstrong	130	489	3.8	4
Perrin	110	456	4.1	3
Lytle	104	408	3.9	1
Keyworth	83	311	3.7	1
Jensen	40	143	3.6	1
Morton	31	125	4.0	4
Weese	11	56	5.1	1
Penrose	4	24	6.0	0
Upchurch	1	19	19.0	1
Dolbin	2	12	6.0	0
Kiick	1	1	1.0	0
Dilts	1	0	0.0	0
Moses	5	−1	−0.2	0

Receiving

Last Name	No.	Yds	Avg	TD
Odoms	37	429	12	3
Moses	27	539	20	4
Dolbin	26	443	17	3
Armstrong	18	128	7	0
Lytle	17	198	12	1
Upchurch	12	245	20	2
Keyworth	11	48	4	0
Perrin	6	106	18	1
Jensen	4	63	16	0
Egloff	2	27	14	0
Kiick	2	14	7	0
Turner	1	25	25	1

Punt Returns

Last Name	No.	Yds	Avg	TD
Upchurch	51	653	13	1
Pane	6	48	8	0
Schultz	1	11	11	0

Kickoff Returns

Last Name	No.	Yds	Avg	TD
Upchurch	20	456	23	0
Schultz	6	135	23	0
Perrin	3	72	24	0
Pane	1	16	16	0
Keyworth	1	15	15	0
Hyde	1	15	15	0
Grant	1	8	8	0
Nairne	1	1	1	0
Dolbin	0	14	—	0

Passing – Punting – Kicking

PASSING	Att	Comp	%	Yds	Yd/Att	TD	Int—	%	RK
Morton	254	131	42	1929	7.6	14	8—	3	2
Penrose	39	21	54	217	5.6	0	4—	10	
Weese	20	11	55	119	6.0	1	0—	0	

PUNTING	No	Avg
Dilts	90	39.2
Weese	1	38.0

KICKING	XP	Att	%	FG	Att	%
Turner	31	34	91	13	19	68

OAKLAND RAIDERS

Rushing

Last Name	No.	Yds	Avg	TD
van Eeghen	324	1273	3.9	7
Davis	194	787	4.1	5
Banaszak	67	214	3.2	5
Garrett	53	175	3.3	1
Robiskie	22	100	4.5	1
Rae	13	75	5.8	1
Ginn	5	6	1.2	0
Stabler	3	−3	−3.0	0

Receiving

Last Name	No.	Yds	Avg	TD
Casper	48	584	12	6
Branch	33	540	16	6
Biletnikoff	33	446	14	5
Siani	24	344	14	2
Davis	16	124	8	0
van Eeghen	15	135	9	0
Garrett	8	61	8	2
Bradshaw	5	90	18	0
Banaszak	2	14	7	0

Punt Returns

Last Name	No.	Yds	Avg	TD
Colzie	32	334	10	0
Jennings	12	71	6	0

Kickoff Returns

Last Name	No.	Yds	Avg	TD
Garrett	21	420	20	0
Jennings	7	153	22	0
Banaszak	7	119	17	0
Robiskie	6	83	14	0
Ginn	3	74	25	0
Davis	3	63	21	0
Hayes	3	57	19	0
Bankston	1	0	0	0
McCoy	1	0	0	0

Passing – Punting – Kicking

PASSING	Att	Comp	%	Yds	Yd/Att	TD	Int—	%	RK
Stabler	294	169	58	2176	7.4	20	20—	7	4
Rae	30	15	50	162	5.4	1	4—	13	

PUNTING	No	Avg
Guy	59	43.3

KICKING	XP	Att	%	FG	Att	%
Mann	39	42	93	20	29	71

SAN DIEGO CHARGERS

Rushing

Last Name	No.	Yds	Avg	TD
Young	157	543	3.5	4
Woods	118	405	3.4	1
J. Washington	62	217	3.5	0
C. Williams	50	215	4.3	2
Matthews	43	193	4.5	0
Barnes	24	70	2.9	0
Rodgers	3	44	14.7	0
Olander	7	30	4.3	0
Harris	10	13	1.3	2
Fouts	6	13	2.2	0
Fuller	1	7	7.0	1
Bauer	4	4	1.0	0
Owens	1	3	3.0	0
Curran	1	2	2.0	0
Munson	1	2	2.0	0

Receiving

Last Name	No.	Yds	Avg	TD
Young	48	423	9	0
Joiner	35	542	15	6
J. Washington	31	244	8	0
Klein	20	244	12	1
Woods	18	218	12	1
McDonald	13	174	13	0
Rodgers	12	187	16	0
Dorsey	10	198	20	2
Curran	10	123	12	0
Matthews	3	41	14	0
C. Williams	3	20	7	0
Bauer	1	15	15	1
Barnes	1	10	10	0
West	1	3	3	0

Punt Returns

Last Name	No.	Yds	Avg	TD
Fuller	28	360	13	1
Rodgers	15	158	11	0
Dove	1	3	3	0
M. Williams	1	0	0	0
C. Williams	1	0	0	0

Kickoff Returns

Last Name	No.	Yds	Avg	TD
C. Williams	24	481	20	0
Owens	8	132	17	0
Rodgers	4	66	17	0
Woods	1	27	27	0
Middleton	1	20	20	0
Joiner	1	8	8	0

Passing – Punting – Kicking

PASSING	Att	Comp	%	Yds	Yd/Att	TD	Int—	%	RK
Harris	211	109	52	1240	5.9	5	11—	5	12
Fouts	109	69	63	869	8.0	4	6—	6	
Munson	31	20	65	225	7.3	1	1—	3	
Olander	16	7	44	76	4.8	0	2—	13	
J. Washington	1	1	100	32	32.0	1	0—	0	
Woods	1	0	0	0	0.0	0	0—	0	

PUNTING	No	Avg
West	72	37.6

KICKING	XP	Att	%	FG	Att	%
Benirschke	21	24	88	17	23	74

SEATTLE SEAHAWKS

Rushing

Last Name	No.	Yds	Avg	TD
Smith	163	763	4.7	4
Testerman	119	459	3.9	1
Sims	99	369	3.7	5
Hunter	32	179	5.6	1
Zorn	25	141	5.6	1
Benjamin	13	48	3.7	0
Adkins	3	6	2.0	0
Myer	6	1	0.2	0
Weaver	1	−2	−2.0	0

Receiving

Last Name	No.	Yds	Avg	TD
Largent	33	643	19	10
Testerman	31	219	7	4
Smith	30	419	14	2
Fergersen	19	374	20	2
Howard	17	177	10	1
Sims	12	176	15	3
Sawyer	10	105	11	0
McCullum	9	198	22	1
Raible	5	79	16	0
Hunter	5	42	8	0
Benjamin	4	27	7	0

Punt Returns

Last Name	No.	Yds	Avg	TD
Packer	20	131	7	0
Ferguson	8	54	7	0
Largent	4	32	8	0

Kickoff Returns

Last Name	No.	Yds	Avg	TD
Hunter	36	820	23	0
Packer	13	280	22	0
Fergerson	11	240	22	0
Sims	4	52	13	0
Smith	3	56	19	0
Raible	2	19	10	0
Dufek	1	21	21	0
Testerman	1	14	14	0

Passing – Punting – Kicking

PASSING	Att	Comp	%	Yds	Yd/Att	TD	Int—	%	RK
Zorn	251	104	41	1687	6.7	16	19—	8	14
Myer	130	70	54	729	5.6	6	12—	9	
Sims	4	1	25	43	10.8	1	1—	25	
Preece	1	0	0	0	0.0	0	0—	0	
Smith	1	0	0	0	0.0	0	0—	0	

PUNTING	No	Avg
Weaver	58	39.5

KICKING	XP	Att	%	FG	Att	%
Leypoldt	33	37	89	9	18	50

KANSAS CITY CHIEFS

Rushing

Last Name	No.	Yds	Avg	TD
Podolak	133	550	4.1	5
Reed	126	505	4.0	2
Bailey	66	266	4.0	2
Brockington	65	186	2.9	1
Lane	25	79	3.2	1
Livingston	19	78	4.1	1
McNight	11	74	6.7	0
Burks	1	51	51.0	0
Adams	5	21	4.2	0
Morgado	3	12	4.0	0
Marshall	7	11	1.6	0
Brunson	2	8	4.0	0
White	2	−3	−1.5	0

Receiving

Last Name	No.	Yds	Avg	TD
White	48	674	14	5
Podolak	32	313	10	0
Marshall	23	445	19	4
Brockington	21	223	11	1
Brunson	20	295	15	0
Bailey	17	206	12	1
Reed	12	125	10	0
Samuels	5	65	13	0
Lane	3	40	13	0
Morgado	2	21	11	0
McKnight	1	11	11	0
Beckman	1	3	3	0

Punt Returns

Last Name	No.	Yds	Avg	TD
Green	14	115	8	0
Brunson	20	108	5	0
Podolak	2	13	7	0

Kickoff Returns

Last Name	No.	Yds	Avg	TD
McNight	12	305	25	0
Reed	11	239	22	0
Brunson	11	216	20	0
Wesson	7	129	18	0
Bailey	3	46	15	0
Getty	1	15	15	0
Burks	1	15	15	0

Passing – Punting – Kicking

PASSING	Att	Comp	%	Yds	Yd/Att	TD	Int—	%	RK
Livingston	282	143	51	1823	6.5	9	15—	5	11
Adams	92	47	51	691	7.5	2	11—	12	

PUNTING	No	Avg
Wilson	88	39.9

KICKING	XP	Att	%	FG	Att	%
Stenerud	27	28	96	8	18	44

1977 Championship Games

NFC CHAMPIONSHIP GAME
January 1, at Irving, Tex.
(Attendance: 61,968)

SCORING

DALLAS	6	10	0	7—23
MINNESOTA	0	6	0	0—6

First Quarter
Dallas — Richards, 32 yard pass from Staubach
PAT — Kick (no good)

Second Quarter
Dallas — Newhouse, 5 yard rush
PAT — Herrera (Kick)
Minn. — Cox, 12 yard field goal
Minn. — Cox, 37 yard field goal
Dallas — Herrera, 21 yard field goal

Fourth Quarter
Dallas — Dorsett, 11 yard rush
PAT — Herrera (Kick)

TEAM STATISTICS

DALLAS		MINN.
16	First Downs—Total	12
7	First Downs—Rushing	4
7	First Downs—Passing	6
2	First Downs—Penalty	2
1	Fumbles—Number	5
1	Fumbles—Lost Ball	3
5	Penalty—Number	5
84	Yards Penalized	32
0	Missed Field Goals	0
66	Offensive Plays	63
328	Net Yards	214
4.8	Average Gain	3.4
2	Giveaways	4
4	Takeaways	2
+2	Difference	-2

As expected, Dallas had no trouble at all with a young, inexperienced Chicago Bear team that turned the ball over seven times in the Pokes' 37-7 NFC semifinal victory in Irving. But it was a different story in Los Angeles that same day as Minnesota took advantage of a sloppy, mud-infested field to upset the playoff-jinxed Rams 14-7. The Cowboys proceeded to start the new year off on the right foot with a convincing 23-6 victory over the Vikes to put themselves in the Super Bowl.

The Vikings were no match for a Dallas defense led by linemen Harvey Martin, and Ed Jones and OLB Tom Henderson. After holding the Bears' Walter payton to only 60 rushing yards the week before, the Cowboys' "flex" limited Chuck Foreman to just 59. Two minutes into the first quarter, Martin tackled RB Robert Miller hard enough to cause a fumble which the big end recovered on Minnesota's 39-yard line to set up the Cowboys' first score. Robert Newhouse, who enjoyed his second-straight 80-yard playoff game, powered his way to the 32-yard line and the QB Roger Staubach took over, faking a quick screen and throwing long to WR Golden Richards in the endzone. Minnesota's Carl Eller blocked the extra point, but on the Cowboys' next TD drive, the Vikes' usually reliable specialty teams failed to stop punter Danny White's fake and subsequent 14-yard run for a first down. A defensive holding call on FS Paul Krauses moved the ball deeper into Viking territory and Newhouse responded with a five-yard TD romp to make it 13-0.

Martin recovered two fumbles while his opposite number, Jones, was an imposing force against the run. Also helping out defensively was a strong secondary effort that kept the Vikes' top receiver, Ahmad Rashad, under wraps all day with double-team coverage.

INDIVIDUAL STATISTICS

RUSHING

DALLAS	No	Yds	Avg.	MINNESOTA	No	Yds	Avg.
Newhouse	15	81	5.4	Foreman	21	59	2.8
Dorsett	19	71	3.7	Miller	8	5	0.6
D. White	1	14	14.0	S. Johnson	1	2	2.0
Staubach	4	4	1.0		30	66	2.2
	39	170	4.3				

RECEIVING

	No	Yds	Avg.		No	Yds	Avg.
D. Pearson	4	62	15.5	Foreman	5	36	7.2
P. Pearson	3	48	16.0	S. White	3	46	15.3
Richards	2	34	17.0	Rashad	3	18	6.0
Newhouse	2	5	2.5	Miller	2	39	19.5
DuPree	1	16	16.0	Voigt	1	19	19.0
	12	165	13.8		14	158	11.3

PUNTING

	No	Yds	Avg.		No	Yds	Avg.
D. White	8		36.6	Clabo	8		34.7

PUNT RETURNS

	No	Yds	Avg.		No	Yds	Avg.
Hill	3	44	14.7	Moore	3	2	0.7
B. Johnson	2	13	6.5				
	5	57	11.4				

KICKOFF RETURNS

	No	Yds	Avg.		No	Yds	Avg.
Brinson	3	36	12.0	Moore	3	74	24.7
				S. White	1	37	37.0
				Kellar	1	11	11.0
					5	122	24.4

INTERCEPTION RETURNS

	No	Yds	Avg.		No	Yds	Avg.
Henderson	1	1	1.0	N. Wright	1	0	0.0

PASSING

DALLAS	Att.	Comp.	Comp. Pct.	Yds.	Int.	Yds/ Att.	Yds/ Comp.	Yards Lost Tackled
Staubach	23	12	52.2	165	1	7.2	13.8	2—7

MINNESOTA								
Lee	31	14	45.2	158	1	5.1	11.3	2—10

AFC CHAMPIONSHIP GAME
January 1, at Denver
(Attendance: 75,004)

SCORING

DENVER	7	0	7	6—20
OAKLAND	3	0	0	14—17

First Quarter
Oak. — Mann, 20 yard field goal
Den. — Moses, 74 yard pass from Morton
PAT—Turner (kick)

Third Quarter
Den. — Keyworth, 1 yard rush
PAT—Turner (kick)

Fourth Quarter
Oak. — Casper, 7 yard pass from Stabler
PAT—Mann (kick)
Den. — Moses, 12 yard pass from Morton
PAT—No pass—pass failed
Oak. — Casper, 17 yard pass from Stabler
PAT—Mann (kick)

TEAM STATISTICS

DENVER		OAKLAND
16	First Downs—Total	20
6	First Downs—Rushing	6
8	First Downs—Passing	11
2	First Downs—Penalty	3
2	Fumbles—Number	0
0	Fumbles—Lost Ball	0
8	Penalty—Number	2
46	Yards Penalized	6
3	Missed Field Goals	1
58	Offensive Plays	72
308	Net Yards	298
5.3	Average Gain	4.1
1	Giveaways	1
1	Takeaways	1
0	Difference	0

The defending Super Bowl champion Raiders just barely made it to AFC title game with a 37-31 overtime victory at Baltimore in one of the most exciting contests of all-time. The leader changed hands six times and Raider Errol Mann tied the score for the last time when he booted a 22-yard field goal with 26 seconds left in regulation following a clutch 42-yard reception by TE Dave Casper. Casper later scored the game winner on a 10-yard Ken Stabler pass 43 seconds into the second overtime, ending the third longest game in NFL history.

Meanwhile, Denver got past its first hurdle with a 34-21 win over Pittsburgh, after breaking open a 21-21 tie with 13 unanswered points in the fourth quarter. Just as it had done all season, the Broncos' Orange Crush defense provided good field position by forcing four turnovers, including two interceptions by All-Pro OLB Tom Jackson.

Because Oakland had more experience and the Cinderella Broncos were still somewhat of an unknown quantity in many observers' eyes, the Raiders were rated as slight favorites over the team which had beaten them to the AFC West crown. As Oakland repeatedly tried to run to the outside and failed because of the superb lateral movement of the Bronco defense, the momentum swung toward Denver. Although Oakland had taken an early lead on Mann's 20-yard field goal, QB Craig Morton struck two plays later on a 74-yard TD bomb to WR Haven Moses.

After leading 7-3 at halftime, Denver was driving for another score midway through the third quarter when perhaps the most controversial play of the season occurred. With first-and-goal at the Raider two, Rob Lytle took a handoff and vaulted over the left side of his offensive line. He was met head-on by safety Jack Tatum, who jarred the ball loose while Lytle was in mid-air. Raider MG Mike McCoy picked up the loose ball and began to run, but the play was whistled dead. The officials, apparently screened from the fumble, ruled that Denver should keep the ball. Jon Keyworth scored from the one on the next play, and Denver had a 14-3 lead.

Whether that disputed "non-fumble" would have changed the outcome of the game will be debated for years, but it certainly put Oakland at a big disadvantage. The Raiders closed the gap on Stabler's seven-yard TD pass to Casper, but the Morton-Moses duo clicked again on a 12-yard scoring pass. Oakland once again trimmed the deficit to three on a 17-yard pass to the reliable Casper with 3:16 remaining, but Denver ran out the clokc using Lonnie Perrin and Otis Armstrong.

INDIVIDUAL STATISTICS

RUSHING

DENVER	No	Yds	Avg.	OAKLAND	No	Yds	Avg.
Perrin	11	42	3.8	van Eeghen	20	71	3.6
Lytle	7	26	3.7	Banaszak	7	22	3.1
Keyworth	8	19	2.4	Davis	9	1	0.1
Armstrong	7	16	2.3		36	94	2.6
Jensen	1	2	2.0				
Morton	2	-4	-2.0				
Moses	1	-10	-10.0				
	37	91	2.5				

RECEIVING

	No	Yds	Avg.		No	Yds	Avg.
Moses	5	168	33.6	Casper	5	71	14.2
Perrin	2	20	10.0	Biletnikoff	4	38	9.5
Jensen	1	20	20.0	Branch	3	59	19.7
Odoms	1	13	13.0	van Eeghen	2	8	4.0
Keyworth	1	3	3.0	Bradshaw	1	25	25.0
	10	224	22.4	Siani	1	12	12.0
				Banaszak	1	2	2.0
					17	215	12.6

PUNTING

	No	Yds	Avg.		No	Yds	Avg.
Dilts	4		40.8	Guy	5		36.0

PUNT RETURNS

	No	Yds	Avg.		No	Yds	Avg.
Upchurch	2	12	6.0	Garrett	2	5	2.5

KICKOFF RETURNS

	No	Yds	Avg.		No	Yds	Avg.
Upchurch	2	33	16.5	Garrett	3	111	37.0
Schultz	1	20	20.0	Davis	1	25	25.0
Lytle	1	14	14.0		4	136	36.0
	4	67	16.8				

INTERCEPTION RETURNS

	No	Yds	Avg.		No	Yds	Avg.
Swenson	1	14	14.0	Rice	1	11	11.0

PASSING

DENVER	Att.	Comp.	Comp. Pct.	Yds.	Int.	Yds/ Att.	Yds/ Comp	Yards Lost Tackled
Morton	20	10	50.0	224	1	11.2	22.4	1—7

OAKLAND								
Stabler	35	17	48.6	215	1	6.1	12.6	1—11

January 9, at Pasadena
(Attendance 100,421)

All the Silver

Orange was undoubtedly the NFL's most popular color during the 77' season, but after the Dallas Cowboys swept past the Denver Broncos 27-10 in the first Super Bowl played indoors, the game's most vivid scenes had been painted in a solid shade of black and blue.

Most responsible for this setting were the imposing members of the Cowboys' defensive line—safety Randy Hughes notwithstanding—as they ripped away at the left side of Denver's offensive line and pressured quarterback Craig Morton into a miserable performance.

Morton, the NFL's Comeback Player of the Year, completed as many passes to the Cowboys as his own teammates, unintentionally entering his name into the less-distinguished portion of the Super Bowl record book.

In addition to his four interceptions, the game featured the most Super Bowl penalties ever by both teams (20 for 154 yards) as well as most fumbles, both teams (10).

Thanks, however, to the Pokes' inability to capitalize on more than a few scoring opportunities in the first half, as well as Bronco Head Coach Red Miller's decision to replace Morton with Norris Weese with 6:40 left in the third quarter, the game was kept from becoming a Super Bore.

Four plays after Hughes snatched a Morton pass on the Denver 29, Tony Dorsett's three-yard sprint off left tackle put the Cowboys on the scoreboard first with 10:31 gone in the first quarter.

Efren Herrera's 35-yard three-pointer following another interception finished up the first-period scoring, and he also provided the second quarter's only score with a 43-yarder after blowing three straight field goal attempts.

Jim Turner's 47-yarder that barely made it over the cross-bar gave the Broncos their first score early in the third quarter, but the Cowboys extended their lead to 20-3 after a stunning 45-yard TD reception by Butch Johnson as he dove across the goal line to snare QB Roger Staubach's pass.

With Weese adding much-needed mobility to the Denver attack, the Broncs scored their first TD of the game on Rob Lytle's one-yard plunge, one play after ex-Cowboy Jim Jensen galloped 16 yards with a Weese pitchout.

But the game's second exceptional TD reception—Golden Richards' 29-yard, over-the-head catch of Robert Newhouse's option pass while rolling left—made sure the Cinderella Broncos would turn back into a normal old orange pumpkin, at least until next year.

For the first time in Super Bowl history, co-winners were selected as MVP's—White (five tackles, one assist) and DE Harvey Martin (two tackles, two sacks, one deflection).

And while Staubach called a clever game, emphasizing a counteraction passing attack away from Denver's pursuit toward the middle, Dallas' Doomsday defense—and all those black and blue marks—really told the story.

LINEUPS

DALLAS	OFFENSE	DENVER
Richards	WR	Dolbin
Neely	LT	Maurer
Scott	LG	Glassic
Fitzgerald	C	Montler
Rafferty	RG	Howard
Donovan	RT	Minor
DuPree	TE	Odoms
D. Pearson	WR	Moses
Staubach	QB	Morton
Dorsett	RB	Armstrong
Newhouse	RB	Keyworth
	DEFENSE	
Jones	LE	Chavous
Pugh	LT-NT	Carter
R. White	RT-RE	Alzado
Martin	RE-LLB	Swenson
Henderson	LLB-LLB	Rizzo
Bruenig	MLB-RLB	Gradishar
Lewis	RLB-RLB	Jackson
Barnes	LCB	L. Wright
Kyle	RCB	Foley
Waters	SS	Thompson
Harris	FS-WS	Jackson

SUBSTITUTES

DALLAS	OFFENSE	
Brinson	Hill	P. Pearson
Carano	Johnson	Saldi
Cooper	Laidlaw	D. White
Dennison	Lawless	R. Wright
Frederick		
	DEFENSE	
Brown	Hegman	Renfro
Cole	Hughes	Stalls
Gregory	Huther	Washington
	KICKER	
	Herrera	

DENVER	OFFENSE	
Allison	Lytle	Schindler
Egloff	Maples	Schultz
Hyde	Penrose	Upchurch
Jensen	Perrin	Weese
	DEFENSE	
Evans	Nairne	Riley
Grant	Poltl	Smith
Jackson	Rich	Turk
Manor		
	KICKERS	
Dilts		Turner

SCORING

DALLAS	10	3	7	7—27	
DENVER	0	0	10	0—10	

First Quarter
Dallas Dorsett, 3 yard rush 10:31
PAT — Herrera (kick)
Dallas Herrera, 35 yard field goal 13:29

Second Quarter
Dallas Herrera, 43 yard field goal 3:44

Third Quarter
Denver Turner, 47 yard field goal 2:28
Dallas Johnson, 45 yard pass from 8:01
Staubach PAT — Herrera (kick)
Denver Lytle, 1 yard rush 9:21
PAT — Turner (kick)

Fourth Quarter
Dallas Richards, 29 yard pass 7:56
from Newhouse
PAT — Herrera (kick)

TEAM STATISTICS

DALLAS		DENVER
17	First Downs—Total	11
8	First Downs—Rushing	8
8	First Downs—Passing	1
1	First Downs—Penalty	2
6	Fumbles—Number	4
2	Fumbles—Lost Ball	4
12	Penalties—Number	8
94	Yards Penalized	60
3	Missed Field Goals	0
71	Offensive Plays	58
325	Net Yards	156
4.6	Average Gain	2.7
2	Giveaways	8
8	Takeaways	2
+6	Differnece	-6

INDIVIDUAL STATISTICS

RUSHING

DALLAS	No	Yds	Avg.	DENVER	No	Yds	Avg.
Dorsett	15	66	4.4	Lytle	10	35	3.5
Newhouse	14	55	3.9	Armstrong	7	27	3.9
D. White	1	13	13.0	Weese	3	26	8.7
P. Pearson	3	11	3.7	Jensen	1	16	16.0
Staubach	3	6	2.6	Keyworth	5	9	1.8
Laidlaw	1	1	1.0	Perrin	3	8	2.7
Johnson	1	-9	-9.0		29	121	4.2
	38	143	3.8				

RECEIVING

DALLAS	No	Yds	Avg.	DENVER	No	Yds	Avg.
P. Pearson	5	37	7.4	Dolbin	2	24	12.0
DuPree	4	66	16.5	Odoms	2	9	4.5
Newhouse	3	-1	-0.3	Moses	1	21	21.0
Johnson	2	53	26.5	Upchurch	1	9	9.0
Richards	2	38	19.0	Jensen	1	5	5.0
Dorsett	2	11	5.5	Perrin	1	-7	-7.0
D. Pearson	1	13	13.0		8	61	7.6
	19	217	11.4				

PUNTING

DALLAS	No		Avg.	DENVER	No		Avg.
D. White	5		41.6	Dilts	4		38.2

PUNT RETURNS

DALLAS	No	Yds	Avg.	DENVER	No	Yds	Avg.
Hill	1	0	0.0	Upchurch	3	22	7.3
				Schultz	1	0	0.0
					4	2	5.5

KICKOFF RETURNS

DALLAS	No	Yds	Avg.	DENVER	No	Yds	Avg.
Johnson	2	29	14.5	Upchurch	3	94	31.3
Brinson	1	22	22.0	Schultz	2	62	31.0
	3	51	17.0	Jensen	1	17	17.0
					6	173	28.8

INTERCEPTION RETURNS

DALLAS	No	Yds	Avg.	DENVER			
Washington	1	27	27.0	none			
Kyle	1	19	19.0				
Barnes	1	0	0.0				
Hughes	1	0	0.0				
	4	46	11.5				

PASSING

DALLAS	Att.	Comp	Comp Pct.	Yds	Int.	Yds/Att.	Yds/Comp.	Yards Lost Tackled
Staubach	25	17	68.0	183	0	7.5	10.8	
D. White	2	1	50.0	5	0	2.5	5.0	
Newhouse	1	1	100.0	29	0	29.0	29.0	
	28	19	67.9	217	0	7.8	11.4	5—35
DENVER								
Morton	15	4	26.7	39	4	2.6	9.8	2—20
Weese	10	4	40.0	22	0	2.2	5.5	2— 6
	25	8	32.0	61	4	2.4	7.6	4—26

Use Name (Nicknames) – Positions	Team by Year	See Section	Hgt	Wgt	College	Int	Pts
Abramowicz, Dan WR-OE	67-73NO 73-74SF 75Buf	2	6'1"	195	Xavier-Ohio		234
Acks, Ron LB	68-71Atl 72-73NE 74-76GB		6'2"	223	Illinois	2	6
Adamle, Mike HB-FB	71-72KC 73-74NYJ 75-76Chi	23	5'9"	196	Northwestern		38
Adams, Bill OG-OT	72,74-77Buf		6'2"	248	Holy Cross		
Adams, Bob TE-OT	67-71Pit 72JJ 73-74NE 75Den 76-77Atl	2	6'2"	222	U. of Pacific		
Adams, Brent OT	75-76Atl		6'5"	256	Tennessee-Chatanooga		
Adams, Doug LB	71-74Cin		6'	225	Ohio State	3	
Adams, Julius DE-DT	71-77NE		6'3"	259	Texas Southern		
Adams, Pete OG	74Cle 75KJ 76Cle 77JJ		6'4"	260	Southern Calif.		
Adams, Sam OG	72-77NE		6'3"	253	Prairie View		
Adams, Tony QB	75-77KC	1	6'	198	Utah State		
Adkins, Margene WR	70-71Dal 72NO 73NYJ 75WFL	23	5'10"	183	Henderson J.C.		
Adkins, Sam QB	77Sea		6'2"	214	Wichita State		
Aiu, Charles OG	76-77SD		6'2"	251	Hawaii		
Albert, Sergio K	74StL		6'3"	195	U.S. International		
Albrecht, Ted OT-OG	77Chi		6'4"	253	California		
Alexakos, Steve OG	70Den 71NYG		6'2"	260	San Diego State		
Alexander, Dan OG	77NYJ		6'4"	245	Louisiana State		
Alexander, Glenn WR	70Buf		6'3"	205	Grambling		
Alexander, John DE	77Mia		6'2"	250	Rutgers		
Alexander, Willie DB	71-77Hou		6'2"	194	Alcorn A & M	16	6
Allen, Carl DB	77StL		6'	185	Southern Miss.	1	
Allen, Doug LB	74-75Buf		6'2"	228	Penn State	1	
Allen, George	HC66-70LA HC71-77Was				Michigan		
Allen, Grady LB	68-72Atl		6'3"	226	Texas A & M	2	
Allen, Jackie DB	69OakA 70-71Buf 72Phi 73JJ		6'1"	187	Baylor		
Allen, Jeff DB	71StL 72JJ		5'11"	190	Iowa State		
Allen, Jim DB	74-77Pit		6'2"	194	U.C.L.A.	7	
Allen, Nate DB	71-74KC 75SF 76-77Min		5'10"	172	Texas Southern	8	12
Allerman, Kurt LB	77StL		6'3"	222	Penn State		
Allison Henry OG-OT	71-72Phi 75-77StL 77Den		6'3"	257	San Diego State		
Alston, Mack TE	70-72Was 73-76Hou 77Bal	2	6'2"	230	Md. Eastern Shore		72
Alward, Tom G	76TB		6'4"	255	Nebraska		
Alzado, Lyle DE-DT	71-77Den		6'3"	258	Yankton		
Ambrose, Dick (Bam Bam) LB	75-77Cle		6'	235	Virginia		
Amman, Dick DE-DT	72-73Bal		6'5"	242	Florida State		
Amundson, George FB-HB	73-74Hou 75Phi	2	6'3"	215	Iowa State		30
Anderson, Bobby HB-FB	70-73Den 74BN 75Was	23	6'	208	Colorado		66
Anderson, Dick DB	68-69MiaA 70-74Mia 75KJ	3	6'2"	198	Colorado	34	24
	76-77Mia						
Anderson, Donny HB	66-71GB 72-74StL	234	6'3"	212	Texas Tech		336
Anderson, Gary OG	77Det		6'3"	250	Stanford		
Anderson, Jerry DB	77Cin		5'11"	198	Oklahoma		
Anderson, Ken QB	71-77CiN	12	6'1"	210	Augustana		66
Anderson, Preston DB	74Cle		6'1"	183	Rice		
Anderson, Ralph DB	71-72Pit 73NE		6'2"	180	West Texas State	6	2
Anderson, Scott C	74,76Min		6'4"	242	Missouri		
Anderson, Terry WR	77Mia		5'9"	182	Bethune-Cookman		
Anderson, Tim DB	75SF 76Buf		6'	193	Ohio State		
Anderson, Warren WR	77Hou		6'2"	195	W. Virginia State		
Andrews, Al LB	70-71Buf		6'3"	216	New Mexico State	1	
Andrews, Billy LB	67-74Cle 75SD 76-77KC		6'	223	Southeastern La.	7	6
Andrews, John TE-HB	72SD 73-74Bal		6'3"	222	Indiana		6
Andrews, John DE-DT	75-76Mia		6'6"	251	Morgan State		
Ane, Charlie C	75-77KC		6'1"	233	Michigan State		
Anthony, Charles HB	74SD 75KJ		6'1"	230	Southern Calif.	1	
Antoine, Lionel OT	72-76Chi 77KJ		6'6"	260	Southern Illinois		
Archer, Troy DT-DE	76-77NYG		6'4"	250	Colorado		
Armstrong, Otis HB	73-77Den	23	5'10"	196	Purdue		138
Arneson, Jim OG-C	73-74Dal 75Was		6'3"	247	Arizona		
Arneson, Mark LB	72-77StL		6'2"	221	Arizona	5	
Arnold, Francis OG	74Den		6'3"	295	Oregon		
Arnsbarger, Bill	HC74-76NYG				Miami-Ohio		
Arrington, Rick QB	70-72Phi	1	6'2"	230	Tulsa		6
Arthur, Gary TE	70-77NYJ		6'5"	254	Miami-Ohio		
Asher, Bob OT-OG	70Dal 71JJ 72-75Chi		6'5"	254	Vanderbilt		
Ashton, Josh HB-FB	72-74NE 75StL	2	6'1"	204	Tulsa		24
Askea, Mike OT	73Den		6'4"	260	Stanford		
Askon, Bert TE-DE	72Pit 73NO 74WFL 75-77GB		6'3"	223	Texas Southern		6
Atessis, Bill DT-DE	71NE		6'3"	240	Texas		
Athas, Pete DB-WR	71-74NYG 75Cle 75Min 76NO	3	5'11"	185	Tennessee	16	6
Atkins, Bob DB	68-69StL 70-76Hou		6'3"	211	Grambling	19	6
Atkins, Dave HB	73SF 75SD		6'1"	205	Texas-El Paso		6
Atkinson, Al LB	65-69NY-A 70-74NYJ 75KJ		6'1"	229	Villanova	21	
Atkinson, Butch DB	68-69OakA 70-77Oak	3	6'	182	Morris Brown	30	42
Audick, Dan OG	77StL		6'3"	244	Hawaii		
August, Steve OT	77Sea		6'5"	254	Tulsa		
Austin, Darrell OG-C-OT	75-77NYJ		6'4"	251	South Carolina		
Austin, Hise LB	73KC 74WFL 75GB		6'4"	191	Prairie View		
Austin, Ocie DB	70-71Pit		6'3"	200	Utah State	3	
Avellini, Bob QB	75-77Chi	12	6'2"	205	Maryland		18
Avery, Ken LB	67-68NYG 69CinA 70-74Cin 75KC 76JJ		6'1"	225	Southern Miss.	2	
Ayers, John OT-OG	77SF		6'5"	247	West Texas State		
Babb, Charlie DB	72-77Mia		6'	190	Memphis State	8	
Babich, Bob LB	70-72SD 73-77Cle		6'2"	231	Miami-Ohio	6	6
Babinecz, John LB	72-73Dal 74JJ 75Chi		6'1"	222	Villanova	1	
Bachman, Ted DB	76Sea 76Mia		6'	190	New Mexico State		
Bacon, Coy DE-DT	68-72LA 73-75SD 76-77Cin		6'4"	270	Jackson State	2	14
Bahr, Chris K	76-77Cin	5	5'9"	169	Penn State		163
Bailey, Jim DT-DE	70-74Bal 75NYJ 76-77Atl		6'4"	253	Kansas	1	
Bailey, Larry DT	74Atl		6'4"	238	U. of Pacific		
Bailey, Mark FB	77KC	2	6'3"	237	Long Beach State		18
Bailey, Tom HB-FB	71-74Phi 75KJ	2	6'2"	211	Florida State		12
Bain, Bill OT-OG	75GB 76Den 77KJ		6'4"	270	Southern Calif.		
Baker, Ed QB	72Hou		6'2"	198	Lafayette		
Baker, John DE	70NYG		6'5"	260	Norfolk State		
Baker, Melvin WR	74Mia 75NO 75NE		6'	189	Texas Southern		12
	75SD 76Hou 77Buf						
Baker, Tony FB-HB	68-71NO 71-72Phi 73-74LA 75SD	2	5'11"	224	Iowa State		102
Baker, Wayne DT	75SF		6'6"	270	Brigham Young		

Use Name (Nicknames) – Positions	Team by Year	See Section	Hgt	Wgt	College	Int	Pts.
Baldassin, Mike LB	77SF		6'1"	218	Washington		6
Ball, Larry LB	72-74Min 75Det 76TB 77Mia		6'6"	232	Louisville	2	6
Ballou, Mike LB	70Bos		6'3"	235	U.C.L.A.		
Banaszak, John DE	75-77Pit		6'3"	240	Eastern Michigan		
Banaszak, Pete HB-FB	66-69OakA 70-77Oak	2	5'11"	206	Miami (Fla.)		312
Banaszek, Cas OT	67NJ 68-77SF		6'3"	249	Northwestern		
Banks, Tom C-OG	71-77StL		6'1"	242	Auburn		
Banks, Willie OG	68-69Was 70NYG 73NE		6'2"	240	Alcorn A & M		
Bankston, Warren TE-FB	69-72Pit 73-77Oak	2	6'4"	232	Tulane		30
Bannon, Bruce LB	73-74Mia		6'3"	225	Penn State		
Barbaro, Gary DB	76-77KC		6'4"	198	Nicholls	11	6
Barber, Bob DE-DT	76-77GB		6'3"	240	Grambling		
Barber, Mike TE-WR	76-77Hou		6'3"	235	Louisiana Tech		6
Barisich, Carl NT-DT	73-75Cle 76Sea 77Mia		6'4"	255	Princeton		
Barkum, Jerome WR-TE	72-77NYJ	2	6'4"	214	Jackson State		138
Barnes, Al WR	72-73Det 74WFL		6'1"	170	New Mexico State		12
Barnes, Benny DB	72-77Dal		6'1"	190	Stanford	2	4
Barnes, Bruce K	73-74NE	4	5'11"	214	U.C.L.A.		
Barnes, Jeff LB	77Oak		6'2"	215	California		
Barnes, Joe QB	74chi		5'11"	196	Texas Tech		
Barnes, Larry FB-HB	77SD		5'11"	220	Tennessee State		
Barnes, Mike DT-DE	73-77Bal		6'6"	256	Miami (Fla.)		
Barnes, Pete LB	67-68HouA 69SD-A 70-72SD		6'3"	242	Southern U.	15	6
	73-75StL 76-77NE						
Barnes, Rodrigo LB	73-74Dal 74-75NE 75Mia 76Oak		6'1"	215	Rice		
Barney, Lem DB	67-77Det	34	6'1"	189	Jackson State	56	66
Barrett, Jean OT-C-OG	73-77SF		6'6"	252	Tulsa		
Barry, Fred DB	70Pit		5'10"	184	Boston U.		
Bartkowski, Steve QB	75-77Atl	12	6'4"	213	California		18
Barzilauskas, Carl DT	74-77NYJ		6'6"	274	Indiana		
Baschnagel, Brian WR-DB	76-77Chi	23	6'	194	Ohio State		6
Bass, Mike DB	67Det 69-73Was		6'	190	Michigan	30	24
Baska, Rich LB	76-77Den		6'3"	225	U.C.L.A.		
Bateman, Marv K	77Buf	4	6'4"	213	Utah		1
Bauer, Hank HB	77SD		5'10"	195	Calif. Lutheran		6
Baumgartner, Steve DE-DT	73-77NO 77Hou		6'7"	258	Purdue		
Baumhower, Bob NT	77Mia		6'5"	258	Alabama		
Bayless, Tom OG	70NYJ		6'3"	240	Purdue		
Baylor, Raymond DE	74SD		6'5"	263	Texas Southern		
Baylor, Tim DB	76-77Bal		6'6"	191	Morgan State		
Beamer, Tim DB	71Buf		5'11"	185	Johnson C. Smith		
Beamon, Autry DB	75-76Min 77Sea		6'1"	190	East Texas State	8	8
Bean, Bubba HB	76-77Atl	2	5'11"	195	Texas A & M		18
Beard, Tom C	72Buf		6'6"	280	Michigan State		
Beasley, John TE	67-70Min 71JJ 72-73Min 73-74NO	2	6'3"	229	California		84
Beasley, Terry WR	72SF 73SJ 74-75SF	2	5'10"	183	Auburn		18
Beatty, Chuck DB	69-72Pit 72StL		6'2"	203	North Texas State	4	6
Beauchamp, Al LB	68-69CinA 70-75Cin 76StL		6'2"	235	Southern U.	15	18
Beauchamp, Joe DB	66-69SD-A 70-75SD		6'	185	Iowa	23	18
Beaudoin, Doug DB	76-77NE		6'1"	198	Minnesota		
Bebout, Nick OT	73-75Atl 76-77Sea		6'5"	261	Wyoming		
Bechman, Edward TE	77KC		6'4"	223	Florida State		
Beck, Braden K	71Hou		6'2"	200	Stanford		4
Beckman, Tom DE	72StL		6'5"	250	Michigan		
Beeson, Terry LB	77Sea		6'3"	240	Kansas		
Beirne, Jim WR-TE	68-69HouA 70-73Hou 74SD 75-76Hou	2	6'2"	198	Purdue		68
Beisler, Randy OG-DE-OT-DT	66-68Phi 69-74SF 75KC 76JJ		6'4"	249	Indiana	1	
Belk, Bill DE-DT	68-74SF		6'3"	248	Md. Eastern Shore	1	12
Bell, Bill K	71-72Atl 73NE	5	6'1"	191	Kansas		154
Bell, Bob DE-DT	71-73Det 74-77StL		6'4"	251	Cincinnati		6
Bell, Carlos TE	71NO 72JJ		6'5"	238	Houston		
Bell, Eddie WR	70-75NYJ 76SD	2	5'10"	160	Idaho State		72
Bell, Gordon HB	76-77NYG	23	5'9"	180	Michigan		12
Bell, Ricky FB	77TB	2	6'2"	220	Southern Calif.		6
Bell, Theo WR	76Pit 77FJ	3	6'	180	Arizona		6
Belser, Caesar DB-LB	68-69KC-A 70-71KC 74SD		6'	211	Ark.-Pine Bluff		
Belton, Willie HB	71-72Atl 73-74StL	23	5'11"	198	Md. Eastern Shore		6
Benirshke, Rolf K	77SD	5	6'	165	California-Davis		72
Benjamin, Tony FB	77Sea		6'3"	225	Duke		
Bennett, Leeman	HC77Atl				Kentucky		
Benson, Brad OG	77NYG		6'3"	255	Penn State		
Benson, Duane LB	67-69OakA 70-71Oak		6'2"	217	Hamline	3	
	72-73Atl 74-76Hou						
Berger, Ron DE-DT	69BosA 70Bos 71-72NE		6'8"	278	Wayne State		
Bergey, Bill LB	69CinA 70-73Cin 74-77Phi		6'3"	245	Arkansas State	21	
Bergey, Bruce DE	71KC		6'4"	240	U.C.L.A.		
Bernhardt, Roger OG	74NYJ 75KC 76JJ		6'4"	244	Kansas		
Bernich, Ken LB	75NYJ		6'2"	250	Auburn		
Berra, Tim WR	74Bal		5'11"	185	Massachusetts		
Berry, Bob QB	65-67Min 68-71Atl 73-76Min	12	5'11"	189	Oregon		24
Berry, Reggie DB	72-74SD		6'	188	Long Beach State		
Berry, Royce DE	69CinA 70-74Cin 75BW 76Chi		6'3"	247	Houston		12
Bertelsen, Jim FB-HB	72-76LA	23	5'11"	205	Texas		108
Bertuca, Tony LB	74Bal		6'2"	225	Chico State		
Besana, Fred QB	77Buf		6'4"	200	California		
Best, Art HB	77Chi		6'1"	205	Kent State		
Best, Keith LB	72KC		6'3"	220	Kansas State		
Bethea, Elvin DE	68-69HouA 70-77Hou		6'3"	256	N. Carolina A & T		10
Betterson, James FB	77Phi	2	6'	210	North Carolina		6
Bettiga, Mike WR	74SF		6'3"	193	Humboldt State		
Beutler, Tom LB	70Cle 71Bal		6'1"	232	Toledo		
Beverly, David K	74-75Hou 75-77GB	4	6'2"	180	Auburn		
Beverly, Ed WR	73SF		5'11"	168	Arizona State		
Biggs, Verlon DE-DT	65-69NY-A 70NYJ 71-74Was 75KJ		6'4"	267	Jackson State	1	12
Biletnikoff, Fred (Blinky) WR-FL	65-69OakA 70-77Oak	2	6'1"	190	Florida State		450
Billingsley, Ron DT-DE	67-69SD-A 70SD		6'8"	278	Wyoming		
	71-72Hou 73JJ 74WFL						
Bingham, Gregg LB	73-77Hou		6'1"	229	Purdue	14	6
Bishop, Rich NT	76-77NE		6'1"	268	Louisville		
Bitterlich, Don K	76Sea		5'7"	166	Temple		10
Bjorklund, Hank HB	72-74NYJ	2	6'1"	200	Princeton		
Black, Stan DB	77SF		6'	196	Mississippi State		

Use Name (Nicknames) – Positions	Team by Year	See Section	Hgt	Wgt	College	Int	Pts
Black, Tim LB	77StL		6'2"	215	Baylor		
Blackwood, Lyle DB	72-75Cin 76Sea 77Bal	3	6'	191	Texas Christian	12	
Blahak, Joe DB	73Hou 74-75Min 76TB 76NE 77Min		5'9"	186	Nebraska	3	2
Blair, Matt LB	74-77Min		6'5"	230	Iowa State	5	6
Blair, T.C. TE	74Det		6'4"	220	Tulsa		
Blanchard, Dick LB	72NE		6'3"	225	Tulsa	1	
Blanchard, Tom K	71-73NYG 74-77NO	4	6'	187	Oregon		
Blankenship, Greg LB	76Oak 76Pit		6'1"	212	Cal. State-Hayward		
Bleamer, Jeff OT-OG	75-76Phi 77NYJ		6'4"	253	Penn State		
Bleier, Rocky HB	68Pit 69MS	2	5'11"	206	Notre Dame		78
	70Inj from MS 71-77Pit						
Blount, Jeb QB	77TB	1	6'3"	200	Tulsa		
Blount, Mel DB	70-77Pit	3	6'3"	205	Southern U.	35	12
Blue, Forrest C	68-74SF 75-77Bal		6'5"	259	Auburn		
Blue, Luther WR	77Det		5'11"	190	Iowa State		6
Boatwright, Ron DT	74SD		6'5"	262	Oklahoma State		
Boden, Lynn OG	75-77Det		6'5"	270	S. Dakota State		
Bokamper, Kim LB	77Mia		6'6"	245	San Jose State		
Bolinger, Russ OG-OT	76-77Det		6'5"	255	Long Beach State		
Bolton, Andy HB	76Sea 76-77Det		6'1"	205	Fisk		
Bolton, Ron DB	72-75NE 76-77Cle		6'2"	173	Virginia State	24	6
Bonner, Glen HB	74-75SD	2	6'2"	202	Washington		24
Bonness, Rik LB	76Oak 77TB		6'3"	220	Nebraska		
Boone, Dave DE	74Min		6'3"	248	Eastern Michigan		
Boozer, Emerson HB	66-69NY-A 70-75NYJ	23	5'11"	203	Md. Eastern Shore		390
Bordelon, Ken LB	76-77NO		6'4"	231	Louisiana State		
Boryla, Mike QB	74-76Phi 77KJ	12	6'3"	200	Stanford		12
Bosarge, Wade DB	77Mia 77NO		5'10"	175	Tulsa		
Bouggess, Lee FB	70-71Phi 72JJ 73Phi	2	6'2"	210	Louisville		48
Bowdell, Gordon WR	71Den		6'2"	203	Michigan		
Boyd, Dennis DE-DT	77Sea		6'6"	255	Oregon State		
Boyd, Greg DB	73NO 74NE		6'2"	201	Arizona		
Boyd, Greg DE	77NE		6'6"	270	San Diego State		
Boykin, Greg HB	77NO		6'	225	Northwestern		
Bradley, Bill DB	69-76Phi 77StL	34	5'11"	190	Texas	34	6
Bradley, Chuck TE	75-77SD 77Chi		6'6"	243	Oregon		
Bradley, Dave OG	69-71GB 72StL		6'4"	245	Penn State		
Bradley, Ed LB	72-75Pit 76Sea 77SF		6'2"	236	Wake Forest	1	
Bradshaw, Morris WR	74-77Oak	2	6'	196	Ohio State		30
Bradshaw, Terry QB	70-77Pit	12	6'3"	214	Louisiana Tech		162
Bragg, Mike K	68-77Was	4	5'11"	186	Richmond		10
Brahaney, Tom C	73-77StL		6'2"	244	Oklahoma		
Branch, Cliff WR	72-77Oak	2	5'11"	170	Colorado		258
Branstetter, Kent OT	73GB		6'3"	260	Houston		
Braxton, Jim FB	71-77Buf	2	6'2"	237	West Virginia		174
Brazile, Robert LB	75-77Hou		6'4"	237	Jackson State	4	
Breunig, Bob LB	75-77Dal		6'2"	227	Arizona State	1	
Brezina, Greg LB	68-69Atl 70KJ 71-77Atl		6'1"	222	Houston	12	
Briggs, Bob DE-DT	68-69SD-A 70SD 71-73Cle 74KC		6'4"	267	Heidelberg	1	12
Brinkman, Charlie WR	72Cle		6'2"	208	Louisville		
Brinson, Larry FB	77Dal		6'	214	Florida		6
Briscoe, Marlin WR-QB	68DenA 69BufA 70-71Buf	12	5'10"	178	Nebraska-Omaha		198
	72-74Mia 75SD 75Det 76NE						
Brister, Willie TE	74-75NYJ		6'4"	236	Southern U.		
Broadnax, Jerry TE	74Hou 75WFL		6'2"	225	Southern U.		
Brock, Pete OG-C-TE	76-77NE		6'5"	257	Colorado		6
Brockington, John FB	71-77GB 77KC	2	6'1"	225	Ohio State		204
Brooks, Billy WR	76-77Cin	2	6'4"	209	Oklahoma		24
Brooks, Bobby DB	74-76NYG		6'1"	195	Bishop	5	
Brooks, Cliff DB	72-74Cle 75-76Phi 76NYJ 76Buf		6'1"	190	Tennessee State		
Brooks, Larry DT	72-77LA		6'3"	255	Virginia State		
Brooks, Lee DT-DE	70-72Hou 73-76StL		6'5"	256	Texas	1	
Broussard, Steve K	75GB	4	6'	200	Southern Miss.		
Brown, Aaron DE	66KC-A 67JJ 68-69KC-A		6'5"	263	Minnesota	1	6
	70-72KC 73-74GB						
Brown, Bob TE	69-70StL 71Min 72-73NO	2	6'3"	225	Alcorn A & M		6
Brown, Bob DT-DE	66-73GB 74SD 76-77Cin		6'5"	268	Arkansas-Pine Bluff	2	
Brown, Booker OT-OG	75SD 76IL 77SD		6'2"	257	Southern Calif.		
Brown, Boyd TE	74-76Den 77NYG		6'4"	216	Alcorn A & M		
Brown, Carlos QB	75-76GB	1	6'3"	210	Pacific		
Brown, Cedric DB	77TB		6'1"	190	Kent State	2	
Brown, Charlie WR	70Det 71JJ		6'2"	195	Northern Arizona		
Brown, Curtis HB	77Buf		5'10"	203	Missouri		6
Brown, Dave DB	75Pit 76-77Sea	3	6'1"	193	Michigan	8	8
Brown, Dean DB	69Cle 70Mia 71JJ		5'10"	170	Fort Valley State	1	
Brown, Eddie DB	74-75Cle 75-77Was	3	5'11"	186	Tennessee	3	6
Brown, Guy LB	77Dal		6'4"	215	Houston		
Brown, Ken HB-FB	70-75Cle	23	5'10"	204	none		54
Brown, Larry HB	69-76Was	2	5'11"	195	Kansas State		330
Brown, Larry TE-OT	71-77Pit	2	6'4"	230	Kansas		24
Brown, Otto DB	69Dal 70-73NYG		6'1"	187	Prairie View	2	6
Brown, Ray DB	71-77Atl	3	6'2"	203	West Texas State	31	12
Brown, Stan WR	71Cle		5'9"	184	Purdue		
Brown, Terry DB-WR	69-70StL 71JJ 72-75Min 76Cle		6'1"	206	Oklahoma State	7	12
Browne, Gordie OT	74-75NYJ		6'5"	265	Boston College		
Brudinski, Bob LB	77LA		6'4"	230	Ohio State	2	
Bruer, Bob TE	77Chi		6'5"	230	Mankota State		
Brumfield, Jim HB	71Pit		6'1"	195	Indiana State		
Brundige, Bill DT-DE	70-77Was		6'5"	270	Colorado		
Brunet, Bob HB	68,70-73Was 74FJ 75-77Was	2	6'1"	205	Louisiana Tech		24
Brunson, Larry WR	74-77KC	23	5'11"	180	Colorado		30
Brunson, Mike WR	70Atl		6'1"	187	Arizona State		
Brupbacher, Ross LB	70-72,76Chi		6'3"	216	Texas A & M	12	12
Bryan, Bill OG	77Den		6'2"	246	Duke		
Bryant, Bill (Boone) DB	76-77NYG		5'11"	195	Grambling	3	6
Bryant, Bobby DB	68-77Min	3	6'	171	South Carolina	39	24
Bryant, Cullen FB	73-77LA	23	6'1"	228	Colorado		42
Bryant, Hubie WR	70Pit 71-72NE	23	5'10"	170	Minnesota		6
Bryant, Warren OT	77Atl		6'6"	270	Kentucky		
Bryant, Waymond LB	74-77Chi		6'3"	235	Tennessee State	4	

Use Name (Nicknames) – Positions	Team by Year	See Section	Hgt	Wgt	College	Int	Pts
Buchanan, Willie DB	72-77GB		6'	190	San Diego State	12	12
Buckey, Don WR	76NYJ		5'11"	180	N. Carolina State		
Buehler, George OG	69OakA 70-77Oak		6'2"	270	Stanford		
Buetow, Bart (The Mad Scientist) OT	73NYG 76-77Min		6'5"	250	Minnesota		
Buffone, Doug LB	66-77Chi		6'1"	227	Louisville	19	6
Buggs, Danny WR	75-76NYG 76-77Was	2	6'2"	185	West Virginia		6
Buie, Drew WR	69OakA 70-71Oak 72Cin		6'2"	180	Catawba		12
Bujnoch, Glenn OG	76-77Cin		6'5"	256	Texas A & M		
Bulaich, Norm FB-HB	70-72Bal 73-74Phi 75-77Mia	2	6'1"	218	Texas Christian		216
Bull, Scott QB	76-77SF	1	6'5"	213	Arkansas		12
Bunting, John LB	72-77Phi		6'1"	220	North Carolina	4	
Burchfield, Don TE	71NO		6'2"	227	Ball State		
Burke, Mark DB	76Phi		6'1"	175	West Virginia		
Burke, Mike K	74LA	4	5'10"	188	Miami (Fla.)		1
Burks, Randy WR	76Chi		5'11"	170	SE Oklahoma State		6
Burks, Ray LB	77KC		6'3"	217	U.C.L.A.		
Burks, Steve WR	75-77NE	2	6'5"	211	Arkansas State		
Burley, Gary DE	76-77Cin		6'3"	264	Pittsburgh		
Burnham, Lem DE	77Phi		6'4"	228	American International		
Burns, Bob FB	72NYJ	2	6'3"	212	Georgia		6
Burns, Leon FB	71SD 72StL 73JJ	2	6'2"	229	Long Beach State		18
Burns, Mike DB	77SF		6'	181	Southern Calif.		
Burrough, Ken WR	70NO 71-77Hou	2	6'4"	210	Texas Southern		210
Burrow, Jim DB	76GB		5'11"	181	Nebraska		
Burrow, Ken WR	71-75Atl	2	6'	190	San Diego State		126
Burton, Al DE	76-77Hou 77NYJ		6'5"	268	Bethune-Cookman		
Burton, Larry WR	75-77NO	2	6'1"	192	Purdue		24
Bussey, Dexter HB	74-77Det	2	6'1"	206	Texas-Arlington		72
Butler, Bill FB	72-74NO	2	6'2"	212	Kansas State		30
Butler, Bill LB	70Den		6'4"	226	San Fern. Valley		
Butler, Gary TE	73KC 74KJ 75-76Chi 77TB		6'3"	235	Rice		12
Butler, Gerald WR	77KC		6'5"	205	Nicholls State		
Butler, Mike DE	77GB		6'5"	265	Kansas		
Butler, Skip K	71NO 71NYG 72-77Hou	45	6'2"	200	Texas-Arlington		340
Buttle, Greg LB	76-77NYJ		6'2"	232	Penn State	4	12
Butz, Dave DT-DE	73-74StL 75-77Was		6'7"	291	Purdue		
Buzin, Rich OT	68-70NYG 71LA 72Chi		6'4"	250	Penn State		
Byas, Rick DB	74-77Atl		5'9"	178	Wayne State	3	6
Cagle, Jim DT	74Phi		6'5"	255	Georgia		
Cahill, Bill DB	73-74Buf		5'11"	175	Washington		6
Cain, J.V. TE-WR	74-77StL	2	6'4"	224	Colorado		54
Calhoun, Don HB-FB	74-75Buf 75-77NE	2	6'	202	Kansas State		42
Calloway, Ernie DT-DE	69-72Phi 73KJ		6'6"	244	Texas Southern		
Cambal, Dennis TE	73NYJ		6'3"	228	William & Mary		
Cameron, Glenn LB	75-77Cin		6'1"	226	Florida		
Campbell, Carter LB-DE	70SF 71Den 72-73NYG 74-75WFL		6'3"	232	Weber State		
Campbell, Gary LB	77Chi		6'1"	218	Colorado		
Campbell, Joe DE	77NO		6'6"	254	Maryland		
Campbell, Sonny HB	70-71Atl 72JJ	2	5'11"	192	Northern Arizona		12
Campbell, Tommy DB	76Phi		6'	188	Iowa State		
Capone, Warren LB	75Dal 76NO		6'1"	219	Louisiana State		6
Cappelletti, John HB-FB	74-77LA	2	6'1"	217	Penn State		84
Cappelman, Bill QB	70Min 73Det		6'3"	210	Florida State		
Capria, Carl DB	74Det 75NYJ		6'3"	185	Purdue		
Capriola, Glenn FB	77Det		5'11"	219	Boston College		
Carlson, Dean QB	74KC		6'3"	210	Iowa State		
Carlton, Darryl OT	75-76Mia 77TB		6'6"	263	Tampa		
Carmichael, Harold WR	71-77Phi	2	6'7"	225	Southern U.		228
Carpenter, Rob FB	77Hou	2	6'1"	214	Miami (Ohio)		6
Carpenter, Ron DT	70-77Cin		6'4"	261	N. Carolina State		2
Carr, Fred LB	68-77GB		6'5"	239	Texas-El Paso	8	6
Carr, Levert OT-DT-OG	69SD-A 70-71Buf 72-73Hou		6'5"	258	North Central		
Carr, Roger WR	74-77Bal	2	6'3"	196	Louisiana Tech		84
Carrell, Duane K	74Dal 75LA 76-77NYJ 77StL	4	5'10"	183	Florida State		
Carroll, Joe LB	72-73Oak		6'1"	220	Pittsburgh		
Carroll, Ronnie OG	74Hou		6'2"	265	Sam Houston State		
Carson, Harry LB	76-77NYG		6'2"	232	S. Carolina State		
Carter, Allen FB	75-76NE 76NYJ	3	5'11"	208	Southern Calif.		6
Carter, Blanchard OT	77TB		6'4"	250	Nevada-Las Vegas		
Carter, David C	77Hou		6'2"	225	Western Kentucky		
Carter, Jim LB	70-75GB 76BA 77GB		6'3"	239	Minnesota	6	6
Carter, Kent LB	74NE		6'3"	235	Southern, Calif.		
Carter, Louis HB	75Oak 76-77TB	2	5'11"	206	Maryland		18
Carter, Mike WR	70GB 72SD		6'1"	210	Sacramento State		
Carter, Rubin NT-DT	75-77Den		6'	255	Miami (Fla.)		
Carter, Virgil QB	68-69Chi 70-72Cin 73BC	12	6'1"	193	Brigham Young		49
	74WFL 75SD 75-76Chi						
Casanova, Tommy DB	72-77Cin	3	6'2"	197	Louisiana State	17	24
Cash, Rick DE-DT	68Atl 69-70LA 71JJ 72-73NE		6'5"	260	NE Missouri State		
Casper, Dave TE	74-77Oak	2	6'4"	234	Notre Dame		120
Cassady, Craig DB	77NO		5'11"	175	Ohio State		
Caster, Rich TE-WR	70-77NYJ	2	6'5"	226	Jackson State		216
Chambers, Rusty LB	75-76NO 76-77Mia		6'1"	217	Tulane		6
Chambers, Wally DT-DE	73-77Chi		6'6"	254	Eastern Kentucky	1	
Chandler, Al TE	73-74Cin 76-77NE	2	6'2"	230	Oklahoma		18
Chandler, Bob WR	71-77Buf	2	6'	180	Southern Calif.		175
Chandler, Edgar LB	68-69BufA 70-72Buf 73NE		6'3"	227	Georgia	2	8
Chandler, Karl C-OG	74-77NYG		6'5"	250	Princeton		
Chapman, Clarence DB-WR	76-77NO		5'10"	185	Eastern Michigan	1	6
Chapman, Gil WR	75NO	3	5'9"	180	Michigan		
Chapple, Dave K	71Buf 72-74LA 74NE	4	6'	184	Cal.-Santa Barbara		
Charles, John DB	67-69BosA 70Min 71-74Hou		6'1"	199	Purdue	16	12
Chavous, Barney DE	73-77Den		6'3"	252	S. Carolina State		
Cheek, Richard OG	70Buf 71KJ		6'3"	266	Auburn		
Cherry, Stan LB	73Bal		6'5"	200	Morgan State		
Chesson, Wes WR	71-73Atl 74Phi	2	6'2"	192	Duke		
Chester, Ray TE	70-72Oak 73-77Bal	2	6'3"	230	Morgan State		198
Cheyunski, Jim LB	68-69BosA 70Bos 71-72NE		6'2"	222	Syracuse	9	
	73-74Buf 75-76Bal 77GB						

Use Name (Nickmane) – Positions	Team by Year	See Section	Hgt	Wgt	College	Int	Pts
Childs, Henry TE	74Atl 74-77NO	2	6'	222	Kansas State		78
Chomsyzak, Steve DT-C-OT	66NY-A 68-69CinA		6'5"	270	Syracuse		
	72-73Cin						
Christiansen, Bob TE	72Buf		6'4"	230	U.C.L.A.		
Cindrich, Ralph LB	72NE 73-74Hou 74Den 75Hou		6'1"	229	Pittsburgh		
Cipa, Larry QB	74-75NO	1	6'3"	209	Michigan		6
Clabo, Neil K	75-77Min	4	6'2"	200	Tennessee		
Clack, Jim OG-C	71-77Pit		6'3"	250	Wake Forest		
Clark, Al DB	71Det 72-75LA 76Phi		6'	183	Eastern Michigan	3	
Clark, Booby FB	73-77Cin	2	6'2"	244	Bethune-Cookman		162
Clark, Gail LB	73Chi 74NE		6'2"	226	Michigan State		
Clark, Leroy K	76Hou		5'11"	200	Prairie View		
Clark, Mario DB	76-77Buf		6'2"	190	Oregon	9	
Clark, Wayne QB	70,72-73SD 74Cin 75KC	1	6'2"	203	U.S. International		6
Clayborn, Ray DB	77NE	3	6'1"	181	Texas		20
Clements, Vin FB	72-73NYG 74WFL	2	6'3"	213	Connecticut		12
Clemons, Craig DB	72-77Chi		5'11"	191	Iowa	9	6
Cline, Tony DE	70-75Oak 76-77SF		6'2"	239	Miami (Fla.)	3	
Clune, Don WR	74-75NYG 76Sea		6'3"	195	Pennsylvania		
Coady, Rich C-TE	70-74Chi		6'3"	240	Memphis State		6
Cobb, Marvin DB	75-77Cin		6'1"	188	Southern Calif.	9	6
Cobb, Mike TE	77Cin		6'5"	248	Michigan State		
Cockroft, Don K	68-77Cle	45	6'1"	192	Adams State		810
Coder, Ron OG	76-77Sea		6'4"	250	Penn State		
Coffield, Randy LB	76Sea 77JJ		6'3"	215	Florida State		
Colavito, Steve LB	75Phi		6'	225	Wake Forest		
Colbert, Danny DB	74-76SD 77JJ		5'11"	175	Tulsa	2	
Colbert, Rondy DB	75-77NYG 77StL	3	5'9"	165	Lamar U.		6
Cole, Larry DE-DT	68-77Dal		6'4"	250	Hawaii	2	18
Cole, Linzy WR	70Chi 71-72Hou 72Buf	3	5'11"	170	Texas Christian		
Cole, Robin LB-DE	77Pit		6'2"	220	New Mexico		
Coleman, Al DB	68Min 69CinA 70-71Cin		6'1"	185	Tennessee State	1	2
	72-73Phi 74JJ						
Coleman, Dennis LB	71NE		6'3"	225	Mississippi		
Coleman, Don LB	74-75NO 76-77KJ		6'2"	222	Michigan		
Coleman, Fred TE	76Buf		6'4"	240	Northeast La.		
Coleman, Greg K	77Cle	4	6'	178	Florida A & M		
Coleman, Ralph LB	72Dal		6'4"	216	N. Carolina A & T		
Coleman, Ronnie HB	74-77Hou	2	5'10"	197	Alabama A & M		108
Coleman, Steve DE	74Den		6'4"	252	Delaware State		
Collett, Elmer OG	67-72SF 73-77Bal		6'4"	241	San Fran. State		
Collier, Mike HB	75Pit 76KJ 77Buf	23	5'11"	200	Morgan State		24
Collier, Tim DB	76-77KC		6'	166	East Texas State	4	6
Collins, Greg LB	75SF 76Sea 77Buf		6'3"	229	Notre Dame		
Collins, Jerald LB	69BufA 70-71Buf		6'1"	220	Western Michigan		
Collins, Sonny HB	76Atl 77LA	2	6'1"	196	Kentucky		
Colman, Wayne LB	68-69Phi 69-74NO 75BA 76NO		6'1"	227	Temple	3	
Colzie, Neal DB	75-77Oak	3	6'2"	205	Ohio State	7	
Condon, Tom OG	74-77KC		6'3"	240	Boston College		
Conley, Steve LB	72Cin 72StL		6'2"	225	Kansas		
Conn, Dick DB	74Pit 75-77NE		6'	184	Georgia		
Conway, Dave K	71GB		6'	195	Texas		5
Cook, Fred DE	74-77Bal		6'4"	243	Southern Miss.	2	6
Cooke, Bill DT-DE-OT	75GB 76-77SF		6'5"	248	Massachusetts		
Cooney, Mark LB	74GB		6'4"	230	Colorado		
Cooper, Bert LB	76TB		6'1"	242	Florida State		
Cooper, Jim OG-C	77Dal		6'5"	252	Temple		
Cope, Jim LB	76Atl		6'1"	235	Ohio State		
Copeland, Jim OG-C	67-74Cle		6'2"	242	Virginia		
Corano, Glenn QB	77Dal		6'3"	195	Nevada-Las Vegas		
Corbett, Jim TE	77Cin		6'3"	214	Pittsburgh		6
Corbett, Steve OG	75NE 76BQ		6'4"	248	Boston College		
Cornelius, Charles DB	77Mia		5'9"	176	Bethune-Cookman		
Cornell, Bo LB-FB	71-72Cle 73-77Buf		6'1"	218	Washington		6
Coryell, Don	HC73-77StL				Washington		
Coslet, Bruce TE	69CinA 70-76Cin	2	6'3"	226	U. of Pacific		54
Costict, Ray LB	77NE		6'	214	Mississippi State		
Cotney, Mark DB	75Hou 76-77TB		6'	204	Cameron State	4	
Cotton, Craig TE	69-72Det 73Chi 74WFL 75SD	2	6'4"	222	Youngstown		6
Cousino, Brad LB	75Cin 76NYG 77Pit		6'	218	Miami (Ohio)		
Cowlings, Al DE-DT-LB	70-72Buf 73-74Hou 75,77LA		6'5"	251	Southern Calif.		
Cox, Fred K	63-77Min	45	5'10"	200	Pittsburgh		1365
Craig, Neal DB	71-73Cin 74Buf 75-76Cle		6'1"	189	Fisk	8	12
Craig, Reggie WR	75-76KC 77Cle 77Buf		6'	188	Arkansas		
Craig, Steve TE	74-77Min	2	6'3"	231	Northwestern		6
Crangle, Mike DE	72NO		6'4"	243	Tennessee-Martin		
Craven, Bill DB	76Cle 77JJ		5'11"	190	Harvard		
Creech, Bob LB	71-72Phi 73NO		6'3"	226	Texas Christian		
Crennel, Carl LB	70Pit		6'1"	230	West Virginia		
Crist, Chuck DB	72-74NYG 75-77NO		6'2"	205	Penn State	14	
Criter, Ken LB	69DenA 70-74Den		5'11"	223	Wisconsin		2
Croft, Don DT	72Buf 73KJ 74-75Buf 76Det		6'3"	256	Texas-El Paso		
Cromwell, Nolan DB	77LA		6'1"	196	Kansas		
Cronan, Pete LB	77Sea		6'2"	238	Boston College		
Croom, Sylvester C	75NO		6'	235	Alabama		
Crosby, Steve HB	74-76NYG		5'11"	205	Ft. Hays (Kans.) State		
Cross, Randy C	76-77SF		6'3"	249	U.C.L.A.		
Crosswhite, Leon FB	73-74Det 75FJ		6'2"	215	Oklahoma		12
Crowder, Randy DT	74-76Mia		6'2"	236	Penn State		
77 – Ineligible to play pro football							
Crowe, Larry HB	72Phi 75Atl		6'1"	198	Texas Southern		
Croyle, Phil LB	71-73Hou 73Buf		6'3"	220	California		
Crum, Bob DE	74StL		6'5"	240	Arizona		
Crump, Dwayne DB	73-76StL		5'11"	180	Fresno State	1	6
Crusan, Doug OT	68-69MiaA 70-74Mia		6'5"	253	Indiana		
Csonka, Larry FB	68-69MiaA 70-74Mia 75WFL 76-77NYG	2	6'3"	239	Syracuse		294
Culbreath, Jim FB	77GB		6'	209	Oklahoma		
Cullers, Willie DE	74NYG		6'5"	250	Kansas		
Culp, Curley MG-DT-OG	68-69KC-A 70-74KC 74-77Hou		6'1"	265	Arizona State	1	6
Cunningham, Bennie TE	76-77Pit	2	6'4"	252	Clemson		18

Use Name (Nicknames) – Positions	Team by Year	See Section	Hgt	Wgt	College	Int	Pts.
Cunningham, Dick LB-OT	67-69BufA 70-72Buf 73Phi 74JJ		6'2"	238	Arkansas		
Cunningham, Doug HB	67-73SF 74Was	23	5'11"	191	Mississippi		60
Cunningham, Sam (Sam the Bam) FB	73-77NE	2	6'3"	223	Southern Calif.		192
Churchin, Jeff OT-OG	70-71Chi 72Buf		6'6"	258	Florida State		
Cureton, Will QB	75Cle	1	6'3"	200	East Texas State		
Curran, Pat TE	69-74LA 75-77SD	2	6'3"	238	Lakeland		25
Current, Mike OT	67MiaA 67-69DenA 70-75Den 76TB 77Mia		6'4"	266	Ohio State		
Currier, Bill DB	77Hou		6'	190	South Carolina	2	
Curtis, Isaac WR	73-77Cin	2	6'	193	San Diego State		204
Curtis, Mike LB-FB	65-75Bal 76Sea 77Was		6'2"	232	Duke	24	18
Curtis, Tom DB	70-71Bal		6'1"	196	Michigan		
Cusick, Pete NT	75NE 76-77KJ		6'1"	255	Ohio State		
Dalby, Dave C-OG	72-77Oak		6'2"	245	U.C.L.A.		
Dalton, Oakley DT	77NO		6'6"	285	Jackson State		
Damkroger, Maury LB	74-75NE		6'2"	230	Nebraska		
Dandridge, Jerry LB	76GB		6'1"	222	Memphis State		
Danelo, Joe K	75GB 76-77NYG	5	5'9"	166	Washington State		158
Daney, George OG	68-69KC-A 70-74KC		6'3"	240	Texas-El Paso		6
Danielson, Gary QB	76-77Det	1	6'2"	195	Purdue		
Darby, Alvis TE	76Sea 76Hou		6'4"	216	Florida		
Darden, Thom DB	72-74Cle 75KJ 76-77Cle	3	6'2"	194	Michigan	25	12
Darrow, Barry OT	74-77Cle		6'7"	260	Montana		
Davis, Anthony HB	77TB	2	5'10"	190	Southern Calif.		6
Davis, Ben DB	67-68Cle 69JJ 70-73Cle 74-76Det	3	5'11"	183	Defiance	19	12
Davis, Bob QB	67-69HouA 70-72NYJ 73NO 74-75WFL	12	6'3"	205	Virginia		12
Davis, Brad FB	75-76Atl		5'10"	204	Louisiana State		
Davis, Butch DB	70Chi		5'11"	183	Missouri	1	
Davis, Charlie HB	74Cin 75KJ 76TB	2	5'11"	200	Colorado		6
Davis, Charlie DT	74Pit 75-77StL		6'1"	266	Texas Christian		6
Davis, Clarence HB	71-77Oak	23	5'10"	193	Southern Calif.		168
Davis, Dave WR	71-72GB 73Pit 74NO 75BN	2	6'	175	Tennessee State		6
Davis, Dick HB-FB	70Den 70NO	2	5'11"	215	Nebraska		
Davis, Gary HB	76-77Mia	23	5'10"	202	Cal. Poly-SLO		24
Davis, Harrison WR	74SD	2	6'4"	220	Virginia		12
Davis, Henry LB	68-69NYG 70-73Pit 74JJ		6'3"	235	Grambling	4	6
Davis, Jerry DB	75NYJ		5'11"	182	Morris Brown		
Davis, Kyle C	75Dal 76KJ		6'4"	240	Oklahoma		
Davis, Marvin LB	74Hou		6'4"	235	Southern U.		
Davis, Oliver DB	77Cle		6'1"	200	Tennessee State	3	
Davis, Ricky DB	75Cin 76TB 77KC		6'1"	180	Alabama	1	
Davis, Ron OG	73StL 74JJ		6'2"	235	Virginia State		
Davis, Sam OG-OT	67-77Pit		6'1"	251	Allen		
Davis, Sonny HB-FB	71-72Phi	2	5'11"	215	Tennessee State		6
Davis, Stan WR	73Phi		5'10"	180	Memphis State		
Davis, Steve FB-HB	72-74Pit 75-76NYJ	23	6'1"	216	Delaware State		66
Davis, Tony FB-HB	76-77Cin	2	5'10"	210	Nebraska		18
Davis, Vern DB	71Phi		6'4"	208	Western Michigan		
Dawkins, Joe FB-HB	70-71Hou 71-73Den 74-75NYG 76Hou	23	5'11"	221	Wisconsin		96
Dawson, Mike DT	76-77StL		6'4"	272	Arizona		
Dawson, Rhett WR	72Hou 73Min		6'1"	185	Florida State		6
Daykin, Tony LB	77Det		6'1"	215	Georgia Tech		
Dean, Fred DE	75-77SD		6'3"	229	Louisiana Tech	1	12
Dean, Fred OG	77Chi		6'3"	253	Texas Southern		
Dean, Randy QB	77NYG		6'3"	195	Northwestern		
DeBerg, Steve QB	77SF		6'2"	205	San Jose State		
DeBernardi, Fred DE	74KC		6'4"	250	Texas-El Paso		
DeGrenier, Jack FB	74NO	2	6'1"	225	Texas-Arlington		
DeJurnett, Charles DT-DE	76-77SD		6'4"	270	San Jose State		
DeLamielleure, Joe OG	73-77Buf		6'3"	249	Michigan State		
DeLeone, Tom C-OG	72-73Cin 74-77Cle		6'2"	250	Ohio State		
Del Gaizo, Jim QB	72Mia 73GB 74NYG 75Mia	1	6'1"	194	Tampa		
DeLisle, Jim DT	71GB		6'4"	254	Wisconsin		
Deloplaine, Jack HB	76-77Pit		5'10"	205	Salem (W. Va.)		12
Demarie, John OG-C-OT	67-75Cle 76Sea		6'3"	250	Louisiana State		
Demery, Calvin WR	72Min		6'	190	Arizona State		
Demory, Bill QB	73-74NYJ	1	6'2"	195	Arizona		
Dempsey, Tom K	69-70NO 71-74Phi 75-76LA 77Hou	5	6'1"	261	Palomar J.C.		652
DenHerder, Vern DE	71-77Mia		6'6"	251	Central (Iowa)	1	
Dennery, Mike LB	74-75Oak 76Mia		6'	224	Southern Miss.		2
Dennis, Al OG	73SD 76-77Cle		6'4"	250	Grambling		
Dennis, Guy OG-C	69CinA 70-72Cin 73-75Det		6'2"	254	Florida		
Dennison, Doug HB-FB	74-77Dal	2	6'1"	201	Kutztown State		108
Denson, Keith WR	76NYJ		5'8"	165	San Diego State		
Denson, Moses FB-HB	74-75Was	2	6'1"	215	Md Eastern Shore		12
DePoyster, Jerry K	68Det 71-72Oak	45	6'1"	202	Wyoming		27
DeRatt, Jimmy DB	75NO		6'	203	North Carolina		
Detwiller, Chuck DB	70-72SD 73StL 74-75WFL		6'	185	Utah State	1	6
Devine, Dan	HC71-74GB				Minnesota-Duluth		
Devlin, Chris LB	75-76Cin 77NJ		6'3"	225	Penn State	1	
Devlin, Joe OT	76-77Buf		6'4"	258	Iowa		
Dickel, Dan LB	74-77Bal		6'3"	228	Iowa	1	
Dickey, Lynn QB	71Hou 72PJ 73-75Hou 76-77GB	12	6'4"	215	Kansas State		7
Dickinson, Parnell QB	76-77TB	1	6'2"	185	Miss. Valley State		
Dicus, Chuck WR	71-72SD	2	6'	174	Arkansas		18
Didion, John C-LB	69-70Was 71-74NO		6'4"	247	Oregon State		
Dieken, Doug OT	71-77Cle		6'5"	248	Illinois		2
Dierdorf, Dan OT-OG	71-77StL		6'4"	275	Michigan		
Dierking, Scott FB	77NYJ		5'10"	215	Purdue		6
Diggs, Shelton WR	77NYJ		6'1"	190	Southern Calif.		
Dilts, Bucky K	77Den	4	5'9"	190	Georgia		
Dixon, Al TE	77NYG		6'5"	220	Iowa State		
Dobbins, Herb OT	74Phi		6'4"	260	San Diego State		
Dobler, Conrad OG	72-77StL		6'3"	253	Wyoming		6
Dockery, John DB	68-69NY-A 70-71NYJ 72-73Pit		6'	186	Harvard	8	
Dodd, Al WR-DB	67Chi 69-71NO 72JJ 73-74Atl	23	6'	180	NW State-La.		24
Dokes, Phil DE	77Buf		6'4"	258	Oklahoma State		
Dolbin, Jack WR	75-77Den	2	5'10"	181	Wake Forest		48
Domres, Marty QB	69SD-A 70-71SD 72-75Bal 76SF 77NYJ	12	6'4"	219	Columbia		60
Domres, Tom DT-DE	68-69HouA 70-71Hou 71-72Den 73JJ		6'3"	257	Wisconsin		6

Use Name (Nicknames) — Positions	Team by Year	See Section	Hgt	Wgt	College	Int	Pts
Donchez, Tom FB	75Chi		6'2"	216	Penn State		
Donckers, Billy QB	76-77StL		6'1"	206	San Diego State		
Donohoe, Mike TE	68,70-71Atl 73-74GB	2	6'3"	228	San Francisco		12
Donovan, Pat OT	75-77Dal		6'4"	252	Stanford		
Dorris, Andy DE	73-76NO 77Sea 77Hou		6'4"	236	New Mexico State		
Dorsett, Tony HB	77Dal	2	5'11"	192	Pittsburgh		78
Dorsey, Larry WR	76-77SD	2	6'1"	195	Tennessee State		12
Dorsey, Nate DE	73NE		6'4"	240	Miss. Valley State		
Doughty, Glenn WR	72-77Bal	2	6'1"	204	Michigan		114
Douglas, Jay C	73-74SD		6'6"	251	Memphis State		
Douglas, John LB	70-73NYG 74WFL		6'2"	227	Missouri	2	
Douglass, Bobby QB	69-75Chi 75SD 76-77NO	12	6'3"	223	Kansas		133
Douglass, Freddie WR	76TB		5'9"	185	Arkansas		
Douthit, Earl DB	75Chi 76TB		6'2"	188	Iowa		
Dove, Jerome DB	77SD		6'	186	Colorado State	1	
Dowling, Brian QB	72-73NE 74-75WFL 77GB	1	6'2"	207	Yale		18
Dragon, Oscar HB-FB	72SD		6'	214	Arizona State		
Drake, Bill DB-WR	73-74LA		6'1"	195	Oregon		
Dressler, Doug FB	70-72Cin 73KJ 74Chi 75NE 75KC	2	6'3"	225	Chico State		66
Drougas, Tom OT-OG	72-73Bal 74Den 74KC 75-76Mia		6'4"	258	Oregon		
Drungo, Elbert OT-OG	69HouA 70-71Hou 72KJ 73-77Hou		6'5"	259	Tennessee State		
Druschel, Rick OT-OG	74Pit		6'2"	248	N. Carolina State		
Dryer, Fred DE	69-71NYG 72-77LA		6'6"	239	San Diego State	1	10
DuBose, Jimmy FB	76-77TB	2	5'11"	216	Florida		
Dufek, Don DB	76-77Sea		6'	195	Michigan	2	
Duhe, A.J. DE	77Mia		6'4"	247	Louisiana State		
Duhon, Bobby HB	68NYG 69JJ 70-72NYG	23	6'	194	Tulane		36
DuLac, Bill OG	74-75NE		6'4"	260	Eastern Michigan		
Dumler, Doug C	73-75NE 76-77Min		6'3"	243	Nebraska		
Dunbar, Jubilee WR	73NO 74Cle	2	6'	196	Southern U.		24
Duncan, Brian FB-HB	76-77Cle		6'	201	S.M.U.		12
Duncan, Jim DB	69-71Bal	3	6'2"	200	Md. Eastern Shore	2	12
Duncan, Ken K	71GB		6'2"	210	Tulsa		
Dungy, Tony DB	77Pit		6'	188	Minnesota	3	
Dunivan, Tom QB	77Hou		6'3"	210	Texas Tech		
Dunlap, Lenny DB	71Bal 72-74SD 75Det	3	6'1"	197	North Texas State	5	
Dunn, Gary DT	76Pit 77KJ		6'3"	240	Miami (Fla.)		
Dunn, Paul HB-FB	70Cin		6'	210	U.S. International		
Dunstan, Bill DT	73-76Phi 77Buf		6'4"	250	Utah State		6
DuPree, Billy Joe TE	73-77Dal	2	6'4"	227	Michigan State		90
Duranko, Pete DE-DT	67-69Den-A 70Den 71JJ 72-74Den 75JJ		6'2"	249	Notre Dame		
Duren, Clarence DB	73-76StL 77SD		6'1"	190	California	10	
Durko, Sandy DB	70-71Cin 72JJ 73-74NE		6'1"	185	Southern Calif.	7	
Dusek, Brad LB	74-77Was		6'2"	214	Texas A&M	2	12
Dusenberry, Bill DB	70NO		6'2"	198	Johnson C. Smith		
Dutton, John DE	74-77Bal		6'7"	265	Nebraska		
Dvorak, Rick DE	74-77NYG 77Mia		6'4"	240	Wichita State		
Eaglin, Larry DB	73Hou		6'3"	195	S.F. Austin State		6
Earl, Robin FB	77Chi	2	6'5"	247	Washington		6
East, Ron DT-DE	67-70Dal 71-74SD 74WFL 75Cle 76Atl 77Sea		6'4"	244	Montana State		2
Easterling, Ray DB	72-77Atl		6'	192	Richmond	10	
Ebersole, John LB	70-77NYJ		6'3"	236	Penn State	8	
Edwards, Cid FB	68-71StL 72-74SD 75Chi	2	6'2"	230	Tennessee State		114
Edwards, Earl DT-DE	69-72SF 73-75Buf 76-77Cle		6'6"	262	Wichita State		
Edwards, Eddie DT	77Cin		6'4"	256	Miami (Fla.)		
Edwards, Emmett WR	75-76Hou 76Buf		6'1"	189	Kansas		
Edwards, Glen DB	71-77Pit	3	6'	185	Florida A&M	25	12
Edwards, Herman DB	77Phi		6'	194	San Diego State	6	
Egloff, Ron TE	77Den		6'5"	227	Wisconsin		
Ehlers, Tom LB	75-77Phi		6'2"	218	Kentucky	1	
Ehrmann, Joe DT	73-77Bal		6'5"	258	Syracuse		
Eidson, Jim OG-C	76Bal 77JJ		6'3"	264	Mississippi State		
Eischeid, Mike K	66-69OakA 70-71Oak 72-74Min	45	6'	190	Upper Iowa		70
Ekern, Carl LB	76-77LA		6'3"	220	San Jose State		
Elam, Cleveland DT-DE	75-77SF		6'4"	252	Tennessee State		6
Eley, Monroe FB	75Atl 76JJ 77Atl	2	6'2"	210	Arizona State		6
Elia, Bruce LB	75Mia 76-77SF		6'1"	220	Ohio State		
Ellenbogen, Bill OG-OT	76-77NYG		6'5"	258	Virginia Tech		
Eller, Carl DE	64-77Min		6'6"	252	Minnesota	1	10
Elliott, John DT-DE-LB	67-69NY-A 70-73NYJ 74WFL		6'4"	244	Texas		2
Elliott, Lenvil HB	73-77Cin	2	6'	205	NE Missouri State		72
Ellis, Allan DB	73-77Chi		5'10"	181	U.C.L.A.	18	6
Ellis, Clarence DB	72-74Atl 75KJ		5'11"	191	Notre Dame	8	
Ellis, Ken DB	70-75GB 76Hou 76Mia 77Cle	3	5'10"	192	Southern U.	22	30
Ellison, Glenn HB-FB	71Oak		6'1"	215	Arkansas		
Ellison, Mark OG	72-73NYG		6'2"	250	Dayton		
Ellison, Willie HB-FB	67-72LA 73-74KC	23	6'1"	204	Texas Southern		180
Elmendorf, Dave DB	71-77LA	3	6'1"	195	Texas A&M	21	12
Elrod, Jimbo LB	76-77KC		6'	216	Oklahoma	1	
Ely, Larry LB	70-71Cin 74WFL 75Chi		6'1"	230	Iowa	1	
Emerson, Vern OT	69-71StL		6'5"	260	Minnesota-Duluth		
Enderle, Dick OG	69-71Atl 72-75NYG 76SF 76GB		6'1"	250	Minnesota		
Engel, Steve HB-FB	70Cle		6'1"	218	Colorado		
Engels, Rick K	76-77Sea 77Pit	4	5'11"	175	Tulsa		
English, Doug DT	75-77Det		6'5"	248	Texas		2
Enyart, Bill FB	69BufA 70Buf 71Oak 72KJ	2	6'4"	236	Oregon State		24
Ernst, Mike QB	72Cin 73Den		6'1"	190	Fullerton State		
Esposito, Mike HB	76-77Atl	2	6'	184	Boston College	1	12
Estes, Larry DE-DT	70-71NO 72Phi 75-77KC		6'6"	253	Alcorn A&M		
Evans, Charlie FB	71-73NYG 74Was 76KJ	2	6'1"	219	Southern Calif.		78
Evans, Larry LB	76-77Den		6'2"	217	Mississippi	1	
Evans, Mike C	68-73Phi		6'5"	250	Boston College		
Evans, Norm OT	65HouA 66-69MiaA 70-75Mia 76-77Sea		6'5"	248	Texas Christian		6
Evans, Vince QB	77Chi		6'2"	216	Southern Calif.		
Fagan, Julian K	70-72NO 73NYJ	4	6'3"	205	Mississippi		
Fahnhorst, Keith OT	74-77SF		6'6"	260	Minnesota		
Fairbanks, Chuck	HC73-77NE				Michigan State		
Fairchild, Greg OG-C-OT	76-77Cin		6'4"	258	Tulsa		

Use Name (Nicknames) — Positions	Team by Year	See Section	Hgt	Wgt	College	Int	Pts
Fairley, Leonard DB	74Hou		5'11"	200	Alcorn A&M		
Fanning, Mike DT-DE	75-77LA		6'6"	260	Notre Dame		
Fanucci, Mike DE	72Was 73Hou 74GB		6'4"	236	Arizona State		
Farasopoulos, Chris DB	71-73NYJ 74NO	3	5'11"	190	Brigham Young	4	6
Farber, Hap LB	70Min 70NO		6'1"	220	Mississippi		
Farmer, George WR	70-75Chi 75Det	2	6'4"	212	U.C.L.A.		60
Farmer, Karl WR	76-77Atl		5'11"	165	Pittsburgh		
Farr, Mel HB	67-73Det	2	6'2"	208	U.C.L.A.		216
Faumuina, Wilson DT	77Atl		6'5"	275	San Jose State		
Feacher, Ricky WR	76NE 76-77Cle	3	5'10"	174	Miss. Valley State		
Federspiel, Joe LB	72-77NO		6'1"	230	Kentucky	2	
Feller, Happy K	71Phi 72-73NO	5	5'11"	185	Texas		75
Fencik, Gary DB	76-77Chi		6'1"	191	Yale	4	
Fergerson, Duke WR	77Sea	2	6'1"	193	San Diego State		12
Ferguson, Bill LB	73-74NYJ		6'3"	225	San Diego State		
Ferguson, Gene OT-DT	69SD-A 70SD 71-72Hou		6'7"	302	Norfolk State		
Ferguson, Joe QB	73-77Buf	12	6'1"	184	Arkansas		42
Fernandes, Ron DE	76-77Bal		6'4"	247	Eastern Michigan		2
Fernandez, Manny DT-DE	68-69MiaA 70-75Mia 76-77KJ		6'2"	250	Utah		
Ferragamo, Vince QB	77LA		6'3"	208	Nebraska		
Ferrell, Bob FB-HB	76-77SF	2	6'	214	U.C.L.A.		12
Fersen, Paul OT	73NO		6'5"	260	Georgia		
Fest, Cotton DT	72Cle		6'2"	255	Dayton		
Fest, Howard OG-OT-C	68-69CinA 70-75Cin 76TB 77JJ		6'6"	263	Texas		
Fields, Edgar DE	77Atl		6'2"	255	Texas A&M		
Fields, Joe C-OG	75-77NYJ		6'2"	243	Widener		
Files, Jim LB	70-73NYG		6'4"	240	Oklahoma		
Fink, Mike DB	73NO		5'11"	180	Missouri		
Finnie, Roger OT-OG	69NY-A 70-72NYJ 73-77StL		6'3"	247	Florida A&M		
Fisher, Ed OG-C-DE	74-77Hou		6'3"	248	Arizona State		
Fitzgerald, John C-OG	71-77Dal		6'5"	253	Boston College		
Flanagan, Ed C	65-74Det 75-76SD		6'3"	247	Purdue		
Fletcher, Chris DB	70-76SD	3	5'11"	186	Temple	13	6
Flowers, Richmond DB-WR	69-71Dal 71-73NYG 74WFL		6'	181	Tennessee	6	
Foley, Dave OT-C	70-71NYJ 72-77Buf		6'5"	252	Ohio State		
Foley, Steve DB	76-77Den		6'2"	186	Tulane	7	
Foley, Tim DB	70-77Mia		6'	194	Purdue	14	14
Foote, James QB	74,76Hou		6'2"	210	Delaware Valley		
Ford, Charlie DB	71-73Chi 74Phi 75Buf 75NYG 76KJ		6'3"	187	Houston	15	
Ford, James HB-FB	71-72NO 73LJ	2	6'	203	Texas Southern		12
Foreman, Chuck HB-FB	73-77Min	2	6'2"	209	Miami (Fla.)		396
Forrest, Tom OG	74Chi		6'2"	255	Cincinnati		
Forsberg, Fred LB	68DenA 70-73Den 73Buf 74SD		6'1"	233	Washington	5	6
Forte, Ike HB	76-77NE	2	6'	199	Arkansas		24
Forzano, Rick	HC74-76Det				Kent State		
Foster, Eddie WR	77Hou	2	5'10"	185	Houston		
Foster, Will LB	73NE		6'2"	230	Eastern Michigan		6
Fouts, Dan QB	73-77SD	12	6'3"	200	Oregon		18
Fowler, Wayne C	70Buf		6'3"	260	Richmond		
Fox, Tim DB	76-77NE		5'11"	188	Ohio State		6
France, Doug OT	75-77LA		6'5"	164	Ohio State		
Francis, Russ TE	75-77NE	2	6'6"	240	Oregon		66
Francis, Wallace WR	73-74Buf 75-77Atl	23	5'11"	190	Arkansas-Pine Bluff		42
Franckowiak, Mike FB	75-76Den 77Buf		6'3"	219	Central Michigan		
Franklin, Cleveland FB	77Phi		6'2"	216	Baylor		
Franklin, Dennis WR	75-76Det		6'1"	185	Michigan		
Franklin, Willie WR	72Bal		6'2"	195	Oklahoma		
Franks, Dennis C	76-77Phi		6'1"	236	Michigan		
Frazier, Cliff DT	77KC		6'4"	265	U.C.L.A.		
Frederick, Andy OT	77Dal		6'6"	241	New Mexico		
Freelon, Solomon OG	72-74Hou		6'2"	250	Grambling		
Freeman, Steve DB	75-77Buf		5'11"	185	Mississippi State	3	6
Freitas, Jessee QB	74-75SD	1	6'1"	198	San Diego State		
Freitas, Rocky OT	68-77Det		6'6"	271	Oregon State		
Fritsch, Ted C	72-74Atl 75KJ 76-77Was		6'2"	241	St. Norbert		
Fritsch, Toni K	71-73Dal 74KJ 75Dal 76SD 77Hou	5	5'7"	189	none		401
Fritts, Stan FB-HB	75-76Cin	2	6'1"	215	N. Carolina State		78
Frohbose, Bill DB	74Det		6'	185	Miami (Fla.)		
Fryer, Brian WR	76Was 77JJ		6'1"	185	Alberta U.		
Fuggett, Jean TE	72-75Dal 76-77Was	2	6'3"	224	Amherst		108
Fuller, Johnny DB	68-72SF 73-75NO	3	6'	182	Lamar Tech	8	
Fuller, Mike DB	75-77SD	3	5'9"	193	Auburn	7	19
Fultz, Mike DT	77NO		6'5"	278	Nebraska		
Funchess, Tom OT	68-69BosA 70Bos 71-73Hou 74Mia		6'5"	264	Jackson State		
Fuqua, John (Frenchy) HB-FB	69NYG 70-76Pit 77BG	23	5'11"	200	Morgan State		144
Furness, Steve DT-DE	72-77Pit		6'4"	255	Rhode Island		
Gaddis, Robert WR	76Buf		5'11"	178	Miss. Valley State		
Gagnon, Dave HB	74Chi		5'10"	210	Ferris State		
Gaines, Clark FB-HB	76-77NYJ	2	6'1"	197	Wake Forest		54
Gaines, Lawrence FB	76Det 77KJ	2	6'1"	240	Wyoming		30
Galbreath, Tony FB-HB	76-77NO	2	6'1"	225	Missouri		66
Galigher, Ed DT-DE	72-76NYJ 77SF		6'4"	254	U.C.L.A.		
Gallagher, Allen OT	74NE		6'3"	255	Southern Calif.		
Gallagher, Dave DT-DE	74Chi 75-76NYG		6'4"	256	Michigan	1	
Gallagher, Frank OG	67-72Det 73Atl 73Min		6'2"	243	North Carolina		
Gallegos, Chan QB	72Oak		5'9"	175	San Jose State		
Ganas, Rusty DT	71Bal		6'4"	257	South Carolina		
Gant, Reuben TE-WR	74-77Buf	2	6'4"	228	Oklahoma State		42
Gantt, Greg K	74-75NYJ	4	5'11"	188	Alabama		11
Gantt, Jerry OT	70Buf		6'4"	266	N. Car. Central		
Gardin, Ron DB-WR	70-71Bal 73NE	3	5'11"	180	Arizona		6
Garlington, John LB	68-77Cle		6'1"	222	Louisiana State	9	
Garrett, Carl HB	69BosA 70Bos 71-72NE 73-74Chi 75NYJ 76-77Oak	23	5'11"	209	N. Mex. Highlands		210
Garrett, Len TE	71-73GB 73-75NO 75SF		6'3"	230	N. Mex. Highlands		
Garrett, Reggie WR	74-75Pit 76KJ	2	6'1"	174	Eastern Michigan		6
Garrison, Gary WR-OE	66-69SD-A 70-76SD 77Hou	2	6'1"	194	San Diego State		348
Garrison, Walt FB-HB	66-74Dal	23	6'	204	Oklahoma State		234
Garror, Leon DB	72-73Buf		6'	180	Alcorn A&M	1	

Use Name (Nicknames) – Positions	Team by Year	See Section	Hgt	Wgt	College	Int	Pts
Gartner, Chris K	74Cle		6'	170	Indiana		
Gatewood, Tom TE-WR	72-73NYG		6'3"	215	Notre Dame		
Gault, Don QB	70Cle		6'2"	190	Hofstra		
Gay, Blenda DE died due to knife wound – Dec. 1976	74SD 75-76Phi		6'5"	254	Fayetteville State		6
Gaydos, Kent WR	75GB 76JJ		6'6"	228	Florida State		
Geddes, Bob LB	72Den 73-75NE		6'2"	240	U.C.L.A.	2	6
Geddes, Ken LB	71-75LA 76-77Sea		6'3"	235	Nebraska	6	
George, Ed OT	75Bal 76-77Phi		6'4"	270	Wake Forest		
George, Steve DT	74StL 75KJ 76Atl		6'6"	265	Houston		
George, Tim WR	73Cin 74Cle		6'5"	218	Whittier		
Geredine, Tom WR	73-74Atl 76LA	23	6'2"	191	NE Missouri State		12
Gerela, Roy K	69HouA 70Hou 71-77Pit	45	5'10"	185	New Mexico State		814
Germany, Willie WR	72Atl 73Det 74WFL 75Hou 76NE		6'	192	Morgan State	2	6
Gersbach, Carl LB	70Phi 71-72Min 73-74SD 75Chi 76StL		6'1"	230	West Chester State	3	
Getty, Charlie OT-OG	74-77KC		6'4"	260	Penn State		
Giammona, Louie HB	76NYJ 77KJ	2	5'9"	180	Utah State		6
Gibbons, Mike OT	76-77NYG		6'4"	262	SW Oklahoma State		
Gibbs, Donnie K	74NO		6'2"	205	Texas Christian		
Gibbs, Pat DB	72Phi		5'10"	188	Lamar Tech		
Giblin, Robert DB	75NYG 76SJ 77StL		6'2"	208	Houston		
Gibson, Paul DB	72GB		6'2"	195	Texas-El Paso		
Gibson, Reuben HB	77Buf		6'	196	Memphis State		
Gibson, Tom DT	71Oak		6'6"	290	Texas-El Paso		
Giles, Jim TE	77Hou	2	6'3"	225	Alcorn A&M		
Gillette, Walker WR	70-71SD 72-73StL 74-76NYG	2	6'5"	199	Richmond		72
Gilliam, Joe QB	72-75Pit	1	6'2"	187	Tennessee State		6
Gilliam, John WR-HB	67-68NO 69-71StL 72-75Min 76Atl 77Chi 77NO	23	6'1"	192	S. Carolina State		312
Gillingham, Gale OG-DT	66-76GB		6'3"	257	Minnesota		
Ginn, Hubert HB	70-73Mia 73Bal 74-75Mia 76-77Oak	23	5'11"	187	Florida A&M		18
Gipson, Paul HB-FB	69-70Atl 71Det 73NE	2	6'	208	Houston		24
Gladieux, Bob HB	69BosA 70Bos 70Buf 71-72NE	2	5'11"	191	Notre Dame		
Glass, Chip TE	69-73Cle 74NYG	2	6'4"	236	Florida State		30
Glass, Leland WR	72-73GB	2	6'	185	Oregon		6
Glassic, Tom OG	76-77Den		6'4"	251	Virginia		
Glossen, Clyde WR	70Buf		5'11"	175	Texas-El Paso		
Glover, Rich DT	73NYG 74WFL 75Phi		6'1"	242	Nebraska		
Goeddeke, George OG-OT-C	67-69DenA 70-72Den 73JJ		6'3"	250	Notre Dame		
Gofourth, Derrel C	77GB		6'3"	260	Oklahoma State		
Goich, Dan DT-DE	69-70Det 71NO 72-73NYG 74Den		6'4"	258	California		
Golsteyn, Jerry QB	77NYG	1	6'4"	210	Northern Illinois		
Golub, Chris DB	77KC		6'2"	196	Kansas		
Gonzalez, Noe HB	74NE		6'	210	SW Texas State		
Goode, Dan LB	74-77SD		6'2"	230	Kansas	7	
Goodman, Brian OG	73-74Hou 75Den		6'2"	250	U.C.L.A.		
Goodman, Harvey OG	76Den		6'4"	260	Colorado		
Goodman, Les HB-FB	73-74GB	2	5'11"	206	Yankton		6
Goodrum, Charlie OT-OG	73-77Min		6'3"	256	Florida A&M		
Gordon, Dick WR-OE	65-71Chi 72-73LA 73GB 74SD	23	5'11"	190	Michigan State		216
Gordon, Ira OG-OT	70-75SD		6'3"	270	Kansas State		
Gordon, John DT	72Det		6'6"	260	Hawaii		
Gordon, Larry LB	76-77Mia		6'4"	230	Arizona State	1	
Gotshalk, Len OT-OG	72-76Atl 77KJ		6'4"	255	Humboldt State		
Gradishar, Randy LB	74-77Den		6'3"	233	Ohio State	12	9
Graf, Dave LB	75-77Cle		6'2"	215	Penn State	1	
Graff, Neil QB	74-75NE 76Sea 76-77Pit	1	6'3"	201	Wisconsin		
Graham, Tom LB	72-74Den 74KC 75-77SD		6'2"	235	Oregon	7	
Grandberry, Ken HB	74Chi	2	6'	198	Washington State		12
Grannell, Dave TE	74SD		6'4"	230	Arizona State		
Grant, Bob LB	68-70Bal 71Was		6'2"	225	Wake Forest	5	6
Grant, Frank WR	73-77Was	2	5'11"	181	S. Colorado State		108
Grant, John NT-DT-DE	73-76Den		6'3"	237	Southern Calif.		
Grant, Wes DE-DT	70JJ 71Cle 71SD 72Cle 73Hou		6'3"	245	U.C.L.A.		
Gravelle, Gordon OT	72-76Pit 77NYG		6'5"	251	Brigham Young		
Gray, Johnnie DB	75-77GB	3	5'11"	185	Cal. State-Fullerton	6	6
Gray, Leon OT	73-77NE		6'3"	256	Jackson State		
Gray, Mel WR	72-77StL	23	5'9"	172	Missouri		228
Gray, Tim DB	75StL 76-77KC		6'1"	200	Texas A&M	6	12
Green, Arthur HB-FB	72NO		5'11"	198	Albany State		
Green, Dave K	73Hou 73-75Cin 76-77TB	45	5'11"	206	Ohio U.		122
Green, Donnie OT	71-76Buf 77Phi		6'7"	266	Purdue		
Green, Gary DB	77KC		5'11"	184	Baylor	3	
Green, Jessie WR	76GB		6'2"	185	Tulsa		
Green, Joe DB	70-71NYG		5'11"	195	Bowling Green		6
Green, Sammy LB	76-77Sea		6'2"	229	Florida	1	
Green, Van DB	73-76Cle 76Buf		6'1"	192	Shaw	3	12
Green, Woody HB	74-76KC 77KJ	2	6'1"	205	Arizona State		66
Greene, Joe (Mean Joe) DT	69-77Pit		6'4"	272	North Texas State	1	
Greene, Tony DB	71-77Buf		5'10"	170	Maryland	33	14
Greenwood, L.C. DE	69-77Pit		6'5"	245	Arkansas-Pine Bluff		2
Greer, Charlie DB	68-69DenA 70-74Den	3	6'	205	Colorado	17	1
Gregory, Bill DT	71-77Dal		6'5"	254	Wisconsin	1	
Gregory, Jack DE	67-71Cle 72-77NYG		6'6"	250	Tenn.-Chatanooga, Delta State	1	
Gresham, Bob HB	71-72NO 73-74Hou 75-76NYJ	23	5'11"	195	West Virginia		84
Griese, Bob QB	67-69MiaA 70-77Mia	12	6'1"	190	Purdue		42
Griffin, Archie HB	76-77Cin	2	5'9"	192	Ohio State		18
Griffin, Wade OT	77Bal		6'5"	231	Mississippi		
Griggs, Perry WR	77Bal		5'10"	182	Baylor		
Grim, Bob WR	67-71Min 72-74NYG 75Chi 76-77Min	23	6'	197	Oregon State		96
Groce, Bob FB	76Min		6'2"	210	MacAlester		
Grogan, Steve QB	75-77NE	12	6'4"	202	Kansas State		102
Grooms, Elois DE	75-77NO		6'4"	247	Tennessee Tech		6
Gross, Lee C	75-77NO		6'3"	238	Auburn		
Grossman, Randy TE	74-77Pit	2	6'1"	217	Temple		12
Gueno, Jim LB	76-77GB		6'2"	220	Tulane		
Gunn, Jimmy LB	70-75Chi 75NYG 76TB		6'1"	220	Southern Calif.	2	
Guthrie, Grant K	70-71Buf	5	6'	210	Florida State		71
Guy, Ray K	73-77Oak	4	6'3"	193	Southern Miss.		
Haden, Pat QB	76-77LA	12	5'11"	182	Southern Calif.		36

Use Name (Nicknames) – Positions	Team by Year	See Section	Hgt	Wgt	College	Int	Pts
Hagen, Halvor OT-C-OG-DE	69-70Dal 71-72NE 73-75Buf		6'5"	252	Weber State		
Haggerty, Steve DB	75Den		5'10"	175	Nevada-Las Vegas		
Hagins, Isaac WR	76-77TB	2	5'9"	180	Southern U.		
Hairston, Carl DE	76-77Phi		6'3"	245	Md. Eastern Shore		
Hall, Charlie LB	71-77Cle		6'3"	225	Houston	8	12
Hall, Charlie DB	71-76GB		6'1"	193	Pittsburgh	2	
Hall, Randy DB	74Bal 75JJ 76Bal		6'3"	190	Idaho		
Hall, Willie LB	72-73NO 75-77Oak		6'2"	222	Southern Calif.	3	6
Hall, Windlan DB	72-75SF 76-77Min 77Was		5'11"	176	Arizona State	2	12
Halverson, Dean LB	69LA 70Atl 71-72LA 73-75Phi 76JJ		6'2"	223	Washington	1	
Ham, Jack LB	71-77Pit		6'3"	224	Penn State	23	12
Hamilton, Andy WR	73-74KC 75NO	2	6'3"	190	Louisiana State		
Hamilton, Ray (Sugar Bear) NT-DT	73-77NE		6'1"	243	Oklahoma		6
Hamilton, Wes OG	76-77Min		6'3"	255	Tulsa		
Hamlin, Gene C	70Was 71Chi 72Det		6'3"	245	Western Michigan		
Hammond, Bob HB	76-77NYG	23	5'10"	173	Morgan State		24
Hammond, Gary WR-HB	73-76StL	3	5'11"	184	S.M.U.		
Hammond, Wayne DT	76Den		6'5"	255	Montana State		
Hampton, Dave HB-FB	69-71GB 72-76Atl 76Phi	23	6'	207	Wyoming		204
Hanburger, Chris LB	65-77Was		6'2"	218	North Carolina	19	30
Hancock, Mike TE	73-74Was 75JJ		6'4"	220	Idaho State		12
Hand, Larry DT-DE	65-77Was		6'4"	247	Appalachian State	5	18
Hannah, Charles DE	77TB		6'5"	250	Alabama		
Hannah, John OG	73-77NE		6'2"	265	Alabama		6
Hanneman, Craig DE-DT	72-73Pit 74-75NE 76JJ		6'3"	243	Oregon State		
Hannon, Tom DB	77Min		6'	193	Michigan		
Hanratty, Terry QB	69-75Pit 77TB	1	6'1"	206	Notre Dame		6
Hansen, Don LB	66-67Min 69-75Atl 76Sea 76-77GB		6'3"	227	Illinois	10	6
Hanson, Dick DT	71NYG		6'6"	280	N. Dakota State		
Hardee, Billy DB	76Den 77NYJ		6'	185	Virginia Tech	1	
Hardeman, Don FB	75-77Hou	2	6'2"	235	Texas A&I		54
Harden, Lee DB	70GB		5'11"	195	Texas-El Paso		
Hardman, Cedrick DE	70-77SF		6'3"	253	North Texas State		2
Harmon, Clarence HB	77Was	2	5'11"	190	Mississippi State		6
Hardy, Cliff DB	71Chi		6'	187	Michigan State		
Hardy, Ed OG	73SF 74JJ		6'4"	242	Jackson State		
Hardy, Kevin DT-DE	68SF 69DJ 70GB 71-72SD		6'5"	271	Notre Dame		
Hargett, Ed QB	69-72NO 73Hou 74WFL	1	5'11"	187	Texas A&M		6
Hargrove, Jim LB	67Min 68MS 69-70Min 71-72StL		6'3"	229	Howard Payne	1	6
Harky, Steve HB-FB	71-72NYJ	2	6'	215	Georgia Tech		
Harper, Bruce HB-WR	77NYJ	23	5'8"	174	Kutztown State		6
Harper, Roland FB-HB	75-77Chi	2	6'	206	Louisiana Tech		24
Harper, Willie LB	73-77SF		6'2"	212	Nebraska	1	
Harrah, Dennis OG	75-77LA		6'5"	257	Miami (Fla.)		
Harraway, Charlie FB	66-68Cle 69-73Was 74WFL	2	6'2"	221	San Jose State		162
Harrell, Rick C	73NYJ		6'3"	238	Clemson		
Harrell, Will HB	75-77GB	23	5'9"	182	Pacific		54
Harris, Bo LB	75-77Cin		6'3"	226	Louisiana State	4	
Harris, Cliff DB	70-77Dal	3	6'	187	Ouachita Baptist	23	6
Harris, Duriel WR	76-77Mia	2	5'11"	175	New Mexico State		36
Harris, Franco FB-HB	72-77Pit	2	6'2"	228	Penn State		336
Harris, Ike WR	75-77StL	2	6'3"	205	Iowa State		24
Harris, James QB	69BufA, 70-71Buf 73-76LA 77SD	12	6'3"	213	Grambling		60
Harris, Jim DB	70Was 71Cin		5'11"	173	Howard Payne		
Harris, Joe LB	77Was		6'1"	225	Georgia Tech		
Harris, Leroy FB	77Mia	2	5'9"	220	Arkansas State		24
Harris, Paul LB	77TB		6'3"	225	Alabama		
Harris, Richard DE-DT	71-73Phi 74-75Chi 76-77Sea		6'4"	258	Grambling		
Harris, Tony DB	71SF		6'2"	190	Toledo		
Harrison, Dwight DB-WR	71-72Den 72-77Buf	2	6'1"	182	Texas A&I	17	18
Harrison, Glynn FB	76KC		5'11"	190	Georgia		
Harrison, Jim FB	71-74Chi	2	6'4"	236	Missouri		42
Harrison, Kenny WR	76-77SF	2	6'	167	S.M.U.		6
Harrison, Reggie (Booby) FB	74StL 74-77Pit	2	5'11"	218	Cincinnati		48
Hart, Harold HB	74-75Oak 76JJ 77NYG	23	6'	208	Texas Southern		42
Hart, Jeff OT	75SF 76NO		6'5"	259	Oregon State		
Hart, Jim QB	66-77StL	12	6'2"	204	Southern Illinois		84
Hart, Leo QB	71Atl 72Buf		6'4"	203	Duke		
Hart, Tommy DE-LB	68-77SF		6'3"	244	Morris Brown	2	14
Hartenstine, Mike DE	75-77Chi		6'3"	254	Penn State		
Hartle, Greg LB	74-76StL		6'2"	225	Newberry		
Hartwig, Keith WR	77Min 77GB		6'	186	Arizona		
Harvey, Claude LB	70Hou		6'4"	225	Prairie View		
Harvey, Richard DB	70Phi 71NO		6'2"	190	Jackson State		
Hasenhorl, George DT	74NYG		6'1"	260	Ohio State		
Haslerig, Clint WR	74-75Buf 75Min 76NYJ		6'	191	Michigan		
Hasselbeck, Don TE	77NE		6'7"	245	Colorado		24
Hauss, Len C	64-77Was		6'2"	234	Georgia		
Haverdick, Dave DT	70Det		6'4"	245	Morehead State		
Havig, Dennis OG	72-75Atl 76Hou 77GB		6'2"	253	Colorado		
Havrilak, Sam WR-HB-DB	69-73Bal 74NO	2	6'2"	195	Bucknell		42
Hawkins, Nate WR	75Hou		6'1"	190	Nevada-Las Vegas		
Hayden, Leo HB-FB	71Min 72-73StL		6'	211	Ohio State		6
Hayes, Billy DB	72NO		6'1"	175	San Diego State		
Hayes, Bob WR-OE	65-74Dal 75SF	23	6'	187	Florida A&M		456
Hayes, Ed DB	70Phi		6'1"	185	Morgan State	1	
Hayes, Lester DB	77Oak		6'	208	Texas A&M	1	
Hayes, Tom DB	71-75Atl 76SD		6'1"	197	San Diego State	19	36
Hayhoe, Bill OT	69-73GB 74JJ 75BL		6'8"	258	Southern Calif.		
Hayman, Conway OG-OT	75-77Hou		6'3"	261	Delaware		
Hayman, Gary HB	74-75Buf	3	6'1"	200	Penn State		
Haynes, Mike DB	76-77NE	3	6'2"	192	Arizona State	13	12
Haywood, Al FB	75Den		5'11"	215	Bethune-Cookman		
Heater, Don HB	72StL		6'2"	205	Montana State		
Heath, Clayton HB	76Buf 76Mia		5'11"	195	Wake Forest		
Hedberg, Randy QB	77TB	1	6'3"	200	Minot State		
Hefferle, Ernie	HC75NO				Duquesne		
Hefner, Larry LB	72-75GB		6'2"	226	Clemson	1	

Use Name (Nicknames) — Positions	Team by Year	See Section	Hgt	Wgt	College	Int	Pts
Hegman, Mike LB	76-77Dal		6'1"	223	Tennessee State	1	
Heinz, Bob DT-DE-NT	69MiaA 70-74Mia 75KJ 76-77Mia		6'6"	269	U. of Pacific		
Helms, Ken OT-C	77NYJ		6'4"	265	Georgia		
Helton, Darius OG	77KC		6'2"	260	N. Carolina Central		
Henderson, Tom LB	75-77Dal		6'2"	221	Langston	3	14
Hendren, Jerry WR	70Den		6'2"	187	Idaho		
Hentricks, Ted (The Stork) LB	69-73Bal 74GB 75-77Oak		6'7"	218	Miami (Fla.)	19	26
Hennessy, John DE	77NYJ		6'3"	246	Michigan		
Hennigan, Mike LB	73-75Det 76-77NYJ		6'2"	217	Tennessee Tech		
Henry, Wally WR	77Phi		5'8"	170	U.C.L.A.		
Henson, Champ FB	75Cin		6'3"	240	Ohio State		
Hepburn, Lonnie DB	71-72Bal 74Den		5'11"	182	Texas Southern	1	
Herkenhoff, Matt OT	76-77KC		6'4"	255	Minnesota		
Hermeling, Terry OT-OG-DE	70-73Was 74KJ 75-77Was		6'5"	255	Nevada-Reno		
Herosian, Brian DB	73Bal		6'3"	200	Connecticut		
Herrera, Efren K	74Dal 75JJ 76-77Dal	5	5'9"	188	U.C.L.A.		240
Herrmann, Don WR	69-74NYG 75-77NO	2	6'2"	199	Waynesburg		96
Herron, Mack HB	73-75NE 75Atl	23	5'5"	174	Kansas State		96
Hertwig, Craig OT	75-77Det		6'8"	270	Georgia		
Hester, Ray LB	71-73NO		6'2"	215	Tulane		
Hews, Bob OT-DE	71Buf		6'5"	240	Princeton		
Hickman, Dallas DE	76-77Was		6'6"	235	California		
Hicks, John OG	74-77NYG		6'2"	258	Ohio State		
Hicks, R.W. C	75Det		6'4"	250	Humboldt State		
Hicks, Tom LB	76-77Chi		6'4"	230	Illinois	1	
Highsmith, Don HB	70-72Oak 73GB 74-75WFL	2	6'	200	Michigan State		12
Hilgenberg, Wally LB	64-66Det 67JJ 68-77Min		6'3"	228	Iowa	8	14
Hill, Barry DB	75-76Mia		6'3"	185	Iowa State		
Hill, Calvin FB-HB	69-74Dal 75WFL 76-77Was	2	6'3"	228	Yale		282
Hill, David TE	76-77Det	2	6'2"	220	Texas A&I		42
Hill, Ike WR-DB	70-71Buf 73-74Chi 76Mia	23	5'10"	180	Catawba		30
Hill, J.D. WR	71-75Buf 76-77Det	2	6'1"	190	Arizona State		126
Hill, Jim DB	68KJ 69SD-A 70-71SD 72-74GB 75Cle		6'2"	192	Texas A&I	19	6
Hill, John C-OT	72-74NYG 75-77NO		6'2"	245	Lehigh		
Hill, Ralph C	76-77NYG		6'1"	245	Florida A&M		
Hill, Tony WR	77Dal		6'2"	196	Stanford		
Hilton, Ron DE	65-73Bal 74NYG 75Atl		6'6"	240	Jackson State	1	12
Himes, Dick OT	68-77GB		6'4"	250	Ohio State		
Hinton, Eddie WR	69-72Bal 73Hou 74NE	2	6'	200	Oklahoma		72
Hoaglin, Fred C	66-72Cle 73Bal 74-75Hou 76Sea		6'4"	247	Pittsburgh		
Hoban, Mike OG	74Chi		6'2"	235	Michigan		
Hobbs, Bill LB	69-71Phi 72NO		6'	218	Texas A&M		6
Hodgins, Norm DB	74Chi 75JJ		6'1"	190	Louisiana State		
Hoey, George DB	71StL 72-73NE 74SD 75Den 75NYJ		5'10"	174	Michigan		
Hofer, Paul HB	76-77SF	23	6'	194	Mississippi		6
Hogan, Mike FB-HB	76-77Phi	2	6'2"	210	Tenn.-Chattanooga		6
Holden, Sam OT	71NO		6'3"	258	Grambling		
Holden, Steve WR	73-77Cle 77Cin	23	6'	196	Arizona State		24
Holland, John WR	74Min 75-77Buf	2	6'	190	Tennessee State		24
Holland, Vern OT	71-77Cin		6'5"	269	Tennessee State		
Hollas, Hugo DB	70-72NO 73KJ 74SF		6'1"	190	Rice	11	
Holliday, Ron WR	73SD 74-75WFL 76KJ	2	5'9"	168	Pittsburgh		1
Holloman, Gus DB	68-69DenA 70-74NYJ	4	6'3"	195	Houston	8	
Holloway, Glenn OG	70-73Chi 74Cle		6'3"	249	North Texas State		
Hollway, Bob	HC71-72StL				Michigan		
Holman, Willie DE-DT	68-73Chi 73Was		6'4"	250	S. Carolina State		
Holmes, Ernie DT	72-77Pit		6'3"	260	Texas Southern		
Holmes, Mel OG-OT	71-73Pit		6'3"	250	N. Carolina A&T		
Holmes, Mike DB-WR	74-75SF 76Buf 76Mia	23	6'2"	195	Texas Southern	3	6
Holmes, Robert FB	68-69KC-A 70-71KC 71-72Hou 73SD 74WFL 75Hou	23	5'9"	220	Southern U.		162
Holmes, Rudy DB	74Atl		5'10"	178	Duke		
Homan, Dennis WR	68-70Dal 71-72KC	2	6'1"	180	Alabama		12
Holtz, Lou	HC76NYJ				Kent State		
Hooker, Fair WR	69-74Cle 75WFL	2	6'1"	198	Arizona State		48
Hooks, Jim FB	73-76Det	2	5'11"	225	Central State-Okla.		
Hooks, Roland HB	76-77Buf	2	6'	197	N. Carolina State		
Hoopes, Mitch K	75Dal 76SD 76Hou 77Det	4	6'1"	208	Arizona		
Hopkins, Andy HB	71Hou		5'10"	187	S.F. Austin State		
Horn, Bob LB	76-77SD		6'3"	236	Oregon State	2	
Horn, Don QB	67-70GB 71Den 72-73Cle 74SD	1	6'2"	195	San Diego State		6
Hornsby, Ron LB	71-74NYG		6'3"	231	Southeastern La.		
Horton, Greg OG	76-77LA		6'4"	245	Colorado		
Horton, Larry DE-DT	72Chi		6'2"	248	Iowa		
Hoskins, Bob DT-OG	70-75SF 76IL		6'2"	246	Wichita State		
Hoss, Clark TE	72Phi		6'8"	235	Oregon State		
Houston, Bill WR	74Dal		6'3"	208	Jackson State		
Houston, Ken DB	67-69HouA 70-72Hou 73-77Was	3	6'3"	195	Prairie View	46	72
Houston, Rich WR	69-73NYG	23	6'2"	196	East Texas State		42
Howard, Billy DE-DT	74-76Det		6'4"	252	Alcorn A&M		
Howard, Bob DB	67-69SD-A 70-74SD 75-77NE		6'1"	178	San Diego State	31	6
Howard, Gene DB	68-70NO 71-72LA	3	6'	190	Langston	14	12
Howard, Harry DB	76NYJ		6'	189	Ohio State		
Howard, Leroy DB	71Hou		5'11"	175	Bishop		
Howard, Paul OG	73-75Den 76JJ 77Den		6'3"	260	Brigham Young		
Howard, Percy WR	75Dal 76-77JJ		6'4"	210	Austin Peay		
Howard, Ron TE	74-75Dal 76-77Sea	2	6'4"	226	Seattle		6
Howard, Tom LB	77KC		6'2"	208	Texas Tech	1	
Howell, Delles DB	70-72NO 73-75NYJ 77JJ		6'3"	199	Grambling	17	
Howfield, Bobby K	68-69DenA 70Den 71-74NYJ	5	5'9"	180	none		487
Hrivnak, Gary DE	73-75Chi 76JJ		6'5"	252	Purdue		
Hubbard, Marv FB	69OakA 70-75Oak 76SJ 77Det	2	6'1"	224	Colgate		144
Hudson, Bob HB	72GB 73-74Oak	3	5'11"	207	Northeastern La.		
Huff, Gary QB	73-76Chi 77TB	12	6'1"	196	Florida State		12
Huff, Ken OG	75-77Bal		6'4"	260	North Carolina		
Huff, Marty LB	72SF		6'2"	234	Michigan		
Hufnagel, John QB	74-75Den	1	6'1"	194	Penn State		
Hughes, Dennis TE	70-71Pit	2	6'1"	220	Georgia		18
Hughes, Pat LB	70-76NYG 77NO		6'2"	233	Boston U.	9	
Hughes, Randy DB	75-77Dal		6'4"	206	Oklahoma	5	6
Hull, Mike FB-TE	68-70Chi 71-74Was	2	6'3"	220	Southern Calif.		6
Hull, Tom LB	74SF 75GB		6'3"	230	Penn State		
Humm, David QB	75-77Oak	1	6'2"	184	Nebraska		
Humphrey, Claude DE	68-74Atl 75KJ 76-77Atl		6'5"	257	Tennessee State	2	10
Humphrey, Tom C	74KC		6'6"	260	Abilene Christian		
Hunt, Calvin C	71Phi 72-73Hou		6'3"	244	Baylor		
Hunt, Charlie LB	73SF 75WFL 76TB		6'3"	215	Florida State		
Hunt, Ervin DB	70GB		6'2"	190	Fresno State		
Hunt, George K	73Bal 75NYG	5	6'1"	215	Tennessee		112
Hunt, Kevin OT-OG	72GB 73NE 73-77Hou		6'5"	260	Doane		
Hunt, Ron OT	76-77Cin		6'6"	265	Oregon		
Hunt, Sam LB	74-77NE		6'1"	243	S.F. Austin State	7	6
Hunter, Al HB	77Sea	23	5'11"	195	Notre Dame		6
Hunter, James DB	76-77Det		6'3"	195	Grambling	13	6
Hunter, Scott QB	71-73GB 74Buf 76-77Atl	12	6'2"	205	Alabama		72
Hutcherson, Ken LB	74Dal 75SD 76JJ		6'1"	219	Livingston State		
Hutchison, Chuck OG	70-72StL 73-75Cle 76KJ		6'3"	243	Ohio State		
Huther, Bruce LB	77Dal		6'1"	217	New Hampshire		
Hyatt, Freddie WR	68-72StL 73NO		6'3"	203	Auburn		
Hyde, Glenn OT	76-77Den		6'3"	253	Pittsburgh		
Hyland, Bob C-OG-OT	67-69GB 70Chi 71-75NYG 76GB 77NE		6'5"	253	Boston College		
Hynoski, Henry FB	75Cle		6'	210	Temple		
Ilgenfritz, Mark DE	74Cle 75WFL		6'4"	250	Vanderbilt		
Imhof, Martin DE-DT	72StL 74Was 75NE 76Den		6'6"	256	San Diego State		
Irons, Gerald LB	70-75Oak 76-77Cle		6'2"	231	Md. Eastern Shore	11	6
Ivory, Horace HB	77NE		6'	197	Oklahoma		
Isenbarger, John HB-WR	70-73SF 74WFL	2	6'3"	203	Indiana		12
Jackson, Bernie DB	72-76Cin 77Den	3	6'	177	Washington State	10	
Jackson, Bob OG-OT	75-77Cle		6'5"	247	Duke		
Jackson, Ernie DB	72-77NO		5'10"	175	Duke	15	6
Jackson, Harold WR	68LA 69-72Phi 73-77LA	2	5'10"	175	Jackson State		342
Jackson, Honor DB	72-73NE 73-74NYG		6'1"	195	U. of Pacific	5	
Jackson, Jazz HB	74-76NYJ	2	5'8"	169	Western Kentucky		12
Jackson, Joey DE-DT	72-73NYJ 74WFL 77Min		6'4"	263	New Mexico State		
Jackson, Johnny MG	77Phi		6'2"	250	Southern		
Jackson, Larron OG-OT	71-74Den 75-76Atl		6'3"	265	Missouri		
Jackson, Melvin OG	76-77GB		6'1"	267	Southern Calif.		
Jackson, Monte (The Phantom) DB	75-77LA		5'11"	189	San Diego State	17	24
Jackson, Noah OG	75-77Chi		6'2"	267	Tampa		
Jackson, Randy OT	67-74Chi		6'5"	247	Florida		
Jackson, Randy HB-FB	72Buf 73SF 74Phi	2	6'	220	Wichita State		6
Jackson, Rusty K	76LA	4	6'2"	190	Louisiana State		
Jackson, Steve DB	77Oak		6'1"	192	Louisiana State	1	
Jackson, Tom LB	73-77Den		5'11"	221	Louisville	14	12
Jackson, Wilbur FB-HB	74-77SF	2	6'1"	215	Alabama		66
Jacobsen, Larry DT-DE	72-74NYG 75BN		6'6"	260	Nebraska		
Jakowenko, George K	74Oak 76Buf	5	5'9"	175	Syracuse		57
James, John K	72-77Atl	4	6'3"	198	Florida		
James, Po HB	72-75Phi	23	6'1"	202	New Mexico State		36
James, Robert DB-WR	69BufA 70-74Buf 75-76KJ		6'1"	182	Fisk	9	6
Jameson, Larry DT	76TB		6'7"	270	Indiana		
Janet, Ernie OG	72-74Chi 75GB 75Phi 76GJ		6'4"	253	Washington		
Jankowski, Bruce WR	71-72KC		5'11"	185	Ohio State		
Jaqua, John DB	70-72Was 73JJ		6'	190	Lewis and Clark	1	
Jarvis, Bruce C	71-74Buf		6'7"	248	Washington		
Jarvis, David QB	74KC		6'2"	212	Kansas		
Jarvis, Ray WR	71-72Atl 73Buf 74-77Det	2	5'11"	193	Norfolk State		60
Jauron, Dick DB	73-77Det	3	6'	190	Yale	14	6
Jaworski, Ron (The Polish Rifle) QB	74-76LA 77Phi	12	6'2"	187	Youngstown State		54
Jefferson, Roy WR-FL-OE	65-69Pit 70Bal 71-76Was	23	6'2"	194	Utah		318
Jeffrey, Neal QB	76-77SD		6'1"	180	Baylor		
Jenkins, Al OG-OT-DE-DT	69-70Cle 72Mia 73Hou		6'2"	250	Tulsa		
Jenkins, Al WR	75-77Atl	2	5'10"	166	Morris Brown		96
Jenkins, Ed HB	72Mia 73JJ 74NYG 74Buf 74NE		6'2"	210	Holy Cross		
Jenkins, Leon DB	72Det		5'11"	165	West Virginia		
Jennings, Dave K	74-77NYG	4	6'4"	205	St. Lawrence		
Jennings, Rick HB-WR	76Oak 77TB 77SF 77Oak		5'9"	180	Maryland		
Jensen, Jim FB-TE	76Dal 77Den	2	6'3"	235	Iowa		6
Jerome, Jim LB	77NYJ		6'4"	225	Syracuse		
Jessie, Ron WR	71-74Det 75-77LA	23	6'	184	Kansas		140
Jeter, Gary DE	77NYG		6'4"	250	Southern Calif.		
Jiggetts, Dan OT	76-77Chi		6'4"	275	Harvard		
Jilek, Dan LB	76-77Buf		6'2"	216	Michigan	2	
Joachim, Steve QB	76NYJ		6'3"	215	Temple		
Jodat, Jim FB	77LA		5'11"	210	Carthage		12
Johannson, Ove K	77Phi		5'10"	175	Abilene Chrisitan		4
Johns, Freeman WR	76-77LA		6'1"	175	S.M.U.		
Johnson, Al HB-DB	72-74Hou 75NJ 76-77Hou		6'	200	Cincinnati		
Johnson, Andy HB	74-76NE 77KJ	23	6'	204	Georgia		84
Johnson, Bennie DB	70-73Hou 74WFL 76NO	3	5'11"	178	Johnson C. Smith	1	
Johnson, Bill K	70NYG	4	6'4"	208	Livingston		
Johnson, Billy (White Shoes, Box Office) WR	74-77Hou	23	5'9"	170	Widener		114
Johnson, Bob C	68-77Cin		6'5"	260	Tennessee		
Johnson, Butch WR	76-77Dal	23	6'1"	189	Cal-Riverside		18
Johnson, Carl OT-OG	72-73NO		6'3"	248	Nebraska		
Johnson, Cecil LB	77TB		6'2"	220	Pittsburgh	1	
Johnson, Charles MG	77Phi		6'3"	262	Colorado		
Johnson, Cornelius OG	68-73Bal		6'2"	245	Virginia Union		
Johnson, Curtis DB	70-77Mia		6'2"	196	Toledo	19	8
Johnson, Dennis DT-DE	74-77Was		6'4"	260	Delaware	2	
Johnson, Eric DB	77Phi		6'1"	192	Washington State		
Johnson, Essex HB	68-69CinA 70-75Cin 76TB	23	5'9"	197	Grambling		186
Johnson, Ezra DE	77GB		6'4"	240	Morris Brown		
Johnson, Gary DT	75-77SD		6'2"	259	Grambling		
Johnson, Greg DT-MG-DE	77Bal 77Chi 77TB		6'4"	240	Florida State	1	6
Johnson, Ken DE	71-77Cin		6'5"	261	Indiana		
Johnson, Ken QB	77Buf		6'2"	205	Colorado		
Johnson, Kermit HB	75-76SF	2	6'	201	U.C.L.A.		6

Use Name (Nicknames) – Positions	Team by Year	See Section	Hgt	Wgt	College	Int	Pts
Johnson, Len C-OG	70NYG		6'2"	250	St. Cloud State		
Johnson, Levi DB	73-77Det		6'3"	196	Texas A & I	21	30
Johnson, Mark DE-LB	75-76Buf 77Cle		6'2"	239	Missouri		
Johnson, Marshall WR-HB	75Bal 76KJ 77Bal		6'1"	190	Houston		12
Johnson, Monte LB	73-77Oak		6'4"	238	Nebraska	8	
Johnson, Pete FB	77Cin	2	6'	240	Ohio State		24
Johnson, Randy QB	66-70Atl 71-73NYG 74WFL 75Was 76GB	12	6'3"	202	Texas A & I		60
Johnson, Randy OG	77TB		6'2"	255	Georgia		
Johnson, Ron HB	69Cle 70-75NYG	2	6'1"	205	Michigan		330
Johnson, Sammy HB-FB	74-76SF 76-77Min	2	6'	222	North Carolina		54
Johnson, Walter DT	65-76Cle 77Cin		6'3"	268	Los Angeles State	2	14
Joiner, Charlie WR	69HouA 70-72Hou 72-75Cin 76-77SD	2	5'11"	186	Grambling		186
Jolitz, Evan LB	74Cin		6'2"	225	Cincinnati		
Jolley, Gordon OT-OG	72-75Det 76-77Sea		6'5"	244	Utah		
Jolley, Lewis HB-FB	72-73Hou		6'	210	North Carolina		
Jones, Andrew FB	75-76NO	2	6'2"	216	Washington State		6
Jones, Bert QB	73-77Bal	12	6'3"	209	Louisiana State		66
Jones, Bob DB	73-74Cin 75-76Atl		6'2"	193	Virginia Union		
Jones, Broderick DB	77Cle		6'1"	195	Tuskegee	1	
Jones, Calvin DB	73-76Den		5'7"	170	Washington	12	6
Jones, Clint HB	67-72Min 73SD 74JJ	23	6'	206	Michigan State		126
Jones, Cody DT-DE	74-77LA		6'5"	240	San Jose State		
Jones, Dave WR	69-71Cle		6'2"	185	Kansas State		
Jones, Doug DB	73-74KC 75KJ 76-77Buf		6'2"	204	Northridge State	6	
Jones, Ed DB	75Buf		6'	185	Rutgers	3	
Jones, Ed (Too Tall) DE	74-77Dal		6'9"	263	Tennessee State	1	
Jones, Ernie DB	76Sea 77NYG		6'3"	180	Miami (Fla.)	1	
Jones, Greg HB	70-71Buf	2	6'1"	200	U.C.L.A.		18
Jones, Harris OG-C	71SD 72JJ 73-74Hou		6'4"	241	Johnson C. Smith		
Jones, Horace DE	71-75Oak 76KJ 77Sea		6'3"	251	Louisville		
Jones, Jimmie DE	69NY-A 70NYJ 71-73Was		6'3"	215	Wichita State		
Jones, Jimmie HB	74Det	23	5'10"	205	U.C.L.A.		6
Jones, Joe (Turkey) DE	70-71Cle 72KJ 73Cle 74Phi 75-77Cle		6'6"	249	Tennessee State		6
Jones, John QB	75NYG	1	6'1"	180	Fisk		
Jones, June QB	77Atl		6'4"	200	Portland State		
Jones, Ken OT-DE	76-77Buf		6'5"	252	Arkansas State		
Jones, Kim FB	76-77NO		6'4"	241	Colorado State		
Jones, Larry WR-DB	74-77Was	3	5'10"	170	NE Missouri State		12
Jones, Leroy DE	76-77SD		6'8"	260	Norfolk State	2	6
Jones, Mike LB	77Sea		6'2"	214	Jackson State		
Jones, Ray DB	70Phi 71Mia 72SD		6'	187	Southern U.	2	
Jones, Spike K	70Hou 71-74Buf 75-77Phi	4	6'2"	191	Georgia		
Jones, Steve HB	73-74Buf 74-77StL	2	6'	200	Duke		90
Jordan, Bob DT	77Atl		6'6"	255	Memphis State		
Jordan, Curtis DB	76-77TB		6'2"	184	Texas Tech	3	
Jordan, Jeff HB-FB	67-69JJ 70LA 71-72Was		6'1"	215	Washington		
Jordan, Shelby OT	75,77NE		6'7"	260	Washington (Mo.)		
76 ineligible to play Football							
Joyce, Terry K-TE	76-77StL	4	6'6"	229	Missouri Southern		
Juenger, Dave WR	73Chi		6'1"	195	Ohio U.		
Kaczmarek, Mike LB	73Bal		6'4"	235	Southern Illinois		
Kadish, Mike DT	73-77Buf		6'5"	269	Notre Dame		8
Kadziel, Ron LB	72NE		6'4"	230	Stanford		
Kalina, Dave WR	70Pit		6'3"	205	Miami (Fla.)		
Kaminski, Larry C	68-69DenA 70-73Den		6'2"	244	Purdue		
Kampa, Bob DT	73-74Buf		6'4"	249	California		
Kane, Rick HB	77Det	2	5'11"	200	San Jose State		24
Kay, Rick LB	73LA 74KJ 75-77LA 77Atl		6'4"	235	Colorado	1	
Kearney, Jim DB	65-66Det 67-69KC-A 70-75KC 76NO		6'2"	204	Prairie View	23	30
Kearney, Tim LB	72-74Cin 75KC 76TB 76-77StL		6'2"	228	Northern Michigan	1	
Keating, Tom DT	64-65BufA 66-67OakA 68FJ 69OakA 70-72Oak 73Pit 74-75KC		6'3"	246	Michigan		
Keeton, Durwood DB	75NE		5'10"	180	Oklahoma		
Keithley, Gary QB	73,75StL	1 4	6'3"	210	Texas-El Paso		
Kelcher, Louie DT	75-77SD		6'5"	282	S. M. U.		
Kellar, Mark FB	76-77Min		6'	225	Northern Illinois		
Keller, Larry LB	76-77NYJ		6'2"	223	Houston	2	
Keller, Mike LB	72-73Dal		6'4"	220	Michigan		
Kelley, Brian LB	73-77NYG		6'3"	222	Calif. Lutheran	5	
Kellum, Marv LB	74-76Pit 77StL		6'2"	225	Wichita State	2	
Kelly, Jim TE	74Chi		6'4"	210	Tennessee State		
Kelly, Mike TE	70-72Cin 73NO		6'4"	217	Davidson		
Kendrick, Vince FB	74Atl 75KJ 76TB		6'	232	Florida		6
Kennard, Ken MG-DE	77Hou		6'2"	245	San Angelo State		2
Kennedy, Jimmie TE	75-77Bal		6'3"	231	Colorado State		6
Kern, Rex DB	71-73Bal 74Buf		5'11"	190	Ohio State	2	
Kersey, Merritt HB-K	74-75Phi	4	6'1"	205	West Chester State		
Key, Wade OG-OT	70-77Phi		6'4"	245	SW Texas State		
Keyes, Leroy HB-DB	69-72Phi 73KC	2	6'3"	208	Purdue	8	18
Keyworth, Jon FB	74-77Den	2	6'3"	231	Colorado		114
Kiick, Jim HB	68-69MiaA 70-74Mia 75WFL 76-77Den 77Was	2	5'11"	215	Wyoming		198
Killian, Gene OG	74Dal		6'4"	250	Tennessee		
Kimbrough, John WR	77Buf	2	5'10"	165	St. Cloud State		18
Kindle, Greg OG-OT	74-75StL 76-77Atl		6'4"	265	Tennessee State		
Kiner, Steve LB	70Dal 71,73NE 74-77Hou		6'	221	Tennessee	9	2
King, Horace FB	75-77Det	2	5'10"	210	Georgia		18
King, Steve LB	73-77NE		6'4"	234	Tulsa	1	
Kingrea, Rick LB	71-72Cle 73-77NO		6'1"	229	Tulane	1	
Kingsriter, Doug TE	73-75Min		6'2"	222	Minnesota		
Kinney, Jeff FB	72-76KC 76Buf	2	6'2"	215	Nebraska		36
Kinney, Steve OT	73-74Chi		6'5"	257	Utah State		
Kirk, Ernest DE	77Hou		6'2"	265	Howard Payne	1	
Kirkland, Mike QB	76-77Bal		6'1"	195	Arkansas		
Kirksey, Roy OG-OT	71-72NYJ 73-74Phi		6'1"	263	Md. Eastern Shore		
Klecko, Joe DT	77NYJ		6'3"	256	Temple		
Klein, Bob TE	69-76LA 77SD	2	6'5"	236	Southern Calif.		96
Knief, Gayle WR	70Bos		6'3"	205	Morningside		6
Knight, Curt K	69-73Was	5	6'1"	190	Coast Guard		475
Knight, David WR	73-77NYJ	2	6'1"	177	William & Mary		42
Knoff, Kurt DB	77Hou		6'5"	188	Kansas		
Knox, Bill DB	74-76Chi		5'9"	192	Purdue	2	
Knox, Chuck	HC73-76LA				Juniata		
Knutson, Steve OT-OG	76-77GB		6'3"	254	Southern Calif.		
Koch, Greg OT	77GB		6'4"	265	Arkansas		
Koegel, Vic LB	74Cin		6'	215	Ohio State		
Koegel, Warren C	71Oak 72JJ 73Cin 74NYJ		6'3"	253	Penn State		
Kolb, John OT-C	69-77Pit		6'2"	253	Oklahoma State		
Kolen, Mike LB	70-75Mia 76KJ 77Mia		6'2"	220	Auburn	5	
Kollar, Bill MG-DT	74-76Cin 77TB		6'4"	254	Montana State		
Koncar, Mark OT	76-77GB		6'5"	270	Colorado		
Korver, Kelvin DT	73-75Oak 76-77KJ		6'6"	267	Northwestern, Iowa	1	
Kosins, Gary HB-FB	72-74Chi	2	6'1"	216	Dayton		12
Kotar, Doug HB	74-77NYG	23	5'11"	205	Kentucky		90
Kowalkowski, Bob OG	66-76Det 77GB		6'3"	243	Virginia		
Koy, Ted LB-TE-HB-FB	70Oak 71-74Buf	2	6'1"	211	Texas		6
Krakau, Merv LB	73-77Buf		6'1"	239	Iowa State	3	
Kramer, Kent TE	66SF 67NO 69-70Min 71-74Phi	2	6'5"	234	Minnestoa		48
Kramer, Tommy QB	77Min	1	6'1"	199	Rice		
Kratzer, Don WR	73KC		6'3"	194	Missouri Valley		
Krause, Larry HB	70-71GB 72JJ 73-74GB 75SJ	3	6'	208	St. Norbert		6
Krause, Paul DB-FL	64-67Was 68-77Min		6'3"	198	Iowa	78	36
Krepfle, Keith TE	75-77Phi	2	6'3"	225	Iowa State		24
Krevis, Al OT	75Cin 76NYJ		6'6"	263	Boston College		
Krieg, Jim WR	72Den		5'9"	172	Washington		
Kroll, Bob DB	72GB 73JJ		6'1"	195	Northern Michigan		
Kruczek, Mike QB	76-77Pit	1	6'	199	Boston College		12
Krueger, Rolf DE-DT	69-72StL 72-74SF		6'4"	251	Texas A & M		
Kuechenberg, Bob OG-C	70-77Mia		6'3"	251	Notre Dame		
Kuehn, Art C	76-77Sea		6'3"	263	U.C.L.A.		
Kunz, George OT	69-74Atl 75-77Bal		6'5"	259	Notre Dame		
Kunz, Terry FB	76Oak 77JJ		6'1"	215	Colorado		
Kupp, Jake OG	64-65Dal 66Was 67Atl 67-75NO		6'3"	240	Washington		
Kuykendall, Fulton LB	75-77Atl		6'5"	225	U.C.L.A.		
Kuziel, Bob C-OT	72NO 74WFL 75-77Was		6'5"	255	Pittsburgh		
Kwalick, Ted TE	69-74SF 75-77Oak	2	6'4"	226	Penn State		138
Kyle, Aaron DB	76-77Dal		5'10"	183	Wyoming	1	2
Laaveg, Paul OG	70-75Was 76KJ		6'4"	247	Iowa		
LaCrosse, Dave LB	77Pit		6'3"	210	Wake Forest		
Lafary, Dave OT	77NO		6'7"	280	Purdue		
LaGrand, Morris FB	75KC 75NO		6'1"	220	Tampa		6
Lahood, Mike OG	69LA 70StL 71-72LA		6'3"	250	Wyoming		
Laidlaw, Scott FB	75-77Dal	2	6'	205	Stanford		30
Laird, Bruce DB	72-77Bal	3	6'	192	American Inter.	8	2
Lally, Bob LB	76GB		6'2"	230	Cornell		
Lamb, Ron FB	68DenA 68-69CinA 71-72Cin 72Atl	2	6'2"	227	South Carolina		
Lambert, Jack LB	74-77Pit		6'4"	219	Kent State	7	
Landry, Greg QB	68-77Det	12	6'4"	207	Massachusetts		114
Lane, MacArthur FB-HB	68-71StL 72-74GB 75-77KC	2	6'	220	Utah State		222
Langer, Jim C-OG	70-77Mia		6'2"	250	S. Dakota State		
Lanier, Willie LB	67-69KCA 70-77KC		6'1"	245	Morgan State	27	14
Lapham, Dave OG-OT-C	74-77Cin		6'4"	258	Syracuse		
LaPorta, Phil OT	74-75NO		6'4"	256	Penn State		
Largent, Steve WR	76-77Sea	2	5'11"	184	Tulsa		84
Larson, Bill TE	75SF 77Was 77Det		6'3"	225	Colorado State		
Larson, Lynn OT	71Bal		6'4"	254	Kansas State		
Lash, Jim WR	73-76Min 76-77SF	2	6'2"	200	Northwestern		24
Laskey, Bill LB	65BufA 66-67OakA 68FJ 69OakA 70Oak 71-72Bal 73-74Den		6'2"	237	Michigan	7	
Laslavic, Jim LB	73-77Det		6'2"	236	Penn State	6	
Laster, Art OT	70Buf		6'4"	280	Md. Eastern Shore		
Latin, Jerry HB	75-77StL	2	5'10"	189	Northern Illinois		24
Latta, Greg TE	75-77Chi	2	6'3"	228	Morgan State		42
Lavender, Joe (Big Bird) DB	73-75Phi 76-77Was		6'4"	190	San Diego State	16	18
Lawless, Burton OG	75-77Dal		6'4"	250	Florida		
Lawrence, Henry OT-OG	74-77Oak		6'4"	272	Florida A & M		
Lawrence, Larry QB	74-75Oak 76TB	1	6'1"	208	Iowa		
Lawrence, Rolland DB	73-77Atl	3	5'10"	178	Tabor	24	6
Lawson, Odell FB-HB	70Bos 71NE 73-74NO	23	6'2"	212	Langston		
Lawson, Roger HB-FB	72-73Chi	2	6'2"	215	Western Michigan		
Lawson, Steve OG	71-72Cin 73-75Min 76-77SF		6'3"	264	Kansas		
Lazetich, Pete MG-DE-DT-LB	72-74SD 76-77Phi		6'3"	241	Stanford		
Leahy, Bob QB	71Pit		6'2"	205	Coll. of Emporia		
Leahy, Pat K	74-77NYJ	5	6'	198	St. Louis U.		214
Leak, Curtis WR	76TB		5'11"	180	Johnson C. Smith		
Leaks, Roosevelt FB	75-77Bal	2	5'10"	223	Texas		72
Leavitt, Allan K	77Atl 77TB	5	5'11"	176	Georgia		20
Leavitt, Dick OT	76NYG 77KJ		6'3"	285	Bowdoin		
LeClair, Jim LB	72-77Cin		6'2"	233	North Dakota	6	
Lee, Bivian DB	71-75NO		6'3"	200	Prairie View	9	
Lee, Bob QB	69-72Min 73-74Atl 75-77Min	12 4	6'2"	195	U. of Pacific		18
Lee, David K	66-77Bal	4	6'4"	224	Louisiana Tech		
Lee, John DE	76-77SD		6'2"	250	Nebraska		
Lee, Ken LB	71Det 72Buf		6'4"	231	Washington	6	6
Lee, Mike LB	74SD		6'	232	Nevada		
Lee, Ron FB	76-77Bal	2	6'4"	225	West Virginia		24
Lee, Willie DT	76-77KC		6'5"	249	Bethune-Cookman		6
LeFear, Billy HB-WR	72-75Cle 76JJ	23	5'11"	197	Henderson State		
Leigh, Charlie FB-HB	68-69Cle 71-74Mia 74GB	23	5'11"	205	none		12
LeMaster, Frank LB	74-77Phi		6'2"	229	Kentucky	4	6
Lemon, Mike LB	75NO 75Den 76-77TB		6'2"	218	Kansas		
Lenkaitis, Bill (Doctor) C-OG	68-69SD-A 70SD 71-77NE		6'3"	255	Penn State		
Lens, Greg DT	70-71Atl		6'5"	260	Trinity (Texas)		
Leonard, Anthony DB	76-77SF	3	5'11"	168	Virginia Union	1	6
Leonard, Cecil DB	69NY-A 70NYJ		5'11"	165	Tuskegee		
LeVeck, Jack LB	73-74StL 75Cle		6'	224	Ohio U.		
LeVias, Jerry WR	69HouA 70Hou 71-74SD	23	5'10"	177	S.M.U.		84
Lewis, Dave QB-K	70-73Cin	4	6'2"	216	Stanford		
Lewis, Dave LB	77TB		6'4"	230	Southern Calif.	2	

Use Name (Nicknames) – Positions	Team by Year	See Section	Hgt	Wgt	College	Int	Pts
Lewis, D.D. LB	68Dal 69MS 70-77Dal		6'2"	219	Mississippi State	5	6
Lewis, Eddie DB	76-77SF		6'	176	Kansas		
Lewis, Frank WR	71-77Pit	2	6'1"	196	Grambling		102
Lewis, Jess LB	70Hou		6'1"	230	Orange State		
Lewis, Mike DT-DE	71-77Atl		6'3"	253	Arkansas-Pine Bluff	1	2
Lewis, Rich LB	72Hou 73-74Buf 75NYJ		6'3"	217	Portland State		
Lewis, Scott DE	71Hou		6'6"	260	Grambling		
Lewis, Stan DE	75Cle		6'4"	240	Wayne (Neb.)		
Leypoldt, John K	71-76Buf 76-77Sea	5	6'2"	229	none		472
Lick, Dennis OT	76-77Chi		6'3"	270	Wisconsin		
Liggett, Bob DT	70KC		6'2"	255	Nebraska		
Line, Bill DT	72Chi		6'7"	260	S.M.U.		
Lingenfelter, Bob OT	77Cle		6'7"	277	Nebraska		
Linhart, Toni K	72NO 74-77Bal	5	6'	177	none		342
Little, Everett OG	76TB 77Oak		6'4"	265	Houston		
Little, Floyd HB	67-69DenA 70-75Den	23	5'10"	196	Syracuse		324
Little, John DT-DE-MG	70-74NYJ 75-76Hou 77Buf		6'3"	241	Oklahoma State		
Little, Larry OG-OT-DT	67-68SD-A 69MiaA 70-77Mia		6'1"	266	Bethune-Cookman		
Livers, Virgil DB	75-77Chi	3	5'9"	177	Western Kentucky	7	6
Livingston, Mike QB	68-69KC-A 70-77KC	12	6'3"	210	S.M.U.		42
Lloyd, Dan LB	76-77NYG		6'2"	225	Washington		
Lloyd, Jeff DE	76Buf		6'6"	255	West Texas State		
Lockhart, Spider DB	65-75NYG	3	6'2"	176	North Texas State	41	18
Logan, Dave WR	76-77Cle	2	6'4"	226	Colorado		6
Logan, Randy DB	73-77Phi		6'1"	195	Michigan	14	
Lohmeyer, John DE-DT	73KC 74JJ 75-77KC		6'4"	230	Kansas St. Teachers		10
Lomas, Mark DE-DT	70-74NYJ 75FJ 76KJ		6'4"	245	Northern Arizona		
Long, Carson K	77Buf	5	5'10"	210	Pittsburgh		34
Long, Doug DB	77Sea		6'	189	Whitworth		
Long, Ken OG	76Det 77JJ		6'3"	265	Purdue		
Long, Kevin HB	77NYJ	2	6'1"	205	South Carolina		
Long, Mel LB	72-74Cle		6'	228	Toledo		
Longley, Clint QB	74-75Dal 76SD	1	6'1"	194	Abilene Christian		
Longo, Tom DB	69-70NYG 71StL		6'1"	199	Notre Dame		
Lorch, Karl DE	76-77Was		6'3"	257	Southern Calif.		
Lou, Ron C	73Hou 74JJ 75Phi 76Hou		6'2"	240	Arizona State		
Love, Walt WR	73NYG		5'9"	180	Westminister (Utah)		
Lowe, Woodrow LB	76-77SD		6'	227	Alabama	2	
Luce, Derrel LB	75-77Bal		6'3"	226	Baylor	2	6
Luck, Terry QB	77Cle	1	6'3"	205	Nebraska		6
Lueck, Bill OG	68-74GB 75Phi		6'3"	239	Arizona		
Luke, Steve DB	75-77GB		6'2"	205	Ohio State	6	
Luken, Tom OG	72-75Phi 76KJ 77Phi		6'3"	253	Purdue		
Lumpkin, Ron DB	73NYG		6'2"	200	Arizona State		
Lunsford, Mel DE-DT	73-77NE		6'3"	256	Central State-Ohio		
Lurtsema, Bob DE-DT	67-71NYG 72-76Min 76-77Sea		6'6"	250	Western Michigan	1	
Lusk, Herb HB	76-77Phi	2	6'	190	Long Beach State		18
Lyle, Garry DB-HB	68-74Chi		6'2"	197	George Washington	12	
Lyman, Jeff LB	72Buf		6'2"	230	Brigham Young		
Lynch, Fran HB-FB	67-69DenA 70-75Den 76KJ	2	6'1"	203	Hofstra		86
Lynch, Jim LB	67-69KC-A 70-77KC		6'1"	232	Notre Dame	17	6
Lynch, Tom OG	77Sea		6'5"	260	Boston College		
Lyons, Dicky DB	70NO		6'	190	Kentucky	1	
Lyons, Tommy OG-C	71-76Den		6'2"	229	Georgia		
Lytle, Bob HB	77Den	2	6'1"	198	Michigan		12
Mabra, Ron DB	75-76Atl 77NYJ		5'10"	166	Howard		
Macek, Don OG-C	76-77SD		6'3"	253	Boston College		
Mack, Tom OG	66-77LA		6'3"	249	Michigan		
MacLeod, Tom LB	73GB 74-75Bal 76FJ 77Bal		6'3"	226	Minnesota	5	
Madden, John	HC69OakA HC70-77Oak				Cal. St. Polytech		
Maddox, Bob DE-DT	74Cin 76-77KC		6'5"	237	Frostburg State		6
Mahalic, Drew LB	75SD 76-77Phi		6'4"	226	Notre Dame	1	
Maitland, Jack HB	70Bal 71-72NE	2	6'1"	210	Williams		18
Majors, Bobby DB	72Cle		6'1"	193	Tennessee		
Malinchak, Bill WR-OE	66-69Det 70-74,76Was	2	6'1"	198	Indiana		32
Mallory, Irvin DB	71NE		6'1"	196	Virginia Union		
Mallory, Larry DB	76-77NYG		5'11"	185	Tennessee State	2	
Malone, Art FB-HB	70-74Atl 75-76Phi	2	5'11"	213	Arizona State		150
Malone, Benny HB	74-77Mia	2	5'10"	193	Arizona State		90
Manders, Dave C	64-66Dal 67JJ 68-74Dal		6'2"	247	Michigan State		
Mandich, Jim TE-WR	70-77Mia	2	6'3"	223	Michigan		138
Mann, Errol K	68GB 69-76Det 76-77Oak	5	6'	202	North Dakota		777
Manning, Archie QB	71-75NO 76SJ 77NO	12	6'3"	208	Mississippi		90
Manning, Rosie DT	72-75Atl 75Phi		6'5"	257	NE State-Okla.		
Manor, Brian DE	77Den		6'4"	247	Arkansas		
Mansfield, Ray C-DT	63Phi 64-76Pit		6'3"	253	Washington		
Maples, Bobby C-LB	65-69HouA 70Hou 71Pit 72-77Den		6'3"	246	Baylor	1	
Marangi, Gary QB	74-76Buf 77Cle	12	6'1"	202	Boston College		12
Marcol, Chester K	72-77GB	5	6'	190	Hillsdale		411
Marinaro, Ed FB-HB	72-75Min 76NYJ 77Sea	2	6'2"	212	Cornell		78
Marion, Frank LB	77NYG		6'3"	230	Florida A & M		
Markovich, Mark OG-C	74-75SD 76-77Det		6'5"	256	Penn State		
Marsalis, Jim DB	69KC-A 70-75KC 77NO		5'11"	193	Tennessee State	15	
Marshall, Al WR	74NE 75KJ		6'2"	190	Boise State		6
Marshall, Ed WR	71Cin 76NYJ 76-77NYG	2	6'5"	199	Cameron State		18
Marshall, Henry WR	76-77KC	2	6'2"	205	Missouri		42
Marhsall, Larry DB	72-73KC 74Min 74-77Phi	3	5'10"	195	Md. Eastern Shore		
Marshall, Randy DE	70-71Atl		6'5"	237	Linfield		6
Marshall, Tank DT	77NYJ		6'4"	245	Texas A & M		
Martin, Amos LB	72-76Min 77Sea		6'3"	228	Louisville	3	6
Martin, Bob LB	76-77NYJ		6'1"	220	Nebraska	3	
Martin, Dee DB	71NO 72KJ		6'1"	190	Kentucky State	3	
Martin, Don DB	73NE 75KC 76TB		5'11"	186	Yale		
Martin, George DE	75-77NYG		6'4"	245	Oregon	1	6
Martin, Harvey (Beautiful) DE	73-77Dal		6'5"	255	East Texas State	1	
Marvaso, Tommy DB	76-77NYJ		6'1"	191	Cincinnati		
Marvin, Mickey OG	77Oak		6'4"	270	Tennessee		
Marx, Greg DE	73Atl		6'4"	260	Notre Dame		

Use Name (Nicknames) – Positions	Team by Year	See Section	Hgt	Wgt	College	Int	Pts
Maslowski, Matt WR	71LA		6'3"	210	San Diego		6
Mason, Dave DB	73NE 74GB		6'	198	Nebraska		
Mass, Wayne OT	68-70Chi 71Mia 72NE 72Phi		6'4"	243	Clemson		
Massey, Jim DB	74-75NE		5'11"	198	Linfield		
Masters, Bill TE	67-69BufA 70-74Den 75-76KC	2	6'5"	236	Louisiana State		90
Matheson, Bob LB-DE	67-70Cle 71-77Mia		6'4"	238	Duke	11	
Matlock, John C-OT	67NY-A 68CinA 70-71Atl 72Buf		6'4"	250	Miami (Fla.)		
Matson, Pat OG	66-67DenA 68-69CinA 70-74Cin 75GB		6'1"	246	Oregon		
Matthews, Al DB	70-75GB 76Sea 77SF		5'11"	190	Texas A & I	13	12
Matthews, Bo FB	74-77SD	2	6'4"	230	Colorado		66
Matthews, Henry HB	72NE 73NO		6'3"	203	Michigan State		
Matuszak, John (Tooz) DE-DT	73-74Hou 75KC 76-77Oak		6'8"	277	Tampa		6
Mauck, Carl C	69Bal 70Mia 71-74SD 75-77Hou		6'3"	243	Southern Illinois		6
Maurer, Andy OT-OG	70-73Atl 74NO 74-75Min 76SF 77Den		6'3"	265	Oregon		
Mauti, Richard WR	77NO	3	6'	190	Penn State		
Maxon, Alvin HB	74-76NO 77Pit	2	5'11"	203	S.M.U.		42
Maxwell, Bruce HB-FB	70Det		6'1"	220	Arkansas		
Maxwell, Tommy DB	69-70Bal 71-73Oak 74Hou		6'2"	195	Texas A & M	5	
May, Art DE	71NE		6'3"	245	Tuskegee		
May, Ray LB	67-69Pit 70-73Bal 73-75Den		6'1"	230	Southern Calif.	13	6
Mayes, Rufus OT-OG	69Chi 70-77Cin		6'5"	259	Ohio State		
Mayo, Ron TE	73Hou 74Bal		6'3"	223	Morgan State		
Mays, Dave QB	76-77Cle	1	6'1"	204	Texas Southern		
Mazur, John	HC70Bos HC71-72NE				Notre Dame		
McAleney, Ed DE	76Atl 76TB		6'2"	235	Massachusetts		
McAlister, James HB	75-76Phi	2	6'1"	205	U.C.L.A.		18
McBath, Mike DE-OT-DT	68-69BufA 70-72Buf		6'4"	248	Penn State		
McBride, Ron HB	73GB		6'	200	Missouri		
McCaffrey, Mike LB	70Buf		6'3"	235	California		
McCaffrey, Robert C	75GB		6'2"	245	Southern Calif.		
McCall, Bob HB	73NE		6'	205	Arizona		
McCann, Jim K	71-72SF 73NYG 75KC	4	6'2"	165	Arizona State		
McCarren, Larry C	73-77GB		6'3"	247	Illinois		
McCartney, Ron LB	77Atl		6'1"	220	Tennessee		
McCauley, Don HB-FB	71-77Bal	23	6'1"	212	North Carolina		240
McClain, Cliff HB-FB	70-73NYJ	2	6'	217	S. Carolina State		12
McClain, Dewey LB	76-77Atl		6'3"	236	East Central (Okla.)	1	
McClain, Kevin LB	76-77LA		6'2"	233	Colorado State		
McClanahan, Brent FB-HB	73-77Min	23	5'10"	202	Arizona State		60
McClanahan, Randy LB	77Oak		6'5"	225	Southwestern La.		
McClard, Bill K	72SD 73-75NO	5	5'10"	202	Arkansas		109
McCollum, Bubba DT	74Hou		6'	250	Kentucky		
McConnell, Brian LB	73Hou		6'4"	207	Michigan State		
McCoy, Mike MG-DT	70-76GB 77Oak		6'5"	279	Notre Dame	1	6
McCoy, Mike (M.C.) DB	75-77GB		5'11"	183	Colorado	4	
McCrary, Greg TE	75Atl 76LJ 77Atl		6'3"	230	Clark		6
McCray, Prentice DB	74-77NE		6'1"	188	Arizona State	12	12
McCreary, Loaird TE-WR	76-77Mia		6'5"	227	Tennessee State		6
McCrumbly, John LB	75Buf		6'1"	245	Texas A & M		
McCullough, Earl WR	68-73Det 74NO 75WFL	2	5'11"	175	Southern Calif.		114
McCullum, Sam WR	74-75Min 76-77Sea	2	6'2"	203	Montana State		48
McCurry, Dave DB	74NE		6'1"	187	Iowa State		
McCutcheon, Lawrence HB	72-77LA	2	6'1"	205	Colorado State		198
McDaniel, John WR	74-77Cin	2	6'1"	194	Lincoln (Mo.)		6
McDonald, Dwight WR	75-77SD	2	6'2"	187	San Diego State		42
McDonald, Mike LB	76StL		6'2"	215	Catawba		
McFarland, Jim TE	70-74StL 75Mia		6'5"	225	Nebraska		18
McGee, Molly HB	74Atl		5'10"	184	Rhode Island		
McGee, Tony DE-DT	71-73Chi 74-77NE		6'4"	248	Bishop		
McGee, Willie WR	73SD 74-75LA 76-77SF	23	5'11"	179	Alcorn A & M		24
McGeorge, Rich TE	70-77GB	2	6'4"	233	Elon		72
McGill, Mike LB	68-70Min 71-72StL		6'2"	236	Notre Dame	3	6
McGill, Ralph DB	72-77SF	3	5'11"	182	Tulsa	7	12
McGraw, Mike LB	76StL 77Det		6'2"	225	Wyoming		
McGriff, Lee WR	76TB		5'9"	163	Florida		
McInally, Pat WR-K	76-77Cin	2 4	6'6"	205	Harvard		18
McIntyre, Sedrick HB	77Atl		5'10"	190	Auburn		6
McKay, Bob OT-OG	70-75Cle 76-77NE		6'5"	262	Texas		
McKay, John	HC76-77TB				Oregon		
McKay, John WR	76-77TB	2	5'11"	180	Southern Calif.		6
McKenzie, Reggie OG	72-77Buf		6'4"	240	Michigan		
McKinley, Bill DE-LB	71Buf 72JJ		6'1"	240	Arizona		
McKinnely, Phil OT-TE	76-77Atl		6'4"	248	U.C.L.A.		
McKinney, Bill LB	72Chi		6'1"	226	West Texas State		
McKinney, Royce DB	75Buf		6'1"	190	Kentucky State		
McKinnis, Hugh FB	73-75Cle 76Sea	2	6'	219	Arizona State		60
McKoy, Bill LB	70-72Den 74SF		6'3"	233	Purdue		
McLinton, Harold LB	69-77Was		6'2"	235	Southern U.	3	6
McMakin, John TE	72-74Pit 75Det 76Sea	2	6'3"	229	Clemson		24
McMath, Herb DT-DE	76Oak 77GB		6'4"	248	Morningside		
McMillan, Eddie DB	73-75LA 76-77Sea		6'	188	Florida State	12	
McNeil, Pat FB	76-77KC		5'9"	208	Baylor		
McNeill, Fred LB	74-77Min		6'2"	230	U.C.L.A.	2	
McNeill, Rod FB	74-76NO 76TB	23	6'2"	218	Southern Calif.		30
McNeill, Tom K	67-69NO 70Min 71-73Phi	4	6'1"	195	S.F. Austin State		
McNight, Ted HB	77KC		6'1"	203	Minnesota-Duluth		
McQuay, Leon HB	74NYG 75NE 76NO	23	5'9"	197	Tampa		6
McQuilken, Kim QB	74-77Atl	1	6'2"	202	Lehigh		
McShane, Charles LB	77Sea		6'3"	230	Calif. Lutheran		
McVea, Warren HB-WR	68CinA 69KC-A 70-71KC 72KJ 73KC	23	5'10"	182	Houston		78
McVey, John	HC76-77NYG				Miami (Ohio)		
Means, Dave DE	74-75Buf		6'4"	235	SW Missouri State		
Medlin, Dan OG	74-76Oak 77TB		6'4"	255	N. Carolina State		
Medenhall, John DT	72-77NYG		6'1"	255	Grambling	1	
Medenhall, Ken C	71-77Bal		6'3"	241	Oklahoma		
Medenhall, Terry LB	71-72Oak		6'1"	210	San Diego State		
Merlo, Jim LB	73-74NO 75JJ 76-77NO		6'1"	221	Stanford	8	18
Merrow, Jeff DE-DT-LB	75-77Atl 77Oak		6'4"	230	West Virginia		

Use Name (Nicknames) – Positions	Team by Year	See Section	Hgt	Wgt	College	Int	Pts
Metcalf, Terry HB	73-77StL	23	5'10"	185	Long Beach State		216
Meyer, Dennis DB	73Pit		5'11"	186	Arkansas State		
Meyer, Ken	HC77SF				Denison		
Meyers, Jerry DE-DT	76-77Chi		6'4"	245	Northern Illinois		
Mialik, Larry TE	72-74Atl 76SD		6'2"	226	Wisconsin		
Michel, Mike K	77Mia	4	5'10"	177	Stanford		
Middleton, Rick LB	74-75NO 76-77SD		6'2"	230	Ohio State	1	
Middleton, Terdell HB	77GB	2	6'	195	Memphis State		6
Mike-Mayer, Nick K	73-74Atl 77Phi	5	5'8"	187	Temple		286
Mike-Mayer, Steve K	75-76SF 77Det	5	6'	179	Maryland		186
Mikolajczyk, Ron OT-OG	76-77NYG		6'3"	275	Tampa		
Milan, Don QB	75GB 76BW	1	6'3"	196	Cal. Poly-SLO		
Mildren, Jack DB	72-73Bal 74NE		6'1"	200	Oklahoma	3	
Miller, Cleo HB	74-75KC 75-77Cle	23	5'11"	202	Arkansas-Pine Bluff		60
Miller, Jim OG	71-72,74Atl		6'3"	240	Iowa		
Miller, Johnny OG	77SF		6'1"	247	Livingstone		
Miller, Red	HC77Den				Western Illinois		
Miller, Robert FB-HB	75-77Min	2	5'11"	204	Kansas		12
Miller, Terry LB	71-74StL		6'2"	224	Illinois		
Miller, Willie WR	75-76Cle 77HJ		5'9"	172	Colorado State		6
Minor, Claudie OT	74-77Den		6'4"	281	San Diego State		
Mitchell, Dale LB	76-77SF		6'3"	224	Southern Calif.		
Mitchell, Jim TE	69-77Atl	2	6'2"	233	Prairie View		162
Mitchell, Jim DE-DT	70-77Det		6'3"	247	Virginia State	1	2
Mitchell, Ken LB	73-74Atl		6'1"	224	Nevada-Las Vegas		
Mitchell, Leroy DB	67-68BosA 69BQ 70Hou 71-73Den		6'2"	192	Texas Southern	19	6
Mitchell, Lydell HB	72-77Bal	2	5'11"	200	Penn State		246
Mitchell, Mack DE	75-77Cle		6'7"	245	Houston		2
Mitchell, Mark DB	77Phi		6'1"	180	Tulane		
Mitchell, Mel OG-C	76-77Mia 77Det		6'3"	260	Tennessee State		
Mitchell, Tom TE-WR	66OakA 68-73Bal 74-77SF	2	6'2"	219	Bucknell		144
Montgomery, Marv OT	71-76Den 76-77NO		6'6"	255	Southern Calif.	1	
Montgomery, Mike HB-WR	71SD 72-73Dal 74Hou	2	6'2"	208	Kansas State		60
Montgomery, Randy DB	71-73Den 74Chi	3	5'11"	183	Weber State	2	6
Montgomery, Ross FB	69-70Chi	2	6'3"	220	Texas Christian		
Montgomery, Wilbert HB	77Phi	2	5'10"	195	Abilene Christian		18
Montler, Mike C-OT-OG	69BosA 70Bos 71-72NE 73-76Buf 77Den		6'4"	257	Colorado		
Moody, Keith DB	76-77Buf	3	5'11"	171	Syracuse	3	12
Mooers, Doug DT-DE	71-72NO		6'6"	265	Whittier		
Mooney, Ed LB	68-71Det 72JJ 73Bal		6'2"	231	Texas Tech		
Moore, Art NT-OT	73-74NE 75KJ 76-77NE		6'5"	255	Tulsa		
Moore, Bob TE	71-75Oak 76-77TB	2	6'3"	222	Stanford		42
Moore, Derland DT	73-77NO		6'4"	257	Oklahoma	1	
Moore, Jerry DB	71-72Chi 73-74NO		6'3"	208	Arkansas	2	
Moore, Joe HB	71Chi 72JJ 73Chi	2	6'1"	205	Missouri		
Moore, Manfred HB	74-75SF 76TB 76Oak 77Min	3	6'	197	Southern Calif.		12
Moore, Maulty DT	72-74Mia 75Cin 76TB		6'5"	265	Bethune-Cookman		
Moore, Nat WR-HB	74-77Mia	23	5'10"	180	Florida		138
Moore, Randy DT	76Den 77JJ		6'2"	241	Arizona		
Moore, Reynaud DB	71NO		6'2"	190	U.C.L.A.		
Moore, Wayne OT	70-77Mia		6'6"	265	Lamar Tech		
Moore, Zeke DB	67-69HouA 70-77Hou	3	6'2"	195	Lincoln (Mo.)	24	24
Moorehead, Emery WR	77NYG	2	6'2"	210	Colorado		6
Mooring, John OT-C	71-73NYJ 74NO		6'6"	255	Tampa		
Moorman, Mo OG-OT	68-69KC-A 70-73KC		6'5"	252	Texas A & M		
Moresco, Tim DB	77GB		5'11"	176	Syracuse		
Morgado, Arnold HB	77KC		6'	210	Hawaii		
Morgan, Dennis HB	74Dal 75Phi	3	5'11"	198	Western Illinois		6
Morgan, Melvin DB	76-77Cin		6'	181	Miss. Valley State	1	6
Morgan, Stanley WR	77NE	2	5'10"	180	Tennessee		18
Moriarty, Tom DB	77Atl		6'	185	Bowling Green		
Morin, Milt TE	66-75Cle	2	6'4"	243	Massachusetts		96
Morris, Chris OT	72-73Cle 75NO		6'3"	250	Indiana		
Morris, Donny Joe HB	74KC		5'11"	195	North Texas State		
Morris, Jon C	64-69BosA 70Bos 71-74NE 75-77Det		6'4"	247	Holy Cross		
Morris, Mercury HB	69MiaA 70-75Mia 76SD	23	5'10"	190	West Texas State		210
Morris, Wayne FB-HB	76-77StL	2	6'	204	S.M.U.		78
Morrison, Dennis QB	74SF	1	6'3"	211	Kansas State		
Morrison, Don OT	71-77NO		6'5"	255	Texas-Arlington		
Morrison, Reece HB	68-72Cle 72-73Cin 74JJ	23	6'	206	SW Texas State		24
Morriss, Guy C	73-77Phi		6'4"	253	Texas Christian		
Morton, Craig QB	65-74Dal 74-76NYG 77Den	12	6'4"	214	California		60
Morton, Greg DE	77Buf		6'1"	230	Michigan		
Moseley, Mark K	70Phi 71-72Hou 74-77Was	5	5'11"	195	S.F. Austin State		490
Moses, Haven WR	68-69BufA 70-72Buf 72-77Den	2	6'3"	204	San Diego State		246
Mosier, John TE	71Den 72Bal 73NE		6'3"	220	Kansas		
Mosely, Wayne HB	74Buf		6'	190	Alabama A & M		
Moss, Eddie FB-HB	73-76StL 77Was		6'	215	SE Missouri State		6
Moss, Roland TE-FB	69Bal 70SD 70Buf 71NE	2	6'3"	215	Toledo		12
Muckensturm, Jerry LB	76-77Chi		6'4"	226	Arkansas State		
Mucker, Larry WR	77TB		5'11"	190	Arizona State		
Muhlmann, Horst K	69CinA 70-74Cin 75-77Phi	5	6'1"	215	none		681
Mul-Key, Herb HB	72-74Was	23	6'	190	none		12
Mullaney, Mark DE	75-77Min		6'6"	242	Colorado State		
Mullen, Tom OG-OT	74-77NYG		6'3"	248	SW Missouri State		
Mulligan, Wayne C	69-73StL 74-75NYJ 76JJ		6'2"	246	Clemson		
Mullins, Gerry OG-OT	71-77Pit		6'3"	241	Southern Calif.		18
Mumphord, Lloyd DB	69MiaA 70-74Mia 75-77Bal		5'11"	179	Texas Southern	19	18
Muncie, Chuck FB-HB	76-77NO	2	6'3"	220	California		54
Munsey, Nelson DB	72-77Bal		6'1"	188	Wyoming	7	12
Munson, Bill QB	64-67LA 68-75Det 76Sea 77SD	12	6'2"	203	Utah State		18
Murdock, Guy C	72Hou		6'2"	245	Michigan		
Murphy, Mark DB	77Was		6'4"	210	Colgate		
Musso, Johnny HB-FB	75-77Chi	2	5'11"	201	Alabama		38
Myer, Steve QB	76-77Sea	1	6'2"	188	New Mexico		
Myer, Chip WR-FL	67SF 69CinA 70-76Cin	2	6'4"	203	NW State (Okla.)		72
Myers, Tom DB	72-77NO		5'11"	181	Syracuse	16	18
Myrtle Chip LB-TE	67-69DenA 70-72Den 73JJ 74SD		6'4"	224	Maryland	4	2
Nafziger, Dave TE	77TB		6'1"	220	Cal. Poly-SLO		
Nairne, Rob LB	77Den		6'4"	220	Oregon State		
Namath, Joe QB	65-69NY-A 70-76NYJ 77LA	12	6'2"	198	Alabama		48
Naponic, Bob QB	70Hou		6'	190	Illinois		
Naumoff, Paul LB	67-77Det		6'1"	216	Tennessee	5	
Neal, Dan C-OG	73-74Bal 75-77Chi		6'4"	245	Kentucky		
Neal, Lewis WR	73-74Atl	2	6'4"	215	Prairie View		6
Neal, Richard DE-DT	69-72NO 73-77NYJ		6'3"	257	Southern U.		6
Neely, Ralph OT	65-77Dal		6'5"	261	Oklahoma		
Neils, Steve LB	74-77StL		6'2"	216	Minnesota		
Nelson, Bill DT	71-75LA		6'7"	270	Oregon State		
Nelson, Bob LB	75-77Buf		6'4"	232	Nebraska		
Nelson, Dennis OT	70-74Bal 76-77Phi		6'5"	260	Illinois State		
Nelson, Lee DB	76-77StL		5'10"	184	Florida State	4	
Nelson, Ralph HB	75Was 76Sea	2	6'2"	195	none		12
Nelson, Shane LB	77Buf		6'1"	222	Baylor		
Nelson, Steve LB	74-77NE		6'2"	230	N. Dakota State	4	
Nelson, Terry TE	74-77LA	2	6'2"	230	Arkansas-Pine Bluff		18
Nettles, Doug DB	74-75Bal 76SJ 77Bal		6'	178	Vanderbilt	2	2
Neville, Tom OT	65-69BosA 70Bos 71-74NE 75BL 76-77NE		6'4"	250	Mississippi State		
Newhouse, Robert FB-HB	72-77Dal	2	5'10"	203	Houston		90
Newland, Bob WR	71-74NO 75JJ	2	6'2"	190	Oregon		48
Newman, Ed OG	73-77Mia		6'2"	245	Duke		
Newsome, Billy DE	70-72Bal 73-74NO 75-76NYJ 77Chi		6'4"	251	Grambling	3	6
Newton, Bob OG	71-75Chi 76-77Sea		6'4"	256	Nebraska		
Newton, Tom FB	77NYJ		6'	205	California		
Nichols, Robbie LB	70-71Bal		6'3"	220	Tulsa		
Nicholson, Jim OT	74-77KC		6'6"	264	Michigan State		
Niehaus, Steve DT-DE	76-77Sea		6'4"	270	Notre Dame		
Nighswander, Nick C	74Buf		6'	232	Morehead State		
Niland, John OG	66-74Dal 75Phi 76KJ		6'4"	247	Iowa		6
Nix, Kent QB	67-69Pit 70-71Chi 72Hou	12	6'1"	195	Texas Christian		12
Nobis, Tommy LB	66-76Atl		6'2"	237	Texas	12	12
Nock, George HB	69NY-A 70-71NYJ 72Was	2	5'10"	200	Morgan State		66
Nordquist, Mark OG-C	68-74Phi 75-76Chi 76SF		6'4"	245	U. of Pacific		
Nott, Mike QB	76KC		6'3"	203	Santa Clara		
Nottingham, Don (The Human Bowling Ball) FB	71-73Bal 73-77Mia	2	5'10"	210	Kent State		210
Novak, Gary DT	71SD		6'5"	247	Michigan State		
Novak, Jack TE	75Cin 76-77TB	2	6'4"	241	Wisconsin		6
Novak, Ken DT	76-77Bal		6'7"	270	Purdue		
Nugent, Dan OG	76-77Was		6'3"	250	Auburn		
Nunamaker, Julian DE-DT	69BufA 70Buf 71JJ		6'3"	251	Tennessee-Martin		
Nunley, Frank LB	67-76SF		6'2"	230	Michigan	14	
Nuzum, Rick C	77LA		6'4"	238	Kentucky		
Nye, Blaine OG	68-76Dal		6'4"	252	Stanford		
Nystrom, Lee OT	74GB		6'5"	260	Macalester		
Nyvall, Vic HB	70NO		5'10"	185	NW State-La.		
Oates, Brad OT	76-77StL		6'6"	272	Brigham Young		
O'Bradovich, Jim TE	75NYG 76-77SF	2	6'2"	226	Southern Calif.		6
O'Brien, Jim WR	70-72Bal 73Det	2 5	6'	195	Cincinnati		301
O'Dell, Stu LB	74Was 75SJ 76-77Was		6'1"	220	Indiana		
Odom, Steve WR	74-77GB	23	5'8"	172	Utah		78
Odoms, Riley TE	72-77Den	2	6'2"	230	Houston		156
O'Donoghue, Neil K	77Buf		6'6"	204	Auburn		10
Ogle, Rick LB	71StL 72Det		6'3"	230	Colorado		
Okoniewski, Steve DT-DE	72-73Buf 74-75GB 76-77StL 77Cle		6'3"	257	Montana		
Olander, Cliff QB	77SD		6'5"	196	New Mexico State		
Oldham, Ray DB	73-77Bal		6'	195	Middle Tennessee	7	
Olds, Bill FB	73-75Bal 76Sea 76Phi	2	6'1"	224	Nebraska		60
Olerich, Dave LB-TE	67-68SF 69-70StL 71Hou 72-73SF		6'1"	221	San Francisco		
Oliver, Frank DB	75Buf 76TB		6'	194	Kentucky State		
Oliver, Greg HB	73-74Phi		6'	192	Trinity (Texas)		
Olsen, Orrin C	76KC		6'1"	245	Brigham Young		
Olsen, Phil C-DT	71-74LA 75-76Den		6'5"	263	Utah State		
O'Malley, Jim LB	73-75Den		6'1"	230	Notre Dame	1	
O'Neal, Steve WR-K	69NY-A 70-72NYJ 73NO	4	6'3"	185	Texas A & M		
O'Neil, Ed LB	74-77Det		6'3"	237	Penn State	1	18
Onkontz, Dennis LB	70NYJ		6'1"	220	Penn State		
Opperman, Jim LB	75Phi		6'3"	220	Colorado State		
Orduna, Joe HB-FB	72-73NYG 74Bal	2	6'	195	Nebraska		24
Oriard, Mike C-OG	70-73KC		6'4"	223	Notre Dame		
Ortega, Ralph LB	75-77Atl		6'2"	220	Florida	4	6
Orvis, Herb DT-DE	72-77Det		6'5"	245	Colorado		
Osborn, Dave HB-FB	65-75Min 76GB	2	6'	207	North Dakota		216
Osborne, Jim DT	72-77Chi		6'3"	251	Southern U.		
Osborne, Richard TE	76Phi 76NYJ 77Phi		6'3"	230	Texas A & M		6
Osley, Willie DB	74KC		6'	195	Illinois		
Otis, Jim FB	70NO 71-72KC 73-77StL	2	6'	223	Ohio State		84
Outlaw, John DB	68JJ 69BosA 70Bos 71-72NE 73,75-77Phi		5'10"	180	Jackson State	14	12
Overmeyer, Bill LB	72Phi		6'3"	220	Ashland		
Owen, Tom QB	74-75SF 76-77NE	1	6'1"	196	Wichita State		6
Owens, Artie WR	76-77SD	3	5'10"	172	West Virginia		6
Owens, Brig DB	66-77Was		5'11"	190	Cincinnati	36	32
Owens, Burgess DB	73-77NYJ		6'2"	199	Miami (Fla.)	10	18
Owens, Joe DE	70SD 71-75NO 76Hou		6'2"	244	Alcorn A & M	1	4
Owens, Marv WR	73StL 74NYJ		5'11"	205	San Diego State		
Owens, Morris WR	75-76Mia 76-77TB	2	6'	190	Arizona State		54
Owens, Steve FB	70-74Det 75KJ	2	6'2"	217	Oklahoma		132
Owens, Terry OT	66-69SD-A 70-75SD		6'6"	263	Jacksonville St.		
Owens, Tinker WR	76NO 77JJ	2	5'11"	170	Oklahoma		6
Packer, Walter DB	77Sea		5'10"	174	Mississippi State		
Pagac, Fred TE	74Chi 75WFL 76TB		6'	220	Ohio State		
Page, Alan DT	67-77Min		6'5"	248	Notre Dame	1	16
Palewicz, Al LB	73-75KC 77NYJ		6'1"	215	Miami (Fla.)		
Palmer, Dick LB	70Mia 71JJ 72Buf 72-73NO 74Atl		6'2"	229	Kentucky		
Palmer, Gary OT-DT	75KC		6'4"	255	Kansas		
Palmer, Scott DT	71NYJ 72StL		6'3"	243	Texas		

Use Name (Nicknames) — Positions	Team by Year	See Section	Hgt	Wgt	College	Int	Pts
Pane, Chris DB	76-77Den		5'11"	183	New Mexico		
Papale, Vince WR	76-77Phi		6'2"	195	St. Joseph's (Pa.)		
Parish, Don LB	70-71StL 71LA 72Den		6'1"	220	Stanford	1	6
Parker, Artimus DB	74-76Phi 77NYJ		6'3"	208	Southern Calif.	5	
Parker, Joel WR	74-75NO 76JJ 77NO	2	6'5"	213	Florida		36
Parker, Kenny DB	70NYG		6'1"	190	Fordham		
Parker, Willie C-OG	73-77Buf		6'3"	245	North Texas State		
Parks, Billy WR	71SD 72Dal 73-75Hou	2	6'1"	187	Long Beach State		42
Parris, Gary TE	73-74SD 75-77Cle	2	6'2"	226	Florida State		30
Parrish, Lemar DB	70-77Cin	3	5'11"	184	Lincoln (Mo.)	25	78
Parrish, Scott OT	76Den		6'6"	270	Utah State		
Parsley, Cliff K	77Hou	4	6'1"	211	Oklahoma State		
Parson, Ray OT	71Det		6'4"	250	Minnesota		
Parsons, Bob TE	72-77Chi	2 4	6'4"	235	Penn State		24
Partee, Dennis K	68-69SD-A 70-75SD	45	6'2"	218	S.M.U.		
Pastorini, Don (Dante) QB	71-77Hou	12 4	6'3"	210	Santa Clara		48
Pastrana, Al QB	69DenA 70Den	1	6'1"	190	Maryland		6
Pate, Lloyd HB	70Buf	2	6'1"	205	Cincinnati		6
Patrick, Frank QB	70-72GB		6'7"	225	Nebraska		
Patrick, Mike K	75-77NE	4	6'	207	Mississippi State		
Patrick, Wayne FB	68-69BufA 70-72Buf 73KJ	2	6'2"	241	Louisville		36
Patton, Bob C	76Buf		6'1"	245	Delaware		
Patton, Jerry DT	71Min 72-73Buf 74Pit 75NE		6'3"	261	Nebraska	1	
Patulski, Walt DE-DT	72-75Buf 76KJ 77StL		6'6"	260	Notre Dame		
Paul, Harold OT	74Oak		6'5"	245	Oklahoma		
Paul, Whitney DE	76-77KC		6'3"	220	Colorado	1	
Payne, Ken, WR	74-77GB 77Phi	2	6'1"	185	Langston		30
Payton, Eddie (Sweet P) HB	77Cle 77Det	3	5'8"	175	Jackson State		12
Payton, Walter (Sweetness) HB	75-77Chi	2	5'11"	203	Jackson State		216
Pear, Dave MG-DT	75Bal 76-77TB		6'2"	247	Washington		
Pearson, Barry WR	72-73Pit 74-76KC	2	5'11"	185	Northwestern		42
Pearson, Drew WR	73-77Dal	2	6'	181	Tulsa		132
Pearson, Preston HB-DB	67-69Bal 70-74Pit 75-77Dal	23	6'1"	198	Illinois		174
Peay, Francis OT	66-67NYG 68-72GB 73-74KC		6'5"	250	Missouri		
Peiffer, Dan C	75-77Chi		6'3"	254	SE Missouri State		
Pena, Bubba OG	72Cle 73KJ		6'2"	250	Massachusetts		
Penchion, Bobby OG-C	72-73Buf 74-75SF 76Sea		6'5"	256	Alcorn A & M		
Pennywell, Robert LB	77Atl		6'1"	222	Grambling	2	6
Penrose, Craig QB	76-77Den	1	6'3"	214	San Diego State		
Peoples, Woody OG	68-75SF 76KJ 77SF		6'2"	250	Grambling		
Peppler, Pat	HC76Atl						
Percival, Mac K	67-73Chi 74Dal	5	6'4"	219	Texas Tech		466
Pergine, John LB	69-72LA 73-75Was		6'1"	225	Notre Dame		6
Perkins, Johnny WR	77NYG	2	6'2"	205	Abilene Christian		
Perko, Tom LB	76GB		6'3"	233	Pittsburgh		
Perretta, Ralph OG-C	75-77SD		6'2"	251	Purdue		
Perrin, Lonnie FB	76-77Den	2	6'1"	223	Illinois		36
Perry, Rod DB	75-77LA		5'9"	170	Colorado	9	
Perry, Scott DB	76-77Cin		6'	184	Williams		
Person, Ara TE	72StL		6'2"	220	Morgan State		
Pesuit, Wally OG-OT-DE	76Atl 76-77Mia		6'4"	255	Kentucky		
Peters, Tony DB	75-77Cle		6'1"	192	Oklahoma	3	
Peterson, Bill	HC72-73Hou				Ohio Northern		
Peterson, Bill LB-TE	68-69CinA 70-72Cin 75KC		6'3"	228	San Jose State	5	
Peterson, Cal LB	74-75Dal 76TB		6'3"	218	U.C.L.A.	2	
Peterson, Jim LB	74-75LA 76TB		6'5"	235	San Diego State		6
Peterson, Ted C-OT-OG	77Pit		6'5"	244	Eastern Illinois		
Pettigrew, Gary DT-DE	66-73Phi 74NYG		6'4"	252	Stanford		
Pharr, Tommy DB	70Buf		5'10"	187	Mississippi State		
Phillips, Bum	HC75-77Hou				S.F. Austin State		
Phillips, Charlie DB	75-77Oak		6'2"	215	Southern Calif.	9	
Phillips, Jess FB-HB-DB	68-69CinA 70-72Cin 73-74NO 75Oak 76-77NE	23	6'1"	208	Michigan State	3	90
Phillips, Mel DB	66-77SF		6'	190	N. Carolina A & T	12	6
Phillips, Ray LB	77Cin		6'3"	221	Nebraska		
Phillips, Rod FB-TE	75-77LA	2	6'	220	Jackson State		12
Philyaw, Charles (King Kong) DE	76-77Oak		6'9"	270	Texas Southern		
Phipps, Mike QB	70-76Cle 77Chi	12	6'2"	207	Purdue		66
Picard, Bob WR	73-76Phi 76Det		6'1"	196	Eastern Wash. State		
Piccone, Lou WR	74-76NYJ 77Buf	23	5'9"	180	West Liberty State		18
Pickard, Bob WR	74Det		6'	190	Xavier		6
Pierce, Danny HB-FB	70Was		6'3"	215	Memphis State		
Pierson, Reggie DB	76Det 76-77TB		5'11"	185	Arizona Western, Oklahoma State		
Pietrzak, Jim DT	74-75NYG 76KJ 77NYG		6'5"	260	Eastern Michigan		
Pifferini, Bob LB	72-75Chi 77LA		6'2"	226	U.C.L.A.		
Pillers, Lawrence DE	76-77NYJ		6'3"	254	Alcorn A & M		
Pinder, Cyril HB-LB	68-70Phi 71-72Chi 73Dal 74WFL	2	6'2"	218	Illinois		42
Pinkney, Reggie DB	77Det		5'11"	190	East Carolina St.	2	6
Pinney, Ray C-OT	76-77Pit		6'4"	240	Washington		
Piper, Scott WR	76Atl		6'1"	179	Arizona		
Pisarcik, Joe QB	77NYG	12	6'4"	220	New Mexico State		12
Pisarkiewicz, Steve QB	77StL		6'2"	205	Missouri		
Pittman, Charlie HB	70StL 71Bal		6'1"	200	Penn State		
Pitts, Frank WR-OE-FL	65-69KC-A 70KC 71-73Cle 74Oak 75Atl	2	6'2"	198	Southern U.		174
Pitts, John DB	67-69BufA 70-72Buf 73-74Den 75Cle		6'4"	218	Arizona State	10	
Plank, Doug DB	75-77Chi		6'	199	Ohio State	10	
Plummer, Tony DB	70StL 71-73Atl 74LA		5'11"	189	U. of Pacific	1	6
Plunkett, Jim QB	71-75NE 76-77SF	12	6'3"	216	Stanford		60
Podolak, Ed HB	69KC-A 70-77KC	23	6'1"	204	Iowa		240
Pollard, Bob DT-DE	71-77NO		6'3"	246	Weber State		6
Poltl, Randy DB	74Min 75-77Den		6'3"	190	Stanford	1	6
Poole, Larry HB	75-77Cle	2	6'	195	Kent State		30
Poole, Steve LB	76NYJ		6'1"	232	Tennessee		6
Pope, Ken DB	74NE		5'11"	200	Oklahoma		
Porter, Jack C	71SD		6'4"	255	Oklahoma		
Porter, Lewis WR	70KC		5'11"	178	Southern U.		
Porter, Ron LB	67-69Bal 69-72Phi 73Min 74WFL		6'3"	232	Idaho	3	
Potts, Charles DB	72Det		6'3"	210	Purdue		
Pough, Ernest WR	76-77Pit	3	6'1"	174	Texas Southern		6

Use Name (Nicknames) — Positions	Team by Year	See Section	Hgt	Wgt	College	Int	Pts
Powell, Darnell HB	76Buf		6'	197	Tenn.-Chattanooga		
Powell, Jesse LB	69MiaA 70-73Mia		6'1"	214	West Texas State		
Powell, Marvin OT	77NYJ		6'5"	264	Southern Calif.		
Powers, Clyde DB	74-77NYG		6'1"	195	Oklahoma	5	
Pratt, Robert OG	74-77Bal		6'4"	250	North Carolina		6
Preece, Steve DB	69NO 70-72Phi 72Den 73-76LA 77Sea		6'1"	195	Oregon State	14	18
Preston, Ray LB	76-77SD		6'	219	Syracuse		
Price, Elex DT	73-77NO		6'3"	260	Alcorn A & M	1	6
Price, Ernie DE	73-77Det		6'4"	249	Texas A & I		2
Pringle, Alan K	75Det		6'	195	Rice		
Pritchard, Ron LB	69HouA 70-72Hou 72-77Cin		6'1"	231	Arizona State	3	2
Pritchett, Billy FB	75Cle 76-77Atl	2	6'3"	231	West Texas State		6
Profit, Joe HB	71-73Atl 73NO	2	6'	210	Northeast La.		18
Prothro, Tommy	HC71-72LA HC74-77SD				Duke		
Protz, Jack LB	70SD		6'1"	218	Syracuse		
Prout, Bob DB	74Oak 75NYJ		6'1"	187	Knox	1	
Provost, Ted DB	70Min 71StL		6'2"	195	Ohio State		
Pruett, Perry DB	71NE		6'1"	190	North Texas State		
Pruitt, Greg HB	73-77Cle	23	5'10"	189	Oklahoma		168
Pruitt, Mike FB	76-77Cle	2	6'	214	Purdue		6
Puetz, Gary OG-OT	73-77NYJ		6'3"	261	Valparaiso		
Pugh, Jethro DT-DE	65-77Dal		6'6"	256	Elizabeth City State	1	4
Pureifory, Dave DE-DT	72-77GB		6'1"	257	Eastern Michigan		4
Queen, Jeff FB-TE	69SD-A 70-71SD 72-73Oak 74Hou	2	6'1"	221	Morgan State		60
Raba, Bob TE	77NYJ		6'1"	222	Maryland		
Rae, Mike QB	76-77Oak	1	6'	190	Southern Calif.		12
Rafferty, Tom OG-C	76-77Dal		6'3"	250	Penn State		
Ragsdale, George WR-HB	77TB		5'11"	185	N. Carolina A & T		
Raible, Steve WR	76-77Sea		6'2"	195	Georgia Tech		12
Raines, Mike DT-DE	74SF		6'5"	255	Alabama		
Ralston, John	HC72-76Den				California		
Ramsey, Chuck K	77NYJ	4	6'2"	195	Wake Forest		
Ramsey, Steve QB	70NO 71-76Den	12	6'2"	210	North Texas State		12
Randolph, Al DB	66-70SF 71GB 72Det 73Cin 74Buf		6'2"	199	Iowa	11	8
Randolph, Terry DB	77GB		6'	184	American Inter.		
Rashad, Ahmad WR	72-73StL 74Buf 75KJ 76-77Min 72 played as Bobby Moore	2	6'2"	204	Oregon		102
Rasley, Rocky OG	69-70,72-73Det 74NO 75KC		6'3"	252	Oregon State		
Rasmussen, Randy OG	67-69NY-A 70-77NYJ		6'2"	257	Kearney State		6
Rather, Bo WR	73Mia 74-77Chi	2	6'1"	184	Michigan		42
Ratliff, Don DE	75Phi		6'5"	250	Maryland		
Ray, David WR-K	69-74LA	5	6'	195	Alabama		497
Ray, Eddie FB-TE	70Bos 71SD 72-74Atl 76Buf	2	6'1"	237	Louisiana State		66
Rayhle, Fred TE	77Sea		6'5"	216	Tenn.-Chattanooga		
Reamon, Tommy HB	76KC	2	5'10"	192	Missouri		30
Reardon, Kerry DB	71-76KC		5'11"	180	Iowa	14	
Reaves, John QB	72-74Phi 75-77Cin	12	6'3"	209	Florida		18
Reaves, Ken DB	66-73Atl 74NO 74-77StL		6'3"	207	Norfolk State	37	6
Reavis, Dave OT-OG	74-75Pit 76-77TB		6'5"	251	Arkansas		
Redmond, Rudy LB	69-71Atl 72Det 73JJ		6'	190	U. of Pacific	8	6
Reece, Beasley DB	76Dal 77NYG		6'1"	186	North Texas State		
Reece, Danny DB	76-77TB	3	5'11"	189	Southern Calif.		6
Reece, Geoff C	76LA 77Sea		6'4"	247	Washington State		
Reed, Alvin TE	67-69HouA 70-72Hou 73-75Was	2	6'5"	232	Prairie View		84
Reed, Frank DB	76-77Atl		5'11"	193	Washington	3	
Reed, Henry LB-DE	71-74NYG		6'3"	230	Weber State	3	
Reed, James LB	77Phi		6'2"	230	California		
Reed, Joe QB	72-74SF 75-77Det	12	6'1"	195	Mississippi State		12
Reed, Oscar HB-FB	68-74Min 75Atl	2	5'11"	222	Colorado State		66
Reed, Tony HB	77KC	2	5'11"	197	Colorado		12
Reese, Don DE-DT	74-76Mia 77 — Ineligible to play pro-Football		6'6"	255	Jackson State		2
Reese, Steve LB	74-75NYJ 76TB		6'2"	229	Louisville		
Reeves, Marion DB	74Phi		6'1"	195	Clemson		
Reid, Andy HB	76Buf		6'	195	Georgia		
Reid, Bill C	75SF 76KJ		6'1"	242	Stanford		
Reid, Mike DT	70-74Cin		6'3"	255	Penn State		
Reihner, George OG	77Hou		6'4"	263	Penn State		
Reilly, Kevin LB	73-74Phi 75NE		6'2"	220	Villanova	1	
Reinfeldt, Mike DB	76Oak 76-77Hou		6'2"	182	Wisc.-Milwaukee	6	
Renfro, Mel DB	64-77Dal	3	6'	191	Oregon	52	36
Reppond, Mike WR	73Chi		6'	180	Arkansas		
Ressler, Glenn OG-C-OT-DT	65-74Bal		6'3"	247	Penn State		
Reynolds, Jack (Hacksaw) LB	70-77LA		6'1"	232	Tennessee	3	
Reynolds, Tom WR	72NE 73Chi 74JJ	2	6'3"	200	San Diego State		12
Rhodes, Bruce DB	76SF 77JJ		6'	187	San Fran. State	3	
Rhodes, Danny LB	74Bal		6'2"	220	Arkansas		
Rhodes, Ray WR-DB	74-77NYG	2	5'11"	185	Tulsa	2	42
Rhone, Ernest LB	75Mia 76KJ 77Mia		6'2"	212	Henderson St. (Ark.)	2	
Ricardo, Benny K	76Buf 76Det 77SJ	5	5'9"	175	San Diego State		54
Rice, Andy DT	66-67KC-A 67HouA 68-69CinA 70-71SD 72-73Chi 74NYG		6'3"	268	Texas Southern		
Rice, Floyd LB-TE	71-73Hou 73-75SD 76-77Oak		6'3"	223	Alcorn A & M	7	6
Rice, Harold DE	71Oak		6'2"	230	Tennessee State		
Rich, Randy DB	77Det 77Den		5'10"	175	New Mexico		
Richards, Golden WR	73-77Dal	23	6'	182	Hawaii		102
Richardson, Gloster WR-FL	67-69KC-A 70KC 71Dal 72-74Cle	2	6'	200	Jackson State		108
Richardson, John DT	67-69MiaA 70-71Mia 72-73StL		6'2"	254	U.C.L.A.		
Richardson, Mike HB	69HouA 70-71Hou	2	5'11"	193	S.M.U.		20
Richardson, Pete DB	69BufA 70-71Buf		6'1"	197	Dayton	8	
Riggins, John FB	71-75NYJ 76-77Was	2	6'2"	231	Kansas State		222
Riley, Ken DB	69CinA 70-77Cin		6'	182	Florida A & M	40	12
Riley, Larry DB	77Den		5'10"	189	Salem College		
Riley, Preston WR	70-72SF 73NO	2	6'	180	Memphis State		6
Riley, Steve OT	74-77Min		6'6"	258	Southern Calif.		
Rivera, Steve WR	76-77SF 77Chi		5'11"	184	California		
Rivers, Jamie LB	68-73StL 74-75NYJ		6'2"	238	Bowling Green	4	
Rives, Don LB	73-77Chi		6'2"	223	Texas Tech		
Rizzo, Jack HB	73NYG		5'10"	195	Lehigh		
Rizzo, Joe LB	74-77Den		6'1"	221	Kings Point	4	

Use Name (Nicknames) – Positions	Team by Year	See Section	Hgt	Wgt	College	Int	Pts
Roach, Travis OG	74NYJ		6'2"	260	Texas		
Roan, Oscar TE	75-77Cle	2	6'6"	214	S.M.U.		54
Roberson, Vern DB	77Mia		6'1"	195	Grambling	1	
Roberts, Gary OG	70Atl		6'2"	242	Purdue		
Roberts, Guy LB	72-75Hou 76Atl 77Mia		6'1"	218	Maryland	5	
Roberts, Hal K	72StL	4	6'1"	180	Houston		
Roberts, J.D.	HC72-74NO				Oklahoma		
Roberts, Willie DB	73Chi		6'1"	190	Houston		
Robertson, Isiah LB	71-77LA		6'3"	225	Southern U.	18	12
Robinson, Craig OT	72-73NO		6'4"	250	Houston		
Robinson, Glenn DE-LB	75Bal 76-77TB		6'6"	242	Oklahoma State		
Robinson, Jim WR	76-77NYG	23	5'9"	170	Georgia Tech		24
Robinson, Larry HB-FB	73Dal		6'4"	210	Tennessee		
Robinson, Matt QB	77NYJ	1	6'2"	196	Georgia		
Robinson, Paul HB	68-69CinA 70-72Cin	23	6'	199	Arizona		156
	72-73Hou 74WFL						
Robinson, Virgil HB	71-72NO	2	5'11"	195	Grambling		12
Robiskie, Terry FB	77Oak		6'1"	210	Louisiana State		6
Roche, Alden DE	70Den 71-76GB 77Sea		6'4"	255	Southern U.		
Roder, Mirro K	73-74Chi 76TB	5	6'1"	221	none		79
Rodgers, Johnny WR	77SD	2	5'10"	180	Nebraska		
Rodgers, Otis LB	77KC		6'3"	230	Iowa State		
Rodgers, Willie HB-FB	72Hou 73KJ 74-75Hou 76JJ	2	6'	210	Kentucky		50
Rogers, Mel LB	71SD 72SJ 73-74SD 75WFL 76LA 77Chi		6'2"	231	Florida A & M	1	
Rogers, Stan OT	75Den		6'4"	255	Maryland		
Rogers, Steve HB	75NO 76NYJ		6'2"	203	Louisiana State		
Roller, Dave DT	71NYG 74WFL 75-77GB		6'2"	265	Kentucky		
Roman, John OG-OT	76-77NYJ		6'4"	250	Idaho State		
Roman, Nick DE	70-71Cin 72-73Cle		6'3"	235	Ohio State	1	6
Romaniszyn, Jim LB	73-74Cle 76NE 77JJ		6'2"	219	Edinboro State		
Romes, Charles DB	77Buf		6'1"	191	N. Carolina State	1	
Rosecrans, James LB	76NYJ		6'1"	230	Penn State		
Ross, Louis DE	71-72Buf 74WFL 75KC 76JJ		6'6"	248	S. Carolina State		
Ross, Oliver HB-FB	73-75Den 76Sea	23	6'	210	Alabama A & M		
Rossovich, Tim LB	68-71Phi 72-73SD 74-75WFL 76Hou		6'4"	245	Southern Calif.	3	
Rothwell, Fred C	74Det		6'3"	240	Kansas State		
Roussel, Tom LB	68-70Was 71-72NO 73Phi		6'3"	235	Southern Miss.	2	
Rowden, Larry DB	71-72Chi		6'2"	220	Houston		
Rowe, Bob DT-DE	67-75StL 76XJ		6'4"	258	Western Michigan	2	6
Rowe, Dave DT-MG	67-70NO 71-73NE 74-75SD 75-77Oak		6'6"	273	Penn State		
Rowser, John DB	67-69GB 70-73Pit 74-76Den		6'1"	185	Michigan	26	24
Rozumek, Dave LB	76-77KC		6'2"	214	New Hampshire		
Rucker, Reggie WR	70-71Dal 71NYG 71-74NE 75-77Cle	2	6'2"	190	Boston U.		150
Rudnay, Jack C	70-77KC		6'3"	240	Northwestern		
Rudnick, Tim DB	74Bal		5'10"	185	Notre Dame		
Rudolph, Council DE	72Hou 73-75StL 76-77TB		6'3"	253	Kentucky State	1	
Rush, Bob C	77SD		6'5"	258	Memphis State		
Russ, Carl LB	75Atl 76-77NYJ		6'2"	227	Michigan		
Russell, Andy LB	64Pit 65MS 66-77Pit		6'3"	221	Missouri	18	13
Ruud, Tom LB	75-77Buf		6'2"	223	Nebraska		
Ryckman, Billy WR	77Atl		5'11"	172	Louisiana Tech		6
Ryczek, Dan C	73-75Was 76-77TB		6'3"	248	Virginia		
Ryczek, Paul C	74-77Atl		6'2"	232	Virginia		
Rydalch, Ron DT	75-77Chi		6'4"	260	Utah		
Salaam, Abdul DT-DE	76-77NYJ		6'3"	255	Kent State		
76 played as Larry Faulk							
Saldi, Jay TE	76-77Dal	2	6'3"	221	South Carolina		18
Salter, Bryant DB	71-73SD 74-75Was 76Mia 76Sea 76Bal		6'4"	196	Pittsburgh	17	
Sampson, Greg OT-DT-DE	72-77Hou		6'6"	265	Stanford		
Samuels, Andre TE	77KC		6'4"	229	Bethune-Cookman		
Sanders, Charlie TE	68-77Det	2	6'4"	227	Minnesota		186
Sanders, Deac DB	74-76NE 77Phi		6'1"	178	South Dakota	12	6
Sanders, Ken DE	72-77Det		6'5"	243	Howard Payne		
Sanderson, Reggie HB	73Chi		5'10"	206	Stanford		
Sandifer, Bill DT-DE	74-76SF 77Sea		6'6"	270	U.C.L.A.		
Sattlewhite, Howard WR	76NYG 77Was 77Bal		5'11"	185	Sam Houston State		
Saul, Rich (General Hospital) C-OG-OT-LB	70-77LA		6'3"	239	Michigan State		
Saul, Ron OG	70-75Hou 76-77Was		6'2"	254	Michigan State		
Saunders, John DB	72Buf 74-75SF		6'3"	198	Toledo		
Sawyer, John TE	75-76Hou 77Sea	2	6'2"	230	Southern Miss.		12
Sawyer, Ken DB	74Cin		6'	192	Syracuse		
Scales, Dwight WR	76-77LA		6'2"	170	Grambling		12
Scales, Hurles DB	74Chi 74StL 75GB		6'1"	200	North Texas State		
Scarber, Sam FB	75-76SD	2	6'2"	232	New Mexico		24
Schaukowitz, Carl OG	75Den 76JJ		6'2"	237	Penn State		
Schaum, Greg DE	76Dal 77KJ		6'3"	246	Michigan State		
Schindler, Steve OG	77Den		6'3"	252	Boston College		
Schmidt, Terry DB	74-76NO 76-77Chi		6'	177	Ball State	5	6
Schmiesing, Joe DT-DE	68-71StL 72Det 73Bal 74NYJ		6'4"	253	New Mexico State		
Schmit, Bob LB	75-76NYG		6'1"	220	Nebraska		
Schnarr, Steve FB	75Buf		6'2"	218	Otterbein		
Schnellenberger, Howard	HC73-74Bal				Kentucky		
Schnitker, Mike OG	69DenA 70-74Den		6'3"	243	Colorado		
Schoen, Tom DB	70Cle		5'11"	185	Notre Dame		
Schreiber, Larry FB-HB	71-75SF 76Chi 77JJ	2	6'	206	Tennessee Tech		85
Schroy, Ken DB	77NYJ		6'2"	191	Maryland		
Schubert, Steve WR	74NE 75-77Chi	23	5'10"	186	Massachusetts		12
Schultz, John WR	76-77Den		5'10"	183	Maryland		
Schumacher, Kurt OT-OG	75-77NO		6'3"	251	Ohio State		
Scolnik, Glenn WR	73Pit		6'3"	190	Indiana		
Scott, Bo FB	69-74Cle	23	6'3"	213	Ohio State		144
Scott, Bobby QB	73-77NO	12	6'1"	199	Tennessee		6
Scott, Clarence DB	71-77Cle		6'	179	Kansas State	22	18
Scott, Clarence DB	69BosA 70Bos 71-72NE		6'2"	204	Morgan State	1	
Scott, Dave OG-OT	76-77Atl		6'4"	285	Kansas		
Scott, Freddie WR	74-77Bal	2	6'2"	173	Amherst		12
Scott, Herbert OG	75-77Dal		6'2"	250	Virginia Union		
Scott, Jake DB	70-75Mia 76-77Was	3	6'	188	Georgia	42	6
Scott, James WR	76-77Chi	2	6'1"	188	Hemerson Jr. Coll.		54
Scribner, Rick OG	77GB		6'4"	257	Idaho State		

Use Name (Nicknames) – Positions	Team by Year	See Section	Hgt	Wgt	College	Int	Pts
Scribner, Rob HB	73-76LA 77LJ	23	6'	200	U.C.L.A.		24
Seal, Paul TE	74-76NO 77SF	2	6'4"	223	Michigan		36
Seifert, Mike DE	74Cle		6'3"	245	Wisconsin		
Seiler, Paul OT-C	67NY-A 68MS 69NY-A		6'4"	258	Notre Dame		
	70JJ 71-73Oak 74-75WFL						
Seiple, Larry TE-HB	67-69MiaA 70-77Mia	2 4	6'	213	Kentucky		42
Seivers, Larry WR	77Phi		6'4"	204	Tennessee		
Selfridge, Andy LB	72Buf 74-75NYG 76Mia 77NYG		6'4"	220	Virginia	1	
Sellers, Ron WR	69BosA 70Bos 71NE 72Dal 73Mia	2	6'4"	196	Florida State		108
Selmon, Dewey LB-DT	76-77TB		6'1"	252	Oklahoma	2	
Selmon, Leroy DE	76-77TB		6'3"	262	Oklahoma		
Sensibaugh, Mike DB	71-75KC 76-77StL		5'11"	191	Ohio State	27	12
Septien, Raphael K	77LA	5	5'9"	171	Southwestern La.		86
Severson, Jeff DB	72Was 73-74Hou 75Den 76-77StL	3	6'1"	183	Long Beach State	6	
Sevy, Jeff OT-DT-OG-DE	75-77Chi		6'5"	257	California		
Sexton, Brent DB	77Pit		6'1"	190	Elon		
Seymour, Jim WR	70-72Chi	2	6'4"	210	Notre Dame		30
Seymour, Paul TE	73-77Buf	2	6'5"	250	Michigan		18
Shanklin, Ron WR	70-74Pit 75-76Chi	2	6'1"	183	North Texas State		144
Sharp, Rich OT	70-74Pit 72Den		6'3"	264	Washington		
Shaw, Bob WR	70NO		6'	194	Winston-Salem St.		
Shaw, Dennis QB	70-73Buf 74-75StL 76NYG	12	6'2"	212	San Diego State		
Shaw, Pete DB	77SD		5'10"	184	Northwestern		
Shears, Larry DB	71-72Atl		5'10"	185	Lincoln (Mo.)		
Shelby, Willie HB	76-77Cin	3	5'11"	194	Alabama		12
Shell, Art OT	68-69OakA 70-77Oak		6'5"	262	Md. Eastern Shore		
Shell, Donnie DB	74-77Pit		5'11"	191	S. Carolina State	6	
Sheppard, Henry OG-OT	76-77Cle		6'6"	246	S.M.U.		
Sherk, Jerry DT	70-77Cle		6'4"	253	Oklahoma State	3	2
Sherman, Rod WR-FL	67OakA 68CinA 69OakA	23	6'	190	Southern Calif.		40
	70-71Oak 72Den 73LA						
Shields, Billy OT	75-77SD		6'7"	262	Georgia Tech		
Shinners, John OG	69-71NO 72Bal 73-77Cin		6'2"	255	Xavier-Ohio		
Shipp, Ken	HC75NYJ				Middle Tennessee		
Shirk, Gary TE	76-77NYG	2	6'1"	220	Moorehead State		1
Shiver, Sanders LB	76-77Bal		6'2"	222	Carson-Newman		
Shoate, Rod LB	75NE 76KJ 77NE		6'1"	213	Oklahoma		
Shy, Don HB-FB	67-68Pit 69-70NO 70-72Chi 73StL	23	6'1"	209	San Diego State		8
Siani, Mike WR	72-77Oak		6'2"	195	Villanova		7
Siemon, Jeff LB	72-77Min		6'2"	233	Stanford	11	
Sikich, Mike OG	71Cle		6'2"	243	Northwestern		
Simmons, Bob OG-OT	77KC		6'4"	260	Texas		
Simon, Bobby OT-OG	76Hou		6'3"	252	Grambling		
Simone, Mike LB	72-74Den		6'	210	Stanford		
Simonini, Ed LB	76-77Bal		6'	215	Texas A & M	1	
Simons, Keith DT	76-77KC		6'3"	254	Minnesota		
Simonson, Dave OT	74Bal 75NYG 76Hou 76Sea 77Det		6'6"	248	Minnesota		
Simpson, Al OG-OT	75-76NYG		6'5"	255	Colorado State		
Simpson, Bill DB	74-77LA		6'1"	180	Michigan State	16	
Simpson, Mike DB	70-73SF		5'11"	172	Houston	3	
Simpson, Nate HB	77GB	2	5'10"	176	Tennessee State		
Simpson, O.J. (Juice) HB	69BufA 70-77Buf	23	6'2"	211	Southern Calif.		42
Sims, David HB	77Sea	2	6'3"	216	Georgia Tech		4
Sims, Jimmy LB	76TB		6'	195	Southern Calif.		
Sims, Robert DT	77Cle		6'5"	282	S. Carolina State		
Singeltary, Bill LB	74NYG		6'2"	230	Temple		
Singleton, Ron OT	76SD 77SF		6'7"	245	Grambling		
Sipe, Brian QB	74-77Cle	12	6'1"	191	San Diego State		2
Sisemore, Jerry OG-OT	73-77Phi		6'4"	258	Texas		
Sistrunk, Manny DT-DE	70-75Was 76-77Phi		6'5"	268	Arkansas-Pine Bluff		
Sistrunk, Otis DT-DE	72-77Oak		6'4"	268	none	3	
Siwek, Mike DT	70StL		6'3"	260	Western Michigan		
Skorupan, John LB	73-77Buf		6'2"	220	Penn State	2	
Slater, Jackie OG-OT	76-77LA		6'4"	261	Jackson State		
Sledge, Leroy FB	71Hou		6'2"	230	Bakersfield J.C.		
Sloan, Ronnie DT	73StL		6'5"	260	Austin Peay		
Slough, Greg LB	71-72Oak		6'3"	230	Southern Calif.		
Small, Eldridge DB	72-74NYG		6'1"	190	Texas A & I	1	
Small, John LB-OT	70-72Atl 73-74Det 75JJ		6'5"	260	The Citadel		
Smith, Barry WR	73-75GB 76TB	2	6'1"	190	Florida State		2
Smith, Barty FB	74-77GB	2	6'4"	240	Richmond		7
Smith, Blane LB	77GB		6'3"	238	Purdue		
Smith, Bubba DE-DT	67-71Bal 72KJ 73-74Oak 75-76Hou		6'7"	280	Michigan State		
Smith, Charlie HB	68-69OakA 70-74Oak 75SD 76KJ	23	6'1"	205	Utah		20
Smith, Charlie (Home Boy) WR	74-77Phi	2	6'1"	185	Grambling		9
Smith, Dave WR	70-72Pit 72Hou 72KC	2	6'2"	205	Indiana State		4
Smith, Donnell DE	71GB 73-74NE		6'4"	247	Southern U.		
Smith, Ed DE	73-74Den 75KJ		6'5"	241	Colorado College	1	
Smith, Jack DB	71Phi		6'4"	204	Troy State		
Smith, Jerry TE	65-77Was	2	6'2"	209	Arizona State		3
Smith, Jerry	HC71Den				Wisconin		
Smith, Jim WR	77Pit	3	6'2"	205	Michigan		
Smith, John K	74-77NE	5	6'	186	none		3
Smith, Ken TE	73Cle 74JJ		6'4"	225	New Mexico		
Smith, Larry HB	69-73LA 74Was	2	6'3"	220	Florida		
Smith, Laverne HB	77Pit		5'10"	193	Kansas		
Smith, Marty DE	76Buf		6'3"	250	Louisville		
Smith, Ollie WR	73-74Bal 76-77GB	2	6'2"	198	Tennessee		
Smith, Paul DT-DE	68-69DenA 70-77Den		6'3"	253	New Mexico	1	
Smith, Perry DB	73-76GB 77StL		6'1"	196	Colorado State	7	
Smith, Ron DB-FL-HB	65Chi 66-67Atl 68-69LA	23	6'1"	191	Wisconsin	13	
	70-72Chi 73SD 74Oak						
Smith, Royce OG	72-73NO 74-76Atl		6'3"	250	Georgia		
Smith, Sherman FB-HB	76-77Sea	2	6'3"	217	Miami (O)		
Smith, Sid C-OT	70-72KC 73JJ 74Hou		6'4"	260	Southern Calif.		
Smith, Steve OT-DE-TE	66Pit 68-70Min 71-74Phi		6'5"	246	Michigan		
Smith, Tody DE	71-72Dal 73-76Hou 76Buf 77JJ		6'5"	248	Southern Calif.	1	
Sniadecki, Jim LB	69-73SF 74-75WFL		6'2"	224	Indiana	1	
Snider, Mel OG-OT	69-71Atl 72-74GB		6'5"	250	Michigan State		
Snow, Jack WR-OE	65-75LA	2	6'2"	195	Notre Dame		2
Snowden, Cal DE	69-70StL 71Buf 72-73SD		6'4"	247	Indiana		

Use Name (Nicknames) – Position	Team by Year	See Section	Hgt	Wgt	College	Int	Pts
Snyder, Todd WR	70-72Atl	2	6'2"	187	Ohio U.		12
Sodaski, John LB-DB	70-72Pit 73Phi		6'1"	214	Villanova	1	
Solomon, Freddie WR-HB	75-77Mia	23	5'11"	181	Tampa		54
Sorie, Revie OG	75-77Chi		6'2"	263	Illinois		
Sowells, Rich DB	71-76NYJ 77Hou		6'	179	Alcorn A & M	10	6
Spencer, Mo DB	74-76NO 77BQ		6'	175	N. Carolina Central	1	
Spencer, Willie FB	76Min 77NYG	2	6'3"	235	none		18
Speyrer, Cotton WR	72-74Bal 75Mia	23	6'	175	Texas		36
Spicer, Bob LB	73NYJ		6'4"	227	Indiana		
Spillis, John WR	69-71GB	2	6'3"	205	Northern Illinois		6
Spivey, Mike DB	77Chi		6'	194	Colorado		
Spivia, Andy LB	77Atl		6'2"	218	Tennessee		
Spurrier, Steve QB	67-75SF 76TB	12 4	6'2"	202	Florida		12
Stabler, Ken (Snake) QB	70-77Oak	12	6'3"	210	Alabama		24
Staggers, Jon WR	70-71Pit 72-74GB 75Det	23	5'10"	185	Missouri		66
Staggs, Jeff LB-DE	67-69SD-A 70-71SD 73-74StL 74SD		6'2"	242	San Diego State	3	
Staley, Bill DT	68-69CinA 70-72Chi		6'3"	249	Utah State		
Stalls, David DE	77Dal		6'4"	236	Northern Colorado		
Stallworth, John WR	74-77Pit	2	6'2"	183	Alabama A & M		90
Stanback, Haskel HB	74-77Atl	2	6'	210	Tennessee		96
Stanfill, Bill DE	69MiaA 70-76Mia 77ZJ		6'5"	251	Georgia	2	12
Starch, Ken FB	76GB		5'11"	210	Wisconsin		
Starke, George OT	73-77Was		6'5"	249	Columbia		
Staroba, Paul WR	72Cle 73GB		6'3"	204	Michigan		6
Staubach, Roger (The Dodger) QB	69-77Dal	12	6'2"	197	Navy		114
St. Claire, Mike DE	76-77Cle		6'5"	245	Grambling		
Stegent, Larry HB	71StL 72SJ		6'1"	200	Texas A & M		
Stein, Bob LB-DE	69KC-A 70-72KC 73-74LA 75SD 75Min 76JJ		6'2"	235	Minnesota	2	
Steinfort, Fred K	76Oak 77Atl	5	5'11"	180	Boston College		59
Stemrick, Greg DB	75-77Hou		5'11"	185	Colorado State	2	6
Stenerud, Jan K	67-69KC-A 70-77KC	5	6'2"	187	Montana State		1082
Stenger, Brian LB	69-72Pit 73NE		6'4"	226	Notre Dame	3	
Stevens, Dick OT	70-74Phi		6'4"	241	Baylor, Randolph Macon		
Stevens, Howard HB	73-74NO 75-77Bal	23	5'5"	167	Louisville		24
Stevenson, Ricky DB	70Cle		5'11"	188	Arizona		
Stewart, Jimmy DB	77NO		5'11"	190	Tulsa		
Stewart, Wayne TE	69NY-A 70-72NYJ 74SD	2	6'7"	214	California		12
Stidham, Howard LB	77SF		6'2"	214	Tennessee Tech		
Stienke, Jim DB	73Cle 74-77NYG		5'11"	183	SW Texas State	4	6
Stieve, Terry OG	76-77NO		6'2"	242	Wisconsin		
Stillwell, Roger DT-DE	75-77Chi		6'5"	259	Stanford		
Stincic, Tom LB	69-71Dal 72NO		6'2"	229	Michigan	1	
Stingley, Darryl WR	73-77NE	2	6'	194	Purdue		96
Stokes, Tim OT	74LA 75-77Was		6'5"	252	Oregon		
Stolberg, Eric WR	71NE		6'2"	180	Indiana		
Stone, Ken DB-WR	73Buf 73-75Was 76TB 77StL		6'1"	180	Vanderbilt	7	6
Story, Bill OT	75KC		6'3"	245	Southern Illinois		
Stoudt, Cliff QB	77Pit		6'4"	218	Youngstown State		
Stowe, Otto WR	71-72Mia 73Dal 74Den	2	6'2"	188	Iowa State		12
Strachan, Mike HB	75-77NO	2	6'	198	Iowa State		24
Strada, John TE	74KC		6'3"	230	William Jewell		
Strayhorn, Les HB	73-74Dal		5'10"	205	East Carolina		6
Stringer, Art LB	77Hou		6'	223	Ball State	1	
Stringert, Hal DB	75-77SD		5'11"	183	Hawaii	5	
Strock, Don QB	74-77Mia	1	6'5"	210	Virginia Tech		12
Strong, Jim HB-FB	70SF 71-72NO	2	6'1"	204	Houston		18
Stroud, Morris TE	69KC-A 70-74KC	2	6'10"	250	Clark-Ga.		42
Strozier, Art TE	70-71SD		6'2"	220	Kansas State		
tuckey, Henry DB	73-74Mia 75-76NYG		6'1"	180	Missouri	2	
tuddard, Vern WR	71NYJ		5'11"	175	Mississippi		
tudwell, Scott LB	77Min		6'2"	224	Illinois	1	
tukes, Charlie DB	67-72Bal 73-74LA 75KJ		6'3"	212	Md. Eastern Shore	32	6
turt, Fred OG	74Was 76-77NE		6'4"	255	Bowling Green		
uggs, Shafer DB	76-77NYJ		6'1"	197	Ball State	1	
ullivan, Dave WR	73-74Cle		5'11"	185	Virginia		
ullivan, Gerry C-OT	74-77Cle		6'4"	250	Illinois		
ullivan, Jim DT-DE	70Atl		6'4"	240	Lincoln (Mo.)		
ullivan, Pat QB	72-75Atl	1	6'	200	Auburn		
ullivan, Tom (Silky) HB-FB	72-77Phi	2	6'	190	Miami (Fla.)		132
ummerell, Carl QB	74-75NYG	1	6'4"	208	East Carolina State		
ummers, Freddie DB	69-71Cle		6'1"	180	Wake Forest		
ummers, Wilbur K	77Det	4	6'4"	220	Louisville		
umner, Walt DB	69-74Cle		6'1"	188	Florida State	15	6
utherland, Doug DT-DE-OG	70NO 71-77Min		6'3"	250	Wisc. St.-Superior		
utton, Mitch DT	74-75Phi		6'4"	260	Kansas		
wann, Lynn WR	74-77Pit	23	5'10"	180	Southern Calif.		144
weeney, Steve WR	73Oak		6'3"	205	California		
weet, Joe WR	72-73LA 74NE 75SD	2	6'2"	196	Tennessee State		8
wenson, Bob LB	75-77Den		6'3"	222	California	4	
wider, Larry K	77TB		6'2"	193	Pittsburgh		
vift, Doug LB	70-75Mia		6'3"	228	Amherst	5	
willey, Dennis OG-OT	77Min		6'4"	241	Texas A & M		
winney, Clovis DT	70NO 71NYJ		6'3"	240	Arkansas State		
kes, Al WR	71NE		6'3"	180	Florida A & M		
ykes, John HB	72SD		5'11"	195	Morgan State		
ylvester, Steve C-OG-OT	75-77Oak		6'4"	261	Notre Dame		
aro, Richie K	75-77NO	5	5'11"	204	Harvard		170
affoni, Joe OT-OG	67-70Cle 72-73NYG		6'3"	251	West Virginia, Tennessee-Martin		
agge, Jerry QB	72-74GB	12	6'2"	218	Nebraska		18
albert, Diron DT	67-70LA 71-77Was		6'5"	251	Texas		
annen, Steve DB	70-74NYJ 75SJ		6'1"	194	Florida	12	6
anner, John LB	71SD 73-74NE		6'4"	231	Tennessee Tech		6
arver, John FB	72-74NE 75Phi	2	6'3"	224	Colorado		48
atarek, Bob DT	68-69BufA 70-72Buf 72Det		6'4"	260	Miami (Fla.)		
ate, Frank LB	75SD 76JJ		6'3"	225	N. Carolina Central		
ate, John LB	76NYG		6'2"	230	Jackson State		
atum, Jack DB	71-77Oak		5'10"	202	Ohio State	25	6
autolo, Terry LB	76-77Phi		6'2"	235	U.C.L.A.		

Use Name (Nicknames) – Positions	Team by Year	See Section	Hgt	Wgt	College	Int	Pts
Taylor, Altie HB	69-75Det 76Hou	23	5'10"	199	Utah State		180
Taylor, Bruce DB	70-77SF	2	6'	184	Boston U.	18	12
Taylor, Charley WR-HB-OE	64-75Was 76SJ 77Was	2	6'3"	210	Arizona State		540
Taylor, Clifton HB	74,76GB	3	6'	198	Memphis State		12
Taylor, David OT	73-77Bal		6'4"	259	Catawba		
Taylor, Ed DB	75-77NYJ		6'	173	Memphis State	3	
Taylor, Jesse HB	72SD	3	6'	200	Cincinnati		6
Taylor, Joe DB	67-74Chi		6'2"	199	N. Carolina A & T	15	
Taylor, Mike OT	68-69Pit 69-70NO 71Was 73StL		6'4"	247	Southern Calif.		
Taylor, Mike LB	72-73NYJ 74WFL		6'1"	230	Michigan	1	
Taylor, Otis WR-FL-OE	65-69KC-A 70-75KC	2	6'2"	215	Prairie View		360
Taylor, Steve DB	76KC		6'3"	204	Kansas		
Teel, Jim LB	73Det		6'3"	225	Purdue		
Teerlinck, John DT	74-75SD 76KJ		6'5"	248	Western Illinois		
Ten Napel, Garth LB	76-77Det		6'1"	213	Texas A & M		
Testerman, Don FB	76-77Sea	2	6'2"	233	Clemson		42
Thaxton, Jim TE-WR	73-74SD 74Cle 76-77NO	2	6'2"	240	Tennessee State	1	24
Theismann, Joe QB	74-77Was	12	6'	184	Notre Dame		18
Thielemann, R.C. OG-C	77Atl		6'4"	247	Arkansas		
Thomas, Bill FB	72Dal 73Hou 74KC	3	6'2"	225	Boston College		
Thomas, Bob HB	71-72LA 73-74SD	2	5'10"	201	Arizona State		24
Thomas, Bob K	75-77Chi	5	5'10"	176	Notre Dame		189
Thomas, Charlie HB	75KC		5'9"	180	Tennessee State		
Thomas, Donnie LB	76NE		6'2"	245	Indiana		
Thomas, Duane HB-FB	70-71Dal 72HO 73-74Was	2	6'1"	215	West Texas State		144
Thomas, Earl WR-TE	71-73Chi 74-75StL 76Hou	2	6'3"	219	Houston		90
Thomas, Earlie DB	70-74NYJ 75Den		6'1"	190	Colorado State	7	6
Thomas, Emmitt DB	66-69KC-A 70-77KC	3	6'2"	192	Bishop	56	30
Thomas, Ike DB-WR	71Dal 71-73GB 74WFL 75Buf	3	6'2"	194	Bishop	2	12
Thomas, Jimmy HB-WR	69-73SF	2	6'1"	215	Texas-Arlington		72
Thomas, Joe	HC74Bal				Ohio Northern		
Thomas, J.T. DB	73-77Pit		6'2"	196	Florida State	13	12
Thomas, Lee DE	71-72SD 73Cin 75LJ		6'5"	246	Jackson State		
Thomas, Mike HB	75-77Was	2	5'11"	190	Nevada-Las Vegas		126
Thomas, Norris DB	77Mia		5'11"	170	Southern Miss.	3	
Thomas, Pat DB	76-77LA		5'9"	180	Texas A & M	5	
Thomas, Skip (Dr. Death) DB	72-77Oak		6'1"	205	Southern Calif.	17	6
Thomas, Speedy WR	69CinA 70-72Cin 73-74NO	2	6'1"	174	Utah		54
Thomas, Spencer DB	75Was		6'2"	185	Washburn		
Thompson, Audra WR-HB	77GB		6'	186	East Texas State		
Thompson, Bill DB	69DenA 70-77Den	3	6'1"	200	Md. Eastern Shore	26	24
Thompson, Bobby HB	75-76Det	23	5'11"	195	Oklahoma		6
Thompson, Dave OT-C-OG	71-73Det 74-75NO		6'4"	271	Clemson		
Thompson, Leonard WR-HB	75-77Det	2	5'10"	190	Oklahoma State		12
Thompson, Norm DB	71-76StL 77Bal		6'1"	178	Utah	25	24
Thompson, Ricky WR	76-77Bal		6'	173	Baylor		
Thompson (born Symonds), Rocky HB	71-73NYG	23	5'11"	200	West Texas State		18
Thompson, Steve DT-DE	68-69NY-A 70NYJ 71VR 72-73NYJ 74WFL		6'5"	244	Washington		
Thompson, Ted LB	75-77Hou		6'1"	218	S.M.U.		
Thompson, Tommy HB	74SD		6'1"	205	Southern Illinois		
Thompson, Woody FB	75-77Atl	2	6'1"	228	Miami (Fla.)		6
Thoms, Art DT-DE-MG	69OakA 70-75Oak 76KJ 77Phi		6'5"	250	Syracuse	2	6
Thornbladh, Bob LB	74KC		6'1"	220	Michigan		
Thornton, Sidney FB	77Pit	2	5'11"	230	Northwest La.		12
Thrower, Jim DB	70-72Phi 73-74Det 75KJ		6'2"	194	East Texas State		
Tilleman, Mike DT-DE	66Min 67-70NO 71-72Hou 73-76Atl		6'5"	275	Montana		
Tilley, Pat WR	76-77StL	23	5'10"	173	Louisiana Tech		6
Tillman, Andre TE	75-77Mia	2	6'5"	230	Texas Tech		18
Tillman, Faddie DE-DT	72NO		6'5"	230	Boise State		
Tillman, Rusty LB	70-77Was		6'2"	230	Northern Arizona		
Tinker, Gerald WR	74-75Atl 75GB 76KJ		5'9"	173	Kent State		18
Tipton, Dave DE-DT	71-73NYG 74-75SD 75NE 76Sea		6'6"	242	Stanford		
Tipton, Dave NT-DT	75NE 75SD 76NE		6'1"	253	Western Illinois		
Todd, Richard QB	76-77NYJ	12	6'2"	208	Alabama		6
Toews, Loren LB	73-77Pit		6'3"	218	California	2	4
Tolbert, Jim DB	66-69SD-A 70-71SD 72Hou 73-75StL 76SD		6'3"	207	Lincoln (Mo.)	10	
Tom, Mel DE	67-73Phi 73-75Chi		6'4"	247	Hawaii, San Jose		2
Toner, Tom LB	73GB 74BC 75-77GB		6'3"	233	Idaho State	4	2
Toomay, Pat DE	70-74Dal 75Buf 76TB 77Oak		6'5"	245	Vanderbilt	2	6
Torkelson, Eric HB-FB	74-77GB	2	6'2"	194	Connecticut		36
Towle, Steve LB	75-77Mia		6'2"	233	Kansas	1	
Towns, Morris OT	77Hou		6'4"	275	Missouri		
Troup, Bill QB	74Bal 75Phi 76-77Bal		6'5"	218	South Carolina		6
Trumpy, Bob TE-WR	68-69CinA 70-77Cin	2	6'6"	226	Illinois, Utah		210
Tucker, Bob TE	70-77NYG 77Min	2	6'3"	230	Bloomsburg State		150
Turk, Goodwin LB	75NYJ 76-77Den		6'2"	230	Southern U.	2	
Turner, Cecil WR	68-73Chi	23	5'10"	172	Cal. St. Polytech		36
Turner, Clem FB	69CinA 70-72Den	2	6'1"	238	Cincinnati		18
Turner, Jim K-QB	64-69NY-A 70NYJ 71-77Den	5	6'2"	206	Utah State		1304
Turner, J.T. DT	77NYG		6'3"	250	Duke		
Turner, Rocky WR-DB	72-73NYJ		6'	195	Tenn.-Chattanooga		
Twilley, Howard WR-OE	66-69MiaA 70-76Mia	2	5'10"	183	Tulsa		138
Tyler, Maurice DB	72Buf 73-74Den 75SD 76Det 77NYJ		6'	189	Morgan State	5	
Tyler, Wendell HB	77LA	2	5'10"	188	U.C.L.A.		18
Upchurch, Rick WR	75-77Den	23	5'10"	173	Minnesota		78
Uperesa, Tuufuli OG	71Phi		6'3"	255	Montana		
Upshaw, Gene OG-OT	67-69OakA 70-77Oak		6'5"	255	Texas A & I		
Upshaw, Marv DT-DE	68-69Cle 70-75KC 76StL		6'3"	253	Trinity (Texas)	2	6
Vactor, Ted DB	69-73Was 74JJ 75Chi	3	6'	185	Nebraska	2	6
Vanderbundt, Skip LB	69-77SF		6'3"	227	Oregon State	14	18
Van Duyne, Bob OG-OT	74-77Bal		6'5"	243	Idaho		
Van Dyke, Bruce OG	66Phi 67-73Pit 74-76GB		6'2"	248	Missouri		
van Eeghen, Mark FB-HB	74-77Oak	2	6'2"	223	Colgate		78
Van Galder, Tim QB	72StL	1	6'1"	190	Iowa State		
Van Heusen, Bill WR	68-69DenA 70-76Den	2 4	6'1"	200	Maryland		72
Van Horn, Doug OT-OG	66Det 68-77NYG		6'2"	245	Ohio State		
Van Note, Jeff C-OG-LB	69-77Atl		6'2"	245	Kentucky		
Vanoy, Vern DT	71NYG 72GB		6'3"	270	Kansas		

Use Name (Nicknames) – Positions	Team by Year	See Section	Hgt	Wgt	College	Int	Pts
Van Pelt, Brad LB	73-77NYG		6'5"	235	Michigan State	9	
Van Valkenberg, Pete HB	73Buf 74GB 74Chi		6'2"	194	Brigham Young		
Varty, Mike LB	74Was 75Bal		6'1"	223	Northwestern		
Vataha, Randy WR-DB	71-76NE 77GB	2	5'10"	173	Stanford		138
Vella, John OT	72-77Oak		6'4"	258	Southern Calif.		
Vermiel, Dick	HC76-77Phi				San Jose State		
Vertefeuille, Brian OT	74SD		6'3"	252	Idaho State		
Villapiano, Phil LB	71-76Oak 77KJ		6'1"	220	Bowling Green	9	6
Vinyard, Kenny K	70Atl	5	5'10"	190	Texas Tech		50
Vitali, Mark QB	77KC		6'5"	209	Purdue		
Voight, Mike HB	77Hou		6'	214	North Carolina		
Voigt, Stu TE	70-77Min	2	6'1"	223	Wisconsin		96
Volk, Rick DB	67-75Bal 76NYG 77Mia	3	6'3"	195	Michigan	34	6
Waddell, Charles TE	77TB		6'5"	235	North Carolina		
Waddy, Billy WR	77LA	23	5'11"	185	Colorado		6
Wade, Charlie WR	74Chi 75GB 77KC	2	5'10"	163	Tennessee State		6
Wafer, Carl DT	74NYG		6'3"	250	Tennessee State		
Wages, Harmon FB-HB	69-71Atl 72KJ 73Atl	2	6'1"	214	Florida		60
Wagner, Mike DB	71-77Pit		6'1"	201	Western Illinois	24	6
Wagner, Steve DB	76-77GB		6'2"	203	Wisconsin		
Walden, Bobby K	64-67Min 68-77Pit	4	6'	192	Georgia		
Walik, Billy WR	70-72Phi	3	5'11"	180	Villanova		6
Walker, Chuck DT-DE	64-72StL 72-75Atl		6'2"	249	Duke	1	
Walker, Cleo LB-C	70BG 71Atl		6'3"	220	Louisville		
Walker, Donnie DB	73-74Buf 75NYJ	3	6'1"	182	Central St.-Ohio	1	
Walker, Glenn K	77LA	4	6'1"	210	Southern Calif.		
Walker, Louie LB	74Dal		6'1"	216	Colorado State		
Walker, Mike K	73NE	5	6'	190	none		21
Walker, Mike DE	71NO		6'4"	235	Tulane		
Walker, Randy K	74GB 75JJ	4	5'10"	177	NW State La.		
Walker, Rick TE	77Cin		6'3"	237	U.C.L.A.		
Walker, Wesley WR	77NYJ	2	6'	172	California		18
Wallace, Bob TE-WR	68-72Chi	2	6'3"	213	Texas-El Paso		54
Wallace, Jackie DB	74Min 75-76Bal 77LA	3	6'3"	198	Arizona	10	12
Wallace, Rodney OG-OT	71-73Dal 74JJ		6'5"	255	New Mexico		
Wallace, Roger WR	76NYG		5'11"	180	Bowling Green		
Walsh, Ward HB	71-72Hou 72GB	2	6'	213	Colorado		12
Walters, Rod OG	76KC 77JJ		6'3"	258	Iowa		
Walters, Stan OT	72-74Cin 75-77Phi		6'6"	270	Syracuse		
Waltersheid, Len DB	77Chi		5'11"	190	Southern Utah		
Walton, Bruce OT-OG-C	73-75Dal		6'6"	251	U.C.L.A.		
Walton, Chuck OG	67-74Det		6'3"	253	Iowa State		
Walton, John QB	76-77Phi	1	6'2"	210	Elizabeth City St.		
Walton, Larry WR	69-74Det 75KJ 76Det	2	5'11"	182	Arizona State		162
Walton, Wayne OT-OG	71NYG 73-74KC		6'5"	252	Abilene Christian		
Ward, John OG-C-DE	70-73Min 74LJ 75Min 76TB 76Chi		6'4"	258	Oklahoma State		
Warfield, Paul WR	64-69Cle 70-74Mia 75WFL 76-77Cle	2	6'	188	Ohio State		516
Washington, Dave LB-TE	70-71Den 72-74Buf 75-77SF		6'5"	222	Alcorn A & M	6	20
Washington, Eric DB	72-73StL		6'2"	190	Texas-El Paso		
Washington, Gene WR-OE	67-72Min 73Den	2	6'3"	212	Michigan State		156
Washington, Gene WR	69-77SF	2	6'1"	185	Stanford		354
Washington, Joe HB	73Atl		5'9"	180	Illinois State		
Washington, Joe HB	76KJ 77SD	2	5'10"	183	Oklahoma		
Washington, Mark DB	70-77Dal		5'10"	186	Morgan State	13	8
Washington, Mike DB	76-77TB		6'3"	190	Alabama	5	6
Washington, Russ OT-DT	68-69SD-A 70-77SD		6'6"	291	Missouri		
Washington, Ted LB	73-77Hou		6'1"	242	Miss. Valley State	3	
Washington, Vic HB-DB-WR	71-73SF 74Hou 75-76Buf	23	5'10"	196	Wyoming		132
Waters, Charlie DB	70-77Dal		6'1"	194	Clemson	29	18
Watkins, Larry FB-HB	69Det 70-72Phi 73-74Buf 75-77NYG	2	6'2"	226	Alcorn A & M		78
Watson, Allen K	70Pit	5	5'10"	165	Newport-Wales		22
Watson, John OG-OT-C	71-76SF 77NO		6'4"	246	Oklahoma		
Waston, Mike OT	77NO		6'6"	272	Miami (O.)		
Watson, Pete TE	72Cin		6'1"	210	Tufts		
Weatherly, Jim C	76Atl		6'3"	245	none		
Weathers, Carl LB	70-71Oak		6'2"	220	San Diego State		
Weatherspoon, Cephus WR	72NO		6'1"	182	Fort Lewis		
Weaver, Charlie LB	71-77Det		6'2"	220	Southern Calif.	10	
Weaver, Gary LB	73-74Oak 75-77GB		6'1"	224	Fresno State		
Weaver, Herman K	70-76Det 77Sea	4	6'4"	210	Tennessee		
Webb, Jimmy DT	75-77SF		6'5"	247	Mississippi State		
Webster, Cornell DB	77Sea		6'	180	Tulsa	1	
Webster, George LB	67-69HouA 70-72Hou 72-73Pit 74-76NE		6'4"	225	Michigan State	5	
Webster, Mike C-OG	74-77Pit		6'1"	244	Wisconsin		
Webster, Tim K	71GB	5	6'	195	Arkansas		26
Weese, Norris QB	76-77Den	12 4	6'1"	194	Mississippi		6
Weger, Mike DB	67-75Det 76-77Hou		6'2"	197	Bowling Green	17	12
Wehrli, Roger DB	69-77StL	3	6'1"	192	Missouri	29	7
Welch, Claxton HB-FB	69-71Dal 73NE	2	5'11"	202	Oregon		12
Wells, Mike QB	75NYG 77Cin		6'5"	225	Illinois		
Wells, Terry HB	74Hou 75GB	2	5'11"	195	Southern Miss.		
Wender, Jack HB	77TB		6'	210	Fresno State		
Werner, Clyde LB	70KC 71KJ 72-74KC 75FJ 76KC		6'4"	227	Washington	2	
Wersching, Ray K	73-76SD 77SF	5	5'11"	215	California		198
Wesson, Ricky DB	77KC		5'9"	163	S.M.U.		
West, Bill DB	72Den		5'10"	185	Tennessee State		
West, Bob WR	72-73KC 74SF	2	6'4"	218	San Diego State		18
West, Charlie DB	68-73Min 74-77Det	3	6'1"	194	Texas-El Paso	14	6
West, Jeff TE	75StL 76-77SD	4	6'3"	217	Cincinnati		
Westbrook, Don WR	77NE		5'10"	188	Nebraska		
Westbrooks, Greg LB	75-77NO		6'2"	217	Colorado	1	
Wheeler, Wayne WR	74Chi		6'2"	180	Alabama		6
Whitaker, Creston WR	72NO		6'2"	187	North Texas State		
White, Charlie HB-FB	77NYJ	2	6'	222	Bethune-Cookman		12
White, Danny QB	76-77Dal	1 4	6'2"	186	Arizona State		
White, Daryl OG	74Det		6'3"	250	Nebraska		
White, Dwight DE	71-77Pit		6'4"	253	East Texas State	4	4
White, Ed OG-OT	69-77Min		6'2"	265	California		
White, James (Duck) DT	76-77Min		6'3"	263	Oklahoma State		
White, Jan TE	71-72Buf	2	6'2"	216	Ohio State		12
White, Jeff K	73NE	5	5'11"	170	Texas-El Paso		63
White, Jeris DB	74-76Mia 77TB		5'11"	180	Hawaii	6	
White, Jim DE	73NE 74-75Hou 76Sea 76Den		6'3"	257	Colorado State		
White, Lee FB	68-69NY-A 70NYJ 72LA 72SD	2	6'4"	238	Weber State		6
White, Marsh FB	75-76NYG 77BW	2	6'2"	220	Arkansas		12
White, Paul HB	70-71StL		6'	200	Texas-El Paso		
White, Randy DT-LB	75-77Dal		6'4"	243	Maryland		
White, Ray LB	71-72SD 73JJ 75-76StL 77KJ		6'1"	227	Syracuse	2	2
White, Sammie WR	76-77Min	2	5'11"	189	Grambling		114
White, Sherman DE	72-75Cin 76-77Buf		6'5"	252	California	1	2
White, Stan LB	72-77Bal		6'1"	224	Ohio State	23	12
White, Walter TE	75-77KC	2	6'3"	215	Maryland		90
Whitehurst, David QB	77GB	1	6'2"	204	Furman		6
Whitley, Wilson DT	77Cin		6'3"	264	Houston		
Whittington, C.L. DB	74-76Hou 77JJ		6'1"	200	Prairie View	6	6
Wickert, Tom OT-OG	74Mia 75-76NO 77Det 77KC		6'4"	248	Washington State		
Wicks, Bob WR	72StL 74NO		6'3"	200	Utah State		
Widby, Ron K	68-71Dal 72-73GB 74XJ	4	6'4"	212	Tennessee		
67-68 played in A.B.A.							
Wilkerson, Doug OG	70Hou 71-77SD		6'2"	257	N. Carolina Central		
Williams, Ben DE-DT	76-77Buf		6'2"	258	Mississippi		
Williams, Clarence (Sweeny) DE	70-77GB		6'5"	255	Prairie View	1	6
Williams, Clarence FB	77SD	2	5'9"	198	South Carolina		12
Williams, Dave WR-FL	67-71StL 72-73SD 73Pit	2	6'2"	205	Washington		150
Williams, Dave HB-FB	77SF		6'2"	200	Colorado		6
Williams, Del OG-C	67-73NO		6'2"	242	Florida State		
Williams, Del HB	74-77SF	2	6'	196	Kansas		150
Williams, Donnie WR	70LA		6'3"	210	Prairie View		
Williams, Ed FB	74-75Cin 76-77TB	2	6'2"	245	Langston		54
Williams, Eric LB	77StL		6'2"	217	Southern Calif.		
Williams, Gerard DB	76-77Was		6'1"	184	Langston	4	
Williams, Jeff OT	77LA		6'4"	256	Rhode Island		
Williams, Joe HB	71Dal 72NO	2	6'	194	Wyoming		6
Williams, John OT-OG-DE	68-71Bal 72-77LA		6'3"	257	Minnesota		
Williams, Lawrence WR	76-77KC 77Cle	3	5'10"	174	Texas Tech		6
Williams, Mike DB	75-77SD		5'10"	180	Louisiana State	7	
Williams, Perry FB	69-73GB 74Chi	2	6'2"	220	Purdue		12
Williams, Reggie LB	76-77Cin		6'1"	229	Dartmouth	4	12
Williams, Richard WR	72NO		5'11"	170	Abilene Christian		
Williams, Roger DB-WR	71-72LA		5'10"	180	Grambling		
Williams, Sam DB	74-75SD 76Hou		6'2"	190	California	2	
Williams, Steve DE	74Bal		6'6"	260	Western Carolina		
Williams, Tom DT	70-71SD		6'4"	250	California-Davis		
Williams, Walt DB	77Det		6'	185	New Mexico State		
Willingham, Larry DB	71-72StL		6'1"	190	Auburn		
Willis, Fred FB	71-72Cin 72-76Hou 77JJ	2	6'	209	Boston College		138
Willis, Larry DB	73Was		5'11"	170	Texas-El Paso		
Willis, Leonard WR	76Min 77NO 77Buf	3	5'10"	180	Ohio State		
Wilson, Joe HB-FB	73Cin 74NE 75NJ	2	5'10"	210	Holy Cross		
Wilson, Mike OG-OT	69CinA 70Cin 71Buf 75KC		6'1"	243	Dayton		
Wilson, Nemiah DB	65-67DenA 68-69OakA 70-74Oak 75Chi		6'	166	Grambling	27	24
Wilson, Steve OG-OT	76-77TB		6'3"	267	Georgia		
Wilson, Tim FB	77Hou	2	6'3"	220	Maryland		18
Winans, Jeff OG-OT-DT-DE	73-75Buf 76Oak 76NO 77TB		6'5"	263	Southern Calif.		
Windauer, Bill DT-NT	73-74Bal 75Mia 75NYG 76Atl 77Mia		6'3"	248	Iowa		
Windsor, Bob TE	67-71SF 72-75NE	2	6'4"	227	Kentucky		90
Winfield, Vern OG	72-73Phi		6'2"	248	Minnesota		
Winfrey, Stan FB	75-76Mia 77TB 77Mia 77Buf	2	5'11"	223	Arkansas State		12
Winfrey, Carl LB	71Min 72Pit		6'	230	Wisconsin		
Winslow, Doug WR	73NO 76Was		5'11"	180	Drake		
Winston, Dennis LB	77Pit		6'	228	Arkansas	2	
Winther, Wimpy C	71GB 72NO		6'3"	260	Mississippi		
Wirgowski, Dennis DE-DT	70Bos 71-72NE 73Phi		6'5"	253	Purdue	1	
Wise, Phil DB	71-76NYJ 77Min		6'	192	Nebraska-Omaha	4	6
Withrow, Carl C	70SD 71-73GB 74StL		6'	240	Kentucky		
Wittum, Tom K	73-77SF	4	6'1"	191	Northern Illinois		5
Wocjik, Greg DT	71LA 72-73SD 74WFL 75SD		6'6"	268	Southern Calif.		
Wolf, Jim DE	74Pit 76KC		6'3"	240	Prairie View		
Wood, Richard LB	75NYJ 76-77TB		6'2"	215	Southern Calif.	4	12
Woodall, Al QB	69NY-A 70-71NYJ 72JJ 73-74NYJ 75KJ	12	6'5"	202	Duke		
Woodcock, John DE-LB	76-77Det		6'3"	240	Hawaii		
Woods, Don FB-HB	74-77SD	2	6'1"	211	New Mexico		108
Woods, Larry DT	71-72Det 73Mia 74-75NYJ 76Sea		6'6"	265	Tennessee State		
Woods, Robert OT-OG	73-77NYJ 77NO		6'3"	257	Tennessee State		
Woolsey, Roland DB	75Dal 76Sea 77Cle	3	6'1"	182	Boise State	5	
Word, Roscoe DB	74-76NYJ 76Buf 76TB	3	5'11"	170	Jackson State	3	
Wortman, Keith OG-OT-C	72-75GB 76-77StL		6'2"	250	Nebraska		
Wright, Elmo WR	71-74KC 75Hou 75NE	2	6'	190	Houston		42
Wright, George DT	70-71Bal 72Cle		6'3"	262	Sam Houston State		
Wright, Jeff DB	71-77Min		5'11"	190	Minnesota	11	
Wright, Louie DB	75-77Den		6'2"	195	San Jose State	5	6
Wright, Nate DB	69Atl 69-70StL 71-77Min		5'11"	180	San Diego State	24	6
Wright, Rayfield OT-TE	67-77Dal		6'7"	253	Fort Valley State		6
Wyatt, Alvin DB	70Oak 71-72Buf 73Hou 74WFL	3	5'10"	183	Bethune-Cookman	5	18
Wyatt, Doug DB	70-72NO 73-74Det		6'1"	195	Tulsa	8	12
Wyche, Sam QB	68-69CinA 70Cin 71-72Was 74Det 76StL 76Buf	12	6'4"	214	Furman		18
Wycinsky, Craig OG	72Cle		6'3"	243	Michigan		
Wynn, Bill DE	73-76Phi 77Was		6'4"	244	Tennessee State		12
Wysocki, Pete LB	75-77Was		6'2"	225	Western Michigan		
Yanchar, Bill DT	70Cle		6'3"	250	Purdue		
Yankowski, Ron DE	71-77StL		6'5"	240	Kansas State		6
Yarbrough, Jim OT	69-77Det		6'6"	261	Florida		
Yarno, John C	77Sea		6'5"	251	Idaho		
Yary, Ron OT	68-77Min		6'6"	257	Southern Calif.		
Yeates, Jeff DT-DE-OG	74-76Buf 76-77Atl		6'3"	247	Boston College		
Yepremian, Garo K	66-67Det 70-77Mia	5	5'8"	170	none		81[illegible]

Use Name (Nicknames) — Positions	Team by Year	See Section	Hgt	Wgt	College	Int	Pts
Young, Adrian LB	68-72Phi 72Det 73Chi		6'1"	230	Southern Calif.		
Young, Al WR	71-72Pit 73IL		6'1"	195	S. Carolina State		
Young, Bob OG-DT	66-69DenA 70Den 71Hou 72-77StL		6'2"	265	Texas, Howard Payne, SW Texas State		
Young, Charley HB	74-76Dal 77KJ	2	6'1"	213	N. Carolina State		
Young, Charlie TE	73-76Phi 77LA	2	6'4"	236	Southern Calif.		84
Young, James DE	77Hou		6'2"	260	Texas Southern		4
Young, Randy OT	76TB		6'5"	250	Iowa State		
Young, Rickey HB	75-77SD	2	6'2"	195	Jackson State		90
Young, Steve OT	74TB 77Mia		6'8"	271	Colorado		
Young, Wilbur DE-DT	71-77KC		6'6"	289	William Penn	2	6
Young, Willie (Sugar Bear) OT	66-75NYG		6'	259	Grambling		
Young, Willie OT	71-72Buf 73Mia		6'4"	270	Alcorn A & M		
Youngblood, Jack DE	71-77LA		6'4"	251	Florida		2

Use Name (Nicknames) — Positions	Team by Year	See Section	Hgt	Wgt	College	Int	Pts
Youngblood, Jim LB	73-77LA	2	6'3"	239	Tennessee Tech	5	6
Zabel, Steve LB-TE	70-74Phi 75-77NE	2	6'4"	234	Oklahoma	5	9
Zanders, Emanuel OG	74-77NO		6'1"	255	Jackson State		
Zapalas, Bill LB-DE	71-73NYJ		6'4"	225	Texas		
Zaunbrechner, Godfrey C	71-73Min		6'4"	238	Louisiana State		
Zelencik, Connie C-OG	77Buf		6'4"	245	Purdue		
Zeno, Coleman WR	71NYG		6'4"	210	Grambling		
Zimmerman, Don WR	73-76Phi 76GB	2	6'3"	195	Northeast La.		30
Zofko, Mickey HB	71-74Det 74NYG	3	6'3"	195	Auburn		1
Zook, John DE	69-75Atl 76-77StL		6'5"	247	Kansas	4	8
Zorn, Jim QB	76-77Sea	12	6'2"	200	Cal. Poly-Pomona		30

Lifetime Statistics — 1970-1977 Players   Section 1 — PASSING
(All men with 25 or more passing attempts)

Name	Years	Att.	Comp.	Comp. Pct.	Yards	Yds/ Att.	TD	Int.	Pct. Int.
Tony Adams	75-77	240	119	49.6	1711	7.1	7	19	7.9
Ken Anderson	71-77	2127	1208	56.8	15471	7.3	99	69	3.2
Rick Arrington	70-72	204	97	47.5	950	4.7	3	9	4.4
Bob Avellini	75-77	690	339	49.1	4526	6.6	25	44	6.4
Steve Bartkowski	75-77	511	236	46.2	3135	6.1	20	37	7.2
Bob Berry	65-76	1173	661	56.4	9207	7.8	64	64	5.5
Jeb Blount	77	89	37	41.6	522	5.9	0	7	7.9
Mike Boryla	74-76	514	270	52.5	2823	5.5	20	29	5.6
Terry Bradshaw	70-77	2019	1008	49.9	13279	6.6	93	118	5.8
Marlin Briscoe	68-77	233	97	41.6	1697	7.3	14	14	6.0
Carlos Brown	75-76	78	29	37.2	396	5.1	3	6	7.7
Scott Bull	76-77	72	28	38.9	341	4.7	2	6	8.3
Virgil Carter	68-72,75-76	785	425	54.1	5063	6.4	29	31	3.9
Larry Cipa	74-75	92	34	37.0	424	4.6	1	3	3.3
Wayne Clark	70,72-75	120	52	43.3	745	6.2	0	14	11.7
Will Cureton	75	32	10	31.3	95	3.0	1	1	3.1
Gary Danielson	76-77	100	42	42.0	445	4.5	1	5	5.0
Bob Davis	67-73	324	137	42.3	1553	4.8	14	23	7.1
Jim Del Gaizo	72-75	103	44	42.7	648	6.3	4	10	9.7
Bill Demory	73-74	39	12	30.8	159	4.1	2	8	20.5
Lynn Dickey	71,73-77	757	383	50.6	4764	6.3	20	56	7.4
Parnell Dickinson	76-77	39	15	38.5	210	5.4	1	5	12.8
Marty Domres	69-77	809	399	49.3	4904	6.1	27	50	6.2
Bobby Douglass	69-77	1166	502	43.1	6403	5.5	35	63	5.4
Brian Dowling	72-73,77	55	29	52.7	383	7.0	2	1	1.8
Joe Ferguson	73-77	1325	656	49.5	8842	6.7	62	64	4.8
Dan Fouts	73-77	1094	595	54.4	7658	7.0	34	57	5.2
Jesse Freitas	74-75	219	98	44.7	1244	5.7	8	13	5.9
Joe Gilliam	72-75	331	147	44.4	2103	6.4	9	17	5.1
Jerry Golsteyn	77	70	31	44.3	416	5.9	2	8	11.4
Neil Graff	74-77	48	25	52.1	288	6.0	2	3	6.3
Bob Griese	67-77	2784	1541	55.4	20351	7.3	161	141	5.1
Steve Grogan	75-77	881	444	50.4	6041	6.9	46	59	6.7
Pat Haden	76-77	321	184	56.7	2447	7.6	19	10	3.1
Terry Hanratty	69-76	431	165	38.3	2510	5.8	24	35	8.1
Ed Hargett	69-73	437	205	46.9	2727	6.2	11	10	2.3
James Harris	69-71,73-77	1052	560	53.2	7580	7.2	43	49	4.7
Jim Hart	66-77	3424	1725	50.4	23869	7.0	152	167	4.9
Randy Hedberg	77	90	25	27.8	244	2.7	0	10	11.1
Don Horn	67-74	465	232	49.9	3369	7.2	20	36	7.7
Gary Huff	73-77	752	377	50.1	4160	5.5	15	47	6.3
John Hufnagel	74-75	61	22	36.1	357	5.9	1	9	14.8
David Humm	75-77	43	21	48.8	287	6.7	3	2	4.7
Scott Hunter	71-74,76,77	707	317	44.8	4435	6.3	22	37	5.2
Ron Jaworski	74-77	470	220	46.8	2902	6.1	19	29	6.2
Randy Johnson	66-73,75-76	1286	647	50.3	8329	6.5	51	90	7.0
Bert Jones	73-77	1458	820	56.2	11269	7.7	82	62	4.3
John Jones	75	57	16	28.1	181	3.2	1	5	8.8
Gary Keithley	73,75	73	32	43.8	369	5.1	1	5	6.8
Tommy Kramer	77	57	30	52.6	425	7.5	5	4	7.0
Mike Kruczek	76-77	92	53	57.6	777	8.4	0	3	3.3
Greg Landry	68-77	1670	909	54.4	11999	7.2	79	80	4.8
Larry Lawrence	74-76	31	9	29.0	79	2.5	0	4	12.9
Bob Lee	69-77	704	355	50.4	4781	6.8	28	38	5.4
Mike Livingston	68-77	1371	709	51.7	9253	6.7	50	66	4.8
Clint Longley	74-76	68	31	45.6	441	6.5	5	4	5.9
Terry Luck	77	50	25	50.0	316	6.3	1	7	14.0
Archie Manning	71-75,77	1696	862	50.8	9983	5.9	55	87	5.1
Gary Marangi	74-77	283	104	36.7	1373	4.9	12	21	7.4
Dave Mays	76-77	141	76	53.9	898	6.4	6	11	7.8
Kim McQuilken	74-77	268	107	39.9	1113	4.2	4	28	10.4
Don Milan	75	32	15	46.9	181	5.7	1	1	3.1
Dennis Morrison	74	51	21	41.2	227	4.5	1	5	9.8
Craig Morton	65-77	2448	1277	52.2	17962	7.3	123	130	5.3
Bill Munson	64-77	1932	1043	54.0	12537	6.5	80	78	4.0
Steve Myer	76-77	130	70	53.8	729	5.6	6	12	9.2
Joe Namath	65-77	3762	1886	50.1	27663	7.4	173	220	5.8
Kent Nix	67-72	652	301	46.2	3644	5.6	23	49	7.5
Tom Owen	74-77	240	113	47.1	1652	6.9	11	17	7.1
Dan Pastorini	71-77	2076	1064	51.3	12301	5.9	66	104	5.0
Al Pastrana	69-70	75	29	38.7	420	5.6	1	9	12.0
Craig Penrose	76-77	75	37	49.3	482	6.4	3	7	9.3
Mike Phipps	70-77	1322	636	48.1	7705	5.8	40	81	6.1
Joe Pisarcik	77	242	103	42.6	1346	5.6	4	14	5.8
Jim Plunkett	71-77	1994	983	49.3	13217	6.6	84	117	5.9
Mike Rae	76-77	95	50	52.6	579	6.1	7	5	5.3
Steve Ramsey	70-76	921	456	49.5	6437	7.0	35	58	6.3
John Reaves	72-77	395	175	44.3	2365	6.0	11	24	6.1
Joe Reed	72-77	481	211	43.9	2661	5.5	16	30	6.2
Matt Robinson	77	54	20	37.0	310	5.7	2	8	14.8
Bobby Scott	73-77	414	196	47.3	2288	5.5	12	22	5.3
Dennis Shaw	70-76	924	489	52.9	6347	6.9	35	68	7.4
Brian Sipe	74-77	703	394	56.0	4376	6.2	28	38	5.4
Steve Spurrier	67-76	1151	597	51.9	6878	6.0	40	60	5.3
Ken Stabler	70-77	1577	945	59.9	12519	7.9	108	91	5.8
Roger Staubach	69-77	2084	1187	57.0	15924	7.6	101	82	3.9
Ron Strock	74-77	96	49	51.0	601	6.3	5	5	5.2
Pat Sullivan	72-75	220	93	42.3	1155	5.3	5	16	7.3
Carl Summerell	74-75	29	13	44.8	157	5.4	0	5	17.2
Jerry Tagge	72-74	281	136	48.4	1583	5.6	3	17	6.0
Joe Theismann	74-77	378	182	48.1	2374	6.3	17	22	5.8
Richard Todd	76-77	427	198	46.4	2733	6.4	14	29	6.8
Tim Van Galder	72	79	40	50.6	434	5.5	1	7	8.9
John Walton	76-77	28	12	42.9	125	4.5	0	2	7.1
Norris Weese	76-77	67	35	52.2	433	6.5	2	6	9.0
Danny White	76-77	30	17	56.7	248	8.3	2	3	10.0
David Whitehurst	77	105	50	47.6	634	6.0	1	7	6.7
Al Woodall	69-71,73-74	503	246	48.9	2970	5.9	18	23	4.6
Sam Wyche	68-72,74,76	222	116	52.7	1748	7.9	12	9	4.6
Jim Zorn	76-77	690	312	45.2	4258	6.2	28	46	6.7

Lifetime Statistics – 1970–1977 Players   Section 2 – **RUSHING and RECEIVING**
(All men with 25 or more rushing attempts or 10 or more receptions)

Name	Years	RUSHING Att.	Yards	Avg.	TD	RECEIVING Rec.	Yards	Avg.	TD
Dan Abramowicz	67-75	6	95	15.8	0	369	5686	15.4	39
Mike Adamle	71-76	308	1149	3.7	4	53	368	6.9	2
Bob Adams	69-71,73-77	2	7	3.5	0	61	732	12.0	0
Margene Adkins	70-73					19	258	13.6	0
Mack Alston	70-77	2	10	5.0	0	80	923	11.5	12
George Amundson	73-75	74	194	2.6	4	25	212	8.5	1
Bobby Anderson	70-73,75	314	1282	4.1	9	84	861	10.3	2
Donny Anderson	66-74	1197	4696	3.9	41	209	2548	12.2	14
Ken Anderson	71-77	219	1080	4.9	11				
Otis Armstrong	73-77	697	3149	4.5	18	98	1043	10.6	5
Josh Ashton	72-75	257	994	3.9	3	33	320	9.7	1
Bob Avellini	75-77	59	164	2.8	3				
Mark Bailey	77	66	266	4.0	2	17	206	12.1	1
Tom Bailey	71-75	42	186	3.9	15	28	194	6.9	1
Tony Baker	68-75	536	2087	3.9	15	82	685	8.4	2
Pete Banaszak	66-77	921	3635	3.9	47	114	944	8.3	5
Warren Bankston	69-77	167	684	4.1	3	38	283	7.4	2
Jerome Barkum	72-77	3	-3	-1.0	0	168	2691	16.0	23
Steve Bartkowski	75-77	40	18	0.5	3				
Brian Baschnagel	76-77	2	-12	-6.0	0	17	276	16.2	0
Bubba Bean	76	124	428	3.5	2	16	148	9.3	1
John Beasley	67-70,72-74					151	1607	10.6	13
Terry Beasley	72,74-75	2	2	1.0	0	38	570	15.0	3
Tom Beer	67-72					65	1012	15.6	4
Jim Beirne	68-76	1	3	3.0	0	142	2011	14.2	11
Eddie Bell	70-76	3	-12	-4.0	0	118	1774	15.0	12
Gordon Bell	76-77	83	296	3.6	2	29	231	8.0	0
Ricky Bell	77	148	436	2.9	1	11	88	8.0	0
Willie Belton	71-74	78	306	3.9	1	4	21	5.3	0
Bob Berry	65-76	109	409	3.8	4				
Jim Bertelsen	72-76	614	2466	4.0	16	88	1014	11.5	2
James Betterson	77	62	233	3.8	1	4	41	10.3	0
Fred Biletnikoff	65-77					569	8689	15.3	74
Hank Bjorklund	72-74	60	171	2.9	0	8	84	10.5	0
Rocky Bleier	68,71-77	593	2457	4.1	13	67	675	10.1	0
Glen Bonner	74-75	94	319	3.4	3	13	109	8.4	1
Emerson Boozer	66-75	1291	5135	4.0	52	139	1488	10.7	12
Mike Boryla	74-76	43	224	5.2	2				
Lee Bouggess	70-71,73	271	697	2.6	5	78	589	7.6	3
Morris Bradshaw	74-77	2	-1	-0.5	0	13	295	22.7	5
Terry Bradshaw	70-77	308	1795	5.8	27				
Cliff Branch	72-77	6	35	5.8	0	212	3967	18.7	43
Jim Braxton	71-77	691	2769	4.0	23	135	1388	10.3	6
Marlin Briscoe	68-76	49	336	6.9	3	224	3537	15.8	30
John Brockington	71-77	1347	5185	3.8	30	157	1297	8.3	4
Billy Brooks	76-77	3	-17	-5.7	0	55	963	17.5	4
Bob Brown	69-73	1	8	8.0	0	28	448	16.0	1
Ken Brown	70-75	346	1193	3.4	7	58	468	8.1	2
Larry Brown	69-76	1530	5875	3.8	35	238	2485	10.4	20
Larry Brown	71-77					47	635	13.5	4
Bob Brunet	68,70-73,75-77	131	406	3.1	3	24	200	8.3	1
Larry Brunson	74-77	12	63	5.3	0	98	1723	17.6	5
Cullen Bryant	73-77	154	597	3.9	4	28	299	10.7	0
Hubie Bryant	70-72	7	26	3.7	0	22	366	16.6	1
Danny Buggs	75-77	1	0	0.0	0	28	366	13.1	1
Norm Bulaich	70-77	765	3129	4.1	26	200	2621	13.1	10
Steve Burks	75-77	1	2	2.0	0	13	264	20.3	0
Bob Burns	74	40	158	4.0	0	11	83	7.5	1
Leon Burns	71-72	87	292	3.4	3	9	44	4.9	0
Ken Burrough	70-77	14	74	5.3	1	290	4967	17.1	34
Ken Burrow	71-75	6	25	4.2	0	152	2668	17.6	21
Larry Burton	75-77	5	4	0.8	0	35	615	17.6	4
Dexter Bussey	74-77	447	1914	4.3	9	57	533	9.4	3
Bill Butler	72-74	162	655	4.0	1	46	354	7.7	4
J.V. Cain	74-77					76	1014	13.3	9
Don Calhoun	74-77	390	1720	4.4	6	32	329	10.3	1
Sonny Campbell	70-71	57	195	3.4	2	10	132	13.2	0
John Cappelletti	74-77	458	1642	3.6	12	64	565	8.8	2
Harold Carmichael	71-77	6	42	7.0	0	300	4136	13.8	38
Rob Carpenter	77	144	652	4.5	1	23	156	6.8	0
Roger Carr	74-77					98	2233	22.8	14
Louis Carter	75-77	231	665	2.9	3	32	239	7.5	0
Virgil Carter	68-73,75-76	109	640	5.9	8				
Dave Casper	74-77	1	5	5.0	0	110	1372	12.5	20
Rich Caster	70-77	13	65	5.0	0	245	4434	18.1	36
Al Chandler	73-74,76-77					13	126	9.7	3
Bob Chandler	71-77	11	18	1.6	0	251	3418	13.6	29
Wes Chesson	71-74	1	-4	-4.0	0	40	598	15.0	2
Ray Chester	70-77	5	9	1.8	0	252	3696	14.7	33
Henry Childs	74-77	1	16	16.0	0	69	1046	15.2	12
Booby Clark	73-77	739	2791	3.8	25	140	1066	7.6	2
Vin Clements	72-73	103	435	4.2	1	24	247	10.3	1
Ronnie Coleman	74-77	583	1327	2.3	13	84	500	6.0	4
Mike Collier	75-77	52	240	4.6	3	4	30	7.5	0
Sonny Collins	76-77	91	319	3.5	0	4	37	9.3	0
Bruce Coslet	69-76	1	1	1.0	0	61	878	14.4	9
Craig Cotton	69-73,75					28	409	14.6	1
Steve Craig	74-77					14	141	10.1	1
Larry Csonka	68-74,76-77	1580	6933	4.4	46	83	672	8.1	3
Bennie Cunningham	76-77					25	396	15.8	3
Doug Cunningham	67-74	406	1515	3.7	10	137	1171	8.5	0
Sam Cunningham	73-77	932	3832	4.1	26	138	1280	9.3	6
Pat Curran	69-77	30	127	4.2	0	97	1174	12.1	3
Isaac Curtis	73-77	19	71	3.7	0	180	3524	19.6	34
Anthony Davis	77	95	297	3.1	1	8	91	11.4	0

Name	Years	RUSHING Att.	Yards	Avg.	TD	RECEIVING Rec.	Yards	Avg.	TD
Bob Davis	67-73	52	332	6.4	2				
Charlie Davis	74-76	113	482	4.3	1	22	203	9.2	0
Clarence Davis	71-77	790	3636	4.6	25	95	841	8.9	2
Dave Davis	71-74	2	0	0.0	0	11	192	17.5	1
Dick Davis	70	27	94	3.5	0	4	29	7.3	0
Gary Davis	76-77	157	693	4.4	3	26	159	6.1	1
Harrison Davis	74	2	-7	-3.5	0	18	432	24.0	2
Sonny Davis	71-72	47	163	3.5	1	11	46	4.2	0
Steve Davis	72-76	322	1305	4.1	9	33	301	9.1	2
Tony Davis	76-77	63	259	4.1	3	13	112	8.6	0
Joe Dawkins	70-76	698	2661	3.8	13	145	1316	9.1	3
Jack DeGrenier	74	33	110	3.3	0	4	13	3.3	0
Doug Dennison	74-77	292	1037	3.6	18	13	104	8.0	0
Moses Denson	74-75	159	586	3.7	0	39	255	6.5	2
Lynn Dickey	71,73-77	27	66	2.4	1				
Chuck Dicus	71-72	2	-13	-6.5	0	24	316	13.2	3
Al Dodd	67,69-71,73-74	9	50	5.6	0	111	1803	16.2	3
Jack Dolbin	75-77	9	89	9.9	0	67	1218	18.2	7
Marty Domres	69-77	130	679	5.2	10				
Mike Donohoe	68,70-71,73-74					10	106	10.6	2
Tony Dorsett	77	208	1007	4.8	12	29	273	9.4	1
Larry Dorsey	76-77	1	-12	-12.0	0	18	306	17.0	2
Glenn Doughty	72-77	25	203	8.1	0	159	2637	16.6	19
Bobby Douglass	69-77	406	2627	6.5	22	1	-2	-2.0	0
Doug Dressler	70-72,74-75	278	1125	4.0	9	90	695	7.7	2
Jimmy DuBose	76-77	91	346	3.8	0	16	115	7.2	0
Bobby Duhon	68,70-72	221	840	3.8	4	68	717	10.5	1
Jubilee Dunbar	73-74	3	3	1.0	0	29	521	18.0	4
Billy Joe DuPree	73-77	17	107	6.3	0	137	2023	14.8	15
Robin Earl	77	56	235	4.2	1	6	32	5.3	0
Cid Edwards	68-75	698	3006	4.3	15	144	1491	10.4	4
Monroe Eley	75,77	98	276	2.8	1	9	60	6.7	0
Lenvil Elliott	73-77	295	1320	4.5	3	90	821	9.1	9
Willie Ellison	67-74	801	3426	4.3	24	104	888	8.5	6
Bill Enyart	69-71	105	387	3.7	1	54	421	7.8	3
Mike Esposito	76-77	94	418	4.4	2	18	87	4.8	0
Charlie Evans	71-74	205	644	3.1	12	54	470	8.7	1
George Farmer	70-75	4	6	1.5	0	119	1995	16.8	10
Mel Farr	67-73	739	3072	4.2	26	146	1374	9.4	10
Duke Fergerson	77					19	374	19.7	2
Joe Ferguson	73-77	184	700	3.8	7	1	-3	-3.0	0
Bob Ferrell	76-77	50	188	3.8	2	3	21	7.0	0
Jamie Ford	71-72	104	407	3.9	2	8	63	7.9	0
Chuck Foreman	73-77	1209	4915	4.1	45	256	2514	9.8	21
Ike Forte	76-77	87	257	3.0	3	11	97	8.8	1
Eddie Foster	77					15	208	13.9	0
Dan Fouts	73-77	73	343	4.7	3				
Russ Francis	75-77	2	12	6.0	0	77	1232	16.0	11
Wallace Francis	73-77	6	18	3.0	0	41	684	16.7	5
Stan Fritts	75-76	141	575	4.1	11	15	138	9.2	2
Jean Fugett	72-77	7	38	5.4	0	121	1775	14.7	18
John Fuqua	69-76	719	3031	4.2	21	135	1247	9.2	3
Clark Gaines	76-77	315	1319	4.2	6	96	869	9.1	3
Lawrence Gaines	76	155	659	4.3	4	23	130	5.7	1
Tony Galbreath	76-77	304	1214	4.0	10	95	685	7.2	1
Reuben Gant	74-77					62	1016	16.4	7
Carl Garrett	69-77	1031	4197	4.1	28	182	1931	10.6	7
Reggie Garrett	74-75					13	178	13.7	1
Gary Garrison	66-77	12	29	2.4	0	405	7538	18.6	58
Walt Garrison	66-74	899	3886	4.3	30	182	1794	9.9	9
Tom Geredine	73-74,76	2	5	2.5	0	17	323	19.0	2
Louie Giammona	76	39	150	3.8	1	15	145	9.7	0
Jim Giles	77	1	-10	-10.0	0	17	147	8.6	0
Walker Gillette	70-76	1	-4	-4.0	0	153	2291	15.0	12
John Gilliam	67-77	35	293	8.4	2	382	7056	18.5	48
Hubert Ginn	70-77	132	521	3.9	3	9	49	5.4	0
Paul Gipson	69-71,73	123	491	4.0	1	21	240	11.4	3
Bob Gladieux	69-72	65	239	3.7	0	25	252	10.1	0
Chip Glass	69-74					34	642	18.9	5
Leland Glass	72-73	2	13	6.5	0	26	380	14.6	1
Les Goodman	73-74	38	189	5.0	1	7	38	5.4	0
Dick Gordon	65-74	15	90	6.0	0	243	3594	14.8	36
Ken Grandberry	74	144	475	3.3	2	30	212	7.1	0
Frank Grant	73-77	5	27	5.4	0	135	2282	16.9	18
Mel Gray	71-77	4	61	15.3	0	211	4273	20.3	38
Woody Green	74-76	375	1442	3.8	9	58	562	9.7	2
Bob Gresham	71-76	410	1360	3.3	12	90	728	8.1	1
Bob Griese	67-77	240	954	4.0	7				
Archie Griffin	76-77	275	1174	4.3	3	44	378	8.6	0
Bob Grim	67-77	8	137	17.1	0	194	2914	15.0	16
Steve Grogan	75-77	151	831	5.5	16				
Randy Grossman	74-77					49	537	11.0	2
Pat Haden	76-77	54	190	3.5	6				
Isaac Hagins	76-77	1	2	2.0	0	15	196	13.1	0
Andy Hamilton	73-75					16	270	16.9	0
Bob Hammond	76-77	154	577	3.7	3	19	136	7.2	0
Dave Hampton	69-76	1148	4538	4.0	25	119	1156	9.7	6
Don Hardeman	75-77	240	924	3.9	8	23	82	3.6	1
Clarence Harmon	77	94	310	3.3	0	14	119	8.5	1
Steve Harkey	71-72	65	191	2.9	0	14	142	10.1	0
Bruce Harper	77	44	198	4.5	0	21	209	10.0	1
Roland Harper	75-77	367	1535	4.2	3	75	622	8.3	1
Charlie Harraway	66-73	822	3019	3.7	20	158	1304	8.3	7
Will Harrell	75-77	311	934	3.0	5	70	656	9.4	3
Duriel Harris	76-77					56	973	17.4	6

Lifetime Statistics – 1970–1977 Players Section 2 – **RUSHING and RECEIVING** (Continued)
(All men with 25 or more rushing attempts or 10 or more receptions)

		RUSHING				RECEIVING			
Name	**Years**	**Att.**	**Yards**	**Avg.**	**TD**	**Rec.**	**Yards**	**Avg.**	**TD**
Franco Harris	72-77	1435	6295	4.4	53	116	876	7.6	3
Ike Harris	75-77					107	1595	14.9	4
James Harris	69-71,73-77	105	334	3.2	10				
Leroy Harris	77	91	417	4.6	4	7	29	4.1	0
Dwight Harrison	71-77	6	45	7.5	0	20	281	14.1	2
Kenny Harrison	76-77	6	15	2.5	0	18	282	15.7	1
Reggie Harrison	74-77	139	631	4.5	8	7	36	5.1	0
Harold Hart	74-75,77	107	441	4.1	5	7	31	4.4	0
Jim Hart	66-77	122	166	1.4	14				
Sam Havrilak	69-74	73	289	4.0	3	51	761	14.9	4
Bob Hayes	65-75	24	68	2.8	2	371	7414	20.0	71
Don Herrmann	69-77	4	-8	-2.0	0	234	3039	13.0	16
Mack Herron	73-75	354	1298	3.7	9	61	789	12.9	6
Don Highsmith	70-73	94	327	3.5	2	12	143	11.9	0
Calvin Hill	69-74,76-77	1314	5567	4.2	40	164	1613	9.8	7
David Hill	76-77	4	10	2.5	0	51	714	14.0	7
Ike Hill	70-71,73-74,76	3	-14	-4.7	0	22	283	12.9	2
J.D. Hill	71-77	3	14	4.7	0	185	2880	15.6	21
Eddie Hinton	69-74	12	110	9.2	2	111	1822	16.4	10
Paul Hofer	76-77	52	180	3.5	0	9	91	10.1	0
Mike Hogan	76-77	278	1107	4.0	0	34	207	6.1	1
Steve Holden	73-77	3	2	0.7	0	62	927	15.0	4
John Holland	74-77					35	634	18.1	3
Ron Holliday	73	6	70	11.7	0	14	182	13.0	0
Mike Holmes	74-76					17	231	13.6	1
Robert Holmes	68-73,75	639	2510	3.9	23	113	982	8.7	4
Dennis Homan	68-72	2	-3	-1.5	0	37	619	16.7	2
Fair Hooker	69-74					129	1845	14.3	8
Jim Hooks	73-76	67	245	3.7	0	11	64	5.8	0
Roland Hooks	76-77	153	613	4.0	0	22	267	12.1	0
Rich Houston	69-73	3	13	4.3	0	65	1121	17.2	7
Ron Howard	74-77	1	2	2.0	0	54	599	11.1	1
Marv Hubbard	69-75,77	951	4544	4.8	23	85	628	7.4	1
Gary Huff	73-77	47	76	1.6	2				
Dennis Hughes	70-71	1	-4	-4.0	0	24	332	13.8	3
Mike Hull	68-74	77	207	2.7	1	29	127	4.4	0
Al Hunter	77	32	179	5.6	1	5	42	8.4	0
Scott Hunter	71-74,76-77	93	201	2.2	12				
John Isenbarger	70-73	27	80	3.0	0	21	291	13.9	2
Harold Jackson	68-77	40	139	3.5	0	415	7084	17.1	57
Jazz Jackson	74-76	27	91	3.4	0	9	101	11.2	1
Randy Jackson	72-74	30	70	2.3	0	15	58	3.9	1
Wilbur Jackson	74-77	631	2580	4.1	8	95	811	8.5	3
Po James	72-75	328	1215	3.7	4	102	747	7.3	2
Ray Jarvis	71-77	2	13	6.5	0	101	1793	17.8	10
Ron Jaworski	74-77	61	209	3.4	9				
Roy Jefferson	65-76	25	188	7.5	0	451	7539	16.7	52
Al Jenkins	75-77	2	7	3.5	0	118	2144	18.2	16
Jim Jensen	76-77	40	143	3.6	1	4	63	15.8	0
Ron Jessie	71-77	18	100	5.6	2	186	3101	16.7	19
Andy Johnson	74-76	288	1183	4.1	9	63	784	12.4	5
Billy Johnson	74-77	22	207	9.4	2	133	1688	12.7	10
Butch Johnson	76-77	1	-3	-3.0	0	17	219	12.9	3
Essex Johnson	68-76	722	3236	4.5	19	146	1742	11.9	12
Kermit Johnson	75-76	36	124	3.4	1	1	11	11.0	0
Pete Johnson	77	153	585	3.8	4	5	49	9.8	0
Randy Johnson	66-73,75-76	114	573	5.0	10				
Ron Johnson	69-75	1203	4307	3.6	40	213	1977	9.3	15
Sammy Johnson	74-77	195	789	4.0	9	45	378	8.4	0
Charlie Joiner	69-77	7	34	4.9	0	249	4541	18.2	31
Andrew Jones	75-76	43	110	2.6	1	10	52	5.2	0
Bert Jones	73-77	170	1018	6.0	8				
Clint Jones	67-73	602	2178	3.6	20	38	431	11.3	0
Greg Jones	70-71	47	166	3.5	1	24	202	8.4	1
Jimmie Jones	74	32	147	4.6	1	4	35	8.8	0
Steve Jones	73-77	195	812	4.2	13	60	412	6.9	2
Rick Kane	77	124	421	3.4	4	18	186	10.3	0
Vince Kendrick	74,76	18	74	4.1	0	12	86	7.2	1
Leroy Keyes	69-73	125	369	3.0	3	30	270	9.0	0
Jon Keyworth	74-77	468	1759	3.8	17	87	672	7.7	2
Jim Kiick	68-74,76-77	1029	3759	3.7	29	233	2302	9.9	4
John Kimbrough	77					10	207	20.7	2
Horace King	75-77	309	1106	3.6	3	74	482	6.5	0
Jeff Kinney	72-76	353	1285	3.6	5	68	502	7.4	1
Bob Klein	69-77	4	14	3.5	0	148	1850	12.5	16
David Knight	73-77					73	1189	16.3	7
Gary Kosins	72-74	35	100	2.9	1	7	26	3.7	1
Doug Kotar	74-77	545	1985	3.6	15	70	535	7.6	0
Ted Koy	70-74	1	9	9.0	0	11	142	12.9	1
Kent Kramer	66-67,69-74					45	576	12.8	8
Keith Krepfle	75-77					34	626	18.4	4
Ted Kwalick	69-77	19	175	9.2	0	168	2570	15.3	23
Scott Laidlaw	75-77	106	449	4.2	3	54	485	9.0	2
Ron Lamb	68-69,71-72	49	128	2.6	0	8	97	12.1	0
Greg Landry	68-77	384	2473	6.4	19				
Mac Arthur Lane	68-77	1154	4379	3.8	30	251	2507	10.0	7
Steve Largent	76-77	4	-14	-3.5	0	87	1348	15.5	14
Jim Lash	73-77	3	5	1.7	0	91	1464	16.1	3
Jerry Latin	75-77	116	488	4.2	4	15	149	9.9	0
Greg Latta	75-77	2	-8	-4.0	0	60	791	13.2	7
Odell Lawson	70-71,73-74	70	130	1.9	0	13	108	8.3	0
Roger Lawson	72-73	57	176	3.1	1	17	180	10.6	0
Roosevelt Leaks	75-77	218	857	3.9	11	12	87	7.3	1
Bob Lee	69-77	87	203	2.3	3				
Ron Lee	76-77	125	566	4.5	4	11	51	4.6	0

		RUSHING				RECEIVING			
Name	**Years**	**Att.**	**Yards**	**Avg.**	**TD**	**Rec.**	**Yards**	**Avg.**	**TD**
Billy LeFear	72-75	35	143	4.1	0	10	73	7.3	0
Charlie Leigh	68-69,71-74	72	372	5.2	2	9	-4	-0.4	0
Jerry LeVias	69-74	19	161	8.5	0	144	2139	14.9	14
Frank Lewis	71-77	10	152	15.2	1	128	2086	16.3	16
Floyd Little	67-75	1641	6323	3.9	43	215	2712	12.6	9
Mike Livingston	68-77	130	631	4.9	6				
Dave Logan	76-77					24	388	16.2	1
Kevin Long	77	56	170	3.0	0	5	17	3.4	0
Herb Lusk	76-77	113	483	4.3	2	18	221	12.3	1
Fran Lynch	67-75	304	1258	4.1	12	35	357	10.2	2
Bob Lytle	77	104	408	3.9	1	17	198	11.6	1
Jack Maitland	70-72	100	267	2.7	2	14	106	7.6	1
Bill Malinchak	66-76					35	508	14.5	4
Art Malone	70-76	635	2457	3.9	19	161	1465	9.1	6
Benny Malone	74-77	497	2111	4.2	15	17	234	13.8	0
Jim Mandich	70-77					121	1406	11.6	23
Archie Manning	71-77	259	1476	5.7	15	1	-7	-7.0	0
Gary Marangi	74-77	50	328	6.6	2				
Ed Marinaro	72-77	383	1319	3.4	4	146	1176	8.1	7
Ed Marshall	71,76-77					17	362	21.3	3
Henry Marshall	76-77	12	111	9.3	1	51	888	17.4	6
Bill Masters	67-76	18	114	6.3	0	169	2268	13.4	15
Bo Matthews	74-77	255	974	3.8	10	36	271	7.5	0
Alvin Maxson	74-77	356	1261	3.5	6	95	619	6.5	1
James McAlister	75-76	171	600	3.5	1	29	206	7.1	2
Don McCauley	71-77	672	2182	3.2	31	174	1495	8.6	8
Cliff McClain	70-73	79	445	5.6	2	13	151	11.6	0
Brent McClanahan	73-77	343	1152	3.4	6	95	704	7.4	4
Earl McCullough	68-74	8	29	3.6	0	124	2319	18.7	19
Sam McCullum	74-77					50	867	17.3	8
Lawrence McCutcheon	72-77	1244	5523	4.4	23	153	1506	9.8	10
John McDaniel	74-77	2	3	1.5	0	26	459	17.7	1
Dwight McDonald	75-77					43	633	14.7	7
Willie McGee	73-77	4	9	2.3	0	24	446	18.6	4
Rich McGeorge	70-77	1	3	3.0	0	152	2123	14.0	12
Pat McInally	76-77	1	4	4.0	0	17	258	15.2	3
John McKay	76-77					32	466	14.6	1
Hugh McKinnis	73-76	269	960	3.6	10	65	572	8.8	0
John McMakin	72-76	1	0	0.0	0	45	673	15.0	4
Rod McNeill	74-76	110	428	3.9	3	30	235	7.8	2
Leon McQuay	74-76	88	287	3.3	1	9	86	9.6	0
Warren McVea	68-71,73	248	1186	4.8	11	38	358	9.4	2
Terry Metcalf	73-77	748	3438	4.6	24	196	1854	9.5	9
Terdell Middleton	77	35	97	2.8	0	1	27	27.0	0
Cleo Miller	74-77	369	1578	4.3	9	73	605	8.3	1
Robert Miller	75-77	143	531	3.7	1	54	462	8.6	1
Jim Mitchell	69-77	26	187	7.2	1	257	3874	15.1	24
Lydell Mitchell	72-77	1391	5487	3.9	27	298	2528	8.5	14
Tom Mitchell	66,68-77	3	14	4.7	0	239	3181	13.3	24
Mike Montgomery	71-74	96	291	3.1	2	59	835	14.2	7
Ross Montgomery	69-70	77	281	3.6	0	16	83	5.2	0
Wilbert Montgomery	77	45	183	4.1	2	3	18	6.0	0
Bob Moore	71-77	2	23	11.5	0	115	1270	11.0	7
Joe Moore	71,73	87	281	3.2	0	8	39	7.8	0
Nat Moore	74-77	29	210	7.2	1	162	2700	16.7	22
Emery Moorehead	77	1	5	5.0	0	12	143	11.9	1
Stanley Morgan	77	1	10	10.0	0	21	443	21.1	3
Milt Morin	66-75	5	41	8.2	0	271	4208	15.5	16
Mercury Morris	69-76	804	4133	5.1	31	54	543	10.1	1
Wayne Morris	76-77	229	953	4.2	11	32	297	9.3	2
Reece Morrison	68-73	160	526	3.3	2	14	210	15.0	2
Craig Morton	65-77	146	496	3.2	10				
Haven Moses	68-77	18	43	2.4	1	304	5484	18.0	40
Roland Moss	69-71					11	155	14.1	1
Herb Mul-Key	72-74	42	178	4.2	1	4	66	16.5	0
Chuck Muncie	76-77	350	1470	4.2	8	52	520	10.0	1
Bill Munson	64-77	130	548	4.2	3	1	-6	-6.0	0
Johnny Musso	75-77	100	365	3.7	6	7	39	5.6	0
Chip Myers	67,69-76					220	3092	14.1	12
Joe Namath	65-77	71	140	2.0	7				
Lou Neal	73-74	1	-1	-1.0	0	13	230	17.7	1
Ralph Nelson	75-76	83	312	3.8	1	17	154	9.1	1
Terry Nelson	74-77	4	34	8.5	0	36	454	12.6	3
Robert Newhouse	72-77	741	3154	4.3	13	84	629	7.5	2
Bob Newland	71-74	1	6	6.0	0	124	1877	15.1	0
Kent Nix	67-72	43	145	3.4	2				
George Nock	69-72	192	556	2.9	8	24	190	7.9	3
Don Nottingham	71-77	611	2496	4.1	34	67	502	7.5	0
Jack Novak	75-77					12	188	15.7	1
Jim O'Bradovich	75-77					10	92	9.2	1
Jim O'Brien	70-73	3	9	3.0	0	14	305	21.8	2
Steve Odom	74-77	16	205	12.8	1	80	1553	19.4	10
Riley Odoms	72-77	22	213	9.7	2	213	2038	9.6	23
Bill Olds	73-76	287	985	3.4	6	62	372	6.0	4
Joe Orduna	72-74	74	236	3.2	3	11	58	5.3	1
Dave Osborn	65-76	1179	4436	3.7	29	173	1412	8.2	7
Jim Otis	70-77	963	3686	3.8	11	82	511	6.2	3
Morris Owens	75-77	4	0	0.0	0	64	1045	16.3	9
Steve Owens	70-74	635	2451	3.9	20	99	861	8.7	2
Tinker Owens	76					12	241	20.1	1
Joel Parker	74-75,77	2	2	1.0	0	51	585	11.5	6
Billy Parks	71-75	5	77	15.4	0	123	1826	14.8	7
Gary Parris	73-77					30	334	11.1	5
Bob Parsons	72-77	3	4	1.3	0	19	231	12.2	4
Don Pastorini	71-77	171	622	3.6	8				

Lifetime Statistics – 1970–1977 Players   Section 2 – **RUSHING and RECEIVING** (Continued)
(All men with 25 or more rushing attempts or 10 or more receptions)

		RUSHING				RECEIVING			
Name	**Years**	**Att.**	**Yards**	**Avg.**	**TD**	**Rec.**	**Yards**	**Avg.**	**TD**
Lloyd Pate	70	46	162	3.1	1	19	103	5.4	0
Wayne Patrick	68-72	264	1084	4.1	5	96	745	7.8	1
Ken Payne	74-77	1	-2	-2.0	0	103	1395	13.5	5
Walter Payton	75-77	846	3921	4.6	34	75	631	8.4	2
Barry Pearson	72-76	1	1	1.0	0	86	1212	14.1	7
Drew Pearson	73-77	8	59	7.4	0	236	3973	16.8	20
Preston Pearson	67-77	906	3485	3.8	12	161	2023	12.6	14
Johnny Perkins	77					20	279	14.0	0
Lonnie Perrin	76-77	147	564	3.8	5	10	141	14.1	1
Jess Phillips	68-77	888	3568	4.0	13	114	694	6.1	2
Rod Phillips	75-77	88	458	5.2	2	7	38	5.6	0
Mike Phipps	70-77	198	1155	5.8	11				
Lou Piccone	74-77	2	17	8.5	0	36	466	12.9	2
Cyril Pinder	68-73	428	1709	4.0	7	67	556	8.3	0
Joe Pisarcik	77	27	57	2.1	2				
Frank Pitts	68-75	28	257	9.2	1	175	2897	16.6	27
Jim Plunkett	71-77	206	983	4.8	10				
Ed Podolak	69-77	1157	4451	3.8	34	288	2456	8.5	6
Larry Poole	75-77	133	588	4.4	2	32	212	6.6	3
Billy Joe Pritchett	75-77	92	290	3.2	1	17	110	6.5	0
Joe Profit	71-73	133	471	3.5	3	14	130	9.3	0
Greg Pruitt	73-77	849	4062	4.8	22	156	1495	9.6	5
Mike Pruitt	76-77	99	343	3.5	1	11	38	3.5	0
Jeff Queen	69-74	178	596	3.3	5	54	658	12.2	5
Steve Ramsey	70-76	33	108	3.3	2				
Ahmad Rashad	72-74,76-77	9	44	4.9	0	199	2694	13.5	15
Bo Rather	73-77	9	46	5.1	0	90	1412	15.7	7
Eddie Ray	70-74,76	181	691	3.8	9	33	275	8.3	2
Tommy Reamon	76	103	314	3.0	4	10	136	13.6	1
John Reaves	72-77	32	132	4.1	3				
Alvin Reed	67-75	1	0	0.0	0	214	2983	13.9	14
Joe Reed	72-77	81	473	5.8	2				
Oscar Reed	68-75	504	2008	4.0	8	94	677	7.2	3
Tony Reed	77	126	505	4.0	2	12	125	10.4	0
Tom Reynolds	72-73					15	279	18.6	2
Ray Rhodes	74-77	6	0	0.0	0	51	980	19.2	7
Golden Richards	73-77	5	15	3.0	0	89	1648	18.5	16
Gloster Richardson	67-74	5	-8	-1.8	0	92	1976	21.5	18
Mike Richardson	69-71	125	452	3.6	2	38	398	10.5	1
John Riggins	71-77	1158	4655	4.0	28	156	1429	9.2	9
Preston Riley	70-72					21	331	15.8	1
Oscar Roan	75-77					69	773	11.2	9
Jim Robinson	76-77					40	671	16.8	4
Paul Robinson	68-73	737	2947	4.0	24	90	612	6.8	2
Virgil Robinson	71-72	34	97	2.9	1	12	53	4.4	1
Johnny Rodgers	77	3	44	14.7	0	12	187	15.6	0
Willie Rogers	72-75	211	672	3.2	8	30	214	7.1	0
Oliver Ross	73-76	63	173	2.7	0	10	104	10.4	0
Reggie Rucker	70-77	10	54	5.4	0	282	4123	14.6	25
Jay Saldi	76-77					12	114	9.5	2
Charlie Sanders	68-77	4	-6	-1.5	0	336	4817	14.3	31
John Sawyer	75-77					35	457	13.1	2
Sam Scarber	75-76	76	304	4.0	2	26	164	6.3	2
Larry Schreiber	71-76	506	1749	3.5	10	117	982	8.4	4
Steve Schubert	74-77					18	282	15.7	1
Bo Scott	69-74	554	2124	3.8	18	112	826	7.4	7
Bobby Scott	73-77	26	78	3.0	1				
Freddie Scott	74-77	2	12	6.0	0	39	619	15.9	2
James Scott	76-77	2	-4	-2.0	0	76	1321	17.4	9
Rob Scribner	73-76	73	361	4.9	3	6	75	12.5	1
Paul Seal	74-77	5	10	2.0	1	82	1182	14.4	5
Larry Seiple	67-77	15	145	9.7	0	73	934	12.8	7
Ron Sellers	69-73					112	2184	19.5	18
Jim Seymour	70-72	1	-9	-9.0	0	21	385	18.3	5
Paul Seymour	73-77					62	818	13.2	3
Ron Shanklin	70-76	5	2	0.4	0	168	3079	18.3	24
Dennis Shaw	70-76	95	420	4.4	0				
Rod Sherman	67-73	4	20	5.0	0	105	1576	15.0	5
Gary Shirk	76-77					20	332	16.6	3
Don Shy	67-73	457	1577	3.5	10	76	835	11.0	3
Mike Siani	72-77					128	2079	16.2	13
Nate Simpson	77	60	204	3.4	0	5	19	3.8	0
O.J. Simpson	69-77	2123	10183	4.8	57	175	1924	11.0	12
David Sims	77	99	369	3.7	5	12	176	14.7	3
Brian Sipe	74-77	53	189	3.6	4				
Barry Smith	73-76	10	24	2.4	0	46	692	15.0	4
Barty Smith	74-77	332	1171	3.5	11	64	568	8.9	2
Charlie Smith	68-75	858	3351	3.9	24	141	1596	11.3	10
Charlie Smith	74-77	20	123	6.2	1	98	1419	14.5	14
Dave Smith	70-73	2	-4	-2.0	0	109	1457	13.4	7
Jerry Smith	65-77	8	56	7.0	0	421	5496	13.1	60
Larry Smith	69-74	528	2027	3.3	11	149	1176	7.9	5
Ollie Smith	73-74,76-77	1	-3	-3.0	0	44	772	17.5	1
Ron Smith	65-74	8	42	5.3	0	11	227	20.6	0
Sherman Smith	76-77	282	1307	4.6	8	66	803	12.2	3
Jack Snow	65-75	2	3	1.5	0	340	6012	17.7	45
Todd Snyder	70-72					24	330	13.8	2
Freddie Solomon	75-77	14	190	13.6	1	61	973	16.0	5
Willie Spencer	76-77	66	186	2.8	3	4	20	5.0	0
Cotton Speyrer	72-75	1	1	1.0	0	34	535	15.7	5
John Spilis	69-71					27	446	16.5	1
Steve Spurrier	67-76	61	258	4.2	2				
Ken Stabler	70-77	60	141	2.4	3				
Jon Staggers	70-75	8	56	7.0	1	93	1370	14.7	7

		RUSHING				RECEIVING			
Name	**Years**	**Att.**	**Yards**	**Avg.**	**TD**	**Rec.**	**Yards**	**Avg.**	**TD**
John Stallworth	74-77	7	85	11.1	0	89	1587	17.8	14
Haskel Stanback	74-77	554	1872	3.4	15	73	589	8.1	1
Roger Staubach	69-77	331	1910	5.8	19	1	-13	-13.0	0
Howard Stevens	73-77	89	376	4.2	4	17	120	7.1	0
Wayne Stewart	74					19	283	14.9	1
Darryl Stingley	73-77	28	244	8.7	2	110	1883	17.1	14
Mike Strachan	75-77	282	1197	4.2	4	39	272	7.0	0
Otto Stowe	71-74	4	29	7.3	0	43	742	17.3	10
Jim Strong	70-72	134	527	3.9	3	30	201	6.7	0
Morris Stroud	69-74					54	977	18.1	7
Tom Sullivan	72-77	871	3135	3.6	17	161	1266	7.9	5
Lynn Swann	74-77	7	35	5.0	0	138	2294	16.6	23
Joe Sweet	72-75	1	1	1.0	0	10	173	17.3	1
Jerry Tagge	72-74	41	117	2.9	3				
John Tarver	72-75	162	562	3.5	7	34	214	6.3	1
Altie Taylor	69-76	1170	4308	3.7	24	175	1538	8.8	6
Charley Taylor	64-75,77	442	1488	3.4	11	649	9110	14.0	79
Otis Taylor	65-75	30	161	5.4	3	410	7306	17.8	57
Don Testerman	76-77	186	705	3.8	2	56	461	8.2	5
Jim Thaxton	73-74,76,77	2	-13	-6.5	0	32	513	16.0	4
Joe Theismann	74-77	52	292	5.6	3				
Bob Thomas	71-74	120	537	4.5	3	19	155	8.2	1
Duane Thomas	70-71,72-74	453	2038	4.5	21	38	297	7.8	3
Earl Thomas	71-76	6	18	3.0	0	106	1651	15.6	14
Jimmy Thomas	69-73	165	824	5.0	4	67	923	13.8	8
Mike Thomas	75-77	717	2826	3.9	12	96	1018	10.6	9
Speedy Thomas	69-72,74	8	22	2.8	1	19	122	6.4	0
Bobby Thompson	75-76	64	310	4.8	1	29	230	7.9	0
Leonard Thompson	75-77	33	79	2.4	1	10	94	9.4	0
Rocky Thompson	71-73	68	217	3.2	1	16	85	5.3	0
Woody Thompson	75-77	242	877	3.6	1	42	259	6.2	0
Sidney Thornton	77	27	103	3.8	2	1	5	5.0	0
Pat Tilley	76-77					31	471	15.2	1
Andre Tillman	75-77					35	359	10.3	3
Richard Todd	76-77	52	153	2.9	3				
Eric Torkelson	74-77	246	884	3.6	5	38	294	7.7	0
Bob Trumpy	68-77	1	-1	-1.0	0	298	4600	15.4	35
Bob Tucker	70-77	6	6	1.0	1	336	4485	13.3	24
Cecil Turner	68-73	8	13	1.6	0	21	364	17.3	2
Clem Turner	69-72	74	270	3.6	2	21	114	5.4	1
Howard Twilley	66-76					212	3064	14.5	23
Wendell Tyler	77	61	317	5.2	3	1	3	3.0	0
Rick Upchurch	75-77	23	187	8.1	3	42	1021	24.3	5
Mark van Eeghen	74-77	721	3021	4.2	12	48	383	8.0	1
Bill Van Heusen	68-76	13	171	13.2	1	82	1684	20.5	11
Randy Vataha	71-77	6	-2	-0.3	0	188	3164	16.8	23
Stu Voigt	70-77	2	3	1.5	1	158	1728	10.9	15
Billy Waddy	77	2	34	17.0	0	23	355	15.4	1
Charlie Wade	74-75,77	1	-15	-15.0	0	39	683	17.5	1
Harmon Wages	68-71,73	332	1321	4.0	5	85	765	9.0	5
Wesley Walker	77	3	25	8.3	0	35	740	21.1	3
Bob Wallace	68-72	8	45	5.6	0	109	1403	12.9	9
Ward Walsh	71-72	46	165	3.6	0	10	58	5.8	1
Larry Walton	69-74,76	12	101	8.4	1	168	2616	15.6	26
Paul Warfield	64-74,76-77	22	204	9.6	0	427	8565	20.1	85
Gene Washington	67-73					182	3237	17.8	26
Gene Washington	69-77	5	-1	-0.2	0	371	6664	18.0	59
Joe Washington	77	62	217	3.5	0	31	244	7.9	0
Vic Washington	71-76	588	2208	3.8	16	130	1090	8.4	5
Larry Watkins	69-77	448	1711	3.8	12	51	284	5.6	1
Norris Weese	76-77	34	198	5.8	1				
Claxton Welch	69-71,73	26	83	3.2	2	7	21	3.0	0
Terry Wells	74-75	33	139	4.2	0	7	20	2.9	0
Bob West	72-74	2	2	1.0	0	13	230	17.7	2
Charlie White	77	50	151	3.0	1	2	5	2.5	1
Jan White	71-72					25	278	11.1	2
Lee White	68-72	123	389	3.2	0	16	143	8.9	1
Marsh White	75-77	86	313	3.6	2	5	22	4.4	0
Sammie White	76-77	5	-10	-2.0	0	92	1666	18.1	19
Walter White	75-77	4	12	3.0	0	118	2041	17.3	15
Clarence Williams	77	50	215	4.3	2	3	20	6.7	0
Dave Williams	67-73	6	69	11.5	0	183	2768	15.1	25
Del Williams	74-77	669	2966	4.4	20	82	841	10.3	5
Ed Williams	74-77	243	896	3.7	7	56	427	7.6	2
Joe Williams	71-72	52	139	2.7	1	19	175	9.2	0
Perry Williams	69-74	177	547	3.1	1	37	285	7.7	0
Fred Willis	71-76	780	2831	3.6	18	203	1380	6.8	5
Joe Wilson	73-75	25	96	3.8	0	3	38	12.7	0
Tim Wilson	77	99	343	3.5	3	20	107	5.4	0
Bob Windsor	67-75	9	57	6.3	0	185	2307	12.5	14
Stan Winfrey	75-77	55	225	4.1	1	6	55	9.2	1
Al Woodall	69-71,73-74	60	214	3.6	0				
Don Woods	74-77	558	2334	4.2	13	91	892	9.8	5
Elmo Wright	71-75	10	69	6.9	0	70	1116	15.9	6
Sam Wyche	68-72,74,76	45	303	6.7	3	1	5	5.0	0
Charley Young	74-76	131	638	4.9	2	40	391	9.8	2
Charlie Young	73-77	13	69	5.3	1	202	2638	13.1	13
Ricky Young	75-77	457	1922	4.2	13	116	1030	8.9	2
Steve Zabel	70-77	1	-5	-5.0	0	10	123	12.3	3
Don Zimmerman	73-76	1	3	3.0	0	53	601	11.3	5
Jim Zorn	76-77	77	387	5.0	5				

Lifetime Statistics – 1970–1977 Players Section 3 – **PUNT RETURNS and KICKOFF RETURNS**
(All men with 25 or more Punt Returns or 25 or more Kickoff Returns)

		PUNT RETURNS				KICKOFF RETURNS			
Name	Year	No.	Yards	Avg.	TD	No.	Yards	Avg.	TD
Mike Adamle	71-76	1	2	2.0	0	34	636	18.7	0
Margene Adkins	70-73	15	49	3.3	0	81	1784	22.0	0
Bobby Anderson	70-75					30	720	24.0	0
Dick Anderson	68-74,76-77	40	272	6.8	0	7	114	16.3	0
Donny Anderson	66-74	15	222	14.8	1	34	759	22.3	0
Otis Armstrong	73-77					36	858	23.8	0
Pete Athas	71-76	92	818	8.9	0	8	163	20.4	0
Butch Atkinson	68-77	148	1247	8.4	3	76	1893	24.9	0
Lem Barney	67-77	143	1312	9.2	2	50	1274	25.5	1
Brian Baschnagel	76-77	5	56	11.2	0	52	1311	25.2	1
Gordon Bell	76-77	2	1	0.5	0	30	587	19.6	0
Theo Bell	76	39	390	10.0	0				
Willie Belton	71-74	52	283	5.4	0	57	1341	23.5	0
Jim Bertelsen	72-76	74	810	10.9	0	6	120	20.0	0
Lyle Blackwood	73-77	63	318	5.0	0	12	271	22.6	0
Mel Blount	70-77	1	52	52.0	0	35	902	25.8	0
Emerson Boozer	66-75					37	872	23.6	1
Bill Bradley	69-77	122	953	7.8	0	27	564	20.9	0
Dave Brown	75-77	33	291	8.8	0	6	126	21.0	0
Eddie Brown	74-77	115	1166	10.1	1	76	1854	24.4	0
Ken Brown	70-75					44	973	22.1	0
Ray Brown	71-77	60	539	9.0	0				
Larry Brunson	74-77	71	610	8.6	0	24	504	21.0	0
Bobby Bryant	68-77	68	397	5.8	0	22	437	19.9	0
Cullen Bryant	73-77	68	680	10.0	0	66	1760	26.7	3
Hubie Bryant	73-75	19	218	11.5	0	48	1266	26.4	2
Allen Carter	75-76					33	898	27.2	1
Tommy Casanova	72-77	91	794	8.7	1	2	82	41.0	0
Gil Chapman	75	17	207	12.2	0	28	614	21.9	0
Ray Clayborn	77					28	869	31.0	3
Rondy Colbert	75-77	40	310	7.8	1	19	450	23.7	0
Linzy Cole	70-72	35	225	6.4	0	50	1290	25.8	0
Mike Collier	75-77					26	578	22.2	1
Neal Colzie	75-77	121	1437	11.9	0	6	115	19.2	0
Doug Cunningham	67-74	30	272	9.1	0	68	1613	23.7	0
Thom Darden	72-77	45	285	6.3	0				
Ben Davis	67-68,70-76	27	240	8.9	1	35	860	24.6	0
Clarence Davis	71-77					60	1636	27.3	0
Gary Davis	76-77	1	11	11.0	0	40	1031	25.8	0
Steve Davis	72-76					54	1363	25.2	0
Joe Dawkins	70-76	1	0	0.0	0	32	799	25.0	0
Al Dodd	67,69-71,73-74	80	744	9.3	0	38	776	20.4	0
Bobby Duhon	68,70-72	40	286	7.2	1	40	716	17.9	0
Jim Duncan	69-71					42	1369	32.6	2
Lenny Dunlap	71-75	27	291	10.8	0	15	337	22.5	0
Glen Edwards	71-77	99	941	9.5	0	13	257	19.8	0
Ken Ellis	70-77	63	426	6.8	1	41	882	21.5	0
Willie Ellison	67-74					42	1011	24.1	0
Dave Elmendorf	71-77	57	502	8.8	0	2	23	11.5	0
Chris Farasopoulos	71-74	53	481	9.1	1	51	1172	23.0	0
Ricky Feacher	76-77	15	157	10.5	0	35	770	22.0	0
Chris Fletcher	70-76	28	205	7.3	0	28	599	21.4	0
Wallace Francis	73-77					84	2077	24.0	2
Johnny Fuller	68-75	25	114	4.6	0	10	186	18.6	0
Mike Fuller	75-77	97	1206	12.4	2	51	1145	22.5	0
John Fuqua	69-76	12	77	6.4	0	26	496	19.1	0
Ron Gardin	70-71	34	419	12.3	1	25	586	23.4	0
Carl Garrett	69-77	43	487	11.3	0	133	3284	24.7	0
Walt Garrison	66-74					41	813	19.8	0
Tom Geredine	73-74,76					27	611	22.6	0
John Gilliam	67-77	23	94	4.1	0	74	1884	25.5	2
Hubert Ginn	70-77	1	4	4.0	0	50	1105	22.1	0
Dick Gordon	65-74	31	149	4.8	0	79	1925	24.4	0
Johnny Gray	75-77	47	375	8.0	0	2	50	25.0	0
Mel Gray	71-77	9	49	5.4	0	51	1191	23.4	0
Charlie Greer	68-74	55	426	7.7	1	2	41	20.5	0
Bob Gresham	71-76					46	1116	24.3	1
Bob Grim	67-77	59	282	4.8	0	26	549	21.1	0
Bob Hammond	76-77	32	334	10.4	1	21	463	22.0	0
Gary Hammond	73-76	40	291	7.3	0	38	872	22.9	0
Dave Hampton	69-76					113	2923	25.9	3
Bruce Harper	77	34	425	12.5	0	42	1035	24.6	0
Will Harrell	75-77	52	382	7.4	1	6	128	21.3	0
Cliff Harris	70-77	66	418	6.3	0	63	1622	25.7	0
Harold Hart	74-75,77					35	984	28.1	1
Bob Hayes	65-75	104	1158	11.1	3				
Gary Hayman	74-75	27	229	8.5	0	8	179	22.4	0
Mike Haynes	76-77	69	808	11.7	2				
Mack Herron	73-75	84	982	11.7	0	82	1985	24.2	1
Ike Hill	70-71,73-74,76	102	622	6.1	2	21	445	21.2	0
Paul Hofer	76-77					41	962	23.5	0
Steve Holden	73-77	36	238	6.6	0	29	675	23.3	0
Mike Holmes	74-76	9	45	5.0	0	31	761	24.5	0
Robert Holmes	68-75					35	928	26.5	0
Ken Houston	67-77	51	333	6.5	0	3	80	26.7	0
Rich Houston	69-73					35	800	22.9	0
Gene Howard	68-72	22	129	5.9	0	41	975	23.8	0
Bob Hudson	72-74	1	0	0.0	0	25	597	23.9	0
Al Hunter	77					36	820	22.8	0
Bernie Jackson	72-77					96	2298	23.9	0
Po James	72-75					41	962	23.5	0
Dick Jauron	73-77	40	405	10.2	0	19	426	22.4	0
Roy Jefferson	65-76	58	436	7.5	1	5	91	18.2	0
Ron Jessie	71-77					47	1237	26.3	2
Andy Johnson	74-76	6	60	10.0	0	25	491	19.6	0
Benny Johnson	70-73,76					28	550	19.0	0

		PUNT RETURNS				KICKOFF RETURNS			
Name	Years	No.	Yards	Avg.	TD	No.	Yards	Avg.	TD
Billy Johnson	74-77	143	1963	13.7	5	113	2792	24.7	2
Butch Johnson	76-77	95	912	9.6	0	50	1229	24.6	0
Essex Johnson	68-76	51	303	5.9	0	49	1036	21.1	0
Clint Jones	67-73					99	2426	24.5	1
Jimmie Jones	74					38	927	24.4	0
Larry Jones	74-77	62	476	7.7	1	73	1816	24.9	1
Doug Kotar	74-77	4	19	4.8	0	37	830	22.4	0
Larry Krause	70-71,73-75					35	864	24.7	1
Bruce Laird	72-77	60	405	6.8	0	134	3372	25.2	0
Rolland Lawrence	73-77	105	724	6.9	0	29	685	23.6	0
Odell Lawson	70-71,73-74	1	0	0.0	0	28	613	21.9	0
Billy LeFear	72-75	10	56	5.6	0	60	1461	24.4	0
Charlie Leigh	68-69,71-74	50	368	7.4	0	46	1082	23.5	0
Anthony Leonard	76-77	57	447	7.8	1	27	621	23.0	0
Jerry LeVias	69-74	88	687	7.8	0	94	2213	23.5	0
Floyd Little	67-75	81	893	11.0	2	104	2523	24.3	0
Virgil Livers	75-77	76	707	9.3	0	27	543	20.1	0
Spider Lockhart	65-75	64	328	5.1	0	1	19	19.0	0
Larry Marshall	72-77	156	1415	9.1	0	129	3173	24.6	0
Richard Mauti	77	37	281	7.6	0	27	609	22.6	0
Don McCauley	71-77					33	770	23.3	1
Brent McClanahan	73-77					60	1409	23.5	0
Willie McGee	73-77	6	56	9.3	0	49	1115	22.8	0
Ralph McGill	72-77	105	964	9.2	1	27	566	21.0	0
Rod McNeill	74-76	1	0	0.0	0	27	660	24.4	0
Leon McQuay	74-76	9	86	9.6	0	48	1092	22.8	0
Warren McVea	68-71,73					47	1008	21.4	0
Terry Metcalf	73-77	80	921	11.5	1	107	2804	26.2	2
Cleo Miller	74-77					27	374	13.9	0
Randy Montgomery	71-74					33	836	25.3	1
Keith Moody	76-77	31	362	11.7	2	56	1241	22.2	0
Manfred Moore	74-77	88	770	8.8	1	76	1734	22.8	0
Nat Moore	74-77	25	288	11.5	0	33	858	26.0	0
Zeke Moore	67-77	8	93	11.6	0	64	1618	25.3	1
Dennis Morgan	74-75	27	347	12.9	1	42	993	23.6	0
Mercury Morris	69-76	27	171	6.3	0	111	2947	26.5	3
Reece Morrison	68-73	26	182	7.0	0	32	727	22.7	0
Herb Mul-Key	72-74	24	243	10.1	0	54	1505	27.9	1
Steve Odom	74-77	16	191	11.9	1	125	2825	22.6	1
Artie Owens	76-77					33	683	20.7	0
Lemar Parrish	70-77	130	1201	9.2	4	61	1504	24.7	1
Eddie Payton	77	30	290	9.7	1	22	548	24.9	1
Preston Pearson	67-77	7	40	5.7	0	114	2801	24.6	2
Jess Phillips	68-77	2	16	8.0	0	45	1048	23.3	0
Lou Piccone	74-77	48	322	6.7	1	100	2386	23.9	0
Ed Podolak	69-77	86	739	8.6	0	34	697	20.5	0
Ernest Pough	76-77					25	480	19.2	0
Greg Pruitt	73-77	56	659	11.8	0	53	1388	26.2	1
Danny Reese	76-77	51	417	8.2	0	4	102	25.5	0
Mel Renfro	64-77	109	842	7.7	1	85	2246	26.4	2
Golden Richards	73-77	62	502	8.1	1	3	44	14.7	0
Jim Robinson	76-77	31	193	6.2	0	20	444	22.2	0
Paul Robinson	68-73	2	1	0.5	0	40	924	23.1	0
Oliver Ross	73-76					38	792	20.8	0
Steve Schubert	74-77	51	399	7.8	1	15	261	17.4	0
Bo Scott	69-74					25	722	28.9	0
Jake Scott	70-77	130	1357	10.4	1	6	137	22.8	0
Rob Scribner	73-76	45	361	8.0	0	16	392	24.5	0
Jeff Severson	72-77	28	212	7.6	0	9	148	16.4	0
Willie Shelby	76-77	32	216	6.8	0	49	1164	23.8	1
Rod Sherman	67-73	27	212	7.9	0	8	145	18.1	0
Don Shy	67-73	29	202	7.0	0	26	618	23.8	0
O.J. Simpson	69-77					33	990	30.0	1
Charlie Smith	68-75					30	659	22.0	0
Jim Smith	77	36	294	8.2	0	16	381	23.8	0
Ron Smith	65-74	235	1788	7.6	2	275	6922	25.2	3
Freddie Solomon	75-77	71	810	11.4	3	28	633	22.6	0
Cotton Speyrer	72-75	8	54	6.8	0	39	1035	26.5	1
Jon Staggers	70-75	94	792	8.4	3	35	854	24.4	0
Howard Stevens	73-77	163	1559	9.6	0	103	2336	22.7	0
Lynn Swann	74-77	60	740	12.3	1	2	11	6.5	0
Altie Taylor	69-76					27	597	22.1	0
Bruce Taylor	70-77	142	1323	9.3	0	12	190	15.8	0
Clifton Taylor	74,76					30	626	20.9	0
Jesse Taylor	72	1	0	0.0	0	31	676	21.8	0
Bill Thomas	72-74					27	621	23.0	0
Emmitt Thomas	66-77	11	64	5.8	0	29	673	23.2	0
Ike Thomas	71-75					51	1394	27.3	0
Bill Thompson	69-77	156	1811	11.6	0	46	1156	25.1	0
Bobby Thompson	75-76					44	996	22.6	0
Rocky Thompson	71-73					65	1768	27.2	2
Pat Tilley	76-77	28	257	9.2	0				
Cecil Turner	68-73	27	114	4.2	0	108	2616	24.2	4
Rick Upchurch	75-77	117	1501	12.8	5	82	2054	25.0	0
Ted Vactor	69-75	42	290	6.9	0	30	746	24.9	0
Rick Volk	67-77	84	548	6.5	0	2	16	8.0	0
Billy Waddy	77	31	219	7.1	0				
Billy Walik	70-72	28	130	4.6	0	67	1640	24.5	0
Donnie Walker	73-75	68	594	8.7	0	1	20	20.0	0
Jackie Wallace	74-77	31	234	7.5	0	6	92	15.3	0
Vic Washington	71-76					129	3341	25.9	1
Roger Wehrli	69-77	43	310	7.2	0	5	38	7.6	0
Charlie West	68-77	154	1080	7.0	1	84	2103	25.0	0
Lawrence Williams	76-77					50	1206	24.1	0
Leonard Willis	76-77	30	207	6.9	0	32	700	21.9	0
Roland Woolsey	75-77	38	320	8.4	0	13	249	19.2	0
Roscoe Word	74-76	39	293	7.5	0	7	127	18.1	0
Alvin Wyatt	70-73	59	504	8.5	2	60	1480	24.7	0
Mickey Zofko	71-74					30	656	21.9	0

Section 4 — PUNTING

Name	Years	No.	Avg.
Donny Anderson	66-74	387	39.6
Bruce Barnes	73-74	100	37.4
Lem Barney	67-77	113	35.5
Marv Bateman	72-77	401	40.9
Dave Beverly	74-77	325	38.5
Tom Blanchard	71-77	532	41.3
Bill Bradley	69-77	213	39.0
Mike Bragg	68-77	715	40.1
Steve Broussard	75	29	31.8
Mike Burke	74	46	37.0
Skip Butler	71-77	50	36.4
Duane Carrell	74-77	257	38.9
Dave Chapple	71-74	162	40.2
Neil Clabo	75-77	225	39.9
Don Cockroft	68-77	651	40.3
Greg Coleman	77	61	39.2
Fred Cox	63-77	70	38.7
Jerry DePoyster	68,71-72	106	38.2
Bucky Dilts	77	90	39.2
Mike Eischeid	66-74	564	41.3
Rick Engles	76-77	89	37.9
Julian Fagan	70-73	299	40.5
Greg Gantt	74-75	134	36.2
Ray Gerela	69-77	42	40.1
Dave Green	73-77	324	39.9
Ray Guy	73-77	337	43.2
Gus Holloman	68-72	47	39.7
Mitch Hoopes	75-77	123	38.7
Rusty Jackson	76	77	39.0
John James	72-77	515	41.7
Dave Jennings	74-77	318	40.4
Bill Johnson	70	43	39.5
Spike Jones	70-77	592	39.1
Terry Joyce	76-77	86	37.0
Gary Keithley	73,75	66	37.5
Merritt Kersey	74-75	97	32.5
Bob Lee	69-77	156	39.7
David Lee	66-77	746	40.9
Dave Lewis	70-73	285	43.7
Jim McCann	71-73,75	139	37.6
Pat McInally	76-77	143	40.6
Tom McNeill	67-73	317	41.1
Mike Michel	77	35	38.2
Steve O'Neal	69-73	337	40.7
Cliff Parsley	77	77	39.4
Bob Parsons	72-77	366	39.9
Dennis Partee	68-75	519	41.3
Dan Pastorini	71-77	316	39.7
Mike Patrick	75-77	215	38.4
Chuck Ramsey	77	62	37.1
Hal Roberts	74	81	38.7
Larry Seiple	67-77	633	40.0
Steve Spurrier	67-76	230	38.3
Wilbur Summers	77	93	36.8
Bill Van Heusen	68-76	574	41.7
Bobby Walden	64-77	974	41.6
Glenn Walker	77	73	35.2
Randy Walker	74	69	38.4
Herman Weaver	70-77	436	40.6
Morris Weese	76-77	53	35.7
Jeff West	75-77	174	38.3
Danny White	76-77	150	39.1
Ron Widby	68-73	368	42.0
Tom Wittum	73-77	303	41.9

Lifetime Statistics — 1970-1977 Players   Section 5 — KICKING
(All men with 10 or more PAT or Field Goal Attempts)

Section 5 — KICKING

Name	Years	PAT	PAT Att.	PAT Pct.	FG	FG Att.	FG Pct.
Chris Bahr	76-77	64	68	94	33	54	61
Bill Bell	71-73	64	69	93	30	55	55
Rolf Bernishke	77	21	24	88	17	23	74
Skip Butler	71-77	127	133	95	71	132	54
Don Cockroft	68-77	318	330	96	164	245	67
Fred Cox	63-77	519	539	96	282	455	62
Joe Danelo	75-77	59	64	92	33	60	55
Tom Dempsey	69-77	208	233	89	148	241	61
Jerry DePoyster	68,71-72	18	20	90	3	15	20
Happy Feller	71-73	27	28	96	16	43	37
Toni Fritsch	71-73,75-77	149	155	96	84	135	62
Roy Gerela	69-77	301	313	96	171	273	63
Dave Green	73-77	56	65	86	22	42	52
Grant Guthrie	70-71	32	34	94	13	29	45
Efren Herrera	74-77	106	108	98	44	65	68
Bobby Howfield	68-74	193	201	96	98	166	59
George Hunt	73,75	46	53	87	22	39	56
George Jakowenko	74,76	21	24	88	12	17	71
Curt Knight	69-73	172	175	98	101	175	58
Pat Leahy	74-77	79	90	88	45	73	62
Allan Leavitt	77	5	5	100	5	10	50
John Leypoldt	71-77	199	217	92	91	151	60
Toni Linhart	72,74-77	159	164	97	61	96	64
Carson Long	77	13	14	93	7	11	64
Errol Mann	68-77	282	295	96	165	256	64
Chester Marcol	72-77	102	109	94	103	163	63
Bill McClard	72-75	31	32	97	26	51	51
Nick Mike-Mayer	73-77	110	113	97	59	107	55
Steve Mike-Mayer	75-77	72	82	88	38	75	51
Mark Moseley	70-72,74-77	166	176	94	108	179	60
Horst Muhlmann	69-77	245	257	95	154	239	64
Jim O'Brien	70-73	109	112	97	60	108	56
Dennis Partee	68-75	165	173	95	71	121	59
Mac Percival	67-74	163	167	98	101	190	53
David Ray	69-74	167	175	95	110	178	62
Benny Ricardo	76	21	23	91	11	18	61
Mirro Roder	73-74,76	28	29	97	17	32	53
Raphael Septien	77	32	35	91	18	30	60
John Smith	74-77	150	155	97	55	85	65
Fred Steinfort	76-77	29	32	91	10	19	53
Jan Stenerud	67-77	341	354	96	247	383	64
Richie Szaro	75-77	71	77	92	33	51	65
Bob Thomas	75-77	72	82	88	39	75	52
Jim Turner	64-77	458	475	96	280	445	63
Kenny Vinyard	70	23	26	88	9	25	36
Mike Walker	72	15	15	100	2	8	25
Allen Watson	70	7	8	88	5	10	50
Tim Webster	71	8	8	100	6	11	55
Ray Wersching	73-77	72	77	94	42	85	49
Jeff White	73	21	25	84	14	25	56
Garo Yepremian	66-67,70-77	327	341	96	161	247	65

Leaders and Features

The mention of any sport brings certain images to mind. When it comes to pro football the pictures are vivid and swift. Mostly though it is an extreme of functions. For those in love with risk and the dramatics of suddenness, there is nothing more serene than the aerial ballet of a 50-yard pass play. And for those who like to chew their fantasy in small, but certain chunks of yardage, there is nothing more pleasurable than the fullback who eludes a mammoth of flesh in search of four yards of daylight. Yet these two simplified illustrations have not always held true for pro football. If nothing else, football is a game of constant change. Unlike any other major sport, there is no way to compare the football athletes of today's two platoon game with those men who needed a double set of talents in which to sustain their playing careers. This point, for example, could not be any sharper than when one considers Joe Namath attempting to play in the 1940s. But fortunately for Namath, and perhaps even the fans of today who would have been denied the excitement of his precision arm, football is no longer a game of one man for sixty minutes.

It is for this reason that many of the records which appear on the following pages have no continuity with the players of yesteryear and those of the modern game. Field goals, for example, are a modern phenomenon and Lou Groza (who revolutionized the kicking game), is the only pre-1960 player to appear on the list of the top 56 single-season leaders. Yet, on the other hand, in the category of punters, Yale Lary, with a 48.9 average, is the only post-1960 player to make the top ten in the single-season leaders. Of course, the changing hash marks and goal post positions are greatly responsible for these records.

Yet beyond the comparison of any era, more important are the achievements of the men who made up their time, and the fact that whatever the criteria, each contributed the fullest and best of his talents. It is on this basis that each must be measured and appreciated in the light of pro football's changing game.

Section Explanations

The following is an explanation of certain statistical matter which may appear unfamiliar:

Yards per Game — In the category of Yards per Game for individuals, "per game" refers to games played by the team as there is no available statistical information of the games played by the individual.

Passing Ranks — These ranks are determined by the formula used by the National Football League for its official rankings from 1960 to 1971. Each passer who qualifies by having a minimum number of passing attempts is ranked in four categories: Percent Completed, Percent Intercepted, Average Yards per Attempt, and Touchdowns. The four ranks are then added for each passer and the totals are then ranked. This ranking of the sum of the four ranks is the passer's rank.

YEARLY CHAMPIONSHIP GAMES

NATIONAL FOOTBALL LEAGUE (CONFERENCE)

Year	Winner (Share)	Loser (Share)	Score
1933	CHICAGO BEARS ($210.34)	New York Giants ($140.22)	23–21
1934	NEW YORK GIANTS ($621)	Chicago Bears ($414.02)	30–13
1935	DETROIT LIONS ($313.35)	New York Giants ($200.20)	26–7
1936	Green Bay Packers ($250)	Boston Redskins ($180)	21–6
	(At New York)		
1937	Washington Redskins ($225.90)	CHICAGO BEARS ($127.78)	28–21
1938	NEW YORK GIANTS ($504.45)	Green Bay Packers ($368.81)	23–17
1939	GREEN BAY PACKERS ($703.97)	New York Giants ($455.57)	27–0
	(at Milwaukee)		
1940	Chicago Bears ($873)	WASHINGTON REDSKINS ($606)	73–0
1941	CHICAGO BEARS ($430)	New York Giants ($288)	37–9
1942	WASHINGTON REDSKINS ($965)	Chicago Bears ($637)	14–6
1943	CHICAGO BEARS ($1,146)	Washington Redskins ($765)	41–21
1944	Green Bay Packers ($1,449)	NEW YORK GIANTS ($814)	14–7
1945	CLEVELAND RAMS ($1,469)	Washington Redskins ($902)	15–14
1946	Chicago Bears ($1,975)	NEW YORK GIANTS ($1,295)	24–14
1947	CHICAGO CARDINALS ($1,132)	Philadelphia Eagles ($754)	28–21
1948	PHILADELPHIA EAGLES ($1,540)	Chicago Cardinals ($874)	7–0
1949	Philadelphia Eagles ($1,094)	LOS ANGELES RAMS ($739)	14–0
1950	CLEVELAND BROWNS ($1,113)	Los Angeles Rams ($686)	30–28
1951	LOS ANGELES RAMS ($2,108)	Cleveland Browns ($1,483)	24–17
1952	Detroit Lions ($2,274)	CLEVELAND BROWNS ($1,712)	17–7
1953	DETROIT LIONS ($2,424)	Cleveland Browns ($1,654)	17–16
1954	CLEVELAND BROWNS ($2,478)	Detroit Lions ($1,585)	56–10
1955	Cleveland Browns ($3,508)	LOS ANGELES RAMS ($2,316)	38–14
1956	NEW YORK GIANTS ($3,779)	Chicago Bears ($2,485)	47–7
1957	DETROIT LIONS ($4,295)	Cleveland Browns ($2,750)	59–14
1958	Baltimore Colts ($4,718)	NEW YORK GIANTS ($3,111)	*23–17
1959	BALTIMORE COLTS ($4,674)	New York Giants ($3,083)	31–16
1960	PHILADELPHIA EAGLES ($5,116)	Green Bay Packers ($3,105)	17–13
1961	GREEN BAY PACKERS ($5,195)	New York Giants ($3,339)	37–0
1962	Green Bay Packers ($5,888)	NEW YORK GIANTS ($4,166)	16–7
1963	CHICAGO BEARS ($5,899)	New York Giants ($4,218)	14–10
1964	CLEVELAND BROWNS ($8,052)	Baltimore Colts ($5,571)	27–0
1965	GREEN BAY PACKERS ($7,819)	Cleveland Browns ($5,288)	23–12
1966	GREEN BAY PACKERS ($9,813)	DALLAS COWBOYS ($6,527)	34–27
1967	GREEN BAY PACKERS ($7,950)	Dallas Cowboys ($5,299)	21–17
1968	Baltimore Colts ($9,306)	CLEVELAND BROWNS ($5,963)	34–0
1969	MINNESOTA VIKINGS ($7,930)	Cleveland Browns ($5,118)	27–7
1970	Dallas Cowboys ($8,500)	SAN FRANCISCO 49ers ($5,500)	17–10
1971	DALLAS COWBOYS ($8,500)	San Francisco 49ers ($5,500)	14–3
1972	WASHINGTON REDSKINS ($8,500)	Dallas Cowboys ($5,500)	26–3
1973	Minnesota Vikings ($8,500)	DALLAS COWBOYS ($5,500)	27–10
1974	MINNESOTA VIKINGS ($8,500)	Los Angeles Rams ($5,500)	14–10
1975	Dallas Cowboys ($8,500)	LOS ANGELES RAMS ($5,500)	37–7
1976	MINNESOTA VIKINGS ($8,500)	Los Angeles Rams ($5,500)	24–13
1977	DALLAS COWBOYS ($8,500)	Minnesota Vikings ($5,500)	23–6

Note: Home Team in Upper Case.

*—Sudden Death Game

ALL–AMERICAN FOOTBALL CONFERENCE

Year	Winner (Share)	Loser (Share)	Score
1946	CLEVELAND BROWNS ($931.57)	New York Yankees ($645.88)	14–9
1947	Cleveland Browns ($1,191.99)	NEW YORK YANKEES ($794.66)	14–3
1948	CLEVELAND BROWNS ($594.18)	Buffalo Bills ($386.22)	49–7
1949	CLEVELAND BROWNS ($266.11)	San Francisco 49ers ($172.61)	21–7

AMERICAN FOOTBALL LEAGUE (CONFERENCE)

Year	Winner (Share)	Loser (Share)	Score
1960	HOUSTON OILERS ($1,025)	Los Angeles Chargers ($718)	24–16
1961	Houston Oilers ($1,792)	SAN DIEGO CHARGERS ($1,111)	10–3
1962	Dallas Chiefs ($2,206)	HOUSTON OILERS ($1,471)	*21–17
1963	SAN DIEGO CHARGERS ($2,498)	Boston Patriots ($1,596)	51–10
1964	BUFFALO BILLS ($2,668)	San Diego Chargers ($1,738)	20–7
1965	Buffalo Bills ($5,189)	SAN DIEGO CHARGERS ($3,447)	23–0
1966	Kansas City Chiefs ($5,309)	BUFFALO BILLS ($3,799)	31–7
1967	OAKLAND RAIDERS ($6,321)	Houston Oilers ($4,996)	40–7
1968	NEW YORK JETS ($7,007)	Oakland Raiders ($5,349)	27–23
1969	Kansas City Chiefs ($7,755)	OAKLAND RAIDERS ($6,252)	17–7
1970	BALTIMORE COLTS ($8,500)	Oakland Raiders ($5,500)	27–17
1971	MIAMI DOLPHINS ($8,500)	Baltimore Colts ($5,500)	21–0
1972	MIAMI DOLPHINS ($8,500)	PITTSBURGH STEELERS ($5,500)	21–17
1973	MIAMI DOLPHINS ($8,500)	Oakland Raiders ($5,500)	27–10
1974	Pittsburgh Steelers ($8,500)	OAKLAND RAIDERS ($5,500)	24–13
1975	PITTSBURGH STEELERS ($8,500)	Oakland Raiders ($5,500)	16–10
1976	OAKLAND RAIDERS ($8,500)	Pittsburgh Steelers ($5,500)	24–7
1977	DENVER BRONCOS ($8,500)	Oakland Raiders ($5,500)	20–17

COMPOSITE STANDINGS
(All Leagues)

Team	Games	Wins	Losses	Pct.	Total Share
Chiefs	3	3	0	1.000	$15,270
Dolphins	3	3	0	1.000	25,500
Jets	1	1	0	1.000	7,007
Broncos	1	1	0	1.000	8,500
Packers	10	8	2	.800	42,541.78
Lions	5	4	1	.800	10,891.35
Vikings	5	4	1	.800	38,930
Eagles	4	3	1	.750	8,504
Colts	6	4	2	.667	38,169
Bills (AFL)	3	2	1	.667	11,656
Bears	10	6	4	.600	14,197.14
Browns	15	8	7	.533	42,102.85
Cowboys	8	4	4	.500	55,826
Oilers	4	2	2	.500	9,284
Steelers	4	2	2	.500	28,000
Cardinals	2	1	1	.500	2,006
Redskins	7	3	4	.429	12,143.90
Rams	8	2	6	.333	23,818
Raiders	9	2	7	.222	53,922
Giants	14	3	11	.214	26,014.44
Chargers	5	1	4	.200	9,512
49ers	3	0	3	.000	11,172.61
Yankees (AAFC)	2	0	2	.000	1,440.54
Bills (AAFC)	1	0	1	.000	386.22
Patriots	1	0	1	.000	1,596

YEARLY TEAM LEADERS

OFFENSE

YEAR	LGUE	POINTS – PTS/G	FIRST DOWNS	RUSH YARDS YDS/GAME	RUSH AVERAGE	RUSH TD	PASS COMPLETION PERCENTAGE	PASS YARDS YDS/GAME	PASS YARDS/ ATTEMPT	PASS TD	FEWEST INT.	LEAST INT. %	PUNTING AVERAGE	PUNT RETURN AVERAGE	KICKOFF RETURN AVERAGE	YEAR	LGUE
1933	NFL	NYG 244 17.4					Bkn. 46.7									1933	NFL
1934	NFL	ChiB 286 22.0					NYG 40.9									1934	NFL
1935	NFL	ChiB 192 16.0	ChiB 140	ChiB 2096 175		Det. 15	NYG 44.8	G.B. 1545 129	G.B. 6.72	ChiB 13						1935	NFL
1936	NFL	G.B. 248 20.7	Det. 170	Det. 2883 240	Det. 4.73	Det. 22	G.B. 42.4	G.B. 1629 136	ChiB 6.46	ChiB 17 G.B. 17						1936	NFL
1937	NFL	G.B. 220 20.0	Was. 149	Det. 2074 189	Det. 4.30	Det. 12	Was. 44.6	G.B. 1397 127	ChiB 6.97	ChiB 16 G.B. 16	NYG 11	NYG 5.42				1937	NFL
1938	NFL	G.B. 223 20.7	Was. 147	Det. 1893 172	Det. 4.01	NYG 12	NYG 48.9	Was. 1536 140	G.B. 6.98	G.B. 20	Bkn. 8	Bkn. 4.73				1938	NFL
1939	NFL	ChiB 298 27.1	G.B. 149	ChiB 2043 186	ChiB 4.66	ChiB 21	Was. 58.2	ChiB 1965 179	Was. 8.93	Was. 18	NYG 11	NYG 6.21				1939	NFL
1940	NFL	Was. 245 22.2	G.B. 154	ChiB 1818 165	Bkn. 3.92	ChiB 16	Was. 59.0	Was. 1887 172	ChiB 8.19	G.B. 18 Was. 18	Bkn. 13	Phi. 5.52				1940	NFL
1941	NFL	ChiB 396 36.0	ChiB 181	ChiB 2290 208	ChiB 4.63	ChiB 30	G.B. 52.6	ChiB 2002 182	**ChiB 10.21**	ChiB 19	ChiB 11	G.B. 5.14	Was. 45.9	**ChiB 20.2**	Det. 26.5	1941	NFL
1942	NFL	ChiB 376 34.2	G.B. 176	ChiB 1911 174	ChiB 4.07	ChiB 23	Was. 53.3	G.B. 2407 219	ChiB 10.18	G.B. 28	Pit. 11	G.B. 5.45	Was. 44.3	Pit. 15.4	Was. 27.8	1942	NFL
1943	NFL	ChiB 303 30.3	ChiB 161	P-P 1730 173	ChiB 3.89	P-P 18	Was. 54.7	ChiB 2310 231	ChiB 10.09	ChiB 28	NYG 9	NYG 6.04	Was. 43.1	Det. 13.6	Det. 24.9	1943	NFL
1944	NFL	Phi. 267 26.7	G.B. 147	Phi. 1661 166	Phi. 3.92	Phi. 23	Was. 56.9	Was. 2021 202	ChiB 7.45	ChiB 21	Phi. 12	Was. 5.69	Det. 40.5	Det. 14.2	NYG 27.4	1944	NFL
1945	NFL	Phi. 272 27.2	ChiB 164	Cle. 1714 171	Cle. 4.61	Phi. 26	**Was. 64.0**	ChiB 1857 186	Cle. 8.88	Cle. 16	Was. 11	Was. 4.82	Was. 43.3	Det. 14.4	Phi. 24.5	1945	NFL
1946	NFL	ChiB 289 26.3	L.A. 214	G.B. 1765 160	L.A. 4.17	ChiB 19	Phi. 53.5	L.A. 2080 189	ChiB 7.71	L.A. 19	Pit. 13	L.A. 7.36	L.A. 44.4	Pit. 13.5	NYG 26.0	1946	NFL
1946	AAFC	Cle. 423 30.2	L.A. 183	S.F. 2175 155	Buf. 4.08	Cle. 27	L.A. 54.7	Cle. 2266 162	Cle. 9.56	Cle. 22	Cle. 7	Cle. 2.95	Bkn. 46.5	N.Y. 15.3	Chi. 24.5	1946	AAFC
1947	NFL	ChiB 363 30.3	ChiB 263	L.A. 2171 181	L.A. 4.73	ChiB 21 Phi. 21	Was. 55.5	Was. 3336 278	ChiB 8.18	ChiB 29	Was. 18	Was. 4.33	G.B. 43.6	Bos. 15.1	Was. 22.1	1947	NFL
1947	AAFC	Cle. 410 29.8	S.F. 218	N.Y. 2930 209	N.Y. 5.49	N.Y. 27	Cle. 58.8	Cle. 2990 214	Cle. 10.10	Cle. 26	Cle. 12	Cle. 4.05	L.A. 45.0	Bal. 16.5	Buf. 25.6	1947	AAFC
1948	NFL	ChiC 395 32.9	ChiB 242	ChiC 2560 213	ChiC 4.82	ChiC 25	Was. 56.1	Was. 2861 238	Was. 7.95	L.A. 28	ChiC 12	ChiC 4.21	Phi. 45.9	ChiC 19.1	ChiB 25.9	1948	NFL
1948	AAFC	S.F. 495 35.4	Cle. 243	**S.F. 3663 262**	**S.F. 6.07**	S.F. 35	S.F. 56.3	Bal. 2899 207	Bal. 8.53	S.F. 30	Bal. 13	Bal. 3.82	L.A. 47.2	Buf. 16.9	S.F. 24.4	1948	AAFC
1949	NFL	Phi. 364 30.3	ChiB 248	Phi. 2607 217	ChiC 4.56	Phi. 25	L.A. 52.5	ChiB 3055 255	ChiB 7.94	ChiB 24	Phi. 14	Phi. 5.56	L.A. 44.4	ChiC 18.2	NYG 26.0	1949	NFL
1949	AAFC	S.F. 416 34.7	Buf. 184	S.F. 2798 233	S.F. 5.53	S.F. 26	Buf. 57.1	Cle. 2929 244	Cle. 9.90	S.F. 28	Cle. 12	Cle. 4.05	S.F. 45.5	S.F. 15.5	L.A. 23.7	1949	AAFC
1950	NFL	**L.A.** 466 **38.8**	L.A. 278	NYG 2336 195	NYY 4.56	L.A. 28	L.A. 55.8	L.A. 3709 309	L.A. 8.19	L.A. 31	NYG 10	NYG 5.35	Cle. 43.2	G.B. 16.6	Det. 26.7	1950	NFL
1951	NFL	L.A. 392 32.7	L.A. 272	ChiB 2408 201	L.A. 5.19	ChiB 24	Cle. 55.7	L.A. 3296 275	L.A. 8.84	Det. 29	Cle 7	L.A. 5.90	Cle. 45.5	Det. 15.1	NYG 25.9	1951	NFL
1952	NFL	L.A. 349 29.1	Cle. 228	S.F. 1905 159	Cle. 4.53	L.A. 17	S.F. 51.8	Cle. 2839 237	G.B. 7.98	G.B. 26	Phi. 19	Phi. 5.26	Cle. 45.7	Det. 14.9	Pit. 28.9	1952	NFL
1953	NFL	S.F. 372 31.0	Phi. 256	S.F. 2230 186	L.A. 5.04	S.F. 26	Cle. 63.0	Phi. 3357 280	Cle. 10.10	Phi. 25	Cle. 9	Cle. 2.97	Pit. 46.9	G.B. 8.9	NYG 26.3	1953	NFL
1954	NFL	Det. 337 28.1	L.A. 255	S.F. 2498 208	S.F. 5.65	S.F. 28	Cle. 59.0	ChiB 3299 275	L.A. 9.91	Phi. 33	S.F. 12	S.F. 3.53	Pit. 43.2	G.B. 9.9	Cle. 25.3	1954	NFL
1955	NFL	Cle. 349 29.1	ChiB 235	ChiB 2388 199	ChiB 4.90	Cle. 20	Cle. 55.6	Phi. 2696 225	Cle. 9.51	Cle. 21	Cle. 11	Cle. 4.70	L.A. 44.6	ChiC 12.0	Pit. 26.3	1955	NFL
1956	NFL	ChiB 363 30.3	Det. 247	ChiB 2468 206	L.A. 5.15	ChiB 22	Bal. 56.6	L.A. 2601 217	ChiB 8.77	G.B. 21	ChiC 14	NYG 5.09	L.A. 43.1	ChiC 9.5	Pit. 26.1	1956	NFL
1957	NFL	L.A. 307 25.6	L.A. 235	L.A. 2142 179	L.A. 4.52	Cle. 19	S.F. 62.6	Bal. 2608 217	Cle. 9.61	Bal. 25	NYG 12	NYG 4.46	S.F. 44.7	Was. 10.5	S.F. 26.1	1957	NFL
1958	NFL	Bal. 381 31.8	Bal. 253	Cle. 2526 211	Cle. 5.32	Bal. 24 Cle. 24	S.F. 58.2	L.A. 2909 242	Pit. 8.62	Bal. 26	Bal. 11	Bal. 3.11	Was. 45.4	Cle. 8.2	ChiB 25.8	1958	NFL
1959	NFL	Bal. 374 31.2	Bal. 267	Cle. 2149 179	L.A. 4.79	Cle. 20	Cle. 57.6	Bal. 2938 245	NYG 8.72	Bal. 33	Cle. 9	Cle. 3.26	NYG 46.6	ChiC 9.8	L.A. 24.5	1959	NFL
1960	NFL	Cle. 362 30.2	G.B. 237	StL. 2356 196	Cle. 5.04	G.B. 29	Cle. 60.6	Bal. 3164 264	Phi. 8.93	Phi. 29	**Cle. 5**	Cle. 1.89	StL. 44.9	Cle. 9.9	S.F. 27.1	1960	NFL
1960	AFL	N.Y. 382 27.3	N.Y. 286	Dal. 1814 130	Dal. 3.76	Dal. 24	L.A. 51.9	Hou. 3371 241	Hou. 7.39	NYT 32	Dal. 19	Dal. 4.37	L.A. 39.7	Dal. 15.0	Hou. 25.5	1960	AFL
1961	NFL	G.B. 391 27.9	NYG 275	G.B. 2350 168	G.B. 4.96	G.B. 27 S.F. 27	G.B. 57.8	Phi. 3824 273	Phi. 8.91	Phi. 34	Cle. 13	Cle. 4.06	**Det. 47.6**	G.B. 17.8	S.F. 26.6	1961	NFL
1961	AFL	**Hou. 513** 36.6	Hou. 293	Dal. 2183 156	Dal. 4.97	S.D. 24	Hou. 51.0	**Hou. 4568 326**	Hou. 9.17	**Hou. 48**	Bos. 21	Bos. 5.00	Buf. 44.5	N.Y. 17.8	Dal. 27.6	1961	AFL
1962	NFL	G.B. 415 29.6	G.B. 281	G.B. 2460 176	G.B. 4.75	**G.B. 36**	G.B. 60.1	Phi. 3632 259	Phi. 8.49	NYG 35	G.B. 13	G.B. 4.18	S.F. 45.6	Det. 12.9	Was. 28.2	1962	NFL
1962	AFL	Dal. 389 27.8	Den. 270	Buf. 2480 177	Buf. 4.95	Dal. 21	Dal. 60.6	Den. 3739 267	Dal. 8.77	Hou. 32	Bos. 13	Bos. 3.40	Den. 42.9	N.Y. 12.3	Hou. 25.9	1962	AFL
1963	NFL	NYG 448 32.0	NYG 278	Cle. 2639 189	Cle. 5.74	G.B. 22	Bal. 57.3	Bal. 3605 258	NYG 8.35	NYG 39	Bal. 12	Bal. 2.77	Chi. 46.5	Was. 13.0	Was. 26.8	1963	NFL
1963	AFL	S.D. 399 28.5	N/A	S.D. 2201 157	S.D. 5.57	Buf. 21	S.D. 56.4	Hou. 3478 248	Oak. 7.69	Oak. 31	K.C. 22	K.C. 5.01	Den. 44.3	Den. 12.9	Hou. 26.4	1963	AFL
1964	NFL	Bal. 428 30.6	StL. 275	G.B. 2276 163	Cle. 4.97	Bal. 29	G.B. 57.9	Was. 3071 219	Bal. 8.83	Cle. 28	G.B. 6	G.B. 1.87	Min. 46.4	Cle. 15.2	G.B. 25.8	1964	NFL
1964	AFL	Buf. 400 28.6	Hou. 284	Buf. 2040 146	Oak. 4.47	Buf. 25	K.C. 55.3	Oak. 3886 276	Buf. 8.62	K.C. 32	K.C. 21	Hou. 4.90	Den. 43.4	Oak. 13.5	Oak. 25.0	1964	AFL
1965	NFL	S.F. 421 30.1	S.F. 292	Cle. 2331 167	Cle. 4.90	ChiB 27	S.F. 59.9	S.F. 3633 260	Chi. 8.37	S.F. 35	Min. 12	Min. 3.23	S.F. 45.8	Cle. 11.9	Det. 27.2	1965	NFL
1965	AFL	S.D. 340 24.3	S.D. 268	S.D. 1998 143	K.C. 4.19	Buf. 16	S.D. 50.6	S.D. 3379 241	S.D. 8.43	Hou. 25	Oak. 17	Oak. 3.94	NYJ 45.3	S.D. 13.4	Den. 23.4	1965	AFL
1966	NFL	Dal. 445 31.8	Dal. 287	Cle. 2166 155	Cle. 5.22	Dal. 24	G.B. 60.7	Dal. 3331 238	G.B. 8.90	Cle. 33	**G.B. 5**	**G.B. 1.57**	Bal. 45.6	Det. 10.4	Chi. 27.9	1966	NFL
1966	AFL	K.C. 448 32.0	K.C. 266	K.C. 2274 162	K.C. 5.18	Buf. 19 K.C. 19	K.C. 52.8	NYJ 3556 254	K.C. 8.28	K.C. 31	K.C. 15 S.D. 15	S.D. 3.46	Den. 45.2	S.D. 12.2	Den. 26.9	1966	AFL
1967	NFL	L.A. 398 28.4	Bal. 289	Cle. 2139 153	Cle. 4.82	Bal. 21	Bal. 58.0	Was. 3887 278	G.B. 8.33	NYG 33	L.A. 16	Was. 3.23	Atl. 43.7	Cle. 10.2	G.B. 27.0	1967	NFL
1967	AFL	Oak. 468 33.4	NYJ 282	Hou. 2122 152	Hou. 4.46	Oak. 19	K.C. 55.8	NYJ 4128 295	NYJ 8.02	Oak. 33	Den. 18	Den. 4.81	Den. 44.9	Den. 13.5	Den. 25.3	1967	AFL
1968	NFL	Dal. 431 30.8	**Dal. 297**	Chi. 2377 170	Chi. 4.75	Dal. 22	G.B. 59.1	Dal. 3295 235	Bal. 8.62	Bal. 28	Det. 15 G.B. 15	Det. 3.98	Atl. 44.3	Dal. 13.5	Bal. 26.4	1968	NFL
1968	AFL	Oak. 453 32.4	Oak. 287	K.C. 2227 159	Oak. 4.64	NYJ 22	K.C. 57.8	S.D. 3813 272	K.C. 9.23	Oak. 31	Cin. 11	Cin. 3.51	K.C. 45.3	K.C. 14.5	Hou. 23.3	1968	AFL
1969	NFL	Min. 379 27.1	N.O. 282	Dal. 2276 163	Atl. 4.52	Cle. 17 Dal. 17 StL. 17	Was. 61.9	S.F. 3379 241	Dal. 9.05	L.A. 25	L.A. 7	L.A. 1.68	Bal. 45.3	Det. 11.0	Bal. 25.3	1969	NFL
1969	AFL	Oak. 377 26.9	S.D. 275	K.C. 2220 159	S.D. 4.36	K.C. 19	K.C. 55.8	Oak. 3375 241	Cin. 8.83	Oak. 36	Cin. 15	S.D. 4.73	S.D. 44.6	Den. 12.2	K.C. 26.6	1969	AFL
1970	NFC	S.F. 352 25.1	NYG 257	Dal. 2300 164	StL. 4.66	StL. 18	Was. 59.4	S.F. 2990 214	Dal. 8.23	S.F. 25	S.F. 10	S.F. 2.61	N.O. 42.5	S.F. 11.5	L.A. 26.3	1970	NFC
1970	AFC	Bal. 321 22.9	Oak. 270	Mia. 2082 149	Cin. 4.46	Den. 17	K.C. 53.3	Bal. 3087 221	Mia. 7.64	Oak. 28	Cin. 11	Cin. 3.24	Cin. 46.2	K.C. 12.0	Bal. 25.8	1970	AFC
1971	NFC	Dal. 406 29.0	Dal. 288	Det. 2376 170	L.A. 4.65	Dal. 25	Atl. 58.6	NYG 3062 219	Atl. 8.75	Dal. 22	L.A. 11	L.A. 2.97	Phi. 41.9	Was. 9.5	Dal. 27.5	1971	NFC
1971	AFC	Oak. 344 24.6	S.D. 264	Mia. 2429 174	Mia. 5.00	Bal. 23	Cin. 58.6	S.D. 3305 236	K.C. 7.99	S.D. 23	Mia. 10	Cin. 3.01	K.C. 44.8	Mia. 10.5	Mia. 25.2	1971	AFC
1972	NFC	S.F. 353 25.2	NYG 265	Chi. 2360 169	L.A. 4.68	Det. 20	NYG 59.9	S.F. 2888 206	Was. 8.03	S.F. 27	G.B. 9	Min. 3.37	L.A. 44.2	G.B. 14.6	**Chi. 29.4**	1972	NFC
1972	AFC	Mia. 385 27.5	**Oak. 297**	Mia. 2960 211	Pit. 5.07	Mia. 26	Cin. 57.0	NYJ 2930 209	Mia. 8.63	Oak. 23	Cin. 11	Cin. 2.86	K.C. 44.8	Den. 11.1	Bal. 28.1	1972	AFC
1973	NFC	L.A. 388 27.7	L.A. 294	L.A. 2925 209	Dal. 4.46	Atl+LA18	Min. 60.1	Phi. 3236 231	L.A. 6.88	Dal. 26	Min. 9	Phi. 2.71	S.F. 43.8	S.F. 10.6	Was. 26.0	1973	NFC
1973	AFC	Den. 354 25.3	Oak. 288	Buf. 3088 221	Buf. 5.10	Buf. 20	Oak. 58.1	Den. 2706 193	Cin. 6.39	Den. 22	Cin. 12 Mia. 12	Cin. 3.61	K.C. 45.6	S.D. 12.4	N.E. 24.1	1973	AFC
1974	NFC	Was. 320 22.9	Dal. 295	Dal. 2454 175	Dal. 4.53	Dal. 22	Was. 61.5	Was. 2978 213	Dal. 7.42	Min. 22 Was. 22	St. L. 8	St.L. 2.05	N.O. 41.8	Det. 12.6	Was. 25.9	1974	NFC
1974	AFC	Oak. 355 25.4	Pit. 284	Pit. 2417 173	Cin. 4.44	Mia. 25	Cin. 63.5	Cin. 2804 200	Mia. 8.17	Oak. 28	Cin. 13	Cin. 3.68	Oak. 42.2	N.E. 13.3	Cle. 22.9	1974	AFC
1975	NFC	Min. 377 26.9	Min. 314	Dal. 2432 174	St.L. 4.33	St.L. 19	Min. 63.0	Min. 3121 223	Dal. 7.54	Was. 28	Det. 12	Min. 3.14	S.F. 41.9	St.L. 10.3	St.L. 24.3	1975	NFC
1975	AFC	Buf. 420 30.0	**Buf. 318**	Buf. 2974 212	Buf. 5.06	Bal. 28 Oak. 28	Mia. 60.9	Cin. 3497 250	Cin. 8.08	Buf. 28	Bal. 8	Bal. 2.26	Oak. 43.8	Hou. 14.4	Oak. 26.0	1975	AFC
1976	NFC	L.A. 351 25.1	St.L. 307	L.A. 2523 180	Det. 4.29	L.A. 23	Min. 61.1	Min. 2855 204	St.L. 6.93	Det. 20 Was. 20	Min. 10	Min. 2.26	Atl. 42.1	Was. 13.2	Dal. 24.5	1976	NFC
1976	AFC	Bal. 417 29.8	Oak. 302	Pit. 2971 212	N.E. 4.99	Pit. 33	Oak. 63.3	K.C. 2929 209	Bal. 7.50	Oak. 33	Bal. 10	Bal. 2.77	Buf. 42.2	N.E. 13.1	Mia. 24.5	1976	AFC
1977	NFC	Dal. 345 24.6	Dal. 272	Chi. 2811 201	Chi. 4.7	Dal. 21	Min. 58.8	Min. 2692 192	Dal. 7.23	Min. 19	Dal. 10	Dal. 2.69	Atl. 41.2	Phi. 10.4	L.A. 18.9	1977	NFC
1977	AFC	Oak. 351 25.1	Oak. 305	Oak. 2627 188	Mia. 4.6	Oak. 20 Pit. 20	Mia. 58.5	Buf. 2803 200	Pit. 7.72	Sea. 23	Bal. 12 Den. 12	Bal. 3.01	Oak. 43.3	Hou. 15.0	N.E. 26.9	1977	AFC

Bold – designates all time leader

YEARLY TEAM LEADERS
DEFENSE

TEAM	LGUE	POINTS—PTS/G	FIRST DOWNS	RUSH YARDS YARDS/ GAME	RUSH AVERAGE	RUSH TD	PASS COMPLETION PERCENTAGE	PASS YARDS YARDS/ GAME	PASS YARDS/ ATTEMPT	PASS TD	MOST INT.	HIGHEST INT. %	PUNT RETURN AVERAGE	KICKOFF RETURN AVERAGE	TEAM	LGUE
1933	NFL	Bkn. **54** 5.4													1933	NFL
1934	NFL	Det. 59 **4.5**													1934	NFL
1935	NFL	G.B. 96 8.0 NYG 96 8.0					**ChiB 30.4**				ChiB 37	**ChiB 19.1**			1935	NFL
1936	NFL	ChiB 94 7.8					Bos. 31.5				ChiB 35	ChiB 15.4			1936	NFL
1937	NFL	ChiB 100 9.1					Pit. 32.4				NYG 30	NYG 16.5			1937	NFL
1938	NFL	NYG 79 7.2					NYG 34.1				NYG 34	NYG 15.0			1938	NFL
1939	NFL	NYG 85 7.7					Was. 37.0				NYG 35	NYG 15.8			1939	NFL
1940	NFL	Bkn. 120 10.9					ChiC 37.1				G.B. 40	Det. 16.4			1940	NFL
1941	NFL	NYG 114 10.3	Bkn. 110 ChiC 110	ChiB 1076 98	Was. 2.71	Bkn. 6 ChiB 6	ChiB 40.0	Pit. 1168 106	ChiB 5.5	Bkn. 6 NYG 6	ChiB 34	NYG 13.3	Cle. 8.2	Was. 19.4	1941	NFL
1942	NFL	ChiB 84 7.6	ChiB 98	ChiB 519 **47**	ChiB 1.77	ChiB 3	Was. 37.5	Was. 1093 99	**ChiB 4.2**	NYG 4	ChiB 33 G.B. 33	G.B. 13.6	Det. 10.2	Pit. 18.5	1942	NFL
1943	NFL	Was. 137 13.7	P-P 96	P-P 793 79	P-P 2.54	NYG 8	ChiB 31.5	ChiB 980 98	ChiB 4.8	ChiB 8	G.B. 42	G.B. 17.4	Was. 9.5	NYG 19.3	1943	NFL
1944	NFL	NYG 75 7.5	**Phi. 86**	**Phi. 558** 56	**Phi. 1.74**	NYG 6	ChiB 33.2	ChiB 1052 105	NYG 5.0	**NYG 3**	NYG 34	Phi. 14.3	C-P 9.9	Phi. 18.0	1944	NFL
1945	NFL	Was. 121 12.1	Phi. 104	Phi. 817 82	Det. 2.56	Det. 7	Cle. 39.1	Was. 1121 112	Was. 5.4	NYG 6	Bos. 30	Bos. 13.2	Det. 9.8	Det. 16.6	1945	NFL
1946	NFL	Pit. 117 10.6	ChiB 138	ChiB 1044 95	Phi. 2.69	Pit. 9	Pit. 39.5	**Pit. 939 85**	Pit. 5.8	G.B. 6 Pit. 6	ChiB 27	Phi. 11.8	Pit. 7.7	**ChiB 16.0**	1946	NFL
1946	AAFC	Cle. 137 9.8	N.Y. 119	S.F. 873 62	S.F. 2.05	S.F. 7	Cle. 41.8	Cle. 1317 94	Cle. 4.4	Cle. 8	Cle. 41	Cle. 13.7	N.Y. 10.8	Mia. 18.5	1946	AAFC
1947	NFL	G.B. 210 17.5	Pit. 170	Phi. 1329 111	L.A. 3.41	ChiB 6	Pit. 40.2	G.B. 1790 149	G.B. 6.5	G.B. 14 L.A. 14	G.B. 30	G.B. 10.8	ChiC 9.4	ChiB 17.5	1947	NFL
1947	AAFC	Cle. 185 13.2	N.Y. 140	N.Y. 1237 88	N.Y. 3.33	L.A. 9	Cle. 42.6	Cle. 1707 122	Cle. 5.6	Cle. 11	Cle. 32	Cle. 10.6	L.A. 10.8	Bal. 17.0	1947	AAFC
1948	NFL	ChiB 151 12.6	Phi. 158	Phi. 1209 101	Phi. 3.22	Phi. 5	Phi. 41.1	G.B. 1626 135	ChiB 4.9	ChiB 12	NYG 39	NYG 12.5	ChiB 9.2	Pit. 17.8	1948	NFL
1948	AAFC	Cle. 190 13.6	Cle. 171	Cle. 1519 108	Cle. 3.48	Cle. 10	Cle. 44.9	Bkn. 1985 142	Cle. 5.9	Cle. 14	S.F. 32	S.F. 8.6	Bal. 10.3	Chi. 17.5	1948	AAFC
1949	NFL	Phi. 134 11.2	Phi. 148	ChiB 1196 100	ChiB 2.79	Phi. 5	Phi. 39.9	Phi. 1607 134	Phi. 5.3	Pit. 9	ChiC 33	Det. 10.3	L.A. 8.3	Det. 18.7	1949	NFL
1949	AAFC	Cle. 171 14.2	N.Y. 129	N.Y. 1134 94	N.Y. 3.15	N.Y. 8	Cle. 39.5	Cle. 1677 140	Cle. 5.5	Cle. 9	S.F. 32	S.F. 10.1	N.Y. 11.0	L.A. 19.2	1949	AAFC
1950	NFL	Phi. 141 11.7	Phi. 141	Det. 1367 114	NYG 2.93	Phi. 5	Phi. 36.8	Cle. 1581 132	Cle. 5.4	Cle. 8	Bal. 34	Phi. 11.2	Cle. 6.6	Pit. 19.2	1950	NFL
1951	NFL	Cle. 152 12.7	NYG 174	NYG 913 76	NYG 2.33	Cle. 8 NYG 8	Phi. 41.5	Pit. 1687 141	Cle. 6.0	Cle. 10	NYG 41	NYG 10.9	S.F. 6.7	G.B. 18.5	1951	NFL
1952	NFL	Det. 192 16.0	S.F. 167	Det. 1145 95	NYG 3.23	ChiC 8 Det. 8 NYG 8 Pit. 8	Cle. 40.5	Was. 1817 151	S.F. 5.6	Was. 12	L.A. 38	L.A. 10.6	NYG 6.7	Pit. 18.3	1952	NFL
1953	NFL	Cle. 162 13.5	Pit. 184	Phi. 1117 93	Pit. 3.07	Phi. 6	Cle. 42.2	Was. 1950 162	Was. 5.6	Was. 8	Det. 38	Det. 10.7	ChiC 1.5	Pit. 16.3	1953	NFL
1954	NFL	Cle. 162 13.5	Cle. 147	Cle. 1050 88	Cle. 2.82	Cle. 4	Phi. 41.4	Cle. 1784 149	Phi. 5.9	Det. 10	NYG 33	Pit. 10.2	**ChiC 1.2**	G.B. 18.5	1954	NFL
1955	NFL	Cle. 218 18.2	Cle. 171	Cle. 1189 99	Was. 3.26	Was. 8	Cle. 39.0	Pit. 1530 127	Cle. 5.5	S.F. 10	G.B. 31 L.A. 31	G.B. 12.0	Bal. 1.9	L.A. 19.7	1955	NFL
1956	NFL	Cle. 177 14.7	Pit. 167	NYG 1443 120	NYG 3.48	Det. 9	ChiC 44.9	Cle. 1215 101	Cle. 5.4	Cle. 7	ChiC 33	ChiC 11.5	S.F. 3.5	Pit. 19.0	1956	NFL
1957	NFL	Cle. 172 14.3	Pit. 156	Bal. 1174 98	Bal. 3.13	Pit. 7	Cle. 43.4	Cle. 1511 126	Cle. 6.2	Cle. 8	G.B. 30	G.B. 9.6	Det. 1.6	Pit. 20.1	1957	NFL
1958	NFL	NYG 183 15.2	ChiB 168	Bal. 1291 108	NYG 3.61	Cle. 6	NYG 45.7	NYG 2130 177	L.A. 6.0	Bal. 9	Bal. 35	Bal. 9.6	Cle. 2.5	S.F. 17.6	1958	NFL
1959	NFL	NYG 170 14.2	NYG 167	NYG 1261 105	NYG 3.33	NYG 6	Pit. 44.9	NYG 1811 151	NYG 6.0	NYG 11	Bal. 40	Bal. 11.4	**Cle. 1.2**	Pit. 17.5	1959	NFL
1960	NFL	S.F. 205 17.1	StL. 158	StL 1212 101	NYG 3.20	G.B. 7	S.F. 47.8	Chi. 1808 151	Chi. 6.2	Bal. 8	Cle. 31	Phi. 10.6	Bal. 3.2	Was. 17.1	1960	NFL
1960	AFL	Da. 253 18.1	Buf. 225	Dal. 980 70	Dal. 2.32	Hou. 6	Buf. 43.1	Buf. 2461 176	Buf. 5.7	Bos. 19 Buf. 19 Dal. 19	Buf. 33	Buf. 7.7	Dal. 5.8	Den. 20.1	1960	AFL
1961	NFL	NYG 220 15.7	NYG 212	Pit. 1463 104	StL. 3.51	NYG 6	NYG 45.6	Bal. 2320 166	G.B. 6.4	Det. 11	NYG 33	NYG 8.5	Min. 6.0	StL. 20.1	1961	NFL
1961	AFL	S.D. 219 15.6	Buf. 200	Bos. 1041 74	Bos. 2.97	S.D. 7	Hou. 43.0	S.D. 2736 195	Hou. 5.6	Hou. 13	**S.D. 49**	S.D. 10.1	Buf. 6.5	Den. 17.1	1961	AFL
1962	NFL	G.B. 148 10.6	Det. 180	Det. 1231 88	Det. 3.51	G.B. 4	Chi. 46.8	G.B. 2084 149	G.B. 5.9	G.B. 10	G.B. 31	G.B. 8.7	StL. 4.7	G.B. 20.1	1962	NFL
1962	AFL	Dal. 233 16.6	Hou. 217	Dal. 1250 89	Dal. 3.56	Buf. 10	Hou. 43.8	Oak. 2517 180	Hou. 5.9	Dal. 13	Buf. 36	Buf. 8.2	Bos. 4.9	Hou. 21.0	1962	AFL
1963	NFL	Chi. 144 10.3	G.B. 193	Chi. 1442 103	Chi. 3.50	Chi. 7	Chi. 46.5	Chi. 2045 146	Chi. 5.8	G.B. 9	ChiB 36	ChiB 10.2	Dal. 4.9	G.B. 19.3	1963	NFL
1963	AFL	S.D. 256 18.3	N/A	N/A	N/A	N/A	N/A	N/A	N/A	N/A	N/A	N/A	N/A	N/A	1963	AFL
1964	NFL	Bal. 225 16.1	G.B. 197	L.A. 1501 107	Dal. 3.43	Dal. 6	Dal. 45.6	G.B. 1980 141	G.B. 6.2	G.B. 11	Was. 34	Was. 8.4	Dal. 2.7	Cle. 20.2	1964	NFL
1964	AFL	Buf. 242 17.3	Buf. 206	Buf. 913 65	Buf. 3.04	Buf. 4	Buf. 46.6	K.C. 2910 208	S.D. 6.0	Oak. 21	NYT 34	Den. 7.3	Oak. 6.6	Hou. 18.5	1964	AFL
1965	NFL	L.A. 224 16.0	L.A. 208	L.A. 1409 101	L.A. 3.38	Det. 9	Dal. 48.1	G.B. 2316 165	G.B. 6.0	G.B. 11	G.B. 27 Was. 27	Was. 8.5	Was. 4.6	Dal. 19.5	1965	NFL
1965	AFL	Buf. 226 16.1	S.D. 190	S.D. 1094 78	Buf. 3.09	Buf. 5	Hou. 42.5	S.D. 2480 177	S.D. 5.2	Bos. 17	Buf. 32	Hou. 6.5	Bos. 7.0	Oak. 19.8	1965	AFL
1966	NFL	G.B. 163 11.6	L.A. 196	Dal. 1176 84	StL. 3.16	Dal. 6	StL. 44.5	G.B. 2316 165	G.B. 5.9	G.B. 7	Cle. 30	Cle. 7.4	Det. 3.6	StL. 20.4	1966	NFL
1966	AFL	Buf. 255 18.2	Buf. 192	Buf. 1051 75	Buf. 3.06	Buf. 6	Buf. 44.0	S.D. 2386 170	K.C. 5.8	S.D. 13	K.C. 33	Mia. 7.3	NYJ 5.0	Mia. 20.4	1966	AFL
1967	NFL	L.A. 196 14.0	G.B. 183	Dal. 1081 77	L.A. 3.10	Bal. 5	Chi. 42.7	G.B. 1644 117	G.B. 4.9	Det. 11	Bal. 32 L.A. 32	Bal. 8.1	G.B. 1.7	Chi. 20.5	1967	NFL
1967	AFL	Hou. 199 14.2	Oak. 182	Oak. 1129 81	Oak. 3.21	Hou. 7	Oak. 41.2	Buf. 2191 156	Hou. 5.7	Hou. 10	K.C. 31	Mia. 8.0	Mia. 6.5	Hou. 18.6	1967	AFL
1968	NFL	Bal. 144 10.3	L.A. 190	Dal. 1195 85	Dal. 3.24	**Dal. 2**	N.O. 41.8	G.B. 2031 145	Bal. 5.6	Bal. 9	Cle. 32	Cle. 7.3	Bal. 3.3	Chi. 17.9	1968	NFL
1968	AFL	K.C. 170 12.1	N.Y. 178	NYJ 1195 85	NYJ 3.25	K.C. 4	Buf. 42.1	Hou. 2003 143	Hou. 5.6	Hou. 13	K.C. 37	K.C. 8.0	Oak. 5.3	K.C. 19.3	1968	AFL
1969	NFL	Min. 133 9.5	Min. 158	Dal. 1050 75	Min. 3.23	Dal. 3	L.A. 47.0	Min. 2035 145	Min. 5.0	Min. 8	Min. 30	Min. 7.3	G.B. 3.4	Dal. 19.4	1969	NFL
1969	AFL	K.C. 177 12.6	K.C. 181	K.C. 1091 78	K.C. 3.47	K.C. 6	Oak. 38.9	K.C. 2491 178	K.C. 5.8	K.C. 10	K.C. 32	K.C. 7.5	Oak. 4.1	Bos. 19.1	1969	AFL
1970	NFC	Min. 143 10.2	Min. 168	Det. 1152 82	Det. 3.18	Min. 4	StL. 47.9	Min. 1798 128	Min. 4.9	Min. 6	Det. 28 Min. 28	Min. 7.6	NYG 2.9	L.A. 18.1	1970	NFC
1970	AFC	Mia. 228 16.3	Den. 199	NYJ 1283 92	NYJ 3.14	Bal. 6	NYJ 43.1	K.C. 2280 163	K.C. 5.6	S.D. 13	K.C. 31	K.C. 7.6	Cle. 3.6	Bos. 20.5	1970	AFC
1971	NFC	Min. 139 9.9	Min. 194	Dal. 1144 82	Dal. 3.24	**Min. 2**	S.F. 44.6	Atl. 1895 135	Min. 5.0	Atl. 9	Was. 29	Det. 7.2	S.F. 2.3	Was. 17.5	1971	NFC
1971	AFC	Bal. 140 10.0	Bal. 196	Bal. 1113 80	Bal. 3.16	Bal. 8	Den. 42.1	Bal. 2027 145	Bal. 5.6	Bal. 9	Bal. 28	Cin. 8.1	S.D. 2.0	Mia. 20.0	1971	AFC
1972	NFC	Was. 218 15.6	Min. 200	Dal. 1515 108	G.B. 3.42	Dal. 7	Atl. 45.5	Min. 1791 128	Min. 5.4	G.B. 7	Min. 26	Min. 7.9	Was. 2.1	L.A. 18.5	1972	NFC
1972	AFC	Mia. 171 12.2	Mia. 186	Mia. 1548 111	Oak. 3.76	Pit. 6	Buf. 42.5	Cle. 1994 142	Cin. 5.8	Pit. 9	Pit. 28	Buf. 7.5	Mia. 3.9	Hou. 19.5	1972	AFC
1973	NFC	Min. 168 12.0	L.A. 173	Dal. 1471 105	Was. 3.34	Dal. 5 L.A. 5 Min. 5	Atl. 46.6	Atl. 1619 116	Atl. 5.0	Min. 8	Was. 26	NYG 7.3	Dal. 5.2	Min. 19.1	1973	NFC
1973	AFC	Mia. 150 10.7	Min. 168	Oak. 1470 105	Oak. 3.38	Oak. 5	Buf. 45.1	N.E. 1600 114	Mia. 5.0	Mia. 6	Pit. 37	Pit. 10.3	Cin. 4.6	Den. 20.4	1973	AFC
1974	NFC	L.A. 181 12.9	L.A. 186	L.A. 1308 93	Dal. 3.23	L.A. 4	Atl. 45.0	Atl. 1847 132	Was. 5.3	Min. 8	Was. 25	Was. 6.4	Phi. 6.8	Min. 17.4	1974	NFC
1974	AFC	Pit. 189 13.5	Pit. 200	N.E. 1587 113	Pit. 3.41	Mia. 7	Pit. 43.4	Pit. 1872 134	Pit. 5.5	Buf. 11	K.C. 28	Cle. 7.8	Mia. 6.2	Mia. 19.1	1974	AFC
1975	NFC	L.A. 135 9.6	Min. 190	Min. 1532 109	S.F. 3.53	L.A. 4	Dal. 43.4	Min. 1994 142	L.A. 5.5	L.A. 11	Min. 28	Min. 7.8	G.B. 4.9	Min. 19.5	1975	NFC
1975	AFC	Pit. 162 11.6	Pit. 214	Hou. 1680 120	Hou. 3.38	Pit. 8	Oak. 43.0	Cin. 2001 143	Cin. 5.1	Mia. 9 Pit. 9	Oak. 35	Oak. 8.8	Pit. 5.5	Oak. 18.6	1975	AFC
1976	NFC	Min. 176 12.6	Det. 191	L.A. 1564 112	L.A. 3.6	Chi 10 SF 10	Was. 41.2	Min. 1575 113	Dal. 5.7	Min. 8	L.A. 32	L.A. 8.1	G.B. 5.6	Was. 16.4	1976	NFC
1976	AFC	Pit. 138 9.9	Pit. 182	Pit. 1457 104	Pit. 3.2	Pit. 5	Pit. 42.4	Cin. 1758 126	Den. 5.8	Den. 8	Cin. 26	Cin. 7.1	Pit. 5.7	Oak. 18.4	1976	AFC
1977	NFC	Atl. 129 9.2	Atl. 192	Dal. 1651 118	NY G 3.4	Atl. 5	Dal. 41.5	Atl. 1775 127	Dal. 5.4	Chi. 7	Atl. 26	Atl. 8.1	L.A. 4.0	Was. 19.1	1977	NFC
1977	AFC	Den. 148 10.6	Oak. 204	Den. 1531 109	Den. 3.3	Den. 5	Pit. 44.0	S.D. 2088 149	S.D. 5.5	Bal. 10 Mia. 10	Pit. 31	Pit. 8.7	Cin. 6.8	Oak. 15.8	1977	AFC

Bold — designates All-Time Leader

YEARLY PASSING LEADERS

YEAR	LGUE	RANK (NAME · TEAM)	YARDS (NAME · TEAM)	COMPLETIONS (NAME · TEAM)	COMP. PCT. (NAME · TEAM)	TOUCHDOWNS (TEAM · NAME)	YARDS/ATT. (NAME · TEAM)	FEWEST PCT. INT. (NAME · TEAM)	YEAR	LGUE
1933	NFL	Friedman Bkn.	Newman NY G 973	Newman NY G 53	Friedman Bkn. 52.5	Newman NY G 9	Molesworth ChiB. 8.4	Monnett G.B. 6.5	1933	NFL
1934	NFL	Herber G.B.	Herber G.B. 799	Herber G.B. 42	Clark Det. 46.9	Herber G.B. 8	Clark Det. 7.8	Newman NY G 5.5	1934	NFL
1935	NFL	Danowski NY G	Danowski NY G 795	Danowski NY G 57	Danowski NY G 50.4	Danowski NY G 11	Masterson ChiB. 10.4	Not Available	1935	NFL
1936	NFL	Herber G.B.	Herber G.B. 1239	Herber G.B. 77	Clark Det. 53.5	Herber G.B. 11	Herber G.B. 7.2	Monnett G.B. 3.8	1936	NFL
1937	NFL	Monnett G.B.	Baugh Was. 1127	Baugh Was. 81	Monnett G.B. 50.7	Monnett G.B. 9	Masterson ChiB. 8.5	Danowski NY G 3.7	1937	NFL
1938	NFL	Monnett G.B.	Parker Bkn. 865	Danowski NY G 70	Monnett G.B 54.4	Monnett G.B 9	Monnett G.B. 8.2	Parker Bkn. 4.7	1938	NFL
1939	NFL	Filchock Was.	O'Brien Phi. 1324	Hall Cle. 106	Filchock Was. 61.8	Filchock Was. 11	Filchock Was. 12.3	Sloan Det. 2.8	1939	NFL
1940	NFL	Baugh Was.	Baugh Was. 1367	O'Brien Phi. 124	Baugh Was. 62.7	Baugh Was. 12	Luckman ChiB. 9.0	Watkins Phi. 3.5	1940	NFL
1941	NFL	Luckman ChiB.	Isbell G.B. 1479	Isbell G.B. 117	Luckman ChiB. 57.1	Isbell G.B. 15	Luckman ChiB. 9.9	Mallouf ChiC. 4.2	1941	NFL
1942	NFL	Baugh Was.	Isbell G.B. 2021	Isbell G.B. 146	Baugh Was. 58.7	Isbell G.B. 24	O'Rourke ChiB. 10.8	Baugh Was. 4.9	1942	NFL
1943	NFL	Luckman ChiB.	Luckman ChiB. 2194	Baugh Was. 133	Baugh Was. 56.2	Luckman ChiB. 28	Luckman ChiB. 10.9	Comp G.B. 4.3	1943	NFL
1944	NFL	Filchock Was.	Comp G.B. 1159	Filchock Was. 84	Filchock Was. 57.1	Filchock Was. 13	Ronzani ChiB. 8.0	Baugh Was. 5.5	1944	NFL
1945	NFL	Baugh Was.	Luckman ChiB. 1725	Baugh Was. 128	Baugh Was. 70.3	Luckman ChiB. 14 Waterfield Cle. 14	Waterfield Cle. 9.4	Baugh Was. 2.2	1945	NFL
1946	NFL	Luckman ChiB.	Luckman ChiB. 1826	Waterfield L.A. 127	Thompson Phi. 55.3	Waterfield L.A. 18	Luckman ChiB. 8.0	Governali Bos. 5.2	1946	NFL
1946	AAFC	Graham Cle.	Dobbs Bkn. 1886	Dobbs Bkn. 135	O'Rourke L.A. 57.7	Graham Cle. 17	Graham Cle. 10.5	Parker N.Y. 2.6	1946	AAFC
1947	NFL	Baugh Was.	Baugh Was. 2938	Baugh Was. 210	Baugh Was. 59.3	Baugh Was. 25	Luckman ChiB. 8.4	Baugh Was. 4.2	1947	NFL
1947	AAFC	Graham Cle.	Graham Cle. 2753	Schwenk Bal. 168	Graham Cle. 60.6	Graham Cle. 25	Graham Cle. 10.2	Graham Cle. 4.1	1947	AAFC
1948	NFL	Baugh Was.	Baugh Was. 2599	Baugh Was. 185	Baugh Was. 58.7	Thompson Phi. 25	LeForce Det. 9.0	Hardy L.A. 3.3	1948	NFL
1948	AAFC	Tittle Bal.	Graham Cle. 2713	Dobbs L.A. 185	Albert S.F. 58.3	Albert S.F. 29	Tittle Bal. 8.7	Tittle Bal. 3.1	1948	AAFC
1949	NFL	Baugh Was.	Lujack ChiB. 2658	Lujack ChiB. 162	Baugh Was. 56.9	Lujack ChiB. 23	Lujack ChiB. 8.2	Enke Det. 3.5	1949	NFL
1949	AAFC	Graham Cle.	Graham Cle. 2785	Graham Cle. 161	Ratterman Buf. 57.9	Albert S.F. 27	Graham Cle. 9.8	Graham Cle. 3.5	1949	AAFC
1950	NFL	Van Brocklin L.A.	Layne Det. 2323	Tittle Bal. 161	Waterfield L.A. 57.3	Ratterman NY Y 22	Van Brocklin L.A. 8.8	Conerly NY G 5.3	1950	NFL
1951	NFL	Graham Cle.	Layne Det. 2403	Layne Det. 152	Thomason G.B. 56.6	Layne Det. 26	Waterfield L.A. 8.9	Thomason G.B. 4.1	1951	NFL
1952	NFL	Rote G.B.	Graham Cle. 2816	Graham Cle. 181	Van Brocklin L.A. 55.1	Finks Pit. 20 Graham Cle. 20	Van Brocklin L.A. 8.5	Thomason Phi. 4.2	1952	NFL
1953	NFL	Graham Cle.	Graham Cle. 2722	Blanda ChiB. 169	Graham Cle. 64.7	Thomason Phi. 21	Graham Cle. 10.6	Conerly Cle. 3.5	1953	NFL
1954	NFL	Layne Det.	Van Brocklin L.A. 2637	Rote G.B. 180	Graham Cle. 59.2	Burk Phi. 23	Van Brocklin L.A. 10.1	Tittle S.F. 3.1	1954	NFL
1955	NFL	Graham Cle.	Finks Pit. 2270	Finks Pit. 165	Graham Cle. 53.0	Rote G.B. 17 Tittle S.F. 17	Graham Cle. 9.3	Gilmer Det. 3.3	1955	NFL
1956	NFL	Brown ChiB.	Rote G.B. 2203	Rote G.B. 146	Brown ChiB. 57.1	Rote G.B. 18	Brown ChiB. 9.9	Conerly NY G 4.0	1956	NFL
1957	NFL	Unitas Bal.	Unitas Bal. 2550	Unitas Bal. 176	Tittle S.F. 63.1	Unitas Bal. 24	O'Connell Cle. 11.2	Morrall Pit. 4.2	1957	NFL
1958	NFL	Unitas Bal.	Wade L.A. 2875	Van Brocklin Phi. 198	Brodie S.F. 59.9	Unitas Bal. 19	Le Baron Was. 9.4	Unitas Bal. 2.7	1958	NFL
1959	NFL	Conerly NY G	Unitas Bal. 2899	Unitas Bal. 193	Wade L.A. 58.6	Unitas Bal. 32	Conerly NY G 8.8	Conerly NY G 2.1	1959	NFL
1960	NFL	Plum Cle.	Unitas Bal. 3099	Unitas Bal. 190	Plum Cle. 60.4	Unitas Bal. 25	Plum Cle. 9.2	Plum Cle. 2.0	1960	NFL
1960	AFL	Kemp L.A.	Tripucka Den. 3038	Tripucka Den. 248	Flores Oak. 54.0	Dorow NY T 26	Kemp L.A. 7.4	Songin Bos. 3.8	1960	AFL
1961	NFL	Plum Cle.	Jurgensen Phi. 3723	Jurgensen Phi. 235	Plum Cle. 58.6	Jurgensen Phi. 32	Brodie S.F. 9.1	Plum Cle. 3.3	1961	NFL
1961	AFL	Blanda Hou.	Blanda Hou. 3330	Dorow NY T 197	Parilli Bos. 52.5	Blanda Hou. 36	Blanda Hou. 9.2	Songin Bos. 4.3	1961	AFL
1962	NFL	Starr G.B.	Jurgensen Phi. 3261	Wade Chi. 225	Starr G.B. 62.4	Tittle NY G 33	Jurgensen Phi. 8.9	Starr G.B. 3.2	1962	NFL
1962	AFL	Dawson Dal.	Tripuka Den. 2917	Tripuka Den. 240	Dawson Dal. 61.0	Dawson Dal. 29	Dawson Dal. 8.9	Parilli Bos. 3.2	1962	AFL
1963	NFL	Tittle NY G	Unitas Bal. 3481	Unitas Bal. 237	Tittle NY G 60.2	Tittle NY G 36	Tittle NY G 8.6	Unitas Bal. 2.9	1963	NFL
1963	AFL	Rote S.D.	Blanda Hou. 3003	Blanda Hou. 225	Rote S.D. 59.4	Dawson Dal. 26	Rote S.D. 8.7	Wood NY T 5.1	1963	AFL
1964	NFL	Starr G.B.	Johnson StL. 3045	Johnson StL. 223	Bukich Chi. 61.9	Ryan Cle. 25	Unitas Bal. 9.3	Starr G.B. 1.6	1964	NFL
1964	AFL	Dawson K.C.	Parilli Bos. 3465	Blanda Hou. 262	Dawson K.C. 56.2	Parilli Bos. 31	Kemp Buf. 8.5	Dawson K.C. 5.1	1964	AFL
1965	NFL	Bukich ChiB.	Brodie S.F. 3112	Brodie S.F. 242	Brodie S.F. 61.9	Brodie S.F. 30	Unitas Bal. 9.0	Bukich Chi. 2.9	1965	NFL
1965	AFL	Dawson K.C.	Hadl S.D. 2798	Blanda Hou. 186	Dawson K.C. 53.4	Dawson K.C. 21	Hadl S.D. 8.0	Wood Oak. 3.8	1965	AFL
1966	NFL	Starr G.B.	Jurgensen Was. 3209	Jurgensen Was. 254	Starr G.B. 62.2	Ryan Cle. 29	Starr G.B. 9.0	Starr G.B. 1.2	1966	NFL
1966	AFL	Dawson K.C.	Namath NY J 3379	Namath NY J 232	Dawson K.C. 56.0	Dawson K.C. 26	Dawson K.C. 8.9	Trull Hou. 2.9	1966	AFL
1967	NFL	Jurgensen Was.	Jurgensen Was. 3747	Jurgensen Was. 288	Unitas Bal. 58.5	Jurgensen Was. 31	Starr G.B. 8.7	Lamonica Oak. 3.2	1967	NFL
1967	AFL	Lamonica Oak.	Namath NY J 4007	Namath NY J 258	Dawson K.C. 57.7	Lamonica Oak. 30	Namath NY J 8.2	Lamonica Oak. 4.7	1967	AFL
1968	NFL	Morrall Bal.	Brodie S.F. 3020	Brodie S.F. 234	Starr G.B. 63.7	Morrall Bal. 26	Starr G.B. 9.5	Munson Det. 2.4	1968	NFL
1968	AFL	Dawson K.C.	Hadl S.D. 3473	Hadl S.D. 208	Dawson K.C. 58.5	Hadl S.D. 27	Dawson K.C. 9.4	Stofa Cin. 2.8	1968	AFL
1969	NFL	Jurgensen Was.	Jurgensen Was. 3102	Jurgensen Was. 274	Starr G.B. 62.2	Gabriel L.A. 24	Horn G.B. 9.0	Gabriel L.A. 1.8	1969	NFL
1969	AFL	Cook Cin.	Lamonica Oak. 3302	Lamonica Oak. 221	Dawson K.C. 59.0	Lamonica Oak. 34	Cook Cin. 9.4	Hadl S.D. 3.4	1969	AFL
1970	NFC	Brodie S.F.	Brodie S.F. 2941	Brodie S.F. 223	Jurgensen Was. 59.9	Brodie S.F. 24	Morton Dal. 8.8	Brodie S.F. 2.7	1970	NFC
1970	AFC	Lamonica Oak.	Lamonica Oak. 2516	Lamonica Oak. 179	Griese Mia. 58.0	Hadl S.D. 22 Lamonica Oak. 22	Griese Mia. 8.2	Carter Cin. 3.2	1970	AFC
1971	NFC	Staubach Dal.	Brodie S.F. 2642	Tarkenton NY G 226	Berry Atl. 60.2	Brodie S.F. 24	Staubach Dal. 8.9	Staubach Dal. 1.9	1971	NFC
1971	AFC	Griese Mia.	Hadl S.D. 3075	Hadl S.D. 233	Carter Cin. 62.2	Hadl S.D. 21	Dawson K.C. 8.3	Carter Cin. 3.2	1971	AFC
1972	NFC	Tarkenton Min.	Manning N.O. 2781	Manning N.O. 230	Snead NY G 60.3	Kilmer Was. 19	Berry Atl. 7.8	Tarkenton Min. 3.4	1972	NFC
1972	AFC	Morrall Mia.	Namath NY J 2816	Namath NY J 230	Dawson K.C. 57.4	Namath NY J 19	Morrall Mia. 9.1	Anderson Cin. 2.3	1972	AFC
1973	NFC	Gabriel Phi.	Gabriel Phi. 3219	Gabriel Phi. 270	Staubach Dal. 62.6	Gabriel Phi. 23 Staubach Dal. 23	Staubach Dal. 8.5	Tarkenton Min. 2.6	1973	NFC
1973	AFC	Anderson Cin.	Plunkett N.E. 2550	Plunkett N.E. 193	Stabler Oak. 62.7	Stabler Oak. 20 Johnson Den. 20	Stabler Oak. 7.7	Anderson Cin. 3.6	1973	AFC
1974	NFC	Jurgensen Was.	Tarkenton Min. 2598	Hart St.L. 200	Jurgensen Was. 64.1	Hart St.L. 20	Harris L.A. 7.8	Hart St.L. 2.1	1974	NFC
1974	AFC	Anderson Cin.	Anderson Cin. 2667	Anderson Cin. 213	Anderson Cin. 64.9	Stabler Oak. 26	Anderson Cin. 8.1	Anderson Cin. 3.0	1974	AFC
1975	NFC	Tarkenton Min.	Tarkenton Min. 2994	Tarkenton Min. 273	Tarkenton Min. 64.2	Tarkenton Min. 25	Staubach Dal. 7.7	Anderson Min. 3.1	1975	NFC
1975	AFC	Anderson Cin.	Anderson Cin. 3169	Anderson Cin. 228	Dawson K.C. 66.4	Ferguson Buf. 25	Griese Mia. 8.9	Jones Bal. 2.3	1975	AFC
1976	NFC	Harris L.A.	Tarkenton Min. 2961	Tarkenton Min. 255	Tarkenton Min. 61.9	Hart St.L. 18	Harris L.A. 9.2	Douglass N.O. 1.9	1976	NFC
1976	AFC	Stabler Oak.	Jones Bal. 3014	Fouts S.D. 208	Stabler Oak. 66.7	Stabler Oak. 27	Stabler Oak. 9.4	Ferguson Buf. 0.7	1976	AFC
1977	NFC	Staubach Dal.	Staubach Dal. 2620	Staubach Dal. 210	Tarkenton Min. 60.1	Jaworski Phi. 18 Staubach Dal. 18	Staubach Dal. 7.3	Staubach Dal. 2.5	1977	NFC
1977	AFC	Griese Mia.	Ferguson Buf. 2803	Jones Bal. 224	Griese Mia. 58.6	Griese Mia. 22	Bradshaw Pit. 8.0	Jones Bal. 2.8	1977	AFC

YEARLY RUSHING LEADERS

YEAR	LGUE	ATTEMPTS NAME	TEAM		YARDS NAME	TEAM		AVERAGE YARDS NAME	TEAM		TOUCHDOWNS NAME	TEAM		YEAR	LGUE
1933	NFL	Jim Musick	Bos.	173	Jim Musick	Bos.	809	Kink Richards	NY G	6.2	Glenn Presnell	Det.	6	1933	NFL
1934	NFL	Swede Hanson	Phi.	147	Beattie Feathers	ChiB.	1004	Beattie Feathers	ChiB.	9.9	Dutch Clark	Det.	8	1934	NFL
											Beattie Feathers	ChiB.	8		
1935	NFL	Kink Richards	NY G.	149	Doug Russell	ChiC.	499	Ernie Caddel	Det.	5.2	Ernie Caddel	Det.	6	1935	NFL
1936	NFL	Tuffy Leemans	NY G.	206	Tuffy Leemans	NY G.	830	Ernie Caddel	Det.	6.4	Dutch Clark	Det.	7	1936	NFL
1937	NFL	Cliff Battles	Was.	216	Cliff Battles	Was.	874	Ernie Caddel	Det.	5.6	Cliff Battles	Was.	5	1937	NFL
											Dutch Clark	Det.	5		
											Clark Hinkle	G.B.	5		
1938	NFL	Whizzer White	Pit.	152	Whizzer White	Pit.	567	Cecil Isbell	G.B.	5.2	Andy Farkas	Was.	6	1938	NFL
1939	NFL	Andy Farkas	Was.	139	Bill Osmanski	ChiB.	699	Joe Maniaci	ChiB.	7.1	Johnny Drake	Cle.	9	1939	NFL
1940	NFL	Whizzer White	Det.	146	Whizzer White	Det.	514	Banks McFadden	Bkn.	6.3	Johnny Drake	Cle.	9	1940	NFL
1941	NFL	Clarke Hinkle	G.B.	129	Pug Manders	Bkn.	486	George McAfee	ChiB.	7.3	Hugh Gallarneau	ChiB.	8	1941	NFL
1942	NFL	Bill Dudley	Pit.	162	Bill Dudley	Pit.	696	Frank Maznicki	ChiB.	6.4	Gary Famiglietti	ChiB.	8	1942	NFL
1943	NFL	Bill Paschal	NY G.	147	Bill Paschal	NY G.	572	Ward Cuff	NY G.	6.5	Bill Paschal	NY G.	10	1943	NFL
1944	NFL	Bill Paschal	NY G.	196	Bill Paschal	NY G.	737	Al Grygo	ChiB.	6.1	Bill Paschal	NY G.	9	1944	NFL
1945	NFL	Frank Akins	Was.	147	Steve Van Buren	Phi.	832	Fred Gehrke	Cle.	6.3	Steve Van Buren	Phi.	15	1945	NFL
1946	NFL	Bill Dudley	Pit.	146	Bill Dudley	Pit.	604	Elmer Angsman	ChiC.	6.8	Ted Fritsch	G.B.	9	1946	NFL
1946	AAFC	Spec Sanders	N.Y.	140	Spec Sanders	N.Y.	709	Chuck Fenenbock	L.A.	8.4	Len Eshmont	S.F.	6	1946	AAFC
											Don Greenwood	Cle.	6		
											John Kimbrough	L.A.	6		
											Spec Sanders	N.Y.	6		
1947	NFL	Steve Van Buren	Phi.	217	Steve Van Buren	Phi.	1008	Kenny Washington	L.A.	7.4	Steve Van Buren	Phi.	13	1947	NFL
1947	AAFC	Spec Sanders	N.Y.	231	Spec Sanders	N.Y.	1432	Special Delivery Jones	Cle.	7.0	Spec Sanders	N.Y.	18	1947	AAFC
1948	NFL	Steve Van Buren	Phi.	201	Steve Van Buren	Phi.	945	Charlie Trippi	ChiC.	5.4	Steve Van Buren	Phi.	10	1948	NFL
1948	AAFC	Spec Sanders	N.Y.	169	Marion Motley	Cle.	964	Joe Perry	S.F.	7.3	Chet Mutryn	Buf.	10	1948	AAFC
											Joe Perry	S.F.	10		
1949	NFL	Steve Van Buren	Phi.	263	Steve Van Buren	Phi.	1146	Bosh Pritchard	Phi.	6.0	Steve Van Buren	Phi.	11	1949	NFL
1949	AAFC	Bob Hoernschemeyer	Chi.	133	Joe Perry	S.F.	783	Frankie Albert	S.F.	7.1	Marion Motley	Cle.	8	1949	AAFC
											Joe Perry	S.F.	8		
1950	NFL	Joe Geri	Pit.	188	Marion Motley	Cle.	810	Johnny Lujack	ChiB.	6.3	Johnny Lujack	ChiB.	11	1950	NFL
		Steve Van Buren	Phi.	188											
1951	NFL	Eddie Price	NY G.	271	Eddie Price	NY G.	971	Tobin Rote	G.B.	6.9	Rob Goode	Was.	9	1951	NFL
1952	NFL	Eddie Price	NY G.	183	Dan Towler	L.A.	894	Hugh McElhenny	S.F.	7.0	Dan Towler	L.A.	10	1952	NFL
1953	NFL	Joe Perry	S.F.	192	Joe Perry	S.F.	1018	Skeets Quinlan	L.A.	7.3	Joe Perry	S.F.	10	1953	NFL
1954	NFL	Joe Perry	S.F.	173	Joe Perry	S.F.	1049	Hugh McElhenny	S.F.	8.0	Dan Towler	L.A.	11	1954	NFL
1955	NFL	Alan Ameche	Bal.	213	Alan Ameche	Bal.	961	Rick Casares	ChiB.	5.4	Alan Ameche	Bal.	9	1955	NFL
1956	NFL	Rick Casares	ChiB.	234	Rick Casares	ChiB.	1126	Lenny Moore	Bal.	7.5	Rick Casares	ChiB.	12	1956	NFL
1957	NFL	Rick Casares	ChiB.	204	Jimmy Brown	Cle.	942	Lenny Moore	Bal.	5.0	Jimmy Brown	Cle.	9	1957	NFL
1958	NFL	Jimmy Brown	Cle.	257	Jimmy Brown	Cle.	1527	Lenny Moore	Bal.	7.3	Jimmy Brown	Cle.	17	1958	NFL
1959	NFL	Jimmy Brown	Cle.	290	Jimmy Brown	Cle.	1329	Johnny Olszewski	Was.	6.6	Jimmy Brown	Cle.	14	1959	NFL
1960	NFL	Jim Taylor	G.B.	230	Jimmy Brown	Cle.	1257	John David Crow	StL.	5.9	Paul Hornung	G.B.	13	1960	NFL
1960	AFL	Abner Haynes	Dal.	156	Abner Haynes	Dal.	875	Paul Lowe	L.A.	6.3	Abner Haynes	Dal.	9	1960	AFL
											Paul Lowe	L.A.	9		
1961	NFL	Jimmy Brown	Cle.	305	Jimmy Brown	Cle.	1408	Lenny Moore	Bal.	7.0	Jim Taylor	G.B.	15	1961	NFL
1961	AFL	Bill Mathis	NY T.	202	Billy Cannon	Hou.	948	Jack Spikes	Dal.	8.6	Abner Haynes	Dal.	9	1961	AFL
											Paul Lowe	L.A.	9		
1962	NFL	Jim Taylor	G.B.	272	Jim Taylor	G.B.	1474	Amos Marsh	Dal.	5.6	Jim Taylor	G.B.	19	1962	NFL
1962	AFL	Charley Tolar	Hou.	244	Cookie Gilchrist	Buf.	1096	Len Dawson	Dal.	6.6	Cookie Gilchrist	Buf.	13	1962	AFL
											Abner Haynes	Dal.	13		
1963	NFL	Jimmy Brown	Cle.	291	Jimmy Brown	Cle.	1863	Jimmy Brown	Cle.	6.4	Jimmy Brown	Cle.	12	1963	NFL
1963	AFL	Cookie Gilchrist	Buf.	232	Clem Daniels	Oak.	1099	Keith Lincoln	S.D.	6.5	Cookie Gilchrist	Buf.	12	1963	AFL
1964	NFL	Jimmy Brown	Cle.	280	Jimmy Brown	Cle.	1446	Jimmy Brown	Cle.	5.2	Lenny Moore	Bal.	16	1964	NFL
1964	AFL	Cookie Gilchrist	Buf.	230	Cookie Gilchrist	Buf.	981	Mack Lee Hill	K.C.	5.5	Sid Blanks	Hou.	6	1964	AFL
											Cookie Gilchrist	Buf.	6		
											Daryle Lamonica	Buf.	6		
1965	NFL	Jimmy Brown	Cle.	289	Jimmy Brown	Cle.	1544	Timmy Brown	Phi.	5.4	Jimmy Brown	Cle	17	1965	NFL
1965	AFL	Cookie Gilchrist	Buf.	252	Paul Lowe	S.D.	1121	Paul Lowe	S.D.	5.1	Paul Lowe	S.D.	7	1965	AFL
1966	NFL	Bill Brown	Min.	251	Gale Sayers	Chi.	1231	Leroy Kelly	Cle.	5.5	Leroy Kelly	Cle.	15	1966	NFL
1966	AFL	Jim Nance	Bos.	299	Jim Nance	Bos.	1458	Mike Garrett	K.C.	5.5	Jim Nance	Bos.	11	1966	AFL
1967	NFL	Leroy Kelly	Cle.	235	Leroy Kelly	Cle.	1205	Leroy Kelly	Cle.	5.1	Leroy Kelly	Cle.	11	1967	NFL
1967	AFL	Jim Nance	Bos.	269	Jim Nance	Bos.	1216	Brad Hubbert	S.D.	5.5	Emerson Boozer	NY J.	10	1967	AFL
1968	NFL	Leroy Kelly	Cle.	248	Leroy Kelly	Cle.	1239	Gale Sayers	Chi.	6.2	Leroy Kelly	Cle.	16	1968	NFL
1968	AFL	Paul Robinson	Cin.	238	Paul Robinson	Cin.	1023	Dickie Post	S.D.	5.0	Paul Robinson	Cin.	8	1968	AFL
1969	NFL	Gale Sayers	Chi.	236	Gale Sayers	Chi.	1032	Tony Baker	N.O.	4.8	Tom Matte	Bal.	11	1969	NFL
1969	AFL	Jim Nance	Bos.	193	Dickie Post	S.D.	873	Carl Garrett	Bos.	5.0	Jim Kiick	Mia.	9	1969	AFL
1970	NFC	Ron Johnson	NY G.	263	Larry Brown	Was.	1125	Duane Thomas	Dal.	5.3	MacArthur Lane	StL.	11	1970	NFC
1970	AFC	Floyd Little	Den.	209	Floyd Little	Den.	901	John Fuqua	Pit.	5.0	John Fuqua	Pit.	7	1970	AFC
											Jim Nance	Bos.	7		
											Bo Scott	Cle.	7		
1971	NFC	Larry Brown	Was.	253	John Brockington	G.B.	1105	John Brockington	G.B.	5.1	Duane Thomas	Dal.	11	1971	NFC
1971	AFC	Floyd Little	Den.	284	Floyd Little	Den.	1133	Larry Csonka	Mia.	5.4	Leroy Kelly	Cle.	10	1971	AFC
1972	NFC	Ron Johnson	NY G.	298	Larry Brown	Was.	1216	Bobby Douglass	Chi.	6.9	Ron Johnson	NY G.	9	1972	NFC
											Greg Landry	Det.	9		
1972	AFC	O. J. Simpson	Buf.	292	O. J. Simpson	Buf.	1251	Franco Harris	Pit.	5.6	Mercury Morris	Mia.	12	1972	AFC
1973	NFC	Calvin Hill	Dal.	273	John Brockington	G.B.	1144	Bobby Douglass	Chi.	5.6	Donny Anderson	StL.	10	1973	NFC
1973	AFC	O. J. Simpson	Buf.	332	O. J. Simpson	Buf.	2003	Mercury Morris	Mia.	6.4	Floyd Little	Den.	12	1973	AFC
											O. J. Simpson	Buf.	12		
1974	NFC	John Brockington	G.B.	266	Lawrence McCutcheon	L.A.	1109	Terry Metcalf	St.L.	4.7	Tom Sullivan	Phi.	11	1974	NFC
1974	AFC	O.J. Simpson	Buf.	270	Otis Armstrong	Den.	1407	Otis Armstrong	Den.	5.3	Jon Keyworth	Den.	10	1974	AFC
1975	NFC	Chuck Foreman	Min.	280	Jim Otis	St.L.	1076	Del Williams	S.F.	5.4	Chuck Foreman	Min.	13	1975	NFC
1975	AFC	O.J. Simpson	Buf.	329	O.J. Simpson	Buf.	1817	O.J. Simpson	Oak.	5.5	Pete Banaszak	Oak.	16	1975	AFC
											O.J. Simpson	Buf.	16		
1976	NFC	Walter Payton	Chi.	311	Walter Payton	Chi.	1390	Del Williams	S.F.	4.9	Chuck Foreman	Min.	13	1976	NFC
											Walter Payton	Chi.	13		
1976	AFC	O.J. Simpson	Buf.	290	O.J. Simpson	Buf.	1503	Don Calhoun	N.E.	4.8	Franco Harris	Pit.	14	1976	AFC
1977	NFC	Walter Payton	Chi.	339	Walter Payton	Chi.	1852	Walter Payton	Chi.	5.5	Walter Payton	Chi.	14	1977	NFC
1977	AFC	Mark van Edghen	Oak.	324	Mark van Edghen	Oak.	1273	Benny Malone	Mia.	4.8	Franco Harris	Pit.	11	1977	AFC

YEARLY LEADERS

RECEIVING — RECEPTIONS / YARDS / AVERAGE YARDS / TOUCHDOWNS

INTERCEPTIONS

YEAR	LGUE	RECEPTIONS NAME	TEAM		YARDS NAME	TEAM		AVERAGE YARDS NAME	TEAM		TOUCHDOWNS NAME	TEAM		INTERCEPTIONS NAME	TEAM		YEAR	LGUE
1933	NFL	Shipwreck Kelly	Bkn.	22	Paul Moss	Pit.	383	Paul Moss	Pit.	29.5	5 tied with 3 each						1933	NFL
1934	NFL	Red Badgro	NY G	16	Harry Ebding	Det.	257	Harry Ebding	Det.	28.6	Bill Hewitt	Chi B	5				1934	NFL
		Joe Carter	Phi.	16														
1935	NFL	Tod Goodwin	NY G	26	Charley Malone	Bos.	433	Joe Carter	Phi.	23.6	Don Hutson	G.B.	7				1935	NFL
1936	NFL	Don Hutson	G.B.	34	Don Hutson	G.B.	526	Bill Hewitt	Chi B	23.9	Don Hutson	G.B.	8				1936	NFL
1937	NFL	Don Hutson	G.B.	41	Gaynell Tinsley	Chi C	675	Jeff Barrett	Bkn.	23.1	Don Hutson	G.B.	7				1937	NFL
1938	NFL	Gaynell Tinsley	Chi C	41	Don Hutson	G.B.	548	Jim Benton	Cle.	19.9	Don Hutson	G.B.	9				1938	NFL
1939	NFL	Don Hutson	G.B.	34	Don Hutson	G.B.	846	Andy Farkas	Was.	27.3	Jim Benton	Cle.	7				1939	NFL
1940	NFL	Don Looney	Phi.	58	Don Looney	Phi.	707	Paul McDonough	Cle.	26.3	Don Hutson	G.B.	7	Don Hutson	G.B.	6	1940	NFL
														Ace Parker	Bkn.	6		
														Rip Ryan	Det.	6		
1941	NFL	Don Hutson	G.B.	58	Don Hutson	G.B.	738	Ken Kavanaugh	Chi B	28.5	Don Hutson	G.B.	10	Marshall Goldberg	Chi C	7	1941	NFL
														Art Jones	Pit.	7		
1942	NFL	Don Hutson	G.B.	74	Don Hutson	G.B.	1211	Ray McLean	Chi B	30.1	Don Hutson	G.B.	17	Bulldog Turner	Chi B	8	1942	NFL
1943	NFL	Don Hutson	G.B.	47	Don Hutson	G.B.	776	Tony Bova	P–P	24.6	Don Hutson	G.B.	11	Sammy Baugh	Was.	11	1943	NFL
1944	NFL	Don Hutson	G.B.	58	Don Hutson	G.B.	866	Mel Bleeker	Phi.	37.4	Don Hutson	G.B.	9	Howie Livingston	NY G	9	1944	NFL
1945	NFL	Don Hutson	G.B.	47	Jim Benton	Cle.	1067	Frank Liebel	NY G	27.0	Frank Liebel	NY G	10	Roy Zimmerman	Phi.	7	1945	NFL
1946	NFL	Jim Benton	L.A.	63	Jim Benton	L.A.	981	Bill Dewell	Chi C	23.8	Bill Dewell	Chi C	7	Bill Dudley	Pit.	10	1946	NFL
1946	AAFC	Alyn Beals	S.F.	40	Dante Lavelli	Cle.	843	Jim McCarthy	Bkn.	26.9	Alyn Beals	S.F.	10	Tom Colella	Cle.	10	1946	AAFC
		Dante Lavelli	Cle.	40														
1947	NFL	Jim Keane	Chi B	64	Mal Kutner	Chi C	944	Dan Currivan	Bos.	32.6	Ken Kavanaugh	Chi B	13	Frank Reagan	NY G	10	1947	NFL
														Frank Seno	Bos.	10		
1947	AAFC	Mac Speedie	Cle.	67	Mac Speedie	Cle.	1146	Crazy Legs Hirsch	Chi.	28.2	Alyn Beals	S.F.	10	Tom Colella	Cle.	6	1947	AAFC
														Len Eshmont	S.F.	6		
														Bill Killagher	Chi.	6		
1948	NFL	Tom Fears	L.A.	51	Mal Kutner	Chi.C	943	Frank Seno	Bos.	24.8	Mal Kutner	Chi C	14	Dan Sandifer	Was.	13	1948	NFL
1948	AAFC	Mac Speedie	Cle.	58	Billy Hillenbrand	Bal.	970	John North	Bal.	26.0	Alyn Beals	S.F.	14	Otto Schnellbacher	N.Y.	11	1948	AAFC
1949	NFL	Tom Fears	L.A.	77	Bob Mann	Det.	1014	Elbie Nickel	Pit.	24.3	Tom Fears	L.A.	9	Bob Nussbaumer	Chi C	12	1949	NFL
											Ken Kavanaugh	Chi B	9					
											Hugh Taylor	Was.	9					
1949	AAFC	Mac Speedie	Cle.	62	Mac Speedie	Cle.	1028	Bill Boedecker	Cle.	33.7	Alyn Beals	S.F.	12	Jim Cason	S.F.	9	1949	AAFC
1950	NFL	Tom Fears	L.A.	84	Tom Fears	L.A.	1116	Hugh Taylor	Was.	21.4	Bob Shaw	Chi C	12	Spec Sanders	NY Y	13	1950	NFL
1951	NFL	Crazy Legs Hirsch	L.A.	66	Crazy Legs Hirsch	L.A.	1495	Crazy Legs Hirsch	L.A.	22.7	Crazy Legs Hirsch	L.A.	17	Otto Schnellbacher	NY G	11	1951	NFL
1952	NFL	Mac Speedie	Cle.	62	Billy Howton	G.B.	1231	Hugh Taylor	Was.	23.4	Cloyce Box	Det.	15	Night Train Lane	L.A.	14	1952	NFL
1953	NFL	Pete Pihos	Phi.	63	Pete Pihos	Phi.	1049	Bob Boyd	L.A.	22.8	Pete Pihos	Phi.	10	Jack Christiansen	Det.	12	1953	NFL
											Billy Wilson	S.F.	10					
1954	NFL	Pete Pihos	Phi.	60	Bob Boyd	L.A.	1212	Harlon Hill	Chi B	25.0	Harlon Hill	Chi B	12	Night Train Lane	Chi C	10	1954	NFL
		Billy Wilson	S.F.	60														
1955	NFL	Pete Pihos	Phi.	62	Pete Pihos	Phi.	864	Ray Renfro	Cle.	20.8	Harlon Hill	Chi B	9	Will Sherman	L.A.	11	1955	NFL
1956	NFL	Billy Wilson	S.F.	60	Billy Howton	G.B.	1188	Harlon Hill	Chi B	24.0	Billy Howton	G.B.	12	Linden Crow	Chi C	11	1956	NFL
1957	NFL	Billy Wilson	S.F.	52	Ray Berry	Bal.	800	Ray Renfro	Cle.	28.0	Jim Mutscheller	Bal.	8	Jack Butler	Pit.	10	1957	NFL
														Jack Christiansen	Det.	10		
														Milt Davis	Bal.	10		
1958	NFL	Ray Berry	Bal.	56	Del Shofner	L.A.	1097	Jimmy Orr	Pit.	27.6	Ray Berry	Bal.	9	Jimmy Patton	NY G	11	1958	NFL
		Pete Retzlaff	Phi.	56							Tommy McDonald	Phi.	9					
1959	NFL	Ray Berry	Bal.	66	Ray Berry	Bal.	959	Max McGee	G.B.	23.2	Ray Berry	Bal.	14	Milt Davis	Bal.	7	1959	NFL
														Dean Derby	Pit.	7		
														Don Shinnick	Bal.	7		
1960	NFL	Ray Berry	Bal.	74	Ray Berry	Bal.	1298	Buddy Dial	Pit.	24.3	Sonny Randle	St L.	15	Dave Baker	S.F.	10	1960	NFL
														Jerry Norton	St L.	10		
1960	AFL	Lionel Taylor	Den.	92	Bill Groman	Hou.	1473	Bill Groman	Hou.	20.5	Art Powell	NY T	14	Goose Gonsoulin	Den.	11	1960	AFL
1961	NFL	Jim Phillips	L.A.	78	Tommy McDonald	Phi.	1144	Franke Clarke	Dal.	22.4	Tommy McDonald	Phi.	13	Dick Lynch	NY G	9	1961	NFL
1961	AFL	Lionel Taylor	Den.	100	Charley Hennigan	Hou.	1746	Bill Groman	Hou.	23.5	Bill Groman	Hou.	17	Billy Atkins	Buf.	10	1961	AFL
1962	NFL	Bobby Mitchell	Was.	72	Bobby Mitchell	Was.	1384	Frank Clarke	Dal.	22.2	Frank Clarke	Dal.	14	Willie Wood	G.B.	9	1962	NFL
1962	AFL	Lionel Taylor	Den.	77	Art Powell	NY T	1130	Jim Colclough	Bos.	21.7	Chris Burford	Dal.	12	Lee Riley	NY T	11	1962	AFL
1963	NFL	Bobby Joe Conrad	St L.	73	Bobby Mitchell	Was.	1436	Buddy Dial	Pit.	21.6	Terry Barr	Det.	13	Dick Lynch	NY G	9	1963	NFL
											Gary Collins	Cle.	13	Rosey Taylor	Chi B	9		
1963	AFL	Lionel Taylor	Den.	78	Art Powell	Oak.	1304	Clem Daniels	Oak.	22.8	Art Powell	Oak.	16	Freddy Glick	Hou.	12	1963	AFL
1964	NFL	Johnny Morris	Chi.	93	Johnny Morris	Chi.	1200	Gary Ballman	Pit.	19.9	Bobby Mitchell	Was.	10	Paul Krause	Was.	12	1964	NFL
											Johnny Morris	Chi B	10					
											Bucky Pope	L.A.	10					
1964	AFL	Charley Hennigan	Hou.	101	Charley Hennigan	Hou.	1546	Elbert Dubenion	Buf.	27.1	Lance Alworth	S.D.	13	Dainard Paulson	NY T	12	1964	AFL
1965	NFL	Dave Parks	S.F.	80	Dave Parks	S.F.	1344	Bob Hayes	Dal.	21.8	Bob Hayes	Dal.	12	Bobby Boyd	Bal.	9	1965	NFL
											Dave Parks	S.F.	12					
1965	AFL	Lionel Taylor	Den.	85	Lance Alworth	S.D.	1602	Lance Alworth	S.D.	23.2	Lance Alworth	S.D.	14	W. K. Hicks	Hou.	9	1965	AFL
											Don Maynard	NY J	14					
1966	NFL	Charley Taylor	Was.	72	Pat Studstill	Det.	1266	Homer Jones	NY G	21.8	Bob Hayes	Dal.	13	Larry Wilson	St L.	10	1966	NFL
1966	AFL	Lance Alworth	S.D.	73	Lance Alworth	S.D.	1383	Otis Taylor	K.C.	22.4	Lance Alworth	S.D.	13	Bobby Hunt	K.C.	10	1966	AFL
														Johnny Robinson	K.C.	10		
1967	NFL	Charley Taylor	Was.	70	Ben Hawkins	Phi.	1265	Homer Jones	NY G	24.7	Homer Jones	NY G	13	Lem Barney	Det.	10	1967	NFL
														Dave Whitsell	N.O.	10		
1967	AFL	George Sauer	NY J	75	Don Maynard	NY J	1434	Don Maynard	NY J	20.2	Al Denson	Den.	11	Miller Farr	Hou.	10	1967	AFL
											Otis Taylor	K.C.	11	Tom Janik	Buf.	10		
														Dick Westmoreland	Mia.	10		
1968	NFL	Clifton McNeil	S.F.	71	Roy Jefferson	Pit.	1074	Homer Jones	NY G	23.5	Paul Warfield	Cle.	12	Willie Williams	NY G	10	1968	NFL
1968	AFL	Lance Alworth	S.D.	68	Lance Alworth	S.D.	1312	Don Maynard	NY J	22.8	Warren Wells	Oak.	11	Dave Grayson	Oak.	10	1968	AFL
1969	NFL	Dan Abramowicz	N.O.	73	Harold Jackson	Phi.	1116	Lance Rentzel	Dal.	22.3	Lance Rentzel	Dal.	12	Mel Renfro	Dal.	10	1969	NFL
1969	AFL	Lance Alworth	S.D.	64	Warren Wells	Oak.	1260	Warren Wells	Oak.	26.8	Warren Wells	Oak.	14	Emmitt Thomas	K.C.	9	1969	AFL
1970	NFC	Dick Gordon	Chi B	71	Gene Washington	S.F.	1100	John Gilliam	St L.	21.2	Dick Gordon	Chi B	13	Dick LeBeau	Det.	9	1970	NFC
1970	AFC	Marlon Briscoe	Buf.	57	Marlon Briscoe	Buf.	1036	Gary Garrison	S.D.	22.9	Gary Garrison	S.D.	12	Johnny Robinson	K.C.	10	1970	AFC
1971	NFC	Bob Tucker	NY G	59	Gene Washington	S.F.	884	Bob Hayes	Dal.	24.0	Bob Hayes	Dal.	8	Bill Bradley	Phi.	11	1971	NFC
1971	AFC	Fred Biletnikoff	Oak.	61	Otis Taylor	K.C.	1110	Paul Warfield	Mia.	23.2	Paul Warfield	Mia.	11	Ken Houston	Hou.	9	1971	AFC
1972	NFC	Harold Jackson	Phi.	62	Harold Jackson	Phi.	1048	John Gilliam	Min.	22.0	Gene Washington	S.F.	12	Bill Bradley	Phi.	9	1972	NFC
1972	AFC	Fred Biletnikoff	Oak.	58	Rich Caster	NY J	833	Rich Caster	NY J	21.4	Rich Caster	NY J	10	Mike Sensibaugh	K.C.	8	1972	AFC
1973	NFC	Harold Carmichael	Phi.	67	Harold Carmichael	Phi.	1116	Harold Jackson	L.A.	21.9	Harold Jackson	L.A.	13	Bobby Bryant	Min.	7	1973	NFC
1973	AFC	Fred Willis	Hou.	57	Issac Curtis	Cin.	843	Issac Curtis	Cin.	18.7	Paul Warfield	Mia.	11	Dick Anderson	Mia.	8	1973	AFC
														Mike Wagner	Pit.	8		
1974	NFC	Charlie Young	Phi.	63	Drew Pearson	Dal.	1087	Gene Washington	S.F.	21.2	Harold Carmichael	Phi.	8	Ray Brown	Atl.	8	1974	NFC
1974	AFC	Lydell Mitchell	Bal.	72	Cliff Branch	Oak.	1092	Isaac Curtis	Cin.	21.1	Cliff Branch	Oak.	13	Emmitt Thomas	K.C.	12	1974	AFC
1975	NFC	Chuck Foreman	Min.	73	Mel Gray	St.L.	996	Al Jenkins	Atl.	20.2	Mel Gray	St.L.	11	Paul Krause	Min.	10	1975	NFC
1975	AFC	Lydell Mitchell	Bal.	60	Ken Burrough	Hou.	1063	Isaac Curtis	Cin.	21.2	Lynn Swann	Pit.	11	Mel Blount	Pit.	11	1975	AFC
		Reggie Rucker	Cle.	60														
1976	NFC	Drew Pearson	Dal.	58	Sammy White	Min.	906	Ron Jessie	L.A.	22.9	Sammy White	Min.	10	Monte Jackson	L.A.	10	1976	NFC
1976	AFC	MacArthur Lane	K.C.	66	Roger Carr	Bal.	1112	Roger Carr	Bal.	25.9	Cliff Branch	Oak.	12	Ken Riley	Cin.	9	1976	AFC
1977	NFC	Ahmad Rashad	Min.	51	Drew Pearson	Dal.	870	Mel Gray	Stl.	20.6	Henry Childs	N.O.	9	Rolland Lawrence	Atl.	7	1977	NFC
											Sammy White	Min.	9					
1977	AFC	Lydell Mitchell	Bal.	71	Ken Burrough	Hou.	816	Wes Walker	N.O.	21.1	Nat Moore	Mia.	12	Lyle Blackwood	Bal.	10	1977	AFC

YEARLY RETURN LEADERS

		PUNT RETURNS									KICKOFF RETURNS										
		RETURNS			YARDS			AVERAGE YARDS			RETURNS			YARDS			AVERAGE YARDS				
YEAR	LGUE	NAME	TEAM		NAME	TEAM		NAME	TEAM		NAME	TEAM		NAME	TEAM		NAME	TEAM		YEAR	LGUE
1941	NFL	Whizzer White	Det.	19	Whizzer White	Det.	262													1941	NFL
1942	NFL	Merl Condit	Bkn.	21	Bill Dudley	Pit.	271	Ernie Steele	Phi.	26.4	Marshall Golberg	ChiC	15	Marshall Goldberg	ChiC	393	Bill Dudley	Pit.	27.1	1942	NFL
1943	NFL	Andy Farkas	Was.	15	Frankie Sinkwich	Det.	228	Frankie Sinkwich	Det.	20.7	Ken Heineman	Bkn.	16	Ken Heineman	Bkn.	442	Ned Mathews	Det.	35.1	1943	NFL
1944	NFL	Bob Davis	Bos.	22	Bob Davis	Bos.	271	Ernie Steele	Phi.	16.5	John Grigas	C–P	23	John Grigas	C–P	471	Steve Van Buren	Phi.	33.3	1944	NFL
1945	NFL	Steve Bagarus	Was.	21	Steve Bagarus	Was.	251	Fred Gehrke	Cle.	15.0	Frank Seno	ChiC	19	Frank Seno	ChiC	408	Ted Fritsch	G.B.	34.9	1945	NFL
1946	NFL	Bill Dudley	Pit.	27	Bill Dudley	Pit.	385	Gil Steinke	Phi.	14.5	Sonny Karnofsky	Bos.	21	Sonny Karnofsky	Bos.	599	Frank Seno	ChiC	31.4	1946	NFL
1946	AAFC	Ken Casanega	S.F.	18	Chuck Fenenbock	L.A.	299	Chuck Fenenbock	L.A.	18.7	Steve Juzwik	Buf.	21	Chuck Fenenbock	L.A.	479	Monk Gafford	Bkn–Mia	31.4	1946	AAFC
		Bob Seymour	L.A.	18																	
1947	NFL	Walt Slater	Pit.	28	Walt Slater	Pit.	435	Frank Seno	Bos.	17.8	Eddie Saenz	Was.	29	Eddie Saenz	Was.	797	Steve Van Buren	Phi.	29.4	1947	NFL
1947	AAFC	Glenn Dobbs	Bkn–L.A.	19	Glenn Dobbs	Bkn–L.A.	215	Spec Sanders	N.Y.	27.3	Spec Sanders	N.Y.	22	Chet Mutryn	Buf.	691	Chet Mutryn	Buf.	32.9	1947	AAFC
1948	NFL	George McAfee	ChiB	30	George McAfee	ChiB	417	Jerry Davis	ChiC	20.9	Dan Sandifer	Was.	26	Dan Sandifer	Was.	594	Frank Minini	G.B.	30.8	1948	NFL
1948	AAFC	Cliff Lewis	Cle.	26	Herm Wedemeyer	L.A.	368	Tom Casey	N.Y.	25.4	Monk Gafford	Bkn.	23	Monk Gafford	Bkn.	559	Forrest Hall	S.F.	28.4	1948	AAFC
1949	NFL	Vitamin Smith	L.A.	27	Vitamin Smith	L.A.	427	Red Cochran	ChiC	20.9	Eddie Saenz	Was.	24	Don Doll	Det.	536	J. Salschneider	NY G	31.6	1949	NFL
											Dan Sandifer	Was.	24								
1949	AAFC	Pete Layden	N.Y.	29	Jim Cason	S.F.	351	Buddy Young	N.Y.	19.0	Herm Wedemeyer	Bal.	30	Herm Wedemeyer	Bal.	602	Ray Ramsey	Chi.	29.2	1949	AAFC
1950	NFL	George McAfee	ChiB	33	Billy Grimes	G.B.	555	Herb Rich	Bal.	23.0	Don Paul	ChiC	28	Vitamin Smith	L.A.	742	Vitamin Smith	L.A.	33.7	1950	NFL
1951	NFL	Em Tunnell	NY G	34	Em Tunnell	NY G	489	Buddy Young	NY Y	19.3	George Taliaferro	NY Y	27	George Taliaferro	NY Y	622	Lynn Chadnois	Pit.	32.5	1951	NFL
1952	NFL	Bibbles Bawel	Phi.	34	Em Tunnell	NY G	411	J. Christiansen	Det.	21.5	Billy Baggett	Dal.	23	Buddy Young	Dal.	643	Lynn Chadnois	Pit.	35.2	1952	NFL
											Buddy Young	Dal.	23								
1953	NFL	Em Tunnell	NY G	38	Woodley Lewis	L.A.	267	Charlie Trippi	ChiC	11.4	Woodley Lewis	L.A.	32	Woodley Lewis	L.A.	830	Joe Arenas	S.F.	34.4	1953	NFL
1954	NFL	Chet Hanulak	Cle.	27	Veryl Switzer	G.B.	306	Veryl Switzer	G.B.	12.8	Woodley Lewis	L.A.	34	Woodley Lewis	L.A.	836	Billy Reynolds	Cle.	29.5	1954	NFL
1955	NFL	Bert Rechichar	Bal.	30	Ollie Matson	ChiC	245	Ollie Matson	ChiC	18.8	Sid Watson	Pit.	27	Sid Watson	Pit.	716	Al Carmichael	G.B.	29.9	1955	NFL
1956	NFL	Carl Taseff	Bal.	27	Carl Taseff	Bal.	233	Kenny Konz	Cle.	14.4	Al Carmichael	G.B.	33	Al Carmichael	G.B.	927	Tom Wilson	L.A.	31.8	1956	NFL
1957	NFL	Tommy McDonald	Phi.	26	Bert Zagers	Was.	217	Bert Zagers	Was.	15.5	Al Carmichael	G.B.	31	Al Carmichael	G.B.	690	Jon Arnett	L.A.	28.0	1957	NFL
1958	NFL	Carl Taseff	Bal.	29	Jon Arnett	L.A.	223	Jon Arnett	L.A.	12.4	Jimmy Sears	ChiC	32	Jimmy Sears	ChiC	756	Ollie Matson	ChiC	35.5	1958	NFL
1959	NFL	Bill Stacy	ChiC	29	Bill Stacy	ChiC	281	Johnny Morris	ChiB	12.2	Lenny Lyles	S.F.	25	Lenny Lyles	S.F.	565	Abe Woodson	S.F.	29.4	1959	NFL
1960	NFL	Bill Stits	NY G	18	Abe Woodson	S.F.	174	Abe Woodson	S.F.	13.4	Ted Dean	Phi.	26	Ted Dean	Phi.	533	Tom Moore	G.B.	33.1	1960	NFL
											Tom Frankhouser	Dal.	26								
1960	AFL	Al Carmichael	Den.	15	Abner Haynes	Dal.	215	Abner Haynes	Dal.	15.4	Leon Burton	NY T	31	Leon Burton	NY T	897	Ken Hall	Hou.	31.3	1960	AFL
1961	NFL	Johnny Sample	Pit.	26	Johnny Sample	Pit.	283	Willie Wood	G.B.	16.1	Timmy Brown	Phi.	29	Timmy Brown	Phi.	811	Dick Bass	L.A.	30.3	1961	NFL
											Jim Steffen	Was.	29								
1961	AFL	Fred Bruney	Bos.	23	Dick Christy	NY T	383	Dick Christy	NY T	21.3	George Fleming	Oak.	29	Frank Jackson	Dal.	645	Dave Grayson	Oak.	28.3	1961	AFL
1962	NFL	Pat Studstill	Det.	29	Pat Studstill	Det.	457	Pat Studstill	Det.	15.8	Abe Woodson	S.F.	37	Abe Woodson	S.F.	1157	Abe Woodson	S.F.	31.3	1962	NFL
1962	AFL	Leon Burton	Bos.	21	Dick Christy	NY T	250	Dick Christy	NY T	16.7	Dick Christy	NY T	38	Dick Christy	NY T	824	Bobby Jancik	Hou.	30.3	1962	AFL
1963	NFL	Tom Watkins	Det.	32	Tom Watkins	Det.	399	Dick James	Was.	13.4	Timmy Brown	Phi.	33	Timmy Brown	Phi.	945	Abe Woodson	S.F.	32.2	1963	NFL
											Bill Butler	Min.	33								
1963	AFL	Claude Gibson	Oak.	26	Claude Gibson	Oak.	307	Claude Gibson	Oak.	11.8	Bobby Jancik	Hou.	45	Bobby Jancik	Hou.	1317	Bobby Jancik	Hou.	29.3	1963	AFL
1964	NFL	Mel Renfro	Dal.	32	Mel Renfro	Dal.	418	Tom Watkins	Det.	14.9	Mel Renfro	Dal.	40	Mel Renfro	Dal.	1017	Clarence Childs	NY G	29.0	1964	NFL
1964	AFL	Hagood Clarke	Buf.	33	Claude Gibson	Oak.	419	Bobby Jancik	Hou.	18.3	Odell Barry	Den.	47	Odel Barry	Den.	1245	Bo Roberson	Oak.	27.1	1964	AFL
1965	NFL	Alvin Haymond	Bal.	41	Alvin Haymond	Bal.	403	Leroy Kelly	Cle.	15.6	Kermit Alexander	S.F.	32	Kermit Alexander	S.F.	741	Tom Watkins	Det.	34.4	1965	AFL
1965	AFL	Claude Gibson	Oak.	31	Speedy Duncan	S.D.	464	Speedy Duncan	S.D.	15.5	Abner Haynes	Den.	34	Abner Haynes	Den.	901	Abner Haynes	Den.	26.5	1965	AFL
1966	NFL	Alvin Haymond	Bal.	40	Alvin Haymond	Bal.	347	Johnny Roland	StL.	11.1	Ron Smith	Atl.	43	Ron Smith	Atl.	1013	Gale Sayers	Chi.	31.2	1966	NFL
1966	AFL	Rodger Bird	Oak.	37	Rodger Bird	Oak.	323	Speedy Duncan	S.D.	13.2	Bobby Jancik	Hou.	34	Bobby Jancik	Hou.	875	Goldie Sellers	Den.	28.5	1966	AFL
1967	NFL	Doug Cunningham	S.F.	27	Bob Hayes	Dal.	276	Ben Davis	Cle.	12.7	Ron Smith	Atl.	39	Ron Smith	Atl.	976	Travis Williams	G.B.	41.1	1967	NFL
1967	AFL	Rodger Bird	Oak.	46	Rodger Bird	Oak.	612	Floyd Little	Den.	16.9	Noland Smith	K.C.	41	Noland Smith	K.C.	1148	Zeke Moore	Hou.	28.9	1967	AFL
1968	NFL	Roy Jefferson	Pit.	28	Chuck Latourette	StL.	345	Bob Hayes	Dal.	20.8	Chuck Latourette	StL.	46	Chuck Latourette	StL.	1237	Preston Pearson	Bal.	35.1	1968	NFL
		Chuck Latourette	StL.	28																	
1968	AFL	Butch Atkinson	Oak.	36	Butch Atkinson	Oak.	490	Noland Smith	K.C.	15.0	Max Anderson	Buf.	39	Max Anderson	Buf.	971	Butch Atkinson	Oak.	25.1	1968	AFL
1969	NFL	Charlie West	Min.	39	Alvin Haymond	L.A.	435	Alvin Haymond	L.A.	13.2	Preston Pearson	Bal.	31	Bo Scott	Cle.	722	Bobby Williams	Det.	33.1	1969	NFL
1969	AFL	Jerry LeVias	Hou.	35	Jerry LeVias	Hou.	292	Bill Thompson	Den.	11.5	Mercury Morris	Mia.	43	Mercury Morris	Mia.	1136	Bill Thompson	Den.	28.5	1969	AFL
1970	NFC	Alvin Haymond	L.A.	53	Bruce Taylor	S.F.	516	Bruce Taylor	S.F.	12.0	Alvin Haymond	L.A.	35	Alvin Haymond	L.A.	1022	Cecil Turner	Chi.	32.7	1970	NFC
1970	AFC	Hubie Bryant	Pit.	37	Ron Gardin	Bal.	330	Ed Podolak	K.C.	13.5	Mike Battle	NY J	40	Mike Battle	NY J	891	Jim Duncan	Bal.	35.4	1970	AFC
1971	NFC	Bruce Taylor	S.F.	34	Bruce Taylor	S.F.	235	Speedy Duncan	Was.	10.6	Dave Hampton	G.B.	46	Dave Hampton	G.B.	1314	Travis Williams	L.A.	29.7	1971	NFC
1971	AFC	Jake Scott	Mia.	33	Jake Scott	Mia.	318	Leroy Kelly	Cle.	9.7	Linzy Cole	Hou.	32	Linzy Cole	Hou.	834	Mercury Morris	Mia.	28.2	1971	AFC
1972	NFC	Ron Smith	Chi.	26	Jim Bertelsen	L.A.	232	Ken Ellis	G.B.	15.4	Margene Adkins	N.O.	43	Margene Adkins	N.O.	1020	Ron Smith	Chi.	30.8	1972	NFC
1972	AFC	Bruce Laird	Bal.	34	Bruce Laird	Bal.	303	C. Farasopoulos	NY J	10.5	Jesse Taylor	S.D.	31	Bruce Laird	Bal.	843	Bruce Laird	Bal.	29.1	1972	AFC
1973	NFC	Ray Brown	Atl.	40	Ray Brown	Atl.	360	Bruce Taylor	S.F.	13.8	Herb Mul-Key	Was.	36	Herb Mul-Key	Was.	1011	Carl Garrett	Chi.	30.4	1973	NFC
1973	AFC	Butch Atkinson	Oak.	41	Bill Thompson	Den.	366	Ron Smith	S.D.	13.0	Mack Herron	N.E.	41	Mack Herron	N.E.	1092	Wallace Francis	Buf.	29.9	1973	AFC
1974	NFC	Howard Stevens	N.O.	37	Howard Stevens	N.O.	376	Dick Jauron	Det.	16.8	Jimmie Jones	Det.	38	Jimmie Jones	Det.	927	Terry Metcalf	St.L.	31.2	1974	NFC
1974	AFC	Donnie Walker	Buf.	43	Lynn Swann	Pit.	577	Lemar Parrish	Cin.	18.8	Lou Piccone	NYJ	39	Lou Piccone	NYJ	961	Greg Pruitt	Cle.	27.5	1974	AFC
1975	NFC	Larry Jones	Was.	53	Virgil Livers	Chi.	456	Terry Metcalf	St.L.	12.4	Larry Jones	Was.	47	Larry Jones	Was.	1086	Walter Payton	Chi.	31.7	1975	NFC
1975	AFC	Neal Colzie	Oak.	48	Neal Colzie	Oak.	655	Billy Johnson	Hou.	15.3	Rick Upchurch	Den.	40	Rick Upchurch	Den.	1084	Harold Hart	Oak.	30.5	1975	AFC
1976	NFC	Rolland Lawrence	Atl.	54	Eddie Brown	Was.	646	Eddie Brown	Was.	13.5	Eddie Brown	Was.	30	Brian Baschnagel	Chi.	754	Cullen Bryant	L.A.	28.7	1976	NFC
											Larry Marshall	Phi.	30								
											Oliver Ross	Sea.	30								
1976	AFC	Mike Haynes	N.E.	45	Mike Haynes	N.E.	608	Rick Upchurch	Den.	13.7	Lou Piccone	NYJ	31	Willie Shelby	Cin.	761	Duriel Harris	Mia.	32.9	1976	AFC
1977	NFC	Eddie Brown	Was.	57	Larry Marshall	Phi.	489	Larry Marshall	Phi.	10.6	Paul Hofer	SF	36	Paul Hofer	S.F.	871	Wilbert Montgomery	Phi.	26.9	1977	NFC
1977	AFC	Rick Upchurch	Den.	51	Rick Upchurch	Den.	653	Billy Johnson	Hou.	15.4	Bruce Harper	NYJ	42	Bruce Harper	NYJ	1035	Ray Clayborn	NE	31.0	1977	AFC

YEARLY LEADERS

		PUNTING AVERAGE			FIELD GOALS MADE			FIELD GOALS PERCENTAGE			PAT'S MADE			POINTS SCORED				
YEAR	LGUE	NAME	TEAM		NAME	TEAM		NAME	TEAM		NAME	TEAM		NAME	TEAM		YEAR	LGUE
1933	NFL				Jack Manders	Chi B	5				Jack Manders	Chi B	14	Glenn Pressnell	Det.	63	1933	NFL
					Glenn Pressnell	Det.	5				Ken Strong	NY G	14					
					Ken Strong	NY G	5											
1934	NFL				Jack Manders	Chi B	10				Jack Manders	Chi B	31	Jack Manders	Chi B	79	1934	NFL
1935	NFL				Armand Niccolai	Pit.	6				Dutch Clark	Det.	16	Dutch Clark	Det.	55	1935	NFL
					Bill Smith	Chi C	6				Jack Manders	Chi B	16					
1936	NFL				Jack Manders	Chi B	7				Dutch Clark	Det.	19	Dutch Clark	Det.	73	1936	NFL
					Armand Niccolai	Pit.	7											
1937	NFL				Jack Manders	Chi B	8				Riley Smith	Was.	22	Jack Manders	Chi B	69	1937	NFL
1938	NFL				Ward Cuff	NY G	5	Regis Monahan	Det.	80	Ward Cuff	NY G	18	Clarke Hinkle	G.B.	58	1938	NFL
					Ralph Kercheval	Bkn.	5											
1939	NFL	George Faust	Chi C	44	Ward Cuff	NY G	7	Chuck Hanneman	Det.	80	Tiny Engebretsen	G.B.	18	Andy Farkas	Was.	68	1939	NFL
		Sid Luckman	Chi B	44														
1940	NFL	Sammy Baugh	Was.	51.3	Clarke Hinkle	G.B.	9	Clarke Hinkle	G.B.	64	Ace Parker	Bkn.	19	Don Hutson	G.B.	57	1940	NFL
1941	NFL	Sammy Baugh	Was.	48.7	Clarke Hinkle	G.B.	6	Andy Marefos	NY G	80	Don Hutson	G.B.	20	Don Hutson	G.B.	95	1941	NFL
											Bob Snyder	Chi B	20					
1942	NFL	Sammy Baugh	Was.	46.6	Bill Daddio	Chi C	5	Ted Fritsch	G.B.	80	Don Hutson	G.B.	33	Don Hutson	G.B.	138	1942	NFL
								Frank Maznicki	Chi B	80								
1943	NFL	Sammy Baugh	Was.	45.9	Ward Cuff	NY G	3	Don Hutson	G.B.	60	Bob Snyder	Chi B	39	Don Hutson	G.B.	117	1943	NFL
					Don Hutson	G.B.	3											
1944	NFL	Cecil Johnson	Bkn.	42.6	Ken Strong	NY G	6	Ken Strong	NY G	50	Pete Gudauskas	Chi B	36	Don Hutson	G.B.	85	1944	NFL
1945	NFL	Sammy Baugh	Was.	43.3	Joe Aguirre	Was.	7	Ben Agajanian	Phi. + Pit.	100	Don Hutson	G.B.	31	Steve Van Buren	Phi.	110	1945	NFL
											Bob Waterfield	Cle.	31					
1946	NFL	Bob Cifers	Det.	45.6	Ted Fritsch	G.B.	9	Bob Waterfield	L.A.	67	Bob Waterfield	L.A.	37	Ted Fritsch	G.B.	100	1946	NFL
1946	AAFC	Glenn Dobbs	Bkn.	47.8	Lou Groza	Cle.	13	Steve Nemeth	Chi.	75	Lou Groza	Cle.	45	Lou Groza	Cle.	84	1946	AAFC
1947	NFL	George Gulyanics	Chi B	44.8	Ward Cuff	G.B.	7	Pat Harder	Chi C	70	Ray McLean	Chi B	44	Pat Harder	Chi C	102	1947	NFL
					Pat Harder	Chi C	7											
					Bob Waterfield	L.A.	7											
1947	AAFC	Bob Reinhard	L.A.	45.7	Ben Agajanian	L.A.	15	Harvey Johnson	N.Y.	88	Harvey Johnson	N.Y.	49	Spec Sanders	N.Y.	114	1947	AAFC
1948	NFL	Joe Muha	Phi.	47.2	Cliff Patton	Phi.	8	Dick Poillon	Was.	71	Pat Harder	Chi C	53	Pat Harder	Chi C	110	1948	NFL
1948	AAFC	Glenn Dobbs	L.A.	49.1	Rex Grossman	Bal.	10	Joe Vetrano	S.F.	63	Joe Vetrano	S.F.	62	Chet Mutryn	BUF.	96	1948	AAFC
1949	NFL	George Gulyanics	Chi B	47.2	Cliff Patton	Phi.	9	Vinnie Yablonski	Chi C	83	Pat Harder	Chi C	45	Pat Harder	Chi C	102	1949	NFL
					Bob Waterfield	L.A.	9							Choo-Choo Roberts	NY G	102		
1949	AAFC	Frankie Albert	S.F.	48.2	Harvey Johnson	N.Y.	7	Rex Grossman	Bal.	55	Joe Vetrano	S.F.	56	Alyn Beals	S.F.	73	1949	AAFC
1950	NFL	Curley Morrison	Chi B	43.3	Lou Groza	Cle.	13	Lou Groza	Cle.	68	Bob Waterfield	L.A.	54	Doak Walker	Det.	128	1950	NFL
1951	NFL	Horace Gillom	Cle.	45.5	Bob Waterfield	L.A.	13	Bill Dudley	Was.	77	Lou Groza	Cle.	43	Crazy Legs Hirsch	L.A.	102	1951	NFL
											Doak Walker	Det.	43					
1952	NFL	Horace Gillom	Cle.	45.7	Lou Groza	Cle.	19	Bob Waterfield	L.A.	61	Bob Waterfield	L.A.	44	Gordie Soltau	S.F.	94	1952	NFL
1953	NFL	Pat Brady	Pit.	46.9	Lou Groza	Cle.	23	Lou Groza	Cle.	88	Gordie Soltau	S.F.	48	Gordie Soltau	S.F.	114	1953	NFL
1954	NFL	Pat Brady	Pit.	43.2	Lou Groza	Cle.	16	Lou Groza	Cle.	67	Doak Walker	Det.	43	Bobby Walston	Phi.	114	1954	NFL
1955	NFL	Norm Van Brocklin	L.A.	44.6	Fred Cone	G.B.	16	Fred Cone	G.B.	67	Lou Groza	Cle.	44	Doak Walker	Det.	96	1955	NFL
1956	NFL	Norm Van Brocklin	L.A.	43.1	Sam Baker	Was.	17	Bobby Layne	Det.	80	George Blanda	Chi B	45	Bobby Layne	Det.	99	1956	NFL
1957	NFL	Don Chandler	NY G	44.6	Lou Groza	Cle.	15	Bobby Walston	Phi.	75	Paige Cothren	L.A.	38	Sam Baker	Was.	77	1957	NFL
1958	NFL	Sam Baker	Was.	45.4	Paige Cothren	L.A.	14	Paige Cothren	L.A.	56	Steve Myhra	Bal.	48	Jimmy Brown	Cle.	108	1958	NFL
					Tom Miner	Pit.	14											
1959	NFL	Yale Lary	Det.	47.1	Pat Summerall	NY G	20	Pat Summerall	NY G	69	Steve Myhra	Bal.	50	Paul Hornung	G.B.	94	1959	NFL
1960	NFL	Jerry Norton	St L.	45.6	Tommy Davis	S.F.	19	Bobby Walston	Phi.	70	Sam Baker	Cle.	44	Paul Hornung	G.B.	176	1960	NFL
1960	AFL	Paul Maguire	L.A.	40.5	Gene Mingo	Den.	18	Gene Mingo	Den.	64	Bill Shockley	NY T	47	Gene Mingo	Den.	123	1960	AFL
1961	NFL	Yale Lary	Det.	48.4	Steve Myhra	Bal.	21	Lou Groza	Cle.	70	Pat Summerall	NY G	46	Paul Hornung	G.B.	146	1961	NFL
1961	AFL	Billy Atkins	Buf.	45.0	Gino Cappelletti	Bos.	17	George Blanda	Hou.	62	George Blanda	Hou.	64	Gino Cappelletti	Bos.	147	1961	AFL
1962	NFL	Tommy Davis	S.F.	45.6	Lou Michaels	Pitt.	26	Don Chandler	NY G	68	Sam Baker	Dal.	50	Jim Taylor	G.B.	114	1962	NFL
1962	AFL	Jim Fraser	Den.	44.4	Gene Mingo	Den.	27	George Blair	S.D.	85	George Blanda	Hou.	48	Gene Mingo	Den.	137	1962	AFL
1963	NFL	Yale Lary	Det.	48.9	Jim Martin	Bal.	24	Lou Groza	Cle.	65	Don Chandler	NY G	52	Don Chandler	NY G	106	1963	NFL
1963	AFL	Jim Fraser	Den.	46.1	Gino Cappelletti	Bos.	22	George Blair	S.D.	63	Mike Mercer	Oak.	47	Gino Cappelletti	Bos.	113	1963	AFL
1964	NFL	Bobby Walden	Min.	46.4	Jim Bakken	StL.	25	Bruce Gossett	L.A.	75	Lou Michaels	Bal.	53	Lenny Moore	Bal.	120	1964	NFL
1964	AFL	Jim Fraser	Den.	44.7	Gino Cappelletti	Bos.	25	Pete Gogolak	Buf.	66	Tommy Brooker	K.C.	46	Gino Cappelletti	Bos.	155	1964	AFL
1965	NFL	Gary Collins	Cle.	46.7	Fred Cox	Min.	23	Jim Bakken	StL.	68	Tommy Davis	S.F.	52	Gale Sayers	Chi B	132	1965	NFL
											Roger Le Clerc	Chi B	52					
1965	AFL	Jerrel Wilson	K.C.	46.1	Pete Gogolak	Buf.	28	Gino Cappelletti	Bos.	63	Herb Travenio	S.D.	40	Gino Cappelletti	Bos.	132	1965	AFL
1966	NFL	David Lee	Bal.	45.6	Bruce Gossett	L.A.	28	Sam Baker	Phi.	72	Danny Villanueva	Dal.	56	Bruce Gossett	L.A.	113	1966	NFL
1966	AFL	Bob Scarpitto	Den.	45.8	Mike Mercer	Oak. + KC	21	Mike Mercer	Oak + KC	70	Booth Lusteg	Buf.	41	Gino Cappelletti	Bos.	119	1966	AFL
1967	NFL	Billy Lothridge	Atl.	43.7	Jim Bakken	StL.	27	Jim Bakken	StL.	69	Bruce Gossett	L.A.	48	Jim Bakken	StL.	117	1967	NFL
1967	AFL	Bob Scarpitto	Den.	44.9	Jan Stenerud	K.C.	21	George Blanda	Hou.	67	George Blanda	Hou.	56	George Blanda	Hou.	116	1967	AFL
1968	NFL	Billy Lothridge	Atl.	44.3	Mac Percival	Chi.	25	Don Cockroft	Cle.	75	Mike Clark	Dal.	54	Leroy Kelly	Cle.	120	1968	NFL
1968	AFL	Jerrel Wilson	K.C.	45.1	Jim Turner	NY J	34	Jan Stenerud	K.C.	75	George Blanda	Hou.	54	Jim Turner	NY J	145	1968	AFL
1969	NFL	David Lee	Bal.	45.3	Fred Cox	Min.	26	Fred Cox	Min.	70	Don Cockroft	Cle.	45	Fred Cox	Min.	121	1969	NFL
1969	AFL	Dennis Partee	S.D.	44.6	Jim Turner	NY J	32	Jan Stenerud	K.C.	77	George Blanda	Oak.	45	Jim Turner	NY J	129	1969	AFL
1970	NFC	Julian Fagan	N.O.	42.5	Fred Cox	Min.	30	Curt Knight	Was.	74	Errol Mann	Det.	41	Fred Cox	Min.	125	1970	NFC
1970	AFC	Dave Lewis	Cin.	46.2	Jan Stenerud	K.C.	30	Garo Yepremian	Mia.	76	George Blanda	Oak.	36	Jan Stenerud	K.C.	116	1970	AFC
											Jim O'Brien	Bal.	36					
1971	NFC	Tom McNeill	Phi.	42.0	Curt Knight	Was.	29	Tom Dempsey	Phi.	71	Mike Clark	Dal.	47	Curt Knight	Was.	114	1971	NFC
1971	AFC	Dave Lewis	Cin.	44.8	Garo Yepremian	Mia.	28	Garo Yepremian	Mia.	70	George Blanda	Oak.	41	Garo Yepremain	Mia.	117	1971	AFC
1972	NFC	Dave Chapple	L.A.	44.2	Chester Marcol	G.B.	33	Errol Mann	Det.	69	Bruce Gossett	S.F.	41	Chester Marcol	G.B.	128	1972	NFC
1972	AFC	Jerrel Wilson	K.C.	44.8	Roy Gerela	Pit.	28	Don Cockroft	Cle.	82	George Blanda	Oak.	44	Bobby Howfield	NY J	121	1972	AFC
1973	NFC	Tom Wittum	S.F.	43.7	David Ray	L.A.	30	Bruce Gossett	S.F.	79	Toni Fritsch	Dal.	43	David Ray	L.A.	130	1973	NFC
1973	AFC	Jerrel Wilson	K.C.	45.5	Roy Gerela	Pit.	29	Don Cockroft	Cle.	71	Jim Turner	Den.	40	Roy Gerela	Pit.	123	1973	AFC
1974	NFC	Tom Blanchard	N.O.	42.1	Chester Marcol	G.B.	25	Errol Mann	Det.	72	Efren Herrera	Dal.	33	Chester Marcol	G.B.	94	1974	NFC
1974	AFC	Ray Guy	Oak.	42.2	Roy Gerela	Pit.	20	Don Cockroft	Cle.	88	George Blanda	Oak.	44	Roy Gerela	Pit.	93	1974	AFC
1975	NFC	Herman Weaver	Det.	42.0	Toni Fritsch	Dal.	22	Tom Dempsey	L.A.	81	Fred Cox	Min.	46	Chuck Foreman	Min.	132	1975	NFC
1975	AFC	Ray Guy	Oak.	43.8	Jan Stenerud	K.C.	22	Garo Yepremian	Mia.	81	John Leypoldt	Buf.	51	O.J. Simpson	Buf.	138	1975	AFC
											Toni Linhart	Bal.	51					
1976	NFC	John James	Atl.	42.1	Mark Moseley	Was.	22	Efren Herrera	Dal.	78	Tom Dempsey	L.A.	36	Mark Moseley	Was.	97	1976	NFC
								Rick Szaro	N.O.	78								
1976	AFC	Marv Bateman	Buf.	42.8	Jan Stenerud	K.C.	21	Toni Linhart	Bal.	74	Toni Linhart	Bal.	49	Toni Linhart	Bal.	109	1976	AFC
1977	NFC	Tom Blanchard	N.O.	42.4	Mark Moseley	Was.	21	Efren Herrera	Dal.	62	Efren Herrera	Dal.	39	Walter Payton	Chi.	96	1977	NFC
1977	AFC	Ray Guy	Oak.	43.3	Errol Mann	Oak.	20	Rolf Benirschke	S.D.	74	Errol Mann	Oak.	39	Errol Mann	Oak.	99	1977	AFC
								Don Cockroft	Cle.	74								

SINGLE SEASON LEADERS

PASSING

NOTE: (For all single season leaders) – Number after individual name indicates the number of times that individual appears within a specific category; the bold indicates the individual appearing most within a specific category.

COMPLETIONS

1	Sonny Jurgensen–1	Was.	NFL	67	288
2	Sonny Jurgensen–2	Was.	NFL	69	274
3	Fran Tarkenton–**1**	Min.	NFC	75	273
4	Roman Gabriel–1	Phi.	NFC	73	270
5	George Blanda–1	Hou.	AFL	64	262
6	Joe Namath–1	NY J	AFL	67	258
7	Johnny Unitas–1	Bal.	NFL	67	255
	Fran Tarkenton–**2**	Min.	NFC	76	255
9	Sonny Jurgensen–3	Was.	NFL	66	254
10	Frank Tripucka–1	Den.	AFL	60	248
11	John Brodie–1	S.F.	NFL	65	242
12	Frank Tripucka–2	Den.	AFL	62	240
	Norm Snead	Phi.	NFL	67	240
14	Johnny Unitas–2	Bal.	NFL	63	237
15	Sonny Jurgensen–4	Phi.	NFL	61	235
16	John Brodie–2	S.F.	NFL	68	234
17	John Hadl–1	S.D.	AFC	71	233
18	John Brodie–3	S.F.	NFL	68	232
	Joe Namath–2	NY J	AFL	66	232
20	Archie Manning	N.O.	NFC	72	230
21	Johnny Unitas–3	Bal.	NFL	61	229
22	Babe Parilli	Bos.	AFL	64	228
	Ken Anderson–1	Cin	AFC	75	228
24	Fran Tarkenton–**3**	NY G	NFC	71	226
25	Billy Wade	Chi.	NFL	62	225
26	George Blanda–2	Hou.	AFL	63	224
	Bert Jones–1	Bal.	AFC	77	224
28	Charley Johnson–1	St.L.	NFL	64	223
	John Brodie–4	S.F.	NFC	70	223
30	Johnny Unitas–4	Bal.	NFL	62	222
	Charley Johnson–2	St.L.	NFL	63	222
32	Y.A. Tittle–1	NY G	NFL	63	221
	Daryle Lamonica–1	Oak.	AFL	69	221
	Joe Ferguson	Buf.	AFC	77	221
35	Daryle Lamonica–2	Oak.	AFL	67	220
	Fran Tarkenton–**4**	NY G	NFL	69	220
37	Fran Tarkenton–**5**	NY G	NFC	70	219
38	Jim Hart–1	St.L.	NFC	76	218
39	Roman Gabriel–2	L.A.	NFL	66	217
	John Hadl–2	S.D.	AFL	67	217
	Roman Gabriel–3	L.A.	NFL	69	217
42	Fran Tarkenton–**6**	Min.	NFC	72	215
43	Ken Anderson–2	Cin.	AFC	74	213
44	Jack Kemp	L.A.	AFL	60	211
	Roman Gabriel–4	L.A.	NFC	70	211
46	Sammy Baugh	Was.	NFL	47	210
	Roger Staubach–1	Dal.	NFC	77	210
48	John Hadl–3	S.D.	AFL	68	208
	John Brodie–5	S.F.	NFC	71	208
	Dan Fouts	S.D.	AFC	76	208
	Roger Staubach–2	Dal.	NFC	76	208
	Jim Zorn	Sea.	NFC	76	208
53	Sonny Jurgensen–5	Was.	NFL	64	207
	Bert Jones–2	Bal.	AFC	76	207
55	Len Dawson	K.C.	AFL	67	206
	Daryle Lamonica–3	Oak.	AFL	68	206
57	Fran Tarkenton–**7**	NYG	NFL	67	204
58	Terry Bradshaw	Pit.	AFC	71	203
	Bert Jones–3	Bal.	AFC	75	203
60	Sonny Jurgensen–6	Was.	NFC	70	202
61	Al Dorow	NY T	AFL	60	201
62	Y.A. Tittle–2	NY G	NFL	62	200
	John Hadl–4	S.D.	AFL	66	200
	Frank Ryan	Cle.	NFL	66	200
	Jim Hart–2	St.L.	NFC	74	200

COMPLETION PERCENTAGE
(Minimum 100 Attempts)

					Att.	Comp.	Pct.
1	Sammy Baugh–1	Was.	NFL	45	182	128	70.3
2	Ken Stabler–1	Oak.	AFC	76	291	194	66.7
3	Len Dawson–**1**	K.C.	AFC	75	140	93	66.4
4	Len Dawson–**2**	K.C.	AFC	73	101	66	65.3
5	Ken Anderson–1	Cin.	AFC	74	328	213	64.9
6	Otto Graham–1	Cle.	NFL	53	258	167	64.7
7	Fran Tarkenton–1	Min.	NFC	75	425	273	64.2
8	Sonny Jurgensen–1	Was.	NFC	74	167	107	64.1
9	Bart Starr–1	G.B.	NFL	68	171	109	63.7
10	John Brodie–1	S.F.	NFC	72	110	70	63.6
11	Y.A. Tittle–1	S.F.	NFL	57	279	176	63.1
12	Sammy Baugh–2	Was.	NFL	40	177	111	62.7
13	Ken Stabler–2	Oak.	AFC	73	260	163	62.7
14	Roger Staubach–1	Dal.	NFC	73	286	179	62.6
15	Bart Starr–**2**	G.B.	NFL	62	285	178	62.5
16	Bart Starr–**3**	G.B.	NFL	69	148	92	62.2
	Virgil Carter	Cin.	AFC	71	222	138	62.2
18	Bart Starr–**4**	G.B.	NFL	66	251	156	62.2
19	Sonny Jurgensen–2	Was.	NFL	69	442	274	62.0
20	John Brodie–2	S.F.	NFL	65	391	242	61.9
21	Fran Tarkenton–2	Min.	NFC	76	412	255	61.9
22	Rudy Bukich	Chi.	NFL	64	160	99	61.9
23	Bob Griese–1	Mia.	AFC	75	191	118	61.8
24	Fran Tarkenton–3	Min.	NFC	73	274	169	61.7
25	Norm Snead–1	NYG & SF	NFC	74	159	97	61.0
26	Len Dawson–**3**	Dal.	AFL	62	310	189	61.0
27	Otto Graham–2	Cle.	AAFC	47	269	163	60.6
28	Ken Anderson–2	Cin.	AFC	75	377	228	60.5
29	Milt Plum–1	Cle.	NFL	60	250	151	60.4
30	Fran Tarkenton–4	Min.	NFC	77	258	155	60.4
31	Bert Jones–1	Bal.	AFC	76	343	207	60.3
32	Norm Snead–2	NY G	NFC	72	325	196	60.3
33	Y.A. Tittle–2	NY G	NFL	63	367	221	60.2
34	Bob Berry–1	Atl.	NFC	71	226	136	60.2
35	Bob Griese–2	Mia.	AFC	74	253	152	60.1
36	Sonny Jurgensen–3	Was.	NFC	73	145	87	60.0
37	Sonny Jurgensen–4	Was.	NFC	70	337	202	59.9
38	Bart Starr–**5**	G.B.	NFL	64	272	163	59.9
39	John Brodie–3	S.F.	NFL	58	172	103	59.9
40	Roger Staubach–2	Dal.	NFC	71	211	126	59.7
41	Bill Munson	Det.	NFC	75	109	65	59.6
42	Bob Griese–3	Mia.	AFC	76	272	162	59.6
43	Tobin Rote	S.D.	AFL	63	286	170	59.4
44	Sammy Baugh–3	Was.	NFL	47	354	210	59.3
45	Eddie LeBaron	Was.	NFL	57	167	99	59.3
46	Otto Graham–3	Cle.	NFL	54	240	142	59.2
	Lynn Dickey	Hou.	AFC	73	120	71	59.2
48	Len Dawson–**4**	K.C.	AFL	69	166	98	59.0
49	Bert Jones–2	Bal.	AFC	75	344	203	59.0
50	John Brodie–4	S.F.	NFC	70	378	223	59.0
51	Mike Boryla	Phi.	NFC	74	102	60	58.8
52	Sammy Baugh–4	Was.	NFL	48	315	185	58.7
53	Len Dawson–**5**	K.C.	AFC	74	235	138	58.7
54	Roman Gabriel	Phi.	NFC	73	460	270	58.7
55	Sammy Baugh–5	Was.	NFL	42	225	132	58.7
56	Milt Plum–2	Cle.	NFL	59	266	156	58.6
57	Bob Griese–4	Mia.	AFC	77	307	180	58.6
58	Billy Wade–1	L.A.	NFL	59	261	153	58.6
59	Milt Plum–3	Cle.	NFL	61	302	177	58.6
60	Fran Tarkenton–5	NY G	NFC	71	386	226	58.5
61	Billy Kilmer	Was.	NFC	74	234	137	58.5
62	Johnny Unitas–1	Bal.	NFL	67	436	255	58.5
63	Len Dawson–**6**	K.C.	AFL	68	224	131	58.5
64	Ken Stabler–3	Oak.	AFC	75	293	171	58.4
65	Frankie Albert	S.F.	AAFC	48	264	154	58.3
66	Bart Starr–**6**	G.B.	NFL	61	295	172	58.3
67	Sonny Jurgensen–5	Was.	NFL	66	436	254	58.3
68	Charley Conerly	NY G	NFL	59	194	113	58.2
69	Billy Wade–2	L.A.	NFL	60	182	106	58.2
70	Roger Staubach–3	Dal.	NFC	77	361	210	58.2
71	Johnny Unitas–2	Bal.	NFL	65	282	164	58.2
72	Bob Berry–2	Atl.	NFC	70	269	156	58.0
73	Bob Griese–5	Mia.	AFC	70	245	142	58.0

YARDS PASSING

1	Joe Namath–1	NY J	AFL	67	4007
2	Sonny Jurgensen–1	Was.	NFL	67	3747
3	Sonny Jurgensen–2	Phi.	NFL	61	3723
4	Johnny Unitas–**1**	Bal.	NFL	63	3481
5	John Hadl–1	S.D.	AFL	68	3473
6	Babe Parilli	Bos.	AFL	64	3465
7	Johnny Unitas–**2**	Bal.	NFL	67	3428
8	Norm Snead–1	Phi.	NFL	67	3399
9	Joe Namath–2	NY J	AFL	66	3379
10	John Hadl–2	S.D.	AFL	67	3365
11	George Blanda–1	Hou.	AFL	61	3330
12	Daryle Lamonica–1	Oak.	AFL	69	3302
13	George Blanda–2	Hou.	AFL	64	3287
14	Charley Johnson–1	St.L.	NFL	63	3280
15	Sonny Jurgensen–3	Phi.	NFL	62	3261
16	Daryle Lamonica–2	Oak.	AFL	68	3245
17	Daryle Lamonica–3	Oak.	AFL	67	3228
18	Y.A. Tittle–1	NY G	NFL	62	3224
19	Roman Gabriel–1	Phi.	NFC	73	3219
20	Sonny Jurgensen–4	Was.	NFL	66	3209
21	Billy Wade–1	Chi.	NFL	62	3172
22	Ken Anderson	Cin.	AFC	75	3169
23	Joe Namath–3	NY J	AFL	68	3147
24	Y.A. Tittle–2	NY G	NFL	63	3145
25	John Brodie–1	S.F.	NFL	65	3112
26	Bert Jones	Bal.	AFC	76	3104
27	Sonny Jurgensen–5	Was.	NFL	69	3102
28	Johnny Unitas–**3**	Bal.	NFL	60	3099
29	Fran Tarkenton–1	NY G	NFL	67	3088
30	John Hadl–3	S.D.	AFC	71	3075
31	Charley Johnson–2	St.L.	NFL	64	3045
32	Norm Snead–2	Was.	NFL	63	3043
33	Frank Tripucka–1	Den.	AFL	60	3038
34	John Brodie–2	S.F.	NFL	68	3020
35	Jack Kemp–1	L.A.	AFL	60	3018
36	Jim Hart–1	St.L.	NFL	67	3008
37	George Blanda–3	Hou.	AFL	63	3003
38	Fran Tarkenton–2	Min.	NFC	75	2994
39	Johnny Unitas–**4**	Bal.	NFL	61	2990
40	Ed Brown	Pit.	NFL	63	2982
41	Frank Ryan	Cle.	NFL	66	2974
42	Johnny Unitas–**5**	Bal.	NFL	62	2967
43	Fran Tarkenton–3	Min.	NFC	76	2961
44	Jim Hart–2	St.L.	NFC	76	2946
45	John Brodie–3	S.F.	NFC	70	2941
46	Sammy Baugh	Was.	NFL	47	2938
47	Sonny Jurgensen–6	Was.	NFL	64	2934
48	Norm Snead–3	Was.	NFL	62	2926
49	Fran Tarkenton–4	NY G	NFL	69	2918
50	Frank Tripucka–2	Den.	AFL	62	2917
51	Jack Kemp–2	Buf.	AFL	63	2914
52	Earl Morrall	Bal.	NFL	68	2909
53	Johnny Unitas–**6**	Bal.	NFL	59	2899
54	Len Dawson–1	K.C.	AFL	64	2879
55	Billy Wade–2	L.A.	NFL	58	2875
56	John Hadl–4	S.D.	AFL	66	2846
57	Johnny Unitas–**7**	Bal.	NFL	64	2824
58	Otto Graham–1	Cle.	NFL	52	2816
	Joe Namath–4	NY J	AFC	72	2816
60	George Blanda–4	Hou.	AFL	62	2810
	John Brodie–4	S.F.	NFL	66	2810
62	Don Meredith	Dal.	NFL	66	2805
63	John Hadl–5	S.D.	AFL	65	2798
64	Otto Graham–2	Cle.	AAFC	49	2785
65	Archie Manning	N.O.	AFC	72	2781
66	Roman Gabriel–2	L.A.	NFL	67	2779
67	Fran Tarkenton–5	NY G	NFC	70	2777
68	Norm Snead–4	Phi.	NFL	69	2768
69	Len Dawson–2	Dal.	AFL	62	2759
70	Otto Graham–3	Cle.	AAFC	47	2753

YARDS PASSING PER SCHEDULED GAME

1	Joe Namath	NY J	AFL	67	286
2	Sonny Jurgensen–**1**	Was.	NFL	67	268
3	Sonny Jurgensen–**2**	Phi.	NFL	61	266
4	Johnny Unitas–1	Bal.	NFL	60	258
5	Johnny Unitas–2	Bal.	NFL	63	249
6	John Hadl–1	S.D.	AFL	68	248
7	Babe Parilli	Bos.	AFL	64	248
8	Sammy Baugh	Was.	NFL	47	245
9	Johnny Unitas–3	Bal.	NFL	67	245
10	Norm Snead	Phi.	NFL	67	243
11	Johnny Unitas–4	Bal.	NFL	59	242
12	Joe Namath–2	NY J	AFL	66	241
13	John Hadl–2	S.D.	AFL	67	240
14	Billy Wade–1	L.A.	NFL	58	240
15	George Blanda–1	Hou.	AFL	61	238
16	Darlye Lamonica–1	Oak.	AFL	69	236
17	George Blanda–2	Hou.	AFL	64	235
18	Otto Graham–1	Cle.	NFL	52	235
19	Charley Johnson	St.L.	NFL	63	234
20	Sonny Jurgensen–**3**	Phi.	NFL	62	233
21	Otto Graham–2	Cle.	AAFC	49	232
22	Daryle Lamonica–2	Oak.	AFL	68	232
23	Daryle Lamonica–3	Oak.	AFL	67	231
24	Y.A. Tittle–1	NY G	NFL	62	230
25	Roman Gabriel	Phi	NFC	73	230
26	Sonny Jurgensen–**4**	Was.	NFL	66	229
27	Otto Graham–3	Cle.	NFL	53	227
28	Billy Wade–2	Chi.	NFL	62	227
29	Ken Anderson	Cin.	AFC	75	226
30	Sid Luckman	ChiB	NFL	47	226
31	Joe Namath–3	NY J	AFL	68	225
32	Y.A. Tittle–2	NY G	NFL	63	225
33	John Brodie	S.F.	NFL	65	222
34	Johnny Lujack	ChiB	NFL	49	222
35	Bert Jones	Bal.	AFC	76	222
36	Sonny Jurgensen–**5**	Was.	NFL	69	222
37	Fran Tarkenton	NY G	NFL	67	221
38	Norm Van Brocklin	L.A.	NFL	54	220
39	John Hadl–3	S.D.	AFC	71	220

YARDS PER ATTEMPT
(Minimum 100 Attempts)

					Att	Yards	Yd/A
1	Tom O'Connell	Cle.	NFL	57	110	1229	11.2
2	Sid Luckman–1	ChiB	NFL	43	202	2194	10.9
3	Otto Graham–**1**	Cle.	NFL	53	258	2722	10.6
4	Otto Graham–**2**	Cle.	AAFC	46	174	1834	10.5
5	Otto Graham–**3**	Cle.	AAFC	47	269	2753	10.2
6	Norm Van Brocklin	L.A.	NFL	54	260	2637	10.1
7	Bill Nelsen	Pit.	NFL	66	112	1122	10.0
8	Sid Luckman–2	ChiB	NFL	41	119	1181	9.9
9	Ed Brown	ChiB	NFL	56	168	1667	9.9
10	Otto Graham–**4**	Cle.	AAFC	49	285	2785	9.8
11	Sid Luckman–3	ChiB	NFL	42	105	1023	9.7
12	Jacky Lee	Hou.	AFL	61	127	1205	9.5
13	Bart Starr–1	G.B.	NFL	68	171	1617	9.5
14	Len Dawson	K.C.	AFL	68	224	2109	9.4
15	Eddie LeBaron–1	Was.	NFL	58	145	1365	9.4
16	Greg Cook	Cin.	AFL	69	197	1854	9.4
17	Bob Waterfield	Cle.	NFL	45	171	1609	9.4
18	Ken Stabler	Oak.	AFC	76	291	2737	9.4
19	Bob Berry	Atl.	NFL	68	153	1433	9.4
20	Otto Graham–**5**	Cle.	NFL	55	185	1721	9.3
21	Johnny Unitas–1	Bal.	NFL	64	305	2824	9.3
22	James Harris	L.A.	NFC	76	158	1460	9.0
23	George Blanda	Hou.	AFL	61	362	3330	9.2
24	Milt Plum	Cle.	NFL	60	250	2297	9.2
25	Earl Morrall–1	Bal.	NFL	68	317	2909	9.2
26	Sammy Baugh	Was.	NFL	45	182	1669	9.2
27	John Brodie	S.F.	NFL	61	283	2588	9.1
28	Earl Morrall–2	Mia.	AFC	72	150	1360	9.1
29	Bert Jones	Bal.	AFC	76	343	3104	9.0
30	Billy Wade	Chi.	NFL	61	250	2258	9.0
31	Eddie LeBaron–2	Was.	NFL	57	167	1508	9.0
32	Clyde LeForce	Det.	NFL	48	101	912	9.0
33	Bart Starr–2	G.B.	NFL	66	252	2257	9.0
34	Johnny Unitas–2	Bal.	NFL	65	282	2530	9.0
35	Sid Luckman–4	ChiB	NFL	40	105	941	9.0
36	Don Horn	G.B.	NFL	69	168	1505	9.0
37	Ken Anderson	Cin.	AFC	75	377	3169	9.0

SINGLE SEASON LEADERS

PASSING

TOUCHDOWN PASSES

1	George Blanda–1	Hou.	AFL	61	36
	Y.A. Tittle–1	NY G	NFL	63	36
3	Daryle Lamonica–1	Oak.	AFL	69	34
4	Y.A. Tittle–2	NY G	NFL	62	33
5	Johnny Unitas–1	Bal.	NFL	59	32
6	Babe Parilli	Bos.	AFL	64	31
	Sonny Jurgensen–1	Was.	NFL	67	31
8	Len Dawson–1	K.C.	AFL	64	30
	John Brodie–1	S.F.	NFL	65	30
	Daryle Lamonica–2	Oak.	AFL	67	30
11	Frankie Albert–1	S.F.	AAFC	48	29
	Len Dawson–2	Dal.	AFL	62	29
	Frank Ryan–1	Cle.	NFL	66	29
	Norm Snead–1	Phi	NFL	67	29
	Fran Tarkenton–1	NY G	NFL	67	29
16	Sid Luckmn–1	ChiB	NFL	43	28
	Charley Johnson	St.L.	NFL	63	28
	Sonny Jurgensen–2	Was.	NFL	66	28
19	Frankie Albert–2	S.F.	AAFC	49	27
	George Blanda–2	Hou.	AFL	62	27
	John Hadl–1	S.D.	AFL	68	27
	Ken Stabler–1	Oak.	AFC	76	27
23	Bobby Layne–1	Det.	NFL	51	26
	Al Dorow	NY T	AFL	60	26
	Len Dawson–3	K.C.	AFL	63	26
	Len Dawson–4	K.C.	AFL	66	26
	Joe Namath	NY J	AFL	67	26
	Earl Morrall–1	Bal.	NFL	68	26
	Ken Stabler–2	Oak.	AFC	74	26
30	Sammy Baugh–1	Was.	NFL	47	25
	Otto Graham–1	Cle.	AAFC	47	25
	Otto Graham–2	Cle.	AAFC	48	25
	Tommy Thompson	Phi	NFL	48	25
	Johnny Unitas–2	Bal.	NFL	60	25
	Frank Ryan–2	Cle.	NFL	63	25
	Frank Ryan–3	Cle.	NFL	64	25
	Roman Gabriel–1	L.A.	NFL	67	25
	Daryle Lamonica–3	Oak.	AFL	68	25
	Joe Ferguson	Buf.	AFC	75	25
	Fran Tarkenton–2	Min.	NFC	75	25
41	Cecil Isbell	G.B.	NFL	42	24
	Sid Luckman–2	ChiB	NFL	47	24
	Johnny Unitas–3	Bal.	NFL	57	24
	George Blanda–3	Hou.	AFL	60	24
	Frank Tripucka	Den.	AFL	60	24
	Norm VanBrocklin	Phi.	NFL	60	24
	Sonny Jurgensen–3	Phi.	NFL	61	24
	Johnny Unitas–4	Bal.	NFL	61	24
	George Blanda–4	Hou.	AFL	63	24
	Earl Morrall–2	Det.	NFL	63	24
	Sonny Jurgensen–4	Was.	NFL	64	24
	Tom Flores	Oak.	AFL	66	24
	Don Meredith–1	Dal.	NFL	66	24
	Len Dawson–5	K.C.	AFL	67	24
	John Hadl–2	S.D.	AFL	67	24
	Roman Gabriel–2	L.A.	NFL	69	24
	John Brodie–2	S.F.	NFC	70	24
	Bert Jones	Bal.	AFC	76	24
59	Sammy Baugh–2	Was.	NFL	43	23
	Johnny Lujack	ChiB	NFL	49	23
	Adrian Burk	Phi.	NFL	54	23
	Johnny Unitas–5	Bal.	NFL	62	23
	Johnny Unitas–6	Bal.	NFL	65	23
	John Hadl–3	S.D.	AFL	66	23
	Bill Nelsen	Cle.	NFL	69	23
	Fran Tarkenton–3	NY G	NFL	69	23
	Sonny Jurgensen–5	Was.	NFC	70	23
	Roman Gabriel–3	Phi.	NFC	73	23
	Roger Staubach	Dal.	NFC	73	23
	Billy Kilmer	Was.	NFC	75	23
71	George Ratterman–1	Buf.	AAFC	47	22
	Sammy Baugh–3	Was.	NFL	48	22
	Chuck Conerly	NY G	NFL	48	22
	George Ratterman–2	NY Y	NFL	50	22
	Butch Songin	Bos.	AFL	60	22
	Billy Wade	Chi.	NFL	61	22
	Sonny Jurgensen–6	Phi.	NFL	62	22
	Norm Snead–2	Was.	NFL	62	22
	Fran Tarkenton–4	Min.	NFL	62	22
	Fran Tarkenton–5	Min.	NFL	64	22
	Don Meredith–2	Dal.	NFL	65	22
	Earl Morrall–3	NYG	NFL	65	22
	Johnny Unitas–7	Bal.	NFL	66	22
	John Brodie–3	S.F.	NFL	68	22
	Sonny Jurgensen–7	Was.	NFL	69	22
	John Hadl–4	S.D.	AFC	70	22
	Daryle Lamonica–4	Oak.	AFC	70	22
	John Hadl–5	L.A.	NFC	73	22
	Bob Griese	Mia.	AFC	77	22

LOWEST PASS INTERCEPTION PERCENTAGE

(Minimum 100 Attempts)

					Att.	Int.	Pct.
1	Joe Ferguson	Buf.	AFC	76	151	1	0.662
2	Bill Nelsen	Pit.	NFL	66	112	1	0.893
3	Bart Starr–1	G.B.	NFL	66	251	3	1.195
4	Bart Starr–2	G.B.	NFL	64	272	4	1.471
5	Bob Berry	Atl.	NFL	69	124	2	1.612
6	Roman Gabriel–1	L.A.	NFL	69	399	7	1.754
7	Bill Munson–1	Det.	NFC	75	109	2	1.835
8	Roger Staubach–1	Dal.	NFC	71	211	4	1.895
9	Fran Tarkenton–1	Min.	NFC	76	412	8	1.942
10	Fran Tarkenton–2	NY G	NFL	69	409	8	1.955
11	Johnny Unitas–1	Bal.	NFL	64	305	6	1.967
12	Roman Gabriel–2	L.A.	NFL	62	101	2	1.980
13	Scott Hunter	Atl.	NFC	77	151	3	1.987
14	Milt Plum	Cle.	NFL	60	250	5	2.000
15	Chuck Conerly	NYG	NFL	59	194	4	2.062
	Jim Hart	St.L.	NFC	74	388	8	2.062
17	Gary Wood	NYG	NFL	64	143	3	2.098
18	Sammy Baugh	Was.	NFL	45	182	4	2.198
19	Ken Anderson–1	Cin.	AFC	72	301	7	2.325
20	Bert Jones–1	Bal.	AFC	75	344	8	2.326
21	Y.A. Tittle	S.F.	NFL	60	127	3	2.362
22	Edd Hargett–1	N.O.	NFC	71	210	5	2.380
23	Bill Munson–2	Det.	NFC	74	292	7	2.397
24	Bill Munson–3	Det.	NFL	68	329	8	2.431
25	Roger Staubach–2	Dal.	NFC	77	361	9	2.493
26	Fran Tarkenton–3	Min.	NFC	73	274	7	2.554
27	Billy Kilmer	Was.	NFC	74	234	6	2.564
28	Ace Parker	N.Y.	AAFC	46	115	3	2.608
29	Roman Gabriel–3	Phi.	NFC	73	460	12	2.609
30	Bert Jones–2	Bal.	AFC	76	343	9	2.624
31	John Brodie	S.F.	NFC	70	378	10	2.645
32	Johnny Unitas–2	Bal.	NFL	58	263	7	2.662
33	Marty Domres	Bal.	AFC	72	222	6	2.702
34	Greg Landry–1	Det.	NFC	76	291	8	2.749
35	Pat Haden	L.A.	NFC	77	217	6	2.765
36	Bert Jones–3	Bal.	AFC	77	393	11	2.798
37	Dwight Sloan	Det.	NFL	39	107	3	2.803
38	John Stofa	Cin.	AFL	68	177	5	2.824
39	Roman Gabriel–4	L.A.	NFC	71	352	10	2.840
40	Don Trull–1	Hou.	AFL	68	105	3	2.857
	Edd Hargett–2	N.O.	NFC	70	175	5	2.857
	Len Dawson	K.C.	AFC	75	140	4	2.857
43	Otto Graham	Cle.	AAFC	46	174	5	2.873
44	Rudy Bukich	Chi.	NFL	65	312	9	2.885
45	Roman Gabriel–5	L.A.	NFL	65	173	5	2.890
46	Don Trull–2	Hou.	AFL	66	172	5	2.907
47	Greg Landry–2	Det.	NFC	77	240	7	2.917
48	Johnny Unitas–3	Bal.	NFL	63	410	12	2.927
49	Ken Anderson–2	Cin.	AFC	75	377	11	2.938
50	Mike Boryla	Phi.	NFC	74	102	3	2.941
51	Roman Gabriel–6	L.A.	NFC	70	407	12	2.948
52	Sonny Jurgensen–1	Was.	NFC	70	337	10	2.967
53	Roger Staubach–3	Dal	NFC	76	369	11	2.981
54	Sonny Jurgensen–2	Was.	NFC	74	167	5	2.994

INTERCEPTIONS

1	Night Train Lane–1	L.A.	NFL	62	14
2	Dan Sandifer	Was.	NFL	48	13
	Spec Sanders	NY Y	NFL	50	13
4	Bob Nussbaumer	ChiC	NFL	49	12
	Don Doll–1	Det.	NFL	50	12
	Woodley Lewis	L.A.	NFL	50	12
	Fred Glick	Hou.	AFL	63	12
	Paul Krause–1	Min.	NFL	64	12
	Dainard Paulson	NY J	AFL	64	12
	Emmitt Thomas	K.C.	AFC	74	12
11	Sammy Baugh	Was.	NFL	43	11
	Otto Schnellbacher–1	N.Y.	AAFC	48	11
	Don Doll–1	Det.	NFL	49	11
	Otto Schnellbacher–2	NYG	NFL	51	11
	Tom Keane–1	Bal.	NFL	53	11
	Will Sherman	L.A.	NFL	55	11
	Lindon Crow	ChiC	NFL	56	11
	Jimmy Patton	NY G	NFL	58	11
	Goose Gonsoulin	Den.	AFL	60	11
	Lee Riley	NY T	AFL	62	11
	Ron Hall	Bos.	AFL	63	11
	Bill Bradley	Phi.	NFC	71	11
	Mel Blount	Pit.	AFC	75	11
24	Irv Comp	G.B.	NFL	43	10
	Bill Dudley	Pit.	NFL	46	10
	Tom Colella	Cle.	AAFC	46	10
	Frank Seno	Bos.	NFL	47	10
	Frank Reagan	NY G	NFL	47	10
	Em Tunnell	NY G	NFL	49	10
	Howard Hartley	Pit.	NFL	51	10
	Tom Keane–2	Dal.	NFL	52	10
	Don Doll–3	Was.	NFL	53	10
	Ray Ramsey	ChiC	NFL	53	10
	Night Train Lane–2	ChiC	NFL	54	10
	Jack Butler	Pit.	NFL	57	10
	Jack Christiansen	Det.	NFL	57	10
	Milt Davis	Bal.	NFL	57	10
	Dave Baker	S.F.	NFL	60	10
	Jerry Norton	St.L.	NFL	60	10
	Billy Atkins	Buf.	AFL	61	10
	Tommy Morrow	Oak.	AFL	62	10
	Pat Fischer	St.L	NFL	64	10
	Bobby Hunt	K.C.	AFL	66	10
	Larry Wilson	St.L	NFL	66	10
	Johnny Robinson–1	K.C.	AFL	66	10
	Lem Barney	Det.	NFL	67	10
	Miller Farr	Hou.	AFL	67	10
	Tom Janik	Buf.	AFL	67	10
	Dick Westmoreland	Mia.	AFL	67	10
	Dave Whitsell	N.O.	NFL	67	10
	Dave Grayson	Oak.	AFL	68	10
	Willie Williams	NY G	NFL	68	10
	Mel Renfro	Dal.	NFL	69	10
	Johnny Robinson–2	K.C.	AFC	70	10
	Paul Krause–2	Min.	NFC	75	10
	Monte Jackson	L.A.	NFC	76	10
	Lyle Blackwood	Bal.	AFC	77	10

PUNTING AVERAGE

(Minimum 30 Punts)

1	Sammy Baugh–1	Was.	NFL	40	51.3
2	Glenn Dobbs–1	L.A.	AAFC	48	49.1
3	Yale Lary–1	Det.	NFL	63	48.9
4	Sammy Baugh–2	Was.	NFL	41	48.7
5	Yale Lary–2	Det.	NFL	61	48.4
6	Frankie Albert	S.F.	AAFC	49	48.2
7	Glenn Dobbs–2	Bkn.	AAFC	46	47.8
8	Joe Muha	Phi.	NFL	48	47.2
9	Yale Lary–3	Det.	NFL	59	47.1
10	Bobby Joe Green–1	Pit.	NFL	61	47.0
11	Pat Brady	Pit.	NFL	53	46.9
12	Gary Collins	Cle.	NFL	65	46.7
13	Sammy Baugh–3	Was.	NFL	42	46.6
	Don Chandler–1	NY G	NFL	59	46.6
15	Bobby Joe Green–2	Chi.	NFL	63	46.5
16	Bobby Walden–1	Min.	NFL	64	46.4
17	Yale Lary–4	Det.	NFL	64	46.3
18	Dave Lewis	Cin.	AFC	70	46.2
19	Jim Fraser	Den.	AFL	63	46.1
	Jerrel Wilson–1	K.C.	AFL	65	46.1
21	Sammy Baugh–4	Was.	NFL	43	45.9
22	Tommy Davis–1	S.F.	NFL	65	45.8
	Bob Scarpitto	Den.	AFL	66	45.8
24	Horace Gillon–1	Cle.	NFL	52	45.7
	Tommy Davis–2	S.F.	NFL	59	45.7
26	Bob Cifers	Det.	NFL	46	45.6
	Jerry Norton	St.L.	NFL	60	45.6
	Tommy Davis–3	S.F.	NFL	62	45.6
	Don Chandler–2	NY G	NFL	64	45.6
	Tommy Davis–4	S.F.	NFL	64	45.6
	David Lee–1	Bal.	NFL	66	45.6
32	Horace Gillon–2	Cle.	NFL	51	45.5
	Sam Baker–1	Was.	NFL	59	45.5
	Danny Villanueva–1	L.A.	NFL	62	45.5
	Jerrel Wilson–2	K.C.	AFC	73	45.5
36	Bob Reinhard	L.A.	AAFC	46	45.4
	Sam Baker–2	Was.	NFL	58	45.4
	Tommy Davis–5	S.F.	NFL	61	45.4
	Sam Baker–3	Dal.	NFL	62	45.4
	Danny Villanueva–2	L.A.	NFL	63	45.4
	Tommy Davis–6	S.F.	NFL	63	45.4
42	Yale Lary–5	Det.	NFL	62	45.3
	Curley Johnson	NY J	AFL	65	45.3
	David Lee–2	Bal.	NFL	69	45.3
	Ray Guy	Oak.	AFC	73	45.3
46	Bobby Walden–2	Pit.	AFC	70	45.2
47	Sammy Baugh–5	Was.	NFL	46	45.1
	Frank Lambert	Pit.	NFL	65	45.1
	Jerrel Wilson–3	K.C.	AFL	68	45.1
	Billy Van Heusen	Den.	AFC	73	45.1
51	Billy Atkins	Buf.	AFL	61	45.0

SINGLE SEASON LEADERS

RUSHING

ATTEMPTS

1	Walter Payton–1	Chi.	NFC	77	339
2	O.J. Simpson–1	Buf.	AFC	73	332
3	O.J. Simpson–2	Buf.	AFC	75	329
4	Mark van Eeghen	Oak.	AFC	77	324
5	Walter Payton–2	Chi.	NFC	76	311
6	Jimmy Brown–1	Cle.	NFL	61	305
7	Franco Harris–1	Pit.	AFC	77	301
8	Lydell Mitchell–1	Bal.	AFC	77	300
9	Jim Nance–1	Bos.	AFL	66	299
10	Ron Johnson–1	NY G	NFC	72	298
11	Lawr. McCutcheon–1	L.A.	NFC	77	294
12	O.J. Simpson–3	Buf.	AFC	72	292
13	Jimmy Brown–2	Cle.	NFL	63	291
	Lawr. McCutcheon–2	L.A.	NFC	76	291
15	Jimmy Brown–3	Cle.	NFL	59	290
	O.J. Simpson–4	Buf.	AFC	76	290
17	Jimmy Brown–4	Cle.	NFL	65	289
	Lydell Mitchell–2	Bal.	AFC	75	289
	Franco Harris–2	Pit.	AFC	76	289
	Lydell Mitchell–3	Bal.	AFC	76	289
21	Larry Brown–1	Was.	NFC	72	285
22	Floyd Little–1	Den.	AFC	71	284
23	Jimmy Brown–5	Cle.	NFL	64	280
	Chuck Foreman–1	Min.	NFC	75	280
25	Chuck Foreman–2	Min.	NFC	76	278
26	John Brockington–1	G.B.	NFC	72	274
27	Calvin Hill–1	Dal.	NFC	73	273
	Larry Brown–2	Was.	NFC	73	273
29	Jim Taylor–1	G.B.	NFL	62	272
	Mike Garrett	S.D.	AFC	72	272
31	Eddie Price	NY G	NFL	51	271
32	O.J. Simpson–5	Buf.	AFC	74	270
	Sam Cunningham	N.E.	AFC	77	270
	Chuck Foreman–3	Min.	NFC	77	270
35	Jim Nance–2	Bos.	AFL	67	269
	Jim Otis	St. L.	NFC	75	269
	Del Williams–1	S.F.	NFC	77	269
38	John Brockington–2	G.B.	NFC	74	266
39	John Brockington–3	G.B.	NFC	73	265
40	Steve Van Buren	Phi.	NFL	49	263
	Ron Johnson–2	NY G	NFC	70	263
	Dave Hampton–1	Atl.	NFC	73	263
	Otis Armstrong–1	Den.	AFC	74	263
44	Franco Harris–3	Pit.	AFC	75	262
45	Ron Johnson–3	NY G	NFC	73	260
46	J.D. Smith	S.F.	NFL	62	258
47	Jimmy Brown–6	Cle.	NFL	58	257
48	Floyd Little–2	Den.	AFC	73	256
49	Boobie Clark	Cin.	AFC	73	254
	Mike Thomas	Was.	NFC	76	254
51	Larry Brown–3	Was.	NFC	71	253
	Lydell Mitchell–4	Bal.	AFC	73	253
53	Cookie Gilchrist	Den.	AFL	65	252
54	John Henry Johnson	Pit.	NFL	62	251
	Bill Brown	Min.	NFL	66	251
56	Dave Hampton–2	Atl.	NFC	75	250
57	Jim Taylor–2	G.B.	NFL	63	248
	Dick Bass	L.A.	NFL	66	248
	Leroy Kelly	Cle.	NFL	68	248
	Del Williams–2	S.F.	NFC	76	248
61	Otis Armstrong–2	Den.	AFC	76	247
	Haskel Stanback	Atl.	NFC	77	247
63	Steve Owens	Det.	NFC	71	246
64	Calvin Hill–2	Dal.	NFC	72	245
65	Charley Taylor	Hou.	AFL	62	244
	Tom Sullivan	Phi.	NFC	74	244
67	Jim Taylor	G.B.	NFL	61	243

YARDS

1	O.J. Simpson–1	Buf.	AFC	73	2003
2	Jimmy Brown–1	Cle.	NFL	63	1863
3	Walter Payton–1	Chi.	NFC	77	1852
4	O.J. Simpson–2	Buf.	AFC	75	1817
5	Jimmy Brown–2	Cle.	NFL	65	1544
6	Jimmy Brown–3	Cle.	NFL	58	1527
7	O.J. Simpson–3	Buf.	AFC	76	1503
8	Jim Taylor–1	G.B.	NFL	62	1474
9	Jim Nance–1	Bos.	AFL	66	1458
10	Jimmy Brown–4	Cle.	NFL	64	1446
11	Spec Sanders	N.Y.	AAFC	47	1432
12	Jimmy Brown–5	Cle.	NFL	61	1408
13	Otis Armstrong–1	Den.	AFC	74	1407
14	Walter Payton–2	Chi.	NFC	76	1390
15	Jimmy Brown–6	Cle.	NFL	59	1329
16	Jim Taylor–2	G.B.	NFL	61	1307
17	Mark van Eeghen–1	Oak.	AFC	77	1273
18	Jimmy Brown–7	Cle.	NFL	60	1257
19	O.J. Simpson–4	Buf.	AFC	72	1251
20	Franco Harris–1	Pit.	AFC	75	1246
21	Leroy Kelly–1	Cle.	NFL	68	1239
22	Lawr. McCutcheon–1	L.A.	NFC	77	1238
23	Gale Sayers–1	Chi.	NFL	66	1231
24	Jim Nance–2	Bos.	AFL	67	1216
	Larry Brown–1	Was.	NFC	72	1216
26	Leroy Kelly–2	Cle.	NFL	67	1205
27	Del Williams	S.F.	NFC	76	1203
28	Lydell Mitchell–1	Bal.	AFC	76	1200
29	Hoyle Granger	Hou.	AFL	67	1195
30	Lydell Mitchell–2	Bal.	AFC	75	1193
31	Ron Johnson	NY G	NFC	72	1182
32	Jim Taylor–3	G.B.	NFL	64	1169
33	Lawr. McCutcheon–2	L.A.	NFC	76	1168
34	Ron Woods	S.D.	AFC	74	1162
	Franco Harris–2	Pit.	AFC	77	1162
36	Lydell Mitchell–3	Bal.	AFC	77	1159
37	Chuck Foreman–1	Min.	NFC	76	1155
38	Steve Van Buren–1	Phi.	NFL	49	1146
39	John Brockington–1	G.B.	NFC	73	1144
40	Calvin Hill–1	Dal.	NFC	73	1142
41	John Henry Johnson–1	Pit.	NFL	62	1141
	Leroy Kelly–3	Cle.	NFL	66	1141
43	Floyd Little	Den.	AFC	71	1133
44	Franco Harris–3	Pit.	AFC	76	1128
45	Rick Casares	ChiB	NFL	56	1126
46	Larry Brown–2	Was.	NFC	70	1125
	O.J. Simpson–5	Buf.	AFC	74	1125
48	Paul Lowe–1	S.D.	AFL	65	1121
49	Larry Csonka–1	Mia.	AFC	72	1117
50	Chuck Foreman–2	Min.	NFC	77	1112
51	Lawr. McCutcheon–3	L.A.	NFC	74	1109
52	John Brockington–2	G.B.	NFC	71	1105
53	Jim Taylor–4	G.B.	NFL	60	1101
	Mike Thomas	Was.	NFC	76	1101
55	Marv Hubbard	Oak.	AFC	72	1100
56	Clem Daniels	Oak.	AFL	63	1099
57	Lawr. McCutcheon–3	L.A.	NFC	73	1097
58	Cookie Gilchrist	Buf.	AFL	62	1096
59	Dick Bass–1	L.A.	NFL	66	1090
60	Mike Garrett–1	K.C.	AFL	67	1087
61	Greg Pruitt–1	Cle.	AFC	77	1086
62	Jim Otis	St. L.	NFC	75	1076
63	John David Crow	St. L.	NFL	60	1071
64	Chuck Foreman–3	Min.	NFC	75	1070
65	Greg Pruitt–2	Cle.	AFC	75	1067
66	Franco Harris–4	Pit.	AFC	72	1055
67	Tony Canadeo	G.B.	NFL	49	1052
68	Larry Csonka–2	Mia.	AFC	71	1051
69	Joe Perry–1	S.F.	NFL	54	1049
	Abner Haynes	Dal.	AFL	62	1049
71	John Henry Johnson–2	Pit.	NFL	64	1048
72	J.D. Smith	S.F.	NFL	59	1036
	Calvin Hill–2	Dal.	NFC	72	1036
	Rocky Bleier	Pit.	AFC	76	1036
75	Steve Owens	Det.	NFC	71	1035
76	Dick Bass–2	L.A.	NFL	62	1033
77	Gale Sayers–2	Chi.	NFL	69	1032
78	Mike Garrett–2	S.D.	AFC	72	1031
79	Ron Johnson–2	NY G	NFC	70	1027
	John Brockington–3	G.B.	NFC	72	1027
81	Paul Robinson	Cin.	AFL	68	1023
82	Joe Perry–2	S.F.	NFL	53	1018
	Jim Taylor–5	G.B.	NFL	63	1018
84	Sam Cunningham	N.E.	AFC	77	1015
85	Charley Tolar	Hou.	AFL	62	1012
	Mark van Eeghen–2	Oak.	AFC	76	1012
87	Paul Lowe–2	S.D.	AFL	63	1010
88	Steve Van Buren–2	Phi.	NFL	47	1008
	Otis Armstrong–2	Den.	AFC	76	1008
90	Tony Dorsett	Dal.	NFC	77	1007
91	Franco Harris–5	Pit.	AFC	74	1006
92	John Riggins	NY J	AFC	75	1005
93	Beattie Feathers	ChiB	NFL	34	1004
94	Larry Csonka–3	Mia.	AFC	73	1003
95	Dave Hampton	Atl.	NFC	75	1002
96	Willie Ellison	L.A.	NFC	71	1000
	Mercury Morris	Mia.	AFC	72	1000
	Greg Pruitt–3	Cle.	AFC	76	1000

YARDS PER SCHEDULED GAME

1	O.J. Simpson–1	Buf.	AFC	73	143
2	Jimmy Brown–1	Cle.	NFL	63	133
3	Walter Payton–1	Chi.	NFC	77	132
4	O.J. Simpson–2	Buf.	AFC	75	130
5	Jimmy Brown–2	Cle.	NFL	58	127
6	Jimmy Brown–3	Cle.	NFL	59	111
7	Jimmy Brown–4	Cle.	NFL	65	110
8	O.J. Simpson–3	Buf.	AFC	76	107
9	Jim Taylor–1	G.B.	NFL	62	105
10	Jimmy Brown–5	Cle.	NFL	60	105
11	Jim Nance–1	Bos.	AFL	66	104
12	Jimmy Brown–6	Cle.	NFL	64	103
13	Spec Sanders	N.Y.	AAFC	47	102
14	Jimmy Brown–7	Cle.	NFL	61	101
15	Otis Armstrong	Den.	AFC	74	101
16	Walter Payton–2	Chi.	NFC	76	99
17	Steve Van Buren	Phi.	NFL	49	96
18	Rick Casares	ChiB	NFL	56	94
19	Jim Taylor–2	G.B.	NFL	61	93
20	Jim Taylor–3	G.B.	NFL	60	92
21	Mark van Eeghen	Oak.	AFC	77	91
22	O.J. Simpson–4	Buf.	AFC	72	89
23	John David Crow	St. L.	NFL	60	89
24	Franco Harris	Pit.	AFC	75	89
25	Leroy Kelly–1	Cle.	NFL	68	89
26	Lawr. McCutcheon	L.A.	NFC	77	88
27	Gale Sayers	Chi.	NFL	66	88
28	Tony Canadeo	G.B.	NFL	49	88
29	Joe Perry–1	S.F.	NFL	54	87
30	Jim Nance–2	Bos.	AFL	67	87
	Larry Brown	Was.	NFC	72	87
32	J.D. Smith	S.F.	NFL	59	86
	Leroy Kelly–2	Cle.	NFL	67	86
34	Del Williams	S.F.	NFC	76	86
35	Lydell Mitchell–1	Bal.	AFC	76	86
36	Hoyle Granger	Hou.	AFL	67	85
37	Lydell Mitchell–2	Bal.	AFC	75	85
38	Joe Perry–2	S.F.	NFL	53	85

AVERAGE YARDS

(Minimum 100 Attempts)

					Att.	Yards	Avg.
1	Beattie Feathers	ChiB	NFL	34	101	1004	9.94
2	Bobby Douglass	Chi.	NFC	72	141	948	6.87
3	Joe Perry–1	S.F.	AAFC	49	115	783	6.81
4	Dan Towler–1	L.A.	NFL	51	126	854	6.78
5	John Strzykalski–1	S.F.	AAFC	48	141	915	6.46
6	Keith Lincoln	S.D.	AFL	63	128	826	6.45
7	Mercury Morris	Mia.	AFC	73	149	954	6.40
8	Jimmy Brown–1	Cle.	NFL	63	291	1863	6.40
9	John Strzykalski–2	S.F.	AAFC	47	143	906	6.34
10	Paul Lowe–1	L.A.	AFL	60	136	855	6.29
11	Dutch Clark	Det.	NFL	34	122	763	6.25
12	Gale Sayers	Chi.	NFL	68	138	856	6.20
13	Chet Mutryn–1	Buf.	AAFC	47	140	868	6.20
14	Spec Sanders	N.Y.	AAFC	47	231	1432	6.20
15	Marion Motley–2	Cle.	AAFC	48	157	964	6.14
16	Buddy Young	N.Y.	AAFC	47	116	712	6.14
17	Marion Motley–2	Cle.	AAFC	47	146	889	6.09
18	Joe Perry–2	S.F.	NFL	58	125	758	6.06
19	Joe Perry–3	S.F.	NFL	54	173	1049	6.06
20	O.J. Simpson–1	Buf.	AFC	73	332	2003	6.03
21	Jimmy Brown–2	Cle.	NFL	58	257	1527	5.94
22	John David Crow	St. L.	NFL	60	183	1071	5.85
23	Jimmy Brown–3	Cle.	NFL	60	215	1257	5.85
24	Steve Van Buren	Phi.	NFL	45	143	832	5.82
25	Marion Motley–3	Cle.	NFL	50	140	810	5.79
26	Dan Towler–2	L.A.	NFL	53	152	879	5.78
27	Bill Osmanski	ChiB	NFL	39	121	699	5.78
28	Dan Towler–3	L.A.	NFL	52	156	894	5.73
29	Paul Lowe–2	S.D.	AFL	63	177	1010	5.71
30	Bobby Mitchell–1	Cle.	NFL	59	131	743	5.67
31	Franco Harris	Pit.	AFC	72	188	1055	5.61
32	Abner Haynes	Dal.	AFL	60	156	875	5.61
33	Chet Mutryn–2	Buf.	AAFC	48	147	823	5.60
34	Don Calhoun	N.E.	AFC	76	129	721	5.59
35	Eddie Price	NY G	NFL	50	126	703	5.58
36	Amos Marsh	Dal.	NFL	62	144	802	5.57
37	Brad Hubbert	S.D.	AFL	67	116	643	5.54
38	O.J. Simpson–2	Buf.	AFC	75	329	1817	5.52
39	Mack Lee Hill	K.C.	AFL	64	105	576	5.49
40	Swede Hanson	Phi.	NFL	34	147	805	5.48
41	Walter Payton	Chi.	NFC	77	339	1852	5.46
42	Leroy Kelly	Cle.	NFL	66	209	1141	5.46
43	Timmy Brown	Phi.	NFL	65	148	861	5.45
44	Mike Garrett	K.C.	AFL	66	147	801	5.45
45	Curtis McClinton	Dal.	AFL	62	111	604	5.44
46	Bobby Mitchell–2	Cle.	NFL	61	101	548	5.43
47	Frank Akins	Was.	NFL	45	147	797	5.42
48	Nick Pietrosante	Det.	NFL	60	161	872	5.42
49	Don Bosseler	Was.	NFL	59	119	644	5.41
	Jim Taylor	G.B.	NFL	62	272	1472	5.41

TOUCHDOWNS

1	Jim Taylor–1	G.B.	NFL	62	19
2	Spec Sanders	N.Y.	AAFC	47	18
3	Jimmy Brown–1	Cle.	NFL	58	17
	Jimmy Brown–2	Cle.	NFL	65	17
5	Lenny Moore	Bal.	NFL	64	16
	Leroy Kelly–1	Cle.	NFL	68	16
	O.J. Simpson–1	Buf.	AFC	75	16
	Pete Banaszek	Oak.	AFC	75	16
9	Steve Van Buren–1	Phi.	NFL	45	15
	Jim Taylor–2	G.B.	NFL	61	15
	Leroy Kelly–2	Cle.	NFL	66	15
12	Jimmy Brown–3	Cle.	NFL	59	14
	John David Crow	St. L.	NFL	62	14
	Gale Sayers	Chi.	NFL	65	14
	Franco Harris–1	Pit.	AFC	76	14
	Walter Payton–1	Chi.	NFC	77	14
17	Steve Van Buren–2	Phi.	NFL	47	13
	Paul Hornung	G.B.	NFL	60	13
	Jimmy Brown–4	Cle.	NFL	62	13
	Cookie Gilchrist–1	Buf.	AFL	62	13
	Abner Haynes	Dal.	AFL	62	13
	Chuck Foreman–1	Min.	NFC	75	13
	Chuck Foreman–2	Min.	NFC	76	13
	Walter Payton–2	Chi.	NFC	76	13
25	Ernie Nevers	ChiC	NFL	29	12
	Rick Casares–1	ChiB	NFL	56	12
	Jim Taylor–3	G.B.	NFL	64	12
	Jimmy Brown–5	Cle.	NFL	63	12
	Cookie Gilchrist–2	Buf.	AFL	63	12
	Mercury Morris–1	Mia.	AFC	72	12
	Floyd Little	Den.	AFC	73	12
	O.J. Simpson–2	Buf.	AFC	73	12
	Don Nottingham	Mia.	AFC	75	12
	Steve Grogan	N.E.	AFC	76	12
	Tony Dorsett	Dal.	NFC	77	12
36	Steve Van Buren–3	Phi.	NFL	49	11
	Johnny Lujack	ChiB	NFL	50	11
	Dan Towler–1	L.A.	NFL	54	11
	Tobin Rote	G.B.	NFL	56	11
	Jim Taylor–4	G.B.	NFL	60	11
	Jim Nance	Bos.	AFL	66	11
	Leroy Kelly–3	Cle.	NFL	67	11
	Bill Brown	Min.	NFL	68	11
	Tom Matte	Bal.	NFL	69	11
	MacArthur Lane	St. L.	NFC	70	11
	Duane Thomas	Dal.	NFC	71	11
	Emerson Boozer–1	NY J	AFC	72	11
	Tom Sullivan	Phi.	NFC	74	11
	Lydell Mitchell	Bal.	AFC	75	11
	Franco Harris–2	Pit.	AFC	77	11
51	Bill Paschal	NY G	NFL	43	10
	Chet Mutryn	Buf.	AAFC	48	10
	Joe Perry–1	S.F.	AAFC	48	10
	Steve Van Buren–4	Phi.	NFL	48	10
	Dick Hoerner	L.A.	NFL	50	10
	Dan Towler–2	L.A.	NFL	52	10
	Joe Perry–2	S.F.	NFL	53	10
	Rick Casares–2	ChiB	NFL	59	10
	J.D. Smith	S.F.	NFL	59	10
	Billy Kilmer	S.F.	NFL	61	10
	Tommy Mason	Min.	NFL	65	10
	Emerson Boozer–2	NY J	AFL	67	10
	Johnny Roland	St. L.	NFL	67	10
	Leroy Kelly–4	Cle.	AFC	71	10
	Franco Harris–3	Pit.	AFC	72	10
	Donny Anderson	St. L.	NFC	73	10
	Mercury Morris–2	Mia.	AFC	73	10
	Jon Keyworth	Den.	AFC	74	10
	Franco Harris–4	Pit.	AFC	75	10
	Don McCauley	Bal.	AFC	75	10

SINGLE SEASON LEADERS

RECEIVING

RECEPTIONS

1	Charley Hennigan–1	Hou.	AFL	64	101
2	Lionel Taylor–1	Den.	AFL	61	100
3	Johnny Morris	Chi.	NFL	64	93
4	Lionel Taylor–2	Den.	AFL	60	92
5	Lionel Taylor–3	Den.	AFL	65	85
6	Tom Fears–1	L.A.	NFL	50	84
7	Charley Hennigan–2	Hou.	AFL	61	82
8	Dave Parks–1	S.F.	NFL	65	80
9	Jim Phillips	L.A.	NFL	61	78
	Lionel Taylor–4	Den.	AFL	63	78
11	Tom Fears–2	L.A.	NFL	49	77
	Lionel Taylor–5	Den.	AFL	62	77
13	Art Powell–1	Oak.	AFL	64	76
	Lionel Taylor–6	Den.	AFL	64	76
15	Ray Berry–1	Bal.	NFL	61	75
	Mike Ditka	Chi.	NFL	64	75
	George Sauer–1	NY J	AFL	67	75
18	Don Hutson	G.B.	NFL	42	74
	Ray Berry–2	Bal.	NFL	60	74
20	Bobby Joe Conrad	St. L.	NFL	63	73
	Art Powell–2	NY T	AFL	63	73
	Lance Alworth–1	S.D.	AFL	66	73
	Dan Abramowicz	N.O.	NFL	69	73
	Chuck Foreman	Min.	NFC	75	73
25	Bill Groman	Hou.	AFL	60	72
	Don Maynard–1	NY T	AFL	60	72
	Bobby Mitchell–1	Was.	NFL	62	72
	Charley Taylor–1	Was.	NFL	66	72
	Lydell Mitchell–1	Bal.	AFC	74	72
30	Art Powell	NY T	AFL	61	71
	Bake Turner	NY T	AFL	63	71
	Don Maynard–2	NY J	AFL	67	71
	Clifton McNeill	S.F.	NFL	68	71
	Charley Taylor–2	Was.	NFL	69	71
	Dick Gordon	Chi.	NFC	70	71
	Lydell Mitchell–2	Bal.	AFC	77	71
37	Charley Taylor–3	Was.	NFL	67	70
38	Art Powell–4	NY T	AFL	60	69
	Bobby Mitchell–2	Was.	NFL	63	69
	Bill Miller	Buf.	AFL	63	69
	Lance Alworth–2	S.D.	AFL	65	69
42	Del Shofner	NY G	NFL	61	68
	Chris Burford	K.C.	AFL	63	68
	Don Maynard–3	NY J	AFL	65	68
	Lance Alworth–3	S.D.	AFL	68	68
46	Mac Speedie	Cle.	AAFC	47	67
	Tommy McDonald	L.A.	NFL	65	67
	Pat Studstill	Det.	NFL	66	67
	Jack Clancy	Mia.	AFL	67	67
	Jerry Smith	Was.	NFL	67	67
	Roy Jefferson	Pit.	NFL	69	67
	Harold Carmichael	Phi.	NFC	73	67
53	Bob Mann	Det.	NFL	49	66
	Crazy Legs Hirsch	L.A.	NFL	51	66
	Roy Berry–3	Bal.	NFL	59	66
	Terry Barr	Det.	NFL	63	66
	Pete Retzlaff	Phi.	NFL	65	66
	Dave Parks–2	S.F.	NFL	66	66
	George Sauer–2	NY J	AFL	68	66
	MacArthur Lane	K.C.	AFC	76	66
61	Frank Clarke	Dal.	NFL	64	65
	Harold Jackson	Phi.	NFL	69	65

YARDS

1	Charley Hennigan–1	Hou.	AFL	61	1746
2	Lance Alworth–1	S.D.	AFL	65	1602
3	Charley Hennigan–2	Hou.	AFL	64	1546
4	Crazy Legs Hirsch	L.A.	NFL	51	1495
5	Bill Groman–1	Hou.	AFL	60	1473
6	Bobby Mitchell–1	Was.	NFL	63	1436
7	Don Maynard–1	NY J	AFL	67	1434
8	Bobby Mitchell–2	Was.	NFL	62	1384
9	Lance Alworth–2	S.D.	AFL	66	1383
10	Art Powell–1	Oak.	AFL	64	1361
11	Dave Parks	S.F.	NFL	65	1344
12	Lance Alworth–3	S.D.	AFL	68	1312
13	Art Powell–2	NY T	AFL	63	1304
14	Ray Berry	Bal.	NFL	60	1298
15	Otis Taylor–1	K.C.	AFL	66	1297
	Don Maynard–2	NY J	AFL	68	1297
17	Buddy Dial	Pit.	NFL	63	1295
18	Pat Studstill	Det.	NFL	66	1266
19	Don Maynard–3	NY T	AFL	60	1265
	Ben Hawkins	Phi.	NFL	67	1265
21	Warren Wells	Oak.	AFL	69	1260
22	Lionel Taylor–1	Den.	AFL	60	1235
	Lance Alworth–4	S.D.	AFL	64	1235
24	Bob Hayes	Dal.	NFL	66	1232
25	Billy Howton–1	G.B.	NFL	52	1231
26	Don Maynard–4	NY J	AFL	65	1218
27	Bob Boyd	L.A.	NFL	54	1212
28	Don Hutson	G.B.	NFL	42	1211
29	Homer Jones	NY G	NFL	67	1209
30	Lance Alworth–5	S.D.	AFL	63	1206
31	Jackie Smith	St. L.	NFL	67	1205
32	Johnny Morris	Chi.	NFL	64	1200
33	Pete Retzlaff	Phi.	NFL	65	1190
34	George Sauer–1	NY J	AFL	67	1189
35	Billy Howton–2	G.B.	NFL	56	1188
36	Del Shofner–1	NY G	NFL	63	1181
37	Lionel Taylor–2	Den.	AFL	61	1176
38	Bill Groman–2	Hou.	AFL	61	1175
39	Art Powell–3	NY T	AFL	60	1167
40	Sonny Randle	St. L.	NFL	62	1158
41	Mac Speedie	Cle.	AAFC	47	1146
	Tommy McDonald–1	Phi.	NFL	62	1146
43	Tommy McDonald–2	Phi.	NFL	61	1144
44	George Sauer–2	NY J	AFL	68	1141
45	Elbert Dubenion	Buf.	AFL	64	1139
46	Warren Wells–2	Oak.	AFL	68	1137
47	Del Shofner–2	NY G	NFL	62	1133
48	Lionel Taylor–3	Den.	AFL	65	1131
49	Art Powell–4	NY T	AFL	62	1130
50	Charley Frazier	Hou.	AFL	66	1129
51	Harlon Hill–1	ChiB	NFL	56	1128
52	Del Shofner–3	NY G	NFL	61	1125
53	Harlon Hill–2	ChiB	NFL	54	1124
54	Charley Taylor	Was.	NFL	66	1119
55	Tom Fears	L.A.	NFL	50	1116
	Harold Jackson	Phi.	NFL	69	1116
	Harold Carmichael	Phi.	NFC	73	1116
58	Roger Carr	Bal.	AFC	76	1112
59	Cliff Branch	Oak.	AFC	76	1111
60	Otis Taylor–2	K.C.	AFC	71	1110
61	Gary Garrison	S.D.	AFL	68	1103
62	Lionel Taylor–4	Den.	AFL	63	1101
63	Gene Washington	S.F.	NFC	70	1100

YARDS PER SCHEDULED GAME

1	Charley Hennigan–1	Hou.	AFL	61	125
2	Crazy Legs Hirsch	L.A.	NFL	51	125
3	Lance Alworth–1	S.D.	AFL	65	114
4	Charley Hennigan–2	Hou.	AFL	64	110
5	Don Hutson–1	G.B.	NFL	42	110
6	Ray Berry	Bal.	NFL	60	108
7	Jim Benton–1	Cle.	NFL	45	107
8	Bill Groman–1	Hou.	AFL	60	105
9	Billy Howton–1	G.B.	NFL	52	103
10	Bobby Mitchell–1	Was.	NFL	63	103
11	Don Maynard–1	NY J	AFL	67	102
12	Bob Boyd	L.A.	NFL	54	101
13	Billy Howton–2	G.B.	NFL	56	99
14	Bobby Mitchell–2	Was.	NFL	62	99
15	Lance Alworth–2	S.D.	AFL	66	99
16	Art Powell–1	Oak.	AFL	64	97
17	Dave Parks	S.F.	NFL	65	96
18	Harlon Hill–1	ChiB	NFL	56	94
19	Lance Alworth–3	S.D.	AFL	68	94
20	Harlon Hill–2	ChiB	NFL	54	94
21	Art Powell–2	NY T	AFL	63	93
22	Tom Fears–1	L.A.	NFL	50	93
23	Otis Taylor	K.C.	AFL	66	93
	Don Maynard–2	NY J	AFL	68	93
25	Buddy Dial	Pit.	NFL	63	93
26	Del Shofner–1	L.A.	NFL	58	91
27	Pat Studstill	Det.	NFL	66	90
28	Don Maynard–3	NY T	AFL	60	90
	Ben Hawkins	Phi.	NFL	67	90
30	Warren Wells	Oak.	AFL	69	90
31	Jim Benton–2	L.A.	NFL	46	89
32	Lionel Taylor–1	Den.	AFL	60	88
	Lance Alworth–4	S.D.	AFL	64	88
34	Bob Hayes	Dal.	NFL	66	88
35	Pete Pihos	Phi.	NFL	53	87
36	Don Hutson–2	G.B.	NFL	44	87
37	Don Maynard–4	NY J	AFL	65	87
38	Homer Jones	NY G	NFL	67	86
39	Lance Alworth–5	S.D.	AFL	63	86
40	Jackie Smith	St. L.	NFL	67	86
41	Johnny Morris	Chi.	NFL	64	86
42	Mac Speedie	Cle.	AAFC	49	86
43	Pete Retzlaff	Phi.	NFL	65	85
44	George Sauer	NY J	AFL	67	85
45	Bob Mann	Det.	NFL	49	85
46	Tom Fears–2	L.A.	NFL	49	84
47	Del Shofner–2	NY G	NFL	63	84
48	Cloyce Box	Det.	NFL	50	84
49	Lionel Taylor–2	Den.	AFL	61	84
50	Bill Groman–2	Hou.	AFL	61	84
51	Art Powell–3	NY T	AFL	60	83
52	Harry Grant	Phi.	NFL	52	83
53	Don Hutson–3	G.B.	NFL	45	83
54	Sonny Randle	St. L.	NFL	62	83

AVERAGE YARDS
(Minimum 400 Yards)

					Rec.	Yards	Avg.
1	Don Currivan	Bos.	NFL	47	24	782	32.6
2	Ducky Pope	L.A.	NFL	64	25	786	31.4
3	Billy Cannon	Oak.	AFL	66	14	436	31.1
4	Ray McLean–1	ChiB	NFL	42	19	571	30.1
5	Mel Gray	St. L.	NFC	71	18	534	29.7
6	Ray Renfro	Cle.	NFL	57	21	589	28.0
7	Jimmy Orr–1	Pit.	NFL	58	33	910	27.6
8	Andy Farkas	Was.	NFL	39	16	437	27.3
9	Homer Jones–1	NY G	NFL	65	26	709	27.3
10	Elbert Dubenion	Buf.	AFL	64	42	1139	27.1
11	Frank Liebel	NY G	NFL	45	22	593	27.0
12	Warren Wells	Oak.	AFL	69	47	1260	26.8
13	Buddy Dial–1	Pit.	NFL	69	16	428	26.8
14	Bill Van Heusen	Den.	AFC	74	16	421	26.3
15	Earl McCullough	Det.	NFC	71	21	552	26.3
16	Jack Snow	L.A.	NFL	67	28	735	26.3
17	Art Graham	Bos.	AFL	63	21	550	26.2
18	Bob Hayes–1	Dal.	NFC	70	34	889	26.2
19	Ron Sellers	Bos.	AFL	69	27	705	26.1
20	Roger Carr	Bal.	AFC	76	43	1112	25.9
21	Jimmy Orr–2	Bal.	NFL	68	29	743	25.6
22	Ken Kavanaugh	ChiB	NFL	47	32	818	25.6
23	Cloyce Box	Det.	NFL	53	16	403	25.2
24	Paul Warfield	Mia.	AFC	70	28	703	25.1
25	Harlon Hill–1	ChiB	NFL	54	45	1124	25.0
26	Don Hutson	G.B.	NFL	39	34	846	24.9
27	Red Mack	Pit.	NFL	63	25	218	24.7
28	Homer Jones–2	NY G	NFL	67	49	1209	24.7
29	Tony Bova	P-P	NFL	43	17	419	24.6
30	Elbert Nickel–1	Pit.	NFL	49	26	633	24.3
31	Walter White	K.C.	AFC	75	23	559	24.3
32	Buddy Dial–2	Pit.	NFL	60	40	972	24.3
33	Rick Upchurch	Den.	AFC	75	18	436	24.2
34	Ray McLean	ChiB	NFL	43	18	435	24.2
35	Cliff Branch	Oak.	AFC	76	46	1111	24.2
36	Roy Jefferson	Pit.	NFL	66	32	772	24.1
37	Harlon Hill–2	ChiB	NFL	56	47	1128	24.0
	Bob Hayes–2	Dal.	NFC	71	35	840	24.0
39	Elbert Nickel–2	Pit.	NFL	50	22	527	24.0

TOUCHDOWNS

1	Don Hutson	G.B.	NFL	42	17
	Crazy Legs Hirsch	L.A.	NFL	51	17
	Bill Groman–1	Hou.	AFL	61	17
4	Art Powell–1	NY T	AFL	63	16
5	Cloyce Box	Det.	NFL	52	15
	Sonny Randle–1	St. L.	NFL	60	15
7	Mal Kutner	ChiC	NFL	48	14
	Alyn Beals–1	S.F.	AAFC	48	14
	Ray Berry	Bal.	NFL	59	14
	Art Powell–2	NY T	AFL	60	14
	Frank Clarke	Dal.	NFL	62	14
	Lance Alworth–1	S.D.	AFL	65	14
	Don Maynard	NY J	AFL	65	14
	Warren Wells	Oak.	AFL	69	14
15	Ken Kavanaugh	ChiB	NFL	47	13
	Billy Howton–1	G.B.	NFL	52	13
	Tommy McDonald–1	Phi.	NFL	60	13
	Tommy McDonald–2	Phi.	NFL	61	13
	Terry Barr	Det.	NFL	63	13
	Gary Collins–1	Cle.	NFL	63	13
	Lance Alworth–2	S.D.	AFL	64	13
	Lance Alworth–3	S.D.	AFL	66	13
	Bob Hayes–1	Dal.	NFL	66	13
	Homer Jones	NY G	NFL	67	13
	Dick Gordon	Chi.	NFC	70	13
	Harold Jackson	L.A.	NFC	73	13
	Cliff Branch–1	Oak.	AFC	74	13
28	Alyn Beals–2	S.F.	AAFC	49	12
	Bob Shaw	ChiC	NFL	50	12
	Leon Hart	Det.	NFL	51	12
	Hugh Taylor	Was.	NFL	52	12
	Harlon Hill	ChiB	NFL	54	12
	Billy Howton–2	G.B.	NFL	56	12
	Bill Groman–2	Hou.	AFL	60	12
	Lionel Taylor	Den.	AFL	60	12
	Buddy Dial	Pit.	NFL	61	12
	Mike Ditka	Chi.	NFL	61	12
	Charley Hennigan	Hou.	AFL	61	12
	Chris Burford	Dal.	AFL	62	12
	Del Shofner	NY G	NFL	62	12
	Sonny Randle–2	St. L.	NFL	63	12
	Bob Hayes–2	Dal.	NFL	65	12
	Dave Parks	S.F.	NFL	65	12
	Art Powell–3	Oak.	AFL	65	12
	Gary Collins–2	Cle.	NFL	66	12
	Charley Frazier	Hou.	AFL	66	12
	Charley Taylor	Was.	NFL	66	12
	Jerry Smith	Was.	NFL	67	12
	Paul Warfield	Cle.	NFL	68	12
	Fred Biletnikoff	Oak.	AFL	69	12
	Lance Rentzel	Dal.	NFL	69	12
	Gary Garrison	S.D.	AFC	70	12
	Gene Washington–1	S.F.	NFC	70	12
	Gene Washington–2	S.F.	NFC	72	12
	Cliff Branch–2	Oak.	AFC	76	12
	Nat Moore	Mia.	AFC	77	12

SINGLE SEASON LEADERS

POINTS

1	Paul Hornung–1	G.B.	NFL	60	176
2	Gino Cappelletti–1	Bos.	AFL	64	155
3	Gino Cappelletti–2	Bos.	AFL	61	147
4	Paul Hornung–2	G.B.	NFL	61	146
5	Jim Turner–1	NY J	AFL	68	145
6	Don Hutson–1	G.B.	NFL	42	138
	O.J. Simpson	Buf.	AFC	75	138
8	Gene Mingo–1	Den.	AFL	62	137
9	Gale Sayers	Chi.	NFL	65	132
	Gino Cappelletti–3	Bos.	AFL	65	132
	Chuck Foreman	Min.	NFC	75	132
12	Dave Ray–1	L.A.	NFC	73	130
13	Jan Stenerud–1	K.C.	AFL	68	129
	Jim Turner–2	NY J	AFL	69	129
15	Doak Walker	Det.	NFL	50	128
	Gino Cappelletti–4	Bos.	AFL	62	128
	Cookie Gilchrist	Buf.	AFL	62	128
	Chester Marcol	G.B.	NFC	72	128
19	Jimmy Brown	Cle.	NFL	65	126
20	Fred Cox–1	Min.	NFC	70	125
21	Gene Mingo–2	Den.	AFL	60	123
	Roy Gerela–1	Pit.	AFC	73	123
23	Fred Cox–2	Min.	NFL	64	121
	Dave Ray–2	L.A.	NFC	70	121
	Bobby Howfield	NY J	AFC	72	121
26	Lenny Moore	Bal.	NFL	64	120
	Leroy Kelly	Cle.	NFL	68	120
28	Gino Cappelletti–5	Bos.	AFL	66	119
	Jan Stenerud–2	K.C.	AFL	69	119
	Roy Gerela–2	Pit.	AFC	72	119
31	Don Hutson–2	G.B.	NFL	43	117
	Jim Bakken–1	St. L.	NFL	67	117
	George Blanda–1	Oak.	AFL	68	117
	Garo Yepremian–1	Mia.	AFC	71	117
35	George Blanda–2	Oak.	AFL	67	116
	Jan Stenerud–3	K.C.	AFC	70	116
37	George Blanda–3	Hou.	AFL	60	115
	Jim Bakken–2	St. L.	NFL	64	115
	Lou Groza	Cle.	NFL	64	115
	Pete Gogolak	Buf.	AFL	65	115
	Garo Yepremian–2	Mia.	AFC	72	115
42	Spec Sanders	N.Y.	AAFC	47	114
	Gordon Soltau	S.F.	NFL	53	114
	Bobby Walston	Phi.	NFL	54	114
	Jim Taylor	G.B.	NFL	62	114
	Abner Haynes	Dal.	AFL	62	114
	Curt Knight	Was.	NFC	71	114
48	Gino Cappelletti–6	Bos.	AFL	63	113
	Fred Cox–3	Min.	NFL	65	113
	Bruce Gossett	L.A.	NFL	66	113
	Garo Yepremian–3	Mia.	AFC	73	113
52	George Blanda–4	Hou.	AFL	61	112
	Nick Mike-Mayer	Atl.	NFC	73	112
54	Horst Muhlmann	Cin.	AFC	72	111
55	Steve Van Buren	Phi.	NFL	45	110
	Pat Harder	ChiC	NFL	48	110
	Lou Michaels	Pit.	NFL	62	110
	Jan Stenerud–4	K.C.	AFC	71	110

POINTS PER SCHEDULED GAME

1	Paul Hornung–1	G.B.	NFL	60	14.7
2	Don Hutson–1	G.B.	NFL	42	12.5
3	Don Hutson–2	G.B.	NFL	43	11.7
4	Gino Cappelletti–1	Bos.	AFL	64	11.1
5	Steve Van Buren	Phi.	NFL	45	11.0
6	Doak Walker–1	Det.	NFL	50	10.7
7	Gino Cappelletti–2	Bos.	AFL	61	10.5
8	Paul Hornung–2	G.B.	NFL	61	10.4
9	Jim Turner–1	NY J	AFL	68	10.4
10	O.J. Simpson	Buf.	AFC	75	9.9
11	Gene Mingo–1	Den.	AFL	62	9.8
12	Don Hutson–3	G.B.	NFL	45	9.7
13	Gordon Soltau	S.F.	NFL	53	9.5
	Bobby Walston–1	Phi.	NFL	54	9.5
15	Gale Sayers	Chi.	NFL	65	9.4
	Gino Cappelletti–3	Bos.	AFL	65	9.4
	Chuck Foreman	Min.	NFC	75	9.4
18	Dave Ray–1	L.A.	NFC	73	9.3
19	Jan Stenerud–1	K.C.	AFL	68	9.2
	Jim Turner–2	NY J	AFL	69	9.2
21	Pat Harder–1	ChiC	NFL	48	9.2
22	Gino Cappelletti–4	Bos.	AFL	62	9.1
	Cookie Gilchrist	Buf.	AFL	62	9.1
	Chester Marcol	G.B.	NFC	72	9.1
25	Johnny Lujack	ChiB	NFL	50	9.1
26	Lou Groza	Cle.	NFL	53	9.0
	Jimmy Brown–1	Cle.	NFL	58	9.0
	Jimmy Brown–2	Cle.	NFL	65	9.0
29	Fred Cox–1	Min.	NFC	70	8.9
30	Doak Walker–2	Det.	NFL	54	8.8
31	Gene Mingo–2	Den.	AFL	60	8.8
	Roy Gerela–1	Pit.	AFC	73	8.8
33	Bobby Walston–2	Phi.	NFL	60	8.8
34	Fred Cox–2	Min.	NFL	69	8.6
	Dave Ray–2	L.A.	NFC	70	8.6
	Bobby Howfield	NY J	AFC	72	8.6
37	Don Hutson–4	G.B.	NFL	41	8.6
38	Lenny Moore	Bal.	NFL	64	8.6
	Leroy Kelly	Cle.	NFL	68	8.6
40	Don Hutson–5	G.B.	NFL	44	8.5
	Pat Harder–2	ChiC	NFL	47	8.5
	Pat Harder–3	ChiC	NFL	49	8.5
	Choo-Choo Roberts	NY G	NFL	49	8.5
	Crazy Legs Hirsch	L.A.	NFL	51	8.5
	Gino Cappelletti–5	Bos.	AFL	66	8.5
	Jan Stenerud–2	K.C.	AFL	69	8.5
	Roy Gerela–2	Pit.	AFC	72	8.5

FIELD GOALS

1	Jim Turner–1	NY J	AFL	68	34
2	Chester Marcol–1	G.B.	NFC	72	33
3	Jim Turner–2	NY J	AFL	69	32
4	Jan Stenerud–1	K.C.	AFL	68	30
	Jan Stenerud–2	K.C.	AFC	70	30
	Fred Cox–1	Min.	NFC	70	30
	Dave Ray–1	L.A.	NFC	73	30
8	Dave Ray–2	L.A.	NFC	70	29
	Curt Knight–1	Was.	NFC	71	29
	Roy Gerela–1	Pit.	AFC	73	29
11	Pete Gogolak–1	Buf.	AFL	65	28
	Bruce Gossett–1	L.A.	NFL	66	28
	Garo Yepremian–1	Mia.	AFC	71	28
	Roy Gerela–2	Pit.	AFC	72	28
15	Gene Mingo	Den.	AFL	62	27
	Jim Bakken–1	St. L.	NFL	67	27
	Jan Stenerud–3	K.C.	AFL	69	27
	Bobby Howfield	NY J	AFC	72	27
	Horst Muhlmann	Cin.	AFC	72	27
20	Lou Michaels	Pit.	NFL	62	26
	Fred Cox–2	Min.	NFL	69	26
	Jan Stenerud–4	K.C.	AFC	71	26
	Bruce Gossett–2	S.F.	NFC	73	26
	Nick Mike-Mayer	Atl.	NFC	73	26
25	Jim Bakken–2	St. L.	NFL	64	25
	Gino Cappelletti–1	Bos.	AFL	65	25
	Mac Percival	Chi.	NFL	68	25
	Errol Mann–1	Det.	NFL	69	25
	Pete Gogolak–2	NY G	NFC	70	25
	Horst Muhlmann–2	Cin.	AFC	70	25
	Jim Turner–3	Den.	AFC	71	25
	Garo Yepremian–2	Mia.	AFC	73	25
	Chester Marcol–2	G.B.	NFC	74	25
34	Jim Martin	Bal.	NFL	63	24
	Dave Ray–3	L.A.	NFC	72	24
	Garo Yepremian–3	Mia.	AFC	72	24
	Tom Dempsey–1	Phi.	NFC	73	24
	Jan Stenerud–5	K.C.	AFC	73	24
39	Lou Groza–1	Cle.	NFL	53	23
	Fred Cox–3	Min.	NFL	65	23
	Jim Bakken–3	St. L.	NFL	66	23
	Bruce Gossett–3	S.F.	NFC	71	23
	Jim Bakken–4	St. L.	NFC	73	23
	George Blanda	Oak.	AFC	73	23
	Errol Mann–2	Det.	NFC	74	23
46	Gino Cappelletti	Bos.	AFL	63	22
	Lou Groza–2	Cle.	NFL	64	22
	Charlie Gogolak	Was.	NFL	66	22
	Dennis Partee	S.D.	AFL	68	22
	Tom Dempsey–2	N.O.	NFL	69	22
	Bruce Gossett–4	L.A.	NFL	69	22
	Garo Yepremian–4	Mia.	AFC	70	22
	Fred Cox–4	Min.	NFC	71	22
	Errol Mann–3	Det.	NFC	71	22
	Don Cockroft–1	Cle.	AFC	72	22
	Don Cockroft–2	Cle.	AFC	73	22
	Curt Knight–2	Was.	NFC	73	22
	Jim Turner–4	Den.	AFC	73	22
	Toni Fritsch	Dal.	NFC	75	22
	Jan Stenerud–6	K.C.	AFC	75	22
	Mark Moseley	Was.	NFC	76	22

PERCENTAGE – FIELD GOALS MADE

(Minimum Attempts: to 1949=5, 50-59 = 10, 1960 + up = 20)

					Made	Att.	Pct.
1	Lou Groza	Cle.	NFL	53	23	26	88.5
2	Jack Manders	ChiB	NFL	36	7	8	87.5
3	Don Cockroft–1	Cle.	AFC	72	22	27	81.5
4	Roy Gerela	Pit.	AFC	75	17	21	81.0
5	Tom Dempsey	L.A.	NFC	75	21	26	80.8
6	Bobby Layne	Det.	NFL	56	12	15	80.0
	Regis Monahan	Det.	NFL	38	4	5	80.0
	Chuck Hanneman	Det.	NFL	39	4	5	80.0
	Andy Marefos	NY G	NFL	41	4	5	80.0
	Ted Fritsch	G.B.	NFL	42	4	5	80.0
	Frank Maznicki	ChiB	NFL	42	4	5	80.0
12	Jim Bakken–1	St. L.	NFC	75	19	24	79.2
13	Bruce Gossett–1	S.F.	NFC	73	26	33	78.8
14	Efren Herrera	Dal.	NFC	76	18	23	78.3
	Rich Szaro	N.O.	NFC	76	18	23	78.3
16	Jan Stenerud–1	K.C.	AFL	69	27	35	77.1
	Bill Dudley	Was.	NFL	51	10	13	76.9
18	Garo Yepremian	Mia.	AFC	70	22	29	75.9
19	Jan Stenerud–2	K.C.	AFL	67	30	40	75.0
	Jim Turner–1	Den.	AFC	75	21	28	75.0
	Bruce Gossett–2	L.A.	NFL	64	18	24	75.0
	Don Cockroft–2	Cle.	NFL	68	18	24	75.0
	Ray Poole	NY G	NFL	51	12	16	75.0
	Steve Nemeth	Chi.	AAFC	46	9	12	75.0
	Bobby Walston–1	Phi.	NFL	57	9	12	75.0
26	Curt Knight	Was.	NFC	70	20	27	74.1
	Jim Bakken–2	St. L.	NFC	76	20	27	74.1
	Toni Linhart	Bal.	AFC	76	20	27	74.1
29	Jim Turner–2	NY J	AFL	67	34	46	73.9
	Don Cockroft–3	Cle.	AFC	75	17	23	73.9
	Rolf Benirschke	S.D.	AFC	77	17	23	73.9
	Don Cockroft–4	Cle.	AFC	77	17	23	73.9
33	Bobby Howfield–1	NY J	AFC	72	27	37	73.0
34	John Smith–1	N.E.	AFC	74	16	22	72.7
35	Sam Baker	Phi.	NFL	66	18	25	72.0
36	Jim Bakken–3	St. L.	NFC	73	23	32	71.9
	Errol Mann–1	Det.	NFC	74	23	32	71.9
38	Jan Stenerud	K.C.	AFC	70	30	42	71.4
	Errol Mann–2	Oak.	AFC	77	20	28	71.4
	Jim Turner–3	Den.	AFC	76	15	21	71.4
	John Smith–2	N.E.	AFC	77	15	21	71.4
42	Don Cockroft–5	Cle.	AFC	73	22	31	71.0
43	Bobby Howfield–2	NY J	AFC	73	17	24	70.8
	Jan Stenerud–4	K.C.	AFC	74	17	24	70.8
45	Fred Cone	G.B.	NFL	57	12	17	70.6
46	Chris Bahr	Cin.	AFC	77	19	27	70.4
47	Fred Cox	Min.	NFL	69	26	37	70.3
48	Garo Yepremian–2	Mia.	AFC	71	28	40	70.0
	Mike Mercer	Oak. + K.C.	AFL	66	21	30	70.0
	John Leypoldt	Buf.	AFC	73	21	30	70.0
	Bobby Walston–2	Phi.	NFL	60	14	20	70.0
	Pat Harder	ChiC	NFL	47	7	10	70.0

POINTS AFTER TOUCHDOWN

1	George Blanda–1	Hou.	AFL	61	64
2	Joe Vetrano–1	S.F.	AAFC	48	62
3	Joe Vetrano–2	S.F.	AAFC	49	56
	Danny Villanueva	Dal.	NFL	66	56
	George Blanda–2	Oak.	AFL	67	56
6	Bob Waterfield	L.A.	NFL	50	54
	George Blanda–3	Oak.	AFL	68	54
	Mike Clark–1	Dal.	NFL	68	54
9	Pat Harder–1	ChiC	NFL	48	53
	Lou Michaels–1	Bal.	NFL	64	53
11	Don Chandler–1	NY G	NFL	63	52
	Tommy Davis	S.F.	NFL	65	52
	Roger LeClerc	Chi.	NFL	65	52
14	Lou Groza–1	Cle.	AAFC	48	51
	Lou Groza–2	Cle.	NFL	66	51
	John Leypoldt	Buf.	AFC	75	51
	Toni Linhart–1	Bal.	AFC	75	51
18	Cliff Patton	Phi.	NFL	48	50
	Steve Myrha–1	Bal.	NFL	59	50
	Sam Baker–1	Dal.	NFL	62	50
21	Harvey Johnson	N.Y.	AAFC	47	49
	Lou Groza–3	Cle.	NFL	64	49
	Toni Linhart–2	Bal.	AFC	76	49
24	Gordie Soltau	S.F.	NFL	53	48
	Steve Myrha–2	Bal.	NFL	58	48
	Gino Cappelletti	Bos.	AFL	61	48
	George Blanda–4	Hou.	AFL	62	48
	Jim Bakken	St. L.	NFL	65	48
	Bruce Gossett	L.A.	NFL	67	48
	Lou Michaels–2	Bal.	NFL	68	48
31	Bill Shockley	NY T	AFL	60	47
	Don Chandler–2	NY G	NFL	62	47
	Mike Mercer	Oak.	AFL	63	47
	Mike Clark–2	Dal	NFC	71	47
35	Ben Agajanian	L.A.	AFL	60	46
	George Blanda–5	Hou.	AFL	60	46
	Pat Summerall	NY G	NFL	61	46
	Tommy Brooker	K.C.	AFL	64	46
	Pete Gogolak	Buf.	AFL	64	46
	Lou Michaels–3	Bal.	NFL	67	46
	Don Cockroft–1	Cle.	NFL	68	46
	Fred Cox	Min.	NFC	75	46
43	Lou Groza–4	Cle.	AAFC	46	45
	Pat Harder	ChiC	NFL	49	45
	Chet Adams	NY Y	NFL	50	45
	Bobby Walston	Phi.	NFL	53	45
	George Blanda–6	ChiB	NFL	56	45
	Lou Groza–5	Cle.	NFL	65	45
	Sam Baker–2	Phi.	NFL	67	45
	Jan Stenerud	K.C.	AFL	67	45
	Dick Van Raaphorst	S.D.	AFL	67	45
	George Blanda–7	Oak.	AFL	69	45
	Don Cockroft–2	Cle.	NFL	69	45

MOST PAT'S – NO MISSES

1	Joe Vetrano	S.F.	AAFC	49	56
	Danny Villanueva	Dal.	NFL	66	56
3	George Blanda–1	Oak.	AFL	68	54
	Mike Clark–1	Dal.	NFL	68	54
5	Pat Harder	ChiC	NFL	48	53
6	Roger LeClerc	Chi.	NFL	65	52
7	Cliff Patton	Phi.	NFL	48	50
8	Jim Bakken–1	St. L.	NFL	65	48
	Bruce Gossett–1	L.A.	NFL	67	48
10	Mike Mercer	Oak.	AFL	63	47
	Mike Clark–2	Dal.	NFC	71	47
12	Pat Summerall	NY G	NFL	61	46
	Tom Brooker	K.C.	AFL	64	46
14	Lou Groza–1	Cle.	NFL	65	45
	Sam Baker	Phi.	NFL	67	45
	Jan Stenerud	K.C.	AFL	67	45
	Dick Van Raaphorst	S.D.	AFL	67	45
	George Blanda–2	Oak.	AFL	69	45
	Don Cockroft	Cle.	NFL	69	45
20	Tommy Davis	S.F.	NFL	61	44
	Jim Bakken–2	St. L.	NFL	63	44
	Fred Cox–1	Min.	NFL	65	44
	George Blanda–3	Oak.	AFL	72	44
24	Rex Grossman	Bal.	AAFC	48	43
	Lou Groza–2	Cle.	NFL	51	43
	Doak Walker	Det.	NFL	54	43
	Lou Groza–3	Cle.	NFL	67	43
	Jim Turner–1	NY J	AFL	68	43
	Fred Cox–2	Min.	NFL	69	43
	Toni Fritsch	Dal.	NFC	73	43
	Garo Yepremian	Mia.	AFC	74	43
32	Paige Cothren	L.A.	NFL	58	42
33	Paul Hornung–1	G.B.	NFL	60	41
	Paul Hornung–2	G.B.	NFL	61	41
	Errol Mann	Det.	NFC	70	41
36	Jim Bakken–3	St. L.	NFL	64	40
	Herb Traveno	S.D.	AFL	65	40
	Jim Bakken–4	St. L.	NFL	68	40
	Jim Turner–2	Den.	AFC	73	40

SINGLE SEASON LEADERS

PUNT RETURNS

1	Eddie Brown–1	Was.	NFC	77	57
2	Rolland Lawrence–1	Atl.	NFC	76	54
3	Alvin Haymond–1	L.A.	NFC	70	53
	Larry Jones	Was.	NFC	75	53
5	Rolland Lawrence–2	Atl.	NFC	77	51
	Rick Upchurch–1	Den.	AFC	77	51
7	Butch Johnson–1	Dal.	NFC	77	50
8	Neal Colzie–1	Oak.	AFC	75	48
	Eddie Brown–2	Was.	NFC	76	48
10	Manfred Moore	Min.	NFC	77	47
11	Rodger Bird–1	Oak.	AFL	67	46
	Larry Marshall	Phi.	NFC	77	46
13	Mike Haynes	N.E.	AFC	76	45
	Butch Johnson–2	Dal.	NFC	76	45
15	Bruce Taylor	S.F.	NFC	70	43
	Donnie Walker	Buf.	AFC	74	43
17	Alvin Haymond–2	Bal.	NFL	65	41
	Butch Atkinson–1	Oak.	AFC	73	41
	Ron Smith	Oak.	AFC	74	41
	Lynn Swann	Pit.	AFC	74	41
	Virgil Livers	Chi.	NFC	75	41
	Neal Colzie–2	Oak.	AFC	76	41
23	Alvin Haymond–3	Bal.	NFL	66	40
	Ray Brown	Atl.	NFC	73	40
	Billie Johnson–1	Hou.	AFC	75	40
26	Charlie West	Min.	NFL	69	39
	Theo Bell	Pit.	AFC	76	39
	Howard Stevens–1	Bal.	AFC	76	39
	Rick Upchurch–2	Den.	AFC	76	39
30	Em Tunnell	NY G	NFL	53	38
	Roscoe Word	NY J	AFC	74	38
	Billy Johnson–2	Hou.	AFC	76	38
33	Rodger Bird–2	Oak.	NFL	66	37
	Hubie Bryant	Pit.	AFC	70	37
	Howard Stevens–2	N.O.	NFC	74	37
	Johnnie Gray	G.B.	NFC	76	37
	Rich Mauti	N.O.	NFC	77	37
38	Speedy Duncan	S.D.	AFL	67	36
	Butch Atkinson–2	Oak.	AFL	68	36
	Ike Hill	Chi.	NFC	73	36
	Mike Fuller	S.D.	AFC	75	36
	Howard Stevens–3	Bal.	AFC	75	36
43	Woodley Lewis	L.A.	NFL	53	35
	Kermit Alexander	S.F.	NFL	65	35
	Jerry LeVias	Hou.	AFL	69	35
	Mack Herron	N.E.	AFC	74	35
	Pete Athas	N.O.	NFC	76	35
	Tony Leonard	S.F.	NFC	76	35
	Billy Johnson–3	Hou.	AFC	77	35

YARDS

1	Neal Colzie–1	Oak.	AFC	75	655
2	Rick Upchurch–1	Den.	AFC	77	653
3	Eddie Brown–1	Was.	NFC	76	646
4	Rodger Bird	Oak.	AFL	67	612
5	Billy Johnson–1	Hou.	AFC	75	610
6	Mike Haynes	N.E.	AFC	76	608
7	Lynn Swann	Pit.	AFC	74	577
8	Billy Grimes	G.B.	NFL	50	555
9	Billy Johnson–2	Hou.	AFC	77	539
10	Rick Upchurch–2	Den.	AFC	76	536
11	Mack Herron	N.E.	AFC	74	517
12	Bruce Taylor	S.F.	NFC	70	516
13	Butch Atkinson	Oak.	AFL	68	490
14	Em Tunnell–1	NY G	NFL	51	489
	Butch Johnson–1	Dal.	NFC	76	489
	Larry Marshall	Phi.	NFC	77	489
17	Ron Smith–1	Oak.	AFC	74	486
18	Speedie Duncan–1	S.D.	AFL	65	464
19	Pat Studstill	Det.	NFL	62	457
20	Virgil Livers	Chi.	NFC	75	456
21	Eddie Brown–2	Was.	NFC	77	452
22	Neal Colzie–2	Oak.	AFC	76	448
23	Mike Fuller–1	S.D.	AFC	76	436
24	Walt Slater	Pit.	NFL	47	435
	Alvin Haymond–1	L.A.	NFL	69	435
26	Speedie Duncan–2	S.D.	AFL	67	434
27	Vitamin Smith	L.A.	NFL	49	427
28	Bruce Harper	NY J	AFC	77	425
29	Butch Johnson–2	Dal.	NFC	77	423
30	Claude Gibson–1	Oak.	AFL	64	419
31	Mel Renfro	Dal.	NFL	64	418
32	George McAfee	ChiB	NFL	48	417
33	Em Tunnell–2	NY G	NFL	52	411
34	Mike Fuller–2	S.D.	AFC	75	410
35	Billy Johnson–3	Hou.	AFC	74	409
36	Larry Jones	Was.	NFC	75	407
37	Alvin Haymond–2	Bal.	NFL	65	403
	Billy Johnson–4	Hou.	AFC	77	403
39	Tom Watkins	Det.	NFL	63	399
40	Roy Mathews	Phi.	NFL	52	397
41	Howard Stevens–1	Bal.	AFC	75	396
42	Tommy Harmon	L.A.	NFL	47	392
43	Theo Bell	Pit.	AFC	76	390
44	Larry Brunson	K.C.	AFC	76	387
45	Bill Dudley	Pit.	NFL	46	385
46	Donnie Walker	Buf.	AFC	74	384
47	Dick Christie	NY T	AFL	61	383
48	Rickie Harris	Was.	NFL	65	377
49	Alvin Haymond–3	L.A.	NFC	70	376
	Howard Stevens–2	N.O.	NFC	74	376
51	Rolland Lawrence–1	Atl.	NFC	76	372
52	Herm Wedemeyer	L.A.	NFL	48	368
53	John Williams	Was.	NFL	52	366
	Bill Thompson–1	Den.	AFC	73	366
55	Roy Brown	Atl.	NFC	73	360
	Mike Fuller–3	S.D.	AFC	77	360
57	Claude Gibson–2	Oak.	AFL	65	357
58	Ron Smith–2	S.D.	AFC	73	352
	Rolland Lawrence–2	Atl.	NFC	77	352
60	Jim Cason	S.F.	AAFC	49	351
	Woodley Lewis	L.A.	NFL	52	351
62	Bill Thompson–2	Den.	AFC	74	350

AVERAGE RETURN

(Minimum – 1 Return per Game)

					Ret.	Yds.	Avg.
1	Ernie Steele	Phi.	NFL	42	10	264	26.40
2	Herb Rich	Bal.	NFL	50	12	276	23.00
3	Jack Christiansen–1	Det.	NFL	52	15	322	21.47
4	Dick Christy	NY T	AFL	61	18	383	21.28
5	Rex Baumgardner	Buf.	AAFC	48	16	336	21.00
6	Red Cochran	ChiC	NFL	49	15	314	20.93
7	Jerome Davis	ChiC	NFL	48	16	334	20.88
8	Bob Hayes	Dal.	NFL	68	15	312	20.80
9	Frankie Sinkwich	Det.	NFL	43	11	228	20.73
10	Buddy Young	NY Y	NFL	51	12	231	19.25
11	Billy Grimes	G.B.	NFL	50	29	555	19.14
12	Jack Christiansen–2	Det.	NFL	51	18	343	19.06
13	Ollie Matson	ChiC	NFL	55	13	245	18.85
14	Lemar Parrish	Cin.	AFC	74	18	338	18.78
15	Chuck Fenenbock	L.A.	AAFC	46	16	299	18.69
16	Woodley Lewis	L.A.	NFL	52	19	351	18.47
17	Frank Seno	Bos.	NFL	47	12	213	17.75

KICKOFF RETURNS

1	Odell Barry	Den.	AFL	64	47
	Larry Jones	Was.	NFC	75	47
3	Chuck Latourette	St. L.	NFL	68	46
	Dave Hampton	G.B.	NFC	71	46
5	Bobby Jancik–1	Hou.	AFL	63	45
6	Ron Smith–1	Atl.	NFL	66	43
	Mercury Morris	Mia.	AFL	69	43
	Margene Adkins	N.O.	NFC	72	43
9	Steve Odom	G.B.	NFC	75	42
	Bruce Harper	NY J	AFC	77	42
11	Noland Smith	K.C.	AFL	67	41
	Mack Herron	N.E.	AFC	73	41
13	Mel Renfro	Dal.	NFL	64	40
	Mike Battle	NY J	AFL	70	40
	Rick Upchurch	Den.	AFC	75	40
16	Ron Smith–2	Atl.	NFL	67	39
	Max Anderson	Buf.	AFL	68	39
	Lou Piccone	NY J	AFC	74	39
19	Dick Christy	NY T	AFL	62	38
	Bo Roberson–1	Oak.	AFL	63	38
	Jerry LeVias	Hou.	AFL	69	38
	Jimmie Jones	Det.	NFC	74	38
23	Abe Woodson–1	S.F.	NFL	62	37
	Charley Mitchell	Den.	AFL	63	37
	Kermit Alexander–1	S.F.	NFL	66	37
	Cannonball Butler	Atl.	NFL	68	37
	Wallace Francis	Buf.	AFC	74	37
28	Bo Roberson–2	Oak.	AFL	64	36
	Willy Porter	Bos.	AFL	68	36
	Rocky Thompson	NY G	NFC	71	36
	Herb Mul-Key	Was.	NFC	73	36
	Ron Smith–3	S.D.	AFC	73	36
	Paul Hofer	S.F.	NFC	77	36
	Al Hunter	Sea.	AFC	77	36
35	Floyd Little	Den.	AFL	67	35
	Ronnie Blye	NY G	NFL	68	35
	Alvin Haymond	L.A.	NFC	70	35
	Dennis Morgan	Dal.	NFC	74	35
	Terry Metcalf	St. L.	NFC	75	35
	Vic Washington–1	Buf.	AFC	75	35
41	Woodley Lewis–1	L.A.	NFL	54	34
	Clarence Childs–1	NY G	NFL	64	34
	Abner Haynes	Den.	AFL	65	34
	Clarence Childs–2	NY G	NFL	66	34
	Bobby Jancik–2	Hou.	AFL	66	34
	Eddie Brown	Was.	NFC	77	34
47	Al Carmichael	G.B.	NFL	56	33
	Timmy Brown	Phi.	NFL	63	33
	Bill Butler	Min.	NFL	63	33
	Charley Warner–1	Buf.	AFL	66	33
	Vic Washington–2	S.F.	NFC	71	33
	Howard Stevens	N.O.	NFC	74	33
	Billy Johnson	Hou.	AFC	75	33
54	Woodley Lewis–2	L.A.	NFL	53	32
	Jimmy Sears	ChiC	NFL	58	32
	Dick James	Was.	NFL	62	32
	Jerry Robinson	S.D.	AFL	62	32
	Abe Woodson–2	S.F.	NFL	64	32
	J.D. Garrett	Bos.	AFL	64	32
	Kermit Alexander–2	S.F.	NFL	65	32
	Charley Warner–2	Buf.	AFL	65	32
	Butch Atkinson	Oak.	AFL	68	32
	Zeke Moore	Hou.	AFL	68	32
	Billy Walik	Phi.	NFC	70	32
	Linzy Cole	Hou.	AFC	71	32
	Allen Carter	N.E.	AFC	75	32
	Terry Metcalf	St. L.	NFC	77	32

YARDS

1	Bobby Jancik–1	Hou.	AFL	63	1317
2	Dave Hampton	G.B.	NFC	71	1314
3	Odell Barry	Den	AFL	64	1245
4	Chuck Latourette	St. L.	NFL	68	1237
5	Abe Woodson–1	S.F.	NFL	62	1157
6	Noland Smith	K.C.	AFL	67	1148
7	Mercury Morris–1	Mia.	AFL	69	1136
8	Mack Herron	N.E.	AFC	73	1092
9	Larry Jones	Was.	NFC	75	1086
10	Rick Upchurch	Den.	AFC	75	1084
11	Bruce Harper	NY J	AFC	77	1035
12	Steve Odom	G.B.	NFC	75	1034
13	Alvin Haymond	L.A.	NFC	70	1022
14	Margene Adkins	N.O.	NFC	72	1020
15	Mel Renfro	Dal.	NFL	64	1017
16	Ron Smith–1	Atl.	NFL	66	1013
17	Herb Mul-Key	Was.	NFC	73	1011
18	Clarence Childs–1	NY G	NFL	64	987
19	Kermit Alexander	S.F.	NFL	66	984
20	Ron Smith–2	Atl.	NFL	67	976
21	Bo Roberson–1	Oak.	AFL	64	975
22	Max Anderson	Buf.	AFL	68	971
23	Lou Piccone	NY J	AFC	74	961
24	Terry Metcalf	St. L.	NFC	75	960
25	Charley Mitchell	Den.	AFL	63	954
26	Rocky Thompson–1	NY G	NFC	71	947
	Ron Smith–3	S.D.	AFC	73	947
	Wallace Francis	Buf.	AFC	74	947
29	Timmy Brown–1	Phi.	NFL	63	945
30	Floyd Little	Den.	AFL	67	942
31	Jerry LeVias	Hou.	AFL	69	940
32	Abe Woodson–2	S.F.	NFL	63	935
33	Al Carmichael	G.B.	NFL	56	927
	Jimmie Jones	Det.	NFC	74	927
35	Ron Smith–4	Chi.	NFC	72	924
36	Vic Washington–1	Buf.	AFC	75	923
37	Abner Haynes	Den.	AFL	65	901
38	Leon Burton	NY J	AFL	60	897
39	Mike Battle	NY J	AFC	70	891
40	Dick James–1	Was.	NFL	62	889
41	Abe Woodson–3	S.F.	NFL	64	880
42	Allen Carter	N.E.	AFC	75	879
43	Bobby Jancik–2	Hou.	AFL	66	875
44	Ray Clayborn	N.E.	AFC	77	869
45	Paul Hofer	S.F.	NFC	77	863
46	Vic Washington–2	S.F.	NFC	71	858
47	Clarence Childs–2	NY G	NFL	66	855
48	Jack Larscheid	Oak.	AFL	60	852
	Eddie Brown	Was.	NFC	77	852
50	Charley Warner–1	Buf.	AFL	66	846
51	Bruce Laird	Bal.	AFC	72	843
52	Woodley Lewis–1	L.A.	NFL	54	836
53	Linzy Cole	Hou.	AFC	71	834
54	Woodley Lewis–2	Phi.	NFL	62	831
55	Woodley Lewis–2	L.A.	NFL	53	830
	Dick James–2	Was.	NFL	63	830
57	Doug Cunningham	S.F.	NFL	67	826
58	Charley Warner–2	Buf.	AFL	65	825
59	Dick Christy	NY T	AFL	62	824
60	Carver Shannon	L.A.	NFL	63	823
	Cliff Harris	Dal.	NFC	71	823
	Dennis Morgan	Dal.	NFC	74	823
63	Rocky Thompson–2	NY G	NFC	72	821
64	Al Hunter	Sea.	AFC	77	820
65	Willie Porter	Bos.	AFL	68	812
	Mercury Morris–2	Mia.	AFC	70	812
67	Timmy Brown–3	Phi.	NFL	61	811
68	Bo Roberson–2	Oak.	AFL	63	809
69	Billy Walik	Phi.	NFC	70	805
70	Butch Atkinson	Oak.	AFL	68	802
71	Joe Arenas	S.F.	NFL	56	801

AVERAGE RETURN

(Minimum – 1 Return per Game)

					Ret.	Yards	Avg.
1	Travis Williams	G.B.	NFL	67	18	739	41.06
2	Gale Sayers–1	ChiB	NFL	67	16	603	37.69
3	Ollie Matson–1	ChiC	NFL	58	14	479	35.50
4	Speedy Duncan	Bal.	AFC	70	20	707	35.35
5	Lynn Chadnois–1	Pit.	NFL	52	17	599	35.24
6	Preston Pearson	Bal.	NFL	68	15	527	35.13
7	Joe Arenas	S.F.	NFL	53	16	551	34.44
8	Tom Watkins	Det.	NFL	65	17	584	34.35
9	Vitamin Smith	L.A.	NFL	50	22	742	33.73
10	Bobby Williams	Det.	NFL	69	17	563	33.12
11	Tom Moore	G.B.	NFL	60	12	397	33.08
12	Chet Mutryn	Buf.	AAFC	47	21	691	32.90
13	Duriel Harris	Mia.	AFC	76	17	559	32.88
14	Cecil Turner	Chi.	NFC	70	23	752	32.70
15	Lynn Chadnois–2	Pit.	NFL	51	23	752	32.70
16	Abe Woodson–1	S.F.	NFL	63	29	935	32.24
17	Tom Wilson	L.A.	NFL	56	15	477	31.80
18	Gary Ballman	Pit.	NFL	63	22	698	31.73
19	Walter Payton	Chi.	NFC	75	14	444	31.71
20	Jack Salschneider	NY G	NFL	49	15	474	31.60
21	Gale Sayers–2	Chi.	NFL	65	21	660	31.43
22	Frank Zeno	ChiC	NFL	46	13	408	31.38
23	Abe Woodson–2	S.F.	NFL	62	37	1157	31.27
24	Ron Hall	Hou.	AFL	60	19	594	31.26
25	Gale Sayers–3	Chi.	NFL	66	23	718	31.22
26	Ollie Matson–2	ChiC	NFL	52	20	624	31.20
27	Terry Metcalf	St. L.	NFC	74	20	623	31.15
28	Ray Clayborn	N.E.	AFC	77	28	869	31.04
29	Lenny Lyles	S.F.	NFL	60	19	526	30.94
30	Frank Minini	ChiB	NFL	48	12	370	30.83
31	Ron Smith	Chi.	NFC	72	30	924	30.80
32	Alvin Haymond	Bal.	NFL	65	20	614	30.70
33	Buddy Young	NY Y	NFL	51	14	427	30.50
34	Harold Hart	Oak.	AFC	75	17	518	30.47
35	Carl Garrett	Chi.	NFC	73	16	486	30.38
36	Dick Bass	L.A.	NFL	61	23	698	30.35
37	Bobby Jancik	Hou.	AFL	62	24	726	30.25
38	Johnny Counts	NY G	NFL	62	26	784	30.15
39	Lemar Parrish	Cin.	AFC	70	16	482	30.13
40	John Gilliam	N.O.	NFL	67	16	431	30.01
41	Mel Renfro	Dal.	NFL	65	21	630	30.00

LIFETIME LEADERS
PASSING

ATTEMPTS (1250)

Rank	Player	Years	Att.
1	Fran Tarkenton	1961-	5895
2	Johnny Unitas	1956-73	5186
3	John Hadl	1962-	4688
4	Roman Gabriel	1962-	4498
5	John Brodie	1957-73	4491
6	Y.A. Tittle	1948-64	4395
7	Norm Snead	1961-76	4353
8	Sonny Jurgensen	1957-74	4262
9	George Blanda	1949-58,60-75	4007
10	Joe Namath	1965-77	3762
11	Len Dawson	1957-75	3741
12	Bobby Layne	1948-62	3700
13	Jim Hart	1966-	3424
14	Charley Johnson	1961-75	3392
15	Babe Parilli	1952-53,56-58,60-69	3330
16	Bart Starr	1956-71	3149
17	Sammy Baugh	1937-52	2995
18	Jack Kemp	1957,60-67,69	2973
19	Billy Kilmer	1961,62,64,66-	2939
20	Tobin Rote	1950-59,63-64,66	2907
21	Norm Van Brocklin	1949-60	2895
22	Chuck Conerly	1948-61	2833
23	Bob Griese	1967-	2784
24	Earl Morrall	1956-76	2689
25	Otto Graham	1946-55	2626
26	Daryl Lamonica	1963-74	2601
27	Billy Wade	1954-66	2523
28	Craig Morton	1965-	2448
29	Milt Plum	1957-69	2419
30	Don Meredith	1960-68	2308
31	Frank Ryan	1958-70	2133
32	Ken Anderson	1971-	2127
33	Roger Staubach	1969-	2084
34	Dan Pastorini	1971-	2076
35	Terry Bradshaw	1970-	2019
36	Jim Plunkett	1971-	1994
37	Ed Brown	1954-65	1987
38	Bill Munson	1964-	1932
39	Bill Nelsen	1963-72	1905
40	Eddie LeBaron	1952-53,55-63	1796
41	Cotton Davidson	1954,57,60-66,68	1752
42	Frank Tripucka	1949-52,60-63	1743
43	Tom Flores	1960-61,63-69	1715
44	Archie Manning	1971-75,77-	1696
45	Greg Landry	1968-	1670
46	Sid Luckman	1939-50	1657
47	Bob Waterfield	1945-52	1617
48	Ken Stabler	1970-	1577
49	Frankie Albert	1946-52	1564
50	Zeke Bratkowski	1954,57-68,71	1484
51	Bert Jones	1973-	1458
52	Tommy Thompson	1940-42,45-50	1424
53	George Ratterman	1947-56	1396
54	Jim Finks	1949-55	1382
55	Mike Livingston	1968-	1371
56	Lemar McHan	1954-63	1351
57	Bobby Thomason	1949,51-57	1346
58	Joe Ferguson	1973-	1325
59	Mike Phipps	1970-	1322
60	Randy Johnson	1966-73,75-76	1286
61	Pete Beathard	1964-73	1282

COMPLETIONS (800)

Rank	Player	Years	Comp.
1	Fran Tarkenton	1961-	3341
2	Johnny Unitas	1956-73	2830
3	John Brodie	1957-73	2469
4	Sonny Jurgensen	1957-74	2433
5	Y.A. Tittle	1948-64	2427
6	Roman Gabriel	1962-	2366
7	John Hadl	1962-	2363
8	Norm Snead	1961-76	2273
9	Len Dawson	1957-75	2136
10	George Blanda	1949-58,60-75	1911
11	Joe Namath	1965-77	1886
12	Bobby Layne	1948-62	1814
13	Bart Starr	1956-71	1808
14	Charley Johnson	1961-75	1737
15	Jim Hart	1966-	1725
16	Sammy Baugh	1937-52	1693
17	Billy Kilmer	1961-62,64,66-	1562
18	Norm Van Brocklin	1949-60	1553
19	Babe Parilli	1952-53,56-58,60-69	1552
20	Bob Griese	1967-	1541
21	Otto Graham	1946-55	1464
22	Jack Kemp	1957,60-67,69	1437
23	Chuck Conerly	1948-61	1418
24	Earl Morrall	1956-76	1379
25	Billy Wade	1954-66	1370
26	Tobin Rote	1950-59,63-64,66	1329
27	Milt Plum	1957-69	1306
28	Daryl Lamonica	1963-74	1288
29	Craig Morton	1965-	1277
30	Ken Anderson	1971-	1208
31	Roger Staubach	1969-	1187
32	Don Meredith	1960-68	1170
33	Frank Ryan	1958-70	1090
34	Dan Pastorini	1971-	1064
35	Bill Munson	1964-	1043
36	Terry Bradshaw	1970-	1008
37	Jim Plunkett	1971-	983
38	Bill Nelsen	1963-72	963
39	Ed Brown	1954-65	949
40	Ken Stabler	1970-	945
41	Greg Landry	1968-	909
42	Sid Luckman	1939-50	904
43	Eddie LeBaron	1952-53,55-63	897
44	Frank Tripucka	1949-52,60-63	879
45	Archie Manning	1971-75,77-	862
46	Tom Flores	1960-61,63-69	839
47	Frankie Albert	1946-52	831
48	Bert Jones	1973-	820
49	Bob Waterfield	1945-52	813

COMPLETION PERCENTAGE
(All with over 1250 Attempts)

Rank	Player	Years	Att.	Comp.	Pct.
1	Ken Stabler	1970-	1577	945	59.92
2	Bart Starr	1956-71	3149	1808	57.42
3	Lenny Dawson	1957-75	3741	2136	57.10
4	Sonny Jurgensen	1957-74	4262	2433	57.09
5	Roger Staubach	1969-	2084	1187	56.96
6	Ken Anderson	1971-	2127	1208	56.79
7	Fran Tarkenton	1961-	5895	3341	56.68
8	Sammy Baugh	1937-52	2995	1693	56.63
9	Bert Jones	1973-	1458	820	56.24
10	Otto Graham	1946-55	2626	1464	55.75
11	Bob Griese	1967-	2784	1541	55.35
12	Y.A. Tittle	1948-64	4395	2427	55.22
13	John Brodie	1957-73	4491	2469	54.98
14	Johnny Unitas	1956-73	5186	2830	54.57
15	Sid Luckman	1939-50	1657	904	54.46
16	Greg Landry	1968-	1670	909	54.43
17	Billy Wade	1954-66	2523	1370	54.30
18	Milt Plum	1957-69	2419	1306	53.99
19	Bill Munson	1964-	1932	1043	53.98
20	Norm Van Brocklin	1949-60	2895	1553	53.64
21	Billy Kilmer	1961-62,64,66-	2939	1562	53.14
22	Frankie Albert	1946-52	1564	831	53.13
23	George Ratterman	1947-56	1396	737	52.79
24	Ron Gabriel	1962-	4498	2366	52.60
25	Norm Snead	1961-76	4353	2373	52.21
26	Craig Morton	1965-	2448	1277	52.17
27	Mike Livingston	1968-	1371	709	51.71
28	Tommy Thompson	1940-42,45-50	1424	732	51.40
29	Zeke Bratkowski	1954,57-68,71	1484	762	51.35
30	Earl Morrall	1956-76	2689	1379	51.28
31	Dan Pastorini	1971-	2076	1064	51.25
32	Charley Johnson	1961-75	3392	1737	51.21
33	Frank Ryan	1958-70	2133	1090	51.10
34	Bobby Thomason	1949,51-57	1346	687	51.04
35	Archie Manning	1971-75,77-	1696	862	50.83
36	Don Meredith	1960-68	2308	1170	50.69
37	Bill Nelsen	1963-72	1905	963	50.55
38	John Hadl	1962-	4688	2363	50.41
39	Frank Tripucka	1949-52,60-63	1743	879	50.37
40	Jim Hart	1966-	3424	1725	50.37
41	Randy Johnson	1966-73,75-76	1286	647	50.31
42	Bob Waterfield	1945-52	1617	813	50.28
43	Joe Namath	1965-77	3762	1886	50.13
44	Chuck Conerly	1948-61	2833	1418	50.05
45	Eddie LeBaron	1952-53,55-63	1796	897	49.94
46	Terry Bradshaw	1970-	2019	1008	49.93
47	Daryl Lamonica	1963-74	2601	1288	49.52
48	Joe Ferguson	1973-	1325	656	49.51
49	Jim Plunkett	1971-	1994	983	49.30
50	Bobby Layne	1948-62	3700	1814	49.03
51	Tom Flores	1960-61,63-69	1715	839	48.86
52	Jack Kemp	1957,60-67,69	2973	1437	48.33
53	Mike Phipps	1970-	1322	636	48.11
54	Jim Finks	1949-55	1382	661	47.88
55	Ed Brown	1954-65	1987	949	47.77
56	George Blanda	1949-58,60-75	4007	1911	47.69
57	Babe Parilli	1952-53,56-58,60-69	3330	1552	46.61
58	Tobin Rote	1950-59,63-64,66	2907	1329	45.72
59	Lamar McHan	1954-63	1351	610	45.15
60	Pete Bethard	1964-73	1282	575	44.85
61	Cotton Davidson	1954,57,60-66,68	1752	770	43.95

YARDS (10,000)

Rank	Player	Years	Yards
1	Fran Tarkenton	1961-	43535
2	Johnny Unitas	1956-73	40239
3	John Hadl	1962-	33503
4	Y.A. Tittle	1948-64	33070
5	Sonny Jurgensen	1957-74	32224
6	John Brodie	1957-73	31548
7	Norm Snead	1961-76	30797
8	Roman Gabriel	1962-	29444
9	Len Dawson	1957-75	28711
10	Joe Namath	1965-77	27663
11	George Blanda	1949-58,60-75	26920
12	Bobby Layne	1948-62	25967
13	Bart Starr	1956-71	24718
14	Charley Johnson	1961-75	24510
15	Jim Hart	1966-	23869
16	Norm Van Brocklin	1949-60	23611
17	Otto Graham	1946-55	23584
18	Babe Parilli	1952-53,56-58,60-69	22671
19	Sammy Baugh	1937-52	21886
20	Jack Kemp	1957,60-67,69	21222
21	Earl Morrall	1956-76	20809
22	Bob Griese	1967-	20351
23	Billy Kilmer	1961-62,64,66-	20179
24	Chuck Conerly	1948-61	19488
25	Daryl Lamonica	1963-74	19154
26	Tobin Rote	1950-59,63-64,66	18850
27	Billy Wade	1954-66	18530
28	Craig Morton	1965-	17942
29	Milt Plum	1957-69	17536
30	Don Meredith	1960-68	17199
31	Frank Ryan	1958-70	16042
32	Roger Staubach	1969-	15924
33	Ed Brown	1954-65	15600
34	Ken Anderson	1971-	15471
35	Sid Luckman	1939-50	14683
36	Bill Nelsen	1963-72	14165
37	Eddie LeBaron	1952-53,55-63	13399
38	Terry Bradshaw	1970-	13279
39	Jim Plunkett	1971-	13217
40	Bill Munson	1964-	12537
41	Ken Stabler	1970-	12519
42	Dan Pastorini	1971-	12301
43	Greg Landry	1968-	11999
44	Tom Flores	1960-61,63-69	11959
45	Bob Waterfield	1945-52	11849
46	Cotton Davidson	1954,57,60-66,68	11760
47	Bert Jones	1973-	11269
48	Frank Albert	1946-52	10795
49	George Ratterman	1947-56	10473
50	Tommy Thompson	1940-42,45-50	10400
51	Zeke Bratkowski	1954,57-68,71	10345
52	Frank Tripucka	1949-52,60-63	10282

Players active at the end of **1977** are shown in **bold face**.

LIFETIME LEADERS
PASSING

YARDS PER ATTEMPT
(All with over 1250 Attempts)

			Yards	Att.	Y/A
1	Otto Graham	1946-55	23584	2626	8.98
2	Sid Luckman	1939-50	14683	1657	8.86
3	Norm Van Brocklin	1949-60	23611	2895	8.16
4	**Ken Stabler**	**1970-**	**12519**	**1577**	**7.94**
5	Ed Brown	1954-65	15600	1987	7.85
6	Bart Starr	1956-71	24718	3149	7.85
7	Johnny Unitas	1956-73	40239	5186	7.76
8	Earl Morrall	1956-76	20809	2689	7.74
9	**Bert Jones**	**1973-**	**11269**	**1458**	**7.73**
10	Lenny Dawson	1957-75	28711	3741	7.68
11	**Roger Staubach**	**1969-**	**15924**	**2084**	**7.64**
12	Sonny Jurgensen	1957-74	32224	4262	7.56
13	Y.A. Tittle	1948-64	33070	4395	7.52
14	Frank Ryan	1958-70	16042	2133	7.52
15	George Ratterman	1947-56	10473	1396	7.50
16	Eddie LeBaron	1952-53,55-63	13399	1796	7.46
17	Don Meredith	1960-68	17199	2308	7.45
18	Bill Nelsen	1963-72	14165	1905	7.44
19	**Fran Tarkenton**	**1961-**	**43535**	**5895**	**7.39**
20	Daryl Lamonica	1963-74	19154	2601	7.36
21	Joe Namath	1965-77	27663	3762	7.35
22	Billy Wade	1954-66	18530	2523	7.34
23	**Craig Morton**	**1965-**	**17942**	**2448**	**7.34**
24	Bob Waterfield	1945-52	11849	1617	7.33
25	**Bob Griese**	**1967-**	**20351**	**2784**	**7.31**
26	Sammy Baugh	1937-52	21886	2995	7.31
27	Tommy Thompson	1940-42,45-50	10400	1424	7.30
28	**Ken Anderson**	**1971-**	**15471**	**2127**	**7.27**
29	Milt Plum	1957-69	17536	2419	7.25
30	Bobby Layne	1948-62	25967	3700	7.24
31	Charley Johnson	1961-75	24510	3392	7.23
32	**Greg Landry**	**1968-**	**11999**	**1670**	**7.19**
33	**John Hadl**	**1962-**	**33503**	**4688**	**7.15**
34	Jack Kemp	1957,60-67,69	21222	2973	7.14
35	Norm Snead	1961-76	30797	4353	7.07
36	Bobby Thomason	1949,51-57	9480	1346	7.04
37	John Brodie	1957-73	31548	4491	7.03
38	Lamar McHan	1954-63	9449	1351	6.99
39	Zeke Bratkowski	1954,57-68,71	10345	1484	6.98
40	Tom Flores	1960-61,63-69	11959	1715	6.97
41	**Jim Hart**	**1966-**	**23869**	**3424**	**6.97**
42	Frankie Albert	1946-52	10795	1564	6.90
43	Chuck Conerly	1948-61	19488	2833	6.88
44	**Billy Kilmer**	**1961-62,64,66-**	**20179**	**2939**	**6.87**
45	Babe Parilli	1952-53,56-58,60-69	22671	3330	6.81
46	**Mike Livingston**	**1968-**	**9253**	**1371**	**6.75**
47	George Blanda	1949-58,60-75	26920	4007	6.72
48	Cotton Davidson	1954,57,60-66,68	11760	1752	6.71
49	**Joe Ferguson**	**1973-**	**8842**	**1325**	**6.67**
50	**Jim Plunkett**	**1971-**	**13217**	**1994**	**6.63**
51	**Terry Bradshaw**	**1970-**	**13279**	**2019**	**6.58**
52	**Roman Gabriel**	**1962-**	**29444**	**4498**	**6.55**
53	**Bill Munson**	**1964-**	**12537**	**1932**	**6.49**
54	Randy Johnson	1966-73,75-76	8329	1286	6.48
55	Tobin Rote	1950-59,63-64,66	18850	2907	6.45
56	Pete Beathard	1964-73	8176	1282	6.38
57	Jim Finks	1949-53	8622	1382	6.24
58	**Don Pastorini**	**1971-**	**12301**	**2076**	**5.93**
59	Frank Tripucka	1949-52,60-63	10282	1745	5.89
60	**Archie Manning**	**1971-**	**9983**	**1696**	**5.89**
61	**Mike Phipps**	**1970-**	**7705**	**1322**	**5.82**

TOUCHDOWN PASSES (85)

1	**Fran Tarkenton**	**1961-**	**317**
2	Johnny Unitas	1956-73	290
3	Sonny Jurgensen	1957-74	255
4	**John Hadl**	**1962-**	**244**
5	Y.A. Tittle	1948-64	242
6	Len Dawson	1957-75	239
7	George Blanda	1949-58,60-75	236
8	John Brodie	1957-73	214
9	**Roman Gabriel**	**1962-**	**201**
10	Bobby Layne	1948-62	196
	Norm Snead	1961-76	196
12	Sammy Baugh	1937-52	188
13	Babe Parilli	1952-53,56-58,60-69	178
14	Otto Graham	1946-55	174
15	Chuck Conerly	1948-61	173
	Norm Van Brocklin	1949-60	173
	Joe Namath	1965-77	173
18	Charley Johnson	1961-75	170
19	Daryl Lamonica	1963-74	164
20	Earl Morrall	1956-76	161
	Bob Griese	**1967-**	**161**
22	Bart Starr	1956-71	152
	Jim Hart	**1966-**	**152**
24	Frank Ryan	1958-70	149
25	Tobin Rote	1950-59,63-64,66	148
	Billy Kilmer	**1961-62,64,66-**	**148**
27	Sid Luckman	1939-50	137
28	Don Meredith	1960-68	135
29	Milt Plum	1957-69	132
30	Billy Wade	1954-66	124
31	**Craig Morton**	**1965-**	**123**
32	Frank Albert	1946-52	115
33	Jack Kemp	1957,60-67,69	114
34	**Ken Stabler**	**1970-**	**108**
35	Eddie LeBaron	1952-53,55-63	104
36	Ed Brown	1954-65	102
37	**Roger Staubach**	**1969-**	**101**
38	**Ken Anderson**	**1971-**	**99**
39	Bob Waterfield	1945-52	98
	Bill Nelsen	1963-72	98
41	Tom Flores	1960-61,63-69	93
	Terry Bradshaw	**1970-**	**93**
43	Tommy Thompson	1940-42,45-50	91
	George Ratterman	1947-56	91

INTERCEPTIONS (135)

1	George Blanda	1949-58,60-75	277
2	**John Hadl**	**1962-**	**268**
3	Norm Snead	1961-76	257
4	Johnny Unitas	1956-73	253
5	Y.A. Tittle	1948-64	248
6	Bobby Layne	1948-62	243
7	**Fran Tarkenton**	**1961-**	**234**
8	John Brodie	1957-73	224
9	Babe Parilli	1952-53,56-58,60-69	220
	Joe Namath	1965-77	220
11	Sammy Baugh	1937-52	203
12	Tobin Rote	1950-59,63-64,66	191
13	Sonny Jurgensen	1957-74	189
14	Len Dawson	1957-75	183
	Jack Kemp	1957,60-67,69	183
16	Charley Johnson	1961-75	181
17	Norm Van Brocklin	1949-60	178
18	Chuck Conerly	1948-61	167
	Jim Hart	**1966-**	**167**
20	**Roman Gabriel**	**1962-**	**149**
21	Earl Morrall	1956-76	148
22	**Billy Kilmer**	**1961-62,64,66-**	**143**
23	**Bob Griese**	**1967-**	**141**
	Eddie LeBaron	1952-53,55-63	141
25	Bart Starr	1956-71	138
	Daryl Lamonica	1963-74	138
	Ed Brown	1954-65	138
28	Otto Graham	1946-55	135

PERCENT INTERCEPTED
(All with over 1250 Attempts)

			Att.	Int.	Pct.
1	**Ken Anderson**	**1971-**	**2127**	**69**	**3.24**
2	**Roman Gabriel**	**1962-**	**4498**	**149**	**3.31**
3	**Roger Staubach**	**1969-**	**2084**	**82**	**3.93**
4	**Fran Tarkenton**	**1961-**	**5895**	**234**	**3.97**
5	**Bill Munson**	**1964-**	**1932**	**78**	**4.04**
6	**Bert Jones**	**1973-**	**1458**	**62**	**4.25**
7	Bart Starr	1956-71	3149	138	4.38
8	Sonny Jurgensen	1957-74	4262	189	4.44
9	**Greg Landry**	**1968-**	**1670**	**80**	**4.79**
10	Don Meredith	1960-68	2308	111	4.81
11	**Mike Livingston**	**1968-**	**1371**	**66**	**4.81**
12	**Joe Ferguson**	**1973-**	**1325**	**64**	**4.83**
13	**Billy Kilmer**	**1961-62,64,66-**	**2939**	**143**	**4.87**
14	Johnny Unitas	1956-73	5186	253	4.88
15	**Jim Hart**	**1966-**	**3424**	**167**	**4.88**
16	Lenny Dawson	1957-75	3741	183	4.89
17	John Brodie	1957-73	4491	224	4.99
18	**Don Pastorini**	**1971-**	**2076**	**141**	**5.01**
19	**Bob Griese**	**1967-**	**2784**	**104**	**5.06**
20	**Archie Manning**	**1971-**	**1696**	**87**	**5.13**
21	Otto Graham	1946-55	2626	135	5.14
22	Frank Ryan	1958-70	2133	111	5.20
23	Milt Plum	1957-69	2410	127	5.30
24	Bill Nelsen	1963-72	1905	101	5.30
25	**Craig Morton**	**1965-**	**2448**	**130**	**5.31**
26	Daryl Lamonica	1963-74	2601	138	5.31
27	Billy Wade	1954-66	2523	134	5.31
28	Charley Johnson	1961-75	3392	181	5.34
29	Tom Flores	1960-61,63-69	1715	92	5.36
30	Earl Morrall	1956-76	2689	148	5.50
31	Y.A. Tittle	1948-64	4395	248	5.51
32	**John Hadl**	**1962-**	**4688**	**268**	**5.72**
33	**Ken Stabler**	**1970-**	**1577**	**91**	**5.77**
34	**Terry Bradshaw**	**1970-**	**2019**	**118**	**5.84**
35	Joe Namath	1965-77	3762	220	5.85
36	**Jim Plunkett**	**1971-**	**1994**	**117**	**5.87**
37	Chuck Conerly	1948-61	2833	167	5.90
38	Norm Snead	1961-76	4353	257	5.94
39	**Mike Phipps**	**1970**	**1322**	**81**	**6.13**
40	Norm Van Brocklin	1949-60	2895	178	6.15
41	Cotton Davidson	1954,57,60-66,68	1752	108	6.16
42	Jack Kemp	1957,60-67,69	2973	183	6.16
43	Frankie Albert	1946-52	1564	98	6.27
44	Jim Finks	1949-55	1382	88	6.37
45	Pete Beathard	1964-73	1282	84	6.55
46	Bobby Layne	1948-62	3700	243	6.57
47	Tobin Rote	1950-59,63-64,66	2907	191	6.57
48	Babe Parilli	1952-53,56-58,60-69	3330	220	6.61
49	Bobby Thomason	1949,51-57	1346	90	6.69
50	Sammy Baugh	1937-52	2995	203	6.78
51	George Ratterman	1947-56	1396	96	6.88
52	George Blanda	1949-58,60-75	4007	277	6.91
53	Ed Brown	1954-65	1987	138	6.94
54	Randy Johnson	1966-73,75-76	1286	90	7.00
55	Frank Tripucka	1949-52,60-63	1745	124	7.11
56	Tommy Thompson	1940-42,45-50	1424	103	7.23
57	Eddie LeBaron	1952-53,55-63	1796	141	7.85
58	Bob Waterfield	1945-52	1617	127	7.85
59	Sid Luckman	1939-50	1657	131	7.89
60	Lamar McHan	1954-63	1351	108	8.00
61	Zeke Bratkowski	1954,57-68,71	1484	122	8.22

RANK
(All with over 1250 Attempts)

		Comp. Pct.	Yds/ Att.	% TD Passes	Pct. Int.	Total
1	Otto Graham	10	1	5	21	– 37
	Lenny Dawson	3	10	8	16	– 37
3	Sonny Jurgensen	4	12	14	8	– 38
4	**Ken Stabler**	**1**	**4**	**4**	**33**	**– 42**
5	Bart Starr	2	6	39	7	– 54
	Fran Tarkenton	**7**	**19**	**24**	**4**	**– 54**
7	Johnny Unitas	14	7	20	14	– 55
8	**Roger Staubach**	**5**	**11**	**38**	**3**	**– 57**
9	**Bert Jones**	**9**	**9**	**37**	**6**	**– 61**
10	Frank Ryan	33	14	3	22	– 72
11	**Bob Griese**	**11**	**25**	**19**	**19**	**– 74**
12	Sid Luckman	15	2	1	59	– 77
	Y.A. Tittle	12	13	21	31	– 77
14	**Ken Anderson**	**6**	**28**	**43**	**1**	**– 78**
	Norm Van Brocklin	20	3	15	40	– 78
16	Don Meredith	36	17	17	10	– 80
17	Earl Morrall	30	8	13	30	– 81
18	Milt Plum	18	29	22	23	– 92
19	Sammy Baugh	8	26	10	50	– 94
20	George Ratterman	23	15	6	51	– 95
21	**Greg Landry**	**16**	**32**	**41**	**9**	**– 98**
22	Daryl Lamonica	47	20	9	26	– 102
	Billy Wade	17	22	36	27	– 102
24	John Brodie	13	37	40	17	– 107
25	Bill Nelson	37	18	29	24	– 108
	Craig Morton	**26**	**23**	**34**	**25**	**– 108**
27	Frankie Albert	22	42	2	43	– 109
28	**Billy Kilmer**	**21**	**44**	**33**	**13**	**– 111**
29	Tommy Tompson	28	27	7	56	– 118
30	**Roman Gabriel**	**24**	**52**	**47**	**2**	**– 125**
31	Charley Johnson	32	31	35	28	– 126
32	**Bill Munson**	**19**	**53**	**53**	**5**	**– 130**
33	**John Hadl**	**38**	**33**	**28**	**32**	**– 131**
34	Chuck Conerly	44	43	11	37	– 135
35	Eddie LeBaron	45	16	18	57	– 136
	Bob Waterfield	42	24	12	58	– 136
37	**Mike Livingston**	**27**	**46**	**57**	**11**	**– 141**
38	Ed Brown	55	5	30	53	– 143
	Tom Flores	51	40	23	29	– 143
40	**Jim Hart**	**40**	**41**	**48**	**15**	**– 144**
	Norm Snead	25	35	46	38	– 144
	Joe Namath	43	21	45	35	– 144
43	Bobby Thomason	34	36	32	49	– 151
	Joe Ferguson	**48**	**49**	**42**	**12**	**– 151**
45	Bobby Layne	50	30	27	46	– 153
46	**Don Pastorini**	**31**	**58**	**60**	**18**	**– 167**
47	George Blanda	56	47	16	52	– 171
48	**Archie Manning**	**35**	**60**	**59**	**20**	**– 174**
49	Babe Parilli	57	45	25	48	– 175
	Terry Bradshaw	**46**	**51**	**44**	**34**	**– 175**
51	Zeke Bratkowski	29	39	49	61	– 178
52	Lamar McHan	59	38	26	60	– 183
53	Jack Kemp	52	34	56	42	– 184
54	**Jim Plunkett**	**49**	**50**	**51**	**36**	**– 186**
55	Tobin Rote	58	55	31	47	– 191
56	Cotton Davidson	61	48	52	41	– 202
57	Frank Tripucka	39	59	50	55	– 203
58	Randy Johnson	41	54	55	54	– 204
59	Jim Finks	54	57	54	44	– 209
60	**Mike Phipps**	**53**	**61**	**61**	**39**	**– 214**
61	Pete Beathard	60	56	58	45	– 219

Players active at the end of **1977** are shown in **bold face.**

LIFETIME LEADERS
RUSHING

ATTEMPTS (900)

1	Jimmy Brown	1957-65	2359
2	**O.J. Simpson**	**1969-**	**2123**
3	Jim Taylor	1958-67	1941
4	Joe Perry	1948-63	1929
5	Leroy Kelly	1964-73	1727
6	Bill Brown	1961-74	1649
7	Floyd Little	1967-75	1641
8	Ken Willard	1965-74	1622
9	**Larry Csonka**	**1968-74,76-**	**1580**
10	John Henry Johnson	1954-66	1571
11	Larry Brown	1969-76	1530
12	Dan Perkins	1961-68	1500
13	**Franco Harris**	**1972-**	**1435**
14	Rick Casares	1955-66	1431
15	**Lydell Mitchell**	**1972-**	**1391**
16	**John Brockington**	**1971-**	**1347**
17	Jim Nance	1965-71,73	1341
18	Steve Van Buren	1944-51	1320
19	**Calvin Hill**	**1969-74,76-**	**1314**
20	Mike Garrett	1966-73	1308
21	Emerson Boozer	1966-75	1291
22	**Lawrence McCutcheon**	**1972-**	**1244**
23	Tom Matte	1961-71	1240
24	Dick Bass	1960-69	1218
25	**Chuck Foreman**	**1973-**	**1209**
26	Ron Johnson	1969-75	1203
27	Donny Anderson	1966-74	1197
28	Alex Webster	1955-64	1196
29	Dave Osborn	1965-76	1179
30	Altie Taylor	1969-76	1170
	Ollie Matson	1952,54-66	1170
32	**John Riggins**	**1971-**	**1158**
33	John David Crow	1958-68	1157
34	**Ed Podolak**	**1969-**	**1157**
35	**MacArthur Lane**	**1968-**	**1154**
36	Dave Hampton	1969-76	1148
37	Clem Daniels	1960-68	1146
38	Dick Hoak	1961-70	1132
39	Hugh McElhenny	1952-64	1124
40	J.D. Smith	1955-66	1100
41	Lenny Moore	1956-67	1069
42	Bob Hoernschemeyer	1946-55	1059
43	Matt Snell	1964-72	1057
44	Bill Mathis	1960-69	1044
45	Clarke Hinkle	1932-41	1043
46	Tommy Mason	1961-71	1040
47	Abner Haynes	1960-67	1036
48	**Carl Garrett**	**1969-**	**1031**
49	**Jim Kiick**	**1968-74,76-**	**1029**
50	Paul Lowe	1960-61,63-69	1026
51	Tony Canadeo	1941-44,46-52	1025
52	Johnny Roland	1966-73	1015
53	Cookie Gilchrist	1962-67	1010
54	Gale Sayers	1965-71	1001
55	Billy Barnes	1957-63,65-66	994
56	Wendell Hayes	1963,65-74	988
57	Alan Ameche	1955-60	964
	Jon Arnett	1957-66	964
59	**Jim Otis**	**1970-**	**963**
60	Nick Pietrosante	1959-67	955
61	Clarence Peaks	1957-65	951
	Marv Hubbard	**1969-75,77-**	**951**
63	**Sam Cunningham**	**1973-**	**932**
64	**Pete Banaszek**	**1966-**	**921**
65	Tuffy Leemans	1936-43	919
66	Charley Tolar	1960-66	907
67	**Preston Pearson**	**1967-**	**906**
68	Fran Rogel	1950-57	900

YARDS (3350)

1	Jimmy Brown	1957-65	12312
2	**O.J. Simpson**	**1969-**	**10183**
3	Joe Perry	1948-63	9723
4	Jim Taylor	1958-67	8597
5	Leroy Kelly	1964-73	7274
6	**Larry Csonka**	**1968-74,76-**	**6933**
7	John Henry Johnson	1954-66	6803
8	Floyd Little	1967-75	6323
9	**Franco Harris**	**1972-**	**6295**
10	Dan Perkins	1961-68	6217
11	Ken Willard	1965-74	6105
12	Larry Brown	1969-76	5875
13	Steve Van Buren	1944-51	5860
14	Bill Brown	1961-74	5838
15	Rick Casares	1955-66	5787
16	**Calvin Hill**	**1969-74,76-**	**5567**
17	**Lawrence McCutcheon**	**1972-**	**5523**
18	**Lydell Mitchell**	**1972-**	**5487**
19	Mike Garrett	1966-73	5481
20	Dick Bass	1960-69	5417
21	Jim Nance	1965-71,73	5401
22	Hugh McElhenny	1952-64	5281
23	**John Brockington**	**1971-**	**5185**
24	Lenny Moore	1956-67	5174
25	Ollie Matson	1952,54-66	5173
26	Clem Daniels	1960-68	5138
27	Emerson Boozer	1966-75	5135
28	Paul Lowe	1960-61,63-69	4995
29	John David Crow	1958-68	4963
30	Gale Sayers	1965-71	4956
31	**Chuck Foreman**	**1973-**	**4915**
32	Marion Motley	1946-53,55	4720
33	Donny Anderson	1966-74	4696
34	J.D. Smith	1956-66	4672
35	**John Riggins**	**1971-**	**4655**
36	Tom Matte	1961-71	4646
37	Alex Webster	1955-64	4638
38	Abner Haynes	1960-67	4630
39	Bob Hoernschemeyer	1946-55	4548
40	**Marv Hubbard**	**1969-75,77-**	**4544**
41	Dave Hampton	1969-76	4538
42	**Ed Podolak**	**1969-**	**4451**
43	**MacArthur Lane**	**1968-**	**4379**
44	Dave Osborn	1965-76	4336
45	Altie Taylor	1969-76	4358
46	Ron Johnson	1969-75	4307
47	Cookie Gilchrist	1962-67	4293
48	Matt Snell	1964-72	4285
49	Tommy Mason	1961-71	4203
50	Tony Canadeo	1941-44,46-52	4197
	Carl Garrett	**1969-**	**4197**
52	Mercury Morris	1969-77	4133
53	**Greg Pruitt**	**1973-**	**4062**
54	Alan Ameche	1955-60	4045
55	Nick Pietrosante	1959-67	4026
56	Dick Hoak	1961-70	3965
57	**Walter Payton**	**1975-**	**3921**
58	Walt Garrison	1966-74	3886
59	Timmy Brown	1959-68	3862
60	Clarke Hinkle	1932-41	3850
61	John Arnett	1957-66	3833
62	**Sam Cunningham**	**1973-**	**3832**
63	**Jim Kiick**	**1968-74,76-**	**3759**
64	Wendell Hayes	1963,65-74	3758
65	Johnny Roland	1966-73	3750
66	Paul Hornung	1957-62,64-66	3711
67	**Jim Otis**	**1970-**	**3686**
68	**Fran Tarkenton**	**1961-**	**3672**
69	Clarence Peaks	1957-65	3660
70	Hoyle Granger	1966-72	3653
71	Tank Younger	1949-58	3640
72	**Clarence Davis**	**1971-**	**3636**
73	**Pete Banaszek**	**1966-**	**3635**
74	Cliff Battles	1932-37	3613
75	Frank Gifford	1952-60,62-64	3609
76	Bill Mathis	1960-69	3589
77	Tom Woodeshick	1963-72	3577
78	**Jess Phillips**	**1968-**	**3568**
79	Charley Trippi	1947-55	3506
80	Dan Towler	1950-55	3493
81	**Preston Pearson**	**1967-**	**3485**
82	**Terry Metcalf**	**1973-**	**3438**
83	Willie Ellison	1967-74	3426
84	Billy Barnes	1957-63,65-66	3421
85	Johnny Strzykalski	1946-52	3415
86	Les Josephson	1964-67,69-74	3407
87	Keith Lincoln	1961-68	3383
88	Wray Carlton	1960-67	3368
89	Charlie Smith	1968-75	3351

AVERAGE YARDS (4.0)
(Minimum 700 Rushes)

			Att.	Yards	Avg.
1	Marion Motley	1946-53,55	828	4720	5.70
2	Jimmy Brown	1947-65	2359	12312	5.22
3	Mercury Morris	1969-76	804	4133	5.14
4	Joe Perry	1948-63	1929	9723	5.04
5	Gale Sayers	1965-71	1001	4956	4.95
6	Paul Lowe	1960-61,63-69	1026	4995	4.87
7	Lenny Moore	1956-67	1069	5174	4.84
8	**O.J. Simpson**	**1969-**	**2123**	**10183**	**4.80**
9	**Greg Pruitt**	**1973-**	**849**	**4062**	**4.79**
10	**Marv Hubbard**	**1969-75,77-**	**951**	**4544**	**4.78**
11	Tank Younger	1949-58	770	3640	4.73
12	Hugh McElhenny	1952-64	1124	5281	4.70
13	**Walter Payton**	**1975-**	**846**	**3921**	**4.63**
14	**Clarence Davis**	**1971-**	**790**	**3636**	**4.60**
15	**Terry Metcalf**	**1973-**	**748**	**3438**	**4.60**
16	Hoyle Granger	1966-72	805	3653	4.54
17	Clem Daniels	1960-68	1146	5138	4.48
18	Abner Haynes	1960-67	1036	4630	4.47
19	Keith Lincoln	1961-68	759	3383	4.46
20	Dick Bass	1960-69	1218	5417	4.45
21	**Lawrence McCutcheon**	**1972-**	**1244**	**5523**	**4.44**
22	Steve Van Buren	1944-51	1320	5860	4.44
23	Jim Taylor	1958-67	1941	8597	4.43
24	Ollie Matson	1952,54-66	1170	5173	4.42
25	**Larry Csonka**	**1968-74,76-**	**1580**	**6933**	**4.39**
26	**Franco Harris**	**1972-**	**1435**	**6295**	**4.39**
27	Timmy Brown	1959-68	889	3862	4.34
28	John Henry Johnson	1954-66	1571	6803	4.33
29	Walt Garrison	1966-74	899	3886	4.32
30	Frank Gifford	1952-60,62-64	840	3609	4.30
31	Amos Marsh	1961-67	750	3222	4.30
32	Bob Hoernschemeyer	1946-55	1059	4548	4.29
33	John David Crow	1958-68	1157	4963	4.29
34	Tom Woodeshick	1963-72	1836	3577	4.28
35	Willie Ellison	1967-74	801	3426	4.28
36	Les Josephson	1964-67,69-74	797	3407	4.27
37	**Robert Newhouse**	**1972-**	**741**	**3154**	**4.26**
38	Cookie Gilchrist	1962-67	1010	4293	4.25
39	J.D. Smith	1956-66	1100	4672	4.25
40	**Calvin Hill**	**1969-74,76-**	**1314**	**5567**	**4.24**
41	Nick Pietrosante	1959-67	955	4026	4.22
42	John Fuqua	1969-76	719	3031	4.22
43	Leroy Kelly	1964-73	964	4045	4.21
44	Alan Ameche	1955-60	1308	5481	4.20
45	Mike Garrett	1966-73	1308	5481	4.19
46	**Mark van Eeghen**	**1974-**	**721**	**3021**	**4.19**
47	Mel Farr	1967-73	739	3072	4.16
48	Paul Hornung	1957-62,64-66	893	3711	4.16
49	Dan Perkins	1961-68	1500	6217	4.14
50	Cliff Battles	1932-37	873	3613	4.14
51	Wray Carlton	1960-67	819	3368	4.11
52	Curtis McClinton	1962-69	762	3124	4.10
53	Tony Canadeo	1941-44,46-52	1025	4197	4.09
54	**Norm Bulaich**	**1970-**	**765**	**3129**	**4.09**
55	Pat Harder	1946-53	740	3016	4.08
56	**Carl Garrett**	**1969-**	**1031**	**4197**	**4.07**
57	**Chuck Foreman**	**1973-**	**1209**	**4915**	**4.07**
58	Matt Snell	1964-72	1057	4285	4.05
59	Rick Casares	1955-66	1431	5787	4.04
60	Tommy Mason	1961-71	1040	4203	4.04
61	Jim Nance	1965-71,73	1341	5401	4.03
62	**John Riggins**	**1971-**	**1158**	**4655**	**4.02**
63	**Jess Phillips**	**1968-**	**888**	**3568**	**4.02**
64	Don Bosseler	1957-64	775	3112	4.02
65	Dan Lewis	1958-66	800	3205	4.01
66	Hewritt Dixon	1963-70	772	3090	4.00

TOUCHDOWNS (30)

1	Jimmy Brown	1957-67	106
2	Jim Taylor	1958-67	83
3	Leroy Kelly	1964-73	74
4	Joe Perry	1948-63	71
5	Steve Van Buren	1944-51	68
6	Lenny Moore	1956-67	63
7	**O.J. Simpson**	**1969-**	**57**
8	**Franco Harris**	**1972-**	**53**
9	Bill Brown	1961-74	52
	Emerson Boozer	1966-75	52
11	Paul Hornung	1957-62,64-66	50
12	Rick Casares	1955-66	49
13	John Henry Johnson	1954-66	48
14	**Pete Banaszek**	**1966-**	**47**
15	Abner Haynes	1960-67	46
	Larry Csonka	**1968-74,76-**	**46**
17	Tom Matte	1961-72	45
	Jim Nance	1965-71,73	45
	Ken Willard	1965-74	45
	Chuck Foreman	**1973-**	**45**
21	Otto Graham	1946-55	44
22	Dan Towler	1950-55	43
	Floyd Little	1967-75	43
24	Dan Perkins	1961-68	42
25	Donny Anderson	1966-74	41
26	Vern Lewellen	1924-32	40
	Allan Ameche	1955-60	40
	Ollie Matson	1952,54-66	40
	J.D. Smith	1955-66	40
	Jack Kemp	1957,60-67,69	40
	Paul Lowe	1960-61,63-69	40
	Ron Johnson	1969-75	40
	Calvin Hill	**1969-74,76-**	**40**
34	Alex Webster	1955-64	39
	Gale Sayers	1965-71	39
	Y.A. Tittle	1948-64	39
37	Hugh McElhenny	1952-64	38
	John David Crow	1958-68	38
39	Ernie Nevers	1926-27,29-31	37
	Tobin Rote	1950-59,63-64,66	37
	Bill Mathis	1960-69	37
	Cookie Gilchrist	1962-67	37
43	Dutch Clark	1931-32,34-38	36
	Pug Manders	1939-47	36
45	Clarke Hinkle	1932-41	35
	Mike Garrett	1966-73	35
	Larry Brown	1969-76	35
48	Tank Younger	1949-58	34
	Frank Gifford	1952-60,62-64	34
	Dick Bass	1960-69	34
	Ed Podolak	**1969-**	**34**
	Don Nottingham	**1971-**	**34**
	Walter Payton	**1975-**	**34**
54	Pat Harder	1946-53	33
	Spec Sanders	1946-48,50	33
56	Tommy Mason	1961-71	32
57	Ted Fritsch	1942-50	31
	Marion Motley	1946-53,55	31
	Timmy Brown	1959-68	31
	Fran Tarkenton	**1961-**	**31**
	Mercury Morris	1969-77	31
62	Dick Hoerner	1947-52	30
	Joe Marconi	1956-66	30
	Clem Daniels	1960-68	30
	Walt Garrison	1966-74	30
	Roman Gabriel	**1962-**	**30**
	MacArthur Lane	**1968-**	**30**
	John Brockington	**1971-**	**30**

Players active at the end of **1977** are shown in **bold face.**

LIFETIME LEADERS

RECEIVING

RECEPTIONS (250)

1	**Charley Taylor**	**1964-**	**649**
2	Don Maynard	1958, 60-73	633
3	Ray Berry	1955-67	631
4	**Fred Biletnikoff**	**1965-**	**569**
5	Lionel Taylor	1959-68	567
6	Lance Alworth	1962-72	542
7	Bobby Mitchell	1958-68	521
8	Billy Howton	1952-63	503
9	Tommy McDonald	1957-68	495
10	Don Hutson	1935-45	488
11	**Jackie Smith**	**1963-**	**480**
12	Art Powell	1959-68	479
13	Boyd Dowler	1959-69,71	474
14	Pete Retzlaff	1956-66	452
15	Roy Jefferson	1965-76	451
16	Carroll Dale	1960-73	438
17	Mike Ditka	1961-72	427
	Paul Warfield	1964-74,76-77	427
19	Bobby Joe Conrad	1958-69	422
20	**Jerry Smith**	**1965-**	**421**
21	**Harold Jackson**	**1968-**	**415**
22	Charley Hennigan	1960-66	410
	Otis Taylor	1965-74	410
24	Billy Wilson	1951-60	407
25	**Gary Garrison**	**1966-**	**405**
26	Jim Phillips	1958-67	401
27	Tom Fears	1948-56	400
	Jimmy Orr	1958-70	400
29	Joe Morrison	1958-72	395
30	Chris Burford	1960-67	391
31	Crazy Legs Hirsch	1946-57	387
32	Dante Lavelli	1946-56	386
33	**John Gilliam**	**1967-**	**382**
34	Pete Pihos	1947-55	373
35	Bob Hayes	1965-75	371
	Gene Washington	**1969-**	**371**
37	Dan Abramowicz	1967-75	369
38	Frank Gifford	1952-60,62-64	367
39	Sonny Randle	1959-68	365
40	Lenny Moore	1956-67	363
41	Dave Parks	1964-73	360
42	Bernie Casey	1961-68	359
43	Johnny Morris	1958-67	356
	Gail Cogdill	1960-70	356
45	Mac Speedie	1946-52	349
	Del Shofner	1957-67	349
47	Max McGee	1954,57-67	345
48	Jack Snow	1965-75	340
49	**Charlie Sanders**	**1968-**	**336**
	Bob Tucker	**1970-**	**336**
51	Gary Collins	1962-71	331
	John Mackey	1963-72	331
53	Elbie Nickel	1947-57	329
54	Gary Ballman	1962-73	323
55	Bobby Walston	1951-62	311
56	George Sauer	1965-70	309
57	Paul Flatley	1963-70	306
58	Preston Carpenter	1956-67	305
59	**Haven Moses**	**1968-**	**304**
60	Kyle Rote	1951-61	300
	Harold Carmichael	**1971-**	**300**
62	**Bob Trumpy**	**1968-**	**298**
	Lydell Mitchell	**1972-**	**298**
64	Elbert Dubenion	1960-68	296
65	Gino Cappelletti	1960-70	292
66	Frank Clarke	1957-67	291
67	**Ken Burrough**	**1970-**	**290**
68	Jim Benton	1939-40,42-47	288
	Ed Podolak	**1969-**	**288**
70	Jim Gibbons	1958-68	287
	Abner Haynes	1960-67	287
72	Bill Brown	1961-74	286
73	Jim Colclough	1960-68	283
	Reggie Rucker	**1970-**	**282**
75	Ray Renfro	1952-63	281
76	Ken Willard	1965-74	277
77	Hugh Taylor	1947-54	272
78	Milt Morin	1966-75	271
79	Lance Rentzel	1965-72,74	268
80	Hugh McElhenny	1952-64	264
81	Hewritt Dixon	1963-70	263
82	Jimmy Brown	1957-65	262
	Aaron Thomas	1961-70	262
84	Buddy Dial	1959-66	261
	Ben Hawkins	1966-73	261
86	Joe Perry	1948-63	260
	Al Denson	1964-71	260
88	John David Crow	1958-68	258
89	**Jim Mitchell**	**1969-**	**257**
90	**Chuck Foreman**	**1973-**	**256**
91	**Ray Chester**	**1970-**	**252**
92	**Bob Chandler**	**1971-**	**251**
	MacArthur Lane	**1968-**	**251**

YARDS (4500)

1	Don Maynard	1958,60-73	11834
2	Lance Alworth	1962-72	10267
3	Ray Berry	1955-67	9275
4	**Charley Taylor**	**1964-**	**9110**
5	**Fred Biletnikoff**	**1965-**	**8689**
6	Paul Warfield	1964-74,76-77	8565
7	Billy Howton	1952-63	8459
8	Tommy McDonald	1957-68	8380
9	Carroll Dale	1960-73	8277
10	Art Powell	1959-68	8046
11	Don Hutson	1935-45	7981
12	Bobby Mitchell	1958-68	7954
13	**Jackie Smith**	**1963-**	**7918**
14	Jimmy Orr	1958-70	7914
15	Roy Jefferson	1965-76	7539
16	**Gary Garrison**	**1966-**	**7538**
17	Bob Hayes	1965-75	7414
18	Pete Retzlaff	1956-66	7412
19	Otis Taylor	1965-74	7306
20	Boyd Dowler	1959-69,71	7270
21	Lionel Taylor	1959-68	7195
22	**Harold Jackson**	**1968-**	**7084**
23	**John Gilliam**	**1967-**	**7056**
24	Crazy Legs Hirsch	1946-57	7029
25	Charley Hennigan	1960-66	6823
26	**Gene Washington**	**1969-**	**6664**
27	Dante Lavelli	1946-56	6488
28	Del Shofner	1957-67	6470
29	Max McGee	1954,57-67	6346
30	Jim Phillips	1958-67	6044
31	Lenny Moore	1956-67	6039
32	Jack Snow	1965-75	6012
33	Sonny Randle	1959-68	5996
34	Billy Wilson	1951-60	5902
	Bobby Joe Conrad	1958-69	5902
36	Mike Ditka	1961-72	5812
37	Gail Gogdill	1960-70	5696
38	Dan Abramowicz	1967-75	5686
39	Pete Pihos	1947-55	5619
	Dave Parks	1964-73	5619
41	Mac Speedie	1946-52	5602
42	Ray Renfro	1952-63	5508
43	Chris Burford	1960-67	5505
44	**Jerry Smith**	**1965-**	**5496**
45	**Haven Moses**	**1968-**	**5484**
46	Buddy Dial	1959-66	5436
47	Frank Gifford	1952-60,62-64	5434
48	Frank Clarke	1957-67	5426
49	Tom Fears	1948-56	5397
50	Gary Ballman	1962-73	5366
51	Bobby Walston	1951-62	5363
52	Elbert Dubenion	1960-68	5309
53	Gary Collins	1962-71	5299
54	John Mackey	1963-72	5236
55	Hugh Taylor	1947-54	5233
56	Elbie Nickel	1947-57	5131
57	Jim Colclough	1960-68	5101
58	Johnny Morris	1958-67	5059
59	Joe Morrison	1959-72	4993
60	Homer Jones	1964-70	4986
61	**Ken Burrough**	**1970-**	**4967**
62	George Sauer	1965-70	4965
63	Paul Flatley	1963-70	4905
64	Lance Rentzel	1965-72,74	4826
65	**Charlie Sanders**	**1968-**	**4817**
66	Jim Benton	1938-40,42-47	4801
67	Kyle Rote	1951-61	4797
68	Ben Hawkins	1966-73	4762
69	Harlon Hill	1954-62	4717
70	**Bob Trumpy**	**1968-**	**4600**
71	Gino Cappelletti	1960-70	4589
72	Aaron Thomas	1961-70	4554
73	**Charlie Joiner**	**1969-**	**4541**

AVERAGE YARDS (16.0)

(Minimum 200 Receptions)

			Rec.	Yards	Avg.
1	Homer Jones	1964-70	224	4986	22.26
2	Buddy Dial	1959-66	261	5436	20.83
3	**Mel Gray**	**1971-**	**211**	**4273**	**20.25**
4	Harlon Hill	1954-62	233	4717	20.25
5	Paul Warfield	1964-74,76-77	427	8565	20.06
6	Bob Hayes	1965-75	371	7414	19.98
7	Ray Renfro	1952-63	281	5508	19.60
8	Hugh Taylor	1947-54	272	5233	19.24
9	Lance Alworth	1962-72	542	10267	18.94
10	Carroll Dale	1960-73	438	8277	18.90
11	**Cliff Branch**	**1972-**	**212**	**3967**	**18.71**
12	Don Maynard	1958,60-73	633	11834	18.70
13	Frank Clarke	1957-67	291	5426	18.65
14	**Gary Garrison**	**1966-**	**405**	**7538**	**18.61**
15	Del Shofner	1957-67	349	6470	18.54
16	**John Gilliam**	**1967-**	**382**	**7056**	**18.47**
17	Max McGee	1954,57-67	345	6346	18.39
18	Ben Hawkins	1966-73	261	4764	18.25
19	**Charlie Joiner**	**1969-**	**249**	**4541**	**18.24**
20	Crazy Legs Hirsch	1946-57	387	7029	18.16
21	**Rich Caster**	**1970-**	**245**	**4434**	**18.10**
22	**Haven Moses**	**1968-**	**304**	**5484**	**18.04**
23	Jim Colclough	1960-68	283	5101	18.03
24	Lance Rentzel	1965-72,74	268	4826	18.01
25	**Gene Washington**	**1969-**	**371**	**6664**	**17.96**
26	Elbert Dubenion	1960-68	296	5309	17.94
27	Darrell Brewster	1952-60	210	3798	17.90
28	Otis Taylor	1965-74	410	7302	17.82
29	Jack Snow	1965-75	340	6012	17.68
30	Aaron Thomas	1961-70	262	4554	17.38
31	Bob Schnelker	1953-61	211	3667	17.38
32	Jim Doran	1951-61	212	3667	17.30
33	Bobby Walston	1951-62	311	5363	17.24
34	**Ken Burrough**	**1970-**	**290**	**4967**	**17.13**
35	**Harold Jackson**	**1968-**	**415**	**7084**	**17.07**
36	Ray Mathews	1951-60	233	3963	17.01
37	Tommy McDonald	1957-68	495	8380	16.93
38	**Drew Pearson**	**1973-**	**236**	**3973**	**16.83**
39	Billy Howton	1952-63	503	8549	16.82
40	Dante Lavelli	1946-56	386	6488	16.81
41	Art Powell	1959-68	479	8046	16.80
42	Terry Barr	1957-65	227	3810	16.78
43	Jim Mutscheller	1954-61	220	3684	16.75
44	Roy Jefferson	1965-76	451	7539	16.72
45	Jim Benton	1938-40,42-47	288	4801	16.67
46	Charley Hennigan	1960-66	410	6823	16.64
47	Lenny Moore	1956-67	363	6039	16.64
48	Gary Ballman	1962-73	323	5366	16.61
49	Charley Frazier	1962-70	209	3461	16.56
50	**Jackie Smith**	**1963-**	**480**	**7918**	**16.50**
51	Al Denson	1964-71	260	4275	16.44
52	Sonny Randle	1959-68	365	5996	16.43
53	Dave Kocourek	1960-68	249	4090	16.43
54	Pete Retzlaff	1956-66	452	7412	16.40
55	Don Hutson	1935-45	488	7981	16.36
56	Clem Daniels	1960-68	203	3314	16.33
57	Willard Dewreall	1959-64	204	3304	16.20
58	Bake Turner	1962-70	220	3539	16.09
59	George Sauer	1965-70	309	4965	16.07
60	Mac Speedie	1946-52	349	5602	16.05
61	Paul Flatley	1963-70	306	4905	16.03
62	Gary Collins	1962-71	331	5299	16.01
63	Gail Cogdill	1960-70	356	5696	16.00

TOUCHDOWNS (40)

1	Don Hutson	1935-45	100
2	Don Maynard	1958,60-73	88
3	Lance Alworth	1962-72	85
	Paul Warfield	1964-74,76-77	85
5	Tommy McDonald	1957-68	84
6	Art Powell	1959-68	81
7	**Charley Taylor**	**1964-**	**79**
8	**Fred Biletnikoff**	**1965-**	**74**
9	Bob Hayes	1965-75	71
10	Gary Collins	1962-71	70
11	Ray Berry	1955-67	68
12	Jimmy Orr	1958-70	66
13	Bobby Mitchell	1958-68	65
	Sonny Randle	1959-68	65
15	Dante Lavelli	1946-56	62
16	Pete Pihos	1947-55	61
	Billy Howton	1952-63	61
18	Crazy Legs Hirsch	1946-57	60
	Jerry Smith	**1965-**	**60**
20	**Gene Washington**	**1969-**	**59**
21	Hugh Taylor	1947-54	58
	Gary Garrison	**1966-**	**58**
23	Otis Taylor	1965-74	57
	Harold Jackson	**1968-**	**57**
25	Chris Burford	1960-67	54
26	Carroll Dale	1960-73	52
	Roy Jefferson	1965-76	52
28	Del Shofner	1957-67	51
	Charley Hennigan	1960-66	51
30	Ken Kavanaugh	1940-41,45-50	50
	Ray Renfro	1952-63	50
	Max McGee	1954,57-67	50
	Frank Clarke	1957-67	50
34	Alyn Beals	1946-51	49
	Billy Wilson	1951-60	49
36	Kyle Rote	1951-61	48
	Lenny Moore	1956-67	48
	John Gilliam	**1967-**	**48**
39	Pete Retzlaff	1956-66	47
	Joe Morrison	1959-72	47
	Billy Cannon	1960-70	47
42	Bobby Walston	1951-62	46
43	Jim Benton	1938-40,42-47	45
	Lionel Taylor	1959-68	45
	Jack Snow	1965-75	45
46	Buddy Dial	1959-66	44
	Dave Parks	1964-73	44
48	Frank Gifford	1952-60,62-64	43
49	Mike Ditka	1961-72	43
	Cliff Branch	**1972-**	**43**
51	Gino Cappelletti	1960-70	42
	Warren Wells	1964,67-70	42
53	Harlon Hill	1954-62	40
	Jim Mutscheller	1954-61	40
	Boyd Dowler	1959-69,71	40
	Bernie Casey	1961-68	40
	Jackie Smith	**1963-**	**40**
	Haven Moses	**1968-**	**40**

Players active at the end of **1977** are shown in **bold face.**

LIFETIME LEADERS

PUNT RETURNS

(100)

	Player	Years	Ret.
1	Em Tunnell	1948-61	258
2	Alvin Haymond	1964-73	253
3	Ron Smith	1965-74	235
4	Speedie Duncan	1964-74	202
5	Willie Wood	1960-71	187
6	**Howard Stevens**	**1973-**	**163**
7	**Bill Thompson**	**1969-**	**156**
	Larry Marshall	**1972-**	**156**
9	**Charlie West**	**1968-**	**154**
10	**Butch Atkinson**	**1967-**	**148**
11	**Lem Barney**	**1967-**	**143**
	Billy Johnson	**1974-**	**143**
13	**Bruce Taylor**	**1970-**	**142**
14	Woodley Lewis	1950-60	138
15	Kermit Alexander	1963-73	133
16	**Lemar Parrish**	**1970-**	**130**
	Jake Scott	**1970-**	**130**
18	Rickie Harris	1965-72	128
19	Hugh McElhenny	1952-64	126
	Yale Lary	1952-53,56-64	126
21	Bill Dudley	1942,45-51,53	124
	Joe Arenas	1951-57	124
23	Abe Woodson	1958-66	123
24	Al Carmichael	1953-58,60-61	122
	Bill Bradley	**1969-**	**122**
26	**Neal Colzie**	**1975-**	**121**
27	Dick James	1956-65	120
	Jon Arnett	1957-66	120
29	Carl Taseff	1951,53-62	117
	Rick Upchurch	**1975-**	**117**
31	**Eddie Brown**	**1974-**	**115**
32	Don Paul	1950-58	113
33	George McAfee	1940-41,45-50	112
34	Claude Gibson	1961-65	110
35	**Mel Renfro**	**1964-**	**109**
36	**Rolland Lawrence**	**1973-**	**105**
	Ralph McGill	**1972-**	**105**
38	Johnny Morris	1958-67	104
	Bob Hayes	1965-75	104
40	Ike Hill	1970-71,73-74,76	102

YARDS (1000)

	Player	Years	Yards
1	Em Tunnell	1948-61	2209
2	Speedy Duncan	1964-74	2201
3	Alvin Haymond	1964-73	2148
4	**Billy Johnson**	**1974-**	**1963**
5	**Bill Thompson**	**1969-**	**1811**
6	Ron Smith	1965-74	1788
7	**Howard Stevens**	**1973-**	**1559**
8	Bill Dudley	1942,45-51,53	1515
9	**Rick Upchurch**	**1975-**	**1501**
10	**Neal Colzie**	**1975-**	**1437**
11	George McAfee	1940-41,45-50	1431
12	**Larry Marshall**	**1972-**	**1415**
13	Willie Wood	1960-71	1391
14	Claude Gibson	1961-65	1381
15	**Jake Scott**	**1970-**	**1357**
16	**Bruce Taylor**	**1970-**	**1323**
17	**Lem Barney**	**1967-**	**1312**
18	**Butch Atkinson**	**1968-**	**1247**
19	**Mike Fuller**	**1975-**	**1206**
20	**Lemar Parrish**	**1970-**	**1201**
21	**Eddie Brown**	**1974-**	**1166**
22	Bob Hayes	1965-75	1158
23	Jack Christiansen	1951-58	1084
24	**Charlie West**	**1968-**	**1080**
25	Bosh Pritchard	1942,46-49,51	1072
26	Rodger Bird	1966-68	1063
27	Rickie Harris	1965-72	1029
28	Woodley Lewis	1950-60	1026

AVERAGE RETURN (8.0)

(Minimum 75 returns)

	Player	Years	Ret.	Yards	Avg.
1	**Billy Johnson**	**1974-**	**143**	**1963**	**13.73**
2	**Rick Upchurch**	**1975-**	**117**	**1501**	**12.83**
3	George McAfee	1940-41,45-50	112	1431	12.78
4	Jack Christianson	1951-58	85	1084	12.75
5	Claude Gibson	1961-65	110	1381	12.56
6	**Mike Fuller**	**1975-**	**97**	**1206**	**12.43**
7	Bill Dudley	1942,45-51,53	124	1515	12.22
8	**Neal Colzie**	**1975-**	**121**	**1437**	**11.88**
9	Mack Herron	1973-75	84	982	11.69
10	**Bill Thompson**	**1969-**	**156**	**1811**	**11.61**
11	**Terry Metcalf**	**1973-**	**80**	**921**	**11.51**
12	Rodger Bird	1966-68	94	1063	11.31
13	Bosh Pritchard	1942,46-49,51	95	1072	11.28
14	Bob Hayes	1965-75	104	1158	11.13
15	Floyd Little	1967-75	81	893	11.02
16	Speedy Duncan	1964-74	202	2201	10.90
17	Vitamin Smith	1949-53	75	814	10.85
18	Leroy Kelly	1964-73	94	990	10.53
19	**Jake Scott**	**1970-**	**130**	**1357**	**10.44**
20	Abner Haynes	1960-67	85	873	10.27
21	**Eddie Brown**	**1974-**	**115**	**1166**	**10.14**
22	Tom Watkins	1961-65,67-68	96	970	10.10
23	Bill Butler	1959-64	88	850	9.66
24	**Howard Stevens**	**1973-**	**163**	**1559**	**9.56**
25	**Glen Edwards**	**1971-**	**98**	**933**	**9.52**
26	**Bruce Taylor**	**1970-**	**142**	**1323**	**9.32**
27	**Virgil Livers**	**1975-**	**76**	**707**	**9.30**
28	Al Dodd	1967,69-71,73-74	80	744	9.30
29	**Lemar Parrish**	**1970-**	**130**	**1201**	**9.24**
30	Cliff Lewis	1946-51	77	710	9.22
31	**Ralph McGill**	**1975-**	**105**	**964**	**9.18**
32	**Lem Barney**	**1967-**	**143**	**1312**	**9.17**
33	**Larry Marshall**	**1972-**	**156**	**1415**	**9.07**
34	Bill Baird	1963-69	88	787	8.94
35	**Manfred Moore**	**1974-**	**88**	**770**	**8.75**
36	**Tommy Casanova**	**1972-**	**91**	**794**	**8.73**
37	**Ed Podolak**	**1969-**	**86**	**739**	**8.59**
38	Johnny Morris	1958-67	104	893	8.59
39	Em Tunnell	1948-61	258	2209	8.56
40	Alvin Haymond	1964-73	253	2148	8.49
41	**Butch Atkinson**	**1968-**	**149**	**1247**	**8.43**
42	Jon Staggers	1970-75	94	792	8.43
43	Jon Arnett	1957-66	120	981	8.18
44	Rickie Harris	1965-72	128	1029	8.04

TOUCHDOWNS (3)

	Player	Years	TD
1	Jack Christiansen	1951-58	8
2	Em Tunnell	1948-61	5
	Billy Johnson	**1974-**	**5**
	Rick Upchurch	**1975-**	**5**
5	Dick Christy	1958,60-62	4
	Speedy Duncan	1964-74	4
	Lemar Parrish	**1970-**	**4**
8	Dick Todd	1939-40,42,45-48	3
	Ray McLean	1940,42-47	3
	Bill Dudley	1942,45-51,53	3
	Woodley Lewis	1950-60	3
	Ray Mathews	1951-60	3
	Yale Lary	1952-53,56-64	3
	Ollie Matson	1952,54-66	3
	Bert Zagers	1955,57-58	3
	Bobby Mitchell	1958-68	3
	Claude Gibson	1961-65	3
	Tom Watkins	1961-65,67-68	3
	Leroy Kelly	1964-73	3
	Rob Hayes	1965-75	3
	Rickie Harris	1965-72	3
	Butch Atkinson	**1968-**	**3**
	Jon Staggers	1970-75	3
	Freddie Solomon	**1975-**	**3**

KICKOFF RETURNS

(100)

	Player	Years	Ret.
1	Ron Smith	1965-74	275
2	Abe Woodson	1958-66	193
3	Al Carmichael	1953-58,60-61	191
4	Dick James	1956-61	189
5	Timmy Brown	1959-68	184
6	Speedy Duncan	1964-74	180
7	Alvin Haymond	1963-73	170
8	Bobby Jancik	1962-67	158
9	Kermit Alexander	1963-73	153
10	Ollie Matson	1952,54-66	144
11	Joe Arenas	1951-57	139
12	Woodley Lewis	1950-60	137
13	Clarence Childs	1964-68	134
	Bruce Laird	**1972-**	**134**
15	Cannonball Butler	1965-72	133
	Carl Garrett	**1969-**	**133**
17	Bill Butler	1959-64	132
18	Bo Roberson	1961-66	130
19	Vic Washington	1971-76	129
	Larry Marshall	**1972-**	**129**
21	Jon Arnett	1957-66	126
22	Buddy Young	1947-55	125
	Steve Odom	**1974-**	**125**
24	Abner Haynes	1960-67	121
25	Herb Adderley	1961-72	120
26	Dick Christy	1958,60-63	117
27	**Preston Pearson**	**1967-**	**114**
28	Dave Hampton	1969-76	113
	Billy Johnson	**1974-**	**113**
30	Mercury Morris	1969-76	111
31	Dave Grayson	1961-70	110
32	Cecil Turner	1968-73	108
33	Walter Roberts	1964-67,69-70	107
	Terry Metcalf	**1973-**	**107**
35	Floyd Little	1967-75	104
36	**Howard Stevens**	**1973-**	**103**
37	Bobby Mitchell	1958-68	102
	Rickie Harris	1965-72	102
	Travis Williams	1967-71	102
40	Tom Watkins	1961-65,67-68	101
	Al Nelson	1965-73	101
42	**Lou Piccone**	**1974-**	**100**

YARDS (2500)

	Player	Years	Yards
1	Ron Smith	1965-74	6922
2	Abe Woodson	1958-66	5538
3	Al Carmichael	1953-58,60-61	4798
4	Jimmy Brown	1959-68	4781
5	Dick James	1956-61	4676
6	Speedy Duncan	1964-74	4539
7	Alvin Haymond	1963-73	4438
8	Bobby Jancik	1962-67	4185
9	Joe Arenas	1951-57	3798
10	Ollie Matson	1952,54-66	3746
11	Kermit Alexander	1963-73	3586
12	Buddy Young	1947-55	3465
13	Clarence Childs	1964-68	3454
14	**Bruce Laird**	**1972-**	**3372**
15	Vic Washington	1971-76	3341
16	Woodley Lewis	1950-60	3325
17	**Carl Garrett**	**1969-**	**3284**
18	**Larry Marshall**	**1972-**	**3173**
19	Jon Arnett	1957-66	3110
20	Herb Adderley	1961-72	3080
21	Bo Roberson	1961-66	3057
22	Abner Haynes	1960-67	3025
23	Mercury Morris	1969-76	2947
24	Cannonball Butler	1965-72	2931
25	Dave Hampton	1969-76	2923
26	Bill Butler	1959-64	2886
27	**Steve Odom**	**1974-**	**2825**
28	Dave Grayson	1961-70	2804
29	**Terry Metcalf**	**1973-**	**2802**
30	Travis Williams	1967-71	2801
	Preston Pearson	**1967-**	**2801**
32	**Billy Johnson**	**1974-**	**2792**
33	Gale Sayers	1965-71	2781
34	Dick Christie	1958,60-63	2770
35	Walt Roberts	1964-67,69-70	2728
36	Lynn Chadnois	1950-56	2720
37	Bobby Mitchell	1958-68	2690
38	Al Nelson	1965-73	2625
39	Cecil Turner	1968-73	2616
40	Floyd Little	1967-75	2523
41	Tom Watkins	1961-65,67-68	2510

AVERAGE RETURN (25.0)

(Minimum 75 returns)

	Player	Years	Ret.	Yards	Avg.
1	Gale Sayers	1965-71	91	2781	30.56
2	Lynn Chadnois	1950-56	92	2920	29.57
3	Abe Woodson	1958-66	193	5538	28.69
4	Buddy Young	1947-55	125	3465	27.72
5	Travis Williams	1967-71	102	2801	27.46
6	Joe Arenas	1951-57	139	3798	27.32
7	Steve Van Buren	1944-51	76	2030	26.71
8	Lenny Lyles	1958-69	81	2161	26.68
9	Mercury Morris	1964-76	111	2947	26.55
10	Bobby Jancik	1962-67	158	4185	26.49
11	**Mel Renfro**	**1964-**	**85**	**2246**	**26.42**
12	Bobby Mitchell	1958-68	102	2690	26.37
13	**Terry Metcalf**	**1973-**	**107**	**2802**	**26.21**
14	Alvin Haymond	1963-73	170	4438	26.11
15	Noland Smith	1967-69	82	2137	26.06
16	Ollie Matson	1952,54-66	144	3746	26.01
17	Al Nelson	1965-73	101	2625	25.99
18	Timmy Brown	1959-68	184	4781	25.98
19	Vic Washington	1971-76	129	3341	25.90
20	Dave Hampton	1969-76	113	2923	25.87
21	Larry Garron	1960-68	89	2299	25.83
22	Clarence Childs	1964-68	134	3454	25.78
23	Herb Adderley	1961-72	120	3080	25.67
24	Pat Studstill	1962-62,64-72	75	1924	25.65
25	Walter Roberts	1964-67,69-70	107	2728	25.50
26	Dave Grayson	1961-70	110	2804	25.49
27	Charley Warner	1963-66	86	2187	25.43
28	Don Shy	1967-73	180	2047	25.27
29	Speedy Duncan	1964-74	180	4539	25.22
30	Ron Smith	1965-74	275	6922	25.17
31	**Bruce Laird**	**1972-**	**134**	**3372**	**25.16**
32	Al Carmichael	1953-58,60-61	191	4798	25.12
33	Bobby Williams	1966-67,69-71	77	1934	25.12
34	Abner Haynes	1960-67	121	3025	25.06
35	**Rick Upchurch**	**1975-**	**82**	**2054**	**25.05**
26	**Charlie West**	**1968-**	**84**	**2103**	**25.04**

TOUCHDOWNS (3)

	Player	Years	TD
1	Ollie Matson	1952,54-66	6
	Gale Sayers	1965-71	6
	Travis Williams	1967-71	6
4	Bobby Mitchell	1958-68	5
	Abe Woodson	1958-66	5
	Timmy Brown	1959-68	5
7	Buddy Young	1947-55	4
	Cecil Turner	1968-73	4
	Steve Van Buren	1944-51	3
9	Vitamin Smith	1949-53	3
	Lynn Chadnois	1950-56	3
	Lenny Lyles	1958-69	3
	Charley Warner	1963-66	3
	Ron Smith	1965-74	3
	Dave Hampton	1969-76	3
	Mercury Morris	1969-76	3
	Cullen Bryant	**1973-**	**3**
	Ray Clayborn	**1977-**	**3**

Players active at the end of 1977 are shown in **bold face.**

LIFETIME LEADERS
POINTS AFTER TOUCHDOWNS

ATTEMPTS (250)

#	Player	Years	Att	#	Player	Years	Att
1	George Blanda	1949-58,60-75	957	14	Tommy Davis	1959-69	350
2	Lou Groza	1946-59,61-67	834	15	Garo Yepremian	1966-67,70-	341
3	Fred Cox	1963-	539	16	Mike Clark	1963-71,73	338
4	Jim Bakken	1962-	523	17	Bob Waterfield	1945-52	336
5	Jim Turner	1964-	475	18	Don Cockroft	1968-	330
6	Sam Baker	1953,56-69	444	19	Roy Gerela	1969-	313
7	Lou Michaels	1958-69,71	402	20	Gordie Soltau	1945-52	302
8	Bobby Walston	1951-62	384	21	Mike Mercer	1950-58	295
9	Bruce Gossett	1964-74	383	22	Errol Mann	1968-	295
10	Jan Stenerud	1967-	354	23	Pat Summerall	1952-61	265
11	Pete Gogolak	1964-74	354	24	Don Chandler	1956-67	258
12	Gino Cappelletti	1960-70	353	25	Horst Muhlman	1969-	257
13	B. Agajanian	1945,47-49,53-57,60-62,64	351				

GOOD (225)

#	Player	Years	Good	#	Player	Years	Good
1	George Blanda	1949-58,60-75	941	15	Garo Yepremian	1966-67,70-	327
2	Lou Groza	1946-59,61-67	810	16	Mike Clark	1963-71,53	325
3	Fred Cox	1963-	519	17	Don Cockroft	1968-	318
4	Jim Bakken	1962-	507	18	Bob Waterfield	1945-52	315
5	Jim Turner	1964-	458	19	Roy Gerela	1969-	301
6	Sam Baker	1953,56-59	428	20	Mike Mercer	1950-58	288
7	Lou Michaels	1958-69,71	386	21	Gordie Soltau	1945-52	284
8	Bruce Gossett	1964-74	374	22	Errol Mann	1968-	282
9	Bobby Walston	1951-62	365	23	Pat Summerall	1952-61	257
10	Tommy Davis	1959-69	348	24	Don Chandler	1956-67	248
11	Pete Gogolak	1964-74	344	25	Horst Muhlmann	1969-	245
12	B. Agajanian	1945,47-49,53-57,60-62,64	343	26	Danny Villanueva	1960-67	236
13	Gino Cappelletti	1960-70	342				
14	Jan Stenerud	1967-	341				

PERCENT MADE (95.0)
(Minimum 200 Attempts)

#	Player	Years	Good	Att	Pct.	#	Player	Years	Good	Att	Pct.
1	Tommy Davis	1958-69	348	350	99.43	10	Pat Summerall	1952-61	257	265	96.98
2	George Blanda	1949-58,60-75	941	957	98.33	11	Jim Bakken	1962-	507	523	96.94
3	Danny Villanueva	1960-67	236	241	97.92	12	Gino Cappelletti	1960-70	342	353	96.88
4	Ben Agajanian	1945,47-49,53-57,60-62,64	343	351	97.72	13	Jim Turner	1964-	458	475	96.42
5	Bruce Gossett	1964-74	374	383	97.65	14	Gene Mingo	1960-67,69-70	215	223	96.41
6	Mike Mercer	1961-70	288	295	97.62	15	Sam Baker	1953,56-69	428	444	96.39
7	Pete Gogolak	1964-74	344	354	97.18	16	Don Cockroft	1968-	318	330	96.36
8	Lou Groza	1946-59,61-67	810	834	97.12	17	Jan Stenerud	1967-	341	354	96.32
9	Pat Harder	1946-53	198	204	97.05	18	Fred Cox	1962-	519	539	96.29
						19	Roy Gerela	1969-	301	313	96.17

#	Player	Years	Good	Att	Pct.
20	Mike Clark	1963-71,73	325	338	96.15
21	Don Chandler	1956-67	248	258	96.12
22	Bobby Howfield	1968-74	193	201	96.02
23	Lou Michaels	1958-59,71	386	402	96.01
24	Garo Yepremian	1966-67,70-	327	341	95.89
25	Errol Mann	1968-	282	295	95.59
26	Horst Muhlmann	1969-	245	257	95.33
27	Bobby Walston	1951-62	365	384	95.05

FIELD GOALS

ATTEMPTS (125)

#	Player	Years	Att	#	Player	Years	Att
1	George Blanda	1949-58,60-75	638	21	Pat Summerall	1952-61	212
2	Lou Groza	1946-59,61-67	481	22	B. Agajanian	1945,47-49,53-57,60-62,64	204
3	Fred Cox	1963-	455	23	Mike Mercer	1961-70	195
4	Jim Turner	1964-	445	24	Jim Martin	1950-61,63-64	192
5	Jim Bakken	1962-	419	25	Mac Percival	1967-74	190
6	Jan Stenerud	1967-	383	26	Mark Moseley	1970-72,74-	179
7	Bruce Gossett	1964-74	360	27	David Ray	1969-74	178
8	Lou Michaels	1958-69,71	341	28	Curt Knight	1969-73	175
9	Gino Cappelletti	1960-70	333	29	Bobby Howfield	1968-74	166
10	Sam Baker	1953,56-69	316	30	Chester Marcol	1972-	163
11	Pete Gogolak	1964-74	294	31	Don Chandler	1956-67	161
12	Tommy Davis	1958-69	276	32	Danny Villanueva	1960-67	160
13	Roy Gerela	1969-	273	33	Bobby Walston	1951-62	157
14	Errol Mann	1968-	256	34	Roger LeClerc	1960-67	152
15	Garo Yepremian	1966-67,70-	247	35	John Leypoldt	1971-	151
16	Don Cockroft	1968-	245	36	Paul Hornung	1951-62,64-66	140
17	Tom Dempsey	1969-	241	37	Gordie Soltau	1950-58	138
18	Horst Muhlmann	1969-	239	38	Toni Fritsch	1971-73,75-	135
19	Mike Clark	1963-71,73	232	39	Skip Butler	1971-	132
20	Gene Mingo	1960-67,69-70	220	40	Wayne Walker	1958-72	131

GOOD (90)

#	Player	Years	Good	#	Player	Years	Good
1	George Blanda	1949-58,60-75	335	17	Tom Dempsey	1969-	148
2	Fred Cox	1963-	282	18	Mike Clark	1963-71,73	133
3	Jim Turner	1964-	280	19	Tommy Davis	1959-69	130
4	Jim Bakken	1962-	267	20	Gene Mingo	1960-67,69-70	112
5	Lou Groza	1946-59,61-67	264	21	David Ray	1969-74	110
6	Jan Stenerud	1967-	247	22	Mark Moseley	1970-72,74-	108
7	Bruce Gossett	1964-74	219	23	B. Agajanian	1945,47-49,53-57,60-62,64	104
8	Lou Michaels	1958-69,71	187	24	Chester Marcol	1972-	103
9	Sam Baker	1953,56-69	179	25	Mike Mercer	1961-70	102
10	Pete Gogolak	1964-74	173	26	Mac Percival	1967-74	101
11	Gino Cappelletti	1960-70	172	27	Curt Knight	1969-73	101
12	Roy Gerela	1969-	171	28	Pat Summerall	1952-61	100
13	Errol Mann	1968-	165	29	Bobby Howfield	1968-74	98
14	Don Cockroft	1968-	164	30	Don Chandler	1956-67	94
15	Garo Yepremian	1966-67	161	31	Jim Martin	1950-61,63-64	92
16	Horst Muhlmann	1969-	154	32	John Leypoldt	1971-	91

PERCENT MADE (50.0)
(Minimum 100 Attempts)

#	Player	Years	Good	Att	Pct.	#	Player	Years	Good	Att	Pct.
1	Don Cockroft	1968-	164	245	66.94	15	Mark Moseley	1970-72,74-	108	179	60.34
2	Garo Yepremian	1966-67,70-	161	247	65.18	16	John Leypoldt	1971-	91	151	60.26
3	Jan Stenerud	1967-	247	383	64.49	17	Bobby Howfield	1968-74	98	166	59.04
4	Errol Mann	1968-	165	256	64.45	18	Pete Gogolak	1964-74	173	294	58.84
5	Horst Muhlmann	1969-	154	239	64.44	19	Dennis Partee	1968-75	71	121	58.68
6	Jim Bakken	1962-	267	419	63.72	20	Don Chandler	1956-67	94	161	58.38
7	Chester Marcol	1972-	103	163	63.19	21	Fred Cone	1951-57,60	59	102	57.84
8	Jim Turner	1964-	280	445	62.92	22	Curt Knight	1969-73	101	175	57.71
9	Roy Gerela	1969-	171	273	62.64	23	Mike Clark	1963-71,73	133	232	57.32
10	Toni Fritsch	1971-73,75-	84	135	62.22	24	Sam Baker	1953,56-69	179	316	56.64
11	Fred Cox	1963-	282	455	61.98	25	Jim O'Brien	1970-73	60	108	55.55
12	David Ray	1969-74	110	178	61.80	26	Nick Mike-Mayer	1973-	59	107	55.14
13	Tom Dempsey	1969-	148	241	61.41	27	Lou Groza	1946-59,61-67	264	481	54.88
14	Bruce Gossett	1964-74	219	360	60.83	28	Lou Michaels	1958-69,71	187	341	54.83

#	Player	Years	Good	Att	Pct.
29	Bob Waterfield	1945-52	60	110	54.54
30	Skip Butler	1971-	71	132	53.79
31	Mac Percival	1967-74	101	190	53.16
32	Danny Villanueva	1960-67	85	160	53.13
33	George Blanda	1949-58,60-75	335	638	52.51
34	Mike Mercer	1961-70	102	195	52.30
35	Charlie Durkee	1967-68,71-72	52	101	51.48
36	Gino Cappelletti	1960-70	172	333	51.35
37	Ben Agajanian	1945,47-49,53-57,60-62,64	104	204	50.98
38	Bobby Walston	1951-62	80	157	50.95
39	Gene Mingo	1960-67,69-70	112	220	50.90
40	Gordie Saltau	1950-58	70	138	50.72
41	Roger LeClerc	1960-67	76	152	50.00

Players active at the end of **1977** are shown in **bold face**.

LIFETIME LEADERS

POINTS

(3 0 0)

1	George Blanda	1949-58,60-75	2000
2	Lou Groza	1946-59,61-67	1608
3	**Fred Cox**	**1963-**	**1365**
4	**Jim Bakken**	**1962-**	**1320**
5	**Jim Turner**	**1964-**	**1304**
6	Gino Cappelletti	1960-70	1130
7	**Jan Stenerud**	**1967-**	**1082**
8	Bruce Gossett	1964-74	1031
9	Sam Baker	1953,56-69	977
10	Lou Michaels	1958-69,71	955
11	Bobby Walston	1951-62	881
12	Pete Gogolak	1964-74	863
13	Don Hutson	1935-45	823
14	**Roy Gerela**	**1969-**	**814**
15	**Garo Yepremian**	**1966-67,70-**	**810**
	Don Cockroft	**1968-**	**810**
17	**Errol Mann**	**1968-**	**777**
18	Paul Hornung	1957-62,64-66	760
19	Jimmy Brown	1957-65	756
20	Tommy Davis	1959-69	738
21	Mike Clark	1963-71,73	724
22	**Horst Muhlmann**	**1969-**	**681**
23	Lenny Moore	1956-67	678
24	B. Agajanian	1945,47-49,53-57,60-62,64	655
25	**Tom Dempsey**	**1969-**	**652**
26	Gordie Soltau	1950-58	644
27	Gene Mingo	1960-67,69-70	629
28	Mike Mercer	1961-70	594
29	Bob Waterfield	1945-52	573
30	Pat Summerall	1952-61	563
31	Jim Taylor	1958-67	558
32	Bobby Mitchell	1958-68	546
33	Leroy Kelly	1964-73	540
34	**Charley Taylor**	**1964-75,77-**	**540**
35	Doak Walker	1950-55	534
36	Don Maynard	1958,60-73	532
37	Pat Harder	1946-53	531
38	Don Chandler	1956-67	530
39	Lance Alworth	1962-72	524
40	**Paul Warfield**	**1964-74,76-77**	**516**
41	Joe Perry	1948-63	513
42	Tommy McDonald	1957-68	510
43	David Ray	1969-74	497
44	Fred Cone	1951-57,60	494
45	Art Powell	1959-67	492
46	Danny Villanueva	1960-67	491
47	**Mark Moseley**	**1970-72,74-**	**490**
48	Bobby Howfield	1968-74	487
49	Bill Dudley	1942,45-51,53	484
	Frank Gifford	1952-60,62-64	484
51	Curt Knight	1969-73	475
52	Ken Strong	1929-35,39,44-47	473
53	**John Leypoldt**	**1971-**	**472**
54	Mac Percival	1967-74	466
55	Steve Van Buren	1944-51	464
56	Bill Brown	1961-74	456
	Bob Hayes	1965-75	456
58	**Fred Biletnikoff**	**1965-**	**450**
59	John David Crow	1958-68	444
60	Ollie Matson	1952,54-66	438
61	Jim Martin	1950-61,63-64	434
62	Paddy Driscoll	1920-29	421
63	Gary Collins	1962-71	420
	O.J. Simpson	**1969-**	**420**
65	Ward Cuff	1937-47	417
66	Abner Haynes	1960-67	414
67	**Chester Marcol**	**1972-**	**411**
68	Ray Berry	1955-67	408
69	Crazy Legs Hirsch	1946-57	305
70	**Toni Fritsch**	**1971-73,75-**	**401**
71	**Chuck Foreman**	**1973-**	**396**
72	Jimmy Orr	1958-70	390
	Joe Morrison	1959-72	390
	Sonny Randle	1959-68	390
	Emerson Boozer	1966-75	390
76	Bobby Joe Conrad	1958-69	389
77	Timmy Brown	1959-68	384
78	Roger LeClerc	1960-67	382
79	Ted Fritsch	1942-50	380
80	Pete Pihos	1947-55	378
	Dennis Partee	1968-75	378
82	Clarke Hinkle	1932-41	377
83	Dante Lavelli	1946-56	372
	Ken Willard	1965-74	273
85	Dutch Clark	1931-32,34-38	369
86	Jack Manders	1933-40	368
87	Billy Howton	1952-63	366
88	Hugh McElhenny	1952-64	360
	Rick Casares	1955-66	360
	Otis Taylor	1965-76	360
	Jerry Smith	**1965-**	**360**
92	**Gene Washington**	**1969-**	**354**
93	Hugh Taylor	1947-54	348
	Gary Garrison	**1966-**	**348**
95	Wayne Walker	1958-72	345
96	Tom Matte	1961-72	342
	Harold Jackson	**1968-**	**342**
	Toni Linhart	**1972,74-**	**342**
99	**Skip Butler**	**1971-**	**340**
100	Alex Webster	1955-64	336
	Gale Sayers	1965-71	336
	Donny Anderson	1966-74	336
	Franco Harris	**1972-**	**336**
104	Chris Burford	1960-67	332
105	Ray Renfro	1952-63	330
	John Henry Johnson	1954-66	330
	Ron Johnson	1969-75	330
	Larry Brown	1969-76	330
109	Clem Daniels	1960-68	324
	Floyd Little	1967-75	324
111	Roy Jefferson	1965-76	318
112	**John Smith**	**1974-**	**315**
113	Ken Kavanaugh	1940-41,45-50	313
114	Kyle Rote	1951-61	312
	Steve Myrha	1957-61	312
	Carroll Dale	1960-73	312
	Pete Banaszek	**1966-**	**312**
	John Gilliam	**1967-**	**312**
119	Joe Aguirre	1941,43-49	310
120	Max McGee	1954,57-67	306
	Frank Clarke	1957-67	306
	Del Shofner	1957-67	306
	Charlie Hennigan	1960-66	306
124	Ernie Nevers	1926-27,29-31	301
	Vernie Lewellen	1924-32	301
	Jim O'Brien	1970-73	301

INTERCEPTIONS

(3 0)

1	Em Tunnell	1948-61	79
2	**Paul Krause**	**1964-**	**78**
3	Night Train Lane	1952-65	68
4	Dick LeBeau	1959-72	62
5	Bobby Boyd	1960-68	57
	Johnny Robinson	1960-71	57
7	**Pat Fischer**	**1961-**	**56**
	Emmitt Thomas	**1966-**	**56**
	Lem Barney	**1967-**	**56**
10	**Willie Brown**	**1963-**	**53**
11	Jack Butler	1951-59	52
	Bobby Dillon	1952-59	52
	Jimmy Patton	1955-66	52
	Larry Wilson	1960-72	52
	Mel Renfro	**1964-**	**52**
16	Yale Lary	1952-53,56-64	50
	Don Burroughs	1955-64	50
18	Dave Grayson	1961-70	49
19	Richie Petibon	1959-73	48
	Willie Wood	1960-70	48
	Herb Adderley	1961-72	48
22	**Jim Johnson**	**1961-**	**47**
23	Jack Christiansen	1951-58	46
	Dave Whitsell	1958-69	46
	Ed Meador	1959-70	46
	Goose Gonsoulin	1960-67	46
	Ken Houston	**1967-**	**46**
28	Erich Barnes	1958-71	45
	Jim Norton	1960-68	44
30	Warren Lahr	1949-59	44
31	Kermit Alexander	1963-73	44
32	Bobby Hunt	1962-69	42
	Jake Scott	**1970-**	**42**
34	Don Doll	1949-54	41
	Johnny Sample	1958-68	41
	Spider Lockhart	1965-75	41
37	Tom Keane	1948-55	40
	Ed Sharockman	1962-72	40
	Butch Bird	1964-71	40
	W.K. Hicks	1964-72	40
	Ken Riley	**1969-**	**40**
42	**Bobby Bryant**	**1968-**	**39**
43	Lindon Crow	1955-64	38
44	Don Shinnick	1957-69	37
	Dick Lynch	1958-66	37
	Ken Reaves	**1966-**	**37**
47	Jim David	1952-59	36
	Brig Owens	**1966-**	**36**
49	Frank Reagan	1941,46-51	35
	Ray Ramsey	1947-53	35
	Jerry Norton	1954-64	35
	Fred Williamson	1960-67	35
	Miller Farr	1965-73	35
	Willie Williams	1965-73	35
	Mel Blount	**1970-**	**35**
56	Tommy James	1947-56	34
	Jim Cason	1948-52,54-56	34
	Otto Schnellbacher	1948-51	34
	Don Paul	1950-58	34
	Bill Baird	1963-69	34
	Jerry Logan	1963-72	34
	Cornell Green	1962-74	34
	Dick Anderson	**1968-74,76-**	**34**
	Rick Volk	**1967-**	**34**
	Bill Bradley	**1969-**	**34**
66	Irv Comp	1943-49	33
	Jim Smith	1948-53	33
	Andy Nelson	1957-64	33
	Tony Greene	**1971-**	**33**
70	Lowell Wagner	1946-53,55	32
	Tom Landry	1949-55	32
	Rosey Taylor	1961-72	32
	Nick Buoniconti	1962-74,76	32
	Lee Roy Jordon	1963-75	32
	Charlie Stokes	1967-74	32
76	Bert Rechichar	1952-61	31
	Bernie Parrish	1959-66	31
	Bob Howard	**1967-**	**31**
	Ray Brown	**1971-**	**31**
80	Don Hutson	1935-45	30
	Cliff Lewis	1946-51	30
	Kenny Konz	1953-59	30
	Sam Huff	1956-67,69	30
	Willie West	1959,61-70	30
	Mike Bass	1960-68	30
	Butch Atkinson	**1968-**	**30**

PUNTING

PUNTS (2 5 0)

1	**Jerrel Wilson**	**1963-**	**1009**
2	**Bobby Walden**	**1964-**	**974**
3	Bobby Joe Green	1960-73	970
4	Paul Maguire	1960-70	794
5	**David Lee**	**1966-**	**746**
6	**Mike Bragg**	**1968-**	**715**
7	Sam Baker	1953,56-59	701
8	Don Chandler	1956-67	660
9	**Don Cockroft**	**1968-**	**651**
10	**Larry Seiple**	**1968-**	**633**
11	**Spike Jones**	**1970**	**592**
12	Bill Van Heusen	1968-76	574
13	Mike Eischeid	1966-74	564
14	Pat Studstill	1961-62,64-72	560
15	Curley Johnson	1960-69	556
16	Billy Lothridge	1964-72	532
	Tom Blanchard	**1971-**	**532**
18	Norm Van Brocklin	1949-60	523
19	Dennis Partee	1968-75	519
20	Jim Norton	1960-68	518
21	**John James**	**1972-**	**515**
22	Tommy Davis	1959-69	511
23	Yale Lary	1952-53,56-64	503
24	Ed Brown	1954-65	493
25	Horace Gillom	1947-56	492
26	Danny Villaneuva	1960-67	488
27	Adrian Burke	1950-56	474
28	**Herman Weaver**	**1970**	**436**
29	**Marv Bateman**	**1972-**	**401**
30	Jug Girard	1948-57	397
31	Tom Landry	1949-55	389
32	Donny Anderson	1966-74	387
33	Tom Yewcic	1961-66	369
34	King Hill	1958-69	368
	Ron Widby	1968-73	368
36	**Bob Parsons**	**1972-**	**366**
37	Jerry Norton	1954-64	358
38	Sammy Baugh	1937-52	338
	Pat Richter	1963-70	338
40	Steve O'Neal	1969-73	337
	Ray Guy	**1973-**	**337**
42	Gary Collins	1962-71	336
43	**Dave Beverly**	**1974-**	**325**
44	**Dave Green**	**1973-**	**324**
45	**Dave Jennings**	**1974-**	**318**
46	Tom McNeill	1967-73	317
47	**Don Pastorini**	**1971-**	**316**
48	Bob Waterfield	1945-52	315
49	Mike Mercer	1961-70	307
50	**Tom Wittum**	**1973-**	**303**
51	Frankie Albert	1946-52	299
	Julian Fagan	1970-73	299
53	Dave Lewis	1970-73	285
54	Bob Scarpitto	1961-68	282
55	Curley Morrison	1950-56	281
56	Roy Zimmerman	1940-48	278
	Cotton Davidson	1954,57,60-66,68	278
58	Jim Fraser	1962-66,68	271
	Duane Carrell	**1974-**	**257**
60	Max McGee	1954,57-67	256
61	Tom Janik	1963-71	253

PUNTING AVERAGE (42.5)

(Minimum 250 Punts)

1	Sammy Baugh	1937-52	44.9
2	Tommy Davis	1959-69	44.7
3	Yale Lary	1952-53,56-64	44.3
4	Bob Scarpitto	1961-68	44.0
5	Jerry Norton	1954-64	43.8
6	**Jerrel Wilson**	**1963-**	**43.8**
7	Dave Lewis	1960-73	43.7
8	Don Chandler	1956-67	43.5
9	Jim Fraser	1962-66,68	43.3
10	**Ray Guy**	**1973-**	**43.2**
11	Horace Gillom	1947-56	43.1
12	Frankie Albert	1946-52	43.0
13	Norm Van Brocklin	1949-60	42.9
14	Sam Baker	1953,56-59	42.7
15	Danny Villaneuva	1960-67	42.7
16	Bobby Joe Green	1960-73	42.6
17	Curley Johnson	1960-69	42.5

Players active at the end of **1977** are shown in **bold face.**

THE HALL OF FAME

1963

Sammy Baugh - Quarterback, Coach
Bert Bell - NFL Commissioner, Coach, Owner
Johnny Blood (McNally) - Halfback, Coach
Joe Carr - NFL President, Founder
Dutch Clark - Quarterback, Coach
Red Grange - Halfback
George Halas - End, Coach, Owner, Founder
Mel Hein - Center, Coach, League Official
Peter Henry - Tackle, Coach
Cal Hubbard - Tackle
Don Hutson - End
Curly Lambeau - Halfback, Coach, Founder
Tim Mara - Owner
George Preston Marshall - Owner
Bronko Nagurski - Fullback
Ernie Nevers - Fullback, Tailback, Coach
Jim Thorpe - Halfback, Coach,
         First NFL President

1964

Jimmy Conzelman - Quarterback, Coach,
         Owner
Ed Healey - Tackle
Clarke Hinkle - Fullback
Mike Michalske - Guard
Art Rooney - Owner
George Trafton - Center

1965

Guy Chamberlin - End, Coach
Paddy Driscoll - Quarterback, Coach
Danny Fortmann - Guard
Otto Graham - Quarterback, Coach
Sid Luckman - Quarterback
Steve Van Buren - Halfback
Bob Waterfield - Quarterback, Kicker, Coach

1966

Bill Dudley - Halfback, Tailback, Kicker
Joe Guyon - Fullback, Tailback
Arnie Herber - Quarterback
Walt Kiesling - Guard, Coach
George McAfee - Halfback, NFL Official
Steve Owen - Tackle, Coach
Shorty Ray - NFL League Official

1967

Chuck Bednarik - Center, Linebacker
Charles Bidwell - Owner
Paul Brown - Coach, Owner
Bobby Layne - Quarterback
Dan Reeves - Owner
Ken Strong - Halfback, Kicker
Joe Stydahar - Tackle, Coach
Em Tunnell - Defensive Back

1968

Cliff Battles - Halfback, Tailback,
         Coach
Art Donovan - Defensive Tackle
Crazy Legs Hirsch - Halfback, End,
         General Manager
Wayne Millner - End, Coach
Marion Motley - Fullback, Linebacker
Charlie Trippi - Halfback, Quarterback
Alex Wojciechowicz - Center, Linebacker

1969

Turk Edwards - Tackle, Coach
Greasy Neale - Coach, Pre NFL End
Leo Nomellini - Defensive Tackle
Joe Perry - Fullback
Ernie Stautner - Defensive Tackle

1970

Jack Christiansen - Defensive Back,
         Coach
Tom Fears - End, Coach
Hugh McElhenny - Halfback
Pete Pihos - End

1971

Jimmy Brown - Fullback
Bill Hewitt - End
Bruiser Kinard - Tackle
Vince Lombardi - Coach
Andy Robustelli - Defensive End,
         General Manager
Y.A. Tittle - Quarterback
Norm Van Brocklin - Quarterback, Coach

1972

Lamar Hunt - AFL Founder and Owner
Gino Marchetti - Defensive End
Ollie Matson - Halfback
Ace Parker - Tailback, Quarterback

1973

Ray Berry - End
Jim Parker - Offensive Tackle, Guard
Joe Schmidt - Linebacker, Coach

1974

Tony Canadeo - Halfback, Fullback
Bill George - Guard, Linebacker, Tackle
Lou Groza - Kicker, Tackle
Night Train Lane - Defensive Back

1975

Rosey Brown - Offensive Tackle
George Connor - Tackle, Guard, Linebacker
Dante Lavelli - End
Lenny Moore - Halfback, Flanker

1976

Ray Flaherty - End, Coach
Len Ford - End
Jim Taylor - Fullback

1977

Frank Gifford - Halfback
Forrest Gregg - Offensive Tackle, Guard
Gale Sayers - Halfback
Bart Starr - Quarterback
Bill Willis - Guard

1978

Lance Alworth - Wide Receiver
Weeb Ewbank - Coach
Tuffy Leemans - Fullback
Ray Nitschke - Linebacker
Larry Wilson - Defensive Back

THE COLLEGES — PRO FOOTBALL'S FARM SYSTEM

All men who played in the A.A.F.C., the A.F.L., or the N.F.L. since 1920 are tabulated here by the college(s) they attended. The colleges are listed by conference within the 7 N.C.A.A. regions. The current names of the colleges and the current football conferences are shown. Many of the conferences have more member colleges than are shown here since colleges that have not been attended by any pro football players are not listed; so "only" 558 four year colleges in the United States are listed here. Players who attended more than one college were counted for each college they attended.

EAST — 1585

IVY LEAGUE	203	Other East	1159
Pennsylvania	49	Pittsburgh	132
Brown	37	Penn State	124
Dartmouth	24	Syracuse	107
Columbia	23	Boston College	88
Cornell	23	West Virginia	70
Harvard	17	Villanova	64
Princeton	16	Holy Cross	58
Yale	14	Colgate	57
		Georgetown	50
		Duquesne	45
YANKEE CONFERENCE	65	Temple	41
		Bucknell	36
Boston U.	24	N.Y.U.	34
Massachusetts	10	Lafayette	24
Connecticut	9	Rutgers	20
New Hampshire	7	Army	19
Rhode Island	6	George Washington	18
Maine	5	Lehigh	15
Vermont	4	Canisius	13
		Navy	13
		St. Bonaventure	11
METROPOLITAN INTERCOL-		Grove City	9
LEGIATE CONFERENCE	61	Waynesburg	9
		Geneva	8
Fordham	50	Niagara	6
Hofstra	6	St. Francis (Pa.)	6
C.W. Post	2	St. John's (N.Y.)	6
Kings Point	2	St. Vincent	6
Wagner	1	Scranton	6
		Delaware	5
		Manhattan	5
MIDDLE ATLANTIC CONF.	57	Springfield	5
		Trinity (Conn.)	5
Muhlenberg	8	Tufts	5
Western Maryland	8	Gettysburg	4
Ursinus	6	American International	3
Widener	6	Buffalo	3
Albright	5	St. Anselm's	3
Swarthmore	5	Westminster	2
Delaware Valley	4	Arnold	2
Franklin and Marshall	4	Coast Guard	2
Gettysburg	4	C.U.N.Y.-Brooklyn	2
Dickinson	3	C.U.N.Y.-City	2
Lebanon Valley	3	LaSalle	2
Upsala	1	Northeastern	2
		St. Joseph's-Pa.	2
		Clarkson Tech.	1
PENNSYLVANIA CONF.	14	Rochester	1
		Brandeis	1
West Chester	7	Cathedral	1
Indiana State (Pa.)	2	Lincoln (Pa.)	1
Kutztown State	2	Long Island U.	1
Bloomsburg State	1	Middlebury	1
Clarion State	1	Norwich	1
Edinboro State	1	Rider	1
		Worcester Tech	1

INDEPENDENT COLLEGE	
ATHLETIC CONFERENCE	12
Hobart	4
St. Lawrence	4
Alfred	3
Ithaca	1

LITTLE THREE CONF.	8
Amherst	4
Williams	4

NEW ENGLAND F.B. CONF.	4
Providence	4

EASTERN FOOTBALL CONF.	1
Southern Connecticut State	1

MAINE INTERCOLLEGIATE	
ATHLETIC CONF.	1
Bowdoin	1

SOUTH — 2037

SOUTHEASTERN CONF.	752
Alabama	105
Georgia	99
Tennessee	96
Mississippi	94
Louisiana State	92
Auburn	69
Florida	63
Kentucky	61
Mississippi State	43
Vanderbilt	30

ATLANTIC COAST CONF.	307
Maryland	66
Duke	48
Wake Forest	46
North Carolina	45
Clemson	37
Virginia	35
North Carolina State	30

MID-EASTERN ATH. CONF.	98
Morgan State	29
Maryland Eastern Shore	23
North Carolina Central	16
South Carolina State	13
North Carolina A&T	12
Delaware State	3
Howard-D.C.	2

SOUTHERN INTERCOLLEGIATE	
ATHLETIC CONF.	88
Florida A&M	39
Bethune-Cookman	16
Morris Brown	8
Alabama A&M	6
Tuskegee	5
Fisk	4
Fort Valley State	4
Clark-Ga.	3
Alabama State	2
Albany State	1

SOUTHERN CONFERENCE	61
William & Mary	29
V.M.I.	11
East Carolina	5
Furman	5
Appalachian State	4
The Citadel	4
Davidson	3

CENTRAL INTERCOLLEGIATE	
ATHLETIC ASSOCIATION	33
Virginia Union	7
Johnson C. Smith	6
Norfolk State	6
Virginia State	6
Elizabeth City State	3
Hampton Institute	2
Fayetteville State	1
Shaw	1
Winston-Salem State	1

OHIO VALLEY CONF.	29
Tennessee Tech	7
Western Kentucky	6
Murray State	5
Eastern Kentucky	4
Morehead State	3
Middle Tennessee	2
Austin Peay	2

WEST VIRGINIA INTERCOL-	
LEGIATE ATH. CONF.	28
West Virginia Wesleyan	18
Salem	3
West Virginia State	3
Alderson-Broaddus	1
Fairmont State	1
West Liberty State	1
West Virginia Tech	1

GULF SOUTH CONFERENCE	28
Southeastern Louisiana	8
Tennessee-Martin	4
Delta State	3
Livingston State	3
Mississippi College	3
Florence State	2
Nicholls State	2
Troy State	2
Jacksonville State	1

SOUTH ATLANTIC CONF.	22
Catawba	9
Presbyterian	5
Elon	4
Lenoir Rhyne	2
Carson-Newman	1
Newberry	1

COLLEGE ATHLETIC CONF.	18
Centre	15
Southwestern at Memphis	2
Rose-Hulman Tech.	1

Other South	573
Georgia Tech	62
Miami (Fla.)	60
Tennessee State	53
Tulane	44
Florida State	39
Southern Mississippi	37
South Carolina	35
Memphis State	32
Tennessee-Chattanooga	31
Louisville	29
Richmond	22
Catholic	17
Virginia Tech	14
Northwest State-La.	13
Washington & Lee	12
Tampa	11
Samford	9
Morris Harvey	7
Northeast Louisiana	7
Davis & Elkins	6
Kentucky State	6
Allen	4
Mercer	3
Birmingham-Southern	2
Loyola (N. Orl.)	2
Oglethorpe	2
Mount St. Mary's	1
Benedict	1
Edward Waters	1
Frostburg State	1
Guilford	1
Louisiana College	1
Loyola (Balt.)	1
Randolph Macon	1
St. Augustine's	1
Spring Hill	1
Union (Tenn.)	1
Washington (Md.)	1
Western Carolina	1
Wofford	1

MIDWEST — 2414

BIG TEN CONFERENCE	1283
Ohio State	182
Purdue	146
Minnesota	140
Michigan	135
Michigan State	134
Illinois	124
Wisconsin	116
Iowa	107
Indiana	102
Northwestern	97

MID-AMERICAN CONF.	169
Miami-Ohio	42
Ohio U.	23
Toledo	20
Bowling Green	19
Western Michigan	15
Kent State	15
Eastern Michigan	14
Northern Illinois	11
Ball State	7
Central Michigan	3

PRESIDENT'S ATH. CONF.	86
Washington & Jefferson	38
Carnegie-Mellon	21
Case Reserve	14
John Carroll	9
Bethany (W. Va.)	2
Thiel	2

OHIO CONFERENCE	69
Ohio Wesleyan	11
Denison	9
Heidelberg	9
Marietta	8
Wittenberg	8
Baldwin-Wallace	7
Otterbein	5
Wooster	4
Ohio Northern	3
Mt. Union	2
Muskingum	2
Kenyon	1

MIDWEST CONFERENCE	54
Chicago	14
Beloit	9
Ripon	9
Lawrence	7
Knox	4
Carleton	3
Monmouth	3
Cornell College	2
Grinnell	2
Lake Forest	1

MINNESOTA INTERCOLLEGIATE	
ATHLETIC CONFERENCE	45
St. Thomas	18
Hamline	8
Gustavus Adolphus	5
St. Olaf	4
St. John's-Minn.	3
Concordia-Moorhead	3
Macalester	3
Augsburg	1

COLLEGE CONFERENCE OF	
ILLINOIS & WISCONSIN	29
Carroll (Wis.)	9
Illinois Wesleyan	7
Millikin	5
Carthage	3
Augusta	2
Elmhurst	1
North Central	1
North Park	1

INDIANA COLLEGE CONF.	25
DePauw	8
Butler	7
Valparaiso	6
Evansville	2
Indiana Central	1
St. Joseph's-Ind.	1

HOOSIER BUCKEYE CONF.	15
Findlay	5
Wilmington	4
Manchester	3
Bluffton	1
Defiance	1
Earlham	1

WISCONSIN STATE UNIV.	
CONF.	12
Wis. St.-Superior	4
Wis. St.-LaCrosse	3
Wis. St.-Oshkosh	2
Wis. St.-Stevens Point	1
Wisconsin-Platteville	1
Wisconsin-Stout	1

GREAT LAKES INTERCOLLEGIATE	
ATHLETIC CONFERENCE	11
Wayne State	7
Hillsdale	3
Ferris State	1

NORTHERN INTERCOLLEGIATE	
CONFERENCE	7
Minnesota-Duluth	4
St. Cloud State	3

MICHIGAN INTERCOLLEGIATE	
ATHLETIC ASSOCIATION	5
Kalamazoo	4
Olivet	1

UPPER MIDWEST CONF.	3
Loras	3

GATEWAY CONFERENCE	1
Northland	1

ILLINI-BADGER INTER.	
CONFERENCE	1
Lakeland	1

Other Midwest	599
Notre Dame	272
Marquette	65
Detroit	56
Cincinnati	38
Dayton	31
Xavier-Ohio	19
Marshall	15
DePaul	12
Western Illinois	11
St. Mary's (Minn.)	10
Loyola (Chic.)	9
Wabash	8
Youngstown	8
Northern Michigan	7
St. Ambrose	7
Lombard	5
Akron	4
Ashland	3
Central State-Ohio	3
Illinois State	3
St. Norbert	2
Eastern Illinois	2
Parsons	2
Wisconsin-Milwaukee	2
Lewis	1
St. Edmonds	1
St. Viator	1
Detroit Tech	1
Franklin (Ind.)	1
Franklin (Ohio)	1

THE COLLEGES — PRO FOOTBALL'S FARM SYSTEM

MISSOURI VALLEY – 1061

BIG EIGHT CONFERENCE — 614

Nebraska	129
Oklahoma	115
Colorado	81
Missouri	74
Kansas	62
Kansas State	57
Oklahoma State	52
Iowa State	44

MISSOURI VALLEY CONF. — 205

Tulsa	95
West Texas State	27
Wichita State	27
New Mexico State	21
Drake	18
Southern Illinois	16
Indiana State	1

NORTH CENTRAL CONF. — 55

North Dakota	16
South Dakota State	15
North Dakota State	8
South Dakota	8
Morningside	6
Augustana (S.D.)	1
Mankota State	1

MISSOURI INTERCOLLEGIATE ATHLETIC ASS'N. — 23

Lincoln (Mo.)	7
NE Missouri State	5
SE Missouri State	4
SW Missouri State	3
Missouri-Rolla	2
Central Missouri State	1
NW Missouri State	1

OKLAHOMA COLLEGIATE ATHLETIC CONF. — 13

Southwestern State-Okla.	5
East Central State-Okla.	3
Northeastern State-Okla.	3
Northwestern State-Okla.	1
Southeastern State-Okla.	1

KANSAS COLLEGE ATHLETIC CONFERENCE — 10

Bethany (Kan.)	3
St. Mary of the Plains	2
Southwestern (Kan.)	2
McPherson	1
Sterling	1
Tabor	1

IOWA INTERCOLLEGIATE ATHLETIC CONFERENCE — 11

Dubuque	3
Luther	3
Simpson	2
Central (Iowa)	1
Upper Iowa	1
William Penn	1

CENTRAL STATES INTER. CONFERENCE — 8

Pittsburg State	3
Ft. Hays Kansas State	2
Washburn	2
Missouri Southern	1

HEART OF AMERICA CONF. — 8

William Jewell	2
Missouri Valley	2
Ottawa (Kan.)	2
Baker	1
Tarkio	1

NEBRASKA COLLEGE CONF. — 7

Kearney State	3
Wayne State-Neb.	2
Peru State	1
Chadron State	1

NEBRASKA INTERCOLLEGIATE ATHLETIC CONFERENCE — 4

Doane	2
Hastings	2

TRI-STATE INTERCOLLEGIATE ATHLETIC CONFERENCE — 3

Yankton	3

SOUTHWEST – 1155

SOUTHWEST ATH. CONF. — 630

Texas	102
Arkansas	90
S.M.U.	82
Baylor	75
Texas A&M	75
Texas Christian	65
Houston	59
Texas Tech	48
Rice	43

SOUTHWESTERN ATH. CONF. — 236

Grambling	61
Jackson State	41
Texas Southern	37
Southern U.	33
Alcorn A&M	31
Prairie View	25
Mississippi Valley St.	8

LONE STAR CONFERENCE — 85

Texas A&I	18
Abilene Christian	17
East Texas State	16
Howard Payne	9
Southwest Texas State	9
Sam Houston State	8
S.F. Austin State	7
San Angelo State	1

SOUTHLAND CONFERENCE — 61

Louisiana Tech	19
Arkansas State	12
Lamar Tech	10
Texas-Arlington	9
McNeese State	6
Southwestern Louisiana	5

TEXAS INTERCOLLEGIATE ATHLETIC CONFERENCE — 27

Trinity (Texas)	11
Austin	8
McMurry	5
Sul Ross State	2
Tarleton State	1

ARKANSAS INTERCOLL. CONF. — 8

Ouachita Baptist	4
Henderson State	2
Arkansas Tech	1
Arkansas State College	1

Other Southwest — 108

North Texas State	36
Hardin Simmons	26
Arkansas-Pine Bluff	14
Centenary	11
Bishop	7
St. Edward's	3
Wiley	3
Eastern New Mexico	2
St. Mary's (Texas)	2
Corpus Christi	1
Midwestern	1
Paul Quinn	1
Philander Smith	1

NORTH DAKOTA COLLEGIATE ATHLETIC CONFERENCE — 1

Minot State	1

SOUTH DAKOTA INTER-COLLEGIATE CONFERENCE — 1

Dakota Wesleyan	1

Other Missouri Valley — 108

St. Louis	18
Washington-St. L.	12
Bradley	11
Oklahoma City	11
Creighton	10
Central State-Okla.	9
Kansas State Teachers	8
Langston	6
Phillips	6
Nebraska-Omaha	5
St. Benedict's	4
Cameron	3
Coll. of Emporia	2
Oklahoma Baptist	1
Westminster (Mo.)	1
Iowa Wesleyan	1

ROCKY MOUNTAINS – 345

WESTERN ATH. CONF. — 189

Colorado State	46
Utah	43
Texas-El Paso	33
Wyoming	27
Brigham Young	22
New Mexico	18

BIG SKY CONFERENCE — 82

Idaho	27
Montana	17
Montana State	12
Weber State	11
Idaho State	7
Northern Arizona	5
Boise State	3

ROCKY MOUNTAIN ATHLETIC CONFERENCE — 14

New Mexico Highlands	6
Adams State	3
Colorado Mines	2
Fort Lewis	1
Southern Utah	1
Westminster (Utah)	1

FRONTIER CONFERENCE — 2

Eastern Montana	2

Other Rocky Mountain — 58

Utah State	43
Denver	12
Colorado College	2
Regis	1

PACIFIC COAST – 1293

PACIFIC – 10 CONFERENCE — 843

Southern California	203
U.C.L.A.	100
Stanford	89
Washington	80
Oregon	75
Oregon State	71
California	63
Arizona State	62
Washington State	61
Arizona	39

PACIFIC COAST A.A. — 124

U. of the Pacific	48
San Jose State	43
Fresno State	18
Long Beach State	13
Fullerton State	2

CALIFORNIA COLL. A.A. — 29

Calif. State Poly-SLO	13
Los Angeles State	13
Calif. State Poly-Pomona	1
Northridge State	1
Calif.-Riverside	1

FAR WESTERN CONFERENCE — 23

San Francisco State	10
Chico State	4
Humboldt State	4
California-Davis	2
Sacramento State	2
Hayward State	1

SOUTHERN CALIFORNIA INTERCOLLEGIATE CONF. — 13

Whittier	6
Occidental	4
Redlands	3

PACIFIC NORTHWEST CONF. — 11

Linfield	3
Whitworth	2
Willamette	2
College of Idaho	1
Lewis & Clark	1
Pacific (Ore.)	1
Pacific Lutheran	1

EVERGREEN CONFERENCE — 2

Eastern Washington St.	1
Central Washington St.	1

Other Pacific Coast — 248

San Diego State	59
St. Mary's	50
Santa Clara	27
San Francisco	27
Nevada	19
Gonzaga	14
Loyola (L.A.)	12
Hawaii	10
Calif.-Santa Barbara	8
Portland	4
Nevada-Las Vegas	4
Pepperdine	3
U.S. International	3
San Diego	3
Portland State	2
California Lutheran	1
Calif. State-Bakersfield	1
Seattle	1

OTHER PLAYERS – 309

227 players did not attend college

73 players attended community or junior colleges only.

9 players attended college outside the United States.

The Top 20 Colleges

1.	Notre Dame	272
2.	Southern California	203
3.	Ohio State	182
4.	Purdue	146
5.	Minnesota	140
6.	Michigan	135
7.	Michigan State	134
8.	Pittsburgh	132
9.	Nebraska	129
10.	Illinois	124
	Penn State	124
12.	Wisconsin	116
13.	Oklahoma	115
14.	Iowa	107
	Syracuse	107
16.	Alabama	105
17.	Indiana	102
	Texas	102
19.	U.C.L.A.	100
20.	Georgia	99

THE CHANGING GAME

AVERAGE POINTS PER GAME

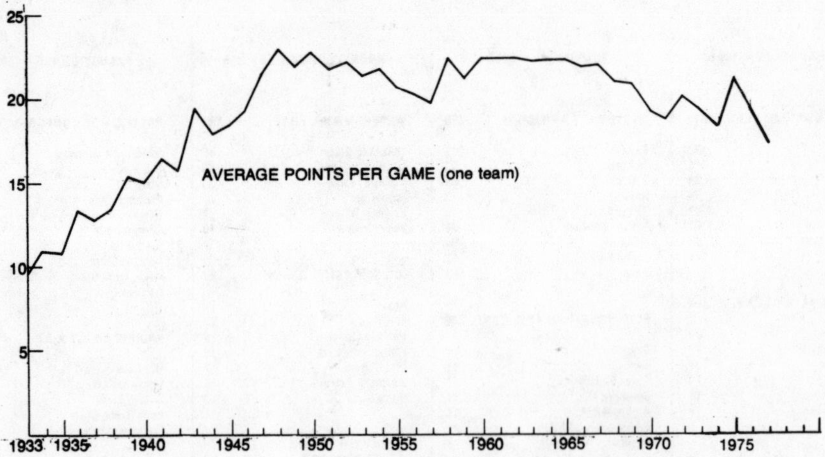

AVERAGE POINTS PER GAME (one team)

AVERAGE NUMBER OF TOUCHDOWNS PER GAME

AVERAGE NUMBER OF TOUCHDOWNS PER GAME (one team)

AVERAGE NUMBER OF FIELD GOALS PER GAME

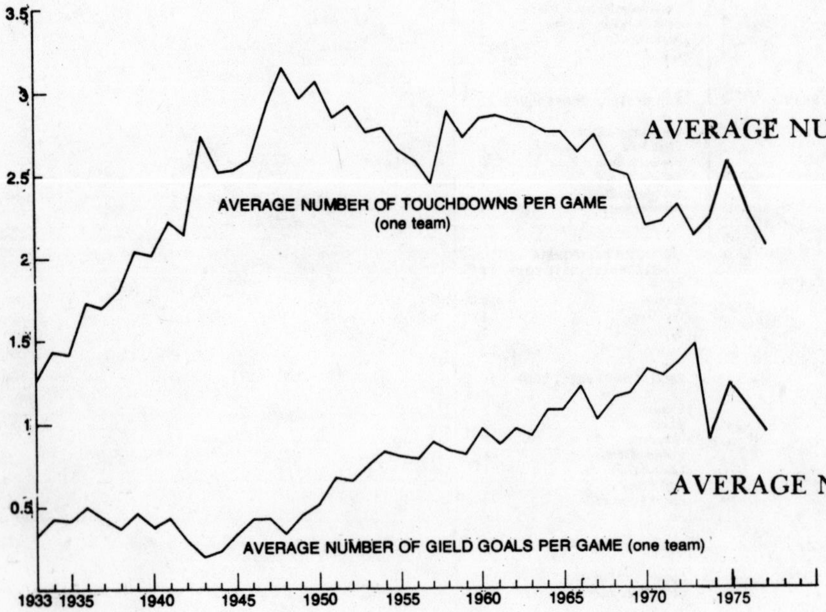

AVERAGE NUMBER OF GIELD GOALS PER GAME (one team)

FIELD GOAL PERCENTAGE
PASSES-PERCENT COMPLETED

PASSES-PERCENT COMPLETED

FIELD GOAL PERCENTAGE

PASSES-PERCENT INTERCEPTED

PASSES-PERCENT INTERCEPTED

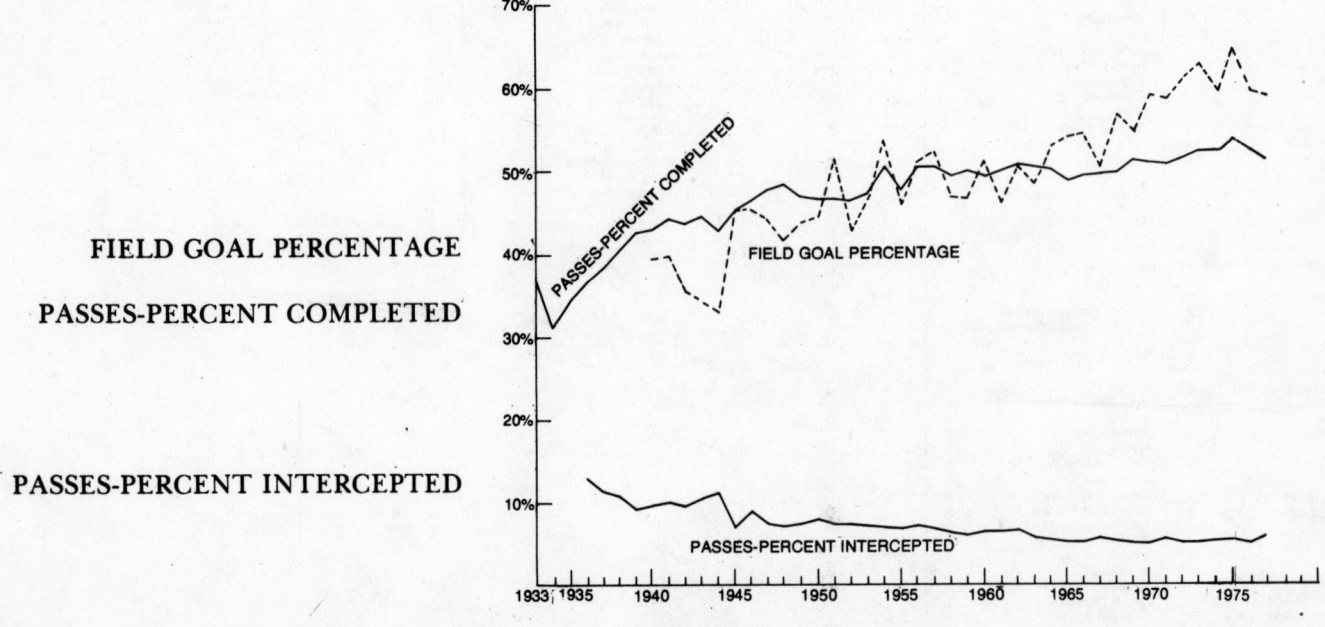